shuf·fle **1.** *v/t* *Karten* mischen; *Papiere etc* umordnen, hierhin oder dorthin legen; ***shuffle one's feet*** schlurfen; *v/i* schlurfen; *Karten* mischen; **2.** Schlurfen *n*, schlurfender Gang; Mischen *n*

Indicating words in *italics*

evening class·es Abendkurs *m*, Abendunterricht *m*
evening dress Gesellschaftsanzug *m*; Frack *m*, Smoking *m*; Abendkleid *n*

Compounds

kultivieren [kʊlti'vi:rən] *v/t (no -ge-, h)* cultivate
Künstler ['kʏnstlɐ] *m* (*-s*; *-*), **Künstlerin** ['kʏnstlərɪn] *f* (-; *-nen*) artist, MUS, THEA *a.* performer

Grammatical information

shy **1.** scheu; schüchtern; **2.** scheuen (***at*** vor *dat*); ***shy away from*** *fig* zurückschrecken vor (*dat*)

Entries divided into grammatical categories

Kumpel ['kʊmpəl] *m* (*-s*; -) miner; F mate, buddy, pal

Register labels

Abschlusszeugnis *n* *Am* diploma, *Br* school-leaving certificate

American and British variants

A B C D E F G H I J K L M N O P Q R S T U V W XY Z

Langenscheidt
Pocket Dictionary

German

German – English
English – German

edited by the
Langenscheidt editorial staff

Munich · Vienna

This dictionary uses the standardised German spelling system valid as of 2006.

Activity section by Jessie McGuire

Printed in Germany

15013

Preface

This new dictionary of English and German is a tool with more than 55,000 references for learners of the German language at beginner's or intermediate level.

Thousands of colloquial and idiomatic expressions have been included and the new German spelling has been used. The user-friendly layout with all headwords in blue allows the user to have quick access to all the words, expressions and their translations.

Clarity of presentation has been a major objective. Is the *mouse* you need for your computer, for example, the same in German as the *mouse* you don't want in the house? This dictionary is rich in sense distinctions like this - and in translation options tied to specific, identified senses.

Vocabulary needs grammar to back it up. In this dictionary you will find extra grammar information on German declension and conjugation as well as on German irregular verb forms.

Another feature is the special quick-reference section listing the States of Germany and Austria and the Cantons of Switzerland, German weights and measures etc.

The additional activity section provides the user with an opportunity to develop language skills with a selection of engaging word puzzles. The games are designed specifically to improve vocabulary, spelling, grammar and comprehension in an enjoyable style.

Designed for a wide variety of uses, this dictionary will be of great value to those who wish to learn German and have fun at the same time.

Contents

Guide for the User

This dictionary endeavors to do everything it can to help you find the words and translations you are looking for as quickly and as easily as possible.

To enable you to get the most out of your dictionary, you will be shown exactly where and how to find the information that will help you choose the right translation in every situation - whether at school or at home, when writing letters, or in everyday conversation.

1. German and English headwords

1.1 When you are looking for a particular word it is important to know that the dictionary entries are arranged in strict **alphabetical order:**

Aa**l** - a**b**
beugen - bi**e**gen
ha**y** - ha**z**e

In the German-English section the umlauts *ä ö ü* are treated as *a o u*. *ß* is treated as *ss*.

1.2 Besides the headwords and their derivatives and compounds, the past tense and past participle of irregular German verbs are also given as individual entries in alphabetical order in the German-English section, e.g. **ging, gegangen.**

1.3 Many German and English proper names and abbreviations are included in the vocabulary.

1.4 How then do you go about finding a particular word? Take a look at the words in bold print at the top of each page. These are the so-called **running heads** and they serve as a guide to tracing your word as quickly as possible. The running head on the top left gives you the first headword on the left-hand page, while the one on the top right gives you the last word on the right-hand page, e.g.

Gesundheit – Glanz

1.5 What about entries comprising hyphenated expressions or two or more words, such as **D-Zug, left-handed** or **mass media?** Expressions of this kind are treated in the same way as single words and thus appear in strict alphabetical order. Should you be unable to find a compound in the dictionary, just break it down into its components and look these up separately. In this way the meaning of many compound expressions can be derived indirectly.

2. Spelling

2.1 Where American and British spelling of a word differs, the American spelling is given first as in

center, *Br* **centre**
center (*Br* **centre) forward**
dialog, *Br* **dialogue**

or in the English-German section as a separate headword, e.g. **theater, defense** etc.

A 'u' or an 'l' in parentheses in a word also indicates variant spellings:

colo(u)red means: *American* **colored,** *British* **coloured**
travel(l)er means: *American* **traveler,** *British* **traveller**

2.2 Word division in a German word is possible after each syllable, e.g.

ein-hül-len, Zu-cker, ba-cken, tes-ten

In the English-German section the centered dots within a headword indicate syllabification breaks.

3. The different typefaces and their functions

3.1 **Bold type** is used for the German and English headwords and for Arabic numerals separating different parts of speech (nouns, transitive and intransitive verbs, adjectives and adverbs etc.) and different grammatical forms of a word:

bieten 1. *v/t* … **2.** *v/i* …
hängen 1. *v/i* (*irr, ge-, h*) hang (***an*** *dat* on…);
2. *v/t* (*ge-, h*) hang (***an*** *acc* on)
feed 1. Futter *n*; … **2.** *v/t* füttern

3.2 *Italics* are used for

a) grammatical and other abbreviations: *v/t, v/i, adj, adv, appr, fig* etc.
b) gender labels (masculine, feminine and neuter): *m, f, n*
c) grammatical references in brackets in the German-English section
d) any additional information preceding or following a translation (including dative or accusative objects):

knacken *v/t and v/i … twig*: snap; *fire, radio*: crackle
Etikett *n* … label (*a. fig*)
Gedanke *m* (*-n; -n*) …
geben (*irr, ge-, h*) …

befolgen ... follow, take (*advice*); observe (*rule etc*)
file ... *Briefe etc* ablegen
labored schwerfällig (*style etc*); mühsam (*breathing etc*)

3.3 ***Boldface italics*** are used for phraseology etc., notes on German grammar and prepositions taken by the headword:

Lage *f* ... ***in der Lage sein zu*** *inf* be able to *inf*
BLZ ... ABBR *of* ***Bankleitzahl***
abheben (*irr*, ***heben***, *sep*, *-ge-*, *h*)
abfahren ... (*irr*, ***fahren***, *sep*, *-ge-*, *sein*) leave, depart (*both*: ***nach*** for)
line ... ***hold the line*** TEL bleiben Sie am Apparat
agree ... sich einigen (***on*** über *acc*)

3.4 Normal type is used for translations of the headwords.

4. Pronunciation

When you have found the headword you are looking for in the German-English section, you will notice that very often this word is followed by certain symbols enclosed in square brackets. This is the phonetic transcription of the word, which tells you how it is pronounced. And one phonetic alphabet has come to be used internationally, namely that of the International Phonetic Association. This phonetic system is known by the abbreviation **IPA.** The symbols used in this dictionary are listed in the following tables on page 8 and 9.

4.1 The length of vowels is indicated by [ː] following the vowel symbol.

4.1.1 Stress is indicated by ['] or [ˌ] preceding the stressed syllable. ['] stands for strong stress, [ˌ] for weak stress:

Kabel ['kaːbəl] - **Kabine** [ka'biːnə]
'nachsehen – Be'sitz – be'sprechen
Jus'tizminisˌterium – Mi'nisterpräsiˌdent

4.1.2 The glottal stop [ʔ] is the forced stop between one word or syllable and a following one beginning with a vowel, as in

Analphabet [anʔalfa'beːt]
beeindrucken [bə'ʔaindrʊkən]

4.2 No transcription of compounds is given if the parts appear as separate entries. Each individual part should be looked up, as with

'**Blumenbeet** (= **Blume** and **Beet**)

4.2.1 If only part of the pronunciation changes or if a compound word consists of a new component, only the pronunciation of the changed or new part is given:

Demonstrant [demɔn'strant]
Demonstration [-stra'tsjoːn]
'**Kinderhort** [-hɔrt]

4.3 Guide to pronunciation for the German-English section

A. Vowels

[a] as in French *carte*: ***Mann*** [man]
[aː] as in *father*: ***Wagen*** ['vaːgən]
[e] as in *bed*: ***Tenor*** [te'noːɐ]
[eː] resembles the first sound in English [eɪ]: ***Weg*** [veːk]
[ə] unstressed e as in *ago*: ***Bitte*** ['bɪtə]
[ɛ] as in *fair*: ***männlich*** ['mɛnlɪç], ***Geld*** [gɛlt]
[ɛː] same sound but long: ***zählen*** ['tsɛːlən]
[ɪ] as in *it*: ***Wind*** [vɪnt]
[i] short, otherwise like [iː]: ***Kapital*** [kapi'taːl]
[iː] long, as in *meet*: ***Vieh*** [fiː]
[ɔ] as in *long*: ***Ort*** [ɔrt]
[o] as in *molest*: ***Moral*** [mo'raːl]
[oː] resembles the English sound in *go* [gəʊ] but without the [ʊ]: ***Boot*** [boːt]
[øː] as in French *feu*. The sound may be acquired by saying [e] through closely rounded lips: ***schön*** [ʃøːn]
[ø] same sound but short: ***ökumenisch*** [øku'meːnɪʃ]
[œ] as in French *neuf*. The sound resembles the English vowel in *her*. Lips, however, must be well rounded as for [ɒ]: ***öffnen*** ['œfnən]
[ʊ] as in *book*: ***Mutter*** ['mʊtɐ]
[u] short, otherwise like [uː]: ***Musik*** [mu'ziːk]
[uː] long, as in *boot*: ***Uhr*** [uːɐ]
[ʏ] short, opener than [yː]: ***Hütte*** ['hʏtə]
[y] almost like the French u as in *sur*. It may be acquired by saying [ɪ] through fairly closely rounded lips: ***Büro*** [by'roː]
[yː] same sound but long: ***führen*** ['fyːrən]

B. Diphthongs

[aɪ] as in like: ***Mai*** [maɪ]
[aʊ] as in *mouse*: ***Maus*** [maʊs]
[ɔʏ] as in *boy*: ***Beute*** ['bɔʏtə], ***Läufer*** ['lɔʏfɐ]

C. Consonants

[b] as in *better*: ***besser*** ['bɛsɐ]

[d] as in *dance*: ***du*** [duː]

[f] as in *find*: ***finden*** ['findən], ***Vater*** ['faːtɐ], ***Philosoph*** [filo'zoːf]

[g] as in *gold*: ***Gold*** [gɔlt]

[ʒ] as in *measure*: ***Genie*** [ʒe'niː]

[h] as in *house* but not aspirated: ***Haus*** [haʊs]

[ç] an approximation to this sound may be acquired by assuming the mouth-configuration for [ɪ] and emitting a strong current of breath: ***Licht*** [lɪçt], ***Mönch*** [mœnç], ***lustig*** ['lʊstɪç]

[x] as in Scottish *loch*. Whereas [ç] is pronounced at the front of the mouth, [x] is pronounced in the throat: ***Loch*** [lɔx]

[j] as in *year*: ***ja*** [jaː]

[k] as in *kick*: ***keck*** [kɛk], ***Tag*** [taːk], ***Chronik*** ['kroːnɪk], ***Café*** [ka'feː]

[l] as in *lump*. Pronounced like English initial „clear l": ***lassen*** ['lasən]

[m] as in *mouse*: ***Maus*** [maʊs]

[n] as in *not*: ***nein*** [naɪn]

[ŋ] as in *sing*, *drink*: ***singen*** ['zɪŋən], ***trinken*** ['trɪŋkən]

[p] as in *pass*: ***Pass*** [pas], ***Trieb*** [triːp], ***obgleich*** [ɔp'glaɪç]

[r] as in *rot*. There are two pronunciations: the frontal or lingual r: ***rot*** [roːt] and the uvular r [ɐ] (unknown in the English language): ***Mauer*** ['maʊɐ]

[s] as in *miss*. Unvoiced when final, doubled, or next a voiceless consonant: ***Glas*** [glaːs], ***Masse*** ['masə], ***Mast*** [mast], ***nass*** [nas]

[z] as in *zero*. S voiced when initial in a word or syllable: ***Sohn*** [zoːn], ***Rose*** ['roːzə]

[ʃ] as in *ship*: ***Schiff*** [ʃɪf], ***Charme*** [ʃarm̍], ***Spiel*** [ʃpiːl], ***Stein*** [ʃtaɪn]

[t] as in *tea*: ***Tee*** [teː], ***Thron*** [troːn], ***Stadt*** [ʃtat], ***Bad*** [baːt], ***Findling*** ['fɪntlɪŋ], ***Wind*** [vɪnt]

[v] as in *vast*: ***Vase*** ['vaːze], ***Winter*** ['vɪntɐ]

[ã, ɛ̃, õ] are nasalized vowels. Examples: ***Ensemble*** [ã'sãːbəl], ***Terrain*** [tɛ'rɛ̃ː], ***Bonbon*** [bõ'bõː]

4.3.1 Phonetic changes in plurals

singular		plural		example
-g	[-k]	-ge	[-gə]	Flug - Flüge
-d	[-t]	-de	[-də]	Grund - Gründe, Abend - Abende
-b	[-p]	-be	[-bə]	Stab - Stäbe
-s	[-s]	-se	[-zə]	Los - Lose
-ch	[-x]	-che	[-çə]	Bach - Bäche
-iv	[-iːf]	-ive	[-iːvə]	Stativ - Stative

4.3.2 The German alphabet

a [aː], b [beː], c [tseː], d [deː], e [eː], f [ɛf], g [geː], h [haː], i [iː], j [jɔt], k [kaː], l [ɛl], m [ɛm], n [ɛn], o [oː], p [peː], q [kuː], r [ɛr], s [ɛs], t [teː], u [uː], v [fau], w [veː], x [ɪks], y ['ʏpsilɔn], z [tsɛt]

4.3.3 List of suffixes

The German suffixes are not transcribed unless they are parts of headwords.

-bar	[-baːɐ]	-isch	[-ɪʃ]
-chen	[-çən]	-ist	[-ɪst]
-d	[-t]	-keit	[-kaɪt]
-de	[-də]	-lich	[-lɪç]
-ei	[-aɪ]	-ling	[-lɪŋ]
-en	[-ən]	-losigkeit	[-loːzɪçkaɪt]
-end	[-ənt]	-nis	[-nɪs]
-er	[-ɐ]	-sal	[-zaːl]
-haft	[-haft]	-sam	[-zaːm]
-heit	[-haɪt]	-schaft	[-ʃaft]
-icht	[-ɪçt]	-sieren	[-ziːrən]
-ie	[-iː]	-ste	[-stə]
-ieren	[-iːrən]	-tät	[-tɛːt]
-ig	[-ɪç]	-tum	[-tuːm]
-ik	[-ɪk]	-ung	[-ʊŋ]
-in	[-ɪn]	-ungs-	[-ʊŋs-]
		-wärts	[-vɛrts]

5. Abbreviations of grammatical terms and subject areas are designed to help the user choose the appropriate headword or translation of a word.

In the dictionary words which are predominantly used in British English are marked by the abbreviation *Br*:

Bürgersteig *m* sidewalk, *Br* pavement
girl guide *Br* Pfadfinderin *f*

List of abbreviations

a.	*also*, auch
ABBR	*abbreviation*, Abkürzung
acc	*accusative (case)*, Akkusativ
adj	*adjective*, Adjektiv
adv	*adverb*, Adverb
AGR	*agriculture*, Landwirtschaft
Am	*American English*, amerikanisches Englisch
ANAT	*anatomy*, Anatomie
appr	*approximately*, etwa
ARCH	*architecture*, Architektur
art	*article*, Artikel
ASTR	*astrology*, Astrologie; *astronomy*, Astronomie
attr	*attributively* , attributiv
AVIAT	*aviation*, Luftfahrt
BIOL	*biology*, Biologie
BOT	*botany*, Botanik
Br	*British English*, britisches Englisch
CHEM	*chemistry*, Chemie
cj	*conjunction*, Konjunktion
coll	*collectively*, als Sammelwort
comp	*comparative*, Komparativ
contp	*contemptuously*, verächtlich
cpds	*compounds*, Zusammensetzungen
dat	*dative (case)*, Dativ
ECON	*economy*, Wirtschaft
EDP	*electronic data processing*, Elektronische Datenverarbeitung
e-e	*a(n)*, eine
e.g.	*for example*, zum Beispiel
ELECTR	*electrical engineering*, Elektrotechnik
e-m	*einem*, to a(n)
e-n	*einen*, a(n)
e-r	*einer*, of a(n), to a(n)
e-s	*eines*, of a(n)
esp.	*especially*, besonders
et., *et.*	etwas, *something*
etc	*et cetera, and so on*, usw., und so weiter

F *colloquial*, umgangssprachlich
f *feminine*, weiblich
fig *figuratively*, übertragen

GASTR *gastronomy*, Kochkunst
gen *genitive* (*case*), Genitiv
GEOGR *geography*, Geografie
GEOL *geology*, Geologie
ger *gerund*, Gerundium
GR *grammar*, Grammatik

h *haben*, have
HIST *history*, Geschichte
HUMOR *humorous*, humorvoll

impers *impersonal*, unpersönlich
indef *indefinite*, unbestimmt
inf *infinitive* (*mood*), Infinitiv
int *interjection*, Interjektion
interr *interrogative*, fragend
irr *irregular*, unregelmäßig

j-m *jemandem*, to someone
j-n *jemanden*, someone
j-s *jemandes*, someone's
JUR *jurisprudence*, Recht

LING *linguistics*, Sprachwissenschaft
LIT *literary*, nur in der Schriftsprache vorkommend

m *masculine*, männlich
MAR *maritime term*, Schifffahrt
MATH *mathematics*, Mathematik
m-e *my*, meine
MED *medicine*, Medizin
METEOR *meteorology*, Meteorologie
MIL *military term*, militärisch
MOT *motoring*, Kraftfahrwesen
m-r *meiner*, of my, to my
mst *mostly* , *usually*, meistens
MUS *music*, Musik

n *neuter*, sächlich
neg! *negative*, *usually considered offensive*, kann als beleidigend empfunden werden
nom *nominative* (*case*), Nominativ
num *numeral*, Zahlwort

OPT *optics*, Optik
O.S., *o.s.* *oneself*, sich

PAINT *painting*, Malerei
PARL *parliamentary term*, parlamentarischer Ausdruck
pass *passive voice*, Passiv
PED *pedagogy*, Schulwesen
pers *personal*, persönlich
PHARM *pharmacy*, Pharmazie
PHIL *philosophy*, Philosophie
PHOT *photography*, Fotografie
PHYS *physics*, Physik
pl *plural*, Plural
POET *poetry*, Dichtung
POL *politics*, Politik
poss *possessive*, besitzanzeigend
POST *post and telecommunications*, Postwesen
pp *past participle*, Partizip Perfekt
pred *predicative*, prädikativ
pres *present*, Präsens
pres p *present participle*, Partizip Präsens
pret *preterit*(*e*), Präteritum
PRINT *printing*, Druckwesen
pron *pronoun*, Pronomen
prp *preposition*, Präposition
PSYCH *psychology*, Psychologie

RAIL *railroad*, *railway*, Eisenbahn
refl *reflexive*, reflexiv
REL *religion*, Religion
RHET *rhetoric*, Rhetorik

s-e *seine*, his, one's
sep *separable*, abtrennbar
sg *singular*, Singular
sl *slang*, Slang
s-m *seinem*, to his, to one's
s-n *seinen*, his, one's
s.o., *s.o.* *someone*, jemand(en)
SPORT *sports*, Sport
s-r *seiner*, of his, of one's, to his, to one's
s-s *seines*, of his, of one's
s.th., *s.th.* *something*, etwas
su *substantive*, Substantiv
subj *subjunctive* (*mood*), Konjunktiv
sup *superlative*, Superlativ

TECH *technology*, Technik
TEL *telegraphy*, Telegrafie; *telephony*, Fernsprechwesen
THEA *theater*, Theater
TV *television*, Fernsehen

u., *u.* *und*, and
UNIV *university*, Hochschulwesen, Studentensprache

V *vulgar*, vulgär, unanständig
v/aux *auxiliary verb*, Hilfsverb
vb *verb*, Verb
VET *veterinary medicine*, Veterinärmedizin, Tiermedizin
v/i *intransitive verb*, intransitives Verb
v/refl *reflexive verb*, reflexives Verb
v/t *transitive verb*, transitives Verb

ZO *zoology*, Zoologie

→ *see*, *refer to*, siehe

® *registered trademark*, eingetragene Marke

6. Translations and phraseology

After the boldface headword in the German-English section, the phonetic transcription of this word, its part of speech label, and its grammar, we finally come to the most important part of the entry: **the translation(s).**

6.1 It is quite rare for a headword to be given just one translation. Usually a word will have several related translations, which are separated by a **comma.**

6.2 Different senses of a word are indicated by

a) **semicolons:**

Fest ... celebration; party; REL festival
balance ... Waage *f*; Gleichgewicht *n*

b) italics for **definitions:**

Läufer ... runner (*a . carpet*); *chess*: bishop
call ... Berufung *f* (***to*** in *ein Amt*; auf *einen Lehrstuhl*)
cake ... Tafel *f Schokolade*, Stück *n Seife*

c) **abbreviations** of subject areas:

Bug *m* ... MAR bow; AVIAT nose
Gespräch *n* talk (*a.* POL); ... TEL call
daisy BOT Gänseblümchen *n*
duck ... ZO Ente *f*

6.2.1 Where a word has fundamentally different meanings, it very often appears as two or more separate entries distinguished by **exponents** or raised figures:

betreten[1] *v/t* ... step on; enter
betreten[2] *adj* embarrassed
Bauer[1] *m* ... farmer
Bauer[2] *n, m* ... (bird)cage
chap[1] ... Riss *m*
chap[2] ... *Br* F Bursche *m*

This does not apply to senses which have directly evolved from the primary meaning of the word.

6.3 When a headword can be several different parts of speech, these are distinguished by boldface **Arabic numerals** (see also the section on p.6, paragraph 3.1 concerning the different typefaces):

geräuschlos **1.** *adj* noiseless (*adjective*)
2. without a sound (*adverb*)

work **1.** Arbeit *f* (*noun*)
2. *v/i* arbeiten (*verb*)

green **1.** grün (*adjective*)
2. Grün *n* (*noun*)

6.3.1 In the German-English section boldface Arabic numerals are also used to distinguish between transitive, intransitive and reflexive verbs (if this affects their translation) and to show that where there is a change of meaning a verb may be differently conjugated:

> **fahren** *(irr, ge-)* **1.** *v/i (sein)* go; *bus etc*: run; … **2.** *v/t (h)* drive *(car etc)* …

If grammatical indications come before the subdivision they refer to all translations that follow:

> **bauen** *(ge-, h)* **1.** *v/t* build …; **2.** *fig v/i*: ***bauen auf*** …

6.3.2 Boldface Arabic numerals are also used to indicate the different meanings of nouns which can occur in more than one gender and to show that where there is a change of meaning a noun may be differently inflected:

> **Halfter 1.** *m, n (-s; -)* halter; **2.** *n (-s; -), f (-; -n)* holster

6.4 Illustrative phrases in boldface italics are generally given within the respective categories of the dictionary article:

> **baden 1.** *v/i* … ***baden gehen*** go swimming; **2.** *v/t* …
> **good 1.** … ***real good*** F echt gut (= *adjective*); **2.** … ***for good*** für immer (= *noun*)

7. Grammatical references

Knowing what to do with the grammatical information available in the dictionary will enable the user to get the most out of this dictionary.

7.1 Verbs (see the list of irregular German verbs on page 662).

Verbs have been treated in the following ways:

a) **bändigen** *v/t (ge-, h)*

The past participle of this word is formed by means of the prefix *ge-* and the auxiliary verb *haben*: ***er hat gebändigt.***

b) **abfassen** *v/t (sep, -ge-, h)*

In conjugation the prefix *ab* must be separated from the primary verb *fassen*: ***sie fasst ab; sie hat abgefasst.***

c) **finden** *v/t (irr, ge-, h)*

irr following a verb means that it is an irregular verb. The principal parts of this particular word can be found as an individual headword in the main part of the German-English section and in the list of irregular German verbs on page 662: ***sie fand; sie hat gefunden.***

d) **abfallen** *v/i (irr,* ***fallen****, sep, -ge-, sein)*

A reference such as *irr*, ***fallen*** indicates that the compound word ***abfallen*** is conjugated in exactly the same way as the primary verb ***fallen*** as given in the list of irregular German verbs on page 662: ***er fiel ab; er ist abgefallen.***

e) **senden** *v/t* ([*irr*,] *ge-*, *h*)

The square brackets indicate that ***senden*** can be treated as a regular or an irregular verb: ***sie sandte*** or ***sie sendete***; ***sie hat gesandt*** or ***sie hat gesendet.***

7.2 Nouns

The inflectional forms (*genitive singular*; *nominative plural*) follow immediately after the indication of gender. No forms are given for compounds if the parts appear as separate headwords.

The horizontal stroke replaces the part of the word which remains unchanged in the inflection:

Affäre *f* (-; *-n*)
Keks *m*, *n* (*-es*; *-e*)
Bau *m* (-[*e*]*s*; *Bauten*)
Blatt *n* (-[*e*]*s*; *Blätter* ['blɛtɐ])

The inflectional forms of German nouns ending in ***-in*** are given in the following ways:

Ärztin *f* (-; *-nen*)
Chemiker(in) (*-s*; *-/-*; *-nen*) = **Chemiker** *m* (*-s*; -) and **Chemikerin** *f* (-; *-nen*)

7.3 Prepositions

If, for instance, a headword (verb, adjective or noun) is governed by certain prepositions, these are given in boldface italics and in brackets together with their English or German translations and placed next to the appropriate translation. If the German or English preposition is the same for all or several translations, it is given only once before or after the first translation and then also applies to the translations which follow it:

abrücken ... **1.** *v/t* (*h*) move away (***von*** from)
befestigen *v/t* (*no -ge-*, *h*) fasten (***an*** *dat* to), fix (to), attach (to)
dissent ... **2.** anderer Meinung sein (***from*** als)
dissimilar (***to***) unähnlich (*dat*); verschieden (von)

With German prepositions which can take the dative or the accusative, the case is given in brackets:

fürchten ... ***sich fürchten*** ... be afraid (***vor*** *dat* of)
bauen ... ***bauen auf*** (*acc*) rely *or* count on

We hope that this somewhat lengthy introduction has shown you that this dictionary contains a great deal more than simple one-to-one translations, and that you are now well-equipped to make the most of all it has to offer.

A

à [a] *prp* **5 Karten à Euro 20** 5 tickets at 20 euros each *or* a piece
Aal [aːl] *m* (-[*e*]*s*; -*e*) zo eel
aalen ['aːlən] *v/refl* (*ge-*, *h*) **sich in der Sonne aalen** bask in the sun
'aal'glatt *fig adj* (as) slippery as an eel
Aas [aːs] *n* (-[*e*]*s*) a) *no pl* carrion, b) F *contp pl* **Äser** beast, *sl* bastard
'Aasgeier *m* zo vulture (*a. fig*)
ab [ap] *prp and adv*: **München ab 13.55** departure from Munich (at) 1.55; **ab 7 Uhr** from 7 o'clock (on); **ab morgen** (**1. März**) starting tomorrow (March 1st); **von jetzt ab** from now on; **ab und zu** now and then; **ein Film ab 18** an X(-rated) film; **ein Knopf ist ab** a button has come off
'abarbeiten *v/t* (*sep*, *-ge-*, *h*) work out *or* off (*debts*); **sich abarbeiten** wear o.s. out
Abart ['apʔart] *f* (-; *en*) variety
abartig ['apʔartɪç] *adj* abnormal
Abb. ABBR *of* **Abbildung** fig., illustration
'Abbau *m* (-[*e*]*s*; *no pl*) mining; TECH dismantling; *fig* overcoming (*of prejudices etc*); reduction (*of expenditure, staff etc*)
'abbauen *v/t* (*sep*, *-ge-*, *h*) mine; TECH dismantle; *fig* overcome (*prejudices etc*); reduce (*expenditure, staff etc*); **sich abbauen** BIOL break down
'abbeißen *v/t* (*irr*, **beißen**, *sep*, *-ge-*, *h*) bite off
'abbeizen *v/t* (*sep*, *-ge-*, *h*) remove *old paint etc* with corrosives
'abbekommen *v/t* (*irr*, **kommen**, *sep*, *no -ge-*, *h*) get off; **s-n Teil** *or* **et. abbekommen** get one's share; **et. abbekommen** *fig* get hurt, get damaged
'abberufen *v/t* (*irr*, **rufen**, *sep*, *no -ge-*, *h*), **'Abberufung** *f* recall
'abbestellen *v/t* (*sep*, *no -ge-*, *h*) cancel one's subscription (*or* order) for
'Abbestellung *f* cancellation
'abbiegen *v/i* (*irr*, **biegen**, *sep*, *-ge-*, *sein*) turn (off); **nach rechts** (**links**) **abbiegen** turn right (left)
'abbilden *v/t* (*sep*, *-ge-*, *h*) show, depict
'Abbildung *f* (-; *-en*) picture, illustration
'Abbitte *f* apology; **j-m Abbitte leisten wegen** apologize to s.o. for
'abblasen F *v/t* (*irr*, **blasen**, *sep*, *-ge-*, *h*) call off, cancel
'abblättern *v/i* (*sep*, *-ge-*, *sein*) *paint etc*: flake off
'abblenden 1. *v/t* (*sep*, *-ge-*, *h*) dim; **2.** *v/i* MOT dim (*Br* dip) the headlights
'Abblendlicht *n* MOT dimmed (*Br* dipped) headlights *pl*, low beam
'abbrechen *v/t* (*irr*, **brechen**, *sep*, *-ge-*) **1.** *v/t* (*h*) break off (*a. fig*); pull down, demolish (*building etc*); strike (*camp, tent*); **2.** *v/i* a) (*sein*) break off, b) (*h*) *fig* stop
'abbremsen *v/t* (*sep*, *-ge-*, *h*) slow down
'abbrennen *v/t* (*irr*, **brennen**, *sep*, *-ge-*) **1.** *v/i* (*sein*) burn down; **2.** *v/t* (*h*) burn down (*building etc*); let *or* set off (*fireworks*)
'abbringen *v/t* (*irr*, **bringen**, *sep*, *-ge-*, *h*) **j-n von e-r Sache abbringen** talk s.o. out of (doing) s.th.; **j-n vom Thema abbringen** get s.o. off a subject
'Abbruch *m* (-[*e*]*s*; *no pl*) breaking off; demolition
'abbruchreif *adj* derelict, due for demolition
'abbuchen *v/t* (*sep*, *-ge-*, *h*) debit (**von** to)
'Abbuchung *f* debit
'abbürsten *v/t* (*sep*, *-ge-*, *h*) brush off (*dust etc*); brush (*coat etc*)
Abc [aːbeːˈtseː] *n* (-; *no pl*) ABC, alphabet
ABC-Waffen *pl* MIL nuclear, biological and chemical weapons
'abdanken *v/i* (*sep*, *-ge-*, *h*) resign; *king etc*: abdicate
'Abdankung *f* (-; *-en*) resignation; abdication
'abdecken *v/t* (*sep*, *-ge-*, *h*) uncover; untile (*roof*); unroof (*house*); clear (*the table*); ECON cover (up)
'abdichten *v/t* (*sep*, *-ge-*, *h*) TECH seal
'abdrängen *v/t* (*sep*, *-ge-*, *h*) push aside
'abdrehen 1. *v/t* (*sep*, *-ge-*, *h*) turn *or* switch off (*light, water etc*); **2.** *v/i* (*a. sein*) *ship, plane*: change one's course
'Abdruck *m* print, mark
'abdrucken *v/t* (*sep*, *-ge-*, *h*) print
'abdrücken (*sep*, *-ge-*, *h*) **1.** *v/t* fire (*gun*); **2.** *v/i* pull the trigger
Abend ['aːbənt] *m* (*-s*; *-e*) evening; **am Abend** in the evening, at night; **heute Abend** tonight; **morgen** (**gestern**) **Abend** tomorrow (last) night; → **bunt**, **essen**
Abendbrot *n* (-[*e*]*s*; *no pl*), **Abendessen** *n* supper, dinner, *Br a.* high tea
Abendkasse *f* THEA *etc* box office
Abendkleid *n* evening dress *or* gown
Abendkurs *m* evening classes *pl*
'Abendland *n* (-[*e*]*s*; *no pl*) West, Occi-

dent
'abendländisch [-lɛndɪʃ] *adj* Western, Occidental
'Abendmahl *n* (-[e]s; *no pl*) *the* (Holy) Communion, *the* Lord's Supper; ***das Abendmahl empfangen*** receive Communion
abends ['a:bənts] *adv* in the evening, at night; ***dienstags abends*** (on) Tuesday evenings
'Abendschule *f* evening classes *pl*, night school
Abenteuer ['a:bəntɔʏɐ] *n* (-*s*; -) adventure (*a. in cpds …ferien, …spielplatz*)
'abenteuerlich *adj* adventurous; *fig* risky; fantastic
Abenteurer ['a:bəntɔʏrɐ] *m* (-*s*; -) adventurer
'Abenteurerin [-rərɪn] *f* (-; -*nen*) adventuress
aber ['a:bɐ] *cj and adv* but; ***oder aber*** or else; ***aber, aber!*** now then!; ***aber nein!*** not at all!
'Aberglaube *m* superstition
abergläubisch ['a:bɐglɔʏbɪʃ] *adj* superstitious
'aberkennen *v/t* (*irr*, ***kennen***, *sep*, *no -ge-*, *h*) ***j-m et. aberkennen*** deprive s.o. of s.th. (*a.* JUR)
'Aberkennung *f* (-; -*en*) deprivation (*a.* JUR)
abermalig ['a:bɐma:lɪç] *adj* repeated
abermals ['a:bɐma:ls] *adv* once more *or* again
'aber'tausend *adj*: ***tausende und abertausende*** thousands upon thousands
'abfahren (*irr*, ***fahren***, *sep*, *-ge-*) **1.** *v/i* (*sein*) leave, depart (*both*: ***nach*** for); F (***voll***) ***abfahren auf*** (*acc*) really go for; **2.** *v/t* (*h*) carry *or* cart away
'Abfahrt *f* departure (***nach*** for), start (for); *skiing*: descent
'Abfahrtslauf *m* downhill skiing (*or* race)
Abfahrtszeit *f* (time of) departure
'Abfall *m* waste, refuse, garbage, trash, *Br a.* rubbish
Abfallbeseitigung *f* waste disposal
Abfalleimer *m* → ***Mülleimer***
'abfallen *v/i* (*irr*, ***fallen***, *sep*, *-ge-*, *sein*) fall (off); *terrain*: slope (down); *fig* fall away (***von*** from); *esp* POL secede (from); ***vom Glauben abfallen*** renounce one's faith; ***abfallen gegen*** compare badly with
'abfällig **1.** *adj* derogatory; **2.** *adv*: ***abfällig von j-m sprechen*** run s.o. down
'Abfallpro,dukt *n* waste product
'abfälschen *v/t* (*sep*, *-ge-*, *h*) SPORT deflect
'abfangen *v/t* (*irr*, ***fangen***, *sep*, *-ge-*, *h*) catch, intercept; MOT, AVIAT right
'abfärben *v/i* (*sep*, *-ge-*, *h*) *color etc*: run, *material*: *a.* bleed; *fig* ***abfärben auf*** (*acc*) rub off on
'abfassen *v/t* (*sep*, *-ge-*, *h*) compose, word, write
'abfertigen *v/t* (*sep*, *-ge-*, *h*) dispatch; *customs*: clear; serve (*customers*); check in (*passengers etc*); ***j-n kurz abfertigen*** be short with s.o.
'Abfertigung *f* dispatch; clearance; check-in
'abfeuern *v/t* (*sep*, *-ge-*, *h*) fire (off); launch (*rocket*)
'abfinden *v/t* (*irr*, ***finden***, *sep*, *-ge-*, *h*) ECON pay off (*creditor*); buy out (*partner*); compensate; ***sich mit e-r Sache abfinden*** put up with s.th.
'Abfindung *f* (-; -*en*) ECON satisfaction; compensation
'abflachen *v/t and v/refl* (*sep*, *-ge-*, *h*) flatten
'abflauen *v/i* (*sep*, *-ge-*, *sein*) *wind etc*: drop (*a. fig*)
'abfliegen *v/i* (*irr*, ***fliegen***, *sep*, *-ge-*, *sein*) AVIAT leave, depart
'abfließen *v/i* (*irr*, ***fließen***, *sep*, *-ge-*, *sein*) flow off, drain (off *or* away)
'Abflug *m* AVIAT departure
'Abfluss *m* (-*es*; *Abflüsse*) a) *no pl* flowing off, b) TECH drain
'Abflussrohr *n* wastepipe, drain(pipe)
'abfragen *v/t* (*sep*, *-ge-*, *h*) quiz *or* question *s.o.* (***über*** *acc* about), test *s.o.* orally
Abfuhr ['apfu:ɐ] *f* (-; -*en*) removal; ***j-m e-e Abfuhr erteilen*** rebuff (F SPORT lick) s.o.
'abführen (*sep*, *-ge-*, *h*) **1.** *v/t* lead *or* take away; ECON pay (over) (***an*** *acc* to); **2.** *v/i* MED move one's bowels; act as a laxative
'abführend *adj*, **'Abführmittel** *n* MED laxative
'abfüllen *v/t* (*sep*, *-ge-*, *h*) bottle; can
'Abgabe *f* (-; -*n*) a) *no pl* handing in, b) SPORT pass, c) ECON rate; duty
'abgabenfrei *adj* tax-free
'abgabenpflichtig *adj* dutiable
'Abgang *m* (-[e]*s*; *Abgänge*) a) *no pl* departure; *Am* graduation, *Br* school-leaving; THEA exit (*a. fig*), b) SPORT dismount
Abgänger ['apgɛŋɐ] *m* (-*s*; -) *Am* graduate, *Br* school-leaver
'Abgas *n* waste gas; *pl* emission(s *pl*); MOT exhaust fumes *pl*
'abgasfrei *adj* emission-free
'Abgasuntersuchung *f* MOT *Am* emissions test, *Br* exhaust emission test
'abgearbeitet *adj* worn out
'abgeben *v/t* (*irr*, ***geben***, *sep*, *-ge-*, *h*) leave (***bei*** with); hand in; deposit (*one's baggage etc*), hand over (*ticket etc*) (***an***

acc to); cast (*vote*); pass (*ball*); *give* off, emit (*heat etc*); make (*offer, statement etc*); ***j-m et. abgeben von*** share s.th. with s.o.; ***sich abgeben mit*** concern o.s. with *s.th.*, associate with *s.o.*

'**abgebrannt** *adj* burnt down; F *fig* broke

abgebrüht *fig adj* hard-boiled

abgedroschen *adj* hackneyed

abgefahren *adj tires*: worn out

abgegriffen *adj* worn

abgehackt *fig adj* disjointed

abgehangen *adj*: ***gut abgehangenes Fleisch*** well-hung meat

abgehärtet *adj* hardened (***gegen*** to)

'**abgehen** *v/i* (*irr*, ***gehen***, *sep*, *-ge-*, *sein*) *train etc*: leave; *mail, goods*: get off; THEA go off (stage); *button etc*: come off; *path etc*: branch off; ***von der Schule abgehen*** leave school; ***abgehen von*** drop (*plan etc*); ***von s-r Meinung abgehen*** change one's mind *or* opinion; ***ihm geht ... ab*** he lacks ...; ***gut abgehen*** end well, pass off well

'**abgehetzt**, **abgekämpft** *adj* exhausted, worn out

abgekartet ['apgəkartət] F *adj*: ***abgekartete Sache*** put-up job

abgelegen *adj* remote, distant

abgemacht *adj* fixed; ***abgemacht!*** it's a deal!

abgemagert *adj* emaciated

abgeneigt *adj*: ***e-r Sache abgeneigt sein*** be averse to s.th.; ***ich wäre nicht abgeneigt, et. zu tun*** I wouldn't mind doing s.th.

abgenutzt *adj* worn out

Abgeordnete ['apgəʔɔrdnətə] *m, f* (*-n; -n*) *Am* representative, congress|man (-woman), *Br* Member of Parliament (ABBR MP)

'**Abgeordnetenhaus** *n Am* House of Representatives, *Br* House of Commons

'**abgepackt** *adj* prepack(ag)ed

'**abgeschieden** *adj* secluded

'**Abgeschiedenheit** *f* (*-; no pl*) seclusion

'**abgeschlossen** *adj* completed; ***abgeschlossene Wohnung*** self-contained apartment (*Br* flat)

abgesehen *adj*: ***abgesehen von*** aside (*Br a.* apart) from; ***ganz abgesehen von*** not to mention, let alone

abgespannt *adj* exhausted, weary

abgestanden *adj* stale

abgestorben *adj* dead (*tree etc*); numb (*leg etc*)

abgestumpft *adj* insensitive, indifferent (***gegen*** to)

abgetragen, **abgewetzt** *adj* worn out; threadbare, shabby

abgewöhnen *v/t* (*sep*, *-ge-*, *h*) ***j-m et. abgewöhnen*** make s.o. give up s.th.; ***sich*** (*dat*) ***das Rauchen abgewöhnen*** stop *or* give up smoking

'**Abgott** *m* idol (*a. fig*)

abgöttisch ['apgœtɪʃ] *adv*: ***j-n abgöttisch lieben*** idolize s.o.

'**abgrasen** *v/t* (*sep*, *-ge-*, *h*) graze; *fig* scour

'**abgrenzen** *v/t* (*sep*, *-ge-*, *h*) mark off; delimit (***gegen*** from)

'**Abgrund** *m* abyss, chasm, gulf (*all a. fig*); ***am Rande des Abgrunds*** *fig* on the brink of disaster

'**abgrund'tief** *adj* abysmal

'**abgucken** F *v/t* (*sep*, *-ge-*, *h*) ***j-m et. abgucken*** learn s.th. from (watching) s.o.; → ***abschreiben***

'**Abguss** *m* cast

'**abhaben** F *v/t* (*irr*, ***haben***, *sep*, *-ge-*, *h*) ***willst du et. abhaben?*** do you want some (of it)? '**abhacken** *v/t* (*sep*, *-ge-*, *h*) chop *or* cut off

'**abhaken** *v/t* (*sep*, *-ge-*, *h*) check (*Br* tick) off; F forget

'**abhalten** *v/t* (*irr*, ***halten***, *sep*, *-ge-*, *h*) hold (*meeting etc*); ***j-n von der Arbeit abhalten*** keep s.o. from his work; ***j-n davon abhalten, et. zu tun*** keep s.o. from doing s.th.

'**abhandeln** *v/t* (*sep*, *-ge-*, *h*) treat (*subject etc*); ***j-m et. abhandeln*** make a deal with s.o. for s.th.

'**Abhandlung** *f* treatise (***über*** *acc* on)

'**Abhang** *m* slope

'**abhängen**[1] *v/t* (*sep*, *-ge-*, *h*) take down (*picture etc*); RAIL *etc* uncouple; F shake *s.o.* off

'**abhängen**[2] *v/i* (*irr*, ***hängen***, *sep*, *-ge-*, *h*) ***abhängen von*** depend on; ***das hängt davon ab*** that depends

abhängig ['aphɛŋɪç] *adj*: ***abhängig von*** dependent on; *a.* addicted to *drugs etc*

'**Abhängigkeit** *f* (*-; -en*) dependence (***von*** on); addiction (to)

'**abhärten** *v/t* (*sep*, *-ge-*, *h*) ***sich abhärten*** harden o.s. (***gegen*** to)

'**abhauen** (*irr*, ***hauen***, *sep*, *-ge-*) **1.** *v/t* (*h*) cut *or* chop off; **2.** F *v/i* (*sein*) make off (***mit*** with), run away (with); ***hau ab!*** beat it!, scram!

'**abheben** (*irr*, ***heben***, *sep*, *-ge-*, *h*) **1.** *v/t* lift *or* take off; pick up (*receiver*); (with)draw (*money*); cut (*cards*); ***sich abheben*** stand out (***von*** among, from), *fig a.* contrast with; **2.** *v/i* cut the cards; answer the phone; *plane*: take (*esp rocket*: lift) off

'**abheften** *v/t* (*sep*, *-ge-*, *h*) file

'**abheilen** *v/i* (*sep*, *-ge-*, *sein*) heal (up)

'**abhetzen** *v/refl* (*sep*, *-ge-*, *h*) wear o.s. out

'**Abhilfe** *f* remedy; ***Abhilfe schaffen*** take remedial measures
'**Abholdienst** *m* pickup service
'**abholen** *v/t (sep, -ge-, h)* pick up, collect; ***j-n von der Bahn abholen*** meet s.o. at the station
'**abholzen** *v/t (sep, -ge-, h)* fell, cut down *(trees)*; deforest *(area)*
'**abhorchen** *v/t (sep, -ge-, h)* MED auscultate, sound
'**abhören** *v/t (sep, -ge-, h)* listen in on, tap *(telephone conversation)*, F bug; → ***abfragen***
'**Abhörgerät** *n* bugging device, F bug
Abitur [abi'tuːɐ] *n (-s; -e)* school-leaving examination (qualifying for university entrance)
'**abjagen** *v/t (sep, -ge-, h)* ***j-m et. abjagen*** recover s.th. from s.o.
'**abkanzeln** F *v/t (sep, -ge-, h)* tell *s.o.* off
'**abkaufen** *v/t (sep, -ge-, h)* ***j-m et. abkaufen*** buy s.th. from s.o.
Abkehr ['apkeːɐ] *f (-; no pl)* break (***von*** with)
'**abkehren** *v/refl (sep, -ge-, h)* ***sich abkehren von*** turn away from
'**abklingen** *v/i (irr,* ***klingen****, sep, -ge-, sein)* fade away; *pain etc*: ease off
'**abklopfen** *v/t (sep, -ge-, h)* MED sound
'**abknallen** F *v/t (sep, -ge-, h)* pick off
'**abknicken** *v/t (sep, -ge-, h)* snap *or* break off; bend
'**abkochen** *v/t (sep, -ge-, h)* boil
'**abkomman,dieren** *v/t (sep, no -ge-, h)* MIL detach (***zu*** for)
'**abkommen** *v/i (irr,* ***kommen****, sep, -ge-, sein)* ***abkommen von*** get off; drop *(plan etc)*; ***vom Thema abkommen*** stray from the point; → ***Weg***
'**Abkommen** *n (-s; -)* agreement, treaty; ***ein Abkommen schließen*** make an agreement
Abkömmling ['apkœmlɪŋ] *m (-s; -e)* descendant
'**abkoppeln** *v/t (sep, -ge-, h)* uncouple (***von*** from); undock *(spacecraft)*
'**abkratzen** *(sep, -ge-)* **1.** *v/t (h)* scrape off; **2.** F *v/i (sein)* kick the bucket
'**abkühlen** *v/t and v/refl (sep, -ge-, h)* cool down *(a. fig)*
'**Abkühlung** *f* cooling
'**abkürzen** *v/t (sep, -ge-, h)* shorten; abbreviate; ***den Weg abkürzen*** take a short cut
'**Abkürzung** *f* abbreviation; short cut
'**abladen** *v/t (irr,* ***laden****, sep, -ge-, h)* unload; dump *(waste etc)*
'**Ablage** *f (-; -n)* a) *no pl* filing, b) filing tray, c) *Swiss* → ***Zweigstelle***
'**ablagern** *(sep, -ge-, h)* **1.** *v/t* season *(wood)*; let *wine* age; GEOL *etc* deposit; ***sich ablagern*** settle, be deposited; **2.** *v/i (a. sein)* season; age
'**Ablagerung** *f (-; -en)* CHEM, GEOL deposit, sediment
'**ablassen** *(irr,* ***lassen****, sep, -ge-, h)* **1.** *v/t* drain off *(liquid)*; let off *(steam)*; drain *(pond etc)*; **2.** *v/i*: ***von et. (j-m) ablassen*** stop doing s.th. (leave s.o. alone)
'**Ablauf** *m (-[e]s; Abläufe)* a) course; process; order of events, b) *no pl* expiration, *Br* expiry, c) → ***Abfluss***
'**ablaufen** *(irr,* ***laufen****, sep, -ge-)* **1.** *v/i (sein) water etc*: run off; *performance etc*: go, proceed; come to an end; *period, passport etc*: expire; *time, record, tape*: run out; *clock*: run down; ***gut ablaufen*** turn out well; **2.** *v/t (h)* wear down
'**ablecken** *v/t (sep, -ge-, h)* lick (off)
'**ablegen** *(sep, -ge-, h)* **1.** *v/t* take off *(clothes)*; file *(letters etc)*; give up *(habit etc)*; take *(examination, oath)*; ***abgelegte Kleider*** cast-offs *pl*; **2.** *v/i* take off one's (hat and) coat; MAR put out, sail
'**Ableger** *m (-s; -)* BOT layer; offshoot *(a. fig)*
'**ablehnen** *v/t (sep, -ge-, h)* refuse; turn down *(application etc)*; PARL reject; object to; condemn
ablehnend *adj* negative
'**Ablehnung** *f (-; -en)* refusal; rejection; objection *(gen* to)
'**ableiten** *v/t (sep, -ge-, h)* divert; LING, MATH derive (***aus*** *dat*, ***von*** from) *(a. fig)*
'**Ableitung** *f* diversion; LING, MATH derivation *(a. fig)*
'**ablenken** *v/t (sep, -ge-, h)* divert (***von*** from); *soccer*: turn away *(ball)*; deflect *(rays etc)*; ***j-n von der Arbeit ablenken*** distract s.o. from his work; ***er lässt sich leicht ablenken*** he is easily diverted
'**Ablenkung** *f* diversion
'**ablesen** *v/t (irr,* ***lesen****, sep, -ge-, h)* read
'**abliefern** *v/t (sep, -ge-, h)* deliver (***bei*** to, at); hand over (to)
'**ablösbar** *adj* detachable
'**ablösen** *v/t (sep, -ge-, h)* detach; take off; take *s.o.'s* place, take over from *s.o.*; *esp* MIL relieve; replace; ***sich ablösen*** take turns *(driving etc)*
'**Ablösesumme** *f* SPORT transfer fee
'**Ablösung** *f* relief
'**abmachen** *v/t (sep, -ge-, h)* remove, take off; settle, arrange
'**Abmachung** *f (-; -en)* arrangement, agreement, deal
'**abmagern** *v/i (sep, -ge-, sein)* get thin
'**Abmagerung** *f (-; -en)* emaciation

'Abmagerungskur *f* slimming diet
'abmähen *v/t (sep, -ge-, h)* mow
'abmalen *v/t (sep, -ge-, h)* copy
'Abmarsch *m (-[e]s; no pl)* start; MIL marching off
'abmar,schieren *v/i (sep, no -ge-, sein)* start; MIL march off
'abmelden *v/t (sep, -ge-, h)* cancel the registration of *(car etc)*; cancel s.o.'s membership *(in a club etc)*; give notice of s.o.'s withdrawal (from school); ***sich abmelden*** give notice of change of address; report off duty
'Abmeldung *f* notice of withdrawal; notice of change of address
'abmessen *v/t (irr, **messen**, sep, -ge-, h)* measure
'Abmessung *f* measurement; *pl* dimensions
'abmon,tieren *v/t (sep, no -ge-, h)* take off; take down; TECH dismantle
'abmühen *v/refl (sep, -ge-, h)* work very hard; try hard *(to do s.th.)*; struggle (***mit*** with)
'abnagen *v/t (sep, -ge-, h)* gnaw (at)
Abnahme ['apna:mə] *f (-; -n)* reduction, decrease; loss *(a. of weight)*; ECON purchase; TECH acceptance
'abnehmbar *adj* removable
'abnehmen *(irr, **nehmen**, sep, -ge-, h)* **1.** *v/t* take off *(a.* MED), remove; pick up *(receiver)*; TECH accept; ECON buy; ***j-m et. abnehmen*** take s.th. (away) from s.o.; **2.** *v/i* decrease, diminish; lose weight; answer the phone; *moon*: wane
'Abnehmer *m (-s; -)* buyer; customer
'Abneigung *f* (***gegen***) dislike (of, for); aversion (to)
abnorm [ap'nɔrm] *adj* abnormal; exceptional, unusual
Abnormität [apnɔrmi'tɛ:t] *f (-; -en)* abnormality
'abnutzen, 'abnützen *v/t and v/refl (sep, -ge-, h)* wear out
'Abnutzung, 'Abnützung *f (-; no pl)* wear (and tear) *(a. fig)*
Abonnement [abɔnə'mã:] *n (-s; -s)* subscription (***auf*** *acc* to)
Abonnent [abɔ'nɛnt] *m (-en; -en)* subscriber; THEA season-ticket holder
abonnieren [abɔ'ni:rən] *v/t (no -ge-, h)* subscribe to
Abordnung *f (-; -en)* delegation
Abort [a'bɔrt] *m (-[e]s; -e)* lavatory, toilet
'abpassen *v/t (sep, -ge-, h)* watch *or* wait for *(s.o., s.th.)*; waylay *s.o. (a. fig)*
'abpfeifen *v/t and v/i (irr, **pfeifen**, sep, -ge-, h)* SPORT blow the final whistle; stop the game
'abplagen *v/refl (sep, -ge-, h)* struggle (***mit*** with)
'abprallen *v/i (sep, -ge-, sein)* rebound, bounce (off); *bullet*: ricochet
'abputzen *v/t (sep, -ge-, h)* wipe off; clean
'abraten *v/i (irr, **raten**, sep, -ge-, h)* ***j-m abraten von*** advise *or* warn s.o. against
'abräumen *v/t (sep, -ge-, h)* clear away; clear *(the table)*
'abrea,gieren *v/t (sep, no -ge-, h)* work off *(one's anger etc)* (***an*** *dat* on); ***sich abreagieren*** F let off steam
'abrechnen *(sep, -ge-, h)* **1.** *v/t* deduct, subtract; claim *(expenses)*; **2.** *v/i*: ***mit j-m abrechnen*** settle accounts *(fig a.* get even) with s.o.
'Abrechnung *f* settlement; F *fig* showdown
'abreiben *v/t (irr, **reiben**, sep, -ge-, h)* rub off; rub down *(body)*; polish
'Abreise *f* departure (***nach*** for)
'abreisen *v/i (sep, -ge-, sein)* depart, leave, start, set out *(all:* ***nach*** for)
'abreißen *(irr, **reißen**, sep, -ge-)* **1.** *v/t (h)* tear *or* pull off; pull down *(building)*; **2.** *v/i (sein)* break; *button etc*: come off
'Abreißka,lender *m* tear-off calendar
'abrichten *v/t (sep, -ge-, h)* train *(animal)*, *a.* break *a horse* in
'abriegeln *v/t (sep, -ge-, h)* block off, cordon off
'Abriss *m (-es; -e)* a) *(no pl)* demolition, b) outline, summary
'abrollen *v/i (sep, -ge-, sein) and v/t (h)* unroll *(a. fig)*
'abrücken *(sep, -ge-)* **1.** *v/t (h)* move away (***von*** from); **2.** *v/i (sein)* draw away (***von*** from); MIL march off
'Abruf *m*: ***auf Abruf*** ECON on call
'abrufen *v/t (irr, **rufen**, sep, -ge-, h)* call away; EDP recall, fetch, retrieve
'abrunden *v/t (sep, -ge-, h)* round (off)
'abrupfen *v/t (sep, -ge-, h)* pluck (off)
abrupt [ap'rupt] *adj* abrupt
'abrüsten *v/i (sep, -ge-, h)* MIL disarm
'Abrüstung *f (-; no pl)* MIL disarmament
'abrutschen *v/i (sep, -ge-, sein)* slide down; slip (off) (***von*** from)
ABS [a:be:'ɛs] → ***Antiblockiersystem***
Absage ['apza:gə] *f (-; -n)* refusal; cancellation
'absagen *(sep, -ge-, h)* **1.** *v/t* call off, cancel *(event etc)*; **2.** *v/i* call off; ***j-m absagen*** *a.* cancel one's appointment with s.o.; decline (the invitation)
'absägen *v/t (sep, -ge-, h)* saw off; F *fig* oust, sack *s.o.*
'absahnen F *v/i (sep, -ge-, h)* cash in
'Absatz *m* paragraph; ECON sales *pl*; *shoe*:

heel; *stairs*: landing
'abschaben *v/t* (*sep*, *-ge-*, *h*) scrape off
'abschaffen *v/t* (*sep*, *-ge-*, *h*) do away with, abolish; repeal (*law*); put an end to (*abuses etc*)
'Abschaffung *f* (*-; no pl*) abolition; repeal
'abschalten (*sep*, *-ge-*, *h*) **1.** *v/t* switch *or* turn off; **2.** F *v/i* relax, switch off
'abschätzen *v/t* (*sep*, *-ge-*, *h*) estimate; assess; size up
abschätzig ['apʃɛtsɪç] *adj* contemptuous; derogatory
Abschaum *m* (*-s; no pl*) scum (*a. fig*)
'Abscheu *m* (*-s; no pl*) disgust (***vor, gegen*** at, for); ***e-n Abscheu haben vor*** abhor, detest; ***Abscheu erregend*** → ***abscheuerregend***
'abscheuerregend *adj* revolting, repulsive
ab'scheulich *adj* abominable, despicable (*a. person*), *a.* atrocious (*crime*)
'abschicken *v/t* (*sep*, *-ge-*, *h*) → ***absenden***
'abschieben *fig v/t* (*irr*, ***schieben***, *sep*, *-ge-*, *h*) push away; get rid of; deport; ***et. auf j-n abschieben*** shove s.th. off on (to) s.o.
Abschied ['apʃiːt] *m* (*-[e]s; -e*) parting, farewell; ***Abschied nehmen*** (***von***) say goodbye (to), take leave (of); ***s-n Abschied nehmen*** resign, retire
'Abschiedsfeier *f* farewell party
'Abschiedskuss *m* goodbye kiss
'abschießen *v/t* (*irr*, ***schießen***, *sep*, *-ge-*, *h*) shoot off (AVIAT down); launch (*rocket*); shoot, kill (*deer*); F pick *s.o.* off; *fig* oust; get rid of *s.o.*
'abschirmen *v/t* (*sep*, *-ge-*, *h*) shield (***gegen*** from); *fig* protect (***gegen*** against, from)
'Abschirmung *f* (*-; -en*) shield, screen; *fig* protection
'abschlachten *v/t* (*sep*, *-ge-*, *h*) slaughter (*a. fig*)
'Abschlag *m* SPORT kickout; ECON down payment
'abschlagen *v/t* (*irr*, ***schlagen***, *sep*, *-ge-*, *h*) knock off; cut off (*head*); cut down (*tree*); refuse (*request etc*), turn *s.th.* down
'abschleifen *v/t* (*irr*, ***schleifen***, *sep*, *-ge-*, *h*) grind off; sand(paper), smooth
'Abschleppdienst *m* MOT emergency road (*Br* breakdown) service
'abschleppen *v/t* (*sep*, *-ge-*, *h*) MOT (give *s.o.* a) tow; *police*: tow away
'Abschleppseil *n* towrope
Abschleppwagen *m Am* tow truck, *Br* breakdown lorry
'abschließen (*irr*, ***schließen***, *sep*, *-ge-*, *h*) **1.** *v/t* lock (up); close, finish; complete; take out (*insurance*); conclude (*research etc*); ***e-n Handel abschließen*** strike a bargain; ***sich abschließen*** shut o.s. off; → ***Wette***; **2.** *v/i* close, finish
abschließend 1. *adj* concluding; final; **2.** *adv*: ***abschließend sagte er*** he concluded by saying
'Abschluss *m* conclusion, close
Abschlussprüfung *f* final examination, finals *pl*, *esp Am a.* graduation; ***s-e Abschlussprüfung machen*** graduate (***an*** *dat* from)
Abschlusszeugnis *n Am* diploma, *Br* school-leaving certificate
'abschmecken *v/t* (*sep*, *-ge-*, *h*) season
'abschmieren *v/t* (*sep*, *-ge-*, *h*) TECH lubricate, grease
'abschminken *v/t* (*sep*, *-ge-*, *h*) ***sich abschminken*** remove one's make-up
'abschnallen *v/t* (*sep*, *-ge-*, *h*) undo; take off (*skis*); ***sich abschnallen*** MOT, AVIAT unfasten one's seat belt
'abschneiden (*irr*, ***schneiden***, *sep*, *-ge-*, *h*) **1.** *v/t* cut (off) (*a. fig*); ***j-m das Wort abschneiden*** cut s.o. short; **2.** *v/i*: ***gut abschneiden*** come off well
'Abschnitt *m* passage, section (*of book etc*); paragraph; MATH, BIOL segment; period (*of time*), stage (*of journey*), phase (*of development*); coupon, slip, stub (*of check etc*)
'abschnittweise *adv* section by section
'abschrauben *v/t* (*sep*, *-ge-*, *h*) unscrew
'abschrecken *v/t* (*sep*, *-ge-*, *h*) deter (***von*** from); GASTR douse *eggs etc* with cold water
abschreckend *adj* deterrent; ***abschreckendes Beispiel*** warning example
'Abschreckung *f* (*-; -en*) deterrence
'abschreiben *v/t* (*irr*, ***schreiben***, *sep*, *-ge-*, *h*) copy; PED crib; ECON write off (*a.* F *fig*)
'Abschrift *f* copy, duplicate
'abschürfen *v/t* (*sep*, *-ge-*, *h*) graze
'Abschürfung *f* (*-; -en*) abrasion
Abschuss *m* launch(ing) (*of rocket*); AVIAT shooting down, downing; kill
Abschussbasis *f* MIL launching base
abschüssig ['apʃʏsɪç] *adj* sloping; steep
'Abschussliste F *f*: ***auf der Abschussliste stehen*** be on the hit list
'Abschussrampe *f* MIL launching pad
'abschütteln *v/t* (*sep*, *-ge-*, *h*) shake off
'abschwächen *v/t* (*sep*, *-ge-*, *h*) lessen, diminish
'abschweifen *fig v/i* (*sep*, *-ge-*, *sein*) digress (***von*** from)
'Abschweifung *f* (*-; -en*) digression
absehbar ['apzeːbaːɐ] *adj* foreseeable; ***in absehbarer*** (***auf absehbare***) ***Zeit*** in the

(for the) foreseeable future
'absehen *v/t* (*irr*, ***sehen***, *sep*, *-ge-*, *h*) foresee; ***es ist kein Ende abzusehen*** there is no end in sight; ***es abgesehen haben auf*** (*acc*) be after; ***absehen von*** refrain from
'abseilen *v/refl* (*sep*, *-ge-*, *h*) descend by a rope, *Br a.* abseil; F make a getaway
abseits ['apzaɪts] *adv and prp* away *or* remote from
'Abseitsfalle *f soccer*: offside trap
abseitsstehen *v/i* (*irr*, ***stehen***, *sep*, *-ge-*, *h*) *soccer*: be offside; *fig* be left out
'absenden *v/t* ([*irr*, ***senden***,] *sep*, *-ge-*, *h*) send (off), dispatch; mail, *esp Br* post (*letter etc*)
'Absender *m* (*-s*; *-*) sender
absetzbar ['apzɛtsbaːɐ] *adj*: ***steuerlich absetzbar*** deductible from tax
'absetzen (*sep*, *-ge-*, *h*) **1.** *v/t* take off (*hat*, *glasses etc*); set *or* put down (*bag etc*); drop (*passenger*); dismiss (*employee*); THEA, *film*: take off; deduct (*from tax*); depose (*king etc*); ECON sell; ***sich absetzen*** CHEM, GEOL settle, be deposited; **2.** *v/i*: ***ohne abzusetzen*** without stopping
'Absetzung *f* (*-*; *-en*) dismissal; deposition; THEA, *film*: withdrawal
'Absicht *f* (*-*; *-en*) intention; ***mit Absicht*** on purpose
'absichtlich **1.** *adj* intentional; **2.** *adv* on purpose
'absitzen (*irr*, ***sitzen***, *sep*, *-ge-*) **1.** *v/i* (*sein*) dismount (***von*** from); **2.** *v/t* (*h*) serve (*sentence*); F sit out (*play etc*)
absolut [apzo'luːt] *adj* absolute
Absolvent [apzɔl'vɛnt] *m* (*-en*; *-en*), **Absol'ventin** *f* (*-*; *-nen*) graduate
absolvieren [apzɔl'viːrən] *v/t* (*no -ge-*, *h*) attend (*school*); complete (*studies*); graduate from (*college etc*)
'absondern *v/t* (*sep*, *-ge-*, *h*) separate; MED, BIOL secrete; ***sich absondern*** cut o.s. off (***von*** from)
'Absonderung *f* (*-*; *-en*) separation; MED, BIOL secretion
absorbieren [apzɔr'biːrən] *v/t* (*no -ge-*, *h*) absorb (*a. fig*)
'abspeichern *v/t* (*sep*, *-ge-*, *h*) EDP store, save
abspenstig ['apʃpɛnstɪç] *adj*: ***j-m die Freundin abspenstig machen*** steal s.o.'s girlfriend
absperren *v/t* (*sep*, *-ge-*, *h*) lock; turn off (*water*, *gas etc*); block off (*road*); cordon off
'Absperrung *f* (*-*; *-en*) barrier; cordon
'abspielen *v/t* (*sep*, *-ge-*, *h*) play (*record etc*); SPORT pass (*the ball*); ***sich abspielen*** happen, take place
'Absprache *f* agreement
'absprechen *v/t* (*irr*, ***sprechen***, *sep*, *-ge-*, *h*) agree upon; arrange; ***j-m die Fähigkeit*** *etc* ***absprechen*** dispute s.o.'s ability *etc*
'abspringen *v/i* (*irr*, ***springen***, *sep*, *-ge-*, *sein*) jump off; AVIAT jump, bail out; *fig* back out (***von*** of)
'Absprung *m* jump; SPORT take-off; *fig* ***den Absprung schaffen*** make it
'abspülen *v/t* (*sep*, *-ge-*, *h*) rinse; wash up
abstammen *v/i* (*sep*, *no past participle*) be descended (***von*** from); CHEM, LING derive
'Abstammung *f* (*-*; *no pl*) descent; derivation
'Abstammungslehre *f* theory of the origin of species
'Abstand *m* distance (*a. fig*); interval; ***Abstand halten*** keep one's distance; *fig* ***mit Abstand*** by far
abstatten ['apʃtatən] *v/t* (*sep*, *-ge-*, *h*) ***j-m e-n Besuch abstatten*** pay a visit to s.o.
'abstauben *v/t* (*sep*, *-ge-*, *h*) dust; F *fig* sponge; swipe
'Abstauber F *m* (*-s*; *-*), **'Abstaubertor** *n* SPORT opportunist goal
'abstechen (*irr*, ***stechen***, *sep*, *-ge-*, *h*) **1.** *v/t* stick (*pig etc*); **2.** *v/i* contrast (***von*** with)
'Abstecher *m* (*-s*; *-*) side-trip, excursion (*a. fig*)
'abstecken *v/t* (*sep*, *-ge-*, *h*) mark out
'abstehen *v/i* (*irr*, ***stehen***, *sep*, *-ge-*, *h*) stick out, protrude; → ***abgestanden***
'absteigen *v/i* (*irr*, ***steigen***, *sep*, *-ge-*, *sein*) get off (*a horse etc*); climb down; stay (***in*** *dat* at); SPORT *Am* be moved down to a lower division, *Br* be relegated
'Absteiger *m* (*-s*; *-*) SPORT *Br* relegated club
'abstellen *v/t* (*sep*, *-ge-*, *h*) put down; leave (*s.th. with s.o.*); turn off (*gas etc*); park (*car*); *fig* put an end to *s.th.*
'Abstellgleis *n* RAIL siding; ***j-n aufs Abstellgleis schieben*** F push s.o. aside
'Abstellraum *m* storeroom
'abstempeln *v/t* (*sep*, *-ge-*, *h*) stamp
'absterben *v/i* (*irr*, ***sterben***, *sep*, *-ge-*, *sein*) die off; *limb*: go numb
Abstieg ['apʃtiːk] *m* (*-[e]s*; *-e*) descent; *fig* decline; SPORT *Br* relegation
'abstimmen *v/i* (*sep*, *-ge-*, *h*) vote (***über*** *acc* on)
'Abstimmung *f* vote; *radio*: tuning
Abstinenzler [apsti'nɛntslɐ] *m* (*-s*; *-*) teetotal(l)er
'Abstoß *m* SPORT goal-kick
'abstoßen *v/t* (*irr*, ***stoßen***, *sep*, *-ge-*, *h*) re-

pel; MED reject; push off (*boat*); F get rid of *s.th.*
abstoßend *fig adj* repulsive
abstrakt [ap'strakt] *adj* abstract
'abstreiten *v/t* (*irr*, **streiten**, *sep*, *-ge-*, *h*) deny
'Abstrich *m* MED smear; *pl* ECON cuts; *fig* reservations
'abstufen *v/t* (*sep*, *-ge-*, *h*) graduate; gradate (*colors*)
'abstumpfen (*sep*, *-ge-*) **1.** *v/t* (*h*) blunt, dull (*a. fig*); **2.** *fig v/i* (*sein*) become unfeeling
'Absturz *m*, **'abstürzen** *v/i* (*sep*, *-ge-*, *sein*) fall; AVIAT, EDP crash
'absuchen *v/t* (*sep*, *-ge-*, *h*) search (**nach** for)
absurd [ap'zʊrt] *adj* absurd, preposterous
Abszess [aps'tsɛs] *m* (*-es*; *-e*) MED abscess
Abt [apt] *m* (*-[e]s*; *Äbte* ['ɛptə]) REL abbot
'abtasten *v/t* (*sep*, *-ge-*, *h*) feel (for); MED palpate; frisk; TECH, EDP scan
'abtauen *v/t* (*sep*, *-ge-*, *h*) defrost
Abtei [ap'tai] *f* (*-*; *-en*) REL abbey
Abteil [ap'tail] *n* (*-[e]s*; *-e*) RAIL compartment
'abteilen *v/t* (*sep*, *-ge-*, *h*) divide; ARCH partition off
Ab'teilung *f* (*-*; *-en*) department (*a.* ECON); ward (*of hospital*); MIL detachment
Ab'teilungsleiter *m* head of (a) department; *Am* floorwalker, *Br* shopwalker
Äbtissin [ɛp'tɪsɪn] *f* (*-*; *-nen*) REL abbess
'abtöten *v/t* (*sep*, *-ge-*, *h*) kill (*bacteria etc*); *fig* deaden (*feelings etc*)
'abtragen *v/t* (*irr*, **tragen**, *sep*, *-ge-*, *h*) wear out (*clothes*); clear away (*dishes etc*); pay off (*debt*)
'Abtrans,port *m* transportation
'abtreiben (*irr*, **treiben**, *sep*, *-ge-*) **1.** *v/i* MED (*h*) have an abortion; MAR, AVIAT (*sein*) be blown off course; **2.** *v/t* (*h*) MED abort
'Abtreibung *f* (*-*; *-en*) abortion; ***e-e Abtreibung vornehmen*** perform an abortion
'abtrennen *v/t* (*sep*, *-ge-*, *h*) detach; separate; MED sever
'abtreten (*irr*, **treten**, *sep*, *-ge-*) **1.** *v/t* (*h*) wear down (*heels*); wipe (*one's feet*); *fig* give up (**an** *acc* to); **2.** *v/i* (*sein*) resign; THEA; exit
'Abtreter *m* (*-s*; *-*) doormat
'abtrocknen (*sep*, *-ge-*, *h*) **1.** *v/t* dry; ***sich abtrocknen*** dry o.s. off; **2.** *v/i* dry the dishes, *Br a.* dry up
abtrünnig ['aptrʏnɪç] *adj* unfaithful, disloyal
'Abtrünnige [-nɪgə] *m*, *f* (*-n*; *-n*) renegade, turncoat
abtun *v/t* (*irr*, **tun**, *sep*, *-ge-*, *h*) dismiss (**als** as), brush *s.o.*, *s.th.* aside
abwägen ['apvɛːgən] *v/t* (*irr*, **wägen**, *sep*, *-ge-*, *h*) weigh (**gegen** against)
'abwählen *v/t* (*sep*, *-ge-*, *h*) vote out
'abwälzen *v/t* (*sep*, *-ge-*, *h*) ***et. auf j-n abwälzen*** shove s.th. off on (to) s.o.
'abwandeln *v/t* (*sep*, *-ge-*, *h*) vary, modify
'abwandern *v/i* (*sep*, *-ge-*, *sein*) migrate (**von** from; **nach** to)
'Abwanderung *f* migration
'Abwandlung *f* modification, variation
'Abwärme *f* TECH waste heat
Abwart ['apvart] *m* (*-s*; *-e*) *Swiss* → ***Hausmeister***
'abwarten (*sep*, *-ge-*, *h*) **1.** *v/t* wait for, await; **2.** *v/i* wait; ***warten wir ab!*** let's wait and see!; ***wart nur ab!*** just wait!
abwärts ['apvɛrts] *adv* down, down-ward(s)
Abwasch ['apvaʃ] *m* (*-[e]s*; *no pl*) ***den Abwasch machen*** do the washing-up
'abwaschbar *adj* washable
'abwaschen (*irr*, **waschen**, *sep*, *-ge-*, *h*) **1.** *v/t* wash off; **2.** *v/i* do the dishes, *Br a.* wash up
'Abwaschwasser *n* dishwater
'Abwasser *n* TECH waste water, sewage
Abwasseraufbereitung *f* TECH sewage treatment
'abwechseln *v/i* (*sep*, *-ge-*, *h*) alternate; ***sich mit j-m abwechseln*** take turns (***bei et.*** at [doing] s.th.)
abwechselnd *adv* by turns
'Abwechslung *f* (*-*; *-en*) change; ***zur Abwechslung*** for a change
'abwechslungsreich *adj* varied; colo(u)rful
'Abweg *m*: ***auf Abwege geraten*** go astray
abwegig ['apveːgɪç] *adj* absurd, unrealistic
'Abwehr *f* (*-*; *no pl*) defen|se, *Br* -ce (*a.* SPORT); warding off (*of blow etc*); save (*of ball*)
'abwehren *v/t* (*sep*, *-ge-*, *h*) ward off (*blow etc*); beat off; SPORT block
'Abwehrfehler *m* SPORT defensive error
Abwehrkräfte *pl* MED resistance
Abwehrspieler *m* SPORT defender
Abwehrstoffe *pl* MED antibodies
'abweichen *v/i* (*irr*, **weichen**, *sep*, *-ge-*, *sein*) deviate (**von** from); digress
'Abweichung *f* (*-*; *-en*) deviation
'abweisen *v/t* (*irr*, **weisen**, *sep*, *-ge-*, *h*) turn away; rebuff; decline, turn down (*request*, *offer etc*)
abweisend *adj* unfriendly
'abwenden *v/t* ([*irr*, **wenden**,] *sep*, *-ge-*, *h*)

turn away (*a.* ***sich abwenden***) (***von*** from); avert (*tragedy etc*)
'abwerfen *v/t* (*irr*, ***werfen***, *sep*, *-ge-*, *h*) throw off; AVIAT drop; BOT shed (*leaves*); ECON yield (*profit*)
'abwerten *v/t* (*sep*, *-ge-*, *h*) ECON devalue
abwertend *fig adj* disparaging
'Abwertung *f* ECON devaluation
'abwesend *adj* absent
'Abwesenheit *f* (*-*; *no pl*) absence
abwickeln *v/t* (*sep*, *-ge-*, *h*) unwind; ECON handle; transact (*business*)
'abwiegen *v/t* (*irr*, ***wiegen***, *sep*, *-ge-*, *h*) weigh (out)
'abwischen *v/t* (*sep*, *-ge-*, *h*) wipe (off)
'Abwurf *m* dropping; *soccer*: throw-out
'abwürgen F *v/t* (*sep*, *-ge-*, *h*) MOT stall; *fig* stifle
'abzahlen *v/t* (*sep*, *-ge-*, *h*) make *monthly etc* payments for; pay off
'abzählen *v/t* (*sep*, *-ge-*, *h*) count
'Abzahlung *f*: ***et. auf Abzahlung kaufen*** *Am* buy s.th. on the instalment plan (*Br* on hire purchase)
'abzapfen *v/t* (*sep*, *-ge-*, *h*) tap, draw off
'Abzeichen *n* badge; medal
'abzeichnen *v/t* (*sep*, *-ge-*, *h*) copy, draw; sign, initial; ***sich abzeichnen*** (begin to) show; stand out (***gegen*** against)
'Abziehbild *n Am* decal, *Br* transfer
'abziehen (*irr*, ***ziehen***, *sep*, *-ge-*) **1.** *v/t* (*h*) take off, remove; MATH subtract; strip (*bed*); take out (*key*); ***das Fell abziehen*** skin; **2.** *v/i* (*sein*) go away; MIL withdraw; *smoke*: escape; *storm*, *clouds*: move off
'Abzug *m* ECON deduction; discount; MIL withdrawal; PRINT copy; PHOT print; *gun*: trigger; TECH vent, outlet; cooker hood
abzüglich ['aptsyːklɪç] *prp* less, minus
'abzweigen (*sep*, *-ge-*) **1.** *v/t* (*h*) divert (*resources etc*) (***für*** to); **2.** *v/i* (*sein*) *path etc*: branch off
'Abzweigung *f* (*-*; *-en*) junction
ach [ax] *int* oh!; ***ach je!*** oh dear!; ***ach so!*** I see; ***ach was!*** *surprised*: really?, *annoyed*: of course not!, nonsense!
Achse ['aksə] *f* (*-*; *-n*) TECH axle; MATH *etc* axis; F ***auf Achse sein*** be on the move
Achsel ['aksəl] *f* (*-*; *-n*) ANAT shoulder; ***die Achseln zucken*** shrug one's shoulders
'Achselhöhle *f* ANAT armpit
acht [axt] *adj* eight; ***heute in acht Tagen*** a week from today, *esp Br* today week; (***heute***) ***vor acht Tagen*** a week ago (today)
Acht *f*: ***Acht geben*** → ***achtgeben***; ***außer Acht lassen*** disregard; ***sich in Acht nehmen*** be careful, look *or* watch out (***vor*** *dat* for)
achtgeben *v/i* (*irr*, ***geben***, *sep*, *-ge-*, *h*) be careful; pay attention (***auf*** *acc* to); take care (***auf*** *acc* of); ***gib acht!*** look *or* watch out!, be careful!
achte ['axtə] *adj* eighth
'achteckig *adj* octagonal
Achtel ['axtəl] *n* (*-s*; *-*) eighth (part)
achten (*ge-*, *h*) **1.** *v/t* respect; **2.** *v/i*: ***achten auf*** (*acc*) pay attention to; keep an eye on; watch; be careful with; ***darauf achten, dass*** see to it that
ächten ['ɛçtən] *v/t* (*ge-*, *h*) ban; *esp* HIST outlaw
Achter ['axtɐ] *m* (*-s*; *-*) *rowing*: eight
'Achterbahn *f* roller coaster
'achtfach *adj and adv* eightfold
'achtlos *adj* careless, heedless
'Achtung *f* (*-*; *no pl*) respect (***vor*** *dat* for); ***Achtung!*** look out!; MIL attention!; ***Achtung! Achtung!*** attention please!; ***Achtung! Fertig! Los!*** On your marks! Get set! Go!; ***Achtung Stufe!*** *Am* caution: step!, *Br* mind the step!
'achtzehn *adj* eighteen
'achtzehnte *adj* eighteenth
achtzig ['axtsɪç] *adj* eighty; ***die achtziger Jahre*** the eighties
achtzigste *adj* eightieth
ächzen ['ɛçtsən] *v/i* (*ge-*, *h*) groan (***vor*** *dat* with)
Acker ['akɐ] *m* (*-s*; *Äcker* ['ɛkɐ]) field
Ackerbau *m* (*-[e]s*; *no pl*) agriculture; farming; ***Ackerbau und Viehzucht*** crop and stock farming
Ackerland *n* (*-[e]s*; *no pl*) farmland
'ackern F *v/i* (*ge-*, *h*) slog (away)
Adapter [a'daptɐ] *m* (*-s*; *-*) TECH adapter
addieren [a'diːrən] *v/t* (*no -ge-*, *h*) add (up)
Addition [adi'tsioːn] *f* (*-*; *-en*) addition, adding up
Adel ['aːdəl] *m* (*-s*; *no pl*) aristocracy
'adeln *v/t* (*ge-*, *h*) ennoble (*a. fig*); *Br* knight
Ader ['aːdɐ] *f* (*-*; *-n*) ANAT blood vessel, vein
Adjektiv ['atjɛktiːf] *n* (*-s*; *-e*) LING adjective
Adler ['aːdlɐ] *m* (*-s*; *-*) ZO eagle
adlig ['aːdlɪç] *adj* noble
Adlige ['aːdlɪgə] *m*, *f* (*-n*; *-n*) noble|man (-woman)
Admiral [atmi'raːl] *m* (*-s*; *-e*) MAR admiral
adoptieren [adɔp'tiːrən] *v/t* (*no -ge-*, *h*) adopt
Adoptivkind [adɔp'tiːf-] *n* adopted child
Adressbuch [a'drɛs-] *n* directory
Adresse [a'drɛsə] *f* (*-*; *-n*) address
adressieren [adrɛ'siːrən] *v/t* (*no -ge-*, *h*)

address (***an*** *acc* to)
Advent [at'vɛnt] *m* (-[*e*]*s*; *no pl*) REL Advent; Advent Sunday
Ad'ventszeit *f* Christmas season
Adverb [at'vɛrp] *n* (-*s*; *Adverbien* [at'vɛrbĭən]) LING adverb
Aerobic [ɛ'ro:bɪk] *n* (-*s*; *no pl*) aerobics
Affäre [a'fɛ:rə] *f* (-; -*n*) affair
Affe ['afə] *m* (-*n*; -*n*) ZO monkey; ape
Affekt [a'fɛkt] *m* (-[*e*]*s*; -*e*) ***im Affekt*** in the heat of passion (*a.* JUR)
affektiert [afɛk'ti:ɐt] *adj* affected
Afrika ['a:frika] Africa
Afrikaner [afri'ka:nɐ] *m* (-*s*; -), **Afri'kanerin** [-nərɪn] *f* (-; -*nen*), **afri'kanisch** *adj* African
After ['aftɐ] *m* (-*s*; -) ANAT anus
AG ABBR *of* ***Aktiengesellschaft*** *Am* (stock) corporation, *Br* PLC, public limited company
Agent [a'gɛnt] *m* (-*en*; -*en*), **A'gentin** *f* (-; -*nen*) agent; POL (secret) agent
Agentur [agɛn'tu:ɐ] *f* (-; -*en*) agency
Aggression [agrɛ'sĭo:n] *f* (-; -*en*) aggression
aggressiv [agrɛ'si:f] *adj* aggressive
Aggressivität [agrɛsivi'tɛ:t] *f* (-; *no pl*) aggressiveness
Agitator [agi'ta:to:ɐ] *m* (-*s*; -*en* [-ta'to:rən]) agitator
ah [a:] *int* ah!
äh [ɛ:] *int* er; *disgusted*: ugh!
aha [a'ha] *int* I see!, oh!
A'ha-Erlebnis *n* aha-experience
Ahn [a:n] *m* (-[*e*]*s*; -*en*; -*en*) ancestor, *pl a.* forefathers
ähneln ['ɛ:nəln] *v/i* (*ge-*, *h*) resemble, look like
ahnen ['a:nən] *v/t* (*ge-*, *h*) suspect; foresee, know
ähnlich ['ɛ:nlɪç] *adj* similar (*dat* to); ***j-m ähnlich sehen*** look like s.o.
'Ähnlichkeit *f* (-; -*en*) likeness, resemblance, similarity (***mit*** to)
'Ahnung *f* (-; -*en*) presentiment, *a.* foreboding; notion, idea; ***ich habe keine Ahnung*** I have no idea
'ahnungslos *adj* unsuspecting, innocent
Ahorn ['a:hɔrn] *m* (-*s*, -*e*) BOT maple
Ähre ['ɛ:rə] *f* (-; -*n*) BOT ear; spike
Aids [eɪdz] *n* (-; *no pl*) MED AIDS
'Aids-Kranke *m*, *f* MED AIDS victim *or* sufferer
Aidstest *m* MED AIDS test
Airbag ['ɛəbæg] *m* (-*s*; -*s*) MOT airbag
Akademie [akade'mi:] *f* (-; -*n*) academy, college
Akademiker(in) [aka'de:mikɐ (-kərɪn)] (-*s*; -/-; -*nen*) university graduate
akademisch [-'de:mɪʃ] *adj* academic
akklimatisieren [aklimati'zi:rən] *v/refl* (*no -ge-*, *h*) acclimatize (***an*** *acc* to)
Akkord [a'kɔrt] *m* (-[*e*]*s*; -*e*) MUS chord; ***im Akkord*** ECON by the piece *or* job
Akkordarbeit *f* ECON piecework
Akkordarbeiter(in) ECON pieceworker
Akkordeon [a'kɔrdeɔn] *n* (-*s*; -*s*) MUS accordion
Ak'kordlohn *m* ECON piece wages
Akku ['aku] F *m* (-*s*; -*s*), **Akkumulator** [akumu'la:to:ɐ] *m* (-*s*; -*en* [-la'to:rən]) TECH (storage) battery, *Br a.* accumulator
Akkusativ ['akuzati:f] *m* (-*s*; -*e*) LING accusative (case)
Akne ['aknə] *f* (-; -*n*) MED acne
Akrobat [akro'ba:t] *m* (-*en*; -*en*), **Akro'batin** *f* (-; -*nen*) acrobat
akro'batisch *adj* acrobatic
Akt [akt] *m* (-[*e*]*s*; -*e*) act(ion); THEA act; PAINT, PHOT nude
Akte ['aktə] *f* (-; -*n*) file; *pl.* files, records; ***zu den Akten legen*** file
'Aktendeckel *m* folder
Aktenkoffer *m* attaché case
Aktenordner *m* file
Aktentasche *f* briefcase
Aktenzeichen *n* reference (number)
Aktie ['aktsĭə] *f* (-; -*n*) ECON share, *esp Am* stock
'Aktiengesellschaft *f* *Am* corporation, *Br* joint-stock company
Aktion [ak'tsĭo:n] *f* (-; -*en*) campaign, drive; MIL *ect* operation; ***in Aktion*** in action
Aktionär [aktsĭo'nɛ:ɐ] *m* (-*s*; -*e*), **Aktio'närin** *f* (-; -*nen*) ECON shareholder, *esp Am* stockholder
aktiv [ak'ti:f] *adj* active
Aktiv ['akti:f] *n* (-*s*; *no pl*) LING active voice
Aktivist [akti'vist] *m* (-*en*; -*en*) *esp* POL activist
Ak'tivurlaub *m* activity vacation
aktualisieren [aktŭali'zi:rən] *v/t* (*no -ge-*, *h*) update
aktuell [aktŭ'ɛl] *adj* topical; current; up-to-date; TV, *radio*: ***e-e aktuelle Sendung*** a current affairs *or* news feature
Akupunktur [akupʊŋk'tu:ɐ] *f* (-; -*en*) MED acupuncture
Akustik [a'kʊstɪk] *f* (-; *no pl*) acoustics
a'kustisch *adj* acoustic
akut [a'ku:t] *adj* urgent (*problem etc*); *a.* MED acute
Akzent [ak'tsɛnt] *m* (-[*e*]*s*; -*e*) accent; stress (*a. fig*)
akzeptabel [aktsɛp'ta:bəl] *adj* acceptable; reasonable (*price etc*)

akzeptieren [aktsɛp'tiːrən] *v/t* (*no -ge-, h*) accept
Alarm [a'larm] *m* (-[*e*]*s*; -*e*) alarm; ***Alarm schlagen*** sound the alarm
Alarmanlage *f* alarm system
Alarmbereitschaft *f*: ***in Alarmbereitschaft*** on standby, on the alert
alarmieren [alar'miːrən] *v/t* (*no -ge-, h*) call; alert
alarmierend *adj* alarming
albern ['albɐn] *adj* silly, foolish
Album ['albʊm] *n* (-*s*; *Alben* ['albən]) album (*a. record*)
Algen ['algən] *pl* BOT algae
Algenpest *f* plague of algae, algal bloom
Algebra ['algəbra] *f* (-; *no pl*) MATH algebra
Alibi ['aːlibi] *n* (-*s*; -*s*) JUR alibi
Alimente [ali'mɛntə] *pl* JUR alimony
Alkohol ['alkohoːl] *m* (-*s*; *no pl*) alcohol
'alkoholfrei *adj* nonalcoholic, soft
Alkoholiker(in) [alko'hoːlikɐ (-kərɪn)] (-*s*; -/-; -*nen*) alcoholic
alko'holisch *adj* alcoholic
Alkoholismus [alkoho'lɪsmʊs] *m* (-; *no pl*) alcoholism
alkoholsüchtig *adj* addicted to alcohol
Alkoholtest *m* MOT breath test
all [al] *indef pron and adj* all; ***alles*** everything; ***alles*** (***Beliebige***) anything; ***alle*** (***Leute***) everybody; anybody; ***alle beide*** both of them; ***wir alle*** all of us; ***alles in allem*** all in all; ***auf alle Fälle*** in any case; ***alle drei Tage*** every three days; → ***Art***, ***Gute***, ***vor***
All *n* (-*s*; *no pl*) universe; (outer) space
alle ['alə] F *adj*: ***alle sein*** be all gone; ***mein Geld ist alle*** I'm out of money
Allee [a'leː] *f* (-; -*n*) avenue
allein [a'lain] *adj and adv* alone; lonely; by o.s.; ***ganz allein*** all alone; ***er hat es ganz allein gemacht*** he did it all by himself; ***allein stehend*** → ***alleinstehend***
Al'leinerziehende *m, f* (-*n*; -*n*) single parent
Alleingang *m*: ***im Alleingang*** single-handedly, solo
alleinig [a'lainɪç] *adj* sole
Al'leinsein *n* (-*s*; *no pl*) loneliness
alleinstehend *adj* single
Allerbeste ['alɐ'bɛstə]: ***der*** (***die, das***) ***Allerbeste*** the best of all, the very best
allerdings ['alɐ'dɪŋs] *adv* however, though; ***allerdings!*** certainly!, *esp Am* F sure!
'aller'erste *adj* very first
Allergie [alɛr'giː] *f* (-; -*n*) MED allergy (***gegen*** to)
allergisch [a'lɛrgɪʃ] *adj* allergic (***gegen*** to)
'aller'hand F *adj* a good deal (of); ***das ist ja allerhand!*** that's a bit much!
'Aller'heiligen *n* REL All Saints' Day
allerlei ['alɐ'lai] *adj* all kinds *or* sorts of
'aller'letzte *adj* last of all, very last
aller'liebst **1.** *adj* (most) lovely; **2.** *adv*: ***am allerliebsten mögen*** like best of all
aller'meiste *adj* (by far the) most
aller'nächste *adj* very next; ***in allernächster Zeit*** in the very near future
aller'neu(e)ste *adj* very latest
'Aller'seelen *n* REL All Souls' Day
allerseits ['alɐ'zaits] *adv* F: ***Tag allerseits!*** hi, everybody!
'aller'wenigst *adv*: ***am allerwenigsten*** least of all
allesamt ['alə'zamt] *adv* all together
'allge'mein **1.** *adj* general; common; universal; **2.** *adv*: ***im Allgemeinen*** in general, generally; ***allgemein verständlich*** intelligible (to all), popular
'Allge'meinbildung *f* general education
'Allge'meinheit *f* (-; *no pl*) (general) public
allgemeinver'ständlich *adj* → ***allgemein***
All'heilmittel *n* cure-all (*a. fig*)
Allianz [a'ljants] *f* (-; -*en*) alliance
Alligator [ali'gaːtoːɐ] *m* (-*s*; -*en*) alligator
Alliierte [ali'iːɐtə]: ***die Alliierten*** *pl* POL the Allies
'all'jährlich *adv* every year; ***alljährlich stattfindend*** annual
all'mächtig *adj* omnipotent; Almighty (*God*)
allmählich [al'mɛːlɪç] **1.** *adj* gradual; **2.** *adv* gradually
'Allradantrieb *m* MOT four-wheel drive
allseitig ['alzaitɪç] *adv*: ***allseitig interessiert sein*** have all-round interests
'Alltag *m* everyday life
'all'täglich *adj* everyday; *fig a.* ordinary
all'wissend *adj* omniscient
'allzu *adv* (all) too; ***allzu viel*** too much
Alm [alm] *f* (-; -*en*) alpine pasture, alp
Almosen ['almoːzən] *n* (-*s*; -) alms
'Alpdruck *m* (-[*e*]*s*; *no pl*) nightmare (*a. fig*)
Alphabet [alfa'beːt] *n* (-[*e*]*s*; -*e*) alphabet
alpha'betisch *adj* alphabetical
alpin [al'piːn] *adj* alpine
'Alptraum *m* nightmare (*a. fig*)
als [als] *cj time*: when; while; *after comp*: than; ***als ich ankam*** when I arrived; ***als Kind*** (***Geschenk***) as a child (present); ***älter als*** older than; ***als ob*** as if, as though; ***nichts als*** nothing but
also ['alzo] *cj* so, therefore; F well, you

know; ***also gut!*** very well (then)!, all right (then)!; ***also doch*** so … after all; ***du willst also gehen*** *etc?* so you want to go *etc?*
alt [alt] *adj* old; HIST ancient; classical (*language*); ***ein 12 Jahre alter Junge*** a twelve-year-old boy
Alt *m* (*-s; no pl*) MUS alto
Altar [al'taːɐ] *m* (*-s; Altäre* [al'tɛːrə]) REL altar
'Alte *m, f* (*-n; -n*) ***der Alte*** the old man (*a. fig*); the boss; ***die Alte*** the old woman (*a. fig*); ***die Alten*** *pl* the old
'Altenheim *n* → ***Altersheim***
'Altenpfleger(in) geriatric nurse
Alter ['altɐ] *n* (*-s; no pl*) age; old age; ***im Alter von …*** at the age of …; ***er ist in deinem Alter*** he's your age
älter ['ɛltɐ] *adj* older; ***mein älterer Bruder*** my elder brother; ***ein älterer Herr*** an elderly gentleman
'altern *v/i* (*ge-, sein*) grow old, age
alternativ [altɛrna'tiːf] *adj* alternative; POL ecological, green; *a.* counter-culture (*movement etc*)
Alternative[1] [altɛrna'tiːvə] *f* (*-; -n*) alternative; option, choice
Alterna'tive[2] *m, f* (*-n; -n*) ecologist, member of the counterculture movement
'Altersgrenze *f* age limit; retirement age
Altersheim *n* old people's home
Altersrente *f* old-age pension
Altersschwäche *f* (*-; no pl*) infirmity; ***an Altersschwäche sterben*** die of old age
Altersversorgung *f* old age pension (scheme)
'Altertum *n* (*-s; no pl*) antiquity
'Altglascon,tainer *m* *Am* glass recycling bin, *Br* bottle bank
'altklug *adj* precocious
'Altlasten *pl* residual pollution
'Altme,tall *n* scrap (metal)
'altmodisch *adj* old-fashioned
'Altöl *n* waste oil
'Altpa,pier *n* waste paper
'altsprachlich *adj*: ***altsprachliches Gymnasium*** *appr* classical secondary school
'Altstadt *f* old town
Altstadtsa,nierung *f* town-cent|er (*Br* -re) rehabilitation
'Altwarenhändler *m* second-hand dealer
Alt'weibersommer *m* Indian summer; gossamer
Aluminium [alu'miːnjʊm] *n* (*-s; no pl*) alumin(i)um
am [am] *prp* at the (*window etc*); *time*: in the (*morning etc*); at the (*weekend etc*); on (*Sunday etc*); ***am 1. Mai*** on May 1st; ***am Tage*** during the day; ***am Himmel*** in the sky; ***am meisten*** most; ***am Leben*** alive
Amateur [ama'tøːɐ] *m* (*-s; -e*) amateur
Amateurfunker *m* radio amateur, F radio ham
Amboss ['ambɔs] *m* (*-es; -e*) anvil
ambulant [ambu'lant] *adv*: ***ambulant behandelt werden*** MED get outpatient treatment
Ambulanz [ambu'lants] *f* (*-; -en*) MED outpatients' department; MOT ambulance
Ameise ['aːmaizə] *f* (*-; -n*) ZO ant
'Ameisenhaufen *m* ZO anthill
Amerika [a'meːrika] America
Amerikaner [ameri'kaːnɐ] *m* (*-s; -*), **Ameri'kanerin** [-nərɪn] *f* (*-; -nen*), **ameri'kanisch** *adj* American
Amnestie [amnɛs'tiː] *f* (*-; -n*), **amnes'tieren** *v/t* (*no -ge-, h*) JUR amnesty
Amok ['aːmɔk] *m*: ***Amok laufen*** run amok
Ampel ['ampəl] *f* (*-; -n*) traffic light(s)
Amphibie [am'fiːbjə] *f* (*-; -n*) ZO amphibian
Ampulle [am'pʊlə] *f* (*-; -n*) ampoule
Amputation [amputa'tsjoːn] *f* (*-; -en*) MED amputation
amputieren [ampu'tiːrən] *v/t* (*no -ge-, h*) MED amputate
Amsel ['amzəl] *f* (*-; -n*) ZO blackbird
Amt [amt] *n* (*-[e]s; Ämter* ['ɛmtɐ]) office, department, *esp Am* bureau; position; duty, function; TEL exchange
'amtlich *adj* official
'Amtsarzt *m* medical examiner (*Br* officer)
Amtseinführung *f* inauguration
Amtsgeheimnis *n* official secret
Amtsgeschäfte *pl* official duties
Amtszeichen *n* TEL dial (*Br* dialling) tone
Amtszeit *f* term (of office)
Amulett [amu'lɛt] *n* (*-[e]s; -e*) amulet, (lucky) charm
amüsant [amy'zant] *adj* amusing, entertaining
amüsieren [amy'ziːrən] *v/t* (*no -ge-, h*) amuse; ***sich amüsieren*** enjoy o.s., have a good time; ***sich amüsieren über*** (*acc*) laugh at
an [an] **1.** *prp*: ***an der Themse*** (***Küste, Wand***) on the Thames (coast, wall); ***an s-m Schreibtisch*** at his desk; ***an der Hand*** by the hand; ***an der Arbeit*** at work; ***an den Hausaufgaben sitzen*** sit over one's homework; ***et. schicken an*** (*acc*) send s.th. to; ***sich lehnen an*** (*acc*) lean against; ***an die Tür*** *etc* ***klopfen*** knock at the door *etc*; ***an e-m Sonntagmorgen*** on a Sunday morning; ***an dem***

Tag, ... on the day ...; ***an Weihnachten*** *etc* at Christmas *etc*; → ***Mangel, Stelle, sterben***; **2.** *adv* on (*a. light etc*); ***von jetzt (da, heute) an*** from now (that time, today) on; ***München an 16.45*** arrival Munich 4.45 p.m.

Anabolikum [ana'bo:likum] *n* (*-s*; *-ka*) PHARM anabolic steroid

analog [ana'lo:k] *adj* analogous

Ana'log... *in cpds* analog(ue) (*computer etc*)

Analphabet [an?alfa'be:t] *m* (*-en*; *-en*), **Analpha'betin** *f* (*-*; *-nen*) illiterate (person)

Analyse [ana'ly:zə] *f* (*-*; *-n*) analysis

analysieren [analy'zi:rən] *v/t* (*no -ge-*, *h*) analy|ze, *Br* -se

Ananas ['ananas] *f* (*-*; *-*, *-se*) BOT pineapple

Anarchie [anar'çi:] *f* (*-*; *-n*) anarchy

Anatomie [anato'mi:] *f* (*-*; *-n*) anatomy

anatomisch [ana'to:mɪʃ] *adj* anatomical

'anbahnen *v/t* (*sep*, *-ge-*, *h*) pave the way for; ***sich anbahnen*** be developing; be impending

'Anbau *m* (*-[e]s*; *-ten*) a) AGR (*no pl*) cultivation, b) ARCH annex, extension

'anbauen *v/t* (*sep*, *-ge-*, *h*) AGR cultivate, grow; ARCH add (***an*** *acc* to), build on

'anbehalten *v/t* (*irr*, ***halten***, *sep*, *no -ge-*, *h*) keep on

an'bei *adv* ECON enclosed

'anbeißen (*irr*, ***beißen***, *sep*, *-ge-*, *h*) **1.** *v/t* take a bite of; **2.** *v/i fish*: bite; *fig* take the bait

'anbellen *v/t* (*sep*, *-ge-*, *h*) bark at

'anbeten *v/t* (*sep*, *-ge-*, *h*) adore, worship (*a. fig*)

'Anbetracht *m*: ***in Anbetracht (dessen, dass)*** considering (that)

'anbetteln *v/t* (*sep*, *-ge-*, *h*) ***j-n um et. anbetteln*** beg s.o. for s.th.

'anbiedern [-bi:dɐn] *v/refl* (*sep*, *-ge-*, *h*) curry favo(u)r (***bei*** with)

'anbieten *v/t* (*irr*, ***bieten***, *sep*, *-ge-*, *h*) offer

'anbinden *v/t* (*irr*, ***binden***, *sep*, *-ge-*, *h*) tie up; ***anbinden an*** (*acc or dat*) tie to

'Anblick *m* sight

'anblicken *v/t* (*sep*, *-ge-*, *h*) look at; glance at

'anbohren *v/t* (*sep*, *-ge-*, *h*) tap

'anbrechen (*irr*, ***brechen***, *sep*, *-ge-*) **1.** *v/t* (*h*) break into (*supplies*); open; **2.** *v/i* (*sein*) begin; *day*: break; *night*: fall

'anbrennen *v/i* (*irr*, ***brennen***, *sep*, *-ge-*, *sein*) burn (*a.* ***anbrennen lassen***)

'anbringen *v/t* (*irr*, ***bringen***, *sep*, *-ge-*, *h*) fix (***an*** *dat* to)

'Anbruch *m* (*-[e]s*; *no pl*) beginning; ***bei Anbruch der Nacht*** at nightfall

'anbrüllen *v/t* (*sep*, *-ge-*, *h*) roar at

Andacht ['andaxt] *f* (*-*; *-en*) REL a) (*no pl*) devotion, b) service; prayers

andächtig ['andɛçtɪç] *adj* REL devout

'andauern *v/i* (*sep*, *-ge-*, *h*) continue, go on, last

andauernd *adj and adv* → ***dauernd***

'Andenken *n* (*-s*; *-*) keepsake; souvenir (*both*: ***an*** *acc* of); ***zum Andenken an*** (*acc*) in memory of

andere ['andərə] *adj and indef pron* other; different; ***mit anderen Worten*** in other words; ***am anderen Morgen*** the next morning; ***et. (nichts) anderes*** s.th. (nothing) else; ***nichts anderes als*** nothing but; ***die anderen*** the others; ***alle anderen*** everybody else

andererseits ['andərɐ'zaits] *adv* on the other hand

ändern ['ɛndɐn] *v/t* (*ge-*, *h*) change; alter (*clothes*); ***ich kann es nicht ändern*** I can't help it; ***sich ändern*** change

'andern'falls *adv* otherwise

anders ['andɐs] *adv* different(ly); ***jemand anders*** somebody else; ***anders werden*** change; ***anders sein (als)*** be different (from); ***es geht nicht anders*** there is no other way

andersherum **1.** *adv* the other way round; **2.** F *adj* queer

anderswo(hin) *adv* elsewhere

anderthalb ['andɐt'halp] *adj* one and a half

'Änderung *f* (*-*; *-en*) change; alteration

'andeuten *v/t* (*sep*, *-ge-*, *h*) hint (at), suggest; indicate; ***j-m andeuten, dass*** give s.o. a hint that

'Andeutung *f* (*-*; *-en*) hint, suggestion

'Andrang *m* (*-[e]s*; *no pl*) crush; ECON rush (***nach*** for), run (***zu, nach*** on)

'andrehen *v/t* (*sep*, *-ge-*, *h*) turn on; F ***j-m et. andrehen*** fob s.th. off on s.o.

'androhen *v/t* (*sep*, *-ge-*, *h*) ***j-m et. androhen*** threaten s.o. with s.th.

'aneignen *v/refl* (*sep*, *-ge-*, *h*) acquire; *esp* JUR appropriate

anei'nander *adv tie etc* together; ***aneinander denken*** think of each other; ***aneinandergeraten*** *v/t* (*irr*, ***geraten***, *sep*, *sein*) clash (***mit*** with)

Anekdote [anɛk'do:tə] *f* (*-*; *-n*) anecdote

'anekeln *v/t* (*sep*, *-ge-*, *h*) disgust, sicken; ***es ekelt mich an*** it makes me sick

'anerkannt *adj* acknowledged, recognized

'anerkennen *v/t* (*irr*, ***kennen***, *sep*, *no -ge-*, *h*) acknowledge, recognize; appreciate

anerkennend *adj* appreciative

'Anerkennung *f* (*-*; *-en*) acknowledg(e)ment, recognition; appreciation

'anfahren (*irr*, ***fahren***, *sep*, *-ge-*) **1.** *v/i* (*sein*) start; **2.** *v/t* (*h*) deliver; MOT *etc* hit, *car etc*: *a.* run into; *fig* ***j-n anfahren*** jump on s.o.

'Anfahrt *f* journey, ride

'Anfall *m* MED fit, attack

'anfallen *v/t* (*irr*, ***fallen***, *sep*, *-ge-*, *h*) attack, assault; *dog*: go for

'anfällig *adj* delicate; ***anfällig für*** susceptible to

'Anfang *m* beginning, start; ***am Anfang*** at the beginning; ***Anfang Mai*** early in May; ***Anfang nächsten Jahres*** early next year; ***Anfang der neunziger Jahre*** in the early nineties; ***er ist Anfang 20*** he is in his early twenties; ***von Anfang an*** from the beginning *or* start

'anfangen *v/t and v/i* (*irr*, ***fangen***, *sep*, *-ge-*, *h*) begin, start; do

'Anfänger *m* (*-s*; -), **'Anfängerin** *f* (-; *-nen*) beginner

'anfangs *adv* at first

'Anfangsbuchstabe *m* initial (letter); ***großer Anfangsbuchstabe*** capital (letter)

Anfangsstadium *n*: ***im Anfangsstadium*** at an early stage

'anfassen *v/t* (*sep*, *-ge-*, *h*) touch; take (hold of); ***sich anfassen*** take each other by the hands; F ***zum Anfassen*** everyman's

'anfechtbar *adj* contestable

'anfechten *v/t* (*irr*, ***fechten***, *sep*, *-ge-*, *h*) contest

'Anfechtung *f* (-; *-en*) contesting

'anfertigen *v/t* (*sep*, *-ge-*, *h*) make, manufacture

'anfeuchten *v/t* (*sep*, *-ge-*, *h*) moisten

'anfeuern *fig v/t* (*sep*, *-ge-*, *h*) cheer

'anflehen *v/t* (*sep*, *-ge-*, *h*) implore

'anfliegen *v/t* (*irr*, ***fliegen***, *sep*, *-ge-*, *h*) AVIAT approach; fly (regularly) to

'Anflug *m* AVIAT approach; *fig* touch

'anfordern *v/t* (*sep*, *-ge-*, *h*) demand; request

'Anforderung *f* (-; *-en*) demand; request; *pl* requirements, qualifications

'Anfrage *f* (-; *-n*) inquiry

'anfragen *v/i* (*sep*, *-ge-*, *h*) inquire (***bei j-m nach et.*** of s.o. about s.th.)

'anfreunden *v/refl* (*sep*, *-ge-*, *h*) make friends (***mit*** with)

'anfühlen *v/refl* (*sep*, *-ge-*, *h*) feel; ***es fühlt sich weich an*** it feels soft

'anführen *v/t* (*sep*, *-ge-*, *h*) lead; state; F fool

'Anführer(in) leader

'Anführungszeichen *pl* quotation marks, inverted commas

'Angabe *f* (-; *-n*) statement; indication; F big talk; *tennis*: service; *pl* information, data; TECH specifications

'angeben (*irr*, ***geben***, *sep*, *-ge-*, *h*) **1.** *v/t* give, state; *customs*: declare; indicate; quote (*price*); **2.** *v/i* F *fig* brag, show off; *tennis*: serve

'Angeber F *m* (*-s*; -) braggart, show-off

Angeberei [ange:bə'rai] F *f* (-; *no pl*) bragging, showing off

angeblich ['ange:plıç] *adj* alleged

angeblich ist er ... he is said to be ...

'angeboren *adj* innate, inborn; MED congenital

'Angebot *n* (-[*e*]*s*, *-e*) offer (*a.* ECON); ***Angebot und Nachfrage*** supply and demand

'angebracht *adj* appropriate

angebunden *adj*: ***kurz angebunden*** curt

angegossen F *adj*: ***wie angegossen sitzen*** fit like a glove

angeheitert *adj* tipsy, *Br a.* (slightly) merry

'angehen (*irr*, ***gehen***, *sep*, *-ge-*, *sein*) **1.** F *v/i light etc*: go on; **2.** *v/t* concern; ***das geht dich nichts an*** that is none of your business

angehend *adj* future; ***angehender Arzt*** doctor-to-be

'angehören *v/i* (*sep*, *no -ge-*, *h*) belong to

'Angehörige *m*, *f* (*-n*; *-n*) relative; member; ***die nächsten Angehörigen*** the next of kin

'Angeklagte *m*, *f* (*-n*; *-n*) JUR defendant

Angel ['aŋəl] *f* (-; *-n*) fishing tackle; TECH hinge

'Angelegenheit *f* (-; *-en*) matter, affair

angelehnt *adj door etc*: ajar

'angelernt *adj* semi-skilled (*worker*)

'Angelhaken *m* fishhook

'angeln (*ge-*, *h*) **1.** *v/i* (***nach*** for) fish, angle (*both a. fig*); **2.** *v/t* catch, hook

'Angelrute *f* fishing rod

'Angelsachse [-zaksə] *m* (*-n*; *-n*), **'angelsächsisch** [-zεksıʃ] *adj* Anglo-Saxon

'Angelschein *m* fishing permit

'Angelschnur *f* fishing line

angemessen *adj* proper, suitable; just (*punishment*); reasonable (*price*)

'angenehm *adj* pleasant, agreeable; ***angenehm!*** pleased to meet you

'angenommen *cj* (let's) suppose, supposing

angeregt *adj* animated; lively

angeschrieben *adj*: ***bei j-m gut (schlecht) angeschrieben sein*** be in s.o.'s good (bad) books

angesehen *adj* respected

'angesichts *prp* (*gen*) in view of

'**Angestellte** *m, f (-n; -n)* employee (***bei*** with), *pl* the staff
'**angetan** *adj*: ***ganz angetan sein von*** be taken with
angetrunken *adj* (slightly) drunk; ***in angetrunkenem Zustand*** under the influence of alcohol
angewandt *adj* applied
angewiesen *adj*: ***angewiesen auf*** *(acc)* dependent (up)on
'**angewöhnen** *v/t (sep, no -ge-, h)* ***sich (j-m) angewöhnen, et. zu tun*** get (s.o.) used to doing s.th.; ***sich das Rauchen angewöhnen*** take to smoking
'**Angewohnheit** *f* habit
Angina [aŋ'giːna] *f (-; -nen)* MED tonsillitis
'**angleichen** *v/t (irr,* ***gleichen****, sep, -ge-, h)* adjust (***an*** *acc* to)
Angler ['aŋlɐ] *m (-s; -)* angler
Anglist [aŋ'glɪst] *m (-en; -en),* **An'glistin** *f (-; -nen)* student of (*or* graduate in) English
'**angreifen** *v/t (irr,* ***greifen****, sep, -ge-, h)* attack (*a.* SPORT *and fig*); affect (*health etc*); touch (*supplies*)
'**Angreifer** *m (-s; -)* attacker, SPORT *a.* offensive player; *esp* POL aggressor
'**angrenzend** *adj* adjacent (***an*** *acc* to)
'**Angriff** *m* attack (*a.* SPORT *and fig*); MIL assault, charge; ***in Angriff nehmen*** set about
'**angriffslustig** *adj* aggressive
Angst [aŋst] *f (-; Ängste* ['ɛŋstə]) fear (***vor*** *dat* of); ***Angst haben*** (***vor*** *dat*) be afraid *or* scared (of); ***j-m Angst einjagen*** frighten *or* scare s.o.; (***hab***) ***keine Angst!*** don't be afraid!
Angsthase F *m* chicken
ängstigen ['ɛŋstɪgən] *v/t (ge-, h)* frighten, scare; ***sich ängstigen*** be afraid (***vor*** *dat* of); be worried (***um*** about)
ängstlich ['ɛŋstlɪç] *adj* timid, fearful; anxious
'**anhaben** F *v/t (irr,* ***haben****, sep, -ge-, h)* have on (*a. light etc*), *a.* wear, be wearing (*dress etc*)
'**anhalten** *(irr,* ***halten****, sep, -ge-, h)* **1.** *v/t* stop; ***den Atem anhalten*** hold one's breath; **2.** *v/i* stop; continue
anhaltend *adj* continual
'**Anhalter** *m (-s; -)* hitchhiker; F ***per Anhalter fahren*** hitchhike
'**Anhaltspunkt** *m* clue
an'hand *prp (gen)* by means of
'**Anhang** *m* a) appendix, b) (*no pl*) relations
'**anhängen** *v/t (sep, -ge-, h)* add; hang up; RAIL, MOT couple (***an*** *acc* to)
'**Anhänger** *m (-s; -)* follower, supporter (*a.* SPORT); pendant; label, tag; MOT trailer
'**anhänglich** *adj* affectionate; *contp* clinging
'**anhäufen** *v/t and v/refl (sep, -ge-, h)* heap up, accumulate
'**Anhäufung** *f (-; -en)* accumulation
'**anheben** *v/t (irr,* ***heben****, sep, -ge-, h)* lift, raise (*a. price*); MOT jack up
'**anheften** *v/t (sep, -ge-, h)* attach, tack (*both*: ***an*** *acc* to)
Anhieb *m*: ***auf Anhieb*** on the first try
'**anhimmeln** F *v/t (sep, -ge-, h)* idolize, worship
'**Anhöhe** *f* rise, hill, elevation
anhören *v/t (sep, -ge-, h)* listen to; ***mit anhören*** overhear; ***es hört sich ... an*** it sounds ...
'**Anhörung** *f (-; -en)* hearing
animieren [ani'miːrən] *v/t (no -ge-, h)* encourage; stimulate
'**ankämpfen** *v/i (sep, -ge-, h)* ***ankämpfen gegen*** fight *s.th.*
'**Ankauf** *m* purchase
Anker ['aŋkɐ] *m (-s; -)* MAR anchor; ***vor Anker gehen*** drop anchor
'**ankern** *v/i (ge-, h)* MAR anchor
'**anketten** *v/t (sep, -ge-, h)* chain up
'**Anklage** *f (-; no pl)* JUR accusation, charge (*a. fig*)
'**anklagen** *v/t (sep, -ge-, h)* JUR accuse (***wegen*** of), charge (with) (*both a. fig.*)
'**anklammern** *v/t (sep, -ge-, h)* clip *s.th.* on; ***sich anklammern*** (***an*** *acc*) cling (to)
Anklang *m*: ***Anklang finden*** meet with approval
'**ankleben** *v/t (sep, -ge-, h)* stick on (***an*** *dat or acc* to)
'**anklicken** *v/t (sep, -ge-, h)* EDP click
'**anklopfen** *v/i (sep, -ge-, h)* knock (***an*** *dat or acc* at)
'**anknipsen** *v/t (sep, -ge-, h)* switch on
'**anknüpfen** *v/t (sep, -ge-, h)* tie (***an*** *acc* to); *fig* begin; ***Beziehungen anknüpfen*** (***zu***) establish contacts (with)
'**ankommen** *v/i (irr,* ***kommen****, sep, -ge-, sein)* arrive; ***nicht gegen j-n ankommen*** be no match for s.o.; ***es kommt*** (***ganz***) ***darauf an*** it (all) depends; ***es kommt darauf an, dass*** what matters is; ***darauf kommt es nicht an*** that doesn't matter; ***es darauf ankommen lassen*** take a chance; ***gut ankommen*** (***bei***) *fig* go down well (with)
'**ankündigen** *v/t (sep, -ge-, h)* announce; advertise
'**Ankündigung** *f* announcement; advertisement
Ankunft ['ankʊnft] *f (-; no pl)* arrival
'**anlächeln**, '**anlachen** *v/t (sep, -ge-, h)*

smile at
ˈ**Anlage** *f* arrangement; facility; plant; TECH system; (stereo *etc*) set; ECON investment; enclosure; *fig* gift; *pl* park, gardens; ***sanitäre Anlagen*** sanitary facilities
Anlass [ˈanlas] *m* (*-es*; *Anlässe* [ˈanlɛsə]) occasion; cause
ˈ**anlassen** *v/t* (*irr*, ***lassen***, *sep*, *-ge-*, *h*) MOT start; F keep on, leave on (*a. light etc*)
ˈ**Anlasser** *m* (*-s*; *-*) MOT starter
anlässlich [ˈanlɛslɪç] *prp* (*gen*) on the occasion of
ˈ**Anlauf** *m* SPORT run-up; *fig* start
ˈ**anlaufen** (*irr*, ***laufen***, *sep*, *-ge-*) **1.** *v/i* (*sein*) run up; *fig* start; *metal*: tarnish; *glasses etc*: steam up; **2.** *v/t* (*h*) MAR call *or* touch at
ˈ**anlegen** (*sep*, *-ge-*, *h*) **1.** *v/t* put on (*dress etc*); lay out (garden *etc*); build (*road etc*); invest (*money*); found (*town etc*); MED apply (*dressing etc*); lay in (*supplies*); ***sich mit j-m anlegen*** pick a quarrel with s.o.; **2.** *v/i* MAR land; moor; ***es anlegen auf*** (*acc*) aim at
ˈ**Anleger** *m* (*-s*; *-*) ECON investor; MAR landing stage
ˈ**anlehnen** *v/t* (*sep*, *-ge-*, *h*) lean (***an*** *acc* against); leave *door etc* ajar; ***sich anlehnen an*** (*acc*) lean against, *fig* lean on *s.o.*
Anleihe [ˈanlaiə] *f* (*-*; *-n*) ECON loan
ˈ**Anleitung** *f* (*-*; *-en*) guidance, instruction; *written* instructions
ˈ**Anliegen** *n* (*-s*; *-*) request; message (*of a film etc*)
Anlieger [ˈanliːgɐ] *m* (*-s*; *-*) resident
ˈ**anlocken** *v/t* (*sep*, *-ge-*, *h*) attract, lure
ˈ**anmachen** *v/t* (*sep*, *-ge-*, *h*) light (*fire etc*); turn on (*light etc*); dress (*salad*); F chat *s.o.* up; turn *s.o.* on
ˈ**anmalen** *v/t* (*sep*, *-ge-*, *h*) paint
ˈ**Anmarsch** *m*: ***im Anmarsch*** on the way
anmaßen *v/t* (*sep*, *-ge-*, *h*) ***sich anmaßen*** assume; claim (*right*); ***sich anmaßen, et. zu tun*** presume to do s.th.
anmaßend *adj* arrogant
ˈ**anmelden** *v/t* (*sep*, *-ge-*, *h*) announce (*visitor*); register (*birth etc*); *customs*: declare; ***sich anmelden*** enrol(l) (*for classes etc*); register (*at a hotel*); ***sich anmelden bei*** make an appointment with (*doctor etc*)
ˈ**Anmeldung** *f* announcement; registration, enrol(l)ment
ˈ**anmerken** *v/t* (*sep*, *-ge-*, *h*) ***j-m et. anmerken*** notice s.th. in s.o.; ***sich et.*** (***nichts***) ***anmerken lassen*** (not) let it show
ˈ**Anmerkung** *f* (*-*; *-en*) note; annotation, footnote
Anmut [ˈanmuːt] *f* (*-*; *no pl*) grace
ˈ**anmutig** *adj* graceful
ˈ**annähen** *v/t* (*sep*, *-ge-*, *h*) sew on (***an*** *acc* to)
ˈ**annähernd** *adv* approximately
ˈ**Annäherung** *f* (*-*; *-en*) approach (***an*** *acc* to)
ˈ**Annäherungsversuche** *pl* advances, F pass
Annahme [ˈanaːmə] *f* (*-*; *-n*) a) (*no pl*) acceptance (*a. fig*), b) assumption
ˈ**annehmbar** *adj* acceptable; reasonable (*price etc*)
ˈ**annehmen** *v/t* (*irr*, ***nehmen***, *sep*, *-ge-*, *h*) accept; suppose; adopt (*child*, *name*); take (*ball*); take on (*color*, *look etc*); ***sich e-r Sache*** *or* ***j-s annehmen*** take care of s.th. *or* s.o.
ˈ**Annehmlichkeiten** *pl* comforts, amenities
Annonce [aˈnõːsə] *f* (*-*; *-n*) advertisement
annullieren [anʊˈliːrən] *v/t* (*no -ge-*, *h*) annul; ECON cancel
anöden [ˈanʔøːdən] F *v/t* (*sep*, *-ge-*, *h*) bore *s.o.* to death
anonym [anoˈnyːm] *adj* anonymous
Anonymität [anonymiˈtɛːt] *f* (*-*; *no pl*) anonymity
Anorak [ˈanorak] *m* (*-s*; *-s*) anorak
ˈ**anordnen** *v/t* (*sep*, *-ge-*, *h*) arrange; give order(s), order
ˈ**Anordnung** *f* (*-*; *-en*) arrangement; direction, order
ˈ**anorganisch** *adj* CHEM inorganic
ˈ**anpacken** F *fig* (*sep*, *-ge-*, *h*) **1.** *v/t* tackle; **2.** *v/i*: ***mit anpacken*** lend a hand
ˈ**anpassen** *v/t* (*sep*, *-ge-*, *h*) adapt, adjust (*both a.* ***sich anpassen***) (*dat*, ***an*** *acc* to)
ˈ**Anpassung** *f* (*-*; *-en*) adaptation, adjustment
ˈ**anpassungsfähig** *adj* adaptable
ˈ**Anpassungsfähigkeit** *f* adaptability
ˈ**Anpfiff** *m* SPORT starting whistle; F *fig* dressing-down
ˈ**anpflanzen** *v/t* (*sep*, *-ge-*, *h*) cultivate, plant
ˈ**Anpflanzung** *f* cultivation
ˈ**anpöbeln** *v/t* (*sep*, *-ge-*, *h*) accost; shout abuse at
anprangern [ˈanpraŋɐn] *v/t* (*sep*, *-ge-*, *h*) denounce
ˈ**anpreisen** *v/t* (*irr*, ***preisen***, *sep*, *-ge-*, *h*) push; plug
ˈ**anproˌbieren** *v/t* (*no -ge-*, *h*) try on
ˈ**anpumpen** F *v/t* (*sep*, *-ge-*, *h*) touch *s.o.* (***um*** for)
ˈ**anraten** *v/t* (*irr*, ***raten***, *sep*, *-ge-*, *h*) advise
ˈ**anrechnen** *v/t* (*sep*, *-ge-*, *h*) charge; allow
ˈ**Anrecht** *n*: ***ein Anrecht haben auf*** (*acc*)

be entitled to
'**Anrede** *f* address
'**anreden** *v/t (sep, -ge-, h)* address (***mit Namen*** by name)
'**anregen** *v/t (sep, -ge-, h)* stimulate; suggest
anregend *adj* stimulating
'**Anregung** *f* stimulation; suggestion
'**Anregungsmittel** *n* PHARM stimulant
'**Anreiz** *m* incentive
'**anrichten** *v/t (sep, -ge-, h)* GASTR prepare, dress; cause, do *(damage etc)*
anrüchig ['anrʏçɪç] *adj* disreputable
'**Anruf** *m* call *(a.* TEL)
Anrufbeantworter *m* TEL answering machine
'**anrufen** *v/t (irr,* ***rufen****, sep, -ge-, h)* TEL call *or* ring up, phone
'**anrühren** *v/t (sep, -ge-, h)* touch; mix
'**Ansage** *f* announcement
'**ansagen** *v/t (sep, -ge-, h)* announce
Ansager ['anza:gɐ] *m (-s; -)*, '**Ansagerin** [-gərɪn] *f (-; -nen)* announcer
'**ansammeln** *v/t and v/refl (sep, -ge-, h)* accumulate
'**Ansammlung** *f* collection, accumulation; crowd
'**Ansatz** *m* start (***zu*** of); attempt (***zu*** at); approach; TECH attachment; MATH set--up; *pl* first signs
'**anschaffen** *v/t (sep, -ge-, h)* get; ***sich et. anschaffen*** buy *or* get (o.s.) s.th.
'**Anschaffung** *f (-; -en)* purchase, buy
'**anschauen** *v/t (sep, -ge-, h)* → ***ansehen***
'**anschaulich** *adj* graphic *(account etc)*
'**Anschauung** *f (-; -en)* (***von***) view (of), opinion (about, of)
'**Anschauungsmateri,al** *n* PED visual aids
'**Anschein** *m (-[e]s; no pl)* appearance; ***allem Anschein nach*** to all appearances; ***den Anschein erwecken, als (ob)*** give the impression of …
'**anscheinend** *adv* apparently
'**anschieben** *v/t (irr,* ***schieben****, sep, -ge-, h)* give a push *(a.* MOT)
'**Anschlag** *m* attack; poster; bill, notice; *typewriter*: stroke; MUS, *swimming*: touch; ***e-n Anschlag auf j-n verüben*** make an attempt on s.o.'s life
Anschlagbrett *n* bulletin *(esp Br* notice) board
'**anschlagen** *(irr,* ***schlagen****, sep, -ge-, h)* **1.** *v/t* post; MUS strike; chip *(cup etc)*; **2.** *v/i dog*: bark; take (effect) *(a.* MED); *swimming*: touch the wall
'**anschließen** *v/t (irr,* ***schließen****, sep, -ge-, h)* ELECTR, TECH connect; ***sich anschließen*** follow; agree with; ***sich j-m or e-r Sache anschließen*** join s.o. or s.th.
anschließend **1.** *adj* following; **2.** *adv* then, afterwards
'**Anschluss** *m* connection; ***im Anschluss an*** *(acc)* following; ***Anschluss finden (bei)*** make contact *or* friends (with); ***Anschluss bekommen*** TEL get through
'**anschmiegen** *v/refl (sep, -ge-, h)* snuggle up (***an*** *acc* to)
'**anschmiegsam** *adj* affectionate
'**anschnallen** *v/t (sep, -ge-, h)* strap on, put on *(a. ski)*; ***sich anschnallen*** AVIAT, MOT fasten one's seat belt
'**anschnauzen** F *v/t (sep, -ge-, h)* tell *s.o.* off, *Am a.* bawl *s.o.* out
'**anschneiden** *v/t (irr,* ***schneiden****, sep, -ge-, h)* cut; *fig* bring up
'**anschrauben** *v/t (sep, -ge-, h)* screw on (***an*** *acc* to)
'**anschreiben** *v/t (irr,* ***schreiben****, sep, -ge-, h)* write on the (black)board; ***j-n anschreiben*** write to s.o.; ***(et.) anschreiben lassen*** buy (s.th.) on credit; → ***angeschrieben***
'**anschreien** *v/t (irr,* ***schreien****, sep, -ge-, h)* shout at
'**Anschrift** *f* address
'**Anschuldigung** *f (-; -en)* accusation
'**anschwellen** *v/i (irr,* ***schwellen****, sep, -ge-, sein)* swell *(a. fig)*
'**anschwemmen** *v/t (sep, -ge-, h)* wash ashore
'**ansehen** *v/t (irr,* ***sehen****, sep, -ge-, h)* look at, have *or* take a look at; watch; see *(all a.* ***sich*** *[dat]* ***ansehen****)*; ***ansehen als*** look upon as; ***et. mit ansehen*** watch *or* witness s.th.; ***man sieht ihm an, dass …*** one can see that …
'**Ansehen** *n (-s; no pl)* reputation
ansehnlich ['anze:nlɪç] *adj* considerable
'**anseilen** *v/t and v/refl (sep, -ge-, h)* rope
'**ansetzen** *(sep, -ge-, h)* **1.** *v/t* put (***an*** *acc* to); put on, add; fix, set *(date etc)*; ***Fett*** *etc* **ansetzen** put on weight *etc*; **2.** *v/i*: ***ansetzen zu*** prepare for *(landing etc)*
'**Ansicht** *f (-; -en)* view, *a.* opinion, *a.* sight; ***der Ansicht sein, dass …*** be of the opinion that …; ***meiner Ansicht nach*** in my opinion; ***zur Ansicht*** ECON on approval
'**Ansichtskarte** *f* picture postcard
Ansichtssache *f* matter of opinion
'**anspannen** *v/t (sep, -ge-, h)* strain
'**Anspannung** *f (-; -en)* strain, exertion
'**anspielen** *v/i (sep, -ge-, h) soccer*: kick off; ***anspielen auf*** *(acc)* allude to, hint at
'**Anspielung** *f (-; -en)* allusion, hint
'**anspitzen** *v/t (sep, -ge-, h)* sharpen
'**Ansporn** *m (-[e]s; no pl)* incentive
'**anspornen** *v/t (sep, -ge-, h)* encourage,

spur *s.o.* on
'Ansprache *f* address, speech; ***e-e Ansprache halten*** deliver an address
'ansprechen *v/t* (*irr*, ***sprechen***, *sep*, *-ge-*, *h*) address, speak to; *fig* appeal to
ansprechend *adj* attractive
'Ansprechpartner *m* s.o. to talk to, contact
'anspringen (*irr*, ***springen***, *sep*, *-ge-*) **1.** *v/i* (*sein*) *engine*: start; **2.** *v/t* (*h*) jump (up)on
'anspritzen *v/t* (*sep*, *-ge-*, *h*) spatter
'Anspruch *m* claim (***auf*** *acc* to) (*a.* JUR); ***Anspruch haben auf*** (*acc*) be entitled to; ***Anspruch erheben auf*** (*acc*) claim; ***Zeit in Anspruch nehmen*** take up time
'anspruchslos *adj* modest; light, undemanding (*reading etc*); *contp* trivial
'anspruchsvoll *adj* demanding; sophisticated, refined (*tastes etc*)
Anstalt ['anʃtalt] *f* (*-; -en*) establishment, institution; mental hospital; ***Anstalten machen zu*** get ready for
'Anstand *m* (*-[e]s; no pl*) decency; manners
'anständig *adj* decent (*a. fig*)
'anstandslos *adv* unhesitatingly; without difficulty
'anstarren *v/t* (*sep*, *-ge-*, *h*) stare at
an'statt *prp* (*gen*) *and cj* instead of
'anstechen *v/t* (*irr*, ***stechen***, *sep*, *-ge-*, *h*) tap (*barrel*)
'anstecken *v/t* (*sep*, *-ge-*, *h*) stick on; put on (*ring*); light; set fire to; MED infect; ***sich bei j-m anstecken*** MED catch s.th. from s.o.
ansteckend *adj* MED infectious, contagious, catching (*all a. fig*)
'Anstecknadel *f* pin, button
'Ansteckung *f* (*-; no pl*) MED infection, contagion
'anstehen *v/i* (*irr*, ***stehen***, *sep*, *-ge-*, *h*) (***nach*** for) stand in line, *Br* queue up
'ansteigen *v/i* (*irr*, ***steigen***, *sep*, *-ge-*, *sein*) rise
'anstellen *v/t* (*sep*, *-ge-*, *h*) engage, employ; TV *etc*: turn on; MOT start; F be up to (*s.th. illegal etc*); make (*inquiries etc*); ***sich anstellen*** line up (***nach*** for), *Br* queue up (for); F (make a) fuss
'Anstellung *f* job, position; ***e-e Anstellung finden*** find employment
Anstieg ['anʃti:k] *m* (*-[e]s; no pl*) rise, increase
'anstiften *v/t* (*sep*, *-ge-*, *h*) incite
'Anstifter *m* instigator
'Anstiftung *f* incitement
'anstimmen *v/t* (*sep*, *-ge-*, *h*) MUS strike up
'Anstoß *m soccer*: kickoff; *fig* initiative, impulse; offen|se, *Br* -ce; ***Anstoß erregen*** give offense (***bei*** to); ***Anstoß nehmen an*** take offense at; ***den Anstoß zu et. geben*** start s.th., initiate s.th.
'anstoßen (*irr*, ***stoßen***, *sep*, *-ge-*) **1.** *v/t* (*h*) nudge *s.o.*; **2.** *v/i* a) (*sein*) knock, bump, b) (*h*) clink glasses; ***anstoßen auf*** (*acc*) drink to *s.o. or s.th.*
anstößig ['anʃtø:sɪç] *adj* offensive
'anstrahlen *v/t* (*sep*, *-ge-*, *h*) illuminate; beam at *s.o.*
'anstreichen *v/t* (*irr*, ***streichen***, *sep*, *-ge-*, *h*) paint; PED mark (*mistakes etc*)
'Anstreicher *m* (house)painter
'anstrengen *v/refl* (*sep*, *-ge-*, *h*) try (hard), make an effort
anstrengend *adj* strenuous, hard
'Anstrengung *f* (*-; -en*) exertion, strain; effort
Ansturm *fig m* (*-[e]s; no pl*) rush (***auf*** *acc* for)
'Anteil *m* share (*a.* ECON), portion; ***Anteil nehmen an*** (*dat*) take an interest in; sympathize with
Anteilnahme [-na:mə] *f* (*-; no pl*) sympathy; interest
Antenne [an'tɛnə] *f* (*-; -n*) antenna, *Br* aerial
Anti..., anti... *in cpds* anti...
Antialko'holiker *m* teetotal(l)er
Anti'babypille F *f* birth control pill, F the pill
Anti'biotikum *n* MED antibiotic
Antiblo'ckiersys͵tem *n* MOT anti-lock braking system
antik [an'ti:k] *adj* antique, HIST *a.* ancient
An'tike *f* (*-; no pl*) ancient world
'Antikörper *m* MED antibody
Antilope [anti'lo:pə] *f* (*-; -n*) ZO antelope
Antipathie [antipa'ti:] *f* (*-; -n*) antipathy
Antiquariat [antikva'rja:t] *n* (*-[e]s; -e*) second-hand bookshop
antiquarisch [anti'kva:rɪʃ] *adj and adv* second-hand
Antiquitäten [antikvi'tɛ:tən] *pl* antiques
Antiquitätenladen *m* antique shop
Antisemit [-ze'mi:t] *m* (*-en; -en*) anti-Semite
antise'mitisch *adj* anti-Semitic
Antisemitismus [-zemi'tɪsmʊs] *m* (*-; no pl*) anti-Semitism
Antrag ['antra:k] *m* (*-[e]s; Anträge* ['antrɛ:gə]) application; PARL motion; proposal; ***Antrag stellen auf*** (*acc*) make an application for; PARL move for
Antragsteller(in) [-ʃtɛlɐ (-lərɪn)] *m* (*-s; -/-; -nen*) applicant; PARL mover
'antreiben (*irr*, ***treiben***, *sep*, *-ge-*) **1.** *v/t* (*h*) TECH drive; urge *s.o.* (on); **2.** *v/i* (*sein*)

float ashore

'antreten (*irr*, ***treten***, *sep*, *-ge-*) **1.** *v/t* (*h*) enter upon (*office etc*); take up (*position*); set out on (*journey*); **2.** *v/i* (*sein*) take one's place; MIL line up

'Antrieb *m* TECH drive (*a. fig*), propulsion; *fig* motive, impulse; ***aus eigenem Antrieb*** of one's own accord

'antun *v/t* (*irr*, ***tun***, *sep*, *-ge-*, *h*) ***j-m et. antun*** do s.th. to s.o.; ***sich et. antun*** lay hands on o.s.

Antwort ['antvɔrt] *f* (-; *-en*) answer (***auf*** *acc* to), reply (to)

'antworten *v/i* (*ge-*, *h*) answer (***j-m*** s.o., ***auf et.*** s.th.), reply (to s.o. *or* s.th.)

'anvertrauen *v/t* (*sep*, *no -ge-*, *h*) ***j-m et. anvertrauen*** (en)trust s.o. with s.th.; confide s.th. to s.o.

'anwachsen *v/i* (*irr*, ***wachsen***, *sep*, *-ge-*, *sein*) BOT take root; *fig* increase

Anwalt ['anvalt] *m* (-[*e*]*s*; *Anwälte* ['anvɛltə]) → ***Rechtsanwalt***

'Anwärter *m* candidate (***auf*** *acc* for)

'anweisen *v/t* (*irr*, ***weisen***, *sep*, *-ge-*, *h*) instruct; direct, order

'Anweisung *f* instruction; order

'anwenden *v/t* ([irr, ***wenden***,] *sep*, *-ge-*, *h*) use; apply (***auf*** *acc* to)

'Anwendung *f* use; application

'anwerben *v/t* (*irr*, ***werben***, *sep*, *-ge-*, *h*) recruit (*a. fig*)

'Anwesen *n* (*-s*; -) estate; property

'anwesend *adj* present

'Anwesenheit *f* (-; *no pl*) presence; PED attendance; ***die Anwesenheit feststellen*** call the roll

'Anwesenheitsliste *f* attendance record (*Br* list)

anwidern ['anviːdɐn] *v/t* (*sep*, *-ge-*, *h*) make *s.o.* sick

'Anzahl *f* (-; *no pl*) number, quantity

'anzahlen *v/t* (*sep*, *-ge-*, *h*) pay on account

'Anzahlung *f* down payment

'anzapfen *v/t* (*sep*, *-ge-*, *h*) tap

'Anzeichen *n* symptom (*a.* MED), sign

Anzeige ['antsaigə] *f* (-; *-n*) advertisement; announcement; JUR information; EDP display; TECH reading

'anzeigen *v/t* (*sep*, *-ge-*, *h*) announce; report to the police; TECH indicate, show

'anziehen *v/t* (*irr*, ***ziehen***, *sep*, *-ge-*, *h*) put on (*dress etc*); dress *s.o.*; *fig* attract, draw; tighten (*screw*); pull (*lever etc*); ***sich anziehen*** get dressed; dress

anziehend *adj* attractive

'Anziehung *f* (-; *no pl*), **'Anziehungskraft** *f* (-; *no pl*) PHYS attraction, *fig a.* appeal

'Anzug *m* suit

anzüglich ['antsyːklɪç] *adj* suggestive (*joke*); personal, offensive (*remark etc*)

'anzünden *v/t* (*sep*, *-ge-*, *h*) light; set on fire

apart [a'part] *adj* striking

Apartment [a'partmənt] *n* (*-s*; *-s*) studio (apartment *or Br* flat)

apathisch [a'paːtɪʃ] *adj* apathetic

Apfel ['apfəl] *m* (*-s*; *Äpfel* ['ɛpfəl]) BOT apple

Apfelmus *n* GASTR apple sauce

Apfelsine [apfəl'ziːnə] *f* (-; *-n*) BOT orange

'Apfelwein *m* cider

Apostel [a'pɔstəl] *m* (*-s*; -) REL apostle

Apostroph [apo'strɔf] *m* (*-s*; *-e*) apostrophe

Apotheke [apo'teːkə] *f* (-; *-n*) pharmacy, drugstore, *Br* chemist's

Apotheker [apo'teːkɐ] *m* (*-s*; -), **Apo'thekerin** *f* (-; *-nen*) pharmacist, druggist, *Br* chemist

App. ABBR *of* ***Apparat*** TEL ext., extension

Apparat [apa'raːt] *m* (-[*e*]*s*; *-e*) apparatus; device; (tele)phone; radio; TV set; camera; POL *etc* machine(ry); ***am Apparat!*** TEL speaking!; ***am Apparat bleiben*** TEL hold the line

Appell [a'pɛl] *m* (*-s*; *-e*) appeal (***an*** *acc* to); MIL roll call

appellieren [apɛ'liːrən] *v/i* (*no -ge-*, *h*) (make an) appeal (***an*** *acc* to)

Appetit [ape'tiːt] *m* (-[*e*]*s*; *no pl*) appetite (***auf*** *acc* for); ***Appetit auf et. haben*** feel like s.th.; ***guten Appetit!*** enjoy your meal!

appe'titanregend *adj* appetizing

Appe'tithappen *m* GASTR appetizer

appe'titlich *adj* appetizing, savo(u)ry, *fig a.* inviting

applaudieren [aplau'diːrən] *v/i* (*no -ge-*, *h*) applaud

Applaus [a'plaus] *m* (*-es*; *no pl*) applause

Aprikose [apri'koːzə] *f* (-; *-n*) BOT apricot

April [a'prɪl] *m* (-[*s*]; *no pl*) April; ***April! April!*** April fool!

Aquaplaning [akva'plaːnɪŋ] *n* (-[*s*]; *no pl*) MOT hydroplaning, *Br* aquaplaning

Aquarell [akva'rɛl] *n* (*-s*; *-e*) watercolo(u)r

Aquarium [a'kvaːrjʊm] *n* (*-s*; *-ien*) aquarium

Äquator [ɛ'kvaːtoːɐ] *m* (*-s*; *no pl*) equator

Ära ['ɛːra] *f* (-; *no pl*) era

Araber ['arabɐ] *m* (*-s*; -), **'Araberin** [-bərɪn] *f* (-; *-nen*) Arab

arabisch [a'raːbɪʃ] *adj* Arabian; Arabic

Arbeit ['arbait] *f* (-; *-en*) work, ECON, POL *a.* labo(u)r; employment, job; PED test; *scientific etc* paper; workmanship; ***bei der Arbeit*** at work; ***zur Arbeit gehen***

or ***fahren*** go to work; ***gute Arbeit leisten*** make a good job of it; ***sich an die Arbeit machen*** set to work
'arbeiten *v/i* (*ge-*, *h*) work (***an*** *dat* at, on)
'Arbeiter *m* (*-s*; -), **'Arbeiterin** *f* (-; *-nen*) worker
'Arbeitgeber *m* (*-s*; -) employer
'Arbeitnehmer *m* (*-s*; -) employee
'Arbeitsamt *n Am* labor office, *Br* job centre
Arbeitsblatt *n* PED worksheet
Arbeitserlaubnis *f* green card, *Br* work permit
'arbeitsfähig *adj* fit for work
'Arbeitsgang *m* TECH operation
Arbeitsgemeinschaft *f* work *or* study group
Arbeitsgericht *n* JUR labor court, *Br* industrial tribunal
Arbeitshose *f* overalls
Arbeitskleidung *f* working clothes
Arbeitskräfte *pl* workers, labo(u)r
'arbeitslos *adj* unemployed, out of work
'Arbeitslose *m*, *f* (*-n*; *-n*) ***die Arbeitslosen*** *pl* the unemployed
'Arbeitslosengeld *n* unemployment compensation (*Br* benefit); ***Arbeitslosengeld beziehen*** F be on the dole
'Arbeitslosigkeit *f* (-; *no pl*) unemployment
'Arbeitsmarkt *m* labo(u)r market
Arbeitsmi,nister *m Am* Secretary of Labor; *Br* Minister of Labour
Arbeitsniederlegung *f* strike, walkout
Arbeitspause *f* break, intermission
Arbeitsplatz *m* workplace; job
'arbeitsscheu *adj* work-shy
'Arbeitsspeicher *m* EDP main memory
Arbeitssuche *f*: ***er ist auf Arbeitssuche*** he is looking for a job
Arbeitssüchtige *m*, *f* workaholic
Arbeitstag *m* workday
'arbeitsunfähig *adj* unfit for work; *permanently* disabled
'Arbeitsweise *f* method (of working)
Arbeitszeit *f* (***gleitende*** flexible) working hours
Arbeitszeitverkürzung *f* fewer working hours
Arbeitszimmer *n* study
Archäologe [arçɛo'lo:gə] *m* (*-n*; *-n*) arch(a)eologist
Archäologie [arçɛolo'gi:] *f* (-; *no pl*) arch(a)eology
Archäo'login *f* (-; *-nen*) arch(a)eologist
Arche ['arçə] *f* (-; *-n*) ark; ***die Arche Noah*** Noah's ark
Architekt [arçi'tɛkt] *m* (*-en*; *-en*), **Archi'tektin** *f* (-; *-nen*) architect
architektonisch [-tɛk'to:nɪʃ] *adj* architectural
Architektur [-tɛk'tu:ɐ] *f* (-; *-en*) architecture
Archiv [ar'çi:f] *n* (*-s*; *-e*) archives; record office
Arena [a're:na] *f* (-; *-nen*) ring
Ärger ['ɛrgɐ] *m* (*-s*; *no pl*) anger (***über*** *acc* at); trouble; F ***j-m Ärger machen*** cause s.o. trouble
'ärgerlich *adj* angry (***über, auf*** *acc* at *s.th.*; with *s.o.*); annoying
'ärgern *v/t* (*ge-*, *h*) annoy; ***sich ärgern*** be annoyed (***über*** *acc* at, about *s.th.*, with *s.o.*)
'Ärgernis *n* (*-ses*; *-se*) nuisance
arglos ['arklo:s] *adj* innocent
Argwohn ['arkvo:n] *m* (*-[e]s*; *no pl*) suspicion (***gegen*** of)
'argwöhnisch [-vø:nɪʃ] *adj* suspicious
Arie ['a:rjə] *f* (-; *-n*) MUS aria
Aristokratie [arɪstokra'ti:] *f* (-; *-n*) aristocracy
arm [arm] *adj* poor; ***die Armen*** the poor
Arm *m* (*-[e]s*; *-e*) ANAT arm; GEOGR branch; F ***j-n auf den Arm nehmen*** pull s.o.'s leg
Armaturen [arma'tu:rən] *pl* TECH instruments; (plumbing) fixtures
Armaturenbrett *n* MOT dashboard
'Armband *n* bracelet
'Armbanduhr *f* wrist-watch
Armee [ar'me:] *f* (-; *-n*) MIL armed forces; army
Ärmel ['ɛrməl] *m* (*-s*; -) sleeve
ärmlich ['ɛrmlɪç] *adj* poor (*a. fig*); shabby
'Armreif(en) *m* bangle
'armselig *adj* wretched, miserable
Armut ['armu:t] *f* (-; *no pl*) poverty; ***Armut an*** (*dat*) lack of
Aroma [a'ro:ma] *n* (*-s*; *-men*) flavo(u)r; aroma
Arrest [a'rɛst] *m* (*-[e]s*; *-e*) PED detention; ***Arrest bekommen*** be kept in
arrogant [aro'gant] *adj* arrogant, conceited
Arsch [arʃ] V *m* (*-es*; *Ärsche* ['ɛrʃə]) ass, *Br* arse
Arschloch V *n* asshole, *Br* arsehole
Art [art] *f* (-; *-en*) way, manner; kind, sort; BIOL species; ***auf diese Art*** (in) this way; ***e-e Art …*** a sort of …; ***Geräte aller Art*** all kinds *or* sorts of tools
'Artenschutz *m* protection of endangered species
Arterie [ar'te:rjə] *f* (-; *-n*) ANAT artery
Ar'terienverkalkung *f* MED arteriosclerosis
Arthritis [ar'tri:tɪs] *f* (-; *-tiden*) MED arthritis

artig ['artɪç] *adj* good, well-behaved; ***sei artig!*** be good!, be a good boy (*or* girl)!
Artikel [ar'tiːkəl] *m* (*-s*; *-*) article
Artillerie ['artɪləriː] *f* (*-*; *no pl*) MIL artillery
Artist [ar'tɪst] *m* (*-en*; *-en*), **Ar'tistin** *f* (*-*; *-nen*) acrobat, (circus) performer
Arznei [aːɐts'nai] *f* (*-*; *-en*), **Arzneimittel** *n* medicine, drug
Arzt [aːɐtst] *m* (*-es*; *Ärzte* ['ɛːɐtstə]) doctor, physician
Ärztin ['ɛːɐtstɪn] *f* (*-*; *-nen*) (lady) doctor *or* physician
'ärztlich *adj* medical; ***sich ärztlich behandeln lassen*** undergo treatment
As [as] *n* (*-*; *-*) MUS A flat
Asbest [as'bɛst] *m* (*-[e]s*; *-e*) asbestos
Asche ['aʃə] *f* (*-*; *-n*) ash(es)
'Aschenbahn *f* SPORT cinder-track, MOT dirt track
Aschenbecher *m* ashtray
Ascher'mittwoch *m* Ash Wednesday
äsen ['ɛːzən] *v/i* (*ge-*, *h*) HUNT feed, browse
Asiat [a'zjaːt] *m* (*-en*; *-en*), **Asi'atin** *f* (*-*; *-nen*) Asian
asi'atisch *adj* Asian, Asiatic
Asien ['aːzjən] *n* (*-s*; *no pl*) Asia
Asket [as'keːt] *m* (*-en*; *-en*), **as'ketisch** *adj* ascetic
'asozial *adj* antisocial
Asphalt [as'falt] *m* (*-s*; *-e*) asphalt
asphaltieren [asfal'tiːrən] *v/t* (*no -ge-*, *h*) (cover with) asphalt
Ass [as] *n* (*-es*; *-e*) ace (*a. tennis and fig*)
aß [aːs] *pret of* ***essen***
Assistent [asɪs'tɛnt] *m* (*-en*; *-en*), **Assis'tentin** *f* (*-*; *-nen*) assistant
Assis'tenzarzt *m Am* intern, *Br* houseman
Ast [ast] *m* (*-es*; *Äste* ['ɛstə]) BOT branch
Astronaut [astro'naut] *m* (*-en*; *-en*), **Astro'nautin** *f* (*-*; *-nen*) astronaut
Astronom [astro'noːm] *m* (*-en*; *-en*) astronomer
Astronomie [-no'miː] *f* (*-*; *no pl*) astronomy
ASU ['aːzu] ABBR *of* ***Abgas-Sonder-Untersuchung*** MOT *Am* emissions test, *Br* exhaust emission test
Asyl [a'zyːl] *n* (*-s*; *-e*) asylum
Asylant [azy'lant] *m* (*-en*; *-en*), **Asy'lantin** *f* (*-*; *-nen*) asylum seeker, (political) refugee
A'sylbewerber(in) asylum seeker
Asylrecht *n* right of (political) asylum
Atelier [ate'ljeː] *n* (*-s*; *-s*) studio
Atem ['aːtəm] *m* (*-s*; *no pl*) breath; ***außer Atem*** out of breath; (***tief***) ***Atem holen*** take a (deep) breath
'atemberaubend *adj* breathtaking
'Atemgerät *n* MED respirator
'atemlos *adj* breathless
'Atempause *f* F breather
'Atemzug *m* breath
Äther ['ɛːtɐ] *m* (*-s*; *no pl*) CHEM ether; *radio etc*: air
Athlet [at'leːt] *m* (*-en*; *-en*), **Ath'letin** *f* (*-*; *-nen*) SPORT athlete
ath'letisch *adj* athletic
Atlas ['atlas] *m* (*-ses*; *-se*, *Atlanten*) atlas
atmen ['aːtmən] *v/i and v/t* (*ge-*, *h*) breathe
Atmosphäre [atmo'sfɛːrə] *f* (*-*; *-n*) atmosphere
'Atmung *f* (*-*; *no pl*) breathing, respiration
Atoll [a'tɔl] *n* (*-s*; *-e*) atoll
Atom [a'toːm] *n* (*-s*; *-e*) atom
A'tom... *in cpds -energie*, *-forschung*, *-kraft*, *-krieg*, *-müll*, *-rakete*, *-reaktor*, *-waffen etc* nuclear ...
atomar [ato'maːɐ] *adj* atomic, nuclear
A'tombombe *f* MIL atom(ic) bomb
A'tomkern *m* PHYS (atomic) nucleus
a'tomwaffenfrei *adj* nuclear-free
Attentat ['atəntaːt] *n* (*-[e]s*; *-e*) assassination attempt, attempt on *s.o.'s* life; ***Opfer e-s Attentats werden*** be assassinated
'Attentäter *m* (*-s*; *-*) assassin
Attest [a'tɛst] *n* (*-[e]s*; *-e*) (doctor's) certificate
Attraktion [atrak'tsjoːn] *f* (*-*; *-en*) attraction
attraktiv [-'tiːf] *adj* attractive
Attrappe [a'trapə] *f* (*-*; *-n*) dummy
Attribut [atri'buːt] *n* (*-[e]s*; *-e*) LING attribute (*a. fig*)
ätzend ['ɛtsənt] *adj* corrosive, caustic (*a. fig*); F gross; ***das ist echt ätzend*** it's the pits
au [au] *int* ouch!; ***au fein!*** oh, good!
Aubergine [obɛr'ʒiːnə] *f* (*-*; *-n*) BOT eggplant, *Br* aubergine
auch [aux] *cj* also, too, as well; ***ich auch*** so am (*or* do) I, F me too; ***auch nicht*** not ... either; ***wenn auch*** even if; ***wo auch*** (***immer***) wherever; ***ist es auch wahr?*** is it really true?
Audienz [au'djɛnts] *f* (*-*; *-en*) audience (***bei*** with)
auf [auf] *prp* (*dat and acc*) *and adv* on; in; at; open; up; ***auf Seite 20*** on page 20; ***auf der Straße*** on (*Br* in) the street; on the road; ***auf der Welt*** in the world; ***auf See*** at sea; ***auf dem Lande*** in the country; ***auf dem Bahnhof*** *etc* at the station *etc*; ***auf Urlaub*** on vacation; ***die Uhr stellen auf*** (*acc*) set the watch to; ***auf***

deutsch in German; ***auf deinen Wunsch*** at your request; ***auf die Sekunde genau*** to the second; ***auf und ab*** up and down

'aufarbeiten *v/t* (*sep*, *-ge-*, *h*) catch up on (*backlog*); refurbish

aufatmen *v/i* (*sep*, *-ge-*, *h*) heave a sigh of relief

'Aufbau *m* (-[*e*]*s*; *no pl*) building (up); structure

'aufbauen *v/t* (*sep*, *-ge-*, *h*) build (up) (*a. fig*); set up; construct

'aufbauschen *v/t* (*sep*, *-ge-*, *h*) exaggerate

aufbekommen *v/t* (*irr*, ***kommen***, *sep*, *no -ge-*, *h*) get *door etc* open; be given (*a task etc*)

aufbereiten *v/t* (*sep*, *no -ge-*, *h*) process, clean, treat

aufbessern *v/t* (*sep*, *-ge-*, *h*) raise (*salary etc*)

aufbewahren *v/t* (*sep*, *no -ge-*, *h*) keep

aufbieten *v/t* (*irr*, ***bieten***, *sep*, *-ge-*, *h*) muster

aufblasen *v/t* (*irr*, ***blasen***, *sep*, *-ge-*, *h*) blow up

aufbleiben *v/i* (*irr*, ***bleiben***, *sep*, *-ge-*, *sein*) stay up; *door etc*: remain open

aufblenden *v/i* (*sep*, *-ge-*, *h*) MOT turn the headlights up

aufblicken *v/i* (*sep*, *-ge-*, *h*) look up (***zu*** at) (*a. fig*)

aufblitzen *v/i* (*sep*, *-ge-*, *h*, *sein*) flash (*a. fig*)

'aufbrausen *v/i* (*sep*, *-ge-*, *sein*) fly into a temper

aufbrausend *adj* irascible

'aufbrechen (*irr*, ***brechen***, *sep*, *-ge-*) **1.** *v/t* (*h*) break *or* force open; **2.** *v/i* (*sein*) burst open; *fig* leave (***nach*** for)

'aufbringen *v/t* (*irr*, ***bringen***, *sep*, *-ge-*, *h*) raise (*money*); muster (*courage etc*); start (*fashion etc*); → ***aufgebracht***

'Aufbruch *m* (-[*e*]*s*; *no pl*) departure, start

'aufbrühen *v/t* (*sep*, *-ge-*, *h*) make

aufbürden *v/t* (*sep*, *-ge-*, *h*) ***j-m et. aufbürden*** burden s.o. with s.th.

aufdecken *v/t* (*sep*, *-ge-*, *h*) uncover

aufdrängen *v/t* (*sep*, *-ge-*, *h*) ***j-m et. aufdrängen*** force s.th. on s.o.; ***sich j-m aufdrängen*** impose on s.o.; ***sich aufdrängen*** *fig* suggest itself

aufdrehen F (*sep*, *-ge-*, *h*) **1.** *v/t* turn on; **2.** *v/i* MOT step on the gas

'aufdringlich *adj* obtrusive

'Aufdruck *m* imprint; *on stamps*: overprint, surcharge

aufei'nander *adv* on top of each other; one after another; ***aufeinanderfolgend*** *adj* successive

Aufenthalt ['aufɛnthalt] *m* (-[*e*]*s*; *-e*) stay; RAIL stop

'Aufenthaltsgenehmigung *f* residence permit

Aufenthaltsraum *m* lounge, recreation room

'auferstehen *v/i* (*irr*, ***stehen***, *sep*, *no -ge-*, *sein*) rise (from the dead)

'Auferstehung *f* (-; *-en*) REL resurrection

'aufessen *v/t* (*irr*, ***essen***, *sep*, *-ge-*, *h*) eat up

'auffahren *v/i* (*irr*, ***fahren***, *sep*, *-ge-*, *sein*) crash (***auf*** *acc* into); *fig* start up

'Auffahrt *f* approach; driveway, *Br* drive

'Auffahrunfall *m* MOT rear-end collision; pileup

'auffallen *v/i* (*irr*, ***fallen***, *sep*, *-ge-*, *sein*) attract attention; ***j-m auffallen*** strike s.o.

'auffallend, **'auffällig** *adj* striking; conspicuous; flashy (*clothes*)

'auffangen *v/t* (*irr*, ***fangen***, *sep*, *-ge-*, *h*) catch (*a. fig*)

'auffassen *v/t* (*sep*, *-ge-*, *h*) understand (***als*** as)

'Auffassung *f* view; interpretation

'auffinden *v/t* (*irr*, ***finden***, *sep*, *-ge-*, *h*) find, discover

'auffordern *v/t* (*sep*, *-ge-*, *h*) ***j-n auffordern, et. zu tun*** ask (*or* tell) s.o. to do s.th.

'Aufforderung *f* request; demand

'auffrischen *v/t* (*sep*, *-ge-*, *h*) freshen up; brush up

'aufführen *v/t* (*sep*, *-ge-*, *h*) THEA *etc* perform, present; state; ***sich aufführen*** behave

'Aufführung *f* THEA *etc* performance; *film*: showing

'Aufgabe *f* task, job; duty; PED task, assignment; MATH problem; *fig* surrender; ***es sich zur Aufgabe machen*** make it one's business

'Aufgang *m* staircase; AST rising

'aufgeben (*irr*, ***geben***, *sep*, *-ge-*, *h*) **1.** *v/t* give up; mail, send, *Br* post; check (*baggage*); PED set, give, assign (*homework etc*); ECON place (*order etc*); **2.** *v/i* give up *or* in

'aufgebracht *adj* furious

aufgedreht F *adj* excited

aufgedunsen ['aufgədunzən] *adj* puffed(-up)

'aufgehen *v/i* (*irr*, ***gehen***, *sep*, *-ge-*, *sein*) open; *sun, dough etc*: rise; MATH come out even; ***in Flammen aufgehen*** go up in flames

'aufgehoben *fig adj*: ***gut aufgehoben sein bei*** be in good hands with

aufgelegt *adj*: ***zu et. aufgelegt sein*** feel

like (doing) s.th.; ***gut*** (***schlecht***) ***aufgelegt*** in a good (bad) mood
aufgeregt *adj* excited; nervous
aufgeschlossen *fig adj* open-minded; ***aufgeschlossen für*** open to
aufgeweckt *fig adj* bright
'aufgreifen *v/t* (*irr*, ***greifen***, *sep*, *-ge-*, *h*) pick up
auf'grund (*gen*) because of
'aufhaben F *v/t* (*irr*, ***haben***, *sep*, *-ge-*, *h*) have on, wear; PED have *homework etc* to do
aufhalten *v/t* (*irr*, ***halten***, *sep*, *-ge-*, *h*) stop, hold up (*a. traffic, thief etc*); keep open; ***sich aufhalten*** (***bei j-m***) stay (with s.o.)
aufhängen *v/t* (*sep*, *-ge-*, *h*) hang (up); ***j-n aufhängen*** hang s.o.
aufheben *v/t* (*irr*, ***heben***, *sep*, *-ge-*, *h*) pick up; keep; abolish (*law etc*); break up (*meeting etc*); ***sich gegenseitig aufheben*** neutralize each other; → ***aufgehoben***
'Aufheben *n* (*-s*; *no pl*) ***viel Aufhebens machen*** make a fuss (***von*** about)
'aufheitern *v/t* (*sep*, *-ge-*, *h*) cheer up; ***sich aufheitern*** *weather*: clear up
aufhelfen *v/i* (*irr*, ***helfen***, *sep*, *-ge-*, *h*) help *s.o.* up
aufhellen *v/t and v/refl* (*sep*, *-ge-*, *h*) brighten
aufhetzen *v/t* (*sep*, *-ge-*, *h*) ***j-n aufhetzen gegen*** set s.o. against
aufholen (*sep*, *-ge-*, *h*) **1.** *v/t* make up for; **2.** *v/i* catch up (***gegen*** with)
aufhorchen *v/i* (*sep*, *-ge-*, *h*) prick (up) one's ears; ***aufhorchen lassen*** make *s.o.* sit up
aufhören *v/i* (*sep*, *-ge-*, *h*) stop, end, finish, quit; ***mit et. aufhören*** stop (doing) s.th.; ***hör(t) auf!*** stop it!
aufkaufen *v/t* (*sep*, *-ge-*, *h*) buy up
'aufklären *v/t* (*sep*, *-ge-*, *h*) clear up, *a.* solve (*crime*); ***j-n aufklären über*** (*acc*) inform s.o. about; ***j-n*** (***sexuell***) ***aufklären*** F tell s.o. the facts of life
'Aufklärung *f* (*-*; *no pl*) clearing up, solution; information; sex education; PHILOS Enlightenment; MIL reconnaissance
'aufkleben *v/t* (*sep*, *-ge-*, *h*) paste *or* stick on
'Aufkleber *m* (*-s*; *-*) sticker
'aufknöpfen *v/t* (*sep*, *-ge-*, *h*) unbutton
'aufkommen *v/i* (*irr*, ***kommen***, *sep*, *-ge-*, *sein*) come up; come into fashion *or* use; *rumo(u)r etc*: arise; ***aufkommen für*** pay (for)
'aufladen *v/t* (*irr*, ***laden***, *sep*, *-ge-*, *h*) load; ELECTR charge
'Auflage *f* edition; circulation
'auflassen F *v/t* (*irr*, ***lassen***, *sep*, *-ge-*, *h*) leave *door etc* open; keep *one's hat etc* on
auflauern *v/i* (*sep*, *-ge-*, *h*) ***j-m auflauern*** waylay s.o.
'Auflauf *m* crowd; GASTR soufflé, pudding
'auflaufen *v/i* (*irr*, ***laufen***, *sep*, *-ge-*, *sein*) MAR run aground
aufleben *v/i* (*sep*, *-ge-*, *sein*) *a.* (***wieder***) ***aufleben lassen*** revive
auflegen (*sep*, *-ge-*, *h*) **1.** *v/t* put on, lay on; **2.** *v/i* TEL hang up
'auflehnen *v/t and v/refl* (*sep*, *-ge-*, *h*) lean (***auf*** *acc* on); ***sich auflehnen*** rebel, revolt (***gegen*** against)
'Auflehnung *f* (*-*; *-en*) rebellion, revolt
'auflesen *v/t* (*irr*, ***lesen***, *sep*, *-ge-*, *h*) pick up (*a. fig*)
aufleuchten *v/i* (*sep*, *-ge-*, *h*) flash (up)
auflisten *v/t* (*sep*, *-ge-*, *h*) list (a. EDP)
auflockern *v/t* (*sep*, *-ge-*, *h*) loosen up; *fig* liven up
'auflösen *v/t* (*sep*, *-ge-*, *h*) dissolve; solve (*a.* MATH); disintegrate
'Auflösung *f* (dis)solution; disintegration
'aufmachen F *v/t* (*sep*, *-ge-*, *h*) open; ***sich aufmachen*** set out
'Aufmachung *f* (*-*; *-en*) get-up
'aufmerksam *adj* attentive (***auf*** *acc* to); thoughtful; ***j-n aufmerksam machen auf*** (*acc*) call s.o.'s attention to
'Aufmerksamkeit *f* (*-*; *-en*) *a*) (*no pl*) attention, b) small present
'aufmuntern *v/t* (*sep*, *-ge-*, *h*) encourage; cheer up
Aufnahme ['aufna:mə] *f* (*-*; *-n*) taking up; reception (*a.* MED *etc*); admission; photo (-graph); recording; *film*: shooting
'aufnahmefähig *adj* receptive (***für*** of)
'Aufnahmegebühr *f* admission fee
Aufnahmeprüfung *f* entrance exam(ination)
'aufnehmen *v/t* (*irr*, ***nehmen***, *sep*, *-ge-*, *h*) take up (*a. post etc*); pick up; put *s.o.* up; hold; take *s.th.* in; receive; PED *etc* admit; PHOT take a picture of; record; take (*the ball*); ***es aufnehmen mit*** be a match for
'aufpassen *v/i* (*sep*, *-ge-*, *h*) pay attention; take care; ***aufpassen auf*** (*acc*) take care of, look after; keep an eye on; ***pass auf!*** look out!
'Aufprall *m* (*-[e]s*; *no pl*) impact
'aufprallen *v/i* (*sep*, *-ge-*, *sein*) ***aufprallen auf*** (*dat or acc*) hit
'aufpumpen *v/t* (*sep*, *-ge-*, *h*) pump up
'aufputschen *v/t* (*sep*, *-ge-*, *h*) pep up
'Aufputschmittel *n* PHARM stimulant, pep pill
'aufraffen *v/refl* (*sep*, *-ge-*, *h*) ***sich aufraffen zu*** bring o.s. to *do s.th.*

aufräumen *v/t (sep, -ge-, h)* tidy up; clear
'aufrecht *adj and adv* upright *(a. fig)*
aufrechterhalten *v/t (irr, **halten**, sep, no -ge-, h)* maintain, keep up
'aufregen *v/t (sep, -ge-, h)* excite, upset; ***sich aufregen*** get excited *or* upset (***über*** *acc* about)
aufregend *adj* exciting
'Aufregung *f* excitement; fuss
'aufreiben *fig v/t (irr, **reiben**, sep, -ge-, h)* wear down
aufreibend *adj* stressful
'aufreißen *v/t (irr, **reißen**, sep, -ge-, h)* tear open; fling *door etc* open; open *one's eyes* wide; F pick *s.o.* up
'aufreizend *adj* provocative
'aufrichten *v/t (sep, -ge-, h)* put up, raise; ***sich aufrichten*** straighten up; sit up
'aufrichtig *adj* sincere; frank
'Aufrichtigkeit *f (-; no pl)* sincerity; frankness
'Aufriss *m (-es; -e)* ARCH elevation
'aufrollen *v/t and v/refl (sep, -ge-, h)* roll up
'Aufruf *m* call; appeal (***zu*** for)
'aufrufen *v/t (irr, **rufen**, sep, -ge-, h)* call on
Aufruhr ['aufruːɐ] *m (-s; no pl)* revolt; riot; turmoil
'Aufrührer *m (-s; -)* rebel; rioter
aufrührerisch ['aufryːrərɪʃ] *adj* rebellious
'aufrunden *v/t (sep, -ge-, h)* round off
'aufrüsten *v/t and v/i (sep, -ge-, h)* (re)arm
'Aufrüstung *f* (re)armament
'aufrütteln *fig v/t (sep, -ge-, h)* shake up, rouse
aufsagen *v/t (sep, -ge-, h)* say; *a.* recite *(poem)*
aufsässig ['aufzɛsɪç] *adj* rebellious
'Aufsatz *m* PED essay, *Am a.* theme; *(newspaper etc)* article; TECH top
'aufsaugen *v/t (sep, -ge-, h)* absorb *(a. fig)*
aufscheuern *v/t (sep, -ge-, h)* chafe
aufschichten *v/t (sep, -ge-, h)* pile up
aufschieben *fig v/t (irr, **schieben**, sep, -ge-, h)* put off, postpone; delay
'Aufschlag *m* impact; ECON extra charge; lapel; cuff, *Br* turnup; *tennis*: service
'aufschlagen *(irr, **schlagen**, sep, -ge-, h)* **1.** *v/t* open *(book, eyes etc)*; pitch *(tent)*; cut *(one's knee etc)*; ***Seite 3 aufschlagen*** open at page 3; **2.** *v/i tennis*: serve; ***auf dem Boden aufschlagen*** hit the ground
'aufschließen *v/t (irr, **schließen**, sep, -ge-, h)* unlock, open
aufschlitzen *v/t (sep, -ge-, h)* slit *or* rip open
'Aufschluss *m* information (***über*** *acc* on)
'aufschnappen F *fig v/t (sep, -ge-, h)* pick up
aufschneiden *(irr, **schneiden**, sep, -ge-, h)* **1.** *v/t* cut open; GASTR cut up; **2.** F *fig v/i* brag, boast, talk big
'Aufschnitt *m (-[e]s; no pl)* GASTR cold cuts, *Br* (slices of) cold meat
'aufschnüren *v/t (sep, -ge-, h)* untie; unlace
aufschrauben *v/t (sep, -ge-, h)* unscrew
aufschrecken *(sep, -ge-)* **1.** *v/t (h)* startle; **2.** *v/i (sein)* start (up)
'Aufschrei *m* yell; scream, outcry *(a. fig)*
'aufschreiben *v/t (irr, **schreiben**, sep, -ge-, h)* write down
aufschreien *v/i (irr, **schreien**, sep, -ge-, h)* cry out, scream
'Aufschrift *f* inscription
'Aufschub *m* postponement; delay; adjournment; respite
'Aufschwung *m* SPORT swing-up; *esp* ECON recovery, upswing; boom
'Aufsehen *n (-s; no pl)* ***Aufsehen erregen*** attract attention; cause a sensation; ***Aufsehen erregend*** → ***aufsehenerregend***
'aufsehenerregend *adj* sensational
'Aufseher *m (-s; -)*, **'Aufseherin** *f (-; -nen)* guard
'aufsetzen *(sep, -ge-, h)* **1.** *v/t* put on; draw up *(letter etc)*; ***sich aufsetzen*** sit up; **2.** *v/i* AVIAT touch down
'Aufsetzer *m (-s; -)* SPORT awkward bouncing ball
'Aufsicht *f (-; no pl)* supervision, control; ***Aufsicht führen*** PED *etc* be on (break) duty; proctor, *Br* invigilate
'Aufsichtsbehörde *f* supervisory board
Aufsichtsrat *m* ECON board of directors; supervisory board
'aufsitzen *v/i (irr, **sitzen**, sep, -ge-, sein)* mount
aufspannen *v/t (sep, -ge-, h)* stretch; put up *(umbrella)*; spread
aufsparen *v/t (sep, -ge-, h)* save
aufsperren *v/t (sep, -ge-, h)* unlock; F open wide
aufspielen *v/refl (sep, -ge-, h)* show off; ***sich aufspielen als*** play
aufspießen *v/t (sep, -ge-, h)* spear, skewer; *animal*: gore
aufspringen *v/i (irr, **springen**, sep, -ge-, sein)* jump up; *door etc*: fly open; *lips etc*: chap
aufspüren *v/t (sep, -ge-, h)* track down
aufstacheln *v/t (sep, -ge-, h)* goad *(s.o. into doing s.th.)*
aufstampfen *v/i (sep, -ge-, h)* stamp (one's foot)

'Aufstand *m* revolt, rebellion
'Aufständische *m, f (-n; -n)* rebel
'aufstapeln *v/t (sep, -ge-, h)* pile up
aufstechen *v/t (irr,* ***stechen****, sep, -ge-, h)* puncture, prick open; MED lance
aufstecken *v/t (sep, -ge-, h)* put up *(hair)*; F *fig* give up
aufstehen *v/i (irr,* ***stehen****, sep, -ge-, sein)* get up, rise
aufsteigen *v/i (irr,* ***steigen****, sep, -ge-, sein)* rise *(a. fig)*; get on *(horse, bicycle)*; be promoted; SPORT *Am a.* be moved up to a higher division
'aufstellen *v/t (sep, -ge-, h)* set up, put up; post *(guard)*; set *(trap, record etc)*; nominate *s.o.*; draw up *(table, list etc)*
'Aufstellung *f* putting up; nomination; list; SPORT line-up
Aufstieg ['aufʃti:k] *m (-[e]s; -e)* ascent, *fig a.* rise
'aufstöbern *fig v/t (sep, -ge-, h)* ferret out
aufstoßen *(irr,* ***stoßen****, sep, -ge-, h)* **1.** *v/t* push open; **2.** *v/i* belch
aufstützen *v/refl (sep, -ge-, h)* lean (***auf*** *acc or dat* on)
aufsuchen *v/t (sep, -ge-, h)* visit; see
'Auftakt *m* MUS upbeat; *fig* prelude
'auftanken *v/t (sep, -ge-, h)* fill up; MOT, AVIAT refuel
auftauchen *v/i (sep, -ge-, sein)* appear; MAR surface
auftauen *v/t (sep, -ge-, h)* thaw; GASTR defrost
aufteilen *v/t (sep, -ge-, h)* divide (up)
Auftrag ['auftra:k] *m (-[e]s; Aufträge* ['auftrɛ:gə]) instructions, order *(a.* ECON); MIL mission; ***im Auftrag von*** on behalf of
auftragen *v/t (irr,* ***tragen****, sep, -ge-, h)* serve (up) *(food)*; apply *(paint)*; ***j-m et. auftragen*** ask *(or* tell) s.o. to do s.th; F ***dick auftragen*** exaggerate
'Auftraggeber *m (-s; -)* principal; customer
'auftreffen *v/i (irr,* ***treffen****, sep, -ge-, sein)* strike, hit
auftreiben F *v/t (irr,* ***treiben****, sep, -ge-, h)* get hold of; raise *(money)*
auftrennen *v/t (sep, -ge-, h)* undo *(seam)*, cut open
auftreten *v/i (irr,* ***treten****, sep, -ge-, sein)* THEA *etc* appear (***als*** *as*); behave, act; occur
'Auftreten *n (-s; no pl)* appearance; behavio(u)r; occurrence
'Auftrieb *m (-[e]s; no pl)* PHYS buoyancy *(a. fig)*; AVIAT lift; *fig* impetus
'Auftritt *m* THEA entrance
'auftun *v/refl (irr,* ***tun****, sep, -ge-, h)* open *(a. fig)*; *abyss:* yawn
auftürmen *v/t (sep, -ge-, h)* pile *or* heap up; ***sich auftürmen*** pile up
aufwachen *v/i (sep, -ge-, sein)* wake up
aufwachsen *v/i (irr,* ***wachsen****, sep, -ge-, sein)* grow up
Aufwand ['aufvant] *m (-[e]s; no pl)* expenditure (***an*** *dat* of), *a.* expense; pomp
aufwändig ['aufwɛndɪç] *adj* costly; extravagant *(lifestyle)*
'aufwärmen *v/t (sep, -ge-, h)* warm up; F *fig contp* bring up
aufwärts ['aufvɛrts] *adv* upward(s); ***aufwärtsgehen*** *v/i (irr,* ***gehen****, sep, -ge-, sein) fig* improve
'aufwecken *v/t (sep, -ge-, h)* wake (up)
aufweichen *v/t (sep, -ge-, h)* soften; soak
aufweisen *v/t (irr,* ***weisen****, sep, -ge-, h)* show, have
aufwenden *v/t ([irr,* ***wenden****,] sep, -ge-, h)* spend (***für*** on); ***Mühe aufwenden*** take pains
aufwendig → ***aufwändig***
'aufwerfen *v/t (irr,* ***werfen****, sep, -ge-, h)* raise *(question etc)*
'aufwerten *v/t (sep, -ge-, h)* ECON revalue; *fig* increase the value of
'Aufwertung *f* revaluation
'aufwickeln *v/t and v/refl (sep, -ge-, h)* wind up, roll up; put *hair* in curlers
aufwiegeln ['aufvi:gəln] *v/t (sep, -ge-, h)* stir up, incite, instigate
'aufwiegen *v/t (irr,* ***wiegen****, sep, -ge-, h)* make up for
Aufwiegler ['aufvi:glɐ] *m (-s; -)* agitator; instigator
'Aufwind *m* upwind; ***im Aufwind*** *fig* on the upswing
'aufwirbeln *v/t (sep, -ge-, h)* whirl up; *fig* ***(viel) Staub aufwirbeln*** make (quite) a stir
aufwischen *v/t (sep, -ge-, h)* wipe up
aufwühlen *fig v/t (sep, -ge-, h)* stir, move
'aufzählen *v/t (sep, -ge-, h)* name (one by one), list
'Aufzählung *f* enumeration, list
'aufzeichnen *v/t (sep, -ge-, h)* TV, *radio etc:* record, tape; draw
'Aufzeichnung *f* recording; *pl* notes
'aufzeigen *v/t (sep, -ge-, h)* show; demonstrate; point out *(mistake etc)*
'aufziehen *(irr,* ***ziehen****, sep, -ge-)* **1.** *v/t (h)* draw *or* pull up; (pull) open; bring up *(child)*; wind (up) *(clock)*; mount *(photo etc)*; ***j-n aufziehen*** tease s.o.; **2.** *v/i (sein)* come up
'Aufzug *m* elevator, *Br* lift; THEA act; F *contp* get-up
'aufzwingen *v/t (irr,* ***zwingen****, sep, -ge-, h)*

j-m et. aufzwingen force s.th. upon s.o.
Augapfel ['auk-] *m* ANAT eyeball
Auge ['augə] *n* (*-s*; *-n*) ANAT eye; ***ein blaues Auge*** a black eye; ***mit bloßem Auge*** with the naked eye; ***mit verbundenen Augen*** blindfold; ***in meinen Augen*** in my view; ***mit anderen Augen*** in a different light; ***aus den Augen verlieren*** lose sight of; ***ein Auge zudrücken*** turn a blind eye; ***unter vier Augen*** in private; F ***ins Auge gehen*** go wrong
'Augenarzt *m* eye specialist
'Augenblick *m* moment, instant
'augenblicklich **1.** *adj* present; immediate; momentary; **2.** *adv* at present, at the moment; immediately
'Augenbraue *f* eyebrow
Augenlicht *n* (*-[e]s*; *no pl*) eyesight
Augenlid *n* eyelid
Augenmaß *n*: ***ein gutes Augenmaß*** a sure eye; ***nach dem Augenmaß*** by the eye
Augenmerk *n*: ***sein Augenmerk richten auf*** (*acc*) turn one's attention to, *fig a.* have in view
Augenschein *m* (*-s*; *no pl*) appearance; ***in Augenschein nehmen*** examine, inspect
Augenzeuge *m* eyewitness
August [au'gust] *m* (*-*; *no pl*) August
Auktion [auk'tsjo:n] *f* (*-*; *-en*) auction
Auktionator [auktsjo'na:to:ɐ] *m* (*-s*; *-en* [-na'to:rən]) auctioneer
Aula ['aula] *f* (*-*; *-s*, *Aulen*) auditorium, *Br* (assembly) hall
aus [aus] *prp* (*dat*) *and adv mst* out of, from; of (*silk etc*); out of (*spite etc*); *light etc*: out, off; *play etc*: over, finished; SPORT out; ***aus dem Fenster*** *etc* out of the window *etc*; ***aus München*** from Munich; ***aus Holz*** (made) of wood; ***aus Mitleid*** out of pity; ***aus Spaß*** for fun; ***aus Versehen*** by mistake; ***aus diesem Grunde*** for this reason; ***von hier aus*** from here; F ***von mir aus!*** I don't care!; ***aus der Mode*** out of fashion; F ***aus sein*** be over; be out; ***aus sein auf*** (*acc*) be out for; be after (*s.o.'s money etc*); ***die Schule*** (***das Spiel***) ***ist aus*** school (the game) is over; ***ein/aus*** TECH on / off
Aus *n*: ***im Aus*** *ball*: out of play
'ausarbeiten *v/t* (*sep*, *-ge-*, *h*) work out; prepare
ausarten *v/i* (*sep*, *-ge-*, *sein*) get out of hand
ausatmen *v/t and v/i* (*sep*, *-ge-*, *h*) breathe out
ausbaden F *v/t* (*sep*, *-ge-*, *h*) ***et. ausbaden müssen*** take the rap for s.th.
'Ausbau *m* (*-[e]s*; *no pl*) extension; completion; removal
'ausbauen *v/t* (*sep*, *-ge-*, *h*) extend; complete; remove; improve
'ausbaufähig *adj*: ***et. ist ausbaufähig*** there is potential for growth *or* development
'ausbessern *v/t* (*sep*, *-ge-*, *h*) mend, repair, F *a.* fix
'Ausbesserung *f* (*-*; *-en*) repair(ing)
'Ausbeute *f* (*-*; *no pl*) gain, profit; yield
'ausbeuten *v/t* (*sep*, *-ge-*, *h*) exploit (*a. contp*)
'Ausbeutung *f* (*-*; *no pl*) exploitation
'ausbilden *v/t* (*sep*, *-ge-*, *h*) train, instruct; ***j-n ausbilden zu*** train s.o. to be
'Ausbilder *m* (*-s*; *-*) instructor
'Ausbildung *f* (*-*; *-en*) training, instruction
'ausbleiben *v/i* (*irr*, ***bleiben***, *sep*, *-ge-*, *sein*) stay out; fail to come; ***es konnte nicht ausbleiben*** it was inevitable
'Ausblick *m* view (***auf*** *acc* of); *fig* outlook (*for*)
'ausbrechen *v/i* (*irr*, ***brechen***, *sep*, *-ge-*, *sein*) break out (*a. fig*); ***in Tränen ausbrechen*** burst into tears
'Ausbrecher *m* (*-s*; *-*) escaped prisoner
'ausbreiten *v/t* (*sep*, *-ge-*, *h*) spread (out); ***sich ausbreiten*** spread
'Ausbreitung *f* (*-*; *no pl*) spreading
'ausbrennen *v/t* (*irr*, ***brennen***, *sep*, *-ge-*, *sein*) burn out
'Ausbruch *m* escape, breakout; outbreak (*of fire etc*); eruption (*of volcano*); (out)-burst (*of resentment etc*)
'ausbrüten *v/t* (*sep*, *-ge-*, *h*) hatch (*a. fig*)
'Ausdauer *f* perseverance, stamina, *esp* SPORT *a.* staying power
'ausdauernd *adj* persevering; SPORT tireless
'ausdehnen *v/t and v/refl* (*sep*, *-ge-*, *h*) stretch; *fig* expand, extend
'Ausdehnung *f* expansion; extension
'ausdenken *v/t* (*irr*, ***denken***, *sep*, *-ge-*, *h*) think *s.th.* up; invent (*a. fig*)
'Ausdruck *m* expression, term; EDP print-out
'ausdrucken *v/t* (*sep*, *-ge-*, *h*) EDP print out
'ausdrücken *v/t* (*sep*, *-ge-*, *h*) stub out (*cigarette etc*); *fig* express
ausdrücklich ['ausdrʏklɪç] *adj* express, explicit
'ausdruckslos *adj* expressionless, blank
ausdrucksvoll *adj* expressive
'Ausdrucksweise *f* language, style
'Ausdünstung *f* (*-*; *-en*) exhalation; perspiration; odo(u)r
auseinander [ausˀai'nandɐ] *adv* apart; separate(d); ***auseinanderbringen*** *v/t* (*irr*, ***bringen***, *sep*, *-ge-*, *h*) separate, ***aus-***

einandergehen *v/i* (*irr*, ***gehen***, *sep*, *-ge-*, *sein*) part; *meeting etc*: break up; *opinions etc*: differ; *married couple*: separate; ***auseinanderhalten*** *v/t* (*irr*, ***halten***, *sep*, *-ge-*, *h*) tell apart; ***auseinandernehmen*** *v/t* (*irr*, ***nehmen***, *sep*, *-ge-*, *h*) take apart (*a. fig*); ***auseinandersetzen*** *v/t* (*irr*, ***setzen***, *sep*, *-ge-*, *h*) explain; ***sich auseinander setzen mit*** *v/refl* deal with; argue with *s.o.*

Ausei'nandersetzung *f* (*-; -en*) argument

'auserlesen *adj* choice, exquisite

'ausfahren (*irr*, ***fahren***, *sep*, *-ge-*) **1.** *v/i* (*sein*) go for a drive *or* ride; **2.** *v/t* (*h*) take *s.o.* out; AVIAT extend (*landing gear*)

'Ausfahrt *f* drive, ride; MOT exit

'Ausfall *m* TECH, MOT, SPORT failure; loss

'ausfallen *v/i* (*irr*, ***fallen***, *sep*, *-ge-*, *sein*) fall out; not take place, be cancelled; TECH, MOT break down, fail; ***gut*** *etc* ***ausfallen*** turn out well *etc*; ***ausfallen lassen*** cancel; ***die Schule fällt aus*** there is no school

'ausfallend, **'ausfällig** *adj* insulting

'ausfertigen *v/t* (*sep*, *-ge-*, *h*) draw up (*contract etc*); make out (*check etc*)

'Ausfertigung *f* drawing up; copy; ***in doppelter Ausfertigung*** in duplicate

'ausfindig *adj*: ***ausfindig machen*** find

ausflippen ['ausflɪpən] F *v/i* (*sep*, *-ge-*, *sein*) freak out

Ausflüchte ['ausflʏçtə] *pl* excuses

'Ausflug *m* trip, excursion, outing

Ausflügler ['ausfly:klɐ] *m* (*-s*; *-*) daytripper

'Ausfluss *m* TECH outlet; MED discharge

'ausfragen *v/t* (*sep*, *-ge-*, *h*) question (***über*** *acc* about); sound out

ausfransen *v/i* (*sep*, *-ge-*, *sein*) fray

ausfressen F *v/t* (*irr*, ***fressen***, *sep*, *-ge-*, *h*) ***et. ausfressen*** be up to no good

Ausfuhr ['ausfu:ɐ] *f* (*-; -en*) ECON export(ation)

'ausführbar *adj* practicable

'ausführen *v/t* (*sep*, *-ge-*, *h*) take *s.o.* out; carry out (*task etc*); ECON export; explain

ausführlich ['ausfy:ɐlɪç] **1.** *adj* detailed; comprehensive; **2.** *adv* in detail

'Ausführlichkeit *f*: ***in aller Ausführlichkeit*** in great detail

'Ausführung *f* execution, performance; type, model, design

'ausfüllen *v/t* (*sep*, *-ge-*, *h*) fill out (*Br* in) (*form*)

'Ausgabe *f* distribution; edition; expense; issue; EDP output

'Ausgang *m* exit, way out; end; result, outcome; TECH, ELECTR output, outlet

'Ausgangspunkt *m* starting point

Ausgangssperre *f* POL curfew

'ausgeben *v/t* (*irr*, ***geben***, *sep*, *-ge-*, *h*) give out; spend; F ***j-m e-n ausgeben*** buy s.o. a drink; ***sich ausgeben als*** pass o.s. off as

'ausgebeult *adj* baggy

ausgebildet *adj* trained, skilled

ausgebucht *adj* booked up

ausgedehnt *adj* extensive

ausgedient *adj*: ***ausgedient haben*** *fig* have had its day

ausgefallen *adj* odd, unusual

ausgeglichen *adj* (well-)balanced

'ausgehen *v/i* (*irr*, ***gehen***, *sep*, *-ge-*, *sein*) go out; end; *hair*: fall out; *money*, *supplies*: run out; ***leer ausgehen*** get nothing; ***ausgehen von*** start from *or* at; come from; ***davon ausgehen, dass*** assume that; ***ihm ging das Geld aus*** he ran out of money

'ausgekocht *fig adj* cunning; out-and-out (*villain etc*)

ausgelassen *fig adj* cheerful; hilarious; ***ausgelassen sein*** be in high spirits

ausgemacht *adj* agreed(-on); downright (*nonsense*)

ausgeprägt *adj* marked, pronounced

ausgerechnet *adv*: ***ausgerechnet er*** he of all people; ***ausgerechnet heute*** today of all days

ausgeschlossen *adj* out of the question

ausgestorben *adj* extinct

ausgesucht *adj* select, choice

ausgewachsen *adj* fullgrown

ausgewogen *adj* (well-)balanced

ausgezeichnet *adj* excellent

ausgiebig ['ausgi:bɪç] *adj* extensive, thorough; substantial (*meal*)

'ausgießen *v/t* (*irr*, ***gießen***, *sep*, *-ge-*, *h*) pour out

'Ausgleich *m* (*-[e]s*; *no pl*) compensation; SPORT even score, *Br* equalization; *tennis*: deuce

'ausgleichen *v/t and v/i* (*irr*, ***gleichen***, *sep*, *-ge-*, *h*) compensate; equalize (*Br a.* SPORT); ECON balance; SPORT make the score even

'Ausgleichssport *m* remedial exercises

Ausgleichstor *n*, **Ausgleichstreffer** *m* SPORT tying point, *Br* equalizer

'ausgraben *v/t* (*irr*, ***graben***, *sep*, *-ge-*, *h*) dig out *or* up (*a. fig*)

'Ausgrabungen *pl* excavations

'ausgrenzen *v/t* (*sep*, *-ge-*, *h*) isolate

'Ausguss *m* (kitchen) sink

'aushalten (*irr*, ***halten***, *sep*, *-ge-*, *h*) **1.** *v/t* bear, stand; keep (*mistress etc*); ***nicht auszuhalten sein*** be unbearable; **2.** *v/i* hold out

aushändigen ['aushɛndɪgən] *v/t* (*sep*, *-ge-*, *h*) hand over
ˈ**Aushang** *m* notice; bulletin
ˈ**aushängen** *v/t* (*sep*, *-ge-*, *h*) hang out, put up; unhinge (*door*)
ˈ**ausheben** *v/t* (*irr*, ***heben***, *sep*, *-ge-*, *h*) dig (*trench*); raid (*place etc*)
aushelfen *v/i* (*irr*, ***helfen***, *sep*, *-ge-*, *h*) help out
ˈ**Aushilfe** *f* (temporary) help
ˈ**Aushilfs...** *in cpds -kellner etc*: temporary
ˈ**ausholen** *v/i* (*sep*, *-ge-*, *h*) ***zum Schlag ausholen*** swing (to strike); *fig* ***weit ausholen*** go far back
aushorchen *v/t* (*sep*, *-ge-*, *h*) sound (***über*** *acc* on)
aushungern *v/t* (*sep*, *-ge-*, *h*) starve out
auskennen *v/refl* (*irr*, ***kennen***, *sep*, *-ge-*, *h*) ***sich auskennen*** (***in*** *dat*) know one's way (about); *fig* know a lot (about)
ausklingen *v/i* (*irr*, ***klingen***, *sep*, *-ge-*, *sein*) draw to a close
ausklopfen *v/t* (*sep*, *-ge-*, *h*) knock out
auskommen *v/i* (*irr*, ***kommen***, *sep*, *-ge-*, *sein*) get by; ***auskommen mit*** manage with *s.th.*; get along with *s.o.*
Auskunft ['auskʊnft] *f* (-; *Auskünfte* ['auskʏnftə]) a) information, b) (*no pl*) information desk; TEL inquiries
ˈ**auslachen** *v/t* (*sep*, *-ge-*, *h*) laugh at (***wegen*** for)
ausladen *v/t* (*irr*, ***laden***, *sep*, *-ge-*, *h*) unload
ˈ**Auslage** *f* window display; *pl* expenses
ˈ**Ausland** *n* (-[*e*]*s*; *no pl*) ***das Ausland*** foreign countries; ***ins Ausland, im Ausland*** abroad
Ausländer ['auslɛndɐ] *m* (-*s*; -) foreigner
Ausländerfeindlichkeit *f* hostility to foreigners, xenophobia
Ausländerin ['auslɛndərɪn] *f* (-; *-nen*) foreigner
ˈ**ausländisch** [-lɛndɪʃ] *adj* foreign
ˈ**Auslandsgespräch** *n* international call
Auslandskorrespondent(in) foreign correspondent
ˈ**auslassen** *v/t* (*irr*, ***lassen***, *sep*, *-ge-*, *h*) leave out; melt (*butter etc*); let out (*seam*); ***s-n Zorn an j-m auslassen*** take it out on s.o.; ***sich auslassen über*** (*acc*) express o.s. on
ˈ**Auslassung** *f* (-; *-en*) omission
ˈ**Auslassungszeichen** *n* LING apostrophe
ˈ**Auslauf** *m* room to move about; *dog*: exercise
ˈ**auslaufen** *v/i* (*irr*, ***laufen***, *sep*, *-ge-*, *sein*) MAR leave port; *pot etc*: leak; *liquid etc*: run out
ˈ**Ausläufer** *m* METEOR ridge, trough; *pl* GEOGR foothills
ˈ**Auslaufmoˌdell** *n* ECON close-out (*Br* phase-out) model
ˈ**auslegen** *v/t* (*sep*, *-ge-*, *h*) lay out; carpet; line (*with paper etc*); display (*goods*); interpret (*text etc*); advance (*money*)
ˈ**Auslegung** *f* (-; *-en*) interpretation
ˈ**ausleihen** *v/t* (*irr*, ***leihen***, *sep*, *-ge-*, *h*) lend (out), loan; ***sich*** (*dat*) ***et. ausleihen*** borrow s.th.
auslernen *v/i* (*sep*, *-ge-*, *h*) complete one's training; ***man lernt nie aus*** we live and learn
ˈ**Auslese** *f* choice, selection; *fig* pick
ˈ**auslesen** *v/t* (*irr*, ***lesen***, *sep*, *-ge-*, *h*) pick out, select; finish (*book etc*)
ˈ**ausliefern** *v/t* (*sep*, *-ge-*, *h*) hand *or* turn over, deliver (up); POL extradite
ˈ**Auslieferung** *f* delivery; extradition
ˈ**ausliegen** *v/i* (*irr*, ***liegen***, *sep*, *-ge-*, *h*) be laid out
auslöschen *v/t* (*sep*, *-ge-*, *h*) put out; *fig* wipe out
auslosen *v/t* (*sep*, *-ge-*, *h*) draw (lots) for
ˈ**auslösen** *v/t* (*sep*, *-ge-*, *h*) TECH release; ransom, redeem; cause, start, trigger *s.th.* off
ˈ**Auslöser** *m* (PHOT shutter) release; trigger
ˈ**ausmachen** *v/t* (*sep*, *-ge-*, *h*) put out (*fire*); turn off (*light etc*); arrange (*date etc*); agree on (*price etc*); make up; amount to; settle (*dispute*); sight, spot; ***macht es Ihnen et. aus*** (, ***wenn...***)***?*** do you mind (if ...)?; ***es macht mir nichts aus*** I don't mind; ***das macht*** (***gar***) ***nichts aus*** that doesn't matter (at all)
ˈ**ausmalen** *v/t* (*sep*, *-ge-*, *h*) paint; ***sich et. ausmalen*** imagine s.th.
ˈ**Ausmaß** *n* extent; *pl* proportions
ausmerzen ['ausmɛrtsən] *v/t* (*sep*, *-ge-*, *h*) eliminate
ausmessen *v/t* (*irr*, ***messen***, *sep*, *-ge-*, *h*) measure
Ausnahme ['ausnaːmə] *f* (-; *-n*) exception
Ausnahmezustand *m* POL state of emergency
ˈ**ausnahmslos** *adv* without exception
ˈ**ausnahmsweise** *adv* by way of exception; just this once
ˈ**ausnehmen** *v/t* (*irr*, ***nehmen***, *sep*, *-ge-*, *h*) clean (*chicken etc*); except; F *contp* fleece *s.o.*
ausnehmend *adv* exceptionally
ˈ**ausnutzen** *v/t* (*sep*, *-ge-*, *h*) use; take advantage of (*a. contp*); exploit
auspacken (*sep*, *-ge-*, *h*) **1.** *v/t* unpack; **2.** F

v/i talk
auspfeifen *v/t* (*irr*, ***pfeifen***, *sep*, *-ge-*, *h*) boo, hiss
ausplaudern *v/t* (*sep*, *-ge-*, *h*) blab out
ausplündern *v/t* (*sep*, *-ge-*, *h*) plunder, rob
auspro͵bieren *v/t* (*sep*, *no -ge-*, *h*) try (out), test
'Auspuff *m* MOT exhaust
Auspuffgase *pl* MOT exhaust fumes
Auspuffrohr *n* MOT exhaust pipe
Auspufftopf *m* MOT muffler, *Br* silencer
'ausquar͵tieren *v/t* (*sep*, *no -ge-*, *h*) move out
ausra͵dieren *v/t* (*sep*, *no -ge-*, *h*) erase; *fig* wipe out
ausran͵gieren *v/t* (*sep*, *no -ge-*, *h*) discard
ausrauben *v/t* (*sep*, *-ge-*, *h*) rob
ausräumen *v/t* (*sep*, *-ge-*, *h*) empty; clear out (*room etc*); *fig* clear up (*doubt etc*)
ausrechnen *v/t* (*sep*, *-ge-*, *h*) work out
'Ausrede *f* excuse
'ausreden (*sep*, *-ge-*, *h*) **1.** *v/i* finish speaking; ***j-n ausreden lassen*** hear s.o. out; **2.** *v/t*: ***j-m et. ausreden*** talk s.o. out of s.th.
'ausreichen *v/i* (*sep*, *-ge-*, *h*) be enough
ausreichend *adj* sufficient, enough; *grade*: (barely) passing, only average, weak, D
'Ausreise *f* departure
'ausreisen *v/i* (*sep*, *-ge-*, *sein*) leave (a *or* one's country)
'Ausreisevisum *n* exit visa
'ausreißen (*irr*, ***reißen***, *sep*, *-ge-*) **1.** *v/t* (*h*) pull *or* tear out; **2.** F *v/i* (*sein*) run away
'Ausreißer *m* (*-s*; *-*) runaway
'ausrenken *v/t* (*sep*, *-ge-*, *h*) MED dislocate
ausrichten *v/t* (*sep*, *-ge-*, *h*) tell *s.o. s.th.*; deliver (*message*); accomplish; arrange (*party etc*); ***richte ihr e-n Gruß von mir aus!*** give her my regards!; ***kann ich et. ausrichten?*** can I take a message
'ausrotten *v/t* (*sep*, *-ge-*, *h*) exterminate
'Ausrottung *f* (*-*; *-en*) extermination
'ausrücken *v/i* (*sep*, *-ge-*, *sein*) F run away; MIL march out
'Ausruf *m* cry, shout
'ausrufen *v/t* (*irr*, ***rufen***, *sep*, *-ge-*, *h*) cry, shout, exclaim; call out (*name*); POL proclaim
'Ausrufung *f* (*-*; *-en*) POL proclamation
'Ausrufungszeichen *n* LING exclamation mark
'ausruhen *v/i*, *v/t and v/refl* (*sep*, *-ge-*, *h*) rest
'ausrüsten *v/t* (*sep*, *-ge-*, *h*) equip
'Ausrüstung *f* equipment
'ausrutschen *v/i* (*sep*, *-ge-*, *sein*) slip
'Aussage *f* statement; JUR evidence
'aussagen *v/t* (*sep*, *-ge-*, *h*) state, declare; JUR testify
ausschalten *v/t* (*sep*, *-ge-*, *h*) switch off; *fig* eliminate
'Ausschau *f*: ***Ausschau halten nach*** → **'ausschauen** *v/i* (*sep*, *-ge-*, *h*) ***Ausschau nach*** look out for, watch out for
'ausscheiden (*irr*, ***scheiden***, *sep*, *-ge-*) **1.** *v/i* (*sein*) be ruled out; SPORT *etc* drop out (***aus*** *dat* of); retire (***aus*** *dat* from *office etc*); ***ausscheiden aus*** (*dat*) leave (*a firm etc*); **2.** *v/t* (*h*) eliminate; MED *etc* secrete, exude
'Ausscheidung *f* elimination (*a.* SPORT); MED secretion
'Ausscheidungs... *in cpds ...spiel etc*: SPORT qualifying ...
'ausschlachten *fig v/t* (*sep*, *-ge-*, *h*) salvage, *Br a.* cannibalize; *contp* exploit
ausschlafen (*irr*, ***schlafen***, *sep*, *-ge-*, *h*) **1.** *v/i* sleep in; **2.** *v/t* sleep off
'Ausschlag *m* MED rash; TECH deflection; ***den Ausschlag geben*** decide it
'ausschlagen (*irr*, ***schlagen***, *sep*, *-ge-*, *h*) **1.** *v/t* knock out (*tooth etc*); *fig* refuse, decline (*offer etc*); **2.** *v/i horse*: kick; BOT bud; TECH deflect
'ausschlaggebend *adj* decisive
'ausschließen *v/t* (*irr*, ***schließen***, *sep*, *-ge-*, *h*) lock out; *fig* exclude; expel; SPORT disqualify
'ausschließlich *adj* exclusive
'Ausschluss *m* exclusion; expulsion; SPORT disqualification; ***unter Ausschluss der Öffentlichkeit*** in closed session
'ausschmücken *v/t* (*sep*, *-ge-*, *h*) decorate; *fig* embellish
ausschneiden *v/t* (*irr*, ***schneiden***, *sep*, *-ge-*, *h*) cut out
'Ausschnitt *m clothing*: neck; (*press*) clipping (*Br* cutting); *fig* part; extract; ***mit tiefem Ausschnitt*** low-necked
'ausschreiben *v/t* (*irr*, ***schreiben***, *sep*, *-ge-*, *h*) write out (*a. check etc*); advertise (*post etc*)
'Ausschreibung *f* advertisement
'Ausschreitungen *pl* violence, riots
'Ausschuss *m* committee, board; TECH (*no pl*) refuse, waste, rejects
'ausschütteln *v/t* (*sep*, *-ge-*, *h*) shake out
ausschütten *v/t* (*sep*, *-ge-*, *h*) pour out (*a. fig*); spill; ECON pay; ***sich vor Lachen ausschütten*** split one's sides
'ausschweifend *adj* dissolute
'Ausschweifung *f* (*-*; *-en*) debauchery, excess
'aussehen *v/i* (*irr*, ***sehen***, *sep*, *-ge-*, *h*) look; ***krank*** (***traurig***) ***aussehen*** look ill (sad); ***aussehen wie ...*** look like ...;

wie sieht er aus? what does he look like? **'Aussehen** *n (-s; no pl)* look(s), appearance
außen ['ausən] *adv* outside; ***nach außen*** (***hin***) outward(s); *fig* outwardly
'Außenbordmotor *m* outboard motor
aussenden *v/t* ([*irr*, ***senden***,] *sep*, *-ge-*, *h*) send out
'Außendienst *m* field service
Außenhandel *m* foreign trade
Außenmi,nister *m Am* Secretary of State, *Br* Foreign Secretary
Außenminis,terium *n Am* State Department, *Br* Foreign Office
Außenpoli,tik *f* foreign affairs; foreign policy
'außenpo,litisch *adj* foreign-policy
'Außenseite *f* outside
'Außenseiter [-zaitɐ] *m (-s; -)* outsider
'Außenspiegel *m* MOT outside rearview mirror
Außenstände *pl* ECON receivables
Außenstelle *f* branch
Außenstürmer *m* SPORT winger
Außenwelt *f* outside world
außer ['ausɐ] **1.** *prp* (*dat*) out of; aside from, *Br* beside(s); except; ***außer sich sein*** be beside o.s. (***vor Freude*** with joy); ***alle außer e-m*** all but one; → ***Betrieb***, ***Gefahr***; **2.** *cj*: ***außer dass*** except that; ***außer wenn*** unless
'außerdem *cj* besides, moreover
äußere ['ɔysərə] *adj* exterior, outer, outward
'Äußere *n (-n; no pl)* exterior, outside; (outward) appearance
'außergewöhnlich *adj* unusual
'außerhalb *prp* (*gen*) *and adv* outside; out of; beyond
'außerirdisch *adj* extraterrestrial
'äußerlich *adj* external, outward
'Äußerlichkeit *f (-; -en)* formality; minor detail
äußern ['ɔysɐn] *v/t* (*ge-*, *h*) utter, express; ***sich äußern*** say s.th.; ***sich äußern zu*** *or* ***über*** (*acc*) express o.s. on
'außer'ordentlich *adj* extraordinary
'außerplanmäßig *adj* unscheduled
äußerst ['ɔysɐst] **1.** *adj* outermost; *fig* extreme; ***im äußersten Fall*** at (the) worst; at (the) most **2.** *adv* extremely
außer'stande *adj*: ***außerstande sein*** be unable
'Äußerung *f (-; -en)* utterance, remark
'aussetzen (*sep*, *-ge-*, *h*) **1.** *v/t* abandon; expose (*dat* to); ***et. auszusetzen haben an*** (*dat*) find fault with; **2.** *v/i* stop, break off; MOT, TECH fail
'Aussicht *f* view (***auf*** *acc* of); *fig* prospect (of), chance (***auf Erfolg*** of success)
'aussichtslos *adj* hopeless, desperate
'Aussichtspunkt *m* vantage point
'aussichtsreich *adj* promising
'Aussichtsturm *m* lookout tower
'Aussiedler *m* resettler, evacuee
'aussitzen *v/t* (*irr*, ***sitzen***, *sep*, *-ge-*, *h*) sit *s.th.* out
aussöhnen ['auszø:nən] *v/refl* (*sep*, *-ge-*, *h*) ***sich aussöhnen*** (***mit***) become reconciled (with), F make it up (with)
'Aussöhnung *f (-; -en)* reconciliation
'aussor,tieren *v/t* (*sep*, *no -ge-*, *h*) sort out
ausspannen (*sep*, *-ge-*, *h*) **1.** *v/t* unharness; **2.** *fig v/i* (take a) rest, relax
'aussperren *v/t* (*sep*, *-ge-*, *h*) lock out (*a.* ECON)
'Aussperrung *f (-; -en)* ECON lock-out
'ausspielen (*sep*, *-ge-*, *h*) **1.** *v/t* play; ***j-n gegen j-n ausspielen*** play s.o. off against s.o.; **2.** *v/i card game*: lead; ***er hat ausgespielt*** *fig* he is done for
ausspio,nieren *v/t* (*sep*, *no -ge-*, *h*) spy out
'Aussprache *f* pronunciation; discussion; *private* heart-to-heart (talk)
'aussprechen *v/t* (*irr*, ***sprechen***, *sep*, *-ge-*, *h*) pronounce; express; ***sich aussprechen für*** (***gegen***) speak for (against); ***sich mit j-m gründlich aussprechen*** have a heart-to-heart talk with s.o.
'Ausspruch *m* saying; remark
'ausspucken *v/i and v/t* (*sep*, *-ge-*, *h*) spit out
ausspülen *v/t* (*sep*, *-ge-*, *h*) rinse
'Ausstand *m* strike, F walkout
'ausstatten *v/t* (*sep*, *-ge-*, *h*) fit out, equip, furnish
'Ausstatung *f (-; -en)* equipment, furnishings; design
'ausstechen *v/t* (*irr*, ***stechen***, *sep*, *-ge-*, *h*) GASTR cut out (*a. fig*); put out (*eyes*)
ausstehen (*irr*, ***stehen***, *sep*, *-ge-*, *h*) **1.** *v/t* stand, endure; F ***ich kann ihn*** (***es***) ***nicht ausstehen*** I can't stand him (it); **2.** *v/i*: (***noch***) ***ausstehen*** be outstanding *or* overdue
'aussteigen *v/i* (*irr*, ***steigen***, *sep*, *-ge-*, *sien*) get out (***aus*** *dat* of); (*a.* ***aussteigen aus*** *dat*) get off *a bus*, *train*; F *fig* drop out
'Aussteiger F *m (-s; -)* drop-out
'ausstellen *v/t* (*sep*, *-ge-*, *h*) exhibit, display, show; make out (*check etc*); issue (*passport*)
'Aussteller *m (-s; -)* exhibitor; issuer; drawer (*of check*)
'Ausstellung *f* exhibition, show
'aussterben *v/i* (*irr*, ***sterben***, *sep*, *-ge-*, *sein*) die out, become extinct (*both a. fig*)
'Aussteuer *f* trousseau; dowry

'**aussteuern** *v/t* (*sep*, *-ge-*, *h*) ELECTR modulate
'**Aussteuerung** *f* ELECTR modulation; level control
Ausstieg ['ausʃtiːk] *m* (*-[e]s*; *-e*) exit; *fig* withdrawal (***aus*** *dat* from)
'**ausstopfen** *v/t* (*sep*, *-ge-*, *h*) stuff; pad
'**Ausstoß** *m* TECH, PHYS discharge, ejection; ECON output
'**ausstoßen** *v/t* (*irr*, ***stoßen***, *sep*, *-ge-*, *h*) TECH, PHYS give off, eject, emit; ECON turn out; give (*cry*, *sigh*); expel
'**ausstrahlen** *v/t* (*sep*, *-ge-*, *h*) radiate (*happiness etc*); TV, *radio*: broadcast, transmit
'**Ausstrahlung** *f* radiation; broadcast; *fig* magnetism, charisma
'**ausstrecken** *v/t* (*sep*, *-ge-*, *h*) stretch (out)
ausstreichen *v/t* (*irr*, ***streichen***, *sep*, *-ge-*, *h*) strike out
ausströmen *v/i* (*sep*, *-ge-*, *sein*) escape (***aus*** *dat* from)
aussuchen *v/t* (*sep*, *-ge-*, *h*) choose, pick
'**Austausch** *m* (*-[e]s*; *no pl*) exchange
'**austauschbar** *adj* exchangeable
'**austauschen** *v/t* (*sep*, *-ge-*, *h*) exchange (***gegen*** for)
'**Austauschschüler(in)** exchange student
'**austeilen** *v/t* (*sep*, *-ge-*, *h*) distribute, hand out; deal (out) (*cards*, *blows*)
Auster ['austɐ] *f* (*-*; *-n*) ZO oyster
'**austragen** *v/t* (*irr*, ***tragen***, *sep*, *-ge-*, *h*) deliver (*mail*); settle (*dispute etc*); hold (*contest etc*); ***das Kind austragen*** have the baby
'**Austragungsort** *m* SPORT venue
Australien [aus'traːljən] Australia
Australier [aus'traːljɐ] *m* (*-s*; *-*), **Aust'ralierin** [-ljərɪn] *f* (*-*; *-nen*), **aust'ralisch** *adj* Australian
'**austreiben** *v/t* (*irr*, ***treiben***, *sep*, *-ge-*, *h*) exorcise; F ***j-m et. austreiben*** cure s.o. of s.th.
austreten (*irr*, ***treten***, *sep*, *-ge-*) **1.** *v/t* (*h*) tread *or* stamp out (*fire*); wear out (*shoes*); **2.** *v/i* (*sein*) escape (***aus*** *dat* from); F go to the bathroom (*Br* toilet); ***austreten aus*** (*dat*) leave (*a club etc*); resign from
austrinken *v/t* (*irr*, ***trinken***, *sep*, *-ge-*, *h*) drink up; empty
'**Austritt** *m* leaving; resignation; escape
'**austrocknen** *v/t* (*sep*, *-ge-*, *h*) *and v/i* (*sein*) dry up
'**ausüben** *v/t* (*sep*, *-ge-*, *h*) practi|ce, *Br* -se; hold (*office*); exercise (*power etc*); exert (*pressure etc*)
'**Ausübung** *f* (*-*; *no pl*) practice; exercise
'**Ausverkauf** *m* ECON (clearance) sale
'**ausverkauft** *adj* ECON, THEA sold out; ***vor ausverkauftem Haus spielen*** play to a full house
'**Auswahl** *f* choice, selection (*both a.* ECON); SPORT representative team
'**auswählen** *v/t* (*sep*, *-ge-*, *h*) choose, select
'**Auswanderer** *m* emigrant
'**auswandern** *v/i* (*sep*, *-ge-*, *sein*) emigrate
'**Auswanderung** *f* emigration
auswärtig ['ausvɛrtɪç] *adj* out-of-town; POL foreign
'**auswärts** *adv* out of town
'**Auswärtssieg** *m* SPORT away victory
Auswärtsspiel *n* SPORT away game
'**auswechseln** *v/t* (*sep*, *-ge-*, *h*) exchange (***gegen*** for); change (*tire*); replace; ***A gegen B auswechseln*** SPORT substitute B for A; ***wie ausgewechselt*** (like) a different person
'**Auswechselspieler** *m* SPORT substitute
'**Ausweg** *m* way out
'**ausweglos** *adj* hopeless
'**Ausweglosigkeit** *f* (*-*; *no pl*) hopelessness
'**ausweichen** *v/i* (*irr*, ***weichen***, *sep*, *-ge-*, *sein*) make way (*dat* for); *fig* avoid *s.o.*; evade (*question*)
ausweichend *adj* evasive
'**ausweinen** *v/refl* (*sep*, *-ge-*, *h*) have a good cry
Ausweis ['ausvais] *m* (*-es*; *-e*) identification (card); card
'**ausweisen** *v/t* (*irr*, ***weisen***, *sep*, *-ge-*, *h*) expel; ***sich ausweisen*** identify o.s.
'**Ausweispa,piere** *pl* documents
'**Ausweisung** *f* (*-*; *-en*) expulsion
'**ausweiten** *fig v/t* (*sep*, *-ge-*, *h*) expand
'**auswendig** *adv* by heart; ***et. auswendig können*** know s.th. by heart; ***auswendig lernen*** memorize; learn by heart
'**auswerfen** *v/t* (*irr*, ***werfen***, *sep*, *-ge-*, *h*) throw out; cast (*anchor*); TECH eject
'**auswerten** *v/t* (*sep*, *-ge-*, *h*) evaluate, analyze, interpret; utilize, exploit
'**Auswertung** *f* evaluation; utilization
'**auswickeln** *v/t* (*sep*, *-ge-*, *h*) unwrap
'**auswirken** *v/refl* (*sep*, *-ge-*, *h*) ***sich auswirken auf*** (*acc*) affect; ***sich positiv auswirken*** have a favo(u)rable effect
'**Auswirkung** *f* effect
'**auswischen** *v/t* (*sep*, *-ge-*, *h*) wipe out
'**auswringen** *v/t* (*irr*, ***wringen***, *sep*, *-ge-*, *h*) wring out
'**Auswuchs** *m* (*-es*; *Auswüchse* ['ausvyːksə]) excrescence; *fig pl* excesses
'**auswuchten** *v/t* (*sep*, *-ge-*, *h*) TECH balance: **auszahlen** *v/t* (*sep*, *-ge-*, *h*) pay (out); pay *s.o.* off; ***sich auswuchten*** pay
auszählen *v/t* (*sep*, *-ge-*, *h*) count; *boxing*:

count out
'Auszahlung *f* payment; paying off
'auszeichnen *v/t* (*sep*, *-ge-*, *h*) price, mark (out) (*goods*); ***sich auszeichnen*** distinguish o.s.; ***j-n mit et. auszeichnen*** award s.th. to s.o.
'Auszeichnung *f* marking; *fig* distinction, hono(u)r; award; decoration
'ausziehen (*irr*, ***ziehen***, *sep*, *-ge-*) **1.** *v/t* (*h*) take off (*coat etc*); pull out (*table etc*); ***sich ausziehen*** undress; **2.** *v/i* (*sein*) move out
'Auszubildende *m*, *f* (*-n*; *-n*) apprentice, trainee
'Auszug *m* move, removal; extract, excerpt; statement (of account)
authentisch [au'tɛntɪʃ] *adj* authentic, genuine
Autismus [au'tɪsmʊs] *m* PSYCH autism
autistisch [au'tɪstɪʃ] *adj* PSYCH autistic
Auto ['auto] *n* (*-s*; *-s*) car, auto(mobile); (***mit dem***) ***Auto fahren*** drive, go by car
'Autobahn *f Am* expressway, *Br* motorway
Autobahndreieck *n* interchange
Autobahngebühr *f* toll
Autobahnkreuz *n* interchange
Autobiogra'phie *f* autobiography
'Autobombe *f* car bomb
Autobus *m* → ***Bus***
Autofähre *f* car ferry
Autofahrer(in) motorist, driver
Autofahrt *f* drive
Autofriedhof F *m* car dump, auto junkyard
Autogramm [auto'gram] *n* autograph
Autogrammjäger *m* autograph hunter
'Autokarte *f* road map
Autokino *n* drive-in theater (*Br* cinema)
Automat [auto'maːt] *m* (*-en*; *-en*) vending (*Br a.* slot) machine; TECH robot; → ***Spielautomat***
Automatik [auto'maːtɪk] *f* (*-*; *no pl*) automatic (system *or* control); MOT automatic transmission; automatic
Automation [automa'tsjoːn] *f* (*-*; *no pl*) automation
auto'matisch *adj* automatic
'Autome,chaniker *m* car mechanic
autonom [auto'noːm] *adj* autonomous
'Autonummer *f* license (*Br* licence) number
Autor ['autoːɐ] *m* (*-s*; *-en* [au'toːrən]) author
'Autorepara,turwerkstatt *f* garage, car repair shop
Autorin [au'toːrɪn] *f* (*-*; *-nen*) author(ess)
autorisieren [autori'ziːrən] *v/t* (*no -ge-*, *h*) authorize
autoritär [autori'tɛːɐ] *adj* authoritarian
Autorität [autori'tɛːt] *f* (*-*; *-en*) authority
'Autotele,fon *n* car phone
Autovermietung *f* car rental (*Br* hire) service
Autowaschanlage *f* car wash
Axt [akst] *f* (*-*; *Äxte* ['ɛkstə]) ax(e)

B

Bach [bax] *m* (*-[e]s*; *Bäche* ['bɛçə]) brook, stream, *Am a.* creek
'Backblech *n* baking sheet
'Backbord *n* (*-s*; *no pl*) MAR port
Backe ['bakə] *f* (*-*; *-n*) ANAT cheek
backen *v/t and v/i* ([*irr*, ***backen***,] *-ge-*, *h*) bake
'Backenzahn *m* ANAT molar (tooth)
Bäcker ['bɛkɐ] *m* (*-s*; *-*) baker; ***beim Bäcker*** at the baker's
Bäckerei [bɛkə'rai] *f* (*-*; *-en*) bakery, baker's (shop)
'Backform *f* baking tin
Backhendl ['bakhɛndl] *Austrian n* (*-s*; *-n*) fried chicken
Backobst *n* dried fruit
Backofen *m* oven
Backpflaume *f* prune
Backpulver *n* baking powder
Backstein *m* brick
backte ['baktə] *pret of* ***backen***
'Backwaren *pl* breads and pastries
Bad [baːt] *n* (*-[e]*; *Bäder* ['bɛːdɐ]) bath; swim; bathroom; → ***Badeort***; ***ein Bad nehmen*** → ***baden 1***
'Badeanstalt *f* swimming pool, public baths
Badeanzug *m* swimsuit
Badehose *f* bathing trunks
Badekappe *f* bathing cap
Bademantel *m* bathrobe
Bademeister *m* pool *or* bath attendant

baden ['ba:dən] (*ge-, h*) **1.** *v/i* bathe, take *or* have a bath; swim; ***baden gehen*** go swimming; **2.** *v/t* bathe (*a.* MED); *Br a.* bath
'Badeort *m* seaside (*or* health) resort
Badetuch *n* bath towel
Badewanne *f* bathtub
Badezimmer *n* bathroom
baff [baf] *adj*: F ***baff sein*** be flabbergasted
Bagatelle [baga'tɛlə] *f* (-; *-n*) trifle
Baga'tellschaden *m* superficial damage
Bagger ['bagɐ] *m* (*-s*; -) TECH excavator; dredge(r)
'baggern *v/i* (*ge-, h*) TECH excavate; dredge
Bahn [ba:n] *f* (-; *-en*) railroad, *Br* railway; train; way, path, course; SPORT track; ***mit der Bahn*** by rail; ***Bahn frei!*** make way!; *cpds* → *a.* ***Eisenbahn***
'bahnbrechend *adj* epoch-making
'Bahndamm *m* railroad (*Br* railway) embankment
'bahnen *v/t* (*ge-, h*) ***den Weg bahnen*** clear the way (*dat* for *s.o. or s.th.*); ***sich e-n Weg bahnen*** force *or* work one's way
'Bahnhof *m* (railroad, *Br* railway) station
Bahnlinie *f* railroad (*Br* railway) line
Bahnsteig [-ʃtaik] *m* (-[*e*]*s*; *-e*) platform
Bahnübergang *m* grade (*Br* level) crossing
Bahre ['ba:rə] *f* (-; *-n*) stretcher; bier
Baisse ['bɛ:sə] *f* (-; *-n*) ECON fall, slump
Bakterien [bak'te:rjən] *pl* MED bacteria, germs
balancieren [balã'si:rən] *v/t and v/i* (*no -ge-, h*) balance
bald [balt] *adv* soon; F almost, nearly; ***so bald wie möglich*** as soon as possible
baldig ['baldıç] *adj* speedy; ***baldige Antwort*** ECON early reply; ***auf (ein) baldiges Wiedersehen!*** see you again soon!
balgen ['balgən] *v/refl* (*ge-, h*) scuffle (***um*** for)
Balken ['balkən] *m* (*-s*; -) beam
Balkon [bal'kɔŋ] *m* (*-s*; *-s, -e* [-'ko:nə]) balcony
Balkontür *f* French window
Ball [bal] *m* (-[*e*]*s*; *Bälle* ['bɛlə]) ball; dance; ***am Ball sein*** SPORT have the ball; ***am Ball bleiben*** *fig* stick to it
Ballade [ba'la:də] *f* (-; *-n*) ballad
Ballast ['balast] *m* (-[*e*]*s*; *no pl*) ballast, *fig a.* burden
Ballaststoffe *pl* MED roughage, bulk
ballen ['balən] *v/t* (*ge-, h*) clench (*fist*)
'Ballen *m* (*-s*; -) bale; ANAT ball
Ballett [ba'lɛt] *n* (-[*e*]*s*; *-e*) ballet
Ballon [ba'lɔŋ] *m* (*-s*; *-s*) balloon
'Ballungsraum *m*, **Ballungszentrum** *n* congested area, conurbation
Balsam ['balza:m] *m* (*-s*; *no pl*) balm
Bambus ['bambʊs] *m* (*-ses*, -; *-se*) BOT bamboo
Bambusrohr *n* BOT bamboo (cane)
banal [ba'na:l] *adj* banal, trite
Banane [ba'na:nə] *f* (-; *-n*) BOT banana
Banause [ba'nauzə] *m* (*-n*; *-n*) philistine
band [bant] *pret of* ***binden***
Band[1] *n* (-[*e*]*s*; *Bänder* ['bɛndɐ]) ribbon; tape; (*hat*) band; ANAT ligament; *fig* tie, link; ***auf Band aufnehmen*** tape; ***am laufenden Band*** *fig* continuously
Band[2] *m* (-[*e*]*s*; *Bände* ['bɛndə]) volume
Bandage [ban'da:ʒə] *f* (-; *-n*) bandage
bandagieren [banda'ʒi:rən] *v/t* (*no -ge-, h*) bandage (up)
'Bandbreite *f* ELECTR bandwidth; *fig* range
Bande ['bandə] *f* (-; *-n*) gang; *billiards*: cushions; *ice hockey*: boards; *bowling*: gutter
'Bänderriss *m* MED torn ligament
bändigen ['bɛndigən] *v/t* (*ge-, h*) tame (*a. fig*); restrain, control (*children etc*)
Bandit [ban'di:t] *m* (*-en*; *-en*) bandit, outlaw
'Bandmaß *n* tape measure
Bandscheibe *f* ANAT (intervertebral) disk (*Br* disc)
Bandscheibenschaden *m*, **Bandscheibenvorfall** *m* MED slipped disk
Bandwurm *m* ZO tapeworm
bange ['baŋə] *adj* afraid; anxious
'Bange *f*: ***j-m Bange machen*** frighten *or* scare s.o.; ***keine Bange!*** (have) no fear!
'bangen *v/i* (*ge-, h*) be anxious *or* worried (***um*** about)
Bank[1] [baŋk] *f* (-; *Bänke* ['bɛŋkə]) bench; F ***durch die Bank*** without exception; ***auf die lange Bank schieben*** put off
Bank[2] *f* (-; *-en*) bank; ***auf der Bank*** in the bank
'Bankangestellte *m, f* bank clerk *or* employee
'Bankautomat *m* → ***Geldautomat***
Bankett [baŋ'kɛt] *n* (-[*e*]*s*; *-e*) banquet
'Bankgeschäfte *pl* banking transactions
Bankier [baŋ'kje:] *m* (*-s*; *-s*) banker
'Bankkonto *n* bank(ing) account
Bankleitzahl *f* A.B.A. number, *Br* bank (sorting) code
Banknote *f* bill, *Br* (bank) note
Bankraub *m* bank robbery
bankrott [baŋ'krɔt] *adj* ECON bankrupt
Bank'rott *m* (-[*e*]*s*; *-e*) ECON bankruptcy; ***Bankrott machen*** go bankrupt

'Bankverbindung *f* account(s), account details
Bann [ban] *m* (-[*e*]*s*; *no pl*) ban; spell
'bannen *v/t* (*ge-*, *h*) ward off; **(*wie*) *gebannt*** spellbound
Banner ['banɐ] *n* (-*s*; -) banner (*a. fig*)
bar [baːɐ] *adj* (in) cash; ***gegen bar*** for cash
Bar *f* (-; -*s*) bar; nightclub
Bär [bɛːɐ] *m* (-*en*; -*en*) ZO bear
Baracke [ba'rakə] *f* (-; -*n*) hut; *contp* shack
Barbar [bar'baːɐ] *m* (-*en*; -*en*) barbarian
barbarisch [bar'baːrɪʃ] *adj* barbarous, *a.* atrocious (*crime etc*)
'Bardame *f* barmaid
'barfuß *adj and adv* barefoot
barg [bark] *pret of* ***bergen***
'Bargeld *n* cash
'bargeldlos *adj* noncash
'Barhocker *m* bar stool
Bariton ['baːritɔn] *m* (-*s*; -*e* [-toːnə]) MUS baritone
Barkasse [bar'kasə] *f* (-; -*n*) MAR launch
barm'herzig *adj* merciful; charitable
Barm'herzigkeit *f* (-; *no pl*) mercy; charity
'Barmixer *m* barman
Barometer [baro'meːtɐ] *n* (-*s*; -) barometer
Baron [ba'roːn] *m* (-*s*; -*e*) baron
Ba'ronin *f* (-; -*nen*) baroness
Barren ['barən] *m* (-*s*; -) bar, ingot, *a. gold, silver* bullion; SPORT parallel bars
Barriere [ba'rjeːrə] *f* (-; -*n*) barrier
Barrikade [bari'kaːdə] *f* (-; -*n*) barricade
barsch [barʃ] *adj* rough, gruff, brusque
Barsch *m* (-[*e*]*s*; -*e*) ZO perch
'Barscheck *m* (negotiable) check, *Br* open cheque
barst [barst] *pret of* ***bersten***
Bart [baːɐt] *m* (-[*e*]*s*; *Bärte* ['bɛːɐtə]) beard; TECH bit; ***sich e-n Bart wachsen lassen*** grow a beard
bärtig ['bɛːɐtɪç] *adj* bearded
'Barzahlung *f* cash payment
Basar [ba'zaːɐ] *m* (-*s*; -*e*) bazaar
Base ['baːzə] *f* (-; -*n*) cousin; CHEM base
basieren [ba'ziːrən] *v/i* (*no -ge-*, *h*) ***basieren auf*** (*dat*) be based on
Basis ['baːzɪs] *f* (-; *Basen*) basis; MIL, ARCH base
Baskenmütze ['baskən-] *f* beret
Bass [bas] *m* (-*es*; *Bässe* ['bɛsə]) MUS bass
Bassin [ba'sɛ̃ː] *n* (-*s*; -*s*) basin; (swimming) pool
Bassist [ba'sɪst] *m* (-*en*; -*en*) MUS bass singer *or* player
Bast [bast] *m* (-[*e*]*s*; -*e*) bast; HUNT velvet
Bastard ['bastart] *m* (-*s*; -*e*) BIOL hybrid; mongrel; V bastard
basteln ['bastəln] (*ge-*, *h*) **1.** *v/i* make *or* repair things o.s.; **2.** *v/t* build, make
Bastler ['bastlɐ] *m* (-*s*; -) home handyman, do-it-yourselfer
bat [baːt] *pret of* ***bitten***
Batik ['baːtɪk] *m* (-*s*; -*en*), *f* (-; -*en*) batik
Batist [ba'tɪst] *m* (-[*e*]*s*; -*e*) cambric
Batterie [batə'riː] *f* (-; -*n*) ELECTR, MIL battery
Bau [bau] *m* (-[*e*]*s*; *Bauten*) a) (*no pl*) building, construction; build, frame, b) building, c) ZO (*pl Baue*) hole, den; ***im Bau*** under construction
Bauarbeiten *pl* construction work; road works
Bauarbeiter *m* construction worker
Bauart *f* style (of construction); type, model
Bauch [baux] *m* (-[*e*]*s*; *Bäuche* ['bɔʏçə]) belly (*a. fig*); ANAT abdomen; F tummy
'bauchig *adj* bulgy
'Bauchlandung *f* AVIAT belly landing
Bauchredner *m* ventriloquist
Bauchschmerzen *pl* stomachache
Bauchtanz *m* belly dancing
bauen ['bauən] (*ge-*, *h*) **1.** *v/t* build, construct, *a.* make (*furniture etc*); **2.** *fig v/i*: ***bauen auf*** (*acc*) rely *or* count on
Bauer[1] ['bauɐ] *m* (-*n*; -*n*) farmer; *chess*: pawn
'Bauer[2] *n*, *m* (-*s*; -) (bird)cage
Bäuerin ['bɔʏərɪn] *f* (-; -*nen*) farmer's wife; farmer
bäuerlich ['bɔʏɐlɪç] *adj* rural; rustic
'Bauernfänger *contp m* trickster, conman
Bauernhaus *n* farmhouse
Bauernhof *m* farm
Bauernmöbel *pl* rustic furniture
'baufällig *adj* dilapidated
'Baufirma *f* builders and contractors
Baugenehmigung *f* building permit
Baugerüst *n* scaffold(ing)
Bauherr *m* owner
Bauholz *n* lumber, *Br a.* timber
Bauinge,nieur *m* civil engineer
Baujahr *n* year of construction; ***Baujahr 1995*** 1995 model
Baukasten *m* box of building blocks (*Br* bricks); TECH construction set; kit
Bauleiter *m* building supervisor
'baulich *adj* structural
Baum [baum] *m* (-[*e*]*s*; *Bäume* ['bɔʏmə]) BOT tree
'Baumarkt *m* do-it-yourself superstore
baumeln ['bauməln] *v/i* (*ge-*, *h*) dangle, swing; ***mit den Beinen baumeln*** dangle one's legs

'Baumschule *f* nursery
Baumstamm *m* trunk; log
Baumwolle *f* cotton
'Bauplan *m* architectural drawing; blueprints
Bauplatz *m* building site
Bausch [bauʃ] *m* (-[*e*]*s*; *-e*) wad, ball; ***in Bausch und Bogen*** lock, stock and barrel
'Bausparkasse *f* building and loan association, *Br* building society
'Baustein *m* brick; (building) block; *fig* element
Baustelle *f* building site; MOT construction zone, *Br* roadworks
Baustil *m* (architectural) style
Baustoff *m* building material
Bautechniker *m* engineer
Bauteil *n* component (part), unit, module
Bauunternehmer *m* building contractor
Bauvorschriften *pl* building regulations
Bauwerk *n* building
Bauzaun *m* hoarding
Bauzeichner *m* draftsman, *Br* draughtsman
Bayern ['baiɐn] Bavaria
Bayer ['baiɐ] *m* (*-n*; *-n*), **Bayerin** ['baiərın] *f* (-; *-nen*), **bay(e)risch** ['bai(ə)rıʃ] *adj* Bavarian
Bazillus [ba'tsılʊs] *m* (-; *-len*) MED bacillus, germ
beabsichtigen [bə'ʔapzıçtıgən] *v/t* (*no -ge-*, *h*) intend, plan; ***es war beabsichtigt*** it was intentional
be'achten *v/t* (*no -ge-*, *h*) pay attention to; observe, follow (*rule etc*); ***beachten Sie, dass ...*** note that ...; ***nicht beachten*** take no notice of; disregard
be'achtlich *adj* remarkable; considerable
Be'achtung *f* (-; *no pl*) attention; consideration; observance
Beamte [bə'ʔamtə] *m* (*-n*; *-n*), **Be'amtin** *f* (-; *-nen*) official; (*police etc*) officer; civil servant
be'ängstigend *adj* alarming
beanspruchen [bə'ʔanʃprʊxən] *v/t* (*no -ge-*, *h*) claim; take up (*time etc*); TECH stress
Be'anspruchung *f* (-; *-en*) claim; TECH stress, strain (*a. fig*)
beanstanden [bə'ʔanʃtandən] *v/t* (*no -ge-*, *h*) complain about; object to
beantragen [bə'ʔantra:gən] *v/t* (*no -ge-*, *h*) apply for; JUR, PARL move (for); propose
be'antworten *v/t* (*no -ge-*, *h*) answer, reply to
be'arbeiten *v/t* (*no -ge-*, *h*) work; AGR till; hew (*stone*); process; be in charge of (*a case etc*); treat (*subject*); revise; THEA adapt (***nach*** from); *esp* MUS arrange; F ***j-n bearbeiten*** work on s.o.
Be'arbeitung *f* (-; *-en*) working; revision; THEA adaptation; *esp* MUS arrangement; TECH processing, treatment
be'atmen *v/t* (*no -ge-*, *h*) MED give artificial respiration to *s.o.*
beaufsichtigen [bə'ʔaufzıçtıgən] *v/t* (*no -ge-*, *h*) supervise; look after
Be'aufsichtigung *f* (-; *-en*) supervision; looking after
be'auftragen *v/t* (*no -ge-*, *h*) commission; instruct; ***beauftragen mit*** put *s.o.* in charge of
Be'auftragte [-tra:ktə] *m, f* (*-n*; *-n*) agent; representative; commissioner
be'bauen *v/t* (*no -ge-*, *h*) build on; AGR cultivate
beben ['be:bən] *v/i* (*ge-*, *h*) shake, tremble; shiver (*all*: ***vor*** with); *earth*: quake
bebildern [bə'bıldɐn] *v/t* (*no -ge-*, *h*) illustrate
Becher ['bɛçɐ] *m* (*-s*; -) cup, mug
Becken ['bɛkən] *n* (*-s*; -) basin, bowl; pool; ANAT pelvis; MUS cymbal(s)
bedacht [bə'daxt] *adj*: ***darauf bedacht sein zu*** *inf* be anxious to *inf*
bedächtig [bə'dɛçtıç] *adj* deliberate; measured
bedang [bə'daŋ] *pret of* ***bedingen***
be'danken *v/refl* (*no -ge-*, *h*) ***sich bei j-m für et. bedanken*** thank s.o. for s.th.
Bedarf [bə'darf] *m* (-[*e*]*s*; *no pl*) need (***an*** *dat* of), want (of); ECON demand (for); ***bei Bedarf*** if necessary
Be'darfshaltestelle *f* request stop
bedauerlich [bə'dauɐlıç] *adj* regrettable
be'dauerlicher'weise *adv* unfortunately
be'dauern *v/t* (*no -ge-*, *h*) feel *or* be sorry for *s.o.*, pity *s.o.*; regret *s.th.*
Be'dauern *n* (*-s*; *no pl*) regret (***über*** *acc* at)
be'dauernswert *adj* pitiable, deplorable
be'decken *v/t* (*no -ge-*, *h*) cover
be'deckt *adj* METEOR overcast
be'denken *v/t* (*irr*, ***denken***, *no -ge-*, *h*) consider, think *s.th.* over
Be'denken *pl* doubts; scruples; objections
be'denkenlos *adv* unhesitatingly; without scruples
be'denklich *adj* doubtful; serious, critical; alarming
Be'denkzeit *f*: ***e-e Stunde Bedenkzeit*** one hour to think it over
be'deuten *v/t* (*no -ge-*, *h*) mean
bedeutend *adj* important; considerable; distinguished
Be'deutung *f* (-; *-en*) meaning; impor-

tance
be'deutungslos *adj* insignificant; meaningless
be'deutungsvoll *adj* significant; meaningful
be'dienen (*no -ge-, h*) **1.** *v/t* serve, wait on *s.o.*; TECH operate, work; ***sich bedienen*** help o.s.; ***bedienen Sie sich!*** help yourself! **2.** *v/i* serve; wait (at table); *card games*: follow suit
Be'dienung *f* (-; *-en*) a) (*no pl*) service, b) waiter, waitress; shop assistant, clerk, c) TECH operation, control
Be'dienungsanleitung *f* operating instructions
bedingen [bə'dɪŋən] *v/t* ([*irr*,] *no -ge-, h*) require; cause; imply, involve
be'dingt *adj*: ***bedingt durch*** caused by, due to
Be'dingung *f* (-; *-en*) condition; *pl* ECON terms; requirements; conditions; ***unter einer Bedingung*** on one condition
be'dingungslos *adj* unconditional
be'drängen *v/t* (*no -ge-, h*) press (hard)
be'drohen *v/t* (*no -ge-, h*) threaten, menace
be'drohlich *adj* threatening
Be'drohung *f* threat, menace (*gen* to)
be'drücken *v/t* (*no -ge-, h*) depress, sadden
bedungen [bə'dʊŋən] *pp of* ***bedingen***
Bedürfnis [bə'dʏrfnɪs] *n* (*-ses*; *-se*) need, necessity (***für, nach*** for)
Bedürfnisanstalt *f* comfort station, *Br* public convenience (*or* toilets)
be'dürftig *adj* needy, poor
be'eilen *v/refl* (*no -ge-, h*) hurry (up)
beeindrucken [bə'ʔaindrʊkən] *v/t* (*no -ge-, h*) impress
beeinflussen [bə'ʔainflʊsən] *v/t* (*no -ge-, h*) influence; affect
beeinträchtigen [bə'ʔaintrɛçtɪgən] *v/t* (*no -ge-, h*) affect, impair
be'end(ig)en *v/t* (*no -ge-, h*) (bring to an) end, finish, conclude, close
beengen [bə'ɛŋən] *v/t* (*no -ge-, h*) make *s.o.* (feel) uncomfortable
be'engt *adj*: ***beengt wohnen*** live in cramped quarters
be'erben *v/t* (*no -ge-, h*) ***j-n beerben*** be s.o.'s heir
beerdigen [bə'ʔeːɐdɪgən] *v/t* (*no -ge-, h*) bury
Be'erdigung *f* (-; *-en*) burial, funeral
Beere ['beːrə] *f* (-; *-n*) BOT berry; grape
Beet [beːt] *n* (-[*e*]*s*; *-e*) bed, patch
befähigen [bə'fɛːɪgən] *v/t* (*no -ge-, h*) enable; qualify (***für, zu*** for)
be'fähigt *adj* (cap)able; ***zu et. befähigt*** fit *or* qualified for s.th.
Be'fähigung *f* (-; *no pl*) qualification(s), (cap)ability
befahl [bə'faːl] *pret of* ***befehlen***
be'fahrbar *adj* passable, practicable; MAR navigable
be'fahren *v/t* (*irr*, ***fahren***, *no -ge-, h*) drive *or* travel on; MAR navigate
be'fallen *v/t* (*irr*, ***fallen***, *no -ge-, h*) attack, seize (*a. fig*)
be'fangen *adj* self-conscious; prejudiced, JUR *a.* bias(s)ed
Be'fangenheit *f* (-; *no pl*) self-consciousness; JUR bias, prejudice
be'fassen *v/refl* (*no -ge-, h*) ***sich befassen mit*** engage *or* occupy o.s. with; work on *s.th.*; deal with *s.o., s.th.*
Befehl [bə'feːl] *m* (-[*e*]*s*; *-e*) order; command (***über*** *acc* of)
be'fehlen *v/t* (*irr, no -ge-, h*) order; command
Be'fehlshaber *m* (*-s*; -) MIL commander
be'festigen *v/t* (*no -ge-, h*) fasten (***an*** *dat* to), fix (to), attach (to); MIL fortify
Be'festigung *f* (-; *-en*) fixing, fastening; MIL fortification
be'feuchten *v/t* (*no -ge-, h*) moisten, damp
be'finden *v/refl* (*irr*, ***finden***, *no -ge-, h*) be (situated)
Be'finden *n* (*-s*; *no pl*) (state of) health
be'flecken *v/t* (*no -ge-, h*) stain; *fig a.* sully
befohlen [bə'foːlən] *pp of* ***befehlen***
be'folgen *v/t* (*no -ge-, h*) follow, take (*advice*); observe (*rule etc*); REL keep
Be'folgung *f* (-; *no pl*) following; observance
be'fördern *v/t* (*no -ge-, h*) carry, transport; haul, ship; promote (***zu*** to)
Be'förderung *f* (-; *-en*) a) (*no pl*) transport(ation); shipment, b) promotion
be'fragen *v/t* (*no -ge-, h*) question, interview
be'freien *v/t* (*no -ge-, h*) free, liberate; rescue; exempt (***von*** from)
Be'freiung *f* (-; *no pl*) liberation; exemption
Befremden [bə'frɛmdən] *n* (*-s*; *no pl*) irritation, displeasure
be'fremdet *adj* irritated, displeased
befreunden [bə'frɔʏndən] *v/refl* (*no -ge-, h*) ***sich befreunden mit*** make friends with; *fig* warm to
be'freundet *adj* friendly; ***befreundet sein*** be friends
befriedigen [bə'friːdɪgən] *v/t* (*no -ge-, h*) satisfy; ***sich selbst befriedigen*** masturbate
befriedigend *adj* satisfactory; *grade*: fair

befriedigt [bə'fri:dɪçt] *adj* satisfied, pleased
Be'friedigung *f* (-; *no pl*) satisfaction
be'fristet *adj* limited (***auf*** *acc* to), temporary
be'fruchten *v/t* (*no -ge-, h*) BIOL fertilize, inseminate
Be'fruchtung *f* (-; *-en*) BIOL fertilization, insemination
Befugnis [bə'fu:knɪs] *f* (-; *-se*) authority; *esp* JUR competence
befugt [bə'fu:kt] *adj* authorized; competent
be'fühlen *v/t* (*no -ge-, h*) feel, touch
Be'fund *m* finding(s) (*a.* MED, JUR)
be'fürchten *v/t* (*no -ge-, h*) fear, be afraid of; suspect
Be'fürchtung *f* (-; *-en*) fear, suspicion
befürworten [bə'fy:ɐvɔrtən] *v/t* (*no -ge-, h*) advocate, speak *or* plead for
Be'fürworter *m* (*-s*; -) advocate
begabt [bə'ga:pt] *adj* gifted, talented
Be'gabung *f* (-; *-en*) gift, talent(s)
begann [bə'gan] *pret of* ***beginnen***
be'geben *v/refl* (*irr*, ***geben***, *no -ge-, h*) ***sich in Gefahr begeben*** expose o.s. to danger
Be'gebenheit *f* (-; *-en*) incident, event
begegnen [bə'ge:gnən] *v/i* (*no -ge-, sein*) meet (*a. fig* ***mit*** with); ***sich begegnen*** meet
Be'gegnung *f* (-; *-en*) meeting, encounter (*a.* SPORT)
be'gehen *v/t* (*irr*, ***gehen***, *no -ge-, h*) walk (on); celebrate (*birthday etc*); commit (*crime*); make (*mistake*); ***ein Unrecht begehen*** do wrong
begehren [bə'ge:rən] *v/t* (*no -ge-, h*) desire
be'gehrenswert *adj* desirable
be'gehrlich *adj* desirous, covetous
begehrt [bə'ge:ɐt] *adj* (very) popular, (much) in demand
begeistern [bə'gaistɐn] *v/t* (*no -ge-, h*) fill with enthusiasm; carry away (*audience*); ***sich begeistern für*** be enthusiastic about
be'geistert *adj* enthusiastic
Be'geisterung *f* (-; *no pl*) enthusiasm
Begierde [bə'gi:ɐdə] *f* (-; *-n*) desire (***nach*** for), appetite (for)
be'gierig *adj* greedy; eager (***nach, auf*** *acc* for; ***zu*** *inf* to *inf*)
be'gießen *v/t* (*irr*, ***gießen***, *no -ge-, h*) water; GASTR baste; F *fig* celebrate *s.th.* (with a drink)
Beginn [bə'gɪn] *m* (*-[e]s*; *no pl*) beginning, start; ***zu Beginn*** at the beginning
be'ginnen *v/t and v/i* (*irr, no -ge-, h*) begin, start
beglaubigen [bə'glaubɪgən] *v/t* (*no -ge-, h*) attest, certify
Be'glaubigung *f* (-; *-en*) attestation, certification
be'gleichen *v/t* (*irr*, ***gleichen***, *no -ge-, h*) pay, settle
be'gleiten *v/t* (*no -ge-, h*) accompany (*a.* MUS ***auf*** *dat* on); ***j-n nach Hause begleiten*** see s.o. home
Be'gleiter(in) (*-s*; *-/-*; *-nen*) companion; MUS accompanist
Be'gleiterscheinung *f* concomitant; MED side effect
Begleitschreiben *n* covering letter
Be'gleitung *f* (-; *-en*) company; *esp* MIL escort; MUS accompaniment
be'glückwünschen *v/t* (*no -ge-, h*) congratulate (***zu*** on)
begnadigen [bə'gna:dɪgən] *v/t* (*no -ge-, h*), **Be'gnadigung** *f* (-; *-en*) JUR pardon; amnesty
begnügen [bə'gny:gən] *v/refl* (*no -ge-, h*) ***sich begnügen mit*** be satisfied with; make do with
begonnen [bə'gɔnən] *pp of* ***beginnen***
be'graben *v/t* (*irr*, ***graben***, *no -ge-, h*) bury (*a. fig*)
Begräbnis [bə'grɛ:pnɪs] *n* (*-ses*; *-se*) burial; funeral
begradigen [bə'gra:dɪgən] *v/t* (*no -ge-, h*) straighten
be'greifen *v/t* (*irr*, ***greifen***, *no -ge-, h*) comprehend, understand
be'greiflich *adj* understandable
be'grenzen *v/t* (*no -ge-, h*) limit, restrict (***auf*** *acc* to)
be'grenzt *adj* limited
Be'griff *m* (*-[e]s*; *-e*) idea, notion; term (*a.* MATH); ***im Begriff sein zu*** *inf* be about to *inf*
be'griffsstutzig *contp adj* F slow on the uptake
be'gründen *v/t* (*no -ge-, h*) give reasons for
be'gründet *adj* well-founded, justified
Be'gründung *f* (-; *-en*) reasons, arguments
be'grünen *v/t* (*no -ge-, h*) landscape
be'grüßen *v/t* (*no -ge-, h*) greet, welcome (*a. fig*)
Be'grüßung *f* (-; *-en*) greeting, welcome
begünstigen [bə'gʏnstɪgən] *v/t* (*no -ge-, h*) favo(u)r
be'gutachten *v/t* (*no -ge-, h*) give an (expert's) opinion on; examine; ***begutachten lassen*** obtain expert opinion on
begütert [bə'gy:tɐt] *adj* wealthy
be'haart *adj* hairy

behäbig [bəˈhɛːbɪç] *adj* slow; portly
beˈhaftet *adj*: ***mit Fehlern behaftet*** flawed
behagen [bəˈhaːgən] *v/i* (*no -ge-, h*) ***j-m behagen*** please *or* suit s.o.
Beˈhagen *n* (*-s; no pl*) pleasure, enjoyment
behaglich [bəˈhaːklɪç] *adj* comfortable; cozy, snug
beˈhalten *v/t* (*irr*, ***halten***, *no -ge-, h*) keep (*fig* ***für sich*** to o.s.); remember
Behälter [bəˈhɛltɐ] *m* (*-s; -*) container, receptacle
beˈhandeln *v/t* (*no -ge-, h*) handle; treat (*a.* MED); ***sich (ärztlich) behandeln lassen*** undergo (medical) treatment
Beˈhandlung *f* (*-; -en*) handling; *a.* MED treatment
beharren [bəˈharən] *v/i* (*no -ge-, h*) insist (***auf*** *dat* on)
beˈharrlich *adj* persistent
behaupten [bəˈhauptən] *v/t* (*no -ge-, h*) claim; pretend
Beˈhauptung *f* (*-; -en*) statement, claim
beˈheben *v/t* (*irr*, ***heben***, *no -ge-, h*) repair (*damage etc*)
beˈheizen *v/t* (*no -ge-, h*) heat
beˈhelfen *v/refl* (*irr*, ***helfen***, *no -ge-, h*) ***sich behelfen mit*** make do with; ***sich behelfen ohne*** do without
Beˈhelfs… *in cpds mst* temporary
beherbergen [bəˈhɛrbɛrgən] *v/t* (*no -ge-, h*) accommodate
beˈherrschen *v/t* (*no -ge-, h*) rule (over), govern; ECON dominate, control; have (a good) command of (*language*); ***sich beherrschen*** control o.s.
Beˈherrschung *f* (*-; no pl*) command, control
beherzigen [bəˈhɛrtsɪgən] *v/t* (*no -ge-, h*) take to heart, mind
beˈhilflich *adj*: ***j-m behilflich sein*** help s.o. (***bei*** with, in)
beˈhindern *v/t* (*no -ge-, h*) hinder; obstruct (*a.* SPORT)
beˈhindert *adj* MED handicapped; disabled
Beˈhinderung *f* (*-; -en*) obstruction; MED handicap
Behörde [bəˈhøːɐdə] *f* (*-; -n*) authority, *mst the* authorities; board
beˈhüten *v/t* (*no -ge-, h*) guard (***vor*** *dat* from)
behutsam [bəˈhuːtzaːm] *adj* careful; gentle
bei [bai] *prp* (*dat*) near; at; with; by; *time:* during; at; ***bei München*** near Munich; ***wohnen bei*** stay (*or* live) with; ***bei mir*** (***ihr***) at my (her) place; ***bei uns*** (***zu Hause***) at home; ***arbeiten bei*** work for; ***e-e Stelle bei*** a job with; ***bei der Marine*** in the navy; ***bei Familie Müller*** at the Müllers'; ***bei Müller*** c/o Müller; ***ich habe kein Geld bei mir*** I have no money with *or* on me; ***bei e-r Tasse Tee*** over a cup of tea; ***wir haben Englisch bei Herrn X*** we have Mr X for English; ***bei Licht*** by light; ***bei Tag*** during the day; ***bei Nacht*** (***Sonnenaufgang***) at night (sunrise); ***bei s-r Geburt*** at his birth; ***bei Regen*** (***Gefahr***) in case of rain (danger); ***bei 100 Grad*** at a hundred degrees; → ***Arbeit***, ***beim***, ***weit***
ˈbeibehalten *v/t* (*irr*, ***halten***, *sep, no -ge-, h*) keep up, retain
ˈbeibringen *v/t* (*irr*, ***bringen***, *sep, no -ge-, h*) teach; tell; inflict (*dat* on)
Beichte [ˈbaiçtə] *f* (*-; -n*) REL confession
ˈbeichten *v/t and v/i* (*ge-, h*) REL confess (*a. fig*)
ˈBeichtstuhl *m* REL confessional
beide [ˈbaidə] *adj and pron* both; ***m-e beiden Brüder*** my two brothers; ***wir beide*** the two of us; both of us; ***keiner von beiden*** neither of them; ***30 beide*** *tennis*: 30 all
beieiˈnander *adv* together
ˈBeifahrer *m* front(-seat) passenger
ˈBeifall *m* (*-[e]s; no pl*) applause; *fig* approval
ˈBeifallssturm *m* (standing) ovation
ˈbeifügen *v/t* (*sep, -ge-, h*) enclose (*dat* with)
beige [beːʃ] *adj* beige
ˈbeigeben (*irr*, ***geben***, *sep, -ge-, h*) **1.** *v/t* add; **2.** F *v/i*: ***klein beigeben*** knuckle under
ˈBeigeschmack *m* smack (***von*** of) (*a. fig*)
Beihilfe *f* aid, allowance; JUR aiding and abetting
Beil [bail] *n* (*-[e]s; -e*) hatchet; ax(e)
ˈBeilage *f* supplement; GASTR side dish; vegetables
ˈbeiläufig *adj* casual
ˈbeilegen *v/t* (*sep, -ge-, h*) add (*dat* to); enclose (with); settle (*dispute*)
ˈBeilegung *f* (*-; -en*) settlement
ˈBeileid *n* (*-[e]s; no pl*) condolence; ***herzliches Beileid*** my deepest sympathy
ˈbeiliegen *v/i* (*irr*, ***liegen***, *sep, -ge-, h*) be enclosed (*dat* with)
beim [baim] *prp*: ***beim Bäcker*** at the baker's; ***beim Sprechen*** *etc* while speaking *etc*; ***beim Spielen*** at play; → *a.* ***bei***
ˈbeimessen *v/t* (*irr*, ***messen***, *sep, -ge-, h*) attach *importance etc* (*dat* to)
Bein [bain] *n* (*-[e]s; -e*) ANAT leg; bone
beinah(e) [ˈbainaː(ə)] *adv* almost, nearly

'Beinbruch *m* MED fracture of the leg
'beipflichten *v/i* (*sep*, *-ge-*, *h*) agree (*dat* with)
be'irren *v/t* (*no -ge-*, *h*) confuse
beisammen [bai'zamən] *adv* together
Bei'sammensein *n*: ***geselliges Beisammensein*** get-together
'Beischlaf *m* JUR sexual intercourse
bei'seite *adv* aside; ***beiseiteschaffen*** *v/t* (*sep*, *-ge-*, *h*) remove; liquidate *s.o.*
'beisetzen *v/t* (*sep*, *-ge-*, *h*) bury
'Beisetzung *f* (*-*; *-en*) funeral
'Beispiel *n* (*-[e]s*; *-e*) example; ***zum Beispiel*** for example, for instance; ***sich an j-m ein Beispiel nehmen*** follow s.o.'s example
'beispielhaft *adj* exemplary
beispiellos *adj* unprecedented, unparaleled
'beispielsweise *adv* such as
beißen ['baisən] *v/t and v/i* (*irr*, *-ge-*, *h*) bite (*a. fig*); ***sich beißen*** *colors*: clash
beißend *adj* biting, pungent (*both a. fig*)
'Beistand *m* (*-[e]s*; *no pl*) assistance
'beistehen *v/i* (*irr*, ***stehen***, *sep*, *-ge-*, *h*) ***j-m beistehen*** assist *or* help s.o.
beisteuern *v/t* (*sep*, *-ge-*, *h*) contribute (***zu*** to)
Beitrag ['baitra:k] *m* (*-[e]s*; *Beiträge* ['baitrɛ:gə]) contribution; dues, *Br* subscription
'beitragen *v/t* (*irr*, ***tragen***, *sep*, *-ge-*, *h*) contribute (***zu*** to)
'beitreten *v/i* (*irr*, ***treten***, *sep*, *-ge-*, *sein*) join
'Beitritt *m* (*-[e]s*; *-e*) joining
'Beiwagen *m* MOT sidecar
bei'zeiten *adv* early, in good time
beizen ['baitsən] *v/t* (*ge-*, *h*) stain (*wood*); pickle (*meat*)
bejahen [bə'ja:ən] *v/t* (*no -ge-*, *h*) answer in the affirmative, affirm
bejahend *adj* affirmative
be'kämpfen *v/t* (*no -ge-*, *h*) fight (against)
bekannt [bə'kant] *adj* (well-)known; familiar; ***et. bekannt geben*** announce s.th.; ***j-n mit j-m bekannt machen*** introduce s.o. to s.o.
Be'kannte *m*, *f* (*-n*; *-n*) acquaintance, *mst* friend
be'kanntgeben *v/t* (*irr*, ***geben***, *sep*, *-ge-*, *h*) → ***bekannt***
be'kanntlich *adv* as you know
be'kanntmachen *v/t* (*sep*, *-ge-*, *h*) → ***bekannt***; **Be'kanntmachung** *f* (*-*; *-en*) announcement
Be'kanntschaft *f* (*-*; *-en*) acquaintance
be'kehren *v/t* (*no -ge-*, *h*) convert
be'kennen *v/t* (*irr*, ***kennen***, *no -ge-*, *h*) confess (*a.* REL); admit; ***sich schuldig bekennen*** JUR plead guilty; ***sich bekennen zu*** profess *s.th.*; claim responsibility for
Be'kennerbrief *m* letter claiming responsibility
Be'kenntnis *n* (*-ses*; *-se*) confession, REL *a.* denomination
be'klagen *v/t* (*no -ge-*, *h*) deplore; ***sich beklagen*** complain (***über*** *acc* about)
be'klagenswert *adj* deplorable
be'kleben *v/t* (*no -ge-*, *h*) stick (*or* paste) on *s.th.*; ***mit Etiketten bekleben*** label *s.th.*
be'kleckern F *v/t* (*no -ge-*, *h*) stain; ***sich bekleckern mit*** spill *s.th.* over o.s.
Be'kleidung *f* (*-*; *-en*) clothing, clothes
be'kommen (*irr*, ***kommen***, *no -ge-*) **1.** *v/t* (*h*) get, receive; MED catch; be having (*baby*); **2.** *v/i* (*sein*) ***j-m*** (***gut***) ***bekommen*** agree with s.o.
bekömmlich [bə'kœmlıç] *adj* wholesome
be'kräftigen *v/t* (*no -ge-*, *h*) confirm
be'kreuzigen *v/refl* (*no -ge-*, *h*) cross o.s.
bekümmert [bə'kʏmɐt] *adj* worried
be'laden *v/t* (*irr*, ***laden***, *no -ge-*, *h*) load, *fig a.* burden
Belag [bə'la:k] *m* (*-[e]s*; *Beläge* [bə'lɛ:gə]) covering; TECH coat(ing); MOT lining; (*road*) surface; MED fur; plaque; GASTR topping; spread; (sandwich) filling
be'lagern *v/t* (*no -ge-*, *h*) MIL besiege (*a. fig*)
Be'lagerung *f* (*-*; *-en*) MIL siege
be'lassen *v/t* (*irr*, ***lassen***, *no -ge-*, *h*) leave; ***es dabei belassen*** leave it at that
be'langlos *adj* irrelevant
be'lastbar *adj* resistant to strain *or* stress; TECH loadable
be'lasten *v/t* (*no -ge-*, *h*) load; *fig* burden; JUR incriminate; pollute; damage; ***j-s Konto belasten mit*** charge *s.th.* to s.o.'s account
belästigen [bə'lɛstıgən] *v/t* (*no -ge-*, *h*) molest; annoy; disturb, bother
Be'lästigung *f* (*-*; *-en*) molestation; annoyance; disturbance
Be'lastung *f* (*-*; *-en*) load (*a.* TECH); *fig* burden; strain; stress; JUR incrimination; pollution, contamination
Be'lastungszeuge *m* JUR witness for the prosecution
be'laufen *v/refl* (*irr*, ***laufen***, *no -ge-*, *h*) ***sich belaufen auf*** (*acc*) amount to
be'lauschen *v/t* (*no -ge-*, *h*) eavesdrop on
be'leben *fig v/t* (*no -ge-*, *h*) stimulate
belebend *adj* stimulating
belebt [bə'le:pt] *adj* busy, crowded
Beleg [bə'le:k] *m* (*-[e]s*; *-e*) proof; receipt;

document
be'legen *v/t* (*no -ge-, h*) cover; reserve (*seat*); prove; enrol(l) for, take (*classes*); GASTR put s.th. on; ***den ersten** etc* ***Platz belegen*** SPORT take first *etc* place
Be'legschaft *f* (-; *-en*) staff
be'legt *adj* taken, occupied; *hotel etc*: full; TEL busy, *Br* engaged; MED coated; ***belegtes Brot*** sandwich
be'lehren *v/t* (*no -ge-, h*) teach, instruct, inform; ***sich belehren lassen*** take advice
beleidigen [bə'laidɪgən] *v/t* (*no -ge-, h*) offend (*a. fig*), insult
beleidigend *adj* offensive, insulting
Be'leidigung *f* (-; *-en*) offense, *Br* offence, insult
be'lesen *adj* well-read
be'leuchten *v/t* (*no -ge-, h*) light (up), illuminate (*a. fig*); *fig* throw light on
Be'leuchtung *f* (-; *-en*) light(ing); illumination
Belgien ['bɛlgjən] Belgium
Belgier ['bɛlgjɐ] *m* (*-s*; -), **'Belgierin** [-gjərɪn] *f* (-; *-nen*), **'belgisch** *adj* Belgian
be'lichten *v/t* (*no -ge-, h*) PHOT expose
Be'lichtungsmesser *m* PHOT exposure meter
Be'lieben *n*: ***nach Belieben*** at will
beliebig [bə'li:bɪç] *adj* any; optional; ***jeder beliebige*** anyone
beliebt [bə'li:pt] *adj* popular (***bei*** with)
Be'liebtheit *f* (-; *no pl*) popularity
be'liefern *v/t* (*no -ge-, h*) supply, furnish (***mit*** with)
Be'lieferung *f* supply
bellen ['bɛlən] *v/i* (*ge-, h*) bark (*a. fig*)
be'lohnen *v/t* (*no -ge-, h*) reward
Be'lohnung *f* (-; *-en*) reward; ***zur Belohnung*** as a reward
be'lügen *v/t* (*irr*, ***lügen***, *no -ge-, h*) ***j-n belügen*** lie to s.o.
belustigen [bə'lʊstɪgən] *v/t* (*no -ge-, h*) amuse
be'lustigt [-tɪçt] *adj* amused
Be'lustigung *f* (-; *-en*) amusement
bemächtigen [bə'mɛçtɪgən] *v/refl* (*no -ge-, h*) get hold of, seize
be'malen *v/t* (*no -ge-, h*) paint
bemängeln [bə'mɛŋəln] *v/t* (*no -ge-, h*) find fault with
bemannt [bə'mant] *adj* manned
be'merkbar *adj* noticeable; ***sich bemerkbar machen*** draw attention to o.s.; begin to show
be'merken *v/t* (*no -ge-, h*) notice; remark
be'merkenswert *adj* remarkable
Be'merkung *f* (-; *-en*) remark (***über*** *acc* about)
be'mitleiden *v/t* (*no -ge-, h*) pity, feel sorry for
be'mitleidenswert *adj* pitiable
be'mühen *v/refl* (*no -ge-, h*) try (hard); ***sich bemühen um*** try to get *s.th.*; try to help *s.o.*; ***bitte bemühen Sie sich nicht!*** please don't bother
Be'mühung *f* (-; *-en*) effort; ***danke für Ihre Bemühungen!*** thank you for your trouble
be'muttern *v/t* (*no -ge-, h*) mother *s.o.*
be'nachbart *adj* neighbo(u)ring
benachrichtigen [bə'na:xrɪçtɪgən] *v/t* (*no -ge-, h*) inform, notify
Be'nachrichtigung *f* (-; *-en*) information, notification
benachteiligen [bə'na:xtailɪgən] *v/t* (*no -ge-, h*) place *s.o.* at a disadvantage; discriminate against *s.o.*
benachteiligt [bə'na:xtailɪçt] *adj* disadvantaged; ***die Benachteiligten*** the underprivileged
Be'nachteiligung *f* (-; *-en*) disadvantage; discrimination
be'nehmen *v/refl* (*irr*, ***nehmen***, *no -ge-, h*) behave (o.s.)
Be'nehmen *n* (*-s*; *no pl*) behavio(u)r; manners
be'neiden *v/t* (*no -ge-, h*) ***j-n um et. beneiden*** envy s.o. s.th.
be'neidenswert *adj* enviable
BENELUX ['be:nelʊks] ABBR *of* ***Belgien, Niederlande, Luxemburg*** Belgium, the Netherlands and Luxembourg
be'nennen *v/t* (*irr*, ***nennen***, *no -ge-, h*) name
Bengel ['bɛŋəl] *m* (*-s*; -) (little) rascal, urchin
benommen [bə'nɔmən] *adj* dazed, F dopey
be'noten *v/t* (*no -ge-, h*) grade, *Br* mark
be'nötigen *v/t* (*no -ge-, h*) need, want, require
be'nutzen *v/t* (*no -ge-, h*) use
Be'nutzer *m* (*-s*; -) user
be'nutzerfreundlich *adj* user-friendly
Be'nutzeroberfläche *f* EDP user interface
Be'nutzung *f* use
Benzin [bɛn'tsi:n] *n* (*-s*; *-e*) gasoline, F gas, *Br* petrol
beobachten [bə'ʔo:baxtən] *v/t* (*no -ge-, h*) watch; observe
Be'obachter *m* (*-s*; -) observer
Be'obachtung *f* (-; *-en*) observation
be'pflanzen *v/t* (*no -ge-, h*) plant (***mit*** with)
bequem [bə'kve:m] *adj* comfortable; easy; lazy
be'quemen *v/refl* (*no -ge-, h*) ***sich beque-***

men zu *inf* bring o.s. to *inf*
Be'quemlichkeit *f* (-; *-en*) a) comfort; ***alle Bequemlichkeiten*** all conveniences, b) (*no pl*) laziness
be'raten *v/t* (*irr*, ***raten***, *no -ge-*, *h*) advise *s.o.*; debate, discuss *s.th.*; ***sich beraten*** confer (***mit j-m*** with s.o.; ***über et.*** on s.th.)
Be'rater *m* (*-s*; -) adviser, consultant
Be'ratung *f* (-; *-en*) advice (*a.* MED); debate; consultation, conference
Be'ratungsstelle *f* counsel(l)ing center (*Br* centre)
be'rauben *v/t* (*no -ge-*, *h*) rob
be'rauschend *adj* intoxicating; F *fig* ***nicht gerade berauschend!*** not so hot!
be'rauscht *fig adj*: ***berauscht von*** drunk with
be'rechnen *v/t* (*no -ge-*, *h*) calculate; ECON charge (***zu*** at)
berechnend *adj* calculating
Be'rechnung *f* calculation (*a. fig*)
berechtigen [bə'rɛçtɪgən] *v/t*: ***j-n berechtigen zu*** entitle (*or* authorize) s.o. to
be'rechtigt [-tɪçt] *adj* entitled (***zu*** to); authorized (to); legitimate
Be'rechtigung *f* (-; *no pl*) right (***zu*** to); authority
Beredsamkeit [bə're:tza:mkait] *f* (-; *no pl*) eloquence
beredt [bə're:t] *adj* eloquent (*a. fig*)
Be'reich *m* (-[*e*]*s*; *-e*) area; range; field
bereichern [bə'raiçɐn] *v/t* (*no -ge-*, *h*) enrich; ***sich bereichern*** get rich (***an*** *dat* on)
Be'reicherung [bə'raiçəruŋ] *f* (-; *no pl*) enrichment
Be'reifung *f* (-; *-en*) (set of) tires (*Br* tyres)
be'reinigen *v/t* (*no -ge-*, *h*) settle
be'reisen *v/t* (*no -ge-*, *h*) tour; cover
bereit [bə'rait] *adj* ready, prepared; willing
be'reiten *v/t* (*no -ge-*, *h*) prepare; cause
be'reithalten *v/t* (*irr*, ***halten***, *sep*, *-ge-*, *h*) have *s.th.* ready; ***sich bereithalten*** stand by
be'reits *adv* already
Be'reitschaft *f* (-; *no pl*) readiness; ***in Bereitschaft*** on standby
Be'reitschaftsdienst *m*: ***Bereitschaftsdienst haben*** *doctor etc*: be on call
be'reitstellen *v/t* (*sep*, *-ge-*, *h*) provide
be'reitwillig *adj* ready, willing
be'reuen *v/t* (*no -ge-*, *h*) repent (of); regret
Berg [bɛrk] *m* (-[*e*]*s*; *-e*) mountain; ***Berge von*** F loads of; ***die Haare standen ihm zu Berge*** his hair stood on end
berg'ab *adv* downhill (*a. fig*)
'Bergarbeiter *m* miner
berg'auf *adv* uphill
'Bergbahn *f* mountain railroad (*Br* railway)
Bergbau *m* (-[*e*]*s*; *no pl*) mining
bergen ['bɛrgən] *v/t* (*irr*, *ge-* *h*) rescue, save *s.o.*; salvage *s.th.*; recover (*body*)
'Bergführer *m* mountain guide
bergig ['bɛrgɪç] *adj* mountainous
'Bergkette *f* mountain range
Bergmann *m* (-[*e*]*s*; *-leute*) miner
Bergrutsch *m* landslide
Bergschuhe *pl* mountain(eering) boots
Bergspitze *f* (mountain) peak
Bergsteigen *n* mountaineering, (mountain) climbing
Bergsteiger *m* (*-s*; -) mountaineer, (mountain) climber
'Bergung *f* (-; *-en*) recovery; rescue
'Bergungsarbeiten *pl* rescue work; salvage operations
'Bergwacht *f* alpine rescue service
'Bergwerk *n* mine
Bericht [bə'rɪçt] *m* (-[*e*]*s*; *-e*) report (***über*** *acc* on), account (of)
be'richten *v/t and v/i* (*no -ge-*, *h*) report (***über*** *acc* on); ***j-m et. berichten*** inform s.o. of s.th.; tell s.o. about s.th.
Be'richterstatter *m* (*-s*; -) reporter; correspondent
Berichterstattung *f* (-; *-en*) report(ing)
berichtigen [bə'rɪçtɪgən] *v/t* (*no -ge-*, *h*) correct
Be'richtigung *f* (-; *-en*) correction
be'rieseln *v/t* (*no -ge-*, *h*) sprinkle
Bernstein ['bɛrnʃtain] *m* (*-s*; *no pl*) amber
bersten ['bɛrstən] *v/i* (*irr*, *-ge-*, *sein*) burst (*fig* ***vor*** *dat* with)
berüchtigt [bə'rʏçtɪçt] *adj* notorious (***wegen*** for)
berücksichtigen [bə'rʏkzɪçtɪgən] *v/t* (*no -ge-*, *h*) take into consideration; ***nicht berücksichtigen*** disregard
Be'rücksichtigung *f*: ***unter Berücksichtigung*** (*gen*) in consideration of
Be'ruf *m* (-[*e*]*s*; *-e*) job, occupation; trade; profession
be'rufen *v/t* (*irr*, ***rufen***, *no -ge-*, *h*) appoint (***zu*** [as] *s.o.*; to *s.th.*); ***sich berufen auf*** (*acc*) refer to
be'ruflich *adj* professional; ***beruflich unterwegs*** away on business
Be'rufs... *in cpds* *...sportler etc*: professional ...
Berufsausbildung *f* vocational (*or* professional) training
Berufsberater *m* careers advisor
Berufsberatung *f* careers guidance
Berufsbezeichnung *f* job designation *or* title
Berufskleidung *f* work clothes

Berufskrankheit *f* occupational disease
Berufsschule *f* vocational school
be'rufstätig *adj*: ***berufstätig sein*** (go to) work, have a job
Be'rufstätige *m, f (-n; -n)* working person, *pl* working people
Be'rufsverkehr *m* rush-hour traffic
Be'rufung *f (-; -en)* appointment (***zu*** to); JUR appeal (***bei*** to); ***unter Berufung auf*** (*acc*) with reference to; on the grounds of
be'ruhen *v/i (no -ge-, h)* ***beruhen auf*** (*dat*) be based on; ***et. auf sich beruhen lassen*** let s.th. rest
beruhigen [bə'ruːɪgən] *v/t (no -ge-, h)* quiet(en), calm, soothe; reassure *s.o.*; ***sich beruhigen*** calm down
beruhigend *adj* reassuring; MED sedative
Be'ruhigung *f (-; -en)* calming (down); soothing; relief
Be'ruhigungsmittel *n* MED sedative; tranquil(l)izer
berühmt [bə'ryːmt] *adj* famous (***wegen*** for)
Be'rühmtheit *f (-; -en)* a) (*no pl*) fame, b) celebrity, star
be'rühren *v/t (no -ge-, h)* touch (*a. fig*); concern
Be'rührung *f (-; -en)* touch; ***in Berührung kommen*** come into contact
Be'rührungsangst *f* fear of contact
Berührungspunkt *m* point of contact
besänftigen [bə'zɛnftɪgən] *v/t (no -ge-, h)* appease, calm, soothe
Be'satzung *f (-; -en)* AVIAT, MAR crew; MIL occupying forces
Be'satzungsmacht *f* MIL occupying power
Besatzungstruppen *pl* MIL occupying forces
be'saufen F *v/refl (irr,* ***saufen****, no -ge-, h)* get drunk, get bombed
be'schädigen *v/t (no -ge-, h)* damage
Be'schädigung *f (-; -en)* damage
be'schaffen *v/t (no -ge-, h)* provide, get; raise (*money*)
Be'schaffenheit *f (-; no pl)* state, condition
beschäftigen [bə'ʃɛftɪgən] *v/t (no -ge-, h)* employ; keep *s.o.* busy; ***sich beschäftigen*** occupy o.s.
be'schäftigt [-tɪçt] *adj* busy, occupied
Be'schäftigte *m, f (-n; -n)* employed person, *pl* employed people
Be'schäftigung *f (-; -en)* employment; occupation
be'schämen *v/t (no -ge-, h)* shame *s.o.*, make *s.o.* feel ashamed
beschämend *adj* shameful; humiliating
be'schämt *adj* ashamed (***über*** *acc* of)
be'schatten *fig v/t (no -ge-, h)* shadow, F tail
Bescheid [bə'ʃait] *m (-[e]s; -e)* answer; JUR decision; information (***über*** *acc* on, about); ***sagen Sie mir Bescheid*** let me know; ***(gut) Bescheid wissen über*** (*acc*) know all about
be'scheiden *adj* modest (*a. fig*); humble
Be'scheidenheit *f (-; no pl)* modesty
bescheinigen [bə'ʃainɪgən] *v/t (no -ge-, h)* certify
Be'scheinigung *f (-; -en)* a) (*no pl*) certification, b) certificate
be'scheißen V *v/t (irr,* ***scheißen****, no -ge-, h)* cheat; ***j-n bescheißen um*** do s.o. out of
be'schenken *v/t (no -ge-, h)* ***j-n (reich) beschenken*** give s.o. (shower s.o. with) presents
Be'scherung *f (-; -en)* distribution of (Christmas) presents; F *fig* mess
be'schichten *v/t (no -ge-, h)* TECH coat
Be'schichtung *f (-; -en)* TECH coat
be'schießen *v/t (irr,* ***schießen****, no -ge-, h)* MIL fire *or* shoot at; bombard (*a.* PHYS), shell
be'schimpfen *v/t (no -ge-, h)* abuse, insult; swear at
Be'schimpfung *f (-; -en)* abuse, insult
be'schissen V *adj* lousy, rotten
Be'schlag *m* TECH metal fitting(s); ***in Beschlag nehmen*** *fig* monopolize *s.o.*; bag; occupy
be'schlagen *(irr,* ***schlagen****, no -ge-)* **1.** *v/t* (*h*) cover; TECH fit, mount; shoe (*horse*); **2.** *v/i* (*sein*) *window etc*: steam up; **3.** *adj* steamed-up; *fig* well-versed (***auf, in*** *dat* in)
Be'schlagnahme [bə'ʃlaːknaːmə] *f (-; -n)* confiscation
be'schlagnahmen *v/t (no -ge-, h)* confiscate
beschleunigen [bə'ʃlɔynɪgən] *v/t and v/i (no -ge-, h)* accelerate, speed up
Be'schleunigung *f (-; -en)* acceleration
be'schließen *v/t (irr,* ***schließen****, no -ge-, h)* decide (on); pass (*law*); conclude
Be'schluss *m* decision
be'schmieren *v/t (no -ge-, h)* smear, soil; scrawl all over; cover *wall etc* with graffiti; spread (*toast etc*)
be'schmutzen *v/t (no -ge-, h)* soil (*a. fig*), dirty
be'schneiden *v/t (irr,* ***schneiden****, no -ge-, h)* clip, cut (*a. fig*); prune; MED circumcise
be'schönigen [bə'ʃøːnɪgən] *v/t (no -ge-, h)* gloss over
beschränken [bə'ʃrɛŋkən] *v/t (no -ge-, h)* confine, limit, restrict; ***sich beschrän-***

ken auf *(acc)* confine o.s. to
be'schränkt *adj* limited; *contp* dense; narrow-minded
Be'schränkung *f* (-; *-en*) limitation, restriction
be'schreiben *v/t* (*irr*, ***schreiben***, *no -ge-*, *h*) describe; write on
Be'schreibung *f* (-; *-en*) description
be'schriften *v/t* (*no -ge-*, *h*) inscribe; mark (*goods*)
Be'schriftung *f* (-; *-en*) inscription
beschuldigen [bə'ʃʊldɪgən] *v/t* (*no -ge-*, *h*) blame; ***j-n e-r Sache beschuldigen*** accuse s.o. of s.th. (*a.* JUR)
Be'schuldigung *f* (-; *-en*) accusation
be'schummeln F *v/t* (*no -ge-*, *h*) cheat
Be'schuss *m*: ***unter Beschuss*** MIL under fire
be'schützen *v/t* (*no -ge-*, *h*) protect, shelter, guard (***vor*** *dat* from)
Be'schützer *m* (*-s*; -) protector
Beschwerde [bə'ʃveːɐdə] *f* (-; *-n*) complaint (***über*** *acc* about; ***bei*** to); *pl* MED complaints, trouble
beschweren [bə'ʃveːrən] *v/t* (*no -ge-*, *h*) weight *s.th.*; ***sich beschweren*** complain (***über*** *acc* about; ***bei*** to)
be'schwerlich *adj* hard, arduous
beschwichtigen [bə'ʃvɪçtɪgən] *v/t* (*no -ge-*, *h*) appease (*a.* POL), calm
be'schwindeln *v/t* (*no -ge-*, *h*) tell a fib *or* lie; cheat
beschwingt [bə'ʃvɪŋt] *adj* buoyant; MUS lively, swinging
beschwipst [bə'ʃvɪpst] F *adj* tipsy
be'schwören *v/t* (*irr*, ***schwören***, *no -ge-*, *h*) swear to; implore; conjure up
beseitigen [bə'zaitɪgən] *v/t* (*no -ge-*, *h*) remove (*a. s.o.*), *a.* dispose of (*waste etc*); eliminate; POL liquidate
Be'seitigung *f* (-; *no pl*) removal; disposal; elimination
Besen ['beːzən] *m* (*-s*; -) broom
'Besenstiel *m* broomstick
besessen [bə'zesən] *adj* obsessed (***von*** by, with); ***wie besessen*** like mad
be'setzen *v/t* (*no -ge-*, *h*) occupy (*a.* MIL); fill (*post etc*); THEA cast; trim; squat in
be'setzt *adj* occupied; *seat*: taken; *bus etc*: full up; TEL busy, *Br* engaged
Be'setztzeichen *n* TEL busy signal, *Br* engaged tone
Be'setzung *f* (-; *-en*) THEA cast; MIL occupation
besichtigen [bə'zɪçtɪgən] *v/t* (*no -ge-*, *h*) visit, see the sights of; inspect
Be'sichtigung *f* (-; *-en*) sightseeing; visit (*gen* to); inspection (of)
be'siedeln *v/t* (*no -ge-*, *h*) settle; colonize; populate
be'siedelt *adj*: ***dicht*** (***dünn***) ***besiedelt*** densely (sparsely) populated
Be'siedlung *f* (-; *-en*) settlement; colonization; population
be'siegeln *v/t* (*no -ge-*, *h*) seal
be'siegen *v/t* (*no -ge-*, *h*) defeat, beat; conquer (*a. fig*)
besinnen *v/refl* (*irr*, ***sinnen***, *no -ge-*, *h*) remember; think (***auf*** *acc* about); ***sich anders besinnen*** change one's mind
be'sinnlich *adj* contemplative
Be'sinnung *f* (-; *no pl*) MED consciousness; (***wieder***) ***zur Besinnung kommen*** MED come round; *fig* come to one's senses
be'sinnungslos *adj* MED unconscious
Be'sitz *m* (*-es*; *no pl*) possession; property; ***Besitz ergreifen von*** take possession of
be'sitzanzeigend *adj* LING possessive
be'sitzen *v/t* (*irr*, ***sitzen***, *no -ge-*, *h*) possess, own
Be'sitzer *m* (*-s*; -) possessor, owner; ***den Besitzer wechseln*** change hands
besoffen [bə'zɔfən] F *adj* drunk, plastered, stoned
besohlen [bə'zoːlən] *v/t* (*no -ge-*, *h*) ***besohlen lassen*** have (re)soled
Be'soldung *f* (-; *-en*) pay; salary
besondere [bə'zɔndərə] *adj* special, particular; peculiar
Be'sonderheit *f* (-; *-en*) peculiarity
be'sonders *adv* especially, particularly; chiefly, mainly
be'sonnen *adj* prudent, level-headed
be'sorgen *v/t* (*no -ge-*, *h*) get, buy; → ***erledigen***
Be'sorgnis [bə'zɔrknɪs] *f* (-; *-se*) concern, alarm, anxiety (***über*** *acc* about, at); ***Besorgnis erregend*** → ***besorgniserregend***
be'sorgniserregend *adj* alarming
besorgt [bə'zɔrkt] *adj* worried, concerned
Be'sorgung *f* (-; *-en*) ***Besorgungen machen*** go shopping
be'spielen *v/t* (*no -ge-*, *h*) make a recording on
be'spitzeln *v/t* (*no -ge-*, *h*) spy on *s.o.*
be'sprechen *v/t* (*irr*, ***sprechen***, *no -ge-*, *h*) discuss, talk *s.th.* over; review (*book etc*)
Be'sprechung *f* (-; *-en*) discussion, talk(s); meeting, conference; review
be'spritzen *v/t* (*no -ge-*, *h*) spatter
besser ['bɛsɐ] *adj and adv* better; ***es ist besser, wir fragen ihn*** we had better ask him; ***immer besser*** better and better; ***es geht ihm besser*** he is better; ***oder bes-***

ser gesagt or rather; ***es besser wissen*** know better; ***es besser machen als*** do better than; ***besser ist besser*** just to be on the safe side
'bessern *v/refl* (*ge-, h*) improve, get better
'Besserung *f* (-; *no pl*) improvement; ***auf dem Wege der Besserung*** on the way to recovery; ***gute Besserung!*** get better soon
'Besserwisser [-vɪsɐ] *m* (-*s*; -) F smart aleck
Be'stand *m* a) (*no pl*) (continued) existence, b) stock; ***Bestand haben*** last, be lasting
be'ständig *adj* constant, steady (*a. character*); settled; ***...beständig*** *in cpds* ...-resistant, ...proof
Be'standsaufnahme *f* ECON stocktaking (*a. fig*); ***Bestandsaufnahme machen*** take stock (*a. fig*)
Be'standteil *m* part, component
be'stärken *v/t* (*no -ge-, h*) confirm, strengthen, encourage (***in*** *dat* in)
bestätigen [bə'ʃtɛːtɪɡən] *v/t* (*no -ge-, h*) confirm; certify; acknowledge (*receipt*); ***sich bestätigen*** prove (to be) true; come true; ***sich bestätigt fühlen*** feel affirmed
Be'stätigung *f* (-; -*en*) confirmation; certificate; acknowledg(e-)ment; letter of confirmation
bestatten [bə'ʃtatən] *v/t* (*no -ge-, h*) bury
Be'stattungsinsti,tut *n* funeral home, *Br* undertakers
be'stäuben *v/t* (*no -ge-, h*) dust; BOT pollinate
beste ['bɛstə] *adj and adv* best; ***am besten*** best; ***welches gefällt dir am besten?*** which one do you like best?; ***am besten nehmen Sie den Bus*** it would be best to take a bus
Beste *m, f* (-*n*; -*n*), *n* (-*n*; *no pl*) *the* best; ***das Beste geben*** do one's best; ***das Beste machen aus*** make the best of; (***nur***) ***zu deinem Besten*** for your own good
be'stechen *v/t* (*irr,* ***stechen****, no -ge-, h*) bribe; fascinate (***durch*** by)
be'stechlich *adj* corrupt
Be'stechung *f* (-; -*en*) bribery, corruption
Be'stechungsgeld *n* bribe
Besteck [bə'ʃtɛk] *n* (-[*e*]*s*; -*e*) (set of) knife, fork and spoon; cutlery
be'stehen (*irr,* ***stehen****, no -ge-, h*) **1.** *v/t* pass (*examination etc*); **2.** *v/i* be, exist; ***bestehen auf*** (*dat*) insist on; ***bestehen aus*** (***in***) (*dat*) consist of (in); ***bestehen bleiben*** last, survive
Be'stehen *n* (-*s*; *no pl*) existence
be'stehlen *v/t* (*irr,* ***stehlen****, no -ge-, h*) ***j-n bestehlen*** steal s.o.'s money *etc*
be'steigen *v/t* (*irr,* ***steigen****, no -ge-, h*) climb; get on *a bus etc*; ascend (*the throne*)
be'stellen *v/t* (*no -ge-, h*) order; book (*room etc*); reserve (*seat etc*); call (*taxi*); give, send (*message etc*); AGR cultivate; ***kann ich et. bestellen?*** can I take a message?; ***bestellen Sie ihm bitte, ...*** please tell him ...
Be'stellschein *m* ECON order form
Be'stellung *f* (-; -*en*) booking; reservation; ECON order; ***auf Bestellung*** to order
'bestenfalls *adv* at best
'bestens *adv* very well
bestialisch [bɛs'tjaːlɪʃ] *adj fig* bestial
Bestie ['bɛstjə] *f* (-; -*n*) beast, *fig a.* brute
be'stimmen *v/t* (*no -ge-, h*) determine, decide; define; choose, pick; ***zu bestimmen haben*** be in charge, F be the boss; ***bestimmt für*** meant for
be'stimmt **1.** *adj* determined, firm; LING definite (*article*); ***bestimmte Dinge*** certain things; **2.** *adv* certainly; ***ganz bestimmt*** definitely; ***er ist bestimmt ...*** he must be ...
Be'stimmung *f* (-; -*en*) regulation; destiny
Be'stimmungsort *m* destination
'Bestleistung *f* SPORT (personal) record
be'strafen *v/t* (*no -ge-, h*) punish
Be'strafung *f* (-; -*en*) punishment
be'strahlen *v/t* (*no -ge-, h*) irradiate (*a.* MED)
Be'strahlung *f* (-; -*en*) irradiation; MED ray treatment, radiotherapy
be'streichen *v/t* (*irr,* ***streichen****, no -ge-, h*) spread
be'streiten *v/t* (*irr,* ***streiten****, no -ge-, h*) challenge; deny; pay for, finance
be'streuen *v/t* (*no -ge-, h*) sprinkle (***mit*** with)
be'stürmen *v/t* (*no -ge-, h*) urge; bombard
be'stürzt *adj* dismayed (***über*** *acc* at)
Be'stürzung *f* (-; *no pl*) consternation, dismay
Besuch [bə'zuːx] *m* (-[*e*]*s*; -*e*) visit (*gen,* ***bei, in*** *dat* to); call (***bei*** on; ***in*** *dat* at); attendance (*gen* at); ***Besuch haben*** have company *or* guests
be'suchen *v/t* (*no -ge-, h*) visit; call on, (go to) see; look *s.o.* up; attend (*meeting etc*); go to (*pub etc*)
Be'sucher(in) (-*s*; -/-; -*nen*) visitor, guest
Be'suchszeit *f* visiting hours
be'sucht *adj*: ***gut*** (***schlecht***) ***besucht*** well (poorly) attended; much (little) frequented
betagt [bə'taːkt] *adj* aged

be'tasten *v/t* (*no -ge-, h*) touch, feel
be'tätigen *v/t* (*no -ge-, h*) TECH operate; apply (*brake*); ***sich betätigen*** be active
Be'tätigung *f* (-; *-en*) activity
betäuben [bə'tɔʏbən] *v/t* (*no -ge-, h*) stun (*a. fig*), daze; MED an(a)esthetize
Be'täubung *f* (-; *-en*) MED an(a)esthetization; an(a)esthesia; *fig* daze, stupor
Be'täubungsmittel *n* MED an(a)esthetic; narcotic
Bete ['beːtə] *f* (-; *-n*) ***rote Bete*** BOT beet, *Br* beetroot
beteiligen [bə'tailɪgən] *v/t* (*no -ge-, h*) ***j-n beteiligen*** give s.o. a share (***an*** *dat* in); ***sich beteiligen*** take part (***an*** *dat*, ***bei*** in), participate (in) (*a.* JUR)
beteiligt [bə'tailɪçt] *adj* concerned; ***beteiligt sein an*** (*dat*) be involved in; ECON have a share in
Be'teiligung *f* (-; *-en*) participation (*a.* JUR, ECON); involvement; share (*a.* ECON)
beten ['beːtən] *v/i* (*ge-, h*) pray (***um*** for), say one's prayers; say grace
beteuern [bə'tɔʏɐn] *v/t* (*no -ge-, h*) protest (*one's innocence etc*)
Beton [be'tɔŋ] *m* (*-s*; *-s*, *-e* [be'toːnə]) concrete
betonen [bə'toːnən] *v/t* (*no -ge-, h*) stress, *fig a.* emphasize
betonieren [beto'niːrən] *v/t* (*no -ge-, h*) (cover with) concrete
Be'tonung *f* (-; *-en*) stress; *fig* emphasis
betören [bə'tøːrən] *v/t* (*no -ge-, h*) infatuate, bewitch
Betr. ABBR *of* ***betrifft*** re
Betracht [bə'traxt] *m*: ***in Betracht ziehen*** take into consideration; ***nicht in Betracht kommen*** be out of the question
be'trachten *v/t* (*no -ge-, h*) look at, *fig a.* view; ***betrachten als*** look upon *or* regard as, consider
Be'trachter *m* (*-s*; -) viewer
beträchtlich [bə'trɛçtlɪç] *adj* considerable
Be'trachtung *f* (-; *-en*) view; ***bei näherer Betrachtung*** on closer inspection
Betrag [bə'traːk] *m* (*-[e]s*; *Beträge* [bə'trɛːgə]) amount, sum
be'tragen (*irr*, ***tragen***, *no -ge-, h*) **1.** *v/t* amount to; **2.** *v/refl* behave (o.s.)
Be'tragen *n* (*-s*; *no pl*) behavio(u)r, conduct
be'trauen *v/t* (*no -ge-, h*) entrust (***mit*** with)
be'treffen *v/t* (*irr*, ***treffen***, *no -ge-, h*) concern; refer to; ***was … betrifft*** as for …, as to …; ***betrifft*** (ABBR ***Betr.***) re
betreffend *adj* concerning; ***die betreffenden Personen*** *etc* the people *etc* concerned
be'treiben *v/t* (*irr*, ***treiben***, *no -ge-, h*) operate, run; go in for (*sport etc*)
be'treten[1] *v/t* (*irr*, ***treten***, *no -ge-, h*) step on; enter; ***Betreten*** (***des Rasens***) ***verboten!*** keep out! (keep off the grass!)
be'treten[2] *adj* embarrassed
betreuen [bə'trɔʏən] *v/t* (*no -ge-, h*) look after, take care of
Be'treuung *f* (-; *no pl*) care (*gen* of, for)
Betrieb [bə'triːp] *m* (*-[e]s*; *-e*) a) business, firm, company, b) (*no pl*) operation, running, c) (*no pl*) rush; ***in Betrieb sein*** (***setzen***) be in (put into) operation; ***außer Betrieb*** out of order; ***im Geschäft war viel Betrieb*** the shop was very busy
Be'triebsanleitung *f* operating instructions
Betriebsberater *m* business consultant
Betriebsferien *pl* company (*Br a.* works) holiday
Betriebsfest *n* annual company fête
Betriebskapi͵tal *n* working capital
Betriebsklima *n* working atmosphere
Betriebskosten *pl* operating costs
Betriebsleitung *f* management
Betriebsrat *m* works council
be'triebssicher *adj* safe to operate
Be'triebsstörung *f* TECH breakdown
Betriebssys͵tem *n* EDP operating system
Betriebsunfall *m* industrial accident
Betriebswirtschaft *f* business administration
be'trinken *v/refl* (*irr*, ***trinken***, *no -ge-, h*) get drunk
betroffen [bə'trɔfən] *adj* affected, concerned; dismayed, shocked
Be'troffenheit *f* (-; *no pl*) dismay, shock
betrübt [bə'tryːpt] *adj* sad, grieved (***über*** *acc* at)
Betrug [bə'truːk] *m* (*-[e]s*; *no pl*) cheat; JUR fraud; deceit
be'trügen *v/t* (*irr*, ***trügen***, *no -ge-, h*) deceive; cheat (***beim Kartenspiel*** at cards); swindle, trick (***um et.*** out of s.th.); be unfaithful to
Be'trüger(in) (*-s*; *-/-*; *-nen*) swindler, trickster
betrunken [bə'trʊŋkən] *adj* drunken; ***betrunken sein*** be drunk
Be'trunkene *m, f* (*-n*; *-n*) drunk
Bett [bɛt] *n* (*-[e]s*; *-en*) bed; ***am Bett*** at the bedside; ***ins Bett gehen*** (***bringen***) go (put) to bed
Bettbezug *m* comforter case, *Br* duvet cover
Bettdecke *f* blanket; quilt
betteln ['bɛtəln] *v/i* (*ge-, h*) beg (***um*** for)
'Bettgestell *n* bedstead

'bettlägerig [-lɛːgərɪç] *adj* bedridden
'Bettlaken *n* sheet
Bettler ['bɛtlɐ] *m* (-*s*; -) beggar
'Bettnässer [-nɛsɐ] *m* (-*s*; -) MED bed wetter
Bettruhe *f* bed rest; ***j-m Bettruhe verordnen*** tell s.o. to stay in bed
Bettvorleger *m* bedside rug
Bettwäsche *f* bed linen
Bettzeug *n* bedding, bedclothes
beugen ['bɔygən] *v/t* (*ge-*, *h*) bend; LING inflect; ***sich beugen*** (***vor*** *dat* to) bend, bow
Beule ['bɔylə] *f* (-; -*n*) MED bump; MOT dent
beunruhigen [bə'ʔʊnruːɪgən] *v/t* (*no -ge-*, *h*) alarm, worry
beurlauben [bə'ʔuːɐlaubən] *v/t* give *s.o.* leave *or* time off; suspend; ***sich beurlauben lassen*** ask for leave
be'urlaubt [-laupt] *adj* on leave
be'urteilen *v/t* (*no -ge-*, *h*) judge (***nach*** by); rate
Be'urteilung *f* (-; -*en*) judg(e)ment; evaluation
Beute ['bɔytə] *f* (-; *no pl*) booty, loot; ZO prey (*a. fig*); HUNT bag; *fig a.* victim
Beutel ['bɔytəl] *m* (-*s*; -) bag; pouch
bevölkern [bə'fœlkɐn] *v/t* (*no -ge-*, *h*) populate
be'völkert *adj* → ***besiedelt***
Be'völkerung *f* (-; -*en*) population
bevollmächtigen [bə'fɔlmɛçtɪgən] *v/t* (*no -ge-*, *h*) authorize
be'vor *cj* before
bevormunden [bə'foːɐmʊndən] *v/t* (*no -ge-*, *h*) patronize
bevorstehen *v/i* (*irr*, ***stehen***, *sep*, *-ge-*, *h*) be approaching; lie ahead; be imminent; ***j-m bevorstehen*** be in store for s.o., await s.o.
be'vorzugen [-tsuːgən] *v/t* (*no -ge-*, *h*) prefer; favo(u)r
Be'vorzugung *f* (-; -*en*) preferential treatment
be'wachen *v/t* (*no -ge-*, *h*) guard, watch over
Be'wacher *m* (-*s*; -) guard; SPORT marker
Be'wachung *f* (-; -*en*) a) (*no pl*) guarding; SPORT marking, b) guard
bewaffnen [bə'vafnən] *v/t* (*no -ge-*, *h*) arm (*a. fig*)
Be'waffnung *f* (-; -*en*) armament; arms
be'wahren *v/t* (*no -ge-*, *h*) keep; ***bewahren vor*** (*dat*) keep *or* save from
be'währen *v/refl* (*no -ge-*, *h*) prove successful; ***sich bewähren als*** prove to be
bewährt [bə'vɛːɐt] *adj* (well-)tried, reliable; experienced
Be'währung *f* (-; -*en*) JUR probation
Be'währungsfrist *f* JUR (period of) probation
Bewährungshelfer *m* JUR probation officer
Bewährungsprobe *f* (acid) test
bewaldet [bə'valdət] *adj* wooded, woody
bewältigen [bə'vɛltɪgən] *v/t* (*no -ge-*, *h*) manage, cope with; cover (*distance*)
be'wandert *adj* (well-)versed (***in*** *dat* in)
be'wässern *v/t* (*no -ge-*, *h*) irrigate
Be'wässerung *f* (-; -*en*) irrigation
bewegen [bə'veːgən] *v/t and v/refl* (*no -ge-*, *h*) move (*a. fig*); ***nicht bewegen!*** don't move!; (*irr*) ***j-n zu et. bewegen*** get s.o. to do s.th.
Be'weggrund *m* motive
beweglich [bə'veːklɪç] *adj* movable; agile; flexible; TECH moving (*parts*)
Be'weglichkeit *f* (-; *no pl*) mobility; agility
be'wegt *adj* rough (*sea*); choked (*voice*); eventful (*life*); *fig* moved, touched
Be'wegung *f* (-; -*en*) movement (*a.* POL); motion (*a.* PHYS); exercise; *fig* emotion; ***in Bewegung setzen*** set in motion
Be'wegungsfreiheit *f* (-; *no pl*) freedom of movement (*fig a.* of action)
be'wegungslos *adj* motionless
Beweis [bə'vais] *m* (-*es*; -*e*) proof (***für*** of); ***Beweis(e)*** evidence (*esp* JUR)
be'weisen *v/t* (*irr*, ***weisen***, *no -ge-*, *h*) prove; show
Be'weismittel *n* JUR (piece of) evidence
Be'weisstück *n* (piece of) evidence, JUR exhibit
be'wenden *v/i*: ***es dabei bewenden lassen*** leave it at that
be'werben *v/refl* (*irr*, ***werben***, *no -ge-*, *h*) ***sich bewerben um*** apply for
Be'wer-ber(in) (-*s*; -/-; -*nen*) applicant
Be'werbung *f* (-; -*en*) application
Be'werbungsschreiben *n* (letter of) application
be'werten *v/t* (*no -ge-*, *h*) assess; judge
Be'wertung *f* (-; -*en*) assessment
bewilligen [bə'vɪlɪgən] *v/t* (*no -ge-*, *h*) grant, allow
be'wirken *v/t* (*no -ge-*, *h*) cause
bewirten [bə'vɪrtən] *v/t* (*no -ge-*, *h*) entertain
be'wirtschaften *v/t* (*no -ge-*, *h*) run; AGR farm
be'wirtschaftet *adj* open (to the public)
Be'wirtung *f* (-; -*en*) catering; service; hospitality
bewog [bə'voːk] *pret of* ***bewegen***
bewogen [bə'voːgən] *pp of* ***bewegen***
be'wohnen *v/t* (*no -ge-*, *h*) live in; inhabit
Be'wohner(in) (-*s*; -/-; -*nen*) inhabitant;

occupant
be'wohnt *adj* inhabited; occupied
bewölken [bə'vœlkən] *v/refl* (*no -ge-, h*) METEOR cloud over (*a. fig*)
be'wölkt *adj* METEOR cloudy, overcast
Be'wölkung *f* (-; *no pl*) METEOR clouds
Bewunderer [bə'vʊndərɐ] *m* (*-s*; -) admirer
be'wundern *v/t* (*no -ge-, h*) admire (***wegen*** for)
be'wundernswert *adj* admirable
Be'wunderung *f* (-; *no pl*) admiration
bewusst [bə'vʊst] *adj* conscious; intentional; ***sich e-r Sache bewusst sein*** be conscious *or* aware of s.th., realize s.th.; ***j-m et. bewusst machen*** make s.o. realize s.th.
be'wusstlos *adj* MED unconscious
be'wusstmachen *v/t* → ***bewusst***
Be'wusstsein *n* (*-s*; *no pl*) MED consciousness; ***bei Bewusstsein*** conscious
be'zahlen *v/t* (*no -ge-, h*) pay; pay for (*a. fig*)
be'zahlt *adj*: ***bezahlter Urlaub*** paid leave; ***es macht sich bezahlt*** it pays
Be'zahlung *f* (-; *no pl*) payment; pay
be'zaubern *v/t* (*no -ge-, h*) charm
bezaubernd *adj* charming, F sweet, darling
be'zeichnen *v/t* (*no -ge-, h*) ***bezeichnen als*** call, describe as
bezeichnend *adj* characteristic, typical (***für*** of)
Be'zeichnung *f* (-; *-en*) name, term
be'zeugen *v/t* (*no -ge-, h*) JUR testify to
be'ziehen *v/t* (*irr*, ***ziehen***, *no -ge-, h*) cover; put clean sheets on (*bed*); move into; receive; subscribe to (*paper etc*); ***beziehen auf*** (*acc*) relate to; ***sich beziehen*** cloud over; ***sich beziehen auf*** (*acc*) refer to
Be'ziehung *f* (-; *-en*) relation (***zu*** to *s.th.*; with *s.o.*); connection (***zu*** with); relationship; respect; ***Beziehungen haben*** have connections
be'ziehungsweise *cj* respectively; or; or rather
Bezirk [bə'tsɪrk] *m* (-[*e*]*s*; *-e*) precinct, *Br a.* district
Bezug [bə'tsuːk] *m* (-[*e*]*s*; *Bezüge* [bə'tsyːgə]) a) cover(ing); case, slip, b) (*no pl*) ECON purchase; subscription (*gen* to), c) *pl* earnings; ***Bezug nehmen auf*** (*acc*) refer to; ***in Bezug auf*** (*acc*) → ***bezüglich***
bezüglich [bə'tsyːklɪç] *prp* (*gen*) regarding, concerning
Be'zugsper,son *f* PSYCH person to relate to, role model
Bezugspunkt *m* reference point
Bezugsquelle *f* source (of supply)
be'zwecken *v/t* (*no -ge-, h*) aim at, intend
be'zweifeln *v/t* (*no -ge-, h*) doubt, question
be'zwingen *v/t* (*irr*, ***zwingen***, *no -ge-, h*) conquer, defeat
Bibel ['biːbəl] *f* (-; *-n*) Bible
Biber ['biːbɐ] *m* (*-s*; -) ZO beaver
Bibliothek [biblio'teːk] *f* (-; *-en*) library
Bibliothekar [bibliote'kaːɐ] *m* (*-s*; *-e*), **Bibliothe'karin** *f* (-; *-nen*) librarian
biblisch ['biːblɪʃ] *adj* biblical
bieder ['biːdɐ] *adj* honest; square
biegen ['biːgən] *v/t* (*irr, ge-, h*) *and v/i* (*sein*) bend (*a.* ***sich biegen***), *road*: *a.* turn; ***um die Ecke biegen*** turn (round) the corner
biegsam ['biːkzaːm] *adj* flexible
'Biegung *f* (-; *-en*) curve
Biene ['biːnə] *f* (-; *-n*) ZO bee
'Bienenkönigin *f* ZO queen (bee)
Bienenkorb *m*, **Bienenstock** *m* (bee)hive
Bienenwachs *n* beeswax
Bier [biːɐ] *n* (-[*e*]*s*; *-e*) beer; ***Bier vom Faß*** draft (*Br* draught) beer
Bierdeckel *m* coaster, beer mat
Bierkrug *m* beer mug, stein
Biest [biːst] F *fig n* (-[*e*]*s*; *-er*) beast; (***kleines***) ***Biest*** brat, little devil, stinker
bieten ['biːtən] (*irr, ge-, h*) **1.** *v/t* offer; ***sich bieten*** present itself; **2.** *v/i auction*: (make a) bid
Bigamie [biga'miː] *f* (-; *-n*) bigamy
Bikini [bi'kiːni] *m* (*-s*; *-s*) bikini
Bilanz [bi'lants] *f* (-; *-en*) ECON balance; *fig* result; ***Bilanz ziehen aus*** (*dat*) *fig* take stock of
Bild [bɪlt] *n* (-[*e*]*s*; *-er* ['bɪldɐ]) picture; image; ***sich ein Bild machen von*** get an idea of
Bildausfall *m* TV blackout
Bildbericht *m* photo(graphic) essay (*Br* report)
bilden ['bɪldən] *v/t* (*ge-, h*) form (*a.* ***sich bilden***); shape; *fig* educate (***sich*** o.s.); be, constitute
'Bilderbuch *n* picture book
'Bildfläche *f*: F ***auf der Bildfläche erscheinen*** (***von der Bildfläche verschwinden***) appear on (disappear from) the scene
'Bildhauer *m* (*-s*; -), **'Bildhauerin** *f* (-; *-nen*) sculptor
'bildlich *adj* graphic; figurative
'Bildnis *n* (*-ses*; *-se*) portrait
'Bildplatte *f* videodisk (*Br* -disc)
'Bildröhre *f* picture tube
'Bildschirm *m* TV screen, EDP *a.* display,

monitor
Bildschirmarbeitsplatz *m* workstation
Bildschirmgerät *n* visual display unit, VDU
Bildschirmschoner *m* (*-s*; -) screen saver
Bildschirmtext *m* videotext, *Br* viewdata
'bild'schön *adj* most beautiful
'Bildung *f* (-; *-en*) a) (*no pl*) education, b) formation
'Bildungs... *in cpds ...chancen, ...reform, ...urlaub etc*: educational ...
Bildungslücke *f* gap in one's knowledge
'Bildunterschrift *f* caption
Billard ['bɪljart] *n* (*-s*; *-e*) billiards, pool
Billardkugel *f* billiard ball
Billardstock *m* cue
Billett [bɪl'jɛt] *n* (*-[e]s*; *-e*) *Swiss* ticket
billig ['bɪlɪç] *adj* cheap (*a. contp*), inexpensive
billigen ['bɪlɪgən] *v/t* (*ge-, h*) approve of
'Billigung *f* (-; *no pl*) approval
Billion [bɪ'ljoːn] *f* (-; *-en*) trillion
bimmeln ['bɪməln] F *v/i* (*ge-, h*) jingle; TEL ring
binär [bi'nɛːɐ] *adj* MATH, PHYS *etc* binary
Binde ['bɪndə] *f* (-; *-n*) bandage; sling; → ***Damenbinde***
Bindegewebe *n* ANAT connective tissue
Bindeglied *n* (connecting) link
'Bindehaut *f* ANAT conjunctiva
Bindehautentzündung *f* MED conjunctivitis
binden (*irr, ge-, h*) **1.** *v/t* bind (*a. book*), tie (***an*** *acc* to); make (*wreath etc*); knot (*tie*); ***sich binden*** bind *or* commit o.s.; **2.** *v/i* bind
'Bindestrich *m* LING hyphen
'Bindewort *n* LING conjunction
Bindfaden ['bɪnt-] *m* string
'Bindung *f* (-; *-en*) tie, link, bond; *skiing*: binding
Binnenhafen ['bɪnən-] *m* inland port
Binnenhandel *m* domestic trade
Binnenmarkt *m*: ***Europäischer Binnenmarkt*** European single market
Binnenschifffahrt *f* inland navigation
Binnenverkehr *m* inland traffic *or* transport
Binse ['bɪnzə] *f* (-; *-n*) BOT rush
'Binsenweisheit *f* (-; *-en*) truism
Bio..., bio... [bio-] *in cpds ...chemie, ...dynamisch, ...sphäre etc*: bio...
Biografie, Biographie [biogra'fiː] *f* (-; *-n*) biography
bio'grafisch, bio'graphisch *adj* biographic(al)
Bioladen ['biːo-] *m* health food shop *or* store
Biologe [bio'loːgə] *m* (*-n*; *-n*) biologist
Biologie [biolo'giː] *f* (-; *no pl*) biology
Bio'login *f* (-; *-nen*) biologist
biologisch [bio'loːgɪʃ] *adj* biological; AGR organic; ***biologisch abbaubar*** biodegradable
'Biorhythmus *m* biorhythms
'Biotechnik *f* (-; *no pl*) biotechnology
Biotop [bio'toːp] *n* (*-s*; *-e*) biotope
Birke ['bɪrkə] *f* (-; *-n*) BOT birch (tree)
Birne ['bɪrnə] *f* (-; *-n*) BOT pear; ELECTR (light) bulb
bis [bɪs] *prp* (*acc*) *and adv and cj time*: till, until, (up) to; *space*: (up) to, as far as; ***von ... bis ...*** from ... to ...; ***bis auf*** (*acc*) except; ***bis zu*** up to; ***bis später!*** see you later!; ***bis jetzt*** up to now, so far; ***bis Montag*** by Monday; ***zwei bis drei*** two or three; ***wie weit ist es bis ...?*** how far is it to ...?
Bischof ['bɪʃɔf] *m* (*-s*; *Bischöfe* ['bɪʃœfə]) REL bishop
bisexuell [bizɛ'ksuɛl] *adj* bisexual
bis'her *adv* up to now, so far; ***wie bisher*** as before
bisherig [bɪs'heːrɪç] *adj* previous
Biskuit [bɪs'kviːt] *n* (*-[e]s*; *-e*) sponge cake (mix)
biss [bɪs] *pret of* ***beißen***
Biss *m* (*-es*; *-e*) bite (*a. fig*)
bisschen ['bɪsçən] *adj and adv*: ***ein bisschen*** a little, a (little) bit (of); ***nicht ein bisschen*** not in the least
Bissen ['bɪsən] *m* (*-s*; -) bite; ***keinen Bissen*** not a thing
bissig ['bɪsɪç] *adj fig* cutting; ***ein bissiger Hund*** a dog that bites; ***Vorsicht, bissiger Hund!*** beware of the dog!
Bistum ['bɪstuːm] *n* (*-s*; *Bistümer* ['bɪstyːmɐ]) REL bishopric, diocese
bis'weilen *adv* at times, now and then
Bit [bɪt] *n* (*-[s]*; *-[s]*) EDP bit
bitte ['bɪtə] *adv* please; ***bitte nicht!*** please don't!; ***bitte (schön)!*** that's all right, not at all, you're welcome; here you are; (***wie***) ***bitte?*** pardon?; ***bitte sehr?*** can I help you?
'Bitte *f* (-; *-n*) request (***um*** for); ***ich habe e-e Bitte (an dich)*** I have a favo(u)r to ask of you
'bitten *v/t* (*irr, ge-, h*) ***j-n um et. bitten*** ask s.o. for s.th.; ***darf ich bitten?*** may I have (the pleasure of) this dance?; → ***Erlaubnis***
bitter ['bɪtɐ] *adj* bitter (*a. fig*), *a.* biting (*cold*)
bitter'kalt *adj* bitterly cold
blähen ['blɛːən] *v/refl* (*ge-, h*) swell
'Blähungen *pl* MED flatulence, *Br a.* wind
blamabel [bla'maːbəl] *adj* embarrassing

Blamage [bla'maːʒə] *f* (-; *-n*) disgrace, shame
blamieren [bla'miːrən] *v/t* (*no -ge-*, *h*) ***j-n blamieren*** make s.o. look like a fool; ***sich blamieren*** make a fool of o.s.
blank [blaŋk] *adj* shining, shiny, bright; polished; F broke
Blanko... ['blaŋko] *in cpds* ECON blank
Bläschen ['blɛːsçən] *n* (*-s*; -) MED vesicle, small blister
Blase ['blaːzə] *f* (-; *-n*) bubble; ANAT bladder; MED blister
'**Blasebalg** *m* (pair of) bellows
'**blasen** *v/t* (*irr*, *ge-*, *h*) blow (*a.* MUS)
'**Blasinstru,ment** *n* MUS wind instrument
Blaska,pelle *f* brass band
Blasrohr *n* blowpipe
blass [blas] *adj* pale (***vor*** with); ***blass werden*** turn pale
Blässe ['blɛsə] *f* (-; *no pl*) paleness, pallor
Blatt [blat] *n* (-[*e*]*s*; *Blätter* ['blɛtɐ]) BOT leaf; piece, sheet (*a.* MUS); (news)paper; *card games*: hand
blättern ['blɛtɐn] *v/i* (*ge-*, *h*) ***blättern in*** (*dat*) leaf through
'**Blätterteig** *m* puff pastry
blau [blau] *adj* blue; F loaded, stoned; ***blaues Auge*** black eye; ***blauer Fleck*** bruise; ***Fahrt ins Blaue*** mystery tour
'**blauäugig** [-ɔʏgɪç] *adj* blue-eyed; *fig* starry-eyed
'**Blaubeere** *f* BOT blueberry, *Br* bilberry
'**blaugrau** *adj* bluish-gray (*Br* -grey)
bläulich ['blɔʏlɪç] *adj* bluish
'**Blaulicht** *n* (-[*e*]*s*; *-er*) flashing light(s)
'**Blauhelme** *pl* MIL UN soldiers
'**blaumachen** F *v/i* (*sep*, *-ge-*, *h*) stay away from work *or* school
'**Blausäure** *f* CHEM prussic acid
Blech [blɛç] *n* (-[*e*]*s*; *-e*) sheet metal; *in cpds* *...dach*, *...löffel etc*: tin ...; *...instrument*: MUS brass ...
'**blechen** F *v/t and v/i* (*ge-*, *h*) shell out
'**Blechbüchse**, **Blechdose** *f* can, *Br a.* tin
Blechschaden *m* MOT bodywork damage
Blei [blai] *n* (-[*e*]*s*; *-e*) lead; ***aus Blei*** leaden
Bleibe ['blaibə] *f* (-; *-n*) place to stay
'**bleiben** *v/i* (*irr*, *ge-*, *sein*) stay, remain; ***bleiben bei*** stick to; F ***et. bleiben lassen*** not do s.th.; ***lass das bleiben!*** stop that!; ***das wirst du schön bleiben lassen!*** you'll do nothing of the sort!; → ***Apparat***, ***ruhig***
bleibend *adj* lasting, permanent
'**bleibenlassen** *v/i* → ***bleiben***
bleich [blaiç] *adj* pale (***vor*** *dat* with)
'**bleichen** *v/t* ([*irr*,] *ge-*, *h*) bleach
bleiern ['blaiɐn] *adj* lead(en *fig*)
'**bleifrei** *adj* MOT unleaded
'**Bleistift** *m* pencil
Bleistiftspitzer *m* pencil sharpener
Blende ['blɛndə] *f* (-; *-n*) blind; PHOT aperture; (***bei***) ***Blende 8*** (at) f-8
'**blenden** *v/t* (*ge-*, *h*) blind, dazzle (*both a. fig*)
blendend *adj* dazzling (*a. fig*); brilliant; ***blendend aussehen*** look great
'**blendfrei** *adj* OPT antiglare
blich [blɪç] *pret of* ***bleichen***
Blick [blɪk] *m* (-[*e*]*s*; *-e*) look (***auf*** *acc* at); view (of); ***flüchtiger Blick*** glance; ***auf den ersten Blick*** at first sight
'**blicken** *v/i* (*ge-*, *h*) look, glance (*both*: ***auf*** *acc*, ***nach*** at)
'**Blickfang** *m* eye-catcher
'**Blickfeld** *n* field of vision
blieb [bliːp] *pret of* ***bleiben***
blies [bliːs] *pret of* ***blasen***
blind [blɪnt] *adj* blind (*a. fig* ***gegen***, ***für*** to; ***vor*** *dat* with); dull (*mirror etc*); ***blinder Alarm*** false alarm; ***blinder Passagier*** stowaway; ***auf e-m Auge blind*** blind in one eye; ***ein Blinder*** a blind man; ***e-e Blinde*** a blind woman; ***die Blinden*** the blind
'**Blinddarm** *m* ANAT appendix
Blinddarmentzündung *f* MED appendicitis
Blinddarmoperati,on *f* MED appendectomy
Blindenhund ['blɪndən-] *m* seeing eye (*Br* guide) dog
Blindenschrift *f* braille
'**Blindgänger** [-gɛŋɐ] *m* (*-s*; -) MIL dud
'**Blindheit** *f* (-; *no pl*) blindness
blindlings ['blɪntlɪŋs] *adv* blindly
'**Blindschleiche** *f* ZO blindworm
blinken ['blɪŋkən] *v/i* (*ge-*, *h*) sparkle, shine; twinkle; flash (a signal); MOT indicate
Blinker ['blɪŋkɐ] *m* (*-s*; -) MOT turn signal, *Br* indicator
blinzeln ['blɪntsəln] *v/i* (*ge-*, *h*) blink (one's eyes)
Blitz [blɪts] *m* (*-es*; *-e*) (flash of) lightning; PHOT flash
Blitzableiter *m* (*-s*; -) lightning conductor
'**blitzen** *v/i* (*ge-*, *h*) flash; ***es blitzt*** it's lightening
'**Blitzgerät** *n* PHOT (electronic) flash
Blitzlampe *f* PHOT flashbulb; flash cube
Blitzlicht *n* (-[*e*]*s*; *-er*) PHOT flash(light)
Blitzschlag *m* lightning stroke
'**blitz'schnell** *adj and adv* like a flash; *attr* split-second
Block [blɔk] *m* (-[*e*]*s*; *Blöcke* ['blœkə]) block; POL, ECON bloc; (*writing*) pad

Blockade [blɔ'kaːdə] *f* (-; -*n*) MAR, MIL blockade
'**Blockflöte** *f* recorder
'**Blockhaus** *n* log cabin
blockieren [blɔ'kiːrən] *v/t and v/i* (*no -ge-*, *h*) block; MOT lock
'**Blockschrift** *f* block letters
blöde ['bløːdə] F *adj* silly, stupid
'**blödeln** *v/i* (*ge-*, *h*) fool *or* clown around
Blödheit ['bløːthait] *f* (-; *no pl*) stupidity
'**Blödsinn** F *m* (-[*e*]*s*; *no pl*) rubbish, nonsense
'**blödsinnig** F *adj* stupid, idiotic
blöken ['bløːkən] *v/i* (*ge-*, *h*) ZO bleat
blond [blɔnt] *adj* blond, fair
Blondine [blɔn'diːnə] *f* (-; -*n*) blonde
bloß [bloːs] **1.** *adj* bare; naked (*eye*); mere; ***bloß legen*** *v/t* (*sep*, *-ge-*, *h*) lay bare, expose; **2.** *adv* only, just, merely
Blöße ['bløːsə] *f* (-; -*n*) nakedness; ***sich e-e Blöße geben*** lay o.s. open to attack *or* criticism
'**bloßlegen** *v/t* → ***bloß***
bloßstellen *v/t* (*sep*, *-ge-*, *h*) expose, compromise, unmask; ***sich bloßstellen*** compromise o.s.
blühen ['blyːən] *v/i* (*ge-*, *h*) (be in) bloom; (be in) blossom; *fig* flourish
Blume ['bluːmə] *f* (-; -*n*) flower; GASTR bouquet; head, froth
'**Blumenbeet** *n* flowerbed
Blumenhändler *m* florist
Blumenkohl *m* BOT cauliflower
Blumenladen *m* flower shop, florist's
Blumenstrauß *m* bunch of flowers; bouquet
Blumentopf *m* flowerpot
Blumenvase *f* vase
Bluse ['bluːzə] *f* (-; -*n*) blouse
Blut [bluːt] *n* (-[*e*]*s*; *no pl*) blood
'**blutarm** *adj* MED an(a)emic (*a. fig*)
'**Blutarmut** *f* MED an(a)emia
Blutbad *n* massacre
Blutbahn *f* ANAT bloodstream
Blutbank *f* (-; -*en*) MED blood bank
'**blutbefleckt** *adj* bloodstained
'**Blutbild** *n* MED blood count
Blutblase *f* MED blood blister
Blutdruck *m* MED blood pressure
Blüte ['blyːtə] *f* (-; -*n*) flower; bloom (*a. fig*); blossom; *fig* height, heyday; ***in*** (***voller***) ***Blüte*** in (full) bloom
'**Blutegel** *m* ZO leech
'**bluten** *v/i* (*ge-*, *h*) bleed (***aus*** *dat* from)
'**Blütenblatt** *n* petal
Blütenstaub *m* pollen
Bluter ['bluːtɐ] *m* (-*s*; -) MED h(a)emophiliac
'**Bluterguss** *m* bruise; MED h(a)ematoma
Blutgefäß *n* ANAT blood vessel
Blutgerinnsel *n* MED blood clot
Blutgruppe *f* MED blood group
Bluthund *m* ZO bloodhound
'**blutig** *adj* bloody; ***blutiger Anfänger*** rank beginner, F greenhorn
'**Blutkörperchen** *n* MED blood corpuscle
Blutkreislauf *m* MED (blood) circulation
Blutlache *f* pool of blood
'**blutleer** *adj* bloodless
'**Blutprobe** *f* MED blood test
'**blutrünstig** [-rʏnstɪç] *adj* bloodthirsty, gory
'**Blutschande** *f* JUR incest
'**Blutspender** *m* blood donor
'**Blutsverwandte** *m, f* blood relation
'**Blutübertragung** *f* MED blood transfusion
'**Blutung** *f* (-; -*en*) MED bleeding, h(a)emorrhage
'**blutunterlaufen** *adj* bloodshot
'**Blutvergießen** *n* (-*s*; *no pl*) bloodshed
Blutvergiftung *f* MED blood poisoning
Blutwurst *f* black sausage (*Br* pudding)
BLZ [beːɛl'tsɛt] ABBR *of* ***Bankleitzahl*** A.B.A. number, *Br* bank (sorting) code
Bö [bøː] *f* (-; -*en*) gust, squall
Bob [bɔp] *m* (-*s*; -*s*) bob(sled)
Bobbahn *f* bob run
Bobfahrer *m* bobber
Bock [bɔk] *m* (-[*e*]*s*; *Böcke* ['bœkə]) ZO buck; he-goat, billy-goat; ram; SPORT buck; F ***e-n Bock schießen*** (make a) blunder; F ***keinen*** (*or* ***null***) ***Bock auf et. haben*** have zero interest in s.th.
'**bocken** *v/i* (*ge-*, *h*) buck; sulk
'**bockig** *adj* obstinate; sulky
'**Bockspringen** *n* leapfrog
Boden ['boːdən] *m* (-*s*; *Böden* ['bøːdən]) ground; AGR soil; bottom; floor; attic
'**Bodenperso,nal** *n* AVIAT ground crew
Bodenre,form *f* land reform
Bodenschätze *pl* mineral resources
Bodenstati,on *f* AVIAT ground control
Bodenturnen *n* floor exercises
Body ['bɔdi] *m* (-*s*; -*s*) bodysuit
bog [boːk] *pret of* ***biegen***
Bogen ['boːgən] *m* (-*s*; *Bögen* ['bøːgən]) bend, curve; MATH arc; ARCH arch; *skiing*: turn; bow; sheet
Bogenschießen *n* archery
Bogenschütze *m* archer
Bohle ['boːlə] *f* (-; -*n*) plank
Bohne ['boːnə] *f* (-; -*n*) BOT bean; ***grüne Bohnen*** green (*Br a.* French) beans
'**Bohnenstange** *f* beanpole (*a.* F)
bohnern ['boːnɐn] *v/t* (*ge-*, *h*) polish, wax
'**Bohnerwachs** *n* floor polish
bohren ['boːrən] *v/t* (*ge-*, *h*) bore, drill (*a.*

dentist)
bohrend *fig adj* piercing (*look*); insistent (*questions etc*)
Bohrer ['bo:rɐ] *m* (*-s*; -) TECH drill
'Bohrinsel *f* oil rig
Bohrloch *n* borehole, well(head)
Bohrmaˌschine *f* (electric) drill
Bohrturm *m* derrick
'Bohrung *f* (-; *-en*) drilling; bore
Boje ['bo:jə] *f* (-; *-n*) MAR buoy
Bolzen ['bɔltsən] *m* (*-s*; -) TECH bolt
bombardieren [bɔmbar'di:rən] *v/t* (*no -ge-*, *h*) bomb; *fig* bombard
Bombe ['bɔmbə] *f* (-; *-n*) bomb; *fig* bombshell
'Bombenangriff *m* air raid
Bombenanschlag *m* bomb attack
Bombenerfolg F *m* roaring success; THEA *etc* smash hit
Bombengeschäft F *n* super deal
'Bombenleger *m* (*-s*; -) bomber
'bombensicher *adj* bombproof
Bomber ['bɔmbɐ] F *m* (*-s*; -) MIL bomber (*a.* SPORT)
Bon [bɔŋ] *m* (*-s*; *-s*) coupon, voucher
Bonbon [bɔŋ'bɔŋ] *m*, *n* (*-s*; *-s*) candy, *Br* sweet
Boot [bo:t] *n* (*-[e]s*; *-e*) boat
'Bootsmann *m* (*-[e]s*; *-leute*) boatswain
Bord[1] [bɔrt] *n* (*-[e]s*; *-e*) shelf
Bord[2] *m*: ***an Bord*** AVIAT, MAR on board; ***über Bord*** MAR overboard; ***von Bord gehen*** MAR disembark
Bordell [bɔr'dɛl] *n* (*-s*; *-e*) brothel, F whorehouse
'Bordkarte *f* AVIAT boarding pass
'Bordstein *m* curb, *Br* kerb
borgen ['bɔrgən] *v/t* (*ge-*, *h*) borrow; ***sich et. von j-m borgen*** borrow s.th. from s.o.; ***j-m et. borgen*** lend s.th. to s.o.
Borke ['bɔrkə] *f* (-; *-n*) BOT bark
borniert [bɔr'ni:ɐt] *adj* narrow-minded
Börse ['bœrzə] *f* (-; *-n*) ECON stock exchange
'Börsenbericht *m* market report
Börsenkurs *m* quotation
Börsenmakler *m* stockbroker
Börsenspekuˌlant *m* stock-jobber
Borste ['bɔrstə] *f* (-; *-n*) bristle
'borstig *adj* bristly
Borte ['bɔrtə] *f* (-; *-n*) border; braid, lace
bösartig ['bø:s-] *adj* vicious; MED malignant
Böschung ['bœʃʊŋ] *f* (-; *-en*) slope, bank; RAIL embankment
böse ['bø:zə] *adj* bad, evil, wicked; angry (***über*** *acc* about; ***auf j-n*** with s.o.), mad (***auf*** *acc* at); ***er meint es nicht böse*** he means no harm
'Böse *n* (*-n*; *no pl*) (the) evil
'Bösewicht *m* (*-[e]s*; *-er*) villain
boshaft ['bo:shaft] *adj* malicious
Bosheit ['bo:shait] *f* (-; *no pl*) malice
'böswillig *adj* malicious, JUR *a.* wil(l)ful
bot [bo:t] *pret of* ***bieten***
Botanik [bo'ta:nɪk] *f* (-; *no pl*) botany
Bo'taniker *m* (*-s*; -) botanist
bo'tanisch *adj* botanical
Bote ['bo:tə] *m* (*-n*; *-n*) messenger
'Botengang *m* errand; ***Botengänge machen*** run errands
Botschaft ['bo:tʃaft] *f* (-; *-en*) message; POL embassy
'Botschafter *m* (*-s*; -) POL ambassador (***in*** *dat* to)
'Botschafterin *f* (-; *-nen*) POL ambassadress (***in*** *dat* to)
Bottich ['bɔtɪç] *m* (*-s*; *-e*) tub, vat
Bouillon [bʊl'jɔŋ] *f* (-; *-s*) consommé, bouillon, broth
Boulevardblatt [bulə'va:ɐ-] *n*, **Boulevardzeitung** *f* tabloid
Bowle ['bo:lə] *f* (-; *-n*) (cold) punch; bowl
boxen ['bɔksən] (*ge-*, *h*) **1.** *v/i* box; **2.** *v/t* punch
'Boxen *n* (*-s*; *no pl*) boxing
Boxer ['bɔksɐ] *m* (*-s*; -) boxer
'Boxhandschuh *m* boxing glove
Boxkampf *m* boxing match, fight
Boxsport *m* boxing
Boykott [bɔʏ'kɔt] *m* (*-[e]s*; *-e*), **boykottieren** [bɔʏkɔ'ti:rən] *v/t* (*no -ge-*, *h*) boycott
brach [bra:x] *pret of* ***brechen***
brachliegend *adj* AGR fallow
brachte ['braxtə] *pret of* ***bringen***
Branche ['brã:ʃə] *f* (-; *-n*) ECON line (of business)
'Branchenverzeichnis *n* TEL yellow pages
Brand [brant] *m* (*-[e]s*; *Brände* ['brɛndə]) fire; ***in Brand geraten*** catch fire; ***in Brand stecken*** set fire to
Brandblase *f* MED blister
branden ['brandən] *v/i* (*ge-*, *sein*) surge (***gegen*** against)
'Brandfleck *m* burn
Brandmal *n* brand
'brandmarken *fig v/t* (*ge-*, *h*) brand, stigmatize
'Brandmauer *f* fire wall
Brandstätte *f*, **Brandstelle** *f* scene of fire
Brandstifter *m* arsonist
Brandstiftung *f* arson
'Brandung *f* (-; *no pl*) surf, surge, breakers
'Brandwunde *f* MED burn; scald
brannte ['brantə] *pret of* ***brennen***
'Branntwein *m* brandy, spirits

braten ['bra:tən] *v/t* (*irr*, *ge-*, *h*) roast; grill, broil; fry; ***am Spieß braten*** roast on a spit, barbecue
'**Braten** *m* (*-s*; *-*) roast (meat); joint
Bratenfett *n* dripping
Bratensoße *f* gravy
'**Bratfisch** *m* fried fish
Brathuhn *n* roast chicken
Bratkar,toffeln *pl* fried potatoes
Bratofen *m* oven
Bratpfanne *f* frying pan
Bratsche ['bra:tʃə] *f* (*-*; *-n*) MUS viola
'**Bratwurst** *f* grilled sausage
Brauch [braux] *m* (*-[e]s*; *Bräuche* ['brɔʏçə]) custom; habit, practice
'**brauchbar** *adj* useful
'**brauchen** *v/t* (*ge-*, *h*) need; require; take (*time*); use; ***wie lange wird er brauchen?*** how long will it take him?; ***du brauchst es nur zu sagen*** just say the word; ***ihr braucht es nicht zu tun*** you don't have to do it; ***er hätte nicht zu kommen brauchen*** he need not have come
brauen ['brauən] *v/t* (*ge-*, *h*) brew
Brauerei [brauə'rai] *f* (*-*; *-en*) brewery
braun [braun] *adj* brown; (sun)tanned; ***braun werden*** (get a) tan
Bräune ['brɔʏnə] *f* (*-*; *no pl*) (sun)tan
'**bräunen** (*ge-*, *h*) **1.** *v/t* brown, tan; **2.** *v/i* (get a) tan
'**Braunkohle** *f* brown coal, lignite
'**bräunlich** *adj* brownish
Brause ['brauzə] *f* (*-*; *-n*) shower; → ***Limonade***
'**brausen** *v/i* a) (*ge-*, *h*) roar, b) (*sein*) rush, c) (*h*) → ***duschen***
Braut [braut] *f* (*-*; *Bräute* ['brɔʏtə]) bride; fiancée
Bräutigam ['brɔʏtɪgam] *m* (*-s*; *-e*) (bride)groom; fiancé
'**Brautjungfer** *f* bridesmaid
Brautkleid *n* wedding-dress
Brautpaar *n* bride and (bride)groom; engaged couple
brav [bra:f] *adj* good; honest; ***sei(d) brav!*** be good!
BRD [be:ˀɛr'de:] ABBR *of* ***Bundesrepublik Deutschland*** FRG, Federal Republic of Germany
brechen ['brɛçən] (*irr*, *ge-*) **1.** *v/t* (*h*) break (*a. fig*); MED vomit; ***sich brechen*** OPT be refracted; ***sich den Arm brechen*** break one's arm; **2.** *v/i* a) (*h*) MED vomit, F throw up, *Br a.* be sick; ***mit j-m brechen*** break with s.o; ***brechend voll*** crammed, packed, b) (*sein*) break, get broken, fracture
'**Brechreiz** *m* MED nausea
'**Brechstange** *f* crowbar
'**Brechung** *f* (*-*; *-en*) OPT refraction
Brei [brai] *m* (*-[e]s*; *-e*) pulp, mash; pap; porridge; pudding
'**breiig** *adj* pulpy, mushy
breit [brait] *adj* wide; broad (*a. fig*)
'**breitbeinig** *adj* with legs (wide) apart
Breite ['braitə] *f* (*-*; *-n*) width, breadth; ASTR, GEOGR latitude
'**breiten** *v/t* (*ge-*, *h*) spread
'**Breitengrad** *m* degree of latitude
Breitenkreis *m* parallel (of latitude)
breitmachen *v/refl* (*sep*, *-ge-*, *h*): ***sich breitmachenmachen*** F spread o.s., take up room
'**Breitwand** *f film*: wide screen
Bremsbelag ['brɛms-] *m* brake lining
Bremse ['brɛmzə] *f* (*-*; *-n*) TECH brake; ZO gadfly
'**bremsen** (*ge-*, *h*) **1.** *v/i* MOT brake, put on the brake(s); slow down; **2.** *v/t* MOT brake; *fig* curb
'**Bremslicht** *n* (*-[e]s*; *-er*) MOT stop light
Bremspe,dal *n* MOT brake pedal
Bremsspur *f* MOT skid marks
Bremsweg *m* MOT stopping distance
'**brennbar** *adj* combustible; (in)flammable
brennen ['brɛnən] (*irr*, *ge-*, *h*) **1.** *v/t* burn; distil(l) (*whisky etc*); bake (*bricks*); **2.** *v/i* burn; be on fire; *wound*, *eyes*: smart, burn; F ***darauf brennen zu*** *inf* be dying to *inf*; ***es brennt!*** fire!
Brenner ['brɛnɐ] *m* (*-s*; *-*) burner
'**Brennholz** *n* firewood
Brennmateri,al *n* fuel
Brennnessel *f* BOT (stinging) nettle
Brennpunkt *m* focus, focal point
Brennspiritus *m* methylated spirit
Brennstab *m* TECH fuel rod
Brennstoff *m* fuel
brenzlig ['brɛntslɪç] *adj* burnt; *fig* hot
Bresche ['brɛʃə] *f* (*-*; *-n*) breach (*a. fig*), gap
Brett [brɛt] *n* (*-[e]s*; *-er*) board
'**Bretterzaun** *m* wooden fence
'**Brettspiel** *n* board game
Brezel ['bre:tsəl] *f* (*-*; *-n*) pretzel
Brief [bri:f] *m* (*-[e]s*; *-e*) letter
Briefbeschwerer *m* (*-s*; *-*) paperweight
Briefbogen *m* sheet of (note)paper
Brieffreund(in) pen pal (*Br* friend)
Briefkasten *m* mailbox, *Br* letterbox
'**brieflich** *adj and adv* by letter
'**Briefmarke** *f* (postage) stamp
Briefmarkensammlung *f* stamp collection
Brieföffner *m* letter opener, *Br* paper knife

Briefpa,pier *n* stationery
Brieftasche *f* wallet
Brieftaube *f* ZO carrier pigeon
Briefträger(in) (*-s; -/-; -nen*) mailman (mailwoman), *Br* postman (postwoman)
Briefumschlag *m* envelope
Briefwahl *f* postal vote
Briefwechsel *m* correspondence
briet [bri:t] *pret of* ***braten***
Brikett [bri'kɛt] *n* (*-s; -s*) briquet(te)
brillant [brɪl'jant] *adj* brilliant
Bril'lant *m* (*-en; -en*) (cut) diamond
Bril'lantring *m* diamond ring
Brille ['brɪlə] *f* (*-; -n*) (pair of) glasses, spectacles; goggles; toilet seat
'Brillenetui *n* eyeglass (*Br* spectacle) case
Brillenträger(in) (*-s; -/-; -nen*) ***Brillenträger sein*** wear glasses
bringen ['brɪŋən] *v/t* (*irr, ge-, h*) bring; take; cause; make (*sacrifice*); yield (*profit*); ***j-n nach Hause bringen*** see (*or* take) s.o. home; ***in Ordnung bringen*** put in order; ***das bringt mich auf e-e Idee*** that gives me an idea; ***j-n dazu bringen, et. zu tun*** get s.o. to do s.th.; ***et. mit sich bringen*** involve s.th.; ***j-n um et. bringen*** deprive s.o. of s.th.; ***j-n zum Lachen bringen*** make s.o. laugh; ***j-n wieder zu sich bringen*** bring s.o. round; ***es zu et.*** (***nichts***) ***bringen*** go far (get nowhere); F ***es bringen*** make it; ***das bringt nichts*** it's no use
Brise ['bri:zə] *f* (*-; -n*) breeze
Brite ['brɪtə] *m* (*-n; -n*), **'Britin** *f* (*-; -nen*) Briton; ***die Briten*** *pl* the British
'britisch *adj* British
bröckeln ['brœkəln] *v/i* (*ge-, h, sein*) crumble
Brocken ['brɔkən] *m* (*-s; -*) piece; lump; rock; GASTR chunk; morsel; ***ein paar Brocken Englisch*** a few scraps of English; F ***ein harter Brocken*** a hard nut to crack
Brombeere ['brɔm-] *f* BOT blackberry
Bronchitis [brɔn'çi:tɪs] *f* (*-; -tiden* [brɔnçi'ti:dən]) MED bronchitis
Bronze ['brõ:sə] *f* (*-; -n*) bronze
Bronzezeit *f* (*-; no pl*) HIST Bronze Age
Brosche ['brɔʃə] *f* (*-; -n*) brooch, pin
broschiert [brɔ'ʃi:ɐt] *adj* paperback
Broschüre [brɔ'ʃy:rə] *f* (*-; -n*) pamphlet; brochure
Brot [bro:t] *n* (*-[e]s; -e*) bread; sandwich; ***ein*** (***Laib***) ***Brot*** a loaf (of bread); ***e-e Scheibe Brot*** a slice of bread; ***sein Brot verdienen*** earn one's living
Brötchen ['brø:tçən] *n* (*-s; -*) roll
'Brotrinde *f* crust
Brot(schneide)ma,schine *f* bread cutter
Bruch [brʊx] *m* (*-[e]s; Brüche* ['bryçə]) break; MED fracture; hernia; MATH fraction; GEOL fault; *fig* breach (*of promise etc*); JUR violation; ***zu Bruch gehen*** be wrecked
Bruchbude F *f* dump, hovel
brüchig ['bryçɪç] *adj* brittle
'Bruchlandung *f* AVIAT crash landing
Bruchrechnung *f* MATH fractional arithmetic, F fractions
'bruchsicher *adj* breakproof
'Bruchstrich *m* MATH fraction bar
Bruchstück *n* fragment
Bruchteil *m* fraction; ***im Bruchteil e-r Sekunde*** in a split second
Bruchzahl *f* MATH fraction(al) number
Brücke ['brʏkə] *f* (*-; -n*) bridge (*a.* SPORT); rug
'Brückenpfeiler *m* pier
Bruder ['bru:dɐ] *m* (*-s; Brüder* ['bry:dɐ]) brother (*a.* REL)
Bruderkrieg *m* civil war
brüderlich ['bry:dɐlɪç] **1.** *adj* brotherly; **2.** *adv*: ***brüderlich teilen*** share and share alike
'Brüderlichkeit *f* (*-; no pl*) brotherhood
'Brüderschaft *f*: ***Brüderschaft trinken*** *agree to use the familiar 'du' form of address*
Brühe ['bry:ə] *f* (*-; -n*) broth; stock; F dishwater; slops; F filthy water, bilge
'Brühwürfel *m* beef cube
brüllen ['brʏlən] *v/i* (*ge-, h*) roar (***vor Lachen*** with laughter); ZO bellow; F bawl; ***brüllendes Gelächter*** roars of laughter
brummen ['brʊmən] *v/i* (*ge-, h*) growl; ZO hum, buzz (*a. engine etc*); *head*: be buzzing
'brummig *adj* grumpy
brünett [bry'nɛt] *adj* brunette, dark-haired
Brunnen ['brʊnən] *m* (*-s; -*) well, spring, fountain
Brunstzeit ['brʊnst-] *f* ZO rutting season
Brust [brʊst] *f* (*-; Brüste* ['brʏstə]) ANAT a) (*no pl*) chest, b) breast(s), bosom
Brustbein *n* ANAT breastbone
Brustbeutel *m* neck pouch, *Br* money bag
brüsten ['brʏstən] *v/refl* (*ge-, h*) boast, brag (***mit*** of)
'Brustkasten *m*, **Brustkorb** *m* ANAT chest, thorax
Brustschwimmen *n* breaststroke
'Brüstung *f* (*-; -en*) parapet
'Brustwarze *f* ANAT nipple
Brut [bru:t] *f* (*-; -en*) ZO brooding; brood (*a.* F), hatch; fry
brutal [bru'ta:l] *adj* brutal
Brutalität [brutali'tɛ:t] *f* (*-; -en*) brutality
'Brutappa,rat *m* ZO incubator

brüten ['bryːtən] *v/i* (*ge-*, *h*) ZO brood, sit (on eggs); ***brüten über*** (*dat*) *fig* brood over
'**Brutkasten** *m* MED incubator
brutto ['bruto] *adv* ECON gross
'**Bruttoeinkommen** *n* ECON gross earnings
Bruttosozi,alpro,dukt *n* ECON gross national product
Bube ['buːbə] *m* (*-n*; *-n*) boy, lad; *card game*: knave, jack
Buch [buːx] *n* (*-[e]s*; *Bücher* ['byːçɐ]) book
Buchbinder *m* (*-s*; *-*) (book)binder
Buchdrucker *m* printer
Buchdruckerei *f* print shop, *Br* printing office
Buche ['buːxə] *f* (*-*; *-n*) BOT beech
'**buchen** *v/t* (*ge-*, *h*) book; ECON enter
Bücherbord ['byːçɐ-] *n* bookshelf
Bücherei [byːçə'rai] *f* (*-*; *-en*) library
'**Bücherre,gal** *n* bookshelf
'**Bücherschrank** *m* bookcase
'**Buchfink** *m* ZO chaffinch
Buchhalter(in) bookkeeper
Buchhaltung *f* (*-*; *no pl*) bookkeeping
Buchhändler(in) bookseller
Buchhandlung *f* bookstore, *Br* bookshop
Buchmacher *m* bookmaker
Büchse ['byksə] *f* (*-*; *-n*) can, *Br* tin; box; rifle
'**Büchsenfleisch** *n* canned (*Br* tinned) meat
Büchsenöffner *m* can (*Br* tin) opener
Buchstabe ['buːxʃtaːbə] *m* (*-n*; *-n*) letter; ***großer*** (***kleiner***) ***Buchstabe*** capital (small) letter
buchstabieren [buːxʃta'biːrən] *v/t* (*no -ge-*, *h*) spell
buchstäblich ['buːxʃtɛːplɪç] *adv* literally
'**Buchstütze** *f* bookend
Bucht ['buxt] *f* (*-*; *-en*) bay; creek, inlet
'**Buchung** *f* (*-*; *-en*) booking; ECON entry
Buckel ['bukəl] *m* (*-s*; *-*) hump, hunch; ***e-n Buckel machen*** hump *or* hunch one's back
bücken ['bykən] *v/refl* (*ge-*, *h*) bend (down), stoop
bucklig ['buklɪç] *adj* hunchbacked
Bucklige ['buklɪgə] *m*, *f* (*-n*; *-n*) hunchback
Bückling ['byklɪŋ] *m* (*-s*; *-e*) smoked herring, *Br* kipper
Buddhismus [bu'dɪsmus] *m* (*-*; *no pl*) Buddhism
Buddhist [bu'dɪst] *m* (*-en*; *-en*), **bud'dhistisch** *adj* Buddhist
Bude ['buːdə] *f* (*-n*; *-n*) stall, booth; hut; F pad, *Br* digs; *contp* shack, dump, hole
Budget [by'dʒeː] *n* (*-s*; *-s*) budget
Büfett [by'fɛt] *n* (*-[e]s*; *-s*, *-e*) counter, bar, buffet; sideboard, cupboard; ***kaltes Büfett*** GASTR cold buffet (meal)
Büffel ['byfəl] *m* (*-s*; *-*) ZO buffalo
'**büffeln** F *v/i* (*ge-*, *h*) grind, cram, swot
Bug [buːk] *m* (*-[e]s*; *-e*) MAR bow; AVIAT nose; ZO, GASTR shoulder
Bügel ['byːgəl] *m* (*-s*; *-*) hanger; bow
Bügelbrett *n* ironing board
Bügeleisen *n* iron
Bügelfalte *f* crease
'**bügelfrei** *adj* no(n)-iron
'**bügeln** *v/t* (*ge-*, *h*) iron, press
buh [buː] *int* boo!
buhen ['buːən] *v/i* (*ge-*, *h*) boo
Bühne ['byːnə] *f* (*-*; *-n*) stage, *fig a.* scene
'**Bühnenbild** *n* (stage) set(ting)
Bühnenbildner(in) (*-s*; *-/-*; *-nen*) stage designer
'**Buhrufe** *pl* boos
Bullauge ['bul-] *n* MAR porthole
'**Bulldogge** *f* ZO bulldog
Bulle ['bulə] *m* (*-n*; *-n*) ZO bull (*a. fig*); F *contp* cop, *pl the* fuzz
Bummel ['buməl] F *m* (*-s*; *-*) stroll
Bummelei [bumə'lai] *f* (*-*; *no pl*) F *contp* dawdling; slackness
'**bummeln** F *v/i* a) (*ge-*, *sein*) stroll, saunter, b) (*ge-*, *h*) *contp* dawdle; ECON go slow
'**Bummelstreik** *m* ECON slowdown, *Br* go-slow (strike)
Bummler ['bumlɐ] F *m* (*-s*; *-*) stroller; *contp* dawdler, slowpoke, *Br* slowcoach
bumsen ['bumzən] *v/i and v/t* (*ge-*, *h*) F → ***krachen***; V screw
Bund[1] [bunt] *m* (*-[e]s*; *Bünde* ['byndə]) union, federation, alliance; association; (waist)band; ***der Bund*** POL the Federal Government; F → ***Bundeswehr***
Bund[2] *n* (*-[e]s*; *-e*) bundle; bunch
Bündel ['byndəl] *n* (*-s*; *-*) bundle
'**bündeln** *v/t* (*ge-*, *h*) bundle (up)
Bundes... ['bundəs-] *in cpds* Federal ...; German ...
Bundesbahn *f* Federal Railroad(s)
Bundesgenosse *m* ally
Bundeskanzler(in) Federal Chancellor
Bundesland *n appr* (federal) state, Land
Bundesliga *f* SPORT First Division
Bundespost *f* Federal Postal Administration
Bundespräsi,dent *m* Federal President
Bundesrat *m* Bundesrat, Upper House of German Parliament
Bundesrepu,blik *f* Federal Republic
Bundesstaat *m* federal state; confederation
Bundesstraße *f* Federal Highway

Bundestag *m* (-[*e*]*s*; *no pl*) Bundestag, Lower House of German Parliament
Bundestrainer *m* coach of the (German) national team
Bundesverfassungsgericht *n* Federal Constitutional Court, *Am appr* Supreme Court
Bundeswehr *f* (-; *no pl*) MIL (German Federal) Armed Forces
bündig ['bʏndɪç] *adj* TECH flush; ***kurz und bündig*** terse(ly); point-blank
Bündnis ['bʏntnɪs] *n* (-*ses*; -*se*) alliance
Bunker ['bʊŋkɐ] *m* (-*s*; -) air-raid shelter, bunker
bunt [bʊnt] *adj* colo(u)red; multicolo(u)red; colo(u)rful (*a. fig*); varied; ***bunter Abend*** evening of entertainment; F ***mir wird's zu bunt*** that's all I can take
'Buntstift *m* colo(u)red pencil, crayon
Bürde ['bʏrdə] *f* (-; -*n*) burden (***für j-n*** to s.o.)
Burg [bʊrk] *f* (-; -*en*) castle
Bürge ['bʏrgə] *m* (-*n*; -*n*) JUR guarantor (*a. fig*)
'bürgen *v/i* (*ge-*, *h*) ***für j-n bürgen*** JUR stand surety for s.o.; ***für et. bürgen*** guarantee s.th.
Bürger ['bʏrgɐ] *m* (-*s*; -), **'Bürgerin** *f* (-; -*nen*) citizen
Bürgerinitia,tive *f* (citizen's *or* local) action group
Bürgerkrieg *m* civil war
'bürgerlich *adj* civil; middle-class; *esp contp* bourgeois; ***bürgerliche Küche*** home cooking
'Bürgerliche *m*, *f* (-*n*; -*n*) commoner
'Bürgermeister *m* mayor
Bürgerrechte *pl* civil rights
Bürgersteig [-ʃtaik] *m* (-[*e*]*s*; -*e*) sidewalk, *Br* pavement
'Bürgschaft *f* (-; -*en*) JUR surety; bail
Büro [by'ro:] *n* (-*s*; -*s*) office
Büroangestellte *m*, *f* (-*n*; -*n*) clerk, office worker
Büroklammer *f* (paper) clip
Bürokrat [byro'kra:t] *m* (-*en*; -*en*) bureaucrat
Bürokratie [byrokra'ti:] *f* (-; -*n*) bureaucracy; *contp* red tape
Bü'rostunden *pl* office hours
Bursche ['bʊrʃə] *m* (-*n*; -*n*) fellow, guy
burschikos [bʊrʃi'ko:s] *adj* (tom)boyish, pert
Bürste ['bʏrstə] *f* (-; -*n*) brush
'bürsten *v/t* (*ge-*, *h*) brush
'Bürstenschnitt *m* crew cut
Bus [bʊs] *m* (-*ses*; -*se*) bus; coach
Busch [bʊʃ] *m* (-[*e*]*s*; *Büsche* ['bʏʃə]) BOT bush, shrub
Büschel ['bʏʃəl] *n* (-*s*; -) bunch; tuft
'buschig *adj* bushy
Busen ['bu:zən] *m* (-*s*; -) ANAT bosom, breast(s)
'Busfahrer *m* bus driver
'Bushaltestelle *f* bus stop
Bussard ['bʊsart] *m* (-*s*; -*e*) ZO buzzard
Buße ['bu:sə] *f* (-; -*n*) REL penance; repentance; ***Buße tun*** do penanc
büßen ['by:sən] *v/t* (*ge-*, *h*) pay *or* suffer for *s.th.*; REL repent
'Bußgeld *n* fine, penalty
'Bußtag *m* REL day of repentance
Büste ['by:stə] *f* (-; -*n*) bust
'Büstenhalter *m* bra
Butter ['bʊtɐ] *f* (-; *no pl*) butter
Butterblume *f* BOT buttercup
Butterbrot *n* (slice *or* piece of) bread and butter; F ***für ein Butterbrot*** for a song
Butterbrotpa,pier *n* greaseproof paper
Butterdose *f* butter dish
Buttermilch *f* buttermilk
b.w. ABBR *of* ***bitte wenden*** PTO, please turn over
bzw. ABBR *of* ***beziehungsweise*** resp., respectively

C

C ABBR *of* ***Celsius*** C, Celsius, centigrade
ca. ABBR *of* ***circa*** approx., approximately
Café [ka'fe:] *n* (-*s*; -*s*) café, coffee house
campen ['kɛmpən] *v/i* (*ge-*, *h*) camp
Camper ['kɛmpɐ] *m* (-*s*; -) camper
Camping... ['kɛmpɪŋ-] *in cpds* ...*bett*, ...*tisch etc* camp ...
Campingbus *m* camper (van *Br*)
Campingplatz *m* campground, *Br* campsite
Catcher ['kɛtʃɐ] *m* (-*s*; -) wrestler
Casino [ka'zi:no] *n* → ***Kasino***

CD [tseː'deː] *f* (-; *-s*) CD, compact disk (*Br* disc)
C'D-ROM *f* CD-ROM
C'D-Spieler *m* CD player
Cellist [tʃɛ'lɪst] *m* (*-en*; *-en*), **Cel'listin** *f* (-; *-nen*) MUS cellist
Cello ['tʃɛlo] *n* (*-s*; *-s*, *Celli*) MUS Cello
Celsius ['tsɛlzjʊs] ***5 Grad Celsius*** (ABBR ***5° C***) five degrees centigrade *or* Celsius
Cembalo ['tʃɛmbalo] *n* (*-s*; *-s*, *-li*) MUS harpsichord
Champagner [ʃam'panjɐ] *m* (*-s*; -) champagne
Champignon ['ʃampɪnjɔŋ] *m* (*-s*; *-s*) BOT mushroom
Chance ['ʃãːsə] *f f* (-; *-n*) chance; ***die Chancen stehen gleich*** (***3 zu 1***) the odds are even (three to one)
'Chancengleichheit *f* equal opportunities
Chaos ['kaːɔs] *n* (-; *no pl*) chaos
Chaot [ka'oːt] *m* (*-en*; *-en*) chaotic person; POL anarchist, *pl a.* lunatic fringe
cha'otisch *adj* chaotic
Charakter [ka'raktɐ] *m* (*-s*; *-e* [-'teːrə]) character, nature
charakterisieren [-teri'ziːrən] *v/t* (*no -ge-*, *h*) characterize, describe (***als*** as)
charakteristisch [-te'rɪstɪʃ] *adj* characteristic, typical (***für*** of)
Cha'rakterzug *m* trait
charmant [ʃar'mant] *adj* charming
Charme [ʃarm] *m* (*-s*; *no pl*) charm
Chassis [ʃa'siː] *n* (-; -) TECH chassis
Chauffeur [ʃɔ'føːɐ] *m* (*-s*; *-e*) chauffeur, driver
Chauvi ['ʃoːvi] *m* (*-s*; *-s*) F male chauvinist (pig)
Chauvinismus [ʃovi'nɪsmʊs] *m* (-; *no pl*) chauvinism, POL *a.* jingoism
Chef [ʃɛf] *m* (*-s*; *-s*) head, chief, F boss
Chefarzt *m* medical director, *Br* senior consultant
Chefsekre,tärin *f* executive secretary
Chemie [çe'miː] *f* (-; *no pl*) chemistry
Chemiefaser *f* synthetic fiber (*Br* fibre)
Chemikalien [çemi'kaːljən] *pl* chemicals
Chemiker(in) ['çeːmikɐ (-kərɪn)] (*-s*; *-/-*; *-nen*) (analytical) chemist
chemisch ['çeːmɪʃ] *adj* chemical; ***chemische Reinigung*** dry cleaning
Chemothera'pie [çemo-] *f* MED chemotherapy
Chiffre ['ʃɪfrə] *f* (-; *-n*) code, cipher; box (number)
chiffrieren [ʃɪ'friːrən] *v/t* (*no -ge-*, *h*) (en)code
China ['çiːna] China
Chinese [çi'neːzə] *m* (*-n*; *-n*), **Chi'nesin** *f* (-; *-nen*), **chi'nesisch** *adj* Chinese
Chinin [çi'niːn] *n* (*-s*; *no pl*) PHARM quinine
Chip [tʃɪp] *m* (*-s*; *-s*) *a.* EDP chip; GASTR *pl* chips, *Br* crisps
Chirurg [çi'rʊrk] *m* (*-en*; *-en*) surgeon
Chirurgie [çirʊr'giː] *f* (-; *-n*) surgery
Chirurgin [çi'rʊrgɪn] *f* (-; *-nen*) surgeon
chirurgisch [çi'rʊrgɪʃ] *adj* surgical
Chlor [kloːɐ] *n* (*-s*; *no pl*) CHEM chlorine
chloren ['kloːrən] *v/t* (*ge-*, *h*) chlorinate
Cholera ['koːlera] *f* (-; *no pl*) MED cholera
cholerisch [ko'leːrɪʃ] *adj* choleric
Cholesterin [çolɛste'riːn] *n* (*-s*; *no pl*) MED cholesterol
Chor [koːɐ] *m* (*-[e]s*; *Chöre* ['køːrə]) MUS choir (*a.* ARCH); ***im Chor*** in chorus
Choral [ko'raːl] *m* (*-s*; *Choräle* [ko'rɛːlə]) MUS, REL chorale, hymn
Christ [krɪst] *m* (*-en*; *-en*) REL Christian
Christbaum *m* Christmas tree
'Christenheit: ***die Christenheit*** REL Christendom
'Christentum *n* (*-s*; *no pl*) REL Christianity
Christin ['krɪstɪn] *f* (-; *-nen*) REL Christian
'Christkind *n* Infant Jesus; Father Christmas, Santa Claus
'christlich *adj* REL Christian
Christus ['krɪstʊs] REL Christ; ***vor Christus*** B.C.; ***nach Christus*** A.D.
Chrom [kroːm] *n* (*-s*; *no pl*) chrome, CHEM *a.* chromium
Chromosom [kromo'zoːm] *n* (*-s*; *-en*) BIOL chromosome
Chronik ['kroːnɪk] *f* (-; *-en*) chronicle
chronisch ['kroːnɪʃ] *adj* MED chronic
chronologisch [krono'loːgɪʃ] *adj* chronological
circa → ***zirka***
City ['sɪtɪ] *f* (-; *-s*) downtown, (city) center, *Br* centre
Clique ['klɪkə] *f* (-; *-n*) F group, set; *contp* clique
Clou [kluː] F *m* (*-s*; *-s*) highlight, climax; ***der Clou daran*** the whole point of it
Compact Disc, **Compact Disk** ['kəmpæktdɪsk] *f* (-; *-s*) compact disk (*Br* disc)
Computer [kɔm'pjuːtɐ] *m* (*-s*; -) computer
Computerausdruck *m* computer printout
com'putergesteuert *adj* computer-controlled
computergestützt *adj* computer-aided
Com'putergrafik *f* computer graphics
computerisieren [kɔmpjutəri'ziːrən] *v/t* (*no -ge-*, *h*) computerize
Com'puterspiel *n* computer game
Computervirus *m* EDP computer virus

Conférencier [kõferã'sjeː] *m* (*-s*; *-s*) master of ceremonies, F emcee, MC, *Br* compère
Cord *etc* → ***Kord*** *etc*
Couch [kautʃ] *f* (*-*; *-s*) couch
Coupé [ku'peː] *n* (*-s*; *-s*) MOT coupé
Coupon → ***Kupon***
Cousin [ku'zɛ̃ː] *m* (*-s*; *-s*), **Cousine** [ku'ziːnə] *f* (*-*; *-n*) cousin
Creme [kreːm] *f* (*-*; *-s*) cream (*a. fig*)
Curry ['kari] *m* (*-s*; *-s*) curry powder
Cursor ['kɜːsə] *m* (*-s*; *-s*) EDP cursor

D

D

da [daː] **1.** *adv space*: there; here; *time*: then, at that time; ***da drüben*** (***draußen, hinten***) over (out, back) there; ***von da aus*** from there; ***das … da*** that … (over there); ***da kommt er*** here he comes; ***da bin ich*** here I am; ***da sein*** be there; exist; ***ist noch … da?*** is any … left?; ***noch nie da gewesen*** unprecedented; ***er ist gleich wieder da*** he'll be right back; ***von da an*** *or* ***ab*** from then on; **2.** *cj* as, since, because
'dabehalten *v/t* (*irr*, ***halten***, *sep*, *no -ge-*, *h*) keep; ***j-n dabehalten*** keep s.o. in
dabei [da'bai] *adv* there, present; near *or* close by; at the same time; included with it; ***dabei sein*** be there; take part; be in on it; ***ich bin dabei!*** count me in!; ***er ist gerade dabei zu gehen*** he's just leaving; ***es ist nichts dabei*** there's nothing to it; there's no harm in it; ***was ist schon dabei?*** (so) what of it?; ***lassen wir es dabei!*** let's leave it at that!
dabeibleiben *v/i* (*irr*, ***bleiben***, *sep*, *-ge-*, *sein*) stick to it
dabeihaben F *v/t* (*irr*, ***haben***, *sep*, *-ge-*, *h*) have with (*or* on) one
'dableiben *v/i* (*irr*, ***bleiben***, *sep*, *-ge-*, *sein*) stay
Dach [dax] *n* (*-[e]s*; *Dächer* ['dɛçɐ]) roof
'Dachboden *m* attic
Dachdecker [-dekɐ] *m* (*-s*; *-*) roofer
Dachfenster *n* dormer window
Dachgepäckträger *m* MOT roof-rack
'Dachgeschoss *n*, **'Dachgeschoß** *Austrian n* attic
Dachgeschosswohnung *f* loft apartment, *Br* attic flat
'Dachkammer *f* garret
Dachluke *f* skylight
Dachpappe *f* roofing felt
Dachrinne *f* gutter
Dachs [daks] *m* (*-es*; *-e*) ZO badger
'Dachstuhl *m* roof framework
dachte ['daxtə] *pret of* ***denken***
'Dachter‚rasse *f* roof terrace
'Dachverband *m* ECON *etc* umbrella organization
Dackel ['dakəl] *m* (*-s*; *-*) ZO dachshund
'dadurch *adv and cj* this *or* that way; for this reason, so; ***dadurch, dass*** due to the fact that
dafür [da'fyːɐ] *adv* for it, for that; instead; in return, in exchange; ***dafür sein*** be in favo(u)r of it; ***er kann nichts dafür*** it is not his fault; ***dafür sorgen, dass*** see to it that
da'gegen *adv and cj* against it; however, on the other hand; ***dagegen sein*** be against (*or* opposed to) it; ***haben Sie et. dagegen, dass ich …?*** do you mind if I …?; ***wenn Sie nichts dagegen haben*** if you don't mind; ***… ist nichts dagegen*** … can't compare
da'heim *adv* at home
'daher *adv and cj* from there; that's why
da'hin *adv* there, to that place; gone, past; ***bis dahin*** till then; up to there
da'hinten *adv* back there
da'hinter *adv* behind it; ***es steckt nichts dahinter*** there is nothing to it; F ***dahinter kommen*** find out (about it)
'dalassen F *v/t* (*irr*, ***lassen***, *sep*, *-ge-*, *h*) leave behind
damalig ['daːmaːlɪç] *adj* then
damals ['daːmaːls] *adv* then, at that time
Dame ['daːmə] *f* (*-*; *-n*) lady; partner; *cards*, *chess*: queen; checkers, *Br* draughts
'Damen… *in cpds* ladies' …; SPORT women's …
Damenbinde *f* sanitary napkin (*Br* towel)
'damenhaft *adj* ladylike
'Damentoi‚lette *f* ladies' room (*Br* toilet), *the* ladies
Damenwahl *f* ladies' choice
damit **1.** ['daːmɪt] *adv* with it *or* that; by it,

D

with it; ***was will er damit sagen?*** what's he trying to say?; ***wie steht es damit?*** how about it?; ***damit einverstanden sein*** have no objections; **2.** [da'mɪt] *cj* so that; in order to *inf*; ***damit nicht*** so as not to *inf*
Damm [dam] *m* (-[*e*]*s*; *Dämme* ['dɛmə]) dam; embankment
dämmerig ['dɛmərɪç] *adj* dim
'Dämmerlicht *n* (-[*e*]*s*; *no pl*) twilight
dämmern ['dɛmɐn] *v/i* (*ge-*, *h*) dawn (*a.* F ***j-m*** on s.o.); get dark *or* dusky
'Dämmerung *f* (-; *-en*) dusk; dawn
Dämon ['dɛːmɔn] *m* (*-s*; *-en* [dɛ'moːnən]) demon
dämonisch [dɛ'moːnɪʃ] *adj* demoniac(al)
Dampf [dampf] *m* (-[*e*]*s*; *Dämpfe* ['dɛmpfə]) steam; PHYS vapo(u)r
'dampfen *v/i* (*ge-*, *h and sein*) steam
dämpfen ['dɛmpfən] *v/t* (*ge-*, *h*) deaden; muffle (*voice*); soften (*light*, *sound*, *blow*); GASTR steam, stew; steam-iron; *fig* put a damper on; curb (*a.* ECON)
Dampfer ['dampfɐ] *m* (*-s*; -) steamer, steamship
'Dampfkochtopf *m* pressure cooker
Dampfma͵schine *f* steam engine
Dampfschiff *n* steamer, steamship
da'nach *adv* after it *or* that; afterwards; for it; according to it; ***ich fragte ihn danach*** I asked him about it; F ***mir ist nicht danach*** I don't feel like it
Däne ['dɛːnə] *m* (*-n*; *-n*) Dane
da'neben *adv* next to it, beside it; besides, as well, at the same time; beside the mark
danebenbenehmen F *v/refl* (*irr*, ***nehmen***, *sep*, *no -ge-*, *h*) step out of line
danebengehen F *v/i* (*irr*, ***gehen***, *sep*, *-ge-*, *sien*) miss (the target); F misfire
'Dänemark Denmark
Dänin ['dɛːnɪn] *f* (-; *-nen*) Danish woman *or* girl
'dänisch *adj* Danish
dank [daŋk] *prp* (*gen*) thanks to
Dank *m* (-[*e*]*s*; *no pl*) thanks; ***Gott sei Dank!*** thank God!; ***vielen Dank!*** many thanks!
'dankbar *adj* grateful (***j-m*** to s.o.); rewarding (*task etc*)
'Dankbarkeit *f* (-; *no pl*) gratitude
'danken *v/i* (*ge-*, *h*) thank (***j-m für et.*** s.o. for s.th.); ***danke*** (***schön***) thank you (very much); (***nein***,) ***danke*** no, thank you; ***nichts zu danken*** not at all
dann [dan] *adv* then; ***dann und wann*** (every) now and then
daran [da'ran] *adv* on it; *die*, *think etc* of it; *believe etc* in it; *suffer etc* from it; → ***liegen***
darauf [da'rauf] *adv* on (top of) it; after (that); *listen*, *drink etc* to it; *proud etc* of it; *wait etc* for it; ***am Tage darauf*** the day after; ***zwei Jahre darauf*** two years later; ***darauf kommt es an*** that's what matters
darauf'hin *adv* after that; as a result
daraus [da'raus] *adv* from (*or* out of) it; ***was ist daraus geworden?*** what has become of it?; ***daraus wird nichts!*** F nothing doing!
Darbietung ['daːɐbiːtʊŋ] *f* (-; *-en*) presentation; performance
darin [da'rɪn] *adv* in it; ['daːrɪn] in that
darlegen ['daːɐ-] *v/t* (*sep*, *-ge-*, *h*) explain, set out
Darlehen ['daːɐleːən] *n* (*-s*; -) loan; ***ein Darlehen geben*** grant a loan
Darm [darm] *m* (-[*e*]*s*; *Därme* ['dɛrmə]) ANAT bowel(s), intestine(s); GASTR skin
Darmgrippe *f* MED intestinal flu
darstellen ['daːɐ-] *v/t* (*sep*, *-ge-*, *h*) represent, show, depict; describe; THEA play, do; trace, graph
'Darsteller(in) (*-s*; *-/-*; *-nen*) THEA performer, actor (actress)
'Darstellung *f* (-; *-en*) representation; description; account; portrayal
darüber [da'ryːbɐ] *adv* over *or* above it; across it; in the meantime; *write*, *talk etc* about it; ***... und darüber*** ... and more; ***darüber werden Jahre vergehen*** that will take years
darum [da'rʊm] *adv and cj* (a)round it; because of it, that's why; ***darum bitten*** ask for it; → ***gehen***
darunter [da'rʊntɐ] *adv* under *or* below it, underneath; among them; including; ***... und darunter*** ... and less; ***was verstehst du darunter?*** what do you understand by it?
das [das] → ***der***
'Dasein *n* (*-s*; *no pl*) life, existence
dass [das] *cj* that; so (that); ***es sei denn, dass*** unless; ***nicht dass ich wüsste*** not that I know of
'dastehen *v/i* (*irr*, ***stehen***, *sep*, *-ge-*, *h*) stand (there)
Datei [da'tai] *f* (-; *-en*) EDP file
Dateiverwaltung *f* EDP file management
Daten ['daːtən] *pl* data (*a.* EDP), facts; particulars
Datenbank *f* (-; *-en*) EDP database, data bank
Datenschutz *m* JUR data protection
Datenspeicher *m* data memory *or* storage
Datenträger *m* data medium *or* carrier

Datenübertragung *f* data transfer
Datenverarbeitung *f* data processing
datieren [da'tiːrən] *v/t and v/i* (*no -ge-, h*) date
Dativ ['daːtiːf] *m* (*-s; -e*) dative (case)
Dattel ['datəl] *f* (*-; -n*) BOT date
Datum ['daːtʊm] *n* (*-s; Daten* ['daːtən]) date; ***welches Datum haben wir heute?*** what's the date today?
Dauer ['dauɐ] *f* (*-; no pl*) duration; continuance; ***auf die Dauer*** in the long run; ***für die Dauer von*** for a period *or* term of; ***von Dauer sein*** last
Dauerarbeitslosigkeit *f* long-term unemployment
Dauerauftrag *m* ECON standing order
Dauergeschwindigkeit *f* MOT *etc* cruising speed
'**dauerhaft** *adj* lasting; durable
'**Dauerkarte** *f* season ticket
Dauerlauf *m* SPORT jogging; ***im Dauerlauf*** at a jog
Dauerlutscher *m* lollipop
dauern *v/i* (*ge-, h*) last, take; → ***lange***
'**Dauerwelle** *f* permanent, *Br* perm
Daumen ['daumən] *m* (*-s; -*) ANAT thumb; F ***j-m den Daumen halten*** keep one's fingers crossed (for s.o.); ***am Daumen lutschen*** suck one's thumb
Daunen ['daunən] *pl* down
'**Daunendecke** *f* eiderdown
da'von *adv* (away) from it; by it; about it; away; of it *or* them; ***et. davon haben*** get s.th. out of it; ***das kommt davon!*** there you are!, that will teach you!
davonkommen *v/i* (*irr*, ***kommen***, *sep, -ge-, sein*) escape, get away
davonlaufen *v/i* (*irr*, ***laufen***, *sep, -ge-, sein*) run away
da'vor *adv* before it; in front of it; *be afraid, warn s.o. etc* of it
da'zu *adv* for it, for that purpose; in addition; ***noch dazu*** into the bargain; ***dazu ist es da*** that's what it's there for; ***Salat dazu?*** a salad with it?; → ***kommen***, ***Lust***
dazugehören *v/i* (*sep, no -ge-, h*) belong to it, be part of it
dazugehörig *adj* belonging to it
dazukommen *v/i* (*irr*, ***kommen***, *sep, -ge-, sein*) join *s.o.*; be added
da'zwischen *adv* between (them); in between; among them
dazwischenkommen *v/i* (*irr*, ***kommen***, *sep, -ge-, sein*) intervene, happen; ***wenn nichts dazwischenkommt*** if all goes well
DB [deː'beː] ABBR *of* ***Deutsche Bahn*** German Rail
dealen ['diːlən] *v/i* (*ge-, h*) F push drugs
Dealer ['diːlɐ] *m* (*-s; -*) drug dealer, F pusher
Debatte [de'batə] *f* (*-; -n*) debate
debattieren [deba'tiːrən] *v/i* (*no -ge-, h*) debate (***über*** *acc* on)
Debüt [de'byː] *n* (*-s; -s*) debut; ***sein Debüt geben*** make your debut
dechiffrieren [deʃɪ'friːrən] *v/t* (*no -ge-, h*) decipher, decode
Deck [dɛk] *n* (*-[e]s; -s*) MAR deck
Decke ['dɛkə] *f* (*-; -n*) blanket; quilt; ARCH ceiling
Deckel ['dɛkəl] *m* (*-s; -*) lid, cover, top
'**decken** *v/t and v/i* (*ge-, h*) cover (*a.* ZO), SPORT *a.* mark; ***sich decken*** (***mit***) coincide (with); → ***Tisch***
'**Deckung** *f* (*-; no pl*) cover; *boxing*: guard; ***in Deckung gehen*** take cover
defekt [de'fɛkt] *adj* defective, faulty; TECH out of order
De'fekt *m* (*-[e]s; -e*) defect, fault
defensiv [defɛn'siːf] *adj*, **Defensive** [-'ziːvə] *f* (*-; no pl*) defensive
definieren [defi'niːrən] *v/t* (*no -ge-, h*) define
Definition [defini'tsjoːn] *f* (*-; -en*) definition
Defizit ['deːfitsɪt] *n* (*-s; -e*) deficit; deficiency
Degen ['deːgən] *m* (*-s; -*) sword; *fencing*: épée
degradieren [degra'diːrən] *v/t* (*no -ge-, h*) degrade (*a. fig*)
dehnbar ['deːnbaːɐ] *adj* flexible, elastic (*a. fig*)
dehnen ['deːnən] *v/t* (*ge-, h*) stretch (*a. fig*)
Deich [daiç] *m* (*-[e]s; -e*) dike
Deichsel ['daiksəl] *f* (*-; -n*) pole, shaft
dein [dain] *poss pron* your; ***deiner, deine, dein(e)s*** yours
deinerseits ['dainɐ'zaits] *adv* on your part
deines'gleichen ['dainəs-] *pron contp* the likes of you
deinetwegen ['dainət'veːgən] *adv* for your sake; because of you
Dekan [de'kaːn] *m* (*-s; -e*), **De'kanin** *f* (*-; -nen*) REL, UNIV dean
Deklination [deklina'tsjoːn] *f* (*-; -en*) LING declension
deklinieren [dekli'niːrən] *v/t* (*no -ge-, h*) decline
Dekolleté [dekɔl'teː] *n* (*-s; -s*) low neckline
Dekorateur [dekora'tøːɐ] *m* (*-s; -e*), **Dekora'teurin** *f* (*-; -nen*) decorator; window dresser
Dekoration [-'tsjoːn] *f* (*-; -en*) decoration;

D

(window) display; THEA scenery
dekorativ [-'ti:f] *adj* decorative
dekorieren [deko'ri:rən] *v/t* (*no -ge-*, *h*) decorate; dress

D

Delfin → ***Delphin***
delikat [deli'ka:t] *adj* delicious, exquisite; *fig* delicate, ticklish
Delikatesse [delika'tɛsə] *f* (-; *-n*) delicacy
Delika'tessenladen *m* delicatessen, F deli
Delphin [dɛl'fi:n] *m* (*-s*; *-e*) ZO dolphin
Dementi [de'mɛnti] *n* (*-s*; *-s*) (official) denial
dementieren [demɛn'ti:rən] *v/t* (*no -ge-*, *h*) deny (officially)
dementsprechend, **demgemäß** ['de:m-] *adv* accordingly
'demnach *adv* according to that
'demnächst *adv* shortly, before long
Demo ['de:mo] F *f* (-; *-s*) demo
Demokrat [demo'kra:t] *m* (*-en*; *-en*) democrat
Demokratie [demokra'ti:] *f* (-; *-n*) democracy
Demo'kratin *f* (-; *-nen*) democrat
demo'kratisch *adj* democratic
demolieren [demo'li:rən] *v/t* (*no -ge-*, *h*) demolish, wreck
Demonstrant [demɔn'strant] *m* (*-en*; *-en*), **Demon'strantin** *f* (-; *-nen*) demonstrator
Demonstration [-stra'tsjo:n] *f* (-; *-en*) demonstration
demonstrieren [-'stri:rən] *v/t and v/i* (*no -ge-*, *h*) demonstrate
demontieren [demɔn'ti:rən] *v/t* (*no -ge-*, *h*) dismantle
demoralisieren [demorali'zi:rən] *v/t* (*no -ge-*, *h*) demoralize
Demoskopie [demosko'pi:] *f* (-; *-n*) public opinion research
Demut ['de:mu:t] *f* (-; *no pl*) humility, humbleness
demütig ['de:my:tɪç] *adj* humble
demütigen ['de:my:tɪgən] *v/t* (*ge-*, *h*) humiliate
'Demütigung *f* (-; *-en*) humiliation
denkbar ['dɛŋkba:ɐ] **1.** *adj* conceivable; **2.** *adv*: ***denkbar einfach*** most simple
denken ['dɛŋkən] *v/t and v/i* (*irr*, *ge-*, *h*) think (***an*** *acc*, ***über*** *acc* of, about); ***daran denken*** (***zu*** *inf*) remember (to *inf*)
'Denkfa,brik *f* think tank
'Denkmal *n* monument; memorial
'denkwürdig *adj* memorable
denn [dɛn] *cj and adv* for, because; ***es sei denn, dass*** unless; ***mehr denn je*** more than ever
dennoch ['dɛnnɔx] *cj* yet, still, nevertheless
Denunziant [denʊn'tsjant] *m* (*-en*; *-en*) informer
denunzieren [-'tsi:rən] *v/t* (*no -ge-*, *h*) inform on *or* against
Deodorant [de'odo'rant] *n* (*-s*; *-e*, *-s*) deodorant
Deponie [depo'ni:] *f* (-; *-n*) dump, waste disposal site
deponieren [depo'ni:rən] *v/t* (*no -ge-*, *h*) deposit, leave
Depot [de'po:] *n* (*-s*; *-s*) depot (*a.* MIL); *Swiss*: deposit
Depression [deprɛ'sjo:n] *f* (-; *-en*) depression (*a.* ECON)
depressiv [deprɛ'si:f] *adj* depressive
deprimieren [depri'mi:rən] *v/t* (*no -ge-*, *h*) depress
deprimierend *adj* depressing
deprimiert [depri'mi:ɐt] *adj* depressed
der [de:ɐ], **die** [di:], **das** [das] **1.** *art* the; **2.** *dem pron* that, this; he, she, it; ***die*** *pl* these, those, they; **3.** *rel pron* who, which, that
'derartig **1.** *adv* so (much); like that; **2.** *adj* such (as this)
derb [dɛrp] *adj* coarse; tough, sturdy
'der'gleichen *dem pron*: ***nichts dergleichen*** nothing of the kind
'der-, **'die-**, **'dasjenige** [-je:nɪgə] *dem pron* the one; ***diejenigen*** *pl* the ones, those
dermaßen ['de:ɐ'ma:sən] *adv* so (much), like that
Dermatologe [dɛrmato'lo:gə] *m* (*-n*; *-n*), **Dermato'login** *f* (-; *-nen*) dermatologist
der-, **die-**, **dasselbe** [-'zɛlbə] *dem pron* the same
Deserteur [dezɛr'tø:ɐ] *m* (*-s*; *-e*) MIL deserter
desertieren [dezɛr'ti:rən] *v/i* (*no -ge-*, *sein*) MIL desert
deshalb ['dɛs'halp] *cj and adv* therefore, for that reason, that is why, so
Desinfektionsmittel [dɛsʔɪnfɛk'tsjo:ns-] *n* MED disinfectant
desinfizieren [dɛsʔɪnfi'tsi:rən] *v/t* (*no -ge-*, *h*) MED disinfect
'Desinteresse *n* (*-s*; *no pl*) indifference
'desinteres,siert *adj* uninterested, indifferent
destillieren [dɛstɪ'li:rən] *v/t* (*no -ge-*, *h*) distil(l)
desto ['dɛsto] *cj and adv* → ***je***
'des'wegen *cj and adv* → ***deshalb***
Detail [de'tai] *n* (*-s*; *-s*) detail
detailliert [deta'ji:ɐt] *adj* detailed
Detektiv [detɛk'ti:f] *m* (*-s*; *-e*) detective
deuten ['dɔʏtən] (*ge-*, *h*) **1.** *v/t* interpret; **2.** *v/i*: ***deuten auf*** (*acc*) point at
'deutlich *adj* clear, distinct, plain

deutsch [dɔytʃ] *adj* German; ***auf Deutsch*** in German
'**Deutsche** *m, f (-n; -n)* German
'**Deutschland** Germany
Devise [de'vi:zə] *f (-; -n)* motto
De'visen *pl* ECON foreign currency
Dezember [de'tsɛmbɐ] *m (-[s]; -)* December
dezent [de'tsɛnt] *adj* discreet, unobtrusive; conservative *(clothes etc)*; soft *(music etc)*
Dezimal... [detsi'ma:l-] MATH *in cpds ...bruch, ...system etc*: decimal ...
Dezimalstelle *f* MATH decimal (place)
DGB [de:ge:'be:] ABBR *of* ***Deutscher Gewerkschaftsbund*** Federation of German Trade Unions
d. h. ABBR *of* ***das heißt*** i. e., that is
Dia ['di:a] *n (-s; -s)* PHOT slide
Diagnose [dia'gno:zə] *f (-; -n)* diagnosis
diagonal [diago'na:l] *adj*, **Diago'nale** *f (-; -n)* diagonal
Dialekt [dia'lɛkt] *m (-[e]s; -e)* dialect
Dialog [dia'lo:k] *m (-[e]s; -e)* dialog, *Br* dialogue
Diamant [dia'mant] *m (-en; -en)* diamond
'**Diapro͵jektor** *m* slide projector
Diät [di'ɛ:t] *f (-; -en)* diet; ***e-e Diät machen*** (***Diät leben***) be on (keep to) a diet
Di'äten *pl* PARL allowance
dich [dɪç] *pers pron* you; ***dich (selbst)*** yourself
dicht [dɪçt] **1.** *adj* dense, *a.* thick *(fog)*; heavy *(traffic)*; F closed, shut; **2.** *adv*: ***dicht an*** *(dat) or* ***bei*** close to
'**dichten** *v/t and v/i (ge-, h)* write (poetry)
Dichter(in) ['dɪçtɐ (-tərɪn)] *(-s; -/-; -nen)* poet; writer
dichterisch ['dɪçtərɪʃ] *adj* poetic; ***dichterische Freiheit*** poetic licen|se, *Br* -ce
'**dichthalten** F *v/i (irr,* ***halten****, sep, -ge-, h)* keep mum
'**Dichtung**[1] *f (-; -en)* TECH seal(ing)
'**Dichtung**[2] *f (-; -en)* poetry
dick [dɪk] *adj* thick; fat; ***es macht dick*** it's fattening
'**Dicke** *f (-; -n)* thickness; fatness;
'**dickfellig** F *adj* thick-skinned
'**dickflüssig** *adj* thick; TECH viscous
Dickicht ['dɪkɪçt] *n (-[e]s; -e)* thicket
'**Dickkopf** *m* stubborn *or* pig-headed person
Dickmilch *f* soured milk
Dieb [di:p] *m (-[e]s; -e* ['di:bə]*)*, **Diebin** ['di:bɪn] *f (-; -nen)* thief
diebisch ['di:bɪʃ] *adj* thievish; *fig* malicious *(glee etc)*
Diebstahl ['di:pʃta:l] *m (-[e]s; -stähle* [-ʃtɛ:lə]*)* theft; JUR *mst* larceny
Diele ['di:lə] *f (-; -n)* board, plank; hallway, *Br a.* hall
dienen ['di:nən] *v/i (ge-, h)* serve (***j-m*** s.o.; ***als*** as)
Diener ['di:nɐ] *m (-s; -)* servant; *fig* bow (***vor*** *dat* to)
Dienst [di:nst] *m (-[e]s; -e)* service; work; ***Dienst haben*** be on duty; ***im (außer) Dienst*** on (off) duty; ***Dienst tuend*** on duty
Dienst... *in cpds ...wagen, ...wohnung etc*: official ..., company ..., business ...
'**Dienstag** *m (-[e]s; -e)* Tuesday
'**Dienstalter** *n* seniority, length of service
'**dienstbereit** *adj* on duty
diensteifrig *adj (contp* over-)eager
'**Dienstgrad** *m* grade, rank (*a.* MIL)
'**Dienstleistung** *f* service
'**dienstlich** *adj* official
'**Dienstreise** *f* business trip
'**Dienststunden** *pl* office hours
'**Dienstweg** *m* official channels
dies [di:s], **dieser** ['di:zɐ], **diese** ['di:zə], **dieses** ['di:zəs] *dem pron* this; this one; ***diese*** *pl* these
diesig ['di:zɪç] *adj* hazy, misty
'**diesjährig** [-jɛ:rɪç] *adj* this year's
'**diesmal** *adv* this time
'**diesseits** [-zaits] *prp (gen)* on this side of
'**Diesseits** *n (-; no pl)* this life *or* world
Dietrich ['di:trɪç] *m (-s; -e)* TECH picklock, skeleton key
Differenz [dɪfə'rɛnts] *f (-; -en)* difference; disagreement
differenzieren [dɪfərɛn'tsi:rən] *v/i (no -ge-, h)* distinguish
Digital... [digi'ta:l] *in cpds ...anzeige, ...uhr etc*: digital ...
Diktat [dɪk'ta:t] *n (-[e]s; -e)* dictation
Diktator [dɪk'ta:to:ɐ] *m (-s; -en)* [dɪkta'to:rən]) dictator
diktatorisch [dɪkta'to:rɪʃ] *adj* dictatorial
Diktatur [dɪkta'tu:ɐ] *f (-; -en)* dictatorship
diktieren [dɪk'ti:rən] *v/t and v/i (no -ge-, h)* dictate
Dik'tiergerät *n* Dictaphone®
Dilettant [dilɛ'tant] *m (-en; -en)* amateur
dilet'tantisch *adj* amateurish
DIN [di:n] ABBR *of* ***Deutsches Institut für Normung*** German Institute for Standardization
Ding [dɪŋ] *n (-[e]s; -e)* thing; ***vor allen Dingen*** above all; F ***ein Ding drehen*** pull a job
'**Dings(bums)** *m, f, n*, **Dingsda** *m, f, n* F thingamajig, whatchamacallit
Dinosaurier [dino'zaurjɐ] *m (-s; -)* ZO dinosaur
Dioxid ['di:ʔɔksy:t] *n (-s; -e)* CHEM dioxide

D

Dioxin [dio'ksi:n] *n* (-*s*; -*e*) CHEM dioxin
Diphtherie [dɪfte'ri:] *f* (-; -*n*) MED diphtheria
Diplom [di'plo:m] *n* (-*s*; -*e*) diploma, degree
Diplom... *in cpds ...ingenieur etc*: qualified ..., graduate ...
Diplomat [diplo'ma:t] *m* (-*en*; -*en*) diplomat
Diplomatie [diploma'ti:] *f* (-; *no pl*) diplomacy
Diplo'matin *f* (-; -*nen*) diplomat
diplo'matisch *adj* diplomatic (*a. fig*)
dir [di:ɐ] *pers pron* (to) you; ***dir* (*selbst*)** yourself
direkt [di'rɛkt] **1.** *adj* direct; TV live; **2.** *adv* direct; *fig* directly, right; TV live; ***direkt gegenüber* (*von*)** right across
Direktion [dirɛk'tsjo:n] *f* (-; -*en*) management
Direktor [di'rɛkto:ɐ] *m* (-*s*; -*en* [dirɛk'to:rən]) director, manager; PED principal, *Br* headmaster
Direktorin [dirɛk'to:rɪn] (-; -*nen*) director, manager; PED principal, *Br* headmistress
Di'rektübertragung *f* TV live transmission *or* broadcast
Dirigent [diri'gɛnt] *m* (-*en*; -*en*) conductor
dirigieren [diri'gi:rən] *v/t and v/i* (*no -ge-, h*) MUS conduct; *fig* direct
Dirne ['dɪrnə] *f* (-; -*n*) prostitute, whore
Disharmo'nie [dɪs-] *f* MUS dissonance (*a. fig*)
dishar'monisch *adj* MUS discordant
Diskette [dɪs'kɛtə] *f* (-; -*n*) EDP diskette, floppy (disk)
Dis'kettenlaufwerk *n* EDP disk drive
Disko ['dɪsko] *f* (-; -*s*) disco
Diskont [dɪs'kɔnt] *m* (-*s*; -*e*) ECON discount
Diskothek [dɪsko'te:k] (-; -*en*) disco, discotheque
diskret [dɪs'kre:t] *adj* discreet
Diskretion [dɪskre'tsjo:n] *f* (-; *no pl*) discretion
diskriminieren [dɪskrimi'ni:rən] *v/t* (*no -ge-, h*) discriminate against
Diskrimi'nierung *f* (-; -*en*) discrimination (***von*** against)
Diskussion [dɪskʊ'sjo:n] *f* (-; -*en*) discussion, debate
Diskussi'onsleiter *m* (panel) chairman
Diskussionsrunde *f*, **Diskussionsteilnehmer** *pl* panel
Diskuswerfen ['dɪskʊs-] *n* (-*s*; *no pl*) SPORT discus throwing
diskutieren [dɪsku'ti:rən] *v/t and v/i* (*no -ge-, h*) discuss
Disqualifikati'on *f* SPORT disqualification (***wegen*** for)
disqualifi'zieren *v/t* (*no -ge-, h*) SPORT disqualify
Dissident [dɪsi'dɛnt] *m* (-*en*; -*en*), **Dissi'dentin** *f* (-; -*nen*) POL dissident
Distanz [dɪs'tants] *f* (-; -*en*) distance
distanzieren [dɪstan'tsi:rən] *v/refl* (*no -ge-, h*) distance o.s. (***von*** from)
Distel ['dɪstəl] *f* (-; -*n*) BOT thistle
Distrikt [dɪs'trɪkt] *m* (-[*e*]*s*; -*e*) district
Disziplin [dɪstsi'pli:n] *f* (-; -*en*) a) (*no pl*) discipline, b) SPORT event
diszipliniert [dɪstsipli'ni:ɐt] *adj* disciplined
divers [di'vɛrs] *adj* various; several
Dividende [divi'dɛndə] *f* (-; -*n*) ECON dividend
dividieren [divi'di:rən] *v/t* (*no -ge-, h*) MATH divide (***durch*** by)
Division [divi'zjo:n] *f* (-; -*en*) MATH, MIL division
DJH [de:jɔt'ha:] ABBR *of* ***Deutsches Jugendherbergswerk*** German Youth Hostel Association
DM [de:'ɛm] ABBR *of* ***Deutsche Mark*** German mark(s)
doch [dɔx] *cj and adv* but, however, yet; ***kommst du nicht* (*mit*)*? - doch!*** aren't you coming? - (oh) yes, I am!; ***ich war es nicht- doch!*** I didn't do it - yes, you did!; ***er kam also doch?*** so he did come after all?; ***du kommst doch?*** you're coming, aren't you?; ***kommen Sie doch herein!*** do come in!; ***wenn doch ...!*** if only ...!
Docht [dɔxt] *m* (-[*e*]*s*; -*e*) wick
Dock [dɔk] *n* (-*s*; -*s*) MAR dock
Dogge ['dɔgə] *f* (-; -*n*) ZO mastiff; Great Dane
Dogma ['dɔgma] *n* (-*s*; *Dogmen* ['dɔgmən]) dogma
dogmatisch [dɔg'ma:tɪʃ] *adj* dogmatic
Dohle ['do:lə] *f* (-; -*n*) ZO (jack)daw
Doktor ['dɔkto:ɐ] *m* (-*s*; -*en* [dɔk'to:rən]) doctor; UNIV doctor's degree
Doktorarbeit *f* UNIV (doctoral *or* PhD) thesis
Dokument [doku'mɛnt] *n* (-[*e*]*s*; -*e*) document
Dokumentar... [dokumɛn'ta:ɐ-] *in cpds ...spiel etc*: documentary ...
Dokumentarfilm *m* documentary (film)
Dolch [dɔlç] *m* (-[*e*]*s*; -*e*) dagger
Dollar ['dɔlar] *m* (-[*s*]; -*s*) dollar
dolmetschen ['dɔlmɛtʃən] *v/i* (*ge-, h*) interpret
'Dolmetscher(in) (-*s*; -/-; -*nen*) interpreter
Dom [do:m] *m* (-[*e*]*s*; -*e*) cathedral
dominierend [domi'ni:rənt] *adj* (pre-)

dominant
Dompteur [dɔmp'tøːɐ] *m* (*-s*; *-e*), **Dompteuse** [dɔmp'tøːzə] *f* (*-*; *-n*) animal tamer *or* trainer
Donner ['dɔnɐ] *m* (*-s*; *no pl*) thunder
'donnern *v/i* (*ge-*, *h*) thunder (*a. fig*)
'Donnerstag *m* (*-[e]s*; *-e*) Thursday
'Donnerwetter F *n* (*-s*; *-*) dressing-down; ***Donnerwetter!*** wow!
doof [doːf] F *adj* stupid, dumb
Doppel ['dɔpəl] *n* (*-s*; *-*) duplicate; *tennis etc*: doubles
Doppel... *in cpds …bett*, *…zimmer etc*: double …
'Doppeldecker [-dɛkɐ] *m* (*-s*; *-*) AVIAT biplane; MOT double-decker (bus)
'Doppelgänger [-gɛŋɐ] *m* (*-s*; *-*) double, look-alike
'Doppelhaus *n* duplex, *Br* pair of semis
Doppelhaushälfte *f* semidetached (house)
'Doppelpass *m soccer*: wall pass
Doppelpunkt *m* LING colon
Doppelstecker *m* ELECTR two-way adapter
doppelt *adj* double; ***doppelt so viel*** (***wie***) twice as much (as)
'Doppelverdiener *pl* two-income family
Dorf [dɔrf] *n* (*-[e]s*; *Dörfer* ['dœrfɐ]) village
Dorfbewohner *m* villager
Dorn [dɔrn] *m* (*-[e]s*; *-en*) BOT thorn (*a. fig*); TECH tongue; spike
'dornig *adj* thorny (*a. fig*)
Dorsch [dɔrʃ] m (*-[e]s*; *-e*) ZO cod(fish)
dort [dɔrt] *adv* there
'dorther *adv* from there
'dorthin *adv* there
Dose ['doːzə] *f* (*-*; *-n*) can, *Br a.* tin
'Dosen... *in cpds* canned, *Br a.* tinned
dösen ['døːzən] F *v/i* (*ge-*, *h*) doze
'Dosenöffner *m* can (*Br* tin) opener
Dosis ['doːzɪs] *f* (*-*; *Dosen*) MED dose
Dotter ['dɔtɐ] *m*, *n* (*-s*; *-*) yolk
Double ['duːbəl] *n* (*-s*; *-s*) *film*: stunt man (*or* woman)
Dozent [do'tsɛnt] *m* (*-en*; *-en*), **Do'zentin** *f* (*-*; *-nen*) (university) lecturer, assistant professor
Dr. ABBR *of* ***Doktor*** Dr., Doctor
Drache ['draxə] *m* (*-n*; *-n*) dragon
'Drachen *m* (*-s*; *-*) kite; SPORT hang glider; ***e-n Drachen steigen lassen*** fly a kite
Drachenfliegen *n* SPORT hang gliding
Draht [draːt] *m* (*-[e]s*; *Drähte* ['drɛːtə]) wire; F ***auf Draht sein*** be on the ball
drahtig ['draːtɪç] *fig adj* wiry
'drahtlos *adj* wireless
'Drahtseil *n* TECH cable; *circus*: tightrope
Drahtseilbahn *f* cable railway
'Drahtzieher *fig m* (*-s*; *-*) wirepuller
drall [dral] *adj* buxom, strapping
Drall *m* (*-[e]s*; *no pl*) twist, spin
Drama ['draːma] *n* (*-s*; *Dramen*) drama
Dramatiker [dra'maːtikɐ] *m* (*-s*; *-*) dramatist, playwright
dra'matisch *adj* dramatic
dran [dran] F *adv* → ***daran***; ***du bist dran*** it's your turn; *fig* you're in for it
drang [draŋ] *pret of* ***dringen***
Drang *m* (*-[e]s*; *no pl*) urge, drive (***nach*** for)
drängeln ['drɛŋəln] F *v/t and v/i* (*ge-*, *h*) push, shove
drängen ['drɛŋən] *v/t and v/i* (*ge-*, *h*) push, shove; ***j-n zu et. drängen*** press *or* urge s.o. to do s.th.; ***sich drängen*** press; force one's way
drängend *adj* pressing
'drankommen F *v/i* (*irr*, ***kommen***, *sep*, *-ge-*, *sein*) have one's turn; ***als erster drankommen*** be first
drastisch ['drastɪʃ] *adj* drastic
drauf [drauf] F *adv* → ***darauf***; ***drauf und dran sein, et. zu tun*** be just about to do s.th.
'Draufgänger [-gɛŋɐ] *m* (*-s*; *-*) daredevil
draus [draus] F *adv* → ***daraus***
draußen ['drausən] *adv* outside; outdoors; ***da draußen*** out there; ***bleib***(***t***) ***draußen!*** keep out!
drechseln ['drɛksəln] *v/t* (*ge-*, *h*) turn (on a lathe)
Drechsler ['drɛkslɐ] *m* (*-s*; *-*) turner
Dreck [drɛk] F *m* (*-[e]s*; *no pl*) dirt; filth (*a. fig*); mud; *fig* trash
dreckig ['drɛkɪç] F *adj* dirty; filthy (*both a. fig*)
Dreharbeiten ['dreː-] *pl film*: shooting
Drehbank *f* (*-*; *-bänke*) TECH lathe
'drehbar *adj* revolving, rotating
'Drehbuch *n film*: script
drehen ['dreːən] *v/t* (*ge-*, *h*) turn; *film*: shoot; roll; ***sich drehen*** turn, rotate; spin; ***sich drehen um*** *fig* be about; → ***Ding***
Dreher ['dreːɐ] *m* (*-s*; *-*) TECH turner
'Drehkreuz *n* turnstile
Drehorgel *f* barrel-organ
Drehort *m film*: location
Drehstrom *m* ELECTR three-phase current
Drehstuhl *m* swivel chair
Drehtür *f* revolving door
'Drehung *f* (*-*; *-en*) turn; rotation
'Drehzahl *f* TECH (number of) revolutions
Drehzahlmesser *m* MOT rev(olution) counter
drei [drai] *adj* three

D

Drei *f* (-; *-en*) three; *grade:* fair, C
'**dreibeinig** *adj* three-legged
dreidimensio,nal *adj* three-dimensional
'**Dreieck** *n* (-[*e*]*s*; *-e*) triangle
'**dreieckig** *adj* triangular
dreierlei ['draiɐ'lai] *adj* three kinds of
'**dreifach** *adj* threefold, triple
'**Dreigang…** TECH *in cpds* three-speed …
Dreikampf *m* SPORT triathlon
Dreirad *n* tricycle
Dreisatz *m* (*-es*; *no pl*) MATH rule of three
Dreisprung *m* (-[*e*]*s*; *no pl*) SPORT triple jump
dreißig ['draisɪç] *adj* thirty
'**dreißigste** *adj* thirtieth
dreist [draist] *adj* brazen, impertinent
'**dreistufig** [-ʃtu:fɪç] *adj* three-stage
'**dreizehn(te)** *adj* thirteen(th)
Dresche ['drɛʃə] F *f* (-; *no pl*) thrashing
'**dreschen** *v/t and v/i* (*irr, ge-, h*) AGR thresh; thrash
'**Dreschma,schine** *f* AGR threshing machine
dressieren [drɛ'si:rən] *v/t* (*no -ge-, h*) train
Dressman ['drɛsmən] *m* (*-s*; *-men*) male model
Dressur [drɛ'su:ɐ] *f* (-; *-en*) training; act
Dressurreiten *n* dressage
dribbeln ['drɪbəln] *v/i* (*ge-, h*), **Dribbling** *n* (*-s*; *-s*) SPORT dribble
drillen ['drɪlən] *v/t* (*ge-, h*) MIL drill (*a. fig*)
Drillinge ['drɪlɪŋə] *pl* triplets
drin [drɪn] F *adv* → ***darin***; ***das ist nicht drin!*** no way!
dringen ['drɪŋən] *v/i* (*irr, ge-, h*) ***dringen auf*** (*acc*) insist on; ***dringen aus*** come from; ***dringen durch*** force one's way through, penetrate, pierce; ***dringen in*** (*acc*) penetrate into; ***darauf dringen, dass*** urge that
dringend *adj* urgent, pressing; strong (*suspicion etc*)
drinnen ['drɪnən] F *adv* inside; indoors
dritte ['drɪtə] *adj* third; ***wir sind zu dritt*** there are three of us; ***die Dritte Welt*** the Third World
'**Drittel** *n* (*-s*; -) third
'**drittens** *adv* thirdly
'**Dritte-Welt-Laden** *m* third world shop
Droge ['dro:gə] *f* (-; *-n*) drug
'**drogenabhängig** *adj* addicted to drugs; ***drogenabhängig sein*** be a drug addict
'**Drogenabhängige** *m, f* (*-n*; *-n*) drug addict
Drogenmissbrauch *m* drug abuse
'**drogensüchtig** → ***drogenabhängig***
'**Drogentote** *m, f* drug victim
Drogerie [drogə'ri:] *f* (-; *-n*) drugstore, *Br* chemist's (shop)
Drogist [dro'gɪst] *m* (*-en*; *-en*), **Dro'gistin** *f* (-; *-nen*) chemist
drohen ['dro:ən] *v/i* (*ge-, h*) threaten, menace
dröhnen ['drø:nən] *v/i* (*ge-, h*) roar
'**Drohung** *f* (-; *-en*) threat (***gegen*** to)
drollig ['drɔlɪç] *adj* funny, droll
Dromedar [dromə'da:ɐ] *n* (*-s*; *-e*) ZO dromedary
drosch [drɔʃ] *pret of* ***dreschen***
Drossel ['drɔsəl] *f* (-; *-n*) ZO thrush
'**drosseln** *v/t* (*ge-, h*) TECH throttle
drüben ['dry:bən] *adv* over there (*a. fig*)
drüber ['drybɐ] F *adv* → ***darüber, drunter***
Druck [drʊk] *m* (-[*e*]*s*; *-e*) pressure; printing; print
'**Druckbuchstabe** *m* block letter
Drückeberger ['drʏkəbɛrgɐ] F *m* (*-s*; -) shirker
'**drucken** *v/t* (*ge-, h*) print; ***et. drucken lassen*** have s.th. printed *or* published
drücken ['drʏkən] (*ge-, h*) **1.** *v/t* press; push; *fig* force down; ***j-m die Hand drücken*** shake hands with s.o.; **2.** *v/i* pinch; **3.** F *v/refl:* ***sich vor et. drücken*** shirk (doing) s.th.
drückend *adj* heavy, oppressive
Drucker ['drʊkɐ] *m* (*-s*; -) printer (*a.* EDP)
Drücker ['drʏkɐ] *m* (*-s*; -) latch; trigger; F hawker
Druckerei [drʊkə'rai] *f* (-; *-en*) printers
'**Druckfehler** *m* misprint
Druckkammer *f* pressurized cabin
Druckknopf *m* snap fastener, *Br* press stud; TECH (push) button
Druckluft *f* TECH compressed air
Drucksache *f* printed (*or* second-class) matter
Druckschrift *f* block letters
Drucktaste *f* TECH push button
drunter ['drʊntɐ] F *adv* → ***darunter***; ***es ging drunter und drüber*** it was absolutely chaotic
Drüse ['dry:zə] *f* (-; *-n*) ANAT gland
Dschungel ['dʒʊŋəl] *m* (*-s*; -) jungle (*a. fig*)
Dschunke ['dʒʊŋkə] *f* (-; *-n*) MAR junk
du [du:] *pers pron* you
Dübel ['dy:bəl] *m* (*-s*; -), '**dübeln** *v/t* (*ge-, h*) TECH dowel
ducken ['dʊkən] *v/refl* (*ge-, h*) duck; *fig* cringe (***vor*** *dat* before); crouch
Duckmäuser ['dʊkmɔʏzɐ] *m* (*-s*; -) coward; yes-man
Dudelsack ['du:dəlzak] *m* MUS bagpipes
Duell [du'ɛl] *n* (*-s*; *-e*) duel
duellieren [duɛ'li:rən] *v/refl* (*no -ge-, h*) fight a duel

Duett [du'ɛt] *n* (-[*e*]*s*; -*e*) MUS duet
Duft [dʊft] *m* (-[*e*]*s*; *Düfte* ['dʏftə]) scent, fragrance, smell (***nach*** of)
'**duften** *v/i* (*ge-*, *h*) smell (***nach*** of)
'**duftend** *adj* fragrant
'**duftig** *adj* dainty
dulden ['dʊldən] *v/t* (*ge-*, *h*) tolerate, put up with; suffer
duldsam ['dʊltzaːm] *adj* tolerant
dumm [dʊm] *adj* stupid, F dumb
'**Dummheit** *f* (-; -*en*) a) (*no pl*) stupidity, ignorance, b) stupid *or* foolish thing
'**Dummkopf** *m contp* fool, blockhead
dumpf [dʊmpf] *adj* dull; *fig* vague
Düne ['dyːnə] *f* (-; -*n*) (sand) dune
Dung [dʊŋ] *m* (-[*e*]*s*; *no pl*) dung, manure
düngen ['dʏŋən] *v/t* (*ge-*, *h*) fertilize; manure
Dünger ['dʏŋɐ] *m* (-*s*; -) fertilizer; manure
dunkel ['dʊŋkəl] *adj* dark (*a. fig*)
'**Dunkelheit** *f* (-; *no pl*) dark(ness)
'**Dunkelkammer** *f* PHOT darkroom
Dunkelziffer *f* number of unreported cases
dünn [dʏn] *adj* thin; weak (*coffee etc*)
Dunst [dʊnst] *m* (-[*e*]*s*; *Dünste* ['dʏnstə]) haze, mist; CHEM vapo(u)r
dünsten ['dʏnstən] *v/t* (*ge-*, *h*) GASTR stew, braise
'**dunstig** *adj* hazy, misty
Duplikat [dupli'kaːt] *n* (-[*e*]*s*; -*e*) duplicate; copy
Dur [duːɐ] *n* (-; *no pl*) MUS major (key)
durch [dʊrç] *prp* (*acc*) *and adv* through; across; MATH divided by; GASTR (well) done; ***durch j-n*** (***et.***) by s.o. (s.th.); ***durch und durch*** through and through
'**durcharbeiten** (*sep*, -*ge*-, *h*) **1.** *v/t* study thoroughly; ***sich durcharbeiten durch*** work (one's way) through a *text etc*; **2.** *v/i* work without a break
durch'aus *adv* absolutely, quite; ***durchaus nicht*** by no means
'**durchblättern** *v/t* (*sep*, -*ge*-, *h*) leaf *or* thumb through
'**Durchblick** *fig m* grasp *of s.th.*
'**durchblicken** *v/i* (*sep*, -*ge*-, *h*) look through; ***durchblicken lassen*** give to understand; ***ich blicke*** (***da***) ***nicht durch*** I don't get it
durch'bohren *v/t* (*no* -*ge*-, *h*) pierce; perforate
'**durchbraten** *v/t* (*irr*, ***braten***, *sep*, -*ge*-, *h*) roast thoroughly
'**durchbrechen**[1] (*irr*, ***brechen***, *sep*, -*ge*-) **1.** *v/t* (*h*) break (in two); **2.** *v/i* (*sein*) break through *or* apart
durch'brechen[2] *v/t* (*irr*, ***brechen***, *no* -*ge*-, *h*) break through
'**durchbrennen** *v/i* (*irr*, ***brennen***, *sep*, -*ge*-, *sein*) ELECTR blow; *reactor*: melt down; F run away
'**durchbringen** *v/t* (*irr*, ***bringen***, *sep*, -*ge*-, *h*) get (MED pull) *s.o.* through; go through *one's money*; support (*family*)
'**Durchbruch** *m* breakthrough (*a. fig*)
durch'dacht *adj* (well) thought-out
'**durchdrehen** (*sep*, -*ge*-, *h*) **1.** *v/i wheels*: spin; F *fig* crack up, flip; **2.** *v/t* GASTR grind, *Br* mince
'**durchdringend** *adj* piercing
durchei'nander *adv* confused; (in) a mess
Durchei'nander *n* (-*s*; *no pl*) confusion, mess; ***Durcheinanderbringen*** *v/t* (*irr*, ***bringen***, *sep*, -*ge*-, *h* confuse, mix up; mess up
durch'fahren[1] *v/t* (*irr*, ***fahren***, *no* -*ge*-, *h*) go (*or* pass, drive) through
'**durchfahren**[2] *v/i* (*irr*, ***fahren***, *sep*, -*ge*-, *sein*) go (*or* pass, drive) through
'**Durchfahrt** *f* passage; ***Durchfahrt verboten*** no thoroughfare
'**Durchfall** *m* MED diarrh(o)ea
'**durchfallen** *v/i* (*irr*, ***fallen***, *sep*, -*ge*-, *sein*) fall through; fail, F flunk (*test etc*); F be a flop; ***j-n durchfallen lassen*** fail (F flunk) s.o.
durchfragen *v/refl* (*sep*, -*ge*-, *h*) ask one's way (***nach, zu*** to)
'**durchführbar** *adj* practicable, feasible
'**durchführen** *v/t* (*sep*, -*ge*-, *h*) carry out, do
'**Durchgang** *m* passage
'**Durchgangs...** *in cpds* *...verkehr etc*: through ...; *...lager etc*: transit ...
'**durchgebraten** *adj* well done
'**durchgehen** (*irr*, ***gehen***, *sep*, -*ge*-, *sein*) **1.** *v/i* go through (*a.* RAIL *and* PARL); *fig* run away (***mit*** with); *horse*: bolt; **2.** *v/t* go *or* look through; ***durchgehen lassen*** tolerate
durchgehend *adj* continuous; ***durchgehender Zug*** through train; ***durchgehend geöffnet*** open all day
'**durchgreifen** *fig v/i* (*irr*, ***greifen***, *sep*, -*ge*-, *h*) take drastic measures
durchgreifend *adj* drastic; radical
'**durchhalten** (*irr*, ***halten***, *sep*, -*ge*-, *h*) **1.** *v/t* keep up; **2.** *v/i* hold out
'**durchhängen** *v/i* (*irr*, ***hängen***, *sep*, -*ge*-, *h*) sag; F have a low
'**durchkämpfen** *v/t* (*sep*, -*ge*-, *h*) fight out; ***sich durchkämpfen*** fight one's way through
'**durchkommen** *v/i* (*irr*, ***kommen***, *sep*, -*ge*-, *sein*) come through (*a.* MED); get through; get along; get away (***mit e-r Lüge*** *etc* with a lie *etc*)

D

durch'kreuzen *v/t* (*no -ge-, h*) cross, thwart
'durchlassen *v/t* (*irr, **lassen**, sep, -ge-, h*) let pass, let through
'durchlässig *adj* permeable (**für** to)
'durchlaufen[1] (*irr, **laufen**, sep, -ge-*) **1.** *v/i* (*sein*) run through; **2.** *v/t* (*h*) wear through
durch'laufen[2] *v/t* (*irr, **laufen**, no -ge-, h*) pass through
'Durchlauferhitzer *m* (*-s; -*) (instant) water heater, *Br a.* geyser
'durchlesen *v/t* (*irr, **lesen**, sep, -ge-, h*) read through
durch'leuchten *v/t* (*no -ge-, h*) MED X-ray; *fig* screen
durchlöchern [-'lœçərn] *v/t* (*no -ge-, h*) perforate, make holes in
'durchmachen F *v/t* (*sep, -ge-, h*) go through; ***viel durchmachen*** suffer a lot; ***die Nacht durchmachen*** make a night of it
'Durchmesser *m* (*-s; -*) diameter
durch'nässen *v/t* (*no -ge-, h*) soak
'durchnehmen *v/t* (*irr, **nehmen**, sep, -ge-, h*) PED do, deal with
'durchpausen *v/t* (*sep, -ge-, h*) trace
durch'queren *v/t* (*no, -ge-, h*) cross
'Durchreiche *f* (*-; -n*) hatch
'Durchreise *f*: ***ich bin nur auf der Durchreise*** I'm only passing through
'durchreisen *v/i* (*sep, -ge-, sein*) travel through
'Durchreisevisum *n* transit visa
'durchreißen (*irr, **reißen**, sep, -ge-*) **1.** *v/t* (*h*) tear (in two); **2.** *v/i* (*sein*) tear, break
durchringen *v/refl* (*irr, **ringen**, sep, -ge-, h*) ***sich durchringen, et. zu tun*** bring o.s. to do s.th.
'Durchsage *f* announcement
durch'schauen *v/t* (*no -ge-, h*) see through *s.o. or s.th.*
'durchscheinen *v/i* (*irr, **scheinen**, sep, -ge-, h*) shine through
durchscheinend *adj* transparent
'durchscheuern *v/t* (*sep, -ge-, h*) chafe; wear through
'durchschlafen *v/i* (*irr, **schlafen**, sep, -ge-, h*) sleep through
'Durchschlag *m* (carbon) copy
durch'schlagen[1] *v/t* (*irr, **schlagen**, no -ge-, h*) cut in two; *bullet etc*: go through, pierce
'durchschlagen[2] (*irr, **schlagen**, sep, -ge-*) **1.** *v/refl* (*h*): ***sich durchschlagen nach*** make one's way to; **2.** *v/i* (*sein*) come through (*a. fig*)
durchschlagend *adj* sweeping; effective
'Durchschlagpa,pier *n* carbon paper
Durchschlagskraft *fig f* force, impact
'durchschneiden *v/t* (*irr, **schneiden**, sep, -ge-, h*) cut (through)
'Durchschnitt *m* average; ***im*** (***über, unter dem***) ***Durchschnitt*** on an (above, below) average; ***im Durchschnitt betragen*** (***verdienen*** *etc*) average
'durchschnittlich **1.** *adj* average; ordinary; **2.** *adv* on an average
'Durchschnitts... *in cpds* average …
'Durchschrift *f* (carbon) copy
'durchsehen *v/t* (*irr, **sehen**, sep, -ge-, h*) look *or* go through; check
durchsetzen *v/t* (*sep, -ge-, h*) put (*or* push) *s.th.* through; ***s-n Kopf durchsetzen*** have one's way; ***sich durchsetzen*** get one's way; be successful; ***sich durchsetzen können*** have authority (***bei*** over)
durch'setzt *adj*: ***durchsetzt mit*** interspersed with
'durchsichtig *adj* transparent (*a. fig*); clear; see-through
'durchsickern *v/i* (*sep, -ge-, sein*) seep through; *fig* leak out
'durchstarten *v/i* (*sep, -ge-, sein*) AVIAT climb and reaccelerate
durch'stechen *v/t* (*irr, **stechen**, no -ge-, h*) pierce
'durchstecken *v/t* (*sep, -ge-, h*) stick through
durchstehen *v/t* (*irr, **stehen**, sep, -ge-, h*) go through
durch'stoßen *v/t* (*irr, **stoßen**, no -ge-, h*) break through
'durchstreichen *v/t* (*irr, **streichen**, sep, -ge-, h*) cross out
durch'suchen *v/t* (*no -ge-, h*) search, F frisk
Durch'suchung *f* (*-; -en*) search
Durch'suchungsbefehl *m* search warrant
durchtrieben [-'tri:bən] *adj* cunning, sly
durch'wachsen *adj* GASTR streaky
'Durchwahl *f* (*-; no pl*) TEL direct dial(l)ing
'durchwählen *v/i* (*sep, -ge-, h*) TEL dial direct
'durchweg [-vɛk] *adv* without exception
durch'weicht *adj* soaked, drenched
durch'wühlen *v/t* (*no -ge-, h*) rummage through
'durchzählen *v/t* (*sep, -ge-, h*) count off (*Br* up)
durchziehen (*irr, **ziehen**, sep, -ge-*) **1.** *v/i* (*sein*) pass through; **2.** *v/t* (*h*) pull *s.th.* through; *fig* carry *s.th.* through (to the end)
durch'zucken *v/t* (*no -ge-, h*) flash through

'Durchzug *m* (-[*e*]*s*; *no pl*) draft, *Br* draught
dürfen ['dʏrfən] **1.** *v/aux* (*irr*, *no -ge-*, *h*) be allowed *or* permitted to *inf*; ***darf ich gehen?*** may I go?; ***ja***(, ***du darfst***) yes, you may; ***du darfst nicht*** you must not, you aren't allowed to; ***dürfte ich …?*** could I …?; ***das dürfte genügen*** that should be enough; **2.** *v/i* (*irr*, *ge-*, *h*) ***er darf*** (***nicht***) he is (not) allowed to *inf*
durfte ['dʊrftə] *pret of* ***dürfen***
dürftig ['dʏrftɪç] *adj* poor; scanty
dürr [dʏr] *adj* dry; barren, arid; skinny
Dürre ['dʏrə] *f* (-; -*n*) a) drought, b) (*no pl*) barrenness
Durst [dʊrst] *m* (-[*e*]*s*; *no pl*) thirst (***auf*** *acc* for); ***Durst haben*** be thirsty
'durstig *adj* thirsty
Dusche ['dʊʃə] *f* (-; -*n*) shower
'duschen *v/refl and v/i* (*ge-*, *h*) have *or* take a shower
Düse ['dyːzə] *f* (-; -*n*) TECH nozzle; jet
'düsen F *v/i* (*ge-*, *sein*) jet
'Düsenantrieb *m* jet propulsion; ***mit Düsenantrieb*** jet-propelled
Düsenflugzeug *n* jet (plane)
Düsenjäger *m* MIL jet fighter
Düsentriebwerk *n* jet engine
düster ['dyːstɐ] *adj* dark, gloomy (*both a. fig*); dim (*light*); *fig* dismal
Dutzend ['dʊtsənt] *n* (-*s*; -*e*) dozen
'dutzendweise *adv* by the dozen
duzen ['duːtsən] *v/t* (*ge-*, *h*) use the familiar 'du' with s.o.; ***sich duzen*** be on 'du' terms
Dynamik [dy'naːmɪk] *f* (-; *no pl*) PHYS dynamics; *fig* dynamism
dy'namisch *adj* dynamic
Dynamit [dyna'miːt] *n* (-*s*; *no pl*) dynamite
Dynamo [dy'anːmo] *m* (-*s*; -*s*) ELECTR dynamo, generator
D-Zug ['deː-] *m* express train

E

Ebbe ['ɛbə] *f* (-; -*n*) ebb, low tide
eben ['eːbən] **1.** *adj* even; flat; MATH plane; ***zu ebener Erde*** on the first (*Br* ground) floor; **2.** *adv* just; ***an eben dem Tag*** on that very day; ***so ist es eben*** that's the way it is; ***gerade eben so*** *or* ***noch*** just barely
'Ebenbild *n* image
'ebenbürtig [-bʏrtɪç] *adj*: ***j-m ebenbürtig sein*** be a match for s.o., be s.o.'s equal
Ebene ['eːbənə] *f* (-; -*n*) GEOGR plain; MATH plane; *fig* level
'ebenerdig *adj and adv* at street level; on the first (*Br* ground) floor
'ebenfalls *adv* as well, too
'Ebenholz *n* ebony
'Ebenmaß *n* (-*es*; *no pl*) symmetry; harmony; regularity
'ebenmäßig *adj* symmetrical; harmonious; regular
'ebenso *adv and cj* just as; as well; ***ebenso wie*** in the same way as; ***ebenso gern***, ***ebenso gut*** just as well; ***ebenso sehr***, ***ebenso viel*** just as much; ***ebenso wenig*** just as little *or* few
Eber ['eːbɐ] *m* (-*s*; -) ZO boar
ebnen ['eːbnən] *v/t* (*ge-*, *h*) even, level; *fig* smooth
Echo ['ɛço] *n* (-*s*; -*s*) echo; *fig* response
echt [ɛçt] *adj* genuine (*a. fig*), real; true; pure; fast (*color*); authentic; F ***echt gut*** real good
'Echtheit *f* (-; *no pl*) genuineness; authenticity
Eckball ['ɛk-] *m* SPORT corner (kick)
Ecke ['ɛkə] *f* (-; -*n*) corner; edge; SPORT ***lange*** (***kurze***) ***Ecke*** far (near) corner; → ***Eckball***
eckig ['ɛkɪç] *adj* square, angular; *fig* awkward
'Eckzahn *m* canine tooth
edel ['eːdəl] *adj* noble; MIN precious
'Edelme,tall *n* precious metal
'Edelstahl *m* stainless steel
'Edelstein *m* precious stone; gem
EDV [eːdeː'fau] ABBR *of* ***Elektronische Datenverarbeitung*** EDP, electronic data processing
Efeu ['eːfɔʏ] *m* (-*s*; *no pl*) BOT ivy
Effekt [ɛ'fɛkt] *m* (-[*e*]*s*; -*e*) effect
effektiv [ɛfɛk'tiːf] **1.** *adj* effective; **2.** *adv* actually
Effektivität [ɛfɛktivi'tɛːt] *f* (-; *no pl*) effectiveness

ef'fektvoll *adj* effective, striking
Effet [ɛ'feː] *m* (*-s*; *-s*) SPORT spin
EG [eː'geː] HIST ABBR *of* ***Europäische Gemeinschaft*** EC, European Community
egal [e'gaːl] F *adj*: ***egal ob*** (***warum, wer*** *etc*) no matter if (why, who, *etc*); ***das ist egal*** it doesn't matter; ***das ist mir egal*** I don't care, it's all the same to me

E

Egge ['ɛgə] *f* (*-*; *-n*), **'eggen** *v/t* (*ge-*, *h*) AGR harrow
Egoismus [ego'ɪsmʊs] *m* (*-*; *no pl*) ego(t)ism
Egoist(in) [ego'ɪst(ɪn)] (*-en*; *-en*/*-*; *-nen*) ego(t)ist
ego'istisch *adj* selfish, ego(t)istic(al)
ehe ['eːə] *cj* before; ***nicht ehe*** not until
Ehe ['eːə] *f* (*-*; *-n*) marriage (***mit*** to)
Eheberatung *f* marriage counseling (*Br* guidance)
Ehebrecher *m* (*-s*; *-*) adulterer
Ehebrecherin *f* (*-*; *-nen*) adulteress
'ehebrecherisch *adj* adulterous
'Ehebruch *m* adultery
Ehefrau *f* wife
Eheleute *pl* married couple
'ehelich *adj* conjugal; JUR legitimate
ehemalig ['eːəmaːlɪç] *adj* former, ex-…
ehemals ['eːəmaːls] *adv* formerly
'Ehemann *m* husband
'Ehepaar *n* (married) couple
eher ['eːɐ] *adv* earlier, sooner; ***je eher, desto lieber*** the sooner the better; ***nicht eher als*** not until *or* before
'Ehering *m* wedding ring
ehrbar ['eːɐbaːɐ] *adj* respectable
Ehre ['eːrə] *f* (*-*; *-n*) hono(u)r; ***zu Ehren*** (***von***) in hono(u)r of
'ehren *v/t* (*ge-*, *h*) hono(u)r; respect
'ehrenamtlich *adj* honorary
'Ehrenbürger *m* honorary citizen
Ehrendoktor *m* UNIV honorary doctor
Ehrengast *m* guest of hono(u)r
Ehrenkodex *m* code of hono(u)r
Ehrenmann *m* man of hono(u)r
Ehrenmitglied *n* honorary member
Ehrenplatz *m* place of hono(u)r
Ehrenrechte *pl* civil rights
Ehrenrettung *f* rehabilitation
'ehrenrührig *adj* defamatory
'Ehrenrunde *f esp* SPORT lap of hono(u)r
Ehrensache *f* point of hono(u)r
Ehrentor *n*, **Ehrentreffer** *m* SPORT consolation goal
'ehrenwert *adj* hono(u)rable
'Ehrenwort *n* (*-[e]s*; *-e*) word of hono(u)r; F ***Ehrenwort!*** cross my heart!
ehrerbietig ['eːɐˀɛɐbiːtɪç] *adj* respectful
Ehrfurcht ['eːɐ-] *f* (*-*; *no pl*) respect (***vor*** *dat* for); awe (of); ***Ehrfurcht gebietend*** awe-inspiring, awesome
'ehrfürchtig [-fʏrçtɪç] *adj* respectful
'Ehrgefühl *n* (*-[e]s*; *no pl*) sense of hono(u)r
'Ehrgeiz *m* ambition
'ehrgeizig *adj* ambitious
'ehrlich *adj* honest; frank; fair
'Ehrlichkeit *f* (*-*; *no pl*) honesty; fairness
'Ehrung *f* (*-*; *-en*) hono(u)r(ing)
'ehrwürdig *adj* venerable
Ei [ai] *n* (*-[e]s*; *Eier* ['aiɐ]) egg; V *pl* balls
Eiche ['aiçə] *f* (*-*; *-n*) oak(-tree)
Eichel ['aiçəl] *f* (*-*; *-n*) BOT acorn; *card games*: club(s); ANAT glans (penis)
eichen ['aiçən] *v/t* (*ge-*, *h*) ga(u)ge
Eichhörnchen ['aiçhœrnçən] *n* (*-s*; *-*) ZO squirrel
Eid [ait] *m* (*-[e]s*; *-e*) oath; ***e-n Eid ablegen*** take an oath
Eidechse ['aidɛksə] *f* (*-*; *-n*) ZO lizard
eidesstattlich ['aidəs-] *adj*: ***eidesstattliche Erklärung*** JUR statutory declaration
'Eidotter *m*, *n* (egg) yolk
'Eierbecher *m* eggcup
Eierkuchen *m* pancake
Eierli,kör *m* eggnog
Eierschale *f* eggshell
Eierstock *m* ANAT ovary
Eieruhr *f* egg timer
Eifer ['aifɐ] *m* (*-s*; *no pl*) zeal, eagerness; ***glühender Eifer*** ardo(u)r
'Eifersucht *f* (*-*; *no pl*) jealousy
'eifersüchtig *adj* jealous (***auf*** *acc* of)
eifrig *adj* eager, zealous; ardent
'Eigelb *n* (*-[e]s*; *-e*) (egg) yolk
eigen ['aigən] *adj* own, of one's own; peculiar; particular, F fussy
…eigen *in cpds staatseigen etc*: …-owned
'Eigenart *f* peculiarity
'eigenartig *adj* peculiar; strange
'Eigenbedarf *m* personal needs
'Eigengewicht *n* dead weight
'eigenhändig [-hɛndɪç] **1.** *adj* personal; **2.** *adv* personally, with one's own hands
'Eigenheim *n* home (of one's own)
Eigenliebe *f* self-love
Eigenlob *n* self-praise
'eigenmächtig *adj* arbitrary
'Eigenname *m* proper noun
'Eigennutz *m* (*-es*; *no pl*) self-interest
'eigennützig [-nʏtsɪç] *adj* selfish
'eigens *adv* (e)specially, expressly
'Eigenschaft *f* (*-*; *-en*) quality; TECH, PHYS, CHEM property; ***in s-r Eigenschaft als*** in his capacity as
'Eigenschaftswort *n* (*-[e]s*; *-wörter*) LING adjective
'Eigensinn *m* (*-[e]s*; *no pl*) stubbornness
'eigensinnig *adj* stubborn, obstinate

eigentlich ['aigəntlıç] **1.** *adj* actual, true, real; exact; **2.** *adv* actually, really; originally
'Eigentor *n* SPORT own goal (*a. fig*)
'Eigentum *n* (-[*e*]*s*; *no pl*) property
Eigentümer ['aıgənty:mɐ] *m* (-*s*; -), **'Eigentümerin** *f* (-; -*nen*) owner, proprietor (proprietress)
'eigentümlich [-ty:mlıç] *adj* peculiar; strange, odd
'Eigentümlichkeit *f* (-; -*en*) peculiarity
'Eigentumswohnung *f* condominium, F condo, *Br* owner-occupied flat
'eigenwillig *adj* wil(l)ful; individual, original (*style etc*)
eignen ['aignən] *v/refl* (*ge-, h*) ***sich eignen für*** be suited *or* fit for
'Eignung *f* (-; *no pl*) suitability; aptitude, qualification
'Eignungsprüfung *f*, **Eignungstest** *m* aptitude test
Eilbote ['ail-] *m*: ***durch Eilboten*** by special delivery
Eilbrief *m* special delivery (*Br* express) letter
Eile ['ailə] *f* (-; *no pl*) haste, hurry
'eilen *v/i* a) (*ge-, sein*) hurry, hasten, rush, b) (*ge-, h*) be urgent
'eilig *adj* hurried, hasty; urgent; ***es eilig haben*** be in a hurry
Eimer ['aimɐ] *m* (-*s*; -) bucket, pail
ein [ain] **1.** *adj* one; **2.** *indef art* a, an; **3.** *adv*: "***einlaus***" "on / off"; ***ein und aus gehen*** come and go; ***nicht mehr ein noch aus wissen*** be at one's wits' end
einander [ai'nandɐ] *pron* each other, one another
'einarbeiten *v/t* (*sep, -ge-, h*) train, acquaint *s.o.* with his work, F break *s.o.* in; ***sich einarbeiten*** work o.s. in
'einarmig [-armıç] *adj* one-armed
einäschern ['ainˀɛʃɐn] *v/t* (*sep, -ge-, h*) cremate
Einäscherung ['ainˀɛʃəruŋ] *f* (-; -*en*) cremation
'einatmen *v/t* (*sep, -ge-, h*) inhale, breathe
'einäugig [-ɔʏgıç] *adj* one-eyed
'Einbahnstraße *f* one-way street
einbalsamieren ['ainbalzami:rən] *v/t* (*no -ge-, h*) embalm
'Einband *m* (-[*e*]*s*; -*bände*) binding, cover
'Einbau *m* (-[*e*]*s*; -*bauten*) installation, fitting; ***Einbau...*** *in cpds ...möbel etc*: built-in ...
'einbauen *v/t* (*sep, -ge-, h*) build in, instal(l), fit
'einberufen *v/t* (*irr*, ***rufen***, *sep, no -ge-, h*) MIL draft, *Br* call up; call (*meeting etc*)
'Einberufung *f* (-; -*en*) MIL draft, *Br* call-up
'einbeziehen *v/t* (*irr*, ***ziehen***, *sep, no -ge-, h*) include
einbiegen *v/i* (*irr*, ***biegen***, *sep, -ge-, sein*) turn (***in*** *acc* into)
'einbilden *v/refl* (*sep, -ge-, h*) imagine; ***sich et. einbilden auf*** (*acc*) be conceited about
'Einbildung *f* (-; *no pl*) imagination, fancy; conceit
'einblenden *v/t* (*sep, -ge-, h*) TV fade in
'Einblick *m* insight (***in*** *acc* into)
'einbrechen *v/i* (*irr*, ***brechen***, *sep, -ge-, sein*) collapse; *winter*: set in; ***einbrechen in*** (*acc*) break into, burgle; fall through (the ice)
'Einbrecher *m* (-*s*; -) burglar
'einbringen *v/t* (*irr*, ***bringen***, *sep, -ge-, h*) bring in; yield (*profit etc*)
'Einbruch *m* burglary; ***bei Einbruch der Nacht*** at nightfall
'einbürgern [-bʏrgɐn] *v/t* (*sep, -ge-, h*) naturalize; ***sich einbürgern*** *fig* come into use
'Einbürgerung *f* (-; -*en*) naturalization
'Einbuße *f* (-; -*n*) loss
'einbüßen *v/t* (*sep, -ge-, h*) lose
'eindämmen [-dɛmən] *v/t* (*sep, -ge-, h*) dam (up), *fig a.* get under control
'eindecken *fig v/t* (*sep, -ge-, h*) provide (***mit*** with)
'eindeutig [-dɔʏtıç] *adj* clear
'eindrehen *v/t* (*sep, -ge-, h*) put *hair* in curlers
'eindringen *v/i* (*irr*, ***dringen***, *sep, -ge-, sein*) ***eindringen in*** (*acc*) enter (*a. fig*); force one's way into; MIL invade
'eindringlich *adj* urgent
'Eindringling *m* (-*s*; -*e*) intruder; MIL invader
'Eindruck *m* impression
'eindrücken *v/t* (*sep, -ge-, h*) break *or* push in
'eindrucksvoll *adj* impressive
eineiig ['ainˀaiıç] *adj* identical (*twins*)
'einein'halb *adj* one and a half
einengen ['ainˀɛŋən] *v/t* (*sep, -ge-, h*) confine, restrict
einer ['ainɐ], **eine** ['ainə], **ein(e)s** ['ain(-ə)s] *indef pron* one
'Einer *m* (-*s*; -) MATH unit; *rowing*: single sculls
einerlei ['ainɐ'lai] *adj*: ***ganz einerlei*** all the same; ***einerlei ob*** no matter if
'Einer'lei *n*: ***das tägliche Einerlei*** the daily grind *or* rut
'einer'seits *adv* on the one hand
'einfach *adj* simple; easy; plain; one-way (*Br* single) (*ticket*)

E

E

'**Einfachheit** *f* (-; *no pl*) simplicity
'**einfädeln** [-fɛːdəln] *v/t* (*sep*, *-ge-*, *h*) thread; F start, set afoot; MOT merge
'**einfahren** (*irr*, ***fahren***, *sep*, *-ge-*) **1.** *v/t* (*h*) MOT run in; bring in (*harvest*); **2.** *v/i* (*sein*) come in, RAIL *a.* pull in
'**Einfahrt** *f* entrance, way in
'**Einfall** *m* idea; MIL invasion
'**einfallen** *v/i* (*irr*, ***fallen***, *sep*, *-ge-*, *sein*) fall in; collapse; MUS join in; ***einfallen in*** (*acc*) MIL invade; ***ihm fiel ein, dass*** it came to his mind that; ***mir fällt nichts ein*** I have no ideas; ***es fällt mir nicht ein*** I can't think of it; ***dabei fällt mir ein*** that reminds me; ***was fällt dir ein?*** what's the idea?
einfältig ['ainfɛltɪç] *adj* simple-minded; stupid
Einfa'milienhaus *n* detached house
'**einfarbig** *adj* solid-colored, *Br* self-coloured
'**einfassen** *v/t* (*sep*, *-ge-*, *h*) border
einfetten *v/t* (*sep*, *-ge-*, *h*) grease
einfinden *v/refl* (*irr*, ***finden***, *sep*, *-ge-*, *h*) appear, arrive
einflechten *fig v/t* (*irr*, ***flechten***, *sep*, *-ge-*, *h*) work in
einfliegen *v/t* (*irr*, ***fliegen***, *sep*, *-ge-*, *h*) fly in
einfließen *v/i* (*irr*, ***fließen***, *sep*, *-ge-*, *sein*) *fig* ***et. einfließen lassen*** slip s.th. in
einflößen *v/t* (*sep*, *-ge-*, *h*) pour (***j-m*** into s.o.'s mouth); *fig* fill with (*awe etc*)
'**Einfluss** *fig m* influence
'**einflussreich** *adj* influential
'**einförmig** [-fœrmɪç] *adj* uniform
'**einfrieren** (*irr*, ***frieren***, *sep*, *-ge-*) **1.** *v/i* (*sein*) freeze (in); **2.** *v/t* (*h*) freeze (*a. fig*)
'**einfügen** *v/t* (*sep*, *-ge-*, *h*) put in; *fig* insert; ***sich einfügen*** fit in; adjust (o.s.) (***in*** *acc* to)
'**Einfügetaste** *f* EDP insert key
einfühlsam ['ainfyːlzaːm] *adj* sympathetic
'**Einfühlungsvermögen** *n* (*-s*; *no pl*) empathy
Einfuhr ['ainfuːɐ] *f* (-; *-en*) ECON a) (*no pl*) importation, b) import
'**einführen** *v/t* (*sep*, *-ge-*, *h*) introduce; install(l) *s.o.*: insert; ECON import
'**Einfuhrstopp** *m* ECON import ban
'**Einführung** *f* (-; *-en*) introduction
'**Einführungs...** *in cpds ...kurs*, *...preis etc*: introductory ...
'**Eingabe** *f* petition; EDP input
Eingabetaste *f* EDP enter *or* return key
'**Eingang** *m* entrance; ECON arrival; receipt
'**eingängig** *adj* catchy (*tune etc*)
'**eingangs** *adv* at the beginning
'**eingeben** *v/t* (*irr*, ***geben***, *sep*, *-ge-*, *h*) MED administer (*dat* to); EDP feed, enter
'**eingebildet** *adj* imaginary; conceited (***auf*** *acc* of)
'**Eingeborene** *m*, *f* (*-n*; *-n*) native
'**Eingebung** *f* (-; *-en*) inspiration; impulse
'**eingefallen** *adj* sunken, hollow
'**eingefleischt** *adj* confirmed
'**eingehen** (*irr*, ***gehen***, *sep*, *-ge-*, *sein*) **1.** *v/i* ECON come in, arrive; BOT, ZO die; *fabric*: shrink; ***eingehen auf*** (*acc*) agree to; go into (*detail*); listen to *s.o.*; **2.** *v/t* enter into (*a contract etc*); make (*a bet*); take (*a risk etc*)
eingehend *adj* thorough; detailed
'**eingemacht** *adj* preserved
eingemeinden ['aingəmaindən] *v/t* (*sep*, *no -ge-*, *h*) incorporate (***in*** *acc* into)
'**eingenommen** *adj* partial (***für*** to); prejudiced (***gegen*** against); ***von sich eingenommen*** full of o.s.
eingeschlossen *adj* locked in; trapped; ECON included
eingeschnappt F *adj* in a huff
eingeschrieben *adj* registered
eingespielt *adj*: (***gut***) ***aufeinander eingespielt sein*** work well together, be a good team
eingestellt *adj*: ***eingestellt auf*** (*acc*) prepared for; ***eingestellt gegen*** opposed to
Eingeweide ['aingəvaidə] *pl* ANAT intestines, guts
'**Eingeweihte** *m*, *f* (*-n*; *-n*) insider
'**eingewöhnen** *v/refl* (*sep*, *no -ge-*, *h*) ***sich eingewöhnen in*** (*acc*) get used to, settle in
'**eingießen** *v/t* (*irr*, ***gießen***, *sep*, *-ge-*, *h*) pour
'**eingleisig** [-glaizɪç] *adj* single-track
'**eingliedern** *v/t* (*sep*, *-ge-*, *h*) integrate
'**Eingliederung** *f* integration
'**eingraben** *v/t* (*irr*, ***graben***, *sep*, *-ge-*, *h*) bury
eingra,vieren *v/t* (*sep*, *no -ge-*, *h*) engrave
'**eingreifen** *v/i* (*irr*, ***greifen***, *sep*, *-ge-*, *h*) step in, interfere
'**Eingriff** *m* intervention, interference; MED operation
'**einhaken** *v/t* (*sep*, *-ge-*, *h*) hook in; ***sich einhaken*** link arms, take s.o.'s arm
'**Einhalt** *m*: ***Einhalt gebieten*** put a stop (*dat* to)
'**einhalten** *v/t* (*irr*, ***halten***, *sep*, *-ge-*, *h*) keep
'**einhängen** (*sep*, *-ge-*, *h*) **1.** *v/t* hang in; TEL hang up (*receiver*); ***sich einhängen*** → ***einhaken***; **2.** *v/i* TEL hang up
'**einheimisch** *adj* native, local; ECON

home, domestic

'Einheimische *m, f (-n; -n)* local, native

'Einheit *f (-; -en)* unit; POL unity

'einheitlich *adj* uniform; homogeneous

'Einheits... *in cpds ...preis etc*: standard

einhellig ['ainhɛlɪç] *adj* unanimous

'einholen *v/t (sep, -ge-, h)* catch up with *(a. fig)*; make up for *lost time*; make *(inquiries)* (**über** *acc* about); seek *(advice)* (**bei** from); ask for *permission etc*; strike *(sail)*; ***einholen gehen*** go shopping

'Einhorn *n* MYTH unicorn

'einhüllen *v/t (sep, -ge-, h)* wrap (up); *fig* shroud

einig ['ainɪç] *adj*: ***sich einig sein*** agree; ***sich nicht einig sein*** disagree, differ

einige ['ainɪgə] *indef pron* some, a few, several

einigen ['ainɪgən] *v/t (ge-, h)* ***sich einigen über*** *(acc)* agree on

einigermaßen ['ainɪgɐ'ma:sən] *adv* quite, fairly; not too bad

'einiges *indef pron* some, something; quite a lot

'Einigkeit *f (-; no pl)* unity; agreement

'Einigung *f (-; -en)* agreement, settlement; POL unification

'einjagen *v/t (sep, -ge-, h)* ***j-m e-n Schrecken einjagen*** give s.o. a fright, frighten *or* scare s.o.

'einjährig [-jɛ:rɪç] *adj* one-year-old; ***einjährige Pflanze*** annual

'einkalku,lieren *v/t (no -ge-, h)* take into account, allow for

'Einkauf *m* purchase; ***Einkäufe machen*** → ***einkaufen*** *2*

'einkaufen *(sep, -ge-, h)* **1.** *v/t* buy, ECON *a.* purchase; **2.** *v/i* go shopping

'Einkaufs... *in cpds* shopping ...

Einkaufsbummel *m* shopping spree

Einkaufspreis *m* ECON purchase price

Einkaufswagen *m* grocery *or* shopping cart, *Br* (supermarket) trolley

Einkaufszentrum *n* (shopping) mall, *Br* shopping centre

'einkehren *v/i (sep, -ge-, sein)* stop (**in** *dat* at)

einklammern *v/t (sep, -ge-, h)* put in brackets

'Einklang *m (-[e]s; no pl)* MUS unison; *fig* harmony

'einkleiden *v/t (sep, -ge-, h)* clothe *(a. fig)*

einklemmen *v/t (sep, -ge-, h)* squeeze, jam; ***eingeklemmt sein*** be stuck, be jammed

einkochen *(sep, -ge-)* **1.** *v/t (h)* preserve; **2.** *v/i (sein)* boil down

'Einkommen *n (-s; -)* income

Einkommensteuererklärung *f* income-tax return

'einkreisen *v/t (sep, -ge-, h)* encircle, surround

Einkünfte ['ainkʏnftə] *pl* income

'einladen *v/t (irr,* ***laden****, sep, -ge-, h)* invite; load

einladend *adj* inviting

'Einladung *f (-; -en)* invitation

'Einlage *f (-; -n)* ECON investment; MED arch support; THEA, MUS interlude

Einlass ['ainlas] *m (-es; no pl)* admission, admittance

'einlassen *v/t (irr,* ***lassen****, sep, -ge-, h)* let in; run *(a bath)*; ***sich einlassen auf*** *(acc)* get involved in; let o.s. in for; agree to; ***sich mit j-m einlassen*** get involved with s.o.

'Einlauf *m* SPORT finish; MED enema

'einlaufen *(irr,* ***laufen****, sep, -ge-)* **1.** *v/i (sein)* come in *(a.* SPORT*)*; *water*: run in; MAR enter port; *fabric*: shrink; **2.** *v/t (h)* break *new shoes* in; ***sich einlaufen*** warm up

'einleben *v/refl (sep, -ge-, h)* settle in

'einlegen *v/t (sep, -ge-, h)* put in; set *(hair)*; GASTR pickle; MOT change into

'Einlegesohle *f* insole

'einleiten *v/t (sep, -ge-, h)* start; introduce; MED induce; TECH dump, discharge *(sewage)*

einleitend *adj* introductory

'Einleitung *f* introduction

'einlenken *v/i (sep, -ge-, h)* come round

einleuchten *v/i (sep, -ge-, h)* be evident, be obvious; ***das leuchtet mir*** (***nicht***) ***ein*** that makes (doesn't make) sense to me

einliefern *v/t (sep, -ge-, h)* take (***ins Gefängnis*** to prison; ***in die Klinik*** to [the] hospital)

einlösen *v/t (sep, -ge-, h)* redeem; cash *(check)*

einmachen *v/t (sep, -ge-, h)* preserve

'einmal *adv* once; some *or* one day, sometime; ***auf einmal*** suddenly; at the same time, at once; ***noch einmal*** once more *or* again; ***noch einmal so ...*** (***wie***) twice as ... (as); ***es war einmal*** once (upon a time) there was; ***haben Sie schon einmal ...?*** have you ever ...?; ***schon einmal dort gewesen sein*** have been there before; ***nicht einmal*** not even

'Einmal... *in cpds* disposable ...

Einmal'eins *n (-; no pl)* multiplication table

einmalig ['ainma:lɪç] *adj* single; *fig* unique; F fabulous

'Einmann... *in cpds* one-man ...

'Einmarsch *m* entry; MIL invasion

E

E

'einmar,schieren *v/i* (*no -ge-, sein*) march in; ***einmarschieren in*** (*acc*) MIL invade
'einmischen *v/refl* (*sep, -ge-, h*) meddle (***in*** *acc* in, with), interfere (with)
'Einmündung *f* junction
'einmütig [-my:tɪç] *adj* unanimous
'Einmütigkeit *f* (-; *no pl*) unanimity
Einnahmen ['ainna:mən] *pl* takings, receipts
'einnehmen *v/t* (*irr*, ***nehmen***, *sep, -ge-, h*) take (*a.* MIL); earn, make
'einnehmend *adj* engaging
'einnicken *v/i* (*sep, -ge-, sein*) doze off
'einnisten *v/refl* (*sep, -ge-, h*) ***sich bei j-m einnisten*** park o.s. on s.o.
'Einöde *f* (-; *-n*) desert, wilderness
'einordnen *v/t* (*sep, -ge-, h*) put in its proper place; file; ***sich einordnen*** MOT get in lane
einpacken *v/t* (*sep, -ge-, h*) pack (up); wrap up
einparken *v/t and v/i* (*sep, -ge-, h*) park (between two cars)
einpferchen *v/t* (*sep, -ge-, h*) pen in; coop up
einpflanzen *v/t* (*sep, -ge-, h*) plant; *fig* implant (*a.* MED)
einplanen *v/t* (*sep, -ge-, h*) allow for
einprägen *v/t* (*sep, -ge-, h*) impress; ***sich et. einprägen*** keep s.th. in mind; memorize s.th.
einquartieren F *v/t* (*no -ge-, h*) put *s.o.* up (***bei j-m*** at s.o.'s place); ***sich einquartieren bei*** (*dat*) move in with
einrahmen *v/t* (*sep, -ge-, h*) frame
einräumen *v/t* (*sep, -ge-, h*) put away; furnish; *fig* grant, concede
einreden (*sep, -ge-, h*) **1.** *v/t*: ***j-m et. einreden*** talk s.o. into (believing) s.th.; **2.** *v/i*: ***auf j-n einreden*** keep on at s.o.
einreiben *v/t* (*irr*, ***reiben***, *sep, -ge-, h*) rub
einreichen *v/t* (*sep, -ge-, h*) hand *or* send in
einreihen *v/t* (*sep, -ge-, h*) place (among); ***sich einreihen*** take one's place
'einreihig [-raiɪç] *adj* single-breasted
'Einreise *f* entry (*a. in cpds*)
'einreisen *v/i* (*sep, -ge-, sein*) enter (***in ein Land*** a country)
'einreißen (*irr*, ***reißen***, *sep, -ge-*) **1.** *v/t* (*h*) tear; pull down; **2.** *v/i* (*sein*) tear; *fig* spread
einrenken *v/t* (*sep, -ge-, h*) MED set; *fig* straighten out
'einrichten *v/t* (*sep, -ge-, h*) furnish; establish; arrange; ***sich einrichten*** furnish one's home; ***sich einrichten auf*** (*acc*) prepare for
'Einrichtung *f* (-; *-en*) furnishings; fittings; TECH installation(s), facilities; institution, facility
'einrücken (*sep, -ge-*) **1.** *v/i* (*sein*) MIL join the forces; march in; **2.** *v/t* (*h*) PRINT indent
eins [ains] *pron and adj* one; one thing; ***es ist alles eins*** it's all the same (thing)
Eins *f* (-; *-en*) one; *grade*: excellent, A
einsam ['ainza:m] *adj* lonely, lonesome; solitary
'Einsamkeit *f* (-; *no pl*) loneliness; solitude
'einsammeln *v/t* (*sep, -ge-, h*) collect
'Einsatz *m* TECH inset, insert; stake(s) (*a. fig*); MUS entry; *fig* effort(s), zeal; use, employment; MIL action, mission; deployment; ***im Einsatz*** in action; ***unter Einsatz des Lebens*** at the risk of one's life
'einsatzbereit *adj* ready for action
einsatzfreudig *adj* dynamic, zealous
'einschalten *v/t* (*sep, -ge-, h*) ELECTR switch *or* turn on; call *s.o.* in; ***sich einschalten*** step in
'Einschaltquote *f* TV rating
'einschärfen *v/t* (*sep, -ge-, h*) urge (***j-m et.*** s.o. to do s.th.)
einschätzen *v/t* (*sep, -ge-, h*) estimate; judge, rate; ***falsch einschätzen*** misjudge
einschenken *v/t* (*sep, -ge-, h*) pour (out)
einschicken *v/t* (*sep, -ge-, h*) send in
einschieben *v/t* (*irr*, ***schieben***, *sep, -ge-, h*) slip in; insert
einschlafen *v/i* (*irr*, ***schlafen***, *sep, -ge-, sein*) fall asleep, go to sleep
einschläfern [-ʃlɛ:fɐn] *v/t* (*sep, -ge-, h*) put to sleep
einschl. ABBR *of* ***einschließlich*** incl., including
'Einschlag *m* strike, impact; *fig* touch
'einschlagen (*irr*, ***schlagen***, *sep, -ge-, h*) **1.** *v/t* knock in (*or* out); break (in), smash; wrap up; take (*road etc*); turn (*wheels*); → ***Laufbahn***; **2.** *v/i lightning etc*: strike; *fig* be a success
'einschlägig [-ʃlɛ:gɪç] *adj* relevant
'einschleusen *fig v/t* (*sep, -ge-, h*) infiltrate (***in*** *acc* into)
einschließen *v/t* (*irr*, ***schließen***, *sep, -ge-, h*) lock in *or* up; enclose; MIL surround, encircle; *fig* include
einschließlich *prp* (*gen*) including, … included
einschmeicheln *v/refl* (*sep, -ge-, h*) ***sich einschmeicheln bei*** ingratiate o.s. with
einschnappen *v/i* (*sep, -ge-, sein*) snap shut; *fig* go into a huff; → ***eingeschnappt***

'einschneidend *fig adj* drastic; farreaching
'Einschnitt *m* cut; notch; *fig* break
'einschränken *v/t (sep, -ge-, h)* restrict, reduce (*both*: ***auf*** *acc* to); cut down on; ***sich einschränken*** economize
'Einschränkung *f (-; -en)* restriction, reduction, cut; ***ohne Einschränkung*** without reservation
'Einschreibebrief *m* registered letter
'einschreiben *v/t (irr,* ***schreiben****, sep, -ge-, h)* enter; book; enrol(l) (*a.* MIL); ***(sich) einschreiben lassen (für)*** enrol(l) (o.s.) (for)
'einschreiten *fig v/i (irr,* ***schreiten****, sep, -ge-, sein)* step in, intervene; ***einschreiten (gegen)*** take (legal) measures (against)
'einschüchtern *v/t (sep, -ge-, h)* intimidate; bully
'Einschüchterung *f (-; -en)* intimidation
'einschulen *v/t (sep, -ge-, h)* ***eingeschult werden*** start school
'Einschuss *m* bullet hole
'einschweißen *v/t (sep, -ge-, h)* shrink-wrap
'einsegnen *v/t (sep, -ge-, h)* REL consecrate; confirm
'Einsegnung *f (-; -en)* REL consecration; confirmation
'einsehen *v/t (irr,* ***sehen****, sep, -ge-, h)* see, realize; ***das sehe ich nicht ein!*** I don't see why!
'Einsehen *n*: ***ein Einsehen haben*** show some understanding
'einseifen *v/t (sep, -ge-, h)* soap; lather; F *fig* ***j-n einseifen*** take s.o. for a ride
'einseitig [-zaitıç] *adj* one-sided; MED, POL, JUR unilateral
'einsenden *v/t ([irr,* ***senden****,] sep, -ge-, h)* send in
'Einsendeschluss *m* closing date (for entries)
'einsetzen *(sep, -ge-, h)* **1.** *v/t* put in, insert; appoint; use, employ; TECH put into service; ECON invest, stake; bet; risk; ***sich einsetzen*** try hard, make an effort; ***sich einsetzen für*** stand up for; **2.** *v/i* set in, start
'Einsicht *f (-; -en)* a) insight, b) *(no pl)* understanding; ***zur Einsicht kommen*** listen to reason; ***Einsicht nehmen in*** *(acc)* take a look at
'einsichtig *adj* understanding; reasonable
'Einsiedler *m (-s; -)* hermit
'einsilbig [-zılbıç] *adj* monosyllabic; *fig* taciturn
'einspannen *v/t (sep, -ge-, h)* harness; TECH clamp, fix; F rope *s.o.* in
einsparen *v/t (sep, -ge-, h)* save, economize on
einsperren *v/t (sep, -ge-, h)* lock *or* shut up
einspielen *v/t (sep, -ge-, h)* bring in; ***sich einspielen*** warm up; *fig* get going; → ***eingespielt***
'Einspielergebnisse *pl film*: box-office returns
'einspringen *v/i (irr,* ***springen****, sep, -ge-, sein)* ***für j-n einspringen*** take s.o.'s place
'Einspritz... *in cpds* MOT fuel-injection
'Einspruch *m* objection (*a.* JUR), protest; POL veto; appeal
'einspurig [-ʃpu:rıç] *adj* RAIL single-track; MOT single-lane
einst [ainst] *adv* once, at one time
'Einstand *m* start; *tennis*: deuce
'einstecken *v/t (sep, -ge-, h)* pocket (*a. fig*); ELECTR plug in; mail, post; *fig* take
einstehen *v/i (irr,* ***stehen****, sep, -ge-, h)* ***einstehen für*** stand up for
einsteigen *v/i (irr,* ***steigen****, sep, -ge-, sein)* get in; get on (*bus etc*); ***alles einsteigen!*** RAIL all aboard!
einstellen *v/t (sep, -ge-, h)* engage, employ, hire; give up; stop; SPORT equal; TECH adjust (***auf*** *acc* to); *radio*: tune in (to); OPT, PHOT focus (on); ***die Arbeit einstellen*** (go on) strike, walk out; ***das Feuer einstellen*** MIL cease fire; ***sich einstellen auf*** *(acc)* adjust to; be prepared for
'Einstellung *f* attitude (***zu*** towards); employment; cessation; TECH adjustment; OPT, PHOT focus(s)ing; *film*: take
'Einstellungsgespräch *n* interview
Einstieg ['ainʃti:k] *m (-[e]s; -e)* entrance, entry (*a.* POL, ECON)
'Einstiegsdroge *f* gateway drug
einstig ['ainstıç] *adj* former, one-time
'einstimmen *v/i (sep, -ge-, h)* MUS join in
'einstimmig [-ʃtımıç] *adj* unanimous
'einstöckig [-ʃtœkıç] *adj* one-storied, *Br* one-storey(ed)
'einstuˌdieren *v/t (no -ge-, h)* THEA rehearse
einstufen *v/t (sep, -ge-, h)* grade, rate
'Einstufungsprüfung *f* placement test
'einstufig [-ʃtu:fıç] *adj* single-stage
'Einsturz *m*, **'einstürzen** *v/i (sep, -ge-, sein)* collapse
'einst'weilen *adv* for the present
'einstweilig [-vailıç] *adj* temporary
'eintauschen *v/t (sep, -ge-, h)* exchange (***gegen*** for)
einteilen *v/t (sep, -ge-, h)* divide (***in*** *acc* into); organize
'einteilig [-tailıç] *adj* one-piece
'Einteilung *f (-; -en)* division; organization; arrangement

'eintönig [-tøːnɪç] *adj* monotonous
'Eintönigkeit *f* (-; *no pl*) monotony
'Eintopf *m* GASTR stew
'Eintracht *f* (-; *no pl*) harmony, unity
'einträchtig *adj* harmonious, peaceful
Eintrag ['aintraːk] *m* (-[*e*]*s*; *Einträge* ['aintrɛːgə]) entry (*a.* ECON), registration
'eintragen *v/t* (*irr*, ***tragen***, *sep*, *-ge-*, *h*) enter (***in*** *acc* in); register (***bei*** with); enrol(l) (with); *fig* earn; ***sich eintragen*** register, *hotel*: *a.* check in
einträglich ['aintrɛːklɪç] *adj* profitable
'eintreffen *v/i* (*irr*, ***treffen***, *sep*, *-ge-*, *sein*) arrive; happen; come true
eintreiben *fig v/t* (*irr*, ***treiben***, *sep*, *-ge-*, *h*) collect
eintreten (*irr*, ***treten***, *sep*, *-ge-*) **1.** *v/i* (*sein*) enter; happen, take place; ***eintreten für*** stand up for, support; ***eintreten in*** (*acc*) join (*club etc*); **2.** *v/t* (*h*) kick in (*door etc*); ***sich et. eintreten*** run s.th. into one's foot
'Eintritt *m* entry; admission; ***Eintritt frei!*** admission free!; ***Eintritt verboten!*** keep out!
'Eintrittsgeld *n* entrance *or* admission (fee)
Eintrittskarte *f* (admission) ticket
'einüben *v/t* (*sep*, *-ge-*, *h*) practise; rehearse
'einverstanden *adj*: ***einverstanden sein*** agree (***mit*** to); ***einverstanden!*** agreed!
'Einverständnis *n* (*-ses*; *no pl*) agreement
Einwand ['ainvant] *m* (-[*e*]*s*; *Einwände* ['ainvɛndə]) objection (***gegen*** to)
'Einwanderer *m*, **'Einwanderin** *f* immigrant
'einwandern *v/t* (*sep*, *-ge-*, *sein*) immigrate
'Einwanderung *f* immigration
'einwandfrei *adj* perfect, faultless
einwärts ['ainvɛrts] *adv* inward(s)
'Einweg... *...rasierer*, *...spritze etc*: disposable
Einwegflasche *f* non-returnable bottle
Einwegpackung *f* throwaway pack
'einweichen *v/t* (*sep*, *-ge-*, *h*) soak
'einweihen *v/t* (*sep*, *-ge-*, *h*) dedicate, *Br* inaugurate; ***j-n einweihen in*** (*acc*) F let s.o. in on
'Einweihung *f* (-; *-en*) dedication, *Br* inauguration
'einweisen *v/t* (*irr*, ***weisen***, *sep*, *-ge-*, *h*) ***j-n einweisen in*** (*acc*) send (*esp* JUR commit) s.o. to; instruct s.o. in, brief s.o. on
'einwenden *v/t* ([*irr*, ***wenden***,] *sep*, *-ge-*, *h*) object (***gegen*** to)
'Einwendung *f* (-; *-en*) objection
'einwerfen *v/t* (*irr*, ***werfen***, *sep*, *-ge-*, *h*) throw in (*a. fig*, SPORT *a. v/i*); break (*window*); mail, *Br* post; insert (*coin*)
'einwickeln *v/t* (*sep*, *-ge-*, *h*) wrap (up); F take *s.o.* in
'Einwickelpa,pier *n* wrapping-paper
einwilligen ['ainvɪlɪgən] *v/i* (*sep*, *-ge-*, *h*) consent (***in*** *acc* to), agree (to)
'Einwilligung *f* (-; *-en*) consent (***in*** *acc* to), agreement
'einwirken *v/i* (*sep*, *-ge-*, *h*) ***einwirken auf*** (*acc*) act (up)on; *fig* work on *s.o.*
'Einwirkung *f* effect, influence
Einwohner ['ainvoːnɐ] *m* (*-s*; -), **'Einwohnerin** *f* (-; *-nen*) inhabitant
'Einwohnermeldeamt *n* registration office
'Einwurf *m* slot; SPORT throw-in
'Einzahl *f* (-; *no pl*) LING singular
'einzahlen *v/t* (*sep*, *-ge-*, *h*) pay in
'Einzahlung *f* payment, deposit
einzäunen ['aintsɔynən] *v/t* (*sep*, *-ge-*, *h*) fence in
Einzel ['aintsəl] *n* (*-s*; -) *tennis*: singles
'Einzel... *in cpds ...bett*, *...zimmer etc*: single ...
Einzelfall *m* special case
Einzelgänger [-gɛŋɐ] *m* (*-s*; -) F loner
Einzelhaft *f* solitary confinement
Einzelhandel *m* retail trade
Einzelhändler *m* retailer
Einzelhaus *n* detached house
'Einzelheit *f* (-; *-en*) detail
'einzeln *adj* single; odd (*shoe etc*); ***Einzelne*** *pl* several, some; ***der Einzelne*** the individual; ***einzeln eintreten*** enter one at a time; ***einzeln angeben*** specify; ***im Einzelnen*** in detail; ***jeder Einzelne*** each and every one
'einziehen (*irr*, ***ziehen***, *sep*, *-ge-*) **1.** *v/t* (*h*) draw in; *esp* TECH retract; duck; strike (*sail etc*); MIL draft, *Br* call up; confiscate; withdraw (*license etc*); make (*inquiries*); **2.** *v/i* (*sein*) move in; march in; soak in
einzig ['aintsɪç] *adj* only; single; ***kein Einziger ...*** not a single ...; ***das Einzige*** the only thing; ***der*** (***die***) ***Einzige*** the only one
einzigartig *adj* unique, singular
'Einzug *m* moving in; entry
Eis [ais] *n* (*-es*; *no pl*) ice; GASTR ice cream; ***Eis am Stiel*** ice lolly
Eisbahn *f* skating rink
Eisbär *m* ZO polar bear
Eisbecher *m* sundae
Eisbein *n* GASTR (pickled) pork knuckles
Eisberg *m* iceberg
Eisbrecher *m* (*-s*; -) MAR icebreaker
Eisdiele *f* ice-cream parlo(u)r
Eisen ['aizən] *n* (*-s*; -) iron

'Eisenbahn *f* railroad, *Br* railway; train set
'Eisenbahner [-baːnɐ] *m* (*-s*; -) railroadman, *Br* railwayman
'Eisenbahnwagen *m* (railroad) car, *Br* coach, railway carriage
'Eisenerz *n* iron ore
Eisengießerei *f* iron foundry
Eisenhütte *f* TECH ironworks
'Eisenwaren *pl* hardware, ironware
Eisenwarenhandlung *f* hardware store, *Br* ironmonger's
eisern ['aizɐn] *adj* iron (*a. fig*), of iron
'eisgekühlt *adj* iced
'Eishockey *n* hockey, *Br* ice hockey
eisig ['aizɪç] *adj* icy (*a. fig*)
'eis'kalt *adj* ice-cold
'Eiskunstlauf *m* (*-[e]s*; *no pl*) figure skating
Eiskunstläufer(in) figure skater
'Eismeer *n* polar sea
Eisre,vue *f* ice show
Eisschnelllauf *m* speed skating
Eisscholle *f* ice floe
Eisverkäufer *m* iceman
Eiswürfel *m* ice cube
Eiszapfen *m* icicle
Eiszeit *f* (-; *no pl*) GEOL ice age
eitel ['aitəl] *adj* vain
'Eitelkeit *f* (-; *no pl*) vanity
Eiter ['aitɐ] *m* (*-s*; *no pl*) MED pus
'Eiterbeule *f* MED abscess, boil
'eitern *v/i* (*ge-*, *h*) MED fester
eitrig ['aitrɪç] *adj* MED purulent, festering
'Eiweiß *n* (*-es*; *no pl*) white of egg; BIOL protein
'eiweißarm *adj* low in protein, low-protein
eiweißreich *adj* rich in protein, high-protein
'Eizelle *f* BIOL egg cell, ovum
Ekel ['eːkəl] **1.** *m* (*-s*; *no pl*) disgust (***vor*** *dat* at), loathing (for); ***Ekel erregend*** → ***ekelhaft***; **2.** F *n* (*-s*; -) beast
ekelerregend *adj* → ***ekelhaft***
'ekelhaft, 'ek(e)lig *adj* sickening, disgusting, repulsive
'ekeln *v/refl and v/impers* (*ge-*, *h*) ***ich ekle mich davor*** it makes me sick
Ekstase [ɛk'staːzə] *f* (-; *-n*) ecstasy
Elan [e'laːn] *m* (*-s*; *no pl*) vigo(u)r
elastisch [e'lastɪʃ] *adj* elastic, flexible
Elch [ɛlç] *m* (*-[e]s*; *-e*) ZO elk; moose
Elefant [ele'fant] *m* (*-en*; *-en*) ZO elephant
Ele'fantenhochzeit F *f* ECON jumbo merger
elegant [ele'gant] *adj* elegant
Eleganz [ele'gants] *f* (-; *no pl*) elegance
Elektriker [e'lɛktrɪkɐ] *m* (*-s*; -) electrician
elektrisch [e'lɛktrɪʃ] *adj* electrical; electric
elektrisieren [elɛktri'ziːrən] *v/t* (*no -ge-*, *h*) electrify
Elektrizität [elɛktritsi'tɛːt] *f* (-; *no pl*) electricity
Elektrizi'tätswerk *n* (electric) power station
Elektrogerät [e'lɛktro-] *n* electric appliance
Elektronik [elɛk'troːnɪk] *f* electronics; electronic system
elektronisch [elɛk'troːnɪʃ] *adj* electronic
E'lektrora,sierer *m* (*-s*; -) electric razor
Elektro'technik *f* electrical engineering
Elektro'techniker *m* electrical engineer
Element [ele'mɛnt] *n* (*-[e]s*; *-e*) element
elementar [elemɛn'taːɐ] *adj* elementary
elend ['eːlɛnt] *adj* miserable
'Elend *n* (*-s*; *no pl*) misery
'Elendsviertel *n* slums
elf [ɛlf] *adj* eleven
Elf *f* (-; *-en*) eleven; *soccer*: team
Elfe ['ɛlfə] *f* (-; *-n*) elf, fairy
'Elfenbein *n* ivory
Elf'meter *m* (*-s*; -) *soccer*: penalty
Elfmeterpunkt *m* penalty spot
Elfmeterschießen *n* penalty shoot-out
'elfte *adj* eleventh
Elite [e'liːtə] *f* (-; *-n*) elite
Ellbogen ['ɛl-] *m* ANAT elbow
Elster ['ɛlstɐ] *f* (-; *-n*) ZO magpie
elterlich ['ɛltɐlɪç] *adj* parental
Eltern ['ɛltɐn] *pl* parents
'Elternhaus *n* (one's parents') home
'elternlos *adj* orphan(ed)
'Elternteil *m* parent
Elternvertretung *f appr* Parent-Teacher Association
Email [e'mai] *n* (*-s*; *-s*), **Emaille** [e'maljə] *f* (-; *-n*) enamel
Emanze [e'mantsə] F *f* (-; *-n*) women's libber
Emanzipation [emantsipa'tsjoːn] *f* (-; *-en*) emancipation; women's lib(eration)
emanzipieren [emantsi'piːrən] *v/refl* (*no -ge-*, *h*) become emancipated
Embargo [ɛm'bargo] *n* (*-s*; *-s*) ECON embargo
Embolie [ɛmbo'liː] *f* (-; *-n*) MED embolism
Embryo ['ɛmbryo] *m* (*-s*; *-en* [ɛmbry'oːnən]) BIOL embryo
Emigrant [emi'grant] *m* (*-en*; *-en*), **Emi'grantin** *f* (-; *-nen*) emigrant, *esp* POL refugee
Emigration [emigra'tsjoːn] *f* (-; *-en*) emigration; ***in der Emigration*** in exile
emigrieren [emi'griːrən] *v/i* (*no -ge-*, *sein*) emigrate

Emission [emɪ'sjo:n] *f* (-; *-en*) PHYS emission; ECON issue
empfahl [ɛm'pfa:l] *pret of* ***empfehlen***
Empfang [ɛm'pfaŋ] *m* (-[*e*]*s*; *Empfänge* [ɛm'pfɛŋə]) reception (*a. radio, hotel*), welcome; receipt (***nach, bei*** on)
emp'fangen *v/t* (*irr*, ***fangen***, *no -ge-, h*) receive; welcome
Emp'fänger(in) (*-s*; *-/-*; *-nen*) receiver (*m a. radio*); addressee
emp'fänglich *adj* susceptible (***für*** to)
Empfängnis [ɛm'pfɛŋnɪs] *f* (-; *no pl*) MED conception
Empfängnisverhütung *f* MED contraception, birth control
Emp'fangsbescheinigung *f* receipt
Empfangsdame *f* receptionist
empfehlen [ɛm'pfe:lən] *v/t* (*irr, no -ge-, h*) recommend
emp'fehlenswert *adj* advisable
Emp'fehlung *f* (-; *-en*) recommendation
empfinden [ɛm'pfɪndən] *v/t* (*irr*, ***finden***, *no -ge-, h*) feel (***als*** ... to be ...)
empfindlich [ɛm'pfɪntlɪç] *adj* sensitive (***für, gegen*** to) (*a.* PHOT, CHEM); tender, delicate; touchy; irritable (*a.* MED); severe (*punishment etc*); ***empfindliche Stelle*** sore spot
Emp'findlichkeit *f* (-; *-en*) sensitivity; PHOT speed; delicacy; touchiness
empfindsam [ɛm'pfɪntza:m] *adj* sensitive
Emp'findung *f* (-; *-en*) sensation; perception; feeling, emotion
empfohlen [ɛm'pfo:lən] *pp of* ***empfehlen***
empor [ɛm'po:ɐ] *adv* up, upward(s)
empören [ɛm'pø:rən] *v/t* (*no -ge-, h*) outrage; shock; ***sich empören*** (***über*** *acc*) be outraged *or* shocked (at)
empörend *adj* shocking, outrageous
Em'porkömmling [-kœmlɪŋ] *contp m* (*-s*; *-e*) upstart
empört [ɛm'pø:ɐt] *adj* indignant (***über*** *acc* at), shocked (at)
Em'pörung *f* (-; *no pl*) indignation
emsig ['ɛmzɪç] *adj* busy
'Emsigkeit *f* (-; *no pl*) activity
Ende ['ɛndə] *n* (*-s*; *no pl*) end; *film*: ending; ***am Ende*** at the end; in the end, finally; ***zu Ende*** over; *time*: up; ***zu Ende gehen*** come to an end; ***zu Ende lesen*** finish reading; ***er ist Ende zwanzig*** he is in his late twenties; ***Ende Mai*** at the end of May; ***Ende der achtziger Jahre*** in the late eighties; *radio*: ***Ende!*** over!
'enden *v/i* (*ge-, h*) (come to an) end; stop, finish; F ***enden als*** end up as
'Endergebnis *n* final result
'endgültig *adj* final, definitive
Endlagerung ['ɛnt-] *f* final disposal (*of radioactive waste*)
'endlich *adv* finally, at last
'endlos *adj* endless
'Endrunde *f*, **Endspiel** *n* SPORT final(s)
Endspurt *m* SPORT final spurt (*a. fig*)
Endstati,on *f* RAIL terminus, terminal
Endsumme *f* (sum) total
'Endung *f* (-; *-en*) LING ending
Energie [enɛr'gi:] *f* (-; *-n*) energy; TECH, ELECTR power; ***Energiesparen*** *n* energy saving, conservation of energy
ener'giebewusst *adj* energy-conscious
Ener'giekrise *f* energy crisis
ener'gielos *adj* lacking in energy
Ener'giequelle *f* source of energy
Energieversorgung *f* power supply
energisch [e'nɛrgɪʃ] *adj* energetic, vigorous
eng [ɛŋ] *adj* narrow; tight; cramped; *fig* close; ***eng beieinander*** close(ly) together
Engagement [ãgaʒə'mã:] *n* (*-s*; *-s*) THEA *etc* engagement; POL commitment
engagieren [ãga'ʒi:rən] *v/t* (*no -ge-, h*) engage; ***sich engagieren für*** be very involved in
engagiert [ãga'ʒi:ɐt] *adj* involved, committed
Enge ['ɛŋə] *f* (-; *no pl*) narrowness; cramped conditions; ***in die Enge treiben*** drive into a corner
Engel ['ɛŋəl] *m* (*-s*; *-*) angel
'England England
Engländer ['ɛŋlɛndɐ] *m* (*-s*; *-*) Englishman; ***die Engländer*** *pl* the English
Engländerin ['ɛŋlɛndərɪn] *f* (-; *-nen*) Englishwoman
'englisch *adj* English; ***auf Englisch*** in English
'Englischunterricht *m* English lesson(s) *or* class(es); teaching of English
'Engpass *m* bottleneck (*a. fig*)
'engstirnig [-ʃtɪrnɪç] *adj* narrow-minded
Enkel ['ɛŋkəl] *m* (*-s*; *-*) grandchild; grandson
'Enkelin *f* (-; *-nen*) granddaughter
enorm [e'nɔrm] *adj* enormous; F terrific
Ensemble [ã'sã:bl] *n* (*-s*; *-s*) THEA company; cast
entarten [ɛnt'ʔa:ɐtən] *v/i* (*no -ge-, sein*),
ent'artet *adj* degenerate
Ent'artung *f* (-; *-en*) degeneration
entbehren [ɛnt'be:rən] *v/t* (*no -ge-, h*) do without; spare; miss
entbehrlich [ɛnt'be:ɐlɪç] *adj* dispensable; superfluous
Ent'behrung *f* (-; *-en*) want, privation
ent'binden (*irr*, ***binden***, *no -ge-, h*) **1.** *v/i* MED have the baby; **2.** *v/t*: ***j-n entbinden***

von** fig* relieve s.o. of; ***entbunden werden von MED give birth to
Ent'bindung *f* (-; *-en*) MED delivery
Ent'bindungsstati,on *f* MED maternity ward
entblößen [ɛnt'blø:sən] *v/t* (*no -ge-, h*) bare, uncover
ent'decken *v/t* (*no -ge-, h*) discover
Ent'decker *m* (*-s*; -), **Ent'deckerin** *f* (-; *-nen*) discoverer
Ent'deckung *f* (-; *-en*) discovery
Ente ['ɛntə] *f* (-; *-n*) ZO duck; F *fig* hoax
ent'ehren *v/t* (*no -ge-, h*) dishono(u)r
enteignen [ɛnt'ʔaignən] *v/t* (*no -ge-, h*) expropriate; dispossess *s.o.*
Ent'eignung *f* (-; *-en*) expropriation; dispossession
ent'erben *v/t* (*no -ge-, h*) disinherit
entern ['ɛntɐn] *v/t* (*ge-, h*) MAR board
entfachen [ɛnt'faxən] *v/t* (*no -ge-, h*) kindle, *fig a.* rouse
entfallen *v/i* (*irr*, ***fallen***, *no -ge-, sein*) be cancelled; ***entfallen auf*** (*acc*) fall to s.o. ('s share); ***es ist mir entfallen*** it has slipped my memory
entfalten *v/t* (*no -ge-, h*) unfold; *fig* develop; ***sich entfalten*** unfold; *fig* develop (***zu*** into)
entfernen [ɛnt'fɛrnən] *v/t* (*no -ge-, h*) remove (*a. fig*); ***sich entfernen*** leave
ent'fernt *adj* distant (*a. fig*); ***weit*** (***zehn Meilen***) ***entfernt*** far (10 miles) away
Ent'fernung *f* (-; *-en*) distance; removal
Ent'fernungsmesser *m* (*-s*; -) PHOT range finder
ent'flammbar *adj* (in)flammable
entfremden [ɛnt'frɛmdən] *v/t* (*no -ge-, h*) estrange (*dat* from)
Ent'fremdung *f* (-; *-en*) estrangement, alienation
ent'führen *v/t* (*no -ge-, h*) kidnap; AVIAT hijack
Ent'führer *m* (*-s*; -) kidnapper; AVIAT hijacker
Ent'führung *f* (-; *-en*) kidnapping; AVIAT hijacking
ent'gegen *prp* (*dat*) *and adv* contrary to; toward(s)
entgegengehen *v/i* (*irr*, ***gehen***, *sep, -ge-, sein*) go to meet
ent'gegengesetzt *adj* opposite
ent'gegenkommen *v/i* (*irr*, ***kommen***, *sep, -ge-, sein*) come to meet; *fig* ***j-m entgegenkommen*** meet s.o. halfway
entgegenkommend *fig adj* obliging
ent'gegennehmen *v/t* (*irr*, ***nehmen***, *sep, -ge-, h*) accept, receive
entgegensehen *v/i* (*irr*, ***sehen***, *sep, -ge-, h*) await; look forward to *s.th.*
entgegensetzen *v/t* (*sep, -ge-, h*) ***j-m Widerstand entgegensetzen*** put up resistance to s.o.
entgegentreten *v/i* (*irr*, ***treten***, *sep, -ge-, sein*) walk towards; oppose; face
entgegnen [ɛnt'ge:gnən] *v/i* (*no -ge-, h*) reply, answer; retort
Ent'gegnung *f* (-; *-en*) reply; retort
ent'gehen *v/i* (*irr*, ***gehen***, *no -ge-, sein*) escape; miss
entgeistert [ɛnt'gaistɐt] *adj* aghast
Entgelt [ɛnt'gɛlt] *n* (*-[e]s*; *-e*) remuneration; fee
entgiften [ɛnt'gɪftən] *v/t* (*no -ge-, h*) decontaminate
entgleisen [ɛnt'glaizən] *v/i* (*no -ge-, sein*) RAIL be derailed; *fig* blunder
ent'gleiten *fig v/i* (*irr*, ***gleiten***, *no -ge-, sein*) get out of control
entgräten [ɛnt'grɛ:tən] *v/t* (*no -ge-, h*) bone, fil(l)et
ent'halten *v/t* (*irr*, ***halten***, *no -ge-, h*) contain, hold; include; ***sich enthalten*** (*gen*) abstain *or* refrain from
ent'haltsam *adj* abstinent; moderate
Ent'haltsamkeit *f* (-; *no pl*) abstinence; moderation
Ent'haltung *f* (-; *-en*) abstention
ent'härten *v/t* (*no -ge-, h*) soften
enthaupten [ɛnt'hauptən] *v/t* (*no -ge-, h*) behead, decapitate
ent'hüllen *v/t* (*no -ge-, h*) uncover; unveil; *fig* reveal, disclose
Ent'hüllung *f* (-; *-en*) unveiling; *fig* revelation, disclosure
Enthusiasmus [ɛntu'zjasmʊs] *m* (-; *no pl*) enthusiasm
Enthusiast(in) [-'zjast(-ɪn)] (*-en, -en*/-; *-nen*) enthusiast; *film*, SPORT F fan
enthusi'astisch *adj* enthusiastic
ent'kleiden *v/t and v/refl* (*no -ge-, h*) undress, strip
ent'kommen *v/i* (*irr*, ***kommen***, *no -ge-, sein*) escape (*dat* from)
ent'korken *v/t* (*no -ge-, h*) uncork
entkräften [ɛnt'krɛftən] *v/t* (*no -ge-, h*) weaken (*a. fig*)
Ent'kräftung *f* (-; *-en*) weakening, exhaustion
ent'laden *v/t* (*irr*, ***laden***, *no -ge-, h*) unload; *esp* ELECTR discharge; ***sich entladen*** *esp* ELECTR discharge; *fig* explode
Ent'ladung *f* (-; *-en*) unloading; *esp* ELECTR discharge; *fig* explosion
ent'lang *prp* (*dat*) *and adv* along; ***hier entlang, bitte!*** this way, please!; ***die Straße*** *etc* ***entlang*** along the street *etc*
entlarven [ɛnt'larfən] *v/t* (*no -ge-, h*) unmask, expose

ent'lassen *v/t* (*irr*, ***lassen***, *no -ge-*, *h*) dismiss, F fire, give *s.o.* the sack; MED discharge; JUR release
Ent'lassung *f* (-; *-en*) dismissal; MED discharge; JUR release
ent'lasten *v/t* (*no -ge-*, *h*) relieve *s.o.* of some of his work; JUR exonerate, clear *s.o.* of a charge; ***den Verkehr entlasten*** relieve the traffic congestion
Ent'lastung *f* (-; *-en*) relief; JUR exoneration
Ent'lastungszeuge *m* JUR witness for the defense (*Br* defence)
ent'laufen *v/i* (*irr*, ***laufen***, *no -ge-*, *sein*) run away (*dat* from)
ent'legen *adj* remote, distant
ent'locken *v/t* (*no -ge-*, *h*) draw, elicit (*dat* from)
ent'lohnen *v/t* (*no -ge-*, *h*) pay (off)
ent'lüften *v/t* (*no -ge-*, *h*) ventilate
entmachten [ɛnt'maxtən] *v/t* (*no -ge-*, *h*) deprive *s.o.* of *his* power
entmilitarisieren [ɛntmilitari'ziːrən] *v/t* (*no -ge-*, *h*) demilitarize
entmündigen [ɛnt'mʏndɪgən] *v/t* (*no -ge-*, *h*) JUR place under disability
entmutigen [ɛnt'muːtɪgən] *v/t* (*no -ge-*, *h*) discourage
ent'nehmen *v/t* (*irr*, ***nehmen***, *no -ge-*, *h*) take (*dat* from); ***entnehmen aus*** (with-)draw from; *fig* gather *or* learn from
ent'puppen *v/refl* (*no -ge-*, *h*) ***sich entpuppen als*** turn out to be
ent'rahmen *v/t* (*no -ge-*, *h*) skim
ent'reißen *v/t* (*irr*, ***reißen***, *no -ge-*, *h*) snatch (away) (*dat* from)
ent'rinnen *v/i* (*irr*, ***rinnen***, *no -ge-*, *sein*) escape (*dat* from)
ent'rollen *v/t* (*no -ge-*, *h*) unroll
ent'rüsten *v/t* (*no -ge-*, *h*) fill with indignation; ***sich entrüsten*** become indignant (***über*** *acc* at *s.th.*, with *s.o.*)
ent'rüstet *adj* indignant (***über*** *acc* at *s.th.*, with *s.o.*;) **Ent'rüstung** *f* (-; *-en*) indignation
Entsafter [ɛnt'zaftɐ] *m* (*-s*; -) juice extractor
ent'salzen *v/t* (*no -ge-*, *h*) desalinize
ent'schädigen *v/t* (*no -ge-*, *h*) compensate
Ent'schädigung *f* (-; *-en*) compensation
ent'schärfen *v/t* (*no -ge-*, *h*) defuse (*a. fig*)
ent'scheiden *v/t and v/i and v/refl* (*irr*, ***scheiden***, *no -ge-*, *h*) decide (***für*** on, in favo[u]r of; ***gegen*** against); settle; ***er kann sich nicht entscheiden*** he can't make up his mind
entscheidend *adj* decisive; crucial
Ent'scheidung *f* (-; *-en*) decision
entschieden [ɛnt'ʃiːdən] *adj* decided, determined, resolute; ***entschieden dafür*** strongly in favo(u)r of it
Ent'schiedenheit *f* (-; *no pl*) determination
ent'schließen *v/refl* (*irr*, ***schließen***, *no -ge-*, *h*) decide, determine, make up one's mind
Ent'schließung *f* (-; *-en*) POL resolution
entschlossen [ɛnt'ʃlɔsən] *adj* determined, resolute
Ent'schlossenheit *f* (-; *no pl*) determination, resoluteness
Ent'schluss *m* decision, resolution
entschlüsseln [ɛnt'ʃlʏsəln] *v/t* (*no -ge-*, *h*) decipher, decode
entschuldigen [ɛnt'ʃʊldɪgən] *v/t* (*no -ge-*, *h*) excuse; ***sich entschuldigen*** apologize (***bei*** to; ***für*** for); excuse o.s.; ***entschuldigen Sie!*** (I'm) sorry!; excuse me!
Ent'schuldigung *f* (-; *-en*) excuse; apology; ***um Entschuldigung bitten*** apologize; ***Entschuldigung!*** (I'm) sorry!; excuse me!
ent'setzen *v/t* (*no -ge-*, *h*) shock; horrify
Ent'setzen *n* (*-s*; *no pl*) horror, terror
ent'setzlich *adj* horrible, dreadful, terrible; atrocious
ent'setzt *adj* shocked; horrified
ent'sichern *v/t* (*no -ge-*, *h*) release the safety catch of
ent'sinnen *v/refl* (*irr*, ***sinnen***, *no -ge-*, *h*) remember, recall
ent'sorgen *v/t* (*no -ge-*, *h*) dispose of
Ent'sorgung *f* (-; *-en*) (waste) disposal
ent'spannen *v/t and v/refl* (*no -ge-*, *h*) relax; ***sich entspannen*** *a.* take it easy; *fig* ease (up)
ent'spannt *adj* relaxed
Ent'spannung *f* (-; *-en*) relaxation; POL détente
ent'spiegelt *adj* OPT non-glare
ent'sprechen *v/i* (*irr*, ***sprechen***, *no -ge-*, *h*) correspond to; answer to *a description*; meet (*requirements etc*)
entsprechend *adj* corresponding (*dat* to); appropriate
Ent'sprechung *f* (-; *-en*) equivalent
ent'springen *v/i* (*irr*, ***springen***, *no -ge-*, *sein*) *river*: rise
entstehen *v/i* (*irr*, ***stehen***, *no -ge-*, *sein*) come into being; arise; emerge, develop; ***entstehen aus*** originate from
Ent'stehung *f* (-; *-en*) origin
ent'stellen *v/t* (*no -ge-*, *h*) disfigure, deform; *fig* distort
Ent'stellung *f* (-; *-en*) disfigurement, deformation, distortion (*a. fig*)
entstört [ɛnt'ʃtøːɐt] *adj* ELECTR interfer-

ence-free
ent'täuschen *v/t* (*no -ge-, h*) disappoint
Ent'täuschung *f* (-; *-en*) disappointment
entwaffnen [ɛnt'vafnən] *v/t* (*no -ge-, h*) disarm
Ent'warnung *f* all clear (signal)
ent'wässern *v/t* (*no -ge-, h*) drain
Ent'wässerung *f* (-; *-en*) drainage; CHEM dehydration
'entweder *cj*: ***entweder ... oder*** either ... or
ent'weichen *v/i* (*irr*, ***weichen***, *no -ge-, sein*) escape (***aus*** from)
ent'weihen *v/t* (*no -ge-, h*) desecrate
ent'wenden *v/t* (*no -ge-, h*) pilfer, steal
ent'werfen *v/t* (*irr*, ***werfen***, *no -ge-, h*) design; draw up
ent'werten *v/t* (*no -ge-, h*) lower the value of (*a. fig*); cancel
Ent'wertung *f* (-; *-en*) devaluation; cancellation
ent'wickeln *v/t and v/refl* (*no -ge-, h*) develop (*a.* PHOT) (***zu*** into)
Ent'wicklung *f* (-; *-en*) development, BIOL *a.* evolution; adolescence, age of puberty
Ent'wicklungshelfer *m*, **Entwicklungshelferin** *f* POL, ECON development aid volunteer; Peace Corps volunteer, *Br* VSO worker
Entwicklungshilfe *f* development aid
Entwicklungsland *n* POL developing country
entwirren [ɛnt'vɪrən] *v/t* (*no -ge-, h*) disentangle (*a. fig*)
ent'wischen *v/i* (*no -ge-, sein*) get away
ent'würdigend *adj* degrading
Ent'wurf *m* outline, (rough) draft, plan; design; sketch
ent'wurzeln *v/t* (*no -ge-, h*) uproot
ent'ziehen *v/t* (*irr*, ***ziehen***, *no -ge-, h*) take away (*dat* from); revoke (*license etc*); deprive of *rights etc*; CHEM extract; ***sich j-m (e-r Sache) entziehen*** evade s.o. (s.th.)
Ent'ziehungsanstalt *f* substance (*Br* drug) abuse clinic
Entziehungskur *f* detoxi(fi)cation (treatment), *a.* F drying out
entziffern [ɛnt'tsɪfɐn] *v/t* (*no -ge-, h*) decipher, make out
ent'zücken *v/t* (*no -ge-, h*) charm, delight
Ent'zücken *n* (*-s*; *no pl*) delight
ent'zückend *adj* delightful, charming, F sweet
ent'zückt *adj* delighted (***über*** *acc*, ***von*** at, with)
Ent'zug *m* withdrawal; revocation
Ent'zugserscheinung *f* MED withdrawal symptom
entzündbar [ɛnt'tsʏntbaːɐ] *adj* (in-)flammable
ent'zünden *v/refl* (*no -ge-, h*) catch fire; MED become inflamed
Ent'zündung *f* (-; *-en*) MED inflammation
ent'zwei *adv* in two, to pieces
Enzyklopädie [ɛntsyklopɛ'diː] *f* (-; *-n*) encyclop(a)edia
Epidemie [epide'miː] *f* (-; *-n*) MED epidemic (disease)
Epilog [epi'loːk] *m* (-[*e*]*s*; *-e* [epi'loːgə]) epilog, *Br* epilogue
episch ['eːpɪʃ] *adj* epic
Episode [epi'zoːdə] *f* (-; *-n*) episode
Epoche [e'pɔxə] *f* (-; *-n*) epoch, period, era
Epos ['eːpɔs] *n* (-; *Epen* ['eːpən]) epic (poem)
er [eːɐ] *pers pron* he; it
Er'achten *n*: ***meines Erachtens*** in my opinion
Erbanlage ['ɛrp-] *f* BIOL genes, genetic code
erbarmen [ɛɐ'barmən] *v/refl* (*no -ge-, h*) ***sich j-s erbarmen*** take pity on s.o.
erbärmlich [ɛɐ'bɛrmlɪç] *adj* pitiful, pitiable; miserable; mean
er'barmungslos *adj* pitiless, merciless
er'bauen *v/t* (*no -ge-, h*) build, construct
Er'bauer *m* (*-s*; -) builder, constructor
er'baulich *adj* edifying
Er'bauung *fig f* (-; *-en*) edification, uplift
Erbe ['ɛrbə] **1.** *m* (*-n*; *-n*) heir; **2.** *n* (*-s*; *no pl*) inheritance, heritage
erben ['ɛrbən] *v/t* (*ge-, h*) inherit
erbeuten [ɛɐ'bɔytən] *v/t* (*no -ge-, h*) MIL capture; *thief*: get away with
'Erbfaktor *m* BIOL gene
Erbin ['ɛrbɪn] *f* (-; *-nen*) heir, heiress
er'bitten *v/t* (*irr*, ***bitten***, *no -ge-, h*) ask for, request
erbittert [ɛɐ'bɪtɐt] *adj* fierce, furious
'Erbkrankheit *f* MED hereditary disease
erblich ['ɛrplɪç] *adj* hereditary
er'blicken *v/t* (*no -ge-, h*) see, catch sight of
erblinden [ɛɐ'blɪndən] *v/i* (*no -ge-, sein*) go blind
er'brechen *v/t and v/refl* (*irr*, ***brechen***, *no -ge-, h*) MED vomit
Erbschaft ['ɛrpʃaft] *f* (-; *-en*) inheritance, heritage
Erbse ['ɛrpsə] *f* (-; *-n*) BOT pea; (***grüne***) ***Erbsen*** green peas
'Erbstück *n* heirloom
Erdapfel ['eːɐt-] *Austrian m* potato
Erdball *m* (-[*e*]*s*; *no pl*) globe
Erdbeben *n* (*-s*; -) earthquake
Erdbeere *f* BOT strawberry
Erdboden *m* earth, ground

E

Erde ['eːɐdə] *f* (-; *-n*) a) (*no pl*) earth, b) ground, soil; → ***eben***
'erden *v/t* (*ge-, h*) ELECTR earth, ground
erdenklich [ɛɐ'dɛŋklɪç] *adj* imaginable
Erdgas ['eːɐt-] *n* natural gas
Erdgeschoss *n*, **Erdgeschoß** *Austrian n* first (*Br* ground) floor
er'dichten *v/t* (*no -ge-, h*) invent, make up
er'dichtet *adj* invented, made-up
erdig ['eːɐdɪç] *adj* earthy
'Erdklumpen *m* clod, lump of earth
Erdkruste *f* earth's crust
Erdkugel *f* globe
Erdkunde *f* (-; *no pl*) geography
Erdleitung *f* ELECTR ground (*Br* earth) connection; underground pipe(line)
Erdnuss *f* BOT peanut
Erdöl *n* (mineral) oil, petroleum
Erdreich *n* ground, earth
erdreisten [ɛɐ'draistən] *v/refl* (*no -ge-, h*) F have the nerve
er'drosseln *v/t* (*no -ge-, h*) throttle
er'drücken *v/t* (*no -ge-, h*) crush (to death)
erdrückend *fig adj* overwhelming
'Erdrutsch *m* (-[*e*]*s*; *-e*) landslide (*a.* POL)
Erdteil *m* GEOGR continent
er'dulden *v/t* (*no -ge-, h*) suffer, endure
'Erdumlaufbahn *f* earth orbit
'Erdung *f* (-; *-en*) ELECTR grounding, *Br* earthing
'Erdwärme *f* GEOL geothermal energy
er'eifern *v/refl* (*no -ge-, h*) get excited
ereignen [ɛɐ'ʔaignən] *v/refl* (*no -ge-, h*) happen, occur
Ereignis [ɛɐ'ʔaignɪs] *n* (*-ses*; *-se*) event, occurrence
er'eignisreich *adj* eventful
Erektion [erɛk'tsjoːn] *f* (-; *-en*) erection
Eremit [ere'miːt] *m* (*-en*; *-en*) hermit, anchorite
er'fahren[1] *v/t* (*irr*, ***fahren***, *no -ge-, h*) hear; learn; experience
er'fahren[2] *adj* experienced
Er'fahrung *f* (-; *-en*) (work) experience
Er'fahrungsaustausch *m* exchange of experience
er'fahrungsgemäß *adv* as experience shows
er'fassen *v/t* (*no -ge-, h*) grasp; record, register; cover, include; EDP collect
er'finden *v/t* (*irr*, ***finden***, *no -ge-, h*) invent
Er'finder(in) (*-s*; -/-; *-nen*) inventor
erfinderisch [ɛɐ'fɪndərɪʃ] *adj* inventive
Er'findung *f* (-; *-en*) invention
Er'findungskraft *f* (-; *no pl*) inventiveness
Erfolg [ɛɐ'fɔlk] *m* (-[*e*]*s*; *-e*) success; result; ***viel Erfolg!*** good luck!; ***Erfolg versprechend*** promising
er'folgen *v/i* (*no -ge-, sein*) happen, take place
er'folglos *adj* unsuccessful; futile
Er'folglosigkeit *f* (-; *no pl*) lack of success
er'folgreich *adj* successful
Er'folgserlebnis *n* sense of achievement
erforderlich [ɛɐ'fɔrdɐlɪç] *adj* necessary, required
er'fordern *v/t* (*no -ge-, h*) require, demand
Erfordernis [ɛɐ'fɔrdɐnɪs] *n* (*-ses*; *-se*) requirement, demand
er'forschen *v/t* (*no -ge-, h*) explore; investigate, study
Er'forscher *m* explorer
Er'forschung *f* exploration
er'freuen *v/t* (*no -ge-, h*) please
erfreulich [ɛɐ'frɔylɪç] *adj* pleasing, pleasant; gratifying
er'freut *adj* pleased (***über*** *acc* at, about); ***sehr erfreut!*** pleased to meet you
er'frieren *v/i* (*irr*, ***frieren***, *no -ge-, sein*) freeze to death
Er'frierung *f* (-; *-en*) MED frostbite
er'frischen *v/t and v/refl* (*no -ge-, h*) refresh (o.s.)
erfrischend *adj* refreshing
Er'frischung *f* (-; *-en*) refreshment
erfroren [ɛɐ'froːrən] *adj* frostbitten; BOT killed by frost
er'füllen *fig v/t* (*no -ge-, h*) fulfil(l); keep (*promise etc*); serve (*purpose etc*); meet (*requirements etc*); ***erfüllen mit*** fill with; ***sich erfüllen*** be fulfilled, come true
Er'füllung *f* (-; *-en*) fulfil(l)ment; ***in Erfüllung gehen*** come true
ergänzen [ɛɐ'gɛntsən] *v/t* (*no -ge-, h*) complement (***einander*** each other); supplement, add
ergänzend *adj* complementary, supplementary
Er'gänzung *f* (-; *-en*) completion; supplement, addition
ergattern [ɛɐ'gatɐn] F *v/t* (*no -ge-, h*) (manage to) get hold of
er'geben (*irr*, ***geben***, *no -ge-, h*) **1.** *v/t* amount *or* come to; **2.** *v/refl* surrender; *fig* arise; ***sich ergeben aus*** result from; ***sich ergeben in*** (*acc*) resign o.s. to
Er'gebenheit *f* (-; *no pl*) devotion
Ergebnis [ɛɐ'geːpnɪs] *n* (*-ses*; *-se*) result, SPORT *a.* score; outcome
er'gebnislos *adj* without result
er'gehen *v/i* (*irr*, ***gehen***, *no -ge-, sein*) *order etc*: be issued (***an*** *acc* to); ***wie ist es dir ergangen?*** how did things go with you?; ***et. über sich ergehen lassen*** (patiently) endure s.th.
ergiebig [ɛɐ'giːbɪç] *adj* productive, rich
Er'giebigkeit *f* (-; *no pl*) (high) yield; productiveness

er'gießen *v/refl* (*irr*, ***gießen***, *no -ge-*, *h*) ***sich ergießen über*** (*acc*) pour down on
er'grauen *v/i* (*no -ge-*, *sein*) turn gray (*Br* grey)
er'greifen *v/t* (*irr*, ***greifen***, *no -ge-*, *h*) seize, grasp, take hold of; take (*measures etc*); take up; *fig* move, touch
ergriffen [ɛɐ'grɪfən] *fig adj* moved
Er'griffenheit *f* (-; *no pl*) emotion
er'gründen *v/t* (*no -ge-*, *h*) find out, fathom
er'haben *adj* raised, elevated; *fig* sublime; ***erhaben sein über*** (*acc*) be above
er'halten[1] *v/t* (*irr*, ***halten***, *no -ge-*, *h*) get, receive; keep, preserve; protect; support, maintain (*family etc*)
er'halten[2] *adj*: ***gut erhalten*** in good condition
erhältlich [ɛɐ'hɛltlɪç] *adj* obtainable, available
Er'haltung *f* (-; *no pl*) preservation; upkeep
er'hängen *v/t* (*no -ge-*, *h*) hang (***sich*** o.s.)
er'heben *v/t* (*irr*, ***heben***, *no -ge-*, *h*) raise (*a. voice*), lift; ***sich erheben*** rise up (***gegen*** against)
erheblich [ɛɐ'heːplɪç] *adj* considerable
Er'hebung *f* (-; *-en*) survey; revolt
erheitern [ɛɐ'haitɐn] *v/t* (*no -ge-*, *h*) cheer up, amuse
erhellen [ɛɐ'hɛlən] *v/t* (*no -ge-*, *h*) light up; *fig* throw light upon
erhitzen [ɛɐ'hɪtsən] *v/t* (*no -ge-*, *h*) heat; ***sich erhitzen*** get hot
er'hoffen *v/t* (*no -ge-*, *h*) hope for
erhöhen [ɛɐ'høːən] *v/t* (*no -ge-*, *h*) raise; increase
Er'höhung *f* (-; *-en*) increase
er'holen *v/refl* (*no -ge-*, *h*) recover; relax, rest
erholsam [ɛɐ'hoːlzaːm] *adj* restful, relaxing
Er'holung *f* (-; *no pl*) recovery; relaxation
Er'holungsheim *n* rest home
erinnern [ɛɐ'ʔɪnɐn] *v/t* (*no -ge-*, *h*) ***j-n erinnern an*** (*acc*) remind s.o. of; ***sich erinnern an*** (*acc*) remember, recall
Erinnerung [ɛɐ'ɪnərʊŋ] *f* (-; *-en*) memory (***an*** *acc* of); remembrance, souvenir; keepsake; ***zur Erinnerung an*** (*acc*) in memory of
erkalten [ɛɐ'kaltən] *v/i* (*no -ge-*, *sein*) cool down (*a. fig*)
erkälten [ɛɐ'kɛltən] *v/refl* (*no -ge-*, *h*) ***sich erkälten*** catch (a) cold; (***stark***) ***erkältet sein*** have a (bad) cold
Er'kältung *f* (-; *-en*) cold
erkennbar [ɛɐ'kɛnbaːɐ] *adj* recognizable
er'kennen *v/t* (*irr*, ***kennen***, *no -ge-*, *h*) recognize (***an*** *dat* by), know (by); see, realize
er'kenntlich *adj*: ***sich*** (***j-m***) ***erkenntlich zeigen*** show (s.o.) one's gratitude
Er'kenntnis *f* (-; *-se*) realization; discovery; *pl* findings
Er'kennungsdienst *m* (police) records department
Erkennungsmelo,die *f* signature tune
Erkennungszeichen *n* badge; AVIAT markings
Erker ['ɛrkɐ] *m* (*-s*; -) ARCH bay
Erkerfenster *n* ARCH bay window
er'klären *v/t* (*no -ge-*, *h*) explain (***j-m*** to s.o.); declare; ***j-n*** (*offiziell*) ***für ... erklären*** pronounce s.o. ...
erklärend *adj* explanatory
erklärlich [ɛɐ'klɛːɐlɪç] *adj* explainable
er'klärt *adj* declared
Er'klärung *f* (-; *-en*) explanation; declaration; definition; ***e-e Erklärung abgeben*** make a statement
er'klingen *v/i* (*irr*, ***klingen***, *no -ge-*, *sein*) (re)sound, ring (out)
erkranken [ɛɐ'kraŋkən] *v/i* (*no -ge-*, *sein*) fall ill, get sick; ***erkranken an*** (*dat*) get
Er'krankung *f* (-; *-en*) illness, sickness
erkunden [ɛɐ'kʊndən] *v/t* (*no -ge-*, *h*) explore
erkundigen [ɛɐ'kʊndɪgən] *v/refl* (*no -ge-*, *h*) inquire (***nach*** about *s.th.*; after *s.o.*); make inquiries (about); ***sich*** (***bei j-m***) ***nach dem Weg erkundigen*** ask (s.o.) the way
Er'kundigung *f* (-; *-en*) inquiry
Er'kundung *f* (-; *-en*) exploration; MIL reconnaissance
Erlagschein [ɛɐ'laːk-] *Austrian m* money-order form
er'lahmen *v/i* (*no -ge-*, *sein*) flag
Erlass [ɛɐ'las] *m* (*-es*; *-e*) decree; JUR remission
er'lassen *v/t* (*irr*, ***lassen***, *no -ge-*, *h*) issue; enact (*bill etc*); ***j-m et. erlassen*** release s.o. from s.th.
erlauben [ɛɐ'laubən] *v/t* (*no -ge-*, *h*) allow, permit; ***sich et. erlauben*** permit o.s. (*or* dare) to do s.th.; treat o.s. to s.th.
Erlaubnis [ɛɐ'laupnɪs] *f* (-; *no pl*) permission; authority; ***um Erlaubnis bitten*** ask s.o.'s permission
Erlaubnisschein *m* permit
erläutern [ɛɐ'lɔytɐn] *v/t* (*no -ge-*, *h*) explain, illustrate
Er'läuterung *f* (-; *-en*) explanation; annotation
Erle ['ɛrlə] *f* (-; *-n*) BOT alder
er'leben *v/t* (*no -ge-*, *h*) experience; go through; see; have; ***das werden wir***

nicht mehr erleben we won't live to see that

Erlebnis [ɛɐ'le:pnɪs] *n* (*-ses*; *-se*) experience; adventure

er'lebnisreich *adj* eventful

erledigen [ɛɐ'le:dɪgən] *v/t* (*no -ge-*, *h*) take care of, do, handle; settle; F finish *s.o.* (*a.* SPORT); do *s.o.* in

erledigt [ɛɐ'le:dɪçt] *adj* finished, settled; F worn out; F ***der ist erledigt!*** he is done for

Er'ledigung *f* (*-*; *-en*) a) (*no pl*) settlement, b) *pl* things to do, shopping

er'legen *v/t* (*no -ge-*, *h*) HUNT shoot

erleichtern [ɛɐ'laɪçtɐn] *v/t* (*no -ge-*, *h*) ease, relieve

er'leichtert *adj* relieved

Er'leichterung [-tərʊŋ] *f* (*-*; *no pl*) relief (***über*** *acc* at)

er'leiden *v/t* (*irr*, ***leiden***, *no -ge-*, *h*) suffer

er'lesen *adj* choice, select

er'leuchten *v/t* (*no -ge-*, *h*) illuminate

er'liegen *v/i* (*irr*, ***liegen***, *no -ge-*, *sein*) succumb to

Er'liegen *n*: ***zum Erliegen kommen*** (***bringen***) come (bring) to a standstill

erlogen [ɛɐ'lo:gən] *adj* false; ***erlogen sein*** be a lie

Erlös [ɛɐ'lø:s] *m* (*-es*; *-e*) proceeds; profit(s)

erlosch [ɛɐ'lɔʃ] *pret of* ***erlöschen***

erloschen [ɛɐ'lɔʃən] **1.** *pp of* ***erlöschen***; **2.** *adj* extinct (*volcano*)

er'löschen *v/i* (*irr*, *no -ge-*, *sein*) go out; *fig* die; JUR lapse, expire

er'lösen *v/t* (*no -ge-*, *h*) deliver, free (*both*: ***von*** from)

Erlöser [ɛɐ'lø:zɐ] *m* (*-s*; *no pl*) REL Savio(u)r

Er'lösung *f* (*-*; *no pl*) REL salvation; relief

ermächtigen [ɛɐ'mɛçtɪgən] *v/t* (*no -ge-*, *h*) authorize

Er'mächtigung *f* (*-*; *-en*) authorization; authority

er'mahnen *v/t* (*no -ge-*, *h*) admonish; reprove, warn (*a.* SPORT)

Er'mahnung *f* (*-*; *-en*) admonition; warning; *esp* SPORT (first) caution

Er'mangelung *f*: ***in Ermangelung*** (*gen*) for want of

ermäßigt [ɛɐ'mɛ:sɪçt] *adj* reduced, cut

Er'mäßigung *f* (*-*; *-en*) reduction, cut

er'messen *v/t* (*irr*, ***messen***, *no -ge-*, *h*) assess; judge

Er'messen *n* (*-s*; *no pl*) discretion; ***nach eigenem Ermessen*** at one's own discretion

er'mitteln (*no -ge-*, *h*) **1.** *v/t* find out; determine; **2.** *v/i esp* JUR investigate

Er'mittlung *f* (*-*; *-en*) finding; JUR investigation

er'möglichen *v/t* (*no -ge-*, *h*) make possible

er'morden *v/t* (*no -ge-*, *h*) murder; *esp* POL assassinate

Er'mordung *f* (*-*; *-en*) murder; *esp* POL assassination

ermüden [ɛɐ'my:dən] (*no -ge-*) **1.** *v/t* (*h*) tire, fatigue; **2.** *v/i* (*sein*) tire, get tired, fatigue (*a.* TECH)

Er'müdung *f* (*-*; *no pl*) fatigue, tiredness

er'muntern [ɛɐ'mʊntɐn] *v/t* (*no -ge-*, *h*) encourage; stimulate

Er'munterung *f* (*-*; *-en*) encouragement; incentive

ermutigen [ɛɐ'mu:tɪgən] *v/t* (*no -ge-*, *h*) encourage

ermutigend *adj* encouraging

Er'mutigung *f* (*-*; *-en*) encouragement

er'nähren *v/t* (*no -ge-*, *h*) feed; support (*family etc*); ***sich ernähren von*** live on

Er'nährer *m* (*-s*; *-*) breadwinner, supporter

Er'nährung *f* (*-*; *no pl*) nutrition, food, diet

er'nennen *v/t* (*irr*, ***nennen***, *no -ge-*, *h*) ***j-n ernennen zu*** appoint s.o. (to be)

Er'nennung *f* (*-*; *-en*) appointment

erneuern [ɛɐ'nɔʏɐn] *v/t* (*no -ge-*, *h*) renew

Er'neuerung *f* (*-*; *-en*) renewal

er'neut **1.** *adj* renewed **2.** *adv* once more

erniedrigen [ɛɐ'ni:drɪgən] *v/t* (*no -ge-*, *h*) humiliate; ***sich erniedrigen*** degrade o.s.

Er'niedrigung *f* (*-*; *-en*) humiliation

ernst [ɛrnst] *adj* serious, earnest; ***ernst nehmen*** take *s.o. or s.th.* seriously

Ernst *m* (*-es*; *no pl*) seriousness, earnest; ***im Ernst***(?) seriously(?); ***ist das dein Ernst?*** are you serious?

'ernsthaft, **'ernstlich** *adj* serious

Ernte ['ɛrntə] *f* (*-*; *-n*) harvest; crop(s)

'Erntedankfest *n* Thanksgiving (Day), *Br* harvest festival

'ernten *v/t* (*ge-*, *h*) harvest, reap (*a. fig*)

er'nüchtern *v/t* (*no -ge-*, *h*) sober, *fig a.* disillusion

Er'nüchterung *f* (*-*; *-en*) sobering up; *fig* disillusionment

Eroberer [ɛɐ'ʔo:bərɐ] *m* (*-s*; *-*) conqueror

erobern [ɛɐ'ʔo:bɐn] *v/t* (*no -ge-*, *h*) conquer

Er'oberung *f* (*-*; *-en*) conquest (*a. fig*)

er'öffnen *v/t* (*no -ge-*, *h*) open; inaugurate; disclose *s.th.* (***j-m*** to s.o.)

Er'öffnung *f* (*-*; *-en*) opening; inauguration; disclosure

erörtern [ɛɐ'ʔœrtɐn] *v/t* (*no -ge-*, *h*) discuss

Er'örterung *f* (-; *-en*) discussion
Erotik [e'ro:tɪk] *f* (-; *no pl*) eroticism
erotisch [e'ro:tɪʃ] *adj* erotic
er'pressen *v/t* (*no -ge-, h*) blackmail; extort
Er'presser(in) (*-s; -/-; -nen*) blackmailer
Er'pressung *f* (-; *-en*) blackmail(ing); extortion
er'proben *v/t* (*no -ge-, h*) try, test
er'raten *v/t* (*irr*, ***raten***, *no -ge-, h*) guess
er'rechnen *v/t* (*no -ge-, h*) calculate, work *s.th.* out
erregbar [ɛɐ're:kba:ɐ] *adj* excitable; irritable
er'regen *v/t* (*no -ge-, h*) excite, *sexually*: *a.* arouse; *fig* rouse; cause; ***sich erregen*** get excited
erregend *adj* exciting, thrilling
Er'reger *m* (*-s; -*) MED germ, virus
Er'regung *f* (-; *-en*) excitement
erreichbar [ɛɐ'raiçba:ɐ] *adj* within reach (*a. fig*); available; ***leicht erreichbar*** within easy reach; ***nicht erreichbar*** out of reach; not available
er'reichen *v/t* (*no -ge-, h*) reach; catch (*train etc*); ***es erreichen, dass ...*** succeed in *doing s.th.*; ***et. erreichen*** get somewhere; ***telefonisch zu erreichen sein*** have a (*Br* be on the) phone
er'richten *v/t* (*no -ge-, h*) put up, erect; *fig* found, *esp* ECON set up
Er'richtung *f* (-; *-en*) erection; *fig* establishment
er'ringen *v/t* (*irr*, ***ringen***, *no -ge-, h*) win, gain; achieve
er'röten *v/i* (*no -ge-, sein*) blush
Errungenschaft [ɛɐ'rʊŋənʃaft] *f* (-; *-en*) achievement; ***m-e neueste Errungenschaft*** my latest acquisition
Ersatz [ɛɐ'zats] *m* (*-es; no pl*) replacement; substitute; surrogate; compensation; damages; ***als Ersatz für*** in exchange for
Ersatzdienst *m* → ***Zivildienst***
Ersatzmann *m* (*-[e]s; -leute*) substitute (*a.* SPORT)
Ersatzmine *f* refill
Ersatzreifen *m* MOT spare tire (*Br* tyre)
Ersatzspieler *m* SPORT substitute
Ersatzteil *n* TECH spare part
er'schaffen *v/t* (*irr*, ***schaffen***, *no -ge-, h*) create
er'schallen *v/i* ([*irr*, ***schallen***,] *no -ge-, sein*) (re)sound, ring (out)
er'scheinen *v/i* (*irr*, ***scheinen***, *no -ge-, sein*) appear, F turn up; be published
Er'scheinen *n* (*-s; no pl*) appearance; publication
Er'scheinung *f* (-; *-en*) appearance; apparition; phenomenon
er'schießen *v/t* (*irr*, ***schießen***, *no -ge-, h*) shoot (dead)
erschlaffen [ɛɐ'ʃlafən] *v/i* (*no -ge-, sein*) go limp; *fig* weaken
er'schlagen *v/t* (*irr*, ***schlagen***, *no -ge-, h*) kill
er'schließen *v/t* (*irr*, ***schließen***, *no -ge-, h*) open up; develop
erschollen [ɛɐ'ʃɔlən] *pp of* ***erschallen***
er'schöpfen *v/t* (*no -ge-, h*) exhaust
er'schöpft *adj* exhausted
Er'schöpfung *f* (-; *no pl*) exhaustion
erschrak [ɛɐ'ʃra:k] *pret of* ***erschrecken*** 2
er'schrecken **1.** *v/t* (*no -ge-, h*) frighten, scare; **2.** *v/i* (*irr, no -ge-, sein*) be frightened (***über*** *acc* at)
erschreckend *adj* alarming; terrible
erschrocken [ɛɐ'ʃrɔkən] *pp of* ***erschrecken*** 2
erschüttern [ɛɐ'ʃʏtɐn] *v/t* (*no -ge-, h*) shake; *fig a.* shock; *fig* move
Er'schütterung *f* (-; *-en*) shock (*a. fig*); TECH vibration
erschweren [ɛɐ'ʃve:rən] *v/t* (*no -ge-, h*) make more difficult; aggravate
er'schwindeln *v/t* (*no -ge-, h*) obtain *s.th.* by fraud; (***sich***) ***et. von j-m erschwindeln*** swindle s.o. out of s.th.
er'schwingen *v/t* (*irr*, ***schwingen***, *no -ge-, h*) afford
er'schwinglich *adj* within one's means, affordable; reasonable (*price*)
er'sehen *v/t* (*irr*, ***sehen***, *no -ge-, h*) see, learn, gather (*all*: ***aus*** from)
ersetzbar [ɛɐ'zɛtsba:ɐ] *adj* replaceable; reparable
er'setzen *v/t* (*no -ge-, h*) replace (***durch*** by); compensate for; ***j-m et. ersetzen*** reimburse s.o. for s.th.
er'sichtlich *adj* evident, obvious
er'sparen *v/t* (*no -ge-, h*) save; ***j-m et. ersparen*** spare s.o. s.th.
Ersparnisse [ɛɐ'ʃpa:ɐnɪsə] *pl* savings
erst [e:ɐrst] *adv* first; at first; ***erst jetzt*** (***gestern***) only now (yesterday); ***erst nächste Woche*** not before *or* until next week; ***es ist erst neun Uhr*** it's only nine o'clock; ***eben erst*** just (now); ***erst recht*** all the more; ***erst recht nicht*** even less; → ***einmal***
er'starren *v/i* (*no -ge-, sein*) stiffen; *fig* freeze
er'starrt *adj* stiff; numb
erstatten [ɛɐ'ʃtatən] *v/t* (*no -ge-, h*) refund, reimburse (***j-m et.*** s.o. for s.th.); ***Bericht erstatten*** (give a) report (***über*** *acc* on); ***Anzeige erstatten*** report to the police

'Erstaufführung *f* THEA first night *or* performance, premiere, *film*: *a.* first run
er'staunen *v/t* (*no -ge-*, *h*) surprise, astonish
Er'staunen *n* (*-s; no pl*) surprise, astonishment; ***in Erstaunen (ver)setzen*** astonish
er'staunlich *adj* surprising, astonishing
er'staunt *adj* astonished
'Erstausgabe *f* first edition
'erst'beste *adj* first; any old
'erste *adj* first; ***auf den ersten Blick*** at first sight; ***fürs Erste*** for the time being; ***als Erste(r)*** first; ***zum ersten Mal(e)*** for the first time; ***am Ersten*** on the first
er'stechen *v/t* (*irr*, ***stechen***, *no -ge-*, *h*) stab
'erstens *adv* first(ly), in the first place
'Erstere: ***der (die, das) Erstere*** the former
er'sticken *v/t* (*no -ge-*, *h*) *and v/i* (*sein*) choke, suffocate
Er'stickung *f* (*-; no pl*) suffocation
'erstklassig [-klasıç] *adj* first-class, F *a.* super
erstmalig [-maːlıç] *adj* first
erstmals [-maːls] *adv* for the first time
er'streben *v/t* (*no -ge-*, *h*) strive after
er'strebenswert *adj* desirable
er'strecken *v/refl* (*no -ge-*, *h*) extend, stretch (***bis, auf*** *acc* to; ***über*** *acc* over); ***sich erstrecken über*** (*acc*) *a.* cover
'Erstschlag *m* MIL first strike
er'suchen *v/t* (*no -ge-*, *h*) request
er'tappen *v/t* (*no -ge-*, *h*) catch; → ***Tat***
er'tönen *v/i* (*no -ge-*, *sein*) (re)sound
Ertrag [ɛɐ'traːk] *m* (*-[e]s; Erträge* [ɛɐ'trɛːgə]) AGR yield, produce, TECH *a.* output; ECON proceeds, returns
er'tragen *v/t* (*irr*, ***tragen***, *no -ge-*, *h*) bear, endure; stand
erträglich [ɛɐ'trɛːklıç] *adj* bearable, tolerable
er'tränken *v/t* (*no -ge-*, *h*) drown
er'trinken *v/i* (*irr*, ***trinken***, *no -ge-*, *sein*) drown
erübrigen [ɛɐ'ʔyːbrıgən] *v/t* (*no -ge-*, *h*) spare; ***sich erübrigen*** be unnecessary
er'wachen *v/i* (*no -ge-*, *sein*) wake (up); *esp fig* awake, awaken
Erw. ABBR *of* ***Erwachsene(r)*** adult(s)
er'wachsen[1] *v/i* (*irr*, ***wachsen***, *no -ge-*, *sein*) arise (***aus*** from)
er'wachsen[2] *adj* grown-up, adult
Er'wachsene *m*, *f* (*-n; -n*) adult; ***nur für Erwachsene!*** adults only!
Er'wachsenenbildung *f* adult education
erwägen [ɛɐ'vɛːgən] *v/t* (*irr*, ***wägen***, *no -ge-*, *h*) consider, think *s.th.* over
Er'wägung *f* (*-; -en*) consideration; ***in Erwägung ziehen*** take into consideration
erwähnen [ɛɐ'vɛːnən] *v/t* (*no -ge-*, *h*) mention
Er'wähnung *f* (*-; -en*) mention(ing)
er'wärmen *v/t and v/refl* (*no -ge-*, *h*) warm (up); *fig* ***sich erwärmen für*** warm to
Er'wärmung *f* (*-; -en*) warming up; ***Erwärmung der Erdatmosphäre*** global warming
er'warten *v/t* (*no -ge-*, *h*) expect; wait for, await
Er'wartung *f* (*-; -en*) expectation, anticipation
er'wartungsvoll *adj and adv* full of expectation, expectant(ly)
er'wecken *fig v/t* (*no -ge-*, *h*) awaken; arouse; → ***Anschein***
er'weisen *v/t* (*irr*, ***weisen***, *no -ge-*, *h*) do (*service etc*); show (*respect etc*); ***sich erweisen als*** prove to be
erweitern [ɛɐ'vaitɐn] *v/t and v/refl* (*no -ge-*, *h*) extend, enlarge; *esp* ECON expand
Er'weiterung *f* (*-; -en*) extension, enlargement, expansion
Erwerb [ɛɐ'vɛrp] *m* (*-[e]s; -e*) acquisition; purchase; income
er'werben *v/t* (*irr*, ***werben***, *no -ge-*, *h*) acquire (*a. fig*); purchase
er'werbslos *adj* unemployed
erwerbstätig *adj* (gainfully) employed, working
erwerbsunfähig *adj* unable to work
Er'werbung *f* (*-; -en*) acquisition; purchase
erwidern [ɛɐ'viːdɐn] *v/t* (*no -ge-*, *h*) reply, answer; return (*visit etc*)
Er'widerung *f* (*-; -en*) reply, answer; return
er'wischen *v/t* (*no -ge-*, *h*) catch, get; ***ihn hat's erwischt*** he's had it
er'wünscht *adj* desired; desirable; welcome
er'würgen *v/t* (*no -ge-*, *h*) strangle
Erz [eːɐts] *n* (*-es; -e*) ore
er'zählen *v/t* (*no -ge-*, *h*) tell; narrate; ***man hat mir erzählt*** I was told
Er'zähler *m* (*-s; -*), **Er'zählerin** *f* (*-; -nen*) narrator
Er'zählung *f* (*-; -en*) (short) story, tale
'Erzbischof *m* REL archbishop
'Erzbistum *n* REL archbishopric
'Erzengel *m* REL archangel
er'zeugen *v/t* (*no -ge-*, *h*) ECON produce (*a. fig*); TECH make, manufacture; ELECTR generate; *fig* cause, create
Er'zeuger *m* (*-s; -*) ECON producer
Er'zeugnis *n* (*-ses; -se*) ECON product (*a. fig*)

Er'zeugung *f (-; -en)* ECON production
er'ziehen *v/t (irr, **ziehen**, no -ge-, h)* bring up, raise; educate; ***j-n zu et. erziehen*** teach s.o. to be *or* to do s.th.
Erzieher [ɛɐ'tsiːɐ] *m (-s; -)*, **Erzieherin** [ɛɐ'tsiːərɪn] *f (-; -nen)* educator; teacher; (qualified) kindergarten teacher
er'zieherisch *adj* educational, pedagogic(al)
Er'ziehung *f (-; no pl)* upbringing; education
Er'ziehungsanstalt *f* reform (*Br* approved) school
Erziehungsberechtigte *m, f (-n; -n)* parent or guardian
Erziehungswesen *n (-s; no pl)* educational system
er'zielen *v/t (no -ge-, h)* achieve; SPORT score
erzogen [ɛɐ'tsoːgən] *adj*: ***gut erzogen sein*** be well-bred; ***schlecht erzogen sein*** be ill-bred
er'zwingen *v/t (irr, **zwingen**, no -ge-, h)* (en)force
es [ɛs] *pers pron* it; he; she; ***es gibt*** there is, there are; ***ich bin es*** it's me; ***ich hoffe es*** I hope so; ***ich kann es*** I can (do it)
Esche ['ɛʃə] *f (-; -n)* BOT ash (tree)
Esel ['eːzəl] *m (-s; -)* ZO donkey, ass (*a.* F)
'Eselsbrücke *f* mnemonic
'Eselsohr *fig n* dog-ear
Eskorte [ɛs'kɔrtə] *f (-; -n)* MIL escort, MAR *a.* convoy
essbar ['ɛsbaːɐ] *adj* eatable; edible
essen ['ɛsən] *v/t and v/i (irr, ge-, h)* eat; ***zu Mittag essen*** (have) lunch; ***zu Abend essen*** have supper (*or* dinner); ***essen gehen*** eat *or* dine out
'Essen *n (-s; -)* food; meal; dish; dinner
'Essensmarke *f* meal ticket
Essenszeit *f* lunchtime; dinner *or* supper time
Essig ['ɛsɪç] *m (-s; -e)* vinegar
'Essiggurke *f* pickled gherkin, pickle
Esslöffel *m* tablespoon
Essstäbchen *pl* chopsticks
Esstisch *m* dining table
Esszimmer *n* dining room
Estrich ['ɛstrɪç] *m (-s; -e)* ARCH flooring, subfloor; *Swiss*: loft, attic, garret
etablieren [eta'bliːrən] *v/refl (no -ge-, h)* establish o.s.
Etage [e'taːʒə] *f (-; -n)* floor, stor(e)y; ***auf der ersten Etage*** on the second (*Br* first) floor
E'tagenbett *n* bunk bed
Etappe [e'tapə] *f (-; -n)* stage, SPORT *a.* leg
Etat [e'taː] *m (-s; -s)* budget
Ethik ['eːtɪk] *f (-; no pl)* ethics
ethisch ['eːtɪʃ] *adj* ethical
ethnisch ['ɛtnɪʃ] *adj* ethnic
Etikett [eti'kɛt] *n (-[e]s; -e[n])* label (*a. fig*); (price) tag
Eti'kette *f (-; -n)* etiquette
etikettieren [etikɛ'tiːrən] *v/t (no -ge-, h)* label
etliche ['ɛtlɪçə] *indef pron* several, quite a few
Etui [ɛt'viː] *n (-s; -s)* case
etwa ['ɛtva] *adv* about, around; perhaps, by any chance; ***nicht etwa, dass*** not that
etwaig ['ɛtvaɪç] *adj* any
etwas ['ɛtvas] **1.** *indef pron* something; anything; **2.** *adj* some; any; **3.** *adv* a little, somewhat
EU [eː'uː] ABBR *of* ***Europäische Union*** EU, European Union
euch [ɔʏç] *pers pron* you; ***euch (selbst)*** yourselves
euer ['ɔʏɐ] *poss pron* your; ***der (die, das) Eu(e)re*** yours
Eule ['ɔʏlə] *f (-; -n)* ZO owl; ***Eulen nach Athen tragen*** carry coals to Newcastle
euresgleichen ['ɔʏrəs'glaɪçən] *pron* people like you, F *contp* the likes of you
Euro... ['ɔʏro] *in cpds ...cheque etc*: Euro...
Europa [ɔʏ'roːpa] Europe; ***Europa...*** *in cpds* European
Europäer [ɔʏro'pɛːɐ] *m (-s; -)*, **Europäerin** [-'pɛːərɪn] *f (-; -nen)*, **euro'päisch** *adj* European; ***Europäische Gemeinschaft*** European Community
Euter ['ɔʏtɐ] *n (-s; -)* udder
ev. ABBR *of* ***evangelisch*** Prot., Protestant
evakuieren [evaku'iːrən] *v/t (no -ge-, h)* evacuate
evangelisch [evaŋ'geːlɪʃ] *adj* REL Protestant; ***evangelisch-lutherisch*** Lutheran
Evangelium [evaŋ'geːljʊm] *n (-s; -lien)* Gospel
eventuell [evɛntu'ɛl] **1.** *adj* possible; **2.** *adv* possibly, perhaps
evtl. ABBR *of* ***eventuell*** poss., possibly
ewig ['eːvɪç] *adj* eternal; F constant, endless; ***auf ewig*** for ever
'Ewigkeit *f (-; no pl)* eternity; F ***eine Ewigkeit*** (for) ages
exakt [ɛ'ksakt] *adj* exact, precise
Ex'aktheit *f (-; no pl)* exactness, precision
Examen [ɛ'ksaːmən] *n (-s; Examina* [ɛ'ksaːmina]) exam, examination
Exekutive [ɛkseku'tiːvə] *f (-; -n)* POL executive (power)
Exemplar [ɛksɛm'plaːɐ] *n (-s; -e)* specimen; copy
exerzieren [ɛksɛr'tsiːrən] *v/i (no -ge-, h)* MIL drill

Exil [ɛ'ksiːl] *n* (*-s*; *-e*) exile
Existenz [ɛksɪs'tɛnts] *f* (*-*; *-en*) existence; living, livelihood
Existenzkampf *m* struggle for survival
Existenzminimum *n* subsistence level
existieren [ɛksɪs'tiːrən] *v/i* (*no -ge-*, *h*) exist; live (***von*** on)
exklusiv [ɛksklu'ziːf] *adj* exclusive, select
exotisch [ɛ'ksoːtɪʃ] *adj* exotic
Expansion [ɛkspan'zjoːn] *f* (*-*; *-en*) expansion
Expedition [ɛkspedi'tsjoːn] *f* (*-*; *-en*) expedition
Experiment [ɛksperi'mɛnt] *n* (*-[e]s*; *-e*), **experimentieren** [ɛksperimɛn'tiːrən] *v/i* (*no -ge-*, *h*) experiment
Experte [ɛks'pɛrtə] *m* (*-n*; *-n*), **Ex'pertin** *f* (*-*; *-nen*) expert (***für*** on)
explodieren [ɛksplo'diːrən] *v/i* (*no -ge-*, *sein*) explode (*a. fig*), burst
Explosion [ɛksplo'zjoːn] *f* (*-*; *-en*) explosion (*a. fig*)
explosiv [-'ziːf] *adj* explosive
Export [ɛks'pɔrt] *m* (*-[e]s*; *-e*) a) (*no pl*) export(ation), b) exports
exportieren [ɛkspɔr'tiːrən] *v/t* (*no -ge-*, *h*) export
Express [ɛks'prɛs] *m* (*-es*; *no pl*) RAIL express; ***per Express*** by special delivery, *Br* express
extra ['ɛkstra] *adv* extra; separately; F on purpose; ***extra für dich*** especially for you
Extra *n* (*-s*; *-s*), **Extrablatt** *n* extra
Extrakt [ɛks'trakt] *m* (*-[e]s*; *-e*) extract
extravagant [ɛkstrava'gant] *adj* flamboyant
extrem [ɛks'treːm] *adj*, **Ex'trem** *n* (*-s*; *-e*) extreme
Extremist(in) [ɛkstre-'mɪst(ɪn)] (*-en*; *-en*/*-*; *-nen*), **extre'mistisch** *adj* extremist, ultra
Exzellenz [ɛkstsɛ'lɛnts] *f* (*-*; *-en*) Excellency
exzentrisch [ɛks'tsɛntrɪʃ] *adj* eccentric
Exzess [ɛks'tsɛs] *m* (*-ses*; *-se*) excess

F

Fa. ABBR *of* ***Firma*** firm; Messrs.
Fabel ['faːbəl] *f* (*-*; *-n*) fable (*a. fig*) **'fabelhaft** *adj* fantastic, wonderful
Fabrik [fa'briːk] *f* (*-*; *-en*) factory, works, shop
Fabrikant [fabri'kant] *m* (*-en*; *-en*) factory owner; manufacturer
Fa'brikarbeiter *m* factory worker
Fabrikat [fabri'kaːt] *n* (*-[e]s*; *-e*) make, brand; product
Fabrikation [fabrika'tsjoːn] *f* (*-*; *-en*) manufacturing, production
Fabrikati'onsfehler *m* flaw
Fa'brikbesitzer *m* factory owner
Fabrikware *f* manufactured product(s)
Fach [fax] *n* (*-[e]s*; *Fächer* ['fɛçɐ]) compartment; pigeonhole; shelf; PED, UNIV subject; → ***Fachgebiet***
Facharbeiter *m* skilled worker
Facharzt *m*, **Fachärztin** *f* specialist (***für*** in)
Fachausbildung *f* professional training
Fachausdruck *m* technical term
Fachbuch *n* specialist book
Fächer ['fɛçɐ] *m* (*-s*; *-*) fan
'Fachfrau *f* expert
Fachgebiet *n* line, field; trade, business
Fachgeschäft *n* dealer (specializing in ...)
Fachhochschule *f appr* (technial) college, *esp Br* polytechnic
Fachkenntnisse *pl* specialized knowledge
'fachkundig *adj* competent, expert
'fachlich *adj* professional, specialized
'Fachlitera,tur *f* specialized literature
Fachmann *m* (*-[e]s*; *-leute*) expert
'fachmännisch [-mɛnɪʃ] *adj* expert
'Fachschule *f* technical school *or* college
fachsimpeln ['faxzɪmpəln] *v/i* (*ge-*, *h*) talk shop
'Fachwerk *n* framework
Fachwerkhaus *n* half-timbered house
Fachzeitschrift *f* (professional *or* specialist) journal
Fackel ['fakəl] *f* (*-*; *-n*) torch
Fackelzug *m* torchlight procession
fade ['faːdə] *adj* GASTR tasteless, flat; stale; *fig* dull, boring
Faden ['faːdən] *m* (*-s*; *Fäden* ['fɛːdən]) thread (*a. fig*)
'fadenscheinig *adj* threadbare; *fig* flimsy

(*excuse etc*)
fähig ['fɛːɪç] *adj* capable (***zu*** of [*doing*] *s.th.*), able (to *do s.th.*)
'**Fähigkeit** *f* (-; *-en*) (cap)ability; talent, gift
fahl [faːl] *adj* pale; ashen (*face*)
fahnden ['faːndən] *v/i* (*ge-*, *h*) search (***nach*** for)
'**Fahndung** *f* (-; *-en*) search
'**Fahndungsliste** *f* wanted list
Fahne ['faːnə] *f* (-; *-n*) flag; *mst fig* banner; F ***e-e Fahne haben*** reek of alcohol
'**Fahnenflucht** *f* (-; *no pl*) MIL desertion
Fahnenstange *f* flagpole, flagstaff
Fahrbahn ['faːɐ-] *f* road(way), pavement; MOT lane
'**fahrbar** *adj* mobile
Fähre ['fɛːrə] *f* (-; *-n*) ferry(boat)
fahren ['faːrən] (*irr*, *ge-*) **1.** *v/i* (*sein*) go; *bus etc*: run; leave; MOT drive; ride; ***mit dem Auto*** (***Zug, Bus*** *etc*) ***fahren*** go by car (train, bus *etc*); ***über e-e Brücke*** *etc* ***fahren*** cross a bridge *etc*; ***mit der Hand über et. fahren*** run one's hand over s.th.; ***was ist denn in dich gefahren?*** what's got into you?; **2.** *v/t* (*h*) drive (*car etc*); ride (*bicycle etc*); carry
Fahrer ['faːrɐ] *m* (*-s*; -) driver
Fahrerflucht *f* hit-and-run offense (*Br* offence)
'**Fahrerin** *f* (-; *-nen*) driver
Fahrgast ['faːɐ-] *m* passenger
Fahrgeld *n* fare
Fahrgelegenheit *f* means of transport(ation)
Fahrgemeinschaft *f* car pool
Fahrgestell *n* MOT chassis; AVIAT → ***Fahrwerk***
Fahrkarte *f* ticket
'**Fahrkartenauto,mat** *m* ticket machine
Fahrkartenentwerter *m* (*-s*; -) ticket-cancel(l)ing machine
Fahrkartenschalter *m* ticket window
'**fahrlässig** *adj* careless, reckless (*a.* JUR); ***grob fahrlässig*** grossly negligent
'**Fahrlehrer** *m* driving instructor
'**Fahrplan** *m* timetable, schedule
'**fahrplanmäßig** **1.** *adj* scheduled; **2.** *adv* according to schedule; on time
'**Fahrpreis** *m* fare
Fahrprüfung *f* driving test
Fahrrad *n* bicycle, F bike
Fahrschein *m* ticket
Fahrschule *f* driving school
Fahrschüler *m* MOT student driver, *Br* learner (driver); PED non-local student
Fahrstuhl *m* elevator, *Br* lift
Fahrstunde *f* driving lesson
Fahrt [faːɐt] *f* (-; *-en*) ride, MOT *a.* drive; trip, journey, MAR voyage, cruise; speed (*a.* MOT); ***in voller Fahrt*** at full speed
Fährte ['fɛːɐtə] *f* (-; *-n*) track (*a. fig*)
'**Fahrtenschreiber** *m* MOT tachograph
'**Fahrwasser** *n* MAR fairway
'**Fahrwerk** *n* AVIAT landing gear
'**Fahrzeug** *n* (-[*e*]*s*; *-e*) vehicle
Fairness ['fɛːɐnɪs] *f* (-; *no pl*) fair play
Faktor ['faktoːɐ] *m* (*-s*; *-en* [fak'toːrən]) factor
Fakultät [fakʊl'tɛːt] *f* (-; *-en*) UNIV faculty, department
Falke ['falkə] *m* (*-n*; *-n*) ZO hawk, falcon
Fall [fal] *m* (-[*e*]*s*; *Fälle* ['fɛlə]) fall; LING, JUR, MED case; ***auf jeden Fall*** in any case; ***auf keinen Fall*** on no account; ***für den Fall, dass …*** in case …; ***gesetzt den Fall, dass*** suppose (that); ***zu Fall bringen*** *fig* defeat
Falle ['falə] *f* (-; *-n*) trap (*a. fig*)
fallen ['falən] *v/i* (*irr*, *ge-*, *sein*) fall (*a. rain etc*), drop; ***fallen lassen*** drop (*a. fig*); MIL be killed (in action); ***ein Tor fiel*** SPORT a goal was scored
fällen ['fɛlən] *v/t* (*ge-*, *h*) fell, cut down (*tree*); JUR pass (*sentence*); make (*a decision etc*)
fällig ['fɛlɪç] *adj* due; payable
'**fallenlassen** ['falәlasən] *v/i* (*irr*, ***fallen***, *no ge-*, *h*) *fig* drop
'**Fallobst** *n* windfall
Fallrückzieher *m soccer*: overhead kick
falls [fals] *cj* if, in case; ***falls nicht*** unless
'**Fallschirm** *m* parachute
Fallschirmjäger *m* MIL paratrooper
Fallschirmspringen *n* MIL parachuting; SPORT skydiving
Fallschirmspringer *m* MIL parachutist; SPORT skydiver
'**Falltür** *f* trapdoor
falsch [falʃ] *adj and adv* wrong; false (*a. fig*); forged; ***falsch gehen*** *watch*: be wrong; ***et. falsch aussprechen*** (***schreiben, verstehen*** *etc*) mispronounce (misspell, misunderstand *etc*) s.th.; ***falsch verbunden!*** TEL sorry, wrong number
fälschen ['fɛlʃən] *v/t* (*ge-*, *h*) forge, fake; counterfeit
'**Fälscher** *m* (*-s*; -) forger
'**Falschgeld** *n* counterfeit *or* false money
Falschmünzer [-mʏntsɐ] *m* (*-s*; -) counterfeiter
Falschspieler *m* cheat
'**Fälschung** *f* (-; *-en*) forgery; counterfeit
'**fälschungssicher** *adj* forgery-proof
Falt… ['falt-] *in cpds …bett, …boot etc*: folding …
Falte ['faltə] *f* (-; -n) fold; wrinkle; pleat; crease

F

'falten *v/t* (*ge-*, *h*) fold
'Faltenrock *m* pleated skirt
Falter ['faltɐ] *m* (*-s*; *-*) zo butterfly
faltig ['faltɪç] *adj* wrinkled
familiär [fami'ljɛːɐ] *adj* personal; informal; ***familiäre Probleme*** family problems
Familie [fa'miːljə] *f* (*-*; *-n*) family (*a.* zo, BOT)
Fa'milienangelegenheit *f* family affair
Familienanschluss *m*: ***Familienanschluss haben*** live as one of the family
Familienname *m* family (*or* last) name, surname
Familienpackung *f* family size (package)
Familienplanung *f* family planning
Familienstand *m* marital status
Familienvater *m* family man
Fanatiker [fa'naːtikɐ] *m* (*-s*; *-*), **Fa'natikerin** *f* (*-*; *-nen*), **fa'natisch** *adj* fanatic
Fanatismus [fana'tɪsmʊs] *m* (*-*; *no pl*) fanaticism
fand [fant] *pret of* ***finden***
Fang [faŋ] *m* (*-*[*e*]*s*; *Fänge* ['fɛŋə]) catch (*a. fig*)
'fangen *v/t* (*irr*, *ge-*, *h*) catch (*a. fig*); ***sich wieder fangen*** get a grip on o.s. again; ***Fangen spielen*** play tag (*Br* catch)
'Fangzahn *m* zo fang
Fantasie [fanta'ziː] *f* (*-*; *-n*) imagination; fantasy
fanta'sielos *adj* unimaginative
fanta'sieren *v/i* (*no -ge-*, *h*) daydream; MED be delirious; F talk nonsense
fanta'sievoll *adj* imaginative
Fantast [fan'tast] *m* (*-en*; *-en*) dreamer
fan'tastisch *adj* fantastic, F *a.* great, terrific
Farbband ['farp-] *n* (typewriter) ribbon
Farbe ['farbə] *f* (*-*; *-n*) colo(u)r; paint; complexion; tan; *card games*: suit
'farbecht *adj* colo(u)r-fast
färben ['fɛrbən] *v/t* (*ge-*, *h*) dye; *esp fig* colo(u)r; ***sich rot färben*** turn red; → ***abfärben***
'farbenblind *adj* colo(u)r-blind
farbenfroh, **farbenprächtig** *adj* colo(u)rful
'Farbfernsehen *n* colo(u)r television
Farbfernseher *m* colo(u)r TV set
Farbfilm *m* colo(u)r film
Farbfoto *n* colo(u)r photo
farbig ['farbɪç] *adj* colo(u)red; stained (*glass*); *fig* colo(u)rful
Farbige ['farbɪgə] *m*, *f* (*-n*; *-n*) → ***Schwarze***
'Farbkasten *m* paintbox
'farblos *adj* colo(u)rless (*a. fig*)
'Farbstift *m* colo(u)red pencil, crayon
'Farbstoff *m* dye; GASTR colo(u)ring
'Farbton *m* shade, tint
'Färbung *f* (*-*; *-en*) colo(u)ring; hue
Farnkraut ['farn-] *n* BOT fern
Fasan [fa'zaːn] *m* (*-*[*e*]*s*; *-e*[*n*]) zo pheasant
Faschismus [fa'ʃɪsmʊs] *m* (*-*; *no pl*) POL fascism
Faschist [fa'ʃɪst] *m* (*-en*; *-en*), **fa'schistisch** *adj* POL fascist
faseln ['faːzəln] F *v/i* (*ge-*, *h*) drivel
Faser ['faːzɐ] *f* (*-*; *-n*) fiber, *Br* fibre; grain
faserig ['faːzərɪç] *adj* fibrous
'fasern *v/i* (*ge-*, *h*) fray
Fass [fas] *n* (*-es*; *Fässer* ['fɛsɐ]) cask, barrel; ***vom Fass*** on tap
Fassade [fa'saːdə] *f* (*-*; *-n*) ARCH facade, front (*a. fig*)
'Fassbier *n* draft (*Br* draught) beer
fassen ['fasən] (*ge-*, *h*) **1.** *v/t* take hold of, grasp; seize; catch (*criminal*); hold, take; set (*jewels*); *fig* grasp, understand; pluck up (*courage*); make (*a decision*); ***sich fassen*** compose o.s.; ***sich kurz fassen*** be brief; ***es ist nicht zu fassen*** that's incredible **2.** *v/i*: ***fassen nach*** reach for
'Fassung *f* (*-*; *-en*) a) setting; frame (*of glasses*); ELECTR socket; draft(ing); wording, version, b) (*no pl*) composure; ***die Fassung verlieren*** lose one's composure; ***j-n aus der Fassung bringen*** put s.o. out
'fassungslos *adj* stunned; speechless
'Fassungsvermögen *n* capacity
fast [fast] *adv* almost, nearly; ***fast nie*** (***nichts***) hardly ever (anything)
fasten ['fastən] *v/i* (*ge-*, *h*) fast
'Fastenzeit *f* REL Lent
'Fastnacht *f* → ***Karneval***
fatal [fa'taːl] *adj* unfortunate; awkward; disastrous
fauchen ['fauxən] *v/i* (*ge-*, *h*) zo hiss
faul [faul] *adj* rotten, bad, GASTR *a.* spoiled; *fig* lazy; F fishy; ***faule Ausrede*** lame excuse
'faulen *v/i* (*ge-*, *h*, *sein*) rot, go bad; decay
faulenzen ['faulɛntsən] *v/i* (*ge-*, *h*) laze, loaf (about)
'Faulenzer(in) [-tsɐ (-tsərɪn)] (*-s*; *-/-*; *-nen*) lazybones; *contp* loafer
'Faulheit *f* (*-*; *no pl*) laziness
faulig ['faulɪç] *adj* rotten
Fäulnis ['fɔylnɪs] *f* (*-*; *no pl*) rottenness, decay (*a. fig*)
'Faulpelz F *m* → ***Faulenzer***
'Faultier *n* zo sloth
Faust [faust] *f* (*-*; *Fäuste* ['fɔystə]) fist; ***auf eigene Faust*** on one's own initiative
Fausthandschuh *m* mitten

Faustregel *f* (***als Faustregel*** as a) rule of thumb
Faustschlag *m* punch
Favorit [favo'riːt] *m* (*-en*; *-en*), **Favo'ritin** *f* (*-*; *-nen*) favo(u)rite
Fax [faks] *n* (*-*; *-[e]*) fax; fax machine
faxen ['faksən] *v/i and v/t* (*ge-*, *h*) fax, send a fax (to)
'Faxgerät *n* fax machine
FCKW [ɛftseːkaː'veː] ABBR *of* ***Fluorchlorkohlenwasserstoff*** chlorofluorocarbon, CFC
Feber ['feːbɐ] *Austrian m* (*-s*; *-*), **Februar** ['feːbruaːɐ] *m* (*-s*; *-e*) February
fechten ['fɛçtən] *v/i* (*irr*, *ge-*, *h*) SPORT fence; *fig* fight
'Fechten *n* (*-s*; *no pl*) SPORT fencing
Fechter(in) ['fɛçtɐ (-tərɪn)] (*-s*; *-/-*; *-nen*) SPORT fencer
Feder ['feːdɐ] *f* (*-*; *-n*) feather; plume; nib; TECH spring
Federball *m* SPORT badminton; shuttlecock
Federbett *n* comforter, *Br* duvet
Federgewicht *n* SPORT featherweight
Federhalter *m* penholder
'feder'leicht *adj* (as) light as a feather
'Federmäppchen [-mɛpçən] *n* (*-s*; *-*) pencil case
'federn (*ge-*, *h*) **1.** *v/i* be springy; **2.** *v/t* TECH spring
federnd *adj* springy, elastic
'Federstrich *m* stroke of the pen
Federung ['feːdərʊŋ] *f* (*-*; *-en*) springs; MOT suspension; ***e-e gute Federung haben*** be well sprung
'Federzeichnung *f* pen-and-ink drawing
Fee [feː] *f* (*-*; *-n*) fairy
fegen ['feːgən] *v/t* (*ge-*, *h*) *and fig v/i* (*sein*) sweep
fehl [feːl] *adj*: ***fehl am Platze*** out of place
'Fehlbetrag *m* deficit
'fehlen *v/i* (*ge-*, *h*) be missing; be absent; ***ihm fehlt*** (***es an***) ... he is lacking ...; ***du fehlst uns*** we miss you; ***was dir fehlt, ist ...*** what you need is ...; ***was fehlt Ihnen?*** what's wrong with you?
Fehler ['feːlɐ] *m* (*-s*; *-*) mistake; fault, TECH *a.* defect, flaw; EDP error
'fehlerfrei *adj* faultless, flawless
'fehlerhaft *adj* faulty; full of mistakes; TECH defective
'Fehlermeldung *f* EDP error message
'Fehlernährung *f* malnutrition
Fehlgeburt *f* MED miscarriage
Fehlgriff *m* mistake; wrong choice
'Fehlschlag *m* failure
'fehlschlagen *v/i* (*irr*, ***schlagen***, *sep*, *-ge-*, *sein*) fail
'Fehlstart *m* false start
Fehltritt *m* slip; *fig* lapse
Fehlzündung *f* MOT backfire (*a.* ***Fehlzündung haben***)
Feier ['faiɐ] *f* (*-*; *-n*) celebration; party
'Feierabend *m* end of a day's work; closing time; evening (at home); ***Feierabend machen*** finish (work), F knock off; ***nach Feierabend*** after work
'feierlich *adj* solemn; festive
'Feierlichkeit *f* (*-*; *-en*) a) (*no pl*) solemnity, b) ceremony
'feiern *v/t and v/i* (*ge-*, *h*) celebrate; have a party
'Feiertag *m* holiday; ***gesetzlicher Feiertag*** public (*or* legal, *Br a.* bank) holiday
feig [faik], **feige** ['faigə] *adj* cowardly; ***feig sein*** be a coward
Feige ['faigə] *f* (*-*; *-n*) BOT *fig*
'Feigheit *f* (*-*; *no pl*) cowardice
'Feigling *m* (*-s*; *-e*) coward
Feile ['failə] *f* (*-*; *-n*), **'feilen** *v/t and v/i* (*ge-*, *h*) file
feilschen ['failʃən] *v/i* (*ge-*, *h*) haggle (***um*** about, over)
fein [fain] *adj* fine; choice, excellent; keen (*ear*); delicate; distinguished, F posh; ***fein!*** good!, okay!
Feind [faint] *m* (*-[e]s*; *-e* ['faində]) enemy (*a. fig*)
Feindbild *n* enemy image
Feindin ['faindɪn] *f* (*-*; *-nen*) enemy
'feindlich *adj* hostile; MIL enemy
'Feindschaft *f* (*-*; *no pl*) hostility
'feindselig *adj* hostile (***gegen*** to)
'Feindseligkeit *f* (*-*; *no pl*) hostility
feinfühlig ['fainfyːlɪç] *adj* sensitive
'Feingefühl *n* (*-[e]s*; *no pl*) sensitiveness
'Feinheit *f* (*-*; *-en*) a) (*no pl*) fineness; keenness; delicacy, b) *pl* niceties
'Feinkostgeschäft *n* delicatessen
Feinme,chaniker *m* precision mechanic
'Feinschmecker *m* (*-s*; *-*) gourmet
feist [faist] *adj* fat, stout
Feld [fɛlt] *n* (*-[e]s*; *-er* ['fɛldɐ]) field (*a. fig*); *chess*: square
Feldarbeit *f* AGR work in the fields; fieldwork
Feldbett *n* cot, *Br* camp bed
Feldflasche *f* water bottle, canteen
Feldlerche *f* ZO skylark
Feldmarschall *m* MIL field marshal
'Feldstecher [-ʃtɛçɐ] *m* (*-s*; *-*) field glasses
'Feldwebel [-veːbəl] *m* (*-s*; *-*) MIL sergeant
'Feldzug *m* MIL campaign (*a. fig*)
Felge ['fɛlgə] *f* (*-*; *-n*) rim; SPORT circle
Fell [fɛl] *n* (*-[e]s*; *-e*) ZO coat; skin, fur
Fels [fɛls] *m* (*-en*; *-en*) rock
'Felsbrocken *m* boulder

F

Felsen ['fɛlzən] *m* (*-s*; *-*) rock
felsig ['fɛlzɪç] *adj* rocky
'**Felsspalte** *f* crevice
'**Felsvorsprung** *m* ledge
feminin [femi'niːn] *adj* feminine (*a.* LING); *contp* effeminate
Feminismus [femi'nɪsmʊs] *m* (*-*; *no pl*) feminism
Feministin [femi'nɪstɪn] *f* (*-*; *-nen*), **femi'nistisch** *adj* feminist
Fenchel ['fɛnçəl] *m* (*-s*; *no pl*) BOT fennel
Fenster ['fɛnstɐ] *n* (*-s*; *-*) window
Fensterbank *f* (*-*; *-bänke*), **Fensterbrett** *n* windowsill
Fensterflügel *m* casement
Fensterladen *m* shutter
Fensterrahmen *m* window frame
Fensterscheibe *f* (window)pane
Ferien ['feːrjən] *pl* vacation, *esp Br* holiday(s *pl*); ***Ferien haben*** be on vacation
Ferienhaus *n* vacation home, cottage
Ferienlager *n* summer camp
Ferienwohnung *f* vacation rental, *Br* holiday apartment
Ferkel ['fɛrkəl] *n* (*-s*; *-*) ZO piglet; F pig
fern [fɛrn] *adj and adv* far(away), far-off, distant; ***von fern*** from a distance
'**Fernamt** *n* telephone exchange
'**Fernbedienung** *f* remote control
'**fernbleiben** *v/i* (*irr*, ***bleiben***, *sep*, *-ge-*, *sein*) stay away (*dat* from)
Ferne ['fɛrnə] *f* (*-*; *no pl*) distance; ***aus der Ferne*** from a distance
ferner ['fɛrnɐ] *adv* further(more); in addition, also
'**Fernfahrer** *m* long-haul truck driver, F trucker, *Br* long-distance lorry driver
Ferngespräch *n* TEL long-distance call
'**ferngesteuert** *adj* remote-controlled; MIL guided (*missile etc*)
'**Fernglas** *n* binoculars
'**fernhalten** *v/t* (*irr*, ***halten***, *sep*, *-ge-*, *h*) keep away (***von*** from)
Fernheizung *f* district heating
Fernkoˌpierer *m* fax machine
Fernkurs *m* correspondence course
Fernlaster F *m* (*-s*; *-*) MOT longhaul truck, *Br* long-distance lorry
Fernlenkung *f* remote control
Fernlicht *n* MOT full (*or* high) beam
'**fernliegen** *v/i* (*irr*, ***liegen***, *sep*, *-ge-*, *h*): ***es liegt mir fernliegen zu*** far be it from me to
'**Fernmeldesatelˌlit** *m* communications satellite
Fernmeldetechnik *f*, **Fernmeldewesen** *n* (*-s*; *no pl*) telecommunications
'**Fernrohr** *n* telescope
Fernschreiben *n*, **Fernschreiber** *m* telex
'**fernsehen** *v/i* (*irr*, ***sehen***, *sep*, *-ge-*, *h*) watch television
'**Fernsehen** *n* (*-s*; *no pl*) television (***im*** on)
'**Fernseher** F *m* (*-s*; *-*) TV (set); TV viewer
'**Fernsehschirm** *m* (TV) screen
Fernsehsendung *f* TV program(me)
Fernsprechamt *n* telephone exchange
'**Fernsteuerung** *f* remote control
'**Fernverkehr** *m* long-distance traffic
Ferse ['fɛrzə] *f* (*-*; *-n*) ANAT heel (*a. fig*)
fertig ['fɛrtɪç] *adj* ready; finished; ***fertig bringen*** manage; *iro* be capable of; ***fertig machen*** finish (*a.* F *s.o.*); get *s.th.* ready; F give *s.o.* hell, do *s.o.* in; ***sich fertig machen*** get ready; ***(mit et.) fertig sein*** have finished (s.th.); ***mit** et.* ***fertig werden*** cope with *a problem etc*; F ***völlig fertig*** dead beat
'**fertigbringen** *v/t* (*irr*, ***bringen***, *sep*, *-ge-*, *h*) → ***fertig***
'**Fertiggericht** *n* ready(-to-serve) meal
Fertighaus *n* prefabricated house, F prefab
'**Fertigkeit** *f* (*-*; *-en*) skill
'**fertigmachen** *v/t* (*irr*, ***bringen***, *sep*, *-ge-*, *h*) → ***fertig***
'**Fertigstellung** *f* (*-*; *no pl*) completion
'**fertigwerden** *v/t* (*irr*, ***bringen***, *sep*, *-ge-*, *sein*) → ***fertig***
fesch [fɛʃ] *Austrian adj* smart, chic
Fessel ['fɛsəl] *f* (*-*; *-n*) shackle (*a. fig*); ANAT ankle
'**fesseln** *v/t* (*ge-*, *h*) bind, tie (up); *fig* fascinate
fest [fɛst] *adj* firm (*a. fig*); solid; fast; *fig* fixed (*date etc*); sound (*sleep*); steady (*girlfriend etc*); ***fest schlafen*** be fast asleep
Fest *n* (*-[e]s*; *-e*) celebration; party; REL festival, feast; → ***froh***
'**festbinden** *v/t* (*irr*, ***binden***, *sep*, *-ge-*, *h*) fasten, tie (***an*** *dat* to)
'**Festessen** *n* banquet, feast
'**festfahren** *v/refl* (*irr*, ***fahren***, *sep*, *-ge-*, *h*) get stuck
'**Festhalle** *f* (festival) hall
'**festhalten** (*irr*, ***halten***, *sep*, *-ge-*, *h*) **1.** *v/i*: ***festhalten an*** (*dat*) stick to; **2.** *v/t* hold on to; hold *s.o. or s.th.* tight; ***sich festhalten an*** (*dat*) hold on to
festigen ['fɛstɪgən] *v/t* (*ge-*, *h*) strengthen; ***sich festigen*** grow firm *or* strong
Festigkeit ['fɛstɪçkait] *f* (*-*; *no pl*) firmness; strength
'**Festland** *n* mainland; *the* Continent
'**festlegen** *v/t* (*sep*, *-ge-*, *h*) fix, set; ***sich festlegen auf*** (*acc*) commit o.s. to *s.th.*
'**festlich** *adj* festive
'**festmachen** *v/t* (*sep*, *-ge-*, *h*) fasten, fix

(**an** *dat* to); MAR moor; ECON fix
'**Festnahme** [-na:mə] *f* (-; -*n*), '**festnehmen** *v/t* (*irr*, ***nehmen***, *sep*, -*ge*-, *h*) arrest
'**Festplatte** *f* EDP hard disk
'**festschrauben** *v/t* (*sep*, -*ge*-, *h*) screw (on) tight
festsetzen *v/t* (*sep*, -*ge*-, *h*) fix
festsitzen *v/i* (*irr*, ***sitzen***, *sep*, -*ge*-, *h*) be stuck; be (left) stranded
'**Festspiele** *pl* festival
'**feststehen** *v/i* (*irr*, ***stehen***, *sep*, -*ge*-, *h*) be certain; *date etc*: be fixed
feststehend *adj* established (*fact etc*); set (*phrase etc*)
'**feststellen** *v/t* (*sep*, -*ge*-, *h*) find (out); establish; see, notice; state; TECH lock, arrest
'**Feststellung** *f* (-; -*en*) finding(s); realization; statement
'**Festtag** *m* holiday; REL religious holiday; F red-letter day
'**Festung** *f* (-; -*en*) fortress
'**Festwertspeicher** *m* EDP read-only memory, ROM
'**Festzug** *m* procession
fett [fɛt] *adj* fat (*a. fig*); PRINT bold; ***fett gedruckt*** boldface, in bold type (*or* print)
Fett *n* (-[*e*]*s*; -*e*) fat; dripping; shortening; TECH grease
'**fettarm** *adj* low-fat, *pred* low in fat
'**Fettfleck** *m* grease spot
fettig ['fɛtɪç] *adj* greasy
'**Fettnäpfchen** *n*: ***ins Fettnäpfchen treten*** put one's foot in it
Fetzen ['fɛtsən] *m* (-*s*; -) shred; rag; scrap (*of paper etc*)
feucht [fɔʏçt] *adj* moist, damp; humid
Feuchtigkeit ['fɔʏçtɪçkait] *f* (-; *no pl*) moisture; dampness; humidity
feudal [fɔʏ'da:l] *adj* POL feudal; F posh, *Br* swish
Feuer ['fɔʏɐ] *n* (-*s*; -) fire (*a. fig*); ***j-m Feuer geben*** give s.o. a light; ***Feuer fangen*** catch fire; *fig* fall for *s.o.*
Feuera͵larm *m* fire alarm
Feuerbestattung *f* cremation
Feuereifer *m* ardo(u)r
'**feuerfest** *adj* fireproof, fire-resistant
'**Feuergefahr** *f* danger of fire
'**feuergefährlich** *adj* inflammable
'**Feuerleiter** *f* fire escape
Feuerlöscher [-lœʃɐ] *m* (-*s*; -) fire extinguisher
Feuermelder [-mɛldɐ] *m* (-*s*; -) fire alarm
feuern ['fɔʏɐn] *v/i and v/t* (*ge*-, *h*) fire (*a.* F *s.o.*)
'**feuer'rot** *adj* blazing red; crimson
'**Feuerschiff** *n* lightship
Feuerstein *m* flint
Feuerwache *f* fire station
Feuerwaffe *f* firearm, gun
Feuerwehr *f* (-; -*en*) fire brigade (*or* department); fire truck (*Br* engine)
Feuerwehrmann *m* (-[*e*]*s*, -*männer*, -*leute*) fireman, fire fighter
Feuerwerk *n* fireworks
Feuerwerkskörper *m* firework, firecracker
Feuerzeug *n* (cigarette) lighter
feurig ['fɔʏrɪç] *adj* fiery, ardent
Fiasko ['fjasko] *n* (-*s*; -*s*) fiasco, (complete) failure
Fibel ['fi:bəl] *f* (-; -*n*) primer, first reader
Fiber ['fi:bɐ] *f* fiber, *Br* fibre
Fiberglas *n* fiberglass, *Br* fibreglass
Fichte ['fɪçtə] *f* (-; -*n*) BOT spruce, F *mst* pine *or* fir (tree)
ficken ['fɪkən] V *v/i and v/t* (*ge*-, *h*) fuck
Fieber ['fi:bɐ] *n* (-*s*; *no pl*) MED temperature, fever (*a. fig*); ***Fieber haben*** (***messen***) have a (take *s.o.'s*) temperature; ***Fieber senkend*** MED antipyretic
'**fieberhaft** *adj* MED feverish (*a. fig*)
'**fiebern** *v/i* (*ge*-, *h*) MED have *or* run a temperature; ***fiebern nach*** *fig* crave for
'**Fieberthermo͵meter** *n* fever (*Br* clinical) thermometer
fiel [fi:l] *pret of* ***fallen***
fies [fi:s] F *adj* mean, nasty
Figur [fi'gu:ɐ] *f* (-; -*en*) figure
Filet [fi'le:] *n* (-*s*; -*s*) GASTR fil(l)et
Filiale [fi'lja:lə] *f* (-; -*n*) branch
Film [film] *m* (-[*e*]*s*; -*e*) film; movie, *esp Br* (motion) picture; *the* movies, *Br the* cinema; ***e-n Film einlegen*** PHOT load a camera
Filmaufnahme *f* filming, shooting; take, shot
filmen ['filmən] (*ge*-, *h*) **1.** *v/t* film, shoot; **2.** *v/i* make a film
'**Filmgesellschaft** *f* motion-picture (*Br* film) company
Filmkamera *f* motion-picture (*Br* film) camera
Filmkas͵sette *f* film magazine, cartridge
Filmpro͵jektor *m* film (*or* movie) projector
Filmregis͵seur *m* film director
Filmschauspieler(in) film (*or* screen, movie) actor (actress)
Filmstudio *n* film studio(s)
Filmthe͵ater *n* → ***Kino***
Filmverleih *m* film distributors
Filmvorführer *m* (-*s*; -) projectionist
Filter ['filtɐ] *m*, *esp* TECH *n* (-*s*; -) filter
'**Filterkaffee** *m* filter coffee
'**filtern** *v/t* (*ge*-, *h*) filter
'**Filterziga͵rette** *f* filter(-tipped) cigarette,

filter tip
Filz [fɪlts] *m* (*-es*; *-e*) felt; F POL corruption, sleaze
'**filzen** F *v/t* (*ge-*, *h*) frisk
'**Filzschreiber** [-ʃraibɐ] *m* (*-s*; -), **Filzstift** *m* felt(-tipped) pen
Finale [fi'naːlə] *n* (*-s*; -) finale; SPORT final(s)
Finanzamt [fi'nants-] *n* tax office; Internal (*Br* Inland) Revenue
Finanzbeamte *m* tax officer
Finanzen [fi'nantsən] *pl* finances
finanziell [finan'tsjɛl] *adj* financial
finanzieren [finan'tsiːrən] *v/t* (*no -ge-*, *h*) finance
Fi'nanzmi,nister *m* minister of finance; Secretary of the Treasury, *Br* Chancellor of the Exchequer
Finanzminis,terium *n* ministry of finance; Treasury Department, *Br* Treasury
Finanzwesen *n* (*-s*; *no pl*) finance
Findelkind ['fɪndəl-] *n* JUR foundling
finden *v/t* (*irr*, *ge-*, *h*) find; think, believe; ***ich finde ihn nett*** I think he's nice; ***wie finden Sie ...?*** how do you like ...?; ***finden Sie (nicht)?*** do (don't) you think so?; ***das wird sich finden*** we'll see
Finder ['fɪndɐ] *m* (*-s*; -) finder
'**Finderlohn** *m* finder's reward
findig ['fɪndɪç] *adj* clever
fing [fɪŋ] *pret of* ***fangen***
Finger ['fɪŋɐ] *m* (*-s*; -) ANAT finger
Fingerabdruck *m* fingerprint
Fingerfertigkeit *f* (*-*; *no pl*) manual skill
Fingerhut *m* thimble; BOT foxglove
Fingernagel *m* ANAT fingernail
Fingerspitze *f* fingertip
Fingerspitzengefühl *n* (*-[e]s*; *no pl*) sure instinct; tact
fingiert [fɪŋ'giːɐt] *adj* faked; fictitious
Fink [fɪŋk] *m* (*-en*; *-en*) ZO finch
Finne ['fɪnə] *m* (*-n*; *-n*), **Finnin** ['fɪnɪn] *f* (*-*; *-nen*) Finn
'**finnisch** *adj* Finnish
Finnland ['fɪn-] Finland
finster ['fɪnstɐ] *adj* dark, gloomy; *fig* grim; shady
'**Finsternis** *f* (*-*; *-se*) darkness, gloom
Finte ['fɪntə] *f* (*-*; *-n*) trick; SPORT feint
Firma ['fɪrma] (*-*; *-men*) firm, company
firmen ['fɪrmən] *v/t* (*ge-*, *h*) REL confirm
'**Firmung** *f* (*-*; *-en*) REL confirmation
First [fɪrst] *m* (*-[e]s*; *-e*) ARCH ridge
Fisch [fɪʃ] *m* (*-[e]s*; *-e*) ZO fish; *pl* ASTR Pisces; ***er ist (ein) Fisch*** he's (a) Pisces
'**Fischdampfer** *m* trawler
fischen ['fɪʃən] *v/t and v/i* (*ge-*, *h*) fish
Fischer ['fɪʃɐ] *m* (*-s*; -) fisherman; ***Fischer...*** *in cpds ...boot*, *...dorf etc*: fishing ...
Fischerei [fɪʃə'rai] *f* (*-*; *no pl*) fishing
'**Fischfang** *m* (*-[e]s*; *no pl*) fishing
Fischgräte *f* fishbone
Fischgrätenmuster *n* herring-bone (pattern)
Fischgründe *pl* fishing grounds
Fischhändler *m* fish dealer, *esp Br* fishmonger
Fischkutter *m* smack
Fischlaich *m* spawn
Fischstäbchen *n* GASTR fish stick (*Br* finger)
Fischzucht *f* fish farming
Fischzug *m* catch, haul (*both a. fig*)
Fisole [fi'zoːlə] *Austrian f* (*-*; *-n*) BOT string bean
Fistel ['fɪstəl] *f* (*-*; *-n*) MED fistula
'**Fistelstimme** *f* falsetto
fit [fɪt] *adj* fit; ***sich fit halten*** keep fit
'**Fitness** *f* (*-*; *no pl*) fitness
Fitnesscenter *n* health club, fitness center, gym
fix [fɪks] *adj* ECON fixed; F quick; F smart, bright; F ***fix und fertig sein*** be dead beat; be a nervous wreck; ***fixe Idee*** PSYCH obsession
fixen ['fɪksən] F *v/i* (*ge-*, *h*) shoot, fix; be a junkie
Fixer ['fɪksɐ] F *m* (*-s*; -) junkie, mainliner
fixieren [fɪ'ksiːrən] *v/t* (*no -ge-*, *h*) fix (*a.* PHOT); stare at *s.o.*
'**Fixstern** *m* ASTR fixed star
FKK [ɛfka:'kaː] ABBR *of* ***Freikörperkultur*** nudism
FK'K-Strand *m* nudist beach
flach [flax] *adj* flat; level, even, plane; *fig* shallow
Fläche ['flɛçə] *f* (*-*; *-n*) surface (*a.* MATH); area (*a.* MATH); expanse, space
'**flächendeckend** *adj* exhaustive
'**Flächeninhalt** *m* MATH (surface) area
Flächenmaß *n* square *or* surface measure
'**Flachland** *n* (*-[e]s*; *no pl*) lowland, plain
Flachs [flaks] *m* (*-es*; *no pl*) BOT flax
flackern ['flakɐn] *v/i* (*ge-*, *h*) flicker
Fladenbrot ['flaːdən-] *n* round flat bread (*or* loaf)
Flagge ['flagə] *f* (*-*; *-n*) flag
'**flaggen** *v/i* (*ge-*, *h*) fly a flag *or* flags
Flak [flak] *f* (*-*; -) MIL anti-aircraft gun
Flamme ['flamə] *f* (*-*; *-n*) flame (*a. fig*)
Flanell [fla'nɛl] *m* (*-s*; *-e*) flannel
Flanke ['flaŋkə] *f* (*-*; *-n*) flank, side; *soccer*: cross; SPORT flank vault
flankieren [flaŋ'kiːrən] *v/t* (*no -ge-*, *h*) flank
Flasche ['flaʃə] *f* (*-*; *-n*) bottle; baby's bot-

tle; F *contp* dead loss
'**Flaschenbier** *n* bottled beer
Flaschenhals *m* neck of a bottle
Flaschenöffner *m* bottle opener
Flaschenpfand *n* (bottle) deposit
Flaschenzug *m* TECH block and tackle, pulley
flatterhaft ['flatɐhaft] *adj* fickle, flighty
flattern ['flatɐn] *v/i* (*ge-*, *sein*) flutter; TECH (*h*) wobble
flau [flau] *adj* queasy; *fig* flat; ECON slack
Flaum [flaum] *m* (*-[e]s*; *no pl*) down, fluff, fuzz
Flausch [flauʃ] *m* (*-es*; *-e*) fleece
flauschig ['flauʃɪç] *adj* fleecy, fluffy
Flausen ['flauzən] F *pl* (funny) ideas
Flaute ['flautə] *f* (*-*; *-n*) MAR calm; ECON slack period
Flechte ['flɛçtə] *f* (*-*; *-n*) plait, braid; BOT, MED lichen
'**flechten** *v/t* (*irr*, *ge-*, *h*) plait, braid (*hair*); weave (*basket*)
Fleck [flɛk] *m* (*-[e]s*; *-e*) stain, mark; speck; dot; blot(ch); *fig* place, spot; patch; ***blauer Fleck*** bruise; ***vom Fleck weg*** on the spot; ***nicht vom Fleck kommen*** not get anywhere
'**Flecken** *m* → ***Fleck***
'**Fleckenentferner** *m* stain remover
'**fleckenlos** *adj* spotless (*a. fig*)
fleckig ['flɛkɪç] *adj* spotted; stained
Fledermaus ['fle:dɐ-] *f* zo bat
Flegel ['fle:gəl] *m* (*-s*; *-*) lout, boor
'**flegelhaft** *adj* loutish
'**Flegeljahre** *pl* awkward age
'**flegeln** F *contp v/refl* (*ge-*, *h*) lounge
flehen ['fle:ən] *v/i* (*ge-*, *h*) beg; pray (***um*** for)
flehentlich ['fle:əntlɪç] *adj* imploring, entreating
Fleisch [flaiʃ] *n* (*-[e]s*; *no pl*) flesh (*a. fig*); GASTR meat; ***Fleisch fressend*** → ***fleischfressend***
Fleischbrühe *f* (meat) broth, consommé
Fleischer ['flaiʃɐ] *m* (*-s*; *-*) butcher
Fleischerei [flaiʃə'rai] *f* (*-*; *-en*) butcher's (shop)
'**fleischfressend** *adj* BOT, ZO carnivorous
'**Fleischhauer** [-hauɐ] *Austrian m* (*-s*; *-*) butcher
fleischig ['flaiʃɪç] *adj* fleshy
'**Fleischklößchen** *n* (*-s*; *-*) meatball
Fleischkon,serven *pl* canned (*Br* tinned) meat
'**fleischlos** *adj* meatless
'**Fleischwolf** *m* meat grinder, *Br* mincer
Fleiß [flais] *m* (*-es*; *no pl*) diligence, hard work
fleißig ['flaisɪç] *adj* diligent, hard-working; ***fleißig sein*** work hard
fletschen ['flɛtʃən] *v/t* (*ge-*, *h*) bare
flexibel [flɛ'ksi:bəl] *adj* flexible
Flexibilität [flɛksibili'tɛ:t] *f* (*-*; *no pl*) flexibility
flicken ['flɪkən] *v/t* (*ge-*, *h*) mend, repair, *a. fig* patch (up)
'**Flicken** *m* (*-s*; *-*) patch
'**Flickwerk** *n* patchwork (*a. fig*)
'**Flickzeug** *n* TECH repair kit
Flieder ['fli:dɐ] *m* (*-s*; *-*) BOT lilac
Fliege ['fli:gə] *f* (*-*; *-n*) ZO fly; bow tie
'**fliegen** *v/i* (*irr*, *ge-*, *sein*) *and v/t* (*h*) fly (*a.* ***fliegen lassen***); F fall; F be fired, F get the sack; be kicked out *of school*; F ***fliegen auf*** (*acc*) really go for; F ***in die Luft fliegen*** blow up
'**Fliegen** *n* (*-s*; *no pl*) flying; aviation
'**Fliegenfänger** *m* flypaper
Fliegenfenster *n* flyscreen
Fliegengewicht *n* SPORT flyweight
Fliegengitter *n* wire mesh (screen)
Fliegenklatsche *f* flyswatter
Fliegenpilz *m* BOT fly agaric
Flieger ['fli:gɐ] *m* (*-s*; *-*) MIL airman; F plane; *cycling*: sprinter
Fliegera,larm *m* air-raid warning
fliehen ['fli:ən] *v/i* (*irr*, *ge-*, *sein*) flee, run away (*both*: ***vor*** *dat* from)
'**Fliehkraft** *f* PHYS centrifugal force
Fliese ['fli:zə] *f* (*-*; *-n*), '**fliesen** *v/t* (*ge-*, *h*) tile
'**Fliesenleger** *m* (*-s*; *-*) tiler
Fließband ['fli:s-] *n* (*-[e]s*; *-bänder*) TECH assembly line; conveyor belt
fließen ['fli:sən] *v/i* (*irr*, *ge-*, *sein*) flow (*a. fig*); run
fließend **1.** *adj* flowing; running; LING fluent; **2.** *adv*: ***er spricht fließend Englisch*** he speaks English fluently *or* fluent English
'**Fließheck** *n* MOT fastback
flimmern ['flɪmɐn] *v/i* (*ge-*, *h*) shimmer; *film*: flicker
flink [flɪŋk] *adj* quick, nimble
Flinte ['flɪntə] *f* (*-*; *-n*) shotgun; F gun
Flipper ['flɪpɐ] F *m* (*-s*; *-*) pinball machine
'**flippern** *v/i* (*ge-*, *h*) play pinball
Flirt [flœrt] *m* (*-s*; *-s*) flirtation
flirten ['flœrtən] *v/i* (*ge-*, *h*) flirt
Flittchen ['flɪtçən] F *n* (*-s*; *-*) floozie
Flitter ['flɪtɐ] *m* (*-s*; *-*) tinsel (*a. fig*), spangles
Flitterwochen *pl* honeymoon
flitzen ['flɪtsən] F *v/i* (*ge-*, *sein*) flit, whizz, shoot
flocht [flɔxt] *pret of* ***flechten***
Flocke ['flɔkə] *f* (*-*; *-n*) flake
flockig ['flɔkɪç] *adj* fluffy, flaky

flog [floːk] *pret of* ***fliegen***
floh [floː] *pret of* ***fliehen***
Floh *m* (-[*e*]*s*; *Flöhe* ['fløːə]) zo flea
'**Flohmarkt** *m* flea market
Florett [flo'rɛt] *n* (-[*e*]*s*; -*e*) foil
florieren [flo'riːrən] *v/i* (*no -ge-, h*) flourish, prosper
Floskel ['flɔskəl] *f* (-; -*n*) empty *or* cliché(d) phrase
floss [flɔs] *pret of* ***fließen***
Floß [floːs] *n* (-*es*; *Flöße* ['fløːsə]) raft, float
Flosse ['flɔsə] *f* (-; -*n*) zo fin, *a.* SPORT flipper
Flöte ['fløːtə] *f* (-; -*n*) MUS flute; recorder
flott [flɔt] *adj* brisk (*pace*); F smart, chic; MAR afloat
Flotte ['flɔtə] *f* (-; -*n*) MAR fleet; navy
'**Flottenstützpunkt** *m* MIL naval base
Fluch [fluːx] *m* (-[*e*]*s*; *Flüche* ['flyːçə]) curse; swear word
fluchen ['fluːxən] *v/i* (*ge-, h*) swear, curse
Flucht [flʊxt] *f* (-; -*en*) flight (***vor*** *dat* from); escape, getaway (***aus*** *dat* from)
'**fluchtartig** *adv* hastily
'**Fluchtauto** *n* getaway car
flüchten ['flʏçtən] *v/i* (*ge-, sein*) flee (***nach, zu*** to), run away; escape, get away
flüchtig ['flʏçtɪç] *adj* quick; superficial; careless; fugitive, *criminal etc*: on the run, at large; ***flüchtiger Blick*** glance; ***flüchtiger Eindruck*** glimpse
'**Flüchtigkeitsfehler** *m* slip
Flüchtling ['flʏçtlɪŋ] *m* fugitive; POL refugee
'**Flüchtlingslager** *n* refugee camp
Flug [fluːk] *m* (-[*e*]*s*; *Flüge* ['flyːgə]) flight; ***im Flug(e)*** rapidly, quickly
Flugabwehrra͵kete *f* MIL anti-aircraft missile
Flugbahn *f* trajectory
Flugball *m tennis*: volley
Flugbegleiter(in) flight attendant
Flugblatt *n* handbill, leaflet
Flugdienst *m* air service
Flügel ['flyːgəl] *m* (-*s*; -) zo wing (*a.* SPORT); TECH blade; *windmill*: sail; MUS grand piano
Flügelmutter *f* TECH wing nut
Flügelschraube *f* TECH thumb screw
Flügelstürmer *m* SPORT wing forward
Flügeltür *f* folding door
'**Fluggast** *m* (air) passenger
flügge ['flʏgə] *adj* full-fledged
'**Fluggesellschaft** *f* airline
Flughafen *m* airport
Fluglinie *f* air route; → ***Fluggesellschaft***
Fluglotse *m* air traffic controller
Flugplan *m* air schedule
Flugplatz *m* airfield, airport
Flugschein *m* (flight) ticket
Flugschreiber *m* (-*s*; -) flight recorder, black box
Flugsicherung *f* air traffic control
Flugverkehr *m* air traffic
'**Flugzeug** *n* (-[*e*]*s*; -*e*) (air)plane, aircraft, *Br a.* aeroplane; ***mit dem Flugzeug*** by air *or* plane
Flugzeugabsturz *m* air *or* plane crash
Flugzeugentführung *f* hijacking, skyjacking
Flugzeughalle *f* hangar
Flugzeugträger *m* MAR MIL aircraft carrier
Flunder ['flʊndɐ] *f* (-; -*n*) zo flounder
flunkern ['flʊŋkɐn] *v/i* (*ge-, h*) fib; brag
Fluor ['fluːoːɐ] *n* (-*s*; *no pl*) CHEM fluorine; fluoride
'**Fluorchlorkohlenwasserstoff** *m* CHEM chlorofluorocarbon, CFC
Flur [fluːɐ] *m* (-[*e*]*s*; -*e*) hall; corridor
Fluss [flʊs] *m* (-*es*; *Flüsse* ['flʏsə]) river; stream; ***im Fluss*** *fig* in (a state of) flux
fluss'abwärts *adv* downstream
fluss'aufwärts *adv* upstream
'**Flussbett** *n* river bed
flüssig ['flʏsɪç] *adj* liquid; melted; *fig* fluent; ECON available
'**Flüssigkeit** *f* (-; -*en*) a) liquid, b) (*no pl*) liquidity; *fig* fluency
'**Flüssigkris͵tallanzeige** *f* liquid crystal display, LCD
'**Flusslauf** *m* course of a river
Flusspferd *n* zo hippopotamus, F hippo
Flussufer *n* riverbank, riverside
flüstern ['flʏstɐn] *v/i and v/t* (*ge-, h*) whisper
Flut [fluːt] *f* (-; -*en*) flood (*a. fig*); high tide; ***es ist Flut*** the tide is in
Flutlicht *n* floodlights
Flutwelle *f* tidal wave
focht [fɔxt] *pret of* ***fechten***
Fohlen ['foːlən] *n* (-*s*; -) zo foal; colt; filly
Föhn[1] [føːn] *m* (-[*e*]*s*; -*e*) hairdrier
Föhn[2] *m* (-[*e*]*s*; -*e*) METEOR foehn, föhn
föhnen ['føːnən] *v/t* (*ge-, h*) blow-dry
Folge ['fɔlgə] *f* (-; -*n*) result, consequence; effect; succession; order; series; TV *etc*: sequel, episode; aftermath; MED aftereffect
folgen ['fɔlgən] *v/i* (*ge-, sein*) follow; obey; ***hieraus folgt, dass*** from this it follows that; ***wie folgt*** as follows
folgend *adj* following, subsequent
folgendermaßen ['fɔlgəndɐ'maːsən] *adv* as follows
'**folgenschwer** *adj* momentous
'**folgerichtig** *adj* logical; consistent
folgern ['fɔlgɐn] *v/t* (*ge-, h*) conclude (***aus***

dat from)
Folgerung ['fɔlgərʊŋ] *f* (-; *-en*) conclusion
folglich ['fɔlklɪç] *cj* consequently, thus, therefore
folgsam ['fɔlkzaːm] *adj* obedient
Folie ['foːljə] *f* (-; *-n*) foil; transparency
Folter ['fɔltɐ] *f* (-; *-n*) torture; ***auf die Folter spannen*** tantalize
'**foltern** *v/t* (*ge-*, *h*) torture, *fig a.* torment
Fön® *m* → ***Föhn***[1]
Fonds [fõː] *m* (-; -) ECON fund
fönen *v/t* → ***föhnen***
Fontäne [fɔn'tɛːnə] *f* (-; *-n*) jet, spout; gush
Förderband ['fœrdɐ-] *n* TECH conveyor belt
Förderkorb *m mining*: cage
fordern ['fɔrdɐn] *v/t* (*ge-*, *h*) demand, *esp* JUR *a.* claim; ECON ask, charge
fördern ['fœrdɐn] *v/t* (*ge-*, *h*) promote; support (*a.* UNIV), sponsor; PED tutor, provide remedial classes for; TECH mine
Forderung ['fɔrdərʊŋ] *f* (-; *-en*) demand; claim (*a.* JUR); ECON charge
Förderung ['fœrdərʊŋ] *f* (-; *-en*) promotion, advancement; support, sponsorship; UNIV *etc*: grant; PED tutoring, remedial classes; TECH mining
Forelle [fo'rɛlə] *f* (-; *-n*) ZO trout
Form [fɔrm] *f* (-; *-en*) form, shape, SPORT *a.* condition; TECH mo(u)ld; ***gut in Form*** in great form
formal [fɔr'maːl] *adj* formal
Formalität [fɔrmali'tɛːt] *f* (-; *-en*) formality
Format [fɔr'maːt] *n* (-[*e*]*s*; *-e*) size; format; *fig* caliber, *Br* calibre
formatieren [fɔrma'tiːrən] *v/t* (*no -ge-*, *h*) EDP format
Forma'tierung *f* (-; *-en*) EDP formatting
Formel ['fɔrməl] *f* (-; *-n*) formula
formell [fɔr'mɛl] *adj* formal
formen ['fɔrmən] *v/t* (*ge-*, *h*) shape, form; *fig* mo(u)ld
'**Formfehler** *m* irregularity
formieren [fɔr'miːrən] *v/t and v/refl* (*no -ge-*, *h*) form (up)
förmlich ['fœrmlɪç] **1.** *adj* formal; *fig* regular; **2.** *adv* formally; *fig* literally
'**formlos** *adj* shapeless; *fig* informal
'**formschön** *adj* well-designed
Formular [fɔrmu'laːɐ] *n* (*-s*; *-e*) form, blank
formulieren [fɔrmu'liːrən] *v/t* (*no -ge-*, *h*) word, phrase; formulate; express
Formu'lierung *f* (-; *-en*) wording, phrasing; formulation; expression, phrase
forsch [fɔrʃ] *adj* dashing
forschen ['fɔrʃən] *v/i* (*ge-*, *h*) research, do research; ***forschen nach*** search for
Forscher ['fɔrʃɐ] *m* (*-s*; -), '**Forscherin** *f* (-; *-nen*) explorer; (research) scientist
Forschung ['fɔrʃʊŋ] *f* (-; *-en*) research (work)
Forst [fɔrst] *m* (-[*e*]*s*; *-e*[*n*]) forest
Förster ['fœrstɐ] *m* (*-s*; -) forester; forest ranger
'**Forstwirtschaft** *f* (-; *no pl*) forestry
fort [fɔrt] *adv* off, away; gone; missing
Fort [foːɐ] *n* (*-s*; *-s*) MIL fort
'**fortbestehen** *v/i* (*irr*, ***stehen***, *sep*, *no -ge-*, *h*) continue
'**fortbewegen** *v/refl* (*sep*, *no -ge-*, *h*) move
'**Fortbewegung** *f* moving; (loco)motion
'**Fortbildung** *f* (-, *no pl*) further education *or* training
'**fortfahren** *v/i* (*irr*, ***fahren***, *sep*, *-ge-*) a) (*sein*) leave, go away, MOT *a.* drive off, b) (*h*) continue, go *or* keep on (***et. zu tun*** doing s.th.)
fortführen *v/t* (*sep*, *-ge-*, *h*) continue, carry on
fortgehen *v/i* (*irr*, ***gehen***, *sep*, *-ge-*, *sein*) go away, leave
'**fortgeschritten** *adj* advanced
'**fortlaufend** *adj* consecutive, successive
'**fortpflanzen** *v/refl* (*sep*, *-ge-*, *h*) BIOL reproduce; *fig* spread
'**Fortpflanzung** *f* BIOL reproduction
'**fortschreiten** *v/i* (*irr*, ***schreiten***, *sep*, *-ge-*, *sein*) advance, proceed, progress
fortschreitend *adj* progressive
'**Fortschritt** *m* progress
'**fortschrittlich** *adj* progressive
'**fortsetzen** *v/t* (*sep*, *-ge-*, *h*) continue, go on with
'**Fortsetzung** *f* (-; *-en*) continuation; *film etc*: sequel; ***Fortsetzung folgt*** to be continued
'**Fortsetzungsro,man** *m* serialized novel
'**fortwährend** *adj* continual, constant
fossil [fɔ'siːl] *adj*, **Fos'sil** *n* (*-s*; *-ien*) GEOL fossil (*a. fig* F)
Foto ['foːto] *n* (*-s*; *-s*) photo(graph); ***ein Foto machen*** (***von***) take a photo (of)
'**Fotoalbum** *n* photo album
'**Fotoappa,rat** *m* camera
Fotograf [foto'graːf] *m* (*-en*; *-en*) photographer
Fotografie [fotogra'fiː] *f* (-; *-n*) a) (*no pl*) photography, b) photograph, picture
fotografieren [fotogra'fiːrən] *v/t and v/i* (*no -ge-*, *h*) take a photo(graph) *or* picture (of); ***sich fotografieren lassen*** have one's picture taken
Foto'grafin *f* (-; *-nen*) photographer
'**Fotohandy** *n* camera phone
Fotoko'pie *f* photocopy

fotoko'pieren *v/t (no -ge-, h)* (photo)copy
'Fotomo,dell *n* model
'Fotozelle *f* photoelectric cell
Fotze ['fɔtsə] V *f (-; -n)* cunt
Foul [faul] *n (-s; -s)* SPORT foul
foulen ['faulən] *v/t and v/i (ge-, h)* SPORT foul
Foyer [foa'je:] *n (-s; -s)* foyer, lobby, lounge
Fr. ABBR *of* ***Frau*** Mrs, Ms
Fracht [fraxt] *f (-; -en)* freight, load, MAR, AVIAT *a.* cargo; ECON freight, *Br* carriage
Frachtbrief *m* RAIL bill of lading (*a.* MAR), *Br* consignment note
Frachter ['fraxtɐ] *m (-s; -)* MAR freighter
Frack [frak] *m (-[e]s; Fräcke* ['frɛkə]) tails, tailcoat
Frage ['fra:gə] *f (-; -n)* question; ***e-e Frage stellen*** ask a question; → ***infrage***
'Fragebogen *m* question(n)aire
'fragen *v/t and v/i (ge-, h)* ask (***nach*** for; ***wegen*** about); ***nach dem Weg (der Zeit) fragen*** ask the way (time); ***sich fragen*** wonder
'Fragewort *n* LING interrogative
Fragezeichen *n* LING question mark
fraglich ['fra:klɪç] *adj* doubtful, uncertain; ... in question
fraglos ['fra:klo:s] *adv* undoubtedly, unquestionably
Fragment [fra'gmɛnt] *n (-[e]s; -e)* fragment
fragwürdig ['fra:k-] *adj* dubious, F shady
Fraktion [frak'tsjo:n] *f (-; -en)* (parliamentary) group *or* party
Frakti'onsführer *m* PARL floor leader, *Br* chief whip
Franc [frã:] *m (-; -s)*, **Franken** ['fraŋkən] *m (-; -)* franc
frankieren [fraŋ'ki:rən] *v/t (no -ge-, h)* stamp; frank
Frankreich ['fraŋkraiç] France
Franse ['franzə] *f (-; -n)* fringe
fransig ['franzɪç] *adj* frayed
Franzose [fran'tso:zə] *m (-n; -n)* Frenchman; ***die Franzosen*** *pl* the French
Französin [fran'tsø:zɪn] *f (-; -nen)* Frenchwoman
französisch [fran'tsø:zɪʃ] *adj* French
fraß [fra:s] *pret of* ***fressen***
Fraß F *contp m (-es; no pl)* muck
Fratze ['fratsə] *f (-; -n)* grimace
Frau [frau] *f (-; -en)* woman; wife; ***Frau X*** Mrs (*or* Ms) X
Frauchen ['frauçən] *n* mistress (*of dog*)
'Frauenarzt *m*, **Frauenärztin** *f* gyn(a)ecologist
Frauenbewegung *f*: ***die Frauenbewegung*** POL women's lib(eration)
'frauenfeindlich *adj* sexist
'Frauenhaus *n* women's shelter (*Br* refuge)
Frauenklinik *f* gyn(a)ecological hospital
Frauenrechtlerin [-rɛçtlərɪn] *f (-; -nen)* feminist
Fräulein ['frɔylain] *n (-s; -)* Miss
'fraulich *adj* womanly, feminine
frech [frɛç] *adj* sassy, *Br* cheeky
'Frechheit *f (-; no pl)* F *Br* cheek
frei [frai] *adj* free (***von*** from, of); independent; freelance; vacant; candid, frank; SPORT unmarked; ***ein freier Tag*** a day off; ***morgen haben wir frei*** there is no school tomorrow; ***im Freien*** outdoors; → ***Fuß***; ***sich frei machen*** undress; ***sich frei machen von*** free o.s. from; → *a.* ***freibekommen, freigeben, freihaben***; ***frei halten*** keep clear (*exit*), → ***freihalten***
'Freibad *n* open-air swimming-pool
'freibekommen *v/t (irr,* ***kommen****, sep, no -ge-, h)* get *a day etc* off
'freiberuflich *adj* freelance, self-employed
'Freiexem,plar *n* free copy
'Freigabe *f (-; no pl)* release
'freigeben *(irr,* ***geben****, sep, -ge-, h)* **1.** *v/t* release; ***e-n Tag*** *etc* ***freigeben*** give a day *etc* off; **2.** *v/i*: ***j-m freigeben*** give s.o. time off
'freigebig [-ge:bɪç] *adj* generous
'Freigepäck *n* AVIAT baggage allowance
'freihaben F *v/i (irr,* ***haben****, sep, -ge-, h)* have a day off (*Br a.* a holiday)
'Freihafen *m* free port
'freihalten *v/t (irr,* ***halten****, sep, -ge-, h)* keep, save (*seat etc*); treat (*s.o.*)
'Freihandel *m* free trade
Freihandelszone *f* free trade area
'freihändig [-hɛndɪç] *adv* with no hands
'Freiheit *f (-; -en)* freedom, liberty; ***sich Freiheiten herausnehmen gegen*** take liberties with
'Freiheitsstrafe *f* JUR prison sentence
'Freikarte *f* free ticket
'freikaufen *v/t (sep, -ge-, h)* ransom
'Freikörperkul,tur *f (-; no pl)* nudism
'freilassen *v/t (irr,* ***lassen****, sep, -ge-, h)* release, set free
'Freilassung *f (-; -en)* release
'Freilauf *m* freewheel (*a.* ***im Freilauf fahren***)
'freilich *adv* indeed, of course
'Freilicht... *in cpds* open-air ...
'freimachen *v/t (sep, -ge-, h) post*: stamp; ***sich freimachen*** undress; ***sich freimachen von*** free o.s. from; → ***frei***; → ***Oberkörper***
'Freimaurer *m* freemason

'**freimütig** [-myːtɪç] *adj* candid, frank
'**freischaffend** *adj* freelance
'**freischwimmen** *v/refl* (*irr*, ***schwimmen***, *sep*, *-ge-*, *h*) pass a 15-minute swimming test
'**freisprechen** *v/t* (*irr*, ***sprechen***, *sep*, *-ge-*, *h*) *esp* REL absolve (***von*** from); JUR acquit (of)
'**Freispruch** *m* JUR acquittal
'**Freistaat** *m* POL free state
'**freistehen** *v/i* (*irr*, ***stehen***, *sep*, *-ge-*, *h*) be unoccupied; SPORT be unmarked; ***es steht dir frei zu*** *inf* you are free to *inf*
freistellen *v/t* (*sep*, *-ge-*, *h*) ***j-n freistellen*** exempt s.o. (***von*** from) (*a.* MIL); ***j-m et. freistellen*** leave s.th. (up) to s.o.
'**Freistil** *m* freestyle
Freistoß *m soccer*: free kick
Freistunde *f* PED free period
Freitag *m* Friday
Freitod *m* suicide
Freitreppe *f* outdoor stairs
Freiübungen *pl* exercises
Freiwild *fig n* fair game
'**freiwillig** *adj* voluntary; ***sich freiwillig melden*** volunteer (***zu*** for)
Freiwillige ['fraivɪlɪgə] *m*, *f* (*-n*; *-n*) volunteer
'**Freizeit** *f* free *or* leisure time
Freizeitgestaltung *f* leisure-time activities
Freizeitkleidung *f* leisurewear
Freizeitpark *m* amusement park
Freizeitzentrum *n* leisure center (*Br* centre)
'**freizügig** *adj* permissive; *film etc*: explicit
fremd [frɛmt] *adj* strange; foreign; unknown; ***ich bin auch fremd hier*** I'm a stranger here myself
'**fremdartig** *adj* strange, exotic
Fremde ['frɛmdə] *m*, *f* (*-n*; *-n*) stranger; foreigner
'**Fremdenführer** *m*, **Fremdenführerin** *f* (*-*; *-nen*) (tourist) guide
Fremdenhass *m* xenophobia
Fremdenlegi̦on *f* Foreign Legion
Fremdenverkehr *m* tourism
Fremdenverkehrsbü̦ro *n* tourist office
Fremdenzimmer *n* guest room; ***Fremdenzimmer*** (***zu vermieten***) rooms to let
'**fremdgehen** F *v/i* (*irr*, ***gehen***, *sep*, *-ge-*, *sein*) be unfaithful (to one's wife *or* husband), play around
'**Fremdkörper** *m* MED foreign body; *fig* alien element
Fremdsprache *f* foreign language
Fremdsprachensekre̦tärin *f* bilingual secretary
'**fremdsprachig**, **fremdsprachlich** *adj* foreign-language
'**Fremdwort** *n* (*-*[*e*]*s*; *-wörter*) foreign word
Frequenz [fre'kvɛnts] *f* (*-*; *-en*) PHYS frequency
Fresse ['frɛsə] V *f* (*-*; *-n*) big (fat) mouth
'**fressen** *v/t* (*irr*, *ge-*, *h*) zo eat, feed on; F gobble (up); *fig* devour
Freude ['frɔʏdə] *f* (*-*; *-n*) joy, delight; pleasure; ***Freude haben an*** (*dat*) take pleasure in
'**Freudengeschrei** *n* shouts of joy, cheers
Freudenhaus F *n* brothel
Freudentag *m* red-letter day
Freudentränen *pl* tears of joy
'**freudestrahlend** *adj* radiant (with joy)
freudig ['frɔʏdɪç] *adj* joyful, cheerful; happy (*event etc*)
freudlos ['frɔʏt-] *adj* joyless, cheerless
freuen ['frɔʏən] *v/t* (*ge-*, *h*) ***es freut mich, dass*** I'm glad *or* pleased (that); ***sich freuen über*** (*acc*) be pleased *or* glad about; ***sich freuen auf*** (*acc*) look forward to
Freund [frɔʏnt] *m* (*-*[*e*]*s*; *-e* ['frɔʏndə]) friend; boyfriend
Freundin ['frɔʏndɪn] *f* (*-*; *-nen*) friend; girlfriend
'**freundlich** *adj* friendly, kind, nice; *fig* cheerful (*room etc*)
'**Freundlichkeit** *f* (*-*; *no pl*) friendliness, kindness
'**Freundschaft** *f* (*-*; *-en*) friendship; ***Freundschaft schließen*** make friends
'**freundschaftlich** *adj* friendly
'**Freundschaftsspiel** *n* SPORT friendly (game)
Frevel ['freːfəl] *m* (*-s*; *-*) outrage (***an*** *dat*, ***gegen*** on)
Frieden ['friːdən] *m* (*-s*; *no pl*) peace; ***im Frieden*** in peacetime; ***lass mich in Frieden!*** leave me alone!
'**Friedensbewegung** *f* peace movement
Friedensforschung *f* peace studies
Friedensverhandlungen *pl* peace negotiations *or* talks
Friedensvertrag *m* peace treaty
friedfertig ['friːt-] *adj* peaceable
'**Friedhof** *m* cemetery, graveyard
'**friedlich** *adj* peaceful
'**friedliebend** *adj* peace-loving
frieren ['friːrən] *v/i* (*irr*, *ge-*, *h*) freeze; ***ich friere*** I am *or* feel cold; I'm freezing
Fries [friːs] *m* (*-es*; *-e*) ARCH frieze
Frikadelle [frika'dɛlə] *f* (*-*; *-n*) meatball
frisch [frɪʃ] *adj* fresh; clean (*shirt etc*); ***frisch gestrichen!*** wet (*or* fresh) paint!
Frische ['frɪʃə] *f* (*-*; *no pl*) freshness
'**Frischhaltebeutel** *m* polythene bag
Frischhaltefolie *f* plastic wrap, *Br* cling

F

film
Friseur [fri'zøːɐ] *m* (*-s*; *-e*) hairdresser; barber
Friseursa,lon *m* hairdresser's (shop), barber's shop
Friseuse [fri'zøːzə] *f* (*-*; *-n*) hairdresser
frisieren [fri'ziːrən] *v/t* (*no -ge-*, *h*) do *s.o.'s* hair; F MOT soup up
Frisör *etc* → ***Friseur*** *etc*

F

Frist [frɪst] *f* (*-*; *-en*) (fixed) period of time; deadline; extension (*a.* ECON)
fristen ['frɪstən] *v/t* (*ge-*, *h*) ***sein Dasein fristen*** scrape a living
'fristlos *adj* without notice
Frisur [fri'zuːɐ] *f* (*-*; *-en*) hairstyle, hairdo
Fritten ['frɪtən] F *pl* fries, *Br* chips
frittieren [fri'tiːrən] *v/t* (*no -ge-*, *h*) deep-fry
frivol [fri'voːl] *adj* frivolous; suggestive
froh [froː] *adj* glad (***über*** *acc* about); cheerful; happy; ***frohes Fest!*** happy holiday!; Merry Christmas!
fröhlich ['frøːlɪç] *adj* cheerful, happy; merry
'Fröhlichkeit *f* (*-*; *no pl*) cheerfulness, merriment
fromm [frɔm] *adj* pious, devout; meek; steady (*horse*); ***frommer Wunsch*** pious hope
Frömmigkeit ['frœmɪçkait] *f* (*-*; *no pl*) religiousness, piety
Fronleichnam ['froːn-] *m* (*-[e]s*; *no pl*) REL Corpus Christi
Front [frɔnt] *f* (*-*; *-en*) front (*a. fig*), ARCH *a.* face, MIL *a.* line; ***in Front liegen*** SPORT be ahead
frontal [frɔn'taːl] *adj* MOT head-on
Fron'talzusammenstoß *m* MOT head-on collision
'Frontantrieb *m* MOT front-wheel drive
fror [froːɐ] *pret of* ***frieren***
Frosch [frɔʃ] *m* (*-[e]s*; *Frösche* ['frœʃə]) ZO frog
Froschmann *m* frogman
Froschperspek,tive *f* worm's-eye view
Froschschenkel *pl* GASTR frog's legs
Frost [frɔst] *m* (*-[e]s*; *Fröste* ['frœstə]) frost
Frostbeule *f* chilblain
frösteln ['frœstəln] *v/i* (*ge-*, *h*) feel chilly, shiver (*a. fig*)
'frostig *adj* frosty, *fig a.* chilly
'Frostschutzmittel *n* MOT antifreeze
Frottee [frɔ'teː] *n*, *m* (*-[s]*; *-s*) terry(-cloth)
frottieren [frɔ'tiːrən] *v/t* (*no -ge-*, *h*) rub down
Frucht [frʊxt] *f* (*-*; *Früchte* ['frʏçtə]) BOT fruit (*a. fig*)
'fruchtbar *adj* BIOL fertile, *esp fig a.* fruitful
'Fruchtbarkeit *f* (*-*; *no pl*) fertility; *fig* fruitfulness
'fruchtlos *adj* fruitless, futile
'Fruchtsaft *m* fruit juice
früh [fryː] *adj and adv* early; ***zu früh kommen*** be early; ***früh genug*** soon enough; ***heute*** (***morgen***) ***früh*** this (tomorrow) morning
'Frühaufsteher *m* (*-s*; *-*) early riser (F bird)
Frühe ['fryːə] *f*: ***in aller Frühe*** (very) early in the morning
früher ['fryːɐ] **1.** *adj* former; previous; **2.** *adv* in former times, at one time; ***früher oder später*** sooner or later; ***ich habe früher*** (***einmal***) ... I used to ...
'frühestens *adv* at the earliest
'Frühgeburt *f* MED premature birth; premature baby
Frühjahr *n* spring
Frühjahrsputz *m* spring cleaning
früh'morgens *adv* early in the morning
'frühreif *adj* precocious
'Frühstück *n* breakfast (***zum*** for)
'frühstücken *v/i* (*ge-*, *h*) (have) breakfast
Frust [frʊst] F *m* (*-[e]s*; *no pl*) frustration
Frustration [frʊstra'tsjoːn] *f* (*-*; *-en*) frustration
frustrieren [frʊs'triːrən] *v/t* (*no -ge-*, *h*) frustrate
frz. ABBR *of* ***französisch*** Fr., French
Fuchs [fʊks] *m* (*-es*; *Füchse* ['fʏksə]) ZO fox (*a. fig*); sorrel
Fuchsjagd *f* foxhunt(ing)
Fuchsschwanz *m* TECH handsaw
'fuchs'teufels'wild F *adj* hopping mad
fuchteln ['fʊxtəln] *v/i* (*ge-*, *h*) ***fuchteln mit*** wave *s.th.* around
Fuge ['fuːgə] *f* (*-*; *-n*) TECH joint; MUS fugue
fügen ['fyːgən] *v/refl* (*ge-*, *h*) submit (***in*** *acc*, *dat* to *s.th.*)
fühlbar ['fyːl-] *fig adj* noticeable; considerable
fühlen ['fyːlən] *v/t and v/i and v/refl* (*ge-*, *h*) feel, *fig a.* sense; ***sich wohl fühlen*** → ***wohlfühlen***
Fühler ['fyːlɐ] *m* (*-s*; *-*) ZO feeler (*a. fig*)
fuhr [fuːɐ] *pret of* ***fahren***
führen ['fyːrən] (*ge-*, *h*) **1.** *v/t* lead; guide; take; run, manage; ECON sell, deal in; keep (*account*, *books etc*); have (*a talk etc*); bear (*name etc*); MIL command; ***j-n führen durch*** show s.o. round; ***sich führen*** conduct o.s.; **2.** *v/i* lead (***zu*** to, *a. fig*), SPORT *a.* be leading, be ahead
führend *adj* leading
Führer ['fyːrɐ] *m* (*-s*; *-*) leader (*a.* POL);

guide; head, chief; guide(book)

'Führerschein *m* MOT driver's license, *Br* driving licence

'Führung *f* (-; -*en*) a) (*no pl*) leadership, control; ECON management, b) (guided) tour; ***gute Führung*** good conduct; ***in Führung gehen*** (***sein***) SPORT take (be in) the lead

'Führungszeugnis *n* certificate of (good) conduct

Fuhrunternehmen ['fuːɐ-] *n* trucking company, *Br* haulage contractors

'Fuhrwerk *n* horse-drawn vehicle

Fülle ['fʏlə] *f* (-; *no pl*) crush; *fig* wealth, abundance; GASTR body

'füllen *v/t and v/refl* (*ge-*, *h*) fill (*a.* MED), stuff (*a.* GASTR)

Füller ['fʏlɐ] *m* (-*s*; -), **'Füllfederhalter** *m* fountain pen

füllig ['fʏlɪç] *adj* stout, portly

'Füllung *f* (-; -*en*) filling (*a.* MED), stuffing (*a.* GASTR)

fummeln ['fʊməln] F *v/i* (*ge-*, *h*) fiddle, tinker (*both*: ***an*** *dat* with); F grope

Fund [fʊnt] *m* (-[*e*]*s*; -*e* ['fʊndə]) discovery; find

Fundament [fʊnda'mɛnt] *n* (-[*e*]*s*; -*e*) ARCH foundation(s), *fig a.* basis

Fundamentalist [fʊndamɛnta'lɪst] *m* (-*en*; -*en*) fundamentalist

'Fundbü,ro *n* lost and found (office), *Br* lost-property office

'Fundgrube *fig f* treasure trove

Fundi ['fʊndi] F *m* (-*s*; -*s*) POL radical Green

fundiert [fʊn'diːɐt] *adj* well-founded (*argument etc*); sound (*knowledge*)

fünf [fʏnf] *adj* five; *grade*: F, N, *Br* fail, poor, E

'Fünfeck *n* (-[*e*]*s*; -*e*) pentagon

'fünffach *adj* fivefold

'Fünfkampf *m* SPORT pentathlon

'Fünflinge *pl* quintuplets

'fünfte *adj* fifth

'Fünftel *n* (-*s*; -) fifth

'fünftens *adv* fifth(ly), in the fifth place

'fünfzehn(te) *adj* fifteen(th)

fünfzig ['fʏnftsɪç] *adj* fifty

'fünfzigste *adj* fiftieth

fungieren [fʊŋ'giːrən] *v/i* (*no -ge-*, *h*) ***fungieren als*** act as, function as

Funk [fʊŋk] *m* (-*s*; *no pl*) radio; ***über*** *or* ***durch Funk*** by radio

'Funkama,teur *m* radio ham

Funke ['fʊŋkə] *m* (-*n*; -*n*) spark; *fig a.* glimmer

funkeln ['fʊŋkəln] *v/i* (*ge-*, *h*) sparkle, glitter; twinkle

'funken *v/t* (*ge-*, *h*) radio, transmit

Funker ['fʊŋkɐ] *m* (-*s*; -) radio operator

'Funkgerät *n* radio set

Funkhaus *n* broadcasting center (*Br* centre)

Funksig,nal *n* radio signal

Funkspruch *m* radio message

Funkstati,on *f* radio station

Funkstreife *f* (radio) patrol car

Funktele,fon *n* cellular phone

Funktion [fʊŋk'tsjoːn] *f* (-; -*en*) function

Funktionär [fʊŋktsjo'nɛːɐ] *m* (-*s*; -*e*) functionary, official (*a.* SPORT)

funktionieren [fʊŋktsjo'niːrən] *v/i* (*no -ge-*, *h*) work

'Funkturm *m* radio tower

'Funkverkehr *m* radio communication

für [fyːɐ] *prp* (*acc*) for; in favo(u)r of; on behalf of; ***für immer*** forever; ***Tag für Tag*** day by day; ***Wort für Wort*** word by word; ***jeder für sich*** everyone by himself; ***was für ...?*** what (kind *or* sort of) ...?; ***das Für und Wider*** the pros and cons

Furche ['fʊrçə] *f* (-; -*n*) furrow; rut

Furcht [fʊrçt] *f* (-; *no pl*) fear, dread (*both*: ***vor*** *dat* of); ***aus Furcht***(, ***dass***) for fear (that); ***Furcht erregend*** → ***furchterregend***

'furchtbar *adj* terrible, awful

fürchten ['fʏrçtən] *v/t and v/i* (*ge-*, *h*) fear, be afraid of; dread; ***fürchten um*** fear for; ***sich fürchten*** be scared; be afraid (***vor*** *dat* of); ***ich fürchte***, ... I'm afraid ...

fürchterlich ['fʏrçtɐlɪç] → ***furchtbar***

'furchterregend *adj* frightening

furchtlos *adj* fearless

furchtsam *adj* timid

fürei'nander *adv* for each other

Furnier [fʊr'niːɐ] *n* (-[*e*]*s*; -*e*), **furnieren** [fʊr'niːrən] *v/t* (*no -ge-*, *h*) veneer

'Fürsorge *f* (-; *no pl*) care; ***öffentliche Fürsorge*** (public) welfare (work)

Fürsorgeempfänger *m* social security beneficiary

'fürsorglich [-zɔrklɪç] *adj* considerate

'Fürsprache *f* intercession (***für*** for; ***bei*** with)

Fürsprech *m* (-[*e*]*s*; -*e*) *Swiss*: lawyer

Fürsprecher(in) advocate (*a. fig*)

Fürst [fʏrst] *m* (-*en*; -*en*) prince

'Fürstentum *n* (-*s*; -*tümer* [-tyːmɐ]) principality

'Fürstin *f* (-; -*nen*) princess

'fürstlich *adj* princely (*a. fig*)

Furt [fʊrt] *f* (-; -*en*) ford

Furunkel [fu'rʊŋkəl] *m* (-*s*; -) MED boil, furuncle

'Fürwort *n* (-[*e*]*s*; -*wörter*) LING pronoun

Furz [fʊrts] *m* (-*es*; -*e*), **'furzen** *v/i* (*ge-*, *h*) fart

Fusion [fu'zjoːn] *f* (-; *-en*) ECON merger, amalgamation
fusionieren [fuzjo'niːrən] *v/i* (*no -ge-*, *h*) ECON merge, amalgamate
Fuß [fuːs] *m* (*-es*; *Füße* ['fyːsə] ANAT foot; stand; stem; ***zu Fuß*** on foot; ***zu Fuß gehen*** walk; ***gut zu Fuß sein*** be a good walker; ***Fuß fassen*** become established; ***auf freiem Fuß*** at large
'**Fußball** *m* a) (*no pl*) soccer, *Br* football, b) soccer ball, *Br* football
'**Fußballer** [-balɐ] *m* (*-s*; -) footballer
'**Fußballfeld** *n* football field
Fußballrowdy *m* (football) hooligan
Fußballspiel *n* soccer *or* football match
Fußballspieler(in) football player, footballer
Fußballtoto *n* football pools
'**Fußboden** *m* floor; flooring
Fußbodenheizung *f* underfloor heating
'**Fußbremse** *f* MOT footbrake
Fussel ['fʊsəl] *f* (-; *-n*), *m* (*-s*; *-[n]*) piece of lint (*Br* fluff); *pl* lint, *Br* fluff
'**fusselig** ['fʊsəlɪç] *adj* linty, *Br* covered in fluff
'**fusseln** *v/i* (*ge-*, *h*) shed a lot of lint (*Br* fluff), F mo(u)lt
'**Fußgänger** [-gɛŋɐ] *m* (*-s*; -), '**Fußgängerin** *f* (-; *-nen*) pedestrian
'**Fußgängerzone** *f* (pedestrian *or* shopping) mall, *Br* pedestrian precinct
'**Fußgeher** *Austrian m* → ***Fußgänger***
'**Fußgelenk** *n* ANAT ankle
Fußmatte *f* doormat
Fußnote *f* footnote
Fußpflege *f* pedicure; MED podiatry, *Br.* chiropody
Fußpfleger(in) podiatrist, *Br* chiropodist
Fußpilz *m* MED athlete's foot
Fußsohle *f* ANAT sole (of the foot)
Fußspur *f* footprint; track
Fußstapfen *pl*: ***in j-s Fußstapfen treten*** follow in s.o.'s footsteps
Fußtritt *m* kick
Fußweg *m* foothpath; ***e-e Stunde Fußweg*** an hour's walk
Futter[1] ['fʊtɐ] *n* (*-s*; *no pl*) AGR feed, fodder, food
'**Futter**[2] *n* (*-s*; -) lining
Futteral [fʊtə'raːl] *n* (*-s*; *-e*) case; cover
füttern[1] ['fʏtɐn] *v/t* (*ge-*, *h*) AGR feed
'**füttern**[2] *v/t* (*ge-*, *h*) line
'**Futternapf** *m* (feeding) bowl
Fütterung ['fʏtərʊŋ] *f* (-; *-en*) feeding (time)
Futur [fu'tuːɐ] *n* (*-s*; *-e*) future (*a.* LING)

G

gab [gaːp] *pret of* ***geben***
Gabe ['gaːbə] *f* (-; *-n*) gift, present; MED dose; *fig* talent, gift; ***milde Gabe*** alms
Gabel ['gaːbəl] *f* (-; *-n*) fork; TEL cradle
'**gabeln** *v/refl* (*ge-*, *h*) fork, branch
'**Gabelstapler** [-ʃtaːplɐ] *m* (*-s*; -) TECH fork-lift (truck)
Gabelung ['gaːbəlʊŋ] *f* (-; *-en*) fork(ing)
gackern ['gakɐn] *v/i* (*ge-*, *h*) cluck, cackle (*a. fig*)
gaffen ['gafən] *v/i* (*ge-*, *h*) gawk, gawp, F rubberneck
Gaffer ['gafɐ] *m* (*-s*; -) F rubberneck(er), *Br* nosy parker
Gage ['gaːʒə] *f* (-; *-n*) fee
gähnen ['gɛːnən] *v/i* (*ge-*, *h*) yawn
Gala ['gaːla] *f* (-; *-s*) gala
galant [ga'lant] *adj* gallant, courteous
Galeere [ga'leːrə] *f* (-; *-n*) MAR galley
Galerie [galə'riː] *f* (-; *-n*) gallery
Galgen ['galgən] *m* (*-s*; -) gallows
Galgenfrist *f* reprieve
Galgenhu,mor *m* gallows humo(u)r
Galgenvogel F *m* crook
Galle ['galə] *f* (-; *-n*) ANAT gall; bile
'**Gallenblase** *f* ANAT gall bladder
Gallenstein *m* MED gallstone
Gallert ['galɐt] *n* (*-[es]*; *-e*), **Gallerte** [ga'lɛrtə] *f* (-; *-n*) jelly
Galopp [ga'lɔp] *m* (*-s*; *-s*, *-e*) gallop
galoppieren [galɔ'piːrən] *v/i* (*no -ge-*, *sein*) gallop
galt [galt] *pret of* ***gelten***
gammeln ['gaməln] F *v/i* (*ge-*, *h*) loaf (about), bum around
Gammler(in) ['gamlɐ (-lərɪn)] F (*-s*; *-/-*; *-nen*) loafer, bum
Gämse ['gɛmzə] *f* (-; *-n*) ZO chamois
gang [gaŋ] *adj*: ***gang und gäbe*** nothing unusual, (quite) usual
Gang [gaŋ] *m* (*-[e]s*; *Gänge* ['gɛŋə]) walk, gait, way *s.o.* walks; ARCH passage, *a.* AVIAT

etc aisle; corridor; MOT gear; GASTR course; ***et. in Gang bringen*** get s.th. going, start s.th.; ***in Gang kommen*** get started; ***im Gang(e) sein*** be (going) on, be in progress; ***in vollem Gang(e)*** in full swing
gängeln ['gɛŋəln] *v/t* (*ge-*, *h*) lead *s.o.* by the nose
gängig ['gɛŋɪç] *adj* current; ECON sal(e)able
'Gangschaltung *f* MOT gears
Ganove [ga'no:və] F *m* (*-n*; *-n*) crook
Gans [gans] *f* (*-*; *Gänse* ['gɛnzə]) ZO goose
Gänseblümchen ['gɛnzə-] *n* BOT daisy
Gänsebraten *m* roast goose
Gänsehaut *f* (*-*; *no pl*) gooseflesh; ***dabei kriege ich e-e Gänsehaut*** F it gives me the creeps
Gänsemarsch *m* (*-[e]s*; *no pl*) single *or* Indian file
Gänserich ['gɛnzərɪç] *m* (*-s*; *-e*) ZO gander
ganz [gants] **1.** *adj* whole, entire, total; F undamaged; full (*hour etc*); ***den ganzen Tag*** all day; ***die ganze Zeit*** all the time; ***auf der ganzen Welt*** all over the world; ***sein ganzes Geld*** all his money; **2.** *adv* completely, totally; very; quite, rather, fairly; ***ganz allein*** all by oneself; ***ganz aus Holz*** *etc* all wood *etc*; ***ganz und gar*** completely, totally; ***ganz und gar nicht*** not at all, by no means; ***ganz wie du willst*** just as you like; ***nicht ganz*** not quite; → ***voll***
Ganze ['gantsə] *n* (*-n*; *no pl*) whole; ***das Ganze*** the whole thing; ***im Ganzen*** in all, altogether; ***im großen Ganzen*** on the whole; ***aufs Ganze gehen*** go all out
gänzlich ['gɛntslɪç] *adv* completely, entirely
'Ganztagsbeschäftigung *f* full-time job
Ganztagsschule *f* all-day school(ing)
gar [ga:ɐ] **1.** *adj* GASTR done; **2.** *adv*: ***gar nicht*** not at all; ***gar nichts*** nothing at all; ***gar zu …*** (a bit) too …
Garage [ga'ra:ʒə] *f* (*-*; *-n*) garage
Garantie [garan'ti:] *f* (*-*; *-n*) guarantee, *esp* ECON warranty
garantieren [garan'ti:rən] *v/t and v/i* (*no -ge-*, *h*) guarantee (***für et.*** s.th.)
Garbe ['garbə] *f* (*-*; *-n*) AGR sheaf
Garde ['gardə] *f* (*-*; *-n*) guard; MIL (the) Guards
Garderobe [gardə'ro:bə] *f* (*-*; *-n*) a) (*no pl*) wardrobe, clothes, b) checkroom, *Br* cloakroom; THEA dressing room
Garde'robenfrau *f* checkroom (*Br* cloakroom) attendant
Garderobenmarke *f* coatcheck (*Br* cloakroom) ticket
Garderobenständer *m* coat stand *or* rack
Gardine [gar'di:nə] *f* (*-*; *-n*) curtain
Gar'dinenstange *f* curtain rod
gären ['gɛ:rən] *v/i* (*[irr*,*] ge-*, *h*, *sein*) ferment, work
Garn [garn] *n* (*-[e]s*; *-e*) yarn; thread; cotton
Garnele [gar'ne:lə] *f* (*-*; *-n*) ZO shrimp; prawn
garnieren [gar'ni:rən] *v/t* (*no -ge-*, *h*) garnish (*a. fig*)
Garnison [garni'zo:n] *f* (*-*; *-en*) MIL garrison, post
Garnitur [garni'tu:ɐ] *f* (*-*, *-en*) set; suite
Garten ['gartən] *m* (*-s*; *Gärten* ['gɛrtən]) garden
Gartenarbeit *f* gardening
Gartenbau *m* (*-[e]s*; *no pl*) horticulture
Gartenerde *f* (garden) mo(u)ld
Gartenfest *n* garden party
Gartengeräte *pl* gardening tools
Gartenhaus *n* summerhouse
Gartenlo,kal *n* beer garden; outdoor restaurant
Gartenschere *f* pruning shears
Gartenstadt *f* garden city
Gartenzwerg *m* (garden) gnome
Gärtner ['gɛrtnɐ] *m* (*-s*; *-*) gardener
Gärtnerei [gɛrtnə'rai] *f* (*-*; *-en*) truck farm, *Br* market garden
'Gärtnerin *f* (*-*; *-nen*) gardener
Gärung ['gɛ:rʊŋ] *f* (*-*; *-en*) fermentation
Gas [ga:s] *n* (*-es*; *-e* ['ga:zə]) gas; ***Gas geben*** MOT accelerate, F step on the gas
'gasförmig [-fœrmɪç] *adj* gaseous
'Gashahn *m* gas valve (*or* cock, *Br* tap)
Gasheizung *f* gas heating
Gasherd *m* gas cooker *or* stove
Gaskammer *f* gas chamber
Gasla,terne *f* gas (street) lamp
Gasleitung *f* gas main
Gasmaske *f* gas mask
Gasofen *m* gas stove
Gaspe,dal *n* MOT gas pedal, *Br* accelerator (pedal)
Gasse ['gasə] *f* (*-*; *-n*) lane, alley
Gast [gast] *m* (*-[e]s*; *Gäste* ['gɛstə]) guest; visitor; customer
'Gastarbeiter *m*, **'Gastarbeiterin** *f* foreign worker
Gästebuch ['gɛstə-] *n* visitors' book
'Gästezimmer *n* guest (*or* spare) room
'gastfreundlich *adj* hospitable
'Gastfreundschaft *f* hospitality
'Gastgeber [-ge:bɐ] *m* (*-s*; *-*) host
'Gastgeberin [-ge:bərɪn] *f* (*-*; *-nen*) hostess
'Gasthaus *n*, **Gasthof** *m* restaurant, inn
gastieren [gas'ti:rən] *v/i* (*no -ge-*, *h*) give

performances; THEA guest, give a guest performance
'gastlich *adj* hospitable
'Gastmannschaft *f* SPORT visiting team
Gastspiel *n* THEA guest performance
Gaststätte *f* restaurant
Gaststube *f* taproom; restaurant
Gastwirt *m* landlord
Gastwirtschaft *f* restaurant, inn
'Gaswerk *n* TECH gasworks
'Gaszähler *m* TECH gas meter
Gatte ['gatə] *m* (*-n*; *-n*) husband
Gatter ['gatɐ] *n* (*-s*; -) fence; gate
Gattin ['gatɪn] *f* (-; *-nen*) wife
Gattung ['gatʊŋ] *f* (-; *-en*) type, class, sort; BIOL genus; species
GAU [gau] (ABBR *of* ***größter anzunehmender Unfall***) *m* (*-[s]*; *no pl*) worst case scenario, *Br* maximum credible accident, MCA
Gaul [gaul] *m* (*-[e]s*; *Gäule* ['gɔʏlə]) nag
Gaumen ['gaumən] *m* (*-s*; -) ANAT palate
Gauner ['gaunɐ] *m* (*-s*; -), **'Gaunerin** *f* (-; *-nen*) F crook
Gaze ['ga:zə] *f* (-; *-n*) gauze
Gazelle [ga'tsɛlə] *f* (-; *-n*) ZO gazelle
geb. ABBR *of* ***geboren*** b., born
Gebäck [gə'bɛk] *n* (*-[e]s*; *-e*) pastry; cookies, *Br* biscuits
ge'backen *pp of* ***backen***
Gebälk [gə'bɛlk] *n* (*-[e]s*; *-e*) timberwork, beams
gebar [gə'ba:ɐ] *pret of* ***gebären***
Gebärde [gə'bɛ:ɐdə] *f* (-; *-n*) gesture
ge'bärden *v/refl* (*no -ge-*, *h*) behave, act (***wie*** like)
gebären [gə'bɛ:rən] *v/t* (*irr*, *no -ge-*, *h*) give birth to
Gebärmutter [gə'bɛ:ɐ-] *f* ANAT uterus, womb
Gebäude [gə'bɔʏdə] *n* (*-s*; -) building, structure
Ge'beine *pl* bones, mortal remains
geben ['ge:bən] *v/t* (*irr*, *ge-*, *h*) give (***j-m et.*** s.o. s.th.); hand, pass; deal (*cards*); make; ***sich geben*** pass; get better; ***von sich geben*** utter, let out; ***j-m die Schuld geben*** blame s.o.; ***es gibt*** there is, there are; ***was gibt es?*** what's up?; what's for *lunch etc?*; TV *etc* what's on?; ***das gibt's nicht*** that can't be true; that's out
Gebet [gə'be:t] *n* (*-[e]s*; *-e*) prayer
ge'beten *pp of* ***bitten***
Gebiet [gə'bi:t] *n* (*-[e]s*; *-e*) region, area; *esp* POL territory; *fig* field
ge'bieterisch *adj* imperious
ge'bietsweise *adv* regionally; ***gebietsweise Regen*** local showers

Gebilde [gə'bɪldə] *n* (*-s*; -) thing, object
gebildet [gə'bɪldət] *adj* educated
Gebirge [gə'bɪrgə] *n* (*-s*; -) mountains
gebirgig [gə'bɪrgɪç] *adj* mountainous
Ge'birgsbewohner *m* mountain-dweller
Gebirgszug *m* mountain range
Ge'biss *n* (*-es*; *-e*) (set of) teeth; (set of) false teeth, denture(s)
ge'bissen *pp of* ***beißen***
Gebläse [gə'blɛ:zə] *n* (*-s*; -) TECH blower, (MOT air) fan
ge'blasen *pp of* ***blasen***
geblichen [gə'blɪçən] *pp of* ***bleichen***
geblieben [gə'bli:bən] *pp of* ***bleiben***
geblümt [gə'bly:mt] *adj* floral
gebogen [gə'bo:gən] **1.** *pp of* ***biegen***; **2.** *adj* bent, curved
geboren [gə'bo:rən] **1.** *pp of* ***gebären***; **2.** *adj* born; ***ein geborener Deutscher*** German by birth; ***geborene Smith*** née Smith; ***ich bin am … geboren*** I was born on the …
geborgen [gə'bɔrgən] **1.** *pp of* ***bergen***; **2.** *adj* safe, secure
Ge'borgenheit *f* (-; *no pl*) safety, security
geborsten [gə'bɔrstən] *pp of* ***bersten***
Gebot [gə'bo:t] *n* (*-[e]s*; *-e*) REL commandment; *fig* rule; necessity; *auction etc*: bid
geboten [gə'bo:tən] *pp of* ***bieten***
gebracht [gə'braxt] *pp of* ***bringen***
gebrannt [gə'brant] *pp of* ***brennen***
ge'braten *pp of* ***braten***
Ge'brauch *m* (*-[e]s*; *no pl*) use; application
ge'brauchen *v/t* (*no -ge-*, *h*) use; employ; ***gut*** (***nicht***) ***zu gebrauchen sein*** be useful (useless); ***ich könnte … gebrauchen*** I could do with …
gebräuchlich [gə'brɔʏçlɪç] *adj* in use; common, usual; current
Ge'brauchsanweisung *f* directions *or* instructions for use
ge'brauchsfertig *adj* ready for use; instant (*coffee etc*)
Ge'brauchsgrafiker *m* commercial artist
ge'braucht *adj* used, ECON *a.* second-hand
Ge'brauchtwagen *m* MOT used *or* second-hand car
Gebrauchtwagenhändler *m* used car dealer
Ge'brechen *n* (*-s*; -) defect, handicap
gebrechlich [gə'brɛçlɪç] *adj* frail; infirm
Ge'brechlichkeit *f* (-; *no pl*) frailty; infirmity
gebrochen [gə'brɔxən] *pp of* ***brechen***
Ge'brüder *pl* brothers
Gebrüll [gə'brʏl] *n* (*-[e]s*; *no pl*) roar(-ing)
Gebühr [gə'by:ɐ] *f* (-; *-en*) charge (*a.* TEL), fee; postage; due

gebührend [gəˈbyːrənt] *adj* due; proper
geˈbührenfrei *adj* free of charge; TEL toll-free, *Br* nonchargeable
gebührenpflichtig *adj* chargeable; ***gebührenpflichtige Straße*** toll road; ***gebührenpflichtige Verwarnung*** fine
gebunden [gəˈbʊndən] **1.** *pp of* ***binden***; **2.** *adj* bound, *fig a.* tied
Geburt [gəˈbuːɐt] *f* (-; *-en*) birth; ***Deutscher von Geburt*** German by birth
Geˈburtenkonˌtrolle *f*, **Geburtenregelung** *f* birth control
geˈburtenschwach *adj* low-birthrate
geburtenstark *adj*: ***geburtenstarke Jahrgänge*** baby boom
Geˈburtenziffer *f* birthrate
gebürtig [gəˈbʏrtɪç] *adj* by birth
Geˈburtsanzeige *f* birth announcement
Geburtsdatum *n* date of birth
Geburtsfehler *m* congenital defect
Geburtshelfer(in) obstetrician
Geburtsjahr *n* year of birth
Geburtsland *n* native country
Geburtsort *m* birthplace
Geburtstag *m* birthday
Geburtstagsfeier *f* birthday party
Geburtstagskind *n* birthday boy (*or* girl)
Geburtsurkunde *f* birth certificate
Gebüsch [gəˈbʏʃ] *n* (-[*e*]*s*; *-e*) bushes, shrubbery
gedacht [gəˈdaxt] *pp of* ***denken***
Gedächtnis [gəˈdɛçtnɪs] *n* (*-ses*; *-se*) memory; ***aus dem Gedächtnis*** from memory; ***zum Gedächtnis an*** (*acc*) in memory (*or* commemoration) of; ***im Gedächtnis behalten*** keep in mind, remember
Gedächtnislücke *f* memory lapse
Gedächtnisschwund *m* MED amnesia; blackout
Gedächtnisstütze *f* memory aid
Gedanke [gəˈdaŋkə] *m* (*-n*; *-n*) thought; idea; ***was für ein Gedanke!*** what an idea!; ***in Gedanken*** absorbed in thought; absent-minded; ***sich Gedanken machen über*** (*acc*) think about; be worried *or* concerned about; ***j-s Gedanken lesen*** read s.o.'s mind
Geˈdankenaustausch *m* exchange of ideas
Gedankengang *m* train of thought
geˈdankenlos *adj* thoughtless
Geˈdankenstrich *m* dash
Gedankenübertragung *f* telepathy
Gedeck [gəˈdɛk] *n* (-[*e*]*s*; *-e*) cover; ***ein Gedeck auflegen*** set a place
gedeihen [gəˈdaiən] *v/i* (*irr*, *no -ge-*, *sein*) thrive, prosper; grow; flourish
geˈdenken *v/i* (*irr*, ***denken***, *no -ge-*, *h*) (*gen*) think of; commemorate; mention
Gedenkfeier [gəˈdɛŋk-] *f* commemoration
Gedenkmiˌnute *f*: ***e-e Gedenkminute*** a moment's (*Br* minute's) silence
Gedenkstätte *f*, **Gedenkstein** *m* memorial
Gedenktafel *f* plaque
Gedicht [gəˈdɪçt] *n* (-[*e*]*s*; *-e*) poem
gediegen [gəˈdiːgən] *adj* solid; tasteful
gedieh [gəˈdiː] *pret of* ***gedeihen***
gediehen [gəˈdiːən] *pp of* ***gedeihen***
Gedränge [gəˈdrɛŋə] *n* (*-s*; -) crowd, F crush
geˈdrängt *fig adj* concise
gedroschen [gəˈdrɔʃən] *pp of* ***dreschen***
geˈdrückt *fig adj* depressed
gedrungen [gəˈdrʊŋən] **1.** *pp of* ***dringen***; **2.** *adj* squat, stocky; thickset
Geduld [gəˈdʊlt] *f* (-; *no pl*) patience
geˈdulden *v/refl* (*no -ge-*, *h*) wait (patiently)
geduldig [gəˈdʊldɪç] *adj* patient
Geˈduldspiel *n* puzzle (*a. fig*)
gedurft [gəˈdʊrft] *pp of* ***dürfen***
geehrt [gəˈʔeːɐt] *adj* hono(u)red; ***Sehr geehrter Herr N.*** Dear Mr N.
geeignet [gəˈʔaignət] *adj* suitable; suited, qualified; right
Gefahr [gəˈfaːɐ] *f* (-; *-en*) danger; threat; risk; ***auf eigene Gefahr*** at one's own risk; ***außer Gefahr*** out of danger, safe
gefährden [gəˈfɛːɐdən] *v/t* (*no -ge-*, *h*) endanger; risk, jeopardize
geˈfahren *pp of* ***fahren***
gefährlich [gəˈfɛːɐlɪç] *adj* dangerous; risky
geˈfahrlos *adj* without risk, safe
Gefährte [gəˈfɛːɐtə] *m* (*-n*; *-n*), **Geˈfährtin** *f* (-; *-nen*) companion
Gefälle [gəˈfɛlə] *n* (*-s*; -) fall, slope, descent; gradient (*a.* PHYS)
geˈfallen 1. *pp of* ***fallen***; **2.** *v/i* (*irr*, ***fallen***, *no -ge-*, *h*) please; ***es gefällt mir (nicht)*** I (don't) like it; ***wie gefällt dir ...?*** how do you like ...?; ***sich et. gefallen lassen*** put up with s.th.
Geˈfallen[1] *m* (*-s*; -) favo(u)r; ***j-n um e-n Gefallen bitten*** ask a favo(u)r of s.o.
Geˈfallen[2] *n*: ***Gefallen finden an*** (*dat*) enjoy, like
geˈfällig *adj* pleasant, agreeable; obliging, kind; ***j-m gefällig sein*** do s.o. a favo(u)r
Geˈfälligkeit *f* (-; *-en*) a) (*no pl*) kindness, b) favo(u)r
geˈfangen 1. *pp of* ***fangen***; **2.** *adj* captive; imprisoned; ***gefangen halten*** keep *s.o.* prisoner; ***gefangen nehmen*** take *s.o.* prisoner; *fig* captivate

G

Ge'fangene *m, f (-n; -n)* prisoner; convict
Ge'fangennahme *f (-; no pl)* capture
Ge'fangenschaft *f (-; no pl)* captivity, imprisonment; ***in Gefangenschaft sein*** be a prisoner of war
Gefängnis [gə'fɛŋnɪs] *n (-ses; -se)* prison, jail, *Br a.* gaol; ***ins Gefängnis kommen*** go to jail *or* prison
Gefängnisdi,rektor *m* governor, warden
Gefängnisstrafe *f* (sentence *or* term of) imprisonment
Gefängniswärter *m* prison guard
Gefäß [gə'fɛːs] *n (-es; -e)* vessel (*a.* ANAT), container
gefasst [gə'fast] *adj* composed; ***gefasst auf*** *(acc)* prepared for
Gefecht [gə'fɛçt] *n (-[e]s; -e)* MIL combat, action
gefedert [gə'feːdɐt] *adj*: ***gut gefedert sein*** MOT have good suspension
gefeit [gə'fait] *adj*: ***gefeit gegen*** immune to
Gefieder [gə'fiːdɐ] *n (-s; -)* ZO plumage, feathers
geflochten [gə'flɔxtən] *pp of* ***flechten***
geflogen [gə'floːgən] *pp of* ***fliegen***
geflohen [gə'floːən] *pp of* ***fliehen***
geflossen [gə'flɔsən] *pp of* ***fließen***
Ge'flügel *n (-s; no pl)* poultry
ge'flügelt *adj*: ***geflügeltes Wort*** saying
gefochten [gə'fɔxtən] *pp of* ***fechten***
Ge'folge *n (-s; -)* entourage, retinue, train
Gefolgschaft [gə'fɔlkʃaft] *f (-; -en)* followers
gefragt [gə'fraːkt] *adj* in demand, popular
gefräßig [gə'frɛːsɪç] *adj* greedy, voracious
Gefreite [gə'fraitə] *m (-n; -n)* MIL private first class, *Br* lance corporal
ge'fressen *pp of* ***fressen***
ge'frieren *v/i (irr,* ***frieren****, no -ge-, sein)* freeze
Gefrierfach [gə'friːɐ-] *n* freezer, freezing compartment
Gefrierfleisch *n* frozen meat
ge'friergetrocknet *adj* freeze-dried
Ge'frierpunkt *m* freezing point
Gefriertruhe *f* freezer, deep-freeze
gefroren [gə'froːrən] *pp of* ***frieren***
Ge'frorene *Austrian n (-n; no pl)* ice cream
Gefüge [gə'fyːgə] *n (-s; -)* structure, texture
gefügig [gə'fyːgɪç] *adj* pliant
Ge'fügigkeit *f (-; no pl)* pliancy
Gefühl [gə'fyːl] *n (-[e]s; -e)* feeling; sense; sensation; emotion
ge'fühllos *adj* insensible, numb; unfeeling, heartless
ge'fühlsbetont *adj* (highly) emotional
ge'fühlvoll *adj* (full of) feeling; tender; sentimental
gefunden [gə'fʊndən] *pp of* ***finden***
gegangen [gə'gaŋən] *pp of* ***gehen***
gegeben [gə'geːbən] *pp of* ***geben***
gegen ['geːgən] *prp (acc)* against, JUR, SPORT *a.* versus; about, around; (in return) for; MED *etc* for; compared with
'Gegen... *in cpds* *...aktion, ...angriff, ...argument, ...frage etc*: counter-...
Gegenbesuch *m* return visit
Gegend ['geːgənt] *f (-; -en)* region, area; countryside; neighbo(u)rhood
gegenei'nander *adv* against one another *or* each other
'Gegenfahrbahn *f* MOT opposite *or* oncoming lane
Gegengewicht *n* counterweight; ***ein Gegengewicht bilden zu et.*** counterbalance s.th.
Gegenkandi,dat *m* rival candidate
Gegenleistung *f* quid pro quo; ***als Gegenleistung*** in return
Gegenlicht *n (-[e]s; no pl)* PHOT back light; ***im*** *or* ***bei Gegenlicht*** against the light
Gegenmaßnahme *f* countermeasure
Gegenmittel *n* MED antidote (*a. fig*)
Gegenpar,tei *f* other side; POL opposition; SPORT opposite side
Gegenrichtung *f* opposite direction
'Gegensatz *m* contrast; opposite; ***im Gegensatz zu*** in contrast to *or* with
'gegensätzlich [-zɛtslɪç] *adj* contrary, opposite
'Gegenseite *f* opposite side
'gegenseitig [-zaitɪç] *adj* mutual
'Gegenseitigkeit *f*: ***auf Gegenseitigkeit beruhen*** be mutual
'Gegenspieler *m*, **Gegenspielerin** *f* SPORT opponent (*a. fig*)
Gegensprechanlage *f* intercom (system)
'Gegenstand *m* object (*a. fig*); *fig* subject
'gegenständlich [-ʃtɛntlɪç] *adj art*: representational
'gegenstandslos *adj* invalid; irrelevant; *art*: abstract, nonrepresentational
'Gegenstimme *f* PARL vote against, no; ***nur drei Gegenstimmen*** only three noes
Gegenstück *n* counterpart
'Gegenteil *n* opposite; ***im Gegenteil*** on the contrary
'gegenteilig *adj* contrary, opposite
gegen'über *adv and prp (dat)* opposite; *fig* to, toward(s); compared with
Gegen'über *n (-s; -)* person opposite; neighbo(u)r across the street

gegen'überstehen *v/i* (*irr*, ***stehen***, *sep*, *-ge-*, *h*) face, be faced with
Gegen'überstellung *f* confrontation
'Gegenverkehr *m* oncoming traffic
'Gegenwart [-vart] *f* (*-*; *no pl*) present (time); presence; LING present (tense)
'gegenwärtig [-vɛrtɪç] **1.** *adj* present, current; **2.** *adv* at present
'Gegenwehr [-veːɐ] *f* (*-*; *no pl*) resistance
Gegenwert *m* equivalent (value)
Gegenwind *m* head wind
'gegenzeichnen *v/t* (*sep*, *-ge-*, *h*) countersign
'Gegenzug *m* countermove; RAIL train coming from the opposite direction
gegessen [gə'gɛsən] *pp of* ***essen***
geglichen [gə'glɪçən] *pp of* ***gleichen***
geglitten [gə'glɪtən] *pp of* ***gleiten***
geglommen [gə'glɔmən] *pp of* ***glimmen***
Gegner ['geːgnɐ] *m* (*-s*; *-*), **'Gegnerin** *f* (*-*; *-nen*) opponent (*a.* SPORT), adversary; MIL enemy
'gegnerisch *adj* opposing; MIL (of the) enemy, hostile
'Gegnerschaft *f* (*-*; *-en*) opposition
gegolten [gə'gɔltən] *pp of* ***gelten***
gegoren [gə'goːrən] *pp of* ***gären***
gegossen [gə'gɔsən] *pp of* ***gießen***
ge'graben *pp of* ***graben***
gegriffen [gə'grɪfən] *pp of* ***greifen***
gehabt [gə'haːpt] *pp of* ***haben***
Gehackte [gə'haktə] *n* → ***Hackfleisch***
Gehalt [gə'halt] **1.** *m* (*-[e]s*; *-e*) content; **2.** *n* (*-[e]s*; *Gehälter* [gə'hɛltɐ]) salary
ge'halten *pp of* ***halten***
Ge'haltsempfänger *m* salaried employee
Gehaltserhöhung *f* raise, *Br* increase *or* rise in salary
ge'haltvoll *adj* substantial; nutritious
gehangen [gə'haŋən] *pp of* ***hängen*** 1
gehässig [gə'hɛsɪç] *adj* malicious, spiteful
Ge'hässigkeit *f* (*-*; *no pl*) malice, spite (-fulness)
ge'hauen *pp of* ***hauen***
Gehäuse [gə'hɔʏzə] *n* (*-s*; *-*) case, box; TECH casing; ZO shell; BOT core
Gehege [gə'heːgə] *n* (*-s*; *-*) enclosure
geheim [gə'haim] *adj* secret; ***et. geheim halten*** keep s.th. (a) secret
Ge'heima,gent *m* secret agent
Geheimdienst *m* secret service
Geheimnis [gə'haimnɪs] *n* (*-ses*; *-se*) secret; mystery
ge'heimnisvoll *adj* mysterious
Ge'heimnummer *f* TEL unlisted (*Br* ex-directory) number
Geheimpoli,zei *f* secret police
Geheimschrift *f* code, cipher
ge'heißen *pp of* **heißen**
gehemmt [gə'hɛmt] *adj* inhibited, self--conscious
gehen ['geːən] *v/i* (*irr*, *ge-*, *sein*) go; walk; leave; TECH work (*a. fig*); ECON sell; *fig* last; ***einkaufen*** (***schwimmen***) ***gehen*** go shopping (swimming); ***gehen wir!*** let's go!; ***wie geht es dir*** (***Ihnen***)***?*** how are you?; ***es geht mir gut*** (***schlecht***) I'm fine (not feeling well); ***gehen in*** (*acc*) go into
gehen nach *road etc*: lead to; *window etc*: face; *fig* go *or* judge by; ***das geht nicht*** that's impossible; ***das geht schon*** that's o.k.; ***es geht nichts über*** (*acc*) ***…*** there is nothing like …; ***worum geht es?*** what is it about?; ***darum geht es*** (***nicht***) that's (not) the point; ***sich gehen nach lassen*** let o.s. go
'gehenlassen *v/refl* (*irr*, ***lassen***, *sep*, *no -ge-*, *h*) → ***gehen***
geheuer [gə'hɔʏɐ] *adj*: ***nicht*** (***ganz***) ***geheuer*** eerie, creepy, F fishy
Geheul [gə'hɔʏl] *n* (*-[e]s*; *no pl*) howling
Ge'hirn *n* (*-[e]s*; *-e*) ANAT brain(s)
Gehirnerschütterung *f* MED concussion (of the brain)
Gehirnschlag *m* MED (cerebral) apoplexy
Gehirnwäsche *f* brainwashing
gehoben [gə'hoːbən] **1.** *pp of* ***heben***; **2.** *adj* elevated; high(er); ***gehobene Stimmung*** high spirits
Gehöft [gə'hœft] *n* (*-[e]s*; *-e*) farm(stead)
geholfen [gə'hɔlfən] *pp of* ***helfen***
Gehölz [gə'hœlts] *n* (*-es*; *-e*) wood, coppice, copse
Gehör [gə'høːɐ] *n* (*-[e]s*; *-e*) (sense of) hearing; ear; ***nach dem Gehör*** by ear; ***sich Gehör verschaffen*** make o.s. heard
ge'horchen *v/i* (*no -ge-*, *h*) obey; ***nicht gehorchen*** disobey
ge'hören *v/i* (*no -ge-*, *h*) belong (*dat or* ***zu*** to); ***gehört dir das?*** is this yours?; ***es gehört sich*** (***nicht***) it is proper *or* right (not done); ***das gehört nicht hierher*** that's not to the point
ge'hörig **1.** *adj* due, proper; necessary; decent; ***zu et. gehörig*** belonging to s.th.; **2.** *adv* properly, thoroughly
ge'hörlos *adj* deaf; ***die Gehörlosen*** the deaf
gehorsam [gə'hoːɐzaːm] *adj* obedient
Ge'horsam *m* (*-s*; *no pl*) obedience
'Gehsteig *m*, **'Gehweg** *m* sidewalk, *Br* pavement
Geier ['gaiɐ] *m* (*-s*; *-*) ZO vulture, buzzard
Geige ['gaigə] *f* (*-*; *-n*) MUS violin, F fiddle; (***auf der***) ***Geige spielen*** play (on) the vi-

G

olin
'**Geigenbogen** *m* MUS (violin) bow
Geigenkasten *m* MUS violin case
'**Geiger** ['gaigɐ] *m* (-*s*; -), **Geigerin** ['gaigərɪn] *f* (-; -*nen*) MUS violinist
'**Geigerzähler** *m* PHYS Geiger counter
geil [gail] *adj* V hot, horny; *contp* lecherous, lewd; BOT rank; F awesome, *Br* brill, ace
Geisel ['gaizəl] *f* (-; -*n*) hostage
Geiselnehmer [-ne:mɐ] *m* (-*s*; -) kidnap(p)er

Geißel ['gaisəl] *fig f* (-; -*n*) scourge
Geist [gaist] *m* (-[*e*]*s*; -*er*) a) (*no pl*) spirit; soul; mind; intellect; wit, b) ghost; ***der Heilige Geist*** REL the Holy Ghost *or* Spirit
Geisterbahn ['gaistɐ-] *f* tunnel of horror, *Br* ghost train
Geisterfahrer F *m* MOT wrong-way driver
'**geisterhaft** *adj* ghostly
'**geistesabwesend** *adj* absent-minded
'**Geistesarbeiter** *m* brainworker
Geistesblitz *m* brainstorm, *Br* brainwave
'**Geistesgegenwart** *f* presence of mind
'**geistesgegenwärtig** *adj* alert; quick-witted
'**geistesgestört** *adj* mentally disturbed, deranged
'**geisteskrank** *adj* mentally ill
'**Geisteskrankheit** *f* mental illness
'**geistesschwach** *adj* feeble-minded
'**Geisteswissenschaften** *pl the* arts, *the* humanities
'**Geisteszustand** *m* mental state
geistig ['gaistɪç] *adj* mental; intellectual; spiritual; ***geistig behindert*** mentally handicapped; ***geistige Getränke*** spirits
'**geistlich** *adj* religious; spiritual; ecclesiastical; clerical
'**Geistliche** *m* (-*n*; -*n*) clergyman; priest; minister; ***die Geistlichen*** the clergy
'**geistlos** *adj* trivial, inane, silly
'**geistreich**, '**geistvoll** *adj* witty, clever
Geiz [gaits] *m* (-*es*; *no pl*) stinginess
'**Geizhals** *m* miser, niggard
geizig ['gaitsɪç] *adj* stingy, miserly
Ge'jammer F *n* (-*s*; *no pl*) wailing, complaining
gekannt [gə'kant] *pp of* ***kennen***
Gekläff [gə'klɛf] F *n* (-[*e*]*s*; *no pl*) yapping
Geklapper [gə'klapɐ] F *n* (-*s*; *no pl*) clatter(ing)
Geklimper F *n* (-*s*; *no pl*) tinkling
geklungen [gə'klʊŋən] *pp of* ***klingen***
gekniffen [gə'knɪfən] *pp of* ***kneifen***
ge'kommen *pp of* ***kommen***
gekonnt [gə'kɔnt] **1.** *pp of* ***können***; **2.** *adj* masterly
gekränkt [gə'krɛŋkt] *adj* hurt, offended
Gekritzel [gə'krɪtsəl] *contp n* (-*s*; *no pl*) scrawl, scribble
gekrochen [gə'krɔxən] *pp of* ***kriechen***
gekünstelt [gə'kʏnstəlt] *adj* affected; artificial
Gelächter [gə'lɛçtɐ] *n* (-*s*; *no pl*) laughter
ge'laden *pp of* ***laden***
Ge'lage *n* (-*s*; -) feast; carouse
Gelände [gə'lɛndə] *n* (-*s*; -) area, country, ground; site; ***auf dem Gelände*** on the premises; ***Gelände...*** *in cpds ...lauf, ...ritt, ...wagen etc*: cross-country ...
Geländer [gə'lɛndɐ] *n* (-*s*; -) banisters; handrail, rail(ing); parapet
ge'lang *pret of* ***gelingen***
ge'langen *v/i* (*no -ge-, sein*) ***gelangen an*** (*acc*) *or* ***nach*** reach, arrive at, get *or* come to; ***gelangen in*** (*acc*) get *or* come into; *fig* ***zu et. gelangen*** gain *or* win *or* achieve s.th.
ge'lassen **1.** *pp of* ***lassen***; **2.** *adj* calm, composed, cool
Gelatine [ʒela'ti:nə] *f* (-; *no pl*) gelatin(e)
ge'laufen *pp of* ***laufen***
ge'läufig *adj* common, current; familiar
gelaunt [gə'launt] *adj*: ***schlecht*** (***gut***) ***gelaunt sein*** be in a bad (good) mood
gelb [gɛlp] *adj* yellow
'**gelblich** *adj* yellowish
'**Gelbsucht** *f* (-; *no pl*) MED jaundice
Geld [gɛlt] *n* (-[*e*]*s*; -*er* ['gɛldɐ]) money; ***zu Geld machen*** turn into cash
'**Geldangelegenheiten** *pl* money *or* financial matters *or* affairs
Geldanlage *f* investment
Geldausgabe *f* expense
Geldauto,mat *m* automatic teller machine, ATM, autoteller, *Br* cash dispenser
Geldbeutel *m*, **Geldbörse** *f* purse
Geldbuße *f* fine, penalty
Geldgeber(in) [-ge:bɐ (-bərɪn)] (-*s*; -/-; -*nen*) financial backer; investor
'**geldgierig** *adj* greedy for money
'**Geldknappheit** *f*, **Geldmangel** *m* lack of money; ECON (financial) stringency
Geldmittel *pl* funds, means, resources
Geldschein *m* bill, *Br* (bank)note
Geldschrank *m* safe
Geldsendung *f* remittance
Geldstrafe *f* fine
Geldstück *n* coin
Geldverlegenheit *f* financial embarrassment
Geldverschwendung *f* waste of money
Geldwaschanlage *f* money laundering scheme
Geldwechsel *m* exchange of money

Geldwechsler [-vɛkslɐ] *m* (*-s*; -) change machine
Gelee [ʒe'leː] *n, m* (*-s*; *-s*) jelly; gel
ge'legen **1.** *pp of* ***liegen***; **2.** *adj* situated, located; *fig* convenient, opportune
Ge'legenheit *f* (-; *-en*) occasion; opportunity, chance; ***bei Gelegenheit*** on occasion
Ge'legenheitsarbeit *f* casual *or* odd job
Gelegenheitsarbeiter *m* casual labo(u)rer, odd-job man
Gelegenheitskauf *m* bargain
gelegentlich [gə'leːgəntlɪç] *adv* occasionally
gelehrig [gə'leːrɪç] *adj* docile
Gelehrsamkeit [gə'leːɐzaːmkait] *f* (-; *no pl*) learning
gelehrt [gə'leːɐt] *adj* learned
Ge'lehrte *m, f* (*-n*; *-n*) scholar, learned man *or* woman
Geleise [gə'laizə] *n* → ***Gleis***
Geleit [gə'lait] *n* (-[*e*]*s*; *-e*) escort
ge'leiten *v/t* (*no -ge-, h*) accompany, conduct, escort
Ge'leitzug *m* MAR, MIL convoy
Gelenk [gə'lɛŋk] *n* (-[*e*]*s*; *-e*) ANAT, TECH joint
ge'lenkig *adj* flexible (*a.* TECH); lithe, supple
gelernt [gə'lɛrnt] *adj* skilled, trained
ge'lesen *pp of* ***lesen***
geliebt [gə'liːpt] *adj* (be)loved, dear
Ge'liebte **1.** *m* (*-n*; *-n*) lover; **2.** *f* (*-n*; *-n*) mistress
geliehen [gə'liːən] *pp of* ***leihen***
gelingen [gə'lɪŋən] *v/i* (*irr, no -ge-, sein*) succeed, manage; turn out well; ***es gelang mir, et. zu tun*** I succeeded in doing (I managed to do) s.th.
Ge'lingen *n* (*-s*; *no pl*) success; ***gutes Gelingen!*** good luck!
gelitten [gə'lɪtən] *pp of* ***leiden***
gelogen [gə'loːgən] *pp of* ***lügen***
gelten ['gɛltən] *v/i and v/t* (*irr, ge-, h*) be worth; *fig* count for; be valid; SPORT count; ECON be effective; ***gelten für*** apply to; ***gelten als*** be regarded *or* looked upon as, be considered *or* supposed to be; ***gelten lassen*** accept (***als*** as)
geltend *adj* accepted; ***geltend machen*** assert; ***s-n Einfluss*** (***bei j-m***) ***geltend machen*** bring one's influence to bear (on s.o.)
'Geltung *f* (-; *no pl*) prestige; weight; ***zur Geltung kommen*** show to advantage
'Geltungsbedürfnis *n* (*-ses*; *no pl*) need for recognition
Gelübde [gə'lʏpdə] *n* (*-s*; -) vow
gelungen [gə'lʊŋən] **1.** *pp of* ***gelingen***; **2.** *adj* successful, a success
gemächlich [gə'mɛːçlɪç] *adj* leisurely
ge'mahlen *pp of* ***mahlen***
Gemälde [gə'mɛːldə] *n* (*-s*; -) painting, picture
Gemäldegale,rie *f* art (*or* picture) gallery
gemäß [gə'mɛːs] *prp* (*dat*) according to
gemäßigt [gə'mɛːsɪçt] *adj* moderate; temperate (*climate etc*)
gemein [gə'main] *adj* mean; dirty, filthy (*joke etc*); BOT, ZO common
Gemeinde [gə'maində] *f* (-; *-n*) POL municipality; local government; REL parish; congregation
Gemeinderat *m* (member of the) city (*Br* local) council
Gemeinderätin [-rɛːtɪn] *f* (-; *-nen*) member of the city (*Br* local) council
Gemeindesteuern *pl* local taxes, *Br* (local) rates
ge'meingefährlich *adj*: ***gemeingefährlicher Mensch*** public enemy
Ge'meinheit *f* (-; *-en*) a) (*no pl*) meanness, b) mean thing (to do *or* say), F dirty trick
ge'meinnützig [-nʏtsɪç] *adj* non-profit, *Br* non-profitmaking
Ge'meinplatz *m* commonplace
ge'meinsam **1.** *adj* common, joint; mutual; **2.** *adv* together
Ge'meinschaft *f* (-; *-en*) community
Ge'meinschaftsarbeit *f* teamwork
Gemeinschaftskunde *f* (-; *no pl*) PED social studies
Gemeinschaftsprodukti,on *f* coproduction
Gemeinschaftsraum *m* recreation room, lounge
Ge'meinsinn *m* (-[*e*]*s*; *no pl*) public spirit; (sense of) solidarity
ge'meinverständlich *adj* popular
Ge'meinwohl *n* public welfare
ge'messen **1.** *pp of* ***messen***; **2.** *adj* measured; formal; grave
Gemetzel [gə'mɛtsəl] *n* (*-s*; -) slaughter, massacre
gemieden [gə'miːdən] *pp of* ***meiden***
Gemisch [gə'mɪʃ] *n* (-[*e*]*s*; *-e*) mixture (*a.* CHEM)
gemocht [gə'mɔxt] *pp of* ***mögen***
gemolken [gə'mɔlkən] *pp of* ***melken***
Gemse → ***Gämse***
Gemurmel [gə'mʊrməl] *n* (*-s*; *no pl*) murmur, mutter
Gemüse [gə'myːzə] *n* (*-s*; -) vegetable(s); greens
Gemüsehändler *m* greengrocer('s)
gemusst [gə'mʊst] *pp of* ***müssen***
Gemüt [gə'myːt] *n* (-[*e*]*s*; *-er*) mind, soul; heart; nature, mentality

ge'mütlich *adj* comfortable, snug, cozy, *Br* cosy; peaceful, pleasant, relaxed; ***mach es dir gemütlich*** make yourself at home
Ge'mütlichkeit *f* (-; *no pl*) snugness, coziness, *Br* cosiness; cozy (*Br* cosy) *or* relaxed atmosphere
Ge'mütsbewegung *f* emotion
ge'mütskrank *adj* emotionally disturbed
Ge'mütszustand *m* state of mind
Gen [ge:n] *n* (*-s*; *-e*) BIOL gene
genannt [gə'nant] *pp of* ***nennen***
genas [gə'na:s] *pret of* ***genesen*** 1
genau [gə'nau] **1.** *adj* exact, precise, accurate; careful, close; strict; ***Genaueres*** further details; **2.** *adv*: ***genau um 10 Uhr*** at 10 o'clock sharp; ***genau der ...*** that very ...; ***genau zuhören*** listen closely; ***es genau nehmen*** (***mit et.***) be particular (about s.th.)
Ge'nauigkeit *f* (-; *no pl*) accuracy, precision, exactness
ge'nauso *adv* → ***ebenso***
genehmigen [gə'ne:mɪgən] *v/t* (*no -ge-, h*) permit, allow; approve
Ge'nehmigung *f* (-; *-en*) permission; approval; permit; licen|se, *Br* -ce
geneigt [gə'naikt] *adj* inclined (***zu*** to)
General [genə'ra:l] *m* (*-s*; *Generäle* [genə'rɛ:lə]) MIL general
Generaldi,rektor *m* ECON president, *Br* chairman
Generalkonsul *m* consul general
Generalkonsu,lat *n* consulate general
Generalprobe *f* THEA dress rehearsal
Generalsekre,tär *m* secretary-general
Generalstab *m* MIL general staff
Generalstreik *m* general strike
Generalversammlung *f* general meeting
Generalvertreter *m* ECON sole agent
Generation [genəra'tsjo:n] *f* (-; *-en*) generation
Generati'onenkon,flikt *m* generation gap
Generator [genə'ra:to:ɐ] *m* (*-s*; *-en* [-ra'to:rən]) ELECTR generator
generell [genə'rɛl] *adj* general, universal
genesen [gə'ne:zən] **1.** *v/i* (*irr, no -ge-, sein*) recover (***von*** from), get well; **2.** *pp of* ***genesen*** 1
Ge'nesung *f* (-; *no pl*) recovery
Genetik [ge'ne:tɪk] *f* (-; *no pl*) BIOL genetics
ge'netisch *adj* BIOL genetic; ***genetischer Fingerabdruck*** genetic fingerprint
genial [ge'nja:l] *adj* brilliant, of genius
Genialität [genjali'tɛ:t] *f* (-; *no pl*) genius
Genick [gə'nɪk] *n* (-[*e*]*s*; *-e*) ANAT (back *or* nape of the) neck
Genie [ʒe'ni:] *n* (*-s*; *-s*) genius
genieren [ʒe'ni:rən] *v/refl* (*no -ge-, h*) be embarrassed
genießen [gə'ni:sən] *v/t* (*irr, no -ge-, h*) enjoy
Genießer [gə'ni:sɐ] *m* (*-s*; -) gourmet
Genitiv ['ge:niti:f] *m* (*-s*; *-e*) LING genitive *or* possessive (case)
genommen [gə'nɔmən] *pp of* ***nehmen***
genormt [gə'nɔrmt] *adj* standardized
genoss [gə'nɔs] *pret of* ***genießen***
Genosse [gə'nɔsə] *m* (*-n*; *-n*) POL comrade; F pal, buddy, *Br* mate
genossen [gə'nɔsən] *pp of* ***genießen***
Ge'nossenschaft *f* (-; *-en*) cooperative
Ge'nossin *f* (-; *-nen*) POL comrade
'Gentechnik *f*, **'Gentechnolo,gie** *f* genetic engineering
genug [gə'nu:k] *adj* enough, sufficient
Genüge [gə'ny:gə] *f*: ***zur Genüge*** (well) enough, sufficiently
ge'nügen *v/i* (*no -ge-, h*) be enough, be sufficient; ***das genügt*** that will do
genügend *adj* enough, sufficient; plenty of
genügsam [gə'ny:kza:m] *adj* easily satisfied; frugal; modest
Ge'nügsamkeit *f* (-; *no pl*) modesty; frugality
Ge'nugtuung *f* (-; *no pl*) satisfaction
Genus ['ge:nʊs] *n* (-; *Genera* ['ge:nera]) LING gender
Genuss [gə'nʊs] *m* (*-es*; *Genüsse* [gə'nʏsə]) a) pleasure, b) (*no pl*) consumption; ***ein Genuss*** a real treat; *food*: *a.* delicious
Genussmittel *n* excise item, *Br* (semi-)luxury
Geografie, **Geographie** [geogra'fi:] *f* (-; *no pl*) geography
geografisch, **geographisch** [geo'gra:fɪʃ] *adj* geographic(al)
Geologe [geo'lo:gə] *m* (*-n*; *-n*) geologist
Geologie [geolo'gi:] *f* (-; *no pl*) geology
Geo'login *f* (-; *-nen*) geologist
geologisch [geo'lo:gɪʃ] *adj* geologic(al)
Geometrie [geome'tri:] *f* (-; *no pl*) geometry
geometrisch [geo'me:trɪʃ] *adj* geometric(al)
Gepäck [gə'pɛk] *n* (-[*e*]*s*; *no pl*) baggage, luggage
Gepäckablage *f* baggage (*or* luggage) rack
Gepäckaufbewahrung *f* baggage room, *Br* left-luggage office
Gepäckkon,trolle *f* baggage check, *Br* luggage inspection
Gepäckschalter *m* baggage (*or* luggage) counter

Gepäckschein *m* baggage check, *Br* luggage ticket
Gepäckträger *m* porter; *bicycle*: carrier
gepanzert [gəˈpantsɐt] *adj* MOT armo(u)red
Gepard [ˈgeːpart] *m* (*-s*; *-e*) ZO cheetah
gepfiffen [gəˈpfɪfən] *pp of* ***pfeifen***
gepflegt [gəˈpfleːkt] *adj* well-groomed, neat; *fig* cultivated
Gepflogenheit [gəˈpfloːgənhait] *f* (*-*; *-en*) habit, custom
Geplapper [gəˈplapɐ] F *n* (*-s*; *no pl*) babbling, chatter(ing)
Geplauder [gəˈplaudɐ] *n* (*-s*; *no pl*) chat (-ting)
Gepolter [gəˈpɔltɐ] *n* (*-s*; *no pl*) rumble
gepriesen [gəˈpriːzən] *pp of* ***preisen***
Gequassel [gəˈkvasəl] F *n* (*-s*; *no pl*), **Gequatsche** [gəˈkvatʃə] F *n* (*-s*; *no pl*) blather, blabber
gequollen [gəˈkvɔlən] *pp of* ***quellen***
gerade [gəˈraːdə] **1.** *adj* straight (*a. fig*); even (*number*); direct; upright, erect (*posture*); **2.** *adv* just; ***nicht gerade*** not exactly; ***das ist es ja gerade!*** that's just it!; ***gerade deshalb*** that's just why; ***gerade rechtzeitig*** just in time; ***warum gerade ich?*** why me of all people?; ***da wir gerade von … sprechen*** speaking of …
Geˈrade *f* (*-n*; *-n*) MATH (straight) line; SPORT straight; ***linke*** (***rechte***) ***Gerade*** *boxing*: straight left (right)
geradeˈaus *adv* straight on *or* ahead
geradeheˈraus *adj* straightforward, frank
geˈradestehen *v/i* (*irr*, ***stehen***, *sep*, *-ge-*, *h*) stand straight; ***geradestehen für*** answer for
geˈradewegs *adv* straight, directly
geˈradezu *adv* simply
gerannt [gəˈrant] *pp of* ***rennen***
Gerät [gəˈrɛːt] *n* (*-[e]s*; *-e*) device; F gadget; appliance; (kitchen) utensil; *radio*, TV set; *coll*, *a.* SPORT *etc* equipment; SPORT apparatus; TECH tool; instrument
geˈraten 1. *pp of* ***raten***; **2.** *v/i* (*irr*, ***raten***, *no -ge-*, *sein*) turn out (***gut*** well); ***geraten an*** (*acc*) come across; ***geraten in*** (*acc*) get into; ***in Brand geraten*** catch fire
Geˈräteturnen *n* apparatus gymnastics
Geˈratewohl *n*: ***aufs Geratewohl*** at random
geräumig [gəˈrɔʏmɪç] *adj* spacious, roomy
Geräusch [gəˈrɔʏʃ] *n* (*-[e]s*; *-e*) sound, noise
geˈräuschlos 1. *adj* noiseless (*a.* TECH); **2.** *adv* without a sound
geˈräuschvoll *adj* noisy
gerben [ˈgɛrbən] *v/t* (*ge-*, *h*) tan
Gerberei [gɛrbəˈrai] *f* (*-*; *-en*) tannery
geˈrecht *adj* just, fair; (*j-m*, *e-r Sache*) ***gerecht werden*** do justice to; meet (*demands etc*)
Geˈrechtigkeit *f* (*-*; *no pl*) justice
Geˈrede F *n* (*-s*; *no pl*) talk; gossip
gereizt [gəˈraitst] *adj* irritable
Geˈreiztheit *f* (*-*; *no pl*) irritability
Gericht[1] [gəˈrɪçt] *n* (*-[e]s*; *-e*) GASTR dish
Geˈricht[2] *n* (*-[e]s*; *-e*) JUR court; ***vor Gericht stehen*** (***stellen***) stand (bring to) trial; ***vor Gericht gehen*** go to court
geˈrichtlich *adj* JUR judicial, legal
Geˈrichtsbarkeit *f* (*-*; *no pl*) JUR jurisdiction
Geˈrichtsgebäude *n* JUR law court(s), courthouse
Gerichtshof *m* JUR law court
Gerichtsmediˌzin *f* JUR forensic medicine
Gerichtssaal *m* JUR courtroom
Gerichtsverfahren *n* JUR lawsuit
Gerichtsverhandlung *f* JUR hearing; trial
Gerichtsvollzieher [-fɔltsiːɐ] *m* (*-s*; *-*) JUR marshal, *Br* bailiff
gerieben [gəˈriːbən] *pp of* ***reiben***
gering [gəˈrɪŋ] *adj* little, small; slight, minor; low; ***gering schätzen*** think little of
geˈringfügig *adj* slight, minor; petty
geˈringschätzen *v/t* (*sep*, *-ge-*, *h*) → ***gering***
geringschätzig [-ʃɛtsɪç] *adj* contemptuous
geˈringst *adj* least; ***nicht im Geringsten*** not in the least
geˈrinnen *v/i* (*irr*, ***rinnen***, *no -ge-*, *sein*) coagulate; curdle; clot
Geˈrippe *n* (*-s*; *-*) skeleton (*a. fig*); TECH framework
gerissen [gəˈrɪsən] **1.** *pp of* ***reißen***; **2.** F *adj* cunning, smart
geritten [gəˈrɪtən] *pp of* ***reiten***
germanisch [gɛrˈmaːnɪʃ] *adj* Germanic
Germanist(in) [gɛrmaˈnɪst(ɪn)] (*-en*; *-en*/*-*; *-nen*) student of (*or* graduate in) German
gern [gɛrn] *adv* willingly, gladly; ***et.*** (***sehr***) ***gern tun*** like (love) to do s.th. *or* doing s.th.; ***ich möchte gern*** I'd like (to); ***gern geschehen!*** not at all, (you're) welcome
gernhaben *v/t* (*irr*, ***haben***, *sep*, *-ge-*, *h*) like, be fond of;
gerochen [gəˈrɔxən] *pp of* ***riechen***
Geröll [gəˈrœl] *n* (*-[e]s*; *-e*) scree; boulders
geronnen [gəˈrɔnən] *pp of* ***rinnen***
Gerste [ˈgɛrstə] *f* (*-*; *-n*) BOT barley
ˈGerstenkorn *n* MED sty(e)
Gerte [ˈgɛrtə] *f* (*-*; *-n*) switch, rod, twig
Geruch [gəˈrʊx] *m* (*-[e]s*; *Gerüche* [gəˈrʏçə]) smell; odo(u)r; scent

G

ge'ruchlos *adj* odo(u)rless
Ge'ruchssinn *m* (sense of) smell
Gerücht [gə'rʏçt] *n* (-[*e*]*s*; -*e*) rumo(u)r
ge'rufen *pp of* ***rufen***
gerührt [gə'ry:ɐt] *adj* touched, moved
Gerümpel [gə'rʏmpəl] *n* (-*s*; *no pl*) lumber, junk
Gerundium [ge'rʊndiʊm] *n* (-*s*; -*ien*) LING gerund
gerungen [gə'rʊŋən] *pp of* ***ringen***
Gerüst [gə'rʏst] *n* (-[*e*]*s*; -*e*) frame(-work); scaffold(ing); stage

G

ge'salzen *pp of* ***salzen***
gesamt [gə'zamt] *adj* whole, entire, total, all
Ge'samt... *in cpds ...ergebnis etc*: *mst* total ...
Gesamtausgabe *f* complete edition
Gesamtschule *f* comprehensive school
gesandt [gə'zant] *pp of* ***senden***
Gesandte [gə'zantə] *m, f* (-*n*; -*n*) POL envoy
Ge'sandtschaft *f* (-; -*en*) legation, mission
Gesang [gə'zaŋ] *m* (-[*e*]*s*; *Gesänge* [gə'zɛŋə]) singing; song; voice
Gesangbuch *n* REL hymn book
Gesang(s)lehrer(in) singing teacher
Gesangverein *m* choral society, glee club
Gesäß [gə'zɛ:s] *n* (-*es*; -*e*) ANAT buttocks, bottom
ge'schaffen *pp of* ***schaffen***[1]
Geschäft [gə'ʃɛft] *n* (-[*e*]*s*; -*e*) business; store, *Br* shop; bargain
ge'schäftig *adj* busy, active
Ge'schäftigkeit *f* (-; *no pl*) activity
ge'schäftlich **1.** *adj* business ...; commercial; **2.** *adv* on business
Ge'schäftsbrief *m* business letter
Geschäftsfrau *f* businesswoman
Geschäftsfreund *m* business friend
Geschäftsführer *m* manager
Geschäftsführung *f* management
Geschäftsinhaber *m* proprietor
Geschäftsmann *m* businessman
ge'schäftsmäßig *adj* businesslike
Ge'schäftsordnung *f* PARL standing orders; rules (of procedure)
Geschäftspartner *m* (business) partner
Geschäftsräume *pl* (business) premises
Geschäftsreise *f* business trip
Geschäftsschluss *m* closing time; ***nach Geschäftsschluss*** *a.* after business hours
Geschäftsstelle *f* office
Geschäftsstraße *f* shopping street
Geschäftsträger *m* POL chargé d'affaires
'ge'schäftstüchtig *adj* efficient, smart
Ge'schäftsverbindung *f* business connection
Geschäftsviertel *n* commercial district; downtown
Geschäftszeit *f* office *or* business hours
Geschäftszweig *m* branch *or* line (of business)
geschah [gə'ʃa:] *pret of* ***geschehen*** 1
geschehen [gə'ʃe:ən] **1.** *v/i* (*irr, no -ge-, sein*) happen, occur, take place; be done; ***es geschieht ihm recht*** it serves him right; **2.** *pp of* ***geschehen*** 1
gescheit [gə'ʃait] *adj* clever, bright, F brainy
Geschenk [gə'ʃɛŋk] *n* (-[*e*]*s*; -*e*) present, gift
Geschenkpackung *f* gift box
Geschichte [gə'ʃɪçtə] *f* (-; -*n*) a) story, b) (*no pl*) history, c) F business, thing
ge'schichtlich *adj* historical
Ge'schichtsschreiber *m* (-*s*; -), **Geschichtswissenschaftler** *m* historian
Geschick [gə'ʃɪk] *n* (-[*e*]*s*; -*e*) fate, destiny; → **Ge'schicklichkeit** *f* (-; *no pl*) skill; dexterity
ge'schickt *adj* skil(l)ful, skilled; dext(e)rous; clever
geschieden [gə'ʃi:dən] **1.** *pp of* ***scheiden***; **2.** *adj* divorced, *marriage*: dissolved
geschienen [gə'ʃi:nən] *pp of* ***scheinen***
Geschirr [gə'ʃɪr] *n* (-[*e*]*s*; -*e*) a) dishes, china, b) (*no pl*) kitchen utensils, pots and pans, crockery, c) harness; ***Geschirr spülen*** wash *or* do the dishes
Ge'schirrspüler *m* (-*s*; -) dishwasher
geschissen [gə'ʃɪsən] *pp of* ***scheißen***
ge'schlafen *pp of* ***schlafen***
ge'schlagen *pp of* ***schlagen***
Geschlecht [gə'ʃlɛçt] *n* (-[*e*]*s*; -*er*) a) (*no pl*) sex, b) kind, species, c) family, line (-age); generation, d) LING gender
Ge'schlechtskrankheit *f* MED venereal disease
Geschlechtsreife *f* puberty
Geschlechtsteile *pl* genitals
Geschlechtstrieb *m* sexual instinct *or* urge
Geschlechtsverkehr *m* (sexual) intercourse
Geschlechtswort *n* LING article
geschlichen [gə'ʃlɪçən] *pp of* ***schleichen***
geschliffen [gə'ʃlɪfən] **1.** *pp of* ***schleifen***[2]; **2.** *adj* cut; *fig* polished
geschlossen [gə'ʃlɔsən] **1.** *pp of* ***schließen***; **2.** *adj* closed
geschlungen [gə'ʃlʊŋən] *pp of* ***schlingen***
Geschmack [gə'ʃmak] *m* (-[*e*]*s*; *Geschmäcke* [gə'ʃmɛkə]) taste (*a. fig*); flavo(u)r; ***Geschmack finden an*** (*dat*) de-

velop a taste for
ge'schmacklos *adj a. fig* tasteless
Ge'schmacklosigkeit *f* (-; *no pl*) tastelessness; ***das war e-e Geschmacklosigkeit*** that was in bad taste
Ge'schmack(s-)sache *f* matter of taste
ge'schmackvoll *adj* tasteful, in good taste
geschmeidig [gəˈʃmaidɪç] *adj* supple, pliant
geschmissen [gəˈʃmɪsən] *pp of* ***schmeißen***
geschmolzen [gəˈʃmɔltsən] *pp of* ***schmelzen***
geschnitten [gəˈʃnɪtən] *pp of* ***schneiden***
geschoben [gəˈʃoːbən] *pp of* ***schieben***
Geschöpf [gəˈʃœpf] *n* (-[*e*]*s*; -*e*) creature
geschoren [gəˈʃoːrən] *pp of* ***scheren***
Geschoss [gəˈʃɔs] *n* (-*es*; -*e*), **Geschoß** [gəˈʃoːs] *Austrian n* (-*es*; -*e*) projectile, missile; stor(e)y, floor
ge'schossen *pp of* ***schießen***
Ge'schrei F *n* (-*s*; *no pl*) shouting, yelling; screams; crying; *fig* fuss
geschrieben [gəˈʃriːbən] *pp of* ***schreiben***
geschrie(e)n [gəˈʃriː(ə)n] *pp of* ***schreien***
geschritten [gəˈʃrɪtən] *pp of* ***schreiten***
geschunden [gəˈʃʊndən] *pp of* ***schinden***
Geschütz [gəˈʃʏts] *n* (-*es*; -*e*) MIL gun, cannon
Geschwader [gəˈʃvaːdɐ] *n* (-*s*; -) MIL MAR squadron; AVIAT group, *Br* wing
Geschwätz [gəˈʃvɛts] F *n* (-*es*; *no pl*) chatter, babble; gossip; *fig* nonsense
ge'schwätzig *adj* talkative; gossipy
geschweige [gəˈʃvaigə] *cj*: ***geschweige (denn)*** let alone
geschwiegen [gəˈʃviːgən] *pp of* ***schweigen***
geschwind [gəˈʃvɪnt] *adj* quick, swift
Geschwindigkeit [gəˈʃvɪndɪçkait] *f* (-; -*en*) speed; fastness, quickness; PHYS velocity; ***mit e-r Geschwindigkeit von …*** at a speed *or* rate of …
Ge'schwindigkeitsbegrenzung *f* speed limit
Geschwindigkeitsüberschreitung *f* MOT speeding
Geschwister [gəˈʃvɪstɐ] *pl* brother(s) and sister(s); JUR siblings
geschwollen [gəˈʃvɔlən] **1.** *pp of* ***schwellen*** 1; **2.** *adj* MED swollen; *fig* bombastic, pretentious, pompous
geschwommen [gəˈʃvɔmən] *pp of* ***schwimmen***
geschworen [gəˈʃvoːrən] *pp of* ***schwören***
Ge'schworene *m, f* (-*n*; -*n*) member of a jury; ***die Geschworenen*** the jury
Geschwulst [gəˈʃvʊlst] *f* (-; *Geschwülste* [gəˈʃvʏlstə]) MED growth, tumo(u)r
geschwunden [gəˈʃvʊndən] *pp of* ***schwinden***
geschwungen [gəˈʃvʊŋən] *pp of* ***schwingen***
Geschwür [gəˈʃvyːɐ] *n* (-*s*; -*e*) MED abscess, ulcer
ge'sehen *pp of* ***sehen***
Geselchte [gəˈzɛlçtə] *Austrian n* (-*n*; *no pl*) GASTR smoked meat
Geselle [gəˈzɛlə] *m* (-*n*; -*n*) journeyman
ge'sellen *v/refl* (*no -ge-, h*) ***sich zu j-m gesellen*** join s.o.
ge'sellig *adj* sociable; ZO *etc* social; ***geselliges Beisammensein*** get-together
Ge'sellin *f* (-; -*nen*) trained woman *hairdresser etc*, journeywoman
Gesellschaft [gəˈzɛlʃaft] *f* (-; -*en*) society; company; party; ECON company, corporation; ***j-m Gesellschaft leisten*** keep s.o. company
ge'sellschaftlich *adj* social
Ge'sellschafts… *in cpds …kritik, …ordnung etc*: social …
Gesellschaftsreise *f* group tour
Gesellschaftsspiel *n* parlo(u)r game
Gesellschaftstanz *m* ballroom dance
gesessen [gəˈzɛsən] *pp of* ***sitzen***
Gesetz [gəˈzɛts] *n* (-*es*; -*e*) JUR law; act
Gesetzbuch *n* JUR code (of law)
Gesetzentwurf *m* PARL bill
ge'setzgebend *adj* JUR legislative
Ge'setzgeber *m* (-*s*; -) JUR legislator
Ge'setzgebung *f* (-; -*en*) JUR legislation
ge'setzlich **1.** *adj* legal; lawful; **2.** *adv*: ***gesetzlich geschützt*** JUR patented, registered
ge'setzlos *adj* lawless
ge'setzmäßig *adj* legal, lawful
gesetzt [gəˈzɛtst] **1.** *adj* staid, dignified; mature (*age*); **2.** *cj*: ***gesetzt den Fall(, dass) …*** supposing (that)
ge'setzwidrig *adj* illegal, unlawful
Gesicht [gəˈzɪçt] *n* (-[*e*]*s*; -*er*) face; ***zu Gesicht bekommen*** catch sight of
Ge'sichtausdruck *m* look, expression
Gesichtfarbe *f* complexion
Gesichtpunkt *m* point of view, aspect, angle
Gesichtzug *m* feature
Gesindel [gəˈzɪndəl] *n* (-*s*; *no pl*) trash, *the* riff-raff
gesinnt [gəˈzɪnt] *adj* minded; ***j-m feindlich gesinnt sein*** be ill-disposed towards s.o.
Ge'sinnung *f* (-; -*en*) mind; attitude; POL conviction(s)

ge'sinnungslos *adj* unprincipled
ge'sinnungstreu *adj* loyal
Ge'sinnungswechsel *m* about-face, *Br* about-turn
gesittet [gə'zɪtət] *adj* civilized, well-mannered
gesoffen [gə'zɔfən] *pp of* ***saufen***
gesogen [gə'zo:gən] *pp of* ***saugen***
gesotten [gə'zɔtən] *pp of* ***sieden***
gespalten [gə'ʃpaltən] *pp of* ***spalten***
Gespann [gə'ʃpan] *n* (-[*e*]*s*; -*e*) team (*a. fig*)
gespannt [gə'ʃpant] *adj* tense (*a. fig*); ***gespannt sein auf*** (*acc*) be anxious to see; ***ich bin gespannt, ob*** (***wie***) I wonder if (how)
Gespenst [gə'ʃpɛnst] *n* (-[*e*]*s*; -*er*) ghost, apparition, *esp fig* specter, *Br* spectre
ge'spenstisch *adj* ghostly, F spooky
gespie(e)n [gə'ʃpi:(ə)n] *pp of* ***speien***
Gespinst [gə'ʃpɪnst] *n* (-[*e*]*s*; -*e*) web, tissue (*both a. fig*)
gesponnen [gə'ʃpɔnən] *pp of* ***spinnen***
Gespött [gə'ʃpœt] *n* (-[*e*]*s*; *no pl*) mockery, ridicule; ***j-n zum Gespött machen*** make a laughingstock of s.o.
Gespräch [gə'ʃprɛ:ç] *n* (-[*e*]*s*; -*e*) talk (*a.* POL), conversation; TEL call
ge'sprächig *adj* talkative
gesprochen [gə'ʃprɔxən] *pp of* ***sprechen***
gesprossen [gə'ʃprɔsən] *pp of* ***sprießen***
gesprungen [gə'ʃprʊŋən] *pp of* ***springen***
Gespür [gə'ʃpy:ɐ] *n* (-*s*; *no pl*) flair, nose
Gestalt [gə'ʃtalt] *f* (-; -*en*) shape, form; figure
ge'stalten *v/t* (*no -ge-*, *h*) arrange; design
Ge'staltung *f* (-; -*en*) arrangement; design; decoration
gestanden [gə'ʃtandən] *pp of* ***stehen***
ge'ständig *adj*: ***geständig sein*** confess; have confessed
Geständnis [gə'ʃtɛntnɪs] *n* (-*ses*; -*se*) confession (*a. fig*)
Gestank [gə'ʃtaŋk] *m* (-[*e*]*s*; *no pl*) stench, stink
gestatten [gə'ʃtatən] *v/t* (*no -ge-*, *h*) allow, permit
Geste ['gɛstə] *f* (-; -*n*) gesture (*a. fig*)
ge'stehen *v/t and v/i* (*irr*, ***stehen***, *no -ge-*, *h*) confess
Ge'stein *n* (-[*e*]*s*; -*e*) rock, stone
Gestell [gə'ʃtɛl] *n* (-[*e*]*s*; -*e*) stand, base, pedestal; shelves; frame
gestern ['gɛstɐn] *adv* yesterday; ***gestern Abend*** last night
gestiegen [gə'ʃti:gən] *pp of* ***steigen***
gestochen [gə'ʃtɔxən] *pp of* ***stechen***
gestohlen [gə'ʃto:lən] *pp of* ***stehlen***
gestorben [gə'ʃtɔrbən] *pp of* ***sterben***
ge'stoßen *pp of* ***stoßen***
gestreift [gə'ʃtraift] *adj* striped
gestrichen [gə'ʃtrɪçən] *pp of* ***streichen***
gestrig ['gɛstrɪç] *adj* yesterday's, of yesterday
gestritten [gə'ʃtrɪtən] *pp of* ***streiten***
Gestrüpp [gə'ʃtrʏp] *n* (-[*e*]*s*; -*e*) brushwood, undergrowth; *fig* jungle, maze
gestunken [gə'ʃtʊŋkən] *pp of* ***stinken***
Gestüt [gə'ʃty:t] *n* (-[*e*]*s*; -*e*) stud
Gesuch [gə'zu:x] *n* (-[*e*]*s*; -*e*) application, request
gesund [gə'zʊnt] *adj* healthy; healthful, *fig a.* sound; ***gesunder Menschenverstand*** common sense; (***wieder***) ***gesund werden*** get well (again), recover
Ge'sundheit *f* (-; *no pl*) health; ***auf j-s Gesundheit trinken*** drink to s.o.'s health; ***Gesundheit!*** bless you!
ge'sundheitlich **1.** *adj*: ***gesundheitlicher Zustand*** state of health; ***aus gesundheitlichen Gründen*** for health reasons; **2.** *adv*: ***gesundheitlich geht es ihm gut*** he is in good health
Ge'sundheitsamt *n* Public Health Department (*Br* Office)
ge'sundheitsschädlich *adj* bad for one's health
Ge'sundheitszeugnis *n* health certificate
Gesundheitszustand *m* state of health
gesungen [gə'zʊŋən] *pp of* ***singen***
gesunken [gə'zʊŋkən] *pp of* ***sinken***
getan [gə'ta:n] *pp of* ***tun***
Getöse [gə'tø:zə] *n* (-*s*; *no pl*) din, (deafening) noise
ge'tragen *pp of* ***tragen***
Getränk [gə'trɛŋk] *n* (-[*e*]*s*; -*e*) drink, beverage
Ge'tränkeauto,mat *m* drinks machine
Getreide [gə'traidə] *n* (-*s*; -) cereals, grain, *Br a.* corn
Getreideernte *f* grain harvest (*or* crop)
ge'treten *pp of* ***treten***
Getriebe [gə'tri:bə] *n* (-*s*; -) MOT transmission
ge'trieben [gə'tri:bən] *pp of* ***treiben***
getroffen [gə'trɔfən] *pp of* ***treffen***
getrogen [gə'tro:gən] *pp of* ***trügen***
getrost [gə'tro:st] *adv* safely
getrunken [gə'trʊŋkən] *pp of* ***trinken***
Getue [gə'tu:ə] F *n* (-*s*; *no pl*) fuss
Getümmel [gə'tʏməl] *n* (-*s*; -) turmoil
Gewächs [gə'vɛks] *n* (-*es*; -*e*) plant; MED growth
ge'wachsen **1.** *pp of* ***wachsen***[1]; **2.** *fig adj*: ***j-m gewachsen sein*** be a match for s.o.; ***e-r Sache gewachsen sein*** be equal to s.th., be able to cope with s.th.

Ge'wächshaus *n* greenhouse, hothouse
gewagt [gə'va:kt] *adj* daring; *fig* risqué
gewählt [gə'vɛ:lt] *adj* refined
Gewähr [gə'vɛ:ɐ] *f*: ***Gewähr übernehmen (für)*** guarantee
ge'währen *v/t* (*no -ge-, h*) grant, allow
ge'währleisten *v/t* (*no -ge-, h*) guarantee
Gewahrsam [gə'va:ɐza:m] *m*: ***et.*** (***j-n***) ***in Gewahrsam nehmen*** take s.th. in safekeeping (s.o. into custody)
Gewalt [gə'valt] *f* (-; *-en*) a) (*no pl*) force, violence, b) power; ***mit Gewalt*** by force; ***höhere Gewalt*** act of God; ***häusliche Gewalt*** domestic violence; ***in s-e Gewalt bringen*** seize by force; ***die Gewalt verlieren über*** (*acc*) lose control over
Gewaltherrschaft *f* tyranny
ge'waltig *adj* powerful, mighty; enormous
ge'waltlos *adj* nonviolent
Ge'waltlosigkeit *f* (-; *no pl*) nonviolence
ge'waltsam **1.** *adj* violent; **2.** *adv* by force; ***gewaltsam öffnen*** force open
ge'walttätig *adj* violent
Ge'walttätigkeit *f* (-; *-en*) a) (*no pl*) violence, b) act of violence
Ge'waltverbrechen *n* crime of violence
Gewand [gə'vant] *n* (-[*e*]*s*; *Gewänder* [gə'vɛndɐ]) robe, gown; REL vestment
gewandt [gə'vant] **1.** *pp of* ***wenden*** (*v/refl*); **2.** *adj* nimble; skil(l)ful; clever
Ge'wandtheit *f* (-; *no pl*) nimbleness; skill; ease
gewann [gə'van] *pret of* ***gewinnen***
ge'waschen *pp of* ***waschen***
Gewässer [gə'vɛsɐ] *n* (-*s*; -) body of water; *pl* waters
Gewebe [gə've:bə] *n* (-*s*; -) fabric; BIOL tissue
Gewehr [gə've:ɐ] *n* (-[*e*]*s*; -*e*) gun; rifle; shotgun
Gewehrkolben *m* (rifle) butt
Gewehrlauf *m* (rifle *or* gun) barrel
Geweih [gə'vai] *n* (-[*e*]*s*; -*e*) ZO antlers, horns
Gewerbe [gə'vɛrbə] *n* (-*s*; -) trade, business
Gewerbeschein *m* trade licen|se, *Br* -ce
Gewerbeschule *f* vocational *or* trade school
gewerblich [gə'vɛrplɪç] *adj* commercial, industrial
gewerbsmäßig [gə'vɛrps-] *adj* professional
Gewerkschaft [gə'vɛrkʃaft] *f* (-; *-en*) labor union, *Br* (trade) union
Ge'werkschaft(l)er *m* (-*s*; -), **Ge'werkschaft(l)erin** *f* (-; *-nen*) labor (*Br* trade) unionist

ge'werkschaftlich *adj*, **Ge'werkschafts...** *in cpds* labor (*Br* trade) union ...
ge'wesen *pp of* ***sein***[1]
gewichen [gə'vɪçən] *pp of* ***weichen***
Gewicht [gə'vɪçt] *n* (-[*e*]*s*; -*e*) weight; importance; ***Gewicht legen auf*** (*acc*) stress
gewiesen [gə'vi:zən] *pp of* ***weisen***
gewillt [gə'vɪlt] *adj* willing, ready
Gewimmel [gə'vɪməl] *n* (-*s*; *no pl*) throng
Gewinde [gə'vɪndə] *n* (-*s*; -) TECH thread; ***ein Gewinde bohren in*** (*acc*) tap
Gewinn [gə'vɪn] *m* (-[*e*]*s*; -*e*) ECON profit (*a. fig*); gain(s); prize; winnings; ***Gewinn bringend*** → ***gewinnbringend***
ge'winnbringend *adj* profitable
ge'winnen *v/t and v/i* (*irr, no -ge-, h*) win; gain
gewinnend *fig adj* winning, engaging
Gewinner [gə'vɪnɐ] *m* (-*s*; -), **Ge'winnerin** *f* (-; *-nen*) winner
Ge'winnzahl *f* winning number
Gewirr [gə'vɪr] *n* (-[*e*]*s*; *no pl*) tangle; maze
gewiss [gə'vɪs] **1.** *adj* certain; **2.** *adv* certainly
Ge'wissen *n* (-*s*; -) conscience
ge'wissenhaft *adj* conscientious
ge'wissenlos *adj* unscrupulous
Ge'wissensbisse *pl* pricks *or* pangs of conscience
Gewissensfrage *f* question of conscience
Gewissensgründe *pl*: ***aus Gewissensgründen*** for reasons of conscience
Ge'wissheit *f* (-; *no pl*) certainty; ***mit Gewissheit*** *know etc* for certain *or* sure
Gewitter [gə'vɪtɐ] *n* (-*s*; -) thunderstorm
Gewitterregen *m* thundershower
Gewitterwolke *f* thundercloud
gewoben [gə'vo:bən] *pp of* ***weben***
gewogen [gə'vo:gən] *pp of* ***wiegen***[1] *and* ***wägen***
gewöhnen [gə'vø:nən] *v/t and v/refl* (*no -ge-, h*) ***sich*** (***j-n***) ***gewöhnen an*** (*acc*) get (s.o.) used to
Gewohnheit [gə'vo:nhait] *f* (-; *-en*) habit (***et. zu tun*** of doing s.th.)
ge'wohnheitsmäßig *adj* habitual
gewöhnlich [gə'vø:nlɪç] *adj* common, ordinary, usual; vulgar, F common
gewohnt [gə'vo:nt] *adj* usual; ***et.*** (***zu tun***) ***gewohnt sein*** be used *or* accustomed to (doing) s.th.
Gewölbe [gə'vœlbə] *n* (-*s*; -) vault
gewölbt [gə'vœlpt] *adj* arched
gewonnen [gə'vɔnən] *pp of* ***gewinnen***
geworben [gə'vɔrbən] *pp of* ***werben***
geworden [gə'vɔrdən] *pp of* ***werden***
geworfen [gə'vɔrfən] *pp of* ***werfen***

gewrungen [gə'vrʊŋən] *pp of* ***wringen***
Gewühl [gə'vy:l] *n* (-[*e*]*s*; *no pl*) crowd, crush
gewunden [gə'vʊndən] **1.** *pp of* ***winden***; **2.** *adj* winding
Gewürz [gə'vʏrts] *n* (-*es*; -*e*) spice
Gewürzgurke *f* pickle(d gherkin)
gewusst [gə'vʊst] *pp of* ***wissen***
gezackt [gə'tsakt] *adj* jagged, serrated
Ge'zeiten *pl* tide(s)
Gezeter [gə'tse:tɐ] *contp n* (-*s*; *no pl*) (shrill) clamo(u)r; nagging
geziert [gə'tsi:ɐt] *adj* affected
gezogen [gə'tso:gən] *pp of* ***ziehen***
Gezwitscher [gə'tsvɪtʃɐ] *n* (-*s*; *no pl*) chirp(ing), twitter(ing)
gezwungen [gə'tsvʊŋən] **1.** *pp of* ***zwingen***; **2.** *adj* forced, unnatural
Gicht [gɪçt] *f* (-; *no pl*) MED gout
Giebel ['gi:bəl] *m* (-*s*; -) gable
Gier [gi:ɐ] *f* (-; *no pl*) greed(iness) (***nach*** for)
gierig ['gi:rɪç] *adj* greedy (***nach, auf*** *acc* for, after)
gießen ['gi:sən] *v/t and v/i* (*irr, ge-, h*) pour; TECH cast; water
Gieße'rei *f* (-; -*en*) TECH foundry
'Gießkanne *f* watering pot (*Br* can)
Gift [gɪft] *n* (-[*e*]*s*; -*e*) poison, ZO *a.* venom (*a. fig*)
'giftig *adj* poisonous; venomous (*a. fig*); poisoned; MED toxic
'Giftmüll *m* toxic waste
Giftmülldepo,nie *f* toxic waste dump
Giftschlange *f* ZO poisonous *or* venomous snake
Giftstoff *m* poisonous *or* toxic substance; pollutant
Giftzahn *m* ZO poison fang
Gigant [gi'gant] *m* (-*en*; -*en*) giant
gi'gantisch *adj* gigantic
ging [gɪŋ] *pret of* ***gehen***
Gipfel ['gɪpfəl] *m* (-*s*; -) top, peak, summit, *fig a.* height
Gipfelkonfe,renz *f* POL summit (meeting *or* conference)
'gipfeln *v/i* (*ge-, h*) culminate (***in*** *dat* in)
Gips [gɪps] *m* (-*es*; -*e*) plaster (of Paris); ***in Gips*** MED in (a) plaster (cast)
Gipsabdruck *m*, **Gipsabguss** *m* plaster cast
'gipsen *v/t* (*ge-, h*) plaster (*a.* F MED)
'Gipsverband *m* MED plaster cast
Giraffe [gi'rafə] *f* (-; -*n*) ZO giraffe
Girlande [gɪr'landə] *f* (-; -*n*) garland, festoon
Girokonto ['ʒi:ro-] *n* checking (*or* current) account; postal check (*Br* giro) account
Gischt [gɪʃt] *m* (-[*e*]*s*; -*e*), *f* (-; -*en*) (sea) spray, spindrift
Gitarre [gi'tarə] *f* (-; -*n*) MUS guitar
Gitarrist [gita'rɪst] *m* (-*en*; -*en*) guitarist
Gitter ['gɪtɐ] *n* (-*s*; -) lattice; grating; F ***hinter Gittern*** (***sitzen***) (be) behind bars
'Gitterbett *n* crib, *Br* cot
'Gitterfenster *n* lattice (window)
Glanz [glants] *m* (-*es*; *no pl*) shine, gloss (*a.* TECH), luster, *Br* lustre, brilliance (*a. fig*); *fig* splendo(u)r, glamo(u)r
glänzen ['glɛntsən] *v/i* (*ge-, h*) shine, gleam; glitter, glisten
glänzend *adj* shining, shiny, bright; PHOT glossy; *fig* brilliant, excellent
'Glanzleistung *f* brilliant achievement
Glanzzeit *f* heyday
Glas [gla:s] *n* (-*es*; *Gläser* ['glɛ:zɐ]) glass
Glaser ['gla:zɐ] *m* (-*s*; -) glazier
gläsern ['glɛ:zɐn] *adj* (of) glass
'Glasfaser *f*, **Glasfiber** *f* glass fiber (*Br* fibre)
Glashütte *f* TECH glassworks
glasieren [gla'zi:rən] *v/t* (*no -ge-, h*) glaze; GASTR ice, frost
glasig ['gla:zɪç] *adj* glassy
'glasklar *adj* crystal-clear (*a. fig*)
'Glasscheibe *f* (glass) pane
Glasur [gla'zu:ɐ] *f* (-; -*en*) glaze; GASTR icing
glatt [glat] *adj* smooth (*a. fig*); slippery; *fig* clear
Glätte ['glɛtə] *f* (-; *no pl*) smoothness (*a. fig*); slipperiness
'Glatteis *n* (glare, *Br* black) ice; ***es herrscht Glatteis*** the roads are icy; F ***j-n aufs Glatteis führen*** mislead s.o.
glätten ['glɛtən] *v/t* (*ge-, h*) smooth; *Swiss*: → ***bügeln***
'glattgehen *v/i* (*irr, sep, -ge-, sein*) F work (out well), go (off) well
Glatze ['glatsə] *f* (-; -*n*) bald head; ***e-e Glatze haben*** be bald
Glaube ['glaubə] *m* (-*ns*; *no pl*) belief, *esp* REL faith (*both*: ***an*** *acc* in)
'glauben *v/t and v/i* (*ge-, h*) believe; think, guess; ***glauben an*** (*acc*) believe in (*a.* REL)
'Glaubensbekenntnis *n* REL creed, profession *or* confession of faith
Glaubenslehre *f*, **Glaubenssatz** *m* dogma, doctrine
glaubhaft ['glauphaft] *adj* credible, plausible
gläubig ['glɔʏbɪç] *adj* religious; devout; ***die Gläubigen*** the faithful
Gläubiger ['glɔʏbɪgɐ] *m* (-*s*; -), **'Gläubigerin** *f* (-; -*nen*) ECON creditor
'glaubwürdig *adj* credible; reliable
gleich [glaiç] **1.** *adj* same; equal (*right etc*);

auf die gleiche Art (in) the same way; ***zur gleichen Zeit*** at the same time; ***das ist mir gleich*** it's all the same to me; ***ganz gleich, wann*** *etc* no matter when *etc*; ***das Gleiche*** the same; ***(ist) gleich …*** MATH equals …, is …; ***gleich bleibend*** → ***gleichbleibend***; ***gleich gesinnt*** like-minded; ***gleich lautend*** → ***gleichlautend***; **2.** *adv* equally, alike; at once, right away; in a moment *or* minute; ***gleich groß (alt)*** of the same size (age); ***gleich nach (neben)*** right after (next to); ***gleich gegenüber*** just opposite *or* across the street; ***es ist gleich 5 Uhr*** it's almost 5 o'clock; ***gleich aussehen (gekleidet sein)*** look (be dressed) alike; ***bis gleich!*** see you soon *or* later!

gleichaltrig ['glaiçʔaltrɪç] *adj* (of) the same age

'**gleichberechtigt** *adj* equal, having equal rights

'**Gleichberechtigung** *f* (-; *no pl*) equal rights

'**gleichbleibend** *adj* constant, steady

'**gleichen** *v/i* (*irr, ge-, h*) (*dat*) be *or* look like

'**gleichfalls** *adv* also, likewise; ***danke, gleichfalls!*** (thanks,) the same to you

'**gleichförmig** [-fœrmɪç] *adj* uniform

'**Gleichgewicht** *n* (-[e]s; *no pl*) balance (*a. fig*)

'**gleichgültig** *adj* indifferent (***gegen*** to); careless; ***das (er) ist mir gleichgültig*** I don't care (for him)

'**Gleichgültigkeit** *f* (-; *no pl*) indifference

'**Gleichheit** *f* (-; *no pl*) equality

'**gleichkommen** *v/i* (*irr*, ***kommen***, *sep, -ge-, sein*) ***e-r Sache gleichkommen*** amount to s.th.; ***j-m gleichkommen*** equal s.o. (***an*** *dat* in)

'**gleichlautend** *adj* identical

'**gleichmäßig** *adj* regular; constant; even

'**gleichnamig** [-na:mɪç] *adj* of the same name

'**Gleichnis** *n* (*-ses; -se*) parable

'**gleichsam** *adv* as it were, so to speak

'**gleichseitig** [-zaitɪç] *adj* MATH equilateral

'**gleichsetzen, gleichstellen** *v/t* (*sep, -ge-, h*) equate (*dat* to, with); put *s.o.* on an equal footing (with)

'**Gleichstrom** *m* ELECTR direct current

'**Gleichung** *f* (-; *-en*) MATH equation

'**gleichwertig** *adj* equally good; ***j-m gleichwertig sein*** be a match for s.o. (*a.* SPORT)

'**gleichzeitig** *adj* simultaneous; ***beide gleichzeitig*** both at the same time

Gleis [glais] *n* (*-es; -e*) RAIL rail(s), track(s), line; platform, gate

gleiten ['glaitən] *v/i* (*irr, ge-, sein*) glide, slide

gleitend *adj*: ***gleitende Arbeitszeit*** flexible working hours, flextime, *Br a.* flexitime

'**Gleitflug** *m* glide

'**Gleitschirmfliegen** *n* paragliding

Gleitschirmflieger *m* paraglider

Gletscher ['glɛtʃɐ] *m* (*-s; -*) glacier

Gletscherspalte *f* crevasse

glich [glɪç] *pret of* ***gleichen***

Glied [gli:t] *n* (*-es; Glieder* ['gli:dɐ]) ANAT limb; penis; TECH link

gliedern ['gli:dɐn] *v/t* (*ge-, h*) structure; divide (***in*** *acc* into)

Gliederung ['gli:dərʊŋ] *f* (-; *-en*) structure, arrangement; outline

'**Gliedmaßen** *pl* ANAT limbs, extremities

glimmen ['glɪmən] *v/i* ([*irr*,] *ge-, h*) glow; smo(u)lder

'**Glimmstängel** F *m* (*-s; -*) cigarette, *Br sl* fag

glimpflich ['glɪmpflɪç] **1.** *adj* lenient, mild; **2.** *adv*: ***glimpflich davonkommen*** get off lightly

glitschig ['glɪtʃɪç] *adj* slippery

glitt [glɪt] *pret of* ***gleiten***

glitzern ['glɪtsɐn] *v/i* (*ge-, h*) glitter, sparkle, glint

global [glo'ba:l] *adj* global

Globus ['glo:bʊs] *m* (-[*ses*]; *-se*) globe

Glocke ['glɔkə] *f* (-; *-n*) bell

'**Glockenblume** *f* bluebell

Glockenspiel *n* chimes

Glockenturm *m* bell tower, belfry

glomm [glɔm] *pret of* ***glimmen***

glorreich ['glo:ɐraiç] *adj* glorious

Glotze ['glɔtsə] F *f* (-; *-n*) TV *the* tube, *Br* goggle box

'**glotzen** F *v/i* (*ge-, h*) goggle, gape, stare

Glück [glʏk] *n* (-[*e*]*s*; *no pl*) (good) luck, fortune; happiness; ***Glück haben*** be lucky; ***zum Glück*** fortunately; ***viel Glück!*** good luck!

Glucke ['glʊkə] *f* (-; *-n*) ZO sitting hen; *fig* hen

gluckern ['glʊkɐn] *v/i* (*ge-, h*) gurgle

'**glücklich** *adj* happy; ***glücklicher Zufall*** lucky chance

'**glücklicher'weise** *adv* fortunately

'**Glücksbringer** *m* (*-s; -*) lucky charm

Glücksfall *m* lucky chance

Glückspfennig *m* lucky penny

Glückspilz *m* lucky fellow

Glücksspiel *n* game of chance; *coll* gambling

Glücksspieler *m* gambler

Glückstag *m* lucky day

'**glückstrahlend** *adj* radiant

'Glückwunsch *m* congratulations; ***herzlichen Glückwunsch!*** congratulations!; happy birthday!
Glühbirne ['gly:-] *f* ELECTR light bulb
glühen ['gly:ən] *v/i* (*ge-*, *h*) glow (*a. fig*)
glühend ['gly:ənt] *adj* glowing; red-hot (*iron*); *fig* burning; ***glühend heiß*** blazing hot
'Glühwein *m* mulled wine
Glut [glu:t] *f* (-; *-en*) (glowing) fire; embers; live coals; *fig* ardo(u)r
'Gluthitze *f* blazing heat
GmbH [ge:ˀɛmbe:'ha:] ABBR *of* ***Gesellschaft mit beschränkter Haftung*** private limited liability company
Gnade ['gna:də] *f* (-; *-n*) mercy, *esp* REL *a.* grace; favo(u)r
'Gnadenfrist *f* reprieve
Gnadengesuch *n* JUR petition for mercy
'gnadenlos *adj* merciless
gnädig ['gnɛ:dɪç] *adj* gracious; *esp* REL merciful
Gold [gɔlt] *n* (-[*e*]*s*; *no pl*) gold
Goldbarren *m* gold bar *or* ingot; *coll* bullion
golden ['gɔldən] *adj* gold; *fig* golden
'Goldfisch *m* zo goldfish
'goldgelb *adj* golden (yellow)
'Goldgräber [-grɛ:bɐ] *m* (*-s*; -) gold digger
Goldgrube *fig f* goldmine, bonanza
goldig ['gɔldɪç] F *adj* sweet, lovely, cute
'Goldmine *f* goldmine
Goldmünze *f* gold coin
Goldschmied *m* goldsmith
Goldstück *n* gold coin
Golf[1] [gɔlf] *m* (-[*e*]*s*; *-e*) GEOGR gulf
Golf[2] *n* (*-s*; *no pl*) SPORT golf
Golfplatz *m* golf course
Golfschläger *m* golf club
Golfspieler *m* golfer
Gondel ['gɔndəl] *f* (-; *-n*) gondola; cabin
Gong ['gɔŋ-] *m* (*-s*; *-s*) gong
gönnen ['gœnən] *v/t* (*ge-*, *h*) ***j-m et. gönnen*** not (be)grudge s.o. s.th.; ***j-m et. nicht gönnen*** (be)grudge s.o. s.th.; ***sich et. gönnen*** allow o.s. s.th., treat o.s. to s.th.
gönnerhaft ['gœnɐhaft] *adj* patronizing
gor [go:ɐ] *pret of* ***gären***
Gorilla [go'rɪla] *m* (*-s*; *-s*) zo gorilla
goss [gɔs] *pret of* ***gießen***
Gosse ['gɔsə] *f* (-; *-n*) gutter (*a. fig*)
Gotik ['go:tɪk] *f* (-; *no pl*) ARCH Gothic style *or* period
'gotisch *adj* Gothic
Gott [gɔt] *m* (-[*e*]*s*; *Götter* ['gœtɐ]) REL God, Lord; MYTH god; ***Gott sei Dank***(!) thank God(!); ***um Gottes Willen!*** for heaven's sake!
'gottergeben *adj* resigned (to the will of God)
'Gottesdienst *m* REL (divine) service
'gottesfürchtig [-fʏrçtɪç] *adj* god-fearing
'Gotteslästerer [-lɛstərɐ] *m* (*-s*; -) blasphemer
'Gotteslästerung *f* (-; *-en*) blasphemy
'Gottheit *f* (-; *-en*) deity, divinity
Göttin ['gœtɪn] *f* (-; *-nen*) goddess
'göttlich ['gœtlɪç] *adj* divine
gott'lob *int* thank God *or* goodness!
'gottlos *adj* godless, wicked
'gottverlassen F *adj* godforsaken
'Gottvertrauen *n* trust in God
Götze ['gœtsə] *m* (*-n*; *-n*), **'Götzenbild** *n* idol
Gouverneur [guvɛr'nø:ɐ] *m* (*-s*; *-e*) governor
Grab [gra:p] *n* (-[*e*]*s*; *Gräber* ['grɛ:bɐ]) grave; tomb
graben ['gra:bən] *v/t and v/i* (*irr*, *ge-*, *h*) dig, zo *a.* burrow
'Graben *m* (*-s*; *Gräben* ['grɛ:bən]) ditch; MIL trench
'Grabmal *n* monument; tomb
Grabrede *f* funeral address
Grabschrift *f* epitaph
Grabstätte *f* burial place; grave, tomb
Grabstein *m* tombstone, gravestone
Grad [gra:t] *m* (-[*e*]*s*; *-e*) degree; MIL *etc* rank, grade; ***15 Grad Kälte*** 15 degrees below zero
Gradeinteilung *f* graduation
graduell [gra'duɛl] *adj* in degree
Graf [gra:f] *m* (*-en*; *-en*) count, *Br* earl
Graffiti [gra'fi:ti] *pl* graffiti
Grafik ['gra:fɪk] *f* (-; *-en*) a) (*no pl*) graphic arts, b) print, c) MATH, TECH graph, diagram, d) (*no pl*) art(work), illustrations, e) (*no pl*) EDP graphics
'Grafiker *m* (*-s*; -), **'Grafikerin** *f* (-; *-nen*) graphic artist
Gräfin ['grɛ:fɪn] *f* (-; *-nen*) countess
grafisch ['gra:fɪʃ] *adj* graphic
Grafologie *f* → ***Graphologie***
'Grafschaft *f* (-; *-en*) county
Gramm [gram] *n* (*-s*; *-e*) gram
Grammatik [gra'matɪk] *f* (-; *-en*) grammar
gram'matisch *adj* grammatical
Granat [gra'na:t] *m* (-[*e*]*s*; *-e*) MIN garnet
Gra'nate *f* (-; *-n*) MIL shell
Gra'natsplitter *m* MIL shell splinter
Granatwerfer *m* MIL mortar
grandios [gran'djo:s] *adj* magnificent, grand
Granit [gra'ni:t] *m* (*-s*; *-e*) granite
Graphik *f etc* → ***Grafik*** *etc*
Graphologie [grafolo'gi:] *f* (-; *no pl*) graphology

Gras [gra:s] *n (-es; Gräser* ['grɛ:zɐ]) grass
grasen ['gra:zən] *v/i (ge-, h)* graze
'**Grashalm** *m* blade of grass
grassieren [gra'si:rən] *v/i (no -ge-, h)* rage, be rife
grässlich ['grɛslɪç] *adj* hideous, atrocious
Gräte ['grɛ:tə] *f (-; -n)* (fish)bone
Gratifikation [gratifika'tsjo:n] *f (-; -en)* gratuity, bonus
gratis ['gra:tɪs] *adv* free (of charge)
Grätsche ['grɛ:tʃə] *f (-; -n)*, '**grätschen** *v/i (ge-, h)* straddle; *soccer*: stride tackle
Gratulant [gratu'lant] *m (-en; -en)*, **Gratu'lantin** *f (-; -nen)* congratulator
Gratulation [-la'tsjo:n] *f (-; -en)* congratulation
gratulieren [-'li:rən] *v/i (no -ge-, h)* congratulate (***j-m zu et.*** s.o. on s.th.); ***j-m zum Geburtstag gratulieren*** wish s.o. many happy returns (of the day)
grau [grau] *adj* gray, *Br* grey
'**Graubrot** *n* rye bread
Gräuel ['grɔʏəl] *m (-s; -)* horror
'**Gräueltat** *f* atrocity
'**grauen** *v/i (ge-, h)* ***mir graut es vor*** *(dat)* I dread (the thought of)
'**Grauen** *n (-s; -)* horror
'**grauenhaft**, '**grauenvoll** *adj* horrible, horrifying
Graupel ['graupəl] *f (-; -n)* sleet, soft hail
grausam ['grauza:m] *adj* cruel
'**Grausamkeit** *f (-; -en)* cruelty
grausig ['grauzɪç] *adj* → ***grauenhaft***
'**Grauzone** *f fig* gray (*Br* grey) area
gravieren [gra'vi:rən] *v/t (no -ge-, h)* engrave
gravierend *adj* serious
Gravur [gra'vu:ɐ] *f (-; -en)* engraving
Grazie ['gra:tsjə] *f (-; no pl)* grace
graziös [gra'tsjø:s] *adj* graceful
greifen ['graifən] *(irr, ge-, h)* **1.** *v/t* seize, grasp, grab, take *or* catch hold of; **2.** *v/i fig* take effect; ***greifen nach*** reach for; grasp at
Greis [grais] *m (-es; -e)* (very) old man
greisenhaft ['graizənhaft] *adj* senile (*a.* MED)
Greisin ['graizɪn] *f (-; -nen)* (very) old woman
grell [grɛl] *adj* glaring; shrill
Grenze ['grɛntsə] *f (-; -n)* border; boundary; *fig* limit
'**grenzen** *v/i (ge-, h)* ***grenzen an*** *(acc)* border on
'**grenzenlos** *adj* boundless
'**Grenzfall** *m* borderline case
Grenzland *n* borderland, frontier
Grenzlinie *f* borderline, POL demarcation line
Grenzstein *m* boundary stone
Grenzübergang *m* frontier crossing (point), checkpoint
Greuel *m* → ***Gräuel***
Grieche ['gri:çə] *m (-n; -n)* Greek
'**Griechenland** Greece
'**Griechin** *f (-; -nen)*, '**griechisch** *adj* Greek
Grieß [gri:s] *m (-es; -e)* semolina
griff [grɪf] *pret of* ***greifen***
Griff *m (-[e]s; -e)* grip, grasp; handle
'**griffbereit** *adj* at hand, handy
Grill [grɪl] *m (-s; -s)* grill
Grille ['grɪlə] *f (-; -n)* zo cricket
'**grillen** *v/t (ge-, h)* grill, barbecue
Grimasse [gri'masə] *f (-; -n)* grimace; ***Grimassen schneiden*** pull faces
grimmig ['grɪmɪç] *adj* grim
grinsen ['grɪnzən] *v/i (ge-, h)* grin (***über*** *acc* at); ***höhnisch*** *or* ***spöttisch grinsen*** (***über*** *acc*) sneer (at)
'**Grinsen** *n (-s; no pl)* grin; ***höhnisches*** *or* ***spöttisches Grinsen*** sneer
Grippe ['grɪpə] *f (-; -n)* MED influenza, F flu
Grips [grɪps] F *m (-es; no pl)* brains
grob [gro:p] **1.** *adj* coarse (*a. fig*); *fig* gross; crude; rude; rough; **2.** *adv*: ***grob geschätzt*** at a rough estimate
'**Grobheit** *f (-; no pl)* coarseness; roughness; rudeness
grölen ['grø:lən] F *v/t and v/i (ge-, h)* bawl
Groll [grɔl] *m (-[e]s; no pl)* grudge, ill will
'**grollen** *v/i (ge-, h)* ***j-m grollen*** bear s.o. a grudge
Groschen ['grɔʃən] *m (-s; -) Austrian* groschen; F ten-pfennig piece, ten pfennigs
groß [gro:s] *adj* big; large (*a. family*); tall; grown-up; F big (*brother etc*); *fig* great (*a. fun, trouble, pain etc*); capital (*letter*); ***großes Geld*** bills, *Br* notes; ***große Ferien*** summer vacation, *Br* summer holiday(s); ***Groß und Klein*** young and old; ***im Großen und Ganzen*** on the whole; F ***groß in et. sein*** be great at (doing) s.th.; ***wie groß ist es?*** what size is it?; ***wie groß bist du?*** how tall are you?
'**großartig** *adj* great, F *a.* terrific
'**Großaufnahme** *f film*: close-up
Größe ['grø:sə] *f (-; -n)* size; height; *esp* MATH quantity; *fig* greatness; celebrity
'**Großeltern** *pl* grandparents
'**großen'teils** *adv* to a large *or* great extent, largely
'**Größenwahn** *m* megalomania (*a. fig*)
'**Großfa,milie** *f* extended family
Großhandel *m* ECON wholesale (trade)
Großhändler *m* ECON wholesale dealer, wholesaler

G

Großhandlung *f* ECON wholesale business
Großindus'trie *f* big industry; big business
Großindustri'elle *m* big industrialist, F tycoon
Großmacht *f* POL great power
Großmarkt *m* ECON hypermarket; wholesale market
Großmaul F *n* braggart
Großmutter *f* grandmother
Großraum *m* conurbation, metropolitan area; ***der Großraum München*** Greater Munich, the Greater Munich area
Großraumflugzeug *n* wide-bodied jet
'großschreiben *v/t* (*irr*, ***schreiben***, *sep*, *-ge-*, *h*) capitalize
'Großschreibung *f* (use of) capitalization
'großsprecherisch [-ʃprɛçərɪʃ] *adj* boastful
'großspurig [-ʃpu:rɪç] *adj* arrogant
'Großstadt *f* big city
'großstädtisch *adj* of *or* in a big city, urban
'größten'teils *adv* mostly, mainly
'großtun *v/i* (*irr*, ***tun***, *sep*, *-ge-*, *h*) show off; ***sich mit et. großtun*** brag about s.th.
'Großvater *m* grandfather
'Großverdiener *m* (*-s*; -) big earner
'Großwild *n* big game
'großziehen *v/t* (*irr*, ***ziehen***, *sep*, *-ge-*, *h*) raise, rear; bring up
'großzügig *adj* generous, liberal; ... on a large scale; spacious
'Großzügigkeit *f* (-; *no pl*) generosity, liberality; spaciousness
grotesk [gro'tɛsk] *adj* grotesque
Grotte ['grɔtə] *f* (-; *-n*) grotto
grub [gru:p] *pret of* ***graben***
Grübchen ['gry:pçən] *n* (*-s*; -) dimple
Grube ['gru:bə] *f* (-; *-n*) pit; mine
Grübelei [gry:bə'lai] *f* (-; *-en*) pondering, musing
grübeln ['gry:bəln] *v/i* (*ge-*, *h*) ponder, muse (***über*** *acc* on, over)
Gruft [grʊft] *f* (-; *Grüfte* ['grʏftə]) tomb, vault
grün [gry:n] *adj* green
Grün *n* (*-s*; -) green; ***im Grünen*** in the country
'Grünanlage *f* park
Grund [grʊnt] *m* (*-[e]s*; *Gründe* ['grʏndə]) reason; cause; ground, AGR *a.* soil; bottom; ***Grund und Boden*** property, land; ***aus diesem Grund(e)*** for this reason; ***von Grund auf*** entirely; ***im Grunde*** (***genommen***) actually, basically; → ***aufgrund***; → ***zugrunde***
'Grund... *in cpds ...bedeutung*, *...bedingung*, *...regel*, *...prinzip*, *...wortschatz* *etc*: *mst* basic ...
Grundbegriffe *pl* basics, fundamentals
Grundbesitz *m* property, land
Grundbesitzer *m* landowner
gründen ['grʏndən] *v/t* (*ge-*, *h*) found (*a. family*), set up, establish; ***sich gründen auf*** (*dat*) be based *or* founded on
Gründer ['grʏndɐ] *m* (*-s*; -), **'Gründerin** *f* (-; *-nen*) founder
'grund'falsch *adj* absolutely wrong
'Grundfläche *f* MATH base; ARCH area
Grundgedanke *m* basic idea
Grundgeschwindigkeit *f* AVIAT ground speed
Grundgesetz *n* POL Basic (Constitutional) Law (for the Federal Republic of Germany)
Grundlage *f* foundation, *fig a.* basis; *pl* (basic) elements
'grundlegend *adj* fundamental, basic
gründlich ['grʏntlɪç] *adj* thorough
'Grundlinie *f* *tennis etc*: base line
'grundlos *adj* groundless, unfounded
'Grundmauer *f* foundation
Grün'donnerstag *m* REL Maundy *or* Holy Thursday
'Grundrechnungsart *f* MATH basic arithmetical operation
Grundriss *m* ARCH ground plan
Grundsatz *m* principle
grundsätzlich ['grʊntzɛtslɪç] **1.** *adj* fundamental; **2.** *adv*: ***ich bin grundsätzlich dagegen*** I am against it on principle
'Grundschule *f* elementary (*or* grade) school, *Br* primary (*or* junior) school
Grundstein *m* ARCH foundation stone; *fig* foundations
Grundstück *n* plot (of land), lot; (building) site; premises
Grundstücksmakler *m* realtor, *Br* real estate agent
'Gründung *f* (-; *-en*) foundation, establishment, setting up
'grundver'schieden *adj* totally different
'Grundwasser *n* ground water
Grundzahl *f* cardinal number
Grundzug *m* main feature, characteristic
Grüne ['gry:nə] *m*, *f* (*-n*; *-n*) POL Green
'Grünfläche *f* green space
'grünlich *adj* greenish
'Grünspan *m* (*-[e]s*; *no pl*) verdigris
grunzen ['grʊntsən] *v/i and v/t* (*ge-*, *h*) grunt
Gruppe ['grʊpə] *f* (-; *-n*) group
'Gruppenreise *f* group tour
gruppieren [grʊ'pi:rən] *v/t* (*no -ge-*, *h*) group, arrange in groups; ***sich gruppieren*** form groups
Grusel... ['gru:zəl-] *in cpds ...film etc*:

horror …
'**gruselig** *adj* eerie, creepy; spine-chilling
'**gruseln** *v/t and v/refl (ge-, h)* ***es gruselt mich*** F it gives me the creeps
Gruß [gruːs] *m (-es; Grüße* ['gryːsə]) greeting(s); MIL salute; ***viele Grüße an*** *(acc)* … give my regards (*or* love) to …; ***mit freundlichen Grüßen*** yours sincerely; ***herzliche Grüße*** best wishes; love
grüßen ['gryːsən] *v/t (ge-, h)* greet, F say hello to; MIL salute; ***grüßen Sie ihn von mir*** give my regards (*or* love) to him
gucken ['gʊkən] *v/i (ge-, h)* look
'**Guckloch** *n* peephole
Güggeli ['gʏgəli] *n (-s; -) Swiss* chicken
gültig ['gʏltɪç] *adj* valid; current
'**Gültigkeit** *f (-; no pl)* validity; ***s-e Gültigkeit verlieren*** expire
Gummi ['gʊmi] *m, n (-s; -[s])* rubber
Gummiband *n (-[e]s; -bänder)* rubber (*esp Br a.* elastic) band
Gummibärchen *pl* gummy bears
Gummibaum *m* BOT rubber tree; rubber plant
Gummibon,bon *m, n* gumdrop
gummieren [gʊ'miːrən] *v/t (no -ge-, h)* gum
'**Gummiknüppel** *m* truncheon
Gummistiefel *m* rubber boot, *esp Br* wellington (boot)
Gummizug *m* elastic
Gunst [gʊnst] *f (-; no pl)* favo(u)r, goodwill; → ***zugunsten***
günstig ['gʏnstɪç] *adj* favo(u)rable (***für*** to); convenient; ***im günstigsten Fall*** at best; ***günstige Gelegenheit*** chance
Gurgel ['gʊrgəl] *f (-; -n)* throat; ***j-m an die Gurgel springen*** fly at s.o.'s throat
'**gurgeln** *v/i (ge-, h)* MED gargle
Gurke ['gʊrkə] *f (-; -n)* BOT cucumber
gurren ['gʊrən] *v/i (ge-, h)* ZO coo
Gurt [gʊrt] *m (-[e]s; -e)* belt (*a.* MOT *and* AVIAT); strap
Gürtel ['gʏrtəl] *m (-s; -)* belt
Gürtelreifen *m* MOT radial (tire, *Br* tyre)
GUS [gʊs, geːˀuː'ˀɛs] ABBR *of* ***Gemeinschaft Unabhängiger Staaten*** CIS, Commonwealth of Independent States
Guss [gʊs] *m (-es; Güsse* ['gʏsə]) downpour; TECH casting; GASTR icing; *fig* ***aus e-m Guss*** of a piece
'**Gusseisen** *n* cast iron
'**gusseisern** *adj* cast-iron
gut [guːt] **1.** *adj* good; fine; ***ganz gut*** not bad; ***also gut!*** all right (then)!; ***schon gut!*** never mind!; (***wieder***) ***gut werden*** come right (again), be all right; ***gute Reise!*** have a nice trip!; ***sei bitte so gut und …*** would you be so good as to *or* good enough to …; ***in et. gut sein*** be good at (doing) s.th.; **2.** *adv* well; *look, taste etc* good; ***du hast es gut*** you are lucky; ***es ist gut möglich*** it may well be; ***es gefällt mir gut*** I (do) like it; ***gut gebaut*** well-built; ***gut gelaunt*** in a good mood; ***gut gemacht!*** well done!; ***mach's gut!*** take care (of yourself)!; ***gut gehen*** go (off) well, work out well *or* all right; ***wenn alles gut geht*** if nothing goes wrong; ***mir geht es gut*** I'm (doing) well
Gut *n (-[e]s; Güter* ['gyːtɐ]) estate; *pl* goods
'**Gutachten** *n (-s; -)* (expert) opinion; certificate
Gutachter ['guːtˀaxtɐ] *m (-s; -)* expert
'**gutartig** *adj* good-natured; MED benign
Gutdünken ['guːtdʏŋkən] *n*: ***nach Gutdünken*** at one's discretion
Gute ['guːtə] *n (-n; no pl)* good; ***Gutes tun*** do good; ***alles Gute!*** all the best!, good luck!
Güte ['gyːtə] *f (-; no pl)* goodness, kindness; ECON quality; F ***meine Güte!*** good gracious!
Güterbahnhof ['gyːtɐ-] *m* freight depot, *Br* goods station
Gütergemeinschaft *f* JUR community of property
Gütertrennung *f* JUR separation of property
Güterverkehr *m* freight (*Br* goods) traffic
Güterwagen *m* freight car, *Br* goods wag(g)on
Güterzug *m* freight (*Br* goods) train
'**gutgläubig** *adj* credulous
'**Guthaben** *n (-s; -)* ECON credit (balance)
'**gutheißen** *v/t (irr,* ***heißen****, sep, -ge-, h)* approve (of)
'**gutherzig** *adj* kind(-hearted)
gütig ['gyːtɪç] *adj* good, kind(ly)
gütlich ['gyːtlɪç] *adv*: ***sich gütlich einigen*** come to an amicable settlement
'**gutmachen** *v/t (sep, -ge-, h)* make up for, repay
'**gutmütig** [-myːtɪç] *adj* good-natured
'**Gutmütigkeit** *f (-; no pl)* good nature
'**Gutsbesitzer** *m,* '**Gutsbesitzerin** *f (-; -nen)* estate owner
'**Gutschein** *m* coupon, *esp Br* voucher
'**gutschreiben** *v/t (irr,* ***schreiben****, sep, -ge-, h)* ***j-m et. gutschreiben*** credit s.th. to s.o.'s account
'**Gutschrift** *f* credit
'**Gutshaus** *n* manor (house)
'**Gutshof** *m* estate, manor
'**gutstehen** *v/refl (irr,* ***stehen****, sep, -ge-, h)*: ***sich gutstehen*** be well off; F ***sich gut mit j-m stehen*** → ***stehen***

G

'Gutsverwalter *m* steward, manager
'gutwillig *adj* willing
Gymnasium [gʏm'naːzjʊm] *n* (*-s; -ien*) high school, *Br appr* grammar school
Gymnastik [gʏm'nastɪk] *f* (*-; no pl*) exercises, gymnastics
gym'nastisch *adj*: ***gymnastische Übungen*** physical exercises
Gynäkologe [gynɛko'loːgə] *m* (*-n; -n*), **Gynäko'login** *f* (*-; -nen*) MED gyn(a)ecologist

Haar [haːɐ] *n* (*-[e]s; -e* ['haːrə]) hair; ***sich die Haare kämmen*** (***schneiden lassen***) comb one's hair (have one's hair cut); ***sich aufs Haar gleichen*** look absolutely identical; ***um ein Haar*** by a hair's breadth
'Haarausfall *m* loss of hair
'Haarbürste *f* hairbrush
haaren ['haːrən] *v/i and v/refl* (*ge-, h*) ZO lose its hair; *fur*: shed hairs
'Haaresbreite *f*: ***um Haaresbreite*** by a hair's breadth
'haarfein *adj* (as) fine as a hair
'Haarfestiger *m* (*-s; -*) setting lotion
'Haargefäß *n* ANAT capillary (vessel)
'haargenau F *adv* precisely; (***stimmt***) ***haargenau!*** dead right!
haarig ['haːrɪç] *adj* hairy
'haarklein F *adv* to the last detail
'Haarklemme *f* bobby pin, *Br* hair clip
Haarnadel *f* hairpin
Haarnadelkurve *f* hairpin bend
Haarnetz *n* hair-net
'haarscharf F *adv* by a hair's breadth
'Haarschnitt *m* haircut
Haarspalterei *f* (*-; no pl*) hair-splitting
Haarspange *f* barrette, *Br* (hair) slide
Haarspray *m, n* hairspray
'haarsträubend *adj* hair-raising
'Haarteil *n* hairpiece
Haartrockner *m* hair dryer
Haarwäsche *f*, **Haarwaschmittel** *n* shampoo
Haarwasser *n* hair tonic
Haarwuchs *m*: ***starken Haarwuchs haben*** have a lot of hair
Haarwuchsmittel *n* hair restorer
haben ['haːbən] *v/t* (*irr, ge-, h*) have (got); ***Hunger haben*** be hungry; ***Durst haben*** be thirsty; ***Ferien*** (***Urlaub***) ***haben*** be on vacation (*Br* holiday); ***er hat Geburtstag*** it's his birthday; ***welche Farbe hat …?*** what colo(u)r is …?; ***zu haben sein*** be available; F ***sich haben*** make a fuss; F ***was hast du?*** what's the matter with you?; F ***da haben wir's!*** there we are!; → ***Datum***
'Haben *n* (*-s; no pl*) ECON credit
Habgier ['haːp-] *f* greed(iness)
'habgierig *adj* greedy
Habicht ['haːbɪçt] *m* (*-s; -e*) ZO hawk
'Habseligkeiten *pl* belongings
Hacke ['hakə] *f* (*-; -n*) AGR hoe; (pick-) axe; ANAT heel
'hacken *v/t* (*ge-, h*) chop; AGR hoe; ZO peck
'Hackentrick *m soccer*: backheeler
Hacker ['hakɐ] *m* (*-s; -*) EDP hacker
'Hackfleisch *n* ground (*Br* minced) meat
Hackordnung *f* ZO pecking order
Hafen ['haːfən] *m* (*-s; Häfen* ['hɛːfən]) harbo(u)r, port
Hafenarbeiter *m* docker, longshoreman
Hafenstadt *f* (sea)port
Hafer ['haːfɐ] *m* (*-s; -*) BOT oats
Haferbrei *m* oatmeal, *Br* porridge
Haferflocken *pl* (rolled) oats
Haferschleim *m* gruel
Haft [haft] *f* (*-; no pl*) JUR confinement, imprisonment; ***in Haft*** under arrest
'haftbar *adj* responsible, JUR liable
'Haftbefehl *m* JUR warrant of arrest
'haften *v/i* (*ge-, h*) stick, adhere (***an*** *dat* to); ***haften für*** JUR answer for, be liable for
Häftling ['hɛftlɪŋ] *m* (*-s; -e*) prisoner, convict
'Haftpflicht *f* JUR liability
Haftpflichtversicherung *f* liability insurance; MOT third party insurance
'Haftung *f* (*-; -en*) responsibility, JUR liability; ***mit beschränkter Haftung*** limited
Hagel ['haːgəl] *m* (*-s; no pl*) hail, *fig a.* shower, volley
'Hagelkorn *n* hailstone

'hageln *v/i (ge-, h)* hail *(a. fig)*
'Hagelschauer *m* hail shower
hager ['ha:gɐ] *adj* lean, gaunt, haggard
Hahn [ha:n] *m (-[e]s; Hähne* ['hɛ:nə]) ZO cock, rooster; TECH (water) tap, faucet
Hähnchen ['hɛ:nçən] *n (-s; -)* ZO chicken
'Hahnenkamm *m* ZO cockscomb
Hai [hai] *m (-[e]s; -e),* **Haifisch** *m* ZO shark
häkeln ['hɛ:kəln] *v/t and v/i (ge-, h)* crochet
Haken ['ha:kən] *m (-s; -)* hook *(a. boxing),* peg; check, *Br* tick; F snag, catch
'Hakenkreuz *n* swastika
halb [halp] *adj and adv* half; ***e-e halbe Stunde*** half an hour; ***ein halbes Pfund*** half a pound; ***zum halben Preis*** at half-price; ***auf halbem Wege (entgegenkommen)*** (meet) halfway; ***halb so viel*** half as much; F ***(mit j-m) halbe-halbe machen*** go halves *or* fifty-fifty (with s.o.); ***halb gar*** GASTR underdone
'Halbbruder *m* half-brother
'Halbdunkel *n* semi-darkness
Halbe ['halbə] *f (-n; -n)* pint (of beer)
'halbfett *adj* GASTR medium-fat; PRINT semi-bold
'Halbfi‚nale *n* SPORT semifinal
'Halbgott *m* demigod
'halbherzig *adj* half-hearted
halbieren [hal'bi:rən] *v/t (no -ge-, h)* halve; MATH bisect
'Halbinsel *f* peninsula
'Halbjahr *n* six months
'halbjährig [-jɛ:rɪç] *adj* six-month
'halbjährlich **1.** *adj* half-yearly; **2.** *adv* half-yearly, twice a year
'Halbkreis *m* semicircle
'Halbkugel *f* hemisphere
'halblaut **1.** *adj* low, subdued; **2.** *adv* in an undertone
'Halbleiter *m* ELECTR semiconductor
'halbmast *adv* (at) half-mast
'Halbmond *m* half-moon, crescent
Halbpensi‚on *f (-; no pl) esp Br* half board
Halbschlaf *m* doze
Halbschuh *m* (low) shoe
Halbschwester *f* half-sister
'halbtags *adv*: ***halbtags arbeiten*** work part-time
'Halbtagsarbeit *f (-; no pl)* part-time job
'Halbtagskraft *f* part-time worker, F part-timer
'halbwegs [-ve:ks] *adv* reasonably
'Halbwüchsige [-vy:ksɪgə] *m, f (-n; -n)* adolescent
'Halbzeit *f* SPORT half (time)
Halbzeitstand *m* SPORT half-time score
Halde ['haldə] *f (-; -n)* slope; dump
half [half] *pret of* ***helfen***
Hälfte ['hɛlftə] *f (-; -n)* half; ***die Hälfte von*** half of
Halfter ['halftɐ] **1.** *m, n (-s; -)* halter; **2.** *n (-s; -), f (-; -n)* holster
Halle ['halə] *f (-; -n)* hall; lounge; ***in der Halle*** SPORT *etc* indoors
'hallen *v/i (ge-, h)* resound, reverberate
'Hallenbad *n* indoor swimming pool
'Hallensport *m* indoor sports
Halm [halm] *m (-[e]s; -e)* BOT blade; ha(u)lm, stalk; straw
Hals [hals] *m (-es; Hälse* ['hɛlzə]) ANAT neck; throat; ***Hals über Kopf*** helter-skelter; F ***sich vom Hals schaffen*** get rid of; F ***es hängt mir zum Hals(e) (he)raus*** I'm fed up with it; *fig* ***bis zum Hals*** up to one's neck
Halsband *n (-[e]s; -bänder)* necklace; collar
Halsentzündung *f* MED sore throat
Halskette *f* necklace
Halsschmerzen *pl*: ***Halsschmerzen haben*** have a sore throat
'halsstarrig [-ʃtarɪç] *adj* stubborn, obstinate
'Halstuch *n* neckerchief; scarf
Halt *m (-[e]s; -e, -s)* a) *(no pl)* hold; support *(a. fig)*; *fig* stability, b) stop
halt [halt] *int* stop!, MIL halt!
'haltbar *adj* durable; GASTR not perishable; *fig* tenable; ***haltbar bis ...*** best before ...
'Haltbarkeitsdatum *n* best-by (*or* best-before) date
halten ['haltən] *(irr, ge-, h)* **1.** *v/t* hold; keep *(animal, promise etc)*; make *(speech)*; give *(lecture)*; take (*Br a.* in) *a paper etc*; SPORT save; ***halten für*** regard as; (mis)take for; ***viel (wenig) halten von*** think highly (little) of; ***sich halten*** last; GASTR keep; ***sich gut halten*** *fig* do well; ***sich halten an*** *(acc)* keep to; **2.** *v/i* hold, last; stop, halt; *ice*: bear; *rope etc*: hold; ***halten zu*** stand by, F stick to
Halter(in) ['hal-tɐ(-tərin)] *(-s; -/-; -nen)* owner; TECH holder
'Haltestelle *f* stop, RAIL *a.* station
'Halteverbot *n* MOT no stopping (area)
'haltlos *adj* unsteady; *fig* baseless
'haltmachen *v/i (sep, -ge-, h)* stop; *fig* ***vor nichts haltmachen*** stop at nothing
'Haltung *f (-; -en)* posture; *fig* attitude (***zu*** towards)
hämisch ['hɛ:mɪʃ] *adj* malicious, sneering
Hammel ['haməl] *m (-s; -)* ZO wether
'Hammelfleisch *n* GASTR mutton
Hammer ['hamɐ] *m (-s; Hämmer* ['hɛmɐ]) hammer *(a.* SPORT)
hämmern ['hɛmɐn] *v/t and v/i (ge-, h)*

hammer
Hämorrhoiden, **Hämorriden** [hɛmɔro'iːdən] *pl* MED h(a)emorrhoids, F *Br* piles
Hampelmann ['hampəl-] *m* jumping jack
Hamster ['hamstɐ] *m* (*-s*; -) ZO hamster
'**hamstern** *v/t and v/i* (*ge-*, *h*) hoard
Hand [hant] *f* (-; *Hände* ['hɛndə]) hand; ***von Hand, mit der Hand*** by hand; ***an Hand von*** (*or gen*) by means of; ***zur Hand*** at hand; ***aus erster*** (***zweiter***) ***Hand*** first-hand (second-hand); ***an die Hand nehmen*** take by the hand; ***sich die Hand geben*** shake hands; ***aus der Hand legen*** lay aside; ***Hand breit*** → ***handbreit***; ***Hand voll*** → ***handvoll***; ***Hände hoch*** (***weg***)***!*** hands up (off)!
Handarbeit *f* a) (*no pl*) manual labo(u)r, b) needlework; ***es ist Handarbeit*** it is handmade
Handball *m* SPORT (European) handball
Handbetrieb *m* TECH manual operation
Handbreit *f* (-; -) hand's breadth
Handbremse *f* MOT handbrake
Handbuch *n* manual, handbook
Händedruck ['hɛndə-] *m* (*-[e]s*; *-drücke*) handshake
Handel ['handəl] *m* (*-s*; *no pl*) commerce, business; trade; market; transaction, deal, bargain; ***Handel treiben*** ECON trade (***mit*** with *s.o.*)
'**handeln** *v/i* (*ge-*, *h*) act, take action; bargain (***um*** for), haggle (over); ***mit j-m handeln*** ECON trade with s.o.; ***handeln mit*** deal in; ***handeln von*** deal with, be about; ***es handelt sich um*** it concerns, it is about; it is a matter of
'**Handelsabkommen** *n* trade agreement
Handelsbank *f* (-; *-banken*) commercial bank
Handelsbi,lanz *f* balance of trade
'**handelseinig** *adj*: ***handelseinig werden*** come to terms
'**Handelsgesellschaft** *f* (trading) company
Handelskammer *f* chamber of commerce
Handelsschiff *n* merchant ship
Handelsschule *f* commercial school
Handelsvertreter *m* (traveling) salesman, *Br* sales representative
Handelsware *f* commodity, merchandise
'**Handfeger** [-feːgɐ] *m* (*-s*; -) handbrush
Handfertigkeit *f* manual skill
'**handfest** *adj* solid
'**Handfläche** *f* ANAT palm
'**handgearbeitet** *adj* handmade
'**Handgelenk** *n* ANAT wrist
Handgepäck *n* hand baggage (*Br* luggage)
Handgra,nate *f* MIL hand grenade
'**handgreiflich** [-graiflɪç] *adj*: ***handgreiflich werden*** turn violent, get tough
'**handhaben** *v/t* (*ge-*, *h*) handle, manage; TECH operate
Händler ['hɛndlɐ] *m* (*-s*; -), '**Händlerin** *f* (-; *-nen*) dealer, trader
'**handlich** *adj* handy, manageable
Handlung ['handlʊŋ] *f* (-; *-en*) act, action; *film etc*: story, plot
'**Handlungsreisende** *m* sales representative, travel(l)ing salesman
Handlungsweise *f* conduct, behavio(u)r
'**Handrücken** *m* ANAT back of the hand
Handschellen *pl* handcuffs; ***j-m Handschellen anlegen*** handcuff s.o.
Handschlag *m* handshake
Handschrift *f* hand(writing)
'**handschriftlich** *adj* handwritten
'**Handschuh** *m* glove
Handspiel *n soccer*: hand ball
Handstand *m* handstand
Handtasche *f* handbag, purse
Handtuch *n* towel
Handvoll *f* handful
Handwagen *m* handcart
Handwerk *n* craft, trade
'**Handwerker** [-vɛrkɐ] *m* (*-s*; -) craftsman; workman
'**Handwerkszeug** *n* (kit of) tools
'**Handwurzel** *f* ANAT wrist
Handy ['hɛndi] *n* (*-s*; *-s*) mobile (phone), cellular phone
Hanf [hanf] *m* (*-es*; *no pl*) BOT hemp; cannabis
Hang [haŋ] *m* (*-[e]s*; *Hänge* ['hɛŋə]) a) slope, b) (*no pl*) *fig* inclination (***zu*** for), tendency (towards)
Hängebrücke ['hɛŋə-] *f* suspension bridge
Hängelampe *f* hanging lamp
Hängematte *f* hammock
hängen ['hɛŋən] **1.** *v/i* (*irr*, *ge-*, *h*) hang (***an*** *dat* on *the wall etc*; from *the ceiling etc*); ***hängen bleiben*** get stuck (*a. fig*); ***hängen bleiben an*** (*dat*) get caught on; ***hängen an*** (*dat*) be fond of; be devoted to; ***alles, woran ich hänge*** everything that is dear to me; **2.** *v/t* (*ge-*, *h*) hang (***an*** *acc* on)
hängenbleiben *v/i* (*irr*, ***bleiben***, *sep*, *-ge-*, *sein*) *fig* get stuck; → ***hängen***
hänseln ['hɛnzəln] *v/t* (*ge-*, *h*) tease (***wegen*** about)
Hanswurst [hans'vʊrst] *m* (*-[e]s*; *-e*) fool, clown
Hantel ['hantəl] *f* (-; *-n*) dumbbell
hantieren [han'tiːrən] *v/i* (*no -ge-*, *h*) ***hantieren mit*** handle; ***hantieren an*** (*dat*) fiddle about with

Happen ['hapən] *m* (-*s*; -) morsel, bite; snack

Hardware ['hɑːdwɛə] *f* (-; -*s*) EDP hardware

Harfe ['harfə] *f* (-; -*n*) MUS harp

Harfenist [harfə'nɪst] *m* (-*en*; -*en*), **Harfe'nistin** *f* (-; -*nen*) MUS harpist

Harke ['harkə] *f* (-; -*n*), **'harken** *v/t* (*ge-*, *h*) rake

harmlos ['harmloːs] *adj* harmless

Harmonie [harmo'niː] *f* (-; -*n*) harmony (*a.* MUS)

harmo'nieren *v/i* (*no -ge-*, *h*) harmonize (***mit*** with)

harmonisch [har'moːnɪʃ] *adj* harmonious

Harn [harn] *m* (-[*e*]*s*; -*e*) MED urine

'Harnblase *f* ANAT (urinary) bladder

'Harnröhre *f* ANAT urethra

Harpune [har'puːnə] *f* (-; -*n*) harpoon

harpunieren [harpu'niːrən] *v/t* (*no -ge-*, *h*) harpoon

hart [hart] **1.** *adj* hard, F *a.* tough; SPORT rough; severe; ***hart gekocht*** hard-boiled; **2.** *adv* hard

Härte ['hɛrtə] *f* (-; -*n*) hardness; toughness; roughness; severity; *esp* JUR hardship

Härtefall *m* case of hardship

'härten *v/t* (*ge-*, *h*) harden

'Hartfaserplatte *f* hardboard

'Hartgeld *n* coin(s)

'hartgesotten [-gəzɔtən] *adj* hard-boiled

'hartherzig *adj* hard-hearted

'hartnäckig [-nɛkɪç] *adj* stubborn, obstinate; persistent

Harz [haːɐts] *n* (-*es*; -*e*) resin; rosin

'harzig *adj* resinous

Hasch [haʃ] F *n* (-*s*; *no pl*) hash

'haschen F *v/i* (*ge-*, *h*) smoke hash

Haschisch ['haʃɪʃ] *n* (-[*s*]; *no pl*) hashish

Hase ['haːzə] *m* (-*n*; -*n*) ZO hare

Haselmaus ['haːzəl-] *f* ZO dormouse

'Haselnuss *f* BOT hazelnut

'Hasenscharte *f* MED harelip

Hass [has] *m* (-*es*; *no pl*) hatred, hate (***auf*** *acc*, ***gegen*** of, for)

hassen ['hasən] *v/t* (*ge-*, *h*) hate

hässlich ['hɛslɪç] *adj* ugly, *fig a.* nasty

Hast [hast] *f* (-; *no pl*) hurry, haste; rush

hasten ['hastən] *v/i* (*ge-*, *sein*) hurry, hasten, rush

'hastig *adj* hasty, hurried

hätscheln ['hɛːtʃəln] *v/t* (*ge-*, *h*) fondle; *contp* pamper

hatte ['hatə] *pret of* ***haben***

Haube ['haubə] *f* (-; -*n*) bonnet (*a. Br* MOT); cap; ZO crest; MOT hood

Hauch [haux] *m* (-[*e*]*s*; -*e*) breath; whiff; *fig* touch, trace

hauchen ['hauxən] *v/t* (*ge-*, *h*) breathe

hauen F *v/t* ([*irr*,] *ge-*, *h*) hit, beat, thrash; TECH hew; ***sich hauen*** (have a) fight

Haufen ['haufən] *m* (-*s*; -) heap, pile (*both a.* F); F crowd

häufen ['hɔʏfən] *v/t* (*ge-*, *h*) heap (up), pile (up); ***sich häufen*** *fig* become more frequent, be on the increase

häufig ['hɔʏfɪç] **1.** *adj* frequent; **2.** *adv* frequently, often

Haupt [haupt] *n* (-[*e*]*s*; *Häupter* ['hɔʏptɐ]) head, *fig a.* leader

Hauptbahnhof *m* main *or* central station

Hauptbeschäftigung *f* chief occupation

Hauptbestandteil *m* chief ingredient

Hauptdarsteller(in) leading actor (actress), lead

Häuptelsa'lat ['hɔʏptəl-] *Austrian m* BOT lettuce

'Hauptfach *n* UNIV major, *Br* main subject

Hauptfilm *m* feature (film)

Hauptgericht *n* GASTR main course

Hauptgewinn *m* first prize

Hauptgrund *m* main reason

Hauptleitung *f* TECH main

Häuptling ['hɔʏptlɪŋ] *m* (-*s*; -*e*) chief

'Hauptmann *m* (-[*e*]*s*; -*leute*) MIL captain

Hauptme'nü *n* EDP main menu

Hauptmerkmal *n* chief characteristic

Hauptper'son F *f* center (*Br* centre) of attention

Hauptquar'tier *n* headquarters

Hauptrolle *f* THEA *etc* lead(ing part)

'Hauptsache *f* main thing *or* point

'hauptsächlich *adj* main, chief, principal

'Hauptsatz *m* LING main clause

Hauptsendezeit *f* TV prime time, *Br* peak time (*or* viewing hours)

Hauptspeicher *m* EDP main memory

Hauptstadt *f* capital

Hauptstraße *f* main street; main road

Hauptverkehrsstraße *f* arterial road

Hauptverkehrszeit *f* rush *or* peak hour(s)

Hauptversammlung *f* general meeting

Hauptwohnsitz *m* main place of residence

Hauptwort *n* (-[*e*]*s*; -*wörter*) LING noun

Haus [haus] *n* (-*es*; *Häuser* ['hɔʏzɐ]) house; building; ***zu Hause*** at home, in; ***nach Hause kommen*** (***bringen***) come *or* get (take) home

Hausangestellte *m*, *f* domestic (servant)

Hausapo'theke *f* medicine cabinet

Hausarbeit *f* housework

Hausarzt *m*, **Hausärztin** *f* family doctor

Hausaufgaben *pl* PED homework, assignment; ***s-e Hausaufgabenn machen*** *a. fig* do one's homework

Hausbar *f* cocktail cabinet

Hausbesetzer *m* (-*s*; -) squatter

H

Hausbesetzung *f* squatting
Hausbesitzer *m* house owner
Hauseinweihung *f* house-warming (party)
hausen ['hauzən] *v/i* (*ge-, h*) live; *fig* play havoc
'**Hausflur** *m* (entrance) hall, hallway
'**Hausfrau** *f* housewife
'**Hausfriedensbruch** *m* JUR trespass
'**hausgemacht** *adj* homemade
'**Haushalt** *m* (-[*e*]*s*; -*e*) household; PARL budget; ***(j-m) den Haushalt führen*** keep house (for s.o.)
'**Haushälterin** [-hɛltərɪn] *f* (-; -*nen*) housekeeper
'**Haushaltsgeld** *n* housekeeping money
Haushaltsplan *m* PARL budget
Haushaltswaren *pl* household articles
'**Hausherr** *m* head of the household; host
Hausherrin *f* lady of the house; hostess
'**haushoch** *adj* huge; crushing (*defeat etc*)
hausieren [hau'ziːrən] *v/i* (*no -ge-, h*) peddle, hawk (***mit et.*** s.th.) (*a. fig*)
Hau'sierer *m* (-*s*; -) pedlar, hawker
häuslich ['hɔʏslɪç] *adj* domestic; home-loving
'**Hausmädchen** *n* (house)maid
Hausmann *m* house husband
Hausmannskost *f* plain fare
Hausmeister *m* caretaker, janitor
Hausmittel *n* household remedy
Hausordnung *f* house rules
Hausrat *m* (-[*e*]*s*; *no pl*) household effects
Hausschlüssel *m* front-door key
Hausschuh *m* slipper
Hausse ['hoːs(ə)] *f* (-; -*n*) ECON rise, boom
'**Haussuchung** *f* (-; -*en*) house search
Haustier *n* domestic animal
Haustür *f* front door
Hausverwaltung *f* property management
Hauswirt *m* landlord
Hauswirtin *f* landlady
Hauswirtschaft *f* (-; *no pl*) housekeeping
Hauswirtschaftslehre *f* domestic science, home economics
Hauswirtschaftsschule *f* domestic science (*or* home economics) school
Haut [haut] *f* (-; *Häute* ['hɔʏtə]) skin; complexion; ***bis auf die Haut durchnässt*** soaked to the skin
Hautabschürfung *f* MED abrasion
Hautarzt *m*, **Hautärztin** *f* dermatologist
Hautausschlag *m* MED rash
'**hauteng** *adj* skin-tight
'**Hautfarbe** *f* colo(u)r of the skin; complexion
Hautkrankheit *f* skin disease
Hautpflege *f* skin care
Hautschere *f* cuticle scissors
Hbf. ABBR *of* ***Hauptbahnhof*** cent. sta., central station
H-Bombe ['haːbɔmbə] *f* MIL H-bomb
Hebamme ['heːpˀamə] *f* (-; -*n*) midwife
Hebebühne ['heːbə-] *f* MOT car hoist
Hebel ['heːbəl] *m* (-*s*; -) TECH lever
heben ['heːbən] *v/t* (*irr, ge-, h*) lift, raise (*a. fig*); heave; hoist; *fig a.* improve; ***sich heben*** rise, go up
Hecht [hɛçt] *m* (-[*e*]*s*; -*e*) ZO pike
'**hechten** *v/i* (*ge-, sein*) dive (***nach*** for); SPORT do a long-fly
Heck [hɛk] *n* (-[*e*]*s*; -*e*) MAR stern; AVIAT tail; MOT rear
Hecke ['hɛkə] *f* (-; -*n*) BOT hedge
'**Heckenrose** *f* BOT dogrose
'**Heckenschütze** *m* MIL sniper
'**Heckscheibe** *f* MOT rear window
Heer [heːɐ] *n* (-[*e*]*s*; -*e*) MIL army, *fig a.* host
Hefe ['heːfə] *f* (-; -*n*) yeast
Heft [hɛft] *n* (-[*e*]*s*; -*e*) notebook; exercise book; booklet; issue, number
heften ['hɛftən] *v/t* (*ge-, h*) fix, fasten, attach (***an*** *acc* to); pin (to); tack, baste; stitch
Hefter ['hɛftɐ] *m* (-*s*; -) stapler; file
heftig ['hɛftɪç] *adj* violent, fierce; heavy
'**Heftklammer** *f* staple
'**Heftpflaster** *n* bandage, Band Aid®, *Br* (adhesive *or* sticking) plaster
Hehl [heːl] *n*: ***kein Hehl aus et. machen*** make no secret of s.th.
Hehler ['heːlɐ] *m* (-*s*; -) JUR receiver of stolen goods, *sl* fence
Hehlerei [heːlə'rai] *f* (-; -*en*) JUR receiving stolen goods
Heide[1] ['haidə] *m* (-*n*; -*n*) REL heathen
'**Heide**[2] *f* (-; -*n*) heath(land)
'**Heidekraut** *n* (-[*e*]*s*; *no pl*) BOT heather, heath
'**Heidenangst** F *f*: ***e-e Heidenangst haben*** be scared stiff
Heidengeld F *n*: ***ein Heidengeld*** a fortune
Heidenlärm F *m*: ***ein Heidenlärm*** a hell of a noise
Heidenspaß F *m*: ***e-n Heidenspaß haben*** have a ball
'**Heidentum** *n* (-*s*; *no pl*) REL heathenism
Heidin ['haidɪn] *f* (-; -*nen*), '**heidnisch** ['haidnɪʃ] *adj* REL heathen
heikel ['haikəl] *adj* delicate, tricky; tender; F fussy
heil [hail] *adj* safe, unhurt; undamaged, whole, intact
Heil *n* (-*s*; *no pl*) REL grace; ***sein Heil versuchen*** try one's luck
Heiland ['hailant] *m* (-[*e*]*s*; *no pl*) REL Sav-

io(u)r, Redeemer
'Heilanstalt *f* sanatorium, sanitarium; mental home
'Heilbad *n* health resort, spa
'heilbar *adj* curable
heilen ['hailən] **1.** *v/t* (*ge-*, *h*) cure; **2.** *v/i* (*ge-*, *sein*) heal (up)
'Heilgym,nastik *f* physiotherapy
heilig ['hailıç] *adj* REL holy; sacred (*a. fig*)
Heilig'abend *m* Christmas Eve
Heilige ['hailıgə] *m*, *f* (*-n*; *-n*) REL saint
heiligen ['hailıgən] *v/t* (*ge-*, *h*) REL sanctify (*a. fig*), hallow
'heiligsprechen *v/t* (*irr*, ***sprechen***, *sep*, *-ge-*, *h*) canonize
'Heiligtum *n* (*-s*; *-tümer* [-ty:mɐ]) REL sanctuary, shrine
'Heilkraft *f* healing *or* curative power
'heilkräftig *adj* curative
'Heilkraut *n* BOT medicinal herb
'heillos *fig adj* utter, hopeless
'Heilmittel *n* remedy, cure (*both a. fig*)
Heilpraktiker(in) [-praktikɐ (-kərın)] (*-s*; *-/-*; *-nen*) nonmedical practitioner
Heilquelle *f* (medicinal) mineral spring
'heilsam *fig adj* salutary
'Heilsar,mee *f* Salvation Army
'Heilung *f* (*-*; *-en*) cure; healing
heim [haim] *adv* home
Heim *n* (*-[e]s*; *-e*) a) (*no pl*) home, b) hostel
Heim... *in cpds ...computer*, *...mannschaft*, *...sieg*, *...spiel etc*: home
Heimat ['haima:t] *f* (*-*; *no pl*) home; home country; home town; ***in der (meiner) Heimat*** at home
'heimatlos *adj* homeless
'Heimatstadt *f* home town
'Heimatvertriebene *m*, *f* expellee
heimisch ['haimıʃ] *adj* home, domestic; BOT, ZO *etc* native; *fig* homelike, hom(e)y; ***sich heimisch fühlen*** feel at home
'Heimkehr [-ke:ɐ] *f* (*-*; *no pl*) return (home)
'heimkehren *v/i* (*sep*, *-ge-*, *sein*) return home, come back
'heimlich *adj* secret
'Heimlichkeit *f* (*-*; *-en*) a) (*no pl*) secrecy, b) *pl* secrets
'Heimreise *f* journey home
'heimsuchen *v/t* (*sep*, *-ge-*, *h*) strike
'heimtückisch *adj* insidious (*a.* MED); treacherous
'heimwärts [-vɛrts] *adv* homeward(s)
'Heimweg *m* way home
'Heimweh *n* (*-s*; *no pl*) homesickness; ***Heimweh haben*** be homesick
'Heimwerker [-vɛrkɐ] *m* (*-s*; *-*) do-it-yourselfer
Heirat ['haira:t] *f* (*-*; *-en*) marriage
heiraten ['haira:tən] *v/t and v/i* (*ge-*, *h*) marry, get married (to)
'Heiratsantrag *m* proposal (of marriage); ***j-m e-n Heiratsantrag machen*** propose to s.o.
Heiratsschwindler *m* marriage impostor
Heiratsvermittler(in) (*-s*; *-/-*; *-nen*) marriage broker
Heiratsvermittlung *f* marriage bureau
heiser ['haizɐ] *adj* hoarse, husky
'Heiserkeit *f* (*-*; *no pl*) hoarseness, huskiness
heiß [hais] *adj* hot, *fig a.* passionate, ardent; ***mir ist heiß*** I am *or* feel hot
heißen ['haisən] *v/i* (*irr*, *ge-*, *h*) be called; mean; ***wie heißen Sie?*** what's your name?; ***wie heißt das?*** what do you call this?; ***was heißt ... auf Englisch?*** what is ... in English?; ***es heißt im Text*** it says in the text; ***das heißt*** that is (ABBR ***d. h.*** i. e.)
heiter ['haitɐ] *adj* cheerful; humorous (*film etc*); METEOR fair; *fig* ***aus heiterem Himmel*** out of the blue
'Heiterkeit *f* (*-*; *no pl*) cheerfulness; amusement
heizbar ['haitsba:ɐ] *adj* heated
heizen ['haitsən] *v/t and v/i* (*ge-*, *h*) heat; ***mit Kohlen heizen*** burn coal
Heizer ['haitsɐ] *m* (*-s*; *-*) MAR, RAIL stoker
'Heizkessel *m* boiler
Heizkissen *n* electric cushion
Heizkörper *m* radiator
Heizkraftwerk *n* thermal power-station
Heizmateri,al *n* fuel
Heizöl *n* fuel oil
'Heizung *f* (*-*; *-en*) heating
Held [hɛlt] *m* (*-en*; *-en* ['hɛldən]) hero
heldenhaft ['hɛldənhaft] *adj* heroic
'Heldentat *f* heroic deed
'Heldentum *n* (*-s*; *no pl*) heroism
Heldin ['hɛldın] *f* (*-*; *-nen*) heroine
helfen ['hɛlfən] *v/i* (*irr*, *ge-*, *h*) help, aid; assist; ***j-m bei et. helfen*** help s.o. with *or* in (doing) s.th.; ***helfen gegen*** MED *etc* be good for; ***er weiß sich zu helfen*** he can manage; ***es hilft nichts*** it's no use
Helfer ['hɛlfɐ] *m* (*-s*; *-*), **'Helferin** *f* (*-*; *-nen*) helper, assistant
'Helfershelfer *contp m* accomplice
hell [hɛl] *adj* bright (*light*, *flame etc*); light (*color etc*); light-colo(u)red (*dress etc*); clear (*voice etc*); pale (*beer*); *fig* bright, clever; ***es wird schon hell*** it's getting light already
hellblau *adj* light blue
hellblond *adj* very fair
hellhörig *adj* quick of hearing; ARCH poorly soundproofed; ***hellhörig werden***

H

prick up one's ears
'Hellseher *m* (-*s*; -), **'Hellseherin** *f* (-; -*nen*) clairvoyant
Helm [hɛlm] *m* (-[*e*]*s*; -*e*) helmet
Hemd [hɛmt] *n* (-[*e*]*s*; -*en* ['hɛmdən]) shirt; vest
Hemdbluse *f* shirt
Hemdblusenkleid *n* shirtwaist, *Br* shirt-waister
Hemisphäre [hemi'sfɛːrə] *f* (-; -*n*) hemisphere
hemmen ['hɛmən] *v/t* (*ge-*, *h*) check, stop; hamper
'Hemmung *f* (-; -*en*) PSYCH inhibition; scruple
'hemmungslos *adj* unrestrained; unscrupulous
Hengst [hɛŋst] *m* (-[*e*]*s*; -*e*) ZO stallion
Henkel ['hɛŋkəl] *m* (-*s*; -) handle
Henker ['hɛŋkɐ] *m* (-*s*; -) hangman, executioner
Henne ['hɛnə] *f* (-; -*n*) ZO hen
her [heːɐ] *adv* here; ***das ist lange her*** that was a long time ago
herab [hɛ'rap] *adv* down
herablassen *fig v/refl* (*irr*, ***lassen***, *sep*, *-ge-*, *h*) condescend
herablassend *adj* condescending
herabsehen *fig v/i* (*irr*, ***sehen***, *sep*, *-ge-*, *h*) ***herabsehen auf*** (*acc*) look down upon
herabsetzen *v/t* (*sep*, *-ge-*, *h*) reduce; *fig* disparage
heran [hɛ'ran] *adv* close, near; ***heran an*** (*acc*) up *or* near to
herangehen *v/i* (*irr*, ***gehen***, *sep*, *-ge-*, *sein*) ***herangehen an*** (*acc*) walk up to; *fig* set about *a task etc*
herankommen *v/i* (*irr*, ***kommen***, *sep*, *-ge-*, *sein*) come near (*a. fig*)
heranwachsen *v/i* (*irr*, ***wachsen***, *sep*, *-ge-*, *sein*) grow (up) (***zu*** into)
He'ranwachsende *m*, *f* (-*n*; -*n*) adolescent
he'ranwinken *v/t* (*sep*, *-ge-*, *h*) hail (*taxi etc*)
herauf [hɛ'rauf] *adv* up (here); upstairs
heraufbeschwören *v/t* (*irr*, ***schwören***, *sep*, *no -ge-*, *h*) call up; bring on, provoke
heraus [hɛ'raus] *adv* out; *fig* ***aus*** (*dat*) ... ***heraus*** out of ...; ***zum Fenster heraus*** out of the window; ***heraus mit der Sprache!*** speak out!, out with it!
herausbekommen *v/t* (*irr*, ***kommen***, *sep*, *no -ge-*, *h*) get out; get back (*change*); *fig* find out
herausbringen *v/t* (*irr*, ***bringen***, *sep*, *-ge-*, *h*) bring out; PRINT publish; THEA stage; *fig* find out
herausfinden (*irr*, ***finden***, *sep*, *-ge-*, *h*) **1.** *v/t* find; *fig* find out, discover; **2.** *v/i* find one's way out
He'rausforderer *m* (-*s*; -) challenger
he'rausfordern *v/t* (*sep*, *-ge-*, *h*) challenge; provoke, F ask for it
He'rausforderung *f* challenge; provocation
he'rausgeben *v/t* (*irr*, ***geben***, *sep*, *-ge-*, *h*) give back; give up; PRINT publish; issue; give change (***auf*** *acc* for)
He'rausgeber(in) [-geːbɐ (-bərɪn)] (-*s*; -/-; -*nen*) publisher
he'rauskommen *v/i* (*irr*, ***kommen***, *sep*, *-ge-*, *sein*) come out; *book*: be published; *stamps*: be issued; ***herauskommen aus*** get out of; F ***groß herauskommen*** be a great success
herausnehmen *v/t* (*irr*, ***nehmen***, *sep*, *-ge-*, *h*) take out; SPORT take *s.o.* off the team; *fig* ***sich et. herausnehmen*** take liberties, go too far
herausputzen *v/t and v/refl* (*sep*, *-ge-*, *h*) spruce (o.s.) up
herausreden *v/refl* (*sep*, *-ge-*, *h*) make excuses; talk one's way out
herausstellen *v/t* (*sep*, *-ge-*, *h*) put out; *fig* emphasize; ***sich herausstellen als*** turn out *or* prove to be
herausstrecken *v/t* (*sep*, *-ge-*, *h*) stick out
heraussuchen *v/t* (*sep*, *-ge-*, *h*) pick out; ***j-m et. heraussuchen*** find s.o. s.th.
herb [hɛrp] *adj* tart; dry (*wine etc*); *fig* harsh; bitter
her'bei *adv* up, over, here
herbeieilen *v/i* (*sep*, *-ge-*, *sein*) come running up
herbeiführen *fig v/t* (*sep*, *-ge-*, *h*) cause, bring about
Herberge ['hɛrbɛrgə] *f* (-; -*n*) inn; lodging; hostel
Herbst [hɛrpst] *m* (-[*e*]*s*; -*e*) fall, autumn
Herd [heːɐt] *m* (-[*e*]*s*; -*e*) ['heːɐdə]) cooker, stove; *fig* center, *Br* centre; MED focus, seat
Herde ['heːɐdə] *f* (-; -*n*) ZO herd (*a. fig contp*); flock (*of sheep, geese etc*)
herein [hɛ'rain] *adv* in (here); ***herein!*** come in!
hereinbrechen *v/i* (*irr*, ***brechen***, *sep*, *-ge-*, *sein*) *night*: fall; ***hereinbrechen über*** (*acc*) befall *s.o.*
hereinfallen F *v/i* (*irr*, ***fallen***, *sep*, *-ge-*, *sein*) be taken in (***auf*** *acc* by)
hereinlegen F *v/t* (*sep*, *-ge-*, *h*) take *s.o.* in
'herfallen *v/i* (*irr*, ***fallen***, *sep*, *-ge-*, *sein*) ***herfallen über*** (*acc*) attack (*a. fig*)
'Hergang *m*: ***j-m den Hergang schildern*** tell s.o. what happened

'hergeben *v/t* (*irr*, ***geben***, *sep*, *-ge-*, *h*) give up, part with; ***sich hergeben zu*** lend o.s. to

Hering ['he:rɪŋ] *m* (*-s*; *-e*) zo herring

'herkommen *v/i* (*irr*, ***kommen***, *sep*, *-ge-*, *sein*) come (here); ***herkommen von*** come from, *fig a.* be caused by

'herkömmlich [-kœmlɪç] *adj* conventional (*a.* MIL)

'Herkunft [-kʊnft] *f* (-; *no pl*) origin; birth, descent

heroisch [he'ro:ɪʃ] *adj* heroic

Herr [hɛr] *m* (*-n*; *-en*) gentleman; master; REL *the* Lord; ***Herr Brown*** Mr Brown; ***Herr der Lage*** master of the situation

'Herrenbekleidung *f* menswear

Herrendoppel *n tennis*: men's doubles

Herreneinzel *n tennis*: men's singles

'herrenlos *adj* abandoned; stray (*dog*)

'Herrentoi,lette *f* men's restroom (*Br* toilet *or* lavatory)

'herrichten *v/t* (*sep*, *-ge-*, *h*) get ready, F fix

herrisch ['hɛrɪʃ] *adj* imperious

herrlich ['hɛrlɪç] *adj* marvel(l)ous, wonderful, F fantastic

'Herrlichkeit *f* (-; *-en*) glory

'Herrschaft *f* (-; *no pl*) rule, power, control (*a. fig*) (***über*** *acc* over); ***die Herrschaft verlieren über*** (*acc*) lose control of

herrschen ['hɛrʃən] *v/i* (*ge-*, *h*) rule; ***es herrschte ...*** there was ...

Herrscher(in) ['hɛrʃɐ (-ʃərɪn)] (*-s*; *-/-*; *-nen*) ruler; sovereign, monarch

'herrschsüchtig *adj* domineering, F bossy

'herrühren *v/i* (*sep*, *-ge-*, *h*) ***herrühren von*** come from, be due to

'herstellen *v/t* (*sep*, *-ge-*, *h*) make, produce; *fig* establish

'Herstellung *f* (-; *no pl*) production; *fig* establishment

'Herstellungskosten *pl* production cost(s)

herüber [hɛ'ry:bɐ] *adv* over (here), across

herum [hɛ'rʊm] *adv* (a)round; F ***anders herum*** the other way round

herumführen *v/t* (*sep*, *-ge-*, *h*) ***j-n*** (***in der Stadt*** *etc*) ***herumführen*** show s.o. (a)round (the town *etc*)

herumkommen F *v/i* (*irr*, ***kommen***, *sep*, *-ge-*, *sein*) (***weit*** *or* ***viel***) ***herumkommen*** get around; ***um et. herumkommen*** *fig* get (a)round s.th.

herumkriegen F *v/t* (*sep*, *-ge-*, *h*) ***j-n zu et. herumkriegen*** get s.o. round to (doing) s.th.

herumlungern F *v/i* (*sep*, *-ge-*, *h*) loaf *or* hang around

herumreichen *v/t* (*sep*, *-ge-*, *h*) pass *or* hand round

herumsprechen *v/refl* (*irr*, ***sprechen***, *sep*, *-ge-*, *h*) get around

herumtreiben F *v/refl* (*irr*, ***treiben***, *sep*, *-ge-*, *h*) gad *or* knock about

He'rumtreiber F *m* (*-s*; -), **He'rumtreiberin** F *f* (-; *-nen*) tramp, loafer

herunter [hɛ'rʊntɐ] *adv* down; downstairs

heruntergekommen *adj* run-down; seedy, shabby

herunterhauen F *v/t* (*sep*, *-ge-*, *h*) ***j-m e-e herunterhauen*** smack *or* slap s.o. ('s face)

heruntermachen F *v/t* (*sep*, *-ge-*, *h*) run *s.o. or s.th.* down

herunterspielen F *v/t* (*sep*, *-ge-*, *h*) play *s.th.* down

hervor [hɛɐ'fo:ɐ] *adv* out of *or* from, forth

hervorbringen *v/t* (*irr*, ***bringen***, *sep*, *-ge-*, *h*) bring out, produce (*a. fig*); yield; utter

hervorgehen *v/i* (*irr*, ***gehen***, *sep*, *-ge-*, *sein*) ***hervorgehen aus*** (*dat*) follow from; ***als Sieger hervorgehen*** come off victorious

hervorheben *v/t* (*irr*, ***heben***, *sep*, *-ge-*, *h*) stress, emphasize

hervorragend *adj* outstanding, excellent, superior; prominent, eminent

hervorrufen *v/t* (*irr*, ***rufen***, *sep*, *-ge-*, *h*) cause, bring about; create

hervorstechend *adj* striking

hervortretend *adj* prominent; protruding, bulging

hervortun *v/refl* (*irr*, ***tun***, *sep*, *-ge-*, *h*) distinguish o.s. (***als*** as)

Herz [hɛrts] *n* (*-ens*; *-en*) ANAT heart (*a. fig*); *cards*: heart(s); ***j-m das Herz brechen*** break s.o.'s heart; ***sich ein Herz fassen*** take heart; ***mit ganzem Herzen*** whole-heartedly; ***schweren Herzens*** with a heavy heart; ***sich et. zu Herzen nehmen*** take s.th. to heart; ***es nicht übers Herz bringen zu*** *inf* not have the heart to *inf*; ***et. auf dem Herzen haben*** have s.th. on one's mind; ***ins Herz schließen*** take to one's heart

Herzanfall *m* heart attack

'Herzenslust *f*: ***nach Herzenslust*** to one's heart's content

Herzenswunsch *m* heart's desire, dearest wish

'Herzfehler *m* cardiac defect

'herzhaft *adj* hearty; savo(u)ry

'herzig *adj* sweet, lovely, cute

'Herzin,farkt *m* MED cardiac infarct(-ion), F *mst* heart attack, coronary

Herzklopfen *n* (*-s*; *no pl*) palpitation; ***er hatte Herzklopfen*** (***vor*** *dat*) his heart was throbbing (with)

H

'herzkrank *adj* suffering from (a) heart disease
'herzlich **1.** *adj* cordial, hearty; warm, friendly; **2.** *adv*: ***herzlich gern*** with pleasure
'herzlos *adj* heartless
Herzog ['hɛrtsoːk] *m* (-*s*; *Herzöge* ['hɛrtsøːgə]) duke
Herzogin ['hɛrtsoːgɪn] *f* (-; -*nen*) duchess
'Herzschlag *m* heartbeat; MED heart failure
Herzschrittmacher *m* MED (cardiac) pacemaker
Herztransplantati,on *f* MED heart transplant
'herzzerreißend *adj* heart-rending
Hetze ['hɛtsə] *f* (-; *no pl*) hurry, rush; POL *etc* agitation, campaign(ing) (***gegen*** against)
'hetzen **1.** *v/t* (*ge-*, *h*) rush; ZO hunt, chase; ***e-n Hund auf j-n hetzen*** set a dog on s.o.; **2.** *v/i* a) (*ge-*, *sein*) hurry, rush, b) (*ge-*, *h*) POL *etc* agitate (***gegen*** against)
'hetzerisch *adj* inflammatory
'Hetzjagd *f* hunt(ing), chase (*a. fig*); *fig* rush
'Hetzkam,pagne *f* POL smear campaign
Heu [hɔʏ] *n* (-[*e*]*s*; *no pl*) hay
'Heuboden *m* hayloft
Heuchelei [hɔʏçə'lai] *f* (-; -*en*) hypocrisy; cant
heucheln ['hɔʏçəln] *v/i and v/t* (*ge-*, *h*) feign, simulate
Heuchler(in) ['hɔʏçlɐ (-lərɪn)] (-*s*; -/-; -*nen*) hypocrite
heuchlerisch ['hɔʏçlərɪʃ] *adj* hypocritical
heuer ['hɔʏɐ] *Austrian adv* this year
Heuer ['hɔʏɐ] *f* (-; -*n*) MAR pay
'heuern *v/t* (*ge-*, *h*) hire, MAR *a.* sign on
heulen ['hɔylən] *v/i* (*ge-*, *h*) howl; F *contp* bawl; MOT roar; *siren*: whine
'Heuschnupfen *m* MED hay fever
'Heuschrecke *f* (-; -*n*) ZO grasshopper; locust
heute ['hɔʏtə] *adv* today; ***heute Abend*** this evening, tonight; ***heute früh, heute Morgen*** this morning; ***heute in acht Tagen*** a week from now; ***heute vor acht Tagen*** a week ago today
heutig ['hɔʏtɪç] *adj* today's; of today, present(-day)
'heutzutage *adv* nowadays, these days
Hexe ['hɛksə] *f* (-; -*n*) witch (*a. fig*); ***alte Hexe*** (old) hag
'hexen *v/i* (*ge-*, *h*) practice witchcraft; F work miracles
'Hexenkessel *m* inferno
Hexenschuss *m* (-*es*; *no pl*) MED lumbago
hieb [hiːp] *pret of* ***hauen***
Hieb [hiːp] *m* (-[*e*]*s*; -*e* ['hiːbə]) blow, stroke; punch; lash, cut; *pl* beating; thrashing
hielt [hiːlt] *pret of* ***halten***
hier [hiːɐ] *adv* here, in this place; present; ***hier entlang!*** this way!
hieran ['hiː'ran] *adv* from *or* in this
hierauf ['hiː'rauf] *adv* on it *or* this; after this, then
hieraus ['hiː'raus] *adv* from *or* out of this
'hier'bei *adv* here, in this case; on this occasion
'hier'durch *adv* by this, hereby, this way
'hier'für *adv* for this
'hier'her *adv* (over) here, this way; ***bis hierher*** so far
hierin ['hiː'rɪn] *adv* in this
'hier'mit *adv* with this
'hier'nach *adv* after this; according to this
hierüber ['hiː'ryːbɐ] *adv* about this (subject)
hierunter ['hiː'rʊntɐ] *adv* under this; among these; *understand etc* by this *or* that
'hier'von *adv* of *or* from this
'hier'zu *adv* for this; to this
hiesig ['hiːzɪç] *adj* local; ***ein Hiesiger*** one of the locals
hieß [hiːs] *pret of* ***heißen***
Hilfe ['hɪlfə] *f* (-; -*n*) help; aid (*a.* ECON), assistance (*a.* MED), relief (***für*** to); ***Erste Hilfe*** first aid; ***um Hilfe rufen*** cry for help; ***Hilfe!*** help!; → ***mithilfe***
Hilfeme,nü *n* EDP help menu
Hilferuf *m* call (*or* cry) for help
Hilfestellung *f* support (*a. fig*)
'hilflos *adj* helpless
hilfreich *adj* helpful
'Hilfsakti,on *f* relief action
'Hilfsarbeiter *m*, **'Hilfsarbeiterin** *f* unskilled worker
'hilfsbedürftig *adj* needy
'hilfsbereit *adj* helpful, ready to help
'Hilfsbereitschaft *f* (-; *no pl*) readiness to help, helpfulness
'Hilfsmittel *n* aid, TECH *a.* device
Hilfsorganisati,on *f* relief organization
Hilfsverb *n* LING auxiliary (verb)
Himbeere ['hɪmbeːrə] *f* BOT raspberry
Himmel ['hɪməl] *m* (-*s*; -) sky; REL heaven (*a. fig*); ***um Himmels willen*** for Heaven's sake; → ***heiter***
'Himmelfahrt REL Ascension (Day)
'Himmelskörper *m* AST celestial body
Himmelsrichtung *f* direction; cardinal point
himmlisch ['hɪmlɪʃ] *adj* heavenly, *fig a.* marvel(l)ous
hin [hɪn] **1.** *adv* there; ***bis hin zu*** as far as;

noch lange hin still a long way off; ***auf s-e Bitte*** (***s-n Rat***) ***hin*** at his request (advice); ***hin und her*** to and fro, back and forth; ***hin und wieder*** now and then; ***hin und zurück*** there and back; RAIL round trip, round-trip ticket, *esp Br* return (ticket); **2.** F *pred adj* ruined; done for; gone
hi'nab *adv* → ***hinunter***
'hinarbeiten *v/i* (*sep, -ge-, h*) ***hinarbeiten auf*** (*acc*) work towards
hi'nauf *adv* up (there); upstairs; ***die Straße*** *etc* ***hinauf*** up the street *etc*
hinaufgehen *v/i* (*irr*, ***gehen***, *sep, -ge-, sein*) go up, *fig a.* rise
hi'naus *adv* out; ***aus … hinaus*** out of …; ***in*** (*acc*) ***… hinaus*** out into …; ***hinaus*** (***mit dir***)***!*** (get) out!, out you go!
hinausgehen *v/i* (*irr*, ***gehen***, *sep, -ge-, sein*) go out(side); ***hinausgehen über*** (*acc*) go beyond; ***hinausgehen auf*** (*acc*) *window etc*: look out onto
hinauslaufen *v/i* (*irr*, ***laufen***, *sep, -ge-, sein*) run out(side); ***hinauslaufen auf*** (*acc*) come *or* amount to
hinausschieben *v/t* (*irr*, ***schieben***, *sep, -ge-, h*) put off, postpone
hinausstellen *v/t* (*sep, -ge-, h*) SPORT send *s.o.* off (the field)
hinauswerfen *v/t* (*irr*, ***werfen***, *sep, -ge-, h*) throw out (***aus*** of), *fig a.* kick out; (give *s.o.* the) sack, fire
hinauswollen *v/i* (*sep, -ge-, h*) ***hinauswollen auf*** (*acc*) aim (*or* drive *or* get) at; ***hoch hinauswollen*** aim high
'Hinblick *m*: ***im Hinblick auf*** (*acc*) in view of, with regard to
'hinbringen *v/t* (*irr*, ***bringen***, *sep, -ge-, h*) take there
hinderlich ['hɪndɐlɪç] *adj* hindering, impeding; ***j-m hinderlich sein*** be in s.o.'s way
hindern ['hɪndɐn] *v/t* (*ge-, h*) hinder, hamper; ***hindern an*** (*dat*) prevent from
Hindernis ['hɪndɐnɪs] *n* (*-ses; -se*) obstacle (*a. fig*)
Hindernisrennen *n* steeplechase
Hindu ['hɪndu] *m* (*-*[*s*]; *-*[*s*]) Hindu
Hinduismus [hɪndu'ɪsmʊs] *m* (*-; no pl*) hinduism
hin'durch *adv* through; ***das ganze Jahr*** *etc* ***hindurch*** throughout the year *etc*
hi'nein *adv* in; ***hinein mit dir!*** in you go!
hineingehen *v/i* (*irr*, ***gehen***, *sep, -ge-, sein*) go in; ***hineingehen in*** (*acc*) go into
'hinfallen *v/i* (*irr*, ***fallen***, *sep, -ge-, sein*) fall (down)
'hinfällig *adj* frail, infirm; invalid
hing [hɪŋ] *pret of* ***hängen*** 1
'Hingabe *f* (*-; no pl*) devotion (***an*** *acc* to)
'hingeben *v/t* (*irr*, ***geben***, *sep, -ge-, h*) give (up); ***sich hingeben*** (*dat*) give o.s. to; devote o.s. to
'hinhalten *v/t* (*irr*, ***halten***, *sep, -ge-, h*) hold out; ***j-n hinhalten*** put s.o. off
hinken ['hɪŋkən] *v/i* a) (*ge-, h*) (walk with a) limp, b) (*ge-, sein*) limp
'hinkommen *v/i* (*irr*, ***kommen***, *sep, -ge-, sein*) get there
hinkriegen F *v/t* (*sep, -ge-, h*) manage
'hinlänglich *adj* sufficient
'hinlegen *v/t* (*sep, -ge-, h*) lay *or* put down; ***sich hinlegen*** lie down
hinnehmen *v/t* (*irr*, ***nehmen***, *sep, -ge-, h*) put up with
'hinreißen *v/t* (*irr*, ***reißen***, *sep, -ge-, h*) carry away
hinreißend *adj* entrancing; breathtaking
'hinrichten *v/t* (*sep, -ge-, h*) execute
'Hinrichtung *f* (*-; -en*) execution
'hinsetzen *v/t* (*sep, -ge-, h*) set *or* put down; ***sich hinsetzen*** sit down
'Hinsicht *f* (*-; no pl*) respect; ***in gewisser Hinsicht*** in a way
'hinsichtlich *prp* (*gen*) with respect *or* regard to
'Hinspiel *n* SPORT first leg
'hinstellen *v/t* (*sep, -ge-, h*) put (down); ***hinstellen als*** make *s.o. or s.th.* appear to be
hinten ['hɪntən] *adv* at the back; MOT in the back; ***von hinten*** from behind
hinter ['hɪntɐ] *prp* (*dat*) behind
'Hinter… *in cpds …achse, …eingang, …rad etc*: rear …
Hinterbein *n* hind leg
Hinterbliebenen [-'bliːbənən] *pl the* bereaved; *esp* JUR surviving dependents
hinterei'nander *adv* one after the other; ***dreimal hintereinander*** three times in a row
'Hintergedanke *m* ulterior motive
hinter'gehen *v/t* (*irr*, ***gehen***, *no -ge-, h*) deceive
'Hintergrund *m* background (*a. fig*)
'Hinterhalt *m* ambush
'hinterhältig [-hɛltɪç] *adj* insidious, underhand(ed)
'Hinterhaus *n* rear building
hinter'her *adv* behind, after; afterwards
'Hinterhof *m* backyard
'Hinterkopf *m* back of the head
hinter'lassen *v/t* (*irr*, ***lassen***, *no -ge-, h*) leave (behind)
Hinter'lassenschaft *f* (*-; -en*) property (left), estate
hinter'legen *v/t* (*no -ge-, h*) deposit (***bei*** with)

H

H

'Hinterlist *f* deceit(fulness); (underhanded) trick
'hinterlistig *adj* deceitful; underhand(ed)
'Hintermann *m* person (car *etc*) behind (one); *fig mst pl* person behind the scenes, brain(s), mastermind
'Hintern F *m* (-*s*; -) bottom, backside, behind, *Br* bum
'hinterrücks [-rʏks] *adv* from behind
'Hinterseite *f* back
Hinterteil F *n* → ***Hintern***
Hintertreppe *f* back stairs
Hintertür *f* back door
hinter'ziehen *v/t* (*irr*, ***ziehen***, *no -ge-, h*) evade (*taxes*)
'Hinterzimmer *n* back room
hi'nüber *adv* over, across; ***hinüber sein*** F be ruined; GASTR be spoilt
hi'nunter *adv* down; downstairs; ***die Straße hinunter*** down the road
Hinweg ['hɪnveːk] *m* way there
hinweg [hɪn'vɛk] *adv*: ***über*** (*acc*) ***… hinweg*** over …
hinwegkommen *v/i* (*irr*, ***kommen*** *sep, -ge-, sein*) ***hinwegkommen über*** (*acc*) get over
hinwegsehen *v/i* (*irr*, ***sehen***, *sep, -ge-, h*) ***hinwegsehen über*** (*acc*) ignore
hinwegsetzen *v/refl* (*sep, -ge-, h*) ***sich hinwegsetzen über*** (*acc*) ignore, disregard
Hinweis ['hɪnvais] *m* (-*es*; -*e*) reference (***auf*** *acc* to); hint, tip (as to, regarding); indication (of), clue (as to)
'hinweisen (*irr*, ***weisen***, *sep, -ge-, h*) **1.** *v/t*: ***j-n hinweisen auf*** (*acc*) draw *or* call s.o.'s attention to; **2.** *v/i*: ***hinweisen auf*** (*acc*) point at *or* to, indicate; *fig* point out, indicate; hint at
'Hinweisschild *n*, **Hinweistafel** *f* sign, notice
'hinwerfen *v/t* (*irr*, ***werfen***, *sep, -ge-, h*) throw down
hinziehen *v/refl* (*irr*, ***ziehen***, *sep, -ge-, h*) extend (***bis zu*** to), stretch (to); drag on
hin'zufügen *v/t* (*sep, -ge-, h*) add (***zu*** to) (*a. fig*)
hinzukommen *v/i* (*irr*, ***kommen***, *sep, -ge-, sein*) be added; ***hinzu kommt, dass*** add to this …, and what is more, …
hinzuziehen *v/t* (*irr*, ***ziehen***, *sep, -ge-, h*) call in, consult
Hirn [hɪrn] *n* (-[*e*]*s*; -*e*) ANAT brain; *fig* brain(s), mind
Hirngespinst *n* fantasy
Hirsch [hɪrʃ] m (-[*e*]*s*; -*e*) ZO stag
Hirschgeweih *n* ZO antlers
Hirschkuh *f* ZO hind
Hirse ['hɪrzə] *f* (-; -*n*) BOT millet
Hirte ['hɪrtə] *m* (-*n*; -*n*) herdsman; shepherd (*a. fig*)
hissen ['hɪsən] *v/t* (*ge-, h*) hoist
Historiker [hɪs'toːrikɐ] *m* (-*s*; -), **His'torikerin** *f* (-; -*nen*) historian
his'torisch *adj* historical; historic (*event etc*)
Hitliste ['hɪtlɪstə] *f* top 40 *etc*, charts
Hitze ['hɪtsə] *f* (-; *no pl*) heat
'Hitzewelle *f* heat wave
'hitzig *adj* hot-tempered, peppery; heated (*debate etc*)
'Hitzkopf *m* hothead
'Hitzschlag *m* MED heatstroke
HIV-negativ [haːʔiː'fau-] *adj* MED HIV negative
HIV-positiv *adj* MED HIV positive
HIV-Positive *m, f* (-*n*; -*n*) MED HIV carrier
H-Milch ['haː-] *f Br* long-life milk
hob [hoːp] *pret of* ***heben***
Hobby ['hɔbi] *n* (-*s*; -*s*) hobby
'Hobby… *in cpds* amateur …
Hobel ['hoːbəl] *m* (-*s*; -) TECH plane
'Hobelbank *f* (-; -*bänke*) TECH carpenter's bench
'hobeln *v/t* (*ge-, h*) TECH plane
hoch [hoːx] *adj and adv* high; tall; *fig* heavy (*fine etc*); distinguished (*guest*); great, old (*age*); deep (*snow*); ***10 hoch 4*** MATH 10 to the power of 4; ***3000 Meter hoch*** *fly etc* at an altitude of 3,000 meters; ***in hohem Maße*** highly, greatly; ***hoch verschuldet*** heavily in debt; F ***das ist mir zu hoch*** that's above me
Hoch *n* (-*s*; -*s*) METEOR high (*a. fig*)
'Hochachtung *f* (deep) respect (***vor*** *dat* for)
'hochachtungsvoll *adv* Yours sincerely
'Hochbau *m* (-[*e*]*s*; *no pl*) ***Hoch- und Tiefbau*** structural and civil engineering
Hochbetrieb F *m* (-[*e*]*s*; *no pl*) rush
'hochdeutsch *adj* High *or* standard German
'Hochdruck *m* high pressure (*a. fig*)
Hochebene *f* plateau, tableland
Hochform *f*: ***in Hochform*** in top form *or* shape
Hochfre,quenz *f* ELECTR high frequency
Hochgebirge *n* high mountains
Hochgenuss *m* real treat
'hochgezüchtet *adj* ZO, TECH highbred, TECH *a.* sophisticated; MOT tuned up, F souped up
'hochhackig [-hakɪç] *adj* high-heeled
'Hochhaus *n* high rise, tower block
Hochkonjunk,tur *f* ECON boom
Hochland *n* highlands
Hochleistungs… *in cpds …sport etc*: high-performance …

'Hochmut *m* arrogance
'hochmütig [-my:tɪç] *adj* arrogant
'Hochofen *m* TECH blast furnace
'hochpro,zentig *adj* high-proof
'Hochrechnung *f* projection; POL computer prediction
Hochsai,son *f* peak (*or* height of the) season
Hochschulabschluss *m* degree
Hochschulausbildung *f* higher education
Hochschule *f* university; college; academy
Hochseefischerei *f* deep-sea fishing
Hochsommer *m* midsummer
Hochspannung *f* ELECTR high tension (*a. fig*) *or* voltage
Hochsprung *m* SPORT high jump
höchst [hø:çst] **1.** *adj* highest, *fig a.* supreme; extreme; **2.** *adv* highly, most, extremely
'Höchst... *in cpds mst* maximum …, top …
'Hochstapler [-ʃta:plɐ] *m* (*-s*; -), **'Hochstaplerin** *f* (-; *-nen*) impostor, swindler
'höchstens *adv* at (the) most, at best
'Höchstform *f* SPORT top form *or* shape
Höchstgeschwindigkeit *f* top speed (***mit*** at); speed limit
Höchstleistung *f* SPORT record (performance); TECH maximum output
Höchstmaß *n* maximum (***an*** *dat* of)
'höchstwahr'scheinlich *adv* most likely *or* probably
'Hochtechnolo,gie *f* high technology, hi tech
'hochtrabend *adj* pompous
'Hochverrat *m* high treason
'Hochwasser *n* high tide; flood
'hochwertig [-ve:ɐtɪç] *adj* high-grade, high-quality
Hochzeit ['hɔxtsait] *f* (-; *-en*) wedding
'Hochzeits... *in cpds …geschenk, …kleid, …tag etc*: wedding …
Hochzeitsreise *f* honeymoon
Hocke ['hɔkə] *f* (-; *-n*) crouch, squat
'hocken *v/i* (*ge-, h*) squat, crouch; F sit
Hocker ['hɔkɐ] *m* (*-s*; -) stool
Höcker ['hœkɐ] *m* (*-s*; -) ZO hump
Hockey ['hɔki] *n* (*-s*; *no pl*) SPORT field hockey, *Br* hockey
Hoden ['ho:dən] *m* (*-s*; -) ANAT testicle
Hof [ho:f] *m* (*-[e]s*; *Höfe* ['hø:fə]) yard; AGR farm; court(yard); court
Hofdame *f* lady-in-waiting
hoffen ['hɔfən] *v/i and v/t* (*ge-, h*) hope (***auf*** *acc* for); trust (in); ***das Beste hoffen*** hope for the best; ***ich hoffe es*** I hope so; ***ich hoffe nicht, ich will es nicht hoffen*** I hope not
'hoffentlich *adv* I hope, let's hope, hopefully
'Hoffnung *f* (-; *-en*) hope (***auf*** *acc* of); ***sich Hoffnungen machen*** have hopes; ***die Hoffnung aufgeben*** lose hope
'hoffnungslos *adj* hopeless
'hoffnungsvoll *adj* hopeful; promising
höflich ['hø:flɪç] *adj* polite, courteous (***zu*** to)
'Höflichkeit *f* (-; *no pl*) politeness, courtesy
Höhe ['hø:ə] *f* (-; *-n*) height; AVIAT, MATH, ASTR, GEOGR altitude; peak (*a. fig*); *fig* amount; level; extent (*of damage etc*); MUS pitch; ***auf gleicher Höhe mit*** on a level with; ***in die Höhe*** up; F ***ich bin nicht ganz auf der Höhe*** I'm not feeling up to the mark
Hoheit ['ho:hait] *f* (-; *no pl*) POL sovereignty; Highness
'Hoheitsgebiet *n* territory
Hoheitsgewässer *pl* territorial waters
Hoheitszeichen *n* national emblem
'Höhenluft *f* mountain air
Höhenmesser *m* altimeter
Höhenruder *n* AVIAT elevator
Höhensonne *f* MED ultraviolet lamp, sunlamp
Höhenzug *m* mountain chain
'Höhepunkt *m* climax, culmination, height, peak; highlight
hohl [ho:l] *adj* hollow (*a. fig*)
Höhle ['hø:lə] *f* (-; *-n*) cave, cavern; ZO hole, burrow; den, lair
'Hohlmaß *n* measure of capacity
Hohlraum *m* hollow, cavity
Hohlspiegel *m* concave mirror
Hohn [ho:n] *m* (*-[e]s*; *no pl*) derision, scorn
'Hohngelächter *n* jeers, jeering laughter
höhnisch ['hø:nɪʃ] *adj* derisive, scornful; ***höhnisches Lächeln*** sneer
holen ['ho:lən] *v/t* (*ge-, h*) (go and) get, fetch, go for; draw (*breath*); call (*s.o., the police etc*); ***holen lassen*** send for; ***sich holen*** catch, get (*a cold etc*); seek (*advice*)
Holland ['hɔlant] Holland, *the* Netherlands
Holländer ['hɔlɛndɐ] *m* (*-s*; -) Dutchman
'Hol'länderin [-dərɪn] *f* (-; *-nen*) Dutchwoman
'holländisch *adj* Dutch
Hölle ['hœlə] *f* (-; *no pl*) hell
'Höllenlärm F *m a* hell of a noise
Holler ['hɔlɐ] *Austrian m* (*-s*; -) BOT elder
höllisch ['hœlɪʃ] *adj* infernal, F hellish
holperig ['hɔlpərɪç] *adj* bumpy (*a. fig*),

rough, uneven; *fig* clumsy (*style etc*)
holpern ['hɔlpɐn] *v/i* (*ge-, sein*) jolt, bump; *fig* be bumpy
Holunder [ho'lʊndɐ] *m* (*-s; -*) BOT elder
Holz [hɔlts] *n* (*-es; Hölzer* ['hœltsɐ]) wood; lumber, *Br a.* timber; ***aus Holz*** (made) of wood, wooden; ***Holz hacken*** chop wood
Holzblasinstru,ment *n* MUS woodwind (instrument)
hölzern ['hœltsɐn] *adj* wooden, *fig a.* clumsy
'Holzfäller [-fɛlɐ] *m* (*-s; -*) woodcutter, lumberjack
Holzhammer *m* mallet; *fig* sledgehammer
holzig ['hɔltsɪç] *adj* woody; stringy
'Holzkohle *f* charcoal
Holzschnitt *m* woodcut
Holzschnitzer *m* wood carver
Holzschuh *m* clog
Holzweg *fig m*: ***auf dem Holzweg sein*** be barking up the wrong tree
Holzwolle *f* wood shavings, excelsior
Holzwurm *m* ZO woodworm
homöopathisch [homøo'pa:tɪʃ] *adj* hom(o)eopathic
homosexuell [homozɛ'ksuɛl] *adj*, **Homosexu'elle** *m, f* (*-n; -n*) homosexual
Honig ['ho:nɪç] *m* (*-s; -e*) honey
'Honigwabe *f* honeycomb
Honorar [hono'ra:ɐ] *n* (*-s; -e*) fee
honorieren [hono'ri:rən] *v/t* (*no -ge-, h*) pay (a fee to); *fig* appreciate, reward
Hopfen ['hɔpfən] *m* (*-s; -*) BOT hop; *brewing*: hops
hoppla ['hɔpla] *int* (wh)oops!
hopsen ['hɔpsən] F *v/i* (*ge-, sein*) hop, jump
Hörappa,rat ['hø:ɐ-] *m* hearing aid
hörbar ['hø:ɐba:ɐ] *adj* audible
horchen ['hɔrçən] *v/i* (*ge-, h*) listen (***auf*** *acc* to); eavesdrop
Horcher ['hɔrçɐ] *m* (*-s; -*) eavesdropper
Horde ['hɔrdə] *f* (*-; -n*) horde (*a.* ZO), *contp a.* mob, gang
hören ['hø:rən] *v/i and v/t* (*ge-, h*) hear; listen to; obey, listen; ***hören auf*** (*acc*) listen to; ***von j-m hören*** hear from (*or* of, about) s.o.; ***er hört schwer*** his hearing is bad; ***hör(t) mal!*** listen!; look (here)!; ***nun*** *or* ***also hör(t) mal!*** wait a minute!, now look *or* listen here!
Hörer ['hø:rɐ] *m* (*-s; -*) listener; TEL receiver
'Hörerin [-rərɪn] *f* (*-; -nen*) listener
Hörfehler ['hø:ɐ-] *m* MED hearing defect
Hörgerät *n* hearing aid
hörig ['hø:rɪç] *adj*: ***j-m hörig sein*** be s.o.'s slave
Horizont [hori'tsɔnt] *m* (*-[e]s; -e*) horizon (*a. fig*); ***s-n Horizont erweitern*** broaden one's mind; ***das geht über meinen Horizont*** that's beyond me
horizontal [horitsɔn'ta:l] *adj* horizontal
Hormon [hɔr'mo:n] *n* (*-s; -e*) hormone
Horn [hɔrn] *n* (*-[e]s; Hörner* ['hœrnɐ]) horn
Hornhaut *f* horny skin, callus(es); ANAT cornea
Hornisse [hɔr'nɪsə] *f* (*-; -n*) ZO hornet
Horoskop [horo'sko:p] *n* (*-s; -e*) horoscope
Hörrohr ['hø:ɐ-] *n* MED stethoscope
Hörsaal *m* lecture hall, auditorium
Hörspiel *n* radio play
Hörweite *f*: ***in*** (***außer***) ***Hörweite*** within (out of) earshot
Höschen ['hø:sçən] *n* (*-s; -*) panties
Hose ['ho:zə] *f* (*-; -n*) (***e-e Hose*** a pair of) pants, *Br* trousers; slacks; shorts
'Hosenanzug *m* pants (*Br* trouser) suit
Hosenrock *m* (***ein Hosenrock*** a pair of) culottes
Hosenschlitz *m* fly
Hosentasche *f* trouser pocket
Hosenträger *pl* (a pair of) suspenders *or Br* braces
Hospital [hɔspi'ta:l] *n* (*-s; -täler* [-'tɛ:lɐ]) hospital
Hostie ['hɔstjə] *f* (*-; -n*) REL host
Hotel [ho'tɛl] *n* (*-s; -s*) hotel
Hoteldi,rektor *m* hotel manager
Hotelfach *n* (*-[e]s; no pl*) hotel business
Hotelzimmer *n* hotel room
HP ABBR *of* ***Halbpension*** half-board
Hr(n). ABBR *of* ***Herrn*** Mr
Hubraum ['hu:p-] *m* MOT cubic capacity
hübsch [hʏpʃ] *adj* pretty, nice(-looking), cute; *fig* nice, lovely
Hubschrauber ['hu:pʃraubɐ] *m* (*-s; -*) helicopter
Hubschrauberlandeplatz *m* heliport
Huf [hu:f] *m* (*-[e]s; -e*) ZO hoof
'Hufeisen *n* horseshoe
Hüfte ['hʏftə] *f* (*-; -n*) ANAT hip
'Hüftgelenk *n* ANAT hip joint
'Hüftgürtel *m* girdle
Hügel ['hy:gəl] *m* (*-s; -*) hill
'hügelig *adj* hilly
'Hügelland *n* downs
Huhn [hu:n] *n* (*-[e]s; Hühner* ['hy:nɐ]) ZO chicken; hen
Hühnchen ['hy:nçən] *n* (*-s; -*) chicken; F ***mit j-m ein Hühnchen zu rupfen haben*** have a bone to pick with s.o.
'Hühnerauge *n* MED corn
Hühnerbrühe *f* chicken broth

Hühnerei *n* hen's egg
Hühnerfarm *f* poultry *or* chicken farm
Hühnerhof *m* poultry *or* chicken yard
Hühnerleiter *f* chicken ladder
Hühnerstall *m* henhouse
huldigen ['hʊldɪgən] *v/i* (*ge-*, *h*) pay homage to; *fig* indulge in
Hülle ['hʏlə] *f* (-; -*n*) cover(ing), wrap(-ping); jacket, *Br* sleeve; sheath; ***in Hülle und Fülle*** in abundance
'**hüllen** *v/t* (*ge-*, *h*) ***hüllen in*** (*acc*) wrap (-up) in, cover in
Hülse ['hʏlzə] *f* (-; -*n*) BOT pod; husk; TECH case
'**Hülsenfrüchte** *pl* pulse
human [hu'ma:n] *adj* humane
humanitär [humani'tɛ:ɐ] *adj* humanitarian
Humanität [humani'tɛ:t] *f* (-; *no pl*) humanity
Hummel ['hʊməl] *f* (-; -*n*) ZO bumblebee
Hummer ['hʊmɐ] *m* (-*s*; -) ZO lobster
Humor [hu'mo:ɐ] *m* (-*s*; *no pl*) humo(u)r; (***keinen***) ***Humor haben*** have a (no) sense of humo(u)r
Humorist [humo'rɪst] *m* (-*en*; -*en*) humorist
humo'ristisch, hu'morvoll *adj* humorous
humpeln ['hʊmpəln] *v/i* a) (*ge-*, *h*) hobble, b) (*ge-*, *sein*) limp
Hund [hʊnt] *m* (-[*e*]*s*; -*e*) ZO dog
Hundehütte ['hʊndə-] *f* doghouse, *Br* kennel
Hundekuchen *m* dog biscuit
Hundeleine *f* lead, leash
'**hunde'müde** *adj* dog-tired
hundert ['hʊndɐt] *adj* a *or* one hundred; ***zu hunderten*** by the hundreds
'**hundertfach** *adj* hundredfold
Hundert'jahrfeier *f* centenary, centennial
'**hundertjährig** [-jɛ:rɪç] *adj* a hundred years old; a hundred years of
'**hundertste** *adj* hundredth
Hündin ['hʏndɪn] *f* (-; -*nen*) ZO bitch
hündisch ['hʏndɪʃ] *adj* doglike, slavish
Hüne ['hy:nə] *m* (-*n*; -*n*) giant
'**Hünengrab** *n* dolmen
Hunger ['hʊŋɐ] *m* (-*s*; *no pl*) hunger; ***Hunger bekommen*** get hungry; ***Hunger haben*** be hungry; ***vor Hunger sterben*** die of starvation, starve to death
'**Hungerlohn** *m* starvation wages
'**hungern** *v/i* (*ge-*, *h*) go hungry, starve
'**Hungersnot** *f* famine
'**Hungerstreik** *m* hunger strike
'**Hungertod** *m* (death from) starvation
hungrig ['hʊŋrɪç] *adj* hungry (***nach, auf*** *acc* for)
Hupe ['hu:pə] *f* (-; -*n*) MOT horn
'**hupen** *v/i* (*ge-*, *h*) MOT sound one's horn, hoot, honk
hüpfen ['hʏpfən] *v/i* (*ge*, *sein*) hop, skip; *ball etc*: bounce
Hürde ['hʏrdə] *f* (-; -*n*) hurdle, *fig a.* obstacle; ZO fold, pen
'**Hürdenlauf** *m* SPORT hurdles
'**Hürdenläufer** *m*, '**Hürdenläuferin** *f* SPORT hurdler
Hure ['hu:rə] *f* (-; -*n*) whore, prostitute
huschen ['hʊʃən] *v/i* (*ge-*, *sein*) flit, dart
hüsteln ['hy:stəln] *v/i* (*ge-*, *h*) cough slightly; *iro* hem
husten ['hu:stən] *v/i* (*ge-*, *h*), '**Husten** *m* (-*s*; *no pl*) cough
'**Hustenbon,bon** *m*, *n* cough drop
Hustensaft *m* PHARM cough syrup
Hut[1] [hu:t] *m* (-[*e*]*s*; *Hüte* ['hy:tə]) hat; ***den Hut aufsetzen*** (***abnehmen***) put on (take off) one's hat
Hut[2] *f*: ***auf der Hut sein*** be on one's guard (***vor*** *dat* against)
hüten ['hy:tən] *v/t* (*ge-*, *h*) guard, protect, watch over; ZO herd, mind; look after; ***das Bett hüten*** be confined to (one's) bed; ***sich hüten vor*** (*dat*) beware of; ***sich hüten, et. zu tun*** be careful not to do s.th.
'**Hutkrempe** *f* (hat) brim
hutschen ['hʊtʃən] *Austrian v/t and v/i* → ***schaukeln***
Hütte ['hʏtə] *f* (-; -*n*) hut; *contp* shack; cottage, cabin; mountain hut; TECH ironworks
Hyäne ['hyɛ:nə] *f* (-; -*n*) ZO hy(a)ena
Hyazinthe [hya'tsɪntə] *f* (-; -*n*) BOT hyacinth
Hydrant [hy'drant] *m* (-*en*; -*en*) hydrant
hydraulisch [hy'draulɪʃ] *adj* hydraulic
Hydrokultur ['hy:dro-] *f* hydroponics
Hygiene [hy'gje:nə] *f* (-; *no pl*) hygiene
hygienisch [hy'gje:nɪʃ] *adj* hygienic
Hypnose [hyp'no:zə] *f* (-; -*n*) hypnosis
Hypnotiseur [hypnoti'zø:ɐ] *m* (-*s*; -*e*) hypnotist
hypnotisieren [hypnoti-'zi:rən] *v/t* (*no -ge-*, *h*) hypnotize
Hypotenuse [hypote'nu:zə] *f* (-; -*n*) MATH hypotenuse
Hypothek [hypo'te:k] *f* (-; -*en*) ECON mortgage; ***e-e Hypothek aufnehmen*** take out a mortgage
Hypothese [hypo'te:zə] *f* (-; -*n*) hypothesis, supposition
hypothetisch [hypo'te:tɪʃ] *adj* hypothetical
Hysterie [hyste'ri:] *f* (-; -*n*) hysteria
hysterisch [hys'te:rɪʃ] *adj* hysterical

H

I

i. A. ABBR *of* ***im Auftrag*** p. p., per procuration
ICE [iːtseːˈʔeː] ABBR *of* ***Intercityexpresszug*** intercity express (train)
ich [ɪç] *pers pron* I; ***ich selbst*** (I) myself; ***ich bin's*** it's me
ideal [ideˈaːl] *adj*, **Ideˈal** *n* (*-s*; *-e*) ideal
Idealismus [ideaˈlɪsmʊs] *m* (*-*; *no pl*) idealism
Ideaˈlist(in) (*-en*; *-en/-*; *-nen*) idealist
Idee [iˈdeː] *f* (*-*; *-n*) idea
identifizieren [idɛntifiˈtsiːrən] *v/t* (*no -ge-*, *h*) identify; ***sich identifizieren mit*** identify with
identisch [iˈdɛntɪʃ] *adj* identical
Identitätskarte [idɛntiˈtɛːts-] *Austrian f* identity card
Ideologe [ideoˈloːgə] *m* (*-n*; *-n*) ideologist
Ideologie [ideoloˈgiː] *f* (*-*; *-n*) ideology
ideoˈlogisch *adj* ideological
idiomatisch [idioˈmaːtɪʃ] *adj* LING idiomatic; ***idiomatischer Ausdruck*** idiom
Idiot [iˈdjoːt] *m* (*-en*; *-en*) idiot
Idiˈotenhügel F *m skiing*: nursery slope
idiˈotisch *adj* idiotic
Idol [iˈdoːl] *n* (*-s*; *-e*) idol
Idyll [iˈdʏl] *n* (*-s*; *-e*), **Iˈdylle** *f* (*-*; *-n*) idyl(l)
iˈdyllisch *adj* idyllic
Igel [ˈiːgəl] *m* (*-s*; *-*) ZO hedgehog
Iglu [ˈiːglu] *m* (*-s*; *-s*) igloo
ignorieren [ɪgnoˈriːrən] *v/t* (*no -ge-*, *h*) ignore, disregard
i. H. ABBR *of* ***im Hause*** on the premises
ihr [iːɐ] *poss pron* her; *pl* their; ***Ihr*** your
ihrerseits [ˈiːrɐzaits] *adv* on her (*pl* their) part
ihresgleichen [ˈiːrəs-] *indef pron* her (*pl* their) equals, people like herself (*pl* themselves)
ihretwegen [ˈiːrət-] *adv* for her (*pl* their) sake
Ikone [iˈkoːnə] *f* (*-*; *-n*) icon (*a.* EDP)
illegal [ˈɪlegaːl] *adj* JUR illegal
illegitim [ɪlegiˈtiːm] *adj* JUR illegitimate
Illusion [ɪluˈzjoːn] *f* (*-*; *-en*) illusion
illusorisch [ɪluˈzoːrɪʃ] *adj* illusory
Illustration [ɪlʊstraˈtsjoːn] *f* (*-*; *-en*) illustration
illustrieren [ɪlʊsˈtriːrən] *v/t* (*no -ge-*, *h*) illustrate
Illustrierte [ɪlʊsˈtriːɐtə] *f* (*-n*; *-n*) magazine
im [ɪm] *prep* in the; ***im Bett*** in bed; ***im Kino*** *etc* at the cinema *etc*; ***im Erdgeschoss*** on the first (*Br* ground) floor; ***im Mai*** in May; ***im Jahre 1997*** in (the year) 1997; ***im Stehen*** (while) standing up; → ***in***
imaginär [imagiˈnɛːɐ] *adj* imaginary
Imbiss [ˈɪmbɪs] *m* (*-es*; *-e*) snack
ˈImbissstube *f* snack bar
imitieren [imiˈtiːrən] *v/t* (*no -ge-*, *h*) imitate
Imker [ˈɪmkɐ] *m* (*-s*; *-*) beekeeper
immatrikulieren [ɪmatrikuˈliːrən] *v/t and v/refl* (*no -ge-*, *h*) UNIV enrol(l), register
immer [ˈɪmɐ] *adv* always, all the time; ***immer mehr*** more and more; ***immer wieder*** again and again; ***für immer*** for ever, for good
ˈImmergrün *n* BOT evergreen
ˈimmerˈhin *adv* after all
ˈimmerˈzu *adv* all the time, constantly
Immigrant [ɪmiˈgrant] *m* (*-en*; *-en*), **Immiˈgrantin** *f* (*-*; *-nen*) immigrant
Immissionen [ɪmɪˈsjoːnən] *pl* (harmful effects of) noise, pollutants *etc*
Immobilien [ɪmoˈbiːliən] *pl* real estate
Immobilienmakler *m* realtor, real estate agent
immun [ɪˈmuːn] *adj* immune (***gegen*** to, against, from); ***immun machen*** → **immunisieren** [ɪmuniˈziːrən] *v/t* (*no -ge-*, *h*) immunize
Immunität [ɪmuniˈtɛːt] *f* (*-*; *no pl*) immunity
Imˈmunschwäche *f* (*-*; *-n*) ***Erworbene Immunschwäche*** MED AIDS
Imperativ [ˈɪmperatiːf] *m* (*-s*; *-e*) LING imperative (mood)
Imperfekt [ˈɪmpɛrfɛkt] *n* (*-s*; *-e*) LING past (tense)
Imperialismus [ɪmperjaˈlɪsmʊs] *m* (*-*; *no pl*) imperialism
Imperialist [ɪmperjaˈlɪst] *m* (*-en*; *-en*), **imperiaˈlistisch** *adj* imperialist
impfen [ˈɪmpfən] *v/t* (*ge-*, *h*) MED vaccinate
ˈImpfpass *m* MED vaccination card
Impfschein *m* MED vaccination certificate
Impfstoff *m* MED vaccine, serum
ˈImpfung *f* (*-*; *-en*) MED vaccination
imponieren [ɪmpoˈniːrən] *v/i* (*no -ge-*, *h*) ***j-m imponieren*** impress s.o.
Import [ɪmˈpɔrt] *m* (*-[e]s*; *-e*) ECON import(ation)
Importeur [ɪmpɔrˈtøːɐ] *m* (*-s*; *-e*) ECON importer

importieren [-'tiːrən] *v/t* (*no -ge-, h*) ECON import
imposant [ɪmpo'zant] *adj* impressive, imposing
imprägnieren [ɪmprɛ'gniːrən] *v/t* (*no -ge-, h*), **imprägniert** [ɪmprɛ'gniːɐt] *adj* waterproof
improvisieren [ɪmprovi'ziːrən] *v/t and v/i* (*no -ge-, h*) improvise
Impuls [ɪm'pʊls] *m* (*-es; -e*) impulse; stimulus
impulsiv [ɪmpʊl'ziːf] *adj* impulsive
imstande [ɪm'ʃtandə] *adj*: ***imstande sein zu*** *inf* be capable of *ger*
in [ɪn] *prp* (*dat and acc*) **1.** in, at; within, inside; into, in; ***überall in*** all over; ***in der Stadt*** in town; ***in der Schule*** at school; ***in die Schule*** to school; ***ins Kino*** to the cinema; ***ins Bett*** to bed; ***warst du schon mal in ...?*** have you ever been to ...?; → ***im***; **2.** in, at, during; ***in dieser*** (***der nächsten***) ***Woche*** this (next) week; ***in diesem Alter*** (***Augenblick***) at this age (moment); ***in der Nacht*** at night; ***heute in acht Tagen*** a week from now; ***heute in e-m Jahr*** this time next year; → ***im***; **3.** in, at; ***gut sein in*** (*dat*) be good at; ***in Eile*** in a hurry; ***in Behandlung*** (***Reparatur***) under treatment (repair); ***ins Deutsche*** into German; → ***im***; **4.** F ***in sein*** be in
'Inbegriff *m* epitome
'inbegriffen *adj* ECON included
in'dem *cj* while, as; by *doing s.th.*
Inder ['ɪndɐ] *m* (*-s; -*), **Inderin** ['ɪndərɪn] *f* (*-; -nen*) Indian
Indian ['ɪndjaːn] *Austrian m* (*-s; -e*) ZO turkey (cock)
Indianer [ɪn'djaːnɐ] *m* (*-s; -*), **Indianerin** [ɪn'djaːnərɪn] *f* (*-; -nen*) Native American, (American) Indian
Indien ['ɪndjən] India
Indikativ ['ɪndikatiːf] *m* (*-s; -e*) LING indicative (mood)
indirekt ['ɪndirɛkt] *adj* indirect, LING *a.* reported
indisch ['ɪndɪʃ] *adj* Indian
indiskret ['ɪndɪskreːt] *adj* indiscreet
Indiskretion [ɪndɪskre'tsjoːn] *f* (*-; -en*) indiscretion
indiskutabel [ɪndɪsku'taːbəl] *adj* out of the question
individuell [ɪndivi'duɛl] *adj*, **Individuum** [ɪndi'viːduʊm] *n* (*-s; -en*) individual
indiz [ɪn'diːts] *n* (*-es; -ien*) indication, sign; *pl* JUR circumstantial evidence
industrialisieren [ɪndʊstriali'ziːrən] *v/t* (*no -ge-, h*) industrialize
Industriali'sierung *f* (*-; no pl*) industrialization
Industrie [ɪndʊs'triː] *f* (*-; -n*) industry
Indus'triegebiet *n* industrial area
industriell [ɪndʊstri'ɛl] *adj* industrial
Industri'elle *m* (*-n; -n*) industrialist
inei'nander *adv* into one another; ***ineinander verliebt*** in love with each other; ***ineinandergreifen*** *v/i* (*irr*, ***greifen***, *sep, -ge-, h*) TECH interlock (*a. fig*)
Infanterie ['ɪnfantəriː] *f* (*-; -n*) MIL infantry
Infanterist ['ɪnfantərɪst] *m* (*-en; -en*) MIL infantryman
Infektion [ɪnfɛk'tsjoːn] *f* (*-; -en*) MED infection
Infekti'onskrankheit *f* infectious disease
Infinitiv ['ɪnfinitiːf] *m* (*-s; -e*) LING infinitive (mood)
infizieren [ɪnfi'tsiːrən] *v/t* (*no -ge-, h*) MED infect
Inflation [ɪnfla'tsjoːn] *f* (*-; -en*) inflation
in'folge *prp* (*gen*) owing to, due to
infolge'dessen *adv* consequently
Informatik [ɪnfɔr'maːtɪk] *f* (*-; no pl*) computer science
Infor'matiker(in) [ɪnfɔr'maːtikɐ (-kərɪn)] (*-s; -/-; -nen*) computer scientist
Information [ɪnfɔrma'tsjoːn] *f* (*-; -en*) information; ***die neuesten Informationen*** the latest information
informieren [ɪnfɔr'miːrən] *v/t* (*no -ge-, h*) inform; ***falsch informieren*** misinform
in'frage: ***infrage stellen*** question; put in jeopardy; ***infrage kommen*** be possible (*person*: eligible); ***nicht infrage kommen*** be out of the question
infrarot ['ɪnfra-] *adj* PHYS infrared
'Infrastruk,tur *f* infrastructure
Ing. ABBR *of* ***Ingenieur*** eng., engineer
Ingenieur [ɪnʒe'njøːɐ] *m* (*-s; -e*), **Inge'nieurin** *f* (*-; -nen*) engineer
Ingwer ['ɪŋvɐ] *m* (*-s; no pl*) ginger
Inhaber ['ɪnhaːbɐ] *m* (*-s; -*), **'Inhaberin** *f* (*-; -nen*) owner, proprietor (proprietress); holder
Inhalt ['ɪnhalt] *m* (*-[e]s; -e*) contents; volume, capacity; *fig* meaning
'Inhaltsangabe *f* summary
Inhaltsverzeichnis *n* table of contents
Initiative [initsja'tiːvə] *f* (*-; -n*) initiative; ***die Initiative ergreifen*** take the initiative
inklusive [ɪnklu'ziːvə] *prp* ECON including
inkonsequent ['ɪnkɔnzekvɛnt] *adj* inconsistent
In-'Kraft-Treten *n* (*-s; no pl*) coming into force, taking effect
'Inland *n* (*-[e]s; no pl*) home (country)
Inlandflug *m* domestic (*or* internal) flight
inländisch ['ɪnlɛndɪʃ] *adj* domestic, home, inland

Inlett ['ınlɛt] *n* (-[*e*]*s*; -*e*) ticking
in'mitten *prp* (*gen*) in the middle of
innen ['ınən] *adv* inside; ***nach innen*** inwards
'Innenarchi,tekt *m*, **Innenarchi,tektin** *f* interior designer
Innenarchitek,tur *f* interior design
Innenmi,nister(in) minister of the interior; Secretary of the Interior, *Br* Home Secretary
Innenminis,terium *n* ministry of the interior; Department of the Interior, *Br* Home Office
Innenpoli,tik *f* domestic politics
'innenpo,litisch *adj* domestic, internal
'Innenseite *f*: ***auf der Innenseite*** (on the) inside
'Innenstadt *f* downtown, (city *or* town) center *or Br* centre
inner ['ınɐ] *adj* inside; *fig* inner; MED, POL internal
Innere ['ınərə] *n* (-*n*; *no pl*) interior, inside
Innereien [ınə'raiən] *pl* GASTR offal
'innerhalb *prp* (*gen*) within
'innerlich *adj* internal (*a.* MED)
innert ['ınɐt] *Swiss prp* (*gen or dat*) within
innig ['ınıç] *adj* tender, affectionate
Innung ['ınʊŋ] *f* (-; -*en*) guild
'inoffiziell *adj* unofficial
ins [ıns] → ***in***
Insasse ['ınzasə] *m* (-*n*; -*n*) inmate; MOT passenger
'Insassenversicherung *f* MOT passenger insurance
'Insassin *f* (-; -*nen*) inmate; MOT passenger
insbe'sondere *adv* (e)specially
'Inschrift *f* inscription, legend
Insekt [ın'zɛkt] *n* (-*s*; -*en*) ZO insect, bug
In'sektenstich *m* insect bite
Insel ['ınzəl] *f* (-; -*n*) island
'Inselbewohner *m* islander
Inserat [ınze'ra:t] *n* (-[*e*]*s*; -*e*) advertisement, F ad
inserieren [ınze'ri:rən] *v/t and v/i* (*no -ge-*, *h*) advertise
insge'heim *adv* secretly
insge'samt *adv* altogether, in all
inso'fern **1.** *adv* as far as that goes; **2.** *cj*: ***insofern als*** in so far as
Inspektion [ınspɛk'tsjo:n] *f* (-; -*en*) inspection; MOT service
Inspektor [ın'spɛkto:ɐ] *m* (-*s*; -*en* [ınspɛk'to:rən]), **Inspek'torin** *f* (-; -*nen*) inspector
inspizieren [ınspi'tsi:rən] *v/t* (*no -ge-*, *h*) inspect
Installateur [ınstala'tø:ɐ] *m* (-*s*; -*e*) plumber; (gas *or* electrical) fitter
installieren [ınsta'li:rən] *v/t* (*no -ge-*, *h*) put in, fit, instal(l)
instand [ın'ʃtant] *adv*: ***instand halten*** keep in good condition *or* repair; TECH maintain; ***instand setzen*** repair
In'standhaltung *f* (-; *no pl*) maintenance
'inständig *adv*: ***j-n inständig bitten*** implore s.o.
In'standsetzung *f* (-; -*en*) repair
Instanz [ın'stants] *f* (-; -*en*) authority; JUR instance
Instinkt [ın'stıŋkt] *m* (-[*e*]*s*; -*e*) instinct
instinktiv [ınstıŋk'ti:f] *adv* instinctively
Institut [ınsti'tu:t] *n* (-[*e*]*s*; -*e*) institute
Institution [ınstitu'tsjo:n] *f* (-; -*en*) institution
Instrument [ınstru'mɛnt] *n* (-[*e*]*s*; -*e*) instrument
inszenieren [ınstse'ni:rən] *v/t* (*no -ge-*, *h*) (put on) stage; *film*: direct; *fig* stage
Insze'nierung *f* (-; -*en*) production
intellektuell [ıntɛlɛk'tuɛl] *adj*, **Intellektu'elle** *m*, *f* (-*n*; -*n*) intellectual, F highbrow
intelligent [ıntɛli'gɛnt] *adj* intelligent
Intelligenz [ıntɛli'gɛnts] *f* (-; -*en*) intelligence
Intelligenzquoti,ent *m* I.Q.
Intendant [ıntɛn'dant] *m* (-*en*; -*en*), **Inten'dantin** *f* (-; -*nen*) THEA *etc* director
intensiv [ıntɛn'zi:f] *adj* intensive; intense
Inten'sivkurs *m* crash course
interessant [ıntərɛ'sant] *adj* interesting
Interesse [ıntə'rɛsə] *n* (-*s*; -*n*) interest (***an*** *dat*, ***für*** in)
Inte'ressengebiet *n* field of interest
Interessent [ıntərɛ'sɛnt] *m* (-*en*; -*en*), **Interes'sentin** *f* (-; -*nen*) interested person; ECON prospect, *Br* prospective buyer
interessieren [ıntərɛ'si:rən] *v/t* (*no -ge-*, *h*) interest (***für*** in); ***sich interessieren für*** take an interest in; be interested in
intern [ın'tɛrn] *adj* internal
Internat [ıntɐ'na:t] *n* (-[*e*]*s*; -*e*) boarding school
internatio'nal [ıntɐ-] *adj* international
Internet ['ıntɐnɛt] *n* (-[*s*]; *no pl*) Internet
Internist [ıntɐ'nıst] *m* (-*en*; -*en*), **Inter'nistin** *f* (-; -*nen*) MED internist
Interpretation [ıntɐpreta'tsjo:n] *f* (-; -*en*) interpretation; analysis
interpretieren [ıntɐpre'ti:rən] *v/t* (*no -ge-*, *h*) interpret, ana|lyze, *Br* -lyse
Interpunktion [ıntɐpʊŋk'tsjo:n] *f* (-; *no pl*) punctuation
Intervall [ıntɐ'val] *n* (-[*e*]*s*; -*e*) interval
intervenieren [ıntɐve'ni:rən] *v/i* (*no -ge-*, *h*) intervene
Interview ['ıntɐvju:] *n* (-*s*; -*s*), **interview-**

en [ɪntɐ'vju:ən] *v/t (no -ge-, h)* interview
intim [ɪn'ti:m] *adj* intimate (***mit*** with) *(a. sexually)*
Intimität [ɪntimi'tɛ:t] *f (-; no pl)* intimacy
In'timsphäre *f* privacy
intolerant ['ɪntolerant] *adj* intolerant (***gegen*** of)
Intoleranz ['ɪntolerants] *f (-; no pl)* intolerance
intransitiv ['ɪntranziti:f] *adj* LING intransitive
Intrige [ɪn'tri:gə] *f (-; -n)* intrigue, scheme, plot
intrigieren [ɪntri'gi:rən] *v/i (no -ge-, h)* (plot and) scheme
Invalide [ɪnva'li:də] *m (-n; -n)* invalid
Inva'lidenrente *f* disability pension
Invalidität [ɪnvalidi'tɛ:t] *f (-; no pl)* disablement, disability
Inventar [ɪnvɛn'ta:ɐ] *n (-s; -e)* inventory, stock
Inventur [ɪnvɛn'tu:ɐ] *f (-; -en)* ECON stocktaking; ***Inventur machen*** take stock
investieren [ɪnvɛs'ti:rən] *v/t (no -ge-, h)* ECON invest *(a. fig)*
Investition [ɪnvɛsti'tsjo:n] *f (-; -en)* ECON investment
inwiefern [ɪnvi'fɛrn] *cj and adv* in what respect *or* way
inwie'weit *cj and adv* to what extent
'Inzucht *f* inbreeding
in'zwischen *adv* meanwhile, in the meantime; by now
irdisch ['ɪrdɪʃ] *adj* earthly, worldly
Ire ['i:rə] *m (-n; -n)* Irishman; *pl* the Irish
irgend ['ɪrgənt] *adv in cpds*: some…; any…; ***wenn irgend möglich*** if at all possible; ***wenn du irgend kannst*** if you possibly can; F ***irgend so ein …*** some …
irgend'ein(e) *indef pron* some(one); any (-one)
irgend'ein(e)s *indef pron* some; any
irgendetwas something; anything
irgendjemand someone, somebody; anyone, anybody
irgend'wann *adv* sometime (or other); (at) any time
irgend'wie *adv* somehow (or other)
irgend'wo *adv* somewhere; anywhere
Irin ['i:rɪn] *f (-; -nen)* Irishwoman
irisch ['i:rɪʃ] *adj* Irish
Irland ['ɪrlant] Ireland
Ironie [iro'ni:] *f (-; no pl)* irony
ironisch [i'ro:nɪʃ] *adj* ironic(al)
irre ['ɪrə] *adj* mad, crazy, insane; confused; F super, terrific
'Irre *m, f (-n; -n)* madman (madwoman), lunatic; ***wie ein Irrer*** like mad *or* a madman
'irreführen *v/t (sep, -ge-, h)* mislead, lead astray
irreführend *adj* misleading
'irregehen *v/i (irr,* ***gehen****, sep, -ge-, sein)* go astray, *fig a.* be wrong
irremachen *v/t (sep, -ge-, h)* confuse
irren ['ɪrən] **1.** *v/refl (ge-, h)* be wrong, be mistaken; ***sich irren*** be wrong; ***sich in et. irren*** get s.th. wrong; **2.** *v/i (ge-, sein)* wander, stray, err
irritieren [ɪri'ti:rən] *v/t (no -ge-, h)* irritate; F confuse
'Irrlicht *n (-[e]s; -er)* will-o'-the-wisp
'Irrsinn *m (-[e]s; no pl)* madness
'irrsinnig *adj* insane, mad; F terrific
Irrtum ['ɪrtu:m] *m (-s; Irrtümer* ['ɪrty:mɐ]) error, mistake; ***im Irrtum sein*** be mistaken
'irrtümlich *adv* by mistake
Ischias ['ɪʃjas] *m, n, f (-; no pl)* MED sciatica
Islam [ɪs'la:m] *m (-[s]; no pl)* Islam
Island ['i:slant] Iceland
Isländer ['i:slɛndɐ] *m (-s; -)*, **'Isländerin** [-dərɪn] *f (-; -nen)* Icelander
'isländisch *adj* Icelandic
Isolierband [izo'li:ɐ-] *n (-[e]s; -bänder)* insulating tape
isolieren [izo'li:rən] *v/t (no -ge-, h)* isolate; ELECTR, TECH insulate
Iso'lierstati,on *f* MED isolation ward
Iso'lierung *f (-; -en)* isolation; ELECTR, TECH insulation
Israel ['ɪsrae:l] Israel
Israeli [ɪsra'e:li] *m (-[s]; -[s]), f (-; -[s])*, **israelisch** [ɪsra'e:lɪʃ] *adj* Israeli
Italien [i'ta:ljən] Italy
Italiener [ita'lje:nɐ] *m (-s; -)*, **Itali'enerin** [-nərɪn] *f (-; -nen)*, **itali'enisch** *adj* Italian

I

J

ja [jaː] *adv* yes, F *a.* yeah; PARL yea, aye; ***wenn ja*** if so; ***da ist er ja!*** well, there he is!; ***ich sagte es Ihnen ja*** I told you so; ***ich bin ja (schließlich) …*** after all, I am …; ***tut es 'ja nicht!*** don't you dare do it!; ***sei 'ja vorsichtig!*** do be careful!; ***vergessen Sie es 'ja nicht!*** be sure not to forget it!; ***ja, weißt du nicht?*** why, don't you know?; ***du kommst doch, ja?*** you're coming, aren't you?
Jacht [jaxt] *f* (*-; -en*) MAR yacht
Jacke ['jakə] *f* (*-; -n*) jacket; coat
Jackett [ʒa'kɛt] *n* (*-s; -s*) jacket, coat
Jagd [jaːkt] *f* (*-; -en*) hunt(ing) (*a. fig*); shoot(ing); *fig* chase; → ***Jagdrevier***; ***auf (die) Jagd gehen*** go hunting *or* shooting; ***Jagd machen auf*** (*acc*) hunt (for); *a.* chase *s.o.*
Jagdaufseher *m* gamekeeper
Jagdflugzeug *n* MIL fighter (plane)
Jagdhund *m* zo hound
Jagdhütte *f* (hunting) lodge
Jagdreˌvier *n* hunting ground
Jagdschein *m* hunting *or* shooting licen|se, *Br* -ce
jagen ['jaːgən] *v/t and v/i* (*ge-, h*) hunt; shoot; *fig* race, dash; hunt, chase; ***j-n aus dem Haus*** *etc* ***jagen*** drive *or* chase s.o. out of the house *etc*
Jäger ['jɛːgɐ] *m* (*-s; -*) hunter, huntsman
Jaguar ['jaːguaːɐ] *m* (*-s; -e*) zo jaguar
jäh [jɛː] *adj* sudden; steep
Jahr [jaːɐ] *n* (*-[e]s; -e* ['jaːrə]) year; ***ein drei viertel Jahr*** nine months; ***einmal im Jahr*** once a year; ***im Jahre 1995*** in (the year) 1995; ***ein 10 Jahre altes Auto*** a ten-year-old car; ***mit 18 Jahren, im Alter von 18 Jahren*** at (the age of) eighteen; ***heute vor e-m Jahr*** a year ago today; ***die 80er-Jahre*** the eighties
jahr'aus *adv*: ***jahraus, jahrein*** year in, year out; year after year
'Jahrbuch *n* yearbook, annual
jahrelang ['jaːrəlaŋ] **1.** *adj* longstanding, (many) years of; **2.** *adv* for (many) years
Jahres… ['jaːrəs-] *in cpds …bericht, …bilanz, …einkommen etc*: annual …
Jahresanfang *m* beginning of the year
Jahresende *n* end of the year
Jahrestag *m* anniversary
Jahreswechsel *m* turn of the year
Jahreszahl *f* date, year
Jahreszeit *f* season, time of (the) year
'Jahrgang *m* age group; PED year, class (***1995*** of '95); GASTR vintage
Jahr'hundert *n* (*-s; -e*) century
Jahrhundertwende *f* turn of the century
jährlich ['jɛːɐlɪç] **1.** *adj* annual, yearly; **2.** *adv* every year, yearly, once a year
'Jahrmarkt *m* fair
Jahr'tausend *n* (*-s; -e*) millennium
Jahr'zehnt *n* (*-[e]s; -e*) decade
'Jähzorn *m* violent (fit of) temper
'jähzornig *adj* hot-tempered
Jalousie [ʒalu'ziː] *f* (*-; -n*) (venetian) blind
Jammer ['jamɐ] *m* (*-s; no pl*) misery; ***es ist ein Jammer*** it is a pity
jämmerlich ['jɛmɐlɪç] *adj* miserable, wretched; pitiful, sorry; ***jämmerlich versagen*** fail miserably
'jammern *v/i* (*ge-, h*) moan, lament (***über*** *acc* over, about); complain (of, about)
jammer'schade *adj*: ***es ist jammerschade, dass*** it's a crying shame that
Janker ['jaŋkɐ] *Austrian m* (*-s; -*) jacket
Jänner ['jɛnɐ] *Austrian m* (*-s; -*), **Januar** ['januaːɐ] *m* (*-[s]; -e*) January
Japan ['jaːpan] Japan
Japaner [ja'paːnɐ] *m* (*-s; -*), **Ja'panerin** [-nərɪn] *f* (*-; -nen*), **ja'panisch** *adj* Japanese
Jargon [ʒar'gõː] *m* (*-s; -s*) jargon; slang
'Jastimme *f* PARL aye, yea
jäten ['jɛːtən] *v/t* (*ge-, h*) weed
Jauche ['jauxə] *f* (*-; -n*) liquid manure
jauchzen ['jauxtsən] *v/i* (*ge-, h*) shout for *or* with joy; exult, rejoice
Jause ['jauzə] *Austrian f* (*-; -n*) snack
ja'wohl *adv* (that's) right, (yes,) indeed
je [jeː] *adv and cj* ever; each; per; ***der beste Film, den ich je gesehen habe*** the best film I have ever seen; ***je zwei (Pfund)*** two (pounds) each; ***drei Mark je Kilo*** three marks per kilo; ***je nach Größe (Geschmack)*** according to size (taste); ***je nachdem(, wie)*** it depends (on how); ***je …, desto …*** the … the …
Jeans [dʒiːnz] *pl, a. f* (*-; -*) (***e-e Jeans*** a pair of) jeans
Jeansjacke *f* denim jacket
jede ['jeːdə], **jeder** ['jeːdɐ], **jedes** ['jeːdəs] *indef pron* every; any; each; either; ***jeder weiß (das)*** everybody knows; ***du kannst jeden fragen*** (you can) ask anyone; ***jeder von uns (euch)*** each of us (you); ***jeder, der*** whoever; ***jeden zweiten Tag*** every other day; ***jeden Augenblick*** any moment now; ***jedes Mal*** every

time; ***jedes Mal wenn*** whenever
'jeden'falls *adv* in any case, anyhow
'jedermann *indef pron* everyone, everybody
'jeder'zeit *adv* any time, always
je'doch *cj* however
je'her *adv*: ***von jeher*** always
jemals ['je:ma:ls] *adv* ever
jemand ['je:mant] *indef pron* someone, somebody; anyone, anybody
jene ['je:nə], **jener** ['je:nɐ], **jenes** ['je:nəs] *dem pron* that (one); *pl* those; ***dies und jenes*** this and that
jenseitig ['je:nzaitɪç] *adj* opposite
jenseits ['je:nzaits] *adv and prp* (*gen*) on the other side (of), beyond (*a. fig*)
'Jenseits *n* (-; *no pl*) next world, hereafter
jetzig ['jɛtsɪç] *adj* present; existing
jetzt [jɛtst] *adv* now, at present; ***bis jetzt*** up to now, so far; ***erst jetzt*** only now; ***jetzt gleich*** right now *or* away; ***für jetzt*** for the present; ***von jetzt an*** from now on
jeweilig ['je:'vailɪç] *adj* respective
jeweils ['je:'vails] *adv* each; at a time
Jh. ABBR *of* ***Jahrhundert*** cent., century
Jochbein ['jɔx-] *n* ANAT cheekbone
Jockei ['dʒɔke] *m* (*-s*; *-s*) jockey
Jod [jo:t] *n* (-[*e*]*s*; *no pl*) CHEM iodine
jodeln ['jo:dəln] *v/i* (*ge-*, *h*) yodel
Joga → ***Yoga***
joggen ['dʒɔgən] *v/i* (*ge-*, *h*) jog
Jogger ['dʒɔgɐ] *m* (*-s*; -) jogger
Jogging ['dʒɔgɪŋ] *n* (*-s*; *no pl*) jogging
Jogginganzug *m* tracksuit
Jogginghose *f* tracksuit trousers
Joghurt, Jogurt ['jo:gʊrt] *m*, *n* (-[*s*]; -[*s*]) yog(h)urt, yoghourt
Johannisbeere [jo'hanɪs-] *f*: ***rote Johannisbeere*** redcurrant; ***schwarze Johannisbeere*** blackcurrant
johlen ['jo:lən] *v/i* (*ge-*, *h*) howl, yell
Jolle ['jɔlə] *f* (-; *-n*) MAR dinghy
Jongleur [ʒõ'glø:ɐ] *m* (*-s*; *-e*) juggler
jonglieren [ʒõ'gli:rən] *v/t and v/i* (*no -ge-*, *h*) juggle
Joule [dʒu:l] *n* (-[*s*]; -) PHYS joule
Journalismus [ʒʊrna'lɪsmʊs] *m* (-; *no pl*) journalism
Journalist(in) [ʒʊrna-'lɪst(ɪn)] (*-en*; *-en*/-; *-nen*) journalist
jr. → ***jun.***
Jubel ['ju:bəl] *m* (*-s*; *no pl*) cheering, cheers; rejoicing
'jubeln *v/i* (*ge-*, *h*) cheer, shout for joy; rejoice
Jubiläum [jubi'lɛ:ʊm] *n* (*-s*; *-läen*) anniversary; ***50-jähriges Jubiläum*** fiftieth anniversary, (golden) jubilee
jucken ['jʊkən] *v/t and v/i* (*ge-*, *h*) itch; ***es juckt mich am …*** my … itches
Jude ['ju:də] *m* (*-n*; *-n*) Jewish person; ***er ist Jude*** he is Jewish
Jüdin ['jy:dɪn] *f* (-; *-nen*) Jewish woman *or* girl; ***sie ist Jüdin*** she is Jewish
jüdisch ['jy:dɪʃ] *adj* Jewish
Judo ['ju:do] *n* (-[*s*]; *no pl*) SPORT judo
Jugend ['ju:gənt] *f* (-; *no pl*) youth; ***die Jugend*** young people
Jugendamt *n* youth welfare office
Jugendarbeitslosigkeit *f* youth unemployment
'jugendfrei *adj*: ***jugendfreier Film*** G(-rated) (*Br* U[-rated]) film; ***nicht jugendfrei*** X-rated
'Jugendfürsorge *f* youth welfare
Jugendgericht *n* JUR juvenile court
Jugendherberge *f* youth hostel
Jugendklub *m* youth club
Jugendkriminali'tät *f* juvenile delinquency
'jugendlich *adj* youthful, young
'Jugendliche *m*, *f* (*-n*; *-n*) young person, *m a.* youth, JUR *a.* juvenile
'Jugendstil *m* (*-s*; *no pl*) Art Nouveau
Jugendstrafanstalt *f* detention center (*Br* centre), reformatory
Jugendverbot *n* for adults only; → ***jugendfrei***
Jugendzentrum *n* youth center (*Br* centre)
Juli ['ju:li] *m* (-[*s*]; *-s*) July
Jumbojet ['jʊmbo-] *m* jumbo (jet)
jun. ABBR *of* ***junior*** Jun., jun., Jnr., Jr., junior
jung [jʊŋ] *adj* young
Junge[1] ['jʊŋə] *m* (*-n*; *-n*) boy; lad; *cards*: jack, knave
'Junge[2] *n* (*-n*; *-n*) ZO young; puppy; kitten; cub; ***Junge bekommen*** *or* ***werfen*** have young
'jungenhaft *adj* boyish
'Jungenstreich *m* boyish prank
jünger ['jʏŋɐ] *adj* younger
'Jünger *m* (*-s*; -) REL disciple (*a. fig*)
Jungfer ['jʊŋfɐ] *f* (-; *-n*) ***alte Jungfer*** old maid
'Jungfernfahrt *f* MAR maiden voyage
Jungfernflug *m* AVIAT maiden flight
'Jungfrau *f* virgin; ASTR Virgo; ***er ist Jungfrau*** he's (a) Virgo
Junggeselle *m* bachelor, single (man)
Junggesellin *f* bachelor girl, single (woman); *esp* JUR spinster
jüngste ['jʏŋstə] *adj* youngest; *fig* latest; ***in jüngster Zeit*** lately, recently; ***das Jüngste Gericht*** the Last Judg(e)ment; ***der Jüngste Tag*** Doomsday
Juni ['ju:ni] *m* (-[*s*]; *-s*) June

J

junior ['ju:njoːɐ] *adj*, **'Junior** *m* (*-s*; *-en* [ju'njo:rən]), **Juni'orin** *f* (*-*; *-nen*) junior (*a.* SPORT)
Jupe [ʒy:p] *Swiss m* (*-s*; *-s*) skirt
Jura ['ju:ra]: ***Jura studieren*** study (the) law
juridisch [ju'ri:dɪʃ] *Austrian* → ***juristisch***
Jurist(in) [ju'rɪst(ɪn)] (*-en*; *-en*/*-*; *-nen*) lawyer; law student
ju'ristisch *adj* legal
Jurorenkomitee [ju'ro:rən-] *Austrian n* → ***Jury***
Jury [ʒy'ri:] *f* (*-*; *-s*) jury
justieren [jʊs'ti:rən] *v/t* (*no -ge-*, *h*) TECH adjust, set
Justiz [jʊs'ti:ts] *f* (*-*; *no pl*) (administration of) justice, (the) law
Justizbeamte *m* judicial officer
Justizirrtum *m* error of justice
Justizmi,nister *m* minister of justice; Attorney General, *Br* Lord Chancellor
Justizminis,terium *n* ministry of justice; Department of Justice
Jute ['ju:tə] *f* (*-*; *no pl*) jute
Juwel [ju've:l] *m*, *n* (*-s*; *-en*) jewel, gem (*both a. fig*); *pl* jewel(le)ry
Juwelier [juve'li:ɐ] *m* (*-s*; *-e*) jewel(l)er

K

Kabarett [kaba'rɛt] *n* (*-s*; *-s*) (political) revue
Kabel ['ka:bəl] *n* (*-s*; *-*) cable
'Kabelfernsehen *n* cable TV
Kabeljau ['ka:bəljau] *m* (*-s*; *-e*, *-s*) ZO cod(fish)
Kabine [ka'bi:nə] *f* (*-*; *-n*) cabin; cubicle; SPORT dressing room; TECH car; TEL *etc* booth
Ka'binenbahn *f* cable railway
Kabinett [kabi'nɛt] *n* (*-s*; *-e*) POL cabinet
Kabis ['ka:bɪs] *Swiss m* (*-*; *no pl*) green cabbage
Kabriolett [kabrio'lɛt] *n* (*-s*; *-s*) MOT convertible
Kachel ['kaxəl] *f* (*-*; *-n*), **'kacheln** *v/t* (*ge-*, *h*) tile
'Kachelofen *m* tiled stove
Kadaver [ka'da:vɐ] *m* (*-s*; *-*) carcass
Kadett [ka'dɛt] *m* (*-en*; *-en*) MIL cadet
Käfer ['kɛ:fɐ] *m* (*-s*; *-*) ZO beetle, bug
Kaffee ['kafe] *m* (*-s*; *-s*) coffee; ***Kaffee kochen*** make coffee; ***Kaffee mit Milch*** white coffee
Kaffeeauto,mat *m* coffee machine
Kaffeebohne *f* coffee bean
Kaffeehaus [ka'fe:-] *Austrian n* café, coffee house
Kaffeekanne *f* coffee pot
Kaffeema,schine *f* cofffeemaker
Kaffeemühle *f* coffee grinder
Käfig ['kɛ:fɪç] *m* (*-s*; *-e*) cage (*a. fig*)
kahl [ka:l] *adj* bald; *fig* bare (*rock*, *wall etc*); barren, bleak (*landscape*)
Kahn [ka:n] *m* (*-[e]s*; *Kähne* ['kɛ:nə]) boat; barge
Kai [kai] *m* (*-s*; *-s*) quay, wharf
Kaiser ['kaizɐ] *m* (*-s*; *-*) emperor
Kaiserin ['kaizərɪn] *f* (*-*; *-nen*) empress
'Kaiserreich *n* empire
Kajüte [ka'jy:tə] *f* (*-*; *-n*) MAR cabin
Kakao [ka'kau] *m* (*-s*; *-s*) cocoa; (hot) chocolate; chocolate milk
Kaktee [kak'te:] *f* (*-*; *-n*), **Kaktus** ['kaktʊs] *m* (*-*; *Kakteen*) BOT cactus
Kalb [kalp] *n* (*-[e]s*; *Kälber* ['kɛlbɐ]) ZO calf
kalben ['kalbən] *v/i* (*ge-*, *h*) calve
'Kalbfleisch *n* veal
'Kalbsbraten *m* roast veal
Kalbsschnitzel *n* veal cutlet; escalope (of veal)
Kaldaunen [kal'daunən] *pl* GASTR tripe
Kalender [ka'lɛndɐ] *m* (*-s*; *-*) calendar
Kalenderjahr *n* calendar year
Kali ['ka:li] *n* (*-s*; *no pl*) CHEM potash
Kaliber [ka'li:bɐ] *n* (*-s*; *-*) caliber, *Br* calibre (*a. fig*)
Kalk [kalk] *m* (*-[e]s*; *-e*) lime; GEOL limestone, chalk; MED calcium
'kalken *v/t* (*ge-*, *h*) whitewash; AGR lime
'kalkig *adj* limy
'Kalkstein *m* limestone
Kalorie [kalo'ri:] *f* (*-*; *-n*) calorie
kalo'rienarm *adj*, **kalorienredu,ziert** *adj* low-calorie, low in calories
kalorienreich *adj* high-calorie, high *or* rich in calories
kalt [kalt] *adj* cold; ***mir ist kalt*** I'm cold; ***es*** (***mir***) ***wird kalt*** it's (I'm) getting cold;

kalt bleiben *fig* keep (one's) cool; ***das lässt mich kalt*** that leaves me cold
'kaltblütig [-blyːtɪç] **1.** *adj* cold-blooded (*a. fig*); **2.** *adv* in cold blood
Kälte ['kɛltə] *f* (-; *no pl*) cold; *fig* coldness; ***vor Kälte zittern*** shiver with cold; ***fünf Grad Kälte*** five degrees below zero
Kälteeinbruch *m* cold snap
Kältegrad *m* degree below zero
Kälteperiˌode *f* cold spell
'kaltmachen F *v/t* (*sep, -ge-, h*) bump off
kam [kaːm] *pret of* ***kommen***
Kamee [ka'meːə] *f* (-; *-n*) cameo
Kamel [ka'meːl] *n* (*-s*; *-e*) ZO camel
Ka'melhaar *n* (-[*e*]*s*; *no pl*) camelhair
Kamera ['kaməra] *f* (-; *-s*) camera
Kamerad [kamə'raːt] *m* (*-en*; *-en* [-'raːdən]) companion, F mate, pal, buddy
Kameradin [-'raːdɪn] *f* (-; *-nen*) companion
Kame'radschaft *f* (-; *no pl*) comradeship
'Kameramann *m* cameraman
'Kamerareˌkorder *m* (*-s*; -) camcorder
Kamille [ka'mɪlə] *f* (-; *-n*) BOT camomile
Kamin [ka'miːn] *m* (*-s*; *-e*) fireplace; chimney (*a.* MOUNT); ***am Kamin*** by the fire (-side)
Kaminkehrer [-keːrɐ] *m* (*-s*; -) chimney sweep
Kaminsims *m, n* mantelpiece
Kamm [kam] *m* (-[*e*]*s*; *Kämme* ['kɛmə]) comb, ZO *a.* crest (*a. fig*)
kämmen ['kɛmən] *v/t* (*ge-, h*) comb; ***sich*** (***die Haare***) ***kämmen*** comb one's hair
Kammer ['kamɐ] *f* (-; *-n*) (small) room; storeroom, closet; garret; POL, ECON chamber; JUR division
'Kammermuˌsik *f* chamber music
'Kammgarn *n* worsted (yarn)
Kampagne [kam'panjə] *f* (-; *-n*) campaign
Kampf [kampf] *m* (-[*e*]*s*; *Kämpfe* ['kɛmpfə]) fight (*a. fig*), struggle (*a. fig*), *esp* MIL combat, battle (*a. fig*); SPORT contest, match; *boxing*: fight, bout; *fig* conflict
'kampfbereit *adj* ready for battle (MIL combat)
kämpfen ['kɛmpfən] *v/i* (*ge-, h*) fight (***gegen*** against; ***mit*** with; ***um*** for) (*a. fig*); struggle (*a. fig*); *fig* contend, wrestle
Kampfer ['kampfɐ] *m* (*-s*; *no pl*) CHEM camphor
Kämpfer ['kɛmpfɐ] *m* (*-s*; -), **'Kämpferin** *f* (-; *-nen*) fighter (*a. fig*)
kämpferisch ['kɛmpfərɪʃ] *adj* fighting, aggressive
'Kampfflugzeug *n* MIL combat aircraft
Kampfkraft *f* (-; *no pl*) fighting strength
Kampfrichter *m* SPORT judge
Kampfsportarten *pl* martial arts
Kanada ['kanada] Canada
Kanadier [ka'naːdjɐ] *m* (*-s*; -), **Ka'nadierin** [-djərɪn] *f* (-; *-nen*), **ka'nadisch** *adj* Canadian
Kanal [ka'naːl] *m* (*-s*; *Kanäle* [ka'nɛːlə]) canal; channel (*a.* TV, TECH, *fig*); sewer, drain; ***der Kanal*** the (English) Channel
Kanalisation [kanaliza'tsjoːn] *f* (-; *-en*) sewerage (system); canalization
kanalisieren [kanali'ziːrən] *v/t* (*no -ge-, h*) sewer; canalize; *fig* channel
Ka'naltunnel *m* Channel Tunnel, F Chunnel
Kanarienvogel [ka'naːrjən-] *m* canary
Kandidat [kandi'daːt] *m* (*-en*; *-en*), **Kandi'datin** *f* (-; *-nen*) candidate
Kandidatur [kandida'tuːɐ] *f* (-; *-en*) candidacy, *Br a.* candidature
kandidieren [kandi'diːrən] *v/i* (*no -ge-, h*) stand *or* run for election; ***kandidieren für …*** run for the office of …
Känguru, Känguruh ['kɛŋguru] *n* (*-s*; *-s*) ZO kangaroo
Kaninchen [ka'niːnçən] *n* (*-s*; -) ZO rabbit
Kanister [ka'nɪstɐ] *m* (*-s*; -) (fuel) can
Kanne ['kanə] *f* (-; *-n*) pot; can
Kannibale [kani'baːlə] *m* (*-n*; *-n*) cannibal
kannte ['kantə] *pret of* ***kennen***
Kanon ['kaːnɔn] *m* (*-s*; *-s*) MUS canon
Kanone [ka'noːnə] *f* (-; *-n*) MIL gun; cannon; F ace, *esp* SPORT *a.* crack
Kante ['kantə] *f* (-; *-n*) edge
'kanten *v/t* (*ge-, h*) set on edge; tilt; edge (*skis*)
'Kanten *m* (*-s*; -) crust
kantig ['kantɪç] *adj* angular, square(d)
Kantine [kan'tiːnə] *f* (-; *-n*) canteen
Kanton [kan'toːn] *m* (*-s*; *-e*) POL canton
Kanu ['kaːnu] *n* (*-s*; *-s*) canoe
Kanüle [ka'nyːlə] *f* (-; *-n*) MED cannula, (drain) tube
Kanzel ['kantsəl] *f* (-; *-n*) REL pulpit; AVIAT cockpit
Kanzlei [kants'lai] *f* (-; *-en*) office
Kanzler ['kantslɐ] *m* (*-s*; -) chancellor
Kanzlerin ['kantslərɪn] *f* (-; *-nen*) chancellor
Kap [kap] *n* (*-s*; *-s*) cape, headland
Kapazität [kapatsi'tɛːt] *f* (-; *-en*) capacity; *fig* authority
Kapelle [ka'pɛlə] *f* (-; *-n*) REL chapel; MUS band
Ka'pellmeister *m* MUS conductor
kapern ['kaːpɐn] *v/t* (*ge-, h*) MAR capture, seize
kapieren [ka'piːrən] F *v/t* (*no -ge-, h*) get; ***kapiert?*** got it?
Kapital [kapi'taːl] *n* (*-s*; *-e, -ien*) ECON capital, funds

Kapitalanlage *f* investment
Kapitalismus [kapita'lɪsmʊs] *m* (-; *no pl*) capitalism
Kapita'list *m* (*-en*; *-en*), **kapita'listisch** *adj* capitalist
Kapi'talverbrechen *n* capital crime, JUR felony
Kapitän [kapi'tɛːn] *m* (*-s*; *-e*) captain (*a.* SPORT)
Kapitel [ka'pɪtəl] *n* (*-s*; *-*) chapter (*a. fig*); F *fig* story
Kapitulation [kapitula'tsjoːn] *f* (-; *-en*) capitulation, surrender (*a. fig*)
kapitulieren [kapitu'liːrən] *v/i* (*no -ge-*, *h*) capitulate, surrender (*a. fig*)
Kaplan [ka'plaːn] *m* (*-s*; *Kapläne* [ka'plɛːnə]) REL curate
Kappe ['kapə] *f* (-; *-n*) cap, TECH *a.* top, hood
'kappen *v/t* (*ge-*, *h*) cut (*rope*); lop, top (*tree*)
Kapsel ['kapsəl] *f* (-; *-n*) capsule
kaputt [ka'pʊt] F *adj* broken (*a. fig*); TECH out of order; *fig* dead beat; ruined; ***kaputt machen*** F *v/t* (*sep*, *-ge-*, *h*) break, wreck (*a. fig*), ruin; *fig* → ***kaputtmachen***; **kaputtgehen** F *v/i* (*irr*, ***gehen***, *sep*, *-ge-*, *sein*) break; MOT *etc* break down; *fig* break up
kaputtmachen *v/t* (*sep*, *-ge-*, *h*) F *fig* wreck, ruin
Kapuze [ka'puːtsə] *f* (-; *-n*) hood; cowl
Karabiner [kara'biːnɐ] *m* (*-s*; *-*) carbine
Karabinerhaken *m* karabiner, snaplink
Karaffe [ka'rafə] *f* (-; *-n*) decanter
Karambolage [karambo'laːʒə] *f* (-; *-n*) collision, crash
Karat [ka'raːt] *n* (*-[e]s*; *-e*) carat
Karate [ka'raːtə] *n* (*-[s]*; *no pl*) SPORT karate
Karawane [kara'vaːnə] *f* (-; *-n*) caravan
Kardinal [kardi'naːl] *m* (*-s*; *Kardinäle* [kardi'nɛːlə]) REL cardinal
Karfiol [kar'fjoːl] *Austrian m* (*-s*; *no pl*) BOT cauliflower
Kar'freitag [kaːɐ-] *m* REL Good Friday
karg [kark], **kärglich** ['kɛrklɪç] *adj* meag|er, *Br* -re, scanty; frugal; poor
kariert [ka'riːɐt] *adj* checked, checkered, *Br* chequered; squared
Karies ['kaːrjɛs] *f* (-; *no pl*) MED (dental) caries
Karikatur [karika'tuːɐ] *f* (-; *-en*) *mst* cartoon, *esp fig* caricature
Karikaturist [karikatu'rɪst] *m* (*-en*; *-en*) cartoonist
karikieren [kari'kiːrən] *v/t* (*no -ge-*, *h*) caricature
Karneval ['karnəval] *m* (*-s*; *-e*, *-s*) carnival
Karo ['kaːro] *n* (*-s*; *-s*) square, check; *cards*: diamonds
Karosserie [karɔsə'riː] *f* (-; *-n*) MOT body
Karotte [ka'rɔtə] *f* (-; *-n*) BOT carrot
Karpfen ['karpfən] *m* (*-s*; *-*) ZO carp
Karre ['karə] *f* (-; *-n*), **'Karren** *m* (*-s*; *-*) cart; wheelbarrow; F MOT jalopy
Karriere [ka'rjeːrə] *f* (-; *-n*) career; ***Karriere machen*** work one's way up, get to the top
Karte ['kartə] *f* (-; *-n*) card; ticket; GEOGR map; chart; GASTR menu; ***gute*** (***schlechte***) ***Karten*** a good (bad) hand
Kartei [kar'tai] *f* (-; *-en*) card index
Karteikarte *f* index *or* file card
'Kartenhaus *n* house of cards (*a. fig*); MAR chartroom
Kartenspiel *n* card game; deck (*Br* pack) of cards
Kartentele,fon *n* cardphone
Kartenvorverkauf *m* advance booking; box office
Kartoffel [kar'tɔfəl] *f* (-; *-n*) BOT potato
Kartoffelbrei *m* mashed potatoes
Kartoffelchips *pl* (potato) chips, *Br* crisps
Kartoffelkloß *m*, **Kartoffelknödel** *m* potato dumpling
Kartoffelpuffer *m* potato fritter
Kartoffelschalen *pl* potato peelings
Kartoffelschäler *m* potato peeler
Karton [kar'tɔŋ] *m* (*-s*; *-s*) cardboard; pasteboard; cardboard box
Karussell [karʊ'sɛl] *n* (*-s*; *-s*) roundabout, car(r)ousel, merry-go-round
Karwoche ['kaːɐ-] *f* REL Holy Week
Kaschmir ['kaʃmiːɐ] *m* (*-s*; *-e*) cashmere
Käse ['kɛːzə] *m* (*-s*; *-*) cheese
Kaserne [ka'zɛrnə] *f* (-; *-n*) barracks
Ka'sernenhof *m* barrack square
käsig ['kɛːzɪç] *adj* cheesy; pasty
Kasino [ka'ziːno] *n* (*-s*; *-s*) casino; MIL (officers') mess
Kasperle ['kaspɐlə] *n*, *m* (*-s*; *-*) Punch
Kasperlethe,ater *n* Punch and Judy show
Kassa ['kasa] *Austrian f* (-; *Kassen*), **Kasse** ['kasə] *f* (-; *-n*) till; cash register; checkout (counter); cash desk; cashier's counter; THEA *etc* box office; F ***gut*** (***knapp***) ***bei Kasse sein*** be flush (be a bit hard up)
'Kassenbeleg *m*, **Kassenbon** *m* sales slip, *Br* receipt
Kassenerfolg *m* THEA *etc* box-office success
Kassenpati,ent *m* MED health plan (*Am* medicaid, *Br* NHS) patient
Kassenschlager F *m* blockbuster
Kassenwart [-vart] *m* (*-[e]s*; *-e*) treasurer
Kassette [ka'sɛtə] *f* (-; *-n*) box, case; MUS,

TV, PHOT *etc* cassette; casket
Kas'setten… *in cpds …rekorder etc*: cassette …
kassieren [ka'siːrən] *v/t and v/i (no -ge-, h)* collect, take (the money)
Kassierer [ka'siːrɐ] *m (-s; -)*, **Kas'siererin** *f (-; -nen)* cashier; teller; collector
Kastanie [kas'taːnjə] *f (-; -n)* BOT chestnut
Kasten ['kastən] *m (-s; Kästen* ['kɛstən]) box (*a.* F TV, SPORT *etc*); case; chest
kastrieren [kas'triːrən] *v/t (no -ge-, h)* MED, VET castrate
Kasus ['kaːzʊs] *m (-; -)* LING case
Katalog [kata'loːk] *m (-[e]s; -e)* catalog(ue *Br*)
Katalysator [kataly'zaːtoːɐ] *m (-s; -en* [-za'toːrən]) CHEM catalyst; MOT catalytic converter
Katapult [kata'pʊlt] *m, n (-[e]s; -e)*, **katapultieren** [katapʊl'tiːrən] *v/t (no -ge-, h)* catapult
katastrophal [katastro'faːl] *adj* disastrous (*a. fig*)
Katastrophe [katas'troːfə] *f (-; -n)* catastrophe, disaster (*a. fig*)
Kata'strophengebiet *n* disaster area
Katastrophenschutz *m* disaster control
Katechismus [katɛ'çɪsmʊs] *m (-; -men)* REL catechism
Kategorie [katego'riː] *f (-; -n)* category
Kater ['kaːtɐ] *m (-s; -)* ZO male cat, tomcat; F hangover
kath. ABBR *of* ***katholisch*** Cath., Catholic
Kathedrale [kate'draːlə] *f (-; -n)* cathedral
Katholik [kato'liːk] *m (-en; -en)*, **Katho'likin** *f (-; -nen)*, **katholisch** [ka'toːlɪʃ] *adj* (Roman) Catholic
Kätzchen ['kɛtsçən] *n (-s; -)* ZO kitten, pussy (*a.* BOT)
Katze ['katsə] *f (-; -n)* ZO cat; kitten
Kauderwelsch ['kaudɐvɛlʃ] *n (-[s]; no pl)* gibberish
kauen ['kauən] *v/t and v/i (ge-, h)* chew
kauern ['kauɐn] *v/i and v/refl (ge-, h)* crouch, squat
Kauf [kauf] *m (-[e]s; Käufe* ['kɔʏfə]) purchase (*a.* ECON), F buy; purchasing, buying; ***ein guter Kauf*** a bargain, F a good buy; ***zum Kauf anbieten*** offer for sale
'kaufen *v/t (ge-, h)* buy (*a. fig*), purchase
Käufer ['kɔʏfɐ] *m (-s; -)*, **'Käuferin** *f (-; -nen)* buyer; customer
'Kauffrau *f (-; -en)* businesswoman
'Kaufhaus *n* department store
Kaufkraft *f (-; no pl)* ECON purchasing power
käuflich ['kɔʏflɪç] *adj* for sale; *fig* venal
'Kaufmann *m (-[e]s; -leute)* businessman; dealer, trader, merchant; storekeeper, *Br mst* shopkeeper; grocer
'kaufmännisch [-mɛnɪʃ] *adj* commercial, business; ***kaufmännischer Angestellter*** clerk
'Kaufvertrag *m* contract of sale
'Kaugummi *m (-s; -s)* chewing gum
kaum [kaum] *adv* hardly; ***kaum zu glauben*** hard to believe
Kaution [kau'tsjoːn] *f (-; -en)* security; JUR bail
Kautschuk ['kautʃʊk] *m (-s; -e)* (india) rubber
Kavalier [kava'liːɐ] *m (-s; -e)* gentleman
Kaviar ['kaːvjar] *m (-s; -e)* caviar(e)
keck [kɛk] *adj* cheeky, saucy, pert
Kegel ['keːgəl] *m (-s; -)* skittle, pin; MATH, TECH cone
Kegelbahn *f* bowling (*esp Br* skittle) alley
'kegelförmig [-fœrmɪç] *adj* conical
'Kegelkugel *f* bowling (*esp Br* skittle) ball
'kegeln *v/i (ge-, h)* bowl, go bowling, *esp Br* play (at) skittles *or* ninepins
Kehle ['keːlə] *f (-; -n)* ANAT throat
'Kehlkopf *m* ANAT larynx
Kehre ['keːrə] *f (-; -n)* (sharp) bend
'kehren *v/t (ge-, h)* sweep; ***j-m den Rücken kehren*** turn one's back on s.o.
Kehricht ['keːrɪçt] *m (-s; no pl)* sweepings
Kehrichtschaufel *f* dustpan
kehrtmachen ['keːɐt-] *v/i (sep, -ge-, h)* turn back
keifen ['kaifən] *v/i (ge-, h)* nag, bitch
Keil [kail] *m (-[e]s; -e)* wedge; gusset
Keiler ['kailɐ] *m (-s; -)* ZO wild boar
'Keilriemen *m* MOT fan belt
Keim [kaim] *m (-[e]s; -e)* BIOL, MED germ; BOT bud, sprout; *fig* seed(s)
'keimen *v/i (ge-, h)* BOT germinate, sprout; *fig* form, grow; stir
'keimfrei *adj* MED sterile
'keimtötend *adj* MED germicidal
'Keimzelle *f* BIOL germ cell
kein [kain] *indef pron* **1.** *adj*: ***kein(e)*** no, not any; ***kein anderer*** no one else; ***kein(e) … mehr*** not any more …; ***kein Geld (keine Zeit) mehr*** no money (time) left; ***kein Kind mehr*** no longer a child; **2.** *su*: ***keiner, keine, kein(e)s*** none, no one, nobody; ***keiner von beiden*** neither (of the two); ***keiner von uns*** none of us
'keines'falls *adv* by no means, under no circumstances
'keineswegs [-'veːks] *adv* by no means, not in the least
'keinmal *adv* not once, not a single time
Keks [keːks] *m, n (-es, -e)* cookie, *Br* biscuit
Kelch [kɛlç] *m (-[e]s; -e)* cup (*a.* BOT); REL chalice

Kelle ['kɛlə] *f* (-; *-n*) GASTR ladle, scoop; TECH trowel; signaling disk
Keller ['kɛlɐ] *m* (*-s*; -) cellar; → **Kellergeschoss** *n*, **Kellergeschoß** *Austrian n* basement
Kellerwohnung *f* basement (apartment, *esp Br* flat)
Kellner ['kɛlnɐ] *m* (*-s*; -) waiter
Kellnerin ['kɛlnərɪn] *f* (-; *-nen*) waitress
keltern ['kɛltɐn] *v/t* (*ge-*, *h*) press
kennen ['kɛnən] *v/t* (*irr*, *ge-*, *h*) know, be acquainted with; ***kennen lernen*** → ***kennenlernen***
'**kennenlernen** *v/t* (*sep*, *-ge-*, *h*) get to know, become acquainted with; meet *s.o.*; ***als ich ihn kennenlernen lernte*** when I first met him
Kenner ['kɛnɐ] *m* (*-s*; -), '**Kennerin** *f* (-; *-nen*) expert
kenntlich ['kɛntlɪç] *adj* recognizable (***an*** *dat* by)
Kenntnis *f* (-; *-se*) knowledge; ***gute Kenntnisse in*** (*dat*) a good knowledge of
'**Kennwort** *n* password
'**Kennzeichen** *n* mark, sign; (distinguishing) feature, characteristic; MOT license (*Br* registration) number
'**kennzeichnen** *v/t* (*ge-*, *h*) mark; *fig* characterize
kentern ['kɛntɐn] *v/i* (*ge-*, *sein*) MAR capsize
Keramik [ke'ra:mɪk] *f* (-; *-en*) ceramics
Kerbe ['kɛrbə] *f* (-; *-n*) notch
Kerker ['kɛrkɐ] *m* (*-s*; -) dungeon
Kerl [kɛrl] F *m* (*-s*; *-e*) fellow, guy; ***armer Kerl*** poor devil; ***ein anständiger Kerl*** a decent sort
Kern [kɛrn] *m* (*-[e]s*; *-e*) BOT pip, seed, stone, kernel; TECH core (*a. fig*); PHYS nucleus
Kern... *in cpds ...energie*, *...forschung*, *...physik*, *...reaktor*, *...technik etc*: nuclear ...
Kernfach *n* PED basic subject
Kernfa͵milie *f* nuclear family
Kerngehäuse *n* BOT core
'**kernge'sund** *adj* F (as) sound as a bell
kernig ['kɛrnɪç] *adj* full of seeds (*Br* pips); *fig* robust; pithy
'**Kernkraft** *f* PHYS nuclear power
Kernkraftgegner *m* anti-nuclear activist
Kernkraftwerk *n* nuclear power station *or* plant
'**kernlos** *adj* BOT seedless
'**Kernspaltung** *f* PHYS nuclear fission
'**Kernwaffen** *pl* MIL nuclear weapons
'**kernwaffenfrei** *adj*: ***kernwaffenfreie Zone*** MIL nuclear-free zone
'**Kernwaffenversuch** *m* MIL nuclear test
'**Kernzeit** *f* ECON core time
Kerze ['kɛrtsə] *f* (-; *-n*) candle; SPORT shoulder stand
kess [kɛs] F *adj* cheeky, saucy, pert
Kessel ['kɛsəl] *m* (*-s*; -) kettle; TECH boiler; tank
Kette ['kɛtə] *f* (-; *-n*) chain (*a. fig*); necklace; ***e-e Kette bilden*** form a line
'**Ketten...** *in cpds ...antrieb*, *...laden*, *...rauchen*, *...raucher*, *...reaktion etc*: chain ...
'**ketten** *v/t* (*ge-*, *h*) chain (***an*** *acc* to)
'**Kettenfahrzeug** *n* tracked vehicle
Ketzer ['kɛtsɐ] *m* (*-s*; -) heretic
Ketzerei [kɛtsə'rai] *f* (-; *-en*) heresy
keuchen ['kɔʏçən] *v/i* (*ge-*, *h*) pant, gasp
'**Keuchhusten** *m* MED whooping cough
Keule ['kɔʏlə] *f* (-; *-n*) club; GASTR leg
keusch [kɔʏʃ] *adj* chaste
'**Keuschheit** *f* (-; *no pl*) chastity
Kfz [ka:ʔɛf'tsɛt] ABBR *of* ***Kraftfahrzeug*** motor vehicle
Kf'z-Brief *m*, **Kf'z-Schein** *m* vehicle registration document
Kf'z-Steuer *f* road *or* automobile tax
Kf'z-Werkstatt *f* garage
KG [ka:'ge:] ABBR *of* ***Kommanditgesellschaft*** ECON limited partnership
kichern ['kɪçɐn] *v/i* (*ge-*, *h*) giggle
Kiebitz ['ki:bɪts] *m* (*-es*; *-e*) ZO peewit, lapwing; F kibitzer
Kiefer[1] ['ki:fɐ] *m* (*-s*; -) ANAT jaw(bone)
'**Kiefer**[2] *f* (-; *-n*) BOT pine(tree)
Kiel [ki:l] *m* (*-[e]s*; *-e*) MAR keel
Kielflosse *f* AVIAT tail fin
Kielraum *m* MAR bilge
Kielwasser *n* (*-s*; -) MAR wake (*a. fig*)
Kieme ['ki:mə] *f* (*-n*; *-n*) ZO gill
Kies [ki:s] *m* (*-es*; *-e*) gravel (*a.* ***mit Kies bestreuen***); F dough
Kiesel ['ki:zəl] *m* (*-s*; -) pebble
Kilo ['ki:lo] *n* (*-s*; -) → ***Kilogramm***
Kilo'gramm [kilo-] *n* kilogram(me)
Kilohertz [-'hɛrts] *n* (-; -) kilohertz
Kilo'meter *m* kilometer, *Br* kilometre
Kilo'watt *n* ELECTR kilowatt
Kind [kɪnt] *n* (*-[e]s*; *-er* ['kɪndɐ]) child; ***ein Kind erwarten*** be expecting a baby
'**Kinderarzt** *m*, **Kinderärztin** *f* p(a)ediatrician
Kindergarten *m* kindergarten, nursery school
Kindergärtnerin [-gɛrtnərɪn] *f* (-; *-nen*) nursery-school *or* kindergarten teacher
Kindergeld *n* child benefit
Kinderhort [-hɔrt] *m* (*-[e]s*; *-e*), **Kinderkrippe** *f* day nursery
Kinderlähmung *f* MED polio(-myelitis)

'kinderlieb *adj* fond of children
'kinderlos *adj* childless
'Kindermädchen *n* nurse(maid), nanny
Kinderspiel *fig n*: ***ein Kinderspiel sein*** be child's play
Kinderstube *fig f* manners, upbringing
Kinderwagen *m* baby carriage, buggy, *Br* pram
Kinderzimmer *n* children's room
Kindesalter ['kɪndəs-] *n* childhood; infancy
Kindesentführung *f* kidnap(p)ing
Kindesmisshandlung *f* child abuse
'Kindheit *f* (-; *no pl*) (***von Kindheit an*** from) childhood
kindisch ['kɪndɪʃ] *adj* childish
'kindlich *adj* childlike
Kinn [kɪn] *n* (-[*e*]*s*; -*e*) ANAT chin
Kinnbacke *f*, **Kinnbacken** *m* (-*s*; -) ANAT jaw(-bone)
Kinnhaken *m boxing*: hook (to the chin), uppercut
Kino ['ki:no] *n* (-*s*; -*s*) a) (*no pl*) motion pictures, *esp Br* cinema, F *the* movies, b) movie theater, *esp Br* cinema
'Kinobesucher *m*, **'Kinogänger** [-gɛŋɐ] *m* (-*s*; -) moviegoer, *Br* cinemagoer
Kippe ['kɪpə] *f* (-; -*n*) F butt, *esp Br* stub; SPORT upstart
'kippen **1.** *v/i* (*ge-*, *sein*) tip *or* topple (over); **2.** *v/t* (*ge-*, *h*) tilt, tip over *or* up
Kirche ['kɪrçə] *f* (-; -*n*) church; ***in die Kirche gehen*** go to church
'Kirchenbuch *n* parish register
Kirchendiener *m* sexton
Kirchengemeinde *f* parish
Kirchenjahr *n* Church *or* ecclesiastical year
Kirchenlied *n* hymn
Kirchenmu,sik *f* sacred *or* church music
Kirchenschiff *n* ARCH nave
Kirchensteuer *f* church tax
Kirchenstuhl *m* pew
Kirchentag *m* church congress
'Kirchgang *m* churchgoing
'Kirchgänger [-gɛŋɐ] *m* (-*s*; -) churchgoer
'kirchlich *adj* church, ecclesiastical
'Kirchturm *m* steeple; spire; church tower
Kirsche ['kɪrʃə] *f* (-; -*n*) BOT cherry
Kissen ['kɪsən] *n* (-*s*; -) pillow; cushion
Kissenbezug *m*, **Kissenhülle** *f* pillowcase, pillowslip
Kiste ['kɪstə] *f* (-; -*n*) box, chest; crate
Kitsch [kɪtʃ] *m* (-[*e*]*s*; *no pl*) kitsch; trash; F slush
'kitschig *adj* kitschy; trashy; slushy
Kitt [kɪt] *m* (-[*e*]*s*; -*e*) cement; putty
Kittel ['kɪtəl] *m* (-*s*; -) smock; overall; MED (white) coat
'kitten *v/t* (*ge-*, *h*) cement; putty
Kitzel ['kɪtsəl] *m* (-*s*; -) tickle, *fig a.* thrill, kick
'kitzeln *v/i and v/t* (*ge-*, *h*) tickle
Kitzler ['kɪtslɐ] *m* (-*s*; -) ANAT clitoris
kitzlig ['kɪtslɪç] *adj* ticklish (*a. fig*)
kläffen ['klɛfən] *v/i* (*ge-*, *h*) yap, yelp
klaffend ['klafənt] *adj* gaping; yawning
Klage ['kla:gə] *f* (-; -*n*) complaint; lament; JUR action, (law)suit
'klagen *v/i* (*ge-*, *h*) complain (***über*** *acc* of, about; ***bei*** to); lament; JUR go to court; ***gegen j-n klagen*** JUR sue s.o.
Kläger ['klɛ:gɐ] *m* (-*s*; -), **'Klägerin** *f* (-; -*nen*) JUR plaintiff
kläglich ['klɛ:klɪç] → ***jämmerlich***
Klamauk [kla'mauk] *m* (-*s*; *no pl*) racket; THEA *etc* slapstick
klamm [klam] *adj* numb; clammy
Klammer ['klamɐ] *f* (-; -*n*) TECH cramp, clamp; clip; clothespin, *Br* (clothes) peg; MED brace; MATH, PRINT bracket(s)
'klammern *v/t* (*ge-*, *h*) fasten *or* clip together; ***sich klammern an*** (*acc*) cling to
klang [klaŋ] *pret of* ***klingen***
Klang *m* (-[*e*]*s*; *Klänge* ['klɛŋə]) sound; tone; clink; ringing
'klangvoll *adj* sonorous; *fig* illustrious
Klappe ['klapə] *f* (-; -*n*) flap; hinged lid; MOT tailgate, *Br* tailboard; TECH, BOT, ANAT valve; F trap
'klappen (*ge-*, *h*) **1.** *v/t*: ***nach oben klappen*** lift up, raise; put *or* fold up; ***nach unten klappen*** lower, put down; ***es lässt sich*** (***nach hinten***) ***klappen*** it folds (backward); **2.** *v/i* clap, clack; F work, work out (well)
Klapper ['klapɐ] *f* (-; -*n*) rattle
'klappern *v/i* (*ge-*, *h*) clatter, rattle (***mit et.*** s.th.)
'Klapperschlange *f* ZO rattlesnake
Klappfahrrad ['klap-] *n* folding bicycle
Klappfenster *n* top-hung window
Klappmesser *n* jack knife, clasp knife
klapprig ['klaprɪç] *adj* MOT rattly, ramshackle; F shaky
'Klappsitz *m* folding *or* tip-up seat
'Klappstuhl *m* folding chair
'Klapptisch *m* folding table
Klaps [klaps] *m* (-*es*; -*e*) slap, pat; smack
klar [kla:ɐ] *adj* clear (*a. fig*); ***ist dir klar, dass …?*** do you realize that …?; ***das ist mir*** (***nicht ganz***) ***klar*** I (don't quite) understand; (***na***) ***klar!*** of course!; ***alles klar?*** everything okay?
Kläranlage ['klɛ:ɐ-] *f* sewage works
klären ['klɛ:rən] *v/t* (*ge-*, *h*) TECH purify, treat; *fig* clear up; settle; SPORT clear
'Klarheit *f* (-; *no pl*) clearness, *fig a.* clarity

K

Klarinette [klari'nɛtə] *f* (-; *-n*) MUS clarinet
'**Klarsicht...** *in cpds* transparent
Klasse ['klasə] *f* (-; *-n*) class (*a.* POL), PED *a.* grade, *Br* form; classroom; F ***klasse sein*** be super, be fantastic
'**Klassenarbeit** *f* (classroom) test
Klassenbuch *n* classbook, *Br* (class) register
Klassenkame,rad *m* classmate
Klassenlehrer(in) homeroom teacher, *Br* form teacher, *a.* form master (mistress)
Klassensprecher *m* class representative
Klassenzimmer *n* classroom
klassifizieren [klasifi'tsiːrən] *v/t* (*no -ge-, h*) classify
'**Klassifi'zierung** *f* (-; *-en*) classification
Klassiker ['klasikɐ] *m* (*-s*; -) classic
klassisch ['klasɪʃ] *adj* classic(al)
Klatsch [klatʃ] F *m* (*-es*; *no pl*) gossip
'**Klatschbase** *f* gossip
'**klatschen** *v/i and v/t* (*ge-, h*) clap, applaud; F slap, bang; splash; F gossip; ***in die Hände klatschen*** clap one's hands
'**klatschhaft** *adj* gossipy
'**Klatschmaul** F *n* (old) gossip
'**klatsch'nass** F *adj* soaking wet
klauben ['klaubən] *Austrian v/t* (*ge-, h*) pick; gather
Klaue ['klauə] *f* (-; *-n*) ZO claw; *pl fig* clutches
klauen ['klauən] F *v/t* (*ge-, h*) pinch
Klausel ['klauzəl] *f* (-; *-n*) JUR clause; condition
Klausur [klau'zuːɐ] *f* (-; *-en*) test (paper), exam(ination)
Klavier [kla'viːɐ] *n* (*-s*; *-e*) MUS piano; ***Klavier spielen*** play the piano
Klavierkon,zert *n* MUS piano concerto; piano recital
Klebeband ['kleːbə-] *n* (*-[e]s*; *-bänder*) adhesive tape
kleben ['kleːbən] (*ge-, h*) **1.** *v/t* glue, paste; stick; **2.** *v/i* stick, cling (***an*** *dat* to) (*a. fig*)
klebrig ['kleːbrɪç] *adj* sticky
Klebstoff ['kleːp-] *m* adhesive; glue
Klebstreifen *m* adhesive tape
kleckern ['klɛkɐn] F (*ge-, h*) **1.** *v/i* make a mess; **2.** *v/t* spill
Klecks [klɛks] F *m* (*-es*; *-e*) (ink)blot; blob
klecksen ['klɛksən] F *v/i* (*ge-, h*) blot, make blots
Klee [kleː] *m* (*-s*; *no pl*) BOT clover
'**Kleeblatt** *n* cloverleaf
Kleid [klait] *n* (*-[e]s*; *-er* ['klaidɐ]) dress; *pl* clothes
kleiden ['klaidən] *v/t* (*ge-, h*) dress, clothe; ***j-n gut kleiden*** suit s.o.; ***sich gut*** *etc* ***kleiden*** dress well *etc*
Kleiderbügel ['klaidɐ-] *m* (coat) hanger
Kleiderbürste *f* clothes brush
Kleiderhaken *m* coat hook
Kleiderschrank *m* wardrobe
Kleiderständer *m* coat stand
Kleiderstoff *m* dress material
'**kleidsam** *adj* becoming
'**Kleidung** *f* (-; *no pl*) clothes, clothing
'**Kleidungsstück** *n* article of clothing
Kleie ['klaiə] *f* (-; *-n*) AGR bran
klein [klain] *adj* small, *esp* F little (*a. finger, brother*); short; ***von klein auf*** from an early age; ***ein klein wenig*** a little bit; ***Groß und Klein*** young and old; ***die Kleinen*** the little ones; ***klein schneiden*** cut up (into small pieces)
'**Kleinanzeige** *f* want ad, *Br* small ad
Kleinbildkamera *f* 35 mm camera
Kleinfa,milie *f* nuclear family
Kleingeld *n* (small) change
Kleinholz *n* matchwood
Kleinigkeit ['klainɪçkait] *f* (-; *-en*) little thing, trifle; little something; ***e-e Kleinigkeit sein*** be nothing, be child's play
'**Kleinkind** *n* baby, infant
'**Kleinkram** F *m* odds and ends
'**kleinlaut** *adj* subdued
'**kleinlich** *adj* small-minded, petty; mean; pedantic, fussy
'**kleinschneiden** *v/t* (*irr*, ***schneiden***, *sep*, *-ge-, h*) → ***klein***
'**Kleinstadt** *f* small town
'**kleinstädtisch** *adj* small-town, provincial
'**Kleintrans,porter** *m* MOT pick-up
'**Kleinwagen** *m* MOT small *or* compact car, F runabout
Kleister ['klaistɐ] *m* (*-s*; -) paste
Klemme ['klɛmə] *f* (-; *-n*) TECH clamp; (hair) clip; F ***in der Klemme sitzen*** be in a fix *or* tight spot
'**klemmen** *v/i and v/t* (*ge-, h*) jam; stick; be stuck, be jammed; ***sich klemmen*** jam one's finger *or* hand
Klempner ['klɛmpnɐ] *m* (*-s*; -) plumber
Klepper ['klɛpɐ] *m* (*-s*; -) ZO nag
Klerus ['kleːrʊs] *m* (-; *no pl*) REL clergy
Klette ['klɛtə] *f* (-; *-n*) BOT bur(r); *fig* leech
klettern ['klɛtɐn] *v/i* (*ge-, sein*) climb; ***auf e-n Baum klettern*** climb (up) a tree
'**Kletterpflanze** *f* BOT climber
Klient [kli'ɛnt] *m* (*-en*; *-en*), **Kli'entin** *f* (-; *-nen*) client
Klima ['kliːma] *n* (*-s*; *-s*) climate, *fig a.* atmosphere
'**Klimaanlage** *f* air-conditioning
klimatisch [kli'maːtɪʃ] *adj* climatic
klimpern ['klɪmpɐn] *v/i* (*ge-, h*) jingle, chink (***mit et.*** s.th.); F MUS strum (away) (***auf*** *dat* on)
Klinge ['klɪŋə] *f* (-; *-n*) blade

Klingel ['klɪŋəl] *f* (-; *-n*) bell
'**Klingelknopf** *m* bell (push)
'**klingeln** *v/i* (*ge-, h*) ring (the bell); ***es klingelt*** the (door)bell is ringing
'**klingen** *v/i* (*irr, ge-, h*) sound; *bell, metal etc*: ring; *glasses etc*: clink
Klinik ['kli:nɪk] *f* (-; *-en*) hospital; clinic
klinisch ['kli:nɪʃ] *adj* clinical
Klinke ['klɪŋkə] *f* (-; *-n*) (door) handle
Klippe ['klɪpə] *f* (-; *-n*) cliff, rock(s); *fig* obstacle
klirren ['klɪrən] *v/i* (*ge-, h*) *window*: rattle; *glasses etc*: clink; *broken glass*: tinkle; *swords*: clash; *keys, coins*: jingle
Klischee [kli'ʃe:] *n* (*-s*; *-s*) cliché
klobig ['klo:bɪç] *adj* bulky, clumsy
klopfen ['klɔpfən] (*ge-, h*) **1.** *v/i heart etc*: beat, throb; knock (***an*** *acc* at, on); tap; pat; ***es klopft*** there's a knock at the door; **2.** *v/t* beat; knock; drive (*nail etc*)
Klosett [klo'zɛt] *n* (*-s*; *-s*) lavatory, toilet
Klosettbrille *f* toilet seat
Klosettpa,pier *n* toilet paper
Kloß [klo:s] *m* (*-es*; *Klöße* ['klø:sə]) clod, lump (*a. fig*); GASTR dumpling
Kloster ['klo:stɐ] *n* (*-s*; *Klöster* ['klø:stɐ]) REL monastery; convent
Klotz [klɔts] *m* (*-es*; *Klötze* ['klœtsə]) block; log
Klub [klʊb] *m* (*-s*; *-s*) club
'**Klubsessel** *m* lounge chair
Kluft [klʊft] *f* (-; *Klüfte* ['klʏftə]) gap (*a. fig*); abyss
klug [klu:k] *adj* intelligent, clever, F bright, smart; wise; ***daraus*** (***aus ihm***) ***werde ich nicht klug*** I don't know what to make of it (him)
'**Klugheit** *f* (-; *no pl*) intelligence, cleverness, F brains; good sense; knowledge
Klumpen ['klʊmpən] *m* (*-s*; -) lump; clod; nugget
'**Klumpfuß** *m* MED club foot
'**klumpig** *adj* lumpy; cloddish
knabbern ['knabɐn] *v/t and v/i* (*ge-, h*) nibble, gnaw
Knabe ['kna:bə] *m* (*-n*; *-n*) boy
'**knabenhaft** *adj* boyish
Knäckebrot ['knɛkə-] *n* crispbread
knacken ['knakən] *v/t and v/i* (*ge-, h*) crack; *twig*: snap; *fire, radio*: crackle
Knacks F *m* (*-es*; *-e*) crack; *fig* defect
Knall [knal] *m* (*-[e]s*; *-e*) bang; crack, report; pop; F ***e-n Knall haben*** be nuts
'**Knallbon,bon** *m, n* cracker
'**knallen** *v/i and v/t* (*ge-, h*) bang; slam; crack; pop; F crash (***gegen*** into); F ***j-m e-e knallen*** slap s.o.('s face)
'**knallig** F *adj* flashy, loud
'**Knallkörper** *m* firecracker

knapp [knap] *adj* scarce; scanty, meager, *Br* meagre (*food, pay etc*); bare (*a. majority etc*); limited (*time etc*); narrow (*escape etc*); tight (*dress etc*); brief; ***knapp an Geld*** (***Zeit*** *etc*) short of money (time *etc*); ***mit knapper Not*** only just, barely
Knappe ['knapə] *m* (*-n*; *-n*) miner
'**knapphalten** *v/t* (*irr*, ***halten***, *sep, -ge-, h*): ***j-n knapphalten halten*** keep s.o. short
'**Knappheit** *f* (-; *no pl*) shortage
Knarre ['knarə] *f* (-; *-n*) rattle; F gun
'**knarren** *v/i* (*ge-, h*) creak
Knast [knast] F *m* (*-[e]s*; *Knäste* ['knɛstə]) *sl* clink
Knastbruder F *m* jailbird
knattern ['knatɐn] *v/i* (*ge-, h*) crackle; MOT roar
Knäuel ['knɔʏəl] *m, n* (*-s*; -) ball; tangle
Knauf [knauf] *m* (*-[e]s*; *Knäufe* ['knɔʏfə]) knob; pommel
knaus(e)rig ['knauz(ə)rɪç] F *adj* stingy
knautschen ['knautʃən] *v/t and v/i* (*ge-, h*) crumple
'**Knautschzone** *f* MOT crumple zone
Knebel ['kne:bəl] *m* (*-s*; -), '**knebeln** *v/t* (*ge-, h*) gag (*a. fig*)
Knecht [knɛçt] *m* (*-[e]s*; *-e*) farmhand; *fig* slave
Knechtschaft *fig f* (-; *no pl*) slavery
kneifen ['knaifən] *v/t and v/i* (*irr, ge-, h*) pinch (***j-m in den Arm*** s.o.'s arm); F chicken out
'**Kneifzange** *f* pincers
Kneipe ['knaipə] F *f* (-; *-n*) saloon, bar, *esp Br* pub
kneten ['kne:tən] *v/t* (*ge-, h*) knead; mo(u)ld
'**Knetmasse** *f* Plasticine®, Play-Doh®
Knick [knɪk] *m* (*-[e]s*; *-e, -s*) fold, crease; bend
'**knicken** *v/t* (*ge-, h*) fold, crease; bend; break; ***nicht knicken!*** do not bend!
Knicks [knɪks] *m* (*-es*; *-e*) curts(e)y; ***e-n Knicks machen*** → '**knicksen** *v/i* (*ge-, h*) curts(e)y (***vor*** *dat* to)
Knie [kni:] *n* (*-s*; - ['kni:ə, kni:]) ANAT knee
Kniebeuge *f* SPORT knee bend
Kniekehle *f* ANAT hollow of the knee
knien [kni:n] *v/i* (*ge-, h*) kneel, be on one's knees (***vor*** *dat* before)
'**Kniescheibe** *f* ANAT kneecap
'**Kniestrumpf** *m* knee(-length) sock
kniff [knɪf] *pret of* ***kneifen***
Kniff *m* (*-[e]s*; *-e*) crease, fold; pinch; trick, knack
kniff(e)lig ['knɪf(ə)lɪç] *adj* tricky
knipsen ['knɪpsən] *v/t and v/i* (*ge-, h*) F PHOT take a picture (of); punch, clip
Knirps [knɪrps] *m* (*-es*; *-e*) little guy

knirschen ['knɪrʃən] *v/i* (*ge-*, *h*) crunch; ***mit den Zähnen knirschen*** grind *or* gnash one's teeth
knistern ['knɪstɐn] *v/i* (*ge-*, *h*) crackle; rustle
knittern ['knɪtɐn] *v/t and v/i* (*ge-*, *h*) crumple, crease, wrinkle
Knoblauch ['kno:plaux] *m* (-[*e*]*s*; *no pl*) BOT garlic
Knöchel ['knœçəl] *m* (-*s*; -) ANAT ankle; knuckle
Knochen ['knɔxən] *m* (-*s*; -) ANAT bone
'Knochenbruch *m* MED fracture
knochig ['knɔxɪç] *adj* bony
Knödel ['knø:dəl] *m* (-*s*; -) dumpling
Knolle ['knɔlə] *f* (-; -*n*) BOT tuber; bulb
Knopf [knɔpf] *m* (-*es*; *Knöpfe* ['knœpfə]), **knöpfen** ['knœpfən] *v/t* (*ge-*, *h*) button
'Knopfloch *n* buttonhole
Knorpel ['knɔrpəl] *m* (-*s*; -) GASTR gristle; ANAT cartilage
knorrig ['knɔrɪç] *adj* gnarled, knotted
Knospe ['knɔspə] *f* (-; -*n*), **'knospen** *v/i* (*ge-*, *h*) BOT bud
knoten [kno:tən] *v/t* (*ge-*, *h*) knot, make a knot in
'Knoten *m* (-*s*; -) knot (*a. fig*)
'Knotenpunkt *m* center, *Br* centre; RAIL junction
knüllen ['knʏlən] *v/t and v/i* (*ge-*, *h*) crumple
Knüller ['knʏlɐ] F *m* (-*s*; -) smash (hit); scoop
knüpfen ['knʏpfən] *v/t* (*ge-*, *h*) tie; weave
Knüppel ['knʏpəl] *m* (-*s*; -) stick, cudgel; truncheon
Knüppelschaltung *f* floor shift
knurren ['knʊrən] *v/i* (*ge-*, *h*) growl, snarl; *fig* grumble (***über*** *acc* at); *stomach*: rumble
knusp(e)rig ['knʊsp(ə)rɪç] *adj* crisp, crunchy
knutschen ['knu:tʃən] F *v/i* (*ge-*, *h*) pet, neck, smooch
k.o. [ka:'ˀo:] *adj* knocked out; *fig* beat
Koalition [koali'tsjo:n] *f* (-; -*en*) *esp* POL coalition
große Koalition grand coalition
Kobold ['ko:bɔlt] *m* (-[*e*]*s*; -*e*) (hob)goblin, imp (*a. fig*)
Koch [kɔx] *m* (-[*e*]*s*; *Köche* ['kœçə]) cook; chef
Kochbuch *n* cookbook, *Br* cookery book
'kochen (*ge-*, *h*) **1.** *v/t* cook; boil (*eggs etc*); make (*coffee etc*); **2.** *v/i* cook, do the cooking; boil (*a. fig*); ***gut kochen*** be a good cook; F ***vor Wut kochen*** boil with rage; ***kochend heiß*** boiling hot
Kocher ['kɔxɐ] *m* (-*s*; -) ELECTR cooker
Köchin ['kœçɪn] *f* (-; -*nen*) cook; chef
'Kochlöffel *m* (wooden) spoon
Kochnische *f* kitchenette
Kochplatte *f* hotplate
Kochsalz *n* common salt
Kochtopf *m* saucepan, pot
Köder ['kø:dɐ] *m* (-*s*; -) bait, decoy (*both a. fig*), lure
'ködern *v/t* (*ge-*, *h*) bait, decoy (*both a. fig*)
Kodex ['ko:dɛks] *m* (-*es*; -, -*e*) code
kodieren [ko'di:rən] *v/t* (*no -ge-*, *h*) (en-)code
Ko'dierung *f* (-; -*en*) (en-) coding
Koffein [kɔfe'i:n] *n* (-*s*; *no pl*) caffeine
Koffer ['kɔfɐ] *m* (-*s*; -) (suit)case; trunk
Kofferradio *n* portable (radio)
Kofferraum *m* MOT trunk, *Br* booth
Kognak ['kɔnjak] *m* (-*s*; -*s*) (French) brandy, cognac
Kohl [ko:l] *m* (-[*e*]*s*; -*e*) BOT cabbage
Kohle ['ko:lə] *f* (-; -*n*) coal; ELECTR carbon; F dough
'Kohlehy,drat *n* carbohydrate
'Kohlen... *in cpds ...dioxid etc*: CHEM carbon ...
Kohlenbergwerk *n* coalmine, colliery
Kohlenofen *m* coal-burning stove
'Kohlensäure *f* CHEM carbonic acid; GASTR F fizz
'kohlensäurehaltig *adj* carbonated, F fizzy
'Kohlenstoff *m* CHEM carbon
Kohlenwasserstoff *m* CHEM hydrocarbon
'Kohlepa,pier *n* carbon paper
Kohlezeichnung *f* charcoal drawing
Kohlrabi [-'ra:bi] *m* (-*s*; -*s*) BOT kohlrabi
Koje ['ko:jə] *f* (-; -*n*) MAR berth, bunk
Kokain [koka'i:n] *n* (-*s*; *no pl*) cocaine
kokettieren [kokɛ'ti:rən] *v/i* (*no -ge-*, *h*) flirt; *fig* ***kokettieren mit*** toy with
Kokosnuss ['ko:kɔs-] *f* BOT coconut
Koks [ko:ks] *m* (-*es*; *no pl*) coke; F dough; *sl* coke, snow
Kolben ['kɔlbən] *m* (-*s*; -) butt; TECH piston
Kolbenstange *f* TECH piston rod
Kolibri ['ko:libri] *m* (-*s*; -*s*) ZO humming bird
Kolleg [kɔ'le:k] *n* (-*s*; -*s*) UNIV course (of lectures)
Kollege [kɔ'le:gə] *m* (-*n*; -*n*), **Kol'legin** *f* (-; -*nen*) colleague
Kollegium [kɔ'le:gjʊm] *n* (-*s*; -*ien*) UNIV faculty, *Br* teaching staff
Kollekte [kɔ'lɛktə] *f* (-; -*n*) REL collection
Kollektion [kɔlɛk'tsjo:n] *f* (-; -*en*) ECON collection; range
kollektiv [kɔlɛk'ti:f] *adj*, **Kollek'tiv** *n* (-*s*; -*e*) collective (*a. in cpds*)

Koller ['kɔlɐ] F *m* (*-s*; *-*) fit; rage
kollidieren [kɔli'di:rən] *v/i* (*no -ge-*, *sein*) collide
Kollision [kɔli'zjo:n] *f* (*-*; *-en*) collision, *fig a.* clash, conflict
Kölnischwasser ['kœlnɪʃ-] *n* (*-s*; *-*) (eau de) cologne
Kolonie [kolo'ni:] *f* (*-*; *-n*) colony
kolonisieren [koloni'zi:rən] *v/t* (*no -ge-*, *h*) colonize
Koloni'sierung *f* (*-*; *-en*) colonization
Kolonne [ko'lɔnə] *f* (*-*; *-n*) column; MIL convoy; gang, crew
Koloss [ko'lɔs] *m* (*-es*; *-e*) colossus, *fig a.* giant (of a man)
kolossal [kolɔ'sa:l] *adj* gigantic
Kombi ['kɔmbi] *m* (*-[s]*; *-s*) MOT station wagon, *Br* estate (car)
Kombination [kɔmbina'tsjo:n] *f* (*-*; *-en*) combination; set; coveralls, *Br* overalls; flying suit; *soccer*: combined move
kombinieren [kɔmbi'ni:rən] (*no -ge-*, *h*) **1.** *v/t* combine; **2.** *v/i* reason
Kombüse [kɔm'by:zə] *f* (*-*; *-n*) MAR galley
Komet [ko'me:t] *m* (*-en*; *-en*) ASTR comet
Komfort [kɔm'fo:ɐ] *m* (*-s*; *no pl*) (modern) conveniences; luxury
komfortabel [kɔmfɔr'ta:bəl] *adj* comfortable; well-appointed; luxurious
Komik ['ko:mɪk] *f* (*-*; *no pl*) humo(u)r; comic effect
Komiker ['ko:mikɐ] *m* (*-s*; *-*) comedian
komisch ['ko:mɪʃ] *adj* comic(al), funny; strange, odd
Komitee [komi'te:] *n* (*-s*; *-s*) committee
Komma ['kɔma] *n* (*-s*; *-s*, *-ta*) comma; ***sechs Komma vier*** six point four
Kommandant [kɔman'dant] *m* (*-en*; *-en*), **Kommandeur** [kɔman'dø:ɐ] *m* (*-s*; *-e*) MIL commander, commanding officer
kommandieren [kɔman'di:rən] *v/i and v/t* (*no -ge-*, *h*) command, be in command of
Kommando [kɔ'mando] *n* (*-s*; *-s*) command; order; MIL commando
Komm'mandobrücke *f* MAR (navigating) bridge
kommen ['kɔmən] *v/i* (*irr*, *ge-*, *sein*) come; arrive; get; reach; ***zu spät kommen*** be late; ***weit kommen*** get far; ***zur Schule kommen*** start school; ***ins Gefängnis kommen*** go to jail; ***kommen lassen*** send for *s.o.*, call *s.o.*; order *s.th.*; ***kommen auf*** (*acc*) think of, hit upon; remember; ***hinter et. kommen*** find s.th. out; ***um et. kommen*** lose s.th.; miss s.th.; ***zu et. kommen*** come by s.th.; ***wieder zu sich kommen*** come round *or* to; ***wohin kommt …?*** where does … go?; ***daher kommt es, dass*** that's why; ***woher kommt es, dass …?*** why is it that …?, F how come …?
'kommenlassen *v/t* (*irr*, ***lassen***, *sep*, *no -ge-*, *h*) → ***kommen***
Kommentar [kɔmɛn'ta:ɐ] *m* (*-s*; *-e*) commentary; ***kein Kommentar!*** no comment
Kommentator [kɔmɛn'ta:to:ɐ] *m* (*-s*; *-en* [-ta'to:rən]), **Kommentatorin** [-ta'to:rɪn] *f* (*-*; *-nen*) commentator
kommentieren [kɔmɛn'ti:rən] *v/t* (*no -ge-*, *h*) comment (on)
kommerzialisieren [kɔmɛrtsjali'zi:rən] *v/t* (*no -ge-*, *h*) commercialize
Kommissar [kɔmɪ'sa:ɐ] *m* (*-s*; *-e*) commissioner; superintendent
Kommission [kɔmɪ'sjo:n] *f* (*-*; *-en*) commission; committee
Kommode [kɔ'mo:də] *f* (*-*; *-n*) bureau, *Br* chest (of drawers)
Kommunal… [kɔmu'na:l-] *in cpds …politik etc*: local …
Kommune [kɔ'mu:nə] *f* (*-*; *-n*) commune
Kommunikation [kɔmunika'tsjo:n] *f* (*-*; *no pl*) communication
Kommunion [kɔmu'njo:n] *f* (*-*; *-en*) REL (Holy) Communion
Kommunismus [kɔmu'nɪsmʊs] *m* (*-*; *no pl*) POL communism
Kommunist [kɔmu'nɪst] *m* (*-en*; *-en*), **Kommu'nistin** *f* (*-*; *-nen*), **kommu'nistisch** *adj* POL communist
Komödie [ko'mø:djə] *f* (*-*; *-n*) comedy; ***Komödie spielen*** put on an act, play-act
kompakt [kɔm'pakt] *adj* compact
Kom'paktanlage *f* stereo system, music center (*Br* centre)
Kompanie [kɔmpa'ni:] *f* (*-*; *-n*) MIL company
Kompass ['kɔmpas] *m* (*-es*; *-e*) compass
kompatibel [kɔmpa'ti:bəl] *adj* compatible (*a.* EDP)
komplett [kɔm'plɛt] *adj* complete
Komplex [kɔm'plɛks] *m* (*-es*; *-e*) complex (*a.* PSYCH)
Kompliment [kɔmpli'mɛnt] *n* (*-[e]s*; *-e*) compliment; ***j-m ein Kompliment machen*** pay s.o. a compliment
Komplize [kɔm'pli:tsə] *m* (*-n*; *-n*) accomplice
komplizieren [kɔmpli'tsi:rən] *v/t* (*no -ge-*, *h*) complicate
kompliziert [kɔmpli'tsi:ɐt] *adj* complicated, complex
Kom'plizin *f* (*-*; *-nen*) accomplice
Komplott [kɔm'plɔt] *n* (*-[e]s*; *-e*) plot, conspiracy
komponieren [kɔmpo'ni:rən] *v/t and v/i* (*no -ge-*, *h*) MUS compose; write

Komponist [kɔmpo'nɪst] *m (-en; -en)* MUS composer
Komposition [kɔmpozi'tsjoːn] *f (-; -en)* MUS composition
Kompott [kɔm'pɔt] *n (-[e]s; -e)* GASTR compot(e), stewed fruit
Kompresse [kɔm'prɛsə] *f (-; -n)* MED compress
komprimieren [kɔmpri'miːrən] *v/t (no -ge-, h)* compress
Kompromiss [kɔmpro'mɪs] *m (-es; -e)* compromise
kompro'misslos *adj* uncompromising
kompromittieren [kɔmpromɪ'tiːrən] *v/t (no -ge-, h)* compromise (***sich*** o.s.)
kompromittierend *adj* compromising
Kondensator [kɔndɛn'zaːtoːɐ] *m (-s; -en [-za'toːrən])* ELECTR capacitor; TECH condenser
kondensieren [kɔndɛn'ziːrən] *v/t (no -ge-, h)* condense
Kondensmilch [kɔn'dɛns-] *f* condensed milk
Kondition [kɔndi'tsjoːn] *f (-; -en)* a) condition, b) *(no pl)* SPORT condition, shape, form; ***gute Kondition*** (great) stamina
konditional [kɔnditsjo'naːl] *adj* LING conditional
Konditi'onstraining *n* fitness training
Konditor [kɔn'diːtoːɐ] *m (-s; -en [-di'toːrən])* confectioner, pastrycook
Konditorei [kɔndito'rai] *f (-; -en)* cake shop; café, tearoom
Konditoreiwaren *pl* confectionery
Kondom [kɔn'doːm] *n, m (-s; -e)* condom
Kondukteur [kɔndʊk'tøːɐ] *Swiss m (-s; -e)* → ***Schaffner***
Konfekt [kɔn'fɛkt] *n (-[e]s; -e)* sweets, chocolates
Konfektion [kɔnfɛk'tsjoːn] *f (-; no pl)* ready-made clothing
Konfekti'ons... *in cpds* ready-made ..., off-the-peg ...
Konferenz [kɔnfe'rɛnts] *f (-; -en)* conference
Konfession [kɔnfɛ'sjoːn] *f (-; -en)* religion, denomination
konfessionell [kɔnfɛsjo'nɛl] *adj* confessional, denominational
Konfessi'onsschule *f* denominational school
Konfirmand [kɔnfɪr'mant] *m (-en; -en)*, **Konfir'mandin** *f (-; -nen)* REL confirmand
Konfirmation [kɔnfɪrma'tsjoːn] *f (-; -en)* REL confirmation
konfirmieren [kɔnfɪr'miːrən] *v/t (no -ge-, h)* confirm
konfiszieren [kɔnfɪs'tsiːrən] *v/t (no -ge-, h)* JUR confiscate
Konfitüre [kɔnfi'tyːrə] *f (-; -n)* jam
Konflikt [kɔn'flɪkt] *m (-[e]s; -e)* conflict
konfrontieren [kɔnfrɔn'tiːrən] *v/t (no -ge-, h)* confront
konfus [kɔn'fuːs] *adj* confused, mixed-up
Kongress [kɔn'grɛs] *m (-es; -e)* convention, *Br* congress
König ['køːnɪç] *m (-s; -e)* king
Königin ['køːnɪgɪn] *f (-; -nen)* queen
königlich ['køːnɪklɪç] *adj* royal
Königreich ['køːnɪk-] *n* kingdom
Konjugation [kɔnjuga'tsjoːn] *f (-; -en)* LING conjugation
konjugieren [kɔnju'giːrən] *v/t (no -ge-, h)* LING conjugate
Konjunktiv ['kɔnjʊŋktiːf] *m (-s; -e)* LING subjunctive (mood)
Konjunktur [kɔnjʊŋk'tuːɐ] *f (-; -en)* economic situation
konkret [kɔn'kreːt] *adj* concrete
Konkurrent [kɔnkʊ'rɛnt] *m (-en; -en)*, **Konkur'rentin** *f (-; -nen)* competitor, rival
Konkurrenz [kɔnkʊ'rɛnts] *f (-; no pl)* competition; ***die Konkurrenz*** one's competitors; ***außer Konkurrenz*** not competing; → ***konkurrenzlos***
konkur'renzfähig *adj* competitive
Konkur'renzkampf *m* competition
konkur'renzlos *adj* without competition, unrival(l)ed
konkurrieren [kɔnkʊ'riːrən] *v/i (no -ge-, h)* compete
Konkurs [kɔn'kʊrs] *m (-es; -e)* ECON, JUR bankruptcy; ***in Konkurs gehen*** go bankrupt
Konkursmasse *f* JUR bankrupt's estate
können ['kœnən] *v/t and v/i (irr, ge-, h), v/aux (irr, no -ge-, h)* can, be able to; may, be allowed to; ***kann ich gehen*** *etc?* can *or* may I go *etc?*; ***du kannst nicht*** you cannot *or* can't; ***ich kann nicht mehr*** I can't go on; I can't manage *or* eat any more; ***es kann sein*** it may be; ***ich kann nichts dafür*** it's not my fault; ***e-e Sprache können*** know *or* speak a language
'Können *n (-s; no pl)* ability, skill
Könner ['kœnɐ] *m (-s; -)*, **'Könnerin** *f (-; -nen)* master, expert; *esp* SPORT ace, crack
konnte ['kɔntə] *pret of* ***können***
konsequent [kɔnze'kvɛnt] *adj* consistent
Konsequenz [kɔnze'kvɛnts] *f (-; -en)* a) *(no pl)* consistency, b) consequence
konservativ [kɔnzɛrva'tiːf] *adj* conservative
Konserven [kɔn'zɛrvən] *pl* canned (*Br a.* tinned) foods

Konservenbüchse *f*, **Konservendose** *f* can, *Br a.* tin
Konservenfa,brik *f* cannery
konservieren [kɔnzɛr'viːrən] *v/t* (*no -ge-*, *h*) preserve
Konser'vierungsmittel *n* preservative
Konsonant [kɔnzo'nant] *m* (*-en*; *-en*) LING consonant
konstruieren [kɔnstru'iːrən] *v/t* (*no -ge-*, *h*) construct; design
Konstrukteur [kɔnstrʊk'tøːɐ] *m* (*-s*; *-e*) TECH designer
Konstruktion [kɔnstrʊk'tsjoːn] *f* (*-*; *-en*) construction
Konsul ['kɔnzʊl] *m* (*-s*; *-n*) consul
Konsulat [kɔnzu'laːt] *n* (*-[e]s*; *-e*) consulate
konsultieren [kɔnzʊl'tiːrən] *v/t* (*no -ge-*, *h*) consult
Konsum[1] [kɔn'zuːm] *m* (*-s*; *no pl*) consumption
Konsum[2] ['kɔnzuːm] *m* (*-s*; *-s*) cooperative (society *or* store), F co-op
Konsument [kɔnzu'mɛnt] *m* (*-en*; *-en*), **Konsu'mentin** *f* (*-*; *-nen*) consumer
Kon'sumgesellschaft *f* consumer society
konsumieren [kɔnzu'miːrən] *v/t* (*no -ge-*, *h*) consume
Kontakt [kɔn'takt] *m* (*-[e]s*; *-e*) contact (*a.* ELECTR); ***Kontakt aufnehmen*** get in touch; ***Kontakt haben*** *or* ***in Kontakt stehen mit*** be in contact *or* touch with; ***den Kontakt verlieren*** lose touch
kon'taktfreudig *adj* sociable
Kon'taktlinsen *pl* OPT contact lenses
Konter ['kɔntɐ] *m* (*-s*; *-*), **'kontern** *v/i* (*ge-*, *h*) counter (*a. fig*)
Kontinent [kɔnti'nɛnt] *m* (*-[e]s*; *-e*) continent
Konto ['kɔnto] *n* (*-s*; *Konten*) account
'Kontoauszug *m* (bank) statement
Kontrast [kɔn'trast] *m* (*-[e]s*; *-e*) contrast (*a.* PHOT, TV *etc*)
Kontrolle [kɔn'trɔlə] *f* (*-*; *-n*) control; supervision; check(up)
Kontrolleur [kɔntrɔ'løːɐ] *m* (*-s*; *-e*), **Kontrol'leurin** *f* (*-*; *-nen*) inspector, RAIL *a.* conductor
kontrollieren [kɔntrɔ'liːrən] *v/t* (*no -ge-*, *h*) check; check up on *s.o.*; control
Kon'trollpunkt *m* checkpoint
Kontroverse [kɔntro'vɛrzə] *f* (*-*; *-n*) controversy
konventionell [kɔnvɛntsjo'nɛl] *adj* conventional
Konversation [kɔnvɛrza'tsjoːn] *f* (*-*; *-en*) conversation
Konversati'onslexikon *n* encyclop(a)edia
Konzentration [kɔntsɛntra'tsjoːn] *f* (*-*; *-en*) concentration
Konzentrati'onslager *n* concentration camp
konzentrieren [kɔntsɛn'triːrən] *v/t and v/refl* (*no -ge-*, *h*) concentrate; ***sich auf et. konzentrieren*** concentrate on s.th.
Konzept [kɔn'tsɛpt] *n* (*-[e]s*; *-e*) (rough) draft; conception; ***j-n aus dem Konzept bringen*** put s.o. out
Konzern [kɔn'tsɛrn] *m* (*-[e]s*; *-e*) ECON combine, group
Konzert [kɔn'tsɛrt] *n* (*-[e]s*; *-e*) MUS concert; concerto
Konzerthalle *f*, **Konzertsaal** *m* concert hall, auditorium
Konzession [kɔntsɛ'sjoːn] *f* (*-*; *-en*) concession; license, *Br* licence
Kopf [kɔpf] *m* (*-[e]s*; *Köpfe* ['kœpfə]) head (*a. fig*); top; *fig a.* brains, mind; ***Kopf hoch!*** chin up!; ***j-m über den Kopf wachsen*** outgrow s.o.; *fig* be too much for s.o.; ***sich den Kopf zerbrechen*** (***über*** *acc*) rack one's brains (over); ***sich et. aus dem Kopf schlagen*** put s.th. out of one's mind; ***Kopf an Kopf*** neck and neck
Kopfball *m* SPORT header; headed goal
Kopfbedeckung *f* headgear; ***ohne Kopfbedeckung*** bareheaded
köpfen ['kœpfən] *v/t* (*ge-*, *h*) behead, decapitate; SPORT head (***ins Tor*** home)
'Kopfende *n* head
Kopfhörer *pl* headphones
Kopfjäger *m* headhunter
Kopfkissen *n* pillow
'kopflos *adj* headless; *fig* panicky
'Kopfrechnen *n* mental arithmetic
Kopfsa,lat *m* BOT lettuce
Kopfschmerzen *pl* headache
Kopfsprung *m* SPORT header
Kopfstand *m* SPORT headstand
Kopftuch *n* scarf, (head)kerchief
kopf'über *adv* headfirst (*a. fig*)
'Kopfweh *n* → ***Kopfschmerzen***
'Kopfzerbrechen *n*: ***j-m Kopfzerbrechen machen*** give s.o. a headache
Kopie [ko'piː] *f* (*-*; *-n*), **ko'pieren** *v/t* (*no -ge-*, *h*) copy
Kopiergerät [ko'piːɐ-] *n* copier
Ko'pierstift *m* indelible pencil
Koppel[1] ['kɔpəl] *f* (*-*; *-n*) paddock
'Koppel[2] *n* (*-s*; *-*) MIL belt
'koppeln *v/t* (*ge-*, *h*) couple; dock
Koralle [ko'ralə] *f* (*-*; *-n*) ZO coral
Korb [kɔrp] *m* (*-[e]s*; *Körbe* ['kœrbə]) basket
Korbmöbel *pl* wicker furniture
Kord [kɔrt] *m* (*-[e]s*; *-e*) corduroy

K

Kordel ['kɔrdəl] *f* (-; -*n*) cord
'**Kordhose** *f* corduroys
Korinthe [ko'rɪntə] *f* (-; -*n*) currant
Kork [kɔrk] *m* (-[*e*]*s*; -*e*) BOT cork
'**Korkeiche** *f* BOT cork oak
Korken ['kɔrkən] *m* (-*s*; -) cork
Korkenzieher [-tsiːɐ] *m* (-*s*; -) corkscrew
Korn[1] [kɔrn] *n* (-[*e*]*s*; *Körner* ['kœrnɐ]) BOT a) grain; seed, b) (*no pl*) grain, *Br a.* corn, c) (*pl* -*e*) TECH front sight
Korn[2] F *m* (-[*e*]*s*; -*e*) (grain) schnapps
körnig ['kœrnɪç] *adj* grainy
Körper ['kœrpɐ] *m* (-*s*; -) body (*a.* PHYS, CHEM), MATH *a.* solid, **Körperbau** *m* (-[*e*]*s*; *no pl*) build, physique
'**körperbehindert** *adj* (physically) disabled *or* handicapped
'**Körpergeruch** *m* body odo(u)r, BO
Körpergröße *f* height
Körperkraft *f* physical strength
'**körperlich** *adj* physical
'**Körperpflege** *f* personal hygiene
'**Körperschaft** *f* (-; -*en*) corporation, (corporate) body
'**Körperteil** *m* part of the body
Körperverletzung *f* JUR bodily injury
korrekt [kɔ'rɛkt] *adj* correct
Korrektur [kɔrɛk'tuːɐ] *f* (-; -*en*) correction; PED *etc* grading, *Br* marking
Korrespondent [kɔrɛspɔn'dɛnt] *m* (-*en*; -*en*), **Korrespon'dentin** *f* (-; -*nen*) correspondent
Korrespondenz [-'dɛnts] *f* (-; -*en*) correspondence
korrespondieren [-'diːrən] *v/i* (*no -ge-, h*) correspond (***mit*** with)
Korridor ['kɔridoːɐ] *m* (-*s*; -*e*) corridor; hall
korrigieren [kɔri'giːrən] *v/t* (*no -ge-, h*) correct; PED *etc* grade, *Br* mark
korrupt [kɔ'rʊpt] *adj* corrupt(ed)
Korruption [kɔrʊp'tsjoːn] *f* (-; -*en*) corruption
Korsett [kɔr'zɛt] *n* (-*s*; -*s*) corset (*a. fig*)
Kosename ['koːzə-] *m* pet name
Kosmetik [kɔs'meːtɪk] *f* (-; *no pl*) beauty culture; cosmetics, toiletries
Kosmetikerin [kɔs'meːtikərɪn] *f* (-; -*nen*) beautician, cosmetician
Kost [kɔst] *f* (-; *no pl*) food, diet; board
'**kostbar** *adj* precious, valuable; costly
'**Kostbarkeit** *f* (-; -*en*) precious object, treasure (*a. fig*)
kosten[1] ['kɔstən] *v/t* (*ge-, h*) cost, be; *fig* take (*time etc*); ***was*** *or* ***wie viel kostet ...?*** how much it ...?
'**kosten**[2] *v/t* (*ge-, h*) taste, try
'**Kosten** *pl* cost(s); price; expenses; charges; ***auf j-s Kosten*** at s.o.'s expense
'**kostenlos 1.** *adj* free; **2.** *adv* free of charge
köstlich ['kœstlɪç] *adj* delicious; *fig* priceless; ***sich köstlich amüsieren*** have great fun, F have a ball
'**Kostprobe** *f* taste, sample (*a. fig*)
'**kostspielig** *adj* expensive, costly
Kostüm [kɔs'tyːm] *n* (-*s*; -*e*) costume, dress; suit
Kostümfest *n* fancy-dress ball
Kot [koːt] *m* (-[*e*]*s*; *no pl*) excrement, ZO *a.* droppings
Kotelett [kotə'lɛt] *n* (-*s*; -*s*) chop, cutlet
Koteletten [kotə'lɛtən] *pl* sideburns
'**Kotflügel** *m* MOT fender, *Br* wing
kotzen ['kɔtsən] V *v/i* (*ge-, h*) puke
Krabbe ['krabə] *f* (-; -*n*) ZO shrimp; prawn
krabbeln ['krabəln] *v/i* (*ge-, sein*) crawl
Krach [krax] *m* (-[*e*]*s*; *Kräche* ['krɛçə]) a) crash, bang, b) (*no pl*) noise, c) F quarrel, fight
'**krachen** *v/i* (*ge-, h*) crack, bang, crash
Kracher ['kraxɐ] *m* (-*s*; -) (fire)cracker
krächzen ['krɛçtsən] *v/t and v/i* (*ge-, h*) croak
Kraft [kraft] *f* (-; *Kräfte* ['krɛftə]) strength, force (*a.* POL), power (*a.* ELECTR, TECH, POL); ***in Kraft sein*** (***setzen, treten***) JUR *etc* be in (put into, come into) force
Kraftbrühe *f* GASTR consommé, clear soup
Kraftfahrer(in) driver, motorist
Kraftfahrzeug *n* motor vehicle
kräftig ['krɛftɪç] *adj* strong (*a. fig*), powerful; substantial (*food*); good
'**kraftlos** *adj* weak, feeble
'**Kraftprobe** *f* test of strength
Kraftstoff *m* MOT fuel
Kraftverschwendung *f* waste of energy
Kraftwerk *n* power station
Kragen ['kraːgən] *m* (-*s*; -) collar
Krähe ['krɛːə] *f* (-; -*n*) ZO crow
krähen ['krɛːən] *v/i* (*ge-, h*) crow
Krake ['kraːkə] *m* (-*n*; -*n*) ZO octopus
Kralle ['kralə] *f* (-; -*n*) ZO claw (*a. fig*)
'**krallen** *v/refl* (*ge-, h*) cling (***an*** *acc* on), clutch (at)
Kram [kraːm] F *m* (-[*e*]*s*; *no pl*) stuff, (one's) things
Krampf [krampf] *m* (-[*e*]*s*; *Krämpfe* ['krɛmpfə]) MED cramp; spasm, convulsion
Krampfader *f* MED varicose vein
'**krampfhaft** *fig adj* forced (*smile etc*); desperate (*attempt etc*)
Kran [kraːn] *m* (-[*e*]*s*; *Kräne* ['krɛːnə]) TECH crane
Kranich ['kraːnɪç] *m* (-*s*; -*e*) ZO crane
krank [kraŋk] *adj* ill, sick; ***krank werden*** get sick, *Br* fall ill

'Kranke *m, f (-n; -n)* sick person, patient; ***die Kranken*** the sick
kränken ['krɛŋkən] *v/t (ge-, h)* hurt *(s.o.'s* feelings), offend
'Krankenbett *n* sickbed
Krankengeld *n* sickness benefit
Krankengymˌnastik *f* physiotherapy
Krankenhaus *n* hospital
Krankenkasse *f* health insurance scheme; ***in e-r Krankenkasse sein*** be a member of a health insurance scheme *or* plan
Krankenpflege *f* nursing
Krankenpfleger *m* male nurse
Krankenschein *m* health insurance certificate
Krankenschwester *f* nurse
Krankenversicherung *f* health insurance
Krankenwagen *m* ambulance
Krankenzimmer *n* sickroom
'krankhaft *adj* morbid *(a. fig)*
'Krankheit *f (-; -en)* illness, sickness, disease
'Krankheitsserreger *m* germ
kränklich ['krɛŋklɪç] *adj* sickly, ailing
Kränkung ['krɛŋkʊŋ] *f (-; -en)* insult, offense, *Br* offence
Kranz [krants] *m (-es; Kränze* ['krɛntsə]) wreath; *fig* ring, circle
krass [kras] *adj* crass, gross; blunt
Krater ['kra:tɐ] *m (-s; -)* crater
kratzen ['kratsən] *v/t and v/refl (ge-, h)* scratch (o.s.); scrape (**von** off)
Kratzer ['kratsɐ] *m (-s; -)* scratch *(a.* MED)
kraulen ['kraulən] **1.** *v/t (ge-, h)* stroke; run one's fingers through; **2.** *v/i (ge-, sein)* SPORT do the crawl
kraus [kraus] *adj* curly *(hair)*; wrinkled
Krause ['krauzə] *f (-; -n)* ruff; friz(z)
kräuseln ['krɔʏzəln] *v/t and v/refl (ge-, h)* curl, friz(z); *water:* ripple
Kraut [kraut] *n (-[e]s; Kräuter* ['krɔʏtɐ]) BOT herb; tops, leaves; cabbage
Krawall [kra'val] *m (-s; -e)* riot; F row, racket
Krawatte [kra'vatə] *f (-; -n)* tie
kreativ [krea'ti:f] *adj* creative
Kreativität [kreativi'tɛ:t] *f (-; no pl)* creativity
Kreatur [krea'tu:ɐ] *f (-; -en)* creature
Krebs [kre:ps] *m* ZO crayfish; MED cancer; AST Cancer; ***sie ist (ein) Krebs*** she's (a) Cancer; ***Krebs erregend*** → ***krebserregend***
Krebs... MED cancerous
krebserregend *adj* MED carcinogenic
Krebsgeschwulst *f* MED carcinoma
Krebskranke *m, f* cancer patient
Kredit [kre'di:t] *m (-[e]s; -e)* ECON credit; loan
Kredithai *m* loan shark
Kreditkarte *f* credit card, *pl coll* F plastic money
Kreide ['kraidə] *f (-; -n)* chalk; crayon
Kreis [krais] *m (-es; -e)* circle *(a. fig)*; POL district, county
Kreisbahn *f* AST orbit
kreischen ['kraiʃən] *v/i (ge-, h)* screech; squeal
Kreisel ['kraizəl] *m (-s; -)* (spinning) top; PHYS gyro(scope)
'kreiseln *v/i (ge-, h, sein)* spin around
kreisen ['kraizən] *v/i (ge-, h, sein)* (move in a) circle, revolve, rotate; circulate
'kreisförmig [-fœrmɪç] *adj* circular
'Kreislauf *m* MED, ECON circulation; BIOL cycle *(a. fig)*, TECH, ELECTR *a.* circuit
Kreislaufstörungen *pl* MED circulatory trouble
'Kreissäge *f* circular saw
Kreisverkehr *m* traffic circle, *Br* roundabout
Krempe ['krɛmpə] *f (-; -n)* brim
Kren [kre:n] *Austrian m (-[e]s; no pl)* GASTR horseradish
Krepp [krɛp] *m (-s; -s)* crepe
Kreuz [krɔʏts] *n (-es; -e)* cross *(a. fig)*; ANAT (small of the) back; *cards:* club(s); MUS sharp; ***über Kreuz*** crosswise; F ***j-n aufs Kreuz legen*** take s.o. in
kreuzen ['krɔʏtsən] **1.** *v/t and v/refl (ge-, h)* cross; clash; **2.** *v/i (ge-, sein)* MAR cruise
Kreuzer ['krɔʏtsɐ] *m (-s; -)* MAR cruiser
'Kreuzfahrer *m* HIST crusader
'Kreuzfahrt *f* MAR cruise
kreuzigen ['krɔʏtsɪgən] *v/t (ge-, h)* crucify
'Kreuzigung *f (-; -en)* crucifixion
'Kreuzotter *f* ZO adder
'Kreuzschmerzen *pl* backache
'Kreuzung *f (-; -en)* RAIL, MOT crossing, junction; intersection, crossroads; BIOL cross(breed)ing; cross(breed); *fig* cross
'Kreuzverhör *n* JUR cross-examination; ***ins Kreuzverhör nehmen*** cross-examine
'kreuzweise *adv* crosswise, crossways
'Kreuzworträtsel *n* crossword (puzzle)
Kreuzzug HIST *m* crusade
kriechen ['kri:çən] *v/i (irr, ge-, sein)* creep, crawl; *fig* ***vor j-m kriechen*** toady to s.o.
Kriecher ['kri:çɐ] *contp m (-s; -)* toady
'Kriechspur *f* MOT slow lane
Krieg [kri:k] *m (-[e]s; -e* ['kri:gə]) war; ***Krieg führen gegen*** be at war with
kriegen ['kri:gən] F *v/t (ge-, h)* get; catch
Krieger ['kri:gɐ] *m (-s; -)* warrior
'Kriegerdenkmal *n* war memorial
kriegerisch ['kri:gərɪʃ] *adj* warlike, mar-

K

tial
'Kriegführung *f* (-; *no pl*) warfare
'Kriegsbeil *fig n*: ***das Kriegsbeil begraben*** bury the hatchet
Kriegsdienstverweigerer *m* (-*s*; -) conscientious objector
Kriegserklärung *f* declaration of war
Kriegsgefangene *m* prisoner of war, P.O.W.
Kriegsgefangenschaft *f* captivity
Kriegsrecht *n* JUR martial law
Kriegsschauplatz *m* theater (*Br* theatre) of war
Kriegsschiff *n* warship
Kriegsteilnehmer *m* (war) veteran, *Br* ex-serviceman
Kriegstreiber [-traibɐ] *m* (-*s*; -) POL warmonger
Kriegsverbrechen *n* war crime
Kriegsverbrecher *m* war criminal
Krimi ['kriːmi] F *m* (-*s*; -*s*) (crime) thriller, detective novel
Kriminalbeamte [krimi'naːl-] *m* detective, plain-clothesman
Kriminalpolizei *f* criminal investigation department
Kriminalroman *m* → ***Krimi***
kriminell [krimi'nɛl] adj, **Krimi'nelle** *m, f* (-*n*; -*n*) criminal
Krippe ['krɪpə] *f* (-; -*n*) crib, manger (*a.* REL); REL crèche, *Br* crib
Krise ['kriːzə] *f* (-; -*n*) crisis
'Krisenherd *m esp* POL trouble spot
Kristall[1] [krɪs'tal] *m* (-*s*; -*e*) crystal
Kris'tall[2] *n* (*s*; *no pl*), **Kristallglas** *n* crystal
kristallisieren [krɪstali'ziːrən] *v/i and v/refl* (*no* -*ge*-, *h*) crystallize
Kriterium [kri'teːrjʊm] *n* (-*s*; -*ien*) criterion (***für*** of)
Kritik [kri'tiːk] *f* (-; -*en*) criticism; THEA, MUS *etc* review, critique; ***gute Kritiken*** a good press; ***Kritik üben an*** (*dat*) criticize
Kritiker(in) ['kriːtikɐ (-kərɪn)] (-*s*; -/-; -*nen*) critic
kri'tiklos *adj* uncritical
kritisch ['kriːtɪʃ] *adj* critical (*a. fig*) (***gegenüber*** of)
kritisieren [kriti'ziːrən] *v/t* (*no* -*ge*-, *h*) criticize
kritzeln ['krɪtsəln] *v/t and v/i* (*ge*-, *h*) scrawl, scribble
kroch [krɔx] *pret of* ***kriechen***
Krokodil [kroko'diːl] *n* (-*s*; -*e*) ZO crocodile
Krone ['kroːnə] *f* (-; -*n*) crown; coronet
krönen ['krøːnən] *v/t* (*ge*-, *h*) crown; ***j-n zum König krönen*** crown s.o. king
'Kronleuchter *m* chandelier
'Kronprinz *m* crown prince
'Kronprin,zessin *f* crown princess
'Krönung *f* (-; -*en*) coronation; *fig* crowning event, climax, high point
Kropf [krɔpf] *m* (-[*e*]*s*; *Kröpfe* ['krœpfə]) MED goiter, *Br* goitre; ZO crop
Kröte ['krøːtə] *f* (-; -*n*) ZO toad
Krücke ['krʏkə] *f* (-; -*n*) crutch
Krug [kruːk] *m* (-[*e*]*s*; *Krüge* ['kryːgə]) jug, pitcher; mug, stein; tankard
Krümel ['kryːməl] *m* (-*s*; -) crumb
krümelig ['kryːməlɪç] *adj* crumbly
'krümeln *v/t and v/i* (*ge*-, *h*) crumble
krumm [krʊm] *adj* crooked (*a. fig*), bent
'krummbeinig [-bainɪç] *adj* bow-legged
krümmen ['krʏmən] *v/t* (*ge*-, *h*) bend (*a.* TECH), crook; ***sich krümmen*** bend; writhe (with pain)
'Krümmung *f* (-; -*en*) bend, curve; GEOGR, MATH, MED curvature
Krüppel ['krʏpəl] *m* (-*s*; -) cripple
Kruste ['krʊstə] *f* (-; -*n*) crust
Kto. ABBR *of* ***Konto*** a/c, account
Kübel ['kyːbəl] *m* (-*s*; -) bucket, pail; tub
Kubikmeter [ku'biːk-] *n, m* cubic meter (*Br* metre)
Kubikwurzel *f* MATH cube root
Küche ['kʏçə] *f* (-; -*n*) kitchen; GASTR cooking, cuisine; ***kalte*** (***warme***) ***Küche*** cold (hot) meals
Kuchen ['kuːxən] *m* (-*s*; -) cake; tart, pie
'Küchengeräte *pl* kitchen utensils (*or* appliances)
Küchengeschirr *n* kitchen crockery, kitchenware
Küchenherd *m* cooker
Küchenschrank *m* (kitchen) cupboard
Kuckuck ['kʊkʊk] *m* (-*s*; -*s*) ZO cuckoo
Kufe ['kuːfə] *f* (-; -*n*) runner; AVIAT skid
Kugel ['kuːgəl] *f* (-; -*n*) ball; bullet; MATH, GEOGR sphere; SPORT shot
'kugelförmig [-fœrmɪç] *adj* ballshaped, *esp* ASTR, MATH spheric(al)
'Kugelgelenk *n* TECH, ANAT ball (and socket) joint
'Kugellager *n* TECH ball bearing
'kugeln *v/i* (*ge*-, *sein*) *and v/t* (*h*) roll
'Kugelschreiber [-ʃraibɐ] *m* (-*s*; -) ballpoint (pen)
'kugelsicher *adj* bulletproof
'Kugelstoßen *n* (-*s*; *no pl*) SPORT shot put(ting)
'Kugelstoßer [-ʃtoːsɐ] *m* (-*s*; -), **'Kugelstoßerin** [-ʃtoːsərɪn] *f* (-; -*nen*) SPORT shot-putter
Kuh [kuː] *f* (-; *Kühe* ['kyːə]) ZO cow
kühl [kyːl] *adj* cool (*a. fig*)
'Kühle *f* (-; *no pl*) cool(ness)

K

'kühlen *v/t (ge-, h)* cool; chill; refrigerate; refresh
Kühler ['kyːlɐ] *m (-s; -)* MOT radiator
'Kühlerhaube *f* MOT hood, *Br* bonnet
'Kühlmittel *n* coolant
'Kühlraum *m* cold-storage room
'Kühlschrank *m* fridge, refrigerator
'Kühltruhe *f* deep-freeze, freezer
'Kühlwasser *n* MOT cooling water
kühn [kyːn] *adj* bold
'Kühnheit *f (-; no pl)* boldness
'Kuhstall *m* cowshed
Küken ['kyːkən] *n (-s; -)* ZO chick (*a. fig*)
Kukuruz ['kʊkurʊts] *Austrian m* → ***Mais***
Kuli ['kuːli] F *m (-s; -s)* ballpoint
Kulissen [ku'lɪsən] *pl* THEA wings; scenery; ***hinter den Kulissen*** backstage, *esp fig* behind the scenes
Kult [kʊlt] *m (-[e]s; -e)* cult; rite, ritual (act)
kultivieren [kʊlti'viːrən] *v/t (no -ge-, h)* cultivate
Kultur [kʊl'tuːɐ] *f (-; -en)* culture (*a.* BIOL), civilization; AGR cultivation
Kul'turbeutel *m* toilet bag
kulturell [kʊltu'rɛl] *adj* cultural
Kul'turgeschichte *f* history of civilization
Kulturvolk *n* civilized people
Kulturzentrum *n* cultural center (*Br* centre)
Kultusmi,nister ['kʊltʊs-] *m* minister of education and cultural affairs
Kummer ['kʊmɐ] *m (-s; no pl)* grief, sorrow; trouble, worry; ***Kummer haben mit*** have trouble *or* problems with
kümmerlich ['kʏmɐlɪç] *adj* miserable; poor, scanty
kümmern ['kʏmɐn] *v/refl and v/t (ge-, h)* ***sich kümmern um*** look after, take care of, mind; care *or* worry about, be interested in
Kumpel ['kʊmpəl] *m (-s; -)* miner; F mate, buddy, pal
Kunde ['kʊndə] *m (-n; -n)* customer, client
'Kundendienst *m* after-sales service; (customer) service; service department; TECH servicing
Kundgebung ['kʊntgeːbʊŋ] *f (-; -en)* meeting, rally, demonstration
kündigen ['kʏndɪgən] *v/i and v/t (ge-, h)* cancel; ***j-m kündigen*** give s.o. his / her / one's notice; dismiss s.o., F sack *or* fire s.o.
'Kündigung *f (-; -en)* cancellation; (period of) notice
Kundin ['kʊndɪn] *f (-; -nen)* customer, client
Kundschaft ['kʊntʃaft] *f (-; -en)* customers, clients
Kunst [kʊnst] *f (-; Künste* ['kʏnstə]*)* art; skill
Kunst... *in cpds ...herz, ...leder, ...licht etc*: artificial ...
Kunstakade,mie *f* academy of arts
Kunstausstellung *f* art exhibition
Kunstdünger *m* AGR artificial fertilizer
Kunsterziehung *f* PED art (education)
Kunstfaser *f* man-made *or* synthetic fiber (*Br* fibre)
Kunstfehler *m* professional blunder
Kunstfliegen *n* stunt flying, aerobatics
Kunstgeschichte *f* history of art
Kunstgewerbe *n*, **Kunsthandwerk** *n* arts and crafts
Künstler ['kʏnstlɐ] *m (-s; -)*, **Künstlerin** ['kʏnstlərɪn] *f (-; -nen)* artist, MUS, THEA *a.* performer
künstlerisch ['kʏnstlərɪʃ] *adj* artistic
künstlich ['kʏnstlɪç] *adj* artificial; false; synthetic; man-made
'Kunstschwimmen *n* water ballet
Kunstseide *f* rayon
Kunstspringen *n* springboard diving
Kunststoff *m* plastic
Kunststück *n* trick, stunt, *esp fig* feat
Kunstturnen *n* gymnastics
Kunstturner *m* gymnast
'kunstvoll *adj* artistic; elaborate
'Kunstwerk *n* work of art
Kupfer ['kʊpfɐ] *n (-s; no pl)* copper (***aus*** of)
Kupferstich *m* copperplate (engraving)
Kupon [ku'põː] *m (-s; -s)* coupon
Kuppe ['kʊpə] *f (-; -n)* (rounded) hilltop; ANAT head
Kuppel ['kʊpəl] *f (-; -n)* ARCH dome; cupola
Kuppelei [kʊpə'lai] *f (-; -en)* JUR procuring
'kuppeln *v/i (ge-, h)* MOT put the clutch in *or* out
Kupplung ['kʊplʊŋ] *f (-; -en)* MOT clutch
Kur [kuːɐ] *f (-; -en)* course of treatment; cure
Kür [kyːɐ] *f (-; -en)* SPORT free skating; free exercises
Kurbel ['kʊrbəl] *f (-; -n)* crank, handle
'kurbeln *v/t (ge-, h)* crank; wind (up *etc*)
'Kurbelwelle *f* TECH crankshaft
Kürbis ['kʏrbɪs] *m (-ses; -se)* BOT pumpkin, gourd, squash
'Kurgast *m* visitor
kurieren [ku'riːrən] *v/t (no -ge-, h)* cure (***von*** of)
kurios [ku'rjoːs] *adj* curious, odd, strange
'Kürlauf *m* SPORT free skating
'Kurort *m* health resort, spa
Kurpfuscher ['kuːɐpfʊʃɐ] *m (-s; -)* quack (doctor)

K

Kurs [kʊrs] *m (-es; -e)* AVIAT, MAR course *(a. fig)*; PED *etc* class(es); ECON (exchange) rate; (stock) price
Kursbuch *n* railroad *(Br* railway) guide
Kürschner ['kʏrʃnɐ] *m (-s; -)* furrier
kursieren [kʊr'ziːrən] *v/i (no -ge-, h)* circulate *(a. fig)*
Kurve ['kʊrvə] *f (-; -n)* curve *(a.* MATH *and fig)*; bend, turn
'**kurvenreich** *adj* winding, full of bends; F curvaceous
kurz [kʊrts] *adj* short; brief; ***kurze Hose*** shorts; (***bis***) ***vor kurzem*** (until) recently; (***erst***) ***seit kurzem*** (only) for a short time; ***kurz vorher*** (***darauf***) shortly before (after[wards]); ***kurz vor uns*** just ahead of us; ***kurz nacheinander*** in quick succession; ***kurz fortgehen*** *etc* go away for a short time *or* a moment; ***kurz gesagt*** in short; ***zu kurz kommen*** go short; ***kurz angebunden*** curt
'**Kurzarbeit** *f* ECON short time
'**kurzarbeiten** *v/i (sep, ge-, h)* ECON work short time
'**kurzatmig** [-ʔaːtmɪç] *adj* short of breath
Kürze ['kʏrtsə] *f (-; no pl)* shortness; brevity; ***in Kürze*** soon, shortly, before long
'**kürzen** *v/t (ge-, h)* shorten (***um*** by); abridge; cut, reduce *(a.* MATH)
kurzerhand ['kʊrtsɐ'hant] *adv* without hesitation, on the spot
'**kurzfassen** *v/refl (sep, -ge-, h)*: ***sich kurzfassen*** be brief, put it briefly
'**kurzfristig** **1.** *adj* short-term; **2.** *adv* at short notice
'**Kurzgeschichte** *f* short story
'**kurzlebig** [-leːbɪç] *adj* short-lived
kürzlich ['kʏrtslɪç] *adv* recently, not long ago
'**Kurznachrichten** *pl* news summary
Kurzschluss *m* ELECTR short circuit, F short
Kurzschrift *f* shorthand
'**kurzsichtig** *adj* nearsighted, *Br* shortsighted
'**Kurzstrecke** *f* short distance
'**Kürzung** *f (-; -en)* cut, reduction *(a.* MATH)
'**Kurzwaren** *pl* notions, *Br* haberdashery
'**kurzweilig** [-vailɪç] *adj* entertaining
'**Kurzwelle** *f* PHYS, *radio*: short wave
kuschelig ['kʊʃəlɪç] F *adj* cozy, *Br* cosy, snug
kuscheln ['kʊʃəln] *v/refl (ge-, h)* snuggle, cuddle (***an*** *acc* up to; ***in*** *acc* in)
Kusine *f* → ***Cousine***
Kuss [kʊs] *m (-es; Küsse* ['kʏsə]) kiss
'**kussecht** *adj* kiss-proof
küssen ['kʏsən] *v/t (ge-, h)* kiss
Küste ['kʏstə] *f (-; -n)* coast, shore; ***an der Küste*** on the coast; ***an die Küste*** ashore
'**Küstengewässer** *pl* coastal waters
Küstenschifffahrt *f* coastal shipping
Küstenschutz *m*, **Küstenwache** *f* coast guard
Küster ['kʏstɐ] *m (-s; -)* REL verger, sexton
Kutsche ['kʊtʃə] *f (-; -n)* carriage, coach
Kutscher ['kʊtʃɐ] *m (-s; -)* coachman
Kutte ['kʊtə] *f (-; -n)* (monk's) habit
Kutteln ['kʊtəln] *pl* GASTR tripe
Kutter ['kʊtɐ] *m (-s; -)* MAR cutter
Kuvert [ku'veːɐ] *n (-s; -s)* envelope
Kybernetik [kybɛr'neːtɪk] *f (-; no pl)* cybernetics

L

labil [la'biːl] *adj* unstable
Labor [la'boːɐ] *n (-s; -e)* laboratory, F lab
Laborant(in) [labo'rant(ɪn)] *(-en; -en/-; -nen)* laboratory assistant
Labyrinth [laby'rɪnt] *n (-[e]s; -e)* labyrinth, maze *(both a. fig)*
Lache ['laxə] *f (-; -n)* pool, puddle
lächeln ['lɛçəln] *v/i (ge-, h)*, '**Lächeln** *n (-s; no pl)* smile
lachen ['laxən] *v/i (ge-, h)* laugh (***über*** *acc* at)
'**Lachen** *n (-s; no pl)* laugh(-ter); ***j-n zum Lachen bringen*** make s.o. laugh
lächerlich ['lɛçɐlɪç] *adj* ridiculous; ***lächerlich machen*** ridicule, make fun of; ***sich lächerlich machen*** make a fool of o.s.
Lachs [laks] *m (-es; -e)* ZO salmon
Lack [lak] *m (-[e]s; -e)* varnish; lacquer; MOT paint(work)
lackieren [la'kiːrən] *v/t (no -ge-, h)* varnish; lacquer; paint *(a.* MOT)
'**Lackschuhe** *pl* patent-leather shoes
Ladefläche ['laːdə-] *f* loading space

'Ladegerät *n* ELECTR battery charger
'Ladehemmung *f* MIL jam
laden ['la:dən] *v/t (irr, ge-, h)* load; ELECTR charge; EDP boot (up); *fig* ***et. auf sich laden*** burden o.s. with s.th.
'Laden *m (-s; Läden* ['lɛ:dən]) store, *Br* shop; shutter
Ladendieb *m* shoplifter
Ladendiebstahl *m* shoplifting
Ladeninhaber *m* storekeeper, *Br* shopkeeper
Ladenkasse *f* till
Ladenschluss *m* closing time; ***nach Ladenschluss*** after hours
Ladentisch *m* counter
'Laderampe *f* loading platform *or* ramp
'Laderaum *m* loading space; MAR hold
'Ladung *f (-; -en)* load, freight; AVIAT, MAR cargo; ELECTR, MIL charge; ***e-e Ladung ...*** a load of ...
lag [la:k] *pret of* ***liegen***
Lage ['la:gə] *f (-; -n)* situation, position *(both a. fig)*; location; layer; round *(of beer etc)*; ***in schöner (ruhiger) Lage*** beautifully (peacefully) situated; ***in der Lage sein zu*** *inf* be able to *inf*, be in a position to *inf*
Lager ['la:gɐ] *n (-s; -)* bed; camp *(a. fig)*; ECON stock, store; GEOL deposit; TECH bearing; ***et. auf Lager haben*** have s.th. in store *(a. fig for s.o.)*
Lagerfeuer *n* campfire
Lagerhaus *n* warehouse
'lagern *(ge-, h)* **1.** *v/i* camp; ECON be stored; **2.** *v/t* store, keep; MED lay, rest; ***kühl lagern*** keep in a cool place
'Lagerraum *m* storeroom
Lagerung ['la:gəruŋ] *f (-; no pl)* storage
Lagune [la'gu:nə] *f (-; -n)* lagoon
lahm [la:m] *adj* lame
lahmen ['la:mən] *v/i (ge-, h)* be lame (***auf*** *dat* in)
'lahmlegen *v/t (sep, -ge-, h)* → ***lähmen***;
lähmen ['lɛ:mən] *v/t (ge-, h)* paralyze, *Br* paralyse; bring *traffic etc* to a standstill
'Lähmung *f (-; -en)* MED paralysis
Laib [laip] *m (-[e]s; -e* ['laibə]) loaf
Laich [laiç] *m (-[e]s; -e)*, **laichen** ['laiçən] *v/i (ge-, h)* spawn
Laie ['laɪə] *m (-n; -n)* layman; amateur
'laienhaft *adj* amateurish
'Laienspiel *n* amateur play
Laken ['la:kən] *n (-s; -)* sheet; bath towel
Lakritze [la'krɪtsə] *f (-; -n)* liquorice
lallen ['lalən] *v/i and v/t (ge-, h)* speak drunkenly; *baby*: babble
Lamm [lam] *n (-[e]s; Lämmer* ['lɛmɐ]) ZO lamb
Lammfell *n* lambskin
Lampe ['lampə] *f (-; -n)* lamp, light; bulb
'Lampenfieber *n* stage fright
'Lampenschirm *m* lampshade
Lampion [lam'pjõ:] *m (-s; -s)* Chinese lantern
Land [lant] *n (-[e]s; Länder* ['lɛndɐ]) land; country; AGR ground, soil; ECON land, property; ***an Land gehen*** MAR go ashore; ***auf dem Lande*** in the country; ***aufs Land fahren*** go into the country; ***außer Landes gehen*** go abroad
Landarbeiter *m* farmhand
Landbevölkerung *f* country *or* rural population
Landebahn ['landə-] *f* AVIAT runway
land'einwärts *adv* up-country, inland
landen ['landən] *v/i (ge-, sein)* land; *fig* ***landen in*** *(dat)* end up in
'Landenge *f* neck of land, isthmus
'Landeplatz *m* AVIAT landing field
Länderspiel ['lɛndɐ-] *n* SPORT international match
'Landesgrenze *f* national border
Landesinnere *n* interior
Landesre,gierung *f* Land *(Austrian* Provincial) government
Landessprache *f* national language
'landesüblich *adj* customary
'Landesverrat *m* treason
Landesverräter *m* traitor (to one's country)
Landesverteidigung *f* national defen|se, *Br* -ce
'Landflucht *f* rural exodus
Landfriedensbruch *m* JUR breach of the public peace
Landgericht *n* JUR *appr* regional superior court
Landgewinnung *f* reclamation of land
Landhaus *n* country house, cottage
Landkarte *f* map
Landkreis *m* district
'landläufig *adj* customary, current, common
ländlich ['lɛntlɪç] *adj* rural; rustic
'Landrat *m*, **Landrätin** [-rɛ:tɪn] *f (-; -nen)* *appr* District Administrator
Landratte F *f* MAR landlubber
'Landschaft *f (-; -en)* countryside; scenery; *esp* PAINT landscape
'landschaftlich *adj* scenic
'Landsmann *m (-[e]s; -leute)* (fellow) countryman
'Landsmännin [-mɛnɪn] *f (-; -nen)* fellow countrywoman
'Landstraße *f* country (*or* ordinary) road
Landstreicher(in) tramp
Landstreitkräfte *pl* MIL land forces
Landtag *m* Land parliament

ˈ**Landung** *f* (-; *-en*) landing, AVIAT *a.* touchdown
ˈ**Landungssteg** *m* MAR gangway
ˈ**Landvermesser** [-fɛɐmɛsɐ] *m* (-*s*; -) land surveyor
Landvermessung *f* (-; *-en*) land surveying
Landweg *m*: ***auf dem Landwege*** by land
Landwirt(in) farmer
ˈ**Landwirtschaft** *f* (-; *no pl*) agriculture, farming
ˈ**landwirtschaftlich** *adj* agricultural
ˈ**Landzunge** *f* GEOGR promontory, spit
lang [laŋ] *adj and adv* long; F tall; ***drei Jahre*** (***einige Zeit***) ***lang*** for three years (some time); ***den ganzen Tag lang*** all day long; ***seit langem*** for a long time; ***vor langer Zeit*** (a) long (time) ago; ***über kurz oder lang*** sooner or later; ***lang ersehnt*** long-hoped-for; ***lang erwartet*** long-awaited; ***gleich lang*** the same length
ˈ**langatmig** [-ʔaːtmɪç] *adj* long-winded
lange [ˈlaŋə] *adv* (for a) long (time); ***es ist schon lange her***(, ***seit***) it has been a long time (since); (***noch***) ***nicht lange her*** not long ago; ***noch lange hin*** still a long way off; ***es dauert nicht lange*** it won't take long; ***ich bleibe nicht lange fort*** I won't be long; ***wie lange noch?*** how much longer?
Länge [ˈlɛŋə] *f* (-; *-n*) length; GEOGR longitude; ***der Länge nach*** (at) full length; (***sich***) ***in die Länge ziehen*** stretch (*a. fig*)
langen [ˈlaŋən] F *v/i* (*ge-*, *h*) reach (***nach*** for); be enough; ***mir langt es*** I've had enough, *fig a.* I'm sick of it
ˈ**Längengrad** *m* GEOGR degree of longitude
Längenmaß *n* linear measure
ˈ**Langeweile** *f* (-; *no pl*) boredom; ***Langeweile haben*** be bored; ***aus Langeweile*** to pass the time
ˈ**langfristig** *adj* long-term
ˈ**langjährig** [-jɛːrɪç] *adj* longstanding; ***langjährige Erfahrung*** many years of experience
ˈ**Langlauf** *m* (-[*e*]*s*; *no pl*) SPORT cross-country (skiing)
ˈ**langlebig** [-leːbɪç] *adj* long-lived
länglich [ˈlɛŋlɪç] *adj* longish, oblong
längs [lɛŋs] **1.** *prp* (*gen*) along(side); **2.** *adv* lengthwise
ˈ**langsam** *adj* slow; ***langsamer werden*** *or* ***fahren*** slow down
ˈ**Langschläfer** [-ʃlɛːfɐ] *m* (-*s*; -), **Langschläferin** [-fərɪn] *f* (-; *-nen*) late riser
Langspielplatte *f* long-playing record, *mst* LP
längst [lɛŋst] *adv* long ago *or* before; ***längst vorbei*** long past; ***ich weiß es längst*** I have known it for a long time
längstens [ˈlɛŋstəns] *adv* at (the) most
ˈ**Langstrecken...** *in cpds* long-distance ...; AVIAT, MIL long-range ...
ˈ**langweilen** *v/t* (*ge-*, *h*) bore; ***sich langweilen*** be bored
ˈ**langweilig** [-vailɪç] *adj* boring, dull; ***langweilige Person*** bore
ˈ**Langwelle** *f* PHYS, *radio*: long wave
ˈ**langwierig** [-viːrɪç] *adj* lengthy, protracted (*a.* MED)
Lanze [ˈlantsə] *f* (-; *-n*) lance, spear
Lappalie [laˈpaːljə] *f* (-; *-n*) trifle
Lappen [ˈlapən] *m* (-*s*; -) (piece of) cloth; rag (*a. fig*)
läppisch [ˈlɛpɪʃ] *adj* silly; ridiculous
Lärche [ˈlɛrçə] *f* (-; *-n*) BOT larch
Lärm [lɛrm] *m* (-*s*; *no pl*) noise
lärmen [ˈlɛrmən] *v/i* (*ge-*, *h*) be noisy
lärmend *adj* noisy
Larve [ˈlarfə] *f* (-; *-n*) mask; ZO larva
las [laːs] *pret of* ***lesen***
lasch [laʃ] F *adj* slack, lax
Lasche [ˈlaʃə] *f* (-; *-n*) flap; tongue
Laser [ˈleːzɐ] *m* (-*s*; -) PHYS laser
Laserdrucker *m* EDP laser printer
Laserstrahl *m* PHYS laser beam
Lasertechnik *f* laser technology
lassen [ˈlasən] *v/t* (*irr*, *ge-*, *h*) *and v/aux* (*irr*, *no -ge-*, *h*) let, leave; ***j-n et. tun lassen*** let s.o. do s.th.; allow s.o. to do s.th.; make s.o. do s.th.; ***j-n*** (***et.***) ***zu Hause lassen*** leave s.o. (s.th.) at home; ***j-n allein*** (***in Ruhe***) ***lassen*** leave s.o. alone; ***sich die Haare schneiden lassen*** have *or* get one's hair cut; ***sein Leben lassen*** (***für***) lose (give) one's life (for); ***rufen lassen*** send for, call in; ***es lässt sich machen*** it can be done; ***lass alles so, wie*** (***wo***) ***es ist*** leave everything as (where) it is; ***er kann das Rauchen*** *etc* ***nicht lassen*** he can't stop smoking *etc*; ***lass das!*** stop it! → ***grüßen***, ***kommen***
lässig [ˈlɛsɪç] *adj* casual; careless
Last [last] *f* (-; *-en*) load, burden, weight (*all a. fig*); ***j-m zur Last fallen*** be a burden to s.o.; ***j-m et. zur Last legen*** charge s.o. with s.th.
lasten [ˈlastən] *v/i* (*ge-*, *h*) ***lasten auf*** (*dat*) *a. fig* weigh *or* rest (up)on
ˈ**Lastenaufzug** *m* freight elevator, *Br* goods lift
Laster[1] [ˈlastɐ] *m* (-*s*; -) → ***Lastwagen***
ˈ**Laster**[2] *n* (-*s*; -) vice
lästern [ˈlɛstɐn] *v/i* (*ge-*, *h*) ***lästern über*** (*acc*) run down
lästig [ˈlɛstɪç] *adj* troublesome, annoying;

(j-m) lästig sein be a nuisance (to s.o.)
'Lastkahn *m* barge
Lasttier *n* pack animal
Lastwagen *m* MOT truck, *Br a.* lorry
Lastwagenfahrer *m* MOT truck (*Br a.* lorry) driver, trucker
Latein [la'tain] *n* (*-s; no pl*) Latin
La'teina,merika Latin America
La'teinameri,kaner(in), **la'teinameri,kanisch** *adj* Latin American
la'teinisch *adj* Latin
Laterne [la'tɛrnə] *f* (*-; -n*) lantern; streetlight
La'ternenpfahl *m* lamppost
Latte ['latə] *f* (*-; -n*) lath; pale; SPORT bar
'Lattenzaun *m* paling, picket fence
Lätzchen ['lɛtsçən] *n* (*-s; -*) bib
Laub [laup] *n* (*-[e]s; no pl*) foliage, leaves
'Laubbaum *m* deciduous tree
Laube ['laubə] *f* (*-; -n*) arbo(u)r
'Laubfrosch *m* ZO tree frog
'Laubsäge *f* fretsaw
Lauch [laux] *m* (*-[e]s; -e*) BOT leek
Lauer ['lauɐ] *f*: ***auf der Lauer liegen*** *or* ***sein*** lie in wait
'lauern *v/i* (*ge-, h*) lurk; ***lauern auf*** (*acc*) lie in wait for
Lauf [lauf] *m* (*-[e]s; Läufe* ['lɔʏfə]) run; course; *gun*: barrel; ***im Lauf(e) der Zeit*** in the course of time
Laufbahn *f* career
Laufdiszi,plin *f* SPORT track event
laufen ['laufən] *v/i and v/t* (*irr, ge-, sein*) run (*a.* TECH, MOT, ECON); walk; *fig* work, run; ***j-n laufen lassen*** let s.o. go; let s.o. off
laufend **1.** *fig adj* present, current (*a.* ECON); continual; ***auf dem Laufenden sein*** be up to date; **2.** *adv* continuously; regularly; always
'laufenlassen *v/t* (*irr*, ***lassen***, *sep, no -ge-, h* → ***laufen***
Läufer ['lɔʏfɐ] *m* (*-s; -*) runner (*a. carpet*); *chess*: bishop
'Läuferin *f* (*-; -nen*) runner
'Laufgitter *n* playpen
Laufmasche *f* run, *Br* ladder
Laufschritt *m*: ***im Laufschritt*** on the double
Laufschuhe *pl* walking shoes; SPORT trainers
Laufsteg *m* footbridge; TECH, *fashion*: catwalk; MAR gangway
Lauge ['laugə] *f* (*-; -n*) suds; CHEM lye
Laune ['launə] *f* (*-; -n*) mood, temper; ***gute*** (***schlechte***) ***Laune haben*** be in a good (bad) mood *or* temper
launenhaft, **'launisch** *adj* moody; bad-tempered
Laus [laus] *f* (*-; Läuse* ['lɔʏzə]) ZO louse
Lauschangriff ['lauʃ-] *m* bugging operation
lauschen ['lauʃən] *v/i* (*ge-, h*) listen (*dat* to); eavesdrop
lauschig ['lauʃɪç] *adj* snug, cozy, *Br* cosy
laut[1] [laut] **1.** *adj* loud; noisy; **2.** *adv* loud(ly); ***laut vorlesen*** read (out) aloud; (***sprich***) ***lauter, bitte!*** speak up, please!
laut[2] *prp* (*gen or dat*) according to
Laut *m* (*-[e]s; -e*) sound, noise
lauten ['lautən] *v/i* (*ge-, h*) read; be
läuten ['lɔʏtən] *v/i and v/t* (*ge-, h*) ring; ***es läutet*** (***an der Tür***) the (door)bell is ringing
lauter ['lautɐ] *adv* sheer (*nonsense etc*); nothing but; (so) many
'lautlos *adj* silent, soundless; hushed
'Lautschrift *f* phonetic transcription
'Lautsprecher *m* TECH (loud)speaker
'Lautstärke *f* loudness, ELECTR *a.* (sound) volume; ***mit voller Lautstärke*** (at) full blast
Lautstärkeregler *m* volume control
lauwarm ['lau-] *adj* lukewarm (*a. fig*)
Lava ['la:va] *f* (*-; Laven*) GEOL lava
Lavabo [la'va:bo] *Swiss n* → ***Waschbecken***
Lavendel [la'vɛndəl] *m* (*-s; -*) BOT lavender
Lawine [la'vi:nə] *f* (*-; -n*) avalanche
Lazarett [latsa'rɛt] *n* (*-[e]s; -e*) (military) hospital
leben ['le:bən] (*ge-, h*) **1.** *v/i* live; be alive; ***von et. leben*** live on s.th.; **2.** *v/t* live
'Leben *n* (*-s; -*) life; ***am Leben bleiben*** stay alive; survive; ***am Leben sein*** be alive; ***ums Leben bringen*** kill; ***sich das Leben nehmen*** take one's (own) life, commit suicide; ***ums Leben kommen*** lose one's life, be killed; ***um sein Leben laufen*** (***kämpfen***) run (fight) for one's life; ***das tägliche Leben*** everyday life; ***mein Leben lang*** all my life
'lebend *adj* living
lebendig [le'bɛndɪç] *adj* living, alive; *fig* lively
'Lebensabend *m* old age, the last years of one's life
Lebensbedingungen *pl* living conditions
Lebensdauer *f* life-span; TECH (service) life
Lebenserfahrung *f* experience of life
Lebenserwartung *f* life expectancy
'lebensfähig *adj* MED viable (*a. fig*)
'Lebensgefahr *f* mortal danger; ***in*** (***unter***) ***Lebensgefahr*** in danger (at the risk) of one's life
'lebensgefährlich *adj* dangerous (to life),

perilous
'lebensgroß *adj* life-size(d)
'Lebensgröße *f*: ***e-e Statue in Lebensgröße*** a life-size(d) statue
'Lebenshaltungskosten *pl* cost of living
'lebenslänglich 1. *adj* lifelong; ***lebenslängliche Freiheitsstrafe*** JUR life sentence; **2.** *adv* for life
'Lebenslauf *m* personal record, curriculum vitae
'lebenslustig *adj* fond of life
'Lebensmittel *pl* food(stuffs); groceries
Lebensmittelgeschäft *n* grocery, supermarket
'lebensmüde *adj* tired of life
'Lebensnotwendigkeit *f* vital necessity
Lebensretter(in) lifesaver, rescuer
Lebensstandard *m* standard of living
Lebensunterhalt *m* livelihood; ***s-n Lebensunterhalt verdienen*** earn one's living (***als*** as; ***mit*** out of, by)
Lebensversicherung *f* life insurance
Lebensweise *f* way of life
'lebenswichtig *adj* vital, essential
'Lebenszeichen *n* sign of life
'Lebenszeit *f* lifetime; ***auf Lebenszeit*** for life
Leber ['le:bɐ] *f* (-; *-n*) ANAT liver
Leberfleck *m* mole
Lebertran *m* cod-liver oil
'Lebewesen *n* living being, creature
lebhaft ['le:phaft] *adj* lively; heavy (*traffic etc*)
'Lebkuchen *m* gingerbread
'leblos *adj* lifeless (*a. fig*)
'Lebzeiten *pl*: ***zu s-n Lebzeiten*** in his lifetime
lechzen ['lɛçtsən] *v/i* (*ge-, h*) ***lechzen nach*** thirst for
leck [lɛk] *adj* leaking, leaky
Leck *n* (-[*e*]*s*; *-s*) leak
lecken[1] ['lɛkən] *v/t and v/i* (*ge-, h*) *a.* ***lecken an*** (*dat*) lick
'lecken[2] *v/i* (*ge-, h*) leak
lecker ['lɛkɐ] *adj* delicious, tasty, F yummy
'Leckerbissen *m* delicacy, treat (*a. fig*)
Leder ['le:dɐ] *n* (*-s*; -) leather
'ledern *adj* leather(n)
'Lederwaren *pl* leather goods
ledig ['le:dɪç] *adj* single, unmarried
lediglich ['le:dɪklɪç] *adv* only, merely
Lee [le:] *f* (-; *no pl*) MAR lee; ***nach Lee*** leeward
leer [le:ɐ] **1.** *adj* empty (*a. fig*); vacant (*house etc*); blank (*page etc*); ELECTR dead, *Br* flat; ***leer stehend*** unoccupied, vacant; **2.** *adv*: ***leer laufen*** TECH idle
Leere ['le:rə] *f* (-; *no pl*) emptiness (*a. fig*)
'leeren *v/t and v/refl* (*ge-, h*) empty
'Leergut *n* empties
'Leerlauf *m* TECH idling; neutral (gear); *fig* running on the spot
'Leertaste *f* space bar
'Leerung *f* (-; *-en*) *post* collection
legal [le'ga:l] *adj* legal, lawful
legalisieren [legali'zi:rən] *v/t* (*no -ge-, h*) legalize
Legali'sierung *f* (-; *-en*) legalization
Legasthenie [legaste'ni:] *f* (-; *-n*) PSYCH dyslexia, F word blindness
Legastheniker [legas'te:nikɐ] *m* (*-s*; -), **Legas'thenikerin** *f* (-; *-nen*) PSYCH dyslexic
legen ['le:gən] *v/t and v/i* (*ge-, h*) lay (*a. eggs*); place, put; set (*hair*); ***sich legen*** lie down; *fig* calm down; *pain*: wear off
Legende [le'gɛndə] *f* (-; *-n*) legend
leger [le'ʒe:ɐ] *adj* casual, informal
Legislative [legɪsla'ti:və] *f* (-; *-n*) legislative power
legitim [legi'ti:m] *adj* legitimate
Lehm [le:m] *m* (-[*e*]*s*; *-e*) loam; clay
lehmig ['le:mɪç] *adj* loamy, F muddy
Lehne ['le:nə] *f* (-; *-n*) back(rest); arm(-rest)
'lehnen *v/t and v/i* lean (*a.* ***sich lehnen***) rest (***an*** *acc*, ***gegen*** against; ***auf*** *acc* on); ***sich aus dem Fenster lehnen*** lean out of the window
'Lehnsessel *m*, **'Lehnstuhl** *m* armchair, easy chair
Lehrbuch ['le:ɐ-] *n* textbook
Lehre ['le:rə] *f* (-; *-n*) science; theory; REL, POL teachings, doctrine; moral; ECON apprenticeship; ***in der Lehre sein*** be apprenticed (***bei*** to); ***das wird ihm e-e Lehre sein*** that will teach him a lesson
'lehren *v/t* (*ge-, h*) teach, instruct; show
Lehrer ['le:rɐ] *m* (*-s*; -) teacher, instructor, *Br a.* master
Lehrerausbildung *f* teacher training
Lehrerin ['le:rərɪn] *f* (-; *-nen*) (lady) teacher, *Br a.* mistress
'Lehrerkol,legium *n* (teaching) staff
Lehrerzimmer *n* staff *or* teachers' room
'Lehrgang *m* course (of instruction *or* study); training course
Lehrherr *m* master
Lehrjahr *n* year (of apprenticeship)
Lehrling ['le:ɐlɪŋ] *m* (*-s*; *-e*) apprentice, trainee
'Lehrmeister *m*, **Lehrmeisterin** *f* master; *fig* teacher
Lehrmittel *pl* teaching aids
Lehrplan *m* curriculum, syllabus
Lehrprobe *f* demonstration lesson
'lehrreich *adj* informative, instructive

'**Lehrstelle** *f* apprenticeship; vacancy for an apprentice
Lehrstuhl *m* professorship
Lehrtochter *Swiss f* apprentice
Lehrvertrag *m* indenture(s)
Lehrzeit *f* apprenticeship
Leib [laip] *m* (-[*e*]*s*; *Leiber* ['laibɐ]) body; belly, ANAT abdomen; stomach; ***bei lebendigem Leibe*** alive; ***mit Leib und Seele*** (with) heart and soul
Leibeserziehung ['laibəs-] *f* PED physical education, ABBR PE
Leibeskräfte *pl*: ***aus Leibeskräften*** with all one's might
'**Leibgericht** *n* GASTR favo(u)rite dish
leibhaftig [laip'haftɪç] *adj*: ***der leibhaftige Teufel*** the devil incarnate; ***leibhaftiges Ebenbild*** living image; ***ich sehe ihn noch leibhaftig vor mir*** I can see him (before me) now
'**leiblich** *adj* physical
'**Leibrente** *f* life annuity
Leibwache *f*, **Leibwächter** *m* bodyguard
Leibwäsche *f* underwear
Leiche ['laiçə] *f* (-; -*n*) (dead) body, corpse
'**leichen'blass** *adj* deadly pale
'**Leichenhalle** *f* mortuary
Leichenschauhaus *n* morgue
Leichenverbrennung *f* cremation
Leichenwagen *m* hearse
leicht [laiçt] *adj* light (*a. fig*); easy, simple; slight, minor; TECH light(weight); ***leicht möglich*** quite possible; ***leicht gekränkt*** easily offended; ***es fällt mir*** (***nicht***) ***leicht*** (***zu*** *inf*) I find it easy (difficult) (to *inf*); ***das ist leicht gesagt*** it's not as easy as that; ***es geht leicht kaputt*** it breaks easily; ***leicht verständlich*** easy to understand
'**Leichtath,let** *m* SPORT (track-and-field) athlete
Leichtath,letik *f* SPORT track and field (events), athletics
Leichtath,letin *f* SPORT (track-and-field) athlete
Leichtgewicht *n* SPORT lightweight
'**leichtgläubig** *adj* credulous
Leichtigkeit ['laiçtɪçkait] *f*: ***mit Leichtigkeit*** easily, with ease
'**leichtlebig** [-leːbɪç] *adj* happy-go-lucky
'**Leichtme,tall** *n* light metal
'**leichtnehmen** *v/t* (*irr*, ***nehmen***, *sep*, -*ge*-, *h*): ***et. leichtnehmen*** not worry about s.th.; make light of s.th.; ***nimm's leichtnehmen!*** never mind!, don't worry about it!
'**Leichtsinn** *m* (-[*e*]*s*; *no pl*) carelessness; recklessness
'**leichtsinnig** *adj* careless; reckless
'**leichtverständlich** *adj* → ***leicht***
Leid [lait] *n* (-[*e*]*s*; *no pl*) sorrow, grief; pain; ***es tut mir Leid*** I'm sorry (***um*** for; ***wegen*** about; ***dass ich zu spät komme*** for being late)
leiden ['laidən] *v/t and v/i* (*irr*, *ge*-, *h*) suffer (***an*** *dat*, ***unter*** *dat* from); ***j-n gut leiden können*** like s.o.; ***ich kann … nicht leiden*** I don't like …; I can't stand …
'**Leiden** *n* (-*s*; -) suffering(s); MED disease
'**Leidenschaft** *f* (-; -*en*) passion
'**leidenschaftlich** *adj* passionate; vehement
'**Leidensgenosse** *m*, '**Leidensgenossin** *f* fellow sufferer
leider ['laidɐ] *adv* unfortunately; ***leider ja*** (***nein***) I'm afraid so (not)
'**leidlich** *adj* passable, F so-so
'**Leidtragende** *m*, *f* (-*n*; -*n*) mourner; ***er ist der Leidtragende dabei*** he is the one who suffers for it
'**Leidwesen** *n*: ***zu m-m Leidwesen*** to my regret
Leierkasten ['laiɐ-] *m* barrel organ
Leierkastenmann *m* organ grinder
leiern ['laiɐn] *v/i and v/t* (*ge*-, *h*) crank (up); *fig* drone
Leihbücherei ['lai-] *f* public library
leihen ['laiən] *v/t* (*irr*, *ge*-, *h*) lend; rent (*Br* hire) out; borrow (***von*** from); rent, hire
'**Leihgebühr** *f* rental, lending fee
Leihhaus *n* pawnshop, pawnbroker's (shop)
Leihmutter F *f* surrogate mother
Leihwagen *m* MOT rented (*Br* hire) car
'**leihweise** *adv* on loan
Leim [laim] *m* (-[*e*]*s*; -*e*), **leimen** ['laimən] *v/t* (*ge*-, *h*) glue
Leine ['lainə] *f* (-; -*n*) line; lead, leash
Leinen ['lainən] *n* (-*s*; -) linen; canvas; ***in Leinen gebunden*** clothbound
'**Leinenschuh** *m* canvas shoe
'**Leinsamen** *m* BOT linseed
Leintuch *n* (linen) sheet
Leinwand *f* linen; PAINT canvas; screen
leise ['laizə] *adj* quiet, *a.* low, soft (*voice*, *a. music etc*); *fig* slight, faint; ***leiser stellen*** turn (the volume) down
Leiste ['laistə] *f* (-; -*n*) ledge; ANAT groin
'**leisten** *v/t* (*ge*-, *h*) do, work; achieve, accomplish; render (*service etc*); take (*oath*); ***gute Arbeit leisten*** do a good job; ***sich et. leisten*** treat o.s. to s.th.; ***ich kann es mir*** (***nicht***) ***leisten*** I can('t) afford it
'**Leistung** *f* (-; -*en*) performance; achievement, PED *a.* (piece of) work, result, TECH *a.* output; service; benefit
'**Leistungsdruck** *m* (-[*e*]*s*; *no pl*) pressure,

stress
'leistungsfähig *adj* efficient; (physically) fit
'Leistungsfähigkeit *f* (-; *no pl*) efficiency (*a.* TECH, ECON); fitness
'Leistungskon,trolle *f* (achievement *or* proficiency) test
Leistungskurs *m* PED *appr* special subject
Leistungssport *m* competitive sport(s)
Leitar,tikel ['lait-] *m* editorial, *esp Br* leader, leading article
leiten ['laitən] *v/t* (*ge-, h*) lead, guide (*a. fig*), conduct (*a.* PHYS, MUS); run (*a.* PED), be in charge of, manage; TV *etc* direct; host
leitend *adj* leading; PHYS conductive; ***leitende Stellung*** key position; ***leitender Angestellter*** executive
Leiter[1] ['laitɐ] *f* (-; *-n*) ladder
'Leiter[2] *m* (*-s*; -) leader; conductor (*a.* PHYS, MUS); ECON *etc* head, manager; chairman; → ***Schulleiter***
Leiterin ['laitərɪn] *f* (-; *-nen*) leader; head; chairwoman
'Leitfaden *m* manual, guide
Leitplanke *f* MOT guardrail, *Br* crash barrier
Leitspruch *m* motto
'Leitung *f* (-; *-en*) ECON management; head office; administration; chairmanship; organization; THEA *etc* direction; TECH main, pipe(s); ELECTR, TEL line; ***die Leitung haben*** be in charge; ***unter der Leitung von*** MUS conducted by
'Leitungsrohr *n* pipe
'Leitungswasser *n* tap water
Lektion [lɛk'tsjo:n] *f* (-; *-en*) lesson
Lektüre [lɛk'ty:rə] *f* (-; *-n*) reading (matter); PED reader
Lende ['lɛndə] *f* (-; *-n*) ANAT loin; GASTR sirloin
lenken ['lɛŋkən] *v/t* (*ge-, h*) steer, drive; *fig* guide *s.o.*; direct (*traffic etc*)
Lenker ['lɛŋkɐ] *m* (*-s*; -) handlebar
'Lenkrad *n* MOT steering wheel
'Lenkung *f* (-; *-en*) MOT steering (system)
Leopard [leo'part] *m* (*-en*; *-en*) ZO leopard
Lerche ['lɛrçə] *f* (-; *-n*) ZO lark
lernen ['lɛrnən] *v/t and v/i* (*ge-, h*) learn; study; ***er lernt leicht*** he is a quick learner; ***lesen lernen*** learn (how) to read
'Lernmittelfreiheit *f* free books *etc*
lesbar ['le:sba:ɐ] *adj* readable
Lesbierin ['lɛsbjərɪn] *f* (-; *-nen*), **lesbisch** ['lɛsbɪʃ] *adj* lesbian
Lesebuch ['le:zə-] *n* reader
'Leselampe *f* reading lamp
lesen ['le:zən] *v/i and v/t* (*irr, ge-, h*) read; AGR harvest
'lesenswert *adj* worth reading
Leser ['le:zɐ] *m* (*-s*; -) reader
'Leseratte F *f* bookworm
'Leserbrief *m* letter to the editor
'Leserin *f* (-; -nen) reader
'leserlich *adj* legible
'Lesestoff *m* reading matter
'Lesezeichen *n* bookmark
'Lesung *f* (-; *-en*) reading (*a.* PARL)
Letzt [lɛtst] *f*: ***zu guter Letzt*** in the end
letzte ['lɛtstə] *adj* last; latest; ***zum letzten Mal(e)*** for the last time; ***in letzter Zeit*** recently; ***als Letzter ankommen*** *etc* arrive *etc* last; ***Letzter sein*** be last (*a.* SPORT); ***das ist das Letzte!*** that's the limit!
'letztens *adv* finally; ***erst letztens*** just recently
letztere ['lɛtstərə] *adj* latter; ***der (die, das) Letztere*** the latter
Leuchtanzeige ['lɔyçt-] *f* luminous *or* LED display light
leuchten ['lɔyçtən] *v/i* (*ge-, h*) shine; glow
'Leuchten *n* (*-s*; *no pl*) shining; glow
'leuchtend *adj* shining (*a. fig*); bright
Leuchter ['lɔyçtɐ] *m* (*-s*; -) candlestick
'Leuchtfarbe *f* luminous paint
Leuchtre,klame *f* neon sign(s)
Leucht(stoff)röhre *f* ELECTR fluorescent lamp
Leuchtturm *m* lighthouse
Leuchtziffer *f* luminous figure
leugnen ['lɔygnən] *v/t and v/i* (*ge-, h*) deny (***et. getan zu haben*** having done s.th.)
Leute ['lɔytə] *pl* people, F folks
Leutnant ['lɔytnant] *m* (*-s*; *-s*) MIL second lieutenant
Lexikon ['lɛksikɔn] *n* (*-s*; *-ka*, *-ken*) encyclop(a)edia; dictionary
Libelle [li'bɛlə] *f* (-; *-n*) ZO dragonfly
liberal [libe'ra:l] *adj* liberal
Libero ['li:bero] *m* (*-s*; *-s*) *soccer*: sweeper
licht ['lɪçt] *adj* bright; *fig* lucid
Licht *n* (*-[e]s*; *-er* ['lɪçtɐ]) a) light, b) (*no pl*) brightness; ***Licht machen*** switch *or* turn on the light(s)
'Lichtbild *n* photo(graph); slide
Lichtbildervortrag *m* slide lecture
Lichtblick *m* ray of hope; bright moment
'lichtempfindlich *adj* sensitive to light; PHOT sensitive
'Lichtempfindlichkeit *f* (light) sensitivity; PHOT speed
lichten ['lɪçtən] *v/t* (*ge-, h*) clear; ***den Anker lichten*** MAR weigh anchor; ***sich lichten*** get thin(ner); *fig* be thinning (out)
'Lichtgeschwindigkeit *f* speed of light
Lichtgriffel *m* light pen
Lichthupe *f* MOT (headlight) flash(er); ***die Lichthupe betätigen*** flash one's lights

Lichtjahr *n* light year
Lichtma,schine *f* MOT generator
Lichtorgel *f* colo(u)r organ
Lichtpause *f* blueprint
Lichtschacht *m* well
Lichtschalter *m* (light) switch
'lichtscheu *fig adj* shady
'Lichtschutzfaktor *m* sun protection factor, SPF
Lichtstrahl *m* ray *or* beam of light (*a. fig*)
'Lichtung *f* (-; *-en*) clearing
Lid [liːt] *n* (-[*e*]*s*; *Lider* ['liːdɐ]) ANAT (eye)-lid
Lidschatten *m* eye shadow
lieb [liːp] *adj* dear; sweet; nice, kind; good; ***lieb gewinnen*** get fond of; ***lieb haben*** love, be fond of
Liebe ['liːbə] *f* (-; *no pl*) love (***zu*** of, for); ***aus Liebe zu*** out of love for; ***Liebe auf den ersten Blick*** love at first sight
'lieben *v/t* (*ge-*, *h*) love, *a.* be in love with *s.o.*; make love to
'liebenswert *adj* lovable, charming, sweet
'liebenswürdig *adj* kind
'Liebenswürdigkeit *f* (-; *no pl*) kindness
lieber ['liːbɐ] *adv* rather, sooner; ***lieber haben*** prefer, like better; ***ich möchte lieber*** (***nicht***) ***...*** I'd rather (not) ...; ***du solltest lieber*** (***nicht***) ***...*** you had better (not) ...
'Liebesbrief *m* love letter
Liebeserklärung *f*: ***j-m e-e Liebeserklärung machen*** declare one's love to s.o.
Liebeskummer *m*: ***Liebeskummer haben*** be lovesick
Liebespaar *n* lovers
'liebevoll *adj* loving, affectionate
'liebgewinnen *v/t* (*irr*, ***gewinnen***, *sep*, *h*) → ***lieb***
'liebhaben *v/t* (*irr*, ***haben***, *sep*, *-ge-*, *h*) → ***lieb***
Liebhaber ['liːphaːbɐ] *m* (*-s*; -) lover (*a. fig*); ***Liebhaber...*** *in cpds ...preis, ...stück etc*: collector's ...
Liebhaberei [liːphaːbə'rai] *f* (-; *-en*) hobby
Liebkosung [liːp'koːzʊŋ] *f* (-; *-en*) caress
'lieblich *adj* lovely, charming, sweet (*a. wine*)
'Liebling *m* (*-s*; *-e*) darling; favo(u)rite
'Lieblings... *in cpds mst* favo(u)rite
'lieblos *adj* unloving, cold; unkind (*words etc*); *fig* careless
Lied [liːt] *n* (-[*e*]*s*; *-er* ['liːdɐ]) song; tune
liederlich ['liːdɐlɪç] *adj* slovenly, sloppy
Liedermacher ['liːdɐ-] *m* (*-s*; -) singer-songwriter
lief [liːf] *pret of* ***laufen***
Lieferant [lifə'rant] *m* (*-en*; *-en*) ECON supplier
lieferbar ['liːfɐbaːɐ] *adj* ECON available
'Lieferfrist *f* ECON term of delivery
liefern ['liːfɐn] *v/t* (*ge-*, *h*) ECON deliver; ***j-m et. liefern*** supply s.o. with s.th.
Lieferung ['liːfərʊŋ] *f* (-; *-en*) ECON delivery; supply
'Lieferwagen *m* MOT (delivery) van
Liege ['liːgə] *f* (-; *-n*) couch
liegen ['liːgən] *v/i* (*irr*, *ge-*, *h*) lie, *a.* be (situated); (***krank***) ***im Bett liegen*** be (ill) in bed; ***nach Osten*** (***der Straße***) ***liegen*** face east (the street); ***daran liegt es***(, ***dass***) that's (the reason) why; ***es*** (***er***) ***liegt mir nicht*** F it (he) is not my cup of tea; ***mir liegt viel*** (***wenig***) ***daran*** it means a lot (doesn't mean much) to me; ***liegen bleiben*** stay in bed; be left behind; ***liegen lassen*** leave (behind); F ***j-n links liegen lassen*** ignore s.o., give s.o. the cold shoulder
'liegenbleiben *v/i* (*irr*, ***bleiben***, *sep*, *-ge-*, *sein*) → ***liegen***
liegenbleibenlassen *v/i* (*irr*, ***lassen***, *sep*, *no -ge-*, *h*) → ***liegen***
'Liegesitz *m* reclining seat
Liegestuhl *m* deckchair
Liegestütz *m* (*-es*; *-e*) SPORT push-up, *Br* press-up
Liegewagen *m* RAIL couchette
lieh [liː] *pret of* ***leihen***
ließ [liːs] *pret of* ***lassen***
Lift [lɪft] *m* (-[*e*]*s*; *-e*, *-s*) elevator, *Br* lift; ski lift
Liga ['liːga] *f* (-; *Ligen*) league, SPORT *a.* division
Likör [li'køːɐ] *m* (*-s*; *-e*) liqueur
lila ['liːla] *adj* purple, violet
Lilie ['liːljə] *f* (-; *-n*) BOT lily
Liliputaner [lilipu'taːnɐ] *m* (*-s*; -) dwarf, midget
Limonade [limo'naːdə] *f* (-; *-n*) pop; lemon soda, *Br* lemonade
Limousine [limu'ziːnə] *f* (-; *-n*) MOT sedan, *Br* saloon car; limousine
Linde ['lɪndə] *f* (-; *-n*) BOT lime (tree), linden
lindern ['lɪndɐn] *v/t* (*ge-*, *h*) relieve, ease, alleviate
Linderung ['lɪndərʊŋ] *f* (-; *no pl*) relief, alleviation
Lineal [line'aːl] *n* (*-s*; *-e*) ruler
Linie ['liːnjə] *f* (-; *-n*) line; ***auf s-e Linie achten*** watch one's weight
'Linienflug *m* AVIAT scheduled flight
Linienrichter *m* SPORT linesman
'linientreu *adj* POL: ***linientreu sein*** follow the party line
linieren [li'niːrən], **liniieren** [lini'iːrən] *v/t*

L

(*no -ge-, h*) rule, line
linke ['lɪŋkə] *adj* left (*a.* POL); ***auf der linken Seite*** on the left(-hand side)
'**Linke** *m, f* (*-n; -n*) POL leftist, left-winger
linkisch ['lɪŋkɪʃ] *adj* awkward, clumsy
links [lɪŋks] *adv* on the left (*a.* POL); on the wrong side; ***nach links*** (to the) left; ***links von*** to the left of
Links... *in cpds ...verkehr etc*: left-hand
Links'außen *m* (-; -) SPORT outside left, left wing
'**Linkshänder** [-hɛndɐ] *m* (*-s*; -), '**Linkshänderin** *f* (-; *-nen*) left-hander
'**Linksradi,kale** *m, f* (*-n*; *-n*) POL left-wing extremist
Linse ['lɪnzə] *f* (-; *-n*) BOT lentil; OPT lens
Lippe ['lɪpə] *f* (-; *-n*) ANAT lip
'**Lippenstift** *m* lipstick
liquidieren [likvi'di:rən] *v/t* (*no -ge-, h*) ECON liquidate (*a.* POL)
lispeln ['lɪspəln] *v/i* (*ge-, h*) (have a) lisp
List [lɪst] *f* (-; *-en*) a) trick, b) (*no pl*) cunning
Liste ['lɪstə] *f* (-; *-n*) list; roll
listig ['lɪstɪç] *adj* cunning, tricky, sly
Liter ['li:tɐ] *n, m* (*-s*; -) liter, *Br* litre
literarisch [lɪtə'ra:rɪʃ] *adj* literary
Literatur [lɪtəra'tu:ɐ] *f* (-; *-en*) literature
Literatur... *in cpds ...kritik etc*: *mst* literary
Litfaßsäule ['lɪtfas-] *f* advertising pillar
litt [lɪt] *pret of* ***leiden***
Lizenz [li'tsɛnts] *f* (-; *-en*) license, *Br* licence
Lkw, LKW ['ɛlkave] *m* (*-[s]*; -) ABBR *of* ***Lastkraftwagen*** truck, *Br a.* lorry
Lob [lo:p] *n* (*-[e]s*; *no pl*), **loben** ['lo:bən] *v/t* (*ge-, h*) praise
'**lobenswert** *adj* praiseworthy, laudable
Loch [lɔx] *n* (*-[e]s*; *Löcher* ['lœçɐ]) hole (*a. fig*); puncture
lochen ['lɔxən] *v/t* (*ge-, h*) punch (*a.* TECH)
Locher ['lɔxɐ] *m* (*-s*; -) punch
Locke ['lɔkə] *f* (-; *-n*) curl; lock
locken[1] ['lɔkən] *v/t and v/refl* (*ge-, h*) curl
locken[2] *v/t* (*ge-, h*) lure, entice, *fig a.* attract, tempt
'**Lockenkopf** *m* curly head
Lockenwickler [-vɪklɐ] *m* (*-s*; -) curler, roller
locker ['lɔkɐ] *adj* loose; slack; *fig* relaxed
'**lockern** *v/t* (*ge-, h*) loosen, slacken; relax (*a. fig*); ***sich lockern*** loosen, (be)come loose; SPORT limber up; *fig* relax
lockig ['lɔkɪç] *adj* curly, curled
'**Lockvogel** *m* decoy (*a. fig*)
lodern ['lo:dɐn] *v/i* (*ge-, h*) blaze, flare
Löffel ['lœfəl] *m* (*-s*; -) spoon; ladle
'**löffeln** *v/t* (*ge-, h*) spoon up

log [lo:k] *pret of* ***lügen***
Logbuch ['lɔk-] *n* MAR log
Loge ['lo:ʒə] *f* (-; *-n*) THEA box; lodge
Logik ['lo:gɪk] *f* (-; *no pl*) logic
logisch ['lo:gɪʃ] *adj* logical
'**logischer'weise** *adv* obviously
Lohn [lo:n] *m* (*-[e]s*; *Löhne* ['lø:nə]) ECON wages, pay(ment); *fig* reward
Lohnempfänger *m* wageworker, *Br* wage earner
lohnen ['lo:nən] *v/refl* (*ge-, h*) be worth (-while), pay; ***es*** (***die Mühe***) ***lohnt sich*** it's worth it (the trouble); ***das Buch*** (***der Film***) ***lohnt sich*** the book (film) is worth reading (seeing)
lohnend *adj* paying; *fig* rewarding
'**Lohnerhöhung** *f* raise, *Br* increase in wages, rise
Lohnsteuer *f* income tax
Lohnstopp *m* wage freeze
Lohntüte *f* pay packet
Loipe ['lɔypə] *f* (-; *-n*) (cross-country) course
Lokal [lo'ka:l] *n* (*-s*; *-e*) restaurant; bar, saloon, *esp Br* pub
Lo'kal... *in cpds mst* local
Lok [lɔk] *f* (-; *-s*) → ***Lokomotive***
Lokführer *m* RAIL engineer, *Br* train driver
Lokomotive [lokomo'ti:və] *f* (-; *-n*) RAIL engine
Lorbeer ['lɔrbe:ɐ] *m* (*-s*; *-en*) BOT laurel; GASTR bay leaf
Lore ['lo:rə] *f* (-; *-n*) TECH tipcart
los [lo:s] *adj and adv* off; *dog etc*: loose; ***los sein*** be rid of; ***was ist los?*** what's the matter?, F what's up?; what's going on (here)?; ***hier ist nicht viel los*** there's nothing much going on here; F ***da ist was los!*** that's where the action is!; F ***also los!*** okay, let's go!
Los [lo:s] *n* (*-es*; *-e* ['lo:zə]) lot, *fig a.* fate; (lottery) ticket, number
'**losbinden** *v/t* (*irr*, ***binden***, *sep, -ge-, h*) untie
Löschblatt ['lœʃ-] *n* blotting paper
löschen ['lœʃən] *v/t* (*ge-, h*) extinguish, put out; quench (*thirst*); blot (*ink*); wipe off *the blackboard*; erase, EDP *a.* delete; slake (*lime*); MAR unload
'**Löschpa,pier** *n* blotting paper
lose ['lo:zə] *adj* loose
Lösegeld ['lø:zə-] *n* ransom
losen ['lo:zən] *v/i* (*ge-, h*) draw lots (***um*** for)
lösen ['lø:zən] *v/t* (*ge-, h*) undo (*knot etc*); loosen, relax; TECH release; take off; solve (*problem etc*); settle (*conflict etc*); buy, get (*ticket etc*); dissolve (*a.* CHEM);

sich lösen come loose *or* undone; *fig* free o.s. (***von*** from)
'losfahren *v/i* (*irr*, ***fahren***, *sep*, *-ge-*, *sein*) leave; drive off
losgehen *v/i* (*irr*, ***gehen***, *sep*, *-ge-*, *sein*) leave; start, begin; *shot etc*: go off; ***auf j-n losgehen*** go for s.o.; ***ich gehe jetzt los*** I'm off now
losketten *v/t* (*sep*, *-ge-*, *h*) unchain
loskommen *v/i* (*irr*, ***kommen***, *sep*, *-ge-*, *sein*) get away (***von*** from)
loslassen *v/t* (*irr*, ***lassen***, *sep*, *-ge-*, *h*) let go; ***den Hund loslassen auf*** (*acc*) set the dog on
loslegen F *v/i* (*sep*, *-ge-*, *h*) get cracking
löslich ['lø:slıç] *adj* CHEM soluble
'losmachen *v/t* (*sep*, *-ge-*, *h*) → ***lösen***
losreißen *v/t* (*irr*, ***reißen***, *sep*, *-ge-*, *h*) tear off; ***sich losreißen*** break away; *esp fig* tear o.s. away (*both*: ***von*** from)
lossagen *v/refl* (*sep*, *-ge-*, *h*) ***sich lossagen von*** break with
losschlagen *v/i* (*irr*, ***schlagen***, *sep*, *-ge-*, *h*) strike (***auf j-n*** out at s.o.)
losschnallen *v/t* (*sep*, *-ge-*, *h*) unbuckle; ***sich losschnallen*** MOT, AVIAT unfasten one's seatbelt
losstürzen *v/i* (*sep*, *-ge-*, *sein*) ***losstürzen auf*** (*acc*) rush at
Losung ['lo:zʊŋ] *f* (*-*; *-en*) MIL password; *fig* slogan
Lösung ['lø:zʊŋ] *f* (*-*; *-en*) solution (*a. fig*); settlement
'Lösungsmittel *n* solvent
'loswerden *v/t* (*irr*, ***werden***, *sep*, *-ge-*, *sein*) get rid of; spend (*money*); lose
'losziehen *v/i* (*irr*, ***ziehen***, *sep*, *-ge-*, *sein*) set out, take off, march away
Lot [lo:t] *n* (*-[e]s*; *-e*) plumbline
löten ['lø:tən] *v/t* (*ge-*, *h*) TECH solder
Lotion [lo'tsjo:n] *f* (*-*; *-en*) lotion
Lotse ['lo:tsə] *m* (*-n*; *-n*), **'lotsen** *v/t* (*ge-*, *h*) MAR pilot
Lotterie [lɔtə'ri:] *f* (*-*; *-n*) lottery
Lotteriegewinn *m* prize
Lotterielos *n* lottery ticket
Lotto ['lɔto] *n* (*-s*; *-s*) lotto, bingo; *Br* national lottery; *in Germany*: Lotto; (***im***) ***Lotto spielen*** do Lotto
Lottoschein *m* Lotto coupon
Lottoziehung *f* Lotto draw
Löwe ['lø:və] *m*(*-n*; *-n*) ZO lion; AST Leo; ***er ist*** (***ein***) ***Löwe*** he's (a) Leo
'Löwenzahn *m* BOT dandelion
Löwin ['lø:vın] *f* (*-*; *-nen*) ZO lioness
loyal [loa'ja:l] *adj* loyal, faithful
Luchs [lʊks] *m* (*-es*; *-e*) ZO lynx
Lücke ['lʏkə] *f* (*-*; *-n*) gap (*a. fig*)
'Lückenbüßer *m* stopgap
'lückenhaft *adj* full of gaps; *fig* incomplete
'lückenlos *adj* without a gap; *fig* complete
'Lückentest *m* PSYCH completion *or* fill-in test
lud [lu:t] *pret of* ***laden***
Luft [lʊft] *f* (*-*; *no pl*) air; ***an der frischen Luft*** (out) in the fresh air; (***frische***) ***Luft schöpfen*** get a breath of fresh air; ***die Luft anhalten*** catch (*esp fig a.* hold) one's breath; ***tief Luft holen*** take a deep breath; ***in die Luft sprengen*** (F ***fliegen***) blow up
'Luftangriff *m* air raid
Luftballon *m* balloon
Luftbild *n* aerial photograph *or* view
Luftblase *f* air bubble
Luftbrücke *f* airlift
'luftdicht *adj* airtight
'Luftdruck *m* (*-[e]s*; *no pl*) PHYS, TECH air pressure
lüften ['lʏftən] *v/t and v/i* (*ge-*, *h*) air, ventilate; *fig* reveal
'Luftfahrt *f* (*-*; *no pl*) aviation, aeronautics
Luftfeuchtigkeit *f* (atmospheric) humidity
Luftgewehr *n* airgun
'luftig *adj* airy; breezy; light (*dress etc*)
'Luftkissen *n* air cushion
Luftkissenfahrzeug *n* hovercraft
Luftkrankheit *f* air-sickness
Luftkrieg *m* air warfare
Luftkurort *m* (climatic) health resort
'luftleer *adj*: ***luftleerer Raum*** vacuum
'Luftlinie *f*: ***50 km Luftlinie*** 50 km as the crow flies
Luftpost *f* air mail
Luftpumpe *f* air pump; bicycle pump
Luftröhre *f* ANAT windpipe, trachea
Luftschlange *f* streamer
Luftschloss *n* castle in the air
Luftsprünge *pl*: ***Luftsprünge machen vor Freude*** jump for joy
'Lüftung *f* (*-*; *-en*) airing; TECH ventilation
'Luftveränderung *f* change of air
Luftverkehr *m* air traffic
Luftverschmutzung *f* air pollution
Luftwaffe *f* MIL air force
Luftweg *m*: ***auf dem Luftweg*** by air
Luftzug *m* draft, *Br* draught
Lüge ['ly:gə] *f* (*-*; *-n*) lie
'lügen *v/i* (*irr*, *ge-*, *h*) lie, tell a lie *or* lies; ***das ist gelogen*** that's a lie
Lügner(in) ['ly:gnɐ (-nərın)] (*-s*; *-/-*; *-nen*) liar
'lügnerisch [-nərıʃ] *adj* false
Luke ['lu:kə] *f* (*-*; *-n*) hatch; skylight
Lümmel ['lʏməl] F *m* (*-s*; *-*) rascal
lumpen ['lʊmpən] F *v/t*: ***sich nicht lum-***

L

pen lassen be generous
'**Lumpen** *m* (*-s*; *-*) rag; ***in Lumpen*** in rags
Lumpenpack F *n sl* bastards
lumpig ['lʊmpɪç] F *adj*: ***für lumpige zwei Mark*** for a paltry two marks
Lunge ['lʊŋə] *f* (*-*; *-n*) ANAT lungs; (***auf***) ***Lunge rauchen*** inhale
'**Lungenentzündung** *f* MED pneumonia
Lungenflügel *m* ANAT lung
Lungenzug *m*: ***e-n Lungenzug machen*** inhale
Lupe ['luːpə] *f* (*-*; *-n*) magnifying glass; ***unter die Lupe nehmen*** scrutinize (closely)
Lust [lʊst] *f* (*-*; *Lüste* ['lʏstə]) a) (*no pl*) desire, interest; pleasure, delight, b) lust; ***Lust haben auf et.*** (***et. zu tun***) feel like (doing) s.th.; ***hättest du Lust auszugehen?*** would you like to go out?, how about going out?; ***ich habe keine Lust*** I don't feel like it, I'm not in the mood for it; ***die Lust an et. verlieren*** (***j-m die Lust an et. nehmen***) (make s.o.) lose all interest in s.th.
lüstern ['lʏstɐn] *adj* greedy (***nach*** for)
lustig ['lʊstɪç] *adj* funny; cheerful; ***er ist sehr lustig*** he is full of fun; ***es war sehr lustig*** it was great fun; ***sich lustig machen über*** (*acc*) make fun of
'**lustlos** *adj* listless, indifferent
'**Lustmord** *m* sex murder
'**Lustspiel** *n* THEA comedy
lutschen ['lʊtʃən] *v/i and v/t* (*ge-*, *h*) suck
Luv [luːf] *f* (*-*; *no pl*) MAR windward, weather side
luxuriös [lʊksu'rjøːs] *adj* luxurious
Luxus ['lʊksʊs] *m* (*-*; *no pl*) luxury
Luxusarˌtikel *m* luxury (article)
Luxusausführung *f* deluxe version
Luxushoˌtel *n* five-star (*or* luxury) hotel
Lymphdrüse ['lʏmf-] *f* ANAT lymph gland
lynchen ['lʏnçən] *v/t* (*ge-*, *h*) lynch
Lyrik ['lyːrɪk] *f* (*-*; *no pl*) poetry
Lyriker ['lyːrikɐ] *m* (*-s*; *-*), '**Lyrikerin** *f* (*-*; *-nen*) (lyric) poet
lyrisch ['lyːrɪʃ] *adj* lyrical (*a. fig*)

M

machbar ['maxbaːɐ] *adj* feasible
machen ['maxən] *v/t* (*ge-*, *h*) do; make; GASTR make, prepare; fix (*a. fig*); be, come to, amount to; take, pass (*test etc*); make, go on (*a trip etc*); ***Hausaufgaben machen*** do one's homework; ***da*** (***-gegen***) ***kann man nichts machen*** it can't be helped; ***mach, was du willst!*** do as you please!; (***nun***) ***mach mal*** *or* ***schon!*** hurry up!, come on *or* along now!; ***mach's gut!*** take care (of yourself)!, good luck!; (***das***) ***macht nichts*** it doesn't matter; ***mach dir nichts d(a)raus!*** never mind!, don't worry!; ***das macht mir nichts aus*** I don't mind *or* care; ***was*** *or* ***wie viel macht das?*** how much is it?; ***sich et.*** (***nichts***) ***machen aus*** (not) care about; (not) care for
'**Machenschaften** *pl* machinations; ***unsaubere Machenschaften*** sleaze (*esp* POL)
Macher ['maxɐ] *m* (*-s*; *-*) man of action, doer
Macho ['matʃo] *m* (*-s*; *-s*) macho
Macht [maxt] *f* (*-*; *Mächte* ['mɛçtə]) power (***über*** *acc* of); ***an der Macht*** in power; ***mit aller Macht*** with all one's might
'**Machthaber** [-haːbɐ] *m* (*-s*; *-*) POL ruler
mächtig ['mɛçtɪç] *adj* powerful, mighty (*a.* F); enormous, huge
'**Machtkampf** *m* struggle for power
'**machtlos** *adj* powerless
'**Machtmissbrauch** *m* abuse of power
Machtpoliˌtik *f* power politics
Machtübernahme *f* takeover
Machtwechsel *m* transition of power
Mädchen ['mɛːtçən] *n* (*-s*; *-*) girl; maid
'**mädchenhaft** *adj* girlish
'**Mädchenname** *m* girl's name; maiden name
Mädchenschule *f* girls' school
Made ['maːdə] *f* (*-*; *-n*) ZO maggot; worm
Mädel ['mɛːdəl] *n* (*-s*; *-s*) girl
'**madig** *adj* maggoty, worm-eaten; F'**madigmachen** *v/t* (*sep*, *-ge-*, *h*): F ***j-m et. madig*** spoil s.th. for s.o.
Magazin [maga'tsiːn] *n* (*-s*; *-e*) magazine (*a.* MIL, PHOT, TV); store(room), warehouse
Magd [maːkt] *f* (*-*; *Mägde* ['mɛːktə]) (female) farmhand
Magen ['maːgən] *m* (*-s*; *Mägen* ['mɛːgən])

M

ANAT stomach
Magenbeschwerden *pl* MED stomach trouble
Magengeschwür *n* MED (stomach) ulcer
Magenschmerzen *pl* stomachache
mager ['maːgɐ] *adj* lean, thin, skinny; GASTR low-fat (*cheese*), lean (*meat*), skim (*milk*); *fig* meager, *Br* meagre
Magie [ma'giː] *f* (-; *no pl*) magic
magisch ['maːgɪʃ] *adj* magic(al)
Magister [ma'gɪstɐ] *m* (-*s*; -) UNIV Master of Arts *or* Science; *Austrian* → ***Apotheker***
Magistrat [magɪs'traːt] *m* (-[*e*]*s*; -*e*) municipal council
Magnet [ma'gneːt] *m* (-[*e*]*s*, -*en*; -*e*[*n*]) magnet (*a. fig*)
Magnet... *in cpds* ...*band*, ...*feld*, ...*nadel etc*: magnetic ...
mag'netisch *adj* magnetic (*a. fig*)
magnetisieren [magneti'ziːrən] *v/t* (*no -ge-*, *h*) magnetize
Mahagoni [maha'goːni] *n* (-*s*; *no pl*) mahogany
mähen ['mɛːən] *v/t* (*ge-*, *h*) mow; cut; AGR reap
'Mähdrescher [-drɛʃɐ] *m* (-*s*; -) AGR combine (harvester)
mahlen ['maːlən] *v/t* (*irr*, *ge-*, *h*) grind; mill
'Mahlzeit *f* (-; -*en*) meal; feed(ing)
Mähne ['mɛːnə] *f* (-; -*n*) ZO mane (*a.* F)
mahnen ['maːnən] *v/t* (*ge-*, *h*) remind; ECON send *s.o.* a reminder
'Mahngebühr *f* reminder fee
'Mahnmal *n* memorial
'Mahnung *f* (-; -*en*) reminder
Mai [mai] *m* (-[*e*]*s*; -*e*) May; ***der Erste Mai*** May Day
Maibaum *m* maypole
Maiglöckchen *n* BOT lily of the valley
Maikäfer *m* ZO cockchafer
Mais [mais] *m* (-*es*; -*e*) BOT corn, *Br* maize
Majestät [majɛs'tɛːt] *f*: ***Seine*** (***Ihre***, ***Eure***) ***Majestät*** His (Her, Your) Majesty
majes'tätisch *adj* majestic
Majonäse *f* → ***Mayonnaise***
Major [ma'joːɐ] *m* (-*s*; -*e*) MIL major
makaber [ma'kaːbɐ] *adj* macabre
Makel ['maːkəl] *m* (-*s*; -) blemish (*a. fig*)
mäkelig ['mɛːkəlɪç] F *adj* picky, *esp Br* choos(e)y
'makellos *adj* immaculate (*a. fig*)
mäkeln ['mɛːkəln] F *v/i* (*ge-*, *h*) carp, pick, nag (***an*** *dat* at)
Makler ['maːklɐ] *m* (-*s*; -) ECON real estate agent; broker
Maklergebühr *f* fee, commission
'Maklerin *f* (-; -*nen*) ECON → ***Makler***
mal [maːl] *adv* MATH times, multiplied by; F → ***einmal***; ***12 mal 5 ist*** (***gleich***) ***60*** 12 times *or* multiplied by 5 is *or* equals 60; ***ein 7 mal 4 Meter großes Zimmer*** a room 7 meters by 4
Mal[1] *n* (-[*e*]*s*; -*e*) time; ***zum ersten*** (***letzten***) ***Mal***(***e***) for the first (last) time; ***mit e-m Mal***(***e***) all of a sudden; ***ein für alle Mal***(***e***) once and for all
Mal[2] *n* mark
malen ['maːlən] *v/t* (*ge-*, *h*) paint
Maler ['maːlɐ] *m* (-*s*; -) painter
Malerei [maːlə'rai] *f* (-; -*en*) painting
Malerin ['maːlərɪn] *f* (-; -*nen*) (woman) painter
'malerisch *fig adj* picturesque
'Malkasten *m* paintbox
'malnehmen → ***multiplizieren***
Malz [malts] *n* (-*es*; *no pl*) malt
'Malzbier *n* malt beer
Mama ['mama] F *f* (-; -*s*) mom(my), *Br* mum(my)
Mammut ['mamʊt] *n* (-*s*; -*e*, -*s*) ZO mammoth
man [man] *indef pron* you, one; they, people; ***wie schreibt man das?*** how do you spell it?; ***man sagt, dass*** they *or* people say (that); ***man hat mir gesagt*** I was told
Manager ['mɛnɪdʒɐ] *m* (-*s*; -), **'Managerin** *f* (-; -*nen*) ECON executive; SPORT manager
manch [manç], **mancher** ['mançɐ], **manche** ['mançə], **manches** ['mançəs] *indef pron* (*mst pl*) some; quite a few, many
'manchmal *adv* sometimes, occasionally
Mandant [man'dant] *m* (-*en*; -*en*), **Man'dantin** *f* (-; -*nen*) JUR client
Mandarine [manda'riːnə] *f* (-; -*n*) BOT tangerine
Mandat [man'daːt] *n* (-[*e*]*s*; -*e*) POL mandate; seat
Mandatar [manda'taːɐ] *Austrian m* → ***Abgeordnete***
Mandel ['mandəl] *f* (-; -*n*) BOT almond; ANAT tonsil
Mandelentzündung *f* MED tonsillitis
Manege [ma'neːʒə] *f* (-; -*n*) (circus) ring
Mangel[1] ['maŋəl] *m* (-*s*; *Mängel* ['mɛŋəl]) a) (*no pl*) lack (***an*** *dat* of), shortage, b) TECH defect, fault; shortcoming; ***aus Mangel an*** (*dat*) for lack of
'Mangel[2] *f* (-; -*n*) mangle
'mangelhaft *adj* poor (*quality etc*); defective (*goods etc*); PED poor, unsatisfactory, failing
'mangeln *v/t* (*ge-*, *h*) mangle
'mangels *prp* (*gen*) for lack *or* want of
'Mangelware *f*: ***Mangelware sein*** be scarce
Manie [ma'niː] *f* (-; -*n*) mania (*a. fig*)
Manieren [ma'niːrən] *pl* manners

manierlich [ma'niːɐlɪç] *adv*: ***sich manierlich betragen*** behave (decently)
Manifest [mani'fɛst] *n* (-[*e*]*s*; -*e*) manifesto
manipulieren [manipu'liːrən] *v/t* (*no -ge-*, *h*) manipulate
Mann [man] *m* (-[*e*]*s*; *Männer* ['mɛnɐ]) man; husband
Männchen ['mɛnçən] *n* (-*s*; -) ZO male
'Manndeckung *f* SPORT man-to-man marking
Mannequin ['manəkɛ̃ː] *n* (-*s*; -*s*) model
mannigfach ['manɪçfax], **'mannigfaltig** *adj* many and various
männlich ['mɛnlɪç] *adj* BIOL male; masculine (*a.* LING)
'Mannschaft *f* (-; -*en*) SPORT team; MAR, AVIAT crew
Manöver [ma'nøːvɐ] *n* (-*s*; -), **manövrieren** [manø'vriːrən] *v/i* (*no -ge-*, *h*) maneuver, *Br* manoeuvre
Mansarde [man'zardə] *f* (-; -*n*) room *or* apartment in the attic
Manschette [man'ʃɛtə] *f* (-; -*n*) cuff; TECH gasket
Man'schettenknopf *m* cuff-link
Mantel ['mantəl] *m* (-*s*; *Mäntel* ['mɛntəl]) coat; *tire*: casing, *bicycle*: tire (*Br* tyre) cover; TECH jacket, shell
Manuskript [manu'skrɪpt] *n* (-[*e*]*s*; -*e*) manuscript; copy
Mappe ['mapə] *f* (-; -*n*) briefcase; school bag, satchel; folder
Märchen ['mɛːrçən] *n* (-*s*; -) fairytale (*a. fig*)
Märchenland *n* (-[*e*]*s*; *no pl*) fairyland
Marder ['mardɐ] *m* (-*s*; -) ZO marten
Margarine [marga'riːnə] *f* (-; *no pl*) margarine
Margerite [margə'riːtə] *f* (-; -*n*) BOT marguerite
Marienkäfer [ma'riːən-] *m* ZO lady bug, *Br* ladybird
Marihuana [mari'huaːna] *n* (-*s*; *no pl*) marijuana, *sl* grass
Marihuanaziga,rette *f sl* joint
Marille [ma'rɪlə] *Austrian f* (-; -*n*) BOT apricot
Marine [ma'riːnə] *f* (-; -*n*) MIL navy
ma'rineblau *adj* navy blue
Marionette [marjo'nɛtə] *f* (-; -*n*) puppet (*a. fig*)
Mario'nettenthe,ater *n* puppet show
Mark[1] [mark] *f* (-; -) mark
Mark[2] *n* (-[*e*]*s*; *no pl*) marrow; BOT pulp
Marke ['markə] *f* (-; -*n*) ECON brand; TECH make; trademark; stamp; badge, tag; mark
markieren [mar'kiːrən] *v/t* (*no -ge-*, *h*) mark (*a.* SPORT); F *fig* act
Mar'kierung *f* (-; -*en*) mark
Markise [mar'kiːzə] *f* (-; -*n*) awning, sun blind
Markt [markt] *m* (-[*e*]*s*; *Märkte* ['mɛrktə]) ECON market; ***auf den Markt bringen*** put on the market
Marktplatz *m* market place
Marktwirtschaft *f* market economy
Marmelade [marmə'laːdə] *f* (-; -*n*) jam
Marmor ['marmoːɐ] *m* (-*s*; -*e*) marble
Marsch[1] [marʃ] *m* (-[*e*]*s*; *Märsche* ['mɛrʃə]) march (*a.* MUS)
Marsch[2] *f* (-; -*en*) GEOGR marsh, fen
Marschall ['marʃal] *m* (-*s*; *Marschälle* ['marʃɛlə]) MIL marshal
'Marschbefehl *m* MIL marching orders
marschieren [mar'ʃiːrən] *v/i* (*no -ge-*, *sein*) march
Marsmensch ['mars-] *m* Martian
Marter ['martɐ] *f* (-; -*n*) torture
'martern *v/t* (*ge-*, *h*) torture
'Marterpfahl *m* stake
Martinshorn ['martiːns-] *n* (police *etc*) siren
Märtyrer ['mɛrtyrɐ] *m* (-*s*; -), **'Märtyrerin** *f* (-; -*nen*) martyr (*a. fig*)
Marxismus [mar'ksɪsmʊs] *m* (-; *no pl*) POL Marxism
Marxist [mar'ksɪst] *m* (-*en*; -*en*), **mar'xistisch** *adj* POL Marxist
März [mɛrts] *m* (-[*es*]; -*e*) March
Marzipan [martsi'paːn] *n* (-*s*; -*e*) marzipan
Masche ['maʃə] *f* (-; -*n*) stitch; mesh; F trick
'Maschendraht *m* wire netting
Maschine [ma'ʃiːnə] *f* (-; -*n*) machine; MOT engine; AVIAT plane; motorcycle; ***Maschine schreiben*** type
Ma'schinenbau *m* (-[*e*]*s*; *no pl*) mechanical engineering
Maschinengewehr *n* MIL machinegun
ma'schinenlesbar *adj* EDP machine-readable
Ma'schinenöl *n* engine oil
Maschinenpis,tole *f* MIL submachine gun, machine pistol
Maschinenschaden *m* engine trouble *or* failure
Maschinenschlosser *m* (engine) fitter
Masern ['maːzɐn] *pl* MED measles
Maserung ['maːzərʊŋ] *f* (-; -*en*) grain
Maske ['maskə] *f* (-; -*n*) mask (*a.* EDP)
'Maskenball *m* fancy-dress ball
'Maskenbildner [-bɪldnɐ] *m* (-*s*; -), **'Maskenbildnerin** *f* (-; -*nen*) THEA *etc* make-up artist
maskieren [mas'kiːrən] *v/t* (*no -ge-*, *h*) mask; ***sich maskieren*** put on a mask

maskulin [masku'liːn] *adj* masculine (*a.* LING)
maß [maːs] *pret of* ***messen***
Maß[1] *n* (*-es*; *-e*) measure (***für*** of); dimensions, measurements, size; *fig* extent, degree; ***Maße und Gewichte*** weights and measures; ***nach Maß*** (***gemacht***) made to measure; ***in gewissem*** (***hohem***) ***Maße*** to a certain (high) degree; ***in zunehmendem Maße*** increasingly; ***Maß halten*** → ***maßhalten***
Maß[2] *f* (-; -[*e*]) liter (*Br* litre) of beer
Massage [ma'saːʒə] *f* (-; *-n*) massage
Massaker [ma'saːkɐ] *n* (*-s*; -) massacre
Masse ['masə] *f* (-; *-n*) mass; substance; bulk; F ***e-e Masse*** *Geld etc* loads *or* heaps of; ***die*** (***breite***) ***Masse***, POL ***die Massen*** *pl* the masses
'Maßeinheit *f* unit of measure(ment)
'Massen... *in cpds ...medien, ...mörder etc*: mass ...
Massenandrang *m* crush
'massenhaft F *adv* masses *or* loads of
'Massenkarambo,lage *f* MOT pileup
Massenprodukti,on *f* ECON mass production
Masseur [ma'søːɐ] *m* (*-s*; *-e*) masseur
Masseurin [ma'søːrɪn] *f* (-; *-nen*), **Masseuse** [ma'søːzə] *f* (-; *-n*) masseuse
'maßgebend, **'maßgeblich** [-geːplɪç] *adj* authoritative
'maßhalten *v/i* (*irr*, ***halten***, *sep*, *-ge-*, *h*) be moderate (***in*** *dat* in)
massieren [ma'siːrən] *v/t* (*no -ge-*, *h*) massage
massig ['masɪç] *adj* massive, bulky
mäßig ['mɛːsɪç] *adj* moderate; poor
mäßigen ['mɛːsɪgən] *v/t and v/refl* (*ge-*, *h*) moderate
'Mäßigung *f* (-; *no pl*) moderation; restraint
massiv [ma'siːf] *adj* solid
Mas'siv *n* (*-s*; *-e*) GEOL massif
'Maßkrug *m* beer mug, stein
'maßlos *adj* immoderate; gross (*exaggeration*)
'Maßnahme [-naːmə] *f* (-; *-n*) measure, step
'Maßregel *f* rule
'maßregeln *v/t* (*ge-*, *h*) reprimand; discipline
'Maßstab *m* scale; *fig* standard; ***im Maßstab 1:10*** on the scale of 1:10
maßstabgetreu *adj* true to scale
'maßvoll *adj* moderate
Mast[1] [mast] *m* (*-[e]s*; *-en*) MAR, TECH mast
Mast[2] *f* (-; *-en*) AGR fattening
'Mastdarm *m* ANAT rectum
mästen ['mɛstən] *v/t* (*ge-*, *h*) AGR fatten; F stuff *s.o.*
masturbieren [mastʊr'biːrən] *v/i* (*no -ge-*, *h*) masturbate
Match [mɛtʃ] *n* (*-[e]s*; *-s*, *-e*) game, *Br* match
Matchball *m tennis*: match point
Material [mate'rjaːl] *n* (*-s*; *-ien*) material (*a. fig*); TECH materials
Materialismus [materja'lɪsmʊs] *m* (-; *no pl*) PHILOS materialism
Materialist [-'lɪst] *m* (*-en*; *-en*) materialist
materia'listisch *adj* materialistic
Materie [ma'teːrjə] *f* (-; *-n*) matter (*a. fig*); *fig* subject (matter)
materiell [mate'rjɛl] *adj* material
Mathematik [matema'tiːk] *f* (-; *no pl*) mathematics
Mathematiker [mate'maːtikɐ] *m* (*-s*; -) mathematician
mathe'matisch *adj* mathematical
Matinee [mati'neː] *f* (-; *-n*) THEA *etc* morning performance
Matratze [ma'tratsə] *f* (-; *-n*) mattress
Matrize [ma'triːtsə] *f* (-; *-n*) stencil
Matrose [ma'troːzə] *m* (*-n*; *-n*) MAR sailor, seaman
Matsch [matʃ] F *m* (*-[e]s*; *no pl*) mud, slush
'matschig *adj* muddy, slushy
matt [mat] *adj* weak; exhausted, worn out; dull, pale (*color*); PHOT mat(t); frosted (*glass*); *chess*: checkmate
Matte ['matə] *f* (-; *-n*) mat
Mattigkeit ['matɪçkait] *f* (-; *no pl*) exhaustion, weakness
'Mattscheibe *f* screen; PHOT focus(s)ing screen; F (boob) tube, *Br* telly, box
Matura [ma'tuːra] *Austrian, Swiss f* → ***Abitur***
Mauer ['mauɐ] *f* (-; *-n*) wall
Mauerblümchen *fig n* wallflower
Mauerwerk *n* (*-[e]s*; *no pl*) masonry, brickwork
'mauern *v/i* (*ge-*, *h*) lay bricks
Maul [maul] *n* (*-[e]s*; *Mäuler* ['mɔylɐ]) ZO mouth; *sl* ***halt's Maul!*** shut up!
maulen ['maulən] F *v/i* (*ge-*, *h*) grumble, sulk, pout
'Maulkorb *m* muzzle (*a. fig*)
Maultier *n* mule
Maulwurf *m* ZO mole
Maulwurfshaufen *m*, **Maulwurfshügel** *m* molehill
Maurer ['maurɐ] *m* (*-s*; -) bricklayer
Maurerkelle *f* trowel
Maurermeister *m* master bricklayer
Maurerpo,lier *m* foreman bricklayer
Maus [maus] *f* (-; *Mäuse* ['mɔyzə]) ZO mouse (*a.* EDP)

'Mausefalle ['mauzə-] *f* mousetrap
Mauser ['mauzɐ] *f* (-; *no pl*) ZO mo(u)lt (-ing); ***in der Mauser sein*** be mo(u)lting
Maut [maut] *Austrian f* (-; *-en*) toll
Mautstraße *f* turnpike, toll road
maximal [maksi'ma:l] **1.** *adj* maximum; **2.** *adv* at (the) most
Maximum ['maksimʊm] *n* (*-s*; *-ma*) maximum
Mayonnaise [majɔ'nɛ:zə] *f* (-; *-n*) GASTR mayonnaise
Mäzen [mɛ'tse:n] *m* (*-s*; *-e*) patron; SPORT sponsor
Mechanik [me'ça:nɪk] *f* (-; *-en*) a) (*no pl*) PHYS mechanics, b) TECH mechanism
Mechaniker [me'ça:nikɐ] *m* (*-s*; -) mechanic
mechanisch [me'ça:nɪʃ] *adj* TECH mechanical
mechanisieren [meçani'zi:rən] *v/t* (*no -ge-*, *h*) mechanize
Mechani'sierung *f* (-; *-en*) mechanization
Mechanismus [meça'nɪsmʊs] *m* (-; *-men*) TECH mechanism; works
meckern ['mɛkɐn] *v/i* (*ge-*, *h*) ZO bleat; F grumble, bitch (***über*** *acc* at, about)
Medaille [me'daljə] *f* (-; *-n*) medal
Me'daillengewinner *m* medal(l)ist
Medaillon [medal'jõ:] *n* (*-s*; *-s*) locket
Medien ['me:djən] *pl* mass media; teaching aids; audio-visual aids
Medikament [medika'mɛnt] *n* (*-[e]s*; *-e*) drug; medicine
meditieren [medi'ti:rən] *v/i* (*no -ge-*, *h*) meditate (***über*** *acc* on)
Medizin [medi'tsi:n] *f* (-; *-en*) a) (*no pl*) (science of) medicine, b) medicine, remedy (***gegen*** for)
Mediziner [medi'tsi:nɐ] *m* (*-s*; -), **Medi'zinerin** *f* (-; *-nen*) (medical) doctor; UNIV medical student
medizinisch [medi'tsi:nɪʃ] *adj* medical
Meer [me:ɐ] *n* (*-[e]s*; *-e* ['me:rə]) sea (*a. fig*), ocean
Meerenge *f* GEOGR straits
Meeresboden ['me:rəs-] *m* seabed
Meeresfrüchte *pl* GASTR seafood
Meeresspiegel *m* sea level
'Meerjungfrau *f* MYTH mermaid
'Meerrettich *m* (*-s*; *-e*) horseradish
'Meerschweinchen [-ʃvainçən] *n* (*-s*; -) ZO guinea pig
Megabyte [mega'bait] *n* EDP megabyte
Mehl [me:l] *n* (*-[e]s*; *-e*) flour; meal
mehlig ['me:lɪç] *adj* mealy
'Mehlspeise *Austrian f* sweet (dish)
mehr [me:ɐ] *indef pron and adv* more; ***immer mehr*** more and more; ***nicht mehr*** no longer, not any longer (*or* more); ***noch mehr*** even more; ***es ist kein ... mehr da*** there isn't any ... left
'mehrdeutig [-dɔʏtɪç] *adj* ambiguous
mehrere ['me:rərə] *adj and indef pron* several
'Mehrheit *f* (-; *-en*) majority
'Mehrkosten *pl* extra costs
'mehrmals *adv* several times
'Mehrwegflasche *f* returnable (*or* deposit) bottle
Mehrwertsteuer *f* ECON value-added tax (ABBR VAT)
Mehrzahl *f* (-; *no pl*) majority; LING plural (form)
'Mehrzweck... *in cpds ...fahrzeug etc*: multi-purpose ...
meiden ['maidən] *v/t* (*irr*, *ge-*, *h*) avoid
Meile ['mailə] *f* (-; *-n*) mile
'meilenweit *adv* (for) miles
mein [main] *poss pron and adj* my; ***das ist meiner*** (***meine, mein[e]s***) that's mine
'Meineid *m* JUR perjury
meinen ['mainən] *v/t* (*ge-*, *h*) think, believe; mean; say; ***meinen Sie wirklich?*** do you (really) think so?; ***wie meinen Sie das?*** what do you mean by that?; ***sie meinen es gut*** they mean well; ***ich habe es nicht so gemeint*** I didn't mean it; ***wie meinen Sie?*** (I beg your) pardon?
meinet'wegen ['mainət-] *adv* for my sake; because of me; F I don't mind *or* care!
'Meinung *f* (-; *-en*) opinion (***über*** *acc*, ***von*** about, of); ***meiner Meinung nach*** in my opinion; ***der Meinung sein, dass*** be of the opinion that, feel *or* believe that; ***s-e Meinung äußern*** express one's opinion; ***s-e Meinung ändern*** change one's mind; ***ich bin Ihrer*** (***anderer***) ***Meinung*** I (don't) agree with you; ***j-m die Meinung sagen*** give s.o. a piece of one's mind
'Meinungsaustausch *m* exchange of views (***über*** *acc* on)
Meinungsforscher *m* pollster
Meinungsfreiheit *f* (-; *no pl*) freedom of speech *or* opinion
Meinungsumfrage *f* opinion poll
Meinungsverschiedenheit *f* disagreement (***über*** *acc* about)
Meise ['maizə] *f* (-; *-n*) ZO titmouse
Meißel ['maisəl] *m* (*-s*; -) chisel
'meißeln *v/t and v/i* (*ge-*, *h*) chisel, carve
meist [maist] **1.** *adj* most; ***das meiste*** (***davon***) most of it; ***die meisten*** (***von ihnen***) most of them; ***die meisten Leute*** most people; ***die meiste Zeit*** most of the time; **2.** *adv* → ***meistens***; ***am meisten*** (the)

most; most (of all)
meistens ['maistəns] *adv* usually; most of the time
Meister ['maistɐ] *m* (-*s*; -) master (*a. fig*); SPORT champion, F champ
'**meisterhaft** **1.** *adj* masterly; **2.** *adv* in a masterly manner *or* way
'**Meisterin** *f* (-; -*nen*) master (*a. fig*); SPORT champion
meistern ['maistɐn] *v/t* (*ge-*, *h*) master
'**Meisterschaft** *f* (-; -*en*) a) (*no pl*) mastery, b) SPORT championship, cup; title
'**Meisterstück** *n*, **Meisterwerk** *n* masterpiece
Melancholie [melaŋko'li:] *f* (-; -*n*) melancholy
melancholisch [melaŋ'ko:lɪʃ] *adj* melancholy; ***melancholisch sein*** feel depressed, F have the blues
Melange [me'lã:ʒə] *Austrian f* (-; -*n*) coffee with milk
melden ['mɛldən] (*ge-*, *h*) **1.** *v/t* report *s.th.* *or s.o.* (***bei*** to); *radio etc*: announce, report; ***j-m et. melden*** notify s.o. of s.th.; **2.** *v/refl*: ***sich melden*** report (***bei*** to, ***für, zu*** for); register (***bei*** with); PED *etc*: put up one's hand; TEL answer the phone; SPORT enter (***für, zu*** for); volunteer (***für, zu*** for)
'**Meldung** *f* (-; -*en*) report, news, announcement; information, notice; notification; registration (***bei*** with); SPORT entry (***für, zu*** for)
melken ['mɛlkən] *v/t* ([*irr*,] *ge-*, *h*) milk
Melodie [melo'di:] *f* (-; -*n*) MUS melody, tune
melodisch [me'lo:dɪʃ] *adj* MUS melodious, melodic
Melone [me'lo:nə] *f* (-; -*n*) BOT melon; F derby, *Br* bowler (hat)
Memoiren [me'moa:rən] *pl* memoirs
Menge ['mɛŋə] *f* (-; -*n*) amount, quantity; MATH set; F ***e-e Menge Geld*** plenty (*or* lots) of money; → ***Menschenmenge***
'**Mengenlehre** *f* (-; *no pl*) MATH set theory; PED new math(ematics)
Mensa ['mɛnza] *f* (-; -*s*, *Mensen*) cafeteria, *Br* refectory, canteen
Mensch [mɛnʃ] *m* (-*en*; -*en*) human being; man; person, individual; *pl* people; mankind; ***kein Mensch*** nobody; ***Mensch!*** wow!
Menschenaffe *m* ZO ape
Menschenfresser *m* cannibal
Menschenfreund *m* philanthropist
Menschenhandel *m* slave trade
Menschenkenntnis *f*: ***Menschenkenntnis haben*** know human nature
Menschenleben *n* human life
'**menschenleer** *adj* deserted
'**Menschenmenge** *f* crowd
Menschenrechte *pl* human rights
Menschenseele *f*: ***keine Menschenseele*** not a (living) soul
'**menschenunwürdig** *adj* degrading; *housing etc*: unfit for human beings
'**Menschenverstand** *m*: ***gesunder Menschenverstand*** common sense
Menschenwürde *f* human dignity
Menschheit: ***die Menschheit*** mankind, the human race
'**menschlich** *adj* human; humane
'**Menschlichkeit** *f* (-; *no pl*) humanity
Menstruation [mɛnstrua'tsjo:n] *f* (-; -*en*) MED menstruation
Mentalität [mɛntali'tɛ:t] *f* (-; -*en*) mentality
Menü [me'ny:] *n* (-*s*; -*s*) set meal (*or* lunch); EDP menu
Meridian [meri'dja:n] *m* (-*s*; -*e*) GEOGR, ASTR meridian
merkbar ['mɛrkba:ɐ] *adj* marked, distinct; noticeable
'**Merkblatt** *n* leaflet
merken ['mɛrkən] *v/t* (*ge-*, *h*) notice; feel; find (out), discover; ***sich et. merken*** remember s.th., keep *or* bear s.th. in mind
'**merklich** *adj* → ***merkbar***
'**Merkmal** *n* sign; feature, trait
'**merkwürdig** *adj* strange, odd, curious
'**merkwürdiger'weise** *adv* strangely enough
messbar ['mɛsba:ɐ] *adj* measurable
'**Messbecher** *m* measuring cup
Messe ['mɛsə] *f* (-; -*n*) ECON fair; REL mass; MIL, MAR mess
messen ['mɛsən] *v/t* (*irr*, *ge-*, *h*) measure; take (*temperature etc*); ***sich nicht mit j-m messen können*** be no match for s.o.; ***gemessen an*** (*dat*) compared with
Messer ['mɛsɐ] *n* (-*s*; -) knife; ***bis aufs Messer*** to the knife; ***auf des Messers Schneide stehen*** be on a razor edge, be touch and go (***ob*** whether)
Messerstecherei [-ʃtɛçə'rai] *f* (-; -*en*) knife fight
'**Messerstich** *m* stab (with a knife)
Messing ['mɛsɪŋ] *n* (-*s*; -*e*) brass
'**Messinstru,ment** *n* measuring instrument
'**Messung** *f* (-; -*en*) measuring; reading
Metall [me'tal] *n* (-*s*; -*e*) metal
metallen [me'talən], **me'tallisch** *adj* metallic
Me'tallwaren *pl* hardware
Metamorphose [metamɔr'fo:zə] *f* (-; -*n*) metamorphosis
Metastase [meta'sta:zə] *f* (-; -*n*) MED me-

tastasis

Meteor [mete'oːɐ] *m* (*-s*; *-e*) ASTR meteor

Meteorit [meteo'riːt] *m* (*-en*; *-e*[*n*]) ASTR meteorite

Meteorologe [meteoro'loːgə] *m* (*-n*; *-n*) meteorologist

Meteorologie [meteorolo'giː] *f* (*-*; *no pl*) meteorology

Meteoro'login *f* (*-*; *-nen*) meteorologist

Meter ['meːtɐ] *n, m* (*-s*; *-*) meter, *Br* metre

Metermaß *n* tape measure

Methode [me'toːdə] *f* (*-*; *-n*) method, TECH *a.* technique

methodisch [me'toːdɪʃ] *adj* methodical

metrisch ['meːtrɪʃ] *adj* metric; ***metrisches Maßsystem*** metric system

Metropole [metro'poːlə] *f* (*-*; *-n*) metropolis

Metzger ['mɛtsgɐ] *m* (*-s*; *-*) butcher

Metzgerei [mɛtsgə'rai] *f* (*-*; *-en*) butcher's (shop)

Meute ['mɔʏtə] *f* (*-*; *-n*) pack (of hounds); *fig* mob, pack

Meuterei [mɔʏtə'rai] *f* (*-*; *-en*) mutiny

Meuterer ['mɔʏtərɐ] *m* (*-s*; *-*) mutineer

meutern ['mɔʏtɐn] *v/i* (*ge-*, *h*) mutiny (***gegen*** against)

MEZ ABBR *of* ***Mitteleuropäische Zeit*** CET, Central European Time

M

miau [mi'au] *int* ZO meow, *Br* miaow

miauen [mi'auən] *v/i* (*no -ge-*, *h*) ZO meow, *Br* miaow

mich [mɪç] *pers pron* me; ***mich*** (***selbst***) myself

mied [miːt] *pret of* ***meiden***

Mieder ['miːdɐ] *n* (*-s*; *-*) corset(s); bodice

Miederhöschen *n* pantie girdle

Miederwaren *pl* foundation garments

Miene ['miːnə] *f* (*-*; *-n*) expression, look, air; ***gute Miene zum bösen Spiel machen*** grin and bear it

mies [miːs] F *adj* rotten, lousy

Miete ['miːtə] *f* (*-*; *-n*) rent; hire charge; ***zur Miete wohnen*** be a tenant; lodge (***bei*** with)

'mieten *v/t* (*ge-*, *h*) rent; (take on) lease; AVIAT, MAR charter; ***ein Auto*** *etc* ***mieten*** rent (*Br* hire) a car *etc*

Mieter(in) ['miːtɐ (-tərɪn)] (*-s*; *-/-*; *-nen*) tenant, lodger

'Mietshaus *n* apartment building *or* house, *Br* block of flats, tenement

'Mietvertrag *m* lease (contract)

'Mietwohnung *f* apartment, *Br* (rented) flat

Migräne [mi'grɛːnə] *f* (*-*; *-n*) MED migraine

Mikro ['miːkro] F *n* (*-s*; *-s*) mike

Mikro... ['miːkro-] *in cpds ...chip*, *...computer*, *...elektronik*, *...film*, *...prozessor etc*: micro...

Mikrofon [mikro'foːn] *n* (*-s*; *-e*) microphone

Mikroskop [mikro'skoːp] *n* (*-s*; *-e*) microscope

mikro'skopisch *adj* microscopic(al)

Mikrowelle ['miːkro-] F *f*, **'Mikrowellenherd** *m* microwave oven

Milbe ['mɪlbə] *f* (*-*; *-n*) ZO mite

Milch [mɪlç] *f* (*-*; *no pl*) milk

Milchgeschäft *n* dairy, creamery

Milchglas *n* frosted glass

milchig ['mɪlçɪç] *adj* milky

'Milchkaffee *m* white coffee

Milchkännchen *n* (milk) jug

Milchkanne *f* milk can

Milchmann F *m* milkman

Milchmixgetränk *n* milk shake

Milchpro,dukte *pl* dairy products

Milchpulver *n* powdered milk

Milchreis *m* rice pudding

Milchstraße *f* ASTR Milky Way, Galaxy

Milchtüte *f* milk carton

Milchwirtschaft *f* dairy farming

Milchzahn *m* milk tooth

mild [mɪlt] *adj* mild, soft; gentle

milde ['mɪldə] *adv* mildly; ***milde ausgedrückt*** to put it mildly

'Milde *f* (*-*; *no pl*) mildness, gentleness; leniency, mercy

mildern ['mɪldɐn] *v/t* (*ge-*, *h*) lessen, soften

mildernd *adj*: ***mildernde Umstände*** JUR mitigating circumstances

'mildtätig *adj* charitable

Milieu [mi'ljøː] *n* (*-s*; *-s*) environment; social background

Militär [mili'tɛːɐ] *n* (*-s*; *no pl*) *the* military, armed forces; army

Militärdienst *m* (*-*[*e*]*s*; *no pl*) military service

Militärdikta,tur *f* military dictatorship

Militärgericht *n* court martial

militärisch [mili'tɛːrɪʃ] *adj* military

Militarismus [milita'rɪsmʊs] *m* (*-*; *no pl*) militarism

Militarist [milita'rɪst] *m* (*-en*; *-en*) militarist

milita'ristisch *adj* militaristic

'Mili'tärre'gierung *f* military government

Milliarde [mɪ'ljardə] *f* (*-*; *-n*) billion, *Br old use a.* a thousand million(s)

Millimeter ['mɪlimeːtɐ] *n, m* (*-s*; *-*) millimet|er, *Br* -re

Millimeterpa,pier *n* graph paper

Million [mɪ'lioːn] *f* (*-*; *-en*) million

Millionär [mɪljo'nɛːɐ] *m* (*-s*; *-e*), **Millio'närin** *f* (*-*; *-nen*) millionaire

Milz [mɪlts] *f* (*-*; *no pl*) ANAT spleen

Mimik ['mi:mɪk] *f* (-; *no pl*) facial expression
minder ['mɪndɐ] **1.** *adj* → ***geringer, weniger***; **2.** *adv* less; ***nicht minder*** no less
'**Minderheit** *f* (-; *-en*) minority
'**minderjährig** [-jɛ:rɪç] *adj*: ***minderjährig sein*** be under age, be a minor
'**Minderjährige** [-jɛ:rɪgə] *m, f* (*-n; -n*) minor
'**Minderjährigkeit** *f* (-; *no pl*) minority
'**minderwertig** *adj* inferior, of inferior quality
'**Minderwertigkeit** *f* (-; *no pl*) inferiority; ECON inferior quality
'**Minderwertigkeitskom,plex** *m* PSYCH inferiority complex
mindest ['mɪndəst] *adj* least; ***das Mindeste*** the (very) least; ***nicht im Mindesten*** not in the least, not at all
'**Mindest...** *in cpds ...alter, ...einkommen, ...lohn etc*: minimum ...
mindestens ['mɪndəstəns] *adv* at least
'**Mindesthaltbarkeitsdatum** *n* pull date, *Br* best-before (*or* best-by, sell-by) date
Mindestmaß *n* minimum; ***auf ein Mindestmaß herabsetzen*** reduce to a minimum
Mine ['mi:nə] *f* (-; *-n*) mine (*a.* MAR, MIL); lead; cartridge; refill
Mineral [minə'ra:l] *n* (*-s; -e, -ien*) mineral
Mineralogie [mineralo'gi:] *f* (-; *no pl*) mineralogy
Mine'ralöl *n* mineral oil
Mine'ralwasser *n* mineral water
Miniatur [minja'tu:ɐ] *f* (-; *-en*) miniature
Minigolf ['mɪni-] *n* miniature (*Br* crazy) golf
minimal [mini'ma:l] *adj, adv* minimal; minimum; at least
Minimum ['mi:nimʊm] *n* (*-s; -ma*) minimum
Minirock ['mɪni-] *m* miniskirt
Minister [mi'nɪstɐ] *m* (*-s; -*), **Mi'nisterin** *f* (-; *-nen*) minister, secretary, *Br a.* secretary of state
Ministerium [minɪs'te:riʊm] *n* (*-s; -ien*) ministry, department, *Br a.* office
Mi'nisterpräsi,dent *m*, **Mi'nisterpräsi,dentin** *f* prime minister
minus ['mi:nʊs] *adv* MATH minus; ***bei 10 Grad minus*** at 10 degrees below zero
Minute [mi'nu:tə] *f* (-; *-n*) minute
Mi'nutenzeiger *m* minute hand
Mio ABBR *of* ***Million(en)*** m, million
mir [mi:ɐ] *pers pron* (to) me
Mischbatte,rie ['mɪʃ-] *f* mixing faucet, *Br* mixer tap
'**Mischbrot** *n* wheat and rye bread
mischen ['mɪʃən] *v/t* (*ge-, h*) mix; blend (*tea etc*); shuffle (*cards*); ***sich mischen*** mingle *or* mix (***unter*** with)
'**Mischling** *m* (*-s; -e*) *esp contp* half-caste; BOT, ZO hybrid; mongrel
'**Mischmasch** F *m* (*-[e]s; -e*) hotchpotch, jumble
'**Mischma,schine** *f* TECH mixer
Mischpult *n radio*, TV: mixer, mixing console
'**Mischung** *f* (-; *-en*) mixture; blend; assortment
'**Mischwald** *m* mixed forest
miserabel [mizə'ra:bəl] F *adj* lousy, rotten
miss'achten [mɪs-] *v/t* (*no -ge-, h*) disregard, ignore; despise
Miss'achtung *f* disregard; contempt; neglect (*all*: *gen* of)
'**Missbildung** *f* (-; *-en*) deformity, malformation
miss'billigen *v/t* (*no -ge-, h*) disapprove of
'**Missbrauch** *m* abuse (*a.* JUR); misuse
miss'brauchen *v/t* (*no -ge-, h*) abuse; misuse
miss'deuten *v/t* (*no -ge-, h*) misinterpret
'**Misserfolg** *m* failure; F flop
'**Missernte** *f* bad harvest, crop failure
miss'fallen *v/i* (*irr*, ***fallen***, *no -ge-, h*) ***j-m missfallen*** displease s.o.
'**Missfallen** *n* (*-s; no pl*) displeasure, dislike
'**missgebildet** *adj* deformed, malformed
'**Missgeburt** *f* deformed child *or* animal; freak
'**Missgeschick** *n* (*-[e]s; -e*) mishap
miss'glücken *v/i* (*no -ge-, sein*) fail
miss'gönnen *v/t* (*no -ge-, h*) ***j-m et. missgönnen*** envy s.o. s.th.
'**Missgriff** *m* mistake
miss'handeln *v/t* (*no -ge-, h*) ill-treat, maltreat (*a. fig*); batter
Miss'handlung *f* ill-treatment, maltreatment, *esp* JUR assault and battery
Mission [mɪ'sjo:n] *f* (-; *-en*) mission (*a.* POL *and fig*)
Missionar(in) [mɪsjo'na:ɐ (-'na:rɪn)] (*-s; -e/-; -nen*) missionary
'**Missklang** *m* dissonance, discord (*both a. fig*)
'**Misskre,dit** *m* discredit
misslang [mɪs'laŋ] *pret of* ***misslingen***
misslingen [mɪs'lɪŋən] *v/i* (*irr, no -ge-, sein*) fail
misslungen [mɪs'lʊŋən] *pp of* ***misslingen***; ***das ist mir misslungen*** I've bungled it
'**missmutig** *adj* bad-tempered, grumpy, glum
miss'raten **1.** *v/i* (*irr*, ***raten***, *no -ge-, sein*)

fail; turn out badly; **2.** *adj* wayward
miss'trauen *v/i (no -ge-, h)* distrust
'Misstrauen *n (-s; no pl)* distrust, suspicion (*both*: ***gegenüber*** of)
'Misstrauensantrag *m* PARL motion of no confidence
Misstrauensvotum *n* PARL vote of no confidence
misstrauisch ['mɪstrauɪʃ] *adj* distrustful, suspicious
'Missverhältnis *n* disproportion
'Missverständnis *n (-ses; -se)* misunderstanding
'missverstehen *v/t (irr,* ***stehen****, no -ge-, h)* misunderstand
'Misswahl *f* beauty contest *or* competition
Mist [mɪst] *m (-[e]s; no p)* AGR dung, manure; F trash, rubbish
'Mistbeet *n* AGR hotbed
Mistel ['mɪstəl] *f (-; -n)* BOT mistletoe
'Mistgabel *f* AGR dung fork
'Misthaufen *m* AGR manure heap
mit [mɪt] *prp (dat) and adv* with; ***mit Gewalt*** by force; ***mit Absicht*** on purpose; ***mit dem Auto*** (***der Bahn*** *etc*) by car (train *etc*); ***mit 20 Jahren*** at (the age of) 20; ***mit 100 Stundenkilometern*** at 100 kilometers per hour; ***mit einem Mal(e)*** all of a sudden; (all) at the same time; ***mit lauter Stimme*** in a loud voice; ***mit anderen Worten*** in other words; ***ein Mann mit dem Namen …*** a man by the name of …; ***j-n mit Namen kennen*** know s.o. by name; ***mit der Grund dafür, dass*** one of the reasons why; ***mit der Beste*** one of the best
'Mitarbeit *f* cooperation; assistance; PED activity, class participation
'Mitarbeiter *m*, **'Mitarbeiterin** *f* colleague; employee; assistant; ***freie(r) Mitarbeiter(in)*** freelance
'mitbekommen F *v/t (irr,* ***kommen****, sep, no -ge-, h)* get; catch
mitbenutzen *v/t (sep, no -ge-, h)* share
'Mitbestimmungsrecht *n* (right of) codetermination, worker participation
Mitbewerber(in) (rival) competitor; fellow applicant
Mitbewohner(in) roommate, *Br* flatmate
'mitbringen *v/t (irr,* ***bringen****, sep, -ge-, h)* bring *s.th. or s.o.* with one; ***j-m et. mitbringen*** bring s.o. s.th.
Mitbringsel ['mɪtbrɪŋzəl] F *n (-s; -)* little present; souvenir
'Mitbürger *m*, **'Mitbürgerin** *f* fellow citizen
mitei'nander *adv* with each other, with one another; together, jointly
'miterleben *v/t (sep, no -ge-, h)* live to see
'Mitesser *m* MED blackhead
'mitfahren *v/i (irr,* ***fahren****, sep, -ge-, sein)* ***mit j-m mitfahren*** drive *or* go with s.o.; ***j-n mitfahren lassen*** give s.o. a lift
'Mitfahrgelegenheit *f* lift
Mitfahrzen,trale *f* car pool(ing) service
'mitfühlend *adj* sympathetic
'mitgeben *v/t (irr,* ***geben****, sep, -ge-, h)* ***j-m et. mitgeben*** give s.o. s.th. (to take along)
'Mitgefühl *n (-[e]s; no pl)* sympathy
'mitgehen *v/i (irr,* ***gehen****, sep, -ge-, sein)* ***mit j-m mitgehen*** go *or* come along with s.o.; F ***et. mitgehen lassen*** walk off with s.th.
'Mitgift *f (-; -en)* dowry
'Mitglied *n* member (***bei*** of)
'Mitgliedsbeitrag *m* subscription
'Mitgliedschaft *f (-; -en)* membership
'mithaben *v/t (irr,* ***haben****, sep, -ge-, h)* ***ich habe kein Geld mit*** I haven't got any money with me *or* on me
'Mithilfe *f (-; no pl)* assistance, help, cooperation (***bei*** in; ***von*** of)
mit'hilfe *prp*: ***mithilfe von*** (*or gen*) with the help of, *fig a.* by means of
'mithören *v/t (sep, -ge-, h)* listen in to; overhear
'Mitinhaber *m*, **'Mitinhaberin** *f* joint owner
'mitkommen *v/i (irr,* ***kommen****, sep, -ge-, sein)* come along (***mit*** with); *fig* keep pace (***mit*** with), follow; PED get on, keep up (with the class)
'Mitlaut *m* LING consonant
'Mitleid *n (-[e]s; no pl)* pity (***mit*** for); ***aus Mitleid*** out of pity; ***Mitleid haben mit*** feel sorry for
mitleidig ['mɪtlaidɪç] *adj* compassionate, sympathetic
'mitleidslos *adj* pitiless
'mitmachen *(sep, -ge-, h)* **1.** *v/i* join in; **2.** *v/t* take part in; follow (*a fashion etc*); F go through
'Mitmenschen: ***die Mitmenschen*** one's fellow human beings; people
'mitnehmen *v/t (irr,* ***nehmen****, sep, -ge-, h)* take *s.th. or s.o.* with one; ***j-n*** (***im Auto***) ***mitnehmen*** give s.o. a lift
'mitreden *v/t (sep, -ge-, h)* ***et. mitzureden haben*** (***bei***) have a say (in)
'mitreißen *v/t (irr,* ***reißen****, sep, -ge-, h)* drag along; *fig* carry away (*mst passive*)
mitreißend *fig adj* electrifying (*speech etc*)
'mitschneiden *v/t (irr,* ***schneiden****, sep, -ge-, h) radio*, TV record, tape(-record)
'mitschreiben *(irr,* ***schreiben****, sep, -ge-, h)* **1.** *v/t* take down; take, do (*a test*); **2.**

v/i take notes
'Mitschuld *f* (-; *no pl*) partial responsibility
'mitschuldig *adj*: ***mitschuldig sein*** be partly to blame (***an*** *dat* for)
'Mitschüler *m*, **'Mitschülerin** *f* classmate; schoolmate, fellow student
'mitspielen *v/i* (*sep*, *-ge-*, *h*) SPORT, MUS play; join in *a game etc*; ***in e-m Film*** *etc* ***mitspielen*** be *or* appear in a film *etc*
'Mitspieler *m*, **'Mitspielerin** *f* partner, SPORT *a.* team-mate
Mittag ['mɪtaːk] *m* (-*s*; -*e*) noon, midday; ***heute Mittag*** at noon today; ***zu Mittag essen*** (have) lunch
Mittagessen *n* lunch; ***was gibt es zum Mittagessen?*** what's for lunch?
'mittags *adv* at noon; ***12 Uhr mittags*** 12 o'clock noon
'Mittagspause *f* lunch break
Mittagsruhe *f* midday rest
Mittagsschlaf *m* after-dinner nap
Mittagszeit *f* lunchtime
Mitte ['mɪtə] *f* (-; *no pl*) middle; center, *Br* centre (*a.* POL); ***Mitte Juli*** in the middle of July; ***Mitte dreißig*** in one's mid thirties
'mitteilen *v/t* (*sep*, *-ge-*, *h*) ***j-m et. mitteilen*** inform s.o. of s.th.
'mitteilsam *adj* communicative
'Mitteilung *f* (-; *-en*) report, information, message
Mittel ['mɪtəl] *n* (-*s*; -) means, way; measure; PHARM remedy (***gegen*** for) (*a. fig*); average; MATH mean; PHYS medium; *pl* means, money
'Mittelalter *n* (-*s*; *no pl*) Middle Ages
'mittelalterlich *adj* medi(a)eval
'Mittelding *n* cross (***zwischen*** between)
Mittelfeld *n* SPORT midfield
Mittelfeldspieler(in) midfield player, midfielder
Mittelfinger *m* ANAT middle finger
'mittelfristig *adj* medium-term
'Mittelgewicht *n* (-[*e*]*s*; *no pl*) SPORT middleweight (class)
'mittelgroß *adj* of medium height; medium-sized
'Mittelklasse *f* middle class (*a.* MOT)
Mittellinie *f* SPORT halfway line
'mittellos *adj* without means
'mittelmäßig *adj* average
'Mittelpunkt *m* center, *Br* centre (*a. fig*)
'mittels *prp* (*gen*) by (means of), through
'Mittelschule *f* → ***Realschule***
'Mittelstrecke *f* SPORT middle distance
Mittelstreckenra,kete *f* MIL medium-range missile
Mittelstreifen *m* MOT median strip, *Br* central reservation
Mittelstufe *f* PED junior highschool, *Br* middle school
Mittelstürmer(in) SPORT center (*Br* centre) forward
Mittelweg *m* middle course
Mittelwelle *f radio*: medium wave (ABBR AM)
Mittelwort *n* (-[*e*]*s*; *-wörter*) LING participle
mitten ['mɪtən] *adv*: ***mitten in*** (***auf, unter*** *dat*) in the midst *or* middle of
mitten'drin F *adv* right in the middle
mitten'durch F *adv* right through (the middle); right in two
Mitternacht ['mɪtɐ-] *f* midnight
mittlere ['mɪtlərə] *adj* middle, central; average, medium
mittlerweile ['mɪtlɐ'vailə] *adv* meanwhile, (in the) meantime
Mittwoch ['mɪtvɔx] *m* (-[*s*]; -*e*) Wednesday
mit'unter *adv* now and then
'Mitverantwortung *f* share of the responsibility
'mitwirken *v/i* (*sep*, *-ge-*, *h*) take part (***bei*** in)
'Mitwirkende *m*, *f* (-*n*; -*n*) THEA, MUS performer; *pl* THEA the cast
'Mitwirkung *f* (-; *no pl*) participation
mixen ['mɪksən] *v/t* (*ge-*, *h*) mix
'Mixbecher *m* shaker
Mixer ['mɪksɐ] *m* (-*s*; -) mixer
'Mixgetränk *n* mixed drink, cocktail, shake
Möbel ['møːbəl] *pl* furniture
Möbelspediti,on *f* removal firm
Möbelstück *n* piece of furniture
Möbelwagen *m* moving (*Br* furniture) van
mobil [mo'biːl] *adj* mobile; ***mobil machen*** MIL mobilize
Mobiliar [mobi'ljaːɐ] *n* (-*s*; *no pl*) furniture
Mo'biltele,fon *n* mobile phone
möblieren [mø'bliːrən] *v/t* (*no -ge-*, *h*) furnish
mochte ['mɔxtə] *pret of* ***mögen***
Mode ['moːdə] *f* (-; -*n*) fashion; ***in Mode*** in fashion; ***Mode sein*** be in fashion, F be in; ***die neueste Mode*** the latest fashion; ***mit der Mode gehen*** follow the fashion; ***in*** (***aus der***) ***Mode kommen*** come into (go out of) fashion
Modell [mo'dɛl] *n* (-*s*; -*e*) model; ***j-m Modell stehen*** *or* ***sitzen*** pose *or* sit for s.o.
Modellbau *m* model construction
Modellbaukasten *m* model construction kit
Modelleisenbahn *f* model railway

M

modellieren [mode'li:rən] *v/t* (*no -ge-, h*) model
Modem ['mo:dɛm] *m, n* (*-s; -s*) EDP modem
'Modenschau *f* fashion show
Moderator [mode'ra:to:ɐ] *m* (*-s; -en* [modera'to:rən]), **Modera'torin** *f* (*-; -nen*) TV *etc* presenter, host, anchorman (anchorwoman)
moderieren [mode'ri:rən] *v/t* (*no -ge-, h*) TV *etc* present, host
moderig ['mo:dərıç] *adj* musty, mo(u)ldy
modern[1] ['mo:dɐn] *v/i* (*ge-, h, sein*) mo(u)ld, rot, decay
modern[2] [mo'dɛrn] *adj* modern; fashionable
modernisieren [modɛrni'zi:rən] *v/t* (*no -ge-, h*) modernize, bring up to date
'Modeschmuck *m* costume jewel(le)ry
Modeschöpfer(in) fashion designer
Modewaren *pl* fashionwear
Modewort *n* (*-[e]s; -wörter*) vogue word, F in word
Modezeichner(in) fashion designer
Modezeitschrift *f* fashion magazine
modisch ['mo:dıʃ] *adj* fashionable, stylish
Modul[1] [mo'du:l] *n* (*-s; -e*) EDP module
Modul[2] ['mo:dʊl] *m* (*-s;-n*) MATH, TECH module
Mofa ['mo:fa] *n* (*-s; -s*) (small) moped, motorized bicycle
mogeln ['mo:gəln] F *v/i* (*ge-, h*) cheat; crib
mögen ['mø:gən] *v/t* (*irr, ge-, h*) *and v/aux* (*irr, no -ge-, h*) like; ***er mag sie*** (***nicht***) he likes (doesn't like) her; ***lieber mögen*** like better, prefer; ***nicht mögen*** dislike; ***was möchten Sie?*** what would you like?; ***ich möchte, dass du es weißt*** I'd like you to know (it); ***ich möchte lieber bleiben*** I'd rather stay; ***es mag sein*** (, ***dass***) it may be (that)
möglich ['mø:klıç] **1.** *adj* possible; ***alle möglichen*** all sorts of; ***sein Möglichstes tun*** do what one can; do one's utmost; ***nicht möglich!*** you don't say (so)!; ***so bald*** (***schnell, oft***) ***wie möglich*** as soon (quickly, often) as possible; **2.** *adv*: ***möglichst bald*** *etc* as soon *etc* as possible
'möglicher'weise *adv* possibly
'Möglichkeit *f* (*-; -en*) possibility; opportunity; chance; ***nach Möglichkeit*** if possible
Mohammedaner [mohame'da:nɐ] *m* (*-s; -*), **mohamme'danisch** *adj* Muslim
Mohn [mo:n] *m* (*-[e]s; -e*) BOT poppy
Möhre ['mø:rə] *f* (*-; -n*), **Mohrrübe** ['mo:ɐ-] *f* BOT carrot
Molch [mɔlç] *m* (*-[e]s; -e*) ZO salamander
Mole ['mo:lə] *f* (*-; -n*) MAR mole, jetty
Molekül [mole'ky:l] *n* (*-s; -e*) CHEM molecule
molk [mɔlk] *pret of* ***melken***
Molkerei [mɔlkə'rai] *f* (*-; -en*) dairy
Moll [mɔl] *n* (*-; no pl*) MUS minor (key); ***a-Moll*** A minor
mollig ['mɔlıç] F *adj* snug, cozy, *Br* cosy; plump, chubby
Moment [mo'mɛnt] *m* (*-[e]s; -e*) moment; (***e-n***) ***Moment bitte!*** just a moment please!; ***im Moment*** at the moment
Monarch [mo'narç] *m* (*-en; -en*) monarch
Monarchie [monar'çi:] *f* (*-; -n*) monarchy
Monarchin [mo'narçın] *f* (*-; -nen*) monarch
Monarchist [monar'çıst] *m* (*-en; -en*) monarchist
Monat ['mo:nat] *m* (*-[e]s; -e*) month; ***zweimal im*** *or* ***pro Monat*** twice a month
'monatelang *adv* for months
'monatlich *adj and adv* monthly
'Monatsbinde *f* sanitary napkin (*Br* towel)
Monatskarte *f* commuter ticket, *Br* (monthly) season ticket
Mönch [mœnç] *m* (*-[e]s; -e*) monk; friar
Mond [mo:nt] *m* (*-[e]s; -e* ['mo:ndə]) moon
Mondfinsternis *f* lunar eclipse
'mondhell *adj* moonlit
'Mondlandefähre *f* lunar module
Mondlandung *f* moon landing
Mondoberfläche *f* moon surface, lunar soil
Mondschein *m* (*-[e]s; no pl*) moonlight
Mondsichel *f* crescent
Mondumkreisung *f*, **Mondumlaufbahn** *f* lunar orbit
Monitor ['mo:nito:ɐ] *m* (*-s; -en* [moni'to:rən]) TV *etc* monitor
Monolog [mono'lo:k] *m* (*-[e]s; -e*) monolog(ue *Br*)
Monopol [mono'po:l] *n* (*-s; -e*) ECON monopoly
monoton [mono'to:n] *adj* monotonous
Monotonie [monoto'ni:] *f* (*-; -n*) monotony
Monoxid ['mo:nɔksi:t] *n* CHEM monoxide
Monster ['mɔnstɐ] *n* (*-s; -*) monster
Montag ['mo:nta:k] *m* (*-[e]s; -e*) Monday
Montage [mɔn'ta:ʒə] *f* (*-; -n*) TECH assembly; installation; ***auf Montage sein*** be away on a field job
Montageband *n* (*-[e]s; -bänder*) TECH assembly line
Montagehalle *f* TECH assembly shop

Monteur [mɔn'tøːɐ] *m* (*-s; -e*) TECH fitter; *esp* MOT, AVIAT mechanic
montieren [mɔn'tiːrən] *v/t* (*no -ge-, h*) TECH assemble; fit, attach; instal(l)
Moor [moːɐ] *n* (*-[e]s; -e*) bog, moor(-land)
moorig ['moːrɪç] *adj* boggy
Moos [moːs] *n* (*-es; -e*) BOT moss
moosig ['moːzɪç] *adj* mossy
Moped ['moːpɛt] *n* (*-s; -s*) moped
Mops [mɔps] *m* (*-es; Möpse* ['mœpsə]) ZO pug(dog)
Moral [mo'raːl] *f* (*-; no pl*) morals, moral standards; MIL *etc* morale
mo'ralisch *adj* moral
moralisieren [morali'ziːrən] *v/i* (*no -ge-, h*) moralize
Morast [mo'rast] *m* (*-[e]s; -e*) morass; mire, mud
Mord [mɔrt] *m* (*-[e]s; -e* ['mɔrdə]) murder (***an*** *dat* of); ***e-n Mord begehen*** commit murder
Mordanschlag *m esp* POL assassination attempt
Mörder ['mœrdɐ] *m* (*-s; -*), **'Mörderin** *f* (*-; -nen*) murderer; (hired) killer; *esp* POL assassin
'Mordkommissi,on *f* homicide division, *Br* murder squad
Mordpro,zess *m* JUR murder trial
'Mordsangst F *f*: ***e-e Mordsangst haben*** be scared stiff
Mordsglück F *n* stupendous luck
Mordskerl F *m* devil of a fellow
Mordswut F *f*: ***e-e Mordswut haben*** be in a hell of a rage
'Mordverdacht *m* suspicion of murder
Mordversuch *m* attempted murder
morgen ['mɔrgən] *adv* tomorrow; ***morgen Abend (früh)*** tomorrow night (morning); ***morgen Mittag*** at noon tomorrow; ***morgen in e-r Woche*** a week from tomorrow; ***morgen um diese Zeit*** this time tomorrow; ***... von morgen*** tomorrow's ..., ... of tomorrow
'Morgen *m* (*-s; -*) morning; AGR acre; ***heute Morgen*** this morning; ***am (frühen) Morgen*** (early) in the morning; ***am nächsten Morgen*** the next morning
Morgenessen *Swiss n* breakfast
Morgengrauen *n* dawn; ***im*** *or* ***bei Morgengrauen*** at dawn
Morgenland *n* (*-[e]s; no pl*) Orient
Morgenmantel *m*, **Morgenrock** *m* dressing gown
'morgens *adv* in the morning; ***von morgens bis abends*** from morning till night
morgig ['mɔrgɪç] *adj* tomorrow's ...
Morphium ['mɔrfjʊm] *n* (*-s; no pl*) PHARM morphine
morsch [mɔrʃ] *adj* rotten; ***morsch werden*** rot
Morsealpha,bet ['mɔrzə-] *n* Morse code
Mörser ['mœrzɐ] *m* (*-s; -*) mortar (*a.* MIL)
'Morsezeichen *n* Morse signal
Mörtel ['mœrtəl] *m* (*-s; -*) mortar
Mosaik [moza'iːk] *n* (*-s; -en*) mosaic
Mosa'ikstein *m* piece
Moschee [mɔ'ʃeː] *f* (*-; -n*) mosque
Moskito [mɔs'kiːto] *m* (*-s; -s*) ZO mosquito
Moslem ['mɔslɛm] *m* (*-s; -s*), **moslemisch** [mɔs'leːmɪʃ] *adj*, **Moslime** [-'liːmə] *f* (*-; -n*) Muslim
Most [mɔst] *m* (*-[e]s; -e*) grape juice; cider
Motiv [mo'tiːf] *n* (*-s; -e*) motive; PAINT, MUS motif
Motivation [motiva'tsjoːn] *f* (*-; -en*) motivation
motivieren [moti'viːrən] *v/t* (*no -ge-, h*) motivate
Motor ['moːtoːɐ, mo'toːɐ] *m* (*-s; -en* [mo'toːrən]) motor, engine
Motorboot *n* motor boat
Motorhaube *f* hood, *Br* bonnet
motorisieren [motori'ziːrən] *v/t* (*no -ge-, h*) motorize
'Motorleistung *f* (engine) performance
Motorrad *n* motorcycle, F motorbike; ***Motorrad fahren*** ride a motorcycle
Motorradfahrer(in) motorcyclist, biker
Motorroller *m* (motor) scooter
Motorsäge *f* power saw
Motorschaden *m* engine trouble (*or* failure)
Motte ['mɔtə] *f* (*-; -n*) ZO moth
'Mottenkugel *f* mothball
'mottenzerfressen *adj* moth-eaten
Motto ['mɔto] *n* (*-s; -s*) motto
Möwe ['møːvə] *f* (*-; -n*) ZO (sea)gull
Mücke ['mʏkə] *f* (*-; -n*) ZO gnat, midge, mosquito; ***aus e-r Mücke e-n Elefanten machen*** make a mountain out of a molehill
'Mückenstich *m* gnat bite
müde ['myːdə] *adj* tired; weary; sleepy; ***müde sein (werden)*** be (get) tired (*fig* ***e-r Sache*** of s.th.)
'Müdigkeit *f* (*-; no pl*) tiredness
Muff [mʊf] *m* (*-[e]s; -e*) muff
Muffe ['mʊfə] *f* (*-; -n*) TECH sleeve, socket
Muffel ['mʊfəl] F *m* (*-s; -*) sourpuss
muff(e)lig ['mʊf(ə)lɪç], **muffig** ['mʊfɪç] F *adj* musty; *contp* sulky, sullen
Mühe ['myːə] *f* (*-; -n*) trouble; effort; difficulty (***mit*** with *s.th.*); ***(nicht) der Mühe wert*** (not) worth the trouble; ***j-m Mühe machen*** give s.o. trouble; ***sich Mühe geben*** try hard; ***sich die Mühe sparen*** save o.s. the trouble; ***mit Mühe und Not***

(just) barely
'mühelos *adv* without difficulty
mühen ['my:ən] *v/refl (ge-, h)* struggle, work hard
'mühevoll *adj* laborious
Mühle ['my:lə] *f (-; -n)* mill; morris
Mühsal ['my:za:l] *f (-; -e)* toil
mühsam ['my:za:m], **'mühselig 1.** *adj* laborious; **2.** *adv* with difficulty
Mulatte [mu'latə] *m (-n; -n)*, **Mu'lattin** *f (-; -nen)* mulatto
Mulde ['mʊldə] *f (-; -n)* hollow
Mull [mʊl] *m (-[e]s; -e)* muslin; *esp* MED gauze
Müll [mʏl] *m (-s; no pl)* garbage, trash, *Br* refuse, rubbish
Müllabfuhr *f* garbage (*Br* refuse) collection
Müllbeseitigung *f* waste disposal
Müllbeutel *m* garbage bag, *Br* dustbin liner
'Mullbinde *f* MED gauze bandage
'Müllcon,tainer *m* garbage (*Br* rubbish) skip
Mülldepo,nie *f* dump
Mülleimer *m* garbage can, *Br* dustbin
Müllfahrer *m* garbage man, *Br* dustman
Müllhalde *f* dump
Müllhaufen *m* garbage (*Br* rubbish) heap
Müllkippe *f* dump
Müllschlucker *m* garbage (*Br* refuse) chute
Mülltonne *f* garbage can, *Br* dustbin
Müllverbrennungsanlage *f* (waste) incineration plant
Müllwagen *m* garbage truck, *Br* dustcart
Multiplikation [mʊltiplika'tsjo:n] *f (-; -en)* MATH multiplication
multiplizieren [mʊltipli'tsi:rən] *v/t (no -ge-, h)* MATH multiply (***mit*** by)
Mumie ['mu:mjə] *f (-; -n)* mummy
Mumps [mʊmps] *m, f (-; no pl)* MED mumps
Mund [mʊnt] *m (-[e]s; Münder* ['mʏndɐ]) mouth; F ***den Mund vollnehmen*** talk big; ***halt den Mund!*** shut up!
Mundart *f* dialect
münden ['mʏndən] *v/i (ge-, h, sein)* ***münden in*** *(acc) river etc*: flow into; *road etc*: lead into
'Mundgeruch *m* bad breath
'Mundhar,monika *f* MUS mouth organ, harmonica
mündig ['mʏndɪç] *adj* emancipated; ***mündig (werden)*** JUR (come) of age
mündlich ['mʏntlɪç] *adj* oral; verbal
'Mundstück *n* mouthpiece; tip
'Mündung *f (-; -en) river*: mouth; *gun*: muzzle
'Mundwasser *n* mouthwash
Mundwerk F *n*: ***ein gutes Mundwerk haben*** have the gift of the gab; ***ein loses Mundwerk*** a loose tongue
Mundwinkel *m* corner of the mouth
'Mund-zu-'Mund-Beatmung *f (-; -en)* MED mouth-to-mouth resuscitation, F kiss of life
Munition [muni'tsjo:n] *f (-; -en)* ammunition
munkeln ['mʊŋkəln] F *v/t (ge-, h)* ***man munkelt, dass*** rumo(u)r has it that
Münster ['mʏnstɐ] *n (-s; -)* cathedral, minster
munter ['mʊntɐ] *adj* awake; lively; merry
Münze ['mʏntsə] *f (-; -n)* coin; medal
'Münzeinwurf *m* (coin) slot
Münzfernsprecher *m* pay phone
Münztank (auto,mat) *m* coin-operated (gas, *Br* petrol) pump
Münzwechsler *m* (-s; -) change machine
mürbe ['mʏrbə] *adj* tender; brittle; GASTR crisp
'Mürbeteig *m* short pastry; shortcake
Murmel ['mʊrməl] *f (-; -n)* marble
'murmeln *v/t and v/i (ge-, h)* murmur
'Murmeltier *n* ZO marmot
murren ['mʊrən] *v/i (ge-, h)* complain (***über*** *acc* about)
mürrisch ['mʏrɪʃ] *adj* sullen; grumpy
Mus [mu:s] *n (-es; -e)* mush; stewed fruit
Muschel ['mʊʃəl] *f (-; -n)* ZO mussel; shell
Museum [mu'ze:ʊm] *n (-s; Museen)* museum
Musik [mu'zi:k] *f (-; no pl)* music
musikalisch [muzi'ka:lɪʃ] *adj* musical
Mu'sikanlage *f* hi-fi *or* stereo set
Musikauto,mat *m*, **Musikbox** *f* juke box
Musiker ['mu:zikɐ] *m (-s; -)*, **'Musikerin** *f (-; -nen)* musician
Mu'sikinstru,ment *n* musical instrument
Musikka,pelle *f* band
Musikkas,sette *f* music cassette
Musiklehrer(in) music teacher
Musikstunde *f* music lesson
musisch ['mu:zɪʃ] *adv*: ***musisch interessiert (begabt)*** fond of (gifted for) fine arts and music
musizieren [muzi'tsi:rən] *v/i (no -ge-, h)* make music
Muskat [mʊs'ka:t] *m (-[e]s; -e)*, **Muskatnuss** *f* BOT nutmeg
Muskel ['mʊskəl] *m (-s; -n)* ANAT muscle
Muskelkater F *m* aching muscles
Muskelzerrung *f* MED pulled muscle
muskulös [mʊsku'lø:s] *adj* muscular, brawny
Müsli ['my:sli] *n (-s; -)* GASTR granola, *Br* muesli

Muss *n* (-; *no pl*) necessity; ***es ist ein Muss*** it is a must
Muße ['muːsə] *f* (-; *no pl*) leisure; spare time
müssen ['mʏsən] *v/i* (*irr, ge-, h*) *and v/aux* (*irr, no -ge-, h*) must, have (got) to; ***du musst den Film sehen!*** you must see the film!; ***ich muss jetzt*** (***m-e***) ***Hausaufgaben machen*** I have (got) to do my homework now; ***sie muss krank sein*** she must be ill; ***du musst es nicht tun*** you need not do it; ***das müsstest du*** (***doch***) ***wissen*** you ought to know (that); ***sie müsste zu Hause sein*** she should (ought to) be (at) home; ***das müsste schön sein!*** that would be nice!; ***du hättest ihm helfen müssen*** you ought to have helped him
müßig ['myːsɪç] *adj* idle; useless
musste ['mʊstə] *pret of* ***müssen***
Muster ['mʊstɐ] *n* (-*s*; -) pattern; sample; model
'**mustergültig**, **musterhaft** *adj* exemplary; ***sich mustergültig benehmen*** behave perfectly
'**Musterhaus** *n* showhouse
'**mustern** *v/t* (*ge-, h*) eye *s.o.*; size *s.o.* up; MIL ***gemustert werden*** F have one's medical
Musterung ['mʊstərʊŋ] *f* (-; -*en*) MIL medical (examination for military service)
Mut [muːt] *m* (-[*e*]*s*; *no pl*) courage; ***j-m Mut machen*** encourage s.o.; ***den Mut verlieren*** lose courage; → ***zumute***
mutig ['muːtɪç] *adj* courageous, brave
'**mutlos** *adj* discouraged
'**mutmaßen** *v/t* (*ge-, h*) speculate
'**mutmaßlich** *adj* probable; presumed
'**Mutprobe** *f* test of courage
Mutter ['mʊtɐ] *f* (-; *Mütter* ['mʏtɐ]) mother; TECH nut
Mutterboden *m*, **Muttererde** *f* AGR topsoil
mütterlich ['mʏtɐlɪç] *adj* motherly
'**mütterlicherseits** *adv*: ***Onkel*** *etc* ***mütterlicherseits*** maternal uncle *etc*
'**Mutterliebe** *f* motherly love
'**mutterlos** *adj* motherless
'**Muttermal** *n* birthmark, mole
Muttermilch *f* mother's milk
Mutterschaftsurlaub *m* maternity leave
Mutterschutz *m* JUR legal protection of expectant and nursing mothers
Muttersöhnchen *contp n* sissy
Muttersprache *f* mother tongue
Muttersprachler [-ʃpraːxlɐ] *m* (-*s*; -) native speaker
Muttertag *m* Mother's Day
Mutti ['mʊti] F *f* (-; -*s*) mom(my), *esp Br* mum(my)
'**mutwillig** *adj* wanton
Mütze ['mʏtsə] *f* (-; -*n*) cap
MwSt ABBR *of* ***Mehrwertsteuer*** VAT, value-added tax
mysteriös [mʏste'rjøːs] adj mysterious
mystisch ['mʏstɪʃ] *adj* mystic(al)
mythisch ['myːtɪʃ] *adj* mythical
Mythologie [mytolo'giː] *f* (-; -*n*) mythology
Mythos ['myːtɔs] *m* (-; *Mythen*) myth

N

N

N ABBR *of* ***Nord***(***en***) N, north
na [na] *int* well; ***na und?*** so what?; ***na gut!*** all right then; ***na ja*** (oh) well; ***na***(***, na***)***!*** come on!, come now!; ***na so*** (***et***)***was!*** what do you know!, *Br* I say!; ***na, dann nicht!*** oh, forget it!; ***na also!*** there you are!; ***na, warte!*** just you wait!
Nabe ['naːbə] *f* (-; -*n*) TECH hub
Nabel ['naːbəl] *m* (-*s*; -) ANAT navel
'**Nabelschnur** *f* ANAT umbilical chord
nach [naːx] *prp* (*dat*) *and adv* to, toward(s), for; after; *time*: after, past; according to, by; ***nach Hause*** home; ***abfahren nach*** leave for; ***nach rechts*** (***Süden***) to the right (south); ***nach oben*** up (-stairs); ***nach unten*** down(stairs); ***nach vorn*** (***hinten***) to the front (back); ***der Reihe nach*** one after the other; ***s-e Uhr nach dem Radio stellen*** set one's watch by the radio; ***nach m-r Uhr*** by my watch; ***suchen*** (***fragen***) ***nach*** look (ask) for; ***nach Gewicht*** (***Zeit***) by weight (the hour); ***riechen*** (***schmecken***) ***nach*** smell (taste) of; ***nach und nach*** gradually; ***nach wie vor*** as before, still
'**nachahmen** [-aːmən] *v/t* (*sep, -ge-, h*) imitate, copy; take off
'**Nachahmung** *f* (-; -*en*) imitation

Nachbar ['naxbaːɐ] *m* (*-n*; *-n*), **'Nachbarin** *f* (-; *-nen*) neighbo(u)r
'Nachbarschaft *f* (-; *no pl*) neighbo(u)rhood, vicinity
'Nachbau *m* (-[*e*]*s*; *-ten*) TECH reproduction
'nachbauen *v/t* (*sep*, *-ge-*, *h*) copy, reproduce
'Nachbildung *f* (-; *-en*) copy, imitation; replica; dummy
'nachblicken *v/i* (*sep*, *-ge-*, *h*) look after
nach'dem *cj* after, when; ***je nachdem wie*** depending on how
'nachdenken *v/i* (*irr*, ***denken***, *sep*, *-ge-*, *h*) think; ***nachdenken über*** (*acc*) think about, think *s.th.* over
'nachdenklich *adj* thoughtful; ***es macht e-n nachdenklich*** it makes you think
'Nachdruck[1] *m* (-[*e*]*s*; *no pl*) emphasis, stress
'Nachdruck[2] (-[*e*]*s*; *-e*) reprint
'nachdrucken *v/t* (*sep*, *-ge-*, *h*) reprint
'nachdrücklich [-drʏklɪç] *adj* emphatic; forceful; ***nachdrücklich raten*** (***empfehlen***) advise (recommend) strongly
'nacheifern *v/i* (*sep*, *-ge-*, *h*) ***j-m nacheifern*** emulate s.o.
nachei'nander *adv* one after the other, in (*or* by) turns
'nacherzählen *v/t* (*sep*, *no -ge-*, *h*) retell
'Nacherzählung *f* (-; *-en*) PED reproduction
'Nachfolge *f* (-; *no pl*) succession; ***j-s Nachfolge antreten*** succeed s.o.
'nachfolgen *v/i* (*sep*, *-ge-*, *sein*) (*dat*) succeed *s.o.*
'Nachfolger(in) [-fɔlgɐ (-gərɪn)] (*-s*; *-/-*; *-nen*) successor
'nachforschen *v/i* (*sep*, *-ge-*, *h*) investigate
'Nachforschung *f* (-; *-en*) investigation, inquiry
'Nachfrage *f* (-; *-n*) inquiry; ECON demand
'nachfragen *v/i* (*sep*, *-ge-*, *h*) inquire, ask
'nachfühlen *v/t* (*sep*, *-ge-*, *h*) ***j-m et. nachfühlen*** understand how s.o. feels
nachfüllen *v/t* (*sep*, *-ge-*, *h*) refill
nachgeben *v/i* (*irr*, ***geben***, *sep*, *-ge-*, *h*) give (way); *fig* give in
'Nachgebühr *f* (-; *-en*) *post* surcharge
'nachgehen *v/i* (*irr*, ***gehen***, *sep*, *-ge-*, *sein*) follow (*a. fig*); *watch*: be slow; ***e-r Sache nachgehen*** investigate s.th.; ***s-r Arbeit nachgehen*** go about one's work
'Nachgeschmack *m* (-[*e*]*s*; *no pl*) aftertaste (*a. fig*)
'nachgiebig [-giːbɪç] *adj* yielding, soft (*both a. fig*)
'Nachgiebigkeit *f* (-; *no pl*) yieldingness, softness (*both a. fig*)
'nachhaltig [-haltɪç] *adj* lasting, enduring
nach'hause → ***Haus***
nach'her *adv* afterwards; ***bis nachher!*** see you later!, so long!
'Nachhilfe *f* help, assistance; PED → **Nachhilfestunden** *pl*, **Nachhilfeunterricht** *m* PED private lesson(s), coaching
'nachholen *v/t* (*sep*, *-ge-*, *h*) make up for, catch up on
'Nachkomme *m* (*-n*; *-n*) descendant, *pl esp* JUR issue
'nachkommen *v/i* (*irr*, ***kommen***, *sep*, *-ge-*, *sein*) follow, come later; (*dat*) comply with
'Nachkriegs... *in cpds* postwar ...
Nachlass ['naːxlas] *m* (*-es*; *-lässe* [-lɛsə]) ECON reduction, discount; JUR estate
'nachlassen *v/i* (*irr*, ***lassen***, *sep*, *-ge-*, *h*) decrease, diminish, go down; *effect etc*: wear off; *student etc*: slacken one's effort; *interest etc*: flag; *health etc*: fail, deteriorate
'nachlässig *adj* careless, negligent
'nachlaufen *v/i* (*irr*, ***laufen***, *sep*, *-ge-*, *sein*) run after
nachlesen *v/t* (*irr*, ***lesen***, *sep*, *-ge-*, *h*) look up
nachmachen *v/t* (*sep*, *-ge-*, *h*) imitate, copy; counterfeit, forge
'Nachmittag *m* afternoon; ***heute Nachmittag*** this afternoon
'nachmittags *adv* in the afternoon
Nachnahme ['naːxnaːmə] *f* (-; *-n*) ECON cash on delivery; ***per Nachnahme schicken*** send C.O.D.
'Nachname *m* surname, last (*or* family) name
Nachporto *n* surcharge
'nachprüfen *v/t* (*sep*, *-ge-*, *h*) check (up), make sure (of)
'nachrechnen *v/t* (*sep*, *-ge-*, *h*) check
'Nachrede *f*: ***üble Nachrede*** malicious gossip; JUR defamation (of character), slander
Nachricht ['naːxrɪçt] *f* (-; *-en*) news; message; report; information, notice; *pl* news (report), newscast; ***e-e gute*** (***schlechte***) ***Nachricht*** good (bad) news; ***Sie hören Nachrichten*** here is the news
'Nachrichtendienst *m* news service; MIL intelligence service
Nachrichtensatel,lit *m* communications satellite
Nachrichtensprecher(in) newscaster, *esp Br* newsreader
Nachrichtentechnik *f* telecommunications
'Nachruf *m* obituary
'nachrüsten *v/i* (*sep*, *-ge-*, *h*) POL, MIL close

N

the armament gap

nachsagen *v/t* (*sep*, *-ge-*, *h*) ***j-m Schlechtes nachsagen*** speak badly of s.o.; ***man sagt ihm nach, dass er …*** he is said to *inf*

'Nachsai,son *f* off-peak season; ***in der Nachsaison*** out of season

'nachschlagen (*irr*, ***schlagen***, *sep*, *-ge-*, *h*) **1.** *v/t* look up; **2.** *v/i*: ***nachschlagen in*** (*dat*) consult

'Nachschlagewerk *n* reference book

'Nachschlüssel *m* duplicate (*or* skeleton) key

Nachschrift *f* postcript; dictation

Nachschub *m esp* MIL supplies

'nachsehen (*irr*, ***sehen***, *sep*, *- ge-*, *h*) **1.** *v/i* follow with one's eyes; (have a) look; ***nachsehen ob*** (go and) see whether; **2.** *v/t* look *or* go over *or* through; correct, mark; *check* (*a.* TECH)

nachsenden *v/t* ([*irr*, ***senden***,] *sep*, *-ge-*, *h*) send on, forward; ***bitte nachsenden!*** *post* please forward!

'Nachsilbe *f* LING suffix

'nachsitzen *v/i* (*irr*, ***sitzen***, *sep*, *-ge-*, *h*) stay in (after school), be kept in; ***nachsitzen lassen*** keep in, detain

'Nachspann *m* (*-*[*e*]*s*; *-e*) *film*: credits *pl*

'Nachspiel *n* sequel, consequences

'nachspielen *v/i* (*sep*, *-ge-*, *h*) SPORT ***5 Minuten nachspielen lassen*** allow 5 minutes for injury time

'Nachspielzeit *f esp soccer*: injury time

'nachspio,nieren *v/i* (*no -ge-*, *h*) spy (up)-on

nachsprechen *v/t* (*irr*, ***sprechen***, *sep*, *-ge-*, *h*) ***j-m et. nachsprechen*** say *or* repeat s.th. after s.o.

nächst'beste ['nɛːçst-] *adj* first, F any old; next-best, second-best

nächste ['nɛːçstə] *adj* next; nearest (*a. relative*); ***in den nächsten Tagen*** (***Jahren***) in the next few days (years); ***in nächster Zeit*** in the near future; ***was kommt als Nächstes?*** what comes next?; ***der Nächste, bitte!*** next please!

'nachstehen *v/i* (*irr*, ***stehen***, *sep*, *-ge-*, *h*) ***j-m in nichts nachstehen*** be in no way inferior to s.o.

'nachstellen (*sep*, *-ge-*, *h*) **1.** *v/t* put back (*watch*); TECH (re)adjust; **2.** *v/i*: ***j-m nachstellen*** be after s.o.

'Nachstellung *f* (*-*; *-en*) persecution

'Nächstenliebe *f* charity

Nacht [naxt] *f* (*-*; *Nächte* ['nɛçtə]) night; ***Tag und Nacht*** night and day; ***die ganze Nacht*** all night (long); ***heute Nacht*** tonight; last night

'Nachtdienst *m* night duty; ***Nachtdienst haben*** PHARM be open all night

'Nachteil *m* disadvantage, drawback; ***im Nachteil sein*** be at a disadvantage (***gegenüber*** compared with)

'nachteilig [-tailɪç] *adj* disadvantageous

'Nachtessen *Swiss n* → ***Abendbrot***

Nachtfalter *m* ZO moth

Nachthemd *n* nightgown, nightdress, F nightie; nightshirt

Nachtigall ['naxtigal] *f* (*-*; *-en*) ZO nightingale

'Nachtisch *m* (*-*[*e*]*s*; *no pl*) dessert; sweet

nächtlich ['nɛçtlɪç] *adj* nightly; at *or* by night

'Nachtlo,kal *n* nightclub

Nachtrag ['naːxtraːk] *m* (*-*[*e*]*s*; *-träge* [-trɛːgə]) supplement

'nachtragen *fig v/t* (*irr*, ***tragen***, *sep*, *-ge-*, *h*) ***j-m et. nachtragen*** bear s.o. a grudge

'nachtragend *adj* unforgiving

'nachträglich [-trɛːklɪç] *adj* additional; later; belated

nachts *adv* at night, in the night(time)

'Nachtschicht *f* night shift; ***Nachtschicht haben*** be on night shift

'nachtschlafend *adj*: ***zu nachtschlafender Zeit*** in the middle of the night

'Nachttisch *m* bedside table

'Nachttopf *m* chamber pot

'Nachtwächter *m* night watchman

'nachwachsen *v/i* (*irr*, ***wachsen***, *sep*, *-ge-*, *sein*) grow again

'Nachwahl *f* PARL special election, *Br* by-election

Nachweis ['naːxvais] *m* (*-es*; *-e*) proof, evidence

'nachweisbar *adj* demonstrable; *esp* CHEM *etc* detectable

'nachweisen *v/t* (*irr*, ***weisen***, *sep*, *-ge-*, *h*) prove; *esp* CHEM *etc* detect

'nachweislich *adv* as can be proved

'Nachwelt *f* (*-*; *no pl*) posterity

Nachwirkung *f* aftereffect(s), *pl a.* aftermath

Nachwort *n* (*-*[*e*]*s*; *-worte*) epilog(ue)

'Nachwuchs *m* (*-es*; *no pl*) young talent, F new blood

Nachwuchs… *in cpds …autor*, *…schauspieler etc*: talented *or* promising young …, up-and-coming …

'nachzahlen *v/t* (*sep*, *-ge-*, *h*) pay extra

nachzählen *v/t* (*sep*, *-ge-*, *h*) count over (again), check

'Nachzahlung *f* additional *or* extra payment

Nachzügler ['naːxtsyːklɐ] *m* (*-s*; *-*) straggler, latecomer

Nacken ['nakən] *m* (*-s*; *-*) ANAT (back *or* nape of the) neck

N

Nackenstütze *f* headrest
nackt [nakt] *adj* naked; *esp* PAINT, PHOT nude; bare (*a. fig*); *fig* plain; ***völlig nackt*** stark naked; ***sich nackt ausziehen*** strip; ***nackt baden*** swim in the nude; ***j-n nackt malen*** paint s.o. in the nude
Nadel ['na:dəl] *f* (-; *-n*) needle; pin; brooch
Nadelbaum *m* BOT conifer(ous tree)
Nadelöhr *n* eye of a needle
Nadelstich *m* pinprick (*a. fig*)
Nagel ['na:gəl] *m* (*-s*; *Nägel* ['nɛ:gəl]) nail; ***an den Nägeln kauen*** bite one's nails
Nagellack *m* nail varnish *or* polish
'**nageln** *v/t* (*ge-*, *h*) nail (***an*** *acc*, ***auf*** *acc* to)
'**nagel'neu** F *adj* brand-new
'**Nagelpflege** *f* manicure
nagen ['na:gən] (*ge-*, *h*) **1.** *v/i* gnaw (***an*** *dat* at); ***an e-m Knochen nagen*** pick a bone; **2.** *v/t* gnaw
'**Nagetier** *n* ZO rodent
'**Nahaufnahme** *f* PHOT *etc* close-up
nahe [na:ə] *adj* near, close (***bei*** to); nearby; ***nahe kommen*** (*dat*) come close to; *fig* →***nahekommen***; →***nahelegen***; →***naheliegen***; →***naheliegend***
Nähe ['nɛ:ə] *f* (-; *no pl*) nearness; neighbo(u)rhood, vicinity; ***in der Nähe des Bahnhofs*** near the station; ***ganz in der Nähe*** quite near, close by; ***in deiner Nähe*** near you
nahegehen *v/i* (*irr*, ***gehen***, *sep*, *-ge-*, *sein*): ***j-m nahegehen*** affect s.o. deeply
'**nahekommen** *v/i* (*irr*, ***kommen***, *sep*, *-ge-*, *sein*) *fig* come close to
'**nahelegen** *v/t* (*sep*, *-ge-*, *h*) suggest
'**naheliegen** *v/i* (*irr*, ***liegen***, *sep*, *-ge-*, *h*) seem likely
'**naheliegend** *adj* likely, obvious
nahen ['na:ən] *v/i* (*ge-*, *sein*) approach
nähen ['nɛ:ən] *v/t and v/i* (*ge-*, *h*) sew; make
Nähere ['nɛ:ərə] *n* (*-n*; *no pl*) details, particulars
nähern ['nɛ:ɐn] *v/refl* (*ge-*, *h*) approach, get near(er) *or* close(r) (*dat* to)
'**nahezu** *adv* nearly, almost
'**Nähgarn** *n* (sewing) cotton
'**Nahkampf** *m* MIL close combat
nahm [na:m] *pret of* ***nehmen***
'**Nähma,schine** *f* sewing machine
'**Nähnadel** *f* (sewing) needle
nähren ['nɛ:rən] *v/t* (*ge-*, *h*) feed; *fig* nurture
nahrhaft ['na:ɐhaft] *adj* nutritious, nourishing
Nährstoff ['nɛ:ɐ-] *m* nutrient
Nahrung ['na:rʊŋ] *f* (-; *no pl*) food, nourishment; AGR feed; diet
'**Nahrungsmittel** *pl* food(stuffs)
Nährwert ['nɛ:ɐ-] *m* nutritional value
Naht [na:t] *f* (-; *Nähte* ['nɛ:tə]) seam; MED suture
'**Nahverkehr** *m* local traffic
'**Nahverkehrszug** *m* local *or* commuter train
'**Nähzeug** *n* sewing kit
naiv [na'i:f] *adj* naive
Naivität [naivi'tɛ:t] *f* (-; *no pl*) naivety
Name ['na:mə] *m* (*-ns*; *-n*) name; ***im Namen von*** on behalf of; ***nur dem Namen nach*** in name only
'**namenlos** *adj* nameless, *fig a.* unspeakable
'**namens** *adv* by (the) name of, named, called
'**Namenstag** *m* name day
Namensvetter *m* namesake
Namenszug *m* signature
namentlich ['na:məntlɪç] *adj and adv* by name
nämlich ['nɛ:mlɪç] *adv* that is (to say), namely; you see *or* know
nannte ['nantə] *pret of* ***nennen***
Napf [napf] *m* (*-[e]s*; *Näpfe* ['nɛpfə]) bowl, basin
Narbe ['narbə] *f* (-; *-n*) scar
narbig ['narbɪç] *adj* scarred
Narkose [nar'ko:zə] *f* (-; *-n*) MED an(a)esthesia; ***in Narkose*** under an an(a)esthetic
Narr [nar] *m* (*-en*; *-en*) fool; ***j-n zum Narren halten*** fool s.o.
'**narrensicher** *adj* foolproof
närrisch ['nɛrɪʃ] *adj* foolish; ***närrisch vor*** (*dat*) mad with
Narzisse [nar'tsɪsə] *f* (-; *-n*) BOT daffodil
nasal [na'za:l] *adj* nasal
naschen ['naʃən] *v/i and v/t* (*ge-*, *h*) nibble (***an*** *dat* at); ***gern naschen*** have a sweet tooth
Naschereien [naʃə'raiən] *pl* dainties, goodies, sweets
'**naschhaft** *adj* sweet-toothed
Nase ['na:zə] *f* (-; *-n*) ANAT nose (*a. fig*); ***sich die Nase putzen*** blow one's nose; ***in der Nase bohren*** pick one's nose; F ***die Nase voll haben*** (***von***) be fed up (with)
'**Nasenbluten** *n* MED nosebleed
Nasenloch *n* nostril
Nasenspitze *f* tip of the nose
Nashorn *n* ZO rhinoceros, F rhino
nass [nas] *adj* wet; ***triefend nass*** soaking (wet)
Nässe ['nɛsə] *f* (-; *no pl*) wet(-ness)
'**nässen** (*ge-*, *h*) **1.** *v/t* wet; **2.** *v/i* MED weep
'**nasskalt** *adj* damp and cold, raw

Nation [na'tsjoːn] *f* (-; *-en*) nation
national [natsjo'naːl] *adj* national
Natio'nalhymne *f* national anthem
Nationalismus [natsjona'lɪsmʊs] *m* (-; *no pl*) nationalism
Nationalität [natsjonali'tɛːt] *f* (-; *-en*) nationality
Natio'nalmannschaft *f* SPORT national team
Nationalpark *m* national park
Natio'nalsozia,lismus *m* HIST National Socialism, *contp* Nazism
Natio'nalsozia,list *m*, **natio'nalsozia,listisch** *adj* HIST National Socialist, *contp* Nazi
Natter ['natɐ] *f* (-; *-n*) ZO adder, viper (*a. fig*)
Natur [na'tuːɐ] *f* (-; *-en*) nature; ***von Natur (aus)*** by nature
Naturalismus [natura'lɪsmʊs] *m* (-; *no pl*) naturalism
Na'turereignis *n*, **Naturerscheinung** *f* natural phenomenon
Naturforscher *m* naturalist
Naturgeschichte *f* natural history
Naturgesetz *n* law of nature
na'turgetreu *adj* true to life; lifelike
Na'turkata,strophe *f* (natural) catastrophe *or* disaster, act of God
natürlich [na'tyːɐlɪç] **1.** *adj* natural; **2.** *adv* naturally, of course
Na'turschätze *pl* natural resources
Naturschutz *m* nature conservation; ***unter Naturschutz*** protected
Naturschützer [-ʃʏtsɐ] *m* (-*s*; -) conservationist
Naturschutzgebiet *n* nature reserve; national park
Naturvolk *n* primitive race
Naturwissenschaft *f* (natural) science
n. Chr. ABBR *of* ***nach Christus*** AD, Anno Domini
Nebel ['neːbəl] *m* (-*s*; -) fog; mist; haze; smoke
Nebelhorn *n* foghorn
Nebelleuchte *f* MOT fog light
neben ['neːbən] *prp* (*dat and acc*) beside, next to; besides, apart from; compared with; ***neben anderem*** among other things; ***setz dich neben mich*** sit by me *or* by my side
neben'an *adv* next door
neben'bei *adv* in addition, at the same time; ***nebenbei (gesagt)*** by the way
'Nebenberuf *m* second job, sideline
'nebenberuflich *adv* as a sideline
'Nebenbuhler [-buːlɐ] *m* (-*s*; -), **'Nebenbuhlerin** *f* (-; *-nen*) rival
'nebenei'nander *adv* side by side; next (door) to each other; ***nebeneinander bestehen*** coexist
'Nebeneinkünfte *pl*, **Nebeneinnahmen** *pl* extra money
Nebenfach *n* PED *etc* minor (subject), *Br* subsidiary subject
Nebenfluss *m* tributary
Nebengebäude *n* next-door *or* adjoining building; annex(e)
Nebenhaus *n* house next door
Nebenkosten *pl* extras
Nebenmann *m*: ***dein Nebenmann*** the person next to you
Nebenpro,dukt *n* by-product
Nebenrolle *f* THEA supporting role, minor part (*a. fig*); cameo (role)
Nebensache *f* minor matter; ***das ist Nebensache*** that's of little *or* no importance
'nebensächlich *adj* unimportant
'Nebensatz *m* LING subordinate clause
Nebenstelle *f* TEL extension
Nebenstraße *f* side street; minor road
Nebenstrecke *f* RAIL branch line
Nebentisch *m* next table
Nebenverdienst *m* extra earnings
Nebenwirkung *f* side effect
Nebenzimmer *n* adjoining room
neblig ['neːblɪç] *adj* foggy; misty; hazy
necken ['nɛkən] *v/t* (*ge-*, *h*) tease
Neckerei [nɛkə'rai] *f* (-; *-en*) teasing
'neckisch *adj* playful, teasing
Neffe ['nɛfə] *m* (-*n*; *-n*) nephew
negativ ['neːgatiːf] *adj* negative
'Negativ *n* (-*s*; *-e*) PHOT negative
Neger ['neːgɐ] *m* (-*s*; -), **Negerin** ['neːgərɪn] *f* (-; *-nen*) → ***Schwarze***
nehmen ['neːmən] *v/t* (*irr*, *ge-*, *h*) take (*a. **sich nehmen***); ***j-m et. nehmen*** take s.th. (away) from s.o. (*a. fig*); ***sich e-n Tag frei nehmen*** take a day off; ***j-n an die Hand nehmen*** take s.o. by the hand
Neid [nait] *m* (-*es*; *no pl*) envy; ***reiner Neid*** sheer envy; ***neidisch*** ['naidɪʃ] *adj* envious (***auf*** *acc* of)
Neige ['naigə] *f*: ***zur Neige gehen*** draw to its close; run out
'neigen (*ge-*, *h*) **1.** *v/t and refl* bend, incline; **2.** *v/i*: ***zu et. neigen*** tend to (do) s.th.
'Neigung *f* (-; *-en*) inclination (*a. fig*), slope, incline; *fig* tendency
nein [nain] *adv* no
Nektar ['nɛktaːɐ] *m* (-*s*; *-e*) BOT nectar
Nelke ['nɛlkə] *f* (-; *-n*) BOT carnation; GASTR clove
nennen ['nɛnən] *v/t* (*irr*, *ge-*, *h*) name, call; mention; ***sich nennen*** call o.s., be called; ***man nennt ihn …*** he is called …;

N

das nenne ich ...! that's what I call ...!
'**nennenswert** *adj* worth mentioning
Nenner ['nɛnɐ] *m* (*-s*; *-*) MATH denominator
'**Nennwert** *m* ECON nominal *or* face value; ***zum Nennwert*** at par
Neo..., **neo...** [neo-] *in cpds ...faschist etc*: neo-...
Neon ['neːɔn] *n* (*-s*; *no pl*) CHEM neon
'**Neonröhre** *f* neon tube
Nepp [nɛp] F *m* (*-s*; *no pl*) rip-off
neppen ['nɛpən] F *v/t* (*ge-*, *h*) fleece, rip *s.o.* off
Nerv [nɛrf] *m* (*-s*; *-en*) ANAT nerve; ***j-m auf die Nerven fallen*** *or* ***gehen*** get on s.o.'s nerves; ***die Nerven behalten*** (***verlieren***) keep (lose) one's head
nerven ['nɛrfən] F *v/t and v/i* (*ge-*, *h*) be a pain in the neck (***j-n*** to s.o.)
'**Nervenarzt** *m*, '**Nervenärztin** *f* neurologist
'**nervenaufreibend** *adj* nerve-racking
'**Nervenbelastung** *f* nervous strain
Nervenkitzel *m* thrill, F kick(s)
'**nervenkrank** *adj* mentally ill
'**Nervensäge** F *f* pain in the neck
Nervensys,tem *n* nervous system
Nervenzusammenbruch *m* nervous breakdown
nervös [nɛr'vøːs] *adj* nervous
Nervosität [nɛrvozi'tɛːt] *f* (*-*; *no pl*) nervousness
Nerz [nɛrts] *m* (*-es*; *-e*) ZO mink
Nessel ['nɛsəl] *f* (*-*; *-n*) BOT nettle
Nest [nɛst] *n* (*-[e]s*; *-er* ['nɛstɐ]) ZO nest; F *contp* one-horse town
nett [nɛt] *adj* nice; kind; ***so nett sein und et.*** (*or* ***et. zu***) ***tun*** be so kind as to do s.th.
netto ['nɛto] *adv* ECON net
Netz [nɛts] *n* (*-es*; *-e*) net; RAIL, TEL, EDP network; ELECTR mains; ***am Netz sein*** EDP be in the network
Netzhaut *f* ANAT retina
Netzkarte *f* RAIL area season ticket
neu [nɔʏ] *adj* new; fresh; *fig* modern; ***neuere Sprachen*** modern languages; ***neueste Nachrichten*** (***Mode***) latest news (fashion); ***von neuem*** anew, afresh; ***seit neu(st)em*** since (very) recently; ***viel Neues*** a lot of new things; ***was gibt es Neues?*** what's the news?, what's new?
'**neuartig** *adj* novel
'**Neubau** *m* (*-[e]s*; *-ten*) new building
Neubaugebiet *n* new housing estate
neuerdings ['nɔʏɐ'dɪŋs] *adv* lately, recently
Neuerer ['nɔʏərɐ] *m* (*-s*; *-*) innovator
'**Neuerung** *f* (*-*; *-en*) innovation
'**Neugestaltung** *f* reorganization, reformation
'**Neugier** *f*, **Neugierde** ['nɔʏgiːɐdə] *f* (*-*; *no pl*) curiosity
'**neugierig** *adj* curious (***auf*** *acc* about); F *contp* nos(e)y; ***ich bin neugierig, ob*** I wonder if
'**Neugierige** [-giːrɪgə] *contp pl* rubbernecks
'**Neuheit** *f* (*-*; *-en*) novelty
Neuigkeit ['nɔʏɪçkait] *f* (*-*; *-en*) (piece of) news
'**Neujahr** *n* New Year('s Day); ***Prost Neujahr!*** Happy New Year!
'**neulich** *adv* the other day
Neuling ['nɔʏlɪŋ] *m* (*-s*; *-e*) newcomer, F greenhorn
'**neumodisch** *contp adj* newfangled
'**Neumond** *m* new moon
neun [nɔʏn] *adj* nine
'**neunte** *adj* ninth
'**Neuntel** *n* (*-s*; *-*) ninth (part)
'**neuntens** *adv* ninthly
'**neunzehn** *adj* nineteen
'**neunzehnte** *adj* nineteenth
'**neunzig** *adj* ninety
'**neunzigste** *adj* ninetieth
Neurose [nɔʏ'roːzə] *f* (*-*; *-n*) MED neurosis
neurotisch [nɔʏ'roːtɪʃ] *adj* MED neurotic
'**neusprachlich** *adj* modern-language
neutral [nɔʏ'traːl] *adj* neutral
Neutralität [nɔʏtrali'tɛːt] *f* (*-*; *no pl*) neutrality
Neutronen... [nɔʏ'troːnən-] PHYS *in cpds ...bombe etc*: neutron ...
Neutrum ['nɔʏtrʊm] *n* (*-s*; *-tra*) LING neuter
'**Neuverfilmung** *f* remake
'**neuwertig** *adj* as good as new
'**Neuzeit** *f* (*-*; *no pl*) modern times
nicht [nɪçt] *adv* not; ***überhaupt nicht*** not at all; ***nicht (ein)mal, gar nicht erst*** not even; ***nicht mehr*** not any more *or* longer; ***sie ist nett*** (***wohnt hier***), ***nicht*** (***wahr***)***?*** she's nice (lives here), isn't (doesn't) she?; ***nicht so ... wie*** not as ... as; ***noch nicht*** not yet; ***nicht besser*** (***als***) no (*or* not any) better (than); ***ich*** (***auch***) ***nicht*** I don't *or* I'm not (either); (***bitte***) ***nicht!*** (please) don't!
'**Nicht...** *in cpds ...mitglied*, *...schwimmer etc*: *mst* non-...
Nichtbeachtung *f* disregard; non-observance
Nichte ['nɪçtə] *f* (*-*; *-n*) niece
nichtig ['nɪçtɪç] *adj* trivial; JUR void, invalid
'**Nichtraucher** *m*, '**Nichtraucherin** *f* non-

smoker

nichts *indef pron* nothing, not anything; ***nichts (anderes) als*** nothing but; ***gar nichts*** nothing at all; F ***das ist nichts*** that's no good; ***nichts sagend*** meaningless

Nichts *n (-s; no pl)* nothing(ness); ***aus dem Nichts*** *appear etc* from nowhere; *build etc* from nothing

nichtsdesto'weniger *adv* nevertheless

'nichtsnutzig [-nʊtsɪç] *adj* good-for-nothing, worthless

'nichtssagend *adj* meaningless

'Nichtstuer [-tuːɐ] *m (-s; -)* do-nothing, F bum

nicken ['nɪkən] *v/i (ge-, h)* nod (one's head)

nie [niː] *adv* never, at no time; ***fast nie*** hardly ever; ***nie und nimmer*** never ever

nieder ['niːdɐ] **1.** *adj* low; **2.** *adv* down

'Niedergang *m (-[e]s; no pl)* decline

'niedergeschlagen *adj* depressed, (feeling) down

'Niederlage *f* defeat, F beating

'niederlassen *v/refl (irr,* ***lassen****, sep, -ge-, h)* settle (down); ECON set up (***als*** as)

'Niederlassung *f (-; -en)* ECON establishment; branch

'niederlegen *v/t (sep, -ge-, h)* lay down (*a. office etc*); ***die Arbeit niederlegen*** (go on) strike, down tools, F walk out; ***sich niederlegen*** lie down; go to bed

niedermetzeln *v/t (sep, -ge-, h)* massacre

'Niederschlag *m* METEOR rain(fall); PHYS fallout; CHEM precipitate; *boxing*: knock-down

'niederschlagen *v/t (irr,* ***schlagen****, sep, -ge-, h)* knock down; cast down (*eyes*); *fig* put down (*revolt etc*); JUR quash; ***sich niederschlagen*** CHEM precipitate

'niederschmettern *fig v/t (sep, -ge-, h)* shatter, crush

'niederträchtig *adj* base, mean

Niederung ['niːdərʊŋ] *f (-; -en)* lowland(s)

niedlich ['niːtlɪç] *adj* pretty, sweet, cute

niedrig ['niːdrɪç] *adj* low (*a. fig*); *fig* light (*sentence etc*); ***niedrig fliegen*** fly low

niemals ['niːmaːls] → ***nie***

niemand ['niːmant] *indef pron* nobody, no one, not anybody; ***niemand von ihnen*** none of them

'Niemandsland *n (-[e]s; no pl)* no-man's-land

Niere ['niːrə] *f (-; -n)* ANAT kidney

nieseln ['niːzəln] *v/i (ge-, h)* drizzle

'Nieselregen *m* drizzle

niesen ['niːzən] *v/i (ge-, h)* sneeze

Niete[1] ['niːtə] *f (-; -n)* TECH rivet

'Niete[2] *f (-; -n)* blank; F failure

Nikolaustag ['nɪkolaus-] *m* St. Nicholas' Day

Nikotin [niko'tiːn] *n (-s; no pl)* CHEM nicotine

Nilpferd ['niːl-] *n* ZO hippopotamus, F hippo

Nippel ['nɪpəl] *m (-s; -)* TECH nipple

nippen ['nɪpən] *v/i (ge-, h)* sip (***an*** *dat* at)

nirgends ['nɪrgənts] *adv* nowhere

Nische ['niːʃə] *f (-; -n)* niche, recess

nisten ['nɪstən] *v/i (ge-, h)* ZO nest

'Nistplatz *m* ZO nesting place

Niveau [ni'voː] *n (-s; -s)* level, *fig a.* standard

Nixe ['nɪksə] *f (-; -n)* water nymph, mermaid

noch [nɔx] *adv* still; ***noch nicht*** not yet; ***noch nie*** never before; ***er hat nur noch 5 Mark (Minuten)*** he has only 5 marks (minutes) left; ***(sonst) noch et.?*** anything else?; ***ich möchte noch et. (Tee)*** I'd like some more (tea); ***noch ein(e, -n)…, bitte*** another …, please; ***noch einmal*** once more *or* again; ***noch zwei Stunden*** another two hours, two hours to go; ***noch besser (schlimmer)*** even better (worse); ***noch gestern*** only yesterday; ***und wenn es noch so … ist*** however (*or* no matter how) … it may be

'nochmalig [-maːlɪç] *adj* new, renewed

'nochmals *adv* once more *or* again

Nockerl ['nɔkɐl] *Austrian n (-s; -n)* GASTR small dumpling

Nomade [no'maːdə] *m (-n; -n)*, **No'madin** *f (-; -nen)* nomad

Nominativ ['noːminatiːf] *m (-s; -e)* LING nominative (case)

nominieren [nomi'niːrən] *v/t (no -ge-, h)* nominate

Nonne ['nɔnə] *f (-; -n)* REL nun

'Nonnenkloster *n* REL convent

Norden ['nɔrdən] *m (-s; no pl)* north; ***nach Norden*** north(wards)

nordisch ['nɔrdɪʃ] *adj* northern; SPORT ***nordische Kombination*** Nordic Combined

nördlich ['nœrtlɪç] **1.** *adj* north(ern); northerly; **2.** *adv*: ***nördlich von*** north of

Nordlicht ['nɔrt-] *n (-[e]s; -er)* ASTR northern lights

Nord'osten *m* northeast

nord'östlich *adj* northeast(ern); northeasterly

'Nordpol *m* North Pole

Nord'westen *m* northwest

nord'westlich *adj* northwest(ern); northwesterly

'Nordwind *m* north wind

nörgeln ['nœrgəln] *v/i (ge-, h)* nag (***an*** *dat*

N

at)
Nörgler ['nœrglɐ] *m* (-*s*; -), '**Nörglerin** *f* (-; -*nen*) nagger
Norm [nɔrm] *f* (-; -*en*) standard, norm
normal [nɔr'maːl] *adj* normal; F ***nicht ganz normal*** not quite right in the head
Nor'mal... *esp* TECH *in cpds ...maß, ...zeit etc*: standard ...
Normalben,zin *n* regular (gas, *Br* petrol)
normalerweise [nɔr'maːlɐ'vaizə] *adv* normally, usually
normalisieren [nɔrmali'ziːrən] *v/refl* (*no -ge-, h*) return to normal
normen ['nɔrmən] *v/t* (*ge-, h*) standardize
Norwegen ['nɔrveːgən] Norway
Norweger ['nɔrveːgɐ] *m* (-*s*; -), '**Norwegerin** [-gərɪn] *f* (-; -*nen*), '**norwegisch** *adj* Norwegian
Not [noːt] *f* (-; *Nöte* ['nøːtə]) need; want; poverty; hardship, misery; difficulty; emergency; distress; ***Not leidend*** needy; ***in Not sein*** be in trouble; ***zur Not*** if need be, if necessary
Notar [no'taːɐ] *m* (-*s*; -*e*), **No'tarin** *f* (-; -*nen*) JUR notary (public)
'**Notaufnahme** *f* MED emergency room, *Br* casualty
Notausgang *m* emergency exit
Notbehelf *m* (-[*e*]*s*; -*e*) makeshift, expedient
Notbremse *f* emergency brake
Notdienst *m* emergency duty
'**notdürftig** *adj* scanty; temporary
Note ['noːtə] *f* (-; -*n*) note (*a.* MUS *and* POL); ECON bill, *esp Br* (bank)note; PED grade, *Br* mark; *pl* MUS (sheet) music; ***Noten lesen*** read music
Notebook ['noutbuk] *n* (-*s*; -*s*) EDP notebook
'**Notendurchschnitt** *m* PED *etc* average
'**Notenständer** *m* music stand
'**Notfall** *m* emergency
'**notfalls** *adv* if necessary
'**notgedrungen** *adv*: ***et. notgedrungen tun*** be forced to do s.th.
notieren [no'tiːrən] *v/t* (*no -ge-, h*) make a note of, note (down); ECON quote
nötig ['nøːtɪç] *adj* necessary; ***nötig haben*** need; ***nötig brauchen*** need badly; ***das Nötigste*** the (bare) necessities *or* essentials
nötigen ['nøːtɪgən] *v/t* (*ge-, h*) force, compel; press, urge
'**Nötigung** *f* (-; -*en*) coercion; JUR intimidation
Notiz [no'tiːts] *f* (-; -*en*) note; ***keine Notiz nehmen von*** take no notice of, ignore; ***sich Notizen machen*** take notes
Notizblock *m* memo pad, *Br* notepad
Notizbuch *n* notebook
'**Notlage** *f* awkward (*or* difficult) situation; difficulties; emergency
'**notlanden** *v/i* (*-ge-, sein*) AVIAT make an emergency landing
'**Notlandung** *f* AVIAT emergency landing
'**Notlösung** *f* expedient
'**Notlüge** *f* white lie
notorisch [no'toːrɪʃ] *adj* notorious
'**Notruf** *m* TEL emergency call
Notrufsäule *f* TEL emergency phone
Notsig,nal *n* emergency *or* distress signal
Notstand *m* state of (national) emergency
Notstandsgebiet *n* disaster area; ECON depressed area
Notstandsgesetze *pl* POL emergency laws
Notverband *m* MED emergency dressing
'**Notwehr** *f* (-; *no pl*) JUR self-defense, *Br* self-defence
'**notwendig** *adj* necessary
'**Notwendigkeit** *f* (-; -*en*) necessity
'**Notzucht** *f* (-; *no pl*) JUR rape
Novelle [no'vɛlə] *f* (-; -*n*) novella; PARL amendment
November [no'vɛmbɐ] *m* (-[*s*]; -) November
Nr. ABBR *of* ***Nummer*** No., no., number
Nu [nuː] *m*: ***im Nu*** in no time
Nuance ['nyãːsə] *f* shade
nüchtern ['nʏçtɐn] *adj* sober (*a. fig*); matter-of-fact; ***auf nüchternen Magen*** on an empty stomach; ***nüchtern werden*** (***machen***) sober up
'**Nüchternheit** *f* (-; *no pl*) sobriety
Nudel ['nuːdəl] *f* (-; -*n*) noodle
nuklear [nukle'aːɐ] *adj* nuclear
null [nʊl] *adj* zero, *Br* nought; TEL 0; SPORT nil, nothing; *tennis*: love; ***null Grad*** zero degrees; ***null Fehler*** no mistakes; ***gleich Null sein*** be nil
'**Nulldi,ät** *f* low-calorie (*or* F starvation) diet
Nullpunkt *m* zero (point *or fig* level)
Nullta,rif *m* free fare(s); ***zum Nulltarif*** free (of charge)
Numerus clausus ['nuːmerʊs 'klauzʊs] *m* (-; *no pl*) UNIV restricted admission(s)
Nummer ['nʊmɐ] *f* (-; -*n*) number; issue; size
nummerieren [nʊmə'riːrən] *v/t* (*no -ge-, h*) number
'**Nummernschild** *n* MOT license plate, *Br* numberplate
nun [nuːn] *adv* now; well
nur [nuːɐ] *adv* only, just; merely; nothing but; ***er tut nur so*** he's just pretending; ***nur so*** (***zum Spaß***) just for fun; ***warte nur!*** just you wait!; ***mach nur!, nur zu!*** go ahead!; → ***Erwachsene***

N

Nuss [nʊs] *f* (-; *Nüsse* ['nʏsə]) BOT nut
Nussbaum *m* walnut (tree)
Nussknacker *m* nutcracker
Nussschale *f* nutshell
Nüstern ['nʏstɐn] *pl* ZO nostrils
Nutte ['nʊtə] F *f* (-; *-n*) hooker, *sl* tart
Nutzanwendung ['nʊts-] *f* practical application
'nutzbar *adj* usable; ***nutzbar machen*** utilize; exploit; harness
'nutzbringend *adj* profitable, useful
nütze ['nʏtsə] *adj* useful; ***zu nichts nütze sein*** be (of) no use; be good for nothing
Nutzen ['nʊtsən] *m* (-*s*; -) use; profit, gain; advantage; ***Nutzen ziehen aus*** (*dat*) benefit *or* profit from *or* by; ***zum Nutzen von*** (*or gen*) for the benefit of
'nutzen, 'nützen (*ge-, h*) **1.** *v/i*: ***j-m nutzen*** be of use to s.o.; ***es nützt nichts*** (***es zu tun***) it's no use (doing it); **2.** *v/t* use, make use of; take advantage of
nützlich ['nʏtslɪç] *adj* useful, helpful; advantageous; ***sich nützlich machen*** make o.s. useful
'nutzlos *adj* useless, (of) no use
'Nutzung *f* (-; *-en*) use, utilization
Nylon® ['nailɔn] *n* (-*s*; *no pl*) nylon
Nylonstrümpfe *pl* nylon stockings
Nymphe ['nʏmfə] *f* (-; *-n*) nymph

O

O ABBR *of* ***Osten*** E, east
o *int* oh!; ***o weh!*** oh dear!
o. Ä. ABBR *of* ***oder Ähnliche(s)*** or the like
Oase [o'a:zə] *f* (-; *-n*) oasis (*a. fig*)
ob [ɔp] *cj* whether, if; ***als ob*** as if, as though; ***und ob!*** and how!, you bet!
Obacht ['o:baxt] *f*: ***Obacht geben auf*** (*acc*) pay attention to; (***gib***) ***Obacht!*** watch out!
Obdach ['ɔpdax] *n* (-[*e*]*s*; *no pl*) shelter
'obdachlos *adj* homeless, without shelter
'Obdachlose *m, f* (-*n*; *-n*) homeless person
'Obdachlosena,syl *n* shelter for the homeless
Obduktion [ɔpdʊk'tsjo:n] *f* (-; *-en*) MED autopsy
obduzieren [ɔpdu'tsi:rən] *v/t* (*no -ge-, h*) MED perform an autopsy on
oben ['o:bən] *adv* above; up; on (the) top; at the top (*a. fig*); on the surface; upstairs; ***da oben*** up there; ***von oben bis unten*** from top to bottom (*or* toe); ***links oben*** (at the) top left; ***siehe oben*** see above; F ***oben ohne*** topless; ***von oben herab*** *fig* patronizing(ly), condescending(ly); ***oben erwähnt*** *or* ***genannt*** above-mentioned
oben'an *adv* at the top
oben'auf *adv* on the top; on the surface; F feeling great
oben'drein *adv* besides, into the bargain, at that
oben'hin *adv* superficially
Ober ['o:bɐ] *m* (-*s*; -) waiter
'Oberarm *m* ANAT upper arm
Oberarzt *m*, **Oberärztin** *f* assistant medical director
Oberbefehl *m* MIL supreme command
Oberbegriff *n* generic term
Oberbürgermeister *m* mayor, *Br* Lord Mayor
obere ['o:bərə] *adj* upper, top, *fig a.* superior
'Oberfläche *f* surface (*a. fig*) (***an*** *dat* on)
'oberflächlich *adj* superficial
'oberhalb *prp* (*gen*) above
'Oberhand *f*: ***die Oberhand gewinnen*** (***über*** *acc*) get the upper hand (of)
Oberhaupt *n* head, chief
Oberhaus *n* (-*es*; *no pl*) *Br* PARL House of Lords
Oberhemd *n* shirt
Oberherrschaft *f* (-; *no pl*) supremacy
Oberin ['o:bərɪn] *f* (-; *-nen*) REL Mother Superior
'oberirdisch *adj* above ground; ELECTR overhead
'Oberkellner *m* head waiter
Oberkiefer *m* ANAT upper jaw
Oberkörper *m* upper part of the body; ***den Oberkörper frei machen*** strip to the waist
Oberleder *n* uppers
Oberleitung *f* chief management; ELECTR overhead contact line
Oberlippe *f* ANAT upper lip
Obers ['o:bɐs] *Austrian n* (-; *no pl*) GASTR

cream

'Oberschenkel *m* ANAT thigh

'Oberschule *f appr* highschool, *Br* grammar school

Oberst ['oːbɐst] *m* (*-en*; *-en*) MIL colonel

oberste ['oːbɐstə] *adj* up(per)most, top (-most); highest; *fig* chief, first

'Oberstufe *f appr* senior highschool, *Br appr* senior classes

Oberteil *n* top

ob'gleich *cj* (al)though

Obhut ['ɔphuːt] *f* (-; *no pl*) care, charge; ***in s-e Obhut nehmen*** take care *or* charge of

obig ['oːbɪç] *adj* above(-mentioned)

Objekt [ɔp'jɛkt] *n* (-[*e*]*s*; *-e*) object (*a.* LING); ECON property

objektiv [ɔpjɛk'tiːf] *adj* objective; impartial, unbias(s)ed

Objek'tiv *n* (*-s*; *-e*) PHOT (object) lens

Objektivität [ɔpjɛktivi'tɛːt] *f* (-; *no pl*) objectivity; impartiality

Oblate [o'blaːtə] *f* (-; *-n*) wafer; REL host

obligatorisch [obliga'toːrɪʃ] *adj* compulsory

Oboe [o'boːə] *f* (-; *-n*) MUS oboe

Oboist [obo'ɪst] *m* (*-en*; *-en*) MUS oboist

Observatorium [ɔpzɛrva'toːrjʊm] *n* (*-s*; *-ien*) ASTR observatory

Obst [oːpst] *n* (-[*e*]*s*; *no pl*) fruit

Obstgarten *m* orchard

Obstkon,serven *pl* canned fruit

Obstladen *m* fruit store, *esp Br* fruiterer's (shop)

Obsttorte *f* fruit pie (*Br* flan)

obszön [ɔps'tsøːn] *adj* obscene, filthy

ob'wohl *cj* (al)though

Occasion [ɔka'zjoːn] *Swiss f* (-; *-en*) bargain, good buy

Ochse ['ɔksə] *m* (*-n*; *-n*) ZO ox, bullock; F blockhead

od. ABBR *of* ***oder*** or

öde ['øːdə] *adj* deserted, desolate; waste; *fig* dull, dreary, tedious

oder ['oːdɐ] *cj* or; ***oder aber*** or else, otherwise; ***oder vielmehr*** or rather; ***oder so*** or so; ***er kommt doch, oder?*** he's coming, isn't he?; ***du kennst ihn ja nicht, oder doch?*** you don't know him, or do you?

Ofen ['oːfən] *m* (*-s*; *Öfen* ['øːfən]) stove; oven; TECH furnace

Ofenheizung *f* stove heating

Ofenrohr *n* stovepipe

offen ['ɔfən] **1.** *adj* open (*a. fig*); vacant (*post*); *fig* frank; **2.** *adv*: ***offen gesagt*** frankly (speaking); ***offen s-e Meinung sagen*** speak one's mind (freely); ***offen stehen*** be open; ECON be outstanding

'offenbar *adj* obvious, evident; apparent

offenbaren [-'baːrən] *v/t* (*ge-*, *h*) reveal, disclose, show

Offen'barung *f* (-; *-en*) revelation

'Offenheit *f* (-; *no pl*) openness, frankness

'offenherzig *adj* open-hearted, frank, candid; *fig* revealing (*dress*)

'offensichtlich *adj* → ***offenbar***

offensiv [ɔfɛn'ziːf] adj, **Offensive** [ɔfɛn'ziːvə] *f* (-; *-n*) offensive

'offenstehen *v/i* (*irr*, ***stehen***, *sep*, *-ge-*, *h*): ***j-m offenstehen*** *fig* be open to s.o.

öffentlich ['œfəntlɪç] *adj* public; ***öffentliche Verkehrsmittel*** *pl* public transport; ***öffentliche Schulen*** *pl* public (*Br* state) schools; ***öffentlich auftreten*** appear in public

'Öffentlichkeit *f* (-; *no pl*) *the* public; ***in aller Öffentlichkeit*** in public, openly; ***an die Öffentlichkeit bringen*** make public

offiziell [ɔfi'tsjɛl] *adj* official

Offizier [ɔfi'tsiːɐ] *m* (*-s*; *-e*) MIL (commissioned) officer

öffnen ['œfnən] *v/t and v/refl* (*ge-*, *h*) open

Öffner ['œfnɐ] *m* (*-s*; -) opener

'Öffnung *f* (-; *-en*) opening

'Öffnungszeiten *pl* business *or* office hours

oft [ɔft] *adv* often, frequently

oh [oː] *int* o(h)!

ohne ['oːnə] *prp* (*acc*) *and cj* without; ***ohne mich!*** count me out!; ***ohne ein Wort*** (***zu sagen***) without (saying) a word

ohne'gleichen *adv* unequal(l)ed, unparalleled

ohne'hin *adv* anyhow, anyway

Ohnmacht ['oːnmaxt] *f* (-; *-en*) MED unconsciousness; *fig* helplessness; ***in Ohnmacht fallen*** faint, pass out

'ohnmächtig *adj* MED unconscious; *fig* helpless; ***ohnmächtig werden*** faint, pass out

Ohr [oːɐ] *n* (-[*e*]*s*; *-en* ['oːrən]) ANAT ear; F ***j-n übers Ohr hauen*** cheat s.o.; ***bis über die Ohren verliebt*** (***verschuldet***) head over heels in love (over your head in debt)

Öhr [øːɐ] *n* (-[*e*]*s*; *-e* ['øːrə]) eye

Ohrenarzt ['oːrən-] *m* ear specialist

'ohrenbetäubend *adj* deafening

'Ohrenschmerzen *pl* earache

Ohrenschützer *pl* earmuffs

Ohrenzeuge *m* earwitness

'Ohrfeige *f* slap in the face (*a. fig*)

'ohrfeigen [-faigən] *v/t* (*ge-*, *h*) ***j-n ohrfeigen*** slap s.o.'s face

'Ohrläppchen [-lɛpçən] *n* (*-s*; -) ANAT earlobe

Ohrring *m* earring
oje [o'je:] *int* oh dear!, dear me!
Ökologe [øko'lo:gə] *m* (*-n*; *-n*) ecologist
Ökologie [økolo'gi:] *f* (-; *no pl*) ecology
ökologisch [øko'lo:gɪʃ] *adj* ecological
Ökonomie [økono'mi:] *f* (-; *no pl*) economy; ECON economics
ökonomisch [øko'no:mɪʃ] *adj* economical; ECON economic
Ökosys'tem ['ø:ko-] *n* ecosystem
Oktave [ɔk'ta:və] *f* (-; *-n*) MUS octave
Oktober [ɔk'to:bɐ] *m* (-[*s*]; -) October
ökumenisch [øku'me:nɪʃ] *adj* REL ecumenical
Öl [ø:l] *n* (-[*e*]*s*; *Öle*) oil; petroleum; ***nach Öl bohren*** drill for oil; ***auf Öl stoßen*** strike oil
'Ölbaum *m* BOT olive (tree)
Oldtimer ['ouldtaɪmə] *m* (*-s*; -) MOT veteran car
ölen ['ø:lən] *v/t* (*ge-*, *h*) oil, TECH *a.* lubricate
'Ölfarbe *f* oil (paint)
Ölfeld *n* oilfield
Ölförderland *n* oil-producing country
Ölförderung *f* oil production
Ölgemälde *n* oil painting
Ölheizung *f* oil heating
ölig ['ø:lɪç] *adj* oily, greasy (*both a. fig*)
oliv [o'li:f] *adj* olive
Olive [o'li:və] *f* (-; *-n*) BOT olive
'Ölleitung *f* (oil) pipeline
Ölmesstab *m* MOT dipstick
Ölpest *f* oil pollution
Ölquelle *f* oil well
Ölsar'dine *f* canned (*Br a.* tinned) sardine
Öltanker *m* MAR oil tanker
Ölteppich *m* oil slick
Ölstand *m* oil level
'Ölung *f* (-; *no pl*) oiling, TECH *a.* lubrication; ***Letzte Ölung*** REL extreme unction
'Ölwanne *f* MOT oil pan, *Br* sump
Ölwechsel *m* MOT oil change
Ölzeug *n* oilskins
Olympia... [o'lʏmpja-] *in cpds ...mannschaft*, *...medaille etc*: Olympic ...
Olympiade [olʏm'pja:də] *f* (-; *-n*) SPORT Olympic Games, Olympics
Oma ['o:ma] F *f* (-; *-s*) grandma
Omi ['o:mi] F *f* (-; *-s*) granny
Omnibus ['ɔmnibʊs] *m* → ***Bus***
onanieren [ona'ni:rən] *v/i* (*no -ge-*, *h*) masturbate
Onkel ['ɔŋkəl] *m* (*-s*; -) uncle
Online... ['ɔnlain-] EDP online ...
Opa ['o:pa] F *m* (*-s*; *-s*) grandpa
Oper ['o:pɐ] *f* (-; *-n*) MUS opera; opera (house)
Operation [opəra'tsjo:n] *f* (-; *-en*) MED operation; ***e-e Operation vornehmen*** perform an operation
Operati'onssaal *m* MED operating room (*Br* theatre)
Operette [opə'rɛtə] *f* (-; *-n*) MUS operetta
operieren [opə'ri:rən] (*no -ge-*, *h*) **1.** *v/t* MED ***j-n operieren*** operate on s.o. (***wegen*** for); ***operiert werden*** be operated on, have an operation; ***sich operieren lassen*** undergo an operation; **2.** *v/i* MED, MIL operate; proceed
'Opernsänger(in) opera singer
Opfer ['ɔpfɐ] *n* (*-s*; -) sacrifice; offering; victim; ***ein Opfer bringen*** make a sacrifice; (*dat*) ***zum Opfer fallen*** fall victim to
'opfern *v/t and v/i* (*ge-*, *h*) sacrifice
Opium ['o:pjʊm] *n* (*-s*; *no pl*) opium
Opposition [ɔpozi'tsjo:n] *f* (-; *-en*) opposition (*a.* PARL)
Optik ['ɔptɪk] *f* (-; *no pl*) optics; PHOT optical system
Optiker ['ɔptikɐ] *m* (*-s*; -), **'Optikerin** *f* (-; *-nen*) optician
optimal [ɔpti'ma:l] *adj* optimum, best
Optimismus [ɔpti'mɪsmʊs] *m* (-; *no pl*) optimism
Optimist(in) [ɔpti'mɪst(ɪn)] (*-en*; *-en*/-; *-nen*) optimist
opti'mistisch *adj* optimistic
Option [ɔp'tsjo:n] *f* (-; *-en*) option
optisch ['ɔptɪʃ] *adj* optical
Orange [o'rã:ʒə] *f* (-; *-n*) BOT orange
Orchester [ɔr'kɛstɐ] *n* (*-s*; -) MUS orchestra
Orchidee [ɔrçi'de:] *f* (-; *-n*) bot orchid
Orden ['ɔrdən] *m* (*-s*; -) medal, decoration; *esp* REL order
'Ordensschwester *f* REL sister, nun
ordentlich ['ɔrdəntlɪç] **1.** *adj* tidy, neat, orderly; proper; thorough; decent (*a.* F); respectable; full (*member etc*); JUR ordinary; reasonable (*performance etc*); F good, sound; **2.** *adv*: ***s-e Sache ordentlich machen*** do a good job; ***sich ordentlich benehmen*** (***anziehen***) behave (dress) properly *or* decently
ordinär [ɔrdi'nɛ:ɐ] *adj* vulgar; common
ordnen ['ɔrdnən] *v/t* (*ge-*, *h*) put in order; arrange, sort (out); file; settle
Ordner ['ɔrdnɐ] *m* (*-s*; -) file; folder; attendant, guard
'Ordnung *f* (-; *no pl*) order; orderliness, tidiness; arrangement; system, set-up; class; ***in Ordnung*** all right; TECH *etc* in (good) order; ***in Ordnung bringen*** put right (*a. fig*); tidy up; repair, fix (*a. fig*); (***in***) ***Ordnung halten*** keep (in) order; ***et. ist nicht in Ordnung*** (***mit***) there is s.th. wrong (with)

O

'ordnungsgemäß **1.** *adj* correct, regular; **2.** *adv* duly, properly
'Ordnungsstrafe *f* JUR fine, penalty
Ordnungszahl *f* MATH ordinal number
Organ [ɔr'ga:n] *n* (*-s*; *-e*) organ
Organempfänger *m* MED organ recipient
Organhandel *m* sale of (transplant) organs
Organisation [ɔrganiza'tsjo:n] *f* (*-*; *-en*) organization
Organisator [ɔrgani'za:to:ɐ] *m* (*-s*; *-en* [-za'to:rən]) organizer
Organisa'torin *f* (*-*; *-nen*) organizer
organisatorisch [-za'to:rɪʃ] *adj* organizational
organisch [ɔr'ga:nɪʃ] *adj* organic
organisieren [ɔrgani'zi:rən] *v/t* organize; F get (hold of); ***sich organisieren*** organize; ECON unionize
organisiert [ɔrgani'zi:ɐt] *adj* organized; ECON unionized
Organismus [ɔrga'nɪsmʊs] *m* (*-*; *-men*) BIOL organism
Organist [ɔrga'nɪst] *m* (*-en*; *-en*), **Orga'nistin** *f* (*-*; *-nen*) MUS organist
Or'ganspender *m* MED (organ) donor
Orgasmus [ɔr'gasmʊs] *m* (*-*; *-men*) orgasm
Orgel ['ɔrgəl] *f* (*-*; *-n*) MUS organ
'Orgelpfeife *f* MUS organ pipe
Orgie ['ɔrgjə] *f* (*-*; *-n*) orgy
Orientale [orjɛn'ta:lə] *m* (*-n*; *-n*), **Orien'talin** *f* (*-*; *-nen*), **orien'talisch** *adj* oriental
orientieren [orjɛn'ti:rən] *v/t* (*no -ge-*, *h*) inform (***über*** *acc* about), brief (on); ***sich orientieren*** orient(ate) o.s. (*a. fig*) (***nach*** by); inform o.s.
Orien'tierung *f* (*-*; *no pl*) orientation, *fig a.* information; ***die Orientierung verlieren*** lose one's bearings
Orien'tierungssinn *m* (*-[e]s*; *no pl*) sense of direction
original [origi'na:l] *adj* original; real, genuine; TV live
Origi'nal *n* (*-s*; *-e*) original; *fig* real (*or* quite a) character
Origi'nal... *in cpds ...aufnahme, ...ausgabe etc*: original ...
Originalübertragung *f* live broadcast *or* program(me)
originell [origi'nɛl] *adj* original; ingenious; witty
Orkan [ɔr'ka:n] *m* (*-[e]s*; *-e*) hurricane
or'kanartig *adj* violent; *fig* thunderous
Ort [ɔrt] *m* (*-[e]s*; *-e*) place; village, (small) town; spot, point; scene; ***vor Ort*** *mining*: at the (pit) face; *fig* in the field, on the spot
orten ['ɔrtən] *v/t* (*ge-*, *h*) locate, spot
orthodox [ɔrto'dɔks] *adj* orthodox
Orthographie [ɔrtogra'fi:] *f* (*-*; *-n*) orthography
Orthopäde [ɔrto'pɛ:də] *m* (*-n*; *-n*), **Ortho'pädin** *f* (*-*; *-nen*) MED orthop(a)edic specialist
örtlich ['œrtlɪç] *adj* local
'Ortsbestimmung *f* AVIAT, MAR location; LING adverb of place
'Ortschaft *f* → ***Ort***
'Ortsgespräch *n* TEL local call
'Ortskenntnis *f*: ***Ortskenntnis besitzen*** know a place
'Ortsnetz *n* TEL local exchange
'Ortszeit *f* local time
Öse ['ø:zə] *f* (*-*; *-n*) eye; eyelet
Ostblock ['ɔst-] *m* (*-[e]s*; *no pl*) HIST POL East(ern) Bloc
Osten ['ɔstən] *m* (*-s*; *no pl*) east; POL *the* East; ***nach Osten*** east(wards)
Osterei ['o:stɐ-] *n* Easter egg
Osterhase *m* Easter bunny *or* rabbit
Ostern ['o:stɐn] *n* (*-*; *-*) Easter (***zu, an*** at); ***frohe Ostern!*** Happy Easter!
Österreicher ['ø:stəraiçe] *m* (*-s*; *-*), **'Österreicherin** [-raiçərɪn] *f* (*-*; *-nen*), **'österreichisch** *adj* Austrian
östlich ['œstlɪç] **1.** *adj* east(ern); easterly; **2.** *adv*: ***östlich von*** (to the) east of
ostwärts ['ɔstvɛrts] *adv* east(wards)
'Ostwind *m* east wind
Otter ['ɔtɐ] ZO **1.** *m* (*-s*; *-*) otter; **2.** *f* (*-*; *-n*) adder, viper
outen ['autən] *v/t* (*ge-*, *h*) out
Ouvertüre [uvɛr'ty:rə] *f* (*-*; *-n*) MUS overture
oval [o'va:l] adj, **O'val** *n* (*-s*; *-e*) oval
Oxid [ɔ'ksi:t] *n* (*-[e]s*; *-e* [ɔ'ksi:də]) CHEM oxide
oxidieren [ɔksi'di:rən] *v/t* (*no -ge-*, *h*) *and v/i* (*h*, *sein*) CHEM oxidize
Oxyd *n* → ***Oxid***
Ozean ['o:tsea:n] *m* (*-s*; *-e*) ocean, sea
Ozon [o'tso:n] *n* (*-s*; *no pl*) CHEM ozone
o'zonfreundlich *adj* ozone-friendly
O'zonloch *n* ozone hole
Ozonschicht *f* ozone layer
Ozonschild *m* ozone shield
Ozonwerte *pl* ozone levels

P

paar [paːɐ] *indef pron*: ***ein paar*** a few, some, F a couple of; ***ein paar Mal*** a few times
Paar *n* (-[*e*]*s*; -*e*) pair; couple; ***ein Paar*** (***neue***) ***Schuhe*** a (new) pair of shoes
paaren ['paːrən] *v/t and v/refl* (*ge-*, *h*) ZO mate; *fig* combine
'Paarlauf *m* SPORT pair skating
'Paarung *f* (-; -*en*) ZO mating, copulation; SPORT matching
'paarweise *adv* in pairs, in twos
Pacht [paxt] *f* (-; -*en*) lease; rent
'pachten *v/t* (*ge-*, *h*) (take on) lease
Pächter ['pɛçtɐ] *m* (-*s*; -), **'Pächterin** *f* (-; -*nen*) leaseholder; AGR tenant
'Pachtvertrag *m* lease
Pachtzins *m* rent
Pack[1] [pak] *m* → ***Packen***
Pack[2] *contp n* (-[*e*]*s*; *no pl*) rabble
Päckchen ['pɛkçən] *n* (-*s*; -) pack, *Br* packet; small parcel
packen ['pakən] *v/t and v/i* (*ge-*, *h*) pack; make up (*parcel etc*); grab, seize (***an*** *dat* by); *fig* grip
'Packen *m* (-*s*; -) pack, pile (*a. fig*)
Packer ['pakɐ] *m* (-*s*; -) packer; removal man
'Packpa,pier *n* packing *or* brown paper
'Packung *f* (-; -*en*) package, box; pack, *Br* packet
Pädagoge [pɛda'goːgə] *m* (-*n*; -*n*), **Päda'gogin** *f* (-; -*nen*) teacher; education(al)ist
päda'gogisch *adj* pedagogic, educational; ***pädagogische Hochschule*** college of education
Paddel ['padəl] *n* (-*s*; -) paddle
'Paddelboot *n* canoe
'paddeln *v/i* (*ge-*, *h*, *sein*) paddle, canoe
Page ['paːʒə] *m* (-*n*; -*n*) page(boy)
Paket [pa'keːt] *n* (-[*e*]*s*; -*e*) package; parcel
Paketkarte *f* parcel post slip, *Br* parcel mailing form
Paketpost *f* parcel post
Paketschalter *m* parcel counter
Paketzustellung *f* parcel delivery
Pakt [pakt] *m* (-[*e*]*s*; -*e*) POL pact
Palast [pa'last] *m* (-[*e*]*s*; *Paläste* [pa'lɛstə]) palace
Palme ['palmə] *f* (-; -*n*) BOT palm (tree)
Palm'sonntag *m* REL Palm Sunday
Pampelmuse ['pampəlmuːzə] *f* (-; -*n*) BOT grapefruit
paniert [pa'niːɐt] *adj* GASTR breaded
Panik ['paːnɪk] *f* (-; -*en*) panic; ***in Panik geraten*** (***versetzen***) panic; ***in Panik*** panic-stricken, F panicky
panisch ['paːnɪʃ] *adj*: ***panische Angst*** mortal terror
Panne ['panə] *f* (-; -*n*) breakdown, MOT *a.* engine trouble; *fig* mishap
'Pannenhilfe *f* MOT breakdown service
Panter, Panther ['pantɐ] *m* (-*s*; -) ZO panther
Pantoffel [pan'tɔfəl] *m* (-*s*; -*n*) slipper
Pantoffelheld F *m* henpecked husband
Pantomime [panto'miːmə] THEA **1.** *f* (-; -*n*) mime, dumb show; **2.** *m* (-*n*; -*n*) mime (artist)
panto'mimisch *adv*: ***pantomimisch darstellen*** mime
Panzer ['pantsɐ] *m* (-*s*; -) armo(u)r (*a. fig*); MIL tank; ZO shell
Panzerglas *n* bulletproof glass
'panzern *v/t* (*ge-*, *h*) armo(u)r; → ***gepanzert***
'Panzerschrank *m* safe
Panzerung ['pantsərʊŋ] *f* (-; -*en*) armo(u)r plating
Papa [pa'paː] F *m* (-*s*; -*s*) dad(dy), pa
Papagei [papa'gai] *m* (-*en*; -*en*) ZO parrot
Papeterie [papɛtə'riː] *Swiss f* (-; -*n*) stationer('s shop)
Papier [pa'piːɐ] *n* (-*s*; -*e*) paper; *pl* papers, documents; identification (paper)
Pa'pier... *in cpds* ...*geld*, ...*handtuch*, ...*serviette*, ...*tüte etc*: *mst* paper ...
Papiergeschäft *n* stationer('s store, *Br* shop)
Papierkorb *m* wastepaper basket
Papierkrieg F *m* red tape
Papierschnitzel *pl* scraps of paper
Papierwaren *pl* stationery
Pappe ['papə] *f* (-; -*n*) cardboard, pasteboard
Pappel ['papəl] *f* (-; -*n*) BOT poplar
'Pappkar,ton *m* cardboard box, carton
Pappteller *m* paper plate
Paprika ['paprika] *m* (-*s*; -[*s*]) a) BOT sweet pepper, b) (*no pl*) GASTR paprika
Papst [paːpst] *m* (-[*e*]*s*; *Päpste* ['pɛːpstə]) pope
'päpstlich *adj* papal
Parade [pa'raːdə] *f* (-; -*n*) parade; *soccer etc*: save; *boxing*, *fencing*: parry
Paradeiser [para'daizɐ] *Austrian m* (-*s*; -) BOT tomato
Paradies [para'diːs] *n* (-*es*; -*e*) paradise

paradiesisch [para'di:zɪʃ] *fig adj* heavenly, delightful
paradox [para'dɔks] *adj* paradoxical
Paragraph [para'gra:f] *m (-en; -en)* JUR article, section; paragraph
parallel [para'le:l] adj, **Paral'lele** *f (-; -n)* parallel
Parasit [para'zi:t] *m (-en; -en)* parasite
Parfüm [par'fy:m] *n (-s; -s)* perfume, *Br a.* scent
Parfümerie [parfymə'ri:] *f (-; -n)* perfumery
parfümieren [parfy'mi:rən] *v/t (no -ge-, h)* perfume, scent; ***sich parfümieren*** put on perfume
parieren [pa'ri:rən] *v/t and v/i (no -ge-, h)* SPORT parry, *fig a.* counter (***mit*** with); pull up (*horse*); obey
Park [park] *m (-s; -s)* park
parken ['parkən] *v/i and v/t (ge-, h)* MOT park; ***Parken verboten!*** no parking!
Parkett [par'kɛt] *n (-[e]s; -e, -s)* parquet (floor); THEA orchestra, *Br* stalls; dance floor
'Parkgebühr *f* parking fee
Park(hoch-)haus *n* parking garage, *Br* multi-storey car park
parkieren [par'ki:rən] *Swiss v/t and v/i* → ***parken***
'Parkkralle *f* wheel clamp
Parklücke *f* parking space
Parkplatz *m* parking lot, *Br* car park; → ***Parklücke***; ***e-n Parkplatz suchen (finden)*** look for (find) somewhere to park the car
Parkscheibe *f* parking disk (*Br* disc)
Parksünder *m* parking offender
Parkuhr *f* MOT parking meter
Parkwächter *m* park keeper; MOT parking lot (*Br* car park) attendant
Parlament [parla'mɛnt] *n (-[e]s; -e)* parliament
parlamentarisch [parlamɛn'ta:rɪʃ] *adj* parliamentary
Parodie [paro'di:] *f (-; -n)*, **paro'dieren** *v/t (no -ge-, h)* parody
Parole [pa'ro:lə] *f (-n; -n)* MIL password; *fig* watchword, POL *a.* slogan
Partei [par'tai] *f (-; -en)* party (*a.* POL); ***j-s Partei ergreifen*** take sides with s.o., side with s.o.
par'teiisch *adj* partial (***für*** to); prejudiced (***gegen*** against)
par'teilos *adj* POL independent
Par'teimitglied *n* POL party member
Parteipro,gramm *n* POL platform
Parteitag *m* POL convention
Parteizugehörigkeit *f* POL party membership
Parterre [par'tɛrə] *n (-s; -s)* first (*Br* ground) floor
Partie [par'ti:] *f (-; -n)* game, SPORT *a.* match; part, passage (*a.* MUS); ***e-e gute*** *etc* ***Partie sein*** be a good *etc* match
Partisan [parti'za:n] *m (-s; -en; -en)*, **Par'ti'sanin** *f (-; -nen)* MIL partisan, guerilla
Partitur [parti'tu:ɐ] *f (-; -en)* MUS score
Partizip [parti'tsi:p] *n (-s; -ien)* LING participle
Partner ['partnɐ] *m (-s; -)*, **'Partnerin** *f (-; -nen)* partner
'Partnerschaft *f (-; -en)* partnership
'Partnerstadt *f* twin town
paschen ['paʃən] *Austrian v/t and v/i (ge-, h)* smuggle
Pascher ['paʃɐ] *Austrian m (-s; -)* smuggler
Pass [pas] *m (-es; Pässe* ['pɛsə]) passport; SPORT, GEOGR pass; ***langer Pass*** SPORT long ball
Passage [pa'sa:ʒə] *f (-; -n)* passage
Passagier [pasa'ʒi:ɐ] *m (-s; -e)* passenger
Passagierflugzeug *n* passenger plane; airliner
Passa'gierin *f (-; -nen)* passenger
Passah ['pasa] *n (-s; no pl)*, **'Passahfest** *n* REL Passover
Passant [pa'sant] *m (-en; -en)*, **Pas'santin** *f (-; -nen)* passerby
'Passbild *n* passport photo(graph)
passen ['pasən] **1.** *v/i (ge-, h)* fit (***j-m*** s.o.; ***auf*** *or* ***für*** *or* ***zu et.*** s.th.); suit (***j-m*** s.o.), be convenient; *cards*, SPORT pass; ***passen zu*** go with, match; ***sie passen gut zueinander*** they are well suited to each other; ***passt es Ihnen morgen?*** would tomorrow suit you *or* be all right (with you)?; ***das (es) passt mir gar nicht*** I don't like that (him) at all; ***das passt (nicht) zu ihm*** that's just like him (not like him, not his style)
passend *adj* fitting; matching; suitable, right
passierbar [pa'si:ɐba:ɐ] *adj* passable
passieren [pa'si:rən] *(no -ge-)* **1.** *v/i (sein)* happen; **2.** *v/t (h)* pass (through)
Pas'sierschein *m* pass, permit
Passion [pa'sjo:n] *f (-; -en)* passion; REL Passion
passiv ['pasi:f] *adj* passive
'Passiv *n (-s; no pl)* LING passive (voice)
Paste ['pastə] *f (-; -n)* paste
Pastell [pas'tɛl] *n (-[e]s; -e)* PAINT pastel
Pastete [pas'te:tə] *f (-; -n)* GASTR pie
Pate ['pa:tə] *m (-n; -n)* godfather
'Patenkind *n* godchild
'Patenschaft *f (-; -en)* sponsorship
Patent [pa'tɛnt] *n (-[e]s; -e)* patent; MIL

commission
Patentamt *n* patent office
Patentanwalt *m* JUR patent agent
patentieren [patɛn'tiːrən] *v/t* (*no -ge-, h*) patent; **(*sich*) *et. patentieren lassen*** take out a patent for s.th.
Pa'tentinhaber *m* patentee
pathetisch [pa'teːtɪʃ] *adj* pompous
Patient [pa'tsjɛnt] *m* (*-en; -en*), **Pa'tientin** *f* (*-; -nen*) MED patient
Patin ['paːtɪn] *f* (*-; -nen*) godmother
Patriot [patri'oːt] *m* (*-en; -en*) patriot
patri'otisch *adj* patriotic
Patrone [pa'troːnə] *f* (*-; -n*) cartridge
Patrouille [pa'trʊljə] *f* (*-; -n*) MIL patrol
patroullieren [patrʊl'jiːrən] *v/i* (*no -ge-, h*) MIL patrol
Patsche ['patʃə] F *f*: ***in der Patsche sitzen*** be in a fix *or* jam
'patschen F *v/i* (*ge-, h*) (s)plash
'patsch'nass *adj* soaking wet
patzen ['patsən] F *v/i* (*ge-, h*), **Patzer** ['patsɐ] F *m* (*-s; -*) blunder
Pauke ['paukə] *f* (*-; -n*) MUS bass drum; kettledrum
'pauken F *v/i and v/t* (*ge-, h*) cram
Pauschale [pau'ʃaːlə] *f* (*-; -n*) lump sum
Pau'schalgebühr *f* flat rate
Pauschalreise *f* package tour
Pauschalurteil *n* sweeping judg(e)ment
Pause[1] ['pauzə] *f* (*-; -n*) recess, *Br* break, *esp* THEA, SPORT intermission, *Br* interval; pause; rest (*a.* MUS)
'Pause[2] *f* (*-; -n*) TECH tracing
'pausen *v/t* (*ge-, h*) TECH trace
'pausenlos *adj* uninterrupted, nonstop
'Pausenzeichen *n radio*: interval signal; PED bell
pausieren [pau'ziːrən] *v/i* (*no -ge-, h*) pause, rest
Pavian ['paːvjaːn] *m* (*-s; -e*) ZO baboon
Pavillon ['pavɪljɔŋ] *m* (*-s; -s*) pavilion
Pazifist [patsi'fɪst] *m* (*-en; -en*), **Pazi'fistin** *f* (*-; -nen*), **pazi'fistisch** *adj* pacifist
PC [peː'tseː] *m* (*-[s]; -[s]*) ABBR *of* ***personal computer*** PC
Pech [pɛç] *n* (*-s; no pl*) pitch; F bad luck
Pechsträhne F *f* run of bad luck
Pechvogel F *m* unlucky fellow
pedantisch [pe'dantɪʃ] *adj* pedantic, fussy
Pegel ['peːgəl] *m* (*-s; -*) level (*a. fig*)
peilen ['pailən] *v/t* (*ge-, h*) sound
peinigen ['painɪgən] *v/t* (*ge-, h*) torment
Peiniger ['painɪgɐ] *m* (*-s; -*) tormentor
peinlich ['painlɪç] *adj* embarrassing; ***peinlich genau*** meticulous (***bei, in*** *dat* in); ***es war mir peinlich*** I was *or* felt embarrassed
Peitsche ['paitʃə] *f* (*-; -n*), **'peitschen** *v/t* (*ge-, h*) whip
'Peitschenhieb *m* lash
Pelle ['pɛlə] *f* (*-; -n*) skin; peel
'pellen *v/t* (*ge-, h*) peel
'Pellkar,toffeln *pl* potatoes (boiled) in their jackets
Pelz [pɛlts] *m* (*-es; -e*) fur; skin
'pelzgefüttert *adj* fur-lined
'Pelzgeschäft *n* fur(rier's) store (*Br* shop)
pelzig ['pɛltsɪç] *adj* furry; MED furred
'Pelzmantel *m* fur coat
'Pelztiere *pl* furred animals, furs
Pendel ['pɛndəl] *n* (*-s; -*) pendulum
'pendeln *v/i* (*ge-, h*) swing; RAIL *etc* shuttle; commute
'Pendeltür *f* swing door
'Pendelverkehr *m* RAIL *etc* shuttle service; commuter traffic
Pendler(in) ['pɛndlɐ (-lərɪn)] (*-s; -/-; -nen*) RAIL *etc* commuter
Penis ['peːnɪs] *m* (*-s; -se*) ANAT penis
Penner ['pɛnɐ] F *m* (*-s; -*) tramp, bum
Pension [pã'sjoːn] *f* (*-; -en*) (old age) pension; boarding-house, private hotel; ***in Pension sein*** be retired
Pensionär(in) [pãsjo'nɛːɐ (-'nɛːrɪn)] (*-s; -e/-; -nen*) (old age) pensioner; boarder
Pensionat [pãsjo'naːt] *n* (*-[e]s; -e*) boarding school
pensionieren [pãsjo'niːrən] *v/t* (*no -ge-, h*) pension (off); ***sich pensionieren lassen*** retire
Pensio'nierung *f* (*-; -en*) retirement
Pensionist [pãsjo'nɪst] *Austrian, Swiss m* (*-en; -en*) (old age) pensioner
Pensi'onsgast *m* boarder
Pensum ['pɛnzʊm] *n* (*-s; Pensen, Pensa*) (work) quota, stint
per [pɛr] *prp* (*acc*) per; by
perfekt [pɛr'fɛkt] *adj* perfect; ***perfekt machen*** settle
'Perfekt *n* (*-s; -e*) LING present perfect
Pergament [pɛrga'mɛnt] *n* (*-[e]s; -e*) parchment
Periode [pe'rjoːdə] *f* (*-; -n*) period, MED *a.* menstruation
periodisch [pe'rjoːdɪʃ] *adj* periodic(al)
Peripherie [perife'riː] *f* (*-; -n*) periphery, outskirts
Peripheriegeräte *pl* EDP peripheral equipment
Perle ['pɛrlə] *f* (*-; -n*) pearl; bead
'perlen *v/i* (*ge-, h*) sparkle, bubble
'Perlenkette *f* pearl necklace
'Perlmuschel *f* ZO pearl oyster
Perlmutt ['pɛrlmʊt] *n* (*-s; no pl*) mother-of-pearl
Perron [pɛ'rõː] *m* (*-s; -s*) *Swiss* platform

Perser ['pɛrzɐ] *m* (*-s*; *-*) Persian; Persian carpet
Perserin ['pɛrzərɪn] *f* (*-*; *-nen*) Persian (woman)
Persien ['pɛrzjən] Persia
persisch ['pɛrzɪʃ] *adj* Persian
Person [pɛr'zoːn] *f* (*-*; *-en*) person, THEA *etc a.* character; ***ein Tisch für drei Personen*** a table for three
Personal [pɛrzo'naːl] *n* (*-s*; *no pl*) staff, personnel; ***zu wenig Personal haben*** be understaffed
Personalabbau *m* staff reduction
Personalabteilung *f* personnel department
Personalausweis *m* identity card
Personalchef *m* staff manager
Personalien [pɛrzo'naːljən] *pl* particulars, personal data
Perso'nalpro,nomen *n* LING personal pronoun
Per'sonen(kraft)wagen (ABBR **PKW**) *m* (*Br a.* motor)car, auto(mobile)
Personenzug *m* passenger train; local *or* commuter train
personifizieren [pɛrzonifi'tsiːrən] *v/t* (*no -ge-, h*) personify
persönlich [pɛr'zøːnlɪç] *adj* personal
Per'sönlichkeit *f* (*-*; *-en*) personality
Perücke [pe'rʏkə] *f* (*-*; *-n*) wig
pervers [pɛr'vɛrs] *adj* perverted; ***perverser Mensch*** pervert
Pessimismus [pɛsi'mɪsmʊs] *m* (*-*; *no pl*) pessimism
Pessimist(in) [pɛsi'mɪst(ɪn)] (*-en*; *-en/-*; *-nen*) pessimist
pessi'mistisch *adj* pessimistic
Pest [pɛst] *f* (*-*; *no pl*) MED plague
Pestizid [pɛsti'tsiːt] *n* (*-s*; *-e*) pesticide
Petersilie [peːtɐ'ziːljə] *f* (*-*; *-n*) BOT parsley
Petroleum [pe'troːleʊm] *n* (*-s*; *no pl*) kerosene, *Br* paraffin
Petroleumlampe *f* kerosene (*Br* paraffin) lamp
petzen ['pɛtsən] F *v/i* (*ge-, h*) tell tales, *Br a.* sneak
Pfad [pfaːt] *m* (*-[e]s*; *-e* ['pfaːdə]) path, track
Pfadfinder *m* boy scout
Pfadfinderin [-fɪndərɪn] *f* (*-*; *-nen*) girl scout, *Br* girl guide
Pfahl [pfaːl] *m* (*-[e]s*; *Pfähle* ['pfɛːlə]) stake; post; pole
Pfand [pfant] *n* (*-[e]s*; *Pfänder* ['pfɛndɐ]) security; pawn, pledge; deposit; forfeit
'Pfandbrief *m* ECON mortgage bond
pfänden ['pfɛndən] *v/t* (*ge-, h*) seize
'Pfandhaus *n* → ***Leihhaus***
'Pfandleiher [-laiɐ] *m* (*-s*; *-*) pawnbroker
'Pfandschein *m* pawn ticket
'Pfändung *f* (*-*; *-en*) JUR seizure
Pfanne ['pfanə] *f* (*-*; *-n*) pan, skillet
'Pfannkuchen *m* pancake
Pfarrbezirk ['pfar-] *m* parish
Pfarrer ['pfarɐ] *m* (*-s*; *-*) vicar; pastor; (parish) priest
'Pfarrgemeinde *f* parish
Pfarrhaus *n* parsonage; rectory, vicarage
Pfarrkirche *f* parish church
Pfau [pfau] *m* (*-[e]s*; *-en*) ZO peacock
Pfeffer ['pfɛfɐ] *m* (*-s*; *-*) pepper
Pfefferkuchen *m* gingerbread
Pfefferminze [-mɪntsə] *f* (*-*; *no pl*) BOT peppermint
'pfeffern *v/t* (*ge-, h*) pepper
'Pfefferstreuer *m* (*-s*; *-*) pepper caster
pfeffrig ['pfɛfrɪç] *adj* peppery
Pfeife ['pfaifə] *f* (*-*; *-n*) whistle; pipe (*a.* MUS)
'pfeifen *v/i and v/t* (*irr, ge-, h*) whistle (***j-m*** to s.o.); F ***pfeifen auf*** (*acc*) not give a damn about
Pfeil [pfail] *m* (*-[e]s*; *-e*) arrow
Pfeiler ['pfailɐ] *m* (*-s*; *-*) pillar; pier
Pfennig ['pfɛnɪç] *m* (*-s*; *-e*) pfennig; *fig* penny
Pferch [pfɛrç] *m* (*-[e]s*; *-e*) fold, pen
'pferchen *v/t* (*ge-, h*) cram (***in*** *acc* into)
Pferd [pfeːɐrt] *n* (*-[e]s*; *-e*) ZO horse (*a.* SPORT); ***zu Pferde*** on horseback
Pferdegeschirr ['pfeːɐdə-] *n* harness
Pferdekoppel *f* paddock
Pferderennen *n* horserace
Pferdestall *m* stable
Pferdestärke *f* TECH horsepower
Pferdewagen *m* (horse-drawn) carriage
pfiff [pfɪf] *pret of* ***pfeifen***
Pfiff *m* (*-[e]s*; *-e*) whistle
pfiffig ['pfɪfɪç] *adj* smart
Pfingsten ['pfɪŋstən] *n* (*-*; *-*) REL Pentecost, *Br* Whitsun (***zu, an*** at)
Pfingst'montag *m* REL Whit Monday
'Pfingstrose *f* BOT peony
Pfingst'sonntag *m* REL Pentecost, *Br* Whit Sunday
Pfirsich ['pfɪrzɪç] *m* (*-s*; *-e*) BOT peach
Pflanze ['pflantsə] *f* (*-*; *-n*) plant; ***Pflanzen fressend*** ZO herbivorous
'pflanzen *v/t* (*ge-, h*) plant
'Pflanzenfett *n* vegetable fat
'pflanzlich *adj* vegetable
'Pflanzung *f* (*-*; *-en*) plantation
Pflaster ['pflastɐ] *n* (*-s*; *-*) pavement; MED Band-Aid®, *Br* plaster
'pflastern *v/t* (*ge-, h*) pave
'Pflasterstein *m* paving stone
Pflaume ['pflaumə] *f* (*-*; *-n*) BOT plum
Pflege ['pfleːgə] *f* (*-*; *no pl*) care; MED

P

nursing; *fig* cultivation; TECH maintenance; ***j-n in Pflege nehmen*** take s.o. into one's care; ***Pflege...*** *in cpds ...eltern, ...kind, ...sohn etc*: foster ...; *...heim, ...kosten, ...personal etc*: nursing ...

'pflegebedürftig *adj* needing care

'Pflegefall *m* constant-care patient

'pflegeleicht *adj* wash-and-wear, easy-care

'pflegen *v/t* (*ge-*, *h*) care for, look after, *esp* MED *a.* nurse; TECH maintain; *fig* cultivate; keep up (*custom etc*); ***sie pflegte zu sagen*** she used to *or* would say

Pfleger ['pfle:gɐ] *m* (*-s*; *-*) male nurse

Pflegerin ['pfle:gərɪn] *f* (*-*; *-nen*) nurse

'Pflegestelle *f* nursing place

Pflicht [pflɪçt] *f* (*-*; *-en*) duty (***gegen*** to); SPORT compulsory events

'pflichtbewusst *adj* conscientious

'Pflichtbewusstsein *n* sense of duty

Pflichterfüllung *f* performance of one's duty

Pflichtfach *n* PED compulsory subject

'pflichtgemäß, pflichtgetreu *adj* dutiful

pflichtvergessen *adv*: ***pflichtvergessen handeln*** neglect one's duty

'Pflichtversicherung *f* compulsory insurance

Pflock ['pflɔk] *m* (*-[e]s*; *Pflöcke* ['pflœkə]) peg, pin; plug

pflücken ['pflʏkən] *v/t* (*ge-*, *h*) pick, gather

Pflug [pflu:k] *m* (*-[e]s*; *Pflüge* ['pfly:gə]), **pflügen** ['pfly:gən] *v/t and v/i* (*ge-*, *h*) plow, *Br* plough

Pforte ['pfɔrtə] *f* (*-*; *-n*) gate, door, entrance

Pförtner ['pfœrtnɐ] *m* (*-s*; *-*) doorman, doorkeeper, porter

Pfosten ['pfɔstən] *m* (*-s*; *-*) post

Pfote ['pfo:tə] *f* (*-*; *-n*) ZO paw (*a.* F)

pfropfen ['pfrɔpfən] *v/t* (*ge-*, *h*) stopper; cork; plug; AGR graft; F cram, stuff

'Pfropfen *m* (*-s*; *-*) stopper; cork; plug; MED clot

pfui [pfui] *int* ugh!; *audience*: boo!

Pfund [pfʊnt] *n* (*-[e]s*; *-e* ['pfʊndə]) pound (*453,59 g*); pound (sterling); ***10 Pfund*** ten pounds

'pfundweise *adv* by the pound

pfuschen ['pfʊʃən] F *v/i* (*ge-*, *h*), **Pfuscherei** [pfʊʃə'rai] F *f* (*-*; *-en*) bungle, botch

Pfütze ['pfʏtsə] *f* (*-*; *-n*) puddle, pool

Phänomen [fɛno'me:n] *n* (*-s*; *-e*) phenomenon

phänomenal [fɛnome'na:l] *adj* phenomenal

Phantasie *etc* → ***Fantasie*** *etc*

pharmazeutisch [farma'tsɔytɪʃ] *adj* pharmaceutic(al)

Phase ['fa:zə] *f* (*-*; *-n*) phase (*a.* ELECTR), stage

Philosoph [filo'zo:f] *m* (*-en*; *-en*) philosopher

Philosophie [filozo'fi:] *f* (*-*; *-n*) philosophy

philosophieren [filozo'fi:rən] *v/i* (*no -ge-*, *h*) philosophize (***über*** *acc* on)

Philo'sophin *f* (*-*; *-nen*) (woman) philosopher

philosophisch [filo'zo:fɪʃ] *adj* philosophical

phlegmatisch [flɛ'gma:tɪʃ] *adj* phlegmatic

Phonetik [fo'ne:tɪk] *f* (*-*; *no pl*) phonetics

pho'netisch *adj* phonetic

Phosphor ['fɔsfo:ɐ] *m* (*-s*; *-e*) CHEM phosphorus

Photo... → ***Foto...***

Phrase ['fra:zə] *contp f* (*-*; *-n*) cliché (phrase)

Physik [fy'zi:k] *f* (*-*; *no pl*) physics

physikalisch [fyzi'ka:lɪʃ] *adj* physical

Physiker ['fy:zikɐ] *m* (*-s*; *-*), **'Physikerin** *f* (*-*; *-nen*) physicist

physisch ['fy:zɪʃ] *adj* physical

Pianist [pja'nɪst] *m* (*-en*; *-en*), **Pia'nistin** *f* (*-*; *-nen*) MUS pianist

Piano ['pja:no] *n* (*-s*; *-s*) MUS piano

Picke ['pɪkə] *f* (*-*; *-n*) TECH pick(axe)

Pickel[1] ['pɪkəl] *m* (*-s*; *-*) TECH pick(axe)

'Pickel[2] *m* (*-s*; *-*) MED pimple

pickelig ['pɪkəlɪç] *adj* MED pimpled, pimply

picken ['pɪkən] *v/i and v/t* (*ge-*, *h*) ZO peck, pick

Picknick ['pɪknɪk] *n* (*-s*; *-e*, *-s*) picnic

'picknicken *v/i* (*ge-*, *h*) (have a) picnic

piekfein ['pi:k-] F *adj* posh

piep(s)en ['pi:p(s)ən] *v/i* (*ge-*, *h*) chirp, cheep; ELECTR bleep

Pietät [pje'tɛ:t] *f* (*-*; *no pl*) reverence; piety

pie'tätlos *adj* irreverent

pie'tätvoll *adj* reverent

Pik [pi:k] *n* (*-[s]*; *-[s]*) *cards*: spade(s)

pikant [pi'kant] *adj* piquant, spicy (*both a. fig*)

Pilger ['pɪlgɐ] *m* (*-s*; *-*) pilgrim

'Pilgerfahrt *f* pilgrimage

'Pilgerin *f* (*-*; *-nen*) pilgrim

'pilgern *v/i* (*ge-*, *sein*) (go on a) pilgrimage

Pille ['pɪlə] *f* (*-*; *-n*) pill; F ***die Pille nehmen*** be on the pill

Pilot [pi'lo:t] *m* (*-en*; *-en*), **Pi'lotin** *f* (*-*; *-nen*) pilot

Pilz [pɪlts] *m* (*-es*; *-e*) BOT mushroom (*a.*

P

fig); toadstool; MED fungus; ***Pilze suchen*** (***gehen***) go mushrooming
Pinguin ['pɪŋguiːn] *m* (*-s*; *-e*) ZO penguin
pinkeln ['pɪŋkəln] F *v/i* (*ge-*, *h*) (have a) pee, piddle
Pinsel ['pɪnzəl] *m* (*-s*; -) (paint)brush
'**Pinselstrich** *m* brushstroke
Pinzette [pɪn'tsɛtə] *f* (-; *-n*) tweezers
Pionier [pjo'niːɐ] *m* (*-s*; *-e*) pioneer, MIL *a.* engineer
Pirat [pi'raːt] *m* (*-en*; *-en*) pirate
Pisse ['pɪsə] V *f* (-; *no pl*), '**pissen** V *v/i* (*ge-*, *h*) piss
Piste ['pɪstə] *f* (-; *-n*) course; AVIAT runway
Pistole [pɪs'toːlə] *f* (-; *-n*) pistol, gun
Pkw, **PKW** ['peːkaːveː] ABBR *of* ***Personenkraftwagen*** (*Br a.* motor)car, automobile
Plache ['plaxə] *Austrian f* (-; *-n*) awning, tarpaulin
placieren *etc* → ***platzieren*** *etc*
plädieren [plɛ'diːrən] *v/i* (*no -ge-*, *h*) JUR plead (***für*** for)
Plädoyer [plɛdoa'jeː] *n* (*-s*; *-s*) JUR final speech, pleading
Plage ['plaːgə] *f* (-; *-n*) trouble, misery; plague; nuisance, F pest
'**plagen** *v/t* (*ge-*, *h*) trouble; bother; pester; ***sich plagen*** toil, drudge
Plakat [pla'kaːt] *n* (*-[e]s*; *-e*) poster, placard, bill
Plakette [pla'kɛtə] *f* (-; *-n*) plaque, badge
Plan [plaːn] *m* (*-[e]s*; *Pläne* ['plɛːnə]) plan; intention
Plane ['plaːnə] *f* (-; *-n*) awning, tarpaulin
'**planen** *v/t* (*ge-*, *h*) plan, make plans for
Planet [pla'neːt] *m* (*-en*; *-en*) ASTR planet
planieren [pla'niːrən] *v/t* (*no -ge-*, *h*) TECH level, plane, grade
Planke ['plaŋkə] *f* (-; *-n*) plank, (thick) board
plänkeln ['plɛŋkəln] *v/i* (*ge-*, *h*) skirmish
'**planlos** *adj* without plan; aimless
'**planmäßig** **1.** *adj* scheduled (*arrival etc*); **2.** *adv* according to plan
Plan(t)schbecken ['planʃ-] *n* paddling pool
plan(t)schen ['planʃən] *v/i* (*ge-*, *h*) splash
Plantage [plan'taːʒə] *f* (-; *-n*) plantation
Plappermaul ['plapɐ-] F *n* chatterbox
plappern ['plapɐn] F *v/i* (*ge-*, *h*) chatter, prattle, babble, jabber
plärren ['plɛrən] F *v/i and v/t* (*ge-*, *h*) blubber; bawl; *radio*: blare
Plastik[1] ['plastɪk] *f* (-; *-en*) sculpture
'**Plastik**[2] *n* (*-s*; *no pl*) plastic; ***Plastik...*** *in cpds …besteck etc*: plastic …
plastisch ['plastɪʃ] *adj* plastic; three-dimensional; *fig* graphic
Platin ['plaːtiːn] *n* (*-s*; *no pl*) platinum
plätschern ['plɛtʃɐn] *v/i* (*ge-*, *h*) ripple (*a. fig*), splash
platt [plat] *adj* flat, level, even; *fig* trite; F flabbergasted
Platte ['platə] *f* (-; *-n*) sheet, plate; slab; board; panel; MUS record, disk, *Br* disc; EDP disk; GASTR dish; F bald pate; ***kalte Platte*** GASTR plate of cold cuts (*Br* meats)
plätten ['plɛtən] *v/t* (*ge-*, *h*) iron, press
'**Plattenspieler** *m* record player
Plattenteller *m* turntable
'**Plattform** *f* platform
'**Plattfuß** *m* MED flat foot
'**Plattheit** *fig f* (-; *-en*) triviality; platitude
Plättli ['plɛtli] *Swiss n* (*-s*; *-s*) tile
Platz [plats] *m* (*-es*; *Plätze* ['plɛtsə]) place, spot; site; room, space; square; circus; seat; ***es ist*** (***nicht***) ***genug Platz*** there's (there isn't) enough room; ***Platz machen für*** make room for; make way for; ***Platz nehmen*** take a seat, sit down; ***ist dieser Platz noch frei?*** is this seat taken?; ***j-n vom Platz stellen*** SPORT send s.o. off; ***auf eigenem Platz*** SPORT at home; ***auf die Plätze, fertig, los!*** SPORT on your marks, get set, go!
'**Platzanweiser** *m* (*-s*; -) usher
Platzanweiserin *f* (-; *-nen*) usherette
Plätzchen ['plɛtsçən] *n* (*-s*; -) (little) place, spot; GASTR cookie, *Br* biscuit
platzen ['platsən] *v/i* (*ge-*, *sein*) burst (*a. fig*); crack, split; explode (*a. fig* ***vor*** *dat* with), blow up; F come to grief *or* nothing, fall through, blow up, *sl* go phut; break up
platzieren [pla'tsiːrən] *v/t* (*no -ge-*, *h*) place; ***sich platzieren*** SPORT be placed
Plat'zierung *f* (-; *-en*) place, placing
'**Platzkarte** *f* reservation (ticket)
Plätzli ['plɛtsli] *Swiss n* (*-s*; -) cutlet
'**Platzpa,trone** *f* blank (cartridge)
Platzregen *m* cloudburst, downpour
Platzreser,vierung *f* seat reservation
Platzverweis *m*: ***e-n Platzverweis erhalten*** SPORT be sent off
Platzwart *m* (*-s*; *-e*) SPORT groundkeeper, *Br* groundsman
Platzwunde *f* MED cut, laceration
Plauderei [plaudə'rai] *f* (-; *-en*) chat
plaudern ['plaudɐn] *v/i* (*ge-*, *h*) (have a) chat
plauschen ['plauʃən] *Austrian v/i* (have a) chat
pleite ['plaitə] F *adj* broke
'**Pleite** F *f* (-; *-n*) bankruptcy; *fig* flop
pleitegehen go broke
Plombe ['plɔmbə] *f* (-; *-n*) TECH seal; MED

filling
plombieren [plɔm'biːrən] *v/t* (*no -ge-, h*) TECH seal; MED fill
plötzlich ['plœtslɪç] **1.** *adj* sudden; **2.** *adv* suddenly, all of a sudden
plump [plʊmp] *adj* clumsy
plumps *int* thud, plop
plumpsen ['plʊmpsən] *v/i* (*ge-, sein*) thud, plop, flop
Plunder ['plʊndɐ] F *m* (*-s; no pl*) trash, junk
Plünderer ['plʏndərɐ] *m* (*-s; -*) looter, plunderer
plündern ['plʏndɐn] *v/i and v/t* (*ge-, h*) plunder, loot
Plural ['pluːraːl] *m* (*-s; -e*) LING plural
plus [plʊs] *adv* plus
Plusquamperfekt ['plʊskvampɛrfɛkt] *n* (*-s; -e*) LING past perfect
Pneu [pnɔʏ] *Swiss m* (*-s; -s*) tire, *Br* tyre
Po [poː] F *m* (*-s; -s*) bottom, behind
Pöbel ['pøːbəl] *m* (*-s; no pl*) mob, rabble
pochen ['pɔxən] *v/i* (*ge-, h*) knock, rap (*both*: ***an*** *acc* at)
Pocke ['pɔkə] *f* (*-; -n*) MED pock
'Pocken *pl* MED smallpox
Pockenimpfung *f* MED smallpox vaccination
Podest [po'dɛst] *n, m* (*-[e]s; -e*) platform; *fig* pedestal
Podium ['poːdjʊm] *n* (*-s; -ien*) podium, platform
'Podiumsdiskussi,on *f* panel discussion
Poesie [poe'ziː] *f* (*-; -n*) poetry
Poet [po'eːt] *m* (*-en; -en*), **Po'etin** *f* (*-; -nen*) poet
poetisch [po'eːtɪʃ] *adj* poetic(al)
Pointe ['poɛ̃ːtə] *f* (*-; -n*) point, punch line
Pokal [po'kaːl] *m* (*-s; -e*) goblet; SPORT cup
Pokalendspiel *n* SPORT cup final
Pokalsieger *m* SPORT cup winner
Pokalspiel *n* SPORT cup tie
pökeln ['pøːkəln] *v/t* (*ge-, h*) salt
Pol [poːl] *m* (*-s; -e*) GEOGR pole
polar [po'laːɐ] *adj* polar
Pole ['poːlə] *m* (*-n; -n*) Pole
'Polen Poland
Polemik [po'leːmɪk] *f* (*-; -en*) polemic(s)
po'lemisch *adj* polemic(al)
polemisieren [polemi'ziːrən] *v/i* (*no -ge-, h*) polemize
Police [po'liːsə] *f* (*-; -n*) policy
Polier [po'liːɐ] *m* (*-s; -e*) TECH foreman
polieren [po'liːrən] *v/t* (*no -ge-, h*) polish
Polin ['poːlɪn] *f* (*-; -nen*) Pole, Polish woman
Politik [poli'tiːk] *f* (*-; no pl*) politics; policy (*a. fig*)
Politiker(in) [po'liːtikɐ (-kərɪn)] (*-s; -/-; -nen*) politician
politisch [po'liːtɪʃ] *adj* political
politisieren [politi'ziːrən] *v/i* (*no -ge-, h*) talk politics
Polizei [poli'tsai] *f* (*-; no pl*) police
Polizeiauto *n* police car
Polizeibeamte *m*, **-in** *f* police officer
poli'zeilich *adj* (of *or* by the) police
Poli'zeiprä,sidium *n* police headquarters
Polizeire,vier *n* police station; precinct, *Br* district
Polizeischutz *m*: ***unter Polizeischutz*** under police guard
Polizeistreife *f* police patrol
Polizeistunde *f* closing time
Polizeiwache *f* police station
Polizist [poli'tsɪst] *m* (*-en; -en*) policeman
Poli'zistin *f* (*-; -nen*) policewoman
polnisch ['pɔlnɪʃ] *adj* Polish
Polster ['pɔlstɐ] *n* (*-s; -*) upholstery; cushion; pad(ding); *fig* bolster
Polstergarni,tur *f* three-piece suite
Polstermöbel *pl* upholstered furniture
'polstern *v/t* (*ge-, h*) upholster; pad
'Polstersessel *m* easy chair, armchair
Polsterstuhl *m* upholstered chair
Polsterung ['pɔlstərʊŋ] *f* (*-; -en*) upholstery; padding
poltern ['pɔltɐn] *v/i* (*ge-, h*) rumble; *fig* bluster
Pommes frites [pɔm'frɪt] *pl* French fries, French fried potatoes, *Br* chips
Pomp [pɔmp] *m* (*-[e]s; no pl*) pomp
pompös [pɔm'pøːs] *adj* showy
Pony[1] ['pɔni] *n* (*-s; -s*) ZO pony
'Pony[2] *m* (*-s; -s*) fringe, bangs
Popgruppe ['pɔp-] *f* MUS pop group
'Popmu,sik *f* pop music
populär [popu'lɛːɐ] *adj* popular
Popularität [populari'tɛːt] *f* (*-; no pl*) popularity
Pore ['poːrə] *f* (*-; -n*) pore
Porno ['pɔrno] F *m* (*-s; -s*), **Pornofilm** *m* porn (film), blue movie
Pornoheft *n* porn magazine
porös [po'røːs] *adj* porous
Portemonnaie [pɔrtmɔ'neː] *n* (*-s; -s*) purse
Portier [pɔr'tjeː] *m* (*-s; -s*) doorman, porter
Portion [pɔr'tsjoːn] *f* (*-; -en*) portion, share; helping, serving
Portmonee *n* → ***Portemonnaie***
Porto ['pɔrto] *n* (*-s; -s, -ti*) postage
Porträt [pɔr'trɛː] *n* (*-s; -s*) portrait
porträtieren [pɔrtrɛ'tiːrən] *v/t* (*no -ge-, h*) portray
Portugal ['pɔrtugal] Portugal
Portugiese [pɔrtu'giːzə] *m* (*-n; -n*), **Por-**

tu'giesin *f* (-; *-nen*), **portu'giesisch** *adj* Portuguese
Porzellan [pɔrtsɛ'la:n] *n* (*-s*; *-e*) china, porcelain
Posaune [po'zaunə] *f* (-; *-n*) MUS trombone; *fig* trumpet
Pose ['po:zə] *f* (-; *-n*) pose, attitude
Position [pozi'tsjo:n] *f* (-; *-en*) position (*a. fig*)
positiv ['po:ziti:f] *adj* positive
possessiv [pɔsɛ'si:f] *adj* LING possessive
Posses'sivpro,nomen *n* LING possessive pronoun
Post [pɔst] *f* (-; *no pl*) mail, *esp Br* post; letters; ***mit der Post*** by post *or* mail
Postamt *n* post office
Postanweisung *f* money order
Postbeamte *m*, **-in** *f* post office clerk
Postbote *m* mailman, *Br* postman
Posten ['pɔstən] *m* (*-s*; -) post; job, position; MIL sentry; ECON item; lot, parcel
'Postfach *n* (PO) box
postieren [pɔs'ti:rən] *v/t* (*no -ge-*, *h*) post, station, place; ***sich postieren*** station o.s.
'Postkarte *f* postcard
'Postkutsche *f* stagecoach
'postlagernd *adj* (in care of) general delivery, *Br* poste restante
'Postleitzahl *f* zip code, *Br* post(al) code
Postmi,nister *m* Postmaster General
Postscheck *m* postal check (*Br* cheque)
Postsparbuch *n* post-office savings book
Poststempel *m* postmark
'postwendend *adv* by return mail, *Br* by return (of post)
'Postwertzeichen *n* (postage) stamp
Postzustellung *f* postal *or* mail delivery
Potenz [po'tɛnts] *f* (-; *-en*) a) (*no pl*) MED potency, b) MATH power
Pracht [praxt] *f* (-; *no pl*) splendo(u)r, magnificence
prächtig ['prɛçtɪç] *adj* splendid, magnificent, *fig a.* great, super
Prädikat [prɛdi'ka:t] *n* (-[*e*]*s*; *-e*) LING predicate
prägen ['prɛ:gən] *v/t* (*ge-*, *h*) stamp, coin (*a. fig*)
prahlen ['pra:lən] *v/i* (*ge-*, *h*) brag, boast (*both*: ***mit*** of), talk big, show off
Prahler ['pra:lɐ] *m* (*-s*; -) boaster, braggart
Prahlerei [pra:lə'rai] *f* (-; *-en*) boasting, bragging
'prahlerisch *adj* boastful; showy
Praktikant [prakti'kant] *m* (*-en*; *-en*), **Prakti'kantin** *f* (-; *-nen*) trainee
Praktiken ['praktikən] *pl* practices
'Praktikum *n* (*-s*; *-ka*) practical training
'praktisch 1. *adj* practical; useful, handy; ***praktischer Arzt*** general practitioner; **2.** *adv* practically; virtually
praktizieren [prakti'tsi:rən] *v/t* (*no -ge-*, *h*) practice (*Br* practise) medicine *or* law
Prälat [prɛ'la:t] *m* (*-en*; *-en*) REL prelate
Praline [pra'li:nə] *f* (-; *-n*) chocolate
prall [pral] *adj* tight; well-rounded; bulging; blazing (*sun*)
prallen ['pralən] *v/i* (*ge-*, *sein*) ***prallen gegen*** (*or* ***auf*** *acc*) crash *or* bump into
Prämie ['prɛ:mjə] *f* (-; *-n*) premium; prize; bonus
prämieren [prɛ'mi:rən], **prämiieren** [prɛmi'i:rən] *v/t* (*no -ge-*, *h*) award a prize to
Pranke ['praŋkə] *f* (-; *-n*) ZO paw (*a.* F)
Präparat [prɛpa'ra:t] *n* (-[*e*]*s*; *-e*) preparation
präparieren [prɛpa'ri:rən] *v/t* (*no -ge-*, *h*) prepare; MED, BOT, ZO dissect
Präposition [prɛpozi'tsjo:n] *f* (-; *-en*) LING preposition
Prärie [prɛ'ri:] *f* (-; *-n*) prairie
Präsens ['prɛ:zɛns] *n* (-; *-sentia* [prɛ'zɛntsja]) LING present (tense)
präsentieren [prɛzɛn'ti:rən] *v/t* (*no -ge-*, *h*) present; offer
Präservativ [prɛzɛrva'ti:f] *n* (*-s*; *-e*) condom
Präsident [prɛzi'dɛnt] *m* (*-en*; *-en*), **Präsi'dentin** *f* (-; *-nen*) president; chairman (chairwoman)
präsidieren [prɛzi'di:rən] *v/i* preside (***in*** *dat* over)
Präsidium [prɛ'zi:djʊm] *n* (*-s*; *-ien*) presidency
prasseln ['prasəln] *v/i* (*ge-*, *h*) *rain etc*: patter; *fire*: crackle
Präteritum [prɛ'te:ritʊm] *n* (*-s*; *-ta*) LING past (tense)
Praxis ['praksɪs] *f* (-; *Praxen*) a) (*no pl*) practice (*a.* MED, JUR), b) MED doctor's office, *Br* surgery
Präzedenzfall [prɛtse'dɛnts-] *m* precedent
präzis [prɛ'tsi:s], **präzise** [prɛ'tsi:zə] *adj* precise
Präzision [prɛtsi'zjo:n] *f* (-; *no pl*) precision
predigen ['pre:dɪgən] *v/i and v/t* (*ge-*, *h*) preach
Prediger ['pre:dɪgɐ] *m* (*-s*; -), **'Predigerin** *f* (-; *-nen*) preacher
Predigt ['pre:dɪçt] *f* (-; *-en*) sermon
Preis [prais] *m* (*-es*; *-e*) price (*a. fig*); prize; *film etc*: award; reward; ***um jeden Preis*** at all costs
'Preisausschreiben *n* competition
Preiselbeere ['praizəl-] *f* BOT cranberry
preisen ['praizən] *v/t* (*irr*, *ge-*, *h*) praise
'Preiserhöhung *f* rise *or* increase in

P

price(s)
'preisgeben *v/t* (*irr*, ***geben***, *sep*, *-ge-*, *h*) abandon; reveal, give away
'preisgekrönt *adj* prize-winning; *film etc*: award-winning
'Preisgericht *n* jury
Preislage *f* price range
Preisliste *f* price list
Preisnachlass *m* discount
Preisrätsel *n* competition
Preisrichter(in) judge
Preisschild *n* price tag
Preisstopp *m* price freeze
Preisträger(in) prizewinner
'preiswert *adj* cheap
prellen ['prɛlən] *v/t* (*ge-*, *h*) *fig* cheat (**um** out of); ***sich et. prellen*** MED bruise s.th.
'Prellung *f* (-; *-en*) MED contusion, bruise
Premiere [prə'mjeːrə] *f* (-; *-n*) THEA *etc* first night, première
Premiermi,nister [prə'mjeː-] *m*, **Pre'mi-ermi,nisterin** *f* prime minister
Presse ['prɛsə] *f* (-; *-n*) a) (*no pl*) press, b) squeezer
Presse... *in cpds* *...agentur*, *...konferenz*, *...fotograf etc*: press ...
Pressefreiheit *f* freedom of the press
Pressemeldung *f* news item
'pressen *v/t* (*ge-*, *h*) press; squeeze
'Pressetri,büne *f* press box
Pressevertreter *m* reporter
'Pressluft *f* compressed air
Pressluft... *in cpds* *...bohrer*, *...hammer etc*: pneumatic ...
Prestige [prɛs'tiːʒə] *n* (*-s*; *no pl*) prestige
Prestigeverlust *m* loss of prestige *or* face
Preuße ['prɔʏsə] *m* (*-n*; *-n*), **'Preußin** *f* (-; *-nen*), **'preußisch** *adj* Prussian
prickeln ['prɪkəln] *v/i* (*ge-*, *h*) prickle; tingle
pries [priːs] *pret of* ***preisen***
Priester ['priːstɐ] *m* (*-s*; -) priest
Priesterin ['priːstərɪn] *f* (-; *-nen*) priestess
'priesterlich *adj* priestly
prima ['priːma] F *adj* great, super
primär [pri'mɛːɐ] *adj* primary
Primararzt [pri'maːɐ-] *Austrian* *m* → ***Oberarzt***
Primarschule *Swiss* *f* → ***Grundschule***
Primel ['priːməl] *f* (-; *-n*) BOT primrose
primitiv [primi'tiːf] *adj* primitive
Prinz [prɪnts] *m* (*-en*; *-en*) prince
Prinzessin [prɪn'tsɛsɪn] *f* (-; *-nen*) princess
'Prinzgemahl *m* prince consort
Prinzip [prɪn'tsiːp] *n* (*-s*; *-ien*) principle (***aus*** on; ***im*** in)
prinzipiell [prɪntsi'pjɛl] *adv* as a matter of principle
Prise ['priːzə] *f* (-; *-n*) ***e-e Prise Salz*** *etc* a pinch of salt *etc*
Prisma ['prɪsma] *n* (*-s*; *-men*) prism
Pritsche ['prɪtʃə] *f* (-; *-n*) plank bed; MOT platform
privat [pri'vaːt] *adj* private; personal
Pri'vat... *in cpds* *...leben*, *...schule*, *...detektiv etc*: private ...
Privatangelegenheit *f* personal *or* private matter *or* affair; ***das ist m-e Privatangelegenheit*** that's my own business
Privileg [privi'leːk] *n* (*-[e]s*; *-gien* [privi'leːgjən]) privilege
pro [proː] *prp* (*acc*) per; ***2 Mark pro Stück*** two marks each
Pro *n*: ***das Pro und Kontra*** the pros and cons
Probe ['proːbə] *f* (-; *-n*) trial, test; sample; THEA rehearsal; MATH proof; ***auf Probe*** on probation; ***auf die Probe stellen*** put to the test
Probea,larm *m* test alarm, fire drill
Probeaufnahmen *pl* *film*: screen test
Probefahrt *f* test drive
Probeflug *m* test flight
'proben *v/i and v/t* (*ge-*, *h*) THEA *etc* rehearse
'probeweise *adv* on trial; on probation
'Probezeit *f* (time of) probation
probieren [pro'biːrən] *v/t* (*no -ge-*, *h*) try; taste
Problem [pro'bleːm] *n* (*-s*; *-e*) problem
problematisch [proble'maːtɪʃ] *adj* problematic(al)
Produkt [pro'dʊkt] *n* (*-[e]s*; *-e*) product (*a.* MATH); result
Produktion [prodʊk'tsjoːn] *f* (-; *-en*) production; output
produktiv [prodʊk'tiːf] *adj* productive
Produktivität [prodʊktivi'tɛːt] *f* (-; *no pl*) productivity
Produzent [produ'tsɛnt] *m* (*-en*; *-en*), **Produ'zentin** *f* (-; *-nen*) producer
produzieren [produ'tsiːrən] *v/t* (*no -ge-*, *h*) produce
professionell [profɛsjo'nɛl] *adj* professional
Professor [pro'fɛsoːɐ] *m* (*-s*; *-en* [profɛ'soːrən]), **Profes'sorin** *f* (-; *-nen*) professor
Professur [profɛ'suːɐ] *f* (-; *-en*) professorship, chair (***für*** of)
Profi ['proːfi] *m* (*-s*; *-s*) pro
Profi... *in cpds* *...boxer*, *...fußballer etc*: professional
Profil [pro'fiːl] *n* (*-s*; *-e*) profile; MOT tread
profilieren [profi'liːrən] *v/refl* (*no -ge-*, *h*) distinguish o.s.
Profit [pro'fiːt] *m* (*-[e]s*; *-e*) profit

P

profitieren [profi'ti:rən] *v/i* (*no -ge-, h*) profit (***von** or **bei et.*** from *or* by s.th.)
Prognose [pro'gno:zə] *f* (-; *-n*) prediction; METEOR forecast; MED prognosis
Programm [pro'gram] *n* (*-s*; *-e*) program(me *Br*), TV *a.* channel; EDP program
Programmfehler *m* EDP program error, bug
programmieren [progra'mi:rən] *v/t* (*no -ge-, h*) program (*a.* EDP)
Programmierer [progra'mi:rɐ] *m* (*-s*; -), **Program'miererin** *f* (-; *-nen*) EDP programmer
Projekt [pro'jɛkt] *n* (-[*e*]*s*; *-e*) project
Projektion [projɛk'tsjo:n] *f* (-; *-en*) projection
Projektor [pro'jɛkto:ɐ] *m* (*-s*; *-en* [projɛk'to:rən]) projector
proklamieren [prokla'mi:rən] *v/t* (*no -ge-, h*) proclaim
Prokurist [proku'rɪst] *m* (*-en*; *-en*), **Proku'ristin** *f* (-; *-nen*) authorized signatory
Proletarier [prole'ta:rjɐ] *m* (*-s*; -), **proletarisch** [-'ta:rɪʃ] *adj* proletarian
Prolog [pro'lo:k] *m* (-[*e*]*s*; *-e*) prologue
Promillegrenze [pro'mɪlə-] *f* (blood) alcohol limit
prominent [promi'nɛnt] *adj* prominent
Prominenz [promi'nɛnts] *f* (-; *no pl*) notables; high society
Promotion [promo'tsjo:n] *f* (-; *-en*) UNIV doctorate
promovieren [promo'vi:rən] *v/i* (*no -ge-, h*) do one's doctorate
prompt [prɔmpt] *adj* prompt; quick
Pronomen [pro'no:mən] *n* (*-s*; *-mina*) LING pronoun
Propeller [pro'pɛlɐ] *m* (*-s*; -) propeller
Prophet [pro'fe:t] *m* (*-en*; *-en*) prophet
pro'phetisch *adj* prophetic
prophezeien [profe'tsaiən] *v/t* (*no -ge-, h*) prophesy, predict
Prophe'zeiung *f* (-; *-en*) prophecy, prediction
Proportion [propɔr'tsjo:n] *f* (-; *-en*) proportion
Proporz [pro'pɔrts] *m* (*-es*; *-e*) POL proportional representation
Prosa ['pro:za] *f* (-; *no pl*) prose
Prospekt [pro'spɛkt] *m* (-[*e*]*s*; *-e*) prospectus; brochure, pamphlet
prost [pro:st] *int* cheers!
Prostituierte [prostitu'i:ɐtə] *f* (*-n*; *-n*) prostitute
Protest [pro'tɛst] *m* (-[*e*]*s*; *-e*) protest; ***aus Protest*** in (*or* as a) protest
Protestant [protɛs'tant] *m* (*-en*; *-en*), **Protes'tantin** *f* (-; *-nen*), **protes'tantisch** *adj* REL Protestant
protestieren [protɛs'ti:rən] *v/i* (*no -ge-, h*) protest
Prothese [pro'te:zə] *f* (-; *-n*) MED artificial limb; denture
Protokoll [proto'kɔl] *n* (*-s*; *-e*) record, minutes; protocol; ***(das) Protokoll führen*** take *or* keep the minutes; ***zu Protokoll nehmen*** JUR record
Protokollführer *m* keeper of the minutes
protokollieren [protokɔ'li:rən] *v/t and v/i* (*no -ge-, h*) take the minutes (of); JUR record
protzen ['prɔtsən] F *v/i* (*ge-, h*) show off (***mit et.*** s.th.)
protzig ['prɔtsɪç] *adj* showy, flashy
Proviant [pro'vjant] *m* (*-s*; *no pl*) provisions, food
Provinz [pro'vɪnts] *f* (-; *-en*) province; *fig* country
provinziell [provɪn'tsjɛl] *adj* provincial (*a. contp*)
Provision [provi'zjo:n] *f* (-; *-en*) ECON commission
provisorisch [provi'zo:rɪʃ] *adj* provisional, temporary
provozieren [provo'tsi:rən] *v/t* (*no -ge-, h*) provoke
Prozent [pro'tsɛnt] *n* (-[*e*]*s*; *-e*) per cent; F *pl* discount
Prozentsatz *m* percentage
prozentual [protsɛn'tua:l] *adj* proportional; ***prozentualer Anteil*** percentage
Prozess [pro'tsɛs] *m* (*-es*; *-e*) process (*a.* TECH, CHEM *etc*); JUR action; lawsuit, case; trial; ***j-m den Prozess machen*** take s.o. to court; ***e-n Prozess gewinnen*** (***verlieren***) win (lose) a case
prozessieren [protsɛ'si:rən] *v/i* (*no -ge-, h*) JUR go to court; ***gegen j-n prozessieren*** bring an action against s.o., take s.o. to court
Prozession [protsɛ'sjo:n] *f* (-; *-en*) procession
Prozessor [pro'tsɛso:ɐ] *m* (*-s*; *-en* [protsɛ'so:rən]) EDP processor
prüde ['pry:də] *adj* prudish; ***prüde sein*** be a prude
prüfen ['pry:fən] *v/t* (*ge-, h*) PED *etc* examine, test (*a.* TECH); check; inspect (*a.* TECH); *fig* consider
prüfend *adj* searching
Prüfer ['pry:fɐ] *m* (*-s*; -), **'Prüferin** *f* (-; *-nen*) PED *etc* examiner; *esp* TECH tester
Prüfling ['pry:flɪŋ] *m* (*-s*; *-e*) candidate
'Prüfstein *m* touchstone (***für*** of)
'Prüfung *f* (-; *-en*) examination, F exam; test; check(ing), inspection; ***e-e Prüfung machen*** (***bestehen, nicht bestehen***) take (pass, fail) an exam(ination)

'Prüfungsarbeit *f* examination *or* test paper
Prügel ['pry:gəl] F *pl* (***e-e Tracht***) ***Prügel bekommen*** get a (good) beating *or* hiding *or* thrashing
Prüge'lei F *f* (-; *-en*) fight
'prügeln F *v/t* (*ge-*, *h*) beat, flog; ***sich prügeln*** (have a) fight
'Prügelstrafe *f* corporal punishment
Prunk [prʊŋk] *m* (-[*e*]*s*; *no pl*) splendo(u)r, pomp
'prunkvoll *adj* splendid, magnificent
PS [pe:'ˀɛs] ABBR *of* ***Pferdestärke*** horsepower, HP
Psalm [psalm] *m* (*-s*; *-en*) REL psalm
Pseudonym [psɔʏdo'ny:m] *n* (*-s*; *-e*) pseudonym
pst [pst] *int* sh!, ssh!; psst!
Psyche ['psy:çə] *f* (-; *-n*) mind, psyche
Psychiater [psy'çja:tɐ] *m* (*-s*; -), **Psy'chiaterin** *f* (-; *-nen*) psychiatrist
psychiatrisch [psy'çja:trɪʃ] *adj* psychiatric
psychisch ['psy:çɪʃ] *adj* mental, MED *a.* psychic
Psychoana'lyse [psyço-] *f* psychoanalysis
Psychologe [psyço'lo:gə] *m* (*-n*; *-n*) psychologist (*a. fig*)
Psychologie [psyçolo'gi:] *f* (-; *no pl*) psychology
Psycho'login *f* (-; *-nen*) psychologist
psycho'logisch *adj* psychological
Psychose [psy'ço:zə] *f* (-; *-n*) MED psychosis
psychosomatisch [psyçozo'ma:tɪʃ] *adj* MED psychosomatic
Pubertät [pubɛr'tɛ:t] *f* (-; *no pl*) puberty
Publikum ['pu:blikʊm] *n* (*-s*; *no pl*) audience, TV *a.* viewers, *radio*: *a.* listeners; SPORT crowd, spectators; ECON customers; public
publizieren [publi'tsi:rən] *v/t* (*no -ge-*, *h*) publish
Pudding ['pʊdɪŋ] *m* (*-s*; *-e*, *-s*) pudding, *esp Br* blancmange
Pudel ['pu:dəl] *m* (*-s*; -) ZO poodle
Puder ['pu:dɐ] *m* (*-s*; -) powder
'Puderdose *f* powder compact
'pudern *v/t* (*ge-*, *h*) powder; ***sich pudern*** powder one's face
'Puderzucker *m* confectioner's (*Br* icing) sugar
Puff[1] [pʊf] F *m* (*-s*; *-s*) brothel
Puff[2] *m* (-[*e*]*s*; *Püffe* ['pʏfə]) hump; poke
Puffer ['pʊfɐ] *m* (*-s*; -) RAIL buffer (*a. fig*)
'Puffmais *m* popcorn
Pulli ['pʊli] F *m* (*-s*; *-s*) (light) sweater
Pullover [pʊ'lo:vɐ] *m* (*-s*; -) sweater, pullover
Puls [pʊls] *m* (*-es*; *-e*) MED pulse; pulse rate
Pulsader *f* ANAT artery
pulsieren [pʊl'zi:rən] *v/i* (*no -ge-*, *h*) MED pulsate (*a. fig*)
Pult [pʊlt] *n* (-[*e*]*s*; *-e*) desk
Pulver ['pʊlvɐ] *n* (*-s*; -) powder; F cash, *sl* dough
pulv(e)rig ['pʊlv(ə)rɪç] *adj* powdery
pulverisieren [pʊlveri'zi:rən] *v/t* (*no -ge-*, *h*) pulverize
'Pulverkaffee *m* instant coffee
'Pulverschnee *m* powder snow
pumm(e)lig ['pʊm(ə)lɪç] F *adj* chubby, plump, tubby
Pumpe ['pʊmpə] *f* (-; *-n*) TECH pump
'pumpen *v/i and v/t* TECH pump; F lend; borrow
Punker ['paŋkɐ] F *m* (*-s*; -), **'Punkerin** *f* (-; *-nen*) punk
Punkt [pʊŋkt] *m* (-[*e*]*s*; *-e*) point (*a. fig*); dot; full stop, period; *fig* spot, place; ***um Punkt zehn*** (***Uhr***) at ten (o'clock) sharp; ***nach Punkten gewinnen*** *etc* SPORT win *etc* on points
punktieren [pʊŋk'ti:rən] *v/t* (*no -ge-*, *h*) dot; MED puncture
pünktlich ['pʏŋktlɪç] *adj* punctual; ***pünktlich sein*** be on time
'Pünktlichkeit *f* (-; *no pl*) punctuality
'Punktsieger *m* SPORT winner on points
Punktspiel *n* SPORT league game
Pupille [pu'pɪlə] *f* (-; *-n*) ANAT pupil
Puppe ['pʊpə] *f* (-; *-n*) doll, F *a.* chick; THEA puppet (*a. fig*); MOT dummy; ZO chrysalis, pupa
'Puppenspiel *n* puppet show
Puppenstube *f* doll's house
Puppenwagen *m* doll carriage, *Br* doll's pram
pur [pu:ɐ] *adj* pure (*a. fig*); *whisky etc*: straight, *Br* neat
Purpur ['pʊrpʊr] *m* (*-s*; *no pl*) crimson
'purpurrot *adj* crimson
Purzelbaum ['pʊrtsəl-] *m* somersault; ***e-n Purzelbaum schlagen*** turn a somersault
purzeln ['pʊrtsəln] *v/i* (*ge-*, *sein*) tumble
Pute ['pu:tə] *f* (-; *-n*) ZO turkey (hen)
Puter ['pu:tɐ] *m* (*-s*; -) ZO turkey (cock)
Putsch [pʊtʃ] *m* (-[*e*]*s*; *-e*) putsch, coup (d'état)
'putschen *v/i* (*ge-*, *h*) revolt, make a putsch
Putz [pʊts] *m* (*-es*; *no pl*) ARCH plaster (-ing); ***unter Putz*** ELECTR concealed
putzen ['pʊtsən] (*ge-*, *h*) **1.** *v/t* clean; polish; wipe; ***sich die Nase putzen*** blow

one's nose; ***sich die Zähne putzen*** brush one's teeth; **2.** *v/i* do the cleaning; ***putzen (gehen)*** work as a cleaner
'**Putzfrau** *f* cleaner, cleaning woman *or* lady
putzig ['pʊtsɪç] *adj* funny, cute
'**Putzlappen** *m* cleaning rag
'**Putzmittel** *n* clean(s)er; polish
Puzzle ['pazəl] *n* (-*s*; -*s*) jigsaw (puzzle)
Pyjama [py'dʒaːma] *m* (-*s*; -*s*) pajamas, *Br* pyjamas
Pyramide [pyra'miːdə] *f* (-; -*n*) pyramid

Q

Quacksalber ['kvakzalbɐ] *m* (-*s*; -) quack (doctor)
Quadrat [kva'draːt] *n* (-[*e*]*s*; -*e*) square; ***ins Quadrat erheben*** MATH square; ***Quadrat...*** *in cpds ...meile, ...meter, ...wurzel, ...zahl etc*: square ...
qua'dratisch *adj* square; MATH quadratic
quaken ['kvaːkən] *v/i* (*ge-*, *h*) *duck*: quack; *frog*: croak
quäken ['kvɛːkən] *v/i* (*ge-*, *h*) squeak
Qual [kvaːl] *f* (-; -*en*) pain, torment, agony; anguish
quälen ['kvɛːlən] *v/t* (*ge-*, *h*) torment (*a. fig*); torture; *fig* pester, plague
Qualifikation [kvalifika'tsjoːn] *f* (-; -*en*) qualification
Qualifikati'ons... *in cpds ...spiel etc*: qualifying ...
qualifizieren [kvalifi'tsiːrən] *v/t and v/refl* (*no -ge-*, *h*) qualify
Qualität [kvali'tɛːt] *f* (-; -*en*) quality
qualitativ [kvalita'tiːf] *adj and adv* in quality
Quali'täts... *in cpds ...arbeit, ...waren etc*: high-quality ...
Qualm [kvalm] *m* (-[*e*]*s*; *no pl*) (thick) smoke
qualmen ['kvalmən] *v/i* (*ge-*, *h*) smoke; F be a heavy smoker
'**qualvoll** *adj* very painful; agonizing
Quantität [kvanti'tɛːt] *f* (-; -*en*) quantity
quantitativ [kvantita'tiːf] *adj and adv* in quantity
Quantum ['kvantʊm] *n* (-*s*; *Quanten*) amount, *fig a.* share
Quarantäne [karan'tɛːnə] *f* (-; -*n*) (***unter Quarantäne stellen*** put in) quarantine
Quark [kvark] *m* (-*s*; *no pl*) curd, cottage cheese
Quartal [kvar'taːl] *n* (-*s*; -*e*) quarter (of a year)
Quartett [kvar'tɛt] *n* (-[*e*]*s*; -*e*) MUS quartet(te)
Quartier [kvar'tiːɐ] *n* (-*s*; -*e*) accommodation; *Swiss*: quarter
Quarz [kvaːɐts] *m* (-*es*; -*e*) MIN quartz
Quatsch [kvatʃ] F *m* (-[*e*]*s*; *no pl*) nonsense, rubbish, *sl* rot, crap, bullshit; ***Quatsch machen*** fool around; joke, F kid
quatschen ['kvatʃən] F *v/i* (*ge-*, *h*) talk rubbish; chat
Quecksilber ['kvɛkzɪlbɐ] *n* (-*s*; *no pl*) mercury, quicksilver
Quelle ['kvɛlə] *f* (-; -*n*) spring, source (*a. fig*), well, *fig a.* origin
'**quellen** *v/i* (*irr, ge-, sein*) pour (***aus*** from)
'**Quellenangabe** *f* reference
quengeln ['kvɛŋəln] F *v/i* (*ge-*, *h*) whine
quer [kveːɐ] *adv* across; crosswise; ***kreuz und quer*** all over the place; ***kreuz und quer durch Deutschland fahren*** travel all over Germany
Quere ['kveːrə] *f*: F ***j-m in die Quere kommen*** get in s.o.'s way
Querfeld'einlauf *m* SPORT cross-country race
'**Querlatte** *f* SPORT crossbar
'**Querschläger** *m* MIL ricochet
'**Querschnitt** *m* cross-section (*a. fig*)
'**querschnitt(s)gelähmt** *adj* MED paraplegic
'**Querstraße** *f* intersecting road; ***zweite Querstraße rechts*** second turning on the right
Querulant [kveru'lant] *m* (-*en*; -*en*), **Queru'lantin** *f* (-; -*nen*) querulous person
quetschen ['kvɛtʃən] *v/t and v/refl* (*ge-*, *h*) squeeze; MED bruise (o.s.)
'**Quetschung** *f* (-; -*en*) MED bruise
quiek(s)en ['kviːk(s)ən] *v/i* (*ge-*, *h*) squeak, squeal
quietschen ['kviːtʃən] *v/i* (*ge-*, *h*) squeal; screech; squeak, creak
quitt [kvɪt] *adj*: ***mit j-m quitt sein*** be quits

or even with s.o. (*a. fig*)
quittieren [kvɪ'tiːrən] *v/t* (*no -ge-, h*) ECON give a receipt for
'**Quittung** *f* (-; *-en*) receipt; *fig* answer
quoll [kvɔl] *pret of* ***quellen***
Quote ['kvoːtə] *f* (-; *-n*) quota; share; rate
'**Quotenregelung** *f* quota system
Quotient [kvo'tsjɛnt] *m* (*-en*; *-en*) MATH quotient

R

Rabatt [ra'bat] *m* (-[*e*]*s*; *-e*) ECON discount, rebate
Rabe ['raːbə] *m* (*-n*; *-n*) ZO raven
rabiat [ra'bjaːt] *adj* rough, tough
Rache ['raxə] *f* (-; *no pl*) revenge; ***aus Rache für*** in revenge for
Rachen ['raxən] *m* (*-s*; -) ANAT throat
rächen ['rɛçən] *v/t* (*ge-, h*) avenge *s.th.*; revenge *s.o.*; ***sich an j-m für et. rächen*** revenge o.s. *or* take revenge on s.o. for s.th.
Rächer ['rɛçɐ] *m* (*-s*; -) avenger
rachsüchtig ['rax-] *adj* revengeful, vindictive
Rad [raːt] *n* (-[*e*]*s*; *Räder* ['rɛːdɐ]) wheel; bicycle, F bike; ***Rad fahren*** cycle, ride a bicycle, F bike; ***ein Rad schlagen*** *peacock*: spread its tail; SPORT turn a (cart)-wheel
Radar [ra'daːɐ] *m, n* (*-s*; *-e*) radar
Radarfalle *f* MOT speed trap
Radarkon͵trolle *f* MOT radar speed check
Radarschirm *m* radar screen
Radarstati͵on *f* radar station
radeln ['raːdəln] F *v/i* (*ge-, sein*) bike
Rädelsführer ['rɛːdəls-] *m* ringleader
Räderwerk ['rɛːdɐ-] *n* TECH gearing
'**Radfahrer** *m* (*-s*; -), '**Radfahrerin** *f* (-; *-nen*) cyclist
radieren [ra'diːrən] *v/t* (*no -ge-, h*) erase, rub out; *art*: etch
Radiergummi [ra'diːɐ-] *m* eraser, *Br a.* rubber
Ra'dierung *f* (-; *-en*) *art*: etching
Radieschen [ra'diːsçən] *n* (*-s*; -) BOT (red) radish
radikal [radi'kaːl] *adj*, **Radi'kale** *m, f* (*-n*; *-n*) radical
Radikalismus [radika'lɪsmʊs] *m* (-; *no pl*) radicalism
Radio ['raːdjo] *n* (*-s*; *-s*) radio; ***im Radio*** on the radio; ***Radio hören*** listen to the radio
radioak'tiv [radjo-] *adj* PHYS radioactive; ***radioaktiver Niederschlag*** fall-out
Radioaktivi'tät *f* (-; *no pl*) radioactivity
'**Radiowecker** *m* clock radio
Radius ['raːdjʊs] *m* (*-s*; *Radien*) radius
'**Radkappe** *f* hubcap
Radrennbahn *f* cycling track
Radrennen *n* cycle race
Radsport *m* cycling
Radsportler *m* cyclist
Radweg *m* cycle track *or* path, bikeway
raffen ['rafən] *v/t* (*ge-, h*) gather up; ***an sich raffen*** grab
Raffinerie [rafinə'riː] *f* (-; *-n*) CHEM refinery
Raffinesse [rafi'nɛsə] *f* (-; *-n*) a) (*no pl*) shrewdness, b) refinement
raffiniert [rafi'niːɐt] *adj* refined (*a. fig*); *fig* shrewd, clever
ragen ['raːgən] *v/i* (*ge-, h*) tower (up), rise (high)
Rahe ['raːə] *f* (-; *-n*) MAR yard
Rahm [raːm] *m* (-[*e*]*s*; *no pl*) cream
rahmen ['raːmən] *v/t* (*ge-, h*) frame; PHOT mount
'**Rahmen** *m* (*-s*; -) frame; *fig* framework; setting; scope; ***aus dem Rahmen fallen*** be out of the ordinary
Rakete [ra'keːtə] *f* (-; *-n*) rocket, MIL *a.* missile; ***ferngelenkte Rakete*** guided missile; ***e-e Rakete abfeuern*** (***starten***) launch a rocket *or* missile
Ra'ketenantrieb *m* rocket propulsion; ***mit Raketenantrieb*** rocket-propelled
Raketenbasis *f* MIL rocket *or* missile base *or* site
rammen ['ramən] *v/t* (*ge-, h*) ram; MOT *etc* hit, collide with
Rampe ['rampə] *f* (-; *-n*) (loading) ramp
'**Rampenlicht** *n* (-[*e*]*s*; *no pl*) THEA footlights; *fig* limelight
Ramsch [ramʃ] F *m* (*-es*; *no pl*) junk
Rand [rant] *m* (-[*e*]*s*; *Ränder* ['rɛndɐ]) edge, border; brink (*a. fig*); rim; brim; margin; ***am Rand(e) des Ruins*** *etc* on the brink of ruin *etc*

randalieren [randa'li:rən] *v/i (no -ge-, h)* kick up a racket
Randalierer [randa'li:rɐ] *m (-s; -)* rowdy, hooligan
'**Randbemerkung** *f* marginal note; *fig* comment
Randgruppe *f* fringe group
'**randlos** *adj* rimless
'**Randstreifen** *m* MOT shoulder
rang [raŋ] *pret of* ***ringen***
Rang *m (-[e]s; Ränge* ['rɛŋə]) position, rank (*a.* MIL); THEA balcony, *Br* circle; *pl* SPORT terraces
rangieren [raŋ'ʒi:rən] *(no -ge-, h)* **1.** *v/t* RAIL switch, *Br* shunt; **2.** *fig v/i* rank (***vor j-m*** before s.o.)
'**Rangordnung** *f* hierarchy
Ranke ['raŋkə] *f (-; -n)* BOT tendril
'**ranken** *v/refl (ge-, h)* BOT creep, climb
rann [ran] *pret of* ***rinnen***
rannte ['rantə] *pret of* ***rennen***
Ranzen ['rantsən] *m (-s; -)* knapsack; satchel
ranzig ['rantsɪç] *adj* rancid, rank
Rappe ['rapə] *m (-n; -n)* ZO black horse
rar [ra:ɐ] *adj* rare, scarce
Rarität [rari'tɛ:t] *f (-; -en)* a) curiosity, b) *(no pl)* rarity
rasch [raʃ] *adj* quick, swift; prompt
rascheln ['raʃəln] *v/i (ge-, h)* rustle
rasen ['ra:zən] *v/i* a) *(ge-, sein)* F MOT race, tear, speed, b) *(ge-, h)* rage; ***rasen vor Begeisterung*** roar with enthusiasm
'**Rasen** *m (-s; -)* lawn, grass
'**rasend** *adj* breakneck; raging; agonizing; splitting; thunderous
'**Rasenmäher** *m* lawn mower
Rasenplatz *m* lawn; *tennis*: grass court
Raserei [ra:zə'rai] *f (-; -en)* a) *(no pl)* frenzied rage; frenzy, madness, b) F MOT reckless driving
Rasierappa,rat [ra'zi:ɐ-] *m* (safety) razor; *esp* ***elektrischer Rasierapparat*** shaver
Rasiercreme *f* shaving cream
rasieren [ra'zi:rən] *v/t and v/refl (no -ge-, h)* shave
Ra'sierklinge *f* razor blade
Rasiermesser *n* (straight) razor
Rasierpinsel *m* shaving brush
Rasierseife *f* shaving soap
Rasierwasser *n* aftershave (lotion)
Rasse ['rasə] *f (-; -n)* race; ZO breed
'**Rassehund** *m* ZO pedigree dog
Rassel ['rasəl] *f (-; -n)*, '**rasseln** *v/i (ge-, h)* rattle
'**Rassen...** *in cpds ...diskriminierung, ...konflikt, ...probleme etc*: *mst* racial ...
Rassentrennung *f* POL (racial) segregation; HIST apartheid
Rassenunruhen *pl* race riots
rassig ['rasɪç] *adj* classy
rassisch ['rasɪʃ] *adj* racial
Rassismus [ra'sɪsmʊs] *m (-; no pl)* POL racism
Ras'sist(in) *(-en; -en/-; -nen)*, **ras'sistisch** *adj* POL racist
Rast [rast] *f (-; -en)* rest, stop; break
rasten ['rastən] *v/i (ge-, h)* rest, stop, take a break
'**rastlos** *adj* restless
'**Rastplatz** *m* resting place; MOT rest area, *Br* lay-by
'**Raststätte** *f* MOT service area
Rasur [ra'zu:ɐ] *f (-; -en)* shave
Rat [ra:t] *m (-[e]s; Räte* ['rɛ:tə]) a) *(no pl)* (piece of) advice, b) council; ***j-n um Rat fragen*** ask s.o.'s advice; ***j-s Rat befolgen*** take s.o.'s advice
Rate ['ra:tə] *f (-; -n)* rate; ECON instal(l)-ment; ***auf Raten*** by instal(l)ments
raten ['ra:tən] *v/t and v/i (irr, ge-, h)* advise; guess; solve; ***j-m zu et. raten*** advise s.o. to do s.th.; ***rate mal!*** (have a) guess!
'**Ratenzahlung** *f* → ***Abzahlung***
'**Rateteam** *n* TV *etc* panel
'**Ratgeber** [-ge:bɐ] *m (-s; -)*, '**Ratgeberin** *f (-; -nen)* adviser, counsel(l)or; *m* guide (***über*** *acc* to)
'**Rathaus** *n* city (*Br* town) hall
ratifizieren [ratifi'tsi:rən] *v/t (no -ge-, h)* ratify
Ration [ra'tsjo:n] *f (-; -en)* ration
rational [ratsjo'na:l] *adj* rational
rationell [ratsjo'nɛl] *adj* efficient; economical
rationieren [ratsjo'ni:rən] *v/t (no -ge-, h)* ration
'**ratlos** *adj* at a loss
'**ratsam** *adj* advisable, wise
'**Ratschlag** *m* piece of advice; ***ein paar gute Ratschläge*** some good advice
Rätsel ['rɛ:tsəl] *n (-s; -)* puzzle; riddle (*both a. fig*); mystery
'**rätselhaft** *adj* puzzling; mysterious
Ratte ['ratə] *f (-; -n)* ZO rat (*a. contp*)
rattern ['ratɐn] *v/i (ge-, h, sein)* rattle, clatter
rau [rau] *adj* rough, rugged (*both a. fig*); harsh; chapped; sore
Raub [raup] *m (-[e]s; no pl)* robbery; loot, booty; prey
Raubbau *m (-[e]s; no pl)* overexploitation (***an*** *dat* of); ***Raubbau mit s-r Gesundheit treiben*** ruin one's health
rauben ['raubən] *v/t (ge-, h)* rob, steal; kidnap; ***j-m et. rauben*** rob s.o. of s.th. (*a. fig*)
Räuber ['rɔʏbɐ] *m (-s; -)* robber

'Raubfisch *m* predatory fish
Raubmord *m* murder with robbery
Raubmörder *m* murderer and robber
Raubtier *n* beast of prey
Raubüberfall *m* holdup, (armed) robbery; mugging
Raubvogel *m* bird of prey
Raubzug *m* raid
Rauch [raux] *m* (-[*e*]*s*; *no pl*) smoke; CHEM *etc* fume
rauchen ['rauxən] *v/i and v/t* (*ge-, h*) smoke; CHEM *etc* fume; ***Rauchen verboten!*** no smoking; ***Pfeife rauchen*** smoke a pipe
Raucher(in) ['rauxɐ (-xərɪn)] (*-s*; *-/-*; *-nen*) smoker (*m a.* RAIL)
Räucher... ['rɔʏçɐ-] *in cpds* *...aal*, *...speck etc*: smoked ...
'räuchern *v/t* (*ge-, h*) smoke
'Räucherstäbchen *n* joss stick
'Rauchfahne *f* trail of smoke
rauchig ['rauxɪç] *adj* smoky
'Rauchwaren *pl* tobacco products; furs
Rauchzeichen *n* smoke signal
Räude ['rɔʏdə] *f* (*-; -n*) VET mange
'räudig *adj* VET mangy
raufen ['raufən] (*ge-, h*) **1.** *v/t*: ***sich die Haare raufen*** tear one's hair; **2.** *v/i* fight, scuffle
Rauferei [raufə'rai] *f* (*-; -en*) fight, scuffle
Raum [raum] *m* (-[*e*]*s*; *Räume* ['rɔʏmə]) room; space; area; (outer) space
Raumanzug *m* spacesuit
Raumdeckung *f* SPORT zone marking
räumen ['rɔʏmən] *v/t* (*ge-, h*) leave, move out of; check out of; clear (***von*** of); evacuate (*a.* MIL); ***s-e Sachen in ...*** (*acc*) ***räumen*** put one's things (away) in ...
'Raumfahrer F *m* spaceman
Raumfahrt *f* (*-; no pl*) space travel *or* flight; astronautics
Raumfahrt... *in cpds* *...technik*, *...zentrum etc*: space ...
Raumfähre *f* space shuttle
Raumflug *m* space flight
Rauminhalt *m* volume
Raumkapsel *f* space capsule
Raumla,bor *n* space lab
räumlich ['rɔʏmlɪç] *adj* three-dimensional
'Raumschiff *n* spacecraft; spaceship
Raumsonde *f* space probe
Raumstati,on *f* space station
'Räumung *f* (*-; -en*) clearance; evacuation (*a.* MIL); JUR eviction
'Räumungsverkauf *m* ECON clearance sale
raunen ['raunən] *v/i* (*ge-, h*) whisper, murmur
Raupe ['raupə] *f* (*-; -n*) ZO caterpillar, TECH *a.* track
'Raupenschlepper *m* MOT caterpillar tractor
'Raureif *m* hoarfrost
raus [raus] F *int* get out (of here)!
Rausch [rauʃ] *m* (*-es*; *Räusche* ['rɔʏʃə]) drunkenness, intoxication; F high; *fig* ecstasy; ***e-n Rausch haben*** be drunk; ***s-n Rausch ausschlafen*** sleep it off
rauschen ['rauʃən] *v/i* a) (*ge-, h*) *water etc*: rush; *brook*: murmur; *storm*: roar, b) (*ge-, sein*) sweep
rauschend *adj* thunderous (*applause*); ***rauschendes Fest*** lavish celebration
'Rauschgift *n* drug(s), narcotic(s)
Rauschgiftdezer,nat *n* narcotics *or* drugs squad
Rauschgifthandel *m* drug traffic(king)
Rauschgifthändler *m* drug trafficker, F pusher
räuspern ['rɔʏspɐn] *v/refl* (*ge-, h*) clear one's throat
Razzia ['ratsja] *f* (*-; -ien*) raid, roundup
Reagenzglas [rea'gɛnts-] *n* CHEM test tube
reagieren [rea'giːrən] *v/i* (*no -ge-, h*) CHEM, MED react (***auf*** *acc* to), *fig a.* respond (to)
Reaktion [reak'tsjoːn] *f* (*-; -en*) CHEM, MED, PHYS, POL reaction (***auf*** *acc* to), *fig a.* response (to)
Reaktor [re'aktoːɐ] *m* (*-s*; *-en* [reak'toːrən]) PHYS (nuclear *or* atomic) reactor
real [re'aːl] *adj* real; concrete
realisieren [reali'ziːrən] *v/t* (*no -ge-, h*) realize
Realismus [rea'lɪsmʊs] *m* (*-; no pl*) realism
rea'listisch *adj* realistic
Realität [reali'tɛːt] *f* (*-; no pl*) reality
Re'alschule *f appr* (junior) highschool, *Br* secondary (modern) school
Rebe ['reːbə] *f* (*-; -n*) BOT vine
Rebell [re'bɛl] *m* (*-en; -en*) rebel
rebellieren [rebɛ'liːrən] *v/i* (*no -ge-, h*) rebel, revolt, rise (*all*: ***gegen*** against)
Re'bellin *f* (*-; -nen*) rebel
re'bellisch *adj* rebellious
Rebhuhn ['reːp-] *n* ZO partridge
'Rebstock *m* BOT vine
Rechen ['rɛçən] *m* (*-s; -*), **'rechen** *v/t* (*ge-, h*) rake
'Rechenaufgabe *f* MATH (arithmetical) problem
Rechenfehler *m* MATH arithmetical error, miscalculation
Rechenma,schine *f* calculator; computer
'Rechenschaft *f*: ***Rechenschaft ablegen***

R

über (*acc*) account for; ***zur Rechenschaft ziehen*** call to account (***wegen*** for)
'**Rechenschieber** *m* MATH slide rule
Rechenwerk *n* EDP arithmetic unit
Rechenzentrum *n* computer center (*Br* centre)
rechnen ['rɛçnən] *v/i and v/t* (*ge-*, *h*) calculate, reckon; work out, do sums; count; ***rechnen mit*** *fig* expect; count on; ***mit mir kannst du nicht rechnen!*** count me out!
'**Rechnen** *n* (*-s*; *no pl*) arithmetic
Rechner ['rɛçnɐ] *m* (*-s*; -) calculator; computer
'**rechnerabhängig** *adj* EDP online
rechnerisch ['rɛçnərɪʃ] *adj* arithmetical
'**rechnerunabhängig** *adj* EDP offline
'**Rechnung** *f* (-; *-en*) MATH calculation; problem, sum; ECON invoice, bill, check; ***die Rechnung, bitte!*** can I have the check, please?; ***das geht auf m-e Rechnung*** that's on me
recht [rɛçt] **1.** *adj* right; correct; POL right-wing; ***auf der rechten Seite*** on the right(-hand side); ***mir ist es recht*** I don't mind; **2.** *adv* right(ly), correctly; rather, quite; ***ich weiß nicht recht*** I don't really know; ***es geschieht ihm recht*** it serves him right; ***erst recht*** all the more; ***erst recht nicht*** even less; ***du kommst gerade recht*** (***zu***) you're just in time (for); ***j-m recht geben*** agree with s.o.; ***recht haben*** be right
Recht *n* (-[*e*]*s*; *-e*) a) right, claim (*both*: ***auf*** *acc* to), b) (*no pl*) JUR law; justice; ***gleiches Recht*** equal rights; ***Recht haben*** → ***recht***; ***j-m Recht geben*** → ***recht***; ***im Recht sein*** be in the right; ***er hat es mit*** (***vollem***) ***Recht getan*** he was (perfectly) right to do so; ***ein Recht auf et. haben*** be entitled to s.th.
'**Rechteck** *n* (-[*e*]*s*; *-e*) rectangle
'**rechteckig** *adj* rectangular
'**rechtfertigen** *v/t* (*ge-*, *h*) justify
'**Rechtfertigung** *f* (-; *-en*) justification
'**rechtlich** *adj* JUR legal
'**rechtlos** *adj* without rights; outcast
'**rechtmäßig** *adj* JUR lawful; legitimate; legal
'**Rechtmäßigkeit** *f* (-; *no pl*) JUR lawfulness, legitimacy
rechts [rɛçts] *adv* on the right(-hand side); ***nach rechts*** to the right
Rechts... *in cpds* POL right-wing ...
Rechtsanspruch *m* legal claim (***auf*** *acc* to)
Rechtsanwalt *m*, **Rechtsanwältin** [-anvɛltɪn] *f* (-; *-nen*) lawyer
Rechts'außen *m* (-; -) *soccer*: outside right
'**rechtschaffen** *adj* honest
'**Rechtschreibfehler** *m* spelling mistake
Rechtschreibung *f* (-; *no pl*) spelling, orthography
'**rechtsextre,mistisch** *adj* POL extreme right
'**Rechtsfall** *m* JUR (law) case
'**Rechtshänder** [-hɛndɐ] *m* (*-s*; -), '**Rechtshänderin** *f* (-; *-nen*) right-handed person; ***sie ist Rechtshänderin*** she is right-handed
'**Rechtsprechung** *f* (-; *no pl*) jurisdiction
'**rechtsradi,kal** *adj* POL extreme right-wing
'**Rechtsschutz** *m* legal protection; legal costs insurance
'**rechtswidrig** *adj* JUR illegal, unlawful
'**rechtwink(e)lig** *adj* rectangular
'**rechtzeitig** **1.** *adj* punctual; **2.** *adv* in time (***zu*** for)
Reck [rɛk] *n* (-[*e*]*s*; *-e*) horizontal bar
recken ['rɛkən] *v/t* (*ge-*, *h*) stretch; ***sich recken*** stretch o.s.
recyceln [ri'saikəln] *v/t* (*no -ge-*, *h*) recycle
Recyclingpa,pier [ri'saiklɪŋ-] *n* recycled paper
Redakteur [redak'tøːɐ] *m* (*-s*; *-e*), **Redak'teurin** *f* (-; *-nen*) editor
Redaktion [redak'tsjoːn] *f* (-; *-en*) a) (*no pl*) editing, b) editorial staff, editors, c) editorial office *or* department
redaktionell [redaktsjo'nɛl] *adj* editorial
Rede ['reːdə] *f* (-; *-n*) speech, address; talk (***von*** of); ***e-e Rede halten*** make a speech; ***direkte*** (***indirekte***) ***Rede*** LING direct (reported *or* indirect) speech; ***j-n zur Rede stellen*** take s.o. to task; ***nicht der Rede wert*** not worth mentioning
'**redegewandt** *adj* eloquent
reden ['reːdən] *v/i and v/t* (*ge-*, *h*) talk, speak (*both*: ***mit*** to; ***über*** *acc* about, of); ***ich möchte mit dir reden*** I'd like to talk to you; ***die Leute reden*** people talk; ***j-n zum Reden bringen*** make s.o. talk
'**Redensart** *f* saying, phrase
redlich ['reːtlɪç] *adj* upright, honest; ***sich redlich(e) Mühe geben*** do one's best
Redner ['reːdnɐ] *m* (*-s*; -), '**Rednerin** *f* (-; *-nen*) speaker
'**Rednerpult** *n* speaker's desk
redselig ['reːtzeːlɪç] *adj* talkative
reduzieren [redu'tsiːrən] *v/t* (*no -ge-*, *h*) reduce (***auf*** *acc* to)
Reeder ['reːdɐ] *m* (*-s*; -) shipowner
Reederei [reːdə'rai] *f* (-; *-en*) shipping

R

company
reell [re'ɛl] *adj* reasonable, fair (*price*); real (*chance*); solid (*firm*)
Referat [refe'ra:t] *n* (-[*e*]*s*; -*e*) paper; report; lecture; ***ein Referat halten*** read a paper
Referendar [referɛn'da:ɐ] *m* (-*s*; -*e*), **Referen'darin** *f* (-; -*nen*) *appr* trainee teacher
Referent [refe'rɛnt] *m* (-*en*; -*en*), **Refe'rentin** *f* (-; -*nen*) speaker
Referenz [refe'rɛnts] *f* (-; -*en*) reference
referieren [refe'ri:rən] *v/i* (*no -ge-*, *h*) (give a) report *or* lecture (***über*** *acc* on)
reflektieren [reflɛk'ti:rən] *v/t and v/i* (*no -ge-*, *h*) reflect (*fig* ***über*** *acc* [up]on)
Reflex [re'flɛks] *m* (-*es*; -*e*) reflex
reflexiv [reflɛ'ksi:f] *adj* LING reflexive
Reform [re'fɔrm] *f* (-; -*en*) reform
Reformator [refɔr'ma:to:ɐ] *m* (-*s*; -*en* [-ma'to:rən]), **Reformer(in)** [re'fɔrmɐ (-mərɪn)] (-*s*; -/-; -*nen*) reformer
Re'formhaus *n* health food store (*Br* shop)
reformieren [refɔr'mi:rən] *v/t* (*no -ge-*, *h*) reform
Refrain [rə'frɛ̃:] *m* (-*s*; -*s*) refrain, chorus
Regal [re'ga:l] *n* (-*s*; -*e*) shelf (unit), shelves
rege ['re:gə] *adj* lively; busy; active
Regel ['re:gəl] *f* (-; -*n*) rule; MED period, menstruation; ***in der Regel*** as a rule
'regelmäßig *adj* regular
regeln ['re:gəln] *v/t* (*ge-*, *h*) regulate, TECH *a.* adjust; ECON settle
'regelrecht *adj* regular (*a.* F)
'Regeltechnik *f* control engineering
'Regelung *f* (-; -*en*) regulation; adjustment; ECON settlement; TECH control
'regelwidrig *adj* against the rule(s); SPORT unfair; ***regelwidriges Spiel*** foul play
regen ['re:gən] *v/t and v/refl* (*ge-*, *h*) move, stir
'Regen *m* (-*s*; -) rain; ***starker Regen*** heavy rain(fall)
Regenbogen *m* rainbow
Regenbogenhaut *f* ANAT iris
Regenguss *m* (heavy) shower, downpour
Regenmantel *m* raincoat
Regenschauer *m* shower
Regenschirm *m* umbrella
Regentag *m* rainy day
Regentropfen *m* raindrop
Regenwald *m* rain forest
Regenwasser *n* rainwater
Regenwetter *n* rainy weather
Regenwurm *m* ZO earthworm
Regenzeit *f* rainy season, the rains
Regie [re'ʒi:] *f* (-; *no pl*) THEA, *film etc*: direction; ***unter der Regie von*** directed by
Re'gieanweisung *f* stage direction
regieren [re'gi:rən] (*no -ge-*, *h*) **1.** *v/i* reign; **2.** *v/t* govern (*a.* LING), rule
Re'gierung *f* (-; -*en*) government, administration; reign
Re'gierungsbezirk *m* administrative district
Regierungschef *m* head of government
Regierungswechsel *m* change of government
Regime [re'ʒi:m] *n* (-*s*; -) POL regime
Re'gimekritiker *m* POL dissident
Regiment [regi'mɛnt] *n* (-[*e*]*s*; -*er*) a) (*no pl*) rule (*a. fig*), b) MIL regiment
Regisseur [reʒɪ'sø:ɐ] *m* (-*s*; -*e*), **Regis'seurin** *f* (-; -*nen*) THEA, *film etc*: director, THEA *Br a.* producer
Register [re'gɪstɐ] *n* (-*s*; -) register (*a.* MUS), record; index
registrieren [regɪs'tri:rən] *v/t* (*no -ge-*, *h*) register, record; *fig* note
Registrierkasse [regɪs'tri:ɐ-] *f* cash register
Reglement [reglə'mã:] *n* (-*s*; -*s*) regulation, order, rule
Regler ['re:glɐ] *m* (-*s*; -) TECH control
regnen ['re:gnən] *v/i* (*ge-*, *h*) rain (*a. fig*); ***es regnet in Strömen*** it's pouring with rain
'regnerisch *adj* rainy
regulär [regu'lɛ:ɐ] *adj* regular; normal
regulierbar [regu'li:ɐba:ɐ] *adj* adjustable; controllable
regulieren [regu'li:rən] *v/t* (*no -ge-*, *h*) regulate, adjust; control
'Regung *f* (-; -*en*) movement, motion; emotion; impulse
'regungslos *adj* motionless
Reh [re:] *n* (-[*e*]*s*; -*e*) ZO deer, roe; doe; GASTR venison
rehabilitieren [rehabili'ti:rən] *v/t* (*no -ge-*, *h*) rehabilitate
'Rehbock *m* ZO (roe)buck
Rehkeule *f* GASTR leg of venison
Rehkitz *n* ZO fawn
Reibe ['raibə] *f* (-; -*n*), **Reibeisen** ['raip-] *n* (-*s*; -) grater, rasp
reiben ['raibən] *v/i and v/t* (*irr*, *ge-*, *h*) rub; grate, grind; ***sich die Augen*** (***Hände***) ***reiben*** rub one's eyes (hands)
'Reibung *f* (-; -*en*) TECH *etc* friction
'reibungslos *adj* TECH *etc* frictionless; *fig* smooth
reich [raiç] *adj* rich (***an*** *dat* in), wealthy; abundant
Reich *n* (-[*e*]*s*; -*e*) empire, kingdom (*a.* REL, BOT, ZO); *fig* world
reichen ['raiçən] (*ge-*, *h*) **1.** *v/t* reach;

R

hand, pass; give, hold out (*one's hand*); **2.** *v/i* last, do; ***reichen bis*** reach *or* come up to; ***das reicht*** that will do; F ***mir reicht's!*** I've had enough
'reichhaltig *adj* rich
'reichlich 1. *adj* rich, plentiful; plenty of; **2.** *adv* rather; generously
'Reichtum *m* (*-s; no pl*) wealth (***an*** *dat* of) (*a. fig*)
'Reichweite *f* reach; AVIAT, MIL *etc* range; ***in (außer) (j-s) Reichweite*** within (out of) (s.o.'s) reach
reif [raif] *adj* ripe, *esp fig* mature
Reif *m* (*-[e]s; no pl*) white frost, hoarfrost
Reife ['raifə] *f* (*-; no pl*) ripeness, *esp fig* maturity
'reifen *v/i* (*ge-, sein*) ripen, mature (*both a. fig*)
Reifen ['raifən] *m* (*-s; -*) hoop; MOT *etc* tire, *Br* tyre
Reifenpanne *f* MOT flat tire (*Br* tyre), puncture, F flat
'Reifeprüfung *f* → ***Abitur***
'reiflich *adj* careful
Reihe ['raiə] *f* (*-; -n*) line, row; number; series; ***der Reihe nach*** in turn; ***ich bin an der Reihe*** it's my turn
'Reihenfolge *f* order
'Reihenhaus *n* row (*Br* terraced) house
'reihenweise *adv* in rows; F *fig* by the dozen
Reiher ['raiɐ] *m* (*-s; -*) ZO heron
Reim [raim] *m* (*-[e]s; -e*) rhyme
reimen ['raimən] *v/t and v/refl* (*ge-, h*) rhyme (***auf*** *acc* with)
rein [rain] *adj* pure (*a. fig*); clean; *fig* clear (*conscience*); plain (*truth*); mere, sheer, nothing but
'Reinfall F *m* flop; let-down
'Reingewinn *m* ECON net profit
'reinhauen F *v/i* (*sep, -ge-, h*) tuck in
'Reinheit *f* (*-; no pl*) purity (*a. fig*); cleanness
reinigen ['rainɪgən] *v/t* (*ge-, h*) clean; cleanse (*a.* MED); dry-clean; *fig* purify
'Reinigung *f* (*-; -en*) clean(s)ing; *fig* purification; (dry) cleaners; ***chemische Reinigung*** dry cleaning; dry cleaner's
'Reinigungsmittel *n* cleaning agent, cleaner, detergent
'reinlich *adj* clean; cleanly
'reinrassig *adj* ZO purebred, pedigree; thoroughbred
'Reinschrift *f* fair copy
Reis [rais] *m* (*-es; -e*) BOT rice
Reise ['raizə] *f* (*-; -n*) trip; journey; tour; MAR voyage; ***auf Reisen sein*** be travel(l)ing; ***e-e Reise machen*** take a trip; ***gute Reise!*** have a nice trip!
Reiseandenken *n* souvenir
Reisebü,ro *n* travel agency *or* bureau
Reiseführer *m* guide(book)
Reisegesellschaft *f* tourist party; tour operator
Reisekosten *pl* travel(l)ing expenses
Reisekrankheit *f* travel sickness
Reiseleiter(in) tour guide *or* manager, *Br* courier
'reisen *v/i* (*ge-, sein*) travel; ***durch Frankreich reisen*** tour France; ***ins Ausland reisen*** go abroad
'Reisende *m, f* (*-n; -n*) travel(l)er; tourist; passenger
'Reisepass *m* passport
Reisescheck *m* travel(l)er's check (*Br* cheque)
Reisetasche *f* travel(l)ing bag, holdall
Reisig ['raizɪç] *n* (*-s; no pl*) brushwood
Reißbrett ['rais-] *n* drawing board
reißen ['raisən] (*irr, ge-*) **1.** *v/t* (*h*) tear (***in Stücke*** to pieces), rip; pull, drag; ZO kill; F crack (*jokes*); SPORT knock down; ***an sich reißen*** seize, snatch, grab; **2.** *v/i* (*sein*) break, burst; ***sich um et. reißen*** scramble for (*or* to get) s.th.
reißend *adj* torrential
Reißer ['raisɐ] F *m* (*-s; -*) thriller; hit
reißerisch ['raisərɪʃ] *adj* sensational, loud
'Reißverschluss *m* zipper; ***den Reißverschluss an et. öffnen (schließen)*** unzip (zip up) s.th.
Reißzwecke *f* thumbtack, *Br* drawing pin
reiten ['raitən] (*irr, ge-*) **1.** *v/i* (*sein*) ride, go on horseback; **2.** *v/t* (*h*) ride
'Reiten *n* (*-s; no pl*) horseback riding
Reiter ['raitɐ] *m* (*-s; -*) rider, horseman
Reiterin ['raitərɪn] *f* (*-; -nen*) rider, horsewoman
'Reitpferd *n* saddle *or* riding horse
Reiz [raits] *m* (*-es; -e*) charm, attraction, appeal; thrill; MED, PSYCH stimulus; ***(für j-n) den Reiz verlieren*** lose one's appeal (for s.o.)
'reizbar *adj* irritable, excitable
reizen ['raitsən] (*ge-, h*) **1.** *v/t* irritate (*a.* MED), annoy; ZO bait; provoke; appeal to, attract; tempt; challenge; **2.** *v/i cards*: bid
'reizend *adj* charming, delightful; lovely, sweet, cute
'reizlos *adj* unattractive
'Reizung *f* (*-; -en*) irritation (*a.* MED)
'reizvoll *adj* attractive; challenging
'Reizwort *n* (*-[e]s; -wörter*) emotive word
rekeln ['rɛːkəln] F *v/refl* (*ge-, h*) loll
Reklamation [reklama'tsjoːn] *f* (*-; -en*) complaint
Reklame [re'klaːmə] *f* (*-; -n*) advertising,

R

publicity; advertisement, F ad; ***Reklame machen für*** advertise, promote
reklamieren [rekla'mi:rən] *v/i* (*no -ge-, h*) complain (***wegen*** about), protest (against)
Rekord [re'kɔrt] *m* (-[*e*]*s*; -*e*) record; ***e-n Rekord aufstellen*** set *or* establish a record
Rekrut [re'kru:t] *m* (-*en*; -*en*) MIL recruit
rekrutieren [rekru'ti:rən] *v/t* (*no -ge-, h*) recruit
Rektor ['rɛkto:ɐ] *m* (-*s*; -*en* [rɛk'to:rən]) principal, *Br* headmaster; UNIV president, *Br* rector
Rektorin [rɛk'to:rɪn] *f* (-; -*nen*) principal, *Br* headmistress; UNIV president, *Br* rector
relativ [rela'ti:f] *adj* relative
Relief [re'ljɛf] *n* (-*s*; -*s*) relief
Religion [reli'gjo:n] *f* (-; -*en*) religion
religiös [reli'gjø:s] *adj* religious
Reling ['re:lɪŋ] *f* (-; -*s*) MAR rail
Reliquie [re'li:kvjə] *f* (-; -*n*) relic
Rempelei [rɛmpə'lai] F *f* (-; -*en*), **rempeln** ['rɛmpəln] F *v/t* (*ge-, h*) jostle
Rennbahn ['rɛn-] *f* racecourse, racetrack; cycling track
'Rennboot *n* racing boat; speedboat
rennen ['rɛnən] *v/i and v/t* (*irr, ge-, sein*) run
'Rennen *n* (-*s*; -) race (*a. fig*); heat
'Rennfahrer *m*, **Rennfahrerin** *f* racing driver; racing cyclist
Rennläufer *m* ski racer
Rennpferd *n* racehorse, racer
Rennrad *n* racing bicycle, racer
Rennsport *m* racing
Rennstall *m* racing stable
Rennwagen *m* race (*Br* racing) car, racer
renommiert [renɔ'mi:ɐt] *adj* renowned
renovieren [reno'vi:rən] *v/t* (*no -ge-, h*) renovate, F do up; redecorate
rentabel [rɛn'ta:bəl] *adj* ECON profitable, paying
Rente ['rɛntə] *f* (-; -*n*) (old age) pension; ***in Rente gehen*** retire
'Rentenalter *n* retirement age
Rentenversicherung *f* pension scheme
Rentier ['rɛnti:ɐ] *n* (-*s*; -*e*) ZO reindeer
rentieren [rɛn'ti:rən] *v/refl* (*no -ge-, h*) ECON pay; *fig* be worth it
Rentner ['rɛntnɐ] *m* (-*s*; -), **'Rentnerin** [-nərɪn] *f* (-; -*nen*) (old age) pensioner
Reparatur [repara'tu:ɐ] *f* (-; -*en*) repair
Reparaturwerkstatt *f* repair shop; MOT garage
reparieren [repa'ri:rən] *v/t* (*no -ge-, h*) repair, mend, F fix
Reportage [repɔr'ta:ʒə] *f* (-; -*n*) report
Reporter [re'pɔrtɐ] *m* (-*s*; -), **Re'porterin** *f* (-; -*nen*) reporter
Repräsentant [reprɛzɛn'tant] *m* (-*en*; -*en*) representative
Repräsentantenhaus *n* PARL House of Representatives
Repräsen'tantin *f* (-; -*nen*) representative
repräsentieren [reprɛzɛn'ti:rən] *v/t* (*no -ge-, h*) represent
Repressalie [reprɛ'sa:ljə] *f* (-; -*n*) reprisal
Reproduktion [reproduk'tsjo:n] *f* (-; -*en*) reproduction, print
reproduzieren [reprodu'tsi:rən] *v/t* (*no -ge-, h*) reproduce
Reptil [rɛp'ti:l] *n* (-*s*; -*ien*) ZO reptile
Republik [repu'bli:k] *f* (-; -*en*) republic
Republikaner [republi'ka:nɐ] *m* (-*s*; -), **Republi'kanerin** *f* (-; -*nen*), **republi'kanisch** *adj* POL republican
Reservat [rezɛr'va:t] *n* (-[*e*]*s*; -*e*) (p)reserve; reservation
Reserve [re'zɛrvə] *f* (-; -*n*) reserve (*a.* MIL)
Reserve... *in cpds …kanister, …rad etc*: spare …
reservieren [rezɛr'vi:rən] *v/t* (*no -ge-, h*) reserve (*a.* ***reservieren lassen***); ***j-m e-n Platz reservieren*** keep *or* save a seat for s.o.
reserviert [rezɛr'vi:ɐt] *adj* reserved (*a. fig*); aloof
Reser'viertheit *f* (-; *no pl*) aloofness
Residenz [rezi'dɛnts] *f* (-; -*en*) residence
Resignation [rezɪgna'tsjo:n] *f* (-; *no pl*) resignation
resignieren [rezɪ'gni:rən] *v/i* (*no -ge-, h*) give up
resigniert [rezɪ'gni:ɐt] *adj* resigned
Resoziali'sierung *f* (-; -*en*) rehabilitation
Respekt [re'spɛkt] *m* (-[*e*]*s*; *no pl*) respect (***vor*** *dat* for)
respektieren [respɛk'ti:rən] *v/t* (*no -ge-, h*) respect
re'spektlos *adj* irreverent, disrespectful
re'spektvoll *adj* respectful
Ressort [rɛ'so:ɐ] *n* (-*s*; -*s*) department, province
Rest [rɛst] *m* (-[*e*]*s*; -*e*) rest; *pl* remains, remnants; GASTR leftovers; F ***das gab ihm den Rest*** that finished him (off)
Restaurant [rɛsto'rã:] *n* (-*s*; -*s*) restaurant
restaurieren [rɛsto'ri:rən] *v/t* (*no -ge-, h*) restore
'Restbetrag *m* remainder
'restlich *adj* remaining
'restlos *adv* completely
Resultat [rezʊl'ta:t] *n* (-[*e*]*s*; -*e*) result (*a.* SPORT), outcome
Retorte [re'tɔrtə] *f* (-; -*n*) CHEM retort
Re'tortenbaby F *n* test-tube baby

retten ['rɛtən] *v/t (ge-, h)* save, rescue (*both*: ***aus*** *dat*, ***vor*** *dat* from)
Retter ['rɛtɐ] *m (-s; -)*, **'Retterin** *f (-; -nen)* rescuer
Rettich ['rɛtɪç] *m (-s; -e)* BOT radish
'Rettung *f (-; -en)* rescue (***aus*** *dat*, ***vor*** *dat* from); ***das war s-e Rettung*** that saved him
'Rettungsboot *n* lifeboat
Rettungsmannschaft *f* rescue party
Rettungsring *m* life belt, life buoy
Rettungsschwimmer *m* lifeguard
Reue ['rɔʏə] *f (-; no pl)* remorse, repentance (*both*: ***über*** *acc* for)
reumütig ['rɔʏmy:tɪç] *adj* repentant
Revanche [re'vã:ʃ(ə)] *f (-; -n)* revenge
revanchieren [revã'ʃi:rən] *v/refl (no -ge-, h)* have one's revenge (***bei, an*** *dat* on); make it up (***bei j-m*** to s.o.)
Revers [re've:ɐ] *n, m (-; -)* lapel
revidieren [revi'di:rən] *v/t (no -ge-, h)* revise; ECON audit
Revier [re'vi:ɐ] *n (-s; -e)* district; ZO territory (*a. fig*); → ***Polizeirevier***
Revision [revi'zjo:n] *f (-; -en)* revision; ECON audit; JUR appeal
Revolte [re'vɔltə] *f (-; -n)*, **revoltieren** [revɔl'ti:rən] *v/i (no -ge-, h)* revolt
Revolution [revolu'tsjo:n] *f (-; -en)* revolution
revolutionär [revolutsjo'nɛ:ɐ] *adj*, **Revolutio'när(in)** *(-s; -e/-; -nen)* revolutionary
Revolver [re'vɔlvɐ] *m (-s; -)* revolver, F gun
Revue [re'vy:] *f (-; -n)* THEA (musical) show
Rezept [re'tsɛpt] *n (-[e]s; -e)* MED prescription; GASTR recipe (*a. fig*)
Rezession [retsɛ'sjo:n] *f (-; -en)* ECON recession
Rhabarber [ra'barbɐ] *m (-s; no pl)* BOT rhubarb
rhetorisch [re'to:rɪʃ] *adj* rhetorical
Rheuma ['rɔʏma] *n (-s; no pl)* MED rheumatism
rhythmisch ['rʏtmɪʃ] *adj* rhythmic(al)
Rhythmus ['rʏtmʊs] *m (-; -men)* rhythm
Ribisel ['ri:bi:zəl] *Austrian f (-; -[n])* → ***Johannisbeere***
richten ['rɪçtən] *v/t (ge-, h)* fix; get *s.th.* ready, prepare; do (*room, one's hair*); (***sich***) ***richten an*** (*acc*) address (o.s.) to; put *a question* to; ***richten auf*** (*acc*) direct *or* turn to; point *or* aim *camera, gun etc* at; ***richten gegen*** direct against; ***sich richten nach*** go by, act according to; follow (*fashion etc*); depend on; ***ich richte mich ganz nach dir*** I leave it to you
Richter ['rɪçtɐ] *m (-s; -)*, **'Richterin** *f (-; -nen)* judge
'richterlich *adj* judicial
'Richtgeschwindigkeit *f* MOT recommended speed
richtig ['rɪçtɪç] **1.** *adj* right; correct, proper; true; real; **2.** *adv*: ***richtig nett*** (***böse***) really nice (angry); ***et. richtig machen*** do s.th. right; ***m-e Uhr geht richtig*** my watch is right
'Richtigkeit *f (-; no pl)* correctness
richtigstellen *v/t (sep, -ge-, h) fig* put *or* set right
'Richtlinien *pl* guidelines
Richtpreis *m* ECON recommended price
'Richtung *f (-; -en)* direction; POL leaning; PAINT *etc* style
'richtungslos *adj* aimless, disorient(at)ed
'richtungweisend *adj* pioneering
rieb [ri:p] *pret of* ***reiben***
riechen ['ri:çən] *v/i and v/t (irr, ge-, h)* smell (***nach*** of; ***an*** *dat* at)
rief [ri:f] *pret of* ***rufen***
Riegel ['ri:gəl] *m (-s; -)* bolt, bar
Riemen ['ri:mən] *m (-s; -)* strap; TECH belt; MAR oar
Riese ['ri:zə] *m (-n; -n)* giant (*a. fig*)
rieseln ['ri:zəln] *v/i (ge-, sein)* trickle; *rain*: drizzle; *snow*: fall gently
'Riesen... *in cpds mst* giant ..., gigantic ..., enormous ...
Riesenerfolg *m* huge success, *film etc*: *a.* smash hit
'riesengroß, **'riesenhaft** → ***riesig***
'Riesenrad *n* Ferris wheel
riesig ['ri:zɪç] *adj* enormous, gigantic, giant
'Riesin *f (-; -nen)* giantess (*a. fig*)
riet [ri:t] *pret of* ***raten***
Riff [rɪf] *n (-[e]s; -e)* GEOGR reef
Rille ['rɪlə] *f (-; -n)* groove
Rind [rɪnt] *n (-[e]s; -er* ['rɪndɐ]) ZO cow, *pl* cattle; GASTR beef
Rinde ['rɪndə] *f (-; -n)* BOT bark; GASTR rind; crust
Rinderbraten ['rɪndɐ-] *m* roast beef
Rinderherde *f* herd of cattle
'Rindfleisch *n* GASTR beef
Rind(s)leder *n* cowhide
Rindvieh *n* ZO cattle
Ring [rɪŋ] *m (-[e]s; -e)* ring (*a. fig*); MOT ring road; *subway etc*: circle (line)
'Ringbuch *n* loose-leaf *or* ring binder
ringeln ['rɪŋəln] *v/refl (ge-, h)* curl, coil (*a.* ZO)
'Ringelnatter *f* ZO grass snake
'Ringelspiel *Austrian n* → ***Karussell***
ringen ['rɪŋən] *(irr, ge-, h)* **1.** *v/i* SPORT wrestle (***mit*** with), *fig a.* struggle (against, with; ***um*** for); ***nach Atem rin-***

R

gen gasp (for breath); **2.** *v/t* wring
'Ringen *n* (*-s; no pl*) SPORT wrestling
Ringer ['rɪŋɐ] *m* (*-s; -*) SPORT wrestler
'ringförmig [-fœrmɪç] *adj* circular
'Ringkampf *m* SPORT wrestling match
'Ringrichter *m* SPORT referee
rings *adv*: ***rings um*** around
'ringshe'rum, 'rings'um, 'ringsum'her *adv* all around; everywhere
Rinne ['rɪnə] *f* (*-; -n*) groove, channel; gutter
'rinnen *v/i* (*irr, ge-, sein*) run; flow, stream
Rinnsal ['rɪnza:l] *n* (*-s; -e*) trickle
'Rinnstein *m* gutter
Rippe ['rɪpə] *f* (*-; -n*) ANAT rib
'Rippenfell *n* ANAT pleura
Rippenfellentzündung *f* MED pleurisy
'Rippenstoß *m* nudge in the ribs
Risiko ['ri:ziko] *n* (*-s; -s, -ken*) risk; ***ein (kein) Risiko eingehen*** take a risk (no risks); ***auf eigenes Risiko*** at one's own risk
riskant [rɪs'kant] *adj* risky
riskieren [rɪs'ki:rən] *v/t* (*no -ge-, h*) risk
riss [rɪs] *pret of* ***reißen***
Riss *m* (*-es; -e*) tear, rip, split (*a. fig*); crack; MED chap, laceration
rissig ['rɪsɪç] *adj* chapped; cracky, cracked
Rist [rɪst] *m* (*-es; -e*) ANAT instep
ritt [rɪt] *pret of* ***reiten***
Ritt *m* (*-[e]s; -e*) ride (on horseback)
Ritter ['rɪtɐ] *m* (*-s; -*) knight; ***j-n zum Ritter schlagen*** knight s.o.
'ritterlich *fig adj* chivalrous
Ritz [rɪts] *m* (*-es; -e*), **Ritze** ['rɪtsə] *f* (*-; -n*) crack, chink; gap
Rivale [ri'va:lə] *m* (*-n; -n*), **Ri'valin** *f* (*-; -nen*) rival
rivalisieren [rivali'zi:rən] *v/i* (*no -ge-, h*) compete
Rivalität [rivali'tɛ:t] *f* (*-; -en*) rivalry
rk., r.-k. ABBR *of* ***römisch-katholisch*** RC, Roman Catholic
Robbe ['rɔbə] *f* (*-; -n*) ZO seal
Robe ['ro:bə] *f* (*-; -n*) robe, gown
Roboter ['rɔbɔtɐ] *m* (*-s; -*) robot
robust [ro'bʊst] *adj* robust, strong, tough
roch [rɔx] *pret of* ***riechen***
röcheln ['rœçəln] (*ge-, h*) **1.** *v/i* moan; **2.** *v/t* gasp
Rock [rɔk] *m* (*-[e]s; Röcke* ['rœkə]) skirt
Rodelbahn ['ro:dəl-] *f* toboggan run
rodeln ['ro:dəln] *v/i* (*ge-, sein*) sled(ge), coast; SPORT toboggan
'Rodelschlitten *m* sled(ge); toboggan
roden ['ro:dən] *v/t* (*ge-, h*) clear; stub
Rogen ['ro:gən] *m* (*-s; -*) (hard) roe
Roggen ['rɔgən] *m* (*-s; -*) BOT rye
roh [ro:] *adj* raw; rough; *fig* brutal; ***mit roher Gewalt*** with brute force
'Rohbau *m* (*-[e]s; -ten*) carcass
'Rohkost *f* raw vegetables and fruit
'Rohling *m* (*-s; -e*) TECH blank; *fig* brute
'Rohmateri,al *n* raw material
'Rohöl *n* crude (oil)
Rohr [ro:ɐ] *n* (*-[e]s; -e* ['ro:rə]) TECH pipe, tube; duct; BOT reed; cane
Röhre ['rø:rə] *f* (*-; -n*) pipe, tube (*a.* TV), TV *etc* valve
'Rohrleitung *f* duct, pipe(s); plumbing; pipeline
Rohrstock *m* cane
Rohrzucker *m* cane sugar
'Rohstoff *m* raw material
Rollbahn ['rɔl-] *f* AVIAT runway
Rolle ['rɔlə] *f* (*-; -n*) roll (*a.* SPORT), TECH *a.* roller; coil; caster, castor; THEA part, role (*both a. fig*); ***e-e Rolle Garn*** a spool of thread, *Br* a reel of cotton; ***das spielt keine Rolle*** that doesn't matter, that makes no difference; ***Geld spielt k-e Rolle*** money is no object
'rollen *v/i* (*ge-, sein*) *and v/t* (*ge-, h*) roll
Roller ['rɔlɐ] *m* (*-s; -*) (motor) scooter
'Rollfilm *m* PHOT roll film
Rollkragen *m* turtleneck, *esp Br* polo neck
Rollladen *m* rolling shutter
Rollo ['rɔlo] *n* (*-s; -s*) shades, *Br* (roller) blind
'Rollschuh *m* roller skate; ***Rollschuh laufen*** roller-skate
Rollschuhbahn *f* roller-skating rink
Rollschuhläufer *m* roller skater
'Rollstuhl *m* wheelchair
'Rolltreppe *f* escalator
Roman [ro'ma:n] *m* (*-s; -e*) novel
Romanik [ro'ma:nɪk] *f* (*-; no pl*) ARCH Romanesque (style *or* period)
romanisch [ro'ma:nɪʃ] *adj* LING Romance; ARCH Romanesque
Romanist [roma'nɪst] *m* (*-en; -en*), **Roma'nistin** *f* (*-; -nen*) student of Romance languages
Ro'manschriftsteller *m*, **Ro'manschriftstellerin** *f* novelist
Romantik [ro'mantɪk] *f* (*-; no pl*) romance; HIST Romanticism
romantisch [ro'mantɪʃ] *adj* romantic
Römer ['rø:mɐ] *m* (*-s; -*), **'Römerin** *f* (*-; -nen*), **römisch** ['rø:mɪʃ] *adj* Roman
Rommee ['rɔme] *n* (*-s; -s*) rummy
röntgen ['rœntgən] *v/t* (*ge-, h*) MED X-ray
'Röntgenappa,rat *m* MED X-ray apparatus
Röntgenaufnahme *f*, **Röntgenbild** *n* MED X-ray

Röntgenstrahlen *pl* PHYS X-rays
Röntgenuntersuchung *f* MED X-ray
rosa ['roːza] *adj* pink; *fig* rose-colo(u)red
Rose ['roːzə] *f* (-; *-n*) BOT rose
'Rosenkohl *m* BOT Brussels sprouts
'Rosenkranz *m* REL rosary
rosig ['roːzɪç] *adj* rosy (*a. fig*)
Rosine [ro'ziːnə] *f* (-; *-n*) raisin
'Rosshaar *n* (-[*e*]*s*; *no pl*) horsehair
Rost [rɔst] *m* (-[*e*]*s*; *-e*) a) (*no pl*) CHEM rust, b) TECH grate; GASTR grid(iron), grill
rosten ['rɔstən] *v/i* (*ge-*, *sein*) rust
rösten ['rœstən] *v/t* (*ge-*, *h*) roast (*a.* F); toast; fry
'Rostfleck *m* rust stain
'rostfrei *adj* rustproof, stainless
'rostig *adj* rusty
rot [roːt] *adj* red (*a.* POL); ***rot glühend*** red-hot; ***rot werden*** blush; ***in den roten Zahlen*** ECON in the red
Rot *n* (*-s*; -) red; ***die Ampel steht auf Rot*** the lights are red; ***bei Rot*** at red
'rotblond *adj* sandy(-haired)
Röte ['røːtə] *f* (-; *no pl*) redness, red (colo[u]r); *fig* blush
Röteln ['røːtəln] *pl* MED German measles
röten ['røːtən] *v/refl* (*ge-*, *h*) redden; flush
'rothaarig *adj* red-haired
'Rothaarige *m*, *f* (*-n*; *-n*) redhead
rotieren [ro'tiːrən] *v/i* (*no -ge-*, *h*) rotate
'Rotkehlchen *n* (*-s*; -) ZO robin
'Rotkohl *m* BOT red cabbage
rötlich ['røːtlɪç] *adj* reddish
'Rotstift *m* red crayon *or* pencil
Rotwein *m* red wine
Rotwild *n* ZO (red) deer
Rotznase [rɔts-] F *f* snotty nose
Route ['ruːtə] *f* (-; *-n*) route
Routine [ru'tiːnə] *f* (-; *no pl*) routine; experience
Routinesache *f* routine (matter)
routiniert [ruti'niːɐt] *adj* experienced
Rübe ['ryːbə] *f* (-; *-n*) BOT turnip; (sugar) beet
Rubin [ru'biːn] *m* (*-s*; *-e*) MIN ruby
Rübli ['ryːpli] *Swiss n* (*-s*; -) BOT carrot
Rubrik [ru'briːk] *f* (-; *-en*) heading; column
Ruck [rʊk] *m* (-[*e*]*s*; *-e*) jerk, jolt, start; *fig* POL swing
Rückantwortschein ['rʏk-] *m* reply coupon
'ruckartig *adj* jerky, abrupt
'rückbezüglich *adj* LING reflexive
'Rückblende *f* flashback (***auf*** *acc* to)
'Rückblick *m* review (***auf*** *acc* of); ***im Rückblick*** in retrospect
rücken ['rʏkən] **1.** *v/t* (*ge-*, *h*) move, shift, push; **2.** *v/i* (*ge-*, *sein*) move; move over; ***näher rücken*** approach
'Rücken *m* (*-s*; -) ANAT back (*a. fig*)
Rückendeckung *fig f* backing, support
Rückenlehne *f* back(rest)
Rückenmark *n* ANAT spinal cord
Rückenschmerzen *pl* backache
Rückenschwimmen *n* backstroke
Rückenwind *m* following wind, tailwind
Rückenwirbel *m* ANAT dorsal vertebra
'Rückerstattung *f* (-; *-en*) refund
Rückfahrkarte *f* round-trip ticket, *Br a.* return (ticket)
Rückfahrt *f* return trip; ***auf der Rückfahrt*** on the way back
Rückfall *m* relapse
'rückfällig *adj*: ***rückfällig werden*** relapse
'Rückflug *m* return flight
'Rückgabe *f* (-; *no pl*) return
'Rückgang *m* drop, fall; ECON recession
'rückgängig *adj*: ***rückgängig machen*** cancel
'Rückgewinnung *f* (-; *no pl*) recovery
Rückgrat *n* ANAT spine, backbone (*both a. fig*)
Rückhalt *m* (-[*e*]*s*; *no pl*) support
Rückhand *f*, **Rückhandschlag** *m tennis*: backhand
Rückkauf *m* ECON repurchase
Rückkehr ['rʏkkeːɐ] *f* (-; *no pl*) return; ***nach s-r Rückkehr aus ...*** on his return from ...
'Rückkopplung *f* ELECTR feedback (*a. fig*)
Rücklage *f* (-; *-n*) reserve(s); savings
Rücklauf *m* TECH rewind
'rückläufig *adj* falling, downward
'Rücklicht *n* (-[*e*]*s*; *-er*) MOT rear light, taillight
rücklings ['rʏklɪŋs] *adv* backward(s); from behind
'Rückporto *n* return postage
'Rückreise *f* → ***Rückfahrt***
Rucksack ['rʊkzak] *m* rucksack, backpack
Rucksacktou,rismus *m* backpacking
Rucksacktou,rist *m* backpacker
'Rückschlag *m* SPORT return; *fig* setback
Rückschluss *m* conclusion
Rückschritt *m fig* step back(ward)
Rückseite *f* back; reverse; flip side
Rücksendung *f* return
'Rücksicht *f* (-; *-en*) consideration, regard; ***aus*** (***ohne***) ***Rücksicht auf*** (*acc*) out of (without any) consideration *or* regard for; ***Rücksicht nehmen auf*** (*acc*) show consideration for
'rücksichtslos *adj* inconsiderate (***gegen*** of), thoughtless (of); ruthless; reckless
'rücksichtsvoll *adj* considerate (***gegen*** of), thoughtful

ˈRücksitz *m* MOT back seat
Rückspiegel *m* MOT rear-view mirror
Rückspiel *n* SPORT return match
Rückstand *m* CHEM residue; ***mit der Arbeit (e-m Tor) im Rückstand sein*** be behind with one's work (down by one goal)
ˈrückständig *adj* backward; underdeveloped; ***rückständige Miete*** arrears of rent
ˈRückstau *m* MOT tailback
Rückstelltaste *f* backspace key
Rücktriff *m* resignation; withdrawal; TECH → **Rücktrittbremse** *f* coaster (*Br* back-pedal) brake
rückwärts [ˈrʏkvɛrts] *adv* backward(s); ***rückwärts aus*** (*dat*) ***… fahren*** back out of …; ***rückwärts in*** (*acc*) ***… fahren*** back into …
ˈRückwärtsgang *m* MOT reverse (gear)
ˈRückweg *m* way back
ˈruckweise *adv* jerkily, in jerks
ˈrückwirkend *adj* retroactive
ˈRückwirkung *f* reaction (***auf*** *acc* upon)
Rückzahlung *f* repayment
Rückzieher *m* (*-s*; *-*) *soccer*: overhead kick; F ***e-n Rückzieher machen*** back (*or* chicken) out (***von*** of)
Rückzug *m* retreat
Rüde [ˈryːdə] *m* (*-n*; *-n*) ZO male (dog *ect*)
Rudel [ˈruːdəl] *n* (*-s*; *-*) ZO pack; herd
Ruder [ˈruːdɐ] *n* (*-s*; *-*) AVIAT, MAR rudder; SPORT oar; ***am Ruder*** at the helm (*a. fig*)
Ruderboot *n* rowing boat, rowboat
Ruderer [ˈruːdərɐ] *m* (*-s*; *-*) rower, oarsman
ˈRuderin *f* (*-*; *-nen*) rower, oarswoman
ˈrudern *v/i and v/t* (*ge-*, *h*) row
ˈRuderreˌgatta *f* (rowing) regatta, boat race
Rudersport *m* rowing
Ruf [ruːf] *m* (*-[e]s*; *-e*) call (*a. fig*); cry, shout; *fig* reputation
ˈrufen *v/i and v/t* (*irr*, *ge-*, *h*) call (*a. doctor etc*); cry, shout; ***rufen nach*** call for (*a. fig*); ***rufen lassen*** send for; ***um Hilfe rufen*** call *or* cry for help
ˈRufnummer *f* telephone number
ˈRufweite *f*: ***in*** (***außer***) ***Rufweite*** within (out of) call(ing distance)
Rüge [ˈryːgə] *f* (*-*; *-n*) reproof, reproach (*both*: ***wegen*** for)
ˈrügen *v/t* (*ge-*, *h*) reprove, reproach
Ruhe [ˈruːə] *f* (*-*; *no pl*) quiet, calm; silence; rest; peace; calm(ness); ***zur Ruhe kommen*** come to rest; ***j-n in Ruhe lassen*** leave s.o. in peace; ***lass mich in Ruhe!*** leave me alone!; ***et. in Ruhe tun*** take one's time (doing s.th.); ***die Ruhe behalten*** F keep (one's) cool, play it cool; ***sich zur Ruhe setzen*** retire; ***Ruhe, bitte!*** (be) quiet, please!
ˈruhelos *adj* restless
ˈruhen *v/i* (*ge-*, *h*) rest (***auf*** *dat* on)
ˈRuhepause *f* break
Ruhestand *m* (*-[e]s*; *no pl*) retirement
Ruhestörer *m* (*-s*; *-*) *esp* JUR disturber of the peace
Ruhetag *m* a day's rest; ***Montag Ruhetag*** closed on Mondays
ruhig [ˈruːɪç] *adj* quiet; silent; calm; cool; TECH smooth; ***ruhig bleiben*** F keep (one's) cool, play it cool
Ruhm [ruːm] *m* (*-[e]s*; *no pl*) fame, *esp* POL, MIL *etc* glory
rühmen [ˈryːmən] *v/t* (*ge-*, *h*) praise (***wegen*** for); ***sich e-r Sache rühmen*** boast of s.th.
rühmlich [ˈryːmlɪç] *adj* laudable, praiseworthy
ˈruhmlos *adj* inglorious
ˈruhmreich *adj* glorious
Ruhr [ruːɐ] *f* (*-*; *no pl*) MED dysentery
Rühreier [ˈryːɐˀaiɐ] *pl* scrambled eggs
rühren [ˈryːrən] *v/t* (*ge-*, *h*) stir; move (*a. fig*); *fig* touch, affect; ***das rührt mich gar nicht*** that leaves me cold; ***rührt euch!*** MIL (stand) at ease!
rührend *fig adj* touching, moving; very kind
rührig [ˈryːrɪç] *adj* active, busy
rührselig [ˈryːɐ-] *adj* sentimental
ˈRührung *f* (*-*; *no pl*) emotion
Ruin [ruˈiːn] *m* (*-s*; *no pl*) ruin
Ruine [ruˈiːnə] *f* (*-*; *-n*) ruin
ruinieren [ruiˈniːrən] *v/t* (*no -ge-*, *h*) ruin
rülpsen [ˈrʏlpsən] *v/i* (*ge-*, *h*), **Rülpser** [ˈrʏlpsɐ] *m* (*-s*; *-*) belch
Rumäne [ruˈmɛːnə] *m* (*-n*; *-n*) Romanian
Rumänien Romania
Ruˈmänin *f* (*-*; *-nen*), **ruˈmänisch** *adj* Romanian
Rummel [ˈrʊməl] F *m* (*-s*; *no pl*) (hustle and) bustle; F ballyhoo
Rummelplatz F *m* amusement park, fairground
rumoren [ruˈmoːrən] *v/i* (*no -ge-*, *h*) rumble
Rumpelkammer [ˈrʊmpəl-] F *f* lumber room
rumpeln [ˈrʊmpəln] F *v/i* (*ge-*, *h*, *sein*) rumble
Rumpf [rʊmpf] *m* (*-es*; *Rümpfe* [ˈrʏmpfə]) ANAT trunk; MAR hull; AVIAT fuselage
rümpfen [ˈrʏmpfən] *v/t* (*ge-*, *h*) ***die Nase rümpfen*** turn up one's nose (***über*** *acc* at), sneer (at)
rund [rʊnt] **1.** *adj* round (*a. fig*); **2.** *adv* about; ***rund um*** (a)round

R

'**Rundblick** *m* panorama
Runde ['rʊndə] *f* (-; -*n*) round (*a. fig and* SPORT); *racing*: lap; ***s-e Runde machen in*** (*dat*) patrol; ***die Runde machen*** go the round(s)
'**Rundfahrt** *f* tour (***durch*** round)
'**Rundfunk** *m* (-*s*; *no pl*) radio; broadcasting corporation; ***im Rundfunk*** on the radio; ***im Rundfunk übertragen*** *or* ***senden*** broadcast
Rundfunkhörer(in) listener, *pl a.* (radio) audience
Rundfunksender *m* broadcasting *or* radio station
'**Rundgang** *m* tour (***durch*** of)
'**rundhe'raus** *adv* frankly, plainly
'**rundhe'rum** *adv* all around
'**rundlich** *adj* plump, chubby
'**Rundreise** *f* tour (***durch*** of)
Rundschau *f* review
Rundschreiben *n* circular (letter)
Rundspruch *Swiss m* → ***Rundfunk***
'**Rundung** *f* (-; -*en*) curve
'**rundweg** [-'vɛk] *adv* flatly, plainly
runter ['rʊntɐ] F *adv* → ***herunter***
Runzel ['rʊntsəl] *f* (-; -*n*) wrinkle
runz(e)lig ['rʊnts(ə)lɪç] *adj* wrinkled
'**runzeln** *v/t* (*ge-*, *h*) ***die Stirn runzeln*** frown (***über*** *acc* at)
Rüpel ['ryːpəl] *m* (-*s*; -) lout
rupfen ['rʊpfən] *v/t* (*ge-*, *h*) pluck
Rüsche ['ryːʃə] *f* (-; -*n*) frill, ruffle
Ruß ['ruːs] *m* (-*es*; *no pl*) soot
Russe ['rʊsə] *m* (-*n*; -*n*) Russian
Rüssel ['rʏsəl] *m* (-*s*; -) ZO trunk; snout
rußen ['ruːsən] *v/i* (*ge-*, *h*) smoke
rußig ['ruːsɪç] *adj* sooty
Russin ['rʊsɪn] *f* (-; -*nen*), **russisch** ['rʊsɪʃ] *adj* Russian
'**Russland** Russia
rüsten ['rʏstən] (*ge-*, *h*) **1.** *v/i* MIL arm; **2.** *v/refl* get ready, prepare (***zu, für*** for); arm o.s. (***gegen*** for)
rüstig ['rʏstɪç] *adj* vigorous, sprightly
rustikal [rʊsti'kaːl] *adj* rustic
'**Rüstung** *f* (-; -*en*) MIL armament; armo(u)r
'**Rüstungsindus,trie** *f* armament industry
Rüstungswettlauf *m* arms race
'**Rüstzeug** *n* equipment
Rute ['ruːtə] *f* (-; -*n*) rod (*a. fig*), switch
Rutschbahn ['rʊtʃ-] *f*, **Rutsche** ['rʊtʃə] *f* (-; -*n*) slide, chute
'**rutschen** *v/i* (*ge-*, *sein*) slide, slip; glide; MOT *etc* skid
rutschig ['rʊtʃɪç] *adj* slippery
'**rutschsicher** *adj* MOT *etc* non-skid
rütteln ['rʏtəln] (*ge-*, *h*) **1.** *v/t* shake; **2.** *v/i* jolt; ***an der Tür rütteln*** rattle at the door

S

S ABBR *of* ***Süd(en)*** S, south
S. ABBR *of* ***Seite*** p., page
s. ABBR *of* ***siehe*** see
Saal [zaːl] *m* (-[*e*]*s*; *Säle* ['zɛːlə]) hall
Saat [zaːt] *f* (-; -*en*) a) (*no pl*) sowing, b) seed(s) (*a. fig*); crop(s)
Sabbat ['zabat] *m* (-*s*; -*e*) sabbath (day)
sabbern ['zabɐn] F *v/i* (*ge-*, *h*) slobber, slaver
Säbel ['zɛːbəl] *m* (-*s*; -) saber, *Br* sabre (*a.* SPORT), sword
'**säbeln** F *v/t* (*ge-*, *h*) cut, hack
Sabotage [zabo'taːʒə] *f* (-; -*n*) sabotage
Saboteur [zabo'tøːɐ] *m* (-*s*; -*e*) saboteur
sabotieren [zabo'tiːrən] *v/t* (*no -ge-*, *h*) sabotage
Sachbearbeiter ['zax-] *m*, **Sachbearbeiterin** *f* official in charge
Sachbeschädigung *f* damage to property
Sachbuch *n* specialized book, *pl coll* nonfiction
'**sachdienlich** *adj*: ***sachdienliche Hinweise*** relevant information
Sache ['zaxə] *f* (-; -*n*) thing; matter, business; issue, problem, question; cause; JUR matter, case; *pl* things, clothes; ***zur Sache kommen*** (***bei der Sache bleiben***) come (keep) to the point; ***nicht zur Sache gehören*** be irrelevant
'**sachgerecht** *adj* proper
'**Sachkenntnis** *f* expert knowledge
'**sachkundig** *adj* expert
'**sachlich** *adj* matter-of-fact, businesslike; unbias(s)ed, objective; practical, technical; ***sachlich richtig*** factually correct
sächlich ['zɛçlɪç] *adj* LING neuter
'**Sachre,gister** *n* (subject) index

'Sachschaden *m* damage to property
sacht [zaxt] *adj* soft, gentle; slow
'Sachverhalt *m* (-[*e*]*s*; -*e*) facts (of the case)
Sachverstand *m* know-how
Sachverständige *m*, *f* (-*n*; -*n*) expert; JUR expert witness
Sachwert *m* (-[*e*]*s*; *no pl*) real value
Sachzwänge *pl* inherent necessities
Sack [zak] *m* (-[*e*]*s*; *Säcke* ['zɛkə]) sack, bag; V balls
sacken ['zakən] F *v/i* (*ge-*, *sein*) sink
'Sackgasse *f* blind alley (*a. fig*), dead end (*a. fig*), *fig* impasse
Sadismus [za'dɪsmʊs] *m* (-; *no pl*) sadism
Sadist [za'dɪst] *m* (-*en*; -*en*) sadist
sa'distisch *adj* sadistic
säen ['zɛːən] *v/t and v/i* (*ge-*, *h*) sow (*a. fig*)
Safari [za'faːri] *f* (-; -*s*) safari
Safaripark *m* wildlife reserve, safari park
Saft [zaft] *m* (-[*e*]*s*; *Säfte* ['zɛftə]) juice; BOT sap (*both a. fig*)
saftig ['zaftɪç] *adj* juicy (*a. fig*); lush; F fancy (*prices etc*)
Sage ['zaːgə] *f* (-; -*n*) legend, myth
Säge ['zɛːgə] *f* (-; -*n*) saw
'Sägemehl *n* sawdust
sagen ['zaːgən] *v/i and v/t* (*ge-*, *h*) say; ***j-m et. sagen*** tell s.o. s.th.; ***die Wahrheit sagen*** tell the truth; ***er lässt dir sagen*** he asked me to tell you; ***sagen wir …*** (let's) say …; ***man sagt, er sei reich*** he is said to be rich; ***er lässt sich nichts sagen*** he will not listen to reason; ***das hat nichts zu sagen*** it doesn't matter; ***et.*** (***nichts***) ***zu sagen haben*** (***bei***) have a say (no say) (in); ***sagen wollen mit*** mean by; ***das sagt mir nichts*** it doesn't mean anything to me; ***unter uns gesagt*** between you and me
sägen ['zɛːgən] *v/t and v/i* (*ge-*, *h*) saw
'sagenhaft *adj* legendary; F fabulous, incredible, fantastic
'Sägespäne *pl* sawdust
'Sägewerk *n* sawmill
sah [zaː] *pret of* ***sehen***
Sahne ['zaːnə] *f* (-; *no pl*) cream
Saison [zɛ'zõː] *f* (-; -*s*) season; ***in der Saison*** in season
sai'sonbedingt *adj* seasonal
Saite ['zaitə] *f* (-; -*n*) MUS string, chord (*a. fig*)
'Saiteninstru‚ment *n* MUS string(ed) instrument
Sakko ['zako] *m*, *n* (-*s*; -*s*) (sports) jacket, sport(s) coat
Sakristei [zakrɪs'tai] *f* (-; -*en*) REL vestry, sacristy
Salat [za'laːt] *m* (-[*e*]*s*; -*e*) BOT lettuce; GASTR salad
Salatsauce *f* salad dressing
Salbe ['zalbə] *f* (-; -*n*) ointment
'Salbung *f* (-; -*en*) unction
'salbungsvoll *adj* unctuous
Saldo ['zaldo] *m* (-*s*; -*s*, -*di*) ECON balance
Salon [za'lõː] *m* (-*s*; -*s*) salon; MAR saloon; drawing room
salopp [za'lɔp] *adj* casual; *contp* sloppy
Salpeter [zal'peːtɐ] *m* (-*s*; *no pl*) CHEM salt|peter (*Br* -petre), niter, *Br* nitre
Salto ['zalto] *m* (-*s*; -*s*, -*ti*) somersault
Salut [za'luːt] *m* (-[*e*]*s*; -*e*) MIL salute; ***Salut schießen*** fire a salute
salutieren [zalu'tiːrən] *v/i* (*no -ge-*, *h*) MIL (give a) salute
Salve ['zalvə] *f* (-; -*n*) MIL volley (*a. fig*); salute
Salz [zalts] *n* (-*es*; -*e*) salt
'Salzbergwerk *n* salt mine
salzen ['zaltsən] *v/t* ([*irr*,] *ge-*, *h*) salt
salzfrei ['zaltsfrai] *adj* salt-free, no-salt *diet*
salzig ['zaltsɪç] *adj* salty
'Salzkar‚toffeln *pl* boiled potatoes
Salzsäure *f* (-; *no pl*) CHEM hydrochloric acid
Salzstange *f* pretzel (*Br* salt) stick
Salzstreuer *m* (-*s*; -) salt shaker, *Br* salt cellar
Salzwasser *n* salt water
Same ['zaːmə] *m* (-*n*; -*n*), **'Samen** *m* (-*s* -) BOT seed (*a. fig*); BIOL sperm, semen
'Samenbank *f* (-; -*en*) MED, VET sperm bank
Samenerguss *m* ejaculation
Samenkorn *n* BOT seedcorn
Sammel… ['zaməl-] *in cpds …begriff*, *…bestellung*, *…konto etc*: collective …
Sammelbüchse *f* collecting box
'sammeln *v/t* (*ge-*, *h*) collect; gather, pick; accumulate; ***sich sammeln*** assemble; *fig* compose o.s.
Sammler ['zamlɐ] *m* (-*s*; -), **'Sammlerin** *f* (-; -*nen*) collector
'Sammlung *f* (-; -*en*) collection
Samstag ['zamstaːk] *m* (-[*e*]*s*; -*e*) Saturday
samt [zamt] *prp* (*dat*) together *or* along with
Samt *m* (-[*e*]*s*; -*e*) velvet
sämtlich ['zɛmtlɪç] *adj*: ***sämtliche*** *pl* all the; the complete *works etc*
Sanatorium [zana'toːrjʊm] *n* (-*s*; -*ien*) sanatorium, sanitarium
Sand [zant] *m* (-[*e*]*s*; -*e*) sand
Sandale [zan'daːlə] *f* (-; -*n*) sandal
Sandalette [zanda'lɛtə] *f* (-; -*n*) high-heeled sandal

S

'Sandbahn *f* SPORT dirt track
Sandbank *f* (-; *-bänke*) sandbank
Sandboden *m* sandy soil
Sandburg *f* sandcastle
sandig ['zandɪç] *adj* sandy
'Sandmann *m*, **Sandmännchen** *n* sandman
Sandpa,pier *n* sandpaper
Sandsack *m* sand bag
Sandstein *m* sandstone
Sandstrand *m* sandy beach
sandte ['zantə] *pret of* ***senden***
'Sanduhr *f* hourglass
sanft [zanft] *adj* gentle, soft; mild; easy (*death*)
'sanftmütig [-myːtɪç] *adj* gentle, mild
sang [zaŋ] *pret of* ***singen***
Sänger ['zɛŋɐ] *m* (-*s*; -), **Sängerin** ['zɛŋərɪn] *f* (-; *-nen*) singer
sanieren [za'niːrən] *v/t* (*no -ge-, h*) redevelop (*a.* ECON), rehabilitate (*a.* ARCH)
Sa'nierung *f* (-; *-en*) redevelopment, rehabilitation
Sa'nierungsgebiet *n* redevelopment area
sanitär [zani'tɛːɐ] *adj* sanitary
Sanitäter [zani'tɛːtɐ] *m* (-*s*; -) paramedic; MIL medic, *Br* medical orderly
sank [zaŋk] *pret of* ***sinken***
Sankt [zaŋkt] Saint, ABBR St
Sardelle [zar'dɛlə] *f* (-; *-n*) ZO anchovy
Sardine [zar'diːnə] *f* (-; *-n*) ZO sardine
Sarg [zark] *m* (-[*e*]*s*; *Särge* ['zɛrgə]) casket, *esp Br* coffin
Sarkasmus [zar'kasmʊs] *m* (-; *no pl*) sarcasm
sar'kastisch *adj* sarcastic
saß [zaːs] *pret of* ***sitzen***
Satan ['zaːtan] *m* (-*s*; *-e*) Satan; *fig* devil
Satellit [zatɛ'liːt] *m* (*-en*; *-en*) satellite (*a. fig*); ***über Satellit*** by *or* via satellite
Satel'liten... *in cpds* *...bild*, *...staat*, *...stadt*, *...-TV*: satellite ...
Satin [za'tɛ̃ː] *m* (-*s*; -*s*) satin; sateen
Satire [za'tiːrə] *f* (-; *-n*) satire (***auf*** *acc* upon)
Satiriker [za'tiːrikɐ] *m* (-*s*; -) satirist
sa'tirisch *adj* satiric(al)
satt [zat] *adj* F full (up); ***ich bin satt*** I've had enough, F I'm full (up); ***sich satt essen*** eat one's fill (***an*** *dat* of)
Sattel ['zatəl] *m* (-*s*; *Sättel* ['zɛtəl]) saddle
'satteln *v/t* (*ge-, h*) saddle
'Sattelschlepper *m* MOT semi-trailer truck, *Br* articulated lorry
'satthaben *v/t* (*irr*, ***haben***, *sep*, *-ge-, h*) F be tired *or* F sick of, be fed up with
sättigen ['zɛtɪgən] (*ge-, h*) **1.** *v/t* satisfy; feed; CHEM, PHYS saturate; **2.** *v/i* be substantial, be filling
'Sättigung *f* (-; *-en*) satiety; CHEM, ECON saturation (*a. fig*)
Sattler ['zatlɐ] *m* (-*s*; -) saddler
Sattlerei [zatlə'rai] *f* (-; *-en*) saddlery
Satz [zats] *m* (-*es*; *Sätze* ['zɛtsə]) leap; LING sentence; *tennis etc*: set; ECON rate; MUS movement
Satzaussage *f* LING predicate
Satzbau *m* (-[*e*]*s*; *no pl*) LING syntax; construction
Satzgegenstand *m* LING subject
Satzung ['zatsʊŋ] *f* (-; *-en*) statute
'Satzzeichen *n* LING punctuation mark
Sau [zau] *f* (-; *Säue* ['zɔʏə]) ZO sow; HUNT wild sow; F swine, pig
sauber ['zaubɐ] *adj* clean (*a.* F fig); pure; neat (*a. fig*), tidy; decent; *iro* fine, nice; ***sauber halten*** keep clean (***sich*** o.s.); ***sauber machen*** clean (up)
'Sauberkeit *f* (-; *no pl*) clean(li)ness; tidiness, neatness; purity; decency
'saubermachen *v/t and v/i* (*sep*, *-ge-, h*) → ***sauber***
säubern ['zɔʏbɐn] *v/t* (*ge-, h*) clean (up); cleanse (*a.* MED); ***säubern von*** clear (POL *a.* purge) of
'Säuberung(sakti,on) *f* POL purge
sauer ['zauɐ] *adj* sour (*a. fig*), acid (*a.* CHEM); GASTR pickled; F mad (***auf*** *acc* at), cross (with); ***sauer werden*** turn sour; F get mad; ***saurer Regen*** acid rain
säuerlich ['zɔʏɐlɪç] *adj* sharp; F wry
'Sauerstoff *m* (-[*e*]*s*; *no pl*) CHEM oxygen
Sauerstoffgerät *n* MED oxygen apparatus
Sauerstoffzelt *n* MED oxygen tent
'Sauerteig *m* leaven
saufen ['zaufən] *v/t and v/i* (*irr*, *ge-, h*) ZO drink; F booze
Säufer(in) ['zɔʏfɐ (-fərɪn)] F (-*s*; -/-; *-nen*) drunkard, F boozer
saugen ['zaugən] *v/i and v/t* ([*irr*,] *ge-, h*) suck (***an et.*** [at] s.th.)
säugen ['zɔʏgən] *v/t* (*ge-, h*) suckle (*a.* ZO), nurse, breastfeed
'Säugetier *n* mammal
saugfähig ['zauk-] *adj* absorbent
Säugling ['zɔʏklɪŋ] *m* (-*s*; *-e*) baby, infant
'Säuglingsheim *n* (baby) nursery
Säuglingspflege *f* infant care
Säuglingsschwester *f* baby nurse
Säuglingsstati,on *f* neonatal care unit
Säuglingssterblichkeit *f* infant mortality
Säule ['zɔʏlə] *f* (-; *-n*) column; pillar (*a. fig*)
'Säulengang *m* colonnade
Saum [zaum] *m* (-[*e*]*s*; *Säume* ['zɔʏmə]) hem(line); seam
säumen ['zɔʏmən] *v/t* (*ge-, h*) hem; border, edge; line

S

Sauna ['zauna] *f* (-; -*s*, *Saunen*) sauna
Säure ['zɔʏrə] *f* (-; -*n*) CHEM acid
'säurehaltig [-haltɪç] *adj* acid
sausen ['zauzən] *v/i* a) (*ge-*, *sein*) F rush, dash, b) (*ge-*, *h*) *ears*: buzz; *wind*: howl
'Saustall *m* pigsty (*a.* F *contp*)
Saxophon [zakso'foːn] *n* (-*s*; -*e*) MUS saxophone, F sax
S-Bahn ['ɛsbaːn] *f* rapid transit, *Br* suburban train
Schabe ['ʃaːbə] *f* (-; -*n*) ZO cockroach
'schaben *v/t* (*ge-*, *h*) scrape (**von** from)
schäbig ['ʃɛːbɪç] *adj* shabby, *fig a.* mean
Schablone [ʃa'bloːnə] *f* (-; -*n*) stencil; *fig* stereotype
Schach [ʃax] *n* (-*s*; *no pl*) chess; ***Schach!*** check!; ***Schach und matt!*** checkmate!; ***j-n in Schach halten*** keep s.o. in check
Schachbrett *n* chessboard
Schachfeld *n* square
Schachfi,gur *f* chessman, piece
schach'matt *adj*: ***j-n schachmatt setzen*** checkmate s.o.
'Schachspiel *n* (game of) chess; chessboard and men
Schacht [ʃaxt] *m* (-[*e*]*s*; *Schächte* ['ʃɛçtə]) shaft, *mining*: *a.* pit
Schachtel ['ʃaxtəl] *f* (-; -*n*) box; carton; ***e-e Schachtel Zigaretten*** a pack (*esp Br* packet) of cigarettes
'Schachzug *m* move (*a. fig*)
schade ['ʃaːdə] *pred adj*: ***es ist schade*** it's a pity; ***wie schade!*** what a pity *or* shame!; ***zu schade sein für*** be too good for
Schädel ['ʃɛːdəl] *m* (-*s*; -) ANAT skull
Schädelbruch *m* MED fracture of the skull
schaden ['ʃaːdən] *v/i* (*ge-*, *h*) damage, do damage to, harm, hurt; ***der Gesundheit schaden*** be bad for one's health; ***das schadet nichts*** it doesn't matter; ***es könnte ihm nicht schaden*** it wouldn't hurt him
'Schaden *m* (-*s*; *Schäden* ['ʃɛːdən]) damage (**an** *dat* to); *esp* TECH trouble, defect (*a.* MED); *fig* disadvantage; ECON loss; ***j-m Schaden zufügen*** do s.o. harm
Schadenersatz *m* damages; ***Schadenersatz leisten*** pay damages
Schadenfreude *f*: ***Schadenfreude empfinden über*** (*acc*) gloat over
'schadenfroh *adv* gloatingly
schadhaft ['ʃaːthaft] *adj* damaged; defective, faulty; leaking (*pipes*)
schädigen ['ʃɛːdɪgən] *v/t* (*ge-*, *h*) damage, harm
schädlich ['ʃɛːtlɪç] *adj* harmful, injurious; bad (for your health)
Schädling ['ʃɛːtlɪŋ] *m* (-*s*; -*e*) BIOL pest
'Schädlingsbekämpfung *f* pest control
Schädlingsbekämpfungsmittel *n* pesticide
Schadstoff ['ʃaːt-] *m* harmful substance; pollutant
'schadstoffarm *adj* MOT low-emission
Schaf [ʃaːf] *n* (-[*e*]*s*; -*e*) ZO sheep
'Schafbock *m* ZO ram
Schäfer ['ʃɛːfɐ] *m* (-*s*; -) shepherd
Schäferhund *m* sheepdog; ***Deutscher Schäferhund*** German shepherd, *esp Br* Alsatian
'Schaffell *n* sheepskin; ZO fleece
schaffen¹ ['ʃafən] *v/t* (*irr*, *ge-*, *h*) create
'schaffen² (*ge-*, *h*) **1.** *v/t* cause, bring about; manage, get *s.th.* done; take; ***es schaffen*** make it, *a.* succeed; **2.** *v/i* work; ***j-m zu schaffen machen*** cause s.o. trouble; ***sich zu schaffen machen an*** (*dat*) tamper with
Schaffner ['ʃafnɐ] *m* (-*s*; -), **'Schaffnerin** *f* (-; -*nen*) conductor; *Br* RAIL guard
Schafott [ʃa'fɔt] *n* (-[*e*]*s*; -*e*) scaffold
Schaft [ʃaft] *m* (-[*e*]*s*; *Schäfte* ['ʃɛftə]) shaft; stock; shank; leg
'Schafwolle *f* sheep's wool
'Schafzucht *f* sheep breeding
schäkern ['ʃɛːkɐn] *v/i* (*ge-*, *h*) joke; flirt
schal [ʃaːl] *adj* stale, flat, *fig a.* empty
Schal *m* (-*s*; -*s*) scarf
Schale ['ʃaːlə] *f* (-; -*n*) bowl, dish; GASTR shell; peel, skin
schälen ['ʃɛːlən] *v/t* (*ge-*, *h*) peel, pare; ***sich schälen*** *skin*: peel (off)
Schall [ʃal] *m* (-[*e*]*s*; -*e*) sound
Schalldämpfer *m* silencer (*a. Br* MOT), MOT muffler
'schalldicht *adj* soundproof
schallen ['ʃalən] *v/i* ([*irr*,] *ge-*, *h*) sound; ring (out); ***schallendes Gelächter*** roars of laughter
'Schallgeschwindigkeit *f* speed of sound
Schallmauer *f* sound barrier
Schallplatte *f* record, disk, *Br* disc
Schallwelle *f* PHYS sound wave
schalten ['ʃaltən] *v/i and v/t* (*ge-*, *h*) switch, turn; MOT shift (*esp Br* change) gear; F get it; react
Schalter ['ʃaltɐ] *m* (-*s*; -) counter; RAIL ticket window; AVIAT desk; ELECTR switch
'Schalthebel *m* MOT gear lever; TECH, AVIAT control lever; ELECTR switch lever
Schaltjahr *n* leap year
Schalttafel *f* ELECTR switchboard, control panel
Schaltuhr *f* time switch
'Schaltung *f* (-; -*en*) MOT gearshift; ELECTR circuit
Scham [ʃaːm] *f* (-; *no pl*) shame; ***vor***

S

Scham with shame
schämen ['ʃɛːmən] *v/refl* (*ge-*, *h*) be *or* feel ashamed (*gen*, ***wegen*** of); ***du solltest dich*** (***was***) ***schämen!*** you ought to be ashamed of yourself!
'Schamgefühl *n* (-[*e*]*s*; *no pl*) sense of shame
Schamhaare *pl* pubic hair
'schamhaft *adj* bashful
'schamlos *adj* shameless; indecent
Schande ['ʃandə] *f* (-; *no pl*) shame, disgrace
schänden ['ʃɛndən] *v/t* (*ge-*, *h*) disgrace; desecrate; rape
Schandfleck ['ʃant-] *m* eyesore
schändlich ['ʃɛntlɪç] *adj* disgraceful
'Schandtat *f* atrocity
Schanze ['ʃantsə] *f* (-; *-n*) SPORT ski jump
Schar [ʃaːɐ] *f* (-; *-en* ['ʃaːrən]) troop, band; F horde; crowd; ZO flock
'scharen *v/refl* (*ge-*, *h*) ***sich scharen um*** gather round
scharf [ʃarf] *adj* sharp (*a. fig*), PHOT *a.* in focus; clear; savage, fierce (*dog*); live (*ammunition*), armed (*bomb etc*); GASTR hot; F hot, sexy; F ***scharf sein auf*** (*acc*) be keen on; ***scharf*** (***ein***)***stellen*** PHOT focus; F ***scharfe Sachen*** hard liquor
Schärfe ['ʃɛrfə] *f* (-; *-n*) sharpness (*a.* PHOT); *fig* severity, fierceness
'schärfen *v/t* (*ge-*, *h*) sharpen
'Scharfrichter *m* executioner
Scharfschütze *m* sharpshooter; sniper
'scharfsichtig *adj* sharp-sighted; *fig* clear-sighted
'Scharfsinn *m* (-[*e*]*s*; *no pl*) acumen
'scharfsinnig *adj* sharp-witted, shrewd
'scharfstellen *v/t* (*sep*, *-ge-*, *h*) → ***scharf***
Scharlach ['ʃarlax] *m* (*-s*; *no pl*) scarlet; MED scarlet fever
'scharlachrot *adj* scarlet
Scharlatan ['ʃarlatan] *m* (*-s*; *-e*) charlatan, fraud
Scharnier [ʃar'niːɐ] *n* (*-s*; *-e*) TECH hinge
Schärpe ['ʃɛrpə] *f* (-; *-n*) sash
scharren ['ʃarən] *v/i* (*ge-*, *h*) scrape, scratch
schartig ['ʃartɪç] *adj* jagged, notchy
Schaschlik ['ʃaʃlɪk] *m*, *n* (*-s*; *-s*) GASTR shish kebab
Schatten ['ʃatən] *m* (*-s*; -) shadow (*a. fig*); shade; ***im Schatten*** in the shade
'schattenhaft *adj* shadowy
Schattierung [ʃa'tiːrʊŋ] *f* (-; *-en*) shade; *fig* colo(u)r
schattig ['ʃatɪç] *adj* shady
Schatz [ʃats] *m* (*-es*; *Schätze* ['ʃɛtsə]) treasure; *fig* darling
Schatzamt *n* POL Treasury Department, *Br* Treasury
schätzen ['ʃɛtsən] *v/t* (*ge-*, *h*) estimate, value (*both*: ***auf*** *acc* at); appreciate; think highly of; F reckon, guess
'Schatzkammer *f* treasury (*a. fig*)
Schatzkanzler *m* Chancellor of the Exchequer
Schatzmeister(in) treasurer
'Schätzung *f* (-; *-en*) estimate; valuation
Schau [ʃau] *f* (-; *-en*) show, exhibition; ***zur Schau stellen*** exhibit, display
Schauder ['ʃaudɐ] *m* (*-s*; -) shudder
'schauderhaft *adj* horrible, dreadful
'schaudern *v/i* (*ge-*, *h*) shudder, shiver (*both*: ***vor*** *dat* with)
schauen ['ʃauən] *v/i* (*ge-*, *h*) look (***auf*** *acc* at)
Schauer ['ʃauɐ] *m* (*-s*; -) METEOR shower; shudder, shiver
Schauergeschichte *f* horror story (*a. fig*)
'schauerlich *adj* dreadful, horrible
Schaufel ['ʃaufəl] *f* (-; *-n*) shovel; dustpan
'schaufeln *v/t* (*ge-*, *h*) shovel; dig
'Schaufenster *n* shop window
Schaufensterauslage *f* window display
Schaufensterbummel *m*: ***e-n Schaufensterbummel machen*** go window-shopping
Schaufensterdekorati͵on *f* window dressing
Schaukel ['ʃaukəl] *f* (-; *-n*) swing
'schaukeln (*ge-*, *h*) **1.** *v/i* swing; *boat etc*: rock; **2.** *v/t* rock
'Schaukelpferd *n* rocking horse
Schaukelstuhl *m* rocking chair, rocker
'Schaulustige [-lʊstɪgə] *pl* (curious) onlookers, F rubbernecks
Schaum [ʃaum] *m* (-[*e*]*s*; *Schäume* ['ʃɔʏmə]) foam; GASTR froth, head; lather; spray
schäumen ['ʃɔʏmən] *v/i* (*ge-*, *h*) foam (*a. fig*), froth; lather; spray
'Schaumgummi *m* foam rubber
schaumig ['ʃaumɪç] *adj* foamy, frothy
'Schaumlöscher *m* foam extinguisher
'Schauplatz *m* scene
'Schaupro͵zess *m* JUR show trial
schaurig ['ʃaurɪç] *adj* creepy; horrible
'Schauspiel *n* THEA play; *fig* spectacle
'Schauspieler(in) actor (actress)
'Schauspielschule *f* drama school
'Schausteller [-ʃtɛlɐ] *m* (*-s*; -) showman
Scheck [ʃɛk] *m* (*-s*; *-s*) ECON check, *Br* cheque
Scheckheft *n* checkbook, *Br* chequebook
scheckig ['ʃɛkɪç] *adj* spotty
'Scheckkarte *f* check cashing (*Br* cheque) card

scheffeln ['ʃɛfəln] F *v/t* (*ge-, h*) rake in
Scheibe ['ʃaibə] *f* (-; *-n*) disk, *Br* disc; slice; pane; target
'**Scheibenbremse** *f* MOT disk (*Br* disc) brake
Scheibenwischer *m* MOT windshield (*Br* windscreen) wiper
Scheide ['ʃaidə] *f* (-; *-n*) sheath; scabbard; ANAT vagina
'**scheiden** (*irr, ge-*) **1.** *v/t* (*h*) separate, part (*both*: ***von*** from); divorce; ***sich scheiden lassen*** get a divorce, ***von j-m***: divorce s.o.; **2.** *v/i* (*sein*) part; ***scheiden aus*** (*dat*) retire from
'**Scheideweg** *m* crossroads
'**Scheidung** *f* (-; *-en*) divorce
'**Scheidungsklage** *f* JUR divorce suit
Schein[1] [ʃain] *m* (-[*e*]*s*; *-e*) certificate; blank, *Br* form; bill, *Br* note
Schein[2] *m* (-[*e*]*s*; *no pl*) light; *fig* appearance; ***et.*** (***nur***) ***zum Schein tun*** (only) pretend to do s.th.
'**scheinbar** *adj* seeming, apparent
scheinen ['ʃainən] *v/i* (*irr, ge-, h*) shine; *fig* seem, appear, look
'**scheinheilig** *adj* hypocritical
'**Scheinwerfer** *m* searchlight; MOT headlight; THEA spotlight
Scheiß... ['ʃais-] V *in cpds* damn ..., fucking ..., *esp Br* bloody ...
Scheiße ['ʃaisə] V *f* (-; *no pl*), '**scheißen** V *v/i* (*irr, ge-, h*) shit, crap
Scheit [ʃait] *n* (-[*e*]*s*; *-e*) piece of wood
Scheitel ['ʃaitəl] *m* (*-s*; -) parting
'**scheiteln** *v/t* (*ge-, h*) part
Scheiterhaufen ['ʃaitɐ-] *m* pyre; HIST stake
scheitern ['ʃaitɐn] *v/i* (*ge-, sein*) fail, go wrong
Schelle ['ʃɛlə] *f* (-; *-n*) (little) bell; TECH clamp, clip
Schellfisch ['ʃɛl-] *m* ZO haddock
Schelm [ʃɛlm] *m* (-[*e*]*s*; *-e*) rascal
schelmisch ['ʃɛlmɪʃ] *adj* impish
Schema ['ʃeːma] *n* (*-s*; *-s, -ta*) pattern, system
schematisch [ʃe'maːtɪʃ] *adj* schematic; mechanical
Schemel ['ʃeːməl] *m* (*-s*; -) stool
schemenhaft ['ʃeːmən-] *adj* shadowy
Schenkel ['ʃɛŋkəl] *m* (*-s*; -) ANAT thigh; shank; MATH leg
schenken ['ʃɛŋkən] *v/t* (*ge-, h*) give (as a present) (***zu*** for)
'**Schenkung** *f* (-; *-en*) JUR donation
Scherbe ['ʃɛrbə] *f* (-; *-n*), '**Scherben** *m* (*-s*; -) (broken) piece, fragment
Schere ['ʃeːrə] *f* (-; *-n*) scissors; ZO claw
scheren[1] ['ʃeːrən] *v/t* (*irr, ge-, h*) ZO shear; BOT clip; cut
'**scheren**[2] *v/refl* (*ge-, h*) ***sich scheren um*** bother about
Scherereien [ʃeːrə'raiən] *pl* trouble, bother
Schermaus ['ʃeːɐ-] *Austrian f* ZO mole
Scherz [ʃɛrts] *m* (*-es*; *-e*) joke; ***im*** (***zum***) ***Scherz*** for fun
scherzen ['ʃɛrtsən] *v/i* (*ge-, h*) joke (***über*** *acc* at)
'**scherzhaft** *adj* joking; ***scherzhaft gemeint*** meant as a joke
scheu [ʃɔʏ] *adj* shy (*a.* ZO); bashful; ***scheu machen*** frighten
Scheu *f* (-; *no pl*) shyness; awe
scheuen ['ʃɔʏən] (*ge-, h*) **1.** *v/i* shy (***vor*** *dat* at), take fright (at); **2.** *v/t* shun, avoid; fear; ***sich scheuen, et. zu tun*** be afraid of doing s.th.
scheuern ['ʃɔʏɐn] *v/t and v/i* (*ge-, h*) scrub, scour; chafe
'**Scheuertuch** *n* floor cloth
'**Scheuklappen** *pl* blinders, *Br* blinkers (*both a. fig*)
'**scheumachen** *v/t* (*sep, -ge-, h*) → ***scheu***
Scheune ['ʃɔʏnə] *f* (-; *-n*) barn
Scheusal ['ʃɔʏzaːl] *n* (*-s*; *-e*) monster (*a. fig*); *fig* beast
scheußlich ['ʃɔʏslɪç] *adj* horrible (*a.* F), atrocious
Schicht [ʃɪçt] *f* (-; *-en*) layer; coat; film; ECON shift; class
schichten ['ʃɪçtən] *v/t* (*ge-, h*) arrange in layers, pile up
'**schichtweise** *adv* in layers
schick [ʃɪk] *adj* smart, chic, stylish
schicken ['ʃɪkən] *v/t* (*ge-, h*) send (***nach, zu*** to); ***das schickt sich nicht*** that isn't done
Schickeria [ʃɪkə'riːa] F *f* (-; *no pl*) smart set, beautiful people, trendies
Schickimicki [ʃɪki'mɪki] F *contp m* (*-s*; *-s*) trendy
Schicksal ['ʃɪkzaːl] *n* (*-s*; *-e*) fate, destiny; lot
Schiebedach ['ʃiːbə-] *n* MOT sliding roof, sunroof
Schiebefenster *n* sliding window; sash window
schieben ['ʃiːbən] *v/t* (*irr, ge-, h*) push
Schieber ['ʃiːbɐ] *m* (*-s*; -) TECH slide; bolt; F profiteer
'**Schiebetür** *f* sliding door
'**Schiebung** F *f* (-; *-en*) swindle, fix (*a.* SPORT)
schied [ʃiːt] *pret of* ***scheiden***
Schiedsrichter ['ʃiːts-] *m*, '**Schiedsrichterin** *f soccer*: referee; *tennis*: umpire; judge, *esp pl a.* jury

schief [ʃiːf] *adj* crooked, not straight; sloping, oblique (*a.* MATH); leaning; *fig* false
Schiefer [ˈʃiːfɐ] *m* (-*s*; -) GEOL slate
ˈ**Schiefertafel** *f* slate
ˈ**schiefgehen** *v/i* (*irr*, ***gehen***, *sep*, *-ge-*, *sein*) F go wrong
schielen [ˈʃiːlən] *v/i* (*ge-*, *h*) squint, be cross-eyed
schien [ʃiːn] *pret of* ***scheinen***
Schienbein [ˈʃiːn-] *n* ANAT shin(bone)
Schiene [ˈʃiːnə] *f* (-; *-n*) TECH *etc* rail; MED splint
ˈ**schienen** *v/t* (*ge-*, *h*) MED splint
Schießbude [ˈʃiːs-] *f* shooting gallery
schießen [ˈʃiːsən] *v/i and v/t* (*irr*, *ge-*, *h*) shoot, fire (*both*: ***auf*** *acc* at); SPORT score
Schießerei [ʃiːsəˈrai] *f* (-; *-en*) shooting; gunfight
ˈ**Schießpulver** *n* gunpowder
Schießscharte *f* MIL loophole, embrasure
Schießscheibe *f* target
Schießstand *m* shooting range
Schiff [ʃɪf] *n* (-[*e*]*s*; *-e*) MAR ship, boat; ARCH nave; ***mit dem Schiff*** by boat
Schiffahrt *f* → ***Schifffahrt***
ˈ**schiffbar** *adj* navigable
ˈ**Schiffbau** *m* (-[*e*]*s*; *no pl*) shipbuilding
ˈ**Schiffbruch** *m* shipwreck (*a. fig*); ***Schiffbruch erleiden*** be shipwrecked
Schiffer [ˈʃɪfɐ] *m* (-*s*; -) sailor; skipper
ˈ**Schifffahrt** *f* (-; *no pl*) shipping, navigation
ˈ**Schiffsjunge** *m* ship's boy
Schiffsladung *f* shipload; cargo
Schiffsschraube *f* (ship's) propeller
Schiffswerft *f* shipyard
Schikane [ʃiˈkaːnə] *f* (-; *-n*) *a. pl* harassment; ***aus reiner Schikane*** out of sheer spite; F ***mit allen Schikanen*** with all the trimmings
schikanieren [ʃikaˈniːrən] *v/t* (*no -ge-*, *h*) harass; bully
Schild[1] [ʃɪlt] *n* (-[*e*]*s*; *-er* [ˈʃɪldɐ]) sign, plate
Schild[2] *m* (-[*e*]*s*; *-e*) shield
ˈ**Schilddrüse** *f* ANAT thyroid (gland)
schildern [ˈʃɪldɐn] *v/t* (*ge-*, *h*) describe; depict, portray
Schilderung [ˈʃɪldərʊŋ] *f* (-; *-en*) description, portrayal; account
ˈ**Schildkröte** *f* ZO tortoise; turtle
Schilf [ʃɪlf] *n* (-[*e*]*s*; *no pl*) BOT reed(s)
schillern [ˈʃɪlɐn] *v/i* (*ge-*, *h*) be iridescent
schillernd *adj* iridescent; *fig* dubious
Schimmel [ˈʃɪməl] *m* ZO white horse; BOT mo(u)ld
schimm(e)lig [ˈʃɪm(ə)lɪç] *adj* mo(u)ldy, musty
ˈ**schimmeln** *v/i* (*ge-*, *h*, *sein*) go mo(u)ldy
Schimmer [ˈʃɪmɐ] *m* (-*s*; -) glimmer (*a. fig*), gleam, *fig a.* trace, touch
ˈ**schimmern** *v/i* (*ge-*, *h*) shimmer, glimmer, gleam
Schimpanse [ʃɪmˈpanzə] *m* (-*n*; *-n*) ZO chimpanzee
schimpfen [ˈʃɪmpfən] *v/i and v/t* (*ge-*, *h*) scold (***mit j-m*** s.o.); F tell *s.o.* off, bawl *s.o.* out; ***schimpfen über*** (*acc*) complain about
ˈ**Schimpfwort** *n* swearword
Schindel [ˈʃɪndəl] *f* (-; *-n*) shingle
schinden [ˈʃɪndən] *v/t* (*irr*, *ge-*, *h*) maltreat; slave-drive; ***sich schinden*** drudge, slave away
Schinder [ˈʃɪndɐ] *m* (-*s*; -) slave driver
Schinderei [ʃɪndəˈrai] *f* (-; *-en*) slavery, drudgery
Schinken [ˈʃɪŋkən] *m* (-*s*; -) ham
Schippe [ˈʃɪpə] *f* (-; *-n*), ˈ**schippen** *v/t* (*ge-*, *h*) shovel
Schirm [ʃɪrm] *m* (-[*e*]*s*; *-e*) umbrella; sunshade; TV, EDP *etc*: screen; shade; peak, visor
Schirmherr(in) patron, sponsor
Schirmherrschaft *f* patronage, sponsorship; ***unter der Schirmherrschaft von*** under the auspices of
Schirmmütze *f* peaked cap
Schirmständer *m* umbrella stand
schiss [ʃɪs] *pret of* scheißen
Schlacht [ʃlaxt] *f* (-; *-en*) battle (***bei*** of)
ˈ**schlachten** *v/t* (*ge-*, *h*) slaughter, kill, butcher
Schlachter [ˈʃlaxtɐ] *m* (-*s*; -) butcher
ˈ**Schlachtfeld** *n* MIL battlefield, battleground
Schlachthaus *n*, **Schlachthof** *m* slaughterhouse
Schlachtplan *m* MIL plan of action (*a. fig*)
Schlachtschiff *n* MIL battleship
Schlacke [ˈʃlakə] *f* (-; *-n*) cinders; GEOL, METALL slag
Schlaf [ʃlaːf] *m* (-[*e*]*s*; *no pl*) sleep; ***e-n leichten*** (***festen***) ***Schlaf haben*** be a light (sound) sleeper; F *fig* ***im Schlaf*** blindfold
ˈ**Schlafanzug** *m* pajamas, *Br* pyjamas
Schläfe [ˈʃlɛːfə] *f* (-; *-n*) ANAT temple
schlafen [ˈʃlaːfən] *v/i* (*irr*, *ge-*, *h*) sleep (*a. fig*); ***schlafen gehen, sich schlafen legen*** go to bed; ***fest schlafen*** be fast asleep; ***j-n schlafen legen*** put s.o. to bed *or* to sleep
schlaff [ʃlaf] *adj* slack (*a. fig*); flabby; limp
ˈ**Schlafgelegenheit** *f* sleeping accommodation

Schlafkrankheit *f* MED sleeping sickness
Schlaflied *n* lullaby
'**schlaflos** *adj* sleepless
'**Schlaflosigkeit** *f* (-; *no pl*) sleeplessness, MED insomnia
'**Schlafmittel** *n* MED sleeping pill(s)
'**Schlafmütze** *fig f* sleepyhead; slowpoke, *Br* slowcoach
schläfrig ['ʃlɛːfrɪç] *adj* sleepy, drowsy
'**Schlafsaal** *m* dormitory
Schlafsack *m* sleeping bag
Schlafta͵blette *f* sleeping pill
'**schlaftrunken** *adj* (very) drowsy
'**Schlafwagen** *m* RAIL sleeping car, sleeper
Schlafwandler(in) [-vandlɐ (-lərɪn)] (-*s*; -/-; -*nen*) sleepwalker, somnambulist
Schlafzimmer *n* bedroom
Schlag [ʃlaːk] *m* (-[*e*]*s*; *Schläge* ['ʃlɛːgə]) blow (*a. fig*); slap; punch; pat, tap; *a. tennis*: stroke; ELECTR shock (*a. fig*); MED beat; *pl* beating; → ***Schlaganfall***
Schlagader *f* ANAT artery
Schlaganfall *m* MED (apoplectic) stroke
'**schlagartig** **1.** *adj* sudden, abrupt; **2.** *adv* all of a sudden, abruptly
'**Schlagbaum** *m* barrier
'**Schlagbohrer** *m* TECH percussion drill
schlagen ['ʃlaːgən] (*irr, ge-, h*) **1.** *v/t* hit, beat (*a.* GASTR *and fig*), strike, knock; fell, cut (down); ***sich schlagen*** fight (***um*** over); ***sich geschlagen geben*** admit defeat; **2.** *v/i* hit, beat (*a. heart etc*), strike (*a. clock*), knock; ***an*** *or* ***gegen et. schlagen*** hit s.th., bump *or* crash into s.th.
Schlager ['ʃlaːgɐ] *m* (-*s*; -) MUS hit (*a. fig*), (pop) song
Schläger ['ʃlɛːgɐ] *m* (-*s*; -) *tennis etc*: racket; *table tennis*, *cricket*, *baseball*: bat; *golf*: club; *hockey*: stick; *contp* thug
Schlägerei [ʃlɛːgə'rai] *f* (-; -*en*) fight, brawl
'**schlagfertig** *adj* quick-witted; ***schlagfertige Antwort*** (witty) repartee
'**Schlaginstru͵ment** *n* MUS percussion instrument
Schlagkraft *f* (-; *no pl*) striking power (*a.* MIL)
Schlagloch *n* pot-hole
Schlagobers *Austrian n*, **Schlagsahne** *f* whipped cream
Schlagseite *f* MAR list; ***Schlagseite haben*** be listing
Schlagstock *m* baton, truncheon
Schlagwort *n* catchword, slogan
Schlagzeile *f* headline
'**Schlagzeug** *n* MUS drums
'**Schlagzeuger** [-tsɔʏgɐ] *m* (-*s*; -) MUS drummer
schlaksig ['ʃlaːksɪç] *adj* lanky, gangling
Schlamm [ʃlam] *m* (-[*e*]*s*; -*e*) mud
schlammig ['ʃlamɪç] *adj* muddy
Schlampe ['ʃlampə] F *f* (-; -*n*) slut
schlampig ['ʃlampɪç] F *adj* sloppy
schlang [ʃlaŋ] *pret of* ***schlingen***
Schlange ['ʃlaŋə] *f* (-; -*n*) ZO snake, serpent (*a. fig*); *fig* line, *esp Br* queue; ***Schlange stehen*** line up, stand in line, *esp Br* queue (up) (***nach*** for)
schlängeln ['ʃlɛŋəln] *v/refl* (*ge-, h*) wind *or* weave (one's way), *person*: worm one's way
'**Schlangenlinie** *f* serpentine line; ***in Schlangenlinien fahren*** weave
schlank [ʃlaŋk] *adj* slim, slender; ***j-n schlank machen*** make s.o. look slim; ***schlanke Unternehmensstruktur*** ECON lean management
'**Schlankheitskur** *f*: ***e-e Schlankheitskur machen*** be slimming
'**schlankmachen** *v/t* (*sep*, -*ge*-, *h*): ***j-n schlankmachen*** → ***schlank***
schlapp [ʃlap] F *adj* worn out; weak
Schlappe ['ʃlapə] F *f* (-; -*n*) setback, beating
'**schlappmachen** F *v/i* (*sep*, -*ge*-, *h*) flake out
'**Schlappschwanz** F *m* weakling, wimp
schlau [ʃlau] *adj* clever, smart, bright; sly, cunning, crafty
Schlauch [ʃlaux] *m* (-[*e*]*s*; *Schläuche* ['ʃlɔʏçə]) tube; hose
Schlauchboot *n* (inflatable *or* rubber) dinghy
Schlaufe ['ʃlaufə] *f* (-; -*n*) loop
schlecht [ʃlɛçt] *adj* bad; poor; ***mir ist*** (***wird***) ***schlecht*** I feel (I'm getting) sick to my stomach; ***schlecht aussehen*** look ill; ***sich schlecht fühlen*** feel bad; ***schlecht werden*** GASTR go bad; ***es geht ihm sehr schlecht*** he is in a bad way; ***schlecht gelaunt*** in a bad temper *or* mood, bad-tempered; F ***j-n schlecht machen*** run s.o. down, backbite s.o.
'**schlechtmachen** *v/t* (*sep*, -*ge*-, *h*): F ***j-n schlechtmachen machen*** run s.o. down, backbite s.o.
schleichen ['ʃlaiçən] *v/i* (*irr, ge-, sein*) creep (*a. fig*), sneak
'**Schleichweg** *m* secret path
'**Schleichwerbung** *f* plugging; ***für et. Schleichwerbung machen*** plug s.th.
Schleier ['ʃlaiɐ] *m* (-*s*; -) veil (*a. fig*); haze
'**schleierhaft** *adj*: F ***es ist mir schleierhaft*** it's a mystery to me
Schleife ['ʃlaifə] *f* (-; -*n*) bow; ribbon; AVIAT, EDP, ELECTR, GEOGR loop
schleifen[1] ['ʃlaifən] *v/t and v/i* (*ge-, h*)

S

drag (along); rub
'schleifen² *v/t (irr, ge-, h)* grind (*a.* TECH), sharpen; sand(paper); cut; F drill *s.o.* hard
Schleifer ['ʃlaifɐ] *m (-s; -)*, **'Schleifma͵schine** *f* TECH grinder
'Schleifpa͵pier *n* sandpaper
'Schleifstein *m* grindstone; whetstone
Schleim [ʃlaim] *m (-[e]s; -e)* slime; MED mucus
'Schleimhaut *f* ANAT mucous membrane
schleimig ['ʃlaimɪç] *adj* slimy (*a. fig*); MED mucous
schlemmen ['ʃlɛmən] *v/i (ge-, h)* feast
schlendern ['ʃlɛndɐn] *v/i (ge-, sein)* stroll, saunter, amble
schlenkern ['ʃlɛŋkɐn] *v/i and v/t (ge-, h)* dangle, swing (***mit den Armen*** one's arms)
schleppen ['ʃlɛpən] *v/t (ge-, h)* drag (*a. fig*); MOT, MAR tow; ***sich schleppen*** drag (on)
schleppend *adj* dragging; *fig* drawling
Schlepper ['ʃlɛpɐ] *m (-s; -)* MAR tug; MOT tractor
'Schlepplift *m* T-bar (lift), drag lift, ski tow
Schlepptau *n* tow-rope; ***im (ins) Schlepptau*** in tow (*a. fig*)
Schleuder ['ʃlɔydɐ] *f (-; -n)* catapult, slingshot; TECH spin drier
'schleudern *(ge-, h)* **1.** *v/t* fling, hurl (*both a. fig*); spin-dry; **2.** *v/i* MOT skid
'Schleudersitz *m* AVIAT ejection (*esp Br* ejector) seat
schleunigst ['ʃlɔynɪçst] *adv* immediately
Schleuse ['ʃlɔyzə] *f (-; -n)* sluice; lock
schlich [ʃlɪç] *pret of* ***schleichen***
schlicht [ʃlɪçt] *adj* plain, simple
schlichten ['ʃlɪçtən] *v/t (ge-, h)* settle
'Schlichtung *f (-; -en)* settlement
schlief [ʃliːf] *pret of* ***schlafen***
schließen ['ʃliːsən] *v/t and v/i (irr, ge-, h)* shut, close (down); *fig* close, finish; ***schließen aus*** *(dat)* conclude from; ***nach ... zu schließen*** judging by ...
Schließfach ['ʃliːs-] *n* safe-deposit box; RAIL *etc*: (left luggage) locker
schließlich ['ʃliːslɪç] *adv* finally; eventually, in the end; after all
schliff [ʃlɪf] *pret of* ***schleifen²***
Schliff *m (-[e]s; -e)* cut; polish (*a. fig*)
schlimm [ʃlɪm] *adj* bad; awful; ***das ist nicht*** *or* ***halb so schlimm*** it's not as bad as that; ***das Schlimme daran*** the bad thing about it
'schlimmsten'falls *adv* at (the) worst
Schlinge ['ʃlɪŋə] *f (-; -n)* loop; noose; HUNT snare (*a. fig*); MED sling

Schlingel ['ʃlɪŋəl] *m (-s; -)* rascal
schlingen ['ʃlɪŋən] *v/t (irr, ge-, h)* wind, twist; tie; wrap (***um*** [a]round); gobble; ***sich um et. schlingen*** wind (a)round s.th.
schlingern ['ʃlɪŋɐn] *v/i (ge-, h)* MAR roll
'Schlingpflanze *f* BOT creeper, climber
Schlips [ʃlɪps] *m (-es; -e)* necktie, *esp Br* tie
schlitteln ['ʃlɪtəln] *Swiss v/i (ge-, sein)* go sledging, go tobogganing
Schlitten ['ʃlɪtən] *m (-s; -)* sled, *Br* sledge; sleigh; SPORT toboggan; ***Schlitten fahren*** go sledging, go tobogganing
Schlittschuh ['ʃlɪt-] *m* ice-skate (*a.* ***Schlittschuh laufen***)
Schlittschuhläufer(in) ice-skater
Schlitz [ʃlɪts] *m (-es; -e)* slit; slot
schlitzen ['ʃlɪtsən] *v/t ge-, h)* slit, slash
schloss [ʃlɔs] *pret of* ***schließen***
Schloss *n (-es; Schlösser* ['ʃlœsɐ]*)* TECH lock; ARCH castle, palace; ***ins Schloss fallen*** *door*: slam shut; ***hinter Schloss und Riegel*** locked up, under lock and key
Schlosser ['ʃlɔsɐ] *m (-s; -)* metalworker; locksmith
Schlosserei [ʃlɔsə'rai] *f (-; -en)* metalwork shop
schlottern ['ʃlɔtɐn] *v/i (ge-, h)* shake, tremble (*both*: ***vor*** *dat* with); bag
Schlucht [ʃlʊxt] *f (-; -en)* canyon, gorge, ravine
schluchzen ['ʃlʊxtsən] *v/i (ge-, h)*, **Schluchzer** ['ʃlʊxtsɐ] *m (-s; -)* sob
Schluck [ʃlʊk] *m (-[e]s; -e)* draught, swallow; sip; gulp
'Schluckauf *m (-s; no pl)* hiccups; ***(e-n) Schluckauf haben*** have (the) hiccups
schlucken ['ʃlʊkən] *v/t and v/i (ge-, h)* swallow (*a. fig*)
'Schluckimpfung *f* MED oral vaccination
schlug [ʃluːk] *pret of* ***schlagen***
Schlummer ['ʃlʊmɐ] *m (-s; no pl)* slumber
'schlummern *v/i (ge-, h)* lie asleep; *fig* slumber
schlüpfen ['ʃlʏpfən] *v/i (ge-, sein)* slip, slide; ZO hatch (out)
Schlüpfer ['ʃlʏpfɐ] *m (-s; -)* briefs, panties
schlüpfrig ['ʃlʏpfrɪç] *adj* slippery; *contp* risqué, off-colo(u)r
Schlupfwinkel ['ʃlʊpf-] *m* hiding place
schlurfen ['ʃlʊrfən] *v/i (ge-, sein)* shuffle (along)
schlürfen ['ʃlʏrfən] *v/t and v/i (ge-, h)* slurp
Schluss [ʃlʊs] *m (-es; no pl)* end; conclusion; ending; ***Schluss machen*** finish; break up; ***Schluss machen mit*** stop

s.th., put an end to *s.th.*; ***zum Schluss*** finally; (***ganz***) ***bis zum Schluss*** to the (very) end; ***Schluss für heute!*** that's all for today!
Schlüssel ['ʃlʏsəl] *m* (*-s*; -) key (***für, zu*** to)
Schlüsselbein *n* ANAT collarbone
Schlüsselblume *f* BOT cowslip, primrose
Schlüsselbund *m, n* bunch of keys
Schlüsselkind F *n* latchkey child
Schlüsselloch *n* keyhole
Schlüsselwort *n* keyword, EDP *a.* password
'Schlussfolgerung *f* conclusion
schlüssig ['ʃlʏsɪç] *adj* conclusive; ***sich schlüssig werden*** make up one's mind (***über*** *acc* about)
'Schlusslicht *n* MOT *etc*: tail-light
Schlusspfiff *m* SPORT final whistle
Schlussphase *f* final stage(s)
Schlussverkauf *m* ECON (end-of-season) sale
schmächtig ['ʃmɛçtɪç] *adj* slight, thin, frail
schmackhaft ['ʃmakhaft] *adj* tasty
schmal [ʃmaːl] *adj* narrow; thin, slender (*a. fig*)
schmälern ['ʃmɛːlɐn] *v/t* (*ge-, h*) detract from
'Schmalfilm *m* cinefilm
'Schmalspur *f* RAIL narrow ga(u)ge
'Schmalspur… *fig in cpds* small-time …
Schmalz [ʃmalts] *n* (*-es*; *-e*) grease; lard
schmalzig ['ʃmaltsɪç] F *adj* schmaltzy, mushy, *Br* soapy
schmarotzen [ʃma'rɔtsən] F *v/i* (*no -ge-, h*) sponge (***bei*** on)
Schmarotzer [ʃma'rɔtsɐ] *m* (*-s*; -) BOT, ZO parasite, *fig a.* sponger
schmatzen ['ʃmatsən] *v/i* smack (one's lips), eat noisily
schmecken ['ʃmɛkən] *v/i and v/t* (*ge-, h*) taste (***nach*** of); ***gut*** (***schlecht***) ***schmecken*** taste good (bad); (***wie***) ***schmeckt dir …?*** (how) do you like …? (*a. fig*); ***es schmeckt süß*** (***nach nichts***) it has a sweet (no) taste
Schmeichelei [ʃmaiçə'lai] *f* (-; *-en*) flattery
'schmeichelhaft *adj* flattering
'schmeicheln *v/i* (*ge-, h*) flatter (***j-m*** s.o.)
Schmeichler(in) ['ʃmaiçlɐ (-lərɪn)] (*-s*; -/-; *-nen*) flatterer
schmeichlerisch ['ʃmaiçlərɪʃ] *adj* flattering
schmeißen ['ʃmaisən] F *v/t and v/i* (*irr, ge-, h*) throw, chuck; slam; ***mit Geld um sich schmeißen*** throw one's money about
'Schmeißfliege *f* ZO blowfly, bluebottle
schmelzen ['ʃmɛltsən] *v/i* (*irr, ge-, sein*) *and v/t* (*h*) melt; thaw; TECH smelt
'Schmelzofen *m* (s)melting furnace
Schmelztiegel *m* melting pot (*a. fig*)
Schmerz [ʃmɛrts] *m* (*-es*; *-en*) pain (*a. fig*), ache; *fig* grief, sorrow
schmerzen ['ʃmɛrtsən] *v/i and v/t* (*ge-, h*) hurt (*a. fig*), ache; *esp fig* pain
'schmerzfrei *adj* without pain
'schmerzhaft *adj* painful
'schmerzlich *adj* painful, sad
'schmerzlos *adj* painless
'Schmerzmittel *n* PHARM painkiller
'schmerzstillend *adj* painkilling
Schmetterling ['ʃmɛtɐlɪŋ] *m* (*-s*; *-e*) ZO butterfly
schmettern ['ʃmɛtɐn] (*ge-, h*) **1.** *v/t* smash (*a. tennis*); F MUS belt out; **2.** *v/i* a) (*sein*) crash, slam, b) MUS blare
Schmied [ʃmiːt] *m* (*-[e]s*; *-e*) (black-)smith
Schmiede ['ʃmiːdə] *f* (-; *-n*) forge, smithy
'Schmiedeeisen *n* wrought iron
'schmieden *v/t* (*ge-, h*) forge; *fig* make (*plans etc*)
schmiegen ['ʃmiːgən] *v/refl* (*ge-, h*) ***sich schmiegen an*** (*acc*) snuggle up to; *dress etc*: cling to
Schmiere ['ʃmiːrə] *f* (-; *-n*) grease
'schmieren *v/t* (*ge-, h*) TECH grease, oil, lubricate; spread (*butter etc*); *contp* scribble, scrawl
Schmiererei [ʃmiːrə'rai] *f* (-; *-en*) scrawl; graffiti
schmierig ['ʃmiːrɪç] *adj* greasy; dirty; filthy; *contp* slimy
Schmiermittel ['ʃmiːɐ-] *n* TECH lubricant
Schminke ['ʃmɪŋkə] *f* (-; *-n*) make-up (*a.* THEA)
'schminken *v/t* (*ge-, h*) make *s.o.* up; ***sich schminken*** make o.s. *or* one's face up
Schmirgelpa,pier ['ʃmɪrgəl-] *n* emery paper
schmiss [ʃmɪs] *pret of* ***schmeißen***
schmollen ['ʃmɔlən] *v/i* (*ge-, h*) sulk, be sulky, pout
schmolz [ʃmɔlts] *pret of* ***schmelzen***
schmoren ['ʃmoːrən] *v/t and v/i* (*ge-, h*) GASTR braise, stew (*a. fig*)
Schmuck [ʃmʊk] *m* (*-[e]s*; *no pl*) jewel(le)ry, jewels; decoration(s), ornament(s)
schmücken ['ʃmʏkən] *v/t* (*ge-, h*) decorate
'schmucklos *adj* unadorned; plain
'Schmuckstück *n* piece of jewel(le)ry; *fig* gem
Schmuggel ['ʃmʊgəl] *m* (-; *no pl*), **Schmuggelei** [ʃmʊgə'lai] *f* (-; *-en*) smug-

S

gling
'**schmuggeln** *v/t and v/i (ge-, h)* smuggle
'**Schmuggelware** *f* smuggled goods
Schmuggler ['ʃmʊglɐ] *m (-s; -)* smuggler
schmunzeln ['ʃmʊntsəln] *v/i (ge-, h)* smile to o.s.
schmusen ['ʃmuːzən] F *v/i (ge-, h)* (kiss and) cuddle, smooch
Schmutz [ʃmʊts] *m (-es; no pl)* dirt, filth, *fig a.* smut
Schmutzfleck *m* smudge
schmutzig ['ʃmʊtsɪç] *adj* dirty, filthy (*both a. fig*); ***schmutzig werden, sich schmutzig machen*** get dirty
Schnabel ['ʃnaːbəl] *m (-s; Schnäbel* ['ʃnɛːbəl]) zo bill, beak
Schnalle ['ʃnalə] *f (-; -n)* buckle
'**schnallen** *v/t (ge-, h)* buckle; ***et. schnallen an*** (*acc*) strap s.th. to
schnalzen ['ʃnaltsən] *v/i (ge-, h)* snap one's fingers; click one's tongue
schnappen ['ʃnapən] *(ge-, h)* **1.** *v/i* snap, snatch (*both*: ***nach*** at); F ***nach Luft schnappen*** gasp for breath; **2.** F *v/t* catch
'**Schnappschuss** *m* PHOT snapshot
Schnaps [ʃnaps] *m (-es; Schnäpse* ['ʃnɛpsə]) spirits, schnapps, F booze
schnarchen ['ʃnarçən] *v/i (ge-, h)* snore
schnarren ['ʃnarən] *v/i (ge-, h)* rattle; *voice*: rasp
schnattern ['ʃnatɐn] *v/i (ge-, h)* zo cackle; chatter (*a.* F)
schnauben ['ʃnaubən] *v/i and v/t (ge-, h)* snort; ***sich die Nase schnauben*** blow one's nose
schnaufen ['ʃnaufən] *v/i (ge-, h)* breathe hard, pant, puff
Schnauze ['ʃnautsə] *f (-; -n)* zo snout, mouth, muzzle; F AVIAT, MOT nose; TECH spout; V trap, kisser; V ***die Schnauze halten*** keep one's trap shut
Schnecke ['ʃnɛkə] *f (-; -n)* zo snail; slug
'**Schneckenhaus** *n* zo snail shell
Schneckentempo *n*: ***im Schneckentempo*** at a snail's pace
Schnee [ʃneː] *m (-s; no pl)* snow (*a. sl*); ***Schnee räumen*** remove snow
Schneeball *m* snowball
Schneeballschlacht *f* snowball fight
'**schneebedeckt** *adj* snow-capped
'**Schneefall** *m* snowfall
Schneeflocke *f* snowflake
Schneegestöber [-gəʃtøːbɐ] *n (-s; -)* snow flurry
Schneeglöckchen *n* BOT snowdrop
Schneegrenze *f* snow line
Schneemann *m* snowman
Schneematsch *m* slush
Schneemo͵bil *n* snowmobile
Schneepflug *m* snowplow, *Br* snowplough
Schneeregen *m* sleet
Schneesturm *m* snowstorm, blizzard
Schneeverwehung *f* snowdrift
'**schnee'weiß** *adj* snow-white
Schneewittchen [ʃneː'vɪtçən] *n (-s; no pl)* Snow White
Schneid [ʃnait] F *m (-[e]s; no pl)* grit, guts
Schneidbrenner *m* TECH cutting torch
Schneide ['ʃnaidə] *f (-; -n)* edge
'**schneiden** *v/t and v/i (irr, ge-, h)* cut (*a. fig*), *film etc*: *a.* edit; GASTR carve
Schneider ['ʃnaidɐ] *m (-s; -)* tailor
Schneiderei [ʃnaidə'rai] *f (-; -en)* a) (*no pl*) tailoring, dressmaking, b) tailor's *or* dressmaker's shop
'**Schneiderin** *f (-; -nen)* dressmaker; seamstress
'**schneidern** *v/i and v/t (ge-, h)* do dressmaking; make, sew
'**Schneidezahn** *m* incisor
schneidig ['ʃnaidɪç] *adj* dashing; smart
schneien ['ʃnaiən] *v/i (ge-, h)* snow
schnell [ʃnɛl] *adj* fast, quick; prompt; rapid; ***es geht schnell*** it won't take long; (***mach***[***t***]) ***schnell!*** hurry up!
'**Schnell...** *in cpds ...dienst, ...paket, ...zug etc*: *mst* express ...
schnellen ['ʃnɛlən] *v/t (ge-, h) and v/i (ge-, sein)* shoot, spring
'**Schnellhefter** *m* folder
Schnelligkeit ['ʃnɛlɪçkait] *f (-; no pl)* speed; quickness, rapidity
'**Schnellimbiss** *m* snack bar
Schnellstraße *f* expressway, thruway, *Br* motorway
schnetzeln ['ʃnɛtsəln] *esp Swiss v/t (ge-, h)* GASTR chop up
Schnippchen ['ʃnɪpçən] *n*: F ***j-m ein Schnippchen schlagen*** outwit s.o.
schnippisch ['ʃnɪpɪʃ] *adj* sassy, pert
schnipsen ['ʃnɪpsən] *v/i (ge-, h)* snap one's fingers
schnitt [ʃnɪt] *pret of* ***schneiden***
Schnitt *m (-[e]s; -e)* cut (*a. fig*); average
'**Schnittblumen** *pl* cut flowers
Schnitte ['ʃnɪtə] *f (-; -n)* slice; open sandwich
schnittig ['ʃnɪtɪç] *adj* stylish; MOT sleek
Schnittlauch *m* BOT chives
Schnittmuster *n* pattern
Schnittpunkt *m* (point of) intersection
Schnittstelle *f film etc*: cut; EDP interface
Schnittwunde *f* MED cut
Schnitzel[1] ['ʃnɪtsəl] *n (-s; -)* GASTR cutlet; ***Wiener Schnitzel*** schnitzel
'**Schnitzel**[2] *n, m (-s; -)* chip; scrap
schnitzen ['ʃnɪtsən] *v/t (ge-, h)* carve, cut

(in wood)
Schnitzer ['ʃnɪtsɐ] *m* (*-s*; *-*) (wood) carver
Schnitzerei [ʃnɪtsə'rai] *f* (*-*; *-en*) (wood) carving
Schnorchel ['ʃnɔrçəl] *m* (*-s*; *-*), '**schnorcheln** *v/i* (*ge-*, *h*) snorkel
Schnörkel ['ʃnœrkəl] *m* (*-s*; *-*) flourish; ARCH scroll
schnorren ['ʃnɔrən] F *v/t* (*ge-*, *h*) mooch, *Br* cadge
schnüffeln ['ʃnʏfəln] *v/i* (*ge-*, *h*) sniff (***an*** *dat* at); F snoop (about *or* around)
Schnuller ['ʃnʊlɐ] *m* (*-s*; *-*) pacifier, *Br* dummy
Schnulze ['ʃnʊltsə] F *f* (*-*; *-n*) tearjerker; schmal(t)zy song
'**Schnulzensänger** F *m*, '**Schnulzensängerin** *f* crooner
schnulzig ['ʃnʊltsɪç] F *adj* schmal(t)zy
Schnupfen ['ʃnʊpfən] *m* (*-s*; *-*) MED cold; ***e-n Schnupfen haben (bekommen)*** have a (catch [a]) cold
'**Schnupftabak** *m* snuff
schnuppern ['ʃnʊpɐn] *v/i* (*ge-*, *h*) sniff (***an et.*** [at] s.th.)
Schnur [ʃnuːɐ] *f* (*-*; *Schnüre* ['ʃnyːrə]) string, cord; ELECTR flex
Schnürchen ['ʃnyːɐçən] *n*: ***wie am Schnürchen*** like clockwork
schnüren ['ʃnyːrən] *v/t* (*ge-*, *h*) lace (up); tie up
'**schnurgerade** *adv* dead straight
'**schnurlos** *adj*: ***schnurloses Telefon*** cordless phone
Schnürlsamt ['ʃnyːɐl-] *Austrian m* corduroy
Schnurrbart ['ʃnʊr-] *m* m(o)ustache
schnurren ['ʃnʊrən] *v/i* (*ge-*, *h*) purr
Schnürschuh ['ʃnyːɐ-] *m* laced shoe
Schnürsenkel [-zɛŋkəl] *m* (*-s*; *-*) shoestring, *Br* shoelace
schnurstracks ['ʃnuːɐ'ʃtraks] *adv* direct(ly), straight; straight away
schob [ʃoːp] *pret of* ***schieben***
Schober ['ʃoːbɐ] *m* (*-s*; *-*) haystack, hayrick; barn
Schock [ʃɔk] *m* (*-[e]s*; *-s*) MED shock; ***unter Schock stehen*** be in (a state of) shock
schocken ['ʃɔkən] F *v/t* (*ge-*, *h*) shock
schockieren [ʃɔ'kiːrən] *v/t* (*no -ge-*, *h*) shock
Schokolade [ʃoko'laːdə] *f* (*-*; *-n*) chocolate; ***e-e Tafel Schokolade*** a bar of chocolate
scholl [ʃɔl] *pret of* ***schallen***
Scholle ['ʃɔlə] *f* (*-*; *-n*) clod; (ice)floe; ZO flounder, *Br* plaice
schon [ʃoːn] *adv* already; ever; even; ***schon damals*** even then; ***schon 1968*** as early as 1968; ***schon der Gedanke*** the very idea; ***ist sie schon da (zurück)?*** has she come (is she back) yet?; ***habt ihr schon gegessen?*** have you eaten yet?; ***bist du schon einmal dort gewesen?*** have you ever been there?; ***ich wohne hier schon seit zwei Jahren*** I've been living here for two years now; ***ich kenne ihn schon, aber*** I do know him, but; ***er macht das schon*** he'll do it all right; ***schon gut!*** never mind!, all right!
schön [ʃøːn] **1.** *adj* beautiful, lovely; METEOR *a.* fine, fair; nice (*a.* F *iro*); ***(na,) schön*** all right; **2.** *adv*: ***schön warm (kühl)*** nice and warm (cool); ***ganz schön teuer (schnell)*** pretty expensive (fast); ***j-n ganz schön erschrecken (überraschen)*** give s.o. quite a start (surprise)
schonen ['ʃoːnən] *v/t* (*ge-*, *h*) take care of, go easy on (*a.* TECH); spare; ***sich schonen*** take it easy; save o.s. *or* one's strength
schonend **1.** *adj* gentle; mild; **2.** *adv*: ***schonend umgehen mit*** take (good) care of; handle with care; go easy on
'**Schönheit** *f* (*-*; *-en*) beauty
'**Schönheitspflege** *f* beauty care
'**Schonung** *f* (*-*; *-en*) a) (*no pl*) (good) care; rest; preservation, b) tree nursery
'**schonungslos** *adj* relentless, brutal
schöpfen ['ʃœpfən] *v/t* (*ge-*, *h*) scoop, ladle; draw (*water*); → ***Luft***, ***Verdacht***
Schöpfer ['ʃœpfɐ] *m* (*-s*; *-*), '**Schöpferin** *f* (*-*; *-nen*) creator
schöpferisch ['ʃœpfərɪʃ] *adj* creative
'**Schöpfung** *f* (*-*; *-en*) creation
schor [ʃoːɐ] *pret of* ***scheren***
Schorf [ʃɔrf] *m* (*-[e]s*; *-e*) MED scab
Schornstein ['ʃɔrnʃtain] *m* chimney; MAR, RAIL funnel
Schornsteinfeger *m* chimneysweep
schoss [ʃɔs] *pret of* ***schießen***
Schoß [ʃoːs] *m* (*-es*; *Schöße* ['ʃøːsə]) lap; womb
Schote ['ʃoːtə] *f* (*-*; *-n*) BOT pod, husk
Schotte ['ʃɔtə] *m* (*-n*; *-n*) Scot(sman); *pl* the Scots, the Scottish (people)
Schotter ['ʃɔtɐ] *m* (*-s*; *-*) gravel, road metal
Schottin ['ʃɔtɪn] *f* (*-*; *-nen*) Scotswoman
'**schottisch** *adj* Scots, Scottish; Scotch
'**Schottland** Scotland
schräg [ʃrɛːk] **1.** *adj* slanting, sloping, oblique; diagonal; **2.** *adv*: ***schräg gegenüber*** diagonally opposite
Schramme ['ʃramə] *f* (*-*; *-n*), '**schrammen**

v/t and v/i (ge-, h) scratch (*a.* MED)
Schrank [ʃraŋk] *m (-[e]s; Schränke* [ˈʃrɛŋkə]) cupboard; closet; wardrobe
Schranke [ˈʃraŋkə] *f (-; -n)* barrier (*a. fig*), RAIL *a.* gate; JUR bar; *pl* limits, bounds
ˈschrankenlos *fig adj* boundless
ˈSchrankenwärter *m* RAIL gatekeeper
ˈSchrankwand *f* wall units
Schraube [ˈʃraubə] *f (-; -n)*, **ˈschrauben** *v/t (ge-, h)* TECH screw
ˈSchraubenschlüssel *m* TECH spanner, wrench
Schraubenzieher *m* TECH screwdriver
Schraubstock [ˈʃraup-] *m* vise, *Br* vice
Schreck [ʃrɛk] *m (-[e]s; -e)* fright, shock; ***j-m e-n Schreck einjagen*** give s.o. a fright, scare s.o.
Schrecken [ˈʃrɛkən] *m (-s; -)* terror, fright; horror(s)
ˈSchreckensnachricht *f* dreadful news
ˈschreckhaft *adj* jumpy; skittish
ˈschrecklich *adj* awful, terrible; horrible, dreadful, atrocious
Schrei [ʃrai] *m (-[e]s; -e)* cry, shout, yell, scream (*all:* ***um, nach*** for)
schreiben [ˈʃraibən] *v/t and v/i (irr, ge-, h)* write (***j-m*** to s.o.; ***über*** *acc* about); type; spell; ***falsch schreiben*** misspell; ***wie schreibt man ...?*** how do you spell ...?
ˈSchreiben *n (-s; -)* letter
ˈSchreibfehler *m* spelling mistake
Schreibheft *n* exercise book
Schreibkraft *f* typist
Schreibmaˌschine *f* typewriter
Schreibmateriˌal *n* writing materials, stationery
Schreibschutz *m* EDP write *or* file protection
Schreibtisch *m* desk
ˈSchreibung *f (-; -en)* spelling
ˈSchreibwaren *pl* stationery
Schreibwarengeschäft *n* stationer's, stationery shop
ˈSchreibzenˌtrale *f* typing pool
schreien [ˈʃraiən] *v/i and v/t (irr, ge-, h)* cry, shout, yell, scream (*all:* ***um, nach*** [out] for); ***schreien vor Schmerz*** (***Angst***) cry out with pain (in terror); ***es war zum Schreien*** it was a scream
schreiend *fig adj* loud (*colors*); flagrant (*abuse etc*), glaring (*injustices etc*)
Schreiner [ˈʃrainɐ] *m (-s; -)* → ***Tischler***
schreiten [ˈʃraitən] *v/i (irr, ge-, sein)* stride
schrie [ʃriː] *pret of* ***schreien***
schrieb [ʃriːp] *pret of* ***schreiben***
Schrift [ʃrɪft] *f (-; -en)* (hand)writing, hand; PRINT type; character, letter; *pl* works, writings; ***die Heilige Schrift*** REL the Scriptures
Schriftart *f* script; PRINT typeface
Schriftdeutsch *n* standard German
ˈschriftlich *adj* written; ***schriftlich übersetzen*** translate in writing
ˈSchriftsteller [-ʃtɛlɐ] *m (-s; -)*, **ˈSchriftstellerin** *f (-; -nen)* author, writer
ˈSchriftverkehr *m*, **Schriftwechsel** *m* correspondence
Schriftzeichen *n* character, letter
schrill [ʃrɪl] *adj* shrill (*a. fig*), piercing
schritt [ʃrɪt] *pret of* ***schreiten***
Schritt *m (-[e]s; -e)* step (*a. fig*); pace; *fig* ***Schritte unternehmen*** take steps; ***Schritt fahren!*** MOT dead slow
Schrittmacher *m* SPORT pacemaker (*a.* MED), pacesetter
ˈschrittweise *adv* step by step, gradually
schroff [ʃrɔf] *adj* steep; jagged; *fig* gruff
Schrot [ʃroːt] *m, n (-[e]s; -e)* a) *(no pl)* coarse meal, b) HUNT (small) shot; pellet
Schrotflinte *f* shotgun
Schrott [ʃrɔt] *m (-[e]s; -e)* scrap (metal)
ˈSchrotthaufen *m* scrap heap
ˈSchrottplatz *m* scrapyard
schrubben [ˈʃrubən] *v/t (ge-, h)* scrub, scour
schrumpfen [ˈʃrumpfən] *v/i (ge-, sein)* shrink
Schub [ʃuːp] *m (-[e]s; Schübe* [ˈʃyːbə]) → ***Schubkraft***
Schubfach *n* drawer
Schubkarren *m* wheelbarrow
Schubkasten *m* drawer
Schubkraft *f* PHYS, TECH thrust
Schublade *f* drawer
Schubs [ʃups] F *m (-es; -e)*, **schubsen** [ˈʃupsən] F *v/t (ge-, h)* push
schüchtern [ˈʃʏçtɐn] *adj* shy, bashful
ˈSchüchternheit *f (-; no pl)* shyness, bashfulness
schuf [ʃuːf] *pret of* ***schaffen***[1]
Schuft [ʃuft] *m (-[e]s; -e) contp* bastard
schuften [ˈʃuftən] F *v/i (ge-, h)* slave away, drudge
Schuh [ʃuː] *m (-[e]s; -e)* shoe; ***j-m et. in die Schuhe schieben*** put the blame for s.th. on s.o.
Schuhanzieher *m* shoehorn
Schuhcreme *f* shoe polish
Schuhgeschäft *n* shoe store (*Br* shop)
Schuhlöffel *m* shoehorn
Schuhmacher *m* shoemaker
Schuhputzer [-putsɐ] *m (-s; -)* shoeshine boy
ˈSchulabbrecher *m (-s; -)* dropout
Schulabgänger [-apgɛŋɐ] *m (-s; -)* school leaver
Schulamt *n* school board, *Br* education authority

S

Schularbeit *f* schoolwork; *pl* homework
Schulbesuch *m* (school) attendance
Schulbildung *f* education
Schulbuch *n* textbook
Schuld [ʃʊlt] *f* (-; *-en* [ˈʃʊldən]) a) (*no pl*) JUR guilt, *esp* REL sin, b) *mst pl* debt; ***j-m die Schuld* (*an et.*) *geben*** blame s.o. (for s.th.); ***es ist* (*nicht*) *deine Schuld*** it is(n't) your fault; ***Schulden haben* (*machen*)** be in (run into) debt; → ***zuschulden***
ˈ**schuldbewusst** *adj*: ***schuldbewusste Miene*** guilty look
schulden [ˈʃʊldən] *v/t* (*ge-, h*) ***j-m et. schulden*** owe s.o. s.th.
schuldig [ˈʃʊldɪç] *adj esp* JUR guilty (***an*** *dat* of); responsible *or* to blame (for); ***j-m et. schuldig sein*** owe s.o. s.th.
Schuldige [ˈʃʊldɪgə] *m, f* (*-n; -n*) culprit; JUR guilty person, offender
ˈ**schuldlos** *adj* innocent
Schuldner [ˈʃʊldnɐ] *m* (*-s; -*)
ˈ**Schuldnerin** *f* (*-; -nen*) debtor
ˈ**Schuldschein** *m* ECON promissory note, IOU (= I owe you)
Schule [ˈʃuːlə] *f* (*-; -n*) school (*a. fig*); ***höhere Schule*** *appr* (senior) high school, *Br* secondary school; ***auf*** *or* ***in der Schule*** at school; ***in die*** *or* ***zur Schule gehen* (*kommen*)** go to (start) school
ˈ**schulen** *v/t* (*ge-, h*) train, school
Schüler [ˈʃyːlɐ] *m* (*-s; -*) student, schoolboy, *esp Br a.* pupil
Schüleraustausch *m* student exchange (program[me])
Schülerin [ˈʃyːlərɪn] *f* (*-; -nen*) student, schoolgirl, *esp Br a.* pupil
ˈ**Schülervertretung** *f appr* student government (*Br* council)
ˈ**Schulferien** *pl* vacation, *Br* holidays
Schulfernsehen *n* educational TV
Schulfunk *m* schools programmes
Schulgebäude *n* school (building)
Schulgeld *n* school fee(s), tuition
Schulheft *n* exercise book
Schulhof *m* school yard, playground
Schulkameˌrad *m* schoolfellow
Schulleiter *m* principal, *Br* headmaster, head teacher
Schulleiterin *f* principal, *Br* headmistress
Schulmappe *f* schoolbag; satchel
Schulordnung *f* school regulations
ˈ**schulpflichtig** *adj*: ***schulpflichtiges Kind*** school--age child
ˈ**Schulschiff** *n* training ship
Schulschluss *m* end of school (*or* term); ***nach Schulschluss*** after school
Schulschwänzer [-ʃvɛntsɐ] *m* (*-s; -*) truant
Schulstunde *f* lesson, class, period
Schultasche *f* schoolbag
Schulter [ˈʃʊltɐ] *f* (*-; -n*) ANAT shoulder
ˈ**Schulterblatt** *n* ANAT shoulder-blade
ˈ**schulterfrei** *adj* strapless
ˈ**schultern** *v/t* (*ge-, h*) shoulder
ˈ**Schultertasche** *f* shoulder bag
ˈ**Schulwesen** *n* (*-s; no pl*) education(al system)
schummeln [ˈʃʊməln] F *v/i* (*ge-, h*) cheat
Schund [ʃʊnt] *m* (*-[e]s; no pl*) trash, rubbish, junk
schund [ʃʊnt] *pret of* ***schinden***
Schuppe [ˈʃʊpə] *f* (*-; -n*) ZO scale; *pl* MED dandruff
ˈ**Schuppen** *m* (*-s; -*) shed, *esp* F *contp* shack
schuppig [ˈʃʊpɪç] *adj* ZO scaly
schüren [ˈʃyːrən] *v/t* (*ge-, h*) stir up (*a. fig*)
schürfen [ˈʃyrfən] *v/i* (*ge-, h*) prospect (***nach*** for)
ˈ**Schürfwunde** *f* MED graze, abrasion
Schurke [ˈʃʊrkə] *m* (*-n; -n*) *esp* THEA *etc* villain
Schurwolle [ˈʃuːɐ-] *f* virgin wool
Schürze [ˈʃyrtsə] *f* (*-; -n*) apron
Schuss [ʃʊs] *m* (*-es; Schüsse* [ˈʃysə]) shot; GASTR dash; SPORT shot, *soccer*: *a.* strike; *skiing*: schuss (*a.* ***Schuss fahren***); *sl* shot, fix; F ***gut in Schuss sein*** be in good shape
Schüssel [ˈʃysəl] *f* (*-; -n*) bowl, dish; basin
ˈ**Schusswaffe** *f* firearm
Schusswunde *f* MED gunshot *or* bullet wound
Schuster [ˈʃuːstɐ] *m* (*-s; -*) shoemaker
Schutt [ʃʊt] *m* (*-[e]s; no pl*) rubble, debris
ˈ**Schüttelfrost** *m* MED shivering fit, *the* shivers
schütteln [ˈʃytəln] *v/t* (*ge-, h*) shake
schütten [ˈʃytən] *v/t* (*ge-, h*) pour; throw
Schutz [ʃʊts] *m* (*-es; no pl*) protection (***gegen, vor*** *dat* against), defense, *Br* defence (against, from); shelter (from); safeguard (against); cover
Schutzblech *n* fender, *Br* mudguard
Schutzbrille *f* goggles
Schütze [ˈʃytsə] *m* (*-n; -n*) MIL rifleman; hunter; SPORT scorer; ASTR Sagittarius; ***er ist* (*ein*) *Schütze*** he's (a) Sagittarius; ***ein guter Schütze*** a good shot
schützen [ˈʃytsən] *v/t* (*ge-, h*) protect (***gegen, vor*** *dat* against, from), defend (against, from), guard (against, from); shelter (from); safeguard
ˈ**Schutzengel** *m* guardian angel
ˈ**Schützengraben** *m* MIL trench
ˈ**Schutzgeld** *n* protection money
Schutzgelderpressung *f* protection

S

racket
ˈ**Schutzhaft** *f* JUR protective custody
Schutzheilige *m, f* patron (saint)
Schutzimpfung *f* MED protective inoculation; vaccination
Schutzkleidung *f* protective clothing
Schützling [ˈʃʏtslɪŋ] *m (-s; -e)* protégé(e)
ˈ**schutzlos** *adj* unprotected; defenseless, *Br* defenceless
ˈ**Schutzmaßnahme** *f* safety measure
Schutzpaˌtron *m* REL patron (saint)
Schutzumschlag *m* dust cover
Schutzzoll *m* ECON protective duty (*or* tariff)
schwach [ʃvax] *adj* weak (*a. fig*); poor; faint; delicate, frail; ***schwächer werden*** grow weak; decline; fail; fade
Schwäche [ˈʃvɛçə] *f* weakness (*a. fig*); MED infirmity; *fig* drawback, shortcoming; ***e-e Schwäche haben für*** be partial to
ˈ**schwächen** *v/t (ge-, h)* weaken (*a. fig*); lessen
ˈ**schwächlich** *adj* weakly, feeble; delicate, frail
ˈ**Schwächling** *m (-s; -e)* weakling (*a. fig*), softy, sissy
ˈ**schwachsinnig** *adj* feeble-minded; F stupid, idiotic
ˈ**Schwachstrom** *m* ELECTR low-voltage current
Schwager [ˈʃva:gɐ] *m (-s; Schwäger* [ˈʃvɛ:gɐ]) brother-in-law
Schwägerin [ˈʃvɛ:gərɪn] *f (-; -nen)* sister-in-law
Schwalbe [ˈʃvalbə] *f (-; -n)* ZO swallow; *soccer*: dive
Schwall [ʃval] *m (-[e]s; -e)* gush, *esp fig a.* torrent
schwamm [ʃvam] *pret of* ***schwimmen***
Schwamm *m (-[e]s; Schwämme* [ˈʃvɛmə]) sponge; BOT fungus; F dry rot
Schwammerl [ˈʃvamɐl] *Austrian m (-s; -[n])* → ***Pilz***
schwammig [ˈʃvamɪç] *adj* spongy; puffy; *fig* woolly
Schwan [ʃva:n] *m (-[e]s; Schwäne* [ˈʃvɛ:nə]) ZO swan
schwand [ʃvant] *pret of* ***schwinden***
schwang [ʃvaŋ] *pret of* ***schwingen***
schwanger [ˈʃvaŋɐ] *adj* pregnant
ˈ**Schwangerschaft** *f (-; -en)* pregnancy
ˈ**Schwangerschaftsabbruch** *m* abortion
schwanken [ˈʃvaŋkən] *v/i (ge-, h)* sway, roll (*a.* MAR); stagger; *fig* ***schwanken zwischen ... und ...*** waver between ... and ...; *prices*: range from ... to ...
ˈ**Schwankung** *f (-; -en)* change, variation (*a.* ECON)
Schwanz [ʃvants] *m (-es; Schwänze* [ˈʃvɛntsə]) ZO tail (*a.* AVIAT, ASTR); V cock
schwänzen [ˈʃvɛntsən] *v/i and v/t (ge-, h)* (***die Schule***) ***schwänzen*** play truant (F hooky)
Schwarm [ʃvarm] *m (-[e]s; Schwärme* [ˈʃvɛrmə]) swarm; crowd, F bunch; ZO shoal, school; F dream; idol
schwärmen [ˈʃvɛrmən] *v/i* a) *(ge-, sein)* ZO swarm, b) *(ge-, h)* ***schwärmen für*** be mad about; dream of; have a crush on *s.o.*; ***schwärmen von*** rave about
Schwarte [ˈʃvartə] *f (-; -n)* rind; F *contp* (old) tome
schwarz [ʃvarts] *adj* black (*a. fig*); ***Schwarzes Brett*** bulletin board, *Br* notice board; ***schwarz auf weiß*** in black and white
ˈ**Schwarzarbeit** *f (-; no pl)* illicit work
ˈ**Schwarzbrot** *n* rye bread
Schwarze [ˈʃvartsə] *m, f (-n; -n)* black (man *or* woman); *pl* the Blacks
schwärzen [ˈʃvɛrtsən] *v/t (ge-, h)* blacken
ˈ**Schwarzfahrer** *m* fare dodger
Schwarzhändler *m* black marketeer
Schwarzmarkt *m* black market
Schwarzseher *m* pessimist; (TV) license (*Br* licence) dodger
Schwarzˈweiß... *in cpds ...film, ...fernseher etc*: black-and-white ...
schwatzen [ˈʃvatsən], **schwätzen** [ˈʃvɛtsən] *v/i (ge-, h)* chat(ter); PED talk
Schwätzer [ˈʃvɛtsɐ] *contp m (-s; -)*, ˈ**Schwätzerin** *f (-; -nen)* loudmouth
schwatzhaft [ˈʃvatshaft] *adj* chatty
Schwebebahn [ˈʃve:bə-] *f* cableway, ropeway
Schwebebalken *m* SPORT beam
schweben [ˈʃve:bən] *v/i (ge-, h)* be suspended; ZO, AVIAT hover (*a. fig*); glide; *esp* JUR be pending; ***in Gefahr schweben*** be in danger
Schwede [ˈʃve:də] *m (-n; -n)* Swede
Schweden [ˈʃve:dən] Sweden
Schwedin [ˈʃve:dɪn] *f (-; -nen)* Swede
ˈ**schwedisch** *adj* Swedish
Schwefel [ˈʃve:fəl] *m (-s; no pl)* CHEM sulfur, *Br* sulphur
Schwefelsäure *f* CHEM sulfuric (*Br* sulphuric) acid
Schweif [ʃvaif] *m (-[e]s; -e)* ZO tail (*a.* ASTR)
schweifen [ˈʃvaifən] *v/i (ge-, sein)* wander (*a. fig*), roam
schweigen [ˈʃvaigən] *v/i (irr, ge-, h)* be silent
ˈ**Schweigen** *n (-s; no pl)* silence
ˈ**schweigend** *adj* silent
schweigsam [ˈʃvaikza:m] *adj* quiet, taci-

S

turn, reticent
Schwein [ʃvain] *n* (-[*e*]*s*; -*e*) ZO pig, hog; F *contp* (filthy) pig; swine, bastard; F ***Schwein haben*** be lucky
'**Schweinebraten** *m* roast pork
'**Schweinefleisch** *n* pork
Schweinerei [ʃvainə'rai] F *f* (-; -*en*) mess; *fig* dirty trick; dirty *or* crying shame; filth(y story *or* joke)
'**Schweinestall** *m* pigsty (*a. fig*)
'**schweinisch** F *adj* filthy, obscene
'**Schweinsleder** *n* pigskin
Schweiß [ʃvais] *m* (-*es*; *no pl*) sweat, perspiration
schweißen *v/t* (*ge*-, *h*) TECH weld
Schweißer *m* (-*s*; -) TECH welder
'**schweißgebadet** *adj* soaked in sweat
'**Schweißgeruch** *m* body odo(u)r, BO
Schweiz [ʃvaits] Switzerland
Schweizer ['ʃvaitsɐ] *m* (-*s*; -), *adj* Swiss
Schweizerin ['ʃvaitsərɪn] *f* (-; -*nen*) Swiss woman *or* girl
schweizerisch ['ʃvaitsərɪʃ] *adj* Swiss
schwelen ['ʃveːlən] *v/i* (*ge*-, *h*) smo(u)lder (*a. fig*)
schwelgen ['ʃvɛlgən] *v/i* (*ge*-, *h*) ***schwelgen in*** (*dat*) revel in
Schwelle ['ʃvɛlə] *f* (-; -*n*) threshold (*a. fig*); RAIL tie, *Br* sleeper
'**schwellen** **1.** *v/i* (*irr*, *ge*-, *sein*) swell; **2.** *v/t* (*ge*-, *h*) swell
'**Schwellung** *f* (-; -*en*) MED swelling
Schwemme ['ʃvɛmə] *f* (-; -*n*) ECON glut, oversupply
'**schwemmen** *v/t* (*ge*-, *h*) ***an Land schwemmen*** wash ashore
Schwengel ['ʃvɛŋəl] *m* (-*s*; -) clapper; handle
schwenken ['ʃvɛŋkən] *v/t* (*ge*-, *h*) *and v/i* (*ge*-, *sein*) swing, wave
schwer [ʃveːɐ] **1.** *adj* heavy; *fig* difficult, hard; GASTR strong, rich; MED *etc* serious, severe; heavy, violent (*storm etc*); ***schwere Zeiten*** hard times; ***es schwer haben*** have a bad time; ***100 Pfund schwer sein*** weigh a hundred pounds; **2.** *adv*: ***schwer arbeiten*** work hard; → ***schwerfallen***; → ***hören***; ***schwer beschädigt*** → ***schwerbeschädigt***; ***schwer verdaulich*** indigestible, heavy (*both a. fig*); ***schwer verständlich*** difficult *or* hard to understand; ***schwer verwundet*** seriously wounded
'**schwerbeschädigt** *adj* seriously disabled
Schwere ['ʃveːrə] *f* (-; *no pl*) weight (*a. fig*); *fig* seriousness
'**schwerfallen** *v/i* (*irr*, ***fallen***, *sep*, -*ge*-, *sein*): ***j-m schwerfallen*** be difficult for s.o.; ***es fällt ihm schwer zu …*** he finds it difficult to …
'**schwerfällig** *adj* awkward, clumsy
'**Schwergewicht** *n* (-[*e*]*s*; *no pl*) heavyweight; *fig* (main) emphasis
'**schwerhörig** *adj* hard of hearing
'**Schwerindusˌtrie** *f* heavy industry
Schwerkraft *f* (-; *no pl*) PHYS gravity
Schwermeˌtall *n* heavy metal
'**schwermütig** [-myːtɪç] *adj* melancholy; ***schwermütig sein*** have the blues
'**Schwerpunkt** *m* center (*Br* centre) of gravity; *fig* (main) emphasis
Schwert [ʃveːɐt] *n* (-[*e*]*s*; -*er*) sword
'**Schwerverbrecher** *m* dangerous criminal, JUR felon
'**schwerverdaulich** *adj* → ***schwer***
schwerverständlich *adj* → ***schwer***
schwerverˌwundet *adj* → ***schwer***
'**schwerwiegend** *fig adj* weighty, serious
Schwester ['ʃvɛstɐ] *f* (-; -*n*) sister, REL *a.* nun; MED nurse
schwieg [ʃviːk] *pret of* ***schweigen***
Schwieger… ['ʃviːgɐ-] *in cpds* *…eltern*, *…mutter*, *…sohn etc*: …-in-law
Schwiele ['ʃviːlə] *f* (-; -*n*) MED callus
schwielig ['ʃviːlɪç] *adj* horny
schwierig ['ʃviːrɪç] *adj* difficult, hard
'**Schwierigkeit** *f* (-; -*en*) difficulty, trouble; ***in Schwierigkeiten geraten*** get *or* run into trouble; ***Schwierigkeiten haben, et. zu tun*** have difficulty in doing s.th.
Schwimmbad ['ʃvɪm-] *n* (indoor) swimming pool
schwimmen ['ʃvɪmən] *v/i* (*irr*, *ge*-, *sein*) swim; float; ***schwimmen gehen*** go swimming
'**Schwimmflosse** *f* swimfin, *Br* flipper
Schwimmgürtel *m* swimming belt
Schwimmhaut *f* ZO web
Schwimmlehrer *m* swimming instructor
Schwimmweste *f* life jacket
Schwindel ['ʃvɪndəl] *m* (-*s*; *no pl*) MED giddiness, dizziness; F swindle, fraud; ***Schwindel erregend*** dizzy
'**schwindelerˌregend** *adj* dizzy
'**schwindeln** F *v/i* (*ge*-, *h*) fib, tell fibs
schwinden ['ʃvɪndən] *v/i* (*irr*, *ge*-, *sein*) dwindle, decline
Schwindler ['ʃvɪndlɐ] F *m* (-*s*; -), '**Schwindlerin** *f* (-; -*nen*) swindler, crook; liar
schwindlig ['ʃvɪndlɪç] *adj* MED dizzy, giddy; ***mir ist schwindlig*** I feel dizzy
Schwinge ['ʃvɪŋə] *f* (-; -*n*) ZO wing
'**schwingen** *v/i and v/t* (*irr*, *ge*-, *h*) swing; wave; PHYS oscillate; vibrate
'**Schwingung** *f* (-; -*en*) PHYS oscillation;

vibration

Schwips [ʃvɪps] F *m*: ***e-n Schwips haben*** be tipsy

schwirren [ˈʃvɪrən] *v/i* a) (*ge-*, *sein*) whirr, whizz, *esp* ZO buzz (*a. fig*), b) (*ge-*, *h*) ***mir schwirrt der Kopf*** my head is buzzing

schwitzen [ˈʃvɪtsən] *v/i* (*ge-*, *h*) sweat, perspire

schwoll [ʃvɔl] *pret of* ***schwellen*** 1

schwor [ʃvoːɐ] *pret of* ***schwören***

schwören [ˈʃvøːrən] *v/t and v/i* (*irr*, *ge-*, *h*) swear; JUR take an *or* the oath; *fig* ***schwören auf*** (*acc*) swear by

schwul [ʃvuːl] F *adj* gay; *contp* queer

schwül [ʃvyːl] *adj* sultry (*a. fig*), close

schwülstig [ˈʃvʏlstɪç] *adj* bombastic, pompous

Schwung [ʃvʊŋ] *m* (-[*e*]*s*; *Schwünge* [ˈʃvʏŋə]) swing; *fig* verve, pep; drive; ***in Schwung kommen*** get going; ***et. in Schwung bringen*** get s.th. going

ˈ**schwungvoll** *adj* full of energy *or* verve; MUS swinging

Schwur [ʃvuːɐ] *m* (-[*e*]*s*; *Schwüre* [ˈʃvyːrə]) oath

Schwurgericht *n* JUR jury court

sechs [zɛks] *adj* six; *grade*: F, *Br a.* poor

ˈ**Sechseck** *n* (-[*e*]*s*; *-e*) hexagon

ˈ**sechseckig** *adj* hexagonal

ˈ**sechsfach** *adj* sixfold

ˈ**sechsmal** *adv* six times

Sechsˈtagerennen *n* SPORT six-day race

ˈ**sechstägig** [-tɛːgɪç] *adj* lasting *or* of six days

ˈ**sechste** *adj* sixth

Sechstel [ˈzɛkstəl] *n* (*-s*; -) sixth (part)

ˈ**sechstens** *adv* sixthly, in the sixth place

sechzehn(te) [ˈzɛçtseːn(tə)] *adj* sixteen(th)

sechzig [ˈzɛçtsɪç] *adj* sixty

ˈ**sechzigste** *adj* sixtieth

See[1] [zeː] *m* (*-s*; *-n*) lake

See[2] *f* (-; *no pl*) sea, ocean; ***auf See*** at sea; ***auf hoher See*** on the high seas; ***an der See*** at the seaside; ***zur See gehen (fahren)*** go to sea (be a sailor); ***in See stechen*** put to sea

Seebad *n* seaside resort

Seefahrt *f* navigation

Seegang *m* (-[*e*]*s*; *no pl*): ***hoher Seegang*** heavy sea

Seehafen *m* seaport

Seehund *m* ZO seal

Seekarte *f* nautical chart

ˈ**seekrank** *adj* seasick

ˈ**Seekrankheit** *f* seasickness

Seele [ˈzeːlə] *f* (-; *-n*) soul (*a. fig*)

ˈ**seelenlos** *adj* soulless

ˈ**Seelenruhe** *f* peace of mind; ***in aller Seelenruhe*** as cool as you please

seelisch [ˈzeːlɪʃ] *adj* mental

ˈ**Seelsorge** *f* (-; *no pl*) pastoral care

ˈ**Seelsorger** [-zɔrgɐ] *m* (*-s*; -), ˈ**Seelsorgerin** *f* (-; *-nen*) pastor

ˈ**Seemacht** *f* sea power

Seemann *m* (-[*e*]*s*; *-leute*) seaman, sailor

Seemeile *f* nautical mile

Seenot *f* (-; *no pl*) distress (at sea)

Seenotkreuzer *m* MAR rescue cruiser

Seeräuber *m* pirate

Seereise *f* voyage, cruise

Seerose *f* BOT water lily

Seesack *m* kit bag

Seeschlacht *f* MIL naval battle

Seestreitkräfte *pl* MIL naval forces, navy

ˈ**seetüchtig** *adj* seaworthy

ˈ**Seewarte** *f* naval observatory

Seeweg *m* sea route; ***auf dem Seeweg*** by sea

Seezeichen *n* seamark

Seezunge *f* ZO sole

Segel [ˈzeːgəl] *n* (*-s*; -) sail

Segelboot *n* sailboat, *Br* sailing boat

Segelfliegen *n* gliding

Segelflugzeug *n* glider

ˈ**segeln** *v/i* (*ge-*, *sein*) sail, SPORT *a.* yacht

ˈ**Segelschiff** *n* sailing ship; sailing vessel

Segelsport *m* sailing, yachting

Segeltuch *n* canvas, sailcloth

Segen [ˈzeːgən] *m* (*-s*; -) blessing (*a. fig*)

Segler [ˈzeːglɐ] *m* (*-s*; -) yachtsman

Seglerin [ˈzeːglərɪn] *f* (-; *-nen*) yachtswoman

segnen [ˈzeːgnən] *v/t* (*ge-*, *h*) bless

ˈ**Segnung** *f* (-; *-nen*) blessing

Sehbeteiligung [ˈzeː-] *f* (TV) ratings

sehen [ˈzeːən] *v/i and v/t* (*irr*, *ge-*, *h*) see; watch; notice; ***sehen nach*** look after; look for; ***sich sehen lassen*** show up; ***das sieht man*** (***kaum***) it (hardly) shows; ***siehst du*** (you) see; I told you; ***siehe oben*** (***unten, Seite …***) see above (below, page …)

ˈ**sehenlassen** *v/refl* (*irr*, ***lassen***, *sep*, *no -ge-*, *h*) → ***sehen***

ˈ**sehenswert** *adj* worth seeing

ˈ**Sehenswürdigkeit** *f* (-; *-en*) place *etc* worth seeing, sight, *pl* sights

ˈ**Sehkraft** *f* (-; *no pl*) eyesight, vision

Sehne [ˈzeːnə] *f* (-; *-n*) ANAT sinew; string

sehnen [ˈzeːnən] *v/refl* (*ge-*, *h*) long (***nach*** for), yearn (for); ***sich danach sehnen zu*** *inf* be longing to *inf*

ˈ**Sehnerv** *m* ANAT optic nerve

sehnig [ˈzeːnɪç] *adj* sinewy, GASTR *a.* stringy

sehnlichst [ˈzeːnlɪçst] *adj* dearest

ˈ**Sehnsucht** *f*, ˈ**sehnsüchtig** *adj* longing,

S

yearning
sehr [zeːɐ] *adv before adj and adv*: very; *with verbs*: very much, greatly
'Sehtest *m* sight test
seicht [zaiçt] *adj* shallow (*a. fig*)
Seide ['zaidə] *f* (-; *-n*), **'seiden** *adj* silk
'Seidenpa,pier *n* tissue paper
'Seidenraupe *f* zo silkworm
seidig ['zaidıç] *adj* silky
Seife ['zaifə] *f* (-; *-n*) soap
'Seifenblase *f* soap bubble
Seifenlauge *f* (soap)suds
Seifenoper *f* TV soap opera
Seifenschale *f* soap dish
Seifenschaum *m* lather
seifig ['zaifıç] *adj* soapy
Seil [zail] *n* (-[*e*]*s*; *-e*) rope
'Seilbahn *f* cable railway
'seilspringen *v/i* (*only inf*) skip
sein[1] [zain] *v/i* (*irr, ge-, sein*) be; exist; ***et. sein lassen*** stop *or* quit (doing) s.th.
sein[2] *poss pron* his, her, its; ***seiner, seine, sein(e)s*** his, hers
Sein *n* (*-s*; *no pl*) being; existence
seinerseits ['zainɐzaits] *adv* for his part
seiner'zeit *adv* then, in those days
seines'gleichen ['zainəs-] *pron* his equals
seinet'wegen ['zainət-] → ***meinetwegen***
'seinlassen *v/t* (*irr, sep, -ge-, h*): ***et. seinlassen*** → ***sein***
seit [zait] *prp and cj* since; ***seit 1982*** since 1982; ***seit drei Jahren*** for three years (now); ***seit langem*** (***kurzem***) for a long (short) time
seit'dem **1.** *adv* since then, since that time, ever since; **2.** *cj* since
Seite ['zaitə] *f* (-; *-n*) side (*a. fig*); page; ***auf der linken Seite*** on the left(-hand side); *fig* ***auf der e-n*** (***anderen***) ***Seite*** on the one (other) hand
'Seitenansicht *f* side view, profile
Seitenblick *m* sidelong glance
Seitenhieb *m* sideswipe
Seitenlinie *f esp soccer*: touchline
seitens ['zaitəns] *prp* (*gen*) on the part of, by
'Seitensprung F *m*: ***e-n Seitensprung machen*** cheat (on one's wife *or* husband)
'Seitenstechen *n* (*-s*; *no pl*) MED a stitch (in the side)
'seitlich *adj* side ..., at the side(s)
'seitwärts [-vɛrts] *adv* sideways, to the side
Sekretär [zekre'tɛːɐ] *m* (*-s*; *-e*) secretary; bureau
Sekretariat [-ta'rjaːt] *n* (-[*e*]*s*; *-e*) (secretary's) office
Sekretärin [-'tɛːrın] *f* (-; *-nen*) secretary
Sekt [zɛkt] *m* (-[*e*]*s*; *-e*) sparkling wine, champagne
Sekte ['zɛktə] *f* (-; *-n*) sect
Sektion [zɛk'tsjoːn] *f* (-; *-en*) section; MED autopsy
Sektor ['zɛktoːɐ] *m* (*-s*; *-en* [zɛk'toːrən]) sector; *fig* field
Sekunde [ze'kʊndə] *f* (-; *-n*) second; ***auf die Sekunde*** to the second
Se'kundenzeiger *m* second(s) hand
selbe ['zɛlbə] *adj* same
selber ['zɛlbɐ] *pron* → ***selbst 1***
selbst [zɛlbst] **1.** *pron*: ***ich*** (***du*** *etc*) ***selbst*** I (you *etc*) myself (yourself *etc*); ***mach es selbst*** do it yourself; ***et. selbst tun*** do s.th. by oneself; ***von selbst*** by itself; ***selbst gemacht*** homemade; **2.** *adv* even
'Selbstachtung *f* self-respect
'selbständig *etc* → ***selbstständig*** *etc*
'Selbstbedienung(sladen *m*) *f* self-service (store, *Br* shop)
Selbstbefriedigung *f* masturbation
Selbstbeherrschung *f* self-control
Selbstbestimmung *f* self-determination
'selbstbewusst *adj* self-confident, self-assured
'Selbstbewusstsein *n* self-confidence
'Selbstbildnis *n* self-portrait
Selbsterhaltungstrieb *m* survival instinct
Selbsterkenntnis *f* (-; *no pl*) self-knowledge
'selbstgerecht *adj* self-righteous
'Selbsthilfe *f* self-help
Selbsthilfegruppe *f* self-help group
Selbstkostenpreis *m*: ***zum Selbstkostenpreis*** ECON at cost (price)
'selbstkritisch *adj* self-critical
'Selbstlaut *m* LING vowel
'selbstlos *adj* unselfish
'Selbstmord *m*, **Selbstmörder(in)** suicide
'selbstmörderisch *adj* suicidal
'selbstsicher *adj* self-confident, self-assured
'selbstständig *adj* independent, self-reliant; self-employed
'Selbstständigkeit *f* (-; *no pl*) independence
'Selbststudium *n* (*-s*; *no pl*) self-study
'selbstsüchtig *adj* selfish, ego(t)istic(al)
selbsttätig *adj* automatic
'Selbsttäuschung *f* self-deception
'selbstverständlich **1.** *adj* natural; ***das ist selbstverständlich*** that's a matter of course; **2.** *adv* of course, naturally; ***selbstverständlich!*** *a.* by all means!
'Selbstverständlichkeit *f* (-; *-en*) matter

of course
'Selbstverteidigung *f* self-defense, *Br* self-defence
Selbstvertrauen *n* self-confidence, self-reliance
Selbstverwaltung *f* self-government, autonomy
Selbstwähldienst *m* TEL automatic long-distance dial(l)ing service
'selbstzufrieden *adj* self-satisfied
selchen ['zɛlçən] *Austrian* → ***räuchern***
selig ['ze:lɪç] *adj* REL blessed; late; *fig* overjoyed
Sellerie ['zɛləri] *m* (-*s*; -[*s*]), *f* (-; -) BOT celeriac; celery
selten ['zɛltən] **1.** *adj* rare; ***selten sein*** be rare, be scarce; **2.** *adv* rarely, seldom
'Seltenheit *f* (-; *no pl*) rarity
seltsam ['zɛltza:m] *adj* strange, odd
Semester [ze'mɛstɐ] *n* (-*s*; -) UNIV semester, *esp Br* term
Semikolon [zemi'ko:lɔn] *n* (-*s*; -*s*) LING semicolon
Seminar [zemi'na:ɐ] *n* (-*s*; -*e*) UNIV department; seminar; REL seminary; teacher training college
sen. ABBR *of* ***senior*** sen., Sen., Sr, Snr, senior
Senat [ze'na:t] *m* (-[*e*]*s*; -*e*) senate
Senator [ze'na:to:ɐ] *m* (-*s*; -*en* [zena'to:rən]), **Sena'torin** *f* (-; -*nen*) senator
Sendemast *m* ELECTR mast
senden ['zɛndən] *v/t* ([*irr*,] *ge*-, *h*) send (***mit der Post*** by mail, *Br* by post); ELECTR broadcast, transmit, *a.* televise
Sender ['zɛndɐ] *m* (-*s*; -) radio *or* television station; ELECTR transmitter
'Sendereihe *f* TV *or* radio series
Sendeschluss *m* close-down, F sign-off
Sendezeichen *n* call letters (*Br* sign)
Sendezeit *f* air time
'Sendung *f* (-; -*en*) broadcast, program(-me), *a.* telecast; ECON consignment, shipment; ***auf Sendung sein*** be on the air
Senf [zɛnf] *m* (-[*e*]*s*; -*e*) mustard (*a.* BOT)
senil [ze'ni:l] *adj* senile
Senilität [zenili'tɛ:t] *f* (-; *no pl*) senility
Senior ['ze:njo:ɐ] **1.** *m* (-*s*; -*en* [ze'njo:rən]) senior (*a.* SPORT); senior citizen; **2.** *adj* senior
Seni'orenheim *n* old people's home
Seni'orin *f* (-; -*nen*) senior citizen
Senke ['zɛŋkə] *f* (-; -*n*) GEOGR depression, hollow
'senken *v/t* (*ge*-, *h*) lower (*a. one's voice*), *a.* bow (*one's head*); ECON *a.* reduce, cut; ***sich senken*** drop, go *or* come down
'senkrecht *adj* vertical
Sensation [zɛnza'tsjo:n] *f* (-; -*en*) sensation
sensationell [zɛnzatsjo'nɛl] *adj*, **Sensa-ti'ons...** *in cpds* ...*blatt etc*: sensational (...)
Sense ['zɛnzə] *f* (-; -*n*) AGR scythe
sensibel [zɛn'zi:bəl] *adj* sensitive
sensibilisieren [zɛnzibili'zi:rən] *v/t* (*no -ge-*, *h*) sensitize (***für*** to)
sentimental [zɛntimɛn'ta:l] *adj* sentimental
Sentimentalität [zɛntimɛntali'tɛ:t] *f* (-; -*en*) sentimentality
September [zɛp'tɛmbɐ] *m* (-[*s*]; -) September
Serenade [zere'na:də] *f* (-; -*n*) MUS serenade
Serie ['ze:rjə] *f* (-; -*n*) series, TV *etc a.* serial; set; ***in Serie*** *produce etc* in series
'serienmäßig *adj* series(-produced); standard
'Seriennummer *f* serial number
Serienwagen *m* MOT standard-type car
seriös [ze'rjø:s] *adj* respectable; honest; serious
Serum ['ze:rʊm] *n* (-*s*; -*ren*, -*ra*) serum
Service[1] [zɛr'vi:s] *n* (-[*s*]; -) set; service
Service[2] ['zø:ɐvɪs] *m*, *n* (-; -*s*) service
servieren [zɛr'vi:rən] *v/t* (*no -ge-*, *h*) serve
Serviererin [zɛr'vi:rərɪn] *f* (-; -*nen*) waitress
Serviertochter [zɛr'vi:ɐ-] *Swiss f* waitress
Serviette [zɛr'vjɛtə] *f* (-; -*n*) napkin, *esp Br* serviette
Servobremse ['zɛrvo-] *f* MOT servo *or* power brake
Servolenkung *f* MOT servo(-assisted) *or* power steering
Sessel ['zɛsəl] *m* (-*s*; -) armchair, easy chair
Sessellift *m* chair lift
sesshaft ['zɛshaft] *adj*: ***sesshaft werden*** settle (down)
Set [zɛt] *n*, *m* (-*s*; -*s*) place mat
setzen ['zɛtsən] *v/t and v/i* (*ge*-, *h*) put, set (*a.* PRINT, AGR, MAR), AGR *a.* plant; place; seat *s.o.*; ***setzen über*** (*acc*) jump over; cross (*river*); ***setzen auf*** (*acc*) bet on, back; ***sich setzen*** sit down; CHEM *etc* settle; ***sich setzen auf*** (*acc*) get on, mount; ***sich setzen in*** (*acc*) get into; ***sich zu j-m setzen*** sit beside *or* with s.o.; ***setzen Sie sich bitte!*** take *or* have a seat!
Setzer ['zɛtsɐ] *m* (-*s*; -) PRINT compositor, typesetter
Setzerei [zɛtsə'rai] *f* (-; -*en*) PRINT composing room
Seuche ['zɔyçə] *f* (-; -*n*) epidemic (disease)

seufzen ['zɔʏftsən] *v/i (ge-, h),* **Seufzer** ['zɔʏftsɐ] *m (-s; -)* sigh
Sexismus [zɛ'ksɪsmʊs] *m (-; no pl)* sexism
Sexist [zɛ'ksɪst] *m (-en; -en),* **se'xistisch** *adj* sexist
Sexual... [zɛ'ksua:l-] *in cpds ...erziehung, ...leben, ...trieb etc:* sex(ual) ...
Sexualverbrechen *n* sex crime
sexuell [zɛ'ksuɛl] *adj* sexual; ***sexuelle Belästigung*** (sexual) harassment
sexy ['zɛksi] *adj* sexy
sezieren [ze'tsi:rən] *v/t (no -ge-, h)* MED dissect *(a. fig)*; perform an autopsy on
Showgeschäft ['ʃou-] *n (-[e]s; no pl)* show business
sich [zɪç] *refl pron* oneself; himself, herself, itself; *pl* themselves; yourself, *pl* yourselves; ***sich ansehen*** look at oneself; look at each other
Sichel ['zɪçəl] *f (-; -n)* AGR sickle; ASTR crescent
sicher ['zɪçɐ] **1.** *adj* safe (***vor*** *dat* from), secure (from); *esp* TECH proof (***gegen*** against); *fig* certain, sure; reliable; **(*sich*)** ***sicher sein*** be sure (***e-r Sache*** of s.th.; ***dass*** that); **2.** *adv* safely; ***sicher!*** of course, sure(ly); certainly; probably; ***du hast (bist) sicher ...*** you must have (be) ...
'Sicherheit *f (-; -en)* a) *(no pl)* security *(a.* MIL, POL, ECON); safety *(a.* TECH); *fig* certainty; skill; **(*sich*)** ***in Sicherheit bringen*** get to safety, b) ECON cover
'Sicherheits... *esp* TECH *in cpds ...glas, ...nadel, ...schloss etc:* safety ...
Sicherheitsgurt *m* seat belt, safety belt
Sicherheitsmaßnahme *f* safety (POL security) measure
'sicherlich *adv* → ***sicher*** *2*
'sichern *v/t (ge-, h)* protect, safeguard; secure *(a.* MIL, TECH); EDP save; ***sich sichern*** secure o.s. (***gegen, vor*** *dat* against, from)
'sicherstellen *v/t (sep, -ge-, h)* secure; guarantee
Sicherung ['zɪçərʊŋ] *f (-; -en)* securing; safeguard(-ing); TECH safety device; ELECTR fuse
'Sicherungskasten *m* ELECTR fuse box
Sicherungsko,pie *f* EDP backup; ***e-e Sicherungskopie machen (von)*** back up
Sicht [zɪçt] *f (-; no pl)* visibility; view; ***in Sicht kommen*** come into sight *or* view; ***auf lange Sicht*** in the long run
'sichtbar *adj* visible
sichten ['zɪçtən] *v/t (ge-, h)* sight; *fig* sort (through *or* out)
'Sichtkarte *f* season ticket
'sichtlich *adv* visibly
'Sichtweite *f* visibility; ***in (außer) Sichtweite*** within (out of) sight
sickern ['zɪkɐn] *v/i (ge-, sein)* trickle, ooze, seep
sie [zi:] *pers pron* she; it; *pl* they; ***Sie*** you
Sieb [zi:p] *n (-[e]s; -e)* sieve; strainer
sieben[1] ['zi:bən] *v/t (ge-, h)* sieve, sift
'sieben[2] *adj* seven
Sieben'meter *m* SPORT penalty shot *or* throw
siebte ['zi:ptə] *adj,* **'Siebtel** *n (-s; -)* seventh
siebzehn(te) ['zi:p-] *adj* seventeen(th)
siebzig ['zi:ptsɪç] *adj* seventy
'siebzigste *adj* seventieth
siedeln ['zi:dəln] *v/i (ge-, h)* settle
sieden ['zi:dən] *v/t and v/i ([irr,] ge-, h)* boil, simmer
'Siedepunkt *m* boiling point *(a. fig)*
Siedler ['zi:dlɐ] *m (-s; -)* settler
Siedlung ['zi:dlʊŋ] *f (-; -en)* settlement; housing development
Sieg [zi:k] *m (-[e]s; -e)* victory, SPORT *a.* win
Siegel ['zi:gəl] *n (-s; -)* seal, signet
'Siegellack *m* sealing wax
'siegeln *v/t (ge-, h)* seal
siegen ['zi:gən] *v/i (ge-, h)* win
Sieger ['zi:gɐ] *m (-s; -),* **Siegerin** ['zi:gərɪn] *f (-; -nen)* winner
'siegreich *adj* winning; victorious
Signal [zɪ'gna:l] *n (-s; -e),* **signalisieren** [zɪgnali'zi:rən] *v/t (no -ge-, h)* signal
signieren [zɪ'gni:rən] *v/t (no -ge-, h)* sign
Silbe ['zɪlbə] *f (-; -n)* syllable
'Silbentrennung *f* LING syllabification
Silber ['zɪlbɐ] *n (-s; no pl)* silver; silverware
'silbergrau *adj* silver-gray *(Br* -grey)
'Silberhochzeit *f* silver wedding
'silbern *adj* silver
Silhouette [zi'luɛtə] *f (-; -n)* silhouette; skyline
Silikon [zili'ko:n] *n (-s; -e)* CHEM silicone
Silizium [zi'li:tsjʊm] *n (-s; no pl)* CHEM silicon
Silvester [zɪl'vɛstɐ] *n (-s; -)* New Year's Eve
Sims [zɪms] *m, n (-es; -e)* ledge; windowsill
simulieren [zimu'li:rən] *v/t and v/i* TECH *etc* simulate; sham
simultan [zimʊl'ta:n] *adj* simultaneous
Sinfonie [zɪnfo'ni:] *f (-; -n)* MUS symphony
singen ['zɪŋən] *v/t and v/i (irr, ge-, h)* sing (***richtig [falsch]*** in [out of] tune)
Singular ['zɪŋgula:ɐ] *m (-s; -e)* LING singular

Singvogel ['zɪŋ-] *m* zo songbird
sinken ['zɪŋkən] *v/i* (*irr, ge-, sein*) sink (*a. fig*), go down (*a.* ECON), ASTR *a.* set; *prices etc*: fall, drop
Sinn [zɪn] *m* (-[*e*]*s*; -*e*) sense (***für*** of); mind; meaning; point, idea; ***im Sinn haben*** have in mind; ***es hat keinen Sinn*** (***zu warten*** *etc*) it's no use *or* good (waiting *etc*)
'**Sinnbild** *n* symbol
'**sinnentstellend** *adj* distorting
Sinnesorgan ['zɪnəs-] *n* sense organ
Sinnestäuschung *f* hallucination
Sinneswandel *m* change of mind
'**sinnlich** *adj* sensuous; sensory; sensual
'**Sinnlichkeit** *f* (-; *no pl*) sensuality
'**sinnlos** *adj* senseless; useless
'**sinnverwandt** *adj* synonymous
'**sinnvoll** *adj* meaningful; useful; wise, sensible
Sintflut ['zɪnt-] *f* *the* Flood
Sippe ['zɪpə] *f* (-; -*n*) (extended) family, clan
Sirene [zi're:nə] *f* (-; -*n*) siren
Sirup ['zi:rʊp] *m* (-*s*; -*e*) sirup, *Br* syrup; treacle, molasses
Sitte ['zɪtə] *f* (-; -*n*) custom, tradition; *pl* morals; manners
'**Sittenlosigkeit** *f* (-; *no pl*) immorality
'**Sittenpoli,zei** *f* vice squad
'**sittenwidrig** *adj* immoral
'**Sittlichkeitsverbrechen** *n* sex crime
Situation [zitua'tsjo:n] *f* (-; -*en*) situation; position
Sitz [zɪts] *m* (-*es*; -*e*) seat; fit
Sitzblo,ckade *f* sit-down demonstration
sitzen ['zɪtsən] *v/i* (*irr, ge-, h*) sit (***an*** *dat* at; ***auf*** *dat* on); be; fit; F do time; ***sitzen bleiben*** keep one's seat; PED have to repeat a year; F ***sitzen bleiben auf*** (*dat*) be left with; F ***j-n sitzen lassen*** leave s.o. in the lurch, let s.o. down
'**sitzenbleiben** *v/i* (*irr*, ***bleiben***, *sep, -ge-, sein*) → ***sitzen***
sitzenlassen *v/i* (*irr*, ***lassen***, *sep, no -ge-, sein*) *a. fig* → ***sitzen***
'**Sitzplatz** *m* seat
'**Sitzstreik** *m* sit-down strike
'**Sitzung** *f* (-; -*en*) session (*a.* PARL), meeting, conference
Skala ['ska:la] *f* (-; -*en*) scale, *fig a.* range
Skalp [skalp] *m* (-*s*; -*e*), **skalpieren** [skal'pi:rən] *v/t* (*no -ge-, h*) scalp
Skandal [skan'da:l] *m* (-*s*; -*e*) scandal; ***ein Skandal sein*** be scandalous
skandalös [skanda'lø:s] *adj* scandalous, shocking
Skelett [ske'lɛt] *n* (-[*e*]*s*; -*e*) skeleton
Skepsis ['skɛpsɪs] *f* (-; *no pl*) skepticism, *Br* scepticism
Skeptiker ['skɛptikɐ] *m* (-*s*; -) skeptic, *Br* sceptic
skeptisch ['skɛptɪʃ] *adj* skeptical, *Br* sceptical
Ski [ʃi:] *m* (-*s*; -*er* ['ʃi:ɐ]) ski; ***Ski laufen*** *or* ***fahren*** ski
Skifahrer(in) skier
Skifliegen *n* ski flying
Skilift *m* ski lift
Skipiste *f* ski run
Skischuh *m* ski boot
Skisport *m* skiing
Skispringen *n* ski jumping
Skizze ['skɪtsə] *f* (-; -*n*), **skizzieren** [skɪ'tsi:rən] *v/t* (*no -ge-, h*) sketch
Sklave ['skla:və] *m* (-*n*; -*n*) slave (*a. fig*)
Sklaverei [skla:və'rai] *f* (-; *no pl*) slavery
'**Sklavin** *f* (-; -*nen*) slave (*a. fig*)
'**sklavisch** *adj* slavish (*a. fig*)
Skonto ['skɔnto] *m, n* (-*s*; -*s*) ECON (cash) discount
Skorpion [skɔr'pjo:n] *m* (-*s*; -*e*) zo scorpion; ASTR Scorpio; ***er ist*** (***ein***) ***Skorpion*** he's (a) Scorpio
Skrupel ['skru:pəl] *m* (-*s*; -) scruple, qualm
'**skrupellos** *adj* unscrupulous
Skulptur [skʊlp'tu:ɐ] *f* (-; -*en*) sculpture
Slalom ['sla:lɔm] *m* (-*s*; -*s*) slalom
Slawe ['sla:və] *m* (-*n*; -*n*), '**Slawin** *f* (-; -*nen*) Slav
'**slawisch** *adj* Slav(ic)
Slip [slɪp] *m* (-*s*; -*s*) briefs, panties
'**Slipeinlage** *f* panty liner
Slipper ['slɪpɐ] *m* (-*s*; -) loafer, *esp Br* slip-on (shoe)
Slowake [slo'va:kə] *m* (-*n*; -*n*) Slovak
Slowakei [slova'kai] *f* Slovakia
Slo'wakin *f* (-; -*nen*), **slo'wakisch** *adj* Slovak
Smaragd [sma'rakt] *m* (-[*e*]*s*; -*e*) MIN, **sma'ragdgrün** *adj* emerald
Smoking ['smo:kɪŋ] *m* (-*s*; -*s*) tuxedo, *Br* dinner jacket
Snob [snɔp] *m* (-*s*; -*s*) snob
Snobismus [sno'bɪsmʊs] *m* (-; *no pl*) snobbery
sno'bistisch *adj* snobbish
so [zo:] **1.** *adv* so; like this *or* that, this *or* that way; thus; such; (***nicht***) ***so groß wie*** (not) as big as; ***so ein***(***e***) such a; ***so sehr*** so (F that) much; ***und so weiter*** and so on; ***oder so et.*** or s.th. like that; ***oder so*** or so; ***so, fangen wir an!*** well *or* all right, let's begin!; F ***so weit sein*** be ready; ***es ist so weit*** it's time; ***so genannt*** so-called; ***doppelt so viel*** twice as much; ***so viel wie möglich*** as much

S

as possible; **2.** *cj* so, therefore; ***so dass*** so that; **3.** *int*: ***so!*** all right!, o.k.!; that's it!; ***ach so!*** I see
s.o. ABBR *of* ***siehe oben*** see above
so'bald [zo-] *cj* as soon as
Socke ['zɔkə] *f* (-; *-n*) sock
Sockel ['zɔkəl] *m* (*-s*; -) base; pedestal
Sodbrennen ['zo:t-] *n* (*-s*; *no pl*) MED heartburn
soeben [zo'e:bən] *adv* just (now)
Sofa ['zo:fa] *n* (*-s*; *-s*) sofa, settee, davenport
sofern [zo'fɛrn] *cj* if, provided that; ***sofern nicht*** unless
soff [zɔf] *pret of* ***saufen***
sofort [zo'fɔrt] *adv* at once, immediately, right away
So'fortbildkamera *f* PHOT instant camera
Software ['zɔftwɛ:ɐ] *f* EDP software
Softwarepa,ket *n* software package
sog [zo:k] *pret of* ***saugen***
Sog *m* (-[*e*]*s*; *-e*) suction, MAR *a.* wake
sogar [zo'ga:ɐ] *adv* even
Sohle ['zo:lə] *f* (-; *-n*) sole; *mining*: floor
Sohn [zo:n] *m* (-[*e*]*s*; *Söhne* ['zø:nə]) son
Sojabohne ['zo:ja-] *f* BOT soybean
so'lange [zo-] *cj* as long as
Solar... [zo'la:ɐ-] *in cpds ...energie etc*: solar ...
solch [zɔlç] *dem pron* such, like this *or* that
Sold [zɔlt] *m* (-[*e*]*s*; *-e*) MIL pay
Soldat [zɔl'da:t] *m* (*-en*; *-en*), **Sol'datin** *f* (-; *-nen*) soldier
Söldner ['zœldnɐ] *m* (*-s*; -) MIL mercenary
Sole ['zo:lə] *f* (-; *-n*) brine, salt water
solidarisch [zoli'da:rɪʃ] *adj*: ***sich solidarisch erklären mit*** declare one's solidarity with
solide [zo'li:də] *adj* solid, *fig a.* sound; reasonable (*prices*); steady (*person*)
Solist [zo'lɪst] *m* (*-en*; *-en*), **So'listin** *f* (-; *-nen*) soloist
Soll [zɔl] *n* (-[*s*]; -[*s*]) ECON debit; target, quota; ***Soll und Haben*** debit and credit
sollen ['zɔlən] *v/i* (*ge-*, *h*) *and v/aux* (*irr*, *no -ge-*, *h*) be to; be supposed to; **(*was*) *soll ich ...?*** (what) shall I ...?; ***du solltest* (*nicht*) *...*** you should(n't) ...; you ought(n't) to; ***was soll das?*** what's the idea?
Solo ['zo:lo] *n* (*-s*, *-s*, *Soli*) *esp* MUS solo; SPORT solo attempt *etc*
so'mit [zo-] *cj* thus, so, consequently
Sommer ['zɔmɐ] *m* (*-s*; -) summer (time); ***im Sommer*** in (the) summer
Sommerferien *pl* summer vacation (*Br* holidays)
Sommerfrische *f* summer resort
'sommerlich *adj* summery
'Sommersprosse *f* freckle
'sommersprossig *adj* freckled
'Sommerzeit *f* summertime; daylight saving (*Br* summer) time
Sonate [zo'na:tə] *f* (-; *-n*) MUS sonata
Sonde ['zɔndə] *f* (-; *-n*) probe (*a.* MED)
Sonder... ['zɔndɐ-] *in cpds ...angebot, ...ausgabe, ...flug, ...preis, ...wunsch, ...zug etc*: special ...
'sonderbar *adj* strange, F funny
'Sonderling *m* (*-s*; *-e*) eccentric
'Sondermüll *m* hazardous (*or* special toxic) waste
Sondermülldepo,nie *f* special waste dump
sondern ['zɔndɐn] *cj* but; ***nicht nur ..., sondern auch ...*** not only ... but also ...
'Sonderschule *f* special school (for the handicapped *etc*)
Sonnabend ['zɔn-] *m* Saturday
Sonne ['zɔnə] *f* (-; *-n*) sun
sonnen ['zɔnən] *v/refl* (*ge-*, *h*) sunbathe
'Sonnenaufgang *m* (***bei Sonnenaufgang*** at) sunrise
'Sonnenbad *n*: ***ein Sonnenbad nehmen*** sunbathe
Sonnenbank *f* (-; *-bänke*) sunbed
Sonnenblume *f* BOT sunflower
Sonnenbrand *m* sunburn
Sonnenbräune *f* suntan
Sonnenbrille *f* sunglasses
Sonnencreme *f* suntan lotion, *Br* sun cream
Sonnenener,gie *f* solar energy
Sonnenfinsternis *f* solar eclipse
'sonnen'klar F *adj* (as) clear as daylight
'Sonnenkol,lektor *m* solar panel
Sonnenlicht *n* (-[*e*]*s*, *no pl*) sunlight
Sonnenöl *n* suntan oil
Sonnenschein *m* sunshine
Sonnenschirm *m* sunshade
Sonnenschutz *m* suntan lotion
Sonnenseite *f* sunny side (*a. fig*)
Sonnenstich *m* sunstroke
Sonnenstrahl *m* sunbeam
Sonnensys,tem *n* solar system
Sonnenuhr *f* sundial
Sonnenuntergang *m* sunset
sonnig ['zɔnɪç] *adj* sunny (*a. fig*)
Sonntag ['zɔn-] *m* Sunday; **(*am*) *Sonntag*** on Sunday
'sonntags *adv* on Sundays
'Sonntagsfahrer *contp m* MOT Sunday driver
sonst [zɔnst] *adv* else; otherwise, or (else); normally, usually; ***sonst noch et. (jemand)?*** anything (anyone) else?; ***sonst noch Fragen?*** any other ques-

S

tions?; ***sonst nichts*** nothing else; ***alles wie sonst*** everything as usual; ***nichts ist wie sonst*** nothing is as it used to be
'sonstig *adj* other
Sopran [zo'praːn] *m* (*-s*; *-e*) MUS, **Sopranistin** [zopra'nɪstɪn] *f* (*-*; *-nen*) MUS soprano
Sorge ['zɔrgə] *f* (*-*; *-n*) worry; sorrow; trouble; care; ***sich Sorgen machen*** (***um***) worry *or* be worried (about); ***keine Sorge!*** don't worry!
sorgen ['zɔrgən] (*ge-*, *h*) **1.** *v/i*: ***sorgen für*** care for, take care of; ***dafür sorgen, dass*** see (to it) that; **2.** *v/refl*: ***sich sorgen um*** worry *or* be worried about
'Sorgenkind *n* problem child
Sorgfalt ['zɔrkfalt] *f* (*-*; *no pl*) care
sorgfältig ['zɔrkfɛltɪç] *adj* careful
sorglos ['zɔrk-] *adj* carefree; careless
Sorte ['zɔrtə] *f* (*-*; *-n*) sort, kind, type
sortieren [zɔr'tiːrən] *v/t* (*no -ge-*, *h*) sort; arrange
Sortiment [zɔrti'mɛnt] *n* (*-[e]s*; *-e*) ECON assortment
Soße ['zoːsə] *f* (*-*; *-n*) sauce; gravy
sott [zɔt] *pret of* ***sieden***
Souffleur [zu'fløːɐ] *m* (*-s*; *-e*), **Souffleuse** [zu'fløːzə] *f* (*-*; *-n*) THEA prompter
soufflieren [zu'fliːrən] *v/i* (*no -ge-*, *h*) THEA prompt (***j-m*** s.o.)
souverän [zuvə'rɛːn] *adj* POL sovereign
Souveränität [zuvərɛni'tɛːt] *f* (*-*; *no pl*) POL sovereignty
so'viel [zo-] *cj* as far as; → ***so***
so'weit *cj* as far as; → ***so***
so'wie *cj* as well as, and … as well; as soon as
sowie'so *adv* anyway, anyhow, in any case
Sowjet [zɔ'vjɛt] *m* (*-s*; *-s*), **sow'jetisch** *adj* HIST Soviet
so'wohl [zo-] *cj*: ***sowohl Lehrer als*** (***auch***) ***Schüler*** both teachers and students
sozial [zo'tsjaːl] *adj* social
Sozi'al… *in cpds …arbeiter, …demokrat, …versicherung etc*: social …
Sozialhilfe *f* welfare, *Br* social security; ***Sozialhilfe beziehen*** be on welfare (*Br* social security)
Sozialismus [zotsja'lɪsmʊs] *m* (*-*; *no pl*) socialism
Sozialist(in) (*-en/-*; *-en/ -nen*), **sozia'listisch** *adj* socialist
Sozi'alkunde *f* PED social studies
Sozi'alstaat *m* welfare state
Soziologe [zotsjo'loːgə] *m* (*-n*; *-n*) sociologist
Soziologie [zotsjolo'giː] *f* (*-*; *no pl*) sociology
Sozio'login *f* (*-*; *-nen*) sociologist
soziologisch [zotsjo'loːgɪʃ] *adj* sociological
sozu'sagen *adv* so to speak
Spagat [ʃpa'gaːt] *m*: ***Spagat machen*** do the splits
Spalier [ʃpa'liːɐ] *n* (*-s*; *-e*) BOT espalier; MIL *etc* lane
Spalt [ʃpalt] *m* (*-[e]s*; *-e*) crack, gap
Spalte ['ʃpaltə] *f* (*-*; *-n*) → ***Spalt***; PRINT column
'spalten *v/t* (*[irr,] ge-*, *h*) split (*a. fig*); POL divide; ***sich spalten*** split (up)
'Spaltung *f* (*-*; *-en*) split(ting); PHYS fission; *fig* split; POL division
Span [ʃpaːn] *m* (*-[e]s*; *Späne* ['ʃpɛːnə]) chip; *pl* TECH shavings
Spange ['ʃpaŋə] *f* (*-*; *-n*) clasp
Spaniel ['ʃpaːnjəl] *m* (*-s*; *-s*) ZO spaniel
Spanien ['ʃpaːnjən] Spain
Spanier ['ʃpaːnjɐ] *m* (*-s*; *-*), **Spanierin** ['ʃpaːnjərɪn] *f* (*-*; *-nen*) Spaniard
spanisch ['ʃpaːnɪʃ] *adj* Spanish
spann [ʃpan] *pret of* ***spinnen***
Spann *m* (*-[e]s*; *-e*) ANAT instep
Spanne ['ʃpanə] *f* (*-*; *-n*) span
'spannen (*ge-*, *h*) **1.** *v/t* stretch, tighten; put up (*line*); cock (*gun*); draw, bend (*bow*); **2.** *v/i* be (too) tight
spannend *adj* exciting, thrilling, gripping
'Spannung *f* (*-*; *-en*) tension (*a.* TECH, POL, PSYCH); ELECTR voltage; *fig* suspense, excitement
'Spannweite *f* span, *fig a.* range
Sparbuch ['ʃpaːɐ-] *n* savings book
Sparbüchse *f esp Br* money box
sparen ['ʃpaːrən] *v/i and v/t* (*ge-*, *h*) save; economize; ***sparen für*** *or* ***auf*** (*acc*) save up for
Sparer(in) ['ʃpaːrɐ (-rərɪn)] (*-s*; *-/-*; *-nen*) saver
'Sparschwein(chen) *n* piggy bank
Spargel ['ʃpargəl] *m* (*-s*; *-*) BOT asparagus
'Sparkasse *f* savings bank
'Sparkonto *n* savings account
spärlich ['ʃpɛːɐlɪç] *adj* sparse, scant; scanty; poor (*attendance*)
sparsam ['ʃpaːɐzaːm] *adj* economical (***mit*** of); ***sparsam leben*** lead a frugal life; ***sparsam umgehen mit*** use sparingly; go easy on
'Sparsamkeit *f* (*-*; *no pl*) economy
Spaß [ʃpaːs] *m* (*-es*; *Späße* ['ʃpɛːsə]), *Austrian a.* **Spass** fun; joke; ***aus*** (***nur zum***) ***Spaß*** (just) for fun; ***es macht viel*** (***keinen***) ***Spaß*** it's great (no) fun; ***j-m den Spaß verderben*** spoil s.o.'s fun; ***er macht nur Spaß*** he is only joking (F kidding); ***keinen Spaß verstehen*** have no

S

sense of humo(u)r**spaßen** ['ʃpaːsən] *v/i* (*ge-, h*) joke
spaßig ['ʃpaːsɪç] *adj* funny
'**Spaßvogel** *m* joker
spät [ʃpɛːt] *adj and adv* late; ***am späten Nachmittag*** late in the afternoon; ***wie spät ist es?*** what time is it?; ***von früh bis spät*** from morning till night; (***fünf Minuten***) ***zu spät kommen*** be (five minutes) late; ***bis später!*** see you (later)!; → ***früher***
Spaten ['ʃpaːtən] *m* (*-s; -*) spade
'**spätestens** *adv* at the latest
Spatz [ʃpats] *m* (*-en; -en*) ZO sparrow
spazieren [ʃpa'tsiːrən]: ***spazieren fahren*** go (take *s.o.*) for a drive; take *s.o.* out; ***spazieren gehen*** go for a walk
Spazierfahrt [ʃpa'tsiːɐ-] *f* drive, ride
Spa'ziergang *m* walk; ***e-n Spaziergang machen*** go for a walk
Spa'ziergänger(in) [-gɛŋɐ (-ŋərɪn)] (*-s; -/-; -nen*) walker
Specht [ʃpɛçt] *m* (*-[e]s; -e*) ZO woodpecker
Speck [ʃpɛk] *m* (*-[e]s; -e*) bacon
speckig ['ʃpɛkɪç] *fig adj* greasy
Spediteur [ʃpedi'tøːɐ] *m* (*-s; -e*) shipping agent; remover
Spedition [ʃpedi'tsjoːn] *f* (*-; -en*) shipping agency; moving (*Br* removal) firm
Speer [ʃpeːɐ] *m* (*-[e]s; -e*) spear; SPORT javelin
Speiche ['ʃpaiçə] *f* (*-; -n*) spoke
Speichel ['ʃpaiçəl] *m* (*-s; no pl*) saliva, spit
Speicher ['ʃpaiçɐ] *m* (*-s; -*) storehouse; tank, reservoir; ARCH attic; EDP memory, store
Speicherdichte *f* EDP bit density
Speicherkapazi'tät *f* EDP memory capacity
'**speichern** *v/t* (*ge-, h*) store (up)
Speicherung ['ʃpaiçərʊŋ] *f* (*-; -en*) storage
speien ['ʃpaiən] *v/t* (*irr, ge-, h*) spit; spout; *volcano etc*: belch
Speise ['ʃpaizə] *f* (*-; -n*) food; dish
Speiseeis *n* ice cream
Speisekammer *f* larder, pantry
Speisekarte *f* menu
'**speisen** (*ge-, h*) **1.** *v/i* dine; **2.** *v/t* feed (*a.* ELECTR *etc*)
'**Speiseröhre** *f* ANAT gullet
Speisesaal *m* dining hall
Speisewagen *m* RAIL diner, *esp Br* dining car
Spekulant [ʃpeku'lant] *m* (*-en; -en*) ECON speculator
Spekulation [ʃpekula'tsjoːn] *f* (*-; -en*) speculation, ECON *a.* venture
spekulieren [ʃpeku'liːrən] *v/i* (*no -ge-, h*) ECON speculate (***auf*** *acc* on; ***mit*** in)
Spende ['ʃpɛndə] *f* (*-; -n*) gift; contribution; donation
'**spenden** *v/t* (*ge-, h*) give (*a. fig*); donate (*a.* MED)
Spender ['ʃpɛndɐ] *m* (*-s; -*) giver; donor (*a.* MED), **Spenderin** *f* (*-; -nen*) donor (*a.* MED)
spendieren [ʃpɛn'diːrən] *v/t* (*no -ge-, h*) ***j-m et. spendieren*** treat s.o. to s.th.
Spengler ['ʃpɛŋlɐ] *Austrian m* → ***Klempner***
Sperling ['ʃpɛrlɪŋ] *m* (*-s; -e*) ZO sparrow
Sperre ['ʃpɛrə] *f* (*-; -n*) barrier, RAIL *a.* gate; *fig* stop; TECH lock(ing device); barricade; SPORT suspension; PSYCH mental block; ECON embargo
'**sperren** *v/t* (*ge-, h*) close; ECON embargo; cut off; stop (*check*); SPORT suspend; obstruct; ***sperren in*** (*acc*) lock (up) in
'**Sperrholz** *n* plywood
Sperrmüllabfuhr *f* removal of bulky refuse
'**Sperrung** *f* (*-; -en*) closing
Spesen ['ʃpeːzən] *pl* expenses
Spezi ['ʃpeːtsi] F *m* (*-s; -[s]*) buddy, pal
Spezialausbildung [ʃpe'tsjaːl-] *f* special training
Spezialgebiet *n* special field, special(i)ty
Spezialgeschäft *n* specialized shop *or* store
spezialisieren [ʃpetsjali'ziːrən] *v/refl* (*no -ge-, h*) specialize (***auf*** *acc* in)
Spezialist(in) [ʃpetsja'lɪst(ɪn)] (*-en; -en/-; -nen*) specialist
Spezialität [ʃpetsjali'tɛːt] *f* (*-; -en*) special(i)ty
speziell [ʃpe'tsjɛl] *adj* specific, particular
spezifisch [ʃpe'tsiːfɪʃ] *adj* specific; ***spezifisches Gewicht*** specific gravity
Sphäre ['sfɛːrə] *f* (*-; -n*) sphere (*a. fig*)
spicken ['ʃpɪkən] (*ge-, h*) **1.** *v/t* GASTR lard (*a. fig*); **2.** F *v/i* PED crib
spie [ʃpiː] *pret of* ***speien***
Spiegel ['ʃpiːgəl] *m* (*-s; -*) mirror (*a. fig*)
'**Spiegelbild** *n* reflection (*a. fig*)
'**Spiegelei** *n* GASTR fried egg
'**spiegel'glatt** *adj* glassy; icy
'**spiegeln** *v/i and v/t* (*ge-, h*) reflect (*a. fig*); shine; ***sich spiegeln*** be reflected (*a. fig*)
'**Spiegelung** *f* (*-; -en*) reflection
Spiel [ʃpiːl] *n* (*-[e]s; -e*) game (*a. fig*); match; play (*a.* THEA *etc*); gambling; *fig* gamble; ***auf dem Spiel stehen*** be at stake; ***aufs Spiel setzen*** risk
spielen ['ʃpiːlən] *v/i and v/t* (*ge-, h*) play (*a. fig*) (***um*** for); THEA act; perform; gam-

S

ble; do (*the pools etc*); ***Klavier** etc **spielen*** play the piano *etc*
'spielend *fig adv* easily
Spieler ['ʃpiːlɐ] *m* (*-s*; -), **Spielerin** ['ʃpiːlərɪn] *f* (-; *-nen*) player; gambler
'Spielfeld *n* (playing) field, pitch
Spielca,sino *n* casino
Spielfilm *m* feature film
Spielhalle *f* amusement arcade, game room
Spielkame,rad(in) playmate
Spielkarte *f* playing card
Spielka,sino *n* casino
Spielmarke *f* counter, chip
Spielplan *m* THEA *etc* program(me)
Spielplatz *m* playground
Spielraum *fig m* play, scope
Spielregel *f* rule (of the game)
Spielsachen *pl* toys
Spielstand *m* score
Spieluhr *f* music (*Br* musical) box
Spielverderber(in) (*-s*; *-/-*; *-nen*) spoilsport
Spielwaren *pl* toys
Spielzeit *f* THEA, SPORT season; playing (*film*: running) time
'Spielzeug *n* toy(s); ***Spielzeug...*** *in cpds ...pistole etc*: toy ...
Spieß [ʃpiːs] *m* (*-es*; *-e*) MIL spear; GASTR spit; skewer
spießen ['ʃpiːsən] *v/t* (*ge-*, *h*) skewer
Spießer ['ʃpiːsɐ] F *contp m* (*-s*; -), **'spießig** F *contp adj* philistine
Spinat [ʃpi'naːt] *m* (*-[e]s*; *-e*) BOT spinach
Spind [ʃpɪnt] *n*, *m* (*-[e]s*; *-e*) locker
Spindel ['ʃpɪndəl] *f* (-; *-n*) spindle
Spinne ['ʃpɪnə] *f* (-; *-n*) ZO spider
'spinnen (*irr*, *ge-*, *h*) **1.** *v/t* spin (*a. fig*); **2.** F *contp v/i* be nuts; talk nonsense
Spinner ['ʃpɪnɐ] *m* (*-s*; -), **'Spinnerin** *f* (-; *-nen*) spinner; F *contp* nut, crackpot
'Spinnrad *n* spinning wheel
'Spinnwebe *f* (-; *-n*) cobweb
Spion [ʃpjoːn] *m* (*-s*; *-e*) spy
Spionage [ʃpjo'naːʒə] *f* (-; *no pl*) espionage
spionieren [ʃpjo'niːrən] *v/i* (*no -ge-*, *h*) spy; F snoop
Spi'onin *f* (-; *-nen*) spy
Spirale [ʃpi'raːlə] *f* (-; *-n*), **spi'ralförmig** [-fœrmɪç] *adj* spiral
Spirituosen [ʃpiri'tuoːzən] *pl* spirits
Spiritus ['ʃpiːritus] *m* spirit
Spital [ʃpi'taːl] *Austrian*, *Swiss n* (*-s*; *Spitäler* [ʃpi'tɛːlɐ]) hospital
spitz [ʃpɪts] *adj* pointed (*a. fig*); MATH acute; ***spitze Zunge*** sharp tongue
'Spitzbogen *m* ARCH pointed arch
Spitze ['ʃpɪtsə] *f* (-; *-n*) point; tip; ARCH spire; BOT, GEOGR top; head (*a. fig*); lace; F MOT top speed; ***spitze sein*** F be super, be (the) tops; ***an der Spitze*** at the top (*a. fig*)
Spitzel ['ʃpɪtsəl] *m* (*-s*; -) informer, F stoolpigeon
spitzen ['ʃpɪtsən] *v/t* (*ge-*, *h*) point, sharpen; purse; ZO prick up (*its ears*)
'Spitzen... *in cpds* top ...; hi-tech ...
Spitzentechnolo,gie *f* high technology, hi tech
'spitzfindig *adj* quibbling
'Spitzfindigkeit *f* (-; *-en*) subtlety
'Spitzhacke *f* pickax(e), pick
'Spitzname *m* nickname
Splitter ['ʃplɪtɐ] *m* (*-s*; -), **'splittern** *v/i* (*ge-*, *h*, *sein*) splinter
'splitter'nackt F *adj* stark naked
sponsern ['ʃpɔnzɐn] *v/t* (*ge-*, *h*) sponsor
Sponsor ['ʃpɔnzɐ] *m* (*-s*; *-en* [ʃpɔn'zoːrən]) sponsor
spontan [ʃpɔn'taːn] *adj* spontaneous
Sporen ['ʃpoːrən] *pl* spurs (*a.* ZO); BIOL spores
Sport [ʃpɔrt] *m* (*-[e]s*; *no pl*) sport(s); PED physical education; ***Sport treiben*** do sports
'Sport... *in cpds ...ereignis*, *...geschäft*, *...hemd*, *...verein*, *...zentrum etc*: *mst* sports ...
Sportkleidung *f* sportswear
'Sportler ['ʃpɔrtlɐ] *m* (*-s*; -), **Sportlerin** ['ʃpɔrtlərɪn] *f* (-; *-nen*) athlete
'sportlich *adj* athletic; casual, sporty
'Sportnachrichten *pl* sports news
Sportplatz *m* sports grounds
Sporttauchen *n* scuba diving
Sportwagen *m* stroller, *Br* pushchair; MOT sports car
Spott [ʃpɔt] *m* (*-[e]s*, *no pl*) mockery; derision
'spott'billig F *adj* dirt cheap
spotten ['ʃpɔtən] *v/i* (*ge-*, *h*) mock (***über*** *acc* at), scoff (at); make fun (of)
Spötter ['ʃpœtɐ] *m* (*-s*; -) mocker, scoffer
'spöttisch *adj* mocking, derisive
'Spottpreis *m*: ***für e-n Spottpreis*** dirt cheap
sprach [ʃpraːx] *pret of **sprechen***
Sprache ['ʃpraːxə] *f* (-; *-n*) language (*a. fig*); speech; ***zur Sprache kommen*** (***bringen***) come up (bring *s.th.* up)
'Sprachfehler *m* speech defect
Sprachgebrauch *m* usage
Sprachla,bor *n* language laboratory
Sprachlehre *f* grammar
Sprachlehrer(in) language teacher
'sprachlich **1.** *adj* language ...; **2.** *adv*: ***sprachlich richtig*** grammatically cor-

S

rect
'sprachlos *adj* speechless
'Sprachrohr *fig n* mouthpiece
Sprachunterricht *m* language teaching
Sprachwissenschaft *f* linguistics
sprang [ʃpraŋ] *pret of* ***springen***
Spraydose ['ʃpre:-] *f* spray can, aerosol (can)
Sprechanlage ['ʃprɛç-] *f* intercom
sprechen ['ʃprɛçən] *v/t and v/i (irr, ge-, h)* speak (***j-n, mit j-m*** to s.o.); talk (to) (*both*: ***über*** *acc*, ***von*** about, of); ***nicht zu sprechen sein*** be busy
Sprecher(in) ['ʃprɛçɐ (-çərɪn)] (*-s*; *-/-*; *-nen*) speaker; announcer; spokesman (spokeswoman)
'Sprechstunde *f* office hours; MED office (*Br* consulting) hours, *Br* surgery
'Sprechzimmer *n* office, *Br a.* consulting room
spreizen ['ʃpraitsən] *v/t (ge-, h)* spread
sprengen ['ʃprɛŋən] *v/t (ge-, h)* blow up; blast; sprinkle; water; *fig* break up
'Sprengkopf *m* MIL warhead
'Sprengstoff *m* MIL explosive
'Sprengung *f* (*-; -en*) blasting; blowing up
sprenkeln ['ʃprɛŋkəln] *v/t (ge-, h)* speck (-le), spot, dot
Spreu [ʃprɔʏ] *f* (*-; no pl*) chaff (*a. fig*)
Sprichwort ['ʃprɪç-] *n* proverb, saying
'sprichwörtlich *adj* proverbial (*a. fig*)
sprießen ['ʃpri:sən] *v/i (irr, ge-, sein)* BOT sprout
'Springbrunnen *m* fountain
springen ['ʃprɪŋən] *v/i (irr, ge-, sein)* jump, leap; *ball etc*: bounce; SPORT dive; *glass etc*: crack; break; burst; ***in die Höhe (zur Seite) springen*** jump up (aside)
Springer ['ʃprɪŋɐ] *m* (*-s; -*) jumper; diver; *chess*: knight
'Springflut *f* spring tide
'Springreiten *n* show jumping
Spritze ['ʃprɪtsə] *f* (*-; -n*) MED injection, F shot; syringe
'spritzen 1. *v/i and v/t (ge-, h)* splash; spray (*a.* TECH, AGR); MED inject; give *s.o.* an injection of; **2.** *v/i (ge-, sein)* spatter; gush (***aus*** from)
Spritzer ['ʃprɪtsɐ] *m* (*-s; -*) splash; dash
'Spritzpis,tole *f* TECH spray gun
'Spritztour F *f* MOT spin
spröde ['ʃprø:də] *adj* brittle (*a. fig*); rough
spross [ʃprɔs] *pret of* ***sprießen***
Sprosse ['ʃprɔsə] *f* (*-; -n*) rung
Spruch [ʃprʊx] *m* (*-[e]s; Sprüche* ['ʃprʏçə]) saying; decision
Spruchband *n* banner
Sprudel ['ʃpru:dəl] *m* (*-s; -*) mineral water
'sprudeln *v/i (ge-, sein)* bubble
Sprühdose ['ʃpry:-] *f* spray can, aerosol (can)
sprühen ['ʃpry:ən] *v/t and v/i (ge-, h)* spray; throw out (*sparks*)
'Sprühregen *m* drizzle
Sprung [ʃprʊŋ] *m* (*-[e]s; Sprünge* ['ʃprʏŋə]) jump, leap; SPORT dive; crack, fissure
Sprungbrett *n* SPORT diving board; springboard; *fig* stepping stone
Sprungschanze *f* ski jump
Spucke ['ʃpʊkə] F *f* (*-; no pl*) spit
'spucken *v/i and v/t (ge-, h)* spit; F throw up
Spuk [ʃpu:k] *m* (*-[e]s; -e*) apparition, ghost
spuken ['ʃpu:kən] *v/i (ge-, h)* ***spuken in*** (*dat*) haunt; ***hier spukt es*** this place is haunted
Spule ['ʃpu:lə] *f* (*-; -n*) spool, reel; bobbin; ELECTR coil
'spulen *v/t (ge-, h)* spool, wind, reel
spülen ['ʃpy:lən] *v/t and v/i (ge-, h)* wash up, do the dishes; rinse; flush the toilet
'Spülma,schine *f* dishwasher
Spur [ʃpu:ɐ] *f* (*-; -en*) track(s); trail; print; lane; trace (*a. fig*); ***j-m auf der Spur sein*** be on s.o.'s trail
spüren ['ʃpy:rən] *v/t (ge-, h)* feel, sense; notice
'spurlos *adv* without leaving a trace
'Spurweite *f* RAIL ga(u)ge; MOT track
St. ABBR *of* ***Sankt*** St, Saint
Staat [ʃta:t] *m* (*-[e]s; -en*) state; POL government
'Staatenbund *m* confederacy, confederation
'staatenlos *adj* stateless
'staatlich 1. *adj* state …; public, national; **2.** *adv*: ***staatlich geprüft*** qualified, registered
'Staatsangehörige *m, f* national, citizen, subject
Staatsangehörigkeit *f* (*-; no pl*) nationality
Staatsanwalt *m* JUR district attorney, *Br* (public) prosecutor
Staatsbesuch *m* official *or* state visit
Staatsbürger(in) citizen
Staatschef *m* head of state
Staatsdienst *m* civil (*or* public) service
'staatseigen *adj* state-owned
'Staatsfeind *m* public enemy
'staatsfeindlich *adj* subversive
'Staatshaushalt *m* budget
Staatskasse *f* treasury
Staatsmann *m* statesman
Staatsoberhaupt *n* head of (the) state
Staatssekre,tär(in) undersecretary of

state
Staatsstreich *m* coup d'état
Staatsvertrag *m* treaty
Staatswissenschaft *f* political science
Stab [ʃtaːp] *m* (-[*e*]*s*; *Stäbe* ['ʃtɛːbə]) staff (*a. fig*); bar; SPORT, MUS baton; SPORT pole
Stäbchen ['ʃtɛːpçən] *pl* chopstick
'**Stabhochsprung** *m* SPORT pole vault
stabil [ʃta'biːl] *adj* stable (*a.* ECON, POL); solid, strong; sound
stabilisieren [ʃtabili'ziːrən] *v/t* (*no -ge-, h*) stabilize
Stabilität [-'tɛːt] *f* (-; *no pl*) stability
stach [ʃtaːx] *pret of* ***stechen***
Stachel ['ʃtaxəl] *m* (-*s*; -*n*) BOT, ZO spine, prick; ZO sting
Stachelbeere *f* BOT gooseberry
Stacheldraht *m* barbed wire
stachelig ['ʃtaxəlɪç] *adj* prickly
'**Stachelschwein** *n* ZO porcupine
Stadel ['ʃtaːdəl] *Austrian m* (-*s*; -[*n*]) barn
Stadion ['ʃtaːdjɔn] *n* (-*s*; -*ien*) stadium
Stadium ['ʃtaːdjʊm] *n* (-*s*; -*ien*) stage, phase
Stadt [ʃtat] *f* (-; *Städte* ['ʃtɛːtə]) town; city; ***die Stadt Berlin*** the city of Berlin; ***in die Stadt fahren*** go downtown, *esp Br* go (in)to town
Stadtbahn *f* urban railway
Städter ['ʃtɛːtɐ] *m* (-*s*; -), '**Städterin** *f* (-; -*nen*) city dweller, F townie, *often contp* city slicker
'**Stadtgebiet** *n* urban area
Stadtgespräch *fig n* talk of the town
städtisch ['ʃɛːtɪʃ] *adj* urban; POL municipal
'**Stadtplan** *m* city map
Stadtrand *m* outskirts
Stadtrat *m* town council; city councilman, *Br* town council(l)or
Stadtrundfahrt *f* sightseeing tour
Stadtstreicher(in) city vagrant
Stadtteil *m*, **Stadtviertel** *n* quarter
Staffel ['ʃtafəl] *f* (-; -*n*) SPORT relay race *or* team; MIL, AVIAT squadron
Staffelei [ʃtafə'lai] *f* (-; -*en*) PAINT easel
'**staffeln** *v/t* (*ge-, h*) grade, scale
stahl [ʃtaːl] *pret of* ***stehlen***
Stahl *m* (-[*e*]*s*; *Stähle* ['ʃtɛːlə]) steel
'**Stahlwerk** *n* steelworks
stak [ʃtaːk] *pret of* ***stecken*** 2
Stall [ʃtal] *m* (-[*e*]*s*; *Ställe* ['ʃtɛlə]) stable
'**Stallknecht** *m* stableman
Stamm [ʃtam] *m* (-[*e*]*s*; *Stämme* ['ʃtɛmə]) BOT stem (*a.* LING), trunk; tribe, stock; *fig* regulars; ***Stamm...*** *in cpds* *...gast, ...kunde, ...spieler etc*: regular ...
Stammbaum *m* family tree; ZO pedigree
stammeln ['ʃtaməln] *v/t* (*ge-, h*) stammer
stammen ['ʃta,ən] *v/i* (*ge-, h*) ***stammen aus*** (***von***) come from; be from; ***stammen von*** *work of art etc*: be by
'**Stammformen** *pl* LING principal parts, *mst* tenses
stämmig ['ʃtɛmɪç] *adj* sturdy; stout
'**Stammkneipe** F *f Br* local
stampfen ['ʃtampfən] (*ge-, h*) **1.** *v/t* mash; **2.** *v/i* stamp (***mit dem Fuß*** one's foot)
stand [ʃtant] *pret of* ***stehen***
Stand *m* (-[*e*]*s*; *Stände* ['ʃtɛndə]) a) (*no pl*) stand(ing), standing *or* upright position; footing, foothold; ASTR position; TECH *etc*: height, level (*a. fig*); reading; SPORT score; *racing*: standings; *fig* state; social standing, status, b) stand, stall, c) class; profession; ***auf den neuesten Stand bringen*** bring up to date; ***e-n schweren Stand haben*** have a hard time (of it); → ***außerstande***; → ***imstande***; → ***instand***; → ***zustande***
Standard ['ʃtandart] *m* (-*s*; -*s*) standard
'**Standbild** *n* statue
Ständchen ['ʃtɛntçən] *n* (-*s*; -) MUS serenade
Ständer ['ʃtɛndɐ] *m* (-*s*; -) stand; rack
Standesamt ['ʃtandəs-] *n* marriage license bureau, *Br* registry office
'**standesamtlich** *adj*: ***standesamtliche Trauung*** civil marriage
'**Standesbeamte** *m*, **-in** *f* civil magistrate, *Br* registrar
'**Standfoto** *n* still
'**standhaft** *adj* steadfast, firm; ***standhaft bleiben*** resist temptation
'**standhalten** *v/i* (*irr*, ***halten***, *sep*, *-ge-, h*) withstand, resist
ständig ['ʃtɛndɪç] *adj* constant; permanent (*address*)
'**Standlicht** *n* (-[*e*]*s*; *no pl*) MOT parking light
Standort *m* position; location; MIL post, garrison
Standpauke F *f*: ***j-m e-e Standpauke halten*** give s.o. a talking-to
Standplatz *m* stand
Standpunkt *m* (point of) view, standpoint
Standrecht *n* (-[*e*]*s*; *no pl*) MIL martial law
Standspur *f* MOT (*Br* hard) shoulder
Standuhr *f* grandfather clock
Stange ['ʃtaŋə] *f* (-; -*n*) pole; staff; rod, bar; carton (*of cigarettes*)
Stängel ['ʃtɛŋəl] *m* (-*s*; -) BOT stalk, stem
stank [ʃtaŋk] *pret of* ***stinken***
Stanniol [ʃta'njoːl] *n* (-*s*; -*e*) tin foil
Stanze ['ʃtantsə] *f* (-; -*n*), '**stanzen** *v/t* (*ge-, h*) TECH punch
Stapel ['ʃtaːpəl] *m* (-*s*; -) pile, stack; heap; ***vom Stapel lassen*** MAR launch (*a. fig*);

S

vom Stapel laufen MAR be launched
'Stapellauf *m* MAR launch
'stapeln *v/t* (*ge-*, *h*) pile (up), stack
stapfen ['ʃtapfən] *v/i* (*ge-*, *sein*) trudge
Star[1] [ʃtaːɐ] *m* (-[*e*]*s*; *-e*) ZO starling; MED cataract
Star[2] *m* (*-s*; *-s*) THEA *etc*: star
starb [ʃtarp] *pret of* ***sterben***
stark [ʃtark] **1.** *adj* strong (*a.* GASTR); powerful; *fig* heavy; F super, great; **2.** *adv*: ***stark beeindruckt*** greatly impressed; ***stark beschädigt*** badly damaged
Stärke ['ʃtɛrkə] *f* (-; *-n*) a) (*no pl*) strength, power; intensity, b) degree, c) CHEM starch
'stärken *v/t* (*ge-*, *h*) strengthen (*a. fig*); starch; ***sich stärken*** take some refreshment
'Starkstrom *m* ELECTR high-voltage (*or* heavy) current
Stärkung *f* (-; *-en*) strengthening; refreshment
'Stärkungsmittel *n* MED tonic
starr [ʃtar] *adj* stiff; rigid (*a.* TECH); frozen (*face*); ***starrer Blick*** (fixed) stare; ***starr vor Kälte*** (***Entsetzen***) frozen (scared) stiff
'starren *v/i* (*ge-*, *h*) stare (***auf*** *acc* at)
'starrköpfig [-kœpfɪç] *adj* stubborn, obstinate
'Starrsinn *m* (-[*e*]*s*; *no pl*) stubbornness, obstinacy
Start [ʃtart] *m* (-[*e*]*s*; *-s*) start (*a. fig*); AVIAT take-off; *rocket*: lift-off
'Startbahn *f* AVIAT runway
'startbereit *adj* ready to start; AVIAT ready for take-off
starten ['ʃtartən] *v/i* (*ge-*, *sein*) *and v/t* (*ge-*, *h*) start (*a.* F); AVIAT take off; lift off; launch (*a. fig*)
Station [ʃta'tsjoːn] *f* (-; *-en*) station; MED ward
stationär [ʃtatsjo'nɛːɐ] *adj*: ***stationärer Patient*** MED in-patient
stationieren [ʃtatsjo'niːrən] *v/t* (*no -ge-*, *h*) MIL station; deploy
Stationsvorsteher *m* RAIL stationmaster
Statist [ʃta'tɪst] *m* (*-en*; *-en*) THEA extra
Statistik [ʃta'tɪstɪk] *f* (-; *-en*) statistics
Sta'tistiker [-tikɐ] *m* (*-s*; -) statistician
sta'tistisch *adj* statistical
Stativ [ʃta'tiːf] *n* (*-s*; *-e*) PHOT tripod
statt [ʃtat] *prp* instead of; ***statt et. zu tun*** instead of doing s.th.
statt'dessen instead
Stätte ['ʃtɛtə] *f* (-; *-n*) place; scene
'stattfinden *v/i* (*irr*, ***finden***, *sep*, *-ge-*, *h*) take place; happen
'stattlich *adj* imposing; handsome
Statue ['ʃtaːtuə] *f* (-; *-n*) statue
Statur [ʃta'tuːɐ] *f* (-; *-en*) build
Status ['ʃtaːtʊs] *m* (-; -) state; status
Statussym,bol *n* status symbol
Statuszeile *f* EDP status line
Stau [ʃtau] *m* (-[*e*]*s*; *-s*, *-e*) MOT traffic jam *or* congestion
Staub [ʃtaup] *m* (-[*e*]*s*; TECH *-e*, *Stäube* ['ʃtɔʏbə]) dust (*a.* ***Staub wischen***)
'Staubecken *n* reservoir
stauben ['ʃtaubən] *v/i* (*ge-*, *h*) give off *or* make dust
staubig ['ʃtaubɪç] *adj* dusty
'staubsaugen *v/i and v/t* (*ge-*, *h*) vacuum, F *Br* hoover
'Staubsauger *m* vacuum cleaner, F *Br* hoover
'Staubtuch *n* duster
'Staudamm *m* dam
Staude ['ʃtaudə] *f* (-; *-n*) BOT herbacious plant
stauen ['ʃtauən] *v/t* (*ge-*, *h*) dam up; ***sich stauen*** MOT *etc* be stacked up
staunen ['ʃtaunən] *v/i* (*ge-*, *h*) be astonished *or* surprised (***über*** *acc* at)
'Staunen *n* (*-s*; *no pl*) astonishment, amazement
Staupe ['ʃtaupə] *f* (-; *-n*) VET distemper
'Stausee *m* reservoir
stechen ['ʃtɛçən] *v/i and v/t* (*irr*, *ge-*, *h*) prick; ZO sting, bite; stab; pierce; ***mit et. stechen in*** (*acc*) stick s.th. in(to); ***sich stechen*** prick o.s.
stechend *fig adj* piercing (*look*); stabbing (*pain*)
'Stechuhr *f* time clock
Steckbrief ['ʃtɛk-] *m* JUR „wanted" poster
'steckbrieflich *adv*: ***er wird steckbrieflich gesucht*** JUR a warrant is out against him
'Steckdose *f* ELECTR (wall) socket
stecken ['ʃtɛkən] (*ge-*, *h*) **1.** *v/t* stick; put; *esp* TECH insert (***in*** *acc* into); pin (***an*** *acc* to, on); AGR set, plant; **2.** *v/i* ([*irr*]) be; stick, be stuck; ***stecken bleiben*** get stuck
'steckenbleiben *v/i* (*irr*, ***bleiben***, *sep*, *-ge-*, *sein*) *fig* get stuck
'Steckenpferd *n* hobby horse; *fig* hobby
Stecker ['ʃtɛkɐ] *m* (*-s*; -) ELECTR plug
'Steckkon,takt *m* ELECTR plug (connection)
Stecknadel *f* pin
Steckplatz *m* EDP slot
Steg [ʃteːk] *m* (-[*e*]*s*; *-e*) footbridge
Stegreif ['ʃteːkraif] *m*: ***aus dem Stegreif*** extempore, ad-lib; ***aus dem Stegreif sprechen*** *or* ***spielen*** *etc* extemporize, ad-lib

stehen ['ʃteːən] *v/i* (*irr, ge-, h*) stand; be; stand up; ***es steht ihr*** it suits (*or* looks well on) her; ***wie steht es*** (*or* ***das Spiel***)***?*** what's the score?; ***hier steht, dass*** it says here that; ***wo steht das?*** where does it say so *or* that?; ***sich schlecht stehen*** be badly off; F ***sich gut mit j-m stehen*** get along well with s.o.; ***wie steht es mit ...?*** what about ...?; F ***darauf stehe ich*** it turns me on; ***stehen bleiben*** stop; *esp* TECH come to a standstill (*a. fig*); ***stehen lassen*** leave (untouched); leave behind; ***alles stehen und liegen lassen*** drop everything; ***sich e-n Bart stehen lassen*** grow a beard

'**stehenbleiben** *v/i* (*irr,* ***bleiben***, *sep, -ge-, sein*) → ***stehen***

stehenlassen *v/t* (*irr,* ***lassen***, *sep, no -ge-, h*) → ***stehen***

'**Stehkragen** *m* stand-up collar

Stehlampe *f* floor (*Br* standard) lamp

Stehleiter *f* step ladder

stehlen ['ʃteːlən] *v/t and v/i* (*irr, ge-, h*) steal (*a. fig* ***sich stehlen***)

'**Stehplatz** *m* standing ticket; *pl* standing room

steif [ʃtaif] *adj* stiff (***vor*** *dat* with)

Steigbügel ['ʃtaik-] *m* stirrup

steigen ['ʃtaigən] *v/i* (*irr, ge-, sein*) go, step; climb (*a.* AVIAT); *fig* rise, go up; ***steigen in*** (***auf***) (*acc*) get on (*bus, bike etc*); ***steigen aus*** (***von***) get off (*bus, horse etc*); ***aus dem Bett steigen*** get out of bed

steigern ['ʃtaigɐn] *v/t* (*ge-, h*) raise, increase; heighten; improve; LING compare; ***sich steigern*** improve, get better

Steigerung ['ʃtaigərʊŋ] *f* (*-; -en*) rise, increase; heightening; improvement; LING comparison

'**Steigung** *f* (*-; -en*) gradient; slope

steil [ʃtail] *adj* steep (*a. fig*)

Stein [ʃtain] *m* (*-[e]s; -e*) stone (*a.* BOT, MED), rock

Steinbock *m* ZO rock goat; ASTR Capricorn; ***er ist*** (***ein***) ***Steinbock*** he's (a) Capricorn

Steinbruch *m* quarry

steinern ['ʃtainɐn] *adj* (of) stone; *fig* stony

'**Steingut** *n* (*-[e]s; -e*) earthenware

steinig ['ʃtainɪç] *adj* stony

steinigen ['ʃtainɪgən] *v/t* (*ge-, h*) stone

'**Steinkohle** *f* (hard) coal

'**Steinmetz** [-mɛts] *m* (*-en; -en*) stonemason

'**Steinzeit** *f* (*-; no pl*) Stone Age

Stellage [ʃtɛ'laːʒə] *Austrian f* (*-; -n*) stand, rack, shelf

Stelle ['ʃtɛlə] *f* (*-; -n*) place; spot; point; job; authority; MATH figure; ***freie Stelle*** vacancy, opening; ***auf der*** (***zur***) ***Stelle*** on the spot; ***an erster Stelle stehen*** (***kommen***) be (come) first; ***an j-s Stelle*** in s.o.'s place; ***ich an deiner Stelle*** if I were you

'**stellen** *v/t* (*ge-, h*) put; set (*trap, clock, task etc*); turn (*up, down etc*); ask (*question*); provide; corner, hunt down (*criminal etc*); ***sich stellen*** give o.s. up, turn o.s. in; ***sich gegen*** (***hinter***) ***j-n stellen*** *fig* oppose (back) s.o.; ***sich schlafend*** *etc* ***stellen*** pretend to be asleep *etc*; ***stell dich dorthin!*** (go and) stand over there!

'**Stellenangebot** *n* vacancy; ***ich habe ein Stellenangebot*** I was offered a job

Stellenanzeige *f* job ad(vertisement), employment ad

Stellengesuch *n* application for a job

'**stellenweise** *adv* partly, in places

'**Stellung** *f* (*-; -en*) position; post, job; ***Stellung nehmen zu*** comment on, give one's opinion of

Stellungnahme [-naːmə] *f* (*-; -n*) comment, opinion (*both:* ***zu*** on)

'**stellungslos** *adj* unemployed, jobless

'**stellvertretend** *adj* acting, deputy, vice-...

'**Stellvertreter(in)** (*-s; -/-; -nen*) representative; deputy

Stelze ['ʃtɛltsə] *f* (*-; -n*) stilt

'**stelzen** *v/i* (*ge-, sein*) stalk

stemmen ['ʃtɛmən] *v/t* (*ge-, h*) lift (*weight*); ***sich stemmen gegen*** press o.s. against; *fig* resist *or* oppose *s.th.*

Stempel ['ʃtɛmpəl] *m* (*-s; -*) stamp; postmark; hallmark; BOT pistil

'**Stempelkissen** *n* ink pad

'**stempeln** (*ge-, h*) **1.** *v/t* stamp; cancel; hallmark; **2.** F *v/i:* ***stempeln gehen*** be on the dole

Stengel → ***Stängel***

Stenografie [ʃtenogra'fiː] *f* (*-; -n*) shorthand

stenogra'fieren *v/t* (*no -ge-, h*) take down in shorthand

Stenogramm [ʃteno'gram] *n* (*-[e]s; -e*) shorthand notes

Stenotypistin [-ty'pɪstɪn] *f* (*-; -nen*) shorthand typist

Steppdecke ['ʃtɛp-] *f* quilt

steppen ['ʃtɛpən] (*ge-, h*) **1.** *v/t* quilt; stitch; **2.** *v/i* tap dance

'**Stepptanz** *m* tap dancing

Sterbebett ['ʃtɛrbə-] *n* deathbed

'**Sterbeklinik** *f* MED hospice

sterben ['ʃtɛrbən] *v/i* (*irr, ge-, sein*) die (***an*** *dat* of) (*a. fig*); ***im Sterben liegen*** be dying

S

sterblich ['ʃtɛrplɪç] *adj* mortal
'**Sterblichkeit** *f* (-; *no pl*) mortality
Stereo ['ʃteːreo] *n* (-*s*; -*s*) stereo
steril [ʃte'riːl] *adj* sterile
Sterilisation [ʃteriliza'tsjoːn] *f* (-; -*en*) sterilization
sterilisieren [ʃterili'ziːrən] *v/t* (*no -ge-*, *h*) sterilize
Stern [ʃtɛrn] *m* (-[*e*]*s*; -*e*) star (*a. fig*)
'**Sternbild** *n* ASTR constellation; sign of the zodiac
'**Sternchen** *n* (-*s*; -) PRINT asterisk
'**Sternenbanner** *n* Star-Spangled Banner, Stars and Stripes
'**Sternenhimmel** *m* starry sky
'**sternklar** *adj* starry
'**Sternkunde** *f* (-; *no pl*) astronomy
Sternschnuppe *f* (-; -*n*) shooting *or* falling star
Sternwarte *f* (-; -*n*) observatory
stetig ['ʃteːtɪç] *adj* continual, constant; steady
stets [ʃteːts] *adv* always
Steuer[1] ['ʃtɔʏɐ] *n* (-*s*; -) MOT (steering) wheel; MAR helm, rudder
'**Steuer**[2] *f* (-; -*n*) tax (***auf*** *acc* on)
'**Steuerbeamte** *m* revenue officer
Steuerberater *m* tax adviser
'**Steuerbord** *n* MAR starboard
'**Steuererklärung** *f* tax return
Steuerermäßigung *f* tax allowance
'**steuerfrei** *adj* tax-free
'**Steuerhinterziehung** *f* tax evasion
'**Steuerknüppel** *m* AVIAT control column *or* stick
Steuermann *m* MAR helmsman; *rowing*: cox, coxswain
'**steuern** *v/t and v/i* (*ge-*, *h*) steer, AVIAT, MAR *a.* navigate, pilot, MOT *a.* drive; TECH control (*a. fig*); *fig* direct
'**steuerpflichtig** *adj* taxable
'**Steuerrad** *n* MOT steering wheel
'**Steuerruder** *n* MAR helm, rudder
'**Steuersenkung** *f* tax reduction
Steuerung ['ʃtɔʏərʊŋ] *f* (-; -*en*) steering (system); ELECTR, TECH control (*a. fig*)
'**Steuerzahler** *m*, '**Steuerzahlerin** *f* taxpayer
Stich [ʃtɪç] *m* (-[*e*]*s*; -*e*) prick; ZO sting, bite; stab; stitch; *cards*: trick; engraving; ***im Stich lassen*** desert *or* abandon *s.o.*, *s.th.*, leave *s.o.* in the lurch, let *s.o.* down
Stichelei [ʃtɪçə'lai] F *f* (-; -*en*) dig, gibe
sticheln ['ʃɪçəln] F *v/i* (*ge-*, *h*) make digs, gibe (***gegen*** at)
'**Stichflamme** *f* jet of flame
'**stichhaltig** *adj* valid, sound; watertight; ***nicht stichhaltig sein*** F not hold water
'**Stichprobe** *f* spot check
Stichtag *m* cutoff date; deadline
Stichwahl *f* POL run-off
Stichwort *n* a) (-[*e*]*s*; -*e*) THEA cue, b) (-[*e*]*s*; -*wörter*) headword; ***Stichworte*** *pl* notes; ***das Wichtigste in Stichworten*** an outline of the main points
Stichwortverzeichnis *n* index
Stichwunde *f* MED stab
sticken ['ʃtɪkən] *v/t and v/i* (*ge-*, *h*) embroider
Stickerei [ʃtɪkə'rai] *f* (-; -*en*) embroidery
stickig ['ʃtɪkɪç] *adj* stuffy
'**Stickstoff** *m* (-[*e*]*s*; *no pl*) CHEM nitrogen
Stief... [ʃtiːf-] *in cpds …mutter etc*: step…
Stiefel ['ʃtiːfəl] *m* (-*s*; -) boot
'**Stiefmütterchen** [-mʏtɐçən] *n* (-*s*; -) BOT pansy
stieg [ʃtiːk] *pret of* ***steigen***
Stiege ['ʃtiːgə] *Austrian f* (-; -*n*) → ***Treppe***
Stiel [ʃtiːl] *m* (-[*e*]*s*; -*e*) handle; stick; stem; BOT stalk
Stier [ʃtiːɐ] *m* (-[*e*]*s*; -*e*) ZO bull; ASTR Taurus; ***er ist*** (***ein***) ***Stier*** he's (a) Taurus
'**Stierkampf** *m* bullfight
stieß [ʃtiːs] *pret of* ***stoßen***
Stift [ʃtɪft] *m* (-[*e*]*s*; -*e*) pen; pencil; crayon; TECH pin; peg
stiften ['ʃtɪftən] *v/t* (*ge-*, *h*) donate; *fig* cause
'**Stiftung** *f* (-; -*en*) donation
Stil [ʃtiːl] *m* (-[*e*]*s*; -*e*) style (*a. fig*); ***in großem Stil*** in (grand) style; *fig* on a large scale
stilistisch [ʃti'lɪstɪʃ] *adj* stylistic
still [ʃtɪl] *adj* quiet, silent; still; ***sei***(***d***) ***still!*** be quiet!; ***halt still!*** keep still!; ***sich still verhalten*** keep quiet (*or* still)
Stille ['ʃtɪlə] *f* (-; *no pl*) silence, quiet(-ness); ***in aller Stille*** quietly; secretly
Stilleben *n* → ***Stillleben***
stillen ['ʃtɪlən] *v/t* (*ge-*, *h*) nurse, breastfeed; *fig* relieve (*pain*); satisfy (*curiosity etc*); quench (*one's thirst*)
'**stillhalten** *v/i* (*irr*, ***halten***, *sep*, -*ge-*, *h*) keep still
'**Stillleben** *n* PAINT still life
'**stilllegen** *v/t* (*sep*, -*ge-*, *h*) close down
'**stillos** *adj* lacking style, tasteless
'**stillschweigend** *adj* tacit
'**Stillstand** *m* (-[*e*]*s*; *no pl*) standstill, stop, *fig a.* stagnation (*a.* ECON); deadlock
'**stillstehen** *v/i* (*irr*, ***stehen***, *sep*, -*ge-*, *h*) (have) stop(ped), (have) come to a standstill
'**Stilmöbel** *pl* period furniture
'**stilvoll** *adj* stylish; ***stilvoll sein*** have style
'**Stimmband** *n* ANAT vocal cord
'**stimmberechtigt** *adj* entitled to vote
Stimme ['ʃtɪmə] *f* (-; -*n*) voice; POL vote;

sich der Stimme enthalten abstain
'stimmen (*ge-, h*) **1.** *v/i* be right, be true, be correct; POL vote (***für*** for; ***gegen*** against); ***es stimmt et. nicht*** (***damit*** *or* ***mit ihm***) there's s.th. wrong (with it *or* him); **2.** *v/t* MUS tune; ***j-n traurig*** *etc* ***stimmen*** make s.o. sad *etc*
'Stimmenthaltung *f* abstention
'Stimmrecht *n* right to vote
'Stimmung *f* (-; *-en*) mood; atmosphere; feeling
'stimmungsvoll *adj* atmospheric
'Stimmzettel *m* ballot (paper)
stinken ['ʃtɪŋkən] *v/i* (*irr, ge-, h*) stink (*a. fig*) (***nach*** of)
Stipendium [ʃti'pɛndjʊm] *n* (*-s; -ien*) UNIV scholarship, grant
stippen ['ʃtɪpən] *v/t* (*ge-, h*) dip
'Stippviˌsite F *f* flying visit
Stirn [ʃtɪrn] *f* (-; *-en*) ANAT forehead; ***die Stirn runzeln*** frown
stöbern ['ʃtøːbɐn] F *v/i* (*ge-, h*) rummage (about)
stochern ['ʃtɔxɐn] *v/i* (*ge-, h*) ***im Feuer stochern*** poke the fire; ***im Essen stochern*** pick at one's food; ***in den Zähnen stochern*** pick one's teeth
Stock [ʃtɔk] *m* (-[*e*]*s*; *Stöcke* ['ʃtœkə]) stick; cane; ARCH stor(e)y, floor; ***im ersten Stock*** on the second (*Br* first) floor
'stock'dunkel F *adj* pitch-dark
stocken ['ʃtɔkən] *v/i* (*ge-, h*) stop (short); falter; *traffic*: be jammed
stockend 1. *adj* halting; **2.** *adv*: ***stockend lesen*** stumble through a text; ***stockend sprechen*** speak haltingly
'Stockfleck *m* mo(u)ld stain
'Stockung *f* (-; *-en*) holdup, delay
'Stockwerk *n* stor(e)y, floor
Stoff [ʃtɔf] *m* (-[*e*]*s*; *-e*) material, stuff (*a.* F); fabric, textile; cloth; CHEM, PHYS *etc* substance; *fig* subject (matter)
'stofflich *adj* material
'Stofftier *n* soft toy animal
'Stoffwechsel *m* BIOL metabolism
stöhnen ['ʃtøːnən] *v/i* (*ge-, h*) groan, moan (*a. fig*)
Stollen ['ʃtɔlən] *m* (*-s*; -) tunnel, gallery
stolpern ['ʃtɔlpɐn] *v/i* (*ge-, sein*) stumble (***über*** *acc* over), trip (over) (*both a. fig*)
stolz [ʃtɔlts] *adj* proud (***auf*** *acc* of)
Stolz *m* (*-es; no pl*) pride (***auf*** *acc* in)
stolzieren [ʃtɔl'tsiːrən] *v/i* (*no -ge-, sein*) strut, stalk
stopfen ['ʃtɔpfən] *v/t* (*ge-, h*) darn, mend; stuff, fill (*a. pipe*)
Stoppel ['ʃtɔpəl] *f* (-; *-n*) stubble
'Stoppelbart F *m* stubbly beard
'stoppelig *adj* stubbly, bristly
'Stoppelzieher *Austrian m* corkscrew
stoppen ['ʃtɔpən] *v/i and v/t* (*ge-, h*) stop (*a. fig*); *esp* SPORT time
'Stopplicht *n* (-[*e*]*s*; *-er*) MOT stop light
Stoppschild *n* stop sign
Stoppuhr *f* stopwatch
Stöpsel ['ʃtœpsəl] *m* (*-s*; -) stopper; plug
Storch [ʃtɔrç] *m* (-[*e*]*s*; *Störche* ['ʃtœrçəl]) ZO stork
stören ['ʃtøːrən] *v/t and v/i* (*ge-, h*) disturb; trouble; bother, annoy; be in the way; ***lassen Sie sich nicht stören!*** don't let me disturb you!; ***darf ich Sie kurz stören?*** may I trouble you for a minute?; ***es*** (***er***) ***stört mich nicht*** it (he) doesn't bother me, I don't mind (him); ***stört es Sie***(, ***wenn ich rauche***)***?*** do you mind (my smoking *or* if I smoke)?
'Störenfried [-friːt] *m* (-[*e*]*s*; *-e*) troublemaker; intruder
Störfall ['ʃtøːɐ-] *m* TECH accident
störrisch ['ʃtœrɪʃ] *adj* stubborn, obstinate
'Störung *f* (-; *-en*) disturbance; trouble (*a.* TECH); TECH breakdown; TV, *radio*: interference
Stoß [ʃtoːs] *m* (*-es*; *Stöße* ['ʃtøːsə]) push, shove; thrust; kick; butt; blow, knock; shock; MOT jolt; bump, *esp* TECH, PHYS impact; pile, stack
'Stoßdämpfer *m* MOT shock absorber
stoßen ['ʃtoːsən] *v/t* (*irr, ge-, h*) *and v/i* (*sein*) push, shove; thrust; kick; butt; knock, strike; pound; ***stoßen gegen*** *or* ***an*** (*acc*) bump *or* run into *or* against; ***sich den Kopf stoßen*** (***an*** *dat*) knock one's head (against); ***stoßen auf*** (*acc*) strike (*oil etc*); *fig* come across; meet with
'stoßgesichert *adj* shockproof, shock-resistant
'Stoßstange *f* MOT bumper
'Stoßzahn *m* ZO tusk
'Stoßzeit *f* rush hour, peak hours
stottern ['ʃtɔtɐn] *v/i and v/t* (*ge-, h*) stutter
Str. ABBR *of* ***Straße*** St, Street; Rd, Road
'Strafanstalt *f* prison, penitentiary
'strafbar *adj* punishable, penal; ***sich strafbar machen*** commit an offense (*Br* offence)
Strafe ['ʃtraːfə] *f* (-; *-n*) punishment; JUR, ECON, SPORT penalty (*a. fig*); fine; ***20 Mark Strafe zahlen müssen*** be fined 20 marks; ***zur Strafe*** as a punishment
'strafen *v/t* (*ge-, h*) punish
straff [ʃtraf] *adj* tight; *fig* strict
'straffrei *adj*: ***straffrei ausgehen*** go unpunished
'Strafgefangene *m, f* prisoner, convict
Strafgesetz *n* criminal law

sträflich ['ʃtrɛːflɪç] **1.** *adj* inexcusable; **2.** *adv*: ***sträflich vernachlässigen*** neglect badly
'Strafmi,nute *f* SPORT penalty minute
Strafpro,zess *m* JUR criminal action, trial
Strafraum *m* SPORT penalty area (F box)
Strafstoß *m* SPORT penalty kick
Straftat *f* JUR criminal offense (*Br* offence); crime
Strafzettel *m* ticket
Strahl [ʃtraːl] *m* (-[*e*]*s*, -*en*) ray (*a. fig*); beam; flash; jet
strahlen ['ʃtraːlən] *v/i* (*ge-*, *h*) radiate; shine (brightly); *fig* beam (***vor*** with)
'Strahlen... *in cpds* PHYS \133*schutz etc*: radiation ...
'Strahlung *f* (-; -*en*) PHYS radiation
Strähne ['ʃtrɛːnə] *f* (-; -*n*) strand; streak
stramm [ʃtram] *adj* tight
strammstehen MIL stand to attention
strampeln ['ʃtrampəln] *v/i* (*ge-*, *h*) kick
Strand [ʃtrant] *m* (-[*e*]*s*; *Strände* ['ʃtrɛndə]) beach; ***am Strand*** on the beach
stranden ['ʃtrandən] *v/i* (*ge-*, *sein*) MAR strand; *fig* fail
'Strandgut *n* flotsam and jetsam (*a. fig*)
Strandkorb *m* roofed wicker beach chair
Strang [ʃtraŋ] *m* (-[*e*]*s*; *Stränge* ['ʃtrɛŋə]) rope; *esp* ANAT cord
Strapaze [ʃtra'paːtsə] *f* (-; -*n*) strain, exertion, hardship
strapazieren [ʃtrapa'tsiːrən] *v/t* (*no -ge-*, *h*) wear *s.o. or s.th.* out, be hard on
strapazierfähig *adj* longwearing, *Br* hardwearing
strapaziös [ʃtrapa'tsjøːs] *adj* strenuous
Straße ['ʃtraːsə] *f* (-; -*n*) road; street; GEOGR strait; ***auf der Straße*** on the road; on (*Br a.* in) the street
'Straßenarbeiten *pl* roadworks
Straßenbahn *f* streetcar, *Br* tram
Straßenca,fé *n* sidewalk (*Br* pavement) café
Straßenkarte *f* road map
Straßenkehrer [-keːrɐ] *m* (-*s*; -) street sweeper
Straßenkreuzung *f* crossroads; intersection
Straßenlage *f* MOT roadholding
Straßenrand *m* roadside; ***am Straßenrand*** at *or* by the roadside
Straßensperre *f* road block
strategisch [ʃtra'teːgɪʃ] *adj* strategic
sträuben ['ʃtrɔʏbən] *v/t and v/refl* (*ge-*, *h*) ruffle (up); bristle (up); ***sich sträuben gegen*** struggle against
Strauch [ʃtraux] *m* (-[*e*]*s*; *Sträucher* ['ʃtrɔʏçɐ]) BOT shrub, bush
straucheln ['ʃtrauxəln] *v/i* (*ge-*, *sein*) stumble
Strauß[1] [ʃtraus] *m* (-*es*; -*e*) ZO ostrich
Strauß[2] *m* (-*es*; *Sträuße* ['ʃtrɔʏsə]) bunch, bouquet
Strebe ['ʃtreːbə] *f* (-; -*n*) prop, stay (*a.* AVIAT, MAR)
'streben *v/i* (*ge-*, *h*) strive (***nach*** for, after)
Streber ['ʃtreːbɐ] *m* (-*s*; -) pusher; PED *etc* grind, *Br* swot
strebsam ['ʃtreːp-] *adj* ambitious
Strecke ['ʃtrɛkə] *f* (-; -*n*) distance (*a.* SPORT, MATH), way; route; RAIL line; SPORT course; stretch; ***zur Strecke bringen*** kill; *esp fig* hunt down
'strecken *v/t* (*ge-*, *h*) stretch (out), extend
Streich [ʃtraiç] *m* (-[*e*]*s*; -*e*) trick, prank, practical joke; ***j-m e-n Streich spielen*** play a trick *or* joke on s.o.
streicheln ['ʃtraiçəln] *v/t* (*ge-*, *h*) stroke, caress
streichen ['ʃtraiçən] *v/t and v/i* (*irr*, *ge-*, *h*) paint; spread; cross out; cancel; MAR strike; MUS bow; ***mit der Hand streichen über*** (*acc*) run one's hand over; ***streichen durch*** roam (*acc*)
Streicher(in) ['ʃtraiçɐ (-çərɪn)] (-*s*; -/-; -*nen*) MUS string player, *pl the* strings
'Streichholz *n* match
Streichinstru,ment *n* MUS string instrument
Streichor,chester *n* MUS string orchestra
'Streichung *f* (-; -*en*) cancellation; cut
Streife ['ʃtraifə] *f* (-; -*n*) patrol; ***auf Streife gehen*** go on patrol; ***auf Streife sein in*** (*dat*) patrol
'streifen *v/t and v/i* (*ge-*, *h*) touch, brush (against); MOT scrape against; graze; slip (***von*** off); *fig* touch on; ***streifen durch*** roam (*acc*), wander through
'Streifen *m* (-*s*; -) stripe; strip
'Streifenwagen *m* squad (*Br* patrol) car
'Streifschuss *m* MED graze
'Streifzug *m* tour (***durch*** of)
Streik [ʃtraik] *m* (-[*e*]*s*; -*s*) strike, walkout; ***wilder Streik*** wildcat strike
'Streikbrecher *m* strikebreaker, *Br* blackleg, *contp* scab
streiken ['ʃtraikən] *v/i* (*ge-*, *h*) (go *or* be on) strike; F *fig* refuse (to work etc)
'Streikende *m*, *f* (-*n*; -*n*) striker
'Streikposten *m* picket
Streit [ʃtrait] *m* (-[*e*]*s*; -*e*) quarrel; argument; fight; POL *etc* dispute; ***Streit anfangen*** pick a fight *or* quarrel; ***Streit suchen*** be looking for trouble
streiten ['ʃtraitən] *v/i and v/refl* (*irr*, *ge-*, *h*) quarrel, argue, fight (*all*: ***wegen, über*** *acc* about, over); ***sich streiten um*** fight for

S

'Streitfrage *f* (point at) issue
streitig ['ʃtraitɪç] *adj*: ***j-m et. streitig machen*** dispute s.o.'s right to s.th.
'Streitkräfte *pl* MIL (armed) forces
'streitshüctig *adj* quarrelsome
streng [ʃtrɛŋ] *adj* strict; severe; harsh; rigid; ***streng genommen*** strictly speaking
Strenge ['ʃtrɛŋə] *f* (-; *no pl*) strictness; severity; harshness; rigidity
'strenggläubig *adj* REL orthodox
Stress [ʃtrɛs] *m* (-*es*; *no pl*) stress; ***im Stress*** under stress
Streu [ʃtrɔʏ] *f* (-; -*en*) AGR litter
'streuen *v/t and v/i* (*ge-*, *h*) scatter (*a.* PHYS); spread; sprinkle; grit
streunen ['ʃtrɔʏnən] *v/i* (*ge-*, *sein*), **streunend** *adj* stray
strich [ʃtrɪç] *pret of* ***streichen***
Strich *m* (-[*e*]*s*; -*e*) line; stroke; F redlight district; F ***auf den Strich gehen*** walk the streets
Strichkode *m* bar code
Strichjunge F *m* male prostitute
'strichweise *adv* in parts; ***strichweise Regen*** scattered showers
Strick [ʃtrɪk] *m* (-[*e*]*s*; -*e*) cord; rope
stricken ['ʃtrɪkən] *v/t and v/i* (*ge-*, *h*) knit
'Strickjacke *f* cardigan
Strickleiter *f* rope ladder
Stricknadel *f* knitting needle
Strickwaren *pl* knitwear
Strickzeug *n* knitting (things)
Striemen ['ʃtri:mən] *m* (-*s*; -) welt, weal
stritt [ʃtrɪt] *pret of* ***streiten***
strittig ['ʃtrɪtɪç] *adj* controversial; ***strittiger Punkt*** point at issue
Stroh [ʃtro:] *n* (-[*e*]*s*; *no pl*) straw; thatch
Strohdach *n* thatch(ed) roof
Strohhalm *m* straw
Strohhut *m* straw hat
Strohwitwe F *f* grass widow
Strohwitwer F *m* grass widower
Strom [ʃtro:m] *m* (-[*e*]*s*; *Ströme* ['ʃtrø:mə]) (large) river; current (*a.* ELECTR); ***ein Strom von*** a stream of (*a. fig*); ***es gießt in Strömen*** it's pouring (with rain)
strom'ab(wärts) *adv* downstream
strom'auf(wärts) *adv* upstream
'Stromausfall *m* ELECTR power failure, blackout
strömen ['ʃtrø:mən] *v/i* (*ge-*, *sein*) stream (*a. fig*), flow, run; pour (*a. fig*)
'Stromkreis *m* ELECTR circuit
'stromlinienförmig *adj* streamlined
'Stromschnelle *f* (-; -*n*) GEOGR rapid
'Stromstärke *f* ELECTR amperage
'Strömung *f* (-; -*en*) current, *fig a.* trend
Strophe ['ʃtro:fə] *f* (-; -*n*) stanza, verse

S

strotzen ['ʃtrɔtsən] *v/i* (*ge-*, *h*) ***strotzen von*** be full of, abound with; ***strotzen vor*** (*dat*) be bursting with
Strudel ['ʃtru:dəl] *m* (-*s*; -) whirlpool (*a. fig*), eddy
Struktur [ʃtrʊk'tu:ɐ] *f* (-; -*en*) structure, pattern
Strumpf [ʃtrʊmpf] *m* (-[*e*]*s*; *Strümpfe* ['ʃtrʏmpfə]) stocking
'Strumpfhose *f* pantyhose, *Br* tights
struppig ['ʃtrʊpɪç] *adj* shaggy
Stück [ʃtʏk] *n* (-[*e*]*s*; -*e*) piece; part; lump; AGR head (*a. pl*); THEA play; ***2 Mark das Stück*** 2 marks each; ***im*** *or* ***am Stück*** in one piece; ***in Stücke schlagen*** (***reißen***) smash (tear) to pieces
'stückweise *adv* bit by bit (*a. fig*); ECON by the piece
Student [ʃtu'dɛnt] *m* (-*en*; -*en*), **Stu'dentin** *f* (-; -*nen*) student
Studie ['ʃtu:djə] *f* (-; -*n*) study (***über*** *acc* of)
'Studienplatz *m* university *or* college place
studieren [ʃtu'di:rən] *v/t and v/i* (*no -ge-*, *h*) study, be a student (of) (***an*** *dat* at)
Studium ['ʃtu:djʊm] *n* (-*s*; -*ien*) studies; ***das Studium der Medizin*** *etc* the study of medicine etc
Stufe ['ʃtu:fə] *f* (-; -*n*) step; level; stage
'Stufenbarren *m* SPORT uneven parallel bars
Stuhl [ʃtu:l] *m* (-[*e*]*s*; *Stühle* ['ʃty:lə]) chair; MED stool
Stuhlgang *m* (-[*e*]*s*; *no pl*) MED (bowel) movement
Stuhllehne *f* back of a chair
stülpen ['ʃtʏlpən] *v/t* (*ge-*, *h*) put (***auf*** *acc*, ***über*** *acc* over, on)
stumm [ʃtʊm] *adj* dumb, mute; *fig* silent
Stummel ['ʃtʊməl] *m* (-*s*; -) stub, stump, butt
'Stummfilm *m* silent film
Stümper ['ʃtʏmpɐ] F *m* (-*s*; -) bungler
stumpf [ʃtʊmpf] *adj* blunt, dull (*a. fig*)
Stumpf *m* (-[*e*]*s*; *Stümpfe* ['ʃtʏmpfə]) stump, stub
'stumpfsinnig *adj* dull; monotonous
Stunde ['ʃtʊndə] *f* (-; -*n*) hour; PED class, lesson; period
'Stundenkilo,meter *m* kilometer (*Br* kilometre) per hour
'stundenlang **1.** *adj*: ***nach stundenlangem Warten*** after hours of waiting; **2.** *adv* for hours (and hours)
'Stundenlohn *m* hourly wage
Stundenplan *m* schedule, *Br* timetable
'stundenweise *adv* by the hour
'Stundenzeiger *m* hour hand

stündlich [ˈʃtʏntlɪç] **1.** *adj* hourly; **2.** *adv* hourly, every hour
Stupsnase [ˈʃtʊps-] F *f* snub nose
stur [ʃtuːɐ] F *adj* pigheaded
Sturm [ʃtʊrm] *m* (-[*e*]*s*; *Stürme* [ˈʃtʏrmə]) storm (*a. fig*)
stürmen [ˈʃtʏrmən] *v/t* (*ge-, h*) *and v/i* (*ge-, sein*) storm; SPORT attack; rush
Stürmer(in) [ˈʃtʏrmɐ (-mərɪn)] (-*s*; -/-; -*nen*) SPORT forward; *esp soccer*: striker
stürmisch [ˈʃtʏrmɪʃ] *adj* stormy; *fig* wild, vehement
Sturz [ʃtʊrts] *m* (-*es*; *Stürze* [ˈʃtʏrtsə]) fall (*a. fig*); POL etc: overthrow
stürzen [ˈʃtʏrtsən] **1.** *v/i* (*ge-, sein*) fall; crash; rush, dash; ***schwer stürzen*** have a bad fall; **2.** *v/t* (*ge-, h*) throw; POL etc: overthrow; ***j-n ins Unglück stürzen*** ruin s.o.; ***sich stürzen aus*** throw o.s. out of; ***sich stürzen auf*** (*acc*) throw o.s. at
ˈ**Sturzflug** *m* AVIAT nosedive
ˈ**Sturzhelm** *m* crash helmet
Stute [ˈʃtuːtə] *f* (-; -*n*) ZO mare
Stütze [ˈʃtʏtsə] *f* (-; -*n*) support, prop; *fig a.* aid
stutzen [ˈʃtʊtsən] (*ge-, h*) **1.** *v/t* trim, clip; **2.** *v/i* stop short; (begin to) wonder
stützen [ˈʃtʏtsən] *v/t* (*ge-, h*) support (*a. fig*); ***sich stützen auf*** (*acc*) lean on; *fig* be based on
ˈ**Stützpfeiler** *m* ARCH supporting column
Stützpunkt *m* MIL base (*a. fig*)
Styropor® [ʃtyroˈpoːɐ] *n* (-*s*; *no pl*) Styrofoam®, *Br* polystyrene
s. u. ABBR *of* ***siehe unten*** see below
Subjekt [zʊpˈjɛkt] *n* (-[*e*]*s*; -*e*) LING subject; *contp* character
subjektiv [zʊpjɛkˈtiːf] *adj* subjective
Substantiv [ˈzʊpstantiːf] *n* (-*s*; -*e*) LING noun
Substanz [zʊpˈstants] *f* (-; -*en*) substance (*a. fig*)
subtrahieren [zʊptraˈhiːrən] *v/t* (*no -ge-, h*) MATH subtract
Subtraktion [zʊptrakˈtsjoːn] *f* (-; -*en*) MATH subtraction
subventionieren [zʊpvɛntsjoˈniːrən] *v/t* (*no -ge-, h*) subsidize
Suche [ˈzuːxə] *f* (-; *no pl*) search (***nach*** for); ***auf der Suche nach*** in search of
ˈ**suchen** *v/t and v/i* (*ge-, h*) look for; search for; ***gesucht: …*** wanted: …; ***was hat er hier zu suchen?*** what's he doing here?; ***er hat hier nichts zu suchen*** he has no business to be here
Sucher [ˈzuːxɐ] *m* (-*s*; -) PHOT viewfinder
Sucht [zʊxt] *f* (-; *Süchte* [ˈzʏçtə]) addiction (***nach*** to); mania (for)
süchtig [ˈzʏçtɪç] *adj*: ***süchtig sein*** be addicted to *drugs etc*, be a *drug etc* addict
Süchtige [ˈzʏçtɪgə] *m, f* (-*n*; -*n*) addict
Süden [ˈzyːdən] *m* (-*s*; *no pl*) south; ***nach Süden*** south(wards)
Südfrüchte [ˈzyːt-] *pl* tropical *or* southern fruits
ˈ**südlich** **1.** *adj* south(ern); southerly; **2.** *adv*: ***südlich von*** (to the) south of
Südˈosten *m* southeast
südˈöstlich *adj* southeast(ern); southeasterly
ˈ**Südpol** *m* South Pole
ˈ**südwärts** [-vɛrts] *adv* southward(s)
Südˈwesten *m* southwest
südˈwestlich *adj* southwest(ern); southwesterly
ˈ**Südwind** *m* south wind
Sülze [ˈzʏltsə] *f* (-; -*n*) GASTR jellied meat
Summe [ˈzʊmə] *f* (-; -*n*) sum (*a. fig*); amount; (sum) total
summen [ˈzʊmən] *v/i and v/t* (*ge-, h*) buzz, hum
summieren [zʊˈmiːrən] *v/refl* (*no -ge-, h*) add up (***auf*** *acc* to)
Sumpf [zʊmpf] *m* (-*es*; *Sümpfe* [ˈzʏmpfə]) swamp, bog
ˈ**sumpfig** *adj* swampy, marshy
Sünde [ˈzʏndə] *f* (-; -*n*) sin (*a. fig*)
ˈ**Sündenbock** F *m* scapegoat
Sünder [ˈzʏndɐ] *m* (-*s*; -), ˈ**Sünderin** *f* (-; -*nen*) sinner
sündig [ˈzʏndɪç] *adj* sinful
sündigen [ˈzʏndɪgən] *v/i* (*ge-, h*) (commit a) sin
Super… [ˈzuːpɐ-] *in cpds …macht etc*: *mst* super…
ˈ**Super** *n* (-*s*; *no pl*), **Superbenˌzin** *n* super *or* premium (gasoline), *Br* four-star (petrol)
Superlativ [ˈzuːpɐlatiːf] *m* (-*s*; -*e*) LING superlative (*a. fig*)
ˈ**Supermarkt** *m* supermarket
Suppe [ˈzʊpə] *f* (-; -*n*) soup
ˈ**Suppen…** *in cpds …löffel, …teller, …küche etc*: soup …
Surfbrett [ˈzøːɐf-] *n* sail board; surfboard
ˈ**surfen** *v/i* (*ge-, h*) go surfing
surren [ˈzʊrən] *v/i* (*ge-, h*) whirr; buzz
süß [zyːs] *adj* sweet, sugary (*both a. fig*)
Süße [ˈzyːsə] *f* (-; *no pl*) sweetness
ˈ**süßen** *v/t* (*ge-, h*) sweeten
Süßigkeiten [ˈzyːsɪçkaitən] *pl* sweets, candy
ˈ**süßlich** *adj* sweetish; *contp* mawkish, sugary
ˈ**süßˈsauer** *adj* GASTR sweet-and-sour
ˈ**Süßstoff** *m* sweetener
ˈ**Süßwasser** *n* fresh water
Symbol [zymˈboːl] *n* (-*s*; -*e*) symbol

Symbolik [zʏm'boːlɪk] *f* (-; *no pl*) symbolism
sym'bolisch *adj* symbolic(al)
Symmetrie [zʏme'triː] *f* (-; *-n*) symmetry
symmetrisch [zʏ'meːtrɪʃ] *adj* symmetric(al)
Sympathie [zʏmpa'tiː] *f* (-; *-n*) liking (***für*** for); sympathy
Sympathisant(in) [zʏmpati'zant(ɪn)] (*-en*; *-en*/-; *-nen*) sympathizer
sympathisch [zʏm'paːtɪʃ] *adj* nice, likable; ***er ist mir sympathisch*** I like him
Symphonie [zʏmfo'niː] *f* (-; *-n*) *etc* → ***Sinfonie***
Symptom [zʏmp'toːm] *n* (*-s*; *-e*) symptom
Synagoge [zyna'goːgə] *f* (-; *-n*) synagogue
synchron [zʏn'kroːn] *adj* TECH synchronous
synchronisieren [zʏnkroni'ziːrən] *v/t* (*no -ge-, h*) synchronize; *film etc*: dub
synonym [zyno'nyːm] *adj* synonymous
Syno'nym *n* (*-s*; *-e*) synonym
Synthese [zʏn'teːzə] *f* (-; *-n*) synthesis
synthetisch [zʏn'teːtɪʃ] *adj* synthetic
System [zʏs'teːm] *n* (*-s*; *-e*) system
systematisch [zʏste'maːtɪʃ] *adj* systematic, methodical
Sys'temfehler *m* EDP system error
Szene ['stseːnə] *f* (-; *-n*) scene (*a. fig*)
Szenerie [stsenə'riː] *f* (-; *-n*) scenery; setting

T

Tabak ['taːbak] *m* (*-s*; *-e*) tobacco
Tabakgeschäft *n* tobacconist's
Tabakwaren *pl* tobacco products
Tabelle [ta'bɛlə] *f* (-; *-n*) table (*a.* MATH, SPORT)
Ta'bellenkalkulati,on *f* EDP spreadsheet
Tabellenplatz *m* SPORT position
Tablett [ta'blɛt] *n* (*-[e]s*; *-s*) tray
Tablette [ta'blɛtə] *f* (-; *-n*) tablet
tabu [ta'buː] *adj*, **Ta'bu** *n* (*-s*; *-s*) taboo
Tabulator [tabu'laːtoːɐ] *m* (*-s*; *-en* [-la'toːrən]) tabulator
Tachometer [taxo'meːtɐ] *m*, *n* (*-s*; -) MOT speedometer
Tadel ['taːdəl] *m* (*-s*; -) blame; censure, reproof, rebuke
'tadellos *adj* faultless; blameless; excellent; perfect
'tadeln *v/t* (*ge-, h*) criticize, blame; censure, reprove, rebuke (*all*: ***wegen*** for)
Tafel ['taːfəl] *f* PED *etc*: blackboard; (bulletin, *esp Br* notice) board; sign; tablet, plaque; GASTR bar (*of chocolate*)
täfeln ['tɛːfəln] *v/t* (*ge-, h*) panel
'Täfelung *f* (-; *-en*) panel(l)ing
Taft [taft] *m* (*-[e]s*; *-e*) taffeta
Tag [taːk] *m* (*-[e]s*; *-e* ['taːgə]) day; daylight; ***welchen Tag haben wir heute?*** what day is it today?; ***heute*** (***morgen***) ***in 14 Tagen*** two weeks from today (tomorrow); ***e-s Tages*** one day; ***den ganzen Tag*** all day; ***am Tage*** during the day; ***Tag und Nacht*** night and day; ***am helllichten Tag*** in broad daylight; ***ein freier Tag*** a day off; ***guten Tag!*** hello!, hi!; how do you do?; (***j-m***) ***guten Tag sagen*** say hello (to s.o.); F ***sie hat ihre Tage*** she has her period; ***unter Tage*** underground; → ***zutage***
Tagebau ['taːgə-] *m* (*-[e]s*; *-e*) opencast mining
Tagebuch *n* diary; ***Tagebuch führen*** keep a diary
'tagelang *adv* for days
'tagen *v/i* (*ge-, h*) meet, hold a meeting; JUR be in session
'Tagesanbruch *m*: ***bei Tagesanbruch*** at daybreak, at dawn
Tagesgespräch *n* talk of the day
Tageskarte *f* day ticket; GASTR menu for the day
Tageslicht *n* (*-[e]s*; *no pl*) daylight
Tagesmutter *f* childminder
Tagesordnung *f* agenda
Tagesstätte *f* day care center (*Br* centre)
Tagestour *f* day trip
Tageszeit *f* time of day; ***zu jeder Tageszeit*** at any hour
Tageszeitung *f* daily (paper)
'tageweise *adv* by the day
täglich ['tɛːklɪç] *adj and adv* daily
'Tagschicht *f* ECON day shift
'tagsüber *adv* during the day
'Tagung *f* (-; *-en*) conference
Taille ['taljə] *f* (-; *-n*) waist; waistline
tailliert [ta'jiːɐt] *adj* waisted, tapered

T

Takelage [takə'laːʒə] *f* (-; -*n*) MAR rigging
Takt [takt] *m* (-[*e*]*s*; -*e*) a) (*no pl*) MUS time, measure, beat, b) MUS bar, c) MOT stroke, d) (*no pl*) tact; ***den Takt halten*** MUS keep time
Taktik ['taktɪk] *f* (-; -*en*) MIL tactics (*a. fig*)
'taktisch *adj* tactical
'taktlos *adj* tactless
'Taktstock *m* MUS baton
'Taktstrich *m* MUS bar
'taktvoll *adj* tactful
Tal [taːl] *n* (-[*e*]*s*; *Täler* ['tɛːlɐ]) valley
Talar [ta'laːɐ] *m* (-*s*; -*e*) robe, gown
Talent [ta'lɛnt] *n* (-[*e*]*s*; -*e*) talent (*a. person*), gift
talentiert [talɛn'tiːɐt] *adj* talented, gifted
Talg [talk] *m* (-[*e*]*s*; -*e*) tallow; GASTR suet
Talisman ['taːlɪsman] *m* (-*s*; -*e*) talisman, charm
Talkmaster ['tɔːk-] *m* (-*s*; -) TV talk (*Br* chat) show host
Talkshow [-ʃoʊ] *f* (-; -*s*) TV talk (*Br* chat) show
'Talsperre *f* dam, barrage
Tampon ['tampɔn] *m* (-*s*; -*s*) tampon
Tandler ['tandlɐ] *Austrian m* (-*s*; -) second-hand dealer
Tang [taŋ] *m* (-[*e*]*s*; -*e*) BOT seaweed
Tank [taŋk] *m* (-*s*; -*s*) tank
tanken ['taŋkən] *v/t* (*ge-*, *h*) get some gasoline (*Br* petrol), fill up
Tanker ['taŋkɐ] *m* (-*s*; -) MAR tanker
'Tankstelle *f* filling (*or* gas, *Br* petrol) station
'Tankwart *m* (-[*e*]*s*; -*e*) gas station (*Br* petrol pump) attendant
Tanne ['tanə] *f* (-; -*n*) BOT fir (tree)
'Tannenbaum *m* Christmas tree
'Tannenzapfen *m* BOT fir cone
Tante ['tantə] *f* (-; -*n*) aunt; ***Tante Lindy*** Aunt Lindy
Tante-Emma-Laden F *m* mom-and-pop store, *Br* corner shop
Tantiemen [tã'tjeːmən] *pl* royalties
Tanz [tants] *m* (-*es*; *Tänze* ['tɛntsə]), **tanzen** ['tantsən] *v/i* (*ge-*, *h*, *sein*) *and v/t* (*ge-*, *h*) dance
Tänzer ['tɛntsɐ] *m* (-*s*; -), **Tänzerin** ['tɛntsərɪn] *f* (-; -*nen*) dancer
'Tanzfläche *f* dance floor
Tanzkurs *m* dancing lessons
Tanzmu,sik *f* dance music
Tanzschule *f* dancing school
Tapete [ta'peːtə] *f* (-; -*n*), **tapezieren** [tape'tsiːrən] *v/t* (*no -ge-*, *h*) wallpaper
tapfer ['tapfɐ] *adj* brave; courageous
'Tapferkeit *f* (-; *no pl*) bravery; courage
Tarif [ta'riːf] *m* (-[*e*]*s*; -*e*) rate(s), tariff; (wage) scale
Tariflohn *m* standard wage(s)
Tarifverhandlungen *pl* wage negotiations, collective bargaining
tarnen ['tarnən] *v/t* (*ge-*, *h*) camouflage; *fig* disguise
'Tarnung *f* (-; -*en*) camouflage
Tasche ['taʃə] *f* (-; -*n*) bag; pocket
'Taschenbuch *n* paperback
Taschendieb *m* pickpocket
Taschengeld *n* allowance, *Br* pocket money
Taschenlampe *f* flashlight, *Br* torch
Taschenmesser *n* penknife, pocketknife
Taschenrechner *m* pocket calculator
Taschenschirm *m* telescopic umbrella
Taschentuch *n* handkerchief, F hankie
Taschenuhr *f* pocket watch
Tasse ['tasə] *f* (-; -*n*) cup; ***e-e Tasse Tee*** *etc* a cup of tea *etc*
Tastatur [tasta'tuːɐ] *f* (-; -*en*) keyboard, keys
Taste ['tastə] *f* (-; -*n*) key
tasten ['tastən] (*ge-*, *h*) **1.** *v/i* grope (***nach*** for), feel (for); fumble (for); **2.** *v/t* touch, feel; ***sich tasten*** feel *or* grope (*a. fig*) one's way
'Tastentele,fon *n* push-button phone
'Tastsinn *m* (-[*e*]*s*; *no pl*) sense of touch
tat [taːt] *pret of* ***tun***
Tat *f* (-; -*en*) act, deed; action; JUR offense, *Br* offence; ***j-n auf frischer Tat ertappen*** catch s.o. in the act
'tatenlos *adj* inactive, passive
Täter ['tɛːtɐ] *m* (-*s*; -), **'Täterin** *f* (-; -*nen*) culprit; JUR offender
tätig ['tɛːtɪç] *adj* active; busy; ***tätig sein bei*** be employed with; ***tätig werden*** act, take action
'Tätigkeit *f* (-; -*en*) activity; work; occupation, job; ***in Tätigkeit*** in action
'Tatkraft *f* (-; *no pl*) energy
'tatkräftig *adj* energetic, active
tätlich ['tɛːtlɪç] *adj* violent; ***tätlich werden gegen*** assault
'Tätlichkeiten *pl* (acts of) violence; JUR assault (and battery)
'Tatort *m* JUR scene of the crime
tätowieren [tɛto'viːrən] *v/t* (*no -ge-*, *h*), **Täto'wierung** *f* (-; -*en*) tattoo
'Tatsache *f* fact
'tatsächlich **1.** *adj* actual, real; **2.** *adv* actually, in fact; really
tätscheln ['tɛːtʃəln] *v/t* (*ge-*, *h*) pat, pet
Tatze ['tatsə] *f* (-; -*n*) ZO paw (*a. fig*)
Tau[1] [tau] *n* (-[*e*]*s*; -*e*) rope
Tau[2] *m* (-[*e*]*s*; *no pl*) dew
taub [taup] *adj* deaf (*fig* ***gegen*** to); numb, benumbed
Taube ['taubə] *f* (-; -*n*) ZO pigeon; *esp fig*

dove
'Taubenschlag *m* pigeonhouse
'Taubheit *f* (-; *no pl*) deafness; numbness
'taubstumm *adj* deaf-and-dumb
'Taubstumme *m, f* (-*n*; -*n*) deaf mute
tauchen ['tauxən] **1.** *v/i* (*ge-, h, sein*) dive (***nach*** for); SPORT skin-dive; *submarine*: *a.* submerge; stay underwater; **2.** *v/t* (*h*) dip (***in*** *acc* into); duck
Taucher ['tauxɐ] *m* (-*s*; -) (SPORT skin) diver
'Tauchsport *m* skin diving
tauen ['tauən] *v/i* (*ge-, sein*) *and v/t* (*ge-, h*) thaw, melt
Taufe ['taufə] *f* (-; -*n*) baptism, christening
'taufen *v/t* (*ge-, h*) baptize, christen
'Taufpate *m* godfather
'Taufpatin *f* godmother
'Taufschein *m* certificate of baptism
taugen ['taugən] *v/i* (*ge-, h*) be good *or* fit *or* of use *or* suited (*all*: ***zu, für*** for); ***nichts taugen*** be no good; F ***taugt es was?*** is it any good?
tauglich ['tauklɪç] *adj esp* MIL fit (for service)
Taumel ['tauməl] *m* (-*s*; *no pl*) dizziness; rapture, ecstasy
'taumelig *adj* dizzy
'taumeln *v/i* (*ge-, sein*) stagger, reel
Tausch [tauʃ] *m* (-[*e*]*s*; -*e*) exchange, F swap
tauschen ['tauʃən] *v/t* (*ge-, h*) exchange, F swap (*both*: ***gegen*** for); switch; change; ***ich möchte nicht mit ihm tauschen*** I wouldn't like to be in his shoes
täuschen ['tɔʏʃən] *v/t* (*ge-, h*) deceive, fool; delude; cheat; *a.* SPORT feint; ***sich täuschen*** deceive o.s.; be mistaken; ***sich täuschen lassen von*** be taken in by; ***täuschende Ähnlichkeit*** striking similarity
'Täuschung *f* (-; -*en*) deception; delusion; JUR deceit; *a.* PED cheating
tausend ['tauzənt] *adj* a thousand
'tausendst *adj* thousandth
'Tausendstel *n* (-*s*; -) thousandth (part)
'Tautropfen *m* dewdrop
'Tauwetter *n* thaw
'Tauziehen *n* (-*s*; *no pl*) SPORT tug-of-war (*a. fig*)
Taxi ['taksi] *n* (-*s*; -*s*) taxi(cab), cab
taxieren [ta'ksiːrən] *v/t* (*no -ge-, h*) rate, estimate (***auf*** *acc* at)
'Taxistand *m* cabstand, *esp Br* taxi rank
Technik ['tɛçnɪk] *f* (-; -*en*) a) (*no pl*) technology, engineering, b) technique (*a.* SPORT *etc*), MUS execution
Techniker ['tɛçnikɐ] *m* (-*s*; -), **'Technikerin** *f* (-; -*nen*) engineer; technician (*a.* SPORT *etc*)
technisch ['tɛçnɪʃ] *adj* technical; technological; ***technische Hochschule*** school *etc* of technology
Technologie [tɛçnolo'giː] *f* (-; -*n*) technology
technologisch [tɛçno'loːgɪʃ] *adj* technological
Tee [teː] *m* (-*s*; -*s*) tea; (***e-n***) ***Tee trinken*** have some tea; (***e-n***) ***Tee machen*** *or* ***kochen*** make some tea
Teebeutel *m* teabag
Teekanne *f* teapot
Teelöffel *m* teaspoon
Teer [teːɐ] *m* (-[*e*]*s*; -*e*), **teeren** ['teːrən] *v/t* (*ge-, h*) tar
'Teesieb *n* tea strainer
'Teetasse *f* teacup
Teich [taiç] *m* (-[*e*]*s*; -*e*) pool, pond
Teig [taik] *m* (-[*e*]*s*; -*e*) dough, paste
teigig ['taigɪç] *adj* doughy, pasty
'Teigwaren *pl* pasta
Teil [tail] *m, n* (-[*e*]*s*; -*e*) part; portion, share; component; ***zum Teil*** partly, in part
Teil… *in cpds …erfolg etc*: partial …
'teilbar *adj* divisible
'Teilchen *n* (-*s*; -) particle
teilen ['tailən] *v/t* (*ge-, h*) divide; share
'teilhaben *v/i* (*irr*, ***haben***, *sep*, *-ge-, h*) ***teilhaben an*** (*dat*) (have a) share in
'Teilhaber(in) [-haːbɐ (-bərɪn)] (-*s*; -/-; -*nen*) ECON partner
'Teilnahme [-naːmə] *f* (-; *no pl*) participation (***an*** *dat* in); *fig* interest (in); sympathy (for)
'teilnahmslos *adj* indifferent; *esp* MED apathetic
'Teilnahmslosigkeit *f* (-; *no pl*) indifference; apathy
'teilnehmen *v/i* (*irr*, ***nehmen***, *sep*, *-ge-, h*) ***teilnehmen an*** (*dat*) take part *or* participate in; share (in)
'Teilnehmer(in) [-neːmɐ (-mərɪn)] (-*s*; -/-; -*nen*) participant; UNIV student; SPORT competitor
teils *adv* partly
'Teilstrecke *f* stage, leg
'Teilung *f* (-; -*en*) division
'teilweise *adv* partly, in part
'Teilzahlung *f* → ***Abzahlung, Rate***
Teint [tɛ̃ː] *m* (-*s*; -*s*) complexion
Tel. ABBR *of* ***Telefon*** tel., telephone
Telefon [tele'foːn] *n* (-*s*; -*e*) telephone, phone; ***am Telefon*** on the (tele)phone; ***Telefon haben*** have a (*Br* be on the) (tele)phone; ***ans Telefon gehen*** answer the (tele)phone
Telefonanruf *m* (tele)phone call

Telefonanschluss *m* telephone connection
Telefonappa,rat *m* telephone, phone
Telefonat [telefo'na:t] *n* (-[*e*]*s*; -*e*) → ***Telefongespräch***
Tele'fonbuch *n* telephone directory, phone book
Telefongebühr *f* telephone charge
Telefongespräch *n* (tele)phone call
telefonieren [telefo'ni:rən] *v/i* (*no -ge-, h*) (tele)phone; be on the phone; ***mit j-m telefonieren*** talk to s.o. on the phone
telefonisch [tele'fo:nɪʃ] **1.** *adj* telephonic, telephone ...; **2.** *adv* by (tele)phone, over the (tele)phone
Telefonist [telefo'nɪst] *m* (-*en*; -*en*), **Telefo'nistin** *f* (-; -*nen*) (telephone) operator
Tele'fonkarte *f* phonecard
Telefonleitung *f* telephone line
Telefonnetz *n* telephone network
Telefonnummer *f* (tele)phone number
Telefonzelle *f* (tele)phone booth, *esp Br* (tele)phone box, *Br* call box
Telefonzen,trale *f* switchboard
telegrafieren [telegra'fi:rən] *v/t and v/i* (*no -ge-, h*) telegraph, wire; cable
telegrafisch [tele'gra:fɪʃ] *adj and adv* by telegraph, by wire, by cable
Telegramm [tele'gram] *n* (-*s*; -*e*) telegram, wire, cable(gram)
Teleobjektiv ['te:lə-] *n* telephoto lens
Telephon *n* → ***Telefon***
Teletext ['te:lə-] *m* teletext
Teller ['tɛlɐ] *m* (-*s*; -) plate
Tellerwäscher [-vɛʃɐ] *m* (-*s*; -) dishwasher
Tempel ['tɛmpəl] *m* (-*s*; -) temple
Temperament [tɛmpəra'mɛnt] *n* (-[*e*]*s*; -*e*) temper(ament); life, F pep
tempera'mentlos *adj* lifeless, dull
temperamentvoll *adj* full of life *or* F pep
Temperatur [tɛmpəra'tu:ɐ] *f* (-; -*en*) temperature; ***j-s Temperatur messen*** take s.o.'s temperature
Tempo ['tɛmpo] *n* (-*s*; -*s*, -*pi*) speed; MUS time; ***mit Tempo*** ... at a speed of ... an hour
Tendenz [tɛn'dɛnts] *f* (-; -*en*) tendency, trend; leaning
tendenziös [tɛndɛn'tsjø:s] *adj* tendentious
tendieren [tɛn'di:rən] *v/i* (*no -ge-, h*) tend (***zu*** towards; ***dazu, et. zu tun*** to do s.th.)
Tennis ['tɛnɪs] *n* (-; *no pl*) tennis
Tennisplatz *m* tennis court
Tennisschläger *m* tennis racket
Tennisspieler(in) tennis player
Tenor [te'no:ɐ] *m* (-*s*; *Tenöre* [te'nø:rə]) MUS tenor
Teppich ['tɛpɪç] *m* (-*s*; -*e*) carpet
'Teppichboden *m* fitted carpet, wall-to-wall carpeting
Termin [tɛr'mi:n] *m* (-*s*; -*e*) date; deadline; engagement; ***e-n Termin vereinbaren*** (***einhalten, absagen***) make (keep, cancel) an appointment
Terminal ['tø:ɐminəl] a) *m, n* (-*s*; -*s*) AVIAT terminal, b) *n* (-*s*; -*s*) EDP terminal
Terrasse [tɛ'rasə] *f* (-; -*n*) terrace
ter'rassenförmig [-fœrmɪç] *adj* terraced, in terraces
Terrine [tɛ'ri:nə] *f* (-; -*n*) tureen
Territorium [tɛri'to:rjʊm] *n* (-*s*; -*ien*) territory
Terror ['tɛro:ɐ] *m* (-*s*; *no pl*) terror
terrorisieren [tɛrori'zi:rən] *v/t* (*no -ge-, h*) terrorize
Terrorismus [tɛro'rɪsmʊs] *m* (-; *no pl*) terrorism
Terrorist(in) [-'rɪst(ɪn)] (-*en*; -*en*/-; -*nen*), **terro'ristisch** *adj* terrorist
Testament [tɛsta'mɛnt] *n* (-[*e*]*s*; -*e*) (last) will; JUR last will and testament
testamentarisch [tɛstamɛn'ta:rɪʃ] *adv* by will
Testa'mentsvollstrecker *m* executor
Testbild ['tɛst-] *n* TV test card
testen ['tɛstən] *v/t* (*no -ge-, h*) test
'Testpi,lot *m* test pilot
Tetanus ['te:tanʊs] *m* (-; *no pl*) MED tetanus
teuer ['tɔʏɐ] *adj* expensive; ***wie teuer ist es?*** how much is it?
Teufel ['tɔʏfəl] *m* (-*s*; -) devil (*a. fig*); ***wer*** (***wo, was***) ***zum Teufel ...?*** who (where, what) the hell ...?
'Teufelskerl F *m* devil of a fellow
'Teufelskreis *m* vicious circle
teuflisch ['tɔʏflɪʃ] *adj* devilish, diabolic(al)
Text [tɛkst] *m* (-[*e*]*s*; -*e*) text; MUS words, lyrics
Texter ['tɛkstɐ] *m* (-*s*; -), **'Texterin** *f* (-; -*nen*) MUS songwriter
Textil... [tɛks'ti:l-] *in cpds* textile ...
Textilien [tɛks'ti:ljən] *pl* textiles
'Textverarbeitung *f* EDP word processing
'Textverarbeitungsgerät *n* EDP word processor
Theater [te'a:tɐ] *n* (-*s*; -) theater, *Br* theatre; F ***Theater machen*** (***um***) make a fuss (about)
Theaterbesucher *m* theatergoer, *Br* theatregoer
Theaterkarte *f* theater (*Br* theatre) ticket
Theaterkasse *f* box office
Theaterstück *n* play
Thema ['te:ma] *n* (-*s*; *Themen*) subject, topic; MUS theme; ***das Thema wechseln***

change the subject
Theologe [teo'lo:gə] *m* (*-n*; *-n*) theologian
Theologie [teolo'gi:] *f* (*-*; *-n*) theology
Theo'login *f* (*-*; *-nen*) theologian
theo'logisch *adj* theological
Theoretiker [teo're:tikɐ] *m* (*-s*; *-*) theorist
theo'retisch *adj* theoretical
Theorie [teo'ri:] *f* (*-*; *-n*) theory
Therapeut [tera'pɔʏt] *m* (*-en*; *-en*), **The'ra'peutin** *f* (*-*; *-nen*) therapist
Therapie [-'pi:] *f* (*-*; *-n*) therapy
Thermometer [tɛrmo'me:tɐ] *n* (*-s*; *-*) thermometer
Thermosflasche® ['tɛrmɔs-] *f* thermos®
These ['te:zə] *f* (*-*; *-n*) thesis
Thon [to:n] *Swiss m* (*-s*; *-s*) tuna (fish)
Thrombose [trɔm'bo:zə] *f* (*-*; *-n*) MED thrombosis
Thron [tro:n] *m* (*-[e]s*; *-e*) throne
'Thronfolger [-fɔlgɐ] *m* (*-s*; *-*), **'Thronfolgerin** [-fɔlgərɪn] *f* (*-*; *-nen*) successor to the throne
Thunfisch ['tu:n-] *m* tuna (fish)
Tick [tɪk] F *m* (*-[e]s*; *-s*) quirk
ticken ['tɪkən] *v/i* (*ge-*, *h*) tick
Tiebreak, Tie-Break ['taɪbreɪk] *m*, *n tennis*: tiebreak(er)
tief [ti:f] *adj* deep (*a. fig*); low
Tief *n* (*-s*; *-s*) METEOR depression (*a.* PSYCH, ECON), low (*a. fig*)
Tiefe ['ti:fə] *f* (*-*; *-n*) depth (*a. fig*)
'Tiefebene *f* lowland(s)
Tiefflieger *m* low-flying air plane
Tiefgang *m* MAR draft, *Br* draught; *fig* depth
Tiefga,rage *f* parking *or* underground garage, *Br* underground car park
'tiefgekühlt *adj* deep-frozen
'Tiefkühlfach *n* freezing compartment
Tiefkühlschrank *m*, **Tiefkühltruhe** *f* freezer, deep-freeze
Tiefkühlkost *f* frozen foods
Tier [ti:ɐ] *n* (*-[e]s*; *-e*) animal; F ***hohes Tier*** bigwig, big shot
Tierarzt *m*, **-ärztin** *f* veterinarian, *Br* veterinary surgeon, F vet
Tierfreund *m* animal lover
Tiergarten *m* → ***Zoo***
Tierheim *n* animal shelter
tierisch ['ti:rɪʃ] *adj* animal; *fig* bestial, brutish
'Tierkreis *m* ASTR zodiac
Tierkreiszeichen *n* sign of the zodiac
'Tiermedi,zin *f* veterinary medicine
Tierquäle'rei *f* cruelty to animals
'Tierreich *n* animal kingdom
Tierschutz *m* protection of animals
Tierschutzverein *m* society for the prevention of cruelty to animals
Tierversuch *m* MED experiment with animals
Tiger ['ti:gɐ] *m* (*-s*; *-*) zo tiger
Tigerin ['ti:gərɪn] *f* (*-*; *-nen*) zo tigress
tilgen ['tɪlgən] *v/t* (*ge-*, *h*) ECON pay off
Tinte ['tɪntə] *f* (*-*; *-n*) ink
'Tintenfisch *m* zo squid
Tipp [tɪp] *m* (*-s*; *-s*) hint, tip; tip-off; ***j-m e-n Tipp geben*** tip s.o. off
tippen ['tɪpən] *v/i and v/t* (*ge-*, *h*) tap; type; F guess; do *lotto etc*
Tisch [tɪʃ] *m* (*-[e]s*; *-e*) table; ***am Tisch sitzen*** sit at the table; ***bei Tisch*** at table; ***den Tisch decken*** (***abräumen***) lay (clear) the table
Tischdecke *f* tablecloth
Tischgebet *n* REL grace: ***das Tischgebet sprechen*** say grace
Tischler ['tɪʃlɐ] *m* (*-s*; *-*) joiner; cabinet-marker
'Tischplatte *f* tabletop
Tischrechner *m* desktop computer
Tischtennis *n* table tennis
Tischtuch *n* tablecloth
Titel ['ti:təl] *m* (*-s*; *-*) title
Titelbild *n* cover picture
Titelblatt *n*, **Titelseite** *f* title page; cover, front page
Toast [to:st] *m* (*-[e]s*; *-s*), **toasten** ['to:stən] *v/t* (*ge-*, *h*) toast
toben ['to:bən] *v/i* (*ge-*, *h*) rage (*a. fig*); romp
tobsüchtig ['to:p-] *adj* raving mad
'Tobsuchtsanfall *m* tantrum
Tochter ['tɔxtɐ] *f* (*-*; *Töchter* ['tœçtɐ]) daughter
Tochtergesellschaft *f* ECON subsidiary (company)
Tod [to:t] *m* (*-[e]s*; *no pl*) death (*a. fig*) (***durch*** from)
tod... *in cpds ...ernst*, *...müde*, *...sicher*: dead ...
Todesängste ['to:dəs-] *pl*: ***Todesängste ausstehen*** be scared to death
Todesanzeige *f* obituary (notice)
Todesfall *m* (case of) death
Todeskampf *m* agony
Todesopfer *n* casualty
Todesstrafe *f* JUR capital punishment; death penalty
Todesursache *f* cause of death
Todesurteil *n* JUR death sentence
'Todfeind *m* deadly enemy
'tod'krank *adj* mortally ill
tödlich ['tø:tlɪç] *adj* fatal; deadly; *esp fig* mortal
'Todsünde *f* mortal *or* deadly sin
Toilette [toa'lɛtə] *f* (*-*; *-n*) bathroom, *Br* toilet, lavatory; *pl* rest rooms, *Br* ladies'

T

or men's rooms
Toi'letten... *in cpds ...papier, ...seife etc*: toilet ...
Toilettentisch *m* dressing table
tolerant [tole'rant] *adj* tolerant (***gegen*** of, towards)
Toleranz [tole'rants *f* (-; *-en*) tolerance (*a.* TECH)
tolerieren [tole'ri:rən] *v/t* (*no -ge-, h*) tolerate
toll [tɔl] *adj* wild; F great, fantastic
'tollkühn *adj* daredevil
'Tollwut *f* VET rabies
'tollwütig [-vy:tɪç] *adj* VET rabid
Tomate [to'ma:tə] *f* (-; *-n*) BOT tomato
Ton[1] [to:n] *m* (-[*e*]*s*; *-e*) clay
Ton[2] *m* (-[*e*]*s*; *Töne* ['tø:nə]) tone (*a.* MUS, PAINT), PAINT *a.* shade; sound (*a.* TV, *film*); note; stress; ***kein Ton*** not a word
Tonabnehmer *m* ELECTR pickup
Tonart *f* MUS key
Tonband *n* (-[*e*]*s*; *-bänder*) (recording) tape
Tonbandgerät *n* tape recorder
tönen ['tø:nən] (*ge-, h*) **1.** *v/i* sound, ring; **2.** *v/t* tinge, tint, shade
'Tonfall *m* tone (of voice); accent
Tonfilm *m* sound film
Tonkopf *m* ELECTR (magnetic) head
Tonlage *f* MUS pitch
Tonleiter *f* MUS scale
Tonne ['tɔnə] *f* (-; *-n*) barrel; (metric) ton
'Tontechniker *m* sound engineer
'Tönung *f* (-; *-en*) tint, tinge, shade
Topf [tɔpf] *m* (-[*e*]*s*; *Töpfe* ['tœpfə]) pot; saucepan
Topfen ['tɔpfən] *Austrian m* (*-s; no pl*) GASTR curd(s)
Töpfer ['tœpfɐ] *m* (*-s*; -) potter
Töpferei [tœpfə'rai] *f* (-; *-en*) pottery
'Töpferin *f* (-; *-nen*) potter
'Töpferscheibe *f* potter's wheel
'Töpferware *f* pottery, earthenware
Tor [to:ɐ] *n* (-[*e*]*s*; *-e*) gate; *soccer etc*: goal; ***ein Tor schießen*** score (a goal); ***im Tor stehen*** keep goal
Torf [tɔrf] *m* (-[*e*]*s*; *-e*) peat
'Torfmull *m* peat dust
'Torhüter [-hy:tɐ] *m* → ***Torwart***
torkeln ['tɔrkəln] F *v/i* (*ge-, h, sein*) reel, stagger
'Torlatte *f* SPORT crossbar
'Torlinie *f* SPORT goal line
torpedieren [tɔrpe'di:rən] *v/t* (*no -ge-, h*) MIL torpedo (*a. fig*)
'Torpfosten *m* SPORT goalpost
Torraum *m* SPORT goalmouth
Torschuss *m* SPORT shot at goal
Torschütze *m* SPORT scorer
Torte ['tɔrtə] *f* (-; *-n*) pie, *esp Br* flan; cream cake, gateau
'Torwart [-vart] *m* (-[*e*]*s*; *-e*) SPORT goalkeeper, F goalie
tosen ['to:zən] *v/i* (*ge-, h*) roar; thunder
tosend *adj* thunderous (*applause*)
tot [to:t] *adj* dead (*a. fig*); late; ***tot geboren*** MED stillborn; ***tot umfallen*** drop dead
total [to'ta:l] *adj* total, complete
totalitär [totali'tɛ:ɐ] *adj* POL totalitarian
'Tote *m, f* (*-n; -n*) dead man *or* woman; (dead) body, corpse; *mst pl* casualty; *pl the* dead
töten ['tø:tən] *v/t* (*ge-, h*) kill
'Totenbett *n* deathbed
'toten'blass *adj* deadly pale
'Totengräber [-grɛ:bɐ] *m* (*-s*; -) gravedigger
Totenkopf *m* skull; skull and crossbones
Totenmaske *f* death mask
Totenmesse *f* REL mass for the dead, requiem (*a.* MUS)
Totenschädel *m* skull
Totenschein *m* death certificate
'toten'still *adj* deathly still
'totlachen F *v/refl* (*sep, -ge-, h*) kill o.s. laughing
Toto ['to:to] *m*, F *n* (*-s; -s*) football pools
'Totschlag *m* (-[*e*]*s*; *no pl*) JUR manslaughter
'totschlagen *v/t* (*irr*, ***schlagen***, *sep, -ge-, h*) kill; ***j-n totschlagen*** beat s.o. to death; ***die Zeit totschlagen*** kill time
'totschweigen *v/t* (*irr*, ***schweigen***, *sep, -ge-, h*) hush up
Toupet [tu'pe:] *n* (*-s; -s*) toupee
toupieren [tu'pi:rən] *v/t* (*no -ge-, h*) *Br* backcomb
Tour [tu:ɐ] *f* (-; *-en*) tour (***durch*** of), trip; excursion; TECH turn, revolution; ***auf Touren kommen*** MOT pick up speed; F ***krumme Touren*** underhand methods
Touren... ['tu:rən-] *in cpds ...rad etc*: touring ...
Tourismus [tu'rɪsmʊs] *m* (-; *no pl*) tourism
Tourismusgeschäft *n* tourist industry
Tourist [tu'rɪst] *m* (*-en; -en*), **Tou'ristin** *f* (-; *-nen*) tourist
tou'ristisch *adj* touristic
Tournee [tʊr'ne:] *f* (-; *-s, -n*) tour; ***auf Tournee gehen*** go on tour
Trab [tra:p] *m* (-[*e*]*s*; *no pl*) trot
Trabant [tra'bant] *m* (*-en; -en*) ASTR satellite
Tra'bantenstadt *f* satellite town
traben ['tra:bən] *v/i* (*ge-, sein*) trot
Traber ['tra:bɐ] *m* (*-s*; -) ZO trotter

T

'**Trabrennen** *n* trotting race
Tracht [traxt] *f* (-; *-en*) costume; uniform; dress; F ***e-e Tracht Prügel*** a thrashing
trächtig ['trɛçtɪç] *adj* zo with young, pregnant
Tradition [tradi'tsjoːn] *f* (-; *-en*) tradition
traditionell [traditsjo'nɛl] *adj* traditional
traf [traːf] *pret of* ***treffen***
Trafik [tra'fɪk] *Austrian f* (-; *-en*) → ***Tabakgeschäft***
Trafikant [trafi'kant] *Austrian m* (*-en*; *-en*) tobacconist
Tragbahre ['traːk-] *f* stretcher
'**tragbar** *adj* portable; wearable; *fig* bearable; *person*: acceptable
Trage ['traːgə] *f* (-; *-n*) stretcher
träge ['trɛːgə] *adj* lazy, indolent; PHYS inert (*a. fig*)
tragen [traːgən] (*irr*, *ge-*, *h*) **1.** *v/t* carry; wear; *fig* bear; ***sich gut tragen*** wear well; **2.** *v/i* BOT bear fruit; *fig* hold
tragend *adj* ARCH supporting; THEA leading
Träger ['trɛːgɐ] *m* (*-s*; -) carrier; porter; (shoulder) strap; TECH support; ARCH girder; *fig* bearer
'**trägerlos** *adj* strapless
'**Tragetasche** *f* carrier bag; carrycot
'**tragfähig** *adj* load-bearing; *fig* sound
'**Tragfläche** *f* AVIAT wing
Trägheit ['trɛːkhait] *f* (-; *no pl*) laziness, indolence; PHYS inertia (*a. fig*)
Tragik ['traːgɪk] *f* (-; *no pl*) tragedy
tragisch ['traːgɪʃ] *adj* tragic
Tragödie [tra'gøːdjə] *f* (-; *-n*) tragedy
'**Tragriemen** *m* strap; sling
'**Tragweite** *f* range; *fig* significance
Trainer ['trɛːnɐ] *m* (*-s*; -), '**Trainerin** *f* (-; *-nen*) SPORT trainer, coach
trainieren [trɛ'niːrən] *v/i and v/t* (*no -ge-*, *h*) SPORT train, coach
'**Training** *n* (*-s*; *-s*) training
'**Trainingsanzug** *m* track suit
Traktor ['traktoːɐ] *m* (*-s*; *-en* [trak'toːrən]) MOT tractor
trällern ['trɛlɐn] *v/t and v/i* (*ge-*, *h*) warble, trill
Tram [tram] *Austrian f* (-; *-s*), *Swiss n* (*-s*; *-s*) streetcar, *Br* tram
trampeln ['trampəln] *v/i* (*ge-*, *h*) trample, stamp
'**Trampelpfad** *m* beaten track
trampen ['trɛmpən] *v/i* (*ge-*, *sein*) hitchhike
Tramper(in) ['trɛmpɐ (-pərɪn)] (*-s*; *-/-*; *-nen*) hitchhiker
Träne ['trɛːnə] *f* (-; *-n*) tear; ***in Tränen ausbrechen*** burst into tears
'**tränen** *v/i* (*ge-*, *h*) water
'**Tränengas** *n* tear gas
trank [traŋk] *pret of* ***trinken***
Tränke ['trɛŋkə] *f* (-; *-n*) watering place
'**tränken** *v/t* (*ge-*, *h*) zo water; soak, drench
Transfer [trans'feːɐ] *m* (*-s*; *-s*) transfer (*a.* SPORT)
Transformator [transfɔr'maːtoːɐ] *m* (*-s*; *-en* [-ma'toːrən]) ELECTR transformer
Transfusion [transfu'zjoːn] *f* (-; *-en*) MED transfusion
Transistor [tran'zɪstoːɐ] *m* (*-s*; *-en* [-zɪs'toːrən]) ELECTR transistor
Transit [tran'ziːt] *m* (*-s*; *-e*) transit
transitiv ['tranzitiːf] *adj* LING transitive
transparent [transpa'rɛnt] *adj* transparent
Transpa'rent *n* (-[*e*]*s*; *-e*) banner
Transplantation [transplanta'tsjoːn] *f* (-; *-en*), **transplantieren** [-'tiːrən] *v/t* (*no -ge-*, *h*) MED transplant
Transport [trans'pɔrt] *m* (-[*e*]*s*; *-e*) transport; shipment
transportabel [transpɔr'taːbəl], **trans'portfähig** *adj* transportable
transportieren [transpɔr'tiːrən] *v/t* (*no -ge-*, *h*) transport, ship, carry, MOT *a.* haul
Trans'portmittel *n* (means of) transport(ation)
Transportunternehmen *n* hauler, *Br* haulier
Trapez [tra'peːts] *n* (*-es*; *-e*) MATH trapezoid, *Br* trapezium; SPORT trapeze
trappeln ['trapəln] *v/i* (*ge-*, *sein*) clatter; patter
trat [traːt] *pret of* ***treten***
Traube ['traubə] *f* (-; *-n*) BOT bunch of grapes; grape; *pl* grapes; *fig* cluster
Traubensaft *m* grape juice
'**Traubenzucker** *m* glucose
trauen ['trauən] (*ge-*, *h*) **1.** *v/t* marry; **2.** *v/i* trust (***j-m*** s.o.); ***sich trauen, et. zu tun*** dare (to) do s.th.; ***ich traute meinen Augen nicht*** I couldn't believe my eyes
Trauer ['trauɐ] *f* (-; *no pl*) grief, sorrow; mourning; ***in Trauer*** in mourning
Trauerfall *m* death
Trauerfeier *f* funeral service
Trauermarsch *m* MUS funeral march
'**trauern** *v/i* (*ge-*, *h*) mourn (***um*** for)
'**Trauerrede** *f* funeral oration
'**Trauerzug** *m* funeral procession
träufeln ['trɔʏfəln] *v/t* (*ge-*, *h*) drip, trickle
Traum [traum] *m* (-[*e*]*s*; *Träume* ['trɔʏmə]) dream (*a. fig*)
Traum... *in cpds ...beruf, ...mann etc*: dream ..., ... of one's dreams
träumen ['trɔʏmən] *v/i and v/t* (*ge-*, *h*) dream (*a. fig*) (***von*** about, of); ***schlecht***

träumen have bad dreams
Träumer ['trɔʏmɐ] *m* (-*s*; -) dreamer (*a. fig*)
Träumerei [trɔʏmə'rai] *fig f* (day)-dream(s), reverie (*a.* MUS)
träumerisch ['trɔʏmərɪʃ] *adj* dreamy
traurig ['traurɪç] *adj* sad (***über*** *acc*, ***wegen*** about)
'**Traurigkeit** *f* (-; *no pl*) sadness
Trauring ['trau-] *m* wedding ring
'**Trauschein** *m* marriage certificate
'**Trauung** *f* (-; -*en*) marriage, wedding
'**Trauzeuge** *m*, '**Trauzeugin** *f* witness to a marriage
Trecker ['trɛkɐ] *m* (-*s*; -) MOT tractor
Treff [trɛf] F *m* (-*s*; -*s*) meeting place
treffen ['trɛfən] *v/t and v/i* (*irr, ge-, h*) hit (*a. fig*); hurt; meet *s.o.*; take (*measures etc*); ***nicht treffen*** miss; ***sich treffen*** (***mit j-m***) meet (s.o.); ***gut treffen*** PHOT *etc*: capture well
'**Treffen** *n* (-*s*; -) meeting
'**treffend 1.** *adj* apt (*remark etc*); **2.** *adv*: ***treffend gesagt*** well put
Treffer ['trɛfɐ] *m* (-*s*; -) hit (*a. fig*); SPORT goal; win
'**Treffpunkt** *m* meeting place
Treibeis ['traip-] *n* drift ice
treiben ['traibən] (*irr, ge-*) **1.** *v/t* (*h*) drive (*a.* TECH *and fig*); SPORT *etc*: do; push, press *s.o.*; BOT put forth; F do, be up to; **2.** *v/i* (*sein*) drift (*a. fig*), float; BOT shoot (up); ***sich treiben lassen*** drift along (*a. fig*); ***treibende Kraft*** driving force
'**Treiben** *n* (-*s*; *no pl*) doings, goingson; ***geschäftiges Treiben*** bustle
'**treibenlassen** *v/refl* (*irr*, ***lassen***, *sep, no -ge-, h*) → ***treiben***
'**Treibhaus** *n* hothouse
Treibhausef‚fekt *m* greenhouse effect
Treibholz *n* driftwood
Treibriemen *m* TECH driving belt
Treibsand *m* quicksand
Treibstoff *m* fuel
trennen ['trɛnən] *v/t* (*ge-, h*) separate; sever; part; divide (*a.* LING, POL); segregate; TEL disconnect; ***sich trennen*** separate (***von*** from), part (*a. fig*); ***sich trennen von*** part with *s.th.*; leave *s.o.*
'**Trennung** *f* (-; -*en*) separation; division; segregation
'**Trennwand** *f* partition
Treppe ['trɛpə] *f* (-; -*n*) staircase, stairs
'**Treppenabsatz** *m* landing
Treppengeländer *n* banisters
Treppenhaus *n* staircase; hall
Tresor [tre'zoːɐ] *m* (-*s*; -*e*) safe; strongroom, vault
treten ['treːtən] *v/i and v/t* (*irr, ge-, h*) kick; step (***aus*** out of; ***in*** *acc* into; ***auf*** *acc* on[-to]); pedal (away)
treu [trɔʏ] *adj* faithful (*a. fig*); loyal; devoted
Treue ['trɔʏə] *f* (-; *no pl*) fidelity, faithfulness, loyalty
'**Treuhänder** [-hɛndɐ] *m* (-*s*; -) JUR trustee
'**treulos** *adj* faithless, disloyal, unfaithful (*all*: ***gegen*** to)
Tribüne [tri'byːnə] *f* (-; -*n*) platform; stand
Trichter ['trɪçtɐ] *m* (-*s*; -) funnel; crater
Trick [trɪk] *m* (-*s*; -*s*) trick
Trickaufnahme *f* trick shot
Trickbetrüger(in) confidence trickster
trieb [triːp] *pret of* ***treiben***
Trieb *m* (-[*e*]*s*; -*e* ['triːbə]) BOT (young) shoot, sprout; *fig* impulse, drive; sex drive
Triebfeder *f* mainspring (*a. fig*)
triefen ['triːfən] *v/i* (*ge-, h*) drip, be dripping (***von*** with)
triftig ['trɪftɪç] *adj* weighty; good
Trikot [tri'koː] *n* (-*s*; -*s*) SPORT shirt, jersey; leotard
Triller ['trɪlɐ] *m* (-*s*; -) MUS trill
'**trillern** *v/i and v/t* (*ge-, h*) trill; ZO warble
trimmen ['trɪmən] *v/refl* (*ge-, h*) keep fit
'**Trimmpfad** *m* fitness trail
trinkbar ['trɪŋkbaːɐ] *adj* drinkable
trinken ['trɪŋkən] *v/t and v/i* (*irr, ge-, h*) drink (***auf*** *acc* to); have; ***et. zu trinken*** a drink
Trinker(in) ['trɪŋkɐ (-kərɪn)] (-*s*; -/-; -*nen*) drinker, alcoholic
'**Trinkgeld** *n* tip; ***j-m*** (***e-e Mark***) ***Trinkgeld geben*** tip s.o. (one mark)
Trinkspruch *m* toast
Trinkwasser *n* drinking water
Trio ['triːo] *n* (-*s*; -*s*) MUS trio (*a. fig*)
trippeln ['trɪpəln] *v/i* (*ge-, sein*) mince
Tripper ['trɪpɐ] *m* (-*s*; -) MED gonorrh(o)ea
Tritt [trɪt] *m* (-[*e*]*s*; -*e*) kick; step
'**Trittbrett** *n* step; MOT running board
'**Trittleiter** *f* stepladder
Triumph [tri'ʊmf] *m* (-[*e*]*s*; -*e*) triumph
triumphal [triʊm'faːl] *adj* triumphant
triumphieren [triʊm'fiːrən] *v/i* (*no -ge-, h*) triumph (***über*** *acc* over)
trocken ['trɔkən] *adj* dry (*a. fig*)
'**Trocken...** *in cpds* dried ...; drying ...
'**Trockenhaube** *f* hairdryer
'**Trockenheit** *f* (-; *no pl*) dryness; AGR drought
'**trockenlegen** *v/t* (*sep, -ge-, h*) drain; change (*a baby*)
trocknen ['trɔknən] *v/t* (*ge-, h*) *and v/i* (*sein*) dry
Trockner ['trɔknɐ] *m* (-*s*; -) dryer
Troddel ['trɔdəl] *f* (-; -*n*) tassel

Trödel ['trøːdəl] *m* (*-s; no pl*) junk
trödeln ['trøːdəln] *v/i* (*ge-, h*) dawdle
Trödler ['trøːdlɐ] *m* (*-s; -*) junk dealer; dawdler
trog [troːk] *pret of* ***trügen***
Trog *m* (*-[e]s; Tröge* ['trøːgə]) trough
Trommel ['trɔməl] *f* (*-; -n*) MUS drum (*a.* TECH)
Trommelfell *n* ANAT eardrum
'trommeln *v/i and v/t* (*ge-, h*) drum
Trommler ['trɔmlɐ] *m* (*-s; -*) drummer
Trompete [trɔm'peːtə] *f* (*-; -n*) MUS trumpet
trom'peten *v/i and v/t* (*no -ge-, h*) trumpet (*a.* ZO)
Trompeter [trɔm'peːtɐ] *m* (*-s; -*) trumpeter
Tropen ['troːpən]: ***die Tropen*** *pl* the tropics
'Tropen... *in cpds* tropical ...
Tropf [trɔpf] *m* (*-[e]s; Tröpfe* ['trœpfə]) MED drip
Tröpfchen ['trœpfçən] *n* (*-s; -*) droplet
tröpfeln ['trœpfəln] *v/i and v/t* (*ge-, h*) drip; ***es tröpfelt*** it's spitting
tropfen ['trɔpfən] *v/i and v/t* (*ge-, h*) drip, drop
'Tropfen *m* (*-s; -*) drop (*a. fig*); ***ein Tropfen auf den heißen Stein*** a drop in the bucket
'tropfenweise *adv* in drops, drop by drop
Trophäe [tro'fɛːə] *f* (*-; -n*) trophy (*a. fig*)
tropisch ['troːpɪʃ] *adj* tropical
Trosse ['trɔsə] *f* (*-; -n*) cable
Trost [troːst] *m* (*-[e]s; no pl*) comfort, consolation; ***ein schwacher Trost*** cold comfort
trösten ['trøːstən] *v/t* (*ge-, h*) comfort, console; ***sich trösten*** console o.s. (***mit*** with)
tröstlich ['trøːstlɪç] *adj* comforting
'trostlos *adj* miserable; desolate
Trott [trɔt] *m* (*-[e]s; -e*) trot; F ***der alte Trott*** the old routine
Trottel ['trɔtəl] F *m* (*-s; -*) dope
trottelig ['trɔtəlɪç] F *adj* dopey
trotten ['trɔtən] *v/i* (*ge-, sein*) trot
Trottinett ['trɔtinɛt] *Swiss n* (*-s; -e*) scooter
Trottoir [trɔ'toaːɐ] *Swiss n* (*-s; -e, -s*) sidewalk, *Br* pavement
trotz [trɔts] *prp* (*gen*) in spite of, despite
Trotz *m* (*-es; no pl*) defiance; ***j-m zum Trotz*** to spite s.o.
'trotzdem *adv* in spite of it, nevertheless, F anyhow, anyway
trotzen ['trɔtsən] *v/i* (*ge-, h*) defy (*dat s.o. or s.th.*); sulk
trotzig ['trɔtsɪç] *adj* defiant; sulky
trüb [tryːp], **trübe** ['tryːbə] *adj* cloudy; muddy; dim; dull, *fig a.* gloomy
Trubel ['truːbəl] *m* (*-s; no pl*) (hustle and) bustle
trüben ['tryːbən] *v/t* (*ge-, h*) cloud; *fig* spoil, mar
Trübsal ['tryːpzaːl] *f*: ***Trübsal blasen*** mope
'trübselig *adj* sad, gloomy; dreary
'Trübsinn *m* (*-[e]s; no pl*) melancholy, gloom, low spirits
'trübsinnig *adj* melancholy, gloomy
trug [truːk] *pret of* ***tragen***
trügen ['tryːgən] (*irr, ge-, h*) **1.** *v/t* deceive; **2.** *v/i* be deceptive
trügerisch ['tryːgərɪʃ] *adj* deceptive
'Trugschluss *m* fallacy
Truhe ['truːə] *f* (*-; -n*) chest
Trümmer ['trʏmɐ] *pl* ruins; debris; pieces, bits
Trumpf [trʊmpf] *m* (*-[e]s; Trümpfe* ['trʏmpfə]) trump (card) (*a. fig*); ***Trumpf sein*** be trumps; *fig* ***s-n Trumpf ausspielen*** play one's trump card
Trunkenheit ['trʊŋkənhait] *f* (*-; no pl*) *esp* JUR; ***Trunkenheit am Steuer*** drunk (*Br* drink) driving
'Trunksucht *f* (*-; no pl*) alcoholism
Trupp [trʊp] *m* (*-s; -s*) band, party; group
Truppe ['trʊpə] *f* (*-; -n*) MIL troop, *pl* troops, forces; THEA company, troupe
'Truppengattung *f* MIL branch (of service)
Truppenübungsplatz *m* training area
Truthahn ['truːt-] *m* ZO turkey
Tscheche ['tʃɛçə] *m* (*-n; -n*) Czech
Tschechien ['tʃɛçjən] Czech Republic
'Tschechin *f* (*-; -nen*) Czech
'tschechisch *adj* Czech; ***Tschechische Republik*** Czech Republic
Tube ['tuːbə] *f* (*-; -n*) tube
Tuberkulose [tubɛrku'loːzə] *f* (*-; -n*) MED tuberculosis
Tuch [tuːx] *n* (*-[e]s*) a) (*pl -e*) cloth, b) (*pl Tücher* ['tyːçɐ]) scarf
'Tuchfühlung *f*: ***auf Tuchfühlung*** in close contact
tüchtig ['tʏçtɪç] *adj* (cap)able, competent; skil(l)ful; efficient; F *fig* good
'Tüchtigkeit *f* (*-; no pl*) (cap)ability, qualities; skill; efficiency
tückisch ['tʏkɪʃ] *adj* malicious; MED insidious; treacherous
tüfteln ['tʏftəln] F *v/i* (*ge-, h*) puzzle (***an*** *dat* over)
Tugend ['tuːgənt] *f* (*-; -en*) virtue (*a. fig*)
Tulpe ['tʊlpə] *f* (*-; -n*) BOT tulip
Tumor ['tuːmoːɐ] *m* (*-s; -en* [tu'moːrən]) MED tumo(u)r
Tümpel ['tʏmpəl] *m* (*-s; -*) pool
Tumult [tu'mʊlt] *m* (*-[e]s; -e*) tumult, up-

roar
tun [tuːn] *v/t and v/i* (*irr, ge-, h*) do; take (*a step etc*); F put; ***zu tun haben*** have work to do; be busy; ***ich weiß*** (***nicht***), ***was ich tun soll*** *or* ***muss*** I (don't) know what to do; ***so tun, als ob*** pretend to *inf*
Tünche ['tʏnçə] *f* (-; *-n*), '**tünchen** *v/t* (*ge-, h*) whitewash
Tunfisch *m* → ***Thunfisch***
Tunke ['tʊŋkə] *f* (-; *-n*) sauce
Tunnel ['tʊnəl] *m* (*-s*; -) tunnel
Tüpfelchen ['tʏpfəlçən] *n*: ***das Tüpfelchen auf dem i*** the icing on the cake
tupfen ['tʊpfən] *v/t* (*ge-, h*) dab
'**Tupfen** *m* (*-s*; -) dot, spot
Tupfer ['tʊpfɐ] *m* (*-s*; -) MED swab
Tür [tyːɐ] *f* (-; *-en* ['tyːrən]) door (*a. fig*); ***die Tür***(***en***) ***knallen*** slam the door(s); F ***j-n vor die Tür setzen*** throw s.o. out; ***Tag der offenen Tür*** open house (*Br* day)
Turban ['tʊrbaːn] *m* (*-s*; *-e*) turban
Turbine [tʊr'biːnə] *f* (-; *-n*) TECH turbine
Turbolader ['tʊrbolaːdɐ] *m* (*-s*; -) MOT turbo(charger)
Türke ['tʏrkə] *m* (*-n*; *-n*) Turk
Türkei [tʏr'kai] *f* Turkey
Türkin ['tʏrkɪn] *f* (-; *-nen*) Turk(ish woman)
'**türkisch** *adj* Turkish
'**Türklingel** *f* doorbell
Türklinke *f* door handle
Türknauf *m* doorknob
Turm [tʊrm] *m* (*-[e]s*; *Türme* ['tʏrmə]) tower; steeple; *chess*: castle, rook
türmen ['tʏrmən] *v/t* (*ge-, h*) pile up (*a.* ***sich türmen***)
'**Turmspitze** *f* spire
'**Turmspringen** *n* SPORT platform diving
turnen ['tʊrnən] *v/i* (*ge-, h*) SPORT do gymnastics
'**Turnen** *n* (*-s*; *no pl*) SPORT gymnastics; PED physical education (ABBR PE)
Turner ['tʊrnɐ] *m* (*-s*; -), **Turnerin** ['tʊrnərɪn] *f* (-; *-nen*) SPORT gymnast
'**Turnhalle** *f* gymnasium, F gym
'**Turnhemd** *n* gym shirt
'**Turnhose** *f* gym shorts
Turnier [tʊr'niːɐ] *n* (*-s*; *-e*) tournament
Tur'niertanz *m* ballroom dancing
'**Turnlehrer(in)** gym(nastics) *or* PE teacher
Turnschuh *m* sneaker, *Br* trainer
Turnverein *m* gymnastics club
'**Türpfosten** *m* doorpost
Türrahmen *m* doorframe
Türschild *n* doorplate
Türsprechanlage *f* entryphone
Tusche ['tʊʃə] *f* (-; *-n*) Indian ink; watercolo(u)r
'**Tuschkasten** *m* paintbox
Tüte ['tyːtə] *f* (-; *-n*) (paper *or* plastic) bag; ***e-e Tüte ...*** a bag of ...
TÜV [tʏf] ABBR *of* ***Technischer Überwachungs-Verein*** *Br appr* MOT (test), compulsory car inspection; (***nicht***) ***durch den TÜV kommen*** pass (fail) its *or* one's MOT
Typ [tyːp] *m* (*-s*; *-en*) type; model; F fellow, guy
Type ['tyːpə] *f* (-; *-n*) TECH type; F character
Typhus ['tyːfʊs] *m* (-; *no pl*) MED typhoid (fever)
typisch ['tyːpɪʃ] *adj* typical (***für*** of)
Tyrann [ty'ran] *m* (*-en*; *-en*) tyrant
Tyrannei [tyra'nai] *f* (-; *-en*) tyranny
tyrannisch [ty'ranɪʃ] *adj* tyrannical
tyrannisieren [tyrani'ziːrən] *v/t* (*no -ge-, h*) tyrannize, bully

U

u. a. ABBR *of* ***unter anderem*** among other things; ***und andere*** and others
U-Bahn ['uːbaːn] *f* underground, subway, *in London*: tube
übel ['yːbəl] *adj* bad; ***mir ist übel*** I feel sick; ***et. übel nehmen*** be offended by s.th.; ***übel riechend*** foul-smelling, foul
'**Übel** *n* (*-s*; -) evil
'**Übelkeit** *f* (-; *-en*) nausea
'**übelnehmen** *v/t* (*irr*, ***nehmen***, *sep, -ge-, h*) → ***übel***
'**Übeltäter** *m*, '**Übeltäterin** *f esp iro* culprit
üben ['yːbən] *v/t and v/i* (*ge-, h*) practice, *Br* practise; ***Klavier*** *etc* ***üben*** practice the piano *etc*
über ['yːbɐ] *prp* (*dat or acc*) over; above (*a. fig*); more than; across; *fig* about, of, *lecture etc a.* on; ***sprechen*** (***nachdenken*** *etc*) ***über*** (*acc*) talk (think *etc*) about; ***über Nacht bleiben*** stay overnight; ***über***

München nach Rom to Rome via Munich
über'all *adv* everywhere; ***überall in …*** *(dat) a.* throughout …, all over …
über'anstrengen *v/t and v/refl (no -ge-, h)* overstrain (o.s.)
über'arbeiten *v/t (no -ge-, h)* revise; ***sich überarbeiten*** overwork o.s.
'überaus *adv* most, extremely
'überbelichten *v/t (no -ge-, h)* PHOT overexpose
über'bieten *v/t (irr,* ***bieten****, no -ge-, h) at auction*: outbid (***um*** by); *fig* beat, *a.* outdo *s.o.*
'Überblick *m* view; *fig* overview (***über*** *acc* of); general idea, outline
über'blicken *v/t (no -ge-, h)* overlook; *fig* be able to calculate
über'bringen *v/t (irr,* ***bringen****, no -ge-, h)* deliver
Über'bringer(in) *(-s; -/-; -nen)* ECON bearer
über'brücken *v/t (no -ge-, h)* bridge *(a. fig)*
überdacht [-'daxt] *adj* roofed, covered
über'dauern *v/t (no -ge-, h)* outlast, survive
über'denken *v/t (irr,* ***denken****, no -ge-, h)* think *s.th.* over
'überdimensio,nal *adj* oversized
'Überdosis *f* MED overdose
'überdrüssig [-drʏsɪç] *adj*: ***überdrüssig sein*** be weary *or* sick *(gen* of)
'überdurchschnittlich *adj* above--average
übereifrig *adj* overzealous
über'eilen *v/t (no -ge-, h)* rush; ***nichts übereilen!*** don't rush things!
über'eilt *adj* rash, hasty
überei'nander *adv* on top of each other; *talk etc* about one another
übereinanderschlagen *v/t (irr,* ***schlagen****, sep, -ge-, h)*: ***die Beine übereinanderschlagen*** cross one's legs
über'einkommen *v/i (irr,* ***kommen****, sep, -ge-, sein)* agree
Über'einkommen *n (-s; -),* **Über'einkunft** *f (-; -künfte)* agreement
über'einstimmen *v/i (sep, -ge-, h)* tally, correspond (with); ***mit j-m übereinstimmen*** agree with s.o. (***in*** *dat* on)
Über'einstimmung *f (-; -en)* agreement; correspondence; ***in Übereinstimmung mit*** in accordance with
über'fahren *v/t (irr,* ***fahren****, no -ge-, h)* run *s.o.* over, knock *s.o.* down
'Überfahrt *f* MAR crossing
'Überfall *m* assault (***auf*** *acc* on); hold-up (on, of); mugging (of); MIL raid (on); invasion (of)
über'fallen *v/t (irr,* ***fallen****, no -ge-, h)* attack, assault; hold up; mug; MIL raid; invade
'überfällig *adj* overdue
über'fliegen *v/t (irr,* ***fliegen****, no -ge-, h)* fly over *or* across; *fig* glance over, skim (through)
'überfließen *v/i (irr,* ***fließen****, sep, -ge-, sein)* overflow
'Überfluss *m (-es; no pl)* abundance (***an*** *dat* of); affluence; ***im Überfluss haben*** abound in
'überflüssig *adj* superfluous
über'fluten *v/t (no -ge-, h)* flood *(a. fig)*
über'fordern *v/t (no -ge-, h)* overtax
überfragt [-'fraːkt] *adj*: F ***da bin ich überfragt*** you've got me there
über'führen *v/t (no -ge-, h)* transport; JUR convict (***e-r Tat*** of a crime)
Über'führung *f (-; -en)* transfer; JUR conviction; MOT overpass, *Br* flyover; footbridge
über'füllt *adj* overcrowded, packed
über'füttern *v/t (no -ge-, h)* overfeed
'Übergang *m* crossing; *fig* transition
über'geben *v/t (irr,* ***geben****, no -ge-, h)* hand over; MIL surrender; ***sich übergeben*** vomit
über'gehen[1] *v/t (irr,* ***gehen****, no -ge-, h)* pass over, ignore
'übergehen[2] *v/i (irr,* ***gehen****, sep, -ge-, sein)* pass (***zu*** on to); ***übergehen in*** *(acc)* change *or* turn (in)to
'übergeschnappt F *adj* cracked
'Übergewicht *n* (***Übergewicht haben*** be) overweight; *fig* predominance
'übergewichtig *adj* overweight
'überglücklich *adj* overjoyed
'übergreifen *v/i (irr,* ***greifen****, sep, -ge-, h)* ***übergreifen auf*** *(acc)* spread to
'Übergriff *m* infringement (***auf*** *acc* of); (act of) violence
'Übergröße *f* outsize; ***in Übergrößen*** outsized, oversize(d)
über'handnehmen *v/i (irr,* ***nehmen****, sep, -ge-, h)* become rampant
über'häufen *v/t (no -ge-, h)* swamp; shower
über'haupt *adv* … at all; anyway; ***überhaupt nicht*** (***nichts***) not (nothing) at all
überheblich [-'heːplɪç] *adj* arrogant
Über'heblichkeit *f (-; no pl)* arrogance
über'hitzen *v/t (no -ge-, h)* overheat *(a. fig)*
überhöht [-'høːt] *adj* excessive
über'holen *v/t (no -ge-, h)* pass, overtake *(a.* SPORT); TECH overhaul, service
über'holt *adj* outdated, antiquated

über'hören *v/t* (*no -ge-, h*) miss, not catch *or* get; ignore
'überirdisch *adj* supernatural
über'kleben *v/t* (*no -ge-, h*) paste up, cover
'überkochen *v/i* (*sep, -ge-, sein*) boil over
über'kommen *v/t* (*irr*, ***kommen***, *no -ge-, h*) ***… überkam ihn*** he was seized with *or* overcome by …
über'laden *v/t* (*irr*, ***laden***, *no -ge-, h*) overload (*a.* ELECTR); *fig* clutter
über'lassen *v/t* (*irr*, ***lassen***, *no -ge-, h*) ***j-m et. überlassen*** let s.o. have s.th., leave s.th. to s.o. (*a. fig*); ***j-n sich selbst überlassen*** leave s.o. to himself; ***j-n s-m Schicksal überlassen*** leave s.o. to his fate
über'lasten *v/t* (*no -ge-, h*) overload (*a.* ELECTR); *fig* overburden
'überlaufen[1] *v/i* (*irr*, ***laufen***, *sep, -ge-, sein*) run *or* flow over; MIL desert
über'laufen[2] *v/t* (*irr*, ***laufen***, *no -ge-, h*) ***es überlief mich heiß und kalt*** I went hot and cold
über'laufen[3] *adj* overcrowded
'Überläufer *m* MIL deserter; POL defector
über'leben *v/t and v/i* (*no -ge-, h*) survive (*a. fig*); live through *s.th.*
Über'lebende *m, f* (*-n; -n*) survivor
'überlebensgroß *adj* larger than life
über'legen[1] *v/t and v/i* (*no -ge-, h*) think about *s.th.*, think *s.th.* over; consider; ***lassen Sie mich überlegen*** let me think; ***ich habe es mir*** (***anders***) ***überlegt*** I've made up (changed) my mind
über'legen[2] *adj* superior (***j-m*** to s.o.)
Über'legenheit *f* (*-; no pl*) superiority
über'legt *adj* deliberate; prudent
Über'legung *f* (*-; -en*) consideration, reflection
'überleiten *v/i* (*sep, -ge-, h*) ***überleiten zu*** lead up *or* over to
über'liefern *v/t* (*no -ge-, h*) hand down, pass on
Über'lieferung *f* (*-; -en*) tradition
über'listen *v/t* (*no -ge-, h*) outwit
'Übermacht *f* (*-; no pl*) superiority; *esp* MIL superior forces; ***in der Übermacht sein*** be superior in numbers
'übermächtig *adj* superior; *fig* overpowering
'Übermaß *n* (*-es; no pl*) excess (***an*** *dat* of)
'übermäßig *adj* excessive
'übermenschlich *adj* superhuman
über'mitteln *v/t* (*no -ge-, h*) convey
'übermorgen *adv* the day after tomorrow
über'müdet *adj* overtired
'übermütig [-myːtɪç] *adj* high-spirited
'übernächst *adj* *the* next but one; ***übernächste Woche*** the week after next
übernachten [-'naxtən] *v/i* (*no -ge-, h*) stay overnight (***bei j-m*** at s.o.'s [house], with s.o.), spend the night (at, with)
Über'nachtung *f* (*-; -en*) night; ***Übernachtung und Frühstück*** bed and breakfast
Übernahme ['yːbɐnaːmə] *f* (*-; -n*) taking (over); adoption
'überna͵türlich *adj* supernatural
über'nehmen *v/t* (*irr*, ***nehmen***, *no -ge-, h*) take over; adopt; take (*responsibility etc*); undertake *to do*
über'prüfen *v/t* (*no -ge-, h*) check, examine; verify; *esp* POL screen
Über'prüfung *f* check, examination; verification; screening
über'queren *v/t* (*no -ge-, h*) cross
über'ragen *v/t* (*no -ge-, h*) tower above (*a. fig*)
über'ragend *adj* outstanding
überraschen [yːbɐ'raʃən] *v/t* (*no -ge-, h*) surprise; ***j-n bei et. überraschen*** *a.* catch s.o. doing s.th.
Über'raschung *f* (*-; -en*) surprise
über'reden *v/t* (*no -ge-, h*) persuade (***et. zu tun*** to do s.th.); ***j-n zu et. überreden*** talk s.o. into (doing) s.th.
Über'redung *f* (*-; no pl*) persuasion
'überregio͵nal *adj* national
über'reichen *v/t* (*no -ge-, h*) present, hand *s.th.* over (*dat* to)
über'reizen *v/t* (*no -ge-, h*) overexcite
über'reizt *adj* overwrought, F on edge
'Überrest *m* remains; *pl* relics; GASTR leftovers
über'rumpeln *v/t* (*no -ge-, h*) (take *s.o.* by) surprise
über'runden *v/t* (*no -ge-, h*) SPORT lap
übersät [-'zɛːt] *adj*: ***übersät mit*** strewn with *garbage*; studded with *stars*
übersättigt [-'zɛtɪçt] *adj* sated, surfeited
'Überschall… *in cpds* supersonic …
über'schatten *v/t* (*no -ge-, h*) overshadow (*a. fig*)
über'schätzen *v/t* (*no -ge-, h*) overrate, overestimate
'Überschlag *m* AVIAT loop; SPORT somersault; ECON rough estimate
'überschlagen[1] (*irr*, ***schlagen***, *sep, -ge-*) **1.** *v/t* (*h*) cross (*one's legs*); **2.** *v/i* (*sein*) *fig* ***überschlagen in*** (*acc*) turn into
über'schlagen[2] (*no -ge-, h*) **1.** *v/t* skip; ECON make a rough estimate of; **2.** *v/refl* turn (right) over; go head over heels; *voice*: break
'überschnappen F *v/i* (*no -ge-, sein*) crack up
über'schneiden *v/refl* (*irr*, ***schneiden***, *no*

U

-ge-, h) overlap *(a. fig)*; intersect
über'schreiben *v/t (irr,* ***schreiben****, no -ge-, h)* make *s.th.* over *(dat* to)
über'schreiten *v/t (irr,* ***schreiten****, no -ge-, h)* cross; *fig* go beyond; pass; break *(the speed limit etc)*
'Überschrift *f* heading, title; headline; caption
'Überschuss *m*, **'überschüssig** [-ʃʏsɪç] *adj* surplus
über'schütten *v/t (no -ge-, h)* ***überschütten mit*** cover with; shower with; heap *s.th.* on
'überschwänglich [-ʃvɛŋlɪç] *adj* effusive
über'schwemmen *v/t (no -ge-, h)*, **Über'schwemmung** *f (-; -en)* flood
'überschwenglich → ***überschwänglich***
'Übersee: ***in (nach) Übersee*** oversea
über'sehen *v/t (irr,* ***sehen****, no -ge-, h)* overlook; ignore
über'setzen[1] *v/t (no -ge-, h)* translate (***in*** *acc* into)
'übersetzen[2] *(sep, -ge-)* **1.** *v/i (h, sein)* cross (***über e-n Fluss*** a river); **2.** *v/t (h)* take over
Übersetzer [-'zɛtsɐ] *m (-s; -)*, **Über'setzerin** *f (-; -nen)* translator
Über'setzung *f (-; -en)* translation (***aus*** *dat* from; ***in*** *acc* into)
'Übersicht *f (-; -en)* overview (***über*** *acc* of); outline, summary
'übersichtlich *adj* clear(ly arranged)
'übersiedeln *v/i (sep, -ge-, sein)* move (***nach*** to)
'Übersied(e)lung *f* move
über'spannen *v/t (no -ge-, h)* span
über'spannt *fig adj* eccentric; extravagant
über'spielen *v/t (no -ge-, h)* record; tape; *fig* cover up
über'spitzt *adj* exaggerated
über'springen *v/t (irr,* ***springen****, no -ge-, h)* jump (over), *esp* SPORT *a.* clear; *fig* skip
über'stehen[1] *v/t (irr,* ***stehen****, no -ge-, h)* get over; survive *(a. fig)*, live through
'überstehen[2] *v/i (irr,* ***stehen****, sep, -ge-, h)* jut out
über'steigen *fig v/t (irr,* ***steigen****, no -ge-, h)* exceed
über'stimmen *v/t (no -ge-, h)* outvote
'überstreifen *v/t (sep, -ge-, h)* slip *s.th.* on
überströmen *v/i (sep, -ge-, sein)* overflow (***vor*** *dat* with)
'Überstunden *pl* overtime; ***Überstunden machen*** work overtime
über'stürzen *v/t (no -ge-, h)* ***et. überstürzen*** rush things; ***sich überstürzen*** *events*: follow in rapid succession
über'stürzt *adj* (over)hasty; rash
über'teuert *adj* overpriced
über'tönen *v/t (no -ge-, h)* drown (out)
über'tragbar *adj* transferable; MED contagious
über'tragen[1] *adj* figurative
über'tragen[2] *v/t (irr,* ***tragen****, no -ge-, h)* broadcast, *a.* televise; translate; MED, TECH transmit; MED transfuse *(blood)*; JUR, ECON transfer
Über'tragung *f (-; -en) radio,* TV broadcast; transmission; translation; MED transfusion; JUR, ECON transfer
über'treffen *v/t (irr,* ***treffen****, no -ge-, h)* outstrip, outdo, surpass, beat
über'treiben *v/i and v/t (irr,* ***treiben****, no -ge-, h)* exaggerate; overdo
Über'treibung *f (-; -en)* exaggeration
'übertreten[1] *v/i (irr,* ***treten****, sep, -ge-, sein)* ***übertreten zu*** go over to, REL convert to
über'treten[2] *(irr,* ***treten****, no -ge-, h)* **1.** *v/t* break, violate; **2.** *v/i* SPORT foul (a jump *or* throw)
Über'tretung *f (-; -en)* violation, JUR *a.* offen|se, *Br* -ce
'Übertritt *m* change (***zu*** to); REL, POL conversion (to)
übervölkert [-'fœlkɐt] *adj* overpopulated
über'wachen *v/t (no -ge-, h)* supervise, oversee; control; observe
Über'wachung *f (-; -en)* supervision, control; observance; surveillance
überwältigen [-'vɛltɪgən] *v/t (no -ge-, h)* overwhelm, overpower, *fig a.* overcome
überwältigend *adj* overwhelming, overpowering
über'weisen *v/t (irr,* ***weisen****, no -ge-, h)* ECON transfer (***an j-n*** to s.o.'s account); remit; MED refer (***an*** *acc* to)
Über'weisung *f (-; -en)* ECON transfer; remittance; MED referral
'überwerfen[1] *v/t (irr,* ***werfen****, sep, -ge-, h)* slip *s.th.* on
über'werfen[2] *v/refl (irr,* ***werfen****, no -ge-, h)* ***sich überwerfen (mit j-m)*** fall out with each other (with s.o.)
über'wiegen *v/i (irr,* ***wiegen****, no -ge-, h)* predominate
überwiegend *adj* predominant; vast *(majority)*
über'winden *v/t (irr,* ***winden****, no -ge-, h)* overcome *(a. fig)*; defeat; ***sich überwinden zu*** *inf* bring o.s. to *inf*
überwintern [-'vɪntɐn] *v/i (no -ge-, h)* spend the winter (***in*** *dat* in)
über'wuchern *v/t (no -ge-, h)* overgrow
'Überzahl *f (-; no pl)* majority; ***in der Überzahl sein*** outnumber *s.o.*
über'zeugen *v/t (no -ge-, h)* convince (***von*** of), persuade; ***sich überzeugen, dass*** make sure that; ***sich selbst über-***

U

zeugen (go and) see for o.s.
überzeugt [-ˈtsɔʏkt] *adj* convinced; ***überzeugt sein*** *a.* be *or* feel (quite) sure
Überˈzeugung *f* (-; *-en*) conviction
ˈüberziehen[1] *v/t* (*irr*, ***ziehen***, *sep*, *-ge-*, *h*) put *s.th.* on
überˈziehen[2] *v/t* (*irr*, ***ziehen***, *no*, *-ge-*, *h*) TECH *etc* cover; ECON overdraw
Überˈziehungskreˌdit *m* ECON overdraft (facility)
ˈÜberzug *m* cover; coat(ing)
üblich [ˈyːplɪç] *adj* usual, normal; ***es ist üblich*** it's the custom; ***wie üblich*** as usual
ˈU-Boot *n* submarine
übrig [ˈyːbrɪç] *adj* remaining; ***die Übrigen*** *pl* the others, the rest; ***übrig sein*** (***haben***) be (have) left; ***übrig bleiben*** be left, remain; ***es bleibt mir nichts anderes übrig*** (***als zu*** *inf*) there is nothing else I can do (but *inf*); ***übrig lassen*** leave
übrigens [ˈyːbrɪgəns] *adv* by the way
ˈübriglassen *v/i* (*irr*, ***lassen***, *sep*, *-ge-*, *sein*) (*a. fig*) → ***übrig***
Übung [ˈyːbʊŋ] *f* (-; *-en*) exercise; practice; ***in*** (***aus der***) ***Übung*** in (out of) practice
Ufer [ˈuːfɐ] *n* (*-s*; -) shore; bank; ***ans Ufer*** ashore
Uhr [uːɐ] *f* (-; *-en* [ˈuːrən]) clock; watch; ***um vier Uhr*** at four o'clock
ˈUhrarmband *n* watchstrap
Uhrmacher *m* (*-s*; -) watchmaker
Uhrwerk *n* clockwork
Uhrzeiger *m* hand
Uhrzeigersinn *m*: ***im Uhrzeigersinn*** clockwise; ***entgegen dem Uhrzeigersinn*** counterclockwise, *Br* anticlockwise
Uhu [ˈuːhu] *m* (*-s*; *-s*) zo eagle owl
UKW [uːkaːˈveː] ABBR *of* ***Ultrakurzwelle*** VHF, very high frequency
Ulk [ʊlk] *m* (*-s*; *-e*) joke; hoax
ulkig [ˈʊlkɪç] *adj* funny
Ulme [ˈʊlmə] *f* (-; *-n*) BOT elm
Ultimatum [ʊltiˈmaːtʊm] *n* (*-s*; *-ten*) ultimatum; ***j-m ein Ultimatum stellen*** deliver an ultimatum to s.o.
um [ʊm] *prp* (*acc*) *and cj* (a)round; at; about, around; ***um Geld*** for money; ***um e-e Stunde*** (***10 cm***) by an hour (10 cm); ***um ... willen*** for the sake of ...; ***um zu*** *inf* (in order) to *inf*; ***um sein*** F be over; ***die Zeit ist um*** time's up; → ***umso***
umarmen [ʊmˈʔarmən] *v/t* (*no -ge-*, *h*) (*a.* ***sich umarmen***) embrace, hug
Umˈarmung *f* (-; *-en*) embrace, hug
ˈUmbau *m* (-[*e*]*s*; *-e*, *-ten*) rebuilding, reconstruction
ˈumbauen *v/t* (*sep*, *-ge-*, *h*) rebuild, reconstruct
ˈumbinden *v/t* (*irr*, ***binden***, *sep*, *-ge-*, *h*) put *s.th.* on
umblättern *v/i* (*sep*, *-ge-*, *h*) turn (over) the page
umbringen *v/t* (*irr*, ***bringen***, *sep*, *-ge-*, *h*) kill; ***sich umbringen*** kill o.s.
umbuchen *v/t* (*sep*, *-ge-*, *h*) change; ECON transfer (***auf*** *acc* to)
umdenken *v/i* (*irr*, ***denken***, *sep*, *-ge-*, *h*) change one's way of thinking
umdispoˌnieren *v/i* (*sep*, *no -ge-*, *h*) change one's plans
umdrehen *v/t* (*sep*, *-ge-*, *h*) turn (round); ***sich umdrehen*** turn round
Umˈdrehung *f* (-; *-en*) turn; PHYS, TECH rotation, revolution
umeiˈnander *adv care etc* about *or* for each other
ˈumfahren[1] *v/t* (*irr*, ***fahren***, *sep*, *-ge-*, *h*) run down
umˈfahren[2] *v/t* (*irr*, ***fahren***, *no -ge-*, *h*) drive (MAR sail) round
ˈumfallen *v/i* (*irr*, ***fallen***, *sep*, *-ge-*, *sein*) fall down *or* over; collapse; ***tot umfallen*** drop dead
ˈUmfang *m* circumference; size; extent; ***in großem Umfang*** on a large scale
ˈumfangreich *adj* extensive; voluminous
umˈfassen *fig v/t* (*no -ge-*, *h*) cover; include
umfassend *adj* comprehensive; complete
ˈumformen *v/t* (*sep*, *-ge-*, *h*) turn, change; ELECTR, LING, MATH *a.* transform, convert (*all:* ***in*** *acc* [in]to)
ˈUmformer *m* (*-s*; -) ELECTR converter
ˈUmfrage *f* opinion poll
ˈUmgang *m* (-[*e*]*s*; *no pl*) company; ***Umgang haben mit*** associate with; ***beim Umgang mit*** when dealing with
ˈumgänglich [-gɛŋlɪç] *adj* sociable
ˈUmgangsformen *pl* manners
Umgangssprache *f* colloquial speech; ***die englische Umgangssprache*** colloquial English
umˈgeben *v/t* (*irr*, ***geben***, *no -ge-*, *h*) surround (***mit*** with)
Umˈgebung *f* (-; *-en*) surroundings; environment
ˈumgehen[1] *v/i* (*irr*, ***gehen***, *sep*, *-ge-*, *sein*) ***umgehen mit*** deal with, handle; ***umgehen können mit*** have a way with, be good with
umˈgehen[2] *v/t* (*irr*, ***gehen***, *no -ge-*, *h*) avoid; bypass
ˈumgehend *adv* immediately
Umˈgehungsstraße *f* bypass; beltway, *Br*

U

ring road
umgekehrt ['ʊmgəkeːɐt] **1.** *adj* reverse; opposite; ***(genau) umgekehrt*** (just) the other way round; **2.** *adv* the other way round; ***und umgekehrt*** and vice versa
'umgraben *v/t* (*irr*, ***graben***, *sep*, *-ge-*, *h*) dig (up), break up
'Umhang *m* cape
'umhängen *v/t* (*sep*, *-ge-*, *h*) put around *or* over s.o.'s shoulders *etc*; rehang
'umhauen *v/t* (*irr*, ***hauen***, *sep*, *-ge-*, *h*) fell, cut down; F knock *s.o.* out
um'her *adv* (a)round, about
um'herstreifen *v/i* (*sep*, *-ge-*, *sein*) roam *or* wander around
'umkehren (*sep*, *-ge-*) **1.** *v/i* (*sein*) turn back; **2.** *v/t* (*h*) reverse
'Umkehrung *f* (-; *-en*) reversal (*a. fig*)
'umkippen (*sep*, *-ge-*) **1.** *v/t* (*h*) tip over, upset; **2.** *v/i* (*sein*) fall down *or* over, overturn
um'klammern *v/t* (*no -ge-*, *h*), **Um'klammerung** *f* (-; *-en*) clasp, clutch, clench
'Umkleideka,bine *f* changing cubicle
Umkleideraum *m esp* SPORT changing *or* locker room; THEA dressing room
'umkommen *v/i* (*irr*, ***kommen***, *sep*, *-ge-*, *sein*) be killed (***bei*** in), die (in); F ***umkommen vor*** (*dat*) be dying with
'Umkreis *m*: ***im Umkreis von*** within a radius of
um'kreisen *v/t* (*no -ge-*, *h*) circle; ASTR revolve around; *satellite etc*: orbit
'umkrempeln *v/t* (*sep*, *-ge-*, *h*) roll up
'Umlauf *m* circulation; PHYS, TECH rotation; ECON circular; ***im (in) Umlauf sein (bringen)*** be in (put into) circulation, circulate
Umlaufbahn *f* ASTR orbit
'umlaufen *v/i* (*irr*, ***laufen***, *sep*, *-ge-*, *sein*) circulate
umlegen *v/t* (*sep*, *-ge-*, *h*) put on; move; share (*expenses etc*); TECH pull; F do *s.o.* in, bump *s.o.* off
'umleiten *v/t* (*sep*, *-ge-*, *h*) divert
'Umleitung *f* (-; *-en*) detour, *Br* diversion
'umliegend *adj* surrounding
'umpacken *v/t* (*sep*, *-ge-*, *h*) repack
'umpflanzen *v/t* (*sep*, *-ge-*, *h*) repot
umranden [ʊm'randən] *v/t* (*no -ge-*, *h*), **Um'randung** *f* (-; *-en*) edge, border
'umräumen *v/t* (*sep*, *-ge-*, *h*) rearrange
'umrechnen *v/t* (*sep*, *-ge-*, *h*) convert (***in*** *acc* into)
'Umrechnung *f* (-; *-en*) conversion
'Umrechnungskurs *m* exchange rate
'umreißen *v/t* (*irr*, ***reißen***, *sep*, *-ge-*, *h*) knock *s.o.* down
um'ringen *v/t* (*no -ge-*, *h*) surround
'Umriss *m* outline (*a. fig*), contour
'umrühren *v/t* (*sep*, *-ge-*, *h*) stir
umrüsten *v/t* (*sep*, *-ge-*, *h*) TECH convert (***auf*** *acc* to)
umsatteln F *v/i* (*sep*, *-ge-*, *h*) ***umsatteln von ... auf*** (*acc*) ... switch from ... to ...
'Umsatz *m* ECON sales
'umschalten *v/t and v/i* (*sep*, *-ge-*, *h*) switch (over) (***auf*** *acc* to) (*a. fig*)
'Umschlag *m* envelope; cover, wrapper; jacket; cuff, *Br* turn-up; MED compress; ECON handling
'umschlagen (*irr*, ***schlagen***, *sep*, *-ge-*) **1.** *v/t* (*h*) cut down, fell; turn up; turn down; ECON handle; **2.** *v/i* (*sein*) turn over; *fig* change (suddenly)
'Umschlagplatz *m* trading center (*Br* centre)
'umschnallen *v/t* (*sep*, *-ge-*, *h*) buckle on
'umschreiben[1] *v/t* (*irr*, ***schreiben***, *sep*, *-ge-*, *h*) rewrite
um'schreiben[2] *v/t* (*irr*, ***schreiben***, *no -ge-*, *h*) paraphrase
Um'schreibung *f* (-; *-en*) paraphrase
'Umschrift *f* transcription
'umschulen *v/t* (*sep*, *-ge-*, *h*) retrain; transfer to another school
umschwärmt [ʊm'ʃvɛrmt] *adj* idolized
'Umschwung *m* (drastic) change, *esp* POL *a.* swing
um'segeln *v/t* (*no -ge-*, *h*) sail round; circumnavigate
'umsehen *v/refl* (*irr*, ***sehen***, *sep*, *-ge-*, *h*) look around (***in e-m Laden*** a shop; ***nach*** for); look back (***nach*** at); ***sich umsehen nach*** be looking for
umsetzen *v/t* (*sep*, *-ge-*, *h*) move (*a.* PED); ECON sell; ***umsetzen in*** (*acc*) convert (in)-to; ***in die Tat umsetzen*** put into action; ***sich umsetzen*** change places
'umsiedeln *v/i* (*sep*, *-ge-*, *sein*) *and v/t* (*h*) resettle; → ***umziehen***
'Umsied(e)lung *f* (-; *-en*) resettlement
'Umsiedler *m* (*-s*; -) resettler
'umso 1. ***je später*** *etc*, ***umso schlechter*** *etc* the later *etc* the worse *etc*; **2.** ***umso besser*** so much the better
um'sonst *adv* free (of charge), for nothing; F for free; *fig* in vain
um'spannen *v/t* (*no -ge-*, *h*) span (*a. fig*)
'umspringen *v/i* (*irr*, ***springen***, *sep*, *-ge-*, *sein*) shift, change (suddenly) (*a. fig*); ***umspringen mit*** treat (badly)
'Umstand *m* circumstance; fact; detail; ***unter diesen (keinen) Umständen*** under the (no) circumstances; ***unter Umständen*** possibly; ***keine Umstände machen*** not cause *s.o.* any trouble; not go to

any trouble; no put o.s. out; ***in anderen Umständen sein*** be expecting
umständlich ['ʊmʃtɛntlɪç] *adj* awkward; complicated; long-winded; ***das ist (mir) viel zu umständlich*** that's far too much trouble (for me)
'Umstandskleid *n* maternity dress
Umstandswort *n* (-[*e*]*s*; *-wörter*) LING adverb
'Umstehende: ***die Umstehenden*** *pl* the bystanders
'umsteigen *v/i* (*irr*, ***steigen***, *sep*, *-ge-*, *sein*) change (***nach*** for), RAIL *a.* change trains (for)
'umstellen *v/t* (*sep*, *-ge-*, *h*) change (***auf*** *acc* to), make a change *or* changes in, *esp* TECH *a.* switch (over) (to), convert (to); adjust (to); rearrange (*a. furniture*), reorganize; reset (*watch*); ***sich umstellen auf*** (*acc*) change *or* switch (over) to; adjust (o.s.) to, get used to
'Umstellung *f* (-; *-en*) change; switch, conversion; adjustment; rearrangement, reorganization
'umstimmen *v/t* (*sep*, *-ge-*, *h*) ***j-n umstimmen*** change s.o.'s mind
'umstoßen *v/t* (*irr*, ***stoßen***, *sep*, *-ge-*, *h*) knock over, upset (*a. fig*)
umstritten [ʊm'ʃtrɪtən] *adj* controversial
'Umsturz *m* overthrow
'umstürzen *v/i* (*sep*, *-ge-*, *sein*) overturn, fall over
'Umtausch *m*, **'umtauschen** *v/t* (*sep*, *-ge-*, *h*) exchange (***gegen*** for)
'umwälzend *adj* revolutionary
'Umwälzung *f* (-; *-en*) radical change
'umwandeln *v/t* (*sep*, *-ge-*, *h*) turn (***in*** *acc* into), transform (into), *esp* CHEM, ELECTR, PHYS *a.* convert ([in]to)
'Umwandlung *f* (-; *-en*) transformation, conversion
'Umweg *m* roundabout route *or* way (*a. fig*), *esp* MOT *a.* detour; ***ein Umweg von 10 Minuten*** ten minutes out of the way; *fig* ***auf Umwegen*** in a roundabout way
'Umwelt *f* (-; *no pl*) environment
'Umwelt... *in cpds mst* environmental ...
Umweltforschung *f* ecology
'umweltfreundlich *adj* environment-friendly, non-polluting
umweltschädlich *adj* harmful, noxious, polluting
'Umweltschutz *m* conservation, environmental protection, pollution control
Umweltschützer *m* environmentalist, conservationist
Umweltschutzpa͵pier *n* recycled paper
Umweltsünder *m* (environmental) polluter
Umweltverschmutzer *m* (*-s*; -) polluter
Umweltverschmutzung *f* (environmental) pollution
Umweltzerstörung *f* ecocide
'umziehen (*irr*, ***ziehen***, *sep* *-ge-*) **1.** *v/i* (*sein*) move (***nach*** to); **2.** *v/refl* (*h*) change (one's clothes)
umzingeln [ʊm'tsɪŋəln] *v/t* (*no -ge-*, *h*) surround, encircle
'Umzug *m* move (***nach*** to), removal (to); parade
unabhängig ['ʊn-] *adj* independent (***von*** of); ***unabhängig davon, ob*** (***was***) regardless of whether (what)
'Unabhängigkeit *f* (-; *no pl*) independence (***von*** from)
'unabsichtlich *adj* unintentional; ***et. unabsichtlich tun*** do s.th. by mistake
unab'wendbar *adj* inevitable
'unachtsam *adj* careless, negligent
'Unachtsamkeit *f* (-; *no pl*) carelessness, negligence
unan'fechtbar *adj* incontestable
'unangebracht *adj* inappropriate; ***unangebracht sein*** be out of place
unangemessen *adj* unreasonable; inadequate
unangenehm *adj* unpleasant; embarrassing
unan'nehmbar *adj* unacceptable
Unannehmlichkeiten ['ʊnˀanneːmlɪçkaitən] *pl* trouble, difficulties
'unansehnlich *adj* unsightly
'unanständig *adj* indecent, obscene
unan'tastbar *adj* inviolable
'unappetitlich *adj* unappetizing
Unart ['ʊnˀart] *f* (-; *-en*) bad habit
'unartig *adj* naughty, bad
'unaufdringlich *adj* unobtrusive
'unauffällig *adj* inconspicuous, unobtrusive
unauf'findbar *adj* not to be found, untraceable
'unaufgefordert *adv* without being asked, of one's own accord
unaufhörlich [ʊnˀauf'høːɐlɪç] *adj* continuous
'unaufmerksam *adj* inattentive
'Unaufmerksamkeit *f* (-; *no pl*) inattention, inattentiveness
'unaufrichtig *adj* insincere
unauslöschlich [ʊnˀaus'lœʃlɪç] *adj* indelible
unausstehlich [-'ʃteːlɪç] *adj* unbearable
'unbarmherzig *adj* merciless
'unbeabsichtigt *adj* unintentional
unbeachtet *adj* unnoticed
unbeaufsichtigt *adj* unattended

U

unbebaut *adj* undeveloped
unbedacht [-bədaxt] *adj* thoughtless
unbedenklich 1. *adj* safe; **2.** *adv* without hesitation
unbedeutend *adj* insignificant; minor
unbedingt 1. *adj* unconditional, absolute; **2.** *adv* by all means, absolutely; *need etc* badly
unbefahrbar *adj* impassable
unbefangen *adj* unprejudiced, unbias(s)ed; unembarrassed
unbefriedigend *adj* unsatisfactory
unbefriedigt *adj* dissatisfied
unbegabt *adj* untalented
unbegreiflich *adj* inconceivable, incomprehensible
unbegrenzt *adj* unlimited, boundless
unbegründet *adj* unfounded
'Unbehagen *n* (*-s*; *no pl*) uneasiness, discomfort
'unbehaglich *adj* uneasy, uncomfortable
unbehelligt [ʊnbə'hɛlɪçt] *adj* unmolested
'unbeherrscht *adj* uncontrolled, lacking self-control
unbeholfen [-bəhɔlfən] *adj* clumsy, awkward
unbeirrt *adj* unwavering
unbekannt *adj* unknown
'Unbekannte *f* (-; *-n*) MATH unknown quantity
'unbekümmert *adj* light-hearted, cheerful
unbelehrbar *adj*: ***er ist unbelehrbar*** he'll never learn
unbeliebt *adj* unpopular; ***er ist überall unbeliebt*** nobody likes him
unbemannt *adj* unmanned
unbemerkt *adj* unnoticed
unbenutzt *adj* unused
unbequem *adj* uncomfortable; inconvenient
unberechenbar *adj* unpredictable
unberechtigt *adj* unauthorized; unjustified
unbeschädigt *adj* undamaged
unbescheiden *adj* immodest
unbe'schränkt *adj* unlimited; absolute (*power*)
unbeschreiblich [-bə'ʃraiplɪç] *adj* indescribable
unbe'sehen *adv* unseen
unbesiegbar [-bə'ziːbaːɐ] *adj* invincible
'unbesonnen *adj* thoughtless, imprudent; rash
unbe'spielbar *adj* SPORT unplayable
unbeständig *adj* unstable; METEOR changeable, unsettled
unbestätigt *adj* unconfirmed
unbe'stechlich *adj* incorruptible
'unbestimmt *adj* indefinite (*a.* LING); uncertain; vague
unbe'streitbar *adj* indisputable
unbestritten [-bə'ʃtrɪtən] *adj* undisputed
'unbeteiligt *adj* not involved; indifferent
unbetont *adj* unstressed
unbeugsam [ʊn'bɔʏkzaːm] *adj* inflexible
'unbewacht *adj* unwatched, unguarded (*a. fig*)
unbewaffnet *adj* unarmed
unbeweglich *adj* immovable; motionless
unbe'wohnbar *adj* uninhabitable
'unbewohnt *adj* uninhabited; unoccupied, vacant
'unbewusst *adj* unconscious
unbe'zahlbar *fig adj* invaluable, priceless
'unbezahlt *adj* unpaid
'unblutig 1. *adj* bloodless; **2.** *adv* without bloodshed
'unbrauchbar *adj* useless
und [ʊnt] *cj* and; F ***na und?*** so what?
'undankbar *adj* ungrateful (***gegen*** to); thankless
'Undankbarkeit *f* (-; *no pl*) ingratitude, ungratefulness
undefi'nierbar *adj* undefinable
un'denkbar *adj* unthinkable
'undeutlich *adj* indistinct; inarticulate; *fig* vague
'undicht *adj* leaky
'unduldsam *adj* intolerant
'Unduldsamkeit *f* (-; *no pl*) intolerance
undurch'dringlich *adj* impenetrable
undurch'führbar *adj* impracticable
'undurchlässig *adj* impervious, impermeable
undurchsichtig *adj* opaque; *fig* mysterious
'uneben *adj* uneven
'Unebenheit *f* a) (-; *no pl*) unevenness, b) (-; *-en*) bump
'unecht *adj* false; artificial; imitation …; F *contp* fake, phon(e)y
'unehelich *adj* illegitimate
'unehrenhaft *adj* dishono(u)rable
'unehrlich *adj* dishonest
'uneigennützig *adj* unselfish
'uneinig *adj*: (***sich***) ***uneinig sein*** disagree (***über*** *acc* on)
'Uneinigkeit *f* (-; *no pl*) disagreement; dissension
unein'nehmbar *adj* impregnable
'unempfänglich *adj* insusceptible (***für*** to)
unempfindlich *adj* insensitive (***gegen*** to)
un'endlich *adj* infinite; endless, never-ending
Un'endlichkeit *f* (-; *no pl*) infinity (*a. fig*)
unentbehrlich [ʊnʔɛnt'beːɐlɪç] *adj* indispensable

unentgeltlich [-'gɛltlɪç] *adj and adv* free (of charge)
'unentschieden *adj* undecided; ***unentschieden enden*** SPORT end in a draw *or* tie; ***es steht unentschieden*** the score is even
'Unentschieden *n* (*-s*; *-*) SPORT draw, tie
'unentschlossen *adj* irresolute
unent'schuldbar *adj* inexcusable
unentwegt [ʊnʔɛnt'veːkt] *adv* untiringly; continuously
'unerfahren *adj* inexperienced
unerfreulich *adj* unpleasant
unerfüllt *adj* unfulfilled
unergiebig *adj* unproductive
unerheblich *adj* irrelevant (***für*** to); insignificant
unerhört ['ʊnʔɛːɐ'høːɐt] *adj* outrageous
'unerkannt *adj* unrecognized
unerklärlich *adj* inexplicable
unerlässlich *adj* essential, indispensable
unerlaubt *adj* unallowed; unauthorized
unerledigt *adj* unsettled (*a.* ECON)
uner'messlich *adj* immeasurable
unermüdlich [ʊnʔɛɐ'myːtlɪç] *adj* indefatigable; untiring
uner'reichbar *adj* inaccessible; *esp fig* unattainable
uner'reicht *adj* unequal(l)ed
unersättlich [ʊnʔɛɐ'zɛtlɪç] *adj* insatiable
'unerschlossen *adj* undeveloped
unerschöpflich [ʊnʔɛɐ'ʃœpflɪç] *adj* inexhaustible
unerschütterlich [-'ʃʏtɐlɪç] *adj* imperturbable
unerschwinglich [-'ʃvɪŋlɪç] *adj* exorbitant; ***für j-n unerschwinglich sein*** be beyond s.o.'s means
unersetzlich [-'zɛtslɪç] *adj* irreplaceable
unerträglich [-'trɛːklɪç] *adj* unbearable
'unerwartet *adj* unexpected
'unerwünscht *adj* unwanted
'unfähig *adj* incompetent; incapable (***zu tun*** of doing), unable (to *inf*)
'Unfähigkeit *f* (*-*; *no pl*) incompetence; incapacity, inability
'Unfall *m* accident; crash
'Unfallstelle *f* scene of the accident
un'fehlbar *adj* infallible (*a.* REL); unfailing
unförmig ['ʊnfœrmɪç] *adj* shapeless; misshapen; monstrous
'unfrankiert *adj* unstamped
'unfrei *adj* not free; *post* unpaid
'unfreiwillig *adj* involuntary; unconscious (*humor*)
'unfreundlich *adj* unfriendly (***zu*** to), unkind (to); *fig* cheerless
'Unfrieden *m* (*-s*; *no pl*) discord; ***Unfrieden stiften*** make mischief
'unfruchtbar *adj* infertile
'Unfruchtbarkeit *f* (*-*; *no pl*) infertility
Unfug ['ʊnfuːk] *m* (*-[e]s*; *no pl*) nonsense; ***Unfug treiben*** be up to mischief, fool around
Ungar ['ʊŋgar] *m* (*-n*; *-n*), **'Ungarin** *f* (*-*; *-nen*), **'ungarisch** *adj* Hungarian
'Ungarn Hungary
'ungastlich *adj* inhospitable
'ungeachtet *prp* (*gen*) regardless of; despite
ungeahnt *adj* unthought-of
ungebeten *adj* uninvited, unasked
ungebildet *adj* uneducated
ungeboren *adj* unborn
ungebräuchlich *adj* uncommon, unusual
ungebührlich [-gəbyːɐlɪç] *adj* unseemly
ungebunden *fig adj* free, independent; ***frei und ungebunden*** footloose and fancy-free
ungedeckt *adj* ECON uncovered; SPORT unmarked
'Ungeduld *f* (*-*; *no pl*) impatience
'ungeduldig *adj* impatient
'ungeeignet *adj* unfit; unqualified; inappropriate
ungefähr ['ʊngəfɛːɐ] **1.** *adj* approximate; rough; **2.** *adv* approximately, roughly, about, around, ... or so; ***so ungefähr*** something like that
'ungefährlich *adj* harmless; safe
'ungeheuer *adj* enormous (*a. fig*), huge, vast
'Ungeheuer *n* (*-s*; *-*) monster (*a. fig*)
unge'heuerlich *adj* monstrous
'ungehindert *adj and adv* unhindered
'ungehobelt *fig adj* uncouth, rough
'ungehörig *adj* improper, unseemly
'ungehorsam *adj* disobedient
Ungehorsam *m* (*-s*; *no pl*) disobedience
'ungekocht *adj* uncooked
ungekünstelt *adj* unaffected
ungekürzt *adj* unabridged
ungelegen *adj* inconvenient; ***j-m ungelegen kommen*** be inconvenient for s.o.
ungelenk ['ʊngəlɛŋk] *adj* awkward, clumsy
'ungelernt *adj* unskilled
'ungemütlich *adj* uncomfortable; F ***ungemütlich werden*** get nasty
'ungenau *adj* inaccurate; *fig* vague
'Ungenauigkeit *f* (*-*; *-en*) inaccuracy
ungeniert ['ʊnʒeniːɐt] *adj* uninhibited
'ungenießbar *adj* uneatable; undrinkable; F unbearable
ungenügend *adj* insufficient; PED poor, unsatisfactory; *grade*: *a.* F
ungepflegt *adj* neglected; untidy, unkempt

ungerade *adj* uneven; odd
ungerecht *adj* unfair, unjust
'Ungerechtigkeit *f* (-; *no pl*) injustice, unfairness
'ungern *adv* unwillingly; ***et. ungern tun*** hate *or* not like to do s.th.
'ungeschehen *adj*: ***ungeschehen machen*** undo
ungeschickt *adj* awkward, clumsy
ungeschliffen *adj* uncut (*diamond etc*); unpolished (*a. fig*)
ungeschminkt *adj* without make-up; *fig* unvarnished, plain (*truth*)
ungesetzlich *adj* illegal, unlawful
ungestört *adj* undisturbed
ungestraft *adj*: ***ungestraft davonkommen*** get off unpunished (F scot-free)
ungesund *adj* unhealthy (*a. fig*)
ungeteilt *adj* undivided (*a. fig*)
Ungetüm ['ʊngətyːm] *n* (-*s*; -*e*) monster, *fig a.* monstrosity
'ungewiss *adj* uncertain; ***j-n im Ungewissen lassen*** keep s.o. in the dark (***über*** *acc* about)
'Ungewissheit *f* (-; *no pl*) uncertainty
'ungewöhnlich *adj* unusual
'ungewohnt *adj* strange, unfamiliar;
Ungeziefer ['ʊngətsiːfɐ] *n* (-*s*; *no pl*) vermin
'ungezogen *adj* naughty, bad; spoilt
'ungezwungen *adj* relaxed, informal; easygoing
'ungläubig *adj* incredulous, unbelieving (*a.* REL)
unglaublich [ʊn'glauplɪç] *adj* incredible, unbelievable
'unglaubwürdig *adj* implausible; unreliable (*witness etc*)
'ungleich *adj* unequal, different; unlike
ungleichmäßig *adj* uneven; irregular
'Unglück *n* (-[*e*]*s*; -*e*) a) (*no pl*) bad luck, misfortune; misery, b) accident; disaster
'unglücklich *adj* unhappy, miserable; unfortunate
'unglücklicher'weise *adv* unfortunately
'ungültig *adj* invalid; ***für ungültig erklären*** JUR invalidate
'Ungunst *f*: ***zu Ungunsten → zuungunsten***
'ungünstig *adj* unfavo(u)rable; disadvantageous
'ungut *adj*: ***ungutes Gefühl*** misgivings (***bei et.*** about s.th.); ***nichts für ungut!*** no offense (*Br* offence) meant!
'unhaltbar *adj* untenable; intolerable; SPORT unstoppable
'unhandlich *adj* unwieldy
'unhar,monisch *adj* MUS discordant
'Unheil *n* (-*s*; *no pl*) mischief; evil; disaster
'unheilbar *adj* MED incurable
'unheilvoll *adj* disastrous; sinister
'unheimlich *adj* creepy, spooky, eerie; F tremendous; F ***unheimlich gut*** terrific, fantastic
'unhöflich *adj* impolite; rude
'Unhöflichkeit *f* (-; *no pl*) impoliteness; rudeness
un'hörbar *adj* inaudible
'unhygienisch *adj* insanitary
Uniform [uni'fɔrm] *f* (-; -*en*) uniform
'uninteressant *adj* uninteresting
uninteressiert ['ʊnʔɪntərɛsiːɐt] *adj* uninterested (***an*** *dat* in)
Union [u'njoːn] *f* (-; -*en*) union
Universität [univɛrzi'tɛːt] *f* (-; -*en*) university
Universum [uni'vɛrzʊm] *n* (-*s*; *no pl*) universe
Unke ['ʊŋkə] *f* (-; -*n*) ZO toad
'unkenntlich *adj* unrecognizable
'Unkenntnis *f* (-; *no pl*) ignorance
'unklar *adj* unclear; uncertain; confused, muddled; ***im Unklaren sein*** (***lassen***) be (leave *s.o.*) in the dark
'unklug *adj* imprudent, unwise
'Unkosten *pl* expenses, costs
'Unkraut *n* (-[*e*]*s*; *no pl*) weed(s); ***Unkraut jäten*** weed (the garden)
unkündbar ['ʊnkʏntbaːɐ] *adj* permanent (*post*)
'unlängst *adv* lately, recently
'unleserlich *adj* illegible
'unlogisch *adj* illogical
un'lösbar *adj* insoluble
'unmännlich *adj* unmanly, effeminate
'unmäßig *adj* excessive
'Unmenge *f* vast quantity *or* number(s) (***von*** of), F loads (of), tons (of)
'Unmensch *m* monster, brute
'unmenschlich *adj* inhuman, cruel
'Unmenschlichkeit *f* (-; -*en*) a) (*no pl*) inhumanity, b) cruelty
un'merklich *adj* imperceptible
'unmissverständlich *adj* unmistakable
'unmittelbar 1. *adj* immediate, direct; **2.** *adv*: ***unmittelbar nach*** (***hinter***) right after (behind)
'unmöbliert *adj* unfurnished
'unmodern *adj* out of fashion *or* style
'unmöglich 1. *adj* impossible; **2.** *adv*: ***ich kann es unmöglich tun*** I can't possibly do it
'unmoralisch *adj* immoral
'unmündig *adj* JUR under age
'unmusikalisch *adj* unmusical
'unnachahmlich *adj* inimitable
'unnachgiebig *adj* unyielding
'unnachsichtig *adj* strict, severe

unnahbar [ʊnˈnaːbaːɐ] *adj* standoffish, cold
ˈ**unnatürlich** *adj* unnatural (*a. fig*); affected
ˈ**unnötig** *adj* unnecessary, needless
unnütz [ˈʊnnʏts] *adj* useless
ˈ**unordentlich** *adj* untidy; ***unordentlich sein*** *room etc*: be (in) a mess
ˈ**Unordnung** *f* (-; *no pl*) disorder, mess
ˈ**unparteiisch** *adj* impartial, unbias(s)ed
ˈ**Unparteiische** *m, f* (-*n*; -*n*) SPORT referee
ˈ**unpassend** *adj* unsuitable; improper; inappropriate
ˈ**unpassierbar** *adj* impassable
unpässlich [ˈʊnpɛslɪç] *adj* indisposed
ˈ**unpersönlich** *adj* impersonal (*a.* LING)
ˈ**unpolitisch** *adj* unpolitical
ˈ**unpraktisch** *adj* impractical
ˈ**unpünktlich** *adj* unpunctual
ˈ**unrecht** *adj* wrong; ***unrecht haben*** be wrong; ***j-m unrecht tun*** do s.o. wrong
ˈ**Unrecht** *n* (-[*e*]*s*; *no pl*) injustice, wrong; ***zu Unrecht*** wrong(ful)ly; ***Unrecht haben*** → ***unrecht***; ***unrecht tun*** → ***unrecht***
ˈ**unrechtmäßig** *adj* unlawful
ˈ**unregelmäßig** *adj* irregular (*a.* LING)
ˈ**Unregelmäßigkeit** *f* (-; -*en*) irregularity
ˈ**unreif** *adj* unripe; *fig* immature
ˈ**Unreife** *fig f* immaturity
ˈ**unrein** *adj* unclean; impure (*a.* REL)
ˈ**Unreinheit** *f* (-; -*en*) impurity
ˈ**unrichtig** *adj* incorrect, wrong
ˈ**Unruhe** *f* (-; -*n*) a) (*no pl*) restlessness, unrest (*a.* POL); anxiety, alarm, b) *pl* disturbances, riots
ˈ**unruhig** *adj* restless; uneasy; worried, alarmed; MAR rough
uns [ʊns] *pers pron* (to) us; each other; ***uns*** (***selbst***) (to) ourselves; ***ein Freund von uns*** a friend of ours
ˈ**unsachgemäß** *adj* improper
unsachlich *adj* unobjective
unsanft *adj* rude, rough
unsauber *adj* unclean, *esp fig a.* impure; SPORT unfair; *fig* underhand
unschädlich *adj* harmless
unscharf *adj* PHOT blurred, out of focus
unˈschätzbar *adj* inestimable, invaluable
ˈ**unscheinbar** *adj* inconspicuous; plain
unschicklich *adj* indecent
unschlüssig *adj* irresolute; undecided
unschön *adj* unsightly; *fig* unpleasant
ˈ**Unschuld** *f* (-; *no pl*) innocence; *fig* virginity
ˈ**unschuldig** *adj* innocent (***an*** *dat* of)
ˈ**unselbstständig** *adj* dependent on others
ˈ**Unselbstständigkeit** *f* lack of independence, dependence on others
unser [ˈʊnzɐ] *poss pron* our; ***unserer, unsere, unseres*** ours
ˈ**unsicher** *adj* unsafe, insecure; self-conscious; uncertain
ˈ**Unsicherheit** *f* (-; -*en*) a) (*no pl*) insecurity, unsafeness; self-consciousness, b) uncertainty
ˈ**unsichtbar** *adj* invisible
ˈ**Unsinn** *m* (-[*e*]*s*; *no pl*) nonsense
ˈ**unsinnig** *adj* nonsensical, stupid; absurd
ˈ**Unsitte** *f* bad habit; abuse
ˈ**unsittlich** *adj* immoral, indecent
ˈ**unsozial** *adj* unsocial
ˈ**unsportlich** *adj* unathletic; *fig* unfair
ˈ**unsterblich 1.** *adj* immortal (*a. fig*); **2.** *adv*: ***unsterblich verliebt*** madly in love (***in*** *acc* with)
ˈ**Unsterblichkeit** *f* immortality
ˈ**Unstimmigkeit** *f* (-; -*en*) discrepancy; *pl* disagreements
ˈ**unsympathisch** *adj* disagreeable; ***er*** (***es***) ***ist mir unsympathisch*** I don't like him (it)
ˈ**untätig** *adj* inactive; idle
ˈ**Untätigkeit** *f* (-; *no pl*) inactivity
ˈ**untauglich** *adj* unfit (*a.* MIL); incompetent
unˈteilbar *adj* indivisible
unten [ˈʊntən] *adv* (down) below, down (*a.* ***nach unten***); downstairs; ***unten auf*** (*dat*) at the bottom of *the page etc*; ***siehe unten*** see below; ***von oben bis unten*** from top to bottom
unter [ˈʊntɐ] *prp* under; below (*a. fig*); among; *fig* less than; ***unter anderem*** among other things; ***unter uns*** (***gesagt***) between you and me; ***unter Wasser*** underwater
ˈ**Unterarm** *m* ANAT forearm
ˈ**unterbelichtet** *adj* PHOT underexposed
unterbesetzt *adj* understaffed
ˈ**Unterbewusstsein** *n* subconscious; ***im Unterbewusstsein*** subconsciously
unterˈbieten *v/t* (*irr*, ***bieten***, *no* -*ge*-, *h*) underbid; undercut; beat (*record*)
unterˈbinden *fig v/t* (*irr*, ***binden***, *no* -*ge*-, *h*) put a stop to; prevent
unterˈbrechen *v/t* (*irr*, ***brechen***, *no* -*ge*-, *h*) interrupt
Unterˈbrechung *f* (-; -*en*) interruption
ˈ**unterbringen** *v/i* (*irr*, ***bringen***, *sep*, -*ge*-, *h*) accommodate, put *s.o.* up; find a place for, put (***in*** *acc* into)
ˈ**Unterbringung** *f* (-; -*en*) accommodation
unterˈdessen *adv* in the meantime, meanwhile
unterˈdrücken *v/t* (*no* -*ge*-, *h*) oppress; suppress
Unterˈdrücker *m* (-*s*; -) oppressor

Unter'drückung *f* (-; *-en*) oppression; suppression
untere ['ʊntərə] *adj* lower (*a. fig*)
'unterentwickelt *adj* underdeveloped
'unterernährt *adj* undernourished, underfed
'Unterernährung *f* (-; *no pl*) undernourishment, malnutrition
Unter'führung *f* (-; *-en*) underpass, *Br a.* subway
'Untergang *m* ASTR setting; MAR sinking; *fig* downfall; decline; fall
'untergehen *v/i* (*irr*, ***gehen***, *sep*, *-ge-*, *sein*) go down (*a. fig*), ASTR *a.* set, MAR *a.* sink
'untergeordnet *adj* subordinate, inferior; secondary
'Untergewicht *n* (-[*e*]*s*; *no pl*), **'untergewichtig** *adj* underweight
unter'graben *fig v/t* (*irr*, **graben**, *no -ge-*, *h*) undermine
'Untergrund *m* subsoil; POL underground; ***in den Untergrund gehen*** go underground
Untergrundbahn *f* → ***U-Bahn***
'unterhalb *prp* (*gen*) below, under
'Unterhalt *m* (-[*e*]*s*; *no pl*) support, maintenance (*a.* JUR)
unter'halten *v/t* (*irr*, ***halten***, *no -ge-*, *h*) entertain; support; ***sich unterhalten*** (***mit***) talk (to, with); ***sich*** (***gut***) ***unterhalten*** enjoy o.s., have a good time
unter'haltsam *adj* entertaining
Unter'haltung *f* (-; *-en*) talk, conversation; entertainment
Unter'haltungsindus,trie *f* show business
'Unterhändler *m* negotiator
Unterhaus *n* (*-es*; *no pl*) *Br* PARL House of Commons
Unterhemd *n* undershirt, *Br* vest
Unterholz *n* (*-es*; *no pl*) undergrowth
Unterhose *f* shorts, *esp Br* underpants, panties, *Br* pants; ***e-e lange Unterhose, lange Unterhosen*** (a pair of) long johns
'unterirdisch *adj* underground
'Unterkiefer *m* ANAT lower jaw
'Unterkleid *n* slip
'unterkommen *v/i* (*irr*, ***kommen***, *sep*, *-ge-*, *sein*) find accommodation; find work *or* a job (***bei*** with)
Unterkunft ['ʊntɐkʊnft] *f* (-; *-künfte* [-kʏnftə]) accommodation, lodging(s); MIL quarters; ***Unterkunft und Verpflegung*** board and lodging
'Unterlage *f* TECH base; *pl* documents; data
unter'lassen *v/t* (*irr*, ***lassen***, *no -ge-*, *h*) omit, fail to do *s.th.*; stop *or* quit doing *s.th.*
Unter'lassung *f* (-; *-en*) omission (*a.* JUR)
'unterlegen[1] *v/t* (*sep*, *-ge-*, *h*) underlay
unter'legen[2] *adj* inferior (*dat* to)
Unter'legenheit *f* (-; *no pl*) inferiority
'Unterleib *m* ANAT abdomen, belly
unter'liegen *v/i* (*irr*, ***liegen***, *no -ge-*, *sein*) be defeated (***j-m*** by s.o.), lose (to s.o.); *fig* be subject to
'Unterlippe *f* ANAT lower lip
'Untermieter *m*, **'Untermieterin** *f* roomer, *Br* lodger
unter'nehmen *v/t* (*irr*, ***nehmen***, *no -ge-*, *h*) make, take, go on *a trip etc*; ***et. unternehmen*** do s.th. (***gegen*** about *s.th.*), take action (against *s.o.*)
Unter'nehmen *n* (*-s*; -) firm, business; venture; undertaking, enterprise; MIL operation
Unter'nehmensberater(in) management consultant
Unter'nehmer *m* (*-s*; -) businessman, entrepreneur; employer
Unter'nehmerin *f* (-; *-nen*) businesswoman
unter'nehmungslustig *adj* active, dynamic; adventurous
'Unteroffizier *m* MIL non-commissioned officer
'unterordnen *v/t and v/refl* (*sep*, *-ge-*, *h*) subordinate (o.s.) (*dat* to)
Unter'redung *f* (-; *-en*) talk(s)
Unterricht ['ʊntɐrɪçt] *m* (-[*e*]*s*; *no pl*) instruction, teaching; PED school, classes, lessons
unter'richten *v/i and v/t* (*no -ge-*, *h*) teach; give lessons; inform (***über*** *acc* of)
'Unterrichtsstunde *f* lesson, PED *a.* class, period
'Unterrock *m* slip
unter'sagen *v/t* (*no -ge-*, *h*) prohibit
unter'schätzen *v/t* (*no -ge-*, *h*) underestimate; underrate
unter'scheiden *v/t and v/i* (*irr*, ***scheiden***, *no -ge-*, *h*) distinguish (***zwischen*** between; ***von*** from); tell apart; ***sich unterscheiden*** differ (***von*** from; ***in*** *dat* in; ***durch*** by)
Unter'scheidung *f* (-; *-en*) distinction
Unterschied ['ʊntɐʃiːt] *m* (-[*e*]*s*; *-e*) difference; ***im Unterschied zu*** unlike, as opposed to
'unterschiedlich *adj* different; varying
unter'schlagen *v/t* (*irr*, ***schlagen***, *no -ge-*, *h*) embezzle
Unter'schlagung *f* (-; *-en*) embezzlement
Unterschlupf ['ʊntɐʃlʊpf] *m* (-[*e*]*s*; *no pl*) hiding place
unter'schreiben *v/t and v/i* (*irr*, ***schreiben***, *no -ge-*, *h*) sign
'Unterschrift *f* signature; caption

'Unterseeboot *n* → ***U-Boot***
Untersetzer ['ʊntɐzɛtsɐ] *m* (*-s; -*) coaster; saucer
unter'setzt *adj* thickset, stocky
'Unterstand *m* shelter, MIL *a.* dugout
unter'stehen (*irr*, ***stehen***, *no -ge-*, *h*) **1.** *v/i* (*dat*) be under (the control of); **2.** *v/refl* dare; ***unterstehen Sie sich (et. zu tun)!*** don't you dare ([to] do s.th.)!
'unterstellen[1] *v/t* (*sep*, *-ge-*, *h*) put *s.th.* in; store; ***sich unterstellen*** take shelter
unter'stellen[2] *v/t* (*no -ge-*, *h*) assume; ***j-m unterstellen, dass er …*** insinuate that s.o. …
Unter'stellung *f* (*-; -en*) insinuation
unter'streichen *v/t* (*irr*, ***streichen***, *no -ge-*, *h*) underline (*a. fig*)
unter'stützen *v/t* (*no -ge-*, *h*) support; back (up)
Unter'stützung *f* (*-; -en*) support; aid; welfare (payments)
unter'suchen *v/t* (*no -ge-*, *h*) examine (*a.* MED), investigate (*a.* JUR); search; CHEM analyze
Unter'suchung *f* (*-; -en*) examination (*a.* MED), investigation (*a.* JUR), *a.* (medical) checkup; CHEM analysis
Unter'suchungsgefangene *m, f* JUR prisoner on remand
Untersuchungsgefängnis *n* JUR remand prison
Untersuchungshaft *f*: ***in Untersuchungshaft sein*** JUR be on remand
Untersuchungsrichter *m* JUR examining magistrate
Untertan ['ʊntɐta:n] *m* (*-s; -en*) subject
'Untertasse *f* saucer
'untertauchen (*sep*, *-ge-*) **1.** *v/i* (*sein*) dive, submerge; *fig* disappear; *esp* POL go underground; **2.** *v/t* (*h*) duck
'Unterteil *n, m* lower part, bottom
unter'teilen *v/t* (*no -ge-*, *h*) subdivide
Unter'teilung *f* (*-; -en*) subdivision
'Untertitel *m* subtitle, *film*: *a.* caption
'Unterton *m* undertone
Unter'treibung *f* (*-; -en*) understatement
'untervermieten *v/t* (*no -ge-*, *h*) sublet
unter'wandern *v/t* (*no -ge-*, *h*) infiltrate
'Unterwäsche *f* underwear
'Unterwasser… *in cpds* underwater …
unterwegs [ʊntɐ've:ks] *adv* on the *or* one's way (***nach*** to)
unter'weisen *v/t* (*irr*, ***weisen***, *no -ge-*, *h*) instruct
Unter'weisung *f* (*-; -en*) instruction
'Unterwelt *f* (*-; no pl*) underworld
unter'werfen *v/t* (*irr*, ***werfen***, *no -ge-*, *h*) subject (*dat* to); subjugate; ***sich unterwerfen*** submit (to)
Unter'werfung *f* (*-; -en*) subjection; submission (***unter*** *acc* to)
unterwürfig [ʊntɐ'vʏrfɪç] *adj* servile
unter'zeichnen *v/t* (*no -ge-*, *h*) sign
Unter'zeichnete *m, f* (*-n; -n*) *the* undersigned
Unter'zeichnung *f* (*-; -en*) signing
'unterziehen[1] *v/t* (*irr*, ***ziehen***, *sep*, *-ge-*, *h*) put *s.th.* on underneath
unter'ziehen[2] *v/t* (*irr*, ***ziehen***, *no -ge-*, *h*) ***sich*** *e-r Behandlung, Prüfung etc* ***unterziehen*** undergo (*treatment etc*), take (*an examination etc*)
'Untiefe *f* shallow, shoal
un'tragbar *adj* unbearable, intolerable
un'trennbar *adj* inseparable
'untreu *adj* unfaithful (*dat* to)
un'tröstlich *adj* inconsolable
untrüglich [ʊn'try:klɪç] *adj* unmistakable
'Untugend *f* vice, bad habit
'unüberlegt *adj* thoughtless
unübersichtlich *adj* blind (*bend etc*)
unübertrefflich [ʊnˀy:bɐ'trɛflɪç] *adj* unsurpassable, matchless
unübertroffen [-'trɔfən] *adj* unequal(l)ed
unüberwindlich [-'vɪntlɪç] *adj* insuperable, invincible
unumgänglich [ʊnˀʊm'gɛŋlɪç] *adj* inevitable
unumschränkt [-'ʃrɛŋkt] *adj* unlimited; POL absolute
unumstritten [-'ʃtrɪtən] *adj* undisputed
unumwunden [-'vʊndən] *adv* straight out, frankly
ununterbrochen ['ʊnˀʊntɐbrɔxən] *adj* uninterrupted; continuous
unver'änderlich *adj* unchanging
unver'antwortlich *adj* irresponsible
unver'besserlich *adj* incorrigible
unver'bindlich *adj* noncommittal, ECON not binding
unver'daulich *adj* indigestible (*a. fig*)
'unverdient *adj* undeserved
'unverdünnt *adj* undiluted; straight
unver'einbar *adj* incompatible
'unverfälscht *adj* unadulterated
'unverfänglich *adj* harmless
'unverfroren *adj* brazen, impertinent
'unvergänglich *adj* immortal, eternal
unver'gesslich *adj* unforgettable
'unver'gleichlich *adj* incomparable
'unverhältnismäßig *adv* disproportionately; ***unverhältnismäßig hoch*** excessive
'unverheiratet *adj* unmarried, single
unverhofft ['ʊnfɛɐhɔft] *adj* unhoped-for; unexpected
unverhohlen ['ʊnfɛɐho:lən] *adj* undisguised, open

'unverkäuflich *adj* not for sale; unsal(e)-able
unver'kennbar *adj* unmistakable
'unverletzt *adj* unhurt
unvermeidlich [ʊnfɛɐ'maitlɪç] *adj* inevitable
'unvermindert *adj* undiminished
'unvermittelt *adj* abrupt, sudden
'Unvermögen *n* (*-s; no pl*) inability, incapacity
'unvermutet *adj* unexpected
'unvernünftig *adj* unreasonable; foolish
'unverschämt *adj* rude, impertinent; outrageous (*price etc*)
'Unverschämtheit *f* (*-; -en*) impertinence; ***die Unverschämtheit haben zu*** *inf* have the nerve to *inf*
'unverschuldet *adj* through no fault of one's own
unversehens ['ʊnfɛɐze:əns] *adv* unexpectedly, all of a sudden
'unversehrt *adj* unhurt; undamaged
unversöhnlich *adj* irreconcilable (*a. fig*), implacable
unversorgt *adj* unprovided for
unverständlich *adj* unintelligible; ***es ist mir unverständlich*** I can't see how *or* why, F it beats me
unversucht *adj*: ***nichts unversucht lassen*** leave nothing undone
unver'wundbar *adj* invulnerable
unverwüstlich [ʊnfɛɐ'vy:stlɪç] *adj* indestructible
unverzeihlich [-'tsailɪç] *adj* inexcusable
unverzüglich [-'tsy:klɪç] **1.** *adj* immediate, prompt; **2.** *adv* immediately, without delay
'unvollendet *adj* unfinished
'unvollkommen *adj* imperfect
'unvollständig *adj* incomplete
'unvorbereitet *adj* unprepared
'unvoreingenommen *adj* unprejudiced, unbias(s)ed
'unvorhergesehen *adj* unforeseen
'unvorhersehbar *adj* unforeseeable
'unvorsichtig *adj* careless
'Unvorsichtigkeit *f* (*-; no pl*) carelessness
unvor'stellbar *adj* unthinkable
'unvorteilhaft *adj* unbecoming
'unwahr *adj* untrue
'Unwahrheit *f* untruth
'unwahrscheinlich *adj* improbable, unlikely; F fantastic
unwegsam ['ʊnve:kza:m] *adj* difficult, rough (*terrain*)
unweigerlich [ʊn'vaigɐlɪç] *adv* inevitably
'unweit *prp* (*gen*) not far from
'Unwetter *n* (*-s; -*) disastrous (thunder)-storm
'unwichtig *adj* unimportant
unwiderlegbar [ʊnvi:dɐ'le:kba:ɐ] *adj* irrefutable
unwiderruflich [-'ru:flɪç] *adj* irrevocable
unwiderstehlich [-'ʃte:lɪç] *adj* irresistible
'Unwille(n) *m* indignation (***über*** *acc* at)
'unwillig *adj* indignant (***über*** *acc* at); unwilling, reluctant
'unwillkürlich *adj* involuntary
'unwirklich *adj* unreal
'unwirksam *adj* ineffective
unwirsch ['ʊnvɪrʃ] *adj* surly, gruff
unwirtlich ['ʊnvɪrtlɪç] *adj* inhospitable
'unwirtschaftlich *adj* uneconomic(al)
'unwissend *adj* ignorant
'Unwissenheit *f* (*-; no pl*) ignorance
'unwohl *adj* unwell; uneasy
'unwürdig *adj* unworthy (*gen* of)
unzählig [ʊn'tsɛ:lɪç] *adj* innumerable, countless
unzer'brechlich *adj* unbreakable
unzer'reißbar *adj* untearable
unzer'störbar *adj* indestructible
unzer'trennlich *adj* inseparable
'Unzucht *f* (*-; no pl*) sexual offense (*Br* offence)
'unzüchtig *adj* indecent; obscene
'unzufrieden *adj* discontent(ed) (***mit*** with), dissatisfied (with)
'Unzufriedenheit *f* discontent, dissatisfaction
'unzugänglich *adj* inaccessible
'unzulänglich *adj* inadequate
'unzulässig *adj* inadmissible
unzu'mutbar *adj* unacceptable; unreasonable
'unzurechnungsfähig *adj* JUR irresponsible
'Unzurechnungsfähigkeit *f* (*-; no pl*) JUR irresponsibility
'unzureichend *adj* insufficient
'unzusammenhängend *adj* incoherent
'unzuverlässig *adj* unreliable, untrustworthy; uncertain
üppig ['ʏpɪç] *adj* luxuriant, lush (*both a. fig*); voluptuous, luscious; opulent; rich
uralt ['u:ɐˀalt] *adj* ancient (*a. iro*)
Uran [u'ra:n] *n* (*-s; no pl*) uranium
'Uraufführung *f* première, first performance (*film*: showing)
urbar ['u:ɐba:ɐ] *adj* arable; ***urbar machen*** cultivate; reclaim
'Urbevölkerung *f*, **'Ureinwohner** *pl* aboriginal inhabitants; *in Australia*: Aborigines
'Urenkel *m* great-grandson
'Urenkelin *f* great-granddaughter
'Urgroß... *in cpds* *...eltern*, *...mutter*, *...vater*: great-grand...

U

Urheberrechte ['u:ɐhe:bɐ-] *pl* copyright (*an dat* on, for)
Urin [u'ri:n] *m* (*-s; -e*) urine
urinieren [uri'ni:rən] *v/i* (*no -ge-, h*) urinate
Urkunde ['u:ɐkʊndə] *f* (-; *-n*) document; diploma
'Urkundenfälschung *f* forgery of documents
Urlaub ['u:ɐlaup] *m* (*-[e]s; -e*) vacation, *Br* holiday(s); MIL leave; ***in** or **im Urlaub sein*** (***auf Urlaub gehen***) be (go) on vacation (*Br* holiday); ***e-n Tag*** (***ein paar Tage***) ***Urlaub nehmen*** take a day (a few days) off
Urlauber(in) ['u:ɐlaubɐ (-bərɪn)] (*-s; -/-; -nen*) vacationist, vacationer, *Br* holidaymaker
Urne ['ʊrnə] *f* (-; *-n*) urn; ballot box
'Ursache *f* (-; *-n*) cause; reason; ***keine Ursache!*** not at all, you're welcome
'Ursprung *m* origin
ursprünglich ['u:ɐʃprʏŋlɪç] *adj* original; natural, unspoilt
Urteil ['ʊrtail] *n* (*-[e]s; -e*) judg(e)ment; JUR sentence; ***sich ein Urteil bilden*** form a judg(e)ment (***über** acc* about)
'urteilen *v/i* (*ge-, h*) judge (***über j-n, et.*** s.o., s.th.; ***nach*** by)
'Urwald *m* primeval forest; jungle
urwüchsig ['u:ɐvy:ksɪç] *adj* coarse, earthy
'Urzeit *f* prehistoric times
usw. ABBR *of* ***und so weiter*** etc, and so on
Utensilien [utɛn'zi:ljən] *pl* utensils
Utopie [uto'pi:] *f* (-; *-n*) illusion
utopisch [u'to:pɪʃ] *adj* utopian; fantastic

V

Vagabund [vaga'bʊnt] *m* (*-en; -en*) vagabond, tramp, F bum
vage ['va:gə] *adj* vague
Vakuum ['va:kuʊm] *n* (*-s; -kua, -kuen*) vacuum
Vampir ['vampi:ɐ] *m* (*-s; -e*) ZO vampire (*a. fig*)
Vanille [va'nɪljə] *f* (-; *no pl*) vanilla
variabel [va'rja:bəl] *adj* variable
Variante [va'rjantə] *f* (-; *-n*) variant
Variation [varja'tsio:n] *f* (-; *-en*) variation
Varietee, *a.* **Varieté** [varje'te:] *n* (*-s; -s*) vaudeville, *Br* variety theatre, music hall
variieren [vari'i:rən] *v/i and v/t* (*no -ge-, h*) vary
Vase ['va:zə] *f* (-; *-n*) vase
Vater ['fa:tɐ] *m* (*-s; Väter* ['fɛ:tɐ]) father
'Vaterland *n* native country
'Vaterlandsliebe *f* patriotism
väterlich ['fɛ:tɐlɪç] *adj* fatherly, paternal
'Vaterschaft *f* (-; *-en*) JUR paternity
'Vater'unser *n* (*-s;* -) REL Lord's Prayer
v. Chr. ABBR *of* ***vor Christus*** BC, before Christ
V-Ausschnitt ['fau-] *m* V-neck
Vegetarier [vege'ta:rjɐ] *m* (*-s;* -), **Vege'tarierin** *f* (-; *-nen*), **vegetarisch** [vege'ta:rɪʃ] *adj* vegetarian
Vegetation [vegeta'tsjo:n] *f* (-; *-en*) vegetation
vegetieren [vege'ti:rən] *v/i* (*no -ge-, h*) vegetate
Veilchen ['failçən] *n* (*-s;* -) BOT violet
Velo ['ve:lo] *Swiss n* (*-s; -s*) bicycle, F bike
Ventil [vɛn'ti:l] *n* (*-s; -e*) TECH valve; *fig* vent, outlet
Ventilation [vɛntila'tsjo:n] *f* (-; *-en*) ventilation
Ventilator [vɛnti'la:to:ɐ] *m* (*-s; -en* [-la'to:rən]) fan
verabreden [fɛɐ'ʔap-] *v/t* (*no -ge-, h*) agree (up)on, arrange; appoint, fix; ***sich verabreden*** make a date (*or* an appointment) (***mit*** with)
Ver'abredung *f* (-; *-en*) appointment; date
ver'abreichen *v/t* (*no -ge-, h*) give; MED administer
verabscheuen *v/t* (*no -ge-, h*) loathe, detest
verabschieden [fɛɐ'ʔapʃi:dən] *v/t* (*no -ge-, h*) say goodbye to (*a.* ***sich verabschieden von***); dismiss; JUR pass
Ver'abschiedung *f* (-; *-en*) dismissal; JUR passing
ver'achten *v/t* (*no -ge-, h*) despise
verächtlich [fɛɐ'ʔɛçtlɪç] *adj* contemptuous
Ver'achtung *f* (-; *no pl*) contempt
verallgemeinern [fɛɐ'ʔalgə'mainɐn] *v/t* (*no -ge-, h*) generalize

ver'altet *adj* antiquated, out of date
Veranda [ve'randa] *f* (-; *-den*) porch, *Br* veranda(h)
veränderlich [fɛɐ'ʔɛndɐlɪç] *adj* changeable (*a.* METEOR), variable (*a.* MATH, LING)
ver'ändern *v/t and v/refl* (*no -ge-*, *h*), **Ver'änderung** *f* change
verängstigt [fɛɐ'ʔɛŋstɪçt] *adj* frightened, scared
ver'anlagen *v/t* (*no -ge-*, *h*) ECON assess
veranlagt [fɛɐ'ʔanla:kt] *adj* inclined (***zu, für*** to); ***künstlerisch*** (***musikalisch***) ***veranlagt sein*** have a gift *or* bent for art (music)
Ver'anlagung *f* (-; *-en*) (pre)disposition (*a.* MED); talent, gift; ECON assessment
ver'anlassen *v/t* (*no -ge-*, *h*) make arrangements (*or* arrange) for *s.th.*; ***j-n zu et. veranlassen*** make s.o. do s.th.
Ver'anlassung *f* (-; *-en*) cause (***zu*** for)
ver'anschaulichen *v/t* (*no -ge-*, *h*) illustrate
ver'anschlagen *v/t* (*no -ge-*, *h*) estimate (***auf*** *acc* at)
ver'anstalten *v/t* (*no -ge-*, *h*) arrange, organize; hold, give (*concert, party etc*)
Ver'anstaltung *f* (-; *-en*) event, SPORT *a.* meet, *Br* meeting
ver'antworten *v/t* (*no -ge-*, *h*) take the responsibility for
ver'antwortlich *adj* responsible; ***j-n verantwortlich machen für*** hold s.o. responsible for
Ver'antwortung *f* (-; *no pl*) responsibility; ***auf eigene Verantwortung*** at one's own risk; ***j-n zur Verantwortung ziehen*** call s.o. to account
Ver'antwortungsgefühl *n* (-[*e*]*s*; *no pl*) sense of responsibility
ver'antwortungslos *adj* irresponsible
ver'arbeiten *v/t* (*no -ge-*, *h*) process; *fig* digest; ***et. verarbeiten zu*** manufacture (*or* make) s.th. into
ver'ärgern *v/t* (*no -ge-*, *h*) make *s.o.* angry, annoy
ver'armt *adj* impoverished
ver'arschen *v/t* (*no -ge-*, *h*) ***j-n verarschen*** take the piss out of s.o.
Verb [vɛrp] *n* (*-s*; *-en* ['vɛrbən]) LING verb
Verband [fɛɐ'bant] *m* (*-es*; *Verbände* [fɛɐ'bɛndə]) MED dressing, bandage; ECON association; MIL formation, unit
Verband(s)kasten *m* MED first-aid kit *or* box
Verband(s)zeug *n* MED dressing material
ver'bannen *v/t* (*no -ge-*, *h*) banish (*a. fig*), exile
Ver'bannung *f* (-; *-en*) banishment, exile
verbarrika'dieren *v/t* (*no -ge-*, *h*) barricade; block
ver'bergen *v/t* (*irr*, ***bergen***, *no -ge-*, *h*) hide (*a.* ***sich verbergen***), conceal
ver'bessern *v/t* (*no -ge-*, *h*) improve; correct
Ver'besserung *f* (-; *-en*) improvement; correction
ver'beugen *v/refl* (*no -ge-*, *h*), **Ver'beugung** *f* (-; *-en*) bow (***vor*** to)
ver'biegen *v/t* (*irr*, ***biegen***, *no -ge-*, *h*) twist
ver'bieten *v/t* (*irr*, ***bieten***, *no -ge-*, *h*) forbid; prohibit; → ***verboten***
ver'billigen *v/t* (*no -ge-*, *h*) reduce in price
verbilligt [-'bɪlɪçt] *adj* reduced, at reduced prices
verbinden *v/t* (*irr*, ***binden***, *no -ge-*, *h*) MED dress, bandage; bandage *s.o.* up; *a.* TECH connect, join, link (up); TEL put *s.o.* through (***mit*** to); combine (*a.* CHEM ***sich verbinden***); *fig* unite; associate; ***j-m die Augen verbinden*** blindfold s.o.; ***damit sind beträchtliche Kosten verbunden*** that involves considerable cost(s *pl*); ***falsch verbunden!*** wrong number!
verbindlich [fɛɐ'bɪntlɪç] *adj* obligatory, compulsory (*a.* PED); obliging
Ver'bindlichkeit *f* (-; *-en*) a) (*no pl*) obligingness, b) *pl* ECON liabilities
Ver'bindung *f* (-; *-en*) connection; combination; CHEM compound; UNIV fraternity, *Br* society; ***sich in Verbindung setzen mit*** get in touch with; ***in Verbindung stehen*** (***bleiben***) be (keep) in touch
verbissen [fɛɐ'bɪsən] *adj* dogged
ver'bittert *adj* bitter, embittered
verblassen [fɛɐ'blasən] *v/i* (*no -ge-*, *sein*) fade (*a. fig*)
Verbleib [fɛɐ'blaip] *m* (-[*e*]*s*; *no pl*) whereabouts
ver'bleiben *v/i* (*irr*, ***bleiben***, *no -ge-*, *sein*) remain
verbleit [fɛɐ'blait] *adj* leaded
ver'blendet *fig adj* blind
Ver'blendung *fig f* (-; *-en*) blindness
verblichen [fɛɐ'blɪçən] *adj* faded
verblüffen [fɛɐ'blʏfən] *v/t* (*no -ge-*, *h*) amaze, F flabbergast
Ver'blüffung *f* (-; *-en*) amazement
ver'blühen *v/i* (*no -ge-*, *sein*) fade, wither (*both a. fig*)
ver'bluten *v/i* (*no -ge-*, *sein*) MED bleed to death
verborgen [fɛɐ'bɔrgən] *adj* hidden, concealed; ***im Verborgenen*** in secret
Verbot [fɛɐ'bo:t] *n* (-[*e*]*s*; *-e*) prohibition, ban (on *s.th.*)
ver'boten *adj*: ***Rauchen verboten*** no smoking

Ver'brauch *m* (-[*e*]*s*; *no pl*) consumption (***an*** *dat* of)
ver'brauchen *v/t* (*no -ge-, h*) consume, use up
Verbraucher [fɛɐ'brauxɐ] *m* (-*s*; -), **Ver'braucherin** *f* (-; *-nen*) consumer
Verbraucherschutz *m* consumer protection
Ver'brechen *n* (-*s*; -) crime; ***ein Verbrechen begehen*** commit a crime
Ver'brecher(in) (-*s*; -/-; *-nen*), **ver'brecherisch** *adj* criminal
ver'breiten *v/t and v/refl* (*no -ge-, h*) spread (***in*** *dat*, ***über*** *acc* over, through); circulate
verbreitern [fɛɐ'braitɐn] *v/t and v/refl* (*no -ge-, h*) widen, broaden
Ver'breitung *f* (-; *no pl*) spread(ing); circulation
ver'brennen *v/i* (*irr*, ***brennen***, *no -ge-, sein*) *and v/t* (*h*) burn (up); cremate
Ver'brennung *f* (-; *-en*) burning; cremation; TECH combustion; MED burn
ver'bringen *v/t* (*irr*, ***bringen***, *no -ge-, h*) spend, pass
verbrüdern [fɛɐ'bry:dɐn] *v/refl* (*no -ge-, h*) fraternize
Verbrüderung [fɛɐ'bry:dərʊŋ] *f* (-; *-en*) fraternization
ver'brühen *v/t* (*no -ge-, h*) scald
ver'buchen *v/t* (*no -ge-, h*) book
verbünden [fɛɐ'bʏndən] *v/refl* (*no -ge-, h*) ally o.s. (***mit*** to, with)
Ver'bündete *m, f* (-*n*; -*n*) ally (*a. fig*)
ver'bürgen *v/refl* (*no -ge-, h*) ***sich verbürgen für*** vouch for, guarantee
ver'büßen *v/t* (*no -ge-, h*) ***e-e Strafe verbüßen*** serve a sentence, serve time
verchromt [fɛɐ'kro:mt] *adj* chromium-plated
Verdacht [fɛɐ'daxt] *m* (-[*e*]*s*; *-e*) suspicion; ***Verdacht schöpfen*** become suspicious
verdächtig [fɛɐ'dɛçtɪç] *adj* suspicious, suspect
Verdächtige [fɛɐ'dɛçtɪgə] *m, f* (-*n*; -*n*) suspect
ver'dächtigen *v/t* (*no -ge-, h*) suspect (***j-n e-r Tat*** s.o. of [doing] s.th.)
Ver'dächtigung *f* (-; *-en*) suspicion
verdammen [fɛɐ'damən] *v/t* (*no -ge-, h*) condemn (***zu*** to), damn (*a.* REL)
Ver'dammnis *f* (-; *no pl*) REL damnation
ver'dammt **1.** *adj* damned, F *a.* damn, darn(ed), *Br sl a.* bloody; F ***verdammt (noch mal)!*** damn (it)!; **2.** *adv*: ***verdammt gut*** *etc* damn (*Br sl a.* bloody) good *etc*
Ver'dammung *f* (-; *-en*) condemnation; REL damnation
ver'dampfen *v/t* (*no -ge-, h*) and *v/i* (*sein*) evaporate
ver'danken *v/t* (*no -ge-, h*) ***j-m*** (***e-m Umstand***) ***et. verdanken*** owe s.th. to s.o. (s.th.)
verdarb [fɛɐ'darp] *pret of* ***verderben***
verdauen [fɛɐ'dauən] *v/t* (*no -ge-, h*) digest (*a. fig*)
ver'daulich *adj* digestible; ***leicht*** (***schwer***) ***verdaulich*** easy (hard) to digest
Ver'dauung *f* (-; *no pl*) digestion
Ver'deck *n* (-[*e*]*s*; *-e*) top
ver'decken *v/t* (*no -ge-, h*) cover (up) (*a. fig*)
ver'denken *v/t* (*irr*, ***denken***, *no -ge-, h*) ***ich kann es ihm nicht verdenken***(, ***dass er …***) I can't blame him (for *doing*)
verderben [fɛɐ'dɛrbən] (*irr*, *no -ge-*) **1.** *v/i* (*sein*) spoil (*a. fig*); GASTR go bad; **2.** *v/t* (*h*) spoil (*a. fig*), ruin; ***sich den Magen verderben*** upset one's stomach
Ver'derben *n* (-*s*; *no pl*) ruin
verderblich [fɛɐ'dɛrplɪç] *adj* perishable; ***leicht verderbliche Lebensmittel*** perishables
ver'dichten *v/t* (*no -ge-, h*) compress, condense
ver'dienen *v/t* (*no -ge-, h*) earn, make; *fig* deserve
Ver'dienst[1] *m* (-[*e*]*s*; *-e*) earnings; salary; wages; gain, profit
Ver'dienst[2] *n* (-[*e*]*s*; *-e*) merit; ***es ist sein Verdienst, dass*** it is thanks to him that
ver'dient *adj* (well-)deserved
ver'doppeln *v/t and v/refl* (*no -ge-, h*) double
verdorben [fɛɐ'dɔrbən] **1.** *pp of* ***verderben***; **2.** *adj* GASTR spoilt, bad (*both a. fig*); MED upset
verdorren [fɛɐ'dɔrən] *v/i* (*no -ge-, sein*) wither, dry up
ver'drängen *v/t* (*no -ge-, h*) supplant, supersede; replace; PHYS displace; PSYCH repress, suppress
ver'drehen *v/t* (*no -ge-, h*) twist, *fig a.* distort; ***die Augen verdrehen*** roll one's eyes; ***j-m den Kopf verdrehen*** turn s.o.'s head
ver'dreht F *fig adj* mixed up
ver'dreifachen *v/t and v/refl* (*no -ge-, h*) treble, triple
verdrießen [fɛɐ'dri:sən] *v/t* (*irr, no -ge-, h*) annoy
verdrießlich [fɛɐ'dri:slɪç] *adj* glum, morose, sullen
verdross [fɛɐ'drɔs] *pret of* ***verdrießen***
verdrossen [fɛɐ'drɔsən] **1.** *pp of* ***verdrießen***; **2.** *adj* grumpy, sullen

Verdruss [fɛɐ'drʊs] *m* (*-es*; *-e*) annoyance
ver'dummen (*no -ge-*) **1.** *v/t* (*h*) make stupid, stultify; **2.** *v/i* (*sein*) become stultified
ver'dunkeln *v/t and v/refl* (*no -ge-, h*) darken; black out; *fig* obscure
Ver'dunk(e)lung *f* (*-; -en*) darkening; blackout; JUR collusion
ver'dünnen *v/t* (*no -ge-, h*) dilute
ver'dunsten *v/i* (*no -ge-, sein*) evaporate
ver'dursten *v/i* (*no -ge-, sein*) die of thirst
verdutzt [fɛɐ'dʊtst] *adj* puzzled
ver'edeln *v/t* (*no -ge-, h*) BOT graft; TECH process, refine
Ver'ed(e)lung *f* (*-; -en*) BOT grafting; TECH processing, refinement
ver'ehren *v/t* (*no -ge-, h*) admire; adore, worship (*both a. fig*), *esp* REL *a.* revere, venerate
Ver'ehrer(in) (*-s; -/-; -nen*) admirer, *esp film etc*: *a.* fan
Ver'ehrung *f* (*-; no pl*) admiration; adoration, worship; *esp* REL reverence, veneration
vereidigen [fɛɐ'ʔaidɪgən] *v/t* (*no -ge-, h*) swear *s.o.* in; JUR put *s.o.* under an oath
Verein [fɛɐ'ʔain] *m* (*-[e]s; -e*) club (*a.* SPORT); society, association
vereinbar [fɛɐ'ʔainbaːɐ] *adj* compatible (***mit*** with)
vereinbaren [fɛɐ'ʔainbaːrən] *v/t* (*no -ge-, h*) agree (up)on, arrange
Ver'einbarung *f* (*-; -en*) agreement, arrangement
ver'einen → ***vereinigen***
ver'einfachen *v/t* (*no -ge-, h*) simplify
Ver'einfachung *f* (*-; -en*) simplification
ver'einheitlichen *v/t* (*no -ge-, h*) standardize
ver'einigen *v/t and v/refl* (*no -ge-, h*) unite (***zu*** into); combine, join
Ver'einigung *f* (*-; -en*) union; combination; alliance
ver'einsamen *v/i* (*no -ge-, sein*) become lonely *or* isolated
vereinzelt [fɛɐ'ʔaintsəlt] *adj* occasional, odd; ***vereinzelt Regen*** scattered showers
ver'eiteln *v/t* (*no -ge-, h*) prevent; frustrate
ver'enden *v/i* (*no -ge-, sein*) *esp* zo die, perish
ver'engen *v/t and v/refl* (*no -ge-, h*) narrow
ver'erben *v/t* (*no -ge-, h*) ***j-m et. vererben*** leave (BIOL transmit) s.th. to s.o.; ***sich vererben*** (***auf*** *acc*) be passed on *or* down (to) (*a.* BIOL *and fig*)
Ver'erbung *f* (*-; no pl*) BIOL heredity
Ver'erbungslehre *f* BIOL genetics
verewigen [fɛɐ'ʔeːvɪgən] *v/t* (*no -ge-, h*) immortalize
ver'fahren (*irr,* ***fahren****, no -ge-*) **1.** *v/i* (*sein*) proceed; ***verfahren mit*** deal with; **2.** *v/refl* (*h*) MOT get lost
Ver'fahren *n* (*-s; -*) procedure, method, *esp* TECH *a.* technique, way; JUR (legal) proceedings (***gegen*** against)
Ver'fall *m* (*-[e]s; no pl*) decay (*a. fig*); dilapidation; *fig* decline; ECON *etc* expiry
ver'fallen (*irr,* ***fallen****, no -ge-, sein*) **1.** *v/i* decay (*a. fig*), dilapidate; *esp fig* decline; ECON expire; MED waste away; become addicted to; (***wieder***) ***verfallen in*** (*acc*) fall (back) into; ***verfallen auf*** (*acc*) hit (up)on; **2.** *adj* decayed; dilapidated; ***j-m verfallen sein*** be s.o.'s slave
Ver'fallsdatum *n* expiry date; GASTR pull date, *Br* best-before (*or* best-by) date; PHARM sell-by date
ver'fälschen *v/t* (*no -ge-, h*) falsify; distort; GASTR adulterate
verfänglich [fɛɐ'fɛŋlɪç] *adj* delicate, tricky; embarrassing, compromising
ver'färben *v/refl* (*no -ge-, h*) discolo(u)r
ver'fassen *v/t* (*no -ge-, h*) write
Verfasser [fɛɐ'fasɐ] *m* (*-s; -*), **Ver'fasserin** *f* (*-; -nen*) author
Ver'fassung *f* (*-; -en*) state (of health *or* of mind), condition; POL constitution
ver'fassungsmäßig *adj* POL constitutional
verfassungswidrig *adj* unconstitutional
ver'faulen *v/i* (*no -ge-, sein*) rot, decay
ver'fechten *v/t* (*irr,* ***fechten****, no -ge-, h*), **Ver'fechter(in)** (*-s; -/-; -nen*) advocate
ver'fehlen *v/t* (*no -ge-, h*) miss (***sich*** each other)
Ver'fehlung *f* (*-; -en*) offense, *Br* offence
verfeinden [fɛɐ'faindən] *v/refl* (*no -ge-, h*) become enemies
ver'feindet *adj* hostile; ***verfeindet sein*** be enemies
verfeinern [fɛɐ'fainɐn] *v/t and v/refl* (*no -ge-, h*) refine
ver'filmen *v/t* (*no -ge-, h*) film
Ver'filmung *f* (*-; -en*) filming; film version
ver'flechten *v/t* (*irr,* ***flechten****, no -ge-, h*) intertwine (*a.* ***sich verflechten***)
ver'fluchen *v/t* (*no -ge-, h*) curse
ver'flucht → ***verdammt***
ver'folgen *v/t* (*no -ge-, h*) pursue (*a. fig*); chase, hunt (*both a. fig*); POL, REL persecute; follow (*track etc*); *fear etc*: haunt *s.o.*; ***j-n gerichtlich verfolgen*** prosecute s.o.
Verfolger [fɛɐ'fɔlgɐ] *m* (*-s; -*) pursuer; persecutor

Ver'folgung *f* (-; *-en*) pursuit (*a. cycling*); chase, hunt; persecution; ***gerichtliche Verfolgung*** prosecution
ver'frachten *v/t* (*no -ge-, h*) freight, ship; F bundle *s.o., s.th.* (***in*** *acc* into)
verfremden [fɛɐ'frɛmdən] *v/t* (*no -ge-, h*) *esp art*: alienate
ver'früht *adj* premature
verfügbar [fɛɐ'fy:kba:ɐ] *adj* available
ver'fügen (*no -ge-, h*) **1.** *v/t* decree, order; **2.** *v/i*: ***verfügen über*** (*acc*) have at one's disposal
Ver'fügung *f* (-; *-en*) a) decree, order, b) (*no pl*) disposal; ***j-m zur Verfügung stehen*** (***stellen***) be (place) at s.o. 's disposal
ver'führen *v/t* (*no -ge-, h*) seduce (***et. zu tun*** into doing s.th.)
Ver'führer *m* (*-s*; -) seducer
Ver'führerin *f* (-; *-nen*) seductress
ver'führerisch *adj* seductive; tempting
Ver'führung *f* (-; *-en*) seduction
vergangen [fɛɐ'gaŋən] *adj* gone, past; ***im vergangenen Jahr*** last year
Ver'gangenheit *f* (-; *no pl*) past; LING past tense
vergänglich [fɛɐ'gɛŋlɪç] *adj* transitory, transient
vergasen [fɛɐ'ga:zən] *v/t* (*no -ge-, h*) gas; CHEM gasify
Vergaser [fɛɐ'ga:zɐ] *m* (*-s*; -) MOT carburet(t)or
vergaß [fɛɐ'ga:s] *pret of* ***vergessen***
ver'geben *v/t* (*irr*, ***geben***, *no -ge-, h*) give away (*a. fig*); award (*prize etc*); forgive
ver'gebens *adv* in vain
vergeblich [fɛɐ'ge:plɪç] **1.** *adj* futile; **2.** *adv* in vain
Ver'gebung *f* (-; *-en*) forgiveness, pardon
ver'gehen (*irr*, ***gehen***, *no -ge-, sein*) **1.** *v/i time etc*: go by, pass; *pain, effect etc*: wear off; ***vergehen vor*** (*dat*) be dying with; ***wie die Zeit vergeht!*** how time flies!; **2.** *v/refl* ***sich vergehen an*** (*dat*) violate; rape
Vergehen *n* (*-s*; -) JUR offen|se, *Br* -ce
ver'gelten *v/t* (*irr*, ***gelten***, *no -ge-, h*) repay; reward
Ver'geltung *f* (-; *-en*) retaliation (*a.* MIL)
vergessen [fɛɐ'gɛsən] **1.** *v/t* (*irr*, *no -ge-, h*) forget; leave; **2.** *pp of* ***vergessen*** 1
Ver'gessenheit *f*: ***in Vergessenheit geraten*** fall into oblivion
vergesslich [fɛɐ'gɛslɪç] *adj* forgetful
vergeuden [fɛɐ'gɔʏdən] *v/t* (*no -ge-, h*), **Ver'geudung** *f* (-; *-en*) waste
vergewaltigen [fɛɐgə'valtɪgən] *v/t* (*no -ge-, h*) rape, violate (*a. fig*)
Verge'waltigung *f* (-; *-en*) rape, violation (*a. fig*)
vergewissern [fɛɐgə'vɪsɐn] *v/refl* (*no -ge-, h*) make sure (***e-r Sache*** of s.th.; ***ob*** whether; ***dass*** that)
ver'gießen *v/t* (*irr*, ***gießen***, *no -ge-, h*) shed (*blood, tears*); spill
ver'giften *v/t* (*no -ge-, h*) poison (*a. fig*); contaminate
Ver'giftung *f* (-; *-en*) poisoning (*a. fig*); contamination
ver'gittert *adj* barred (*window etc*)
Ver'gleich *m* (*-[e]s*; *-e*) comparison; JUR compromise
ver'gleichbar *adj* comparable (***mit*** to, with)
ver'gleichen *v/t* (*irr*, ***gleichen***, *no -ge-, h*) compare (***mit*** with *or* to); ***... ist nicht zu vergleichen mit*** ... cannot be compared to; ... cannot compare with; ***verglichen mit*** compared to *or* with
ver'gleichsweise *adv* comparatively, relatively
ver'glühen *v/i* (*no -ge-, sein*) burn out (*or* up)
vergnügen [fɛɐ'gny:gən] *v/refl* (*no -ge-, h*) enjoy o.s. (***mit et.*** doing s.th.)
Ver'gnügen *n* (*-s*; -) pleasure, enjoyment, fun; ***mit Vergnügen*** with pleasure; ***viel Vergnügen!*** have fun!, have a good time!
vergnügt [fɛɐ'gny:kt] *adj* cheerful
Ver'gnügung *f* (-; *-en*) pleasure, amusement, entertainment
Ver'gnügungspark *m* amusement park
ver'gnügungssüchtig *adj* pleasure-seeking
Ver'gnügungsviertel *n* nightlife district
ver'golden *v/t* (*no -ge-, h*) gild
vergöttern [fɛɐ'gœtɐn] *v/t* (*no -ge-, h*) idolize, adore
ver'graben *v/t* (*irr*, ***graben***, *no -ge-, h*) bury (*a. fig*)
ver'greifen *v/refl* (*irr*, ***greifen***, *no -ge-, h*) ***sich vergreifen an*** (*dat*) lay hands on
vergriffen [fɛɐ'grɪfən] *adj* out of print
vergrößern [fɛɐ'grø:sɐn] *v/t* (*no -ge-, h*) enlarge (*a.* PHOT); increase; OPT magnify; ***sich vergrößern*** increase, grow, expand
Ver'größerung *f* (-; *-en*) increase; PHOT enlargement; OPT magnification
Ver'größerungsglas *n* OPT magnifying glass
Vergünstigung [fɛɐ'gʏnstɪgʊŋ] *f* (-; *-en*) privilege
vergüten [fɛɐ'gy:tən] *v/t* (*no -ge-, h*) reimburse, pay (for)
Ver'gütung *f* (-; *-en*) reimbursement
ver'haften *v/t* (*no -ge-, h*), **Ver'haftung** *f* (-; *-en*) arrest
ver'halten[1] *v/refl* (*irr*, ***halten***, *no -ge-, h*) behave, conduct o.s., act; ***sich ruhig ver-***

V

halten keep quiet
ver'halten[2] *adj* restrained; subdued
Ver'halten *n* (*-s; no pl*) behavio(u)r, conduct
Ver'haltensforschung *f* behavio(u)ral science
ver'haltensgestört *adj* disturbed, maladjusted
Verhältnis [fɛɐ'hɛltnɪs] *n* (*-ses; -se*) relationship, relations; attitude; proportion, relation, *esp* MATH ratio; F affair; *pl* circumstances, conditions; ***über j-s Verhältnisse*** beyond s.o.'s means
ver'hältnismäßig *adv* comparatively, relatively
Ver'hältniswort *n* (-[*e*]*s*; *-wörter*) LING preposition
ver'handeln *no* (*-ge-, h*) **1.** *v/i* negotiate; **2.** *v/t* JUR hear
Ver'handlung *f* (*-; -en*) negotiation, talk; JUR hearing; trial
Ver'handlungsbasis *f* ECON asking price
ver'hängen *v/t* (*no -ge-, h*) cover (***mit*** with); impose (***über*** *acc* on)
Verhängnis [fɛɐ'hɛŋnɪs] *n* (*-ses; -se*) fate; disaster
ver'hängnisvoll *adj* fatal, disastrous
verharmlosen [fɛɐ'harmlo:zən] *v/t* (*no -ge-, h*) play *s.th.* down
verhärmt [fɛɐ'hɛrmt] *adj* careworn
ver'hasst *adj* hated; hateful
ver'hätscheln *v/t* (*no -ge-, h*) coddle, pamper, spoil
ver'hauen F *v/t* (*no -ge-, h*) spank
verheerend [fɛɐ'he:rənt] *adj* disastrous
ver'heilen *v/i* (*no -ge-, sein*) heal (up)
verheimlichen [fɛɐ'haimlɪçən] *v/t* (*no -ge-, h*) hide, conceal
ver'heiraten *v/t* (*no -ge-, h*) marry (*s.o.* off) (***mit*** to); ***sich verheiraten*** get married
ver'heiratet *adj* married (***mit*** to)
ver'heißungsvoll *adj* promising
ver'helfen *v/i* (*irr*, ***helfen***, *no -ge-, h*) ***j-m zu et. verhelfen*** help s.o. to get s.th.
ver'herrlichen *v/t* (*no -ge-, h*) glorify, *contp a.* idolize
Ver'herrlichung *f* (*-; -en*) glorification
ver'hexen *v/t* (*no -ge-, h*) bewitch
ver'hindern *v/t* (*no -ge-, h*) prevent (***dass j. et. tut*** s.o. from doing s.th.)
ver'hindert *adj* unable to come; F ***ein verhinderter …*** a would-be …
Ver'hinderung *f* (*-; -en*) prevention
ver'höhnen *v/t* (*no -ge-, h*) deride, mock (at), jeer (at)
Verhör [fɛɐ'hø:ɐ] *n* (-[*e*]*s*; *-e*) JUR interrogation
ver'hören (*no -ge-, h*) **1.** *v/t* interrogate, question; **2.** *v/refl* get it wrong
ver'hüllen *v/t* (*no -ge-, h*) cover, veil
ver'hungern *v/i* (*no -ge-, sein*) die of hunger, starve (to death)
Ver'hungern *n* (*-s; no pl*) starvation
ver'hüten *v/t* (*no -ge-, h*) prevent
Ver'hütung *f* (*-; -en*) prevention
Ver'hütungsmittel *n* MED contraceptive
ver'irren *v/refl* (*no -ge-, h*) get lost, lose one's way, go astray (*a. fig*)
Ver'irrung *f* (*-; -en*) aberration
ver'jagen *v/t* (*no -ge-, h*) chase *or* drive away
verjähren [fɛɐ'jɛ:rən] *v/i* (*no -ge-, sein*) JUR come under the statute of limitations
ver'jährt *adj* JUR statute-barred
verjüngen [fɛɐ'jʏŋən] *v/t* (*no -ge-, h*) make *s.o.* (look) younger, rejuvenate; ***sich verjüngen*** ARCH, TECH taper (off)
ver'kabeln *v/t* (*no -ge-, h*) ELECTR cable
Ver'kauf *m* sale
ver'kaufen *v/t* (*no -ge-, h*) sell; ***zu verkaufen*** for sale; ***sich gut verkaufen*** sell well
Ver'käufer *m* (*-s; -*) (sales)clerk, salesman, *Br* shop assistant; ECON seller
Ver'käuferin *f* (*-; -nen*) (sales)clerk, saleslady, *Br* shop assistant
ver'käuflich *adj* for sale; ***schwer verkäuflich*** hard to sell
Verkehr [fɛɐ'ke:ɐ] *m* (*-s; no pl*) traffic; transportation, *Br* transport; *fig* contact, dealings; intercourse; circulation; ***starker*** (***schwacher***) ***Verkehr*** heavy (light) traffic
ver'kehren (*no -ge-, h*) **1.** *v/i bus etc*: run; ***verkehren in*** (*dat*) frequent; ***verkehren mit*** associate *or* mix with; have intercourse with; **2.** *v/t* turn (***in*** *acc* into); ***ins Gegenteil verkehren*** reverse
Ver'kehrsader *f* arterial road
Verkehrsampel *f* traffic light(s)
Verkehrsbehinderung *f* hold--up, delay; JUR obstruction of traffic
Verkehrsde,likt *n* traffic offense (*Br* offence)
Verkehrsflugzeug *n* airliner
Verkehrsfunk *m* traffic bulletin
Verkehrsinsel *f* traffic island
Verkehrsmeldung *f* traffic announcement, flash
Verkehrsmi,nister *m* minister of transportation
Verkehrsminis,terium *n* ministry of transportation
Verkehrsmittel *n* means of transportation; ***öffentliche Verkehrsmittel*** public transportation
Verkehrsopfer *n* road casualty
Verkehrspoli,zei *f* traffic police

Verkehrsrowdy *m* F road hog
ver'kehrssicher *adj* MOT roadworthy
Ver'kehrssicherheit *f* MOT road safety; roadworthiness
Verkehrsstau *m* traffic jam
Verkehrssünder(in) F traffic offender
Verkehrsteilnehmer(in) road user
Verkehrsunfall *m* traffic accident; (car) crash
Verkehrsunterricht *m* traffic instruction
Verkehrszeichen *n* traffic sign
ver'kehrt *adj and adv* wrong; upside down; inside out
ver'kennen *v/t* (*irr*, ***kennen***, *no -ge-*, *h*) mistake, misjudge
ver'klagen *v/t* (*no -ge-*, *h*) JUR sue (***auf*** *acc*, ***wegen*** for)
ver'klappen *v/t* (*no -ge-*, *h*) dump (into the sea)
ver'kleben *v/t* (*no -ge-*, *h*) glue (together)
ver'kleiden *v/t* (*no -ge-*, *h*) disguise (***als*** as), dress *s.o.* up (as); TECH cover, (en-)case; panel; ***sich verkleiden*** disguise o.s., dress (o.s.) up
Ver'kleidung *f* (-; *-en*) disguise; TECH cover, encasement; panel(l)ing; MOT fairing
verkleinern [fɛɐ'klainɐn] *v/t* (*no -ge-*, *h*) make smaller, reduce, diminish
Ver'kleinerung [fɛɐ'klainərʊŋ] *f* (-; *-en*) reduction
ver'klingen *v/i* (*irr*, ***klingen***, *no -ge-*, *sein*) die away
ver'knallt F *adj*: ***verknallt sein in*** (*acc*) be madly in love with, have a crush on
ver'knoten *v/t* (*no -ge-*, *h*) knot
ver'knüpfen *v/t* (*no -ge-*, *h*) knot together; *fig* connect, combine
ver'kohlen *v/i* (*no -ge-*, *sein*) char
ver'kommen **1.** *v/i* (*irr*, ***kommen***, *no -ge-*, *sein*) become run-down *or* dilapidated; go to seed; GASTR go bad; **2.** *adj* run-down, dilapidated; neglected; depraved, rotten (to the core)
ver'korken *v/t* (*no -ge-*, *h*) cork (up)
ver'körpern *v/t* (*no -ge-*, *h*) personify; embody; *esp* THEA impersonate
ver'kriechen *v/refl* (*irr*, ***kriechen***, *no -ge-*, *h*) hide
ver'krümmt *adj* crooked, curved (*a.* MED)
ver'krüppelt *adj* crippled
ver'kümmern *v/i* (*no -ge-*, *sein*) BIOL become stunted
ver'kümmert *adj* BIOL stunted
verkünden [fɛɐ'kʏndən] *v/t* (*no -ge-*, *h*) announce; proclaim; JUR pronounce; REL preach
Ver'kündung *f* (-; *-en*) announcement; proclamation; JUR pronouncement; REL preaching
ver'kürzen *v/t* (*no -ge-*, *h*) shorten; reduce
ver'laden *v/t* (*irr*, ***laden***, *no -ge-*, *h*) load (***auf*** *acc* onto; ***in*** *acc* into)
Verlag [fɛɐ'la:k] *m* (-[*e*]*s*; *-e* [-'la:gə]) publishing house *or* company, publisher(s)
ver'lagern *v/t and v/refl* (*no -ge-*, *h*) shift (***auf*** *acc* to)
ver'langen *v/t* (*no -ge-*, *h*) ask for; demand; claim; charge; take, call for
Ver'langen *n* (*-s*; -) desire (***nach*** for); longing (for), yearning (for); ***auf Verlangen*** by request; ECON on demand
verlängern [fɛɐ'lɛŋɐn] *v/t* (*no -ge-*, *h*) lengthen, make longer; prolong, extend (*a.* ECON)
Verlängerung [fɛɐ'lɛŋərʊŋ] *f* (-; *-en*) lengthening; prolongation, extension; SPORT overtime, *Br* extra time
ver'langsamen *v/t and v/refl* (*no -ge-*, *h*) slacken, slow down (*both a. fig*)
ver'lassen (*irr*, ***lassen***, *no -ge-*, *h*) **1.** *v/t* leave; abandon, desert; **2.** *v/refl*: ***sich verlassen auf*** (*acc*) rely *or* depend on
verlässlich [fɛɐ'lɛslɪç] *adj* reliable, dependable
Ver'lauf *m* course
ver'laufen (*irr*, ***laufen***, *no -ge-*) **1.** *v/i* (*sein*) run; go; end (up); **2.** *v/refl* (*h*) get lost, lose one's way
ver'leben *v/t* (*no -ge-*, *h*) spend; have
ver'legen[1] *v/t* (*no -ge-*, *h*) move; mislay; TECH lay; put off, postpone; publish
ver'legen[2] *adj* embarrassed
Ver'legenheit *f* (-; *-en*) a) (*no pl*) embarrassment, b) embarrassing situation
Verleger [fɛɐ'le:gɐ] *m* (*-s*; -), **Ver'legerin** *f* (-; *-nen*) publisher
Verleih [fɛɐ'lai] *m* (-[*e*]*s*; *-e*) a) (*no pl*) hire, rental, b) *film*: distributor(s)
ver'leihen *v/t* (*irr*, ***leihen***, *no -ge-*, *h*) lend, loan; MOT *etc* rent (*Br* hire) out; award (*prize etc*); grant (*privilege etc*)
Ver'leihung *f* (-; *-en*) award(ing), presentation; grant(ing)
ver'leiten *v/t* (*no -ge-*, *h*) ***j-n zu et. verleiten*** make s.o. do s.th., lead s.o. to do s.th.
ver'lernen *v/t* (*no -ge-*, *h*) forget
ver'lesen (*irr*, ***lesen***, *no -ge-*, *h*) **1.** *v/t* read (*or* call) out; **2.** *v/refl* make a slip (in reading); misread *s.th.*
verletzen [fɛɐ'lɛtsən] *v/t* (*no -ge-*, *h*) hurt, injure, *fig a.* offend; ***sich verletzen*** hurt o.s., get hurt
verletzend *adj* offensive
Ver'letzte *m*, *f* (*-n*; *-n*) injured person; *pl* *the* injured
Ver'letzung *f* (-; *-en*) injury, *esp pl a.* hurt; JUR violation
ver'leugnen *v/t* (*no -ge-*, *h*) deny; re-

nounce

verleumden [fɛɐ'lɔʏmdən] *v/t* (*no -ge-, h*) defame; JUR slander, libel

ver'leumderisch *adj* JUR slanderous, libel(l)ous

Ver'leumdung *f* (-; *-en*) JUR slander; libel

ver'lieben *v/refl* (*no -ge-, h*) fall in love (***in*** *acc* with)

verliebt [fɛɐ'liːpt] *adj* in love (***in*** *acc* with); amorous (*look etc*)

Ver'liebte *m, f* (*-n*; *-n*) lover

verlieren [fɛɐ'liːrən] *v/t and v/i* (*irr, no -ge-, h*) lose

Ver'lierer(in) (*-s*; *-/-*; *-nen*) loser

ver'loben *v/refl* (*no -ge-, h*) get engaged (***mit*** to)

Verlobte [fɛɐ'loːptə] **1.** *m* (*-n*; *-n*) fiancé; **2.** *f* (*-n*; *-n*) fiancée

Ver'lobung *f* (-; *-en*) engagement

ver'locken *v/t* (*no -ge-, h*) tempt

verlockend *adj* tempting

Ver'lockung *f* (-; *-en*) temptation

verlogen [fɛɐ'loːgən] *adj* untruthful, lying

verlor [fɛɐ'loːɐ] *pret of* ***verlieren***

verloren [fɛɐ'loːrən] **1.** *pp of* ***verlieren***; **2.** *adj* lost; wasted; ***verloren gehen*** be *or* get lost

ver'lorengehen *v/i* (*irr,* ***gehen****, sep, -ge-, sein*) → ***verloren***

ver'losen *v/t* (*no -ge-, h*) raffle (off)

Ver'losung *f* (-; *-en*) raffle

Verlust [fɛɐ'lʊst] *m* (*-[e]s*; *-e*) loss (*a. fig*); *pl esp* MIL casualties

ver'machen *v/t* (*no -ge-, h*) leave, will

Vermächtnis [fɛɐ'mɛçtnɪs] *n* (*-ses*; *-se*) legacy (*a. fig*)

ver'markten *v/t* (*no -ge-, h*) market, merchandize

Ver'marktung *f* (-; *-en*) marketing, merchandizing

ver'mehren *v/t and v/refl* increase (***um*** by), multiply (by) (*a.* BIOL); BIOL reproduce, *esp* ZO *a.* breed

Ver'mehrung *f* (-; *-en*) increase; BIOL reproduction

vermeidbar [fɛɐ'maitbaːɐ] *adj* avoidable

ver'meiden *v/t* (*irr,* ***meiden****, no -ge-, h*) avoid

vermeintlich [fɛɐ'maintlɪç] *adj* supposed, alleged

ver'mengen *v/t* (*no -ge-, h*) mix, mingle, blend

Vermerk [fɛɐ'mɛrk] *m* (*-[e]s*; *-e*) note

ver'merken *v/t* (*no -ge-, h*) make a note of

ver'messen[1] *v/t* (*irr,* ***messen****, no -ge-, h*) measure; survey

ver'messen[2] *adj* presumptuous

Ver'messung *f* (-; *-en*) measuring; surveying

ver'mieten *v/t* (*no -ge-, h*) let, rent, lease (out); rent (*Br* hire) out (*cars etc*); ***zu vermieten*** for rent, *Br* to let, for hire

Ver'mieter *n* (*-s*; -) landlord

Ver'mieterin *f* (-; *-nen*) landlady

Ver'mietung *f* (-; *-en*) letting, renting

ver'mischen *v/t and v/refl* (*no -ge-, h*) mix, mingle, blend (***mit*** with)

ver'mischt *adj* mixed; miscellaneous

vermissen [fɛɐ'mɪsən] *v/t* (*no -ge-, h*) miss

ver'misst *adj* missing; ***die Vermissten*** *pl* the missing

ver'mitteln (*no -ge-, h*) **1.** *v/t* arrange; give, convey (*impression etc*); ***j-m et. vermitteln*** get *or* find s.o. s.th.; **2.** *v/i* mediate (***zwischen*** between)

Ver'mittler *m* (*-s*; -) mediator, go-between; ECON agent, broker

Ver'mittlung *f* (-; *-en*) mediation; arrangement; agency, office; (telephone) exchange; operator

ver'modern *v/i* (*no -ge-, sein*) rot, mo(u)lder

Ver'mögen *n* (*-s*; -) fortune, property, possessions; ECON assets

ver'mögend *adj* well-to-do, well-off

vermummen [fɛɐ'mʊmən] *v/refl* (*no -ge-, h*) mask o.s., disguise o.s.

vermuten [fɛɐ'muːtən] *v/t* (*no -ge-, h*) suppose, expect, think, guess

ver'mutlich *adv* probably

Ver'mutung *f* (-; *-en*) supposition; speculation

vernachlässigen [fɛɐ'naːxlɛsɪgən] *v/t* (*no -ge-, h*), **Ver'nachlässigung** *f* (-; *-en*) neglect

ver'narben *v/i* (*no -ge-, sein*) scar over; *fig* heal

ver'narrt *adj*: ***vernarrt in*** (*acc*) mad *or* crazy about

ver'nehmen *v/t* (*irr,* ***nehmen****, no -ge-, h*) JUR question, interrogate

ver'nehmlich *adj* clear, distinct

Ver'nehmung *f* (-; *-en*) JUR interrogation, examination

ver'neigen *v/refl* (*no -ge-, h*), **Ver'neigung** *f* (-; *-en*) bow (***vor*** *dat* to) (*a. fig*)

ver'neinen (*no -ge-, h*) **1.** *v/t* deny; **2.** *v/i* say no, answer in the negative

verneinend *adj* negative

Ver'neinung *f* (-; *-en*) denial, negative (*a.* LING)

ver'nichten *v/t* (*no -ge-, h*) destroy

vernichtend *adj* devastating (*a. fig*); crushing

Ver'nichtung *f* (-; *-en*) destruction; extermination

Vernunft [fɛɐ'nʊnft] *f* (-; *no pl*) reason; ***Vernunft annehmen*** listen to reason; ***j-n zur Vernunft bringen*** bring s.o. to reason
vernünftig [fɛɐ'nʏnftɪç] *adj* sensible, reasonable (*a.* ECON); F decent
ver'öden *v/i* (*no -ge-, sein*) become deserted
ver'öffentlichen *v/t* (*no -ge-, h*) publish
Ver'öffentlichung *f* (-; *-en*) publication
ver'ordnen *v/t* (*no -ge-, h*) order, MED *a.* prescribe (***gegen*** for)
Ver'ordnung *f* (-; *-en*) order; MED prescription
ver'pachten *v/t* (*no -ge-, h*) lease
Ver'pächter *m* lessor
ver'packen *v/t* (*no -ge-, h*) pack (up); TECH package; wrap up
Ver'packung *f* (-; *-en*) pack(ag)ing; wrapping
Ver'packungsmüll *m* superfluous packaging
ver'passen *v/t* (*no -ge-, h*) miss
ver'patzen F *v/t* (*no -ge-, h*) mess up, spoil
verpesten [fɛɐ'pɛstən] *v/t* (*no -ge-, h*) pollute, foul, contaminate; stink up (*Br* out)
ver'petzen F *v/t* (*no -ge-, h*) ***j-n verpetzen*** tell on s.o. (***bei*** to)
ver'pfänden *v/t* (*no -ge-, h*) pawn; *fig* pledge
ver'pflanzen *v/t* (*no -ge-, h*), **Ver'pflanzung** *f* (-; *-en*) transplant (*a.* MED)
ver'pflegen *v/t* (*no -ge-, h*) feed
Ver'pflegung *f* (-; *-en*) food
ver'pflichten *v/t* (*no -ge-, h*) oblige; engage; ***sich verpflichten, et. zu tun*** undertake (ECON agree) to do s.th.
ver'pflichtet *adj*: ***verpflichtet sein*** (***sich verpflichtet fühlen***) ***et. zu tun*** be (feel) obliged to do s.th.
Ver'pflichtung *f* (-; *-en*) obligation; duty; ECON, JUR liability; engagement, commitment
ver'pfuschen F *v/t* (*no -ge-, h*) bungle, botch
ver'plappern *v/refl* (*no -ge-, h*) blab
verpönt [fɛɐ'pø:nt] *adj* taboo
ver'prügeln F *v/t* (*no -ge-, h*) beat *s.o.* up
Ver'putz *m* (*-es; no pl*), **ver'putzen** *v/t* (*no -ge-, h*) ARCH plaster
verquollen [fɛɐ'kvɔlən] *adj face etc*: puffy, swollen; *wood*: warped
Verrat [fɛɐ'ra:t] *m* (-[*e*]*s*; *no pl*) betrayal (***an*** *dat* of); treachery (to); JUR treason (to)
ver'raten *v/t* (*irr*, ***raten***, *no -ge-, h*) betray, give away (*both a. fig*); ***sich verraten*** betray o.s., give o.s. away
Verräter [fɛɐ'rɛ:tɐ] *m* (*-s*; -), **Ver'räterin** *f* (-; *-nen*) traitor
verräterisch [fɛɐ'rɛ:tərɪʃ] *adj* treacherous; *fig* telltale
ver'rechnen (*no -ge-, h*) **1.** *v/t* offset (***mit*** against); **2.** *v/refl* miscalculate, make a mistake (*a. fig*); ***sich um e-e Mark verrechnen*** be one mark out
Ver'rechnungsscheck *m* ECON voucher check, *Br* crossed cheque
ver'regnet *adj* rainy
ver'reisen *v/i* (*no -ge-, sein*) go away (***geschäftlich*** on business)
ver'reist *adj* away (***geschäftlich*** on business)
verrenken [fɛɐ'rɛŋkən] *v/t* (*no -ge-, h*) MED dislocate, luxate; ***sich et. verrenken*** MED dislocate s.th.; ***sich den Hals verrenken*** crane one's neck
Ver'renkung *f* (-; *-en*) MED dislocation, luxation
ver'richten *v/t* (*no -ge-, h*) do, perform, carry out
ver'riegeln *v/t* (*no -ge-, h*) bolt, bar
verringern [fɛɐ'rɪŋɐn] *v/t* (*no -ge-, h*) decrease, lessen (*both a.* ***sich verringern***), reduce, cut down
Ver'ringerung *f* (-; *-en*) reduction, decrease
ver'rosten *v/t* (*no -ge-, sein*) rust, get rusty (*a. fig*)
verrotten [fɛɐ'rɔtən] *v/i* (*no -ge-, sein*) rot
ver'rottet *adj* rotten
ver'rücken *v/t* (*no -ge-, h*) move, shift
ver'rückt *adj* mad, crazy (*both a. fig* ***nach*** about); ***wie verrückt*** like mad; ***verrückt werden*** go mad, go crazy; ***j-n verrückt machen*** drive s.o. mad
Ver'rückte *m, f* (*-n; -n*) madman (madwoman), lunatic, maniac (*all a.* F)
Ver'rücktheit *f* (-; *-en*) a) (*no pl*) madness, craziness, b) crazy thing
Ver'ruf *m*: ***in Verruf bringen*** bring discredit (up)on; ***in Verruf kommen*** get into discredit
ver'rufen *adj* disreputable, notorious
ver'rutschen *v/i* (*no -ge-, sein*) slip, get out of place
Vers [fɛrs] *m* (*-es; -e* ['fɛrzə]) verse; line
ver'sagen (*no -ge-, h*) **1.** *v/i* fail (*a.* MED), MOT *etc a.* break down; *gun etc*: misfire; **2.** *v/t* deny, refuse
Ver'sagen *n* (*-s; no pl*) failure
Ver'sager *m* (*-s*; -) failure
ver'salzen *v/t* (*no -ge-, h*) oversalt
ver'sammeln *v/t* (*no -ge-, h*) gather, assemble; ***sich versammeln*** *a.* meet
Ver'sammlung *f* (-; *-en*) assembly, meeting
Versand [fɛɐ'zant] *m* (-[*e*]*s*; *no pl*) dis-

patch, shipment; ***Versand...*** *in cpds* *...haus, ...katalog etc*: mail-order ...
ver'säumen *v/t* (*no -ge-, h*) miss; ***versäumen et. zu tun*** fail to do s.th.
Versäumnis [fɛɐ'zɔʏmnɪs] *n* (*-ses; -se*) omission
ver'schaffen *v/t* (*no -ge-, h*) get, find; ***sich verschaffen*** *a.* obtain
ver'schämt *adj* bashful
ver'schanzen *v/refl* (*no -ge-, h*) entrench o.s. (*a. fig* ***hinter*** behind)
ver'schärfen *v/t* (*no -ge-, h*) aggravate; tighten up; increase; ***sich verschärfen*** get worse
ver'schenken *v/t* (*no -ge-, h*) give away (*a. fig*)
ver'scherzen *v/t* (*no -ge-, h*) forfeit
ver'scheuchen *v/t* (*no -ge-, h*) chase away (*a. fig*)
ver'schicken *v/t* (*no -ge-, h*) send off, *esp* ECON *a.* dispatch
ver'schieben *v/t* (*irr*, ***schieben***, *no -ge-, h*) move, shift (*a.* ***sich verschieben***); postpone, put off
Ver'schiebung *f* (*-; -en*) shift(ing); postponement
verschieden [fɛɐ'ʃiːdən] *adj* different (***von*** from); ***verschiedene ...*** *pl* various ..., several...
verschiedenartig *adj* different; various
Ver'schiedenheit *f* (*-; -en*) difference
ver'schiedentlich *adv* repeatedly
ver'schiffen *v/t* (*no -ge-, h*) ship
Ver'schiffung *f* (*-; -en*) shipment
ver'schimmeln *v/i* (*no -ge-, sein*) get mo(u)ldy
ver'schlafen (*irr*, ***schlafen***, *no -ge-, h*) **1.** *v/i* oversleep; **2.** *v/t* sleep through; **3.** *adj* sleepy (*a. fig*)
Ver'schlag *m* shed
ver'schlagen[1] *v/t* (*irr*, ***schlagen***, *no -ge-, h*) ***j-m den Atem verschlagen*** take s.o.'s breath away; ***j-m die Sprache verschlagen*** leave s.o. speechless; ***es hat ihn nach X verschlagen*** he ended up in X
ver'schlagen[2] *adj* sly, cunning
verschlechtern [fɛɐ'ʃlɛçtɐn] *v/t and v/refl* (*no -ge-, h*) make (*refl* get) worse, worsen, deteriorate
Ver'schlechterung *f* (*-; -en*) deterioration; change for the worse
ver'schleiern *v/t* (*no -ge-, h*) veil (*a. fig*)
Verschleiß [fɛɐ'ʃlais] *m* (*-es; no pl*) wear (and tear)
ver'schleißen *v/t* (*irr, no -ge-, h*) wear out
ver'schleppen *v/t* (*no -ge-, h*) carry off; POL displace; draw out, delay; MED neglect
ver'schleudern *v/t* (*no -ge-, h*) waste; ECON sell dirt cheap
ver'schließen *v/t* (*irr*, ***schließen***, *no -ge-, h*) close (*a. fig one's eyes*); lock (up)
ver'schlingen *v/t* (*irr*, ***schlingen***, *no -ge-, h*) devour (*a. fig*); gulp (down)
verschliss [fɛɐ'ʃlɪs] *pret of* ***verschleißen***
verschlissen [fɛɐ'ʃlɪsən] *pp of* ***verschleißen***
verschlossen [fɛɐ'ʃlɔsən] *adj* closed; *fig* aloof, reserved
Ver'schlossenheit *f* (*-; no pl*) aloofness
ver'schlucken (*no -ge-, h*) **1.** *v/t* swallow (*fig* up); **2.** *v/refl* choke; ***ich habe mich verschluckt*** it went down the wrong way
Ver'schluss *m* fastener; clasp; catch; lock; cover, lid; cap, top; PHOT shutter; ***unter Verschluss*** under lock and key
ver'schlüsseln *v/t* (*no -ge-, h*) (en)code, (en)cipher
verschmähen [fɛɐ'ʃmɛːən] *v/t* (*no -ge-, h*) disdain, scorn
ver'schmelzen *v/i* (*irr*, ***schmelzen***, *no -ge-, sein*) *and v/t* (*h*) merge, fuse (*both a.* ECON, POL *etc*), melt
Ver'schmelzung *f* (*-; -en*) fusion (*a. fig*)
ver'schmerzen *v/t* (*no -ge-, h*) get over *s.th.*
ver'schmieren *v/t* (*no -ge-, h*) smear, smudge
verschmitzt [fɛɐ'ʃmɪtst] *adj* mischievous
ver'schmutzen (*no -ge-*) **1.** *v/t* (*h*) soil, dirty; pollute; **2.** *v/i* (*sein*) get dirty; get polluted
ver'schnaufen F *v/i and v/refl* (*no -ge-, h*) stop for breath
ver'schneit *adj* snow-covered, snowy
Ver'schnitt *m* blend; waste
verschnupft [fɛɐ'ʃnʊpft] *adj*: ***verschnupft sein*** MED have a cold; F be in a huff
ver'schnüren *v/t* (*no -ge-, h*) tie up
verschollen [fɛɐ'ʃɔlən] *adj* missing; JUR presumed dead
ver'schonen *v/t* (*no -ge-, h*) spare; ***j-n mit et. verschonen*** spare s.o. s.th.
verschönern [fɛɐ'ʃøːnɐn] *v/t* (*no -ge-, h*) embellish
Verschönerung [fɛɐ'ʃøːnərʊŋ] *f* (*-; -en*) embellishment
verschossen [fɛɐ'ʃɔsən] *adj* faded; F ***verschossen sein in*** (*acc*) have a crush on
verschränken [fɛɐ'ʃrɛŋkən] *v/t* (*no -ge-, h*) fold; cross (*one's legs*)
ver'schreiben (*irr*, ***schreiben***, *no -ge-, h*) **1.** *v/t* MED prescribe (***gegen*** for); **2.** *v/refl* make a slip of the pen
ver'schreibungspflichtig *adj* PHARM available on prescription only
verschroben [fɛɐ'ʃroːbən] *adj* eccentric,

V

odd
ver'schrotten *v/t* (*no -ge-, h*) scrap
ver'schüchtert *adj* intimidated
ver'schulden *v/t* (*no -ge-, h*) be responsible for, cause, be the cause of; ***sich verschulden*** get into debt
ver'schuldet *adj* in debt
ver'schütten *v/t* (*no -ge-, h*) spill; bury *s.o.* (alive)
verschwägert [fɛɐ'ʃvɛːgɐt] *adj* related by marriage
ver'schweigen *v/t* (*irr*, ***schweigen***, *no -ge-, h*) keep *s.th.* a secret, hide
verschwenden [fɛɐ'ʃvɛndən] *v/t* (*no -ge-, h*) waste
Verschwender [fɛɐ'ʃvɛndɐ] *m* (*-s; -*) spendthrift
verschwenderisch [fɛɐ'ʃvɛndərɪʃ] *adj* wasteful, extravagant; lavish
Ver'schwendung *f* (*-; -en*) waste
verschwiegen [fɛɐ'ʃviːgən] *adj* discreet; hidden, secret
Ver'schwiegenheit *f* (*-; no pl*) secrecy, discretion
ver'schwimmen *v/i* (*irr*, ***schwimmen***, *no -ge-, sein*) become blurred
ver'schwinden *v/i* (*irr*, ***schwinden***, *no -ge-, sein*) disappear, vanish; F ***verschwinde!*** beat it!
Ver'schwinden *n* (*-s; no pl*) disappearance
verschwommen [fɛɐ'ʃvɔmən] *adj* blurred (*a.* PHOT), *fig a.* vague, hazy
ver'schwören *v/refl* (*irr*, ***schwören***, *no -ge-, h*) conspire, plot
Verschwörer [fɛɐ'ʃvøːrɐ] *m* (*-s; -*) conspirator
Ver'schwörung *f* (*-; -en*) conspiracy, plot
verschwunden [fɛɐ'ʃvʊndən] *adj* missing
ver'sehen (*irr*, ***sehen***, *no -ge-, h*) **1.** *v/t* hold (*an office etc*); ***versehen mit*** provide with; **2.** *v/refl* make a mistake
Ver'sehen *n* (*-s; -*) mistake, error; ***aus Versehen*** → **versehentlich** [fɛɐ'zeːəntlɪç] *adv* by mistake, unintentionally
Versehrte [fɛɐ'zeːɐtə] *m, f* (*-n; -n*) disabled person
ver'sengen *v/t* (*no -ge-, h*) singe, scorch
ver'senken *v/t* (*no -ge-, h*) sink; ***sich versenken in*** (*acc*) become absorbed in
versessen [fɛɐ'zɛsən] *adj*: ***versessen auf*** (*acc*) keen on, mad *or* crazy about
ver'setzen *v/t* (*no -ge-, h*) move, shift; transfer; PED promote, *Br* move *s.o.* up; give (*s.o. a kick etc*); pawn; AGR transplant; F ***j-n versetzen*** stand s.o. up; ***j-n in die Lage versetzen zu*** *inf* put s.o. in a position to *inf*, enable s.o. to *inf*; ***sich in j-s Lage versetzen*** put o.s. in s.o.'s place
Ver'setzung *f* (*-; -en*) transfer; PED promotion
ver'seuchen *v/t* (*no -ge-, h*) contaminate
Ver'seuchung *f* (*-; -en*) contamination
ver'sichern *v/t* (*no -ge-, h*) ECON insure (***bei*** with); assure (***j-m et.*** s.o. of s.th.), assert; ***sich versichern*** insure o.s.; make sure (***dass*** that)
Ver'sicherte *m, f* (*-n; -n*) *the* insured
Ver'sicherung *f* (*-; -en*) insurance; assurance, assertion
Ver'sicherungsgesellschaft *f* insurance company
Versicherungspo,lice *f*, **Versicherungsschein** *m* insurance policy
ver'sickern *v/i* (*no -ge-, sein*) trickle away
ver'siegeln *v/t* (*no -ge-, h*) seal
ver'siegen *v/i* (*no -ge-, sein*) dry up, run dry
ver'silbern *v/t* (*no -ge-, h*) silver-plate; F turn *s.th.* into cash
ver'sinken *v/i* (*irr*, ***sinken***, *no -ge-, sein*) sink; → ***versunken***
Version [vɛr'zjoːn] *f* (*-; -en*) version
'Versmaß *n* meter, *Br* metre
versöhnen [fɛɐ'zøːnən] *v/t* (*no -ge-, h*) reconcile; ***sich*** (***wieder***) ***versöhnen*** make it up (***mit*** with)
ver'söhnlich *adj* conciliatory
Ver'söhnung *f* (*-; -en*) reconciliation; *esp* POL appeasement
ver'sorgen *v/t* (*no -ge-, h*) provide (***mit*** with), supply (with); support; take care of, look after
Ver'sorgung *f* (*-; no pl*) supply (***mit*** with); support; care
ver'späten *v/refl* (*no -ge-, h*) be late
ver'spätet *adj* belated, late, RAIL *etc a.* delayed
Ver'spätung *f* (*-; -en*) being *or* coming late, RAIL *etc* delay; ***20 Minuten Verspätung haben*** be 20 minutes late
ver'speisen *v/t* (*no -ge-, h*) eat (up)
ver'sperren *v/t* (*no -ge-, h*) bar, block (up), obstruct (*a. view*); lock
ver'spielen *v/t* (*no -ge-, h*) lose
ver'spielt *adj* playful
ver'spotten *v/t* (*no -ge-, h*) make fun of, ridicule
ver'sprechen (*irr*, ***sprechen***, *no -ge-, h*) **1.** *v/t* promise (*a. fig*); ***sich zu viel versprechen*** (***von***) expect too much (of); **2.** *v/refl* make a mistake *or* slip
Ver'sprechen *n* (*-s; -*) promise; ***ein Versprechen geben*** (***halten, brechen***) make (keep, break) a promise
Ver'sprecher F *m* (*-s; -*) slip (of the tongue)

ver'staatlichen *v/t* (*no -ge-, h*) ECON nationalize

Ver'staatlichung *f* (-; *-en*) ECON nationalization

Verstädterung [fɛɐ'ʃtɛːtəruŋ] *f* (-; *-en*) urbanization

Verstand [fɛɐ'ʃtant] *m* (-[*e*]*s*; *no pl*) mind, intellect; reason, (common) sense; intelligence, brains; ***nicht bei Verstand*** out of one's mind, not in one's right mind; ***den Verstand verlieren*** go out of one's mind

verstandesmäßig [fɛɐ'ʃtandəsmɛːsɪç] *adj* rational

ver'ständig *adj* reasonable, sensible

verständigen [fɛɐ'ʃtɛndɪgən] *v/t* (*no -ge-, h*) inform (***von*** of), notify (of); call (*doctor, police etc*); ***sich verständigen*** communicate; come to an agreement (***über*** *acc* on)

Ver'ständigung *f* (-; *no pl*) communication (*a.* TEL); agreement

verständlich [fɛɐ'ʃtɛntlɪç] *adj* audible; intelligible; comprehensible; understandable; ***schwer*** (***leicht***) ***verständlich*** difficult (easy) to understand; ***j-m et. verständlich machen*** make s.th. clear to s.o.; ***sich verständlich machen*** make o.s. understood

Verständnis [fɛɐ'ʃtɛntnɪs] *n* (*-ses; no pl*) comprehension, understanding; sympathy; (***viel***) ***Verständnis haben*** be (very) understanding; ***Verständnis haben für*** understand; appreciate

ver'ständnislos *adj* uncomprehending; blank (*look etc*)

ver'ständnisvoll *adj* understanding, sympathetic; knowing (*look etc*)

ver'stärken *v/t* (*no -ge-, h*) reinforce (*a.* TECH, MIL); strengthen (*a.* TECH); *radio*, PHYS amplify; intensify

Ver'stärker *m* (*-s*; -) amplifier

Ver'stärkung *f* (-; *-en*) strengthening; reinforcement(s MIL); amplification; intensification

ver'stauben *v/i* (*no -ge-, sein*) get dusty

verstauchen [fɛɐ'ʃtauxən] *v/t* (*no -ge-, h*), **Ver'stauchung** *f* (-; *-en*) MED sprain

ver'stauen *v/t* (*no -ge-, h*) stow away

Versteck [fɛɐ'ʃtɛk] *n* (-[*e*]*s*; *-e*) hiding place, hideout, hideaway

ver'stecken *v/t and v/refl* (*no -ge-, h*) hide (*a. fig*); ***Verstecken spielen*** play (at) hide-and-seek

ver'stehen *v/t* (*irr*, ***stehen***, *no -ge-, h*) understand, F get; catch; see; realize; know; ***es verstehen zu*** *inf* know how to *inf*; ***zu verstehen geben*** give *s.o.* to understand, suggest; ***ich verstehe!*** I see!; ***falsch verstehen*** misunderstand; ***was verstehen Sie unter ...?*** what do you mean *or* understand by ...?; ***sich*** (***gut***) ***verstehen*** get along (well) (***mit*** with); ***es versteht sich von selbst*** it goes without saying

ver'steifen (*no -ge-, h*) **1.** *v/t* stiffen (*a.* ***sich versteifen***); TECH strut, brace; **2.** *v/refl*: ***sich auf et. versteifen*** insist on (doing) s.th.

ver'steigern *v/t* (*no -ge-, h*) auction off

Ver'steigerung *f* (-; *-en*) auction (sale)

ver'steinern *v/i* (*no -ge-, sein*) petrify (*a. fig*)

ver'stellbar *adj* adjustable

ver'stellen *v/t* (*no -ge-, h*) block; move; set *s.th.* wrong *or* the wrong way; TECH adjust, regulate; disguise (*one's voice etc*); ***sich verstellen*** pretend

Ver'stellung *f* (-; *no pl*) disguise, make-believe, (false) show

ver'steuern *v/t* (*no -ge-, h*) pay duty *or* tax on

verstiegen [fɛɐ'ʃtiːgən] *adj* high-flown

ver'stimmen *v/t* (*no -ge-, h*) MUS put out of tune; *fig* annoy

ver'stimmt *adj* annoyed; MUS out of tune; MED upset

Ver'stimmung *f* (-; *-en*) annoyance

verstockt [fɛɐ'ʃtɔkt] *adj* stubborn, obstinate

verstohlen [fɛɐ'ʃtoːlən] *adj* furtive, stealthy

ver'stopfen *v/t* (*no -ge-, h*) plug (up); block, jam; MED constipate

ver'stopft *adj* MED constipated

Ver'stopfung *f* (-; *-en*) block(age); MED constipation

verstorben [fɛɐ'ʃtɔrbən] *adj* late, deceased

Ver'storbene *m, f* (*-n; -n*) *the* deceased; ***die Verstorbenen*** the deceased

verstört [fɛɐ'ʃtøːɐt] *adj* upset; distracted; wild (*look etc*)

Ver'stoß *m* offense, *Br* offence (***gegen*** against), violation (of)

ver'stoßen (*irr*, ***stoßen***, *no -ge-, h*) **1.** *v/t* expel (***aus*** from); disown; **2.** *v/i*: ***verstoßen gegen*** offend against, violate

ver'strahlt *adj* (radioactively) contaminated

ver'streichen (*irr*, ***streichen***, *no -ge-*) **1.** *v/i* (*sein*) *time*: pass, go by; *date*: expire; **2.** *v/t* (*h*) spread

ver'streuen *v/t* (*no -ge-, h*) scatter

verstümmeln [fɛɐ'ʃtʏməln] *v/t* (*no -ge-, h*) mutilate (*a. fig*)

Ver'stümmelung *f* (-; *-en*) mutilation (*a. fig*)

ver'stummen *v/i* (*no -ge-, sein*) grow silent; stop; die down
Versuch [fɛɐ'zuːx] *m* (*-[e]s; -e*) attempt, try; trial, test; PHYS experiment; ***mit et. (j-m) e-n Versuch machen*** give s.th. (s.o.) a try
ver'suchen *v/t* (*no -ge-, h*) try, attempt; taste; REL tempt; ***es versuchen*** have a try (at it)
Ver'suchs... *in cpds ...bohrung etc*: test ..., trial ...
Versuchska'ninchen *n* guinea pig
Versuchsstadium *n* experimental stage
Versuchstier *n* laboratory *or* test animal
ver'suchsweise *adv* by way of trial
Ver'suchung *f* (*-; -en*) temptation; ***j-n in Versuchung führen*** tempt s.o.
versunken [fɛɐ'zʊŋkən] *fig adj*: ***versunken in*** (*acc*) absorbed *or* lost in
ver'süßen *v/t* (*no -ge-, h*) sweeten
ver'tagen *v/t and v/refl* (*no -ge-, h*) adjourn
Ver'tagung *f* (*-; -en*) adjournment
ver'tauschen *v/t* (*no -ge-, h*) exchange (***mit*** for)
verteidigen [fɛɐ'taidɪgən] *v/t* (*no -ge-, h*) defend (***sich*** o.s.)
Verteidiger(in) [fɛɐ'taidɪgɐ (-gərɪn)] (*-s; -/-; -nen*) defender, SPORT *a.* back; *fig* advocate
Ver'teidigung *f* (*-; -en*) defense, *Br* defence
Ver'teidigungs... *in cpds ...politik etc*: *mst* defense ..., *Br* defence ...
Verteidigungsmi'nister *m* Secretary of Defense, *Br* Minister of Defence
Verteidigungsminis'terium *n* Department of Defense, *Br* Ministry of Defence
ver'teilen *v/t* (*no -ge-, h*) distribute; hand out
Ver'teiler *m* (*-s; -*) distributor
Ver'teilung *f* (*-; -en*) distribution
ver'tiefen *v/t and v/refl* (*no -ge-, h*) deepen (*a. fig*); ***sich vertiefen in*** (*acc*) become absorbed in
Ver'tiefung *f* (*-; -en*) hollow, depression, dent; *fig* deepening
vertikal [vɛrti'kaːl] *adj*, **Verti'kale** *f* (*-; -n*) vertical
ver'tilgen *v/t* (*no -ge-, h*) exterminate; F consume
Ver'tilgung *f* (*-; no pl*) extermination
vertonen [fɛɐ'toːnən] *v/t* (*no -ge-, h*) set to music
Vertrag [fɛɐ'traːk] *m* (*-[e]s; Verträge* [fɛɐ'trɛːgə]) contract; POL treaty
ver'tragen *v/t* (*irr*, ***tragen***, *no -ge-, h*) endure, bear, stand; ***ich kann ... nicht vertragen*** ... doesn't agree with me; I can't stand ...; ***er kann viel vertragen*** he can take a lot; he can hold his drink; F ***ich (es) könnte ... vertragen*** I (it) could do with ...; ***sich (gut) vertragen*** get along (well) (***mit*** with); ***sich wieder vertragen*** make it up
ver'traglich *adv* by contract
verträglich [fɛɐ'trɛːklɪç] *adj* easy to get on with; GASTR (easily) digestible
ver'trauen *v/i* (*no -ge-, h*) trust (***auf*** *acc* in)
Ver'trauen *n* (*-s; no pl*) confidence, trust, faith; ***im Vertrauen (gesagt)*** between you and me; ***wenig Vertrauen erweckend aussehen*** inspire little confidence
Ver'trauensfrage *f*: ***die Vertrauensfrage stellen*** PARL ask for a vote of confidence
Vertrauenssache *f*: ***das ist Vertrauenssache*** that is a matter of confidence
Vertrauensstellung *f* position of trust
ver'trauensvoll *adj* trustful, trusting
Ver'trauensvotum *n* PARL vote of confidence
ver'trauenswürdig *adj* trustworthy
ver'traulich *adj* confidential; familiar
ver'traut *adj* familiar; close
Ver'traute *m, f* (*-n; -n*) confidant(e *f*)
Ver'trautheit *f* (*-; no pl*) familiarity
ver'treiben *v/t* (*irr*, ***treiben***, *no -ge-, h*) drive *or* chase away (*a. fig*); pass (*the time*); ECON sell; ***vertreiben aus*** drive out of
Ver'treibung *f* (*-; -en*) expulsion (***aus*** from)
ver'treten *v/t* (*irr*, ***treten***, *no -ge-, h*) substitute for, replace, stand in for; POL, ECON represent, PARL *a.* sit for; JUR act for *s.o.*; ***j-s Sache vertreten*** JUR plead s.o.'s cause; ***die Ansicht vertreten, dass*** argue that; ***sich den Fuß vertreten*** sprain one's ankle; F ***sich die Beine vertreten*** stretch one's legs
Ver'treter *m* (*-s; -*), **Ver'treterin** *f* (*-; -nen*) substitute, deputy; POL, ECON representative, ECON *a.* agent; MED locum
Ver'tretung *f* (*-; -en*) substitution, replacement; substitute, stand-in, *a.* supply teacher; ECON, POL representation
Vertrieb [fɛɐ'triːp] *m* (*-[e]s; no pl*) ECON sale, distribution
Vertriebene [fɛɐ'triːbənə] *m, f* (*-n; -n*) POL expellee, refugee
ver'trocknen *v/i* (*no -ge-, sein*) dry up
ver'trödeln F *v/t* (*no -ge-, h*) dawdle away, waste
ver'trösten *v/t* (*no -ge-, h*) put *s.o.* off
ver'tuschen F *v/t* (*no -ge-, h*) cover up
ver'übeln *v/t* (*no -ge-, h*) take amiss; ***ich kann es ihr nicht verübeln*** I can't blame

her for it
ver'üben *v/t* (*no -ge-, h*) commit
verunglücken [fɛɐ'ʔʊnglʏkən] *v/i* (*no -ge-, sein*) have an accident; *fig* go wrong; ***tödlich verunglücken*** die in an accident
ver'ursachen *v/t* (*no -ge-, h*) cause
ver'urteilen *v/t* (*no -ge-, h*) condemn (***zu*** to) (*a. fig*), sentence (to), convict (***wegen*** of)
Ver'urteilung *f* (-; *-en*) condemnation (*a. fig*)
ver'vielfachen *v/t* (*no -ge-, h*) multiply
vervielfältigen [fɛɐ'fiːlfɛltɪgən] *v/t* (*no -ge-, h*) copy, duplicate
Ver'vielfältigung *f* (-; *-en*) duplication; copy
ver'vollkommnen *v/t* (*no -ge-, h*) perfect; improve
vervollständigen [fɛɐ'fɔlʃtɛndɪgən] *v/t* (*no -ge-, h*) complete
ver'wachsen *adj* MED deformed, crippled; *fig* ***verwachsen mit*** deeply rooted in, bound up with
ver'wackelt F *adj* PHOT blurred
ver'wahren *v/t* (*no -ge-, h*) keep (in a safe place); ***sich verwahren gegen*** protest against
verwahrlost [fɛɐ'vaːɐloːst] *adj* uncared-for, neglected
ver'walten *v/t* (*no -ge-, h*) manage, *esp* POL *a.* administer
Ver'walter *m* (*-s*; -) manager; administrator
Ver'waltung *f* (-; *-en*) administration, management
Ver'waltungs... *in cpds ...gericht, ...kosten etc*: administrative ...
ver'wandeln *v/t* (*no -ge-, h*) change, turn (*both a.* ***sich verwandeln***), *esp* PHYS, CHEM *a.* transform, convert (*all*: ***in*** *acc* into)
Ver'wandlung *f* (-; *-en*) change, transformation; conversion
verwandt [fɛɐ'vant] *adj* related (***mit*** to)
Ver'wandte *m, f* (*-n*; *-n*) relative; (***alle***) ***m-e Verwandten*** (all) my relatives *or* relations; ***der nächste Verwandte*** the next of kin
Ver'wandtschaft *f* (-; *-en*) a) relationship, b) (*no pl*) relations
ver'warnen *v/t* (*no -ge-, h*) *Br* caution; SPORT book
Ver'warnung *f* (-; *-en*) *Br* caution; SPORT booking
ver'waschen *adj* washed-out
ver'wässern *v/t* (*no -ge-, h*) water down (*a. fig*)
ver'wechseln *v/t* (*no -ge-, h*) confuse (***mit*** with), mix up (with), mistake (for)
Ver'wechs(e)lung *f* (-; *-en*) mistake, F mix-up
ver'wegen *adj* daring, bold
Ver'wegenheit *f* (-; *no pl*) boldness, daring
ver'weichlicht *adj* soft
ver'weigern *v/t* (*no -ge-, h*) refuse; disobey
Ver'weigerung *f* (-; *-en*) denial, refusal
ver'weilen *v/i* (*no -ge-, h*) stay; *fig* rest
Verweis [fɛɐ'vais] *m* (*-es*; *-e*) reprimand, reproof; reference (***auf*** *acc* to)
ver'weisen *v/t* (*irr*, ***weisen***, *no -ge-, h*) refer (***auf*** *acc*, ***an*** *acc* to); expel (*gen* from)
ver'welken *v/i* (*no -ge-, sein*) wither, *fig a.* fade
ver'wenden *v/t* (*no -ge-, h*) use; spend (*time etc*) (***auf*** *acc* on)
Ver'wendung *f* (-; *-en*) use; ***keine Verwendung haben für*** have no use for
ver'werfen *v/t* (*irr*, ***werfen***, *no -ge-, h*) drop, give up; reject
ver'werten *v/t* (*no -ge-, h*) use, make use of
verwesen [fɛɐ'veːzən] *v/i* (*no -ge-, sein*), **Ver'wesung** *f* (-; *no pl*) decay
ver'wickeln *fig v/t* (*no -ge-, h*) involve; ***sich verwickeln in*** (*acc*) get caught in
ver'wickelt *fig adj* complicated; ***verwickelt sein*** (***werden***) ***in*** (*acc*) be (get) involved in
Ver'wicklung *fig f* (-; *-en*) involvement; complication
ver'wildern *v/i* (*no -ge-, sein*) grow (*or* run) wild
ver'wildert *adj* wild (*a. fig*), overgrown
ver'winden *v/t* (*irr*, ***winden***, *no -ge-, h*) get over *s.th.*
ver'wirklichen *v/t* (*no -ge-, h*) realize; ***sich verwirklichen*** come true; ***sich selbst verwirklichen*** fulfil(l) o.s.
Ver'wirklichung *f* (-; *-en*) realization
ver'wirren *v/t* (*no -ge-, h*) tangle (up); *fig* confuse
ver'wirrt *fig adj* confused
Ver'wirrung *fig f* (-; *-en*) confusion
ver'wischen *v/t* (*no -ge-, h*) blur (*a. fig*); cover (*track etc*)
verwittern [fɛɐ'vɪtɐn] *v/i* (*no -ge-, sein*) GEOL weather
ver'witwet *adj* widowed
verwöhnen [fɛɐ'vøːnən] *v/t* (*no -ge-, h*) spoil
ver'wöhnt *adj* spoilt
verworren [fɛɐ'vɔrən] *adj* confused, muddled; complicated
verwundbar [fɛɐ'vʊntbaːɐ] *adj* vulnerable (*a. fig*)
ver'wunden *v/t* (*no -ge-, h*) wound

ver'wunderlich *adj* surprising
Verwunderung [fɛɐ'vʊndərʊŋ] *f* (-; *no pl*) (***zu m-r etc Verwunderung*** to my *etc*) surprise
Ver'wundete m, *f* (*-n*; *-n*) wounded (person), casualty
Ver'wundung *f* (-; *-en*) wound, injury
ver'wünschen *v/t* (*no -ge-, h*), **Ver'wünschung** *f* (-; *-en*) curse
ver'wüsten *v/t* (*no -ge-, h*) lay waste, devastate, ravage
Ver'wüstung *f* (-; *-en*) devastation, ravage
ver'zählen *v/refl* (*no -ge-, h*) count wrong
verzärteln [fɛɐ'tsɛrtəln] *v/t* (*no -ge-, h*) coddle, pamper
ver'zaubern *v/t* (*no -ge-, h*) enchant, *fig a.* charm; ***verzaubern in*** (*acc*) turn into
ver'zehren *v/t* (*no -ge-, h*) consume (*a. fig*)
ver'zeichnen *v/t* (*no -ge-, h*) record, keep a record of, list; *fig* achieve; suffer
Ver'zeichnis *n* (*-ses*; *-se*) list, catalog(ue); record, register; index
verzeihen [fɛɐ'tsaiən] *v/t and v/i* (*irr, no -ge-, h*) forgive *s.o.*; pardon, excuse *s.th.*
ver'zeihlich *adj* pardonable
Ver'zeihung *f* (-; *no pl*) pardon; ***(j-n) um Verzeihung bitten*** apologize (to s.o.); ***Verzeihung!*** (I'm) sorry!; excuse me!
ver'zerren *v/t* (*no -ge-, h*) distort (*a. fig*); ***sich verzerren*** become distorted
Ver'zerrung *f* (-; *-en*) distortion
Verzicht [fɛɐ'tsɪçt] *m* (-[*e*]*s*; *-e*) renunciation (***auf*** *acc* of); *mst* giving up, doing without *etc*
ver'zichten *v/i* (*no -ge-, h*) ***verzichten auf*** (*acc*) do without; give up; renounce (*a.* JUR)
verzieh [fɛɐ'tsiː] *pret of* ***verzeihen***
ver'ziehen (*irr*, ***ziehen***, *no -ge-*) **1.** *v/i* (*sein*) move (***nach*** to); **2.** *v/t* (*h*) spoil; ***das Gesicht verziehen*** make a face; ***sich verziehen*** *wood*: warp; *storm etc*: pass (over); F disappear; **3.** *pp of* ***verzeihen***
ver'zieren *v/t* (*no -ge-, h*) decorate
Ver'zierung *f* (-; *-en*) decoration, ornament
ver'zinsen *v/t* (*no -ge-, h*) pay interest on; ***sich verzinsen*** yield interest
Ver'zinsung *f* (-; *-en*) interest
ver'zögern *v/t* (*no -ge-, h*) delay; ***sich verzögern*** be delayed
Ver'zögerung *f* (-; *-en*) delay
ver'zollen *v/t* (*no -ge-, h*) pay duty on; ***et. (nichts) zu verzollen haben*** have s.th. (nothing) to declare
verzückt [fɛɐ'tsʏkt] *adj* ecstatic
Ver'zückung *f* (-; *-en*) ecstasy; ***in Verzückung geraten*** go into ecstasies *or* raptures (***wegen, über*** *acc* over)
Verzug [fɛɐ'tsuːk] *m* (-[*e*]*s*; *no pl*) delay; ECON default
ver'zweifeln *v/i* (*no -ge-, h*) despair (***an*** *dat* of)
ver'zweifelt *adj* desperate, despairing
Ver'zweiflung *f* (-; *no pl*) despair; ***j-n zur Verzweiflung bringen*** drive s.o. to despair
verzweigen [fɛɐ'tsvaigən] *v/refl* (*no -ge-, h*) branch
verzwickt [fɛɐ'tsvɪkt] F *adj* tricky
Veteran [vete'raːn] *m* (*-en*; *-en*) MIL veteran (*a. fig*)
Veterinär [veteri'nɛːɐ] *m* (*-s*; *-e*), **Veteri'närin** *f* (-; *-nen*) veterinarian, *Br* veterinary surgeon, F vet
Veto ['veːto] *n* (*-s*; *-s*) veto; ***(s)ein Veto einlegen gegen*** veto
Vetter ['fɛtɐ] *m* (*-s*; *-n*) cousin
'Vetternwirtschaft *f* (-; *no pl*) nepotism
vgl. ABBR *of* ***vergleiche*** cf., confer
VHS ABBR *of* ***Volkshochschule*** adult education program(me); adult evening classes
Vibration [vibra'tsjoːn] *f* (-; *-en*) vibration
vibrieren [vi'briːrən] *v/i* (*no -ge-, h*) vibrate
Video ['viːdeo] *n* (*-s*; *-s*) video (*a. in cpds …aufnahme, …clip, …kamera, …kassette, …recorder etc*); ***auf Video aufnehmen*** video(tape), tape
Videoband *n* videotape
Videotext *m* teletext
Videothek [video'teːk] *f* (-; *-en*) video (-tape) library; video store (*Br* shop)
Vieh [fiː] *n* (-[*e*]*s*; *no pl*) cattle; ***20 Stück Vieh*** 20 head of cattle
Viehbestand *m* livestock
Viehhändler *m* cattle dealer
'viehisch *contp adj* bestial, brutal
'Viehmarkt *m* cattle market
Viehzucht *f* cattle breeding, stockbreeding
Viehzüchter *m* cattle breeder, stockbreeder
viel [fiːl] *adj and adv* a lot (of), plenty (of), F lots of; ***viele*** many; ***nicht viel*** not much; ***nicht viele*** not many; ***sehr viel*** a great deal (of); ***sehr viele*** very many, a lot (of); ***das viele Geld*** all that money; ***ziemlich viel*** quite a lot (of); ***ziemlich viele*** quite a few; ***viel besser*** much better; ***viel teurer*** much more expensive; ***e-r zu viel*** one too many; ***viel zu viel*** far too much; ***viel zu wenig*** not nearly enough; ***viel lieber*** much rather; ***wie viel*** how much (*pl* many); ***viel beschäftigt*** very busy; ***viel sagend*** meaningful; ***viel***

versprechend promising
'**vieldeutig** [-dɔʏtɪç] *adj* ambiguous
vielerlei ['fiːlɐ'lai] *adj* all kinds *or* sorts of
'**vielfach** **1.** *adj* multiple; **2.** *adv* in many cases, (very) often
'**Vielfalt** *f* (-; *no pl*) (great) variety (*gen* of)
'**vielfarbig** *adj* multicolo(u)red
vielleicht [fi'laiçt] *adv* perhaps, maybe; ***vielleicht ist er …*** he may *or* might be …
'**vielmals** *adv*: (***ich***) ***danke*** (***Ihnen***) ***vielmals*** thank you very much; ***entschuldigen Sie vielmals*** I'm very sorry, I do apologize
viel'mehr *cj* rather
'**vielsagend** *adj* meaningful
vielversprechend *adj* promising
'**vielseitig** [-zaitɪç] *adj* versatile
'**Vielseitigkeit** *f* (-; *no pl*) versatility
vier [fiːɐ] *adj* four; ***zu viert sein*** be four; ***auf allen vieren*** on all fours; ***unter vier Augen*** in private, privately
'**Vierbeiner** [-bainɐ] *m* (-*s*; -) zo quadruped, four-legged animal
'**vierbeinig** *adj* four-legged
'**Viereck** *n* quadrangle, quadrilateral
'**viereckig** *adj* quadrangular, square
Vierer ['fiːrɐ] *m* (-*s*; -) *rowing*: four
'**vierfach** *adj* fourfold; ***vierfache Ausfertigung*** four copies
'**vierfüßig** [-fyːsɪç] *adj* four-footed
'**Vierfüßler** [-fyːslɐ] *m* (-*s*; -) zo quadruped
'**vierhändig** [-hɛndɪç] *adj* MUS four-handed
'**vierjährig** [-jɛːrɪç] *adj* four-year-old, of four
Vierlinge ['fiːɐlɪŋə] *pl* quadruplets, quads
'**viermal** *adv* four times
'**Vierradantrieb** *m* MOT four-wheel drive
'**vierseitig** [-zaitɪç] *adj* MATH quadrilateral
'**vierspurig** [-ʃpuːrɪç] *adj* MOT four-lane
'**vierstöckig** [-ʃtœkɪç] *adj* four-storied, *Br* four-storey …
'**Viertaktmotor** *m* four-stroke engine
vierte ['fiːɐtə] *adj* fourth
Viertel ['fɪrtəl] *n* (-*s*; -) fourth (part); quarter; (***ein***) ***Viertel vor*** (***nach***) (a) quarter to (past)
Viertelfi,nale *n* SPORT quarter finals
Viertel'jahr *n* three months
'**vierteljährlich** **1.** *adj* quarterly; **2.** *adv* every three months, quarterly
vierteln ['fɪrtəln] *v/t* (*ge-*, *h*) quarter
'**Viertelnote** *f* MUS quarter note, *Br* crotchet
Viertelpfund *n* quarter of a pound
Viertel'stunde *f* quarter of an hour
viertens ['fiːɐtəns] *adv* fourthly
vierzehn ['fɪrtseːn] *adj* fourteen; ***vierzehn Tage*** two weeks, *esp Br a.* a fortnight
'**vierzehnte** *adj* fourteenth
vierzig ['fɪrtsɪç] *adj* forty
'**vierzigste** *adj* fortieth
Villa ['vɪla] *f* (-; *Villen*) villa
violett [vio'lɛt] *adj* violet, purple
Violine [vio'liːnə] *f* (-; -*n*) MUS violin
Virtuelle Realität [vɪr'tuɛlə] *f* EDP virtual reality, Cyberspace
virtuos [vɪr'tuoːs] *adj* virtuoso …, masterly
Virtuose [vɪr'tuoːzə] *m* (-*n*; -*n*) virtuoso
Virtuosität [vɪrtuozi'tɛːt] *f* (-; *no pl*) virtuosity
Virus ['viːrʊs] *n*, *m* (-; *Viren*) MED virus
Visier [vi'ziːɐ] *n* (-*s*; -*e*) sights; visor
Vision [vi'zjoːn] *f* (-; -*en*) vision
Visite [vi'ziːtə] *f* (-; -*n*) MED round
Vi'sitenkarte *f* (visiting) card
Visum ['viːzʊm] *n* (-*s*; *Visa*) visa
vital [vi'taːl] *adj* vigorous
Vitalität [vitali'tɛːt] *f* (-; *no pl*) vigo(u)r
Vitamin [vita'miːn] *n* (-*s*; -*e*) vitamin
Vitrine [vi'triːnə] *f* (-; -*n*) (glass) cabinet; showcase
Vize… ['fiːtsə-] *in cpds* vice(-)…
Vogel ['foːgəl] *m* (-*s*; *Vögel* ['føːgəl]) zo bird; F ***den Vogel abschießen*** take the cake
'**Vogelbauer** *n* birdcage
'**vogelfrei** *adj* outlawed
'**Vogelfutter** *n* birdseed
Vogelgrippe *f* bird flu, avian flu
Vogelkunde *f* ornithology
Vogelkäfig *m* birdcage
vögeln ['føːgəln] V *v/t and v/i* (*ge-*, *h*) screw
'**Vogelnest** *n* bird's nest
Vogelperspektive *f* bird's-eye view
Vogelscheuche *f* scarecrow (*a. fig*)
Vogelschutzgebiet *n* bird sanctuary
Vogelwarte *f* ornithological station
Vogelzug *m* bird migration
Vokabel [vo'kaːbəl] *f* (-; -*n*) word; *pl* → **Vokabular** [vokabu'laːɐ] *n* (-*s*; -*e*) vocabulary
Vokal [vo'kaːl] *m* (-*s*; -*e*) LING vowel
Volant [vo'lãː] *Austrian m* → ***Lenkrad***
Volk [fɔlk] *n* (-[*e*]*s*; *Völker* ['fœlkɐ]) people, nation; *the* people; zo swarm; ***ein Mann aus dem Volke*** a man of the people
Völkerkunde ['fœlkɐ-] *f* ethnology
Völkermord *m* genocide
Völkerrecht *n* (-[*e*]*s*; *no pl*) international law
Völkerwanderung *f* migration of peoples; F mass exodus

V

'Volksabstimmung *f* POL referendum
Volksfest *n* funfair
Volkshochschule *f* adult evening classes
Volkslied *n* folk song
Volksmund *m*: ***im Volksmund*** in the vernacular
Volksmu,sik *f* folk music
Volksrepu,blik *f* people's republic
Volksschule HIST *f* → ***Grundschule***
Volkssport *m* popular sport
Volkssprache *f* vernacular
Volksstamm *m* tribe, race
Volkstanz *m* folk dance
Volkstracht *f* national costume
'volkstümlich [-tyːmlɪç] *adj* popular, folk …; traditional
'Volksversammlung *f* public meeting
Volkswirt *m* economist
Volkswirtschaft *f* (national) economy; → **Volkswirtschaftslehre** *f* economics
Volkszählung *f* census
voll [fɔl] **1.** *adj* full (*a. fig*); full up (*a.* F); F plastered; thick, rich (*hair*); ***voller*** full of, filled with, *a.* covered with *dirt etc*; **2.** *adv* fully; completely, totally, wholly; *pay etc* in full, the full price; *hit etc* full, straight, right; ***voll entwickelt*** fully developed; (***nicht***) ***für voll nehmen*** (not) take seriously
'vollauf *adv* perfectly, quite
'vollauto,matisch *adj* fully automatic
'Vollbart *m* (full) beard
'Vollbeschäftigung *f* full employment
'Vollblut... *in cpds* full-blooded (*a. fig*)
'Vollblüter [-blyːtɐ] *m* (*-s; -*) zo thoroughbred
voll'bringen *v/t* (*irr*, ***bringen***, *no -ge-, h*) accomplish, achieve; perform
'Volldampf *m* full steam; F ***mit Volldampf*** (at) full blast
voll'enden *v/t* (*no -ge-, h*) finish, complete
voll'endet *adj* completed; *fig* perfect
vollends ['fɔlɛnts] *adv* completely
Voll'endung *f* (*-; no pl*) finishing, completion; *fig* perfection
voll'führen *v/t* (*no -ge-, h*) perform
'vollfüllen *v/t* (*sep, -ge-, h*) (***gießen***) fill (up)
'Vollgas *n* (*-es; no pl*) MOT full throttle; ***Vollgas geben*** F step on it
völlig ['fœlɪç] **1.** *adj* complete, absolute, total; **2.** *adv* completely; ***völlig unmöglich*** absolutely impossible
'volljährig [-jɛːrɪç] *adj* JUR ***volljährig sein*** (***werden***) be (come) of age; ***noch nicht volljährig*** under age
'Volljährigkeit *f* (*-; no pl*) JUR majority
voll'kommen *adj* perfect; → ***völlig***
Voll'kommenheit *f* (*-; no pl*) perfection
'Vollkornbrot *n* wholemeal bread
'vollmachen *v/t* (*sep, -ge-, h*) fill (up); F soil, dirty; ***um das Unglück voll zu machen*** to crown it all
Vollmacht *f* (*-; -en*) full power(s), authority; JUR power of attorney; ***Vollmacht haben*** be authorized
Vollmilch *f* full-cream milk
Vollmond *m* full moon
'vollpacken *v/t* (*sep, -ge-, h*) load (***mit*** with) (*a. fig*)
'Vollpensi,on *f* full board
'vollschlank *adj* plump
'vollständig *adj* complete; → ***völlig***
'vollstopfen *v/t* (*sep, -ge-, h*) stuff, *fig a.* cram, pack (*all*: ***mit*** with)
voll'strecken *v/t* (*no -ge-, h*) JUR execute
Voll'streckung *f* (*-; -en*) JUR execution
'volltanken *v/t* (*sep, -ge-, h*): ***bitte volltanken!*** MOT fill her up, please!
'Volltreffer *m* direct hit; bull's eye (*a. fig*)
Vollversammlung *f* plenary session
'vollwertig *adj* full
'Vollwertkost *f* wholefoods
vollzählig ['fɔltsɛːlɪç] *adj* complete
voll'ziehen *v/t* (*irr*, ***ziehen***, *no -ge-, h*) execute; perform; ***sich vollziehen*** take place
Voll'ziehung *f* (*-; no pl*), **Voll'zug** *m* (*-[e]s; no pl*) execution
Volontär [volɔn'tɛːɐ] *m* (*-s; -e*), **Volon'tärin** *f* (*-; -nen*) unpaid trainee
Volt [vɔlt] *n* (*-; -*) ELECTR volt
Volumen [vo'luːmən] *n* (*-s; -, -mina*) volume; size
von [fɔn] *prp* from; *instead of gen*: of; *passive*: by; about *s.o. or s.th.*; ***südlich von*** south of; ***weit von*** far from; ***von Hamburg*** from Hamburg; ***von nun an*** from now on; ***ein Freund von mir*** a friend of mine; ***die Freunde von Alice*** Alice's friends; ***ein Brief*** (***Geschenk***) ***von Tom*** a letter (gift) from Tom; ***ein Buch*** (***Bild***) ***von Orwell*** (***Picasso***) a book (painting) by Orwell (Picasso); ***der König*** (***Bürgermeister*** *etc*) ***von ...*** the King (Mayor *etc*) of …; ***ein Kind von 10 Jahren*** a child of ten; ***müde von der Arbeit*** tired from work; ***es war nett*** (***gemein***) ***von dir*** it was nice (mean) of you; ***reden*** (***hören***) ***von*** talk (hear) about *or* of; ***von Beruf*** (***Geburt***) by profession (birth); ***von selbst*** by itself; ***von mir aus!*** I don't mind *or* care
von'stattengehen *v/i* (*irr*, ***gehen***, *sep, -ge-, sein*) go, come off
vor [foːɐ] *prp* (*dat and acc*) in front of; outside; before; … ago; with, for; ***vor der Klasse*** in front of the class; ***vor***

der Schule in front of *or* outside the school; before school; ***vor kurzem (e-r Stunde)*** a short time (an hour) ago; ***5 Minuten vor 12*** five (minutes) to twelve; ***vor j-m liegen*** be *or* lie ahead of s.o. (*a. fig and* SPORT); ***vor sich hin*** *smile etc* to o.s.; ***sicher vor*** safe from; ***vor Kälte*** with cold; ***vor Angst*** for fear; ***vor allem*** above all; ***vor sich gehen*** go on, happen
'Vorabend *m* eve (*a. fig*)
'Vorahnung *f* presentiment, foreboding
voran [fo'ran] *adv* at the head (*dat* of), in front (of), before; ***Kopf voran*** head first
vorangehen *v/i* (*irr*, ***gehen***, *sep*, *-ge-*, *sein*) go in front *or* first; *esp fig* lead the way
vorankommen *v/i* (*irr*, ***kommen***, *sep*, *-ge-*, *sein*) get on *or* along (*a. fig*), make headway
'Voranzeige *f* preannouncement; *film*: trailer
'vorarbeiten *v/i* (*sep*, *-ge-*, *h*) work in advance; *fig* pave the way
'Vorarbeiter *m* foreman
voraus [fo'raus] *adv* ahead (*dat* of); ***im Voraus*** in advance, beforehand
vo'rausgehen *v/i* (*irr*, ***gehen***, *sep*, *-ge-*, *sein*) precede; → ***vorangehen***
vo'rausgesetzt *cj*: ***vorausgesetzt, dass*** provided that
Vo'raussage *f* (-; *-n*) prediction; METEOR forecast
vo'raussagen *v/t* (*sep*, *-ge-*, *h*) predict; forecast
vo'rausschicken *v/t* (*sep*, *-ge-*, *h*) send on ahead
voraussehen *v/t* (*irr*, ***sehen***, *sep*, *-ge-*, *h*) foresee, see *s.th.* coming
vo'raussetzen *v/t* (*sep*, *-ge-*, *h*) assume; take *s.th.* for granted
Vo'raussetzung *f* (-; *-en*) condition, prerequisite; assumption; ***die Voraussetzungen erfüllen*** meet the requirements
Vo'raussicht *f* (-; *no pl*) foresight; ***aller Voraussicht nach*** in all probability
vo'raussichtlich *adv* probably; ***er kommt voraussichtlich morgen*** he is expected to arrive tomorrow
Vo'rauszahlung *f* advance payment
'Vorbedeutung *f* omen
'Vorbedingung *f* prerequisite
Vorbehalt ['fo:ɐbəhalt] *m* (-[*e*]*s*; *-e*) reservation
'vorbehalten **1.** *v/t* (*irr*, ***halten***, *sep*, *no -ge-*, *h*) ***sich (das Recht) vorbehalten zu*** *inf* reserve the right to *inf*; **2.** *adj* reserved
'vorbehaltlos **1.** *adj* unconditional; **2.** *adv* without reservation
vor'bei *adv time*: over, past; finished; gone; *space*: past, by; ***jetzt ist alles vorbei*** it's all over now; ***vorbei!*** missed!
vorbeifahren *v/i* (*irr*, ***fahren***, *sep*, *-ge-*, *sein*) go (*or* drive) past (***an*** *dat s.o. or s.th.*), pass (*s.o. or s.th.*)
vorbeigehen *v/i* (*irr*, ***gehen***, *sep*, *-ge-*, *sein*) walk past; *a. fig* go by, pass; *shot etc*: miss
vorbei kommen *v/i* (*irr*, ***kommen***, *sep*, *-ge-*, *sein*) pass (***an*** *dat s.th.*); get past (*an obstacle etc*); F drop in (***bei j-m*** on s.o.); *fig* avoid
vorbeilassen *v/t* (*irr*, ***lassen***, *sep*, *-ge-*, *h*) let *s.o.* pass
'Vorbemerkung *f* preliminary remark
'vorbereiten *v/t and v/refl* (*sep*, *no -ge-*, *h*) prepare (***auf*** *acc* for)
'Vorbereitung *f* (-; *-en*) preparation (***auf*** *acc* for)
'vorbestellen *v/t* (*sep*, *no -ge-*, *h*) book (*or* order) in advance; reserve (*room*, *seat etc*)
'Vorbestellung *f* (-; *-en*) advance booking; reservation
'vorbestraft *adj*: ***vorbestraft sein*** have a police record
'vorbeugen (*sep*, *-ge-*, *h*) **1.** *v/i* prevent (***e-r Sache*** s.th.); **2.** *v/refl* bend forward
vorbeugend *adj* preventive, MED *a.* prophylactic
'Vorbeugung *f* (-; *-en*) prevention
'Vorbild *n* model, pattern; ***(j-m) ein Vorbild sein*** set an example (to s.o.); ***sich j-n zum Vorbild nehmen*** follow s.o.'s example
'vorbildlich *adj* exemplary
'Vorbildung *f* education(al background)
'vorbringen *v/t* (*irr*, ***bringen***, *sep*, *-ge-*, *h*) bring forward; say, state
vorda,tieren *v/t* (*no -ge-*, *h*) antedate; postdate
Vorder... ['fɔrdɐ-] *in cpds ...achse*, *...rad*, *...sitz*, *...tür*, *...zahn etc*: front ...
vordere ['fɔrdərə] *adj* front
'Vordergrund *m* foreground (*a. fig*)
Vordermann *m*: ***mein Vordermann*** the man *or* boy in front of me
Vorderseite *f* front (side); head
'vordränge(l)n *v/refl* (*sep*, *-ge-*, *h*) cut into line, *Br* jump the queue
vordringen *v/i* (*irr*, ***dringen***, *sep*, *-ge-*, *sein*) advance; ***vordringen (bis) zu*** work one's way through to (*a. fig*)
vordringlich **1.** *adj* (most) urgent; **2.** *adv*: ***et. vordringlich behandeln*** give s.th. priority
'Vordruck *m* (-[*e*]*s*; *-e*) form, blank
'voreilig *adj* hasty, rash, precipitate; ***vor-***

eilige Schlüsse ziehen jump to conclusions
'voreingenommen *adj* prejudiced, bias(s)ed
'Voreingenommenheit *f* (-; *no pl*) prejudice, bias
'vorenthalten *v/t* (*irr*, ***halten***, *sep*, *no -ge-*, *h*) keep back, withhold (*both*: ***j-m et.*** s.th. from s.o.)
'Vorentscheidung *f* preliminary decision
'vorerst *adv* for the present, for the time being
Vorfahr ['fo:ɐfa:ɐ] *m* (*-en*; *-en*) ancestor
'vorfahren *v/i* (*irr*, ***fahren***, *sep*, *-ge-*, *sein*) drive up (*or* on)
'Vorfahrt *f* (-; *no pl*) right of way, priority
'Vorfall *m* incident, occurrence, event
'vorfallen *v/i* (*irr*, ***fallen***, *sep*, *-ge-*, *sein*) happen, occur
vorfinden *v/t* (*irr*, ***finden***, *sep*, *-ge-*, *h*) find
'Vorfreude *f* anticipation
'vorführen *v/t* (*sep*, *-ge-*, *h*) show, present; perform (*trick etc*); demonstrate; JUR bring (***j-m*** before s.o.)
'Vorführer *m* demonstrator
'Vorführung *f* presentation, show(ing); performance; demonstration; JUR production
'Vorführwagen *m* MOT demonstrator, *Br* demonstration car
'Vorgabe *f* handicap
'Vorgang *m* event, occurrence, happening; file, record(s); BIOL, TECH process; ***e-n Vorgang schildern*** give an account of what happened
Vorgänger(in) ['fo:ɐgɛŋɐ (-ŋərɪn)] (*-s*; *-/-*; *-nen*) predecessor
'Vorgarten *m* front yard (*Br* garden)
'vorgeben *v/t* (*irr*, ***geben***, *sep*, *-ge-*, *h*) SPORT give; *fig* use *s.th.* as a pretext
'Vorgebirge *n* foothills
'vorgefasst *adj* preconceived
'vorgefertigt *adj* prefabricated
'Vorgefühl *n* presentiment
'vorgehen *v/i* (*irr*, ***gehen***, *sep*, *-ge-*, *sein*) go on; come first; act; JUR sue (***gegen j-n*** s.o.); proceed; *watch*: be fast
'Vorgehen *n* (*-s*; *no pl*) procedure
'vorgeschichtlich *adj* prehistoric
'Vorgeschmack *m* foretaste (***auf*** *acc* of)
Vorgesetzte *m*, *f* (*-n*; *-n*) superior, F boss
'vorgestern *adv* the day before yesterday
'vorgreifen *v/i* (*irr*, ***greifen***, *sep*, *-ge-*, *h*) anticipate *s.o. or s.th.*
'vorhaben *v/t* (*irr*, ***haben***, *sep*, *-ge-*, *h*) plan, intend; ***haben Sie heute Abend et. vor?*** have you anything on tonight?; ***was hat er jetzt wieder vor?*** what is he up to now?
'Vorhaben *n* (*-s*; *-*) plan(s), intention; TECH, ECON *a.* project
'Vorhalle *f* (entrance) hall, lobby
'vorhalten (*irr*, ***halten***, *sep*, *-ge-*, *h*) **1.** *v/t*: ***j-m et. vorhalten*** hold s.th. in front of s.o.; *fig* blame s.o. for (doing) s.th.; **2.** *v/i* last
'Vorhaltungen *pl* reproaches; ***j-m Vorhaltungen machen*** (***für et.***) reproach s.o. (with s.th., for being ...)
'Vorhand *f* (-; *no pl*) *tennis*: forehand
vorhanden [fo:ɐ'handən] *adj* available; in existence; ***vorhanden sein*** exist; ***es ist nichts mehr vorhanden*** there's nothing left
Vor'handensein *n* (*-s*; *no pl*) existence
'Vorhang *m* curtain
'Vorhängeschloss *n* padlock
vor'her *adv* before, earlier; in advance, beforehand
vor'herbestimmen *v/t* (*sep*, *no -ge-*, *h*) predetermine
vorherig [fo:ɐ'he:rɪç] *adj* previous
'Vorherrschaft *f* (-; *no pl*) predominance
'vorherrschen *v/i* (*sep*, *-ge-*, *h*) predominate, prevail
'vorherrschend *adj* predominant, prevailing
vor'hersehbar *adj* foreseeable
vor'hersehen *v/t* (*irr*, ***sehen***, *sep*, *-ge-*, *h*) foresee
vor'hin *adv* a (little) while ago
'Vorhut *f* (-; *-en*) MIL vanguard
vorig ['fo:rɪç] *adj* last; former, previous
vorjährig ['fo:ɐjɛ:rɪç] *adj* of last year, last year' ...
'Vorkämpfer *m*, **'Vorkämpferin** *f* champion, pioneer
Vorkehrungen ['fo:ɐke:rʊŋən] *pl*: ***Vorkehrungen treffen*** take precautions
'Vorkenntnisse *pl* previous knowledge *or* experience (***in*** *dat* of)
'vorkommen *v/i* (*irr*, ***kommen***, *sep*, *-ge-*, *sein*) be found; happen; ***es kommt mir ... vor*** it seems ... to me
'Vorkommen *n* (*-s*; *-*) MIN deposit(s)
Vorkommnis ['fo:ɐkɔmnɪs] *n* (*-ses*; *-se*) occurrence, incident, event
'Vorkriegs... *in cpds* prewar ...
'vorladen *v/t* (*irr*, ***laden***, *sep*, *-ge-*, *h*) JUR summon
'Vorladung *f* (-; *-en*) JUR summons
'Vorlage *f* model; pattern; copy; presentation; PARL bill; *soccer etc*: pass
'vorlassen *v/t* (*irr*, ***lassen***, *sep*, *-ge-*, *h*) let *s.o.* go first; let *s.o.* pass; ***vorgelassen werden*** be admitted (***bei*** to)
'Vorlauf *m* *recorder*: fast-forward; SPORT (preliminary) heat

ˈ**Vorläufer** *m* forerunner, precursor
ˈ**vorläufig** **1.** *adj* provisional, temporary; **2.** *adv* for the present, for the time being
ˈ**vorlaut** *adj* pert, cheeky
ˈ**Vorleben** *n* (*-s*; *no pl*) former life, past
ˈ**vorlegen** *v/t* (*sep*, *-ge-*, *h*) present; produce; show
ˈ**Vorleger** *m* (*-s*; *-*) rug; mat
ˈ**vorlesen** *v/t* (*irr*, ***lesen***, *sep*, *-ge-*, *h*) read out (aloud); ***j-m et. vorlesen*** read s.th. to s.o.
ˈ**Vorlesung** *f* (*-*; *-en*) lecture (***über*** *acc* on; ***vor*** *dat* to); ***e-e Vorlesung halten*** (give a) lecture
ˈ**vorletzte** *adj* last but one; ***vorletzte Nacht*** (***Woche***) the night (week) before last
ˈ**vorliebnehmen** *v/i* (*irr*, ***nehmen***, *sep*, *-ge-*, *h*) ***mit*** make do with
ˈ**Vorliebe** *f* (*-*; *-n*) preference, special liking
ˈ**vorliegen** *v/i* (*irr*, ***liegen***, *sep*, *-ge-*, *h*) ***es liegen*** (***keine***) ***… vor*** there are (no) …; ***was liegt gegen ihn vor?*** what is he charged with?
vorliegend *adj* present, in question
ˈ**vorlügen** *v/t* (*irr*, ***lügen***, *sep*, *-ge-*, *h*) ***j-m et. vorlügen*** tell s.o. lies
vormachen *v/t* (*sep*, *-ge-*, *h*) ***j-m et. vormachen*** show s.th. to s.o., show s.o. how to do s.th.; *fig* fool s.o.
ˈ**Vormachtstellung** *f* supremacy
ˈ**Vormarsch** *m* MIL advance (*a. fig*)
ˈ**vormerken** *v/t* (*sep*, *-ge-*, *h*) ***j-n vormerken*** put s.o.'s name down
ˈ**Vormittag** *m* morning; ***heute Vormittag*** this morning
ˈ**vormittags** *adv* in the morning; ***sonntags vormittags*** on Sunday mornings
ˈ**Vormund** *m* (*-*[*e*]*s*; *-e*) JUR guardian
Vormundschaft *f* (*-*; *-en*) JUR guardianship
vorn [fɔrn] *adv* in front; ***nach vorn*** forward; ***von vorn*** from the front; from the beginning; ***j-n von vorn(e) sehen*** see s.o.'s face; ***noch einmal von vorn(e)*** (***anfangen***) (start) all over again
ˈ**Vorname** *m* first *or* Christian name, forename
vornehm [ˈfoːɐneːm] *adj* distinguished; noble; fashionable, exclusive, F smart, posh; ***die vornehme Gesellschaft*** (high) society; ***vornehm tun*** put on airs
ˈ**vornehmen** *v/t* (*irr*, ***nehmen***, *sep*, *-ge-*, *h*) carry out, do; make (*changes etc*); ***sich et. vornehmen*** decide *or* resolve to do s.th.; make plans for s.th.; ***sich fest vorgenommen haben zu*** *inf* have the firm intention to *inf*, be determined to *inf*
ˈ**vornherein** *adv*: ***von vornherein*** from the start *or* beginning

ˈ**Vorort** *m* suburb
Vorort(s)zug *m* suburban *or* local *or* commuter train
ˈ**Vorposten** *m* outpost (*a.* MIL)
ˈ**vorprogramˌmieren** *v/t* (*sep*, *no -ge-*, *sein*) (pre)program(me); *fig* ***das war vorprogrammiert*** that was bound to happen
ˈ**Vorrang** *m* (*-*[*e*]*s*; *no pl*) precedence (***vor*** *dat* over), priority (over)
ˈ**Vorrat** *m* (*-*[*e*]*s*; *-räte*) store, stock, supply (*all*: ***an*** *dat* of); GASTR provisions; ECON resources, reserves; ***e-n Vorrat anlegen an*** (*dat*) stockpile
vorrätig [ˈfoːɐrɛːtɪç] *adj* available; ECON in stock
ˈ**Vorrecht** *n* privilege
ˈ**Vorredner** *m* previous speaker
ˈ**Vorrichtung** *f* TECH device
ˈ**vorrücken** (*sep*, *-ge-*) **1.** *v/t* (*h*) move forward; **2.** *v/i* (*sein*) advance
ˈ**Vorrunde** *f* SPORT preliminary round
ˈ**vorsagen** *v/i* (*sep*, *-ge-*, *h*) ***j-m vorsagen*** prompt s.o.
ˈ**Vorsaiˌson** *f* off-peak season
ˈ**Vorsatz** *m* resolution; intention; JUR intent
vorsätzlich [ˈfoːɐzɛtslɪç] *adj* intentional; *esp* JUR wil(l)ful
ˈ**Vorschau** *f* preview (***auf*** *acc* of), *film*, TV *a.* trailer
ˈ**Vorschein** *m*: ***zum Vorschein bringen*** produce; *fig* bring out; ***zum Vorschein kommen*** appear; *fig* come to light
ˈ**vorschieben** *v/t* (*irr*, ***schieben***, *sep*, *-ge-*, *h*) push forward; slip (*bolt*); *fig* use as a pretext
vorschießen F *v/t* (*irr*, ***schießen***, *sep*, *-ge-*, *h*) advance (*money*)
ˈ**Vorschlag** *m* suggestion, proposal (*a.* PARL *etc*); ***den Vorschlag machen*** → ˈ**vorschlagen** *v/t* (*irr*, ***schlagen***, *sep*, *-ge-*, *h*) suggest, propose
ˈ**Vorschlussrunde** *f* SPORT semifinal
ˈ**vorschnell** *adj* hasty, rash
ˈ**vorschreiben** *fig v/t* (*irr*, ***schreiben***, *sep*, *-ge-*, *h*) prescribe; tell; ***ich lasse mir nichts vorschreiben*** I won't be dictated to
ˈ**Vorschrift** *f* rule, regulation; instruction, direction; ***Dienst nach Vorschrift machen*** work to rule
ˈ**vorschriftsmäßig** *adj* correct, proper
vorschriftswidrig *adj and adv* contrary to regulations
ˈ**Vorschub** *m*: ***Vorschub leisten*** (*dat*) encourage; JUR aid and abet
ˈ**Vorschul…** *in cpds* pre-school …
ˈ**Vorschule** *f* preschool

'**Vorschuss** *m* advance
'**vorschützen** *v/t* (*sep*, *-ge-*, *h*) use *s.th.* as a pretext
'**vorsehen** (*irr*, ***sehen***, *sep*, *-ge-*, *h*) **1.** *v/t* plan; JUR provide; ***vorsehen für*** intend (*or* designate) for; **2.** *v/refl* be careful, take care, watch out (***vor*** *dat* for)
'**Vorsehung** *f* (-; *no pl*) providence
'**vorsetzen** *v/t* (*sep*, *-ge-*, *h*) ***j-m et. vorsetzen*** put s.th. before s.o.; offer s.o. s.th.
'**Vorsicht** *f* (-; *no pl*) caution, care; ***Vorsicht!*** look *or* watch out!, (be) careful!; ***Vorsicht, Stufe!*** mind the step!
'**vorsichtig** *adj* careful, cautious
'**vorsichtshalber** [-halbɐ] *adv* to be on the safe side
'**Vorsichtsmaßnahme** *f* precaution, precautionary measure; ***Vorsichtsmaßnahmen treffen*** take precautions
'**Vorsilbe** *f* LING prefix
'**vorsingen** *v/t and v/i* (*irr*, ***singen***, *sep*, *-ge-*, *h*) ***j-m et. vorsingen*** sing s.th. to s.o.; (have an) audition
'**Vorsitz** *m* chair(manship), presidency; ***den Vorsitz haben*** (***übernehmen***) be in (take) the chair, preside (***bei*** over, at)
'**Vorsitzende** *m*, *f* (*-n*; *-n*) chairman (chairwoman), president
'**Vorsorge** *f* (-; *no pl*) precaution; ***Vorsorge treffen*** take precautions
Vorsorgeuntersuchung *f* MED preventive checkup
'**vorsorglich** **1.** *adj* precautionary; **2.** *adv* as a precaution
'**Vorspann** *m* (-[*e*]*s*; *-e*) *film etc*: credits
'**Vorspeise** *f* hors d'œuvre, *Br* starter
'**Vorspiel** *n* MUS prelude (*a. fig*); foreplay
'**vorspielen** *v/t* (*sep*, *-ge-*, *h*) ***j-m et. vorspielen*** play s.th. to s.o.
'**vorsprechen** (*irr*, ***sprechen***, *sep*, *-ge-*, *h*) **1.** *v/t* pronounce (***j-m*** for s.o.); **2.** *v/i* call (***bei*** at); THEA (have an) audition
'**vorspringen** *fig v/i* (*irr*, ***springen***, *sep*, *-ge-*, *sein*) project, protrude (*both a.* ARCH)
'**Vorsprung** *m* ARCH projection; SPORT lead; ***e-n Vorsprung haben*** be leading (***von*** by); *esp fig* ***e-n Vorsprung von zwei Jahren haben*** be two years ahead
'**Vorstadt** *f* suburb
'**Vorstand** *m* ECON board (of directors); managing committee (*of a club etc*)
'**vorstehen** *v/i* (*irr*, ***stehen***, *sep*, *-ge-*, *h*) project, protrude
'**vorstellen** *v/t* (*sep*, *-ge-*, *h*) introduce (***sich*** o.s.; ***j-n j-m*** s.o. to s.o.); put *watch* forward (***um*** by); *fig* mean; ***sich et.*** (***j-n als ...***) ***vorstellen*** imagine s.th. (s.o. as ...); ***so stelle ich mir ... vor*** that's my idea of ...; ***sich vorstellen bei*** have an interview with *a firm etc*
'**Vorstellung** *f* (-; *-en*) introduction; interview; THEA performance, *film etc*: *a.* show; idea; expectation
'**Vorstellungskraft** *f* (-; *no pl*), **Vorstellungsvermögen** *n* (*-s*; *no pl*) imagination
Vorstopper ['foːɐʃtɔpɐ] *m* (*-s*; -) SPORT center (*Br* centre) back
'**Vorstoß** *m* MIL advance; *fig* attempt
'**Vorstrafe** *f* previous conviction
'**vorstrecken** *v/t* (*sep*, *-ge-*, *h*) advance (*money*)
'**Vorstufe** *f* preliminary stage
'**vortäuschen** *v/t* (*sep*, *-ge-*, *h*) feign, fake
'**Vorteil** *m* advantage (*a.* SPORT); benefit, profit; ***die Vorteile und Nachteile*** the pros and cons
'**vorteilhaft** *adj* advantageous, profitable
'**Vorteilsregel** *f* SPORT advantage rule
Vortrag ['foːɐtraːk] *m* (-[*e*]*s*; *Vorträge* ['foːɐtrɛːgə]) talk, *esp* UNIV lecture; MUS *etc* recital; ***e-n Vortrag halten*** give a talk *or* lecture (***vor*** *dat* to; ***über*** *acc* on)
'**vortragen** *v/t* (*irr*, ***tragen***, *sep*, *-ge-*, *h*) express, state; MUS *etc* perform, play; recite (*poem etc*)
'**vortreten** *v/i* (*irr*, ***treten***, *sep*, *-ge-*, *sein*) step forward; *fig* protrude, stick out
'**Vortritt** *m* (-[*e*]*s*; *no pl*) precedence; ***j-m den Vortritt lassen*** let s.o. go first
vorüber [fo'ryːbɐ] *adv*: ***vorüber sein*** be over
vorübergehen *v/i* (*irr*, ***gehen***, *sep*, *-ge-*, *sein*) pass, go by
vorübergehend *adj* temporary
'**Vorübung** *f* preparatory exercise
'**Voruntersuchung** *f* JUR, MED preliminary examination
'**Vorurteil** *n* prejudice
'**vorurteilslos** *adj* unprejudiced, unbias(s)ed
'**Vorverkauf** *m* THEA advance booking
'**vorverlegen** *v/t* (*sep*, *no -ge-*, *h*) advance
'**Vorwahl** *f* TEL area (*Br* STD *or* dialling) code; POL primary, *Br* preliminary election
'**Vorwand** *m* pretext, excuse
vorwärts ['foːɐvɛrts] *adv* forward, on (-ward), ahead; ***vorwärts!*** come on!, let's go!
'**vorwärtskommen** *v/i* (*irr*, ***kommen***, *sep*, *-ge-*, *sein*) make headway (*a. fig*)
vorweg [foːɐ'vɛk] *adv* beforehand
vor'wegnehmen *v/t* (*irr*, ***nehmen***, *sep*, *-ge-*, *h*) anticipate
'**vorweisen** *v/t* (*irr*, ***weisen***, *sep*, *-ge-*, *h*) produce, show; ***et. vorweisen können***

boast s.th.
vorwerfen *fig v/t (irr,* ***werfen****, sep, -ge-, h)* ***j-m et. vorwerfen*** reproach s.o. with s.th.
'**vorwiegend** *adv* predominantly, chiefly, mainly, mostly
'**vorwitzig** *adj* cheeky, pert
'**Vorwort** *n (-[e]s; -e)* foreword; preface
'**Vorwurf** *m* reproach; ***j-m Vorwürfe machen (wegen)*** reproach s.o. (for)
'**vorwurfsvoll** *adj* reproachful
'**Vorzeichen** *n* omen, sign *(a.* MATH)
'**vorzeigen** *v/t (sep, -ge-, h)* show; produce
'**vorzeitig** *adj* premature, early
'**vorziehen** *v/t (irr,* ***ziehen****, sep, -ge-, h)* draw; *fig* prefer
'**Vorzimmer** *n* anteroom; outer office; *Austrian* → ***Hausflur***
'**Vorzug** *m* advantage; merit
vorzüglich [foːɐ'tsyːklıç] *adj* excellent, exquisite
'**vorzugsweise** *adv* preferably
Votum ['voːtʊm] *n (-s; -ta, -ten)* vote
VP ABBR *of* ***Vollpension*** full board; (full) board and lodging
vulgär [vʊl'gɛːɐ] *adj* vulgar
Vulkan [vʊl'kaːn] *m (-s; -e)* volcano
Vulkanausbruch *m* volcanic eruption
vul'kanisch *adj* volcanic

W

W ABBR *of* ***West(en)*** W, west; ***Watt*** W, watt(s)
Waage ['vaːgə] *f (-; -n)* scale(s *Br*); balance; ASTR Libra; ***sich die Waage halten*** balance each other; ***er ist (e-e) Waage*** he's (a) Libra
'**waagerecht** *adj* horizontal
Waagschale ['vaːk-] *f* scale
Wabe ['vaːbə] *f (-; -n)* honeycomb
wach [vax] *adj* awake; ***wach rütteln*** rouse; *fig* → ***wachrütteln***; ***wach werden*** wake (up), *esp fig* → ***wachwerden***
Wache ['vaxə] *f (-; -n)* guard *(a.* MIL); sentry; MAR, MED *etc* watch; police station; ***Wache haben*** be on guard (MAR watch); ***Wache halten*** keep watch
'**wachen** *v/i (ge-, h)* (keep) watch (***über*** *acc* over)
'**Wachhund** *m* watchdog
'**Wachmann** *m (-[e]s; -männer, -leute)* watchman; *Austrian* → ***Polizist***
Wacholder [va'xɔldɐ] *m (-s; -)* BOT juniper
'**wachrufen** *v/t (irr,* ***rufen****, sep, -ge-, h)* call up, evoke
wachrütteln *v/t (sep, -ge-, h) fig* rouse *(a. fig)*
Wachs [vaks] *n (-es; -e)* wax
wachsam ['vaxzaːm] *adj* watchful, on one's guard, vigilant
'**Wachsamkeit** *f (-; no pl)* watchfulness, vigilance
wachsen[1] ['vaksən] *v/i (irr, ge-, sein)* grow *(a.* ***sich wachsen lassen****), fig a.* increase
'**wachsen**[2] *v/t (ge-, h)* wax
'**Wachsfi,gurenkabi,nett** *n* waxworks
Wachstuch *n* oilcloth
'**Wachstum** *n (-s; no pl)* growth, *fig a.* increase
Wachtel ['vaxtəl] *f (-; -n)* ZO quail
Wächter ['vɛçtɐ] *m (-s; -)* guard
'**Wachtmeister** *m (-s; no pl)* patrolman, *Br* (police) constable
'**Wach(t)turm** *m* watchtower
'**wachwerden** *v/i (irr,* ***werden****, sep, -ge-, sein) fig* awake; → ***wach***
wackelig ['vakəlıç] *adj* shaky *(a. fig)*; loose *(tooth)*
'**wackeln** *v/i (ge-, h)* shake; *table etc*: wobble; *tooth*: be loose; PHOT move; ***wackeln mit*** waggle
Wade ['vaːdə] *f (-; -n)* ANAT calf
Waffe ['vafə] *f (-; -n)* weapon *(a. fig)*, *pl a.* arms
Waffel ['vafəl] *f (-; -n)* waffle; wafer
'**Waffengewalt** *f*: ***mit Waffengewalt*** by force of arms
Waffenschein *m* gun license (*Br* licence)
Waffenstillstand *m* armistice *(a. fig)*; truce
wagen ['vaːgən] *v/t (ge-, h)* dare; risk; ***sich wagen*** venture
'**Wagen** *m (-s; -)* MOT car; RAIL car, *Br* carriage
wägen ['vɛːgən] *lit v/t (irr, ge-, h)* weigh *(one's words etc)*
'**Wagenheber** *m* TECH jack
Wagenladung *f* cartload
Waggon [va'gõː] *m (-s, -s)* (railroad) car, *Br* (railway) carriage; freight car, *Br* goods waggon

Wagnis ['va:knɪs] *n* (*-ses*; *-se*) venture, risk
Wa'gon *m* → ***Waggon***
Wahl [va:l] *f* (*-*; *-en*) choice; alternative; selection; POL election; voting, poll; vote; ***die Wahl haben*** (***s-e Wahl treffen***) have the (make one's) choice; ***keine*** (***andere***) ***Wahl haben*** have no choice *or* alternative
'wahlberechtigt *adj* POL entitled to vote
'Wahlbeteiligung *f* POL poll, (voter) turnout; ***hohe*** (***niedrige***) ***Wahlbeteiligung*** heavy (light) poll
'Wahlbezirk *m* → ***Wahlkreis***
wählen ['vɛ:lən] *v/t and v/i* (*ge-*, *h*) choose, pick, select; POL vote (for); elect; TEL dial
'Wähler *m* (*-s*; *-*) voter
'Wahlergebnis *n* election result
wählerisch ['vɛ:lərɪʃ] *adj* F picky (***in*** *dat* about), *esp Br* choos(e)y
'Wählerschaft *f* (*-*; *-en*) electorate, voters
'Wahlfach *n* PED *etc* elective, optional subject
Wahlka,bine *f* voting (*esp Br* polling) booth
Wahlkampf *m* election campaign
Wahlkreis *m* electoral district, *Br* constituency
Wahllo,kal *n* polling place (*Br* station)
'wahllos *adj* indiscriminate
'Wahlpro,gramm *n* election platform
Wahlrecht *n* (*-[e]s*; *no pl*) (right to) vote, suffrage, franchise
Wahlrede *f* election speech
'Wählscheibe *f* TEL dial
'Wahlsieg *m* election victory
Wahlsieger *m* election winner
Wahlspruch *m* motto
Wahlurne *f* ballot box
Wahlversammlung *f* election rally
'Wahnsinn *m* (*-[e]s*; *no pl*) madness (*a.* F), insanity
'wahnsinnig 1. *adj* mad (*a.* F), insane, F *a.* crazy; F awful, terrible; **2.** F *adv* terribly, awfully; madly (*in love*)
'Wahnsinnige *m*, *f* (*-n*; *-n*) madman (madwoman), lunatic, maniac (*all a.* F)
'Wahnvorstellung *f* delusion, hallucination
wahr [va:ɐ] *adj* true; real; genuine
wahren ['va:rən] *v/t* (*ge-*, *h*) protect; ***den Schein wahren*** keep up appearances
während ['vɛ:rənt] **1.** *prp* (*gen*) during; **2.** *cj* while; whereas
'wahrhaft, **wahr'haftig** *adv* really, truly
'Wahrheit *f* (*-*; *-en*) truth
'wahrheitsgemäß, **wahrheitsgetreu** *adj* true, truthful
wahrheitsliebend *adj* truthful
wahrnehmbar ['va:ɐne:mba:ɐ] *adj* noticeable, perceptible
'wahrnehmen *v/t* (*irr*, ***nehmen***, *sep*, *-ge-*, *h*) perceive, notice; seize, take (*chance etc*); look after (*s.o.'s interests etc*)
'Wahrnehmung *f* (*-*; *-en*) perception
'wahrsagen *v/i* (sep, -ge-, h) ***j-m wahrsagen*** tell s.o. his fortune; ***sich wahrsagen lassen*** have one's fortune told
'Wahrsager [-za:gɐ] *m* (*-s*; *-*), **'Wahrsagerin** [-za:gərɪn] *f* (*-*; *-nen*) fortune-teller
wahr'scheinlich 1. *adj* probable, likely; **2.** *adv* probably, (very *or* most) likely; ***wahrscheinlich gewinnt er*** (***nicht***) he is (not) likely to win
Wahr'scheinlichkeit *f* (*-*; *-en*) probability, likelihood
Währung ['vɛ:rʊŋ] *f* (*-*; *-en*) currency
'Währungs... *in cpds ...politik*, *...reform etc*: monetary ...
'Wahrzeichen *n* landmark
Waise ['vaizə] *f* (*-*; *-n*) orphan; ***Waise werden*** be orphaned
'Waisenhaus *n* orphanage
Wal [va:l] *m* (*-[e]s*; *-e*) ZO whale
Wald [valt] *m* (*-[e]s*; *Wälder* ['vɛldɐ]) wood(s), forest
Waldbrand *m* forest fire
'waldreich *adj* wooded
'Waldsterben *n* dying of forests
'Walfang *m* whaling
'Walfänger *m* whaler
Walkman® *m* (*-s*; *-men*) personal stereo, Walkman®
Wall [val] *m* (*-[e]s*; *Wälle* ['vɛlə]) mound; MIL rampart
Wallach ['valax] *m* (*-[e]s*; *-e*) ZO gelding
wallen ['valən] *v/i* (*ge-*, *sein*) flow
'Wallfahrer *m*, **'Wallfahrerin** *f* pilgrim
'Wallfahrt *f* pilgrimage
'Walnuss *f* BOT walnut
'Walross *n* ZO walrus
Walze ['valtsə] *f* (*-*; *-n*) roller; cylinder; TECH, MUS barrel
'walzen *v/t* (*ge-*, *h*) roll (*a.* TECH)
wälzen ['vɛltsən] *v/t* (*ge-*, *h*) roll (*a.* ***sich wälzen***); *fig* turn *s.th.* over in one's mind
Walzer ['valtsɐ] *m* (*-s*; *-*) MUS waltz (*a.* ***Walzer tanzen***)
wand [vant] *pret of* ***winden***
Wand *f* (*-*; *Wände* ['vɛndə]) wall, *fig a.* barrier
Wandale [van'da:lə] *m* (*-n*; *-n*) vandal
Wandalismus [vanda'lɪsmʊs] *m* (*-*; *no pl*) vandalism
Wandel ['vandəl] *m* (*-s*; *no pl*), **'wandeln** *v/t and v/refl* (*ge-*, *h*) change
Wanderer ['vandərɐ] *m* (*-s*; *-*), **'Wanderin**

f (-; *-nen*) hiker
wandern ['vandɐn] *v/i* (*ge-*, *sein*) hike; ramble (about); *eyes etc*: roam, wander
'Wanderpo,kal *m* challenge cup
Wanderpreis *m* challenge trophy
Wanderschuhe *pl* walking shoes
Wandertag *m* (school) outing *or* excursion
'Wanderung *f* (-; *-en*) walking tour, hike; zo *etc* migration
'Wandgemälde *n* mural
Wandka,lender *m* wall calendar
Wandkarte *f* wallchart
Wandlung ['vandlʊŋ] *f* (-; *-en*) change
'Wandschrank *m* closet, *Br* built-in cupboard
Wandtafel *f* blackboard
wandte ['vantə] *pret of* ***wenden***
'Wandteppich *m* tapestry
Wange ['vaŋə] *f* (-; *-n*) ANAT cheek
Wankelmotor ['vaŋkəl-] *m* rotary piston *or* Wankel engine
wankelmütig ['vaŋkəlmy:tɪç] *adj* fickle
wanken ['vaŋkən] *v/i* (*ge-*, *sein*) stagger, reel; *fig* rock
wann [van] *interr adv* when, (at) what time; ***seit wann?*** (for) how long?, since when?
Wanne ['vanə] *f* (-; *-n*) tub (*a.* F); bath(tub)
Wanze ['vantsə] *f* (-; *-n*) zo bug (*a.* F)
Wapitihirsch [va'pi:ti-] *m* zo elk
Wappen ['vapən] *n* (*-s*; -) (coat of) arms
'Wappenkunde *f* heraldry
wappnen ['vapnən] *fig v/refl* (*ge-*, *h*) arm o.s.
war [va:ɐ] *pret of* ***sein***[1]
warb [varp] *pret of* ***werben***
Ware ['va:rə] *f* (-; *-n*) *coll mst* goods; article; product
'Warenhaus *n* department store
Warenlager *n* stock
Warenprobe *f* sample
Warenzeichen *n* trademark
warf [varf] *pret of* ***werfen***
warm [varm] *adj* warm (*a. fig*); GASTR hot; ***schön warm*** nice and warm; ***warm halten*** keep warm; ***warm machen*** warm (up)
Wärme ['vɛrmə] *f* (-; *no pl*) warmth; PHYS heat
Wärmeiso,lierung *f* heat insulation
'wärmen *v/t* (*ge-*, *h*) warm
'Wärmflasche *f* hot-water bottle
'warmherzig *adj* warm-hearted
'warmmachen *v/t* (*sep*, *-ge-*, *h*) → ***warm***
Warm'wasserbereiter *m* (*-s*; -) water heater
Warmwasserversorgung *f* hot-water supply
'Warnblinkanlage *f* MOT warning flasher
Warndreieck *n* MOT warning triangle
warnen ['varnən] *v/t* (*ge-*, *h*) warn (***vor*** *dat* of, against); ***j-n davor warnen, et. zu tun*** warn s.o. not to do s.th.
'Warnschild *n* danger sign
Warnsig,nal *n* warning signal
Warnstreik *m* token strike
'Warnung *f* (-; *-en*) warning
warten[1] ['vartən] *v/i* (*ge-*, *h*) wait (***auf*** *acc* for); *j-n* ***warten lassen*** keep *s.o.* waiting
'warten[2] *v/t* (*ge-*, *h*) TECH service, maintain
Wärter ['vɛrtɐ] *m* (*-s*; -), **'Wärterin** *f* (-; *-nen*) attendant; zo keeper
'Warteliste *f* waiting list
Wartesaal *m*, **Wartezimmer** *n* waiting room
'Wartung *f* (-; *-en*) TECH maintenance
warum [va'rʊm] *interr adv* why
Warze ['vartsə] *f* (-; *-n*) MED wart
was [vas] **1.** *interr pron* what; ***was gibt's?*** what is it?, F what's up?; what's for lunch *etc?*; ***was soll's?*** so what?; ***was machen Sie?*** what are you doing?; what do you do?; ***was kostet ...?*** how much is ...?; ***was für ...?*** what kind *or* sort of ...?; ***was für e-e Farbe*** (***Größe***)***?*** what colo(u)r (size)?; ***was für ein Unsinn*** what nonsense!; ***was für e-e gute Idee!*** what a good idea!; **2.** *rel pron* what; ***was*** (***auch***) ***immer*** whatever; ***alles, was ich habe*** (***brauche***) all I have (need); ***ich weiß nicht, was ich tun*** (***sagen***) ***soll*** I don't know what to do (say); ***..., was mich ärgerte...***, which made me angry; **3.** F *indef pron* → ***etwas***
waschbar ['vaʃba:ɐ] *adj* washable
'Waschbecken *n* washbowl, *Br* washbasin
Wäsche ['vɛʃə] *f* (-; *-n*) a) washing, b) (*no pl*) laundry; linen; underwear; ***in der Wäsche*** in the wash; ***schmutzige Wäsche waschen*** wash one's dirty linen in public
'waschecht *adj* washable; fast (*color*); *fig* trueborn, genuine
'Wäscheklammer *f* clothespin, *Br* clothes peg
Wäscheleine *f* clothesline
waschen ['vaʃən] *v/t and v/refl* (*irr*, *ge-*, *h*) wash; ***sich die Haare*** (***Hände***) ***waschen*** wash one's hair (hands)
Wäscherei [vɛʃə'rai] *f* (-; *-en*) laundry
'Waschlappen *m* washcloth, *Br* flannel, facecloth
Waschma,schine *f* washing machine, F washer
'waschma,schinenfest *adj* machine-

washable
Waschmittel *n*, **Waschpulver** *n* washing powder
Waschraum *m* lavatory, washroom
Waschsa,lon *m* laundromat, *Br* launderette
Waschstraße *f* MOT car wash
Wasser ['vasɐ] *n* (*-s*; -) water
Wasserball *m* beach ball; SPORT water polo
Wasserbett *n* water bed
Wasserdampf *m* steam
'**wasserdicht** *adj* waterproof; *esp* MAR watertight (*a. fig*)
'**Wasserfall** *m* waterfall; falls
Wasserfarbe *f* water colo(u)r
Wasserflugzeug *n* seaplane
Wassergraben *m* SPORT water jump
Wasserhahn *m* tap, faucet
wässerig ['vɛsərɪç] *adj* watery; ***j-m den Mund wässerig machen*** make s.o.'s mouth water
'**Wasserkessel** *m* kettle
Wasserklo,sett *n* water closet, W.C.
Wasserkraft *f* (-; *no pl*) water power
Wasserkraftwerk *n* hydroelectric power station *or* plant
Wasserlauf *m* watercourse
Wasserleitung *f* waterpipe(s)
Wassermangel *m* (*-s*; *no pl*) water shortage
Wassermann *m* (-[*e*]*s*; *no pl*) ASTR Aquarius; ***er ist*** (***ein***) ***Wassermann*** he's (an) Aquarius
'**wassern** *v/i* (*ge-*, *h*) AVIAT touch down on water; *spacecraft*: splash down
wässern ['vɛsɐn] *v/t* (*ge-*, *h*) water; AGR irrigate; GASTR soak; PHOT rinse
'**Wasserpflanze** *f* BOT aquatic plant
'**Wasserrohr** *n* TECH water pipe
'**Wasserscheide** *f* GEOGR watershed
'**wasserscheu** *adj* afraid of water
'**Wasserski 1.** *m* water ski; **2.** *n* (*-s*; *no pl*) water skiing; ***Wasserski fahren*** water-ski
Wasserspiegel *m* water level
Wassersport *m* water *or* aquatic sports, aquatics
Wasserspülung *f* TECH flushing cistern; ***Toilette mit Wasserspülung*** (flush) toilet, W.C.
Wasserstand *m* water level
Wasserstoff *m* (-[*e*]*s*; *no pl*) CHEM hydrogen
Wasserstoffbombe *f* MIL hydrogen bomb, H-bomb
Wasserstrahl *m* jet of water
Wasserstraße *f* waterway
Wassertier *n* aquatic animal
Wasserverschmutzung *f* water pollution
Wasserversorgung *f* water supply
Wasserwaage *f* (*Br* spirit) level
Wasserweg *m* waterway; ***auf dem Wasserweg*** by water
Wasserwelle *f* water wave
Wasserwerk(e *pl*) *n* waterworks
Wasserzeichen *n* watermark
waten ['vaːtən] *v/i* (*ge-*, *sein*) wade
watscheln ['vaːtʃəln] *v/i* (*ge-*, *sein*) waddle
Watt[1] [vat] *n* (*-s*; -) ELECTR watt
Watt[2] *n* (-[*e*]*s*; *-en*) GEOGR mud flats
Watte ['vatə] *f* (-; *-n*) cotton wool
wattiert [va'tiːɐt] *adj* padded; quilted
weben ['veːbən] *v/t and v/i* ([*irr*,] *ge-*, *h*) weave
Weber ['veːbɐ] *m* (*-s*; -) weaver
Weberei [veːbə'rai] *f* (-; *-en*) weaving mill
'**Weberin** *f* (-; *-nen*) weaver
Webstuhl ['veːp-] *m* loom
Wechsel ['vɛksəl] *m* (*-s*; -) change; exchange; ECON bill of exchange; allowance
'**Wechselgeld** *n* (small) change
wechselhaft *adj* changeable
'**Wechseljahre** *pl* MED menopause
'**Wechselkurs** *m* ECON exchange rate
'**wechseln** *v/t and v/i* (*ge-*, *h*) change; exchange; vary
wechselnd *adj* varying
'**wechselseitig** [-zaitɪç] *adj* mutual, reciprocal
'**Wechselstrom** *m* ELECTR alternating current
Wechselstube *f* ECON exchange office
Wechselwirkung *f* interaction
wecken ['vɛkən] *v/t* (*ge-*, *h*) wake (up), F call; *fig* awaken (*memories etc*); rouse (*s.o.'s curiosity etc*)
Wecker ['vɛkɐ] *m* (*-s*; -) alarm (clock)
wedeln ['veːdəln] *v/i* (*ge-*, *h*) wave (***mit et.*** s.th.); *skiing*: wedel; ***mit dem Schwanz wedeln*** wag its tail
weder ['veːdɐ] *cj*: ***weder … noch …*** neither … nor …
Weg [veːk] *m* (- [*e*]*s*, *-e* ['veːgə]) way (*a. fig*); road (*a. fig*); path; route; walk; ***auf friedlichem*** (***legalem***) ***Wege*** by peaceful (legal) means; ***j-m aus dem Weg gehen*** get (*fig* keep) out of s.o.'s way; ***j-n aus dem Weg räumen*** put s.o. out of the way; ***vom Weg abkommen*** lose one's way; → ***halb***
weg [vɛk] *adv* away; gone; off; F in raptures (***von*** over, about); ***Finger weg!*** (keep your) hands off!; ***nichts wie weg!*** let's get out of here!; F ***weg sein*** be out
wegbleiben F *v/i* (*irr*, ***bleiben***, *sep*, *-ge-*,

sein) stay away; be left out
wegbringen F *v/t (irr,* ***bringen****, sep, -ge-, h)* take away; ***wegbringen von*** get *s.o.* away from
wegen ['ve'gən] *prp (gen)* because of; for the sake of; due *or* owing to; JUR for
wegfahren ['vɛk-] *(irr,* ***fahren****, sep, -ge-)* **1.** *v/i (sein)* leave; **2.** *v/t (h)* take away, remove
'**wegfallen** *v/i (irr,* ***fallen****, sep, -ge-, sein)* be dropped; stop, be stopped
Weggang ['vɛk-] *m (-[e]s; no pl)* leaving
'**weggehen** *v/i (irr,* ***gehen****, sep, -ge-, sein)* go away *(a. fig)*, leave; *stain etc*: come off; ECON sell
wegjagen ['vɛk-] *v/t (sep, -ge-, h)* drive *or* chase away
wegkommen F *v/i (irr,* ***kommen****, sep, -ge-, sein)* get away; get lost; ***gut wegkommen*** come off well; ***mach, dass du wegkommst!*** get out of here!, *sl* get lost!
weglassen *v/t (irr,* ***lassen****, sep, -ge-, h)* let *s.o.* go; leave *s.th.* out
weglaufen *v/i (irr,* ***laufen****, sep, -ge-, sein)* run away (**[vor]** ***j-m*** from s.o.) *(a. fig)*
weglegen *v/t (sep, -ge-, h)* put away
wegnehmen *v/t (irr,* ***nehmen****, sep, -ge-, h)* take away (**von** from); take up *(room, time)*; steal *(a. s.o.'s girlfriend etc)*; ***j-m et. wegnehmen*** take s.th. (away) from s.o.
wegräumen *v/t (sep, -ge-, h)* clear away, remove
wegschaffen *v/t (sep, -ge-, h)* remove
wegschicken *v/t (sep, -ge-, h)* send away *or* off
wegsehen *v/i (irr,* ***sehen****, sep, -ge-, h)* look away
wegsetzen *v/t (sep, -ge-, h)* move
Wegweiser ['veːkvaizɐ] *m (-s; -)* signpost; *fig* guide
Wegwerf... ['vɛkvɛrf-] *in cpds ...geschirr, ...besteck, ...rasierer etc*: throwaway ..., disposable ...; *...flasche etc*: non-returnable ...
'**wegwerfen** *v/t (irr,* ***werfen****, sep, -ge-, h)* throw away
wegwischen ['vɛk-] *v/t (sep, -ge-, h)* wipe off
wegziehen *(irr,* ***ziehen****, sep, -ge-)* **1.** *v/i (sein)* move away; **2.** *v/t (h)* pull away
weh [veː] *adv*: ***weh tun*** → ***wehtun***
wehen ['veːən] *v/i (ge-, h)* blow; wave
'**Wehen** *pl* MED labo(u)r
wehmütig ['veːmyːtɪç] *adj* melancholy; wistful
Wehr[1] [veːɐ] *n (-[e]s; -e* ['veːrə]) weir
Wehr[2] *f*: ***sich zur Wehr setzen*** → ***wehren***
'**Wehrdienst** *m (-[e]s; no pl)* military service
Wehrdienstverweigerer *m (-s; -)* conscientious objector
wehren ['veːrən] *v/refl (ge-, h)* defend o.s. (***gegen*** against), fight *(a. fig* ***gegen et.*** s.th.)
'**wehrlos** *adj* defenseless, *Br* defenceless; *fig* helpless
'**Wehrpflicht** *f (-; no pl)* compulsory military service
'**wehrpflichtig** *adj* liable to military service
'**Wehrpflichtige** *m (-n; -n)* draftee, *Br* conscript
'**wehtun** hurt (***j-m*** s.o.; *fig* s.o.'s feelings); be aching; ***sich*** **(*am Finger*)** ***wehtun*** hurt o.s. (hurt one's finger)
Weib [vaip] *n (-[e]s; -er* ['vaibɐ]) *contp* woman; bitch
'**Weibchen** *n (-s; -)* ZO female
weibisch ['vaibɪʃ] *adj* effeminate, F sissy
'**weiblich** *adj* female; feminine *(a.* LING)
weich [vaiç] *adj* soft *(a. fig)*, tender; GASTR done; soft-boiled *(egg)*; ***weich werden*** soften; *fig* give in
Weiche ['vaiçə] *f (-; -n)* RAIL switch, points
weichen ['vaiçən] *v/i (irr, ge-, sein)* give way *(dat* to), yield (to); go (away)
'**weichlich** *adj* soft, effeminate, F sissy
'**Weichling** *m (-s; -e)* weakling, F softy, sissy
'**weichmachen** *v/t (sep, -ge-, h)*: F ***j-n weichmachen*** soften s.o. up
'**Weichspüler** *m (-s; -)* fabric softener
'**Weichtier** *n* ZO mollusk, *Br* mollusc
Weide[1] ['vaidə] *f (-; -n)* BOT willow
'**Weide**[2] *f (-; -n)* AGR pasture; ***auf die*** **(*der*)** ***Weide*** to (at) pasture
'**Weideland** *n* pasture(land), range
'**weiden** *v/t and v/i (ge-, h)* graze, pasture; *fig* ***sich weiden an*** *(dat)* feast on; *contp* gloat over
weigern ['vaigɐn] *v/refl (ge-, h)* refuse
Weigerung ['vaigərʊŋ] *f (-; -en)* refusal
Weihe ['vaiə] *f (-; -n)* REL consecration; ordination
'**weihen** *v/t (ge-, h)* consecrate; ***zum Priester weihen*** ordain *s.o.* priest
Weiher ['vaiɐ] *m (-s; -)* pond
Weihnachten ['vainaxtən] *n (-; -)* Christmas, F Xmas
'**Weihnachtsabend** *m* Christmas Eve
Weihnachtsbaum *m* Christmas tree
Weihnachtseinkäufe *pl* Christmas shopping
Weihnachtsgeschenk *n* Christmas present
Weihnachtslied *n* (Christmas) carol
Weihnachtsmann *m* Father Christmas,

Santa Claus
Weihnachtsmarkt *m* Christmas fair
Weihnachtstag *m* Christmas Day; ***zweiter Weihnachtstag*** day after Christmas, *esp Br* Boxing Day
Weihnachtszeit *f* Christmas season
'Weihrauch *m* REL incense
Weihwasser *n (-s; no pl)* REL holy water
weil [vail] *cj* because; since, as
'Weilchen *n*: ***ein Weilchen*** a little while
Weile ['vailə] *f*: ***e-e Weile*** a while
Wein [vain] *m (-[e]s; -e)* wine; BOT vine
Wein(an)bau *m (-[e]s; no pl)* wine growing
Weinbeere *f* grape
Weinberg *m* vineyard
Weinbrand *m* brandy
weinen ['vainən] *v/i (ge-, h)* cry (***vor*** *dat* with; ***nach*** for; ***wegen*** about, over); weep (***um*** for, over; ***über*** *acc* at; ***vor*** *dat* for, with)
weinerlich ['vainɐlɪç] *adj* tearful; whining
'Weinfass *n* wine cask *or* barrel
Weinflasche *f* wine bottle
Weinhändler *m* wine merchant
Weinhauer *Austrian m* → ***Winzer***
Weinkarte *f* wine list
Weinkeller *m* wine cellar *or* vault, vaults
Weinkellerei *f* winery
Weinkenner *m* wine connoisseur
Weinlese *f* vintage
Weinpresse *f* wine press
Weinprobe *f* wine tasting
Weinrebe *f* BOT vine
'weinrot *adj* claret
'Weinstock *m* BOT vine
'Weintraube *f* → ***Traube***
weise ['vaizə] *adj* wise
'Weise *f (-; -n)* way; MUS tune; ***auf diese (die gleiche) Weise*** this (the same) way; ***auf m-e (s-e) Weise*** my (his) way
weisen ['vaizən] *v/t and v/i (irr, ge-, h)* show; ***j-n von der Schule weisen*** expel s.o. from school; ***weisen auf*** *(acc)* point to *or* at; ***von sich weisen*** reject; repudiate
Weisheit ['vaishait] *f (-; -en)* wisdom; ***mit s-r Weisheit am Ende sein*** be at one's wit's end
'Weisheitszahn *m* wisdom tooth
weismachen ['vais-] F *v/t*: ***j-m weismachen, dass*** make s.o. believe that; ***du kannst mir nichts weismachen*** you can't fool me
weiß [vais] *adj* white; ***weiß werden*** *or* ***machen*** whiten
'Weißbrot *n* white bread
'Weiße *m, f (-n; -n)* white, white man (woman), *pl the* whites
'weißen *v/t (ge-, h)* whitewash
'Weißkohl *m*, **'Weißkraut** *n* BOT (green, *Br* white) cabbage
'weißlich *adj* whitish
'weißmachen *v/t (sep, -ge-, h)* → ***weiß***
'Weißwein *m* white wine
Weisung ['vaizʊŋ] *f (-; -en)* instruction, directive
weit [vait] **1.** *adj* wide, *clothes*: *a.* big; long *(way, trip etc)*; **2.** *adv* far, a long way *(a. time and fig)*; ***weit weg*** far away (***von*** from); ***von weitem*** from a distance; ***weit und breit*** far and wide; ***bei weitem*** by far; ***bei weitem nicht so …*** not nearly as …; ***weit über*** *(acc)* well over; ***weit besser*** far *or* much better; ***zu weit gehen*** go too far; ***es weit bringen*** go far; ***wir haben es weit gebracht*** we have come a long way; ***weit blickend*** *fig* farsighted; ***weit reichend*** far-reaching; ***weit verbreitet*** widespread
'weit'ab *adv* far away (***von*** from)
'weit'aus *adv* (by) far, much
Weite ['vaitə] *f (-; -n)* width; vastness, expanse; *esp* SPORT distance
'weiten *v/t and v/refl (ge-, h)* widen
weiter ['vaitɐ] *adv* on, further; (***mach***) ***weiter!*** go on!; (***geh***) ***weiter!*** move on!; ***und so weiter*** and so on *or* forth, et cetera; ***nichts weiter*** nothing else
weiterarbeiten *v/i (sep, -ge-, h)* go on working
weiterbilden *v/refl (sep, -ge-, h)* improve one's knowledge; continue one's education *or* training
'Weiterbildung *f (-; no pl)* further education *or* training
weitere ['vaitərə] *adj* further, additional; ***alles Weitere*** the rest; ***bis auf weiteres*** until further notice; ***ohne weiteres*** easily; ***Weiteres*** more, (further) details
'weitergeben *v/t (irr,* ***geben****, sep, -ge-, h)* pass *(dat,* ***an*** *acc* to) *(a. fig)*
weitergehen *v/i (irr,* ***gehen****, sep, -ge-, sein)* move on; *fig* continue, go on
'weiter'hin *adv* further(more); ***et. weiterhin tun*** go on doing s.th., continue to do s.th.
'weiterkommen *v/i (irr,* ***kommen****, sep, -ge-, sein)* get on *(fig* in life)
weiterleben *v/i (sep, -ge-, h)* live on, *fig a.* survive
weitermachen *v/t and v/i (sep, -ge-, h)* go *or* carry on, continue
'Weiterverkauf *m* resale
'weitgehend **1.** *adj* considerable; **2.** *adv* largely
weitläufig *adj* spacious; distant *(relative)*
weitsichtig *adj* MED farsighted *(a. fig)*, *Br*

longsighted
'**Weitsprung** *m* broad (*Br* long) jump
'**Weitwinkelobjek,tiv** *n* PHOT wide-angle lens
Weizen ['vaitsən] *m* (*-s*; -) BOT wheat
welche ['vɛlçə], **welcher** ['vɛlçɐ], **welches** ['vɛlçəs] **1.** *interr pron* what, which; ***welcher?*** which one?; ***welcher von beiden?*** which of the two?; **2.** *rel pron* who, that; which, that; **3.** F ***welche*** *indef pron* some, any
welk [vɛlk] *adj* faded, withered; flabby
welken ['vɛlkən] *v/i* (*ge-, sein*) fade, wither
Wellblech ['vɛl-] *n* corrugated iron
Welle ['vɛlə] *f* (*-; -n*) wave (*a.* PHYS *and fig*); TECH shaft
'**wellen** *v/t and v/refl* (*ge-, h*) wave
'**Wellenlänge** *f* ELECTR wavelength
'**Wellensittich** [-zɪtɪç] *m* (*-s; -e*) ZO budgerigar, F budgie
wellig ['vɛlɪç] *adj* wavy
Welt [vɛlt] *f* (*-; -en*) world; ***die ganze Welt*** the whole world; ***auf der ganzen Welt*** all over *or* throughout the world; ***das beste*** *etc* ... ***der Welt*** the best *etc* ... in the world, the world's best *etc* ...; ***zur Welt kommen*** be born; ***zur Welt bringen*** give birth to
'**Weltall** *n* universe
'**weltberühmt** *adj* world-famous
Weltergewicht ['vɛltɐ-] *n* (*-[e]s; no pl*), '**Weltergewichtler** *m* (*-s;* -) SPORT welterweight
'**weltfremd** *adj* naive, unrealistic
'**Weltfriede(n)** *m* world peace
'**Weltgeschichte** *f* world history
'**weltklug** *adj* worldlywise
'**Weltkrieg** *m* world war; ***der Zweite Weltkrieg*** World War II
'**Weltkugel** *f* globe
'**weltlich** *adj* worldly
'**Weltlitera,tur** *f* world literature
Weltmacht *f* POL world power
Weltmarkt *m* ECON world market
Weltmeer *n* ocean
Weltmeister(in) world champion
Weltmeisterschaft *f* world championship; *esp soccer*: World Cup
Weltraum *m* (*-[e]s; no pl*) (outer) space
Weltreich *n* empire
Weltreise *f* world trip
Weltre,kord *m* world record
Weltruf *m* (***von Weltruf*** of) worldwide reputation
Weltstadt *f* metropolis
Weltuntergang *m* end of the world
'**weltweit** *adj* worldwide
'**Weltwirtschaft** *f* world economy
'**Weltwirtschaftskrise** *f* worldwide economic crisis
'**Weltwunder** *n* wonder of the world
Wende ['vɛndə] *f* (*-; -n*) turn (*a. swimming*); change
Wendekreis *m* ASTR, GEOGR tropic; MOT turning circle
Wendeltreppe ['vɛndəl-] *f* spiral staircase
'**wenden** *v/t and v/i* (*ge-, h*) *and v/refl* (*[irr,] ge-, h*) turn (***nach*** to; ***gegen*** against); MOT turn (round); GASTR turn over; ***sich an j-n um Hilfe wenden*** turn to s.o. for help; ***bitte wenden*** please turn over, pto
'**Wendepunkt** *m* turning point
wendig ['vɛndɪç] *adj* MOT, MAR maneuverable, *Br* manoeuvrable; *fig* nimble
'**Wendung** *f* (*-; -en*) turn, *fig a.* change; expression, phrase
wenig ['veːnɪç] *indef pron and adv* little; ***wenig(e)*** *pl* few; ***nur wenige*** only few; only a few; (***in***) ***weniger als*** (in) less than; ***am wenigsten*** least of all; ***er spricht wenig*** he doesn't talk much; (***nur***) ***ein*** (***klein***) ***wenig*** (just) a little (bit)
'**wenigstens** *adv* at least
wenn [vɛn] *cj* when; if; ***wenn ... nicht*** if ... not, unless; ***wenn auch*** (al)though, even though; ***wie*** *or* ***als wenn*** as though, as if; ***wenn ich nur ... wäre!*** if only I were ...!; ***wenn auch noch so ...*** no matter how ...; ***und wenn nun ...?*** what if ...?
wer [veːɐ] **1.** *interr pron* who, which; ***wer von euch?*** which of you?; **2.** *rel pron* who; ***wer auch*** (***immer***) who(so)ever; **3.** F *indef pron* somebody, anybody
Werbeabteilung ['vɛrbə-] *f* publicity department
Werbeagen,tur *f* advertising agency
Werbefeldzug *m* advertising campaign
Werbefernsehen *n* commercial television
Werbefilm *m* promotion(al) film
Werbefunk *m* radio commercials
werben ['vɛrbən] (*irr, ge-, h*) **1.** *v/i* advertise (***für et.*** s.th.), promote (s.th.), give *s.th. or s.o.* publicity; *esp* POL make propaganda (***für*** for), canvass (for); ***werben um*** court (*a. fig*); **2.** *v/t* recruit; canvass, solicit
'**Werbesendung** *f*, '**Werbespot** [-ʃpɔt] *m* (*-s; -s*) (TV) commercial
'**Werbung** *f* (*-; no pl*) advertising, (sales) promotion; *a.* POL *etc* publicity, propaganda; recruitment; ***Werbung machen für et.*** advertise s.th.
Werdegang ['veːɐdə-] *m* career
werden ['veːɐdən] *v/i* (*irr, ge-, sein*) *and v/aux* become, get; turn, go; grow; turn

out; ***wir werden*** we will (*or* shall), we are going to; ***geliebt werden*** be loved (***von*** by); ***was willst du werden?*** what do you want to be?; ***mir wird schlecht*** I'm going to be sick; F ***es wird schon wieder*** (***werden***) it'll be all right

werfen ['vɛrfən] *v/i and v/t* (*irr, ge-, h*) throw (*a.* zo) ([***mit***] ***et. nach*** s.th. at); drop (*bombs*); cast (*shadow*)

Werft [vɛrft] *f* (-; *-en*) MAR shipyard, dockyard

Werk [vɛrk] *n* (-[*e*]*s*; *-e*) work, deed; TECH mechanism; ECON works, factory; ***ans Werk gehen*** set *or* go to work

Werkbank *f* (-; *-bänke*) TECH workbench

Werkmeister *m* TECH foreman

'Werkstatt *f* (-; *-stätten*) workshop; MOT garage

'Werktag *m* workday

'werktags *adv* on workdays

'werktätig *adj* working

'Werkzeug *n* tool (*a. fig*); *coll* tools; instrument

Werkzeugmacher *m* toolmaker

wert [veːɐt] *adj* worth; ***die Mühe*** (***e-n Versuch***) ***wert*** worth the trouble (a try); *fig* ***nichts wert*** no good

Wert *m* (-[*e*]*s*; *-e*) value, *esp fig a.* worth; use; *pl* data, figures; ***... im Wert***(***e***) ***von 20 Dollar*** 20 dollars' worth of ...; ***großen Wert legen auf*** (*acc*) set great store by

werten ['veːɐtən] *v/t* (*ge-, h*) value; *a.* SPORT rate, judge

'Wertgegenstand *m* article of value

'wertlos *adj* worthless

'Wertpa,piere *pl* securities

'Wertsachen *pl* valuables

'Wertung *f* (-; *-en*) valuation; *a.* SPORT rating, judging; score, points

'wertvoll *adj* valuable

Wesen ['veːzən] *n* (*-s*; -) being, creature; *fig* essence; nature, character; ***viel Wesens machen um*** make a fuss about

'wesentlich *adj* essential; considerable; ***im Wesentlichen*** on the whole

weshalb [vɛs'halp] *interr adv* → ***warum***

Wespe ['vɛspə] *f* (-; *-n*) zo wasp

Weste ['vɛstə] *f* (-; *-n*) vest, *Br* waistcoat

Westen ['vɛstən] *m* (*-s*; *no pl*) west; POL West

Western ['vɛstɐn] *m* (*-s*; -) western

'westlich **1.** *adj* western; westerly; POL West(ern); **2.** *adv*: ***westlich von*** (to the) west of

'Westwind *m* west(erly) wind

Wettbewerb ['vɛtbəvɛrp] *m* (-[*e*]*s*; *-e*) competition (*a.* ECON), contest

'Wettbü,ro *n* betting office

Wette ['vɛtə] *f* (-; *-n*) bet; ***e-e Wette abschließen*** make a bet; ***um die Wette laufen*** *etc* race (***mit j-m*** s.o.)

'wetteifern *v/i* (*ge-, h*) compete (***mit*** with; ***um*** for)

'wetten *v/i and v/t* (*ge-, h*) bet; ***mit j-m um 10 Dollar wetten*** bet s.o. ten dollars; ***wetten auf*** (*acc*) bet on, back

Wetter ['vɛtɐ] *n* (*-s*; -) weather

'Wetterbericht *m* weather report

'Wetterfahne *f* weather vane

'wetterfest *adj* weatherproof

'Wetterkarte *f* weather chart

Wetterlage *f* weather situation

Wetterleuchten *n* sheet lightning

Wettervorhersage *f* weather forecast

Wetterwarte *f* weather station

'Wettkampf *m* competition, contest

Wettkämpfer(in) contestant, competitor

Wettlauf *m* race (*a. fig* ***mit*** against)

Wettläufer(in) runner

'wettmachen *v/t* (*sep, -ge-, h*) make up for

'Wettrennen *n* race

'Wettrüsten *n* (*-s*; *no pl*) arms race

'Wettstreit *m* contest, competition

wetzen ['vɛtsən] *v/t* (*ge-, h*) whet, sharpen

wich [vɪç] *pret of* ***weichen***

wichtig ['vɪçtɪç] *adj* important

'Wichtigkeit *f* (-; *no pl*) importance

'wickeln *v/t* (*ge-, h*) change (*baby*); ***wickeln in*** (*acc*) wrap in; ***wickeln um*** wrap (a)round

Widder ['vɪdɐ] *m* (*-s*; -) zo ram; ASTR Aries; ***er ist*** (***ein***) ***Widder*** he's (an) Aries

wider ['viːdɐ] *prp* (*acc*) ***wider Willen*** against one's will; ***wider Erwarten*** contrary to expectations

'Widerhaken *m* barb

'widerhallen *v/i* (*sep, -ge-, h*) resound (***von*** with)

wider'legen *v/t* (*no -ge-, h*) refute, disprove

'widerlich *adj* sickening, disgusting

'widerrechtlich *adj* illegal, unlawful

'Widerruf *m* JUR revocation; withdrawal

wider'rufen *v/t* (*irr,* ***rufen****, no -ge-, h*) revoke; withdraw

Widersacher ['viːdɐzaxɐ] *m* (*-s*; -) adversary, rival

'Widerschein *m* reflection

wider'setzen *v/refl* (*no -ge-, h*) (*dat*) oppose, resist

'widersinnig *adj* absurd

widerspenstig ['viːdɐʃpɛnstɪç] *adj* unruly, stubborn

'widerspiegeln *v/t* (*sep, -ge-, h*) reflect (*a. fig*); ***sich widerspiegeln in*** (*dat*) be reflected in

wider'sprechen *v/i* (*irr,* ***sprechen****, no -ge-, h*) (*dat*) contradict

W

'**Widerspruch** *m* contradiction
widersprüchlich ['viːdɐʃprʏçlɪç] *adj* contradictory
'**widerspruchslos** *adv* without contradiction
'**Widerstand** *m* resistance (*a.* ELECTR), opposition; ***Widerstand leisten*** offer resistance (*dat* to)
'**widerstandsfähig** *adj* resistant (*a.* TECH)
wider'stehen *v/i* (*irr*, ***stehen***, *no -ge-, h*) (*dat*) resist
wider'streben *v/i* (*no -ge-, h*) ***es widerstrebt mir, dies zu tun*** I hate doing *or* to do that
widerstrebend *adv* reluctantly
widerwärtig ['viːdɐvɛrtɪç] *adj* disgusting
'**Widerwille** *m* aversion (***gegen*** to), dislike (of, for); disgust (at)
'**widerwillig** *adj* reluctant, unwilling
widmen ['vɪtmən] *v/t* (*ge-, h*) dedicate
'**Widmung** *f* (*-; -en*) dedication
wie [viː] **1.** *interr adv* how; ***wie geht es Gordon?*** how is Gordon?; ***wie ist er?*** what's he like?; ***wie ist das Wetter?*** what's the weather like?; ***wie heißen Sie?*** what's your name?; ***wie nennt man ...?*** what do you call ...?; ***wie wäre (ist, steht) es mit ...?*** what *or* how about ...?; ***wie viele ...?*** how many ...?; **2.** *cj* like; as; ***wie neu (verrückt)*** like new (mad); ***doppelt so ... wie*** twice as ... as; ***wie (zum Beispiel)*** such as, like; ***wie üblich*** as usual; ***wie er sagte*** as he said; ***ich zeige (sage) dir, wie (...)*** I'll show (tell) you how (...)
wieder ['viːdɐ] *adv* again; *in cpds often* re...; ***immer wieder*** again and again; ***wieder aufbauen*** reconstruct; ***wieder aufnehmen*** resume; ***wieder beleben*** MED resuscitate, revive (*a. fig*); ***wieder erkennen*** recognize (***an*** *dat* by); ***wieder finden*** find (what one has lost); *fig* regain; ***wieder gutmachen*** make up for; ***wieder herstellen*** restore; ***wieder sehen*** see *or* meet again; ***wieder verwendbar*** reusable; ***wieder verwerten*** TECH recycle
Wieder'aufbau *m* (*-[e]s; no pl*) reconstruction, rebuilding
Wieder'aufbereitung *f* TECH recycling, reprocessing (*a.* NUCL)
Wieder'aufbereitungsanlage *f* TECH reprocessing plant
Wieder'aufleben *n* (*-s; no pl*) revival
Wieder'aufnahme *f* (*-; no pl*) resumption
'**wiederbekommen** *v/t* (*irr*, ***kommen***, *sep, no -ge-, h*) get back
'**Wiederbelebung** *f* (*-; -en*) MED resuscitation
Wiederbelebungsversuch *m* MED attempt at resuscitation
'**wiederbringen** *v/t* (*irr*, ***bringen***, *sep, -ge-, h*) bring back; return
Wieder'einführung *f* reintroduction
'**Wiederentdeckung** *f* rediscovery
'**Wiedergabe** *f* TECH reproduction, playback
'**wiedergeben** *v/t* (*irr*, ***geben***, *sep, -ge-, h*) give back, return; *fig* describe; TECH play back, reproduce
Wieder'gutmachung *f* (*-; -en*) reparation
'**wiederholen**[1] *v/t* (*sep, -ge-, h*) (go and) get *s.o. or s.th.* back
wieder'holen[2] *v/t* (*no -ge-, h*) repeat; PED revise, review; THEA replay; ***sich wiederholen*** repeat o.s. (*a. fig*)
wieder'holt *adv* repeatedly, several times
Wieder'holung *f* (*-; -en*) repetition; PED review; TV *etc* rerun; SPORT replay
Wiederkehr ['viːdɐkeːɐ] *f* (*-; no pl*) return; recurrence
'**wiederkehren** *v/i* (*sep, -ge-, sein*) return; recur
'**wiederkommen** *v/i* (*irr*, ***kommen***, *sep, -ge-, sein*) come back, return
'**Wiedersehen** *n* (*-s; -*) seeing *s.o.* again; reunion; ***auf Wiedersehen!*** goodbye!
wiederum ['viːdərʊm] *adv* again; on the other hand
'**Wiedervereinigung** *f* reunion, *esp* POL *a.* reunification
Wiederverkauf *m* resale
Wiederverwendung *f* reuse
Wiederverwertung *f* (*-; -en*) TECH recycling
Wiederwahl *f* POL re-election
Wiege ['viːgə] *f* (*-; -n*) cradle
wiegen[1] ['viːgən] *v/t and v/i* (*irr, ge-, h*) weigh
'**wiegen**[2] *v/t* (*ge-, h*) rock (***in den Schlaf*** to sleep)
'**Wiegenlied** *n* lullaby
wiehern ['viːɐn] *v/i* (*ge-, h*) ZO neigh
wies [viːs] *pret of* ***weisen***
Wiese ['viːzə] *f* (*-; -n*) meadow
Wiesel ['viːzəl] *n* (*-s; -*) ZO weasel
wieso [vi'zoː] *interr adv* → ***warum***
wievielt [vi'fiːlt] *adj*: ***zum wievielten Male?*** how many times?
wild [vɪlt] *adj* wild (*a. fig*) (F ***auf*** *acc* about); violent; ***wilder Streik*** wildcat strike
Wild *n* (*-[e]s; no pl*) HUNT game; GASTR *mst* venison
Wildbach *m* torrent
Wilde ['vɪldə] *m, f* (*-n; -n*) savage; F ***wie ein Wilder*** like mad
Wilderer ['vɪldərɐ] *m* (*-s; -*) poacher

'wildern *v/i (ge-, h)* poach
'Wildhüter *m* gamekeeper
'Wildkatze *f* zo wild cat
'Wildleder *n* suede
'Wildnis *f (-; -se)* wilderness
'Wildpark *m*, **Wildreser,vat** *n* game park *or* reserve
Wildschwein *n* zo wild boar
Wille ['vɪlə] *m (-ns; -n)* will; intention; ***s-n Willen durchsetzen*** have *or* get one's own way; ***j-m s-n Willen lassen*** let s.o. have his (own) way
'willenlos *adj* weak(-willed)
'Willenskraft *f (-; no pl)* willpower; ***durch Willenskraft erzwingen*** will
'willensstark *adj* strong-willed
willig ['vɪlɪç] *adj* willing
will'kommen *adj* welcome (*a.* ***willkommen heißen***) (***in*** *dat* to)
willkürlich ['vɪlkyːɐlɪç] *adj* arbitrary; random
wimmeln ['vɪməln] *v/i (ge-, h)* ***wimmeln von*** be teeming with
wimmern ['vɪmɐn] *v/i (ge-, h)* whimper
Wimpel ['vɪmpəl] *m (-s; -)* pennant
Wimper ['vɪmpɐ] *f (-; -n)* eyelash; ***ohne mit der Wimper zu zucken*** without turning a hair
'Wimperntusche *f* mascara
Wind [vɪnt] *m (-[e]s; -e* ['vɪndə]) wind
Winde ['vɪndə] *f (-; -n)* winch, windlass, hoist
Windel ['vɪndəl] *f (-; -n)* diaper, *Br* nappy
winden ['vɪndən] *v/t (irr, ge-, h)* wind, TECH *a.* hoist; ***sich winden*** wind (one's way); writhe (*with pain etc*)
'Windhund *m* zo greyhound
windig ['vɪndɪç] *adj* windy
'Windmühle *f* windmill
Windpocken *pl* MED chickenpox
Windrichtung *f* direction of the wind
Windschutzscheibe *f* MOT windshield, *Br* windscreen
Windstärke *f* wind force
'windstill *adj*, **'Windstille** *f* calm
'Windstoß *m* gust
'Windsurfen *n* windsurfing
'Windung *f (-; -en)* bend, turn (*a.* TECH)
Wink [vɪŋk] *m (-[e]s; -e)* sign; *fig* hint
Winkel ['vɪŋkəl] *m (-s; -)* corner; MATH angle
'winkelig *adj* angular; crooked
winken ['vɪŋkən] *v/i (ge-, h)* wave (one's hand *etc*), signal; beckon
winseln ['vɪnzəln] *v/i (ge-, h)* whimper, whine
Winter ['vɪntɐ] *m (-s; -)* winter
'winterlich *adj* wintry
'Winterreifen *m* MOT snow tire (*Br* tyre)
Winterschlaf *m* zo hibernation
Winterspiele *pl*: ***Olympische Winterspiele*** SPORT Winter Olympics
Wintersport *m* winter sports
Winzer ['vɪntsɐ] *m (-s; -)* winegrower
winzig ['vɪntsɪç] *adj* tiny, diminutive
Wipfel ['vɪpfəl] *m (-s; -)* (tree)top
Wippe ['vɪpə] *f (-; -n)*, **'wippen** *v/i (ge-, h)* seesaw
wir [viːɐ] *pers pron* we; ***wir drei*** the three of us; F ***wir sind's!*** it's us!
Wirbel ['vɪrbəl] *m (-s; -)* whirl (*a. fig*); ANAT vertebra
'wirbeln *v/i (ge-, sein)* whirl
'Wirbelsäule *f* ANAT spinal column, spine
Wirbelsturm *m* cyclone, tornado
Wirbeltier *n* vertebrate
Wirbelwind *m* whirlwind
wirken ['vɪrkən] *(ge-, h)* **1.** *v/i* work; be effective (***gegen*** against); look; ***anregend*** *etc* ***wirken*** have a stimulating *etc* effect (***auf*** *acc* [up]on); ***wirken als*** act as; **2.** *v/t* weave; *fig* work (*miracles etc*)
wirklich ['vɪrklɪç] *adj* real, actual; true, genuine
'Wirklichkeit *f (-; -en)* reality; ***in Wirklichkeit*** in reality, actually
wirksam ['vɪrkzaːm] *adj* effective
'Wirkung *f (-; -en)* effect
'wirkungslos *adj* ineffective
'wirkungsvoll *adj* effective
wirr [vɪr] *adj* confused, mixed-up; *hair*: tousled
Wirren ['vɪrən] *pl* disorder, confusion
Wirrwarr ['vɪrvar] *m (-s; no pl)* confusion, mess, welter
Wirt [vɪrt] *m (-[e]s; -e)* landlord
'Wirtin *f (-; -nen)* landlady
'Wirtschaft *f (-; -en)* ECON, POL economy; business; → ***Gastwirtschaft***
'wirtschaften *v/i (ge-, h)* keep house; manage one's money *or* affairs *or* business; economize; ***gut*** (***schlecht***) ***wirtschaften*** be a good (bad) manager
'Wirtschafterin *f (-; -nen)* housekeeper
'wirtschaftlich *adj* economic; economical
'Wirtschafts... ECON *in cpds ...gemeinschaft, ...gipfel, ...krise, ...system, ...wunder etc*: economic ...
'Wirtshaus *n* → ***Gastwirtschaft***
wischen ['vɪʃən] *v/t (ge-, h)* wipe; ***Staub wischen*** dust
wispern ['vɪspɐn] *v/t and v/i (ge-, h)* whisper
wissbegierig ['vɪs-] *adj* curious
wissen ['vɪsən] *v/t and v/i (irr, ge-, h)* know; ***ich möchte wissen*** I'd like to know, I wonder; ***soviel ich weiß*** as far as I know; ***weißt du*** you know; ***weißt***

du noch? (do you) remember?; ***woher weißt du das?*** how do you know?; ***man kann nie wissen*** you never know; ***ich will davon*** (***von ihm***) ***nichts wissen*** I don't want anything to do with it (him)

'Wissen *n* (*-s*; *no pl*) knowledge; know-how; ***m-s Wissens*** as far as I know

'Wissenschaft *f* (*-*; *-en*) science

'Wissenschaftler *m* (*-s*; *-*), **'Wissenschaftlerin** *f* (*-*; *-nen*) scientist

'wissenschaftlich *adj* scientific

'wissenswert *adj* worth knowing; ***Wissenswertes*** useful facts; ***alles Wissenswerte*** (***über*** *acc*) all you need to know (about)

wittern ['vɪtɐn] *v/t* (*ge-*, *h*) scent, smell (*both a. fig*)

Witwe ['vɪtvə] *f* (*-*; *-n*) widow

Witwer ['vɪtvɐ] *m* (*-s*; *-*) widower

Witz [vɪts] *m* (*-es*; *-e*) joke; ***Witze reißen*** crack jokes

witzig ['vɪtsɪç] *adj* funny; witty

wo [voː] *adv* where; ***wo ... doch*** when, although

wob [voːp] *pret of* ***weben***

wobei [vo'bai] *adv*: ***wobei bist du?*** what are you at?; ***wobei mir einfällt*** which reminds me

Woche ['vɔxə] *f* (*-*; *-n*) week

'Wochen... *in cpds ...lohn*, *...markt*, *...zeitung etc*: weekly ...

Wochenende *n* weekend; ***am Wochenende*** on (*Br* at) the weekend

'wochenlang **1.** *adj*: ***wochenlanges Warten*** (many) weeks of waiting; **2.** *adv* for weeks

'Wochenschau *f film*: newsreel

'Wochentag *m* weekday

wöchentlich ['vœçəntlɪç] **1.** *adj* weekly; **2.** *adv* weekly, every week; ***einmal wöchentlich*** once a week

wodurch [vo'durç] *adv* how; through which

wofür [vo'fyːɐ] *adv* for which; ***wofür?*** what (...) for?

wog [voːk] *pret of* ***wiegen***[1] *and* ***wägen***

Woge ['voːgə] *f* (*-*; *-n*) wave, *esp fig a.* surge; breaker

'wogen *v/i* (*ge-*, *h*) surge, heave (*both a. fig*)

woher [vo'heːɐ] *adv* where ... from; ***woher weißt du*** (***das***)***?*** how do you know?

wohin [vo'hɪn] *adv* where (... to)

wohl [voːl] *adv and cj* well; probably, I suppose; ***sich wohl fühlen*** → ***wohlfühlen***; ***wohl oder übel*** willy-nilly, whether you *etc* like it or not; ***wohl kaum*** hardly

Wohl *n* (*-[e]s*; *no pl*) well-being; ***auf j-s Wohl trinken*** drink to s.o.('s health); ***zum Wohl!*** to your health!; F cheers!

'wohlbehalten *adv* safely

'Wohlfahrtsstaat *m* welfare state

'wohlgemerkt *adv* mind you

wohlgenährt *adj* well-fed

wohlgesinnt *adj*: ***j-m wohlgesinnt sein*** be well-disposed towards s.o.

wohlhabend *adj* well-off, well-to-do

'wohlfühlen *v/refl* (*sep*, *-ge-*, *h*): ***sich wohlfühlen*** feel well, be well; feel good; feel at home (***bei*** with); ***ich fühle mich nicht wohl*** I don't feel well

wohlig ['voːlɪç] *adj* snug, cozy, *Br* cosy

'Wohlstand *m* (*-[e]s*; *no pl*) prosperity, affluence

Wohlstandsgesellschaft *f* affluent society

'Wohltat *f* (*-*; *no pl*) pleasure; relief; blessing

'Wohltäter(in) benefactor (benefactress)

'wohltätig *adj* charitable; ***für wohltätige Zwecke*** for charity

'Wohltätigkeits... *in cpds ...ball*, *...konzert etc*: charity ...

'wohltun *v/i* (*irr*, **tun**, *sep*, *-ge-*, *h*): ***j-m wohltun*** do s.o. good

'wohlverdient *adj* well-deserved

'wohlwollend *adj* benevolent

wohnen ['voːnən] *v/i* (*ge-*, *h*) live (***in*** *dat* in; ***bei j-m*** with s.o.); stay (***in*** *dat* at; ***bei*** with)

'Wohngebiet *n* residential area

'Wohngemeinschaft *f*: (***mit j-m***) ***in e-r Wohngemeinschaft leben*** share an apartment (*Br* a flat) *or* a house (with s.o.)

wohnlich ['voːnlɪç] *adj* comfortable, snug, cozy, *Br* cosy

'Wohnmo,bil *n* (*-s*; *-e*) camper, motor home (*Br* caravan)

'Wohnsiedlung *f* housing development (*Br* estate)

Wohnsitz *m* residence; ***ohne festen Wohnsitz*** of no fixed abode

'Wohnung *f* (*-*; *-en*) apartment, *Br* flat; ***m-e*** *etc* ***Wohnung*** my *etc* place

'Wohnungsamt *n* housing office

Wohnungsbau *m* (*-[e]s*; *no pl*) house building

Wohnungsnot *f* housing shortage

'Wohnwagen *m* trailer, *Br* caravan; mobile home

'Wohnzimmer *n* sitting *or* living room

wölben ['vœlbən] *v/refl* (*ge-*, *h*), **'Wölbung** *f* (*-*; *-en*) vault, arch

Wolf [vɔlf] *m* (*-[e]s*; *Wölfe* ['vœlfə]) zo wolf

Wolke ['vɔlkə] *f* (*-*; *-n*) cloud

'Wolkenbruch *m* cloudburst

'**Wolkenkratzer** *m (-s; -)* skyscraper
'**wolkenlos** *adj* cloudless
wolkig ['vɔlkɪç] *adj* cloudy, clouded
Woll... [vɔl-] *in cpds ...schal, ...socken etc*: wool(l)en ...
Wolldecke *f* blanket
Wolle ['vɔlə] *f (-; -n)* wool
wollen ['vɔlən] *v/t and v/i (ge-, h) and v/aux (no -ge-, h)* want (to); ***lieber wollen*** prefer; ***wollen wir (gehen*** *etc)?* shall we (go *etc*)?; ***wollen Sie bitte ...*** will *or* would you please ...; ***wie (was, wann) du willst*** as (whatever, whenever) you like; ***sie will, dass ich komme*** she wants me to come; ***ich wollte, ich wäre (hätte) ...*** I wish I were (had) ...
womit [vo'mɪt] *adv* with which; ***womit?*** what ... with?
Wonne ['vɔnə] *f (-; -n)* joy, delight
woran [vo'ran] *adv*: ***woran denkst du?*** what are you thinking of?; ***woran liegt es, dass ...?*** how is it that ...?; ***woran sieht man, welche (ob) ...?*** how can you tell which (if) ...?
worauf [vo'rauf] *adv* after which; on which; ***worauf?*** what ... on?; ***worauf wartest du?*** what are you waiting for?
woraus [vo'raus] *adv* from which; ***woraus ist es?*** what's it made of?
worin [vo'rɪn] *adv* in which; ***worin?*** where?
Wort [vɔrt] *n (-[e]s; -e, Wörter* ['vœrtɐ]) word; ***mit anderen Worten*** in other words; ***sein Wort geben (halten, brechen)*** give (keep, break) one's word; ***j-n beim Wort nehmen*** take s.o. at his word; ***ein gutes Wort einlegen für*** put in a good word for; ***j-m ins Wort fallen*** cut s.o. short
'**Wortart** *f* LING part of speech
Wörterbuch ['vœrtɐ-] *n* dictionary
Wörterverzeichnis *n* vocabulary, list of words
'**Wortführer** *m* spokesman
'**Wortführerin** *f* spokeswoman
'**wortkarg** *adj* taciturn
wörtlich ['vœrtlɪç] *adj* literal; ***wörtliche Rede*** LING direct speech
'**Wortschatz** *m* vocabulary
Wortspiel *n* pun
Wortstellung *f* LING word order
worüber [vo'ry:bɐ] *adv* about which; ***worüber lachen Sie?*** what are you laughing at *or* about?
worum [vo'rʊm] *adv* about which; ***worum handelt es sich?*** what is it about?
worunter [vo'rʊntɐ] *adv* among which; ***worunter?*** what ... under?
wovon [vo'fɔn] *adv* about which; ***wovon redest du?*** what are you talking about?
wovor [vo'fo:ɐ] *adv* of which; ***wovor hast du Angst?*** what are you afraid of?
wozu [vo'tsu:] *adv*: ***wozu er mir rät*** what he advised me to do; ***wozu?*** what (...) for?; why?
Wrack [vrak] *n (-[e]s; -s)* MAR wreck (*a. fig*)
wrang [vraŋ] *pret of* ***wringen***
wringen ['vrɪŋən] *v/t (irr, ge-, h)* wring
Wucher ['vu:xɐ] *m (-s; no pl)* usury
Wucherer ['vu:xərɐ] *m (-s; -)* usurer
'**wuchern** *v/i (ge-, h)* grow (*fig* be) rampant
Wucherung ['vu:xərʊŋ] *f (-; -en)* MED growth
Wuchs [vu:ks] *m (-es; no pl)* growth; build
wuchs [vu:ks] *pret of* ***wachsen***[1]
Wucht [vʊxt] *f (-; no pl)* force; impact
wuchtig ['vʊxtɪç] *adj* massive; powerful
wühlen ['vy:lən] *v/i (ge-, h)* dig; zo root; rummage (***in*** *dat* in, through)
Wulst [vʊlst] *m (-es; Wülste* ['vʏlstə)], *f (-; Wülste)* bulge; roll (*of fat*)
wulstig ['vʊlstɪç] *adj* bulging; thick
wund [vʊnt] *adj* MED sore; ***wunde Stelle*** MED sore; ***wunder Punkt*** *fig* sore point
Wunde ['vʊndə] *f (-; -n)* MED wound
Wunder ['vʊndɐ] *n (-s; -)* miracle, *fig a.* wonder; ***Wunder wirken*** work wonders; ***(es ist) kein Wunder, dass du müde bist*** no wonder you are tired
'**wunderbar** *adj* wonderful, marvel(l)ous
'**Wunderkind** *n* infant prodigy
'**wunderlich** *adj* funny, odd; senile
'**wundern** *v/refl (ge-, h)* be surprised *or* astonished (***über*** *acc* at)
'**wundervoll** *adj* wonderful
'**Wundstarrkrampf** *m (-es; no pl)* MED tetanus
Wunsch [vʊnʃ] *m (-[e]s; Wünsche* ['vʏnʃə]) wish; request; ***auf j-s Wunsch*** at s.o.'s request; ***auf eigenen Wunsch*** at one's own request; ***(je) nach Wunsch*** as desired
wünschen ['vʏnʃən] *v/t (ge-, h)* wish; ***sich et. (zu Weihnachten*** *etc*) ***wünschen*** want s.th. (for Christmas *etc*); ***das habe ich mir (schon immer) gewünscht*** that's what I (always) wanted; ***alles, was man sich nur wünschen kann*** everything one could wish for; ***ich wünschte, ich wäre (hätte) ...*** I wish I were (had) ...
'**wünschenswert** *adj* desirable
wurde ['vʊrdə] *pret of* ***werden***
Würde ['vʏrdə] *f (-; -n)* dignity
'**würdelos** *adj* undignified
'**Würdenträger** *m* dignitary

'**würdevoll** *adj* dignified
würdig ['vʏrdɪç] *adj* worthy (*gen* of); dignified
würdigen ['vʏrdɪgən] *v/t* (*ge-, h*) appreciate; ***j-n keines Blickes würdigen*** ignore s.o. completely
'**Würdigung** *f* (-; *-en*) appreciation
Wurf [vʊrf] *m* (-[*e*]*s*; *Würfe* ['vʏrfə]) throw; ZO litter
Würfel ['vʏrfəl] *m* (*-s*; -) cube (*a.* MATH); dice
'**würfeln** *v/i* (*ge-, h*) throw dice (***um*** for); play dice; GASTR dice; ***e-e Sechs würfeln*** throw a six
'**Würfelzucker** *m* lump sugar
'**Wurfgeschoss** *n* missile
würgen ['vʏrgən] *v/i and v/t* (*ge-, h*) choke; throttle *s.o.*
Wurm [vʊrm] *m* (-[*e*]*s*; *Würmer* ['vʏrmɐ]) ZO worm
wurmen ['vʊrmən] F *v/t* (*ge-, h*) gall *s.o.*
'**wurmstichig** ['vʊrmʃtɪçɪç] *adj* worm-eaten
Wurst [vʊrst] *f* (-; *Würste* ['vʏrstə]) sausage
Würstchen ['vʏrstçən] *n* (*-s*; -) small sausage, frankfurter, wiener; hot dog
Würze [vʏrtsə] *f* (-; *-n*) spice (*a. fig*)
Wurzel ['vʊrtsəl] *f* (-; *-n*) root (*a.* MATH); ***Wurzeln schlagen*** take root (*a. fig*)
'**wurzeln** *v/i* (*ge-, h*) ***wurzeln in*** (*dat*) be rooted in (*a. fig*)
'**würzen** *v/t* (*ge-, h*) spice, season, flavo(u)r
würzig ['vʏrtsɪç] *adj* spicy, well-seasoned
wusch [vu:ʃ] *pret of* ***waschen***
wusste ['vʊstə] *pret of* ***wissen***
Wust [vu:st] F *m* (-[*e*]*s*; *no pl*) tangled mass
wüst [vy:st] *adj* waste; confused; wild, dissolute
Wüste ['vy:stə] *f* (-; *-n*) desert
Wut [vu:t] *f* (-; *no pl*) rage, fury; ***e-e Wut haben*** be furious (***auf*** *acc* with)
'**Wutanfall** *m* fit of rage
wüten ['vy:tən] *v/i* (*ge-, h*) rage (*a. fig*)
wütend *adj* furious (***auf*** *acc* with; ***über*** *acc* at), F mad (at)
'**wutschnaubend** *adj* fuming

X, Y

X-Beine ['ɪksbainə] *pl* knock-knees; ***sie hat X-Beine*** she's knock-kneed
x-beinig ['ɪksbainɪç] *adj* knock-kneed
x-be'liebig *adj*: ***jede(r, -s) x-Beliebige ...*** any ... you like, F any old ...
'**x-mal** F *adv* umpteen times
x-te ['ɪkstə] *adj*: ***zum x-ten Male*** for the umpteenth time
Xylophon [ksylo'fo:n] *n* (*-s*; *-e*) MUS xylophone
Yacht [jaxt] *f* (-; *-en*) MAR yacht
Yoga ['jo:ga] *m, n* (-[*s*]; *no pl*) yoga

Z

Zacke ['tsakə] *f* (-; *-n*), '**Zacken** *m* (*-s*; -) (sharp) point; tooth
zackig ['tsakɪç] *adj* serrated; jagged; *fig* smart
zaghaft ['tsa:khaft] *adj* timid
zäh [tsɛ:] *adj* tough (*a. fig*)
zähflüssig *adj* thick, viscous; *fig* slow-moving (*traffic*)
Zähigkeit ['tsɛ:ɪçkait] *f* (-; *no pl*) toughness, *fig a.* stamina
Zahl [tsa:l] *f* (-; *-en*) number; figure
'**zahlbar** *adj* payable (***an*** *acc* to; ***bei*** at)
zählbar ['tsɛ:lba:ɐ] *adj* countable
zahlen ['tsa:lən] *v/i and v/t* (*ge-, h*) pay; ***zahlen, bitte!*** the check (*Br* bill), please!
zählen ['tsɛ:lən] *v/t and v/i* (*ge-, h*) count

(**bis** up to; *fig* **auf** *acc* on); **zählen zu** rank with *the best etc*
'**zahlenmäßig** **1.** *adj* numerical; **2.** *adv*: **j-m zahlenmäßig überlegen sein** outnumber s.o.
Zähler ['tsɛːlɐ] *m* (*-s*; *-*) counter (*a.* TECH); MATH numerator; ELECTR *etc* meter
'**Zahlkarte** *f post* deposit (*Br* paying-in) slip
'**zahllos** *adj* countless
'**Zahlmeister** *m* MIL paymaster; MAR purser
'**zahlreich** **1.** *adj* numerous; **2.** *adv* in great number
'**Zahltag** *m* payday
'**Zahlung** *f* (*-*; *-en*) payment
'**Zählung** *f* (*-*; *-en*) count; POL census
'**Zahlungsaufforderung** *f* request for payment
Zahlungsbedingungen *pl* terms of payment
Zahlungsbefehl *m* order to pay
'**zahlungsfähig** *adj* solvent
'**Zahlungsfrist** *f* term of payment
Zahlungsmittel *n* currency; **gesetzliches Zahlungsmittel** legal tender
Zahlungsschwierigkeiten *pl* financial difficulties
Zahlungster,min *m* date of payment
'**zahlungsunfähig** *adj* insolvent
'**Zählwerk** *n* TECH counter
'**Zahlwort** *n* LING numeral
zahm [tsaːm] *adj* tame (*a. fig*)
zähmen ['tsɛːmən] *v/t* (*ge-*, *h*) tame (*a. fig*)
'**Zähmung** *f* (*-*; *no pl*) taming
Zahn [tsaːn] *m* (*-[e]s*; *Zähne* ['tsɛːnə]) tooth, TECH *a.* cog
Zahnarzt *m*, **Zahnärztin** *f* dentist, dental surgeon
Zahnbürste *f* toothbrush
Zahncreme *f* toothpaste
zahnen ['tsaːnən] *v/i* (*ge-*, *h*) cut one's teeth, teethe
'**Zahnfleisch** *n* gums
'**zahnlos** *adj* toothless
'**Zahnlücke** *f* gap between the teeth
Zahnmedi,zin *f* dentistry
Zahnpasta, **Zahnpaste** *f* toothpaste
Zahnradbahn *f* rack railroad
Zahnschmerzen *pl* toothache
Zahnspange *f* MED brace
Zahnstein *m* tartar
Zahnstocher *m* (*-s*; *-*) toothpick
Zange ['tsaŋə] *f* (*-*; *-n*) TECH pliers; pincers; tongs; MED forceps; ZO pincer
zanken ['tsaŋkən] *v/refl* (*ge-*, *h*) quarrel (**wegen** about; **um** over), fight, argue (about; over)
zänkisch ['tsɛŋkɪʃ] *adj* quarrelsome
Zäpfchen ['tsɛpfçən] *n* (*-s*; *-*) ANAT uvula; PHARM suppository
zapfen ['tsapfən] *v/t* (*ge-*, *h*) tap
'**Zapfen** *m* (*-s*; *-*) faucet, *Br* tap; TECH peg, pin; bung; tenon; pivot; BOT cone
'**Zapfenstreich** *m* MIL tattoo, taps
'**Zapfhahn** *m* faucet, *Br* tap; MOT nozzle
Zapfsäule *f* MOT gasoline (*Br* petrol) pump
zappelig ['tsapəlɪç] *adj* fidgety
zappeln ['tsapəln] *v/i* (*ge-*, *h*) fidget, wriggle
zappen ['zɛpən] F *v/i* (*ge-*, *h*) TV zap
zart [tsaːɐt] *adj* tender; gentle; **zart fühlend** sensitive
'**Zartgefühl** *n* (*-[e]s*; *no pl*) delicacy (of feeling), sensitivity, tact
zärtlich ['tsɛːɐtlɪç] *adj* tender, affectionate (**zu** with)
'**Zärtlichkeit** *f* (*-*; *-en*) a) (*no pl*) tenderness, affection, b) caress
Zauber ['tsaubɐ] *m* (*-s*; *-*) magic, spell, charm (*all a. fig*), *fig* enchantment
Zauberei [tsaubə'rai] *f* (*-*; *-en*) magic, witchcraft
Zauberer ['tsaubərɐ] *m* (*-s*; *-*) magician, sorcerer, wizard (*a. fig*)
'**zauberhaft** *fig adj* enchanting, charming
Zauberin ['tsaubərɪn] *f* (*-*; *-nen*) sorceress
'**Zauberkraft** *f* magic power
Zauberkünstler *m* magician, conjurer
Zauberkunststück *n* conjuring trick
'**zaubern** (*ge-*, *h*) **1.** *v/i* practise magic; do conjuring tricks; **2.** *v/t* conjure (up)
'**Zauberspruch** *m* spell
zaudern ['tsaudɐn] *v/i* (*ge-*, *h*) hesitate
Zaum [tsaum] *m* (*-[e]s*; *Zäume* ['tsɔʏmə]) bridle; **im Zaum halten** control (**sich** o.s.), keep in check
zäumen ['tsɔʏmən] *v/t* (*ge-*, *h*) bridle
'**Zaumzeug** *n* (*-[e]s*; *-e*) bridle
Zaun [tsaun] *m* (*-[e]s*; *Zäune* ['tsɔʏnə]) fence
Zaungast *m* onlooker
Zaunpfahl *m* pale
z. B. ABBR *of* **zum Beispiel** e.g., for example, for instance
Zebra ['tseːbra] *n* (*-s*; *-s*) ZO zebra
'**Zebrastreifen** *m* MOT zebra crossing
Zeche ['tsɛçə] *f* (*-*; *-n*) check, *Br* bill; (coal) mine, pit; **die Zeche bezahlen müssen** F have to foot the bill
Zeh [tseː] *m* (*-s*; *-en*), **Zehe** ['tseːə] *f* (*-*; *-n*) ANAT toe; **große** (**kleine**) **Zeh** big (little) toe
'**Zehennagel** *m* ANAT toenail
'**Zehenspitze** *f* tip of the toe; **auf Zehenspitzen gehen** (walk on) tiptoe

zehn [tse:n] *adj* ten
'zehnfach *adj* tenfold
'zehnjährig [-jɛ:rıç] *adj* ten-year-old (*boy etc*); ten-year *anniversary etc*; *absence etc* of ten years
Zehnkampf *m* SPORT decathlon
'zehnmal *adv* ten times
'zehnte *adj* tenth
'Zehntel *n* (-*s*; -) tenth
'zehntens *adv* tenthly
Zeichen ['tsaiçən] *n* (-*s*; -) sign; mark; signal; ***zum Zeichen*** *gen* as a token of
Zeichenblock *m* sketch pad
Zeichenbrett *n* drawing board
Zeichendreieck *n* MATH set square
Zeichenfolge *f* EDP string
Zeichenlehrer(in) art teacher
Zeichensetzung *f* (-; *no pl*) LING punctuation
Zeichensprache *f* sign language
Zeichentrickfilm *m* (animated) cartoon
zeichnen ['tsaiçnən] *v/i and v/t* (*ge-, h*) draw; mark (*a. fig*); sign; *fig* leave its mark on *s.o.*
'Zeichnen *n* (-*s*; *no pl*) drawing; PED art
'Zeichner ['tsaiçnɐ] *m* (-*s*; -) *mst* graphic artist; draftsman, *Br* draughtsman
'Zeichnung *f* (-; -*en*) drawing; diagram; ZO marking
Zeigefinger ['tsaigə-] *m* ANAT forefinger, index finger
zeigen ['tsaigən] (*ge-, h*) **1.** *v/t* show (*a.* ***sich zeigen***); **2.** *v/i*: ***zeigen nach*** point to; (***mit dem Finger***) ***zeigen auf*** (*acc*) point (one's finger) at
Zeiger ['tsaigɐ] *m* (-*s*; -) hand; TECH pointer, needle
'Zeigestock *m* pointer
Zeile ['tsailə] *f* (-; -*n*) line (*a.* TV); ***j-m ein paar Zeilen schreiben*** drop s.o. a line
Zeit [tsait] *f* (-; -*en*) time; age, era; LING tense; ***vor einiger Zeit*** some time ago, a while ago; ***in letzter Zeit*** lately, recently; ***in der*** (*or* ***zur***) ***Zeit*** *gen* in the days of; ***... aller Zeiten*** ... of all time; ***die Zeit ist um*** time's up; ***e-e Zeit lang*** for some time, for a while; ***sich Zeit lassen*** take one's time; ***es wird Zeit, dass ...*** it's time to *inf*; ***das waren noch Zeiten*** those were the days; ***Zeit raubend*** → ***zeitraubend***; → ***zurzeit***
'Zeitabschnitt *m* period (of time)
Zeitalter *n* age
Zeitbombe *f* time bomb (*a. fig*)
Zeitdruck *m*: ***unter Zeitdruck stehen*** be pressed for time
Zeitfahren *n* (-*s*; *no pl*) *cycling*: time trials
'zeitgemäß *adj* modern, up-to-date
'Zeitgenosse *m*, **'Zeitgenossin** *f*, **'zeitgenössisch** [-gənœsıʃ] *adj* contemporary
'Zeitgeschichte *f* (-; *no pl*) contemporary history
Zeitgewinn *m* (-[*e*]*s*; *no pl*) gain of time
Zeitkarte *f* season ticket
'Zeitlang *f* → ***Zeit***
zeit'lebens *adv* all one's life
'zeitlich **1.** *adj* time ...; **2.** *adv*: ***et. zeitlich planen*** *or* ***abstimmen*** time s.th.
'zeitlos *adj* timeless; classic
'Zeitlupe *f*: ***in Zeitlupe*** in slow motion
Zeitnot *f*: ***in Zeitnot sein*** be pressed for time
Zeitpunkt *m* moment
Zeitraffer *m*: ***im Zeitraffer*** in quick motion
'zeitraubend *adj* time-consuming
'Zeitraum *m* period (of time)
'Zeitschrift *f* magazine
Zeitung ['tsaituŋ] *f* (-; -*en*) (news)paper
'Zeitungsabonne,ment *n* subscription to a paper
Zeitungsar,tikel *m* newspaper article
Zeitungsausschnitt *m* (newspaper) clipping (*Br* cutting)
Zeitungsjunge *m* paper boy
Zeitungskiosk *m* newspaper kiosk
Zeitungsno,tiz *f* press item
Zeitungspa,pier *n* newspaper
Zeitungsstand *m* newsstand
Zeitungsverkäufer(in) newsdealer, *Br* news vendor
'Zeitverlust *m* (-[*e*]*s*; *no pl*) loss of time
'Zeitverschiebung *f* AVIAT time lag
'Zeitverschwendung *f* waste of time
'Zeitvertreib [-fɛɐtraip] *m* (-[*e*]*s*; -*e*) pastime; ***zum Zeitvertreib*** to pass the time
zeitweilig ['tsaitvailıç] *adj* temporary
'zeitweise *adv* at times, occasionally
'Zeitwort *n* (-[*e*]*s*; -*wörter*) LING verb
'Zeitzeichen *n* *radio*: time signal
'Zeitzünder *m* MIL time fuse
Zelle ['tsɛlə] *f* (-; -*n*) cell
Zellstoff ['tsɛl-] *m*, **Zellulose** [tsɛlu'lo:zə] *f* (-; -*n*) TECH cellulose
Zelt [tsɛlt] *n* (-[*e*]*s*; -*e*) tent
zelten ['tsɛltən] *v/i* (*ge-, h*) camp
'Zeltlager *n* camp
'Zeltplatz *m* campsite
Zement [tse'mɛnt] *m* (-[*e*]*s*; -*e*), **zementieren** [tsemɛn'ti:rən] *v/t* (*no -ge-, h*) cement
Zenit [tse'ni:t] *m* (-[*e*]*s*; *no pl*) zenith
zensieren [tsɛn'zi:rən] *v/t* (*no -ge-, h*) censor; PED mark, grade
Zensor ['tsɛnzo:ɐ] *m* (-*s*; -*en* [tsɛn'zo:rən]) censor
Zensur [tsɛn'zu:ɐ] *f* (-; -*en* [tsɛn'zu:rən])

a) (*no pl*) censorship, b) PED mark, grade
Zentimeter [tsɛnti'meːtɐ] *n*, *m* (*-s*; *-*) centimeter, *Br* centimetre
Zentner ['tsɛntnɐ] *m* (*-s*; *-*) 50 kilograms, metric hundredweight
zentral [tsɛn'traːl] *adj* central
Zentrale [tsɛn'traːlə] *f* (*-*; *-n*) head office; headquarters; TEL switchboard; TECH control room
Zen'tralheizung *f* central heating
Zentralverriegelung *f* MOT central locking
Zentrum ['tsɛntrʊm] *n* (*-s*; *Zentren*) center, *Br* centre
Zepter ['tsɛptɐ] *n* (*-s*; *-*) scepter, *Br* sceptre
zer'brechen *v/i* (*irr*, ***brechen***, *no -ge-*, *sein*) *and v/t* (*h*) break; → ***Kopf***
zer'brechlich *adj* fragile
zer'bröckeln *v/t* (*no -ge-*, *h*) *and v/i* (*sein*) crumble
zer'drücken *v/t* (*no -ge-*, *h*) crush
Zeremonie [tseremo'niː] *f* (*-*; *-n*) ceremony
zeremoniell [tseremo'njɛl] *adj*, **Zeremoni'ell** *n* (*-s*; *-e*) ceremonial
Zer'fall *m* (*-[e]s*; *no pl*) disintegration, decay
zer'fallen *v/i* (*irr*, ***fallen***, *no -ge-*, *sein*) disintegrate, decay; ***zerfallen in*** (*acc*) break up into
zer'fetzen *v/t* (*no -ge-*, *h*) tear to pieces
zer'fressen *v/t* (*irr*, ***fressen***, *no -ge-*, *h*) eat (holes in); CHEM corrode
zer'gehen *v/i* (*irr*, ***gehen***, *no -ge-*, *sein*) melt, dissolve
zer'hacken *v/t* (*no -ge-*, *h*) chop (*a.* ELECTR)
zerknirscht [tsɛɐ'knɪrʃt] *adj* remorseful
zer'knittern *v/t* (*no -ge-*, *h*) (c)rumple, crease
zer'knüllen *v/t* (*no -ge-*, *h*) crumple up
zer'kratzen *v/t* (*no -ge-*, *h*) scratch
zer'krümeln *v/t* (*no -ge-*, *h*) crumble
zer'lassen *v/t* (*irr*, ***lassen***, *no -ge-*, *h*) melt
zer'legen *v/t* (*no -ge-*, *h*) take apart *or* to pieces; TECH dismantle; GASTR carve; CHEM, LING, *fig* analyze, *Br* analyse
zer'lumpt *adj* ragged, tattered
zer'mahlen *v/t* (*no -ge-*, *h*) grind
zer'mürben *v/t* (*no -ge-*, *h*) wear down
zer'quetschen *v/t* (*no -ge-*, *h*) crush
Zerrbild ['tsɛɐ-] *n* caricature
zer'reiben *v/t* (*irr*, ***reiben***, *no -ge-*, *h*) rub to powder, pulverize
zer'reißen (*irr*, ***reißen***, *no -ge-*) **1.** *v/t* (*h*) tear up *or* to pieces; ***sich die Hose zerreißen*** tear one's trousers; **2.** *v/i* (*sein*) tear; break
zerren ['tsɛrən] (*ge-*, *h*) **1.** *v/t* tug, drag, pull (*a.* MED); **2.** *v/i*: ***zerren an*** (*dat*) tug (*or* strain) at
'Zerrung *f* (*-*; *-en*) MED pulled muscle
zerrütten [tsɛɐ'rʏtən] *v/t* (*no -ge-*, *h*) ruin
zer'rüttet *adj*: ***zerrüttete Ehe*** (***Verhältnisse***) broken marriage (home)
zer'sägen *v/t* (*no -ge-*, *h*) saw up
zerschellen [-'ʃɛlən] *v/i* (*no -ge-*, *sein*) be smashed, AVIAT *a.* crash
zer'schlagen 1. *v/t* (*irr*, ***schlagen***, *no -ge-*, *h*) smash (to pieces); *fig* smash; ***sich zerschlagen*** come to nothing; **2.** *adj*: ***sich zerschlagen fühlen*** be (all) worn out, F be dead beat
zer'schmettern *v/t* (*no -ge-*, *h*) smash (to pieces), shatter (*a. fig*)
zer'schneiden *v/t* (*irr*, ***schneiden***, *no -ge-*, *h*) cut (up)
zer'setzen *v/t* (*no -ge-*, *h*) CHEM decompose (*a.* ***sich zersetzen***); *fig* corrupt, undermine
zer'splittern *v/t* (*no -ge-*, *h*) *and v/i* (*sein*) split (up), splinter; shatter
zer'springen *v/i* (*irr*, ***springen***, *no -ge-*, *sein*) crack; shatter
zer'stampfen *v/t* (*no -ge-*, *h*) pound; GASTR mash
zer'stäuben *v/t* (*no -ge-*, *h*) spray
Zerstäuber [tsɛɐ'ʃtɔʏbɐ] *m* (*-s*; *-*) atomizer, sprayer
zer'stören *v/t* (*no -ge-*, *h*) destroy, ruin (*both a. fig*)
Zer'störer *m* (*-s*; *-*) destroyer (*a.* MAR)
zer'störerisch *adj* destructive
Zer'störung *f* (*-*; *-en*) destruction
zer'streuen *v/t and v/refl* (*no -ge-*, *h*) scatter, disperse; break up (*crowd etc*); *fig* take s.o.'s (*refl* one's) mind off things
zer'streut *fig adj* absent-minded
Zer'streutheit *f* (*-*; *no pl*) absent-mindedness
Zer'streuung *fig f* (*-*; *-en*) diversion, distraction
zer'stückeln *v/t* (*no -ge-*, *h*) cut up *or* (in)to pieces; dismember (*body*)
Zertifikat [tsɛrtifi'kaːt] *n* (*-[e]s*; *-e*) certificate
zer'treten *v/t* (*irr*, ***treten***, *no -ge-*, *h*) crush (*a. fig*)
zer'trümmern *v/t* (*no -ge-*, *h*) smash
zerzaust [tsɛɐ'tsaust] *adj* tousled, dishevel(l)ed
Zettel ['tsɛtəl] *m* (*-s*; *-*) slip (of paper); note; label, sticker
Zeug [tsɔʏk] *n* (*-[e]s*; *-e*) stuff (*a.* F); things; ***er hat das Zeug dazu*** he's got what it takes; ***dummes Zeug*** nonsense
Zeuge ['tsɔʏgə] *m* (*-n*; *-n*) witness

'zeugen[1] *v/i* (*ge-*, *h*) JUR give evidence (**für** for); *fig* **zeugen von** testify to
'zeugen[2] *v/t* (*ge-*, *h*) BIOL procreate; father
'Zeugenaussage *f* JUR testimony, evidence
Zeugenbank *f* (-; *-bänke*) JUR witness stand (*Br* box)
'Zeugin *f* (-; *-nen*) JUR (female) witness
Zeugnis ['tsɔyknɪs] *n* (*-ses*; *-se*) report card, *Br* (school) report; certificate, diploma; reference; *pl* credentials
'Zeugung *f* (-; *-en*) BIOL procreation
z. H(d). ABBR *of* **zu Händen** attn, attention
Zickzack ['tsɪktsak] *m* (-[*e*]*s*; *-e*) (*a.* **im Zickzack fahren**) zigzag
Ziege ['tsi:gə] *f* (-; *-n*) ZO (nanny) goat; F *contp* (**blöde**) **Ziege** (silly old) cow
Ziegel ['tsi:gəl] *m* (*-s*; -) brick; tile
'Ziegeldach *n* tiled roof
Ziegelei [tsi:gə'lai] *f* (-; *-en*) brickyard
'Ziegelstein *m* brick
'Ziegenbock *m* ZO billy goat
Ziegenleder *n* kid (leather)
Ziegenpeter [-pe:tɐ] *m* (*-s*; -) MED mumps
ziehen ['tsi:ən] (*irr*, *-ge-*) **1.** *v/t* (*h*) pull, draw; take off *one's hat* (**vor** *dat* to) (*a. fig*); AGR grow; pull *or* take out (**aus** of); **j-n ziehen an** (*dat*) pull s.o. by; **auf sich ziehen** attract (*attention etc*); **sich ziehen** run; stretch; → **Länge**, **Erwägung**; **2.** *v/i* a) (*h*) pull (**an** *dat* at), b) (*sein*) move; ZO *etc* migrate; go; travel; wander, roam; **es zieht** there's a draft (*Br* draught)
Ziehharmonika ['tsi:harmo:nika] *f* (-; *-s*) MUS accordion
'Ziehung *f* (-; *-en*) draw
Ziel [tsi:l] *n* (-[*e*]*s*; *-e*) aim, target, mark (*all a. fig*), *fig a.* goal, objective; destination; SPORT finish; **sich ein Ziel setzen** set o.s. a goal; **sein Ziel erreichen** reach one's goal; **sich zum Ziel gesetzt haben, et. zu tun** aim to do *or* at doing s.th.
'Zielband *n* (-[*e*]*s*; *-bänder*) SPORT tape
zielen ['tsi:lən] *v/i* (*ge-*, *h*) (take) aim (**auf** *acc* at)
'Ziellinie *f* SPORT finishing line
'ziellos *adj* aimless
'Zielscheibe *f* target, *fig a.* object
zielstrebig ['tsi:lʃtre:bɪç] *adj* purposeful, determined
ziemlich ['tsi:mlɪç] **1.** *adj* quite a; **2.** *adv* rather, fairly, quite, F pretty; **ziemlich viele** quite a few
Zierde ['tsi:ɐdə] *f* (-; *-n*) (**zur** as a) decoration
zieren ['tsi:rən] *v/t* (*ge-*, *h*) decorate; **sich zieren** be coy; make a fuss
zierlich ['tsi:ɐlɪç] *adj* dainty; petite
Zierpflanze ['tsi:ɐ-] *f* ornamental plant
Ziffer ['tsɪfɐ] *f* (-; *-n*) figure
'Zifferblatt *n* dial, face
Zigarette [tsiga'rɛtə] *f* (-; *-n*) cigarette
Ziga'rettenauto,mat *m* cigarette machine
Zigarettenstummel *m* cigarette end, stub, butt
Zigarre [tsi'garə] *f* (-; *-n*) cigar
Zigeuner [tsi'gɔynɐ] *m* (*-s*; -), **Zi'geunerin** [-nərɪn] *f* (-; *-nen*) gypsy, *Br* gipsy
Zimmer ['tsɪmɐ] *n* (*-s*; -) room; apartment
Zimmereinrichtung *f* furniture
Zimmermädchen *n* (chamber)maid
Zimmermann *m* carpenter
'zimmern *v/t* (*ge-*, *h*) build, make
'Zimmerpflanze *f* indoor plant
Zimmerservice *m* room service
Zimmersuche *f*: **auf Zimmersuche sein** be looking (*or* hunting) for a room
Zimmervermittlung *f* accommodation office
zimperlich ['tsɪmpɐlɪç] *adj* prudish; soft, F sissy
Zimt [tsɪmt] *m* (-[*e*]*s*; *-e*) cinnamon
Zink ['tsɪŋk] *n* (-[*e*]*s*; *no pl*) CHEM zinc
Zinke ['tsɪŋkə] *f* (-; *-n*) tooth; prong
Zinn [tsɪn] *n* (-[*e*]*s*; *no pl*) CHEM tin; pewter
Zins [tsɪns] *m* (*-es*; *-en*) ECON interest (*a. pl*); **3% Zinsen bringen** bear interest at 3%
'zinslos *adj* ECON interest-free
'Zinssatz *m* ECON interest rate
Zipfel ['tsɪpfəl] *m* (*-s*; -) corner; point; tail; GASTR end
Zipfelmütze *f* pointed cap
zirka ['tsɪrka] *adv* about, approximately
Zirkel ['tsɪrkəl] *m* (*-s*; -) circle (*a. fig*); MATH compasses, dividers
zirkulieren [tsɪrku'li:rən] *v/i* (*no -ge-*, *h*) circulate
Zirkus ['tsɪrkʊs] *m* (-; *-se*) circus
zirpen ['tsɪrpən] *v/i* (*ge-*, *h*) chirp
zischen ['tsɪʃən] *v/i and v/t* (*ge-*, *h*) hiss; *fat etc*: sizzle; *fig* whiz(z)
ziselieren [tsizə'li:rən] *v/t* (*no -ge-*, *h*) TECH chase
Zitat [tsi'ta:t] *n* (-[*e*]*s*; *-e*) quotation, F quote
zitieren [tsi'ti:rən] *v/t* (*no -ge-*, *h*) quote, cite (*a.* JUR), JUR summon
Zitrone [tsi'tro:nə] *f* (-; *-n*) BOT lemon
Zi'tronenlimo,nade *f* lemon soda *or* pop, *Br* (fizzy) lemonade
Zitronensaft *m* lemon juice
Zitronenschale *f* lemon peel
zitterig ['tsɪtərɪç] *adj* shaky
zittern ['tsɪtɐn] *v/i* (*ge-*, *h*) tremble, shake (*both*: **vor** *dat* with)
zivil [tsi'vi:l] *adj* civil, civilian

Zi'vil *n* (*-s; no pl*) civilian clothes; ***Polizist in Zivil*** plainclothes policeman
Zi'vildienst *m* MIL alternative service (*in lieu of military service*)
Zivilisation [tsiviliza'tsjo:n] *f* (*-; -en*) civilization
zivilisieren [tsivili'zi:rən] *v/t* (*no -ge-, h*) civilize
Zivilist [tsivi'lɪst] *m* (*-en; -en*) civilian
Zi'vilrecht *n* (*-[e]s; no pl*) JUR civil law
Zi'vilschutz *m* civil defen|se, *Br* -ce
Znüni ['tsny:ni] *Swiss m, n* (*-s; -*) mid-morning snack, tea (*or* coffee) break
zog [tso:k] *pret of* ***ziehen***
zögern ['tsø:gɐn] *v/i* (*ge-, h*) hesitate
'Zögern *n* (*-s; no pl*) hesitation
Zoll[1] [tsɔl] *m* (*-[e]s; -*) inch
Zoll[2] *m* (*-[e]s; Zölle* ['tsœlə]) a) (*no pl*) customs, b) duty
'Zollabfertigung *f* customs clearance
'Zollbeamte *m* customs officer
'Zollerklärung *f* customs declaration
'zollfrei *adj* duty-free
'Zollkon,trolle *f* customs examination
'zollpflichtig *adj* liable to duty
'Zollstock *m* (folding) rule
Zone ['tso:nə] *f* (*-; -n*) zone
Zoo [tso:] *m* (*-s; -s*) zoo
'Zoohandlung *f* pet shop
Zoologe [tsoo'lo:gə] *m* (*-n; -n*) zoologist
Zoologie [tsoolo'gi:] *f* (*-; no pl*) zoology
Zoo'login *f* (*-; -nen*) zoologist
zoo'logisch *adj* zoological
Zopf [tsɔpf] *m* (*-[e]s; Zöpfe* ['tsœpfə]) plait; pigtail
Zorn [tsɔrn] *m* (*-[e]s; no pl*) anger
zornig ['tsɔrnɪç] *adj* angry
Zote ['tso:tə] *f* (*-; -n*) filthy joke, obscenity
zottelig ['tsɔtəlɪç] *adj* shaggy
z. T. ABBR *of* ***zum Teil*** partly
zu [tsu:] **1.** *prp* (*dat*) to, toward(s); at; *purpose*: for; ***zu Fuß*** (***Pferd***) on foot (horseback); ***zu Hause*** (***Ostern*** *etc*) at home (Easter *etc*); ***zu Weihnachten*** *give etc* for Christmas; ***Tür*** (***Schlüssel***) ***zu …*** door (key) to …; ***zu m-r Überraschung*** to my surprise; ***wir sind zu dritt*** there are three of us; ***zu zweien*** two by two; ***zu e-r Mark*** at *or* for one mark; SPORT ***1 zu 1*** one all; ***2 zu 1 gewinnen*** win two one, win by two goals *etc* to one; → ***zum***, ***zur***; **2.** *adv* too; F closed, shut; ***ein zu großes Risiko*** too much of a risk; ***zu viel*** too much, too many; ***zu wenig*** too little, too few; **3.** *cj* to; ***es ist zu erwarten*** it is to be expected
Zubehör ['tsu:bəhø:ɐ] *n* (*-[e]s; -e*) accessories
'zubereiten *v/t* (*sep, no -ge-, h*) prepare
'Zubereitung *f* (*-; -en*) preparation
'zubinden *v/t* (*irr*, ***binden***, *sep, -ge-, h*) tie (up)
zubleiben *v/i* (*irr*, ***bleiben***, *sep, -ge-, sein*) stay shut
zublinzeln *v/i* (*sep, -ge-, h*) (*dat*) wink at
'Zubringer *m* (*-s; -*), **Zubringerstraße** *f* MOT feeder (road), access road
Zucht [tsʊxt] *f* (*-; -en*) breed; ZO breeding; BOT cultivation
züchten ['tsʏçtən] *v/t* (*ge-, h*) ZO breed; BOT grow, cultivate
Züchter(in) ['tsʏçtɐ (-tərɪn)] *m* (*-s; -/-; -nen*) ZO breeder; BOT grower
'Zuchtperle *f* culture(d) pearl
zucken ['tsʊkən] *v/i* (*ge-, h*) jerk; twitch (***mit et.*** s.th.); wince; *lightning*: flash
zücken ['tsʏkən] *v/t* (*ge-, h*) draw (*weapon*); F pull out (*one's wallet etc*)
Zucker ['tsʊkɐ] *m* (*-s; -*) sugar
Zuckerdose *f* sugar bowl
Zuckerguss *m* icing, frosting
'zuckerkrank *adj*, **'Zuckerkranke** *m, f* (*-n; -n*) MED diabetic
'Zuckerkrankheit *f* MED diabetes
'Zuckermais *m* sweet corn
'zuckern *v/t* (*ge-, h*) sugar
'Zuckerrohr *n* BOT sugarcane
'Zuckerrübe *f* BOT sugar beet
'Zuckerwatte *f* candy floss
'Zuckerzange *f* sugar tongs
'Zuckung *f* (*-; -en*) twitch(ing); tic; convulsion, spasm
'zudecken *v/t* (*sep, -ge-, h*) cover (up)
zudem [tsu'de:m] *adv* besides, moreover
'zudrehen *v/t* (*sep, -ge-, h*) turn off; ***j-m den Rücken zudrehen*** turn one's back on s.o.
'zudringlich *adj*: ***zudringlich werden*** F get fresh (***j-m gegenüber*** with s.o.)
'zudrücken *v/t* (*sep, -ge-, h*) close, push *s.th.* shut; → ***Auge***
zuerst [tsu'ʔe:ɐst] *adv* first; at first; first (of all), to begin with
'Zufahrt *f* approach; drive(way)
'Zufahrtsstraße *f* access road
'Zufall *m* chance; ***durch Zufall*** by chance, by accident
'zufallen *v/i* (*irr*, ***fallen***, *sep, -ge-, sein*) *door etc*: slam (shut); *fig* fall to *s.o.*; ***mir fallen die Augen zu*** I can't keep my eyes open
'zufällig **1.** *adj* accidental, chance …; **2.** *adv* by accident, by chance; ***zufällig tun*** happen to do
'Zuflucht *f*: ***Zuflucht suchen*** (***finden***) look for (find) refuge *or* shelter (***vor*** *dat* from; ***bei*** with); (***s-e***) ***Zuflucht nehmen zu*** resort to
zufrieden [tsu'fri:dən] *adj* content(ed),

satisfied; ***zufrieden stellen*** satisfy; ***zufrieden stellend*** satisfactory
Zu'friedenheit *f* (-; *no pl*) contentment, satisfaction
zu'friedengeben *v/refl* (*irr*, ***geben***, *sep*, *-ge-*, *h*): ***sich zufriedengeben mit*** content o.s. with
zufriedenlassen *v/t* (*irr*, ***lassen***, *sep*, *-ge-*, *h*) leave s.o. alone
zufriedenstellen *v/t* (*sep*,*-ge-*, *h*) satisfy
zufriedenstellend *adj* satisfactory
'zufrieren *v/i* (*irr*, ***frieren***, *sep*, *-ge-*, *sein*) freeze up *or* over
'zufügen *v/t* (*sep*, *-ge-*, *h*) do, cause; ***j-m Schaden zufügen*** *a.* harm s.o.
Zufuhr ['tsu:fu:ɐ] *f* (-; *-en*) supply
Zug [tsu:k] *m* (-[*e*]*s*; *Züge* ['tsy:gə]) RAIL train; procession, line; parade; *fig* feature; trait; tendency; *chess etc*: move (*a. fig*); *swimming*: stroke; pull (*a.* TECH), PHYS *a.* tension; *smoking*: puff; draft, *Br* draught; PED stream; ***im Zuge*** *gen* in the course of; ***in e-m Zug*** at one go; ***Zug um Zug*** step by step; ***in groben Zügen*** in broad outlines
'Zugabe *f* addition; THEA encore
'Zugang *m* access (*a. fig*)
'zugänglich [-gɛŋlıç] *adj* accessible (***für*** to) (*a. fig*)
'Zugbrücke *f* drawbridge
'zugeben *v/t* (*irr*, ***geben***, *sep*, *-ge-*, *h*) add; *fig* admit
'zugehen *v/i* (*irr*, ***gehen***, *sep*, *-ge-*, *sein*) F *door etc*: close, shut; ***zugehen auf*** (*acc*) walk up to, approach (*a. fig*); ***es geht auf 8 Uhr zu*** it's getting on for 8; ***es ging lustig zu*** we had a lot of fun
'Zugehörigkeit *f* (-; *no pl*) membership
Zügel ['tsy:gəl] *m* (*-s*; -) rein (*a. fig*)
'zügeln **1.** *v/t* (*ge-*, *h*) curb, control, bridle; **2.** *Swiss v/i* (*ge-*, *sein*) move
'Zugeständnis *n* concession
'zugestehen *v/t* (*irr*, ***stehen***, *sep*, *no -ge-*, *h*) concede, grant
'zugetan *adj* attached (*dat* to)
'Zugführer *m* RAIL conductor, *Br* guard
zugig ['tsu:gıç] *adj* drafty, *Br* draughty
'Zugkraft *f* a) TECH traction, b) (*no pl*) attraction, draw, appeal
'zugkräftig *adj*: ***zugkräftig sein*** be a draw
zu'gleich [tsu-] *adv* at the same time
'Zugluft *f* (-; *no pl*) draft, *Br* draught
'Zugma,schine *f* MOT tractor
'zugreifen *v/i* (*irr*, ***greifen***, *sep*, *-ge-*, *h*) grab (at) it; *fig* grab the opportunity; ***greifen Sie zu!*** help yourself!; ***mit zugreifen*** lend a hand
'Zugriffscode *m* EDP access code
'Zugriffszeit *f* EDP access time
zugrunde [tsu'grʊndə] *adv*: ***zugrunde gehen*** (***an*** *dat*) perish (of); ***e-r Sache et. zugrunde legen*** base s.th. on s.th.; ***zugrunde richten*** ruin
zugunsten [tsu'gʊnstən] *prp* (*gen*) in favo(u)r of
zu'gute [tsu-] *adv*: ***zugute halten*** → ***zugutehalten***; ***zugute kommen*** → ***zugutekommen***; **zugutehalten** *v/t* (*irr*, ***halten***, *sep*, *-ge-*, *h*): ***j-m et. zugute*** give s.o. credit for s.th.; make allwances for s.o.'s …
zugutekommen *v/t* (*irr*, ***kommen***, *sep*, *-ge-*, *sein*): ***j-m zugutekommen*** be for the benefit of s.o. **'Zugvogel** *m* zo bird of passage
'zuhalten *v/t* (*irr*, ***halten***, *sep*, *-ge-*, *h*) keep shut; ***sich die Ohren*** (***Augen***) ***zuhalten*** cover one's ears (eyes) with one's hands; ***sich die Nase zuhalten*** hold one's nose
Zuhälter ['tsu:hɛltɐ] *m* (*-s*; -) pimp
Zuhause [tsu'hauzə] *n* (*-s*; *no pl*) home
zu'hause *adv* → ***Haus***
'zuhören *v/i* (*sep*, *-ge-*, *h*) listen (*dat* to)
'Zuhörer *m*, **'Zuhörerin** *f* listener, *pl a. the* audience
'zujubeln *v/i* (*sep*, *-ge-*, *h*) cheer
'zukleben *v/t* (*sep*, *-ge-*, *h*) seal
'zuknöpfen *v/t* (*sep*, *-ge-*, *h*) button (up)
'zukommen *v/i* (*irr*, ***kommen***, *sep*, *-ge-*, *sein*) ***zukommen auf*** (*acc*) come up to; *fig* be ahead of; ***die Dinge auf sich zukommen lassen*** wait and see
Zukunft ['tsu:kʊnft] *f* (-; *no pl*) future (*a.* LING)
'zukünftig **1.** *adj* future; **2.** *adv* in future
'zulächeln *v/i* (*sep*, *-ge-*, *h*) smile at
'Zulage *f* bonus
'zulangen F *v/i* (*sep*, *-ge-*, *h*) tuck in
'zulassen *v/t* (*irr*, ***lassen***, *sep*, *-ge-*, *h*) F keep *s.th.* closed; *fig* allow; MOT *etc* license, register; ***j-n zu et. zulassen*** admit s.o. to s.th.
'zulässig *adj* admissible (*a.* JUR); ***zulässig sein*** be allowed
'Zulassung *f* (-; *-en*) admission; MOT *etc* license, *Br* licence
'zulegen *v/t* (*sep*, *-ge-*, *h*) add; F ***sich … zulegen*** get o.s. *s.th.*; adopt (*name*)
zu'letzt [tsu-] *adv* in the end; *come etc* last; finally; ***wann hast du ihn zuletzt gesehen?*** when did you last see him?
zu'liebe [tsu-] *adv*: ***j-m zuliebe*** for s.o.'s sake
zum [tsʊm] *prp* ***zu dem*** → ***zu***; ***zum ersten Mal*** for the first time; *et.* ***zum Kaffee*** *s.th.* with one's coffee; ***zum Schwimmen*** *etc* ***gehen*** go swimming *etc*
'zumachen F (*sep*, *-ge-*, *h*) **1.** *v/t* close,

shut; button (up); **2.** *v/i* close (down)

'**zumauern** *v/t* (*sep*, *-ge-*, *h*) brick *or* wall up

zumutbar ['tsu:mu:tba:ɐ] *adj* reasonable

zu'mute [tsu-] *adv*: ***mir ist ... zumute*** I feel ...

'**zumuten** *v/t* (*sep*, *-ge-*, *h*) ***j-m et. zumuten*** expect s.th. of s.o.; ***sich zu viel zumuten*** overtax o.s.

'**Zumutung** *f*: ***das ist e-e Zumutung*** that's asking *or* expecting a bit much

zu'nächst [tsu-] *adv* → ***zuerst***

'**zunageln** *v/t* (*sep*, *-ge-*, *h*) nail up

'**zunähen** *v/t* (*sep*, *-ge-*, *h*) sew up

Zunahme ['tsu:na:mə] *f* (*-*; *-n*) increase

'**Zuname** *m* surname

zünden ['tsʏndən] *v/i* (*ge-*, *h*) kindle; ELECTR, MOT ignite, fire

zündend *fig adj* stirring

Zünder ['tsʏndɐ] *m* (*-s*; *-*) MIL fuse; *pl Austrian* matches

Zündholz ['tsʏnt-] *n* match

Zündkerze *f* MOT spark plug

Zündschlüssel *m* MOT ignition key

Zündschnur *f* fuse

'**Zündung** *f* (*-*; *-en*) MOT ignition

'**zunehmen** *v/i* (*irr*, ***nehmen***, *sep*, *-ge-*, *h*) increase (***an*** *dat* in); put on weight; *moon*: wax; *days*: grow longer

'**Zuneigung** *f* (*-*; *-en*) affection

Zunft [tsʊnft] HIST *f* (*-*; *Zünfte* ['tsʏnftə]) guild

Zunge [tsʊŋə] *f* (*-*; *-n*) ANAT tongue; ***es liegt mir auf der Zunge*** it's on the tip of my tongue

züngeln ['tsʏŋəln] *v/i* (*ge-*, *h*) *flames*: lick, flicker

'**Zungenspitze** *f* tip of the tongue

'**zunicken** *v/i* (*sep*, *-ge-*, *h*) (*dat*) nod at

zunutze [tsu'nʊtsə] *adv*: ***sich et. zunutze machen*** make (good) use of s.th.; take advantage of s.th.

zupfen [tsʊpfən] *v/t and v/i* (*ge-*, *h*) pull (***an*** *dat* at), pick, pluck (at) (*a.* MUS)

zur [tsu:ɐ] *prp* ***zu der*** → ***zu***; ***zur Schule*** (***Kirche***) ***gegen*** go to school (church); ***zur Hälfte*** half (of it *or* them); ***zur Belohnung*** *etc* as a reward *etc*

'**zurechnungsfähig** *adj* JUR responsible

'**Zurechnungsfähigkeit** *f* (*-*; *no pl*) JUR responsibility

zu'rechtfinden *v/refl* (*irr*, ***finden***, *sep*, *-ge-*, *h*) find one's way; *fig* cope, manage

zurechtkommen *v/i* (*irr*, ***kommen***, *sep*, *-ge-*, *sein*) get along (***mit*** with); cope (with)

zurechtlegen *v/t* (*sep*, *-ge-*, *h*) arrange; *fig* ***sich et. zurechtlegen*** think s.th. out

zurechtmachen F *v/t* (*sep*, *-ge-*, *h*) get ready, prepare, fix; ***sich zurechtmachen*** do o.s. up

zurechtrücken *v/t* (*sep*, *-ge-*, *h*) put *s.th.* straight (*a. fig*)

zu'rechtweisen *v/t* (*irr*, ***weisen***, *sep*, *-ge-*, *h*), **Zu'rechtweisung** *f* reprimand

'**zureden** *v/i* (*sep*, *-ge-*, *h*) ***j-m zureden*** encourage s.o.

zureiten *v/t* (*irr*, ***reiten***, *sep*, *-ge-*, *h*) break in

zurichten F *fig v/t* (*sep*, *-ge-*, *h*) ***übel zurichten*** batter, *a.* beat *s.o.* up badly, *a.* make a mess of *s.th.*, ruin

zurück [tsu'rʏk] *adv* back; behind (*a. fig*)

zurückbehalten *v/t* (*irr*, ***halten***, *sep*, *no -ge-*, *h*) keep back, retain

zurückbekommen *v/t* (*irr*, ***kommen***, *sep*, *no -ge-*, *h*) get back

zurückbleiben *v/i* (*irr*, ***bleiben***, *sep*, *-ge-*, *sein*) stay behind, be left behind; fall behind (*a.* PED *etc*)

zurückblicken *v/i* (*sep*, *-ge-*, *h*) look back (***auf*** *acc* at, *fig* on)

zurückbringen *v/t* (*irr*, ***bringen***, *sep*, *-ge-*, *h*) bring *or* take back, return

zurückda,tieren *v/t* (*sep*, *no -ge-*, *h*) backdate (***auf*** *acc* to)

zurückfallen *fig v/i* (*irr*, ***fallen***, *sep*, *-ge-*, *sein*) fall behind, SPORT *a.* drop back

zurückfinden *v/i* (*irr*, ***finden***, *sep*, *-ge-*, *h*) find one's way back (***nach, zu*** to); *fig* return (to)

zurückfordern *v/t* (*sep*, *-ge-*, *h*) reclaim

zurückführen *v/t* (*sep*, *-ge-*, *h*) lead back; ***zurückführen auf*** (*acc*) attribute to

zurückgeben *v/t* (*irr*, ***geben***, *sep*, *-ge-*, *h*) give back, return

zurückgeblieben *fig adj* backward; retarded

zurückgehen *v/i* (*irr*, ***gehen***, *sep*, *-ge-*, *sein*) go back, return; *fig* decrease; go down, drop

zurückgezogen *fig adj* secluded

zurückgreifen *v/i* (*irr*, ***greifen***, *sep*, *-ge-*, *h*) ***zurückgreifen auf*** (*acc*) fall back (up)on

zu'rückhalten (*irr*, ***halten***, *sep*, *-ge-*, *h*) **1.** *v/t* hold back; **2.** *v/refl* control o.s.; be careful

zurückhaltend *adj* reserved

Zu'rückhaltung *f* (*-*; *no pl*) reserve

zu'rückkehren *v/i* (*sep*, *-ge-*, *sein*) return

zurückkommen *v/i* (*irr*, ***kommen***, *sep*, *-ge-*, *sein*) come back, return (*both fig* ***auf*** *acc* to)

zurücklassen *v/t* (*irr*, ***lassen***, *sep*, *-ge-*, *h*) leave (behind)

zurücklegen *v/t* (*sep*, *-ge-*, *h*) put back; put aside, save (*money*); cover, do (*miles*)

zurücknehmen *v/t* (*irr*, ***nehmen***, *sep*, *-ge-*, *h*) take back (*a. fig*)
zurückrufen (*irr*, ***rufen***, *sep*, *-ge-*, *h*) **1.** *v/t* call back (*a.* TEL); ECON recall; ***ins Gedächtnis zurückrufen*** recall; **2.** *v/i* TEL call back
zurückschlagen (*irr*, ***schlagen***, *sep*, *-ge-*, *h*) **1.** *v/t* beat off; *tennis*: return; fold back; **2.** *v/i* hit back; MIL retaliate (*a. fig*)
zurückschrecken *v/i* (*sep*, *-ge-*, *sein*) ***zurückschrecken vor*** (*dat*) shrink from; ***vor nichts zurückschrecken*** stop at nothing
zurücksetzen *v/t* (*sep*, *-ge-*, *h*) MOT back (up); *fig* neglect *s.o.*
zurückstehen *v/i* (*irr*, ***stehen***, *sep*, *-ge-*, *h*) stand aside
zurückstellen *v/t* (*sep*, *-ge-*, *h*) put back (*a. watch*); put aside; MIL defer
zurückstrahlen *v/t* (*sep*, *-ge-*, *h*) reflect
zurücktreten *v/i* (*irr*, ***treten***, *sep*, *-ge-*, *sein*) step *or* stand back; resign (***von e-m Amt*** [***Posten***] one's office [post]); ECON, JUR withdraw (***von*** from)
zurückweichen *v/i* (*irr*, ***weichen***, *sep*, *-ge-*, *sein*) fall back (*a.* MIL)
zurückweisen *v/t* (*irr*, ***weisen***, *sep*, *-ge-*, *h*) turn down; JUR dismiss
zurückzahlen *v/t* (*sep*, *-ge-*, *h*) pay back (*a. fig*)
zurückziehen *v/t* (*irr*, ***ziehen***, *sep*, *-ge-*, *h*) draw back; *fig* withdraw; ***sich zurückziehen*** retire, withdraw, MIL *a.* retreat
'Zuruf *m* shout
'zurufen *v/t* (*irr*, ***rufen***, *sep*, *-ge-*, *h*) ***j-m et. zurufen*** shout s.th. to s.o.
zur'zeit *adv* at the moment, at present
'Zusage *f* promise; assent
'zusagen *v/i and v/t* (*sep*, *-ge-*, *h*) accept (an invitation); (*dat*) suit, appeal to; ***s-e Hilfe zusagen*** promise to help
zusammen [tsu'zamən] *adv* together; ***alles zusammen*** (all) in all; ***das macht zusammen …*** that makes … altogether
Zu'sammenarbeit *f* (-; *no pl*) cooperation; ***in Zusammenarbeit mit*** in collaboration with
zu'sammenarbeiten *v/i* (*sep*, *-ge-*, *h*) cooperate, collaborate
zu'sammenbeißen *v/t* (*irr*, ***beißen***, *sep*, *-ge-*, *h*) ***die Zähne zusammenbeißen*** clench one's teeth
zu'sammenbrechen *v/i* (*irr*, ***brechen***, *sep*, *-ge-*, *sein*) break down, collapse (*both a. fig*)
Zu'sammenbruch *m* breakdown, collapse
zu'sammenfallen *v/i* (*irr*, ***fallen***, *sep*, *-ge-*, *sein*) coincide
zusammenfalten *v/t* (*sep*, *-ge-*, *h*) fold up
zu'sammenfassen *v/t* (*sep*, *-ge-*, *h*) summarize, sum up
Zu'sammenfassung *f* (-; *-en*) summary
zu'sammenfügen *v/t* (*sep*, *-ge-*, *h*) join (together)
zusammengesetzt *adj* compound
zusammenhalten *v/i and v/t* (*irr*, ***halten***, *sep*, *-ge-*, *h*) hold together (*a. fig*); F stick together
Zu'sammenhang *m* (-[*e*]*s*; *-hänge*) connection; context; ***im Zusammenhang stehen*** (***mit***) be connected (with)
zu'sammenhängen *v/i* (*irr*, ***hängen***, *sep*, *-ge-*, *h*) be connected
zusammenhängend *adj* coherent
zu'sammenhang(s)los *adj* incoherent, disconnected
zu'sammenklappen *v/i* (*sep*, *-ge-*, *sein*) *and v/t* (*h*) TECH fold up; F break down
zusammenkommen *v/i* (*irr*, ***kommen***, *sep*, *-ge-*, *sein*) meet
Zu'sammenkunft [-kʊnft] *f* (-; *-künfte* [-kʏnftə]) meeting
zu'sammenlegen (*sep*, *-ge-*, *h*) **1.** *v/t* combine; fold up; **2.** *v/i* club together
zusammennehmen *v/t* (*irr*, ***nehmen***, *sep*, *-ge-*, *h*) muster (up); ***sich zusammennehmen*** pull o.s. together
zusammenpacken *v/t* (*sep*, *-ge-*, *h*) pack up
zusammenpassen *v/i* (*sep*, *-ge-*, *h*) harmonize; match
zusammenrechnen *v/t* (*sep*, *-ge-*, *h*) add up
zusammenreißen F *v/refl* (*irr*, ***reißen***, *sep*, *-ge-*, *h*) pull o.s. together
zusammenrollen *v/t* (*sep*, *-ge-*, *h*) roll up; ***sich zusammenrollen*** coil up
zusammenrotten [-rɔtən] *v/refl* (*sep*, *-ge-*, *h*) band together
zusammenrücken (*sep*, *-ge-*) **1.** *v/t* (*h*) move closer together; **2.** *v/i* (*sein*) move up
zusammenschlagen *v/t* (*irr*, ***schlagen***, *sep*, *-ge-*, *h*) clap (*hands*); click (*one's heels*); beat *s.o.* up; smash (up)
zu'sammenschließen *v/refl* (*irr*, ***schließen***, *sep*, *-ge-*, *h*) join, unite
Zu'sammenschluss *m* union
zu'sammenschreiben *v/t* (*irr*, ***schreiben***, *sep*, *-ge-*, *h*) write in one word
zusammenschrumpfen *v/i* (*sep*, *-ge-*, *sein*) shrink
zu'sammensetzen *v/t* (*sep*, *-ge-*, *h*) put together; TECH assemble; ***sich zusammensetzen aus*** (*dat*) consist of, be composed of
Zu'sammensetzung *f* (-; *-en*) composi-

tion; CHEM, LING compound; TECH assembly
zu'sammenstellen *v/t (sep, -ge-, h)* put together; arrange
Zu'sammenstoß *m* collision *(a. fig)*, crash; impact; *fig* clash
zu'sammenstoßen *v/i (irr,* ***stoßen****, sep, -ge-, sein)* collide *(a. fig)*; *fig* clash; ***zusammenstoßen mit*** run *or* bump into; *fig* have a clash with
zu'sammentreffen *v/i (irr,* ***treffen****, sep, -ge-, sein)* meet, encounter; coincide (***mit*** with)
Zu'sammentreffen *n (-s; -)* meeting; coincidence; encounter
zu'sammentreten *v/i (irr,* ***treten****, sep, -ge-, sein)* meet
zusammentun *v/refl (irr,* ***tun****, sep, -ge-, h)* join (forces), F team up
zusammenwirken *v/i (sep, -ge-, h)* combine
zusammenzählen *v/t (sep, -ge-, h)* add up
zusammenziehen *(irr,* ***ziehen****, sep, -ge-)* **1.** *v/t and v/refl (h)* contract; **2.** *v/i (sein)* move in (***mit*** with)
zusammenzucken *v/i (sep, -ge-, sein)* wince, flinch
'Zusatz *m* addition; *chemical etc* additive; ***Zusatz…*** *in cpds mst* additional …, supplementary …; auxiliary …
zusätzlich ['tsu:zɛtslɪç] *adj* additional, extra
'zuschauen *v/i (sep, -ge-, h)* look on (***bei et.*** at s.th.); ***j-m zuschauen*** watch s.o. (***bei et.*** doing s.th.)
Zuschauer ['tsu:ʃauɐ] *m (-s; -)*, **'Zuschauerin** *f (-; -nen)* spectator; TV viewer, *pl a. the* audience
'Zuschauerraum *m* auditorium
'Zuschlag *m* extra charge; RAIL *etc* excess fare; bonus; *auction*: knocking down
'zuschlagen *v/i (irr,* ***schlagen****, sep, -ge-, sein) and v/t (h) door etc*: slam *or* bang shut; *boxing etc*: hit, strike (a blow); *fig* act; ***j-m et. zuschlagen*** *auction*: knock s.th. down to s.o.
'zuschließen *v/t (irr,* ***schließen****, sep, -ge-, h)* lock (up)
zuschnallen *v/t (sep, -ge-, h)* buckle (up)
zuschnappen *v/i (sep, -ge-)* a) *(h) dog*: snap, b) *(sein) door etc*: snap shut
zuschneiden *v/t (irr,* ***schneiden****, sep, -ge-, h)* cut out; cut (to size)
zuschnüren *v/t (sep, -ge-, h)* tie *(or* lace) up
zuschrauben *v/t (sep, -ge-, h)* screw shut
zuschreiben *v/t (irr,* ***schreiben****, sep, -ge-, h)* ascribe *or* attribute *(dat* to)
'Zuschrift *f* letter
zuschulden [tsu'ʃʊldən] *adv*: ***sich et. (nichts) zuschulden kommen lassen*** do s.th. (nothing) wrong
'Zuschuss *m* allowance; subsidy
'zuschütten *v/t (sep, -ge-, h)* fill up
'zusehen → ***zuschauen***
zusehends ['tsu:se:ənts] *adv* noticeably; rapidly
'zusetzen *(sep, -ge-, h)* **1.** *v/t* add; lose *(money)*; **2.** *v/i* lose money; ***j-m zusetzen*** press s.o. (hard)
'zuspielen *v/t (sep, -ge-, h)* SPORT pass
'zuspitzen *v/t (sep, -ge-, h)* point; ***sich zuspitzen*** become critical
'Zuspruch *m (-[e]s; no pl)* encouragement; words of comfort
'Zustand *m* condition, state, F shape
zustande [tsu'ʃtandə] *adv*: ***zustande bringen*** bring about, manage (to do); ***zustande kommen*** come about; ***es kam nicht zustande*** it didn't come off
'zuständig *adj* responsible (***für*** for), in charge (of)
'zustehen *v/i (irr,* ***stehen****, sep, -ge-, h)* ***j-m steht et. (zu tun) zu*** s.o. is entitled to (do) s.th.
'zustellen *v/t (sep, -ge-, h) post*: deliver
'Zustellung *f post*: delivery
'zustimmen *v/i (sep, -ge-, h)* agree *(dat* to *s.th.*; with *s.o.)*
'Zustimmung *f* approval, consent; ***(j-s) Zustimmung finden*** meet with (s.o.'s) approval
'zustoßen *v/i (irr,* ***stoßen****, sep, -ge-, sein)* ***j-m zustoßen*** happen to s.o.
zutage [tsu'ta:gə] *adv*: ***zutage bringen (kommen)*** bring (come) to light
'Zutaten *pl* ingredients
'zuteilen *v/t (sep, -ge-, h)* assign, allot
'Zuteilung *f (-; -en)* allotment; ration
'zutragen *v/refl (irr,* ***tragen****, sep, -ge-, h)* happen
'zutrauen *v/t (sep, -ge-, h)* ***j-m et. zutrauen*** credit s.o. with s.th.; ***sich zu viel zutrauen*** overrate o.s.
zutraulich ['tsu:traulɪç] *adj* trusting; zo friendly
'zutreffen *v/i (irr,* ***treffen****, sep, -ge-, h)* be true; ***zutreffen auf*** *(acc)* apply to, go for
zutreffend *adj* true, correct
'zutrinken *v/i (irr,* ***trinken****, sep, -ge-, h)* ***j-m zutrinken*** drink to s.o.
'Zutritt *m (-[e]s; no pl)* admission; access; ***Zutritt verboten!*** no admittance!
zu'ungunsten *adv* to *s.o.'s* disadvantage
zuverlässig ['tsu:fɛɐlɛsɪç] *adj* reliable, dependable; safe
'Zuverlässigkeit *f (-; no pl)* reliability, dependability

Zuversicht ['tsu:fɛɐzɪçt] *f* (-; *no pl*) confidence
'**zuversichtlich** *adj* confident, optimistic
zuviel → ***zu***
zu'vor [tsu-] *adv* before, previously; first
zu'vorkommen *v/i* (*irr*, ***kommen***, *sep*, *-ge-*, *sein*) anticipate; prevent; ***j-m zuvorkommen*** *a.* F beat s.o. to it
zuvorkommend *adj* obliging; polite
Zuwachs ['tsu:vaks] *m* (*-es*; *no pl*) increase, growth
'**zuwachsen** *v/i* (*irr*, ***wachsen***, *sep*, *-ge-*, *sein*) become overgrown; MED close
zu'weilen [tsu-] *adv* occasionally, now and then
'**zuweisen** *v/t* (*irr*, ***weisen***, *sep*, *-ge-*, *h*) assign
'**zuwenden** *v/t and v/refl* ([*irr*, ***wenden***,] *sep*, *-ge-*, *h*) turn to (*a. fig*)
'**Zuwendung** *f* (-; *-en*) a) payment, b) (*no pl*) attention; (loving) care, love, affection
zuwenig → ***zu***
'**zuwerfen** *v/t* (*irr*, ***werfen***, *sep*, *-ge-*, *h*) slam (shut); ***j-m et. zuwerfen*** throw s.o. s.th.; ***j-m e-n Blick zuwerfen*** cast a glance at s.o.
zu'wider [tsu-] *adj*: ***... ist mir zuwider*** I hate *or* detest ...
zuwiderhandeln *v/i* (*sep*, *-ge-*, *h*) (*dat*) act contrary to; violate
'**zuwinken** *v/i* (*sep*, *-ge-*, *h*) wave to; signal to
zuzahlen *v/t* (*sep*, *-ge-*, *h*) pay extra
zuziehen (*irr*, ***ziehen***, *sep*, *-ge-*) **1.** *v/t* (*h*) draw (*curtains etc*); pull tight; *fig* consult; ***sich zuziehen*** MED catch; **2.** *v/i* (*sein*) move in
zuzüglich ['tsu:tsy:klɪç] *prp* (*gen*) plus
Zvieri ['tsfi:ri] *Swiss m, n* (*-s*; *-s*) afternoon snack, tea *or* coffee break
zwang [tsvaŋ] *pret of* ***zwingen***
Zwang *m* (*-[e]s*; *Zwänge* ['tsvɛŋə]) compulsion, constraint; restraint; coercion; force; ***Zwang sein*** be compulsory
zwängen ['tsvɛŋən] *v/t* (*ge-*, *h*) press, squeeze, force
'**zwanglos** *adj* informal; casual
'**Zwanglosigkeit** *f* (-; *no pl*) informality
'**Zwangsarbeit** *f* JUR hard labo(u)r
Zwangsherrschaft *f* (-; *no pl*) despotism, tyranny
Zwangslage *f* predicament
'**zwangsläufig** *adv* inevitably
'**Zwangsmaßnahme** *f* sanction
Zwangsvollstreckung *f* JUR compulsory execution
Zwangsvorstellung *f* PSYCH obsession
'**zwangsweise** *adv* by force
zwanzig ['tsvantsɪç] *adj* twenty
'**zwanzigste** *adj* twentieth
zwar [tsva:ɐ] *adv*: ***ich kenne ihn zwar, aber ...*** I do know him, but ..., I know him all right, but ...; ***und zwar*** that is (to say), namely
Zweck [tsvɛk] *m* (*-[e]s*; *-e*) purpose, aim; ***s-n Zweck erfüllen*** serve its purpose; ***es hat keinen Zweck*** (***zu warten*** *etc*) it's no use (waiting *etc*)
'**zwecklos** *adj* useless
'**zweckmäßig** *adj* practical; wise; TECH, ARCH functional
'**Zweckmäßigkeit** *f* (-; *no pl*) practicality, functionality
zwecks *prp* (*gen*) for the purpose of
zwei [tsvai] *adj* two
'**zweibeinig** [-bainɪç] *adj* two-legged
'**Zweibettzimmer** *n* twin-bedded room
'**zweideutig** [-dɔytɪç] *adj* ambiguous; off-colo(u)r
Zweier ['tsvaiɐ] *m* (*-s*; -) *rowing*: pair
zweierlei ['tsvaiɐ'lai] *adj* two kinds of
'**zweifach** *adj* double, twofold
Zweifa'milienhaus *n* duplex, *Br* two-family house
Zweifel ['tsvaifəl] *m* (*-s*; -) doubt
'**zweifelhaft** *adj* doubtful, dubious
'**zweifellos** *adv* undoubtedly, no *or* without doubt
'**zweifeln** *v/i* (*ge-*, *h*) ***zweifeln an*** (*dat*) doubt *s.th.*, have one's doubts about
Zweig [tsvaik] *m* (*-[e]s*; *-e*) BOT branch (*a. fig*); twig
Zweiggeschäft *n*, **Zweigniederlassung** *f*, **Zweigstelle** *f* branch
'**zweijährig** [-jɛ:rɪç] *adj* two-year-old, of two (years)
'**Zweikampf** *m* duel
'**zweimal** *adv* twice
'**zweimalig** *adj* (twice) repeated
'**zweimotorig** [-moto:rɪç] *adj* twin-engined
zweireihig [-raiɪç] *adj* double-breasted (*suit*)
zweischneidig *adj* double-edged, two-edged (*both a. fig*)
zweiseitig [-zaitɪç] *adj* two-sided; reversible; POL bilateral; EDP double-sided
'**Zweisitzer** [-zɪtsɐ] *m* (*-s*; -) *esp* MOT two-seater
'**zweisprachig** [-ʃpra:xɪç] *adj* bilingual
zweistimmig [-ʃtɪmɪç] *adj* MUS ... for two voices
zweistöckig [-ʃtœkɪç] *adj* two-storied, *Br* two-storey ...
zweit [tsvait] *adj* second; ***ein zweiter ...*** another ...; ***jede(r, -s) zweite ...*** every other ...; ***aus zweiter Hand*** second-

hand; ***wir sind zu zweit*** there are two of us

'zweitbeste *adj* second-best

'zweiteilig *adj* two-piece (*suit etc*)

zweitens ['tsvaitəns] *adv* secondly

'zweitklassig [-klasɪç] adj, **'zweitrangig** [-raŋɪç] *adj* second-class *or* -rate

Zwerchfell ['tsvɛrç-] *n* ANAT diaphragm

Zwerg [tsvɛrk] *m* (-[*e*]*s*; -*e* ['tsvɛrgə]) dwarf; gnome; *fig* midget; ***Zwerg...*** *in cpds* BOT dwarf ...; ZO pygmy ...

Zwetsch(g)e ['tsvɛtʃ(g)ə] *f* (-; -*n*) BOT plum

zwicken ['tsvikən] *v/t and v/i* (*ge*-, *h*) pinch, nip

Zwieback ['tsvi:bak] *m* (-[*e*]*s*; -*e*, -*bäcke* [-bɛkə]) rusk, zwieback

Zwiebel ['tsvi:bəl] *f* (-; -*n*) GASTR onion; BOT bulb

Zwiegespräch ['tsvi:-] *n* dialog(ue)

'Zwielicht *n* (-[*e*]*s*; *no pl*) twilight

'Zwiespalt *m* (-[*e*]*s*; -*e*) conflict

'zwiespältig [-ʃpɛltɪç] *adj* conflicting

'Zwietracht *f* (-; *no pl*) discord

Zwilling ['tsvɪlɪŋ] *m* (-*s*; -*e*) twin; *pl* ASTR Gemini; ***er ist*** (***ein***) ***Zwilling*** he's (a) Gemini

'Zwillingsbruder *m* twin brother

Zwillingsschwester *f* twin sister

Zwinge ['tsvɪŋə] *f* (-; -*n*) TECH clamp

zwingen ['tsvɪŋən] *v/t* (*irr*, *ge*-, *h*) force, compel

zwingend *adj* compelling; cogent

Zwinger ['tsvɪŋɐ] *m* (-*s*; -) kennels

zwinkern ['tsvɪŋkɐn] *v/i* (*ge*-, *h*) wink, blink

Zwirn [tsvɪrn] *m* (-[*e*]*s*; -*e*) thread, yarn, twist

zwischen ['tsvɪʃən] *prp* (*dat and acc*) between; among

'zwischen'durch F *adv* in between

'Zwischenergebnis *n* intermediate result

Zwischenfall *m* incident

Zwischenhändler *m* ECON middleman

Zwischenlandung *f* AVIAT stopover; ***ohne Zwischenlandung*** nonstop

'Zwischenraum *m* space, interval

Zwischenruf *m* (loud) interruption; *pl* heckling

Zwischenrufer *m* (-*s*; -) heckler

Zwischenspiel *n* interlude

Zwischenstati̦on *f* stop(over); ***Zwischenstation machen*** (***in*** *dat*) stop over (in)

Zwischenwand *f* partition (wall)

Zwischenzeit *f*: ***in der Zwischenzeit*** in the meantime, meanwhile

Zwist [tsvɪst] *m* (-[*e*]*s*; -*e*) discord

zwitschern ['tsvɪtʃɐn] *v/i* (*ge*-, *h*) twitter, chirp

Zwitter ['tsvɪtɐ] *m* (-*s*; -) BIOL hermaphrodite

zwölf [tsvœlf] *adj* twelve; ***um zwölf*** (***Uhr***) at twelve (o'clock); at noon; at midnight

'zwölfte *adj* twelfth

Zyankali [tsya:n'ka:li] *n* (-*s*; *no pl*) CHEM potassium cyanide

Zyklus ['tsy:klʊs] *m* (-; -*klen*) cycle; series, course

Zylinder [tsi'lɪndɐ] *m* (-*s*; -) top hat; MATH, TECH cylinder

zylindrisch [tsi'lɪndrɪʃ] *adj* cylindrical

Zyniker ['tsy:nikɐ] *m* (-*s*; -) cynic

zynisch ['tsy:nɪʃ] *adj* cynical

Zynismus [tsy'nɪsmʊs] *m* (-; -*men*) cynicism

Zypresse [tsy'prɛsə] *f* (-; -*n*) BOT cypress

Zyste ['tsʏstə] *f* (-; -*n*) MED cyst

z.Z(t). ABBR *of* ***zur Zeit*** at the moment, at present

Activity & Reference Section

The following section contains three parts, each of which will help you in your learning:

Games and puzzles to help you learn to use this dictionary and practice your German-language skills. You'll learn about the different features of this dictionary and how to look something up effectively.

Basic words and expressions to reinforce your learning and help you master the basics.

A short grammar reference to help you use the language correctly.

Using Your Dictionary

Using a bilingual dictionary is important if you want to speak, read or write in a foreign language. Unfortunately, if you don't understand the symbols in your dictionary or the structure of the entries, you'll make mistakes.

What kind of mistakes? Think of some of the words you know in English that sound or look alike. For example, think about the word *ring*. How many meanings can you think of for the word *ring*? Try to list at least three:

a. ____

b. ____

c. ____

Now look up *ring* in the English side of the dictionary. There are more than ten German words that correspond to the single English word *ring*. Some of these German words are listed below in scrambled form.

Unscramble the jumbled German words, then draw a line connecting each German word with the appropriate English meaning or context.

German jumble

1. LKGENNLI
2. NGRI
3. EGAEMN
4. FEANRNU
5. GRNIBXO
6. EIKRS

English meanings

a. a circle around something

b. the action a bell or telephone does (to ring)

c. jewelry worn on the finger

d. the boxing venue

e. one of the venues at a circus

f. the action of calling someone

With so many German words to choose from, each meaning something different, you must be careful to choose the right one to fit the context of your translation. Using the wrong word can make it hard for people to understand you. Imagine the confusing sentences you would make if you never looked beyond the first translation.

For example:

The boxer wearily entered the circle.

She always wore the circle left to her by her grandmother.

I was waiting for the phone to circle when there was a knock at the door.

If you choose the wrong meaning, you simply won't be understood. Mistakes like these are easy to avoid once you know what to look for when using your dictionary. The following pages will review the structure of your dictionary and show you how to pick the right word for your context. Read the tips and guidelines, then complete the puzzles and exercises to practice what you have learned.

Identifying Headwords

If you are looking for a single word in the dictionary, you simply look for that word's location in alphabetical order. However, if you are looking for a phrase, or an object that is described by several words, you will have to decide which word to look up.

Two-word terms are listed by their first word. If you are looking for the German equivalent of *shooting star*, you will find it under *shooting*.

So-called phrasal verbs, verbs used in combination with other words, are found in a block under the main verb. The phrasal verbs *go ahead*, *go at*, *go for*, *go on*, *go out*, and *go up* are all found in a block after *go*.

Idiomatic expressions are found under the key word in the expression. The phrase *give someone a ring*, meaning to call someone, is found in the entry for *ring*.

Headwords referring specifically to males or females with the same profession or nationality are listed together in alphabetical order. In German, a male dancer is called a **Tänzer** and a female dancer is a **Tänzerin**. Both of the words are found in alphabetical order under the masculine form, **Tänzer**.

Find the following words and phrases in your bilingual dictionary. Identify the headword that each is found under. Then, try to find all of the headwords in the word-search puzzle on the next page.

1. get the message
2. be in shock
3. give someone a break
4. make a dash for
5. with no strings attached
6. be mixed up with
7. minor key
8. get away with
9. it's going to rain
10. take advantage of
11. charakterisieren
12. 20 Minuten Verspätung haben
13. Hund
14. sich wahrsagen lassen
15. Apotheke

V	X	R	T	R	G	F	Z	N	A	M	D	N	V	W
K	E	V	V	N	E	P	R	C	D	I	D	Y	I	M
A	O	R	I	V	D	K	H	C	V	N	A	E	M	Y
G	K	R	S	A	C	A	E	G	A	O	I	O	E	U
Z	T	N	S	P	R	W	M	H	N	R	G	B	G	Q
S	F	H	K	A	Ä	X	D	W	T	E	O	Y	A	N
E	D	R	K	X	G	T	M	X	A	O	O	B	S	V
W	U	T	I	M	I	P	U	P	G	B	P	C	S	M
Z	E	D	N	U	H	M	A	N	E	Z	Z	A	E	P
R	H	K	J	B	O	Z	N	Q	G	I	E	N	M	T
N	E	G	A	S	R	H	A	W	S	H	O	C	K	E
C	Z	E	A	M	K	E	Q	Z	W	Q	U	Z	Q	G
M	Z	K	N	P	S	A	A	J	D	G	M	I	J	D
F	G	W	K	N	Z	O	P	K	F	N	O	G	X	W
N	P	E	K	C	O	O	P	V	Z	A	P	V	W	N

Alphabetization

The entries in a bilingual dictionary are in alphabetical order. If words begin with the same letter or letters, they are alphabetized from A to Z using the first unique letter in each word.

Umlauts **ä**, **ö**, and **ü** are treated the same as **a**, **o**, and **u**. If they are in a list together, the non-umlauted form goes before the umlauted one (**schon**, **schön**). The "**eszet**" (**ß**) is alphabetized as if it were **ss**.

Rewrite the following words in alphabetical order. Next to each word also write the number associated with it. Then follow that order to connect the dots on the next page. Not all of the dots will be used, only those whose numbers appear in the word list.

zu	1
anrufen	4
zusammen	8
schön	11
Jacke	16
Gast	22
Tante	28
interessant	33
hin und zurück	34
Badehose	35
Öl	37
Weißwein	38
Regenschirm	40
trinken	46
kommen	82
fahren	49
Ohrring	53
langsam	54
jährlich	56
Regenmantel	64
Gasthaus	65
schon	68
Mechanikerin	72
Museum	73
Flughafen	76
Bäckerei	78
können	47
Computer	84
Elefant	87
danke	90
wissen	93
Bad	98
Volkswagen	99

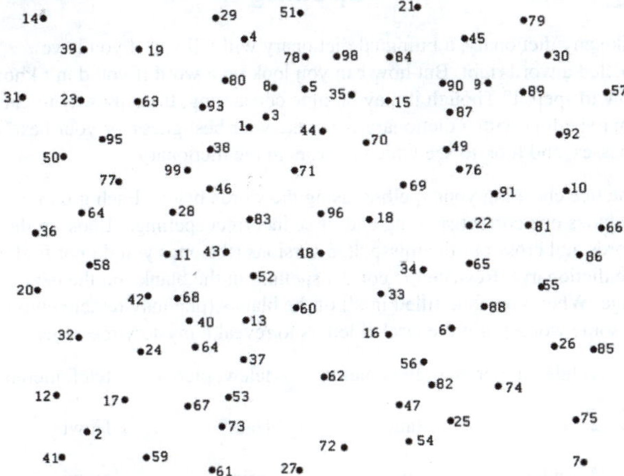

Welches Land sehen Sie?

___ ___ ___ ___ ___ ___ ___ ___ ___ ___ ___

Spelling

Like any dictionary, a bilingual dictionary will tell you if you have spelled a word right. But how can you look up a word if you don't know how to spell it? Though it may be time consuming, the only way to check your spelling with a dictionary is to take your best guess, or your best guesses, and look to see which appears in the dictionary.

Practice checking your spelling using the words below. Each group includes one correct spelling and three incorrect spellings. Look up the words and cross out the misspelled versions (the ones you do not find in the dictionary). Rewrite the correct spelling in the blanks on the next page. When you have filled in all of the blanks (one may remain empty in some words), use the circled letters to reveal a mystery message.

1.	telephonieren	televonieren	telewonieren	telefonieren
2.	Hout	Haut	Häut	Howt
3.	gruhn	gruin	grün	greun
4.	Universität	Universitat	Universitaat	Universiteet
5.	Addrese	Addresse	Adrässe	Adresse
6.	Meßer	Mezser	Mezzer	Messer
7.	Räzel	Retsel	Rätsel	Reezel
8.	Hilfe	Hülfe	Hilpe	Helfe
9.	Esszimmer	Ässzimmer	Eßzimmer	Eszimmer
10.	Tish	Tisch	Tich	Tichs
11.	Shild	Schildt	Schild	Schilt

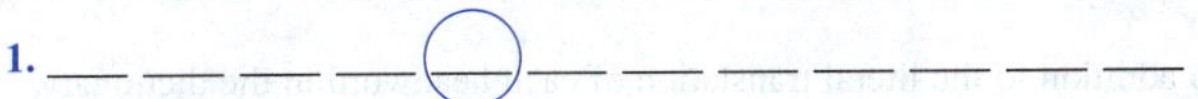

1. ___ ___ ___ ___ ___ ___ ___ ___ ___ ___ ___ ___

2. ___ ___ ___ ___

3. ___ ___ ___ ___ ___

4. ___ ___ ___ ___ ___ ___ ___ ___ ___ ___ ___ ___

5. ___ ___ ___ ___ ___ ___ ___ ___

6. ___ ___ ___ ___ ___ ___

7. ___ ___ ___ ___ ___ ___

8. ___ ___ ___ ___ ___

9. ___ ___ ___ ___ ___ ___ ___ ___ ___

10. ___ ___ ___ ___ ___

11. ___ ___ ___ ___ ___ ___

___ ___ ___ ___ ___ ___ ___ ___ ___ ___ ___ !

1 2 3 4 5 6 7 8 9 10 11

Entries in Context

In addition to the literal translation of each headword in the dictionary, entries sometimes include compound words or phrases using that word.

Solve the crossword puzzle below using the correct word in context.

Hint: Each clue contains key words that will help you find the answer. Look up the key words in each clue. You'll find the answers in expressions within each entry.

ACROSS

3. You need to stay away from him. You must **von ihm** __________.
4. __________ (nowadays), many women have careers. This may not have been the case with previous generations.
6. Needing a light for her candle, she asked the man: **"Haben Sie ______?"**
10. The woman chased after the pickpocket, yelling **"Halt! ______!"**
12. I'm sorry. **Es tut mir ________.**
13. To answer the telephone is **ans Telefon** _____________.
14. The sign indicating a one-way street reads _________________.
15. She was so sad. She went home with a heavy heart, _______**Herzens**.

DOWN

1. Last but not least! **"Nicht __________, nicht zu vergessen."**
2. Those bright ornaments catch my eye. They **fallen ins** ________.
3. I had heard that my friend had been ill, so I asked how he was. I said: "__________ ______________?" (4 words)
5. I'd prefer to eat on the open-air patio, **im** ____________.
7. When the Germans fall in love, they ______________ **sich.**
8. In order to reach my ideal weight, I must **25 Pfund** __________.

9. What a pity! **Wie ________!**

11. I wondered what time it was; I asked a friend, **"Wie ________ ist es?"**

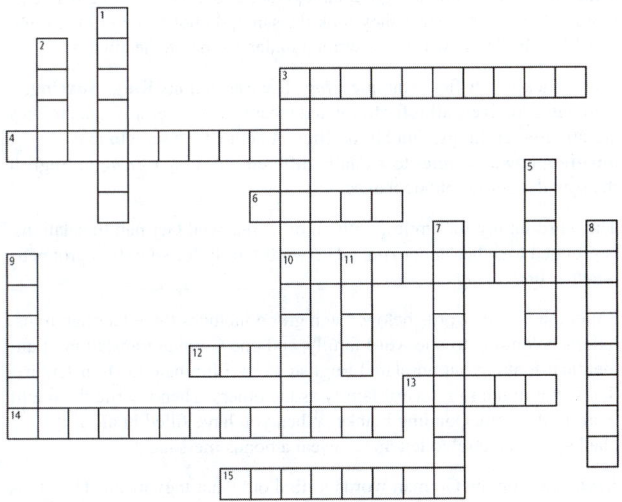

Word Families

Some English words have several related meanings that are represented by different words in German. These related meanings belong to the same word family and are grouped together under a single English headword. Other words, while they look the same, do not belong to the same word family. These words are written under a separate headword.

Think back to our first example, *ring*. The translations **Ring**, **Boxring**, **Manege** and **Kreis** all refer to related meanings of *ring* in English. They are all circular things, though in different contexts. **Klingeln** and **anrufen**, however, refer to a totally different meaning of *ring* in English: the sound a bell or phone makes.

The word family for circles, with all of its nuanced German translations, is grouped together under *ring*[1]. The word family for sounds is grouped together under *ring*[2].

Study the lists of words below. Each group includes three German translations belonging to one word family, and one German translation of an identical-looking but unrelated English word. Eliminate the translation that is not in the same word family as the others. Then rewrite the misfit word in the corresponding blanks. When you have filled in all of the blanks, use the circled letters to reveal a bonus message.

Hint: Look up the German words to find out what they mean. Then look up those translations in the English-German side of your dictionary to find the word family that contains the German words.

1. klingeln	Manege	Ring	Kreis
2. leicht	unbedeutend	beleidigen	gering
3. stampfen	Briefmarke	trampeln	stempeln
4. Pause	ausruhen	rasten	Rest
5. Menge	Messe	Masse	Mehrzahl
6. stecken	Stock	Schläger	Zweig

1. ___ ___ ___ ___ ___ ___ ___ ___

2. ___ ___ ___ ___ ___ ___ ___ ___ ___ ___

3. ___ ___ ___ ___ ___ ___ ___ ___ ___ ___

4. ___ ___ ___ ___

5. ___ ___ ___ ___ ___

6. ___ ___ ___ ___ ___ ___ ___

___ ___ ___ ___ ___ ___ !

1 2 3 4 5 6

Running Heads

Running heads are the words printed in blue at the top of each page. The running head on the left tells you the first headword on the left-hand page. The running head on the right tells you the last headword on the right-hand page. All the words that fall in alphabetical order between the two running heads appear on those two dictionary pages.

Look up the running head on the page where each headword appears, and write it in the space provided. Then unscramble the jumbled running heads and match them with what you wrote.

Headword	Running head	Jumbled running head
1. Bart	BANKVERBINDUNG	UFRATZPU
2. Dunkelheit	______	IUJN
3. Gesundheit	______	DORK
4. Jugend	______	MENRUDCHKMO
5. Kartoffel	______	TRAUSSIMNE
6. konventionell	______	RADIESCHISPA
7. mitbringen	______	STSON
8. Nachmittag	______	BEUTANSCHGAL
9. Pass	______	SINNUNGELOSS
10. quatschen	______	VERGNUDNIBBNAK
11. Software	______	BRACHAN
12. Taxistand	______	PITAKALLANAEG

Pronunciation

Though German has more vowel sounds than English, pronunciation in the two languages is similar. Refer to the pronunciation guide in this dictionary to see equivalent sounds across the two languages. Study the guide to familiarize yourself with the symbols used to give pronunciations in this dictionary.

Practice recognizing pronunciations as they are written in the dictionary. Look at each of the pronunciations below, then connect it to its correct English or German spelling.

1. frend	**A.** Imbiss
2. ˈevri	**B.** language
3. æpl	**C.** Bad
4. naïf	**D.** every
5. ˈlægwidʒ	**E.** selig
6. baːt	**F.** friend
7. ˈɪmbɪs	**G.** Fang
8. ˈzeˑliç	**H.** knife
9. faŋ	**I.** gekränkt
10. gəˈkrɛŋkt	**J.** apple

Parts of Speech

In German and English, words are categorized into different ***parts of speech***. These labels tell us what function a word performs in a sentence. In this dictionary, the part of speech is given before a word's definition.

Nouns are people, places or things. ***Verbs*** describe actions. ***Adjectives*** describe nouns in sentences. For example, the adjective *pretty* tells you about the noun *girl* in the phrase *a pretty girl*. ***Adverbs*** also describe, but they modify verbs, adjectives, and other adverbs. The adverb *quickly* tells you more about how the action is carried out in the phrase *ran quickly*. Adjectives usually take endings when used in a German sentence. Adverbs do not. Most adjectives are also used as adverbs. *The fast (adj) runners ran fast (adv) to the finish line.* The only way to identify whether a particular word is an adjective or adverb is to observe its use in the sentence.

Prepositions specify relationships in time and space. They are words such as *in*, *on*, *before*, or *with*. ***Articles*** are words that accompany nouns. Words like *the* and *a* or *an* modify the noun, marking it as specific or general, and known or unknown.

Conjunctions are words like *and*, *but*, and *if* that join phrases and sentences together. ***Pronouns*** take the place of nouns in a sentence.

The following activity uses words from the dictionary in a Sudoku-style puzzle. In Sudoku puzzles, the numbers 1 to 9 are used to fill in grids. All digits 1 to 9 must appear, but cannot be repeated, in each square, row, and column.

In the following puzzles, you are given a set of words for each part of the grid. Look up each word to find out its part of speech. Then arrange the words within the square so that, in the whole puzzle, you do not repeat any part of speech within a column or row.

Hint: If one of the words given in the puzzle is a noun, then you know that no other nouns can be put in that row or column of the grid. Use the process of elimination to figure out where the other parts of speech can go.

Let's try a small puzzle first. Use the categories noun *n*, verb *v*, adjective/adverb *adj*/*adv*, and preposition *prep* to solve this puzzle. Each section corresponds to one quarter of the puzzle.

Section 1

denken, Hund, schwarz, mit

Section 2

Euro, auf, machen, toll

Section 3

ehrlich, vor, Bilder, spielen

Section 4

Lotterie, staatlich, **schaden**, nach

denken (v)			**Euro** (n)
		schaden (v)	
ehrlich (adj/adv)			

Now try a larger puzzle. For this puzzle, use the categories noun *n*, verb *v*, adjective/adverb *adj/adv*, preposition *prep*, article *art*, and pronoun *pro*. The sections are numbered from top left to bottom right.

Section 1

Aufzug, attraktiv, **steigen**, **wir**, ein, über

Section 2

andere, ehe, **sortieren**, **Bilder**, das, sie

Section 3

mit, Käse, **planen**, mild, **er**, **eine**

Section 4

schreiben, **exklusiv**, du, die, **Lampen**, ohne

Section 5

nach, diskret, Etappe, wohnen, **ich**, **der**

Section 6

Familie, **ihm**, **zwischen**, gut, kaufen, einen

wir (pron)		**steigen** (v)	**Bilder** (n)		
Aufzug (n)					**sortieren** (v)
	planen (v)			**Lampen** (n)	
eine (art)	**er** (pron)			**exklusiv** (adj/adv)	
nach (prep)		**der** (art)			**ihm** (pron)
		ich (pron)	**zwischen** (prep)		

Pluralization of Nouns

There are sixteen different patterns used to pluralize German nouns. You can familiarize yourself with them in the appendix of this dictionary. The plural form is indicated in parentheses after the gender of the noun in its dictionary entry. First you see an **–s**, **-(e)s** or **–es**. That indicates the genitive form of the noun (the form that says *of the*...). Following that is the abbreviated indicator of the plural form. The symbol **–e** means that the word adds an **–e** to become plural. Many feminine nouns add **–en** in the plural. Many masculine and neuter nouns add an umlaut on the stem vowel and then an **–e**.

Write the plurals of the nouns in the list and then check your spelling by finding them in the following word search.

Singular	***Plural***
1. Kind	____________________
2. Mutter	____________________
3. Hund	____________________
4. Bruder	____________________
5. Auto	____________________
6. Frau	____________________
7. Haus	____________________
8. Gericht	____________________
9. Arbeiter	____________________
10. Lehrerin	____________________

A	F	A	A	E	S	M	J	Z	M	O	D	R	Q	T
D	R	L	B	U	T	O	H	K	C	C	G	E	Z	G
F	A	I	V	X	E	H	T	E	M	O	K	T	H	A
P	U	E	D	N	U	H	C	U	W	K	E	I	Y	T
U	E	I	Z	Q	M	H	A	I	A	S	O	E	H	Q
K	N	L	I	M	Ü	T	T	E	R	V	F	B	X	H
X	H	I	N	B	Q	B	F	Q	D	E	D	R	N	J
J	I	M	Z	Z	F	S	A	G	B	S	G	A	R	H
W	Q	V	W	F	B	K	R	V	M	R	A	O	Ä	O
N	E	N	N	I	R	E	R	H	E	L	Ü	U	T	B
B	E	U	T	A	D	S	J	L	S	L	S	D	Y	T
B	B	J	W	N	V	M	Z	N	N	E	R	A	E	X
D	T	D	I	W	P	L	E	Q	R	Z	S	J	H	R
K	P	K	Q	B	V	K	A	K	J	E	T	P	T	B
D	P	Y	O	X	T	C	J	Y	L	V	Y	Y	I	R

Gender

German nouns are easily recognizable. They are always capitalized, even in the middle of a sentence. They all belong to one of three groups: masculine, feminine, or neuter. A noun's gender is indicated in an entry after the headword or pronunciation with **m** for masculine, **f** for feminine, and **n** for neuter.

Look up the words listed below and mark the gender of each word. Then use the genders to lead you through the puzzle: if a word is masculine, go left; if a word is feminine, go right; if a word is neuter, go up.

	m (go left)	*f* (go right)	*n* (go up)
1. Gericht			
2. Katze			
3. Mond			
4. Sonne			
5. Wagen			
6. Kuchen			
7. Großmutter			
8. Freundschaft			
9. Aufzug			
10. Frühstück			
11. Person			
12. Professor			
13. Bestellung			
14. Reis			

Start

Adjectives

In German, adjectives take different endings in order to agree in gender and number with the noun they modify. In most cases, an **–e** is added to the adjective for the feminine form, and an **–n** is added for the plural form. A table of adjective endings can be found in the appendix of this dictionary.

Use the dictionary to determine whether the nouns in the following phrases are masculine or feminine, singular or plural. Then write in the correct form of the adjective to complete the phrase. We have added the correct endings for you. Check your answers against the word search. The correct forms will be found in the puzzle with their endings.

1. a friendly smile = ein ____________es Lächeln

2. a blonde woman = eine ____________e Frau

3. an important message = eine _______________e Nachricht

4. public school = ________________e Schule

5. the green car = der ______________e Wagen

6. an unforgettable picnic = ein _______________es Picknick

7. a pretty girl = ein _________es Mädchen

8. in a good book = in einem ______________en Buch

9. an interesting speaker = ein _____________er Redner

10. a German piano player = ein ___________er Klavierspieler

11. a heavy backback = ein ____________er Rucksack

U	E	T	R	Y	G	M	I	E	S	X	O	V	J	X
K	N	H	O	E	A	C	N	F	C	V	H	L	Z	M
S	H	V	M	D	N	N	T	R	H	D	V	V	C	D
F	L	X	E	X	O	U	E	Y	W	G	R	G	Z	E
W	W	Q	F	R	Y	P	R	X	E	F	Q	S	G	H
L	I	M	T	N	G	S	E	G	R	N	M	V	O	C
W	L	C	M	N	C	E	S	R	E	E	G	N	B	I
F	M	N	H	H	K	I	S	S	R	T	R	F	J	L
Q	B	W	Ö	T	B	X	A	S	L	U	J	D	L	T
Z	C	N	Q	H	I	H	N	F	L	G	Y	S	E	N
Q	E	X	Q	J	F	G	T	W	O	I	E	K	T	E
S	E	D	N	O	L	B	E	V	Z	I	C	F	C	F
N	D	U	R	F	U	S	R	M	B	T	O	H	X	F
S	E	H	C	I	L	D	N	U	E	R	F	I	E	Ö
D	E	U	T	S	C	H	E	R	K	L	E	B	C	S

Verbs

Verbs are listed in the dictionary in their infinitive form. To use the verb in a sentence, you must conjugate it and use the form that agrees with the sentence's subject.

Most verbs are regular and conjugate like the chart in the appendix of this dictionary. A few are irregular and require a vowel change in the present tense. A list of all irregular verbs can also be found in the appendix.

For this puzzle, conjugate the given verbs in the present tense. Use the context and the subject pronoun to determine the person and number of the form you need. The correct answer fits in the crossword spaces provided.

ACROSS

2. Am Samstag ____________ es auch einen Gemüsemarkt in der Marburger Straße. **geben**

4. Das Kind ____________ mit seinen Freunden ins Kino. **gehen**

6. Zur gleichen Zeit __________ ich in die Stadt einkaufen. **fahren**

7. Der Film __________ den Kindern gut. Sie wollen ihn ein zweites Mal sehen. **gefallen**

9. Die Nachbarin ____________ dem Ehepaar zum Hochzeitstag. **gratulieren**

12. Was ____________ ich meinen Eltern zum Hochzeitstag? Zwei Schiffskarten für eine Kreuzfahrt im Mittelmeer. **schenken**

13. Wir ____________ drei Dutzend Eier, da wir backen wollen. **kaufen**

14. Mein Vater ____________ seine neue Digitalkamera auf die Reise mit. **nehmen**

17. Die Suppe __________ der Familie sehr gut und ist sehr gesund. **schmecken**

18. Die Feier war so toll, dass alle Gäste nächstes Jahr wieder kommen __________ . **wollen**

DOWN

1. Die Kinder __________ den Film “Superman” am Samstag an. **sehen**

3. Der Supermarkt __________ Eier zum halben Preis an. **bieten**

5. Mein Mann ___________ den Kindern immer bei den Hausaufgaben. Er ist Lehrer. **helfen**

6. Die Großeltern ___________ am Sonntag ihren fünfzigsten Hochzeitstag. **feiern**

8. Meine Nachbarn ___________ den Brokkoli vom Leoni-Markt. **mögen**

10. Bevor sie wegfahren, ___________ sie uns immer an und verabschieden sich. **rufen**

11. Katarina ___________ früh nach Hause gehen und ihre Hausaufgaben für Montag machen. **müssen**

12. Morgen ___________ die ganze Familie nach Ulm zu den Großeltern. **fahren**

16. Meine 10-jährige Tochter ___________ jeden Abend in ihr Tagebuch. **schreiben**

17. Seine Bilder ___________ sehr gut geworden. **sein**

19. Mein Babysitter muss heute schon früh gehen, also ___________ ich nur 15 Minuten auf der Fete. **bleiben**

1 2 3 4 5 6 7 8 9 10 11 12 13 14 15 16 17 18 19

When you are reading German, you face a different challenge. You see a conjugated verb in context and need to determine what its infinitive is in order to understand its meaning.

Often you will see a preposition at the end of the sentence with no object. That's called a separable prefix and is considered part of the verb. **Ich rufe meine Mutter jetzt an.** The verb is **anrufen**. The prefix **an** is separated from the verb in the sentence, but must be added back onto the infinitive in order to insure that you find the correct meaning.

For the next puzzle, you will see conjugated verbs in the sentences. Figure out which verb the conjugated form represents, and write the infinitive (the headword form) in the puzzle.

ACROSS

2. Das Kind **versteckte** seinen Teddybär unter seinem Kopfkissen.
3. Machst du eine Diät? Du **siehst** gut **aus**.
6. Das brave Kind **gehorcht** seinen Eltern immer.
8. Gerd und Gerlinde **kamen** drei Stunden zu spät **an**.
10. Matthias **weiß**, wie wir hinkommen.
11. Wir **rufen** unsere Tante um sechs Uhr **an**.
13. Sie **steht** jeden Morgen um 7.30 **auf**.
16. Der Film **gefällt** den Kindern.
17. Sie **isst** jeden Abend zusammen mit ihrer Familie.
18. Das Telefon **klingelt** sehr laut.

DOWN

1. Carsten **bestellt** ein Käsebrot mit einem Glas Bier.
4. Die Katze **schläft** in der Sonne.
5. Ich **verstehe** nicht, was der Lehrer sagt.
7. Der König **heiratet** seine Prinzessin am Dienstag in der Schlosskapelle.
9. **Kannst** du mir helfen?
12. Du **hast verloren**!

14. Ich **sehe** dich hinter der Couch!

15. Die Schauspielerinnen **sind** sehr hübsch.

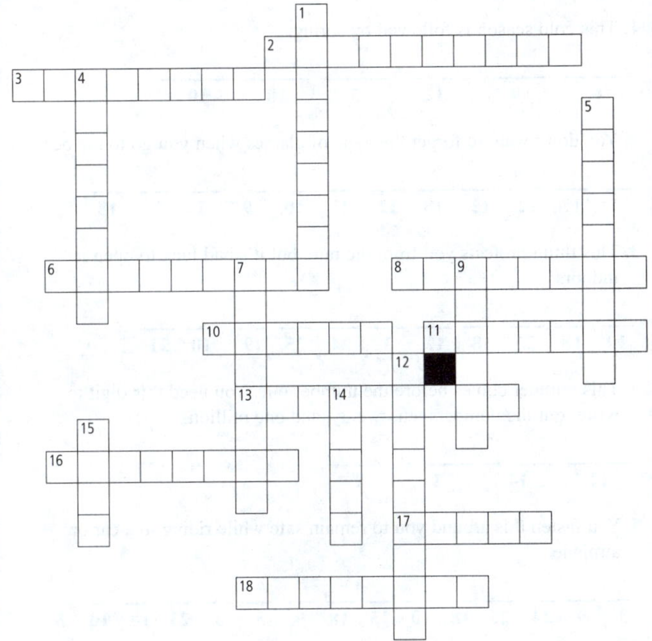

Riddles

Solve the following riddles in English. Then write the German translation of the answer on the lines.

1. This cold season is followed by spring.

___ ___ ___ ___ ___ ___
6 9 12 5 18 10

2. You don't want to forget this type of glasses when you go to the beach.

___ ___ ___ ___ ___ ___ ___ ___ ___ ___ ___ ___
3 17 12 12 18 12 11 10 9 1 1 18

3. This thing protects you from the rain, but it's bad luck to open it indoors!

___ ___ ___ ___ ___ ___ ___ ___ ___ ___ ___
10 18 23 18 12 3 24 25 9 10 21

4. This number comes before the number one. You need this digit to write out the numbers ten, twenty, and one million.

___ ___ ___ ___
12 14 1 1

5. You fasten this around you to remain safe while riding in a car or airplane.

___ ___ ___ ___ ___ ___ ___ ___ ___ ___ ___ ___ ___ ___ ___
3 9 24 25 18 10 25 18 9 5 3 23 14 10 5

6. If you are injured or very ill, you should go to this place.

___ ___ ___ ___ ___ ___ ___ ___ ___ ___ ___
7 10 15 12 7 18 12 25 15 14 3

7. This mode of transportation has only two wheels. It is also good exercise!

___ ___ ___ ___ ___ ___ ___
13 15 25 10 10 15 2

8. This large mammal lives in the ocean.

___ ___ ___
6 15 1

9. This person is your mother's mother.

___ ___ ___ ___ ___ ___ ___ ___ ___ ___
23 10 17 27 21 14 5 5 18 10

10. There are twelve of these in a year.

___ ___ ___ ___ ___ ___
21 17 12 15 5 18

11. Snow White bit into this red fruit and fell into a long slumber.

___ ___ ___ ___ ___
15 4 13 18 1

12. This professional brings letters and packages to your door.

___ ___ ___ ___ ___ ___ ___ ___ ___ ___ ___
11 10 9 18 13 5 10 8 23 18 10

13. This midday meal falls between breakfast and dinner.

___ ___ ___ ___ ___ ___ ___ ___ ___ ___ ___
21 9 5 5 15 23 18 3 3 18 12

14. A very young cat is referred to as this.

___ ___ ___ ___ ___ ___ ___ ___
7 8 5 16 24 25 28 12

15. An archer uses a bow and this.

___ ___ ___ ___ ___
4 13 18 9 1

16. My mother was married to this relative of mine when she was twenty-three.

___ ___ ___ ___ ___
19 15 5 18 10

Cryptogram

Write the letter that corresponds to each number in the spaces. When you are done, read the German message. It's a quote from a famous German author and expresses our wish that you look forward to your German language experience.

21	15	12		21	14	3	3		9	21	21
18	10		18	5	6	15	3		25	15	11
18	12		6	17	10	15	14	13		21	15
12		3	9	24	25		13	10	18	14	5
	16	9	5	15	5		19	17	12		18
2	14	15	10	2		21	Ö	10	9	7	18

”___ ___ ___   ___ ___ ___ ___   ___ ___ ___ ___ ___

___ ___ ___ ___ ___   ___ ___ ___ ___ ___ ,

___ ___ ___ ___ ___ ___   ___ ___ ___   ___ ___ ___ ___

___ ___ ___ ___ ___ . “   ___ ___ ___ ___ ___

___ ___ ___

___ ___ ___ ___ ___ ___   ___ ___ ___ ___ ___ ___

Answer Key

Using Your Dictionary

a–c. Answers will vary

1. klingeln, b
2. Ring, c
3. Manege, e
4. anrufen, f
5. Boxring, d
6. Kreis, a

Identifying Headwords

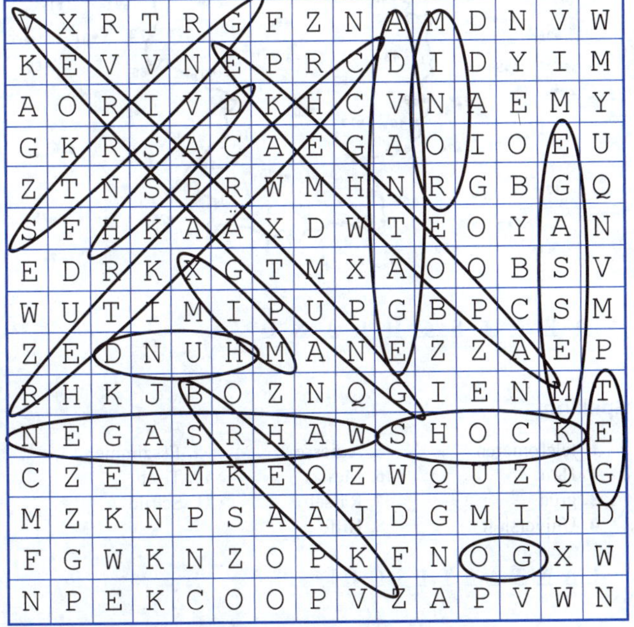

Alphabetization

anrufen, Bäckerei, Bad, Badehose, Computer, danke, Elefant, fahren, Flughafen, Gast, Gasthaus, hin und zurück, interessant, Jacke, jährlich, kommen, können, langsam, Mechanikerin, Museum, Ohrring, Öl, Regenmantel, Regenschirm, schon, schön, Tante, trinken, Volkswagen, Weißwein, wissen, zu, zusammen

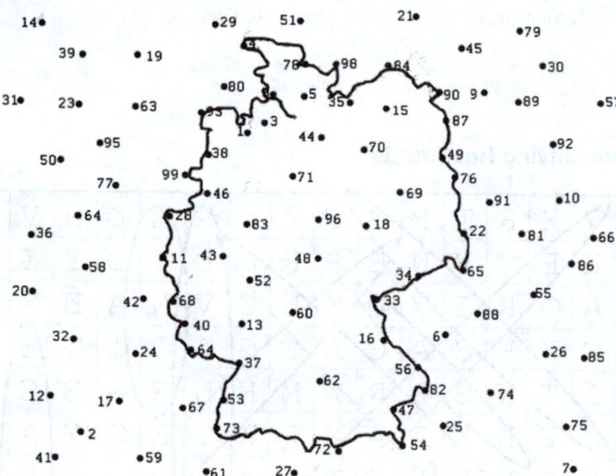

D E U T S C H L A N D

Spelling

1. telefonieren
2. Haut
3. grün
4. Universität
5. Adresse
6. Messer
7. Rätsel
8. Hilfe
9. Esszimmer
10. Tisch
11. Schild

F A N T A S T I S C H!

Entries in Context

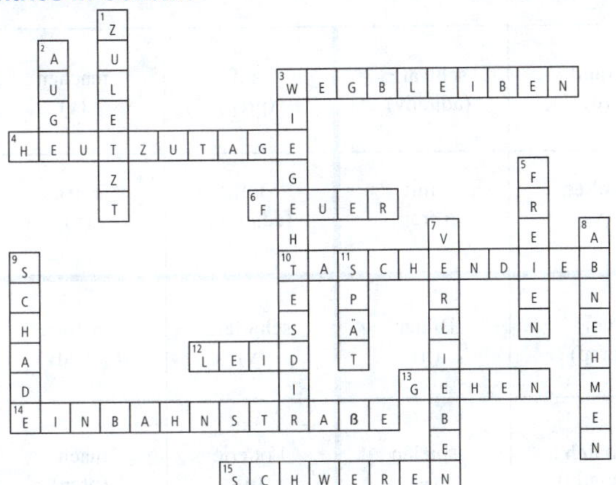

Word Families

1. **k**lingeln
2. be**l**eidigen
3. Briefm**a**rke
4. Re**s**t
5. Mes**s**e
6. st**e**cken

K L A S S E!

Pronunciation

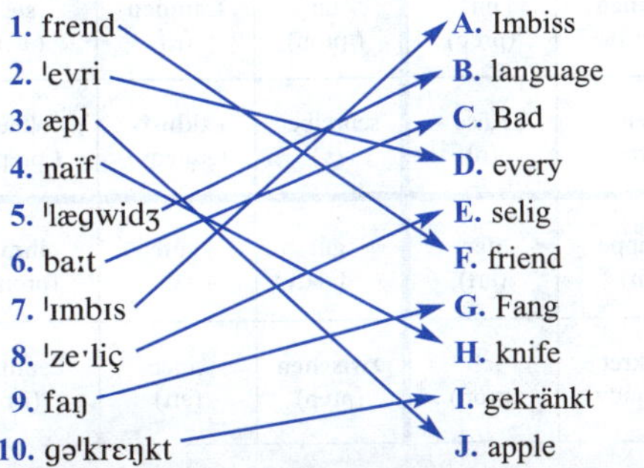

Parts of Speech

Hund (n)	schwarz (adj/adv)	auf (prep)	machen (v)
denken (v)	mit (prep)	toll (adj/adv)	**Euro** (n)
vor (prep)	Bilder (n)	**schaden** (v)	staatlich (adj/adv)
ehrlich (adj/adv)	spielen (v)	Lotterie (n)	nach (prep)

wir (pron)	**ein** (art)	**steigen** (v)	**Bilder** (n)	ehe (prep)	andere (adj/adv)
Aufzug (n)	**über** (prep)	attraktiv (adj/adv)	das (art)	sie (pron)	**sotieren** (v)
mild (adj/adv)	**planen** (v)	mit (prep)	du (pron)	**Lampen** (n)	sie (art)
eine (art)	**er** (pron)	Käse (n)	schreiben (v)	**exklusiv** (adj/adv)	ohne (prep)
nach (prep)	Etappe (n)	**der** (art)	gut (adj/adv)	kaufen (v)	**ihm** (pron)
wohnen (v)	diskret (adj/adv)	**ich** (pron)	**zwischen** (prep)	einen (art)	Familie (n)

Pluralization of Nouns

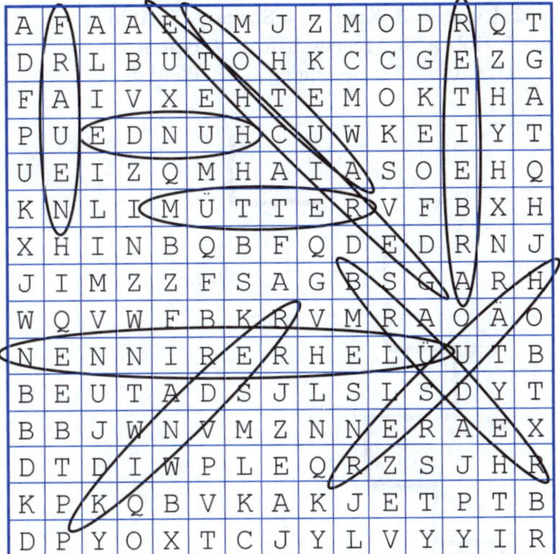

Kinder, Mütter, Hunde, Brüder, Autos, Frauen, Häuser, Gerichte, Arbeiter, Lehrerinnen

Gender

1. Gericht *n* **2.** Katze *f* **3.** Kind *n* **4.** Sonne *f* **5.** Auto *n*
6. Kuchen *m* **7.** Holz *n* **8.** Freundschaft *f* **9.** Bett *n*
10. Person *f* **11.** Brot *n* **12.** Bestellung *f* **13.** Pferd *n*

Running Heads

Headword	Running head	Jumbled running head
1. Bart	BANKVERBINDUNG	UFRATZPU
2. Dunkelheit	DURCHKOMMEN	IUJN
3. Gesundheit	GESINNUNGSLOS	DORK
4. Jugend	JUNI	MENRUDCHKMO
5. Kartoffel	KAPITALANLAGE	TRAUSSIMNE
6. konventionell	KORD	RADIESCHISPA
7. mitbringen	MISSTRAUEN	STSON
8. Nachmittag	NACHBAR	BEUTANSCHGAL
9. Pass	PARADIESISCH	SINNUNGELOSS
10. quatschen	PUTZFRAU	VERGNUDNIBBNAK
11. Software	SONST	BRACHAN
12. Taxistand	TAUBENSCHLAG	PITAKALLANAEG

Adjectives

1. ein freundliches Lächeln
2. eine blonde Frau
3. eine wichtige Nachricht
4. öffentliche Schule
5. der grüne Wagen
6. ein unvergessliches Picknick
7. ein schönes Mädchen
8. in einem guten Buch
9. ein interessanter Redner
10. ein deutscher Klavierspieler
11. ein schwerer Rucksack

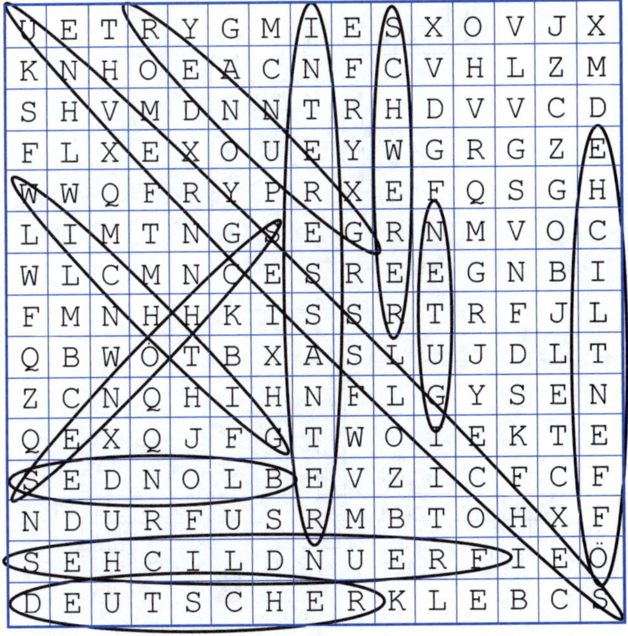

Verbs

Riddles

1. Winter
2. Sonnenbrille
3. Regenschirm
4. null
5. Sicherheitsgurt
6. Krankenhaus
7. Fahrrad
8. Wal
9. Großmutter
10. Monate
11. Apfel
12. Briefträger
13. Mittagessen
14. Kätzchen
15. Pfeil
16. Vater

Cryptogram

21 M	15 A	12 N		21 M	14 U	3 S	3 S		9 I	21 M	21 M
18 E	10 R		18 E	5 T	6 W	15 A	3 S		25 H	15 A	11 B
18 E	12 N		6 W	17 O	10 R	15 A	14 U	13 F		21 M	15 A
12 N		3 S	9 I	24 C	25 H		13 F	10 R	18 E	14 U	5 T
	16 Z	9 I	5 T	15 A	5 T		19 V	17 O	12 N		18 E
2 D	14 U	15 A	10 R	2 D		21 M	Ö	10 R	9 I	7 K	18 E

„Man muss immer etwas haben, worauf man sich freut.“ Zitat von Eduard Mörike.

Eduard Mörike was a German lyrical poet who lived from 1805–1875 and wrote that, “One must always have something to look forward to.” We hope that you look forward to learning German and to working with this dictionary.

BASIC GERMAN PHRASES & GRAMMAR

Pronunciation

In this section we have used a simplified phonetic system to represent the sounds of German. Simply read the pronunciation as if it were English.

Stress

Generally, as in English, the first syllable is stressed in German, except when short prefixes are added to the beginning of the word. Then the second syllable is stressed (e.g. **bewegen** *to move*, **gesehen** *seen*).

BASIC PHRASES

Essential

Good afternoon!	**Guten Tag!**	goo-ten tahk
Good evening!	**Guten Abend!**	goo-ten ah-bent
Goodbye!	**Auf Wiedersehen!**	owf vee-duh-zay-en
…, please!	**…, bitte!**	bit-tuh
Thank you!	**Danke!**	dahn-kuh
Yes.	**Ja.**	yah
No.	**Nein.**	nine
Sorry!	**Entschuldigung!**	ent-shool-dee-goong
Where are the restrooms?	**Wo ist die Toilette?**	vo ist dee toi-let-tuh
When?	**Wann?**	vahn
What?	**Was?**	vahs
Where?	**Wo?**	vo
Here.	**Hier.**	here
There.	**Dort.**	dawt
On the right.	**Rechts.**	rekhts
On the left.	**Links.**	linx
Do you have …?	**Haben Sie …?**	hah-ben zee
I'd like …	**Ich möchte …**	ikh merkh-tuh
How much is that?	**Was kostet das?**	wahs kaws-tet dahs
Where is …?	**Wo ist …?**	vo ist
Where can I get …?	**Wo gibt es …?**	vo gheept es

Communication Difficulties

Do you speak English?	**Sprechen Sie Englisch?**	shpre-khen zee ayng-lish
Does anyone here speak English?	**Spricht hier jemand Englisch?**	shprikht here yay-mahnt ayng-lish
Did you understand that?	**Haben Sie das verstanden?**	hah-ben zee dahs fair-stahn-den
I understand.	**Ich habe verstanden.**	ikh hah-beh fair-shtahnd-den
I didn't understand that.	**Ich habe das nicht verstanden.**	ikh hah-beh dahs nikht fair-shtahn-den
Could you speak a bit more slowly, please?	**Könnten Sie bitte etwas langsamer sprechen?**	kern-ten zee bit-tuh et-vahs lahng-zah-mer shpre-khen
Could you please repeat that?	**Könnten Sie das bitte wiederholen?**	kern-ten zee dahs bit-tuh veeder-ho-len
What's that in German?	**Wie heißt das auf Deutsch?**	vee highst dahs owf doitch
What does … mean?	**Was bedeutet …?**	vahs buh-doi-tet
Could you write it down for me, blease?	**Könnten Sie es mir bitte aufschreiben?**	kern-ten zee es meer bit-tuh owf-shry-ben

Greetings

Good morning!	**Guten Morgen!**	goo-ten maw-ghen
Good afternoon!	**Guten Tag!**	goo-ten tahk
Good evening!	**Guten Abend!**	goo-ten ah-bent
Goodnight!	**Gute Nacht!**	goo-tuh nakht
Hello!	**Hallo!**	hah-lo
How are you?	**Wie geht es Ihnen / dir?**	vee gate es ee-nen / deer
Fine, thanks. And you?	**Danke, gut. Und Ihnen / dir?**	dahn-kuh goot oont eenen / deer
I'm afraid I have to go.	**Es tut mir Leid, aber ich muss gehen.**	es toot meer lite ah-buh ikh moos gain
Goodbye!	**Auf Wiedersehen!**	owf vee-duh-zay-en
See you soon / tomorrow!	**Bis bald / morgen!**	bis bahlt / maw-ghen
Bye!	**Tschüs!**	chews

It was nice meeting you.	**Schön, Sie / dich kennen gelernt zu haben.**	shern zee / dikh ken-nen guh-lairnt tsoo hah-ben
Have a good trip!	**Gute Reise!**	goo-tuh reye-suh

Meeting People

What's your name?	**Wie heißen Sie / heißt du?**	vee high-sen zee / highst doo
My name is …	**Ich heiße …**	ikh high-suh
May I introduce …	**Darf ich bekannt machen? Das ist …**	dahf ikh buh-kahnt mah-khen dahs ist
– my husband.	**mein Mann.**	mighn mahn
– my wife.	**meine Frau.**	migh-nuh frow
– my boyfriend.	**mein Freund.**	mighn froint
– my girlfriend.	**meine Freundin.**	migh-nuh froin-din
Where are you from?	**Woher sind Sie?**	vo-hair zind zee
I'm from …	**Ich komme aus …**	ikh kom-uh ows
– the US.	**den USA.**	dane oo-es-ah
– Canada.	**Kanada.**	kah-nah-dah
– the UK.	**Großbritannien.**	gross-brit-tahn-ee-en

Expressing Likes and Dislikes

Very good!	**Sehr gut!**	zair goot
I'm very happy.	**Ich bin sehr zufrieden!**	ikh bin zair tsoo-free-den
I like that.	**Das gefällt mir.**	dahs guh-felt meer
What a shame!	**Wie schade!**	vee shah-duh
I'd rather …	**Ich würde lieber …**	ikh vewr-duh lee-buh …
I don't like it.	**Das gefällt mir nicht.**	dahs guh-felt meer nikht
I'd rather not.	**Das möchte ich lieber nicht.**	dahs merkh-tuh ikh lee-buh nisht
Certainly not.	**Auf keinen Fall.**	owf keye-nen fahl

Expressing Requests and Thanks

Thank you very much.	**Vielen Dank.**	fee-len dahnk
Thanks, you too.	**Danke, gleichfalls.**	dahn-kuh gleyekh-fahls
May I?	**Darf ich?**	dahf ikh
Please, …	**Bitte, …**	bit-tuh
No, thank you.	**Nein, danke.**	nine dahn-kuh
Could you help me, please?	**Könnten Sie mir bitte helfen?**	kern-ten zee meer bit-tuh hel-fen
Thank you, that's very nice of you.	**Vielen Dank, das ist sehr nett von Ihnen.**	fee-len dahnk dahs ist zair net fun ee-nen
Thank you very much for all your trouble / help.	**Vielen Dank für Ihre Mühe / Hilfe.**	fee-len dahnk fewr ee-ruh mew-uh / hil-fuh
You're welcome.	**Gern geschehen.**	gehrn guh-shay-en
Sorry!	**Entschuldigung!**	ent-shool-dee-goong
Excuse me!	**Entschuldigen Sie!**	ent-shool-dee-ghen zee
I'm sorry about that.	**Das tut mir Leid.**	dahs toot meer lite
Don't worry about it!	**Macht nichts!**	makht nikhts
How embarrassing!	**Das ist mir sehr unangenehm.**	dahs ist meer zair oon-ahn-guh-name
It was a misunderstanding.	**Das war ein Missverständnis.**	dahs vah eye-n miss-fair-shtent-niss

GRAMMAR

Regular Verbs and Their Tenses

The past is often expressed by using *to have* **haben** + past participle. The future is formed with **werden** + infinitive.

Infinitive:	**kaufen** *to buy*		**arbeiten** *to work*
Past Participle:	**gekauft** *bought*		**gearbeitet** *worked*

	Present	***Past***	***Future***
ich *I*	**kaufe**	**habe gekauft**	**werde kaufen**
du *you inform.*	**kaufst**	**hast gekauft**	**wirst kaufen**
Sie *you form.*	**kaufen**	**haben gekauft**	**werden kaufen**
er/sie/es *he/she/it*	**kauft**	**hat gekauft**	**wird kaufen**
wir *we*	**kaufen**	**haben gekauft**	**werden kaufen**
ihr *you pl. inform.*	**kauft**	**habt gekauft**	**werdet kaufen**
Sie *you pl. form.*	**kaufen**	**haben gekauft**	**werden kaufen**
sie *they*	**kaufen**	**haben gekauft**	**werden kaufen**

Irregular verbs have to be memorized. Verbs that indicate movement are conjugated with *to be* **sein**, e.g. *to go* **gehen**:

	Present	***Past***	***Future***
ich *I*	**gehe**	**bin gegangen**	**werde gehen**
du *you inform.*	**gehst**	**bist gegangen**	**wirst gehen**
Sie *you form.*	**gehen**	**sind gegangen**	**werden gehen**
er/sie/es *he/she/it*	**geht**	**ist gegangen**	**wird gehen**
wir *we*	**gehen**	**sind gegangen**	**werden gehen**
ihr *you pl. inform.*	**geht**	**seid gegangen**	**werdet gehen**
Sie *you pl. form.*	**gehen**	**sind gegangen**	**werden gehen**
sie *they*	**gehen**	**sind gegangen**	**werden gehen**

To express future, usually the present tense is used together with a time adverb: *I'll work tomorrow.* **Ich arbeite morgen.**

Nouns and Articles

All nouns are written with a capital letter. Their definite articles indicate their gender: **der** (masculine = m), **die** (feminine = f), **das** (neuter = n). The plural article is always **die**, regardless of gender.

Examples:	***Singular***	***Plural***
	der Mann *the man*	**die Männer** *the men*
	die Frau *the woman*	**die Frauen** *the women*
	das Kind *the child*	**die Kinder** *the children*

The indefinite article also indicates the gender of the noun: **ein** (m, n), **eine** (f). There is no indefinite article in the plural.

Examples:	***Singular***	***Plural***
	ein Zug *a train*	**Züge** *trains*
	eine Karte *a map*	**Karten** *maps*

Possessives also relate to the gender of the noun that follows.

Nominative (m, n/f)	***Accusative (n/f/m)***	***Dative (m, n/f)***
mein/e *my*	**mein/e/en** *my*	**meinem / meiner** *my*
dein/e *your inform.*	**dein/e/en** *your*	**deinem / deiner** *your*
Ihr/e *your form.*	**Ihr/e/en** *your*	**Ihrem / Ihrer** *your*
sein/e *his*	**sein/e/en** *his*	**seinem / seiner** *his*
ihr/e *her*	**ihr/e/en** *her*	**ihrem / ihrer** *her*
sein/e *its*	**sein/e/en** *its*	**seinem / seiner** *its*
unser/e *our*	**unser/e/en** *our*	**unserem / unserer** *our*
euer/e *your pl. inform.*	**euer/e/en** *your*	**eurem / eurer** *your*
Ihr/e *your pl. form.*	**Ihr/e/en** *your*	**Ihrem / Ihrer** *your*
ihr/e *their*	**ihr/e/en** *their*	**ihrem / ihrer** *their*

Examples:		
	Wo ist meine Fahrkarte?	*Where is my ticket?*
	Ihr Taxi ist hier.	*Your taxi is here.*
	Hier ist euer Pass.	*Here is your passport.*

Word Order

The conjugated verb comes after the subject and before the object. When a sentence doesn't begin with a subject, the word order changes.

Examples:		
	Er ist in Berlin.	*He is in Berlin.*
	Heute ist er in Berlin.	*Today he is in Berlin.*
	Wir sind in Berlin gewesen.	*We were in Berlin.*

Questions are formed by reversing the order of subject and verb.

Examples:	**Haben Sie Bücher?**	*Do you have books?*
	Wie ist das Wetter?	*How is the weather?*
	Seid ihr in Köln gewesen?	*Have you been to Cologne?*

Negations

Negative sentences are formed by adding **nicht** (*not*) to that part of the sentence which is to be negated.

Examples:	**Wir rauchen nicht.**	We don't smoke.
	Der Bus fährt nicht ab.	The bus doesn't leave.
	Warum schreibst du nicht?	Why don't you write?

If a noun is used, the negation is made by adding **kein**. Its ending is defined by the noun's gender.

Examples:	**Ich trinke kein Bier.**	*I don't drink beer.*
	Wir haben keine Einzelzimmer.	*We don't have any single rooms.*
	Gibt es keinen Zimmerservice?	*Is there no room service?*

Imperatives (Command Form)

du *you sing. inform.*	**Geh!** *Go!*	**Sei still!** *Be quiet!*
ihr *you pl. inform.*	**Geht!** *Go!*	**Seid still!** *Be quiet!*
Sie *you sing./pl. form.*	**Gehen Sie!** *Go!*	**Seien Sie still!** *Be quiet!*
wir *we*	**Gehen wir!** *Let's go!*	**Seien wir still!** *Let's be quiet!*

Examples:	**Hört mal alle zu!**	*Listen everybody!*
	Seid nicht so laut!	*Don't be so noisy!*

Pronouns

Pronouns serve as substitutes for nouns and relate to their gender.

Nominative	***Accusative***	***Dative***
ich *I*	**mich** *me*	**mir** *me*
du *you inform.*	**dich** *you*	**dir** *you*
Sie *you form.*	**Sie** *you*	**Ihnen** *you*

er *he*	**ihn** *him*	**ihm** *him*
sie *she*	**sie** *her*	**ihr** *her*
es *it*	**es** *it*	**ihm** *him*
wir *we*	**uns** *us*	**uns** *us*
ihr *you pl. inform.*	**euch** *you*	**euch** *you*
Sie *you pl. form.*	**Sie** *you*	**Ihnen** *you*
sie *they*	**sie** *them*	**ihnen** *them*

Examples:	**Ich sehe sie.**	*I see them.*
	Hören Sie mich?	*Do you hear me?*

Adjectives

Adjectives describe nouns. Their endings depend on the case.

Examples:	**Wir haben ein altes Auto.**	*We have an old car.*
	Wo ist mein neuer Koffer?	*Where is my new suitcase?*
	Gute Arbeit, Richard!	*Good work, Richard!*

Adverbs and Adverbial Expressions

In German, adverbs are usually identical with adjectives. They describe verbs but, unlike adjectives, their endings don't change.

Examples:	**Linda fährt sehr langsam.**	*Linda drives very slowly.*
	Robert ist sehr nett.	*Robert is very nice.*
	Sie sprechen gut Deutsch.	*You speak German well.*

Some common adverbial time expressions:

zurzeit	*presently*
bald	*soon*
immer noch	*still*
nicht mehr	*not anymore*

Comparisons and Superlatives

Most German adjectives add **–er** for their comparative and **–(e)st** for their superlative. The following list contains only a small selection to illustrate formation and irregularities.

Adjective	*Comparative*	*Superlative*
klein *small, little*	**kleiner** *smaller*	**am kleinsten** *the smallest*
billig *cheap*	**billiger** *cheaper*	**am billigsten** *the cheapest*
neu *new*	**neuer** *newer*	**am neusten** *the newest*
schlecht *bad*	**schlechter** *worse*	**am schlechtesten** *the worst*
groß *big, large*	**größer** *bigger*	**am größten** *the biggest*
alt *old*	**älter** *older*	**am ältesten** *the oldest*
lang *long*	**länger** *longer*	**am längsten** *the longest*
kurz *short*	**kürzer** *shorter*	**am kürzesten** *the shortest*
gut *good*	**besser** *better*	**am besten** *the best*
teuer *expensive*	**teurer** *more expensive*	**am teuersten** *the most expensive*

Examples:	**Diese Postkarten sind billiger.**	*These postcards are cheaper.*
	Wo ist der beste Buchladen?	*Where is the best bookstore?*

A

A, a A, a *n*; ***from A to Z*** von A bis Z
A *grade* Eins
a *before vowel*: **an** *indef art* ein(e); per, pro, je; ***not a(n)*** kein(e); ***all of a size*** alle gleich groß; ***100 dollars a year*** 100 Dollar im Jahr; ***twice a week*** zweimal die *or* in der Woche
a·back: ***taken aback*** überrascht, verblüfft; bestürzt
a·ban·don aufgeben, preisgeben; verlassen; überlassen; ***be found abandoned*** MOT *etc* verlassen aufgefunden werden
a·base erniedrigen, demütigen
a·base·ment Erniedrigung *f*, Demütigung *f*
a·bashed verlegen
ab·at·toir *Br* Schlachthof *m*
ab·bess REL Äbtissin *f*
ab·bey REL Kloster *n*; Abtei *f*
ab·bot REL Abt *m*
ab·bre·vi·ate (ab)kürzen
ab·bre·vi·a·tion Abkürzung *f*, Kurzform *f*
ABC Abc *n*, Alphabet *n*
ab·di·cate *Amt*, *Recht etc* aufgeben, verzichten auf (*acc*); ***abdicate (from) the throne*** abdanken
ab·di·ca·tion Verzicht *m*; Abdankung *f*
ab·do·men ANAT Unterleib *m*
ab·dom·i·nal ANAT Unterleibs…
ab·duct JUR *j-n* entführen
ab·er·ra·tion Verirrung *f*
a·bet → ***aid 1***
ab·hor verabscheuen
ab·hor·rence Abscheu *m* (***of*** vor *dat*)
ab·hor·rent zuwider (***to*** *dat*); abstoßend
a·bide *v/i*: ***abide by the law*** *etc* sich an das Gesetz *etc* halten; *v/t*: ***he can't abide him*** er kann ihn nicht ausstehen
a·bil·i·ty Fähigkeit *f*
ab·ject verächtlich, erbärmlich; ***in abject poverty*** in äußerster Armut
ab·jure abschwören; entsagen (*dat*)
a·blaze in Flammen; *fig* glänzend, funkelnd (***with*** vor *dat*)
a·ble fähig; geschickt; ***be able to*** *inf* in der Lage sein zu *inf*, können
a·ble-bod·ied kräftig
ab·norm·al abnorm, ungewöhnlich; anomal
a·board an Bord; ***all aboard!*** MAR alle Mann *or* Reisenden an Bord!; RAIL alles einsteigen!; ***aboard a bus*** in e-m Bus; ***go aboard a train*** in e-n Zug einsteigen
a·bode *a.* ***place of abode*** Aufenthaltsort *m*, Wohnsitz *m*; ***of*** *or* ***with no fixed abode*** ohne festen Wohnsitz
a·bol·ish abschaffen, aufheben
ab·o·li·tion Abschaffung *f*, Aufhebung *f*
A-bomb → ***atom(ic) bomb***
a·bom·i·na·ble abscheulich, scheußlich
a·bom·i·nate verabscheuen
a·bom·i·na·tion Abscheu *m*
ab·o·rig·i·nal **1.** eingeboren, Ur…; **2.** Ureinwohner *m*
ab·o·rig·i·ne Ureinwohner *m*
a·bort *v/t* abbrechen (*a.* MED *Schwangerschaft*); MED *Kind* abtreiben; *v/i* fehlschlagen, scheitern; MED e-e Fehlgeburt haben
a·bor·tion MED Fehlgeburt *f*; Schwangerschaftsabbruch *m*, Abtreibung *f*; ***have an abortion*** abtreiben (lassen)
a·bor·tive misslungen, erfolglos
a·bound reichlich vorhanden sein; Überfluss haben, reich sein (***in*** an *dat*); voll sein (***with*** von)
a·bout **1.** *prp* um (… herum); bei (*dat*); (irgendwo) herum in (*dat*); um, gegen, etwa; im Begriff, dabei; über (*acc*); ***I had no money about me*** ich hatte kein Geld bei mir; **2.** *adv* herum, umher; in der Nähe; etwa, ungefähr
a·bove **1.** *prp* über (*dat or acc*), oberhalb (*gen*); *fig* über, erhaben über (*acc*); ***above all*** vor allem; **2.** *adv* oben; darüber; **3.** *adj* obig, oben erwähnt
a·breast nebeneinander; ***keep abreast of, be abreast of*** *fig* Schritt halten mit
a·bridge (ab-, ver)kürzen
a·bridg(e)·ment Kürzung *f*; Kurzfassung *f*
a·broad im *or* ins Ausland; überall(hin); ***the news soon spread abroad*** die Nachricht verbreitete sich rasch
a·brupt abrupt; jäh; schroff
ab·scess MED Abszess *m*
ab·sence Abwesenheit *f*; Mangel *m*
ab·sent **1.** abwesend; fehlend; nicht vorhanden; ***be absent*** fehlen (***from school*** in der Schule; ***from work*** am Arbeitsplatz); **2.** ***absent o.s. from*** fernbleiben (*dat*) *or* von
ab·sent-mind·ed zerstreut, geistesabwesend
ab·so·lute absolut; unumschränkt; vollkommen; unbedingt; CHEM rein, unvermischt
ab·so·lu·tion REL Absolution *f*

ab·solve freisprechen, lossprechen
ab·sorb absorbieren, aufsaugen, einsaugen; *fig* ganz in Anspruch nehmen
ab·sorb·ing *fig* fesselnd, packend
ab·stain sich enthalten (***from*** *gen*)
ab·ste·mi·ous enthaltsam; mäßig
ab·sten·tion Enthaltung *f*; POL Stimmenthaltung *f*
ab·sti·nence Abstinenz *f*, Enthaltsamkeit *f*
ab·sti·nent abstinent, enthaltsam
ab·stract **1.** abstrakt; **2.** *das* Abstrakte; Auszug *m*; **3.** abstrahieren; entwenden
ab·stract·ed *fig* zerstreut
ab·strac·tion Abstraktion *f*; abstrakter Begriff
ab·surd absurd; lächerlich
a·bun·dance Überfluss *m*; Fülle *f*; Überschwang *m*
a·bun·dant reich, reichlich
a·buse **1.** Missbrauch *m*; Beschimpfung(en *pl*) *f*; ***abuse of drugs*** Drogenmissbrauch *m*; ***abuse of power*** Machtmissbrauch *m*; **2.** missbrauchen; beschimpfen
a·bu·sive beleidigend, Schimpf…
a·but (an)grenzen (***on*** an *acc*)
a·byss Abgrund *m* (*a. fig*)
ac·a·dem·ic **1.** Hochschullehrer *m*; **2.** akademisch
a·cad·e·mi·cian Akademiemitglied *n*
a·cad·e·my Akademie *f*; ***academy of music*** Musikhochschule *f*
ac·cede: ***accede to*** zustimmen (*dat*); *Amt* antreten; *Thron* besteigen
ac·cel·e·rate *v/t* beschleunigen; *v/i* schneller werden, MOT *a.* beschleunigen, Gas geben
ac·cel·e·ra·tion Beschleunigung *f*
ac·cel·e·ra·tor MOT Gaspedal *n*
ac·cent **1.** Akzent *m* (*a.* LING); **2.** → **accen·tu·ate** akzentuieren, betonen
ac·cept annehmen; akzeptieren; hinnehmen
ac·cept·a·ble annehmbar; *person*: tragbar
ac·cept·ance Annahme *f*; Aufnahme *f*
ac·cess Zugang *m* (***to*** zu); *fig* Zutritt *m* (***to*** bei, zu); EDP Zugriff *m* (***to*** auf *acc*); ***easy of access*** zugänglich (*person*)
ac·ces·sa·ry → ***accessory***
ac·cess code EDP Zugriffskode *m*
ac·ces·si·ble (leicht) zugänglich
ac·ces·sion (Neu)Anschaffung *f* (***to*** für); Zustimmung *f* (***to*** zu); Antritt *m* (*e-s Amtes*); ***accession to power*** Machtübernahme *f*; ***accession to the throne*** Thronbesteigung *f*
ac·ces·so·ry JUR Komplize *m*, Komplizin *f*, Mitschuldige *m, f*; *mst pl* Zubehör *n*, *fashion*: *a.* Accessoires *pl*, TECH *a.* Zubehörteile *pl*
ac·cess road Zufahrts- *or* Zubringerstraße *f*
access time EDP Zugriffszeit *f*
ac·ci·dent Unfall *m*, Unglück *n*, Unglücksfall *m*; NUCL Störfall *m*; ***by accident*** zufällig
ac·ci·den·tal zufällig; versehentlich
ac·claim feiern (***as*** als)
ac·cla·ma·tion lauter Beifall; Lob *n*
ac·cli·ma·tize (sich) akklimatisieren *or* eingewöhnen
ac·com·mo·date unterbringen; Platz haben für, fassen; anpassen (***to*** *dat or* an *acc*)
ac·com·mo·da·tion Unterkunft *f*, Unterbringung *f*
accommodation of·fice Zimmervermittlung *f*
ac·com·pa·ni·ment MUS Begleitung *f*
ac·com·pa·ny begleiten (*a.* MUS)
ac·com·plice JUR Komplize *m*, Komplizin *f*, Helfershelfer(in)
ac·com·plish erreichen; leisten
ac·com·plished fähig, tüchtig
ac·com·plish·ment Fähigkeit *f*, Talent *n*
ac·cord **1.** Übereinstimmung *f*; ***of one's own accord*** von selbst; ***with one accord*** einstimmig; **2.** übereinstimmen (***with*** mit)
ac·cord·ance: ***in accordance with*** entsprechend (*dat*)
ac·cord·ing: ***according to*** laut; nach
ac·cord·ing·ly folglich, also; (dem)entsprechend
ac·cost *j-n* ansprechen
ac·count **1.** ECON Rechnung *f*, Berechnung *f*; Konto *n*; Rechenschaft *f*; Bericht *m*; ***by all accounts*** nach allem, was man so hört; ***of no account*** ohne Bedeutung; ***on no account*** auf keinen Fall; ***on account of*** wegen; ***take into account, take account of*** in Betracht *or* Erwägung ziehen, berücksichtigen; ***turn s.th. to (good) account*** et. (gut) ausnutzen; ***keep accounts*** die Bücher führen; ***call to account*** zur Rechenschaft ziehen; ***give (an) account of*** Rechenschaft ablegen über (*acc*); ***give an account of*** Bericht erstatten über (*acc*); **2.** *v/i*: ***account for*** Rechenschaft über *et.* ablegen; (sich) erklären
ac·count·a·ble verantwortlich; erklärlich
ac·coun·tant ECON Buchhalter(in)
ac·count·ing ECON Buchführung *f*
acct ABBR *of* ***account*** Konto *n*
ac·cu·mu·late (sich) (an)häufen *or* ansammeln

ac·cu·mu·la·tion Ansammlung *f*
ac·cu·mu·la·tor ELECTR Akkumulator *m*
ac·cu·ra·cy Genauigkeit *f*
ac·cu·rate genau
ac·cu·sa·tion Anklage *f*; Anschuldigung *f*, Beschuldigung *f*
ac·cu·sa·tive *a.* ***accusative case*** LING Akkusativ *m*
ac·cuse JUR anklagen; beschuldigen (***of*** *gen*); ***the accused*** der *or* die Angeklagte, die Angeklagten *pl*
ac·cus·er JUR Ankläger(in)
ac·cus·ing anklagend, vorwurfsvoll
ac·cus·tom gewöhnen (***to*** an *acc*)
ac·cus·tomed gewohnt, üblich; gewöhnt (***to*** an *acc*, zu *inf*)
ace Ass *n* (*a. fig*); ***have an ace in the hole*** (*Br* ***up one's sleeve***) *fig* (noch) e-n Trumpf in der Hand haben; ***within an ace*** um ein Haar
ache **1.** schmerzen, wehtun; **2.** *anhaltender* Schmerz
a·chieve zustande bringen; *Ziel* erreichen
a·chieve·ment Zustandebringen *n*, Leistung *f*, Ausführung *f*
ac·id **1.** sauer; *fig* beißend, bissig; **2.** CHEM Säure *f*
a·cid·i·ty Säure *f*
ac·id rain saurer Regen
ac·knowl·edge anerkennen; zugeben; *Empfang* bestätigen
ac·knowl·edg(e)·ment Anerkennung *f*; (Empfangs)Bestätigung *f*; Eingeständnis *n*
a·corn BOT Eichel *f*
a·cous·tics Akustik *f*
ac·quaint bekannt machen; ***acquaint s.o. with s.th.*** j-m et. mitteilen; ***be acquainted with*** kennen
ac·quaint·ance Bekanntschaft *f*; Bekannte *m*, *f*
ac·quire erwerben; sich aneignen
ac·qui·si·tion Erwerb *m*; Anschaffung *f*, Errungenschaft *f*
ac·quit JUR freisprechen (***of*** von); ***acquit o.s. well*** s-e Sache gut machen
ac·quit·tal JUR Freispruch *m*
a·cre Acre *m* (*4047 qm*)
ac·rid scharf, beißend
ac·ro·bat Akrobat(in)
ac·ro·bat·ic akrobatisch
a·cross **1.** *adv* hinüber, herüber; (quer) durch; drüben, auf der anderen Seite; über Kreuz; **2.** *prp* (quer) über (*acc*); (quer) durch; auf der anderen Seite von (*or gen*), jenseits (*gen*); über (*dat*); ***come across, run across*** *fig* stoßen auf (*acc*)
act **1.** *v/i* handeln; sich verhalten *or* benehmen; (ein)wirken; funktionieren; (Theater) spielen; *v/t* THEA spielen (*a. fig*), *Stück* aufführen; ***act as*** fungieren als; **2.** Handlung *f*, Tat *f*; JUR Gesetz *n*; THEA Akt *m*
act·ing THEA Spiel(en) *n*
ac·tion Handlung *f* (*a.* THEA), Tat *f*; *film etc*: Action *f*; Funktionieren *n*; (Ein-) Wirkung *f*; JUR Klage *f*, Prozess *m*; MIL Gefecht *n*, Einsatz *m*; ***take action*** handeln
ac·tive aktiv; tätig, rührig; lebhaft (*a.* ECON), rege; wirksam
ac·tiv·ist *esp* POL Aktivist(in)
ac·tiv·i·ty Tätigkeit *f*; Aktivität *f*; Betriebsamkeit *f*; *esp* ECON Lebhaftigkeit *f*
activity va·ca·tion Aktivurlaub *m*
ac·tor Schauspieler *m*
ac·tress Schauspielerin *f*
ac·tu·al wirklich, tatsächlich, eigentlich
ac·u·men Scharfsinn *m*
ac·u·punc·ture MED Akupunktur *f*
a·cute akut (*shortage, pain etc*); brennend (*problem etc*); scharf (*hearing etc*); scharfsinnig; MATH spitz (*angle*)
ad F → ***advertisement***
ad·a·mant unerbittlich
a·dapt anpassen (***to*** *dat or* an *acc*); *Text* bearbeiten (***from*** nach); TECH umstellen (***to*** auf *acc*); umbauen (***to*** für)
a·dapt·a·ble anpassungsfähig
ad·ap·ta·tion Anpassung *f*; Bearbeitung *f*
a·dapt·er, a·dapt·or ELECTR Adapter *m*
add *v/t* hinzufügen; ***add up*** zusammenzählen, addieren; *v/i*: ***add to*** vermehren, beitragen zu, hinzukommen zu; ***add up*** MATH ergeben; F sich summieren; *fig* e-n Sinn ergeben; ***add up to*** *fig* hinauslaufen auf (*acc*)
ad·der zo Natter *f*
ad·dict Süchtige *m*, *f*; ***alcohol*** (***drug***) ***addict*** Alkoholsüchtige (Drogen- *or* Rauschgiftsüchtige); (*Fußball- etc*) Fanatiker(in), (*Film- etc*)Narr *m*
ad·dic·ted süchtig, abhängig (***to*** von); ***be addicted to alcohol*** (***drugs***) alkoholsüchtig (drogenabhängig *or* -süchtig) sein
ad·dic·tion Sucht *f*, Süchtigkeit *f*
ad·di·tion Hinzufügen *n*; Zusatz *m*; Zuwachs *m*; ARCH Anbau *m*; MATH Addition *f*; ***in addition*** außerdem; ***in addition to*** außer (*dat*)
ad·di·tion·al zusätzlich
ad·dress **1.** *Worte* richten (***to*** an *acc*), *j-n* anreden *or* ansprechen; **2.** Adresse *f*, Anschrift *f*; Rede *f*, Ansprache *f*
ad·dress·ee Empfänger(in)
ad·ept erfahren, geschickt (***at, in*** in *dat*)

ad·e·qua·cy Angemessenheit *f*
ad·e·quate angemessen
ad·here (*to*) kleben, haften (an *dat*); *fig* festhalten (an *dat*)
ad·her·ence Anhaften *n*; *fig* Festhalten *n*
ad·her·ent Anhänger(in)
ad·he·sive **1.** klebend; **2.** Klebstoff *m*
adhesive plas·ter MED Heftpflaster *n*
adhesive tape Klebeband *n*, Klebstreifen *m*; MED Heftpflaster *n*
ad·ja·cent angrenzend, anstoßend (*to* an *acc*); benachbart
ad·jec·tive LING Adjektiv *n*, Eigenschaftswort *n*
ad·join (an)grenzen an (*acc*)
ad·journ *v/t* verschieben, (*v/i* sich) vertagen
ad·journ·ment Vertagung *f*, Verschiebung *f*
ad·just anpassen; TECH einstellen, regulieren
ad·just·a·ble TECH verstellbar, regulierbar
ad·just·ment Anpassung *f*; TECH Einstellung *f*
ad-lib aus dem Stegreif (sprechen *or* spielen)
ad·min·is·ter verwalten; PHARM geben, verabreichen; ***administer justice*** Recht sprechen
ad·min·is·tra·tion Verwaltung *f*; POL Regierung *f*; Amtsperiode *f*
ad·min·is·tra·tive Verwaltungs…
ad·min·is·tra·tor Verwaltungsbeamte *m*
ad·mi·ra·ble bewundernswert; großartig
ad·mi·ral MAR Admiral *m*
ad·mi·ra·tion Bewunderung *f*
ad·mire bewundern; verehren
ad·mir·er Verehrer *m*
ad·mis·si·ble zulässig
ad·mis·sion Eintritt *m*, Zutritt *m*; Aufnahme *f*; Eintrittsgeld *n*; Eingeständnis *n*; ***admission free*** Eintritt frei
ad·mit *v/t* zugeben; (her)einlassen (***to, into*** in *acc*), eintreten lassen; zulassen (***to*** zu)
ad·mit·tance Einlass *m*, Eintritt *m*, Zutritt *m*; ***no admittance*** Zutritt verboten
ad·mon·ish ermahnen; warnen (***of, against*** vor *dat*)
a·do Getue *n*, Lärm *m*; ***without more*** *or* ***further ado*** ohne weitere Umstände
ad·o·les·cence Jugend *f*, Adoleszenz *f*
ad·o·les·cent **1.** jugendlich, heranwachsend; **2.** Jugendliche *m*, *f*
a·dopt adoptieren; übernehmen; ***adopted child*** Adoptivkind *n*
a·dop·tion Adoption *f*
a·dop·tive par·ents Adoptiveltern *pl*
a·dor·a·ble F bezaubernd, entzückend
ad·o·ra·tion Anbetung *f*, Verehrung *f*
a·dore anbeten, verehren
a·dorn schmücken, zieren
a·dorn·ment Schmuck *m*, Verzierung *f*
a·droit geschickt
ad·ult **1.** erwachsen; **2.** Erwachsene *m*, *f*; ***adults only*** nur für Erwachsene!
adult ed·uca·tion Erwachsenenbildung *f*
a·dul·ter·ate verfälschen, *Wein* panschen
a·dul·ter·er Ehebrecher *m*
a·dul·ter·ess Ehebrecherin *f*
a·dul·ter·ous ehebrecherisch
a·dul·ter·y Ehebruch *m*
ad·vance **1.** *v/i* vordringen, vorrücken (*a. time*); Fortschritte machen; *v/t* vorrücken; *Termin etc* vorverlegen; *Argument etc* vorbringen; *Geld* vorstrecken, F vorschießen; (be)fördern; *Preis* erhöhen; *Wachstum etc* beschleunigen; **2.** Vorrücken *n*, Vorstoß *m* (*a. fig*); Fortschritt *m*; ECON Vorschuss *m*; Erhöhung *f*; ***in advance*** im Voraus
ad·vanced fortgeschritten; ***advanced for one's years*** weit *or* reif für sein Alter
ad·vance·ment Fortschritt *m*, Verbesserung *f*
ad·van·tage Vorteil *m* (*a.* SPORT); ***advantage rule*** SPORT Vorteilsregel *f*; ***take advantage of*** ausnutzen
ad·van·ta·geous vorteilhaft
ad·ven·ture Abenteuer *n*, Wagnis *n*
ad·ven·tur·er Abenteurer *m*
ad·ven·tur·ess Abenteu(r)erin *f*
ad·ven·tur·ous abenteuerlich; verwegen, kühn
ad·verb LING Adverb *n*, Umstandswort *n*
ad·ver·sa·ry Gegner(in)
ad·ver·tise ankündigen, bekannt machen; inserieren; Reklame machen (für)
ad·ver·tise·ment Anzeige *f*, Inserat *n*
ad·ver·tis·ing **1.** Reklame *f*, Werbung *f*; **2.** Reklame…, Werbe…
advertising a·gen·cy Werbeagentur *f*
advertising cam·paign Werbefeldzug *m*
ad·vice Rat(schlag) *m*; ECON Benachrichtigung *f*; ***take medical advice*** e-n Arzt zu Rate ziehen; ***take my advice*** hör auf mich
ad·vice cen·ter, *Br* **advice cen·tre** Beratungsstelle *f*
ad·vis·ab·le ratsam
ad·vise *v/t j-n* beraten; *j-m* raten; *esp* ECON benachrichtigen, avisieren; *v/i* sich beraten
ad·vis·er *esp Br*, **ad·vis·or** Berater *m*
ad·vi·so·ry beratend
ad·vo·cate **1.** befürworten, verfechten; **2.** Befürworter(in), Verfechter(in)
aer·i·al **1.** luftig; Luft…; **2.** Antenne *f*

aer·i·al pho·to·graph, aerial view Luftaufnahme *f*, Luftbild *n*
aer·o... Aero..., Luft...
aer·o·bics SPORT Aerobic *n*
aer·o·drome *esp Br* Flugplatz *m*
aer·o·dy·nam·ic aerodynamisch
aer·o·dy·nam·ics Aerodynamik *f*
aer·o·nau·tics Luftfahrt *f*
aer·o·plane *Br* Flugzeug *n*
aer·o·sol Spraydose *f*, Sprühdose *f*
aes·thet·ic *etc* → ***esthetic*** *etc*
a·far: ***from afar*** von weit her
af·fair Angelegenheit *f*, Sache *f*; F Ding *n*, Sache *f*; Affäre *f*
af·fect beeinflussen; MED angreifen, befallen; bewegen, rühren; e-e Vorliebe haben für; vortäuschen
af·fec·tion Liebe *f*, Zuneigung *f*
af·fec·tion·ate liebevoll, herzlich
af·fil·i·ate *als Mitglied* aufnehmen; angliedern
af·fin·i·ty Affinität *f*; (geistige) Verwandtschaft; Neigung *f* (***for, to*** zu)
af·firm versichern; beteuern; bestätigen
af·fir·ma·tion Versicherung *f*; Beteuerung *f*; Bestätigung *f*
af·fir·ma·tive **1.** bejahend; **2.** ***answer in the affirmative*** bejahen
af·fix (***to***) anheften, ankleben (an *acc*), befestigen (an *dat*); beifügen, hinzufügen (*dat*)
af·flict heimsuchen, plagen; ***afflicted with*** geplagt von, leidend an (*dat*)
af·flic·tion Gebrechen *n*; Elend *n*, Not *f*
af·flu·ence Überfluss *m*; Wohlstand *m*
af·flu·ent reich, reichlich
affluent so·ci·e·ty Wohlstandsgesellschaft *f*
af·ford sich leisten; gewähren, bieten; ***I can afford it*** ich kann es mir leisten
af·front **1.** beleidigen; **2.** Beleidigung *f*
a·float MAR flott, schwimmend; ***set afloat*** MAR flottmachen; *fig Gerücht etc* in Umlauf setzen
a·fraid: ***be afraid of*** sich fürchten *or* Angst haben vor (*dat*); ***I'm afraid she won't come*** ich fürchte, sie wird nicht kommen; ***I'm afraid I must go now*** leider muss ich jetzt gehen
a·fresh von neuem
Af·ri·ca Afrika *n*
Af·ri·can **1.** afrikanisch; **2.** Afrikaner(in)
af·ter **1.** *adv* hinterher, nachher, danach; **2.** *prp* nach; hinter (*dat*) (... her); ***after all*** schließlich (doch); **3.** *cj* nachdem; **4.** *adj* später; Nach...
after ef·fect MED Nachwirkung *f* (*a. fig*)
af·ter·glow Abendrot *n*
af·ter·math Nachwirkungen *pl*, Folgen *pl*
af·ter·noon Nachmittag *m*; ***this afternoon*** heute Nachmittag; ***good afternoon!*** guten Tag!
af·ter·taste Nachgeschmack *m*
af·ter·thought nachträglicher Einfall
af·ter·ward, *Br* **af·ter·wards** nachher, später
a·gain wieder; wiederum; ferner; ***again and again, time and again*** immer wieder; ***as much again*** noch einmal so viel
a·gainst gegen; an (*dat or acc*); ***as against*** verglichen mit; ***he was against it*** er war dagegen
age **1.** (Lebens)Alter *n*; Zeit(alter *n*) *f*; Menschenalter *n*; (***old***) ***age*** (hohes) Alter; ***at the age of*** im Alter von; *s.o.* ***your age*** in deinem *or* Ihrem Alter; (***come***) ***of age*** mündig *or* volljährig (werden); ***be over age*** die Altersgrenze überschritten haben; ***under age*** minderjährig; unmündig; ***wait for ages*** F e-e Ewigkeit warten; **2.** alt werden *or* machen
a·ged[1] alt, betagt
aged[2]: ***aged twenty*** 20 Jahre alt
age·less zeitlos; ewig jung
a·gen·cy Agentur *f*; Geschäftsstelle *f*, Büro *n*
a·gen·da Tagesordnung *f*
a·gent Agent *m* (*a.* POL), Vertreter *m*; (*Grundstücks- etc*)Makler *m*; CHEM Wirkstoff *m*, Mittel *n*
ag·glom·er·ate (sich) zusammenballen; (sich) (an)häufen
ag·gra·vate erschweren, verschlimmern; F ärgern
ag·gre·gate **1.** sich belaufen auf (*acc*); **2.** gesamt; **3.** Gesamtmenge *f*, Summe *f*; TECH Aggregat *n*
ag·gres·sion Angriff *m*
ag·gres·sive aggressiv, Angriffs...; *fig* energisch
ag·gres·sor Angreifer *m*
ag·grieved verletzt, gekränkt
a·ghast entgeistert, entsetzt
ag·ile flink, behend
a·gil·i·ty Flinkheit *f*, Behendigkeit *f*
ag·i·tate *v/t fig* aufregen, aufwühlen; *Flüssigkeit* schütteln; *v/i* POL agitieren, hetzen (***against*** gegen)
ag·i·ta·tion Aufregung *f*; POL Agitation *f*
ag·i·ta·tor POL Agitator *m*
a·glow: ***be aglow*** strahlen (***with*** vor)
a·go: ***a year ago*** vor e-m Jahr
ag·o·ny Qual *f*; Todeskampf *m*
a·gree *v/i* übereinstimmen; sich vertragen; einig werden, sich einigen (***on*** über *acc*); übereinkommen; ***agree to*** zustimmen (*dat*), einverstanden sein mit
a·gree·a·ble (***to***) angenehm (für); über-

einstimmend (mit)
a·gree·ment Übereinstimmung *f*; Vereinbarung *f*; Abkommen *n*
ag·ri·cul·tur·al landwirtschaftlich
ag·ri·cul·ture Landwirtschaft *f*
a·ground MAR gestrandet; ***run aground*** stranden, auf Grund laufen
a·head vorwärts, voraus; vorn; ***go ahead!*** nur zu!, mach nur!; ***straight ahead*** geradeaus
aid **1.** unterstützen, *j-m* helfen (***in*** bei); fördern; ***he was accused of aiding and abetting*** JUR er wurde wegen Beihilfe angeklagt; **2.** Hilfe *f*, Unterstützung *f*
AIDS, **Aids** MED Aids *n*; ***person with AIDS*** Aids-Kranke *m, f*
ail kränklich sein
ail·ment Leiden *n*
aim **1.** *v/i* zielen (***at*** auf *acc*, nach); ***aim at*** *fig* beabsichtigen; ***be aiming to do s.th.*** vorhaben, et. zu tun; *v/t*: ***aim at*** *Waffe etc* richten auf *or* gegen (*acc*); **2.** Ziel *n* (*a. fig*); Absicht *f*; ***take aim at*** zielen auf (*acc*) *or* nach
aim·less ziellos
air[1] **1.** Luft *f*; Luftzug *m*; Miene *f*, Aussehen *n*; ***by air*** auf dem Luftwege; ***in the open air*** im Freien; ***on the air*** im Rundfunk *or* Fernsehen; ***be on the air*** senden; in Betrieb sein; ***go off the air*** die Sendung beenden (*person*); sein Programm beenden (*station*); ***give o.s. airs, put on airs*** vornehm tun; **2.** (aus)lüften; *fig* an die Öffentlichkeit bringen; erörtern
air[2] MUS Arie *f*, Weise *f*, Melodie *f*
air·bag MOT Airbag *m*
air·base MIL Luftstützpunkt *m*
air·bed Luftmatratze *f*
air·borne AVIAT in der Luft; MIL Luftlande...
air·brake TECH Druckluftbremse *f*
air·bus AVIAT Airbus *m*, Großraumflugzeug *n*
air-con·di·tioned mit Klimaanlage
air-con·di·tion·ing Klimaanlage *f*
air·craft car·ri·er MAR, MIL Flugzeugträger *m*
air·field Flugplatz *m*
air force MIL Luftwaffe *f*
air host·ess AVIAT Stewardess *f*
air jack·et Schwimmweste *f*
air·lift AVIAT Luftbrücke *f*
air·line AVIAT Fluggesellschaft *f*
air·lin·er AVIAT Verkehrsflugzeug *n*
air·mail Luftpost *f*; ***by airmail*** mit Luftpost
air·man MIL Flieger *m*
air·plane Flugzeug *n*
air·pock·et AVIAT Luftloch *n*
air pol·lu·tion Luftverschmutzung *f*
air·port Flughafen *m*
air raid MIL Luftangriff *m*
air-raid pre·cau·tions MIL Luftschutz *m*
air-raid shel·ter MIL Luftschutzraum *m*
air route AVIAT Flugroute *f*
air·sick luftkrank
air·space Luftraum *m*
air·strip (behelfsmäßige) Start- und Landebahn
air ter·mi·nal Flughafenabfertigungsgebäude *n*
air·tight luftdicht
air time Sendezeit *f*
air traf·fic AVIAT Flugverkehr *m*
air-traf·fic con·trol AVIAT Flugsicherung *f*
air-traffic con·trol·ler AVIAT Fluglotse *m*
air·way AVIAT Fluggesellschaft *f*
air·wor·thy AVIAT flugtüchtig
air·y luftig
aisle ARCH Seitenschiff *n*; Gang *m*
a·jar halb offen, angelehnt
a·kin verwandt (***to*** mit)
a·lac·ri·ty Bereitwilligkeit *f*
a·larm **1.** Alarm(zeichen *n*) *m*; Wecker *m*; Angst *f*; **2.** alarmieren; beunruhigen
alarm clock Wecker *m*
al·bum Album *n* (*a. record*)
al·bu·mi·nous BIOL eiweißhaltig
al·co·hol Alkohol *m*
al·co·hol·ic **1.** alkoholisch; **2.** Alkoholiker(in)
al·co·hol·ism Alkoholismus *m*, Trunksucht *f*
a·lert **1.** wachsam; munter; **2.** Alarm *m*; Alarmbereitschaft *f*; ***on the alert*** auf der Hut; in Alarmbereitschaft; **3.** warnen (***to*** vor *dat*), alarmieren
al·ga BOT Alge *f*
al·ge·bra MATH Algebra *f*
al·i·bi JUR Alibi *n*
a·li·en **1.** ausländisch; fremd; **2.** Ausländer(in); Außerirdische *m, f*
a·li·en·ate veräußern; entfremden; *esp art*: verfremden
a·li·en·a·tion Entfremdung *f*; *esp art*: Verfremdung *f*
a·light **1.** in Flammen; **2.** aussteigen; absteigen, absitzen; zo sich niederlassen; AVIAT landen
a·lign (sich) ausrichten (***with*** nach)
a·like **1.** *adj* gleich; **2.** *adv* gleich, ebenso
al·i·men·ta·ry nahrhaft
alimentary ca·nal ANAT Verdauungskanal *m*
al·i·mo·ny JUR Unterhalt *m*
a·live lebendig; (noch) am Leben; lebhaft; ***alive and kicking*** gesund und munter; ***be alive with*** wimmeln von

all 1. *adj* all; ganz; jede(r, -s); 2. *pron* alles; alle *pl*; 3. *adv* ganz, völlig; ***all at once*** auf einmal; ***all the better*** desto besser; ***all but*** beinahe, fast; ***all in*** F fertig, ganz erledigt; ***all right*** in Ordnung; ***for all that*** dessen ungeachtet, trotzdem; ***for all I know*** soviel ich weiß; ***at all*** überhaupt; ***not at all*** überhaupt nicht; ***the score was two all*** das Spiel stand zwei zu zwei
all-A·mer·i·can typisch amerikanisch; die ganzen USA vertretend
al·lay beruhigen; lindern
al·le·ga·tion *unerwiesene* Behauptung
al·lege behaupten
al·leged angeblich, vermeintlich
al·le·giance Treue *f*
al·ler·gic MED allergisch (***to*** gegen)
al·ler·gy MED Allergie *f*
al·le·vi·ate mildern, lindern
al·ley (enge *or* schmale) Gasse; Garten-, Parkweg *m*; *bowling*: Bahn *f*
al·li·ance Bündnis *n*
al·li·ga·tor zo Alligator *m*
al·lo·cate zuteilen, anweisen
al·lo·ca·tion Zuteilung *f*
al·lot zuteilen, an-, zuweisen
al·lot·ment Zuteilung *f*; Parzelle *f*
al·low erlauben, bewilligen, gewähren; zugeben; ab-, anrechnen, vergüten; ***allow for*** einplanen, berücksichtigen (*acc*)
al·low·a·ble erlaubt, zulässig
al·low·ance Erlaubnis *f*; Bewilligung *f*; Taschengeld *n*, Zuschuss *m*; Vergütung *f*; *fig* Nachsicht *f*; ***make allowance(s) for s.th.*** et. berücksichtigen
al·loy TECH 1. Legierung *f*; 2. legieren
all-round vielseitig
all·round·er Alleskönner *m*; Allroundsportler *m*, -spieler *m*
al·lude anspielen (***to*** auf *acc*)
al·lure locken, an-, verlocken
al·lure·ment Verlockung *f*
al·lu·sion Anspielung *f*
all-wheel drive MOT Allradantrieb *m*
al·ly 1. (sich) vereinigen, verbünden (***to, with*** mit); 2. Verbündete *m, f*, Bundesgenosse *m*, Bundesgenossin *f*; ***the Allies*** MIL die Alliierten *pl*
al·might·y allmächtig; ***the Almighty*** REL der Allmächtige
al·mond BOT Mandel *f*
al·most fast, beinah(e)
alms Almosen *n*
a·loft (hoch) (dr)oben
a·lone allein; ***let alone, leave alone*** in Ruhe lassen, bleiben lassen; ***let alone ...*** geschweige denn ...
a·long 1. *adv* weiter, vorwärts; da; dahin; ***all along*** die ganze Zeit; ***along with*** (zusammen) mit; ***come along*** mitkommen, mitgehen; ***get along*** vorwärtskommen, weiterkommen; auskommen, sich vertragen (***with s.o.*** mit j-m); ***take along*** mitnehmen; 2. *prp* entlang (*dat*), längs (*gen*)
a·long·side Seite an Seite; neben
a·loof abseits; reserviert, zurückhaltend, verschlossen
a·loof·ness Reserviertheit *f*; Verschlossenheit *f*
a·loud laut
al·pha·bet Alphabet *n*
al·pine (Hoch)Gebirgs..., alpin
al·read·y bereits, schon
al·right → ***all right***
Al·sa·tian *esp Br* zo Deutscher Schäferhund
al·so auch, ferner
al·tar REL Altar *m*
al·ter ändern, sich (ver)ändern; ab-, umändern
al·ter·a·tion Änderung *f* (***to*** an *dat*), Veränderung *f*
al·ter·nate 1. abwechseln (lassen); 2. abwechselnd
al·ter·nat·ing cur·rent ELECTR Wechselstrom *m*
al·ter·na·tion Abwechslung *f*; Wechsel *m*
al·ter·na·tive 1. alternativ, wahlweise; 2. Alternative *f*, Wahl *f*, Möglichkeit *f*
al·though obwohl, obgleich
al·ti·tude Höhe *f*; ***at an altitude of*** in e-r Höhe von
al·to·geth·er im Ganzen, insgesamt; ganz (und gar), völlig
al·u·min·i·um *Br*, **a·lu·mi·num** Aluminium *n*
al·ways immer, stets
am, AM ABBR *of* ***before noon*** (*Latin* ***ante meridiem***) morgens, vorm., vormittags
a·mal·gam·ate (sich) zusammenschließen, ECON *a.* fusionieren
a·mass anhäufen, aufhäufen
am·a·teur Amateur(in); Dilettant(in); Hobby...
a·maze in Erstaunen setzen, verblüffen
a·maze·ment Staunen *n*, Verblüffung *f*
a·maz·ing erstaunlich
am·bas·sa·dor POL Botschafter *m* (***to*** in *e-m Land*)
am·bas·sa·dress POL Botschafterin *f* (***to*** in *e-m Land*)
am·ber Bernstein *m*
am·bi·gu·i·ty Zwei-, Mehrdeutigkeit *f*
am·big·u·ous zwei-, mehr-, vieldeutig
am·bi·tion Ehrgeiz *m*
am·bi·tious ehrgeizig, strebsam
am·ble 1. Passgang *m*; 2. im Passgang gehen *or* reiten; schlendern

am·bu·lance Krankenwagen *m*
am·bush 1. Hinterhalt *m*; ***be** or **lie in ambush for s.o.*** j-m auflauern; **2.** auflauern (*dat*); überfallen
a·men *int* REL amen
a·mend verbessern, berichtigen; PARL abändern, ergänzen
a·mend·ment Bess(e)rung *f*; Verbesserung *f*; PARL Abänderungsantrag *m*, Ergänzungsantrag *m*; Zusatzartikel *m* zur Verfassung
a·mends (Schaden)Ersatz *m*; ***make amends*** Schadenersatz leisten, es wieder gutmachen; ***make amends to s.o. for s.th.*** j-n für et. entschädigen
a·men·i·ty *often pl* Annehmlichkeiten *pl*
A·mer·i·ca Amerika *n*
A·mer·i·can 1. amerikanisch; **2.** Amerikaner(in)
A·mer·i·can·is·m LING Amerikanismus *m*
A·mer·i·can·ize (sich) amerikanisieren
A·mer·i·can plan Vollpension *f*
a·mi·a·ble liebenswürdig, freundlich
am·i·ca·ble freundschaftlich, *a.* JUR gütlich
a·mid(st) inmitten (*gen*), (mitten) in *or* unter
a·miss verkehrt, falsch, übel; ***take s.th. amiss*** et. übel nehmen, et. verübeln
am·mo·ni·a CHEM Ammoniak *n*
am·mu·ni·tion Munition *f*
am·nes·ty JUR **1.** Amnestie *f*; **2.** begnadigen
a·mok: ***run amok*** Amok laufen
a·mong(st) (mitten) unter, zwischen
am·o·rous verliebt
a·mount 1. (**to**) sich belaufen (auf *acc*); hinauslaufen (auf *acc*); **2.** Betrag *m*, (Gesamt)Summe *f*; Menge *f*
am·per·age ELECTR Stromstärke *f*
am·ple weit, groß, geräumig; reich, reichlich, beträchtlich
am·pli·fi·ca·tion Erweiterung *f*; PHYS Verstärkung *f*
am·pli·fi·er ELECTR Verstärker *m*
am·pli·fy erweitern; ELECTR verstärken
am·pli·tude Umfang *m*, Weite *f*, Fülle *f*; ELECTR, PHYS Amplitude *f*
am·pu·tate MED amputieren
a·muck → ***amok***
a·muse (**o.s.** sich) amüsieren, unterhalten, belustigen
a·muse·ment Unterhaltung *f*, Vergnügen *n*, Zeitvertreib *m*
amusement park Vergnügungspark *m*, Freizeitpark *m*
a·mus·ing amüsant, unterhaltend
an → ***a***
an·a·bol·ic ster·oid PHARM Anabolikum *n*
a·nae·mi·a *Br* → ***anemia***
an·aes·thet·ic *Br* → ***anesthetic***
a·nal ANAT anal, Anal…
a·nal·o·gous analog, entsprechend
a·nal·o·gy Analogie *f*, Entsprechung *f*
an·a·lyse *esp Br*, **an·a·lyze** analysieren; zerlegen
a·nal·y·sis Analyse *f*
an·arch·y Anarchie *f*, Gesetzlosigkeit *f*; Chaos *n*
a·nat·o·mize MED zerlegen; zergliedern
a·nat·o·my MED Anatomie *f*; Zergliederung *f*, Analyse *f*
an·ces·tor Vorfahr *m*, Ahn *m*
an·ces·tress Vorfahrin *f*, Ahnfrau *f*
an·chor MAR **1.** Anker *m*; ***at anchor*** vor Anker; **2.** verankern
an·chor·man TV Moderator *m*
an·chor·wom·an TV Moderatorin *f*
an·cho·vy ZO Anschovis *f*, Sardelle *f*
an·cient 1. alt, antik; uralt; **2.** ***the ancients*** HIST die Alten, die antiken Klassiker
and und
an·ec·dote Anekdote *f*
a·ne·mi·a MED Blutarmut *f*, Anämie *f*
an·es·thet·ic MED **1.** betäubend, Narkose…; **2.** Betäubungsmittel *n*
an·gel Engel *m*
an·ger 1. Zorn *m*, Ärger *m* (**at** über *acc*); **2.** erzürnen, (ver)ärgern
an·gle[1] Winkel *m* (*a.* MATH)
an·gle[2] angeln (**for** nach)
an·gler Angler(in)
An·gli·can REL **1.** anglikanisch; **2.** Anglikaner(in)
An·glo-Sax·on 1. angelsächsisch; **2.** Angelsachse *m*
an·gry zornig, verärgert, böse (**at, with** über *acc*, mit *dat*)
an·guish Qual *f*, Schmerz *m*
an·gu·lar winkelig; knochig
an·i·mal 1. Tier *n*; **2.** tierisch
animal lov·er Tierfreund *m*
animal shel·ter Tierheim *n*
an·i·mate beleben; aufmuntern, anregen
an·i·mat·ed lebendig; lebhaft, angeregt
animated car·toon Zeichentrickfilm *m*
an·i·ma·tion Lebhaftigkeit *f*; Animation *f*, Herstellung *f* von (Zeichen-)Trickfilmen; EDP bewegtes Bild
an·i·mos·i·ty Animosität *f*, Feindseligkeit *f*
an·kle ANAT (Fuß)Knöchel *m*
an·nals Jahrbücher *pl*
an·nex 1. anhängen; annektieren; **2.** Anhang *m*; ARCH Anbau *m*
an·ni·ver·sa·ry Jahrestag *m*; Jahresfeier *f*
an·no·tate mit Anmerkungen versehen;

kommentieren
an·nounce ankündigen; bekannt geben; *radio*, TV ansagen; durchsagen
an·nounce·ment Ankündigung *f*; Bekanntgabe *f*; *radio*, TV Ansage *f*; Durchsage *f*
an·nounc·er *radio*, TV Ansager(in), Sprecher(in)
an·noy ärgern; belästigen
an·noy·ance Störung *f*, Belästigung *f*; Ärgernis *n*
an·noy·ing ärgerlich, lästig
an·nu·al **1.** jährlich, Jahres…; **2.** einjährige Pflanze; Jahrbuch *n*
an·nu·i·ty (Jahres)Rente *f*
an·nul für ungültig erklären, annullieren
an·nul·ment Annullierung *f*, Aufhebung *f*
an·o·dyne MED **1.** schmerzstillend; **2.** schmerzstillendes Mittel
a·noint REL salben
a·nom·a·lous anomal
a·non·y·mous anonym
an·o·rak Anorak *m*
an·oth·er ein anderer; ein Zweiter; noch eine(r, -s)
an·swer **1.** *v/t et.* beantworten; *j-m* antworten; entsprechen (*dat*); *Zweck* erfüllen; TECH *dem Steuer* gehorchen; JUR *e-r Vorladung* Folge leisten; *e-r Beschreibung* entsprechen; ***answer the bell*** *or* ***door*** (die Tür) aufmachen; ***answer the telephone*** ans Telefon gehen; *v/i* antworten (***to*** auf *acc*); entsprechen (***to*** *dat*); ***answer s.o. back*** freche Antworten geben; widersprechen; ***answer for*** einstehen für; **2.** Antwort *f* (***to*** auf *acc*)
an·swer·a·ble verantwortlich
an·swer·ing ma·chine TEL Anrufbeantworter *m*
ant ZO Ameise *f*
an·tag·o·nism Feindschaft *f*
an·tag·o·nist Gegner(in)
an·tag·o·nize bekämpfen; sich *j-n* zum Feind machen
Ant·arc·tic antarktisch
an·te·ced·ent vorhergehend, früher (***to*** als)
an·te·lope ZO Antilope *f*
an·ten·na[1] ZO Fühler *m*
an·ten·na[2] ELECTR Antenne *f*
an·te·ri·or vorhergehend, früher (***to*** als); vorder
an·them MUS Hymne *f*
an·ti… Gegen…, gegen … eingestellt, Anti…, anti…
an·ti·air·craft MIL Fliegerabwehr…, Flugabwehr…
an·ti·bi·ot·ic MED Antibiotikum *n*
an·ti·bod·y BIOL Antikörper *m*, Abwehrstoff *m*
an·tic·i·pate voraussehen, ahnen; erwarten; zuvorkommen; vorwegnehmen
an·tic·i·pa·tion (Vor)Ahnung *f*; Erwartung *f*; Vorwegnahme *f*; Vorfreude *f*; ***in anticipation*** im Voraus
an·ti·clock·wise *Br* entgegen dem Uhrzeigersinn
an·tics Mätzchen *pl*
an·ti·dote Gegengift *n*, Gegenmittel *n*
an·ti-for·eign·er vi·o·lence Gewalt *f* gegen Ausländer
an·ti·freeze Frostschutzmittel *n*
an·ti-lock brak·ing sys·tem MOT Antiblockiersystem *n* (ABBR ***ABS***)
an·ti·mis·sile MIL Raketenabwehr…
an·ti·nu·cle·ar ac·tiv·ist Kernkraftgegner(in)
an·tip·a·thy Abneigung *f*
an·ti·quat·ed veraltet
an·tique **1.** antik, alt; **2.** Antiquität *f*
an·tique deal·er Antiquitätenhändler(in)
antique shop *esp Br*, **antique store** Antiquitätenladen *m*
an·tiq·ui·ty Altertum *n*, Vorzeit *f*
an·ti·sep·tic MED **1.** antiseptisch; **2.** antiseptisches Mittel
ant·lers ZO Geweih *n*
a·nus ANAT After *m*
an·vil Amboss *m*
anx·i·e·ty Angst *f*, Sorge *f*
anx·ious besorgt, beunruhigt (***about*** wegen); begierig, gespannt (***for*** auf *acc*); bestrebt (***to do*** zu tun)
an·y **1.** *adj and pron* (irgend)eine(r, -s), (irgend)welche(r, -s); (irgend)etwas; jede(r, -s) (beliebige); einige *pl*, welche *pl*; ***not any*** keiner; **2.** *adv* irgend(wie), ein wenig, (noch) etwas
an·y·bod·y (irgend)jemand; jeder
an·y·how irgendwie; trotzdem, jedenfalls; wie dem auch sei
an·y·one → ***anybody***
an·y·thing (irgend)etwas; alles; ***anything but*** alles andere als; ***anything else?*** sonst noch etwas?; ***not anything*** nichts
an·y·way → ***anyhow***
an·y·where irgendwo(hin); überall
a·part einzeln, für sich; beiseite; ***apart from*** abgesehen von
a·part·heid POL Apartheid *f*, Politik *f* der Rassentrennung
a·part·ment Wohnung *f*
apartment build·ing, **apartment house** Mietshaus *n*
ap·a·thet·ic apathisch, teilnahmslos, gleichgültig
ap·a·thy Apathie *f*, Teilnahmslosigkeit *f*

ape ZO (Menschen)Affe *m*
ap·er·ture Öffnung *f*
a·pi·a·ry Bienenhaus *n*
a·piece für jedes Stück, pro Stück, je
a·pol·o·gize sich entschuldigen (***for*** für; ***to*** bei)
a·pol·o·gy Entschuldigung *f*; Rechtfertigung *f*; ***make an apology*** (***for s.th.***) sich (für et.) entschuldigen
ap·o·plex·y MED Schlaganfall *m*, F Schlag *m*
a·pos·tle REL Apostel *m*
a·pos·tro·phe LING Apostroph *m*
ap·pal(l) erschrecken, entsetzen
ap·pal·ling erschreckend, entsetzlich
ap·pa·ra·tus Apparat *m*, Vorrichtung *f*, Gerät *n*
ap·par·ent offenbar; anscheinend; scheinbar
ap·pa·ri·tion Erscheinung *f*, Gespenst *n*
ap·peal **1.** JUR Berufung *or* Revision einlegen, Einspruch erheben, Beschwerde einlegen; appellieren, sich wenden (***to*** an *acc*); ***appeal to*** gefallen (*dat*), zusagen (*dat*), wirken auf (*acc*); *j-n* dringend bitten (***for*** um); **2.** JUR Revision *f*, Berufung *f*; Beschwerde *f*; Einspruch *m*; Appell *m* (***to*** an *acc*), Aufruf *m*; Wirkung *f*, Reiz *m*; Bitte *f* (***to*** an *acc*; ***for*** um); ***appeal for mercy*** JUR Gnadengesuch *n*
ap·peal·ing flehend; ansprechend
ap·pear (er)scheinen; sich zeigen; *öffentlich* auftreten; sich ergeben *or* herausstellen
ap·pear·ance Erscheinen *n*; Auftreten *n*; Äußere *n*, Erscheinung *f*, Aussehen *n*; Anschein *m*, äußerer Schein; ***keep up appearances*** den Schein wahren; ***to*** *or* ***by all appearances*** allem Anschein nach
ap·pease besänftigen, beschwichtigen; *Durst etc* stillen; *Neugier* befriedigen
ap·pend an-, hinzu-, beifügen
ap·pend·age Anhang *m*; Anhängsel *n*
ap·pen·di·ci·tis MED Blinddarmentzündung *f*
ap·pen·dix Anhang *m*; *a.* ***vermiform appendix*** ANAT Wurmfortsatz *m*, Blinddarm *m*
ap·pe·tite (***for***) Appetit *m* (auf *acc*); *fig* Verlangen *n* (nach)
ap·pe·tiz·er Appetithappen *m*, appetitanregendes Gericht *or* Getränk
ap·pe·tiz·ing appetitanregend
ap·plaud applaudieren, Beifall spenden; loben
ap·plause Applaus *m*, Beifall *m*
ap·ple BOT Apfel *m*
ap·ple cart: ***upset s.o.'s apple cart*** F j-s Pläne über den Haufen werfen
ap·ple pie (*warmer*) gedeckter Apfelkuchen
ap·ple·pie or·der: F ***in applepie order*** in schönster Ordnung
ap·ple sauce Apfelmus *n*; *sl* Schmus *m*, Quatsch *m*
ap·pli·ance Vorrichtung *f*; Gerät *n*; Mittel *n*
ap·plic·a·ble anwendbar (***to*** auf *acc*)
ap·pli·cant Antragsteller(in), Bewerber(in) (***for*** um)
ap·pli·ca·tion Anwendung *f* (***to*** auf *acc*); Bedeutung *f* (***to*** für); Gesuch *n* (***for*** um); Bewerbung *f* (***for*** um)
ap·ply *v/t* (***to***) (auf)legen, auftragen (auf *acc*); anwenden (auf *acc*); verwenden (für); ***apply o.s. to*** sich widmen (*dat*); *v/i* (***to***) passen, zutreffen, sich anwenden lassen (auf *acc*); gelten (für); sich wenden (an *acc*); ***apply for*** sich bewerben um, *et.* beantragen
ap·point bestimmen, festsetzen; verabreden; ernennen (***s.o.*** *governor* j-n zum ...); berufen (***to*** auf *e-n Posten*)
ap·point·ment Bestimmung *f*; Verabredung *f*; Termin *m*; Ernennung *f*, Berufung *f*; Stelle *f*
appointment book Terminkalender *m*
ap·por·tion verteilen, zuteilen
ap·prais·al (Ab)Schätzung *f*
ap·praise (ab)schätzen, taxieren
ap·pre·cia·ble nennenswert, spürbar
ap·pre·ci·ate *v/t* schätzen, würdigen; dankbar sein für; *v/i* im Wert steigen
ap·pre·ci·a·tion Würdigung *f*; Dankbarkeit *f*; (richtige) Beurteilung; ECON Wertsteigerung *f*
ap·pre·hend ergreifen, fassen; begreifen; befürchten
ap·pre·hen·sion Ergreifung *f*, Festnahme *f*; Besorgnis *f*
ap·pre·hen·sive ängstlich, besorgt (***for*** um; ***that*** dass)
ap·pren·tice **1.** Auszubildende *m, f*, Lehrling *m*, *Swiss* Lehrtochter *f*; **2.** in die Lehre geben
ap·pren·tice·ship Lehrzeit *f*, Lehre *f*, Ausbildung *f*
ap·proach **1.** *v/i* näher kommen, sich nähern; *v/t* sich nähern (*dat*); herangehen *or* herantreten an (*acc*); **2.** (Heran)Nahen *n*; Einfahrt *f*, Zufahrt *f*, Auffahrt *f*; Annäherung *f*; Methode *f*
ap·pro·ba·tion Billigung *f*, Beifall *m*
ap·pro·pri·ate **1.** sich aneignen; verwenden; PARL bewilligen; **2.** (***for, to***) angemessen (*dat*), passend (für, zu)
ap·prov·al Billigung *f*; Anerkennung *f*,

Beifall *m*
ap·prove billigen, anerkennen
ap·proved bewährt
ap·prox·i·mate annähernd, ungefähr
a·pri·cot BOT Aprikose *f*
A·pril (ABBR ***Apr***) April *m*
a·pron Schürze *f*
apron strings: ***be tied to one's mother's apron strings*** an Mutters Schürzenzipfel hängen
apt geeignet, passend; treffend; begabt; ***apt to*** geneigt zu
ap·ti·tude (***for***) Begabung *f* (für), Befähigung *f* (für), Talent *n* (zu)
ap·ti·tude test Eignungsprüfung *f*
aq·ua·plan·ing *Br* MOT Aquaplaning *n*
a·quar·i·um Aquarium *n*
A·quar·i·us ASTR Wassermann *m*; ***he*** (***she***) ***is*** (***an***) ***Aquarius*** er (sie) ist (ein) Wassermann
a·quat·ic Wasser…
a·quat·ic plant Wasserpflanze *f*
a·quat·ics, **a·quat·ic sports** Wassersport *m*
aq·ue·duct Aquädukt *m*
Ar·ab Araber(in)
A·ra·bi·a Arabien *n*
Ar·a·bic **1.** arabisch; **2.** LING Arabisch *n*
ar·a·ble AGR anbaufähig; Acker…
ar·bi·tra·ry willkürlich, eigenmächtig
ar·bi·trate entscheiden, schlichten
ar·bi·tra·tion Schlichtung *f*
ar·bi·tra·tor Schiedsrichter *m*; Schlichter *m*
ar·bo(u)r Laube *f*
arc Bogen *m*; ELECTR Lichtbogen *m*
ar·cade Arkade *f*; Lauben-, Bogengang *m*; Durchgang *m*, Passage *f*
arch[1] **1.** Bogen *m*; Gewölbe *n*; **2.** (sich) wölben; krümmen
arch[2] erste(r, -s), oberste(r, -s), Haupt…, Erz…
arch[3] schelmisch
ar·cha·ic veraltet
arch·an·gel Erzengel *m*
arch·bish·op REL Erzbischof *m*
ar·cher Bogenschütze *m*
ar·cher·y Bogenschießen *n*
ar·chi·tect Architekt(in)
ar·chi·tec·ture Architektur *f*
ar·chives Archiv *n*
arch·way (Bogen)Gang *m*
arc·tic arktisch, nördlich, Polar…
ar·dent feurig, glühend; *fig* leidenschaftlich, heftig; eifrig
ar·do(u)r Leidenschaft *f*, Glut *f*, Feuer *n*; Eifer *m*
are *du* bist, *wir or sie or Sie* sind, *ihr* seid
ar·e·a (Boden)Fläche *f*; Gegend *f*, Gebiet *n*; Bereich *m*
ar·e·a code TEL Vorwahl(nummer) *f*
Ar·gen·ti·na Argentinien *n*
Ar·gen·tine **1.** argentinisch; **2.** Argentinier(in)
a·re·na Arena *f*
ar·gue argumentieren; streiten; diskutieren
ar·gu·ment Argument *n*; Wortwechsel *m*, Auseinandersetzung *f*
ar·id dürr, trocken (*a. fig*)
Ar·ies ASTR Widder *m*; ***he*** (***she***) ***is*** (***an***) ***Aries*** er (sie) ist (ein) Widder
a·rise entstehen; auftauchen, auftreten
ar·is·toc·ra·cy Aristokratie *f*, Adel *m*
ar·is·to·crat Aristokrat(in), Adlige *m, f*
ar·is·to·crat·ic aristokratisch, adlig
a·rith·me·tic[1] Rechnen *n*
ar·ith·met·ic[2] arithmetisch, Rechen…
ar·ith·met·ic u·nit EDP Rechenwerk *n*
ark Arche *f*; ***Noah's ark*** die Arche Noah
arm[1] ANAT Arm *m*; Armlehne *f*; ***keep s.o. at arm's length*** sich j-n vom Leibe halten
arm[2] MIL (sich) bewaffnen; (auf)rüsten
ar·ma·ment MIL Bewaffnung *f*; Aufrüstung *f*
arm·chair Lehnstuhl *m*, Sessel *m*
ar·mi·stice MIL Waffenstillstand *m*
ar·mo(u)r **1.** MIL Rüstung *f*, Panzer *m* (*a. fig*, ZO); **2.** panzern
ar·mo(u)red car gepanzertes Fahrzeug
arm·pit ANAT Achselhöhle *f*
arms Waffen *pl*; Waffengattung *f*
arms con·trol Rüstungskontrolle *f*
arms race Wettrüsten *n*, Rüstungswettlauf *m*
ar·my MIL Armee *f*, Heer *n*
a·ro·ma Aroma *n*, Duft *m*
ar·o·mat·ic aromatisch, würzig
a·round **1.** *adv* (rings)herum, (rund-) herum, ringsumher, überall; umher, herum; in der Nähe; da; **2.** *prp* um, um… herum, rund um; in (*dat*) … herum; ungefähr, etwa
a·rouse (auf)wecken; *fig* aufrütteln, erregen
ar·range (an)ordnen; festlegen, festsetzen; arrangieren (*a.* MUS); vereinbaren; MUS, THEA bearbeiten
ar·range·ment Anordnung *f*; Vereinbarung *f*; Vorkehrung *f*; MUS Arrangement *n*, Bearbeitung *f* (*a.* THEA)
ar·rears Rückstand *m*, Rückstände *pl*
ar·rest JUR **1.** Verhaftung *f*, Festnahme *f*; **2.** verhaften, festnehmen
ar·riv·al Ankunft *f*; Erscheinen *n*; Ankömmling *m*; ***arrivals*** AVIAT, RAIL *etc* 'Ankunft' (*timetable*)

ar·rive (an)kommen, eintreffen, erscheinen; ***arrive at*** *fig* erreichen (*acc*), kommen zu
ar·ro·gance Arroganz *f*, Überheblichkeit *f*
ar·ro·gant arrogant, überheblich
ar·row Pfeil *m*
ar·row·head Pfeilspitze *f*
ar·se·nic CHEM Arsen *n*
ar·son JUR Brandstiftung *f*
art **1.** Kunst *f*; **2.** Kunst…; ***art exhibition*** Kunstausstellung *f*; → ***arts***
ar·ter·i·al ANAT Schlagader…
ar·te·ri·al road Hauptverkehrsstraße *f*, Verkehrsader *f*
ar·ter·i·o·scle·ro·sis MED Arteriosklerose *f*, Arterienverkalkung *f*
ar·te·ry ANAT Arterie *f*, Schlagader *f*; (Haupt)Verkehrsader *f*
art·ful schlau, verschmitzt
art gal·le·ry Gemäldegalerie *f*
ar·thri·tis MED Arthritis *f*, Gelenkentzündung *f*
ar·ti·choke BOT Artischocke *f*
ar·ti·cle Artikel *m* (*a.* LING)
ar·tic·u·late **1.** deutlich (aus)sprechen; **2.** deutlich ausgesprochen; gegliedert
ar·tic·u·lat·ed Gelenk…; ***articulated lorry*** *Br* MOT Sattelschlepper *m*
ar·tic·u·la·tion (deutliche) Aussprache; TECH Gelenk *n*
ar·ti·fi·cial künstlich, Kunst…; ***artificial person*** juristische Person
ar·til·le·ry MIL Artillerie *f*
ar·ti·san Handwerker *m*
art·ist Künstler(in)
ar·tis·tic künstlerisch, Kunst…
art·less schlicht; naiv
arts Geisteswissenschaften *pl*; ***Arts Department***, *Br* ***Faculty of Arts*** philosophische Fakultät
as **1.** *adv* so, ebenso; wie; als; **2.** *cj* (gerade) wie, so wie; ebenso wie; als, während; obwohl, obgleich; da, weil; ***as … as*** (eben)so … wie; ***as for, as to*** was … (an-)betrifft; ***as from*** von *e-m Zeitpunkt* an, ab; ***as it were*** sozusagen; ***as Hamlet*** THEA als Hamlet
as·bes·tos Asbest *m*
as·cend (auf)steigen; ansteigen; besteigen
as·cen·dan·cy, as·cen·den·cy Überlegenheit *f*; Einfluss *m*
as·cen·sion Aufsteigen *n* (*esp* ASTR); Aufstieg *m*
As·cen·sion (Day) REL Himmelfahrt(stag *m*) *f*
as·cent Aufstieg *m*; Besteigung *f*; Steigung *f*
as·cet·ic asketisch
a·sep·tic MED **1.** aseptisch, keimfrei; **2.** aseptisches Mittel
ash[1] BOT Esche *f*; Eschenholz *n*
ash[2] *a.* ***ashes*** Asche *f*
a·shamed beschämt; ***be ashamed of*** sich schämen für (*or gen*)
ash·en Aschen…; aschfahl, aschgrau
a·shore am *or* ans Ufer *or* Land
ash·tray Asch(en)becher *m*
Ash Wednes·day Aschermittwoch *m*
A·sia Asien *n*
A·sian, A·si·at·ic **1.** asiatisch; **2.** Asiat(in)
a·side beiseite (*a.* THEA), seitwärts; ***aside from*** abgesehen von
ask *v/t* fragen (***s.th.*** nach et.); verlangen (***of, from s.o.*** von j-m); bitten (***s.o.*** [***for***] ***s.th.*** j-n um et.; ***that*** darum, dass); erbitten; ***ask*** (***s.o.***) ***a question*** (j-m) e-e Frage stellen; *v/i* ***ask for*** bitten um; fragen nach; ***he asked for it*** *or* ***for trouble*** er wollte es ja so haben; ***to be had for the asking*** umsonst zu haben sein
a·skance: ***look askance at s.o.*** j-n schief *or* misstrauisch ansehen
a·skew schief
a·sleep schlafend; ***be*** (***fast, sound***) ***asleep*** (fest) schlafen; ***fall asleep*** einschlafen
as·par·a·gus BOT Spargel *m*
as·pect Lage *f*; Aspekt *m*, Seite *f*, Gesichtspunkt *m*
as·phalt **1.** Asphalt *m*; **2.** asphaltieren
as·pic GASTR Aspik *m*, Gelee *n*
as·pi·rant Bewerber(in)
as·pi·ra·tion Ambition *f*, Bestrebung *f*
as·pire streben (***to, after*** nach)
ass zo Esel *m*
as·sail angreifen; ***be assailed with doubts*** von Zweifeln befallen werden
as·sail·ant Angreifer(in)
as·sas·sin (*esp* politischer) Mörder, Attentäter *m*
as·sas·sin·ate *esp* POL ermorden; ***be assassinated*** e-m Attentat *or* Mordanschlag zum Opfer fallen
as·sas·sin·a·tion (***of***) (*esp* politischer) Mord (an *dat*), Ermordung *f* (*gen*), Attentat *n* (auf *acc*)
as·sault **1.** Angriff *m*, Überfall *m*; **2.** angreifen, überfallen
as·sem·blage Ansammlung *f*; TECH Montage *f*
as·sem·ble (sich) versammeln; TECH montieren
as·sem·bly Versammlung *f*, Gesellschaft *f*; TECH Montage *f*
assembly line TECH Fließband *n*
as·sent **1.** Zustimmung *f*; **2.** (***to***) zustim-

men (*dat*); billigen (*acc*)
as·sert behaupten; geltend machen; ***assert o.s.*** sich behaupten, sich durchsetzen
as·ser·tion Behauptung *f*; Erklärung *f*; Geltendmachung *f*
as·sess *Kosten etc* festsetzen; *Einkommen etc* (zur Steuer) veranlagen (***at*** mit); *fig* abschätzen, beurteilen
as·sess·ment Festsetzung *f*; (Steuer-) Veranlagung *f*; *fig* Einschätzung *f*
as·set ECON Aktivposten *m*; *fig* Plus *n*, Gewinn *m*; *pl* ECON Aktiva *pl*; JUR Vermögen(smasse *f*) *n*; Konkursmasse *f*
as·sid·u·ous emsig, fleißig
as·sign an-, zuweisen; bestimmen; zuschreiben
as·sign·ment An-, Zuweisung *f*; Aufgabe *f*; Auftrag *m*; JUR Abtretung *f*; Übertragung *f*
as·sim·i·late (sich) angleichen *or* anpassen (***to, with*** *dat*)
as·sim·i·la·tion Assimilation *f*, Angleichung *f*, Anpassung *f* (*all*: ***to*** an *acc*)
as·sist *j-m* beistehen, helfen; *j-n* unterstützen
as·sist·ance Beistand *m*, Hilfe *f*
as·sist·ant **1.** stellvertretend, Hilfs…; **2.** Assistent(in), Mitarbeiter(in); (***shop***) ***assistant*** *Br* Verkäufer(in)
as·so·ci·ate **1.** vereinigen, verbinden, zusammenschließen; assoziieren; ***associate with*** verkehren mit; **2.** Teilhaber(in)
as·so·ci·a·tion Vereinigung *f*, Verbindung *f*; Verein *m*
as·sort sortieren, aussuchen, zusammenstellen
as·sort·ment ECON (***of***) Sortiment *n* (von), Auswahl *f* (an *dat*)
as·sume annehmen, voraussetzen; übernehmen
as·sump·tion Annahme *f*, Voraussetzung *f*; Übernahme *f*; ***the Assumption*** REL Mariä Himmelfahrt *f*
as·sur·ance Zusicherung *f*, Versicherung *f*; *esp Br* (Lebens)Versicherung *f*; Sicherheit *f*, Gewissheit *f*; Selbstsicherheit *f*
as·sure *j-m* versichern; *esp Br j-s Leben* versichern
as·sured **1.** sicher; **2.** *esp Br* Versicherte *m*, *f*
as·sur·ed·ly ganz gewiss
as·te·risk PRINT Sternchen *n*
asth·ma MED Asthma *n*
as·ton·ish in Erstaunen setzen; ***be astonished*** erstaunt sein (***at*** über *acc*)
as·ton·ish·ing erstaunlich
as·ton·ish·ment (Er)Staunen *n*, Verwunderung *f*
as·tound verblüffen
a·stray: ***go astray*** vom Weg abkommen; *fig* auf Abwege geraten; irregehen; ***lead astray*** *fig* irreführen; verleiten
a·stride rittlings (***of*** auf *dat*)
as·trin·gent MED **1.** adstringierend; **2.** Adstringens *n*
as·trol·o·gy Astrologie *f*
as·tro·naut Astronaut *m*, (Welt)Raumfahrer *m*
as·tron·o·my Astronomie *f*
as·tute scharfsinnig; schlau
a·sun·der auseinander, entzwei
a·sy·lum Asyl *n*; ***right of asylum*** Asylrecht *n*
a·sy·lum seek·er Asylant(in), Asylbewerber(in)
at *prp place*: in, an, bei, auf; *direction*: auf, nach, gegen, zu; *occupation*: bei, beschäftigt mit, in; *manner, state*: in, bei, zu, unter; *price etc*: für, um; *time*, *age*: um, bei; ***at the baker's*** beim Bäcker; ***at the door*** an der Tür; ***at school*** in der Schule; ***at 10 dollars*** für 10 Dollar; ***at 18*** mit 18 (Jahren); ***at the age of*** im Alter von; ***at 8 o'clock*** um 8 Uhr
a·the·ism Atheismus *m*
ath·lete SPORT (Leicht)Athlet(in)
ath·let·ic SPORT athletisch
ath·let·ics SPORT (Leicht)Athletik *f*
At·lan·tic **1.** *a.* ***Atlantic Ocean*** *der* Atlantik; **2.** atlantisch
at·mo·sphere Atmosphäre *f* (*a. fig*)
at·mo·spher·ic atmosphärisch
at·oll Atoll *n*
at·om Atom *n*
atom bomb Atombombe *f*
a·tom·ic atomar, Atom…
atomic age Atomzeitalter *n*
atomic bomb Atombombe *f*
atomic en·er·gy Atomenergie *f*
atomic pile Atomreaktor *m*
atomic pow·er Atomkraft *f*
atomic-pow·ered atomgetrieben
atomic waste Atommüll *m*
atomic weight CHEM Atomgewicht *n*
at·om·ize atomisieren; *Flüssigkeit* zerstäuben
at·om·iz·er Zerstäuber *m*
a·tone: ***atone for*** büßen für, *et.* sühnen
a·tone·ment Buße *f*, Sühne *f*
a·tro·cious grässlich; grausam
a·troc·i·ty Scheußlichkeit *f*; Greueltat *f*
at sign EDP at-Zeichen *n*
at·tach *v/t* (***to***) anheften, ankleben (an *acc*), befestigen, anbringen (an *dat*); *Wert*, *Wichtigkeit etc* beimessen (*dat*); ***be attached to*** *fig* hängen an
at·tach·ment Befestigung *f*; Bindung *f* (***to***

an *acc*); Anhänglichkeit *f* (**to** an *acc*)
at·tack **1.** angreifen; **2.** Angriff *m*; MED Anfall *m*
at·tempt **1.** versuchen; **2.** Versuch *m*; ***an attempt on s.o.'s life*** ein Mordanschlag *or* Attentat auf j-n
at·tend *v/t* (ärztlich) behandeln; *Kranke* pflegen; teilnehmen an (*dat*), *Schule, Vorlesung etc* besuchen; *fig* begleiten; *v/i* anwesend sein; erscheinen; ***attend to*** *j-n* (*im Laden*) bedienen; ***are you being attended to?*** werden Sie schon bedient?; ***attend to s.th.*** etwas erledigen
at·tend·ance Dienst *m*, Bereitschaft *f*; Pflege *f*; Anwesenheit *f*, Erscheinen *n*; Besucher *pl*, Teilnehmer *pl*; Besuch(erzahl *f*) *m*, Beteiligung *f*
at·tend·ant Begleiter(in); Aufseher(in); (*Tank-*)Wart *m*
at·ten·tion Aufmerksamkeit *f* (*a. fig*); ***pay attention*** aufpassen
at·ten·tive aufmerksam
at·tic Dachboden *m*; Dachkammer *f*
at·ti·tude (Ein)Stellung *f*; Haltung *f*
at·tor·ney Bevollmächtigte *m, f*; JUR (Rechts)Anwalt *m*, (Rechts)Anwältin *f*; ***power of attorney*** Vollmacht *f*
At·tor·ney Gen·e·ral JUR Justizminister; *Br* erster Kronanwalt
at·tract anziehen; *Aufmerksamkeit* erregen; *fig* reizen
at·trac·tion Anziehung *f*, Anziehungskraft *f*, Reiz *m*; Attraktion *f*, THEA *etc* Zugnummer *f*, Zugstück *n*
at·trac·tive anziehend; attraktiv; reizvoll
at·trib·ute[1] zuschreiben (**to** *dat*); zurückführen (**to** auf *acc*)
at·tri·bute[2] Attribut *n* (*a.* LING), Eigenschaft *f*, Merkmal *n*
at·tune: ***attune to*** *fig* einstellen auf (*acc*)
au·ber·gine BOT Aubergine *f*
au·burn kastanienbraun
auc·tion **1.** Auktion *f*, Versteigerung *f*; **2.** *mst* ***auction off*** versteigern
auc·tion·eer Auktionator *m*
au·da·cious unverfroren, dreist
au·dac·i·ty Unverfrorenheit *f*, Dreistigkeit *f*
au·di·ble hörbar
au·di·ence Publikum *n*, Zuhörer *pl*, Zuschauer *pl*, Besucher *pl*, Leser(kreis *m*) *pl*; Audienz *f*
au·di·o·vis·u·al aids audiovisuelle Unterrichtsmittel *pl*
au·dit ECON **1.** Buchprüfung *f*; **2.** prüfen
au·di·tion MUS Vorsingen *n*; THEA Vorsprechen *n*; ***have an audition*** vorsingen, THEA vorsprechen
au·di·tor ECON Buchprüfer *m*; UNIV Gasthörer(in)
au·di·to·ri·um Zuhörer-, Zuschauerraum *m*; Vortrags-, Konzertsaal *m*
Aug ABBR *of* ***August*** Aug., August *m*
au·ger TECH großer Bohrer
Au·gust (ABBR ***Aug***) August *m*
aunt Tante *f*
au pair (girl) Au-pair-Mädchen *n*
aus·pic·es: ***under the auspices of*** unter der Schirmherrschaft (*gen*)
aus·tere streng; enthaltsam; dürftig; einfach, schmucklos
Aus·tra·li·a Australien
Aus·tra·li·an **1.** australisch; **2.** Australier(in)
Aus·tri·a Österreich *n*
Aus·tri·an **1.** österreichisch; **2.** Österreicher(in)
au·then·tic authentisch; zuverlässig; echt
au·thor Urheber(in); Autor(in), Verfasser(in), Schriftsteller(in)
au·thor·ess Autorin *f*, Verfasserin *f*, Schriftstellerin *f*
au·thor·i·ta·tive gebieterisch, herrisch; maßgebend
au·thor·i·ty Autorität *f*; Nachdruck *m*, Gewicht *n*; Vollmacht *f*; Einfluss *m* (**over** auf *acc*); Ansehen *n*; Quelle *f*; Autorität *f*, Kapazität *f*; *mst pl* Behörde *f*
au·thor·ize *j-n* autorisieren, ermächtigen, bevollmächtigen
au·thor·ship Urheberschaft *f*
au·to Auto *n*
au·to... auto..., selbst..., Auto..., Selbst...
au·to·bi·og·ra·phy Autobiografie *f*
au·to·graph Autogramm *n*
au·to·mat® Automatenrestaurant *n*
au·to·mate automatisieren
au·to·mat·ic **1.** automatisch; **2.** Selbstladepistole *f*, -gewehr *n*; Auto *n* mit Automatik
automatic tel·ler ma·chine (ABBR ***ATM***) Geld-, Bankautomat *m*
au·to·ma·tion TECH Automation *f*
au·tom·a·ton Roboter *m*
au·to·mo·bile Auto *n*, Automobil *n*
au·ton·o·my POL Autonomie *f*
au·top·sy MED Autopsie *f*
au·to·tel·ler Geld-, Bankautomat *m*
au·tumn Herbst *m*
au·tum·nal herbstlich, Herbst...
aux·il·i·a·ry helfend, Hilfs...
a·vail: ***to no avail*** vergeblich
a·vail·a·ble verfügbar, vorhanden; erreichbar; ECON lieferbar, vorrätig, erhältlich
av·a·lanche Lawine *f*
av·a·rice Habsucht *f*

av·a·ri·cious habgierig
a·venge rächen
a·veng·er Rächer(in)
av·e·nue Allee *f*; Boulevard *m*, Prachtstraße *f*
av·e·rage **1.** Durchschnitt *m*; **2.** durchschnittlich, Durchschnitts…
a·verse abgeneigt (***to*** *dat*)
a·ver·sion Widerwille *m*, Abneigung *f*
a·vert abwenden (*a. fig*)
avian flu Vogelgrippe *f*
a·vi·a·ry Vogelhaus *n*, Voliere *f*
a·vi·a·tion Luftfahrt *f*
a·vi·a·tor Flieger *m*
av·id gierig (***for*** nach); begeistert
av·o·ca·do BOT Avocado *f*
a·void (ver)meiden; ausweichen
a·void·ance Vermeidung *f*
a·vow·al Bekenntnis *n*, (Ein)Geständnis *n*
a·wait erwarten, warten auf (*acc*)
a·wake **1.** wach, munter; **2.** *a.* **a·waken** *v/t* (auf)wecken; *v/i* aufwachen, erwachen;
a·wak·en·ing Erwachen *n*
a·ward **1.** Belohnung *f*; Preis *m*, Auszeichnung *f*; **2.** zuerkennen, *Preis etc* verleihen
a·ware: ***be aware of s.th.*** von etwas wissen, sich e-r Sache bewusst sein; ***become aware of s.th.*** etwas merken
a·way weg, fort; (weit) entfernt; immer weiter, d(a)rauflos; SPORT Auswärts…;
away match SPORT Auswärtsspiel *n*
awe **1.** Furcht *f*, Scheu *f*; **2.** *j-m* (Ehr)-Furcht *or* großen Respekt einflößen
aw·ful furchtbar, schrecklich
awk·ward ungeschickt, linkisch; unangenehm; unhandlich, sperrig; ungünstig, ungelegen
awl Ahle *f*, Pfriem *m*
aw·ning Plane *f*; Markise *f*
a·wry schief
ax(e) Axt *f*, Beil *n*
ax·is MATH *etc* Achse *f*
ax·le TECH (Rad)Achse *f*, Welle *f*
ay(e) PARL Jastimme *f*
A-Z *Br appr* Stadtplan *m*
az·ure azurblau, himmelblau

B

B, b B, b *n*
b ABBR *of* ***born*** geb., geboren
bab·ble **1.** stammeln; plappern, schwatzen; plätschern; **2.** Geplapper *n*, Geschwätz *n*
babe kleines Kind, Baby *n*; F Puppe *f*
ba·boon ZO Pavian *m*
ba·by **1.** Baby *n*, Säugling *m*, kleines Kind; F Puppe *f*; **2.** Baby…, Kinder…; klein
baby bug·gy, **baby car·riage** Kinderwagen *m*
ba·by·hood Säuglingsalter *n*
ba·by·ish *contp* kindisch
ba·by-mind·er *Br* Tagesmutter *f*
ba·by·sit babysitten
ba·by·sit·ter Babysitter(in)
bach·e·lor Junggeselle *m*
back **1.** Rücken *m*; Rückseite *f*; (Rück)-Lehne *f*; hinterer *or* rückwärtiger Teil; SPORT Verteidiger *m*; **2.** *adj* Hinter…, Rück…, hintere(r, -s), rückwärtig; ECON rückständig; alt, zurückliegend; **3.** *adv* zurück, rückwärts; **4.** *v/t* mit e-m Rücken versehen; wetten *or* setzen auf (*acc*); *a.* ***back up*** unterstützen; zurückbewegen; MOT zurückstoßen mit; ***back up*** EDP e-e Sicherungskopie machen von; *v/i often* ***back up*** sich rückwärts bewegen, zurückgehen *or* -fahren, MOT *a.* zurückstoßen; ***back in(to a parking space)*** MOT rückwärts einparken; ***back up*** EDP e-e Sicherungskopie machen
back·ache Rückenschmerzen *pl*
back·bite verleumden, schlechtmachen
back·bone ANAT Rückgrat *n* (*a. fig*)
back·break·ing erschöpfend, mörderisch
back·chat *Br* freche Antwort(en *pl*)
back·comb *Br* toupieren
back door Hintertür *f*; *fig* Hintertürchen *n*
back·er Unterstützer *m*, Geldgeber *m*
back·fire MOT Früh- *or* Fehlzündung haben; *fig* fehlschlagen
back·ground Hintergrund *m*
back·hand SPORT Rückhand *f*, Rückhandschlag *m*
back·heel·er *soccer*: Hackentrick *m*
back·ing Unterstützung *f*
back num·ber alte Nummer
back·pack *großer* Rucksack
back·pack·er Rucksacktourist(in)
back·pack·ing Rucksacktourismus *m*

back-ped·al brake *Br* Rücktritt *m*, Rücktrittbremse *f*
back seat MOT Rücksitz *m*
back·side Gesäß *n*, F Hintern *m*, Po *m*
back·space (key) EDP Rücktaste *f*
back stairs Hintertreppe *f*
back street Seitenstraße *f*
back·stroke Rückenschwimmen *n*
back talk freche Antwort(en *pl*)
back·track *fig* e-n Rückzieher machen
back·up Unterstützung *f*; TECH Ersatzgerät *n*; EDP Backup *n*, Sicherungskopie *f*; MOT Rückstau *m*
back·ward 1. *adj* Rück…, Rückwärts…; zurückgeblieben; rückständig; ***a backward glance*** ein Blick zurück; **2.** *adv a.* ***backwards*** rückwärts, zurück
back·yard Garten *m* hinter dem Haus; *Br* Hinterhof *m*
ba·con Speck *m*
bac·te·ri·a BIOL Bakterien *pl*
bad schlecht, böse, schlimm; ***go bad*** schlecht werden, verderben; ***he is in a bad way*** es geht ihm schlecht; ***he is badly off*** es geht ihm finanziell schlecht; ***badly wounded*** schwer verwundet; ***want badly*** dringend brauchen
badge Abzeichen *n*; Dienstmarke *f*
bad·ger 1. ZO Dachs *m*; **2.** *j-n* plagen, *j-m* zusetzen
bad·min·ton Federball(spiel *n*) *m*, SPORT Badminton *n*
bad-tempered schlecht gelaunt
bag 1. Beutel *m*, Sack *m*; Tüte *f*; Tasche *f*; ***bag and baggage*** (mit) Sack und Pack; **2.** in e-n Beutel *etc* tun; in Beutel verpacken *or* abfüllen; HUNT zur Strecke bringen; schlottern; *a.* ***bag out*** sich bauschen
bag·gage (Reise)Gepäck *n*
baggage car RAIL Gepäckwagen *m*
baggage check Gepäckschein *m*
baggage claim AVIAT Gepäckausgabe *f*
baggage room RAIL Gepäckaufbewahrung *f*
bag·gy bauschig; ausgebeult
bag·pipes MUS Dudelsack *m*
bail 1. Bürge *m*; JUR Kaution *f*; ***be out on bail*** gegen Kaution auf freiem Fuß sein; ***go*** *or* ***stand bail for s.o.*** für j-n Kaution stellen; **2. *bail out*** JUR *j-n* gegen Kaution freibekommen; AVIAT (mit dem Fallschirm) abspringen
bai·liff (Guts)Verwalter *m*; *Br* JUR Gerichtsvollzieher *m*
bait 1. Köder *m* (*a. fig*); **2.** mit e-m Köder versehen; *fig* ködern
bake backen, im (Back)Ofen braten; TECH brennen; dörren
bak·er Bäcker *m*
bak·er·y Bäckerei *f*
bak·ing pow·der Backpulver *n*
bal·ance 1. Waage *f*; Gleichgewicht *n* (*a. fig*); ECON Bilanz *f*; Saldo *m*, Kontostand *m*, Guthaben *n*; Restbetrag *m*; ***keep one's balance*** das Gleichgewicht halten; ***lose one's balance*** das Gleichgewicht verlieren; *fig* die Fassung verlieren; ***balance of payments*** ECON Zahlungsbilanz *f*; ***balance of power*** POL Kräftegleichgewicht *n*; ***balance of trade*** ECON Handelsbilanz *f*; **2.** *v/t* abwägen; im Gleichgewicht halten, balancieren; ECON ausgleichen; *v/i* balancieren; ECON sich ausgleichen; ***balance each other*** sich die Waage halten
bal·ance sheet ECON Bilanz *f*
bal·co·ny Balkon *m* (*a.* THEA)
bald kahl
bale[1] ECON Ballen *m*
bale[2]: ***bale out*** *Br* AVIAT (mit dem Fallschirm) abspringen
bale·ful hasserfüllt
balk 1. Balken *m*; **2.** stutzen; scheuen
ball[1] **1.** Ball *m*; Kugel *f*; ANAT (Hand-, Fuß)Ballen *m*; Knäuel *m, n*; Kloß *m*; ***start the ball rolling*** den Stein ins Rollen bringen; ***play ball*** F mitmachen; ***long ball*** SPORT langer Pass; **2.** ballen; sich zusammenballen
ball[2] Ball *m*, Tanzveranstaltung *f*
bal·lad Ballade *f*
bal·last 1. Ballast *m*; **2.** mit Ballast beladen
ball bear·ing TECH Kugellager *n*
bal·let Ballett *n*
bal·lis·tics MIL Ballistik *f*
bal·loon 1. Ballon *m*; Sprech-, Denkblase *f*; **2.** sich (auf)blähen
bal·lot 1. Stimmzettel *m*; (geheime) Wahl; **2.** (***for***) stimmen (für), (in geheimer Wahl) wählen (*acc*)
ballot box Wahlurne *f*
ballot pa·per Stimmzettel *m*
ball·point (pen) Kugelschreiber *m*, F Kuli *m*
ball·room Ballsaal *m*, Tanzsaal *m*
balls V Eier *pl*
balm Balsam *m* (*a. fig*)
balm·y lind, mild
ba·lo·ney F Quatsch *m*
bal·us·trade Balustrade *f*, Brüstung *f*, Geländer *n*
bam·boo BOT Bambus(rohr *n*) *m*
bam·boo·zle F betrügen, *j-n* übers Ohr hauen
ban 1. (amtliches) Verbot, Sperre *f*; REL Bann *m*; **2.** verbieten
ba·nal banal, abgedroschen

ba·na·na BOT Banane *f*
band **1.** Band *n*; Streifen *m*; Schar *f*, Gruppe *f*; *contp* Bande *f*; (Musik)Kapelle *f*, (Tanz-, Unterhaltungs)Orchester *n*, (*Jazz-, Rock*)Band *f*; **2.** ***band together*** sich zusammentun *or* -rotten
ban·dage MED **1.** Bandage *f*; Binde *f*; Verband *m*; (Heft)Pflaster *n*; **2.** bandagieren; verbinden
'**Band-Aid**® MED (Heft)Pflaster *n*
b & b, B & B ABBR *of* ***bed and breakfast*** Übernachtung *f* mit Frühstück
ban·dit Bandit *m*
band·lead·er MUS Bandleader *m*
band·mas·ter MUS Kapellmeister *m*
ban·dy krumm
ban·dy-legged säbelbeinig, o-beinig
bang **1.** heftiger Schlag; Knall *m*; *mst pl* Pony *m*; **2.** dröhnend (zu)schlagen
ban·gle Armreif *m*, Fußreif *m*
ban·ish verbannen
ban·ish·ment Verbannung *f*
ban·is·ter *a. pl* Treppengeländer *n*
ban·jo MUS Banjo *n*
bank[1] ECON **1.** Bank *f* (*a.* MED); **2.** *v/t* bei e-r Bank einzahlen; *v/i* ein Bankkonto haben (***with*** bei)
bank[2] (Erd)Wall *m*; Böschung *f*; (*Fluss-etc*)Ufer *n*; (*Sand-, Wolken*)Bank *f*
bank ac·count Bankkonto *n*
bank bill Banknote *f*, Geldschein *m*
bank·book Sparbuch *n*
bank code ECON Bankleitzahl *f*
bank·er Bankier *m*, Banker *m*; ***banker's card*** Scheckkarte *f*
bank hol·i·day *Br* gesetzlicher Feiertag *m*
bank·ing ECON **1.** Bankgeschäft *n*, Bankwesen *n*; **2.** Bank…
bank note *Br* → ***bank bill***
bank rate ECON Diskontsatz *m*
bank·rupt JUR **1.** Konkursschuldner *m*; **2.** bankrott; ***go bankrupt*** in Konkurs gehen, Bankrott machen; **3.** *j-n, Unternehmen* Bankrott machen
bank·rupt·cy JUR Bankrott *m*, Konkurs *m*
bank sort·ing code → ***bank code***
ban·ner Transparent *n*
banns Aufgebot *n*
ban·quet Bankett *n*
ban·ter necken
bap·tism REL Taufe *f*
bap·tize REL taufen
bar **1.** Stange *f*, Stab *m*; SPORT (Tor-, Quer-, Sprung)Latte *f*; Riegel *m*; Schranke *f*, Sperre *f*; *fig* Hindernis *n*; (*Gold- etc*)Barren *m*; MUS Taktstrich *m*; *ein* Takt *m*; dicker Strich; JUR (Gerichts)Schranke *f*; JUR Anwaltschaft *f*; Bar *f*; Lokal *n*, Imbissstube *f*; *pl* Gitter *n*; ***a bar of chocolate*** ein Riegel *or* e-e Tafel Schokolade; ***a bar of soap*** ein Stück Seife; **2.** zuriegeln, verriegeln; versperren; einsperren; (ver)hindern); ausschließen
barb Widerhaken *m*
bar·bar·i·an **1.** barbarisch; **2.** Barbar(in)
bar·be·cue **1.** Bratrost *m*, Grill *m*; Barbecue *n*; **2.** auf dem Rost *or* am Spieß braten, grillen
barbed wire Stacheldraht *m*
bar·ber (Herren)Friseur *m*, (-)Frisör *m*
bar code Strichkode *m*
bare **1.** nackt, bloß; kahl; leer; **2.** entblößen
bare·faced unverschämt, schamlos
bare·foot, bare·foot·ed barfuß
bare·head·ed barhäuptig
bare·ly kaum
bar·gain **1.** Geschäft *n*, Handel *m*; vorteilhaftes Geschäft, Gelegenheitskauf *m*; ***a (dead) bargain*** spottbillig; ***it's a bargain!*** abgemacht!; ***into the bargain*** obendrein; **2.** (ver)handeln
bargain sale Verkauf *m* zu herabgesetzten Preisen; Ausverkauf *m*
barge **1.** Lastkahn *m*; **2.** ***barge in*** F hereinplatzen (***on*** bei)
bark[1] BOT Borke *f*, Rinde *f*
bark[2] **1.** bellen; ***bark up the wrong tree*** F auf dem Holzweg sein; an der falschen Adresse sein; **2.** Bellen *n*
bar·ley BOT Gerste *f*; Graupe *f*
barn Scheune *f*; (Vieh)Stall *m*
ba·rom·e·ter Barometer *n*
bar·on Baron *m*; Freiherr *m*
bar·on·ess Baronin *f*; Freifrau *f*
bar·racks MIL Kaserne *f*; *contp* Mietskaserne *f*
bar·rage Staudamm *m*; MIL Sperrfeuer *n*; *fig* (Wort- *etc*)Schwall *m*
bar·rel Fass *n*, Tonne *f*; (*Gewehr*)Lauf *m*; TECH Trommel *f*, Walze *f*
bar·rel or·gan MUS Drehorgel *f*
bar·ren unfruchtbar; trocken
bar·rette Haarspange *f*
bar·ri·cade **1.** Barrikade *f*; **2.** verbarrikadieren; sperren
bar·ri·er Schranke *f* (*a. fig*), Barriere *f*, Sperre *f*; Hindernis *n*
bar·ris·ter *Br* JUR Barrister *m*
bar·row Karre *f*
bar·ter **1.** Tausch(handel) *m*; **2.** tauschen (***for*** gegen)
base[1] gemein
base[2] **1.** Basis *f*; Grundlage *f*; Fundament *n*; Fuß *m*; MIL Standort *m*; MIL Stützpunkt *m*; **2.** gründen, stützen (***on*** auf *acc*)
base[3] CHEM Base *f*
base·ball SPORT Baseball(spiel *n*) *m*

base·board Scheuerleiste *f*
base·less grundlos
base·line *tennis etc*: Grundlinie *f*
base·ment ARCH Fundament *n*; Kellergeschoss *n*
bash·ful scheu, schüchtern
ba·sic[1] **1.** Grund…, grundlegend; **2.** *pl* Grundlagen *pl*
ba·sic[2] CHEM basisch
ba·sic·al·ly im Grunde
ba·sin Becken *n*, Schale *f*, Schüssel *f*; Tal-, Wasser-, Hafenbecken *n*
ba·sis Basis *f*; Grundlage *f*
bask sich sonnen (*a. fig*)
bas·ket Korb *m*
bas·ket·ball SPORT Basketball(spiel *n*) *m*
bass[1] MUS Bass *m*
bass[2] ZO (Fluss-, See)Barsch *m*
bas·tard Bastard *m*
baste[1] GASTR mit Fett begießen
baste[2] (an)heften
bat[1] ZO Fledermaus *f*; ***as blind as a bat*** stockblind
bat[2] *baseball, cricket* **1.** Schlagholz *n*, Schläger *m*; F ***right off the bat*** sofort; **2.** am Schlagen sein
batch Stapel *m*, Stoß *m*
batch pro·cessing EDP Stapelverarbeitung *f*
bate: ***with bated breath*** mit angehaltenem Atem
bath 1. (Wannen)Bad *n*; *pl* Bad *n*, Badeanstalt *f*; Badeort *m*; ***have a bath*** *Br*, ***take a bath*** baden, ein Bad nehmen; **2.** *Br v/t j-n* baden; *v/i* baden, ein Bad nehmen
bathe *v/t* baden (*a.* MED); *v/i* baden, ein Bad nehmen; schwimmen
bath·ing 1. Baden *n*; **2.** Bade…
bath·ing suit → ***swimsuit***
bath·robe Bademantel *m*; Morgenrock *m*, Schlafrock *m*
bath·room Badezimmer *n*; Toilette *f*
bath·tub Badewanne *f*
bat·on Stab *m*; MUS Taktstock *m*; Schlagstock *m*, Gummiknüppel *m*
bat·tal·i·on MIL Bataillon *n*
bat·ten Latte *f*
bat·ter[1] heftig schlagen; misshandeln; verbeulen; ***batter down, batter in*** einschlagen
bat·ter[2] GASTR Rührteig *m*
bat·ter[3] *baseball, cricket*: Schläger *m*, Schlagmann *m*
bat·ter·y ELECTR Batterie *f*; JUR Tätlichkeit *f*, Körperverletzung *f*; ***assault and battery*** JUR tätliche Beleidigung
bat·ter·y charg·er ELECTR Ladegerät *n*
bat·ter·y·op·e·rat·ed ELECTR batteriebetrieben
bat·tle 1. MIL Schlacht *f* (***of*** bei); *fig* Kampf *m* (***for*** um); **2.** kämpfen
bat·tle·field, bat·tle·ground MIL Schlachtfeld *n*
bat·tle·ments ARCH Zinnen *pl*
bat·tle·ship MIL Schlachtschiff *n*
baulk → ***balk***
Ba·va·ri·a Bayern *n*
Ba·var·i·an 1. bay(e)risch; **2.** Bayer(in)
bawd·y obszön
bawl brüllen, schreien; ***bawl s.o. out*** mit j-m schimpfen
bay[1] GEOGR Bai *f*, Bucht *f*; ARCH Erker *m*
bay[2] *a.* ***bay tree*** BOT Lorbeer(baum) *m*
bay[3] **1.** ZO bellen, Laut geben; **2.** ***hold or keep at bay*** *j-n* in Schach halten; *et.* von sich fernhalten
bay[4] **1.** rotbraun; **2.** ZO Braune *m*
bay·o·net MIL Bajonett *n*
bay·ou GEOGR sumpfiger Flussarm
bay win·dow ARCH Erkerfenster *n*
ba·zaar Basar *m*
BC ABBR *of* ***before Christ*** v. Chr., vor Christus
be sein; *to form the passive*: werden; stattfinden; ***he wants to be a doctor*** *etc* er möchte Arzt *etc* werden; ***how much are the shoes?*** was kosten die Schuhe?; ***that's five dollars*** das macht *or* kostet fünf Dollar; ***she is reading*** sie liest gerade; ***there is, there are*** es gibt
beach Strand *m*
beach ball Wasserball *m*
beach bug·gy MOT Strandbuggy *m*
beach·wear Strandkleidung *f*
bea·con Leucht-, Signalfeuer *n*
bead (*Glas-, Schweiß- etc*)Perle *f*; *pl* REL Rosenkranz *m*
bead·y klein, rund und glänzend
beak ZO Schnabel *m*; TECH Tülle *f*
beam 1. Balken *m*; (Licht)Strahl *m*; AVIAT *etc* Peil-, Leit-, Richtstrahl *m*; **2.** ausstrahlen; strahlen (*a. fig* ***with*** vor *dat*)
bean BOT Bohne *f*; ***be full of beans*** F aufgekrazt sein; → ***spill*** *1*
bear[1] ZO Bär *m*
bear[2] tragen; zur Welt bringen, gebären; ertragen, aushalten; ***I can't bear him (it)*** ich kann ihn (es) nicht ausstehen *or* leiden; ***bear out*** bestätigen
bear·a·ble erträglich
beard Bart *m*; BOT Grannen *pl*
beard·ed bärtig
bear·er Träger(in); ECON Überbringer(in), Inhaber(in)
bear·ing Ertragen *n*; Betragen *n*; (Körper)Haltung *f*; *fig* Beziehung *f*; Lage *f*, Richtung *f*, Orientierung *f*; ***take one's bearings*** sich orientieren; ***lose one's***

bearings die Orientierung verlieren
beast (*a. wildes*) Tier; Bestie *f*
beast·ly scheußlich
beast of prey ZO Raubtier *n*
beat 1. schlagen; (ver)prügeln; besiegen; übertreffen; F ***beat s.o. to it*** j-m zuvorkommen; ***beat it!*** F hau ab!; ***that beats all!*** das ist doch der Gipfel *or* die Höhe!; ***that beats me*** F das ist mir zu hoch; ***beat about the bush*** wie die Katze um den heißen Brei herumschleichen; ***beat down*** ECON drücken, herunterhandeln; ***beat s.o. up*** j-n zusammenschlagen; **2.** Schlag *m*; MUS Takt(schlag) *m*; *jazz*: Beat *m*; Pulsschlag *m*; Runde *f*, Revier *n*; **3.** (***dead***) ***beat*** F wie erschlagen, fix und fertig
beat·en track Trampelpfad *m*; ***off the beaten track*** ungewohnt, ungewöhnlich
beat·ing (Tracht *f*) Prügel *pl*
beau·ti·cian Kosmetikerin *f*
beau·ti·ful schön
beaut·y Schönheit *f*; ***Sleeping Beauty*** Dornröschen *n*
beauty care Schönheitspflege *f*
beauty par·lo(u)r, beauty sal·on Schönheitssalon *m*
bea·ver ZO Biber *m*; Biberpelz *m*
be·cause weil; ***because of*** wegen (*gen*)
beck·on (zu)winken (*dat*)
be·come *v/i* werden (***of*** aus); *v/t* sich schicken für; *j-m* stehen, *j-n* kleiden
be·com·ing passend; schicklich; kleidsam
bed 1. Bett *n*; ZO Lager *n*; AGR Beet *n*; Unterlage *f*; ***bed and breakfast*** Zimmer *n* mit Frühstück; **2. *bed down*** sein Nachtlager aufschlagen
bed·clothes Bettwäsche *f*
bed·ding Bettzeug *n*; AGR Streu *f*
bed·lam Tollhaus *n*
bed·rid·den bettlägerig
bed·room Schlafzimmer *n*
bed·side: ***at the bedside*** am (*a. Kranken*)Bett
bed·side lamp Nachttischlampe *f*
bed·sit F, **bed·sit·ter, bed·sit·ting room** *Br* möbliertes Zimmer; Einzimmerappartement *n*
bed·spread Tagesdecke *f*
bed·stead Bettgestell *n*
bed·time Schlafenszeit *f*
bee ZO Biene *f*; ***have a bee in one's bonnet*** F e-n Fimmel *or* Tick haben
beech BOT Buche *f*
beech·nut BOT Buchecker *f*
beef GASTR Rindfleisch *n*
beef·bur·ger GASTR *Br* Hamburger *m*
beef tea GASTR (Rind)Fleischbrühe *f*
beef·y F bullig
bee·hive Bienenkorb *m*, Bienenstock *m*
bee·keep·er Imker *m*
bee·line: ***make a beeline for*** F schnurstracks losgehen auf (*acc*)
beep·er TECH Piepser *m*
beer Bier *n*
beet BOT Runkelrübe *f*, Rote Bete, Rote Rübe
bee·tle ZO Käfer *m*
beet·root BOT *Br* Rote Bete, Rote Rübe
be·fore 1. *adv space*: vorn, voran; *time*: vorher, früher, schon (früher); **2.** *cj* bevor, ehe, bis; **3.** *prp* vor
be·fore·hand zuvor, im Voraus, vorweg
be·friend sich *j-s* annehmen
beg *v/t et.* erbitten (***of s.o.*** von j-m); betteln um; *j-n* bitten; *v/i* betteln; (dringend) bitten
be·get (er)zeugen
beg·gar 1. Bettler(in); F Kerl *m*; **2. *it beggars all description*** es spottet jeder Beschreibung
be·gin beginnen, anfangen
be·gin·ner Anfänger(in)
be·gin·ning Beginn *m*, Anfang *m*
be·grudge missgönnen
be·guile täuschen; betrügen (***of, out of*** um); sich *die Zeit* vertreiben
be·half: ***in*** (*Br* ***on***) ***behalf of*** im Namen von (*or gen*)
be·have sich (gut) benehmen
be·hav·io(u)r Benehmen *n*, Betragen *n*, Verhalten *n*
be·hav·io(u)r·al sci·ence PSYCH Verhaltensforschung *f*
be·head enthaupten
be·hind 1. *adv* hinten, dahinter; zurück; **2.** *prp* hinter (*dat or acc*); **3.** F Hinterteil *n*, Hintern *m*
beige beige
be·ing Sein *n*, Dasein *n*, Existenz *f*; (Lebe)Wesen *n*, Geschöpf *n*; *j-s* Wesen *n*, Natur *f*
be·lat·ed verspätet
belch 1. aufstoßen, rülpsen; *a.* ***belch out*** speien, ausstoßen; **2.** Rülpser *m*
bel·fry Glockenturm *m*, -stuhl *m*
Bel·gium Belgien *n*
Bel·gian 1. belgisch; **2.** Belgier(in)
be·lief Glaube *m* (***in*** an *acc*)
be·liev·a·ble glaubhaft
be·lieve glauben (***in*** an *acc*); ***I couldn't believe my ears*** (***eyes***) ich traute m-n Ohren (Augen) nicht
be·liev·er REL Gläubige *m, f*
be·lit·tle *fig* herabsetzen
bell Glocke *f*; Klingel *f*
bell·boy *Br*, **bell·hop** (Hotel)Page *m*

bel·lig·er·ent kriegerisch; streitlustig, aggressiv; Krieg führend
bel·low **1.** brüllen; **2.** Gebrüll *n*
bel·lows Blasebalg *m*
bel·ly **1.** Bauch *m*; Magen *m*; **2.** ***belly out*** (an)schwellen lassen; bauschen
bel·ly·ache F Bauchweh *n*
be·long gehören; ***belong to*** gehören *dat or* zu
be·long·ings Habseligkeiten *pl*, Habe *f*
be·loved **1.** (innig) geliebt; **2.** Geliebte *m, f*
be·low **1.** *adv* unten; **2.** *prp* unter (*dat or acc*)
belt **1.** Gürtel *m*; Gurt *m*; GEOGR Zone *f*, Gebiet *n*; TECH (Treib)Riemen *m*; **2.** ***belt out*** MUS schmettern; *a.* ***belt up*** den Gürtel (*gen*) zumachen; ***belt up*** MOT sich anschnallen
belt·ed mit e-m Gürtel
belt·way Umgehungsstraße *f*; Ringstraße *f*
be·moan betrauern, beklagen
bench Sitzbank *f*, Bank *f* (*a.* SPORT); TECH Werkbank *f*; JUR Richterbank *f*; Richter *m or pl*
bend **1.** Biegung *f*, Kurve *f*; ***drive s.o. round the bend*** F j-n noch wahnsinnig machen; **2.** (sich) biegen *or* krümmen; neigen; beugen; *fig* richten (***to, on*** auf *acc*)
be·neath → ***below***
ben·e·dic·tion REL Segen *m*
ben·e·fac·tor Wohltäter *m*
be·nef·i·cent wohltätig
ben·e·fi·cial wohltuend, zuträglich, nützlich
ben·e·fit **1.** Nutzen *m*, Vorteil *m*; Wohltätigkeitsveranstaltung *f*; (*Sozial-, Versicherungs- etc*)Leistung *f*; (*Arbeitslosen- etc*)Unterstützung *f*; (*Kranken- etc*)Geld *n*; **2.** nützen; ***benefit by, benefit from*** Vorteil haben von *or* durch, Nutzen ziehen aus
be·nev·o·lence Wohlwollen *n*
be·nev·o·lent wohltätig; wohlwollend
be·nign MED gutartig
bent **1.** ***bent on doing*** entschlossen zu tun; **2.** Hang *m*, Neigung *f*; Veranlagung *f*
ben·zene CHEM Benzol *n*
ben·zine CHEM Leichtbenzin *n*
be·queath JUR vermachen
be·quest JUR Vermächtnis *n*
be·reave berauben
be·ret Baskenmütze *f*
ber·ry BOT Beere *f*
berth **1.** MAR Liege-, Ankerplatz *m*; Koje *f*; RAIL (Schlafwagen)Bett *n*; **2.** MAR festmachen, anlegen
be·seech (inständig) bitten (um); anflehen
be·set heimsuchen; ***beset with difficulties*** mit vielen Schwierigkeiten verbunden
be·side *prp* neben (*dat or acc*); ***beside o.s.*** außer sich (***with*** vor); ***beside the point, beside the question*** nicht zur Sache gehörig
be·sides **1.** *adv* außerdem; **2.** *prp* abgesehen von, außer (*dat*)
be·siege belagern
be·smear beschmieren
be·spat·ter bespritzen
best **1.** *adj* beste(r, -s) höchste(r, -s), größte(r, -s), meiste; ***best before*** GASTR haltbar bis; **2.** *adv* am besten; **3.** *der, die, das* Beste; ***all the best!*** alles Gute!, viel Glück!; ***to the best of ...*** nach bestem ...; ***make the best of*** das Beste machen aus (*dat*); ***at best*** bestenfalls; ***be at one's best*** in Hoch- *or* Höchstform sein
best-be·fore date, best-by date Mindesthaltbarkeitsdatum *n*
bes·ti·al *fig* tierisch, bestialisch
be·stow geben, verleihen (***on*** *dat*)
best-sell·er Bestseller *m*
bet **1.** Wette *f*; ***make a bet*** e-e Wette abschließen; **2.** wetten; ***bet s.o. ten dollars*** mit j-m um zehn Dollar wetten; ***you bet*** F und ob!
be·tray verraten (*a. fig*); verleiten
be·tray·al Verrat *m*
be·tray·er Verräter(in)
bet·ter **1.** *adj* besser; ***he is better*** es geht ihm besser; ***better and better*** immer besser; **2.** *das* Bessere; ***get the better of*** die Oberhand gewinnen über (*acc*); *et.* überwinden; **3.** *adv* besser; mehr; ***do better than*** es besser machen als; ***know better*** es besser wissen; ***so much the better*** desto besser; ***you had better go*** *Br*, F ***you better go*** es wäre besser, wenn du gingest; ***better off*** (finanziell) besser gestellt; ***he is better off than I am*** es geht ihm besser als mir; **4.** *v/t* verbessern; *v/i* sich bessern
be·tween **1.** *adv* dazwischen; ***in between*** zwischendurch; F ***few and far between*** (ganz) vereinzelt; **2.** *prp* zwischen (*dat or acc*); unter (*dat*); ***between you and me*** unter uns *or* im Vertrauen (gesagt)
bev·el TECH abkanten, abschrägen
bev·er·age Getränk *n*
bev·y zo Schwarm *m*, Schar *f*
be·ware (***of***) sich in Acht nehmen (vor *dat*), sich hüten (vor *dat*); ***beware of the dog!*** Vorsicht, bissiger Hund!

be·wil·der verwirren
be·wil·der·ment Verwirrung *f*
be·witch bezaubern, verhexen
be·yond **1.** *adv* darüber hinaus; **2.** *prp* jenseits (*gen*); über … (*acc*) hinaus
bi… zwei, zweifach, zweimal
bi·as Neigung *f*; Vorurteil *n*
bi·as(s)ed voreingenommen; JUR befangen
bi·ath·lete SPORT Biathlet *m*
bi·ath·lon SPORT Biathlon *n*
bib (Sabber)Lätzchen *n*
Bi·ble Bibel *f*
bib·li·cal biblisch, Bibel…
bib·li·og·ra·phy Bibliografie *f*
bi·car·bon·ate *a.* ***bicarbonate of soda*** CHEM doppeltkohlensaures Natron
bi·cen·te·na·ry *Br*, **bi·cen·ten·ni·al** Zweihundertjahrfeier *f*
bi·ceps ANAT Bizeps *m*
bick·er sich zanken *or* streiten
bi·cy·cle Fahrrad *n*
bid **1.** *auction*: bieten; **2.** ECON Gebot *n*, Angebot *n*
bi·en·ni·al zweijährlich; BOT zweijährig
bi·en·ni·al·ly alle zwei Jahre
bier (Toten)Bahre *f*
big groß; dick, stark; ***talk big*** F den Mund voll nehmen
big·a·my Bigamie *f*
big busi·ness Großunternehmertum *n*
big·head F Angeber *m*
big shot, **big·wig** F hohes Tier
bike F **1.** (Fahr)Rad *n*; **2.** Rad fahren
bik·er Motorradfahrer(in); Radfahrer(in), Radler(in)
bi·lat·er·al bilateral
bile Galle *f* (*a. fig*)
bi·lin·gual zweisprachig
bill[1] ZO Schnabel *m*
bill[2] ECON Rechnung *f*; POL (Gesetzes-) Vorlage *f*; JUR (An)Klageschrift *f*; Plakat *n*; Banknote *f*, (Geld)Schein *m*
bill·board Reklametafel *f*
bill·fold Brieftasche *f*
bil·li·ards Billard(spiel) *n*
bil·li·on Milliarde *f*
bill of de·liv·er·y ECON Lieferschein *m*
bill of ex·change ECON Wechsel *m*
bill of sale JUR Verkaufsurkunde *f*
bil·low **1.** Woge *f*; (*Rauch- etc*) Schwaden *m*; **2.** *a.* ***billow out*** sich bauschen *or* blähen
bil·ly goat ZO Ziegenbock *m*
bin (großer) Behälter
bi·na·ry MATH, PHYS *etc* binär, Binär…
bi·na·ry code EDP Binärcode *m*
bi·na·ry num·ber MATH Binärzahl *f*
bind *v/t* (an-, ein-, um-, auf-, fest-, ver-) binden; *a.* vertraglich binden, verpflichten; einfassen; *v/i* binden
bind·er (*esp Buch*)Binder(in); Einband *m*; Aktendeckel *m*
bind·ing **1.** bindend, verbindlich; **2.** Einband *m*; Einfassung *f*, Borte *f*
bin·go Bingo *n*
bi·noc·u·lars, Fern-, Opernglas *n*
bi·o·chem·is·try Biochemie *f*
bi·o·de·gra·da·ble biologisch abbaubar, umweltfreundlich
bi·og·ra·pher Biograf *m*
bi·og·ra·phy Biografie *f*
bi·o·log·i·cal biologisch
bi·ol·o·gist Biologe *m*, Biologin *f*
bi·ol·o·gy Biologie *f*
bi·o·rhythms Biorhythmus *m*
bi·o·tope Biotop *n*
bi·ped ZO Zweifüßer *m*
birch BOT Birke *f*
bird ZO Vogel *m*
bird·cage Vogelkäfig *m*
bird flu Vogelgrippe *f*
bird of pas·sage ZO Zugvogel *m*
bird of prey ZO Raubvogel *m*
bird sanc·tu·a·ry Vogelschutzgebiet *n*
bird·seed Vogelfutter *n*
bird's-eye view Vogelperspektive *f*
bi·ro® Kugelschreiber *m*
birth Geburt *f*; Herkunft *f*; ***give birth to*** gebären, zur Welt bringen
birth cer·tif·i·cate Geburtsurkunde *f*
birth con·trol Geburtenregelung *f*
birth control pill MED Antibabypille *f*
birth·day Geburtstag *m*; ***happy birthday!*** alles Gute *or* herzlichen Glückwunsch zum Geburtstag!
birth·mark Muttermal *n*
birth·place Geburtsort *m*
birth·rate Geburtenziffer *f*
bis·cuit *Br* Keks *m*, *n*, Plätzchen *n*
bi·sex·u·al bisexuell
bish·op REL Bischof *m*; *chess*: Läufer *m*
bish·op·ric REL Bistum *n*
bi·son ZO Bison *m*; Wisent *m*
bit Bisschen *n*, Stück(chen) *n*; Gebiss *n* (*am Zaum*); (Schlüssel)Bart *m*; EDP Bit *n*; ***a*** (***little***) ***bit*** ein (kleines) bisschen
bitch ZO Hündin *f*; F *contp* Miststück *n*, Schlampe *f*
bit den·si·ty EDP Speicherdichte *f*
bite **1.** Beißen *n*; Biss *m*; Bissen *m*, Happen *m*; TECH Fassen *n*, Greifen *n*; **2.** (an)beißen; ZO stechen; GASTR brennen; *fig* schneiden (*cold etc*); beißen (*smoke etc*); TECH fassen, greifen
bit·ter bitter; *fig* verbittert
bit·ters GASTR Magenbitter *m*
biz F → ***business***

black **1.** schwarz; dunkel; finster; ***have s.th. in black and white*** et. schwarz auf weiß haben *or* besitzen; ***be black and blue*** blaue Flecken haben; ***beat s.o. black and blue*** j-n grün und blau schlagen; **2.** schwärzen; ***black out*** verdunkeln; **3.** Schwarz *n*; Schwärze *f*; Schwarze *m, f*
black·ber·ry BOT Brombeere *f*
black·bird ZO Amsel *f*
black·board (Schul-, Wand)Tafel *f*
black box AVIAT Flugschreiber *m*
black cur·rant BOT schwarze Johannisbeere
black·en *v/t* schwärzen; *fig* anschwärzen; *v/i* schwarz werden
black eye blaues Auge, Veilchen *n*
black·head MED Mitesser *m*
black ice Glatteis *n*
black·ing schwarze Schuhwichse
black·leg *Br* Streikbrecher *m*
black·mail **1.** Erpressung *f*; **2.** *j-n* erpressen
black·mail·er Erpresser(in)
black mar·ket Schwarzmarkt *m*
black·ness Schwärze *f*
black·out Verdunkelung *f*; Black-out *n, m*; ELECTR Stromausfall *m*; Ohnmacht *f*
black pud·ding GASTR Blutwurst *f*
black sheep *fig* schwarzes Schaf
black·smith Schmied *m*
blad·der ANAT Blase *f*
blade TECH Blatt *n*, Schaufel *f*; Klinge *f*; Schneide *f*; BOT Halm *m*
blame **1.** Tadel *m*; Schuld *f*; **2.** tadeln; ***be to blame for*** schuld sein an (*dat*)
blame·less untadelig
blanch *v/t* bleichen; GASTR blanchieren; *v/i* erbleichen, bleich werden
blank **1.** leer; unausgefüllt, unbeschrieben; ECON Blanko…; verdutzt; **2.** Leere *f*; leerer Raum, Lücke *f*; unbeschriebenes Blatt, Formular *n*; *lottery*: Niete *f*
blank car·tridge Platzpatrone *f*
blank check (*Br* **cheque**) ECON Blankoscheck *m*
blan·ket **1.** (Woll)Decke *f*; **2.** zudecken
blare brüllen, plärren (*radio etc*), schmettern (*trumpet*)
blas·pheme lästern
blas·phe·my Gotteslästerung *f*
blast **1.** Windstoß *m*; MUS Ton *m*; TECH Explosion *f*; Druckwelle *f*; Sprengung *f*; **2.** sprengen; *fig* zunichtemachen; ***blast off (into space)*** in den Weltraum schießen; ***blast off*** abheben, starten (*rocket*); ***blast!*** verdammt!; ***blast you!*** der Teufel soll dich holen!; ***blasted*** verdammt, verflucht
blast fur·nace TECH Hochofen *m*
blast-off Start *m* (*of a rocket*)
bla·tant offenkundig, eklatant
blaze **1.** Flamme(n *pl*) *f*, Feuer *n*; heller Schein; *fig* Ausbruch *m*; **2.** brennen, lodern; leuchten
blaz·er Blazer *m*
bla·zon Wappen *n*
bleach bleichen
bleak öde, kahl; rau; *fig* trüb, freudlos, finster
blear·y trübe, verschwommen
bleat ZO **1.** Blöken *n*; **2.** blöken
bleed *v/i* bluten; *v/t* MED zur Ader lassen; F schröpfen
bleed·ing MED Blutung *f*; Aderlass *m*
bleep **1.** Piepton *m*; **2.** *j-n* anpiepsen
bleep·er *Br* F Piepser *m*
blem·ish **1.** (*a.* Schönheits)Fehler *m*; Makel *m*; **2.** entstellen
blend **1.** (sich) (ver)mischen; GASTR verschneiden; **2.** Mischung *f*; GASTR Verschnitt *m*
blend·er Mixer *m*, Mixgerät *n*
bless segnen; preisen; ***be blessed with*** gesegnet sein mit; (***God***) ***bless you!*** alles Gute!; Gesundheit!; ***bless me!, bless my heart!, bless my soul!*** F du meine Güte!
bless·ed selig, gesegnet; F verflixt
bless·ing Segen *m*
blight BOT Mehltau *m*
blind **1.** blind (*fig* ***to*** gegen[über]); unübersichtlich; **2.** Rouleau *n*, Rollo *n*; ***the blind*** die Blinden *pl*; **3.** blenden; *fig* blind machen (***to*** für, gegen)
blind al·ley Sackgasse *f*
blind·ers Scheuklappen *pl*
blind·fold **1.** blindlings; **2.** *j-m* die Augen verbinden; **3.** Augenbinde *f*
blind·ly *fig* blindlings
blind·ness Blindheit *f*; Verblendung *f*
blind·worm ZO Blindschleiche *f*
blink **1.** Blinzeln *n*; **2.** blinzeln, zwinkern; blinken
blink·ers *Br* Scheuklappen *pl*
bliss Seligkeit *f*, Wonne *f*
blis·ter MED, TECH **1.** Blase *f*; **2.** Blasen hervorrufen auf (*dat*); Blasen ziehen *or* TECH werfen
blitz MIL **1.** heftiger Luftangriff; **2.** schwer bombardieren
bliz·zard Blizzard *m*, Schneesturm *m*
bloat·ed (an)geschwollen, (auf)gedunsen; *fig* aufgeblasen
bloat·er GASTR Bückling *m*
blob Klecks *m*
block **1.** Block *m*, Klotz *m*; Baustein *m*,

(Bau)Klötzchen *n*; (*Schreib-, Notiz-*) Block *m*; (Häuser)Block *m*; TECH Verstopfung *f*; *fig geistige etc* Sperre; ***block (of flats)*** *Br* Wohn-, Mietshaus *n*; **2.** *a.* ***block up*** (ab-, ver)sperren, blockieren, verstopfen
block·ade **1.** Blockade *f*; **2.** blockieren
block·bust·er F Kassenmagnet *m*, Kassenschlager *m*
block·head F Dummkopf *m*
block let·ters Blockschrift *f*
blond **1.** Blonde *m*; **2.** blond; hell (*skin*)
blonde **1.** blond; **2.** Blondine *f*
blood Blut *n*; ***in cold blood*** kaltblütig
blood bank MED Blutbank *f*
blood clot MED Blutgerinnsel *n*
blood cor·pus·cle MED Blutkörperchen *n*
blood·cur·dling grauenhaft
blood do·nor MED Blutspender(in)
blood group MED Blutgruppe *f*
blood·hound ZO Bluthund *m*
blood pres·sure MED Blutdruck *m*
blood·shed Blutvergießen *n*
blood·shot blutunterlaufen
blood·thirst·y blutdürstig
blood ves·sel ANAT Blutgefäß *n*
blood test MED Blutprobe *f*
blood·y blutig; *Br* F verdammt, verflucht
bloom **1.** Blume *f*, Blüte *f*; *fig* Blüte(zeit) *f*; **2.** blühen; *fig* (er)strahlen
blos·som **1.** Blüte *f*; **2.** blühen; *fig* ***blossom into*** erblühen zu
blot **1.** Klecks *m*; *fig* Makel *m*; **2.** beklecksen
blotch Klecks *m*; Hautfleck *m*
blotch·y fleckig
blot·ter (Tinten)Löscher *m*
blot·ting pa·per Löschpapier *n*
blouse Bluse *f*
blow[1] Schlag *m* (*a. fig*), Stoß *m*
blow[2] *v/i* blasen, wehen; keuchen, schnaufen; explodieren; platzen (*tire*); ELECTR durchbrennen; ***blow up*** in die Luft fliegen; explodieren; *v/t*: ***blow one's nose*** sich die Nase putzen; ***blow one's top*** F an die Decke gehen (*vor Wut*); ***blow out*** ausblasen; ***blow up*** sprengen; PHOT vergrößern
blow-dry föhnen
blow·fly ZO Schmeißfliege *f*
blow·pipe Blasrohr *n*
blow-up PHOT Vergrößerung *f*
blud·geon Knüppel *m*
blue **1.** blau; F melancholisch, traurig, schwermütig; **2.** Blau *n*; ***out of the blue*** *fig* aus heiterem Himmel
blue·ber·ry BOT Blau-, Heidelbeere *f*
blue·bot·tle ZO Schmeißfliege *f*
blue-col·lar work·er Arbeiter(in)
blues MUS Blues *m*; F Melancholie *f*; ***have the blues*** F den Moralischen haben
bluff[1] Steilufer *n*
bluff[2] **1.** Bluff *m*; **2.** bluffen
blu·ish bläulich
blun·der **1.** Fehler *m*, F Schnitzer *m*; **2.** e-n (groben) Fehler machen; verpfuschen, F verpatzen
blunt stumpf; *fig* offen
blunt·ly freiheraus
blur [blɜː] **1.** *v/t* verwischen; verschmieren; PHOT, TV verwackeln, verzerren; *fig* trüben; **2.** *v/i* verschwimmen (*a. fig*)
blurt: ***blurt out*** herausplatzen mit
blush **1.** Erröten *n*, Schamröte *f*; **2.** erröten, rot werden
blus·ter brausen (*wind*); *fig* poltern, toben
BMX ABBR *of* ***bicycle motocross*** Querfeldeinrennen *n*
BMX bike BMX-Rad *n*
BO ABBR → ***body odo(u)r***
boar ZO Eber *m*; Keiler *m*
board **1.** Brett *n*; (Anschlag)Brett *n*; Konferenztisch *m*; Ausschuss *m*, Kommission *f*; Behörde *f*; Verpflegung *f*; Pappe *f*, Karton *m*; SPORT (Surf)Board *n*; ***on board a train*** in e-m Zug; **2.** *v/t* dielen, verschalen; beköstigen; an Bord gehen; MAR entern; RAIL *etc* einsteigen in; *v/i* in Kost sein, wohnen
board·er Kostgänger(in); Pensionsgast *m*; Internatsschüler(in)
board game Brettspiel *n*
board·ing card AVIAT Bordkarte *f*
boarding house Pension *f*, Fremdenheim *n*
boarding school Internat *n*
board of di·rec·tors ECON Aufsichtsrat *m*
Board of Trade Handelskammer *f*; *Br* Handelsministerium *n*
board·walk Strandpromenade *f*
boast **1.** Prahlerei *f*; **2.** ***(of, about)*** sich rühmen (*gen*), prahlen (mit)
boat Boot *n*; Schiff *n*
bob **1.** Knicks *m*; kurzer Haarschnitt; *Br* HIST F Schilling *m*; **2.** *v/t* *Haar* kurz schneiden; *v/i* sich auf und ab bewegen; knicksen
bob·bin Spule *f* (*a.* ELECTR)
bob·sleigh SPORT Bob *m*
bod·ice Mieder *n*; Oberteil *n*
bod·i·ly körperlich
bod·y Körper *m*, Leib *m*; Leiche *f*; JUR Körperschaft *f*; Hauptteil *m*; MOT Karosserie *f*; MIL Truppenkörper *m*
bod·y·guard Leibwache *f*; Leibwächter *m*
bod·y o·do(u)r (ABBR ***BO***) Körpergeruch

m

body stock·ing Body *m*

bod·y·work MOT Karosserie *f*

Boer **1.** Bure *m*; **2.** Buren…

bog Sumpf *m*, Morast *m*

bo·gus falsch; Schwindel…

boil[1] MED Geschwür *n*, Furunkel *m*, *n*

boil[2] **1.** kochen, sieden; **2.** Kochen *n*, Sieden *n*

boil·er (Dampf)Kessel *m*; Boiler *m*

boil·er suit Overall *m*

boil·ing point Siedepunkt *m* (*a. fig*)

bois·ter·ous ungestüm; heftig, laut; lärmend

bold kühn, verwegen; keck, dreist, unverschämt; steil; PRINT fett; ***as bold as brass*** F frech wie Oskar; *words* ***in bold print*** fett gedruckt

bold·ness Kühnheit *f*, Verwegenheit *f*; Dreistigkeit *f*

bol·ster **1.** Keilkissen *n*; **2.** ***bolster up*** *fig* (unter)stützen, *j-m* Mut machen

bolt **1.** Bolzen *m*; Riegel *m*; Blitz(strahl) *m*; plötzlicher Satz, Fluchtversuch *m*; **2.** *adv*: ***bolt upright*** kerzengerade; **3.** *v/t* verriegeln; F hinunterschlingen; *v/i* davonlaufen, ausreißen; ZO scheuen, durchgehen

bomb **1.** Bombe *f*; ***the bomb*** die Atombombe; **2.** bombardieren

bom·bard bombardieren

bomb·er AVIAT Bomber *m*; Bombenleger *m*

bomb·proof bombensicher

bomb·shell Bombe *f* (*a. fig*)

bo·nan·za *fig* Goldgrube *f*

bond Bund *m*, Verbindung *f*; ECON Schuldverschreibung *f*, Obligation *f*; ***in bond*** ECON unter Zollverschluss

bond·age Hörigkeit *f*

bonds *fig* Bande *pl*

bone **1.** ANAT Knochen *m*, *pl a.* Gebeine *pl*; ZO Gräte *f*; ***bone of contention*** Zankapfel *m*; ***have a bone to pick with s.o.*** mit j-m ein Hühnchen zu rupfen haben; ***make no bones about*** nicht lange fackeln mit; **2.** die Knochen auslösen (aus); entgräten

bon·fire Feuer *n* im Freien; Freudenfeuer *n*

bon·net Haube *f*; *Br* Motorhaube *f*

bo·nus ECON Bonus *m*, Prämie *f*; Gratifikation *f*

bon·y knöchern; knochig

boo *int* buh!; THEA ***boo off the stage***, *soccer*: ***boo off the park*** auspfeifen

boobs *sl* Titten *pl*

boo·by F Trottel *m*

book **1.** Buch *n*; Heft *n*; Liste *f*; Block *m*; **2.** buchen; eintragen; SPORT verwarnen; *Fahrkarte etc* lösen; *Platz etc* (vor)bestellen, reservieren lassen; *Gepäck* aufgeben; ***book in*** *esp Br* sich (*im Hotel*) eintragen; ***book in at*** absteigen in (*dat*); ***booked up*** ausgebucht, ausverkauft, belegt

book·case Bücherschrank *m*

book·ing Buchen *n*, (Vor)Bestellung *f*; SPORT Verwarnung *f*

booking clerk Schalterbeamte *m*, -beamtin *f*

booking of·fice Fahrkartenausgabe *f*, -schalter *m*; THEA Kasse *f*

book·keep·er ECON Buchhalter(in)

book·keep·ing ECON Buchhaltung *f*, Buchführung *f*

book·let Büchlein *n*, Broschüre *f*

book·mak·er Buchmacher *m*

book·mark(·er) Lesezeichen *n*

book·sell·er Buchhändler(in)

book·shelf Bücherregal *n*

book·shop *esp Br*, **book·store** Buchhandlung *f*

book·worm *fig* Bücherwurm *m*

boom[1] ECON **1.** Boom *m*, Aufschwung *m*, Hochkonjunktur *f*, Hausse *f*; **2.** e-n Boom erleben

boom[2] MAR Baum *m*, Spiere *f*; TECH (Kran)Ausleger *m*; *film*, TV (Mikrofon)-Galgen *m*

boom[3] dröhnen, donnern

boor·ish ungehobelt

boost **1.** hochschieben; ECON in die Höhe treiben; ankurbeln; ELECTR verstärken; TECH erhöhen; *fig* stärken, Auftrieb geben (*dat*); **2.** Erhöhung *f*; Auftrieb *m*; ELECTR Verstärkung *f*

boot[1] Stiefel *m*; *Br* MOT Kofferraum *m*

boot[2]: ***boot*** **(*up*)** EDP laden

boot[3]: ***to boot*** obendrein

boot·ee (*Damen*)Halbstiefel *m*

booth (Markt- *etc*)Bude *f*; (Messe-) Stand *m*; (Wahl- *etc*)Kabine *f*; (Telefon)Zelle *f*

boot·lace Schnürsenkel *m*

boot·y Beute *f*

booze F **1.** saufen; **2.** Zeug *n*; Sauferei *f*

bor·der **1.** Rand *m*, Saum *m*, Einfassung *f*; Rabatte *f*; Grenze *f*; **2.** einfassen; (um)säumen; grenzen (***on*** an *acc*)

bore[1] **1.** Bohrloch *n*; TECH Kaliber *n*; **2.** bohren

bore[2] **1.** Langweiler *m*; langweilige *or* lästige Sache; **2.** *j-n* langweilen; ***be bored*** sich langweilen

bore·dom Lang(e)weile *f*

bor·ing langweilig

bo·rough Stadtteil *m*; Stadtgemeinde *f*; Stadtbezirk *m*

bor·row (sich) *et.* borgen *or* (aus)leihen
bos·om Busen *m*; *fig* Schoß *m*
boss F **1.** Boss *m*, Chef *m*; **2.** *a.* ***boss about, boss around*** herumkommandieren
boss·y F herrisch
bo·tan·i·cal botanisch
bot·a·ny Botanik *f*
botch **1.** Pfusch *m*; **2.** verpfuschen
both beide(s); ***both … and …*** sowohl … als (auch) …
both·er **1.** Belästigung *f*, Störung *f*, Plage *f*, Mühe *f*; **2.** belästigen, stören, plagen; ***don't bother!*** bemühen Sie sich nicht!
bot·tle **1.** Flasche *f*; **2.** in Flaschen abfüllen
bottle bank *Br* Altglascontainer *m*
bot·tle·neck *fig* Engpass *m*
bot·tle o·pen·er Flaschenöffner *m*
bot·tom unterster Teil, Boden *m*, Fuß *m*, Unterseite *f*; Grund *m*; F Hintern *m*, Popo *m*; ***be at the bottom of s.th.*** hinter e-r Sache stecken; ***get to the bottom of s.th.*** e-r Sache auf den Grund gehen
bough Ast *m*, Zweig *m*
boul·der Geröllblock *m*, Findling *m*
bounce **1.** aufprallen *or* aufspringen (lassen); springen, hüpfen, stürmen; ECON F platzen (*check*); **2.** Sprung *m*, Satz *m*; F Schwung *m*
bounc·ing kräftig, stramm
bound[1] unterwegs (***for*** nach)
bound[2] *mst pl* Grenze *f*, *fig a.* Schranke *f*
bound[3] **1.** Sprung *m*, Satz *m*; **2.** springen, hüpfen; auf-, abprallen
bound·a·ry Grenze *f*
bound·less grenzenlos
boun·te·ous, boun·ti·ful freigebig, reichlich
boun·ty Freigebigkeit *f*; großzügige Spende *f*; Prämie *f*
bou·quet Bukett *n* (*a.* GASTR), Strauß *m*; GASTR Blume *f*
bout SPORT (*Box-, Ring*)Kampf *m*; MED Anfall *m*
bou·tique Boutique *f*
bow[1] **1.** Verbeugung *f*; **2.** *v/i* sich verbeugen *or* verneigen (***to*** vor *dat*); *fig* sich beugen *or* unterwerfen (***to*** *dat*); *v/t* biegen; beugen, neigen
bow[2] MAR Bug *m*
bow[3] Bogen *m*; Schleife *f*
bow·els ANAT Darm *m*; Eingeweide *pl*
bowl[1] Schale *f*, Schüssel *f*, Napf *m*; (*Zucker*)Dose *f*; Becken *n*; (*Pfeifen-*) Kopf *m*
bowl[2] **1.** (*Bowling-, Kegel- etc*)Kugel *f*; **2.** kegeln; rollen (*bowling ball*); *cricket*: werfen
bow-leg·ged o-beinig
bowl·er[1] Bowlingspieler(in); Kegler(in)
bowl·er[2], *a.* **bowler hat** *esp Br* Bowler *m*, F Melone *f*
bowl·ing Bowling *n*; Kegeln *n*; ***go bowling*** kegeln
bowling al·ley Kegelbahn *f*
bowling ball Kegelkugel *f*
box[1] Kasten *m*, Kiste *f*; Büchse *f*, Dose *f*, Kästchen *n*; Schachtel *f*; Behälter *m*; TECH Gehäuse *n*; Postfach *n*; *Br* (Telefon)Zelle *f*; JUR Zeugenstand *m*; THEA Loge *f*; MOT, ZO Box *f*
box[2] **1.** SPORT boxen; F ***box s.o.'s ears*** j-n ohrfeigen; **2.** F ***a box on the ear*** e-e Ohrfeige
box[3] [bɒks] BOT Buchsbaum *m*
box·er Boxer *m*
box·ing Boxen *n*, Boxsport *m*
Box·ing Day *Br* der zweite Weihnachtsfeiertag
box num·ber Chiffre(nummer) *f*
box of·fice Theaterkasse *f*
boy Junge *m*, Knabe *m*, Bursche *m*
boy·cott **1.** boykottieren; **2.** Boykott *m*
boy·friend Freund *m*
boy·hood Knabenjahre *pl*, Jugend(-zeit) *f*
boy·ish jungenhaft
boy scout Pfadfinder *m*
bra BH *m* (*Büstenhalter*)
brace **1.** TECH Strebe *f*, Stützbalken *m*; (Zahn)Klammer *f*, (-)Spange *f*; **2.** TECH verstreben, versteifen, stützen
brace·let Armband *n*
brac·es *Br* Hosenträger *pl*
brack·et TECH Träger *m*, Halter *m*, Stütze *f*; PRINT Klammer *f*; (*esp Alters-, Steuer*)-Klasse *f*; ***lower income bracket*** niedrige Einkommensgruppe
brack·ish brackig, salzig
brag prahlen (***about*** mit)
brag·gart Prahler *m*, F Angeber *m*
braid **1.** Zopf *m*; Borte *f*, Tresse *f*; **2.** flechten; mit Borte besetzen
brain ANAT Gehirn *n*, *often pl fig a.* Verstand *m*, Intelligenz *f*, Kopf *m*
brain·storm Geistesblitz *m*
brain·wash *j-n* e-r Gehirnwäsche unterziehen
brain·wash·ing Gehirnwäsche *f*
brain·wave *Br* Geistesblitz *m*
brain·y F gescheit
braise GASTR schmoren
brake TECH **1.** Bremse *f*; **2.** bremsen
brake·light MOT Bremslicht *n*
bram·ble BOT Brombeerstrauch *m*
bran AGR Kleie *f*
branch **1.** Ast *m*, Zweig *m*; *fig* Fach *n*; Linie *f* (*des Stammbaumes*); ECON Zweig-

stelle *f*, Filiale *f*; **2.** sich verzweigen; abzweigen
brand **1.** ECON (Schutz-, Handels)Marke *f*, Warenzeichen *n*; Markenname *m*; Sorte *f*, Klasse *f*; Brandmal *n*; **2.** einbrennen; brandmarken
bran·dish schwingen
brand name ECON Markenname *m*
brand-new nagelneu
bran·dy Kognak *m*, Weinbrand *m*
brass Messing *n*; F Unverschämtheit *f*
brass band MUS Blaskapelle *f*
bras·sière Büstenhalter *m*
brat *contp* Balg *m*, *n*, Gör *n*
brave **1.** tapfer, mutig, unerschrocken; **2.** trotzen; mutig begegnen (*dat*)
brav·er·y Tapferkeit *f*
brawl **1.** Krawall *m*; Rauferei *f*; **2.** Krawall machen; raufen
brawn·y muskulös
bray **1.** zo Eselsschrei *m*; **2.** zo schreien; *fig* wiehern
bra·zen unverschämt, unverfroren, frech
Bra·zil Brasilien *n*
Bra·zil·ian **1.** brasilianisch; **2.** Brasilianer(in)
breach **1.** Bruch *m*; *fig* Verletzung *f*; MIL Bresche *f*; **2.** e-e Bresche schlagen in (*acc*)
bread Brot *n*; ***brown bread*** Schwarzbrot *n*; ***know which side one's bread is buttered*** F s-n Vorteil (er)kennen
breadth Breite *f*
break **1.** Bruch *m*; Lücke *f*; Pause *f* (*Br a.* PED), Unterbrechung *f*; (plötzlicher) Wechsel, Umschwung *m*; (*Tages*)Anbruch *m*; ***bad break*** F Pech *n*; ***lucky break*** F Dusel *m*, Schwein *n*; ***give s.o. a break*** F j-m e-e Chance geben; ***take a break*** e-e Pause machen; ***without a break*** ununterbrochen; **2.** *v/t* (ab-, auf-, durch-, zer)brechen; zerschlagen, kaputt machen; zo *a.* ***break in*** zähmen, abrichten, zureiten; *Gesetz*, *Vertrag etc* brechen; *Kode etc* knacken; *schlechte Nachricht* (schonend) beibringen; *v/i* brechen (*a. fig*); (zer-)brechen, (zer)reißen, kaputtgehen; anbrechen (*Tag*); METEOR umschlagen; *fig* ausbrechen (***into*** in *Tränen etc*); ***break away*** ab-, losbrechen; sich losmachen *or* losreißen; ***break down*** ein-, niederreißen, *Haus* abbrechen; zusammenbrechen (*a. fig*); versagen; MOT e-e Panne haben; *fig* scheitern; ***break in*** einbrechen, eindringen; ***break into*** einbrechen in (*ein Haus etc*); ***break off*** abbrechen, *fig a.* Schluss machen mit; ***break out*** ausbrechen; ***break through*** durchbrechen; *fig* den Durchbruch schaffen; ***break up*** abbrechen, beenden, schließen; (sich) auflösen; *fig* zerbrechen, auseinandergehen
break·a·ble zerbrechlich
break·age Bruch *m*
break·a·way **1.** Trennung *f*; **2.** Splitter…
break·down Zusammenbruch *m* (*a. fig*); TECH Maschinenschaden *m*; MOT Panne *f*; ***nervous breakdown*** MED Nervenzusammenbruch *m*
breakdown lor·ry *Br* MOT Abschleppwagen *m*
breakdown ser·vice *Br* MOT Pannendienst *m*, Pannenhilfe *f*
breakdown truck *Br* MOT Abschleppwagen *m*
break·fast **1.** Frühstück *n*; ***have breakfast*** → **2.** frühstücken
break·through *fig* Durchbruch *m*
break·up Aufhebung *f*; Auflösung *f*
breast ANAT Brust *f*; Busen *m*; *fig* Herz *n*; ***make a clean breast of s.th.*** et. offen (ein)gestehen
breast·stroke Brustschwimmen *n*
breath Atem(zug) *m*; Hauch *m*; ***be out of breath*** außer Atem sein; ***waste one's breath*** in den Wind reden
breath·a·lyse *Br*, **breath·a·lyze** F (ins Röhrchen) blasen *or* pusten lassen
breath·a·lys·er® *Br*, **breath·alyz·er®** Alkoholtestgerät *n*, F Röhrchen *n*
breathe atmen
breath·less atemlos
breath·tak·ing atemberaubend
breech·es Kniebund-, Reithosen *pl*
breed **1.** zo Rasse *f*, Zucht *f*; **2.** *v/t* BOT, zo züchten; *v/i* BIOL sich fortpflanzen
breed·er Züchter(in); Zuchttier *n*; PHYS Brüter *m*
breed·ing BIOL Fortpflanzung *f*; (Tier-)Zucht *f*; *fig* Erziehung *f*; (gutes) Benehmen
breeze Brise *f*
breth·ren *esp* REL Brüder *pl*
brew brauen; *Tee* zubereiten, aufbrühen
brew·er (Bier)Brauer *m*
brew·er·y Brauerei *f*
bri·ar → ***brier***
bribe **1.** Bestechungsgeld *n*, -geschenk *n*; Bestechung *f*; **2.** bestechen
brib·er·y Bestechung *f*
brick **1.** Ziegel(stein) *m*, Backstein *m*; *Br* Baustein *m*, (Bau)Klötzchen *n*
brick·lay·er Maurer *m*
brick·yard Ziegelei *f*
brid·al Braut…
bride Braut *f*
bride·groom Bräutigam *m*
brides·maid Brautjungfer *f*

bridge 1. Brücke *f*; 2. e-e Brücke schlagen über (*acc*); *fig* überbrücken
bri·dle 1. Zaum *m*; Zügel *m*; 2. (auf)zäumen; zügeln
bridle path Reitweg *m*
brief 1. kurz, bündig; 2. instruieren, genaue Anweisungen geben (*dat*)
brief·case Aktenmappe *f*
briefs Slip *m*
bri·er BOT Dornstrauch *m*; Wilde Rose
bri·gade MIL Brigade *f*
bright hell, glänzend; klar; heiter; lebhaft; gescheit
bright·en *v/t a.* ***brighten up*** heller machen, aufhellen, erhellen; aufheitern; *v/i a.* ***brighten up*** sich aufhellen
bright·ness Helligkeit *f*; Glanz *m*; Heiterkeit *f*; Gescheitheit *f*
brill *Br* F super, toll
bril·liance, bril·lian·cy Glanz *m*; *fig* Brillanz *f*
bril·liant 1. glänzend; hervorragend, brillant; 2. Brillant *m*
brim 1. Rand *m*; Krempe *f*; 2. bis zum Rande füllen *or* voll sein
brim·ful(l) randvoll
brine Sole *f*; Lake *f*
bring bringen, mitbringen, herbringen; *j-n* dazu bringen (***to do*** zu tun); ***bring about*** zustande bringen; bewirken; ***bring forth*** hervorbringen; ***bring off*** *et.* fertigbringen, schaffen; ***bring on*** verursachen; ***bring out*** herausbringen; ***bring round*** *Ohnmächtigen* wieder zu sich bringen; *Kranken* wieder auf die Beine bringen; ***bring up*** auf-, großziehen; erziehen; zur Sprache bringen
brink Rand *m* (*a. fig*)
brisk flott; lebhaft; frisch
bris·tle 1. Borste *f*; (Bart)Stoppel *f*; 2. *a.* ***bristle up*** sich sträuben; zornig werden; strotzen, wimmeln (***with*** von)
bris·tly stoppelig, Stoppel…
Brit F Brite *m*, Britin *f*
Brit·ain Britannien *n*
Brit·ish britisch; ***the British*** die Briten *pl*
Brit·on Brite *m*, Britin *f*
brit·tle spröde, zerbrechlich
broach *Thema* anschneiden
broad breit; weit; hell; deutlich (*hint etc*); derb (*humor etc*); stark (*accent*); allgemein; weitherzig; liberal
broad·cast 1. im Rundfunk *or* Fernsehen bringen, ausstrahlen, übertragen; senden; 2. *radio*, TV Sendung *f*
broad·cast·er Rundfunk-, Fernsehsprecher(in)
broad·en verbreitern, erweitern
broad jump SPORT Weitsprung *m*
broad·mind·ed liberal
bro·cade Brokat *m*
bro·chure Broschüre *f*, Prospekt *m*
brogue fester Straßenschuh
broil grillen
broke F pleite, abgebrannt
bro·ken zerbrochen, kaputt; gebrochen (*a. fig*); zerrüttet
brok·en-heart·ed verzweifelt, untröstlich
bro·ker ECON Makler *m*
bron·chi·tis MED Bronchitis *f*
bronze 1. Bronze *f*; 2. bronzefarben; Bronze…
brooch Brosche *f*
brood ZO 1. Brut *f*; 2. Brut…; 3. brüten (*a. fig*)
brook Bach *m*
broom Besen *m*
broth GASTR Fleischbrühe *f*
broth·el Bordell *n*
broth·er Bruder *m*; ***brother(s) and sister(s)*** Geschwister *pl*
broth·er·hood REL Bruderschaft *f*
broth·er-in-law Schwager *m*
broth·er·ly brüderlich
brow ANAT (Augen)Braue *f*; Stirn *f*; GEOGR Rand *m*
brow·beat einschüchtern
brown 1. braun; 2. Braun *n*; 3. bräunen; braun werden
browse grasen, weiden; *fig* schmökern
bruise 1. MED Quetschung *f*, blauer Fleck; 2. quetschen; anstoßen; MED e-e Quetschung *or* e-n blauen Fleck bekommen
brunch Brunch *m*
brush 1. Bürste *f*; Pinsel *m*; ZO (*Fuchs*)-Rute *f*; Scharmützel *n*; Unterholz *n*; 2. bürsten; fegen; streifen; ***brush against s.o.*** j-n streifen; ***brush away, brush off*** wegbürsten, abwischen; ***brush aside, brush away*** *et.* abtun; ***brush up (on)*** *fig* aufpolieren, auffrischen
brush·wood Gestrüpp *n*, Unterholz *n*
brusque brüsk, barsch
Brus·sels sprouts BOT Rosenkohl *m*
bru·tal brutal, roh
bru·tal·i·ty Brutalität *f*
brute 1. brutal; ***with brute force*** mit roher Gewalt; 2. Vieh *n*; F Untier *n*, Scheusal *n*; Rohling *m*
brut·ish *fig* tierisch
bub·ble 1. Blase *f*; 2. sprudeln
buck[1] 1. ZO Bock *m*; 2. bocken
buck[2] F Dollar *m*
buck·et Eimer *m*, Kübel *m*
buck·le 1. Schnalle *f*, Spange *f*; 2. *a.* ***buckle up*** zu-, festschnallen; ***buckle on*** anschnallen
buck·skin Wildleder *n*

bud 1. BOT Knospe *f*; *fig* Keim *m*; **2.** knospen, keimen
bud·dy F Kamerad *m*; Kumpel *m*, Spezi *m*
budge *v/i* sich (von der Stelle) rühren; *v/t* (vom Fleck) bewegen
bud·ger·i·gar zo Wellensittich *m*
bud·get Budget *n*, Etat *m*; PARL Haushaltsplan *m*
bud·gie F → ***budgerigar***
buf·fa·lo zo Büffel *m*
buff·er TECH Puffer *m*
buf·fet[1] schlagen; ***buffet about*** durchrütteln, durchschütteln
buf·fet[2] Büfett *n*, Anrichte *f*
buf·fet[3] (*Frühstücks- etc*)Büfett *n*; Theke *f*
bug 1. zo Wanze *f* (*a.* F *fig*); Insekt *n*; EDP Programmfehler *m*; **2.** F Wanzen anbringen in (*dat*); F ärgern
bug·ging de·vice Abhörgerät *n*
bugging op·e·ra·tion Lauschangriff *m*
bug·gy Kinderwagen *m*; MOT Buggy *m*
bu·gle MUS Wald-, Signalhorn *n*
build 1. (er)bauen, errichten; **2.** Körperbau *m*, Figur *f*, Statur *f*
build·er Erbauer *m*; Bauunternehmer *m*
build·ing 1. (Er)Bauen *n*; Bau *m*, Gebäude *n*; **2.** Bau…
building site Baustelle *f*
built-in eingebaut, Einbau…
built-up: ***built-up area*** bebautes Gelände *or* Gebiet; geschlossene Ortschaft
bulb BOT Zwiebel *f*, Knolle *f*; ELECTR (Glüh)Birne *f*
bulge 1. (Aus)Bauchung *f*, Ausbuchtung *f*; **2.** sich (aus)bauchen; hervorquellen
bulk Umfang *m*, Größe *f*, Masse *f*; Großteil *m*; ***in bulk*** ECON lose, unverpackt; en gros
bulk·y sperrig
bull zo Bulle *m*, Stier *m*
bull·dog zo Bulldogge *f*
bull·doze planieren; F einschüchtern
bull·doz·er TECH Bulldozer *m*, Planierraupe *f*
bul·let Kugel *f*
bul·le·tin Bulletin *n*, Tagesbericht *m*
bul·le·tin board Schwarzes Brett
bul·let·proof kugelsicher
bull·fight Stierkampf *m*
bul·lion Gold-, Silberbarren *m*
bul·lock zo Ochse *m*
bull's-eye: ***hit the bull's-eye*** ins Schwarze treffen (*a. fig*)
bul·ly 1. tyrannische Person, Tyrann *m*; **2.** einschüchtern, tyrannisieren
bul·wark Bollwerk *n* (*a. fig*)
bum F **1.** Gammler *m*; Tippelbruder *m*, Vagabund *m*; Nichtstuer *m*; **2.** *v/t* schnorren; ***bum around*** herumgammeln
bum·ble·bee zo Hummel *f*
bump 1. heftiger Schlag *or* Stoß; Beule *f*; Unebenheit *f*; **2.** stoßen; rammen, auf *ein Auto* auffahren; zusammenstoßen; holpern; ***bump into*** *fig j-n* zufällig treffen; F ***bump s.o. off*** j-n umlegen
bump·er MOT Stoßstange *f*
bump·y holp(e)rig
bun süßes Brötchen; (Haar)Knoten *m*
bunch Bund *n*, Bündel *n*; F Verein *m*, Haufen *m*; ***bunch of flowers*** Blumenstrauß *m*; ***bunch of grapes*** Weintraube *f*; ***bunch of keys*** Schlüsselbund *m*, *n*
bun·dle 1. Bündel *n* (*a. fig*), Bund *n*; **2.** *v/t a.* ***bundle up*** bündeln
bun·ga·low Bungalow *m*
bun·gee elastisches Seil
bun·gee jump·ing Bungeespringen *n*
bun·gle 1. Pfusch *m*; **2.** (ver)pfuschen
bunk Koje *f*; → **bunk bed** Etagenbett *n*
bun·ny Häschen *n*
buoy 1. MAR Boje *f*; **2.** ***buoy up*** *fig* Auftrieb geben (*dat*)
bur·den 1. Last *f*; Bürde *f*; **2.** belasten
bu·reau *Br* Schreibtisch *m*; (Spiegel-)Kommode *f*; Büro *n*
bu·reauc·ra·cy Bürokratie *f*
burg·er GASTR Hamburger *m*
bur·glar Einbrecher *m*
bur·glar·ize einbrechen in (*acc*)
bur·glar·y Einbruch *m*
bur·gle *Br* → ***burglarize***
bur·i·al Begräbnis *n*
bur·ly stämmig, kräftig
burn 1. MED Verbrennung *f*, Brandwunde *f*; verbrannte Stelle; **2.** (ver-, an-)brennen; ***burn down*** ab-, niederbrennen; ***burn out*** ausbrennen; ***burn up*** auflodern; verbrennen; verglühen (*rocket etc*)
burn·ing brennend (*a. fig*)
burp F rülpsen, aufstoßen; ein Bäuerchen machen (lassen)
bur·row 1. zo Bau *m*; **2.** graben; sich eingraben *or* vergraben
burst 1. Bersten *n*; Riss *m*; *fig* Ausbruch *m*; **2.** *v/i* bersten, (zer)platzen; zerspringen; explodieren; ***burst from*** sich losreißen von; ***burst in on*** *or* ***upon s.o.*** bei j-m hereinplatzen; ***burst into tears*** in Tränen ausbrechen; ***burst out*** *fig* herausplatzen; *v/t* (auf)sprengen
bur·y begraben, vergraben; beerdigen
bus Omnibus *m*, Bus *m*
bus driv·er Busfahrer *m*
bush Busch *m*; Gebüsch *n*
bush·el Bushel *m*, Scheffel *m* (*Am 35,24 l*, *Br 36,37 l*)
bush·y buschig
busi·ness Geschäft *n*; Arbeit *f*, Beschäf-

tigung *f*, Beruf *m*, Tätigkeit *f*; Angelegenheit *f*; Sache *f*, Aufgabe *f*; ***business of the day*** Tagesordnung *f*; ***on business*** geschäftlich, beruflich; ***you have no business doing*** (*or* ***to do***) ***that*** Sie haben kein recht, das zu tun; ***that's none of your business*** das geht Sie nichts an; → ***mind*** 2

busi·ness hours Geschäftszeit *f*

busi·ness·like geschäftsmäßig, sachlich

busi·ness·man Geschäftsmann *m*

busi·ness trip Geschäftsreise *f*

busi·ness·wom·an Geschäftsfrau *f*

bus stop Bushaltestelle *f*

bust[1] Büste *f*

bust[2]: ***go bust*** F pleitegehen

bus·tle **1.** geschäftiges Treiben; **2.** ***bustle about*** geschäftig hin und her eilen

bus·y **1.** beschäftigt; geschäftig; fleißig (***at*** bei, an *dat*); belebt (*street*); arbeitsreich (*dat*); TEL besetzt; **2.** (*mst* ***busy o.s.*** sich) beschäftigen (***with*** mit)

bus·y·bod·y aufdringlicher Mensch, Gschaftlhuber *m*

bus·y sig·nal TEL Besetztzeichen *n*

but **1.** *cj* aber, jedoch; sondern; außer, als; ohne dass; dennoch; ***but then*** and(e)rerseits; ***he could not but laugh*** er musste einfach lachen; **2.** *prp* außer (*dat*); ***all but him*** alle außer ihm; ***the last but one*** der Vorletzte; ***the next but one*** der Übernächste; ***nothing but*** nichts als; ***but for*** wenn nicht … gewesen wäre, ohne; **3.** der (die *or* das) nicht; ***there is no one but knows*** es gibt niemand, der es nicht weiß; **4.** *adv* nur; erst, gerade; ***all but*** fast, beinahe

butch·er **1.** Fleischer *m*, Metzger *m*; **2.** (*fig* ab)schlachten

but·ler Butler *m*

butt[1] **1.** (*Gewehr*)Kolben *m*; (*Zigarren etc*)Stummel *m*, (*Zigaretten*)Kippe *f*; (Kopf)Stoß *m*; **2.** (mit dem Kopf) stoßen; ***butt in*** F sich einmischen (***on*** in *acc*)

butt[2] Wein-, Bierfaß *n*; Regentonne *f*

but·ter **1.** Butter *f*; **2.** mit Butter bestreichen

but·ter·cup BOT Butterblume *f*

but·ter·fly ZO Schmetterling *m*, Falter *m*

but·tocks ANAT Gesäß *n*, F *or* ZO Hinterteil *n*

but·ton **1.** Knopf *m*; Button *m*, (Anstecker)-Plakette *f*, Abzeichen *n*; **2.** *mst* ***button up*** zuknöpfen

but·ton·hole Knopfloch *n*

but·tress Strebepfeiler *m*

bux·om drall, stramm

buy **1.** F Kauf *m*; **2.** (an-, ein)kaufen (***of, from*** von; ***at*** bei); *Fahrkarte* lösen; ***buy out*** *j-n* abfinden, auszahlen; *Firma* aufkaufen; ***buy up*** aufkaufen

buy·er Käufer(in); ECON Einkäufer(in)

buzz **1.** Summen *n*, Surren *n*; Stimmengewirr *n*; **2.** *v/i* summen, surren; ***buzz off!*** F schwirr ab!, hau ab!

buz·zard ZO Bussard *m*

buzz·er ELECTR Summer *m*

by **1.** *prp* (nahe *or* dicht) bei *or* an, neben (***side by side*** Seite an Seite); vorbei *or* vorüber an; *time*: bis um, bis spätestens (***be back by 9.30*** sei um 9 Uhr 30 zurück); während, bei (***by day*** bei Tage); per, mit (***by bus*** mit dem Bus; ***by rail*** per Bahn); nach, …weise (***by the dozen*** dutzendweise); nach, gemäß (***by my watch*** nach *or* auf m-r Uhr); von (***by nature*** von Natur aus); von, durch (***a play by …*** ein Stück von …; ***by o.s.*** allein); um (***by an inch*** um e-n Zoll); MATH mal (***2 by 4***); *geteilt* durch (***6 by 3***); **2.** *adv* vorbei, vorüber (***go by*** vorbeigehen, -fahren; *time*: vergehen); beiseite (***put by*** beiseitelegen, zurücklegen); ***by and large*** im Großen und Ganzen

by… Neben…; Seiten…

bye, bye-bye *int* F Wiedersehen!, tschüs(s)!

by-e·lec·tion PARL Nachwahl *f*

by·gone **1.** vergangen; **2.** ***let bygones be bygones*** lass(t) das Vergangene ruhen

by·pass **1.** Umgehungsstraße *f*; MED Bypass *m*; **2.** umgehen; vermeiden

by-prod·uct Nebenprodukt *n*

by·road Nebenstraße *f*

by·stand·er Zuschauer(in), *pl die* Umstehenden *pl*

byte EDP Byte *n*

by·way Nebenstraße *f*

by·word Inbegriff *m*; ***be a byword for*** stehen für

C

C

C, c C, c *n*
C ABBR *of* ***Celsius*** C, Celsius; ***centigrade*** hundertgradig
c ABBR *of* ***cent(s)*** Cent *m or pl*; ***century*** Jh., Jahrhundert *n*; ***circa*** ca., zirca, ungefähr; ***cubic*** Kubik…
cab Droschke *f*, Taxi *n*; RAIL Führerstand *m*; MOT Fahrerhaus *n*, *a.* TECH Führerhaus *n*
cab·a·ret Varieteedarbietung(en *pl*) *f*
cab·bage BOT Kohl *m*
cab·in Hütte *f*; MAR Kabine *f*, Kajüte *f*; AVIAT Kanzel *f*
cab·i·net Schrank *m*, Vitrine *f*; POL Kabinett *n*
cab·i·net-mak·er Kunsttischler *m*
cab·i·net meet·ing POL Kabinettssitzung *f*
ca·ble **1.** Kabel *n*; (Draht)Seil *n*; **2.** telegrafieren; *j-m Geld* telegrafisch anweisen; TV verkabeln
ca·ble car Kabine *f*; Wagen *m*
ca·ble·gram (Übersee)Telegramm *n*
ca·ble rail·way Drahtseil-, Kabinenbahn *f*
cable tel·e·vi·sion, cable TV Kabelfernsehen *n*
cab rank, cab·stand Taxi-, Droschkenstand *m*
cack·la ZO **1.** Gegacker *n*, Geschnatter *n*; **2.** gackern, schnattern
cac·tus BOT Kaktus *m*
ca·dence MUS Kadenz *f*; (Sprech-) Rhythmus *m*
ca·det MIL Kadett *m*
cadge *Br* F schnorren
caf·é, caf·e Café *n*
caf·e·te·ri·a Cafeteria *f*, Selbstbedienungsrestaurant *n*, *a.* Kantine *f*, UNIV Mensa *f*
cage **1.** Käfig *m*; *mining*: Förderkorb *m*; **2.** einsperren
cake **1.** Kuchen *m*, Torte *f*; Tafel *f Schokolade*, Stück *n Seife*; F ***take the cake*** den Vogel abschießen; **2.** ***caked with mud*** schmutzverkrustet
ca·lam·i·ty großes Unglück, Katastrophe *f*
cal·cu·late *v/t* kalkulieren; be-, aus-, errechnen; F vermuten; *v/i*: ***calculate on*** rechnen mit *or* auf (*acc*), zählen auf (*acc*)
cal·cu·la·tion Berechnung *f* (*a. fig*); ECON Kalkulation *f*; *fig* Überlegung *f*
cal·cu·la·tor TECH (Taschen)Rechner *m*
cal·en·dar Kalender *m*
calf[1] ANAT Wade *f*
calf[2] ZO Kalb *n*
calf·skin Kalb(s)fell *n*
cal·i·ber, *esp Br* **cal·i·bre** Kaliber *n*
call **1.** Ruf *m*; TEL Anruf *m*, Gespräch *n*; Ruf *m*, Berufung *f* (**to** in *ein Amt*; auf *e-n Lehrstuhl*); Aufruf *m*, Aufforderung *f*; Signal *n*; (kurzer) Besuch; ***on call*** auf Abruf; ***be on call*** MED Bereitschaftsdienst haben; ***make a call*** telefonieren; **2.** *v/t* (herbei)rufen; (ein)berufen; TEL *j-n* anrufen; *j-n* berufen, ernennen (**to** zu); nennen; *Aufmerksamkeit* lenken (**to** auf *acc*); ***be called*** heißen; ***call s.o. names*** j-n beschimpfen, j-n beleidigen; *v/i* rufen; TEL anrufen; e-n (kurzen) Besuch machen (***on s.o., at s.o.'s*** [***house***] bei j-m); ***call at a port*** MAR e-n Hafen anlaufen; ***call for*** rufen nach; *et.* anfordern; *et.* abholen; ***to be called for*** postlagernd; ***call on*** sich an *j-n* wenden (**for** wegen); appellieren an (*acc*) (***to do*** zu tun); ***call on s.o.*** j-n besuchen
call box *Br* Telefonzelle *f*
call·er Besucher(in); TEL Anrufer(in)
call girl Callgirl *n*
call-in → ***phone-in***
call·ing Berufung *f*; Beruf *m*
cal·lous schwielig; *fig* gefühllos
cal·lus Schwiele *f*
calm **1.** still, ruhig; **2.** (Wind)Stille *f*, Ruhe *f*; **3.** *often* ***calm down*** besänftigen, (sich) beruhigen
cal·o·rie Kalorie *f*; ***high*** *or* ***rich in calories*** kalorienreich; ***low in calories*** kalorienarm, kalorienreduziert
cal·o·rie-con·scious kalorienbewusst
calve ZO kalben
cam·cor·der Camcorder *m*, Kamerarekorder *m*
cam·el ZO Kamel *n*
cam·e·o Kamee *f*; THEA, *film*: kleine Nebenrolle, kurze Szene
cam·e·ra Kamera *f*, Fotoapparat *m*
cam·o·mile BOT Kamille *f*
cam·ou·flage **1.** Tarnung *f*; **2.** tarnen
camp **1.** (*Zelt- etc*)Lager *n*; **2.** lagern; ***camp out*** zelten, campen
cam·paign **1.** MIL Feldzug *m* (*a. fig*); *fig* Kampagne *f*, Aktion *f*; POL Wahlkampf *m*; **2.** *fig* kämpfen (**for** für; ***against*** gegen)
camp bed *Br*, **camp cot** Feldbett *n*
camp·er (van) Campingbus *m*, Wohnmobil *n*

camp·ground, **camp·site** Lagerplatz *m*; Zeltplatz *m*, Campingplatz *m*
cam·pus Campus *m*, Universitätsgelände *n*
can[1] *v/aux ich* kann, *du* kannst *etc*; dürfen, können
can[2] **1.** Kanne *f*; (Blech-, Konserven-) Dose *f*, (-)Büchse *f*; **2.** einmachen, eindosen
Can·a·da Kanada *n*
Ca·na·di·an **1.** kanadisch; **2.** Kanadier(in)
ca·nal Kanal *m* (*a.* ANAT)
ca·nar·y ZO Kanarienvogel *m*
can·cel (durch-, aus)streichen; entwerten; rückgängig machen; absagen; ***be cancel(l)ed*** ausfallen
Can·cer ASTR Krebs *m*; ***he*** (***she***) ***is*** (***a***) ***Cancer*** er (sie) ist (ein) Krebs
can·cer MED Krebs *m*
can·cer·ous MED Krebs…, krebsbefallen
can·cer pa·tient MED Krebskranke *m, f*
can·did aufrichtig, offen
can·di·date Kandidat(in) (***for*** für), Bewerber(in) (***for*** um)
can·died kandiert
can·dle Kerze *f*; Licht *n*; ***burn the candle at both ends*** mit s-r Gesundheit Raubbau treiben
can·dle·stick Kerzenleuchter *m*, Kerzenständer *m*
can·do(u)r Aufrichtigkeit *f*, Offenheit *f*
can·dy **1.** Kandis(zucker) *m*; Süßigkeiten *pl*; **2.** kandieren
candy floss Zuckerwatte *f*
candy store Süßwarengeschäft *n*
cane BOT Rohr *n*; (Rohr)Stock *m*
ca·nine Hunde…
canned Dosen…, Büchsen…; ***canned fruit*** Obstkonserven *pl*
can·ne·ry Konservenfabrik *f*
can·ni·bal Kannibale *m*
can·non MIL Kanone *f*
can·ny schlau
ca·noe **1.** Kanu *n*, Paddelboot *n*; **2.** Kanu fahren, paddeln
can·on Kanon *m*; Regel *f*
can o·pen·er Dosen-, Büchsenöffner *m*
can·o·py Baldachin *m*
cant Jargon *m*; Phrase(n *pl*) *f*
can·tan·ker·ous F zänkisch, mürrisch
can·teen *esp Br* Kantine *f*; MIL Feldflasche *f*; Besteck(kasten *m*) *n*
can·ter **1.** Kanter *m*; **2.** kantern
can·vas Segeltuch *n*; Zelt-, Packleinwand *f*; Segel *pl*; PAINT Leinwand *f*; Gemälde *n*
can·vass **1.** POL Wahlfeldzug *m*; ECON Werbefeldzug *m*; **2.** *v/t* eingehend untersuchen *or* erörtern *or* prüfen; POL werben um (*Stimmen*); *v/i* POL e-n Wahlfeldzug veranstalten
can·yon GEOGR Cañon *m*, Schlucht *f*
cap **1.** Kappe *f*; Mütze *f*; Haube *f*; Zündkapsel *f*; **2.** (mit e-r Kappe *etc*) bedecken; *fig* krönen; übertreffen
ca·pa·bil·i·ty Fähigkeit *f*
cap·a·ble fähig (***of*** zu)
ca·pac·i·ty (Raum)Inhalt *m*; Fassungsvermögen *n*; Kapazität *f*; Aufnahmefähigkeit *f*; (TECH Leistungs)Fähigkeit *f* (***for*** *ger* zu *inf*); ***in my capacity as*** in meiner Eigenschaft als
cape[1] GEOGR Kap *n*, Vorgebirge *n*
cape[2] Cape *n*, Umhang *m*
ca·per **1.** Kapriole *f*, Luftsprung *m*; ***cut capers*** → **2.** Freuden- *or* Luftsprünge machen
ca·pil·la·ry ANAT Haar-, Kapillargefäß *n*
cap·i·tal **1.** ECON Kapital *n*; Hauptstadt *f*; Großbuchstabe *m*; **2.** Kapital…; Tod(es)…; Haupt…; großartig, prima
capital crime JUR Kapitalverbrechen *n*
cap·i·tal·ism ECON Kapitalismus *m*
cap·i·tal·ist ECON Kapitalist *m*
cap·i·tal·ize großschreiben; ECON kapitalisieren
cap·i·tal let·ter Großbuchstabe *m*
capital pun·ish·ment JUR Todesstrafe *f*
ca·pit·u·late kapitulieren (***to*** vor *dat*)
ca·pri·cious launisch
Cap·ri·corn ASTR Steinbock *m*; ***he*** (***she***) ***is*** (***a***) ***Capricorn*** er (sie) ist (ein) Steinbock
cap·size MAR *v/i* kentern; *v/t* zum Kentern bringen
cap·sule Kapsel *f*
cap·tain (An)Führer *m*; MAR, ECON Kapitän *m*; AVIAT Flugkapitän *m*; MIL Hauptmann *m*; SPORT (Mannschafts-) Kapitän *m*, Spielführer *m*
cap·tion Überschrift *f*, Titel *m*; Bildunterschrift *f*; *film*: Untertitel *m*
cap·ti·vate *fig* gefangen nehmen, fesseln
cap·tive **1.** gefangen; gefesselt; ***hold captive*** gefangen halten; **2.** Gefangene *m, f*
cap·tiv·i·ty Gefangenschaft *f*
cap·ture **1.** Eroberung *f*; Gefangennahme *f*; **2.** fangen, gefangen nehmen; erobern; erbeuten; MAR kapern
car Auto *n*, Wagen *m*; (Eisenbahn-, Straßenbahn)Wagen *m*; Gondel *f* (*of a balloon etc*); Kabine *f*; ***by car*** mit dem Auto, im Auto
car·a·mel Karamell *m*; Karamelle *f*
car·a·van Karawane *f*; *Br* Wohnwagen *m*
caravan site Campingplatz *m* für Wohnwagen
car·a·way BOT Kümmel *m*
car·bine MIL Karabiner *m*
car·bo·hy·drate CHEM Kohle(n)hydrat *n*

car bomb Autobombe *f*
car·bon CHEM Kohlenstoff *m*; → ***carbon copy, carbon paper***
car·bon cop·y Durchschlag *m*
car·bon pa·per Kohlepapier *n*
car·bu·ret·(t)or MOT Vergaser *m*
car·case *Br*, **car·cass** Kadaver *m*, Aas *n*; GASTR Rumpf *m*
car·cin·o·genic MED karzinogen, krebserregend
car·ci·no·ma MED Krebsgeschwulst *f*
card Karte *f*; ***play cards*** Karten spielen; ***have a card up one's sleeve*** *fig* (noch) e-n Trumpf in der Hand haben
card·board Pappe *f*
cardboard box Pappschachtel *f*, Pappkarton *m*
car·di·ac MED Herz…
cardiac pace·mak·er MED Herzschrittmacher *m*
car·di·gan Strickjacke *f*
car·di·nal **1.** Grund…, Haupt…, Kardinal…; scharlachrot; **2.** REL Kardinal *m*
car·di·nal num·ber MATH Kardinalzahl *f*, Grundzahl *f*
card in·dex Kartei *f*
card phone Kartentelefon *n*
card·sharp·er Falschspieler *m*
car dump Autofriedhof *m*
care **1.** Sorge *f*; Sorgfalt *f*; Vorsicht *f*; Obhut *f*, Pflege *f*; ***needing care*** MED pflegebedürftig; ***medical care*** ärztliche Behandlung; ***take care of*** aufpassen auf (*acc*); versorgen; ***with care!*** Vorsicht!; **2.** Lust haben (***to*** *inf* zu *inf*); ***care about*** sich kümmern um; ***care for*** sorgen für, sich kümmern um; sich etwas machen aus; ***I don't care!*** F meinetwegen!; ***I couldn't care less*** F es ist mir völlig egal
ca·reer **1.** Karriere *f*, Laufbahn *f*; **2.** Berufs…; Karriere…; **3.** rasen
ca·reers ad·vice Berufsberatung *f*
careers ad·vi·sor Berufsberater *m*
careers guidance Berufsberatung *f*
careers of·fice Berufsberatungsstelle *f*
careers of·fi·cer Berufsberater *m*
care·free sorgenfrei, sorglos
care·ful vorsichtig; sorgsam bedacht (***of*** auf *acc*); sorgfältig; ***be careful!*** pass auf!
care·less nachlässig, unachtsam; leichtsinnig, unvorsichtig; sorglos
care·less·ness Nachlässigkeit *f*, Unachtsamkeit *f*; Leichtsinn *m*; Sorglosigkeit *f*
ca·ress **1.** Liebkosung *f*; Zärtlichkeit *f*; **2.** liebkosen, streicheln
care·tak·er Hausmeister *m*; (Haus- *etc*)-Verwalter *m*
care·worn abgehärmt, verhärmt
car fer·ry Autofähre *f*
car·go Ladung *f*
car hire *Br* Autovermietung *f*
car·i·ca·ture **1.** Karikatur *f*, Zerrbild *n*; **2.** karikieren
car·i·ca·tur·ist Karikaturist *m*
car·ies, *a.* ***dental caries*** MED Karies *f*
car me·chan·ic Automechaniker *m*
car·mine Karmin(rot) *n*
car·na·tion BOT Nelke *f*
car·nap·per F Autoentführer *m*
car·ni·val Karneval *m*
car·niv·o·rous ZO fleischfressend
car·ol Weihnachtslied *n*
carp[1] ZO Karpfen *m*
carp[2] nörgeln
car park *esp Br* Parkplatz *m*; Parkhaus *n*
car·pen·ter Zimmermann *m*
car·pet **1.** Teppich *m*; ***fitted carpet*** Teppichboden *m*; ***sweep s.th. under the carpet*** *fig* et. unter den Teppich kehren; **2.** mit Teppich(boden) auslegen
car phone Autotelefon *n*
car pool Fahrgemeinschaft *f*
car pool(-ing) ser·vice Mitfahrzentrale *f*
car·port MOT überdachter Abstellplatz
car rent·al Autovermietung *f*
car re·pair shop Autoreparaturwerkstatt *f*
car·riage Beförderung *f*, Transport *m*; Transportkosten *pl*; Kutsche *f*; *Br* RAIL (Personen)Wagen *m*; (Körper-)Haltung *f*
car·riage·way Fahrbahn *f*
car·ri·er Spediteur *m*; Gepäckträger *m* (*on a bicycle*); MIL Flugzeugträger *m*
car·ri·er bag *Br* Trag(e)tasche *f*, -tüte *f*
car·ri·on **1.** Aas *n*; **2.** Aas…
car·rot BOT Karotte *f*, Mohrrübe *f*
car·ry *v/t* bringen, führen, tragen (*a. v/i*), fahren, befördern; (bei sich) haben *or* tragen; *Ansicht* durchsetzen; *Gewinn, Preis* davontragen; *Ernte, Zinsen* tragen; (weiter)führen, *Mauer* ziehen; *Antrag* durchbringen; ***be carried*** PARL *etc* angenommen werden; ***carry the day*** den Sieg davontragen; ***carry s.th. too far*** et. übertreiben, et. zu weit treiben; ***get carried away*** *fig* die Kontrolle über sich verlieren; sich hinreißen lassen; ***carry forward, carry over*** ECON übertragen; ***carry on*** fortsetzen, weiterführen; ECON betreiben; ***carry out, carry through*** aus-, durchführen
car·ry·cot *Br* (Baby)Trag(e)tasche *f*
cart **1.** Karren *m*; Wagen *m*; Einkaufswagen *m*; ***put the cart before the horse*** *fig* das Pferd beim Schwanz aufzäumen; **2.** karren
car·ti·lage ANAT Knorpel *m*
cart·load Wagenladung *f*

C

car·ton Karton *m*; ***a carton of cigarettes*** e-e Stange Zigaretten
car·toon Cartoon *m, n*; Karikatur *f*; Zeichentrickfilm *m*
car·toon·ist Karikaturist *m*
car·tridge Patrone *f* (*a.* MIL); (Film-) Patrone *f*, (Film)Kassette *f*; Tonabnehmer *m*
cart·wheel: ***turn cartwheels*** Rad schlagen
carve GASTR vorschneiden, zerlegen; TECH schnitzen; meißeln
carv·er (Holz)Schnitzer *m*; Bildhauer *m*; GASTR Tranchierer *m*; Tranchiermesser *n*
carv·ing Schnitzerei *f*
car wash Autowäsche *f*; (Auto)Waschanlage *f*, Waschstraße *f*
cas·cade Wasserfall *m*
case[1] **1.** Behälter *m*; Kiste *f*, Kasten *m*; Etui *n*; Gehäuse *n*; Schachtel *f*; (*Glas-*)Schrank *m*; (*Kissen*)Bezug *m*; TECH Verkleidung *f*; **2.** in ein Gehäuse *or* Etui stecken; TECH verkleiden
case[2] Fall *m* (*a.* JUR), LING *a.* Kasus *m*; MED (Krankheits)Fall *m*, Patient(in); Sache *f*, Angelegenheit *f*
case·ment Fensterflügel *m*; → **casement window** Flügelfenster *n*
cash 1. Bargeld *n*; Barzahlung *f*; ***cash down*** gegen bar; ***cash on delivery*** Lieferung *f* gegen bar; (per) Nachnahme *f*; **2.** einlösen
cash·book ECON Kassenbuch *n*
cash desk Kasse *f*
cash dis·pens·er *esp Br* Geld-, Bankautomat *m*
cash·ier Kassierer(in)
cash·less bargeldlos
cash ma·chine Geld-, Bankautomat *m*
cash·mere Kaschmir *m*
cash·point *Br* → ***cash machine***
cash reg·is·ter Registrierkasse *f*
cas·ing (Schutz)Hülle *f*; Verschalung *f*, Verkleidung *f*, Gehäuse *n*
cask Fass *n*
cas·ket Kästchen *n*; Sarg *m*
cas·sette (*Film-, Band-, Musik*)Kassette *f*
cassette deck Kassettendeck *n*
cassette player Kassettenrekorder *m*
cassette ra·di·o Radiorekorder *m*
cassette re·cord·er Kassettenrekorder *m*
cas·sock REL Soutane *f*
cast 1. Wurf *m*; TECH Guss(form *f*) *m*; Abguss *m*, Abdruck *m*; Schattierung *f*, Anflug *m*; Form *f*, Art *f*; Auswerfen *n* (*of a fishing line etc*); THEA Besetzung *f*; **2.** (ab-, aus-, hin-, um-, weg)werfen; ZO abwerfen (*skin*); verlieren (*teeth*); verwerfen; gestalten; TECH gießen; *a.* ***cast up*** ausrechnen, zusammenzählen; THEA *Stück* besetzen; *Rollen* verteilen (***to*** an *acc*); ***cast lots*** losen (***for*** um); ***cast away*** wegwerfen; ***be cast down*** niedergeschlagen sein; ***cast off*** *Kleidung* ausrangieren; MAR losmachen; *Freund etc* fallen lassen; *knitting*: abketten; *v/i*: ***cast about for, cast around for*** suchen (nach), *fig a.* sich umsehen nach
cas·ta·net Kastagnette *f*
cast·a·way Schiffbrüchige *m, f*
caste Kaste *f* (*a. fig*)
cast·er Laufrolle *f*; *Br* (*Salz-, Zucker-etc*)Streuer *m*
cast i·ron Gusseisen *n*
cast-i·ron gusseisern
cas·tle Burg *f*, Schloss *n*; *chess*: Turm *m*
cast·or → ***caster***
cast·or oil PHARM Rizinusöl *n*
cas·trate kastrieren
cas·u·al zufällig; gelegentlich; flüchtig; lässig
cas·u·al·ty Unfall *m*; Verunglückte *m, f*, Opfer *n*; MIL Verwundete *m*; Gefallene *m*; ***casualties*** Opfer *pl*, MIL *mst* Verluste *pl*
casualty (de·part·ment) MED Notaufnahme *f*
casualty ward MED Unfallstation *f*
cas·u·al wear Freizeitkleidung *f*
cat ZO Katze *f*
cat·a·log, *esp Br* **cat·a·logue 1.** Katalog *m*; Verzeichnis *n*, Liste *f*; **2.** katalogisieren
cat·a·lyt·ic con·vert·er MOT Katalysator *m*
cat·a·pult *Br* Schleuder *f*; Katapult *n, m*
cat·a·ract Wasserfall *m*; Stromschnelle *f*; MED grauer Star
ca·tarrh MED Katarr(h) *m*
ca·tas·tro·phe Katastrophe *f*
catch 1. Fangen *n*; Fang *m*, Beute *f*; Halt *m*, Griff *m*; TECH Haken *m* (*a. fig*); (Tür)Klinke *f*; Verschluss *m*; **2.** *v/t* (auf-, ein)fangen; packen, fassen, ergreifen; überraschen, ertappen; *Blick etc* auffangen; F *Zug etc* (noch) kriegen, erwischen; *et.* erfassen, verstehen; *Atmosphäre etc* einfangen; sich *e-e Krankheit* holen; ***catch (a) cold*** sich erkälten; ***catch the eye*** ins Auge fallen; ***catch s.o.'s eye*** j-s Aufmerksamkeit auf sich lenken; ***catch s.o. up*** j-n einholen; ***be caught up in*** verwickelt sein in (*acc*); *v/i* sich verfangen, hängen bleiben; fassen, greifen; TECH ineinandergreifen; klemmen; einschnappen; ***catch up with*** einholen
catch·er Fänger *m*
catch·ing packend; MED ansteckend (*a. fig*)

catch·word Schlagwort *n*; Stichwort *n*
catch·y MUS eingängig
cat·e·chis·m REL Katechismus *m*
cat·e·go·ry Kategorie *f*
ca·ter: ***cater for*** Speisen und Getränke liefern für; *fig* sorgen für
cat·er·pil·lar ZO Raupe *f*
Cat·er·pil·lar® MOT Raupenfahrzeug *n*
Caterpillar trac·tor® MOT Raupenschlepper *m*
cat·gut MUS Darmsaite *f*
ca·the·dral Dom *m*, Kathedrale *f*
Cath·o·lic REL **1.** katholisch; **2.** Katholik(in)
cat·kin BOT Kätzchen *n*
cat·tle Vieh *n*
cattle breed·er Viehzüchter *m*
cattle breed·ing Viehzucht *f*
cattle dealer Viehhändler *m*
cattle mar·ket Viehmarkt *m*
ca(u)l·dron großer Kessel
cau·li·flow·er BOT Blumenkohl *m*
cause **1.** Ursache *f*; Grund *m*; Sache *f*; **2.** verursachen; veranlassen
cause·less grundlos
cau·tion **1.** Vorsicht *f*; Warnung *f*; Verwarnung *f*; **2.** warnen; verwarnen; JUR belehren
cau·tious behutsam, vorsichtig
cav·al·ry HIST MIL Kavallerie *f*
cave **1.** Höhle *f*; **2.** *v/i*: ***cave in*** einstürzen
cav·ern (große) Höhle
cav·i·ty Höhle *f*; MED Loch *n*
caw ZO **1.** krächzen; **2.** Krächzen *n*
CD ABBR *of* ***compact disk*** CD *f*
CD play·er CD-Spieler *m*
CD-ROM ABBR *of* ***compact disk read-only memory*** CD-ROM
CD vid·e·o CD-Video *n*
cease aufhören; beenden
cease·fire MIL Feuereinstellung *f*; Waffenruhe *f*
cease·less unaufhörlich
cei·ling (Zimmer)Decke *f*; ECON Höchstgrenze *f*, oberste Preisgrenze
cel·e·brate feiern
cel·e·brat·ed gefeiert, berühmt (***for*** für, wegen)
cel·e·bra·tion Feier *f*
ce·leb·ri·ty Berühmtheit *f*
cel·e·ry BOT Sellerie *m*, *f*
ce·les·ti·al himmlisch
cel·i·ba·cy Ehelosigkeit *f*
cell BIOL Zelle *f*, ELECTR *a.* Element *n*
cel·lar Keller *m*
cel·list MUS Cellist(in)
cel·lo MUS (Violon)Cello *n*
cel·lo·phane® Cellophan® *n*
cel·lu·lar BIOL Zell(en)…
cel·lu·lar phone Handy *n*
Cel·tic keltisch
ce·ment **1.** Zement *m*; Kitt *m*; **2.** zementieren; (ver)kitten
cem·e·tery Friedhof *m*
cen·sor **1.** Zensor *m*; **2.** zensieren
cen·sor·ship Zensur *f*
cen·sure **1.** Tadel *m*, Verweis *m*; **2.** tadeln
cen·sus Volkszählung *f*
cent Hundert *n*; Cent *m* (*1/100 Dollar*); ***per cent*** Prozent *n*
cen·te·na·ry Hundertjahrfeier *f*, hundertjähriges Jubiläum
cen·ten·ni·al **1.** hundertjährig; **2.** → ***centenary***
cen·ter **1.** Zentrum *n*, Mittelpunkt *m*; *soccer*: Flanke *f*; **2.** (sich) konzentrieren; zentrieren
center back *soccer*: Vorstopper *m*
center for·ward SPORT Mittelstürmer(in)
center of grav·i·ty PHYS Schwerpunkt *m*
cen·ti·grade: ***10 degrees centigrade*** 10 Grad Celsius
cen·ti·me·ter, *Br* **cen·ti·me·tre** Zentimeter *m*, *n*
cen·ti·pede ZO Tausendfüß(l)er *m*
cen·tral zentral; Haupt…, Zentral…; Mittel…
central heat·ing Zentralheizung *f*
cen·tral·ize zentralisieren
cen·tral lock·ing MOT Zentralverriegelung *f*
central res·er·va·tion *Br* MOT Mittelstreifen *m*
cen·tre *Br* → ***center***
cen·tu·ry Jahrhundert *n*
ce·ram·ics Keramik *f*, keramische Erzeugnisse *pl*
ce·re·al **1.** Getreide…; **2.** BOT Getreide *n*; Getreidepflanze *f*; GASTR Getreideflocken *pl*, Frühstückskost *f*
cer·e·bral ANAT Gehirn…
cer·e·mo·ni·al **1.** zeremoniell; **2.** Zeremoniell *n*
cer·e·mo·ni·ous zeremoniell; förmlich
cer·e·mo·ny Zeremonie *f*; Feier *f*, Feierlichkeit *f*; Förmlichkeit(en *pl*) *f*
cer·tain sicher, gewiss; zuverlässig; bestimmt; gewisse(r, -s)
cer·tain·ly sicher, gewiss; *int* sicherlich, bestimmt, natürlich
cer·tain·ty Sicherheit *f*, Bestimmtheit *f*, Gewissheit *f*
cer·tif·i·cate Zeugnis *n*; Bescheinigung *f*; ***certificate of (good) conduct*** Führungszeugnis *n*; ***General Certificate of Education advanced level (A level)*** *Br* PED *appr* Abitur(zeugnis) *n*; ***General Certificate of Education ordinary level***

(***O level***) *Br* PED *appr* mittlere Reife; ***medical certificate*** ärztliches Attest
cer·ti·fy *et.* bescheinigen; beglaubigen
cer·ti·tude Sicherheit *f*, Bestimmtheit *f*, Gewissheit *f*
CET ABBR *of* ***Central European Time*** MEZ, mitteleuropäische Zeit
cf (*Latin* ***confer***) ABBR *of* ***compare*** vgl., vergleiche
CFC ABBR *of* ***chlorofluorocarbon*** FCKW, Fluorchlorkohlenwasserstoff *m*
chafe *v/t* warm reiben; aufreiben, wund reiben; *v/i* (sich durch)reiben, scheuern
chaff AGR Spreu *f*; Häcksel *n*
chaf·finch zo Buchfink *m*
chag·rin **1.** Ärger *m*; **2.** ärgern
chain **1.** Kette *f*; *fig* Fessel *f*; **2.** (an)ketten; fesseln
chain re·ac·tion Kettenreaktion *f*
chain-smoke F Kette rauchen
chain-smok·er Kettenraucher(in)
chain-smok·ing Kettenrauchen *n*
chain store Kettenladen *m*
chair Stuhl *m*; UNIV Lehrstuhl *m*; ECON *etc* Vorsitz *m*; ***be in the chair*** den Vorsitz führen
chair lift Sessellift *m*
chair·man Vorsitzende *m*, Präsident *m*; Diskussionsleiter *m*; ECON *Br* Generaldirektor *m*
chair·man·ship Vorsitz *m*
chair·wom·an Vorsitzende *f*, Präsidentin *f*; Diskussionsleiterin *f*
chal·ice REL Kelch *m*
chalk **1.** Kreide *f*; **2.** mit Kreide schreiben *or* zeichnen
chal·lenge **1.** Herausforderung *f*; **2.** herausfordern
chal·len·ger Herausforderer *m*
cham·ber TECH, PARL *etc* Kammer *f*
cham·ber·maid Zimmermädchen *n*
cham·ber of com·merce ECON Handelskammer *f*
cham·ois zo Gämse *f*
cham·ois (leath·er) Fensterleder *n*
champ F SPORT → ***champion***
cham·pagne Champagner *m*
cham·pi·on **1.** Verfechter(in), Fürsprecher(in); SPORT Meister(in); **2.** verfechten, eintreten für
cham·pi·on·ship SPORT Meisterschaft *f*
chance **1.** Zufall *m*; Chance *f*, (günstige) Gelegenheit; Aussicht *f* (***of*** auf *acc*); Möglichkeit *f*; Risiko *n*; ***by chance*** zufällig; ***take a chance*** es darauf ankommen lassen; ***take no chances*** nichts riskieren (wollen); **2.** zufällig; **3.** F riskieren
chan·cel·lor Kanzler(in)
chan·de·lier Kronleuchter *m*
change **1.** Veränderung *f*, Wechsel *m*; Abwechslung *f*; Wechselgeld *n*; Kleingeld *n*; ***for a change*** zur Abwechslung; ***change for the better*** (***worse***) Bess(e)rung *f* (Verschlechterung *f*); **2.** *v/t* (ver)ändern, umändern; (aus)wechseln; (aus-, ver-) tauschen (***for*** gegen); umbuchen; MOT, TECH schalten; ***change over*** umschalten; umstellen; ***change trains*** umsteigen; *v/i* sich (ver)ändern, wechseln; sich umziehen
change·a·ble veränderlich
change ma·chine Münzwechsler *m*
change·o·ver Umstellung *f* (***to*** auf *acc*)
chang·ing room *esp* SPORT Umkleidekabine *f*, Umkleideraum *m*
chan·nel **1.** Kanal *m* (*a. fig*); (*Fernseh- etc*)Kanal *m*, (*Fernseh- etc*)Programm *n*; *fig* Weg *m*; **2.** *fig* lenken
Chan·nel Tun·nel Kanaltunnel *m*, Eurotunnel *m*
chant **1.** (Kirchen)Gesang *m*; Singsang *m*; **2.** in Sprechchören rufen
cha·os Chaos *n*
chap[1] **1.** Riss *m*; **2.** rissig machen *or* werden; aufspringen
chap[2] *Br* F Bursche *m*, Kerl *m*
chap·el ARCH Kapelle *f*; REL Gottesdienst *m*
chap·lain REL Kaplan *m*
chap·ter Kapitel *n*
char verkohlen
char·ac·ter Charakter *m*; Ruf *m*, Leumund *m*; Schriftzeichen *n*, Buchstabe *m*; *novel etc*: Figur *f*, Gestalt *f*; THEA Rolle *f*
char·ac·ter·is·tic **1.** charakteristisch (***of*** für); **2.** Kennzeichen *n*
char·ac·ter·ize charakterisieren
char·coal Holzkohle *f*
charge **1.** *v/t* ELECTR (auf)laden; *Gewehr etc* laden; *j-n* beauftragen (***with*** mit); *j-n* beschuldigen *or* anklagen (***with*** *e-r Sache*) (*a.* JUR); ECON berechnen, verlangen, fordern (***for*** für); MIL angreifen; stürmen; ***charge s.o. with s.th.*** ECON j-m et. in Rechnung stellen; *v/i*: ***charge at s.o.*** auf j-n losgehen; **2.** Ladung *f* (*a.* ELECTR *etc*); (Spreng)Ladung *f*; Beschuldigung *f*, *a.* JUR Anklage(-punkt *m*) *f*; ECON Preis *m*; Forderung *f*; Gebühr *f*; *a. pl* Unkosten *pl*, Spesen *pl*; Verantwortung *f*; Schützling *m*, Mündel *n*, *m*; ***free of charge*** kostenlos; ***be in charge of*** verantwortlich sein für; ***take charge of*** die Leitung *etc* übernehmen, die Sache in die Hand nehmen
char·i·ot HIST Streit-, Triumphwagen *m*
cha·ris·ma Charisma *n*, Ausstrahlung *f*,

C

Ausstrahlungskraft *f*
char·i·ta·ble wohltätig
char·i·ty Nächstenliebe *f*; Wohltätigkeit *f*; Güte *f*, Nachsicht *f*; milde Gabe
char·la·tan Scharlatan *m*; Quacksalber *m*, Kurpfuscher *m*
charm **1.** Zauber *m*; Charme *m*, Reiz *m*; Talisman *m*, Amulett *n*; **2.** bezaubern, entzücken
charm·ing charmant, bezaubernd
chart (*See-*, *Himmels-*, *Wetter*)Karte *f*; Diagramm *n*, Schaubild *n*; *pl* MUS Charts *pl*, Hitliste(n *pl*) *f*
char·ter **1.** Urkunde *f*; Charta *f*; Chartern *n*; **2.** chartern, mieten
char·ter flight Charterflug *m*
char·wom·an Putzfrau *f*, Raumpflegerin *f*
chase **1.** Jagd *f*; Verfolgung *f*; **2.** *v/t* jagen, hetzen; Jagd machen auf (*acc*); TECH ziselieren; *v/i* rasen, rennen
chasm Kluft *f*, Abgrund *m*
chaste keusch; schlicht
chas·tise züchtigen
chas·ti·ty Keuschheit *f*
chat **1.** Geplauder *n*, Schwätzchen *n*, Plauderei *f*; **2.** plaudern
chat show *Br* TV Talkshow *f*
chat show host *Br* TV Talkmaster *m*
chat·ter **1.** plappern; schnattern; klappern; **2.** Geplapper *n*; Klappern *n*
chat·ter·box F Plappermaul *n*
chat·ty gesprächig
chauf·feur Chauffeur *m*
chau·vi F Chauvi *m*
chau·vin·ist Chauvinist *m*; F ***male chauvinist pig*** Chauvi *m*; *contp* Chauvischwein *n*
cheap billig; *fig* schäbig, gemein
cheap·en (sich) verbilligen; *fig* herabsetzen
cheat **1.** Betrug *m*, Schwindel *m*; Betrüger(in); **2.** betrügen; F schummeln
check **1.** Schach(stellung *f*) *n*; Hemmnis *n*, Hindernis *n* (***on*** für); Einhalt *m*; Kontrolle *f* (***on*** *gen*); Kontrollabschnitt *m*, -schein *m*; Gepäckschein *m*; Garderobenmarke *f*; ECON Scheck *m* (***for*** über); Häkchen *n* (*on a list etc*); ECON Kassenzettel *m*, Rechnung *f*; karierter Stoff; **2.** *v/i* (plötzlich) innehalten; ***check in*** sich (*in e-m Hotel*) anmelden; einstempeln; AVIAT einchecken; ***check out*** (*aus e-m Hotel*) abreisen; ausstempeln; ***check up*** (***on***) F (*e-e Sache*) nachprüfen, (*e-e Sache*, *j-n*) überprüfen; *v/t* hemmen, hindern, aufhalten; zurückhalten; checken, kontrollieren, überprüfen; *auf e-r Liste* abhaken; *Mantel etc* in der Garderobe abgeben; *Gepäck* aufgeben
check card ECON Scheckkarte *f*
checked kariert
check·ers Damespiel *n*
check-in Anmeldung *f*; Einstempeln *n*; AVIAT Einchecken *n*
check-in coun·ter, check-in desk AVIAT Abfertigungsschalter *m*
check·ing ac·count ECON Girokonto *n*
check·list Check-, Kontrollliste *f*
check·mate **1.** (Schach)Matt *n*; **2.** (schach)matt setzen
check-out Abreise *f*; Ausstempeln *n*
check-out coun·ter Kasse *f*
check·point Kontrollpunkt *m*
check·room Garderobe *f*; Gepäckaufbewahrung *f*
check·up Überprüfung *f*; MED Check-up *m*, Vorsorgeuntersuchung *f*
cheek ANAT Backe *f*, Wange *f*; *Br* Unverschämtheit *f*
cheek·y *Br* frech
cheer **1.** Stimmung *f*, Fröhlichkeit *f*; Hoch *n*, Hochruf *m*, Beifall *m*, Beifallsruf *m*; *pl* SPORT Anfeuerungsrufe *pl*; ***three cheers!*** dreimal hoch!; ***cheers!*** prost!; **2.** *v/t* mit Beifall begrüßen; *a.* ***cheer on*** anspornen; *a.* ***cheer up*** aufheitern; *v/i* hoch rufen, jubeln; *a.* ***cheer up*** Mut fassen; ***cheer up!*** Kopf hoch!
cheer·ful vergnügt
cheer·i·o *int Br* F tschüs(s)!
cheer·lead·er SPORT Einpeitscher *m*, Cheerleader *m*
cheer·less freudlos; unfreundlich
cheer·y vergnügt
cheese Käse *m*
chee·tah zo Gepard *m*
chef Küchenchef *m*; Koch *m*
chem·i·cal **1.** chemisch; **2.** Chemikalie *f*
chem·ist Chemiker(in); Apotheker(in); Drogist(in)
chem·is·try Chemie *f*
chem·ist's shop Apotheke *f*; Drogerie *f*
chem·o·ther·a·py MED Chemotherapie *f*
cheque *Br* ECON Scheck *m*; ***crossed cheque*** Verrechnungsscheck *m*
cheque ac·count *Br* Girokonto *n*
cheque card *Br* Scheckkarte *f*
cher·ry BOT Kirsche *f*
chess Schach(spiel) *n*; ***a game of chess*** e-e Partie Schach
chess·board Schachbrett *n*
chess·man, chess·piece Schachfigur *f*
chest Kiste *f*; Truhe *f*; ANAT Brust *f*, Brustkasten *m*; ***get s.th. off one's chest*** F sich et. von der Seele reden
chest·nut **1.** BOT Kastanie *f*; **2.** kastanienbraun
chest of drawers Kommode *f*

chew (zer)kauen
chew·ing gum Kaugummi *m*
chic schick, *Austrian* fesch
chick zo Küken *n*, junger Vogel; F Biene *f*, Puppe *f* (*girl*)
chick·en zo Huhn *n*; Küken *n*; GASTR (*Brat*)Hähnchen *n*, (*Brat*)Hühnchen *n*
chick·en·heart·ed furchtsam, feige
chick·en pox MED Windpocken *pl*
chic·o·ry BOT Chicorée *m*, *f*
chief 1. oberste(r, -s), Ober…, Haupt…, Chef…; wichtigste(r, -s); **2.** Chef *m*; Häuptling *m*
chief·ly hauptsächlich
chil·blain MED Frostbeule *f*
child Kind *n*; ***from a child*** von Kindheit an; ***with child*** schwanger
child a·buse JUR Kindesmisshandlung *f*
child ben·e·fit *Br* Kindergeld *n*
child·birth Geburt *f*, Niederkunft *f*
child·hood Kindheit *f*; ***from childhood*** von Kindheit an
child·ish kindlich; kindisch
child·like kindlich
child·mind·er Tagesmutter *f*
chill 1. kalt, frostig, kühl (*a. fig*); **2.** Frösteln *n*; Kälte *f*, Kühle *f* (*a. fig*); MED Erkältung *f*; **3.** abkühlen; *j-n* frösteln lassen; kühlen
chill·y kalt, frostig, kühl (*a. fig*)
chime 1. Glockenspiel *n*; Geläut *n*; **2.** läuten; schlagen (*clock*)
chim·ney Schornstein *m*
chim·ney sweep Schornsteinfeger *m*
chimp F, **chim·pan·zee** zo Schimpanse *m*
chin ANAT Kinn *n*; ***chin up!*** Kopf hoch!, halt die Ohren steif!
chi·na Porzellan *n*
Chi·na China *n*
Chi·nese 1. chinesisch; **2.** Chinese *m*, Chinesin *f*; LING Chinesisch *n*; ***the Chinese*** die Chinesen *pl*
chink Ritz *m*, Spalt *m*
chip 1. Splitter *m*, Span *m*, Schnitzel *n*, *m*; dünne Scheibe; Spielmarke *f*; EDP Chip *m*; **2.** *v/t* schnitzeln; anschlagen, abschlagen; *v/i* abbröckeln
chips (Kartoffel)Chips *pl*; *Br* Pommes frites *pl*, F Fritten *pl*
chi·rop·o·dist Fußpfleger(in), Pediküre *f*
chirp zo zirpen, zwitschern, piepsen
chis·el 1. Meißel *m*; **2.** meißeln
chit-chat Plauderei *f*
chiv·al·rous ritterlich
chive(s) BOT Schnittlauch *m*
chlo·ri·nate *Wasser etc* chloren
chlo·rine CHEM Chlor *n*
chlo·ro·fluo·ro·car·bon (ABBR ***CFC***) CHEM Fluorchlorkohlenwasserstoff *m* (ABBR ***FCKW***)
chlor·o·form MED **1.** Chloroform *n*; **2.** chloroformieren
choc·o·late Schokolade *f*; Praline *f*; *pl* Pralinen *pl*, Konfekt *n*
choice 1. Wahl *f*; Auswahl *f*; **2.** auserlesen, ausgesucht, vorzüglich
choir ARCH, MUS Chor *m*
choke 1. *v/t* (er)würgen, (*a. v/i*) ersticken; ***choke back*** *Ärger etc* unterdrücken, *Tränen* zurückhalten; ***choke down*** hinunterwürgen; *a.* ***choke up*** verstopfen; **2.** MOT Choke *m*, Luftklappe *f*
cho·les·te·rol MED Cholesterin *n*
choose (aus)wählen, aussuchen
choos·(e)y *esp Br* wählerisch
chop 1. Hieb *m*, (Handkanten)Schlag *m*; GASTR Kotelett *n*; **2.** *v/t* (zer)hacken, hauen; ***chop down*** fällen; *v/i* hacken
chop·per Hackmesser *n*, Hackbeil *n*; F Hubschrauber *m*
chop·py unruhig (*sea*)
chop·stick Essstäbchen *n*
cho·ral MUS Chor…
cho·rale MUS Choral *m*
chord MUS Saite *f*; Akkord *m*
chore schwierige *or* unangenehme Aufgabe; *pl* Hausarbeit *f*
cho·rus MUS Chor *m*; Kehrreim *m*, Refrain *m*; Tanzgruppe *f*
Christ REL Christus *m*
chris·ten REL taufen
chris·ten·ing REL **1.** Taufe *f*; **2.** Tauf…
Chris·tian REL **1.** christlich; **2.** Christ(in)
Chris·ti·an·i·ty REL Christentum *n*
Chris·tian name Vorname *m*
Christ·mas Weihnachten *n and pl*; ***at Christmas*** zu Weihnachten
Christmas Day erster Weihnachtsfeiertag
Christmas Eve Heiliger Abend
chrome Chrom *n*
chro·mi·um CHEM Chrom *n*
chron·ic chronisch; ständig, (an)dauernd
chron·i·cle Chronik *f*
chron·o·log·i·cal chronologisch
chro·nol·o·gy Zeitrechnung *f*; Zeitfolge *f*
chub·by F rundlich, pumm(e)lig; pausbäckig
chuck F werfen, schmeißen; ***chuck out*** *j-n* rausschmeißen; *et.* wegschmeißen; ***chuck up*** *Job etc* hinschmeißen
chuck·le 1. ***chuckle*** (***to o.s.***) (stillvergnügt) in sich hineinlachen; **2.** leises Lachen
chum F Kamerad *m*, Kumpel *m*
chum·my F dick befreundet
chump Holzklotz *m*; F Trottel *m*
chunk Klotz *m*, Klumpen *m*
Chun·nel F → ***Channel Tunnel***

C

church 1. Kirche *f*; 2. Kirch…, Kirchen…
church ser·vice REL Gottesdienst *m*
church·yard Kirchhof *m*
churl·ish grob, flegelhaft
churn 1. Butterfass *n*; 2. buttern; *Wellen* aufwühlen, peitschen
chute Stromschnelle *f*; Rutsche *f*, Rutschbahn *f*; F Fallschirm *m*
ci·der *a.* ***hard cider*** Apfelwein *m*; **(*sweet*) *cider*** Apfelmost *m*, Apfelsaft *m*
ci·gar Zigarre *f*
cig·a·rette Zigarette *f*
cinch F todsichere Sache
cin·der Schlacke *f*; *pl* Asche *f*
Cin·de·rel·la Aschenbrödel *n*, Aschenputtel *n*
cin·der track SPORT Aschenbahn *f*
cin·e·cam·e·ra (Schmal)Filmkamera *f*
cin·e·film Schmalfilm *m*
cin·e·ma *Br* Kino *n*; Film *m*
cin·na·mon Zimt *m*
ci·pher Geheimschrift *f*, Chiffre *f*; Null *f* (*a. fig*)
cir·cle 1. Kreis *m*; THEA Rang *m*; *fig* Kreislauf *m*; 2. (um)kreisen
cir·cuit Kreislauf *m*; ELECTR Stromkreis *m*; Rundreise *f*; SPORT Zirkus *m*; ***short circuit*** ELECTR Kurzschluss *m*
cir·cu·i·tous gewunden; weitschweifig; ***circuitous route*** Umweg *m*
cir·cu·lar 1. kreisförmig; Kreis…; 2. Rundschreiben *n*; Umlauf *m*; (Post-) Wurfsendung *f*
cir·cu·late *v/i* zirkulieren, im Umlauf sein; *v/t* in Umlauf setzen
cir·cu·lat·ing li·bra·ry Leihbücherei *f*
cir·cu·la·tion (*a.* Blut)Kreislauf *m*, Zirkulation *f*; ECON Umlauf *m*; *newspaper etc*: Auflage *f*
cir·cum·fer·ence (Kreis)Umfang *m*
cir·cum·nav·i·gate umschiffen, umsegeln
cir·cum·scribe MATH umschreiben; *fig* begrenzen
cir·cum·spect umsichtig, vorsichtig
cir·cum·stance Umstand *m*; *pl* (Sach-) Lage *f*, Umstände *pl*; Verhältnisse *pl*; ***in** or **under no circumstances*** unter keinen Umständen, auf keinen Fall; ***in** or **under the circumstances*** unter diesen Umständen
cir·cum·stan·tial ausführlich; umständlich
circumstantial ev·i·dence JUR Indizien *pl*, Indizienbeweis *m*
cir·cus Zirkus *m*
CIS ABBR *of* ***Commonwealth of Independent States*** *die* GUS, *die* Gemeinschaft unabhängiger Staaten
cis·tern Wasserbehälter *m*; Spülkasten *m*

ci·ta·tion Zitat *n*; JUR Vorladung *f*
cite zitieren; JUR vorladen
cit·i·zen Bürger(in); Städter(in); Staatsangehörige *m, f*
cit·i·zen·ship Staatsangehörigkeit *f*
cit·y 1. (Groß)Stadt *f*; ***the City*** die (Londoner) City; 2. städtisch, Stadt…
city cen·tre *Br* Innenstadt *f*, City *f*
city coun·cil·(l)or Stadtrat *m*, Stadträtin *f*
city hall Rathaus *n*; Stadtverwaltung *f*
city slick·er *often contp* Städter(in), Stadtmensch *m*
city va·grant Stadtstreicher(in), Nichtsesshafte *m, f*
civ·ic städtisch, Stadt…
civ·ics PED Staatsbürgerkunde *f*
civ·il staatlich, Staats…; (staats)bürgerlich, Bürger…; zivil, Zivil…; JUR zivilrechtlich; höflich
ci·vil·i·an Zivilist *m*
ci·vil·i·ty Höflichkeit *f*
civ·i·li·za·tion Zivilisation *f*, Kultur *f*
civ·i·lize zivilisieren
civ·il rights (Staats)Bürgerrechte *pl*
civil rights ac·tiv·ist Bürgerrechtler(in)
civil rights move·ment Bürgerrechtsbewegung *f*
civ·il ser·vant Staatsbeamte *m*, -beamtin *f*
civil ser·vice Staatsdienst *m*
civil war Bürgerkrieg *m*
clad gekleidet
claim 1. Anspruch *m*; Anrecht *n* (***to*** auf *acc*); Forderung *f*; Behauptung *f*; Claim *m*; 2. beanspruchen; fordern; behaupten
clair·voy·ant 1. hellseherisch; 2. Hellseher(in)
clam·ber (mühsam) klettern
clam·my feuchtkalt, klamm
clam·o(u)r 1. Geschrei *n*, Lärm *m*; 2. lautstark verlangen (***for*** nach)
clamp TECH Zwinge *f*
clan Clan *m*, Sippe *f*
clan·des·tine heimlich
clang klingen, klirren; erklingen lassen
clank 1. Gerassel *n*, Geklirr *n*; 2. rasseln *or* klirren (mit)
clap 1. Klatschen *n*; Schlag *m*, Klaps *m*; 2. schlagen *or* klatschen (mit)
clar·et roter Bordeaux(wein); Rotwein *m*
clar·i·fy *v/t* (auf)klären, klarstellen; *v/i* sich (auf)klären, klar werden
clar·i·net MUS Klarinette *f*
clar·i·ty Klarheit *f*
clash 1. Zusammenstoß *m*; Konflikt *m*; 2. zusammenstoßen; *fig* nicht zusammenpassen *or* harmonieren
clasp 1. Haken *m*, Schnalle *f*; Schloss *n*, (Schnapp) Verschluss *m*; Umklamme-

rung *f*; **2.** einhaken, zuhaken; ergreifen, umklammern

clasp knife Taschenmesser *n*

class 1. Klasse *f*; (Bevölkerungs-) Schicht *f*; (Schul)Klasse *f*; (Unterrichts)Stunde *f*; Kurs *m*; Jahrgang *m*; **2.** (in Klassen) einteilen, einordnen, einstufen

clas·sic 1. Klassiker *m*; **2.** klassisch

clas·si·cal klassisch

clas·sic car Klassiker *m*

clas·si·fi·ca·tion Klassifizierung *f*, Einteilung *f*

clas·si·fied klassifiziert; MIL, POL geheim

classified ad Kleinanzeige *f*

clas·si·fy klassifizieren, einstufen

class·mate Mitschüler(in)

class·room Klassenzimmer *n*

clat·ter 1. Geklapper *n*; **2.** klappern (mit)

clause JUR Klausel *f*, Bestimmung *f*; LING Satz(teil *n*) *m*

claw 1. zo Klaue *f*, Kralle *f*; (*Krebs-*) Schere *f*; **2.** (zer)kratzen; umkrallen, packen

clay Ton *m*, Lehm *m*

clean 1. *adj* rein; sauber, glatt, eben; *sl* clean; **2.** *adv* völlig, ganz und gar; **3.** reinigen, säubern, putzen; ***clean out*** reinigen; ***clean up*** gründlich reinigen; aufräumen

clean·er Rein(e)machefrau *f*, (*Fenster- etc*)Putzer *m*; Reinigungsmittel *n*, Reiniger *m*; ***take to the cleaners*** *et.* zur Reinigung bringen; F *j-n* ausnehmen

clean·ing: ***do the cleaning*** sauber machen, putzen

cleaning la·dy, cleaning wom·an Putzfrau *f*

clean·li·ness Reinlichkeit *f*

clean·ly 1. *adv* sauber; **2.** *adj* reinlich

cleanse reinigen, säubern

cleans·er Putzmittel *n*, Reinigungsmittel *n*, Reiniger *m*

clear 1. klar; hell; rein; deutlich; frei (***of*** von); ECON Netto…, Rein…; **2.** *v/t* reinigen, säubern; *Wald* lichten, roden; wegräumen (*a.* ***clear away***); *Tisch* abräumen; räumen, leeren; *Hindernis* nehmen; SPORT klären; ECON verzollen; JUR freisprechen; EDP löschen; *v/i* klar *or* hell werden; METEOR aufklaren; sich verziehen (*fog*); ***clear out*** aufräumen; ausräumen, entfernen; F abhauen; ***clear up*** aufräumen; *Verbrechen etc* aufklären; METEOR aufklaren

clear·ance Räumung *f*; TECH lichter Abstand; Freigabe *f*

clearance sale ECON Räumungsverkauf *m*, Ausverkauf *m*

clear·ing Lichtung *f*

cleave spalten

cleav·er Hackmesser *n*

clef MUS Schlüssel *m*

cleft Spalt *m*, Spalte *f*

clem·en·cy Milde *f*, Nachsicht *f*

clem·ent mild (*a.* METEOR)

clench *Lippen etc* (fest) zusammenpressen; *Zähne* zusammenbeißen; *Faust* ballen

cler·gy REL Klerus *m*, *die* Geistlichen *pl*

cler·gy·man REL Geistliche *m*

clerk Verkäufer(in); (Büro- *etc*)Angestellte *m*, *f*, (Bank-, Post)Beamte *m*, (-)Beamtin *f*

clev·er klug, gescheit; geschickt

click 1. Klicken *n*; **2.** *v/i* klicken; zu-, einschnappen; *mit der Zunge* schnalzen; *v/t* klicken *or* einschnappen lassen; mit *der Zunge* schnalzen; ***click on*** EDP anklicken

cli·ent JUR Klient(in), Mandant(in); Kunde *m*, Kundin *f*, Auftraggeber(in)

cliff Klippe *f*, Felsen *m*

cli·mate Klima *n*

cli·max Höhepunkt *m*; Orgasmus *m*

climb klettern; (er-, be)steigen; ***climb (up) a tree*** auf e-n Baum klettern

climb·er Kletterer *m*, Bergsteiger(in); BOT Kletterpflanze *f*

clinch 1. TECH sicher befestigen; (ver-)nieten; *boxing*: umklammern (*v/i* clinchen); *fig* entscheiden; ***that clinched it*** damit war die Sache entschieden; **2.** *boxing*: Clinch *m*

cling (***to***) festhalten (an *dat*), sich klammern (an *acc*); sich (an)schmiegen (an *acc*)

cling·film® *esp Br* Frischhaltefolie *f*

clin·ic Klinik *f*

clin·i·cal klinisch

clink 1. Klirren *n*, Klingen *n*; *sl* Knast *m*; **2.** klingen *or* klirren (lassen); klimpern mit

clip[1] **1.** ausschneiden; *Schafe etc* scheren; **2.** Schnitt *m*; Schur *f*; (*Film- etc*) Ausschnitt *m*; (*Video*)Clip *m*

clip[2] **1.** (Heft-, Büro- *etc*)Klammer *f*; (*Ohr*)Klipp *m*; **2.** *a.* ***clip on*** anklammern

clip·per: (***a pair of***) ***clippers*** (e-e) (*Nagel- etc*)Schere *f*, Haarschneidemaschine *f*

clip·pings Abfälle *pl*, Schnitzel *pl*; (*Zeitungs- etc*)Ausschnitte *pl*

clit·o·ris ANAT Klitoris *f*

cloak 1. Umhang *m*; **2.** *fig* verhüllen

cloak·room *Br* Garderobe *f*; Toilette *f*

clock 1. (*Wand-*, *Stand-*, *Turm*)Uhr *f*; ***9 o'clock*** 9 Uhr; **2.** SPORT Zeit stoppen; ***clock in, clock on*** einstempeln; ***clock out, clock off*** ausstempeln

clock ra·di·o Radiowecker *m*

clock·wise im Uhrzeigersinn

C

clock·work Uhrwerk *n*; ***like clockwork*** wie am Schnürchen
clod (Erd)Klumpen *m*
clog **1.** (Holz)Klotz *m*; Holzschuh *m*; **2.** *a.* ***clog up*** verstopfen
clois·ter ARCH Kreuzgang *m*; REL Kloster *n*
close **1.** *adj* geschlossen; knapp (*result etc*); genau, gründlich (*inspection etc*); eng (anliegend); stickig, schwül; eng (*friend*), nah (*relative*); ***keep a close watch on*** scharf im Auge behalten (*acc*); **2.** *adv* eng, nahe, dicht; ***close by*** ganz in der Nähe, nahe *or* dicht bei; **3.** Ende *n*, (Ab)Schluss *m*; ***come or draw to a close*** sich dem Ende nähern; Einfriedung *f*; **4.** *v/t* (ab-, ver-, zu)schließen, zumachen; ECON schließen; *Straße* (ab)sperren; *v/i* sich schließen; schließen, zumachen; enden, zu Ende gehen; ***close down*** *Geschäft etc* schließen, *Betrieb* stilllegen; *radio*, TV das Programm beenden, Sendeschluss haben; ***close in*** bedrohlich nahe kommen; hereinbrechen (*night*); ***close up*** (ab-, ver-, zu)schließen; aufschließen, aufrücken
closed geschlossen, F *pred* zu
clos·et (Wand)Schrank *m*
close-up PHOT, *film*: Großaufnahme *f*
clos·ing date Einsendeschluss *m*
clos·ing time Laden-, Geschäftsschluss *m*; Polizeistunde *f* (*of a pub*)
clot **1.** Klumpen *m*, Klümpchen *n*; ***clot of blood*** MED Blutgerinnsel *n*; **2.** gerinnen; Klumpen bilden
cloth Stoff *m*, Tuch *n*; Lappen *m*
cloth·bound in Leinen gebunden
clothe (an-, be)kleiden; einkleiden
clothes Kleider *pl*, Kleidung *f*; Wäsche *f*
clothes bas·ket Wäschekorb *m*
clothes·horse Wäscheständer *m*
clothes·line Wäscheleine *f*
clothes peg *Br*, **clothes·pin** Wäscheklammer *f*
cloth·ing (Be)Kleidung *f*
cloud **1.** Wolke *f*; *fig* Schatten *m*; **2.** (sich) bewölken; (sich) trüben
cloud·burst Wolkenbruch *m*
cloud·less wolkenlos
cloud·y bewölkt; trüb; *fig* unklar
clout F Schlag *m*; POL Einfluss *m*
clove[1] GASTR (Gewürz)Nelke *f*; ***clove of garlic*** Knoblauchzehe *f*
clo·ven hoof ZO Huf *m* der Paarzeher
clo·ver BOT Klee *m*
clown Clown *m*, Hanswurst *m*
club **1.** Keule *f*; Knüppel *m*; SPORT Schlagholz *n*; (*Golf*)Schläger *m*; Klub *m*; *pl card game*: Kreuz *n*; **2.** einknüppeln auf (*acc*), niederknüppeln
club·foot MED Klumpfuß *m*
cluck ZO **1.** gackern; glucken; **2.** Gackern *n*; Glucken *n*
clue Anhaltspunkt *m*, Fingerzeig *m*, Spur *f*
clump **1.** Klumpen *m*; (*Baum- etc* -) Gruppe *f*; **2.** trampeln
clum·sy unbeholfen, ungeschickt, plump
clus·ter **1.** BOT Traube *f*, Büschel *n*; Haufen *m*; **2.** sich drängen
clutch **1.** Griff *m*; TECH Kupplung *f*; *fig* Klaue *f*; **2.** (er)greifen; umklammern
clut·ter *fig* überladen
c/o ABBR *of* ***care of*** c/o, (wohnhaft) bei
Co ABBR *of* ***company*** ECON Gesellschaft *f*
coach **1.** Reisebus *m*; *Br* RAIL (Personen)-Wagen *m*; Kutsche *f*; SPORT Trainer(in); PED Nachhilfelehrer(in); **2.** SPORT trainieren; PED *j-m* Nachhilfeunterricht geben
coach·man Kutscher *m*
co·ag·u·late gerinnen (lassen)
coal (Stein)Kohle *f*; ***carry coals to Newcastle*** F *Br* Eulen nach Athen tragen
co·a·li·tion POL Koalition *f*; Bündnis *n*, Zusammenschluss *m*
coal·mine, **coal·pit** Kohlengrube *f*
coarse grob; rau; derb; ungeschliffen; gemein
coast **1.** Küste *f*; **2.** MAR die Küste entlangfahren; im Leerlauf (*car*) *or* im Freilauf (*bicycle*) fahren; rodeln
coast·er brake Rücktritt(bremse *f*) *m*
coast·guard (Angehörige *m* der) Küstenwache *f*
coast·line Küstenlinie *f*, -strich *m*
coat **1.** Mantel *m*; ZO Pelz *m*, Fell *n*; (*Farb- etc*)Überzug *m*, Anstrich *m*, Schicht *f*; **2.** (an)streichen, überziehen, beschichten
coat hang·er Kleiderbügel *m*
coat·ing (*Farb- etc*)Überzug *m*, Anstrich *m*; Schicht *f*; Mantelstoff *m*
coat of arms Wappen(schild *m*, *n*) *n*
coax überreden, beschwatzen
cob Maiskolben *m*
cob·bled: ***cobbled street*** Straße *f* mit Kopfsteinpflaster
cob·bler (Flick)Schuster *m*
cob·web Spinn(en)gewebe *n*
co·caine Kokain *n*
cock **1.** ZO Hahn *m*; V Schwanz *m*; **2.** aufrichten; ***cock one's ears*** die Ohren spitzen
cock·a·too ZO Kakadu *m*
cock·chaf·er ZO Maikäfer *m*
cock·eyed F schielend; (krumm und) schief
Cock·ney Cockney *m*, waschechter Londoner

cock·pit AVIAT Cockpit *n*
cock·roach ZO Schabe *f*
cock·sure F übertrieben selbstsicher
cock·tail Cocktail *m*
cock·y großspurig, anmaßend
co·co BOT Kokospalme *f*
co·coa Kakao *m*
co·co·nut BOT Kokosnuss *f*
co·coon (*Seiden*)Kokon *m*
cod ZO Kabeljau *m*, Dorsch *m*
COD ABBR *of* ***collect*** (*Br* ***cash***) ***on delivery*** per Nachnahme
cod·dle verhätscheln, verzärteln
code **1.** Kode *m*; **2.** verschlüsseln, chiffrieren; kodieren
cod·fish → ***cod***
cod·ing Kodierung *f*
cod-liv·er oil Lebertran *m*
co·ed·u·ca·tion PED Gemeinschaftserziehung *f*
co·ex·ist gleichzeitig *or* nebeneinander bestehen *or* leben
co·ex·ist·ence Koexistenz *f*
cof·fee Kaffee *m*; ***black*** (***white***) ***coffee*** Kaffee ohne (mit) Milch
coffee bar *Br* Café *n*; Imbissstube *f*
coffee bean Kaffeebohne *f*
coffee grind·er Kaffeemühle *f*
coffee machine Kaffeeautomat *m*
cof·fee·mak·er Kaffeemaschine *f*
cof·fee pot Kaffeekanne *f*
coffee shop Café *n*; Imbissstube *f*
coffee ta·ble Couchtisch *m*
cof·fin Sarg *m*
cog TECH (Rad)Zahn *m*; → **cog·wheel** TECH Zahnrad *n*
co·her·ence, **co·her·en·cy** Zusammenhang *m*
co·her·ent zusammenhängend
co·he·sion Zusammenhalt *m*
co·he·sive (fest) zusammenhaltend
coif·fure Frisur *f*
coil **1.** *a.* ***coil up*** aufrollen, (auf)wickeln; sich zusammenrollen; **2.** Spirale *f* (*a.* TECH, MED); Rolle *f*, Spule *f*
coin **1.** Münze *f*; **2.** prägen
co·in·cide zusammentreffen; übereinstimmen
co·in·ci·dence (zufälliges) Zusammentreffen; Zufall *m*
coin-op·e·rat·ed: ***coin-operated*** (***gas***, *Br* ***petrol***) ***pump*** Münztank(automat) *m*
coke Koks *m* (*a.* F *cocaine*)
Coke® F Coke *n*, Cola *n*, *f*, Coca *n*, *f*
cold **1.** kalt; **2.** Kälte *f*; MED Erkältung *f*; ***catch*** (***a***) ***cold*** sich erkälten; ***have a cold*** erkältet sein
cold-blood·ed kaltblütig
cold cuts GASTR Aufschnitt *m*
cold-heart·ed kaltherzig
cold·ness Kälte *f*
cold sweat Angstschweiß *m*; ***he broke out in a cold sweat*** ihm brach der Angstschweiß aus
cold war POL kalter Krieg
cold wave METEOR Kältewelle *f*
cole·slaw Krautsalat *m*
col·ic MED Kolik *f*
col·lab·o·rate zusammenarbeiten
col·lab·o·ra·tion Zusammenarbeit *f*; ***in collaboration with*** gemeinsam mit
col·lapse **1.** zusammenbrechen (*a. fig*), einstürzen; umfallen; *fig* scheitern; **2.** Einsturz *m*; *fig* Zusammenbruch *m*
col·lap·si·ble Klapp…, zusammenklappbar
col·lar **1.** Kragen *m*; (*Hunde- etc*)Halsband *n*; **2.** beim Kragen packen; *j-n* festnehmen, F schnappen
col·lar·bone ANAT Schlüsselbein *n*
col·league Kollege *m*, Kollegin *f*, Mitarbeiter(in)
col·lect *v/t* (ein)sammeln; *Daten* erfassen; *Geld* kassieren; *j-n or et.* abholen; *Gedanken etc* sammeln; *v/i* sich (ver-)sammeln
col·lect·ed *fig* gefasst
col·lect·ing box Sammelbüchse *f*
col·lec·tion Sammlung *f*; ECON Eintreibung *f*; REL Kollekte *f*; Abholung *f*
col·lec·tive gesammelt; Sammel…; ***collective bargaining*** ECON Tarifverhandlungen
col·lec·tive·ly insgesamt; zusammen
col·lec·tor Sammler(in); Steuereinnehmer *m*; ELECTR Stromabnehmer *m*
col·lege College *n*; Hochschule *f*; höhere Lehranstalt
col·lide zusammenstoßen, kollidieren (*a. fig*)
col·lie·ry Kohlengrube *f*
col·li·sion Zusammenstoß *m*, Kollision *f* (*a. fig*)
col·lo·qui·al umgangssprachlich
co·lon LING Doppelpunkt *m*
colo·nel MIL Oberst *m*
co·lo·ni·al·is·m POL Kolonialismus *m*
col·o·nize kolonisieren, besiedeln
col·o·ny Kolonie *f*
col·o(u)r **1.** Farbe *f*; *pl* MIL Fahne *f*; MAR Flagge *f*; ***what colo(u)r is …?*** welche Farbe hat …?; **2.** *v/t* färben; anmalen, bemalen, anstreichen; *fig* beschönigen; *v/i* sich (ver)färben; erröten
col·o(u)r bar Rassenschranke *f*
col·o(u)r-blind farbenblind
col·o(u)red bunt; farbig
col·o(u)r·fast farbecht

col·o(u)r film PHOT Farbfilm *m*
col·o(u)r·ful farbenprächtig; *fig* farbig, bunt
col·o(u)r·ing Färbung *f*; Farbstoff *m*; Gesichtsfarbe *f*
col·o(u)r·less farblos
col·o(u)r line Rassenschranke *f*
col·o(u)r set Farbfernseher *m*
colo(u)r tel·e·vi·sion Farbfernsehen *n*
colt ZO (Hengst)Fohlen *n*
col·umn Säule *f*; PRINT Spalte *f*; MIL Kolonne *f*
col·umn·ist Kolumnist(in)
comb 1. Kamm *m*; **2.** kämmen; striegeln
com·bat 1. Kampf *m*; ***single combat*** Zweikampf *m*; **2.** kämpfen gegen, bekämpfen
com·ba·tant MIL Kämpfer *m*
com·bi·na·tion Verbindung *f*, Kombination *f*
com·bine 1. (sich) verbinden; **2.** ECON Konzern *m*; AGR *a.* ***combine harvester*** Mähdrescher *m*
com·bus·ti·ble 1. brennbar; **2.** Brennstoff *m*, Brennmaterial *n*
com·bus·tion Verbrennung *f*
come kommen; ***to come*** künftig, kommend; ***come and go*** kommen und gehen; ***come to see*** besuchen; ***come about*** geschehen, passieren; ***come across*** auf *j-n or et.* stoßen; ***come along*** mitkommen, mitgehen; ***come apart*** auseinanderfallen; ***come away*** sich lösen, ab-, losgehen (*button etc*); ***come back*** zurückkommen; ***come by s.th.*** zu et. kommen; ***come down*** herunterkommen (*a. fig*); einstürzen; sinken (*prices*); überliefert werden; ***come down with*** F erkranken an (*dat*); ***come for*** abholen kommen, kommen wegen; ***come forward*** sich melden; ***come from*** kommen aus; kommen von; ***come home*** nach Hause (*Austrian, Swiss a.* nachhause) kommen; ***come in*** hereinkommen; eintreffen (*news*); einlaufen (*train*); ***come in!*** herein!; ***come loose*** sich ablösen, abgehen; ***come off*** ab-, losgehen (*button etc*); ***come on!*** los!, vorwärts!, komm!; ***come out*** herauskommen; ***come over*** vorbeikommen (*visitor*); ***come round*** vorbeikommen (*visitor*); wieder zu sich kommen; ***come through*** durchkommen; *Krankheit etc* überstehen, überleben; ***come to*** sich belaufen auf (*acc*); wieder zu sich kommen; ***come up to*** entsprechen (*dat*), heranreichen an (*acc*)
come·back Come-back *n*
co·me·di·an Komiker *m*
com·e·dy Komödie *f*, Lustspiel *n*
come·ly attraktiv, gut aussehend
com·fort 1. Komfort *m*, Bequemlichkeit *f*; Trost *m*; ***cold comfort*** schwacher Trost; **2.** trösten
com·for·ta·ble komfortabel, behaglich, bequem; tröstlich
com·fort·er Tröster *m*; *esp Br* Schnuller *m*; Steppdecke *f*
com·fort·less unbequem; trostlos
com·fort sta·tion Bedürfnisanstalt *f*
com·ic komisch; Komödien…, Lustspiel…
com·i·cal komisch, spaßig
com·ics Comics *pl*, Comic-Hefte *pl*
com·ma LING Komma *n*
com·mand 1. Befehl *m*; Beherrschung *f*; MIL Kommando *n*; **2.** befehlen; MIL kommandieren; verfügen über (*acc*); beherrschen
com·mand·er MIL Kommandeur *m*, Befehlshaber *m*
commander in chief MIL Oberbefehlshaber *m*
com·mand·ment REL Gebot *n*
com·mand mod·ule Kommandokapsel *f*
com·man·do MIL Kommando *n*
com·mem·o·rate gedenken (*gen*)
com·mem·o·ra·tion: ***in commemoration of*** zum Gedenken *or* Gedächtnis an (*acc*)
com·mem·o·ra·tive Gedenk…, Erinnerungs…
com·ment 1. (***on***) Kommentar *m* (zu); Bemerkung *f* (zu); Anmerkung *f* (zu); ***no comment!*** kein Kommentar!; **2.** *v/i* ***comment on*** e-n Kommentar abgeben zu, sich äußern über (*acc*); *v/t* bemerken (***that*** dass)
com·men·ta·ry Kommentar *m* (***on*** zu)
com·men·ta·tor Kommentator *m*, *radio*, TV *a.* Reporter *m*
com·merce ECON Handel *m*
com·mer·cial 1. ECON Handels…, Geschäfts…; kommerziell, finanziell; **2.** *radio*, TV Werbespot *m*, Werbesendung *f*
commercial art Gebrauchsgrafik *f*
commercial art·ist Gebrauchsgrafiker(in)
com·mer·cial·ize kommerzialisieren
com·mer·cial tel·e·vi·sion Werbefernsehen *n*; kommerzielles Fernsehen
com·mis·e·rate: ***commiserate with*** Mitleid empfinden mit
com·mis·e·ra·tion Mitleid *n* (***for*** mit)
com·mis·sion 1. Auftrag *m*; Kommission *f*, Ausschuss *m*; ECON Kommission *f*, Provision *f*; Begehung *f* (*of a crime*); **2.** beauftragen; *et.* in Auftrag geben
com·mis·sion·er Beauftragte *m, f*; Kommissar(in)

com·mit anvertrauen, übergeben (***to*** *dat*); JUR *j-n* einweisen (***to*** in *acc*); *Verbrechen* begehen; *j-n* verpflichten (***to*** zu), *j-n* festlegen (***to*** auf *acc*)

com·mit·ment Verpflichtung *f*; Engagement *n*

com·mit·tal JUR Einweisung *f*

com·mit·tee Komitee *n*, Ausschuss *m*

com·mod·i·ty ECON Ware *f*, Artikel *m*

com·mon 1. gemeinsam, gemeinschaftlich; allgemein; alltäglich; gewöhnlich, einfach; 2. Gemeindeland *n*; ***in common*** gemeinsam (***with*** mit)

com·mon·er Bürgerliche *m, f*

com·mon law (ungeschriebenes englisches) Gewohnheitsrecht

Com·mon Mar·ket ECON, POL HIST Gemeinsamer Markt

com·mon·place 1. Gemeinplatz *m*; 2. alltäglich; abgedroschen

Com·mons: ***the Commons, the House of Commons*** *Br* PARL das Unterhaus

com·mon sense gesunder Menschenverstand

Com·mon·wealth: ***the Commonwealth (of Nations)*** das Commonwealth

com·mo·tion Aufregung *f*; Aufruhr *m*, Tumult *m*

com·mu·nal Gemeinde…; Gemeinschafts…

com·mune Kommune *f*

com·mu·ni·cate *v/t* mitteilen; *v/i* sich besprechen; sich in Verbindung setzen (***with s.o.*** mit j-m); (durch e-e Tür) verbunden sein

com·mu·ni·ca·tion Mitteilung *f*; Verständigung *f*, Kommunikation *f*; Verbindung *f*; *pl* Kommunikationsmittel *pl*; Verkehrswege *pl*

com·mu·ni·ca·tions sat·el·lite Nachrichtensatellit *m*

com·mu·ni·ca·tive mitteilsam, gesprächig

Com·mu·nion *a.* ***Holy Communion*** REL (heilige) Kommunion, Abendmahl *n*

com·mu·nis·m POL Kommunismus *m*

com·mu·nist POL 1. Kommunist(in); 2. kommunistisch

com·mu·ni·ty Gemeinschaft *f*; Gemeinde *f*

com·mute JUR Strafe *mildernd* umwandeln; RAIL *etc* pendeln

com·mut·er Pendler(in)

commuter train Pendlerzug *m*, Nahverkehrszug *m*

com·pact 1. Puderdose *f*; MOT Kleinwagen *m*; 2. *adj* kompakt; eng, klein; knapp (*style*)

compact car MOT Kleinwagen *m*

compact disk (ABBR ***CD***) Compact Disc *f*, CD *f*

compact disk play·er CD-Player *m*, CD--Spieler *m*

com·pan·ion Begleiter(in); Gefährte *m*, Gefährtin *f*; Gesellschafter(in); Handbuch *n*, Leitfaden *m*

com·pan·ion·ship Gesellschaft *f*

com·pa·ny Gesellschaft *f*, ECON *a.* Firma *f*; MIL Kompanie *f*; THEA Truppe *f*; ***keep s.o. company*** j-m Gesellschaft leisten

com·pa·ra·ble vergleichbar

com·par·a·tive 1. vergleichend; verhältnismäßig; 2. *a.* ***comparative degree*** LING Komparativ *m*

com·par·a·tive·ly vergleichsweise; verhältnismäßig

com·pare 1. *v/t* vergleichen; ***compared with*** im Vergleich zu; *v/i* sich vergleichen lassen; 2. ***beyond compare, without compare*** unvergleichlich

com·pa·ri·son Vergleich *m*

com·part·ment Fach *n*; RAIL Abteil *n*

com·pass Kompass *m*; ***pair of compasses*** Zirkel *m*

com·pas·sion Mitleid *n*

com·pas·sion·ate mitleidig

com·pat·i·ble vereinbar; ***be compatible (with)*** passen (zu), zusammenpassen; EDP *etc* kompatibel sein (mit)

com·pat·ri·ot Landsmann *m*, Landsmännin *f*

com·pel (er)zwingen

com·pel·ling bezwingend

com·pen·sate *j-n* entschädigen; *et.* ersetzen; ausgleichen

com·pen·sa·tion Ersatz *m*; Ausgleich *m*; Schadenersatz *m*, Entschädigung *f*; Bezahlung *f*, Gehalt *n*

com·pere *Br* Conférencier *m*

com·pete sich (mit)bewerben (***for*** um); konkurrieren; SPORT (am Wettkampf) teilnehmen

com·pe·tence Können *n*, Fähigkeit *f*

com·pe·tent fähig, tüchtig; fachkundig, sachkundig

com·pe·ti·tion Wettbewerb *m*; Konkurrenz *f*

com·pet·i·tive konkurrierend

com·pet·i·tor Mitbewerber(in); Konkurrent(in); SPORT (Wettbewerbs-)Teilnehmer(in)

com·pile kompilieren, zusammentragen, zusammenstellen

com·pla·cence, com·pla·cen·cy Selbstzufriedenheit *f*, Selbstgefälligkeit *f*

com·pla·cent selbstzufrieden, selbstgefällig

com·plain sich beklagen *or* beschweren

(***about*** über *acc*; ***to*** bei); klagen (***of*** über *acc*)
com·plaint Klage *f*, Beschwerde *f*; MED Leiden *n*, *pl* MED *a.* Beschwerden *pl*
com·ple·ment **1.** Ergänzung *f*; **2.** ergänzen
com·ple·men·ta·ry (sich) ergänzend
com·plete **1.** vollständig; vollzählig; **2.** vervollständigen; beenden, abschließen
com·ple·tion Vervollständigung *f*; Abschluss *m*
completion test PSYCH Lückentext *m*
com·plex **1.** zusammengesetzt; komplex, vielschichtig; **2.** Komplex *m* (*a.* PSYCH)
com·plex·ion Gesichtsfarbe *f*, Teint *m*
com·plex·i·ty Komplexität *f*, Vielschichtigkeit *f*
com·pli·ance Einwilligung *f*; Befolgung *f*; ***in compliance with*** gemäß (*dat*)
com·pli·ant willfährig
com·pli·cate komplizieren
com·pli·cat·ed kompliziert
com·pli·ca·tion Komplikation *f* (*a.* MED)
com·plic·i·ty JUR Mitschuld *f*, Mittäterschaft *f* (***in*** an *dat*)
com·pli·ment **1.** Kompliment *n*; Empfehlung *f*; Gruß *m*; **2.** *v/t* *j-m* ein Kompliment *or* Komplimente machen (***on*** über *acc*)
com·ply (***with***) einwilligen (in *acc*); (*e-e Abmachung etc*) befolgen
com·po·nent Bestandteil *m*; TECH, ELECTR Bauelement *n*
com·pose zusammensetzen, -stellen; MUS komponieren; verfassen; ***be composed of*** bestehen *or* sich zusammensetzen aus; ***compose o.s.*** sich beruhigen
com·posed ruhig, gelassen
com·pos·er MUS Komponist(in)
com·po·si·tion Zusammensetzung *f*; MUS Komposition *f*; PED Aufsatz *m*
com·po·sure Fassung *f*, (Gemüts)Ruhe *f*
com·pound[1] Lager *n*; Gefängnishof *m*; (Tier)Gehege *n*
com·pound[2] **1.** Zusammensetzung *f*; Verbindung *f*; LING zusammengesetztes Wort; **2.** zusammengesetzt; ***compound interest*** ECON Zinseszinsen *pl*; **3.** *v/t* zusammensetzen; steigern, *esp* verschlimmern
com·pre·hend begreifen, verstehen
com·pre·hen·si·ble verständlich
com·pre·hen·sion Verständnis *n*; Begriffsvermögen *n*, Verstand *m*; ***past comprehension*** unfassbar, unfasslich
com·pre·hen·sive **1.** umfassend; **2.** *a.* ***comprehensive school*** *Br* Gesamtschule *f*
com·press zusammendrücken, -pressen;
compressed air Druckluft *f*
com·pres·sion PHYS Verdichtung *f*; TECH Druck *m*
com·prise einschließen, umfassen; bestehen aus
com·pro·mise **1.** Kompromiss *m*; **2.** *v/t* bloßstellen, kompromittieren; *v/i* e-n Kompromiss schließen
com·pro·mis·ing kompromittierend; verfänglich
com·pul·sion Zwang *m*
com·pul·sive zwingend, Zwangs…; PSYCH zwanghaft
com·pul·so·ry obligatorisch; Pflicht…, Zwangs…
com·punc·tion Gewissensbisse *pl*; Reue *f*; Bedenken *pl*
com·pute berechnen; schätzen
com·put·er Computer *m*, Rechner *m*
com·put·er-aid·ed computergestützt
computer-con·trolled computergesteuert
com·put·er game Computerspiel *n*
computer graph·ics Computergrafik *f*
com·put·er·ize (sich) auf Computer umstellen; computerisieren; mit Hilfe e-s Computers errechnen *or* zusammenstellen
com·put·er pre·dic·tion Hochrechnung *f*
computer sci·ence Informatik *f*
computer sci·en·tist Informatiker *m*
computer vi·rus EDP Computervirus *m*
com·rade Kamerad *m*; (Partei)Genosse *m*
con[1] → ***contra***
con[2] F reinlegen, betrügen
con·ceal verbergen; verheimlichen
con·cede zugestehen, einräumen
con·ceit Einbildung *f*, Dünkel *m*
con·ceit·ed eingebildet (***of*** auf *acc*)
con·cei·va·ble denkbar, begreiflich
con·ceive *v/i* schwanger werden; *v/t Kind* empfangen; sich *et.* vorstellen *or* denken
con·cen·trate (sich) konzentrieren
con·cept Begriff *m*; Gedanke *m*
con·cep·tion Vorstellung *f*, Begriff *m*; BIOL Empfängnis *f*
con·cern **1.** Angelegenheit *f*; Sorge *f*; ECON Geschäft *n*, Unternehmen *n*; **2.** betreffen, angehen; beunruhigen
con·cerned besorgt; beteiligt (***in*** an *dat*)
con·cern·ing *prp* betreffend, hinsichtlich (*gen*), was … (*acc*) (an)betrifft
con·cert MUS Konzert *n*
con·cert hall Konzerthalle *f*, -saal *m*
con·ces·sion Zugeständnis *n*; Konzession *f*
con·cil·i·a·to·ry versöhnlich, vermittelnd
con·cise kurz, knapp

con·cise·ness Kürze *f*
con·clude schließen, beenden; *Vertrag etc* abschließen; *et.* folgern, schließen (***from*** aus); ***to be concluded*** Schluss folgt
con·clu·sion (Ab)Schluss *m*, Ende *n*; Abschluss *m* (*of a contract etc*); (Schluss)Folgerung *f*; → ***jump***
con·clu·sive schlüssig
con·coct (zusammen)brauen; *fig* aushecken, ausbrüten
con·coc·tion Gebräu *n*; *fig* Erfindung *f*
con·crete[1] konkret
con·crete[2] **1.** Beton *m*; **2.** Beton…; **3.** betonieren
con·cur übereinstimmen
con·cur·rence Zusammentreffen *n*; Übereinstimmung *f*
con·cus·sion MED Gehirnerschütterung *f*
con·demn verurteilen (*a.* JUR); verdammen; für unbrauchbar *or* unbewohnbar *etc* erklären; ***condemn to death*** JUR zum Tode verurteilen
con·dem·na·tion Verurteilung *f* (*a.* JUR); Verdammung *f*
con·den·sa·tion Kondensation *f*; Zusammenfassung *f*
con·dense kondensieren; zusammenfassen
con·densed milk Kondensmilch *f*
con·dens·er TECH Kondensator *m*
con·de·scend sich herablassen
con·de·scend·ing herablassend, gönnerhaft
con·di·ment Gewürz *n*, Würze *f*
con·di·tion **1.** Zustand *m*; (*körperlicher or* Gesundheits)Zustand *m*; SPORT Kondition *f*, Form *f*; Bedingung *f*; *pl* Verhältnisse *pl*, Umstände *pl*; ***on condition that*** unter der Bedingung, dass; ***out of condition*** in schlechter Verfassung, in schlechtem Zustand; **2.** bedingen; in Form bringen
con·di·tion·al **1.** (***on***) bedingt (durch), abhängig (von); **2.** *a.* ***conditional clause*** LING Bedingungs-, Konditionalsatz *m*; *a.* ***conditional mood*** LING Konditional *m*
con·do → ***condominium***
con·dole kondolieren (***with*** *dat*)
con·do·lence Beileid *n*
con·dom Kondom *n*, *m*
con·do·min·i·um Eigentumswohnanlage *f*; Eigentumswohnung *f*
con·done verzeihen, vergeben
con·du·cive dienlich, förderlich (***to*** *dat*)
con·duct **1.** Führung *f*; Verhalten *n*, Betragen *n*; **2.** führen; PHYS leiten; MUS dirigieren; ***conducted tour*** Führung *f* (***of*** durch)
con·duc·tor Führer *m*, Leiter *m*; (*Bus-, Straßenbahn*)Schaffner *m*; RAIL Zugbegleiter *m*; MUS Dirigent *m*; PHYS Leiter *m*; ELECTR Blitzableiter *m*
cone Kegel *m*; GASTR Eistüte *f*; BOT Zapfen *m*
con·fec·tion Konfekt *n*
con·fec·tion·er Konditor *m*
con·fec·tion·e·ry Süßigkeiten *pl*, Süß-, Konditoreiwaren *pl*; Konfekt *n*; Konditorei *f*; Süßwarengeschäft *n*
con·fed·e·ra·cy (Staaten)Bund *m*; ***the Confederacy*** HIST die Konföderation
con·fed·er·ate **1.** verbündet; **2.** Verbündete *m*, Bundesgenosse *m*; **3.** (sich) verbünden
con·fed·er·a·tion Bund *m*, Bündnis *n*; (Staaten)Bund *m*
con·fer *v/t Titel etc* verleihen (***on*** *dat*); *v/i* sich beraten
con·fe·rence Konferenz *f*
con·fess gestehen; beichten
con·fes·sion Geständnis *n*; REL Beichte *f*
con·fes·sion·al REL Beichtstuhl *m*
con·fes·sor REL Beichtvater *m*
con·fi·dant(e) Vertraute *m* (*f*)
con·fide: ***confide s.th. to s.o.*** j-m et. anvertrauen; ***confide in s.o.*** sich j-m anvertrauen
con·fi·dence Vertrauen *n*; Selbstvertrauen *n*
confidence man → ***conman***
confidence trickster Trickbetrüger *m*
con·fi·dent überzeugt, zuversichtlich
con·fi·den·tial vertraulich
con·fine begrenzen, beschränken; einsperren; ***be confined of*** entbunden werden von
con·fine·ment Haft *f*; Beschränkung *f*; MED Entbindung *f*
con·firm bestätigen; bekräftigen; REL konfirmieren, firmen
con·fir·ma·tion Bestätigung *f*; REL Konfirmation *f*, Firmung *f*
con·fis·cate beschlagnahmen
con·fis·ca·tion Beschlagnahme *f*
con·flict **1.** Konflikt *m*, Zwiespalt *m*; **2.** im Widerspruch stehen (***with*** zu)
con·flict·ing widersprüchlich, zwiespältig
con·form (sich) anpassen (***to*** *dat*, an *acc*)
con·found verwirren, durcheinanderbringen
con·front gegenübertreten, -stehen (*dat*); sich stellen (*dat*); konfrontieren
con·fron·ta·tion Konfrontation *f*
con·fuse verwechseln; verwirren
con·fused verwirrt; verlegen; verworren
con·fu·sion Verwirrung *f*; Verlegenheit *f*; Verwechslung *f*

C

con·geal erstarren (lassen); gerinnen (lassen)
con·gest·ed überfüllt; verstopft
con·ges·tion MED Blutandrang *m*; *a.* ***traffic congestion*** Verkehrsstockung *f*, Verkehrsstörung *f*, Verkehrsstau *m*
con·grat·u·late beglückwünschen, *j-m* gratulieren
con·grat·u·la·tion Glückwunsch *m*; ***congratulations!*** ich gratuliere!, herzlichen Glückwunsch!
con·gre·gate (sich) versammeln
con·gre·ga·tion REL Gemeinde *f*
con·gress Kongress *m*; ***Congress*** PARL der Kongress
Con·gress·man PARL Kongressabgeordnete *m*
Con·gress·wom·an PARL Kongressabgeordnete *f*
con·ic, con·i·cal *esp* TECH konisch, kegelförmig
co·ni·fer BOT Nadelbaum *m*
con·jec·ture **1.** Vermutung *f*; **2.** vermuten
con·ju·gal ehelich
con·ju·gate LING konjugieren, beugen
con·ju·ga·tion LING Konjugation *f*, Beugung *f*
con·junc·tion Verbindung *f*; LING Konjunktion *f*, Bindewort *n*
con·junc·ti·vi·tis MED Bindehautentzündung *f*
con·jure zaubern; *Teufel etc* beschwören; ***conjure up*** heraufbeschwören (*a. fig*)
con·jur·er *esp Br* → ***conjuror***
con·jur·ing trick Zauberkunststück *n*
con·jur·or Zauberer *m*, Zauberin *f*, Zauberkünstler(in)
con·man Betrüger *m*; Hochstapler *m*
con·nect verbinden; ELECTR anschließen, zuschalten; RAIL, AVIAT *etc* Anschluss haben (***with*** an *acc*)
con·nect·ed verbunden; (logisch) zusammenhängend (*speech etc*); ***be well connected*** gute Beziehungen haben
con·nec·tion, *Br* **con·nex·ion** Verbindung *f*, Anschluss *m* (*a.* ELECTR, RAIL, AVIAT, TEL); Zusammenhang *m*; *mst pl* Beziehungen *pl*, Verbindungen *pl*; Verwandte *pl*
con·quer erobern; (be)siegen
con·quer·or Eroberer *m*
con·quest Eroberung *f* (*a. fig*); erobertes Gebiet
con·science Gewissen *n*
con·sci·en·tious gewissenhaft; Gewissens…
con·sci·en·tious·ness Gewissenhaftigkeit *f*
con·sci·en·tious ob·jec·tor MIL Wehrdienstverweigerer *m*
con·scious MED bei Bewusstsein; bewusst; ***be conscious of*** sich bewusst sein (*gen*)
con·scious·ness Bewusstsein *n* (*a.* MED)
con·script MIL **1.** einberufen; **2.** Wehrpflichtige *m*
con·scrip·tion MIL Einberufung *f*; Wehrpflicht *f*
con·se·crate REL weihen; widmen
con·se·cra·tion REL Weihe *f*
con·sec·u·tive aufeinanderfolgend; fortlaufend
con·sent **1.** Zustimmung *f*; **2.** einwilligen, zustimmen
con·se·quence Folge *f*, Konsequenz *f*; Bedeutung *f*
con·se·quent·ly folglich, daher
con·ser·va·tion Erhaltung *f*; Naturschutz *m*; Umweltschutz *m*; ***conservation area*** (Natur)Schutzgebiet *n*
con·ser·va·tion·ist Naturschützer(in); Umweltschützer(in)
con·ser·va·tive **1.** erhaltend; konservativ; vorsichtig; **2.** ***Conservative*** POL Konservative *m, f*
con·ser·va·to·ry Treibhaus *n*, Gewächshaus *n*; Wintergarten *m*
con·serve erhalten
con·sid·er *v/t* nachdenken über (*acc*); betrachten als, halten für; sich überlegen, erwägen; in Betracht ziehen, berücksichtigen; *v/i* nachdenken, überlegen
con·sid·e·ra·ble ansehnlich, beträchtlich
con·sid·e·ra·bly bedeutend, ziemlich, (sehr) viel
con·sid·er·ate rücksichtsvoll
con·sid·e·ra·tion Erwägung *f*, Überlegung *f*; Berücksichtigung *f*; Rücksicht (-nahme) *f*; ***take into consideration*** in Erwägung *or* in Betracht ziehen
con·sid·er·ing in Anbetracht (der Tatsache, dass)
con·sign ECON *Waren* zusenden
con·sign·ment ECON (Waren)Sendung *f*; Zusendung *f*
con·sist: ***consist in*** bestehen in (*dat*); ***consist of*** bestehen aus
con·sis·tence, con·sis·ten·cy Konsistenz *f*, Beschaffenheit *f*; Übereinstimmung *f*; Konsequenz *f*
con·sis·tent übereinstimmend, vereinbar (***with*** mit); konsequent; SPORT *etc*: beständig
con·so·la·tion Trost *m*
con·sole trösten
con·sol·i·date festigen; *fig* zusammenschließen, -legen
con·so·nant LING Konsonant *m*, Mitlaut

C

m
con·spic·u·ous deutlich sichtbar; auffallend
con·spi·ra·cy Verschwörung *f*
con·spi·ra·tor Verschwörer *m*
con·spire sich verschwören
con·sta·ble *Br* Polizist *m*
con·stant konstant, gleichbleibend; (be)ständig, (an)dauernd
con·stant-care pa·tient MED Pflegefall *m*
con·ster·na·tion Bestürzung *f*
con·sti·pat·ed MED verstopft
con·sti·pa·tion MED Verstopfung *f*
con·sti·tu·en·cy POL *Br* Wählerschaft *f*; Wahlkreis *m*
con·sti·tu·ent (wesentlicher) Bestandteil; POL Wähler(in)
con·sti·tute ernennen, einsetzen; bilden, ausmachen
con·sti·tu·tion POL Verfassung *f*; Konstitution *f*, körperliche Verfassung
con·sti·tu·tion·al konstitutionell; POL verfassungsmäßig
con·strained gezwungen, unnatürlich
con·strict zusammenziehen
con·stric·tion Zusammenziehung *f*
con·struct bauen, errichten, konstruieren
con·struc·tion Konstruktion *f*; Bau *m*, Bauwerk *n*; ***under construction*** im Bau (befindlich)
construction site Baustelle *f*
con·struc·tive konstruktiv
con·struc·tor Erbauer *m*, Konstrukteur *m*
con·sul Konsul *m*
con·su·late Konsulat *n*
consulate gen·e·ral Generalkonsulat *n*
con·sul gen·e·ral Generalkonsul *m*
con·sult *v/t* konsultieren, um Rat fragen; in *e-m Buch* nachschlagen; *v/i* (sich) beraten
con·sul·tant (fachmännischer) Berater; *Br* Facharzt *m*
con·sul·ta·tion Konsultation *f*, Beratung *f*, Rücksprache *f*
con·sult·ing beratend
consulting hours *Br* MED Sprechstunde *f*
consulting room *Br* MED Sprechzimmer *n*
con·sume *v/t Essen etc* zu sich nehmen, verzehren (*a. fig*); verbrauchen, konsumieren; zerstören, vernichten
con·sum·er ECON Verbraucher(in)
consumer so·ci·e·ty Konsumgesellschaft *f*
con·sum·mate **1.** vollendet; **2.** vollenden; *Ehe* vollziehen
con·sump·tion Verbrauch *m*
cont ABBR *of* ***continued*** Forts., Fortsetzung *f*; fortgesetzt
con·tact **1.** Berührung *f*; Kontakt *m*; Ansprechpartner(in), Kontaktperson *f* (*a.* MED); ***make contacts*** Verbindungen anknüpfen *or* herstellen; **2.** sich in Verbindung setzen mit, Kontakt aufnehmen mit
contact lens Kontaktlinse *f*, -schale *f*, Haftschale *f*
con·ta·gious MED ansteckend (*a. fig*)
con·tain enthalten; *fig* zügeln, zurückhalten
con·tain·er Behälter *m*; ECON Container *m*
con·tain·er·ize ECON auf Containerbetrieb umstellen; in Containern transportieren
con·tam·i·nate verunreinigen; infizieren, vergiften; (*a.* radioaktiv) verseuchen; ***radioactively contaminated*** verstrahlt; ***contaminated soil*** Altlasten *pl*
con·tam·i·na·tion Verunreinigung *f*; Vergiftung *f*; (*a.* radioaktive) Verseuchung
contd ABBR *of* ***continued*** (→ ***cont***)
con·tem·plate (nachdenklich) betrachten; nachdenken über (*acc*); erwägen, beabsichtigen
con·tem·pla·tion (nachdenkliche) Betrachtung; Nachdenken *n*
con·tem·pla·tive nachdenklich
con·tem·po·ra·ry **1.** zeitgenössisch; **2.** Zeitgenosse *m*, Zeitgenossin *f*
con·tempt Verachtung *f*
con·temp·ti·ble verachtenswert
con·temp·tu·ous geringschätzig, verächtlich
con·tend kämpfen, ringen (***for*** um; ***with*** mit)
con·tend·er *esp* SPORT Wettkämpfer(in)
con·tent[1] Gehalt *m*, Aussage *f*, *pl* Inhalt *m*; (***table of***) ***contents*** Inhaltsverzeichnis *n*
con·tent[2] **1.** zufrieden; **2.** befriedigen; ***content o.s.*** sich begnügen
con·tent·ed zufrieden
con·tent·ment Zufriedenheit *f*
con·test **1.** (Wett)Kampf *m*; Wettbewerb *m*; **2.** sich bewerben um; bestreiten, *a.* JUR anfechten
con·tes·tant Wettkämpfer(in), (Wettkampf)Teilnehmer(in)
con·text Zusammenhang *m*
con·ti·nent Kontinent *m*, Erdteil *m*; ***the Continent*** *Br* das (europäische) Festland
con·ti·nen·tal kontinental, Kontinental…
con·tin·gen·cy Möglichkeit *f*, Eventualität *f*; ***contingency plan*** Notplan *m*
con·tin·gent **1.** ***be contingent on*** abhängen von; **2.** Kontingent *n* (*a.* MIL)
con·tin·u·al fortwährend, unaufhörlich

C

con·tin·u·a·tion Fortsetzung *f*; Fortbestand *m*, Fortdauer *f*
con·tin·ue *v/t* fortsetzen, fortfahren mit; beibehalten; ***to be continued*** Fortsetzung folgt; *v/i* fortdauern; andauern, anhalten; fortfahren, weitermachen
con·ti·nu·i·ty Kontinuität *f*
con·tin·u·ous ununterbrochen
continuous form LING Verlaufsform *f*
con·tort verdrehen; verzerren
con·tor·tion Verdrehung *f*; Verzerrung *f*
con·tour Umriss *m*
con·tra wider, gegen
con·tra·band ECON Schmuggelware *f*
con·tra·cep·tion MED Empfängnisverhütung *f*
con·tra·cep·tive MED **1.** empfängnisverhütend; **2.** Verhütungsmittel *n*
con·tract **1.** Vertrag *m*; **2.** (sich) zusammenziehen; sich *e-e Krankheit* zuziehen; e-n Vertrag abschließen; sich vertraglich verpflichten
con·trac·tion Zusammenziehung *f*
con·trac·tor *a.* ***building contractor*** Bauunternehmer *m*
con·tra·dict widersprechen (*dat*)
con·tra·dic·tion Widerspruch *m*
con·tra·dic·to·ry (sich) widersprechend
con·tra·ry **1.** entgegengesetzt (***to*** *dat*); gegensätzlich; ***contrary to expectations*** wider Erwarten; **2.** Gegenteil *n*; ***on the contrary*** im Gegenteil
con·trast **1.** Gegensatz *m*; Kontrast *m*; **2.** *v/t* gegenüberstellen, vergleichen; *v/i* sich abheben (***with*** von, gegen); im Gegensatz stehen (***with*** zu)
con·trib·ute beitragen, beisteuern; spenden (***to*** für)
con·tri·bu·tion Beitrag *m*; Spende *f*
con·trib·u·tor Beitragende *m, f*; Mitarbeiter(in)
con·trib·u·to·ry beitragend
con·trite zerknirscht
con·trive zustande bringen; es fertig bringen
con·trol **1.** Kontrolle *f*, Herrschaft *f*, Macht *f*, Gewalt *f*, Beherrschung *f*; Aufsicht *f*; TECH Steuerung *f*; *mst pl* TECH Steuervorrichtung *f*; ***get*** (***have, keep***) ***under control*** unter Kontrolle bringen (haben, halten); ***get out of control*** außer Kontrolle geraten; ***lose control of*** die Herrschaft *or* Gewalt *or* Kontrolle verlieren über; **2.** beherrschen, die Kontrolle haben über (*acc*); *e-r Sache* Herr werden, (erfolgreich) bekämpfen; kontrollieren, überwachen; ECON (staatlich) lenken, *Preise* binden; ELECTR, TECH steuern, regeln, regulieren
control desk ELECTR Schalt-, Steuerpult *n*
control pan·el ELECTR Schalttafel *f*
control tow·er AVIAT Kontrollturm *m*, Tower *m*
con·tro·ver·sial umstritten
con·tro·ver·sy Kontroverse *f*, Streit *m*
con·tuse MED sich *et.* prellen *or* quetschen
con·tu·sion MED Prellung *f*, Quetschung *f*
con·va·lesce gesund werden, genesen
con·va·les·cence Rekonvaleszenz *f*, Genesung *f*
con·va·les·cent **1.** genesend; **2.** Rekonvaleszent(in), Genesende *m, f*
con·vene (sich) versammeln; zusammenkommen; *Versammlung* einberufen
con·ve·ni·ence Annehmlichkeit *f*, Bequemlichkeit *f*; *Br* Toilette *f*; ***all*** (***modern***) ***conveniences*** aller Komfort; ***at your earliest convenience*** möglichst bald
con·ve·ni·ent bequem; günstig, passend
con·vent REL (Nonnen)Kloster *n*
con·ven·tion Zusammenkunft *f*, Tagung *f*, Versammlung *f*; Abkommen *n*; Konvention *f*, Sitte *f*
con·ven·tion·al herkömmlich, konventionell
con·verge konvergieren; zusammenlaufen, -strömen
con·ver·sa·tion Gespräch *n*, Unterhaltung *f*
con·ver·sa·tion·al Unterhaltungs…; ***conversational English*** Umgangsenglisch *n*
con·verse sich unterhalten
con·ver·sion Umwandlung *f*, Verwandlung *f*; Umbau *m*; Umstellung *f* (***to*** auf *acc*); REL Bekehrung *f*, Übertritt *m*; MATH Umrechnung *f*
conversion ta·ble Umrechnungstabelle *f*
con·vert (sich) umwandeln *or* verwandeln; umbauen (***into*** zu); umstellen (***to*** auf *acc*); REL *etc* (sich) bekehren; MATH umrechnen
con·vert·er ELECTR Umformer *m*
con·ver·ti·ble **1.** umwandelbar, verwandelbar; ECON konvertierbar; **2.** MOT Kabrio(lett) *n*
con·vey befördern, transportieren, bringen; überbringen, übermitteln; *Ideen etc* mitteilen, vermitteln
con·vey·ance Beförderung *f*, Transport *m*; Übermittlung *f*; Verkehrsmittel *n*
con·vey·or belt TECH Förderband *n*
con·vict **1.** Verurteilte *m, f*; Strafgefangene *m, f*; **2.** JUR (***of***) überführen (*gen*); verurteilen (wegen)
con·vic·tion Überzeugung *f*; JUR Verurteilung *f*

con·vince überzeugen
con·voy **1.** MAR Geleitzug *m*, Konvoi *m*; MOT (Wagen)Kolonne *f*; (Geleit-) Schutz *m*; **2.** Geleitschutz geben (*dat*), eskortieren
con·vul·sion MED Zuckung *f*, Krampf *m*
con·vul·sive MED krampfhaft, krampfartig, konvulsiv
coo zo gurren (*a. fig*)
cook **1.** Koch *m*; Köchin *f*; **2.** kochen; F *Bericht etc* frisieren; ***cook up*** F sich ausdenken, erfinden
cook·book Kochbuch *n*
cook·er *Br* Ofen *m*, Herd *m*
cook·e·ry Kochen *n*; Kochkunst *f*
cook·e·ry book *Br* Kochbuch *n*
cook·ie (süßer) Keks, Plätzchen *n*
cook·ing GASTR Küche *f*
cook·y → ***cookie***
cool **1.** kühl; *fig* kalt(blütig), gelassen; abweisend; gleichgültig; F klasse, prima, cool; **2.** Kühle *f*; F (Selbst)Beherrschung *f*; **3.** (sich) abkühlen; ***cool down, cool off*** sich beruhigen
coon F zo Waschbär *m*
coop **1.** Hühnerstall *m*; **2.** ***coop up, coop in*** einsperren, einpferchen
co-op F Co-op *m*
co·op·e·rate zusammenarbeiten; mitwirken, helfen
co·op·e·ra·tion Zusammenarbeit *f*; Mitwirkung *f*, Hilfe *f*
co·op·e·ra·tive **1.** zusammenarbeitend; kooperativ, hilfsbereit; ECON Gemeinschafts…, Genossenschafts…; **2.** *a.* ***co-operative society*** Genossenschaft *f*; Co-op *m*, Konsumverein *m*; *a.* ***cooperative store*** Co-op *m*, Konsumladen *m*
co·or·di·nate **1.** koordinieren, aufeinander abstimmen; **2.** koordiniert, gleichgeordnet
co·or·di·na·tion Koordinierung *f*, Koordination *f*; harmonisches Zusammenspiel
cop F Bulle *m*
cope: ***cope with*** gewachsen sein (*dat*), fertigwerden mit
cop·i·er Kopiergerät *n*, Kopierer *m*
co·pi·ous reich(lich); weitschweifig
cop·per **1.** MIN Kupfer *n*; Kupfermünze *f*; **2.** kupfern, Kupfer…
cop·pice, **copse** Gehölz *n*
cop·y **1.** Kopie *f*; Abschrift *f*; Nachbildung *f*; Durchschlag *m*; Exemplar *n*; (*Zeitungs*)Nummer *f*; PRINT Satzvorlage *f*; ***fair copy*** Reinschrift *f*; **2.** kopieren; abschreiben, e-e Kopie anfertigen von; EDP *Daten* übertragen; nachbilden; nachahmen
cop·y·book Schreibheft *n*
cop·y·ing Kopier…
cop·y·right Urheberrecht *n*, Copyright *n*
cor·al zo Koralle *f*
cord **1.** Schnur *f* (*a.* ELECTR), Strick *m*; Kordsamt *m*; **2.** ver-, zuschnüren
cor·di·al[1] Fruchtsaftkonzentrat *n*; MED Stärkungsmittel *n*
cor·di·al[2] herzlich
cor·di·al·i·ty Herzlichkeit *f*
cord·less schnurlos
cord·less phone schnurloses Telefon
cor·don **1.** Kordon *m*, Postenkette *f*; **2.** ***cordon off*** abriegeln, absperren
cor·du·roy Kord *m*; (***a pair of***) ***corduroys*** (e-e) Kordhose
core **1.** Kerngehäuse *n*; Kern *m*, *fig a. das* Innerste; **2.** entkernen
core time ECON Kernzeit *f*
cork **1.** Kork(en) *m*; **2.** *a.* ***cork up*** zu-, verkorken
cork·screw Korkenzieher *m*
corn[1] **1.** Korn *n*, Getreide *n*; *a.* ***Indian corn*** Mais *m*; **2.** pökeln
corn[2] MED Hühnerauge *n*
cor·ner **1.** Ecke *f*; Winkel *m*; *esp* MOT Kurve *f*; *soccer*: Eckball *m*, Ecke *f*; *fig* schwierige Lage, Klemme *f*; **2.** Eck…; **3.** in die Ecke (*fig* Enge) treiben
corner kick *soccer*: Eckball *m*, Eckstoß *m*
corner shop *Br* Tante-Emma-Laden *m*
cor·net MUS Kornett *n*; *Br* GASTR Eistüte *f*
corn·flakes Cornflakes *pl*
cor·nice ARCH Gesims *n*, Sims *m*
cor·o·na·ry **1.** ANAT Koronar…; **2.** F MED Herzinfarkt *m*
cor·o·na·tion Krönung *f*
cor·o·net Adelskrone *f*
cor·po·ral MIL Unteroffizier *m*
cor·po·ral pun·ish·ment körperliche Züchtigung
cor·po·rate gemeinsam; Firmen…
cor·po·ra·tion JUR Körperschaft *f*; Stadtverwaltung *f*; ECON (Aktien)Gesellschaft *f*
corpse Leichnam *m*, Leiche *f*
cor·pu·lent beleibt
cor·ral **1.** Korral *m*, Hürde *f*, Pferch *m*; **2.** *Vieh* in e-n Pferch treiben
cor·rect **1.** korrekt, richtig, *a.* genau (*time*); **2.** korrigieren, verbessern, berichtigen
cor·rec·tion Korrektur *f*, Verbess(e)rung *f*; Bestrafung *f*
cor·rect·ness Richtigkeit *f*
cor·re·spond (***with, to***) entsprechen (*dat*), übereinstimmen (mit); korrespondieren (***with*** mit)
cor·re·spon·dence Übereinstimmung *f*;

C

Korrespondenz *f*, Briefwechsel *m*
correspondence course Fernkurs *m*
cor·re·spon·dent **1.** entsprechend; **2.** Briefpartner(in); Korrespondent(in)
cor·re·spon·ding entsprechend
cor·ri·dor Korridor *m*, Gang *m*
cor·rob·o·rate bekräftigen, bestätigen
cor·rode zerfressen; CHEM korrodieren; rosten
cor·ro·sion CHEM Korrosion *f*; Rost *m*
cor·ro·sive CHEM ätzend; *fig* nagend, zersetzend
cor·ru·gat·ed i·ron Wellblech *n*
cor·rupt **1.** korrupt, bestechlich, käuflich; *moralisch* verdorben; **2.** bestechen; *moralisch* verderben
cor·rupt·i·ble korrupt, bestechlich, käuflich
cor·rup·tion Verdorbenheit *f*; Unredlichkeit *f*; Korruption *f*; Bestechlichkeit *f*; Bestechung *f*
cor·set Korsett *n*
cos·met·ic **1.** kosmetisch, Schönheits…; **2.** kosmetisches Mittel, Schönheitsmittel *n*
cos·me·ti·cian Kosmetiker(in)
cos·mo·naut Kosmonaut *m*, (Welt-) Raumfahrer *m*
cos·mo·pol·i·tan **1.** kosmopolitisch; **2.** Weltbürger(in)
cost **1.** Preis *m*; Kosten *pl*; Schaden *m*; **2.** kosten
cost·ly kostspielig; teuer erkauft
cost of liv·ing Lebenshaltungskosten *pl*
cos·tume Kostüm *n*, Kleidung *f*, Tracht *f*
costume jew·el·(le)ry Modeschmuck *m*
co·sy *Br* → ***cozy***
cot Feldbett *n*; *Br* Kinderbett *n*
cot·tage Cottage *n*, (kleines) Landhaus; Ferienhaus *n*, Ferienhäuschen *n*
cot·ton **1.** Baumwolle *f*; Baumwollstoff *m*; (Baumwoll)Garn *n*, (Baumwoll-) Zwirn *m*; (Verband)Watte *f*; **2.** baumwollen, Baumwoll…
cot·ton·wood BOT *e-e* amer. Pappel
cot·ton wool *Br* (Verband)Watte *f*
couch Couch *f*, Sofa *n*; Liege *f*
cou·chette RAIL Liegewagenplatz *m*; *a.* ***couchette coach*** Liegewagen *m*
cou·gar ZO Puma *m*
cough **1.** Husten *m*; **2.** husten
coun·cil Rat *m*, Ratsversammlung *f*
council house *Br* gemeindeeigenes Wohnhaus
coun·cil·(l)or Ratsmitglied *n*, Stadtrat *m*, Stadträtin *f*
coun·sel **1.** Beratung *f*; Rat(schlag) *m*; *Br* JUR (Rechts)Anwalt *m*; ***counsel for the defense*** (*Br* ***defence***) Verteidiger *m*; ***counsel for the prosecution*** Anklagevertreter *m*; **2.** *j-m* raten; zu *et.* raten; ***counseling center*** (*Br* ***counselling centre***) Beratungsstelle *f*
coun·sel·(l)or (*Berufs- etc*)Berater(in); JUR (Rechts)Anwalt *m*
count¹ Graf *m*
count² **1.** Zählung *f*; JUR Anklagepunkt *m*; **2.** *v/t* (ab-, auf-, aus-, nach-, zusammen)zählen; aus-, berechnen; *fig* halten für, betrachten als; *v/i* zählen; gelten; ***count ten*** bis zehn zählen; ***count down*** *Geld* hinzählen; den Count-down durchführen für, letzte (Start)Vorbereitungen treffen für; ***count on*** zählen auf (*acc*), sich verlassen auf (*acc*), sicher rechnen mit
count·down Count-down *m*, *n*, letzte (Start)Vorbereitungen *pl*
coun·te·nance Gesichtsausdruck *m*; Fassung *f*, Haltung *f*
count·er¹ TECH Zähler *m*; *Br* Spielmarke *f*
coun·ter² Ladentisch *m*; Theke *f*; (Bank-, Post)Schalter *m*
coun·ter³ **1.** (ent)gegen, Gegen…; **2.** entgegentreten (*dat*), entgegnen (*dat*), bekämpfen; abwehren
coun·ter·act entgegenwirken (*dat*); neutralisieren
coun·ter·bal·ance **1.** Gegengewicht *n*; **2.** ein Gegengewicht bilden zu, ausgleichen
coun·ter·clock·wise entgegen dem Uhrzeigersinn
coun·ter·es·pi·o·nage Spionageabwehr *f*
coun·ter·feit **1.** falsch, gefälscht; **2.** Fälschung *f*; **3.** *Geld, Unterschrift etc* fälschen
counterfeit mon·ey Falschgeld *n*
coun·ter·foil Kontrollabschnitt *m*
coun·ter·mand *Befehl etc* widerrufen; *Ware* abbestellen
coun·ter·pane Tagesdecke *f*
coun·ter·part Gegenstück *n*; genaue Entsprechung
coun·ter·sign gegenzeichnen
coun·tess Gräfin *f*
count·less zahllos
coun·try **1.** Land *n*, Staat *m*; Gegend *f*, Landschaft *f*; ***in the country*** auf dem Lande; **2.** Land…, ländlich
coun·try·man Landbewohner *m*; Bauer *m*; *a.* ***fellow countryman*** Landsmann *m*
coun·try road Landstraße *f*
coun·try·side (ländliche) Gegend; Landschaft *f*
coun·try·wom·an Landbewohnerin *f*; Bäuerin *f*; *a.* ***fellow countrywoman*** Landsmännin *f*
coun·ty (Land)Kreis *m*; *Br* Grafschaft *f*

county seat Kreis(haupt)stadt *f*
county town *Br* Grafschaftshauptstadt *f*
coup Coup *m*; Putsch *m*
cou·ple **1.** Paar *n*; ***a couple of*** F ein paar; **2.** (zusammen)koppeln; TECH kuppeln; zo (sich) paaren
cou·pon Gutschein *m*; Kupon *m*, Bestellzettel *m*
cour·age Mut *m*
cou·ra·geous mutig, beherzt
cou·ri·er Kurier *m*, Eilbote *m*; Reiseleiter *m*
course AVIAT, MAR Kurs *m* (*a. fig*); SPORT (*Renn*)Bahn *f*, (*Renn*)Strecke *f*, (*Golf*)-Platz *m*; Verlauf *m*; GASTR Gang *m*; Reihe *f*, Zyklus *m*; Kurs *m*, Lehrgang *m*; ***of course*** natürlich, selbstverständlich; ***the course of events*** der Gang der Ereignisse, der Lauf der Dinge
court **1.** Hof *m*; kleiner Platz; SPORT Platz *m*, (Spiel)Feld *n*; JUR Gericht *n*, Gerichtshof *m*; ***go to court*** JUR prozessieren; ***take s.o. to court*** JUR gegen j-n prozessieren; j-m den Prozess machen; **2.** *j-m* den Hof machen; werben um
cour·te·ous höflich
cour·te·sy Höflichkeit *f*; ***by courtesy of*** mit freundlicher Genehmigung von (*or gen*)
court·house Gerichtsgebäude *n*
court·ier Höfling *m*
court·ly höfisch; höflich
court mar·tial MIL Kriegsgericht *n*
court-mar·tial MIL vor ein Kriegsgericht stellen
court·room Gerichtssaal *m*
court·ship Werben *n*
court·yard Hof *m*
cous·in Cousin *m*, Vetter *m*; Cousine *f*, Kusine *f*
cove kleine Bucht
cov·er **1.** Decke *f*; Deckel *m*; (Buch-)Deckel *m*, Einband *m*; Umschlag *m*; Titelseite *f*; Hülle *f*; Überzug *m*, Bezug *m*; Schutzhaube *f*, Schutzplatte *f*; Abdeckhaube *f*; Briefumschlag *m*; GASTR Gedeck *n*; Deckung *f*; Schutz *m*; *fig* Tarnung *f*; ***take cover*** in Deckung gehen; ***under plain cover*** in neutralem Umschlag; ***under separate cover*** mit getrennter Post; **2.** (be-, zu)decken; einschlagen, einwickeln; verbergen; decken, schützen; ECON (ab)decken; versichern; *Thema* erschöpfend behandeln; *radio*, TV berichten über (*acc*); sich über *e-e Fläche etc* erstrecken; *Strecke* zurücklegen; SPORT *Gegenspieler* decken; *j-n* beschatten; ***cover up*** ab-, zudecken; *fig* verheimlichen, vertuschen; ***cover up for s.o.*** j-n decken
cov·er·age Berichterstattung *f* (**of** über *acc*)
cov·er girl Covergirl *n*, Titelblattmädchen *n*
cov·er·ing Decke *f*; Überzug *m*; Hülle *f*; (*Fußboden*)Belag *m*
cov·er sto·ry Titelgeschichte *f*
cow[1] zo Kuh *f*
cow[2] einschüchtern
cow·ard **1.** feig(e); **2.** Feigling *m*
cow·ard·ice Feigheit *f*
cow·ard·ly feig(e)
cow·boy Cowboy *m*
cow·er kauern; sich ducken
cow·herd Kuhhirt *m*
cow·hide Rind(s)leder *n*
cow·house Kuhstall *m*
cowl Mönchskutte *f*; Kapuze *f*; TECH Schornsteinkappe *f*
cow·shed Kuhstall *m*
cow·slip BOT Schlüsselblume *f*; Sumpfdotterblume *f*
cox, **cox·swain** Bootsführer *m*; *rowing*: Steuermann *m*
coy schüchtern, scheu
coy·ote zo Kojote *m*, Präriewolf *m*
co·zy **1.** behaglich, gemütlich; **2.** → ***egg cosy***, ***tea cosy***
CPU ABBR *of* ***central processing unit*** EDP Zentraleinheit *f*
crab zo Krabbe *f*, Taschenkrebs *m*
crack **1.** Knall *m*; Sprung *m*, Riss *m*; Spalt(e *f*) *m*, Ritze *f*; (heftiger) Schlag; **2.** erstklassig; **3.** *v/i* krachen, knallen, knacken; (zer)springen; überschnappen (*voice*); *a.* ***crack up*** zusammenbrechen; F ***crack up*** überschnappen; ***get cracking*** F loslegen; *v/t* knallen mit (*Peitsche*), knacken mit (*Fingern*); zerbrechen; *Nuss*, F *Kode*, *Safe etc* knacken; ***crack a joke*** e-n Witz reißen
crack·er GASTR Cracker *m*, Kräcker *m*; Schwär-mer *m*, Knallfrosch *m*, Knallbonbon *m*, *n*
crack·le knattern, knistern, prasseln
cra·dle **1.** Wiege *f*; **2.** wiegen; betten
craft[1] Boot(e *pl*) *n*, Schiff(e *pl*) *n*; Flugzeug(e *pl*) *n*; (Welt)Raumfahrzeug(e *pl*) *n*
craft[2] Handwerk *n*, Gewerbe *n*; Schlauheit *f*, List *f*
crafts·man (Kunst)Handwerker *m*
craft·y gerissen, listig, schlau
crag Klippe *f*, Felsenspitze *f*
cram *v/t* (voll)stopfen; nudeln, mästen; mit *j-m* pauken; *v/i* pauken, büffeln (**for** für)
cramp **1.** MED Krampf *m*; TECH Klammer

C

f; *fig* Fessel *f*; **2.** einengen, hemmen
cran·ber·ry BOT Preiselbeere *f*
crane[1] TECH Kran *m*
crane[2] **1.** ZO Kranich *m*; **2.** den Hals recken; ***crane one's neck*** sich den Hals verrenken (***for*** nach)
crank **1.** TECH Kurbel *f*; TECH Schwengel *m*; F Spinner *m*, komischer Kauz; **2.** (an)kurbeln
crank·shaft TECH Kurbelwelle *f*
crank·y wack(e)lig; verschroben; schlecht gelaunt
cran·ny Riss *m*, Ritze *f*
crape Krepp *m*, Flor *m*
crash **1.** Krach *m*, Krachen *n*; MOT Unfall *m*, Zusammenstoß *m*; AVIAT Absturz *m*; ECON Zusammenbruch *m*, (Börsen)Krach *m*; **2.** *v/t* zertrümmern; e-n Unfall haben mit; AVIAT abstürzen mit; *v/i* krachend einstürzen, zusammenkrachen; *esp* ECON zusammenbrechen; krachen (***against, into*** gegen); MOT zusammenstoßen, verunglücken; AVIAT abstürzen; **3.** Schnell…, Sofort…
crash bar·ri·er MOT Leitplanke *f*
crash course Schnell-, Intensivkurs *m*
crash di·et radikale Schlankheitskur
crash hel·met Sturzhelm *m*
crash-land AVIAT e-e Bruchlandung machen (mit)
crash land·ing AVIAT Bruchlandung *f*
crate (Latten)Kiste *f*
cra·ter Krater *m*; Trichter *m*
crave sich sehnen (***for, after*** nach)
crav·ing heftiges Verlangen
craw·fish → ***crayfish***
crawl **1.** Kriechen *n*; **2.** kriechen; krabbeln; kribbeln; wimmeln (***with*** von); *swimming*: kraulen; ***it makes my skin crawl*** F mir läuft e-e Gänsehaut über den Rücken
cray·fish ZO Flusskrebs *m*
cray·on Zeichen-, Buntstift *m*
craze Verrücktheit *f*, F Fimmel *m*; ***be the craze*** Mode sein
cra·zy verrückt (***about*** nach)
creak knarren, quietschen
cream **1.** GASTR Rahm *m*, Sahne *f*; Creme *f*; *fig* Auslese *f*, Elite *f*; **2.** creme(farben)
cream·y sahnig; weich
crease **1.** (Bügel)Falte *f*; **2.** (zer)knittern
cre·ate (er)schaffen; hervorrufen; verursachen
cre·a·tion Schöpfung *f*
cre·a·tive schöpferisch
cre·a·tor Schöpfer *m*
crea·ture Geschöpf *n*; Kreatur *f*
crèche (Kinder)Krippe *f*; (Weihnachts)Krippe *f*
cre·den·tials Beglaubigungsschreiben *n*; Referenzen *pl*; Zeugnis *n*; Ausweis *m*, Ausweispapiere *pl*
cred·i·ble glaubwürdig
cred·it **1.** Glaube(n) *m*; Ruf *m*, Ansehen *n*; Verdienst *n*; ECON Kredit *m*; Guthaben *n*; ***credit*** (***side***) Kredit(seite *f*) *n*, Haben *n*; ***on credit*** auf Kredit; **2.** *j-m* glauben; *j-m* trauen; ECON gutschreiben; ***credit s.o. with s.th.*** j-m et. zutrauen; j-m et. zuschreiben
cred·i·ta·ble achtbar, ehrenvoll (***to*** für)
cred·it card ECON Kreditkarte *f*
cred·i·tor ECON Gläubiger *m*
cred·its *film*: Vorspann *m*, Nachspann *m*
cred·it·wor·thy ECON kreditwürdig
cred·u·lous leichtgläubig
creed REL Glaubensbekenntnis *n*
creek Bach *m*; *Br* kleine Bucht
creep kriechen; schleichen (*a. fig*); ***creep in*** (sich) hinein- *or* hereinschleichen; sich einschleichen (*mistake etc*); ***it makes my flesh creep*** mir läuft e-e Gänsehaut über den Rücken
creep·er BOT Kriech-, Kletterpflanze *f*
creep·y unheimlich
cre·mate verbrennen, einäschern
cres·cent Halbmond *m*
cress BOT Kresse *f*
crest ZO Haube *f*, Büschel *n*; (*Hahnen-*)Kamm *m*; Bergrücken *m*, Kamm *m*; (*Wellen*)Kamm *m*; Federbusch *m*; ***family crest*** Familienwappen *n*
crest·fal·len niedergeschlagen
cre·vasse GEOL (Gletscher)Spalte *f*
crev·ice GEOL Riss *m*, Spalte *f*
crew AVIAT, MAR Besatzung *f*, Crew *f*, MAR Mannschaft *f*
crib **1.** (Futter)Krippe *f*; Kinderbettchen *n*; *esp Br* (Weihnachts)Krippe *f*; F PED Spickzettel *m*; **2.** F abschreiben, spicken
crick: ***a crick in one's back*** (***neck***) ein steifer Rücken (Hals)
crick·et[1] ZO Grille *f*
crick·et[2] SPORT Kricket *n*
crime JUR Verbrechen *n*; *coll* Verbrechen *pl*
crime nov·el Kriminalroman *m*
crim·i·nal **1.** kriminell; Kriminal…, Straf…; **2.** Verbrecher(in), Kriminelle *m, f*
crimp kräuseln
crim·son karmesinrot; puterrot
cringe sich ducken
crin·kle **1.** Falte *f*, Fältchen *n*; **2.** (sich) kräuseln; knittern
crip·ple **1.** Krüppel *m*; **2.** zum Krüppel machen; *fig* lähmen
cri·sis Krise *f*

crisp knusp(e)rig, mürbe; frisch, knackig (*vegetable*); scharf, frisch (*air*); kraus (*hair*)
crisp·bread Knäckebrot *n*
crisps *a.* ***potato crisps*** *Br* (Kartoffel)-Chips *pl*
criss-cross **1.** Netz *n* sich schneidender Linien; **2.** kreuz und quer ziehen durch; kreuz und quer (ver)laufen
cri·te·ri·on Kriterium *n*
crit·ic Kritiker(in)
crit·i·cal kritisch; bedenklich
crit·i·cis·m Kritik *f* (***of*** an *dat*)
crit·i·cize kritisieren; kritisch beurteilen; tadeln
cri·tique Kritik *f*, Besprechung *f*, Rezension *f*
croak ZO krächzen; quaken (*both a. fig*)
cro·chet **1.** Häkelei *f*; Häkelarbeit *f*; **2.** häkeln
crock·e·ry Geschirr *n*
croc·o·dile ZO Krokodil *n*
cro·ny F alter Freund
crook **1.** Krümmung *f*; Hirtenstab *m*; F Gauner *m*; **2.** (sich) krümmen *or* biegen
crook·ed gekrümmt krumm; F unehrlich, betrügerisch
croon schmachtend singen; summen
croon·er Schnulzensänger(in)
crop **1.** AGR (Feld)Frucht *f*; Ernte *f*; ZO Kropf *m*; kurzer Haarschnitt; kurz geschnittenes Haar; **2.** ZO abfressen, abweiden; *Haar* kurz schneiden; ***crop up*** *fig* plötzlich auftauchen
cross **1.** Kreuz *n* (*a. fig*); BIOL Kreuzung *f*; *soccer*: Flanke *f*; **2.** böse, ärgerlich; **3.** (sich) kreuzen; *Straße* überqueren; *Plan etc* durchkreuzen; BIOL kreuzen; ***cross off, cross out*** ausstreichen, durchstreichen; ***cross o.s.*** sich bekreuzigen; ***cross one's arms*** die Arme verschränken; ***cross one's legs*** die Beine übereinanderschlagen; ***keep one's fingers crossed*** den Daumen drücken
cross·bar SPORT Tor-, Querlatte *f*
cross·breed Mischling *m*, Kreuzung *f*
cross-coun·try Querfeldein…, Gelände…; ***cross-country skiing*** Skilanglauf *m*
cross-ex·am·i·na·tion JUR Kreuzverhör *n*
cross-ex·am·ine JUR ins Kreuzverhör nehmen
cross-eyed: ***be cross-eyed*** schielen
cross·ing (*Straßen- etc*)Kreuzung *f*; Straßenübergang *m*; *Br* Fußgängerüberweg *m*; MAR Überfahrt *f*
cross·road Querstraße *f*
cross·roads (Straßen)Kreuzung *f*; *fig* Scheideweg *m*
cross-sec·tion Querschnitt *m*
cross·walk Fußgängerüberweg *m*
cross·wise kreuzweise
cross·word (puz·zle) Kreuzworträtsel *n*
crotch ANAT Schritt *m*
crotch·et MUS *Br* Viertelnote *f*
crouch **1.** sich ducken; **2.** Hockstellung *f*
crow **1.** ZO Krähe *f*; Krähen *n*; **2.** krähen
crow·bar TECH Brecheisen *n*
crowd **1.** (Menschen)Menge *f*; Masse *f*; Haufen *m*; **2.** sich drängen; *Straßen etc* bevölkern; vollstopfen
crowd·ed überfüllt, voll
crown **1.** Krone *f*; **2.** krönen; *Zahn* überkronen; ***to crown it all*** zu allem Überfluss
cru·cial entscheidend, kritisch
cru·ci·fix REL Kruzifix *n*
cru·ci·fix·ion REL Kreuzigung *f*
cru·ci·fy REL kreuzigen
crude roh, unbearbeitet; *fig* roh, grob
crude (oil) Rohöl *n*
cru·el grausam; roh, gefühllos
cru·el·ty Grausamkeit *f*; ***cruelty to animals*** Tierquälerei *f*; ***society for the prevention of cruelty to animals*** Tierschutzverein *m*; ***cruelty to children*** Kindesmisshandlung *f*
cru·et Essig-, Ölfläschchen *n*
cruise **1.** Kreuzfahrt *f*, Seereise *f*; **2.** kreuzen, e-e Kreuzfahrt *or* Seereise machen; AVIAT, MOT mit Reisegeschwindigkeit fliegen *or* fahren
cruise mis·sile MIL Marschflugkörper *m*
cruis·er Kreuzfahrtschiff *n*; MIL MAR Kreuzer *m*; (Funk)Streifenwagen *m*
crumb Krume *f*, Krümel *m*
crum·ble zerkrümeln, zerbröckeln
crum·ple *v/t* zerknittern; *v/i* knittern; zusammengedrückt werden
crumple zone MOT Knautschzone *f*
crunch geräuschvoll (zer)kauen; knirschen
cru·sade HIST Kreuzzug *m* (*a. fig*)
crush **1.** Gedränge *n*; ***have a crush on s.o.*** für j-n schwärmen, F in j-n verknallt sein; **2.** *v/t* zerquetschen, zermalmen, zerdrücken; TECH zerkleinern, zermahlen; auspressen; *fig* nieder-, zerschmettern, vernichten; *v/i* sich drängen
crush bar·ri·er Barriere *f*, Absperrung *f*
crust (Brot)Kruste *f*, (Brot)Rinde *f*
crus·ta·cean ZO Krebs-, Krusten-, Schalentier *n*
crust·y krustig
crutch Krücke *f*
cry **1.** Schrei *m*, Ruf *m*; Geschrei *n*; Weinen *n*; **2.** schreien, rufen (***for*** nach); weinen; heulen, jammern

C

crypt Gruft *f*, Krypta *f*
crys·tal Kristall *m*; Uhrglas *n*
crys·tal·line kristallen
crys·tal·lize kristallisieren
cub ZO Junge *n*
cube Würfel *m* (*a.* MATH); PHOT Blitzwürfel *m*; MATH Kubikzahl *f*
cube root MATH Kubikwurzel *f*
cu·bic, **cu·bi·cal** würfelförmig; kubisch; Kubik...
cu·bi·cle Kabine *f*
cuck·oo ZO Kuckuck *m*
cu·cum·ber BOT Gurke *f*; ***(as) cool as a cucumber*** F eiskalt, kühl und gelassen
cud AGR wiedergekäutes Futter; ***chew the cud*** wiederkäuen; *fig* überlegen
cud·dle *v/t* an sich drücken; schmusen mit; *v/i*: ***cuddle up*** sich kuscheln *or* schmiegen (***to*** an *acc*)
cud·gel **1.** Knüppel *m*; **2.** prügeln
cue[1] THEA *etc* Stichwort *n* (*a. fig*); *fig* Wink *m*
cue[2] *billiards*: Queue *n*
cuff[1] Manschette *f*; (Hosen-, *Br* Ärmel-) Aufschlag *m*
cuff[2] **1.** Klaps *m*; **2.** *j-m* e-n Klaps geben
cuff link Manschettenknopf *m*
cui·sine GASTR Küche *f*
cul·mi·nate gipfeln (***in*** in *dat*)
cu·lottes (***a pair of*** ein) Hosenrock
cul·prit Schuldige *m*, *f*, Täter(in)
cul·ti·vate AGR anbauen, bebauen; kultivieren; *Freundschaft etc* pflegen
cul·ti·vat·ed AGR bebaut; *fig* gebildet, kultiviert
cul·ti·va·tion AGR Kultivierung *f*, Anbau *m*; *fig* Pflege *f*
cul·tu·ral kulturell; Kultur...
cul·ture Kultur *f* (*a.* BIOL); ZO Zucht *f*
cul·tured kultiviert; gezüchtet, Zucht...
cum·ber·some lästig, hinderlich; klobig
cu·mu·la·tive sich (an)häufend, anwachsend; Zusatz...
cun·ning **1.** schlau, listig; **2.** List *f*, Schlauheit *f*
cup **1.** Tasse *f*; Becher *m*; Schale *f*; Kelch *m*; SPORT Cup *m*, Pokal *m*; **2.** *die Hand* hohl machen; ***she cupped her chin in her hand*** sie stützte das Kinn in die Hand
cup·board (Geschirr-, Speise-, *Br a.* Wäsche-, Kleider)Schrank *m*
cup·board bed Schrankbett *n*
cup fi·nal SPORT Pokalendspiel *n*
cu·po·la ARCH Kuppel *f*
cup tie SPORT Pokalspiel *n*
cup win·ner SPORT Pokalsieger *m*
cur Köter *m*; Schurke *m*
cu·ra·ble MED heilbar
cu·rate REL Hilfsgeistliche *m*
cu·ra·tive heilkräftig; ***curative power*** Heilkraft *f*
curb **1.** Kandare *f* (*a. fig*); Bordstein *m*; **2.** an die Kandare legen (*a. fig*); *fig* zügeln
curd *a. pl* Dickmilch *f*, Quark *m*
cur·dle *v/t Milch* gerinnen lassen; *v/i* gerinnen, dick werden; ***the sight made my blood curdle*** bei dem Anblick erstarrte mir das Blut in den Adern
cure **1.** MED Kur *f*; (Heil)Mittel *n*; Heilung *f*; **2.** MED heilen; GASTR pökeln; räuchern; trocknen
cur·few MIL Ausgangsverbot *n*, -sperre *f*
cu·ri·o Rarität *f*
cu·ri·os·i·ty Neugier *f*; Rarität *f*
cu·ri·ous neugierig; wissbegierig; seltsam, merkwürdig
curl **1.** Locke *f*; **2.** (sich) kräuseln *or* locken
curl·er Lockenwickler *m*
curl·y gekräuselt; gelockt, lockig
cur·rant BOT Johannisbeere *f*; GASTR Korinthe *f*
cur·ren·cy ECON Währung *f*; ***foreign currency*** Devisen *pl*
cur·rent **1.** laufend; gegenwärtig, aktuell; üblich, gebräuchlich; ***current events*** Tagesereignisse *pl*; **2.** Strömung *f*, Strom *m* (*both a. fig*); ELECTR Strom *m*
current ac·count *Br* ECON Girokonto *n*
cur·ric·u·lum Lehr-, Stundenplan *m*
curriculum vi·tae Lebenslauf *m*
cur·ry[1] GASTR Curry *m*, *n*
cur·ry[2] *Pferd* striegeln
curse **1.** Fluch *m*, Verwünschung *f*; **2.** (ver)fluchen, verwünschen
curs·ed verflucht
cur·sor EDP Cursor *m*
cur·so·ry flüchtig, oberflächlich
curt knapp; barsch, schroff
cur·tail *Ausgaben etc* kürzen; *Rechte* beschneiden
cur·tain **1.** Vorhang *m*, Gardine *f*; ***draw the curtains*** die Vorhänge auf- *or* zuziehen; **2.** ***curtain off*** mit Vorhängen abteilen
curt·s(e)y **1.** Knicks *m*; **2.** knicksen (***to*** vor *dat*)
cur·va·ture Krümmung *f*
curve **1.** Kurve *f*; Krümmung *f*, Biegung *f*; **2.** (sich) krümmen *or* biegen
cush·ion **1.** Kissen *n*, Polster *n*; **2.** polstern; *Stoß etc* dämpfen
cuss **1.** Fluch *m*; **2.** (ver)fluchen
cus·tard Eiercreme *f*, Vanillesoße *f*
cus·to·dy JUR Haft *f*; Sorgerecht *n*
cus·tom Brauch *m*, Gewohnheit *f*; ECON Kundschaft *f*
cus·tom·a·ry üblich

D

cus·tom-built nach Kundenangaben gefertigt
cus·tom·er Kunde *m*, Kundin *f*, Auftraggeber(in)
cus·tom house Zollamt *n*
cus·tom-made maßgefertigt, Maß…
cus·toms Zoll *m*
customs clear·ance Zollabfertigung *f*
customs of·fi·cer, customs of·fi·cial Zollbeamte *m*
cut 1. Schnitt *m*; MED Schnittwunde *f*; GASTR Schnitte *f*, Stück *n*; (Zu)Schnitt *m* (*clothes*); TECH Schnitt *m*, Schliff *m*; Haarschnitt *m*; *fig* Kürzung *f*, Senkung *f*; *cards*: Abheben *n*; **2.** schneiden; ab-, an-, auf-, aus-, be-, durch-, zer-, zuschneiden; *Edelstein etc* schleifen; *Gras* mähen, *Bäume* fällen, *Holz* hacken; MOT *Kurve* schneiden; *Löhne etc* kürzen; *Preise* herabsetzen, senken; *Karten* abheben; ***cut one's teeth*** Zähne bekommen, zahnen; ***cut s.o. (dead)*** *fig* F j-n schneiden; ***cut s.o.*** *or* ***s.th. short*** j-n *or* et. unterbrechen, j-m ins Wort fallen; ***cut across*** quer durch … gehen; ***cut back*** *Pflanze* beschneiden, stutzen; einschränken; ***cut down*** *Bäume* fällen; verringern, einschränken, reduzieren; ***cut in*** F sich einmischen, unterbrechen; ***cut in on s.o.*** MOT j-n schneiden; ***cut off*** abschneiden; unterbrechen, trennen; *Strom etc* sperren; ***cut out*** (her)ausschneiden; *Kleid etc* zuschneiden; ***be cut out for*** wie geschaffen sein für; ***cut up*** zerschneiden
cut·back Kürzung *f*
cute F schlau; niedlich, süß
cu·ti·cle Nagelhaut *f*
cut·le·ry (Ess)Besteck *n*
cut·let GASTR Kotelett *n*; (*Kalbs-, Schweine*)Schnitzel *n*; Hacksteak *n*
cut·off date Stichtag *m*
cut-price, cut-rate ECON herabgesetzt, ermäßigt; Billig…
cut·ter Zuschneider *m*; (*Glas-, Diamant*)-Schleifer *m*; Schneidemaschine *f*, -werkzeug *n*; *film*: Cutter(in); MAR Kutter *m*
cut·throat 1. Mörder *m*; Killer *m*; **2.** mörderisch
cut·ting 1. schneidend; scharf; TECH Schneid(e)…, Fräs…; **2.** Schneiden *n*; BOT Steckling *m*; *esp Br* Ausschnitt *m*
cut·tings Schnipsel *pl*; Späne *pl*
cut·ting torch TECH Schneidbrenner *m*
Cy·ber·space → ***virtual reality***
cy·cle[1] Zyklus *m*; Kreis(lauf) *m*
cy·cle[2] **1.** Fahrrad *n*; **2.** Rad fahren
cy·cle path, cycle track (Fahr)Radweg *m*
cy·cling Radfahren *n*
cy·clist Radfahrer(in); Motorradfahrer(in)
cy·clone Wirbelsturm *m*
cyl·in·der Zylinder *m*, TECH *a.* Walze *f*, Trommel *f*
cyn·ic Zyniker(in)
cyn·i·cal zynisch
cyn·i·cism Zynismus *m*
cy·press BOT Zypresse *f*
cyst MED Zyste *f*
czar → ***tsar***
Czech 1. tschechisch; ***Czech Republic*** Tschechien *n*, Tschechische Republik; **2.** Tscheche *m*, Tschechin *f*; LING Tschechisch *n*

D

D, d D, d *n*
d ABBR *of* ***died*** gest., gestorben
dab 1. Klecks *m*, Spritzer *m*; **2.** betupfen, abtupfen
dab·ble bespritzen; ***dabble at, dabble in*** sich oberflächlich *or contp* in dilettantischer Weise beschäftigen mit
dachs·hund ZO Dackel *m*
dad F, **dad·dy** F Papa *m*, Vati *m*
dad·dy long·legs ZO Schnake *f*; Weberknecht *m*
daf·fo·dil BOT gelbe Narzisse
dag·ger Dolch *m*; ***be at daggers drawn*** *fig* auf Kriegsfuß stehen (***with*** mit)
dai·ly 1. täglich; ***the daily grind*** *or* ***rut*** das tägliche Einerlei; **2.** Tageszeitung *f*; Putzfrau *f*
dain·ty 1. zierlich, reizend; wählerisch; **2.** Leckerbissen *m*
dair·y Molkerei *f*; Milchwirtschaft *f*; Milchgeschäft *n*
dai·sy BOT Gänseblümchen *n*
dal·ly: ***dally about*** herumtrödeln
dam 1. (Stau)Damm *m*; **2.** *a.* ***dam up*** stau-

en, eindämmen

dam·age **1.** Schaden *m*, (Be)Schädigung *f*; *pl* JUR Schadenersatz *m*; **2.** (be)schädigen

D

dam·ask Damast *m*

damn **1.** verdammen; verurteilen; ***damn (it)!*** F verflucht!, verdammt!; **2.** *adj and adv* F → ***damned***; **3.** ***I don't care a damn*** F das ist mir völlig gleich(gültig) *or* egal

dam·na·tion Verdammung *f*; REL Verdammnis *f*

damned F verdammt

damn·ing vernichtend, belastend

damp **1.** feucht, klamm; **2.** Feuchtigkeit *f*; **3.** *a.* **damp·en** an-, befeuchten; dämpfen

damp·ness Feuchtigkeit *f*

dance **1.** Tanz *m*; Tanzveranstaltung *f*; **2.** tanzen

danc·er Tänzer(in)

danc·ing **1.** Tanzen *n*; **2.** Tanz…

dan·de·li·on BOT Löwenzahn *m*

dan·druff (Kopf)Schuppen *pl*

Dane Däne *m*, Dänin *f*

dan·ger Gefahr *f*; ***be out of danger*** außer Lebensgefahr sein

danger ar·e·a Gefahrenzone *f*, Gefahrenbereich *m*

dan·ger·ous gefährlich

dan·ger zone → ***danger area***

dan·gle baumeln (lassen)

Da·nish **1.** dänisch; **2.** LING Dänisch *n*

dank feucht, nass(kalt)

dare *v/i* es wagen, sich (ge)trauen; ***I dare say*** ich glaube wohl; allerdings; ***how dare you!*** was fällt dir ein!; untersteh dich!; *v/t et.* wagen

dare·dev·il Draufgänger *m*

dar·ing **1.** kühn, verwegen, waghalsig; **2.** Mut *m*, Kühnheit *f*, Verwegenheit *f*

dark **1.** dunkel; finster; *fig* düster, trüb(e); geheim(nisvoll); **2.** Dunkel *n*, Dunkelheit *f*; ***before (at, after) dark*** vor (bei, nach) Einbruch der Dunkelheit; ***keep s.o. in the dark about s.th.*** j-n über et. im Ungewissen lassen

Dark Ag·es *das* frühe Mittelalter

dark·en (sich) verdunkeln *or* verfinstern

dark·ness Dunkelheit *f*, Finsternis *f*

dark·room PHOT Dunkelkammer *f*

dar·ling **1.** Liebling *m*; **2.** lieb; F goldig

darn stopfen, ausbessern

dart **1.** Wurfpfeil *m*; Sprung *m*, Satz *m*; ***darts*** Darts *n*; **2.** *v/t* werfen, schleudern; *v/i* schießen, stürzen

dart·board Dartsscheibe *f*

dash **1.** Schlag *m*; Klatschen *n*; GASTR Prise *f* (*of salt*), Schuss *m* (*of rum etc*), Spritzer *m* (*of lemon etc*); Gedankenstrich *m*; SPORT Sprint *m*; *fig* Anflug *m*; ***a dash of blue*** ein Stich ins Blaue; ***make a dash for*** losstürzen auf (*acc*); **2.** *v/t* schleudern, schmettern; *Hoffnung etc* zerstören, zunichtemachen; *v/i* stürmen; ***dash off*** davonstürzen

dash·board MOT Armaturenbrett *n*

dash·ing schneidig, forsch

da·ta Daten *pl* (*a.* EDP), Angaben *pl*

data bank, **data·base** EDP Datenbank *f*

data cap·ture Datenerfassung *f*

data car·rier Datenträger *m*

data in·put Dateneingabe *f*

data me·di·um Datenträger *m*

data mem·o·ry Datenspeicher *m*

data output Datenausgabe *f*

data pro·cess·ing Datenverarbeitung *f*

data pro·tec·tion JUR Datenschutz *m*

data stor·age Datenspeicher *m*

data trans·fer Datenübertragung *f*

date[1] BOT Dattel *f*

date[2] Datum *n*; Zeit *f*, Zeitpunkt *m*; Termin *m*; Verabredung *f*; F (Verabredungs-) Partner(in); ***out of date*** veraltet, unmodern; ***up to date*** zeitgemäß, modern, auf dem Laufenden; **1.** datieren; F sich verabreden mit, (aus)gehen mit

dat·ed veraltet, überholt

da·tive *a.* ***dative case*** LING Dativ *m*, dritter Fall

daub (be)schmieren

daugh·ter Tochter *f*

daugh·ter-in-law Schwiegertochter *f*

daunt entmutigen

dav·en·port Sofa *n*

daw zo Dohle *f*

daw·dle F (herum)trödeln

dawn **1.** (Morgen)Dämmerung *f*; ***at dawn*** bei Tagesanbruch; **2.** dämmern; ***dawn on*** *fig j-m* dämmern

day Tag *m*; *often pl* (Lebens)Zeit *f*; ***any day*** jederzeit; ***these days*** heutzutage; ***the other day*** neulich; ***the day after tomorrow*** übermorgen; ***the day before yesterday*** vorgestern; ***open all day*** durchgehend geöffnet; ***let's call it a day!*** machen wir Schluss für heute!, Feierabend!

day·break Tagesanbruch *m*

day care cen·ter (*Br* **cen·tre**) → ***day nursery***

day·dream **1.** Tag-, Wachtraum *m*; **2.** (mit offenen Augen) träumen

day·dream·er Träumer(in)

day·light Tageslicht *n*; ***in broad daylight*** am helllichten Tag

day nur·se·ry (Kinder)Tagesstätte *f*

day off freier Tag

day re·turn *Br* Tagesrückfahrkarte *f*

day·time: ***in the daytime*** am Tag, bei Ta-

ge
daze 1. blenden; betäuben; **2. *in a daze*** benommen, betäubt
dead 1. tot; unempfindlich (***to*** für); matt; blind (*window etc*); erloschen; ECON flau; tot (*capital etc*); völlig, total; ***dead stop*** völliger Stillstand; ***drop dead*** tot umfallen; **2.** *adv* völlig, total; plötzlich, abrupt; genau, direkt; ***dead slow*** MOT Schritt fahren!; ***dead tired*** todmüde; **3. *the dead*** die Toten *pl*; ***in the dead of winter*** im tiefsten Winter; ***in the dead of night*** mitten in der Nacht
dead·en abstumpfen; (ab)schwächen; dämpfen
dead end Sackgasse *f* (*a. fig*)
dead heat SPORT totes Rennen
dead·line letzter (Ablieferungs)Termin; Stichtag *m*
dead·lock *fig* toter Punkt
dead·locked *fig* festgefahren
dead loss Totalverlust *m*; F ***he's a dead loss*** er ist e-e Niete
dead·ly tödlich
deaf 1. taub; **2. *the deaf*** die Tauben *pl*
deaf-and-dumb taubstumm
deaf·en taub machen; betäuben
deaf-mute Taubstumme *m, f*
deal 1. F Geschäft *n*, Handel *m*; Menge *f*; ***it's a deal!*** abgemacht!; ***a good deal*** ziemlich viel; ***a great deal*** sehr viel; **2.** *v/t* (aus-, ver-, zu)teilen; *j-m Karten* geben; *j-m e-n Schlag* versetzen; *v/i* handeln (***in*** mit *e-r Ware*); *sl* dealen; *cards*: geben; ***deal with*** sich befassen mit, behandeln; ECON Handel treiben mit, Geschäfte machen mit
deal·er ECON Händler(in); *cards*: Geber(in); *sl* Dealer *m*
deal·ing *mst pl* Umgang *m*, Beziehungen *pl*
dean REL, UNIV Dekan *m*
dear 1. teuer; lieb; ***Dear Sir*** Sehr geehrter Herr …; **2.** Liebste *m, f*, Schatz *m*; ***my dear*** m-e Liebe, mein Lieber; **3.** *int* (***oh***) ***dear!, dear dear!, dear me!*** F du liebe Zeit!, ach herrje!
dear·est sehnlichst
dear·ly innig, von ganzem Herzen; ECON teuer
death Tod *m*; Todesfall *m*
death·bed Sterbebett *n*
death cer·tif·i·cate Totenschein *m*
death·ly tödlich; ***deathly still*** totenstill
death war·rant JUR Hinrichtungsbefehl *m*; *fig* Todesurteil *n*
de·bar: ***debar s.o. from*** j-n ausschließen aus
de·base erniedrigen; mindern
de·ba·ta·ble umstritten
de·bate 1. Debatte *f*, Diskussion *f*; **2.** debattieren, diskutieren
deb·it ECON **1.** Soll *n*; (Konto)Belastung *f*; ***debit and credit*** Soll und Haben *n*; **2.** *j-n, ein Konto* belasten
deb·ris Trümmer *pl*, Schutt *m*
debt Schuld *f*; ***be in debt*** Schulden haben, verschuldet sein; ***be out of debt*** schuldenfrei sein; ***get into debt*** sich verschulden, Schulden machen
debt·or Schuldner(in)
de·bug TECH, EDP Fehler beseitigen
de·but Debüt *n*
Dec ABBR *of* ***December*** Dez., Dezember *m*
dec·ade Jahrzehnt *n*
dec·a·dent dekadent
de·caf·fein·at·ed koffeinfrei
de·camp F verschwinden
de·cant abgießen; umfüllen
de·cant·er Karaffe *f*
de·cath·lete SPORT Zehnkämpfer *m*
de·cath·lon SPORT Zehnkampf *m*
de·cay 1. zerfallen; verfaulen; kariös *or* schlecht werden (*tooth*); **2.** Zerfall *m*; Verfaulen *n*
de·cease *esp* JUR Tod *m*, Ableben *n*
de·ceased *esp* JUR **1. *the deceased*** der *or* die Verstorbene; die Verstorbenen *pl*; **2.** verstorben
de·ceit Betrug *m*; Täuschung *f*
de·ceit·ful betrügerisch
de·ceive betrügen; täuschen
de·ceiv·er Betrüger(in)
De·cem·ber (ABBR ***Dec***) Dezember *m*
de·cen·cy Anstand *m*
de·cent anständig; F annehmbar, (ganz) anständig; F nett
de·cep·tion Täuschung *f*
de·cep·tive trügerisch; ***be deceptive*** täuschen, trügen
de·cide (sich) entscheiden; bestimmen; beschließen, sich entschließen
de·cid·ed entschieden; bestimmt; entschlossen
dec·i·mal MATH **1.** *a.* ***decimal fraction*** Dezimalbruch *m*; **2.** Dezimal…
de·ci·pher entziffern
de·ci·sion Entscheidung *f*; Entschluss *m*; Entschlossenheit *f*; ***make a decision*** e-e Entscheidung treffen; ***reach*** *or* ***come to a decision*** zu e-m Entschluss kommen
de·ci·sive entscheidend; ausschlaggebend; entschieden
deck 1. MAR Deck *n*; Spiel *n*, Pack *m* (Spiel)Karten; **2. *deck out*** schmücken
deck·chair Liegestuhl *m*
dec·la·ra·tion Erklärung *f*; Zollerklärung

D

f
de·clare erklären; deklarieren, verzollen
de·clen·sion LING Deklination *f*
de·cline **1.** abnehmen, zurückgehen; fallen; verfallen; (höflich) ablehnen; LING deklinieren; **2.** Abnahme *f*, Rückgang *m*, Verfall *m*
de·cliv·i·ty (Ab)Hang *m*
de·clutch MOT auskuppeln
de·code entschlüsseln
de·com·pose zerlegen; (sich) zersetzen; verwesen
de·con·tam·i·nate entgasen, entgiften, entseuchen, entstrahlen
de·con·tam·i·na·tion Entseuchung *f*
dec·o·rate verzieren, schmücken; tapezieren; (an)streichen; dekorieren
dec·o·ra·tion Verzierung *f*, Schmuck *m*, Dekoration *f*; Orden *m*
dec·o·ra·tive dekorativ; Zier…
dec·o·ra·tor Dekorateur *m*; Maler *m* und Tapezierer *m*
dec·o·rous anständig
de·co·rum Anstand *m*
de·coy **1.** Lockvogel *m* (*a*, *fig*); Köder *m* (*a. fig*); **2.** ködern; locken (***into*** in *acc*); verleiten (***into*** zu)
de·crease **1.** Abnahme *f*; **2.** abnehmen; (sich) vermindern
de·cree **1.** Dekret *n*, Erlass *m*, Verfügung *f*; *esp* JUR Entscheid *m*, Urteil *n*; **2.** verfügen
ded·i·cate widmen
ded·i·cat·ed engagiert
ded·i·ca·tion Widmung *f*; Hingabe *f*
de·duce ableiten; folgern
de·duct *Betrag* abziehen (***from*** von)
de·duct·i·ble: ***tax-deductible*** steuerlich absetzbar
de·duc·tion Abzug *m*; (Schluss-)Folgerung *f*, Schluss *m*
deed Tat *f*; Heldentat *f*; JUR (Übertragungs)Urkunde *f*
deep **1.** tief (*a. fig*); **2.** Tiefe *f*
deep·en (sich) vertiefen, *fig a.* (sich) verstärken
deep freeze **1.** tiefkühlen, einfrieren; **2.** Tiefkühl-, Gefriertruhe *f*
deep-fro·zen tiefgefroren
deep fry frittieren
deep·ness Tiefe *f*
deer zo Hirsch *m*; Reh *n*
de·face entstellen; unleserlich machen; ausstreichen
def·a·ma·tion Verleumdung *f*
de·fault **1.** JUR Nichterscheinen *n* vor Gericht; SPORT Nichtantreten *n*; ECON Verzug *m*; **2.** s-n Verpflichtungen nicht nachkommen, ECON *a.* im Verzug sein; JUR nicht vor Gericht erscheinen; SPORT nicht antreten
de·feat **1.** Niederlage *f*; **2.** besiegen, schlagen; vereiteln, zunichtemachen
de·fect Defekt *m*, Fehler *m*; Mangel *m*
de·fec·tive mangelhaft; schadhaft, defekt
de·fence *Br* → ***defense***
de·fence·less *Br* → ***defenseless***
de·fend (***from, against***) verteidigen (gegen), schützen (vor *dat*, gegen)
de·fen·dant Angeklagte *m, f*; Beklagte *m, f*
de·fend·er Verteidiger(in); SPORT Abwehrspieler(in)
de·fense Verteidigung *f* (*a.* MIL, JUR, SPORT), Schutz *m*; SPORT Abwehr *f*; ***witness for the defense*** Entlastungszeuge *m*
de·fense·less schutzlos, wehrlos
de·fen·sive **1.** Defensive *f*, Verteidigung *f*, Abwehr *f*; **2.** defensiv; Verteidigungs…, Abwehr…
de·fer aufschieben, verschieben
de·fi·ance Herausforderung *f*; Trotz *m*
de·fi·ant herausfordernd; trotzig
de·fi·cien·cy Unzulänglichkeit *f*; Mangel *m*
de·fi·cient mangelhaft, unzureichend
def·i·cit ECON Defizit *n*, Fehlbetrag *m*
de·file beschmutzen
de·fine definieren; erklären, bestimmen
def·i·nite bestimmt; endgültig, definitiv
def·i·ni·tion Definition *f*, Bestimmung *f*, Erklärung *f*
de·fin·i·tive endgültig, definitiv
de·flect *v/t* ablenken; *Ball* abfälschen; *v/i* abweichen
de·form entstellen, verunstalten
de·formed deformiert, verunstaltet; verwachsen
de·for·mi·ty Missbildung *f*
de·fraud betrügen (***of*** um)
de·frost *v/t Windschutzscheibe etc* entfrosten; *Kühlschrank etc* abtauen, *Tiefkühlkost etc* auftauen; *v/i* ab-, auftauen
deft geschickt, gewandt
de·fy herausfordern; trotzen (*dat*)
de·gen·e·rate **1.** entarten; **2.** entartet
deg·ra·da·tion Erniedrigung *f*
de·grade erniedrigen, demütigen
de·gree Grad *m*; Stufe *f*; (akademischer) Grad; ***by degrees*** allmählich; ***take one's degree*** e-n akademischen Grad erwerben, promovieren
de·hy·drate austrocknen; TECH das Wasser entziehen (*dat*)
de·i·fy vergöttern; vergöttlichen
deign sich herablassen
de·i·ty Gottheit *f*

de·jec·ted niedergeschlagen, mutlos, deprimiert
de·jec·tion Niedergeschlagenheit *f*
de·lay **1.** Aufschub *m*; Verzögerung *f*; RAIL *etc* Verspätung *f*; **2.** ver-, aufschieben; verzögern; aufhalten; ***be delayed*** sich verzögern; RAIL *etc* Verspätung haben
del·e·gate **1.** abordnen, delegieren; *Vollmachten etc* übertragen; **2.** Delegierte *m, f*, bevollmächtigter Vertreter
del·e·ga·tion Übertragung *f*; Abordnung *f*, Delegation *f*
de·lete (aus)streichen; EDP löschen
de·lib·e·rate absichtlich, vorsätzlich; bedächtig, besonnen
de·lib·e·ra·tion Überlegung *f*; Beratung *f*; Bedächtigkeit *f*
del·i·ca·cy Delikatesse *f*, Leckerbissen *m*; Zartheit *f*; Feingefühl *n*, Takt *m*
del·i·cate delikat (*a. fig*), schmackhaft; zart; fein; zierlich; zerbrechlich; heikel; empfindlich
del·i·ca·tes·sen Delikatessen *pl*, Feinkost *f*; Feinkostgeschäft *n*
de·li·cious köstlich
de·light **1.** Vergnügen *n*, Entzücken *n*; **2.** entzücken, erfreuen; ***delight in*** (große) Freude haben an (*dat*)
de·light·ful entzückend
de·lin·quen·cy Kriminalität *f*
de·lin·quent **1.** straffällig; **2.** Straffällige *m, f*; → ***juvenile 1***
de·lir·i·ous MED im Delirium, fantasierend
de·lir·i·um MED Delirium *n*
de·liv·er ausliefern, (ab)liefern; *Briefe* zustellen; *Rede etc* halten; befreien, erlösen; ***be delivered of*** MED entbunden werden von
de·liv·er·ance Befreiung *f*
de·liv·er·er Befreier(in)
de·liv·er·y (Ab-, Aus)Lieferung *f*; *post* Zustellung *f*; Halten *n* (*e-r Rede*); Vortrag(sweise *f*) *m*; MED Entbindung *f*
de·liv·er·y van *Br* MOT Lieferwagen *m*
dell kleines Tal
de·lude täuschen
del·uge Überschwemmung *f*; *fig* Flut *f*
de·lu·sion Täuschung *f*; Wahn(vorstellung *f*) *m*
de·mand **1.** Forderung *f* (***for*** nach); Anforderung *f* (***on*** an *acc*); Nachfrage *f* (***for*** nach), Bedarf *m* (***for*** an *dat*); ***on demand*** auf Verlangen; **2.** verlangen, fordern; (*fordernd*) fragen nach; erfordern
de·mand·ing anspruchsvoll
de·men·ted wahnsinnig
dem·i... Halb..., halb...
de·mil·i·ta·rize entmilitarisieren
dem·o F Demo *f*
de·mo·bi·lize demobilisieren
de·moc·ra·cy Demokratie *f*
dem·o·crat Demokrat(in)
dem·o·crat·ic demokratisch
de·mol·ish demolieren; ab-, ein-, niederreißen; zerstören
dem·o·li·tion Demolierung *f*; Niederreißen *n*, Abbruch *m*
de·mon Dämon *m*; Teufel *m*
dem·on·strate demonstrieren; beweisen; zeigen; vorführen
dem·on·stra·tion Demonstration *f*, *a.* Kundgebung *f*, *a.* Vorführung *f*
demonstration car *Br* Vorführwagen *m*
de·mon·stra·tive: ***be demonstrative*** s-e Gefühle (offen) zeigen
dem·on·stra·tor Demonstrant(in); Vorführer(in); MOT Vorführwagen *m*
de·mor·al·ize demoralisieren
de·mote degradieren
de·mure ernst, zurückhaltend
den zo Höhle *f* (*a. fig*); F Bude *f*
de·ni·al Ablehnung *f*; Leugnen *n*; Verweigerung *f*; ***official denial*** Dementi *n*
den·ims Jeans *pl*
Den·mark Dänemark *n*
de·nom·i·na·tion REL Konfession *f*; ECON Nennwert *m*
de·note bezeichnen; bedeuten
de·nounce (öffentlich) anprangern
dense dicht; *fig* beschränkt, begriffsstutzig
den·si·ty Dichte *f*
dent **1.** Beule *f*, Delle *f*; **2.** ver-, einbeulen
den·tal Zahn...
dental plaque Zahnbelag *m*
dental plate (Zahn)Prothese *f*
dental surgeon Zahnarzt *m*, Zahnärztin *f*
den·tist Zahnarzt *m*, Zahnärztin *f*
den·tures (Zahn)Prothese *f*, (künstliches) Gebiss
de·nun·ci·a·tion Denunziation *f*
de·nun·ci·a·tor Denunziant(in)
de·ny abstreiten, bestreiten, dementieren, (ab)leugnen; *j-m et.* verweigern, abschlagen
de·o·do·rant De(s)odorant *n*, Deo *n*
de·part abreisen; abfahren, abfliegen; abweichen (***from*** von)
de·part·ment Abteilung *f*, UNIV *a.* Fachbereich *m*; POL Ministerium *n*
De·part·ment of De·fense Verteidigungsministerium *n*
Department of the En·vi·ron·ment *Br* Umweltministerium *n*
Department of the In·te·ri·or Innenministerium *n*
Department of State *a.* ***State Depart-***

D

ment Außenministerium *n*
de·part·ment store Kaufhaus *n*, Warenhaus *n*
de·par·ture Abreise *f*; RAIL *etc* Abfahrt *f*; AVIAT Abflug *m*; *fig* Abweichung *f*; ***departures*** 'Abfahrt'
departure gate AVIAT Flugsteig *m*
departure lounge AVIAT Abflughalle *f*
de·pend: ***depend on*** sich verlassen auf (*acc*); abhängen von; angewiesen sein auf (*acc*); ***that depends*** das kommt darauf an
de·pend·a·ble zuverlässig
de·pend·a·bil·i·ty Zuverlässigkeit *f*
de·pen·dant Angehörige *m, f*
de·pen·dence Abhängigkeit *f*; Vertrauen *n*
de·pen·dent **1.** (***on***) abhängig (von); angewiesen (auf *acc*); **2.** → ***dependant***
de·plor·a·ble bedauerlich, beklagenswert
de·plore beklagen, bedauern
de·pop·u·late entvölkern
de·port ausweisen, *Ausländer a.* abschieben; deportieren
de·pose *j-n* absetzen; JUR unter Eid erklären
de·pos·it **1.** absetzen, abstellen; CHEM, GEOL (sich) ablagern *or* absetzen; deponieren, hinterlegen; ECON *Betrag* anzahlen; **2.** CHEM Ablagerung *f*, GEOL *a.* (*Erz- etc*)Lager *n*; Deponierung *f*, Hinterlegung *f*; ECON Anzahlung *f*; ***make a deposit*** e-e Anzahlung leisten (***on*** für)
dep·ot Depot *n*; Bahnhof *m*
de·prave *moralisch* verderben
de·pre·ci·ate an Wert verlieren
de·press (nieder)drücken; deprimieren, bedrücken
de·pressed deprimiert, niedergeschlagen; ECON flau (*market*); Not leidend (*industry*)
depressed ar·e·a ECON Notstandsgebiet *n*
de·press·ing deprimierend, bedrückend
de·pres·sion Depression *f*, Niedergeschlagenheit *f*; ECON Depression *f*, Flaute *f*; Senke *f*, Vertiefung *f*; METEOR Tief (-druckgebiet) *n*
de·prive: ***deprive s.o. of s.th.*** j-m et. entziehen *or* nehmen
de·prived benachteiligt
dept, **Dept** ABBR *of* ***department*** Abt., Abteilung *f*
depth **1.** Tiefe *f*; **2.** Tiefen…
dep·u·ta·tion Abordnung *f*
dep·u·tize: ***deputize for s.o.*** j-n vertreten
dep·u·ty (Stell)Vertreter(in); PARL Abgeordnete *m, f*; *a.* ***deputy sheriff*** Hilfssheriff *m*
de·rail: ***be derailed*** entgleisen
de·ranged geistesgestört
der·by F Melone *f*
der·e·lict heruntergekommen, baufällig
de·ride verhöhnen, verspotten
de·ri·sion Hohn *m*, Spott *m*
de·ri·sive höhnisch, spöttisch
de·rive herleiten (***from*** von); (sich) ableiten (***from*** von); abstammen (***from*** von); ***derive pleasure from*** Freude finden *or* haben an (*dat*)
der·ma·tol·o·gist Dermatologe *m*, Hautarzt *m*
de·rog·a·to·ry abfällig, geringschätzig
der·rick TECH Derrickkran *m*; MAR Ladebaum *m*; TECH Bohrturm *m*
de·scend herab-, hinabsteigen, herunter-, hinuntersteigen, -gehen, -kommen; AVIAT niedergehen; abstammen, herkommen (***from*** von); ***descend on*** herfallen über (*acc*); überfallen (*acc*) (*visitor etc*)
de·scen·dant Nachkomme *m*
de·scent Herab-, Hinuntersteigen *n*, -gehen *n*; AVIAT Niedergehen *n*; Gefälle *n*; Abstammung *f*, Herkunft *f*
de·scribe beschreiben
de·scrip·tion Beschreibung *f*, Schilderung *f*; Art *f*, Sorte *f*
de·scrip·tive beschreibend; anschaulich
des·e·crate entweihen
de·seg·re·gate die Rassentrennung aufheben in (*dat*)
de·seg·re·ga·tion Aufhebung *f* der Rassentrennung
des·ert[1] **1.** Wüste *f*; **2.** Wüsten…
de·sert[2] *v/t* verlassen, im Stich lassen; *v/i* MIL desertieren
de·sert·er MIL Deserteur *m*
de·ser·tion (JUR *a.* böswilliges) Verlassen; MIL Fahnenflucht *f*
de·serve verdienen
de·serv·ed·ly verdientermaßen
de·serv·ing verdienstvoll
de·sign **1.** Design *n*, Entwurf *m*, (TECH Konstruktions)Zeichnung *f*; Design *n*, Muster *n*; (*a.* böse)Absicht; **2.** entwerfen, TECH konstruieren; gestalten; ausdenken; bestimmen, vorsehen (***for*** für)
des·ig·nate *et. or j-n* bestimmen
de·sign·er Designer(in); TECH Konstrukteur *m*; (*Mode*)Schöpfer(in)
de·sir·a·ble erwünscht, wünschenswert; begehrenswert
de·sire **1.** Wunsch *m*, Verlangen *n*, Begierde *f* (***for*** nach); **2.** wünschen; begehren
de·sist Abstand nehmen (***from*** von)
desk Schreibtisch *m*; Pult *n*; Empfang *m*, Rezeption *f*; Schalter *m*
desk·top com·put·er Desktop-Computer *m*, Tischcomputer *m*, Tischrechner *m*

desktop pub·lish·ing (ABBR ***DTP***) EDP Desktop-Publishing *n*
des·o·late einsam, verlassen; trostlos
de·spair 1. Verzweiflung *f*; ***drive s.o. to despair*** j-n zur Verzweiflung bringen; 2. verzweifeln (***of*** an *dat*)
de·spair·ing verzweifelt
de·spatch → ***dispatch***
des·per·ate verzweifelt; F hoffnungslos, schrecklich
des·per·a·tion Verzweiflung *f*
des·pic·a·ble verachtenswert, verabscheuungswürdig
de·spise verachten
de·spite trotz (*gen*)
de·spon·dent mutlos, verzagt
des·pot Despot *m*, Tyrann *m*
des·sert Nachtisch *m*, Dessert *n*
des·ti·na·tion Bestimmung *f*; Bestimmungsort *m*
des·tined bestimmt; MAR *etc* unterwegs (***for*** nach)
des·ti·ny Schicksal *n*
des·ti·tute mittellos
de·stroy zerstören, vernichten; *Tier* töten, einschläfern
de·stroy·er Zerstörer(in); MAR MIL Zerstörer *m*
de·struc·tion Zerstörung *f*, Vernichtung *f*
de·struc·tive zerstörend, vernichtend; zerstörerisch
de·tach (ab-, los)trennen, (los)lösen
de·tached einzeln, frei *or* allein stehend; unvoreingenommen; distanziert; ***detached house*** Einzelhaus *n*
de·tach·ment (Los)Lösung *f*, (Ab-) Trennung *f*; MIL (Sonder)Kommando *n*
de·tail 1. Detail *n*, Einzelheit *f*; MIL (Sonder)Kommando *n*; ***in detail*** ausführlich; 2. genau schildern; MIL abkommandieren
de·tailed detailliert, ausführlich
de·tain aufhalten; JUR in (Untersuchungs)Haft behalten
de·tect entdecken, (heraus)finden
de·tec·tion Entdeckung *f*
de·tec·tive Kriminalbeamte *m*, Detektiv *m*
detective nov·el, detective sto·ry Kriminalroman *m*
de·ten·tion JUR Haft *f*; PED Nachsitzen *n*
de·ter abschrecken (***from*** von)
de·ter·gent Reinigungs-, Wasch-, Geschirrspülmittel *n*
de·te·ri·o·rate (sich) verschlechtern, nachlassen; verderben
de·ter·mi·na·tion Entschlossenheit *f*, Bestimmtheit *f*; Entschluss *m*; Feststellung *f*, Ermittlung *f*
de·ter·mine *et.* beschließen, bestimmen; feststellen, ermitteln; (sich) entscheiden; sich entschließen
de·ter·mined entschlossen
de·ter·rence Abschreckung *f*
de·ter·rent 1. abschreckend; 2. Abschreckungsmittel *n*
de·test verabscheuen
de·throne entthronen
de·to·nate *v/t* zünden; *v/i* detonieren, explodieren
de·tour Umweg *m*; Umleitung *f*
de·tract: ***detract from*** ablenken von; schmälern (*acc*)
de·tri·ment Nachteil *m*, Schaden *m*
deuce *cards etc*: Zwei *f*; *tennis*: Einstand *m*
de·val·u·a·tion Abwertung *f*
de·val·ue abwerten
dev·a·state verwüsten
dev·a·stat·ing verheerend, vernichtend; F umwerfend, toll
de·vel·op (sich) entwickeln; *Naturschätze, Bauland* erschließen, *Altstadt etc* sanieren
de·vel·op·er PHOT Entwickler *m*; (Stadt)-Planer *m*
de·vel·op·ing Entwicklungs…
developing coun·try, developing nation Entwicklungsland *n*
de·vel·op·ment Entwicklung *f*; Erschließung *f*, Sanierung *f*
de·vi·ate abweichen (***from*** von)
de·vi·a·tion Abweichung *f*
de·vice Vorrichtung *f*, Gerät *n*; Plan *m*, Trick *m*; ***leave s.o. to his own devices*** j-n sich selbst überlassen
dev·il Teufel *m* (*a. fig*)
dev·il·ish teuflisch
de·vi·ous abwegig; gewunden; unaufrichtig; ***devious route*** Umweg *m*
de·vise (sich) ausdenken
de·void: ***devoid of*** ohne (*acc*)
de·vote widmen (***to*** *dat*)
de·vot·ed ergeben; hingebungsvoll; eifrig, begeistert
dev·o·tee begeisterter Anhänger
de·vo·tion Ergebenheit *f*; Hingabe *f*; Frömmigkeit *f*, Andacht *f*
de·vour verschlingen
de·vout fromm; sehnlichst, innig
dew Tau *m*
dew·y taufeucht, taufrisch
dex·ter·i·ty Gewandtheit *f*
dex·ter·ous, dex·trous gewandt
di·a·bol·i·cal teuflisch
di·ag·nose diagnostizieren
di·ag·no·sis Diagnose *f*
di·ag·o·nal 1. diagonal; 2. Diagonale *f*

D

di·a·gram Diagramm *n*, grafische Darstellung
di·al **1.** Zifferblatt *n*; TEL Wählscheibe *f*; TECH Skala *f*; **2.** TEL wählen; ***dial direct*** durchwählen (***to*** nach); ***direct dial(l)ing*** Durchwahl *f*
di·a·lect Dialekt *m*, Mundart *f*
di·al·ling code *Br* TEL Vorwahl(nummer) *f*
di·a·log, *Br* **di·a·logue** Dialog *m*, (Zwie-)Gespräch *n*
di·am·e·ter Durchmesser *m*; ***in diameter*** im Durchmesser
di·a·mond Diamant *m*; Raute *f*, Rhombus *m*; *cards*: Karo *n*
di·a·per Windel *f*
di·a·phragm ANAT Zwerchfell *n*; OPT Blende *f*; TEL Membran(e) *f*
di·ar·rh(o)e·a MED Durchfall *m*
di·a·ry Tagebuch *n*
dice **1.** Würfel *m*; **2.** GASTR in Würfel schneiden; würfeln
dic·tate diktieren; *fig* vorschreiben
dic·ta·tion Diktat *n*
dic·ta·tor Diktator *m*
dic·ta·tor·ship Diktatur *f*
dic·tion Ausdrucksweise *f*, Stil *m*
dic·tion·a·ry Wörterbuch *n*
die[1] sterben; zo eingehen, verenden; ***die of hunger*** verhungern; ***die of thirst*** verdursten; ***die away*** sich legen (*wind*); verklingen (*sound*); ***die down*** nachlassen; herunterbrennen; schwächer werden; ***die out*** aussterben (*a. fig*)
die[2] Würfel *m*
di·et **1.** Diät *f*; Nahrung *f*, Kost *f*; ***be on a diet*** Diät leben; ***put s.o. on a diet*** j-m e-e Diät verordnen; **2.** Diät leben
di·e·ti·cian Diätassistent(in)
dif·fer sich unterscheiden; anderer Meinung sein (***with, from*** als); abweichen
dif·fe·rence Unterschied *m*; Differenz *f*; Meinungsverschiedenheit *f*
dif·fe·rent verschieden; andere(r, -s); anders (***from*** als)
dif·fe·ren·ti·ate (sich) unterscheiden
dif·fi·cult schwierig
dif·fi·cul·ty Schwierigkeit *f*, *pl* Unannehmlichkeiten *pl*
dif·fi·dence Schüchternheit *f*
dif·fi·dent schüchtern
dif·fuse **1.** *fig* verbreiten; **2.** diffus; *esp* PHYS zerstreut; weitschweifig
dif·fu·sion CHEM, PHYS (Zer)Streuung *f*
dig **1.** graben; ***dig (up)*** umgraben; ***dig (up or out)*** ausgraben (*a. fig*); ***dig s.o. in the ribs*** j-m e-n Rippenstoß geben; **2.** F Puff *m*, Stoß *m*; Seitenhieb *m* (***at*** auf *acc*)
di·gest **1.** verdauen; ***digest well*** leicht verdaulich sein; **2.** Abriss *m*; Auslese *f*, Auswahl *f*
di·gest·i·ble verdaulich
di·ges·tion Verdauung *f*
di·ges·tive verdauungsfördernd; Verdauungs…
dig·ger (*esp* Gold)Gräber *m*
di·git Ziffer *f*; ***three-digit number*** dreistellige Zahl
di·gi·tal digital, Digital…
dig·i·tal clock, **digital watch** Digitaluhr *f*
dig·ni·fied würdevoll, würdig
dig·ni·ta·ry Würdenträger(in)
dig·ni·ty Würde *f*
di·gress abschweifen
dike[1] **1.** Deich *m*, Damm *m*; Graben *m*; **2.** eindeichen, eindämmen
dike[2] *sl* Lesbe *f*
di·lap·i·dat·ed verfallen, baufällig, klapp(e)rig
di·late (sich) ausdehnen *or* (aus)weiten; *Augen* weit öffnen
dil·a·to·ry verzögernd, hinhaltend; langsam
dil·i·gence Fleiß *m*
dil·i·gent fleißig, emsig
di·lute **1.** verdünnen; *fig* verwässern; **2.** verdünnt; *fig* verwässert
dim **1.** (halb)dunkel, düster; undeutlich, verschwommen; schwach, trüb(e) (*light*); **2.** (sich) verdunkeln *or* verdüstern; (sich) trüben; undeutlich werden; ***dim one's headlights*** MOT abblenden
dime Zehncentstück *n*
di·men·sion Dimension *f*, Maß *n*, Abmessung *f*; *pl a.* Ausmaß *n*
di·min·ish (sich) vermindern *or* verringern
di·min·u·tive klein, winzig
dim·ple Grübchen *n*
din Getöse *n*, Lärm *m*
dine essen, speisen; ***dine in*** zu Hause essen; ***dine out*** auswärts essen, essen gehen
din·er Speisende *m, f*; Gast *m*; Speiselokal *n*; RAIL Speisewagen *m*
din·ghy MAR Jolle *f*; Dingi *n*; Beiboot *n*; Schlauchboot *n*
din·gy schmutzig, schmudd(e)lig
din·ing car RAIL Speisewagen *m*
din·ing room Ess-, Speisezimmer *n*
din·ner (Mittag-, Abend)Essen *n*; Diner *n*, Festessen *n*
dinner jack·et Smoking *m*
dinner par·ty Dinnerparty *f*, Abendgesellschaft *f*
dinner ser·vice, **dinner set** Speiseservice *n*, Tafelgeschirr *n*
din·ner·time Essens-, Tischzeit *f*

di·no F → ***dinosaur***
di·no·saur zo Dinosaurier *m*
dip **1.** *v/t* (ein)tauchen; senken; schöpfen; ***dip one's headlights*** *Br* MOT abblenden; *v/i* (unter)tauchen; sinken; sich neigen, sich senken; **2.** (Ein-, Unter-)Tauchen *n*; F kurzes Bad; Senkung *f*, Neigung *f*, Gefälle *n*; GASTR Dip *m*
diph·ther·i·a MED Diphtherie *f*
di·plo·ma Diplom *n*
di·plo·ma·cy Diplomatie *f*
dip·lo·mat Diplomat *m*
dip·lo·mat·ic diplomatisch
dip·per Schöpfkelle *f*
dire schrecklich; höchste(r, -s), äußerste(r, -s)
di·rect **1.** *adj* direkt; gerade; unmittelbar; offen, aufrichtig; **2.** *adv* direkt, unmittelbar; **3.** richten; lenken, steuern; leiten; anordnen; *j-n* anweisen; *j-m* den Weg zeigen; *Brief* adressieren; Regie führen bei
direct cur·rent ELECTR Gleichstrom *m*
direct train durchgehender Zug
di·rec·tion Richtung *f*; Leitung *f*, Führung *f*; *film etc*: Regie *f*; *mst pl* Anweisung *f*, Anleitung *f*; ***directions for use*** Gebrauchsanweisung *f*; ***sense of direction*** Ortssinn *m*
direction in·di·ca·tor MOT Fahrtrichtungsanzeiger *m*, Blinker *m*
di·rec·tive Anweisung *f*
di·rect·ly **1.** *adv* sofort; **2.** *cj* F sobald, sowie
di·rec·tor Direktor *m*; *film etc*: Regisseur(in)
di·rec·to·ry Adressbuch *n*
di·rect speech LING wörtliche Rede
dirt Schmutz *m*; (lockere) Erde
dirt cheap F spottbillig
dirt·y **1.** schmutzig (*a. fig*); **2.** *v/t* beschmutzen; *v/i* schmutzig werden, schmutzen
dis·a·bil·i·ty Unfähigkeit *f*
dis·a·bled **1.** arbeitsunfähig, erwerbsunfähig, invalid(e); MIL kriegsversehrt; *körperlich or geistig* behindert; **2.** ***the disabled*** die Behinderten *pl*
dis·ad·van·tage Nachteil *m*; Schaden *m*
dis·ad·van·ta·geous nachteilig, ungünstig
dis·a·gree nicht übereinstimmen; uneinig sein; nicht bekommen (***with s.o.*** j-m)
dis·a·gree·a·ble unangenehm
dis·a·gree·ment Verschiedenheit *f*, Unstimmigkeit *f*, Uneinigkeit *f*; Meinungsverschiedenheit *f*
dis·ap·pear verschwinden
dis·ap·pear·ance Verschwinden *n*
dis·ap·point *j-n* enttäuschen; *Hoffnungen etc* zunichtemachen
dis·ap·point·ing enttäuschend
dis·ap·point·ment Enttäuschung *f*
dis·ap·prov·al Missbilligung *f*
dis·ap·prove missbilligen; dagegen sein
dis·arm *v/t* entwaffnen (*a. fig*); *v/i* MIL, POL abrüsten
dis·ar·ma·ment Entwaffnung *f*; MIL, POL Abrüstung *f*
dis·ar·range in Unordnung bringen
dis·ar·ray Unordnung *f*
di·sas·ter Unglück *n*, Unglücksfall *m*, Katastrophe *f*
disaster ar·e·a Katastrophen-, Notstandsgebiet *n*
disaster con·trol Katastrophenschutz *m*
di·sas·trous katastrophal, verheerend
dis·be·lief Unglaube *m*; Zweifel *m* (***in*** an *dat*)
dis·be·lieve *et.* bezweifeln, nicht glauben
disc *Br* → ***disk***
dis·card *Karten* ablegen, *Kleidung etc a.* ausrangieren; *Freund etc* fallen lassen
di·scern wahrnehmen, erkennen
di·scern·ing kritisch, scharfsichtig
di·scern·ment Scharfblick *m*
dis·charge **1.** *v/t* entladen, ausladen; *j-n* befreien, entbinden; *j-n* entlassen; *Gewehr etc* abfeuern; von sich geben, ausströmen, -senden, -stoßen; MED absondern; *Pflicht etc* erfüllen; *Zorn etc* auslassen (***on*** an *dat*); *v/i* ELECTR sich entladen; sich ergießen, münden (*river*); MED eitern; **2.** MAR Entladung *f*; MIL Abfeuern *n*; Ausströmen *n*; MED Absonderung *f*, Ausfluss *m*; Ausstoßen *n*; ELECTR Entladung *f*; Entlassung *f*; Erfüllung *f* (*e-r Pflicht*)
di·sci·ple Schüler *m*; Jünger *m*
dis·ci·pline **1.** Disziplin *f*; **2.** disziplinieren; ***well disciplined*** diszipliniert; ***badly disciplined*** disziplinlos, undiszipliniert
dis·claim abstreiten, bestreiten; *Verantwortung* ablehnen; JUR verzichten auf (*acc*)
dis·close bekannt geben *or* machen; enthüllen, aufdecken
dis·clo·sure Enthüllung *f*
dis·co Disko *f*
dis·col·o(u)r (sich) verfärben
dis·com·fort **1.** Unbehagen *n*; Unannehmlichkeit *f*; **2.** *j-m* Unbehagen verursachen
dis·con·cert aus der Fassung bringen
dis·con·nect trennen (*a.* ELECTR); TECH auskuppeln; ELECTR *Gerät* abschalten; *Gas, Strom, Telefon* abstellen; TEL *Gespräch* unterbrechen
dis·con·nect·ed zusammenhang(s)los

D

dis·con·so·late untröstlich
dis·con·tent Unzufriedenheit *f*
dis·con·tent·ed unzufrieden
dis·con·tin·ue aufgeben, aufhören mit; unterbrechen
dis·cord Uneinigkeit *f*, Zwietracht *f*, Zwist *m*; MUS Missklang *m*
dis·cord·ant nicht übereinstimmend; MUS unharmonisch, misstönend
dis·co·theque Diskothek *f*
dis·count ECON Diskont *m*; Preisnachlass *m*, Rabatt *m*, Skonto *m*, *n*
dis·cour·age entmutigen; abschrecken, abhalten, *j-m* abraten (***from*** von)
dis·cour·age·ment Entmutigung *f*; Abschreckung *f*
dis·course **1.** Unterhaltung *f*, Gespräch *n*; Vortrag *m*; **2.** e-n Vortrag halten (***on*** über *acc*)
dis·cour·te·ous unhöflich
dis·cour·te·sy Unhöflichkeit *f*
dis·cov·er entdecken; ausfindig machen, (heraus)finden
dis·cov·e·ry Entdeckung *f*
dis·cred·it **1.** Zweifel *m*; Misskredit *m*, schlechter Ruf; ***bring discredit (up)on*** in Verruf bringen; **2.** nicht glauben; in Misskredit bringen
di·screet besonnen, vorsichtig; diskret, verschwiegen
di·screp·an·cy Diskrepanz *f*, Widerspruch *m*
di·scre·tion Ermessen *n*, Gutdünken *n*; Diskretion *f*, Verschwiegenheit *f*
di·scrim·i·nate unterscheiden; ***discriminate against*** benachteiligen, diskriminieren
di·scrim·i·nat·ing kritisch, urteilsfähig
di·scrim·i·na·tion unterschiedliche (*esp* nachteilige) Behandlung; Diskriminierung *f*, Benachteiligung *f*; Urteilsfähigkeit *f*
dis·cus SPORT Diskus *m*
di·scuss diskutieren, erörtern, besprechen
di·scus·sion Diskussion *f*, Besprechung *f*
dis·cus throw SPORT Diskuswerfen *n*
discus throw·er SPORT Diskuswerfer(in)
dis·ease Krankheit *f*
dis·eased krank
dis·em·bark von Bord gehen (lassen); MAR *Waren* ausladen
dis·en·chant·ed: ***be disenchanted with*** sich keine Illusionen mehr machen über (*acc*)
dis·en·gage (sich) frei machen; losmachen; TECH auskuppeln, loskuppeln
dis·en·tan·gle entwirren; (sich) befreien
dis·fa·vo(u)r Missfallen *n*; Ungnade *f*
dis·fig·ure entstellen
dis·grace **1.** Schande *f*; Ungnade *f*; **2.** Schande bringen über (*acc*), *j-m* Schande bereiten
dis·grace·ful schändlich; skandalös
dis·guise **1.** verkleiden (***as*** als); *Stimme etc* verstellen; *et.* verbergen, verschleiern; **2.** Verkleidung *f*; Verstellung *f*; Verschleierung *f*; ***in disguise*** maskiert, verkleidet; *fig* verkappt; ***in the disguise of*** verkleidet als
dis·gust **1.** Ekel *m*, Abscheu *m*; **2.** (an)ekeln; empören, entrüsten
dis·gust·ing ekelhaft
dish **1.** flache Schüssel; (Servier)Platte *f*; GASTR Gericht *n*, Speise *f*; ***the dishes*** das Geschirr; ***wash*** *or* ***do the dishes*** abspülen, abwaschen; **2.** ***dish out*** F austeilen; *often* ***dish up*** *Speisen* anrichten, auftragen; F *Geschichte etc* auftischen
dish·cloth Geschirrtuch *n*
dis·heart·en entmutigen
di·shev·el(l)ed zerzaust
dis·hon·est unehrlich, unredlich
dis·hon·est·y Unehrlichkeit *f*; Unredlichkeit *f*
dis·hon·o(u)r **1.** Schande *f*; **2.** Schande bringen über (*acc*); ECON *Wechsel* nicht honorieren *or* einlösen
dis·hon·o(u)·ra·ble schändlich, unehrenhaft
dish·wash·er Tellerwäscher *m*, Spüler(in); TECH Geschirrspülmaschine *f*, Geschirrspüler *m*
dish·wa·ter Spülwasser *n*
dis·il·lu·sion **1.** Ernüchterung *f*, Desillusion *f*; **2.** ernüchtern, desillusionieren; ***be disillusioned with*** sich keine Illusionen mehr machen über (*acc*)
dis·in·clined abgeneigt
dis·in·fect MED desinfizieren
dis·in·fec·tant Desinfektionsmittel *n*
dis·in·her·it JUR enterben
dis·in·te·grate (sich) auflösen; verfallen, zerfallen
dis·in·terest·ed uneigennützig, selbstlos; objektiv, unvoreingenommen
disk Scheibe *f*; (Schall)Platte *f*; Parkscheibe *f*; EDP Diskette *f*; ANAT Bandscheibe *f*; ***slipped disk*** MED Bandscheibenvorfall *m*
disk drive EDP Diskettenlaufwerk *n*
disk·ette EDP Floppy *f*, Diskette *f*
disk jock·ey Diskjockey *m*
disk park·ing MOT Parken *n* mit Parkscheibe
dis·like **1.** Abneigung *f*, Widerwille *m* (***of, for*** gegen); ***take a dislike to s.o.*** gegen j-n e-e Abneigung fassen; **2.** nicht leiden

können, nicht mögen

dis·lo·cate MED sich *den Arm etc* verrenken *or* ausrenken

dis·loy·al treulos, untreu

dis·mal trüb(e), trostlos, elend

dis·man·tle TECH demontieren

dis·may 1. Schreck(en) *m*, Bestürzung *f*; ***in dismay, with dismay*** bestürzt; ***to my dismay*** zu m-r Bestürzung; **2.** *v/t* erschrecken, bestürzen

dis·miss *v/t* entlassen; wegschicken; ablehnen; *Thema etc* fallen lassen; JUR abweisen

dis·miss·al Entlassung *f*; Aufgabe *f*; JUR Abweisung *f*

dis·mount *v/i* absteigen, absitzen (***from*** von); *v/t* demontieren; TECH auseinandernehmen

dis·o·be·di·ence Ungehorsam *m*

dis·o·be·di·ent ungehorsam

dis·o·bey nicht gehorchen, ungehorsam sein (gegen)

dis·or·der Unordnung *f*; Aufruhr *m*; MED Störung *f*

dis·or·der·ly unordentlich; ordnungswidrig; unruhig; aufrührerisch

dis·or·gan·ize durcheinanderbringen; desorganisieren

dis·own nicht anerkennen; *Kind* verstoßen; ablehnen

di·spar·age verächtlich machen, herabsetzen; gering schätzen

di·spar·i·ty Ungleichheit *f*; ***disparity of*** *or* ***in age*** Altersunterschied *m*

dis·pas·sion·ate leidenschaftslos; objektiv

di·spatch 1. schnelle Erledigung; (Ab)-Sendung *f*; Abfertigung *f*; Eile *f*; (Eil)-Botschaft *f*; Bericht *m*; **2.** schnell erledigen; absenden, abschicken, *Telegramm* aufgeben, abfertigen

di·spel *Menge etc* zerstreuen (*a. fig*), *Nebel* zerteilen

di·spen·sa·ble entbehrlich

di·spen·sa·ry Werks-, Krankenhaus-, Schul-, MIL Lazarettapotheke *f*

dis·pen·sa·tion Austeilung *f*; Befreiung *f*; Dispens *m*; *göttliche* Fügung

di·spense austeilen; *Recht* sprechen; *Arzneien* zubereiten und abgeben; ***dispense with*** auskommen ohne; überflüssig machen

di·spens·er Spender *m*, *a.* Abroller *m* (*for adhesive tape etc*), (*Briefmarken-etc*)Automat *m*

di·sperse verstreuen; (sich) zerstreuen

di·spir·it·ed entmutigt

dis·place verschieben; ablösen, entlassen; *j-n* verschleppen; ersetzen; verdrängen

dis·play 1. Entfaltung *f*; (Her)Zeigen *n*; (protzige) Zurschaustellung; EDP Display *n*, Bildschirm *m*, Datenanzeige *f*; ECON Display *n*, Auslage *f*; ***be on display*** ausgestellt sein; **2.** entfalten; zur Schau stellen; zeigen

dis·please *j-m* missfallen

dis·pleased ungehalten

dis·plea·sure Missfallen *n*

dis·pos·a·ble Einweg…; Wegwerf…

dis·pos·al Beseitigung *f*, Entsorgung *f*; Endlagerung *f*; Verfügung(srecht *n*) *f*; ***be (put) at s.o.'s disposal*** j-m zur Verfügung stehen (stellen)

dis·pose *v/t* (an)ordnen, einrichten; geneigt machen, bewegen; *v/i*: ***dispose of*** verfügen über (*acc*); erledigen; loswerden; wegschaffen, beseitigen; *Abfall, a. Atommüll etc* entsorgen

dis·posed geneigt; …gesinnt

dis·po·si·tion Veranlagung *f*

dis·pos·sess enteignen, vertreiben; berauben (***of*** *gen*)

dis·pro·por·tion·ate(·ly) unverhältnismäßig

dis·prove widerlegen

di·spute 1. Disput *m*, Kontroverse *f*; Streit *m*; Auseinandersetzung *f*; **2.** streiten (über *acc*); bezweifeln

dis·qual·i·fy unfähig *or* untauglich machen; für untauglich erklären; SPORT disqualifizieren

dis·re·gard 1. Nichtbeachtung *f*; Missachtung *f*; **2.** nicht beachten

dis·rep·u·ta·ble übel; verrufen

dis·re·pute schlechter Ruf

dis·re·spect Respektlosigkeit *f*; Unhöflichkeit *f*

dis·re·spect·ful respektlos; unhöflich

dis·rupt unterbrechen

dis·sat·is·fac·tion Unzufriedenheit *f*

dis·sat·is·fied unzufrieden (***with*** mit)

dis·sect MED sezieren, zerlegen, zergliedern (*a. fig*)

dis·sen·sion Meinungsverschiedenheit(en *pl*) *f*, Differenz(en *pl*) *f*; Uneinigkeit *f*

dis·sent 1. abweichende Meinung; **2.** anderer Meinung sein (***from*** als)

dis·sent·er Andersdenkende *m, f*

dis·si·dent Andersdenkende *m, f*; POL Dissident(in), Regime-, Systemkritiker(-in)

dis·sim·i·lar (***to***) unähnlich (*dat*); verschieden (von)

dis·sim·u·la·tion Verstellung *f*

dis·si·pate (sich) zerstreuen; verschwenden

D

dis·si·pat·ed ausschweifend, zügellos
dis·so·ci·ate trennen; ***dissociate o.s.*** sich distanzieren (***from*** von)
dis·so·lute → ***dissipated***
dis·so·lu·tion Auflösung *f*
dis·solve (sich) auflösen
dis·suade *j-m* abraten (***from*** von)
dis·tance **1.** Abstand *m*; Entfernung *f*; Ferne *f*; Strecke *f*; *fig* Distanz *f*, Zurückhaltung *f*; ***at a distance*** von weitem; in einiger Entfernung; ***keep s.o. at a distance*** j-m gegenüber reserviert sein; **2.** hinter sich lassen
distance race SPORT Langstreckenlauf *m*
distance run·ner SPORT Langstreckenläufer(in), Langstreckler(in)
dis·tant entfernt; fern, Fern…; distanziert
dis·taste Widerwille *m*, Abneigung *f*
dis·taste·ful ekelerregend; unangenehm; ***be distasteful to s.o.*** j-m zuwider sein
dis·tem·per VET Staupe *f*
dis·tend (sich) (aus)dehnen; (auf)blähen; sich weiten
dis·til(l) destillieren
dis·tinct verschieden; deutlich, klar
dis·tinc·tion Unterscheidung *f*; Unterschied *m*; Auszeichnung *f*; Rang *m*
dis·tinc·tive unterscheidend; kennzeichnend, bezeichnend
dis·tin·guish unterscheiden; auszeichnen; ***distinguish o.s.*** sich auszeichnen
dis·tin·guished berühmt; ausgezeichnet; vornehm
dis·tort verdrehen; verzerren
dis·tract ablenken
dis·tract·ed beunruhigt, besorgt; (***by, with*** vor *dat*) außer sich, wahnsinnig
dis·trac·tion Ablenkung *f*; Zerstreuung *f*; Wahnsinn *m*; ***drive s.o. to distraction*** j-n wahnsinnig machen
dis·traught → ***distracted***
dis·tress **1.** Leid *n*, Kummer *m*, Sorge *f*; Not(lage) *f*; **2.** beunruhigen, mit Sorge erfüllen
dis·tressed Not leidend
distressed ar·e·a Notstandsgebiet *n*
dis·tress·ing besorgniserregend
dis·trib·ute ver-, aus-, zuteilen; ECON *Waren* vertreiben, absetzen; *Filme* verleihen
dis·tri·bu·tion Ver-, Aus-, Zuteilung *f*; ECON Vertrieb *m*, Absatz *m*; *film*: Verleih *m*
dis·trict Bezirk *m*; Gegend *f*
dis·trust **1.** Misstrauen *n*; **2.** misstrauen (*dat*)
dis·trust·ful misstrauisch
dis·turb stören; beunruhigen
dis·turb·ance Störung *f*; Unruhe *f*; ***disturbance of the peace*** JUR Störung *f* der öffentlichen Sicherheit und Ordnung; ***cause a disturbance*** für Unruhe sorgen; ruhestörenden Lärm machen
dis·turbed geistig gestört; verhaltensgestört
dis·used nicht mehr benutzt (*machinery etc*), stillgelegt (*colliery etc*)
ditch Graben *m*
di·van Diwan *m*
divan bed Bettcouch *f*
dive **1.** (unter)tauchen; *vom Sprungbrett* springen; e-n Hecht- *or* Kopfsprung machen; hechten (***for*** nach); e-n Sturzflug machen; **2.** *swimming*: Springen *n*; Kopfsprung *m*, Hechtsprung *m*; *soccer*: Schwalbe *f*; AVIAT Sturzflug *m*; F Spelunke *f*
div·er Taucher(in); SPORT Wasserspringer(in)
di·verge auseinanderlaufen; abweichen
di·ver·gence Abweichung *f*
di·ver·gent abweichend
di·verse verschieden; mannigfaltig
di·ver·si·fy verschieden(artig) *or* abwechslungsreich gestalten
di·ver·sion Ablenkung *f*; Zeitvertreib *m*; *Br* MOT Umleitung *f*
di·ver·si·ty Verschiedenheit *f*; Mannigfaltigkeit *f*
di·vert ablenken; *j-n* zerstreuen, unterhalten; *Br Verkehr* umleiten
di·vide **1.** *v/t* teilen; ver-, aus-, aufteilen; trennen; MATH dividieren, teilen (***by*** durch); *v/i* sich teilen; sich aufteilen; MATH sich dividieren *or* teilen lassen (***by*** durch); **2.** GEOGR Wasserscheide *f*
di·vid·ed geteilt; ***divided highway*** Schnellstraße *f*
div·i·dend ECON Dividende *f*
di·vid·ers (***a pair of dividers*** ein) Stechzirkel *m*
di·vine göttlich
di·vine ser·vice REL Gottesdienst *m*
div·ing **1.** Tauchen *n*; SPORT Wasserspringen *n*; **2.** Taucher…
div·ing·board Sprungbrett *n*
div·ing·suit Taucheranzug *m*
di·vin·i·ty Gottheit *f*; Göttlichkeit *f*; Theologie *f*
di·vis·i·ble teilbar
di·vi·sion Teilung *f*; Trennung *f*; Abteilung *f*; MIL, MATH Division *f*
di·vorce **1.** (Ehe)Scheidung *f*; ***get a divorce*** sich scheiden lassen (***from*** von); **2.** JUR *j-n*, *Ehe* scheiden; ***get divorced*** sich scheiden lassen
di·vor·cee Geschiedene *m*, *f*
DIY ABBR → ***do-it-yourself***
DIY store Baumarkt *m*

diz·zy schwind(e)lig
do *v/t* tun, machen; (zu)bereiten; *Zimmer* aufräumen; *Geschirr* abwaschen; *Wegstrecke* zurücklegen, schaffen; ***do you know him? no, I don't*** kennst du ihn? nein; ***what can I do for you?*** was kann ich für Sie tun?, womit kann ich (Ihnen) dienen?; ***do London*** F London besichtigen; ***have one's hair done*** sich die Haare machen *or* frisieren lassen; ***have done reading*** fertig sein mit Lesen; *v/i* tun, handeln; sich befinden; genügen; ***that will do*** das genügt; ***how do you do?*** guten Tag!; ***do be quick*** beeil dich doch; ***do you like New York? I do*** gefällt Ihnen New York? ja; ***she works hard, doesn't she?*** sie arbeitet viel, nicht wahr?; ***do well*** s-e Sache gut machen; gute Geschäfte machen; ***do away with*** beseitigen, weg-, abschaffen; ***do s.o. in*** F j-n umlegen; ***I'm done in*** F ich bin geschafft; ***do up*** *Kleid etc* zumachen; *Haus etc* instand setzen; *Päckchen* zurechtmachen; ***do o.s. up*** sich zurechtmachen; ***I could do with …*** ich könnte … brauchen *or* vertragen; ***do without*** auskommen *or* sich behelfen ohne
doc F → ***doctor***
do·cile gelehrig; fügsam
dock[1] stutzen, kupieren
dock[2] **1.** MAR Dock *n*; Kai *m*, Pier *m*; JUR Anklagebank *f*; **2.** *v/t* MAR (ein)docken; *Raumschiff* koppeln; *v/i* MAR anlegen; andocken, ankoppeln (*Raumschiff*)
dock·er Dock-, Hafenarbeiter *m*
dock·ing Docking *n*, Ankopp(e)lung *f*
dock·yard MAR Werft *f*
doc·tor Doktor *m* (*a.* UNIV), Arzt *m*, Ärztin *f*
doc·tor·al: ***doctoral thesis*** UNIV Doktorarbeit *f*
doc·trine Doktrin *f*, Lehre *f*
doc·u·ment **1.** Urkunde *f*; **2.** (urkundlich) belegen
doc·u·men·ta·ry **1.** urkundlich; *film etc*: Dokumentar…; **2.** Dokumentarfilm *m*
dodge (rasch) zur Seite springen, ausweichen; F sich drücken (vor *dat*)
dodg·er Drückeberger *m*
doe zo (Reh)Geiß *f*, Ricke *f*
dog **1.** zo Hund *m*; **2.** *j-n* beharrlich verfolgen
dog-eared mit Eselsohren (*book*)
dog·ged verbissen, hartnäckig
dog·ma Dogma *n*; Glaubenssatz *m*
dog·mat·ic dogmatisch
do-it-your·self **1.** Heimwerken *n*; **2.** Heimwerker…
do-it-your·self·er Heimwerker *m*
dole **1.** milde Gabe; *Br* F Stempelgeld *n*; ***go*** *or* ***be on the dole*** *Br* F stempeln gehen; **2.** ***dole out*** sparsam ver- *or* austeilen
dole·ful traurig, trübselig
doll Puppe *f*
dol·lar Dollar *m*
dol·phin zo Delphin *m*
dome Kuppel *f*
do·mes·tic **1.** häuslich; inländisch, einheimisch; zahm; **2.** Hausangestellte *m, f*
domestic an·i·mal Haustier *n*
do·mes·ti·cate *Tier* zähmen
do·mes·tic flight AVIAT Inlandsflug *m*
domestic mar·ket ECON Binnenmarkt *m*
domestic trade ECON Binnenhandel *m*
domestic vi·olence häusliche Gewalt
dom·i·cile Wohnsitz *m*
dom·i·nant dominierend, (vor)herrschend
dom·i·nate beherrschen; dominieren
dom·i·na·tion (Vor)Herrschaft *f*
dom·i·neer·ing herrisch, tyrannisch
do·nate schenken; stiften; spenden (*a.* MED)
do·na·tion Schenkung *f*
done getan; erledigt; fertig; GASTR gar
don·key zo Esel *m*
do·nor Spender(in) (*a.* MED)
do-noth·ing F Nichtstuer *m*
doom **1.** Schicksal *n*, Verhängnis *n*; **2.** verurteilen, verdammen
Dooms·day der Jüngste Tag
door Tür *f*; Tor *n*; ***next door*** nebenan
door·bell Türklingel *f*
door han·dle Türklinke *f*
door·keep·er Pförtner *m*
door·knob Türknauf *m*
door·mat (Fuß)Abtreter *m*
door·step Türstufe *f*
door·way Türöffnung *f*
dope **1.** F Stoff *m* (*Rauschgift*); Betäubungsmittel *n*; SPORT Dopingmittel *n*; *sl* Trottel *m*; **2.** F *j-m* Stoff geben; SPORT dopen
dope test SPORT Dopingkontrolle *f*
dor·mant schlafend, ruhend; untätig
dor·mi·to·ry Schlafsaal *m*; Studentenwohnheim *n*
dor·mo·bile® Campingbus *m*, Wohnmobil *n*
dor·mouse zo Haselmaus *f*
dose **1.** Dosis *f*; **2.** *j-m* e-e Medizin geben
dot **1.** Punkt *m*; Fleck *m*; ***on the dot*** F auf die Sekunde pünktlich; **2.** punktieren; tüpfeln; *fig* sprenkeln; ***dotted line*** punktierte Linie
dote: ***dote on*** vernarrt sein in (*acc*)
dot·ing vernarrt

D

doub·le **1.** doppelt; Doppel...; zweifach; **2.** Doppelte *n*; Doppelgänger(in); *film*, TV Double *n*; **3.** (sich) verdoppeln; *film*, TV *j-n* doubeln; *a.* ***double up*** falten; *Decke* zusammenlegen; ***double back*** kehrtmachen; ***double up with*** sich krümmen vor (*dat*)
dou·ble-breast·ed zweireihig
dou·ble-check genau nachprüfen
dou·ble chin Doppelkinn *n*
dou·ble-cross ein doppeltes *or* falsches Spiel treiben mit
dou·ble-deal·ing **1.** betrügerisch; **2.** Betrug *m*
dou·ble-deck·er Doppeldecker *m*
dou·ble-edged zweischneidig (*a. fig*); zweideutig
dou·ble fea·ture *film*: Doppelprogramm *n*
dou·ble-park MOT in zweiter Reihe parken
dou·bles *esp tennis*: Doppel *n*; ***men's doubles*** Herrendoppel *n*; ***women's doubles*** Damendoppel *n*
dou·ble-sid·ed EDP zweiseitig
doubt **1.** *v/i* zweifeln; *v/t* bezweifeln; misstrauen (*dat*); **2.** Zweifel *m*; ***be in doubt about*** Zweifel haben an (*dat*); ***no doubt*** ohne Zweifel
doubt·ful zweifelhaft
doubt·less ohne Zweifel
douche **1.** Spülung *f* (*a.* MED); Spülapparat *m*; **2.** spülen (*a.* MED)
dough Teig *m*
dough·nut *appr* Krapfen *m*, Berliner Pfannkuchen, Schmalzkringel *m*
dove ZO Taube *f*
dow·dy unelegant; unmodern
dow·el TECH Dübel *m*
down[1] Daunen *pl*; Flaum *m*
down[2] **1.** *adv* nach unten, herunter, hinunter, herab, hinab, abwärts; unten; **2.** *prp* herab, hinab, herunter, hinunter; ***down the river*** flussabwärts; **3.** *adj* nach unten gerichtet; deprimiert, niedergeschlagen; ***down platform*** Abfahrtsbahnsteig *m* (*in London*); ***down train*** Zug *m* (von London fort); **4.** *v/t* niederschlagen; *Flugzeug* abschießen; F *Getränk* runterkippen; ***down tools*** die Arbeit niederlegen, in den Streik treten
down·cast niedergeschlagen
down·fall Platzregen *m*; *fig* Sturz *m*
down·heart·ed niedergeschlagen
down·hill **1.** *adv* bergab; **2.** *adj* abschüssig; *skiing*: Abfahrts...; **3.** Abhang *m*; *skiing*: Abfahrt *f*
down pay·ment ECON Anzahlung *f*
down·pour Regenguss *m*, Platzregen *m*
down·right **1.** *adv* völlig, ganz und gar, ausgesprochen; **2.** *adj* glatt (*lie etc*); ausgesprochen
downs Hügelland *n*
down·stairs die Treppe herunter *or* hinunter; (nach) unten
down·stream stromabwärts
down-to-earth realistisch
down·town **1.** *adv* im *or* ins Geschäftsviertel; **2.** *adj* im Geschäftsviertel (gelegen *or* tätig); **3.** Geschäftsviertel *n*, Innenstadt *f*, City *f*
down·ward(s) abwärts, nach unten
down·y flaumig
dow·ry Mitgift *f*
doze **1.** dösen, ein Nickerchen machen; **2.** Nickerchen *n*
doz·en Dutzend *n*
drab trist; düster; eintönig
draft **1.** Entwurf *m*; (Luft)Zug *m*; Zugluft *f*; Zug *m*, Schluck *m*; MAR Tiefgang *m*; ECON Tratte *f*, Wechsel *m*; MIL Einberufung *f*; ***beer on draft, draft beer*** Bier *n* vom Fass, Fassbier *n*; **2.** entwerfen; *Brief etc* aufsetzen; MIL einberufen
draft·ee MIL Wehr(dienst)pflichtige *m*
drafts·man TECH Zeichner *m*
drafts·wom·an TECH Zeichnerin *f*
draft·y zugig
drag **1.** Schleppen *n*, Zerren *n*; *fig* Hemmschuh *m*; F *et.* Langweiliges; **2.** schleppen, zerren, ziehen, schleifen; *a.* ***drag behind*** zurückbleiben, nachhinken; ***drag on*** weiterschleppen; *fig* sich dahinschleppen; *fig* sich in die Länge ziehen
drag lift Schlepplift *m*
drag·on MYTH Drache *m*
drag·on·fly ZO Libelle *f*
drain **1.** Abfluss(kanal) *m*, Abflussrohr *n*; Entwässerungsgraben *m*; **2.** *v/t* abfließen lassen; entwässern; austrinken, leeren; *v/i*: ***drain off, drain away*** abfließen, ablaufen
drain·age Abfließen *n*, Ablaufen *n*, Entwässerung *f*; Entwässerungsanlage *f*, -system *n*
drain·pipe Abflussrohr *n*
drake ZO Enterich *m*, Erpel *m*
dram Schluck *m*
dra·ma Drama *n*
dra·mat·ic dramatisch
dram·a·tist Dramatiker *m*
dram·a·tize dramatisieren
drape **1.** drapieren; in Falten legen; **2.** *mst* ***drapes*** Vorhänge *pl*
drap·er·y *Br* Textilien *pl*
dras·tic drastisch, durchgreifend
draught *Br* → ***draft***
draughts *Br* Damespiel *n*

D

draughts·man *etc* → ***draftsman*** *etc*
draugh·ty *Br* → ***drafty***
draw 1. *v/t* ziehen; *Vorhänge* auf-, zuziehen; *Atem* holen; *Tee* ziehen lassen; *fig Menge* anziehen; *Interesse* auf sich ziehen; zeichnen; *Geld* abheben; *Scheck* ausstellen; *v/i* ziehen; SPORT unentschieden spielen; ***draw back*** zurückweichen; ***draw near*** sich nähern; ***draw out*** *Geld* abheben; *fig* in die Länge ziehen; ***draw up*** *Schriftstück* aufsetzen; MOT (an)halten; vorfahren; **2.** Ziehen *n*; *lottery*: Ziehung *f*; SPORT Unentschieden *n*; Attraktion *f*, Zugnummer *f*
draw·back Nachteil *m*, Hindernis *n*
draw·bridge Zugbrücke *f*
draw·er[1] Schublade *f*, Schubfach *n*
draw·er[2] Zeichner(in); ECON Aussteller(-in)
draw·ing Zeichnen *n*; Zeichnung *f*
drawing board Reißbrett *n*
drawing pin *Br* Reißzwecke *f*, Reißnagel *m*, Heftzwecke *f*
drawing room → ***living room***; Salon *m*
drawl gedehnt sprechen
drawn abgespannt; SPORT unentschieden
dread 1. (große) Angst, Furcht *f*; **2.** (sich) fürchten
dread·ful schrecklich, furchtbar
dream 1. Traum *m*; **2.** träumen
dream·er Träumer(in)
dream·y träumerisch, verträumt
drear·y trübselig; trüb(e); langweilig
dredge 1. (Schwimm)Bagger *m*; **2.** (aus)baggern
dredg·er (Schwimm)Bagger *m*
dregs Bodensatz *m*; *fig* Abschaum *m*
drench durchnässen
dress 1. Kleidung *f*; Kleid *n*; **2.** (sich) ankleiden *or* anziehen; schmücken, dekorieren; zurechtmachen; GASTR zubereiten, *Salat* anmachen; MED *Wunde* verbinden; *Haare* frisieren; ***get dressed*** sich anziehen; ***dress s.o. down*** F j-m e-e Standpauke halten; ***dress up*** (sich) fein machen; sich kostümieren *or* verkleiden
dress cir·cle THEA erster Rang
dress de·sign·er Modezeichner(in)
dress·er Anrichte *f*; Toilettentisch *m*
dress·ing An-, Zurichten *n*; Ankleiden *n*; MED Verband *m*; GASTR Dressing *n*, Füllung *f*
dressing-down F Standpauke *f*
dress·ing gown *esp Br* Morgenrock *m*, -mantel *m*; SPORT Bademantel *m*
dressing room THEA *etc* (Künstler)Garderobe *f*; SPORT (Umkleide)Kabine *f*
dressing ta·ble Toilettentisch *m*
dress·mak·er (Damen)Schneider(in)
dress re·hears·al THEA *etc* Generalprobe *f*
drib·ble tröpfeln (lassen); sabbern, geifern; *soccer*: dribbeln
dried getrocknet, Dörr…
dri·er → ***dryer***
drift 1. (Dahin)Treiben *n*; (Schnee)Verwehung *f*; Schnee-, Sandwehe *f*; *fig* Tendenz *f*; **2.** (dahin)treiben; wehen; sich häufen
drill 1. TECH Bohrer *m*; MIL Drill *m* (*a. fig*), Exerzieren *n*; **2.** bohren; MIL drillen (*a. fig*)
drill·ing site TECH Bohrgelände *n*, Bohrstelle *f*
drink 1. Getränk *n*; **2.** trinken; ***drink to s.o.*** j-m zuprosten *or* zutrinken
drink-driv·ing *Br* Trunkenheit *f* am Steuer
drink·er Trinker(in)
drinks ma·chine Getränkeautomat *m*
drip 1. Tröpfeln *n*; MED Tropf *m*; **2.** tropfen *or* tröpfeln (lassen); triefen
drip-dry bügelfrei
drip·ping Bratenfett *n*
drive 1. Fahrt *f*; Aus-, Spazierfahrt *f*; Zufahrt(sstraße) *f*; (private) Auffahrt; TECH Antrieb *m*; EDP Laufwerk *n*; MOT (*Links-etc*)Steuerung *f*; PSYCH Trieb *m*; *fig* Kampagne *f*; *fig* Schwung *m*, Elan *m*, Dynamik *f*; **2.** *v/t* treiben; *Auto etc* fahren, lenken, steuern; (im Auto *etc*) fahren; TECH (an)treiben; *a.* ***drive off*** vertreiben; *v/i* treiben; (Auto) fahren; ***drive off*** wegfahren; ***what are you driving at?*** F worauf wollen Sie hinaus?
drive-in 1. Auto…; ***drive-in cinema*** *Br*, ***drive-in motion-picture theater*** Autokino *n*; **2.** Autokino *n*; Drive-in-Restaurant *n*; Autoschalter *m*, Drive-in-Schalter *m*
driv·el 1. faseln; **2.** Geschwätz *n*, Gefasel *n*
driv·er MOT Fahrer(in); (*Lokomotiv-*) Führer *m*
driv·er's li·cense Führerschein *m*
driv·ing (an)treibend; TECH Antriebs…, Treib…, Trieb…; MOT Fahr…
driv·ing force *fig* Triebkraft *f*
driv·ing li·cence *Br* Führerschein *m*
driv·ing test Fahrprüfung *f*
driz·zle 1. Sprühregen *m*; **2.** sprühen, nieseln
drone 1. zo Drohne *f* (*a. fig*); **2.** summen; dröhnen
droop (schlaff) herabhängen
drop 1. Tropfen *m*; Fallen *n*, Fall *m*; *fig* Fall *m*, Sturz *m*; Bonbon *m*, *n*; ***fruit drops*** Drops *pl*; **2.** *v/t* tropfen (lassen); fallen lassen(*a. fig*); *Brief* einwerfen;

D

Fahrgast absetzen; senken; ***drop s.o. a few lines*** j-m ein paar Zeilen schreiben; *v/i* tropfen; herab-, herunterfallen; umsinken, fallen; ***drop in*** (kurz) hereinschauen; ***drop off*** abfallen; zurückgehen, nachlassen; F einnicken; ***drop out*** herausfallen; aussteigen (***of*** aus); *a.* ***drop out of school*** (***university***) die Schule (das Studium) abbrechen
drop·out Drop-out *m*, Aussteiger *m*; (Schul-, Studien)Abbrecher *m*
drought Trockenkeit *f*, Dürre *f*
drown *v/t* ertränken; überschwemmen; *fig* übertönen; *v/i* ertrinken
drow·sy schläfrig; einschläfernd
drudge sich (ab)placken, schuften, sich schinden
drudg·e·ry (stumpfsinnige) Plackerei *or* Schinderei *or* Schufterei
drug 1. Arzneimittel *n*, Medikament *n*; Droge *f*, Rauschgift *n*; ***be on drugs*** drogenabhängig *or* drogensüchtig sein; ***be off drugs*** clean sein; **2.** *j-m* Medikamente geben; *j-n* unter Drogen setzen; ein Betäubungsmittel beimischen (*dat*); betäuben (*a. fig*)
drug a·buse Drogenmissbrauch *m*; Medikamentenmissbrauch *m*
drug ad·dict Drogenabhängige *m, f*, Drogensüchtige *m, f*; ***be a drug addict*** drogenabhängig *or* drogensüchtig sein
drug·gist Apotheker(in); Inhaber(in) e-s Drugstores
drug·store Apotheke *f*; Drugstore *m*
drug vic·tim Drogentote *m, f*
drum 1. MUS Trommel *f*; ANAT Trommelfell *n*; *pl* MUS Schlagzeug *n*; **2.** trommeln
drum·mer MUS Trommler *m*; Schlagzeuger *m*
drunk 1. *adj* betrunken; ***get drunk*** sich betrinken; **2.** Betrunkene *m, f*; → ***drunkard***
drunk·ard Trinker(in), Säufer(in)
drunk driv·ing Trunkenheit *f* am Steuer
drunk·en betrunken
drunken driv·ing *Br* Trunkenheit *f* am Steuer
dry 1. trocken, GASTR *a.* herb; F durstig; **2.** trocknen; dörren; ***dry out*** trocknen; e-e Entziehungskur machen, F trocken werden; ***dry up*** austrocknen; versiegen
dry-clean chemisch reinigen
dry clean·er's chemische Reinigung
dry·er TECH Trockner *m*
dry goods Textilien *pl*
du·al doppelt, Doppel…
dual car·riageway *Br* Schnellstraße *f*
dub *Film* synchronisieren
du·bi·ous zweifelhaft
duch·ess Herzogin *f*
duck 1. ZO Ente *f*; Ducken *n*; F Schatz *m*; **2.** (unter)tauchen; (sich) ducken
duck·ling ZO Entchen *n*
due 1. zustehend; gebührend; angemessen; ECON fällig; ***due to*** wegen (*gen*); ***be due to*** zurückzuführen sein auf (*acc*); **2.** *adv* direkt, genau (*nach Osten etc*)
du·el Duell *n*
dues Gebühren *pl*; Beitrag *m*
du·et MUS Duett *n*
duke Herzog *m*
dull 1. dumm; träge, schwerfällig; stumpf; matt (*eyes etc*); schwach (*hearing*); langweilig; abgestumpft, teilnahmslos; dumpf; trüb(e); ECON flau; **2.** stumpf machen *or* werden; (sich) trüben; mildern, dämpfen; *Schmerz* betäuben; *fig* abstumpfen
du·ly ordnungsgemäß; gebührend; rechtzeitig
dumb stumm; sprachlos; F doof, dumm, blöd
dum(b)·found·ed verblüfft, sprachlos
dum·my Attrappe *f*; Kleider-, Schaufensterpuppe *f*; MOT Dummy *m*, Puppe *f*; *Br* Schnuller *m*
dump 1. *v/t* (hin)plumpsen *or* (hin)fallen lassen; auskippen; *Schutt etc* abladen; *Schadstoffe in e-n Fluss etc* einleiten, *im Meer* verklappen (***into*** in); ECON *Waren* zu Dumpingpreisen verkaufen; **2.** Plumps *m*; Schuttabladeplatz *m*, Müllkippe *f*, Müllhalde *f*, (Müll)Deponie *f*
dump·ing ECON Dumping *n*, Ausfuhr *f* zu Schleuderpreisen
dune Düne *f*
dung AGR **1.** Dung *m*; **2.** düngen
dun·geon (Burg)Verlies *n*
dupe betrügen, täuschen
du·plex 1. doppelt, Doppel…; **2.** *a.* ***duplex apartment*** Maisonette *f*, Maisonettewohnung *f*; *a.* ***duplex house*** Doppel-, Zweifamilienhaus *n*
du·pli·cate 1. doppelt; ***duplicate key*** Zweit-, Nachschlüssel *m*; **2.** Duplikat *n*; Zweit-, Nachschlüssel *m*; **3.** doppelt ausfertigen; kopieren, vervielfältigen
du·plic·i·ty Doppelzüngigkeit *f*
dur·a·ble haltbar; dauerhaft
du·ra·tion Dauer *f*
du·ress Zwang *m*
dur·ing während
dusk (Abend)Dämmerung *f*
dusk·y dämmerig, düster (*a. fig*); schwärzlich
dust 1. Staub *m*; **2.** *v/t* abstauben; (be)streuen; *v/i* Staub wischen, abstauben
dust·bin *Br* Abfall-, Mülleimer *m*; Ab-

fall-, Mülltonne *f*
dustbin lin·er *Br* Müllbeutel *m*
dust·cart *Br* Müllwagen *m*
dust·er Staubtuch *n*
dust cov·er, dust jack·et Schutzumschlag *m*
dust·man *Br* Müllmann *m*
dust·pan Kehrichtschaufel *f*
dust·y staubig
Dutch 1. *adj* holländisch, niederländisch; **2.** *adv*: ***go Dutch*** getrennte Kasse machen; **3.** LING Holländisch *n*, Niederländisch *n*; ***the Dutch*** die Holländer *pl*, die Niederländer *pl*
Dutch·man Holländer *m*, Niederländer *m*
Dutch·wom·an Holländerin *f*, Niederländerin *f*
du·ti·a·ble ECON zollpflichtig
du·ty Pflicht *f*; Ehrerbietung *f*; ECON Abgabe *f*; Zoll *m*; Dienst *m*; ***on duty*** diensthabend; ***be on duty*** Dienst haben; ***be off duty*** dienstfrei haben
du·ty-free zollfrei
dwarf 1. Zwerg(in); **2.** verkleinern, klein erscheinen lassen
dwell wohnen; *fig* verweilen (***on*** bei)
dwell·ing Wohnung *f*
dwin·dle (dahin)schwinden, abnehmen
dye 1. Farbe *f*; ***of the deepest dye*** *fig* von der übelsten Sorte; **2.** färben
dy·ing 1. sterbend; Sterbe…; **2.** Sterben *n*; ***dying of forests*** Waldsterben *n*
dyke → ***dike***[1, 2]
dy·nam·ic dynamisch, kraftgeladen
dy·nam·ics Dynamik *f*
dy·na·mite 1. Dynamit *n*; **2.** (mit Dynamit) sprengen
dys·en·te·ry MED Ruhr *f*
dys·pep·si·a MED Verdauungsstörung *f*

E

E, e E, e *n*
each jede(r, -s); ***each other*** einander, sich; je, pro Person, pro Stück
ea·ger begierig; eifrig
ea·ger·ness Begierde *f*; Eifer *m*
ea·gle ZO Adler *m*; HIST Zehndollarstück *n*
ea·gle-eyed scharfsichtig
ear BOT Ähre *f*; ANAT Ohr *n*; Öhr *n*; Henkel *m*; ***keep an ear to the ground*** die Ohren offen halten
ear·ache Ohrenschmerzen *pl*
ear·drum ANAT Trommelfell *n*
earl *englischer* Graf
ear·lobe ANAT Ohrläppchen *n*
ear·ly früh; Früh…; Anfangs…, erste(r, -s); bald(ig); ***as early as May*** schon im Mai; ***as early as possible*** so bald wie möglich; ***early on*** schon früh, frühzeitig
ear·ly bird Frühaufsteher(in)
ear·ly warn·ing sys·tem MIL Frühwarnsystem *n*
ear·mark 1. Kennzeichen *n*; Merkmal *n*; **2.** kennzeichnen; zurücklegen (***for*** für)
earn verdienen; einbringen
ear·nest 1. ernst, ernstlich, ernsthaft; ernst gemeint; **2.** Ernst *m*; ***in earnest*** im Ernst; ernsthaft
earn·ings Einkommen *n*
ear·phones Ohrhörer *pl*; Kopfhörer *pl*
ear·piece TEL Hörmuschel *f*
ear·ring Ohrring *m*
ear·shot: ***within (out of) earshot*** in (außer) Hörweite
earth 1. Erde *f*; Land *n*; **2.** *v/t* ELECTR erden
earth·en irden
earth·en·ware Steingut(geschirr) *n*
earth·ly irdisch, weltlich; F denkbar
earth·quake Erdbeben *n*
earth·worm ZO Regenwurm *m*
ease 1. Bequemlichkeit *f*; (Gemüts)Ruhe *f*; Sorglosigkeit *f*; Leichtigkeit *f*; ***at (one's) ease*** ruhig, entspannt; unbefangen; ***be or feel ill at ease*** sich (in s-r Haut) nicht wohlfühlen; **2.** *v/t* erleichtern; beruhigen; *Schmerzen* lindern; *v/i mst* ***ease off, ease up*** nachlassen; sich entspannen (*situation etc*)
ea·sel Staffelei *f*
east 1. Ost, Osten *m*; **2.** *adj* östlich, Ost…; **3.** *adv* nach Osten, ostwärts
Eas·ter Ostern *n*; Oster…
Easter bun·ny Osterhase *m*
Easter egg Osterei *n*
eas·ter·ly östlich, Ost…
east·ern östlich, Ost…
east·ward(s) östlich, nach Osten
eas·y leicht; einfach; bequem; gemäch-

lich, gemütlich; ungezwungen; ***go easy on*** schonen, sparsam umgehen mit; ***go easy, take it easy*** sich Zeit lassen; ***take it easy!*** immer mit der Ruhe!
eas·y chair Sessel *m*
eas·y·go·ing gelassen; ungezwungen
eat essen; (zer)fressen; ***eat out*** essen gehen; ***eat up*** aufessen
eat·a·ble essbar, genießbar
eat·er Esser(in)
eaves Dachrinne *f*, Traufe *f*
eaves·drop (heimlich) lauschen *or* horchen; ***eavesdrop on*** belauschen
ebb 1. Ebbe *f*; **2.** zurückgehen; ***ebb away*** abnehmen
ebb tide Ebbe *f*
eb·o·ny Ebenholz *n*
ec ABBR *of* ***Eurocheque*** *Br* Eurocheque *m*
ec·cen·tric 1. exzentrisch; **2.** Exzentriker *m*, Sonderling *m*
ec·cle·si·as·tic, **ec·cle·si·as·ti·cal** geistlich, kirchlich
ech·o 1. Echo *n*; **2.** widerhallen; *fig* echoen, nachsprechen
e·clipse ASTR (*Sonnen-*, *Mond*)Finsternis *f*; *fig* Niedergang *m*
e·co·cide Umweltzerstörung *f*
e·co·lo·gi·cal ökologisch, Umwelt…
e·col·o·gist Ökologe *m*
e·col·o·gy Ökologie *f*
ec·o·nom·ic Wirtschafts…, wirtschaftlich; ***economic growth*** Wirtschaftswachstum *n*
e·co·nom·i·cal wirtschaftlich, sparsam
e·co·nom·ics Volkswirtschaft(slehre) *f*
e·con·o·mist Volkswirt *m*
e·con·o·mize sparsam wirtschaften (mit)
e·con·o·my 1. Wirtschaft *f*; Wirtschaftlichkeit *f*, Sparsamkeit *f*; Einsparung *f*; **2.** Spar…
e·co·sys·tem Ökosystem *n*
ec·sta·sy Ekstase *f*, Verzückung *f*
ec·stat·ic verzückt
ed·dy 1. Wirbel *m*; **2.** wirbeln
edge 1. Schneide *f*; Rand *m*; Kante *f*; Schärfe *f*; ***be on edge*** nervös *or* gereizt sein; **2.** schärfen; (um)säumen; (sich) drängen
edge·ways, **edge·wise** seitlich, von der Seite
edg·ing Einfassung *f*; Rand *m*
edg·y scharf(kantig); F nervös; F gereizt
ed·i·ble essbar, genießbar
e·dict Edikt *n*
ed·i·fice Gebäude *n*
ed·it *Text* herausgeben, redigieren; EDP editieren; *Zeitung* als Herausgeber leiten
e·di·tion (*Buch*)Ausgabe *f*; Auflage *f*
ed·i·tor Herausgeber(in); Redakteur(in)
ed·i·to·ri·al 1. Leitartikel *m*; **2.** Redaktions…
EDP ABBR *of* ***electronic data processing*** EDV, elektronische Datenverarbeitung
ed·u·cate erziehen; unterrichten
ed·u·cat·ed gebildet
ed·u·ca·tion Erziehung *f*; (Aus)Bildung *f*; Bildungs-, Schulwesen *n*; ***Ministry of Education*** *appr Unterrichtsministerium*
ed·u·ca·tion·al erzieherisch, pädagogisch, Erziehungs…; Bildungs…
ed·u·ca·tion·(al·)ist Pädagoge *m*
eel zo Aal *m*
ef·fect (Aus)Wirkung *f*; Effekt *m*, Eindruck *m*; *pl* ECON Effekten *pl*; ***be in effect*** in Kraft sein; ***in effect*** in Wirklichkeit; ***take effect*** in Kraft treten
ef·fec·tive wirksam; eindrucksvoll; tatsächlich
ef·fem·i·nate verweichlicht; weibisch
ef·fer·vesce brausen, sprudeln
ef·fer·ves·cent sprudelnd, schäumend
ef·fi·cien·cy Leistung *f*; Leistungsfähigkeit *f*; ***efficiency measure*** ECON Rationalisierungsmaßnahme *f*
ef·fi·cient wirksam; leistungsfähig, tüchtig
ef·flu·ent Abwasser *n*, Abwässer *pl*
ef·fort Anstrengung *f*, Bemühung *f* (***at*** um); Mühe *f*; ***without effort*** → ***ef·fort·less*** mühelos, ohne Anstrengung
ef·fron·te·ry Frechheit *f*
ef·fu·sive überschwänglich
egg[1] Ei *n*; ***put all one's eggs in one basket*** alles auf eine Karte setzen
egg[2]: ***egg on*** anstacheln
egg co·sy *Br* Eierwärmer *m*
egg·cup Eierbecher *m*
egg·head F Eierkopf *m*
egg·plant BOT Aubergine *f*
egg·shell Eierschale *f*
egg tim·er Eieruhr *f*
e·go·is·m Egoismus *m*, Selbstsucht *f*
e·go·ist Egoist(in)
E·gypt Ägypten *n*
E·gyp·tian 1. ägyptisch; **2.** Ägypter(in)
ei·der·down Eiderdaunen *pl*; Daunendecke *f*
eight 1. acht; **2.** Acht *f*
eigh·teen 1. achtzehn; **2.** Achtzehn *f*
eigh·teenth achtzehnte(r, -s)
eight·fold achtfach
eighth 1. achte(r, -s); **2.** Achtel *n*
eighth·ly achtens
eigh·ti·eth achtzigste(r, -s)
eigh·ty 1. achtzig; ***the eighties*** die Achtzigerjahre; **2.** Achtzig *f*
ei·ther jede(r, -s) (*von zweien*): eine(r, -s)

E

(*von zweien*); beides; ***either ... or*** entweder ... oder; ***not either*** auch nicht
e·jac·u·late *v/t Samen* ausstoßen; *v/i* ejakulieren, e-n Samenerguss haben
e·jac·u·la·tion Samenerguss *m*
e·ject *j-n* hinauswerfen; TECH ausstoßen, auswerfen
eke: ***eke out*** *Vorräte etc* strecken; *Einkommen* aufbessern; ***eke out a living*** sich (mühsam) durchschlagen
e·lab·o·rate **1.** sorgfältig (aus)gearbeitet; kompliziert; **2.** sorgfältig ausarbeiten
e·lapse verfließen, verstreichen
e·las·tic **1.** elastisch, dehnbar; ***elastic band*** *Br* → **2.** Gummiring *m*, Gummiband *n*
e·las·ti·ci·ty Elastizität *f*
e·lat·ed begeistert (***at, by*** von)
el·bow **1.** Ellbogen *m*; (scharfe) Biegung; TECH Knie *n*; ***at one's elbow*** bei der Hand; **2.** mit dem Ellbogen (weg)stoßen; ***elbow one's way through*** sich (mit den Ellbogen) e-n Weg bahnen durch
el·der[1] **1.** ältere(r, -s); **2.** der, die Ältere; (Kirchen)Älteste(r) *m*
el·der[2] BOT Holunder *m*
el·der·ly ältlich, ältere(r, -s)
el·dest älteste(r, -s)
e·lect **1.** gewählt; **2.** (aus-, er)wählen
e·lec·tion Wahl *f*
election vic·to·ry POL Wahlsieg *m*
election win·ner POL Wahlsieger *m*
e·lec·tor Wähler(in); POL Wahlmann *m*; HIST Kurfürst *m*
e·lec·to·ral Wähler..., Wahl...; ***electoral college*** POL Wahlmänner *pl*; ***electoral district*** POL Wahlkreis *m*
elec·to·rate POL Wähler(schaft *f*) *pl*
e·lec·tric elektrisch, Elektro...
e·lec·tri·cal elektrisch; Elektro...
electrical en·gi·neer Elektroingenieur *m*, Elektrotechniker *m*
electrical en·gi·neer·ing Eletrotechnik *f*
e·lec·tric chair elektrischer Stuhl
e·lec·tri·cian Elektriker *m*
e·lec·tri·ci·ty Elektrizität *f*
e·lec·tric ra·zor Elektrorasierer *m*
e·lec·tri·fy elektrifizieren; elektrisieren (*a. fig*)
e·lec·tro·cute auf dem elektrischen Stuhl hinrichten; durch elektrischen Strom töten
e·lec·tron Elektron *n*
e·lec·tron·ic elektronisch, Elektronen...
electronic da·ta pro·cess·ing elektronische Datenverarbeitung
e·lec·tron·ics Elektronik *f*
el·e·gance Eleganz *f*
el·egant elegant; geschmackvoll; erstklassig
el·e·ment CHEM Element *n*; Urstoff *m*; (Grund)Bestandteil *m*; *pl* Anfangsgründe *pl*, Grundlage(n *pl*) *f*; Elemente *pl*, Naturkräfte *pl*
el·e·men·tal elementar; wesentlich
el·e·men·ta·ry elementar; Anfangs...
elementary school Grundschule *f*
el·e·phant ZO Elefant *m*
el·e·vate erhöhen; *fig* erheben
el·evat·ed erhöht; *fig* gehoben, erhaben
el·e·va·tion Erhebung *f*; Erhöhung *f*; Höhe *f*; Erhabenheit *f*
el·e·va·tor TECH Lift *m*, Fahrstuhl *m*, Aufzug *m*
e·lev·en **1.** elf; **2.** Elf *f*
e·leventh **1.** elfte(r, -s); **2.** Elftel *n*
elf Elf *m*, Elfe *f*; Kobold *m*
e·li·cit *et.* entlocken (***from*** *dat*); ans (Tages)Licht bringen
el·i·gi·ble infrage kommend, geeignet, annehmbar, akzeptabel
e·lim·i·nate entfernen, beseitigen; ausscheiden
e·lim·i·na·tion Entfernung *f*, Beseitigung *f*; Ausscheidung *f*
é·lite Elite *f*; Auslese *f*
elk ZO Elch *m*; Wapitihirsch *m*
el·lipse MATH Ellipse *f*
elm BOT Ulme *f*
e·lon·gate verlängern
e·lope (mit s-m *or* s-r Geliebten) ausreißen *or* durchbrennen
el·o·quent redegewandt, beredt
else sonst, weiter; andere(r, -s)
else·where anderswo(hin)
e·lude geschickt entgehen, ausweichen, sich entziehen (*all*: *dat*); *fig* nicht einfallen (*dat*)
e·lu·sive schwer fassbar
e·ma·ci·ated abgezehrt, ausgemergelt
em·a·nate ausströmen; ausgehen (***from*** von)
em·a·na·tion Ausströmen *n*; *fig* Ausstrahlung *f*
e·man·ci·pate emanzipieren
e·ma·ci·pa·tion Emanzipation *f*
em·balm (ein)balsamieren
em·bank·ment (Bahn-, Straßen-) Damm *m*; (Erd)Damm *m*; Uferstraße *f*
em·bar·go ECON Embargo *n*, (Hafen-, Handels)Sperre *f*
em·bark AVIAT, MAR an Bord nehmen *or* gehen, MAR *a.* (sich) einschiffen; *Waren* verladen; ***embark on*** *et.* anfangen, *et.* beginnen
em·bar·rass in Verlegenheit bringen, verlegen machen, in e-e peinliche Lage bringen

E

em·bar·rass·ing unangenehm, peinlich; verfänglich
em·bar·rass·ment Verlegenheit *f*
em·bas·sy POL Botschaft *f*
em·bed (ein)betten, (ein)lagern
em·bel·lish verschönern; *fig* ausschmücken, beschönigen
em·bers Glut *f*
em·bez·zle unterschlagen
em·bez·zle·ment Unterschlagung *f*
em·bit·ter verbittern
em·blem Sinnbild *n*; Wahrzeichen *n*
em·bod·y verkörpern; enthalten
em·bo·lis·m MED Embolie *f*
em·brace 1. (sich) umarmen; einschließen; **2.** Umarmung *f*
em·broi·der (be)sticken; *fig* ausschmücken
em·broi·der·y Stickerei *f*; *fig* Ausschmückung *f*
em·broil verwickeln (***in*** in *acc*)
e·mend *Texte* verbessern, korrigieren
em·e·rald 1. Smaragd *m*; **2.** smaragdgrün
e·merge auftauchen; sich herausstellen *or* ergeben
e·mer·gen·cy 1. Not *f*, Notlage *f*, Notfall *m*, Notstand *m*; ***state of emergency*** POL Ausnahmezustand *m*; **2.** Not…
emergency brake Notbremse *f*
emergency call Notruf *m*
emergency ex·it Notausgang *m*
emergency land·ing AVIAT Notlandung *f*
emergency num·ber Notruf(nummer *f*) *m*
emergency room MED Notaufnahme *f*
em·i·grant Auswanderer *m*, *esp* POL Emigrant(in)
em·i·grate auswandern, *esp* POL emigrieren
em·i·gra·tion Auswanderung *f*, *esp* POL Emigration *f*
em·i·nence Berühmtheit *f*, Bedeutung *f*; ***Eminence*** REL Eminenz *f*
em·i·nent hervorragend, berühmt; bedeutend
eminently ganz besonders, äußerst
e·mis·sion Ausstoß *m*, Ausstrahlung *f*, Ausströmen *n*
emission-free abgasfrei
e·mit aussenden, ausstoßen, ausstrahlen, ausströmen; von sich geben
e·mo·tion (Gemüts)Bewegung *f*, Gefühl *n*, Gefühlsregung *f*; Rührung *f*
e·mo·tion·al emotional; gefühlsmäßig; gefühlsbetont
e·mo·tion·al·ly emotional, gefühlsmäßig; ***emotionally disturbed*** seelisch gestört
e·mo·tion·less gefühllos
e·mo·tive word PSYCH Reizwort *n*
em·pe·ror Kaiser *m*
em·pha·sis Gewicht *n*; Nachdruck *m*
em·pha·size nachdrücklich betonen
em·phat·ic nachdrücklich; deutlich; bestimmt
em·pire Reich *n*, Imperium *n*; Kaiserreich *n*
em·pir·i·cal erfahrungsgemäß
em·ploy 1. beschäftigen, anstellen; an-, verwenden, gebrauchen; **2.** Beschäftigung *f*; ***in the employ of*** angestellt bei;
em·ploy·ee Angestellte *m*, *f*, Arbeitnehmer(in)
em·ploy·er Arbeitgeber(in)
em·ploy·ment Beschäftigung *f*, Arbeit *f*
employment ad Stellenanzeige *f*
employment of·fice Arbeitsamt *n*
em·pow·er ermächtigen; befähigen
em·press Kaiserin *f*
emp·ti·ness Leere *f* (*a. fig*)
emp·ty 1. leer (*a. fig*); **2.** leeren, ausleeren, entleeren; sich leeren
em·u·late wetteifern mit; nacheifern (*dat*); es gleichtun (*dat*)
e·mul·sion Emulsion *f*
en·a·ble befähigen, es *j-m* ermöglichen; ermächtigen
en·act *Gesetz* erlassen; verfügen
e·nam·el 1. Email *n*, Emaille *f*; ANAT (Zahn)Schmelz *m*; Glasur *f*, Lack *m*; Nagellack *m*; **2.** emaillieren; glasieren; lackieren
en·am·o(u)red: ***enamo(u)red of*** verliebt in (*acc*)
en·camp·ment *esp* MIL (Feld)Lager *n*
en·cased: ***encased in*** gehüllt in (*acc*)
en·chant bezaubern
en·chant·ing bezaubernd
en·chant·ment Bezauberung *f*; Zauber *m*
en·cir·cle einkreisen, umzingeln; umfassen, umschlingen
en·close einschließen, umgeben; beilegen, beifügen
en·clo·sure Einzäunung *f*; Anlage *f*
en·code verschlüsseln, chiffrieren; kodieren
en·com·pass umgeben
en·coun·ter 1. Begegnung *f*; Gefecht *n*; **2.** begegnen (*dat*); auf *Schwierigkeiten etc* stoßen; mit *j-m feindlich* zusammenstoßen
en·cour·age ermutigen; fördern
en·cour·age·ment Ermutigung *f*; Anfeuerung *f*; Unterstützung *f*
en·cour·ag·ing ermutigend
en·croach (***on***) eingreifen (in *j-s Recht etc*), eindringen (in *acc*); über Gebühr in Anspruch nehmen (*acc*)
en·croach·ment Ein-, Übergriff *m*

en·cum·ber belasten; (be)hindern
en·cum·brance Belastung *f*
en·cy·clo·p(a)e·di·a Enzyklopädie *f*
end 1. Ende *n*; Ziel *n*, Zweck *m*; ***no end of*** unendlich viel(e), unzählige; ***at the end of May*** Ende Mai; ***in the end*** am Ende, schließlich; ***on end*** aufrecht; ***stand on end*** zu Berge stehen (*hair*); ***to no end*** vergebens; ***go off the deep end*** F *fig* in die Luft gehen; ***make (both) ends meet*** durchkommen, finanziell über die Runden kommen; **2.** enden; beend(-ig)en
en·dan·ger gefährden
en·dear beliebt machen (***to s.o.*** bei j-m)
en·dear·ing gewinnend; liebenswert
en·dear·ment: ***words of endearment, endearments*** zärtliche Worte *pl*
en·deav·o(u)r 1. Bestreben *n*, Bemühung *f*; **2.** sich bemühen
end·ing Ende *n*; Schluss *m*; LING Endung *f*
en·dive BOT Endivie *f*
end·less endlos, unendlich; TECH ohne Ende
en·dorse ECON *Scheck etc* indossieren; *et.* vermerken (***on*** auf der Rückseite); billigen
en·dorse·ment Vermerk *m*; ECON Indossament *n*, Giro *n*
en·dow *fig* ausstatten; ***endow s.o. with s.th.*** j-m et. stiften
en·dow·ment Stiftung *f*; *mst pl* Begabung *f*, Talent *n*
en·dur·ance Ausdauer *f*; ***beyond endurance, past endurance*** unerträglich
en·dure ertragen
end us·er Endverbraucher *m*
en·e·my 1. Feind *m*; **2.** feindlich
en·er·get·ic energisch; tatkräftig
en·er·gy Energie *f*
en·er·gy cri·sis Energiekrise *f*
en·er·gy-sav·ing energiesparend
en·er·gy sup·ply Energieversorgung *f*
en·fold einhüllen; umfassen
en·force (mit Nachdruck, *a.* gerichtlich) geltend machen; *Gesetz etc* durchführen; durchsetzen, erzwingen
en·force·ment ECON, JUR Geltendmachung *f*; Durchsetzung *f*, Erzwingung *f*
en·fran·chise *j-m* das Wahlrecht verleihen
en·gage *v/t j-s Aufmerksamkeit* auf sich ziehen; TECH einrasten lassen; MOT *e-n Gang* einlegen; *j-n* einstellen, anstellen, *Künstler* engagieren; *v/i* TECH einrasten, greifen; ***engage in*** sich einlassen auf (*acc*) *or* in (*acc*); sich beschäftigen mit
en·gaged verlobt (***to*** mit); beschäftigt (***in, on*** mit); besetzt (*a. Br* TEL); ***engaged tone*** *or* ***signal*** *Br* TEL Besetztzeichen *n*
en·gage·ment Verlobung *f*; Verabredung *f*; MIL Gefecht *n*
en·gag·ing einnehmend; gewinnend
en·gine Maschine *f*; Motor *m*; RAIL Lokomotive *f*
engine driv·er *Br* RAIL Lokomotivführer *m*
en·gi·neer 1. Ingenieur *m*, Techniker *m*, Mechaniker *m*; RAIL Lokomotivführer *m*; MIL Pionier *m*; **2.** bauen; *fig* (geschickt) in die Wege leiten
en·gi·neer·ing Technik *f*, Ingenieurwesen *n*, Maschinen- und Gerätebau *m*
En·gland England *n*
En·glish 1. englisch; **2.** LING Englisch *n*; ***the English*** die Engländer *pl*; ***in plain English*** *fig* unverblümt
Eng·lish·man Engländer *m*
Eng·lish·wom·an Engländerin *f*
en·grave (ein)gravieren, (ein)meißeln, (ein)schnitzen; *fig* einprägen
en·grav·er Graveur *m*
en·grav·ing (Kupfer-, Stahl)Stich *m*; Holzschnitt *m*
en·grossed: ***engrossed in*** (voll) in Anspruch genommen von, vertieft *or* versunken in (*acc*)
en·hance erhöhen, verstärken, steigern
e·nig·ma Rätsel *n*
en·ig·mat·ic rätselhaft
en·joy sich erfreuen an (*dat*); genießen; ***did you enjoy it?*** hat es Ihnen gefallen?; ***enjoy o.s.*** sich amüsieren, sich gut unterhalten; ***enjoy yourself!*** viel Spaß!; ***I enjoy my dinner*** es schmeckt mir
en·joy·a·ble angenehm, erfreulich
en·joy·ment Vergnügen *n*, Freude *f*; Genuss *m*
en·large (sich) vergrößern *or* erweitern, ausdehnen; PHOT vergrößern; sich verbreiten *or* auslassen (***on*** über *acc*)
en·large·ment Erweiterung *f*; Vergrößerung *f* (*a.* PHOT)
en·light·en aufklären, belehren
en·light·en·ment Aufklärung *f*
en·list MIL *v/t* anwerben; *v/i* sich freiwillig melden; ***enlisted men*** Unteroffiziere *pl* und Mannschaften *pl*
en·liv·en beleben
en·mi·ty Feindschaft *f*
en·no·ble adeln; veredeln
e·nor·mi·ty Ungeheuerlichkeit *f*
e·nor·mous ungeheuer
e·nough genug
en·quire, en·qui·ry → ***inquire, inquiry***
en·rage wütend machen
en·raged wütend (***at*** über *acc*)
en·rap·ture entzücken, hinreißen

E

en·rap·tured entzückt, hingerissen
en·rich bereichern; anreichern
en·rol(l) (sich) einschreiben *or* eintragen; UNIV (sich) immatrikulieren
en·sign MAR *esp* (National)Flagge *f*; MIL Leutnant *m* zur See
en·sue (darauf-, nach)folgen
en·sure sichern
en·tail mit sich bringen, zur Folge haben
en·tan·gle verwickeln
en·ter *v/t* hinein-, hereingehen, -kommen, -treten in (*acc*), eintreten, einsteigen in (*acc*), betreten; einreisen in (*acc*); MAR, RAIL einlaufen, einfahren in (*acc*); eindringen in (*acc*); *Namen etc* eintragen, einschreiben; SPORT melden, nennen (***for*** für); *fig* eintreten in (*acc*), beitreten (*dat*); EDP eingeben; *v/i* eintreten, herein-, hineinkommen, herein-, hineingehen; THEA auftreten; sich eintragen *or* einschreiben *or* anmelden (***for*** für); SPORT melden, nennen (***for*** für)
en·ter key EDP Eingabetaste *f*
en·ter·prise Unternehmen *n* (*a.* ECON); ECON Unternehmertum *n*; Unternehmungsgeist *m*
en·ter·pris·ing unternehmungslustig; wagemutig; kühn
en·ter·tain unterhalten; bewirten
en·ter·tain·er Entertainer(in), Unterhaltungskünstler(in)
en·ter·tain·ment Unterhaltung *f*; Entertainment *n*; Bewirtung *f*
en·thral(l) fesseln, bezaubern
en·throne inthronisieren
en·thu·si·asm Begeisterung *f*, Enthusiasmus *m*
en·thu·si·ast Enthusiast(in)
en·thu·si·as·tic begeistert, enthusiastisch
en·tice (ver)locken
en·tice·ment Verlockung *f*, Reiz *m*
en·tire ganz, vollständig; ungeteilt
en·tire·ly völlig; ausschließlich
en·ti·tle betiteln; berechtigen (***to*** zu)
en·ti·ty Einheit *f*
en·trails ANAT Eingeweide *pl*
en·trance Eintreten *n*, Eintritt *m*; Eingang *m*, Zugang *m*; Zufahrt *f*; Einlass *m*, Eintritt *m*, Zutritt *m*
en·trance ex·am(·i·na·tion) Aufnahmeprüfung *f*
entrance fee Eintritt *m*, Eintrittsgeld *n*; Aufnahmegebühr *f*
en·treat inständig bitten, anflehen
en·trea·ty dringende *or* inständige Bitte
en·trench MIL verschanzen (*a. fig*)
en·tre·pre·neur ECON Unternehmer(in)
en·tre·pre·neu·ri·al ECON unternehmerisch
en·trust anvertrauen (***s.th. to s.o.*** j-m et.); *j-n* betrauen (***with*** mit)
en·try Eintreten *n*, Eintritt *m*; Einreise *f*; Beitritt *m* (***into*** zu); Einlass *m*, Zutritt *m*; Zugang *m*, Eingang *m*, Einfahrt *f*; Eintrag(ung *f*) *m*; Stichwort *n*; SPORT Nennung *f*, Meldung *f*; ***no entry!*** Zutritt verboten!, MOT keine Einfahrt!
en·try per·mit Einreiseerlaubnis *f*, -genehmigung *f*
en·try·phone Türsprechanlage *f*
en·try vi·sa Einreisevisum *n*
en·twine ineinander schlingen
e·nu·me·rate aufzählen
en·vel·op (ein)hüllen, einwickeln
en·ve·lope Briefumschlag *m*
en·vi·a·ble beneidenswert
en·vi·ous neidisch
en·vi·ron·ment Umgebung *f*, *a.* Milieu *n*; Umwelt *f*
en·vi·ron·men·tal Milieu...; Umwelt...
en·vi·ron·mental·ist Umweltschützer(in)
en·vi·ron·men·tal law Umweltschutzgesetz *n*
environmental pol·lu·tion Umweltverschmutzung *f*
en·vi·ron·ment friend·ly umweltfreundlich
en·vi·rons Umgebung *f*
en·vis·age sich *et.* vorstellen
en·voy Gesandte *m*, Gesandtin *f*
en·vy **1.** Neid *m*; **2.** beneiden
ep·ic **1.** episch; **2.** Epos *n*
ep·i·dem·ic MED **1.** seuchenartig; ***epidemic disease*** → **2.** Epidemie *f*, Seuche *f*
ep·i·der·mis ANAT Oberhaut *f*
ep·i·lep·sy MED Epilepsie *f*
ep·i·log, *Br* **ep·i·logue** Epilog *m*, Nachwort *n*
e·pis·co·pal REL bischöflich
ep·i·sode Episode *f*
ep·i·taph Grabinschrift *f*
e·poch Epoche *f*, Zeitalter *n*
eq·ua·ble ausgeglichen (*a.* METEOR)
e·qual **1.** gleich; gleichmäßig; ***equal to*** *fig* gewachsen (*dat*); ***equal opportunities*** Chancengleichheit *f*; ***equal rights for women*** Gleichberechtigung *f* der Frau; **2.** Gleiche *m*, *f*; **3.** gleichen (*dat*)
e·qual·i·ty Gleichheit *f*
e·qual·i·za·tion Gleichstellung *f*; Ausgleich *m*
e·qual·ize gleichmachen, gleichstellen, angleichen; SPORT ausgleichen
e·qual·iz·er SPORT Ausgleich *m*, Ausgleichstor *n*, -treffer *m*
eq·ua·nim·i·ty Gleichmut *m*
e·qua·tion MATH Gleichung *f*
e·qua·tor Äquator *m*

e·qui·lib·ri·um Gleichgewicht *n*
e·quip ausrüsten
e·quip·ment Ausrüstung *f*, Ausstattung *f*; TECH Einrichtung *f*; *fig* Rüstzeug *n*
e·quiv·a·lent **1.** gleichwertig, äquivalent; gleichbedeutend (***to*** mit); **2.** Äquivalent *n*, Gegenwert *m*
e·ra Zeitrechnung *f*; Zeitalter *n*
e·rad·i·cate ausrotten
e·rase ausradieren, ausstreichen, löschen (*a.* EDP); *fig* auslöschen
e·ras·er Radiergummi *m*
e·rect **1.** aufrecht; **2.** aufrichten; *Denkmal etc* errichten; aufstellen
e·rec·tion Errichtung *f*; MED Erektion *f*
er·mine ZO Hermelin *n*
e·rode GEOL erodieren
e·ro·sion GEOL Erosion *f*
e·rot·ic erotisch
err (sich) irren
er·rand Botengang *m*, Besorgung *f*; ***go on an errand, run an errand*** e-e Besorgung machen
errand boy Laufbursche *m*
er·rat·ic sprunghaft, unstet, unberechenbar
er·ro·ne·ous irrig
er·ror Irrtum *m*, Fehler *m* (*a.* EDP); ***in error*** irrtümlicherweise; ***error of judg(e)ment*** Fehleinschätzung *f*; ***errors excepted*** ECON Irrtümer vorbehalten
error mes·sage EDP Fehlermeldung *f*
e·rupt ausbrechen (*volcano etc*); durchbrechen (*teeth*)
e·rup·tion (*Vulkan-*) Ausbruch *m*; MED Ausschlag *m*
ESA ABBR *of* ***European Space Agency*** Europäische Weltraumbehörde
es·ca·late eskalieren; ECON steigen, in die Höhe gehen
es·ca·la·tion Eskalation *f*
es·ca·la·tor Rolltreppe *f*
es·ca·lope GASTR (*esp* Wiener) Schnitzel *n*
es·cape **1.** entgehen (*dat*); entkommen, entrinnen (*both dat*); entweichen; *j-m* entfallen; **2.** Entrinnen *n*; Entweichen *n*, Flucht *f*; ***have a narrow escape*** mit knapper Not davonkommen
es·cape chute AVIAT Notrutsche *f*
es·cape key EDP Escape-Taste *f*
es·cort **1.** MIL Eskorte *f*; Geleit(schutz *m*) *n*; **2.** MIL eskortieren; AVIAT, MAR Geleit (-schutz) geben; geleiten
es·cutch·eon Wappenschild *m*, *n*
es·pe·cial besondere(r, -s);
es·pe·cial·ly besonders
es·pi·o·nage Spionage *f*
es·pla·nade (*esp* Strand)Promenade *f*
es·say Aufsatz *m*, kurze Abhandlung, Essay *m*, *n*
es·sence Wesen *n*; Essenz *f*; Extrakt *m*
es·sen·tial **1.** wesentlich; unentbehrlich; **2.** *mst pl das* Wesentliche
es·sen·tial·ly im Wesentlichen, in der Hauptsache
es·tab·lish einrichten, errichten; ***establish o.s.*** sich etablieren *or* niederlassen; beweisen, nachweisen
es·tab·lish·ment Einrichtung *f*, Errichtung *f*; ECON Unternehmen *n*, Firma *f*; ***the Establishment*** das Establishment, die etablierte Macht, die herrschende Schicht
es·tate (großes) Grundstück, Landsitz *m*, Gut *n*; JUR Besitz *m*, (Erb)Masse *f*, Nachlass *m*; ***housing estate*** (Wohn)Siedlung *f*; ***industrial estate*** Industriegebiet *n*; ***real estate*** Liegenschaften *pl*
estate a·gent *Br* Grundstücks-, Immobilienmakler *m*
estate car *Br* MOT Kombiwagen *m*
es·teem **1.** Achtung *f*, Ansehen *n* (***with*** bei); **2.** achten, (hoch) schätzen
es·thet·ic ästhetisch
es·thet·ics Ästhetik *f*
es·ti·mate **1.** (ab-, ein)schätzen; veranschlagen; **2.** Schätzung *f*; (Kosten)Voranschlag *m*
es·ti·ma·tion Meinung *f*; Achtung *f*, Wertschätzung *f*
es·tranged entfremdet
es·trange·ment Entfremdung *f*
es·tu·a·ry weite Flussmündung
etch ätzen; radieren
etch·ing Radierung *f*; Kupferstich *m*
e·ter·nal ewig
e·ter·ni·ty Ewigkeit *f*
e·ther Äther *m*
e·the·re·al ätherisch (*a. fig*)
eth·i·cal sittlich, ethisch
eth·ics Sittenlehre *f*, Ethik *f*
eu·ro Euro *m*
Eu·ro·cheque *Br* Eurocheque *m*
Eu·rope Europa *n*
Eu·ro·pe·an **1.** europäisch; **2.** Europäer(in)
European Com·mu·ni·ty (ABBR ***EC***) Europäische Gemeinschaft (ABBR EG)
e·vac·u·ate entleeren; evakuieren; *Haus etc* räumen
e·vade (geschickt) ausweichen (*dat*); umgehen
e·val·u·ate schätzen; abschätzen, bewerten, beurteilen
e·vap·o·rate verdunsten, verdampfen (lassen)
evaporated milk Kondensmilch *f*
e·vap·o·ra·tion Verdunstung *f*, Verdamp-

fung *f*
e·va·sion Umgehung *f*, Vermeidung *f*; (*Steuer*)Hinterziehung *f*; Ausflucht *f*
e·va·sive ausweichend; ***be evasive*** ausweichen
eve Vorabend *m*; Vortag *m*; ***on the eve of*** unmittelbar vor (*dat*), am Vorabend (*gen*)
e·ven **1.** *adj* eben, gleich; gleichmäßig; ausgeglichen; glatt; gerade (*Zahl*); ***get even with s.o.*** es j-m heimzahlen; **2.** *adv* selbst, sogar, auch; ***not even*** nicht einmal; ***even though, even if*** wenn auch; **3.** ***even out*** sich einpendeln; sich ausgleichen
eve·ning Abend *m*; ***in the evening*** am Abend, abends
evening class·es Abendkurs *m*, Abendunterricht *m*
evening dress Gesellschaftsanzug *m*; Frack *m*, Smoking *m*; Abendkleid *n*
e·ven·song REL Abendgottesdienst *m*
e·vent Ereignis *n*; Fall *m*; SPORT Disziplin *f*; SPORT Wettbewerb *m*; ***at all events*** auf alle Fälle; ***in the event of*** im Falle (*gen*)
e·vent·ful ereignisreich
e·ven·tu·al(·ly) schließlich
ev·er immer (wieder); je(mals); ***ever after, ever since*** seitdem; ***ever so*** F sehr, noch so; ***for ever*** für immer, auf ewig; ***Yours ever, …, Ever yours, …*** Viele Grüße, dein(e) *or* Ihr(e), …; ***have you ever been to Boston?*** bist du schon einmal in Boston gewesen?
ev·er·green **1.** immergrün; unverwüstlich, *esp* immer wieder gern gehört; **2.** immergrüne Pflanze; MUS Evergreen *m, n*
ev·er·last·ing ewig
ev·er·more: (***for***) ***evermore*** für immer
ev·ery jede(r, -s); alle(r, -s); ***every now and then*** von Zeit zu Zeit, dann und wann; ***every one of them*** jeder von ihnen; ***every other day*** jeden zweiten Tag, alle zwei Tage
ev·ery·bod·y jeder(mann)
ev·ery·day Alltags…
ev·ery·one jeder(mann)
ev·ery·thing alles
ev·ery·where überall(hin)
e·vict JUR zur Räumung zwingen; *j-n* gewaltsam vertreiben
ev·i·dence Beweis(material *n*) *m*, Beweise *pl*; (Zeugen)Aussage *f*; ***give evidence*** (als Zeuge) aussagen
ev·i·dent augenscheinlich, offensichtlich
e·vil **1.** übel, schlimm, böse; **2.** Übel *n*; *das* Böse
e·vil-mind·ed bösartig
e·voke (herauf)beschwören; *Erinnerungen* wachrufen
ev·o·lu·tion Entwicklung *f*; BIOL Evolution *f*
e·volve (sich) entwickeln
ewe ZO Mutterschaf *n*
ex *prp* ECON ab; ***ex works*** ab Werk
ex… Ex…, ehemalig
ex·act **1.** exakt, genau; **2.** fordern, verlangen
ex·act·ing streng, genau; aufreibend, anstrengend
ex·act·ly exakt, genau; ***exactly!*** ganz recht!, genau!
ex·act·ness Genauigkeit *f*
ex·ag·ge·rate übertreiben
ex·ag·ge·ra·tion Übertreibung *f*
ex·am F Examen *n*
ex·am·i·na·tion Examen *n*, Prüfung *f*; Untersuchung *f*; JUR Vernehmung *f*, Verhör *n*
ex·am·ine untersuchen; JUR vernehmen, verhören; PED *etc* prüfen (***in*** in *dat*; ***on*** über *acc*)
ex·am·ple Beispiel *n*; Vorbild *n*, Muster *n*; ***for example*** zum Beispiel
ex·as·pe·rate wütend machen
ex·as·pe·rat·ing ärgerlich
ex·ca·vate ausgraben, ausheben, ausschachten
ex·ceed überschreiten; übertreffen
ex·ceed·ing übermäßig
ex·ceed·ing·ly außerordentlich, überaus
ex·cel *v/t* übertreffen; *v/i* sich auszeichnen
ex·cel·lence ausgezeichnete Qualität
Ex·cel·lency Exzellenz *f*
ex·cel·lent ausgezeichnet, hervorragend
ex·cept **1.** ausnehmen, ausschließen; **2.** *prp* ausgenommen, außer; ***except for*** abgesehen von, bis auf (*acc*)
ex·cept·ing *prp* ausgenommen
ex·cep·tion Ausnahme *f*; Einwand *m* (***to*** gegen); ***make an exception*** e-e Ausnahme machen; ***take exception to*** Anstoß nehmen an (*dat*); ***without exception*** ohne Ausnahme, ausnahmslos
ex·cep·tion·al außergewöhnlich
ex·cep·tion·al·ly ungewöhnlich, außergewöhnlich
ex·cerpt Auszug *m*
ex·cess **1.** Übermaß *n*; Überschuss *m*; Ausschweifung *f*; **2.** Mehr…
excess baggage AVIAT Übergepäck *n*
excess fare (Fahrpreis)Zuschlag *m*
ex·ces·sive übermäßig, übertrieben
ex·cess lug·gage → ***excess baggage***
excess post·age Nachgebühr *f*
ex·change **1.** (aus-, ein-, um)tauschen (***for*** gegen); wechseln; **2.** (Aus-, Um-) Tausch *m*; (*esp* Geld)Wechsel *m*; ECON *a.* ***bill of***

exchange Wechsel *m*; Börse *f*; Wechselstube *f*; TEL Fernsprechamt *n*; ECON ***foreign exchange(s)*** Devisen *pl*; ***rate of exchange*** → ***exchange rate***
exchange of·fice Wechselstube *f*
exchange rate Wechselkurs *m*
exchange student Austauschschüler(in), Austauschstudent(in)
Ex·cheq·uer: ***Chancellor of the Exchequer*** *Br* Finanzminister *m*
ex·cise Verbrauchssteuer *f*
ex·ci·ta·ble reizbar, (leicht) erregbar
ex·cite erregen, anregen; reizen
ex·cit·ed erregt, aufgeregt
ex·cite·ment Aufregung *f*, Erregung *f*
ex·cit·ing erregend, aufregend, spannend
ex·claim (aus)rufen
ex·cla·ma·tion Ausruf *m*, (Auf)Schrei *m*
exclamation mark *Br*, **exclamation point** Ausrufe-, Ausrufungszeichen *n*
ex·clude ausschließen
ex·clu·sion Ausschließung *f*, Ausschluss *m*
ex·clu·sive ausschließlich; exklusiv; Exklusiv…; ***exclusive of*** abgesehen von, ohne
ex·com·mu·ni·cate REL exkommunizieren
ex·com·mu·ni·ca·tion REL Exkommunikation *f*
ex·cre·ment Kot *m*
ex·crete MED ausscheiden
ex·cur·sion Ausflug *m*
ex·cu·sa·ble entschuldbar
ex·cuse 1. entschuldigen; ***excuse me*** entschuldige(n Sie); **2.** Entschuldigung *f*
ex·di·rec·to·ry num·ber *Br* TEL Geheimnummer *f*
ex·e·cute ausführen; vollziehen; MUS vortragen; hinrichten; JUR *Testament* vollstrecken
ex·e·cu·tion Ausführung *f*; Vollziehung *f*; JUR (Zwangs-) Vollstreckung *f*; Hinrichtung *f*; MUS Vortrag *m*; ***put*** *or* ***carry a plan into execution*** e-n Plan ausführen *or* verwirklichen
ex·e·cu·tion·er JUR Henker *m*, Scharfrichter *m*
ex·ec·u·tive 1. vollziehend, ausübend, POL Exekutiv…; ECON leitend; **2.** POL Exekutive *f*, vollziehende Gewalt; ECON *der, die* leitende Angestellte
ex·em·pla·ry vorbildlich
ex·em·pli·fy veranschaulichen
ex·empt 1. befreit, frei; **2.** ausnehmen, befreien
ex·er·cise 1. Übung *f*; Ausübung *f*; PED Übung(sarbeit) *f*, Schulaufgabe *f*; MIL Manöver *n*; (körperliche) Bewegung; ***do one's exercises*** Gymnastik machen; ***take exercise*** sich Bewegung machen; **2.** üben; ausüben; (sich) bewegen; sich Bewegung machen; MIL exerzieren
ex·er·cise book Schul-, Schreibheft *n*
ex·ert *Einfluss etc* ausüben; ***exert o.s.*** sich anstrengen *or* bemühen
ex·er·tion Ausübung *f*; Anstrengung *f*, Strapaze *f*
ex·hale ausatmen; *Gas, Geruch etc* verströmen; *Rauch* ausstoßen
ex·haust 1. erschöpfen; *Vorräte* ver-, aufbrauchen; **2.** TECH Auspuff *m*; *a.* ***exhaust fumes*** TECH Auspuff-, Abgase *pl*
ex·haust·ed erschöpft, aufgebraucht (*supplies*), vergriffen (*book*)
ex·haus·tion Erschöpfung *f*
ex·haus·tive erschöpfend
ex·haust pipe TECH Auspuffrohr *n*
ex·hib·it 1. ausstellen; vorzeigen; *fig* zeigen, zur Schau stellen; **2.** Ausstellungsstück *n*; JUR Beweisstück *n*
ex·hi·bi·tion Ausstellung *f*; Zurschaustellung *f*
ex·hil·a·rat·ing erregend, berauschend
ex·hort ermahnen
ex·ile 1. Exil *n*; im Exil Lebende *m, f*; **2.** ins Exil schicken
ex·ist existieren; vorhanden sein; leben; bestehen
ex·ist·ence Existenz *f*; Vorhandensein *n*, Vorkommen *n*; Leben *n*, Dasein *n*
ex·ist·ent vorhanden
ex·it 1. Abgang *m*; Ausgang *m*; (Autobahn)Ausfahrt *f*; Ausreise *f*; **2.** *v/i* verlassen; EDP (das Programm) beenden; ***exit Macbeth*** THEA Macbeth (geht) ab
ex·o·dus Auszug *m*; Abwanderung *f*; ***general exodus*** allgemeiner Aufbruch
ex·on·e·rate entlasten, entbinden, befreien
ex·or·bi·tant übertrieben, maßlos; unverschämt (*price etc*)
ex·or·cize *böse Geister* beschwören, austreiben (***from*** aus); befreien (***of*** von)
ex·ot·ic exotisch; fremd(artig)
ex·pand ausbreiten; (sich) ausdehnen *or* erweitern; ECON *a.* expandieren
ex·panse weite Fläche, Weite *f*
ex·pan·sion Ausbreitung *f*; Ausdehnung *f*, Erweiterung *f*
ex·pan·sive mitteilsam
ex·pat·ri·ate *j-n* ausbürgern, *j-m* die Staatsangehörigkeit aberkennen
ex·pect erwarten; F annehmen; ***be expecting*** in anderen Umständen sein
ex·pec·tant erwartungsvoll; ***expectant mother*** werdende Mutter
ex·pec·ta·tion Erwartung *f*; Hoffnung *f*,

Aussicht *f*
ex·pe·dient **1.** zweckdienlich, zweckmäßig; ratsam; **2.** (Hilfs)Mittel *n*, (Not)Behelf *m*
ex·pe·di·tion Expedition *f*, (Forschungs)-Reise *f*
ex·pe·di·tious schnell

E

ex·pel (***from***) vertreiben (aus); ausweisen (aus); ausschließen (von, aus)
ex·pen·di·ture Ausgaben *pl*, (Kosten-) Aufwand *m*
ex·pense Ausgaben *pl*; *pl* ECON Unkosten *pl*, Spesen *pl*, Auslagen *pl*; ***at the expense of*** auf Kosten (*gen*)
ex·pen·sive kostspielig, teuer
ex·pe·ri·ence **1.** Erfahrung *f*; (Le-bens)-Praxis *f*; Erlebnis *n*; **2.** erfahren, erleben
ex·pe·rienced erfahren
ex·per·i·ment **1.** Versuch *m*; ***experiment with animals*** MED Tierversuch *m*; **2.** experimentieren
ex·per·i·men·tal Versuchs…
ex·pert **1.** erfahren, geschickt; fachmännisch; **2.** Fachmann *m*; Sachverständige *m, f*
ex·pi·ra·tion Ablauf *m*, Ende *n*; Verfall *m*
ex·pire ablaufen, erlöschen; verfallen
ex·plain erklären
ex·pla·na·tion Erklärung *f*
ex·pli·cit ausdrücklich; ausführlich; offen, deutlich; (***sexually***) ***explicit*** freizügig (*film etc*)
ex·plode *v/t* zur Explosion bringen; *v/i* explodieren; *fig* ausbrechen (***with*** in *acc*), platzen (***with*** vor); *fig* sprunghaft ansteigen
ex·ploit **1.** (Helden)Tat *f*; **2.** ausbeuten; *fig* ausnutzen
ex·ploi·ta·tion Ausbeutung *f*, Auswertung *f*, Verwertung *f*, Abbau *m*
ex·plo·ra·tion Erforschung *f*
ex·plore erforschen
ex·plor·er Forscher(in); Forschungsreisende *m, f*
ex·plo·sion Explosion *f*; *fig* Ausbruch *m*; *fig* sprunghafter Anstieg
ex·plo·sive **1.** explosiv; *fig* aufbrausend; *fig* sprunghaft ansteigend; **2.** Sprengstoff *m*
ex·po·nent MATH Exponent *m*, Hochzahl *f*; Vertreter(in), Verfechter(in)
ex·port ECON **1.** exportieren, ausführen; **2.** Export *m*, Ausfuhr *f*; *mst pl* Export-, Ausfuhrartikel *m*
ex·por·ta·tion ECON Ausfuhr *f*
ex·port·er ECON Exporteur *m*
ex·pose aussetzen; PHOT belichten; *Waren* ausstellen; *j-n* entlarven, bloßstellen, *et.* aufdecken
ex·po·si·tion Ausstellung *f*
ex·po·sure Aussetzen *n*, Ausgesetztsein *n* (***to*** *dat*); *fig* Bloßstellung *f*, Aufdeckung *f*, Enthüllung *f*, Entlarvung *f*; PHOT Belichtung *f*; PHOT Aufnahme *f*; ***die of exposure*** an Unterkühlung sterben
exposure me·ter PHOT Belichtungsmesser *m*
ex·press **1.** ausdrücklich, deutlich; Express…, Eil…; **2.** Eilbote *m*; Schnellzug *m*; ***by express*** → **3.** *adv* durch Eilboten; als Eilgut; **4.** äußern, ausdrücken
ex·pres·sion Ausdruck *m*
ex·pres·sion·less ausdruckslos
ex·pres·sive ausdrucksvoll; ***be expressive of*** *et.* ausdrücken
ex·press let·ter *Br* Eilbrief *m*
ex·press·ly ausdrücklich, eigens
ex·press train Schnellzug *m*
ex·press·way Schnellstraße *f*
ex·pro·pri·ate JUR enteignen
ex·pul·sion (***from***) Vertreibung *f* (aus); Ausweisung *f* (aus)
ex·pur·gate reinigen
ex·qui·site erlesen; fein
ex·tant noch vorhanden
ex·tem·po·re aus dem Stegreif
ex·tem·po·rize aus dem Stegreif sprechen *or* spielen
ex·tend (aus)dehnen, (aus)weiten; *Hand etc* ausstrecken; *Betrieb etc* vergrößern, ausbauen; *Frist, Pass etc* verlängern; sich ausdehnen *or* erstrecken
ex·tend·ed fam·i·ly Großfamilie *f*
ex·ten·sion Ausdehnung *f*; Vergrößerung *f*, Erweiterung *f*; (Frist)Verlängerung *f*; ARCH Erweiterung *f*, Anbau *m*; TEL Nebenanschluss *m*, (-)Apparat *m*; *a.* ***extension cord*** (*Br* ***lead***) ELECTR Verlängerungskabel *n*, -schnur *f*
ex·ten·sive ausgedehnt, umfassend
ex·tent Ausdehnung *f*; Umfang *m*, (Aus)-Maß *n*, Grad *m*; ***to some extent, to a certain extent*** bis zu e-m gewissen Grade; ***to such an extent that*** so sehr, dass
ex·ten·u·ate abschwächen, mildern; beschönigen; ***extenuating circumstances*** JUR mildernde Umstände *pl*
ex·te·ri·or **1.** äußerlich, äußere(r, -s), Außen…; **2.** *das* Äußere; Außenseite *f*; äußere Erscheinung
ex·ter·mi·nate ausrotten (*a. fig*), vernichten, *Ungeziefer, Unkraut a.* vertilgen
ex·ter·nal äußere(r, -s), äußerlich, Außen…
ex·tinct erloschen; ausgestorben
ex·tinc·tion Erlöschen *n*; Aussterben *n*, Untergang *m*; Vernichtung *f*, Zerstörung *f*

ex·tin·guish (aus)löschen; vernichten
ex·tin·guish·er (*Feuer*)Löscher *m*
ex·tort erpressen (***from*** von)
ex·tra **1.** *adj* zusätzlich, Extra…, Sonder…; ***be extra*** gesondert berechnet werden; **2.** *adv* extra, besonders; ***charge extra for*** *et.* gesondert berechnen; **3.** Sonderleistung *f*; *esp* MOT Extra *n*; Zuschlag *m*; Extrablatt *n*; THEA, *film*: Statist(in)
ex·tract **1.** Auszug *m*; **2.** (heraus)ziehen; herauslocken; ableiten, herleiten
ex·trac·tion (Heraus)Ziehen *n*; Herkunft *f*
ex·tra·dite ausliefern; *j-s* Auslieferung erwirken;
ex·tra·di·tion Auslieferung *f*
extra·or·di·na·ry außerordentlich; ungewöhnlich; Sonder…
ex·tra pay Zulage *f*
ex·tra·ter·res·tri·al außerirdisch
ex·tra time SPORT (Spiel)Verlängerung *f*
ex·trav·a·gance Übertriebenheit *f*; Verschwendung *f*; Extravaganz *f*
ex·trav·a·gant übertrieben, überspannt; verschwenderisch; extravagant
ex·treme **1.** äußerste(r, -s), größte(r, -s), höchste(r, -s); außergewöhnlich; ***extreme right*** POL rechtsextrem(istisch); ***extreme right wing*** POL rechtsradikal; **2.** *das* Äußerste; Extrem *n*; höchster Grad
ex·treme·ly äußerst, höchst
ex·trem·ism POL Extremismus *m*
ex·trem·ist POL Extremist(in)
ex·trem·i·ties Gliedmaßen *pl*, Extremitäten *pl*
ex·trem·i·ty *das* Äußerste; höchste Not; äußerste Maßnahme
ex·tri·cate herauswinden, herausziehen, befreien
ex·tro·vert Extrovertierte *m*, *f*
ex·u·be·rance Fülle *f*; Überschwang *m*
ex·u·be·rant reichlich, üppig; überschwänglich; ausgelassen
ex·ult frohlocken, jubeln
eye **1.** ANAT Auge *n*; Blick *m*; Öhr *n*; Öse *f*; ***see eye to eye with s.o.*** mit j-m völlig übereinstimmen; ***be up to the eyes in work*** bis über die Ohren in Arbeit stecken; ***with an eye to s.th.*** im Hinblick auf et.; **2.** ansehen; mustern
eye·ball ANAT Augapfel *m*
eye·brow ANAT Augenbraue *f*
eye-catch·ing ins Auge fallend, auffallend
eye doc·tor F Augenarzt *m*, -ärztin *f*
eye·glass·es *a.* ***pair of eyeglasses*** Brille *f*
eye·lash ANAT Augenwimper *f*
eye·lid ANAT Augenlid *n*
eye·lin·er Eyeliner *m*
eye-o·pen·er: ***that was an eye-opener to me*** das hat mir die Augen geöffnet
eye shad·ow Lidschatten *m*
eye·sight Augen(licht *n*) *pl*, Sehkraft *f*
eye·sore F Schandfleck *m*
eye spe·cial·ist Augenarzt *m*, -ärztin *f*
eye·strain Ermüdung *f or* Überanstrengung *f* der Augen
eye·wit·ness Augenzeuge *m*, -zeugin *f*

F

F, f F, f *n*
fa·ble Fabel *f*; Sage *f*
fab·ric Gewebe *n*, Stoff *m*; Struktur *f*
fab·ri·cate fabrizieren (*mst fig*)
fab·u·lous sagenhaft, der Sage angehörend; fabelhaft
fa·cade, fa·çade ARCH Fassade *f*
face **1.** Gesicht *n*; Gesichtsausdruck *m*, Miene *f*; (Ober)Fläche *f*; Vorderseite *f*; Zifferblatt *n*; ***face to face with*** Auge in Auge mit; ***save*** (***lose***) ***one's face*** das Gesicht wahren (verlieren); ***on the face of it*** auf den ersten Blick; ***pull a long face*** ein langes Gesicht machen; ***have the face to do s.th.*** die Stirn haben, et. zu tun; **2.** *v/t* ansehen; gegenüberstehen (*dat*); (hinaus)gehen auf (*acc*); die Stirn bieten (*dat*); einfassen; ARCH bekleiden; *v/i*: ***face about*** sich umdrehen
face·cloth, *Br* **face flan·nel** Waschlappen *m*
face·lift Facelifting *n*, Gesichtsstraffung *f*; *fig* Renovierung *f*, Verschönerung *f*
fa·ce·tious witzig
fa·cial **1.** Gesichts…; **2.** Gesichtsbehand-

lung *f*
fa·cile leicht; oberflächlich
fa·cil·i·tate erleichtern
fa·cil·i·ty Leichtigkeit *f*; Oberflächlichkeit *f*; *mst pl* Erleichterung(en *pl*) *f*; Einrichtung(en *pl*) *f*, Anlage(n *pl*) *f*
fac·ing TECH Verkleidung *f*; *pl* Besatz *m*
fact Tatsache *f*, Wirklichkeit *f*, Wahrheit *f*; Tat *f*; *pl* Daten; ***in fact*** in der Tat, tatsächlich
fac·tion *esp* POL Splittergruppe *f*; Zwietracht *f*
fac·ti·tious künstlich
fac·tor Faktor *m*
fac·to·ry Fabrik *f*
fac·ul·ty Fähigkeit *f*; Kraft *f*; *fig* Gabe *f*; UNIV Fakultät *f*; Lehrkörper *m*
fad Mode *f*, Modeerscheinung *f*, -torheit *f*; (vorübergehende) Laune
fade (ver)welken (lassen); verschießen, verblassen (*color*); schwinden; immer schwächer werden (*person*); *film, radio,* TV ***fade in*** auf- *or* eingeblendet werden; auf- *or* einblenden; ***fade out*** aus- *or* abgeblendet werden; aus- *or* abblenden; ***faded jeans*** ausgewaschene Jeans *pl*
fail **1.** *v/i* versagen; misslingen, fehlschlagen; versiegen; nachlassen; durchfallen (*candidate*); *v/t* im Stich lassen; *j-n in e-r Prüfung* durchfallen lassen; **2.** ***without fail*** mit Sicherheit, ganz bestimmt
fail·ure Versagen *n*; Fehlschlag *m*, Misserfolg *m*; Versäumnis *n*; Versager *m*, F Niete *f*
faint **1.** schwach, matt; **2.** ohnmächtig werden, in Ohnmacht fallen (***with*** vor); **3.** Ohnmacht *f*
faint-heart·ed verzagt
fair[1] gerecht, ehrlich, anständig, fair; recht gut, ansehnlich; schön (*weather*); klar (*sky*); blond (*hair*); hell (*skin*); ***play fair*** fair spielen; *fig* sich an die Spielregeln halten
fair[2] (Jahr)Markt *m*; Volksfest *n*; Ausstellung *f*, Messe *f*
fair game *fig* Freiwild *n*
fair·ground Rummelplatz *m*
fair·ly gerecht; ziemlich
fair·ness Gerechtigkeit *f*, Fairness *f*
fair play SPORT *and fig* Fair Play *n*, Fairness *f*
fai·ry Fee *f*; Zauberin *f*; Elf *m*, Elfe *f*
fai·ry·land Feen-, Märchenland *n*
fai·ry sto·ry, fairy tale Märchen *n* (*a. fig*)
faith Glaube *m*; Vertrauen *n*
faith·ful treu (***to*** *dat*); ***Yours faithfully*** Hochachtungsvoll (*letter*)
faith·less treulos
fake **1.** Schwindel *m*; Fälschung *f*; Schwindler *m*; **2.** fälschen; imitieren, nachmachen; vortäuschen, simulieren; **3.** gefälscht; fingiert
fal·con ZO Falke *m*
fall **1.** Fallen *n*, Fall *m*; Sturz *m*; Verfall *m*; Einsturz *m*; Herbst *m*; ECON Sinken *n* (*of prices etc*); Gefälle *n*; *mst pl* Wasserfall *m*; **2.** fallen, stürzen; ab-, einfallen; sinken; sich legen (*wind*); *in e-n Zustand* verfallen; ***fall ill, fall sick*** krank werden; ***fall in love with*** sich verlieben in (*acc*); ***fall short of*** *den Erwartungen etc* nicht entsprechen; ***fall back*** zurückweichen; ***fall back on*** *fig* zurückgreifen auf (*acc*); ***fall for*** hereinfallen auf (*acc*); F sich in *j-n* verknallen; ***fall off*** zurückgehen (*business, demand etc*), nachlassen; ***fall on*** herfallen über (*acc*); ***fall out*** sich streiten (***with*** mit); ***fall through*** durchfallen (*a. fig*); ***fall to*** reinhauen, tüchtig zugreifen
fal·la·cious trügerisch
fal·la·cy Trugschluss *m*
fall guy F *der* Lackierte, *der* Dumme
fal·li·ble fehlbar
fall·ing star Sternschnuppe *f*
fall·out Fall-out *m*, radioaktiver Niederschlag
fal·low ZO falb; AGR brach(liegend)
false falsch
false·hood, false·ness Falschheit *f*; Unwahrheit *f*
false start Fehlstart *m*
fal·si·fi·ca·tion (Ver)Fälschung *f*
fal·si·fy (ver)fälschen
fal·si·ty Falschheit *f*, Unwahrheit *f*
fal·ter schwanken; stocken (*voice*); stammeln; *fig* zaudern
fame Ruf *m*, Ruhm *m*
famed berühmt (***for*** wegen)
fa·mil·i·ar **1.** vertraut; gewohnt; familiär; **2.** Vertraute *m, f*
fa·mil·i·ar·i·ty Vertrautheit *f*; (plumpe) Vertraulichkeit
fa·mil·i·ar·ize vertraut machen
fam·i·ly **1.** Familie *f*; **2.** Familien…, Haus…; ***be in the family way*** F in anderen Umständen sein
family al·low·ance → ***child benefit***
family doc·tor Hausarzt *m*
family name Familien-, Nachname *m*
family plan·ning Familienplanung *f*
family tree Stammbaum *m*
fam·ine Hungersnot *f*; Knappheit *f* (***of*** an *dat*)
fam·ished verhungert; ***be famished*** F am Verhungern sein
fa·mous berühmt
fan[1] **1.** Fächer *m*; Ventilator *m*; **2.** (zu-)fä-

cheln; anfachen; *fig* entfachen
fan[2] (*Sport- etc*)Fan *m*
fa·nat·ic Fanatiker(in)
fa·nat·i·cal fanatisch
fan belt TECH Keilriemen *m*
fan·ci·er BOT, ZO Liebhaber(in), Züchter(in)
fan·ci·ful fantastisch
fan club Fanklub *m*
fan·cy **1.** Fantasie *f*; Einbildung *f*; plötzlicher Einfall, Idee *f*; Laune *f*; Vorliebe *f*, Neigung *f*; **2.** ausgefallen; Fantasie…; **3.** sich vorstellen; sich einbilden; ***fancy that!*** stell dir vor!, denk nur!; sieh mal einer an!
fan·cy ball Kostümfest *n*, Maskenball *m*
fancy dress (Masken)Kostüm *n*
fan·cy-free → ***footloose***
fan·cy goods Modeartikel *pl*, -waren *pl*
fan·cy·work Stickerei *f*
fang ZO Reiß-, Fangzahn *m*; Hauer *m*; Giftzahn *m*
fan mail Fanpost *f*, Verehrerpost *f*
fan·tas·tic fantastisch
fan·ta·sy Fantasie *f*
far **1.** *adj* fern, entfernt, weit; **2.** *adv* fern; weit; (sehr) viel; ***as far as*** bis; ***in so far as*** insofern als
far·a·way weit entfernt
fare **1.** Fahrgeld *n*; Fahrgast *m*; Verpflegung *f*, Kost *f*; **2.** *gut* leben; ***he fared well*** es (er)ging ihm gut
fare dodg·er Schwarzfahrer(in)
fare·well **1.** *int* lebe(n Sie) wohl!; **2.** Abschied *m*, Lebewohl *n*
far·fetched *fig* weit hergeholt, gesucht
farm **1.** Bauernhof *m*, Gut *n*, Gehöft *n*, Farm *f*; **2.** *Land, Hof* bewirtschaften
farm·er Bauer *m*, Landwirt *m*, Farmer *m*
farm·hand Landarbeiter(in)
farm·house Bauernhaus *n*
farm·ing **1.** Acker…, landwirtschaftlich; **2.** Landwirtschaft *f*
farm·stead Bauernhof *m*, Gehöft *n*
farm·yard Wirtschaftshof *m*
far-off entfernt, fern
far right POL rechtsgerichtet
far·sight·ed weitsichtig, *fig a.* weitblickend
fas·ci·nate faszinieren
fas·ci·nat·ing faszinierend
fas·ci·na·tion Zauber *m*, Reiz *m*, Faszination *f*
fas·cism POL Faschismus *m*
fas·cist POL **1.** Faschist *m*; **2.** faschistisch
fash·ion Mode *f*; Art *f* und Weise *f*; ***be in fashion*** in Mode sein; ***out of fashion*** unmodern; **1.** formen, gestalten
fash·ion·a·ble modisch, elegant; in Mode
fash·ion pa·rade, fashion show Mode(n)-schau *f*
fast[1] **1.** Fasten *n*; **2.** fasten
fast[2] schnell; fest; treu; echt, beständig (*color*); flott; ***be fast*** vorgehen (*watch*)
fast·back MOT (Wagen *m* mit) Fließheck *n*
fast breed·er (re·ac·tor) PHYS Schneller Brüter
fas·ten befestigen, festmachen, anheften, anschnallen, anbinden, zuknöpfen, zu-, verschnüren; *Blick etc* richten (***on*** auf *acc*); sich festmachen *or* schließen lassen
fas·ten·er Verschluss *m*
fast food Schnellgericht(e *pl*) *n*
fast-food res·tau·rant Schnellimbiss *m*, Schnellgaststätte *f*
fas·tid·i·ous anspruchsvoll, heikel, wählerisch, verwöhnt
fast lane MOT Überholspur *f*
fat **1.** fett; dick; fettig, fetthaltig; **2.** Fett *n*; ***be low in fat*** fettarm sein
fa·tal tödlich; verhängnisvoll, fatal (***to*** für)
fa·tal·i·ty Verhängnis *n*; tödlicher Unfall; (Todes)Opfer *n*
fate Schicksal *n*; Verhängnis *n*
fa·ther Vater *m*
Fa·ther Christ·mas *esp Br* der Weihnachtsmann, der Nikolaus
fa·ther·hood Vaterschaft *f*
fa·ther-in-law Schwiegervater *m*
fa·ther·less vaterlos
fa·ther·ly väterlich
fath·om **1.** MAR Faden *m*; **2.** MAR loten; *fig* ergründen
fath·om·less unergründlich
fa·tigue **1.** Ermüdung *f*; Strapaze *f*; **2.** ermüden
fat·ten dick *or contp* fett machen *or* werden; mästen
fat·ty fett; fettig
fau·cet TECH (Wasser)Hahn *m*
fault Fehler *m*; Defekt *m*; Schuld *f*; ***find fault with*** et. auszusetzen haben an (*dat*); ***be at fault*** Schuld haben
fault·less fehlerfrei, fehlerlos
fault·y fehlerhaft, TECH *a.* defekt
fa·vo(u)r **1.** Gunst *f*; Gefallen *m*; Begünstigung *f*; ***in favo(u)r of*** zu Gunsten von (*or gen*); ***do s.o. a favo(u)r*** j-m e-n Gefallen tun; **2.** begünstigen; bevorzugen, vorziehen; wohlwollend gegenüberstehen; SPORT favorisieren
fa·vo(u)r·a·ble günstig
fa·vo(u)r·ite **1.** Liebling *m*; SPORT Favorit *m*; **2.** Lieblings…
fawn **1.** ZO (Reh)Kitz *n*; Rehbraun *n*; **2.** rehbraun
fax **1.** Fax *n*; **2.** faxen; ***fax s.th. (through)***

F

to s.o. j-m et. faxen
fax (ma·chine) Faxgerät *n*
fear **1.** Furcht *f* (**of** vor *dat*); Befürchtung *f*; Angst *f*; **2.** (be)fürchten; sich fürchten vor (*dat*)
fear·ful furchtsam; furchtbar
fear·less furchtlos
fea·si·ble durchführbar
feast **1.** REL Fest *n*, Feiertag *m*; Festessen *n*; *fig* Fest *n*, (Hoch)Genuss *m*; **2.** *v/t* festlich bewirten; *v/i* sich gütlich tun (**on** an *dat*), schlemmen
feat große Leistung; (Helden)Tat *f*
fea·ther **1.** Feder *f*; *a. pl* Gefieder *n*; ***birds of a feather*** Leute vom gleichen Schlag; ***birds of a feather flock together*** Gleich und Gleich gesellt sich gern; ***that is a feather in his cap*** darauf kann er stolz sein; **2.** mit Federn polstern *or* schmücken; *Pfeil* fiedern
feath·er·bed verhätscheln
feath·er·brained F hohlköpfig
feath·ered zo gefiedert
feath·er·weight SPORT Federgewicht *n*, Federgewichtler *m*; Leichtgewicht *n* (*person*)
feath·er·y gefiedert; federleicht
fea·ture **1.** (Gesichts)Zug *m*; (charakteristisches) Merkmal; *radio*, TV *etc* Feature *n*; Haupt-, Spielfilm *m*; **2.** groß herausbringen; *film*: in der Hauptrolle zeigen
feature film Haupt-, Spielfilm *m*
Feb ABBR *of* ***February*** Febr., Februar *m*
Feb·ru·a·ry (ABBR ***Feb***) Februar *m*
fed·e·ral POL Bundes…
Fed·e·ral Re·pub·lic of Ger·man·y *die* Bundesrepublik Deutschland (ABBR ***BRD***)
fed·e·ra·tion POL Bundesstaat *m*; Föderation *f*, Staatenbund *m*; ECON, SPORT *etc* (Dach)Verband *m*
fee Gebühr *f*; Honorar *n*; (Mitglieds-) Beitrag *m*; Eintrittsgeld *n*
fee·ble schwach
feed **1.** Futter *n*; Nahrung *f*; Fütterung *f*; TECH Zuführung *f*, Speisung *f*; **2.** *v/t* füttern; ernähren; TECH *Maschine* speisen; EDP eingeben; AGR weiden lassen; ***be fed up with s.o.*** (***s.th.***) j-n (et.) satthaben; ***well fed*** wohlgenährt; *v/i* (fr)essen; sich ernähren; weiden
feed·back ELECTR Feed-back *n*, Rückkopplung *f*; *radio*, TV Reaktion *f*
feed·er Esser *m*
feed·er road Zubringer(straße *f*) *m*
feed·ing bot·tle (Saug)Flasche *f*
feel **1.** (sich) fühlen; befühlen; empfinden; sich anfühlen; ***feel sorry for s.o.*** j-n bedauern *or* bemitleiden; **2.** Gefühl *n*; Empfindung *f*
feel·er zo Fühler *m*
feel·ing Gefühl *n*
feign *Interesse etc* vortäuschen, *Krankheit a.* simulieren
feint Finte *f*
fell niederschlagen; fällen
fel·low **1.** Gefährte *m*, Gefährtin *f*, Kamerad(in); Gegenstück *n*; F Kerl *m*; ***old fellow*** F alter Knabe; ***the fellow of a glove*** der andere Handschuh; **2.** Mit…
fellow be·ing Mitmensch *m*
fellow cit·i·zen Mitbürger *m*
fellow coun·try·man Landsmann *m*
fel·low·ship Gemeinschaft *f*; Kameradschaft *f*
fel·low trav·el·(l)er Mitreisende *m*, *f*, Reisegefährte *m*, -gefährtin *f*; POL Mitläufer(in)
fel·on JUR Schwerverbrecher *m*
fel·o·ny JUR (schweres) Verbrechen, Kapitalverbrechen *n*
felt Filz *m*
felt pen, felt tip, felt-tip(ped) pen Filzstift *m*, Filzschreiber *m*
fe·male **1.** weiblich; **2.** *contp* Weib *n*, Weibsbild *n*; zo Weibchen *n*
fem·i·nine weiblich, Frauen…; feminin
fem·i·nism Feminismus *m*
fem·i·nist **1.** Feminist(in); **2.** feministisch
fen Fenn *n*, Sumpf-, Marschland *n*
fence **1.** Zaun *m*; *sl* Hehler *m*; **2.** *v/t*: ***fence in*** einzäunen, umzäunen; einsperren; ***fence off*** abzäunen; *v/i* SPORT fechten
fenc·er SPORT Fechter *m*
fenc·ing **1.** Einfriedung *f*; SPORT Fechten *n*; **2.** Fecht…
fend: ***fend off*** abwehren; ***fend for o.s.*** für sich selbst sorgen
fend·er Schutzvorrichtung *f*; Schutzblech *n*; MOT Kotflügel *m*; Kamingitter *n*, Kaminvorsetzer *m*
fen·nel BOT Fenchel *m*
fer·ment **1.** Ferment *n*; Gärung *f*; **2.** gären (lassen)
fer·men·ta·tion Gärung *f*
fern BOT Farn(kraut *n*) *m*
fe·ro·cious wild; grausam
fe·ro·ci·ty Wildheit *f*
fer·ret **1.** zo Frettchen *n*; *fig* Spürhund *m*; **2.** herumstöbern; ***ferret out*** aufspüren, aufstöbern
fer·ry **1.** Fähre *f*; **2.** übersetzen
fer·ry·boat Fährboot *n*, Fähre *f*
fer·ry·man Fährmann *m*
fer·tile fruchtbar; reich (**of, in** an *dat*)
fer·til·i·ty Fruchtbarkeit *f* (*a. fig*)
fer·ti·lize fruchtbar machen; befruchten; AGR düngen

fer·ti·liz·er AGR (*esp* Kunst)Dünger *m*, Düngemittel *n*
fer·vent glühend, leidenschaftlich
fer·vo(u)r Glut *f*; Inbrunst *f*
fes·ter MED eitern
fes·ti·val Fest *n*; Festival *n*, Festspiele *pl*
fes·tive festlich
fes·tiv·i·ty Festlichkeit *f*
fes·toon Girlande *f*
fetch holen; *Preis* erzielen; *Seufzer* ausstoßen
fetch·ing F reizend
fete, fête **1.** Fest *n*; ***village fete*** Dorffest *n*; **2.** feiern
fet·id stinkend
fet·ter **1.** Fessel *f*; **2.** fesseln
feud Fehde *f*
feud·al Feudal…, Lehns…
feu·dal·ism Feudalismus *m*, Feudal-, Lehnssystem *n*
fe·ver MED Fieber *n*
fe·ver·ish MED fieb(e)rig, fieberhaft (*a. fig*)
few wenige; ***a few*** ein paar, einige; ***no fewer than*** nicht weniger als; ***quite a few, a good few*** e-e ganze Menge
fi·an·cé Verlobte *m*
fi·an·cée Verlobte *f*
fi·as·co Fiasko *n*
fib F **1.** Flunkerei *f*, Schwindelei *f*; **2.** schwindeln, flunkern
fi·ber, *Br* **fi·bre** Faser *f*
fi·ber·glass TECH Fiberglas *n*, Glasfaser *f*
fi·brous faserig
fick·le wankelmütig; unbeständig
fic·tion Erfindung *f*; Prosaliteratur *f*, Belletristik *f*; Romane *pl*
fic·tion·al erdichtet; Roman…
fic·ti·tious erfunden, fiktiv
fid·dle **1.** Fiedel *f*, Geige *f*; ***play first (second) fiddle*** *esp fig* die erste (zweite) Geige spielen; ***(as) fit as a fiddle*** kerngesund; **2.** MUS fiedeln; *a.* ***fiddle about or around (with)*** herumfingern (an *dat*), spielen (mit)
fid·dler Geiger(in)
fi·del·i·ty Treue *f*; Genauigkeit *f*
fid·get F nervös machen; (herum)zappeln
fid·get·y zapp(e)lig, nervös
field Feld *n*; SPORT Spielfeld *n*; Arbeitsfeld *n*; Gebiet *n*; Bereich *m*; ***field of vision*** OPT Gesichtsfeld *n*
field e·vents SPORT Sprung- und Wurfdisziplinen *pl*
field glass·es *a.* ***pair of field glasses*** Feldstecher *m*, Fernglas *n*
field mar·shal MIL Feldmarschall *m*
field·work praktische (wissenschaftliche) Arbeit, *a.* Arbeit *f* im Gelände; ECON Feldarbeit *f*
fiend Satan *m*, Teufel *m*; F (*Frischluft-etc*)Fanatiker(in)
fiend·ish teuflisch, boshaft
fierce wild; scharf; heftig
fierce·ness Wildheit *f*, Schärfe *f*; Heftigkeit *f*
fi·er·y feurig; hitzig
fif·teen **1.** fünfzehn; **2.** Fünfzehn *f*
fif·teenth fünfzehnte(r, -s)
fifth **1.** fünfte(r, -s); **2.** Fünftel *n*
fifth·ly fünftens
fif·ti·eth fünfzigste(r, -s)
fif·ty **1.** fünfzig; **2.** Fünfzig *f*
fif·ty-fif·ty F halbe-halbe
fig BOT Feige *f*
fight **1.** Kampf *m*; MIL Gefecht *n*; Schlägerei *f*; *boxing*: Kampf *m*, Fight *m*; **2.** *v/t* bekämpfen; kämpfen gegen *or* mit, SPORT *a.* boxen gegen; *v/i* kämpfen, sich schlagen; SPORT boxen
fight·er Kämpfer *m*; SPORT Boxer *m*, Fighter *m*; *a.* ***fighter plane*** MIL Jagdflugzeug *n*
fight·ing Kampf *m*
fig·u·ra·tive bildlich
fig·ure **1.** Figur *f*; Gestalt *f*; Zahl *f*, Ziffer *f*; Preis *m*; ***be good at figures*** ein guter Rechner sein; **2.** *v/t* abbilden, darstellen; F meinen, glauben; sich *et.* vorstellen; ***figure out*** *Problem* lösen, F rauskriegen; verstehen; ***figure up*** zusammenzählen; *v/i* erscheinen, vorkommen; ***figure on*** rechnen mit
figure skat·er Eiskunstläufer(in)
figure skat·ing Eiskunstlauf *m*
fil·a·ment ELECTR Glühfaden *m*
filch F klauen, stibitzen
file[1] **1.** Ordner *m*; Karteikasten *m*; Akte *f*, Akten *pl*; Ablage *f*; EDP Datei *f*; Reihe *f*; MIL Rotte *f*; ***on file*** bei den Akten; **2.** *v/t Briefe etc* ablegen, zu den Akten nehmen, einordnen; *Antrag* einreichen, *Berufung* einlegen; *v/i* hintereinander marschieren
file[2] TECH **1.** Feile *f*; **2.** feilen
file man·age·ment EDP Dateiverwaltung *f*
file pro·tec·tion EDP Schreibschutz *m*
fil·et GASTR Filet *n*
fi·li·al kindlich, Kindes…
fil·ing Ablegen *n*
fil·ing cab·i·net Aktenschrank *m*
fill **1.** (sich) füllen; an-, aus-, erfüllen, vollfüllen; *Pfeife* stopfen; *Zahn* füllen, plombieren; ***fill in*** einsetzen; ***fill out*** (*Br* ***in***) *Formular* ausfüllen; ***fill up*** vollfüllen; sich füllen; ***fill her up!*** F MOT volltanken, bitte!; **2.** Füllung *f*; ***eat one's fill*** sich satt essen

fil·let → ***filet***
fill·ing Füllung *f*; MED (Zahn)Füllung *f*, Plombe *f*
filling sta·tion Tankstelle *f*
fil·ly zo Stutenfohlen *n*
film 1. Häutchen *n*; Membran(e) *f*; Film *m* (*a.* PHOT); ***take*** *or* ***shoot a film*** e-n Film drehen; **2.** (ver)filmen; sich verfilmen lassen
film star *esp Br* Filmstar *m*
fil·ter 1. Filter *m*; **2.** filtern
fil·ter tip Filter *m*; Filterzigarette *f*
fil·ter-tipped: ***filtertipped cigarette*** Filterzigarette *f*
filth Schmutz *m*
filth·y schmutzig; *fig* unflätig
fin zo Flosse *f*; SPORT Schwimmflosse *f*
fi·nal 1. letzte(r, -s); End…, Schluss…; endgültig; **2.** SPORT Finale *n*; *mst pl* Schlussexamen *n*, -prüfung *f*
fi·nal dis·pos·al Endlagerung *f*
fi·nal·ist SPORT Finalist(in)
fi·nal·ly endlich, schließlich; endgültig
fi·nal whis·tle SPORT Schlusspfiff *m*, Abpfiff *m*
fi·nance 1. Finanzwesen *n*; *pl* Finanzen *pl*; **2.** finanzieren
fi·nan·cial finanziell
fi·nan·cier Finanzier *m*
finch zo Fink *m*
find 1. finden; (an)treffen; herausfinden; JUR *j-n* für (*nicht*) *schuldig* erklären; beschaffen, besorgen; ***find out*** *v/t et.* herausfinden; *v/i* es herausfinden; **2.** Fund *m*, Entdeckung *f*
find·ings Befund *m*; JUR Feststellung *f*, Spruch *m*
fine[1] **1.** *adj* fein; schön; ausgezeichnet, großartig; ***I'm fine*** mir geht es gut; **2.** *adv* F sehr gut, bestens
fine[2] **1.** Geldstrafe *f*, Bußgeld *n*; **2.** zu e-r Geldstrafe verurteilen
fin·ger 1. ANAT Finger *m*; → ***cross*** 3; **2.** betasten, (herum)fingern an (*dat*)
fin·ger·nail ANAT Fingernagel *m*
fin·ger·print Fingerabdruck *m*
fin·ger·tip Fingerspitze *f*
fin·i·cky pedantisch; wählerisch
fin·ish 1. (be)enden, aufhören (mit); *a.* ***finish off*** vollenden, zu Ende führen, erledigen, *Buch etc* auslesen; *a.* ***finish off, finish up*** aufessen, austrinken; **2.** Ende *n*, Schluss *m*; SPORT Endspurt *m*, Finish *n*; Ziel *n*; Vollendung *f*, letzter Schliff
fin·ish·ing line SPORT Ziellinie *f*
Fin·land Finnland *n*
Finn Finne *m*, Finnin *f*
Finn·ish 1. finnisch; **2.** LING Finnisch *n*
fir *a.* ***fir tree*** BOT Tanne *f*
fir cone BOT Tannenzapfen *m*
fire 1. Feuer *n*; ***be on fire*** in Flammen stehen, brennen; ***catch fire*** Feuer fangen, in Brand geraten; ***set on fire, set fire to*** anzünden; **2.** *v/t* anzünden, entzünden; *fig* anfeuern; abfeuern; *Ziegel etc* brennen; F *j-n* rausschmeißen; heizen; *v/i* Feuer fangen (*a. fig*); feuern
fire a·larm Feueralarm *m*; Feuermelder *m*
fire·arms Schusswaffen *pl*
fire bri·gade *Br* Feuerwehr *f*
fire·bug F Feuerteufel *m*
fire·crack·er Knallfrosch *m*; Knallbonbon *m*, *n*
fire de·part·ment Feuerwehr *f*
fire en·gine *Br* Löschfahrzeug *n*
fire es·cape Feuerleiter *f*, -treppe *f*
fire ex·tin·guish·er Feuerlöscher *m*
fire fight·er Feuerwehrmann *m*
fire·guard *Br* Kamingitter *n*
fire hy·drant *Br* Hydrant *m*
fire·man Feuerwehrmann *m*; Heizer *m*
fire·place (offener) Kamin
fire·plug Hydrant *m*
fire·proof feuerfest
fire-rais·ing *Br* Brandstiftung *f*
fire·screen Kamingitter *n*
fire ser·vice *Br* Feuerwehr *f*
fire·side (offener) Kamin
fire sta·tion Feuerwache *f*
fire truck Löschfahrzeug *n*
fire·wood Brennholz *n*
fire·works Feuerwerk *n*
fir·ing squad MIL Exekutionskommando *n*
firm[1] fest; hart; standhaft
firm[2] Firma *f*
first 1. *adj* erste(r, -s); beste(r, -s); **2.** *adv* erstens; zuerst; ***first of all*** an erster Stelle; zu allererst; **3.** Erste(r, -s); ***at first*** zuerst, anfangs; ***from the first*** von Anfang an
first aid MED Erste Hilfe
first aid box, first aid kit Verband(s)kasten *m*
first·born erstgeborene(r, -s), älteste(r, -s)
first class RAIL *etc* 1. Klasse
first-class erstklassig
first floor Erdgeschoss *n*, *Br* erster Stock; → ***second floor***
first·hand aus erster Hand
first leg SPORT Hinspiel *n*
first·ly erstens
first name Vorname *m*
first-rate erstklassig
firth Förde *f*, Meeresarm *m*
fish 1. zo Fisch *m*; **2.** fischen, angeln
fish·bone Gräte *f*
fish·er·man Fischer *m*

fish·e·ry Fischerei *f*
fish fin·ger *Br* GASTR Fischstäbchen *n*
fish·hook Angelhaken *m*
fish·ing Fischen *n*, Angeln *n*
fishing line Angelschnur *f*
fishing rod Angelrute *f*
fishing tack·le Angelgerät *n*
fish·mon·ger *esp Br* Fischhändler *m*
fish stick GASTR Fischstäbchen *n*
fish·y Fisch…; F verdächtig
fis·sion PHYS Spaltung *f*
fis·sure GEOL Spalt *m*, Riss *m*
fist Faust *f*
fit[1] **1.** geeignet, passend; tauglich; SPORT fit, (gut) in Form; ***keep fit*** sich fit halten; **2.** *v/t* passend machen (***for*** für), anpassen; TECH einpassen, einbauen; anbringen; ***fit in*** *j-m* e-n Termin geben, *j-n*, *et.* einschieben; *a.* ***fit on*** anprobieren; *a.* ***fit out*** ausrüsten, ausstatten, einrichten (***with*** mit); *a.* ***fit up*** einrichten (***with*** mit); montieren, installieren; *v/i* passen, sitzen (*dress etc*); **3.** Sitz *m*
fit[2] MED Anfall *m*; ***give s.o. a fit*** F j-n auf die Palme bringen; j-m e-n Schock versetzen
fit·ful unruhig (*sleep etc*)
fit·ness Tauglichkeit *f*; *esp* SPORT Fitness *f*, (gute) Form
fitness cen·ter (*Br* **cen·tre**) Fitnesscenter *n*
fit·ted zugeschnitten; ***fitted carpet*** Spannteppich *m*, Teppichboden *m*; ***fitted kitchen*** Einbauküche *f*
fit·ter Monteur *m*; Installateur *m*
fit·ting 1. passend; schicklich; **2.** Montage *f*, Installation *f*; *pl* Ausstattung *f*; Armaturen *pl*
five 1. fünf; **2.** Fünf *f*
fix 1. befestigen, anbringen (***to*** an *dat*); *Preis* festsetzen; fixieren; *Blick etc* richten (***on*** auf *acc*); *Aufmerksamkeit etc* fesseln; reparieren, in Ordnung bringen (*a. fig*); *Essen* zubereiten; **2.** F Klemme *f*; *sl* Fix *m*
fixed fest; starr
fix·ings GASTR Beilagen *pl*
fix·ture Inventarstück *n*; ***lighting fixture*** Beleuchtungskörper *m*
fizz zischen, sprudeln
flab·ber·gast F verblüffen; ***be flabbergasted*** F platt sein
flab·by schlaff
flac·cid schlaff, schlapp
flag[1] **1.** Fahne *f*, Flagge *f*; **2.** beflaggen
flag[2] **1.** (Stein)Platte *f*, Fliese *f*; **2.** mit (Stein)Platten *or* Fliesen belegen, fliesen
flag[3] nachlassen, erlahmen
flag·pole, **flag·staff** Fahnenstange *f*
flag·stone (Stein)Platte *f*, Fliese *f*
flake 1. Flocke *f*; Schuppe *f*; **2.** *mst* ***flake off*** abblättern; F ***flake out*** schlappmachen
flak·y flockig; blätt(e)rig
flak·y pas·try GASTR Blätterteig *m*
flame 1. Flamme *f* (*a. fig*); ***be in flames*** in Flammen stehen; **2.** flammen, lodern
flam·ma·ble TECH brennbar, leicht entzündlich, feuergefährlich
flan GASTR Obst-, Käsekuchen *m*
flank 1. Flanke *f*; **2.** flankieren
flan·nel Flanell *m*; *Br* Waschlappen *m*; *pl Br* Flanellhose *f*
flap 1. Flattern *n*, (Flügel)Schlag *m*; Klappe *f*; **2.** mit *den Flügeln etc* schlagen; flattern
flare 1. flackern; sich weiten; ***flare up*** aufflammen; *fig* aufbrausen; **2.** Lichtsignal *n*
flash 1. Aufblitzen *n*, Aufleuchten *n*, Blitz *m*; *radio etc*: Kurzmeldung *f*; PHOT F Blitz *m*; F Taschenlampe *f*; ***like a flash*** wie der Blitz; ***in a flash*** im Nu; ***a flash of lightning*** ein Blitz; **2.** (auf)blitzen *or* aufleuchten (lassen); zucken; rasen, flitzen
flash·back *film*: Rückblende *f*
flash freeze GASTR schnell einfrieren
flash·light PHOT Blitzlicht *n*; Taschenlampe *f*
flash·y protzig; auffallend
flask Taschenflasche *f*
flat[1] **1.** flach, eben, platt; schal; ECON flau; MOT platt (*tire*); **2.** *adv* ***fall flat*** danebengehen; ***sing flat*** zu tief singen; **3.** Fläche *f*, Ebene *f*; flache Seite; Flachland *n*, Niederung *f*; MOT Reifenpanne *f*
flat[2] *Br* Wohnung *f*
flat-foot·ed plattfüßig
flat·mate *Br* Mitbewohner(in)
flat·ten (ein)ebnen; abflachen; *a.* ***flatten out*** flach(er) werden
flat·ter schmeicheln (*dat*)
flat·ter·er Schmeichler(in)
flat·ter·y Schmeichelei *f*
fla·vo(u)r 1. Geschmack *m*; Aroma *n*; Blume *f*; *fig* Beigeschmack *m*; Würze *f*; **2.** würzen
fla·vo(u)r·ing Würze *f*, Aroma *n*
flaw Fehler *m*, TECH *a.* Defekt *m*
flaw·less einwandfrei, tadellos
flax BOT Flachs *m*
flea zo Floh *m*
flea mar·ket Flohmarkt *m*
fleck Fleck(en) *m*; Tupfen *m*
fledged zo flügge
fledg(e)·ling zo Jungvogel *m*; *fig* Grünschnabel *m*
flee fliehen; meiden

fleece 1. Vlies *n*, *esp* Schafsfell *n*; 2. F *j-n* neppen
fleet MAR Flotte *f*
flesh Fleisch *n*
flesh·y fleischig; dick
flex[1] *esp* ANAT biegen
flex[2] *esp Br* ELECTR (Anschluss-, Verlängerungs)Kabel *n*, (-)Schnur *f*
flex·i·ble flexibel, biegsam; *fig* anpassungsfähig; ***flexible working hours*** Gleitzeit *f*

F

flex·i·time *Br*, **flex·time** Gleitzeit *f*
flick schnippen; schnellen
flick·er 1. flackern; TV flimmern; 2. Flackern *n*; TV Flimmern *n*
fli·er AVIAT Flieger *m*; Reklamezettel *m*
flight Flucht *f*; Flug *m* (*a. fig*); *zo* Schwarm *m*; *a.* ***flight of stairs*** Treppe *f*; ***put to flight*** in die Flucht schlagen; ***take*** (***to***) ***flight*** die Flucht ergreifen
flight at·tend·ant AVIAT Flugbegleiter(in)
flight·less *zo* flugunfähig
flight re·cord·er AVIAT Flugschreiber *m*
flight·y flatterhaft
flim·sy dünn; zart; *fig* fadenscheinig
flinch (zurück)zucken, zusammenfahren; zurückschrecken (***from*** vor *dat*)
fling 1. werfen, schleudern; ***fling o.s.*** sich stürzen; ***fling open*** (***to***) *Tür etc* aufreißen (zuschlagen); 2. ***have a fling*** sich austoben; ***have a fling at*** es versuchen *or* probieren mit
flint Feuerstein *m*
flip schnippen, schnipsen; *Münze* hochwerfen
flip·pant respektlos, F schnodd(e)rig
flip·per *zo* Flosse *f*; Schwimmflosse *f*
flirt 1. flirten; 2. ***be a flirt*** gern flirten
flir·ta·tion Flirt *m*
flit flitzen, huschen
float 1. *v/i* (auf dem Wasser) schwimmen, (im Wasser) treiben; schweben; *a.* ECON in Umlauf sein; *v/t* schwimmen *or* treiben lassen; MAR flottmachen; ECON *Wertpapiere etc* in Umlauf bringen; *Währung* floaten, den Wechselkurs (*gen*) freigeben; 2. Festwagen *m*
float·ing 1. schwimmend, treibend; ECON umlaufend; frei (*exchange rate*); frei konvertierbar (*currency*); 2. ECON Floating *n*
float·ing vot·er POL Wechselwähler(in)
flock 1. *zo* Herde *f* (*a.* REL); Menge *f*, Schar *f*; 2. *fig* strömen
floe (treibende) Eisscholle
flog prügeln, schlagen
flog·ging Tracht *f* Prügel
flood 1. *a.* ***flood tide*** Flut *f*; Überschwemmung *f*; 2. überfluten, überschwemmen
flood·gate Schleusentor *n*
flood·lights ELECTR Flutlicht *n*
floor 1. (Fuß)Boden *m*; Stock *m*, Stockwerk *n*, Etage *f*; Tanzfläche *f*; → ***first floor***, ***second floor***; ***take the floor*** das Wort ergreifen; 2. e-n (Fuß)Boden legen in; zu Boden schlagen; *fig* F *j-n* umhauen
floor·board (Fußboden)Diele *f*
floor cloth Putzlappen *m*
floor·ing (Fuß)Bodenbelag *m*
floor lamp Stehlampe *f*
floor lead·er PARL Fraktionsführer *m*
floor-length bodenlang
floor show Nachtklubvorstellung *f*
floor·walk·er Aufsicht *f*
flop 1. sich (hin)plumpsen lassen; F durchfallen, danebengehen, ein Reinfall sein; 2. Plumps *m*; F Flop *m*, Reinfall *m*, Pleite *f*; Versager *m*
flop·py (disk) EDP Floppy Disk *f*, Diskette *f*
flor·id rot, gerötet
flor·ist Blumenhändler(in)
floun·der[1] *zo* Flunder *f*
floun·der[2] zappeln; strampeln; *fig* sich verhaspeln
flour (feines) Mehl
flour·ish 1. Schnörkel *m*; MUS Tusch *m*; 2. *v/i* blühen, gedeihen; *v/t* schwenken
flow 1. fließen, strömen; wallen; 2. Fluß *m*, Strom *m* (*both a. fig*)
flow·er 1. Blume *f*; Blüte *f* (*a. fig*); 2. blühen
flow·er·bed Blumenbeet *n*
flow·er·pot Blumentopf *m*
fluc·tu·ate schwanken
fluc·tu·a·tion Schwankung *f*
flu F MED Grippe *f*
flue Rauchfang *m*, Esse *f*
flu·en·cy Flüssigkeit *f*; (Rede)Gewandtheit *f*
flu·ent flüssig; gewandt; ***speak fluent French*** fließend Französisch sprechen
fluff 1. Flaum *m*; Staubflocke *f*; 2. *zo* aufplustern
fluff·y flaumig
flu·id 1. flüssig; 2. Flüssigkeit *f*
flunk F durchfallen (lassen)
flu·o·res·cent fluoreszierend
flu·o·ride CHEM Fluor *n*
flu·o·rine CHEM Fluor *n*
flur·ry Windstoß *m*; (*Regen-*, *Schnee-*) Schauer *m*; *fig* Aufregung *f*, Unruhe *f*
flush 1. (Wasser)Spülung *f*; Erröten *n*; Röte *f*; 2. *v/t a.* ***flush out*** (aus)spülen; ***flush down*** hinunterspülen; ***flush the toilet*** spülen; *v/i* erröten, rot werden; spülen; 3. ***be flush*** F gut bei Kasse sein
flus·ter 1. nervös machen *or* werden; 2. Nervosität *f*

flute MUS **1.** Flöte *f*; **2.** (auf der) Flöte spielen
flut·ter **1.** flattern; **2.** Flattern *n*; *fig* Erregung *f*
flux *fig* Fluss *m*
fly[1] ZO Fliege *f*
fly[2] Hosenschlitz *m*; Zeltklappe *f*
fly[3] fliegen (lassen); stürmen, stürzen; flattern, wehen; (ver)fliegen (*time*); *Drachen* steigen lassen; ***fly at s.o.*** auf j-n losgehen; ***fly into a passion** or **rage*** in Wut geraten
fly·er → ***flier***
fly·ing fliegend; Flug…
flying sau·cer fliegende Untertasse
flying squad Überfallkommando *n*
flying vis·it F Stippvisite *f*
fly·o·ver *Br* (Straßen-, Eisenbahn-) Überführung *f*
fly·screen Fliegenfenster *n*
fly·weight *boxing*: Fliegengewicht *n*, Fliegengewichtler *m*
fly·wheel TECH Schwungrad *n*
foal ZO Fohlen *n*
foam **1.** Schaum *m*; **2.** schäumen
foam ex·tin·guish·er Schaumlöscher *m*, -löschgerät *n*
foam rub·ber Schaumgummi *m*
foam·y schaumig
fo·cus **1.** Brennpunkt *m*, *fig a.* Mittelpunkt *m*; OPT, PHOT Scharfeinstellung *f*; **2.** OPT, PHOT scharf einstellen; *fig* konzentrieren (***on*** auf *acc*)
fod·der AGR (Trocken)Futter *n*
foe POET Feind *m*, Gegner *m*
fog (dichter) Nebel
fog·gy neb(e)lig; *fig* nebelhaft
foi·ble (kleine) Schwäche
foil[1] Folie *f*; *fig* Hintergrund *m*
foil[2] vereiteln
foil[3] *fencing*: Florett *n*
fold[1] **1.** Falte *f*; Falz *m*; **2.** …fach, …fältig; **3.** (sich) falten; falzen; *Arme* verschränken; einwickeln; *often* ***fold up*** zusammenfalten, -legen, -klappen
fold[2] AGR Schafhürde *f*, Pferch *m*; REL Herde *f*
fold·er Aktendeckel *m*; Schnellhefter *m*; Faltprospekt *m*, -blatt *n*, Broschüre *f*
fold·ing zusammenlegbar; Klapp…
folding bed Klappbett *n*
folding bi·cy·cle Klapprad *n*
folding boat Faltboot *n*
folding chair Klappstuhl *m*
folding door(s) Falttür *f*
fo·li·age BOT Laub *n*, Laubwerk *n*
folk **1.** Leute *pl*; *pl* F *m-e etc* Leute *pl*; **2.** Volks…
folk·lore Volkskunde *f*; Volkssagen *pl*; Folklore *f*
folk mu·sic Volksmusik *f*
folk song Volkslied *n*; Folksong *m*
fol·low folgen (*dat*); folgen auf (*acc*); befolgen; verfolgen; *s-m Beruf etc* nachgehen; ***follow through*** *Plan etc* bis zum Ende durchführen; ***follow up*** *e-r Sache* nachgehen; *e-e Sache* weiterverfolgen; ***as follows*** wie folgt
fol·low·er Nachfolger(in); Verfolger(in); Anhänger(in)
fol·low·ing **1.** Anhängerschaft *f*, Anhänger *pl*; Gefolge *n*; ***the following*** das Folgende; die Folgenden *pl*; **2.** folgende(r, -s); **3.** im Anschluss an (*acc*)
fol·ly Torheit *f*
fond zärtlich; vernarrt (***of*** in *acc*); ***be fond of*** gernhaben, lieben
fon·dle liebkosen; streicheln; (ver)hätscheln
fond·ness Zärtlichkeit *f*; Vorliebe *f*
font REL Taufstein *m*, Taufbecken *n*
food Nahrung *f*, Essen *n*; Nahrungs-, Lebensmittel *pl*; AGR Futter *n*
fool **1.** Narr *m*, Närrin *f*, Dummkopf *m*; ***make a fool of s.o.*** j-n zum Narren halten; ***make a fool of o.s.*** sich lächerlich machen; **2.** zum Narren halten; betrügen (***out of*** um); ***fool about, fool around*** herumtrödeln; Unsinn machen, herumalbern
fool·har·dy tollkühn
fool·ish dumm, töricht; unklug
fool·ish·ness Dummheit *f*
fool·proof kinderleicht; todsicher
foot **1.** ANAT Fuß *m* (*a. linear measure = 30,48 cm*); Fußende *n*; ***on foot*** zu Fuß; **2.** F *Rechnung* bezahlen; ***have to foot the bill*** die Zeche bezahlen müssen; ***foot it*** zu Fuß gehen
foot·ball Football(spiel *n*) *m*; *Br* Fußball(-spiel *n*) *m*; Football-Ball *m*; *Br* Fußball *m*
foot·bal·ler *Br* Fußballer *m*
foot·ball hoo·li·gan *Br* Fußballrowdy *m*
football play·er *Br* Fußballspieler *m*
foot·bridge Fußgängerbrücke *f*
foot·fall Tritt *m*, Schritt *m*
foot·hold fester Stand, Halt *m*
foot·ing Halt *m*, Stand *m*; *fig* Grundlage *f*, Basis *f*; ***be on a friendly footing with s.o.*** ein gutes Verhältnis zu j-m haben; ***lose one's footing*** den Halt verlieren
foot·lights THEA Rampenlicht(er *pl*) *n*
foot·loose frei, unbeschwert; ***footloose and fancy-free*** frei und ungebunden
foot·note Fußnote *f*
foot·path (Fuß)Pfad *m*, (Fuß)Weg *m*
foot·print Fußabdruck *m*, *pl a.* Fußspur(en *pl*) *f*

F

F

foot·sore: ***be footsore*** wunde Füße haben
foot·step Tritt *m*, Schritt *m*; Fußstapfe *f*
foot·wear Schuhwerk *n*, Schuhe *pl*
fop Geck *m*, F Fatzke *m*
for 1. *prp mst* für; *purpose*, *direction*: zu; nach; *warten*, *hoffen etc* auf (*acc*); *sich sehnen etc* nach; *cause*: aus, vor (*dat*), wegen; *time*: ***for three days*** drei Tage (lang); seit drei Tagen; *distance*: ***I walked for a mile*** ich ging eine Meile (weit); *exchange*: (an)statt; als; ***I for one*** ich zum Beispiel; ***for sure*** sicher!, gewiss!; **2.** *cj* denn, weil
for·age *a.* ***forage about*** (herum)stöbern, (-)wühlen (***in*** in *dat*; ***for*** nach)
for·ay MIL Einfall *m*, Überfall *m*; *fig* Ausflug *m* (***into*** *politics* in *die Politik*)
for·bid verbieten; hindern
for·bid·ding abstoßend
force 1. Stärke *f*, Kraft *f*, Gewalt *f*, Wucht *f*; ***the*** (***police***) ***force*** die Polizei; (***armed***) ***forces*** MIL Streitkräfte *pl*; ***by force*** mit Gewalt; ***come*** *or* ***put into force*** in Kraft treten *or* setzen; **2.** *j-n* zwingen; *et.* erzwingen; zwängen; drängen; *Tempo* beschleunigen; ***force s.th. on s.o.*** j-m et. aufzwingen *or* aufdrängen; ***force o.s. on s.o.*** sich j-m aufdrängen; ***force open*** aufbrechen
forced erzwungen; gezwungen, gequält
forced land·ing AVIAT Notlandung *f*
force·ful energisch, kraftvoll; eindrucksvoll, überzeugend
for·ceps MED Zange *f*
for·ci·ble gewaltsam; eindringlich
ford 1. Furt *f*; **2.** durchwaten
fore 1. vorder, Vorder…; vorn; **2.** Vorderteil *m*, Vorderseite *f*, Front *f*
fore·arm ANAT Unterarm *m*
fore·bear *mst pl* Vorfahren *pl*, Ahnen *pl*
fore·bod·ing (böses) Vorzeichen; (*böse*) (Vor)Ahnung
fore·cast 1. voraussagen, vorhersehen; *Wetter* vorhersagen; **2.** Voraussage *f*; METEOR Vorhersage *f*
fore·fa·ther Vorfahr *m*
fore·fin·ger ANAT Zeigefinger *m*
fore·foot ZO Vorderfuß *m*
fore·gone con·clu·sion ausgemachte Sache; ***be a foregone conclusion*** *a.* von vornherein feststehen
fore·ground Vordergrund *m*
fore·hand SPORT **1.** Vorhand *f*, Vorhandschlag *m*; **2.** Vorhand…
fore·head ANAT Stirn *f*
for·eign fremd, ausländisch, Außen…, Auslands…
foreign af·fairs Außenpolitik *f*
foreign aid Auslandshilfe *f*
for·eign·er Ausländer(in)
for·eign lan·guage Fremdsprache *f*
foreign min·is·ter POL Außenminister *m*
For·eign Of·fice *Br* POL Außenministerium *n*
for·eign pol·i·cy Außenpolitik *f*
For·eign Sec·re·ta·ry *Br* POL Außenminister *m*
for·eign trade ECON Außenhandel *m*
for·eign work·er Gastarbeiter(in)
fore·knowl·edge vorherige Kenntnis
fore·leg ZO Vorderbein *n*
fore·man TECH Vorarbeiter *m*, Polier *m*; Werkmeister *m*; JUR Sprecher *m*
fore·most vorderste(r, -s), erste(r, -s)
fore·name Vorname *m*
fo·ren·sic JUR Gerichts…
forensic me·di·cine Gerichtsmedizin *f*
fore·run·ner Vorläufer(in)
fore·see vorhersehen, voraussehen
fore·see·a·ble vorhersehbar
fore·shad·ow ahnen lassen, andeuten
fore·sight Weitblick *m*; (weise) Voraussicht
for·est Wald *m* (*a. fig*); Forst *m*
fore·stall *et.* vereiteln; *j-m* zuvorkommen
for·est·er Förster *m*
for·est·ry Forstwirtschaft *f*
fore·taste Vorgeschmack *m*
fore·tell vorhersagen
for·ev·er, for ev·er für immer
fore·wom·an TECH Vorarbeiterin *f*
fore·word Vorwort *n*
for·feit verwirken; einbüßen
forge 1. Schmiede *f*; **2.** fälschen; schmieden
forg·er Fälscher *m*
for·ge·ry Fälschen *n*; Fälschung *f*
for·ge·ry-proof fälschungssicher
for·get vergessen
for·get·ful vergesslich
for·get-me-not BOT Vergissmeinnicht *n*
for·give vergeben, verzeihen
for·give·ness Verzeihung *f*; Vergebung *f*
for·giv·ing versöhnlich; nachsichtig
fork 1. Gabel *f*; **2.** (sich) gabeln
fork·lift truck MOT Gabelstapler *m*
form 1. Form *f*; Gestalt *f*; Formular *n*, Vordruck *m*; *Br* (Schul)Klasse *f*; Formalität *f*; Kondition *f*, Verfassung *f*; ***in great form*** gut in Form; **2.** (sich) formen, (sich) bilden, gestalten
for·mal förmlich; formell
for·mal dress Gesellschaftskleidung *f*
for·mal·i·ty Förmlichkeit *f*; Formalität *f*
for·mat 1. Aufmachung *f*; Format *n*; **2.** EDP formatieren
for·ma·tion Bildung *f*

form·a·tive bildend; gestaltend; ***formative years*** Entwicklungsjahre *pl*
for·mat·ting EDP Formatierung *f*
for·mer **1.** früher; ehemalig; **2.** ***the former*** der *or* die *or* das Erstere
for·mer·ly früher
for·mi·da·ble furchterregend; gewaltig, riesig, gefährlich, schwierig
form mas·ter *Br* Klassenlehrer *m*, -leiter *m*
form mis·tress *Br* Klassenlehrerin *f*, -leiterin *f*
form teach·er *Br* Klassenlehrer(in), Klassenleiter(in)
for·mu·la Formel *f*; Rezept *n*
for·mu·late formulieren
for·sake aufgeben; verlassen
for·swear abschwören, entsagen (*dat*)
fort MIL Fort *n*, Festung *f*
forth weiter, fort; (her)vor; ***and so forth*** und so weiter
forth·com·ing bevorstehend, kommend; in Kürze erscheinend (*book*) *or* anlaufend (*film*)
for·ti·eth vierzigste(r, -s)
for·ti·fi·ca·tion Befestigung *f*
for·ti·fy MIL befestigen; *fig* (ver)stärken
for·ti·tude (innere) Kraft *or* Stärke
fort·night *esp Br* vierzehn Tage
for·tress MIL Festung *f*
for·tu·i·tous zufällig
for·tu·nate glücklich; ***be fortunate*** Glück haben
for·tu·nate·ly glücklicherweise
for·tune Vermögen *n*; (glücklicher) Zufall, Glück *n*; Schicksal *n*
for·tune-tell·er Wahrsager(in)
for·ty **1.** vierzig; ***have forty winks*** F ein Nickerchen machen; **2.** Vierzig *f*
for·ward **1.** *adv* nach vorn, vorwärts; **2.** *adj* Vorwärts…; fortschrittlich; vorlaut, dreist; **3.** *soccer*: Stürmer *m*; **4.** befördern, (ver)senden, schicken; *Brief etc* nachsenden
for·ward·ing a·gent Spediteur *m*
fos·sil GEOL Fossil *n* (*a.* F), Versteinerung *f*
fos·ter-child Pflegekind *n*
fos·ter-par·ents Pflegeeltern *pl*
foul **1.** stinkend, widerlich; verpestet, schlecht (*air, water*); GASTR verdorben, faul; schmutzig, verschmutzt; METEOR stürmisch, schlecht; SPORT regelwidrig; *esp Br* F mies;**2.** SPORT Foul *n*, Regelverstoß *m*; ***vicious foul*** böses *or* übles Foul; **3.** beschmutzen, verschmutzen; SPORT foulen
found[1] gründen; stiften
found[2] TECH gießen
foun·da·tion ARCH Grundmauer *f*, Fundament *n*; *fig* Gründung *f*, Errichtung *f*; (gemeinnützige) Stiftung; *fig* Grundlage *f*, Basis *f*
found·er[1] Gründer(in); Stifter(in)
foun·der[2] MAR sinken; *fig* scheitern
found·ling JUR Findelkind *n*
foun·dry TECH Gießerei *f*
foun·tain Springbrunnen *m*; (*Wasser-*) Strahl *m*
fountain pen Füllfederhalter *m*
four **1.** vier; **2.** Vier *f*; *rowing*: Vierer *m*; ***on all fours*** auf allen vieren
four star *Br* F Super *n*
four-star pet·rol *Br* Superbenzin *n*
four-stroke en·gine Viertaktmotor *m*
four·teen **1.** vierzehn; **2.** Vierzehn *f*
four·teenth vierzehnte(r, -s)
fourth **1.** vierte(r, -s); **2.** Viertel *n*
fourth·ly viertens
four-wheel drive MOT Vierradantrieb *m*
fowl zo Geflügel *n*
fox zo Fuchs *m*
fox·glove BOT Fingerhut *m*
fox·y schlau, gerissen
frac·tion Bruchteil *m*; MATH Bruch *m*
frac·ture MED **1.** (Knochen)Bruch *m*; **2.** brechen
fra·gile zerbrechlich
frag·ment Bruchstück *n*
fra·grance Wohlgeruch *m*, Duft *m*
fra·grant wohlriechend, duftend
frail gebrechlich; zerbrechlich; zart, schwach
frail·ty Zartheit *f*; Gebrechlichkeit *f*; Schwäche *f*
frame **1.** Rahmen *m*; (*Brillen- etc*)Gestell *n*; Körper(bau) *m*; ***frame of mind*** (Gemüts)Verfassung *f*, (-)Zustand *m*; **2.** (ein)rahmen; bilden, formen, bauen; *a.* ***frame up*** F *j-m* et. anhängen
frame-up F abgekartetes Spiel; Intrige *f*
frame·work TECH Gerüst *n*; *fig* Struktur *f*, System *n*
franc Franc *m*; Franken *m*
France Frankreich *n*
fran·chise POL Wahlrecht *n*; ECON Konzession *f*
frank **1.** frei(mütig), offen; ***frankly (speaking)*** offen gesagt; **2.** *Brief* freistempeln
frank·fur·ter GASTR Frankfurter (Würstchen *n*) *f*
frank·ness Offenheit *f*
fran·tic hektisch; ***be frantic*** außer sich sein
fra·ter·nal brüderlich
frat·er·nize sich verbrüdern
frat·er·ni·za·tion Verbrüderung *f*
fra·ter·ni·ty Brüderlichkeit *f*; Vereinigung

f, Zunft *f*; UNIV Verbindung *f*
fraud Betrug *m*; F Schwindel *m*
fraud·u·lent betrügerisch
fray ausfransen, (sich) durchscheuern
freak 1. Missgeburt *f*; Laune *f*; *in cpds* F …freak *m*, …fanatiker *m*; Freak *m*, irrer Typ; ***freak of nature*** Laune *f* der Natur; **2.** F *a.* ***freak out*** durchdrehen, die Nerven verlieren
freck·le Sommersprosse *f*
freck·led sommersprossig
free 1. frei; ungehindert; ungebunden; kostenlos, zum Nulltarif; freigebig; ***free and easy*** zwanglos; sorglos; ***set free*** freilassen; **2.** befreien; freilassen
free·dom Freiheit *f*
free fares Nulltarif *m*
free·lance frei, freiberuflich tätig, freischaffend
Free·ma·son Freimaurer *m*
free skat·ing Kür *f*
free·style SPORT Freistil *m*
free time Freizeit *f*
free trade ECON Freihandel *m*
free trade ar·e·a ECON Freihandelszone *f*
free·way Schnellstraße *f*
free·wheel im Freilauf fahren
freeze 1. *v/i* (ge)frieren; erstarren; *v/t* gefrieren lassen; GASTR einfrieren (*a.* ECON), tiefkühlen; **2.** Frost *m*, Kälte *f*; ECON, POL Einfrieren *n*; ***wage freeze, freeze on wages*** ECON Lohnstopp *m*
freeze-dried gefriergetrocknet
freeze-dry gefriertrocknen
freez·er Gefriertruhe *f*, Tiefkühl-, Gefriergerät *n*; Gefrierfach *n*
freez·ing eisig; Gefrier…
freezing com·part·ment Gefrierfach *n*
freezing point Gefrierpunkt *m*
freight 1. Fracht *f*; Frachtgebühr *f*; **2.** Güter…; **3.** beladen; verfrachten
freight car RAIL Güterwagen *m*
freight·er MAR Frachter *m*, Frachtschiff *n*; AVIAT Transportflugzeug *n*
freight train Güterzug *m*
French 1. französisch; **2.** LING Französisch *n*; ***the French*** die Franzosen *pl*
French doors Terrassen-, Balkontür *f*
French fries GASTR Pommes frites *pl*
French·man Franzose *m*
French win·dows → ***French doors***
French·wom·an Französin *f*
fren·zied wahnsinnig, rasend (***with*** vor *dat*); hektisch
fren·zy Wahnsinn *m*; Ekstase *f*; Raserei *f*
fre·quen·cy Häufigkeit *f*; ELECTR Frequenz *f*
fre·quent 1. häufig; **2.** (oft) besuchen
fresh frisch; neu; unerfahren; frech; ***get fresh (with s.o.)*** (j-m gegenüber) zudringlich werden
fresh·en auffrischen (*wind*); ***freshen (o.s.) up*** sich frisch machen
fresh·man UNIV Student(in) im ersten Jahr
fresh·ness Frische *f*; Frechheit *f*
fresh wa·ter Süßwasser *n*
fresh·wa·ter Süßwasser…
fret sich Sorgen machen;
fret·ful verärgert, gereizt; quengelig
FRG ABBR *of* ***Federal Republic of Germany*** Bundesrepublik *f* Deutschland
Fri ABBR *of* ***Friday*** Fr., Freitag *m*
fri·ar REL Mönch *m*
fric·tion TECH *etc* Reibung *f* (*a. fig*)
Fri·day (ABBR ***Fri***) Freitag *m*; ***on Friday*** (am) Freitag; ***on Fridays*** freitags
fridge F Kühlschrank *m*
friend Freund(in); Bekannte *m, f*; ***make friends with*** sich anfreunden mit, Freundschaft schließen mit
friend·ly 1. freund(schaft)lich; **2.** *esp Br* SPORT Freundschaftsspiel *n*
friend·ship Freundschaft *f*
fries F GASTR Fritten *pl*
frig·ate MAR Fregatte *f*
fright Schreck(en) *m*; ***look a fright*** F verboten aussehen
fright·en erschrecken; ***be frightened*** erschrecken (***at, by, of*** vor *dat*); Angst haben (***of*** vor *dat*)
fright·ful schrecklich, fürchterlich
fri·gid PSYCH frigid(e); kalt, frostig
frill Krause *f*, Rüsche *f*
fringe 1. Franse *f*; Rand *m*; Pony *m*; **2.** mit Fransen besetzen
fringe ben·e·fits ECON Gehalts-, Lohnnebenleistungen *pl*
fringe e·vent Randveranstaltung *f*
fringe group *soziale* Randgruppe *f*
frisk herumtollen; F *j-n* filzen, durchsuchen
frisk·y lebhaft, munter
frit·ter: ***fritter away*** *Geld etc* vertun, *Zeit* vertrödeln, *Geld, Kräfte* vergeuden
fri·vol·i·ty Frivolität *f*, Leichtfertigkeit *f*
friv·o·lous frivol, leichtfertig
friz·zle F GASTR verbrutzeln
frizz·y gekräuselt, kraus
fro: ***to and fro*** hin und her
frock REL Kutte *f*
frog zo Frosch *m*
frog·man Froschmann *m*, MIL *a.* Kampfschwimmer *m*
frol·ic herumtoben, herumtollen
from von; aus; von … aus *or* her; von … (an), seit; aus, vor (*dat*); ***from 9 to 5 (o'clock)*** von 9 bis 5 (Uhr)

front **1.** Vorderseite *f*; Front *f* (*a.* MIL); ***at the front, in front*** vorn; ***in front of*** vor; ***be in front*** in Führung sein; **2.** Vorder…; **3.** *a.* ***front on, front to(wards)*** gegenüberstehen, gegenüberliegen
front·age ARCH (Vorder)Front *f*
front cov·er Titelseite *f*
front door Haustür *f*, Vordertür *f*
front en·trance Vordereingang *m*
fron·tier **1.** (Landes)Grenze *f*; HIST Grenzland *n*, Grenze *f*; **2.** Grenz…
front-page F wichtig, aktuell
front-wheel drive MOT Vorderradantrieb *m*
frost **1.** Frost *m*; *a.* ***hoar frost, white frost*** Reif *m*; **2.** mit Reif überziehen; *Glas* mattieren; GASTR glasieren, mit Zuckerguss überziehen; mit (Puder)Zucker bestreuen
frost·bite MED Erfrierung *f*
frost·bit·ten MED erfroren
frost·ed glass Matt-, Milchglas *n*
frost·y eisig, frostig (*a. fig*)
froth **1.** Schaum *m*; **2.** schäumen; zu Schaum schlagen
froth·y schäumend; schaumig
frown **1.** Stirnrunzeln *n*; ***with a frown*** stirnrunzelnd; **2.** *v/i* die Stirn runzeln
fro·zen *adj* (eis)kalt; (ein-, zu)gefroren; Gefrier…
fro·zen foods Tiefkühlkost *f*
fru·gal sparsam; bescheiden; einfach
fruit Frucht *f*; Früchte *pl*; Obst *n*
fruit·er·er Obsthändler *m*
fruit·ful fruchtbar
fruit·less unfruchtbar; erfolglos
fruit juice Fruchtsaft *m*
fruit·y fruchtartig; fruchtig (*wine*)
frus·trate vereiteln; frustrieren
frus·tra·tion Vereitelung *f*; Frustration *f*
fry braten; ***fried eggs*** Spiegeleier *pl*; ***fried potatoes*** Bratkartoffeln *pl*
fry·ing pan Bratpfanne *f*
fuch·sia BOT Fuchsie *f*
fuck V ficken, vögeln; ***fuck off!*** verpiss dich!; ***get fucked!*** der Teufel soll dich holen!
fuck·ing V Scheiß…, verflucht; ***fucking hell!*** verdammte Scheiße!
fudge GASTR Fondant *m*
fu·el **1.** Brennstoff *m*; MOT Treib-, Kraftstoff *m*; **2.** MOT, AVIAT (auf)tanken
fu·el in·jec·tion en·gine MOT Einspritzmotor *m*
fu·gi·tive **1.** flüchtig (*a. fig*); **2.** Flüchtling *m*
ful·fil *Br*, **ful·fill** erfüllen; vollziehen
ful·fil·(l)ing befriedigend
ful·fil(l)·ment Erfüllung *f*, Ausführung *f*
full **1.** voll; ganz; Voll…; ***full of*** voll von, voller; ***full (up)*** (voll) besetzt (*bus etc*); F voll, satt; ***house full!*** THEA ausverkauft!; ***full of o.s.*** (ganz) von sich eingenommen; **2.** *adv* völlig, ganz; **3.** ***in full*** vollständig, ganz; ***write out in full*** *Wort etc* ausschreiben
full board Vollpension *f*
full dress Gesellschaftskleidung *f*
full-fledged zo flügge; *fig* richtig
full-grown ausgewachsen
full-length in voller Größe; bodenlang; abendfüllend (*film etc*)
full moon Vollmond *m*
full stop LING Punkt *m*
full time SPORT Spielende *n*
full-time ganztägig, Ganztags…
full-time job Ganztagsbeschäftigung *f*
ful·ly voll, völlig, ganz
ful·ly-fledged *Br* → ***full-fledged***
ful·ly-'grown *Br* → ***full-grown***
fum·ble tasten; fummeln
fume wütend sein
fumes Dämpfe *pl*, Rauch *m*; Abgase *pl*
fum·ing wutschnaubend
fun Scherz *m*, Spaß *m*; ***for fun*** aus *or* zum Spaß; ***make fun of*** sich lustig machen über (*acc*), verspotten
func·tion **1.** Funktion *f*; Aufgabe *f*; Veranstaltung *f*; **2.** funktionieren
func·tion·a·ry Funktionär *m*
func·tion key EDP Funktionstaste *f*
fund ECON Fonds *m*; Geld(mittel *pl*) *n*
fun·da·men·tal **1.** Grund…, grundlegend; **2.** ***fundamentals*** Grundlage *f*, Grundbegriffe *pl*
fun·da·men·tal·ist Fundamentalist *m*
fu·ne·ral Begräbnis *n*, Beerdigung *f*
funeral march MUS Trauermarsch *m*
funeral o·ration Trauerrede *f*
funeral pro·ces·sion Trauerzug *m*
funeral ser·vice Trauerfeier *f*
fun·fair Rummelplatz *m*
fun·gus BOT Pilz *m*, Schwamm *m*
fu·nic·u·lar *a.* ***funicular railway*** (Draht)-Seilbahn *f*
funk·y F irre, schräg, schrill
fun·nel Trichter *m*; MAR, RAIL Schornstein *m*
fun·nies F Comics *pl*
fun·ny komisch, lustig, spaßig; sonderbar
fur Pelz *m*, Fell *n*; MED Belag *m*; TECH Kesselstein *m*
fu·ri·ous wütend
furl *Fahne*, *Segel* aufrollen, einrollen; *Schirm* zusammenrollen
fur·nace TECH Schmelzofen *m*, Hochofen *m*; (Heiz)Kessel *m*
fur·nish einrichten, möblieren; liefern;

F

versorgen, ausrüsten, ausstatten (***with*** mit)
fur·ni·ture Möbel *pl*; ***sectional furniture*** Anbaumöbel *pl*
furred MED belegt, pelzig
fur·ri·er Kürschner *m*
fur·row **1.** Furche *f*; **2.** furchen
fur·ry pelzig; flauschig
fur·ther **1.** weiter; **2.** fördern, unterstützen
further ed·u·ca·tion *Br* Fortbildung *f*, Weiterbildung *f*
fur·ther·more *fig* weiter, überdies
fur·ther·most entfernteste(r, -s), äußerste(r, -s)
fur·tive heimlich, verstohlen
fu·ry Wut *f*, Zorn *m*
fuse **1.** Zünder *m*; ELECTR Sicherung *f*; Zündschnur *f*; **2.** schmelzen; ELECTR durchbrennen
fuse box ELECTR Sicherungskasten *m*
fu·se·lage (Flugzeug)Rumpf *m*
fu·sion Verschmelzung *f*, Fusion *f*; PHYS ***nuclear fusion*** Kernfusion *f*
fuss **1.** (unnötige) Aufregung; Wirbel *m*, F Theater *n*; **2.** sich (unnötig) aufregen; viel Aufhebens machen (***about*** um, von)
fuss·y aufgeregt, hektisch; kleinlich, pedantisch; heikel, wählerisch
fus·ty muffig; *fig* verstaubt
fu·tile nutzlos, zwecklos
fu·ture **1.** (zu)künftig; **2.** Zukunft *f*; LING Futur *n*, Zukunft *f*; ***in future*** in Zukunft, künftig
fuzz feiner Flaum
fuzz·y kraus, wuschelig; unscharf, verschwommen; flaumig, flauschig

G

G, g G, g *n*
gab F Geschwätz *n*; ***have the gift of the gab*** ein gutes Mundwerk haben
gab·ar·dine Gabardine *m*
gab·ble **1.** Geschnatter *n*, Geschwätz *n*; **2.** schnattern, schwatzen
ga·ble ARCH Giebel *m*
gad: F ***gad about*** (viel) unterwegs sein (in *dat*), sich herumtreiben
gad·fly ZO Bremse *f*
gad·get TECH Apparat *m*, Gerät *n*, Vorrichtung *f*; *often contp* technische Spielerei
gag **1.** Knebel *m* (*a. fig*); F Gag *m*; **2.** knebeln; *fig* mundtot machen
gage **1.** Eichmaß *n*; TECH Messgerät *n*, Lehre *f*; TECH Stärke *f*, Dicke *f*; RAIL Spur(weite) *f*; **2.** TECH eichen; (ab-, aus-)messen
gai·e·ty Fröhlichkeit *f*
gain **1.** gewinnen; erreichen, bekommen; zunehmen an (*dat*); vorgehen (um) (*watch*); ***gain speed*** schneller werden; ***gain 5 pounds*** 5 Pfund zunehmen; ***gain in*** zunehmen an (*dat*); **2.** Gewinn *m*; Zunahme *f*; ***gain of time*** Zeitgewinn *m*
gait Gang *m*, Gangart *f*; Schritt *m*
gai·ter Gamasche *f*
gal F Mädchen *n*
ga·la **1.** Festlichkeit *f*; Gala(veranstaltung) *f*; **2.** Gala…
gal·ax·y ASTR Milchstraße *f*, Galaxis *f*
gale Sturm *m*
gall[1] Frechheit *f*
gall[2] **1.** wund geriebene Stelle; **2.** wund reiben *or* scheuern; *fig* (ver)ärgern
gal·lant tapfer; galant, höflich
gal·lan·try Tapferkeit *f*; Galanterie *f*
gall blad·der ANAT Gallenblase *f*
gal·le·ry Galerie *f*; Empore *f*
gal·ley MAR Galeere *f*; Kombüse *f*; *a.* ***galley proof*** PRINT Fahne *f*, Fahnenabzug *m*
gal·lon Gallone *f* (*3,79 l, Br 4,55 l*)
gal·lop **1.** Galopp *m*; **2.** galoppieren (lassen)
gal·lows Galgen *m*
gal·lows hu·mo(u)r Galgenhumor *m*
ga·lore in rauen Mengen
gam·ble **1.** (um Geld) spielen; **2.** Glücksspiel *n*
gam·bler (Glücks)Spieler(in)
gam·bol **1.** Luftsprung *m*; **2.** (herum-)tanzen, (herum)hüpfen
game (Karten-, Ball- *etc*)Spiel *n*; (einzelnes) Spiel (*a. fig*); HUNT Wild *n*; Wildbret *n*; *pl* Spiele *pl*; PED Sport *m*
game·keep·er Wildhüter *m*
game park, **game re·serve** Wildpark *m*; Wildreservat *n*
gan·der ZO Gänserich *m*
gang **1.** (Arbeiter)Trupp *m*; Gang *f*, Bande *f*; Clique *f*; Horde *f*; **2.** ***gang up*** sich

zusammentun, *contp* sich zusammenrotten
gan·gling schlaksig
gang·ster Gangster *m*
gang war, **gang war·fare** Bandenkrieg *m*
gang·way Gang *m*; AVIAT, MAR Gangway *f*
gaol, **gaol·bird**, **gaol·er** *Br* → ***jail*** *etc*
gap Lücke *f*; Kluft *f*; Spalte *f*
gape gähnen; klaffen; gaffen
gar·age **1.** Garage *f*; (Reparatur)Werkstatt *f* (und Tankstelle *f*); **2.** *Auto* in e-r Garage ab- *or* unterstellen; *Auto* in die Garage fahren
gar·bage Abfall *m*, Müll *m*
garbage bag Müllbeutel *m*
garbage can Abfalleimer *m*, Mülleimer *m*; Abfalltonne *f*, Mülltonne *f*
garbage truck Müllwagen *m*
gar·den Garten *m*
gar·den·er Gärtner(in)
gar·den·ing Gartenarbeit *f*
gar·gle gurgeln
gar·ish grell, auffallend
gar·land Girlande *f*
gar·lic BOT Knoblauch *m*
gar·ment Kleidungsstück *n*; Gewand *n*
gar·nish GASTR garnieren
gar·ret Dachkammer *f*
gar·ri·son MIL Garnison *f*
gar·ter Strumpfband *n*; Sockenhalter *m*; Strumpfhalter *m*, Straps *m*
gas Gas *n*; F Benzin *n*, Sprit *m*
gas·e·ous gasförmig
gash klaffende Wunde
gas·ket TECH Dichtung(sring *m*) *f*
gas me·ter Gasuhr *f*, Gaszähler *m*
gas·o·lene, **gas·o·line** Benzin *n*
gasolene pump Zapfsäule *f*
gasp **1.** keuchen, röcheln; ***gasp (for breath)*** nach Atem ringen, F nach Luft schnappen; **2.** Keuchen *n*, Röcheln *n*
gas sta·tion Tankstelle *f*
gas stove Gasofen *m*, Gasherd *m*
gas·works TECH Gaswerk *n*
gate Tor *n*; Pforte *f*; Schranke *f*, Sperre *f*; AVIAT Flugsteig *m*
gate·crash F uneingeladen kommen (zu); sich ohne zu bezahlen hineinschmuggeln (in *acc*)
gate·post Tor-, Türpfosten *m*
gate·way Tor(weg *m*) *n*, Einfahrt *f*
gate·way drug Einstiegsdroge *f*
gath·er *v/t* sammeln, *Informationen* einholen, einziehen; *Personen* versammeln; ernten, pflücken; zusammenziehen, kräuseln; *fig* folgern, schließen (***from*** aus); ***gather speed*** schneller werden; *v/i* sich (ver)sammeln; sich (an)sammeln
gath·er·ing Versammlung *f*; Zusammenkunft *f*
gau·dy auffällig, bunt, grell; protzig
gauge *Br* → ***gage***
gaunt hager; ausgemergelt
gaunt·let Schutzhandschuh *m*
gauze Gaze *f*; MED Bandage *f*, Binde *f*
gav·el Hammer *m*
gaw·ky linkisch
gay **1.** lustig, fröhlich; bunt, (farben-)prächtig; F schwul; **2.** F Schwule *m*
gaze **1.** (starrer) Blick; **2.** starren; ***gaze at*** starren auf (*acc*), anstarren
ga·zette Amtsblatt *n*
ga·zelle ZO Gazelle *f*
gear TECH Getriebe *n*; MOT Gang *m*; *mst in cpds* Vorrichtung *f*, Gerät *n*; F Kleidung *f*, Aufzug *m*; ***shift*** (*esp Br* ***change***) ***gear(s)*** MOT schalten; ***shift*** (*esp Br* ***change***) ***into second gear*** MOT in den zweiten Gang schalten
gear·box MOT Getriebe *n*
gear le·ver *Br*, **gear shift**, **gear stick** *Br* MOT Schalthebel *m*
Gei·ger count·er PHYS Geigerzähler *m*
geld·ing ZO Wallach *m*
gem Edelstein *m*
Gem·i·ni ASTR Zwillinge *pl*; ***he (she) is (a) Gemini*** er (sie) ist (ein) Zwilling
gen·der LING Genus *n*, Geschlecht *n*
gene BIOL Gen *n*, Erbfaktor *m*
gen·e·ral **1.** allgemein; Haupt…, General…; **2.** MIL General *m*; ***in general*** im Allgemeinen
general de·liv·er·y: ***(in care of) general delivery*** postlagernd
general e·lec·tion *Br* POL Parlamentswahlen *pl*
gen·e·ral·ize verallgemeinern
gen·er·al·ly im Allgemeinen, allgemein
gen·e·ral prac·ti·tion·er (ABBR ***GP***) *appr* Arzt *m or* Ärztin *f* für Allgemeinmedizin
gen·e·rate erzeugen
gen·e·ra·tion Erzeugung *f*; Generation *f*
gen·e·ra·tor ELECTR Generator *m*; MOT Lichtmaschine *f*
gen·e·ros·i·ty Großzügigkeit *f*
gen·e·rous großzügig; reichlich
ge·net·ic genetisch
genetic code BIOL Erbanlage *f*
genetic en·gin·eer·ing Gentechnologie *f*
genetic fin·ger·print genetischer Fingerabdruck
ge·net·ics BIOL Genetik *f*, Vererbungslehre *f*
ge·ni·al freundlich
gen·i·tive *a.* ***genitive case*** LING Genitiv *m*, zweiter Fall
ge·ni·us Genie *n*
gen·o·cide Völkermord *m*

G

gent F *esp Br* Herr *m*; ***gents*** *Br* F Herrenklo *n*
gen·tle sanft, zart, sacht; mild
gen·tle·man Gentleman *m*; Herr *m*
gen·tle·man·ly gentlemanlike, vornehm
gen·tle·ness Sanftheit *f*, Zartheit *f*; Milde *f*
gen·try *Br* niederer Adel; Oberschicht *f*
gen·u·ine echt; aufrichtig
ge·og·ra·phy Geografie *f*
ge·ol·o·gy Geologie *f*
ge·om·e·try Geometrie *f*

G

germ BIOL, BOT Keim *m*; MED Bazillus *m*, Bakterie *f*, (Krankheits)Erreger *m*
Ger·man 1. deutsch; **2.** Deutsche *m*, *f*; LING Deutsch *n*
German shep·herd ZO Deutscher Schäferhund
Ger·man·y Deutschland *n*
ger·mi·nate BIOL, BOT keimen (lassen)
ger·und LING Gerundium *n*
ges·tic·u·late gestikulieren
ges·ture Geste *f*, Gebärde *f*
get *v/t* bekommen, erhalten; sich *et.* verschaffen *or* besorgen; erwerben, sich aneignen; holen; bringen; F erwischen; F kapieren, verstehen; *j-n* dazu bringen (***to do*** zu tun); *with pp*: lassen; ***get one's hair cut*** sich die Haare schneiden lassen; ***get going*** in Gang bringen; ***get s.th. by heart*** et. auswendig lernen; ***get s.th. ready*** et. fertig machen; ***have got*** haben; ***have got to*** müssen; *v/i* kommen, gelangen; *with pp or adj*: werden; ***get tired*** müde werden, ermüden; ***get going*** in Gang kommen; *fig* in Schwung kommen; ***get home*** nach Hause kommen; ***get ready*** sich fertig machen; ***get about*** herumkommen; sich herumsprechen *or* verbreiten (*rumor etc*); ***get ahead of*** übertreffen (*acc*); ***get along*** vorwärts-, vorankommen; auskommen (***with*** mit *j-m*); zurechtkommen (***with*** mit *et.*); ***get at*** herankommen an (*acc*); ***what is he getting at?*** worauf will er hinaus?; ***get away*** loskommen; entkommen; ***get away with*** davonkommen mit; ***get back*** zurückkommen; *et.* zurückbekommen; ***get in*** hinein-, hereinkommen; einsteigen (in *acc*); ***get off*** aussteigen (aus); davonkommen (***with*** mit); ***get on*** einsteigen (in *acc*); → ***get along***; ***get out*** herausgehen, hinausgehen; aussteigen (***of*** aus); *et.* herausbekommen; ***get over s.th.*** über et. hinwegkommen; ***get to*** kommen nach; ***get together*** zusammenkommen; ***get up*** aufstehen
get·a·way Flucht *f*; ***getaway car*** Fluchtauto *n*
get·up Aufmachung *f*
gey·ser GEOL Geysir *m*; *Br* TECH Durchlauferhitzer *m*
ghast·ly grässlich; schrecklich; (toten-) bleich
gher·kin Gewürzgurke *f*
ghet·to Getto *n*
ghost Geist *m*, Gespenst *n*; *fig* Spur *f*
ghost·ly geisterhaft
gi·ant 1. Riese *m*; **2.** riesig
gib·ber·ish Kauderwelsch *n*
gib·bet Galgen *m*
gibe 1. spotten (***at*** über *acc*); **2.** höhnische Bemerkung, Stichelei *f*
gib·lets GASTR Hühner-, Gänseklein *n*
gid·di·ness MED Schwindel(gefühl *n*) *m*
gid·dy schwindelerregend; ***I feel giddy*** mir ist schwind(e)lig
gift Geschenk *n*; Talent *n*
gift·ed begabt
gig F MUS Gig *m*, Auftritt *m*, Konzert *n*
gi·gan·tic gigantisch, riesenhaft, riesig, gewaltig
gig·gle 1. kichern; **2.** Gekicher *n*
gild vergolden
gill ZO Kieme *f*; BOT Lamelle *f*
gim·mick F Trick *m*; Spielerei *f*
gin Gin *m*
gin·ger 1. Ingwer *m*; **2.** rötlich *or* gelblich braun;
gin·ger·bread Lebkuchen *m*, Pfefferkuchen *m*
gin·ger·ly behutsam, vorsichtig
gip·sy *Br* → ***gypsy***
gi·raffe ZO Giraffe *f*
gir·der TECH Tragbalken *m*
gir·dle Hüfthalter *m*, Hüftgürtel *m*
girl Mädchen *n*
girl·friend Freundin *f*
girl guide *Br* Pfadfinderin *f*
girl·hood Mädchenjahre *pl*, Jugend *f*, Jugendzeit *f*
girl·ish mädchenhaft; Mädchen…
girl scout Pfadfinderin *f*
gi·ro *Br* Postgirodienst *m*
gi·ro ac·count *Br* Postgirokonto *n*
gi·ro cheque *Br* Postscheck *m*
girth (Sattel)Gurt *m*; (*a.* Körper)Umfang *m*
gist *das* Wesentliche, Kern *m*
give geben; schenken; spenden; *Leben* hingeben, opfern; *Befehl etc* geben, erteilen; *Hilfe* leisten; *Schutz* bieten; *Grund etc* angeben; THEA *etc* geben, aufführen; *Vortrag* halten; *Schmerzen* bereiten, verursachen; *Grüße etc* übermitteln; ***give her my love*** bestelle ihr herzliche Grüße von mir; ***give birth to*** zur Welt bringen; ***give s.o. to understand that***

j-m zu verstehen geben, dass; ***give way*** nachgeben; *Br* MOT die Vorfahrt lassen (*dat*); ***give away*** hergeben, weggeben, verschenken; *j-n, et.* verraten; ***give back*** zurückgeben; ***give in*** *Gesuch etc* einreichen; *Prüfungsarbeit etc* abgeben; nachgeben; aufgeben; ***give off*** *Geruch* verbreiten; ausstoßen; ausströmen, verströmen; ***give on*(*to*)** führen auf *or* nach, gehen nach; ***give out*** aus-, verteilen; *esp Br* bekannt geben; zu Ende gehen (*supplies, strength etc*); F versagen (*engine etc*); ***give up*** aufgeben; aufhören mit; *j-n* ausliefern; ***give o.s. up*** sich (freiwillig) stellen (***to the police*** der Polizei)

give-and-take beiderseitiges Entgegenkommen, Kompromiss(bereitschaft *f*) *m*

giv·en: ***be given to*** neigen zu (*dat*)

giv·en name Vorname *m*

gla·cial eisig; Eis…

gla·ci·er Gletscher *m*

glad froh, erfreut; ***be glad of*** sich freuen über (*acc*)

glad·ly gern(e)

glam·o(u)r Zauber *m*, Glanz *m*

glam·o(u)r·ous bezaubernd, reizvoll

glance **1.** (schneller *or* flüchtiger) Blick (***at*** auf *acc*); ***at a glance*** auf e-n Blick; **2.**(schnell *or* flüchtig) blicken (***at*** auf *acc*)

gland ANAT Drüse *f*

glare **1.** grell scheinen *or* leuchten; wütend starren; ***glare at s.o.*** j-n wütend anstarren; **2.** greller Schein, grelles Leuchten; wütender Blick

glar·ing *fig* schreiend

glass **1.** Glas *n*; (Trink)Glas *n*; Glas(-gefäß) *n*; (Fern-, Opern)Glas *n*; *Br* F Spiegel *m*; *Br* Barometer *n*; (***a pair of***) ***glasses*** (e-e) Brille; **2.** gläsern; Glas…; **3.** ***glass in, glass up*** verglasen

glass case Vitrine *f*; Schaukasten *m*

glass·ful *ein* Glas (voll)

glass·house Gewächs-, Treibhaus *n*

glass·ware Glaswaren *pl*

glass·y gläsern; glasig

glaze **1.** *v/t* verglasen; glasieren; *v/i*: *a.* ***glaze over*** glasig werden (*eyes*); **2.** Glasur *f*

gla·zi·er Glaser *m*

gleam **1.** schwacher Schein, Schimmer *m*; **2.** leuchten, schimmern

glean *v/t* sammeln; *v/i* Ähren lesen

glee Fröhlichkeit *f*

glee club Gesangverein *m*

glee·ful ausgelassen, fröhlich

glen enges Bergtal *n*

glib gewandt; schlagfertig

glide **1.** gleiten; segeln; **2.** Gleiten *n*; AVIAT Gleitflug *m*

glid·er Segelflugzeug *n*

glid·ing Segelfliegen *n*

glim·mer **1.** schimmern; **2.** Schimmer *m*

glimpse **1.** (nur) flüchtig zu sehen bekommen; **2.** flüchtiger Blick

glint **1.** glitzern, glänzen; **2.** Glitzern *n*, Glanz *m*

glis·ten glitzern, glänzen

glit·ter **1.** glitzern, funkeln, glänzen; **2.** Glitzern *n*, Funkeln *n*, Glanz *m*

gloat: ***gloat over*** sich hämisch *or* diebisch freuen über (*acc*)

gloat·ing hämisch, schadenfroh

glo·bal Welt…, global, weltumspannend; umfassend

global warm·ing Erwärmung *f* der Erdatmosphäre

globe (Erd)Kugel *f*; Globus *m*

gloom Düsterkeit *f*; Dunkelheit *f*; düstere *or* gedrückte Stimmung

gloom·y düster; hoffnungslos; niedergeschlagen; trübsinnig, trübselig

glo·ri·fi·ca·tion Verherrlichung *f*

glo·ri·fy verherrlichen

glo·ri·ous ruhmreich, glorreich; herrlich, prächtig

glo·ry Ruhm *m*; Herrlichkeit *f*, Pracht *f*

gloss **1.** Glanz *m*; LING Glosse *f*; **2.** ***gloss over*** beschönigen, vertuschen

glos·sa·ry Glossar *n*

gloss·y glänzend

glove Handschuh *m*

glove com·partment MOT Handschuhfach *n*

glow **1.** glühen; **2.** Glühen *n*; Glut *f*

glow·er finster blicken

glow-worm ZO Glühwürmchen *n*

glu·cose Traubenzucker *m*

glue **1.** Leim *m*; **2.** kleben

glum bedrückt

glut·ton *fig* Vielfraß *m*

glut·ton·ous gefräßig, unersättlich

gnarled knorrig; knotig (*hands etc*)

gnash knirschen (mit)

gnat ZO (Stech)Mücke *f*

gnaw (zer)nagen; (zer)fressen

gnome Gnom *m*; Gartenzwerg *m*

go **1.** gehen, fahren, reisen (***to*** nach); (fort)gehen; gehen, führen (***to*** nach) (*road etc*); sich erstrecken, gehen (***to*** bis zu); verkehren, fahren (*bus etc*); TECH gehen, laufen, funktionieren; vergehen (*time*); harmonieren (***with*** mit), passen (***with*** zu); ausgehen, ablaufen, ausfallen; werden (***go mad***; ***go blind***); ***be going to*** *inf* im Begriff sein zu *inf*, *tun* wollen, *tun* werden; ***go shares*** teilen; ***go swimming*** schwimmen gehen; ***it is going to rain*** es gibt Regen; ***I must be going*** ich muss gehen; ***go for a walk*** e-n Spaziergang machen, spazieren gehen; ***go to bed*** ins Bett gehen; ***go to school*** zur Schule gehen; ***go to see*** besuchen; ***let go*** loslassen; ***go after*** nachlaufen (*dat*); sich bemühen um; ***go ahead*** vorangehen; vorausgehen, vorausfahren; ***go ahead with*** beginnen mit; fortfahren mit; ***go at*** losgehen auf (*acc*); ***go away*** weggehen; ***go between*** vermitteln zwischen (*dat*); ***go by*** vorbeigehen, vorbeifahren; vergehen (*time*); *fig* sich halten an (*acc*), sich richten nach; ***go down*** untergehen (*sun*); ***go for*** holen; ***go in*** hineingehen; ***go in for an examination*** e-e Prüfung machen; ***go off*** fortgehen, weggehen; losgehen (*gun etc*); ***go on*** weitergehen, weiterfahren; *fig* fortfahren (***doing*** zu tun); *fig* vor sich gehen, vorgehen; ***go out*** hinausgehen; ausgehen (***with*** mit); ausgehen (*light etc*); ***go through*** durchgehen, durchnehmen; durchmachen; ***go up*** steigen; hinaufgehen, -steigen; ***go without*** sich behelfen ohne, auskommen ohne; **2.** F Schwung *m*, Schmiss *m*; *esp Br* F Versuch *m*; ***it's my go*** *esp Br* F ich bin dran *or* an der Reihe; ***it's a go!*** F abgemacht!; ***have a go at s.th.*** *Br* F et. probieren; ***be all the go*** *Br* F große Mode sein

goad *fig* anstacheln

go-a·head[1]: ***get the go-ahead*** grünes Licht bekommen; ***give s.o. the go-ahead*** j-m grünes Licht geben

go-a·head[2] *Br* zielstrebig; unternehmungslustig

goal Ziel *n* (*a. fig*); SPORT Tor *n*; ***keep goal*** im Tor stehen; ***score a goal*** ein Tor schießen *or* erzielen; ***consolation goal*** Ehrentreffer *m*; ***own goal*** Eigentor *n*, Eigentreffer *m*; ***shot at goal*** Torschuss *m*

goal·ie F, **goal·keep·er** SPORT Torwart *m*, Torhüter *m*

goal kick *soccer*: Abstoß *m*

goal line SPORT Torlinie *f*

goal·mouth SPORT Torraum *m*

goal·post SPORT Torpfosten *m*

goat ZO Ziege *f*, Geiß *f*

gob·ble schlingen; *mst* ***gobble up*** verschlingen (*a. fig*)

go-be·tween Vermittler(in), Mittelsmann *m*

gob·lin Kobold *m*

god REL ***God*** Gott *m*; *fig* Abgott *m*

god·child Patenkind *n*

god·dess Göttin *f*

god·fa·ther Pate *m* (*a. fig*), Taufpate *m*

god·for·sak·en *contp* gottverlassen

god·head Gottheit *f*

god·less gottlos

god·like gottähnlich; göttlich

god·moth·er (Tauf)Patin *f*

god·pa·rent (Tauf)Pate, (Tauf)Patin *f*

god·send Geschenk *n* des Himmels

gog·gle glotzen

gog·gle box *Br* F TV Glotze *f*

gog·gles Schutzbrille *f*

go·ings-on F Treiben *n*, Vorgänge *pl*

gold **1.** Gold *n*; **2.** golden

gold·en *mst fig* golden, goldgelb

gold·finch ZO Stieglitz *m*

gold·fish ZO Goldfisch *m*

gold·smith Goldschmied *m*

golf **1.** Golf(spiel) *n*; **2.** Golf spielen

golf club Golfschläger *m*; Golfklub *m*

golf course, **golf links** Golfplatz *m*

gon·do·la Gondel *f*

gone *adj* fort; F futsch; vergangen; tot; F hoffnungslos

good **1.** gut; artig; gütig; gründlich; ***good at*** geschickt *or* gut in (*dat*); ***real good*** F echt gut; **2.** Nutzen *m*, Wert *m*; *das* Gute; ***do (no) good*** (nichts) nützen; ***for good*** für immer; F ***what good is …?*** was nützt …?

good·by(e) **1.** ***wish s.o. goodby, say goodby to s.o.*** j-m Auf Wiedersehen sagen; **2.** *int* (auf) Wiedersehen!

Good Fri·day REL Karfreitag *m*

good-hu·mo(u)red gut gelaunt; gutmütig

good-look·ing gut aussehend

good-na·tured gutmütig

good·ness Güte *f*; ***thank goodness!*** Gott sei Dank!; ***(my) goodness!, goodness gracious!*** du meine Güte!, du lieber Himmel!; ***for goodness' sake*** um Himmels willen!; ***goodness knows*** weiß der Himmel

goods ECON Waren *pl*, Güter *pl*

good·will gute Absicht, guter Wille; ECON Firmenwert *m*

good·y F Bonbon *m*, *n*

goose ZO Gans *f*

goose·ber·ry BOT Stachelbeere *f*

goose·flesh, **goose pim·ples** *fig* Gänsehaut *f*

go·pher ZO Taschenratte *f*; Ziesel *m*

gore durchbohren, aufspießen

gorge **1.** ANAT Kehle *f*, Schlund *m*; GEOGR enge (Fels)Schlucht; **2.** verschlingen; schlingen, (sich) vollstopfen

gor·geous prächtig

go·ril·la ZO Gorilla *m*

gor·y F blutrünstig

gosh *int* F Mensch!, Mann!

gos·ling ZO junge Gans

go-slow *Br* ECON Bummelstreik *m*

Gos·pel REL Evangelium *n*

gos·sa·mer Altweibersommer *m*
gos·sip **1.** Klatsch *m*, Tratsch *m*; Klatschbase *f*; **2.** klatschen, tratschen
gos·sip·y geschwätzig; voller Klatsch und Tratsch (*letter etc*)
Goth·ic ARCH **1.** gotisch; ***Gothic novel*** Schauerroman *m*; **2.** Gotik *f*
gourd BOT Kürbis *m*
gout MED Gicht *f*
gov·ern *v/t* regieren; lenken, leiten; *v/i* herrschen
gov·ern·ess Erzieherin *f*
gov·ern·ment Regierung *f*; Staat *m*
gov·er·nor Gouverneur *m*; Direktor *m*, Leiter *m*; F Alte *m*
gown Kleid *n*; Robe *f*, Talar *m*
grab **1.** packen, (hastig *or* gierig) ergreifen, fassen; **2.** (hastiger *or* gieriger) Griff; TECH Greifer *m*
grace **1.** Anmut *f*, Grazie *f*; Anstand *m*; ECON Frist *f*, Aufschub *m*; Gnade *f*; REL Tischgebet *n*; **2.** zieren, schmücken
grace·ful anmutig
grace·less ungraziös
gra·cious gnädig
gra·da·tion Abstufung *f*
grade **1.** Grad *m*, Rang *m*; Stufe *f*; ECON Qualität *f*; RAIL *etc* Steigung *f*, Gefälle *n*; PED Klasse *f*; Note *f*, Zensur *f*; **2.** sortieren, einteilen; abstufen
grade cross·ing RAIL schienengleicher Bahnübergang
grade school Grundschule *f*
gra·di·ent *Br* RAIL *etc* Steigung *f*, Gefälle *n*
grad·u·al stufenweise, allmählich
grad·u·al·ly nach und nach; allmählich
grad·u·ate **1.** UNIV Hochschulabsolvent(in), Akademiker(in); Graduierte *m*, *f*; PED Schulabgänger(in); **2.** abstufen, staffeln; UNIV graduieren; PED die Abschlussprüfung bestehen
grad·u·a·tion Abstufung *f*, Staffelung *f*; UNIV Graduierung *f*; PED Absolvieren *n* (***from*** *gen*)
graf·fi·ti Graffiti *pl*, Wandschmierereien *pl*
graft **1.** MED Transplantat *n*; AGR Pfropfreis *n*; **2.** MED *Gewebe* verpflanzen, transplantieren; AGR pfropfen
grain (Samen-, *esp* Getreide)Korn *n*; Getreide *n*; (*Sand- etc*)Körnchen *n*, (-)Korn *n*; Maserung *f*; ***go against the grain for s.o.*** *fig* j-m gegen den Strich gehen
gram Gramm *n*
gram·mar Grammatik *f*
gram·mar school Grundschule *f*; *Br appr* (humanistisches) Gymnasium
gram·mat·i·cal grammatisch, Grammatik…
gramme → ***gram***
gra·na·ry Kornspeicher *m*
grand **1.** *fig* großartig; erhaben; groß; Groß…, Haupt…; **2.** F Riese *m* (*1000 dollars or pounds*)
grand·child Enkel *m*, Enkelin *f*
grand·daugh·ter Enkelin *f*
gran·deur Größe *f*, Erhabenheit *f*; Großartigkeit *f*
grand·fa·ther Großvater *m*
gran·di·ose großartig
grand·moth·er Großmutter *f*
grand·par·ents Großeltern *pl*
grand·son Enkel *m*
grand·stand SPORT Haupttribüne *f*
gran·ny F Oma *f*
grant **1.** bewilligen, gewähren; *Erlaubnis etc* geben; *Bitte etc* erfüllen; *et.* zugeben; ***take s.th. for granted*** et. als selbstverständlich betrachten *or* hinnehmen; **2.** Stipendium *n*; Bewilligung *f*, Unterstützung *f*
gran·u·lat·ed körnig, granuliert; ***granulated sugar*** Kristallzucker *m*
gran·ule Körnchen *n*
grape BOT Weinbeere *f*, Weintraube *f*
grape·fruit BOT Grapefruit *f*, Pampelmuse *f*
grape·vine BOT Weinstock *m*
graph grafische Darstellung
graph·ic grafisch; anschaulich; ***graphic arts*** Grafik *f*
graph·ics EDP Grafik *f*
grap·ple: ***grapple with*** kämpfen mit, *fig a.* sich herumschlagen mit
grasp **1.** (er)greifen, packen; *fig* verstehen, begreifen; **2.** Griff *m*; Reichweite *f* (*a. fig*); *fig* Verständnis *n*
grass Gras *n*; Rasen *m*; Weide(land *n*) *f*; *sl.* Grass *n* (*marijuana*)
grass·hop·per ZO Heuschrecke *f*
grass roots POL Basis *f*
grass wid·ow Strohwitwe *f*
grass wid·ow·er Strohwitwer *m*
gras·sy grasbedeckt, Gras…
grate **1.** (Kamin)Gitter *n*; (Feuer)Rost *m*; **2.** reiben, raspeln; knirschen (mit); ***grate on s.o.'s nerves*** an j-s Nerven zerren
grate·ful dankbar
grat·er Reibe *f*
grat·i·fi·ca·tion Befriedigung *f*; Freude *f*
grat·i·fy erfreuen; befriedigen
grat·ing[1] kratzend, knirschend, quietschend; schrill; unangenehm
grat·ing[2] Gitter(werk) *n*
grat·i·tude Dankbarkeit *f*
gra·tu·i·tous unentgeltlich; freiwillig
gra·tu·i·ty Abfindung *f*; Gratifikation *f*;

Trinkgeld *n*
grave[1] ernst; (ge)wichtig; gemessen
grave[2] Grab *n*
grave·dig·ger Totengräber *m*
grav·el **1.** Kies *m*; **2.** mit Kies bestreuen
grave·stone Grabstein *m*
grave·yard Friedhof *m*
grav·i·ta·tion PHYS Gravitation *f*, Schwerkraft *f*
grav·i·ty PHYS Schwerkraft *f*; Ernst *m*
gra·vy Bratensaft *m*; Bratensoße *f*
gray **1.** grau; **2.** Grau *n*; **3.** grau machen *or* werden
gray·hound ZO Windhund *m*
graze[1] *Vieh* weiden (lassen); (ab)weiden; (ab)grasen
graze[2] **1.** streifen; schrammen; *Haut* (ab-, auf)schürfen, (auf)schrammen; **2.** Abschürfung *f*, Schramme *f*; Streifschuss *m*
grease **1.** Fett *n*; TECH Schmierfett *n*, Schmiere *f*; **2.** (ein)fetten; TECH schmieren
greas·y fett(ig), ölig; speckig; schmierig
great groß; Ur(groß)…; F großartig, super
Great Brit·ain Großbritannien *n*
great-grand·child Urenkel(in)
great-grand·par·ents Urgroßeltern *pl*
great·ly sehr
great·ness Größe *f*
Greece Griechenland *n*
greed Gier *f*
greed·y gierig (***for*** auf *acc*, nach); habgierig; gefräßig
Greek **1.** griechisch; **2.** Grieche *m*, Griechin *f*; LING Griechisch *n*
green **1.** grün; *fig* grün, unerfahren; **2.** Grün *n*; Grünfläche *f*, Rasen *m*; *pl* grünes Gemüse, Blattgemüse *n*
green·back F Dollar *m*
green belt Grüngürtel *m*
green card Arbeitserlaubnis *f*
green·gro·cer *esp Br* Obst- und Gemüsehändler(in)
green·horn F Greenhorn *n*, Grünschnabel *m*
green·house Gewächs-, Treibhaus *n*
greenhouse ef·fect Treibhauseffekt *m*
green·ish grünlich
greet grüßen
greet·ing Begrüßung *f*, Gruß *m*; *pl* Grüße *pl*
gre·nade MIL Granate *f*
grey *Br* → ***gray***
grid Gitter *n*; ELECTR *etc* Versorgungsnetz *n*; Gitter(netz) *n* (*map etc*)
grid·i·ron Bratrost *m*
grief Kummer *m*
griev·ance (Grund *m* zur) Beschwerde *f*; Missstand *m*
grieve *v/t* betrüben, bekümmern; *v/i* bekümmert sein; ***grieve for*** trauern um
griev·ous schwer, schlimm
grill **1.** grillen; **2.** Grill *m*; Bratrost *m*; GASTR *das* Gegrillte *n*
grim grimmig; schrecklich; erbittert; F schlimm
gri·mace **1.** Fratze *f*, Grimasse *f*; **2.** Grimassen schneiden
grime Schmutz *m*; Ruß *m*
grim·y schmutzig; rußig
grin **1.** Grinsen *n*; **2.** grinsen
grind **1.** *v/t* (zer)mahlen, zerreiben, zerkleinern; *Messer etc* schleifen; *Fleisch* durchdrehen; ***grind one's teeth*** mit den Zähnen knirschen; *v/i* F schuften; pauken, büffeln; **2.** Schinderei *f*, F Schufterei *f*; ***the daily grind*** das tägliche Einerlei
grind·er (Messer- *etc*)Schleifer *m*; TECH Schleifmaschine *f*; TECH Mühle *f*
grind·stone Schleifstein *m*
grip **1.** packen (*a. fig*); **2.** Griff *m*; *fig* Gewalt *f*, Herrschaft *f*; Reisetasche *f*
grip·ping spannend
gris·ly grässlich, schrecklich
gris·tle GASTR Knorpel *m*
grit **1.** Kies *m*, (grober) Sand; *fig* Mut *m*; **2.** streuen; ***grit one's teeth*** die Zähne zusammenbeißen
griz·zly (bear) ZO Grislibär *m*, Graubär *m*
groan **1.** stöhnen, ächzen; **2.** Stöhnen *n*, Ächzen *n*
gro·cer Lebensmittelhändler *m*
gro·cer·ies Lebensmittel *pl*
gro·cer·y Lebensmittelgeschäft *n*
grog·gy F groggy, schwach *or* wackelig (auf den Beinen)
groin ANAT Leiste *f*, Leistengegend *f*
groom **1.** Pferdepfleger *m*, Stallbursche *m*; Bräutigam *m*; **2.** *Pferde* versorgen, striegeln; pflegen
groove Rinne *f*, Furche *f*; Rille *f*, Nut *f*
grope tasten; F *Mädchen* befummeln
gross **1.** dick, feist; grob, derb; ECON Brutto…; **2.** Gros *n*
gro·tesque grotesk
ground[1] gemahlen (*coffee etc*); ***ground meat*** Hackfleisch *n*
ground[2] **1.** (Erd)Boden *m*, Erde *f*; Boden *m*, Gebiet *n*; SPORT (*Spiel*)Platz *m*; ELECTR Erdung *f*; (Boden)Satz *m*; *fig* Beweggrund *m*; *pl* Grundstück *n*, Park *m*, Gartenanlage *f*; ***on the ground(s) of*** aufgrund (*gen*); ***hold*** *or* ***stand one's ground*** sich behaupten; **2.** MAR auflaufen; ELECTR erden; *fig* gründen, stützen
ground crew AVIAT Bodenpersonal *n*
ground floor *esp Br* Erdgeschoss *n*

ground forc·es MIL Bodentruppen *pl*, Landstreitkräfte *pl*
ground·hog ZO Amer. Waldmurmeltier *n*
ground·ing ELECTR Erdung *f*; Grundlagen *pl*, Grundkenntnisse *pl*
ground·keep·er SPORT Platzwart *m*
ground·less grundlos
ground·nut *Br* BOT Erdnuss *f*
grounds·man *Br* SPORT Platzwart *m*
ground staff *Br* AVIAT Bodenpersonal *n*
ground sta·tion Bodenstation *f*
ground·work *fig* Grundlage *f*, Fundament *n*
group **1.** Gruppe *f*; **2.** (sich) gruppieren
group·ie F Groupie *n*
group·ing Gruppierung *f*
grove Wäldchen *n*, Gehölz *n*
grov·el (am Boden) kriechen
grow *v/i* wachsen; (allmählich) werden; ***grow up*** aufwachsen, heranwachsen; *v/t* BOT anpflanzen, anbauen, züchten; ***grow a beard*** sich e-n Bart wachsen lassen
grow·er Züchter *m*, Erzeuger *m*
growl knurren, brummen
grown-up **1.** erwachsen; **2.** Erwachsene *m*, *f*
growth Wachsen *n*, Wachstum *n*; Wuchs *m*, Größe *f*; *fig* Zunahme *f*, Anwachsen *n*; MED Gewächs *n*, Wucherung *f*
grub **1.** ZO Larve *f*, Made *f*; F Futter *n*; **2.** graben
grub·by schmudd(e)lig
grudge **1.** missgönnen (***s.o. s.th.*** j-m et.); **2.** Groll *m*
grudg·ing·ly widerwillig
gru·el Haferschleim *m*
gruff grob, schroff, barsch, unwirsch
grum·ble murren, F meckern (***über*** *acc* about, at); ***grumble at*** schimpfen über (*acc*)
grump·y F schlecht gelaunt, mürrisch, missmutig, verdrießlich, verdrossen
grun·gy F schmudd(e)lig-schlampig; MUS schlecht und laut
grunt **1.** grunzen; brummen; stöhnen; **2.** Grunzen *n*; Stöhnen *n*
guar·an·tee **1.** Garantie *f*; Kaution *f*, Sicherheit *f*; **2.** (sich ver)bürgen für; garantieren
guar·an·tor JUR Bürge *m*, Bürgin *f*
guar·an·ty JUR Garantie *f*; Sicherheit *f*
guard **1.** Wache *f*, (Wacht)Posten *m*, Wächter *m*; Wärter *m*, Aufseher *m*; Wache *f*, Bewachung *f*; *Br* Zugbegleiter *m*; Schutz(vorrichtung *f*) *m*; Garde *f*; ***be on guard*** Wache stehen; ***be on*** (***off***) ***one's guard*** (nicht) auf der Hut sein; **2.** *v/t* bewachen, (be)schützen (***from*** vor *dat*); *v/i* sich hüten *or* in Acht nehmen *or* schützen (***against*** vor *dat*)
guard·ed vorsichtig, zurückhaltend
guard·i·an **1.** JUR Vormund *m*; **2.** Schutz…
guard·i·an·ship JUR Vormundschaft *f*
gue(r)·ril·la MIL Guerilla *m*
gue(r)·ril·la war·fare Guerillakrieg *m*
guess **1.** (er)raten; vermuten; schätzen; glauben, meinen; **2.** Vermutung *f*
guess·work (reine) Vermutung(en *pl*)
guest Gast *m*
guest·house (Hotel)Pension *f*, Fremdenheim *n*
guest·room Gäste-, Fremdenzimmer *n*
guf·faw **1.** schallendes Gelächter; **2.** schallend lachen
guid·ance Führung *f*; (An)Leitung *f*
guide **1.** (Reise-, Fremden)Führer(in); (Reise- *etc*)Führer *m* (*book*); Handbuch (***to*** *gen*); ***a guide to London*** ein London-Führer; **2.** leiten; führen; lenken
guide·book (Reise- *etc*)Führer *m*
guid·ed tour Führung *f*
guide·lines Richtlinien *pl* (***on*** *gen*)
guild HIST Gilde *f*, Zunft *f*
guile·less arglos
guilt Schuld *f*
guilt·less schuldlos, unschuldig (***of*** an *dat*)
guilt·y schuldig (***of*** *gen*); schuldbewusst
guin·ea pig ZO Meerschweinchen *n*; *fig* Versuchsperson *f*, F Versuchskaninchen *n*
guise *fig* Gestalt *f*, Maske *f*
gui·tar MUS Gitarre *f*
gulch GEOGR tiefe Schlucht, Klamm *f*
gulf GEOGR Golf *m*; *fig* Kluft *f*
gull ZO Möwe *f*
gul·let ANAT Speiseröhre *f*; Gurgel *f*, Kehle *f*
gulp **1.** (großer) Schluck; **2.** *often* ***gulp down*** *Getränk* hinunterstürzen, *Speise* hinunterschlingen
gum[1] ANAT *mst pl* Zahnfleisch *n*
gum[2] **1.** Gummi *m*, *n*; Klebstoff *m*; Kaugummi *m*; (Frucht)Gummi *m*; **2.** kleben
gump·tion F Grips *m*; Schneid *m*
gun **1.** Gewehr *n*; Pistole *f*, Revolver *m*; Geschütz *n*, Kanone *f*; **2.** ***gun down*** niederschießen
gun·fight Feuergefecht *n*, Schießerei *f*
gun·fire Schüsse *pl*; MIL Geschützfeuer *n*
gun li·cence *Br*, **gun li·cense** Waffenschein *m*
gun·man Bewaffnete *m*
gun·point: ***at gunpoint*** mit vorgehaltener Waffe, mit Waffengewalt
gun·pow·der Schießpulver *n*
gun·run·ner Waffenschmuggler *m*
gun·run·ning Waffenschmuggel *m*

G

gun·shot Schuss *m*; ***within (out of) gunshot*** in (außer) Schussweite
gur·gle 1. gurgeln, gluckern, glucksen; **2.** Gurgeln *n*, Gluckern *n*, Glucksen *n*
gush 1. strömen, schießen (***from*** aus); **2.** Schwall *m*, Strom *m* (*a. fig*)
gust Windstoß *m*, Bö *f*
gust F Eingeweide *pl*; Schneid *m*, Mumm *m*
gut·ter Gosse *f* (*a. fig*), Rinnstein *m*; Dachrinne *f*
guy F Kerl *m*, Typ *m*
guz·zle F saufen; fressen
gym F Fitnesscenter *n*; → ***gymnasium***; → ***gymnastics***
gym·na·si·um Turn-, Sporthalle *f*
gym·nast Turner(in)
gym·nas·tics Turnen *n*, Gymnastik *f*
gym shirt Turnhemd *n*
gym shorts Turnhose *f*
gy·n(a)e·col·o·gist Gynäkologe *m*, Gynäkologin *f*, Frauenarzt *m*, -ärztin *f*
gy·n(a)e·col·o·gy Gynäkologie *f*, Frauenheilkunde *f*
gyp·sy Zigeuner *m*, Zigeunerin *f*
gy·rate kreisen, sich (im Kreis) drehen, (herum)wirbeln

H

H

H, h H, h *n*
hab·it (An)Gewohnheit *f*; *esp* (Ordens-) Tracht *f*; ***get into (out of) the habit of smoking*** sich das Rauchen angewöhnen (abgewöhnen)
ha·bit·u·al gewohnheitsmäßig, Gewohnheits…
hack[1] hacken
hack[2] *contp* Schreiberling *m*
hack[3] *contp* Klepper *m*
hack·er EDP Hacker *m*
hack·neyed abgedroschen
had·dock zo Schellfisch *m*
h(a)e·mor·rhage MED Blutung *f*
hag hässliches altes Weib, Hexe *f*
hag·gard abgespannt; verhärmt, abgehärmt; hager
hag·gle feilschen, handeln
hail 1. Hagel *m*; **2.** hageln
hail·stone Hagelkorn *n*
hail·storm Hagelschauer *m*
hair *einzelnes* Haar; *coll* Haar *n*, Haare *pl*; ***let one's hair down*** F aus sich herausgehen; ***without turning a hair*** ohne mit der Wimper zu zucken
hair·breadth → ***hair's breadth***
hair·brush Haarbürste *f*
hair·cut Haarschnitt *m*
hair·do F Frisur *f*
hair·dress·er Friseur(in)
hair·dri·er, hair·dry·er Trockenhaube *f*; Haartrockner *m*, Föhn *m*
hair·grip *Br* Haarklammer *f*, Haarklemme *f*
hair·less ohne Haare, kahl
hair·pin Haarnadel *f*
hairpin bend MOT Haarnadelkurve *f*
hair-rais·ing haarsträubend
hair's breadth: ***by a hair's breadth*** um Haaresbreite
hair slide *Br* Haarspange *f*
hair-split·ting Haarspalterei *f*
hair·spray Haarspray *m*, *n*
hair·style Frisur *f*
hair styl·ist Hair-Stylist *m*, Damenfriseur *m*
hair·y behaart, haarig
half 1. Hälfte *f*; ***go halves*** halbe-halbe machen, teilen; **2.** halb; ***half an hour*** e-e halbe Stunde; ***half a pound*** ein halbes Pfund; ***half past ten*** halb elf (Uhr); ***half way up*** auf halber Höhe
half-breed Halbblut *n*
half-broth·er Halbbruder *m*
half-caste *esp contp* Mischling *m*
half-heart·ed halbherzig
half time SPORT Halbzeit *f*
half time score SPORT Halbzeitstand *m*
half·way halb; auf halbem Weg, in der Mitte
halfway line *soccer*: Mittellinie *f*
half-wit·ted schwachsinnig
hal·i·but zo Heilbutt *m*
hall Halle *f*, Saal *m*; Flur *m*, Diele *f*; *esp Br* Herrenhaus *n*; *Br* UNIV Speisesaal *m*; *Br* ***hall of residence*** Studentenheim *n*
hall·mark *fig* Kennzeichen *n*
Hal·low·e'en Abend *m* vor Allerheiligen
hal·lu·ci·na·tion Halluzination *f*
hall·way Halle *f*, Diele *f*; Korridor *m*

ha·lo ASTR Hof *m*; Heiligenschein *m*
halt 1. Halt *m*; **2.** (an)halten
hal·ter Halfter *m*, *n*
halt·ing zögernd, stockend
halve halbieren
ham Schinken *m*; ***ham and eggs*** Schinken mit (Spiegel)Ei
ham·burg·er GASTR Hamburger *m*; Rinderhack *n*
ham·let Weiler *m*
ham·mer 1. Hammer *m*; **2.** hämmern
ham·mock Hängematte *f*
ham·per[1] (Deckel)Korb *m*; Präsentkorb *m*; Wäschekorb *m*
ham·per[2] (be)hindern
ham·ster ZO Hamster *m*
hand 1. Hand *f* (*a. fig*); Handschrift *f*; (Uhr)Zeiger *m*; *often in cpds* Arbeiter *m*; Fachmann *m*; *card game*: Blatt *n*, Karten *pl*; ***hand in glove*** ein Herz und eine Seele; ***change hands*** den Besitzer wechseln; ***give** or **lend a hand*** mit zugreifen, *j-m* helfen (***with*** by); ***shake hands with*** *j-m* die Hand schütteln *or* geben; ***at hand*** in Reichweite; nahe; bei der *or* zur Hand; ***at first hand*** aus erster Hand; ***by hand*** mit der Hand; ***on the one hand*** einerseits; ***on the other hand*** andererseits; ***on the right hand*** rechts; ***hands off!*** Hände weg!; ***hands up!*** Hände hoch!; **2.** aushändigen, (über)geben, (über)reichen; ***hand around*** herumreichen; ***hand down*** weitergeben, überliefern; ***hand in*** *Prüfungsarbeit etc* abgeben; *Bericht*, *Gesuch etc* einreichen; ***hand on*** weiterreichen, weitergeben; überliefern; ***hand out*** austeilen, verteilen; ***hand over*** übergeben, aushändigen (***to*** *dat*); ***hand up*** hinauf-, heraufreichen
hand·bag Handtasche *f*
hand bag·gage Handgepäck *n*
hand·ball SPORT Handball *m*; *soccer*: Handspiel *n*
hand·book Handbuch *n*
hand·bill Handzettel *m*, Flugblatt *n*
hand·brake TECH Handbremse *f*
hand·cart Handwagen *m*
hand·cuffs Handschellen *pl*
hand·ful Handvoll *f*; F Plage *f*
hand gre·nade MIL Handgranate *f*
hand·i·cap 1. Handikap *n*, MED *a.* Behinderung *f*, SPORT *a.* Vorgabe *f*; → ***mental handicap, physical handicap***; **2.** behindern, benachteiligen
hand·i·capped 1. gehandikapt, behindert, benachteiligt; → ***mental, physical***; **2.** ***the handicapped*** MED die Behinderten *pl*
hand·ker·chief Taschentuch *n*
han·dle 1. Griff *m*; Stiel *m*; Henkel *m*; Klinke *f*; ***fly off the handle*** F wütend werden; **2.** anfassen, berühren; hantieren *or* umgehen mit; behandeln
han·dle·bar(s) Lenkstange *f*
hand lug·gage Handgepäck *n*
hand·made handgearbeitet
hand·out Almosen *n*; Handzettel *m*; Hand-out *n*, Informationsmaterial *n*
hand·rail Geländer *n*
hand·shake Händedruck *m*
hand·some gut aussehend; *fig* ansehnlich, beträchtlich (*sum etc*)
hands-on praktisch
hand·spring Handstandüberschlag *m*
hand·stand Handstand *m*
hand·writ·ing Handschrift *f*
hand·writ·ten handgeschrieben
hand·y zur Hand; geschickt; handlich, praktisch; nützlich; ***come in handy*** sich als nützlich erweisen; (sehr) gelegen kommen
hand·y·man Handwerker *m*; ***be a handyman*** *a.* handwerklich geschickt sein
hang (auf-, be-, ein)hängen; *Tapete* ankleben; *j-n* (auf)hängen; ***hang o.s.*** sich erhängen; ***hang about, hang around*** herumlungern; ***hang on*** sich klammern (***to*** an *acc*) (*a. fig*), festhalten (***to*** *acc*); TEL am Apparat bleiben; ***hang up*** TEL einhängen, auflegen; ***she hung up on me*** sie legte einfach auf
han·gar Hangar *m*, Flugzeughalle *f*
hang·er Kleiderbügel *m*
hang glid·er SPORT (Flug)Drachen *m*; Drachenflieger(in)
hang glid·ing SPORT Drachenfliegen *n*
hang·ing 1. Hänge…; **2.** (Er)Hängen *n*
hang·ings Tapete *f*, Wandbehang *m*, Vorhang *m*
hang·man Henker *m*
hang·nail MED Niednagel *m*
hang·o·ver Katzenjammer *m*, Kater *m*
han·ker F sich sehnen (***after, for*** nach)
han·kie, han·ky F Taschentuch *n*
hap·haz·ard willkürlich, planlos, wahllos
hap·pen (zufällig) geschehen; sich ereignen, passieren, vorkommen
hap·pen·ing Ereignis *n*, Vorkommnis *n*; Happening *n*
hap·pi·ly glücklich(erweise)
hap·pi·ness Glück *n*
hap·py glücklich; erfreut
hap·py-go-luck·y unbekümmert, sorglos
ha·rangue 1. (Straf)Predigt *f*; **2.** *v/t j-m* e-e Strafpredigt halten
har·ass ständig belästigen; schikanieren; aufreiben, zermürben

har·ass·ment ständige Belästigung; Schikane(n *pl*) *f*; → ***sexual harassment***
har·bo(u)r 1. Hafen *m*; Zufluchtsort *m*; **2.** *j-m* Zuflucht *or* Unterschlupf gewähren; *Groll etc* hegen
hard hart (*a. fig*); fest; schwer, schwierig; heftig, stark; streng (*a. winter*); *fig* nüchtern (*facts etc*); ***give s.o. a hard time*** j-m das Leben schwer machen; ***hard of hearing*** schwerhörig; ***be hard on s.th.*** et. strapazieren; ***hard up*** F in (Geld)Schwierigkeiten, knapp bei Kasse; F ***the hard stuff*** die harten Sachen (*alcohol, drugs*)
hard·back gebundene Ausgabe
hard-boiled GASTR hart (gekocht); F *fig* hart, unsentimental, nüchtern
hard cash Bargeld *n*; klingende Münze
hard core harter Kern
hard-core zum harten Kern gehörend; hart
hard court *tennis*: Hartplatz *m*
hard·cov·er 1. gebunden; **2.** Hard Cover *n*, gebundene Ausgabe
hard cur·ren·cy ECON harte Währung
hard disk EDP Festplatte *f*
hard·en härten; hart machen *or* werden; (sich) abhärten
hard hat Schutzhelm *m*
hard-head·ed nüchtern, praktisch; starrköpfig, dickköpfig
hard-heart·ed hartherzig
hard la·bo(u)r JUR Zwangsarbeit *f*
hard line *esp* POL harter Kurs
hard-line *esp* POL hart, kompromisslos
hard·ly kaum
hard·ness Härte *f*; Schwierigkeit *f*
hard·ship Not *f*; Härte *f*; Strapaze *f*
hard shoul·der *Br* MOT Standspur *f*
hard·top MOT Hardtop *n*, *m*
hard·ware Eisenwaren *pl*; Haushaltswaren *pl*; EDP Hardware *f*
hard·wear·ing strapazierfähig
har·dy zäh, robust, abgehärtet; BOT winterhart, winterfest
hare ZO Hase *m*
hare·bell BOT Glockenblume *f*
hare·brained verrückt
hare·lip MED Hasenscharte *f*
harm 1. Schaden *m*; **2.** verletzen; schaden (*dat*)
harm·ful schädlich
harm·less harmlos
har·mo·ni·ous harmonisch
har·mo·nize harmonieren; in Einklang sein *or* bringen
har·mo·ny Harmonie *f*
har·ness 1. (*Pferde- etc*)Geschirr *n*; ***die in harness*** *fig* in den Sielen sterben; **2.** anschirren; anspannen (***to*** an *acc*)
harp 1. MUS Harfe *f*; **2.** MUS Harfe spielen; F ***harp on*** (***about***) herumreiten auf (*dat*)
har·poon 1. Harpune *f*; **2.** harpunieren
har·row AGR **1.** Egge *f*; **2.** eggen
har·row·ing quälend, qualvoll, erschütternd
harsh rau; grell; streng; schroff, barsch
hart ZO Hirsch *m*
har·vest 1. Ernte(zeit) *f*; (Ernte)Ertrag *m*; **2.** ernten
har·vest·er MOT Mähdrescher *m*
hash[1] GASTR Haschee *n*; F ***make a hash of s.th.*** et. verpfuschen
hash[2] F Hasch *n*
hash browns GASTR Brat-, Röstkartoffeln *pl*
hash·ish Haschisch *n*
hasp TECH Haspe *f*
haste Eile *f*, Hast *f*
has·ten *j-n* antreiben; (sich be)eilen; *et.* beschleunigen
hast·y eilig, hastig, überstürzt; voreilig
hat Hut *m*
hatch[1]: *a.* ***hatch out*** ZO ausbrüten; ausschlüpfen
hatch[2] Durchreiche *f*; AVIAT, MAR Luke *f*
hatch·back MOT (Wagen *m* mit) Hecktür *f*
hatch·et Beil *n*; ***bury the hatchet*** das Kriegsbeil begraben
hate 1. Hass *m*; **2.** hassen
hate·ful verhasst; abscheulich
ha·tred Hass *m*
haugh·ty hochmütig, überheblich
haul 1. ziehen, zerren; schleppen; befördern, transportieren; **2.** Ziehen *n*; Fischzug *m*, *fig* F *a.* Fang *m*; Beförderung *f*, Transport *m*; Transportweg *m*
haul·age Beförderung *f*, Transport *m*
haul·er, *Br* **haul·i·er** Transportunternehmer *m*
haunch ANAT Hüfte *f*, Hüftpartie *f*, Hinterbacke *f*; GASTR Keule *f*
haunt 1. spuken in (*dat*); häufig besuchen; *fig* verfolgen, quälen; **2.** häufig besuchter Ort; Schlupfwinkel *m*
haunt·ing quälend; unvergesslich, eindringlich
have *v/t* haben; erhalten, bekommen; essen, trinken; ***have breakfast*** frühstücken; ***have a cup of tea*** e-n Tee trinken); *with inf*: müssen (***I have to go now*** ich muss jetzt gehen); *with object and pp*: lassen (***I had my hair cut*** ich ließ mir die Haare schneiden); ***have back*** zurückbekommen; ***have on*** *Kleidungsstück* anhaben, *Hut* aufhaben; *v/aux* haben; *v/i* oft *ten* sein; ***I have come*** ich bin gekommen
ha·ven Hafen *m* (*mst fig*)
hav·oc Verwüstung *f*, Zerstörung *f*; ***play***

havoc with verwüsten, zerstören; *fig* verheerend wirken auf (*acc*)
hawk[1] ZO Habicht *m*, Falke *m*
hawk[2] hausieren mit; auf der Straße verkaufen
hawk·er Hausierer(in); Straßenhändler(in); Drücker(in)
haw·thorn BOT Weißdorn *m*
hay Heu *n*
hay fe·ver MED Heuschnupfen *m*
hay·loft Heuboden *m*
hay·stack Heuhaufen *m*
haz·ard Gefahr *f*, Risiko *n*
haz·ard·ous gewagt, gefährlich, riskant
hazardous waste Sonder-, Giftmüll *m*
haze Dunst(schleier) *m*
ha·zel 1. BOT Hasel(nuss)strauch *m*; **2.** (hasel)nussbraun
ha·zel·nut BOT Haselnuss *f*
haz·y dunstig, diesig; *fig* unklar, verschwommen
H-bomb H-Bombe *f*, Wasserstoffbombe *f*
he 1. er; **2.** Er *m*; ZO Männchen *n*; ***he-goat*** Ziegenbock *m*
head 1. Kopf *m*; (Ober)Haupt *n*; Chef *m*; (An)Führer(in), Leiter(in); Spitze *f*; Kopf(ende *n*) *m*; Kopf *m* (*of a page, nail etc*); Vorderseite *f*; Überschrift *f*; ***20 dollars a head*** *or* ***per head*** zwanzig Dollar pro Kopf *or* Person; ***40 head (of cattle)*** 40 Stück (Vieh); ***heads or tails?*** Kopf oder Zahl?; ***at the head of*** an der Spitze (*gen*); ***head over heels*** kopfüber; bis über beide Ohren (*verliebt sein*); ***bury one's head in the sand*** den Kopf in den Sand stecken; ***get it into one's head that …*** es sich in den Kopf setzen, dass; ***lose one's head*** den Kopf *or* die Nerven verlieren;**2.** Ober…, Haupt…, Chef…, oberste(r, -s), erste(r, -s); **3.** *v/t* anführen, an der Spitze stehen von (*or gen*); voran-, vorausgehen (*dat*); (an)führen, leiten; *soccer*: köpfen; *v/i* (***for***) gehen, fahren (nach); lossteuern, losgehen (auf *acc*); MAR Kurs halten (auf *acc*)
head·ache Kopfweh *n*
head·band Stirnband *n*
head·dress Kopfschmuck *m*
head·er Kopfsprung *m*; *soccer*: Kopfball *m*
head·first kopfuber, mit dem Kopf voran; *fig* ungestüm, stürmisch
head·gear Kopfbedeckung *f*
head·ing Überschrift *f*, Titel(zeile *f*) *m*
head·land Landspitze *f*, Landzunge *f*
head·light MOT Scheinwerfer *m*
head·line Schlagzeile *f*; ***news headlines*** *radio*, TV *das* Wichtigste in Schlagzeilen
head·long kopfüber; *fig* ungestüm
head·mas·ter *Br* PED Direktor *m*, Rektor *m*
head·mis·tress *Br* PED Direktorin *f*, Rektorin *f*
head-on frontal, Frontal…; ***head-on collision*** MOT Frontalzusammenstoß *m*
head·phones Kopfhörer *pl*
head·quar·ters (ABBR ***HQ***) MIL Hauptquartier *n*; Zentrale *f*
head·rest MOT Kopfstütze *f*
head·set Kopfhörer *pl*
head start SPORT Vorgabe *f*, Vorsprung *m* (*a. fig*)
head·strong halsstarrig
head teach·er → ***headmaster, headmistress, principal***
head·wa·ters GEOGR Quellgebiet *n*
head·way Fortschritt(e *pl*) *m*; ***make headway*** (gut) vorankommen
head·word Stichwort *n*
head·y zu Kopfe steigend, berauschend
heal heilen; ***heal over, heal up*** (zu)heilen
heal·ing Heilung *f*; ***healing power*** Heilkraft *f*
health Gesundheit *f*
health cer·tif·i·cate Gesundheitszeugnis *n*
health club Fitnessklub *m*, Fitnesscenter *n*
health food Reform-, Biokost *f*
health food shop *Br*, **health food store** Reformhaus *n*, Bioladen *m*
health·ful gesund; heilsam
health in·su·rance Krankenversicherung *f*
health re·sort Kurort *m*
health service Gesundheitsdienst *m*
health·y gesund
heap 1. Haufe(n) *m*; **2.** *a.* ***heap up*** aufhäufen, *fig a.* anhäufen
hear hören; anhören, *j-m* zuhören; *Zeugen* vernehmen; *Lektion* abhören
hear·er (Zu)Hörer(in)
hear·ing Gehör *n*; Hören *n*; JUR Verhandlung *f*; JUR Vernehmung *f*; *esp* POL Hearing *n*, Anhörung *f*; ***within (out of) hearing*** in (außer) Hörweite
hear·ing aid Hörgerät *n*
hear·say Gerede *n*; ***by hearsay*** vom Hörensagen *n*
hearse Leichenwagen *m*
heart ANAT Herz *n* (*a. fig*); Kern *m*; *card games*: Herz(karte *f*) *n*, *pl* Herz *n*; ***lose heart*** den Mut verlieren; ***take heart*** sich ein Herz fassen; ***take s.th. to heart*** sich et. zu Herzen nehmen; ***with a heavy heart*** schweren Herzens
heart·ache Kummer *m*
heart at·tack MED Herzanfall *m*; Herzin-

H

farkt *m*
heart·beat Herzschlag *m*
heart·break Leid *n*, großer Kummer
heart·break·ing herzzerreißend
heart·brok·en gebrochen, verzweifelt
heart·burn MED Sodbrennen *n*
heart·en ermutigen
heart fail·ure MED Herzversagen *n*
heart·felt innig, tief empfunden
hearth Kamin *m*
heart·less herzlos
heart·rend·ing herzzerreißend
heart trans·plant MED Herzverpflanzung *f*, Herztransplantation *f*
heart·y herzlich; gesund; herzhaft
heat 1. Hitze *f*; PHYS Wärme *f*; Eifer *m*; ZO Läufigkeit *f*; SPORT (Einzel)Lauf *m*; ***preliminary heat*** Vorlauf *m*; **2.** *v/t* heizen; *a.* ***heat up*** erhitzen, aufwärmen; *v/i* sich erhitzen (*a. fig*)
heat·ed geheizt; heizbar; erhitzt, *fig a.* erregt
heat·er Heizgerät *n*, Heizkörper *m*
heath Heide *f*, Heideland *n*
hea·then REL **1.** Heide *m*, Heidin *f*; **2.** heidnisch
heath·er BOT Heidekraut *n*; Erika *f*
heat·ing 1. Heizung *f*; **2.** Heiz…
heat·proof hitzebeständig
heat shield Hitzeschild *m*
heat·stroke MED Hitzschlag *m*
heat wave Hitzewelle *f*
heave *v/t* (hoch)stemmen, (hoch)hieven; *Anker* lichten; *Seufzer* ausstoßen; *v/i* sich heben und senken, wogen
heav·en Himmel *m*
heav·en·ly himmlisch
heav·y schwer; stark (*rain, smoker, drinker, traffic etc*); hoch (*fine, taxes etc*); schwer (verdaulich); drückend, lastend; Schwer…
heav·y cur·rent ELECTR Starkstrom *m*
heav·y-du·ty TECH Hochleistungs…; strapazierfähig
heav·y-hand·ed ungeschickt
heav·y·weight *boxing*: Schwergewicht *n*, Schwergewichtler *m*
He·brew 1. hebräisch; **2.** Hebräer(in); LING Hebräisch *n*
heck·le *Redner* durch Zwischenrufe *or* Zwischenfragen stören
heck·ler Zwischenrufer *m*
heck·ling Zwischenrufe
hec·tic hektisch
hedge 1. Hecke *f*; **2.** *v/t*: *a.* ***hedge in*** mit e-r Hecke einfassen; *v/i fig* ausweichen
hedge·hog ZO Stachelschwein *n*; *Br* Igel *m*
hedge·row Hecke *f*
heed 1. beachten, Beachtung schenken (*dat*); **2.** ***give*** *or* ***pay heed to, take heed of*** → 1
heed·less: ***be heedless of*** nicht beachten, *Warnung etc* in den Wind schlagen
heel 1. ANAT Ferse *f*; Absatz *m*; ***down at heel*** *fig* abgerissen; heruntergekommen; **2.** Absätze machen auf (*acc*)
hef·ty kräftig, stämmig; mächtig (*blow etc*), gewaltig; F saftig (*prices, fine etc*)
heif·er ZO Färse *f*, junge Kuh
height Höhe *f*; (Körper)Größe *f*; Anhöhe *f*; *fig* Höhe(punkt *m*) *f*
height·en erhöhen; vergrößern
heir Erbe *m*; ***heir to the throne*** Thronerbe *m*, Thronfolger *m*
heir·ess Erbin *f*
heir·loom Erbstück *n*
hel·i·cop·ter AVIAT Hubschrauber *m*, Helikopter *m*
hel·i·port AVIAT Hubschrauberlandeplatz *m*
hell 1. Hölle *f*; ***a hell of a noise*** F ein Höllenlärm; ***what the hell …?*** F was zum Teufel …?; ***raise hell*** F e-n Mordskrach schlagen; **2.** Höllen…; **3.** *int* F verdammt!, verflucht!
hell·ish F höllisch
hel·lo *int* hallo!
helm MAR Ruder *n*, Steuer *n*
hel·met Helm *m*
helms·man MAR Steuermann *m*
help 1. Hilfe *f*; Hausangestellte *f*; ***a call*** *or* ***cry for help*** ein Hilferuf, ein Hilfeschrei; **2.** helfen; ***help o.s.*** sich bedienen, zulangen; ***I cannot help it*** ich kann es nicht ändern; ***I could not help laughing*** ich musste einfach lachen
help·er Helfer(in)
help·ful hilfreich; nützlich
help·ing Portion *f*
help·less hilflos
help·less·ness Hilflosigkeit *f*
help men·u EDP Hilfemenü *n*
hel·ter-skel·ter 1. *adv* holterdiepolter, Hals über Kopf; **2.** *adj* überstürzt
helve Stiel *m*, Griff *m*
Hel·ve·tian Schweizer …
hem 1. Saum *m*; **2.** säumen; ***hem in*** einschließen
hem·i·sphere GEOGR Halbkugel *f*, Hemisphäre *f*
hem·line Saum *m*
hem·lock BOT Schierling *m*
hemp BOT Hanf *m*
hem·stitch Hohlsaum *m*
hen ZO Henne *f*, Huhn *n*; Weibchen *n*
hence daher; ***a week hence*** in e-r Woche
hence·forth von nun an

hen house Hühnerstall *m*
hen·pecked hus·band Pantoffelheld *m*
her sie; ihr; ihr(e); sich
her·ald **1.** HIST Herold *m*; **2.** ankündigen
her·ald·ry Wappenkunde *f*, Heraldik *f*
herb BOT Kraut *n*; Heilkraut *n*
her·ba·ceous BOT krautartig; ***herbaceous plant*** Staudengewächs *n*
herb·al BOT Kräuter…, Pflanzen…
her·bi·vore ZO Pflanzenfresser *m*
herd **1.** Herde *f* (*a. fig*), Rudel *n*; **2.** *v/t Vieh* hüten; *v/i*: *a.* ***herd together*** in e-r Herde leben; sich zusammendrängen
herds·man Hirt *m*
here hier; hierher; ***here you are*** hier (bitte); ***here's to you!*** auf dein Wohl!
here·a·bout(s) hier herum, in dieser Gegend
here·af·ter **1.** künftig; **2.** *das* Jenseits
here·by hiermit
he·red·i·ta·ry BIOL erblich, Erb…
he·red·i·ty BIOL Erblichkeit *f*; ererbte Anlagen *pl*, Erbmasse *f*
here·in hierin
here·of hiervon
her·e·sy REL Ketzerei *f*
her·e·tic REL Ketzer(in)
here·up·on hierauf, darauf(hin)
here·with hiermit
her·i·tage Erbe *n*
her·maph·ro·dite BIOL Zwitter *m*
her·met·ic TECH hermetisch
her·mit Einsiedler *m*
he·ro Held *m*
he·ro·ic heroisch, heldenhaft, Helden…
her·o·in Heroin *n*
her·o·ine Heldin *f*
her·o·is·m Heldentum *n*
her·on ZO Reiher *m*
her·ring ZO Hering *m*
hers ihrs, ihre(r, -s)
her·self sie selbst, ihr selbst; sich (selbst); ***by herself*** von selbst, allein, ohne Hilfe
hes·i·tant zögernd, zaudernd, unschlüssig
hes·i·tate zögern, zaudern, unschlüssig sein, Bedenken haben
hes·i·ta·tion Zögern *n*, Zaudern *n*, Unschlüssigkeit *f*; ***without hesitation*** ohne zu zögern, bedenkenlos
hew hauen, hacken; ***hew down*** fällen, umhauen
hey *int* F he!, heda!
hey·day Höhepunkt *m*, Gipfel *m*; Blüte (-zeit) *f*
hi *int* F hallo!
hi·ber·nate ZO Winterschlaf halten
hic·cough, **hic·cup** **1.** Schluckauf *m*; **2.** den Schluckauf haben
hide[1] (sich) verbergen, verstecken; verheimlichen
hide[2] Haut *f*, Fell *n*
hide-and-seek Versteckspiel *n*
hide·a·way F Versteck *n*
hid·e·ous abscheulich, scheußlich
hide·out Versteck *n*
hid·ing[1] F Tracht *f* Prügel
hid·ing[2]: ***be in hiding*** sich versteckt halten; ***go into hiding*** untertauchen
hid·ing place Versteck *n*
hi-fi Hi-Fi *n*, Hi-Fi-Gerät *n*, -Anlage *f*
high **1.** hoch; groß (*hopes etc*); GASTR angegangen; F blau; F high; ***be in high spirits*** in Hochstimmung sein; ausgelassen *or* übermütig sein; **2.** METEOR Hoch *n*; Höchststand *m*; High School *f*
high·brow F **1.** Intellektuelle *m*, *f*; **2.** (betont) intellektuell
high-cal·o·rie kalorienreich
high-class erstklassig
high·er ed·u·ca·tion Hochschulausbildung *f*
high fi·del·i·ty High Fidelity *f*
high·grade hochwertig; erstklassig
high-hand·ed anmaßend, eigenmächtig
high-heeled hochhackig
high jump SPORT Hochsprung *m*
high jump·er SPORT Hochspringer(in)
high·land Hochland *n*
high·light **1.** Höhe-, Glanzpunkt *m*; **2.** hervorheben
high·ly *fig* hoch; ***think highly of*** viel halten von
high·ly-strung reizbar, nervös
high·ness *mst fig* Höhe *f*; ***Highness*** Hoheit *f* (*title*)
high-pitched schrill; steil (*roof*)
high-pow·ered TECH Hochleistungs…; *fig* dynamisch
high-pres·sure METEOR, TECH Hochdruck…
high-rank·ing hochrangig
high rise Hochhaus *n*
high road *esp Br* Hauptstraße *f*
high school High School *f*
high sea·son Hochsaison *f*
high so·ci·e·ty High Society *f*
high-spir·it·ed übermütig, ausgelassen
high street *Br* Hauptstraße *f*
high tea *Br* frühes Abendessen
high tech·nol·o·gy Hochtechnologie *f*
high ten·sion ELECTR Hochspannung *f*
high tide Flut *f*
high time: ***it is high time*** es ist höchste Zeit
high wa·ter Hochwasser *n*
high·way Highway *m*, Haupt(verkehrs)-straße *f*
High·way Code *Br* Straßenverkehrsord-

nung *f*
hi·jack 1. *Flugzeug* entführen; *j-n*, *Geldtransport etc* überfallen; **2.** (Flugzeug-) Entführung *f*; Überfall *m*
hi·jack·er Räuber *m*; (Flugzeug)Entführer(in)
hike 1. wandern; **2.** Wanderung *f*
hik·er Wanderer *m*, Wanderin *f*
hik·ing Wandern *n*
hi·lar·i·ous ausgelassen
hi·lar·i·ty Ausgelassenheit *f*
hill Hügel *m*, Anhöhe *f*
hill·bil·ly *contp* Hinterwäldler *m*
hill·ock kleiner Hügel
hill·side (Ab)Hang *m*
hill·top Hügelspitze *f*
hill·y hügelig
hilt Heft *n*, Griff *m*
him ihn; ihm; F er; sich
him·self er *or* ihm *or* ihn selbst; sich; sich (selbst); ***by himself*** von selbst, allein, ohne Hilfe
hind[1] zo Hirschkuh *f*
hind[2] Hinter…
hin·der hindern (***from*** an *dat*); hemmen
hind·most hinterste(r, -s), letzte(r, -s)
hin·drance Hindernis *n*
Hin·du Hindu *m*
Hin·du·ism Hinduismus *m*
hinge 1. TECH (Tür)Angel *f*, Scharnier *n*; **2.** ***hinge on*** *fig* abhängen von
hint 1. Wink *m*, Andeutung *f*; Tipp *m*; Anspielung *f*; ***take a hint*** e-n Wink verstehen; **2.** andeuten; anspielen (***at*** auf *acc*)
hip[1] ANAT Hüfte *f*
hip[2] BOT Hagebutte *f*
hip·po F → **hip·po·pot·a·mus** zo Flusspferd *n*, Nilpferd *n*
hire 1. *Br Auto etc* mieten, *Flugzeug etc* chartern; *j-n* anstellen; *j-n* engagieren, anheuern; ***hire out*** *Br* vermieten; **2.** Miete *f*; Lohn *m*; ***for hire*** zu vermieten; frei
hire car *Br* Leih-, Mietwagen *m*
hire pur·chase: ***on hire purchase*** *Br* ECON auf Abzahlung, auf Raten
his sein(e); seins, seine(r, -s)
hiss 1. zischen; fauchen (*cat*); auszischen; **2.** Zischen *n*; Fauchen *n*
his·to·ri·an Historiker(in)
his·tor·ic historisch, geschichtlich (bedeutsam)
his·tor·i·cal historisch, geschichtlich (belegt *or* überliefert); Geschichts…; ***historical novel*** historischer Roman
his·to·ry Geschichte *f*; ***history of civilization*** Kulturgeschichte *f*; ***contemporary history*** Zeitgeschichte *f*
hit 1. schlagen; treffen (*a. fig*); MOT *etc j-n*, *et.* anfahren, *et.* rammen; F ***hit it off*** (***with s.o.***) sich (mit j-m) gut vertragen; ***hit on*** (zufällig) auf *et.* stoßen, *et.* finden; **2.** Schlag *m*; *fig* (Seiten)Hieb *m*; (Glücks-) Treffer *m*; Hit *m*
hit-and-run: ***hit-and-run driver*** (unfall)flüchtiger Fahrer; ***hit-and-run offense*** (*Br* ***offence***) Fahrerflucht *f*
hitch 1. befestigen, festmachen, festhaken, anbinden, ankoppeln (***to*** an *acc*); ***hitch up*** hochziehen; ***hitch a ride*** *or* ***lift*** im Auto mitgenommen werden; **2.** Ruck *m*, Zug *m*; Schwierigkeit *f*, Haken *m*; ***without a hitch*** glatt, reibungslos;
hitch·hike per Anhalter fahren, trampen
hitch·hik·er Anhalter(in), Tramper(in)
hi-tech → ***high tech***
HIV: ***HIV carrier*** HIV-Positive *m, f*; ***HIV negative*** HIV-negativ; ***HIV positive*** HIV-positiv
hive Bienenstock *m*; Bienenschwarm *m*
hoard 1. Vorrat *m*, Schatz *m*; **2.** *a.* ***hoard up*** horten, hamstern
hoard·ing Bauzaun *m*; *Br* Reklametafel *f*
hoar·frost (Rau)Reif *m*
hoarse heiser, rau
hoax 1. Falschmeldung *f*; (übler) Scherz; **2.** *j-n* hereinlegen
hob·ble humpeln, hinken
hob·by Hobby *n*, Steckenpferd *n*
hob·by·horse Steckenpferd *n* (*a. fig*)
hob·gob·lin Kobold *m*
ho·bo F Landstreicher *m*
hock[1] weißer Rheinwein
hock[2] zo Sprunggelenk *n*
hock·ey SPORT Eishockey *n*; *esp Br* Hockey *n*
hodge·podge Mischmasch *m*
hoe AGR **1.** Hacke *f*; **2.** hacken
hog zo (Haus-, Schlacht)Schwein *n*
hoist 1. hochziehen; hissen; **2.** TECH Winde *f*, (Lasten)Aufzug *m*
hold 1. halten; festhalten; *Gewicht etc* tragen, aushalten; zurück-, abhalten (***from*** von); *Wahlen*, *Versammlung etc* abhalten; *Stellung* halten; SPORT *Meisterschaft etc* austragen; *Aktien*, *Rechte etc* besitzen; *Amt* bekleiden; *Platz* einnehmen; *Rekord* halten; fassen, enthalten; Platz bieten für; der Ansicht sein (***that*** dass); halten für; *fig* fesseln, in Spannung halten; (sich) festhalten; anhalten, andauern (*a. fig*); ***hold one's ground, hold one's own*** sich behaupten; ***hold the line*** TEL am Apparat bleiben; ***hold responsible*** verantwortlich machen; ***hold still*** still halten; ***hold s.th. against s.o.*** j-m et. vorhalten *or* vorwerfen; j-m et. übel nehmen *or* nachtragen; ***hold back*** (sich) zurückhalten; *fig* zurückhalten mit; ***hold***

on (sich) festhalten (***to*** an *dat*); aus-, durchhalten; andauern; TEL am Apparat bleiben; ***hold out*** aus-, durchhalten; reichen (*supplies etc*); ***hold up*** hochheben; hochhalten; hinstellen (***as*** als); aufhalten, verzögern; *j-n, Bank etc* überfallen; **2.** Griff *m*, Halt *m*; Stütze *f*, Gewalt *f*, Macht *f*, Einfluss *m*; MAR Laderaum *m*, Frachtraum *m*; ***catch*** (***get, take***) ***hold of s.th.*** et. ergreifen, et. zu fassen bekommen

hold·er TECH Halter *m*; *esp* ECON Inhaber(in)

hold·ing Besitz *m*

holding com·pa·ny ECON Holding-, Dachgesellschaft *f*

hold-up (Verkehrs)Stockung *f*; (bewaffneter) (Raub)Überfall

hole 1. Loch *n*; Höhle *f*, Bau *m*; *fig* F Klemme *f*; **2.** durchlöchern

hol·i·day Feiertag *m*; freier Tag; *esp Br mst pl* Ferien *pl*, Urlaub *m*; ***be on holiday*** im Urlaub sein, Urlaub machen

holiday home Ferienhaus *n*, Ferienwohnung *f*

hol·i·day·mak·er Urlauber(in)

hol·i·ness Heiligkeit *f*; ***His Holiness*** Seine Heiligkeit

hol·ler F schreien

hol·low 1. hohl; **2.** Hohlraum *m*, (Aus-)Höhlung *f*; Mulde *f*, Vertiefung *f*; **3.** ***hollow out*** aushöhlen

hol·ly BOT Stechpalme *f*

hol·o·caust Massenvernichtung *f*, Massensterben *n*, (*esp* Brand)Katastrophe *f*; ***the Holocaust*** HIST der Holocaust

hol·ster (Pistolen)Halfter *m, n*

ho·ly heilig

ho·ly wa·ter REL Weihwasser *n*

Ho·ly Week REL Karwoche *f*

home 1. Heim *n*; Haus *n*; Wohnung *f*; Zuhause *n*; Heimat *f*; ***at home*** zu Hause; ***make oneself at home*** es sich bequem machen; ***at home and abroad*** im In- und Ausland; **2.** *adj* häuslich, Heim… (*a.* SPORT); inländisch, Inlands…; Heimat…; **3.** *adv* heim, nach Hause; zu Hause; daheim; *fig* ins Ziel, ins Schwarze; ***return home*** heimkehren; ***strike home*** sitzen, treffen

home ad·dress Privatanschrift *f*

home com·put·er Heimcomputer *m*

home·less heimatlos; obdachlos; ***homeless person*** Obdachlose *m, f*; ***shelter for the homeless*** Obdachlosenasyl *n*

home·ly einfach; unscheinbar, reizlos

home·made selbst gemacht, Hausmacher…

home mar·ket ECON Binnenmarkt *m*

Home Of·fice *Br* POL Innenministerium *n*

Home Sec·re·ta·ry *Br* POL Innenminister *m*

home·sick: ***be homesick*** Heimweh haben

home·sick·ness Heimweh *n*

home team SPORT Gastgeber *pl*

home·ward *adj* Heim…, Rück…

home·ward(s) *adv* nach Hause

home·work Hausaufgabe(n *pl*) *f*; ***do one's homework*** s-e Hausaufgaben machen (*a. fig*)

hom·i·cide JUR Mord *m*; Totschlag *m*; Mörder(in)

hom·i·cide squad Mordkommission *f*

ho·mo·ge·ne·ous homogen, gleichartig

ho·mo·sex·u·al 1. homosexuell; **2.** Homosexuelle *m, f*

hone TECH fein schleifen

hon·est ehrlich, rechtschaffen; aufrichtig

hon·es·ty Ehrlichkeit *f*, Rechtschaffenheit *f*; Aufrichtigkeit *f*

hon·ey Honig *m*; Liebling *m*, Schatz *m*

hon·ey·comb (Honig)Wabe *f*

hon·eyed *fig* honigsüß

hon·ey·moon 1. Flitterwochen *pl*, Hochzeitsreise *f*; **2.** ***be honeymooning*** auf Hochzeitsreise sein

hon·ey·suck·le BOT Geißblatt *n*

honk MOT hupen

hon·or·ar·y Ehren…; ehrenamtlich

hon·o(u)r 1. Ehre *f*; Ehrung *f*, Ehre(n *pl*) *f*; *pl* besondere Auszeichnung(en *pl*); ***Your Hono(u)r*** JUR Euer Ehren; **2.** ehren; auszeichnen; ECON *Scheck etc* honorieren, einlösen

hon·o(u)r·a·ble ehrenvoll, ehrenhaft; ehrenwert

hood Kapuze *f*; MOT Verdeck *n*; (Motor-)Haube *f*; TECH (Schutz)Haube *f*

hood·lum F Rowdy *m*; Ganove *m*

hood·wink *j-n* hinters Licht führen

hoof zo Huf *m*

hook 1. Haken *m*; Angelhaken *m*; ***by hook or by crook*** F mit allen Mitteln; **2.** an-, ein-, fest-, zuhaken; angeln (*a. fig*)

hooked krumm, Haken…; F süchtig (***on*** nach) (*a. fig*); ***hooked on heroin*** (***television***) heroinsüchtig (fernsehsüchtig)

hook·er F Nutte *f*

hook·y: ***play hooky*** F (die Schule) schwänzen

hoo·li·gan Rowdy *m*

hoo·li·gan·ism Rowdytum *n*

hoop Reif(en) *m*

hoot 1. zo Schrei *m* (*a. fig*); MOT Hupen *n*; **2.** *v/i* heulen; johlen; zo schreien; MOT hupen; *v/t* auspfeifen, auszischen

Hoo·ver® *Br* **1.** Staubsauger *m*; **2.** *mst*

hoover (staub)saugen
hop[1] **1.** hüpfen, hopsen; hüpfen über (*acc*); ***be hopping mad*** F e-e Stinkwut haben; **2.** Sprung *m*
hop[2] BOT Hopfen *m*
hope **1.** Hoffnung *f* (***of*** auf *acc*); **2.** hoffen (***for*** auf *acc*); ***hope for the best*** das Beste hoffen; ***I hope so, let's hope so*** hoffentlich
hope·ful: ***be hopeful that*** hoffen, dass
hope·ful·ly hoffnungsvoll; hoffentlich
hope·less hoffnungslos; verzweifelt
horde Horde *f* (*often contp*)
ho·ri·zon Horizont *m*
hor·i·zon·tal horizontal, waag(e)recht
hor·mone BIOL Hormon *n*
horn zo Horn *n*, *pl* Geweih *n*; MOT Hupe *f*
hor·net zo Hornisse *f*
horn·y schwielig; V geil
hor·o·scope Horoskop *n*
hor·ri·ble schrecklich, furchtbar, scheußlich
hor·rid *esp Br* grässlich, abscheulich; schrecklich
hor·rif·ic schrecklich, entsetzlich
hor·ri·fy entsetzen
hor·ror Entsetzen *n*; Abscheu *m*, Horror *m*; F Gräuel *m*
horse zo Pferd *n*; Bock *m*, Gestell *n*; ***wild horses couldn't drag me there*** keine zehn Pferde bringen mich dort hin
horse·back: ***on horseback*** zu Pferde, beritten
horse chest·nut BOT Rosskastanie *f*
horse·hair Rosshaar *n*
horse·man (geübter) Reiter
horse·pow·er TECH Pferdestärke *f*
horse race Pferderennen *n*
horse rac·ing Pferderennen *n or pl*
horse·rad·ish BOT Meerrettich *m*
horse·shoe Hufeisen *n*
horse·wom·an (geübte) Reiterin
hor·ti·cul·ture Gartenbau *m*
hose[1] Schlauch *m*
hose[2] Strümpfe *pl*, Strumpfwaren *pl*
ho·sier·y Strumpfwaren *pl*
hos·pice Sterbeklinik *f*
hos·pi·ta·ble gastfreundlich
hos·pi·tal Krankenhaus *n*, Klinik *f*; ***in the hospital*** im Krankenhaus
hos·pi·tal·i·ty Gastfreundschaft *f*
hos·pi·tal·ize ins Krankenhaus einliefern *or* einweisen
host[1] **1.** Gastgeber *m*; BIOL Wirt *m*; *radio*, TV Talkmaster *m*, Showmaster *m*, Moderator(in); ***your host was …*** durch die Sendung führte Sie …; **2.** *radio*, TV F *Sendung* moderieren
host[2] Menge *f*, Masse *f*
host[3] REL *often* ***Host*** Hostie *f*
hos·tage Geisel *m*, *f*; ***take s.o. hostage*** j-n als Geisel nehmen
hos·tel *esp Br* UNIV (Wohn)Heim *n*; *mst* ***youth hostel*** Jugendherberge *f*
host·ess Gastgeberin *f*; Hostess *f* (*a.* AVIAT); AVIAT Stewardess *f*
hos·tile feindlich; feindselig (***to*** gegen); ***hostile to foreigners*** ausländerfeindlich
hos·til·i·ty Feindseligkeit *f* (***to*** gegen); ***hostility to foreigners*** Ausländerfeindlichkeit *f*
hot heiß (*a. fig and sl*); GASTR scharf; warm (*meal*); *fig* hitzig, heftig; ganz neu *or* frisch (*news etc*); ***I am or feel hot*** mir ist heiß
hot·bed Mistbeet *n*; *fig* Brutstätte *f*
hotch·potch *Br* → ***hodgepodge***
hot dog GASTR Hot Dog *n*, *m*
ho·tel Hotel *n*
hot·head Hitzkopf *m*
hot·house Treib-, Gewächshaus *n*
hot line POL heißer Draht; TEL Hotline *f*
hot·plate Kochplatte *f*
hot spot *esp* POL Unruhe-, Krisenherd *m*
hot spring Thermalquelle *f*
hot-tem·pered jähzornig
hot-wa·ter bot·tle Wärmflasche *f*
hound zo Jagdhund *m*
hour Stunde *f*; *pl* (*Arbeits*)Zeit *f*, (*Geschäfts*)Stunden *pl*
hour·ly stündlich
house **1.** Haus *n*; **2.** unterbringen
house·bound ans Haus gefesselt
house·break·ing Einbruch *m*
house·hold **1.** Haushalt *m*; **2.** Haushalts…
house hus·band Hausmann *m*
house·keep·er Haushälterin *f*
house·keep·ing Haushaltung *f*, Haushaltsführung *f*
house·maid Hausangestellte *f*, Hausmädchen *n*
house·man *Br* MED Assistenzarzt *m*, -ärztin *f*
House of Lords *Br* PARL Oberhaus *n*
house plant Zimmerpflanze *f*
house-warm·ing Hauseinweihung *f*, Einzugsparty *f*
house·wife Hausfrau *f*
house·work Hausarbeit *f*
hous·ing Wohnung *f*
housing de·vel·opment, *Br* **housing es·tate** Wohnsiedlung *f*
hov·er schweben; herumlungern; *fig* schwanken
hov·er·craft Hovercraft *n*, Luftkissenfahrzeug *n*
how wie; ***how are you?*** wie geht es dir?;

how about …? wie steht's mit …?, wie wäre es mit …?; ***how do you do?*** guten Tag!; ***how much?*** wie viel?; ***how many*** wie viele?
how·ev·er **1.** *adv* wie auch (immer); **2.** *cj* jedoch
howl **1.** heulen; brüllen, schreien; **2.** Heulen *n*
howl·er F grober Schnitzer
hub TECH (Rad)Nabe *f*; *fig* Mittelpunkt *m*, Angelpunkt *m*
hub·bub Stimmengewirr *n*; Tumult *m*
hub·by F (Ehe)Mann *m*
huck·le·ber·ry BOT amerikanische Heidelbeere
hud·dle: ***huddle together*** (sich) zusammendrängen; ***huddled up*** zusammengekauert
hue[1] Farbe *f*; (Farb)Ton *m*
hue[2]: ***hue and cry*** *fig* großes Geschrei, heftiger Protest
huff: ***in a huff*** verärgert, verstimmt
hug **1.** (sich) umarmen; an sich drücken; **2.** Umarmung *f*
huge riesig, riesengroß
hulk F Koloss *m*; sperriges Ding; ***a hulk of a man*** ein ungeschlachter Kerl
hull **1.** BOT Schale *f*, Hülse *f*; MAR Rumpf *m*; **2.** enthülsen, schälen
hul·la·ba·loo Lärm *m*, Getöse *n*
hul·lo *int* hallo!
hum summen; brummen
hu·man **1.** menschlich, Menschen…; **2.** *a.* ***human being*** Mensch *m*
hu·mane human, menschlich
hu·man·i·tar·i·an humanitär, menschenfreundlich
hu·man·i·ty die Menschheit, die Menschen *pl*; Humanität *f*, Menschlichkeit *f*; *pl* Geisteswissenschaften *pl*; Altphilologie *f*
hu·man·ly: ***humanly possible*** menschenmöglich
hu·man rights Menschenrechte *pl*
hum·ble **1.** demütig; bescheiden; **2.** demütigen
hum·ble·ness Demut *f*
hum·drum eintönig, langweilig
hu·mid feucht, nass
hu·mid·i·ty Feuchtigkeit *f*
hu·mil·i·ate demütigen, erniedrigen
hu·mil·i·a·tion Demütigung *f*, Erniedrigung *f*
hu·mil·i·ty Demut *f*
hum·ming·bird ZO Kolibri *m*
hu·mor·ous humorvoll, komisch
hu·mo(u)r **1.** Humor *m*; Komik *f*; **2.** *j-m* s-n Willen lassen; eingehen auf (*acc*)
hump ZO Höcker *m*; MED Buckel *m*
hump·back(ed) → ***hunchback(ed)***
hunch **1.** → ***hump***; dickes Stück; (Vor)-Ahnung *f*; **2.** *a.* ***hunch up*** krümmen; ***hunch one's shoulders*** die Schultern hochziehen
hunch·back Buckel *m*; Bucklige *m*, *f*
hunch·backed buck(e)lig
hun·dred **1.** hundert; **2.** Hundert *f*
hun·dredth **1.** hundertste(r, -s); **2.** Hundertstel *n*
hun·dred·weight *appr* Zentner *m* (*= 50,8 kg*)
Hun·ga·ri·an **1.** ungarisch; **2.** Ungar(in); LING Ungarisch *n*
Hun·ga·ry Ungarn *n*
hun·ger **1.** Hunger *m* (*a. fig* ***for*** nach); **2.** *fig* hungern (***for, after*** nach)
hun·ger strike Hungerstreik *m*
hun·gry hungrig
hunk dickes *or* großes Stück
hunt **1.** jagen; Jagd machen auf (*acc*); verfolgen; suchen (***for, after*** nach); ***hunt down*** zur Strecke bringen; ***hunt for*** Jagd machen auf (*acc*); ***hunt out, hunt up*** aufspüren; **2.** Jagd *f* (*a. fig*), Jagen *n*; Verfolgung *f*; Suche *f* (***for, after*** nach)
hunt·er Jäger *m*; Jagdpferd *n*
hunt·ing **1.** Jagen *n*; **2.** Jagd…
hunt·ing ground Jagdrevier *n*
hur·dle SPORT Hürde *f* (*a. fig*)
hur·dler SPORT Hürdenläufer(in)
hur·dle race SPORT Hürdenrennen *n*
hurl schleudern; ***hurl abuse at s.o.*** j-m Beleidigungen ins Gesicht schleudern
hur·rah, hur·ray *int* hurra!
hur·ri·cane Hurrikan *m*, Wirbelsturm *m*; Orkan *m*
hur·ried eilig, hastig, übereilt
hur·ry **1.** *v/t* schnell *or* eilig befördern *or* bringen; *often* ***hurry up*** *j-n* antreiben, hetzen; *et.* beschleunigen; *v/i* eilen, hasten; ***hurry (up)*** sich beeilen; ***hurry up!*** (mach) schnell!; **2.** (große) Eile, Hast *f*; ***be in a hurry*** es eilig haben
hurt verletzen, verwunden (*a. fig*); schmerzen, wehtun; schaden (*dat*)
hurt·ful verletzend
hus·band (Ehe)Mann *m*
hush **1.** *int* still!; **2.** Stille *f*; **3.** zum Schweigen bringen; ***hush up*** vertuschen, totschweigen
hush mon·ey Schweigegeld *n*
husk BOT **1.** Hülse *f*, Schote *f*, Schale *f*; **2.** enthülsen, schälen
hus·tle **1.** (*in aller Eile*) *wohin* bringen *or* schicken; hasten, hetzen; sich beeilen; **2.** ***hustle and bustle*** Gedränge *n*; Gehetze *n*; Betrieb *m*, Wirbel *m*
hut Hütte *f*

hutch Stall *m*
hy·a·cinth BOT Hyazinthe *f*
hy·(a)e·na ZO Hyäne *f*
hy·brid BIOL Mischling *m*, Kreuzung *f*
hy·drant Hydrant *m*
hy·draul·ic hydraulisch
hy·draul·ics hydraulik *f*
hy·dro... Wasser...
hy·dro·car·bon CHEM Kohlenwasserstoff *m*
hy·dro·chlor·ic ac·id CHEM Salzsäure *f*
hy·dro·foil MAR Tragflächenboot *n*, Tragflügelboot *n*
hy·dro·gen CHEM Wasserstoff *m*
hydrogen bomb Wasserstoffbombe
hy·dro·plane AVIAT Wasserflugzeug *n*; MAR Gleitboot *n*
hy·dro·plan·ing MOT Aquaplaning *n*
hy·e·na ZO Hyäne *f*
hy·giene Hygiene *f*
hy·gien·ic hygienisch
hymn Kirchenlied *n*, Choral *m*
hype F **1.** *a.* ***hype up*** (übersteigerte) Publicity machen für; **2.** (übersteigerte) Publicity; ***media hype*** Medienrummel *m*
hy·per... hyper..., übermäßig
hy·per·mar·ket *Br* Groß-, Verbrauchermarkt *m*
hy·per·sen·si·tive überempfindlich (***to*** gegen)
hy·phen Bindestrich *m*
hy·phen·ate mit Bindestrich schreiben
hyp·no·tize hypnotisieren
hy·po·chon·dri·ac Hypochonder *m*
hy·poc·ri·sy Heuchelei *f*
hyp·o·crite Heuchler(in)
hyp·o·criti·cal heuchlerisch, scheinheilig
hy·poth·e·sis Hypothese *f*
hys·te·ri·a MED Hysterie *f*
hys·ter·i·cal hysterisch
hys·ter·ics hysterischer Anfall; ***go into hysterics*** hysterisch werden

I

I, i I, i *n*
I ich; ***it is I*** ich bin es
ice 1. Eis *n*; **2.** *Getränke etc* mit *or* in Eis kühlen; GASTR glasieren, mit Zuckerguss überziehen; ***iced over*** zugefroren (*lake etc*); ***iced up*** vereist (*road*)
ice age Eiszeit *f*
ice·berg Eisberg *m* (*a. fig*)
ice·bound eingefroren
ice cream (Speise)Eis *n*
ice-cream par·lo(u)r Eisdiele *f*
ice cube Eiswürfel *m*
iced eisgekühlt
ice floe Eisscholle *f*
ice hock·ey SPORT Eishockey *n*
ice lol·ly *Br* Eis *n* am Stiel
ice rink (Kunst)Eisbahn *f*
ice skate Schlittschuh *m*
ice-skate Schlittschuh laufen
ice show Eisrevue *f*
i·ci·cle Eiszapfen *m*
ic·ing GASTR Glasur *f*, Zuckerguss *m*; ***the icing on the cake*** das Tüpfelchen auf dem i
i·con REL Ikone *f*; EDP Ikone *f*, (Bild)-Symbol *n*
i·cy eisig; vereist
ID ABBR *of* ***identity*** Identität *f*; ***ID card*** (Personal)Ausweis *m*
i·dea Idee *f*, Vorstellung *f*, Begriff *m*; Gedanke *m*, Idee *f*; ***have no idea*** keine Ahnung haben
i·deal 1. ideal; **2.** Ideal *n*
i·deal·ism Idealismus *m*
i·deal·ize idealisieren
i·den·ti·cal identisch (***to, with*** mit)
identical twins eineiige Zwillinge *pl*
i·den·ti·fi·ca·tion Identifizierung *f*
identification (pa·pers) Ausweis(papiere *pl*) *m*
i·den·ti·fy identifizieren; ***identify o.s.*** sich ausweisen
i·den·ti·kit® pic·ture *Br* JUR Phantombild *n*
i·den·ti·ty Identität *f*
identity card (Personal)Ausweis *m*
i·de·o·log·i·cal ideologisch
i·de·ol·o·gy Ideologie *f*
id·i·om Idiom *n*, idiomatischer Ausdruck, Redewendung *f*
id·i·o·mat·ic idiomatisch
id·i·ot MED Idiot(in), *contp a.* Trottel *m*
id·i·ot·ic MED idiotisch, F *a.* blödsinnig, schwachsinnig
i·dle 1. untätig; faul, träge; nutzlos; leer, hohl (*talk*); TECH stillstehend, außer Be-

trieb; MOT leerlaufend, im Leerlauf; **2.** faulenzen; MOT leerlaufen; *mst* ***idle away*** *Zeit* vertrödeln
i·dol Idol *n* (*a. fig*); Götzenbild *n*
i·dol·ize abgöttisch verehren, vergöttern
i·dyl·lic idyllisch
if wenn, falls; ob; ***if I were you*** wenn ich du wäre
ig·loo Iglu *m*, *n*
ig·nite anzünden, (sich) entzünden; MOT zünden
ig·ni·tion MOT Zündung *f*
ig·ni·tion key MOT Zündschlüssel *m*
ig·no·rance Unkenntnis *f*, Unwissenheit *f*
ig·no·rant: ***be ignorant of s.th.*** et. nicht wissen *or* kennen, nichts wissen von et.
ig·nore ignorieren, nicht beachten
ill krank; schlimm, schlecht; ***fall ill, be taken ill*** krank werden, erkranken
ill-ad·vised schlecht beraten; unklug
ill-bred schlecht erzogen; ungezogen
il·le·gal verboten; JUR illegal, ungesetzlich; ***illegal parking*** Falschparken *n*
il·le·gi·ble unleserlich
il·le·git·i·mate unehelich; unrechtmäßig
ill feel·ing Verstimmung *f*; ***cause ill feeling*** böses Blut machen
ill-hu·mo(u)red schlecht gelaunt
il·li·cit unerlaubt, verboten
il·lit·e·rate ungebildet
ill-man·nered ungehobelt, ungezogen
ill-na·tured boshaft, bösartig
ill·ness Krankheit *f*
ill-tem·pered schlecht gelaunt
ill-timed ungelegen, unpassend
ill-treat misshandeln
il·lu·mi·nate beleuchten
il·lu·mi·nat·ing aufschlussreich
il·lu·mi·na·tion Beleuchtung *f*; *pl* Illumination *f*, Festbeleuchtung *f*
il·lu·sion Illusion *f*, Täuschung *f*
il·lu·sive, **il·lu·so·ry** illusorisch, trügerisch
il·lus·trate illustrieren; bebildern; erläutern, veranschaulichen
il·lus·tra·tion Erläuterung *f*; Illustration *f*; Bild *n*, Abbildung *f*
il·lus·tra·tive erläuternd
il·lus·tri·ous berühmt
ill will Feindschaft *f*
im·age Bild *n*; Ebenbild *n*; Image *n*; bildlicher Ausdruck, Metapher *f*
im·age·ry Bildersprache *f*, Metaphorik *f*
i·ma·gi·na·ble vorstellbar, denkbar
i·ma·gi·na·ry eingebildet, imaginär
i·ma·gi·na·tion Einbildung(skraft) *f*; Vorstellungskraft *f*, -vermögen *n*
i·ma·gi·na·tive ideenreich, einfallsreich; fantasievoll
i·ma·gine sich *j-n or et.* vorstellen; sich *et.* einbilden
im·bal·ance Unausgewogenheit *f*; POL *etc* Ungleichgewicht *n*
im·be·cile Idiot *m*, Trottel *m*
im·i·tate nachahmen, nachmachen, imitieren
im·i·ta·tion **1.** Nachahmung *f*, Imitation *f*; **2.** nachgemacht, unecht, künstlich, Kunst…
im·mac·u·late unbefleckt, makellos; tadellos, fehlerlos
im·ma·te·ri·al unwesentlich, unerheblich (***to*** für)
im·ma·ture unreif
im·mea·su·ra·ble unermesslich
im·me·di·ate unmittelbar; sofortig, umgehend; nächste(r, -s) (*family*)
im·me·di·ate·ly unmittelbar; sofort
im·mense riesig, *fig a.* enorm, immens
im·merse (ein)tauchen; ***immerse o.s. in*** sich vertiefen in (*acc*)
im·mer·sion Eintauchen *n*
im·mer·sion heat·er Tauchsieder *m*
im·mi·grant Einwanderer *m*, Einwanderin *f*, Immigrant(in)
im·mi·grate einwandern, immigrieren (***into*** in *dat*)
im·mi·gra·tion Einwanderung *f*, Immigration *f*
im·mi·nent nahe bevorstehend; ***imminent danger*** drohende Gefahr
im·mo·bile unbeweglich
im·mod·e·rate maßlos
im·mod·est unbescheiden; schamlos, unanständig
im·mor·al unmoralisch
im·mor·tal **1.** unsterblich; **2.** Unsterbliche *m*, *f*
im·mor·tal·i·ty Unsterblichkeit *f*
im·mo·va·ble unbeweglich; *fig* unerschütterlich; hart, unnachgiebig
im·mune MED immun (***to*** gegen); geschützt (***from*** vor, gegen)
immune sys·tem MED Immunsystem *n*
im·mu·ni·ty MED Immunität *f*
im·mu·nize MED immunisieren, immun machen (***against*** gegen)
imp Kobold *m*; F Racker *m*
im·pact Zusammenprall *m*, Anprall *m*; Aufprall *m*; Wucht *f*; *fig* (Ein)Wirkung *f*, (starker) Einfluss (***on*** auf *acc*)
im·pair beeinträchtigen
im·part (***to*** *dat*) mitteilen; vermitteln
im·par·tial unparteiisch, unvoreingenommen
im·par·ti·al·i·ty Unparteilichkeit *f*, Objektivität *f*
im·pass·a·ble unpassierbar

im·passe *fig* Sackgasse *f*; ***reach an impasse*** in e-e Sackgasse geraten
im·pas·sioned leidenschaftlich
im·pas·sive teilnahmslos; ungerührt; gelassen
im·pa·tience Ungeduld *f*
im·pa·tient ungeduldig
im·peach JUR anklagen (***for, of, with*** *gen*); JUR anfechten; infrage stellen, in Zweifel ziehen
im·pec·ca·ble untadelig, einwandfrei
im·pede (be)hindern
im·ped·i·ment Hindernis *n* (***to*** für); Behinderung *f*
im·pel antreiben; zwingen
im·pend·ing nahe bevorstehend, drohend
im·pen·e·tra·ble undurchdringlich; *fig* unergründlich
im·per·a·tive **1.** unumgänglich, unbedingt erforderlich; gebieterisch; LING Imperativ...; **2.** *a.* ***imperative mood*** LING Imperativ *m*, Befehlsform *f*
im·per·cep·ti·ble nicht wahrnehmbar, unmerklich
im·per·fect **1.** unvollkommen; mangelhaft; **2.** *a.* ***imperfect tense*** LING Imperfekt *n*, 1. Vergangenheit
im·pe·ri·al·ism POL Imperialismus
im·pe·ri·al·ist POL Imperialist *m*
im·per·il gefährden
im·pe·ri·ous herrisch, gebieterisch
im·per·me·a·ble undurchlässig
im·per·son·al unpersönlich
im·per·so·nate *j-n* imitieren, nachahmen; verkörpern, THEA *etc* darstellen
im·per·ti·nence Unverschämtheit *f*, Frechheit *f*
im·per·ti·nent unverschämt, frech
im·per·tur·ba·ble unerschütterlich, gelassen
im·per·vi·ous undurchlässig; *fig* unzugänglich (***to*** für)
im·pe·tu·ous ungestüm, heftig; impulsiv; vorschnell
im·pe·tus TECH Antrieb *m*, Impuls *m*
im·pi·e·ty Gottlosigkeit *f*; Pietätlosigkeit *f*, Respektlosigkeit *f* (***to*** gegenüber)
im·pinge: ***impinge on*** sich auswirken auf (*acc*), beeinflussen (*acc*)
im·pi·ous gottlos; pietätlos, respektlos (***to*** gegenüber)
im·plac·a·ble unversöhnlich
im·plant MED implantieren, einpflanzen; *fig* einprägen
im·plau·si·ble unglaubwürdig
im·ple·ment **1.** Werkzeug *n*, Gerät *n*; **2.** ausführen
im·pli·cate *j-n* verwickeln, hineinziehen (***in*** in *acc*)
im·pli·ca·tion Verwicklung *f*; Folge *f*; Andeutung *f*
im·pli·cit vorbehaltlos, bedingungslos; impliziert, (stillschweigend *or* mit) inbegriffen
im·plore *j-n* anflehen; *et.* erflehen
im·ply implizieren, einbeziehen, mit enthalten; andeuten; bedeuten
im·po·lite unhöflich
im·pol·i·tic unklug
im·port ECON **1.** importieren, einführen; **2.** Import *m*, Einfuhr *f*
im·por·tance Wichtigkeit *f*, Bedeutung *f*
im·por·tant wichtig, bedeutend
im·por·ta·tion → ***import*** *2*
im·port du·ty ECON Einfuhrzoll *m*
im·port·er ECON Importeur *m*
im·pose auferlegen, aufbürden (***on*** *dat*); *Strafe* verhängen (***on*** gegen); *et.* aufdrängen, aufzwingen (***on*** *dat*); ***impose o.s. on s.o.*** sich j-m aufdrängen
im·pos·ing imponierend, eindrucksvoll, imposant
im·pos·si·bil·i·ty Unmöglichkeit *f*
im·pos·si·ble unmöglich
im·pos·ter, *Br* **im·pos·tor** Betrüger(in), *esp* Hochstapler(in)
im·po·tence Unvermögen *n*, Unfähigkeit *f*; Hilflosigkeit *f*; MED Impotenz *f*
im·po·tent unfähig; hilflos; MED impotent
im·pov·e·rish arm machen; ***be impoverished*** verarmen; verarmt sein
im·prac·ti·ca·ble undurchführbar; unpassierbar
im·prac·ti·cal unpraktisch; undurchführbar
im·preg·na·ble uneinnehmbar
im·preg·nate imprägnieren, tränken; BIOL schwängern
im·press aufdrücken, einprägen (*a. fig*); *j-n* beeindrucken; ***be impressed with*** beeindruckt sein von
im·pres·sion Eindruck *m*; Abdruck *m*; ***under the impression that*** in der Annahme, dass
im·pres·sive eindrucksvoll
im·print **1.** (auf)drücken (***on*** auf *acc*); ***imprint s.th. on s.o.'s memory*** j-m et. ins Gedächtnis einprägen; **2.** Abdruck *m*, Eindruck *m*; PRINT Impressum *n*
im·pris·on JUR inhaftieren
im·pris·on·ment Freiheitsstrafe *f*, Gefängnis(strafe *f*) *n*, Haft *f*
im·prob·a·ble unwahrscheinlich
im·prop·er ungeeignet, unpassend; unanständig, unschicklich; unrichtig
im·pro·pri·e·ty Unschicklichkeit *f*
im·prove *v/t* verbessern; *Wert etc* erhöhen, steigern; ***improve on*** übertreffen; *v/i*

sich (ver)bessern, besser werden, sich erholen
im·prove·ment (Ver)Bess(e)rung *f*; Steigerung *f*; Fortschritt *m* (**on** gegenüber *dat*)
im·pro·vise improvisieren
im·pru·dent unklug
im·pu·dence Unverschämtheit *f*
im·pu·dent unverschämt
im·pulse Impuls *m* (*a. fig*); Anstoß *m*, Anreiz *m*
im·pul·sive impulsiv
im·pu·ni·ty: ***with impunity*** straflos, ungestraft
im·pure unrein (*a.* REL), schmutzig; *fig* schlecht, unmoralisch
im·pu·ri·ty Unreinheit *f*
im·pute: ***impute s.th. to s.o.*** j-n e-r Sache bezichtigen; j-m et. unterstellen
in 1. *prp place*: in (*dat or acc*), an (*dat*), auf (*dat*): ***in New York*** in New York; ***in the street*** auf der Straße; ***put it in your pocket*** steck es in deine Tasche; *time*: in (*dat*), an (*dat*): ***in 1999*** 1999; ***in two hours*** in zwei Stunden; ***in the morning*** am Morgen; *state, manner*: in (*dat*), auf (*acc*), mit; ***in English*** auf Englisch; *activity*: in (*dat*), bei, auf (*dat*): ***in crossing the road*** beim Überqueren der Straße; *author*: bei: ***in Shakespeare*** bei Shakespeare; *direction*: in (*acc, dat*), auf (*acc*), zu: ***have confidence in*** Vertrauen haben zu; *purpose*: in (*dat*), zu, als: ***in defense of*** zur Verteidigung *or* zum Schutz von; *material*: in (*dat*), aus, mit: ***dressed in blue*** in Blau (gekleidet); *amount etc*: in, von, aus, zu: ***three in all*** insgesamt *or* im Ganzen drei; ***one in ten*** eine(r, -s) von zehn; nach, gemäß: ***in my opinion*** m-r Meinung nach; **2.** *adv* innen, drinnen; hinein, herein; da, (an)gekommen; da, zu Hause; **3.** *adj* F in (Mode)
in·a·bil·i·ty Unfähigkeit *f*
in·ac·ces·si·ble unzugänglich, unerreichbar (**to** für *or dat*)
in·ac·cu·rate ungenau
in·ac·tive untätig
in·ac·tiv·i·ty Untätigkeit *f*
in·ad·e·quate unangemessen; unzulänglich, ungenügend
in·ad·mis·si·ble unzulässig, unstatthaft
in·ad·ver·tent unbeabsichtigt, versehentlich; ***inadvertently*** *a.* aus Versehen
in·an·i·mate leblos; langweilig
in·ap·pro·pri·ate unpassend, ungeeignet (**for, to** für)
in·apt ungeeignet, unpassend
in·ar·tic·u·late unartikuliert, undeutlich (ausgesprochen), unverständlich; unfähig(, deutlich) zu sprechen
in·at·ten·tive unaufmerksam
in·au·di·ble unhörbar
in·au·gu·ral 1. Eröffnungs…, Antritts…; ***inaugural speech*** → **2.** Antrittsrede *f*
in·au·gu·rate *j-n* (feierlich) (in sein Amt) einführen; einweihen, eröffnen; einleiten
in·au·gu·ra·tion Amtseinführung *f*; Einweihung *f*, Eröffnung *f*; Beginn *m*; ***Inauguration Day*** Tag *m* der Amtseinführung des neu gewählten Präsidenten der USA
in·born angeboren
in·cal·cu·la·ble unberechenbar; unermesslich
in·can·des·cent (weiß) glühend
in·ca·pa·ble unfähig (**of** zu *inf or gen*), nicht imstande (***of doing*** zu tun)
in·ca·pa·ci·tate unfähig *or* untauglich machen
in·ca·pac·i·ty Unfähigkeit *f*, Untauglichkeit *f*
in·car·nate leibhaftig; personifiziert
in·cau·tious unvorsichtig
in·cen·di·a·ry Brand…; *fig* aufwiegelnd, aufhetzend
in·cense[1] REL Weihrauch *m*
in·cense[2] in Wut bringen, erbosen
in·cen·tive Ansporn *m*, Anreiz *m*
in·ces·sant ständig, unaufhörlich
in·cest Inzest *m*, Blutschande *f*
inch 1. Inch *m* (2,54 *cm*), Zoll *m* (*a. fig*); ***by inches, inch by inch*** allmählich; ***every inch*** durch und durch; **2.** (sich) zentimeterweise *or* sehr langsam bewegen
in·ci·dence Vorkommen *n*
in·ci·dent Vorfall *m*, Ereignis *n*; POL Zwischenfall *m*
in·ci·den·tal nebensächlich, Neben…; beiläufig
in·ci·den·tal·ly nebenbei bemerkt, übrigens
in·cin·e·rate verbrennen
in·cin·e·ra·tor TECH Verbrennungsofen *m*; Verbrennungsanlage *f*
in·cise einschneiden; aufschneiden; einritzen, einschnitzen
in·ci·sion (Ein)Schnitt *m*
in·ci·sive schneidend, scharf; *fig* treffend
in·ci·sor ANAT Schneidezahn *m*
in·cite anstiften; aufwiegeln, aufhetzen
in·cite·ment Anstiftung *f*; Aufhetzung *f*, Aufwieg(e)lung *f*
in·clem·ent rau
in·cli·na·tion Neigung *f* (*a. fig*)
in·cline 1. *v/i* sich neigen (***to, towards*** nach); *fig* neigen (***to, towards*** zu); *v/t* neigen; *fig* veranlassen; **2.** Gefälle *n*;

(Ab)Hang *m*

in·close, **in·clos·ure** → ***enclose***, ***enclosure***

in·clude einschließen, enthalten; aufnehmen (***in*** in *e-e Liste etc*); ***the group included several …*** zu der Gruppe gehörten einige …; ***tax included*** inklusive Steuer

in·clud·ing einschließlich

in·clu·sion Einschluss *m*, Einbeziehung *f*

in·clu·sive einschließlich, inklusive (***of*** *gen*); ***be inclusive of*** einschließen (*acc*)

in·co·her·ent unzusammenhängend, unklar, unverständlich

in·come ECON Einkommen *n*, Einkünfte *pl*

income tax ECON Einkommensteuer *f*

in·com·ing hereinkommend; ankommend; nachfolgend, neu; ***incoming mail*** Posteingang *m*

in·com·mu·ni·ca·tive verschlossen

in·com·pa·ra·ble unvergleichlich; unvergleichbar

in·com·pat·i·ble unvereinbar; unverträglich; inkompatibel

in·com·pe·tence Unfähigkeit *f*; Inkompetenz *f*

in·com·pe·tent unfähig; nicht fachkundig *or* sachkundig; unzuständig, inkompetent

in·com·plete unvollständig; unvollendet

in·com·pre·hen·si·ble unbegreiflich, unfassbar

in·com·pre·hen·sion Unverständnis *n*

in·con·cei·va·ble unbegreiflich, unfassbar; undenkbar

in·con·clu·sive nicht überzeugend; ergebnislos, erfolglos

in·con·gru·ous nicht übereinstimmend; unvereinbar

in·con·se·quen·tial unbedeutend

in·con·sid·e·ra·ble unbedeutend

in·con·sid·er·ate unüberlegt; rücksichtslos

in·con·sis·tent unvereinbar; widersprüchlich; inkonsequent

in·con·so·la·ble untröstlich

in·con·spic·u·ous unauffällig

in·con·stant unbeständig, wankelmütig

in·con·test·a·ble unanfechtbar

in·con·ti·nent MED inkontinent

in·con·ve·ni·ence 1. Unbequemlichkeit *f*; Unannehmlichkeit *f*, Ungelegenheit *f*; **2.** *j-m* lästig sein; *j-m* Umstände machen

in·con·ve·ni·ent unbequem; ungelegen, lästig

in·cor·po·rate (sich) vereinigen *or* zusammenschließen; (mit) einbeziehen; enthalten; eingliedern; *Ort* eingemeinden; ECON, JUR als Aktiengesellschaft eintragen (lassen)

in·cor·po·rat·ed com·pa·ny ECON Aktiengesellschaft *f*

in·cor·po·ra·tion Vereinigung *f*, Zusammenschluss *m*; Eingliederung *f*; Eingemeindung *f*; ECON, JUR Eintragung *f* als Aktiengesellschaft

in·cor·rect unrichtig, falsch; inkorrekt

in·cor·ri·gi·ble unverbesserlich

in·cor·rup·ti·ble unbestechlich

in·crease 1. zunehmen, (an)wachsen; steigen; vergrößern, vermehren, erhöhen; **2.** Vergrößerung *f*, Erhöhung *f*, Zunahme *f*, Zuwachs *m*, (An)Wachsen *n*, Steigerung *f*

in·creas·ing·ly immer mehr; ***increasingly difficult*** immer schwieriger

in·cred·i·ble unglaublich

in·cre·du·li·ty Ungläubigkeit *f*

in·cred·u·lous ungläubig, skeptisch

in·crim·i·nate *j-n* belasten

in·cu·bate ausbrüten

in·cu·ba·tor Brutapparat *m*; MED Brutkasten *m*

in·cur sich *et.* zuziehen, auf sich laden; *Schulden* machen; *Verluste* erleiden

in·cu·ra·ble unheilbar

in·cu·ri·ous nicht neugierig, gleichgültig, uninteressiert

in·cur·sion (feindlicher) Einfall; Eindringen *n*

in·debt·ed (zu Dank) verpflichtet; ECON verschuldet

in·de·cent unanständig, anstößig; JUR unsittlich, unzüchtig; ***indecent assault*** JUR Sittlichkeitsverbrechen *n*

in·de·ci·sion Unentschlossenheit *f*

in·de·ci·sive unentschlossen; unentschieden; unbestimmt, ungewiss

in·deed 1. *adv* in der Tat, tatsächlich, wirklich; allerdings; ***thank you very much indeed!*** vielen herzlichen Dank!; **2.** *int* ach wirklich?

in·de·fat·i·ga·ble unermüdlich

in·de·fen·si·ble unhaltbar

in·de·fi·na·ble undefinierbar, unbestimmbar

in·def·i·nite unbestimmt; unbegrenzt

in·def·i·nite·ly auf unbestimmte Zeit

in·del·i·ble unauslöschlich (*a. fig*); ***indelible pencil*** Tintenstift *m*

in·del·i·cate taktlos; unfein, anstößig

in·dem·ni·fy *j-n* entschädigen, *j-m* Schadenersatz leisten (***for*** für)

in·dem·ni·ty Entschädigung *f*

in·dent (ein)kerben, auszacken; PRINT *Zeile* einrücken

in·de·pen·dence Unabhängigkeit *f*; Selbstständigkeit *f*; ***Independence Day*** Unabhängigkeitstag *m*
in·de·pen·dent unabhängig; selbstständig
in·de·scri·ba·ble unbeschreiblich
in·de·struc·ti·ble unzerstörbar; unverwüstlich
in·de·ter·mi·nate unbestimmt; unklar, vage
in·dex Index *m*, (Inhalts-, Namens-, Stichwort)Verzeichnis *n*, (Sach)Register *n*; (An)Zeichen *n*; ***cost of living index*** Lebenshaltungsindex *m*
in·dex card Karteikarte *f*
in·dex fin·ger ANAT Zeigefinger *m*
In·di·a Indien *n*
In·di·an **1.** indisch; *neg!* indianisch, Indianer…; **2.** Inder(in); ***American Indian*** Indianer(in)
Indian corn BOT Mais *m*
Indian file: ***in Indian file*** im Gänsemarsch
Indian sum·mer Altweibersommer *m*, Nachsommer *m*
in·di·a rub·ber Gummi *n*, *m*; Radiergummi *m*
in·di·cate deuten *or* zeigen auf (*acc*); TECH anzeigen; MOT blinken; *fig* hinweisen *or* hindeuten auf (*acc*); andeuten
in·di·ca·tion (An)Zeichen *n*, Hinweis *m*, Andeutung *f*, Indiz *n*
in·dic·a·tive *a.* ***indicative mood*** LING Indikativ *m*
in·di·ca·tor TECH Anzeiger *m*; MOT Richtungsanzeiger *m*, Blinker *m*
in·dict JUR anklagen (***for*** wegen)
in·dict·ment JUR Anklage *f*
in·dif·fer·ence Gleichgültigkeit *f*
in·dif·fer·ent gleichgültig (***to*** gegen); mittelmäßig
in·di·gent arm
in·di·ges·ti·ble unverdaulich
in·di·ges·tion MED Verdauungsstörung *f*, Magenverstimmung *f*
in·dig·nant entrüstet, empört, ungehalten (***about, at, over*** über *acc*)
in·dig·na·tion Entrüstung *f*, Empörung *f* (***about, at, over*** über *acc*)
in·dig·ni·ty Demütigung *f*, unwürdige Behandlung
in·di·rect indirekt; ***by indirect means*** *fig* auf Umwegen
in·dis·creet unbesonnen, unbedacht; indiskret
in·dis·cre·tion Unbesonnenheit *f*; Indiskretion *f*
in·dis·crim·i·nate kritiklos; wahllos
in·di·spen·sa·ble unentbehrlich, unerlässlich
in·dis·posed indisponiert, unpässlich; abgeneigt
in·dis·po·si·tion Unpässlichkeit *f*; Abneigung *f* (***to do*** zu tun)
in·dis·pu·ta·ble unbestreitbar, unstreitig
in·dis·tinct undeutlich; unklar, verschwommen
in·dis·tin·guish·a·ble nicht zu unterscheiden(d) (***from*** von)
in·di·vid·u·al **1.** individuell, einzeln, Einzel…; persönlich; **2.** Individuum *n*, Einzelne *m*, *f*
in·di·vid·u·al·ism Individualismus *m*
in·di·vid·u·al·ist Individualist(in)
in·di·vid·u·al·i·ty Individualität *f*, (persönliche) Note
in·di·vid·u·al·ly einzeln, jede(r, -s) für sich; individuell
in·di·vis·i·ble unteilbar
in·dom·i·ta·ble unbezähmbar, nicht unterzukriegen(d)
in·door Haus…, Zimmer…, Innen…, SPORT Hallen…
in·doors im Haus, drinnen; ins Haus (hinein); SPORT in der Halle
in·dorse → ***endorse*** *etc*
in·duce *j-n* veranlassen; verursachen, bewirken
in·duce·ment Anreiz *m*
in·duct einführen, -setzen
in·duc·tion Herbeiführung *f*; Einführung *f*, Einsetzung *f*; ELECTR Induktion *f*
in·dulge nachsichtig sein gegen; *e-r Neigung etc* nachgeben; ***indulge in s.th.*** sich et. gönnen *or* leisten
in·dul·gence Nachsicht *f*; Luxus *m*; REL Ablass *m*
in·dul·gent nachsichtig, nachgiebig
in·dus·tri·al industriell, Industrie…, Gewerbe…, Betriebs…
in·dus·tri·al ar·e·a Industriegebiet *n*
in·dus·tri·al·ist Industrielle *m*, *f*
in·dus·tri·al·ize industrialisieren
in·dus·tri·ous fleißig
in·dus·try Industrie(zweig *m*) *f*; Gewerbe(zweig *m*) *n*; Fleiß *m*
in·ed·i·ble ungenießbar, nicht essbar
in·ef·fec·tive, **in·ef·fec·tu·al** unwirksam, wirkungslos; unfähig, untauglich
in·ef·fi·cient ineffizient; unfähig, untauglich; unrationell, unwirtschaftlich
in·el·e·gant unelegant
in·el·i·gi·ble nicht berechtigt
in·ept unpassend; ungeschickt; albern, töricht
in·e·qual·i·ty Ungleichheit *f*
in·ert PHYS träge (*a. fig*); inaktiv
in·er·tia PHYS Trägheit *f* (*a. fig*)
in·es·cap·a·ble unvermeidlich

I

in·es·sen·tial unwesentlich, unwichtig (***to*** für)
in·es·ti·ma·ble unschätzbar
in·ev·i·ta·ble unvermeidlich
in·ev·i·ta·bly zwangsläufig
in·ex·act ungenau
in·ex·cu·sa·ble unverzeihlich, unentschuldbar
in·ex·haus·ti·ble unerschöpflich; unermüdlich
in·ex·o·ra·ble unerbittlich
in·ex·pe·di·ent unzweckmäßig; nicht ratsam
in·ex·pen·sive billig, preiswert
in·ex·pe·ri·ence Unerfahrenheit *f*
in·ex·pe·ri·enced unerfahren
in·ex·pert unerfahren; ungeschickt
in·ex·plic·a·ble unerklärlich
in·ex·pres·si·ble unaussprechlich, unbeschreiblich
in·ex·pres·sive ausdruckslos
in·ex·tri·ca·ble unentwirrbar
in·fal·li·ble unfehlbar
in·fa·mous berüchtigt; schändlich, niederträchtig
in·fa·my Ehrlosigkeit *f*; Schande *f*; Niedertracht *f*
in·fan·cy frühe Kindheit; ***be in its infancy*** *fig* in den Kinderschuhen stecken
in·fant Säugling *m*; kleines Kind, Kleinkind *n*
in·fan·tile kindlich; Kindes…, Kinder…; infantil, kindisch
in·fan·try MIL Infanterie *f*
in·fat·u·at·ed vernarrt (***with*** in *acc*)
in·fect MED *j-n, et.* infizieren, *j-n* anstecken (*a. fig*); verseuchen, verunreinigen
in·fec·tion MED Infektion *f*, Ansteckung *f* (*a. fig*)
in·fec·tious MED infektiös, ansteckend (*a. fig*)
in·fer folgern, schließen (***from*** aus)
in·fer·ence (Schluss)Folgerung *f*, (Rück)-Schluss *m*
in·fe·ri·or 1. untergeordnet (***to*** *dat*), niedriger (***to*** als); weniger wert (***to*** als); minderwertig; ***be inferior to s.o.*** j-m untergeordnet sein; j-m unterlegen sein; **2.** Untergebene *m, f*
in·fe·ri·or·i·ty Unterlegenheit *f*; Minderwertigkeit *f*
inferiority com·plex PSYCH Minderwertigkeitskomplex *m*
in·fer·nal höllisch, Höllen…
in·fer·no Inferno *n*, Hölle *f*
in·fer·tile unfruchtbar
in·fest verseuchen, befallen; *fig* überschwemmen (***with*** mit)
in·fi·del·i·ty (*esp* eheliche) Untreue
in·fil·trate einsickern in (*acc*); einschleusen (***into*** in *acc*); POL unterwandern
in·fi·nite unendlich
in·fin·i·tive *a.* ***infinitive mood*** LING Infinitiv *m*, Nennform *f*
in·fin·i·ty Unendlichkeit *f*
in·firm schwach, gebrechlich
in·fir·ma·ry Krankenhaus *n*; PED *etc* Krankenzimmer *n*
in·fir·mi·ty Schwäche *f*, Gebrechlichkeit *f*
in·flame entflammen (*mst fig*); erregen; ***become inflamed*** MED sich entzünden
in·flam·ma·ble brennbar, leicht entzündlich; feuergefährlich
in·flam·ma·tion MED Entzündung *f*
in·flam·ma·to·ry MED entzündlich; *fig* aufrührerisch, Hetz…
in·flate aufpumpen, aufblasen, aufblähen (*a. fig*); ECON *Preise etc* in die Höhe treiben
in·fla·tion ECON Inflation *f*
in·flect LING flektieren, beugen
in·flec·tion LING Flexion *f*, Beugung *f*
in·flex·i·ble unbiegsam, starr (*a. fig*); *fig* inflexibel, unbeweglich, unbeugsam
in·flex·ion *Br* → ***inflection***
in·flict (***on***) *Leid, Schaden etc* zufügen (*dat*); *Wunde etc* beibringen (*dat*); *Strafe* auferlegen (*dat*), verhängen (über *acc*); aufbürden, aufdrängen (*dat*)
in·flic·tion Zufügung *f*; Verhängung *f*; Plage *f*
in·flu·ence 1. Einfluss *m*; **2.** beeinflussen
in·flu·en·tial einflussreich
in·flux Zustrom *m*, Zufluss *m*, (*Waren-*) Zufuhr *f*
in·form benachrichtigen, unterrichten (***of*** von), informieren (***of*** über *acc*); ***inform against*** *or* ***on s.o.*** j-n anzeigen; j-n denunzieren
in·for·mal formlos, zwanglos
in·for·mal·i·ty Formlosigkeit *f*; Ungezwungenheit *f*
in·for·ma·tion Auskunft *f*, Information *f*; Nachricht *f*
information (su·per·)highway EDP Datenautobahn *f*
in·for·ma·tive informativ; lehrreich; mitteilsam
in·form·er Denunziant(in); Spitzel *m*
in·fra·struc·ture Infrastruktur *f*
in·fre·quent selten
in·fringe: ***infringe on*** *Rechte, Vertrag etc* verletzen, verstoßen gegen
in·fu·ri·ate wütend machen
in·fuse *Tee* aufgießen
in·fu·sion Aufguss *m*; MED Infusion *f*
in·ge·ni·ous genial; einfallsreich; raffiniert

in·ge·nu·i·ty Genialität *f*; Einfallsreichtum *m*
in·gen·u·ous offen, aufrichtig; naiv
in·got (*Gold- etc*)Barren *m*
in·gra·ti·ate: ***ingratiate o.s. with s.o.*** sich bei j-m beliebt machen
in·grat·i·tude Undankbarkeit *f*
in·gre·di·ent Bestandteil *m*; GASTR Zutat *f*
in·hab·it bewohnen, leben in (*dat*)
in·hab·it·a·ble bewohnbar
in·hab·i·tant Bewohner(in); Einwohner(in)
in·hale einatmen, MED *a.* inhalieren
in·her·ent innewohnend, eigen (***in*** *dat*)
in·her·it erben
in·her·i·tance Erbe *n*
in·hib·it hemmen (*a.* PSYCH), (ver)hindern
in·hib·it·ed PSYCH gehemmt
in·hi·bi·tion PSYCH Hemmung *f*
in·hos·pi·ta·ble ungastlich; unwirtlich (*region etc*)
in·hu·man unmenschlich
in·hu·mane inhuman, menschenunwürdig
in·im·i·cal feindselig (***to*** gegen); nachteilig (***to*** für)
in·im·i·ta·ble unnachahmlich
i·ni·tial **1.** anfänglich, Anfangs…; **2.** Initiale *f*, (großer) Anfangsbuchstabe
i·ni·tial·ly am *or* zu Anfang, anfänglich
i·ni·ti·ate in die Wege leiten, ins Leben rufen; einführen
i·ni·ti·a·tion Einführung *f*
i·ni·tia·tive Initiative *f*, erster Schritt; ***take the initiative*** die Initiative ergreifen; ***on one's own initiative*** aus eigenem Antrieb
in·ject MED injizieren, einspritzen
in·jec·tion MED Injektion *f*, Spritze *f*
in·ju·di·cious unklug, unüberlegt
in·junc·tion JUR gerichtliche Verfügung
in·jure verletzen, verwunden; schaden (*dat*); kränken
in·jured **1.** verletzt; **2.** ***the injured*** die Verletzten *pl*
in·ju·ri·ous schädlich; ***be injurious to*** schaden (*dat*); ***injurious to health*** gesundheitsschädlich
in·ju·ry MED Verletzung *f*; Kränkung *f*
injury time *Br esp soccer*: Nachspielzeit *f*
in·jus·tice Ungerechtigkeit *f*; Unrecht *n*; ***do s.o. an injustice*** j-m unrecht tun
ink Tinte *f*
ink·ling Andeutung *f*; dunkle *or* leise Ahnung
ink pad Stempelkissen *n*
ink·y Tinten…; tinten-, pechschwarz
in·laid eingelegt, Einlege…; ***inlaid work*** Einlegearbeit *f*
in·land **1.** *adj* inländisch, einheimisch; ECON Binnen…; **2.** *adv* landeinwärts
In·land Rev·e·nue *Br* Finanzamt *n*
in·lay Einlegearbeit *f*; MED (Zahn)Füllung *f*, Plombe *f*
in·let GEOGR schmale Bucht; TECH Eingang *m*, Einlass *m*
in-line skate Inliner *m*, Inline Skate *m*
in·mate Insasse *m*, Insassin *f*; Mitbewohner(in)
in·most innerste(r, -s) (*a. fig*)
inn Gasthaus *n*, Wirtshaus *n*
in·nate angeboren
in·ner innere(r, -s); Innen…; verborgen
in·ner·most → ***inmost***
in·nings *cricket*, *baseball*: Spielzeit *f*
inn·keep·er Gastwirt(in)
in·no·cence Unschuld *f*; Harmlosigkeit *f*; Naivität *f*
in·no·cent unschuldig; harmlos; arglos, naiv
in·noc·u·ous harmlos
in·no·va·tion Neuerung *f*
in·nu·en·do (versteckte) Andeutung *f*
in·nu·me·ra·ble unzählig, zahllos
i·noc·u·late MED impfen
i·noc·u·la·tion MED Impfung *f*
in·of·fen·sive harmlos
in·op·e·ra·ble MED inoperabel, nicht operierbar; undurchführbar (*plan etc*)
in·op·por·tune inopportun, unangebracht, ungelegen
in·or·di·nate unmäßig
in·pa·tient MED stationärer Patient, stationäre Patientin
in·put Input *m*, *n*, EDP *a.* (Daten)Eingabe *f*, ELECTR *a.* Eingangsleistung *f*
in·quest JUR gerichtliche Untersuchung
in·quire fragen *or* sich erkundigen (nach); ***inquire into*** *et.* untersuchen, prüfen
in·quir·ing forschend; wissbegierig
in·quir·y Erkundigung *f*, Nachfrage *f*; Untersuchung *f*; Ermittlung *f*; ***make inquiries*** Erkundigungen einziehen
in·qui·si·tion (amtliche) Untersuchung; Verhör *n*; ***Inquisition*** REL HIST Inquisition *f*
in·quis·i·tive neugierig, wissbegierig
in·roads (***in***[***to***], ***on***) Eingriff *m* (in *acc*), Übergriff *m* (auf *acc*)
in·sane geisteskrank, wahnsinnig
in·san·i·ta·ry unhygienisch
in·san·i·ty Geisteskrankheit *f*, Wahnsinn *m*
in·sa·tia·ble unersättlich
in·scrip·tion Inschrift *f*, Aufschrift *f*; Widmung *f*
in·scru·ta·ble unerforschlich, unergründlich

in·sect zo Insekt *n*
in·sec·ti·cide Insektenvertilgungsmittel *n*, Insektizid *n*
in·se·cure unsicher; nicht sicher *or* fest
in·sen·si·ble unempfindlich (***to*** gegen); bewusstlos; unempfänglich (***of, to*** für), gleichgültig (***of, to*** gegen); unmerklich
in·sen·si·tive unempfindlich (***to*** gegen); unempfänglich (***of, to*** für), gleichgültig (***of, to*** gegen)
in·sep·a·ra·ble untrennbar; unzertrennlich
in·sert **1.** einfügen, einsetzen, einführen, (hinein)stecken, *Münze* einwerfen; inserieren; **2.** (Zeitungs)Beilage *f*, (Buch)-Einlage *f*
in·ser·tion Einfügen *n*, Einsetzen *n*, Einführen *n*, Hineinstecken *n*; Einfügung *f*; Einwurf *m*; Anzeige *f*, Inserat *n*
in·sert key EDP Einfügetaste *f*
in·shore an *or* nahe der Küste; Küsten…
in·side **1.** Innenseite *f*; *das* Innere; ***turn inside out*** umkrempeln; auf den Kopf stellen; **2.** *adj* innere(r, -s), Innen…; Insider…; **3.** *adv* im Inner(e)n, innen, drinnen; ***inside of*** F innerhalb (*gen*); **4.** *prp* innerhalb, im Inner(e)n
in·sid·er Insider(in), Eingeweihte *m, f*
in·sid·i·ous heimtückisch
in·sight Einsicht *f*, Einblick *m*; Verständnis *n*
in·sig·ni·a Insignien *pl*; Abzeichen *pl*
in·sig·nif·i·cant bedeutungslos; unbedeutend
in·sin·cere unaufrichtig
in·sin·u·ate andeuten, anspielen auf (*acc*); unterstellen; ***insinuate that s.o. …*** j-m unterstellen, dass er …
in·sin·u·a·tion Anspielung *f*, Andeutung *f*, Unterstellung *f*
in·sip·id geschmacklos, fad
in·sist bestehen, beharren (***on*** auf *dat*)
in·sis·tence Bestehen *n*, Beharren *n*; Beharrlichkeit *f*
in·sis·tent beharrlich, hartnäckig
in·sole Einlegesohle *f*; Brandsohle *f*
in·so·lent unverschämt
in·sol·u·ble unlöslich (*substance etc*); unlösbar (*problem etc*)
in·sol·vent ECON zahlungsunfähig, insolvent
in·som·ni·a Schlaflosigkeit *f*
in·spect untersuchen, prüfen, nachsehen; besichtigen, inspizieren
in·spec·tion Prüfung *f*, Untersuchung *f*, Kontrolle *f*; Inspektion *f*
in·spec·tor Aufsichtsbeamte *m*, Inspektor *m*; (Polizei)Inspektor *m*, (Polizei)-Kommissar *m*
in·spi·ra·tion Inspiration *f*, (plötzlicher) Einfall
in·spire inspirieren, anregen; *Gefühl etc* auslösen
in·stall TECH installieren, einrichten, aufstellen, einbauen, *Leitung* legen; *j-n in ein Amt etc* einsetzen
in·stal·la·tion TECH Installation *f*, Einrichtung *f*, Einbau *m*; TECH *fertige* Anlage *f*; *fig* Einsetzung *f*, Einführung *f*
in·stall·ment, in·stal·ment *Br* ECON Rate *f*; (Teil)Lieferung *f*; Fortsetzung *f*; *radio*, TV Folge *f*
in·stall·ment plan: ***buy on the installment plan*** ECON auf Abzahlung *or* Raten kaufen
in·stance Beispiel *n*; (besonderer) Fall; JUR Instanz *f*; ***for instance*** zum Beispiel
in·stant **1.** Moment *m*, Augenblick *m*; **2.** sofortig, augenblicklich
in·stan·ta·ne·ous sofortig, augenblicklich; ***death was instantaneous*** der Tod trat sofort ein
in·stant cam·e·ra PHOT Sofortbildkamera *f*
instant cof·fee GASTR Pulver-, Instantkaffee *m*
in·stant·ly sofort, augenblicklich
in·stead stattdessen, dafür; ***instead of*** anstelle von, (an)statt
in·step ANAT Spann *m*, Rist *m*
in·sti·gate anstiften; aufhetzen; veranlassen
in·sti·ga·tor Anstifter(in); (Auf)Hetzer(in)
in·stil *Br*, **in·still** beibringen, einflößen (***into*** *dat*)
in·stinct Instinkt *m*
in·stinc·tive instinktiv
in·sti·tute Institut *n*
in·sti·tu·tion Institution *f*, Einrichtung *f*; Institut *n*; Anstalt *f*
in·struct unterrichten, -weisen; ausbilden, schulen; informieren; anweisen
in·struc·tion Unterricht *m*; Ausbildung *f*, Schulung *f*, Unterweisung *f*; Anweisung *f*, Instruktion *f*; EDP Befehl *m*; ***instructions for use*** Gebrauchsanweisung *f*; ***operating instructions*** Bedienungsanleitung *f*
in·struc·tive instruktiv, lehrreich
in·struc·tor Lehrer *m*; Ausbilder *m*
in·struc·tress Lehrerin *f*; Ausbilderin *f*
in·stru·ment Instrument *n* (*a.* MUS); Werkzeug *n* (*a. fig*)
in·stru·men·tal MUS Instrumental…; behilflich; ***be instrumental in*** beitragen zu
in·sub·or·di·nate aufsässig
in·sub·or·di·na·tion Auflehnung *f*, Auf-

sässigkeit *f*
in·suf·fe·ra·ble unerträglich, unausstehlich
in·suf·fi·cient unzulänglich, ungenügend
in·su·lar Insel…; *fig* engstirnig
in·su·late isolieren
in·su·la·tion Isolierung *f*; Isoliermaterial *n*
in·sult **1.** Beleidigung *f*; **2.** beleidigen
in·sur·ance Versicherung *f*; Versicherungssumme *f*; Absicherung *f* (***against*** gegen)
insurance com·pa·ny Versicherungsgesellschaft *f*
insurance pol·i·cy Versicherungspolice *f*
in·sure versichern (***against*** gegen)
in·sured: ***the insured*** der *or* die Versicherte
in·sur·gent **1.** aufständisch; **2.** Aufständische *m, f*
in·sur·moun·ta·ble *fig* unüberwindlich
in·sur·rec·tion Aufstand *m*
in·tact intakt, unversehrt, unbeschädigt, ganz
in·take (*Nahrungs- etc*)Aufnahme *f*; (Neu)Aufnahme(n *pl*) *f*, (Neu)Zugänge *pl*; TECH Einlass(öffnung *f*) *m*
in·te·gral ganz, vollständig; wesentlich
in·te·grate (sich) integrieren; zusammenschließen; eingliedern, einbeziehen; ***integrated circuit*** ELECTR integrierter Schaltkreis
in·te·gra·tion Integration *f*
in·teg·ri·ty Integrität *f*; Vollständigkeit *f*; Einheit *f*
in·tel·lect Intellekt *m*, Verstand *m*
in·tel·lec·tual **1.** intellektuell, Verstandes…, geistig; **2.** Intellektuelle *m, f*
in·tel·li·gence Intelligenz *f*; nachrichtendienstliche Informationen *pl*
in·tel·li·gent intelligent, klug
in·tel·li·gi·ble verständlich (***to*** für)
in·tem·per·ate unmäßig
in·tend beabsichtigen, vorhaben, planen; ***intended for*** bestimmt für *or* zu
in·tense intensiv, stark, heftig
in·ten·si·fy intensivieren; (sich) verstärken
in·ten·si·ty Intensität *f*
in·ten·sive intensiv, gründlich
intensive care u·nit MED Intensivstation *f*
in·tent **1.** gespannt, aufmerksam; ***intent on*** fest entschlossen zu (*dat*); konzentriert auf (*acc*); **2.** Absicht *f*, Vorhaben *n*
in·ten·tion Absicht *f*; JUR Vorsatz *m*
in·ten·tion·al absichtlich, vorsätzlich
in·ter bestatten
in·ter… zwischen, Zwischen…; gegenseitig, einander
in·ter·act aufeinander (ein)wirken, sich gegenseitig beeinflussen
in·ter·ac·tion Wechselwirkung *f*
in·ter·cede vermitteln, sich einsetzen (***with*** bei; ***for*** für)
in·ter·cept abfangen
in·ter·ces·sion Fürsprache *f*
in·ter·change **1.** austauschen; **2.** Austausch *m*; MOT Autobahnkreuz *n*
in·ter·com Sprechanlage *f*
in·ter·course Verkehr *m*; *a.* ***sexual intercourse*** (Geschlechts)Verkehr *m*
in·terest **1.** Interesse *n* (***in*** an *dat*, für); Wichtigkeit *f*, Bedeutung *f*; Vorteil *m*, Nutzen *m*; ECON Anteil *m*, Beteiligung *f*; ECON Zins(en *pl*) *m*; ***take an interest in*** sich interessieren für; **2.** interessieren (***in*** für *et*)
in·terest·ed interessiert (***in*** an *dat*); ***be interested in*** sich interessieren für
in·terest·ing interessant
in·terest rate ECON Zinssatz *m*
in·ter·face EDP Schnittstelle *f*
in·ter·fere sich einmischen (***with*** in *acc*); stören
in·ter·fer·ence Einmischung *f*; Störung *f*
in·te·ri·or **1.** innere(r, -s), Innen…; Binnen…; Inlands…; **2.** *das* Innere; Interieur *n*; POL innere Angelegenheiten *pl*; → ***Department of the Interior***
interior dec·o·ra·tor Innenarchitekt(in)
in·ter·ject *Bemerkung* einwerfen
in·ter·jec·tion Einwurf *m*; Ausruf *m*; LING Interjektion *f*
in·ter·lace (sich) (ineinander) verflechten
in·ter·lop·er Eindringling *m*
in·ter·lude Zwischenspiel *n*; Pause *f*; ***interludes of bright weather*** zeitweilig schön
in·ter·me·di·a·ry Vermittler(in), Mittelsmann *m*
in·ter·me·di·ate in der Mitte liegend, Mittel…, Zwischen…; PED für fortgeschrittene Anfänger
in·ter·ment Beerdigung *f*, Bestattung *f*
in·ter·mi·na·ble endlos
in·ter·mis·sion Unterbrechung *f*; THEA *etc* Pause *f*
in·ter·mit·tent mit Unterbrechungen, periodisch (auftretend); ***intermittent fever*** MED Wechselfieber *n*
in·tern[1] internieren
in·tern[2] Assistenzarzt *m*, -ärztin *f*
in·ter·nal innere(r, -s); einheimisch, Inlands…
in·ter·nal-com·bus·tion en·gine Verbrennungsmotor *m*
in·ter·na·tion·al **1.** international; Auslands…; **2.** SPORT Internationale *m, f*, Na-

tionalspieler(in); internationaler Wettkampf; Länderspiel *n*
international call TEL Auslandsgespräch *n*
international law JUR Völkerrecht *n*
In·ter·net Internet *n*
in·tern·ist MED Internist *m*
in·ter·per·son·al zwischenmenschlich
in·ter·pret interpretieren, auslegen, erklären; dolmetschen
in·ter·pre·ta·tion Interpretation *f*, Auslegung *f*
in·ter·pret·er Dolmetscher(in)
in·ter·ro·gate verhören, vernehmen; (be)-fragen
in·ter·ro·ga·tion Verhör *n*, Vernehmung *f*; Frage *f*
in·ter·rog·a·tive LING Interrogativ…, Frage…
in·ter·rupt unterbrechen
in·ter·rup·tion Unterbrechung *f*
in·ter·sect (durch)schneiden; sich schneiden *or* kreuzen
in·ter·sec·tion Schnittpunkt *m*; (Straßen)Kreuzung *f*
in·ter·sperse einstreuen, hier und da einfügen
in·ter·state **1.** zwischenstaatlich; **2.** *a.* ***interstate highway*** Autobahn *f*
in·ter·twine (sich ineinander) verschlingen, sich verflechten
in·ter·val Intervall *n* (*a.* MUS), Abstand *m*; *Br* Pause *f* (*a.* THEA *etc*); ***at regular intervals*** in regelmäßigen Abständen
in·ter·vene eingreifen, einschreiten, intervenieren; dazwischenkommen
in·ter·ven·tion Eingreifen *n*, Einschreiten *n*, Intervention *f*
in·ter·view **1.** Interview *n*; Einstellungsgespräch *n*; **2.** interviewen; ein Einstellungsgespräch führen mit
in·ter·view·ee Interviewte *m, f*
in·ter·view·er Interviewer(in)
in·ter·weave (miteinander) verweben
in·tes·tate: ***die intestate*** JUR ohne Hinterlassung e-s Testaments sterben
in·tes·tine ANAT Darm *m*; *pl* Eingeweide *pl*; ***large intestine*** Dickdarm *m*; ***small intestine*** Dünndarm *m*
in·ti·ma·cy Intimität *f*, Vertrautheit *f*; (*a. plumpe*) Vertraulichkeit; intime (*sexuelle*) Beziehungen *pl*
in·ti·mate **1.** intim (*a. sexually*); vertraut, eng (*friends etc*); (*a.* plump)vertraulich; innerste(r, -s); gründlich, genau (*knowledge etc*); **2.** Vertraute *m, f*
in·tim·i·date einschüchtern
in·tim·i·da·tion Einschüchterung *f*
in·to in (*acc*), in (*acc*) … hinein; gegen (*acc*); MATH in (*acc*); ***4 into 20 goes five times*** 4 geht fünfmal in 20
in·tol·e·ra·ble unerträglich
in·tol·e·rance Intoleranz *f*, Unduldsamkeit (***of*** gegen)
in·tol·e·rant intolerant, unduldsam (***of*** gegen)
in·to·na·tion MUS Intonation *f*, LING *a.* Tonfall *m*
in·tox·i·cat·ed berauscht, betrunken
in·tox·i·ca·tion Rausch *m* (*a. fig*)
in·trac·ta·ble eigensinnig; schwer zu handhaben(d)
in·tran·si·tive LING intransitiv
in·tra·ve·nous MED intravenös
in tray: ***in the in tray*** im Posteingang *etc*
in·trep·id unerschrocken
in·tri·cate verwickelt, kompliziert
in·trigue **1.** Intrige *f*; **2.** faszinieren, interessieren; intrigieren
in·tro·duce vorstellen (***to*** *dat*), *j-n* bekannt machen (***to*** mit); einführen
in·tro·duc·tion Vorstellung *f*; Einführung *f*; Einleitung *f*, Vorwort *n*; ***letter of introduction*** Empfehlungsschreiben *n*
in·tro·duc·to·ry Einführungs…; einleitend, Einleitungs…
in·tro·spec·tion Selbstbeobachtung *f*
in·tro·vert PSYCH introvertierter Mensch
in·tro·vert·ed PSYCH introvertiert, in sich gekehrt
in·trude (sich) aufdrängen; stören; ***am I intruding?*** störe ich?
in·trud·er Eindringling *m*, Störenfried *m*
in·tru·sion Störung *f*
in·tru·sive aufdringlich
in·tu·i·tion Intuition *f*
in·tu·i·tive intuitiv
In·u·it *a.* ***Innuit*** Inuit *m*, Eskimo *m*
in·un·date überschwemmen, überfluten (*a. fig*)
in·vade eindringen in (*acc*), einfallen in (*acc*), MIL *a.* einmarschieren in (*acc*); *fig* überlaufen, überschwemmen
in·vad·er Eindringling *m*
in·va·lid[1] **1.** krank; invalid(e); **2.** Kranke *m; f*; Invalide *m, f*
in·val·id[2] (rechts)ungültig
in·val·i·date JUR für ungültig erkären
in·val·u·a·ble *fig* unschätzbar, unbezahlbar
in·var·i·a·ble unveränderlich
in·var·i·a·bly ausnahmslos
in·va·sion Invasion *f* (*a.* MIL), Einfall *m*, MIL *a.* Einmarsch *m*; *fig* Eingriff *m*, Verletzung *f*
in·vec·tive Schmähung(en *pl*) *f*, Beschimpfung(en *pl*) *f*
in·vent erfinden

in·ven·tion Erfindung *f*
in·ven·tive erfinderisch; einfallsreich
in·ven·tor Erfinder(in)
in·ven·tory Inventar *n*, Bestand *m*; Bestandsliste *f*; Inventur *f*
in·verse **1.** umgekehrt; **2.** Umkehrung *f*, Gegenteil *n*
in·ver·sion Umkehrung *f*; LING Inversion *f*
in·vert umkehren
in·ver·te·brate ZO **1.** wirbellos; **2.** wirbelloses Tier
in·vert·ed com·mas LING Anführungszeichen *pl*
in·vest ECON investieren, anlegen
in·ves·ti·gate untersuchen; überprüfen; Untersuchungen *or* Ermittlungen anstellen (***into*** über *acc*), nachforschen
in·ves·ti·ga·tion Untersuchung *f*; Ermittlung *f*, Nachforschung *f*
in·ves·ti·ga·tor: ***private investigator*** Privatdetektiv *m*
in·vest·ment ECON Investition *f*, (Kapital)Anlage *f*
in·ves·tor ECON Anleger *m*
in·vet·e·rate unverbesserlich; hartnäckig
in·vid·i·ous gehässig, boshaft, gemein
in·vig·o·rate stärken, beleben
in·vin·ci·ble unbesiegbar; unüberwindlich
in·vi·o·la·ble unantastbar
in·vis·i·ble unsichtbar
in·vi·ta·tion Einladung *f*; Aufforderung *f*
in·vite einladen; auffordern; *Gefahr etc* herausfordern; ***invite s.o. in*** j-n hereinbitten
in·vit·ing einladend, verlockend
in·voice ECON **1.** (Waren)Rechnung *f*; **2.** in Rechnung stellen, berechnen
in·voke flehen um; *Gott etc* anrufen; beschwören
in·vol·un·ta·ry unfreiwillig; unabsichtlich; unwillkürlich
in·volve verwickeln, hineinziehen (***in*** in *acc*); *j-n, et.* angehen, betreffen; zur Folge haben, mit sich bringen
in·volved kompliziert, verworren
in·volve·ment Verwicklung *f*; Beteiligung *f*
in·vul·ne·ra·ble unverwundbar; *fig* unanfechtbar
in·ward **1.** *adj* innere(r, -s), innerlich; **2.** *adv mst* ***inwards*** einwärts, nach innen
i·o·dine CHEM Jod *n*
i·on PHYS Ion *n*
IOU (= ***I owe you***) Schuldschein *m*
IQ ABBR *of* ***intelligence quotient*** IQ, Intelligenzquotient *m*
I·ran Iran *m*
I·ra·ni·an **1.** iranisch; **2.** Iraner(in); LING Iranisch *n*
I·raq Irak *m*
I·ra·qi **1.** irakisch; **2.** Iraker(in); LING Irakisch *n*
i·ras·ci·ble jähzornig
i·rate zornig, wütend
Ire·land Irland *n*
ir·i·des·cent schillernd
i·ris ANAT Regenbogenhaut *f*, Iris *f*; BOT Schwertlilie *f*, Iris *f*
I·rish **1.** irisch; **2.** LING Irisch *n*; ***the Irish*** die Iren *pl*
I·rish·man Ire *m*
I·rish·wom·an Irin *f*
i·ron **1.** Eisen *n*; Bügeleisen *n*; ***strike while the iron is hot*** *fig* das Eisen schmieden, solange es heiß ist; **2.** eisern (*a. fig*), Eisen…, aus Eisen; **3.** bügeln; ***iron out*** ausbügeln
I·ron Cur·tain POL HIST Eiserner Vorhang
i·ron·ic, **i·ron·i·cal** ironisch, spöttisch
i·ron·ing board Bügelbrett *n*
i·ron·mon·ger *Br* Eisenwarenhändler *m*
i·ron·works TECH Eisenhütte *f*
i·ron·y Ironie *f*
ir·ra·tion·al irrational, unvernünftig
ir·rec·on·ci·la·ble unversöhnlich; unvereinbar
ir·re·cov·e·ra·ble unersetzlich; unwiederbringlich
ir·re·fut·a·ble unwiderlegbar
ir·reg·u·lar unregelmäßig; ungleichmäßig; regelwidrig, vorschriftswidrig
ir·rel·e·vant irrelevant, unerheblich, belanglos (***to*** für)
ir·rep·a·ra·ble irreparabel, nicht wieder gutzumachen(d)
ir·re·place·a·ble unersetzlich
ir·re·pres·si·ble nicht zu unterdrücken(d); unbezähmbar
ir·re·proach·a·ble einwandfrei, untadelig
ir·re·sist·i·ble unwiderstehlich
ir·res·o·lute unentschlossen
ir·re·spec·tive: ***irrespective of*** ohne Rücksicht auf (*acc*); unabhängig von
ir·re·spon·si·ble unverantwortlich; verantwortungslos
ir·re·trie·va·ble unwiederbringlich, unersetzlich
ir·rev·e·rent respektlos
ir·rev·o·ca·ble unwiderruflich, endgültig
ir·ri·gate bewässern
ir·ri·ga·tion Bewässerung *f*
ir·ri·ta·ble reizbar
ir·ri·tant Reizmittel *n*
ir·ri·tate reizen; (ver)ärgern
ir·ri·tat·ing ärgerlich
ir·ri·ta·tion Reizung *f*; Verärgerung *f*; Är-

ger *m* (**at** über *acc*)
is *er, sie, es* ist
Is·lam der Islam
is·land Insel *f*; *a.* ***traffic island*** Verkehrsinsel *f*
is·land·er Inselbewohner(in)
isle POET Insel *f*
i·so·late absondern; isolieren
i·so·lat·ed isoliert, abgeschieden; einzeln; ***become isolated*** vereinsamen
i·so·la·tion Isolierung *f*, Absonderung *f*
isolation ward MED Isolierstation *f*
Is·rael Israel *n*
Is·rae·li **1.** israelisch; **2.** Israeli *m, f*
is·sue **1.** Streitfrage *f*, Streitpunkt *m*; Ausgabe *f*; Erscheinen *n*; JUR Nachkommen(schaft *f*) *pl*; *fig* Ausgang *m*, Ergebnis *n*; ***be at issue*** zur Debatte stehen; ***point at issue*** strittiger Punkt; ***die without issue*** kinderlos sterben; **2.** *v/t Zeitung etc* herausgeben; *Banknoten etc* ausgeben; *Dokument etc* ausstellen; *v/i* herauskommen, hervorkommen; herausfließen, herausströmen
it es; *s.th. previously mentioned*: es, er, ihn, sie
I·tal·i·an **1.** italienisch; **2.** Italiener(in); LING Italienisch *n*
i·tal·ics PRINT Kursivschrift *f*
It·a·ly Italien *n*
itch **1.** Jucken *n*, Juckreiz *m*; **2.** jucken, kratzen; ***I itch all over*** es juckt mich überall; ***be itching for s.th.*** F et. unbedingt (haben) wollen; ***be itching to*** *inf* F darauf brennen zu *inf*
itch·y juckend; kratzend
i·tem Punkt *m* (*on the agenda etc*), Posten *m* (*on a list*); Artikel *m*, Gegenstand *m*; (*Presse-, Zeitungs*)Notiz *f*, (*a. radio*, TV) Nachricht *f*, Meldung *f*
i·tem·ize einzeln angeben *or* aufführen
i·tin·e·ra·ry Reiseweg *m*, Reiseroute *f*; Reiseplan *m*
its sein(e), ihr(e)
it·self sich; sich selbst; selbst; ***by itself*** (für sich) allein; von selbst; ***in itself*** an sich
i·vo·ry Elfenbein *n*
i·vy BOT Efeu *m*

J

J, j J, j *n*
jab **1.** (hinein)stechen, (hinein)stoßen; **2.** Stich *m*, Stoß *m*
jab·ber F (daher)plappern
jack **1.** TECH Hebevorrichtung *f*; MOT Wagenheber *m*; *cards*: Bube *m*; **2.** ***jack up*** *Auto* aufbocken
jack·al ZO Schakal *m*
jack·ass ZO Esel *m* (*a. fig*)
jack·daw ZO Dohle *f*
jack·et Jacke *f*, Jackett *n*; TECH Mantel *m*; (Schutz)Umschlag *m*; (*Platten-*)Hülle *f*; ***jacket potatoes, potatoes (boiled) in their jackets*** Pellkartoffeln *pl*
jack knife **1.** Klappmesser *n*; **2.** zusammenklappen, -knicken
jack-of-all-trades Hansdampf *m* in allen Gassen
jack·pot Jackpot *m*, Haupttreffer *m*; ***hit the jackpot*** F den Jackpot gewinnen; *fig* das große Los ziehen
jade MIN Jade *m, f*; Jadegrün *n*
jag Zacken *m*
jag·ged gezackt, zackig; schartig
jag·u·ar ZO Jaguar *m*
jail **1.** Gefängnis *n*; **2.** einsperren
jail·bird F Knastbruder *m*
jail·er Gefängnisaufseher *m*
jail·house Gefängnis *n*
jam[1] Konfitüre *f*, Marmelade *f*
jam[2] **1.** *v/t* (hinein)pressen, (hinein-) quetschen, (hinein)zwängen, *Menschen a.* (hinein)pferchen; (ein)klemmen, (ein)quetschen; *a.* ***jam up*** blockieren, verstopfen; *Funkempfang* stören; ***jam on the brakes*** MOT voll auf die Bremse treten; *v/i* sich (hinein)drängen *or* (hinein-) quetschen; TECH sich verklemmen, *brake*: blockieren; **2.** Gedränge *n*; TECH Blockierung *f*; Stauung *f*, Stockung *f*; ***traffic jam*** Verkehrsstau *m*; ***be in a jam*** F in der Klemme stecken
jamb (Tür-, Fenster)Pfosten *m*
jam·bo·ree Jamboree *n*, Pfadfindertreffen *n*; Fest *n*
Jan ABBR *of* ***January*** Jan., Januar *m*
jan·gle klimpern *or* klirren (mit)
jan·i·tor Hausmeister *m*

Jan·u·a·ry (ABBR *of* ***Jan***) Januar *m*
Ja·pan Japan *n*
Jap·a·nese **1.** japanisch; **2.** Japaner(in); LING Japanisch *n*; ***the Japanese*** die Japaner *pl*
jar[1] **1.** Gefäß *n*, Krug *m*; (Marmelade- *etc*)-Glas *n*
jar[2]: ***jar on*** wehtun (*dat*)
jar·gon Jargon *m*, Fachsprache *f*
jaun·dice MED Gelbsucht *f*
jaunt **1.** Ausflug *m*, MOT Spritztour *f*; **2.** e-n Ausflug *or* e-e Spritztour machen
jaun·ty unbeschwert, unbekümmert; flott
jav·e·lin SPORT Speer *m*; ***javelin*** (***throw***), ***throwing the javelin*** SPORT Speerwerfen *n*
jav·e·lin throw·er SPORT Speerwerfer(in)
jaw ANAT Kiefer *m*; *pl* ZO Rachen *m*, Maul *n*; TECH Backen *pl*; ***lower jaw*** ANAT Unterkiefer *m*; ***upper jaw*** ANAT Oberkiefer
jaw·bone ANAT Kieferknochen *m*
jay ZO Eichelhäher *m*
jay·walk·er unachtsamer Fußgänger
jazz MUS Jazz *m*
jazz·y F poppig
jeal·ous eifersüchtig (***of*** auf acc); neidisch
jeal·ous·y Eifersucht *f*; Neid *m*
jeans Jeans *pl*
jeer **1.** (***at***) höhnische Bemerkung(en) machen (über *acc*); höhnisch lachen (über *acc*); ***jeer*** (***at***) verhöhnen; **2.** höhnische Bemerkung; Hohngelächter *n*
jel·lied GASTR in Aspik, in Sülze
jel·ly Gallert(e *f*) *n*; GASTR Gelee *n*; Aspik *m*, *n*, Sülze *f*; Götterspeise *f*
jelly ba·by *Br* Gummibärchen *n*
jelly bean Gummi-, Geleebonbon *m*, *n*
jel·ly·fish ZO Qualle *f*
jeop·ar·dize gefährden
jerk **1.** ruckartig ziehen an (*dat*); (zusammen)zucken; sich ruckartig bewegen; **2.** (plötzlicher) Ruck; Sprung *m*, Satz *m*; MED Zuckung *f*
jerk·y ruckartig; holprig; rüttelnd
jer·sey Pullover *m*
jest **1.** Scherz *m*, Spaß *m*; **2.** scherzen, spaßen
jest·er HIST (Hof)Narr *m*
jet **1.** (Wasser-, Gas- *etc*)Strahl *m*; TECH Düse *f*; AVIAT Jet *m*; **2.** (heraus-, hervor)-schießen (***from*** aus); AVIAT F jetten
jet en·gine AVIAT Düsen-, Strahltriebwerk *n*
jet plane AVIAT Düsenflugzeug *n*, Jet *m*
jet-pro·pelled AVIAT mit Düsenantrieb, Düsen…
jet pro·pul·sion AVIAT Düsen-, Strahlantrieb *m*
jet·ty MAR (Hafen)Mole *f*
Jew Jude *m*, Jüdin *f*
jew·el Juwel *n*, *m*, Edelstein *m*
jew·el·er, *Br* **jew·el·ler** Juwelier *m*
jew·el·lery *Br*, **jew·el·ry** Juwelen *pl*; Schmuck *m*
Jew·ess Jüdin *f*
Jew·ish jüdisch
jif·fy: F ***in a jiffy*** im Nu, sofort
jig·saw Laubsäge *f*; → **jig·saw puz·zle** Puzzle(spiel) *n*
jilt *Mädchen* sitzen lassen; *e-m Liebhaber* den Laufpass geben
jin·gle **1.** klimpern (mit), bimmeln (lassen; **2.** Klimpern *n*, Bimmeln *n*; Werbesong *m*, Werbespruch *m*
jit·ters: F ***the jitters*** Bammel *m*, e-e Heidenangst
jit·ter·y F nervös; ängstlich
job **1.** (*einzelne*) Arbeit; Beruf *m*, Beschäftigung *f*, Stellung *f*, Stelle *f*, Arbeit *f*, Job *m* (*a.* EDP); Arbeitsplatz *m*; Aufgabe *f*, Sache *f*, Angelegenheit *f*; *a.* ***job work*** Akkordarbeit *f*; ***by the job*** im Akkord; ***out of a job*** arbeitslos; **2.** ***job around*** jobben
job ad, **job ad·ver·tise·ment** Stellenanzeige *f*
job·ber *Br* ECON Börsenspekulant *m*
job cen·tre *Br* Arbeitsamt *n*
job hop·ping häufiger Arbeitsplatzwechsel
job·hunt·ing Arbeitssuche *f*; ***be jobhunting*** auf Arbeitssuche sein
job·less arbeitslos
jock·ey Jockei *m*
jog **1.** stoßen an (*acc*) *or* gegen, *j-n* anstoßen; *mst* ***jog along***, ***jog on*** dahintrotten, dahinzuckeln; SPORT joggen; **2.** (leichter) Stoß, Stups *m*; Trott *m*; SPORT Trimmtrab *m*
jog·ger SPORT Jogger(in)
jog·ging SPORT Joggen *n*, Jogging *n*
join **1.** *v/t* verbinden, vereinigen, zusammenfügen; sich anschließen (*dat or* an *acc*), sich gesellen zu; eintreten in (*acc*), beitreten; teilnehmen *or* sich beteiligen an (*dat*), mitmachen bei; ***join in*** einstimmen in; *v/i* sich vereinigen *or* verbinden; ***join in*** teilnehmen *or* sich beteiligen (an *dat*), mitmachen (bei); **2.** Verbindungsstelle *f*, Naht *f*
join·er Tischler *m*, Schreiner *m*
joint **1.** Verbindungs-, Nahtstelle *f*; ANAT, TECH Gelenk *n*; BOT Knoten *m*; *Br* GASTR Braten *m*; F Laden *m*; Bude *f*, Spelunke *f*; *sl* Joint *m*; ***out of joint*** MED ausgerenkt; *fig* aus den Fugen; **2.** gemeinsam, gemeinschaftlich; Mit…
joint·ed gegliedert; Glieder…

J

joint-stock com·pa·ny *Br* ECON Kapital- *or* Aktiengesellschaft *f*
joint ven·ture ECON Gemeinschaftsunternehmen *n*
joke 1. Witz *m*; Scherz *m*, Spaß *m*; ***practical joke*** Streich *m*; ***play a joke on s.o.*** j-m e-n Streich spielen; **2.** scherzen, Witze machen
jok·er Spaßvogel *m*, Witzbold *m*; *cards*: Joker *m*
jol·ly 1. *adj* lustig, fröhlich, vergnügt; **2.** *adv Br* F ganz schön; ***jolly good*** prima
jolt 1. e-n Ruck *or* Stoß geben; durchrütteln, durchschütteln; rütteln, holpern (*vehicle*); *fig* aufrütteln; **2.** Ruck *m*, Stoß *m*; *fig* Schock *m*
joss stick Räucherstäbchen *n*
jos·tle (an)rempeln; dränge(l)n
jot 1. ***not a jot*** keine Spur; **2.** ***jot down*** sich schnell *et.* notieren
joule PHYS Joule *n*
jour·nal Journal *n*; (Fach)Zeitschrift *f*; Tagebuch *n*
jour·nal·ism Journalismus *m*
jour·nal·ist Journalist(in)
jour·ney 1. Reise *f*; **2.** reisen
jour·ney·man Geselle *m*
joy Freude *f*; ***for joy*** vor Freude
joy·ful freudig; erfreut
joy·less freudlos, traurig
joy·stick AVIAT Steuerknüppel *m*; EDP Joystick *m*
jub·i·lant jubelnd, überglücklich
ju·bi·lee Jubiläum *n*
judge 1. JUR Richter(in); SPORT Kampf-, Schieds-, Preisrichter(in); *fig* Kenner(in); **2.** JUR *Fall* verhandeln; urteilen, ein Urteil fällen; beurteilen, einschätzen
judg·ment JUR Urteil *n*; Urteilsvermögen *n*; Meinung *f*, Ansicht *f*; göttliches (Straf)Gericht; ***the Last Judgment*** REL das Jüngste Gericht
Judgment Day, *a.* ***Day of Judgment*** REL Tag *m* des Jüngsten Gerichts, Jüngster Tag
ju·di·cial JUR gerichtlich, Justiz…; richterlich
ju·di·cia·ry JUR Richter *pl*
ju·di·cious klug, weise
ju·do SPORT Judo *n*
jug Krug *m*; Kanne *f*, Kännchen *n*
jug·gle jonglieren (mit); ECON *Bücher etc* frisieren
jug·gler Jongleur *m*
juice Saft *m*; MOT F Sprit *m*
juic·y saftig; F pikant (*story etc*); F gepfeffert (*price etc*)
juke·box Musikbox *f*, Musikautomat *m*
Jul ABBR *of* ***July*** Juli *m*
Ju·ly (ABBR ***Jul***) Juli *m*
jum·ble 1. *a.* ***jumble together, jumble up*** durcheinanderbringen *or* durcheinanderwerfen; **2.** Durcheinander *n*
jumble sale *Br* Wohltätigkeitsbasar *m*
jum·bo 1. riesig, Riesen…; **2.** AVIAT F Jumbo *m*
jumbo jet AVIAT Jumbo-Jet *m*
jum·bo-sized riesig
jump 1. *v/i* springen; hüpfen; zusammenzucken, -fahren, hochfahren (***at*** bei); ***jump at the chance*** mit beiden Händen zugreifen; ***jump to conclusions*** voreilige Schlüsse ziehen; *v/t* (hinweg)springen über (*acc*); überspringen; ***jump the queue*** *Br* sich vordränge(l)n; ***jump the lights*** bei Rot über die Kreuzung fahren; **2.** Sprung *m*
jump·er[1] SPORT (*Hoch- etc*)Springer(in)
jump·er[2] Trägerrock *m*, Trägerkleid *n*; *Br* Pullover *m*
jump·ing jack Hampelmann *m*
jump·y nervös
Jun ABBR *of* ***June*** Juni *m*
junc·tion (Straßen)Kreuzung *f*; RAIL Knotenpunkt *m*
junc·ture: ***at this juncture*** zu diesem Zeitpunkt
June (ABBR ***Jun***) Juni *m*
jun·gle Dschungel *m*
ju·ni·or 1. junior; jüngere(r, -s); untergeordnet; SPORT Junioren…, Jugend…; **2.** Jüngere *m, f*
junior school *Br* Grundschule *f* (*for children aged 7 to 11*)
junk[1] MAR Dschunke *f*
junk[2] F Trödel *m*; Schrott *m*; Abfall *m*; *sl* Stoff *m*
junk food F Junk-Food *n*
junk·ie, junk·y *sl* Junkie *m*, Fixer(in)
junk·yard Schuttabladeplatz *m*; Schrottplatz *m*; ***auto junkyard*** Autofriedhof *m*
jur·is·dic·tion JUR Gerichtsbarkeit *f*; Zuständigkeit(sbereich *m*) *f*
ju·ris·pru·dence Rechtswissenschaft *f*
ju·ror JUR Geschworene *m, f*
ju·ry JUR *die* Geschworenen *pl*; SPORT *etc* Jury *f*, Preisrichter *pl*
ju·ry·man JUR Geschworene *m*
ju·ry·wom·an JUR Geschworene *f*
just 1. *adj* gerecht; berechtigt; angemessen; **2.** *adv* gerade, (so)eben; genau, eben; gerade (noch), ganz knapp; nur, bloß; ***just about*** ungefähr, etwa; ***just like that*** einfach so; ***just now*** gerade (jetzt), (so)eben
jus·tice Gerechtigkeit *f*; JUR Richter *m*; ***Justice of the Peace*** Friedensrichter *m*; ***court of justice*** Gericht *n*, Gerichts-

hof *m*
jus·ti·fi·ca·tion Rechtfertigung *f*
jus·ti·fy rechtfertigen
just·ly mit *or* zu Recht
jut: ***jut out*** vorspringen, herausragen
ju·ve·nile 1. jugendlich; Jugend…; **2.** Jugendliche *m, f*
juvenile court JUR Jugendgericht *n*
juvenile de·lin·quen·cy JUR Jugendkriminalität *f*
juvenile de·lin·quent JUR straffälliger Jugendlicher, jugendlicher Straftäter

K

K, k K, k *n*
kan·ga·roo ZO Känguru *n*
ka·ra·te SPORT Karate *n*
keel MAR **1.** Kiel *m*; **2.** ***keel over*** umschlagen, kentern
keen scharf (*a. fig*); schneidend (*cold*); heftig, stark; lebhaft (*interest*); groß (*appetite etc*); begeistert, leidenschaftlich; ***keen on*** versessen *or* scharf auf (*acc*)
keep 1. *v/t* (auf-, fest-, zurück)halten; (bei)behalten, bewahren; *Gesetze etc* einhalten, befolgen; *Ware* führen; *Geheimnis* für sich behalten; *Versprechen, Wort* halten; ECON *Buch* führen; aufheben, aufbewahren; abhalten, hindern (***from*** von); *Tiere* halten; *Bett* hüten; ernähren, erhalten, unterhalten; ***keep early hours*** früh zu Bett gehen; ***keep one's head*** die Ruhe bewahren; ***keep one's temper*** sich beherrschen; ***keep s.o. company*** j-m Gesellschaft leisten; ***keep s.th. from s.o.*** j-m et. vorenthalten *or* verschweigen *or* verheimlichen; ***keep time*** richtig gehen (*watch*); MUS Takt halten; *v/i* bleiben; sich halten; ***keep going*** weitergehen; ***keep smiling*** immer nur lächeln!; ***keep (on) talking*** weitersprechen
keep (*on*) *trying* es weiterversuchen, es immer wieder versuchen; ***keep s.o. waiting*** j-n warten lassen; ***keep away*** (sich) fernhalten (***from*** von); ***keep back*** zurückhalten (*a. fig*); ***keep from doing s.th.*** et. nicht tun; ***keep in*** *Schüler(in)* nachsitzen lassen; ***keep off*** (sich) fern halten; ***keep off!*** Betreten verboten!; ***keep on*** *Kleidungsstück* anbehalten, anlassen, *Hut* aufbehalten; *Licht* brennen lassen; ***keep on doing*** fortfahren zu tun; ***keep out*** nicht hinein- *or* hereinlassen; ***keep out!*** Zutritt verboten!; ***keep to*** sich halten an (*acc*); ***keep up*** *fig* aufrechterhalten; *Mut* nicht sinken lassen; fortfahren mit, weitermachen; ***keep s.o. up*** j-n nicht schlafen lassen; ***keep it up*** so weitermachen; ***keep up with*** Schritt halten mit; ***keep up with the Joneses*** nicht hinter den Nachbarn zurückstehen (wollen); **1.** (Lebens)Unterhalt *m*; ***for keeps*** F für immer
keep·er Wärter(in), Wächter(in), Aufseher(in); *mst in cpds*: Inhaber(in), Besitzer(in)
keep·ing Verwahrung *f*; Obhut *f*; ***be in (out of) keeping with …*** (nicht) übereinstimmen mit …
keep·sake Andenken *n*
keg Fässchen *n*, kleines Fass
ken·nel Hundehütte *f*; ***kennels*** Hundezwinger *m*; Hundepension *f*
kerb *Br* → ***curb***
ker·chief (Hals-, Kopf)Tuch *n*
ker·nel BOT Kern *m* (*a. fig*)
ker·o·sene Petroleum *n*
ket·tle Kessel *m*
ket·tle·drum MUS (Kessel)Pauke *f*
key 1. Schlüssel *m* (*a. fig*); (*Schreibmaschinen-, Klavier- etc*)Taste *f*; MUS Tonart *f*; **2.** Schlüssel…; **3.** anpassen (***to*** an *acc*); ***key in*** EDP *Daten* eingeben; ***keyed up*** nervös, aufgeregt, überdreht
key·board Tastatur *f*
key·hole Schlüsselloch *n*
key·note MUS Grundton *m*; *fig* Grundgedanke *m*, Tenor *m*
key ring Schlüsselring *m*
key·stone ARCH Schlussstein *m*; *fig* Grundpfeiler *m*
key·word Schlüssel-, Stichwort *n*
kick 1. (mit dem Fuß) stoßen, treten, e-n Tritt geben *or* versetzen (*dat*); *soccer*: schießen, treten, kicken; strampeln; ausschlagen (*horse*); ***kick off*** von sich schleudern; *soccer*: anstoßen; ***kick out*** F rausschmeißen; ***kick up*** hochschleudern; ***kick up a fuss or row*** F Krach

schlagen; **2.** (Fuß)Tritt *m*; Stoß *m*; *soccer*: Schuss *m*; ***free kick*** Freistoß *m*; ***for kicks*** F zum Spaß; ***they get a kick out of it*** es macht ihnen e-n Riesenspaß

kick·off *soccer*: Anstoß *m*

kick·out *soccer*: Abschlag *m*

kid[1] zo Zicklein *n*, Kitz *n*; Ziegenleder *n*; F Kind *n*; ***kid brother*** F kleiner Bruder

kid[2] *v/t j-n* auf den Arm nehmen; ***kid s.o.*** j-m et. vormachen; *v/i* Spaß machen; ***he is only kidding*** er macht ja nur Spaß; ***no kidding!*** im Ernst!

kid gloves Glacéhandschuhe *pl* (*a. fig*)

kid·nap entführen, kidnappen

kid·nap·(p)er Entführer(in), Kidnapper(in)

kid·nap·(p)ing Entführung *f*, Kidnapping *n*

kid·ney ANAT Niere *f*

kidney bean BOT Kidneybohne *f*, rote Bohne

kidney ma·chine MED künstliche Niere

kill töten (*a. fig*), umbringen, ermorden; vernichten; zo schlachten; HUNT erlegen, schießen; ***be killed in an accident*** tödlich verunglücken; ***kill time*** die Zeit totschlagen

kill·er Mörder(in), Killer(in)

kill·ing mörderisch, tödlich

kill·joy Spielverderber *m*

kiln TECH Brennofen *m*

ki·lo F Kilo *n*

kil·o·gram(me) Kilogramm *n*

kil·o·me·ter, *Br* **kil·o·me·tre** Kilometer *m*

kilt Kilt *m*, Schottenrock *m*

kin Verwandtschaft *f*, Verwandte *pl*; ***next of kin*** *der*, *die* nächste Verwandte, *die* nächsten Angehörigen *pl*

kind[1] freundlich, liebenswürdig, nett; herzlich

kind[2] Art *f*, Sorte *f*; Wesen *n*; ***all kinds of*** alle möglichen, allerlei; ***nothing of the kind*** nichts dergleichen; ***kind of*** F ein bisschen

kin·der·gar·ten Kindergarten *m*

kind-heart·ed gütig

kin·dle anzünden, (sich) entzünden; *Interesse etc* wecken

kind·ly **1.** *adj* freundlich, liebenswürdig, nett; **2.** *adv* → 1; freundlicherweise, liebenswürdigerweise, netterweise

kind·ness Freundlichkeit *f*, Liebenswürdigkeit *f*; Gefälligkeit *f*

kin·dred verwandt; ***kindred spirits*** Gleichgesinnte *pl*

king König *m*

king·dom Königreich *n*; REL Reich *n* Gottes; *fig* Reich *n*; ***animal kingdom*** Tierreich *n*; ***vegetable kingdom*** Pflanzenreich *n*

king·ly königlich

king-size(d) Riesen…

kink Knick *m*; *fig* Tick *m*, Spleen *m*

kink·y spleenig; pervers

ki·osk Kiosk *m*; *Br* Telefonzelle *f*

kip·per GASTR Räucherhering *m*

kiss **1.** Kuss *m*; **2.** (sich) küssen

kit Ausrüstung *f*; Arbeitsgerät *n*, Werkzeug(e *pl*) *n*; Werkzeugtasche *f*, -kasten *m*; Bastelsatz *m*

kit bag Seesack *m*

kitch·en **1.** Küche *f*; **2.** Küchen…

kitch·en·ette Kleinküche *f*, Kochnische *f*

kitch·en gar·den Küchen-, Gemüsegarten *m*

kite Drachen *m*; zo Milan *m*; ***fly a kite*** e-n Drachen steigen lassen

kit·ten zo Kätzchen *n*

knack Kniff *m*, Trick *m*, F Dreh *m*; Geschick *n*, Talent *n*

knave *card games*: Bube *m*, Unter *m*

knead kneten; massieren

knee ANAT Knie *n*; TECH Knie(stück) *n*

knee·cap ANAT Kniescheibe *f*

knee-deep knietief, bis an die Knie (reichend)

knee joint ANAT Kniegelenk *n* (*a.* TECH)

kneel knien (***to*** vor *dat*)

knee-length knielang

knell Totenglocke *f*

knick·er·bock·ers Knickerbocker *pl*, Kniehosen *pl*

knick·ers *Br* F (Damen)Schlüpfer *m*

knick-knack Nippsache *f*

knife **1.** Messer *n*; **2.** mit e-m Messer stechen *or* verletzen; erstechen

knight **1.** Ritter *m*; *chess*: Springer *m*; **2.** zum Ritter schlagen

knight·hood Ritterwürde *f*, -stand *m*

knit *v/t* stricken; *a.* ***knit together*** zusammenfügen, verbinden; ***knit one's brows*** die Stirn runzeln; *v/i* stricken; MED zusammenwachsen

knit·ting **1.** Stricken *n*; Strickzeug *n*; **2.** Strick…

knitting nee·dle Stricknadel *f*

knit·wear Strickwaren *pl*

knob Knopf *m*, Knauf *m*, *runder* Griff; GASTR Stück(chen) *n*

knock **1.** schlagen, stoßen; pochen, klopfen; ***knock at the door*** an die Tür klopfen; ***knock about, knock around*** herumstoßen; F sich herumtreiben; F herumliegen; ***knock down*** *Gebäude etc* abreißen; umstoßen, umwerfen; niederschlagen; anfahren, umfahren; überfahren; mit *dem Preis* heruntergehen; *auction*: *et.* zuschlagen (***to s.o.*** j-m); ***be***

knocked down überfahren werden; ***knock off*** herunter-, abschlagen; F *et.* hinhauen; F aufhören (mit); F Feierabend *or* Schluss machen; ***knock out*** herausschlagen, -klopfen, *Pfeife* ausklopfen; *j-n* bewusstlos schlagen; *boxing*: k.o. schlagen; *fig* betäuben (*drug etc*); *fig* F umhauen, schocken; ***knock over*** umwerfen, umstoßen; überfahren; ***be knocked over*** überfahren werden; **2.** Schlag *m*, Stoß *m*; Klopfen *n*; ***there is a knock*** (***on*** [*Br* ***at***] ***the door***) es klopft

knock·er Türklopfer *m*

knock-kneed x-beinig

knock·out *boxing*: K.o. *m*

knoll Hügel *m*

knot 1. Knoten *m*; BOT Astknoten *m*; MAR Knoten *m*, Seemeile *f*; **2.** (ver-)knoten, (ver)knüpfen

knot·ty knotig; knorrig; *fig* verwickelt, kompliziert

know wissen; können; kennen; erfahren, erleben; (wieder) erkennen; verstehen; ***know French*** Französisch können; ***know one's way around*** sich auskennen in (*a place etc*); ***know all about it*** genau Bescheid wissen; ***get to know*** kennenlernen; ***know one's business, know the ropes, know a thing or two, know what's what*** F sich auskennen, Erfahrung haben; ***you know*** wissen Sie

know-how Know-how *n*, (Sach-, Spezial-)Kenntnis(se *pl*) *f*

know·ing klug, gescheit; schlau; verständnisvoll

know·ing·ly wissend; wissentlich, absichtlich, bewusst

knowl·edge Kenntnis(se *pl*) *f*; Wissen *n*; ***to my knowledge*** meines Wissens; ***have a good knowledge of*** viel verstehen von, sich gut auskennen in (*dat*)

knowl·edge·a·ble: ***be very knowledgeable about*** viel verstehen von

knuck·le 1. ANAT (Finger)Knöchel *m*; **2.** ***knuckle down to work*** sich an die Arbeit machen

Krem·lin: POL ***the Kremlin*** der Kreml

L

L, l L, l *n*

L ABBR *of* ***large*** (***size***) groß

lab F Labor *n*

la·bel 1. Etikett *n*, (Klebe- *etc*)Zettel *m*, (-)Schild(chen) *n*; (Schall)Plattenfirma *f*; **2.** etikettieren, beschriften; *fig* abstempeln als

la·bor 1. (schwere) Arbeit; Mühe *f*; Arbeiter *pl*, Arbeitskräfte *pl*; MED Wehen *pl*; **2.** (schwer) arbeiten; sich bemühen, sich abmühen, sich anstrengen

la·bor·a·to·ry Labor(atorium) *n*

laboratory assis·tant Laborant(in)

la·bored schwerfällig (*style etc*); mühsam (*breathing etc*)

la·bor·er (*esp* Hilfs)Arbeiter *m*

la·bo·ri·ous mühsam; schwerfällig

la·bor u·ni·on Gewerkschaft *f*

la·bour *Br* → ***labor***

Labour *Br* POL die Labour Party

la·boured, **la·bour·er** *Br* → ***labored***, ***laborer***

La·bour Par·ty *Br* POL Labour Party *f*

lace 1. Spitze *f*; Borte *f*; Schnürsenkel *m*; **2.** ***lace up*** (zu-, zusammen)schnüren; *Schuh* zubinden; ***laced with brandy*** mit e-m Schuss Weinbrand

la·ce·rate zerschneiden, zerkratzen, aufreißen; *j-s Gefühle* verletzen

lack 1. (***of***) Fehlen *n* (von), Mangel *m* (an *dat*); **2.** *v/t* nicht haben; ***he lacks money*** es fehlt ihm an Geld; *v/i* ***be lacking*** fehlen; ***he is lacking in courage*** ihm fehlt der Mut

lack·lus·ter, *Br* **lack·lus·tre** glanzlos, matt

la·con·ic lakonisch, wortkarg

lac·quer 1. Lack *m*; Haarspray *m*, *n*; **2.** lackieren

lad Bursche *m*, Junge *m*

lad·der Leiter *f*; *Br* Laufmasche *f*

lad·der·proof (lauf)maschenfest

la·den (schwer) beladen

la·dle 1. (Schöpf-, Suppen)Kelle *f*, Schöpflöffel *m*; **2.** ***ladle out*** *Suppe* austeilen

la·dy Dame *f*; ***Lady*** Lady *f*; ***lady doctor*** Ärztin *f*; ***Ladies' room***, *Br* ***Ladies***(**'**) Damentoilette *f*

la·dy·bird zo Marienkäfer *m*

la·dy·like damenhaft

lag **1.** *mst* ***lag behind*** zurückbleiben; **2.** → ***time lag***
la·ger Lagerbier *n*
la·goon Lagune *f*
lair ZO Lager *n*, Höhle *f*, Bau *m*
la·i·ty Laien *pl*
lake See *m*
lamb ZO **1.** Lamm *n*; **2.** lammen
lame **1.** lahm (*a. fig*); **2.** lähmen
la·ment **1.** jammern, (weh)klagen; trauern; **2.** Jammer *m*, (Weh)Klage *f*
lam·en·ta·ble beklagenswert; kläglich
lam·en·ta·tion (Weh)Klage *f*
lam·i·nat·ed laminiert, geschichtet, beschichtet
laminated glass Verbundglas *n*
lamp Lampe *f*; Laterne *f*
lamp·post Laternenpfahl *m*
lamp·shade Lampenschirm *m*
lance Lanze *f*
land **1.** Land *n*, AGR *a.* Boden *m*, POL *a.* Staat *m*; ***by land*** auf dem Landweg; **2.** landen, MAR *a.* anlegen; *Güter* ausladen, MAR *a.* löschen
land a·gent AGR Gutsverwalter *m*
land·ed Land..., Grund...; ***landed gentry*** Landadel *m*; ***landed property*** Grundbesitz *m*
land·ing AVIAT Landung *f*, Landen *n*, MAR *a.* Anlegen *n*; Treppenabsatz *m*
landing field AVIAT Landeplatz *m*
landing gear AVIAT Fahrgestell *n*
landing stage MAR Landungsbrücke *f*, -steg *m*
landing strip AVIAT Landeplatz *m*
land·la·dy Vermieterin *f*; Wirtin *f*
land·lord Vermieter *m*; Wirt *m*; Grundbesitzer *m*
land·lub·ber MAR *contp* Landratte *f*
land·mark Wahrzeichen *n*; *fig* Meilenstein *m*
land·own·er Grundbesitzer(in)
land·scape Landschaft *f* (*a. paint*)
land·slide Erdrutsch *m* (*a.* POL); ***a landslide victory*** POL ein überwältigender Wahlsieg
land·slip (kleiner) Erdrutsch
lane (Feld)Weg *m*; Gasse *f*, Sträßchen *n*; MAR Fahrrinne *f*; AVIAT Flugschneise *f*; SPORT (*einzelne*) Bahn; MOT (Fahr-) Spur *f*; ***change lanes*** MOT die Spur wechseln; ***get in lane*** MOT sich einordnen
lan·guage Sprache *f*
language la·bor·a·to·ry Sprachlabor *n*
lan·guid matt; träg(e)
lank glatt
lank·y schlaksig
lan·tern Laterne *f*
lap[1] Schoß *m*
lap[2] SPORT **1.** Runde *f*; ***lap of hono(u)r*** Ehrenrunde *f*; **2.** *Gegner* überrunden; e-e Runde zurücklegen
lap[3] *v/t*: ***lap up*** auflecken, aufschlecken; *v/i* plätschern
la·pel Revers *n, m*, Aufschlag *m*
lapse **1.** Versehen *n*, (kleiner) Fehler *or* Irrtum; Vergehen *n*; Zeitspanne *f*; JUR Verfall *m*; ***lapse of memory, memory lapse*** Gedächtnislücke *f*; **2.** verfallen; JUR verfallen, erlöschen
lar·ce·ny JUR Diebstahl *m*
larch BOT Lärche *f*
lard **1.** Schweinefett *n*, Schweineschmalz *n*; **2.** *Fleisch* spicken
lar·der Speisekammer *f*, -schrank *m*
large groß; beträchtlich, reichlich; umfassend, weitgehend; ***at large*** in Freiheit, auf freiem Fuß; *fig* (sehr) ausführlich; in der Gesamtheit
large·ly großenteils, größtenteils
large-mind·ed aufgeschlossen, tolerant
large·ness Größe *f*
lar·i·at Lasso *n, m*
lark[1] ZO Lerche *f*
lark[2] F Jux *m*, Spaß *m*
lark·spur BOT Rittersporn *m*
lar·va ZO Larve *f*
lar·yn·gi·tis MED Kehlkopfentzündung *f*
lar·ynx ANAT Kehlkopf *m*
las·civ·i·ous geil, lüstern
la·ser PHYS Laser *m*
laser beam PHYS Laserstrahl *m*
laser print·er EDP Laserdrucker *m*
laser tech·nol·o·gy Lasertechnik *f*
lash **1.** Peitschenschnur *f*; (Peitschen-) Hieb *m*; Wimper *f*; **2.** peitschen (mit); (fest)binden; schlagen; ***lash out*** (wild) um sich schlagen
las·so Lasso *n, m*
last[1] **1.** *adj* letzte(r, -s); vorige(r, -s); ***last but one*** vorletzte(r, -s); ***last night*** gestern Abend; letzte Nacht; **2.** *adv* zuletzt, an letzter Stelle; ***last but not least*** nicht zuletzt, nicht zu vergessen; **3.** *der, die, das* Letzte; ***at last*** endlich; ***to the last*** bis zum Schluss
last[2] (an-, fort)dauern; (sich) halten; (aus)reichen
last[3] (Schuhmacher)Leisten *m*
last·ing dauerhaft; beständig
last·ly zuletzt, zum Schluss
latch **1.** Schnappriegel *m*; Schnappschloss *n*; **2.** einklinken, zuklinken
latch·key Haus-, Wohnungsschlüssel *m*
late spät; jüngste(r, -s), letzte(r, -s), frühere(r, -s), ehemalig; verstorben; ***be late*** zu spät kommen, sich verspäten; RAIL *etc* Verspätung haben; ***as late as*** noch, erst;

of late kürzlich; ***later on*** später
late·ly kürzlich
lath Latte *f*, Leiste *f*
lathe TECH Drehbank *f*
la·ther 1. (Seifen)Schaum *m*; **2.** *v/t* einseifen; *v/i* schäumen
Lat·in LING **1.** lateinisch; südländisch; **2.** Latein(isch) *n*
Latin A·mer·i·ca Lateinamerika *n*
Latin A·mer·i·can 1. lateinamerikanisch; **2.** Lateinamerikaner(in)
lat·i·tude GEOGR Breite *f*
lat·ter Letztere(r, -s)
lat·tice Gitter(werk) *n*
lau·da·ble lobenswert
laugh 1. lachen (***at*** über *acc*); ***laugh at s.o. a.*** j-n auslachen; **2.** Lachen *n*, Gelächter *n*
laugh·a·ble lächerlich, lachhaft
laugh·ter Lachen *n*, Gelächter *n*
launch¹ 1. MAR vom Stapel lassen; MIL abschießen, *Rakete a.* starten; *fig Projekt etc* in Gang setzen, starten; **2.** MAR Stapellauf *m*; MIL Abschuss *m*, Start *m*
launch² MAR Barkasse *f*
launch pad → ***launching pad***
launch·ing → ***launch¹*** 2
launching pad Abschussrampe *f*
launching site Abschussbasis *f*
laun·der *Wäsche* waschen (und bügeln); F *esp Geld* waschen
laun·der·ette, laun·drette *esp Br*, **laun·dro·mat®** Waschsalon *m*
laun·dry Wäscherei *f*; Wäsche *f*
laur·el BOT Lorbeer *m* (*a. fig*)
la·va GEOL Lava *f*
lav·a·to·ry Toilette *f*, Klosett *n*; ***public lavatory*** Bedürfnisanstalt *f*
lav·en·der BOT Lavendel *m*
lav·ish 1. sehr freigebig, verschwenderisch; **2.** ***lavish s.th. on s.o.*** j-n mit et. überhäufen *or* überschütten
law Gesetz(e *pl*) *n*; Recht *n*, Rechtssystem *n*; Rechtswissenschaft *f*, Jura; F Bullen *pl* (*police*); F Bulle *m* (*policeman*); Gesetz *n*, Vorschrift *f*; ***law and order*** Recht *or* Ruhe und Ordnung
law-a·bid·ing gesetzestreu
law·court Gericht *n*, Gerichtshof *m*
law·ful gesetzlich; rechtmäßig, legitim; rechtsgültig
law·less gesetzlos; gesetzwidrig; zügellos
lawn Rasen *m*
lawn·mow·er Rasenmäher *m*
law·suit JUR Prozess *m*
law·yer JUR (Rechts)Anwalt *m*, (Rechts)-Anwältin *f*
lax locker, schlaff; lax, lasch
lax·a·tive MED **1.** abführend; **2.** Abführmittel *n*
lay¹ REL weltlich; Laien…
lay² *v/t* legen; *Teppich* verlegen; belegen, auslegen (***with*** mit); *Tisch* decken; *zo Eier* legen; vorlegen (***before*** *dat*), bringen (***before*** vor *acc*); *Schuld etc* zuschreiben, zur Last legen (*dat*); *v/i zo* (Eier) legen; ***lay aside*** beiseitelegen, zurücklegen; ***lay off*** *Arbeiter* (*esp* vorübergehend) entlassen; *Arbeit* einstellen; ***lay open*** darlegen; ***lay out*** ausbreiten, auslegen; *Garten etc* anlegen; entwerfen, planen; PRINT das Layout (*gen*) machen; ***lay up*** anhäufen, (an)sammeln; ***be laid up*** das Bett hüten müssen
lay-by *Br* MOT Parkbucht *f*, Parkstreifen *m*; Parkplatz *m*, Rastplatz *m*
lay·er Lage *f*, Schicht *f*; BOT Ableger *m*
lay·man Laie *m*
lay-off ECON (*esp* vorübergehende) Entlassung
lay·out Grundriss *m*, Lageplan *m*; PRINT Layout *n*, Gestaltung *f*
la·zy faul, träg(e)
LCD ABBR *of* ***liquid crystal display*** Flüssigkristallanzeige *f*
lead¹ 1. *v/t* führen; (an)führen, leiten; dazu bringen, veranlassen (***to do*** zu tun); *v/i* führen; vorangehen; SPORT an der Spitze *or* in Führung liegen; ***lead off*** anfangen, beginnen; ***lead on*** *j-m* et. vormachen *or* weismachen; ***lead to*** *fig* führen zu; ***lead up to*** *fig* (allmählich) führen zu; **2.** Führung *f*; Leitung *f*; Spitzenposition *f*; Vorbild *n*, Beispiel *n*; THEA Hauptrolle *f*; Hauptdarsteller(in); (Hunde-)Leine *f*; Hinweis *m*, Tipp *m*, Anhaltspunkt *m*; SPORT *and fig* Führung *f*, Vorsprung *m*; ***be in the lead*** in Führung sein; ***take the lead*** in Führung gehen, die Führung übernehmen
lead² CHEM Blei *n*; MAR Lot *n*
lead·ed verbleit, bleihaltig
lead·en bleiern (*a. fig*), Blei…
lead·er (An)Führer(in), Leiter(in); Erste *m, f*; *Br* Leitartikel *m*
lead·er·ship Führung *f*, Leitung *f*
lead-free bleifrei
lead·ing leitend; führend; Haupt…
leaf 1. BOT, PRINT Blatt *n*; (*Tür- etc*)Flügel *m*; (*Tisch*)Klappe *f*, Ausziehplatte *f*; **2.** ***leaf through*** durchblättern
leaf·let Hand-, Reklamezettel *m*; Prospekt *m*
league POL Bund *m*; SPORT Liga *f*
leak 1. lecken, leck sein; tropfen; ***leak out*** auslaufen; *fig* durchsickern; **2.** Leck *n*, undichte Stelle (*a. fig*)
leak·age Auslaufen *n*

leak·y leck, undicht
lean[1] (sich) lehnen; (sich) neigen; ***lean on*** sich verlassen auf (*acc*)
lean[2] **1.** mager (*a. fig*); **2.** GASTR das Magere
lean man·age·ment ECON schlanke Unternehmensstruktur
leap 1. springen; ***leap at*** *fig* sich stürzen auf (*acc*); **2.** Sprung *m*
leap·frog Bockspringen *n*
leap year Schaltjahr *n*
learn (er)lernen; erfahren, hören
learn·ed gelehrt
learn·er Anfänger(in); Lernende *m, f*; ***learner driver*** *Br* MOT Fahrschüler(in)
learn·ing Gelehrsamkeit *f*
lease 1. Pacht *f*, Miete *f*; Pacht-, Mietvertrag *m*; **2.** pachten, mieten; leasen; ***lease out*** verpachten, vermieten
leash (Hunde)Leine *f*
least 1. *adj* geringste(r, -s), mindeste(r, -s), wenigste(r, -s); **2.** *adv* am wenigsten; ***least of all*** am allerwenigsten; **3.** *das* Mindeste, *das* wenigste; ***at least*** wenigstens; ***to say the least*** gelinde gesagt
leath·er 1. Leder *n*; **2.** ledern; Leder…
leave 1. *v/t* (hinter-, über-, ver-, zurück-) lassen, übrig lassen; liegen *or* stehen lassen, vergessen; vermachen, vererben; ***be left*** übrig bleiben, übrig sein; *v/i* (fort-, weg)gehen, abreisen, abfahren, abfliegen; ***leave alone*** allein lassen; *j-n, et.* in Ruhe lassen; ***leave behind*** zurücklassen; ***leave on*** anlassen; ***leave out*** draußen lassen; auslassen, weglassen; **2.** Erlaubnis *f*; Urlaub *m*; Abschied *m*; ***on leave*** auf Urlaub
leav·en Sauerteig *m*
leaves BOT Laub *n*
leav·ings Überreste *pl*
lech·er·ous geil, lüstern
lec·ture 1. UNIV Vorlesung *f* (***über*** *acc* on); Vortrag *m*; Strafpredigt *f*; **2.** *v/i* UNIV e-e Vorlesung *or* Vorlesungen halten (***über*** *acc* on; ***vor*** *dat* to); e-n Vortrag *or* Vorträge halten; *v/t j-m* e-e Strafpredigt halten
lec·tur·er UNIV Dozent(in); Redner(in)
ledge Leiste *f*, Sims *m, n*
leech ZO Blutegel *m*
leek BOT Lauch *m*, Porree *m*
leer 1. anzüglicher *or* lüsterner Seitenblick; **2.** anzüglich *or* lüstern blicken *or* schielen (***at*** nach)
left 1. *adj* linke(r, -s), Links…; **2.** *adv* links; ***turn left*** (sich) nach links wenden; MOT links abbiegen; **3.** *die* Linke (*a.* POL, *boxing*), linke Seite; ***on the left*** links, auf der linken Seite; ***to the left*** (nach) links; ***keep to the left*** sich links halten; links fahren
left-hand linke(r, -s)
left-hand drive MOT Linkssteuerung *f*
left-hand·ed linkshändig; für Linkshänder; ***be left-handed*** Linkshänder(in) sein
left lug·gage of·fice *Br* RAIL Gepäckaufbewahrung *f*
left·o·vers (Speise)Reste *pl*
left-wing POL dem linken Flügel angehörend, links…, Links…
leg ANAT Bein *n*; GASTR Keule *f*; MATH Schenkel *m*; ***pull s.o.'s leg*** F j-n auf den Arm nehmen; ***stretch one's*** sich die Beine vertreten
leg·a·cy *fig* Vermächtnis *n*, Erbe *n*
le·gal legal, gesetzmäßig; gesetzlich, rechtlich; juristisch, Rechts…
le·gal·ize legalisieren
le·gal·i·za·tion Legalisierung *f*
le·gal pro·tec·tion Rechtsschutz *m*
le·ga·tion POL Gesandtschaft *f*
le·gend Legende *f*, Sage *f*
le·gen·da·ry legendär
le·gi·ble leserlich
le·gis·la·tion Gesetzgebung *f*
le·gis·la·tive POL **1.** gesetzgebend, legislativ; **2.** Legislative *f*, gesetzgebende Gewalt
le·gis·la·tor POL Gesetzgeber *m*
le·git·i·mate legitim; gesetzmäßig, rechtmäßig; ehelich
lei·sure freie Zeit; Muße *f*; ***at leisure*** ohne Hast
leisure cen·tre *Br* Freizeitzentrum *n*
lei·sure·ly gemächlich
lei·sure time Freizeit *f*
lei·sure-time ac·tiv·i·ties Freizeitbeschäftigung *f*, -gestaltung *f*
lei·sure·wear Freizeitkleidung *f*
lem·on BOT **1.** Zitrone *f*; **2.** Zitronen…
lem·on·ade Zitronenlimonade *f*
lend *j-m et.* (ver-, aus)leihen
length Länge *f*; Strecke *f*; (Zeit)Dauer *f*; ***at length*** ausführlich
length·en verlängern, länger machen; länger werden
length·ways, length·wise der Länge nach
length·y sehr lang
le·ni·ent mild(e), nachsichtig
lens ANAT, PHOT, PHYS Linse *f*; PHOT Objektiv *n*
Lent REL Fastenzeit *f*
len·til BOT Linse *f*
Le·o ASTR Löwe *m*; ***he*** (***she***) ***is*** (***a***) ***Leo*** er (sie) ist (ein) Löwe
leop·ard ZO Leopard *m*

le·o·tard (Tänzer)Trikot *n*
lep·ro·sy MED Lepra *f*
les·bi·an **1.** lesbisch; **2.** Lesbierin *f*, F Lesbe *f*
less **1.** *adj and adv* kleiner, geringer, weniger; **2.** *prp* weniger, minus, abzüglich
less·en (sich) vermindern *or* verringern; abnehmen; herabsetzen
less·er kleiner, geringer
les·son Lektion *f*; (Unterrichts)Stunde *f*; *fig* Lehre *f*; *pl* Unterricht *m*
let lassen; *esp Br* vermieten, verpachten; ***let alone*** *j-n, et.* in Ruhe lassen; geschweige denn; ***let down*** hinunterlassen, herunterlassen; *Kleider* verlängern; *j-n* im Stich lassen, F *j-n* sitzen lassen; enttäuschen; ***let go*** loslassen; ***let o.s. go*** sich gehenlassen; ***let's go*** gehen wir!; ***let in*** (her)einlassen; ***let o.s. in for s.th.*** sich et. einbrocken, sich auf et. einlassen
le·thal tödlich; Todes...
leth·ar·gy Lethargie *f*
let·ter Buchstabe *m*; PRINT Type *f*; Brief *m*
let·ter·box *esp Br* Briefkasten *m*
let·ter car·ri·er Briefträger *m*
let·tuce BOT (*esp* Kopf)Salat *m*
leu·k(a)e·mia MED Leukämie *f*
lev·el **1.** *adj* eben; gleich (*a. fig*); ausgeglichen; ***be level with*** auf gleicher Höhe sein mit; ***my level best*** F mein Möglichstes; **2.** Ebene *f* (*a. fig*), ebene Fläche; Höhe *f* (*a.* GEOGR), (*Wasser- etc*)Spiegel *m*, (-)Stand *m*, (-)Pegel *m*; Wasserwaage *f*; *fig* Niveau *n*, Stufe *f*; ***sea level*** Meeresspiegel *m*; ***on the level*** F ehrlich, aufrichtig; **3.** (ein)ebnen, planieren; dem Erdboden gleichmachen; ***level at*** *Waffe* richten auf (*acc*); *Beschuldigungen* erheben gegen (*acc*); **4.** *adv*: ***level with*** in Höhe (*gen*)
lev·el cross·ing *Br* schienengleicher Bahnübergang
lev·el-head·ed vernünftig, nüchtern
le·ver Hebel *m*
lev·y **1.** Steuer *f*, Abgabe *f*; **2.** *Steuern* erheben
lewd geil, lüstern; unanständig, obszön
li·a·bil·i·ty ECON, JUR Verpflichtung *f*, Verbindlichkeit *f*; ECON, JUR Haftung *f*, Haftpflicht *f*; Neigung *f* (***to*** zu), Anfälligkeit *f* (***to*** für)
li·a·ble ECON, JUR haftbar, haftpflichtig; ***be liable for*** haften für; ***be liable to*** neigen zu, anfällig sein für
li·ar Lügner(in)
li·bel JUR **1.** (*schriftliche*) Verleumdung *or* Beleidigung; **2.** (*schriftlich*) verleumden *or* beleidigen
lib·e·ral **1.** liberal (*a.* POL), aufgeschlossen; großzügig; reichlich; **2.** Liberale *m, f* (*a.* POL)
lib·e·rate befreien
lib·e·ra·tion Befreiung *f*
lib·e·ra·tor Befreier *m*
lib·er·ty Freiheit *f*; ***take liberties with*** sich Freiheiten gegen *j-n* herausnehmen; willkürlich mit *et.* umgehen; ***be at liberty*** frei sein
Li·bra ASTR Waage *f*; ***he*** (***she***) ***is*** (***a***) ***Libra*** er (sie) ist (eine) Waage
li·brar·i·an Bibliothekar(in)
li·bra·ry Bibliothek *f*; Bücherei *f*
li·cence **1.** *Br* → ***license*** *1*; **2.** e-e Lizenz *or* Konzession erteilen (*dat*); *behördlich* genehmigen
li·cense **1.** Lizenz *f*, Konzession *f*; (*Führer-, Jagd-, Waffen- etc*)Schein *m*; **2.** *Br* → ***licence*** *2*
li·cense plate MOT Nummernschild *n*
li·chen BOT Flechte *f*
lick **1.** Lecken *n*; Salzlecke *f*; **2.** *v/t* ab-, auflecken; F verdreschen, verprügeln; F schlagen, besiegen; *v/i* lecken; züngeln (*flames*)
lic·o·rice Lakritze *f*
lid Deckel *m*; ANAT (Augen)Lid *n*
lie[1] **1.** lügen; ***lie to s.o.*** j-n belügen, j-n anlügen; **2.** Lüge *f*; ***tell lies, tell a lie*** lügen; ***give the lie to*** *j-n, et.* Lügen strafen
lie[2] **1.** liegen; ***let sleeping dogs lie*** schlafende Hunde soll man nicht wecken; ***lie behind*** *fig* dahinter stecken; ***lie down*** sich hinlegen; **2.** Lage *f* (*a. fig*)
lie-down *Br* F Nickerchen *n*
lie-in: ***have a lie-in*** *esp Br* F sich gründlich ausschlafen
lieu: ***in lieu of*** anstelle von (*or gen*)
lieu·ten·ant MIL Leutnant *m*
life Leben *n*; JUR lebenslängliche Freiheitsstrafe; ***all her life*** ihr ganzes Leben lang; ***for life*** fürs (ganze) Leben; *esp* JUR lebenslänglich
life as·sur·ance *Br* → ***life insurance***
life belt Rettungsgürtel *m*
life·boat Rettungsboot *n*
life·guard Bademeister *m*; Rettungsschwimmer *m*
life im·pris·on·ment JUR lebenslängliche Freiheitsstrafe
life in·sur·ance Lebensversicherung *f*
life jack·et Schwimmweste *f*
life·less leblos; matt, schwung-, lustlos
life·like lebensecht
life·long lebenslang
life pre·serv·er Schwimmweste *f*; Rettungsgürtel *m*
life sen·tence JUR lebenslängliche Frei-

L

heitsstrafe
life·time Lebenszeit *f*
lift **1.** *v/t* (hoch-, auf)heben; erheben; *Verbot etc* aufheben; *Gesicht etc* liften, straffen; F klauen; *v/i* sich heben, steigen (*a. fog*); ***lift off*** starten (*rocket*), AVIAT abheben; **2.** (Hoch-, Auf)Heben *n*; PHYS, AVIAT Auftrieb *m*; *Br* Lift *m*, Aufzug *m*, Fahrstuhl *m*; ***give s.o. a lift*** j-n (im Auto) mitnehmen; F j-n aufmuntern, j-m Auftrieb geben
lift-off Start *m*, Abheben *n*
lig·a·ment ANAT Band *n*
light[1] **1.** Licht *n* (*a. fig*); Beleuchtung *f*; Schein *m*; Feuer *n*; *fig* Aspekt *m*; *Br mst pl* (Verkehrs)Ampel *f*; ***do you have*** (*Br* ***have you got***) ***a light?*** haben Sie Feuer?; **2.** *v/t* beleuchten, erleuchten; *a.* ***light up*** anzünden; *v/i* sich entzünden; ***light up*** *fig* aufleuchten; **3.** hell, licht
light[2] leicht (*a. fig*); ***make light of s.th.*** et. leichtnehmen; et. bagatellisieren
light·en[1] *v/t* erhellen; aufhellen; *v/i* hell(er) werden, sich aufhellen
light·en[2] leichter machen *or* werden; erleichtern
light·er Anzünder *m*; Feuerzeug *n*
light-head·ed (leicht) benommen; leichtfertig, töricht
light-heart·ed fröhlich, unbeschwert
light·house Leuchtturm *m*
light·ing Beleuchtung *f*
light·ness Leichtheit *f*; Leichtigkeit *f*
light·ning Blitz *m*; ***like lightning*** wie der Blitz; (***as***) ***quick as lightning*** blitzschnell
light·ning con·duc·tor *Br*, **lightning rod** ELECTR Blitzableiter *m*
light·weight SPORT Leichtgewicht *n*, Leichtgewichtler *m*
like[1] **1.** *v/t* gernhaben, mögen; ***I like it*** es gefällt mir; ***I like her*** ich kann sie gut leiden; ***how do you like it?*** wie gefällt es dir?, wie findest du es?; ***I like that!*** *iro* das hab ich gern!; ***I should*** *or* ***would like to know*** ich möchte gern wissen; *v/i* wollen; (***just***) ***as you like*** (ganz) wie du willst; ***if you like*** wenn du willst; **2.** ***likes and dislikes*** Neigungen und Abneigungen *pl*
like[2] **1.** gleich; wie; ähnlich; ***like that*** so; ***feel like*** Lust haben auf (*acc*) *or* zu; ***what is he like?*** wie ist er?; ***that is just like him!*** das sieht ihm ähnlich!; **2.** *der, die, das* Gleiche; ***his like*** seinesgleichen; ***the like*** dergleichen; ***the likes of you*** Leute wie du
like·li·hood Wahrscheinlichkeit *f*
like·ly **1.** *adj* wahrscheinlich; geeignet; **2.** *adv* wahrscheinlich; ***not likely!*** F bestimmt nicht!
like·ness Ähnlichkeit *f*; Abbild *n*
like·wise ebenso
lik·ing Vorliebe *f*
li·lac **1.** lila; **2.** BOT Flieder *m*
lil·y BOT Lilie *f*
lil·y of the val·ley BOT Maiglöckchen *n*
limb ANAT (*Körper*)Glied *n*; BOT Ast *m*
lime[1] Kalk *m*
lime[2] BOT Linde *f*; Limone *f*
lime·light *fig* Rampenlicht *n*
lim·it **1.** Limit *n*, Grenze *f*; ***within limits*** in Grenzen; ***off limits*** Zutritt verboten (***to*** für); ***that is the limit!*** F das ist der Gipfel!, das ist (doch) die Höhe!; ***go to the limit*** bis zum Äußersten gehen; **2.** beschränken (***to*** auf *acc*)
lim·i·ta·tion Beschränkung *f*; *fig* Grenze *f*; JUR Verjährung *f*
lim·it·ed beschränkt, begrenzt; ***limited*** (***liability***) ***company*** *Br* ECON Gesellschaft *f* mit beschränkter Haftung
lim·it·less grenzenlos
limp[1] **1.** hinken, humpeln; **2.** Hinken *n*, Humpeln *n*
limp[2] schlaff, schlapp, F lappig
line[1] **1.** Linie *f*, Strich *m*; Zeile *f*; Falte *f*, Runzel *f*; Reihe *f*; (Menschen-, *a.* Auto)-Schlange *f*; (Abstammungs)Linie *f*; (*Verkehrs-*, *Eisenbahn- etc*)Linie *f*, Strecke *f*; (*Flug- etc*)Gesellschaft *f*; *esp* TEL Leitung *f*; MIL Linie *f*; Fach *n*, Gebiet *n*, Branche *f*; SPORT (*Ziel- etc*)Linie *f*; Leine *f*; Schnur *f*; Linie *f*, Richtung *f*; *fig* Grenze *f*; *pl* THEA Rolle *f*, Text *m*; ***the line*** der Äquator; ***draw the line*** Halt machen, die Grenze ziehen (***at*** bei); ***the line is busy*** *or* ***engaged*** TEL die Leitung ist besetzt; ***hold the line*** TEL bleiben Sie am Apparat; ***stand in line*** anstehen, Schlange stehen (***for*** um, nach); **2.** lin(i)ieren; *Gesicht* zeichnen, (zer)furchen; *Straße etc* säumen; ***line up*** (sich) in e-r Reihe *or* Linie aufstellen, SPORT sich aufstellen; sich anstellen (***for*** um, nach)
line[2] *Kleid etc* füttern; TECH auskleiden, ausschlagen; MOT *Bremsen etc* belegen
lin·e·ar linear; Längen…
lin·en **1.** Leinen *n*; (*Bett-*, *Tisch- etc* -) Wäsche *f*; **2.** leinen, Leinen…
lin·en clos·et, *Br* **linen cup·board** Wäscheschrank *m*
lin·er MAR Linienschiff *n*; AVIAT Verkehrsflugzeug *n*
lines·man SPORT Linienrichter *m*
lines·wom·an SPORT Linienrichterin *f*
line-up SPORT Aufstellung *f*; Gegenüberstellung *f* (zur Identifizierung)

L

lin·ger verweilen, sich aufhalten; *a.* ***linger on*** dahinsiechen; ***linger on*** noch dableiben; *fig* fortleben
lin·ge·rie Damenunterwäsche *f*
lin·ing Futter(stoff *m*) *n*; TECH Auskleidung *f*; MOT (*Brems- etc*)Belag *m*
link **1.** (Ketten)Glied *n*; Manschettenknopf *m*; *fig* (Binde)Glied *n*, Verbindung *f*; **2.** *a.* ***link up*** (sich) verbinden
links → ***golf links***
link·up Verbindung *f*
lin·seed BOT Leinsamen *m*
lin·seed oil Leinöl *n*
li·on ZO Löwe *m*
li·on·ess ZO Löwin *f*
lip ANAT Lippe *f*; (*Tassen- etc*)Rand *m*; F Unverschämtheit *f*
lip·stick Lippenstift *m*
liq·ue·fy (sich) verflüssigen
liq·uid **1.** Flüssigkeit *f*; **2.** flüssig
liq·ui·date liquidieren (*a.* ECON); *Schulden* tilgen
liq·uid·ize zerkleinern, pürieren
liq·uid·iz·er Mixgerät *n*, Mixer *m*
liq·uor *Br* alkoholische Getränke *pl*, Alkohol *m*; Schnaps *m*, Spirituosen *pl*
liq·uo·rice *Br* → ***licorice***
lisp **1.** lispeln; **2.** Lispeln *n*
list **1.** Liste *f*, Verzeichnis *n*; MAR Schlagseite *f*; **2.** (in e-e Liste) eintragen, erfassen; MAR ***be listing*** Schlagseite haben
lis·ten hören; ***listen in*** Radio hören; ***listen in to*** *et.* im Radio (an)hören; ***listen in on*** *Telefongespräch etc* abhören *or* mithören; ***listen to*** anhören (*acc*), zuhören (*dat*); hören auf (*acc*)
lis·ten·er Zuhörer(in); (Rundfunk-)Hörer(in)
list·less teilnahmslos, lustlos
li·ter Liter *m*, *n*
lit·e·ral (wort)wörtlich; genau; prosaisch
lit·e·ra·ry literarisch, Literatur…
lit·e·ra·ture Literatur *f*
lithe geschmeidig, gelenkig
li·tre *Br* → ***liter***
lit·ter **1.** (*esp Papier*)Abfall *m*; AGR Streu *f*; ZO Wurf *m*; Trage *f*; Sänfte *f*; **2.** *et.* herumliegen lassen in (*dat*) *or* auf (*dat*); ***be littered with*** übersät sein mit
lit·ter bas·ket, **litter bin** Abfallkorb *m*
lit·tle **1.** *adj* klein; wenig; ***the little ones*** die Kleinen *pl*; **2.** *adv* wenig, kaum; **3.** Kleinigkeit *f*; ***a little*** ein wenig, ein bisschen; ***little by little*** (ganz) allmählich, nach und nach; ***not a little*** nicht wenig
live[1] leben; wohnen (***with*** bei); ***live to see*** erleben; ***live on*** leben von; weiterleben; ***live up to*** *s-n Grundsätzen etc* gemäß leben; *Erwartungen etc* entsprechen; ***live with*** mit *j-m* zusammenleben; mit *et.* leben
live[2] **1.** *adj* lebend, lebendig; richtig, echt; ELECTR Strom führend; *radio*, TV Direkt…, Live-…; **2.** *adv* direkt, original, live
live·li·hood (Lebens)Unterhalt *m*
live·li·ness Lebhaftigkeit *f*
live·ly lebhaft, lebendig; aufregend
liv·er ANAT Leber *f* (*a.* GASTR)
liv·e·ry Livree *f*
live·stock Vieh *n*, Viehbestand *m*
liv·id bläulich; F fuchsteufelswild
liv·ing **1.** lebend; ***the living image of*** das genaue Ebenbild (*gen*); **2.** Leben *n*, Lebensweise *f*; Lebensunterhalt *m*; ***the living*** die Lebenden *pl*; ***standard of living*** Lebensstandard *m*; ***earn*** *or* ***make a living*** (sich) s-n Lebensunterhalt verdienen
liv·ing room Wohnzimmer *n*
liz·ard ZO Eidechse *f*
load **1.** Last *f* (*a. fig*); Ladung *f*; Belastung *f*; **2.** *j-n* überhäufen (***with*** mit); *Schusswaffe* laden; ***load a camera*** e-n Film einlegen; *a.* ***load up*** (auf-, be-, ein)laden
loaf[1] Laib *m* (Brot); Brot *n*
loaf[2] *a.* ***loaf about, loaf around*** F herumlungern
loaf·er Müßiggänger(in)
loam Lehm *m*
loam·y lehmig
loan **1.** (Ver)Leihen *n*; ECON Kredit *m*, Darlehen *n*; Leihgabe *f*; ***on loan*** leihweise; **2.** ***loan s.o. s.th., loan s.th. to s.o.*** j-m et. (aus)leihen; et. an j-n verleihen
loan shark ECON Kredithai *m*
loath: ***be loath to do s.th.*** et. nur (sehr) ungern tun
loathe verabscheuen, hassen
loath·ing Abscheu *m*
lob *esp tennis*: Lob *m*
lob·by **1.** Vorhalle *f*; THEA, *film*: Foyer *n*; Wandelhalle *f*; POL Lobby *f*, Interessengruppe *f*; **2.** POL *Abgeordnete etc* beeinflussen
lobe ANAT, BOT Lappen *m*
lob·ster ZO Hummer *m*
lo·cal **1.** örtlich, Orts…, lokal, Lokal…; **2.** Ortsansässige *m*, *f*, Einheimische *m*, *f*; *Br* F Stammkneipe *f*
local call TEL Ortsgespräch *n*
local e·lec·tions POL Kommunalwahlen *pl*
local gov·ern·ment Gemeindeverwaltung *f*
local time Ortszeit *f*
local traf·fic Orts-, Nahverkehr *m*
lo·cate ausfindig machen; orten; ***be located*** gelegen sein, liegen, sich befinden

L

lo·ca·tion Lage *f*; Standort *m*; Platz *m* (***for*** für); *film*, TV Gelände *n* für Außenaufnahmen; ***on location*** auf Außenaufnahme

lock[1] **1.** (*Tür-, Gewehr- etc*)Schloss *n*; Schleuse(nkammer) *f*; Verschluss *m*; Sperrvorrichtung *f*; **2.** *v/t* zu-, verschließen, zu-, versperren (*a.* ***lock up***); umschlingen, umfassen; TECH sperren; *v/i* schließen; abschließbar *or* verschließbar sein; MOT *etc* blockieren; ***lock away*** wegschließen; ***lock in*** einschließen, einsperren; ***lock out*** aussperren; ***lock up*** abschließen; wegschließen; einsperren

lock[2] (Haar)Locke *f*

lock·er Spind *m*, Schrank *m*; Schließfach *n*

locker room *esp* SPORT Umkleidekabine *f*, Umkleideraum *m*

lock·et Medaillon *n*

lock·out ECON Aussperrung *f*

lock·smith Schlosser *m*

lock·up Arrestzelle *f*

lo·cust zo Heuschrecke *f*

lodge **1.** Portier-, Pförtnerloge *f*; (*Jagd-, Ski- etc*)Hütte *f*; Sommer-, Gartenhaus *n*; (*Freimaurer*)Loge *f*; **2.** *v/i* logieren, (*esp* vorübergehend *or* in Untermiete) wohnen; stecken (bleiben) (*bullet etc*); *v/t* aufnehmen, beherbergen, (für die Nacht) unterbringen; *Beschwerde etc* einreichen; *Berufung*, *Protest* einlegen

lodg·er Untermieter(in)

lodg·ing Unterkunft *f*; *pl esp* möbliertes Zimmer

loft (Dach)Boden *m*; Heuboden *m*; Empore *f*; ***(converted) loft*** Loft *m*, Fabriketage *f*

loft·y hoch; erhaben; stolz, hochmütig

log (Holz)Klotz *m*; (*gefällter*) Baumstamm; (Holz)Scheit *n*; → **log·book** MAR Logbuch *n*; AVIAT Bordbuch *n*; MOT Fahrtenbuch *n*

log cab·in Blockhaus *n*, Blockhütte *f*

log·ger·heads: ***be at loggerheads*** sich streiten, sich in den Haaren liegen (***with*** mit)

lo·gic Logik *f*

lo·gic·al logisch

loin GASTR Lende(nstück *n*) *f*; *pl* ANAT Lende *f*

loi·ter trödeln; herumlungern

loll hängen (*head*), heraushängen (*tongue*); ***loll around*** *or* ***about*** F sich rekeln *or* lümmeln

lol·li·pop GASTR Lutscher *m*; *esp Br* Eis *n* am Stiel; ***lollipop man*** *Br* Schülerlotse *m*; ***lollipop woman, lollipop lady*** *Br* Schülerlotsin *f*

lol·ly GASTR F Lutscher *m*; ***ice lolly*** Eis *n* am Stiel

lone·li·ness Einsamkeit *f*

lone·ly einsam; ***become lonely*** vereinsamen

lone·some einsam

long[1] **1.** *adj* lang; weit; langfristig; **2.** *adv* lang(e); ***as*** *or* ***so long as*** solange wie; vorausgesetzt, dass; ***long ago*** vor langer Zeit; ***so long!*** F bis dann!, tschüs(s)!; **3.** (e-e) lange Zeit; ***for long*** lange; ***take long*** lange brauchen *or* dauern

long[2] sich sehnen (***for*** nach)

long-dis·tance Fern…, Langstrecken…

long-distance call TEL Ferngespräch *n*

long-distance run·ner SPORT Langstreckenläufer(in)

long·hand Schreibschrift *f*

long·ing **1.** sehnsüchtig; **2.** Sehnsucht *f*, Verlangen *n*

lon·gi·tude GEOGR Länge *f*

long johns lange Unterhose

long jump SPORT Weitsprung *m*

long-life milk *esp Br* H-Milch *f*

long-play·er, long-play·ing rec·ord Langspielplatte *f*

long-range MIL, AVIAT Fern…, Langstrecken…; langfristig

long·shore·man Dock-, Hafenarbeiter *m*

long·sight·ed *esp Br* weitsichtig, *fig a.* weitblickend

long-stand·ing seit langer Zeit bestehend; alt

long-term langfristig, auf lange Sicht

long wave ELECTR Langwelle *f*

long·wear·ing strapazierfähig

long·wind·ed langatmig

look **1.** sehen, blicken, schauen (***at, on*** auf *acc*, nach); nachschauen, nachsehen; *krank etc* aussehen; nach *e-r Richtung* liegen, gehen (*window etc*); ***look here!*** schau mal (her); hör mal (zu)!; ***look like*** aussehen wie; ***it looks as if*** es sieht (so) aus, als ob; ***look after*** aufpassen auf (*acc*); sich kümmern um, sorgen für, *den Haushalt etc* versehen; ***look ahead*** nach vorne sehen; *fig* vorausschauen; ***look around*** sich umsehen; ***look at*** ansehen; ***look back*** sich umsehen; *fig* zurückblicken; ***look down*** herab-, heruntersehen (*a. fig* ***on s.o.*** auf j-n); ***look for*** suchen; ***look forward to*** sich freuen auf (*acc*); ***look in*** F hereinschauen (***on*** bei); ***look into*** untersuchen, prüfen; ***look on*** zusehen, zuschauen (*dat*); betrachten, ansehen (***as*** als); ***look onto*** liegen zu, (hinaus)gehen auf (*acc*) (*window etc*); ***look out*** hinaus-, heraussehen; aufpassen, sich vorsehen; ausschauen *or*

Ausschau halten (***for*** nach); ***look over*** *et.* durchsehen; *j-n* mustern; ***look round*** sich umsehen; ***look through*** *et.* durchsehen; ***look up*** aufblicken, aufsehen; *et.* nachschlagen; *j-n* aufsuchen; **2.** Blick *m*; Miene *f*, (Gesichts)Ausdruck *m*; (***good***) ***looks*** gutes Aussehen; ***have a look at s.th.*** sich et. ansehen; ***I don't like the look of it*** es gefällt mir nicht

look·ing glass Spiegel *m*

look·out Ausguck *m*; Ausschau *f*; *fig* F Aussicht(en *pl*) *f*; ***be on the lookout for*** Ausschau halten nach; ***that's his own lookout*** F das ist allein seine Sache

loom[1] Webstuhl *m*

loom[2] *a.* ***loom up*** undeutlich sichtbar werden *or* auftauchen

loop **1.** Schlinge *f*, Schleife *f*; Schlaufe *f*; Öse *f*; AVIAT Looping *m*, *n*; EDP Schleife *f*; **2.** (sich) schlingen

loop·hole MIL Schießscharte *f*; *fig* Hintertürchen *n*; ***a loophole in the law*** e-e Gesetzeslücke

loose **1.** los(e); locker; weit; frei; ***let loose*** loslassen; freilassen; **2.** ***be on the loose*** frei herumlaufen

loos·en (sich) lösen *or* lockern; ***loosen up*** SPORT Lockerungsübungen machen

loot **1.** Beute *f*; **2.** plündern

lop *Baum* beschneiden, stutzen; ***lop off*** abhauen, abhacken

lop·sid·ed schief; *fig* einseitig

lord Herr *m*, Gebieter *m*; *Br* Lord *m*; ***the Lord*** REL Gott *m* (der Herr); ***the Lord's Prayer*** REL das Vaterunser; ***the Lord's Supper*** REL das (heilige) Abendmahl; ***House of Lords*** *Br* POL Oberhaus *n*

Lord Mayor *Br* Oberbürgermeister *m*

lor·ry *Br* MOT Last(kraft)wagen *m*, Lastauto *n*, Laster *m*

lose verlieren; verpassen, versäumen; nachgehen (*watch*); ***lose o.s.*** sich verirren; sich verlieren

los·er Verlierer(in)

loss Verlust *m*; Schaden *m*; ***at a loss*** ECON mit Verlust; ***be at a loss*** in Verlegenheit sein (***for*** um)

lost verloren; ***be lost*** sich verirrt haben, sich nicht mehr zurechtfinden (*a. fig*); ***be lost in thought*** in Gedanken versunken sein; ***get lost*** sich verirren; ***get lost!*** *sl* hau ab!

lost-and-found (of·fice), *Br* **lost prop·er·ty of·fice** Fundbüro *n*

lot Los *n*; Parzelle *f*; Grundstück *n*; ECON Partie *f*, Posten *m*; Gruppe *f*, Gesellschaft *f*; Menge *f*, Haufen *m*; Los *n*, Schicksal *n*; ***the lot*** alles, das Ganze; ***a lot of*** F, ***lots of*** F viel, e-e Menge; ***a bad lot*** F ein übler Kerl; ***cast*** *or* ***draw lots*** losen

loth → ***loath***

lo·tion Lotion *f*

lot·te·ry Lotterie *f*

loud laut; *fig* schreiend, grell

loud·mouth *contp* Schwätzer *m*

loud·speak·er Lautsprecher *m*

lounge **1.** Wohnzimmer *n*; Aufenthaltsraum *m*, Lounge *f* (*a.* AVIAT); Wartehalle *f*; **2.** F *contp* sich flegeln; ***lounge about, lounge around*** herumlungern

louse zo Laus *f*

lou·sy verlaust; F miserabel, saumäßig

lout Flegel *m*, Lümmel *m*, Rüpel *m*

lov·a·ble liebenswert; reizend

love **1.** Liebe *f* (***of, for, to, towards*** zu); Liebling *m*, Schatz *m*; *tennis*: null; ***be in love with s.o.*** in j-n verliebt sein; ***fall in love with s.o.*** sich in j-n verlieben; ***make love*** sich lieben, miteinander schlafen; ***give my love to her*** grüße sie herzlich von mir; ***send one's love to*** *j-n* grüßen lassen; ***love from ...*** herzliche Grüße von …; **2.** lieben; gern mögen

love af·fair Liebesaffäre *f*

love·ly (wunder)schön; nett, reizend; F prima

lov·er Liebhaber *m*, Geliebte *m*, *f*; (*Musik- etc*)Liebhaber(in), (-)Freund(in); *pl* Liebende *pl*, Liebespaar *n*

lov·ing liebevoll, liebend

low **1.** *adj* niedrig (*a. fig*); tief (*a. fig*); knapp (*supplies etc*); gedämpft, schwach (*light*); tief (*sound*); leise (*sound, voice*); *fig* gering(schätzig); ordinär; niedergeschlagen, deprimiert; **2.** *adv* niedrig; tief (*a. fig*); leise **3.** METEOR Tief(druckgebiet) *n*; *fig* Tief(punkt *m*) *n*

low·brow F **1.** geistig Anspruchslose *m*, *f*, Unbedarfte *m*, *f*; **2.** geistig anspruchslos, unbedarft

low-cal·o·rie kalorienarm, -reduziert

low-e·mis·sion schadstoffarm

low·er **1.** niedriger; tiefer; untere(r, -s), Unter…; **2.** niedriger machen; herab-, herunterlassen; *Augen, Stimme, Preis etc* senken; *Standard* herabsetzen; *fig* erniedrigen

low-fat fettarm

low-fly·ing plane AVIAT Tiefflieger *m*

low·land Tief-, Flachland *n*

low·ly niedrig

low-necked (tief) ausgeschnitten

low-pitched MUS tief

low-pres·sure METEOR Tiefdruck…; TECH Niederdruck…

low-rise ARCH niedrig (gebaut)

L

low-spir·it·ed niedergeschlagen
low tide Ebbe *f*
low wa·ter Niedrigwasser *n*
loy·al loyal, treu
loy·al·ty Loyalität *f*, Treue *f*
loz·enge MATH Raute *f*, Rhombus *m*; GASTR Pastille *f*
lu·bri·cant TECH Schmiermittel *n*
lu·bri·cate TECH schmieren, ölen
lu·bri·ca·tion TECH Schmieren *n*, Ölen *n*
lu·cid klar
luck Schicksal *n*; Glück *n*; ***bad luck, hard luck, ill luck*** Unglück *n*, Pech *n*; ***good luck*** Glück *n*; ***good luck!*** viel Glück!; ***be in (out of) luck*** (kein) Glück haben
luck·i·ly glücklicherweise, zum Glück
luck·y glücklich, Glücks…; ***be lucky*** Glück haben; ***lucky day*** Glückstag *m*; ***lucky fellow*** Glückspilz *m*
lu·cra·tive einträglich, lukrativ
lu·di·crous lächerlich
lug zerren, schleppen
luge SPORT Rennrodeln *n*; Rennrodel *m*, Rennschlitten *m*
lug·gage *esp Br* (Reise)Gepäck *n*
luggage rack *esp Br* RAIL *etc* Gepäcknetz *n*, Gepäckablage *f*
luggage van *Br* RAIL Gepäckwagen *m*
luke·warm lau(warm); *fig* lau, mäßig, halbherzig
lull 1. beruhigen; sich legen (*storm*); *mst* ***lull to sleep*** einlullen; **2.** Pause *f*; MAR Flaute *f* (*a. fig*)
lul·la·by Wiegenlied *n*
lum·ba·go MED Hexenschuss *m*
lum·ber[1] schwerfällig gehen; (dahin-) rumpeln (*vehicle*)
lum·ber[2] **1.** Bau-, Nutzholz *n*; *esp Br* Gerümpel *n*; **2.** *v/t* ***lumber s.o. with s.th.*** *Br* F j-m et. aufhalsen
lum·ber·jack Holzfäller *m*, -arbeiter *m*
lum·ber mill Sägewerk *n*
lum·ber room *esp Br* Rumpelkammer *f*
lum·ber·yard Holzplatz *m*, Holzlager *n*
lu·mi·na·ry *fig* Leuchte *f*, Koryphäe *f*
lu·mi·nous leuchtend, Leucht…
lu·mi·nous di·splay Leuchtanzeige *f*
lu·mi·nous paint Leuchtfarbe *f*
lump 1. Klumpen *m*; Schwellung *f*, Beule *f*; MED Geschwulst *f*, Knoten *m*; GASTR Stück *n*; ***in the lump*** in Bausch und Bogen, pauschal; **2.** *v/t*: ***lump together*** *fig* zusammenwerfen; in e-n Topf werfen; *v/i* Klumpen bilden, klumpen
lump sug·ar Würfelzucker *m*
lump sum Pauschalsumme *f*
lump·y klumpig
lu·na·cy Wahnsinn *m*
lu·nar ASTR Mond…
lu·nar mod·ule Mond(lande)fähre *f*
lu·na·tic *fig* **1.** wahnsinnig, verrückt; **2.** Wahnsinnige *m, f*, Verrückte *m, f*
lunch, *formal* **lun·cheon 1.** Lunch *m*, Mittagessen *n*; **2.** zu Mittag essen
lunch hour, lunch time Mittagszeit *f*, Mittagspause *f*
lung ANAT Lungenflügel *m*; *pl* die Lunge
lunge sich stürzen (***at*** auf *acc*)
lurch 1. taumeln, torkeln; **2.** ***leave s.o. in the lurch*** j-n im Stich lassen, F j-n sitzen lassen
lure 1. Köder *m*; *fig* Lockung *f*; **2.** ködern, (an)locken
lu·rid grell; grässlich, schauerlich
lurk lauern; ***lurk about, lurk around*** herumschleichen
lus·cious köstlich, lecker; üppig; F knackig
lush saftig, üppig
lust 1. sinnliche Begierde, Lust *f*; Gier *f*; **2.** ***lust after, lust for*** begehren; gierig sein nach
lus·ter, *Br* **lus·tre** Glanz *m*, Schimmer *m*
lus·trous glänzend, schimmernd
lust·y kräftig, robust, vital
lute MUS Laute *f*
Lu·ther·an REL lutherisch
lux·u·ri·ant üppig
lux·u·ri·ate schwelgen (***in*** in *dat*)
lux·u·ri·ous luxuriös, Luxus…
lux·u·ry 1. Luxus *m*; Komfort *m*; Luxusartikel *m*; **2.** Luxus…
lye Lauge *f*
ly·ing lügnerisch, verlogen
lymph MED Lymphe *f*
lynch lynchen
lynch law Lynchjustiz *f*
lynx zo Luchs *m*
lyr·ic 1. lyrisch; **2.** lyrisches Gedicht; *pl* Lyrik *f*; (Lied)Text *m*
lyr·i·cal lyrisch, gefühlvoll; schwärmerisch

L

M

M, m M, m *n*
M ABBR *of* ***medium*** (***size***) mittelgroß
ma F Mama *f*, Mutti *f*
ma'am → ***madam***
ma·cad·am Asphalt *m*
mac·a·ro·ni Makkaroni *pl*
ma·chine **1.** Maschine *f*; **2.** maschinell herstellen
ma·chine·gun Maschinengewehr *n*
ma·chine-read·a·ble EDP maschinenlesbar
ma·chin·e·ry Maschinen *pl*; Maschinerie *f*
ma·chin·ist TECH Maschinist *m*
mach·o *contp* Macho *m*
mack·e·rel zo Makrele *f*
mac·ro... Makro..., (sehr) groß
mad wahnsinnig, verrückt; VET tollwütig; F wütend; *fig* ***be mad about*** wild *or* versessen sein auf (*acc*), verrückt sein nach; ***drive s.o. mad*** j-n verrückt machen; ***go mad*** verrückt werden; ***like mad*** wie verrückt
mad·am gnädige Frau
mad·cap verrückt
mad cow dis·ease VET Rinderwahn (-sinn) *m*
mad·den verrückt *or* rasend machen
mad·den·ing unerträglich; verrückt *or* rasend machend
made: ***made of gold*** aus Gold
made-to-meas·ure maßgeschneidert
made-up geschminkt; erfunden
mad·house *fig* F Irrenhaus *n*
mad·ly wie verrückt; F wahnsinnig, schrecklich
mad·man Verrückte *m*
mad·ness Wahnsinn
mad·wom·an Verrückte *f*
mag·a·zine Magazin *n* (*a.* PHOT, MIL), Zeitschrift *f*; Lagerhaus *n*
mag·got zo Made *f*
Ma·gi: ***the*** (***three***) ***Magi*** die (drei) Weisen aus dem Morgenland, die Heiligen Drei Könige
ma·gic **1.** Magie *f*, Zauberei *f*; Zauber *m*; *fig* Wunder *n*; **2.** *a.* ***magical*** magisch, Zauber...
ma·gi·cian Magier *m*, Zauberer *m*; Zauberkünstler *m*
ma·gis·trate (Friedens)Richter(in)
mag·na·nim·i·ty Großmut *f*
mag·nan·i·mous großmütig
mag·net Magnet *m*
mag·net·ic magnetisch, Magnet...
mag·nif·i·cent großartig, prächtig
mag·ni·fy vergrößern
mag·ni·fy·ing glass Vergrößerungsglas *n*, Lupe *f*
mag·ni·tude Größe *f*; Wichtigkeit *f*
mag·pie zo Elster *f*
ma·hog·a·ny Mahagoni(holz) *n*
maid (Dienst)Mädchen *n*, Hausangestellte *f*; ***maid of all work*** *esp fig* Mädchen *n* für alles; ***maid of hono(u)r*** Hofdame *f*; (erste) Brautjungfer
maid·en Jungfern..., Erstlings...
maid·en name Mädchenname *m*
mail **1.** Post(sendung) *f*; ***by mail*** mit der Post; **2.** mit der Post (zu)schicken, aufgeben, *Brief* einwerfen
mail·bag Postsack *m*; Posttasche *f*
mail·box Briefkasten *m*
mail car·ri·er, **mail·man** Briefträger *m*, Postbote *m*
mail or·der Bestellung *f* bei e-m Versandhaus
mail-or·der firm, **mail-order house** Versandhaus *n*
maim verstümmeln
main **1.** Haupt..., wichtigste(r, -s); hauptsächlich; ***by main force*** mit äußerster Kraft; **2.** *mst pl* Hauptleitung *f*, Hauptgas-, Hauptwasser-, Hauptstromleitung *f*; (Strom)Netz *n*; ***in the main*** in der Hauptsache, im Wesentlichen
main·frame EDP Großrechner *m*
main·land Festland *n*
main·ly hauptsächlich
main mem·o·ry EDP Hauptspeicher *m*; Arbeitsspeicher *m*
main men·u EDP Hauptmenü *n*
main road Haupt(verkehrs)straße *f*
main·spring TECH Hauptfeder *f*; *fig* (Haupt)Triebfeder *f*
main·stay *fig* Hauptstütze *f*
main street Hauptstraße *f*
main·tain (aufrecht)erhalten, beibehalten; instand halten, pflegen, TECH *a.* warten; *Familie etc* unterhalten, versorgen; *et.* behaupten
main·te·nance (Aufrecht)Erhaltung *f*; Instandhaltung *f*, Pflege *f*, TECH *a.* Wartung *f*; Unterhalt *m*
maize *esp Br* BOT Mais *m*
ma·jes·tic majestätisch
ma·jes·ty Majestät *f*; ***His*** (***Her, Your***) ***Majesty*** Seine (Ihre, Eure) Majestät

ma·jor **1.** größere(r, -s), *fig a.* bedeutend, wichtig; JUR volljährig; ***C major*** MUS C-Dur *n*; **2.** MIL Major *m*; JUR Volljährige *m, f*; UNIV Hauptfach *n*; MUS Dur *n*
major gen·e·ral MIL Generalmajor *m*
ma·jor·i·ty Mehrheit *f*, Mehrzahl *f*; JUR Volljährigkeit *f*
ma·jor league *baseball*: oberste Spielklasse
ma·jor road Haupt(verkehrs)straße *f*
make **1.** machen; anfertigen, herstellen, erzeugen; (zu)bereiten; (er)schaffen; ergeben, bilden; machen zu; ernennen zu; *Geld* verdienen; sich erweisen als, abgeben (*person*); schätzen auf (*acc*); *Geschwindigkeit* erreichen; *Fehler* machen; *Frieden etc* schließen; *e-e Rede* halten; F *Strecke* zurücklegen; *with inf*: *j-n* lassen, veranlassen zu, bringen zu, zwingen zu; ***make it*** es schaffen; ***make do with s.th.*** mit et. auskommen, sich mit et. behelfen; ***do you make one of us?*** machen Sie mit?; ***what do you make of it?*** was halten Sie davon?; ***make believe*** vorgeben; ***make friends with*** sich anfreunden mit; ***make good*** wieder gutmachen; *Versprechen etc* halten; ***make haste*** sich beeilen; ***make way*** Platz machen; ***make for*** zugehen auf (*acc*); sich aufmachen nach; ***make into*** verarbeiten zu; ***make off*** sich davonmachen, sich aus dem Staub machen; ***make out*** *Rechnung, Scheck etc* ausstellen; ausmachen, erkennen; aus *j-m, e-r Sache* klug werden; ***make over*** *Eigentum* übertragen; ***make up*** *et.* zusammenstellen; sich *et.* ausdenken, *et.* erfinden; (sich) zurechtmachen *or* schminken; ***make it up*** sich versöhnen *or* wieder vertragen (***with*** mit); ***make up one's mind*** sich entschließen; ***be made up of*** bestehen aus, sich zusammensetzen aus; ***make up for*** nachholen, aufholen; für *et.* entschädigen; **2.** Machart *f*, Bauart *f*; Fabrikat *n*, Marke *f*
make-be·lieve Schein *m*, Fantasie *f*
mak·er Hersteller *m*; ***Maker*** REL Schöpfer *m*
make·shift **1.** Notbehelf *m*; **2.** behelfsmäßig, Behelfs…
make-up Make-up *n*, Schminke *f*; Aufmachung *f*; Zusammensetzung *f*
mak·ing Erzeugung *f*, Herstellung *f*, Fabrikation *f*; ***be in the making*** noch in Arbeit sein; ***have the makings of*** das Zeug haben zu
mal·ad·just·ed nicht angepasst, verhaltensgestört, milieugestört
mal·ad·min·i·stra·tion schlechte Verwaltung; POL Misswirtschaft *f*
mal·con·tent **1.** unzufrieden; **2.** Unzufriedene *m, f*
male **1.** männlich; **2.** Mann *m*; ZO Männchen *n*
male nurse (Kranken)Pfleger *m*
mal·for·ma·tion Missbildung *f*
mal·ice Bosheit *f*; Groll *m*; JUR böse Absicht, Vorsatz *m*
ma·li·cious boshaft; böswillig
ma·lign verleumden
ma·lig·nant bösartig (*a.* MED); boshaft
mall Einkaufszentrum *n*
mal·le·a·ble TECH verformbar; *fig* formbar
mal·let Holzhammer *m*; (Krocket-, Polo)-Schläger *m*
mal·nu·tri·tion Unterernährung *f*; Fehlernährung *f*
mal·o·dor·ous übel riechend
mal·prac·tice Vernachlässigung *f* der beruflichen Sorgfalt; MED falsche Behandlung, (ärztlicher) Kunstfehler
malt Malz *n*
mal·treat schlecht behandeln; misshandeln
mam·mal ZO Säugetier *n*
mam·moth **1.** ZO Mammut *n*; **2.** Mammut…, Riesen…, riesig
mam·my F Mami *f*
man **1.** Mann *m*; Mensch(en *pl*) *m*; Menschheit *f*; F (Ehe)Mann *m*; F Geliebte *m*; (*Schach*)Figur *f*; (*Dame*)Stein *m*; ***the man on*** (*Br* ***in***) ***the street*** der Mann auf der Straße; **2.** (*Raum*)*Schiff etc* bemannen; *Büro etc* besetzen
man·age *v/t* *Betrieb etc* leiten, führen; *Künstler, Sportler etc* managen; *et.* zustande bringen; es fertigbringen (***to do*** zu tun); umgehen (können) mit; mit *j-m, et.* fertigwerden; F *Arbeit, Essen etc* bewältigen, schaffen; *v/i* auskommen (***with*** mit; ***without*** ohne); F es schaffen, zurechtkommen; F es einrichten, es ermöglichen
man·age·a·ble handlich; lenksam
man·age·ment Verwaltung *f*; ECON Management *n*, Unternehmensführung *f*; Geschäftsleitung *f*, Direktion *f*
man·ag·er Verwalter *m*; ECON Manager *m* (*a.* THEA *etc*); Geschäftsführer *m*, Leiter *m*, Direktor *m*; SPORT (Chef-) Trainer *m*; ***be a good manager*** gut *or* sparsam wirtschaften können
man·a·ge·ri·al ECON geschäftsführend, leitend; ***managerial position*** leitende Stellung; ***managerial staff*** leitende Angestellte *pl*
man·ag·ing ECON geschäftsführend, leitend

M

managing di·rec·tor Generaldirektor *m*, leitender Direktor
man·date Mandat *n*; Auftrag *m*; Vollmacht *f*
man·da·to·ry obligatorisch, zwingend
mane ZO Mähne *f* (*a.* F)
ma·neu·ver *a. fig* **1.** Manöver *n*; **2.** manövrieren
mange VET Räude *f*
man·ger AGR Krippe *f*
man·gle **1.** (Wäsche)Mangel *f*; **2.** mangeln; *j-n* übel zurichten, zerfleischen; *fig Text* verstümmeln
mang·y VET räudig; *fig* schäbig
man·hood Mannesalter *n*; Männlichkeit *f*
ma·ni·a Wahnsinn *m*; *fig* (**for**) Sucht *f* (nach), Leidenschaft *f* (für), Manie *f*, Fimmel *m*
ma·ni·ac F Wahnsinnige *m, f*, Verrückte *m, f*; *fig* Fanatiker(in)
man·i·cure Maniküre *f*, Handpflege *f*
man·i·fest **1.** offenkundig; **2.** *v/t* offenbaren, manifestieren
man·i·fold mannigfaltig, vielfältig
ma·nip·u·late manipulieren; (geschickt) handhaben
ma·nip·u·la·tion Manipulation *f*
man·kind die Menschheit, die Menschen *pl*
man·ly männlich
man-made vom Menschen geschaffen, künstlich; ***man-made fiber*** Kunstfaser *f*
man·ner Art *f* (und Weise *f*); Betragen *n*, Auftreten *n*; *pl* Benehmen *n*, Umgangsformen *pl*, Manieren *pl*; Sitten *pl*
ma·noeu·vre *Br* → ***maneuver***
man·or *Br* (Land)Gut *n*; → **man·or house** Herrenhaus *n*
man·pow·er menschliche Arbeitskraft; Arbeitskräfte *pl*
man·sion (herrschaftliches) Wohnhaus
man·slaugh·ter JUR Totschlag *m*, fahrlässige Tötung
man·tel·piece, **man·tel·shelf** Kaminsims *m*
man·u·al **1.** Hand…; mit der Hand (gemacht); **2.** Handbuch *n*
man·u·fac·ture **1.** erzeugen, herstellen; **2.** Herstellung *f*, Fertigung *f*; Erzeugnis *n*, Fabrikat *n*
man·u·fac·tur·er Hersteller *m*, Erzeuger *m*
man·u·fac·tur·ing Herstellungs…
ma·nure AGR **1.** Dünger *m*, Mist *m*, Dung *m*; **2.** düngen
man·u·script Manuskript *n*
man·y **1.** viel(e); ***many a*** manche(r, -s), manch eine(r, -s); ***many times*** oft; ***as many*** ebenso viel(e); **2.** viele; ***a good many*** ziemlich viel(e); ***a great many*** sehr viele
map **1.** (Land- *etc*)Karte *f*; (Stadt- *etc*)Plan *m*; **2.** e-e Karte machen von; auf e-r Karte eintragen; ***map out*** *fig* (bis in die Einzelheiten) (voraus)planen
ma·ple BOT Ahorn *m*
mar beeinträchtigen; verderben
Mar ABBR *of* ***March*** März *m*
mar·a·thon SPORT **1.** *a.* ***marathon race*** Marathonlauf *m*; **2.** Marathon… (*a. fig*)
ma·raud plündern
mar·ble **1.** Marmor *m*; Murmel *f*; **2.** marmorn
march **1.** marschieren; *fig* fortschreiten; **2.** Marsch *m*; *fig* (Fort)Gang *m*; ***the march of events*** der Lauf der Dinge
March (ABBR ***Mar***) März *m*
mare ZO Stute *f*
mar·ga·rine, *Br* F **marge** Margarine *f*
mar·gin Rand *m* (*a. fig*); Grenze *f* (*a. fig*); *fig* Spielraum *m*; (*Gewinn-*, *Verdienst*)-Spanne *f*; ***by a wide margin*** mit großem Vorsprung
mar·gin·al Rand…; ***marginal note*** Randbemerkung *f*
mar·i·hua·na, **mar·i·jua·na** Marihuana *n*
ma·ri·na Boots-, Jachthafen *m*
ma·rine Marine *f*; MIL Marineinfanterist *m*
mar·i·ner Seemann *m*
mar·i·tal ehelich, Ehe…
mar·i·tal sta·tus Familienstand *m*
mar·i·time See…; Küsten…; Schifffahrts…
mark[1] (Deutsche) Mark
mark[2] **1.** Marke *f*, Markierung *f*; (Kenn)-Zeichen *n*, Merkmal *n*; (Körper)Mal *n*; Ziel *n* (*a. fig*); Spur *f* (*a. fig*); Fleck *m*; (*Fabrik-*, *Waren*)Zeichen *n*, (*Schutz-*, *Handels*)Marke *f*; ECON Preisangabe *f*; PED Note *f*, Zensur *f*, Punkt *m*; SPORT Startlinie *f*; *fig* Zeichen *n*; *fig* Norm *f*; ***be up to the mark*** den Anforderungen gewachsen sein (*person*) *or* genügen (*performance etc*); *gesundheitlich* auf der Höhe sein; ***be wide of the mark*** weit danebenschießen; *fig* sich gewaltig irren; weit danebenliegen (*estimate etc*); ***hit the mark*** (das Ziel) treffen; *fig* ins Schwarze treffen; ***miss the mark*** danebenschießen, das Ziel verfehlen (*a. fig*); **2.** markieren, anzeichnen; anzeigen; kennzeichnen; *Waren* auszeichnen; *Preis* festsetzen; Spuren hinterlassen auf (*dat*); Flecken machen auf (*dat*); PED benoten, zensieren; SPORT *Gegenspieler* decken, markieren; ***mark my words*** denk an m-e Worte; ***to mark the occasion*** zur

Feier des Tages; ***mark time*** auf der Stelle treten (*a. fig*); ***mark down*** notieren, vermerken; *im Preis* herabsetzen; ***mark off*** abgrenzen; *auf e-r Liste* abhaken; ***mark out*** *durch Striche etc* markieren; bestimmen (***for*** für); ***mark up*** *im Preis* heraufsetzen

marked deutlich, ausgeprägt

mark·er Markierstift *m*; Lesezeichen *n*; SPORT Bewacher(in)

mar·ket **1.** Markt *m*; Marktplatz *m*; (Lebensmittel)Geschäft *n*, Laden *m*; ECON Absatz *m*, (***for***) Nachfrage *f* (nach), Bedarf *m* (an *dat*); ***on the market*** auf dem Markt *or* im Handel; ***put on the market*** auf den Markt *or* in den Handel bringen; (zum Verkauf) anbieten; **2.** *v/t* auf den Markt *or* in den Handel bringen; verkaufen, vertreiben

mar·ket·a·ble ECON marktgängig

mar·ket gar·den *Br* Gemüse- und Obstgärtnerei *f*

mar·ket·ing ECON Marketing *n*

mark·ing Markierung *f*; zo Zeichnung *f*; SPORT Deckung *f*; ***man-to-man marking*** Manndeckung *f*

marks·man guter Schütze

mar·ma·lade *esp* Orangenmarmelade *f*

mar·mot zo Murmeltier *n*

ma·roon **1.** kastanienbraun; **2.** *auf e-r einsamen Insel* aussetzen; **3.** Leuchtrakete *f*

mar·quee Festzelt *n*

mar·quis Marquis *m*

mar·riage Heirat *f*, Hochzeit *f* (***to*** mit); Ehe *f*; ***civil marriage*** standesamtliche Trauung

mar·ria·ge·a·ble heiratsfähig

mar·riage cer·tif·i·cate Trauschein *m*, Heiratsurkunde *f*

mar·ried verheiratet; ehelich, Ehe…; ***married couple*** Ehepaar *n*; ***married life*** Ehe(leben *n*) *f*

mar·row ANAT (Knochen)Mark *n*; *fig* Kern *m*, *das* Wesentliche

mar·ry *v/t* heiraten; *Paar* trauen; ***be married*** verheiratet sein (***to*** mit); ***get married*** heiraten; sich verheiraten (***to*** mit); *v/i* heiraten

marsh Sumpf(land *n*) *m*, Marsch *f*

mar·shal **1.** MIL Marschall *m*; Bezirkspolizeichef *m*; **2.** ordnen; führen

marsh·y sumpfig

mar·ten zo Marder *m*

mar·tial kriegerisch; Kriegs…, Militär…

martial arts asiatische Kampfsportarten *pl*

martial law Kriegsrecht *n*

mar·tyr REL Märtyrer(in) (*a. fig*)

mar·vel **1.** Wunder *n*; **2.** sich wundern, staunen

mar·vel·(l)ous wunderbar; fabelhaft, fantastisch

mar·zi·pan Marzipan *n*, *m*

mas·ca·ra Wimperntusche *f*

mas·cot Maskottchen *n*

mas·cu·line männlich; Männer…; maskulin (*a.* LING)

mash zerdrücken, zerquetschen

mashed po·ta·toes Kartoffelbrei *m*

mask **1.** Maske *f* (*a.* EDP); **2.** maskieren; *fig* verbergen, verschleiern

masked maskiert; ***masked ball*** Maskenball *m*

ma·son Steinmetz *m*; *mst* ***Mason*** Freimaurer *m*

ma·son·ry Mauerwerk *n*

masque THEA HIST Maskenspiel *n*

mas·que·rade **1.** Maskerade *f* (*a. fig*); Verkleidung *f*; **2.** sich ausgeben (***as*** als, für)

mass **1.** Masse *f*; Menge *f*; Mehrzahl *f*; ***the masses*** die (breite) Masse; **2.** (sich) (an)sammeln *or* (an)häufen; **3.** Massen…

Mass REL Messe *f*

mas·sa·cre **1.** Massaker *n*; **2.** niedermetzeln

mas·sage **1.** Massage *f*; **2.** massieren

mas·seur Masseur *m*

mas·seuse Masseurin *f*, Masseuse *f*

mas·sif (Gebirgs)Massiv *n*

mas·sive massiv; groß, gewaltig

mass me·di·a Massenmedien *pl*

mass-pro·duce serienmäßig herstellen

mass pro·duc·tion Massen-, Serienproduktion *f*

mast MAR Mast *m*; *Br* ELECTR Sendemast *m*

mas·ter **1.** Meister *m* (*a.* PAINT); Herr *m*; *esp Br* Lehrer *m*; Original(kopie *f*) *n*; UNIV Magister *m*; ***Master of Arts*** (ABBR ***MA***) Magister *m* Artium; ***master of ceremonies*** Conférencier *m*; **2.** Meister…; Haupt…; ***master copy*** Originalkopie *f*; ***master tape*** TECH Mastertape *n*, Originaltonband *n*; **3.** Herr sein über (*acc*); *Sprache etc* beherrschen; *Aufgabe etc* meistern

mas·ter key Hauptschlüssel *m*

mas·ter·ly meisterhaft, virtuos

mas·ter·piece Meisterstück *n*, -werk *n*

mas·ter·y Herrschaft *f*; Oberhand *f*; Beherrschung *f*

mas·tur·bate masturbieren, onanieren

mat[1] **1.** Matte *f*; Untersetzer *m*; **2.** sich verfilzen

mat[2] mattiert, matt

match[1] Streichholz *n*, Zündholz *n*

match[2] **1.** *der, die, das* Gleiche; (dazu) passende Sache *or* Person, Gegenstück *n*; (*Fußball- etc*)Spiel *n*, (*Box- etc* -)

Kampf *m*, (*Tennis- etc*)Match *n, m*; Heirat *f*; *gute etc* Partie (*person*); ***be a (no) match for s.o.*** j-m (nicht) gewachsen sein; ***find** or **meet one's match*** s-n Meister finden; **2.** *v/t j-m, e-r Sache* ebenbürtig *or* gewachsen sein, gleichkommen; *j-m, e-r Sache* entsprechen, passen zu; *v/i* zusammenpassen, übereinstimmen, entsprechen; ***gloves to match*** dazu passende Handschuhe

match·box Streichholz-, Zündholzschachtel *f*

match·less unvergleichlich, einzigartig

match·mak·er Ehestifter(in)

match point *tennis etc*: Matchball *m*

mate[1] → ***checkmate***

mate[2] **1.** (Arbeits)Kamerad *m*, (-)Kollege *m*; ZO Männchen *n*, Weibchen *n*; MAR Maat *m*; **2.** zo (sich) paaren

ma·te·ri·al 1. Material *n*, Stoff *m*; ***writing materials*** Schreibmaterial(ien *pl*) *n*; **2.** materiell; leiblich; wesentlich

ma·ter·nal mütterlich, Mutter…; mütterlicherseits

ma·ter·ni·ty 1. Mutterschaft *f*; **2.** Schwangerschafts…, Umstands…

ma·ter·ni·ty leave Mutterschaftsurlaub *m*

maternity ward Entbindungsstation *f*

math F Mathe *f*

math·e·ma·ti·cian Mathematiker *m*

math·e·mat·ics Mathematik *f*

maths *Br* F Mathe *f*

mat·i·née THEA *etc* Nachmittagsvorstellung *f*

ma·tric·u·late (sich) immatrikulieren

mat·ri·mo·ni·al ehelich, Ehe…

mat·ri·mo·ny Ehe *f*, Ehestand *m*

ma·trix TECH Matrize *f*

ma·tron *Br* MED Oberschwester *f*; Hausmutter *f*; Matrone *f*

mat·ter 1. Materie *f*, Material *n*, Substanz *f*, Stoff *m*; MED Eiter *m*; Sache *f*, Angelegenheit *f*; ***printed matter*** Drucksache *f*; ***what's the matter (with you)?*** was ist los (mit dir)?; ***no matter who*** gleichgültig, wer; ***for that matter*** was das betrifft; ***a matter of course*** e-e Selbstverständlichkeit; ***a matter of fact*** e-e Tatsache; ***as a matter of fact*** tatsächlich, eigentlich; ***a matter of form*** e-e Formsache; ***a matter of time*** e-e Frage der Zeit; **2.** von Bedeutung sein (***to*** für); ***it doesn't matter*** es macht nichts

mat·ter-of-fact sachlich, nüchtern

mat·tress Matratze *f*

ma·ture 1. reif (*a. fig*); **2.** (heran)reifen, reif werden

ma·tu·ri·ty Reife *f* (*a. fig*)

maud·lin rührselig

maul übel zurichten; *fig* verreißen

Maun·dy Thurs·day Gründonnerstag *m*

mauve malvenfarbig, mauve

mawk·ish rührselig

max·i… Maxi…, riesig, Riesen…

max·im Grundsatz *m*

max·i·mum 1. Maximum *n*; **2.** maximal, Maximal…, Höchst…

May Mai *m*

may *v/aux ich* kann / mag / darf *etc*, *du* kannst / magst / darfst etc

may·be vielleicht

may·bug ZO Maikäfer *m*

May Day der 1. Mai

may·on·naise Mayonnaise *f*

mayor Bürgermeister *m*

may·pole Maibaum *m*

maze Irrgarten *m*, Labyrinth *n* (*a. fig*)

me mich; mir; F ich

mead·ow Wiese *f*, Weide *f*

mea·ger, *Br* **mea·gre** mager (*a. fig*), dürr; dürftig

meal[1] Mahl(zeit *f*) *n*; Essen *n*

meal[2] Schrotmehl *n*

mean[1] gemein, niederträchtig; geizig, knauserig; schäbig

mean[2] meinen; sagen wollen; bedeuten; beabsichtigen, vorhaben; ***be meant for*** bestimmt sein für; ***mean well (ill)*** es gut (schlecht) meinen

mean[3] **1.** Mitte *f*, Mittel *n*, Durchschnitt *m*; **2.** mittlere(r, -s), Mittel…, durchschnittlich, Durchschnitts…

mean·ing 1. Sinn *m*, Bedeutung *f*; **2.** bedeutungsvoll, bedeutsam

mean·ing·ful bedeutungsvoll; sinnvoll

mean·ing·less sinnlos

means Mittel *n or pl*, Weg *m*; ECON Mittel *pl*, Vermögen *n*; ***by all means*** auf alle Fälle, unbedingt; ***by no means*** keineswegs, auf keinen Fall; ***by means of*** durch, mit

mean·time 1. inzwischen; **2. *in the meantime*** inzwischen

mean·while inzwischen

mea·sles MED Masern *pl*

mea·sur·a·ble messbar

mea·sure 1. Maß *n* (*a. fig*); TECH Messgerät *n*; MUS Takt *m*; *fig* Maßnahme *f*; ***beyond measure*** über alle Maßen; ***in a great measure*** großenteils; ***take measures*** Maßnahmen treffen *or* ergreifen; **2.** (ab-, aus-, ver-)messen; *j-m* Maß nehmen; ***measure up to*** den Ansprüchen (*gen*) genügen

measured gemessen; wohlüberlegt; maßvoll

mea·sure·ment (Ver)Messung *f*; Maß *n*

measurement of ca·pac·i·ty Hohlmaß *n*

mea·sur·ing tape → ***tape measure***
meat GASTR Fleisch *n*; ***cold meat*** kalter Braten
meat·ball GASTR Fleischklößchen *n*
me·chan·ic Mechaniker *m*
me·chan·i·cal mechanisch; Maschinen…
me·chan·ics PHYS Mechanik *f*
mech·a·nism Mechanismus *m*
mech·a·nize mechanisieren
med·al Medaille *f*; Orden *m*
med·al·(l)ist SPORT Medaillengewinner(in)
med·dle sich einmischen (***with, in*** in *acc*)
med·dle·some aufdringlich
me·di·a Medien *pl*
med·i·ae·val → ***medieval***
me·di·an *a.* ***median strip*** MOT Mittelstreifen *m*
me·di·ate vermitteln
me·di·a·tion Vermittlung *f*
me·di·a·tor Vermittler *m*
med·ic MIL Sanitäter *m*
med·i·cal **1.** medizinisch, ärztlich; **2.** ärztliche Untersuchung
med·i·cal cer·tif·i·cate ärztliches Attest
med·i·cated medizinisch
me·di·ci·nal medizinisch, heilkräftig, Heil…
medi·cine Medizin *f*, *a.* Arznei *f*, *a.* Heilkunde *f*
med·i·e·val mittelalterlich
me·di·o·cre mittelmäßig
med·i·tate *v/i* (***on***) nachdenken (über *acc*); meditieren (über *acc*); *v/t* erwägen
med·i·ta·tion Nachdenken *n*; Meditation *f*
med·i·ta·tive nachdenklich
Med·i·ter·ra·ne·an Mittelmeer…
me·di·um **1.** Mitte *f*; Mittel *n*; Medium *n*; **2.** mittlere(r, -s), Mittel…, *a.* mittelmäßig; GASTR medium, halb gar
med·ley Gemisch *n*; MUS Medley *n*, Potpourri *n*
meek sanft(mütig), bescheiden
meet *v/t* treffen, sich treffen mit; begegnen (*dat*); *j-n* kennenlernen; *j-n* abholen; zusammentreffen mit, stoßen *or* treffen auf (*acc*); *Wünschen* entgegenkommen, entsprechen; *e-r Forderung, Verpflichtung* nachkommen; *v/i* zusammenkommen, -treten; sich begegnen, sich treffen; (*feindlich*) zusammenstoßen; SPORT aufeinandertreffen; sich kennenlernen; ***meet with*** zusammentreffen mit; sich treffen mit; stoßen auf (*Schwierigkeiten etc*); erleben, erleiden
meet·ing Begegnung *f*, (Zusammen-)Treffen *n*; Versammlung *f*, Konferenz *f*, Tagung *f*
meeting place Tagungs-, Versammlungsort *m*; Treffpunkt *m*
mel·an·chol·y **1.** Melancholie *f*, Schwermut *f*, Trübsinn *m*; **2.** melancholisch, traurig, trübsinnig, wehmütig
mel·low **1.** reif, weich; sanft, mild (*light*), zart (*colors*); *fig* gereift (*person*); **2.** reifen (lassen) (*a. fig*); weich *or* sanft werden
me·lo·di·ous melodisch
mel·o·dra·mat·ic melodramatisch
mel·o·dy MUS Melodie *f*
mel·on BOT Melone *f*
melt (zer)schmelzen; ***melt down*** einschmelzen
mem·ber Mitglied *n*, Angehörige *m, f*; ANAT Glied *n*, Gliedmaße *f*; (männliches) Glied; ***Member of Parliament*** *Br* Mitglied *n* des Unterhauses, Unterhausabgeordnete *m, f*
mem·ber·ship Mitgliedschaft *f*; Mitgliederzahl *f*
mem·brane Membran(e) *f*
mem·o Memo *n*
mem·oirs Memoiren *pl*
mem·o·ra·ble denkwürdig
me·mo·ri·al Denkmal *n*, Ehrenmal *n*, Gedenkstätte *f* (***to*** für); Gedenkfeier *f* (***to*** für)
mem·o·rize auswendig lernen, sich *et.* einprägen
mem·o·ry Gedächtnis *n*; Erinnerung *f*; Andenken *n*; EDP Speicher *m*; ***in memory of*** zum Andenken an (*acc*)
memory ca·pac·i·ty EDP Speicherkapazität *f*
men·ace **1.** (be)drohen; **2.** (Be)Drohung *f*
mend **1.** *v/t* (ver)bessern; ausbessern, reparieren, flicken; ***mend one's ways*** sich bessern; *v/i* sich bessern; **2.** ausgebesserte Stelle; ***on the mend*** auf dem Wege der Bess(e)rung
men·di·cant REL Bettelmönch *m*
me·ni·al niedrig, untergeordnet
men·in·gi·tis MED Meningitis *f*, Hirnhautentzündung *f*
men·o·pause MED Wechseljahre *pl*
men·stru·ate menstruieren
men·stru·a·tion Menstruation *f*
men·tal geistig, Geistes…; seelisch, psychisch
mental a·rith·me·tic Kopfrechnen *n*
mental hand·i·cap geistige Behinderung
mental hos·pi·tal psychiatrische Klinik
men·tal·i·ty Mentalität *f*
men·tal·ly: ***mentally handicapped*** geistig behindert; ***mentally ill*** geisteskrank
men·tion **1.** erwähnen; ***don't mention it!*** keine Ursache!; **2.** Erwähnung *f*

men·u Speise(n)karte *f*; EDP Menü *n*
me·ow zo miauen
mer·can·tile Handels…
mer·ce·na·ry **1.** geldgierig; **2.** MIL Söldner *m*
mer·chan·dise **1.** Ware(n *pl*) *f*; **2.** vermarkten
mer·chan·dis·ing Vermarktung *f*
mer·chant **1.** (Groß)Händler *m*, (Groß)-Kaufmann *m*; **2.** Handels…
mer·ci·ful barmherzig, gnädig
mer·ci·less unbarmherzig, erbarmungslos
mer·cu·ry CHEM Quecksilber *n*
mer·cy Barmherzigkeit *f*, Erbarmen *n*, Gnade *f*
mere, mere·ly bloß, nur
merge verschmelzen (***into, with*** mit); ECON fusionieren
merg·er ECON Fusion *f*
me·rid·i·an GEOGR Meridian *m*; *fig* Gipfel *m*, Höhepunkt *m*
mer·it **1.** Verdienst *n*; Wert *m*; Vorzug *m*; **2.** verdienen
mer·maid Meerjungfrau *f*, Nixe *f*
mer·ri·ment Fröhlichkeit *f*; Gelächter *n*, Heiterkeit *f*
mer·ry lustig, fröhlich, ausgelassen; ***Merry Christmas!*** fröhliche *or* frohe Weihnachten
mer·ry-go-round Karussell *n*
mesh **1.** Masche *f*; *fig often pl* Netz *n*, Schlingen *pl*; ***be in mesh*** TECH (ineinander)greifen; **2.** TECH (ineinander)greifen; *fig* passen (***with*** zu), zusammenpassen
mess **1.** Unordnung *f*, Durcheinander *n*; Schmutz *m*, F Schweinerei *f*; F Patsche *f*, Klemme *f*; MIL Messe *f*, Kasino *n*; ***make a mess of*** F *fig* verpfuschen, ruinieren, *Pläne etc* über den Haufen werfen; **2.** ***mess about, mess around*** F herumspielen, herumbasteln (***with*** an *dat*); herumgammeln; ***mess up*** in Unordnung bringen, durcheinanderbringen; *fig* F verpfuschen, ruinieren, *Pläne etc* über den Haufen werfen
mes·sage Mitteilung *f*, Nachricht *f*; Anliegen *n*, Aussage *f*; ***can I take a message?*** kann ich etwas ausrichten?; ***get the message*** F kapieren
mes·sen·ger Bote *m*
mess·y unordentlich; unsauber, schmutzig
me·tab·o·lis·m MED Stoffwechsel *m*
met·al Metall *n*
me·tal·lic metallisch; Metall…
met·a·mor·pho·sis Metamorphose *f*, Verwandlung *f*
met·a·phor Metapher *f*
me·tas·ta·sis MED Metastase *f*
me·te·or Meteor *m*
me·te·or·o·log·i·cal meteorologisch, Wetter…, Witterungs…
meteorological of·fice Wetteramt *n*
me·te·o·rol·o·gy Meteorologie *f*, Wetterkunde *f*
me·ter[1] TECH Messgerät *n*, Zähler *m*
me·ter[2] Meter *m*, *n*; Versmaß *n*
meth·od Methode *f*, Verfahren *n*; System *n*
me·thod·i·cal methodisch, systematisch, planmäßig
me·tic·u·lous peinlich genau, übergenau
me·tre *Br* → ***meter***[2]
met·ric metrisch
metric sys·tem metrisches (Maß- und Gewichts)System
met·ro·pol·i·tan … der Hauptstadt
me·trop·o·lis Weltstadt *f*
met·tle Eifer *m*, Mut *m*, Feuer *n*
mew zo miauen
Mex·i·can **1.** mexikanisch; **2.** Mexikaner(in)
Mex·i·co Mexiko *n*
mi·aow zo miauen
mi·cro… Mikro…, (sehr) klein
mi·cro·chip Mikrochip *m*
mi·cro·e·lec·tron·ics Mikroelektronik *f*
mi·cro·film Mikrofilm *m*
mi·cro·or·gan·ism BIOL Mikroorganismus *m*
mi·cro·phone Mikrofon *n*
mi·cro·pro·ces·sor Mikroprozessor *m*
mi·cro·scope Mikroskop *n*
mi·cro·scop·ic mikroskopisch
mi·cro·wave Mikrowelle *f*
microwave ov·en Mikrowellenherd *m*
mid mittlere(r, -s), Mitt(el)…
mid·air: ***in midair*** in der Luft
mid·day **1.** Mittag *m*; **2.** mittägig, Mittag(s)…
mid·dle **1.** mittlere(r, -s), Mittel…; **2.** Mitte *f*
mid·dle-aged mittleren Alters
Mid·dle Ag·es HIST Mittelalter *n*
mid·dle class(·es) Mittelstand *m*
mid·dle·man ECON Zwischenhändler *m*; Mittelsmann *m*
mid·dle name zweiter Vorname *m*
mid·dle-sized mittelgroß
mid·dle·weight *boxing*: Mittelgewicht *n*, Mittelgewichtler *m*
mid·dling F mittelmäßig, Mittel…; leidlich
mid·field *esp soccer*: Mittelfeld *n*
mid·field·er, mid·field play·er *esp soccer*: Mittelfeldspieler *m*
midge zo Mücke *f*

M

midg·et Zwerg *m*, Knirps *m*
mid·night Mitternacht *f*; ***at midnight*** um Mitternacht
midst: ***in the midst of*** mitten in (*dat*)
mid·sum·mer Hochsommer *m*; ASTR Sommersonnenwende *f*
mid·way auf halbem Wege
mid·wife Hebamme *f*
mid·win·ter Mitte *f* des Winters; ASTR Wintersonnenwende *f*; ***in midwinter*** mitten im Winter
might Macht *f*, Gewalt *f*; Kraft *f*
might·y mächtig, gewaltig
mi·grate (aus)wandern, (fort)ziehen (*a.* zo)
mi·gra·tion Wanderung *f* (*a.* zo)
mi·gra·to·ry Wander…; zo Zug…
mike F Mikrofon *n*
mild mild, sanft, leicht
mil·dew BOT Mehltau *m*
mild·ness Milde *f*
mile Meile *f* (*1,6 km*)
mile·age zurückgelegte Meilenzahl *or* Fahrtstrecke; Meilenstand *m*; *a.* ***mileage allowance*** Meilengeld *n*, *appr* Kilometergeld *n*
mile·stone Meilenstein *m* (*a. fig*)
mil·i·tant militant; streitbar, kriegerisch
mil·i·ta·ry **1.** militärisch, Militär…; **2.** ***the military*** das Militär
military gov·ern·ment Militärregierung *f*
military po·lice (ABBR ***MP***) Militärpolizei *f*
mi·li·tia Miliz *f*, Bürgerwehr *f*
milk **1.** Milch *f*; ***it's no use crying over spilt milk*** geschehen ist geschehen; **2.** *v/t* melken; *v/i* Milch geben
milk choc·olate Vollmilchschokolade *f*
milk·man Milchmann *m*
milk pow·der Milchpulver *n*, Trockenmilch *f*
milk shake Milchmixgetränk *n*
milk tooth ANAT Milchzahn *m*
milk·y milchig; Milch…
Milky Way ASTR Milchstraße *f*
mill **1.** Mühle *f*; Fabrik *f*; **2.** *Korn etc* mahlen; *Metall* verarbeiten; *Münze* rändeln
mil·le·pede → ***millipede***
mill·er Müller *m*
mil·let BOT Hirse *f*
mil·li·ner Hutmacherin *f*, Putzmacherin *f*, Modistin *f*
mil·lion Million *f*
mil·lion·aire Millionär(in)
mil·lionth **1.** millionste(r, -s); **2.** Millionstel *n*
mil·li·pede zo Tausendfüß(l)er *m*
mill·stone Mühlstein *m*; ***be a millstone round s.o.'s neck*** *fig* j-m ein Klotz am Bein sein
milt zo Milch *f*
mime **1.** Pantomime *f*; Pantomime *m*; **2.** (panto)mimisch darstellen
mim·ic **1.** mimisch; Schein…; **2.** Imitator *m*; **3.** nachahmen; nachäffen
mim·ic·ry Nachahmung *f*; zo Mimikry *f*
mince **1.** *v/t* zerhacken, (zer)schneiden; ***he does not mince matters*** *or* ***his words*** er nimmt kein Blatt vor den Mund; *v/i* tänzeln, trippeln; **2.** *u.* ***minced meat*** Hackfleisch *n*
minc·er Fleischwolf *m*
mind **1.** Sinn *m*, Gemüt *n*, Herz *n*; Verstand *m*, Geist *m*; Ansicht *f*, Meinung *f*; Absicht *f*, Neigung *f*, Lust *f*; Erinnerung *f*, Gedächtnis *n*; ***be out of one's mind*** nicht (recht) bei Sinnen sein; ***bear*** *or* ***keep in mind*** (immer) denken an (*acc*), *et.* nicht vergessen; ***change one's mind*** es sich anders überlegen, s-e Meinung ändern; ***enter s.o.'s mind*** j-m in den Sinn kommen; ***give s.o. a piece of one's mind*** j-m gründlich die Meinung sagen; ***have*** (***half***) ***a mind to*** *inf* (nicht übel) Lust haben zu *inf*; ***lose one's mind*** den Verstand verlieren; ***make up one's mind*** sich entschließen, e-n Entschluss fassen; ***to my mind*** meiner Ansicht nach; **2.** *v/t* achtgeben auf (*acc*); sehen nach, aufpassen auf (*acc*); et. haben gegen; ***mind the step!*** Vorsicht, Stufe!; ***mind your own business!*** kümmere dich um deine eigenen Angelegenheiten!; ***do you mind if I smoke?***, ***do you mind my smoking?*** haben Sie et. dagegen *or* stört es Sie, wenn ich rauche?; ***would you mind opening the window?*** würden Sie bitte das Fenster öffnen?; ***would you mind coming*** würden Sie bitte kommen?; *v/i* aufpassen; et. dagegen haben; ***mind*** (***you***) wohlgemerkt, allerdings; ***never mind!*** macht nichts!, ist schon gut!; ***I don't mind*** meinetwegen, von mir aus
mind·less gedankenlos, blind; unbekümmert (***of*** um), ohne Rücksicht (***of*** auf *acc*)
mine[1] meins; ***that's mine*** das gehört mir
mine[2] **1.** Bergwerk *n*, Mine *f*, Zeche *f*, Grube *f*; MIL Mine *f*; *fig* Fundgrube *f*; **2.** *v/i* schürfen, graben (***for*** nach); *v/t* *Erz, Kohle* abbauen; MIL verminen
min·er Bergmann *m*, Kumpel *m*
min·e·ral **1.** Mineral *n*; *pl Br* Mineralwasser *n*; **2.** Mineral…
mineral oil Mineralöl *n*
mineral wa·ter Mineralwasser *n*
min·gle *v/t* (ver)mischen; *v/i* sich mischen *or* mengen (***with*** unter)

min·i... Mini..., Klein(st)...; → ***miniskirt***
min·i·a·ture **1.** Miniatur(gemälde *n*) *f*; **2.** Miniatur...; Klein...
miniature cam·e·ra Kleinbildkamera *f*
min·i·mize auf ein Mindestmaß herabsetzen; herunterspielen, bagatellisieren
min·i·mum **1.** Minimum *n*, Mindestmaß *n*; **2.** minimal, Mindest...
min·ing **1.** Bergbau *m*; **2.** Berg(bau)..., Bergwerks...; Gruben...
min·i·skirt Minirock *m*
min·is·ter POL Minister(in); Gesandte *m*; REL Geistliche *m*
min·is·try POL Ministerium *n*; REL geistliches Amt
mink zo Nerz *m*
mi·nor **1.** kleinere(r, -s), *fig a.* unbedeutend, geringfügig; JUR minderjährig; ***A minor*** MUS a-Moll *n*; ***minor key*** MUS Moll(tonart *f*) *n*; **2.** JUR Minderjährige *m*, *f*; UNIV Nebenfach *n*; MUS Moll *n*
mi·nor·i·ty Minderheit *f*; JUR Minderjährigkeit *f*
min·ster *Br* Münster *n*
mint[1] **1.** Münze *f*, Münzanstalt *f*; **2.** prägen
mint[2] BOT Minze *f*
min·u·et MUS Menuett *n*
mi·nus **1.** *prp* minus, weniger; F ohne; **2.** *adj* Minus...; **3.** Minus *n*, *fig a.* Nachteil *m*
min·ute[1] Minute *f*; Augenblick *m*; ***in a minute*** sofort; ***just a minute!*** Moment mal!
mi·nute[2] winzig; sehr genau
min·utes Protokoll *n*; ***take*** (*or* ***keep***) ***the minutes*** (das) Protokoll führen
mir·a·cle Wunder *n*
mi·rac·u·lous wunderbar
mi·rac·u·lous·ly wie durch ein Wunder
mi·rage Luftspiegelung *f*, Fata Morgana *f*
mire Schlamm *m*; ***drag through the mire*** *fig* in den Schmutz ziehen
mir·ror **1.** Spiegel *m*; **2.** (wider)spiegeln (*a. fig*)
mis... miss..., falsch, schlecht
mis·ad·ven·ture Missgeschick *n*; Unglück *n*, Unglücksfall *m*
mis·an·thrope, **mis·an·thro·pist** Menschenfeind(in)
mis·ap·ply falsch an- *or* verwenden
mis·ap·pre·hend missverstehen
mis·ap·pro·pri·ate unterschlagen, veruntreuen
mis·be·have sich schlecht benehmen
mis·cal·cu·late falsch berechnen; sich verrechnen (in *dat*)
miscar·riage MED Fehlgeburt *f*; Misslingen *n*, Fehlschlag(en *n*) *m*; ***miscarriage of justice*** JUR Fehlurteil *n*
mis·car·ry MED e-e Fehlgeburt haben; misslingen, scheitern
mis·cel·la·ne·ous gemischt, vermischt; verschiedenartig
mis·cel·la·ny Gemisch *n*; Sammelband *m*
mis·chief Schaden *m*; Unfug *m*; Übermut *m*
mischief-mak·er Unruhestifter(in)
mis·chie·vous boshaft, mutwillig; schelmisch
mis·con·ceive falsch auffassen, missverstehen
mis·con·duct schlechtes Benehmen; schlechte Führung; Verfehlung *f*
mis·con·strue falsch auslegen, missdeuten
mis·de·mea·no(u)r JUR Vergehen *n*
mis·di·rect fehlleiten, irreleiten; *Brief etc* falsch adressieren
mise-en-scène THEA Inszenierung *f*
mi·ser Geizhals *m*
mis·e·ra·ble erbärmlich, kläglich, elend; unglücklich
mi·ser·ly geizig, F knick(e)rig
mis·e·ry Elend *n*, Not *f*
mis·fire versagen (*gun*); MOT fehlzünden, aussetzen; *fig* danebengehen
mis·fit Außenseiter(in)
mis·for·tune Unglück *n*, Unglücksfall *m*; Missgeschick *n*
mis·giv·ing Befürchtung *f*, Zweifel *m*
mis·guid·ed irregeleitet, irrig, unangebracht
mis·hap Unglück *n*; Missgeschick *n*; ***without mishap*** ohne Zwischenfälle
mis·in·form falsch unterrichten
mis·in·ter·pret missdeuten, falsch auffassen *or* auslegen
mis·lay *et.* verlegen
mis·lead irreführen, täuschen; verleiten
mis·man·age schlecht verwalten *or* führen *or* handhaben
mis·place *et.* an e-e falsche Stelle legen *or* setzen; *et.* verlegen; ***misplaced*** *fig* unangebracht, deplatziert
mis·print **1.** verdrucken; **2.** Druckfehler *m*
mis·read falsch lesen; falsch deuten, missdeuten
mis·rep·re·sent falsch darstellen; entstellen, verdrehen
miss **1.** *v/t* verpassen, versäumen, verfehlen; übersehen, nicht bemerken; überhören; nicht verstehen *or* begreifen; vermissen; *a.* ***miss out*** auslassen, übergehen, überspringen; *v/i* nicht treffen; missglücken; ***miss out on*** *et.* verpassen; **2.** Fehlschuss *m*, Fehlstoß *m*, Fehlwurf *m etc*; Verpassen *n*, Verfehlen *n*
Miss Fräulein *n*

mis·shap·en missgebildet
mis·sile **1.** Geschoss *n*; Rakete *f*; **2.** Raketen…
miss·ing fehlend; ***be missing*** fehlen, verschwunden *or* weg sein; (MIL *a.* ***missing in action***) vermisst; ***be missing*** MIL vermisst sein *or* werden
mis·sion (*Militär- etc*)Mission *f*; *esp* POL Auftrag *m*, Mission *f* (*a.* REL); MIL, AVIAT Einsatz *m*
mis·sion·a·ry REL Missionar *m*
mis·spell falsch buchstabieren *or* schreiben
mis·spend falsch verwenden; vergeuden
mist **1.** (feiner *or* leichter) Nebel; **2.** ***mist over*** sich trüben; ***mist up*** (sich) beschlagen
mis·take **1.** verwechseln (***for*** mit); verkennen, sich irren in (*dat*); falsch verstehen, missverstehen; **2.** Irrtum *m*, Versehen *n*, Fehler *m*; ***by mistake*** aus Versehen, irrtümlich
mis·tak·en irrig, falsch (verstanden); ***be mistaken*** sich irren
mis·tle·toe BOT Mistel *f*
mis·tress Herrin *f*; *esp Br* Lehrerin *f*; Geliebte *f*
mis·trust **1.** misstrauen (*dat*); **2.** Misstrauen *n* (***of*** gegen)
mis·trust·ful misstrauisch
mist·y (leicht) neb(e)lig; *fig* unklar, verschwommen
mis·un·der·stand missverstehen; *j-n* nicht verstehen
mis·un·der·standing Missverständnis *n*
mis·use **1.** missbrauchen; falsch gebrauchen; **2.** Missbrauch *m*
mite zo Milbe *f*; kleines Ding, Würmchen *n*; ***a mite*** F ein bisschen
mi·ter, *Br* **mi·tre** REL Mitra *f*, Bischofsmütze *f*
mitt *baseball*: Fanghandschuh *m*; → **mitten** Fausthandschuh *m*
mix **1.** (ver)mischen, vermengen; *Getränke* mixen; sich (ver)mischen; sich mischen lassen; verkehren (***with*** mit); ***mix well*** kontaktfreudig sein; ***mix up*** zusammenmischen, durcheinander mischen; (völlig) durcheinanderbringen; verwechseln (***with*** mit); ***be mixed up*** verwickelt sein *or* werden (***in*** in *acc*); (*geistig*) ganz durcheinander sein; **2.** Mischung *f*
mixed gemischt (*a. fig*); vermischt, Misch…
mix·er Mixer *m*; TECH Mischmaschine *f*; *radio*, TV *etc*: Mischpult *n*
mix·ture Mischung *f*; Gemisch *n*
mix-up F Verwechs(e)lung *f*
moan **1.** Stöhnen *n*; **2.** stöhnen
moat (Burg-, Stadt)Graben *m*
mob **1.** Mob *m*, Pöbel *m*; **2.** herfallen über (*acc*); *j-n* bedrängen, belagern
mo·bile **1.** beweglich; MIL mobil, motorisiert; *fig* lebhaft; **2.** → ***mobile phone*** *or* ***telephone***
mobile home Wohnwagen *m*
mobile phone, **mobile tel·e·phone** Mobiltelefon *n*, Handy *n*
mo·bil·ize mobilisieren, MIL *a.* mobil machen
moc·ca·sin Mokassin *m*
mock **1.** *v/t* verspotten; nachäffen; *v/i* sich lustig machen, spotten (***at*** über *acc*); **2.** nachgemacht, Schein…
mock·e·ry Spott *m*, Hohn *m*; Gespött *n*
mock·ing·bird zo Spottdrossel *f*
mode (Art *f* und) Weise *f*; EDP Modus *m*, Betriebsart *f*
mod·el **1.** Modell *n*; Muster *n*; Vorbild *n*; Mannequin *n*; Model *n*, (Foto)Modell *n*; TECH Modell *n*, Typ *m*; ***male model*** Dressman *m*; **2.** Modell…, Muster…; **3.** *v/t* modellieren, *a. fig* formen; *Kleider etc* vorführen; *v/i* Modell stehen *or* sitzen; als Mannequin *or* (Foto)Modell *or* Dressman arbeiten
mo·dem EDP Modem *m*, *n*
mod·e·rate **1.** (mittel)mäßig; gemäßigt; vernünftig, angemessen; **2.** (sich) mäßigen
mod·e·ra·tion Mäßigung *f*
mod·ern modern, neu
mod·ern·ize modernisieren
mod·est bescheiden
mod·es·ty Bescheidenheit *f*
mod·i·fi·ca·tion (Ab-, Ver)Änderung *f*
mod·i·fy (ab-, ver)ändern
mod·u·late modulieren
mod·ule TECH Modul *n*, ELECTR *a.* Baustein *m*; (*Kommando- etc*)Kapsel *f*
moist feucht
moist·en *v/t* anfeuchten, befeuchten; *v/i* feucht werden
mois·ture Feuchtigkeit *f*
mo·lar ANAT Backenzahn *m*
mo·las·ses Sirup *m*
mold[1] Schimmel *m*; Moder *m*; Humus (-boden) *m*
mold[2] TECH **1.** (Gieß-, Guss-, Press-) Form *f*; **2.** gießen; formen
mol·der *a.* ***molder away*** vermodern; zerfallen
mold·y verschimmelt, schimm(e)lig; mod(e)rig
mole[1] zo Maulwurf *m*
mole[2] Muttermal *n*, Leberfleck *m*
mole[3] Mole *f*, Hafendamm *m*
mol·e·cule Molekül *n*

M

mole·hill Maulwurfshügel *m*; ***make a mountain out of a molehill*** aus e-r Mücke e-n Elefanten machen
mo·lest belästigen
mol·li·fy besänftigen, beschwichtigen
mol·lusc *Br*, **mol·lusk** ZO Weichtier *n*
mol·ly·cod·dle F verhätscheln, verzärteln
molt (sich) mausern; *Haare* verlieren
mol·ten geschmolzen
mom F Mami *f*, Mutti *f*
mom-and-pop store Tante-Emma-Laden *m*
mo·ment Moment *m*, Augenblick *m*; Bedeutung *f*; PHYS Moment *n*
mo·men·ta·ry momentan, augenblicklich
mo·men·tous bedeutsam, folgenschwer
mo·men·tum PHYS Moment *n*; Schwung *m*
Mon ABBR *of* ***Monday*** Mo., Montag *m*
mon·arch Monarch(in), Herrscher(in)
mon·ar·chy Monarchie *f*
mon·as·tery REL (Mönchs)Kloster *n*
Mon·day (ABBR ***Mon***) Montag *m*; ***on Monday*** (am) Montag; ***on Mondays*** montags
mon·e·ta·ry ECON Währungs…; Geld…
mon·ey Geld *n*
mon·ey·box *Br* Sparbüchse *f*
mon·ey·chang·er (Geld)Wechsler *m*; TECH Wechselautomat *m*
mon·ey or·der Post- *or* Zahlungsanweisung *f*
mon·grel ZO Bastard *m*, *esp* Promenadenmischung *f*
mon·i·tor **1.** Monitor *m*; Kontrollgerät *n*, -schirm *m*; **2.** abhören; überwachen
monk REL Mönch *m*
mon·key **1.** ZO Affe *m*; F (kleiner) Schlingel; ***make a monkey (out) of s.o.*** F j-n zum Deppen machen; **2.** ***monkey about, monkey around*** F (herum)albern; ***monkey about*** *or* ***around with*** F herumspielen mit *or* an (*dat*) herummurksen an (*dat*)
monkey wrench TECH Engländer *m*, Franzose *m*; ***throw a monkey wrench into s.th.*** F et. behindern
mon·o **1.** Mono *n*; F Monogerät *n*; F Monoschallplatte *f*; **2.** Mono…
mon·o… ein…, mono…
mon·o·log, *esp Br* **mon·o·logue** Monolog *m*
mo·nop·o·lize monopolisieren; *fig* an sich reißen
mo·nop·o·ly Monopol *n* (***of*** auf *acc*)
mo·not·o·nous monoton, eintönig
mo·not·o·ny Monotonie *f*
mon·soon Monsun *m*
mon·ster **1.** Monster *n*, Ungeheuer *n* (*a. fig*); Monstrum *n*; **2.** Riesen…
mon·stros·i·ty Ungeheuerlichkeit *f*; Momstrum *n*
mon·strous ungeheuer; *mst contp* ungeheuerlich; scheußlich
month Monat *m*
month·ly **1.** monatlich, Monats…; **2.** Monatsschrift *f*
mon·u·ment Monument *n*, Denkmal *n*
mon·u·ment·al monumental; F kolossal, Riesen…; Gedenk…
moo ZO muhen
mooch F schnorren
mood Stimmung *f*, Laune *f*; ***be in a good (bad) mood*** gute (schlechte) Laune haben, gut (schlecht) aufgelegt sein
mood·y launisch; schlecht gelaunt
moon **1.** ASTR Mond *m*; **2.** ***moon about, moon around*** F herumtrödeln; F ziellos herumstreichen
moon·light Mondlicht *n*, -schein *m*
moon·lit mondhell
moor[1] (Hoch)Moor *n*
moor[2] MAR vertäuen, festmachen
moor·ings MAR Vertäuung *f*; Liegeplatz *m*
moose ZO *nordamerikanischer* Elch
mop **1.** Mopp *m*; F (Haar)Wust *m*; **2.** wischen; ***mop up*** aufwischen
mope Trübsal blasen
mo·ped *Br* MOT Moped *n*
mor·al **1.** moralisch; Moral…, Sitten…; **2.** Moral *f*, Lehre *f*; *pl* Moral *f*, Sitten *pl*
mo·rale Moral *f*, Stimmung *f*
mor·al·ize moralisieren (***about, on*** über *acc*)
mor·bid morbid, krankhaft
more **1.** *adj* mehr; noch (mehr); ***some more tea*** noch etwas Tee; **2.** *adv* mehr; noch; ***more and more*** immer mehr; ***more or less*** mehr oder weniger; ***once more*** noch einmal; ***the more so because*** umso mehr, da; ***more important*** wichtiger; ***more often*** öfter; **3.** Mehr *n* (***of*** an *dat*); ***a little more*** etwas mehr
mo·rel BOT Morchel *f*
more·o·ver außerdem, weiter, ferner
morgue Leichenschauhaus *n*; F (Zeitungs)Archiv *n*
morn·ing Morgen *m*; Vormittag *m*; ***good morning!*** guten Morgen!; ***in the morning*** morgens, am Morgen; vormittags, am Vormittag; ***tomorrow morning*** morgen früh *or* Vormittag
mo·rose mürrisch, verdrießlich
mor·phi·a, **mor·phine** PHARM Morphium *n*
mor·sel Bissen *m*, Happen *m*; ***a morsel of*** ein bisschen
mor·tal **1.** sterblich; tödlich; Tod(es)…; **2.** Sterbliche *m*, *f*

mor·tal·i·ty Sterblichkeit *f*
mor·tar[1] Mörtel *m*
mor·tar[2] Mörser *m*
mort·gage 1. Hypothek *f*; **2.** mit e-r Hypothek belasten, e-e Hypothek aufnehmen auf (*acc*)
mor·ti·cian Leichenbestatter *m*
mor·ti·fi·ca·tion Kränkung *f*; Ärger *m*, Verdruss *m*
mor·ti·fy kränken; ärgern, verdrießen
mor·tu·a·ry Leichenhalle *f*
mo·sa·ic Mosaik *n*
Mos·lem → ***Muslim***
mosque Moschee *f*
mos·qui·to ZO Moskito *m*; Stechmücke *f*
moss BOT Moos *n*
moss·y BOT moosig, bemoost
most 1. *adj* meiste(r, -s), größte(r, -s); die meisten; ***most people*** die meisten Leute; **2.** *adv* am meisten; ***most of all*** am allermeisten; *before adj*: höchst, äußerst; ***the most important point*** der wichtigste Punkt; **3.** *das* meiste, *das* Höchste; das meiste, der größte Teil; die meisten *pl*; ***at (the) most*** höchstens; ***make the most of*** *et.* nach Kräften ausnutzen, das Beste herausholen aus
most·ly hauptsächlich, meist(ens)
mo·tel Motel *n*
moth ZO Motte *f*
moth-eat·en mottenzerfressen
moth·er 1. Mutter *f*; **2.** bemuttern
moth·er coun·try Vaterland *n*, Heimatland *n*; Mutterland *n*
moth·er·hood Mutterschaft *f*
moth·er-in-law Schwiegermutter *f*
moth·er·ly mütterlich
moth·er-of-pearl Perlmutter *f*, *n*, Perlmutt *n*
moth·er tongue Muttersprache *f*
mo·tif Motiv *n*
mo·tion 1. Bewegung *f*; PARL Antrag *m*; ***in quick motion*** *film*: im Zeitraffer; ***in slow motion*** *film*: in Zeitlupe; ***put*** *or* ***set in motion*** in Gang bringen (*a. fig*), in Bewegung setzen; **2.** *v/t j-n* durch e-n Wink auffordern, *j-m* ein Zeichen geben; *v/i* winken
mo·tion·less bewegungslos, unbeweglich
mo·tion pic·ture Film *m*
mo·ti·vate motivieren, anspornen
mo·ti·va·tion Motivation *f*, Ansporn *m*
mo·tive 1. Motiv *n*, Beweggrund *m*; **2.** treibend (*a. fig*)
mot·ley bunt
mo·to·cross SPORT Motocross *n*
mo·tor 1. Motor *m*, *fig a.* treibende Kraft; **2.** Motor…
mo·tor·bike Moped *n*; *Br* F Motorrad *n*
mo·tor·boat Motorboot *n*
mo·tor·cade Auto-, Wagenkolonne *f*
mo·tor·car *Br* Kraftfahrzeug *n*
mo·tor car·a·van *Br* Wohnmobil *n*
mo·tor·cy·cle Motorrad *n*
mo·tor·cy·clist Motorradfahrer(in)
mo·tor home Wohnmobil *n*
mo·tor·ing Autofahren *n*; ***school of motoring*** Fahrschule *f*
mo·tor·ist Autofahrer(in)
mo·tor·ize motorisieren
mo·tor launch Motorbarkasse *f*
mo·tor·way *Br* Autobahn *f*
mot·tled gefleckt, gesprenkelt
mould[1] *Br* → ***mold***[1]
mould[2] *Br* → ***mold***[2]
moul·der *Br* → ***molder***
mould·y *Br* → ***moldy***
moult *Br* → ***molt***
mound Erdhügel *m*, Erdwall *m*
mount 1. *v/t Pferd etc* besteigen, steigen auf (*acc*); montieren; anbringen, befestigen; *Bild etc* aufziehen, aufkleben; *Edelstein* fassen; ***mounted police*** berittene Polizei; *v/i* aufsitzen (*rider*); steigen, *fig a.* (an)wachsen; ***mount up to*** sich belaufen auf (*acc*); **2.** Gestell *n*; Fassung *f*; Reittier *n*, Reitpferd *n*
moun·tain 1. Berg *m*, *pl a.* Gebirge *n*; **2.** Berg…, Gebirgs…
moun·tain bike Mountainbike *n*
moun·tain·eer Bergsteiger(in)
moun·tain·eer·ing Bergsteigen *n*
moun·tain·ous bergig, gebirgig
mourn *v/i* trauern (***for, over*** um); *v/t* betrauern, trauern um
mourn·er Trauernde *m*, *f*
mourn·ful traurig
mourn·ing Trauer *f*; Trauerkleidung *f*
mouse ZO Maus *f* (*a.* EDP)
mous·tache → ***mustache***
mouth Mund *m*; ZO Maul *n*, Schnauze *f*; GEOGR Mündung *f*; Öffnung *f*
mouth·ful *ein* Mundvoll; Bissen *m*
mouth or·gan F Mundharmonika *f*
mouth·piece Mundstück *n*; *fig* Sprachrohr *n*
mouth·wash Mundwasser *n*
mo·va·ble beweglich
move 1. *v/t* (weg)rücken; transportieren; bewegen, rühren (*both a. fig*); *chess etc*: e-n Zug machen mit; PARL beantragen; ***move house*** umziehen; ***move heaven and earth*** Himmel und Hölle in Bewegung setzen; *v/i* sich (fort)bewegen; sich rühren; umziehen (***to*** nach); *chess etc*: e-n Zug machen; ***move away*** weg-, fortziehen; ***move in*** einziehen; ***move off*** sich in Bewegung setzen;

move on weitergehen; ***move out*** ausziehen; **2.** Bewegung *f*; Umzug *m*; *chess etc*: Zug *m*; *fig* Schritt *m*; ***on the move*** in Bewegung; auf den Beinen; ***get a move on!*** F Tempo!, mach(t) schon!, los!
move·a·ble → ***movable***
move·ment Bewegung *f* (*a. fig*); MUS Satz *m*; TECH Werk *n*
mov·ie **1.** Film *m*; Kino *n*; **2.** Film…, Kino…
movie cam·e·ra Filmkamera *f*
movie star Filmstar *m*
movie thea·ter Kino *n*
mov·ing sich bewegend, beweglich; *fig* rührend
moving stair·case Rolltreppe *f*
moving van Möbelwagen *m*
mow mähen
mow·er Mähmaschine *f*, *esp* Rasenmäher *m*
Mr. ABBR *of* ***Mister*** Herr *m*
Mrs. Frau *f*
Ms. Frau *f*
much **1.** *adj* viel; **2.** *adv* sehr; viel; ***much better*** viel besser; ***very much*** sehr; ***I thought as much*** das habe ich mir gedacht; **3.** große Sache; ***nothing much*** nichts Besonderes; ***make much of*** viel Wesens machen von; ***think much of*** viel halten von; ***I am not much of a dancer*** F ich bin kein großer Tänzer
muck F *Br* AGR Mist *m*, Dung *m*; *fig* Dreck *m*, Schmutz *m*; F *contp* Fraß *m*
mu·cus (Nasen)Schleim *m*
mud Schlamm *m*, Matsch *m*; Schmutz *m* (*a. fig*)
mud·dle **1.** Durcheinander *n*; ***be in a muddle*** durcheinander sein; **2.** *a.* ***muddle up*** durcheinanderbringen; ***muddle through*** F sich durchwursteln
mud·dy schlammig, trüb; schmutzig; *fig* wirr
mud·guard Kotflügel *m*; Schutzblech *n*
mues·li Müsli *n*
muff Muff *m*
muf·fle *Ton etc* dämpfen; *often* ***muffle up*** einhüllen, einwickeln
muf·fler (dicker) Schal; MOT Auspufftopf *m*
mug[1] Krug *m*; Becher *m*; große Tasse; F Visage *f*; V Fresse *f*
mug[2] F überfallen und ausrauben
mug·ger F (Straßen)Räuber *m*
mug·ging F Raubüberfall *m*, *esp* Straßenraub *m*
mug·gy schwül
mul·ber·ry BOT Maulbeerbaum *m*; Maulbeere *f*
mule ZO Maultier *n*; Maulesel *m*
mulled: ***mulled wine*** Glühwein *m*
mul·li·on ARCH Mittelpfosten *m*
mul·ti… viel…, mehr…, Mehrfach…, Multi…
mul·ti·cul·tur·al multikulturell
mul·ti·far·i·ous mannigfaltig, vielfältig
mul·ti·lat·e·ral vielseitig; POL multilateral, mehrseitig
mul·ti·me·di·a multimedial
mul·ti·na·tion·al ECON multinationaler Konzern, F Multi *m*
mul·ti·ple **1.** vielfach, mehrfach; **2.** MATH Vielfache *n*
mul·ti·pli·ca·tion Vermehrung *f*; MATH Multiplikation *f*
multiplication table Einmaleins *n*
mul·ti·pli·ci·ty Vielfalt *f*; Vielzahl *f*
mul·ti·ply (sich) vermehren, (sich) vervielfachen; MATH multiplizieren, malnehmen (***by*** mit)
mul·ti·pur·pose Mehrzweck…
mul·ti·sto·rey *Br* mehrstöckig
multistorey car park *Br* Park(hoch)haus *n*
mul·ti·tude Vielzahl *f*
mul·ti·tu·di·nous zahlreich
mum[1] *Br* F Mami *f*, Mutti *f*
mum[2] **1.** *int*: ***mum's the word*** Mund halten!, kein Wort darüber!; **2.** *adj*: ***keep mum*** nichts verraten, den Mund halten
mum·ble murmeln, F nuscheln; mümmeln
mum·mi·fy mumifizieren
mum·my[1] Mumie *f*
mum·my[2] *Br* F Mami *f*, Mutti *f*
mumps MED Ziegenpeter *m*, Mumps *m*
munch mampfen
mun·dane alltäglich; weltlich
mu·ni·ci·pal städtisch, Stadt…, kommunal, Gemeinde…; ***municipal council*** Stadt-, Gemeinderat *m*
mu·ni·ci·pal·i·ty Kommunalbehörde *f*; Stadtverwaltung *f*
mu·ral Wandgemälde *n*
mur·der **1.** Mord *m*, Ermordung *f*; **2.** Mord…; **3.** ermorden; F verschandeln
mur·der·er Mörder *m*
mur·der·ess Mörderin *f*
mur·der·ous mörderisch
murk·y dunkel, finster
mur·mur **1.** Murmeln *n*; Gemurmel *n*; Murren *n*; **2.** murmeln; murren
mus·cle Muskel *m*
mus·cu·lar Muskel…; muskulös
muse[1] (nach)sinnen, (nach)grübeln (***on, over*** über *acc*)
muse[2] *a.* ***Muse*** Muse *f*
mu·se·um Museum *n*
mush Brei *m*, Mus *n*; Maisbrei *m*
mush·room **1.** BOT Pilz *m*, *esp* Champig-

M

non *m*; **2.** rasch wachsen; ***mushroom up*** *fig* (wie Pilze) aus dem Boden schießen
mu·sic Musik *f*; Noten *pl*; ***put*** *or* ***set to music*** vertonen
mu·sic·al 1. musikalisch; Musik…; **2.** Musical *n*
musical box *esp Br* Spieldose *f*
musical in·stru·ment Musikinstrument *n*
mu·sic box Spieldose *f*
music cen·ter (*Br* **cen·ter**) Kompaktanlage *f*
music hall *Br* Varietee(theater) *n*
mu·si·cian Musiker(in)
mu·sic stand Notenständer *m*
musk Moschus *m*
musk·rat ZO Bisamratte *f*; Bisampelz *m*
Mus·lim 1. Muslim *m*, Moslem *m*; **2.** muslimisch, moslemisch
mus·sel ZO (Mies)Muschel *f*
must[1] 1. *v/aux* ich muss, *du* musst *etc*; ***you must not*** (F ***mustn't***) du darfst nicht; **2.** Muss *n*
must[2] Most *m*
mus·tache Schnurrbart *m*
mus·tard Senf *m*
mus·ter 1. ***muster up*** *s-e Kraft etc* aufbieten; *s-n Mut* zusammennehmen; **2.** ***pass muster*** *fig* Zustimmung finden (***with*** bei); den Anforderungen genügen
must·y mod(e)rig, muffig
mu·ta·tion Veränderung *f*; BIOL Mutation *f*
mute 1. stumm; **2.** Stumme *m, f*; MUS Dämpfer *m*
mu·ti·late verstümmeln
mu·ti·la·tion Verstümmelung *f*
mu·ti·neer Meuterer *m*
mu·ti·nous meuternd; rebellisch
mu·ti·ny 1. Meuterei *f*; **2.** meutern
mut·ter 1. murmeln; murren; **2.** Murmeln *n*; Murren *n*
mut·ton GASTR Hammel-, Schaffleisch *n*; ***leg of mutton*** Hammelkeule *f*
mut·ton chop GASTR Hammelkotelett *n*
mu·tu·al gegenseitig; gemeinsam
muz·zle 1. ZO Maul *n*, Schnauze *f*; Mündung *f* (*of a gun*); Maulkorb *m*; **2.** e-n Maulkorb anlegen (*dat*), *fig a. j-n* mundtot machen
my mein(e)
myrrh BOT Myrrhe *f*
myr·tle BOT Myrte *f*
my·self ich, mich *or* mir selbst; mich; mich (selbst); ***by myself*** allein
mys·te·ri·ous rätselhaft, unerklärlich; geheimnisvoll, mysteriös
mys·te·ry Geheimnis *n*, Rätsel *n*; REL Mysterium *n*; ***mystery tour*** Fahrt *f* ins Blaue
mys·tic 1. Mystiker(in); **2.** → **mystic·al** mystisch
mys·ti·fy verwirren, vor ein Rätsel stellen; ***be mystified*** vor e-m Rätsel stehen
myth Mythos *m*, Sage *f*
my·thol·o·gy Mythologie *f*

N

N, n N, n *n*
nab F schnappen, erwischen
na·dir ASTR Nadir *m*; *fig* Tiefpunkt *m*
nag[1] 1. nörgeln; ***nag (at)*** herumnörgeln an (*dat*); **2.** Nörgler(in)
nag[2] F Gaul *m*, Klepper *m*
nail 1. ANAT, TECH Nagel *m*; **2.** (an-)nageln (***to*** an *acc*)
nail pol·ish Nagellack *m*
nail scis·sors Nagelschere *f*
nail var·nish *Br* Nagellack *m*
na·ive, na·ïve naiv (*a. art*)
na·ked nackt, bloß; kahl; *fig* ungeschminkt
nak·ed·ness Nacktheit *f*
name 1. Name *m*; Ruf *m*; ***by name*** mit Namen, namentlich; ***by the name of*** ... namens ...; ***what's your name?*** wie heißen Sie?; ***call s.o. names*** j-n beschimpfen; **2.** (be)nennen; erwähnen; ernennen zu
name·less namenlos; unbekannt
name·ly nämlich
name·plate Namens-, Tür-, Firmenschild *n*
name·sake Namensvetter *m*, Namensschwester *f*
name tag Namensschild *n*
nan·ny Kindermädchen *n*
nan·ny goat ZO Geiß *f*, Ziege *f*
nap 1. Schläfchen *n*; ***have*** *or* ***take a nap*** → **2.** ein Nickerchen machen

nape *mst* ***nape of the neck*** ANAT Genick *n*, Nacken *m*
nap·kin Serviette *f*
nap·py *Br* Windel *f*
nar·co·sis MED Narkose *f*
nar·cot·ic **1.** narkotisch, betäubend, einschläfernd; Rauschgift…; ***narcotic addiction*** Rauschgiftsucht *f*; **2.** Narkotikum *n*, Betäubungsmittel *n*; *often pl* Rauschgift *n*; ***narcotics squad*** Rauschgiftdezernat *n*
nar·rate erzählen; berichten, schildern
nar·ra·tion Erzählung *f*
nar·ra·tive **1.** Erzählung *f*; Bericht *m*, Schilderung *f*; **2.** erzählend
nar·ra·tor Erzähler(in)
nar·row **1.** eng, schmal; beschränkt; knapp; **2.** enger *or* schmäler werden *or* machen, (sich) verengen; beschränken, einschränken
nar·row·ly mit knapper Not
nar·row-mind·ed engstirnig, beschränkt
nar·row·ness Enge *f*; Beschränktheit *f*
na·sal nasal; Nasen…
nas·ty ekelhaft, eklig, widerlich (*smell, sight etc*); abscheulich (*weather etc*); böse, schlimm (*accident etc*); hässlich (*character, behavior etc*); gemein, fies; schmutzig, zotig (*language*)
na·tal Geburts…
na·tion Nation *f*, Volk *n*
na·tion·al **1.** national, National…, Landes…, Volks…; **2.** Staatsangehörige *m, f*
national an·them Nationalhymne *f*
na·tion·al·i·ty Nationalität *f*, Staatsangehörigkeit *f*
na·tion·al·ize ECON verstaatlichen
na·tion·al park Nationalpark *m*
national so·cial·ism HIST POL Nationalsozialismus *m*
national so·cial·ist HIST POL Nationalsozialist *m*
national team SPORT Nationalmannschaft *f*
na·tion-wide landesweit
na·tive **1.** einheimisch, Landes…; heimatlich, Heimat…; eingeboren, Eingeborenen…; angeboren; **2.** Eingeborene *m, f*; Einheimische *m, f*
native lan·guage Muttersprache *f*
native speak·er Muttersprachler(in)
Na·tiv·i·ty REL *die* Geburt Christi
nat·ty F schick, *Austrian* fesch
nat·u·ral natürlich; angeboren; Natur…
natural gas Erdgas *n*
nat·u·ral·ize naturalisieren, einbürgern
nat·u·ral·ly natürlich; von Natur (aus)
nat·u·ral re·sourc·es Boden- u. Naturschätze *pl*
natural sci·ence Naturwissenschaft *f*
na·ture Natur *f*
nature con·ser·va·tion Naturschutz *m*
nature re·serve Naturschutzgebiet *n*
nature trail Naturlehrpfad *m*
naugh·ty unartig; unanständig
nau·se·a Übelkeit *f*, Brechreiz *m*
nau·se·ate: ***nauseate s.o.*** j-m Übelkeit verursachen; *fig* j-n anwidern
nau·se·at·ing ekelerregend, widerlich
nau·ti·cal nautisch, See…
na·val MIL Flotten…, Marine…; See…
naval base MIL Flottenstützpunkt *m*
naval offi·cer MIL Marineoffizier *m*
naval pow·er MIL Seemacht *f*
nave ARCH Mittel-, Hauptschiff *n*
na·vel ANAT Nabel *m* (*a. fig*)
nav·i·ga·ble schiffbar
nav·i·gate MAR befahren; AVIAT, MAR steuern, lenken
nav·i·ga·tion Schifffahrt *f*; AVIAT, MAR Navigation *f*
nav·i·ga·tor AVIAT, MAR Navigator *m*
na·vy (Kriegs)Marine *f*; Kriegsflotte *f*
na·vy blue Marineblau *n*
nay PARL Gegen-, Neinstimme *f*
Na·zi HIST POL *contp* Nazi *m*
Na·zism HIST POL *contp* Nazismus *m*
near **1.** *adj* nahe; kurz; nahe (verwandt); ***in the near future*** in naher Zukunft; ***be a near miss*** knapp scheitern; **2.** *adv* nahe, in der Nähe (*a.* ***near at hand***); nahe (bevorstehend) (*a.* ***near at hand***); beinahe, fast; ***near the station*** *etc* in der Nähe des Bahnhofs *etc*; ***near you*** in deiner Nähe; **3.** *prp* nahe (*dat*), in der Nähe von (*or gen*); **4.** sich nähern, näher kommen (*dat*)
near·by **1.** *adj* nahe (gelegen); **2.** *adv* in der Nähe
near·ly beinahe, fast; annähernd
near·sight·ed kurzsichtig
neat ordentlich; sauber; gepflegt; pur (*whisky etc*)
neb·u·lous verschwommen
ne·ces·sar·i·ly notwendigerweise; ***not necessarily*** nicht unbedingt
ne·ces·sa·ry notwendig, nötig; unvermeidlich
ne·ces·si·tate *et.* erfordern, verlangen
ne·ces·si·ty Notwendigkeit *f*; (dringendes) Bedürfnis; Not *f*
neck **1.** ANAT Hals *m* (*a. of bottle etc*); Genick *n*, Nacken *m*; ***be neck and neck*** F Kopf an Kopf liegen (*a. fig*); ***be up to one's neck in debt*** F bis zum Hals in Schulden stecken; **2.** F knutschen, schmusen
neck·er·chief Halstuch *n*
neck·lace Halskette *f*

neck·let Halskettchen *n*
neck·line Ausschnitt *m*
neck·tie Krawatte *f*, Schlips *m*
née: ***née Smith*** geborene Smith
need **1.** (***of, for***) (dringendes) Bedürfnis (nach), Bedarf *m* (an *dat*); Notwendigkeit *f*; Mangel *m* (***of, for*** an *dat*); Not *f*; ***be in need of s.th.*** et. dringend brauchen; ***in need*** in Not; ***in need of help*** hilfs-, hilfebedürftig; **2.** *v/t* benötigen, brauchen; *v/aux* brauchen, müssen
nee·dle **1.** Nadel *f* (*a.* BOT, MED); Zeiger *m*; **2.** F *j-n* aufziehen, hänseln
need·less unnötig, überflüssig
nee·dle·wom·an Näherin *f*
nee·dle·work Handarbeit *f*
need·y bedürftig, arm
ne·ga·tion Verneinung *f*
neg·a·tive **1.** negativ; verneinend; **2.** Verneinung *f*; PHOT Negativ *n*; ***answer in the negative*** verneinen
ne·glect **1.** vernachlässigen; es versäumen (***doing, to do*** zu tun); **2.** Vernachlässigung *f*; Nachlässigkeit *f*
neg·li·gence Nachlässigkeit *f*, Unachtsamkeit *f*
neg·li·gent nachlässig, unachtsam; lässig, salopp
neg·li·gi·ble unbedeutend
ne·go·ti·ate verhandeln (über *acc*)
ne·go·ti·a·tion Verhandlung *f*
ne·go·ti·a·tor Unterhändler(in)
neigh zo **1.** wiehern; **2.** Wiehern *n*
neigh·bo(u)r Nachbar(in)
neigh·bo(u)r·hood Nachbarschaft *f*, Umgebung *f*
neigh·bo(u)r·ing benachbart, Nachbar…, angrenzend
neigh·bo(u)r·ly (gut)nachbarlich
nei·ther **1.** *adj and pron* keine(r, -s) (von beiden); **2.** *cj* ***neither … nor*** weder … noch
ne·on CHEM Neon *n*
neon lamp Neonlampe *f*
neon sign Neon-, Leuchtreklame *f*
neph·ew Neffe *m*
nep·o·tism *contp* Vetternwirtschaft *f*
nerd F Trottel *m*; Computerfreak *m*
nerve Nerv *m*; Mut *m*, Stärke *f*, Selbstbeherrschung *f*; F Frechheit *f*; ***get on s.o.'s nerves*** j-m auf die Nerven gehen *or* fallen; ***lose one's nerve*** den Mut *or* die Nerven verlieren; ***you've got a nerve!*** F Sie haben Nerven!
nerve·less kraftlos; mutlos; ohne Nerven, kaltblütig
ner·vous nervös; Nerven…
ner·vous·ness Nervosität *f*
nest **1.** Nest *n*; **2.** nisten
nes·tle (sich) schmiegen *or* kuscheln (***against, on*** an *acc*); *a.* ***nestle down*** sich behaglich niederlassen, es sich bequem machen (***in*** in *dat*)
net[1] **1.** Netz *n*; ***net curtain*** Store *m*; **2.** mit e-m Netz fangen *or* abdecken
net[2] **1.** netto, Netto…, Rein…; **2.** netto einbringen
Neth·er·lands *die* Niederlande *pl*
net·tle **1.** BOT Nessel *f*; **2.** F *j-n* ärgern
net·work Netz *n* (*a.* EDP), Netzwerk *n*; (*Straßen- etc*)Netz *n*; *radio*, TV Sendernetz *n*; ***be in the network*** EDP am Netz sein
neu·ro·sis MED Neurose *f*
neu·rot·ic MED **1.** neurotisch; **2.** Neurotiker(in)
neu·ter **1.** LING sächlich; geschlechtslos; **2.** LING Neutrum *n*
neu·tral **1.** neutral; **2.** Neutrale *m*, *f*; *a.* ***neutral gear*** MOT Leerlauf(stellung *f*) *m*
neu·tral·i·ty Neutralität *f*
neu·tral·ize neutralisieren
neu·tron PHYS Neutron *n*
nev·er nie, niemals
nev·er-end·ing endlos, nicht enden wollend, unendlich
nev·er·the·less nichtsdestoweniger, dennoch, trotzdem
new neu; frisch; unerfahren; ***nothing new*** nichts Neues
new·born neugeboren
new·com·er Neuankömmling *m*; Neuling *m*
new·ly kürzlich; neu
news Neuigkeit(en *pl*) *f*, Nachricht(en *pl*) *f*
news·a·gent Zeitungshändler(in)
news·boy Zeitungsjunge *m*, Zeitungsausträger *m*
news bul·le·tin Kurznachricht(en *pl*) *f*
news·cast *radio*, TV Nachrichtensendung *f*
news·cast·er *radio*, TV Nachrichtensprecher(in)
news deal·er Zeitungshändler(in)
news·flash *radio*, TV Kurzmeldung *f*
news·let·ter Rundschreiben *n*
news·pa·per Zeitung *f*
news·print Zeitungspapier *n*
news·read·er *esp Br* → ***newscaster***
news·reel *film*: Wochenschau *f*
news·room Nachrichtenredaktion *f*
news·stand Zeitungskiosk *m*, -stand *m*
news·ven·dor *esp Br* Zeitungsverkäufer(in)
new year Neujahr *n*, *das* neue Jahr; ***New Year's Day*** Neujahrstag *m*; ***New Year's Eve*** Silvester(abend *m*) *m*, *n*

next **1.** *adj* nächste(r, -s); **(*the*) *next day*** am nächsten Tag; ***next door*** nebenan; ***next but one*** übernächste(r, -s); ***next to*** gleich neben *or* nach; beinahe, fast *unmöglich etc*; **2.** *adv* als Nächste(r, -s); demnächst, das nächste Mal; **3.** *der, die, das* Nächste; → ***kin***
next-door (von) nebenan
nib·ble *v/i* knabbern (***at*** an *dat*); *v/t Loch etc* nagen, knabbern (***in*** in *acc*)
nice nett, freundlich; hübsch, schön; *fig* fein (*detail etc*)
nice·ly gut, fein; genau, sorgfältig
ni·ce·ty Feinheit *f*; Genauigkeit *f*
niche Nische *f*
nick **1.** Kerbe *f*; ***in the nick of time*** gerade noch rechtzeitig, im letzten Moment; **2.** (ein)kerben; *j-n* streifen (*bullet*); *Br* F *et.* klauen; *Br* F *j-n* schnappen
nick·el **1.** MIN Nickel *n*; Fünfcentstück *n*; **2.** TECH vernickeln
nick·el-plate TECH vernickeln
nick-nack → ***knick-knack***
nick·name **1.** Spitzname *m*; **2.** *j-m* den Spitznamen … geben
niece Nichte *f*
nig·gard Geizhals *m*
nig·gard·ly geizig, knaus(e)rig; schäbig, kümmerlich
night Nacht *f*; Abend *m*; ***at night, by night, in the night*** in der Nacht, nachts
night·cap Schlummertrunk *m*
night·club Nachtklub *m*, Nachtlokal *n*
night·dress (Damen-, Kinder)Nachthemd *n*
night·fall: ***at nightfall*** bei Einbruch der Dunkelheit
night·gown → ***nightdress***
night·ie F → ***nightdress***
nigh·tin·gale ZO Nachtigall *f*
night·ly (all)nächtlich; (all)abendlich; jede Nacht; jeden Abend
night·mare Albtraum *m* (*a. fig*)
night school Abendschule *f*
night shift Nachtschicht *f*
night·shirt (Herren)Nachthemd *n*
night·time: ***in the nighttime, at nighttime*** nachts
night watch·man Nachtwächter *m*
night·y F → ***nightdress***
nil Nichts *n*, Null *f*; ***our team won two to nil*** *or* ***by two goals to nil*** (***2-0***) unsere Mannschaft gewann zwei zu null (2:0)
nim·ble flink, gewandt; geistig beweglich
nine **1.** neun; ***nine to five*** normale Dienststunden (von 9-5); ***a nine-to-five job*** e-e (An)Stellung mit geregelter Arbeitszeit; **2.** Neun *f*
nine·pins Kegeln *n*
nine·teen **1.** neunzehn; **2.** Neunzehn *f*
nine·teenth neunzehnte(r, -s)
nine·ti·eth neunzigste(r, -s)
nine·ty **1.** neunzig; **2.** Neunzig *f*
ninth **1.** neunte(r, -s); **2.** Neuntel *n*
ninth·ly neuntens
nip[1] **1.** kneifen, zwicken; F flitzen, sausen; ***nip off*** F abknipsen; ***nip in the bud*** *fig* im Keim ersticken; **2.** Kneifen *n*, Zwicken *n*; ***it was nip and tuck*** F es war ganz knapp; ***there's a nip in the air today*** heute ist es ganz schön kalt
nip[2] Schlückchen *n* (*of brandy etc*)
nip·per: (***a pair of***) ***nippers*** (e-e) (Kneif-)Zange *f*
nip·ple ANAT Brustwarze *f*; (Gummi-)Sauger *m*; TECH Nippel *m*
ni·ter, *Br* **ni·tre** CHEM Salpeter *m*
ni·tro·gen CHEM Stickstoff *m*
no **1.** *adv* nein; nicht; **2.** *adj* kein(e); ***no one*** keiner, niemand; ***in no time*** im Nu, im Handumdrehen; **3.** Nein *n*
no·bil·i·ty (Hoch)Adel *m*; *fig* Adel *m*
no·ble adlig; edel, nobel; prächtig
no·ble·man Adlige *m*
no·ble·wom·an Adlige *f*
no·bod·y **1.** niemand, keiner; **2.** *fig* Niemand *m*, Null *f*
no-cal·o·rie di·et Nulldiät *f*
noc·tur·nal nächtlich, Nacht…
nod **1.** nicken (mit); ***nod off*** einnicken; ***have a nodding acquaintance with s.o.*** j-n flüchtig kennen; **2.** Nicken *n*
node BOT, MED Knoten *m*
noise **1.** Krach *m*, Lärm *m*; Geräusch *n*; **2.** ***noise about*** (***abroad, around***) *Gerücht etc* verbreiten
noise·less geräuschlos
nois·y laut, geräuschvoll
no·mad Nomade *m*, Nomadin *f*
nom·i·nal nominell; ***nominal value*** ECON Nennwert *m*
nom·i·nate ernennen; nominieren, (zur Wahl) vorschlagen
nom·i·na·tion Ernennung *f*; Nominierung *f*
nom·i·na·tive *a.* ***nominative case*** LING Nominativ *m*, erster Fall
nom·i·nee Kandidat(in)
non… nicht…, Nicht…, un…
non·al·co·hol·ic alkoholfrei
non·a·ligned POL blockfrei
non·com·mis·sioned of·fi·cer MIL Unteroffizier *m*
non·com·mit·tal unverbindlich
non·con·duc·tor ELECTR Nichtleiter *m*
non·de·script nichtssagend; unauffällig
none **1.** *pron* keine(r, -s), niemand; **2.** *adv* in keiner Weise, keineswegs

non·en·ti·ty *fig* Null *f*
none·the·less nichtsdestoweniger, dennoch, trotzdem
non·ex·ist·ence Nichtvorhandensein *n*, Fehlen *n*
non·ex·ist·ent nicht existierend
non·fic·tion Sachbücher *pl*
non·flam·ma·ble, **non·in·flam·mable** nicht brennbar
non·in·ter·fer·ence, **non·in·ter·vention** POL Nichteinmischung *f*
non·i·ron bügelfrei
no-non·sense nüchtern, sachlich
non·par·ti·san POL überparteilich; unparteiisch
non·pay·ment ECON Nicht(be)zahlung *f*
non·plus verblüffen
non·pol·lut·ing umweltfreundlich
non·prof·it, *Br* **non·prof·it·mak·ing** gemeinnützig
non·res·i·dent **1.** nicht (orts)ansässig; nicht im Hause wohnend; **2.** Nichtansässige *m, f*; nicht im Hause Wohnende *m, f*
non·re·turn·a·ble Einweg…
nonreturnable bot·tle Einwegflasche *f*
non·sense Unsinn *m*, dummes Zeug
non-skid rutschfest, rutschsicher
non·smok·er Nichtraucher(in)
non·smok·ing Nichtraucher…
non·stick mit Antihaftbeschichtung
non·stop nonstop, ohne Unterbrechung; RAIL durchgehend; AVIAT ohne Zwischenlandung; ***nonstop flight*** *a.* Nonstop-Flug *m*
non·u·nion nicht (gewerkschaftlich) organisiert
non·vi·o·lence (Politik *f* der) Gewaltlosigkeit *f*
non·vi·o·lent gewaltlos
noo·dle Nudel *f*
nook Ecke *f*, Winkel *m*
noon Mittag(szeit *f*) *m*; ***at noon*** um 12 Uhr (mittags)
noose Schlinge *f*
nope F ne(e), nein
nor → ***neither*** 2; auch nicht
norm Norm *f*
nor·mal normal
nor·mal·ize (sich) normalisieren
north **1.** Nord, Norden *m*; **2.** *adj* nördlich, Nord…; **3.** *adv* nach Norden, nordwärts
north·east **1.** Nordost, Nordosten *m*; **2.** *a.* ***northeastern*** nordöstlich
nor·ther·ly, **nor·thern** Nord…, nördlich
North Pole Nordpol *m*
north·ward(s) *adv* nördlich, nach Norden
north·west **1.** Nordwest, Nordwesten *m*; **2.** *a.* ***northwestern*** nordwestlich
Nor·way Norwegen *n*

N

Nor·we·gian **1.** norwegisch; **2.** Norweger(in); LING Norwegisch *n*
nose **1.** Nase *f*; ZO Schnauze *f*; *fig* Gespür *n*; **2.** *Auto etc* vorsichtig fahren; *a.* ***nose about, nose around*** *fig* F herumschnüffeln (in *dat*) (***for*** nach)
nose·bleed Nasenbluten *n*; ***have a nosebleed*** Nasenbluten haben
nose·dive AVIAT Sturzflug *m*
nos·ey → ***nosy***
nos·tal·gia Nostalgie *f*
nos·tril ANAT Nasenloch *n*, *esp* ZO Nüster *f*
nos·y F neugierig
not nicht; ***not a*** kein(e)
no·ta·ble bemerkenswert; beachtlich
no·ta·ry *mst* ***notary public*** Notar *m*
notch **1.** Kerbe *f*; GEOL Engpass *m*; **2.** (ein)kerben
note (*mst pl*) Notiz *f*, Aufzeichnung *f*; Anmerkung *f*; Vermerk *m*; Briefchen *n*, Zettel *m*; (diplomatische) Note; Banknote *f*, Geldschein *m*; MUS Note *f*; *fig* Ton *m*; ***take notes*** (***of***) sich Notizen machen (über *acc*)
note·book Notizbuch *n*; EDP Notebook *n*
not·ed bekannt, berühmt (***for*** wegen)
note·pa·per Briefpapier *n*
note·wor·thy bemerkenswert
noth·ing nichts; ***nothing but*** nichts als, nur; ***nothing much*** F nicht viel; ***for nothing*** umsonst; ***to say nothing of*** ganz zu schweigen von; ***there is nothing like*** es geht nichts über (*acc*)
no·tice **1.** Ankündigung *f*, Bekanntgabe *f*, Mitteilung *f*, Anzeige *f*; Kündigung(sfrist) *f*; Beachtung *f*; ***give*** *or* ***hand in one's notice*** kündigen (***to*** bei); ***give s.o. notice*** j-m kündigen; ***give s.o. notice to quit*** j-m kündigen; ***at six months' notice*** mit halbjährlicher Kündigungsfrist; ***take*** (***no***) ***notice of*** (keine) Notiz nehmen von, (nicht) beachten; ***at short notice*** kurzfristig; ***until further notice*** bis auf weiteres; ***without notice*** fristlos; **2.** (es) bemerken; (besonders) beachten *or* achten auf (*acc*)
no·tice·a·ble erkennbar, wahrnehmbar; bemerkenswert
no·tice·board *Br* schwarzes Brett
no·ti·fy *et.* anzeigen, melden, mitteilen; *j-n* benachrichtigen
no·tion Begriff *m*, Vorstellung *f*; Idee *f*
no·tions Kurzwaren *pl*
no·to·ri·ous berüchtigt (***for*** für)
not·with·stand·ing trotz (*gen*)
nought *Br*: ***0.4*** (***nought point four***) 0,4
noun LING Substantiv *n*, Hauptwort *n*
nour·ish (er)nähren; *fig* hegen
nour·ish·ing nahrhaft

nour·ish·ment Ernährung *f*; Nahrung *f*
Nov ABBR *of* ***November*** Nov., November *m*
nov·el **1.** Roman *m*; **2.** (ganz) neu(artig)
nov·el·ist Romanschriftsteller(in)
no·vel·la Novelle *f*
nov·el·ty Neuheit *f*
No·vem·ber (ABBR ***Nov***) November *m*
nov·ice Anfänger(in), Neuling *m*; REL Novize *m*, Novizin *f*
now **1.** *adv* nun, jetzt; ***now and again, (every) now and then*** von Zeit zu Zeit, dann und wann; ***by now*** inzwischen; ***from now (on)*** von jetzt an; ***just now*** gerade eben; **2.** *cj a.* ***now that*** nun da
now·a·days heutzutage
no·where nirgends
nox·ious schädlich
noz·zle TECH Schnauze *f*; Stutzen *m*; Düse *f*; Zapfpistole *f*
nu·ance Nuance *f*
nub springender Punkt
nu·cle·ar Kern..., Atom..., atomar, nuklear, Nuklear...
nuclear en·er·gy PHYS Atomenergie *f*, Kernenergie *f*
nuclear fam·i·ly Kern-, Kleinfamilie *f*
nuclear fis·sion PHYS Kernspaltung *f*
nu·cle·ar-free atomwaffenfrei
nu·cle·ar fu·sion PHYS Kernfusion *f*
nuclear phys·ics Kernphysik *f*
nuclear pow·er PHYS Atomkraft *f*, Kernkraft *f*
nu·cle·ar-pow·ered atomgetrieben
nu·cle·ar pow·er plant ELECTR Atomkraftwerk *n*, Kernkraftwerk *n*
nuclear re·ac·tor PHYS Atomreaktor *m*, Kernreaktor *m*
nuclear war Atomkrieg *m*
nuclear war·head MIL Atomsprengkopf *m*
nuclear waste Atommüll *m*
nuclear weap·ons MIL Atomwaffen *pl*, Kernwaffen *pl*
nu·cle·us BIOL, PHYS Kern *m* (*a. fig*)
nude **1.** nackt; **2.** *art*: Akt *m*
nudge **1.** *j-n* anstoßen, (an)stupsen; **2.** Stups(er) *m*
nug·get (*esp* Gold)Klumpen *m*
nui·sance Plage *f*, Ärgernis *n*; Nervensäge *f*, Quälgeist *m*; ***what a nuisance!*** wie ärgerlich!; ***be a nuisance to s.o.*** j-m lästig fallen, F j-n nerven; ***make a nuisance of o.s.*** den Leuten auf die Nerven gehen *or* fallen
nukes F Atom-, Kernwaffen *pl*
null: ***null and void*** *esp* JUR null und nichtig
numb **1.** starr (***with*** vor), taub; *fig* wie betäubt (***with*** vor); **2.** starr *or* taub machen
num·ber **1.** Zahl *f*, Ziffer *f*; Nummer *f*; (An)Zahl *f*; Ausgabe *f*; (*Bus- etc*)Linie *f*; ***sorry, wrong number*** TEL falsch verbunden!; **2.** nummerieren; zählen; sich belaufen auf (*acc*)
num·ber·less zahllos
num·ber·plate *esp Br* MOT Nummernschild *n*
nu·me·ral Ziffer *f*; LING Zahlwort *n*
nu·me·ra·tor MATH Zähler *m*
nu·me·rous zahlreich
nun REL Nonne *f*
nun·ne·ry REL Nonnenkloster *n*
nurse **1.** (Kranken-, Säuglings)Schwester *f*; Kindermädchen *n*; (Kranken-) Pflegerin *f*; → ***male nurse***; *a.* ***wet nurse*** Amme *f*; **2.** stillen; pflegen; hegen; als Krankenschwester *or* -pfleger arbeiten; ***nurse s.o. back to health*** j-n gesund pflegen
nur·se·ry Tagesheim *n*, Tagesstätte *f*; Baum-, Pflanzschule *f*
nursery rhyme Kinderlied *n*, Kinderreim *m*
nursery school *Br* Vorschule *f*
nursery slope *skiing*: F Idiotenhügel *m*
nurs·ing Stillen *n*; (Kranken)Pflege *f*
nursing bot·tle (Saug)Flasche *f*
nursing home Pflegeheim *n*
nut BOT Nuss *f*; TECH (Schrauben)Mutter *f*; F verrückter Kerl; F Birne *f* (*head*); ***be off one's nut*** F spinnen
nut·crack·er(s) Nussknacker *m*
nut·meg BOT Muskatnuss *f*
nu·tri·ent **1.** Nährstoff *m*; **2.** nahrhaft
nu·tri·tion Ernährung *f*
nu·tri·tious, nu·tri·tive nahrhaft
nut·shell Nussschale *f*; ***(to put it) in a nutshell*** F kurz gesagt, mit e-m Wort
nut·ty voller Nüsse; Nuss...; F verrückt
ny·lon Nylon *n*
nylon stock·ings Nylonstrümpfe *pl*
nymph Nymphe *f*

N

O

O, o O, o *n*
o Null *f*
oaf Lümmel *m*, Flegel *m*
oak BOT Eiche *f*
oar Ruder *n*
oars·man SPORT Ruderer *m*
oars·wom·an SPORT Ruderin *f*
o·a·sis Oase *f* (*a. fig*)
oath Eid *m*, Schwur *m*; Fluch *m*; ***take an oath*** e-n Eid leisten *or* schwören; ***be on*** *or* ***under oath*** JUR unter Eid stehen; ***take the oath*** JUR schwören
oat·meal Hafermehl *n*, Hafergrütze *f*
oats BOT Hafer *m*; ***sow one's wild oats*** sich die Hörner abstoßen
o·be·di·ence Gehorsam *m*
o·be·di·ent gehorsam
o·bese fett, fettleibig
o·bes·i·ty Fettleibigkeit *f*
o·bey gehorchen (*dat*), folgen (*dat*); *Befehl etc* befolgen
o·bit·u·a·ry Nachruf *m*; *a.* ***obituary notice*** Todesanzeige *f*
ob·ject **1.** Objekt *n* (*a.* LING); Gegenstand *m*; Ziel *n*, Zweck *m*, Absicht *f*; **2.** einwenden; et. dagegen haben
ob·jec·tion Einwand *m*, Einspruch *m* (*a.* JUR)
ob·jec·tion·a·ble nicht einwandfrei; unangenehm; anstößig
ob·jec·tive **1.** objektiv, sachlich; **2.** Ziel *n*
ob·jec·tive·ness Objektivität *f*
ob·li·ga·tion Verpflichtung *f*; ***be under an obligation to s.o.*** j-m (zu Dank) verpflichtet sein; ***be under an obligation to do*** verpflichtet sein, *et.* zu tun
ob·lig·a·to·ry verpflichtend, verbindlich
o·blige nötigen, zwingen; (zu Dank) verpflichten; ***oblige s.o.*** j-m e-n Gefallen tun; ***much obliged*** besten Dank
o·blig·ing entgegenkommend, gefällig
o·blique schief, schräg; *fig* indirekt
o·blit·er·ate auslöschen; vernichten, völlig zerstören; verdecken
o·bliv·i·on Vergessen(heit *f*) *n*; ***fall into oblivion*** in Vergessenheit geraten
o·bliv·i·ous: ***be oblivious of*** *or* ***to s.th.*** sich e-r Sache nicht bewusst sein; et. nicht bemerken *or* wahrnehmen
ob·long rechteckig; länglich
ob·nox·ious widerlich
ob·scene obszön, unanständig
ob·scure **1.** dunkel, *fig a.* unklar; unbekannt; **2.** verdunkeln, verdecken
ob·scu·ri·ty Unbekanntheit *f*; Unklarheit *f*
ob·se·quies Trauerfeier(lichkeiten *pl*) *f*
ob·ser·va·ble wahrnehmbar, merklich
ob·ser·vance Beachtung *f*, Befolgung *f*
ob·ser·vant aufmerksam
ob·ser·va·tion Beobachtung *f*, Überwachung *f*; Bemerkung *f* (***on*** über *acc*)
ob·ser·va·to·ry Observatorium *n*, Sternwarte *f*
ob·serve beobachten; überwachen; *Vorschrift etc* beachten, befolgen, einhalten; bemerken, äußern
ob·serv·er Beobachter(in)
ob·sess: ***be obsessed by*** *or* ***with*** besessen sein von
ob·ses·sion PSYCH Besessenheit *f*, fixe Idee, Zwangsvorstellung *f*
ob·ses·sive PSYCH zwanghaft
ob·so·lete veraltet
ob·sta·cle Hindernis *n*
ob·sti·na·cy Starrsinn *m*
ob·sti·nate hartnäckig; halsstarrig, eigensinnig, starrköpfig
ob·struct verstopfen, versperren; blockieren; behindern
ob·struc·tion Verstopfung *f*; Blockierung *f*; Behinderung *f*
ob·struc·tive blockierend; hinderlich
ob·tain erhalten, bekommen, sich *et.* beschaffen
ob·tain·a·ble erhältlich
ob·tru·sive aufdringlich
ob·tuse MATH stumpf; *fig* begriffsstutzig; ***be obtuse*** sich dumm stellen
ob·vi·ous offensichtlich, klar, einleuchtend
oc·ca·sion Gelegenheit *f*; Anlass *m*; Veranlassung *f*; (festliches) Ereignis; ***on the occasion of*** anlässlich (*gen*)
oc·ca·sion·al gelegentlich; vereinzelt
oc·ca·sion·al·ly gelegentlich, manchmal
Oc·ci·dent *der* Westen, *der* Okzident, *das* Abendland
oc·ci·den·tal abendländisch, westlich
oc·cu·pant Bewohner(in); Insasse *m*, Insassin *f*
oc·cu·pa·tion Beruf *m*; Beschäftigung *f*; MIL, POL Besetzung *f*, Besatzung *f*, Okkupation *f*
oc·cu·py in Besitz nehmen, MIL, POL besetzen; *Raum* einnehmen; in Anspruch nehmen; beschäftigen; ***be occupied*** bewohnt sein; besetzt sein (*seat*)

oc·cur sich ereignen; vorkommen; ***it occurred to me that*** es fiel mir ein *or* mir kam der Gedanke, dass
oc·cur·rence Vorkommen *n*; Ereignis *n*; Vorfall *m*
o·cean Ozean *m*, (Welt)Meer *n*
o'clock: (***at***) ***five o'clock*** (um) fünf Uhr
Oct ABBR *of* ***October*** Okt., Oktober *m*
Oc·to·ber (ABBR ***Oct***) Oktober *m*
oc·u·lar Augen…
oc·u·list Augenarzt *m*, Augenärztin *f*
OD F *v/i*: ***OD on heroin*** an e-r Überdosis Heroin sterben
odd sonderbar, seltsam, merkwürdig; einzeln, Einzel…; ungerade (*number*); gelegentlich, Gelegenheits…; ***odd jobs*** Gelegenheitsarbeiten *pl*; F ***30 odd*** (et.) über 30, einige 30
odds (Gewinn)Chancen *pl*; ***the odds are 10 to 1*** die Chancen stehen 10 zu 1; ***the odds are that*** es ist sehr wahrscheinlich, dass; ***against all odds*** wider Erwarten, entgegen allen Erwartungen; ***be at odds*** uneins sein (***with*** mit); ***odds and ends*** Krimskrams *m*
odds-on hoch, klar (*favorite*), aussichtsreichst (*candidate etc*); F ***it's odds-on that*** es sieht ganz so aus, als ob …
ode Ode *f*
o·do(u)r Geruch *m*
o·do(u)r·less geruchlos
of *prp* von; *origin*: von, aus; *material*: aus; um (***cheat s.o. of s.th.*** j-n um et. betrügen); *cause*: an (*dat*) (***die of*** sterben an); aus (***of charity*** aus Nächstenliebe); vor (*dat*) (***be afraid of*** Angst haben vor); auf (*acc*) (***be proud of*** stolz sein auf); über (*acc*) (***be glad of*** sich freuen über); nach (***smell of*** riechen nach); von, über (*acc*) (***speak of s.th.*** von *or* über et. sprechen); an (*acc*) (***think of s.th.*** an et. denken); ***the city of London*** die Stadt London; ***the works of Dickens*** Dickens' Werke; ***your letter of …*** Ihr Schreiben vom …; ***five minutes of twelve*** fünf Minuten vor zwölf
off **1.** *adv* fort(…), weg(…); ab(…), ab, abgegangen (*button etc*); weg, entfernt (***3 miles off***); ELECTR *etc* aus(…), aus-, abgeschaltet; TECH zu; aus(gegangen), alle; aus, vorbei; verdorben (*food*); frei; ***I must be off*** ich muss gehen *or* weg; ***off with you!*** fort mit dir!; ***be off*** ausfallen, nicht stattfinden; ***10% off*** ECON 10% Nachlass; ***off and on*** ab und zu, hin und wieder; ***take a day off*** sich e-n Tag freinehmen; ***be well*** (***badly***) ***off*** gut (schlecht) d(a)ran *or* gestellt *or* situiert sein; **2.** *prp* fort von, weg von, von (…, ab, weg, herunter); abseits von (*or gen*), von … weg; MAR vor *der Küste etc*; ***be off duty*** nicht im Dienst sein, dienstfrei haben; ***be off smoking*** nicht mehr rauchen; **3.** *adj* frei, arbeits-, dienstfrei; *fig* ***have an off day*** e-n schlechten Tag haben
of·fal GASTR Innereien *pl*
off-col·o(u)r schlüpfrig, zweideutig
of·fence *Br* → ***offense***
of·fend beleidigen, kränken; verstoßen (***against*** gegen)
of·fend·er (Übel-, Misse)Täter(in); ***first offender*** JUR nicht Vorbestrafte *m, f*, Ersttäter(in)
of·fense Vergehen *n*, Verstoß *m*; JUR Straftat *f*; Beleidigung *f*, Kränkung *f*; ***take offense*** Anstoß nehmen (***at*** an *dat*)
of·fen·sive **1.** beleidigend, anstößig; widerlich (*smell etc*); MIL Offensiv…, Angriffs…; **2.** MIL Offensive *f* (*a. fig*)
of·fer **1.** *v/t* anbieten (*a.* ECON); *Preis, Möglichkeit etc* bieten; *Preis, Belohnung* aussetzen; sich bereit erklären (***to do*** zu tun); *Widerstand* leisten; *v/i* es *or* sich anbieten; **2.** Angebot *n*
off·hand **1.** *adj* lässig; Stegreif…; ***be offhand with s.o.*** F mit j-m kurz angebunden sein; **2.** *adv* auf Anhieb, so ohne weiteres
of·fice Büro *n*, Geschäftsstelle *f*, (*Anwalts*)Kanzlei *f*; (*esp* öffentliches) Amt, Posten *m*; *mst* ***Office*** *esp Br* Ministerium *n*
office block *Br*, **office build·ing** Bürohaus *n*
office hours Dienstzeit *f*; Geschäfts-, Öffnungszeiten *pl*
of·fi·cer MIL Offizier *m*; (*Polizei- etc*)Beamte *m*, (-)Beamtin *f*
of·fi·cial **1.** Beamte *m*, Beamtin *f*; **2.** offiziell, amtlich, dienstlich
of·fi·ci·ate amtieren
of·fi·cious übereifrig
off-licence *Br* Wein- und Spirituosenhandlung *f*
off·line EDP offline, Offline…, rechnerunabhängig
off-peak: ***off-peak electricity*** Nachtstrom *m*; ***off-peak hours*** verkehrsschwache Stunden *pl*
off sea·son Nebensaison *f*
off·set ECON ausgleichen; verrechnen (***against*** mit)
off·shoot BOT Ableger *m*, Spross *m*
off·shore vor der Küste
off·side SPORT abseits; ***offside position*** Abseitsposition *f*, Abseitsstellung *f*; ***offside trap*** Abseitsfalle *f*

off·spring Nachkomme *m*, Nachkommenschaft *f*
off-the-peg *Br*, **off-the-rack** Konfektions…, … von der Stange
off-the-rec·ord inoffiziell
of·ten oft(mals), häufig
oh *int* oh!
oil 1. Öl *n*; Erdöl *n*; **2.** (ein)ölen, schmieren (*a. fig*)
oil change MOT Ölwechsel *m*
oil·cloth Wachstuch *n*
oil·field Ölfeld *n*
oil paint·ing Ölmalerei *f*; Ölgemälde *n*
oil pan MOT Ölwanne *f*
oil plat·form → ***oilrig***
oil pol·lu·tion Ölpest *f*
oil pro·duc·tion Ölförderung *f*
oil-pro·duc·ing coun·try Ölförderland *n*
oil re·fin·e·ry Erdölraffinerie *f*
oil·rig (Öl)Bohrinsel *f*
oil·skins Ölzeug *n*
oil slick Ölteppich *m*
oil well Ölquelle *f*
oil·y ölig; *fig* schmierig, schleimig
oint·ment Salbe *f*
OK, o·kay F **1.** *adj and int* okay(!), o.k.(!), in Ordnung(!); **2.** genehmigen, *e-r Sache* zustimmen; **3.** Okay *n*, O.K. *n*, Genehmigung *f*, Zustimmung *f*
old 1. alt; **2.** ***the old*** die Alten *pl*
old age (hohes) Alter
old age pen·sion Rente *f*, Pension *f*
old age pen·sion·er Rentner(in), Pensionär(in)
old-fash·ioned altmodisch
old·ish ältlich
old peo·ple's home Altersheim *n*, Altenheim *n*
ol·ive BOT Olive *f*; Olivgrün *n*
O·lym·pic Games SPORT Olympische Spiele *pl*
om·i·nous unheilvoll
o·mis·sion Auslassung *f*; Unterlassung *f*; Versäumnis *n*
o·mit auslassen, weglassen; unterlassen
om·nip·o·tent allmächtig
om·nis·ci·ent allwissend
on 1. *prp* auf (*acc or dat*) (***on the table*** auf dem *or* den Tisch); an (*dat*) (***on the wall*** an der Wand); in (***on TV*** im Fernsehen); *direction, target*: auf (*acc*) … (hin), an (*acc*), nach (*dat*) … (hin) (***march on London*** nach London marschieren); *fig* auf (*acc*) … (hin) (***on demand*** auf Anfrage); *time*: an (*dat*) (***on Sunday*** am Sonntag; ***on the 1st of April*** am 1. April); (gleich) nach, bei (***on his arrival***); *gehörig* zu, *beschäftigt* bei (***be on a committee*** e-m Ausschuss angehören; ***be on the „Daily Mail"*** bei der "Daily Mail" beschäftigt sein); *state*: in (*dat*), auf (*dat*) (***on duty*** im Dienst; ***be on fire*** in Flammen stehen); *subject*: über (*acc*) (***talk on a subject*** über ein Thema sprechen); nach (*dat*) (***on this model*** nach diesem Modell); von (*dat*) (***live on s.th.*** von et. leben); ***on the street*** auf der Straße; ***on a train*** in e-m Zug; ***on hearing it*** als ich *etc* es hörte; ***have you any money on you?*** hast du Geld bei dir?; **2.** *adj and adv* an (-geschaltet) (*light etc*), eingeschaltet (*radio etc*), auf (*faucet etc*); (dar)auf(*legen, -schrauben etc*); an(*haben, -ziehen*) (***have a coat on*** e-n Mantel anhaben); auf (*-behalten*) (***keep one's hat on*** den Hut aufbehalten); weiter(*gehen, -sprechen etc*); ***and so on*** und so weiter; ***on and on*** immer weiter; ***from this day on*** von dem Tage an; ***be on*** THEA gegeben werden; *film*: laufen; *radio*, TV gesendet werden; ***what's on?*** was ist los?
once 1. einmal; einst; ***once again, once more*** noch einmal; ***once in a while*** ab und zu, hin und wieder; ***once and for all*** ein für alle Mal; ***not once*** kein einziges Mal, keinmal; ***at once*** sofort; auf einmal, gleichzeitig; ***all at once*** plötzlich; ***for once*** diesmal, ausnahmsweise; ***this once*** dieses eine Mal; ***once upon a time there was …*** es war einmal …; **2.** sobald
one ein(e); einzig; man; Eins *f*, eins; ***one's*** sein(e); ***one day*** eines Tages; ***one Smith*** ein gewisser Smith; ***one another*** sich (gegenseitig), einander; ***one by one, one after another, one after the other*** e-r nach dem andern; ***I for one*** ich zum Beispiel; ***the little ones*** die Kleinen *pl*
one-horse town F *contp* Nest *n*
one·self sich (selbst); sich selbst; (***all***) ***by oneself*** ganz allein; ***to oneself*** ganz für sich (allein)
one-sid·ed einseitig
one·time ehemalig, früher
one-track mind: ***have a one-track mind*** immer nur dasselbe im Kopf haben
one-two *soccer*: Doppelpass *m*
one-way Einbahn…
one-way street Einbahnstraße *f*
one-way tick·et RAIL *etc* einfache Fahrkarte, AVIAT einfaches Ticket
one-way traf·fic MOT Einbahnverkehr *m*
on·ion BOT Zwiebel *f*
on·line EDP online, Online…, rechnerabhängig
on·look·er Zuschauer(in)
on·ly 1. *adj* einzige(r, -s); **2.** *adv* nur, bloß; erst; ***only yesterday*** erst gestern; **3.** *cj* F

nur, bloß
on·rush Ansturm *m*
on·set Beginn *m*; MED Ausbruch *m*
on·slaught (heftiger) Angriff (*a. fig*)
on·to auf (*acc*)
on·ward(s) *adv* vorwärts, weiter; ***from now onward*** von nun an
ooze *v/i* sickern; ***ooze away*** *fig* schwinden; *v/t* absondern; *fig* ausstrahlen, verströmen
o·paque undurchsichtig; *fig* unverständlich
o·pen 1. offen, *a.* geöffnet, *a.* frei (*country etc*); öffentlich; *fig* offen, *a.* unentschieden, *a.* freimütig; *fig* zugänglich, aufgeschlossen (***to*** für *or dat*); ***open all day*** durchgehend geöffnet; ***in the open air*** im Freien; **2.** *golf, tennis*: offenes Turnier; ***in the open*** im Freien; ***come out into the open*** *fig* an die Öffentlichkeit treten; **3.** *v/t* öffnen, aufmachen, *Buch etc a.* aufschlagen; eröffnen; *v/i* sich öffnen, aufgehen; öffnen, aufmachen (*store*); anfangen, beginnen; ***open into*** führen nach *or* in (*acc*); ***open onto*** hinausgehen auf (*acc*)
o·pen-air im Freien
o·pen-end·ed zeitlich unbegrenzt
o·pen·er (*Dosen- etc*)Öffner *m*
o·pen-eyed mit großen Augen, staunend
o·pen-hand·ed freigebig, großzügig
o·pen-heart·ed offenherzig
o·pen·ing 1. Öffnung *f*; ECON freie Stelle; Eröffnung *f*, Erschließung *f*, Einstieg *m*; **2.** Eröffnungs…; Öffnungs…
o·pen-mind·ed aufgeschlossen
o·pen·ness Offenheit *f*
op·e·ra Oper *f*
opera glass·es Opernglas *n*
opera house Opernhaus *n*, Oper *f*
op·e·rate *v/i* wirksam sein *or* werden; TECH arbeiten, in Betrieb sein, laufen (*machine etc*); MED operieren (***on s.o.*** j-n); *v/t Maschine* bedienen, *Schalter etc* betätigen; *Unternehmen, Geschäft* betreiben, führen
op·e·rat·ing room MED Operationssaal *m*
operating sys·tem EDP Betriebssystem *n*
operating thea·tre *Br* MED Operationssaal *m*
op·e·ra·tion TECH Betrieb *m*, Lauf *m*; Bedienung *f*; ECON Tätigkeit *f*, Unternehmen *n*; MED, MIL Operation *f*; ***in operation*** TECH in Betrieb; ***have an operation*** MED operiert werden
op·e·ra·tive wirksam; MED operativ
op·e·ra·tor TECH Bedienungsperson *f*; EDP Operator *m*; TEL Vermittlung *f*
o·pin·ion Meinung *f*, Ansicht *f*; Gutachten *n* (***on*** über *acc*); ***in my opinion*** meines Erachtens
op·po·nent Gegner(in)
op·por·tune günstig, passend; rechtzeitig
op·por·tu·ni·ty (günstige) Gelegenheit
op·pose sich widersetzen (*dat*)
op·posed entgegengesetzt; ***be opposed to*** gegen … sein
op·po·site 1. Gegenteil *n*, Gegensatz *m*; **2.** *adj* gegenüberliegend; entgegengesetzt; **3.** *adv* gegenüber (***to*** *dat*); **4.** *prp* gegenüber (*dat*)
op·po·si·tion Widerstand *m*, Opposition *f* (*a.* PARL); Gegensatz *m*
op·press unterdrücken
op·pres·sion Unterdrückung *f*
op·pres·sive (be)drückend; hart, grausam; schwül (*weather*)
op·tic Augen…, Seh…; → **op·ti·cal** optisch
op·ti·cian Optiker(in)
op·ti·mism Optimismus *m*
op·ti·mist Optimist(in)
op·ti·mis·tic optimistisch
op·tion Wahl *f*; ECON Option *f*, Vorkaufsrecht *n*; MOT Extra *n*
op·tion·al freiwillig; Wahl…; ***be an optional extra*** MOT gegen Aufpreis erhältlich sein
optional sub·ject PED *etc* Wahlfach *n*
or oder; ***or else*** sonst
o·ral mündlich; Mund…
or·ange 1. BOT Orange *f*, Apfelsine *f*; **2.** orange(farben)
or·ange·ade Orangenlimonade *f*
o·ra·tion Rede *f*, Ansprache *f*
or·a·tor Redner(in)
or·bit 1. Kreisbahn *f*, Umlaufbahn *f*; ***get*** *or* ***put into orbit*** in e-e Umlaufbahn gelangen *or* bringen; **2.** *v/t die Erde etc* umkreisen; *v/i* die Erde *etc* umkreisen, sich auf e-r Umlaufbahn bewegen
or·chard Obstgarten *m*
or·ches·tra MUS Orchester *n*; THEA Parkett *n*
or·chid BOT Orchidee *f*
or·dain: ***ordain s.o.*** (***priest***) j-n zum Priester weihen
or·deal Qual *f*, Tortur *f*
or·der 1. Ordnung *f*; Reihenfolge *f*; Befehl *m*, Anordnung *f*; ECON Bestellung *f*, Auftrag *m*; PARL *etc* (Geschäfts)Ordnung *f*; REL *etc* Orden *m*; ***order to pay*** ECON Zahlungsanweisung *f*; ***in order to*** *inf* um zu *inf*; ***out of order*** TECH nicht in Ordnung, defekt; außer Betrieb; ***make to order*** auf Bestellung *or* nach Maß anfertigen; **2.** *v/t j-m* befehlen (***to do*** zu tun), *et.* befehlen, anordnen; *j-n*

O

schicken, beordern; MED *j-m et.* verordnen; ECON bestellen; *fig* ordnen, in Ordnung bringen; *v/i* bestellen (*in restaurant*)
or·der·ly 1. ordentlich; *fig* gesittet, friedlich; **2.** MED Hilfspfleger *m*
or·di·nal *a.* ***ordinal number*** MATH Ordnungszahl *f*
or·di·nary üblich, gewöhnlich, normal
ore MIN Erz *n*
or·gan ANAT Organ *n* (*a. fig*); MUS Orgel *f*
organ do·nor MED Organspender *m*
organ grind·er Leierkastenmann *m*
organ recip·i·ent MED Organempfänger *m*
or·gan·ic organisch
or·gan·ism Organismus *m*
or·gan·i·za·tion Organisation *f*
or·gan·ize organisieren; sich (gewerkschaftlich) organisieren
or·gan·iz·er Organisator(in)
or·gasm Orgasmus *m*
o·ri·ent 1. ***Orient*** *der* Osten, *der* Orient, *das* Morgenland; **2.** orientieren
o·ri·en·tal 1. orientalisch, östlich; **2.** ***Oriental*** Orientale *m*, Orientalin *f*
o·ri·en·tate orientieren
or·i·gin Ursprung *m*, Abstammung *f*, Herkunft *f*
o·rig·i·nal 1. ursprünglich; Original…; originell; **2.** Original *n*
o·rig·i·nal·i·ty Originalität *f*
o·rig·i·nal·ly ursprünglich; originell
o·rig·i·nate *v/t* schaffen, ins Leben rufen; *v/i* zurückgehen (***from*** auf *acc*), (her)stammen (***from*** von, aus)
or·na·ment 1. Ornament(e *pl*) *n*, Verzierung(en *pl*) *f*, Schmuck *m*; *fig* Zier(de) *f* (***to*** für *or gen*); **2.** verzieren, schmücken (***with*** mit)
or·na·men·tal dekorativ, schmückend, Zier…
or·nate *fig* überladen
or·phan 1. Waise *f*, Waisenkind *n*; **2.** ***be orphaned*** Waise werden
or·phan·age Waisenhaus *n*
or·tho·dox orthodox
os·cil·late PHYS schwingen; *fig* schwanken (***between*** zwischen *dat*)
os·prey ZO Fischadler *m*
os·ten·si·ble angeblich, vorgeblich
os·ten·ta·tion (protzige) Zurschaustellung; Protzerei *f*, Prahlerei *f*
os·ten·ta·tious protzend, prahlerisch
os·tra·cize ächten
os·trich ZO Strauß *m*
oth·er andere(r, -s); ***the other day*** neulich; ***the other morning*** neulich morgens; ***every other day*** jeden zweiten Tag, alle zwei Tage

oth·er·wise anders; sonst
ot·ter ZO Otter *m*
ought *v/aux ich* sollte, *du* solltest *etc*; ***you ought to have done it*** Sie hätten es tun sollen
ounce Unze *f* (*28,35 g*)
our unser
ours unsere(r, -s)
our·selves wir *or* uns selbst; uns (selbst)
oust verdrängen, hinauswerfen (***from*** aus); *j-n s-s Amtes* entheben
out 1. *adv, adj* aus; hinaus(*gehen, -werfen etc*); heraus(*kommen etc*); aus(*brechen etc*); draußen, im Freien; nicht zu Hause; SPORT aus, draußen; aus, vorbei; aus, erloschen; ausverkauft; F out, aus der Mode; ***out of*** aus (… heraus); zu … hinaus; außerhalb von (*or gen*); außer *Reichweite etc*; außer *Atem, Übung etc*; (hergestellt) aus; aus *Furcht etc*; ***be out of bread*** kein Brot mehr haben; ***in nine out of ten cases*** in neun von zehn Fällen; **2.** *prp* F aus (… heraus); zu … hinaus; **3.** outen
out·bal·ance überwiegen
out·bid überbieten
out·board mo·tor Außenbordmotor *m*
out·break MED, MIL Ausbruch *m*
out·build·ing Nebengebäude *n*
out·burst *fig* Ausbruch *m*
out·cast 1. ausgestoßen; **2.** Ausgestoßene *m, f*, Verstoßene *m, f*
out·come Ergebnis *n*
out·cry Aufschrei *m*, Schrei *m* der Entrüstung
out·dat·ed überholt, veraltet
out·dis·tance hinter sich lassen
out·do übertreffen
out·door *adj* im Freien, draußen
out·doors *adv* draußen, im Freien
out·er äußere(r, -s)
out·er·most äußerste(r, -s)
out·er space Weltraum *m*
out·fit Ausrüstung *f*, Ausstattung *f*; Kleidung *f*; F (Arbeits)Gruppe *f*
out·fit·ter Ausstatter *m*; ***men's outfitter*** Herrenausstatter *m*
out·go·ing (aus dem Amt) scheidend
out·grow herauswachsen aus (*dat*); *Angewohnheit etc* ablegen; größer werden als
out·house Nebengebäude *n*
out·ing Ausflug *m*; Outing *n*
out·land·ish befremdlich, sonderbar
out·last überdauern, überleben
out·law HIST Geächtete *m, f*
out·lay (Geld)Auslagen *pl*, Ausgaben *pl*
out·let Abfluss *m*, Abzug *m*; *fig* Ventil *n*
out·line 1. Umriss *m*; Überblick *m*; **2.** umreißen, skizzieren
out·live überleben

O

out·look (Aus)Blick *m*, (Aus)Sicht *f*; Einstellung *f*, Auffassung *f*
out·ly·ing abgelegen, entlegen
out·num·ber in der Überzahl sein; ***be outnumbered by s.o.*** j-m zahlenmäßig unterlegen sein
out-of-date veraltet, überholt
out-of-the-way abgelegen, entlegen; *fig* ungewöhnlich
out·pa·tient MED ambulanter Patient, ambulante Patientin
out·post Vorposten *m*
out·pour·ing (Gefühls)Erguss *m*
out·put ECON Output *m*, Produktion *f*, Ausstoß *m*, Ertrag *m*; EDP (Daten-)Ausgabe *f*
out·rage **1.** Gewalttat *f*, Verbrechen *n*; Empörung *f*; **2.** grob verletzen; *j-n* empören
out·ra·geous abscheulich; empörend, unerhört
out·right **1.** *adj* völlig, gänzlich, glatt (*lie etc*); **2.** *adv* auf der Stelle, sofort; ohne Umschweife
out·run schneller laufen als; *fig* übersteigen, übertreffen
out·set Anfang *m*, Beginn *m*
out·shine überstrahlen, *fig a.* in den Schatten stellen
out·side **1.** Außenseite *f*; SPORT Außenstürmer(in); ***at the*** (***very***) ***outside*** (aller-)höchstens; ***outside left*** (***right***) SPORT Linksaußen (Rechtsaußen) *m*; **2.** *adj* äußere(r, -s), Außen…; **3.** *adv* draußen; heraus, hinaus; **4.** *prp* außerhalb
out·sid·er Außenseiter(in)
out·size **1.** Übergröße *f*; **2.** übergroß
out·skirts Stadtrand *m*, Außenbezirke *pl*
out·spo·ken offen, freimütig
out·spread ausgestreckt, ausgebreitet
out·stand·ing hervorragend; ECON ausstehend; ungeklärt (*problem*); unerledigt (*work*)
out·stay länger bleiben als; → ***welcome*** *4*
out·stretched ausgestreckt
out·strip überholen; *fig* übertreffen
out tray: ***in the out tray*** im Postausgang *etc*
out·vote überstimmen
out·ward **1.** äußere(r, -s); äußerlich; **2.** *adv mst* ***outwards*** auswärts, nach außen
out·ward·ly äußerlich
out·weigh *fig* überwiegen
out·wit überlisten, F reinlegen
out·worn veraltet, überholt
o·val **1.** oval; **2.** Oval *n*
o·va·tion Ovation *f*; ***give s.o. a standing ovation*** j-m stehende Ovationen bereiten, j-m stehend Beifall klatschen
ov·en Backofen *m*, Bratofen *m*
ov·en-read·y bratfertig
o·ver **1.** *prp* über; über (*acc*), über (*acc*) … (hin)weg; über (*dat*), auf der anderen Seite von (*or gen*); über (*acc*), mehr als; **2.** *adv* hinüber, herüber (***to*** zu); drüben; darüber, mehr; zu Ende, vorüber, vorbei; über…, um…: *et.* über(*geben etc*); über (*-kochen etc*); um(*fallen*, *-werfen etc*); herum(*drehen etc*); von Anfang bis Ende, durch(*lesen etc*); (gründlich) über(*legen etc*); (***all***) ***over again*** noch einmal; ***all over*** ganz vorbei; ***over and over*** (***again***) immer wieder; ***over and above*** obendrein, überdies
o·ver·age zu alt
o·ver·all **1.** gesamt, Gesamt…; allgemein; insgesamt; **2.** *Br* Arbeitsmantel *m*, Kittel *m*; (*Br* ***overalls***) Overall *m*, Arbeitsanzug *m*; Arbeitshose *f*
o·ver·awe einschüchtern
o·ver·bal·ance umstoßen, umkippen; das Gleichgewicht verlieren
o·ver·bear·ing anmaßend
o·ver·board MAR über Bord
o·ver·bur·den *fig* überlasten
o·ver·cast bewölkt, bedeckt
o·ver·charge überlasten, ELECTR *a.* überladen; ECON *j-m* zu viel berechnen; *Betrag* zu viel verlangen
o·ver·coat Mantel *m*
o·ver·come überwinden, überwältigen; ***be overcome with emotion*** von s-n Gefühlen übermannt werden
o·ver·crowd·ed überfüllt; überlaufen
o·ver·do übertreiben; GASTR zu lange kochen *or* braten; ***overdone*** *a.* übergar
o·ver·dose Überdosis *f*
o·ver·draft ECON (Konto)Überziehung *f*; *a.* ***overdraft facility*** Überziehungskredit *m*
o·ver·draw ECON *Konto* überziehen (***by*** um)
o·ver·dress (sich) zu fein anziehen; ***overdressed*** overdressed, zu fein angezogen
o·ver·drive MOT Overdrive *m*, Schongang *m*
o·ver·due überfällig
o·ver·eat zu viel essen
o·ver·es·ti·mate zu hoch schätzen *or* veranschlagen; *fig* überschätzen
o·ver·ex·pose PHOT überbelichten
o·ver·feed überfüttern
o·ver·flow **1.** *v/t* überfluten, überschwemmen; *v/i* überlaufen, überfließen; überquellen (***with*** von); **2.** TECH Überlauf *m*; Überlaufen *n*, -fließen *n*
o·ver·grown BOT überwachsen, überwuchert

O

o·ver·hang *v/t* über (*dat*) hängen; *v/i* überhängen
o·ver·haul *Maschine* überholen
o·ver·head **1.** *adv* oben, droben; **2.** *adj* Hoch…, Ober…; ECON ***overhead expenses*** *or* ***costs*** Gemeinkosten *pl*; SPORT Überkopf…; ***overhead kick*** *soccer*: Fallrückzieher *m*; **3.** ECON *esp Br a. pl* Gemeinkosten *pl*
o·ver·hear (zufällig) hören
o·ver·heat·ed überhitzt, überheizt; TECH heiß gelaufen
o·ver·joyed überglücklich
o·ver·lap (sich) überlappen; sich überschneiden
o·ver·leaf umseitig, umstehend
o·ver·load überlasten (*a.* ELECTR), überladen
o·ver·look übersehen; ***overlooking the sea*** mit Blick aufs Meer
o·ver·night **1.** über Nacht; ***stay overnight*** über Nacht bleiben, übernachten; **2.** Nacht…, Übernachtungs…; ***overnight bag*** Reisetasche *f*
o·ver·pass (Straßen-, Eisenbahn-) Überführung *f*
o·ver·pay zu viel (be)zahlen
o·ver·pop·u·lat·ed übervölkert
o·ver·pow·er überwältigen; ***overpowering*** *fig* überwältigend
o·ver·rate überbewerten, überschätzen
o·ver·reach: ***overreach o.s.*** sich übernehmen
o·ver·re·act überreagieren, überzogen reagieren (***to*** auf *acc*)
o·ver·re·ac·tion Überreaktion *f*, überzogene Reaktion
o·ver·ride sich hinwegsetzen über (*acc*)
o·ver·rule *Entscheidung etc* aufheben, *Einspruch etc* abweisen
o·ver·run länger dauern als vorgesehen; *Signal* überfahren; ***be overrun with*** wimmeln von
o·ver·seas **1.** *adj* überseeisch, Übersee…; **2.** *adv* in *or* nach Übersee
o·ver·see beaufsichtigen, überwachen
o·ver·shad·ow *fig* überschatten, in den Schatten stellen
o·ver·sight Versehen *n*
o·ver·size(d) übergroß, überdimensional, in Übergröße(n)
o·ver·sleep verschlafen
o·ver·staffed (personell) überbesetzt
o·ver·state übertreiben
o·ver·state·ment Übertreibung *f*
o·ver·stay länger bleiben als; → ***welcome*** *4*
o·ver·step *fig* überschreiten
o·ver·take überholen; *j-n* überraschen
o·ver·tax zu hoch besteuern; *fig* überbeanspruchen, überfordern
o·ver·throw **1.** *Regierung etc* stürzen; **2.** (Um)Sturz *m*
o·ver·time ECON Überstunden *pl*; SPORT (Spiel)Verlängerung *f*; ***be on overtime, do overtime, work overtime*** Überstunden machen
o·ver·tired übermüdet
o·ver·ture MUS Ouvertüre *f*; Vorspiel *n*
o·ver·turn *v/t* umwerfen, umstoßen; *Regierung etc* stürzen; *v/i* umkippen, MAR kentern
o·ver·view *fig* Überblick *m* (***of*** über *acc*)
o·ver·weight **1.** Übergewicht *n*; **2.** übergewichtig (*person*), zu schwer (***by*** um); ***be five pounds overweight*** fünf Pfund Übergewicht haben
o·ver·whelm überwältigen (*a. fig*)
o·ver·whelm·ing überwältigend
o·ver·work sich überarbeiten; überanstrengen
o·ver·wrought überreizt
o·ver·zeal·ous übereifrig
owe *j-m et.* schulden, schuldig sein; *et.* verdanken
ow·ing: ***owing to*** infolge, wegen
owl ZO Eule *f*
own **1.** eigen; ***my own*** mein Eigentum; ***(all) on one's own*** allein; **2.** besitzen; zugeben, (ein)gestehen
own·er Eigentümer(in), Besitzer(in)
own·er-oc·cu·pied *esp Br* eigengenutzt; ***owner-occupied flat*** Eigentumswohnung *f*
own·er·ship Besitz *m*; Eigentum *n*; Eigentumsrecht *n*
ox ZO Ochse *m*
ox·ide CHEM Oxid *n*, Oxyd *n*
ox·i·dize CHEM oxidieren
ox·y·gen CHEM Sauerstoff *m*
oxygen ap·pa·ra·tus MED Sauerstoffgerät *n*
oxygen tent MED Sauerstoffzelt *n*
oy·ster ZO Auster *f*
o·zone CHEM Ozon *n*
o·zone-friend·ly FCKW-frei, ohne Treibgas
o·zone hole Ozonloch *n*
ozone lay·er Ozonschicht *f*
ozone lev·els Ozonwerte *pl*
ozone shield Ozonschild *m*

O

P

P, p P, p *n*
pace **1.** Tempo *n*, Geschwindigkeit *f*; Schritt *m*; Gangart *f* (*of a horse*); **2.** *v/t* *Zimmer etc* durchschreiten; *a.* ***pace out*** abschreiten; *v/i* (einher)schreiten; ***pace up and down*** auf und ab gehen
pace·mak·er SPORT Schrittmacher(in); MED Herzschrittmacher *m*
pace·set·ter SPORT Schrittmacher(in)
Pa·cif·ic *a.* ***Pacific Ocean*** *der* Pazifik, *der* Pazifische *or* Stille Ozean
pac·i·fi·er Schnuller *m*
pac·i·fist Pazifist(in)
pac·i·fy beruhigen, besänftigen
pack **1.** Pack(en) *m*, Paket *n*, Bündel *n*; Packung *f*, Schachtel *f*; zo Meute *f*; Rudel *n*; *contp* Pack *n*, Bande *f*; MED *etc* Packung *f*; (Karten)Spiel *n*; ***a pack of lies*** ein Haufen Lügen; **2.** *v/t* ein-, zusammenpacken, abpacken, verpacken (*a.* ***pack up***); zusammenpferchen; vollstopfen; *Koffer etc* packen; ***pack off*** F fort-, wegschicken; *v/i* packen; (sich) drängen (***into*** in *acc*); ***pack up*** zusammenpacken; ***send s.o. packing*** j-n fort- *or* wegjagen
pack·age Paket *n*; Packung *f*; ***software package*** EDP Software-, Programmpaket *n*
pack·age deal F Pauschalangebot *n*, -arrangement *n*
package hol·i·day Pauschalurlaub *m*
package tour Pauschalreise *f*
pack·et Päckchen *n*; Packung *f*, Schachtel *f*
pack·ing Packen *n*; Verpackung *f*
pact Pakt *m*, POL *a.* Vertrag *m*
pad **1.** Polster *n*; SPORT (*Knie- etc*)Schützer *m*; (*Schreib- etc*)Block *m*; (*Stempel*)Kissen *n*; zo Ballen *m*; (*Abschuss-*) Rampe *f*; **2.** (aus)polstern, wattieren
pad·ding Polsterung *f*, Wattierung *f*
pad·dle **1.** Paddel *n*; MAR (Rad)Schaufel *f*; **2.** paddeln; plan(t)schen
pad·dock (Pferde)Koppel *f*
pad·lock Vorhängeschloss *n*
pa·gan **1.** Heide *m*, Heidin *f*; **2.** heidnisch
page[1] **1.** Seite *f*; **2.** paginieren
page[2] **1.** (Hotel)Page *m*; **2.** *j-n* ausrufen (lassen)
pag·eant (*a.* historischer) Festzug
pa·gin·ate paginieren
pail Eimer *m*, Kübel *m*
pain **1.** Schmerz(en *pl*) *m*; Kummer *m*; *pl* Mühe *f*, Bemühungen *pl*; ***be in (great) pain*** (große) Schmerzen haben; ***be a pain (in the neck)*** F e-m auf den Wecker gehen; ***take pains*** sich Mühe geben; **2.** *esp fig* schmerzen
pain·ful schmerzhaft, schmerzend; *fig* schmerzlich; peinlich
pain·kill·er Schmerzmittel *n*
pain·less schmerzlos
pains·tak·ing sorgfältig, gewissenhaft
paint **1.** Farbe *f*; Anstrich *m*; **2.** *v/t* anmalen, bemalen; (an)streichen; *Auto etc* lackieren; *v/i* malen
paint·box Malkasten *m*
paint·brush (Maler)Pinsel *m*
paint·er (*a.* Kunst)Maler(in), Anstreicher(in)
paint·ing Malerei *f*; Gemälde *n*, Bild *n*
pair **1.** Paar *n*; ***a pair of …*** ein Paar …, ein(e) …; ***a pair of scissors*** e-e Schere; **2.** *v/i* zo sich paaren; *a.* ***pair off, pair up*** Paare bilden; *v/t a.* ***pair off, pair up*** paarweise anordnen; ***pair off*** *zwei Leute* zusammenbringen, verkuppeln
pa·ja·ma(s) ***(a pair of) pajamas*** (ein) Schlafanzug *m*, (ein) Pyjama *m*
pal Kamerad *m*, F Kumpel *m*, Spezi *m*
pal·ace Palast *m*, Schloss *n*
pal·a·ta·ble schmackhaft (*a. fig*)
pal·ate ANAT Gaumen *m*; *fig* Geschmack *m*
pale[1] **1.** blass, *a.* bleich, *a.* hell (*color*); **2.** blass *or* bleich werden
pale[2] Pfahl *m*; *fig* Grenzen *pl*
pale·ness Blässe *f*
Pal·es·tin·i·an **1.** palästinensisch; **2.** Palästinenser(in)
pal·ings Lattenzaun *m*
pal·i·sade Palisade *f*; *pl* Steilufer *n*
pal·let TECH Palette *f*
pal·lid blass
pal·lor Blässe *f*
palm[1] *a.* ***palm tree*** BOT Palme *f*
palm[2] **1.** ANAT Handfläche *f*; **2.** *et.* in der Hand verschwinden lassen; ***palm s.th. off on s.o.*** F j-m et. andrehen
pal·pa·ble fühlbar, greifbar
pal·pi·tate MED klopfen, pochen
pal·pi·ta·tions MED Herzklopfen *n*
pal·sy MED Lähmung *f*
pal·try armselig
pam·per verwöhnen
pam·phlet Broschüre *f*
pan Pfanne *f*; Topf *m*
pan·a·ce·a Allheilmittel *n*

pan·cake Pfannkuchen *m*
pan·da zo Panda *m*
pan·da car *Br* (Funk)Streifenwagen *m*
pan·de·mo·ni·um Hölle *f*, Höllenlärm *m*, Tumult *m*, Chaos *n*
pan·der Vorschub leisten (***to*** *dat*)
pane (*Fenster*)Scheibe *f*
pan·el 1. (*Tür*)Füllung *f*, (*Wand*)Täfelung *f*; ELECTR, TECH Instrumentenbrett *n*, (*Schalt-*, *Kontroll-* *etc*)Tafel *f*; JUR Liste *f* der Geschworenen; Diskussionsteilnehmer *pl*, Diskussionsrunde *f*; Rateteam *n*; **2.** täfeln
pang stechender Schmerz; ***pangs of hunger*** nagender Hunger; ***pangs of conscience*** Gewissensbisse *pl*
pan·han·dle 1. Pfannenstiel *m*; GEOGR schmaler Fortsatz; **2.** F betteln
pan·ic 1. panisch; **2.** Panik *f*; **3.** in Panik versetzen *or* geraten
pan·ick·y: F ***be panicky*** in Panik sein
pan·ic-strick·en von Panik erfasst *or* erfüllt
pan·o·ra·ma Panorama *n*, Ausblick *m*
pan·sy BOT Stiefmütterchen *n*
pant keuchen, schnaufen, nach Luft schnappen
pan·ther zo Panther *m*; Puma *m*; Jaguar *m*
pan·ties (Damen)Schlüpfer *m*, Slip *m*; Höschen *n*
pan·to·mime THEA Pantomime *f*; *Br* F Weihnachtsspiel *n*
pan·try Speisekammer *f*
pants Hose *f*; *Br* Unterhose *f*; *Br* Schlüpfer *m*
pant·suit Hosenanzug *m*
pan·ty·hose Strumpfhose *f*
pan·ty·lin·er Slipeinlage *f*
pap Brei *m*
pa·pal päpstlich
pa·per 1. Papier *n*; Zeitung *f*; (Prüfungs-)Arbeit *f*; UNIV Klausur(arbeit) *f*; Aufsatz *m*; Referat *n*; Tapete *f*; *pl* (Ausweis)Papiere *pl*; **2.** tapezieren
pa·per·back Taschenbuch *n*, Paperback *n*
pa·per bag (Papier)Tüte *f*
pa·per·boy Zeitungsjunge *m*
pa·per clip Büro-, Heftklammer *f*
pa·per cup Pappbecher *m*
pa·per·hang·er Tapezierer *m*
pa·per knife *Br* Brieföffner *m*
pa·per mon·ey Papiergeld *n*
pa·per·weight Briefbeschwerer *m*
par: ***at par*** zum Nennwert; ***be on a par with*** gleich *or* ebenbürtig sein (*dat*)
par·a·ble Parabel *f*, Gleichnis *n*
par·a·chute Fallschirm *m*
par·a·chut·ist Fallschirmspringer(in)
pa·rade 1. Umzug *m*, *esp* MIL Parade *f*; *fig* Zurschaustellung *f*; ***make a parade of*** *fig* zur Schau stellen; **2.** ziehen (***through*** durch); MIL antreten (lassen), vorbeimarschieren (lassen); zur Schau stellen; ***parade (through)*** stolzieren durch
par·a·dise Paradies *n*
par·af·fin *Br* Petroleum *n*
par·a·glid·er SPORT Gleitschirm *m*; Gleitschirmflieger(in)
par·a·glid·ing SPORT Gleitschirmfliegen *n*
par·a·gon Muster *n* (***of*** an *dat*)
par·a·graph Absatz *m*, Abschnitt *m*; (Zeitungs)Notiz *f*
par·al·lel 1. parallel (***to, with*** zu); **2.** MATH Parallele *f* (*a. fig*); ***without parallel*** ohne Parallele, ohnegleichen; **3.** entsprechen (*dat*), gleichkommen (*dat*)
par·a·lyse *Br*, **par·a·lyze** MED lähmen, *fig a.* lahmlegen, zum Erliegen bringen; ***paralysed with*** *fig* starr *or* wie gelähmt vor (*dat*)
pa·ral·y·sis MED Lähmung *f*, *fig a.* Lahmlegung *f*
par·a·med·ic MED Sanitäter *m*
par·a·mount größte(r, -s), übergeordnet; ***of paramount importance*** von (aller)größter Bedeutung *or* Wichtigkeit
par·a·pet Brüstung *f*
par·a·pher·na·li·a (persönliche) Sachen *pl*; Ausrüstung *f*; *esp Br* F Scherereien *pl*
par·a·phrase 1. umschreiben; **2.** Umschreibung *f*
par·a·site Parasit *m*, Schmarotzer *m*
par·a·troop·er MIL Fallschirmjäger *m*; *pl* Fallschirmjägertruppe *f*
par·boil halb gar kochen, ankochen
par·cel 1. Paket *n*; Parzelle *f*; **2. *parcel out*** aufteilen; ***parcel up*** (als Paket) verpacken
parch ausdörren, austrocknen; vertrocknen
parch·ment Pergament *n*
par·don 1. JUR Begnadigung *f*; ***I beg your pardon*** Entschuldigung!, Verzeihung!; erlauben Sie mal!, ich muss doch sehr bitten!; *a.* ***pardon?*** F (wie) bitte?; **2.** verzeihen; vergeben; JUR begnadigen; ***pardon me*** → ***I beg your pardon***; F (wie) bitte?
par·don·a·ble verzeihlich
pare sich *die Nägel* schneiden; *Apfel etc* schälen
par·ent Elternteil *m*, Vater *m*, Mutter *f*; *pl* Eltern *pl*
par·ent·age Abstammung *f*, Herkunft *f*
pa·ren·tal elterlich
pa·ren·the·ses (runde) Klammer
par·ents-in-law Schwiegereltern *pl*

P

par·ent-teach·er meet·ing PED Elternabend *m*
par·ings Schalen *pl*
par·ish REL Gemeinde *f*
par·ish church REL Pfarrkirche *f*
pa·rish·ion·er REL Gemeindemitglied *n*
park **1.** Park *m*, (Grün)Anlage(n *pl*) *f*; **2.** MOT parken; ***look for somewhere to park the car*** e-n Parkplatz suchen
par·ka Parka *m, f*
park·ing MOT Parken *n*; ***no parking*** Parkverbot, Parken verboten
parking disk Parkscheibe *f*
parking fee Parkgebühr *f*
parking garage Park(hoch)haus *n*
parking lot Parkplatz *m*
parking lot at·tend·ant Parkwächter *m*
parking me·ter Parkuhr *f*
parking of·fender Parksünder(in)
parking space Parkplatz *m*, Parklücke *f*
parking tick·et Strafzettel *m*
par·ley *esp* MIL Verhandlung *f*
par·lia·ment Parlament *n*
par·lia·men·tar·i·an Parlamentarier(in)
par·lia·men·ta·ry parlamentarisch, Parlaments…
par·lo(u)r *mst in cpds* Salon *m*
pa·ro·chi·al REL Pfarr…, Gemeinde…; *fig* engstirnig, beschränkt
par·o·dy **1.** Parodie *f*; **2.** parodieren
pa·role JUR **1.** Hafturlaub *m*; bedingte Haftentlassung; ***he is out on parole*** er hat Hafturlaub; er wurde bedingt entlassen; **2.** ***parole s.o.*** j-m Hafturlaub gewähren; j-n bedingt entlassen
par·quet Parkett *n* (*a.* THEA)
par·quet floor Parkett(fuß)boden *m*
par·rot **1.** ZO Papagei *m* (*a. fig*); **2.** *et.* (wie ein Papagei) nachplappern
par·ry abwehren, parieren
par·si·mo·ni·ous geizig
pars·ley BOT Petersilie *f*
par·son REL Pfarrer *m*
par·son·age REL Pfarrhaus *n*
part **1.** Teil *m*; TECH Teil *n*, Bau-, Ersatzteil *n*; Anteil *m*; Seite *f*, Partei *f*; THEA, *fig* Rolle *f*; MUS Stimme *f*, Partie *f*; GEOGR Gegend *f*, Teil *m*; (Haar)Scheitel *m*; ***for my part*** was mich betrifft; ***for the most part*** größtenteils; meistens; ***in part*** teilweise, zum Teil; ***on the part of*** vonseiten, seitens (*gen*); ***on my part*** von m-r Seite; ***take part in s.th.*** an e-r Sache teilnehmen; ***take s.th. in good part*** et. nicht übel nehmen; **2.** *v/t* trennen; (ab-, zer-)teilen; einteilen; *Haar* scheiteln; ***part company*** sich trennen (***with*** von); *v/i* sich trennen (***with*** von); **3.** *adj* Teil…; **4.** *adv*: **part …, part** teils …, teils
par·tial Teil…, teilweise; parteiisch, voreingenommen (***to*** für)
par·ti·al·i·ty Parteilichkeit *f*, Voreingenommenheit *f*; Schwäche *f*, besondere Vorliebe (***for*** für)
par·tial·ly teilweise, zum Teil
par·tic·i·pant Teilnehmer(in)
par·tic·i·pate teilnehmen, sich beteiligen (*both*: ***in*** an *dat*)
par·tic·i·pa·tion Teilnahme *f*, Beteiligung *f*
par·ti·ci·ple LING Partizip *n*, Mittelwort *n*
par·ti·cle Teilchen *n*
par·tic·u·lar **1.** besondere(r, -s), speziell; genau, eigen, wählerisch; **2.** Einzelheit *f*; *pl* nähere Umstände *pl or* Angaben *pl*; Personalien *pl*; ***in particular*** insbesondere
par·tic·u·lar·ly besonders
part·ing **1.** Trennung *f*, Abschied *m*; *esp Br* (Haar)Scheitel *m*; **2.** Abschieds…
par·ti·san **1.** Parteigänger(in); MIL Partisan(in); **2.** parteiisch
par·ti·tion **1.** Teilung *f*; Trennwand *f*; **2.** ***partition off*** abteilen, abtrennen
part·ly teilweise, zum Teil
part·ner Partner(in), ECON *a.* Teilhaber(in)
part·ner·ship Partnerschaft *f*, ECON *a.* Teilhaberschaft *f*
part-own·er Miteigentümer(in)
par·tridge ZO Rebhuhn *n*
part-time **1.** *adj* Teilzeit…, Halbtags…; ***part-time worker*** → ***part-timer***; **2.** *adv* halbtags
part-tim·er F Teilzeitbeschäftigte *m, f*, Halbtagskraft *f*
par·ty Partei *f* (*a.* POL); (*Arbeits-, Reise-*) Gruppe *f*; (*Rettungs- etc*)Mannschaft *f*; MIL Kommando *n*, Trupp *m*; Party *f*, Gesellschaft *f*; Teilnehmer(in), Beteiligte *m, f*
party line POL Parteilinie *f*
party pol·i·tics Parteipolitik *f*
pass **1.** *v/i* vorbeigehen, -fahren, -kommen, -ziehen *etc* (***by*** an *dat*); übergehen (***to*** auf *acc*), fallen (***to*** an *acc*); vergehen (*pain etc, time*); durchkommen, (die Prüfung) bestehen; gelten (***as, for*** als), gehalten werden (***as, for*** für); PARL Rechtskraft erlangen; unbeanstandet bleiben; SPORT (den Ball) abspielen *or* passen (***to*** zu); *card game*: passen (*a. fig*); ***let s.o. pass*** j-n vorbeilassen; ***let s.th. pass*** et. durchgehen lassen; *v/t* vorbeigehen, -fahren, -fließen, -kommen, -ziehen *etc* an (*dat*); überholen; *Prüfung* bestehen; *Prüfling* durchkommen lassen; (*mit der Hand*) streichen (***over*** über *acc*); *j-m et.* reichen, geben, *et.* weitergeben; SPORT

P

Ball abspielen, passen (***to*** zu); *Zeit* verbringen; PARL *Gesetz* verabschieden; *Urteil* abgeben, fällen, JUR *a.* sprechen (***on*** über *acc*); *fig* hinausgehen über (*acc*), übersteigen, übertreffen; ***pass away*** sterben; ***pass off*** *j-n, et.* ausgeben (***as*** als); *gut etc* verlaufen; ***pass out*** ohnmächtig werden; **2.** Passierschein *m*; Bestehen *n* (*examination*); SPORT Pass *m*, Zuspiel *n*; (*Gebirgs*)Pass *m*; ***free pass*** Frei(fahr)-karte *f*; ***things have come to such a pass that*** F die Dinge haben sich derart zugespitzt, dass; ***make a pass at*** F Annäherungsversuche machen bei

pass·a·ble passierbar, befahrbar; passabel, leidlich

pas·sage Passage *f*, Korridor *m*, Gang *m*; Durchgang *m*; (See-, Flug)Reise *f*; Durchfahrt *f*, Durchreise *f*; Passage *f* (*a.* MUS), Stelle *f*; ***bird of passage*** Zugvogel *m*

pass·book ECON Sparbuch *n*

pas·sen·ger Passagier *m*, Fahrgast *m*, Fluggast *m*, Reisende *m, f*, MOT Insasse *m*, Insassin *f*

pass·er-by Passant(in)

pas·sion Leidenschaft *f*; Wut *f*, Zorn *m*; ***Passion*** REL Passion *f*; ***passions ran high*** die Erregung schlug hohe Wellen

pas·sion·ate leidenschaftlich

pas·sive passiv; LING passivisch

Pass·o·ver REL Passah(fest) *n*

pass·port (Reise)Pass *m*

pass·word Kennwort *n* (*a.* EDP), MIL *a.* Parole *f*, Losung *f*

past **1.** *adj* vergangen; frühere(r, -s); ***be past*** *a.* vorüber sein; ***for some time past*** seit einiger Zeit; ***past tense*** LING Vergangenheit *f*, Präteritum *n*; **2.** *adv* vorüber, vorbei; ***go past*** vorbeigehen; **3.** *prp time*: nach, über (*acc*); über … (*acc*) hinaus; an … (*dat*) vorbei; ***half past two*** halb drei; ***past hope*** hoffnungslos; **4.** Vergangenheit *f* (*a.* LING)

pas·ta Teigwaren *pl*

paste **1.** Paste *f*; Kleister *m*; Teig *m*; **2.** kleben (***to, on*** an *acc*); ***paste up*** ankleben

paste·board Karton *m*, Pappe *f*

pas·tel Pastell(zeichnung *f*) *n*

pas·teur·ize pasteurisieren

pas·time Zeitvertreib *m*, Freizeitbeschäftigung *f*

pas·tor REL Pastor *m*, Pfarrer *m*, Seelsorger *m*

pas·tor·al REL seelsorgerisch, pastoral; ***pastoral care*** Seelsorge *f*

pas·try GASTR (*Blätter-, Mürbe*)Teig *m*; Feingebäck *n*

pastry cook Konditor *m*

pas·ture **1.** Weide(land *n*) *f*; **2.** *v/t* weiden (lassen); *v/i* grasen, weiden

pas·ty[1] *esp Br* GASTR (Fleisch)Pastete *f*

past·y[2] blass, F käsig

pat **1.** Klaps *m*; GASTR Portion *f*; **2.** tätscheln; klopfen

patch **1.** Fleck *m*; Flicken *m*; kleines Stück Land; ***in patches*** stellenweise; **2.** flicken

pa·tent **1.** offenkundig; patentiert; Patent…; **2.** Patent *n*; ***take out a patent for s.th.*** (sich) et. patentieren lassen; **3.** *et.* patentieren lassen

pa·tent·ee Patentinhaber(in)

pa·tent leath·er Lackleder *n*

pa·ter·nal väterlich; väterlicherseits

pa·ter·ni·ty JUR Vaterschaft *f*

path Pfad *m*; Weg *m*

pa·thet·ic mitleiderregend; kläglich, miserabel

pa·tience Geduld *f*; *esp Br* Patience *f*

pa·tient[1] geduldig

pa·tient[2] MED Patient(in)

pat·i·o Terrasse *f*; Innenhof *m*, Patio *m*

pat·ri·ot Patriot(in)

pat·ri·ot·ic patriotisch

pa·trol **1.** Patrouille *f* (*a.* MIL), Streife *f*, Runde *f*; ***on patrol*** auf Patrouille, auf Streife; **2.** abpatrouillieren, auf Streife sein in (*dat*), s-e Runde machen in (*dat*)

pa·trol car (Funk)Streifenwagen *m*

pa·trol·man Streifenpolizist *m*; *Br* motorisierter Pannenhelfer

pa·tron Schirmherr *m*; Gönner *m*, Förderer *m*; (Stamm)Kunde *m*; Stammgast *m*

pat·ron·age Schirmherrschaft *f*; Förderung *f*

pat·ron·ess Schirmherrin *f*; Gönnerin *f*, Förderin *f*

pat·ron·ize fördern; (Stamm)Kunde *or* Stammgast sein bei *or* in (*dat*); gönnerhaft *or* herablassend behandeln

pa·tron saint REL Schutzheilige *m, f*

pat·ter prasseln (*rain*); trappeln (*feet*)

pat·tern **1.** Muster *n* (*a. fig*); Schema *n*; **2.** bilden, formen (***after, on*** nach)

paunch (dicker) Bauch

pau·per Arme *m, f*

pause **1.** Pause *f*; **2.** innehalten, e-e Pause machen

pave pflastern; ***pave the way for*** *fig* den Weg ebnen für

pave·ment Fahrbahn *f*; Belag *m*, Pflaster *n*; *Br* Bürgersteig *m*, Gehsteig *m*

pave·ment ca·fé *Br* Straßencafé *n*

paw **1.** zo Pfote *f*, Tatze *f*; **2.** *v/t Boden* scharren; scharren an (*dat*); F betatschen; *v/i* scharren (***at*** an *dat*)

pawn[1] *chess*: Bauer *m*; *fig* Schachfigur *f*

pawn[2] **1.** verpfänden, versetzen; **2.** ***be in***

P

pawn verpfändet *or* versetzt sein
pawn·bro·ker Pfandleiher *m*
pawn·shop Leihhaus *n*, Pfandhaus *n*
pay 1. *v/t et.* (be)zahlen; *j-n* bezahlen; *Aufmerksamkeit* schenken; *Besuch* abstatten; *Kompliment* machen; ***pay attention*** achtgeben auf (*acc*); PED aufpassen; ***pay cash*** bar bezahlen; *v/i* zahlen; *fig* sich lohnen; ***pay for*** (*fig* für) *et.* bezahlen; *fig* büßen; ***pay in*** einzahlen; ***pay into*** einzahlen auf (*acc*); ***pay off*** *et.* ab(be)-zahlen; *j-n* auszahlen; **2.** Bezahlung *f*, Gehalt *n*, Lohn *m*
pay·a·ble zahlbar, fällig
pay·day Zahltag *m*
pay·ee Zahlungsempfänger(in)
pay en·ve·lope Lohntüte *f*
pay·ing lohnend
pay·mas·ter MIL Zahlmeister *m*
pay·ment (Be)Zahlung *f*
pay pack·et *Br* Lohntüte *f*
pay phone *Br* Münzfernsprecher *m*
pay·roll Lohnliste *f*
pay·slip Lohn-, Gehaltsstreifen *m*
PC ABBR *of* ***personal computer*** PC *m*, Personal Computer *m*; ***PC user*** PC-Benutzer *m*
pea BOT Erbse *f*
peace Friede(n) *m*; Ruhe *f*; JUR öffentliche Ruhe und Ordnung; ***at peace*** in Frieden
peace·a·ble friedlich, friedfertig
peace·ful friedlich
peace·lov·ing friedliebend
peace move·ment Friedensbewegung *f*
peace·time Friedenszeiten *pl*
peach BOT Pfirsich(baum) *m*
pea·cock ZO Pfau *m*, Pfauhahn *m*
pea·hen ZO Pfauhenne *f*
peak Spitze *f*, Gipfel *m*; Schirm *m*; *fig* Höhepunkt *m*, Höchststand *m*
peaked cap Schirmmütze *f*
peak hours Hauptverkehrszeit *f*, Stoßzeit *f*; ELECTR Hauptbelastungszeit *f*
peak time, peak viewing hours *Br* TV Haupteinschaltzeit *f*, Hauptsendezeit *f*, beste Sendezeit
peal 1. (*Glocken*)Läuten *n*; (*Donner-*) Schlag *m*; ***peals of laughter*** schallendes Gelächter; **2.** *a.* ***peal out*** läuten; krachen
pea·nut BOT Erdnuss *f*; *pl* F lächerliche Summe
pear BOT Birne *f*; Birnbaum *m*
pearl 1. Perle *f*; Perlmutter *f*, Perlmutt *n*; **2.** Perlen…
pearl·y perlenartig, Perlen…
peas·ant Kleinbauer *m*
peat Torf *m*
peb·ble Kiesel(stein) *m*
peck picken, hacken; ***peck at one's food*** im Essen herumstochern
pe·cu·li·ar eigen, eigentümlich, typisch; eigenartig, seltsam
pe·cu·li·ar·i·ty Eigenheit *f*; Eigentümlichkeit *f*
ped·a·go·gic pädagogisch
ped·al 1. Pedal *n*; **2.** das Pedal treten; (mit dem Rad) fahren, strampeln
pe·dan·tic pedantisch
ped·dle hausieren (gehen) mit; ***peddle drugs*** mit Drogen handeln
ped·dler Hausierer(in)
ped·es·tal Sockel *m*
pe·des·tri·an 1. Fußgänger(in); **2.** Fußgänger…
pedestrian cross·ing Fußgängerübergang *m*
pedestrian mall, *esp Br* **pedestrian precinct** Fußgängerzone *f*
ped·i·cure Pediküre *f*
ped·i·gree Stammbaum *m* (*a.* ZO)
ped·lar *Br* → ***peddler***
pee F **1.** pinkeln; **2.** ***have*** (*or* ***go for***) ***a pee*** pinkeln (gehen)
peek 1. kurz *or* verstohlen gucken (***at*** auf *acc*); **2.** ***have*** *or* ***take a peek at*** e-n kurzen *or* verstohlenen Blick werfen auf (*acc*)
peel 1. *v/t* schälen; *a.* ***peel off*** abschälen, *Folie*, *Tapete etc* abziehen, ablösen; *Kleid* abstreifen; *v/i a.* ***peel off*** sich lösen (*wallpaper etc*), abblättern (*paint etc*), sich schälen (*skin*); **2.** BOT Schale *f*
peep[1] **1.** kurz *or* verstohlen gucken (***at*** auf *acc*); *mst* ***peep out*** (her)vorschauen; **2.** ***take a peep at*** e-n kurzen *or* verstohlenen Blick werfen auf (*acc*)
peep[2] **1.** Piep(s)en *n*; F Piepser *m*; **2.** piep(s)en
peep·hole Guckloch *n*; (Tür)Spion *m*
peer angestrengt schauen, spähen; ***peer at s.o.*** j-n anstarren
peer·less unvergleichlich, einzigartig
peev·ish verdrießlich, gereizt
peg 1. (Holz)Stift *m*, Zapfen *m*, Pflock *m*; (Kleider)Haken *m*; *Br* (*Wäsche-*) Klammer *f*; (*Zelt*)Hering *m*; ***take s.o. down a peg*** (***or two***) F j-m e-n Dämpfer aufsetzen; **2.** anpflocken; *Wäsche* anklammern, festklammern
pel·i·can ZO Pelikan *m*
pelican cross·ing *Br* Ampelübergang *m*
pel·let Kügelchen *n*; Schrotkorn *n*
pelt[1] *v/t* bewerfen, *v/i*: ***it's pelting*** (***down***), *esp Br* ***it's pelting with rain*** es gießt in Strömen
pelt[2] ZO Fell *n*, Pelz *m*
pel·vis ANAT Becken *n*

pen[1] *(Schreib)*Feder *f*; Füller *m*; Kugelschreiber *m*
pen[2] **1.** Pferch *m*, *(Schaf)*Hürde *f*; **2.** ***pen in, pen up*** *Tiere* einpferchen, *Personen* zusammenpferchen
pe·nal JUR Straf…; strafbar
pe·nal code JUR Strafgesetzbuch *n*
pe·nal·ize bestrafen
pen·al·ty Strafe *f*, SPORT *a.* Strafpunkt *m*; *soccer*: Elfmeter *m*
penalty ar·e·a, penalty box F *soccer*: Strafraum *m*
penalty goal *soccer*: Elfmetertor *n*
penalty kick *soccer*: Elfmeter *m*, Strafstoß *m*
penalty shoot-out *soccer*: Elfmeterschießen *n*
penalty spot *soccer*: Elfmeterpunkt *m*
pen·ance REL Buße *f*
pen·cil **1.** Bleistift *m*; **2.** (mit Bleistift) markieren *or* schreiben *or* zeichnen; *Augenbrauen* nachziehen
pen·cil case Federmäppchen *n*
pen·cil sharp·en·er Bleistiftspitzer *m*
pen·dant, pen·dent (Schmuck)Anhänger *m*
pend·ing **1.** *prp* bis zu; **2.** *adj esp* JUR schwebend
pen·du·lum Pendel *n*
pen·e·trate *v/t* eindringen in *(acc)*; dringen durch, durchdringen; *v/i* eindringen (***into*** in *acc*)
pen·e·trat·ing durchdringend; *fig* scharf; scharfsinnig
pen·e·tra·tion Durchdringen *n*, Eindringen *n*; *fig* Scharfsinn *m*
pen friend *Br* Brieffreund(in)
pen·guin ZO Pinguin *m*
pe·nin·su·la Halbinsel *f*
pe·nis ANAT Penis *m*
pen·i·tence Buße *f*, Reue *f*
pen·i·tent **1.** reuig, bußfertig; **2.** REL Büßer(in)
pen·i·ten·tia·ry (Staats)Gefängnis *n*, Strafanstalt *f*
pen·knife Taschenmesser *n*
pen name Schriftstellername *m*, Pseudonym *n*
pen·nant Wimpel *m*
pen·ni·less (völlig) mittellos
pen·ny *a.* ***new penny*** *Br* Penny *m*
pen pal Brieffreund(in)
pen·sion **1.** Rente *f*, Pension *f*; **2.** ***pension off*** pensionieren, in den Ruhestand versetzen
pen·sion·er Rentner(in), Pensionär(in)
pen·sive nachdenklich
pen·tath·lete SPORT Fünfkämpfer(in)
pen·tath·lon SPORT Fünfkampf *m*
Pen·te·cost REL Pfingsten *n*
pent·house Penthouse *n*, Penthaus *n*
pent-up auf-, angestaut *(emotions)*
pe·o·ny BOT Pfingstrose *f*
peo·ple **1.** Volk *n*, Nation *f*; die Menschen *pl*, die Leute *pl*; Leute *pl*, Personen *pl*; man; ***the people*** das *(gemeine)* Volk; **2.** besiedeln, bevölkern (***with*** mit)
peo·ple's re·pub·lic Volksrepublik *f*
pep F **1.** Pep *m*, Schwung *m*; **2.** *mst* ***pep up*** *j-n or et.* in Schwung bringen, aufmöbeln
pep·per **1.** Pfeffer *m*; BOT Paprikaschote *f*; **2.** pfeffern
pep·per cast·er Pfefferstreuer *m*
pep·per·mint BOT Pfefferminze *f*; Pfefferminz *n*
pep·per·y pfeff(e)rig; *fig* hitzig
pep·pill F Aufputschpille *f*
per per, durch; pro, für, je
per·ceive (be)merken, wahrnehmen; erkennen
per cent, per·cent Prozent *n*
per·cen·tage Prozentsatz *m*; F Prozente *pl*, (An)Teil *m*
per·cep·ti·ble wahrnehmbar, merklich
per·cep·tion Wahrnehmung *f*; Auffassung *f*, Auffassungsgabe *f*
perch[1] **1.** (Sitz)Stange *f*; **2.** (***on***) sich setzen (auf *acc*), sich niederlassen (auf *acc*, *dat*); F hocken (***on*** auf *dat*); ***perch o.s.*** F sich hocken (***on*** auf *acc*)
perch[2] ZO Barsch *m*
per·co·la·tor Kaffeemaschine *f*
per·cus·sion Schlag *m*; Erschütterung *f*; MUS Schlagzeug *n*
percussion drill TECH Schlagbohrer *m*
percussion in·stru·ment MUS Schlaginstrument *n*
pe·remp·to·ry herrisch
pe·ren·ni·al ewig, immer während; BOT mehrjährig
per·fect **1.** perfekt, vollkommen, vollendet; gänzlich, völlig; **2.** vervollkommnen; **3.** *a.* ***perfect tense*** LING Perfekt *n*
per·fec·tion Vollendung *f*; Vollkommenheit *f*, Perfektion *f*
per·fo·rate durchbohren, -löchern
per·form *v/t* verrichten, durchführen, tun; *Pflicht etc* erfüllen; THEA, MUS aufführen, spielen, vortragen; *v/i* THEA *etc* e-e Vorstellung geben, auftreten, spielen
per·form·ance Verrichtung *f*, Durchführung *f*; Leistung *f*; THEA, MUS Aufführung *f*, Vorstellung *f*, Vortrag *m*
per·form·er THEA, MUS Darsteller(in), Künstler(in)
per·fume **1.** Duft *m*; Parfüm *n*; **2.** parfümieren
per·fum·er·y Parfümerie *f*

per·haps vielleicht
per·il Gefahr *f*
per·il·ous gefährlich
pe·ri·od Periode *f*, Zeit *f*, Zeitdauer *f*, Zeitraum *m*, Zeitspanne *f*; (Unterrichts)Stunde *f*; MED Periode *f*; LING Punkt *m*
period fur·ni·ture Stilmöbel *pl*
pe·ri·od·ic periodisch
pe·ri·od·i·cal **1.** periodisch; **2.** Zeitschrift *f*
pe·riph·e·ral EDP Peripheriegerät *n*
peripheral e·quip·ment EDP Peripheriegeräte *pl*
pe·riph·e·ry Peripherie *f*, Rand *m*
per·ish umkommen; GASTR schlecht werden, verderben; TECH verschleißen
per·ish·a·ble leicht verderblich
per·ish·a·bles leicht verderbliche Lebensmittel
per·jure: ***perjure o.s.*** JUR e-n Meineid leisten
per·ju·ry JUR Meineid *m*; ***commit perjury*** e-n Meineid leisten
perk: ***perk up*** *v/i* aufleben, munter werden; *v/t j-n* munter machen, F aufmöbeln
perk·y F munter, lebhaft; keck, selbstbewusst
perm **1.** Dauerwelle *f*; ***get a perm*** → **2.** ***get one's hair permed*** sich e-e Dauerwelle machen lassen
per·ma·nent **1.** (be)ständig, dauerhaft, Dauer…; **2.** *a.* ***permanent wave*** Dauerwelle *f*
per·me·a·ble durchlässig (***to*** für)
per·me·ate durchdringen; dringen (***into*** in *acc*; ***through*** durch)
per·mis·si·ble zulässig, erlaubt
per·mis·sion Erlaubnis *f*
per·mis·sive liberal; (sexuell) freizügig
permissive so·ci·e·ty tabufreie Gesellschaft
per·mit **1.** erlauben, gestatten; **2.** Genehmigung *f*
per·pen·dic·u·lar senkrecht; rechtwink(e)lig (***to*** zu)
per·pet·u·al fortwährend, ständig, ewig
per·plex verwirren
per·plex·i·ty Verwirrung *f*
per·se·cute verfolgen
per·se·cu·tion Verfolgung *f*
per·se·cu·tor Verfolger(in)
per·se·ver·ance Ausdauer *f*, Beharrlichkeit *f*
per·se·vere beharrlich weitermachen
per·sist beharren (***in*** auf *dat*); anhalten
per·sis·tence Beharrlichkeit *f*
per·sis·tent beharrlich; anhaltend
per·son Person *f* (*a.* LING)
per·son·al persönlich (*a.* LING); Personal…; Privat…
personal com·pu·ter (ABBR ***PC***) Personal Computer *m*
personal da·ta Personalien *pl*
per·son·al·i·ty Persönlichkeit *f*; *pl* anzügliche *or* persönliche Bemerkungen *pl*
per·son·al or·ga·ni·zer Notizbuch *n*, Adressbuch *n* und Taschenkalender *m etc* (*in einem*)
personal pro·noun LING Personalpronomen *n*
personal ster·e·o Walkman® *m*
per·son·i·fy personifizieren, verkörpern
per·son·nel Personal *n*, Belegschaft *f*; die Personalabteilung
personnel de·part·ment Personalabteilung *f*
personnel man·ag·er Personalchef *m*
per·spec·tive Perspektive *f*; Fernsicht *f*
per·spi·ra·tion Transpirieren *n*, Schwitzen *n*; Schweiß *m*
per·spire transpirieren, schwitzen
per·suade überreden; überzeugen
per·sua·sion Überredung(skunst) *f*; Überzeugung *f*
per·sua·sive überzeugend
pert keck, kess; schnippisch
per·tain: ***pertain to s.th.*** et. betreffen
per·ti·nent sachdienlich, relevant, zur Sache gehörig
per·turb beunruhigen
per·vade durchdringen, erfüllen
per·verse pervers; eigensinnig
per·ver·sion Verdrehung *f*; Perversion *f*
per·ver·si·ty Perversität *f*; Eigensinn *m*
per·vert **1.** pervertieren; verdrehen; **2.** perverser Mensch
pes·sa·ry MED Pessar *n*
pes·si·mism Pessimismus *m*
pes·si·mist Pessimist(in)
pes·si·mis·tic pessimistisch
pest ZO Schädling *m*; F Nervensäge *f*; F Plage *f*
pest con·trol Schädlingsbekämpfung *f*
pes·ter F *j-n* belästigen, *j-m* keine Ruhe lassen
pes·ti·cide Pestizid *n*, Schädlingsbekämpfungsmittel *n*
pet **1.** (zahmes) (Haus)Tier; *often contp* Liebling *m*; **2.** Lieblings…; Tier…; **3.** streicheln; F Petting machen
pet·al BOT Blütenblatt *n*
pet food Tiernahrung *f*
pe·ti·tion **1.** Eingabe *f*, Gesuch *n*, (schriftlicher) Antrag; **2.** ersuchen; ein Gesuch einreichen (***for*** um), e-n Antrag stellen (***for*** auf *acc*)
pet name Kosename *m*

P

pet·ri·fy versteinern
pet·rol *Br* Benzin *n*
pe·tro·le·um Erdöl *n*, Mineralöl *n*
pet·rol pump *Br* Zapfsäule *f*
petrol station *Br* Tankstelle *f*
pet shop Tierhandlung *f*, Zoogeschäft *n*
pet·ti·coat Unterrock *m*
pet·ting F Petting *n*
pet·tish launisch, gereizt
pet·ty belanglos, unbedeutend, JUR *a.* geringfügig; engstirnig
petty cash Portokasse *f*
petty lar·ce·ny JUR einfacher Diebstahl
pet·u·lant launisch, gereizt
pew (Kirchen)Bank *f*
pew·ter Zinn *n*; *a.* ***pewter ware*** Zinn(-geschirr) *n*
phan·tom Phantom *n*; Geist *m*
phar·ma·cist Apotheker(in)
phar·ma·cy Apotheke *f*
phase Phase *f*
pheas·ant ZO Fasan *m*
phe·nom·e·non Phänomen *n*, Erscheinung *f*
phi·lan·thro·pist Philanthrop(in), Menschenfreund(in)
phil·is·tine F *contp* **1.** Spießer *m*; **2.** spießig
phi·lol·o·gist Philologe *m*, Philologin *f*
phi·lol·o·gy Philologie *f*
phi·los·o·pher Philosoph(in)
phi·los·o·phy Philosophie *f*
phlegm MED Schleim *m*
phone **1.** Telefon *n*; ***answer the phone*** ans Telefon gehen; ***by phone*** telefonisch; ***on the phone*** am Telefon; ***be on the phone*** Telefon haben; am Telefon sein; **2.** telefonieren, anrufen
phone book Telefonbuch *n*
phone booth, *Br* **phone box** Telefonzelle *f*
phone call Anruf *m*, Gespräch *n*
phone·card Telefonkarte *f*
phone-in *radio*, TV Sendung *f* mit telefonischer Zuhörer- *or* Zuschauerbeteiligung
phone num·ber Telefonnummer *f*
pho·net·ics Phonetik *f*
pho·n(e)y F **1.** Fälschung *f*; Schwindler(in); **2.** falsch, gefälscht, unecht; Schein...
phos·pho·rus CHEM Phosphor *m*
pho·to F Foto *n*, Bild *n*; ***in the photo*** auf dem Foto; ***take a photo*** ein Foto machen (***of*** von)
pho·to·cop·i·er Fotokopiergerät *n*
pho·to·cop·y **1.** Fotokopie *f*; **2.** fotokopieren
pho·to·graph **1.** Fotografie *f*; **2.** fotografieren
pho·tog·ra·pher Fotograf(in)
pho·tog·ra·phy Fotografie *f*
phras·al verb LING Verb *n* mit Adverb (und Präposition)
phrase **1.** (Rede)Wendung *f*, Redensart *f*, idiomatischer Ausdruck; **2.** ausdrücken
phrase·book Sprachführer *m*
phys·i·cal **1.** physisch, körperlich; physikalisch; ***physically handicapped*** körperbehindert; **2.** ärztliche Untersuchung
physical ed·u·ca·tion Leibeserziehung *f*, Sport *m*
physical ex·am·i·na·tion ärztliche Untersuchung
physical hand·i·cap Körperbehinderung *f*
physical train·ing Leibeserziehung *f*, Sport *m*
phy·si·cian Arzt *m*, Ärztin *f*
phys·i·cist Physiker(in)
phys·ics Physik *f*
phy·sique Körper(bau) *m*, Statur *f*
pi·a·nist MUS Pianist(in)
pi·an·o MUS Klavier *n*
pick **1.** (auf)hacken; (auf)picken; auflesen, aufnehmen; pflücken; *Knochen* abnagen; bohren *or* stochern in (*dat*); F *Schloss* knacken; aussuchen, auswählen; ***pick one's nose*** in der Nase bohren; ***pick one's teeth*** in den Zähnen (herum)stochern; ***pick s.o.'s pocket*** j-n bestehlen; ***have a bone to pick with s.o.*** mit j-m ein Hühnchen zu rupfen haben; ***pick out*** (sich) *et.* auswählen; ausmachen, erkennen; ***pick up*** aufheben, auflesen, aufnehmen; aufpicken; *Spur* aufnehmen; *j-n* abholen; *Anhalter* mitnehmen; F *Mädchen* aufreißen; *Kenntnisse, Informationen etc* aufschnappen; sich *e-e Krankheit etc* holen; *a.* ***pick up speed*** MOT schneller werden; **2.** (Spitz)-Hacke *f*, Pickel *m*; (Aus)Wahl *f*; ***take your pick*** suchen Sie sich etwas aus
pick-a-back huckepack
pick·ax, *Br* **pick·axe** (Spitz)Hacke *f*, Pickel *m*
pick·et **1.** Pfahl *m*; Streikposten *m*; **2.** Streikposten aufstellen vor (*dat*), mit Streikposten besetzen; Streikposten stehen
picket fence Lattenzaun *m*
picket line Streikpostenkette *f*
pick·le GASTR **1.** Salzlake *f*; Essigsoße *f*; Essig-, Gewürzgurke *f*; *mst pl esp Br* Pickles *pl*; ***be in a*** (***pretty***) ***pickle*** F (ganz schön) in der Patsche sitzen *or* sein *or* stecken; **2.** einlegen
pick·lock Einbrecher *m*; TECH Dietrich *m*

P

pick·pock·et Taschendieb(in)
pick-up Tonabnehmer *m*; Kleintransporter *m*; F (Zufalls)Bekanntschaft *f*
pick·y F wählerisch (***in*** *dat* about)
pic·nic 1. Picknick *n*; **2.** ein Picknick machen, picknicken
pic·ture 1. Bild *n*; Gemälde *n*; PHOT Aufnahme *f*; Film *m*; *pl esp Br* Kino *n*; **2.** darstellen, malen; *fig* sich *j-n, et.* vorstellen
picture book Bilderbuch *n*
picture post·card Ansichtskarte *f*
pic·tur·esque malerisch
pie (*Fleisch- etc*)Pastete *f*; (*mst* gedeckter) (*Apfel- etc*)Kuchen
piece 1. Stück *n*; Teil *n* (*of a machine etc*); Teil *m* (*of a set etc*); *chess*: Figur *f*; *board game*: Stein *m*; (Zeitungs)Artikel *m*, (-)Notiz *f*; ***by the piece*** stückweise; ***a piece of advice*** ein Rat; ***a piece of news*** e-e Neuigkeit; ***give s.o. a piece of one's mind*** j-m gründlich die Meinung sagen; ***go to pieces*** F zusammenbrechen; ***take to pieces*** auseinandernehmen; **2. *piece together*** zusammensetzen, -stückeln; *fig* zusammenfügen
piece·meal schrittweise
piece·work Akkordarbeit *f*; ***do piecework*** im Akkord arbeiten
pier MAR Pier *m*, Landungsbrücke *f*; TECH Pfeiler *m*
pierce durchbohren, durchstechen, durchstoßen; durchdringen
pierc·ing durchdringend, (*Kälte etc a.*) schneidend, (*Schrei a.*) gellend, (*Blick, Schmerz etc a.*) stechend
pi·e·ty Frömmigkeit *f*
pig ZO Schwein *n* (*a.* F); F Ferkel *n*; *sl contp* Bulle *m*
pi·geon ZO Taube *f*
pi·geon·hole 1. Fach *n*; **2.** ablegen
pig·gy F Schweinchen *n*
pig·gy·back huckepack
pig·gy bank Sparschwein(chen) *n*
pig·head·ed dickköpfig, stur
pig·let ZO Ferkel *n*
pig·sty Schweinestall *m*, F *contp* Saustall *m*
pig·tail Zopf *m*
pike[1] ZO Hecht *m*
pike[2] → ***turnpike***
pile[1] **1.** Stapel *m*, Stoß *m*; F Haufen *m*, Menge *f*; (***atomic***) ***pile*** Atommeiler *m*; **2. *pile up*** (an-, auf)häufen, (auf)stapeln, aufschichten; sich anhäufen; MOT F aufeinander auffahren
pile[2] Flor *m*
pile[3] Pfahl *m*
piles *Br* F MED Hämorrhoiden *pl*
pile·up MOT Massenkarambolage *f*
pil·fer stehlen, klauen
pil·grim Pilger(in)
pil·grim·age Pilgerfahrt *f*, Wallfahrt *f*
pill PHARM Pille *f*; ***the pill*** F die (*Antibaby*)-Pille; ***be on the pill*** die Pille nehmen
pil·lar Pfeiler *m*; Säule *f*
pil·li·on MOT Soziussitz *m*
pil·lo·ry 1. HIST Pranger *m*; **2.** *fig* anprangern
pil·low (Kopf)Kissen *n*
pil·low·case, pil·low slip (Kopf)Kissenbezug *m*
pi·lot 1. AVIAT Pilot *m*; MAR Lotse *m*; **2.** Versuchs…, Pilot…; **3.** lotsen; steuern
pilot film TV Pilotfilm *m*
pilot scheme Versuchs-, Pilotprojekt *n*
pimp Zuhälter *m*
pim·ple MED Pickel *m*, Pustel *f*
pin 1. (Steck)Nadel *f*; (*Haar-, Krawatten- etc*)Nadel *f*; Brosche *f*; TECH Bolzen *m*, Stift *m*; *bowling*: Kegel *m*; Pin *m*; (*Wäsche*)Klammer *f*; *Br* (*Reiß-*)Nagel *m*, (-)Zwecke *f*; **2.** (an)heften, anstecken (***to*** an *acc*), befestigen (***to*** an *dat*); pressen, drücken (***against, to*** gegen, an *acc*)
PIN *a.* ***PIN number*** ABBR *of* ***personal identification number*** PIN, persönliche Geheimzahl
pin·a·fore Schürze *f*
pin·ball Flippern *n*; ***play pinball*** flippern
pin·ball ma·chine Flipper(automat) *m*
pin·cers: (***a pair of pincers*** e-e) (Kneif)-Zange
pinch 1. *v/t* kneifen, zwicken; F klauen; *v/i* drücken; **2.** Kneifen *n*, Zwicken *n*; Prise *f*; *fig* Not(lage) *f*
pin·cush·ion Nadelkissen *n*
pine[1] BOT Kiefer *f*, Föhre *f*
pine[2] sich sehnen (***for*** nach)
pine·ap·ple BOT Ananas *f*
pine cone BOT Kiefernzapfen *m*
pine·tree BOT Kiefer *f*, Föhre *f*
pin·ion ZO Schwungfeder *f*
pink 1. rosa(farben); **2.** Rosa *n*; BOT Nelke *f*
pint Pint *n* (*0,47 l, Br 0,57 l*); *Br* F Halbe *f*
pi·o·neer 1. Pionier *m*; **2.** den Weg bahnen (für)
pi·ous fromm, religiös
pip[1] *Br* (*Apfel-, Orangen- etc*)Kern *m*
pip[2] (Piep)Ton *m*
pip[3] *on cards etc*: Auge *n*, Punkt *m*
pipe 1. TECH Rohr *n*, Röhre *f*; (*Tabaks*)-Pfeife *f*; MUS (*Orgel*)Pfeife *f*; *pl Br* F Dudelsack *m*; **2.** (durch Rohre) leiten
pipe·line Rohrleitung *f*; Pipeline *f*
pip·er MUS Dudelsackpfeifer *m*
pip·ing 1. Rohrleitung *f*, Rohrnetz *n*; **2.**

piping hot kochend heiß, siedend heiß
pi·quant pikant (*a. fig*)
pique 1. ***in a fit of pique*** gekränkt, verletzt, pikiert; **2.** kränken, verletzen; ***be piqued*** *a.* pikiert sein
pi·rate 1. Pirat *m*, Seeräuber *m*; **2.** unerlaubt kopieren *or* nachdrucken *or* nachpressen
pi·rate ra·di·o Piratensender *m or pl*
Pis·ces ASTR Fische *pl*; ***he*** (***she***) ***is*** (***a***) ***Pisces*** er (sie) ist (ein) Fisch
piss V **1.** Pisse *f*; ***take the piss out of s.o.*** j-n verarschen; **2.** pissen; ***piss off!*** verpiss dich!
pis·tol Pistole *f*
pis·ton TECH Kolben *m*
pit[1] **1.** Grube *f* (*a.* ANAT), MIN *a.* Zeche *f*; *esp Br* THEA Parkett *n*; *a.* ***orchestra pit*** THEA Orchestergraben *m*; MED (*esp* Pocken)Narbe *f*; *car racing*: Box *f*; ***pit stop*** Boxenstopp *m*; **2.** mit Narben bedecken
pit[2] **1.** BOT Kern *m*, Stein *m*; **2.** entkernen, entsteinen
pitch[1] **1.** *v/t Zelt*, *Lager* aufschlagen; werfen, schleudern; MUS (an)stimmen; *v/i* stürzen, fallen; MAR stampfen; sich neigen (*roof etc*); ***pitch in*** F sich ins Zeug legen; kräftig zulangen; **2.** *esp Br* SPORT (Spiel)Feld *n*; MUS Tonhöhe *f*; *fig* Grad *m*, Stufe *f*; *esp Br* Stand(platz) *m*; MAR Stampfen *n*; Neigung *f* (*of a roof etc*)
pitch[2] Pech *n*
pitch-black, **pitch-dark** pechschwarz; stockdunkel
pitch·er[1] Krug *m*
pitch·er[2] *baseball*: Werfer *m*
pitch·fork Heugabel *f*, Mistgabel *f*
pit·e·ous kläglich
pit·fall Fallgrube *f*; *fig* Falle *f*
pith BOT Mark *n*; weiße innere Haut; *fig* Kern *m*
pith·y markig, prägnant
pit·i·a·ble → ***pitiful***
pit·i·ful mitleiderregend, bemitleidenswert; erbärmlich, jämmerlich
pit·i·less unbarmherzig, erbarmungslos
pit·ta bread Fladenbrot *n*
pit·y 1. Mitleid *n* (***on*** mit); ***it is a*** (***great***) ***pity*** es ist (sehr) schade; ***what a pity!*** wie schade!; **2.** bemitleiden, bedauern
piv·ot 1. TECH Drehzapfen *m*; *fig* Dreh- und Angelpunkt *m*; **2.** sich drehen; ***pivot on*** *fig* abhängen von
pix·el EDP Pixel *m*
piz·za Pizza *f*
plac·ard 1. Plakat *n*; Transparent *n*; **2.** mit Plakaten bekleben
place 1. Platz *m*, Ort *m*, Stelle *f*; Stätte *f*; Haus *n*, Wohnung *f*; Wohnort *m*; (*Arbeits-*, *Lehr*)Stelle *f*; ***in the first place*** erstens; ***in third place*** SPORT *etc* auf dem dritten Platz; ***in place of*** anstelle von (*or gen*); ***out of place*** fehl am Platz; ***take place*** stattfinden; ***take s.o.'s place*** j-s Stelle einnehmen; **2.** stellen, legen, setzen; *Auftrag* erteilen (***with*** *dat*), *Bestellung* aufgeben (***with*** bei); ***be placed*** SPORT sich platzieren (***second*** an zweiter Stelle)
place mat Platzdeckchen *n*, Set *n*, *m*
place·ment test Einstufungsprüfung *f*
place name Ortsname *m*
plac·id ruhig; gelassen
pla·gia·rize plagiieren
plague 1. Seuche *f*; Pest *f*; Plage *f*; **2.** plagen
plaice zo Scholle *f*
plaid Plaid *n or m*
plain 1. *adj* einfach schlicht; klar (und deutlich); offen (und ehrlich); unscheinbar, wenig anziehend; rein, völlig (*nonsense etc*); **2.** *adv* F (ganz) einfach; **3.** Ebene *f*, Flachland *n*
plain choc·olate *Br* (zart)bittere Schokolade
plain-clothes … in Zivil
plain·tiff JUR Kläger(in)
plain·tive traurig, klagend
plait *esp Br* **1.** Zopf *m*; **2.** flechten
plan 1. Plan *m*; **2.** planen; beabsichtigen
plane[1] Flugzeug *n*; ***by plane*** mit dem Flugzeug; ***go by plane*** fliegen
plane[2] **1.** flach, eben; **2.** MATH Ebene *f*; *fig* Stufe *f*, Niveau *n*
plane[3] **1.** Hobel *m*; **2.** hobeln; ***plane down*** abhobeln
plan·et ASTR Planet *m*
plank Planke *f*, Bohle *f*
plank bed Pritsche *f*
plank·ing Planken *pl*
plant 1. BOT Pflanze *f*; ECON Werk *n*, Betrieb *m*, Fabrik *f*; **2.** (an-, ein)pflanzen; bepflanzen; *Garten etc* anlegen; aufstellen, postieren; ***plant s.th. on s.o*** F j-m et. (*Belastendes*) unterschieben
plan·ta·tion Plantage *f*, Pflanzung *f*; Schonung *f*
plant·er Plantagenbesitzer(in), Pflanzer(in); Pflanzmaschine *f*; Übertopf *m*
plaque Gedenktafel *f*; MED Zahnbelag *m*
plas·ter 1. MED Pflaster *n*; (Ver)Putz *m*; *a.* ***plaster of Paris*** Gips *m*; ***have one's leg in plaster*** MED das Bein in Gips haben;**2.** verputzen; bekleben
plaster cast Gipsabguss *m*, Gipsmodell *n*; MED Gipsverband *m*
plas·tic 1. plastisch; Plastik…; **2.** Plastik *n*, Kunststoff *m*; → **plastic mon·ey** F Plas-

tikgeld *n*, Kreditkarten *pl*
plastic wrap Frischhaltefolie *f*
plate 1. Teller *m*; Platte *f*; (*Namens-*, *Nummern- etc*)Schild *n*; (Bild)Tafel *f*; (Druck)Platte *f*; Gegenstände *pl* aus Edelmetall; Doublé *n*, Dublee *n*; **2.** ***plated with gold, gold-plated*** vergoldet
plat·form Plattform *f*; RAIL Bahnsteig *m*; (Redner)Tribüne *f*, Podium *n*; POL Plattform *f*; MOT Pritsche *f*; ***party platform*** POL Parteiprogramm *n*; ***election platform*** POL Wahlprogramm *n*
plat·i·num CHEM Platin *n*
pla·toon MIL Zug *m*
plat·ter (Servier)Platte *f*
plau·si·ble plausibel, glaubhaft
play 1. Spiel *n*; Schauspiel *n*, (Theater)-Stück *n*; TECH Spiel *n*; *fig* Spielraum *m*; ***at play*** beim Spiel(en); ***in play*** im Spiel (*ball*); ***out of play*** im Aus (*ball*); **2.** *v/i* spielen (*a.* SPORT, THEA *etc*); *v/t Karten*, *Rolle*, *Stück etc* spielen, SPORT *Spiel* austragen; ***play s.o.*** SPORT gegen j-n spielen; ***play the guitar*** Gitarre spielen; ***play a trick on s.o.*** j-m e-n Streich spielen; ***play back*** *Ball* zurückspielen (***to*** zu); *Tonband* abspielen; ***play*** *s.th.* ***down*** verharmlosen, herunterspielen; ***play off*** *fig* ausspielen (***against*** gegen); ***play on*** *fig j-s Schwächen* ausnutzen
play·back Play-back *n*, Wiedergabe *f*, Abspielen *n*
play·boy Playboy *m*
play·er MUS, SPORT Spieler(in); TECH Plattenspieler *m*
play·fel·low *Br* → ***playmate***
play·ful verspielt; scherzhaft
play·go·er Theaterbesucher(in)
play·ground Spielplatz *m* (*a. fig*); Schulhof *m*
play·group *Br* Spielgruppe *f*
play·house THEA Schauspielhaus *n*; Spielhaus *n* (*for children*)
play·ing card Spielkarte *f*
play·ing field Sportplatz *m*, Spielfeld *n*
play·mate Spielkamerad(in)
play·pen Laufgitter *n*, Laufstall *m*
play·thing Spielzeug *n*
play·wright Dramatiker(in)
plc, **PLC** *Br* ECON ABBR *of* ***public limited company*** AG, Aktiengesellschaft *f*
plea: ***enter a plea of*** (***not***) ***guilty*** JUR sich schuldig bekennen (s-e Unschuld erklären)
plead *v/i* (dringend) bitten (***for*** um); ***plead*** (***not***) ***guilty*** JUR sich schuldig bekennen (s-e Unschuld erklären); *v/t a.* JUR zu s-r Verteidigung *or* Entschuldigung anführen, geltend machen; ***plead s.o.'s case*** sich für j-n einsetzen; JUR j-n vertreten
pleas·ant angenehm, erfreulich; freundlich; sympathisch
please 1. *j-m* gefallen; *j-m* zusagen, *j-n* erfreuen; zufriedenstellen; ***only to please you*** nur dir zuliebe; ***please o.s.*** tun, was man will; ***please yourself!*** mach, was du willst!; **2.** *int* bitte; (***yes***,) **please** (ja,) bitte; (oh ja,) gerne; ***please come in!*** bitte, treten Sie ein!
pleased erfreut, zufrieden; ***be pleased about*** sich freuen über (*acc*); ***be pleased with*** zufrieden sein mit; ***I am pleased with it*** es gefällt mir; ***be pleased to do s.th.*** et. gern tun; ***pleased to meet you!*** angenehm!
pleas·ing angenehm
plea·sure Vergnügen *n*; ***at*** (***one's***) ***pleasure*** nach Belieben
pleat (Plissee)Falte *f*
pleat·ed skirt Faltenrock *m*
pledge 1. Pfand *n*; *fig* Unterpfand *n*; Versprechen *n*; **2.** versprechen, zusichern
plen·ti·ful reichlich
plen·ty 1. Überfluss *m*; ***in plenty*** im Überfluss, in Hülle und Fülle; ***plenty of*** e-e Menge, viel(e), reichlich; **2.** F reichlich
pleu·ri·sy MED Brustfell-, Rippenfellentzündung *f*
pli·a·ble, **pli·ant** biegsam; *fig* flexibel; *fig* leicht beeinflussbar
pli·ers (***a pair of pliers*** e-e) Beißzange *f*
plight Not *f*, Notlage *f*
plim·soll *Br* Turnschuh *m*
plod *a.* ***plod along*** sich dahinschleppen; ***plod away*** sich abplagen (***at*** mit), schuften
plop F **1.** Plumps *m*, Platsch *m*; **2.** plumpsen, (*ins Wasser*) platschen
plot 1. Stück *n* Land, Parzelle *f*, Grundstück *n*; THEA, *film etc*: Handlung *f*; Komplott *n*, Verschwörung *f*; EDP grafische Darstellung; **2.** *v/i* sich verschwören (***against*** gegen); *v/t* planen; einzeichnen
plot·ter EDP Plotter *m*
plough *Br*, **plow** AGR **1.** Pflug *m*; **2.** (um)-pflügen
plough·share *Br*, **plow·share** AGR Pflugschar *f*
pluck 1. *v/t Geflügel* rupfen; *mst* ***pluck out*** ausreißen, ausrupfen, auszupfen; MUS *Saiten* zupfen; ***pluck up*** (***one's***) ***courage*** Mut *or* sich ein Herz fassen; *v/i* zupfen (***at*** an *dat*); **2.** F Mut *m*, Schneid *m*
pluck·y F mutig
plug 1. Stöpsel *m*; ELECTR Stecker *m*, F Steckdose *f*; F MOT (*Zünd*)Kerze *f*; **2.**

v/t F für *et.* Schleichwerbung machen; *a.* ***plug up*** zustöpseln; zustopfen, verstopfen; ***plug in*** ELECTR anschließen, einstecken
plug·ging F Schleichwerbung *f*
plum BOT Pflaume *f*; Zwetsch(g)e *f*
plum·age Gefieder *n*
plumb **1.** (Blei)Lot *n*; **2.** ausloten, *fig a.* ergründen; ***plumb in*** *esp Br Waschmaschine etc* anschließen; **3.** *adj* lotrecht, senkrecht; **4.** *adv* F (haar)genau
plumb·er Klempner *m*, Installateur *m*
plumb·ing Klempner-, Installateurarbeit *f*; Rohre *pl*, Rohrleitungen *pl*
plume (Schmuck)Feder *f*; Federbusch *m*; (*Rauch*)Fahne *f*
plump **1.** *adj* drall, mollig, rund(lich), F pumm(e)lig; **2.** ***plump down*** fallen *or* plumpsen (lassen)
plum pud·ding *Br* Plumpudding *m*
plun·der **1.** plündern; **2.** Plünderung *f*; Beute *f*
plunge **1.** (ein-, unter)tauchen; (sich) stürzen (***into*** in *acc*); MAR stampfen; **2.** (Kopf)Sprung *m*; ***take the plunge*** *fig* den entscheidenden Schritt wagen
plu·per·fect *a.* ***pluperfect tense*** LING Plusquamperfekt *n*, Vorvergangenheit *f*
plu·ral LING Plural *m*, Mehrzahl *f*
plus **1.** *prp* plus, und, *esp* ECON zuzüglich; **2.** *adj* Plus…; ***plus sign*** MATH Plus *n*, Pluszeichen *n*; **3.** MATH Plus *n* (*a.* F), Pluszeichen *n*; F Vorteil *m*
plush Plüsch *m*
ply[1] *regelmäßig* verkehren, fahren (***between*** zwischen *dat*)
ply[2] *mst in cpds* TECH Lage *f*, Schicht *f*; ***three-ply*** dreifach (*thread etc*); dreifach gewebt (*carpet*)
ply·wood Sperrholz *n*
pm, **PM** ABBR *of* ***after noon*** (*Latin* ***post meridiem***) nachm., nachmittags, abends
pneu·mat·ic Luft…, pneumatisch; TECH Druck…, Pressluft…
pneu·mat·ic drill Pressluftbohrer *m*
pneu·mo·ni·a MED Lungenentzündung *f*
poach[1] GASTR pochieren; ***poached eggs*** verlorene Eier *pl*
poach[2] wildern
poach·er Wilddieb *m*, Wilderer *m*
PO Box Postfach *n*; ***write to PO Box 225*** schreiben Sie an Postfach 225
pock MED Pocke *f*, Blatter *f*
pock·et **1.** (Hosen- *etc*)Tasche *f*; **2.** *adj* Taschen…; **3.** einstecken, in die Tasche stecken; *fig* in die eigene Tasche stecken
pock·et·book Notizbuch *n*; Brieftasche *f*
pock·et cal·cu·la·tor Taschenrechner *m*
pocket knife Taschenmesser *n*
pocket money Taschengeld *n*
pod BOT Hülse *f*, Schote *f*
po·di·a·trist Fußpfleger(in)
po·em Gedicht *n*
po·et Dichter(in)
po·et·ic dichterisch
po·et·i·cal dichterisch
po·et·ic jus·tice *fig* ausgleichende Gerechtigkeit
po·et·ry Gedichte *pl*; Poesie *f* (*a. fig*), Dichtkunst *f*, Dichtung *f*
poi·gnant schmerzlich; ergreifend
point **1.** Spitze *f*; GEOGR Landspitze *f*; LING, MATH, PHYS, SPORT *etc* Punkt *m*; MATH (Dezimal)Punkt *m*; Grad *m*; MAR (*Kompass*)Strich *m*; *fig* Punkt *m*, Stelle *f*, Ort *m*; Zweck *m*; Ziel *n*, Absicht *f*; springender Punkt; Pointe *f*; ***two point five*** (***2.5***) 2,5; ***point of view*** Stand-, Gesichtspunkt *m*; ***be on the point of doing s.th.*** im Begriff sein, et. zu tun; ***to the point*** zur Sache gehörig; ***off*** *or* ***beside the point*** nicht zur Sache gehörig; ***come to the point*** zur Sache kommen; ***that's not the point*** darum geht es nicht; ***what's the point?*** wozu?; ***win on points*** SPORT nach Punkten gewinnen; ***winner on points*** SPORT Punktsieger *m*; **2.** *v/t* (zu)spitzen; *Waffe etc* richten (***at*** auf *acc*); ***point one's finger at s.o.*** (mit dem Finger) auf j-n zeigen; ***point out*** zeigen; *fig* hinweisen *or* aufmerksam machen auf (*acc*); *v/i* (mit dem Finger) zeigen (***at, to*** auf *acc*); ***point to*** nach *e-r Richtung* weisen *or* liegen; *fig* hinweisen auf (*acc*)
point·ed spitz; Spitz…; *fig* scharf (*remark etc*); ostentativ
point·er Zeiger *m*; Zeigestock *m*; ZO Pointer *m*, Vorstehhund *m*
point·less sinnlos, zwecklos
points *Br* RAIL Weiche *f*
poise **1.** (Körper)Haltung *f*; *fig* Gelassenheit *f*; **2.** balancieren; ***be poised*** schweben
poi·son **1.** Gift *n*; **2.** vergiften
poi·son·ous giftig (*a. fig*)
poke **1.** *v/t* stoßen; *Feuer* schüren; stecken; *v/i* ***poke about, poke around*** F (herum-) stöbern, (-)wühlen (***in*** in *dat*); **2.** Stoß *m*
pok·er Schürhaken *m*
pok·y F eng; schäbig
Po·land Polen *n*
po·lar polar
polar bear ZO Eisbär *m*
pole[1] GEOGR Pol *m*
pole[2] Stange *f*; Mast *m*; Deichsel *f*; SPORT (Sprung)Stab *m*
Pole Pole *m*, Polin *f*

P

pole·cat ZO Iltis *m*; F Skunk *m*, Stinktier *n*
po·lem·ic, po·lem·i·cal polemisch
pole star ASTR Polarstern *m*
pole vault SPORT Stabhochsprung *m*, Stabhochspringen *n*
pole-vault SPORT stabhochspringen
pole vault·er SPORT Stabhochspringer(in)
po·lice **1.** Polizei *f*; **2.** überwachen
po·lice car Polizeiauto *n*
po·lice·man Polizist *m*
po·lice of·fi·cer Polizeibeamte *m*, -beamtin *f*, Polizist(in)
police sta·tion Polizeiwache *f*, Polizeirevier *n*
po·lice·wom·an Polizistin *f*
pol·i·cy Politik *f*; Taktik *f*; Klugheit *f*; (Versicherungs)Police *f*
po·li·o MED Polio *f*, Kinderlähmung *f*
pol·ish **1.** polieren; *Schuhe* putzen; ***polish up*** aufpolieren (*a. fig*); **2.** Politur *f*; (*Schuh*)Creme *f*; *fig* Schliff *m*
Pol·ish **1.** polnisch; **2.** LING Polnisch *n*
po·lite höflich
po·lite·ness Höflichkeit *f*
po·lit·i·cal politisch
pol·i·ti·cian Politiker(in)
pol·i·tics Politik *f*
pol·ka MUS Polka *f*
pol·ka-dot gepunktet, getupft
poll **1.** (*Meinungs*)Umfrage *f*; Wahlbeteiligung *f*; *a. pl* Stimmabgabe *f*, Wahl *f*; **2.** befragen; *Stimmen* erhalten
pol·len BOT Pollen *m*, Blütenstaub *m*
poll·ing Stimmabgabe *f*; Wahlbeteiligung *f*
polling booth *esp Br* Wahlkabine *f*
polling day Wahltag *m*
polling place, *esp Br* **polling sta·tion** Wahllokal *n*
polls Wahl *f*; Wahllokal *n*
poll·ster Demoskop(in), Meinungsforscher(in)
pol·lut·ant Schadstoff *m*
pol·lute beschmutzen, verschmutzen; verunreinigen
pol·lut·er *a.* ***environmental polluter*** Umweltsünder(in)
pol·lu·tion (*Luft-, Wasser- etc*)Verschmutzung *f*; Verunreinigung *f*
po·lo SPORT Polo *n*
po·lo neck *a.* ***polo neck sweater*** *esp Br* Rollkragenpullover *m*
pol·yp ZO, MED Polyp *m*
pol·y·sty·rene Styropor® *n*
pom·mel (Sattel- *etc*)Knopf *m*
pomp Pomp *m*, Prunk *m*
pom·pous aufgeblasen, wichtigtuerisch; schwülstig (*speech*)
pond Teich *m*, Weiher *m*
pon·der *v/i* nachdenken (***on, over*** über *acc*); *v/t* überlegen
pon·der·ous schwerfällig; schwer
pon·toon Ponton *m*
pon·toon bridge Pontonbrücke *f*
po·ny ZO Pony *n*
po·ny·tail Pferdeschwanz *m*
poo·dle ZO Pudel *m*
pool[1] Teich *m*, Tümpel *m*; Pfütze *f*, (*Blut- etc*)Lache *f*; (*Schwimm*)Becken *n*, (*Swimming*)Pool *m*
pool[2] **1.** (*Arbeits-, Fahr*)Gemeinschaft *f*; (*Mitarbeiter- etc*)Stab *m*; (*Fuhr*)Park *m*; (*Schreib*)Pool *m*; ECON Pool *m*, Kartell *n*; *card games*: Gesamteinsatz *m*; Poolbillard *n*; **2.** *Geld, Unternehmen etc* zusammenlegen; *Kräfte etc* vereinen
pool hall, pool·room Billardspielhalle *f*
pools *a.* ***football pools*** *Br* (Fußball)Toto *n, m*
poor **1.** arm; dürftig, mangelhaft, schwach; **2.** ***the poor*** die Armen *pl*
poor·ly **1.** *adj esp Br* F kränklich, unpässlich; **2.** *adv* ärmlich, dürftig, schlecht, schwach
pop[1] **1.** *v/t* zerknallen; F schnell *wohin* tun *or* stecken; *v/i* knallen; (zer)platzen; ***pop in*** F auf e-n Sprung vorbeikommen; ***pop off*** F (plötzlich) den Löffel weglegen; ***pop up*** (plötzlich) auftauchen; **2.** Knall *m*; F Limo *f*
pop[2] MUS **1.** Pop *m*; **2.** Schlager…; Pop…
pop[3] F Paps *m*, Papa *m*
pop[4] ABBR *of* ***population*** Einw., Einwohner(zahl *f*) *pl*
pop con·cert MUS Popkonzert *n*
pop·corn Popcorn *n*, Puffmais *m*
Pope REL Papst *m*
pop-eyed F glotzäugig
pop group MUS Popgruppe *f*
pop·lar BOT Pappel *f*
pop mu·sic Popmusik *f*
pop·py BOT Mohn *m*
pop·u·lar populär, beliebt; volkstümlich; allgemein
pop·u·lar·i·ty Popularität *f*, Beliebtheit *f*; Volkstümlichkeit *f*
pop·u·late bevölkern, besiedeln; bewohnen
pop·u·la·tion Bevölkerung *f*
pop·u·lous dicht besiedelt, dicht bevölkert
porce·lain Porzellan *n*
porch überdachter Vorbau; Portal *n*; Veranda *f*
por·cu·pine ZO Stachelschwein *n*
pore[1] Pore *f*
pore[2]: ***pore over*** vertieft sein in (*acc*), *et.* eifrig studieren

pork GASTR Schweinefleisch *n*
porn F → ***porno***
por·no F **1.** Porno *m*; **2.** Porno…
por·nog·ra·phy Pornografie *f*
po·rous porös
por·poise ZO Tümmler *m*
por·ridge Porridge *m*, *n*, Haferbrei *m*
port[1] Hafen *m*; Hafenstadt *f*
port[2] AVIAT, MAR Backbord *n*
port[3] EDP Port *m*, Anschluss *m*
port[4] Portwein *m*
por·ta·ble tragbar
por·ter (Gepäck)Träger *m*; *esp Br* Pförtner *m*, Portier *m*; RAIL Schlafwagenschaffner *m*
port·hole MAR Bullauge *n*
por·tion 1. (An)Teil *m*; GASTR Portion *f*; **2.** ***portion out*** aufteilen, verteilen (***among, between*** unter *acc*)
port·ly korpulent
por·trait Porträt *n*, Bild *n*, Bildnis *n*
por·tray porträtieren; darstellen; schildern
por·tray·al THEA Verkörperung *f*, Darstellung *f*; Schilderung *f*
Por·tu·gal Portugal *n*
Por·tu·guese 1. portugiesisch; **2.** Portugiese *m*, Portugiesin *f*; LING Portugiesisch *n*; ***the Portuguese*** die Portugiesen *pl*
pose 1. *v/t* aufstellen; *Problem*, *Frage* aufwerfen, *Bedrohung*, *Gefahr etc* darstellen; *v/i* Modell sitzen *or* stehen; ***pose as*** sich ausgeben als *or* für; **2.** Pose *f*
posh *esp Br* F schick, piekfein
po·si·tion 1. Position *f*, Lage *f*, Stellung *f* (*a. fig*); Stand *m*; *fig* Standpunkt *m*; **2.** (auf)stellen
pos·i·tive 1. positiv; bestimmt, sicher, eindeutig; greifbar, konkret; konstruktiv; **2.** PHOT Positiv *n*
pos·sess besitzen; *fig* beherrschen
pos·sessed *fig* besessen
pos·ses·sion Besitz *m*; *fig* Besessenheit *f*
pos·ses·sive besitzergreifend; LING possessiv, besitzanzeigend
pos·si·bil·i·ty Möglichkeit *f*
pos·si·ble möglich
pos·si·bly möglicherweise, vielleicht; ***if I possibly can*** wenn ich irgend kann; ***I can't possibly do this*** ich kann das unmöglich tun
post[1] (*Tür-*, *Tor-*, *Ziel- etc*)Pfosten *m*; Pfahl *m*; **1.** *a.* ***post up*** *Plakat etc* anschlagen, ankleben; ***be posted missing*** AVIAT, MAR als vermisst gemeldet werden
post[2] *esp Br* **1.** Post *f*; Postsendung *f*; ***by post*** mit der Post; **2.** mit der Post (zu-) schicken, aufgeben, *Brief* einwerfen

post[3] **1.** Stelle *f*, Job *m*; Posten *m*; **2.** aufstellen, postieren; *esp Br* versetzen, MIL abkommandieren (***to*** nach)
post… nach…, Nach…
post·age Porto *n*
postage stamp Postwertzeichen *n*, Briefmarke *f*
post·al postalisch, Post…
postal or·der *Br* ECON Postanweisung *f*
postal vote POL Briefwahl *f*
post·bag *esp Br* Postsack *m*
post·box *esp Br* Briefkasten *m*
post·card Postkarte *f*; *a.* ***picture postcard*** Ansichtskarte *f*
post·code *Br* Postleitzahl *f*
post·er Plakat *n*; Poster *n*, *m*
poste res·tante *Br* **1.** Abteilung *f* für postlagernde Sendungen; **2.** postlagernd
pos·te·ri·or HUMOR Hinterteil *n*
pos·ter·i·ty die Nachwelt
post-free *esp Br* portofrei
post·hu·mous post(h)um
post·man *esp Br* Briefträger *m*, Postbote *m*
post·mark 1. Poststempel *m*; **2.** (ab-)stempeln
post·mas·ter Postamtsvorsteher *m*
post of·fice Post *f*; Postamt *n*, -filiale *f*
post of·fice box → ***PO Box***
post-paid portofrei
post·pone verschieben, aufschieben
post·pone·ment Verschiebung *f*, Aufschub *m*
post·script Postskript(um) *n*, Nachschrift *f*
pos·ture 1. (Körper)Haltung *f*; Stellung *f*; **2.** *fig* sich aufspielen
post·war Nachkriegs…
post·wom·an *esp Br* Briefträgerin *f*, Postbotin *f*
po·sy Sträußchen *n*
pot 1. Topf *m*; Kanne *f*; Kännchen *n* (*Tee etc*); SPORT F Pokal *m*; **2.** *Pflanze* eintopfen
po·tas·si·um cy·a·nide CHEM Zyankali *n*
po·ta·to Kartoffel *f*; → ***chips, crisps***
pot·bel·ly Schmerbauch *m*
po·ten·cy Stärke *f*; Wirksamkeit *f*, Wirkung *f*; MED Potenz *f*
po·tent PHARM stark; MED potent
po·ten·tial 1. potenziell, möglich; **2.** Potenzial *n*, Leistungsfähigkeit *f*
pot·hole MOT Schlagloch *n*
po·tion Trank *m*
pot·ter[1] *Br*: ***potter about*** herumwerkeln
pot·ter[2] Töpfer(in)
pot·ter·y Töpferei *f*; Töpferware(n *pl*) *f*
pouch Beutel *m* (*a.* ZO); ZO (*Backen-*)Tasche *f*

poul·tice MED (warmer) Umschlag *m*
poul·try Geflügel *n*
pounce **1.** sich stürzen (***on*** auf *acc*); **2.** Satz *m*, Sprung *m*
pound[1] Pfund *n* (*453,59 g*); ***pound*** (***sterling***) (ABBR **£**) Pfund *n*
pound[2] Tierheim *n*; Abstellplatz *m* für (polizeilich) abgeschleppte Fahrzeuge
pound[3] *v/t* zerstoßen, zerstampfen; trommeln *or* hämmern auf (*acc*) *or* an (*acc*) *or* gegen; *v/i* hämmern (***with*** vor *dat*)
pour *v/t* gießen, schütten; ***pour out*** ausgießen, ausschütten; *Getränk* eingießen; *v/i* strömen (*a. fig*)
pout *v/t Lippen* schürzen; *v/i* e-n Schmollmund machen; schmollen
pov·er·ty Armut *f*
pow·der **1.** Pulver *n*; Puder *m*; **2.** pulverisieren; (sich) pudern
powder puff Puderquaste *f*
powder room (Damen)Toilette *f*
pow·er **1.** Kraft *f*; Macht *f*; Fähigkeit *f*, Vermögen *n*; Gewalt *f*; JUR Befugnis *f*, Vollmacht *f*; MATH Potenz *f*; ELECTR Strom *m*; ***in power*** POL an der Macht; **2.** TECH antreiben
power cut ELECTR Stromsperre *f*
power fail·ure ELECTR Stromausfall *m*, Netzausfall *m*
pow·er·ful stark, kräftig; mächtig
pow·er·less kraftlos; machtlos
pow·er plant Elektrizitäts-, Kraftwerk *n*
power pol·i·tics Machtpolitik *f*
power sta·tion *Br* Elektrizitäts-, Kraftwerk *n*
prac·ti·ca·ble durchführbar
prac·ti·cal praktisch
practical joke Streich *m*
prac·ti·cal·ly so gut wie
prac·tice **1.** Praxis *f*; Übung *f*; Gewohnheit *f*, Brauch *m*; ***it is common practice*** es ist allgemein üblich; ***put into practice*** in die Praxis umsetzen; **2.** *v/t* (ein)üben; *als Beruf* ausüben; ***practice law*** (***medicine***) als Anwalt (Arzt) praktizieren; *v/i* praktizieren; üben
prac·ticed geübt (***in*** in *dat*)
prac·tise *Br* → ***practice*** *2*
prac·tised → ***practiced***
prac·ti·tion·er: ***general practitioner*** praktischer Arzt
prai·rie Prärie *f*
prai·rie schoo·ner HIST Planwagen *m*
praise **1.** loben, preisen; **2.** Lob *n*
praise·wor·thy lobenswert
pram *Br* Kinderwagen *m*
prance sich aufbäumen, steigen (*horse*); tänzeln (*horse*); stolzieren
prank Streich *m*
prat·tle: ***prattle on*** plappern (***about*** von)
prawn ZO Garnele *f*
pray beten (***to*** zu; ***for*** für, um)
prayer REL Gebet *n*; *often pl* Andacht *f*; ***the Lord's Prayer*** das Vaterunser
prayer book REL Gebetbuch *n*
preach predigen (***to*** zu, vor *dat*)
preach·er Prediger(in)
pre·am·ble Einleitung *f*
pre·ar·range vorher vereinbaren
pre·car·i·ous prekär, unsicher; gefährlich
pre·cau·tion Vorsichtsmaßnahme *f*; ***as a precaution*** vorsorglich; ***take precautions*** Vorsichtsmaßnahmen treffen
pre·cau·tion·a·ry vorbeugend; vorsorglich
pre·cede voraus-, vorangehen (*dat*)
pre·ce·dence Vorrang *m*
pre·ce·dent Präzedenzfall *m*
pre·cept Regel *f*, Richtlinie *f*
pre·cinct (*Wahl*)Bezirk *m*; (*Polizei*)Revier *n*; *pl* Gelände *n*; *esp Br* (*Einkaufs*)Viertel *n*; (*Fußgänger*)Zone *f*
pre·cious **1.** *adj* kostbar, wertvoll; Edel… (*stone etc*); **2.** *adv*: ***precious little*** F herzlich wenig
pre·ci·pice Abgrund *m*
pre·cip·i·tate **1.** *v/t* (hinunter-, herunter)schleudern; CHEM ausfällen; beschleunigen; stürzen (***into*** in *acc*); *v/i* CHEM ausfallen; **2.** *adj* überstürzt; **3.** CHEM Niederschlag *m*
pre·cip·i·ta·tion CHEM Ausfällung *f*; METEOR Niederschlag *m*; Überstürzung *f*, Hast *f*
pre·cip·i·tous steil (abfallend); überstürzt
pré·cis Zusammenfassung *f*
pre·cise genau, präzis
pre·ci·sion Genauigkeit *f*; Präzision *f*
pre·clude ausschließen
pre·co·cious frühreif; altklug
pre·con·ceived vorgefasst
pre·con·cep·tion vorgefasste Meinung
pre·cur·sor Vorläufer(in)
pred·a·to·ry ZO Raub…
pre·de·ces·sor Vorgänger(in)
pre·des·ti·na·tion Vorherbestimmung *f*
pre·des·tined prädestiniert, vorherbestimmt (***to*** für, zu)
pre·de·ter·mine vorherbestimmen; vorher vereinbaren
pre·dic·a·ment missliche Lage, Zwangslage *f*
pred·i·cate LING Prädikat *n*, Satzaussage *f*
pre·dic·a·tive LING prädikativ
pre·dict vorhersagen, voraussagen
pre·dic·tion Vorhersage *f*, Voraussage *f*; ***computer prediction*** Hochrechnung *f*
pre·dis·pose geneigt machen, einneh-

men (***in favor of*** für); *esp* MED anfällig machen (***to*** für)
pre·dis·po·si·tion: ***predisposition to*** Neigung *f* zu, *esp* MED *a.* Anfälligkeit *f* für
pre·dom·i·nant (vor)herrschend, überwiegend
pre·dom·i·nate vorherrschen, überwiegen; die Oberhand haben
pre·em·i·nent hervorragend, überragend
pre·emp·tive ECON Vorkaufs…; MIL Präventiv…
preen ZO *sich or das Gefieder* putzen
pre·fab F Fertighaus *n*
pre·fab·ri·cate vorfabrizieren, vorfertigen; ***prefabricated house*** Fertighaus *n*
pref·ace **1.** Vorwort *n* (***to*** zu); **2.** *Buch, Rede etc* einleiten (***with*** mit)
pre·fect *Br* PED Aufsichts-, Vertrauensschüler(in)
pre·fer vorziehen (***to*** *dat*), lieber mögen (***to*** als), bevorzugen
pref·e·ra·ble: ***be preferable*** (***to***) vorzuziehen sein (*dat*), besser sein (als)
pref·e·ra·bly vorzugsweise, lieber, am liebsten
pref·e·rence Vorliebe *f* (***for*** für); Vorzug *m*
pre·fix LING Präfix *n*, Vorsilbe *f*
preg·nan·cy MED Schwangerschaft *f*; ZO Trächtigkeit *f*
preg·nant MED schwanger; ZO trächtig
pre·heat *Backofen etc* vorheizen
pre·judge *j-n* vorverurteilen; vorschnell beurteilen
prej·u·dice **1.** Vorurteil *n*, Voreingenommenheit *f*, Befangenheit *f*; ***to the prejudice of*** zum Nachteil *or* Schaden (*gen*); **2.** einnehmen (***in favo[u]r of*** für; ***against*** gegen); schaden (*dat*), beeinträchtigen
prej·u·diced (vor)eingenommen, befangen
pre·lim·i·na·ry **1.** vorläufig, einleitend, Vor…; **2.** *pl* Vorbereitungen *pl*
prel·ude Vorspiel *n* (*a.* MUS)
pre·mar·i·tal vorehelich
pre·ma·ture vorzeitig, verfrüht; *fig* voreilig
pre·med·i·tat·ed JUR vorsätzlich
pre·med·i·ta·tion: ***with premeditation*** JUR vorsätzlich
prem·i·er POL Premier(minister) *m*
prem·i·ere, prem·i·ère THEA *etc* Premiere *f*, Ur-, Erstaufführung *f*
prem·is·es Gelände *n*, Grundstück *n*, (*Geschäfts*)Räume *pl*; ***on the premises*** an Ort und Stelle, im Haus, im Lokal
pre·mi·um Prämie *f*, Bonus *m*
pre·mi·um (gas·o·line) MOT Super *n*, Superbenzin *n*
pre·mo·ni·tion (böse) Vorahnung
pre·oc·cu·pa·tion Beschäftigung *f* (***with*** mit)
pre·oc·cu·pied gedankenverloren, geistesabwesend
pre·oc·cu·py (stark) beschäftigen
prep *Br* F PED Hausaufgabe(n *pl*) *f*
pre·packed, **pre·pack·aged** abgepackt
pre·paid *post* frankiert, freigemacht
prepaid envelope Freiumschlag *m*
prep·a·ra·tion Vorbereitung *f* (***for*** auf *acc*, für); Zubereitung *f*; CHEM, MED Präparat *n*
pre·par·a·to·ry vorbereitend
pre·pare *v/t* vorbereiten; GASTR zubereiten; *v/i*: ***prepare for*** sich vorbereiten auf (*acc*); Vorbereitungen treffen für; sich gefasst machen auf (*acc*)
pre·pared vorbereitet; bereit
prep·o·si·tion LING Präposition *f*, Verhältniswort *n*
pre·pos·sess·ing einnehmend, anziehend
pre·pos·ter·ous absurd; lächerlich, grotesk
pre·pro·gram(me) vorprogrammieren
pre·req·ui·site Vorbedingung *f*, Voraussetzung *f*
pre·rog·a·tive Vorrecht *n*
pre·school Vorschule *f*
pre·scribe *et.* vorschreiben; MED *j-m et.* verschreiben
pre·scrip·tion Verordnung *f*, Vorschrift *f*; MED Rezept *n*
pres·ence Gegenwart *f*, Anwesenheit *f*
presence of mind Geistesgegenwart *f*
pres·ent[1] Geschenk *n*
pre·sent[2] präsentieren; (über)reichen, (über)bringen, (über)geben; schenken; vorbringen, vorlegen; zeigen, vorführen, THEA *etc* aufführen; schildern, darstellen; *j-n, Produkt etc* vorstellen; *Programm etc* moderieren
pres·ent[3] **1.** anwesend; vorhanden; gegenwärtig, jetzig; laufend; vorliegend (*case etc*); ***present tense*** LING Präsens *n*, Gegenwart *f*; **2.** Gegenwart *f*, LING *a.* Präsens *n*; ***at present*** gegenwärtig, zurzeit; ***for the present*** vorerst, vorläufig
pre·sen·ta·tion Präsentation *f*; Überreichung *f*; Vorlage *f*; Vorführung *f*, THEA *etc* Aufführung *f*; Schilderung *f*, Darstellung *f*; Vorstellung *f*; *radio*, TV Moderation *f*
pres·ent-day heutig, gegenwärtig, modern
pre·sent·er *esp Br radio*, TV Moderator(in)
pre·sen·ti·ment (böse) Vorahnung

pres·ent·ly zurzeit, jetzt; *Br* bald
pres·er·va·tion Bewahrung *f*; Erhaltung *f*; GASTR Konservierung *f*
pre·ser·va·tive GASTR Konservierungsmittel *n*
pre·serve 1. bewahren, (be)schützen; erhalten; GASTR konservieren, *Obst etc* einmachen, einkochen; **2.** (*Jagd-*)Revier *n*; *fig* Ressort *n*, Reich *n*; *mst pl* GASTR *das* Eingemachte
pre·side den Vorsitz haben (***at, over*** bei)
pres·i·den·cy POL Präsidentschaft *f*; Amtszeit *f*
pres·i·dent Präsident *m*; ECON Generaldirektor *m*
press 1. *v/t* drücken, pressen; *Frucht* (aus)pressen; drücken auf (*acc*); bügeln; drängen; *j-n* (be)drängen; bestehen auf (*dat*); *v/i* drücken; drängen (*time etc*); (sich) drängen; ***press for*** dringen *or* drängen auf (*acc*); ***press on*** (zügig) weitermachen; **2.** Druck *m* (*a. fig*); (*Wein-etc*)Presse *f*; Bügeln *n*; *die* Presse; *a.* ***printing press*** Druckerpresse *f*
press a·gen·cy Presseagentur *f*
press box Pressetribüne *f*
press con·fe·rence Pressekonferenz *f*
press of·fice Pressebüro *n*, Pressestelle *f*
press of·fi·cer Pressereferent(in)
press·ing dringend
press re·lease Pressemitteilung *f*
press stud *Br* Druckknopf *m*
press-up *esp Br* SPORT Liegestütz *m*
pres·sure PHYS, TECH *etc* Druck *m* (*a. fig*)
pressure cook·er Dampfkochtopf *m*, Schnellkochtopf *m*
pres·tige Prestige *n*, Ansehen *n*
pre·su·ma·bly vermutlich
pre·sume *v/t* annehmen, vermuten; sich erdreisten *or* anmaßen (***to do*** zu tun); *v/i* annehmen, vermuten; anmaßend sein; ***presume on*** *et.* ausnützen, *et.* missbrauchen
pre·sump·tion Annahme *f*, Vermutung *f*; Anmaßung *f*
pre·sump·tu·ous anmaßend, vermessen
pre·sup·pose voraussetzen
pre·sup·po·si·tion Voraussetzung *f*
pre·tence *Br* → ***pretense***
pre·tend vortäuschen, vorgeben; sich verstellen; Anspruch erheben (***to*** auf *acc*); ***she is only pretending*** sie tut nur so
pre·tend·ed vorgetäuscht, gespielt
pre·tense Verstellung *f*, Vortäuschung *f*; Anspruch *m* (***to*** auf *acc*)
pre·ten·sion Anspruch *m* (***to*** auf *acc*); Anmaßung *f*
pre·ter·it(e) LING Präteritum *n*
pre·text Vorwand *m*
pret·ty 1. *adj* hübsch; **2.** *adv* ziemlich, ganz schön
pret·zel Brezel *f*
pre·vail vorherrschen, weit verbreitet sein; siegen (***over, against*** über *acc*)
pre·vail·ing (vor)herrschend
pre·vent verhindern, verhüten, *e-r Sache* vorbeugen; *j-n* hindern (***from*** an *dat*)
pre·ven·tion Verhinderung *f*, Verhütung *f*, Vorbeugung *f*
pre·ven·tive vorbeugend
pre·view *film*, TV Voraufführung *f*; Vorbesichtigung *f*; *film*, TV *etc*: Vorschau *f* (***of*** auf *acc*)
pre·vi·ous vorhergehend, vorausgehend, vorherig, vorig; ***previous to*** bevor, vor (*dat*); ***previous knowledge*** Vorkenntnisse *pl*
pre·vi·ous·ly vorher, früher
pre-war Vorkriegs…
prey 1. ZO Beute *f*, Opfer *n* (*a. fig*); ***be easy prey for*** *or* ***to*** *fig* e-e leichte Beute sein für; **2.** ***prey on*** ZO Jagd machen auf (*acc*); *fig* nagen an (*dat*); ***prey on s.o.'s mind*** j-m keine Ruhe lassen
price 1. Preis *m*; **2.** den Preis festsetzen für; auszeichnen (***at*** mit)
price·less unbezahlbar
price tag Preisschild *n*
prick 1. Stich *m*; V Schwanz *m*; ***pricks of conscience*** Gewissensbisse *pl*; **2.** *v/t* (auf-, durch)stechen, stechen in (*acc*); ***her conscience pricked her*** sie hatte Gewissensbisse; ***prick up one's ears*** die Ohren spitzen; *v/i* stechen
prick·le BOT, ZO Stachel *m*, Dorn *m*
prick·ly stach(e)lig; prickelnd, kribbelnd
pride 1. Stolz *m*; Hochmut *m*; ***take (a) pride in*** stolz sein auf (*acc*); **2. *pride o.s. on*** stolz sein auf (*acc*)
priest REL Priester *m*
prig Tugendbold *m*
prig·gish tugendhaft
prim steif; prüde
pri·mae·val *esp Br* → ***primeval***
pri·ma·ri·ly in erster Linie, vor allem
pri·ma·ry 1. wichtigste(r, -s), Haupt…; grundlegend, elementar, Grund…; Anfangs…, Ur…; **2.** POL Vorwahl *f*
pri·ma·ry school *Br* Grundschule *f*
prime 1. MATH Primzahl *f*; *fig* Blüte(zeit) *f*; ***in the prime of life*** in der Blüte s-r Jahre; ***be past one's prime*** s-e besten Jahre hinter sich haben; **2.** *adj* erste(r, -s), wichtigste(r, -s), Haupt…; erstklassig; **3.** *v/t* TECH grundieren; *j-n* instruieren, vorbereiten
prime min·is·ter (ABBR POL F ***PM***) Premierminister(in), Ministerpräsident(in)

P

prime num·ber MATH Primzahl *f*
prim·er Fibel *f*, Elementarbuch *n*
prime time TV Haupteinschaltzeit *f*, Hauptsendezeit *f*, beste Sendezeit
pri·me·val urzeitlich, Ur...
prim·i·tive erste(r, -s), ursprünglich, Ur...; primitiv
prim·rose BOT Primel *f*, *esp* Schlüsselblume *f*
prince Fürst *m*; Prinz *m*
prin·cess Fürstin *f*; Prinzessin *f*
prin·ci·pal **1.** wichtigste(r, -s), hauptsächlich, Haupt...; **2.** PED Direktor(in), Rektor(in); THEA Hauptdarsteller(in); MUS Solist(in)
prin·ci·pal·i·ty Fürstentum *n*
prin·ci·ple Prinzip *n*, Grundsatz *m*; ***on principle*** grundsätzlich, aus Prinzip
print **1.** PRINT Druck *m* (*a. art*); Gedruckte *n*; (*Finger- etc*)Abdruck *m*; PHOT Abzug *m*; bedruckter Stoff; ***in print*** gedruckt; ***out of print*** vergriffen; **2.** *v/i* drucken; *v/t* (ab-, auf-, be)drucken; in Druckbuchstaben schreiben; *fig* einprägen (***on*** *dat*); *a.* ***print off*** PHOT abziehen; ***print out*** EDP ausdrucken
print·ed mat·ter *post* Drucksache *f*
print·er Drucker *m* (*a.* TECH); ***printer's error*** Druckfehler *m*; ***printer's ink*** Druckerschwärze *f*
print·ers Druckerei *f*
print·ing Drucken *n*; Auflage *f*
printing ink Druckerschwärze *f*
printing press Druckerpresse *f*
print·out EDP Ausdruck *m*
pri·or frühere(r, -s); vorrangig
pri·or·i·ty Priorität *f*, Vorrang *m*; MOT Vorfahrt *f*; ***give s.th. priority*** et. vordringlich behandeln
prise *esp Br* → ***prize***[2]
prism Prisma *n*
pris·on Gefängnis *n*, Strafanstalt *f*
pris·on·er Gefangene *m*, *f*, Häftling *m*; ***hold prisoner, keep prisoner*** gefangen halten; ***take prisoner*** gefangen nehmen
pri·va·cy Intim-, Privatsphäre *f*; Geheimhaltung *f*
pri·vate **1.** privat, Privat...; vertraulich; geheim; ***private parts*** Geschlechtsteile *pl*; **2.** MIL gemeiner Soldat; ***in private*** privat; unter vier Augen
pri·va·tion Entbehrung *f*
priv·i·lege Privileg *n*; Vorrecht *n*
priv·i·leged privilegiert
priv·y: ***be privy to*** eingeweiht sein in (*acc*)
prize[1] **1.** (Sieger-, Sieges)Preis *m*, Prämie *f*, Auszeichnung *f*; (*Lotterie*)Gewinn *m*; **2.** preisgekrönt; Preis...; **3.** (hoch) schätzen
prize[2]: ***prize open*** aufbrechen, aufstemmen
prize·win·ner Preisträger(in)
pro[1] F Profi *m*
pro[2]: ***the pros and cons*** das Pro und Kontra, das Für und Wider
prob·a·bil·i·ty Wahrscheinlichkeit *f*; ***in all probability*** höchstwahrscheinlich
prob·a·ble *adj* wahrscheinlich
prob·a·bly *adv* wahrscheinlich
pro·ba·tion Probe *f*, Probezeit *f*; JUR Bewährung *f*, Bewährungsfrist *f*
pro·ba·tion of·fi·cer JUR Bewährungshelfer(in)
probe **1.** MED, TECH Sonde *f*; *fig* Untersuchung *f* (***into*** *gen*); **2.** sondieren; (gründlich) untersuchen
prob·lem Problem *n*; MATH *etc* Aufgabe *f*
prob·lem·at·ic, prob·lem·at·i·cal problematisch
pro·ce·dure Verfahren *n*, Verfahrensweise *f*, Vorgehen *n*
pro·ceed (weiter)gehen, (weiter)fahren; sich begeben (***to*** nach, zu); *fig* weitergehen; *fig* fortfahren; *fig* vorgehen; ***proceed from*** kommen *or* herrühren von; ***proceed to do s.th.*** sich anschicken *or* daranmachen, et. zu tun
pro·ceed·ing Verfahren *n*, Vorgehen *n*
pro·ceed·ings Vorgänge *pl*, Geschehnisse *pl*; ***start*** *or* ***take*** (***legal***) ***proceedings against*** JUR (gerichtlich) vorgehen gegen
pro·ceeds ECON Erlös *m*, Ertrag *m*, Einnahmen *pl*
pro·cess **1.** Prozess *m*, Verfahren *n*, Vorgang *m*; ***in the process*** dabei; ***be in process*** im Gange sein; ***in process of construction*** im Bau (befindlich); **2.** TECH *etc* bearbeiten, behandeln; EDP *Daten* verarbeiten; PHOT *Film* entwickeln
pro·ces·sion Prozession *f*
pro·ces·sor EDP Prozessor *m*; (*Wort-, Text*)Verarbeitungsgerät *n*
pro·claim proklamieren, ausrufen
proc·la·ma·tion Proklamation *f*, Bekanntmachung *f*
pro·cure (sich) *et.* beschaffen *or* besorgen; verkuppeln
prod **1.** stoßen; *fig* anstacheln, anspornen (***into*** zu); **2.** Stoß *m*
prod·i·gal **1.** verschwenderisch; **2.** F Verschwender(in)
pro·di·gious erstaunlich, großartig
prod·i·gy Wunder *n*; ***child prodigy*** Wunderkind *n*
pro·duce[1] ECON produzieren (*a. film,* TV), herstellen, erzeugen (*a. fig*); hervorholen (***from*** aus); *Ausweis etc* (vor)zeigen;

Beweise etc vorlegen; *Zeugen etc* beibringen; *Gewinn etc* (er)bringen, abwerfen; THEA inszenieren; *fig* hervorrufen, *Wirkung* erzielen
prod·uce[2] *esp* (*Agrar*)Produkt(e *pl*) *n*, (*Agrar*)Erzeugnis(se *pl*) *n*
pro·duc·er Produzent(in) (*a. film*, TV), Hersteller(in); THEA Regisseur(in)
prod·uct Produkt *n*, Erzeugnis *n*
pro·duc·tion ECON Produktion *f* (*a. film*, TV), Erzeugung *f*, Herstellung *f*; Produkt *n*, Erzeugnis *n*; Hervorholen *n*; Vorzeigen *n*, Vorlegen *n*, Beibringung *f*; THEA Inszenierung *f*
pro·duc·tive produktiv (*a. fig*), ergiebig, rentabel; *fig* schöpferisch
pro·duc·tiv·i·ty Produktivität *f*
prof F Prof *m*
pro·fa·na·tion Entweihung *f*
pro·fane 1. (gottes)lästerlich; profan, weltlich; **2.** entweihen
pro·fan·i·ty: ***profanities*** Flüche *pl*, Lästerungen *pl*
pro·fess vorgeben, vortäuschen; behaupten (***to be*** zu sein); erklären
pro·fessed erklärt (*enemy etc*); angeblich
pro·fes·sion (*esp akademischer*) Beruf; Berufsstand *m*
pro·fes·sion·al 1. Berufs…, beruflich; Fach…, fachlich; fachmännisch; professionell; **2.** Fachmann *m*, Profi *m*; Berufsspieler(in), -sportler(in), Profi *m*
pro·fes·sor Professor(in); Dozent(in)
pro·fi·cien·cy Können *n*, Tüchtigkeit *f*
pro·fi·cient tüchtig (***at, in*** in *dat*)
pro·file Profil *n*; ***keep a low profile*** Zurückhaltung üben
prof·it 1. Gewinn *m*, Profit *m*; Vorteil *m*, Nutzen *m*; **2.** ***profit by, profit from*** Nutzen ziehen aus, profitieren von
prof·it·a·ble gewinnbringend, einträglich; nützlich, vorteilhaft
prof·it·eer *contp* Profitmacher *m*, Schieber *m*
prof·it shar·ing ECON Gewinnbeteiligung *f*
prof·li·gate verschwenderisch
pro·found *fig* tief; tiefgründig; profund (*knowledge etc*)
pro·fuse (über)reich; verschwenderisch
pro·fu·sion Überfülle *f*; ***in profusion*** in Hülle und Fülle
prog·e·ny Nachkommen(schaft *f*) *pl*
prog·no·sis MED Prognose *f*
pro·gram 1. Programm *n* (*a.* EDP); *radio*, TV *a.* Sendung *f*; **2.** (vor)programmieren; planen; EDP programmieren
pro·gram·er EDP Programmierer(in)
pro·gramme *Br* → ***program***
'pro·gram·mer *Br* → ***programer***
pro·gress 1. Fortschritt(e *pl*) *m*; ***make slow progress*** (nur) langsam vorankommen; ***be in progress*** im Gange sein; **2.** fortschreiten; Fortschritte machen
pro·gres·sive progressiv, fortschreitend; fortschrittlich
pro·hib·it verbieten; verhindern
pro·hi·bi·tion Verbot *n*
pro·hib·i·tive Schutz… (*Zoll etc*); unerschwinglich
proj·ect[1] Projekt *n*, Vorhaben *n*
pro·ject[2] *v/i* vorspringen, vorragen, vorstehen; *v/t* werfen, schleudern; planen; projizieren
pro·jec·tile Projektil *n*, Geschoss *n*
pro·jec·tion Vorsprung *m*, vorspringender Teil; Werfen *n*, Schleudern *n*; Planung *f*; *film*: Projektion *f*
pro·jec·tion·ist Filmvorführer *m*
pro·jec·tor *film*: Projektor *m*
pro·le·tar·i·an 1. proletarisch; **2.** Proletarier(in)
pro·lif·ic fruchtbar
pro·log, *esp Br* **pro·logue** Prolog *m*
pro·long verlängern
prom·e·nade 1. (Strand)Promenade *f*; **2.** promenieren
prom·i·nent vorspringend, vorstehend; *fig* prominent
pro·mis·cu·ous sexuell freizügig
prom·ise 1. Versprechen *n*; *fig* Aussicht *f*; **2.** versprechen
prom·is·ing vielversprechend
prom·on·to·ry GEOGR Vorgebirge *n*
pro·mote *j-n* befördern; *Schüler* versetzen; ECON werben für; *Boxkampf, Konzert etc* veranstalten; *et.* fördern; ***be promoted*** SPORT *esp Br* aufsteigen (***to*** in *acc*)
pro·mot·er Promoter(in), Veranstalter(in); ECON Verkaufsförderer *m*
pro·mo·tion Beförderung *f*; PED Versetzung *f*; SPORT Aufstieg *m*; ECON Verkaufsförderung *f*, Werbung *f*
pro·mo·tion(·al) film Werbefilm *m*
prompt 1. *j-n* veranlassen (***to do*** zu tun); führen zu, *Gefühle etc* wecken; *j-m* vorsagen; THEA *j-m* soufflieren; **2.** prompt, umgehend, unverzüglich; pünktlich
prompt·er THEA Souffleur *m*, Souffleuse *f*
prone auf dem Bauch *or* mit dem Gesicht nach unten liegend; ***be prone to*** *a.* MED neigen zu, anfällig sein für
prong Zinke *f*; (*Geweih*)Sprosse *f*
pro·noun LING Pronomen *n*, Fürwort *n*
pro·nounce aussprechen; erklären für; JUR *Urteil* verkünden
pro·nun·ci·a·tion Aussprache *f*
proof 1. Beweis(e *pl*) *m*, Nachweis *m*; Pro-

P

be *f*; PRINT Korrekturfahne *f*, *a.* PHOT Probeabzug *m*; **2.** *adj in cpds* …fest, …beständig, …dicht, …sicher; → ***heatproof***, ***soundproof***, ***waterproof***; ***be proof against*** geschützt sein vor (*dat*); **3.** imprägnieren
proof·read PRINT Korrektur lesen
proof·read·er PRINT Korrektor(in)
prop **1.** Stütze *f* (*a. fig*); **2.** *a.* ***prop up*** stützen; *sich or et.* lehnen (***against*** gegen)
prop·a·gate BIOL sich fortpflanzen *or* vermehren; verbreiten
prop·a·ga·tion Fortpflanzung *f*, Vermehrung *f*; Verbreitung *f*
pro·pel (an)treiben
pro·pel·lant, **pro·pel·lent** Treibstoff *m*; Treibgas *n*
pro·pel·ler AVIAT Propeller *m*, MAR *a.* Schraube *f*
pro·pel·ling pen·cil Drehbleistift *m*
pro·pen·si·ty *fig* Neigung *f*
prop·er richtig, passend, geeignet; anständig, schicklich; echt, wirklich, richtig; eigentlich; eigen(tümlich); *esp Br* F ordentlich, tüchtig, gehörig
prop·er name, **proper noun** Eigenname *m*
prop·er·ty Eigentum *n*, Besitz *m*; Landbesitz *m*, Grundbesitz *m*; Grundstück *n*; *fig* Eigenschaft *f*
proph·e·cy Prophezeiung *f*
proph·e·sy prophezeien
proph·et Prophet *m*
pro·por·tion **1.** Verhältnis *n*; (An)Teil *m*; *pl* Größenverhältnisse *pl*, Proportionen *pl*; ***in proportion to*** im Verhältnis zu; **2.** (***to***) in das richtige Verhältnis bringen (mit, zu); anpassen (*dat*)
pro·por·tion·al proportional; → ***proportionate***
pro·por·tion·ate (***to***) im richtigen Verhältnis (zu), entsprechend (*dat*)
pro·pos·al Vorschlag *m*; (Heirats)Antrag *m*
pro·pose *v/t* vorschlagen; beabsichtigen, vorhaben; *Toast* ausbringen (***to*** auf *acc*); ***propose s.o.'s health*** auf j-s Gesundheit trinken; *v/i*: ***propose to*** *j-m* e-n (Heirats)Antrag machen
prop·o·si·tion Behauptung *f*; Vorschlag *m*, ECON *a.* Angebot *n*
pro·pri·e·ta·ry ECON gesetzlich *or* patentrechtlich geschützt; *fig* besitzergreifend
pro·pri·e·tor Eigentümer *m*, Besitzer *m*, Geschäftsinhaber *m*
pro·pri·e·tress Eigentümerin *f*, Besitzerin *f*, Geschäftsinhaberin *f*
pro·pri·e·ty Anstand *m*; Richtigkeit *f*
pro·pul·sion TECH Antrieb *m*
pro·sa·ic prosaisch, nüchtern, sachlich
prose Prosa *f*
pros·e·cute JUR strafrechtlich verfolgen, (gerichtlich) belangen (***for*** wegen)
pros·e·cu·tion JUR strafrechtliche Verfolgung, Strafverfolgung *f*; ***the prosecution*** die Staatsanwaltschaft, die Anklage(behörde)
pros·e·cu·tor *a.* ***public prosecutor*** JUR Staatsanwalt *m*, Staatsanwältin *f*
pros·pect **1.** Aussicht *f* (*a. fig*); Interessent *m*, ECON möglicher Kunde, potenzieller Käufer; **2.** ***prospect for*** *mining*: schürfen nach; bohren nach
pro·spec·tive voraussichtlich
pro·spec·tus (Werbe)Prospekt *m*
pros·per gedeihen; ECON blühen, florieren
pros·per·i·ty Wohlstand *m*
pros·per·ous ECON erfolgreich, blühend, florierend; wohlhabend
pros·ti·tute Prostituierte *f*, Dirne *f*; ***male prostitute*** Strichjunge *m*
pros·trate **1.** hingestreckt; *fig* am Boden liegend; erschöpft; ***prostrate with grief*** gramgebeugt; **2.** niederwerfen; *fig* erschöpfen; *fig* niederschmettern
pros·y langweilig; weitschweifig
pro·tag·o·nist Vorkämpfer(in); THEA Hauptfigur *f*, Held(in)
pro·tect (be)schützen (***from*** vor *dat*; ***against*** gegen)
pro·tec·tion Schutz *m*; F Schutzgeld *n*; ***protection of animals*** Tierschutz; ***protection of endangered species*** Artenschutz *m*
protection money F Schutzgeld *n*
protection rack·et F Schutzgelderpressung *f*
pro·tec·tive (be)schützend; Schutz…
protective cloth·ing Schutzkleidung *f*
protective cus·to·dy JUR Schutzhaft *f*
protective du·ty, **protective tar·iff** ECON Schutzzoll *m*
pro·tec·tor Beschützer *m*; (*Brust- etc* -) Schutz *m*
pro·tec·to·rate POL Protektorat *n*
pro·test **1.** Protest *m*; Einspruch *m*; **2.** *v/i* protestieren (***against*** gegen); *v/t* protestieren gegen; beteuern
Prot·es·tant REL **1.** protestantisch; **2.** Protestant(in)
prot·es·ta·tion Beteuerung *f*; Protest *m* (***against*** gegen)
pro·to·col Protokoll *n*
pro·to·type Prototyp *m*
pro·tract in die Länge ziehen, hinziehen
pro·trude herausragen, vorstehen (***from*** aus)
pro·trud·ing vorstehend (*a. teeth*), vor-

P

springend (*chin*)
proud stolz (***of*** auf *acc*)
prove *v/t* be-, er-, nachweisen; *v/i*: ***prove (to be)*** sich herausstellen *or* erweisen als
prov·en bewährt
prov·erb Sprichwort *n*
pro·vide *v/t* versehen, versorgen, beliefern; zur Verfügung stellen, bereitstellen; JUR vorsehen, vorschreiben (***that*** dass); *v/i*: ***provide against*** Vorsorge treffen gegen; JUR verbieten; ***provide for*** sorgen für; vorsorgen für; JUR *et.* vorsehen
pro·vid·ed: ***provided (that)*** vorausgesetzt(, dass)
pro·vid·er Ernährer(in)
prov·ince Provinz *f*; (Aufgaben-, Wissens)Gebiet *n*
pro·vin·cial **1.** Provinz..., provinziell, *contp* provinzlerisch; **2.** *contp* Provinzler(in)
pro·vi·sion Bereitstellung *f*, Beschaffung *f*; Vorkehrung *f*, Vorsorge *f*; Bestimmung *f*, Vorschrift *f*; *pl* Proviant *m*, Verpflegung *f*; ***with the provision that*** unter der Bedingung, dass
pro·vi·sion·al provisorisch, vorläufig
pro·vi·so Bedingung *f*, Vorbehalt *m*; ***with the proviso that*** unter der Bedingung, dass
prov·o·ca·tion Provokation *f*
pro·voc·a·tive provozierend, (*a. sexually*) aufreizend
pro·voke provozieren, reizen
prowl **1.** *v/i a.* ***prowl about, prowl around*** herumschleichen, herumstreifen; *v/t* durchstreifen; **2.** Herumstreifen *n*
prowl car (Funk)Streifenwagen *m*
prox·im·i·ty Nähe *f*
prox·y (Handlungs)Vollmacht *f*; (Stell)-Vertreter(in), Bevollmächtigte *m, f*; ***by proxy*** durch e-n Bevollmächtigten
prude: ***be a prude*** prüde sein
pru·dence Klugheit *f*, Vernunft *f*; Besonnenheit *f*
pru·dent klug, vernünftig; besonnen
prud·ish prüde
prune[1] BOT (be)schneiden
prune[2] Backpflaume *f*
prus·sic ac·id CHEM Blausäure *f*
pry[1] neugierig sein; ***pry about*** herumschnüffeln; ***pry into*** s-e Nase stecken in (*acc*)
pry[2] → ***prize***[2]
psalm REL Psalm *m*
pseu·do·nym Pseudonym *n*, Deckname *m*
psy·chi·a·trist Psychiater(in)
psy·chi·a·try Psychiatrie *f*
psy·cho·a·nal·y·sis Psychoanalyse *f*
psy·cho·log·i·cal psychologisch
psy·chol·o·gist Psychologe *m*, Psychologin *f*
psy·chol·o·gy Psychologie *f*
psy·cho·so·mat·ic psychosomatisch
pub *Br* Pub *n, m*, Kneipe *f*
pu·ber·ty Pubertät *f*
pu·bic hair Schamhaare *pl*
pub·lic **1.** öffentlich; allgemein bekannt; ***make public*** bekannt machen, an die Öffentlichkeit bringen; **2.** *die* Öffentlichkeit, *das* Publikum; ***in public*** öffentlich, in aller Öffentlichkeit
pub·li·ca·tion Bekanntgabe *f*, Bekanntmachung *f*; Publikation *f*, Veröffentlichung *f*
pub·lic con·ve·ni·ence *Br* öffentliche Bedürfnisanstalt
public en·e·my Staatsfeind *m*
public health öffentliches Gesundheitswesen
public hol·i·day gesetzlicher Feiertag
pub·lic·i·ty Publicity *f*, *a.* Bekanntheit *f*, ECON *a.* Reklame *f*, Werbung *f*
publicity depart·ment Werbeabteilung *f*
pub·lic li·bra·ry Leihbücherei *f*
public rela·tions (ABBR ***PR***) Public Relations *pl*, Öffentlichkeitsarbeit *f*
public school staatliche Schule; *Br* Public School *f*
public trans·port *esp Br*, **public trans·por·tation** öffentliche Verkehrsmittel *pl*
pub·lish bekannt geben *or* machen; publizieren, veröffentlichen; *Buch etc* verlegen, herausgeben
pub·lish·er Verleger(in), Herausgeber(in); Verlag *m*, Verlagshaus *n*
pub·lish·er's, **pub·lish·ers**, **publish·ing house** Verlag *m*, Verlagshaus *n*
puck·er *a.* ***pucker up*** (sich) verziehen, (sich) runzeln
pud·ding *Br* GASTR Nachspeise *f*, Nachtisch *m*; (*Reis- etc*)Auflauf *m*; (*Art*) Fleischpastete *f*; Pudding *m*
pud·dle Pfütze *f*
pu·er·ile infantil, kindisch
puff **1.** *v/i* schnaufen, keuchen; *a.* ***puff away*** paffen (***at*** an *dat*); ***puff up*** (an)-schwellen; *v/t* *Rauch* blasen; ***puff out*** *Kerze etc* ausblasen; *Rauch etc* ausstoßen; *Brust* herausdrücken; **2.** Zug *m*; (*Wind-*) Hauch *m*, (*Wind*)Stoß *m*; (*Puder*)Quaste *f*; F Puste *f*
puffed sleeve Puffärmel *m*
puff pas·try GASTR Blätterteig *m*
puff·y (an)geschwollen; aufgedunsen
pug ZO Mops *m*
puke F (aus)kotzen

P

pull **1.** Ziehen *n*; Zug *m*, Ruck *m*; Anstieg *m*, Steigung *f*; Zuggriff *m*, Zugleine *f*; F Beziehungen *pl*; **2.** ziehen; ziehen an (*dat*); zerren; reißen; *Pflanze* ausreißen; *esp Br Bier* zapfen; *fig* anziehen; ***pull ahead of*** vorbeiziehen an (*dat*), MOT überholen (*acc*); ***pull away*** anfahren (*bus etc*); ***pull down*** *Gebäude* abreißen; ***pull in*** einfahren (*train*); anhalten; ***pull off*** F *et.* zustande bringen, schaffen; ***pull out*** herausziehen (***of*** aus); *Tisch* ausziehen; RAIL abfahren; MOT ausscheren; *fig* sich zurückziehen, aussteigen (***of*** aus); ***pull over*** (s-n Wagen) an die *or* zur Seite fahren; ***pull round*** MED durchbringen; durchkommen; ***pull through*** *j-n* durchbringen; ***pull o.s. together*** sich zusammennehmen, F sich zusammenreißen; ***pull up*** MOT anhalten; (an)halten; ***pull up to, pull up with*** SPORT *j-n* einholen

pull date Mindesthaltbarkeitsdatum *n*

pul·ley TECH Flaschenzug *m*

pull-in *Br* F Raststätte *f*, Rasthaus *n*

pull·o·ver Pullover *m*

pull-up SPORT Klimmzug *m*; ***do a pull-up*** e-n Klimmzug machen

pulp **1.** Fruchtfleisch *n*; Brei *m*; **2.** Schund...; ***pulp novel*** Schundroman *m*

pul·pit Kanzel *f*

pulp·y breiig

pul·sate pulsieren, vibrieren

pulse Puls *m*; Pulsschlag *m*

pul·ver·ize pulverisieren

pu·ma zo Puma *m*

pum·mel mit den Fäusten bearbeiten

pump **1.** Pumpe *f*; (*Zapf*)Säule *f*; **2.** pumpen; F *j-n* aushorchen; ***pump up*** aufpumpen

pump at·tend·ant Tankwart *m*

pump·kin BOT Kürbis *m*

pun **1.** Wortspiel *n*; **2.** Wortspiele *or* ein Wortspiel machen

punch[1] **1.** boxen, (mit der Faust) schlagen; **2.** (Faust)Schlag *m*

punch[2] **1.** lochen; *Loch* stanzen (***in*** in *acc*); ***punch in*** einstempeln; ***punch out*** ausstempeln; **2.** Locher *m*; Lochzange *f*; Locheisen *n*

punch[3] Punsch *m*

Punch *appr* Kasper *m*, Kasperle *n*, *m*; ***be as pleased*** *or* ***proud as Punch*** sich freuen wie ein Schneekönig

Punch and Ju·dy show Kasperletheater *n*

punc·tu·al pünktlich

punc·tu·al·i·ty Pünktlichkeit *f*

punc·tu·ate interpunktieren

punc·tu·a·tion LING Interpunktion *f*

punctuation mark LING Satzzeichen *n*

punc·ture **1.** (Ein)Stich *m*, Loch *n*; MOT Reifenpanne *f*; **2.** durchstechen, durchbohren; ein Loch bekommen, platzen; MOT e-n Platten haben

pun·gent scharf, stechend, beißend (*smell, taste*); scharf, bissig (*remark etc*)

pun·ish *j-n* (be)strafen

pun·ish·a·ble strafbar

pun·ish·ment Strafe *f*; Bestrafung *f*

punk Punk *m* (*a.* MUS); Punk(er) *m*

pu·ny schwächlich

pup zo Welpe *m*, junger Hund

pu·pa zo Puppe *f*

pu·pil[1] Schüler(in)

pu·pil[2] ANAT Pupille *f*

pup·pet Handpuppe *f*; Marionette *f* (*a. fig*)

puppet show Marionettentheater *n*, Puppenspiel *n*

pup·pe·teer Puppenspieler(in)

pup·py zo Welpe *m*, junger Hund

pur·chase **1.** kaufen; *fig* erkaufen; **2.** Kauf *m*; ***make purchases*** Einkäufe machen

pur·chas·er Käufer(in)

pure rein; pur

pure·bred zo reinrassig

pur·ga·tive MED **1.** abführend; **2.** Abführmittel *n*

pur·ga·to·ry REL Fegefeuer *n*

purge **1.** *Partei etc* säubern (***of*** von); **2.** Säuberung *f*, Säuberungsaktion *f*

pu·ri·fy reinigen

pu·ri·tan (HIST ***Puritan***) **1.** Puritaner(in); **2.** puritanisch

pu·ri·ty Reinheit *f*

purl **1.** linke Masche; **2.** links stricken

pur·ple purpurn, purpurrot

pur·pose **1.** Absicht *f*, Vorsatz *m*; Zweck *m*, Ziel *n*; Entschlossenheit *f*; ***on purpose*** absichtlich; ***to no purpose*** vergeblich; **2.** beabsichtigen, vorhaben

pur·pose·ful entschlossen, zielstrebig

pur·pose·less zwecklos; ziellos

pur·pose·ly absichtlich

purr zo schnurren; MOT summen, surren

purse[1] Geldbeutel *m*, Geldbörse *f*, Portemonnaie *n*; Handtasche *f*; SPORT Siegprämie *f*; *boxing*: Börse *f*

purse[2]: ***purse (up) one's lips*** die Lippen schürzen

purs·er MAR Zahlmeister *m*

pur·su·ance: ***in (the) pursuance of his duty*** in Ausübung s-r Pflicht

pur·sue verfolgen; *s-m Studium etc* nachgehen; *Absicht, Politik etc* verfolgen; *Angelegenheit etc* weiterführen

pur·su·er Verfolger(in)

pur·suit Verfolgung *f*; Weiterführung *f*

pur·vey *Lebensmittel etc* liefern

pur·vey·or Lieferant *m*

pus MED Eiter *m*
push 1. stoßen, F schubsen; schieben; *Taste etc* drücken; drängen; (an)treiben; F *Rauschgift* pushen; *fig j-n* drängen (***to do*** zu tun); *fig* Reklame machen für; ***push one's way*** sich drängen (***through*** durch); ***push ahead with*** *Plan etc* vorantreiben; ***push along*** F sich auf die Socken machen; ***push around*** F herumschubsen; ***push for*** drängen auf (*acc*); ***push forward with*** → ***push ahead with***; ***push o.s. forward*** *fig* sich in den Vordergrund drängen *or* schieben; ***push in*** F sich vordrängeln; ***push off!*** F hau ab!; ***push on with*** → ***push ahead with***; ***push out*** *fig j-n* hinausdrängen; ***push through*** *et.* durchsetzen; ***push up*** *Preise etc* hochtreiben; **2.** Stoß *m*, F Schubs *m*; (*Werbe*)-Kampagne *f*; F Durchsetzungsvermögen *n*, Energie *f*, Tatkraft *f*
push but·ton TECH Druckknopf *m*, Drucktaste *f*
push-but·ton TECH (Druck)Knopf…, (Druck)Tasten…; ***push-button (tele)-phone*** Tastentelefon *n*
push·chair *Br* Sportwagen *m*
push·er F *contp* Rauschgifthändler *m*
push·o·ver F Kinderspiel *n*
push-up SPORT Liegestütz *m*
puss F zo Mieze *f*
pus·sy *a.* ***pussy cat*** F Miezekatze *f*
pus·sy·foot: F ***pussyfoot about, pussyfoot around*** leisetreten, sich nicht festlegen wollen
put legen, setzen, stecken, stellen, tun; *j-n in e-e Lage etc, et. auf den Markt, in Ordnung etc* bringen; *et. in Kraft, in Umlauf etc* setzen; SPORT *Kugel* stoßen; unterwerfen, unterziehen (***to*** *dat*); *et.* ausdrücken, *in Worte* fassen; übersetzen (***into German*** ins Deutsche); *Schuld* geben (***on*** *dat*); ***put right*** in Ordnung bringen; ***put s.th. before s.o.*** *fig* j-m et. vorlegen; ***put to bed*** ins Bett bringen; ***put to school*** zur Schule schicken; ***put about*** *Gerüchte* verbreiten, in Umlauf setzen; ***put across*** *et.* verständlich machen; ***put ahead*** SPORT in Führung bringen; ***put aside*** beiseitelegen; *Ware* zurücklegen; *fig* beiseiteschieben; ***put away*** weglegen, wegtun; auf-, wegräumen; ***put back*** zurücklegen, -stellen, -tun; *Uhr* zurückstellen (***by*** um); ***put by*** *Geld* zurücklegen; ***put down*** *v/t* hinlegen, niederlegen, hinsetzen, hinstellen; *j-n* absetzen, aussteigen lassen; (auf-, nieder-) schreiben, eintragen; zuschreiben (***to*** *dat*); *Aufstand* niederschlagen; (*a. v/i*) AVIAT landen; ***put forward*** *Plan etc* vorlegen; *Uhr* vorstellen (***by*** um); *fig* vorverlegen (***two days*** um zwei Tage; ***to*** auf *acc*); ***put in*** *v/t* hineinlegen, -stecken, -stellen, *Kassette etc* einlegen; installieren; *Gesuch etc* einreichen, *Forderung etc a.* geltend machen; *Antrag* stellen; *Arbeit, Zeit* verbringen (***on*** mit); *Bemerkung* einwerfen; *v/i* MAR einlaufen (***at*** in *acc*); ***put off*** *et.* verschieben (***until*** auf *acc*); *j-m* absagen; *j-n* hinhalten (***with*** mit), *j-n* vertrösten; *j-n* aus dem Konzept brimgen; ***put on*** *Kleider etc* anziehen, *Hut, Brille* aufsetzen; *Licht, Radio etc* anmachen, einschalten; *Sonderzug* einsetzen; THEA *Stück etc* herausbringen; *et.* vortäuschen; F *j-n* auf den Arm nehmen; ***put on airs*** sich aufspielen; ***put on weight*** zunehmen; ***put out*** *v/t* hinauslegen, -setzen, -stellen; *Hand etc* ausstrecken; *Feuer* löschen; *Licht, Radio etc* ausmachen (*a. cigarette*), ab-, ausschalten; veröffentlichen, herausgeben; *radio*, TV bringen, senden; *j-n* aus der Fassung bringen; *j-n* verärgern; *j-m* Ungelegenheiten bereiten; *j-m* Umstände machen; sich *den Arm etc* verrenken *or* ausrenken; *v/i* MAR auslaufen; ***put over*** → ***put across***; ***put through*** TEL *j-n* verbinden (***to*** mit); durch-, ausführen; ***put together*** zusammenbauen, -setzen, -stellen; ***put up*** *v/t* hinauflegen, -stellen; *Hand* (hoch)heben; *Zelt etc* aufstellen; *Gebäude* errichten; *Bild etc* aufhängen; *Plakat, Bekanntmachung etc* anschlagen; *Schirm* aufspannen; *zum Verkauf* anbieten; *Preis* erhöhen; *Widerstand* leisten; *Kampf* liefern; *j-n* unterbringen, (bei sich) aufnehmen; *v/i* ***put up at*** absteigen in (*dat*); ***put up with*** sich gefallen lassen; sich abfinden mit
pu·tre·fy (ver)faulen, verwesen
pu·trid faul, verfault, verwest; F scheußlich, saumäßig
put·ty 1. Kitt *m*; **2.** kitten
put-up job F abgekartetes Spiel
puz·zle 1. Rätsel *n*; Geduld(s)spiel *n*; **2.** *v/t j-n* vor ein Rätsel stellen; verwirren; ***be puzzled*** vor e-m Rätsel stehen; ***puzzle out*** herausfinden, herausbringen, F austüfteln; *v/i* sich den Kopf zerbrechen (***about, over*** über *dat or acc*)
pyg·my 1. Pygmäe *m*, Pygmäin *f*; Zwerg(in); **2.** *esp* zo Zwerg…
py·ja·mas *Br* → ***pajamas***
py·lon TECH Hochspannungsmast *m*
pyr·a·mid Pyramide *f*
pyre Scheiterhaufen *m*
py·thon zo Python(schlange) *f*
pyx REL Hostienbehälter *m*

P

Q

Q, q Q, q *n*
quack[1] zo **1.** quaken; **2.** Quaken *n*
quack[2] *a.* ***quack doctor*** Quacksalber *m*, Kurpfuscher *m*
quack·er·y Quacksalberei *f*, Kurpfuscherei *f*
quad·ran·gle Viereck *n*
quad·ran·gu·lar viereckig
quad·ra·phon·ic quadrophon(isch)
quad·rat·ic MATH quadratisch
quad·ri·lat·er·al MATH **1.** vierseitig; **2.** Viereck *n*
quad·ro·phon·ic → ***quadraphonic***
quad·ru·ped zo Vierfüß(l)er *m*; Vierbeiner *m*
quad·ru·ple **1.** vierfach; **2.** (sich) vervierfachen
quad·ru·plets Vierlinge *pl*
quads Vierlinge *pl*
quag·mire Morast *m*, Sumpf *m*
quail zo Wachtel *f*
quaint idyllisch, malerisch
quake **1.** zittern, beben (***with, for*** vor *dat*; ***at*** bei); **2.** F Erdbeben *n*
Quak·er REL Quäker(in)
qual·i·fi·ca·tion Qualifikation *f*, Befähigung *f*, Eignung *f* (***for*** für, zu); Voraussetzung *f*; Einschränkung *f*
qual·i·fied qualifiziert, geeignet, befähigt (***for*** für); berechtigt; bedingt, eingeschränkt
qual·i·fy *v/t* qualifizieren, befähigen (***for*** für, zu); berechtigen (***to do*** zu tun); einschränken, abschwächen, mildern; *v/i* sich qualifizieren *or* eignen (***for*** für; ***as*** als); SPORT sich qualifizieren (***for*** für)
qual·i·ty Qualität *f*; Eigenschaft *f*
qualms Bedenken *pl*, Skrupel *pl*
quan·da·ry: ***be in a quandary about what to do*** nicht wissen, was man tun soll
quan·ti·ty Quantität *f*, Menge *f*
quan·tum PHYS **1.** Quant *n*; **2.** Quanten…
quar·an·tine **1.** Quarantäne *f*; **2.** unter Quarantäne stellen
quar·rel **1.** Streit *m*, Auseinandersetzung *f*; **2.** (sich) streiten
quar·rel·some streitsüchtig, zänkisch
quar·ry[1] Steinbruch *m*
quar·ry[2] HUNT Beute *f*, *a. fig* Opfer *n*
quart Quart *n* (ABBR ***qt***) *(0,95 l, Br 1,14 l)*
quar·ter **1.** Viertel *n*, vierter Teil; Quartal *n*, Vierteljahr *n*; Viertelpfund *n*; Vierteldollar *m*; SPORT (Spiel)Viertel *n*; (Himmels)Richtung *f*, Gegend *f*, Teil *m*; (Stadt)Viertel *n*; GASTR (*esp* Hinter)Viertel *n*; Gnade *f*, Pardon *m*; *pl* Quartier *n*, Unterkunft *f* (*a.* MIL); ***a quarter of an hour*** e-e Viertelstunde; ***a quarter of*** (*Br* ***to***) ***five*** (ein) Viertel vor fünf *(4.45)*; ***a quarter after*** (*Br* ***past***) ***five*** (ein) Viertel nach fünf *(5.15)*; ***at close quarters*** in *or* aus nächster Nähe; ***from official quarters*** von amtlicher Seite; **2.** vierteln; *esp* MIL einquartieren (***on*** bei)
quar·ter·deck MAR Achterdeck *n*
quar·ter·fi·nals SPORT Viertelfinale *n*
quar·ter·ly **1.** vierteljährlich; **2.** Vierteljahresschrift *f*
quar·tet(te) MUS Quartett *n*
quartz MIN Quarz *m*
quartz clock Quarzuhr *f*
quartz watch Quarz(armband)uhr *f*
qua·ver **1.** *v/i* zittern; *v/t et.* mit zitternder Stimme sagen; **2.** Zittern *n*
quay MAR Kai *m*
quea·sy: ***I feel queasy*** mir ist übel *or* F mulmig
queen Königin *f*; *card game, chess*: Dame *f*; F Schwule *m*, Homo *m*
queen bee zo Bienenkönigin *f*
queen·ly wie e-e Königin, königlich
queer komisch, seltsam; F wunderlich; F schwul
quench *Durst* löschen, stillen
quer·u·lous nörglerisch
que·ry **1.** Frage *f*; Zweifel *m*; **2.** infrage stellen, in Zweifel ziehen
quest **1.** Suche *f* (***for*** nach); ***in quest of*** auf der Suche nach; **2.** suchen (***after, for*** nach)
ques·tion **1.** Frage *f*, *a.* Problem *n*, *a.* Sache *f*, *a.* Zweifel *m*; ***only a question of time*** nur e-e Frage der Zeit; ***this is not the point in question*** darum geht es nicht; ***there is no question that, it is beyond question that*** es steht außer Frage, dass; ***there is no question about this*** daran besteht kein Zweifel; ***be out of the question*** nicht infrage kommen; **2.** befragen (***about*** über *acc*); JUR vernehmen, verhören (***about*** zu); bezweifeln, in Zweifel ziehen, infrage stellen
ques·tion·a·ble fraglich, zweifelhaft; fragwürdig
ques·tion·er Fragesteller(in)
ques·tion mark Fragezeichen *n*
question mas·ter *esp Br* Quizmaster *m*

ques·tion·naire Fragebogen *m*
queue *esp Br* **1.** Schlange *f*; → ***jump***; **2.** *mst* ***queue up*** Schlange stehen, anstehen, sich anstellen
quib·ble sich herumstreiten (***with*** mit; ***about, over*** wegen)
quick **1.** *adj* schnell, rasch; aufbrausend, hitzig (*temper*); ***be quick!*** mach schnell!, beeil dich!; **2.** *adv* schnell, rasch; **3.** ***cut s.o. to the quick*** *fig* j-n tief verletzen
quick·en (sich) beschleunigen
quick·sand Treibsand *m*
quick-tem·pered aufbrausend, hitzig
quick-wit·ted schlagfertig; geistesgegenwärtig
qui·et **1.** ruhig, still; ***quiet, please*** Ruhe, bitte; ***be quiet!*** sei still!; **2.** Ruhe *f*, Stille *f*; ***on the quiet*** F heimlich; **3.** *v/t a.* ***quiet down*** *j-n* beruhigen; *v/i a.* ***quiet down*** sich beruhigen
qui·et·en *Br* → ***quiet*** *3*
qui·et·ness Ruhe *f*, Stille *f*
quill ZO (Schwung-, Schwanz)Feder *f*; Stachel *m*
quilt Steppdecke *f*
quilt·ed Stepp…
quince BOT Quitte *f*
quin·ine PHARM Chinin *n*
quint F Fünfling *m*
quin·tes·sence Quintessenz *f*; Inbegriff *m*
quin·tet(te) MUS Quintett *n*
quin·tu·ple **1.** fünffach; **2.** (sich) verfünffachen
quin·tu·plets Fünflinge *pl*
quip **1.** geistreiche *or* witzige Bemerkung; **2.** witzeln, spötteln
quirk Eigenart *f*, Schrulle *f*; ***by some quirk of fate*** durch e-e Laune des Schicksals, durch e-n verrückten Zufall
quit F *v/t* aufhören mit; ***quit one's job*** kündigen; *v/i* aufhören; kündigen
quite ganz, völlig; ziemlich; ***quite a few*** ziemlich viele; ***quite nice*** ganz nett, recht nett; ***quite (so)!*** *esp Br* genau, ganz recht; ***be quite right*** völlig recht haben; ***she's quite a beauty*** sie ist e-e wirkliche Schönheit
quits F quitt (***with*** mit); ***call it quits*** es gut sein lassen
quit·ter: F ***be a quitter*** schnell aufgeben
quiv·er[1] zittern (***with*** vor *dat*; ***at*** bei)
quiv·er[2] Köcher *m*
quiz **1.** Quiz *n*; Prüfung *f*, Test *m*; **2.** ausfragen (***about*** über *acc*)
quiz·mas·ter Quizmaster *m*
quiz·zi·cal spöttisch-fragend
quo·ta Quote *f*, Kontingent *n*
quo·ta·tion Zitat *n*; ECON Notierung *f*; Kostenvoranschlag *m*
quotation marks LING Anführungszeichen *pl*
quote zitieren; *Beispiel etc* anführen; *Preis* nennen; ***be quoted at*** ECON notieren mit
quo·tient MATH Quotient *m*

R

R, r R, r *n*
rab·bi REL Rabbiner *m*
rab·bit ZO Kaninchen *n*
rab·ble Pöbel *m*, Mob *m*
rab·ble-rous·ing Hetz…, aufwieglerisch
rab·id VET tollwütig; *fig* fanatisch
ra·bies VET Tollwut *f*
rac·coon ZO Waschbär *m*
race[1] Rasse *f*, Rassenzugehörigkeit *f*; (*Menschen*)Geschlecht *n*
race[2] **1.** (Wett)Rennen *n*, (Wett)Lauf *m*; **2.** *v/i* an (e-m) Rennen teilnehmen; um die Wette laufen *or* fahren *etc*; rasen, rennen; MOT durchdrehen; *v/t* um die Wette laufen *or* fahren *etc* mit; rasen mit
race car MOT Rennwagen *m*
race·course Rennbahn *f*
race·horse Rennpferd *n*
rac·er Rennpferd *n*; Rennrad *n*, Rennwagen *m*
race ri·ots Rassenunruhen *pl*
race·track Rennbahn *f*
ra·cial rassisch, Rassen…
rac·ing **1.** Rennsport *m*; **2.** Renn…
rac·ing car *Br* MOT Rennwagen *m*
ra·cism Rassismus *m*
ra·cist **1.** Rassist(in); **2.** rassistisch
rack **1.** Gestell *n*, (*Geschirr-, Zeitungs- etc*)Ständer *m*, RAIL (*Gepäck*)Netz *n*, MOT (*Dach*)Gepäckständer *m*; HIST Folter(bank) *f*; **2.** ***be racked by*** *or* ***with*** geplagt *or* gequält werden von; ***rack one's***

brains sich das Hirn zermartern, sich den Kopf zerbrechen
rack·et[1] *tennis etc*: Schläger *m*
rack·et[2] F Krach *m*, Lärm *m*; Schwindel *m*, Gaunerei *f*; *(Drogen- etc)*Geschäft *n*; organisierte Erpressung
rack·et·eer Gauner *m*; Erpresser *m*
ra·coon → ***raccoon***
rac·y spritzig, lebendig; gewagt (*joke*)
ra·dar TECH Radar *m*, *n*
radar screen Radarschirm *m*
radar speed check MOT Radarkontrolle *f*
radar sta·tion Radarstation *f*
radar trap MOT Radarkontrolle *f*
ra·di·al **1.** radial, Radial…, strahlenförmig; **2.** MOT Gürtelreifen *m*
ra·di·al tire, *Br* **radial tyre** → ***radial*** 2
ra·di·ant strahlend, leuchtend (*a. fig* ***with*** vor *dat*)
ra·di·ate ausstrahlen; strahlenförmig ausgehen (***from*** von)
ra·di·a·tion Ausstrahlung *f*
ra·di·a·tor Heizkörper *m*; MOT Kühler *m*
rad·i·cal **1.** radikal (*a.* POL); MATH Wurzel…; **2.** POL Radikale *m*, *f*
ra·di·o **1.** Radio(apparat *m*) *n*; Funk *m*; Funkgerät *n*; ***by radio*** über Funk; ***on the radio*** im Radio; **2.** funken
ra·di·o·ac·tive radioaktiv
radioactive waste Atommüll *m*, radioaktiver Abfall
ra·di·o·ac·tiv·i·ty Radioaktivität *f*
ra·di·o ham Funkamateur *m*
radio play Hörspiel *n*
radio set Radioapparat *m*
radio sta·tion Funkstation *f*; Rundfunksender *m*, -station *f*
radio ther·a·py MED Strahlentherapie *f*, Röntgentherapie *f*
radio tow·er Funkturm *m*
rad·ish BOT Rettich *m*; Radieschen *n*
ra·di·us MATH Radius *m*
raf·fle **1.** Tombola *f*; **2.** *a.* ***raffle off*** verlosen
raft Floß *n*
raf·ter (Dach)Sparren *m*
rag Lumpen *m*, Fetzen *m*; Lappen *m*; ***in rags*** zerlumpt
rage **1.** Wut *f*, Zorn *m*; ***fly into a rage*** wütend werden; ***the latest rage*** F der letzte Schrei; ***be all the rage*** F große Mode sein; **2.** wettern (***against, at*** gegen); wüten, toben
rag·ged zerlumpt; struppig; *fig* stümperhaft
raid **1.** (***on***) Überfall *m* (auf *acc*), MIL *a.* Angriff *m* (gegen); Razzia *f* (in *dat*); **2.** überfallen, MIL *a.* angreifen; e-e Razzia machen in (*dat*)
rail **1.** Geländer *n*; Stange *f*; *(Handtuch)*-Halter *m*; (Eisen)Bahn *f*; RAIL Schiene *f*, *pl a.* Gleis *n*; ***by rail*** mit der Bahn; **2.** ***rail in*** einzäunen; ***rail off*** abzäunen
rail·ing *often pl* (Gitter)Zaun *m*
rail·road Eisenbahn *f*
railroad line Bahnlinie *f*
railroad·man Eisenbahner *m*
railroad sta·tion Bahnhof *m*
rail·way *Br* → ***railroad***
rain **1.** Regen *m*, *pl* Regenfälle *pl*; ***the rains*** die Regenzeit; **(*come*)** ***rain or shine*** *fig* was immer auch geschieht; **2.** regnen; ***it is raining cats and dogs*** F es gießt in Strömen; ***it never rains but it pours*** es kommt immer gleich knüppeldick, ein Unglück kommt selten allein
rain·bow Regenbogen *m*
rain·coat Regenmantel *m*
rain·fall Niederschlag(smenge *f*) *m*
rain for·est GEOGR Regenwald *m*
rain·proof regendicht, wasserdicht
rain·y regnerisch, verregnet, Regen…; ***save s.th. for a rainy day*** et. für schlechte Zeiten zurücklegen
raise **1.** heben; hochziehen; erheben; *Denkmal etc* errichten; *Staub etc* aufwirbeln; *Gehalt, Miete etc* erhöhen; *Geld* zusammenbringen, beschaffen; *Kinder* aufziehen, großziehen; *Tiere* züchten; *Getreide etc* anbauen; *Frage* aufwerfen, *et.* zur Sprache bringen; *Blockade etc, a. Verbot* aufheben; **2.** Lohn- *or* Gehaltserhöhung *f*
rai·sin Rosine *f*
rake **1.** Rechen *m*, Harke *f*; **2.** *v/t*: ***rake*** (***up***) (zusammen)rechen, (zusammen)-harken; F ***rake in*** scheffeln; *v/i*: ***rake about, rake around*** herumstöbern
rak·ish flott, keck, verwegen
ral·ly **1.** (sich) (wieder) sammeln; sich erholen (***from*** von) (*a.* ECON); ***rally round*** sich scharen um; **2.** Kundgebung *f*, (Massen)Versammlung *f*; MOT Rallye *f*; *tennis etc*: Ballwechsel *m*
ram **1.** ZO Widder *m*, Schafbock *m*; TECH Ramme *f*; **2.** rammen
ram·ble **1.** wandern, umherstreifen; abschweifen; **2.** Wanderung *f*
ram·bler Wanderer *m*; BOT Kletterrose *f*
ram·bling weitschweifig; weitläufig
rambling rose BOT Kletterrose *f*
ramp Rampe *f*; MOT (Autobahn)Auffahrt *f*; (Autobahn)Ausfahrt *f*
ram·page **1.** ***rampage through*** (wild *or* aufgeregt) trampeln durch (*elephant etc*); → **2.** ***go on the rampage through*** randalierend ziehen durch

ram·pant: ***be rampant*** wuchern (*plant*); grassieren (***in*** in *dat*)
ram·shack·le baufällig (*building*); klapp(e)rig (*vehicle*)
ranch Ranch *f*; (*Geflügel- etc*)Farm *f*
ranch·er Rancher *m*; (*Geflügel- etc*) Züchter *m*
ran·cid ranzig
ran·co(u)r Groll *m*, Erbitterung *f*
ran·dom **1.** *adj* ziellos, wahllos; zufällig, Zufalls…; ***random sample*** Stichprobe *f*; **2.** ***at random*** aufs Geratewohl
range **1.** Reich-, Schuss-, Tragweite *f*; Entfernung *f*; *fig* Bereich *m*, *a.* Spielraum *m*, *a.* Gebiet *n*; (*Schieß*)Stand *m*, (-)Platz *m*; (*Berg*)Kette *f*; offenes Weidegebiet; ECON Kollektion *f*, Sortiment *n*; Küchenherd *m*; ***at close range*** aus nächster Nähe; ***within range of vision*** in Sichtweite; ***a wide range of …*** eine große Auswahl an … (*dat*); **2.** *v/i*: ***range from … to …, range between … and …*** sich zwischen … und … bewegen (*prices etc*); *v/t* aufstellen, anordnen
range find·er PHOT Entfernungsmesser *m*
rang·er Förster *m*; Ranger *m*
rank[1] **1.** Rang *m* (*a.* MIL), (soziale) Stellung; Reihe *f*; (*Taxi*)Stand *m*; ***of the first rank*** *fig* erstklassig; ***the rank and file*** *fig* die Basis; ***the ranks*** *fig* das Heer, die Masse;**2.** *v/t* rechnen, zählen (***among*** zu); stellen (***above*** über *acc*); *v/i* zählen, gehören (***among*** zu); gelten (***as*** als)
rank[2] BOT (üppig) wuchernd; übel riechend, übel schmeckend; *fig* krass (*outsider*), blutig (*beginner*)
ran·kle *fig* nagen, wehtun, F wurmen
ran·sack durchwühlen, durchsuchen; plündern
ran·som **1.** Lösegeld *n*; **2.** freikaufen, auslösen
rant: ***rant (on) about, rant and rave about*** eifern gegen
rap **1.** Klopfen *n*; Klaps *m*; **2.** klopfen (an *acc*, auf *acc*)
ra·pa·cious habgierig
rape[1] **1.** vergewaltigen; **2.** Vergewaltigung *f*
rape[2] BOT Raps *m*
rap·id schnell, rasch
ra·pid·i·ty Schnelligkeit *f*
rap·ids GEOGR Stromschnellen *pl*
rapt: ***with rapt attention*** mit gespannter Aufmerksamkeit
rap·ture Entzücken *n*, Verzückung *f*; ***go into raptures*** in Verzückung geraten
rare[1] selten, rar; dünn (*air*); F Mords…
rare[2] GASTR blutig (*steak*)
rar·e·fied dünn (*air*)
rar·i·ty Seltenheit *f*; Rarität *f*
ras·cal Schlingel *m*
rash[1] voreilig, vorschnell, unbesonnen
rash[2] MED (Haut)Ausschlag *m*
rash·er dünne Speckscheibe
rasp **1.** raspeln; kratzen; **2.** Raspel *f*; Kratzen *n*
rasp·ber·ry BOT Himbeere *f*
rat ZO Ratte *f* (*a. contp*); F ***smell a rat*** Lunte *or* den Braten riechen
rate **1.** Quote *f*, Rate *f*, (*Geburten-, Sterbe*)Ziffer *f*; (*Steuer-, Zins- etc*)Satz *m*; (*Wechsel*)Kurs *m*; Geschwindigkeit *f*, Tempo *n*; ***at any rate*** auf jeden Fall; **2.** einschätzen, halten (***as*** für); *Lob etc* verdienen; ***be rated as*** gelten als
rate of ex·change ECON (Umrechnungs-, Wechsel)Kurs *m*
rate of in·terest ECON Zinssatz *m*
ra·ther ziemlich; eher, vielmehr, besser gesagt; ***rather!*** *esp Br* F und ob!; ***I would*** *or* ***had rather go*** ich möchte lieber gehen
rat·i·fy POL ratifizieren
rat·ing Einschätzung *f*; *radio*, TV Einschaltquote *f*
ra·ti·o MATH Verhältnis *n*
ra·tion **1.** Ration *f*; **2.** *et.* rationieren; ***ration out*** zuteilen (***to*** *dat*)
ra·tion·al rational; vernunftbegabt; vernünftig; verstandesmäßig
ra·tion·al·i·ty Vernunft *f*
ra·tion·al·ize rational erklären; ECON rationalisieren
rat race F endloser Konkurrenzkampf
rat·tle **1.** klappern; rasseln *or* klimpern (mit); prasseln (***on*** auf *acc*) (*rain etc*); rattern, knattern (*vehicle*); rütteln an (*dat*); F *j-n* verunsichern; ***rattle at*** rütteln an (*dat*); ***rattle off*** F *Gedicht etc* herunterrasseln; F ***rattle on*** quasseln (***about*** über *acc*); F ***rattle through*** *Rede etc* herunterrasseln; **2.** Klappern *n* (*etc* → 1); Rassel *f*, Klapper *f*
rat·tle·snake ZO Klapperschlange *f*
rau·cous heiser, rau
rav·age verwüsten
rav·ag·es Verwüstungen *pl*, *a. fig* verheerende Auswirkungen *pl*
rave fantasieren, irrereden; toben; wettern (***against, at*** gegen); schwärmen (***about*** von)
rav·el (sich) verwickeln *or* verwirren
ra·ven ZO Rabe *m*
rav·e·nous ausgehungert, heißhungrig
ra·vine Schlucht *f*, Klamm *f*
rav·ing mad tobsüchtig
rav·ings irres Gerede, Delirien *pl*
rav·ish·ing *fig* hinreißend

raw GASTR roh, ECON, TECH *a.* Roh…; MED wund; METEOR nasskalt; *fig* unerfahren; ***raw vegetables and fruit*** Rohkost *f*
raw-boned knochig, hager
raw·hide Rohleder *n*
raw ma·te·ri·al Rohstoff *m*
ray Strahl *m*; *fig* Schimmer *m*
ray·on Kunstseide *f*
ra·zor Rasiermesser *n*; Rasierapparat *m*; ***electric razor*** Elektrorasierer *m*
ra·zor blade Rasierklinge *f*
ra·zor('s) edge *fig* kritische Lage; ***be on a razor('s) edge*** auf des Messers Schneide stehen
re… wieder, noch einmal, neu
reach **1.** *v/t* erreichen; reichen *or* gehen bis an (*acc*) *or* zu; ***reach down*** herunter-, hinunterreichen (***from*** von); ***reach out*** *Arm etc* ausstrecken; *v/i* reichen, gehen, sich erstrecken; *a.* ***reach out*** greifen, langen (***for*** nach); ***reach out*** die Hand ausstrecken; **2.** Reichweite *f*; ***within*** (***out of***) ***reach*** in (außer) Reichweite; ***within easy reach*** leicht erreichbar
re·act reagieren (***to*** auf *acc*; CHEM ***with*** mit)
re·ac·tion Reaktion *f* (*a.* CHEM)
re·ac·tor PHYS Reaktor *m*
read lesen; TECH (an)zeigen; *Zähler etc* ablesen; UNIV studieren; deuten, verstehen (***as*** als); sich *gut etc* lesen (lassen); lauten; ***read (s.th.) to s.o.*** j-m (et.) vorlesen; ***read medicine*** Medizin studieren
read·a·ble lesbar; leserlich; lesenswert
read·er Leser(in); Lektor(in); Lesebuch *n*
read·i·ly bereitwillig, gern; leicht, ohne weiteres
read·i·ness Bereitschaft *f*
read·ing **1.** Lesen *n*; Lesung *f* (*a.* PARL); TECH Anzeige *f*, (*Thermometer- etc* -)Stand *m*; Auslegung *f*; **2.** Lese…; ***reading matter*** Lesestoff *m*
re·ad·just TECH nachstellen, korrigieren; ***readjust (o.s.) to*** sich wieder anpassen (*dat*) *or* an (*acc*), sich wieder einstellen auf (*acc*)
read·y bereit, fertig; bereitwillig; im Begriff (***to do*** zu tun); schnell, schlagfertig; ***ready for use*** gebrauchsfertig; ***get ready*** (sich) fertig machen
read·y cash → ***ready money***
read·y-made Konfektions…
read·y meal Fertiggericht *n*
read·y mon·ey Bargeld *n*
real echt; wirklich, tatsächlich, real; F ***for real*** echt, im Ernst
real es·tate Grundbesitz *m*, Immobilien *pl*
real estate a·gent Grundstücks-, Immobilienmakler *m*
re·a·lism Realismus *m*
re·al·ist Realist(in)
re·al·is·tic realistisch
re·al·i·ty Realität *f*, Wirklichkeit *f*
re·a·li·za·tion Erkenntnis *f*; Realisierung *f* (*a.* ECON), Verwirklichung *f*
re·al·ize sich klarmachen, erkennen, begreifen, einsehen; realisieren (*a.* ECON), verwirklichen
real·ly wirklich, tatsächlich; ***well, really!*** ich muss schon sagen!; ***really?*** im Ernst?
realm Königreich *n*; *fig* Reich *n*
real·tor Grundstücks-, Immobilienmakler *m*
reap *Getreide etc* schneiden; *Feld* abernten; *fig* ernten
re·ap·pear wieder erscheinen
rear **1.** *v/t Kind, Tier* aufziehen, großziehen; *Kopf* heben; *v/i* sich aufbäumen (*horse*); **2.** Rückseite *f*, Hinterseite *f*, MOT Heck *n*; ***in*** (*Br* ***at***) ***the rear of*** hinter (*dat*); ***bring up the rear*** die Nachhut bilden; **3.** hinter, Hinter…, Rück…, MOT *a.* Heck…
rear-end col·li·sion MOT Auffahrunfall *m*
rear·guard MIL Nachhut *f*
rear light MOT Rücklicht *n*
re·arm MIL (wieder) aufrüsten
re·ar·ma·ment MIL (Wieder)Aufrüstung *f*
rear·most hinterste(r, -s)
rear·view mir·ror MOT Rückspiegel *m*
rear·ward **1.** *adj* hintere(r, -s), rückwärtig; **2.** *adv a.* ***rearwards*** rückwärts
rear-wheel drive MOT Hinterradantrieb *m*
rear win·dow MOT Heckscheibe *f*
rea·son **1.** Grund *m*; Verstand *m*; Vernunft *f*; ***by reason of*** wegen; ***for this reason*** aus diesem Grund; ***listen to reason*** Vernunft annehmen; ***it stands to reason that*** es leuchtet ein, dass; **2.** *v/i* vernünftig *or* logisch denken; vernünftig reden (***with*** mit); *v/t* folgern, schließen (***that*** dass); ***reason s.o. into*** (***out of***) ***s.th.*** j-m et. einreden (ausreden)
rea·son·a·ble vernünftig; günstig (*price*); ganz gut, nicht schlecht
re·as·sure beruhigen
re·bate ECON Rabatt *m*, (Preis)Nachlass *m*; Rückzahlung *f*
reb·el[1] **1.** Rebell(in); Aufständische *m, f*; **2.** aufständisch
re·bel[2] rebellieren, sich auflehnen (***against*** gegen)
re·bel·lion Rebellion *f*, Aufstand *m*
re·bel·lious rebellisch, aufständisch
re·birth Wiedergeburt *f*
re·bound **1.** abprallen, zurückprallen (***from*** von); *fig* zurückfallen (***on*** auf

acc.); **2.** SPORT Abpraller *m*

re·buff **1.** schroffe Abweisung, Abfuhr *f*; **2.** schroff abweisen

re·build wieder aufbauen (*a. fig*)

re·buke **1.** rügen, tadeln; **2.** Rüge *f*, Tadel *m*

re·call **1.** zurückrufen, abberufen; MOT (in die Werkstatt) zurückrufen; sich erinnern an (*acc*); erinnern an (*acc*); **2.** Zurückrufung *f*, Abberufung *f*; Rückrufaktion *f*; ***have total recall*** das absolute Gedächtnis haben; ***beyond recall, past recall*** unwiederbringlich *or* unwiderruflich vorbei

re·ca·pit·u·late rekapitulieren, (kurz) zusammenfassen

re·cap·ture wieder einfangen (*a. fig*); *Häftling* wieder fassen; MIL zurückerobern

re·cast TECH umgießen; umformen, neu gestalten; THEA *etc* umbesetzen, neu besetzen

re·cede schwinden; ***receding chin*** fliehendes Kinn

re·ceipt *esp* ECON Empfang *m*, Eingang *m*; Quittung *f*; *pl* Einnahmen *pl*

re·ceive bekommen, erhalten; empfangen; *j-n* aufnehmen (***into*** in *acc*); *radio*, TV empfangen

re·ceiv·er Empfänger(in); TEL Hörer *m*; JUR Hehler(in); *a.* ***official receiver*** *Br* JUR Konkursverwalter *m*

re·cent neuere(r, -s); jüngste(r, -s)

re·cent·ly kürzlich, vor kurzem

re·cep·tion Empfang *m*; Aufnahme *f* (***into*** in *acc*); *radio*, TV Empfang *m*; *a.* ***reception desk*** *hotel*: Rezeption *f*, Empfang *m*

re·cep·tion·ist Empfangsdame *f*, -chef *m*; MED Sprechstundenhilfe *f*

re·cep·tive aufnahmefähig; empfänglich (***to*** für)

re·cess Unterbrechung *f*, (Schul)Pause *f*; PARL, JUR Ferien *pl*; Nische *f*

re·ces·sion ECON Rezession *f*

re·ci·pe (Koch)Rezept *n*

re·cip·i·ent Empfänger(in)

re·cip·ro·cal wechselseitig, gegenseitig

re·cip·ro·cate *v/i* TECH sich hin- und herbewegen; sich revanchieren; *v/t Einladung etc* erwidern

re·cit·al Vortrag *m*, (*Klavier- etc*)Konzert *n*, (*Lieder*)Abend *m*; Schilderung *f*

re·ci·ta·tion Aufsagen *n*, Hersagen *n*; Vortrag *m*

re·cite aufsagen, hersagen; vortragen; aufzählen

reck·less rücksichtslos

reck·on *v/t* (aus-, be)rechnen; glauben, schätzen; ***reckon up*** zusammenrechnen; *v/i*: ***reckon on*** rechnen mit; ***reckon with*** rechnen mit; ***reckon without*** nicht rechnen mit

reck·on·ing (Be)Rechnung *f*; ***be out in one's reckoning*** sich verrechnet haben

re·claim zurückfordern; *Gepäck etc* abholen; *dem Meer etc Land* abgewinnen; TECH wiedergewinnen

re·cline sich zurücklehnen

re·cluse Einsiedler(in)

rec·og·ni·tion (Wieder)Erkennen *n*; Anerkennung *f*

rec·og·nize (wieder) erkennen; anerkennen; zugeben, eingestehen

re·coil **1.** zurückschrecken (***from*** vor *dat*); **2.** Rückstoß *m*

rec·ol·lect sich erinnern an (*acc*)

rec·ol·lec·tion Erinnerung *f* (***of*** an *acc*)

rec·om·mend empfehlen (***as*** als; ***for*** für)

rec·om·men·da·tion Empfehlung *f*

rec·om·pense **1.** entschädigen (***for*** für); **2.** Entschädigung *f*

rec·on·cile versöhnen, aussöhnen; in Einklang bringen (***with*** mit)

rec·on·cil·i·a·tion Versöhnung *f*, Aussöhnung *f* (***between*** zwischen *dat*; ***with*** mit)

re·con·di·tion TECH (general)überholen

re·con·nais·sance MIL Aufklärung *f*, Erkundung *f*

re·con·noi·ter, *Br* **re·con·noi·tre** MIL erkunden, auskundschaften

re·con·sid·er noch einmal überdenken

re·con·struct wieder aufbauen (*a. fig*); *Verbrechen etc* rekonstruieren

re·con·struc·tion Wiederaufbau *m*; Rekonstruktion *f*

rec·ord[1] Aufzeichnung *f*; JUR Protokoll *n*; Akte *f*; (Schall)Platte *f*; SPORT Rekord *m*; ***off the record*** inoffiziell; ***have a criminal record*** vorbestraft sein

re·cord[2] aufzeichnen, aufschreiben, schriftlich niederlegen; JUR protokollieren, zu Protokoll nehmen; *auf Schallplatte, Tonband etc* aufnehmen, *Sendung a.* aufzeichnen, mitschneiden

re·cord·er (*Kassetten*)Rekorder *m*; (*Tonband*)Gerät *n*; MUS Blockflöte *f*

re·cord·ing Aufnahme *f*, Aufzeichnung *f*, Mitschnitt *m*

rec·ord play·er Plattenspieler *m*

re·count erzählen

re·cov·er *v/t* wiedererlangen, wiederbekommen, wieder finden; *Kosten etc* wiedereinbringen; *Fahrzeug, Verunglückten etc* bergen; ***recover consciousness*** MED wieder zu sich kommen, das Bewusstsein wiedererlangen; *v/i* sich erholen (***from*** von)

re·cov·er·y Wiedererlangen *n*; Wiederfin-

R

den *n*; Bergung *f*; Genesung *f*; Erholung *f*
rec·re·a·tion Entspannung *f*; Unterhaltung *f*, Freizeitbeschäftigung *f*
re·cruit **1.** MIL Rekrut *m*; Neue *m*, *f*, neues Mitglied; **2.** MIL rekrutieren; *Personal* einstellen; *Mitglieder* werben
rec·tan·gle MATH Rechteck *n*
rec·tan·gu·lar rechteckig
rec·ti·fy ELECTR gleichrichten
rec·tor REL Pfarrer *m*
rec·to·ry REL Pfarrhaus *n*
re·cu·pe·rate sich erholen (***from*** von) (*a. fig*)
re·cur wiederkehren, wieder auftreten
re·cur·rence Wiederkehr *f*
re·cur·rent wiederkehrend
re·cy·cla·ble TECH recycelbar, wiederverwertbar
re·cy·cle TECH *Abfälle* recyceln, wieder verwerten; ***recycled paper*** Recyclingpapier *n*, Umwelt(schutz)-papier *n*
re·cy·cling TECH Recycling *n*, Wiederverwertung *f*
red **1.** rot; **2.** Rot *n*; ***be in the red*** ECON in den roten Zahlen sein
red·breast → ***robin***
Red Cres·cent Roter Halbmond
Red Cross Rotes Kreuz
red·cur·rant BOT Rote Johannisbeere
red·den röten, rot färben; rot werden
red·dish rötlich
re·dec·o·rate *Zimmer etc* neu streichen *or* tapezieren
re·deem *Pfand*, *Versprechen etc* einlösen; REL erlösen
Re·deem·er REL Erlöser *m*, Heiland *m*
re·demp·tion Einlösung *f*; REL Erlösung *f*
re·de·vel·op *Gebäude*, *Stadtteil* sanieren
red-faced verlegen, mit rotem Kopf
red-hand·ed: ***catch s.o. red-handed*** j-n auf frischer Tat ertappen
red·head F Rotschopf *m*, Rothaarige *f*
red-head·ed rothaarig
red her·ring *fig* falsche Fährte *or* Spur
red-hot rot glühend; *fig* glühend; F brandaktuell (*news etc*)
Red In·di·an *contp* Indianer(in)
red-let·ter day Freuden-, Glückstag *m*
red·ness Röte *f*
re·dou·ble verdoppeln
red tape Bürokratismus *m*, F Amtsschimmel *m*
re·duce verkleinern; *Geschwindigkeit*, *Risiko etc* verringern, *Steuern etc* senken, *Preis*, *Waren etc* herabsetzen, reduzieren (***from*** ... ***to*** von ... auf *acc*), *Gehalt etc* kürzen; verwandeln (***to*** in *acc*), machen (***to*** zu); reduzieren, zurückführen (***to*** auf *acc*)
re·duc·tion Verkleinerung *f*; Verringerung *f*, Senkung *f*, Herabsetzung *f*, Reduzierung *f*, Kürzung *f*
re·dun·dant überflüssig
reed BOT Schilf(rohr) *n*
re·ed·u·cate umerziehen
re·ed·u·ca·tion Umerziehung *f*
reef (Felsen)Riff *n*
reek **1.** Gestank *m*; **2.** stinken (***of*** nach)
reel[1] **1.** Rolle *f*, Spule *f*; **2.** ***reel off*** abrollen, abspulen; *fig* herunterrasseln
reel[2] sich drehen; (sch)wanken, taumeln, torkeln; ***my head reeled*** mir drehte sich alles
re-e·lect wieder wählen
re-en·ter wieder eintreten in (*acc*), wieder betreten
re-en·try Wiedereintreten *n*, Wiedereintritt *m*
ref F SPORT Schiri *m*
re·fer: ***refer to*** verweisen *or* hinweisen auf (*acc*); *j-n* verweisen an (*acc*); sich beziehen auf (*acc*); anspielen auf (*acc*); erwähnen (*acc*); nachschlagen in (*dat*)
ref·er·ee SPORT Schiedsrichter *m*, Unparteiische *m*; *boxing*: Ringrichter *m*
ref·er·ence Verweis *m*, Hinweis *m* (***to*** auf *acc*); Verweisstelle *f*; Referenz *f*, Empfehlung *f*, Zeugnis *n*; Bezugnahme *f* (***to*** auf *acc*); Anspielung *f* (***to*** auf *acc*); Erwähnung *f* (***to*** *gen*); Nachschlagen *n* (***to*** in *dat*); ***list of references*** Quellenangabe *f*
reference book Nachschlagewerk *n*
reference li·bra·ry Handbibliothek *f*
reference num·ber Aktenzeichen *n*
ref·e·ren·dum POL Referendum *n*, Volksentscheid *m*
re·fill **1.** wieder füllen, nachfüllen, auffüllen; **2.** (*Ersatz*)Mine *f*; (*Ersatz*)Patrone *f*
re·fine TECH raffinieren; *fig* verfeinern, kultivieren; ***refine on*** verbessern, verfeinern
re·fined TECH raffiniert; *fig* kultiviert, vornehm
re·fine·ment TECH Raffinierung *f*; *fig* Verbess(e)rung *f*, Verfeinerung *f*; Kultiviertheit *f*, Vornehmheit *f*
re·fin·e·ry TECH Raffinerie *f*
re·flect *v/t* reflektieren, zurückwerfen, -strahlen, (wider)spiegeln; ***be reflected in*** sich (wider)spiegeln in (*dat*) (*a. fig*); *v/i* nachdenken (***on*** über *acc*); ***reflect (badly) on*** sich nachteilig auswirken auf (*acc*); ein schlechtes Licht werfen auf (*acc*)
re·flec·tion Reflexion *f*, Zurückwerfung *f*, -strahlung *f*, (Wider)Spiegelung *f* (*a. fig*);

R

Spiegelbild *n*; Überlegung *f*; Betrachtung *f*; ***on reflection*** nach einigem Nachdenken
re·flec·tive reflektierend; nachdenklich
re·flex Reflex *m*
reflex ac·tion Reflexhandlung *f*
reflex cam·e·ra PHOT Spiegelreflexkamera *f*
re·flex·ive LING reflexiv, rückbezüglich
re·form **1.** reformieren, verbessern; sich bessern; **2.** Reform *f* (*a.* POL), Besserung *f*
ref·or·ma·tion Reformierung *f*; Besserung *f*; ***the Reformation*** REL die Reformation
re·form·er *esp* POL Reformer *m*; REL Reformator *m*
re·fract *Strahlen etc* brechen
re·frac·tion (*Strahlen- etc*)Brechung *f*
re·frain[1]: ***refrain from*** sich enthalten (*gen*), unterlassen (*acc*)
re·frain[2] Kehrreim *m*, Refrain *m*
re·fresh (***o.s.*** sich) erfrischen, stärken; *Gedächtnis* auffrischen
re·fresh·ing erfrischend (*a. fig*)
re·fresh·ment Erfrischung *f*
re·fri·ge·rate TECH kühlen
re·fri·ge·ra·tor Kühlschrank *m*
re·fu·el auftanken
ref·uge Zuflucht *f*, Zufluchtsstätte *f*; *Br* Verkehrsinsel *f*
ref·u·gee Flüchtling *m*
ref·u·gee camp Flüchtlingslager *n*
re·fund **1.** Rückzahlung *f*, Rückerstattung *f*; **2.** *Geld* zurückzahlen, zurückerstatten; *Auslagen* ersetzen
re·fur·bish aufpolieren (*a. fig*); renovieren
re·fus·al Ablehnung *f*; Weigerung *f*; Verweigerung *f*
re·fuse[1] *v/t* ablehnen; verweigern; sich weigern, es ablehnen (***to do*** zu tun); *v/i* ablehnen; sich weigern
ref·use[2] Abfall *m*, Abfälle *pl*, Müll *m*
ref·use dump Müllabladeplatz *m*
re·fute widerlegen
re·gain wieder-, zurückgewinnen
re·gale: ***regale s.o. with s.th.*** j-n mit et. erfreuen *or* ergötzen
re·gard **1.** Achtung *f*; Rücksicht *f*; *pl* Grüße *pl*; ***in this regard*** in dieser Hinsicht; ***with regard to*** im Hinblick auf (*acc*); hinsichtlich (*gen*); ***with kind regards*** mit freundlichen Grüßen; **2.** betrachten (*a. fig*), ansehen; ***regard as*** betrachten als, halten für; ***as regards ...*** was ... betrifft
re·gard·ing bezüglich, hinsichtlich (*gen*)
re·gard·less: ***regardless of*** ohne Rücksicht auf (*acc*), ungeachtet (*gen*)
regd ABBR *of* ***registered*** ECON eingetragen; *post* eingeschrieben
re·gen·e·rate (sich) erneuern *or* regenerieren
re·gent Regent(in)
re·gi·ment **1.** MIL Regiment *n*, *fig a.* Schar *f*; **2.** reglementieren, bevormunden
re·gion Gegend *f*, Gebiet *n*, Region *f*
re·gion·al regional, örtlich, Orts...
re·gis·ter **1.** Register *n*, Verzeichnis *n*, (*Wähler- etc*)Liste *f*; **2.** *v/t* registrieren, eintragen (lassen); *Messwerte* anzeigen; *Brief etc* einschreiben lassen; *v/i* sich eintragen (lassen)
re·gis·tered let·ter Einschreib(e)brief *m*, Einschreiben *n*
re·gis·tra·tion Registrierung *f*, Eintragung *f*; MOT Zulassung *f*
registration fee Anmeldegebühr *f*
registration num·ber MOT (polizeiliches) Kennzeichen
re·gis·try Registratur *f*
re·gis·try of·fice *esp Br* Standesamt *n*
re·gret **1.** bedauern; bereuen; **2.** Bedauern *n*; Reue *f*
re·gret·ful bedauernd
re·gret·ta·ble bedauerlich
reg·u·lar **1.** regelmäßig; geregelt, geordnet; richtig; normal; MIL Berufs...; ***regular gas*** (*Br* ***petrol***) MOT Normalbenzin *n*; **2.** F Stammkunde *m*, Stammkundin *f*; Stammgast *m*; SPORT Stammspieler(in); MIL Berufssoldat *m*; MOT Normal(-benzin) *n*
reg·u·lar·i·ty Regelmäßigkeit *f*
reg·u·late regeln, regulieren; TECH einstellen, regulieren
reg·u·la·tion Reg(e)lung *f*, Regulierung *f*; TECH Einstellung *f*; Vorschrift *f*
reg·u·la·tor TECH Regler *m*
re·hears·al MUS, THEA Probe *f*
re·hearse MUS, THEA proben
reign **1.** Regierung *f*, *a. fig* Herrschaft *f*; **2.** herrschen, regieren
re·im·burse *Auslagen* erstatten, vergüten
rein **1.** Zügel *m*; **2.** ***rein in*** *Pferd etc* zügeln; *fig* bremsen
rein·deer ZO Ren *n*, Rentier *n*
re·in·force verstärken
re·in·force·ment Verstärkung *f*
re·in·state *j-n* wieder einstellen (***as*** als; ***in*** in *dat*)
re·in·sure rückversichern
re·it·e·rate (ständig) wiederholen
re·ject *j-n*, *et.* ablehnen, *Bitte* abschlagen, *Plan etc* verwerfen; *j-n* ab-, zurückweisen; MED *Organ etc* abstoßen
re·jec·tion Ablehnung *f*; Verwerfung *f*;

Zurückweisung *f*; MED Abstoßung *f*
re·joice sich freuen, jubeln (***at, over*** über *acc*)
re·joic·ing(s) Jubel *m*
re·join[1] wieder zusammenfügen; wieder zurückkehren zu
re·join[2] erwidern
re·ju·ve·nate verjüngen
re·kin·dle *Feuer* wieder anzünden; *fig* wieder entfachen
re·lapse **1.** zurückfallen, wieder verfallen (***into*** in *acc*); rückfällig werden; MED e-n Rückfall bekommen; **2.** Rückfall *m*
re·late *v/t* erzählen, berichten; in Verbindung *or* Zusammenhang bringen (***to*** mit); *v/i* sich beziehen (***to*** auf *acc*); zusammenhängen (***to*** mit)
re·lat·ed verwandt (***to*** mit)
re·la·tion Verwandte *m, f*; Beziehung *f* (***between*** zwischen *dat*; ***to*** zu); *pl diplomatische, geschäftliche* Beziehungen *pl*; ***in*** *or* ***with relation to*** in Bezug auf (*acc*)
re·la·tion·ship Verwandtschaft *f*; Beziehung *f*, Verhältnis *n*
rel·a·tive[1] Verwandte *m, f*
rel·a·tive[2] relativ, verhältnismäßig; bezüglich (***to*** *gen*); LING Relativ..., bezüglich
rel·a·tive pro·noun LING Relativpronomen *n*, bezügliches Fürwort
re·lax *v/t Muskeln etc* entspannen; *Griff etc* lockern; *fig* nachlassen in (*dat*); *v/i* sich entspannen, *fig a.* ausspannen; sich lockern
re·lax·a·tion Entspannung *f*; Erholung *f*; Lockerung *f*
re·laxed entspannt, zwanglos
re·lay[1] **1.** Ablösung *f*; SPORT Staffel *f*; *radio*, TV Übertragung *f*; ELECTR Relais *n*; **2.** *radio*, TV übertragen
re·lay[2] *Kabel, Teppich* neu verlegen
re·lay race SPORT Staffel *f*
re·lease **1.** entlassen, freilassen; loslassen; freigeben, herausbringen, veröffentlichen; MOT *Handbremse* lösen; *fig* befreien, erlösen; **2.** Entlassung *f*, Freilassung *f*; Befreiung *f*; Freigabe *f*; Veröffentlichung *f*; TECH, PHOT Auslöser *m*; *film*: *often* ***first release*** Uraufführung *f*
rel·e·gate verbannen; ***be relegated*** SPORT absteigen (***to*** in *acc*)
re·lent nachgeben; nachlassen
re·lent·less unbarmherzig; anhaltend
rel·e·vant relevant, erheblich, wichtig; sachdienlich, zutreffend
re·li·a·bil·i·ty Zuverlässigkeit *f*
re·li·a·ble zuverlässig
re·li·ance Vertrauen *n*; Abhängigkeit *f* (***on*** von)
rel·ic Relikt *n*, Überrest *m*; REL Reliquie *f*
re·lief Erleichterung *f*; Unterstützung *f*, Hilfe *f*; Sozialhilfe *f*; Ablösung *f*; Relief *n*
relief map GEOGR Reliefkarte *f*
re·lieve *Schmerz, Not* lindern, *j-n, Gewissen* erleichtern; *j-n* ablösen
re·li·gion Religion *f*
re·li·gious Religions...; religiös; gewissenhaft
rel·ish **1.** *fig* Gefallen *m*, Geschmack *m* (***for*** an *dat*); GASTR Würze *f*; Soße *f*; ***with relish*** mit Genuss; **2.** genießen, sich *et.* schmecken lassen; Geschmack *or* Gefallen finden an (*dat*)
re·luc·tance Widerstreben *n*; ***with reluctance*** widerwillig, ungern
re·luc·tant widerstrebend, widerwillig
re·ly: ***rely on*** sich verlassen auf (*acc*)
re·main **1.** (ver)bleiben; übrig bleiben; **2.** *pl* (Über)Reste *pl*
re·main·der Rest *m*; Restbetrag *m*
re·make **1.** wieder *or* neu machen; **2.** Remake *n*, Neuverfilmung *f*
re·mand JUR **1.** ***be remanded in custody*** in Untersuchungshaft bleiben; **2.** ***be on remand*** in Untersuchungshaft sein; ***prisoner on remand*** Untersuchungsgefangene *m, f*
re·mark **1.** *v/t* bemerken, äußern; *v/i* sich äußern (***on*** über *acc*, zu); **2.** Bemerkung *f*
re·mark·a·ble bemerkenswert; außergewöhnlich
rem·e·dy **1.** (Heil-, Hilfs-, Gegen)Mittel *n*; (Ab)Hilfe *f*; **2.** *Schaden etc* beheben; *Missstand* abstellen; *Situation* bereinigen
re·mem·ber sich erinnern an (*acc*); denken an (*acc*); ***please remember me to her*** grüße sie bitte von mir
re·mem·brance Erinnerung *f*; ***in remembrance of*** zur Erinnerung an (*acc*)
re·mind erinnern (***of*** an *acc*)
re·mind·er Mahnung *f*
rem·i·nis·cences Erinnerungen *pl* (***of*** an *acc*)
rem·i·nis·cent: ***be reminiscent of*** erinnern an (*acc*)
re·mit *Schulden, Strafe* erlassen; *Sünden* vergeben; *Geld* überweisen (***to*** *dat or* an *acc*)
re·mit·tance ECON Überweisung *f* (***to*** an *acc*)
rem·nant (Über)Rest *m*
re·mod·el umformen, umgestalten
re·morse Gewissensbisse *pl*, Reue *f* (***über*** *acc* for)
re·morse·ful zerknirscht, reumütig

R

re·morse·less unbarmherzig
re·mote fern, entfernt; abgelegen, entlegen
remote con·trol TECH Fernlenkung *f*, Fernsteuerung *f*; Fernbedienung *f*
re·mov·al Entfernung *f*; Umzug *m*
re·mov·al van Möbelwagen *m*
re·move *v/t* entfernen (***from*** von); *Hut, Deckel etc* abnehmen; *Kleidung* ablegen; beseitigen, aus dem Weg räumen; *v/i* (um)ziehen (***from*** von; ***to*** nach)
re·mov·er (*Flecken- etc*)Entferner *m*
Re·nais·sance *die* Renaissance
ren·der *berühmt, schwierig, möglich etc* machen; *Dienst* erweisen; *Gedicht, Musikstück* vortragen; übersetzen, übertragen (***into*** in *acc*); *mst* ***render down*** *Fett* auslassen
ren·der·ing *esp Br* → ***rendition***
ren·di·tion MUS *etc* Vortrag *m*; Übersetzung *f*, Übertragung *f*
re·new erneuern; *Gespräch etc* wieder aufnehmen; *Kraft etc* wiedererlangen; *Vertrag, Pass* verlängern (lassen)
re·new·al Erneuerung *f*; Verlängerung *f*
re·nounce verzichten auf (*acc*); *s-m Glauben etc* abschwören
ren·o·vate renovieren
re·nown Ruhm *m*
re·nowned berühmt (***as*** als; ***for*** wegen, für)
rent[1] **1.** Miete *f*; Pacht *f*; Leihgebühr *f*; ***for rent*** zu vermieten, zu verleihen; **2.** mieten, pachten (***from*** von); *a.* ***rent out*** vermieten, verpachten (***to*** an *acc*); ***rented car*** Miet-, Leihwagen *m*
rent[2] Riss *m*
rent·al Miete *f*; Pacht *f*; Leihgebühr *f*; ***rental car*** Miet-, Leihwagen *m*
re·nun·ci·a·tion Verzicht *m* (***of*** auf *acc*); Abschwören *n*
re·pair **1.** reparieren, ausbessern; *fig* wieder gutmachen; **2.** Reparatur *f*; Ausbesserung *f*; *pl* Instandsetzungsarbeiten *pl*; ***beyond repair*** nicht mehr zu reparieren; ***in good*** (***bad***) ***repair*** in gutem (schlechtem) Zustand; ***be under repair*** in Reparatur sein; ***the road is under repair*** an der Straße wird gerade gearbeitet
rep·a·ra·tion Wiedergutmachung *f*; Entschädigung *f*; *pl* POL Reparationen *pl*
rep·ar·tee Schlagfertigkeit *f*; schlagfertige Antwort(en *pl*) *f*
re·pay *et.* zurückzahlen; *Besuch* erwidern; *et.* vergelten; *j-n* entschädigen
re·pay·ment Rückzahlung *f*
re·peal *Gesetz etc* aufheben
re·peat **1.** *v/t* wiederholen; nachsprechen; ***repeat o.s.*** sich wiederholen; *v/i* F aufstoßen (***on s.o.*** j-m) (*food*); **2.** *radio*, TV Wiederholung *f*
re·peat·ed wiederholt
re·peat·ed·ly verschiedentlich
re·pel *Angriff, Feind* zurückschlagen; *Wasser etc, fig j-n* abstoßen
re·pel·lent abstoßend
re·pent bereuen
re·pent·ance Reue *f* (***for*** über *acc*)
re·pen·tant reuig, reumütig
re·per·cus·sion *mst pl* Auswirkungen *pl* (***on*** auf *acc*)
rep·er·toire THEA *etc* Repertoire *n*
rep·er·to·ry the·a·ter (*Br* **the·a·tre**) Repertoiretheater *n*
rep·e·ti·tion Wiederholung *f*
re·place an *j-s* Stelle treten, *j-n*, *et.* ersetzen; TECH austauschen, ersetzen
re·place·ment TECH Austausch *m*; Ersatz *m*
re·plant umpflanzen
re·play **1.** SPORT *Spiel* wiederholen; *Tonband-, Videoaufname etc* abspielen; **2.** SPORT Wiederholung *f*
re·plen·ish (wieder) auffüllen
re·plete satt; angefüllt, ausgestattet (***with*** mit)
rep·li·ca *art*: Originalkopie *f*; Kopie *f*, Nachbildung *f*
re·ply **1.** antworten, erwidern (***to*** auf *acc*); **2.** Antwort *f*, Erwiderung *f* (***to*** auf *acc*); ***in reply to*** (als Antwort) auf (*acc*)
re·ply cou·pon Rückantwortschein *m*
re·ply-paid en·ve·lope Freiumschlag *m*
re·port **1.** Bericht *m*; Meldung *f*, Nachricht *f*; Gerücht *n*; Knall *m*; ***report card*** PED Zeugnis *n*; **2.** berichten (über *acc*); (sich) melden; anzeigen; ***it is reported that*** es heißt, dass; ***reported speech*** LING indirekte Rede
re·port·er Reporter(in), Berichterstatter(in)
re·pose Ruhe *f*; Gelassenheit *f*
re·pos·i·to·ry (Waren)Lager *n*; *fig* Fundgrube *f*, Quelle *f*
rep·re·sent *j-n*, *Wahlbezirk* vertreten; darstellen; hinstellen (***as, to be*** als)
rep·re·sen·ta·tion Vertretung *f*; Darstellung *f*
rep·re·sen·ta·tive **1.** repräsentativ (*a.* POL), typisch (***of*** für); **2.** (Stell)Vertreter(in); ECON (Handels)Vertreter(in); PARL Abgeordnete *m, f*; ***House of Representatives*** Repräsentantenhaus *n*
re·press unterdrücken; PSYCH verdrängen
re·pres·sion Unterdrückung *f*; PSYCH Verdrängung *f*
re·prieve JUR **1.** ***he was reprieved*** er wurde begnadigt; s-e Urteilsvollstreckung

wurde ausgesetzt; **2.** Begnadigung *f*; Vollstreckungsaufschub *m*
rep·ri·mand 1. rügen, tadeln (***for*** wegen); **2.** Rüge *f*, Tadel *m*, Verweis *m*
re·print 1. neu auflegen *or* drucken, nachdrucken; **2.** Neuauflage *f*, Nachdruck *m*
re·pri·sal Repressalie *f*, Vergeltungsmaßnahme *f*
re·proach 1. Vorwurf *m*; **2.** vorwerfen (***s.o. with s.th.*** j-m et.); Vorwürfe machen
re·proach·ful vorwurfsvoll
rep·ro·bate verkommenes Subjekt
re·pro·cess NUCL wieder aufbereiten
re·pro·cess·ing TECH Wiederaufbereitung *f*
reprocessing plant TECH Wiederaufbereitungsanlage *f*
re·pro·duce *v/t Ton etc* wiedergeben; *Bild etc* reproduzieren; ***reproduce o.s.*** → *v/i* BIOL sich fortpflanzen, sich vermehren
re·pro·duc·tion BIOL Fortpflanzung *f*; Reproduktion *f*; Wiedergabe *f*; PED Nacherzählung *f*
re·pro·duc·tive BIOL Fortpflanzungs…
re·proof Rüge *f*, Tadel *m*
re·prove rügen, tadeln (***for*** wegen)
rep·tile ZO Reptil *n*
re·pub·lic Republik *f*
re·pub·li·can 1. republikanisch; **2.** Republikaner(in)
re·pug·nant widerlich, abstoßend
re·pulse 1. *j-n*, *Angebot etc* zurückweisen; MIL *Angriff* zurückschlagen; **2.** MIL Zurückschlagen *n*; Zurückweisung *f*
re·pul·sion Abscheu *m*, Widerwille *m*; PHYS Abstoßung *f*
re·pul·sive abstoßend, widerlich, widerwärtig; PHYS abstoßend
rep·u·ta·ble angesehen
rep·u·ta·tion (guter) Ruf, Ansehen *n*
re·pute (guter) Ruf
re·put·ed angeblich
re·quest 1. (***for***) Bitte *f* (um), Wunsch *m* (nach); ***at the request of s.o., at s.o.'s request*** auf j-s Bitte hin; ***on request*** auf Wunsch; **2.** um *et.* bitten *or* ersuchen; *j-n* bitten, ersuchen (***to do*** zu tun)
re·quest stop *Br* Bedarfshaltestelle *f*
re·quire erfordern; benötigen, brauchen; verlangen; ***if required*** wenn nötig
re·quire·ment Erfordernis *n*, Bedürfnis *n*; Anforderung *f*
req·ui·site 1. erforderlich; **2.** *mst pl* Artikel *pl*; ***toilet requisites*** Toilettenartikel *pl*
req·ui·si·tion 1. Anforderung *f*; MIL Requisition *f*, Beschlagnahme *f*; ***make a requisition for*** *et.* anfordern; **2.** anfordern; MIL requirieren, beschlagnahmen
re·sale Wieder-, Weiterverkauf *m*
re·scind JUR *Gesetz*, *Urteil etc* aufheben
res·cue 1. retten (***from*** aus, vor *dat*); **2.** Rettung *f*; Hilfe *f*; **3.** Rettungs…
re·search 1. Forschung *f*; **2.** forschen; *et.* erforschen
re·search·er Forscher(in)
re·sem·blance Ähnlichkeit *f* (***to*** mit; ***between*** zwischen *dat*)
re·sem·ble ähnlich sein, ähneln (*both: dat*)
re·sent übel nehmen, sich ärgern über (*acc*)
re·sent·ful ärgerlich (***of, at*** über *acc*)
re·sent·ment Ärger *m* (***against, at*** über *acc*)
res·er·va·tion Reservierung *f*, Vorbestellung *f*; Vorbehalt *m*; (*Indianer*)Reservat(ion *f*) *n*; (*Wild*)Reservat *n*
re·serve 1. (sich) *et.* aufsparen (***for*** für); sich vorbehalten; reservieren (lassen), vorbestellen; **2.** Reserve *f* (*a.* MIL); Vorrat *m*; (*Naturschutz-, Wild*)Reservat *n*; SPORT Reservespieler(in); Reserviertheit *f*, Zurückhaltung *f*
re·served zurückhaltend, reserviert
res·er·voir Reservoir *n* (*a. fig* ***of*** an *dat*)
re·set *Uhr* umstellen; *Zeiger etc* zurückstellen (***to*** auf *acc*)
re·set·tle umsiedeln
re·side wohnen, ansässig sein, s-n Wohnsitz haben
res·i·dence Wohnsitz *m*, Wohnort *m*; Aufenthalt *m*; Residenz *f*; ***official residence*** Amtssitz *m*
residence per·mit Aufenthaltsgenehmigung *f*, -erlaubnis *f*
res·i·dent 1. wohnhaft, ansässig; **2.** Bewohner(in), *in a town etc a.* Einwohner(in); (Hotel)Gast *m*; MOT Anlieger(in)
res·i·den·tial Wohn…
residential ar·e·a Wohngebiet *n*, Wohngegend *f*
re·sid·u·al übrig (geblieben), restlich, Rest…
residual pol·lu·tion Altlasten *pl*
res·i·due Rest *m*, CHEM *a.* Rückstand *m*
re·sign *v/i* zurücktreten (***from*** von); *v/t Amt etc* niederlegen; aufgeben; verzichten auf (*acc*); ***resign o.s. to*** sich fügen in (*acc*), sich abfinden mit
res·ig·na·tion Rücktritt *m*; Resignation *f*
re·signed ergeben, resigniert
re·sil·i·ence Elastizität *f*; *fig* Zähigkeit *f*
re·sil·i·ent elastisch; *fig* zäh
res·in Harz *n*
re·sist widerstehen (*dat*); Widerstand leisten, sich widersetzen (*both: dat*)

R

re·sist·ance Widerstand *m* (*a.* ELECTR); MED Widerstandskraft *f*; (*Hitze- etc -*) Beständigkeit *f*, (*Stoß- etc*)Festigkeit *f*; ***line of least resistance*** Weg *m* des geringsten Widerstands
re·sist·ant widerstandsfähig; (*hitze- etc*) beständig, (*stoß- etc*)fest
res·o·lute resolut, entschlossen
res·o·lu·tion Beschluss *m*, PARL *etc a.* Resolution *f*; Vorsatz *m*; Entschlossenheit *f*; Lösung *f*
re·solve **1.** beschließen; *Problem etc* lösen; (sich) auflösen; ***resolve on*** sich entschließen zu; **2.** Vorsatz *m*; Entschlossenheit *f*
res·o·nance Resonanz *f*; voller Klang
res·o·nant voll(tönend); widerhallend
re·sort **1.** Erholungsort *m*, Urlaubsort *m*; ***have resort to*** → **2.** ***resort to*** Zuflucht nehmen zu
re·sound widerhallen (***with*** von)
re·source Mittel *n*, Zuflucht *f*; Ausweg *m*; Einfallsreichtum *m*; *pl* Mittel *pl*; (*natürliche*) Reichtümer *pl*, (*Boden-*, *Natur*)Schätze *pl*
re·source·ful einfallsreich, findig
re·spect **1.** Achtung *f*, Respekt *m* (*both*: ***for*** vor *dat*); Rücksicht *f* (***for*** auf *acc*); Beziehung *f*, Hinsicht *f*; ***with respect to ...*** was ... anbelangt *or* betrifft; ***in this respect*** in dieser Hinsicht; ***give my respects to ...*** e-e Empfehlung an ... (*acc*); **2.** *v/t* respektieren, *a.* achten, *a.* berücksichtigen, beachten
re·spect·a·ble ehrbar, anständig, geachtet; F ansehnlich, beachtlich
re·spect·ful respektvoll, ehrerbietig
re·spec·tive jeweilig; ***we went to our respective places*** jeder ging zu seinem Platz
re·spec·tive·ly beziehungsweise
res·pi·ra·tion Atmung *f*
res·pi·ra·tor Atemschutzgerät *n*
re·spite Pause *f*; Aufschub *m*, Frist *f*; ***without respite*** ohne Unterbrechung
re·splen·dent glänzend, strahlend
re·spond antworten, erwidern (***to*** auf *acc*; ***that*** dass); reagieren, MED *a.* ansprechen (***to*** auf *acc*)
re·sponse Antwort *f*, Erwiderung *f* (***to*** auf *acc*); *fig* Reaktion *f* (***to*** auf *acc*)
re·spon·si·bil·i·ty Verantwortung *f*; ***on one's own responsibility*** auf eigene Verantwortung; ***sense of responsibility*** Verantwortungsgefühl *n*; ***take (full) responsibility for*** die (volle) Verantwortung übernehmen für
re·spon·si·ble verantwortlich; verantwortungsbewusst; verantwortungsvoll
rest[1] **1.** Ruhe(pause) *f*; Erholung *f*; TECH Stütze *f*; (*Telefon*)Gabel *f*; ***have or take a rest*** sich ausruhen; ***set s.o.'s mind at rest*** j-n beruhigen; **2.** *v/i* ruhen; sich ausruhen; lehnen (***against, on*** an *dat*); ***let s.th. rest*** et. auf sich beruhen lassen; ***rest on*** ruhen auf (*dat*) (*a. fig*); *fig* beruhen auf (*dat*); *v/t* (aus)ruhen (lassen); lehnen (***against*** gegen; ***on*** an *acc*)
rest[2] Rest *m*; ***all the rest of them*** alle Übrigen; ***for the rest*** im Übrigen
rest ar·e·a MOT Rastplatz *m*
res·tau·rant Restaurant *n*, Gaststätte *f*
rest·ful ruhig, erholsam
rest home Altenpflegeheim *n*; Erholungsheim *n*
res·ti·tu·tion ECON Rückgabe *f*, Rückerstattung *f*
res·tive unruhig, nervös
rest·less ruhelos, rastlos; unruhig
res·to·ra·tion Wiederherstellung *f*; Restaurierung *f*; Rückgabe *f*, Rückerstattung *f*
re·store wiederherstellen; restaurieren; zurückgeben, -erstatten; ***be restored (to health)*** wieder gesund sein
re·strain (***from***) zurückhalten (von), hindern an (*dat*); ***I had to restrain myself*** ich musste mich beherrschen (***from doing s.th.*** um nicht et. zu tun)
re·strained beherrscht; dezent (*color*)
re·straint Beherrschung *f*, Zurückhaltung *f*; ECON Be-, Einschränkung *f*
re·strict ECON beschränken (***to*** auf *acc*), einschränken
re·stric·tion ECON Be-, Einschränkung *f*; ***without restrictions*** uneingeschränkt
rest room Toilette *f*
re·struc·ture umstrukturieren
re·sult **1.** Ergebnis *n*, Resultat *n*; Folge *f*; ***as a result of*** als Folge von (*or gen*); ***without result*** ergebnislos; **2.** folgen, sich ergeben (***from*** aus); ***result in*** zur Folge haben (*acc*), führen zu
re·sume wieder aufnehmen; fortsetzen; *Platz* wieder einnehmen
re·sump·tion Wiederaufnahme *f*; Fortsetzung *f*
Res·ur·rec·tion REL Auferstehung *f*
re·sus·ci·tate MED wieder beleben
re·sus·ci·ta·tion MED Wiederbelebung *f*
re·tail ECON **1.** Einzelhandel *m*; ***by retail*** im Einzelhandel; **2.** Einzelhandels...; **3.** *adv* im Einzelhandel; **4.** *v/t* im Einzelhandel verkaufen (***at, for*** für); *v/i* im Einzelhandel verkauft werden (***at, for*** für)
re·tail·er ECON Einzelhändler(in)
re·tain (be)halten, bewahren; *Wasser, Wärme* speichern

re·tal·i·ate Vergeltung üben, sich revanchieren
re·tal·i·a·tion Vergeltung *f*, Vergeltungsmaßnahmen *pl*
re·tard verzögern, aufhalten, hemmen; ***(mentally) retarded*** (geistig) zurückgeblieben
retch würgen
re·tell nacherzählen
re·think *et.* noch einmal überdenken
re·ti·cent schweigsam, zurückhaltend
ret·i·nue Gefolge *n*
re·tire *v/i* in Rente *or* Pension gehen, sich pensionieren lassen; sich zurückziehen; ***retire from business*** sich zur Ruhe setzen; *v/t* in den Ruhestand versetzen, pensionieren
re·tired pensioniert, im Ruhestand (lebend); ***be retired*** *a.* in Rente *or* Pension sein
re·tire·ment Pensionierung *f*, Ruhestand *m*
re·tir·ing zurückhaltend
re·tort 1. (scharf) entgegnen *or* erwidern; **2.** (scharfe) Entgegnung *or* Erwiderung
re·touch PHOT retuschieren
re·trace *Tathergang etc* rekonstruieren; ***retrace one's steps*** denselben Weg zurückgehen
re·tract *v/t Angebot* zurückziehen; *Behauptung* zurücknehmen; *Geständnis* widerrufen; TECH, ZO einziehen; *v/i* TECH, ZO eingezogen werden
re·train umschulen
re·tread MOT **1.** *Reifen* runderneuern; **2.** runderneuerter Reifen
re·treat 1. MIL Rückzug *m*; Zufluchtsort *m*; ***beat a (hasty) retreat*** das Feld räumen, F abhauen; **2.** sich zurückziehen; zurückweichen (***from*** vor *dat*)
ret·ri·bu·tion Vergeltung *f*
re·trieve zurückholen, wiederbekommen; *Fehler, Verlust etc* wieder gutmachen; HUNT apportieren
ret·ro·ac·tive JUR rückwirkend
ret·ro·grade rückschrittlich
ret·ro·spect: ***in retrospect*** im Rückblick
ret·ro·spec·tive rückblickend; JUR rückwirkend
re·try JUR *Fall* erneut verhandeln; neu verhandeln gegen *j-n*
re·turn 1. *v/i* zurückkehren, zurückkommen; zurückgehen; ***return to*** auf *ein Thema etc* zurückkommen; in *e-e Gewohnheit etc* zurückfallen; in *e-n Zustand etc* zurückkehren; *v/t* zurückgeben (***to*** *dat*); zurückbringen (***to*** *dat*); zurückschicken, -senden (***to*** *dat or* an *acc*); zurücklegen, -stellen; erwidern; *Gewinn etc* abwerfen; → ***verdict***; **2.** Rückkehr *f*; *fig* Wiederauftreten *n*; Rückgabe *f*; Zurückbringen *n*; Zurückschicken *n*, -senden *n*; Zurücklegen *n*, -stellen *n*; Erwiderung *f*; (*Steuer*)Erklärung *f*; *tennis etc*: Return *m*, Rückschlag *m*; ECON *a. pl* Gewinn *m*; *Br* → ***return ticket***; *Br* ***many happy returns (of the day)*** herzlichen Glückwunsch zum Geburtstag; ***by return (of post)*** umgehend, postwendend; ***in return for*** (als Gegenleistung) für; **3.** *adj* Rück…
re·turn·a·ble *in cpds* Mehrweg…; ***returnable bottle*** Pfandflasche *f*
re·turn key EDP Eingabetaste *f*
return game, return match SPORT Rückspiel *n*
return tick·et *Br* RAIL Rückfahrkarte *f*; AVIAT Rückflugticket *n*
re·u·ni·fi·ca·tion POL Wiedervereinigung *f*
re·u·nion Treffen *n*, Wiedersehensfeier *f*; Wiedervereinigung *f*
re·us·a·ble wieder verwendbar
rev F MOT **1.** Umdrehung *f*; ***rev counter*** Drehzahlmesser *m*; **2.** *a.* ***rev up*** aufheulen (lassen)
re·val·ue ECON *Währung* aufwerten
re·veal den Blick freigeben auf (*acc*), zeigen; *Geheimnis etc* enthüllen, aufdecken
re·veal·ing aufschlussreich (*remark etc*); offenherzig (*dress etc*)
rev·el: ***revel in*** schwelgen in (*dat*); sich weiden an (*dat*)
rev·e·la·tion Enthüllung *f*; REL Offenbarung *f*
re·venge 1. Rache *f*; *esp* SPORT Revanche *f*; ***in revenge for*** aus Rache für; ***take revenge on s.o. for s.th.*** sich an j-m für et. rächen; **2.** rächen
re·venge·ful rachsüchtig
rev·e·nue Staatseinkünfte *pl*, Staatseinnahmen *pl*
re·ver·be·rate nach-, widerhallen
re·vere (ver)ehren
rev·e·rence Verehrung *f*; Ehrfurcht *f* (***for*** vor *dat*)
Rev·e·rend REL Hochwürden *m*
rev·e·rent ehrfürchtig, ehrfurchtsvoll
rev·er·ie (Tag)Träumerei *f*
re·vers·al Umkehrung *f*; Rückschlag *m*
re·verse 1. *adj* umgekehrt; ***in reverse order*** in umgekehrter Reihenfolge; **2.** *Wagen* im Rückwärtsgang fahren *or* rückwärtsfahren; *Reihenfolge etc* umkehren; *Urteil etc* aufheben; *Entscheidung etc* umstoßen; **3.** Gegenteil *n*; MOT Rückwärtsgang *m*; Rückseite *f*, Kehrseite *f* (*of a coin*); Rückschlag *m*

reverse gear MOT Rückwärtsgang *m*
reverse side linke (*Stoff*)Seite
re·vers·i·ble doppelseitig (tragbar)
re·vert: ***revert to*** in *e-n Zustand* zurückkehren; in *e-e Gewohnheit etc* zurückfallen; auf *ein Thema* zurückkommen
re·view **1.** Überprüfung *f*; Besprechung *f*, Kritik *f*, Rezension *f*; MIL Parade *f*; PED (Stoff)Wiederholung *f* (***for*** für *e-e Prüfung*); **2.** überprüfen; besprechen, rezensieren; MIL besichtigen, inspizieren; PED *Stoff* wiederholen (***for*** für *e-e Prüfung*)
re·view·er Kritiker(in), Rezensent(in)
re·vise revidieren, *Ansicht* ändern, *Buch etc* überarbeiten; *Br* PED *Stoff* wiederholen (***for*** für *e-e Prüfung*)
re·vi·sion Revision *f*, Überarbeitung *f*; überarbeitete Ausgabe; *Br* PED (Stoff-) Wiederholung *f* (***for*** für *e-e Prüfung*)
re·viv·al Wiederbelebung *f*; Wiederaufleben *n*
re·vive wieder beleben; wieder aufleben (lassen); *Erinnerungen* wachrufen; MED wieder zu sich kommen; sich erholen
re·voke widerrufen, zurücknehmen, rückgängig machen
re·volt **1.** *v/i* sich auflehnen, revoltieren (***against*** gegen); Abscheu empfinden, empört sein (***against, at, from*** über *acc*); *v/t* mit Abscheu erfüllen, abstoßen; **2.** Revolte *f*, Aufstand *m*
re·volt·ing abscheulich, abstoßend
rev·o·lu·tion Revolution *f*, Umwälzung *f*; ASTR Umlauf *m* (***round*** um); TECH Umdrehung *f*; ***number of revolutions*** Drehzahl *f*; ***revolution counter*** Drehzahlmesser *m*
rev·o·lu·tion·a·ry **1.** revolutionär; Revolutions…; **2.** POL Revolutionär(in)
rev·o·lu·tion·ize revolutionieren
re·volve sich drehen (***on, round*** um); ***revolve around*** *fig* sich drehen um
re·volv·er Revolver *m*
re·volv·ing Dreh…; ***revolving door(s)*** Drehtür *f*
re·vue THEA Revue *f*; Kabarett *n*
re·vul·sion Abscheu *m*
re·ward **1.** Belohnung *f*; **2.** belohnen
re·ward·ing lohnend
re·write neu schreiben, umschreiben
rhap·so·dy MUS Rhapsodie *f*
rhe·to·ric Rhetorik *f*
rheu·ma·tism MED Rheumatismus *m*, F Rheuma *n*
rhi·no F, **rhi·no·ce·ros** ZO Rhinozeros *n*, Nashorn *n*
rhu·barb BOT Rhabarber *m*
rhyme **1.** Reim *m*; Vers *m*; ***without rhyme or reason*** ohne Sinn und Verstand; **2.** (sich) reimen
rhyth·m Rhythmus *m*
rhyth·mic, rhyth·mi·cal rhythmisch
rib ANAT Rippe *f*
rib·bon (*a.* Farb-, Ordens)Band *n*; Streifen *m*; Fetzen *m*
rib cage ANAT Brustkorb *m*
rice BOT Reis *m*
rice pud·ding GASTR Milchreis *m*
rich **1.** reich (***in*** an *dat*); prächtig, kostbar; GASTR schwer; AGR fruchtbar, fett (*soil*); voll (*sound*); satt (*color*); ***rich (in calories)*** kalorienreich; **2.** ***the rich*** die Reichen *pl*
rick (Stroh-, Heu)Schober *m*
rick·ets MED Rachitis *f*
rick·et·y F *fig* gebrechlich; wack(e)lig
rid befreien (***of*** von); ***get rid of*** loswerden
rid·dance: F ***good riddance!*** den (die, das) sind wir Gott sei Dank los!
rid·den *in cpds* geplagt von
rid·dle[1] Rätsel *n*
rid·dle[2] **1.** grobes Sieb, Schüttelsieb *n*; **2.** sieben; durchlöchern, durchsieben
ride **1.** *v/i* reiten; fahren (***on*** auf *e-m Fahrrad etc*; ***on*** *or Br* ***in*** in *e-m Bus etc*); *v/t* reiten (auf *dat*); *Fahrrad, Motorrad* fahren, fahren auf (*dat*); **2.** Ritt *m*; Fahrt *f*
rid·er Reiter(in); (*Motorrad-, Rad*)Fahrer(in)
ridge GEOGR (*Gebirgs*)Kamm *m*, Grat *m*; ARCH (*Dach*)First *m*
rid·i·cule **1.** Spott *m*; **2.** lächerlich machen, spotten über (*acc*), verspotten
ri·dic·u·lous lächerlich
rid·ing Reit…
riff-raff *contp* Gesindel *n*
ri·fle[1] Gewehr *n*
ri·fle[2] durchwühlen
rift Spalt *m*, Spalte *f*; *fig* Riss *m*
rig **1.** *Schiff* auftakeln; ***rig out*** *j-n* ausstaffieren; ***rig up*** F (behelfsmäßig) zusammenbauen (***from*** aus); **2.** MAR Takelage *f*; TECH Bohrinsel *f*; F Aufmachung *f*
rig·ging MAR Takelage *f*
right **1.** *adj* recht; richtig; rechte(r, -s), Rechts…; ***all right!*** in Ordnung!, gut!; ***that's all right!*** das macht nichts!, schon gut!, bitte!; ***that's right!*** richtig!, ganz recht!, stimmt!; ***be right*** recht haben; ***put right, set right*** in Ordnung bringen; berichtigen, korrigieren; **2.** *adv* (nach) rechts; richtig, recht; genau; gerade (-wegs), direkt; ganz, völlig; ***right away*** sofort; ***right now*** im Moment; sofort; ***right on*** geradeaus; ***turn right*** (sich) nach rechts wenden; MOT rechts abbiegen; **3.** Recht *n*; *die* Rechte (*a.* POL, *boxing*), rechte Seite; ***on the right*** rechts,

auf der rechten Seite; ***to the right*** (nach) rechts; ***keep to the right*** sich rechts halten; MOT rechts fahren; **4.** aufrichten; *et.* wieder gutmachen; in Ordnung bringen
right an·gle MATH rechter Winkel
right-an·gled MATH rechtwink(e)lig
right·eous gerecht (*anger etc*)
right·ful rechtmäßig
right-hand rechte(r, -s)
right-hand drive MOT Rechtssteuerung *f*
right-hand·ed rechtshändig; für Rechtshänder; ***be right-handed*** Rechtshänder(in) sein
right·ly richtig; mit Recht
right of way MOT Vorfahrt *f*, Vorfahrtsrecht *n*; Durchgangsrecht *n*
right-wing POL dem rechten Flügel angehörend, Rechts…
rig·id starr, steif; *fig* streng, strikt
rig·a·ma·role Geschwätz *n*; *fig* Theater *n*, Zirkus *m*
rig·or·ous streng; genau
rig·o(u)r Strenge *f*, Härte *f*
rile F ärgern, reizen
rim Rand *m*; TECH Felge *f*
rim·less randlos
rind (*Zitronen- etc*)Schale *f*; (*Käse*)Rinde *f*; (*Speck*)Schwarte *f*
ring[1] **1.** Ring *m*; Kreis *m*; Manege *f*; (Box)Ring *m*; (Spionage- *etc*)Ring *m*; **2.** umringen, umstellen; *Vogel* beringen
ring[2] **1.** läuten; klingeln; klingen (*a. fig*); *Br* TEL anrufen; ***the bell is ringing*** es läutet *or* klingelt; ***ring the bell*** läuten, klingeln; ***ring back*** *Br* TEL zurückrufen; ***ring for*** nach *j-m*, *et.* läuten; *Arzt etc* rufen; ***ring off*** *Br* TEL (den Hörer) auflegen, Schluss machen; ***ring s.o.*** (***up***) j-n *or* bei j-m anrufen; **2.** Läuten *n*, Klingeln *n*; *fig* Klang *m*; *Br* TEL Anruf *m*; F ***give s.o. a ring*** j-n anrufen
ring bind·er Ringbuch *n*
ring fin·ger Ringfinger *m*
ring·lead·er Rädelsführer(in)
ring·let (Ringel)Löckchen *n*
ring road *Br* Umgehungsstraße *f*; Ringstraße *f*
ring·side: ***at the ringside*** *boxing*: am Ring
rink (Kunst)Eisbahn *f*; Rollschuhbahn *f*
rinse *a.* ***rinse out*** (aus)spülen
ri·ot **1.** Aufruhr *m*; Krawall *m*; ***run riot*** randalieren; ***run riot through*** randalierend ziehen durch; **2.** Krawall machen, randalieren
ri·ot·er Aufrührer(in); Randalierer(in)
ri·ot·ous aufrührerisch; randalierend; ausgelassen, wild
rip **1.** *a.* ***rip up*** zerreißen; ***rip open*** aufreißen; F ***rip s.o. off*** j-n neppen; **2.** Riss *m*
ripe reif
rip·en reifen (lassen)
rip-off F Nepp *m*
rip·ple **1.** (sich) kräuseln; plätschern, rieseln; **2.** kleine Welle; Kräuselung *f*; Plätschern *n*, Rieseln *n*
rise **1.** aufstehen, sich erheben; REL auferstehen; aufsteigen (*smoke etc*); sich heben (*curtain, spirits*); ansteigen (*road, river etc*), anschwellen (*river etc*); (an)steigen (*temperature etc*), *prices etc*: *a.* anziehen; stärker werden (*wind etc*); aufgehen (*sun etc, bread etc*); entspringen (*river etc*); *fig* aufsteigen; *fig* entstehen (***from, out of*** aus); *a.* ***rise up*** sich erheben (***against*** gegen); ***rise to the occasion*** sich der Lage gewachsen zeigen; **2.** (An)Steigen *n*; Steigung *f*; Anhöhe *f*; ASTR Aufgang *m*; *Br* Lohn- *or* Gehaltserhöhung *f*; *fig* Anstieg *m*; Aufstieg *m*; ***give rise to*** verursachen, führen zu
ris·er: ***early riser*** Frühaufsteher(in)
ris·ing **1.** Aufstand *m*; **2.** aufstrebend
risk **1.** Gefahr *f*, Risiko *n*; ***at one's own risk*** auf eigene Gefahr; ***at the risk of doing s.th.*** auf die Gefahr hin, et. zu tun; ***be at risk*** gefährdet sein; ***run the risk of doing s.th.*** Gefahr laufen, et. zu tun; ***run a risk, take a risk*** ein Risiko eingehen; **2.** wagen, riskieren
risk·y riskant
rite Ritus *m*; Zeremonie *f*
rit·u·al **1.** rituell; Ritual…; **2.** Ritual *n*
ri·val **1.** Rivale *m*, Rivalin *f*, Konkurrent(in); **2.** Konkurrenz…, rivalisierend; **3.** rivalisieren *or* konkurrieren mit
ri·val·ry Rivalität *f*; Konkurrenz *f*; Konkurrenzkampf *m*
riv·er Fluss *m*; Strom *m*
riv·er·side Flussufer *n*; ***by the riverside*** am Fluss
riv·et **1.** TECH Niet *m*, *n*, Niete *f*; **2.** TECH (ver)nieten; *fig Aufmerksamkeit*, *Blick* richten (***on*** auf *acc*)
road (Auto-, Land)Straße *f*; *fig* Weg *m*; ***on the road*** auf der Straße; unterwegs; THEA auf Tournee
road ac·ci·dent Verkehrsunfall *m*
road·block Straßensperre *f*
road hog F Verkehrsrowdy *m*
road map Straßenkarte *f*
road safe·ty Verkehrssicherheit *f*
road·side Straßenrand *m*; ***at the roadside, by the roadside*** am Straßenrand
road toll Straßenbenutzungsgebühr *f*
road·way Fahrbahn *f*
road works Straßenarbeiten *pl*
road·wor·thi·ness Verkehrssicherheit *f*

R

road·wor·thy verkehrssicher
roam *v/i* (umher)streifen, (-)wandern; *v/t* streifen *or* wandern durch
roar 1. Brüllen *n*, Gebrüll *n*; Brausen *n*, Krachen *n*, Donnern *n*; ***roars of laughter*** brüllendes Gelächter; **2.** brüllen; brausen; donnern (*truck, gun etc*)
roast GASTR **1.** *v/t* braten (*a. v/i*); *Kaffee etc* rösten; **2.** Braten *m*; **3.** *adj* gebraten
roast beef GASTR Rinderbraten *m*
rob *Bank etc* überfallen; *j-n* berauben
rob·ber Räuber *m*
rob·ber·y Raubüberfall *m*, (*Bank-*) Raub *m*, (*Bank*)Überfall *m*
robe *a. pl* Robe *f*, Talar *m*
rob·in ZO Rotkehlchen *n*
ro·bot Roboter *m*
ro·bust robust, kräftig
rock[1] schaukeln, wiegen; erschüttern (*a. fig*)
rock[2] Fels(en) *m*; Felsen *pl*; GEOL Gestein *n*; Felsbrocken *m*; Stein *m*; *Br* Zuckerstange *f*; *pl* Klippen *pl*; F ***on the rocks*** in ernsten Schwierigkeiten (*business etc*); kaputt (*marriage etc*); GASTR mit Eis
rock[3] *a.* ***rock music*** Rock(musik *f*) *m*; → ***rock 'n' roll***
rock·er Kufe *f*; Schaukelstuhl *m*; *Br* Rocker *m*; ***off one's rocker*** F übergeschnappt
rock·et 1. Rakete *f*; **2.** rasen, schießen; *a.* ***rocket up*** hochschnellen, in die Höhe schießen (*prices*)
rock·ing chair Schaukelstuhl *m*
rock·ing horse Schaukelpferd *n*
rock 'n' roll MUS Rock 'n' Roll *m*
rock·y felsig; steinhart
rod Rute *f*; TECH Stab *m*, Stange *f*
ro·dent ZO Nagetier *n*
ro·de·o Rodeo *m, n*
roe ZO *a.* ***hard roe*** Rogen *m*; *a.* ***soft roe*** Milch *f*
roe·buck ZO Rehbock *m*
roe deer ZO Reh *n*
rogue Schurke *m*, Gauner *m*; Schlingel *m*, Spitzbube *m*
ro·guish schelmisch, spitzbübisch
role THEA *etc* Rolle *f* (*a. fig*)
roll 1. *v/i* rollen; sich wälzen; fahren; MAR schlingern; (g)rollen (*thunder*); *v/t et.* rollen; auf-, zusammenrollen; *Zigarette* drehen; ***roll down*** *Ärmel* herunterkrempeln; MOT *Fenster* herunterkurbeln; ***roll out*** ausrollen; ***roll up*** aufrollen; (sich) zusammenrollen; *Ärmel* hochkrempeln; MOT *Fenster* hochkurbeln; **2.** Rolle *f*; GASTR Brötchen *n*, Semmel *f*; Namens-, Anwesenheitsliste *f*; (G)Rollen *n* (*of thunder*); (*Trommel*)Wirbel *m*; MAR Schlingern *n*
roll call Namensaufruf *m*
roll·er (Locken)Wickler *m*; TECH Rolle *f*, Walze *f*
roll·er coast·er Achterbahn *f*
roll·er skate Rollschuh *m*
roll·er-skate Rollschuh laufen
roll·er-skat·ing Rollschuhlaufen *n*
roll·er tow·el Rollhandtuch *n*
roll·ing pin Nudelholz *n*
roll-on Deoroller *m*
Ro·man 1. römisch; **2.** Römer(in)
ro·mance Abenteuer-, Liebesroman *m*; Romanze *f*; Romantik *f*
Ro·mance LING romanisch
Ro·ma·ni·a Rumänien *n*
Ro·ma·ni·an 1. rumänisch; **2.** Rumäne *m*, Rumänin *f*; LING Rumänisch *n*
ro·man·tic 1. romantisch; **2.** Romantiker(in)
ro·man·ti·cism Romantik *f*
romp *a.* ***romp about, romp around*** herumtollen, herumtoben
romp·ers Spielanzug *m*
roof 1. Dach *n*; MOT Verdeck *n*; **2.** mit e-m Dach versehen; ***roof in, roof over*** überdachen
roof·ing felt Dachpappe *f*
roof-rack MOT Dachgepäckträger *m*
rook[1] ZO Saatkrähe *f*
rook[2] *chess*: Turm *m*
rook[3] F *j-n* betrügen (***of*** um)
room 1. Raum *m*, *a.* Zimmer *n*, *a.* Platz *m*; *fig* Spielraum *m*; **2.** wohnen
room·er Untermieter(in)
room·ing-house Fremdenheim *n*, Pension *f*
room·mate Zimmergenosse *m*, -genossin *f*
room ser·vice Zimmerservice *m*
room·y geräumig
roost 1. (Hühner)Stange *f*; ZO Schlafplatz *m*; **2.** auf der Stange *etc* sitzen *or* schlafen
roost·er ZO (Haus)Hahn *m*
root 1. Wurzel *f*; ***take root*** Wurzeln schlagen (*a. fig*); **2.** *v/i* Wurzeln schlagen; wühlen (***for*** nach); ***root about*** herumwühlen (***among*** in *dat*); *v/t* ***root out*** *fig* ausrotten; ***root up*** mit der Wurzel ausreißen
root·ed: ***deeply rooted*** *fig* tief verwurzelt; ***stand rooted to the spot*** wie angewurzelt dastehen
rope 1. Seil *n*; MAR Tau *n*; Strick *m*; (*Perlen- etc*)Schnur *f*; ***give s.o. plenty of rope*** j-m viel Freiheit *or* Spielraum lassen; ***know the ropes*** F sich auskennen; ***show s.o. the ropes*** F j-n einarbeiten; **2.** festbinden (***to*** an *dat or acc*); ***rope***

R

off (durch ein Seil) absperren *or* abgrenzen
rope lad·der Strickleiter *f*
ro·sa·ry REL Rosenkranz *m*
rose **1.** BOT Rose *f*; Brause *f*; **2.** rosarot, rosenrot
ros·trum Redner-, Dirigentenpult *n*
ros·y rosig (*a. fig*)
rot **1.** *v/t* (ver)faulen *or* verrotten lassen; *v/i a.* ***rot away*** (ver)faulen, verrotten, morsch werden; **2.** Fäulnis *f*
ro·ta·ry rotierend, sich drehend; Rotations…, Dreh…
ro·tate rotieren (lassen), (sich) drehen; turnusmäßig (aus-) wechseln
ro·ta·tion Rotation *f*, Drehung *f*; Wechsel *m*
ro·tor TECH Rotor *m*
rot·ten verfault, faul; verrottet, morsch; *fig* miserabel; gemein; ***feel rotten*** F sich mies fühlen
ro·tund rund und dick
rough **1.** *adj* rau; uneben (*road etc*); stürmisch (*sea, crossing, weather*); grob; barsch; hart; grob, ungefähr (*estimate etc*); roh, Roh…; **2.** *adv* ***sleep rough*** im Freien übernachten; ***play rough*** SPORT hart spielen; **3.** *golf*: Rough *n*; ***write it out in rough first*** zuerst ins Unreine schreiben; **4.** ***rough it*** F primitiv *or* anspruchslos leben; ***rough out*** entwerfen, skizzieren; ***rough up*** F *j-n* zusammenschlagen
rough·age MED Ballaststoffe *pl*
rough·cast ARCH Rauputz *m*
rough cop·y Rohentwurf *m*, Konzept *n*
rough draft Rohfassung *f*
rough·en rau werden; rau machen, anrauen, aufrauen
rough·ly grob, *fig a.* ungefähr
rough·neck F Schläger *m*
rough·shod: ***ride roughshod over*** *j-n* rücksichtslos behandeln; sich rücksichtslos über *et.* hinwegsetzen
round **1.** *adj* rund; ***a round dozen*** ein rundes Dutzend; ***in round figures*** aufgerundet, abgerundet, rund(e) …; **2.** *adv* rund(her)um, rings(her)um; überall, auf *or* von *or* nach allen Seiten; ***turn round*** sich umdrehen; ***invite s.o. round*** j-n zu sich einladen; ***round about*** F ungefähr; ***all*** (***the***) ***year round*** das ganze Jahr hindurch *or* über; ***the other way round*** umgekehrt; **3.** *prp* (rund) um, um (*acc* … herum); in *or* auf (*dat*) … herum; ***trip round the world*** Weltreise *f*; **4.** Runde *f*, *a.* Rundgang *m*, MED Visite *f*, *a.* Lage *f* (*beer etc*); Schuss *m*; *esp Br* Scheibe *f* (*bread etc*); MUS Kanon *m*; **5.** rund machen, (ab)runden, *Lippen* spitzen; umfahren, fahren um, *Kurve* nehmen; ***round down*** *Zahl etc* abrunden (***to*** auf *acc*); ***round off*** *Essen etc* abrunden, beschließen (***with*** mit); *Zahl etc* auf- *or* abrunden (***to*** auf *acc*); ***round up*** *Vieh* zusammentreiben; *Leute etc* zusammentrommeln; *Zahl etc* aufrunden (***to*** auf *acc*)
round·a·bout **1.** *Br* MOT Kreisverkehr *m*; *Br* Karussell *n*; **2.** ***take a roundabout route*** e-n Umweg machen; ***in a roundabout way*** *fig* auf Umwegen
round trip Hin- und Rückfahrt *f*; Hin- und Rückflug *m*
round-trip tick·et Rückfahrkarte *f*; Rückflugticket *n*
round·up Razzia *f*
rouse *j-n* wecken; *fig j-n* aufrütteln, wach rütteln; *j-n* erzürnen, reizen
route Route *f*, Strecke *f*, Weg *m*, (*Bus-etc*)Linie *f*
rou·tine **1.** Routine *f*; ***the same old*** (***daily***) ***routine*** das (tägliche) ewige Einerlei; **2.** üblich, routinemäßig, Routine…
rove (umher)streifen, (umher)wandern
row[1] Reihe *f*
row[2] **1.** rudern; **2.** Kahnfahrt *f*
row[3] *Br* F **1.** Krach *m*; (lauter) Streit; **2.** (sich) streiten
row·boat Ruderboot *n*
row·er Ruderer *m*, Ruderin *f*
row house Reihenhaus *n*
row·ing boat *Br* Ruderboot *n*
roy·al königlich, Königs…
roy·al·ty die königliche Familie; Tantieme *f* (***on*** auf *acc*)
rub **1.** *v/t* reiben; abreiben; polieren; ***rub dry*** trocken reiben; ***rub it in*** *fig* F darauf herumreiten; ***rub shoulders with*** F verkehren mit; *v/i* reiben, scheuern (***against, on*** an *dat*); ***rub down*** abreiben, trocken reiben; abschmirgeln, abschleifen; ***rub off*** abreiben; abgehen (*paint etc*); ***rub off on(to)*** *fig* abfärben auf (*acc*); ***rub out*** *Br* ausradieren; **2.** ***give s.th. a rub*** et. abreiben *or* polieren
rub·ber Gummi *n, m*; *esp Br* Radiergummi *m*; Wischtuch *n*; F Gummi *m*
rub·ber band Gummiband *n*
rub·ber din·ghy Schlauchboot *n*
rub·ber·neck F **1.** neugierig gaffen; **2.** *a.* ***rubbernecker*** Gaffer(in), Schaulustige *m, f*
rub·ber·y gummiartig; zäh
rub·bish *Br* Abfall *m*, Abfälle *pl*, Müll *m*; F Schund *m*; Quatsch *m*, Blödsinn *m*
rubbish bin *Br* Mülleimer *m*
rubbish chute *Br* Müllschlucker *m*

rub·ble Schutt *m*; Trümmer *pl*
ru·by Rubin *m*; Rubinrot *n*
ruck·sack *esp Br* Rucksack *m*
rud·der AVIAT, MAR Ruder *n*
rud·dy frisch, gesund
rude unhöflich, grob; unanständig (*joke etc*); bös (*shock etc*)
ru·di·men·ta·ry elementar, Anfangs…; primitiv
ru·di·ments Anfangsgründe *pl*
rue·ful reuevoll, reumütig
ruff Halskrause *f* (*a.* ZO)
ruf·fle 1. kräuseln; *Haar* zerzausen; *Federn* sträuben; ***ruffle s.o.'s composure*** j-n aus der Fassung bringen; **2.** Rüsche *f*
rug Vorleger *m*, Brücke *f*; *esp Br* dicke Wolldecke
rug·by *a.* ***rugby football*** SPORT Rugby *n*
rug·ged GEOGR zerklüftet, schroff; TECH robust, stabil; zerfurcht (*face*)
ru·in 1. Ruin *m*; *mst pl* Ruine(n *pl*) *f*, Trümmer *pl*; **2.** ruinieren, zerstören
ru·in·ous ruinös
rule 1. Regel *f*; Spielregel *f*; Vorschrift *f*; Herrschaft *f*; Lineal *n*; ***against the rules*** regelwidrig; verboten; ***as a rule*** in der Regel; ***as a rule of thumb*** als Faustregel; ***work to rule*** Dienst nach Vorschrift tun; **2.** *v/t* herrschen über (*acc*); *esp* JUR entscheiden; *Papier* lin(i)ieren; *Linie* ziehen; ***be ruled by*** *fig* sich leiten lassen von; beherrscht werden von; ***rule out*** *et.* ausschließen; *v/i* herrschen (***over*** über *acc*); *esp* JUR entscheiden
rul·er Herrscher(in); Lineal *n*
rum Rum *m*
rum·ble rumpeln (*vehicle*); (g)rollen (*thunder*); knurren (*stomach*)
ru·mi·nant ZO Wiederkäuer *m*
ru·mi·nate ZO wiederkäuen
rum·mage F **1.** *a.* ***rummage about*** herumstöbern, herumwühlen (***among, in, through*** in *dat*); **2.** Ramsch *m*
rummage sale Wohltätigkeitsbasar *m*
ru·mo(u)r 1. Gerücht *n*; ***rumo(u)r has it that*** es geht das Gerücht, dass; **2.** ***it is rumo(u)red that*** es geht das Gerücht, dass; ***he is rumo(u)red to be …*** man munkelt, er sei …
rump F Hinterteil *n*
rum·ple zerknittern, zerknüllen, zerwühlen; *Haar* zerzausen
run 1. *v/i* laufen (*a.* SPORT), rennen; fahren, verkehren, gehen (*train, bus etc*); laufen, fließen; zerfließen, zerlaufen (*butter, paint etc*); TECH laufen (*engine*), in Betrieb *or* Gang sein; verlaufen (*road etc*); *esp* JUR gelten, laufen (***for one year*** ein Jahr); THEA *etc* laufen (***for three months*** drei Monate lang); lauten (*text*); gehen (*melody*); POL kandidieren (***for*** für); ***run dry*** austrocknen; ***run low*** knapp werden; ***run short*** knapp werden; ***run short of gas*** (*Br* ***petrol***) kein Benzin mehr haben; *v/t Strecke*, *Rennen* laufen; *Zug*, *Bus* fahren *or* verkehren lassen; *Wasser*, *Maschine etc* laufen lassen; *Geschäft*, *Hotel etc* führen, leiten; *Zeitungsartikel etc* abdrucken, bringen; ***run s.o. home*** F j-n nach Hause bringen *or* fahren; ***be running a temperature*** erhöhte Temperatur *or* Fieber haben; → ***errand***; ***run across*** *j-n* zufällig treffen; stoßen auf (*acc*); ***run after*** hinterherlaufen, nachlaufen (*dat*); ***run along!*** F ab mit dir!; ***run away*** davonlaufen (***from*** vor *dat*); ***run away with*** durchbrennen mit; durchgehen mit (*feelings etc*); ***run down*** MOT anfahren, umfahren; F schlechtmachen; ausfindig machen; ablaufen (*watch*); leer werden (*battery*); ***run in*** *Wagen etc* einfahren; F *Verbrecher* schnappen; ***run into*** laufen *or* fahren gegen; *j-n* zufällig treffen; *fig* geraten in (*acc*); *fig* sich belaufen auf (*acc*); ***run off with*** → ***run away with***; ***run on*** weitergehen, sich hinziehen (***until*** bis); F unaufhörlich reden (***about*** über *acc*, von); ***run out*** ablaufen (*time etc*); ausgehen, zu Ende gehen (*supplies etc*); ***run out of gas*** (*Br* ***petrol***) kein Benzin mehr haben; ***run over*** MOT überfahren; überlaufen, überfließen; ***run through*** überfliegen, durchgehen, durchlesen; ***run up*** *Flagge* hissen; *hohe Rechnung*, *Schulden* machen; ***run up against*** stoßen auf (*acc*); **2.** Lauf *m* (*a.* SPORT); Fahrt *f*; Spazierfahrt *f*; Ansturm *m*, ECON *a.* Run *m* (***on*** auf *acc*); THEA *etc* Laufzeit *f*; Laufmasche *f*; Gehege *n*; Auslauf *m*, (*Hühner*)Hof *m*; SPORT (*Bob-*, *Rodel-*) Bahn *f*; (*Ski*)Hang *m*; ***run of good*** (***bad***) ***luck*** Glückssträhne *f* (Pechsträhne *f*); ***in the long run*** auf die Dauer; ***in the short run*** zunächst; ***on the run*** auf der Flucht
run·a·bout F MOT Stadt-, Kleinwagen *m*
run·a·way Ausreißer(in)
rung Sprosse *f*
run·ner SPORT Läufer(in); Rennpferd *n*; *mst in cpds* Schmuggler(in); (*Schlitten-*, *Schlittschuh*)Kufe *f*; Tischläufer *m*; TECH (Gleit)Schiene *f*; BOT Ausläufer *m*
runner bean *Br* BOT grüne Bohne
run-up SPORT Zweite *m*, *f*, Vizemeister(in)
run·ning 1. Laufen *n*, Rennen *n*; Führung *f*, Leitung *f*; **2.** fließend; SPORT Lauf…; ***two days running*** zwei Tage hintereinander

R

running costs ECON Betriebskosten *pl*, laufende Kosten *pl*
run·ny F flüssig; laufend (*nose*), tränend (*eyes*)
run-off POL Stichwahl *f*
run·way AVIAT Start- und Landebahn *f*, Rollbahn *f*, Piste *f*
rup·ture 1. Bruch *m* (*a.* MED *and fig*), Riss *m*; **2.** bersten, platzen; (zer)reißen; ***rupture o.s.*** MED sich e-n Bruch heben *or* zuziehen
ru·ral ländlich
ruse List *f*, Trick *m*
rush[1] **1.** *v/i* hasten, hetzen, stürmen, rasen; ***rush at*** losstürzen *or* sich stürzen auf (*acc*); ***rush in*** hineinstürzen, hineinstürmen, hereinstürzen, hereinstürmen; ***rush into*** *fig* sich stürzen in (*acc*); *et.* überstürzen; *v/t* antreiben, drängen, hetzen; schnell bringen; *Essen* hinunterschlingen; losstürmen auf (*acc*); ***don't rush it*** lass dir Zeit dabei; **2.** Ansturm *m*; Hast *f*, Hetze *f*; Hochbetrieb *m*; ECON stürmische Nachfrage; ***what's all the rush?*** wozu diese Eile *or* Hetze?
rush[2] BOT Binse *f*
rush hour Rushhour *f*, Hauptverkehrszeit *f*, Stoßzeit *f*
rush-hour traf·fic Stoßverkehr *m*
rusk *esp Br* Zwieback *m*
Rus·sia Russland *n*
Rus·sian 1. russisch; **2.** Russe *m*, Russin *f*; LING Russisch *n*
rust 1. Rost *m*; **2.** *v/t* (ein-, ver)rosten lassen; *v/i* (ein-, ver)rosten
rus·tic ländlich, bäuerlich; rustikal
rus·tle 1. rascheln (mit), knistern; *Vieh* stehlen; **2.** Rascheln *n*
rust·proof rostfrei, nicht rostend
rust·y rostig; *fig* eingerostet
rut[1] **1.** (Rad)Spur *f*, Furche *f*; *fig* (alter) Trott; ***the daily rut*** das tägliche Einerlei; **2.** furchen; ***rutted*** ausgefahren
rut[2] ZO Brunft *f*, Brunst *f*
ruth·less unbarmherzig; rücksichtslos, skrupellos
rye BOT Roggen *m*

S

S, s S, s *n*
S ABBR *of* ***small*** (***size***) klein
sa·ber, *Br* **sa·bre** Säbel *m*
sa·ble ZO Zobel *m*; Zobelpelz *m*
sab·o·tage 1. Sabotage *f*; **2.** sabotieren
sack 1. Sack *m*; ***get the sack*** *Br* F rausgeschmissen werden; ***give s.o. the sack*** *Br* F j-n rausschmeißen; ***hit the sack*** F sich in die Falle *or* Klappe hauen; **2.** in Säcke füllen, einsacken; *Br* F *j-n* rausschmeißen
sack·cloth, **sack·ing** Sackleinen *n*
sac·ra·ment REL Sakrament *n*
sa·cred geistlich (*music etc*); heilig
sac·ri·fice 1. Opfer *n*; **2.** opfern
sac·ri·lege REL Sakrileg *n*; Frevel *m*
sac·ris·ty REL Sakristei *f*
sad traurig; schmerzlich; schlimm
sad·dle 1. Sattel *m*; **2.** satteln
sa·dism Sadismus *m*
sa·dist Sadist(in)
sa·dis·tic sadistisch
sad·ness Traurigkeit *f*
sa·fa·ri Safari *f*
safari park Safaripark *m*
safe 1. sicher; **2.** Safe *m*, *n*, Tresor *m*, Geldschrank *m*
safe con·duct freies Geleit
safe de·pos·it Tresor *m*
safe-de·pos·it box Schließfach *n*
safe·guard 1. Schutz *m* (***against*** gegen, vor *dat*); **2.** schützen (***against, from*** gegen, vor *dat*)
safe·keep·ing sichere Verwahrung
safe·ty 1. Sicherheit *f*; **2.** Sicherheits…
safety belt → ***seat belt***
safety is·land Verkehrsinsel *f*
safety lock Sicherheitsschloss *n*
safety mea·sure Sicherheitsmaßnahme *f*
safety pin Sicherheitsnadel *f*
safety ra·zor Rasierapparat *m*
sag sich senken, absacken; durchhängen; (herab)hängen (*shoulders*); *fig* sinken (*morale*); nachlassen (*interest etc*)
sa·ga·cious scharfsinnig
sa·ga·ci·ty Scharfsinn *m*
sage BOT Salbei *m*, *f*
Sa·git·tar·i·us ASTR Schütze *m*; ***he*** (***she***) ***is*** (***a***) ***Sagittarius*** er (sie) ist (ein) Schütze
sail 1. Segel *n*; Segelfahrt *f*; (*Windmüh-*

*len)*Flügel *m*; ***set sail*** auslaufen (***for*** nach); ***go for a sail*** segeln gehen; **2.** *v/i* MAR segeln, fahren; auslaufen (***for*** nach); gleiten, schweben; ***go sailing*** segeln gehen; *v/t* MAR befahren; *Schiff* steuern, *Boot* segeln
sail·board Surfbrett *n*
sail·boat Segelboot *n*
sail·ing Segeln *n*; Segelsport *m*; ***when is the next sailing to …?*** wann fährt das nächste Schiff nach …?
sailing boat *Br* Segelboot *n*
sailing ship Segelschiff *n*
sail·or Seemann *m*, Matrose *m*; ***be a good*** (***bad***) ***sailor*** (nicht) seefest sein
sail·plane Segelflugzeug *n*
saint Heilige *m, f*
saint·ly heilig, fromm
sake: ***for the sake of …*** um … (*gen*) willen; ***for my sake*** meinetwegen; ***for God's sake*** F um Gottes willen
sal·a·ble verkäuflich
sal·ad Salat *m*
salad dress·ing Dressing *n*, Salatsoße *f*
sal·a·ried: ***salaried employee*** Angestellte *m, f*, Gehaltsempfänger(in)
sal·a·ry Gehalt *n*
sale Verkauf *m*; Absatz *m*, Umsatz *m*; (Saison)Schlussverkauf *m*; Auktion *f*, Versteigerung *f*; ***for sale*** zu verkaufen; ***not for sale*** unverkäuflich; ***be on sale*** verkauft werden, erhältlich sein
sale·a·ble → ***salable***
sales·clerk (Laden)Verkäufer(in)
sales·girl (Laden)Verkäuferin *f*
sales·man Verkäufer *m*; (Handels-) Vertreter *m*
sales rep·re·sen·ta·tive Handlungsreisende *m, f*; (Handels)Vertreter(in)
sales slip ECON Quittung *f*
sales tax ECON Umsatzsteuer *f*
sales·wom·an Verkäuferin *f*; (Handels)-Vertreterin *f*
sa·line salzig, Salz…
sa·li·va Speichel *m*
sal·low gelblich
salm·on ZO Lachs *m*
sal·on (*Schönheits- etc*)Salon *m*
sa·loon *Br* MOT Limousine *f*; HIST Saloon *m*; MAR Salon *m*
sa·loon car *Br* MOT Limousine *f*
salt 1. Salz *n*; **2.** salzen; (ein)pökeln, einsalzen (*a.* ***salt down***); *Straße etc* (mit Salz) streuen; **3.** Salz…; gepökelt; salzig, gesalzen
salt·cel·lar *Br* Salzstreuer *m*
salt·pe·ter, *esp Br* **salt·pe·tre** CHEM Salpeter *m*
salt shak·er Salzstreuer *m*
salt wa·ter Salzwasser *n*
salt·y salzig
sal·u·ta·tion Gruß *m*, Begrüßung *f*; Anrede *f*
sa·lute 1. MIL salutieren; (be-)grüßen; **2.** Gruß *m*; MIL Ehrenbezeugung *f*; Salut *m*
sal·vage 1. Bergung *f*; Bergungsgut *n*; **2.** bergen (***from*** aus); retten (*a. fig*)
sal·va·tion Rettung *f*; REL Erlösung *f*; (Seelen)Heil *n*
Sal·va·tion Ar·my Heilsarmee *f*
salve (Heil)Salbe *f*
same: ***the same*** derselbe, dieselbe, dasselbe; ***all the same*** trotzdem; ***it is all the same to me*** es ist mir ganz egal
sam·ple 1. Muster *n*, Probe *f*; **2.** kosten, probieren
san·a·to·ri·um Sanatorium *n*
sanc·ti·fy heiligen
sanc·tion 1. Billigung *f*, Zustimmung *f*; *mst pl* Sanktionen *pl*; **2.** billigen, sanktionieren
sanc·ti·ty Heiligkeit *f*
sanc·tu·a·ry Zuflucht *f*, Asyl *n*; ZO Schutzgebiet *n*
sand 1. Sand *m*; *pl* Sandfläche *f*; **2.** *Straße etc* mit Sand (be)streuen; TECH schmirgeln
san·dal Sandale *f*
sand·bag Sandsack *m*
sand·bank GEOGR Sandbank *f*
sand·box Sandkasten *m*
sand·cas·tle Sandburg *f*
sand·man Sandmännchen *n*
sand·pa·per Sand-, Schmirgelpapier *n*
sand·pip·er ZO Strandläufer *m*
sand·pit *Br* Sandkasten *m*; Sandgrube *f*
sand·stone GEOL Sandstein *m*
sand·storm Sandsturm *m*
sand·wich 1. Sandwich *n*; **2.** ***be sandwiched between*** eingekeilt sein zwischen (*dat*); ***sandwich s.th. in between*** *fig* et. einschieben zwischen (*acc or dat*)
sand·y sandig; rotblond
sane geistig gesund; JUR zurechnungsfähig; vernünftig
san·i·tar·i·um → ***sanatorium***
san·i·ta·ry hygienisch; Gesundheits…
sanitary nap·kin, *Br* **sanitary tow·el** (Damen)Binde *f*
san·i·ta·tion sanitäre Einrichtungen *pl*; Kanalisation *f*
san·i·ty geistige Gesundheit; JUR Zurechnungsfähigkeit *f*
San·ta Claus der Weihnachtsmann, der Nikolaus
sap[1] BOT Saft *m*
sap[2] schwächen
sap·phire Saphir *m*

sar·casm Sarkasmus *m*
sar·cas·tic sarkastisch
sar·dine ZO Sardine *f*
sash[1] Schärpe *f*
sash[2] Fensterrahmen *m*
sash win·dow Schiebefenster *n*
sas·sy frech
Sat ABBR *of* ***Saturday*** Sa., Samstag *m*, Sonnabend *m*
Sa·tan der Satan
satch·el (Schul)Ranzen *m*; Schultasche *f*
sat·ed *fig* übersättigt
sat·el·lite 1. Satellit *m*; ***by*** *or* ***via satellite*** über Satellit; **2.** Satelliten…; ***satellite dish*** F Satellitenschüssel *f*
sat·in Satin *m*
sat·ire Satire *f*
sat·ir·ic, sat·ir·i·cal satirisch
sat·i·rist Satiriker(in)
sat·ir·ize verspotten
sat·is·fac·tion Befriedigung *f*; Genugtuung *f*, Zufriedenheit *f*
sat·is·fac·to·ry befriedigend, zufriedenstellend
sat·is·fy befriedigen, zufrieden stellen; überzeugen; ***be satisfied that*** davon überzeugt sein, dass
sat·u·rate (durch)tränken (***with*** mit); CHEM sättigen (*a. fig*)
Sat·ur·day Sonnabend *m*, Samstag *m*; ***on Saturday*** (am) Sonnabend *or* Samstag; ***on Saturdays*** sonnabends, samstags
sauce Soße *f*
sauce·pan Kochtopf *m*
sau·cer Untertasse *f*
sauc·y *Br* frech
saun·ter bummeln, schlendern
saus·age Wurst *f*; *a.* ***small sausage*** Würstchen *n*
sav·age 1. wild; unzivilisiert; **2.** Wilde *m, f*
sav·ag·e·ry Wildheit *f*; Rohheit *f*, Grausamkeit *f*
save 1. retten (***from*** vor *dat*); *Geld, Zeit etc* (ein)sparen; *et.* aufheben, aufsparen (***for*** für); *j-m et.* ersparen; EDP (ab)speichern, sichern; SPORT *Schuss* halten, parieren, *Tor* verhindern; **2.** SPORT Parade *f*
sav·er Retter(in); ECON Sparer(in)
sav·ings ECON Ersparnisse *pl*
savings ac·count Sparkonto *n*
savings bank Sparkasse *f*
savings de·pos·it Spareinlage *f*
sa·vio(u)r Retter(in); ***the Savio(u)r*** REL der Erlöser, der Heiland
sa·vo(u)r mit Genuss essen *or* trinken; ***savo(u)r of*** *fig* e-n Beigeschmack haben von
sa·vo(u)r·y schmackhaft
saw 1. Säge *f*; **2.** sägen
saw·dust Sägemehl *n*, Sägespäne *pl*
saw·mill Sägewerk *n*
Sax·on 1. (Angel)Sachse *m*, (Angel-)Sächsin *f*; **2.** (angel)sächsisch
say 1. sagen; aufsagen; *Gebet* sprechen, *Vaterunser* beten; ***say grace*** das Tischgebet sprechen; ***what does your watch say?*** wie spät ist es auf deiner Uhr?; ***he is said to be …*** er soll … sein; ***it says*** es lautet (*letter etc*); ***it says here*** hier heißt es; ***it goes without saying*** es versteht sich von selbst; ***no sooner said than done*** gesagt, getan; ***that is to say*** das heißt; ***(and) that's saying s.th.*** (und) das will was heißen; ***you said it*** du sagst es; ***you can say that again!*** das kannst du laut sagen!; ***you don't say (so)!*** was du nicht sagst!; ***I say*** sag(en Sie) mal!; ich muss schon sagen!; ***I can't say*** das kann ich nicht sagen; **2.** Mitspracherecht *n* (***in*** bei); ***have one's say*** s-e Meinung äußern, zu Wort kommen; ***he always has to have his say*** er muss immer mitreden
say·ing Sprichwort *n*, Redensart *f*; ***as the saying goes*** wie man so (schön) sagt
scab MED, BOT Schorf *m*; *contp* Streikbrecher(in)
scaf·fold (Bau)Gerüst *n*; Schafott *n*
scaf·fold·ing (Bau)Gerüst *n*
scald 1. sich *die Zunge etc* verbrühen; *Milch* abkochen; ***scalding hot*** kochend heiß; **2.** MED Verbrühung *f*
scale[1] **1.** Skala *f* (*a. fig*), Grad- *or* Maßeinteilung *f*; MATH, TECH Maßstab *m* (*a. fig*); Waage *f*; MUS Skala *f*, Tonleiter *f*; *fig* Ausmaß *n*, Umfang *m*; **2.** erklettern; ***scale down*** *fig* verringern; ***scale up*** *fig* erhöhen
scale[2] Waagschale *f*; ***(a pair of) scales*** (e-e) Waage
scale[3] **1.** ZO Schuppe *f*; TECH Kesselstein *m*; ***the scales fell from my eyes*** es fiel mir wie Schuppen von den Augen; **2.** *Fisch* (ab)schuppen
scal·lop ZO Kammmuschel *f*
scalp 1. Kopfhaut *f*; Skalp *m*; **2.** skalpieren
scal·y zo schuppig (*a. fig*)
scamp F Schlingel *m*, (kleiner) Strolch
scam·per trippeln; huschen
scan 1. *et.* absuchen (***for*** nach); *Zeitung etc* überfliegen; EDP, *radar*, TV abtasten, scannen; **2.** MED *etc* Scanning *n*
scan·dal Skandal *m*; Klatsch *m*
scan·dal·ize: ***be scandalized at s.th.*** über et. empört *or* entrüstet sein
scan·dal·ous skandalös; ***be scandalous***

S

a. ein Skandal sein (***that*** dass)
Scan·di·na·vi·a Skandinavien *n*
Scan·di·na·vi·an **1.** skandinavisch; **2.** Skandinavier(in)
scan·ner TECH Scanner *m*
scant dürftig, gering
scant·y dürftig, kärglich, knapp
scape·goat Sündenbock *m*
scar MED **1.** Narbe *f* (*a. fig*); **2.** e-e Narbe *or* Narben hinterlassen auf (*dat*) *or fig* bei *j-m*; ***scar over*** vernarben
scarce knapp (*food etc*); selten; ***be scarce*** Mangelware sein (*a. fig*)
scarce·ly kaum
scar·ci·ty Mangel *m*, Knappheit *f* (***of*** an *dat*)
scare **1.** erschrecken; ***be scared*** Angst haben (***of*** vor *dat*); ***scare away, scare off*** verjagen, -scheuchen; **2.** Schreck(en) *m*; Panik *f*
scare·crow Vogelscheuche *f* (*a. fig*)
scarf Schal *m*; Hals-, Kopf-, Schultertuch *n*
scar·let scharlachrot
scarlet fe·ver MED Scharlach *m*
scarred narbig
scath·ing bissig (*remark etc*); vernichtend (*criticism etc*)
scat·ter (sich) zerstreuen (*crowd*); ausstreuen, verstreuen; auseinanderstieben (*birds etc*)
scat·ter·brained F schusselig, schusslig
scat·tered verstreut; vereinzelt
scav·enge: ***scavenge on*** zo leben von; ***scavenge for*** suchen (nach)
scene Szene *f*; Schauplatz *m*; *pl* THEA Kulissen *pl*
sce·ne·ry Landschaft *f*, Gegend *f*; THEA Bühnenbild *n*, Kulissen *pl*
scent **1.** Duft *m*, Geruch *m*; *esp Br* Parfüm *n*; HUNT Witterung *f*; Fährte *f*, Spur *f* (*a. fig*); **2.** wittern; *esp Br* parfümieren
scent·less geruchlos
scep·ter, *Br* **scep·tre** Zepter *n*
scep·tic, **scep·ti·cal** *Br* → ***skeptic*** *etc*
sched·ule **1.** Aufstellung *f*, Verzeichnis *n*; (*Arbeits-, Stunden-, Zeit- etc*)Plan *m*; Fahr-, Flugplan *m*; ***ahead of schedule*** dem Zeitplan voraus, früher als vorgesehen; ***be behind schedule*** Verspätung haben; im Verzug *or* Rückstand sein; ***on schedule*** (fahr-) planmäßig, pünktlich; **2.** ***the meeting is scheduled for Monday*** die Sitzung ist für Montag angesetzt; ***it is scheduled to take place tomorrow*** es soll morgen stattfinden
sched·uled de·par·ture (fahr)planmäßige Abfahrt
scheduled flight Linienflug *m*
scheme **1.** *esp Br* Programm *n*, Projekt *n*; Schema *n*, System *n*; Intrige *f*, Machenschaft *f*; **2.** intrigieren
schmaltz·y F schnulzig
schnit·zel GASTR Wiener Schnitzel *n*
schol·ar Gelehrte *m*, *f*; UNIV Stipendiat(in)
schol·ar·ly gelehrt
schol·ar·ship Gelehrsamkeit *f*; UNIV Stipendium *n*
school[1] **1.** Schule *f* (*a. fig*); UNIV Fakultät *f*; Hochschule *f*; ***at school*** auf *or* in der Schule; ***go to school*** in die *or* zur Schule gehen; **2.** *j-n* schulen, unterrichten; *Tier* dressieren
school[2] zo Schule *f*, Schwarm *m*
school·bag Schultasche *f*
school·boy Schüler *m*
school·child Schulkind *n*
school·fel·low → ***schoolmate***
school·girl Schülerin *f*
school·ing (Schul)Ausbildung *f*
school·mate Mitschüler(in), Schulkamerad(in)
school·teach·er (Schul)Lehrer(in)
school·yard Schulhof *m*
schoo·ner MAR Schoner *m*
sci·ence Wissenschaft *f*; *a.* ***natural science*** Naturwissenschaft(en *pl*) *f*
science fic·tion (ABBR ***SF***) Sciencefiction *f*
sci·en·tif·ic (natur)wissenschaftlich; exakt, systematisch
sci·en·tist (Natur)Wissenschaftler(in)
sci-fi F Sciencefiction *f*
scis·sors: (***a pair of scissors*** e-e) Schere
scoff **1.** spotten (***at*** über *acc*); **2.** spöttische Bemerkung
scold schimpfen (mit)
scoop **1.** Schöpfkelle *f*; (*Mehl- etc* -) Schaufel *f*; (*Eis- etc*)Portionierer *m*; Kugel *f* (*icecream*); *newspaper, radio,* TV Exklusivmeldung *f*, F Knüller *m*; **2.** schöpfen, schaufeln; ***scoop up*** aufheben, hochheben
scoot·er (Kinder)Roller *m*; (*Motor-*) Roller *m*
scope Bereich *m*; Spielraum *m*
scorch *v/t* ansengen, versengen, verbrennen; ausdörren; *v/i Br* MOT F rasen
score **1.** SPORT (Spiel)Stand *m*, (-)Ergebnis *n*; MUS Partitur *f*; Musik *f*; 20 (Stück); *a.* ***score mark*** Kerbe *f*, Rille *f*; ***what is the score?*** wie steht es *or* das Spiel?; ***the score stood at*** *or* ***was 3-2*** das Spiel stand 3:2; ***keep*** (***the***) ***score*** anschreiben; ***scores of*** e-e Menge; ***four score and ten*** neunzig; ***on that score*** deshalb, in dieser Hinsicht; ***have a score to settle***

S

with s.o. e-e alte Rechnung mit j-m zu begleichen haben; **2.** *v/t* SPORT *Punkte, Treffer* erzielen, *Tor a.* schießen; *Erfolg, Sieg* erringen; MUS instrumentieren; die Musik schreiben zu *or* für; einkerben; *v/i* SPORT e-n Treffer *etc* erzielen, ein Tor schießen; erfolgreich sein
score·board SPORT Anzeigetafel *f*
scor·er SPORT Torschütze *m*, Torschützin *f*; Anschreiber(in)
scorn Verachtung *f*
scorn·ful verächtlich
Scor·pi·o ASTR Skorpion *m*; ***he*** (***she***) ***is*** (***a***) ***Scorpio*** er (sie) ist (ein) Skorpion
Scot Schotte *m*, Schottin *f*
Scotch 1. schottisch; **2.** Scotch *m*
scot-free: F ***get off scot-free*** ungeschoren davonkommen
Scot·land Schottland *n*
Scots schottisch
Scotsman Schotte *m*
Scots·wom·an Schottin *f*
Scot·tish schottisch
scoun·drel Schurke *m*
scour[1] scheuern, schrubben
scour[2] *Gegend* absuchen, durchkämmen (***for*** nach)
scourge 1. Geißel *f* (*a. fig*); **2.** geißeln, *fig a.* heimsuchen
scout 1. *esp* MIL Kundschafter *m*; *Br* motorisierter Pannenhelfer; *a.* ***boy scout*** Pfadfinder *m*; *a.* ***girl scout*** Pfadfinderin *f*; *a.* ***talent scout*** Talentsucher(in); **2.** ***scout about, scout around*** sich umsehen (***for*** nach); *a.* ***scout out*** MIL auskundschaften
scowl 1. finsteres Gesicht; **2.** finster blicken; ***scowl at s.o.*** j-n böse *or* finster anschauen
scram·ble 1. klettern; sich drängeln (***for*** zu); **2.** Kletterei *f*; Drängelei *f*
scram·bled eggs Rührei(er *pl*) *n*
scrap[1] **1.** Stückchen *n*, Fetzen *m*; Altmaterial *n*; Schrott *m*; *pl* Abfall *m*, Speisereste *pl*; **2.** verschrotten; ausrangieren; *Plan etc* aufgeben, fallen lassen
scrap[2] F **1.** Streiterei *f*; Balgerei *f*; **2.** sich streiten; sich balgen
scrap·book Sammelalbum *n*
scrape 1. (ab)kratzen, (ab)schaben; sich *die Knie etc* aufschürfen; *Wagen etc* ankratzen; scheuern (***against*** an *dat*); (entlang)streifen; scharren; **2.** Kratzen *n*; Kratzer *m*, Schramme *f*; *fig* Klemme *f*
scrap heap Schrotthaufen *m*
scrap met·al Altmetall *n*, Schrott *m*
scrap pa·per *esp Br* Schmierpapier *n*
scrap val·ue Schrottwert *m*
scrap·yard Schrottplatz *m*
scratch 1. (zer)kratzen; abkratzen; *s-n Namen etc* einkratzen; (sich) kratzen; scharren; **2.** Kratzer *m*, Schramme *f*; Gekratze *n*; Kratzen *n*; ***from scratch*** F ganz von vorn; **3.** (bunt) zusammengewürfelt
scratch·pad Notiz-, Schmierblock *m*
scratch pa·per Schmierpapier *n*
scrawl 1. kritzeln; **2.** Gekritzel *n*
scraw·ny dürr
scream 1. schreien (***with*** vor *dat*); *a.* ***scream out*** schreien; ***scream with laughter*** vor Lachen brüllen; **2.** Schrei *m*; ***screams of laughter*** brüllendes Gelächter; ***be a scream*** F zum Schreien (komisch) sein
screech 1. kreischen (*a. fig*), (gellend) schreien; **2.** Kreischen *n*; (gellender) Schrei
screen 1. Wand-, Ofen-, Schutzschirm *m*; *film*: Leinwand *f*; *radar*, TV, EDP Bildschirm *m*; Fliegenfenster *n*, -gitter *n*; *fig* Tarnung *f*; **2.** abschirmen; *film* zeigen, *Fernsehprogramm a.* senden; *fig j-n* decken; *fig j-n* überprüfen; ***screen off*** abtrennen
screen·play Drehbuch *n*
screen sav·er EDP Bildschirmschoner *m*
screw 1. TECH Schraube *f*; ***he has a screw loose*** F bei ihm ist e-e Schraube locker; **2.** (an)schrauben (***to*** an *acc*); V bumsen, vögeln; ***screw up*** *Gesicht* verziehen; *Augen* zusammenkneifen; ***screw up one's courage*** sich ein Herz fassen
screw·ball F Spinner(in)
screw·driv·er Schraubenzieher *m*
screw top Schraubverschluss *m*
scrib·ble 1. (hin)kritzeln; **2.** Gekritzel *n*
scrimp: ***scrimp and save*** jeden Pfennig zweimal umdrehen
script Manuskript *n*; film, TV Drehbuch *n*, Skript *n*; THEA Text *m*, Textbuch *n*; Schrift(zeichen *pl*) *f*; *Br* UNIV (schriftliche) Prüfungsarbeit
Scrip·ture *a.* ***the Scriptures*** REL die Heilige Schrift
scroll 1. Schriftrolle *f*; **2.** ***scroll down*** (***up***) EDP zurückrollen (vorrollen)
scro·tum ANAT Hodensack *m*
scrub[1] **1.** schrubben, scheuern; **2.** Schrubben *n*, Scheuern *n*
scrub[2] Gebüsch *n*, Gestrüpp *n*
scru·ple 1. Skrupel *m*, Zweifel *m*, Bedenken *pl*; **2.** Bedenken haben
scru·pu·lous gewissenhaft
scru·ti·nize genau prüfen; mustern
scru·ti·ny genaue Prüfung; prüfender Blick
scu·ba div·ing (Sport)Tauchen *n*
scuf·fle 1. Handgemenge *n*, Rauferei *f*; **2.**

sich raufen
scull **1.** Skull *n*; Skullboot *n*; **2.** rudern, skullen
sculp·tor Bildhauer *m*
sculp·ture **1.** Bildhauerei *f*; Skulptur *f*, Plastik *f*; **2.** hauen, meißeln, formen
scum Schaum *m*; *fig* Abschaum *m*; ***the scum of the earth*** *fig* der Abschaum der Menschheit
scurf (Kopf)Schuppen *pl*
scur·ri·lous beleidigend; verleumderisch
scur·ry huschen; trippeln
scur·vy MED Skorbut *m*
scut·tle: ***scuttle away, scuttle off*** davonhuschen
scythe Sense *f*
sea Meer *n* (*a. fig*), See *f*; ***at sea*** auf See; ***be all*** *or* ***completely at sea*** *fig* F völlig ratlos sein; ***by sea*** auf dem Seeweg; ***by the sea*** am Meer
sea·food GASTR Meeresfrüchte *pl*
sea·gull ZO Seemöwe *f*
seal[1] ZO Robbe *f*, Seehund *m*
seal[2] **1.** Siegel *n*; TECH Plombe *f*; TECH Dichtung *f*; **2.** (ver)siegeln; TECH plombieren; abdichten; *fig* besiegeln; ***sealed envelope*** verschlossener Briefumschlag; ***seal off*** *Gegend etc* abriegeln
sea lev·el: ***above*** (***below***) ***sea level*** über (unter) dem Meeresspiegel
seal·ing wax Siegellack *m*
seam Naht *f*; Fuge *f*; GEOL Flöz *n*
sea·man Seemann *m*
seam·stress Näherin *f*
sea·plane Wasserflugzeug *n*
sea·port Seehafen *m*; Hafenstadt *f*
sea pow·er Seemacht *f*
search **1.** *v/i* suchen (***for*** nach); ***search through*** durchsuchen; *v/t j-n, et.* durchsuchen (***for*** nach); ***search me!*** F keine Ahnung!; **2.** Suche *f* (***for*** nach); Fahndung *f* (***for*** nach); Durchsuchung *f*; ***in search of*** auf der Suche nach
search·ing prüfend (*look*); eingehend (*examination*)
search·light (Such)Scheinwerfer *m*
search par·ty Suchmannschaft *f*
search war·rant JUR Haussuchungs-, Durchsuchungsbefehl *m*
sea·shore Meeresküste *f*
sea·sick seekrank
sea·side: ***at*** *or* ***by the seaside*** am Meer; ***go to the seaside*** ans Meer fahren
sea·side re·sort Seebad *n*
sea·son[1] Jahreszeit *f*; Saison *f*, THEA *etc a.* Spielzeit *f*, (*Jagd-, Urlaubs- etc*)Zeit *f*; ***in*** (***out of***) ***season*** in (außerhalb) der (Hoch)Saison; ***cherries are now in season*** jetzt ist Kirschenzeit; ***Season's Greetings!*** Frohe Weihnachten!; ***with the compliments of the season*** mit den besten Wünschen zum Fest
sea·son[2] *Speise* würzen (***with*** mit); *Holz* ablagern
sea·son·al saisonbedingt, Saison…
sea·son·ing GASTR Gewürz *n*
sea·son tick·et RAIL *etc* Dauer-, Zeitkarte *f*; THEA Abonnement *n*
seat **1.** Sitz(gelegenheit *f*) *m*; (Sitz)Platz *m*; Sitz(fläche *f*) *m*; Hosenboden *m*; Hinterteil *n*; (*Geschäfts-, Regierungs- etc*)-Sitz *m*; PARL Sitz *m*; ***take a seat*** Platz nehmen; ***take one's seat*** s-n Platz einnehmen; **2.** *j-n* setzen; Sitzplätze bieten für; ***be seated*** sitzen; ***please be seated*** bitte nehmen Sie Platz; ***remain seated*** sitzen bleiben
seat belt AVIAT, MOT Sicherheitsgurt *m*; ***fasten one's seat belt*** sich anschnallen
sea ur·chin ZO Seeigel *m*
sea·ward(s) seewärts
sea·weed BOT (See)Tang *m*
sea·wor·thy seetüchtig
sec F Augenblick *m*, Sekunde *f*; ***just a sec*** Augenblick(, bitte)!
se·cede sich abspalten (***from*** von)
se·ces·sion Abspaltung *f*, Sezession *f* (***from*** von)
se·clud·ed abgelegen, abgeschieden (*place*); zurückgezogen (*life*)
se·clu·sion Abgeschiedenheit *f*; Zurückgezogenheit *f*
sec·ond[1] **1.** *adj* zweite(r, -s); ***every second day*** jeden zweiten Tag, alle zwei Tage; ***second to none*** unerreicht, unübertroffen; ***but on second thought*** (*Br* ***thoughts***) aber wenn ich es mir so überlege; **2.** *adv* als Zweite(r, -s); **3.** *der, die, das* Zweite; MOT zweiter Gang; Sekundant *m*; *pl* F ECON Waren *pl* zweiter Wahl; **4.** *Antrag etc* unterstützen
sec·ond[2] Sekunde *f*; *fig* Augenblick *m*, Sekunde *f*; ***just a second*** Augenblick(, bitte)!
sec·ond·a·ry sekundär, zweitrangig; PED höher
sec·ond-best zweitbeste(r, -s)
sec·ond class RAIL *etc* zweiter Klasse
sec·ond-class zweitklassig
sec·ond floor erster (*Br* zweiter) Stock
sec·ond hand Sekundenzeiger *m*
sec·ond-hand aus zweiter Hand; gebraucht; antiquarisch
sec·ond·ly zweitens
sec·ond-rate zweitklassig
se·cre·cy Verschwiegenheit *f*; Geheimhaltung *f*
se·cret **1.** geheim, Geheim…; heimlich;

verschwiegen; **2.** Geheimnis *n*; ***in secret*** heimlich, im Geheimen; ***keep s.th. a secret*** et. geheim halten (***from*** vor *dat*); ***can you keep a secret?*** kannst du schweigen?

se·cret a·gent Geheimagent(in)

sec·re·ta·ry Sekretär(in); POL Minister(in)

Sec·re·ta·ry of State POL Außenminister(in); *Br* Minister(in)

se·crete MED absondern

se·cre·tion MED Sekret *n*; Absonderung *f*

se·cre·tive verschlossen

se·cret·ly heimlich

se·cret ser·vice Geheimdienst *m*

sec·tion Teil *m*; Abschnitt *m*; JUR Paragraf *m*; Abteilung *f*; MATH, TECH Schnitt *m*

sec·tor Sektor *m*, Bereich *m*

sec·u·lar weltlich

se·cure 1. sicher (***against, from*** vor *dat*); **2.** *Tür etc* fest verschließen; *et.* sichern (***against, from*** vor *dat*)

se·cu·ri·ty Sicherheit *f*; *pl* ECON Wertpapiere *pl*

security check Sicherheitskontrolle *f*

security mea·sure Sicherheitsmaßnahme *f*

security risk Sicherheitsrisiko *n*

se·dan MOT Limousine *f*

se·date ruhig, gelassen

sed·a·tive *mst* MED **1.** beruhigend; **2.** Beruhigungsmittel *n*

sed·i·ment (Boden)Satz *m*

se·duce verführen

se·duc·er Verführer(in)

se·duc·tion Verführung *f*

se·duc·tive verführerisch

see[1] *v/i* sehen; nachsehen; ***I see!*** (ich) verstehe!, ach so!; ***you see*** weißt du; ***let me see*** warte mal, lass mich überlegen; ***we'll see*** mal sehen; *v/t* sehen; besuchen; *j-n* aufsuchen, *j-n* konsultieren; ***see s.o. home*** j-n nach Hause bringen *or* begleiten; ***see you!*** bis dann!, auf bald!; ***see about*** sehen nach, sich kümmern um; ***see off*** *j-n* verabschieden (***at*** am *Bahnhof etc*); ***see out*** *j-n* hinausbringen, hinausbegleiten; ***see through*** *j-n, et.* durchschauen; *j-m* hinweghelfen über (*acc*); ***see to it that*** dafür sorgen, dass

see[2] REL Bistum *n*, Diözese *f*; ***Holy See*** *der* Heilige Stuhl

seed 1. BOT Same(n) *m*; AGR Saat *f*, Saatgut *n*; *(Apfel- etc)*Kern *m*; SPORT gesetzter Spieler, gesetzte Spielerin; ***go*** *or* ***run to seed*** BOT schießen; ***go to seed*** F herunterkommen, verkommen; **2.** *v/t* besäen; entkernen; SPORT *Spieler* setzen; *v/i* BOT in Samen schießen

seedless BOT kernlos

seed·y F heruntergekommen

seek *Schutz, Wahrheit etc* suchen

seem scheinen

seem·ing scheinbar

seep sickern

see·saw Wippe *f*, Wippschaukel *f*

seethe schäumen (*a. fig*); *fig* kochen

see-through durchsichtig

seg·ment Teil *m, n*; Stück *n*; Abschnitt *m*; Segment *n*

seg·re·gate trennen

seg·re·ga·tion Rassentrennung *f*

seize *j-n, et.* packen, ergreifen; *Macht etc* an sich reißen; *et.* beschlagnahmen; *et.* pfänden

sei·zure Beschlagnahme *f*; Pfändung *f*; MED Anfall *m*

sel·dom *adv* selten

se·lect 1. (aus)wählen; **2.** ausgewählt; exklusiv

se·lec·tion (Aus)Wahl *f*; ECON Auswahl *f* (***of*** an *dat*)

self Ich *n*, Selbst *n*

self-as·sured selbstbewusst, -sicher

self-cen·tered, *Br* **self-cen·tred** egozentrisch

self-col·o(u)red einfarbig

self-con·fi·dence Selbstbewusstsein *n*, Selbstvertrauen *n*

self-con·fi·dent selbstbewusst

self-con·scious befangen, gehemmt, unsicher

self-con·tained (in sich) abgeschlossen; *fig* verschlossen; ***self-contained flat*** *Br* abgeschlossene Wohnung

self-con·trol Selbstbeherrschung *f*

self-crit·i·cal selbstkritisch

self-de·fence *Br*, **self-de·fense** Selbstverteidigung *f*; ***in self-defence*** in *or* aus Notwehr

self-de·ter·mi·na·tion POL Selbstbestimmung *f*

self-em·ployed selbstständig

self-es·teem Selbstachtung *f*

self-ev·i·dent selbstverständlich; offensichtlich

self-gov·ern·ment POL Selbstverwaltung *f*

self-help Selbsthilfe *f*

self-help group Selbsthilfegruppe *f*

self-im·por·tant überheblich

self-in·dul·gent nachgiebig gegen sich selbst; zügellos

self-in·terest Eigennutz *m*

self·ish selbstsüchtig, egoistisch

self-knowl·edge Selbsterkenntnis *f*

self-pit·y Selbstmitleid *n*

self-por·trait Selbstportät *n*

self-pos·sessed selbstbeherrscht

self-re·li·ant selbstständig
self-re·spect Selbstachtung *f*
self-right·eous selbstgerecht
self-sat·is·fied selbstzufrieden
self-serv·ice **1.** mit Selbstbedienung, Selbstbedienungs…; **2.** Selbstbedienung *f*
self-stud·y Selbststudium *n*
self-suf·fi·cient ECON autark
self-sup·port·ing finanziell unabhängig
self-willed eigensinnig, eigenwillig
sell *v/t* verkaufen; *v/i* verkauft werden (***at, for*** für); sich *gut etc* verkaufen (lassen), gehen; ***sell by …*** mindestens haltbar bis …; ***sell off*** (*esp* billig) abstoßen; ***sell out*** ausverkaufen; ***be sold out*** ausverkauft sein; ***sell up*** *esp Br sein Geschäft etc* verkaufen
sell-by date Mindesthaltbarkeitsdatum *n*
sell·er Verkäufer(in); ***good seller*** ECON gut gehender Artikel
sem·blance Anschein *m* (***of*** von)
se·men MED Samen(flüssigkeit *f*) *m*, Sperma *n*
se·mes·ter UNIV Semester *n*
sem·i… halb…, Halb…
sem·i·cir·cle Halbkreis *m*
sem·i·co·lon LING Semikolon *n*, Strichpunkt *m*
sem·i·con·duc·tor ELECTR Halbleiter *m*
sem·i·de·tached (house) *Br* Doppelhaushälfte *f*
sem·i·fi·nals SPORT Semi-, Halbfinale *n*
sem·i·nar·y Priesterseminar *n*
sem·i·pre·cious: ***semi-precious stone*** Halbedelstein *m*
sem·i·skilled angelernt
sem·o·li·na Grieß *m*
sen·ate POL Senat *m*
sen·a·tor POL Senator *m*
send *et., a. Grüße, Hilfe etc* senden, schicken (***to*** *dat or* an *acc*); *Ware etc* versenden, verschicken (***to*** an *acc*); *j-n* schicken (***to*** ins *Bett etc*); *with adj or pp*: machen: ***send s.o. mad*** j-n wahnsinnig machen; ***send word to s.o.*** j-m Nachricht geben; ***send away*** fort-, wegschicken; *Brief etc* absenden, abschicken; ***send down*** *Preise etc* fallen lassen; ***send for*** nach *j-m* schicken, *j-n* kommen lassen; sich *et.* kommen lassen, *et.* anfordern; ***send in*** einsenden, einschicken, einreichen; ***send off*** fort-, wegschicken; *Brief etc* absenden, abschicken; SPORT *j-n* vom Platz stellen; ***send on*** *Brief etc* nachsenden, nachschicken (***to*** an *acc*); *Gepäck etc* vorausschicken; ***send out*** hinausschicken; *Einladungen etc* verschicken; ***send up*** *Preise etc* steigen lassen
send·er Absender(in)
se·nile senil
se·nil·i·ty Senilität *f*
se·ni·or **1.** senior; älter (***to*** als); dienstälter; rangälter; Ober…; **2.** Ältere *m, f*; UNIV Student(in) im letzten Jahr; ***he is my senior by a year*** er ist ein Jahr älter als ich
senior cit·i·zens ältere Mitbürger *pl*, Senioren *pl*
se·ni·or·i·ty (höheres) Alter; (höheres) Dienstalter; (höherer) Rang
se·ni·or part·ner ECON Seniorpartner *m*
sen·sa·tion Empfindung *f*; Gefühl *n*; Sensation *f*
sen·sa·tion·al F großartig, fantastisch; sensationell, Sensations…
sense **1.** Sinn *m*; Verstand *m*; Vernunft *f*; Gefühl *n*; Bedeutung *f*; ***bring s.o. to his senses*** j-n zur Besinnung *or* Vernunft bringen; ***come to one's senses*** zur Besinnung *or* Vernunft kommen; ***in a sense*** in gewisser Hinsicht; ***make sense*** e-n Sinn ergeben; vernünftig sein; ***sense of duty*** Pflichtgefühl *n*; ***sense of security*** Gefühl *n* der Sicherheit; **2.** fühlen, spüren
sense·less bewusstlos; sinnlos
sen·si·bil·i·ty Empfindlichkeit *f*; *a. pl* Empfindsamkeit *f*, Zartgefühl *n*
sen·si·ble vernünftig; spürbar, merklich; *esp Br* praktisch (*clothes etc*)
sen·si·tive empfindlich; sensibel, empfindsam, feinfühlig
sen·sor TECH Sensor *m*
sen·su·al sinnlich
sen·su·ous sinnlich
sen·tence **1.** LING Satz *m*; JUR Strafe *f*, Urteil *n*; ***pass*** *or* ***pronounce sentence*** das Urteil fällen (***on*** über *acc*); **2.** JUR verurteilen (***to*** zu)
sen·ti·ment Gefühle *pl*; Sentimentalität *f*; *a. pl* Ansicht *f*, Meinung *f*
sen·ti·ment·al sentimental; gefühlvoll
sen·ti·men·tal·i·ty Sentimentalität *f*
sen·try MIL Wache *f*, (Wach[t])Posten *m*
sep·a·ra·ble trennbar
sep·a·rate **1.** (sich) trennen; (auf-, ein-, zer)teilen (***into*** in *acc*); **2.** getrennt, separat; einzeln
sep·a·ra·tion Trennung *f*; (Auf-, Ein-, Zer)Teilung *f*
Sept ABBR *of* ***September*** Sept., September *m*
Sep·tem·ber September *m*
sep·tic MED vereitert, septisch
se·quel Nachfolgeroman *m*, -film *m*, Fortsetzung *f*; *fig* Folge *f*; Nachspiel *n*
se·quence (Aufeinander-, Reihen)Folge

f; *film*, TV Sequenz *f*, Szene *f*; ***sequence of tenses*** LING Zeitenfolge *f*
ser·e·nade MUS **1.** Serenade *f*, Ständchen *n*; **2.** *j-m* ein Ständchen bringen
se·rene klar; heiter; gelassen
ser·geant MIL Feldwebel *m*; (Polizei-)Wachtmeister *m*
se·ri·al **1.** Fortsetzungsroman *m*; (*Rundfunk-*, *Fernseh*)Serie *f*; **2.** serienmäßig, Serien…, Fortsetzungs…
se·ries Serie *f*, Reihe *f*, Folge *f*; (*Buch*)-Reihe *f*; (*Rundfunk-*, *Fernseh*)Serie *f*, Sendereihe *f*
se·ri·ous ernst, ernsthaft; ernstlich; schwer (*illness*, *damage*, *crime etc*); ***be serious*** es ernst meinen (***about*** mit)
se·ri·ous·ness Ernst *m*, Ernsthaftigkeit *f*; Schwere *f*
ser·mon REL Predigt *f*; F Moral-, Strafpredigt *f*
ser·pen·tine gewunden, kurvenreich
ser·rat·ed zackig, gezackt
se·rum MED Serum *n*
ser·vant Diener(in) (*a. fig*); Dienstmädchen *n*; → ***civil servant***
serve **1.** *v/t j-m*, *s-m Land etc* dienen; *Dienstzeit* (*a.* MIL) ableisten, *Amtszeit etc* durchlaufen; *j-n*, *et.* versorgen (***with*** mit); *Essen* servieren; *Alkohol* ausschenken; *j-n* (*im Laden*) bedienen; JUR *Strafe* verbüßen; *e-m Zweck* dienen; *e-n Zweck* erfüllen; JUR *Vorladung etc* zustellen (***on s.o.*** j-m); *tennis etc*: aufschlagen; ***are you being served?*** werden Sie schon bedient?; (***it***) ***serves him right*** F (das) geschieht ihm ganz recht; *v/i esp* MIL dienen; servieren; dienen (***as, for*** als); *tennis etc*: aufschlagen; ***XY to serve*** *tennis etc*: Aufschlag XY; ***serve on a committee*** e-m Ausschuss angehören; **2.** *tennis etc*: Aufschlag *m*
serv·er *tennis etc*: Aufschläger(in); GASTR Servierlöffel *m*
ser·vice **1.** Dienst *m* (***to*** an *dat*); Dienstleistung *f*; (*Post-*, *Staats-*, *Telefon- etc-*) Dienst *m*; (*Zug- etc*)Verkehr *m*; ECON Service *m*, Kundendienst *m*; Bedienung *f*; Betrieb *m*; REL Gottesdienst *m*; TECH Wartung *f*, MOT *a.* Inspektion *f*; (*Tee- etc*) Service *n*; JUR Zustellung *f* (*e-r Vorladung*); *tennis etc*: Aufschlag *m*; *pl* MIL Streitkräfte *pl*; **2.** TECH warten
ser·vice·a·ble brauchbar; strapazierfähig
ser·vice ar·e·a MOT (Autobahn)Raststätte *f*
service charge Bedienung *f*, Bedienungszuschlag *m*
service sta·tion Tankstelle *f*; (Reparatur)Werkstatt *f*
ser·vi·ette *esp Br* Serviette *f*
ser·vile sklavisch (*a. fig*); servil, unterwürfig
serv·ing Portion *f*
ser·vi·tude Knechtschaft *f*; Sklaverei *f*
ses·sion Sitzung *f*; Sitzungsperiode *f*; ***be in session*** JUR, PARL tagen
set **1.** *v/t* setzen, stellen, legen; *in e-n Zustand* versetzen; veranlassen (***doing*** zu tun); TECH einstellen, *Uhr* stellen (***by*** nach), *Wecker* stellen (***for*** auf *acc*); *Tisch* decken; *Preis*, *Termin etc* festsetzen, festlegen; *Rekord* aufstellen; *Edelstein* fassen (***in*** in *dat*); *Ring etc* besetzen (***with*** mit); *Flüssigkeit* erstarren lassen; *Haar* legen; *Knochen* einrenken, einrichten; MUS vertonen; PRINT absetzen; *Aufgabe*, *Frage* stellen; ***set at ease*** beruhigen; ***set an example*** ein Beispiel geben; ***set s.o. free*** j-n freilassen; ***set going*** in Gang setzen; ***set s.o. thinking*** j-m zu denken geben; ***set one's hopes on*** s-e Hoffnung setzen auf (*acc*); ***set s.o.'s mind at rest*** j-n beruhigen; ***set great*** (***little***) ***store by*** großen (geringen) Wert legen auf (*acc*); ***the novel is set in*** der Roman spielt in (*dat*); *v/i* ASTR untergehen; fest werden, erstarren; HUNT vorstehen; ***set about doing s.th.*** sich daranmachen, et. zu tun; ***set about s.o.*** F über j-n herfallen; ***set aside*** beiseitelegen; JUR *Urteil etc* aufheben; ***set back*** verzögern; *j-n*, *et.* zurückwerfen (***by two months*** um zwei Monate); ***set in*** einsetzen; ***set off*** aufbrechen, sich aufmachen; hervorheben, betonen; *et.* auslösen; ***set out*** arrangieren, herrichten; aufbrechen, sich aufmachen; ***set out to do s.th.*** sich daranmachen, et. zu tun; ***set up*** errichten; *Gerät etc* aufbauen; *Firma etc* gründen; *et.* auslösen, verursachen; *j-n* versorgen (***with*** mit); sich niederlassen; ***set o.s. up as*** sich ausgeben für; **2.** *adj* festgesetzt, festgelegt; F bereit, fertig; starr (*smile etc*); ***set lunch*** *or* ***meal*** *Br* Menü *n*; ***set phrase*** feststehender Ausdruck; ***be set on doing s.th.*** (fest) entschlossen sein, et. zu tun; ***be all set*** F startklar sein; **3.** Satz *m*; (*Möbel- etc*)Garnitur *f*, (*Tee- etc*)Service *n*; (*Fernseh-*, *Rundfunk-*)Apparat *m*, (-)Gerät *n*; THEA Bühnenbild *n*; *film*, TV Set *n*, *m*; *tennis etc*: Satz *m*; (Personen)Kreis *m*, Clique *f*; (*Kopf- etc*)Haltung *f*; ***have a shampoo and set*** sich die Haare waschen und legen lassen
set·back Rückschlag *m* (***to*** für)
set·square *Br* Winkel *m*, Zeichendreieck *n*
set·tee Sofa *n*

set·the·o·ry MATH Mengenlehre *f*
set·ting ASTR Untergang *m*; TECH Einstellung *f*; Umgebung *f*; *film etc*: Schauplatz *m*; (*Gold- etc*)Fassung *f*
set·ting lo·tion Haarfestiger *m*
set·tle *v/i* sich niederlassen (***on*** auf *acc or dat*), sich setzen (***on*** auf *acc*) (*a.* ***settle down***); sich niederlassen (***in*** in *dat*); sich legen (*dust*); sich setzen (*coffee etc*); sich senken (*building etc*); sich beruhigen (*person, stomach etc*), sich legen (*a.* ***settle down***); sich einigen; *v/t j-n, Nerven etc* beruhigen; vereinbaren; *Frage etc* klären, entscheiden; *Streit etc* beilegen; *Land* besiedeln; *Leute* ansiedeln; *Rechnung* begleichen, bezahlen; *Konto* ausgleichen; *Schaden* regulieren; *s-e Angelegenheiten* in Ordnung bringen; ***settle o.s.*** sich niederlassen (***on*** auf *acc or dat*), sich setzen (***on*** auf *acc*); ***that settles it*** damit ist der Fall erledigt; ***that's settled then*** das ist also klar; ***settle back*** sich (gemütlich) zurücklehnen; ***settle down*** → *v/i*; sesshaft werden; ***settle down to*** sich widmen (*dat*); ***settle for*** sich zufriedengeben *or* begnügen mit; ***settle in*** sich einleben *or* eingewöhnen; ***settle on*** sich einigen auf (*acc*); ***settle up*** (be)zahlen; abrechnen (***with*** mit)
set·tled fest (*ideas etc*); geregelt (*life*); beständig (*weather*)
set·tle·ment Vereinbarung *f*; Klärung *f*; Beilegung *f*; Einigung *f*; Siedlung *f*; Besiedlung *f*; Begleichung *f*, Bezahlung *f*; ***reach a settlement*** sich einigen
set·tler Siedler(in)
sev·en **1.** sieben; **2.** Sieben *f*
sev·en·teen **1.** siebzehn; **2.** Siebzehn *f*
sev·en·teenth siebzehnte(r, -s)
sev·enth **1.** siebente(r, -s), siebte(r, -s); **2.** Siebentel *n*, Siebtel *n*
sev·enth·ly siebentens, siebtens
sev·en·ti·eth siebzigste(r, -s)
sev·en·ty **1.** siebzig; **2.** Siebzig *f*
sev·er durchtrennen; abtrennen; *Beziehungen* abbrechen; (zer)reißen
sev·er·al mehrere
sev·er·al·ly einzeln, getrennt
se·vere schwer (*injuries, setback etc*); stark (*pain*); hart, streng (*winter*); streng (*person, discipline etc*); scharf (*criticism etc*)
se·ver·i·ty Schwere *f*; Stärke *f*; Härte *f*; Strenge *f*; Schärfe *f*
sew nähen
sew·age Abwasser *n*
sew·age works Kläranlage *f*
sew·er Abwasserkanal *m*
sew·er·age Kanalisation *f*
sew·ing **1.** Nähen *n*; Näharbeit *f*; **2.** Näh…
sewing ma·chine Nähmaschine *f*
sex Geschlecht *n*; Sexualität *f*; Sex *m*; Geschlechtsverkehr *m*
sex·ism Sexismus *m*
sex·ist **1.** sexistisch; **2.** Sexist(in)
sex·ton Küster *m* (und Totengräber *m*)
sex·u·al sexuell, Sexual…, geschlechtlich, Geschlechts…
sexual har·ass·ment sexuelle Belästigung
sexual in·ter·course Geschlechtsverkehr *m*
sex·u·al·i·ty Sexualität *f*
sex·y F sexy, aufreizend
shab·by schäbig
shack Hütte *f*, Bude *f*; F *contp* Schuppen *m*
shack·les Fesseln *pl*, Ketten *pl* (*both a. fig*)
shade **1.** Schatten *m* (*a. fig*); (*Lampen-*)Schirm *m*; Schattierung *f*; Rouleau *n*; *fig* Nuance *f*; ***a shade*** *fig* ein kleines bisschen, e-e Spur; **2.** abschirmen (***from*** gegen); schattieren; ***shade off*** allmählich übergehen (***into*** in *acc*)
shad·ow **1.** Schatten *m* (*a. fig*); ***there's not a*** *or* ***the shadow of a doubt about it*** daran besteht nicht der geringste Zweifel; **2.** *j-n* beschatten
shad·ow·y schattig, dunkel; verschwommen, vage, schemenhaft
shad·y schattig; Schatten spendend; F zwielichtig, fragwürdig
shaft (*Pfeil- etc*)Schaft *m*; (*Hammer- etc*) Stiel *m*; TECH Welle *f*; (*Aufzugs-, Bergwerks- etc*)Schacht *m*; (*Sonnen- etc*) Strahl *m*
shag·gy zottig, struppig
shake **1.** *v/t* schütteln; rütteln an (*dat*); erschüttern; ***shake hands*** sich die Hand geben *or* schütteln; *v/i* zittern, beben, wackeln (***with*** vor *dat*); ***shake down*** herunterschütteln; durchsuchen, F filzen; *Br* F kampieren; ***shake off*** abschütteln; *Erkältung etc* loswerden; ***shake up*** *Kissen etc* aufschütteln; *Flasche, Flüssigkeit* (durch-) schütteln; *fig* erschüttern; **2.** Schütteln *n*; F Milchshake *m*; ***shake of the head*** Kopfschütteln *n*
shake·down F Erpressung *f*; Durchsuchung *f*, Filzung *f*; *Br* (Not)Lager *n*
shak·en *a.* ***shaken up*** erschüttert
shak·y wack(e)lig; zitt(e)rig
shall *v/aux future*: *ich* werde, *wir* werden; *in questions*: soll *ich* …?, sollen *wir* …?; ***shall we go?*** gehen wir?
shal·low seicht, flach, *fig a.* oberflächlich

S

shal·lows seichte *or* flache Stelle, Untiefe *f*
sham **1.** Farce *f*; Heuchelei *f*; **2.** unecht, falsch; vorgetäuscht, geheuchelt; **3.** *v/t Mitgefühl etc* vortäuschen, heucheln; *Krankheit etc* simulieren; *v/i* sich verstellen, heucheln; ***he's only shamming*** er tut nur so
sham·bles F Schlachtfeld *n*, wüstes Durcheinander, Chaos *n*
shame **1.** Scham *f*, Schamgefühl *n*; Schande *f*; ***shame!*** pfui!; ***shame on you!*** pfui!; schäm dich!; ***put to shame*** → **2.** beschämen; Schande machen (*dat*)
shame·faced betreten, verlegen
shame·ful beschämend; schändlich
shame·less schamlos
sham·poo **1.** Shampoo *n*, Schampon *n*, Schampun *n*; Haarwäsche *f*; → ***set*** *3*; **2.** *Haare* waschen; *j-m* die Haare waschen; *Teppich etc* schamponieren
shank TECH Schaft *m*; GASTR Hachse *f*
shan·ty¹ Hütte *f*, Bude *f*
shan·ty² Shanty *n*, Seemannslied *n*
shan·ty·town Elendsviertel *n*
shape **1.** Form *f*; Gestalt *f*; Verfassung *f*, Zustand *m*; ***in good*** (***bad***) ***shape*** in gutem (schlechtem) Zustand; ***in*** (***out of***) ***shape*** SPORT (nicht) gut in Form; ***take shape*** *fig* Gestalt annehmen; **2.** *v/t* formen; gestalten; *v/i a.* ***shape up*** sich *gut etc* machen
shape·less formlos; ausgebeult
shape·ly wohlgeformt
share **1.** Anteil *m* (***in, of*** an *dat*); *esp Br* ECON Aktie *f*; ***go shares*** teilen; ***have a*** (***no***) ***share in*** (nicht) beteiligt sein an (*dat*); **2.** *v/t* (sich) *et.* teilen (***with*** mit); *a.* ***share out*** verteilen (***among, between*** an *acc*, unter *acc*); *v/i* teilen; ***share in*** sich teilen in (*acc*)
share·hold·er *esp Br* ECON Aktionär(in)
shark ZO Hai(fisch) *m*; → ***loan shark***
sharp **1.** *adj* scharf (*a. fig*); spitz; abrupt; schneidend (*wind, frost, command, voice, etc*); beißend (*cold, smell etc*); stechend, heftig (*pain*); gescheit; MUS (*um e-n Halbton*) erhöht; ***C sharp*** MUS Cis *n*; **2.** *adv* scharf, abrupt; MUS zu hoch; pünktlich, genau; ***at eight o'clock sharp*** Punkt 8 (Uhr); ***look sharp*** F sich beeilen; ***look sharp!*** F mach schnell!, Tempo!; F pass auf!, gib Acht!
sharp·en *Messer etc* schärfen, schleifen; *Bleistift etc* spitzen
sharp·en·er (*Messer- etc*)Schärfer *m*; (*Bleistift*)Spitzer *m*
sharp·ness Schärfe *f* (*a. fig*)
sharp·shoot·er Scharfschütze *m*
sharp-sight·ed scharfsichtig
sharp-wit·ted scharfsinnig
shat·ter *v/t* zerschmettern, zerschlagen; *Hoffnungen etc* zerstören; *v/i* zerspringen, zersplittern
shat·ter·ing vernichtend; erschütternd
shat·ter·proof splitterfrei
shave **1.** (sich) rasieren; (glatt) hobeln; *j-n, et.* streifen; **2.** Rasur *f*; ***have a shave*** sich rasieren; ***that was a close shave*** das war knapp, das ist gerade noch einmal gut gegangen!
shav·en kahl geschoren
shav·er (*esp* elektrischer) Rasierapparat *m*
shav·ing **1.** Rasieren *n*; **2.** Rasier…
shaving bag Kulturbeutel *m*
shaving brush Rasierpinsel *m*
shaving cream Rasiercreme *f*
shav·ings Späne *pl*
shawl Umhängetuch *n*; Kopftuch *n*
she **1.** *pron* sie; **2.** Sie *f*; ZO Weibchen *n*; **3.** *adj in cpds* ZO \133weibchen *n*; ***she-bear*** Bärin *f*
sheaf Bündel *n*; AGR Garbe *f*
shear **1.** scheren; **2.** (***a pair of***) ***shears*** (e-e) große Schere
sheath (*Schwert- etc*)Scheide *f*; Hülle *f*; *Br* Kondom *n, m*
sheathe *Schwert etc* in die Scheide stecken; TECH umhüllen, verkleiden, ummanteln
shed¹ Schuppen *m*; Stall *m*
shed² *Tränen etc* vergießen; *Blätter etc* verlieren; *fig Hemmungen etc* ablegen; ***shed its skin*** sich häuten; ***shed a few pounds*** ein paar Pfund abnehmen
sheen Glanz *m*
sheep ZO Schaf *n*
sheep·dog ZO Schäferhund *m*
sheep·ish verlegen
sheep·skin Schaffell *n*
sheer rein, bloß; steil, (fast) senkrecht; hauchdünn
sheet Betttuch *n*, (Bett)Laken *n*, Leintuch *n*; (*Glas-, Metall- etc*)Platte *f*; Blatt *n*, Bogen *m*; weite (*Eis- etc*)Fläche; ***the rain was coming down in sheets*** es regnete in Strömen
sheet light·ning Wetterleuchten *n*
shelf (Bücher-, Wand- *etc*)Brett *n*, (-)Bord *n*; GEOGR Riff *n*; *pl* Regal *n*; ***off the shelf*** gleich zum Mitnehmen
shell **1.** (*Austern-, Eier-, Nuss- etc*)Schale *f*; BOT (*Erbsen- etc*)Hülse *f*; ZO Muschel *f*; (*Schnecken*)Haus *n*; ZO Panzer *m*; MIL Granate *f*; (Geschoss-, Patronen)Hülse *f*; Patrone *f*; TECH Rumpf *m*, Gerippe *n*, ARCH *a.* Rohbau *m*; **2.** schälen, enthül-

S

sen; mit Granaten beschießen

shell·fish zo Schal(en)tier *n*

shel·ter **1.** Zuflucht *f*, Schutz *m*; Unterkunft *f*, Obdach *n*; MIL Unterstand *m*; ***run for shelter*** Schutz suchen; ***take shelter*** sich unterstellen (***under*** unter *dat*); ***bus shelter*** Wartehäuschen *n*; **2.** *v/t* schützen (***from*** vor *dat*); *v/i* sich unterstellen

shelve *v/t Bücher* in ein Regal stellen; *Plan etc* aufschieben, zurückstellen; *v/i* sanft abfallen (*garden etc*)

shep·herd **1.** Schäfer *m*, Hirt *m*; **2.** *j-n* führen

sher·iff Sheriff *m*

shield **1.** Schild *m*; **2.** *j-n* (be)schützen (***from*** vor *dat*); *j-n* decken

shift **1.** *v/t et.* bewegen, schieben, *Möbelstück a.* (ver)rücken; *Schuld etc* (ab-)schieben (***onto*** auf *acc*); ***shift gear(s)*** MOT schalten; *v/i* sich bewegen; umspringen (*wind*); *fig* sich verlagern *or* verschieben *or* wandeln; MOT schalten (***into, to*** in *acc*); ***shift from one foot to the other*** von e-m Fuß auf den anderen treten; ***shift on one's chair*** auf s-m Stuhl *ungeduldig etc* hin und her rutschen; **2.** *fig* Verlagerung *f*, Verschiebung *f*, Wandel *m*; ECON Schicht *f*

shift key TECH Umschalttaste *f*

shift work·er Schichtarbeiter(in)

shift·y F verschlagen

shim·mer schimmern; flimmern

shin **1.** *a.* ***shinbone*** ANAT Schienbein *n*; **2.** ***shin up*** hinaufklettern; ***shin down*** herunterklettern

shine **1.** *v/i* scheinen; leuchten; glänzen (*a. fig*); *v/t Schuhe etc* polieren; **2.** Glanz *m*

shin·gle[1] grober Strandkies

shin·gle[2] (Dach)Schindel *f*

shin·gles MED Gürtelrose *f*

shin·y blank, glänzend

ship **1.** Schiff *n*; **2.** verschiffen; ECON verfrachten, versenden

ship·ment ECON Ladung *f*; Verschiffung *f*, Verfrachtung *f*, Versand *m*

ship·own·er Reeder *m*; Schiffseigner *m*

ship·ping Schifffahrt *f*; Schiffsbestand *m*; ECON Verschiffung *f*, Verfrachtung *f*, Versand *m*

ship·wreck Schiffbruch *m*

ship·wrecked **1.** ***be shipwrecked*** Schiffbruch erleiden; **2.** schiffbrüchig

ship·yard (Schiffs)Werft *f*

shirk sich drücken (vor *dat*)

shirk·er Drückeberger(in)

shirt Hemd *n*

shirt·sleeve **1.** Hemdsärmel *m*; ***in (one's) shirtsleeves*** in Hemdsärmeln, hemdsärmelig; **2.** hemdsärmelig

shish ke·bab GASTR Schaschlik *m*, *n*

shit V **1.** Scheiße *f* (*a. fig*); *fig* Scheiß *m*; **2.** (voll)scheißen

shiv·er **1.** zittern (***with*** vor *dat*); **2.** Schauer *m*; *pl* MED F Schüttelfrost *m*; ***the sight send shivers (up and) down my spine*** bei dem Anblick überlief es mich eiskalt

shoal[1] Untiefe *f*; Sandbank *f*

shoal[2] zo Schwarm *m*

shock[1] **1.** Schock *m* (*a.* MED); Wucht *f*; ELECTR Schlag *m*, (*a.* MED Elektro-)Schock *m*; ***be in (a state of) shock*** unter Schock stehen; **2.** schockieren, empören; *j-m* e-n Schock versetzen

shock[2] (***shock of hair*** Haar)Schopf *m*

shock ab·sorb·er TECH Stoßdämpfer *m*

shock·ing schockierend, empörend, anstößig; F scheußlich

shod·dy minderwertig (*goods*); gemein, schäbig (*trick etc*)

shoe **1.** Schuh *m*; Hufeisen *n*; **2.** *Pferd* beschlagen

shoe·horn Schuhanzieher *m*, -löffel *m*

shoe·lace Schnürsenkel *m*

shoe·mak·er Schuhmacher *m*, Schuster *m*

shoe·shine boy Schuhputzer *m*

shoe store (*Br* **shop**) Schuhgeschäft *n*

shoe·string Schnürsenkel *m*

shoot **1.** *v/t* schießen, HUNT *a.* erlegen; abfeuern, abschießen; erschießen; *Riegel* vorschieben; *j-n* fotografieren, aufnehmen, *Film* drehen; *Heroin etc* spritzen; ***shoot the lights*** MOT bei Rot fahren; *v/i* schießen (***at*** auf *acc*); jagen; *fig* schießen, rasen; *film*, TV drehen, filmen; BOT sprießen, treiben; **2.** BOT Trieb *m*; Jagd *f*; Jagdrevier *n*

shoot·er F Schießeisen *n*

shoot·ing **1.** Schießen *n*; Schießerei *f*; Erschießung *f*; Anschlag *m*; Jagd *f*; *film*, TV Dreharbeiten *pl*, Aufnahmen *pl*; **2.** stechend (*pain*)

shooting gal·le·ry Schießbude *f*

shooting range Schießstand *m*

shooting star ASTR Sternschnuppe *f*

shop **1.** *Br* Laden *m*, Geschäft *n*; Werkstatt *f*; Betrieb *m*; ***talk shop*** fachsimpeln; **2.** *mst* ***go shopping*** einkaufen gehen

shop as·sis·tant *Br* Verkäufer(in)

shop·keep·er *Br* Ladenbesitzer(in), Ladeninhaber(in)

shop·lift·er Ladendieb(in)

shop·lift·ing Ladendiebstahl *m*

shop·per Käufer(in)

shop·ping **1.** Einkauf *m*, Einkaufen *n*; Einkäufe *pl* (*items bought*); ***do one's***

shopping *Br* einkaufen, (s-e) Einkäufe machen; **2.** Einkaufs…
shopping bag Einkaufsbeutel *m*, -tasche *f*
shopping cart Einkaufswagen *m*
shopping cen·ter (*Br* **cen·tre**) Einkaufszentrum *n*
shopping list Einkaufsliste *f*, -zettel *m*
shopping mall Einkaufszentrum *n*
shopping precinct *Br* Fußgängerzone *f*
shopping street Geschäfts-, Ladenstraße *f*
shop stew·ard ECON gewerkschaftlicher Vertrauensmann
shop·walk·er *Br* Aufsicht(sperson) *f*
shop win·dow Schaufenster *n*
shore[1] Küste *f*; (*See*)Ufer *n*; ***on shore*** an Land
shore[2]: ***shore up*** (ab)stützen
short 1. *adj* kurz; klein (*person*); kurz angebunden, barsch, schroff (***with*** zu); GASTR mürbe; ***be short for*** die Kurzform sein von; ***be short of …*** nicht genügend … haben; **2.** *adv* plötzlich, abrupt; ***short of*** außer; ***cut short*** plötzlich unterbrechen; ***fall short of*** *et.* nicht erreichen; ***stop short*** plötzlich innehalten, stutzen; ***stop short of*** *or* ***at*** zurückschrecken vor (*dat*); → ***run 1***; **3.** F Kurzfilm *m*; ELECTR Kurze *m*; ***called … for short*** kurz … genannt; ***in short*** kurz(um)
short·age Knappheit *f*, Mangel *m* (***of*** an *dat*)
short·com·ings Unzulänglichkeiten *pl*, Mängel *pl*, Fehler *pl*
short cut Abkürzung *f*; ***take a short cut*** (den Weg) abkürzen
short·en *v/t* (ab-, ver)kürzen; *v/i* kürzer werden
short·hand Kurzschrift *f*, Stenografie *f*
shorthand typ·ist Stenotypistin *f*
short·ly bald; barsch, schroff; mit wenigen Worten
short·ness Kürze *f*; Schroffheit *f*
shorts *a.* ***pair of shorts*** Shorts *pl*; (Herren-)Unterhose *f*
short·sight·ed *esp Br* kurzsichtig (*a. fig*)
short sto·ry Kurzgeschichte *f*
short-tem·pered aufbrausend, hitzig
short-term ECON kurzfristig
short time ECON Kurzarbeit *f*
short wave ELECTR Kurzwelle *f*
short-wind·ed kurzatmig
shot Schuss *m*; Schrot(kugeln *pl*) *m*, *n*; SPORT Kugel *f*; *guter etc* Schütze *m*; *soccer etc*: Schuss *m*; *basketball etc*: Wurf *m*; *tennis*, *golf*: Schlag *m*; PHOT Schnappschuss *m*, Aufnahme *f*; *film*, TV Aufnahme *f*, Einstellung *f*; MED F Spritze *f*; F Schuss *m* (*of drugs*); *fig* F Versuch *m*; ***a shot of rum*** ein Schluck Rum; ***I'll have a shot at it*** ich probier's mal; ***not by a long shot*** F noch lange nicht; → ***big shot***
shot·gun Schrotflinte *f*
shot·gun wed·ding F Mussheirat *f*
shot put SPORT Kugelstoßen *n*
shot put·ter SPORT Kugelstoßer(in)
shoul·der 1. ANAT Schulter *f*; MOT Standspur *f*; **2.** schultern; *Kosten*, *Verantwortung etc* übernehmen; (mit der Schulter) stoßen
shoulder bag Schulter-, Umhängetasche *f*
shoulder blade ANAT Schulterblatt *n*
shoulder strap Träger *m*; Tragriemen *m*
shout 1. *v/i* rufen, schreien (***for*** nach; ***for help*** um Hilfe); ***shout at s.o.*** j-n anschreien; *v/t* rufen, schreien; **2.** Ruf *m*, Schrei *m*
shove 1. stoßen, F schubsen; *et.* schieben, stopfen; **2.** Stoß *m*, F Schubs *m*
shov·el 1. Schaufel *f*; **2.** schaufeln
show 1. *v/t* zeigen, vorzeigen, anzeigen; *j-n* bringen, führen (***to*** zu); ausstellen; zeigen, *film etc a.* vorführen, TV *a.* bringen; *v/i* zu sehen sein; ***be showing*** gezeigt werden, laufen; ***show around*** herumführen; ***show in*** herein-, hineinführen, herein-, hineinbringen; ***show off*** angeben *or* protzen (mit); vorteilhaft zur Geltung bringen; ***show out*** heraus-, hinausführen, heraus-, hinausbringen; ***show round*** herumführen; ***show up*** *v/t* herauf-, hinaufführen, herauf-, hinaufbringen; sichtbar machen; *j-n* entlarven, bloßstellen; *et.* aufdecken; *j-n* in Verlegenheit bringen; *v/i* zu sehen sein; F aufkreuzen, auftauchen; **2.** THEA *etc* Vorstellung *f*; Show *f*; *radio*, TV Sendung *f*; Ausstellung *f*; Zurschaustellung *f*, Demonstration *f*; *fig leerer* Schein; ***be on show*** ausgestellt *or* zu besichtigen sein; ***steal the show from s.o.*** *fig* j-m die Schau stehlen; ***make a show of*** *Anteilnahme*, *Interesse etc* heucheln; ***put up a poor show*** F e-e schwache Leistung zeigen; ***be in charge of the whole show*** F den ganzen Laden schmeißen; **3.** Muster…
show·biz F, **show busi·ness** Showbusiness *n*, Showgeschäft *n*, Unterhaltungsindustrie *f*
show·case Schaukasten *m*, Vitrine *f*
show·down Kraft-, Machtprobe *f*
show·er 1. (Regen- *etc*)Schauer *m*; (*Funken*)Regen *m*; (*Wasser-*, *Wort- etc*) Schwall *m*; Dusche *f*; (Geschenk-) Party *f*; ***have*** *or* ***take a shower*** duschen; **2.** *v/t*

S

j-n mit et. überschütten *or* überhäufen; *v/i* duschen; ***shower down*** niederprasseln
show jump·er SPORT Springreiter(in)
show jump·ing SPORT Springreiten *n*
show-off F Angeber(in)
show·room Ausstellungsraum *m*
show tri·al JUR Schauprozess *m*
show·y auffallend
shred **1.** Fetzen *m*; **2.** zerfetzen; in (schmale) Streifen schneiden, schnitzeln, schnetzeln; in den Papier- *or* Reißwolf geben
shred·der Schnitzelmaschine *f*; Papier-, Reißwolf *m*
shrewd scharfsinnig; schlau
shriek **1.** (gellend) aufschreien; ***shriek with laughter*** vor Lachen kreischen; **2.** (schriller) Schrei
shrill schrill; *fig* heftig, scharf, lautstark
shrimp ZO Garnele *f*; *fig contp* Knirps *m*
shrine Schrein *m*
shrink **1.** (ein-, zusammen)schrumpfen (lassen); einlaufen; *fig* abnehmen; **2.** F Klapsdoktor *m*
shrink·age Schrumpfung *f*; Einlaufen *n*; *fig* Abnahme *f*
shrink-wrap einschweißen
shriv·el schrumpfen (lassen); runz(e)lig werden (lassen)
shroud **1.** Leichentuch *n*; **2.** *fig* hüllen
Shrove Tues·day Fastnachts-, Faschingsdienstag *m*
shrub Strauch *m*, Busch *m*
shrub·be·ry BOT Strauch-, Buschwerk *n*, Gebüsch *n*
shrug **1.** *a.* ***shrug one's shoulders*** mit den Achseln *or* Schultern zucken; **2.** Achselzucken *n*, Schulterzucken *n*
shuck BOT **1.** Hülse *f*, Schote *f*; Schale *f*; **2.** enthülsen; schälen
shud·der **1.** schaudern; **2.** Schauder *m*
shuf·fle **1.** *v/t Karten* mischen; *Papiere etc* umordnen, hierhin oder dorthin legen; ***shuffle one's feet*** schlurfen; *v/i* schlurfen; *Karten* mischen; **2.** Schlurfen *n*, schlurfender Gang; Mischen *n*
shun *j-n, et.* meiden
shunt *Zug etc* rangieren, verschieben; *a.* ***shunt off*** F *j-n* abschieben (***to*** in *acc*, nach)
shut (sich) schließen; zumachen; ***shut down*** *Fabrik etc* schließen; ***shut off*** *Wasser, Gas, Maschine etc* abstellen; ***shut up*** einschließen; einsperren; *Geschäft* schließen; ***shut up!*** F halt die Klappe!
shut·ter Fensterladen *m*; PHOT Verschluss *m*
shut·tle **1.** Pendelverkehr *m*; (*Raum-*) Fähre *f*, (-)Transporter *m*; TECH Schiffchen *n*; **2.** hin- und herbefördern
shut·tle·cock SPORT Federball *m*
shut·tle ser·vice Pendelverkehr *m*
shy **1.** scheu; schüchtern; **2.** scheuen (***at*** vor *dat*); ***shy away from*** *fig* zurückschrecken vor (*dat*)
shy·ness Scheu *f*; Schüchternheit *f*
sick **1.** krank; ***be sick*** *esp Br* sich übergeben; ***she was*** *or* ***felt sick*** ihr war schlecht; ***get sick*** krank werden; ***be off sick*** krank (geschrieben) sein; ***report sick*** sich krank melden; ***be sick of s.th.*** F et. satthaben; ***it makes me sick*** F mir wird schlecht davon, *a. fig* es ekelt *or* widert mich an; **2.** ***the sick*** die Kranken *pl*
sick·bed Krankenbett *n*
sick·en *v/t j-n* anekeln, anwidern; *v/i esp Br* krank werden
sick·le ['sɪkl] Sichel *f*
sick leave: ***be on sick leave*** krank (geschrieben) sein, wegen Krankheit fehlen
sick·ly kränklich; ungesund; matt; widerlich (*smell etc*)
sick·ness Krankheit *f*; Übelkeit *f*
sickness ben·e·fit *Br* Krankengeld *n*
side **1.** Seite *f*; *esp Br* SPORT Mannschaft *f*; ***side by side*** nebeneinander; ***take sides*** Partei ergreifen (***with*** für; ***against*** gegen); **2.** Seiten…; Neben…; **3.** Partei ergreifen (***with*** für; ***against*** gegen)
side·board Anrichte *f*, Sideboard *n*
side·car MOT Bei-, Seitenwagen *m*
side dish GASTR Beilage *f*
side·long seitlich; Seiten…
sidelong glance Seitenblick *m*
side street Nebenstraße *f*
side·swipe Seitenhieb *m*
side·track *j-n* ablenken; F *et.* abbiegen; RAIL *etc* rangieren, verschieben
side·walk Bürgersteig *m*, Gehsteig *m*
side·walk ca·fé Straßencafé *n*
side·ways seitlich; seitwärts, nach der *or* zur Seite
sid·ing RAIL Nebengleis *n*
si·dle: ***sidle up to s.o.*** sich an j-n heranschleichen
siege MIL Belagerung *f*; ***lay siege to*** belagern (*a. fig*)
sieve **1.** Sieb *n*; **2.** (durch)sieben
sift (durch)sieben; *a.* ***sift through*** *fig* sichten, durchsehen, prüfen
sigh **1.** seufzen; **2.** Seufzer *m*
sight **1.** Sehvermögen *n*, Sehkraft *f*, Augenlicht *n*; Anblick *m*; Sicht(weite) *f*; *pl* Visier *n*; Sehenswürdigkeiten *pl*; ***at sight, on sight*** sofort; ***at the sight of*** beim Anblick von (*or gen*); ***at first sight***

auf den ersten Blick; ***catch sight of*** erblicken; ***know by sight*** vom Sehen kennen; ***lose sight of*** aus den Augen verlieren; ***be*** (***with***)***in sight*** in Sicht sein (*a. fig*); **2.** sichten
sight-read MUS vom Blatt singen *or* spielen
sight·see·ing Sightseeing *n*, Besichtigung *f* von Sehenswürdigkeiten; ***go sightseeing*** sich die Sehenswürdigkeiten anschauen
sightseeing tour Sightseeingtour *f*, Besichtigungstour *f*, (Stadt)Rundfahrt *f*
sight·se·er Tourist(in)
sight test Sehtest *m*
sign **1.** Zeichen *n*; (*Hinweis-*, *Warn- etc*) Schild *n*; *fig* (An)Zeichen *n*; **2.** unterschreiben, unterzeichnen; *Scheck* ausstellen; ***sign in*** sich eintragen; ***sign out*** sich austragen
sig·nal **1.** Signal *n* (*a. fig*); Zeichen *n* (*a. fig*); **2.** (ein) Zeichen geben; signalisieren
sig·na·to·ry Unterzeichner(in)
sig·na·ture Unterschrift *f*; Signatur *f*
signature tune *radio*, TV Kennmelodie *f*
sign·board (Aushänge)Schild *n*
sign·er Unterzeichnete *m*, *f*
sig·net Siegel *n*
sig·nif·i·cance Bedeutung *f*, Wichtigkeit *f*
sig·nif·i·cant bedeutend, bedeutsam, wichtig; bezeichnend
sig·ni·fy bedeuten; andeuten
sign·post Wegweiser *m*
si·lence **1.** Stille *f*; Schweigen *n*; ***silence!*** Ruhe!; ***in silence*** schweigend; ***reduce to silence*** → **2.** zum Schweigen bringen
si·lenc·er TECH Schalldämpfer *m*; *Br* MOT Auspufftopf *m*
si·lent still; schweigend; schweigsam; stumm
silent part·ner ECON stiller Teilhaber
sil·i·con CHEM Silizium *n*
sil·i·cone CHEM Silikon *n*
silk **1.** Seide *f*; **2.** Seiden…
silk·worm ZO Seidenraupe *f*
silk·y seidig; samtig (*voice*)
sill (*Fenster*)Brett *n*
sil·ly **1.** albern, töricht, dumm; **2.** F Dummerchen *n*
sil·ver **1.** Silber *n*; **2.** silbern, Silber…; **3.** versilbern
sil·ver-plat·ed versilbert
sil·ver·ware Tafelsilber *n*
sil·ver·y silberglänzend; *fig* silberhell
sim·i·lar ähnlich (***to*** *dat*)
sim·i·lar·i·ty Ähnlichkeit *f*
sim·i·le Gleichnis *n*, Vergleich *m*
sim·mer leicht kochen, köcheln; ***simmer with*** *fig* kochen vor (*rage etc*), fiebern vor (*excitement etc*); ***simmer down*** F sich beruhigen, F sich abregen
sim·per albern *or* affektiert lächeln
sim·ple einfach, schlicht; leicht; dumm, einfältig; naiv; ***the simple fact is that ...*** es ist einfach e-e Tatsache, dass ...
sim·ple-mind·ed dumm; naiv
sim·pli·ci·ty Einfachheit *f*, Schlichtheit *f*; Dummheit *f*; Naivität *f*
sim·pli·fi·ca·tion Vereinfachung *f*
sim·pli·fy vereinfachen
sim·ply einfach; bloß, nur
sim·u·late vortäuschen; MIL, TECH simulieren
sim·ul·ta·ne·ous simultan, gleichzeitig
sin **1.** Sünde *f*; **2.** sündigen
since **1.** *adv a.* ***ever since*** seitdem, seither; **2.** *prp* seit (*dat*); **3.** *cj* seit(dem); da
sin·cere aufrichtig, ehrlich, offen
sin·cer·i·ty Aufrichtigkeit *f*; Offenheit *f*
sin·ew ANAT Sehne *f*
sin·ew·y sehnig; *fig* kraftvoll
sin·ful sündig, sündhaft
sing singen; ***sing s.th. to s.o.*** j-m et. vorsingen
singe (sich *et.*) ansengen *or* versengen
sing·er Sänger(in)
sing·ing Singen *n*, Gesang *m*
sin·gle **1.** einzig; einzeln, Einzel…; einfach; ledig, unverheiratet; ***in single file*** im Gänsemarsch; **2.** *Br* RAIL *etc* einfache Fahrkarte, AVIAT einfaches Ticket (*both a.* ***single ticket***); Single *f*; Single *m*, Unverheiratete *m*, *f*; **3.** ***single out*** sich herausgreifen
sin·gle-breast·ed einreihig
sin·gle-en·gined AVIAT einmotorig
sin·gle fam·i·ly home Einfamilienhaus *n*
sin·gle fa·ther allein erziehender Vater
sin·gle-hand·ed eigenhändig, allein
sin·gle-lane MOT einspurig
sin·gle-mind·ed zielstrebig, -bewusst
sin·gle moth·er allein erziehende Mutter
sin·gle pa·rent Alleinerziehende *m*, *f*
sin·gle room Einzelzimmer *n*
sin·gles *esp tennis*: Einzel *n*; ***a singles match*** ein Einzel; ***men's singles*** Herreneinzel *n*; ***women's singles*** Dameneinzel *n*
sin·glet *Br* ärmelloses Unterhemd *or* Trikot
sin·gle-track eingleisig, einspurig
sin·gu·lar **1.** einzigartig, einmalig; **2.** LING Singular *m*, Einzahl *f*
sin·is·ter finster, unheimlich
sink **1.** *v/i* sinken, untergehen; sich senken; ***sink in*** eindringen (*a. fig*); *v/t* versenken; *Brunnen etc* bohren; *Zähne etc*

S

vergraben (***into*** in *acc*); **2.** Spülbecken *n*, Spüle *f*; Waschbecken *n*

sin·ner Sünder(in)

sip 1. Schlückchen *n*; **2.** *v/t* nippen an (*dat*) *or* von; schlückchenweise trinken; *v/i* nippen (***at*** an *dat or* von)

sir mein Herr; ***Dear Sir or Madam*** Sehr geehrte Damen und Herren (*address in letters*)

sire zo Vater *m*, Vatertier *n*

si·ren Sirene *f*

sis·sy F Weichling *m*

sis·ter Schwester *f*; *Br* MED Oberschwester *f*; REL (Ordens)Schwester *f*

sis·ter·hood Schwesternschaft *f*

sis·ter-in-law Schwägerin *f*

sis·ter·ly schwesterlich

sit *v/i* sitzen; sich setzen; tagen; *v/t j-n* setzen; *esp Br Prüfung* ablegen, machen; ***sit down*** sich setzen; ***sit for*** *Br Prüfung* ablegen, machen; ***sit in*** ein Sit-in veranstalten; an e-m Sit-in teilnehmen; ***sit in for*** *j-n* vertreten; ***sit in on*** als Zuhörer teilnehmen an (*dat*); ***sit on*** sitzen auf (*dat*) (*a. fig*); ***sit on a committee*** e-m Ausschuss angehören; ***sit out*** *Tanz* auslassen; das Ende (*gen*) abwarten; *Krise etc* aussitzen; ***sit up*** sich *or j-n* aufrichten *or* aufsetzen; aufrecht sitzen; aufbleiben

sit·com → ***situation comedy***

sit-down *a.* ***sit-down strike*** Sitzstreik *m*; *a.* ***sit-down demonstration*** *or* F ***demo*** Sitzblockade *f*

site Platz *m*, Ort *m*, Stelle *f*; (*Ausgrabungs*)Stätte *f*; Baustelle *f*

sit-in Sit-in *n*, Sitzstreik *m*

sit·ting Sitzung *f*

sit·ting room *esp Br* Wohnzimmer *n*

sit·u·at·ed: ***be situated*** liegen, gelegen sein

sit·u·a·tion Lage *f*, Situation *f*

situation com·e·dy TV *etc* Situationskomödie *f*

six 1. sechs; **2.** Sechs *f*

six·teen 1. sechzehn; **2.** Sechzehn *f*

six·teenth sechzehnte(r, -s)

sixth 1. sechste(r, -s); **2.** Sechstel *n*

sixth·ly sechstens

six·ti·eth sechzigste(r, -s)

six·ty 1. sechzig; **2.** Sechzig *f*

size 1. Größe *f*, *fig a.* Ausmaß *n*, Umfang *m*; **2.** ***size up*** F abschätzen

siz(e)·a·ble beträchtlich

siz·zle brutzeln

skate 1. Schlittschuh *m*; Rollschuh *m*; **2.** Schlittschuh laufen, eislaufen; Rollschuh laufen

skate·board Skateboard *n*

skat·er Eisläufer(in), Schlittschuhläufer(in); Rollschuhläufer(in)

skat·ing Eislaufen *n*, Schlittschuhlaufen *n*; Rollschuhlaufen *n*; ***free skating*** Kür *f*, Kürlauf *m*

skating rink (Kunst)Eisbahn *f*; Rollschuhbahn *f*

skel·e·ton Skelett *n*, Gerippe *n*

skep·tic Skeptiker(in)

skep·ti·cal skeptisch

sketch 1. Skizze *f*; THEA *etc* Sketch *m*; **2.** skizzieren

skew·er 1. (Brat)Spieß *m*; **2.** (auf)spießen

ski 1. Ski *m*; **2.** Ski…; **3.** Ski fahren *or* laufen

skid 1. MOT rutschen, schleudern; **2.** MOT Rutschen *n*, Schleudern *n*; TECH Kufe *f*

skid mark(s) MOT Bremsspur *f*

ski·er Skifahrer(in), Skiläufer(in)

ski·ing Skifahren *n*, Skilaufen *n*, Skisport *m*

ski jump (Sprung)Schanze *f*

ski jump·er Skispringer *m*

ski jump·ing Skispringen *n*

skil·ful *Br* → ***skillful***

ski lift Skilift *m*

skill Geschicklichkeit *f*, Fertigkeit *f*

skilled geschickt (***at, in*** in *dat*)

skilled work·er Facharbeiter(in)

skill·ful geschickt

skim *Fett etc* abschöpfen (*a.* ***skim off***); *Milch* entrahmen; (hin)gleiten über (*acc*); *a.* ***skim over, skim through*** *Bericht etc* überfliegen

skim(med) milk Magermilch *f*

skimp *a.* ***skimp on*** sparen an (*dat*)

skimp·y dürftig; knapp

skin 1. ANAT Haut *f*; zo Fell *n*; BOT Schale *f*; **2.** *Tier* abhäuten; *Zwiebel etc* schälen; sich *das Knie etc* aufschürfen

skin-deep (nur) oberflächlich

skin div·ing Sporttauchen *n*

skin·flint Geizhals *m*

skin·ny F dürr, mager

skin·ny-dip F nackt baden

skip 1. *v/i* hüpfen, springen; seilhüpfen, seilspringen; *v/t et.* überspringen, aus lassen; **2.** Hüpfer *m*

skip·per MAR, SPORT Kapitän *m*

skir·mish Geplänkel *n*

skirt 1. Rock *m*; **2.** *a.* ***skirt (a)round*** umgeben; *Problem etc* umgehen

skirt·ing board *Br* Scheuerleiste *f*

ski run Skipiste *f*

ski tow Schlepplift *m*

skit·tle Kegel *m*

skulk sich herumdrücken, herumschleichen

skull ANAT Schädel *m*

skul(l)·dug·ge·ry F fauler Zauber

skunk zo Skunk *m*, Stinktier *n*
sky *a.* ***skies*** Himmel *m*
sky·jack *Flugzeug* entführen
sky·jack·er Flugzeugentführer(in)
sky·lark zo Feldlerche *f*
sky·light Dachfenster *n*
sky·line Skyline *f*, Silhouette *f*
sky·rock·et F hochschnellen, in die Höhe schießen
sky·scrap·er Wolkenkratzer *m*
slab (*Stein- etc*)Platte *f*; dickes Stück
slack 1. locker; ECON flau; *fig* lax, lasch, nachlässig; **2.** bummeln; ***slack off, slack up*** *fig* nachlassen, (*person a.*) abbauen
slack·en *v/t* lockern; verringern; ***slacken speed*** langsamer werden; *v/i* locker werden; *a.* ***slacken off*** nachlassen
slacks F Hose *f*
slag TECH Schlacke *f*
sla·lom SPORT Slalom *m*
slam 1. *a.* ***slam shut*** zuschlagen, F zuknallen; *a.* ***slam down*** F *et.* knallen (***on*** auf *acc*); ***slam on the brakes*** F MOT auf die Bremse steigen; **2.** Zuschlagen *n*; Knall *m*
slan·der 1. Verleumdung *f*; **2.** verleumden
slan·der·ous verleumderisch
slang 1. Slang *m*; Jargon *m*; **2.** *esp Br* F *j-n* wüst beschimpfen
slant 1. schräg legen *or* liegen; sich neigen; **2.** schräge Fläche; Abhang *m*; *fig* Einstellung *f*; ***at or on a slant*** schräg
slant·ing schräg
slap 1. Klaps *m*, Schlag *m*; **2.** e-n Klaps geben (*dat*); schlagen; klatschen (***down on*** auf *acc*; ***against*** gegen)
slap·stick THEA Slapstick *m*, Klamauk *m*
slapstick com·e·dy Slapstickkomödie *f*
slash 1. auf-, zerschlitzen; *Preise* drastisch herabsetzen; *Ausgaben etc* drastisch kürzen; ***slash at*** schlagen nach; **2.** Hieb *m*; Schlitz *m*
slate 1. Schiefer *m*; Schiefertafel *f*; POL Kandidatenliste *f*; **2.** mit Schiefer decken; *j-n* vorschlagen (***for, to be*** als); *et.* planen (***for*** für)
slaugh·ter 1. Schlachten *n*; *fig* Blutbad *n*, Gemetzel *n*; **2.** schlachten; *fig* niedermetzeln
slaugh·ter·house Schlachthaus *n*, Schlachthof *m*
Slav 1. Slawe *m*, Slawin *f*; **2.** slawisch
slave 1. Sklave *m*, Sklavin *f* (*a. fig*); **2.** *a.* ***slave away*** sich abplagen, F schuften
slav·er geifern, sabbern
sla·ve·ry Sklaverei *f*
slav·ish sklavisch
sleaze unsaubere Machenschaften; Kumpanei *f*; F POL Filz *m*
slea·zy schäbig, heruntergekommen; anrüchig
sled 1. (*a.* Rodel)Schlitten *m*; **2.** Schlitten fahren, rodeln
sledge *Br* → ***sled***
sledge·ham·mer TECH Vorschlaghammer *m*
sleek 1. glatt, glänzend; geschmeidig; MOT schnittig; **2.** glätten
sleep 1. Schlaf *m*; ***I couldn't get to sleep*** ich konnte nicht einschlafen; ***go to sleep*** einschlafen (F *a. leg etc*); ***put to sleep*** *Tier* einschläfern; **2.** *v/i* schlafen; ***sleep late*** lang *or* länger schlafen; ***sleep on*** *Problem etc* überschlafen; ***sleep with s.o.*** mit j-m schlafen; *v/t* Schlafgelegenheit bieten für
sleep·er Schlafende *m, f*, Schläfer(in); *Br* RAIL Schwelle *f*; RAIL Schlafwagen *m*
sleep·ing bag Schlafsack *m*
Sleep·ing Beau·ty Dornröschen *n*
sleep·ing car RAIL Schlafwagen *m*
sleeping part·ner *Br* ECON stiller Teilhaber
sleeping pill PHARM Schlaftablette *f*, -mittel *n*
sleeping sick·ness MED Schlafkrankheit *f*
sleep·less schlaflos
sleep·walk·er Schlafwandler(in)
sleep·y schläfrig, müde; verschlafen
sleep·y·head F Schlafmütze *f*
sleet 1. Schneeregen *m*; Graupelschauer *m*; **2.** ***it's sleeting*** es gibt Schneeregen; es graupelt
sleeve Ärmel *m*; TECH Manschette *f*, Muffe *f*; *esp Br* (*Platten*)Hülle *f*
sleeve·less ärmellos
sleigh (*esp* Pferde)Schlitten *m*
sleight of hand Fingerfertigkeit *f*; *fig* (Taschenspieler)Trick *m*
slen·der schlank; *fig* mager, dürftig; schwach (*hope etc*)
slice 1. Scheibe *f*, Stück *n*; *fig* Anteil *m* (***of*** an *dat*); **2.** *a.* ***slice up*** in Scheiben *or* Stücke schneiden; ***slice off*** *Stück* abschneiden (***from*** von)
slick 1. gekonnt; geschickt, raffiniert; glatt (*road etc*); **2.** F (*Öl*)Teppich *m*; **3.** ***slick down*** *Haar* glätten, F anklatschen
slick·er Regenmantel *m*
slide 1. gleiten (lassen); rutschen; schlüpfen; schieben; ***let things slide*** *fig* die Dinge schleifenlassen; **2.** Gleiten *n*, Rutschen *n*; Rutsche *f*, Rutschbahn *f*; TECH Schieber *m*; PHOT Dia *n*; Objektträger *m*; (*Erd- etc*)Rutsch *m*; *Br* (*Haar*)Spange *f*
slide rule Rechenschieber *m*

slide tack·le *soccer*: Grätsche *f*
slid·ing door Schiebetür *f*
slight **1.** leicht, gering(fügig), unbedeutend; **2.** beleidigen, kränken; **3.** Beleidigung *f*, Kränkung *f*
slim **1.** schlank; *fig* gering; **2.** *a.* ***be slimming, be on a slimming diet*** e-e Schlankheitskur machen, abnehmen
slime Schleim *m*
slim·y schleimig (*a. fig*)
sling **1.** aufhängen; F schleudern; **2.** Schlinge *f*; Tragriemen *m*; Tragetuch *n*; Schleuder *f*
slip[1] **1.** *v/i* rutschen, schlittern; ausgleiten, ausrutschen; schlüpfen; *v/t* sich losreißen von; ***slip s.th. into s.o.'s hand*** j-m et. in die Hand schieben; ***slip s.o. s.th.*** j-m et. zuschieben; ***slip s.o.'s attention*** j-m *or* j-s Aufmerksamkeit entgehen; ***slip s.o.'s mind*** j-m entfallen; ***she has slipped a disk*** MED sie hat e-n Bandscheibenvorfall; ***slip by, slip past*** verstreichen (*time*); ***slip off, slip out of*** schlüpfen aus; ***slip on*** überstreifen, schlüpfen in (*acc*); **2.** Ausgleiten *n*, (Aus)Rutschen *n*; Versehen *n*; Unterrock *m*; (*Kissen*)Bezug *m*; ***slip of the tongue*** Versprecher *m*; ***give s.o. the slip*** F j-m entwischen
slip[2] *a.* ***slip of paper*** Zettel *m*
slip·case Schuber *m*
slip-on **1.** *adj* ***slip-on shoe*** → **2.** Slipper *m*
slipped disk MED Bandscheibenvorfall *m*
slip·per Hausschuh *m*, Pantoffel *m*
slip·per·y glatt, rutschig, glitschig
slip road *Br* MOT → ***ramp***
slip·shod schlampig
slit **1.** Schlitz *m*; **2.** schlitzen; ***slit open*** aufschlitzen
slith·er gleiten, rutschen
sliv·er (*Glas- etc*)Splitter *m*
slob·ber sabbern
slo·gan Slogan *m*
sloop MAR Schaluppe *f*
slop **1.** *v/t* verschütten; *v/i* überschwappen; schwappen (***over*** über *acc*); **2.** *a. pl* schlabb(e)riges Zeug; (*Tee-, Kaffee-*)Rest(e *pl*) *m*; *esp Br* Schmutzwasser *n*
slope **1.** (Ab)Hang *m*; Neigung *f*, Gefälle *n*; **2.** sich neigen, abfallen
slop·py schlampig; F gammelig; F rührselig
slot Schlitz *m*, (Münz)Einwurf *m*; EDP Steckplatz *m*
sloth ZO Faultier *n*
slot ma·chine (Waren-, Spiel)Automat *m*
slouch **1.** krumme Haltung; F latschiger Gang; **2.** krumm dasitzen *or* dastehen; F latschen
slough[1]: ***slough off*** *Haut* abstreifen, ZO sich häuten
slough[2] Sumpf *m*, Sumpfloch *n*
Slo·vak **1.** slowakisch; **2.** Slowake *m*, Slowakin *f*; LING Slowakisch *n*
Slo·va·ki·a Slowakei *f*
slov·en·ly schlampig
slow **1.** *adj* langsam; begriffsstutzig; ECON schleppend; ***be (ten minutes) slow*** (zehn Minuten) nachgehen; **2.** *adv* langsam; **3.** *v/t often* ***slow down, slow up*** *Geschwindigkeit* verringern; *v/i often* ***slow down, slow up*** langsamer fahren *or* gehen *or* werden
slow·coach *Br* → ***slowpoke***
slow·down ECON Bummelstreik *m*
slow lane MOT Kriechspur *f*
slow mo·tion PHOT Zeitlupe *f*
slow-mov·ing kriechend (*traffic*)
slow·poke Langweiler(in)
slow·worm ZO Blindschleiche *f*
sludge Schlamm *m*
slug[1] ZO Nacktschnecke *f*
slug[2] F (*Gewehr- etc*)Kugel *f*; Schluck *m* (*whisky etc*)
slug[3] F *j-m* e-n Faustschlag versetzen
slug·gish träge; ECON schleppend
sluice TECH Schleuse *f*
slum *a. pl* Slums *pl*, Elendsviertel *n or pl*
slum·ber POET **1.** schlummern; **2.** *a. pl* Schlummer *m*
slump **1.** ECON stürzen (*prices*), stark zurückgehen (*sales etc*); ***sit slumped over*** zusammengesunken sitzen über (*dat*); ***slump into a chair*** sich in e-n Sessel fallen lassen; **2.** ECON starker Konjunkturrückgang; ***slump in prices*** Preissturz *m*
slur[1] **1.** MUS *Töne* binden; ***slur one's speech*** undeutlich sprechen; lallen; **2.** undeutliche Aussprache
slur[2] **1.** verleumden; **2.** ***slur on s.o.'s reputation*** Rufschädigung *f*
slurp F schlürfen
slush Schneematsch *m*; F Kitsch *m*
slush·y F kitschig
slut Schlampe *f*; Nutte *f*
sly gerissen, schlau, listig; ***on the sly*** heimlich
smack[1] **1.** *j-m* e-n Klaps geben; ***smack one's lips*** sich (geräuschvoll) die Lippen lecken; ***smack down*** F *et.* hinklatschen; **2.** klatschendes Geräusch, Knall *m*; F Schmatz *m* (*kiss*); F Klaps *m*
smack[2]: ***smack of*** *fig* schmecken *or* riechen nach
small **1.** *adj and adv* klein; ***small wonder (that)*** kein Wunder, dass; ***feel small*** *fig* sich klein (und hässlich) vorkommen; **2.** ***small of the back*** ANAT Kreuz *n*
small ad Kleinanzeige *f*

small arms Handfeuerwaffen *pl*
small change Kleingeld *n*
small hours: ***in the small hours*** in den frühen Morgenstunden
small-mind·ed engstirnig; kleinlich
small·pox MED Pocken *pl*
small print *das* Kleingedruckte
small talk Small Talk *m*, *n*, oberflächliche Konversation; ***make small talk*** plaudern
small-time F klein, unbedeutend; *in cpds* Schmalspur…
small town Kleinstadt *f*
smart 1. schick, fesch; smart, schlau, clever; **2.** wehtun; brennen; **3.** (brennender) Schmerz
smart al·eck F Besserwisser(in), Klugscheißer(in)
smart·ness Schick *m*; Schlauheit *f*, Cleverness *f*
smash 1. *v/t* zerschlagen (*a.* ***smash up***); schmettern (*a. tennis etc*); *Aufstand etc* niederschlagen, *Drogenring etc* zerschlagen; ***smash up one's car*** s-n Wagen zu Schrott fahren; *v/i* zerspringen; ***smash into*** prallen an (*acc*) *or* gegen, krachen gegen; **2.** Schlag *m*; *tennis etc*: Schmetterball *m*; → ***smash hit***, ***smash-up***
smash hit Hit *m*
smash-up MOT, RAIL schwerer Unfall
smat·ter·ing: ***have a smattering of English*** ein paar Brocken Englisch können
smear 1. Fleck *m*; MED Abstrich *m*; Verleumdung *f*; **2.** (ein-, ver)schmieren; (sich) verwischen; verleumden
smell 1. *v/i* riechen (***at*** an *dat*); duften; stinken; *v/t* riechen (an *dat*); **2.** Geruch *m*; Gestank *m*; Duft *m*
smell·y übel riechend, stinkend
smelt *Erz* schmelzen
smile 1. Lächeln *n*; **2.** lächeln; ***smile at*** *j-n* anlächeln, *j-m* zulächeln; *j-n*, *et.* belächeln, lächeln über (*acc*); ***smile to o.s.*** schmunzeln
smirk (selbstgefällig *or* schadenfroh) grinsen
smith Schmied *m*
smith·e·reens: ***smash (in)to smithereens*** F in tausend Stücke schlagen *or* zerspringen
smith·y Schmiede *f*
smit·ten verliebt, F verknallt (***with*** in *acc*); ***be smitten by*** *or* ***with*** *fig* gepackt werden von
smock Kittel *m*
smog Smog *m*
smoke 1. Rauch *m*; ***have a smoke*** eine rauchen; **2.** rauchen; räuchern
smok·er Raucher(in); RAIL Raucher *m*, Raucherabteil *n*
smoke·stack Schornstein *m*
smok·ing Rauchen *n*; ***no smoking*** Rauchen verboten
smoking com·part·ment RAIL Raucher *m*, Raucherabteil *n*
smok·y rauchig; verräuchert
smooch F schmusen
smooth 1. glatt (*a. fig*); ruhig (*a. journey etc*); mild (*wine*); *fig* (aal)glatt; **2.** *a.* ***smooth out*** glätten, glatt streichen; ***smooth away*** *Falten etc* glätten; *Schwierigkeiten etc* aus dem Weg räumen; ***smooth down*** glatt streichen
smoth·er ersticken
smo(u)l·der glimmen, schwelen
smudge 1. Schmutzfleck *m*; **2.** (be-, ver)schmieren; (sich) verwischen
smug selbstgefällig
smug·gle schmuggeln (***into*** nach; in *acc*)
smug·gler Schmuggler(in)
smut Rußflocke *f*; Schmutz *m* (*a. fig*)
smut·ty *fig* schmutzig
snack Snack *m*, Imbiss *m*; ***have a snack*** e-e Kleinigkeit essen
snack bar Snackbar *f*, Imbissstube *f*
snag 1. *fig* Haken *m*; **2.** mit *et.* hängen bleiben (***on*** an *dat*)
snail ZO Schnecke *f*
snake ZO Schlange *f*
snap 1. *v/i* (zer)brechen, (zer)reißen; *a.* ***snap shut*** zuschnappen; ***snap at*** schnappen nach; *j-n* anschnauzen; ***snap out of it!*** F Kopf hoch!, komm, komm!; ***snap to it!*** mach fix!; *v/t* zerbrechen; PHOT F knipsen; ***snap one's fingers*** mit den Fingern schnalzen; ***snap one's fingers at*** *fig* keinen Respekt haben vor (*dat*), sich hinwegsetzen über (*acc*); ***snap off*** abbrechen; ***snap up*** *et.* schnell entschlossen kaufen; ***snap it up!*** mach fix!; **2.** Krachen *n*, Knacken *n*, Knall *m*; PHOT F Schnappschuss *m*; Druckknopf *m*; F Schwung *m*; ***cold snap*** Kälteeinbruch *m*
snap fas·ten·er Druckknopf *m*
snap·pish *fig* bissig
snap·py modisch, schick; ***make it snappy!*** F mach fix!
snap·shot PHOT Schnappschuss *m*
snare 1. Schlinge *f*, Falle *f* (*a. fig*); **2.** in der Schlinge fangen; F *et.* ergattern
snarl 1. knurren; ***snarl at s.o.*** j-n anknurren; **2.** Knurren *n*
snatch 1. *v/t et.* packen; *Gelegenheit* ergreifen; *ein paar Stunden Schlaf etc* ergattern; ***snatch s.o.'s handbag*** j-m die Handtasche entreißen; *v/i* ***snatch at*** (schnell) greifen nach; *Gelegenheit* ergreifen; **2.** ***make a snatch at*** (schnell)

greifen nach; ***snatch of conversation*** Gesprächsfetzen *m*
sneak 1. *v/i* (sich) schleichen; *Br* F petzen; *v/t* F stibitzen; **2.** *Br* F Petze *f*
sneak·er Turnschuh *m*
sneer 1. höhnisch *or* spöttisch grinsen (***at*** über *acc*); spotten (***at*** über *acc*); **2.** höhnisches *or* spöttisches Grinsen; höhnische *or* spöttische Bemerkung
sneeze 1. niesen; **2.** Niesen *n*
snick·er kichern (***at*** über *acc*)
sniff 1. *v/i* schniefen; schnüffeln (***at*** an *dat*); ***sniff at*** *fig* die Nase rümpfen über (*acc*); *v/t Klebstoff etc* schnüffeln, *Kokain etc* schnupfen; **2.** Schniefen *n*
snif·fle 1. schniefen; **2.** Schniefen *n*; ***she's got the sniffles*** F ihr läuft dauernd die Nase
snig·ger *esp Br* → ***snicker***
snip 1. Schnitt *m*; **2.** durchschnippeln; ***snip off*** abschnippeln
snipe[1] zo Schnepfe *f*
snipe[2] aus dem Hinterhalt schießen (***at*** auf *acc*)
snip·er Heckenschütze *m*
sniv·el greinen, jammern
snob Snob *m*
snob·bish versnobt
snoop: ***snoop about, snoop around*** F herumschnüffeln
snoop·er F Schnüffler(in)
snooze F **1.** ein Nickerchen machen; **2.** Nickerchen *n*
snore 1. schnarchen; **2.** Schnarchen *n*
snor·kel 1. Schnorchel *m*; **2.** schnorcheln
snort 1. schnauben; **2.** Schnauben *n*
snot·ty nose F Rotznase *f*
snout zo Schnauze *f*, Rüssel *m*
snow 1. Schnee *m* (*a. sl cocaine*); **2.** schneien; ***be snowed in*** *or* ***up*** eingeschneit sein
snow·ball Schneeball *m*
snowball fight Schneeballschlacht *f*
snow·bound eingeschneit
snow-capped schneebedeckt
snow·drift Schneewehe *f*
snow·drop BOT Schneeglöckchen *n*
snow·fall Schneefall *m*
snow·flake Schneeflocke *f*
snow line Schneegrenze *f*
snow·man Schneemann *m*
snow·mo·bile Schneemobil *n*
snow·plough *Br*, **snow·plow** Schneepflug *m*
snow·storm Schneesturm *m*
snow-white schneeweiß
Snow White Schneewittchen *n*
snow·y schneereich; verschneit
snub *j-n* brüskieren, *j-n* vor den Kopf stoßen
snub nose Stupsnase *f*
snuff[1] Schnupftabak *m*
snuff[2] *Kerze* ausdrücken, löschen; ***snuff out*** *Leben* auslöschen
snuf·fle schnüffeln, schniefen
snug gemütlich, behaglich; *clothing*: gut sitzend; eng (anliegend)
snug·gle: ***snuggle up to s.o.*** sich an j-n kuscheln; ***snuggle down in bed*** sich ins Bett kuscheln
so so; deshalb; → ***hope*** 2, ***think***; ***is that so?*** wirklich?; ***an hour or so*** etwa e-e Stunde; ***she is tired - so am I*** sie ist müde - ich auch; ***so far*** bisher
soak *v/t* einweichen (***in*** in *dat*); durchnässen; ***soak up*** aufsaugen; *v/i* sickern
soak·ing *a.* ***soaking wet*** völlig durchnässt, F klatschnass
soap 1. Seife *f*; F → ***soap opera***; **2.** (sich) einseifen
soap op·e·ra *radio*, TV Seifenoper *f*
soap·y Seifen…; seifig; *fig* F schmeichlerisch
soar (hoch) aufsteigen; hochragen; zo, AVIAT segeln, gleiten; *fig* in die Höhe schnellen (*prices etc*)
sob 1. schluchzen; **2.** Schluchzen *n*
so·ber 1. nüchtern (*a. fig*); **2.** ernüchtern; ***sober up*** nüchtern machen *or* werden
so-called sogenannt
soc·cer Fußball *m*
soc·cer hoo·li·gan Fußballrowdy *m*
so·cia·ble gesellig
so·cial sozial, Sozial…; gesellschaftlich, Gesellschafts…; zo gesellig
social dem·o·crat POL Sozialdemokrat(in)
social insur·ance Sozialversicherung *f*
so·cial·ism Sozialismus *m*
so·cial·ist 1. Sozialist(in); **2.** sozialistisch
so·cial·ize *v/i* gesellschaftlich verkehren (***with*** mit); *v/t* sozialisieren
so·cial sci·ence Sozialwissenschaft *f*
social se·cu·ri·ty *Br* Sozialhilfe *f*; ***be on social security*** Sozialhilfe beziehen
social ser·vic·es *esp Br* Sozialeinrichtungen
social work Sozialarbeit *f*
social work·er Sozialarbeiter(in)
so·ci·e·ty Gesellschaft *f*; Verein *m*
so·ci·ol·o·gy Soziologie *f*
sock Socke *f*
sock·et ELECTR Steckdose *f*; Fassung *f*; (Anschluss)Buchse *f*; ANAT (*Augen-*) Höhle *f*
so·da Soda(wasser) *n*; (*Orangen- etc*)Limonade *f*
sod·den aufgeweicht (*ground*); durchweicht (*clothes*)

so·fa Sofa *n*
soft weich; sanft; leise; gedämpft (*light etc*); F leicht, angenehm, ruhig (*job etc*); alkoholfrei (*drink*); F verweichlicht
soft drink Soft Drink *m*, alkoholfreies Getränk
soft·en *v/t* weich machen; *Wasser* enthärten; *Ton, Licht, Stimme etc* dämpfen; ***soften up*** F *j-n* weich machen; *v/i* weich(er) *or* sanft(er) *or* mild(er) werden
soft·heart·ed weichherzig
soft land·ing weiche Landung
soft·ware EDP Software *f*
software pack·age EDP Softwarepaket *n*
soft·y F Softie *m*, Weichling *m*
sog·gy aufgeweicht, matschig
soil[1] Boden *m*, Erde *f*
soil[2] beschmutzen, schmutzig machen
so·lar Sonnen…
solar en·er·gy Solar-, Sonnenenergie *f*
solar pan·el Sonnenkollektor *m*
solar sys·tem Sonnensystem *n*
sol·der TECH (ver)löten
sol·dier Soldat *m*
sole[1] **1.** (Fuß-, Schuh)Sohle *f*; **2.** besohlen
sole[2] zo Seezunge *f*
sole[3] einzig; alleinig, Allein…
sole·ly (einzig und) allein, ausschließlich
sol·emn feierlich; ernst
so·lic·it bitten um
so·lic·i·tous besorgt (***about, for*** um)
sol·id **1.** fest; stabil; massiv; MATH körperlich; gewichtig, triftig (*reason etc*), stichhaltig (*argument etc*); solid(e), gründlich (*work etc*); einmütig, geschlossen; ***a solid hour*** F e-e geschlagene Stunde; **2.** MATH Körper *m*; *pl* feste Nahrung
sol·i·dar·i·ty Solidarität *f*
so·lid·i·fy fest werden (lassen); *fig* (sich) festigen
so·lil·o·quy Selbstgespräch *n*, *esp* THEA Monolog *m*
sol·i·taire Solitär *m*; Patience *f*
sol·i·ta·ry einsam, (*Leben a.*) zurückgezogen, (*Ort etc a.*) abgelegen; einzig
solitary con·fine·ment JUR Einzelhaft *f*
so·lo MUS Solo *n*; AVIAT Alleinflug *m*
so·lo·ist MUS Solist(in)
sol·u·ble CHEM löslich; *fig* lösbar
so·lu·tion CHEM Lösung *f*; *fig* (Auf)Lösung *f*
solve *Fall etc* lösen
sol·vent **1.** ECON zahlungsfähig; **2.** CHEM Lösungsmittel *n*
som·ber, *Br* **som·bre** düster, trüb(e); *fig* trübsinnig
some (irgend)ein; *pl* einige, ein paar; manche; etwas, ein wenig, ein bisschen; ungefähr; ***some 20 miles*** etwa 20 Meilen; ***some more cake*** noch ein Stück Kuchen; ***to some extent*** bis zu e-m gewissen Grade
some·bod·y jemand
some·day eines Tages
some·how irgendwie
some·one jemand
some·place irgendwo, irgendwohin
som·er·sault **1.** Salto *m*; Purzelbaum *m*; ***turn a somersault*** → **2.** e-n Salto machen; e-n Purzelbaum schlagen
some·thing etwas; ***something like*** ungefähr
some·time irgendwann
some·times manchmal
some·what ein bisschen, ein wenig
some·where irgendwo(hin)
son Sohn *m*; ***son of a bitch*** V Scheißkerl *m*
so·na·ta MUS Sonate *f*
song MUS Lied *n*; Gesang *m*; ***for a song*** F für ein Butterbrot
song·bird zo Singvogel *m*
son·ic Schall…
sonic bang *Br*, **sonic boom** Überschallknall *m*
son-in-law Schwiegersohn *m*
son·net Sonett *n*
so·nor·ous sonor, volltönend
soon bald; ***as soon as*** sobald; ***as soon as possible*** so bald wie möglich
soon·er eher, früher; ***sooner or later*** früher oder später; ***the sooner the better*** je eher, desto besser; ***no sooner … than*** kaum … als; ***no sooner said than done*** gesagt, getan
soot Ruß *m*
soothe beruhigen, beschwichtigen (*a.* ***soothe down***); *Schmerzen* lindern, mildern
sooth·ing beruhigend; lindernd
soot·y rußig
sop[1] Beschwichtigungsmittel *n* (***to*** für)
sop[2]: ***sop up*** aufsaugen
so·phis·ti·cat·ed anspruchsvoll, kultiviert; intellektuell; TECH raffiniert, hoch entwickelt
soph·o·more Student(in) im zweiten Jahr
sop·o·rif·ic einschläfernd
sop·ping *a.* ***sopping wet*** F klatschnass
sor·cer·er Zauberer *m*, Hexenmeister *m*, Hexer *m*
sor·cer·ess Zauberin *f*, Hexe *f*
sor·cer·y Zauberei *f*, Hexerei *f*
sor·did schmutzig; schäbig
sore **1.** weh, wund (*a. fig*); entzündet; F *fig* sauer; ***I'm sore all over*** mir tut alles weh; ***sore throat*** Halsentzündung *f*; ***have a sore throat*** *a.* Halsschmerzen haben;

2. wunde Stelle, Wunde *f*
sor·rel[1] BOT Sauerampfer *m*
sor·rel[2] **1.** zo Fuchs *m* (*horse*); **2.** rotbraun
sor·row Kummer *m*, Leid *n*, Schmerz *m*, Trauer *f*
sor·row·ful traurig, betrübt
sor·ry **1.** *adj* traurig, jämmerlich; ***be** or* ***feel sorry for s.o.*** j-n bedauern *or* bemitleiden; ***I'm sorry for her*** sie tut mir leid; ***I am sorry to say*** ich muss leider sagen; ***I'm sorry*** → **2.** *int* (es) tut mir leid!; Entschuldigung!, Verzeihung!; ***sorry?*** *esp Br* wie bitte?
sort **1.** Sorte *f*, Art *f*; ***sort of*** F irgendwie; ***of a sort, of sorts*** F so etwas Ähnliches wie; ***all sorts of things*** alles Mögliche; ***nothing of the sort*** nichts dergleichen; ***what sort of*** (***a***) ***man is he?*** wie ist er?; ***be out of sorts*** F nicht auf der Höhe *or* auf dem Damm sein; ***be completely out of sorts*** SPORT F völlig außer Form sein; **2.** sortieren; ***sort out*** aussortieren; *Problem etc* lösen, *Frage etc* klären
SOS SOS *n*; ***send an SOS*** ein SOS funken; ***SOS call** or* ***message*** SOS-Ruf *m*
soul Seele *f* (*a. fig*); MUS Soul *m*
sound[1] **1.** Geräusch *n*; Laut *m*; PHYS Schall *m*; *radio*, TV Ton *m*; MUS Klang *m*, Sound *m*; **2.** *v/i* (er)klingen, (er)tönen; sich *gut etc* anhören; *v/t* LING (aus)sprechen; MAR (aus)loten; MED abhorchen; ***sound one's horn*** MOT hupen
sound[2] gesund; intakt, in Ordnung; solid(e), stabil, sicher; klug, vernünftig (*person, advice etc*); gründlich (*training etc*); gehörig (*beating*); vernichtend (*defeat*); fest, tief (*sleep*)
sound bar·ri·er Schallgrenze *f*, Schallmauer *f*
sound film Tonfilm *m*
sound·less lautlos
sound·proof schalldicht
sound·track Filmmusik *f*; Tonspur *f*
sound wave Schallwelle *f*
soup **1.** Suppe *f*; **2.** ***soup up*** F *Motor* frisieren
sour **1.** sauer; *fig* mürrisch; **2.** sauer werden (lassen); *fig* trüben, verbittern
source Quelle *f*, *fig a.* Ursache *f*, Ursprung *m*
south **1.** Süd, Süden *m*; **2.** *adj* südlich, Süd…; **3.** *adv* nach Süden, südwärts
south·east **1.** Südost, Südosten *m*; **2.** *a.* **south·east·ern** südöstlich
south·er·ly, **south·ern** südlich, Süd…
south·ern·most südlichste(r, -s)
South Pole Südpol *m*
south·ward(s) südlich, nach Süden
south·west **1.** Südwest, Südwesten *m*; **2.** *a.* **south·west·ern** südwestlich
sou·ve·nir Souvenir *n*, Andenken *n* (***of*** an *acc*)
sove·reign **1.** Monarch(in), Landesherr(in); **2.** POL souverän
sove·reign·ty Souveränität *f*
So·vi·et HIST POL sowjetisch, Sowjet…
sow[1] (aus)säen
sow[2] zo Sau *f*
soy bean BOT Sojabohne *f*
spa (Heil)Bad *n*
space **1.** Raum *m*, Platz *m*; (Welt-) Raum *m*; Zwischenraum *m*; Zeitraum *m*; **2.** *a.* ***space out*** in Abständen anordnen; PRINT sperren
space age Weltraumzeitalter *n*
space bar TECH Leertaste *f*
space cap·sule Raumkapsel *f*
space cen·ter (*Br* **cen·tre**) Raumfahrtzentrum *n*
space·craft (Welt)Raumfahrzeug *n*
space flight (Welt)Raumflug *m*
space·lab Raumlabor *n*
space·man F Raumfahrer *m*; Außerirdische *m*
space probe (Welt)Raumsonde *f*
space re·search (Welt)Raumforschung *f*
space·ship Raumschiff *n*
space shut·tle Raumfähre *f*, Raumtransporter *m*
space sta·tion (Welt)Raumstation *f*
space·suit Raumanzug *m*
space walk Weltraumspaziergang *m*
space·wom·an F (Welt)Raumfahrerin *f*; Außerirdische *f*
spa·cious geräumig
spade Spaten *m*; *card game*: Pik *n*, Grün *n*; ***king of spades*** Pikkönig *m*; ***call a spade a spade*** das Kind beim (rechten) Namen nennen
Spain Spanien *n*
span **1.** Spanne *f*; Spannweite *f*; **2.** *Fluss etc* überspannen; *fig* sich erstrecken über (*acc*)
span·gle **1.** Flitter *m*, Paillette *f*; **2.** mit Flitter *or* Pailletten besetzen; *fig* übersäen (***with*** mit)
Span·iard Spanier(in)
span·iel zo Spaniel *m*
Span·ish **1.** spanisch; **2.** LING Spanisch *n*; ***the Spanish*** die Spanier *pl*
spank *j-m* den Hintern versohlen
spank·ing Tracht *f* Prügel
span·ner *esp Br* Schraubenschlüssel *m*; ***put** or* ***throw a spanner in the works*** F j-m in die Quere kommen
spar *boxing*: sparren (***with*** mit); *fig* sich ein Wortgefecht liefern (***with*** mit)
spare **1.** *j-n*, *et.* entbehren; *Geld*, *Zeit etc*

übrig haben; *keine Kosten, Mühen etc* scheuen; ***spare s.o. s.th.*** j-m et. ersparen; **2.** Ersatz…, Reserve…; überschüssig; **3.** MOT Ersatz-, Reservereifen *m*; *esp Br* → **spare part** TECH Ersatzteil *n, m*
spare room Gästezimmer *n*
spare time Freizeit *f*
spar·ing sparsam; ***use sparingly*** sparsam umgehen mit
spark 1. Funke(n) *m* (*a. fig*); **2.** Funken sprühen
spark·ing plug *Br* → ***spark plug***
spar·kle 1. funkeln, blitzen (***with*** vor *dat*); perlen (*drink*); **2.** Funkeln *n*, Blitzen *n*
spar·kling funkelnd, blitzend; (geist)sprühend, spritzig; ***sparkling wine*** Sekt *m*, Schaumwein *m*
spark plug MOT Zündkerze *f*
spar·row ZO Spatz *m*, Sperling *m*
spar·row·hawk ZO Sperber *m*
sparse spärlich, dünn
spasm MED Krampf *m*; Anfall *m*
spas·mod·ic MED krampfartig; *fig* sporadisch, unregelmäßig
spas·tic MED **1.** spastisch; **2.** Spastiker(in)
spa·tial räumlich
spat·ter (be)spritzen
spawn 1. ZO laichen; *fig* hervorbringen; **2.** ZO Laich *m*
speak *v/i* sprechen, reden (***to, with*** mit; ***about*** über *acc*); sprechen (***to*** vor *dat*; ***about, on*** über *acc*); ***so to speak*** sozusagen; ***speaking!*** TEL am Apparat!; ***speak up*** lauter sprechen; *v/t* sprechen, sagen; *Sprache* sprechen
speak·er Sprecher(in), Redner(in)
spear 1. Speer *m*; **2.** aufspießen; durchbohren
spear·head Speerspitze *f*; MIL Angriffsspitze *f*; SPORT (Sturm-, Angriffs)Spitze *f*
spear·mint BOT Grüne Minze
spe·cial 1. besondere(r, -s); speziell; Sonder…; Spezial…; **2.** Sonderbus *m*, Sonderzug *m*; *radio*, TV Sondersendung *f*; ECON F Sonderangebot *n*; ***be on special*** ECON im Angebot sein
spe·cial·ist Spezialist(in), MED *a.* Facharzt *m*, Fachärztin *f* (***in*** für)
spe·ci·al·i·ty *Br* → ***specialty***
spe·cial·ize sich spezialisieren (***in*** auf *acc*)
spe·cial·ty Spezialgebiet *n*; GASTR Spezialität *f*
spe·cies Art *f*, Spezies *f*
spe·cif·ic konkret, präzis; spezifisch, speziell, besondere(r, -s); eigen (***to*** *dat*)
spe·ci·fy genau beschreiben *or* angeben *or* festlegen
spe·ci·men Exemplar *n*; Probe *f*, Muster *n*
speck kleiner Fleck, (*Staub*)Korn *n*; Punkt *m* (***on the horizon*** am Horizont)
speck·led gefleckt, gesprenkelt
spec·ta·cle Schauspiel *n*; Anblick *m*; (***a pair of***) ***spectacles*** (e-e) Brille
spec·tac·u·lar 1. spektakulär; **2.** große (*Fernseh- etc*)Show
spec·ta·tor Zuschauer(in)
spec·ter (*fig a. Schreck*)Gespenst *n*
spec·tral geisterhaft, gespenstisch
spec·tre *Br* → ***specter***
spec·u·late spekulieren, Vermutungen anstellen (***about, on*** über *acc*); ECON spekulieren (***in*** mit)
spec·u·la·tion Spekulation *f* (*a.* ECON), Vermutung *f*
spec·u·la·tive spekulativ, ECON *a.* Spekulations…
spec·u·la·tor ECON Spekulant(in)
speech Sprache *f*; Rede *f*, Ansprache *f*; ***make a speech*** e-e Rede halten
speech day *Br* PED (Jahres)Schlussfeier *f*
speech·less sprachlos (***with*** vor *dat*)
speed 1. Geschwindigkeit *f*, Tempo *n*, Schnelligkeit *f*; TECH Drehzahl *f*; PHOT Lichtempfindlichkeit *f*; *sl* Speed *n*; MOT *etc* Gang *m*; ***five-speed gearbox*** Fünfganggetriebe *n*; ***at a speed of*** mit e-r Geschwindigkeit von; ***at full*** *or* ***top speed*** mit Höchstgeschwindigkeit; **2.** *v/i* rasen; ***be speeding*** MOT zu schnell fahren; ***speed up*** beschleunigen, schneller werden; *v/t* rasch bringen *or* befördern; ***speed up*** *et.* beschleunigen
speed·boat Rennboot *n*
speed·ing MOT zu schnelles Fahren, Geschwindigkeitsüberschreitung *f*
speed lim·it MOT Geschwindigkeitsbegrenzung *f*, Tempolimit *n*
speed·om·e·ter MOT Tachometer *m, n*
speed trap MOT Radarfalle *f*
speed·y schnell, (*reply etc a.*) prompt
spell[1] *a.* ***spell out*** buchstabieren; (*orthographisch* richtig) schreiben
spell[2] Weile *f*; (*Husten- etc*)Anfall *m*; ***for a spell*** e-e Zeit lang; ***a spell of fine weather*** e-e Schönwetterperiode; ***hot spell*** Hitzewelle *f*
spell[3] Zauber *m* (*a. fig*)
spell·bound wie gebannt
spell·er EDP Speller *m*, Rechtschreibsystem *n*; ***be a good*** (***bad***) ***speller*** in Rechtschreibung gut (schlecht) sein
spell·ing Buchstabieren *n*; Rechtschreibung *f*; Schreibung *f*, Schreibweise *f*
spelling mis·take (Recht)Schreibfehler *m*
spend *Geld* ausgeben (***on*** für); *Urlaub, Zeit* verbringen

spend·ing Ausgaben *pl*
spend·thrift Verschwender(in)
spent verbraucht
sperm BIOL Sperma *n*, Samen *m*
sphere Kugel *f*; *fig* (*Einfluss- etc*)Sphäre *f*, (*Einfluss- etc*)Bereich *m*, Gebiet *n*
spher·i·cal kugelförmig
spice **1.** Gewürz *n*; *fig* Würze *f*; **2.** würzen
spick-and-span blitzsauber
spic·y gut gewürzt, würzig; *fig* pikant
spi·der ZO Spinne *f*
spike **1.** Spitze *f*; Dorn *m*; Stachel *m*; SPORT Spike *m*, Dorn *m*; *pl* Spikes *pl*, Rennschuhe *pl*; **2.** aufspießen
spill **1.** *v/t* ausschütten, verschütten; ***spill the beans*** F alles ausplaudern, singen; → ***milk*** *1*; *v/i fig* strömen (***out of*** aus); ***spill over*** überlaufen; *fig* übergreifen (***into*** auf *acc*); **2.** F Sturz *m*
spin **1.** *v/t* drehen; *Wäsche* schleudern; *Münze* hochwerfen; *Fäden, Wolle etc* spinnen; ***spin out*** *Arbeit etc* in die Länge ziehen; *Geld etc* strecken; *v/i* sich drehen; spinnen; ***my head was spinning*** mir drehte sich alles; ***spin along*** MOT dahinrasen; ***spin round*** herumwirbeln; **2.** (schnelle) Drehung; SPORT Effet *m*; TECH Schleudern *n*; AVIAT Trudeln *n*; ***be in a (flat) spin*** *esp Br* F am Rotieren sein; ***go for a spin*** MOT F e-e Spritztour machen
spin·ach BOT Spinat *m*
spin·al ANAT Rückgrat…
spinal col·umn ANAT Wirbelsäule *f*, Rückgrat *n*
spinal cord, **spinal mar·row** ANAT Rückenmark *n*
spin·dle Spindel *f*
spin·dri·er (Wäsche)Schleuder *f*
spin-dry *Wäsche* schleudern
spin-dry·er → ***spin-drier***
spine ANAT Wirbelsäule *f*, Rückgrat *n*; ZO Stachel *m*, BOT *a.* Dorn *m*; (*Buch-*) Rücken *m*
spin·ning mill TECH Spinnerei *f*
spinning top Kreisel *m*
spinning wheel Spinnrad *n*
spin·ster ältere unverheiratete Frau, *contp* alte Jungfer, spätes Mädchen
spin·y ZO stach(e)lig, BOT *a.* dornig
spi·ral **1.** spiralförmig, Spiral…; **2.** (*a.* ECON *Preis- etc*)Spirale *f*
spi·ral stair·case Wendeltreppe *f*
spire (*Kirch*)Turmspitze *f*
spir·it Geist *m*; Stimmung *f*, Einstellung *f*; Schwung *m*; Elan *m*; CHEM Spiritus *m*; *mst pl* Spirituosen *pl*
spir·it·ed energisch; erregt (*debate etc*)
spir·it·less temperamentlos; mutlos
spir·its Laune *f*, Stimmung *f*; ***be in high spirits*** in Hochstimmung sein; ausgelassen *or* übermütig sein; ***be in low spirits*** niedergeschlagen sein
spir·i·tu·al **1.** geistig; geistlich; **2.** MUS Spiritual *n*
spit[1] **1.** spucken; knistern (*fire*), brutzeln (*meat etc*); *a.* ***spit out*** ausspucken; ***spit at s.o.*** j-n anspucken; ***it is spitting (with rain)*** es tröpfelt; **2.** Spucke *f*
spit[2] (Brat)Spieß *m*; GEOGR Landzunge *f*
spite **1.** Bosheit *f*, Gehässigkeit *f*; ***out of*** *or* ***from pure spite*** aus reiner Bosheit; ***in spite of*** trotz (*gen*); **2.** *j-n* ärgern
spite·ful boshaft, gehässig
spit·ting im·age Ebenbild *n*; ***she is the spitting image of her mother*** sie ist ihrer Mutter wie aus dem Gesicht geschnitten
spit·tle Speichel *m*, Spucke *f*
splash **1.** (be)spritzen; klatschen; plan(t)schen; platschen; ***splash down*** wassern; **2.** Klatschen *n*, Platschen *n*; Spritzer *m*, Spritzfleck *m*; *esp Br* GASTR Spritzer *m*, Schuss *m*
splash·down Wasserung *f*
splay *a.* ***splay out*** *Finger, Zehen* spreizen
spleen ANAT Milz *f*
splen·did großartig, herrlich, prächtig
splen·do(u)r Pracht *f*
splice miteinander verbinden, *Film etc* (zusammen)kleben
splint MED Schiene *f*; ***put in a splint, put in splints*** schienen
splin·ter **1.** Splitter *m*; **2.** (zer)splittern; ***splinter off*** absplittern; *fig* sich abspalten (***from*** von)
split **1.** *v/t* (zer)spalten; zerreißen; *a.* ***split up*** aufteilen (***between*** unter *acc*; ***into*** in *acc*); sich *et.* teilen; ***split hairs*** Haarspalterei treiben; ***split one's sides*** F sich vor Lachen biegen; *v/i* sich spalten; zerreißen; sich teilen (***into*** in *acc*); *a.* ***split up (with)*** Schluss machen (mit), sich trennen (von); **2.** Riss *m*; Spalt *m*; Aufteilung *f*; *fig* Bruch *m*; *fig* Spaltung *f*
split·ting heftig, rasend (*headache etc*)
splut·ter stottern (*a.* MOT); zischen
spoil **1.** *v/t* verderben; ruinieren; *j-n* verwöhnen, *Kind a.* verziehen; *v/i* verderben, schlecht werden; **2.** *mst pl* Beute *f*
spoil·er MOT Spoiler *m*
spoil·sport F Spielverderber(in)
spoke TECH Speiche *f*
spokes·man Sprecher *m*
spokes·wom·an Sprecherin *f*
sponge **1.** Schwamm *m*; Schnorrer(in); *Br* → ***sponge cake***; **2.** *v/t a.* ***sponge down*** (mit e-m Schwamm) abwaschen;

sponge off weg-, abwischen; ***sponge (up)*** aufsaugen, aufwischen (***from*** von); *et.* schnorren (***from, off, on*** von, bei); *v/i* schnorren (***from, off, on*** bei)
sponge cake Biskuitkuchen *m*
spong·er Schnorrer(in)
spong·y schwammig; weich
spon·sor 1. Bürge *m*, Bürgin *f*; Sponsor(in), Geldgeber(in); Spender(in); **2.** bürgen für; sponsern
spon·ta·ne·ous spontan
spook F Geist *m*
spook·y F gespenstisch, unheimlich
spool Spule *f*; ***spool of thread*** Garnrolle *f*
spoon 1. Löffel *m*; **2.** löffeln
spoon-feed *Kind etc* füttern
spoon·ful (*ein*) Löffel (voll)
spo·rad·ic sporadisch, gelegentlich
spore BOT Spore *f*
sport 1. Sport *m*; Sportart *f*; F feiner Kerl; *pl* Sport *m*; **2.** herumlaufen mit; protzen mit
sports Sport…
sports car MOT Sportwagen *m*
sports cen·ter (*Br* **cen·tre**) Sportzentrum *n*
sports·man Sportler *m*
sports·wear Sportkleidung *f*
sports·wom·an Sportlerin *f*
spot 1. Punkt *m*, Tupfen *m*; Fleck *m*; MED Pickel *m*; Ort *m*, Platz *m*, Stelle *f*; *radio*, TV (Werbe)Spot *m*; F Spot *m*; ***a spot of*** *Br* F ein bisschen; ***on the spot*** auf der Stelle, sofort; zur Stelle; an Ort und Stelle, vor Ort; auf der Stelle; ***be in a spot*** F in Schwulitäten sein; ***soft spot*** *fig* Schwäche *f* (***for*** für); ***tender spot*** empfindliche Stelle; ***weak spot*** schwacher Punkt; Schwäche *f*; **2.** entdecken, sehen
spot check Stichprobe *f*
spot·less tadellos sauber; *fig* untad(e)lig
spot·light Spotlight *n*, Scheinwerfer *m*; Scheinwerferlicht *n*
spot·ted getüpfelt; fleckig
spot·ter Beobachter *m*
spot·ty pick(e)lig
spouse Gatte *m*, Gattin *f*, Gemahl(in)
spout 1. *v/t Wasser etc* (heraus)spritzen; *v/i* spritzen (***from*** aus); **2.** Schnauze *f*, Tülle *f*; (*Wasser- etc*)Strahl *m*
sprain MED **1.** sich *et.* verstauchen; **2.** Verstauchung *f*
sprat ZO Sprotte *f*
sprawl ausgestreckt liegen *or* sitzen (*a.* ***sprawl out***); sich ausbreiten
spray 1. (be)sprühen; spritzen; sich *die Haare* sprayen; *Parfüm etc* versprühen, zerstäuben; **2.** Sprühnebel *m*; Gischt *m, f*; Spray *m, n*; → ***sprayer***
spray can → **spray·er** Sprüh-, Spraydose *f*, Zerstäuber *m*
spread 1. *v/t* ausbreiten, *Arme a.* ausstrecken, *Finger etc* spreizen (*all a.* ***spread out***); *Furcht, Krankheit, Nachricht etc* verbreiten, *Gerücht a.* ausstreuen; *Butter etc* streichen (***on*** auf *acc*); *Brot etc* (be)streichen (***with*** mit); *v/i* sich ausbreiten (*a.* ***spread out***); sich erstrecken (***over*** über *acc*); sich verbreiten, übergreifen (***to*** auf *acc*); sich streichen lassen (*butter etc*); **2.** Ausbreitung *f*, Verbreitung *f*; Ausdehnung *f*; Spannweite *f*; GASTR Aufstrich *m*
spread·sheet EDP Tabellenkalkulation *f*, Tabellenkalkulationsprogramm *n*
spree: ***go (out) on a spree*** F e-e Sauftour machen; ***go on a buying*** (*or* ***shopping, spending***) ***spree*** wie verrückt einkaufen
sprig BOT kleiner Zweig
spright·ly lebhaft; rüstig
spring 1. *v/i* springen; ***spring from*** herrühren von; ***spring up*** aufkommen (*wind*); aus dem Boden schießen (*building etc*); *v/t*: ***spring a leak*** ein Leck bekommen; ***spring a surprise on s.o.*** j-n überraschen; **2.** Frühling *m*, Frühjahr *n*; Quelle *f*; TECH Feder *f*; Elastizität *f*; Federung *f*; Sprung *m*, Satz *m*; ***in (the) spring*** im Frühling
spring·board Sprungbrett *n*
spring-clean gründlich putzen, Frühjahrsputz machen (in *dat*)
spring tide Springflut *f*
spring·time Frühling *m*, Frühlingszeit *f*, Frühjahr *n*
spring·y elastisch, federnd
sprin·kle 1. *Wasser etc* sprengen (***on*** auf *acc*); *Salz etc* streuen (***on*** auf *acc*); *et.* (be)sprengen *or* bestreuen (***with*** mit); ***it is sprinkling*** es tröpfelt; **2.** Sprühregen *m*
sprin·kler (*Rasen*)Sprenger *m*; Sprinkler *m*, Berieselungsanlage *f*
sprin·kling: ***a sprinkling of*** ein bisschen, ein paar
sprint SPORT **1.** sprinten; spurten; **2.** Sprint *m*; Spurt *m*
sprint·er SPORT Sprinter(in)
sprite Kobold *m*
sprout BOT **1.** sprießen (*a. fig*), keimen; wachsen lassen; **2.** Spross *m*; (***Brussels***) ***sprouts*** Rosenkohl *m*
spruce[1] BOT Fichte *f*, Rottanne *f*
spruce[2] adrett
spry rüstig, lebhaft
spur 1. Sporn *m* (*a.* ZO); *fig* Ansporn *m* (***to***

zu); ***on the spur of the moment*** spontan; **2.** *e-m Pferd* die Sporen geben; *often* ***spur on*** *fig* anspornen (***to*** zu)
spurt[1] **1.** spurten, sprinten; **2.** plötzliche Aktivität, (*Arbeits*)Anfall *m*; Spurt *m*, Sprint *m*
spurt[2] **1.** spritzen (***from*** aus); **2.** (*Wasser-etc*)Strahl *m*
sput·ter stottern (*a.* MOT); zischen
spy **1.** Spion(in); **2.** spionieren, Spionage treiben (***for*** für); ***spy into*** *fig* herumspionieren in (*dat*); ***spy on*** *j-m* nachspionieren
spy·hole (Tür)Spion *m*
squab·ble (sich) streiten (***about, over*** um, wegen)
squad Mannschaft *f*, Trupp *m*; (*Überfall-etc*)Kommando *n*; Dezernat *n*
squad car (Funk)Streifenwagen *m*
squad·ron MIL, AVIAT Staffel *f*; MAR Geschwader *n*
squal·id schmutzig, verwahrlost, verkommen, armselig
squall Bö *f*
squan·der *Geld, Zeit etc* verschwenden, *Chance* vertun
square **1.** Quadrat *n*; Viereck *n*; *öffentlicher* Platz; MATH Quadrat(zahl *f*) *n*; *board game*: Feld *n*; TECH Winkel(maß *n*) *m*; **2.** quadratisch, Quadrat...; viereckig; rechtwink(e)lig; eckig (*shoulders etc*); *fig* fair, gerecht; ***be (all) square*** quitt sein; **3.** quadratisch *or* rechtwink(e)lig machen (*a.* ***square off*** *or* ***up***); in Quadrate einteilen (*a.* ***square off***); MATH *Zahl* ins Quadrat erheben; *Schultern* straffen; *Konto* ausgleichen; *Schulden* begleichen; *fig* in Einklang bringen *or* stehen (***with*** mit); ***square up*** F abrechnen; ***square up to*** sich *j-m, e-m Problem etc* stellen
square root MATH Quadratwurzel *f*
squash[1] **1.** zerdrücken, zerquetschen; quetschen, zwängen (***into*** in *acc*); ***squash flat*** flach drücken, F platt walzen; **2.** Gedränge *n*; SPORT Squash *n*
squash[2] BOT Kürbis *m*
squat **1.** hocken, kauern; *leer stehendes Haus* besetzen; ***squat down*** sich (hin)kauern *or* (hin)hocken; **2.** gedrungen, untersetzt
squat·ter Hausbesetzer(in)
squaw Squaw *f*
squawk kreischen, schreien; F lautstark protestieren (***about*** gegen)
squeak **1.** piep(s)en (*mouse etc*); quietschen (*door etc*); **2.** Piep(s)en *n*; Piep(s) *m*; Quietschen *n*
squeak·y piepsig (*voice*); quietschend (*door etc*)
squeal **1.** kreischen (***with*** vor *dat*); ***squeal on s.o.*** *fig* F j-n verpfeifen; **2.** Kreischen *n*; Schrei *m*
squeam·ish empfindlich, zart besaitet
squeeze **1.** drücken; auspressen, ausquetschen; (sich) quetschen *or* zwängen (***into*** in *acc*); **2.** Druck *m*; GASTR Spritzer *m*; Gedränge *n*
squeez·er (Frucht)Presse *f*
squid ZO Tintenfisch *m*
squint schielen; blinzeln
squirm sich winden
squir·rel ZO Eichhörnchen *n*
squirt **1.** (be)spritzen; **2.** Strahl *m*
stab **1.** *v/t* niederstechen; ***be stabbed in the arm*** e-n Stich in den Arm bekommen; *v/i* stechen (***at*** nach); **2.** Stich *m*
sta·bil·i·ty Stabilität *f*; *fig* Dauerhaftigkeit *f*; Ausgeglichenheit *f*
sta·bil·ize (sich) stabilisieren
sta·ble[1] stabil; *fig* dauerhaft; ausgeglichen
sta·ble[2] Stall *m*
stack **1.** Stapel *m*, Stoß *m*; ***stacks of, a stack of*** F jede Menge *Arbeit etc*; **2.** stapeln; voll stapeln (***with*** mit); ***stack up*** aufstapeln
sta·di·um SPORT Stadion *n*
staff **1.** Stab *m*; Mitarbeiter(stab *m*) *pl*; Personal *n*, Belegschaft *f*; Lehrkörper *m*; MIL Stab *m*; **2.** besetzen (***with*** mit)
staff room Lehrerzimmer *n*
stag ZO Hirsch *m*
stage **1.** THEA Bühne *f* (*a. fig*); Etappe *f* (*a. fig*), (Reise)Abschnitt *m*; Teilstrecke *f*, Fahrzone *f* (*bus etc*); *fig* Stufe *f*, Stadium *n*, Phase *f*; **2.** THEA inszenieren; veranstalten
stage·coach Postkutsche *f*
stage di·rec·tion THEA Regieanweisung *f*
stage fright Lampenfieber *n*
stage man·ag·er THEA Inspizient *m*
stag·ger **1.** *v/i* (sch)wanken, taumeln, torkeln; *v/t j-n* sprachlos machen, F umhauen; *Arbeitszeit etc* staffeln; **2.** Wanken *n*, Schwanken *n*, Taumeln *n*
stag·nant stehend (*water*); *esp* ECON stagnierend
stag·nate *esp* ECON stagnieren
stain **1.** *v/t* beflecken; (ein)färben; *Holz* beizen; *Glas* bemalen; *v/i* Flecken bekommen, schmutzen; **2.** Fleck *m*; TECH Färbemittel *n*; (*Holz*)Beize *f*; Makel *m*
stained glass Bunt-, Farbglas *n*
stain·less nicht rostend, rostfrei
stair (Treppen)Stufe *f*; *pl* Treppe *f*
stair·case, stair·way Treppe *f*; Treppenhaus *n*

stake[1] **1.** Pfahl *m*, Pfosten *m*; HIST Marterpfahl *m*; **2.** ***stake off, stake out*** abstecken
stake[2] **1.** Anteil *m*, Beteiligung *f* (***in*** an *dat*) (*a.* ECON); (Wett- *etc*)Einsatz *m*; ***be at stake*** *fig* auf dem Spiel stehen; **2.** *Geld etc* setzen (***on*** auf *acc*); *Ruf etc* riskieren, aufs Spiel setzen
stale alt(backen); abgestanden, *beer etc*: *a.* schal, *air etc*: *a.* verbraucht
stalk[1] BOT Stängel *m*, Stiel *m*, Halm *m*
stalk[2] *v/t* sich heranpirschen an (*acc*); verfolgen, hinter *j-m*, *et.* herschleichen; *v/i* stolzieren
stall[1] **1.** (*Obst- etc*)Stand *m*, (*Markt-*)Bude *f*; AGR Box *f*; *pl* REL Chorgestühl *n*; *Br* THEA Parkett *n*; **2.** *v/t Motor* abwürgen; *v/i* MOT absterben
stall[2] *v/i* Ausflüchte machen; Zeit schinden; *v/t j-n* hinhalten; *et.* hinauszögern
stal·li·on ZO (Zucht)Hengst *m*
stal·wart kräftig, robust; *esp* POL treu
stam·i·na Ausdauer *f*; Durchhaltevermögen *n*, Kondition *f*
stam·mer **1.** stottern, stammeln; **2.** Stottern *n*, Stammeln *n*
stamp **1.** *v/i* sta(m)pfen, trampeln; *v/t Pass etc* (ab)stempeln; *Datum etc* aufstempeln (***on*** auf *acc*); *Brief etc* frankieren; *fig j-n* abstempeln (***as*** als, zu); ***stamp one's foot*** aufstampfen; ***stamp out*** *Feuer* austreten; TECH ausstanzen; **2.** (Brief-) Marke *f*; (*Steuer- etc*)Marke *f*; Stempel *m*; ***stamped addressed envelope*** Freiumschlag *m*
stam·pede **1.** ZO wilde Flucht; wilder Ansturm, Massenansturm *m* (***for*** auf *acc*); **2.** *v/i* ZO durchgehen; *v/t* in Panik versetzen
stanch treu, zuverlässig
stand **1.** *v/i* stehen; aufstehen; *fig fest- etc* bleiben; ***stand still*** still stehen; *v/t* stellen (***on*** auf *acc*); aushalten, ertragen; *e-r Prüfung etc* standhalten; *Probe* bestehen; *Chance* haben; *Drink etc* spendieren; ***I can't stand him*** (*or* ***it***) ich kann ihn (*or* das) nicht ausstehen *or* leiden; ***stand around*** herumstehen; ***stand back*** zurücktreten; ***stand by*** danebenstehen; *fig* zu *j-m* halten; zu *et.* stehen; ***stand idly by*** tatenlos zusehen; ***stand down*** verzichten; zurücktreten; JUR den Zeugenstand verlassen; ***stand for*** stehen für, bedeuten; sich *et.* gefallen lassen, *et.* dulden; *esp Br* kandidieren für; ***stand in*** einspringen (***for*** für); ***stand in for s.o.*** *a.* j-n vertreten; ***stand on*** (*fig* be)stehen auf (*dat*); ***stand out*** hervorstechen; sich abheben (***against*** gegen, von); ***stand over*** überwachen, aufpassen auf (*acc*); ***stand together*** zusammenhalten, -stehen; ***stand up*** aufstehen, sich erheben; ***stand up for*** eintreten *or* sich einsetzen für; ***stand up to*** *j-m* mutig gegenübertreten, *j-m* die Stirn bieten; **2.** (*Obst-, Messe- etc*)Stand *m*; (*Schirm-, Noten- etc*) Ständer *m*; SPORT *etc* Tribüne *f*; (*Taxi*)-Stand(platz) *m*; JUR Zeugenstand *m*; ***take a stand*** *fig* Position beziehen (***on*** zu)
stan·dard[1] **1.** Norm *f*, Maßstab *m*; Standard *m*, Niveau *n*; ***standard of living, living standard*** Lebensstandard *m*; **2.** normal, Normal...; durchschnittlich, Durchschnitts...; Standard...
stan·dard[2] Standarte *f*, MOT Stander *m*; HIST Banner *n*
stan·dard·ize vereinheitlichen, *esp* TECH standardisieren, normen
stan·dard lamp *Br* Stehlampe *f*
stand·by **1.** Reserve *f*; AVIAT Stand-by *n*; ***be on standby*** in Bereitschaft stehen; **2.** Reserve..., Not...; AVIAT Stand-by...
stand-in *film*, TV Double *n*; Ersatzmann *m*; Vertreter(in)
stand·ing **1.** stehend; *fig* ständig; → ***ovation***; **2.** Rang *m*, Stellung *f*; Ansehen *n*, Ruf *m*; Dauer *f*; ***of long standing*** alt, seit langem bestehend
standing or·der ECON Dauerauftrag *m*
standing room: ***standing room only*** nur noch Stehplätze
stand·off·ish F (sehr) ablehnend, hochnäsig
stand·point *fig* Standpunkt *m*
stand·still Stillstand *m*; ***be at a standstill*** stehen (*car etc*); ruhen (*production etc*); ***bring to a standstill*** *Auto etc* zum Stehen bringen; *Produktion etc* zum Erliegen bringen
stand-up Steh...; ***stand-up fight*** Schlägerei *f*
stan·za Strophe *f*
sta·ple[1] **1.** Hauptnahrungsmittel *n*; ECON Haupterzeugnis *n*; **2.** Haupt...; üblich
sta·ple[2] **1.** Heftklammer *f*; Krampe *f*; **2.** heften
sta·pler TECH (Draht)Hefter *m*
star **1.** ASTR Stern *m*; PRINT Sternchen *n*; THEA, SPORT *etc* Star *m*; **2.** *v/t* PRINT mit e-m Sternchen kennzeichnen; ***starring ...*** in der Hauptrolle *or* in den Hauptrollen ...; ***a film starring ...*** ein Film mit ... in der Hauptrolle *or* den Hauptrollen; *v/i* die *or* e-e Hauptrolle spielen (***in*** in *dat*)
star·board AVIAT, MAR Steuerbord *n*
starch **1.** (*Kartoffel- etc*)Stärke *f*; stärkereiches Nahrungsmittel; (*Wäsche-*) Stärke *f*; **2.** *Wäsche* stärken

S

stare **1.** starren; ***stare at*** *j-n* anstarren; **2.** (starrer) Blick, Starren *n*
stark **1.** *adj fig* nackt; ***be in stark contrast to*** in krassem Gegensatz stehen zu; **2.** *adv*: F ***stark naked*** splitternackt; ***stark raving mad, stark staring mad*** total verrückt
star·light ASTR Sternenlicht *n*
star·ling ZO Star *m*
star·lit stern(en)klar
star·ry Stern…, Sternen…
star·ry-eyed F blauäugig, naiv
start **1.** *v/i* anfangen, beginnen (*a.* ***start off***); aufbrechen (***for*** nach) (*a.* ***start off, start out***); RAIL *etc* abfahren, MAR ablegen, AVIAT abfliegen, starten; MOT anspringen; TECH anlaufen; SPORT starten; zusammenfahren, -zucken (***at*** bei); ***to start with*** anfangs, zunächst; erstens; ***start from scratch*** ganz von vorn anfangen; *v/t* anfangen, beginnen (*a.* ***start off***); in Gang setzen *or* bringen, *Motor etc a.* anlassen, starten; **2.** Anfang *m*, Beginn *m*, (*esp* SPORT) Start *m*; Aufbruch *m*; Auffahren *n*, Aufschrecken *n*; ***at the start*** am Anfang; SPORT am Start; ***for a start*** erstens; ***from start to finish*** von Anfang bis Ende
start·er SPORT Starter(in); MOT Anlasser *m*, Starter *m*; *esp Br* GASTR F Vorspeise *f*; ***for starters*** zunächst einmal
start·le erschrecken; überraschen, bestürzen
starv·a·tion Hungern *n*; ***die of starvation*** verhungern; ***starvation diet*** F Fasten-, Hungerkur *f*, Nulldiät *f*
starve hungern (lassen); ***starve (to death)*** verhungern (lassen); ***I'm starving!*** *Br* F, ***I'm starved!*** F ich komme um vor Hunger!
state **1.** Zustand *m*; Stand *m*, Lage *f*; POL (Bundes-, Einzel)Staat *m*; *often* ***State*** POL Staat *m*; **2.** Staats…, staatlich; **3.** angeben, nennen; erklären, JUR aussagen (***that*** dass); festlegen, festsetzen
State De·part·ment POL Außenministerium *n*
state·ly gemessen, würdevoll; prächtig
state·ment Statement *n*, Erklärung *f*; Angabe f; JUR Aussage *f*; ECON (*Bank-*, *Konto*)Auszug *m*; ***make a statement*** e-e Erklärung abgeben
state-of-the-art TECH neuest, modernst
states·man POL Staatsmann *m*
stat·ic statisch
sta·tion **1.** (*a. Bus-*, *U-*)Bahnhof *m*, Station *f*; (*Forschungs-*, *Rettungs- etc*)Station *f*; Tankstelle *f*; (*Feuer*)Wache *f*; (*Polizei*)Revier *n*; (*Wahl*)Lokal *n*; *radio*, TV Sender *m*, Station *f*; **2.** aufstellen, postieren; MIL stationieren
sta·tion·ar·y stehend
sta·tion·er Schreibwarenhändler(in)
sta·tion·er's (shop) Schreibwarenhandlung *f*
sta·tion·er·y Schreibwaren *pl*; Briefpapier *n*
sta·tion·mas·ter RAIL Stations-, Bahnhofsvorsteher *m*
sta·tion wag·on MOT Kombiwagen *m*
sta·tis·ti·cal statistisch
stat·is·ti·cian Statistiker *m*
sta·tis·tics Statistik(en *pl*) *f*
stat·ue Statue *f*, Standbild *n*
sta·tus Status *m*, Rechtsstellung *f*; (*Familien*)Stand *m*; Stellung *f*, Rang *m*, Status *m*
status line EDP Statuszeile *f*
stat·ute Gesetz *n*; Statut *n*, Satzung *f*
stat·ute of lim·i·ta·tions JUR Verjährungsfrist *f*; ***come under the statute of limitations*** verjähren
staunch[1] *Br* → ***stanch***
staunch[2] *Blutung* stillen
stay **1.** bleiben (***with s.o.*** bei j-m); wohnen (***at*** in *dat*; ***with s.o.*** bei j-m); ***stay put*** F sich nicht (vom Fleck) rühren; ***stay away*** wegbleiben, sich fernhalten (***from*** von); ***stay up*** aufbleiben; **2.** Aufenthalt *m*; JUR Aussetzung *f*, Aufschub *m*
stead·fast treu, zuverlässig; fest
stead·y **1.** *adj* fest; stabil; ruhig (*hand*), gut (*nerves*); gleichmäßig; **2.** (sich) beruhigen; **3.** *int a.* ***steady on!*** *Br* F Vorsicht!; **4.** *adv*: ***go steady with s.o.*** (fest) mit j-m gehen; **5.** feste Freundin, fester Freund
steak GASTR Steak *n*; (*Fisch*)Filet *n*
steal stehlen (*a. fig*); sich stehlen, (sich) schleichen (***out of*** aus)
stealth: ***by stealth*** heimlich, verstohlen
stealth·y heimlich, verstohlen
steam **1.** Dampf *m*; Dunst *m*; ***let off steam*** Dampf ablassen, *fig a.* sich Luft machen; **2.** Dampf…; **3.** *v/i* dampfen; ***steam up*** beschlagen (*mirror etc*); *v/t* GASTR dünsten, dämpfen
steam·boat Dampfboot *n*, Dampfer *m*
steam·er Dampfer *m*, Dampfschiff *n*; Dampf-, Schnellkochtopf *m*
steam·ship Dampfer *m*, Dampfschiff *n*
steel **1.** Stahl *m*; **2.** ***steel o.s. for*** sich wappnen gegen
steel·work·er Stahlarbeiter *m*
steel·works Stahlwerk *n*
steep[1] steil; *fig* stark (*rise etc*); F happig
steep[2] eintauchen (***in*** in *acc*); *Wäsche* (ein)weichen
stee·ple Kirchturm *m*

S

stee·ple·chase *horse racing*: Hindernisrennen *n*; SPORT Hindernislauf *m*
steer[1] ZO (junger) Ochse
steer[2] steuern, lenken
steer·ing col·umn MOT Lenksäule *f*
steer·ing wheel MOT Lenkrad *n*, *a.* MAR Steuerrad *n*
stein Maßkrug *m*
stem 1. BOT Stiel *m* (*a. of a wine glass etc*), Stängel *m*; LING Stamm *m*; **2. *stem from*** stammen *or* herrühren von
stench Gestank *m*
sten·cil Schablone *f*; PRINT Matrize *f*
ste·nog·ra·pher Stenotypistin *f*
step 1. Schritt *m* (*a. fig*); Stufe *f*; Sprosse *f*; **(*a pair of*) *steps*** (e-e) Tritt- *or* Stufenleiter; ***mind the step!*** Vorsicht, Stufe!; ***step by step*** Schritt für Schritt; ***take steps*** Schritte *or* et. unternehmen; **2.** gehen; treten (***in*** in *acc*; ***on*** auf *acc*); ***step on it, step on the gas*** MOT F Gas geben, auf die Tube drücken; ***step aside*** zur Seite treten; *fig* Platz machen; ***step down*** *fig* Platz machen; ***step up*** *Produktion etc* steigern
step-by-step *fig* schrittweise
step·fa·ther Stiefvater *m*
step·lad·der Tritt-, Stufenleiter *f*
step·moth·er Stiefmutter *f*
steppes GEOGR Steppe *f*
step·ping-stone *fig* Sprungbrett *n* (***to*** für)
ster·e·o 1. Stereo *n*; Stereogerät *n*, Stereoanlage *f*;**2.** Stereo…
stereo sys·tem MUS Kompaktanlage *f*
ster·ile steril (*a. fig*), *a.* unfruchtbar, MED *a.* keimfrei
ste·ril·i·ty Sterilität *f* (*a. fig*), Unfruchtbarkeit *f*
ster·il·ize MED sterilisieren
ster·ling das Pfund Sterling
stern[1] streng
stern[2] MAR Heck *n*
stew 1. *Fleisch, Gemüse* schmoren, *Obst* dünsten; ***stewed apples*** Apfelkompott *n*; **2.** Eintopf *m*; ***be in a stew*** in heller Aufregung sein
stew·ard Ordner *m*; AVIAT, MAR Steward *m*
stew·ard·ess AVIAT, MAR Stewardess *f*
stick[1] trockener Zweig; Stock *m*; ([*Eis*]-*Hockey*)Schläger *m*; (*Besen- etc-*) Stiel *m*; AVIAT (*Steuer*)Knüppel *m*; Stück *n*, Stange *f*, (*Lippen- etc*)Stift *m*, Stäbchen *n*
stick[2] *v/t* mit *e-r Nadel etc* stechen (***into*** in *acc*); *et.* kleben (***on*** auf, an *acc*); an-, festkleben (***with*** mit); stecken; F tun, stellen, setzen, legen; ***I can't stick him*** (*or **it***) *esp Br* F ich kann ihn (*or* das) nicht ausstehen *or* leiden; *v/i* kleben; kleben bleiben (***to*** an *dat*); stecken bleiben; ***stick at nothing*** vor nichts zurückschrecken; ***stick by*** F bleiben bei; F zu *j-m* halten; ***stick out*** vorstehen; abstehen; *et.* ausstrecken *or* vorstrecken; ***stick to*** bleiben bei
stick·er Aufkleber *m*
stick·ing plas·ter *Br* Heftpflaster *n*
stick·y klebrig (***with*** von); F heikel, unangenehm
stiff 1. *adj* steif; F stark (*drink etc*); schwer, hart (*task, penalty etc*); hartnäckig (*resistance*); F happig, gepfeffert, gesalzen (*price*); ***keep a stiff upper lip*** *fig* Haltung bewahren; **2.** *adv* äußerst; höchst; ***be bored stiff*** F sich zu Tode langweilen; ***be scared stiff*** e-e wahnsinnige Angst haben; ***be worried stiff*** sich furchtbare Sorgen machen
stiff·en *v/t Wäsche* stärken; versteifen; verstärken; *v/i* steif werden; sich verhärten *or* versteifen
sti·fle ersticken; *fig* unterdrücken
stile Zauntritt *m*
sti·let·to Stilett *n*
stiletto heel Bleistift-, Pfennigabsatz *m*
still[1] **1.** *adv* (immer) noch, noch immer; *with comparative*: noch; **2.** *cj* dennoch, trotzdem
still[2] **1.** *adj* still; ruhig; GASTR ohne Kohlensäure; **2.** *film*, TV Standfoto *n*
still·born MED tot geboren
still life PAINT Stillleben *n*
stilt Stelze *f*
stilt·ed *fig* gestelzt
stim·u·lant MED Stimulans *n*, Anregungs-, Aufputschmittel *n*; *fig* Anreiz *m*, Ansporn *m* (***to*** für)
stim·u·late MED stimulieren (*a. fig*), anregen, *fig a.* anspornen
stim·u·lus Reiz *m*; *fig* Anreiz *m*, Ansporn *m* (***to*** für)
sting 1. stechen (*insect*); brennen (auf *or* in *dat*); **2.** Stachel *m*; Stich *m*; Brennen *n*, brennender Schmerz
stin·gy F knaus(e)rig, knick(e)rig (*person*); mick(e)rig (*meal etc*)
stink 1. stinken (***of*** nach); ***stink up*** (*Br* ***out***) verpesten; **2.** Gestank *m*
stint: ***stint o.s.*** (***of s.th.***) sich einschränken (mit et.); ***stint*** (***on***) ***s.th.*** sparen mit et.
stip·u·late zur Bedingung machen; festsetzen, vereinbaren
stip·u·la·tion Bedingung *f*; Vereinbarung *f*
stir 1. (um)rühren; (sich) rühren *or* bewegen; *j-n* aufwühlen; ***stir up*** *Unruhe* stiften; *Streit* entfachen; *Erinnerungen* wachrufen; **2. *give s.th. a stir*** et. umrüh-

ren; ***cause*** (*or* ***create***) ***a stir*** für Aufsehen sorgen
stir·rup Steigbügel *m*
stitch 1. Stich *m*; Masche *f*; MED Seitenstechen *n*; **2.** zunähen, *Wunde* nähen (*a.* ***stitch up***); heften
stock 1. Vorrat *m* (***of*** an *dat*); GASTR Brühe *f*; *a.* ***livestock*** Viehbestand *m*; (*Gewehr*)Schaft *m*; *fig* Abstammung *f*, Herkunft *f*; ECON Aktie(n *pl*) *f*; *pl* Aktien *pl*, Wertpapiere *pl*; ***have s.th. in stock*** ECON et. vorrätig *or* auf Lager haben; ***take stock*** ECON Inventur machen; ***take stock of*** *fig* sich klar werden über (*acc*); **2.** ECON *Ware* vorrätig haben, führen; ***stock up*** sich eindecken *or* versorgen (***on, with*** mit); **3.** Serien…; Standard…; stereotyp
stock·breed·er AGR Viehzüchter *m*
stock·breed·ing AGR Viehzucht *f*
stock·brok·er ECON Börsenmakler *m*
stock ex·change ECON Börse *f*
stock·hold·er ECON Aktionär(in)
stock·ing Strumpf *m*
stock mar·ket ECON Börse *f*
stock·pile 1. Vorrat *m* (***of*** an *dat*); **2.** e-n Vorrat anlegen an (*dat*)
stock·still regungslos
stock·tak·ing ECON Inventur *f*; *fig* Bestandsaufnahme *f*
stock·y stämmig, untersetzt
stol·id gleichmütig
stom·ach 1. ANAT Magen *m*; Bauch *m*; *fig* Appetit *m* (***for*** auf *acc*); **2.** vertragen (*a. fig*)
stom·ach·ache MED Magenschmerzen *pl*, Bauchschmerzen *pl*, Bauchweh *n*
stom·ach up·set MED Magenverstimmung *f*
stone 1. Stein *m*, BOT *a.* Kern *m*; (*Hagel*)Korn *n*; **2.** mit Steinen bewerfen; steinigen; entkernen, entsteinen
stone·ma·son Steinmetz *m*
stone·ware Steingut *n*
ston·y steinig; steinern (*face etc*), eisig (*silence*)
stool Hocker *m*, Schemel *m*; MED Stuhl *m*, Stuhlgang *m*
stool·pi·geon F (Polizei)Spitzel *m*
stoop 1. *v/i* sich bücken (*a.* ***stoop down***); gebeugt gehen; ***stoop to*** *fig* sich herablassen *or* hergeben zu; **2.** gebeugte Haltung
stop 1. *v/i* (an)halten, stehen bleiben (*a. watch etc*), stoppen; aufhören; *esp Br* bleiben; ***stop dead*** plötzlich *or* abrupt stehen bleiben; ***stop at nothing*** vor nichts zurückschrecken; ***stop short of doing***, ***stop short at*** *s.th.* zurückschrecken vor (*dat*); *v/t* anhalten, stoppen; aufhören mit; ein Ende machen *or* setzen (*dat*); *Blutung* stillen; *Arbeiten*, *Verkehr etc* zum Erliegen bringen; *et.* verhindern; *j-n* abhalten (***from*** von), hindern (***from*** an *dat*); *Rohr etc* verstopfen (*a.* ***stop up***); *Zahn* füllen, plombieren; *Scheck* sperren (lassen); ***stop by*** vorbeischauen; ***stop in*** vorbeischauen (***at*** bei); ***stop off*** F kurz Halt machen; ***stop over*** kurz Halt machen; Zwischenstation machen; **2.** Halt *m*; (*Bus*)Haltestelle *f*; PHOT Blende *f*; *mst* ***full stop*** LING Punkt *m*
stop·gap Notbehelf *m*
stop·light MOT Bremslicht *n*; rotes Licht
stop·o·ver Zwischenstation *f*; AVIAT Zwischenlandung *f*
stop·page Unterbrechung *f*, Stopp *m*; Verstopfung *f*; Streik *m*; *Br* (Gehalts-, Lohn)Abzug *m*
stop·per Stöpsel *m*
stop sign MOT Stoppschild *n*
stop·watch Stoppuhr *f*
stor·age ECON Lagerung *f*; Lagergeld *n*; EDP Speicher *m*
store 1. (ein)lagern; *Energie* speichern; EDP (ab)speichern, sichern; *a.* ***store up*** sich e-n Vorrat anlegen an (*dat*); **2.** Vorrat *m*; Lager *n*, Lagerhalle *f*, Lagerhaus *n*; Laden *m*, Geschäft *n*, *esp Br* Kaufhaus *n*, Warenhaus *n*; ***set great store by*** großen Wert legen auf (*acc*)
store·house Lagerhaus *n*; *fig* Fundgrube *f*
store·keep·er Ladenbesitzer(in)
store·room Lagerraum *m*
sto·rey *Br* → ***story***[2]
…sto·reyed *Br*, **…sto·ried** mit … Stockwerken, …stöckig
stork zo Storch *m*
storm 1. Unwetter *n*; Gewitter *n*; Sturm *m*; **2.** *v/t* MIL *etc* stürmen; *v/i* stürmen, stürzen
storm·y stürmisch
sto·ry[1] Geschichte *f*; Märchen *n* (*a. fig*); Story *f*, *a.* Handlung *f*, *a.* Bericht *m* (***on*** über *acc*)
sto·ry[2] Stock *m*, Stockwerk *n*, Etage *f*
stout korpulent, vollschlank; *fig* unerschrocken; entschieden
stove Ofen *m*, Herd *m*
stow *a.* ***stow away*** verstauen
stow·a·way AVIAT, MAR blinder Passagier
strad·dle rittlings sitzen auf (*dat*)
strag·gle verstreut liegen *or* stehen; BOT *etc* wuchern; ***straggle in*** F einzeln eintrudeln
strag·gler Nachzügler(in)
strag·gly verstreut (liegend); BOT *etc* wu-

chernd; struppig (*mustache etc*)

straight **1.** *adj* gerade; glatt (*hair*); pur (*whisky etc*); aufrichtig, offen, ehrlich; *sl* hetero(*sexuell*); *sl* clean, sauber; ***put straight*** in Ordnung bringen; **2.** *adv* gerade; genau, direkt; klar; ehrlich, anständig; ***straight ahead*** geradeaus; ***straight off*** F sofort; ***straight on*** geradeaus; ***straight out*** F offen, rundheraus; **3.** SPORT (*Gegen-*, *Ziel*)Gerade *f*

straight·en *v/t* gerade machen, (gerade) richten; ***straighten out*** in Ordnung bringen; *v/i a.* ***straighten out*** gerade werden; ***straighten up*** sich aufrichten

straight·for·ward aufrichtig; einfach

strain **1.** *v/t Seil etc* (an)spannen; *sich*, *Augen etc* überanstrengen; sich *e-n Muskel etc* zerren; *Gemüse*, *Tee etc* abgießen; *v/i* sich anstrengen; ***strain at*** zerren *or* ziehen an (*dat*); **2.** Spannung *f*; Anspannung *f*; Strapaze *f*; *fig* Belastung *f*; MED Zerrung *f*

strained MED gezerrt; gezwungen (*smile etc*); gespannt (*relations*); ***look strained*** abgespannt aussehen

strain·er Sieb *n*

strait GEOGR Meerenge *f*, Straße *f*; *pl fig* Notlage *f*

strait·ened: ***live in straitened circumstances*** in beschränkten Verhältnissen leben

strand Strang *m*; Faden *m*; (*Kabel-*) Draht *m*; (*Haar*)Strähne *f*

strand·ed: ***be stranded*** MAR gestrandet sein; ***be*** (***left***) ***stranded*** *fig* festsitzen (***in*** in *dat*)

strange merkwürdig, seltsam, sonderbar; fremd

strang·er Fremde *m*, *f*

stran·gle erwürgen

strap **1.** Riemen *m*, Gurt *m*; (*Uhr*)Armband *n*; Träger *m*; **2.** festschnallen; anschnallen

stra·te·gic strategisch

strat·e·gy Strategie *f*

stra·tum GEOL Schicht *f* (*a. fig*)

straw Stroh *n*; Strohhalm *m*

straw·ber·ry BOT Erdbeere *f*

stray **1.** (herum)streunen; sich verirren; *fig* abschweifen (***from*** von); **2.** verirrtes *or* streunendes Tier; **3.** verirrt (*bullet*, *dog etc*); streunend (*dog etc*); vereinzelt

streak **1.** Streifen *m*; Strähne *f*; (Charakter)Zug *m*; ***a streak of lightning*** ein Blitz; ***lucky streak*** Glückssträhne *f*; **2.** flitzen; streifen

streak·y streifig; GASTR durchwachsen

stream **1.** Bach *m*; Strömung *f*; *fig* Strom *m*; **2.** strömen; flattern, wehen

stream·er Luft-, Papierschlange *f*; Wimpel *m*; EDP Streamer *m*

street **1.** Straße *f*; ***on*** (*esp Br* ***in***) ***the street*** auf der Straße; **2.** Straßen…

street·car Straßenbahn(wagen *m*) *f*

street sweep·er Straßenkehrer *m*

strength Stärke *f*, Kraft *f*, Kräfte *pl*

strength·en *v/t* (ver)stärken; *v/i* stärker werden

stren·u·ous anstrengend, strapaziös; unermüdlich

stress **1.** *fig* Stress *m*; PHYS, TECH Beanspruchung *f*, Belastung *f*, Druck *m*; LING Betonung *f*; *fig* Nachdruck *m*; **2.** betonen

stress·ful stressig, aufreibend

stretch **1.** *v/t* strecken; (aus)weiten, dehnen; spannen; *fig* es nicht allzu genau nehmen mit; ***stretch out*** ausstrecken; ***be fully stretched*** *fig* richtig gefordert werden; voll ausgelastet sein; *v/i* sich dehnen, *a.* länger *or* weiter werden; sich dehnen *or* recken *or* strecken; sich erstrecken; ***stretch out*** sich ausstrecken; **2.** Dehnbarkeit *f*, Elastizität *f*; Strecke *f*; SPORT (*Gegen-*, *Ziel*)Gerade *f*; Zeit *f*, Zeitraum *m*, Zeitspanne *f*; ***have a stretch*** sich dehnen *or* recken *or* strecken

stretch·er Trage *f*

strick·en schwer betroffen; ***stricken with*** befallen *or* ergriffen von

strict streng, strikt; genau; ***strictly*** (***speaking***) genau genommen

strict·ness Strenge *f*

stride **1.** schreiten, mit großen Schritten gehen; **2.** großer Schritt

strife Streit *m*

strike **1.** *v/t* schlagen; treffen; einschlagen in (*acc*) (*lightning*); *Streichholz* anzünden; MAR auflaufen auf (*acc*); streichen (***from***, ***off*** aus *dat*, von); stoßen auf (*acc*); *j-n* beeindrucken; *j-m* einfallen, in den Sinn kommen; *Münze* prägen; *Saite etc* anschlagen; *Lager*, *Zelt* abbrechen; *Flagge*, *Segel* streichen; ***strike out*** (aus)streichen; ***strike up*** *Lied etc* anstimmen; *Freundschaft etc* schließen; *v/i* schlagen; einschlagen; ECON streiken; ***strike*** (***out***) ***at s.o.*** auf j-n einschlagen; **2.** ECON Streik *m*; (*Öl- etc*)Fund *m*; MIL Angriff *m*; *soccer*: Schuss *m*; ***be on strike*** streiken; ***go on strike*** streiken, in den Streik treten; ***a lucky strike*** ein Glückstreffer

strik·er ECON Streikende *m*, *f*; *soccer*: Stürmer(in)

strik·ing apart; auffallend

string **1.** Schnur *f*, Bindfaden *m*; (*Schürzen-*, *Schuh- etc*)Band *n*; (*Puppenspiel-*)

S

Faden *m*, Draht *m*; (*Perlen- etc*)Schnur *f*; MUS, SPORT Saite *f*; (*Bogen*)Sehne *f*; BOT Faser *f*; EDP Zeichenfolge *f*; *fig* Reihe *f*, Serie *f*; ***the strings*** MUS die Streichinstrumente *pl*, die Streicher *pl*; ***pull a few strings*** *fig* ein paar Beziehungen spielen lassen; ***with no strings attached*** *fig* ohne Bedingungen; **2.** *Perlen etc* aufreihen; *Gitarre etc* besaiten, *Tennisschläger etc* bespannen; *Bohnen* abziehen; **3.** MUS Streich…

string bean BOT grüne Bohne

strin·gent streng

string·y fas(e)rig

strip 1. *v/i*: *a.* ***strip off*** sich ausziehen (***to*** bis auf *acc*); *v/t* ausziehen; *Farbe etc* abkratzen, *Tapete etc* abreißen (***from, off*** von); *a.* ***strip down*** TECH zerlegen, auseinandernehmen; ***strip s.o. of s.th.*** j-m et. rauben *or* wegnehmen; **2.** (*Land-, Papier- etc*)Streifen *m*; Strip *m*

stripe Streifen *m*

striped gestreift

strive: ***strive for*** *or* ***after*** streben nach

stroke 1. streicheln; streichen über (*acc*); **2.** Schlag *m* (*a.* SPORT); MED Schlag(anfall) *m*; (*Pinsel*)Strich *m*; *swimming*: Zug *m*; TECH Hub *m*; → ***four-stroke engine***; ***stroke of lightning*** Blitzschlag *m*; ***a stroke of luck*** *fig* ein glücklicher Zufall, ein Glücksfall

stroll 1. bummeln, spazieren; **2.** Bummel *m*, Spaziergang *m*

stroll·er Bummler(in), Spaziergänger(in); Sportwagen *m*

strong stark (*a.* GASTR, PHARM); kräftig; mächtig; stabil; fest; robust

strong·box (Geld-, Stahl)Kassette *f*

strong·hold Festung *f*; Stützpunkt *m*; *fig* Hochburg *f*

strong-mind·ed willensstark

strong room Tresor(raum) *m*

struc·ture Struktur *f*; (Auf)Bau *m*, Gliederung *f*; Bau *m*, Konstruktion *f*

strug·gle 1. kämpfen, ringen (***with*** mit; ***for*** um); sich abmühen; sich winden, zappeln; ***struggle against*** sich sträuben gegen; **2.** Kampf *m*

strum klimpern auf (*dat*) (*or* ***on*** auf *dat*)

strut[1] stolzieren

strut[2] TECH Strebe *f*; Stütze *f*

stub 1. (*Bleistift-, Zigaretten- etc*)Stummel *m*; Kontrollabschnitt *m*; **2.** sich *die Zehe* anstoßen; ***stub out*** *Zigarette* ausdrücken

stub·ble Stoppeln *pl*

stub·bly stoppelig

stub·born eigensinnig, stur; hartnäckig

stub·born·ness Starrsinn *m*

stuck-up F hochnäsig

stud[1] **1.** (*Kragen-, Manschetten*)Knopf *m*; *soccer*: Stollen *m*; Beschlagnagel *m*; Ziernagel *m*; *pl* MOT Spikes *pl*; **2.** ***be studded with*** besetzt sein mit; übersät sein mit; ***studded tires*** Spikesreifen *pl*

stud[2] Gestüt *n*

stu·dent Student(in); Schüler(in)

stud farm Gestüt *n*

stud horse ZO Zuchthengst *m*

stud·ied wohlüberlegt; gesucht

stu·di·o Studio *n*; Atelier *n*; *a.* ***studio apartment***, *Br* ***studio flat*** Studio *n*, Einzimmerappartement *n*

studio couch Schlafcouch *f*

stu·di·ous fleißig

stud·y 1. Studium *n*; Studie *f*, Untersuchung *f*; Arbeitszimmer *n*; *pl* Studium *n*; ***be in a brown study*** in Gedanken versunken *or* geistesabwesend sein; **2.** studieren; lernen (***for*** für)

stuff 1. Zeug *n*; **2.** (aus)stopfen, stopfen, vollstopfen; füllen (*a.* GASTR); ***stuff o.s.*** F sich vollstopfen

stuff·ing Füllung *f* (*a.* GASTR)

stuff·y stickig; spießig; prüde

stum·ble 1. stolpern (***on, over***, *fig* ***at, over*** über *acc*); ***stumble across, stumble on*** stoßen auf (*acc*); **2.** Stolpern *n*

stump 1. Stumpf *m*; Stummel *m*; **2.** stampfen, stapfen

stump·y F kurz und dick

stun betäuben; *fig* sprachlos machen

stun·ning fantastisch; unglaublich

stunt[1] (*das Wachstum gen*) hemmen; ***stunted*** BIOL verkümmert; ***become stunted*** BIOL verkümmern

stunt[2] (*Film*)Stunt *m*; (*gefährliches*) Kunststück; (*Reklame*)Gag *m*

stunt man *film*, TV Stuntman *m*, Double *n*

stunt wom·an *film*, TV Stuntwoman *f*, Double *n*

stu·pid dumm; F blöd

stu·pid·i·ty Dummheit *f*

stu·por Betäubung *f*; ***in a drunken stupor*** im Vollrausch

stur·dy kräftig, stämmig; *fig* entschlossen, hartnäckig

stut·ter 1. stottern (*a.* MOT); stammeln; **2.** Stottern *n*, Stammeln *n*

sty[1] → ***pigsty***

sty[2], **stye** MED Gerstenkorn *n*

style 1. Stil *m*; Ausführung *f*; Mode *f*; **2.** entwerfen; gestalten

styl·ish stilvoll; modisch, elegant

styl·ist Stilist(in)

Sty·ro·foam® Styropor® *n*

suave verbindlich

sub·con·scious Unterbewusstsein *n*; ***subconsciously*** im Unterbewusstsein

sub·di·vi·sion Unterteilung *f*; Unterabteilung *f*
sub·due unterwerfen; *Ärger etc* unterdrücken
sub·dued gedämpft (*light, voice etc*); ruhig, still (*person*)
sub·ject **1.** Thema *n*; PED, UNIV Fach *n*; LING Subjekt *n*, Satzgegenstand *m*; Untertan(in); Staatsangehörige *m, f*, -bürger(in); **2** *adj*: ***subject to*** anfällig für; ***be subject to*** *a.* neigen zu; ***be subject to*** unterliegen (*dat*); abhängen von; ***prices subject to change*** Preisänderungen vorbehalten; **1.** unterwerfen; ***subject to*** *e-m Test etc* unterziehen; *der Kritik etc* aussetzen
sub·jec·tion Unterwerfung *f*; Abhängigkeit *f* (***to*** von)
sub·ju·gate unterjochen, unterwerfen
sub·junc·tive LING *a.* ***subjunctive mood*** Konjunktiv *m*
sub·lease, **sub·let** untervermieten, weitervermieten
sub·lime großartig; *fig* total
sub·ma·chine gun Maschinenpistole *f*
sub·ma·rine **1.** unterseeisch; **2.** Unterseeboot *n*, U-Boot *n*
sub·merge tauchen; (ein)tauchen (***in*** in *acc*)
sub·mis·sion Einreichung *f*; *boxing etc*: Aufgabe *f*; Unterwerfung *f* (***to*** unter)
sub·mis·sive unterwürfig
sub·mit *Gesuch etc* einreichen (***to*** *dat or* bei); sich fügen (***to*** *dat or* in *acc*); *boxing etc*: aufgeben
sub·or·di·nate **1.** untergeordnet (***to*** *dat*); **2.** Untergebene *m, f*; **3.** ***subordinate to*** unterordnen (*dat*), zurückstellen (hinter *acc*)
subordinate clause LING Nebensatz *m*
sub·scribe *v/t Geld* gegen, spenden (***to*** für); *v/i*: ***subscribe to*** *Zeitung etc* abonnieren
sub·scrib·er Abonnent(in); TEL Teilnehmer(in)
sub·scrip·tion Abonnement *n*; (Mitglieds)Beitrag *m*
sub·se·quent später
sub·side sich senken (*building, road etc*); zurückgehen (*flood, demand etc*), sich legen (*storm, anger etc*)
sub·sid·i·a·ry **1.** Neben…; ***subsidiary question*** Zusatzfrage *f*; **2.** ECON Tochtergesellschaft *f*
sub·si·dize subventionieren
sub·si·dy Subvention *f*
sub·sist leben, existieren (***on*** von)
sub·sis·tence Existenz *f*
sub·stance Substanz *f* (*a. fig*), Stoff *m*; *das* Wesentliche, Kern *m*
sub·stan·dard minderwertig
sub·stan·tial solid (*furniture etc*); beträchtlich (*salary etc*), (*changes etc a.*) wesentlich; reichlich, kräftig (*meal*)
sub·stan·ti·ate beweisen
sub·stan·tive LING Substantiv *n*, Hauptwort *n*
sub·sti·tute **1.** Ersatz *m*; Stellvertreter(in), Vertretung *f*; SPORT Auswechselspieler(in), Ersatzspieler(in); **2.** ***substitute s.th. for s.th.*** et. durch et. ersetzen, et. gegen et. austauschen *or* auswechseln; ***substitute for*** einspringen für, *j-n* vertreten
sub·sti·tu·tion Ersatz *m*; SPORT Austausch *m*, Auswechslung *f*
sub·ter·fuge List *f*
sub·ter·ra·ne·an unterirdisch
sub·ti·tle Untertitel *m*
sub·tle fein (*differences etc*); raffiniert (*plan etc*); scharf (*mind*); scharfsinnig
sub·tract MATH abziehen, subtrahieren (***from*** von)
sub·trac·tion MATH Abziehen *n*, Subtraktion *f*
sub·trop·i·cal subtropisch
sub·urb Vorort *m*, Vorstadt *f*
sub·ur·ban Vorort…, vorstädtisch, Vorstadt…
sub·ver·sive umstürzlerisch, subversiv
sub·way Unterführung *f*; U-Bahn *f*
suc·ceed *v/i* Erfolg haben, erfolgreich sein, (*plan etc a.*) gelingen; ***succeed to*** in *e-m Amt* nachfolgen; ***succeed to the throne*** auf dem Thron folgen; *v/t*: ***succeed s.o. as*** j-s Nachfolger werden als
suc·cess Erfolg *m*
suc·cess·ful erfolgreich
suc·ces·sion Folge *f*; Erb-, Nach-, Thronfolge *f*; ***five times in succession*** fünfmal hintereinander; ***in quick succession*** in rascher Folge
suc·ces·sive aufeinanderfolgend
suc·ces·sor Nachfolger(in); Thronfolger(in)
suc·cu·lent GASTR saftig
such solche(r, -s); derartige(r, -s); so; derart; ***such a*** so ein(e)
suck **1.** *v/t* saugen; lutschen (an *dat*); *v/i* saugen (***at*** an *dat*); **2.** ***have*** *or* ***take a suck at*** saugen *or* lutschen an (*dat*)
suck·er zo Saugnapf *m*, Saugorgan *n*; TECH Saugfuß *m*; BOT Wurzelschössling *m*, Wurzelspross *m*; F Trottel *m*, Simpel *m*; Lutscher *m*
suck·le säugen, stillen
suc·tion (An)Saugen *n*; Saugwirkung *f*

suction pump TECH Saugpumpe *f*
sud·den plötzlich, unvermittelt; ***all of a sudden*** F ganz plötzlich
sud·den·ly plötzlich
suds Seifenschaum *m*
sue JUR *j-n* verklagen (***for*** auf *acc*, wegen); klagen (***for*** auf *acc*)
suede, **suède** Wildleder *n*, Velours(-leder) *n*
su·et GASTR Nierenfett *n*, Talg *m*
suf·fer *v/i* leiden (***from*** an *dat*, unter *dat*); darunter leiden; *v/t* erleiden; *Folgen* tragen
suf·fer·er Leidende *m*, *f*
suf·fer·ing Leiden *n*; Leid *n*
suf·fi·cient genügend, genug, ausreichend; ***be sufficient*** genügen, (aus)reichen
suf·fix LING Suffix *n*, Nachsilbe *f*
suf·fo·cate ersticken
suf·frage POL Wahl-, Stimmrecht *n*
suf·fuse durchfluten (*light etc*); überziehen (*color etc*)
sug·ar **1.** Zucker *m*; **2.** zuckern
sug·ar beet BOT Zuckerrübe *f*
sug·ar bowl Zuckerdose *f*
sug·ar·cane BOT Zuckerrohr *n*
sug·ar tongs Zuckerzange *f*
sug·ar·y süß; *fig* süßlich
sug·gest vorschlagen, anregen; hindeuten *or* hinweisen auf (*acc*), schließen lassen auf (*acc*); andeuten
sug·ges·tion Vorschlag *m*, Anregung *f*; Anflug *m*, Spur *f*; Andeutung *f*; PSYCH Suggestion *f*
sug·ges·tive zweideutig (*remark etc*), vielsagend (*look etc*)
su·i·cide Selbstmord *m*; Selbstmörder(in); ***commit suicide*** Selbstmord begehen
suit **1.** Anzug *m*; Kostüm *n*; *card game*: Farbe *f*; JUR Prozess *m*; ***follow suit*** *fig* dem Beispiel folgen, dasselbe tun; **2.** *v/t j-m* passen (*date etc*); *j-n* kleiden, *j-m* stehen; *et.* anpassen (***to*** *dat*); ***suit s.th., be suited to s.th.*** geeignet sein *or* sich eignen für; ***suit yourself!*** mach, was du willst!
sui·ta·ble passend, geeignet (***for, to*** für)
suit·case Koffer *m*
suite (*Möbel-*, *Sitz*)Garnitur *f*; Suite *f*, Zimmerflucht *f*; MUS Suite *f*; Gefolge *n*
sul·fur CHEM Schwefel *m*
sul·fu·ric ac·id CHEM Schwefelsäure *f*
sulk schmollen, F eingeschnappt sein
sulk·y schmollend, F eingeschnappt
sul·len mürrisch, verdrossen
sul·phur *Br* → ***sulfur***
sul·phu·ric ac·id *Br* → ***sulfuric acid***
sul·try schwül; aufreizend (*look etc*)
sum **1.** Summe *f*; Betrag *m*; (einfache) Rechenaufgabe; ***do sums*** rechnen; **2.** ***sum up*** zusammenfassen; *j-n*, *et.* abschätzen
sum·mar·ize zusammenfassen
sum·ma·ry Zusammenfassung *f*, (kurze) Inhaltsangabe
sum·mer Sommer *m*; ***in (the) summer*** im Sommer
summer camp Ferienlager *n*
summer hol·i·days *Br* Sommerferien *pl*
summer resort Sommerfrische *f*
summer school Ferienkurs *m*
sum·mer·time Sommer *m*, Sommerszeit *f*; ***in (the) summertime*** im Sommer
sum·mer time *esp Br* Sommerzeit *f*
summer va·ca·tion Sommerferien *pl*
sum·mer·y sommerlich, Sommer…
sum·mit Gipfel *m* (*a.* ECON, POL, *fig*)
summit con·fe·rence POL Gipfelkonferenz *f*
summit meet·ing POL Gipfeltreffen *n*
sum·mon auffordern; *Versammlung etc* einberufen; JUR vorladen; ***summon up*** *Kraft, Mut etc* zusammenehmen
sum·mons JUR Vorladung *f*
sump *Br* MOT Ölwanne *f*
sump·tu·ous luxuriös, aufwändig
sun **1.** Sonne *f*; **2.** Sonnen…; **3.** ***sun o.s.*** sich sonnen
Sun ABBR *of* ***Sunday*** So., Sonntag *m*
sun·bathe sich sonnen, ein Sonnenbad nehmen
sun·beam Sonnenstrahl *m*
sun·bed Sonnenbank *f*
sun·burn Sonnenbrand *m*
sun cream Sonnencreme *f*
sun·dae GASTR Eisbecher *m*
Sun·day (ABBR ***Sun***) Sonntag *m*; ***on Sunday*** (am) Sonntag; ***on Sundays*** sonntags
sun·dial Sonnenuhr *f*
sun·dries Diverses, Verschiedenes
sun·dry diverse, verschiedene
sun·glass·es (***a pair of sunglasses*** e-e) Sonnenbrille *f*
sunk·en MAR gesunken, versunken; versenkt; tief liegend; eingefallen (*cheeks*), (*a. eyes*) eingesunken
sun·light Sonnenlicht *n*
sun·lit sonnenbeschienen
sun·ny sonnig
sun·rise Sonnenaufgang *m*; ***at sunrise*** bei Sonnenaufgang
sun·roof Dachterrasse *f*; MOT Schiebedach *n*
sun·set Sonnenuntergang *m*; ***at sunset*** bei Sonnenuntergang
sun·shade Sonnenschirm *m*
sun·shine Sonnenschein *m*

sun·stroke MED Sonnenstich *m*
sun·tan (Sonnen)Bräune *f*
suntan lo·tion Sonnenschutz *m*, Sonnencreme *f*
suntan oil Sonnenöl *n*
su·per F super, spitze, klasse
su·per... Über..., über...
su·per·a·bun·dant überreichlich
su·per·an·nu·at·ed pensioniert, im Ruhestand
su·perb ausgezeichnet
su·per·charg·er MOT Kompressor *m*
su·per·cil·i·ous hochmütig, F hochnäsig
su·per·fi·cial oberflächlich
su·per·flu·ous überflüssig
su·per·hu·man übermenschlich
su·per·im·pose überlagern; *Bild etc* einblenden (***on*** in *acc*)
su·per·in·tend die (Ober)Aufsicht haben über (*acc*), überwachen; leiten
su·per·in·tend·ent Aufsicht *f*, Aufsichtsbeamter *m*, -beamtin *f*; *Br* Kriminalrat *m*
su·pe·ri·or 1. ranghöher (***to*** als); überlegen (***to*** *dat*), besser (***to*** als); ausgezeichnet, hervorragend; überheblich, überlegen; ***Father Superior*** REL Superior *m*; ***Mother Superior*** REL Oberin *f*; 2. Vorgesetzte *m, f*
su·peri·or·i·ty Überlegenheit *f* (***over*** gegenüber)
su·per·la·tive 1. höchste(r, -s), überragend; 2. *a.* ***superlative degree*** LING Superlativ *m*
su·per·mar·ket Supermarkt *m*
su·per·nat·u·ral übernatürlich
su·per·nu·me·ra·ry zusätzlich
su·per·sede ablösen, ersetzen, verdrängen
su·per·son·ic AVIAT, PHYS Überschall...
su·per·sti·tion Aberglaube *m*
su·per·sti·tious abergläubisch
su·per·store Großmarkt *m*
su·per·vene dazwischenkommen
su·per·vise beaufsichtigen, überwachen
su·per·vi·sion Beaufsichtigung *f*, Überwachung *f*; ***under s.o.'s supervision*** unter j-s Aufsicht
su·per·vi·sor Aufseher(in), Aufsicht *f*
sup·per Abendessen *n*; ***have supper*** zu Abend essen; → ***lord***
sup·plant verdrängen
sup·ple gelenkig, geschmeidig, biegsam
sup·ple·ment 1. Ergänzung *f*; Nachtrag *m*, Anhang *m*; Ergänzungsband *m*; (*Zeitungs- etc*)Beilage *f*; 2. ergänzen
sup·ple·men·ta·ry ergänzend, zusätzlich
sup·pli·er ECON Lieferant(in), *a. pl* Lieferfirma *f*
sup·ply 1. liefern; stellen, sorgen für; *j-n, et.* versorgen, ECON beliefern (***with*** mit); 2. Lieferung *f* (***to*** an *acc*); Versorgung *f*; ECON Angebot *n*; *mst pl* Vorrat *m* (***of*** an *dat*), *a.* Proviant *m*, MIL Nachschub *m*; ***supply and demand*** ECON Angebot und Nachfrage
sup·port 1. (ab)stützen, *Gewicht etc* tragen; *Währung* stützen; unterstützen; unterhalten, sorgen für; 2. Stütze *f*; TECH Träger *m*; *fig* Unterstützung *f*
sup·port·er Anhänger(in) (*a.* SPORT), Befürworter(in)
sup·pose 1. annehmen, vermuten; ***be supposed to ...*** sollen; ***what is that supposed to mean?*** was soll denn das?; ***I suppose so*** ich nehme es an, vermutlich; 2. *cj* angenommen; wie wäre es, wenn
sup·posed angeblich, vermeintlich
sup·pos·ing → ***suppose*** *2*
sup·po·si·tion Annahme *f*, Vermutung *f*
sup·pos·i·to·ry PHARM Zäpfchen *n*
sup·press unterdrücken
sup·pres·sion Unterdrückung *f*
sup·pu·rate MED eitern
su·prem·a·cy Vormachtstellung *f*
su·preme höchste(r, -s), oberste(r, -s), Ober...; größte(r, -s)
sur·charge 1. Nachporto *or* e-n Zuschlag erheben (***on*** auf *acc*); 2. Aufschlag *m*, Zuschlag *m* (***on*** auf *acc*); Nach-, Strafporto *n* (***on*** auf *acc*)
sure 1. *adj* sicher; ***sure of o.s.*** selbstsicher; ***sure of winning*** siegessicher; ***sure thing!*** F (aber) klar!; ***be*** *or* ***feel sure*** sicher sein; ***be sure to ...*** vergiss nicht zu ...; ***for sure*** ganz sicher *or* bestimmt; ***make sure that*** sich (davon) überzeugen, dass; ***to be sure*** sicher(lich); 2. *adv* F sicher, klar; ***sure enough*** tatsächlich
sure·ly sicher(lich)
sur·e·ty JUR Bürge *m*, Bürgin *f*; Bürgschaft *f*, Sicherheit *f*; ***stand surety for s.o.*** für j-n bürgen
surf 1. Brandung *f*; 2. SPORT surfen
sur·face 1. Oberfläche *f*; (*Straßen*)Belag *m*; 2. auftauchen; *Straße* mit e-m Belag versehen; 3. Oberflächen...; *fig* oberflächlich; ***surface mail*** gewöhnliche Post
surf·board Surfboard *n*, Surfbrett *n*
surf·er Surfer(in), Wellenreiter(in)
surf·ing Surfen *n*, Wellenreiten *n*
surge 1. *fig* Welle *f*, Woge *f*, (*Gefühls*)Aufwallung *f*; 2. (vorwärts-)drängen; ***surge*** (***up***) aufwallen
sur·geon MED Chirurg(in)
sur·ge·ry MED Chirurgie *f*; operativer Eingriff, Operation *f*; *Br* Sprechzimmer *n*; *Br* Sprechstunde *f*; *a.* ***doctor's sur-***

S

gery Arztpraxis *f*
surgery hours MED *Br* Sprechstunde(n *pl*) *f*
sur·gi·cal MED chirurgisch
sur·ly mürrisch, unwirsch
sure·name Familienname *m*, Nachname *m*, Zuname *m*
sur·pass *Erwartungen etc* übertreffen
sur·plus **1.** Überschuss *m* (***of*** an *dat*); **2.** überschüssig
sur·prise **1.** Überraschung *f*, Verwunderung *f*; ***take s.o. by surprise*** j-n überraschen; **2.** überraschen; ***be surprised at*** *or* ***by*** überrascht sein über (*acc*)
sur·ren·der **1.** *v/i* ***surrender to*** MIL, *a. fig* sich ergeben (*dat*), kapitulieren vor (*dat*); ***surrender to the police*** sich der Polizei stellen; *v/t et.* übergeben, ausliefern (***to*** *dat*); aufgeben, verzichten auf (*acc*); ***surrender o.s. to the police*** sich der Polizei stellen; **2.** MIL Kapitulation *f* (*a. fig*); Aufgabe *f*, Verzicht *m*
sur·ro·gate Ersatz *m*
sur·ro·gate moth·er Leihmutter *f*
sur·round umgeben; umstellen
sur·round·ing umliegend
sur·round·ings Umgebung *f*
sur·vey **1.** (sich) *et.* betrachten (*a. fig*); *Haus etc* begutachten; *Land* vermessen; **2.** Umfrage *f*; Überblick *m* (***of*** über *acc*); Begutachtung *f*; Vermessung *f*
sur·vey·or Gutachter *m*; Land(ver)-messer *m*
sur·viv·al Überleben *n* (*a. fig*); Überbleibsel *n*
survival in·stinct Selbsterhaltungstrieb *m*
survival kit Überlebensausrüstung *f*
survival train·ing Überlebenstraining *n*
sur·vive überleben; *Feuer etc* überstehen; erhalten bleiben *or* sein
sur·vi·vor Überlebende *m, f* (***from, of*** *gen*)
sus·cep·ti·ble empfänglich, anfällig (*both*: ***to*** für)
sus·pect **1.** *j-n* verdächtigen (***of*** *gen*); *et.* vermuten; *et.* anzweifeln, *et.* bezweifeln; **2.** Verdächtige *m, f*; **3.** verdächtig, suspekt
sus·pend *Verkauf, Zahlungen etc* (vorübergehend) einstellen; JUR *Verfahren, Urteil* aussetzen; *Strafe* zur Bewährung aussetzen; *j-n* suspendieren; vorübergehend ausschließen (***from*** aus); SPORT *j-n* sperren; (auf)hängen; ***be suspended*** schweben
sus·pend·er *Br* Strumpfhalter *m*, Straps *m*; Sockenhalter *m*; (*a.* ***a pair of***) ***suspenders*** Hosenträger *pl*
sus·pense Spannung *f*; ***in suspense*** gespannt, voller Spannung
sus·pen·sion (vorübergehende) Einstellung; Suspendierung *f*; vorübergehender Ausschluss; SPORT Sperre *f*; MOT *etc* Aufhängung *f*
suspension bridge Hängebrücke *f*
suspension rail·way *esp Br* Schwebebahn *f*
sus·pi·cion Verdacht *m*; Verdächtigung *f*; Argwohn *m*, Misstrauen *n*; *fig* Hauch *m*, Spur *f*
sus·pi·cious verdächtig; argwöhnisch, misstrauisch; ***become suspicious*** Verdacht schöpfen
sus·tain *j-n* stärken; *Interesse etc* aufrechterhalten; *Schaden, Verlust* erleiden; JUR *e-m Einspruch etc* stattgeben
swab MED **1.** Tupfer *m*; Abstrich *m*; **2.** *Wunde* abtupfen
swad·dle *Baby* wickeln
swag·ger stolzieren
swal·low[1] **1.** schlucken (*a.* F); hinunterschlucken; ***swallow up*** *fig* schlucken, verschlingen; **2.** Schluck *m*
swal·low[2] ZO Schwalbe *f*
swamp **1.** Sumpf *m*; **2.** überschwemmen; ***be swamped with*** *fig* überschwemmt werden mit
swamp·y sumpfig
swan ZO Schwan *m*
swank **1.** F *esp Br* angeben; **2.** F *esp Br* Angeber(in); Angabe *f*; **3.** F piekfein
swank·y F piekfein; *esp Br* angeberisch
swap F **1.** (ein)tauschen; **2.** Tausch *m*
swarm **1.** ZO Schwarm *m* (*a. fig*); **2.** ZO schwärmen, *fig a.* strömen; *a. fig* wimmeln (***with*** von)
swar·thy dunkel (*skin*), dunkelhäutig (*person*)
swas·ti·ka Hakenkreuz *n*
swat *Fliege etc* totschlagen
sway **1.** *v/i* sich wiegen, schaukeln; ***sway between*** *fig* schwanken zwischen (*dat*); *v/t* hin- und herbewegen, schwenken, *s-n Körper* wiegen; beeinflussen; **2.** Schwanken *n*, Schaukeln *n*
swear fluchen; schwören; ***swear at s.o.*** j-n wüst beschimpfen; ***swear by*** *fig* F schwören auf (*acc*); ***swear s.o. in*** JUR j-n vereidigen
sweat **1.** *v/i* schwitzen (***with*** vor *dat*); v/t: ***sweat out*** *Krankheit* ausschwitzen; ***sweat blood*** F sich abrackern (***over*** mit); **2.** Schweiß *m*; F Schufterei *f*; ***get in(to) a sweat*** *fig* F ins Schwitzen geraten *or* kommen
sweat·er Pullover *m*
sweat·shirt Sweatshirt *n*

S

sweat·y schweißig, verschwitzt; nach Schweiß riechend, Schweiß…; schweißtreibend
Swede Schwede *m*, Schwedin *f*
Swe·den Schweden *n*
Swe·dish 1. schwedisch; **2.** LING Schwedisch *n*
sweep 1. *v/t* kehren, fegen; *fig* fegen über (*acc*) (*storm etc*); *Horizont etc* absuchen (***for*** nach); *fig Land etc* überschwemmen; ***sweep along*** mitreißen; *v/i* kehren, fegen; rauschen (*person*); **2.** Kehren *n*, Fegen *n*; Hieb *m*, Schlag *m*; F Schornsteinfeger *m*, Kaminkehrer *m*; ***give the floor a good sweep*** den Boden gründlich kehren *or* fegen; ***make a clean sweep*** gründlich aufräumen; SPORT gründlich abräumen
sweep·er (*Straßen*)Kehrer *m*; Kehrmaschine *f*; *soccer*: Libero *m*
sweep·ing durchgreifend (*changes etc*); pauschal, zu allgemein
sweep·ings Kehricht *m*
sweet 1. süß (*a. fig*); lieblich; lieb; ***sweet nothings*** Zärtlichkeiten *pl*; ***have a sweet tooth*** gern naschen; **2.** *Br* Süßigkeit *f*, Bonbon *m, n*; *Br* Nachtisch *m*
sweet corn *esp Br* BOT Zuckermais *m*
sweet·en süßen
sweet·heart Schatz *m*, Liebste *m, f*
sweet pea BOT Gartenwicke *f*
sweet shop *esp Br* Süßwarengeschäft *n*
swell 1. *v/i a.* ***swell up*** MED (an)schwellen; *a.* ***swell out*** sich blähen; *v/t fig Zahl etc* anwachsen lassen; *a.* ***swell out*** *Segel* blähen; **2.** MAR Dünung *f*; **3.** F klasse
swell·ing MED Schwellung *f*
swel·ter vor Hitze fast umkommen
swerve 1. schwenken (***to the left*** nach links), e-n Schwenk machen; *fig* abweichen (***from*** von); **2.** Schwenk *m*, Schwenkung *f*, MOT *etc a.* Schlenker *m*
swift schnell
swim 1. *v/i* schwimmen; *fig* verschwimmen; ***my head was swimming*** mir drehte sich alles; *v/t Strecke* schwimmen; *Fluss etc* durchschwimmen; **2.** Schwimmen *n*; ***go for a swim*** schwimmen gehen
swim·mer Schwimmer(in)
swim·ming Schwimmen *n*
swimming bath(s) *Br* Schwimmbad *n*, *esp* Hallenbad *n*
swimming cap Badekappe *f*, Bademütze *f*
swimming costume Badeanzug *m*
swimming pool Swimmingpool *m*, Schwimmbecken *n*
swimming trunks Badehose *f*
swim·suit Badeanzug *m*
swin·dle 1. *j-n* beschwindeln (***out of*** um); **2.** Schwindel *m*
swine zo Schwein *n* (*a.* F *fig*)
swing 1. *v/i* (hin- und her)schwingen; sich schwingen; einbiegen, -schwenken (***into*** in *acc*); MUS schwungvoll spielen (*band etc*); Schwung haben (*music*); ***swing round*** sich ruckartig umdrehen; ***swing shut*** zuschlagen (*door etc*); *v/t* et., *die Arme etc* schwingen; **2.** Schwingen *n*; Schaukel *f*; *fig* Schwung *m*; *fig* Umschwung *m*; ***in full swing*** in vollem Gang
swing door Pendeltür *f*
swin·ish ekelhaft
swipe 1. Schlag *m*; **2.** schlagen (***at*** nach)
swirl 1. wirbeln; **2.** Wirbel *m*
swish[1] **1.** *v/i* sausen, zischen; rascheln (*silk etc*); *v/t* mit *dem Schwanz* schlagen; **2.** Sausen *n*, Zischen *n*; Rascheln *n*; Schlagen *n*
swish[2] *Br* feudal, schick
Swiss 1. schweizerisch, eidgenössisch, Schweizer…; **2.** Schweizer(in); ***the Swiss*** die Schweizer *pl*
switch 1. ELECTR, TECH Schalter *m*; RAIL Weiche *f*; Gerte *f*, Rute *f*; *fig* Umstellung *f*; **2.** ELECTR, TECH (um)schalten (*a.* ***switch over***) (***to*** auf *acc*); RAIL rangieren; wechseln (***to*** zu); ***switch off*** abschalten, ausschalten; ***switch on*** anschalten, einschalten
switch·board ELECTR Schalttafel *f*; (Telefon)Zentrale *f*
Swit·zer·land die Schweiz
swiv·el (sich) drehen
swiv·el chair Drehstuhl *m*
swoon in Ohnmacht fallen
swoop 1. *fig* F zuschlagen (*police etc*); *a.* ***swoop down*** zo herabstoßen (***on*** auf *acc*); ***swoop on*** F herfallen über (*acc*); **2.** Razzia *f*
swop F → ***swap***
sword Schwert *n*
syc·a·more BOT Bergahorn *m*; Platane *f*
syl·la·ble Silbe *f*
syl·la·bus PED, UNIV Lehrplan *m*
sym·bol Symbol *n*
sym·bol·ic symbolisch
sym·bol·is·m Symbolik *f*
sym·bol·ize symbolisieren
sym·met·ri·cal symmetrisch
sym·me·try Symmetrie *f*
sym·pa·thet·ic mitfühlend; verständnisvoll; wohlwollend
sym·pa·thize mitfühlen; sympathisieren
sym·pa·thiz·er Sympathisant(in)
sym·pa·thy Mitgefühl *n*; Verständnis *n*
sym·pho·ny MUS Sinfonie *f*
symphony orches·tra MUS Sinfonieor-

chester *n*
sympׅ·tom Symptom *n*
syn·chro·nize *v/t* aufeinander abstimmen; *Uhren, Film* synchronisieren; *v/i* synchron gehen *or* sein
syn·o·nym Synonym *n*
sy·non·y·mous synonym; gleichbedeutend
syn·tax LING Syntax *f*, Satzlehre *f*
syn·the·sis Synthese *f*
syn·thet·ic CHEM synthetisch
synthetic fi·ber (*Br* **fi·bre**) Kunstfaser *f*
Syr·i·a Syrien *n*
sy·ringe MED Spritze *f*
syr·up Sirup *m*
sys·tem System *n*; (*Straßen- etc*)Netz *n*; Organismus *m*
sys·te·mat·ic systematisch
sys·tem er·ror EDP Systemfehler *m*

T

T, t T, t *n*
tab Aufhänger *m*, Schlaufe *f*; Lasche *f*; Etikett *n*, Schildchen *n*; Reiter *m*; F Rechnung *f*
ta·ble 1. Tisch *m*; (Tisch)Runde *f*; Tabelle *f*, Verzeichnis *n*; MATH Einmaleins *n*; ***at table*** bei Tisch; ***at the table*** am Tisch; ***turn the tables (on s.o.)*** *fig* den Spieß umdrehen; **2.** *fig* auf den Tisch legen; *esp fig* zurückstellen
ta·ble·cloth Tischdecke *f*, Tischtuch *n*
ta·ble·land GEOGR Tafelland *n*, Plateau *n*, Hochebene *f*
ta·ble lin·en Tischwäsche *f*
ta·ble·mat Untersetzer *m*
ta·ble·spoon Esslöffel *m*
tab·let PHARM Tablette *f*; Stück *n*; (*Stein- etc*)Tafel *f*
ta·ble ten·nis SPORT Tischtennis *n*
ta·ble·top Tischplatte *f*
ta·ble·ware Geschirr *n* und Besteck *n*
tab·loid Boulevardblatt *n*, -zeitung *f*
tab·loid press Boulevardpresse *f*
ta·boo 1. tabu; **2.** Tabu *n*
tab·u·lar tabellarisch
tab·u·late tabellarisch (an)ordnen
tab·u·la·tor Tabulator *m*
tach·o·graph MOT Fahrtenschreiber *m*
ta·chom·e·ter MOT Drehzahlmesser *m*
ta·cit stillschweigend
ta·ci·turn schweigsam, wortkarg
tack 1. Stift *m*, (Reiß)Zwecke *f*; Heftstich *m*; **2.** heften (***to*** an *acc*); ***tack on*** anfügen (***to*** *dat*)
tack·le 1. *Problem etc* angehen; *soccer etc*: *ballführenden Gegner* angreifen; *j-n* zur Rede stellen (***about*** wegen); **2.** TECH Flaschenzug *m*; (*Angel*)Gerät(e *pl*) *n*; *soccer etc*: Angriff *m*
tack·y klebrig; F schäbig
tact Takt *m*, Feingefühl *n*
tact·ful taktvoll
tac·tics Taktik *f*
tact·less taktlos
tad·pole ZO Kaulquappe *f*
taf·fe·ta Taft *m*
taf·fy Sahnebonbon *m*, *n*, Toffee *n*
tag 1. Etikett *n*; (*Namens-, Preis*)Schild *n*; (Schnürsenkel)Stift *m*; stehende Redensart *f*; *a.* ***question tag*** LING Frageanhängsel *n*; **2.** etikettieren; *Waren* auszeichnen; anhängen; ***tag along*** F mitgehen, mitkommen; ***tag along behind s.o.*** F hinter j-m hertrotten
tail 1. Schwanz *m*; Schweif *m*; hinterer Teil; F Schatten *m*, Beschatter(in); *pl* Rück-, Kehrseite *f*; Frack *m*; ***put a tail on*** *j-n* beschatten lassen; ***turn tail*** *fig* sich auf dem Absatz umdrehen; ***with one's tail between one's legs*** *fig* mit eingezogenem Schwanz; **2.** F *j-n* beschatten; ***tail back*** *esp Br* MOT sich stauen (***to*** bis zu); ***tail off*** schwächer werden, abnehmen, nachlassen
tail·back *esp Br* MOT Rückstau *m*
tail·coat Frack *m*
tail end Ende *n*, Schluss *m*
tail·light MOT Rücklicht *n*
tai·lor 1. Schneider *m*; **2.** schneidern
tai·lor-made Maß...; maßgeschneidert (*a. fig*)
tail pipe TECH Auspuffrohr *n*
tail·wind Rückenwind *m*
taint·ed GASTR verdorben
take 1. *v/t* nehmen; (weg)nehmen; mitnehmen; bringen; MIL, MED einnehmen; *chess etc*: *Figur, Stein* schlagen; *Gefangene, Prüfung etc* machen; UNIV studieren;

Preis etc erringen; *Scheck etc* (an)nehmen; *Rat* annehmen; *et.* hinnehmen; fassen, Platz bieten für; *et.* aushalten, ertragen; PHOT *et.* aufnehmen, *Aufnahme* machen; *Temperatur* messen; *Notiz* machen, niederschreiben; *ein Bad, Zug, Bus, Weg etc* nehmen; *Gelegenheit, Maßnahmen* ergreifen; *Mut* fassen; *Zeit, Geduld etc* erfordern, brauchen; *Zeit* dauern; ***it took her four hours*** sie brauchte vier Stunden; ***I take it that*** ich nehme an, dass; ***take it or leave it*** F mach, was du willst; ***taken all in all*** im Großen (und) Ganzen; ***this seat is taken*** dieser Platz ist besetzt; ***be taken by*** *or* ***with*** angetan sein von; ***be taken ill*** *or* ***sick*** erkranken, krank werden; ***take to bits*** *or* ***pieces*** *et.* auseinandernehmen, zerlegen; ***take the blame*** die Schuld auf sich nehmen; ***take care*** vorsichtig sein, aufpassen; ***take care!*** F mach's gut!; → ***care*** *1*; ***take hold of*** ergreifen; ***take part*** teilnehmen (***in*** an *dat*); → ***part*** *1*; ***take pity on*** Mitleid haben mit; ***take a walk*** e-n Spaziergang machen; ***take my word for it*** verlass dich drauf; → ***advice***, ***bath*** *1*, ***break*** *1*, ***lead***[1] 2, ***message, oath, offense, place*** 1, ***prisoner, risk*** 1, ***seat*** 1, ***step*** 1, ***trouble*** 1, ***turn*** 2, *etc*; *v/i* MED wirken, anschlagen; ***take after*** *j-m* nachschlagen, ähneln; ***take along*** mitnehmen; ***take apart*** auseinandernehmen (*a. fig* F), zerlegen; ***take away*** wegnehmen (***from s.o.*** j-m); ***… to take away*** *Br* … zum Mitnehmen; ***take back*** zurückbringen; zurücknehmen; bei *j-m* Erinnerungen wachrufen; *j-n* zurückversetzen (***to*** in *acc*); ***take down*** herunternehmen, abnehmen; *Hose* herunterlassen; auseinandernehmen, zerlegen; (sich) *et.* aufschreiben *or* notieren; sich *Notizen* machen; ***what do you take me for?*** wofür hältst du mich eigentlich?; ***take from*** *j-m et.* wegnehmen; MATH abziehen von; ***take in*** *j-n* (bei sich) aufnehmen; *fig et.* einschließen; *Kleidungsstück* enger machen; *et.* begreifen; *j-n* hereinlegen, F *j-n* aufs Kreuz legen; ***be taken in by*** hereinfallen auf (*acc*); ***take off*** *Kleidungsstück* ablegen, ausziehen, *Hut etc* abnehmen; *et.* ab-, wegnehmen; abziehen; AVIAT abheben; SPORT abspringen; F sich davonmachen; ***take a day off*** sich e-n Tag freinehmen; ***take on*** *j-n* einstellen; *Arbeit etc* annehmen, übernehmen; *Farbe, Ausdruck etc* annehmen; sich anlegen mit; ***take out*** herausnehmen, *Zahn* ziehen; *j-n* ausführen, ausgehen mit *j-m*; *Versicherung* abschließen; *s-n Frust etc* auslassen (***on*** an *dat*); ***take over*** *Amt, Macht, Verantwortung etc* übernehmen; die Macht übernehmen; ***take to*** Gefallen finden an (*dat*); ***take to doing s.th.*** anfangen, et. zu tun; ***take up*** *Vorschlag etc* aufgreifen; *Zeit etc* in Anspruch nehmen, *Platz* einnehmen; *Erzählung etc* aufnehmen; ***take up doing s.th.*** anfangen, sich mit et. zu beschäftigen; ***take up with*** sich einlassen mit; **2.** *film*, TV Einstellung *f*; F Einnahmen *pl*

take·a·way *Br* **1.** Essen *n* zum Mitnehmen; **2.** Restaurant *n* mit Straßenverkauf

take·off AVIAT Abheben *n*, Start *m*; SPORT Absprung *m*

tak·ings Einnahmen *pl*

tale Erzählung *f*; Geschichte *f*; Lüge *f*, Lügengeschichte *f*, Märchen *n*; ***tell tales*** petzen

tal·ent Talent *n*, Begabung *f*

tal·ent·ed talentiert, begabt

tal·is·man Talisman *m*

talk **1.** *v/i* reden, sprechen, sich unterhalten (***to, with*** mit; ***about*** über *acc*; ***of*** von); ***talk about s.th.*** *a.* et. besprechen; ***s.o. to talk to*** Ansprechpartner(in); *v/t Unsinn etc* reden; reden *or* sprechen *or* sich unterhalten über (*acc*); ***talk s.o. into s.th.*** j-n zu et. überreden; ***talk s.o. out of s.th.*** j-m et. ausreden; ***talk s.th. over*** *Problem etc* besprechen (***with*** mit); ***talk round*** *j-n* bekehren (***to*** zu), umstimmen; **2.** Gespräch *n*, Unterhaltung *f* (***with*** mit; ***about*** über *acc*); Vortrag *m*; Sprache *f*, Sprechweise *f*; Gerede *n*, Geschwätz *n*; ***give a talk*** e-n Vortrag halten (***to*** vor *dat*; ***about, on*** über *acc*); ***be the talk of the town*** Stadtgespräch sein; ***baby talk*** Babysprache *f*, kindliches Gebabbel; → ***small talk***

talk·a·tive gesprächig, redselig

talk·er: ***be a good talker*** gut reden können

talk·ing-to F Standpauke *f*; ***give s.o. a talking-to*** j-m e-e Standpauke halten

talk show TV Talkshow *f*

talk-show host TV Talkmaster *m*

tall groß (*person*), hoch (*building etc*)

tal·low Talg *m*

tal·ly[1] SPORT *etc* Stand *m*; ***keep a tally of*** Buch führen über (*acc*)

tal·ly[2] übereinstimmen (***with*** mit); *a.* ***tally up*** zusammenrechnen, -zählen

tal·on zo Kralle *f*, Klaue *f*

tame **1.** zo zahm; *fig* fad(e), lahm; **2.** zo zähmen (*a. fig*)

tam·per: ***tamper with*** sich zu schaffen machen an (*dat*)

tam·pon MED Tampon *m*

tan 1. *Fell* gerben; bräunen; braun werden; 2. Gelbbraun *n*; (Sonnen)Bräune *f*; 3. gelbbraun
tang (scharfer) Geruch *or* Geschmack
tan·gent MATH Tangente *f*; ***fly or go off at a tangent*** plötzlich (vom Thema) abschweifen
tan·ge·rine BOT Mandarine *f*
tan·gi·ble greifbar, *fig a.* handfest, klar
tan·gle 1. (sich) verwirren *or* verheddern, durcheinanderbringen; durcheinanderkommen; 2. Gewirr *n*, *fig a.* Wirrwarr *m*, Durcheinander *n*
tank MOT *etc* Tank *m*; MIL Panzer *m*
tank·ard (Bier)Humpen *m*
tank·er MAR Tanker *m*, Tankschiff *n*; AVIAT Tankflugzeug *n*; MOT Tankwagen *m*
tan·ner Gerber *m*
tan·ne·ry Gerberei *f*
tan·ta·lize *j-n* aufreizen
tan·ta·liz·ing verlockend
tan·ta·mount: ***be tantamount to*** gleichbedeutend sein mit, hinauslaufen auf (*acc*)
tan·trum Wut-, Tobsuchtsanfall *m*
tap[1] 1. TECH Hahn *m*; ***beer on tap*** Bier *n* vom Fass; 2. *Naturschätze etc* erschließen; *Vorräte etc* angreifen; *Telefon(leitung)* abhören, F anzapfen; *Fass* anzapfen, anstechen
tap[2] 1. mit *den Fingern, Füßen* klopfen, mit *den Fingern* trommeln (**on** auf *acc*); antippen; ***tap s.o. on the shoulder*** j-m auf die Schulter klopfen; ***tap on*** (leicht) klopfen an (*acc*) *or* auf (*acc*) *or* gegen; 2. (leichtes) Klopfen; Klaps *m*
tap dance Stepptanz *m*
tape 1. (schmales) Band; Kleb(e)streifen *m*; (Magnet-, Video-, Ton)Band *n*; (*Video- etc*)Kassette *f*; (Band)Aufnahme *f*; TV Aufzeichnung *f*; SPORT Zielband *n*; → ***red tape***; 2. (auf Band) aufnehmen; TV aufzeichnen; *a.* ***tape up*** (mit Klebeband) zukleben
tape deck Tapedeck *n*
tape meas·ure Bandmaß *n*, Maßband *n*, Messband *n*
ta·per *a.* ***taper off*** spitz zulaufen, sich verjüngen; *fig* langsam nachlassen
tape re·cord·er Tonbandgerät *n*
tape re·cord·ing Tonbandaufnahme *f*
ta·pes·try Gobelin *m*, Wandteppich *m*
tape·worm ZO Bandwurm *m*
taps MIL Zapfenstreich *m*
tap wa·ter Leitungswasser *n*
tar 1. Teer *m*; 2. teeren
tare ECON Tara *f*
tar·get (Schieß-, Ziel)Scheibe *f*; MIL Ziel *n* (*a. fig*), ECON *a.* Soll *n*; *fig* Zielscheibe *f*
target ar·e·a MIL Zielbereich *m*
target group Zielgruppe *f*
tar·iff ECON Zoll(tarif) *m*; *esp Br* Preisverzeichnis *n*
tar·mac Asphalt *m*; AVIAT Rollfeld *n*, Rollbahn *f*
tar·nish *v/i* anlaufen; *v/t Ansehen etc* beflecken
tart[1] *esp Br* Obstkuchen *m*; Obsttörtchen *n*; F Flittchen *n*, *sl* Nutte *f*
tart[2] herb, sauer; scharf (*a. fig*)
tar·tan Tartan *m*; Schottenstoff *m*; Schottenmuster *n*
tar·tar MED Zahnstein *m*; CHEM Weinstein *m*
task Aufgabe *f*; ***take s.o. to task*** *fig* j-n zurechtweisen (**for** wegen)
task force MIL *etc* Sonder-, Spezialeinheit *f*
tas·sel Troddel *f*, Quaste *f*
taste 1. Geschmack *m* (*a. fig*), Geschmackssinn *m*; Kostprobe *f*; Vorliebe *f* (**for** für); 2. *v/t* kosten, probieren; schmecken; *v/i* schmecken (**of** nach)
taste·ful *fig* geschmackvoll
taste·less geschmacklos (*a. fig*)
tast·y schmackhaft
tat·tered zerlumpt
tat·ters Fetzen *pl*; ***in tatters*** zerfetzt, in Fetzen; *fig* ruiniert
tat·too[1] 1. Tätowierung *f*; 2. (ein)tätowieren
tat·too[2] MIL Zapfenstreich *m*
taunt 1. verhöhnen, verspotten; 2. höhnische *or* spöttische Bemerkung
Tau·rus ASTR Stier *m*; ***he (she) is (a) Taurus*** er (sie) ist (ein) Stier
taut straff; *fig* angespannt
taw·dry (billig und) geschmacklos
taw·ny gelbbraun
tax 1. Steuer *f* (**on** auf *acc*); 2. besteuern; *j-s Geduld etc* strapazieren
tax·a·ble steuerpflichtig
tax·a·tion Besteuerung *f*
tax e·va·sion Steuerhinterziehung *f*
tax·i 1. Taxi *n*, Taxe *f*; 2. AVIAT rollen
tax·i driv·er Taxifahrer(in)
tax·i rank, **tax·i stand** Taxistand *m*
tax of·fi·cer Finanzbeamte *m*
tax·pay·er Steuerzahler(in)
tax re·duc·tion Steuersenkung *f*
tax re·turn Steuererklärung *f*
T-bar Bügel *m*; *a.* ***T-bar lift*** Schlepplift *m*
tea Tee *m*; ***have a cup of tea*** e-n Tee trinken; ***make some tea*** e-n Tee machen *or* kochen
tea·bag Teebeutel *m*, Aufgussbeutel *m*
teach lehren, unterrichten (in *dat*); *j-m et.* beibringen; unterrichten (**at** an *dat*)

teach·er Lehrer(in)
tea co·sy Teewärmer *m*
tea·cup Teetasse *f*; ***a storm in a teacup*** *fig* ein Sturm im Wasserglas
team Team *n*, *a.* Arbeitsgruppe *f*, SPORT *a.* Mannschaft *f*, *soccer: a.* Elf *f*
team·ster MOT LKW-Fahrer *m*
team·work Zusammenarbeit *f*, Teamwork *n*; Zusammenspiel *n*
tea·pot Teekanne *f*
tear[1] Träne *f*; ***in tears*** weinend, in Tränen (aufgelöst)
tear[2] **1.** *v/t* zerreißen; sich *et.* zerreißen (***on*** an *dat*); weg-, losreißen (***from*** von); *v/i* (zer)reißen; F rasen, sausen; ***tear down*** *Plakat etc* herunterreißen; *Haus etc* abreißen; ***tear off*** abreißen; sich *Kleidung* vom Leib reißen; ***tear out*** (her)ausreißen; ***tear up*** aufreißen; zerreißen; **2.** Riss *m*
tear·drop Träne *f*
tear·ful weinend; tränenreich
tear·jerk·er F Schnulze *f*
tea·room Teestube *f*
tease necken, hänseln; ärgern
tea·spoon Teelöffel *m*
teat zo Zitze *f*; *Br* (Gummi)Sauger *m*
tech·ni·cal technisch; fachlich, Fach…
tech·ni·cal·i·ty technische Einzelheit; reine Formsache
tech·ni·cian Techniker(in)
tech·nique Technik *f*, Verfahren *n*
tech·nol·o·gy Technologie *f*; Technik *f*
ted·dy bear Teddybär *m*
te·di·ous langweilig, ermüdend
teem: ***teem with*** wimmeln von, strotzen von *or* vor (*dat*)
teen·age(d) im Teenageralter; für Teenager
teen·ag·er Teenager *m*
teens: ***be in one's teens*** im Teenageralter sein
tee·ny(-wee·ny) F klitzeklein, winzig
tee shirt → ***T-shirt***
teethe zahnen
tee·to·tal·(l)er Abstinenzler(in)
tel·e·cast Fernsehsendung *f*
tel·e·com·mu·ni·ca·tions Telekommunikation *f*, Fernmeldewesen *n*
tel·e·gram Telegramm *n*
tel·e·graph **1.** ***by telegraph*** telegrafisch; **2.** telegrafieren
tel·e·graph·ic telegrafisch
te·leg·ra·phy Telegrafie *f*
tel·e·phone **1.** Telefon *n*; **2.** telefonieren; anrufen
telephone booth, **telephone box** *Br* Telefonzelle *f*, Fernsprechzelle *f*
telephone call Telefonanruf *n*, Telefongespräch *n*
telephone di·rec·to·ry → ***phone book***
telephone exchange Fernsprechamt *n*
telephone number Telefonnummer *f*
te·leph·o·nist *esp Br* Telefonist(in)
tel·e·pho·to lens PHOT Teleobjektiv *n*
tel·e·print·er Fernschreiber *m*
tel·e·scope Teleskop *n*, Fernrohr *n*
tel·e·text Teletext *m*, Videotext *m*
tel·e·type·writ·er Fernschreiber *m*
tel·e·vise im Fernsehen übertragen *or* bringen
tel·e·vi·sion **1.** Fernsehen *n*; *a.* ***television set*** Fernsehapparat *m*, -gerät *n*, F Fernseher *m*; ***on television*** im Fernsehen; ***watch television*** fernsehen; **2.** Fernseh…
tel·ex **1.** Telex *n*, Fernschreiben *n*; **2.** telexen (***to*** an *acc*), ein Telex schicken (*dat*)
tell *v/t* sagen; erzählen; erkennen (***by*** an *dat*); *Namen etc* nennen; *et.* anzeigen; *j-m* sagen, befehlen (***to do*** zu tun); ***I can't tell one from the other, I can't tell them apart*** ich kann sie nicht auseinanderhalten; *v/i* sich auswirken (***on*** bei, auf *acc*), sich bemerkbar machen; ***who can tell?*** wer weiß?; ***you can never tell, you never can tell*** man kann nie wissen; ***tell against*** sprechen gegen; von Nachteil sein für; ***tell s.o. off*** F mit j-m schimpfen (***for*** wegen); ***tell on s.o.*** j-n verpetzen *or* verraten
tell·er Kassierer(in)
tell·ing aufschlussreich
tell·tale **1.** verräterisch; **2.** F Petze *f*
tel·ly *Br* F Fernseher *m*
te·mer·i·ty Frechheit *f*, Kühnheit *f*
tem·per **1.** Temperament *n*, Wesen *n*, Wesensart *f*; Laune *f*, Stimmung *f*; TECH Härte(grad *m*) *f*; ***keep one's temper*** sich beherrschen, ruhig bleiben; ***lose one's temper*** die Beherrschung verlieren; **2.** TECH *Stahl* härten
tem·pe·ra·ment Temperament *n*, Naturell *n*, Wesen *n*, Wesensart *f*
tem·pe·ra·men·tal launisch; von Natur aus
tem·pe·rate gemäßigt (*climate, region*)
tem·pe·ra·ture Temperatur *f*; ***have*** *or* ***be running a temperature*** MED erhöhte Temperatur *or* Fieber haben
tem·pest POET (heftiger) Sturm
tem·ple[1] Tempel *m*
tem·ple[2] ANAT Schläfe *f*
tem·po·ral weltlich; LING temporal, der Zeit
tem·po·ra·ry vorübergehend, zeiweilig
tempt *j-n* in Versuchung führen; *j-n* verführen (***to*** zu)

temp·ta·tion Versuchung *f*, Verführung *f*
tempt·ing verführerisch
ten **1.** zehn; **2.** Zehn *f*
ten·a·ble *fig* haltbar
te·na·cious hartnäckig, zäh
ten·ant Pächter(in), Mieter(in)
tend neigen, tendieren (***to*** zu); ***tend upwards*** e-e steigende Tendenz haben
ten·den·cy Tendenz *f*; Neigung *f*
ten·der[1] empfindlich, *fig a.* heikel; GASTR zart, weich; sanft, zart, zärtlich
ten·der[2] RAIL, MAR Tender *m*
ten·der[3] ECON **1.** Angebot *n*; ***legal tender*** gesetzliches Zahlungsmittel; **2.** ein Angebot machen (***for*** für)
ten·der·foot F Neuling *m*, Anfänger *m*
ten·der·loin GASTR zartes Lendenstück
ten·der·ness Zartheit *f*; Zärtlichkeit *f*
ten·don ANAT Sehne *f*
ten·dril BOT Ranke *f*
ten·e·ment Mietshaus *n*, *contp* Mietskaserne *f*
ten·nis Tennis *n*
tennis court Tennisplatz *m*
tennis play·er Tennisspieler(in)
ten·or MUS, JUR Tenor *m*, JUR *a.* Wortlaut *m*, Sinn *m*; Verlauf *m*
tense[1] LING Zeit(form) *f*, Tempus *n*
tense[2] gespannt, straff (*rope etc*), (an)gespannt (*a. fig*); (über)nervös, verkrampft (*person*)
ten·sion Spannung *f* (*a.* ELECTR)
tent Zelt *n*
ten·ta·cle ZO Tentakel *m*, *n*, Fangarm *m*
ten·ta·tive vorläufig; vorsichtig, zaghaft
ten·ter·hooks: ***be on tenterhooks*** wie auf (glühenden) Kohlen sitzen
tenth **1.** zehnte(r, -s); **2.** Zehntel *n*
tenth·ly zehntens
ten·u·ous *fig* lose (*link*, *relationship etc*)
ten·ure Besitz *m*, Besitzdauer *f*; ***tenure of office*** Amtsdauer *f*, Dienstzeit *f*
tep·id lau(warm)
term **1.** Zeit *f*, Zeitraum *m*, Dauer *f*; JUR Laufzeit *f*; PED, UNIV Semester *n*, *esp Br* Trimester *n*; Ausdruck *m*, Bezeichnung *f*; ***term of office*** Amtsdauer *f*, Amtsperiode *f*, Amtszeit *f*; *pl* Bedingungen *pl*; ***be on good*** (***bad***) ***terms with*** gut (schlecht) auskommen mit; ***they are not on speaking terms*** sie sprechen nicht (mehr) miteinander; ***come to terms*** sich einigen (***with*** mit); **2.** nennen, bezeichnen als
ter·mi·nal **1.** End…; letzte(r, -s); MED unheilbar; im Endstadium; ***terminally ill*** unheilbar krank; **2.** RAIL *etc* Endstation *f*; Terminal *m*, *n*; ELECTR Pol *m*; EDP Terminal *n*, Datenendstation *f*
ter·mi·nate *v/t* beenden; *Vertrag* kündigen, lösen; MED *Schwangerschaft* unterbrechen; *v/i* enden; ablaufen (*contract*)
ter·mi·na·tion Beendigung *f*; Kündigung *f*, Lösung *f*; Ende *n*; Ablauf *m*
ter·mi·nus RAIL *etc* Endstation *f*
ter·race Terrasse *f*; Häuserreihe *f*; *mst pl esp Br* SPORT Ränge *pl*
ter·raced house *Br* Reihenhaus *n*
ter·res·tri·al irdisch; Erd…; esp BOT, ZO Land…
ter·ri·ble schrecklich
ter·rif·ic F toll, fantastisch; irre (*speed*, *heat etc*)
ter·ri·fy *j-m* schreckliche Angst einjagen
ter·ri·to·ri·al territorial, Gebiets…
ter·ri·to·ry Territorium *n*, (*a.* Hoheits-, Staats)Gebiet *n*
ter·ror Entsetzen *n*; Schrecken *m*; POL Terror *m*; F Landplage *f*; ***in terror*** in panischer Angst
ter·ror·is·m Terrorismus *m*
ter·ror·ist Terrorist(in)
ter·ror·ize terrorisieren
terse *fig* knapp, kurz (und bündig)
test **1.** Test *m*, Prüfung *f*; Probe *f*; **2.** testen, prüfen; probieren; *j-s Geduld etc* auf e-e harte Probe stellen
tes·ta·ment: ***last will and testament*** JUR Letzter Wille, Testament *n*
test an·i·mal Versuchstier *n*
test card TV Testbild *n*
test drive MOT Probefahrt *f*
tes·ti·cle ANAT Hoden *m*
tes·ti·fy JUR aussagen
tes·ti·mo·ni·al Referenz *f*
tes·ti·mo·ny JUR Aussage *f*; Beweis *m*
test pi·lot AVIAT Testpilot *m*
test tube CHEM Reagenzglas *n*
tes·ty gereizt
tet·a·nus MED Tetanus *m*, Wundstarrkrampf *m*
teth·er **1.** Strick *m*; Kette *f*; ***at the end of one's tether*** *fig* mit s-n Kräften *or* Nerven am Ende sein; **2.** *Tier* anbinden; anketten
text Text *m*
text·book Lehrbuch *n*
tex·tile **1.** Stoff *m*, *pl* Textilien *pl*; **2.** Textil…
tex·ture Textur *f*, Gewebe *n*; Beschaffenheit *f*; Struktur *f*
than als
thank **1.** *j-m* danken, sich bei *j-m* bedanken (***for*** für); ***thank you*** danke; ***thank you very much*** vielen Dank; ***no, thank you*** nein, danke; (***yes***,) ***thank you*** ja, bitte; **2.** ***thanks*** Dank *m*; ***thanks*** danke (schön); ***no, thanks*** nein, danke; ***thanks***

T

to dank (*gen*), wegen (*gen*)
thank·ful dankbar
thank·less undankbar
that **1.** *pron and adj* das; jene(r, -s), der, die, das, derjenige, diejenige, dasjenige; **2.** *relative pron* der, die, das, welche(r, -s); **3.** *cj* dass; **4.** *adv* F so, dermaßen; ***it's that simple*** so einfach ist das
thatch **1.** mit Stroh *or* Reet decken; **2.** (Dach)Stroh *n*, Reet *n*; Strohdach *n*, Reetdach *n*
thaw **1.** (auf)tauen; **2.** Tauwetter *n*; (Auf)-Tauen *n*
the **1.** der, die, das, *pl* die; **2.** *adv*: ***the … the …*** je … desto …; ***the sooner the better*** je eher, desto besser
the·a·ter Theater *n*; UNIV (*Hör*)Saal *m*; MIL (Kriegs)Schauplatz *m*
the·a·ter·go·er Theaterbesucher(in)
the·a·tre *Br* → ***theater***; MED Operationssaal *m*
the·at·ri·cal Theater…; *fig* theatralisch
theft Diebstahl *m*
their ihr(e)
theirs der (die, das) ihrige *or* ihre
them sie (*acc pl*); ihnen (*dat*)
theme Thema *n*
them·selves sie (*acc pl*) selbst; sich (selbst)
then **1.** *adv* dann; da; damals; ***by then*** bis dahin; ***from then on*** von da an; → ***every***, ***now*** *1*, ***there***; **2.** *adj* damalig
the·o·lo·gian Theologe *m*, Theologin *f*
the·ol·o·gy Theologie *f*
the·o·ret·i·cal theoretisch
the·o·rist Theoretiker *m*
the·o·ry Theorie *f*
ther·a·peu·tic therapeutisch; F wohltuend; gesund
ther·a·pist Therapeut(in)
ther·a·py Therapie *f*
there **1.** da, dort; (da-, dort)hin; ***there is, there are*** es gibt, es ist, *pl* es sind; ***there and then*** auf der Stelle; ***there you are*** hier bitte; siehst du!, na also!; **2.** *int* so; siehst du!, na also!; ***there, there*** ist ja gut!
there·a·bout(s) so ungefähr
there·af·ter danach
there·by dadurch
there·fore deshalb, daher; folglich
there·up·on darauf(hin)
ther·mal **1.** thermisch, Thermo…, Wärme…; **2.** Thermik *f*
ther·mom·e·ter Thermometer *n*
ther·mos® Thermosflasche® *f*
the·sis These *f*; UNIV Dissertation *f*, Doktorarbeit *f*
they sie *pl*; man
thick **1.** *adj* dick, (*fog etc a.*) dicht; F dumm; F dick befreundet; ***be thick with*** wimmeln von; ***thick with smoke*** verräuchert; ***that's a bit thick!*** *esp Br* F das ist ein starkes Stück!; **2.** *adv* dick, dicht; ***lay it on thick*** F dick auftragen; **3.** ***in the thick of*** mitten in (*dat*); ***through thick and thin*** durch dick und dünn
thick·en dicker werden, (*fog etc a.*) dichter werden; GASTR eindicken, binden
thick·et Dickicht *n*
thick·head·ed F strohdumm
thick·ness Dicke *f*; Lage *f*, Schicht *f*
thick·set gedrungen, untersetzt
thick-skinned *fig* dickfellig
thief Dieb(in)
thigh ANAT (Ober)Schenkel *m*
thim·ble Fingerhut *m*
thin **1.** *adj* dünn; dürr; spärlich, dürftig; schütter (*hair*); schwach, (*excuse etc a.*) fadenscheinig; **2.** *adv* dünn; **3.** verdünnen; dünner werden, (*fog, hair a.*) sich lichten
thing Ding *n*; Sache *f*; *pl* Sachen *pl*, Zeug *n*; *fig* Dinge *pl*, Lage *f*, Umstände *pl*; ***I couldn't see a thing*** ich konnte überhaupt nichts sehen; ***another thing*** et. anderes; ***the right thing*** das Richtige
thing·a·ma·jig F Dings(bums) *m, f, n*
think *v/i* denken (***of*** an *acc*); nachdenken (***about*** über *acc*); ***I think so*** ich glaube *or* denke schon; ***I'll think about it*** ich überlege es mir; ***think of*** sich erinnern an (*acc*); ***think of doing s.th.*** beabsichtigen *or* daran denken, et. zu tun; ***what do you think of*** *or* ***about … ?*** was halten Sie von …?; *v/t* denken, glauben, meinen; *j-n, et.* halten für; ***think over*** nachdenken über (*acc*), sich *et.* überlegen; ***think up*** sich *et.* ausdenken
think tank Beraterstab *m*, Sachverständigenstab *m*, Denkfabrik *f*
third **1.** dritte(r, -s); **2.** Drittel *n*
third·ly drittens
third-rate drittklassig
Third World Dritte Welt
thirst Durst *m*
thirst·y durstig; ***be thirsty*** Durst haben, durstig sein
thir·teen **1.** dreizehn; **2.** Dreizehn *f*
thir·teenth dreizehnte(r, -s)
thir·ti·eth dreißigste(r, -s)
thir·ty **1.** dreißig; **2.** Dreißig *f*
this diese(r, -s); ***this morning*** heute Morgen; ***this is John speaking*** TEL hier (spricht) John
this·tle BOT Distel *f*
thong (Leder)Riemen *m*
thorn Dorn *m*

T

thorn·y dornig; *fig* schwierig, heikel
thor·ough gründlich, genau; fürchterlich (*mess etc*)
thor·ough·bred zo Vollblüter *m*
thor·ough·fare Hauptverkehrsstraße *f*; ***no thoroughfare!*** Durchfahrt verboten!
though **1.** *cj* obwohl; (je)doch; ***as though*** als ob; **2.** *adv* dennoch, trotzdem
thought Denken *n*; Gedanke *m* (***of*** an *acc*); ***on second thought*** wenn ich es mir (recht) überlege
thought·ful nachdenklich; rücksichtsvoll, aufmerksam
thought·les gedankenlos; rücksichtslos
thou·sand **1.** tausend; **2.** Tausend *n*
thou·sandth **1.** tausendste(r, -s); **2.** Tausendstel *n*
thrash verdreschen, verprügeln; SPORT F *j-m* e-e Abfuhr erteilen; ***thrash about, thrash around*** sich *im Bett etc* hin und her werfen; um sich schlagen; zappeln (*fish*); ***thrash out*** *Problem etc* ausdiskutieren
thrash·ing Dresche *f*, Tracht *f* Prügel
thread **1.** Faden *m* (*a. fig*); Garn *n*; TECH Gewinde *n*; **2.** *Nadel* einfädeln; *Perlen etc* auffädeln, aufreihen
thread·bare abgewetzt, abgetragen; *fig* abgedroschen
threat Drohung *f*; Bedrohung *f*, Gefahr *f* (***to*** *gen or* für)
threat·en (be)drohen
threat·en·ing drohend
three **1.** drei; **2.** Drei *f*
three·fold dreifach
three-ply → ***ply²***
three·score sechzig
three-stage dreistufig
thresh AGR dreschen
thresh·ing ma·chine AGR Dreschmaschine *f*
thresh·old Schwelle *f*
thrift Sparsamkeit *f*
thrift·y sparsam
thrill **1.** prickelndes Gefühl; Nervenkitzel *m*; aufregendes Erlebnis; **2.** *v/t* ***be thrilled*** (ganz) hingerissen sein (***at, about*** von)
thrill·er Thriller *m*, F Reißer *m*
thrill·ing spannend, fesselnd, packend
thrive gedeihen; *fig* blühen, florieren
throat ANAT Kehle *f*, Gurgel *f*; Rachen *m*; Hals *m*; ***clear one's throat*** sich räuspern; → ***sore 1***
throb **1.** hämmern (*machine*), (*heart etc a.*) pochen, schlagen; pulsieren (*pain*); **2.** Hämmern *n*, Pochen *n*, Schlagen *n*
throm·bo·sis MED Thrombose *f*
throne Thron *m*
throng **1.** Schar *f*, Menschenmenge *f*; **2.** sich drängen (in *dat*)
throt·tle **1.** erdrosseln; ***throttle down*** MOT, TECH drosseln, Gas wegnehmen; **2.** TECH Drosselklappe *f*
through **1.** *prp* durch (*acc*); bis (einschließlich); ***Monday through Friday*** von Montag bis Freitag; **2.** *adv* durch; ***through and through*** durch und durch; ***put s.o. through to*** TEL j-n verbinden mit; ***wet through*** völlig durchnässt; **3.** *adj* durchgehend (*train etc*); Durchgangs…
through·out **1.** *prp*: ***throughout the night*** die ganze Nacht hindurch; ***throughout the country*** im ganzen Land, überall im Land; **2.** *adv* ganz, überall; die ganze Zeit (hindurch)
through traf·fic Durchgangsverkehr *m*
through·way *Br* → ***thruway***
throw **1.** werfen; *Hebel etc* betätigen; *Reiter* abwerfen; *Party* geben, F schmeißen; ***throw a four*** e-e Vier würfeln; ***throw off*** *Jacke etc* abwerfen; *Verfolger* abschütteln; *Krankheit* loswerden; ***throw on*** sich *e-e Jacke etc* (hastig) überwerfen; ***throw out*** hinauswerfen; wegwerfen; ***throw up*** *v/t* hochwerfen; F *Job etc* hinschmeißen; F (er)brechen; *v/i* F (sich er)brechen; **2.** Wurf *m*
throw·a·way Wegwerf…, Einweg…
throwaway pack Einwegpackung *f*
throw-in *soccer*: Einwurf *m*
thru F → ***through***
thrum → ***strum***
thrush zo Drossel *f*
thrust **1.** *j-n, et.* stoßen (***into*** in *acc*); *et.* stecken, schieben (***into*** in *acc*); ***thrust at*** stoßen nach; ***thrust s.th. upon s.o.*** j-m et. aufdrängen; **2.** Stoß *m*; MIL Vorstoß *m*; PHYS Schub *m*, Schubkraft *f*
thru·way Schnellstraße *f*
thud **1.** dumpfes Geräusch, Plumps *m*; **2.** plumpsen
thug Verbrecher *m*, Schläger *m*
thumb **1.** ANAT Daumen *m*; **2.** ***thumb a lift or ride*** per Anhalter fahren, trampen (***to*** nach); ***thumb through a book*** ein Buch durchblättern; ***well-thumbed*** abgegriffen
thumb·tack Reißzwecke *f*, Reißnagel *m*, Heftzwecke *f*
thump **1.** *v/t j-m* e-n Schlag versetzen; ***thump out*** *Melodie* herunterhämmern (***on the piano*** auf dem Klavier); *v/i* (heftig) schlagen *or* hämmern *or* pochen (*a. heart*); plumpsen; trampeln; **2.** dumpfes Geräusch, Plumps *m*; Schlag *m*
thun·der **1.** Donner *m*, Donnern *n*; **2.** donnern

thun·der·bolt Blitz *m* und Donner *m*
thun·der·clap Donnerschlag *m*
thun·der·cloud Gewitterwolke *f*
thun·der·ous donnernd (*applause*)
thun·der·storm Gewitter *n*, Unwetter *n*
thun·der·struck wie vom Donner gerührt
Thur(s) ABBR *of* ***Thursday*** Do., Donnerstag *m*
Thurs·day (ABBR ***Thur, Thurs***) Donnerstag *m*; ***on Thursday*** (am) Donnerstag; ***on Thursdays*** donnerstags
thus so, auf diese Weise; folglich, somit; ***thus far*** bisher
thwart durchkreuzen, vereiteln
thyme BOT Thymian *m*
thy·roid (gland) ANAT Schilddrüse *f*
tick[1] **1.** Ticken *n*; Haken *m*, Häkchen *n*; **2.** *v/i* ticken; *v/t mst* ***tick off*** ab-, anhaken
tick[2] zo Zecke *f*
tick[3]: ***on tick*** *Br* F auf Pump
tick·er-tape pa·rade Konfettiparade *f*
tick·et 1. Fahrkarte *f*, Fahrschein *m*; Flugkarte *f*, Flugschein *m*, Ticket *n*; (*Eintritts-*, *Theater- etc*)Karte *f*; (*Gepäck*)-Schein *m*; Etikett *n*, (*Preis- etc* -) Schild *n*; POL Wahl-, Kandidatenliste *f*; (*a.* ***parking ticket***) MOT Strafzettel *m*; **2.** etikettieren; bestimmen, vorsehen (***for*** für)
tick·et-can·cel·(l)ing ma·chine (Fahrschein)Entwerter *m*
tick·et col·lec·tor (Bahnsteig)Schaffner(in)
ticket machine Fahrkartenautomat *m*
ticket of·fice RAIL Fahrkartenschalter *m*
tick·ing Inlett *n*; Matratzenbezug *m*
tick·le kitzeln
tick·lish kitz(e)lig, *fig a.* heikel
tid·al wave Flutwelle *f*
tid·bit Leckerbissen *m*
tide 1. Gezeiten *pl*; Flut *f*; *fig* Strömung *f*, Trend *m*; ***high tide*** Flut *f*; ***low tide*** Ebbe *f*; **2.** ***tide over*** *fig j-m* hinweghelfen über (*acc*); *j-n* über Wasser halten
ti·dy 1. sauber, ordentlich, aufgeräumt; F hübsch, beträchtlich (*Sum etc*); **2.** *a.* ***tidy up*** in Ordnung bringen, (*Zimmer a.*) aufräumen; ***tidy away*** wegräumen, aufräumen
tie 1. Krawatte *f*, Schlips *m*; Band *n*; Schnur *f*; Stimmengleichheit *f*; SPORT Unentschieden *n*; (*Pokal*)Spiel *n*; RAIL Schwelle *f*; *mst pl fig* Bande *pl*; **2.** *v/t* an-, festbinden; (sich) *Krawatte etc* binden; *fig* verbinden; ***the game was tied*** SPORT das Spiel ging unentschieden aus; *v/i*: ***they tied for second place*** SPORT *etc* sie belegten gemeinsam den zweiten Platz; ***tie down*** *fig* (an)binden; *j-n* festlegen (***to*** auf *acc*); ***tie in with*** übereinstimmen mit, passen zu; verbinden *or* koppeln mit; ***tie up*** *Paket etc* verschnüren; *et.* in Verbindung bringen (***with*** mit); *Verkehr etc* lahmlegen; ***be tied up*** ECON fest angelegt sein (***in*** in *dat*)
tie·break(·er) *tennis*: Tie-Break *m*, *n*
tie-in (enge) Verbindung, (enger) Zusammenhang; ECON Kopplungsgeschäft *n*; ***a book movie tie-in*** *appr* das Buch zum Film
tie-on Anhänge…
tie·pin Krawattennadel *f*
tier (Sitz)Reihe *f*; Lage *f*, Schicht *f*; *fig* Stufe *f*
tie-up (enge) Verbindung, (enger) Zusammenhang; ECON Fusion *f*
ti·ger zo Tiger *m*
tight 1. *adj* fest (sitzend), fest angezogen; straff (*rope etc*); eng (*a. dress etc*); knapp (*a. fig*); F knick(e)rig; F blau; ***be in a tight corner*** in der Klemme sein *or* sitzen *or* stecken; **2.** *adv* fest; F gut; ***hold tight*** festhalten; ***sleep tight!*** F schlaf gut!
tight·en festziehen, anziehen; *Seil etc* straffen; ***tighten one's belt*** *fig* den Gürtel enger schnallen; ***tighten up*** (***on***) *Gesetz etc* verschärfen
tight·fist·ed F knick(e)rig
tights (*Tänzer-*, *Artisten*)Trikot *n*; *esp Br* Strumpfhose *f*
ti·gress zo Tigerin *f*
tile 1. (Dach)Ziegel *m*; Fliese *f*, Kachel *f*; **2.** (mit Ziegeln) decken; fliesen, kacheln
til·er Dachdecker *m*; Fliesenleger *m*
till[1] → ***until***
till[2] (Laden)Kasse *f*
tilt 1. kippen; sich neigen; **2.** Kippen *n*; ***at a tilt*** schief, schräg; (***at***) ***full tilt*** F mit Volldampf
tim·ber *Br* Bau-, Nutzholz *n*; Baumbestand *m*, Bäume *pl*; Balken *m*
time 1. Zeit *f*; Uhrzeit *f*; MUS Takt *m*; Mal *n*; ***time after time, time and again*** immer wieder; ***every time I …*** jedes Mal, wenn ich …; ***how many times?*** wie oft?; ***next time*** nächstes Mal; ***this time*** diesmal; ***three times*** dreimal; ***three times four equals*** *or* ***is twelve*** drei mal vier ist zwölf; ***what's the time?*** wie spät ist es?; ***what time?*** um wie viel Uhr?; ***all the time*** die ganze Zeit; ***at all times, at any time*** jederzeit; ***at the time*** damals; ***at the same time*** gleichzeitig; ***at times*** manchmal; ***by the time*** wenn; als; ***for a time*** e-e Zeit lang; ***for the time being*** vorläufig, fürs Erste; ***from time to time*** von Zeit zu Zeit; ***have a good time*** sich gut unterhalten *or* amüsieren; ***in time*** rechtzeitig; ***in no time*** (***at all***) im

Nu; ***on time*** pünktlich; ***some time ago*** vor einiger Zeit; ***to pass the time*** zum Zeitvertreib; ***take one's time*** sich Zeit lassen; **2.** *et.* timen (*a.* SPORT); (ab)stoppen; zeitlich abstimmen, den richtigen Zeitpunkt wählen *or* bestimmen für
time card Stechkarte *f*
time clock Stechuhr *f*
time lag Zeitdifferenz *f*
time-lapse *film*: Zeitraffer…
time·less immer während, ewig; zeitlos
time lim·it Frist *f*
time·ly (recht)zeitig
time sheet Stechkarte *f*
time sig·nal *radio*: Zeitzeichen *n*
time·ta·ble *Br* Fahrplan *m*, Flugplan *m*; Stundenplan *m*; Zeitplan *m*
tim·id ängstlich, furchtsam, zaghaft
tim·ing Timing *n*
tin 1. Zinn *n*; *Br* (Blech-, Konserven)Dose *f*, (-)Büchse *f*; **2.** verzinnen; *Br* einmachen, eindosen
tinc·ture Tinktur *f*
tin·foil Stanniol(papier) *n*; Alufolie *f*
tinge 1. tönen; ***be tinged with*** *fig* e-n Anflug haben von; **2.** Tönung *f*; *fig* Anflug *m*, Spur *f* (**of** von)
tin·gle prickeln, kribbeln
tink·er herumpfuschen, herumbasteln (***at*** an *dat*)
tin·kle bimmeln; klirren
tinned *Br* Dosen…, Büchsen…
tinned fruit *Br* Obstkonserven *pl*
tin o·pen·er *Br* Dosenöffner *m*, Büchsenöffner *m*
tin·sel Lametta *n*; Flitter *m*
tint 1. (Farb)Ton *m*, Tönung *f*; **2.** tönen
ti·ny winzig
tip[1] 1. Spitze *f*; Filter *m*; ***it's on the tip of my tongue*** *fig* es liegt mir auf der Zunge; **2.** mit e-r Spitze versehen
tip[2] 1. *esp Br* (aus)kippen, schütten; kippen; ***tip over*** umkippen; **2.** *esp Br* (*Schutt- etc*)Abladeplatz *m*, (-)Halde *f*; *Br fig* F Saustall *m*
tip[3] 1. Trinkgeld *n*; **2.** *j-m* ein Trinkgeld geben
tip[4] 1. Tipp *m*, Rat(schlag) *m*; **2.** tippen auf (*acc*) (***as*** als); ***tip s.o. off*** j-m e-n Tipp *or* Wink geben
tip·sy angeheitert
tip·toe 1. ***on tiptoe*** auf Zehenspitzen; **2.** auf Zehenspitzen gehen
tire[1] MOT Reifen *m*
tire[2] ermüden, müde machen *or* werden
tired müde; ***be tired of*** *j-n, et.* satt haben
tire·less unermüdlich
tire·some ermüdend; lästig
tis·sue BIOL Gewebe *n*; Papier(taschen)tuch *n*; → **tissue pa·per** Seidenpapier *n*
tit[1] F *contp* Titte *f*
tit[2] ZO Meise *f*
tit·bit *esp Br* → ***tidbit***
tit·il·late *j-n* (*sexuell*) anregen
ti·tle Titel *m*; JUR (Rechts)Anspruch *m* (***to*** auf *acc*)
ti·tle·hold·er SPORT Titelhalter(in)
ti·tle page Titelseite *f*
ti·tle role THEA *etc* Titelrolle *f*
tit·mouse ZO Meise *f*
tit·ter 1. kichern; **2.** Kichern *n*
to 1. *prp* zu; an (*acc*), auf (*acc*), für, in (*acc*), in (*dat*), nach; (im Verhältnis *or* im Vergleich) zu, gegen(über); *extent, limit, degree*: bis, (bis) zu, (bis) an (*acc*); *time*: bis, bis zu, bis gegen, vor (*dat*); ***from Monday to Friday*** von Montag bis Freitag; ***a quarter to one*** (ein) Viertel vor eins, drei viertel eins; ***go to Italy*** nach Italien fahren; ***go to school*** in die *or* zur Schule gehen; ***have you ever been to Rome?*** bist du schon einmal in Rom gewesen?; ***to me*** *etc* mir *etc*; ***here's to you!*** auf Ihr Wohl!, prosit!; **2.** *adv* zu; ***pull to*** *Tür etc* zuziehen; ***come to*** (wieder) zu sich kommen; ***to and fro*** hin und her, auf und ab; **3.** *with infinitive*: zu; *intention, aim*: um zu; ***to go*** gehen; ***easy to learn*** leicht zu lernen; ***… to earn money …*** um Geld zu verdienen
toad ZO Kröte *f*, Unke *f*
toad·stool BOT ungenießbarer Pilz; Giftpilz *m*
toad·y 1. Kriecher(in); **2.** ***toady to s.o.*** *fig* vor j-m kriechen
toast[1] 1. Toast *m*; **2.** toasten; rösten
toast[2] 1. Toast *m*, Trinkspruch *m*; **2.** auf *j-n or j-s* Wohl trinken
toast·er TECH Toaster *m*
to·bac·co Tabak *m*
to·bac·co·nist Tabak(waren)händler(in)
to·bog·gan 1. (Rodel)Schlitten *m*; **2.** Schlitten fahren, rodeln
to·day 1. *adv* heute; heutzutage; ***a week today, today week*** heute in e-r Woche, heute in acht Tagen; **2.** ***today's paper*** die heutige Zeitung, die Zeitung von heute; ***of today, today's*** von heute, heutig
tod·dle auf wack(e)ligen *or* unsicheren Beinen gehen
to-do F *fig* Theater *n*
toe ANAT Zehe *f*; Spitze *f*
toe·nail ANAT Zehennagel *m*
tof·fee, tof·fy Sahnebonbon *m, n*, Toffee *n*
to·geth·er zusammen; gleichzeitig
toi·let Toilette *f*
toilet pa·per Toilettenpapier *n*
toilet roll *esp Br* Rolle *f* Toilettenpapier

to·ken Zeichen *n*; ***as a token, in token of*** als *or* zum Zeichen (*gen*); zum Andenken an (*acc*)
token strike Warnstreik *m*
tol·e·ra·ble erträglich
tol·e·rance Toleranz *f*; Nachsicht *f*
tol·e·rant tolerant (***of, towards*** gegenüber)
tol·e·rate tolerieren, dulden; ertragen
toll[1] Benutzungsgebühr *f*, Maut *f*; ***heavy death toll*** große Zahl an Todesopfern; ***take its toll*** (***on***) *fig* s-n Tribut fordern (von); s-e Spuren hinterlassen (bei)
toll[2] läuten
toll-free TEL gebührenfrei
toll road gebührenpflichtige Straße, Mautstraße *f*
tom F → ***tomcat***
to·ma·to BOT Tomate *f*
tomb Grab *n*; Grabmal *n*; Gruft *f*
tom·boy Wildfang *m*
tomb·stone Grabstein *m*
tom·cat zo Kater *m*
tom·fool·e·ry Unsinn *m*
to·mor·row 1. *adv* morgen; ***a week tomorrow, tomorrow week*** morgen in e-r Woche, morgen in acht Tagen; ***tomorrow morning*** morgen früh; ***tomorrow night*** morgen Abend; **2.** ***the day after tomorrow*** übermorgen; ***of tomorrow, tomorrow's*** von morgen
ton (ABBR ***t, tn***) Tonne *f*
tone 1. Ton *m*; Klang *m*; (Farb)Ton *m*; MUS Note *f*; MED Tonus *m*; *fig* Niveau *n*; **2.** ***tone down*** abschwächen; ***tone up*** *Muskeln etc* kräftigen
tongs (***a pair of tongs*** e-e) Zange *f*
tongue ANAT, TECH Zunge *f*; (*Mutter*)Sprache *f*; Klöppel *m* (*e-r Glocke*); ***hold one's tongue*** den Mund halten
ton·ic Tonikum *n*, Stärkungsmittel *n*; Tonic *n*; MUS Grundton *m*
to·night heute Abend *or* Nacht
ton·sil ANAT Mandel *f*
ton·sil·li·tis MED Mandelentzündung *f*; Angina *f*
too zu; zu, sehr; auch (noch)
tool Werkzeug *n*, Gerät *n*
tool bag Werkzeugtasche *f*
tool box Werkzeugkasten *m*
tool kit Werkzeug *n*
tool·mak·er Werkzeugmacher *m*
tool·shed Geräteschuppen *m*
toot *esp* MOT hupen
tooth Zahn *m*
tooth·ache Zahnschmerzen *pl*, Zahnweh *n*
tooth·brush Zahnbürste *f*
tooth·less zahnlos
tooth·paste Zahncreme *f*, Zahnpasta *f*
tooth·pick Zahnstocher *m*
top[1] **1.** oberer Teil; GEOGR Gipfel *m*, Spitze *f*; BOT Krone *f*, Wipfel *m*; Kopfende *n*, oberes Ende; Oberteil *n*; Oberfläche *f*; Deckel *m*; Verschluss *m*; MOT Verdeck *n*; MOT höchster Gang; ***at the top of the page*** oben auf der Seite; ***at the top of one's voice*** aus vollem Hals; ***on top*** oben(auf); darauf, F drauf; ***on top of*** (oben) auf (*dat or acc*), über (*dat or acc*); **2.** oberste(r, -s); Höchst…, Spitzen…, Top…; **3.** bedecken (***with*** mit); *fig* übersteigen, übertreffen; ***top up*** *Tank etc* auffüllen; F *j-m* nachschenken
top[2] Kreisel *m* (*toy*)
top hat Zylinder *m*
top-heav·y kopflastig (*a. fig*)
top·ic Thema *n*
top·ic·al aktuell
top·ple: *mst* ***topple over*** umkippen; ***topple the government*** die Regierung stürzen
top·sy-tur·vy in e-r heillosen Unordnung
torch *Br* Taschenlampe *f*; Fackel *f*
torch·light Fackelschein *m*; ***torchlight procession*** Fackelzug *m*
tor·ment 1. Qual *f*; **2.** quälen, peinigen, plagen
tor·na·do Tornado *m*, Wirbelsturm *m*
tor·pe·do MIL **1.** Torpedo *m*; **2.** torpedieren (*a. fig*)
tor·rent reißender Strom; *fig* Schwall *m*
tor·ren·tial: ***torrential rain*** sintflutartige Regenfälle *pl*
tor·toise zo Schildkröte *f*
tor·tu·ous gewunden
tor·ture 1. Folter *f*, Folterung *f*; *fig* Qual *f*, Tortur *f*; **2.** foltern; *fig* quälen
toss 1. *v/t* werfen; *Münze* hochwerfen; GASTR schwenken; ***toss off*** F *Bild etc* hinhauen; *v/i a.* ***toss about, toss and turn*** sich *im Schlaf* hin und her werfen; *a.* ***toss up*** e-e Münze hochwerfen; ***toss for s.th.*** um et. losen; ***toss one's head*** den Kopf zurückwerfen; **2.** Wurf *m*; Zurückwerfen *n*; Hochwerfen *n*
tot F Knirps *m*
to·tal 1. völlig, total; ganz, gesamt, Gesamt…; **2.** Gesamtbetrag *m*, -menge *f*; **3.** sich belaufen auf (*acc*); ***total up*** zusammenrechnen, -zählen
tot·ter schwanken, wanken
touch 1. (sich) berühren; anfassen; *Essen etc* anrühren; *fig* herankommen an (*acc*); *fig* rühren; ***touch wood!*** toi, toi, toi!; ***touch down*** AVIAT aufsetzen; ***touch up*** ausbessern; PHOT retuschieren; **2.** Tast-

empfindung *f*; Berührung *f*, MUS *etc* Anschlag *m*; (*Pinsel- etc*)Strich *m*; GASTR Spur *f*; Verbindung *f*, Kontakt *m*; *fig* Note *f*; *fig* Anflug *m*; ***a touch of flu*** e-e leichte Grippe; ***get in touch with s.o.*** sich mit j-m in Verbindung setzen
touch-and-go F kritisch, riskant, prekär; ***it was touch-and-go whether*** es stand auf des Messers Schneide, ob
touch·down AVIAT Aufsetzen *n*, Landung *f*
touched gerührt; F leicht verrückt
touch·ing rührend
touch·line *soccer*: Seitenlinie *f*
touch·stone Prüfstein *m* (***of*** für)
touch·y empfindlich; heikel (*subject etc*)
tough zäh; widerstandsfähig; *fig* hart; schwierig (*problem, negotiations etc*)
tough·en *a.* ***toughen up*** hart *or* zäh machen *or* werden
tour **1.** Tour *f* (***of*** durch), (Rund)Reise *f*, (Rund)Fahrt *f*; Ausflug *m*; Rundgang *m* (***of*** durch); THEA Tournee *f* (*a.* SPORT); ***go on tour*** auf Tournee gehen; → ***conduct*** *2*; **2.** bereisen, reisen durch
tour·is·m Tourismus *m*, Fremdenverkehr *m*
tour·ist **1.** Tourist(in); **2.** Touristen…
tourist class AVIAT, MAR Touristenklasse *f*
tourist in·dus·try Tourismusgeschäft *n*
tourist infor·ma·tion of·fice, tourist of·fice Verkehrsverein *m*
tourist sea·son Reisesaison *f*, Reisezeit *f*
tour·na·ment Turnier *n*
tou·sled zerzaust
tow **1.** *Boot etc* schleppen, *Auto etc a.* abschleppen; **2.** ***give s.o. a tow*** j-n abschleppen; ***take in tow*** *Auto etc* abschleppen
to·ward, *esp Br* **to·wards** auf (*acc*) … zu, (in) Richtung, zu; *time*: gegen; *fig* gegenüber
tow·el **1.** Handtuch *n*, (*Bade- etc*)Tuch *n*; **2.** (mit e-m Handtuch) abtrocknen *or* abreiben
tow·er 1. Turm *m*; **1.** ***tower above, tower over*** überragen
tower block *Br* Hochhaus *n*
tow·er·ing turmhoch; *fig* überragend; ***in a towering rage*** rasend vor Zorn
town Stadt *f*; Kleinstadt *f*; ***go into town*** in die Stadt gehen
town cen·tre *Br* Innenstadt *f*, City *f*
town coun·cil *Br* Stadtrat *m*
town coun·ci(l)·lor *Br* Stadtrat *m*, Stadträtin *f*
town hall Rathaus *n*
town·ie F Städter(in), Stadtmensch *m*
town plan·ner Stadtplaner(in)
town plan·ning Stadtplanung *f*
towns·peo·ple Städter *pl*, Stadtbevölkerung *f*
tow·rope MOT Abschleppseil *n*
tox·ic toxisch, giftig; Gift…
tox·ic waste Giftmüll *m*
tox·ic waste dump Giftmülldeponie *f*
toy **1.** Spielzeug *n*, *pl a.* Spielsachen *pl*, ECON Spielwaren *pl*; **2.** Spielzeug…; Miniatur…; Zwerg…; **3.** ***toy with*** spielen mit (*a. fig*)
trace **1.** (durch)pausen; *j-n*, *et.* ausfindig machen, aufspüren, *et.* finden; *a.* ***trace back*** *et.* zurückverfolgen (***to*** bis zu); ***trace s.th. to*** et. zurückführen auf (*acc*); **2.** Spur *f* (*a. fig*)
track **1.** Spur *f* (*a. fig*), Fährte *f*; Pfad *m*, Weg *m*; RAIL Gleis *n*, Geleise *n*; TECH Raupe *f*, Raupenkette *f*; SPORT (Renn-, Aschen)Bahn *f*, (*Renn*)Strecke *f*; *tape etc*: Spur *f*; Nummer *f* (*on an LP etc*); **2.** verfolgen; ***track down*** aufspüren; auftreiben
track and field SPORT Leichtathletik *f*
track e·vent SPORT Laufdisziplin *f*
track·ing sta·tion Bodenstation *f*
track·suit Trainingsanzug *m*
tract Fläche *f*, Gebiet *n*; ANAT (*Verdauungs*)Trakt *m*, (*Atem*)Wege *pl*
trac·tion Ziehen *n*, Zug *m*
trac·tion en·gine Zugmaschine *f*
trac·tor Traktor *m*, Trecker *m*
trade **1.** Handel *m*; Branche *f*, Gewerbe *n*; (*esp* Handwerks)Beruf *m*; **2.** Handel treiben, handeln; ***trade on*** ausnutzen
trade a·gree·ment Handelsabkommen *n*
trade·mark Warenzeichen *n*
trade name Markenname *m*, Handelsbezeichnung *f*
trade price Großhandelspreis *m*
trad·er Händler(in)
trades·man (Einzel)Händler *m*; Ladeninhaber *m*; Lieferant *m*
trade(s *Br***)**| **u·nion** Gewerkschaft *f*
trade u·nion·ist Gewerkschaftler(in)
tra·di·tion Tradition *f*; Überlieferung *f*
tra·di·tion·al traditionell
traf·fic **1.** Verkehr *m*; (*esp* illegaler) Handel (***in*** mit); **2.** (*esp* illegal) handeln (***in*** mit)
traffic cir·cle MOT Kreisverkehr *m*
traffic in·struc·tion Verkehrsunterricht *m*
traffic is·land Verkehrsinsel *f*
traffic jam (Verkehrs)Stau *m*, Verkehrsstockung *f*
traffic light(s) Verkehrsampel *f*
traffic of·fense (*Br* **of·fence**) Verkehrsdelikt *n*
traffic offend·er Verkehrssünder(in)
traffic reg·ula·tions Straßenverkehrsord-

nung *f*
traffic sign Verkehrszeichen *n*, -schild *n*
traffic sig·nal → ***traffic light(s)***
traffic war·den *Br* Parküberwacher *m*, Politesse *f*
tra·ge·dy Tragödie *f*
tra·gic tragisch
trail 1. *v/t et.* nachschleifen lassen; verfolgen; SPORT zurückliegen hinter (*dat*) (***by*** um); *v/i* sich schleppen; BOT kriechen; SPORT zurückliegen (***by 3-0*** 0:3); ***trail (along) behind s.o.*** hinter j-m herschleifen; **2.** Spur *f* (*a. fig*), Fährte *f*; Pfad *m*, Weg *m*; ***trail of blood*** Blutspur *f*; ***trail of dust*** Staubwolke *f*
trail·er MOT Anhänger *m*; Wohnwagen *m*, Caravan *m*; *film*, TV Trailer *m*, Vorschau *f*
trailer park Standplatz *m* für Wohnwagen
train 1. RAIL Zug *m*; Kolonne *f*, Schlange *f*; Schleppe *f*; *fig* Folge *f*, Kette *f*; ***by train*** mit der Bahn, mit dem Zug; ***train of thought*** Gedankengang *m*; **2.** *v/t j-n* ausbilden (***as*** als, zum), schulen; SPORT trainieren; *Tier* abrichten, dressieren; *Kamera etc* richten (***on*** auf *acc*); *v/i* ausgebildet werden (***as*** als, zum); SPORT trainieren (***for*** für)
train·ee Auszubildende *m, f*
train·er Ausbilder(in); zo Abrichter(in), Dompteur *m*, Dompteuse *f*; SPORT Trainer(in); *Br* Turnschuh *m*
train·ing Ausbildung *f*, Schulung *f*; Abrichten *n*, Dressur *f*; SPORT Training *n*
trait (Charakter)Zug *m*
trai·tor Verräter *m*
tram *Br* Straßenbahn(wagen *m*) *f*
tram·car *Br* Straßenbahnwagen *m*
tramp 1. sta(m)pfen *or* trampeln (durch); **2.** Tramp *m*, Landstreicher *m*, Vagabund *m*; Wanderung *f*; Flittchen *n*
tram·ple (zer)trampeln
trance Trance *f*
tran·quil ruhig, friedlich
tran·quil·(l)i·ty Ruhe *f*, Frieden *m*
tran·quil·(l)ize beruhigen
tran·quil·(l)iz·er PHARM Beruhigungsmittel *n*
trans·act *Geschäft* abwickeln, *Handel* abschließen
trans·ac·tion Abwicklung *f*, Abschluss *m*; Geschäft *n*, Transaktion *f*
trans·at·lan·tic transatlantisch, Transatlantik…, Übersee…
tran·scribe abschreiben, kopieren; *Stenogramm etc* übertragen
tran·script Abschrift *f*, Kopie *f*
tran·scrip·tion Umschreibung *f*, Umschrift *f*; Abschrift *f*, Kopie *f*
trans·fer 1. *v/t* (***to***) *Betrieb etc* verlegen (nach); *j-n* versetzen (nach); SPORT *Spieler* transferieren (zu), abgeben (an *acc*); *Geld* überweisen (an *acc*, auf *acc*); JUR *Eigentum, Recht* übertragen (auf *acc*); *v/i* SPORT wechseln (***to*** zu); umsteigen (***from … to …*** von … auf … *acc*); **2.** Verlegung *f*; Versetzung *f*; SPORT Transfer *m*, Wechsel *m*; ECON Überweisung *f*; JUR Übertragung *f*; Umsteige(fahr)karte *f*
trans·fer·a·ble übertragbar
trans·fixed *fig* versteinert, starr
trans·form umwandeln, verwandeln
trans·for·ma·tion Umwandlung *f*, Verwandlung *f*
trans·form·er ELECTR Transformator *m*
trans·fu·sion MED Bluttransfusion *f*, Blutübertragung *f*
trans·gress verletzen, verstoßen gegen
tran·sient flüchtig, vergänglich
tran·sis·tor Transistor *m*
tran·sit Transit-, Durchgangsverkehr *m*; ECON Transport *m*; ***in transit*** unterwegs, auf dem Transport
tran·si·tion Übergang *m*
tran·si·tive LING transitiv
tran·si·to·ry → ***transient***
trans·late übersetzen (***from English into German*** aus dem Englischen ins Deutsche)
trans·la·tion Übersetzung *f*
trans·la·tor Übersetzer(in)
trans·lu·cent lichtdurchlässig
trans·mis·sion MED Übertragung *f*; *radio*, TV Sendung *f*; MOT Getriebe *n*
trans·mit *Signale* (aus)senden; *radio*, TV senden; PHYS *Wärme etc* leiten, *Licht etc* durchlassen; MED *Krankheit* übertragen
trans·mit·ter Sender *m*
trans·par·en·cy Durchsichtigkeit *f* (*a. fig*); *fig* Durchschaubarkeit *f*; Dia(-positiv) *n*; Folie *f*
trans·par·ent durchsichtig (*a. fig*); *fig* durchschaubar
tran·spire transpirieren, schwitzen; *fig* durchsickern; F passieren
trans·plant 1. umpflanzen, verpflanzen (*a.* MED); MED transplantieren; **2.** MED Transplantation *f*, Verpflanzung *f*; Transplantat *n*
trans·port 1. Transport *m*, Beförderung *f*; Beförderungs-, Verkehrsmittel *n or pl*; MIL Transportschiff *n*, -flugzeug *n*, (*Truppen*)Transporter *m*; **2.** transportieren, befördern
trans·port·a·ble transportabel, transportfähig
trans·por·ta·tion Transport *m*, Beförderung *f*

T

trap **1.** Falle *f* (*a. fig*); ***set a trap for s.o.*** j-m e-e Falle stellen; ***shut one's trap, keep one's trap shut*** F die Schnauze halten; **2.** (in *or* mit e-r Falle) fangen; *fig* in e-e Falle locken; ***be trapped*** eingeschlossen sein
trap·door Falltür *f*; THEA Versenkung *f*
tra·peze Trapez *n*
trap·per Trapper *m*, Fallensteller *m*, Pelztierjäger *m*
trap·pings Rangabzeichen *pl*; *fig* Drum und Dran *n*
trash F Schund *m*; Quatsch *m*, Unsinn *m*; Abfall *m*, Abfälle *pl*, Müll *m*; Gesindel *n*
trash·can Abfall-, Mülleimer *m*; Abfall-, Mülltonne *f*
trash·y Schund…
trav·el **1.** *v/i* reisen; fahren; TECH *etc* sich bewegen; *fig* sich verbreiten; *fig* schweifen, wandern; *v/t* bereisen; *Strecke* zurücklegen, fahren; **2.** Reisen *n*; *pl* (*esp* Auslands)Reisen *pl*
travel a·gen·cy Reisebüro *n*
travel a·gent Reisebüroinhaber(in); Angestellte *m, f* in e-m Reisebüro
travel a·gent's, travel bu·reau Reisebüro *n*
trav·el·(l)er Reisende *m, f*
trav·el·(l)er's check (*Br* **cheque**) Reise-, Travellerscheck *m*
trav·el·(l)ing bag Reisetasche *f*
travel(l)ing expens·es Reisekosten *pl*
trav·el sick·ness Reisekrankheit *f*
trav·es·ty Zerrbild *n*
trawl **1.** Schleppnetz *n*; **2.** mit dem Schleppnetz fischen
trawl·er MAR Trawler *m*
tray Tablett *n*; Ablagekorb *m*
treach·er·ous verräterisch; tückisch
treach·er·y Verrat *m*
trea·cle *esp Br* Sirup *m*
tread **1.** treten (***on*** auf *acc*; in *acc*); *Pfad etc* treten; **2.** Gang *m*; Schritt(e *pl*) *m*; (Reifen)Profil *n*
tread·mill Tretmühle *f* (*a. fig*)
trea·son Landesverrat *m*
trea·sure **1.** Schatz *m*; **2.** sehr schätzen; in Ehren halten
trea·sur·er Schatzmeister(in)
trea·sure trove Schatzfund *m*
Trea·su·ry *Br*, **Treasury De·part·ment** Finanzministerium *n*
treat **1.** *j-n, et.* behandeln; umgehen mit; *et.* ansehen, betrachten (***as*** als); MED *j-n* behandeln (***for*** gegen); *j-n* einladen (***to*** zu); ***treat s.o. to s.th.*** *a.* j-m et. spendieren; ***treat o.s. to s.th.*** sich et. leisten *or* gönnen; ***be treated for*** MED in ärztlicher Behandlung sein wegen; **2.** (besondere) Freude *or* Überraschung; ***this is my treat*** das geht auf meine Rechnung, ich lade dich *etc* ein
trea·tise Abhandlung *f*
treat·ment Behandlung *f*
treat·y Vertrag *m*
tre·ble[1] **1.** dreifach; **2.** (sich) verdreifachen
tre·ble[2] MUS Knabensopran *m*; *radio*: (Ton)Höhe *f*
tree BOT Baum *m*
tre·foil BOT Klee *m*
trel·lis BOT Spalier *n*
trem·ble zittern (***with*** vor *dat*)
tre·men·dous gewaltig, enorm; F klasse, toll
trem·or Zittern *n*; Beben *n*
trench Graben *m*; MIL Schützengraben *m*
trend Trend *m*, Entwicklung *f*, Tendenz *f*; Mode *f*
trend·y F **1.** modern, modisch; ***be trendy*** als schick gelten, in sein; **2.** *esp Br contp* Schickimicki *m*
tres·pass **1.** ***trespass on*** *Grundstück etc* unbefugt betreten; *j-s Zeit etc* über Gebühr in Anspruch nehmen; ***no trespassing*** Betreten verboten!; **2.** unbefugtes Betreten
tres·pass·er: ***trespassers will be prosecuted*** Betreten bei Strafe verboten!
tres·tle Bock *m*, Gestell *n*
tri·al **1.** JUR Prozess *m*, (Gerichts)Verhandlung *f*, (-)Verfahren *n*; Erprobung *f*, Probe *f*, Prüfung *f*, Test *m*; Plage *f*; ***on trial*** auf *or* zur Probe; ***be on trial*** erprobt *or* getestet werden; ***be on trial, stand trial*** vor Gericht stehen (***for*** wegen); ***by way of trial*** versuchsweise; **2.** Versuchs…, Probe…
tri·an·gle Dreieck *n*; Winkel *m*, Zeichendreieck *n*
tri·an·gu·lar dreieckig
tri·ath·lon SPORT Triathlon *n, m*, Dreikampf *m*
trib·al Stammes…
tribe (Volks)Stamm *m*
tri·bu·nal JUR Gericht(shof *m*) *n*
trib·u·ta·ry GEOGR Nebenfluss *m*
trib·ute: ***be a tribute to*** *j-m* Ehre machen; ***pay tribute to*** *j-m* Anerkennung zollen
trick **1.** Trick *m*; (*Karten- etc*)Kunststück *n*; Streich *m*; *card game*: Stich *m*; (merkwürdige) Angewohnheit, Eigenart *f*; ***play a trick on s.o.*** j-m e-n Streich spielen; **2.** Trick…; ***trick question*** Fangfrage *f*; **3.** überlisten, F reinlegen
trick·e·ry Tricks *pl*
trick·le **1.** tröpfeln; rieseln; **2.** Tröpfeln *n*; Rinnsal *n*
trick·ster Betrüger(in), Schwindler(in)

T

trick·y heikel, schwierig; durchtrieben, raffiniert
tri·cy·cle Dreirad *n*
tri·dent Dreizack *m*
tri·fle 1. Kleinigkeit *f*; Lappalie *f*; ***a trifle*** ein bisschen, etwas; **2. *trifle with*** *fig* spielen mit; ***he is not to be trifled with*** er lässt nicht mit sich spaßen
tri·fling geringfügig, unbedeutend
trig·ger Abzug *m*; ***pull the trigger*** abdrücken
trig·ger-hap·py F schießwütig
trill 1. Triller *m*; **2.** trillern
trim 1. *Hecke etc* stutzen, beschneiden, sich *den Bart etc* stutzen; *Kleidungsstück* besetzen (***with*** mit); ***trimmed with fur*** pelzbesetzt, mit Pelzbesatz; ***trim off*** abschneiden; **2. *give s.th. a trim*** et. stutzen, et. (be)schneiden; ***be in good trim*** F gut in Form sein; **3.** gepflegt
trim·mings Besatz *m*; GASTR Beilagen *pl*
Trin·i·ty REL Dreieinigkeit *f*
trin·ket (*esp* billiges) Schmuckstück
trip 1. *v/i* stolpern (***over*** über *acc*); (e-n) Fehler machen; *v/t a.* ***trip up*** *j-m* ein Bein stellen (*a. fig*); **2.** (kurze) Reise; Ausflug *m*, Trip *m* (*a. sl*); Stolpern *n*, Fallen *n*
tripe GASTR Kaldaunen *pl*, Kutteln *pl*
trip·le 1. dreifach; **2.** verdreifachen
trip·le jump SPORT Dreisprung *m*
trip·lets Drillinge *pl*
trip·li·cate 1. dreifach; **2. *in triplicate*** in dreifacher Ausfertigung
tri·pod PHOT Stativ *n*
trip·per *esp Br* (*esp Tages*)Ausflügler(in)
trite abgedroschen, banal
tri·umph 1. Triumph *m*, *fig* Sieg *m* (***over*** über *acc*); **2.** triumphieren (***over*** über *acc*)
tri·um·phal Triumph…
tri·um·phant triumphierend
triv·i·al unbedeutend, bedeutungslos; trivial, alltäglich
trol·ley *esp Br* Einkaufswagen *m*; Gepäckwagen *m*, Kofferkuli *m*; (*Tee- etc*) Wagen *m*; (***supermarket***) ***trolley*** Einkaufswagen *m*; ***shopping trolley*** Einkaufsroller *m*
trol·ley·bus Oberleitungsbus *m*, Obus *m*
trom·bone MUS Posaune *f*
troop 1. Schar *f*; *pl* MIL Truppen *pl*; **2.** (*herein- etc*)strömen; ***troop the colour*** *Br* MIL e-e Fahnenparade abhalten
troop·er MIL Kavallerist *m*; Panzerjäger *m*; Polizist *m*
tro·phy Trophäe *f*
trop·ic ASTR, GEOGR Wendekreis *m*; ***the tropic of Cancer*** der Wendekreis des Krebses; ***the tropic of Capricorn*** der Wendekreis des Steinbocks
trop·i·cal tropisch, Tropen…
trop·ics Tropen *pl*
trot 1. Trab *m*; Trott *m*; **2.** traben (lassen); ***trot along*** F losziehen
trou·ble 1. Schwierigkeit *f*, Problem *n*, Ärger *m*; Mühe *f*; MED Beschwerden *pl*; *a. pl* POL Unruhen *pl*; *pl* Unannehmlichkeiten *pl*; ***be in trouble*** in Schwierigkeiten sein; ***get into trouble*** Schwierigkeiten *or* Ärger bekommen; *j-n* in Schwierigkeiten bringen; ***get*** *or* ***run into trouble*** in Schwierigkeiten geraten; ***have trouble with*** Schwierigkeiten *or* Ärger haben mit; ***put s.o. to trouble*** j-m Mühe *or* Umstände machen; ***take the trouble to do s.th.*** sich die Mühe machen, et. zu tun; **2.** *v/t j-n* beunruhigen; *j-m* Mühe *or* Umstände machen; *j-n* bemühen (***for*** um), bitten (***for*** um; ***to do*** zu tun); ***be troubled by*** geplagt werden von, leiden an (*dat*); *v/i* sich bemühen (***to do*** zu tun), sich Umstände machen (***about*** wegen)
trou·ble·mak·er Störenfried *m*, Unruhestifter(in)
trou·ble·some lästig
trou·ble spot *esp* POL Krisenherd *m*
trough Trog *m*; Wellental *n*
trounce SPORT haushoch besiegen
troupe THEA Truppe *f*
trou·ser: (***a pair of***) ***trousers*** (e-e) Hose *f*
trou·ser suit *Br* Hosenanzug *m*
trous·seau Aussteuer *f*
trout zo Forelle *f*
trow·el (Maurer)Kelle *f*
tru·ant Schulschwänzer(in); ***play truant*** *Br* (die Schule) schwänzen
truce MIL Waffenstillstand *m* (*a. fig*)
truck 1. MOT Lastwagen *m*; Fernlaster *m*; *Br* RAIL (offener) Güterwagen; Transportkarren *m*; **2.** auf *or* mit Lastwagen transportieren
truck driv·er, truck·er MOT Lastwagenfahrer *m*; Fernfahrer *m*
truck farm ECON Gemüse- und Obstgärtnerei *f*
trudge (mühsam) stapfen
true wahr; echt, wirklich; treu (***to*** *dat*); ***be true*** wahr sein, stimmen; ***come true*** in Erfüllung gehen; wahr werden; ***true to life*** lebensecht
tru·ly wahrheitsgemäß; wirklich, wahrhaft; aufrichtig
trump 1. Trumpf(karte *f*) *m*; *pl* Trumpf *m*; **2.** mit e-m Trumpf stechen; ***trump up*** erfinden
trum·pet 1. MUS Trompete *f*; **1.** trompeten; *fig* ausposaunen

trun·cheon (Gummi)Knüppel *m*, Schlagstock *m*
trun·dle *Karren etc* ziehen
trunk (Baum)Stamm *m*; Schrankkoffer *m*; zo Rüssel *m*; ANAT Rumpf *m*; MOT Kofferraum *m*
trunk road *Br* Fernstraße *f*
trunks (*a.* ***a pair of trunks*** e-e) (*Bade*)Hose *f*; SPORT Shorts *pl*
truss 1. *a.* ***truss up*** *j-n* fesseln; GASTR *Geflügel etc* dressieren; **2.** MED Bruchband *n*
trust 1. Vertrauen *n* (***in*** zu); JUR Treuhand *f*; ECON Trust *m*; Großkonzern *m*; ***hold s.th. in trust*** et. treuhänderisch verwalten (***for*** für); ***place s.th. in s.o.'s trust*** j-m et. anvertrauen; **2.** *v/t* (ver)trauen (*dat*); sich verlassen auf (*acc*); (zuversichtlich) hoffen; ***trust him!*** das sieht ihm ähnlich!; *v/i*: ***trust in*** vertrauen auf (*acc*); ***trust to*** sich verlassen auf (*acc*)
trust·ee JUR Treuhänder(in); Sachverwalter(in)
trust·ful, **trust·ing** vertrauensvoll
trust·wor·thy vertrauenswürdig, zuverlässig
truth Wahrheit *f*
truth·ful wahr; wahrheitsliebend
try 1. *v/t* versuchen; *et.* (aus)probieren; JUR (über) *e-e Sache* verhandeln; *j-m* den Prozess machen (***for*** wegen); *j-n, j-s Geduld, Nerven etc* auf e-e harte Probe stellen; ***try*** *s.th.* ***on*** *Kleid etc* anprobieren; ***try*** *s.th.* ***out*** et. ausprobieren; *v/i* es versuchen; ***try for*** *Br*, ***try out for*** sich bemühen um; **2.** Versuch *m*; ***give*** *s.o., s.th.* ***a try*** es mit *j-m, et.* versuchen; ***have a try*** es versuchen
try·ing anstrengend
tsar HIST Zar *m*
T-shirt T-Shirt *n*
tub Bottich *m*, Zuber *m*, Tonne *f*; Becher *m*; F (Bade)Wanne *f*
tub·by F pumm(e)lig
tube Röhre *f* (*a.* ANAT), Rohr *n*; Schlauch *m*; Tube *f*; *Br* F U-Bahn *f* (*in London*); F Röhre *f*, Glotze *f*
tube·less schlauchlos
tu·ber BOT Knolle *f*
tu·ber·cu·lo·sis MED Tuberkulose *f*
tu·bu·lar röhrenförmig
tuck 1. stecken; ***tuck away*** F wegstecken; ***tuck in*** *esp Br* F reinhauen, zulangen; ***tuck up*** (***in bed***) *Kind* ins Bett packen; **2.** Biese *f*; Saum *m*; Abnäher *m*
Tue(s) ABBR *of* ***Tuesday*** Di., Dienstag *m*
Tues·day (ABBR ***Tue, Tues***) Dienstag *m*; ***on Tuesday*** (am) Dienstag; ***on Tuesdays*** dienstags
tuft (*Gras-, Haar- etc*)Büschel *n*
tug 1. zerren *or* ziehen (an *dat or* ***at*** an *dat*); **2.** ***give*** *s.th.* ***a tug*** zerren *or* ziehen an (*dat*)
tug-of-war SPORT Tauziehen *n* (*a. fig*)
tu·i·tion Unterricht *m*; Unterrichtsgebühr(en *pl*) *f*
tu·lip BOT Tulpe *f*
tum·ble 1. fallen, stürzen; purzeln (*a. fig*); **2.** Fall *m*, Sturz *m*
tum·ble·down baufällig
tum·bler (Trink)Glas *n*
tu·mid MED geschwollen
tum·my F Bauch *m*, Bäuchlein *n*
tu·mo(u)r MED Tumor *m*
tu·mult Tumult *m*
tu·mul·tu·ous tumultartig, (*applause etc*) stürmisch
tu·na zo Thunfisch *m*
tune 1. MUS Melodie *f*; ***be out of tune*** verstimmt sein; **2.** *v/t mst* ***tune in*** *Radio etc* einstellen (***to*** auf *acc*); *a.* ***tune up*** MUS stimmen; *a.* ***tune up*** *Motor* tunen; *v/i*: ***tune in*** (das Radio *etc*) einschalten; ***tune up*** MUS (die Instrumente) stimmen
tune·ful melodisch
tune·less unmelodisch
tun·er *radio*, TV Tuner *m*
tun·nel 1. Tunnel *m*; **2.** *Berg* durchtunneln; *Fluss etc* untertunneln
tun·ny zo Thunfisch *m*
tur·ban Turban *m*
tur·bid trüb (*water*); dick, dicht (*smoke etc*); *fig* verworren, wirr
tur·bine TECH Turbine *f*
tur·bo F, **tur·bo·charg·er** MOT Turbolader *m*
tur·bot zo Steinbutt *m*
tur·bu·lent turbulent
tu·reen (Suppen)Terrine *f*
turf 1. Rasen *m*; Sode *f*, Rasenstück *n*; ***the turf*** die (Pferde)Rennbahn; der Pferderennsport; **2.** mit Rasen bedecken
tur·gid MED geschwollen
Turk Türke *m*, Türkin *f*
Tur·key die Türkei
tur·key zo Truthahn *m*, Truthenne *f*, Pute *f*, Puter *m*; ***talk turkey*** F offen *or* sachlich reden
Turk·ish 1. türkisch; **2.** LING Türkisch *n*
tur·moil Aufruhr *m*
turn 1. *v/t* drehen, herum-, umdrehen; (um)wenden; *Seite* umblättern; *Schlauch etc* richten (***on*** auf *acc*); *Antenne* ausrichten (***toward[s]*** auf *acc*); *Aufmerksamkeit* zuwenden (***to*** *dat*); verwandeln (***into*** in *acc*); *Laub etc* färben; *Milch* sauer werden lassen; TECH formen, drechseln; ***turn the corner*** um die Ecke biegen; ***turn loose*** los-, freilassen; ***turn s.o.'s stom-***

ach j-m den Magen umdrehen; → **inside** *1*, **upside down**, **somersault** *1*; *v/i* sich (um)drehen; abbiegen; einbiegen (**onto** auf *acc*; **into** in *acc*); MOT wenden; *blass, sauer etc* werden; sich verwandeln, *fig a.* umschlagen (**into, to** in *acc*); → **left** *2*, **righ** *2*; **turn against** *j-n* aufbringen *or* aufhetzen gegen; *fig* sich wenden gegen; **turn away** (sich) abwenden (**from** von); *j-n* abweisen, wegschicken; **turn back** umkehren; *j-n* zurückschicken; *Uhr* zurückstellen; **turn down** *Radio etc* leiser stellen; *Gas etc* klein(er) stellen; *Heizung etc* runterschalten; *j-n*, *Angebot etc* ablehnen; *Kragen* umschlagen; *Bettdecke* zurückschlagen; **turn in** *v/t* zurückgeben; *Gewinn etc* erzielen, machen; *Arbeit* einreichen, abgeben; **turn o.s. in** sich stellen; *v/i* F sich aufs Ohr legen; **turn off** *v/t Gas, Wasser etc* abdrehen; *Licht, Radio etc* ausmachen, ausschalten; *Motor* abstellen; F *j-n* anwidern; F *j-m* die Lust nehmen; *v/i* abbiegen; **turn on** *Gas, Wasser etc* aufdrehen; *Gerät* anstellen; *Licht, Radio etc* anmachen, an-, einschalten; F *j-n* antörnen, anmachen; **turn out** *v/t Licht* ausmachen, ausschalten; *j-n* hinauswerfen; F *Waren* ausstoßen; *Tasche etc* (aus)leeren; *v/i* kommen (**for** zu); sich erweisen *or* herausstellen als; **turn over** (sich) umdrehen; *Seite* umblättern; wenden; *et.* umkippen; sich *et.* überlegen; *j-n, et.* übergeben (**to** *dat*); *Waren* umsetzen; **turn round** sich umdrehen; **turn one's car round** wenden; **turn to** sich an *j-n* wenden; sich zuwenden (*dat*); **turn up** *Kragen* hochschlagen; *Ärmel, Saum etc* umschlagen; *Radio etc* lauter stellen; *Gas etc* aufdrehen; *fig* auftauchen; **2.** (Um)Drehung *f*; Biegung *f*, Kurve *f*, Kehre *f*; Abzweigung *f*; *fig* Wende *f*, Wendung *f*; **at every turn** auf Schritt und Tritt; **by turns** abwechselnd; **in turn** der Reihe nach; abwechselnd; **it is my turn** ich bin an der Reihe *or* F dran; **make a left turn** (nach) links abbiegen; **take turns** sich abwechseln (**at** bei); **take a turn for the better** (**worse**) sich bessern (sich verschlimmern); **do s.o. a good** (**bad**) **turn** j-m e-n guten (schlechten) Dienst erweisen

turn·coat Abtrünnige *m, f*, Überläufer(in); (**political**) **turncoat** F Wendehals *m*

turn·er Drechsler *m*; Dreher *m*

turn·ing *esp Br* Abzweigung *f*

turn·ing cir·cle MOT Wendekreis *m*

turn·ing point *fig* Wendepunkt *m*

tur·nip BOT Rübe *f*

turn-off Abzweigung *f*

turn·out Besucher(zahl *f*) *pl*, Beteiligung *f*; Wahlbeteiligung *f*; F Aufmachung *f*

turn·o·ver ECON Umsatz *m*; Personalwechsel *m*, Fluktuation *f*

turn·pike (**road**) gebührenpflichtige Schnellstraße

turn·stile Drehkreuz *n*

turn·ta·ble Plattenteller *m*

turn-up *Br* (Hosen)Aufschlag *m*

tur·pen·tine CHEM Terpentin *n*

tur·quoise MIN Türkis *m*

tur·ret ARCH Ecktürmchen *n*; MIL (Panzer)Turm *m*; MAR Gefechtsturm *m*, Geschützturm *m*

tur·tle ZO (See)Schildkröte *f*

tur·tle·dove ZO Turteltaube *f*

tur·tle·neck Rollkragen(pullover) *m*

tusk ZO Stoßzahn *m*; Hauer *m*

tus·sle F Gerangel *n*

tus·sock Grasbüschel *n*

tu·te·lage (An)Leitung *f*; JUR Vormundschaft *f*

tu·tor Privat-, Hauslehrer(in); *Br* UNIV Tutor(in), Studienleiter(in)

tu·to·ri·al *Br* UNIV Tutorenkurs *m*

tux·e·do Smoking *m*

TV 1. TV *n*, Fernsehen *n*; Fernsehgerät *n*, F Fernseher *m*; **on TV** im Fernsehen; **watch TV** fernsehen; **2.** Fernseh…

twang 1. Schwirren *n*; *mst* **nasal twang** näselnde Aussprache; **2.** schwirren (lassen)

tweak F zwicken, kneifen

tweet ZO piep(s)en

tweez·ers (**a pair of tweezers** e-e) Pinzette *f*

twelfth 1. zwölfte(r, -s); **2.** Zwölftel *n*

twelve 1. zwölf; **2.** Zwölf *f*

twen·ti·eth zwanzigste(r, -s)

twen·ty 1. zwanzig; **2.** Zwanzig *f*

twice zweimal

twid·dle (herum)spielen mit (*or* **with** mit); **twiddle one's thumbs** Däumchen drehen

twig BOT dünner Zweig, Ästchen *n*

twi·light (*esp* Abend)Dämmerung *f*; Zwielicht *n*, Dämmerlicht *n*

twin 1. Zwilling *m*; *pl* Zwillinge *pl*; **2.** Zwillings…; doppelt; **3. be twinned with** die Partnerstadt sein von

twin-bed·ded room Zweibettzimmer *n*

twin beds zwei Einzelbetten

twin broth·er Zwillingsbruder *m*

twine 1. Bindfaden *m*, Schnur *f*; **2.** (sich) schlingen *or* winden (**round** um); *a.* **twine together** zusammendrehen

twin-en·gined AVIAT zweimotorig

twinge stechender Schmerz, Stechen *n*; **a twinge of conscience** Gewissensbisse

pl
twin·kle **1.** glitzern (*stars*), (*a. eyes*) funkeln (***with*** vor *dat*); **2.** Glitzern *n*, Funkeln *n*; ***with a twinkle in one's eye*** augenzwinkernd
twin sis·ter Zwillingsschwester *f*
twin town Partnerstadt *f*
twirl **1.** (herum)wirbeln; wirbeln (***round*** über *acc*); **2.** Wirbel *m*
twist **1.** *v/t* drehen; wickeln (***round*** um); *fig* verdrehen; ***twist off*** abdrehen, *Deckel* abschrauben; ***twist one's ankle*** (mit dem Fuß) umknicken, sich den Fuß vertreten; ***her face was twisted with pain*** ihr Gesicht war schmerzverzerrt; *v/i* sich winden, (*river etc a.*) sich schlängeln; **2.** Drehung *f*; Biegung *f*; (*überraschende*) Wendung; MUS Twist *m*
twitch **1.** *v/t* zucken (mit); *v/i* zucken (***with*** vor); zupfen (***at*** an *dat*); **2.** Zucken *n*; Zuckung *f*
twit·ter **1.** zwitschern; **2.** Zwitschern *n*, Gezwitscher *n*; ***be all of a twitter*** F ganz aufgeregt sein
two **1.** zwei; ***the two cars*** die beiden Autos; ***the two of us*** wir beide; ***in twos*** zu zweit, paarweise; ***cut in two*** in zwei Teile schneiden; ***put two and two together*** zwei und zwei zusammenzählen; **2.** Zwei *f*
two-edged zweischneidig
two-faced falsch, heuchlerisch
two·fold zweifach
two·pence *Br* zwei Pence *pl*
two·pen·ny *Br* F für zwei Pence
two-piece zweiteilig; ***two-piece dress*** Jackenkleid *n*
two-seat·er AVIAT, MOT Zweisitzer *m*
two-sid·ed zweiseitig
two-sto·ried, *Br* **two-sto·rey** zweistöckig
two-way traf·fic MOT Gegenverkehr *m*
ty·coon (*Industrie- etc*)Magnat *m*
type **1.** Art *f*, Sorte *f*; Typ *m*; PRINT Type *f*, Buchstabe *m*; **2.** *v/t et.* mit der Maschine schreiben, tippen; *v/i* Maschine schreiben, tippen
type·writ·er Schreibmaschine *f*
type·writ·ten maschine(n)geschrieben
ty·phoid (fe·ver) MED Typhus *m*
ty·phoon Taifun *m*
ty·phus MED Flecktyphus *m*, -fieber *n*
typ·i·cal typisch, bezeichnend (***of*** für)
typ·i·fy typisch sein für, kennzeichnen; verkörpern
typ·ing er·ror Tippfehler *m*
typ·ing pool ECON Schreibzentrale *f*
typ·ist Schreibkraft *f*; Maschinenschreiber(in)
ty·ran·ni·cal tyrannisch
tyr·an·nize tyrannisieren
tyr·an·ny Tyrannei *f*
ty·rant Tyrann(in)
tyre *Br* → ***tire***[1]
tzar → ***tsar***

U

U, u U, u *n*
ud·der zo Euter *n*
ug·ly hässlich (*a. fig*); bös(e), schlimm (*wound etc*)
ul·cer MED Geschwür *n*
ul·te·ri·or: ***ulterior motive*** Hintergedanke *m*
ul·ti·mate letzte(r, -s), End…; höchste(r, -s)
ul·ti·mate·ly letztlich; schließlich
ul·ti·ma·tum Ultimatum *n*; ***deliver an ultimatum to s.o.*** j-m ein Ultimatum stellen
ul·tra·high fre·quen·cy ELECTR Ultrakurzwelle *f*
ul·tra·ma·rine ultramarin
ul·tra·son·ic Ultraschall…
ul·tra·sound PHYS Ultraschall *m*
ul·tra·vi·o·let ultraviolett
um·bil·i·cal cord ANAT Nabelschnur *f*
um·brel·la (Regen)Schirm *m*; *fig* Schutz *m*
um·pire SPORT **1.** Schiedsrichter(in); **2.** als Schiedsrichter(in) fungieren (bei)
un·a·bashed unverfroren
un·a·bat·ed unvermindert
un·a·ble unfähig, außerstande, nicht in der Lage
un·ac·cept·a·ble unzumutbar
un·ac·count·a·ble unerklärlich
un·ac·cus·tomed ungewohnt
un·ac·quaint·ed: ***be unacquainted with s.th.*** et. nicht kennen, mit e-r Sache nicht vertraut sein

un·ad·vised unbesonnen, unüberlegt
un·af·fect·ed natürlich, ungekünstelt; ***be unaffected by*** nicht betroffen sein von
un·aid·ed ohne Unterstützung, (ganz) allein
un·al·ter·a·ble unabänderlich
u·nan·i·mous einmütig; einstimmig
un·an·nounced unangemeldet
un·an·swer·a·ble unwiderlegbar; nicht zu beantworten(d)
un·ap·pe·tiz·ing unappetitlich
un·ap·proach·a·ble unnahbar
un·armed unbewaffnet
un·asked ungestellt (*question*); unaufgefordert, ungebeten (*guest etc*)
un·as·sist·ed ohne (fremde) Hilfe, (ganz) allein
un·as·sum·ing bescheiden
un·at·tached ungebunden, frei
un·at·tend·ed unbeaufsichtigt
un·at·trac·tive unattraktiv, wenig anziehend, reizlos
un·au·thor·ized unberechtigt, unbefugt
un·a·void·a·ble unvermeidlich
un·a·ware: ***be unaware of s.th.*** sich e-r Sache nicht bewusst sein, et. nicht bemerken
un·a·wares: ***catch*** *or* ***take s.o. unawares*** j-n überraschen
un·bal·ance *j-n* aus dem (seelischen) Gleichgewicht bringen
un·bal·anced unausgeglichen, labil
un·bar aufriegeln, entriegeln
un·bear·a·ble unerträglich; *person*: unausstehlich
un·beat·a·ble unschlagbar
un·beat·en ungeschlagen, unbesiegt
un·be·com·ing unvorteilhaft
un·be·known(st): ***unbeknown to s.o.*** ohne j-s Wissen
un·be·liev·a·ble unglaublich
un·bend gerade biegen; sich aufrichten; *fig* aus sich herausgehen, auftauen
un·bend·ing unbeugsam
un·bi·as(s)ed unvoreingenommen; JUR unbefangen
un·bind losbinden
un·blem·ished makellos
un·born ungeboren
un·break·a·ble unzerbrechlich
un·bri·dled *fig* ungezügelt, zügellos; ***unbridled tongue*** lose Zunge
un·bro·ken ununterbrochen; heil, unversehrt; nicht zugeritten (*horse*)
un·buck·le aufschnallen, losschnallen
un·bur·den: ***unburden o.s. to s.o.*** j-m sein Herz ausschütten
un·but·ton aufknöpfen
un·called-for ungerechtfertigt; unnötig; unpassend
un·can·ny unheimlich
un·cared-for vernachlässigt
un·ceas·ing unaufhörlich
un·ce·re·mo·ni·ous brüsk, unhöflich; überstürzt
un·cer·tain unsicher, ungewiss, unbestimmt; vage; METEOR unbeständig
un·cer·tain·ty Unsicherheit *f*, Ungewissheit *f*
un·chain losketten
un·changed unverändert
un·chang·ing unveränderlich
un·char·i·ta·ble unfair
un·checked ungehindert; ungeprüft
un·chris·tian unchristlich
un·civ·il unhöflich
un·civ·i·lized unzivilisiert
un·cle Onkel *m*
un·com·fort·a·ble unbequem; ***feel uncomfortable*** sich unbehaglich fühlen
un·com·mon ungewöhnlich
un·com·mu·ni·ca·tive wortkarg, verschlossen
un·com·pre·hend·ing verständnislos
un·com·pro·mis·ing kompromisslos
un·con·cerned: ***be unconcerned about*** sich keine Gedanken *or* Sorgen machen über (*acc*); ***be unconcerned with*** uninteressiert sein an (*dat*)
un·con·di·tion·al bedingungslos
un·con·firmed unbestätigt
un·con·scious unbewusst; unbeabsichtigt; MED bewusstlos; ***be unconscious of*** sich *e-r Sache* nicht bewusst sein, nicht bemerken
un·con·scious·ness MED Bewusstlosigkeit *f*
un·con·sti·tu·tion·al verfassungswidrig
un·con·trol·la·ble unkontrollierbar; nicht zu bändigen(d); unbändig (*rage etc*)
un·con·trolled unkontrolliert
un·con·ven·tion·al unkonventionell
un·con·vinced: ***be unconvinced*** nicht überzeugt sein (***about*** von)
un·con·vinc·ing nicht überzeugend
un·cooked ungekocht, roh
un·cork entkorken
un·count·a·ble unzählbar
un·coup·le abkoppeln
un·couth *fig* ungehobelt
un·cov·er aufdecken, *fig a.* enthüllen
un·crit·i·cal unkritisch; ***be uncritical of s.th.*** e-r Sache unkritisch gegenüberstehen
unc·tion REL Salbung *f*
unc·tu·ous salbungsvoll
un·cut ungekürzt (*film, novel etc*); ungeschliffen (*diamond etc*)

un·dam·aged unbeschädigt, unversehrt, heil
un·dat·ed undatiert, ohne Datum
un·daunt·ed unerschrocken, furchtlos
un·de·cid·ed unentschieden, offen; unentschlossen
un·de·mon·stra·tive zurückhaltend, reserviert
un·de·ni·a·ble unbestreitbar
un·der **1.** *prp* unter (*dat or acc*); **2.** *adv* unten; darunter
un·der·age minderjährig
un·der·bid unterbieten
un·der·brush → ***undergrowth***
un·der·car·riage AVIAT Fahrwerk *n*, Fahrgestell *n*
un·der·charge zu wenig berechnen; zu wenig verlangen
un·der·clothes, **un·der·cloth·ing** → ***underwear***
un·der·coat Grundierung *f*
un·der·cov·er: ***undercover agent*** verdeckter Ermittler
un·der·cut *j-n* (im Preis) unterbieten
un·der·de·vel·oped unterentwickelt; ***underdeveloped country*** Entwicklungsland *n*
un·der·dog Benachteiligte *m, f*
un·der·done nicht durchgebraten
un·der·es·ti·mate zu niedrig schätzen *or* veranschlagen; *fig* unterschätzen
un·der·ex·pose PHOT unterbelichten
un·der·fed unterernährt
un·der·go erleben, durchmachen; MED sich *e-r Operation etc* unterziehen
un·der·grad F, **un·der·grad·u·ate** Student(in)
un·der·ground **1.** *adv* unterirdisch, unter der Erde; **2.** *adj* unterirdisch; *fig* Untergrund...; **3.** *esp Br* Untergrundbahn *f*, U-Bahn *f*; ***by underground*** mit der U-Bahn
un·der·growth Unterholz *n*
un·der·hand, **un·der·hand·ed** heimlich; hinterhältig
un·der·line unterstreichen (*a. fig*)
un·der·ling *contp* Untergebene *m, f*
un·der·ly·ing zugrunde liegend
un·der·mine unterspülen; *fig* untergraben, unterminieren
un·der·neath **1.** *prp* unter (*dat or acc*); **2.** *adv* darunter
un·der·nour·ished unterernährt
un·der·pants Unterhose *f*
un·der·pass Unterführung *f*
un·der·pay *j-m* zu wenig bezahlen, *j-n* unterbezahlen
un·der·priv·i·leged unterprivilegiert, benachteiligt
un·der·rate unterbewerten, -schätzen
un·der·sec·re·ta·ry POL Staatssekretär *m*
un·der·sell ECON *Ware* verschleudern, unter Wert verkaufen; ***undersell o.s.*** *fig* sich schlecht verkaufen
un·der·shirt Unterhemd *n*
un·der·side Unterseite *f*
un·der·signed: ***the undersigned*** der *or* die Unterzeichnete, die Unterzeichneten *pl*
un·der·size(d) zu klein
un·der·staffed (personell) unterbesetzt
un·der·stand verstehen; erfahren *or* gehört haben (***that*** dass); ***make o.s. understood*** sich verständlich machen; ***am I to understand that*** soll das heißen, dass; ***give s.o. to understand that*** j-m zu verstehen geben, dass
un·der·stand·a·ble verständlich
un·der·stand·ing **1.** Verstand *m*; Verständnis *n*; Abmachung *f*; Verständigung *f*; ***come to an understanding*** e-e Abmachung treffen (***with*** mit); ***on the understanding that*** unter der Voraussetzung, dass; **2.** verständnisvoll
un·der·state untertreiben, untertrieben darstellen
un·der·state·ment Understatement *n*, Untertreibung *f*
un·der·take *et.* übernehmen; sich verpflichten (***to do*** zu tun)
un·der·tak·er Leichenbestatter *m*; Beerdigungs-, Bestattungsinstitut *n*
un·der·tak·ing Unternehmen *n*; Zusicherung *f*
un·der·tone *fig* Unterton *m*; ***in an undertone*** mit gedämpfter Stimme
un·der·val·ue unterbewerten
un·der·wa·ter **1.** *adj* Unterwasser...; **2.** *adv* unter Wasser
un·der·wear Unterwäsche *f*
un·der·weight **1.** Untergewicht *n*; **2.** untergewichtig, zu leicht (***by*** um); ***she is five pounds underweight*** sie hat fünf Pfund Untergewicht
un·der·world Unterwelt *f*
un·de·served unverdient
un·de·sir·a·ble unerwünscht
un·de·vel·oped unerschlossen (*area*); unentwickelt
un·dies F (Damen)Unterwäsche *f*
un·dig·ni·fied würdelos
un·di·min·ished unvermindert
un·dis·ci·plined undiszipliniert
un·dis·cov·ered unentdeckt
un·dis·guised unverhohlen
un·dis·put·ed unbestritten
un·dis·turbed ungestört
un·di·vid·ed ungeteilt

un·do aufmachen, öffnen; *fig* zunichtemachen
un·do·ing: ***be s.o.'s undoing*** j-s Ruin *or* Verderben sein
un·done unerledigt; offen; ***come undone*** aufgehen
un·doubt·ed unbestritten
un·doubt·ed·ly zweifellos, ohne (jeden) Zweifel
un·dreamed-of, **un·dreamt-of** ungeahnt
un·dress sich ausziehen; *j-n* ausziehen
un·due übermäßig
un·du·lat·ing sanft (*hills*)
un·dy·ing ewig
un·earned *fig* unverdient
un·earth ausgraben, *fig a.* ausfindig machen, aufstöbern
un·earth·ly überirdisch; unheimlich; ***at an unearthly hour*** F zu e-r unchristlichen Zeit
un·eas·i·ness Unbehagen *n*
un·eas·y unruhig (*sleep*); unsicher (*peace*); ***feel uneasy*** sich unbehaglich fühlen; ***I'm uneasy about*** mir ist nicht wohl bei
un·e·co·nom·ic unwirtschaftlich
un·ed·u·cat·ed ungebildet
un·e·mo·tion·al leidenschaftslos, kühl, beherrscht
un·em·ployed **1.** arbeitslos; **2.** ***the unemployed*** die Arbeitslosen *pl*
un·em·ploy·ment Arbeitslosigkeit *f*
unemployment ben·e·fit *Br*, **unemployment com·pen·sa·tion** Arbeitslosengeld *n*
un·end·ing endlos
un·en·dur·a·ble unerträglich
un·en·vi·a·ble wenig beneidenswert
un·e·qual ungleich (*a. fig*), unterschiedlich; *fig* einseitig; ***be unequal to*** *e-r Aufgabe etc* nicht gewachsen sein
un·e·qual(l)ed unerreicht, unübertroffen
un·er·ring unfehlbar
un·e·ven uneben; ungleich(mäßig); ungerade (*number*)
un·e·vent·ful ereignislos
un·ex·am·pled beispiellos
un·ex·pec·ted unerwartet
un·ex·posed PHOT unbelichtet
un·fail·ing unerschöpflich; nie versagend
un·fair unfair, ungerecht
un·faith·ful untreu (***to*** *dat*)
un·fa·mil·i·ar ungewohnt; unbekannt; nicht vertraut (***with*** mit)
un·fas·ten aufmachen, öffnen; losbinden
un·fa·vo(u)r·a·ble ungünstig; unvorteilhaft (***for, to*** für); negativ, ablehnend
un·feel·ing gefühllos, herzlos
un·fin·ished unvollendet; unfertig; unerledigt
un·fit nicht fit, nicht in Form; ungeeignet, untauglich; unfähig
un·flag·ging unermüdlich, unentwegt
un·flap·pa·ble F nicht aus der Ruhe zu bringen(d)
un·fold auffalten, auseinanderfalten; darlegen, enthüllen; sich entfalten
un·fore·seen unvorhergesehen, unerwartet
un·for·get·ta·ble unvergesslich
un·for·got·ten unvergessen
un·for·tu·nate unglücklich; unglückselig; bedauerlich
un·for·tu·nate·ly leider
un·found·ed unbegründet
un·friend·ly unfreundlich (***to, towards*** zu)
un·furl *Fahne* aufrollen, entrollen, *Segel* losmachen
un·fur·nished unmöbliert
un·gain·ly linkisch, unbeholfen
un·god·ly gottlos; ***at an ungodly hour*** F zu e-r unchristlichen Zeit
un·gra·cious ungnädig; unfreundlich
un·grate·ful undankbar
un·guard·ed unbewacht; unbedacht, unüberlegt
un·hap·pi·ly unglücklicherweise, leider
un·hap·py unglücklich
un·harmed unversehrt
un·health·y kränklich, nicht gesund; ungesund; *contp* krankhaft, unnatürlich
un·heard: ***go unheard*** keine Beachtung finden, unbeachtet bleiben
un·heard-of noch nie da gewesen, beispiellos
un·hinge: ***unhinge s.o.('s mind)*** *fig* j-n völlig aus dem Gleichgewicht bringen
un·ho·ly F furchtbar, schrecklich
un·hoped-for unverhofft, unerwartet
un·hurt unverletzt
u·ni·corn Einhorn *n*
un·i·den·ti·fied unbekannt, nicht identifiziert
u·ni·fi·ca·tion Vereinigung *f*
u·ni·form **1.** Uniform *f*; **2.** gleichmäßig; einheitlich
u·ni·form·i·ty Einheitlichkeit *f*
u·ni·fy verein(ig)en; vereinheitlichen
u·ni·lat·e·ral *fig* einseitig
un·i·ma·gin·a·ble unvorstellbar
un·i·ma·gin·a·tive fantasielos, einfallslos
un·im·por·tant unwichtig
un·im·pressed: ***remain unimpressed*** unbeeindruckt bleiben (***by*** von)
un·in·formed nicht unterrichtet *or* eingeweiht
un·in·hab·it·a·ble unbewohnbar
un·in·hab·it·ed unbewohnt

un·in·jured unverletzt
un·in·tel·li·gi·ble unverständlich
un·in·ten·tion·al unabsichtlich, unbeabsichtigt
un·in·terest·ed uninteressiert (***in*** an *dat*); ***be uninterested in*** *a.* sich nicht interessieren für
un·in·terest·ing uninteressant
un·in·ter·rupt·ed ununterbrochen
u·nion Vereinigung *f*; Union *f*; Gewerkschaft *f*
u·nion·ist Gewerkschaftler(in)
u·nion·ize (sich) gewerkschaftlich organisieren
u·nique einzigartig; einmalig
u·ni·son: ***in unison*** gemeinsam
u·nit Einheit *f*; PED Unit *f*, Lehreinheit *f*; MATH Einer *m*; TECH (Anbau)Element *n*, Teil *n*; ***unit furniture*** Anbaumöbel *pl*
u·nite verbinden, vereinigen; sich vereinigen *or* zusammentun
u·nit·ed vereinigt, vereint
U·nit·ed King·dom *das* Vereinigte Königreich (*England, Scotland, Wales and Northern Ireland*)
U·nit·ed States of A·mer·i·ca *die* Vereinigten Staaten von Amerika
u·ni·ty Einheit *f*; MATH Eins *f*
u·ni·ver·sal allgemein; universal, universell; Welt...
u·ni·verse Universum *n*, Weltall *n*
u·ni·ver·si·ty Universität *f*, Hochschule *f*
university grad·u·ate Akademiker(in)
un·just ungerecht
un·kempt ungekämmt (*hair*); ungepflegt (*clothes etc*)
un·kind unfreundlich
un·known **1.** unbekannt (***to*** *dat*); **2.** *der, die, das* Unbekannte
unknown quan·ti·ty MATH unbekannte Größe (*a. fig*), Unbekannte *f*
un·law·ful ungesetzlich, gesetzwidrig
un·lead·ed bleifrei
un·learn *Ansichten etc* ablegen, aufgeben
un·less wenn ... nicht, außer wenn ..., es sei denn ...
un·like *prp* im Gegensatz zu; ***he is very unlike his father*** er ist ganz anders als sein Vater; ***that is very unlike him*** das sieht ihm gar nicht ähnlich
un·like·ly unwahrscheinlich
un·lim·it·ed unbegrenzt
un·list·ed: ***be unlisted*** nicht im Telefonbuch stehen
unlisted num·ber TEL Geheimnummer *f*
un·load entladen, abladen, ausladen; MAR *Ladung* löschen
un·lock aufschließen
un·loos·en losmachen; lockern; lösen
un·loved ungeliebt
un·luck·y unglücklich; ***be unlucky*** Pech haben
un·made ungemacht
un·manned unbemannt
un·marked nicht gekennzeichnet; SPORT ungedeckt, frei
un·mar·ried unverheiratet, ledig
un·mask *fig* entlarven
un·matched unübertroffen, unvergleichlich
un·men·tio·na·ble Tabu...; ***be unmentionable*** tabu sein
un·mis·tak·a·ble unverkennbar, unverwechselbar, untrüglich
un·mo·lest·ed unbehelligt
un·moved ungerührt; ***she remained unmoved by it*** es ließ sie kalt
un·mu·si·cal unmusikalisch
un·named ungenannt
un·nat·u·ral unnatürlich; widernatürlich
un·ne·ces·sa·ry unnötig
un·nerve entnerven
un·no·ticed unbemerkt
un·num·bered unnummeriert
un·ob·tru·sive unauffällig, unaufdringlich
un·oc·cu·pied leer (stehend), unbewohnt; unbeschäftigt
un·of·fi·cial inoffiziell
un·pack auspacken
un·paid unbezahlt; *post* unfrei
un·par·al·leled einmalig, beispiellos
un·par·don·a·ble unverzeihlich
un·per·turbed gelassen, ruhig
un·pick *Naht etc* auftrennen
un·placed: ***be unplaced*** SPORT sich nicht platzieren können
un·play·a·ble SPORT unbespielbar
un·pleas·ant unangenehm, unerfreulich; unfreundlich
un·plug den Stecker (*gen*) herausziehen
un·pol·ished unpoliert; *fig* ungehobelt
un·pol·lut·ed sauber, unverschmutzt
un·pop·u·lar unpopulär, unbeliebt
un·pop·u·lar·i·ty Unbeliebtheit *f*
un·prac·ti·cal unpraktisch
un·prac·ticed, *Br* **un·prac·tised** ungeübt
un·pre·ce·dent·ed beispiellos, noch nie da gewesen
un·pre·dict·a·ble unvorhersehbar; unberechenbar (*person*)
un·prej·u·diced unvoreingenommen; JUR unbefangen
un·pre·med·i·tat·ed nicht vorsätzlich; unüberlegt
un·pre·pared unvorbereitet
un·pre·ten·tious bescheiden, einfach, schlicht

un·prin·ci·pled skrupellos, gewissenlos
un·prin·ta·ble nicht druckfähig *or* druckreif
un·pro·duc·tive unproduktiv, unergiebig
un·pro·fes·sion·al unprofessionell; unfachmännisch
un·prof·it·a·ble unrentabel
un·pro·nounce·a·ble unaussprechbar
un·pro·tect·ed ungeschützt
un·proved, un·prov·en unbewiesen
un·pro·voked grundlos
un·pun·ished unbestraft, ungestraft; ***go unpunished*** straflos bleiben
un·qual·i·fied unqualifiziert, ungeeignet (***for*** für); uneingeschränkt
un·ques·tion·a·ble unbestritten
un·ques·tion·ing bedingungslos
un·quote: ***quote ... unquote*** Zitat ... Zitat Ende
un·rav·el (sich) auftrennen (*pullover etc*); entwirren
un·read·a·ble nicht lesenswert, unlesbar, *a.* unleserlich
un·re·al unwirklich
un·rea·lis·tic unrealistisch
un·rea·son·a·ble unvernünftig; übertrieben, unzumutbar
un·rec·og·niz·a·ble nicht wieder zu erkennen(d)
un·re·lat·ed: ***be unrelated*** in keinem Zusammenhang stehen (***to*** mit)
un·re·lent·ing unvermindert
un·re·li·a·ble unzuverlässig
un·re·lieved ununterbrochen, ständig
un·re·mit·ting unablässig, unaufhörlich
un·re·quit·ed: ***unrequited love*** unerwiderte Liebe
un·re·served uneingeschränkt; nicht reserviert
un·rest POL *etc* Unruhen *pl*
un·re·strained hemmungslos, ungezügelt
un·re·strict·ed uneingeschränkt
un·ripe unreif
un·ri·val(l)ed unerreicht, unübertroffen, einzigartig
un·roll (sich) aufrollen *or* entrollen; sich entfalten
un·ruf·fled gelassen, ruhig
un·ru·ly ungebärdig, wild; widerspenstig (*hair*)
un·sad·dle *Pferd* absatteln; *Reiter* abwerfen
un·safe unsicher, nicht sicher
un·said unausgesprochen
un·sal(e)·a·ble unverkäuflich
un·salt·ed ungesalzen
un·san·i·tar·y unhygienisch
un·sat·is·fac·to·ry unbefriedigend
un·sat·u·rat·ed CHEM ungesättigt
un·sa·vo(u)r·y anrüchig, unerfreulich
un·scathed unversehrt, unverletzt
un·screw abschrauben, losschrauben
un·scru·pu·lous skrupellos, gewissenlos
un·seat *Reiter* abwerfen; *j-n* s-s Amtes entheben
un·seem·ly ungebührlich
un·self·ish selbstlos, uneigennützig
un·set·tle durcheinanderbringen; beunruhigen; aufregen
un·set·tled ungeklärt, offen (*question etc*); unsicher (*situation etc*); METEOR unbeständig
un·shak(e)·a·ble unerschütterlich
un·shav·en unrasiert
un·shrink·a·ble nicht eingehend *or* einlaufend
un·sight·ly unansehnlich; hässlich
un·skilled: ***unskilled worker*** ungelernter Arbeiter
un·so·cia·ble ungesellig
un·so·cial: ***work unsocial hours*** außerhalb der normalen Arbeitszeit arbeiten
un·so·lic·it·ed unaufgefordert ein- *or* zugesandt, ECON *a.* unbestellt
un·solved ungelöst (*problem etc*)
un·so·phis·ti·cat·ed einfach, schlicht; TECH unkompliziert
un·sound nicht gesund; nicht in Ordnung; morsch; unsicher, schwach; nicht stichhaltig (*argument etc*); ***of unsound mind*** JUR unzurechnungsfähig
un·spar·ing großzügig, freigebig, verschwenderisch; schonungslos, unbarmherzig
un·speak·a·ble unbeschreiblich, entsetzlich
un·spoiled, un·spoilt unverdorben; nicht verwöhnt *or* verzogen
un·sta·ble instabil; unsicher, schwankend; labil (*person*)
un·stead·y wack(e)lig, schwankend, unsicher; unbeständig; ungleichmäßig, unregelmäßig
un·stop *Abfluss etc* frei machen; *Flasche* entstöpseln
un·stressed LING unbetont
un·stuck: ***come unstuck*** abgehen, sich lösen; *fig* scheitern
un·stud·ied ungekünstelt, natürlich
un·suc·cess·ful erfolglos, ohne Erfolg; vergeblich
un·suit·a·ble unpassend, ungeeignet; unangemessen
un·sure unsicher; ***unsure of o.s.*** unsicher
un·sur·passed unübertroffen
un·sus·pect·ed unverdächtig; unvermutet

un·sus·pect·ing nichts ahnend, ahnungslos
un·sus·pi·cious arglos; unverdächtig, harmlos
un·sweet·ened ungesüßt
un·swerv·ing unbeirrbar, unerschütterlich
un·tan·gle entwirren (*a. fig*)
un·tapped unerschlossen (*resource etc*)
un·teach·a·ble unbelehrbar (*person*); nicht lehrbar
un·ten·a·ble unhaltbar (*theory etc*)
un·think·a·ble undenkbar, unvorstellbar
un·think·ing gedankenlos
un·ti·dy unordentlich
un·tie aufknoten, *Knoten etc* lösen; losbinden
un·til *prp*, *cj* bis; ***not until*** erst; erst wenn, nicht bevor
un·time·ly vorzeitig, verfrüht; unpassend, ungelegen
un·tir·ing unermüdlich
un·told *fig* unermesslich
un·touched unberührt, unangetastet
un·true unwahr, falsch
un·trust·wor·thy unzuverlässig, nicht vertrauenswürdig
un·used[1] unbenutzt, ungebraucht
un·used[2]: ***be unused to s.th.*** an et. nicht gewöhnt sein, et. nicht gewohnt sein; ***be unused to doing s.th.*** es nicht gewohnt sein, et. zu tun
un·u·su·al ungewöhnlich
un·var·nished *fig* ungeschminkt
un·var·y·ing unveränderlich, gleichbleibend
un·veil *Denkmal etc* enthüllen
un·versed unbewandert, unerfahren (***in*** in *dat*)
un·voiced unausgesprochen
un·want·ed unerwünscht, ungewollt
un·war·rant·ed ungerechtfertigt
un·washed ungewaschen
un·wel·come unwillkommen
un·well: ***be*** *or* ***feel unwell*** sich unwohl fühlen *or* nicht wohlfühlen
un·whole·some ungesund (*a. fig*)
un·wield·y unhandlich, sperrig
un·will·ing widerwillig; ungern; ***be unwilling to do s.th.*** et. nicht tun wollen
un·wind (sich) abwickeln; F abschalten, sich entspannen
un·wise unklug
un·wit·ting unwissentlich; unbeabsichtigt
un·wor·thy unwürdig; ***he*** (***she***) ***is unworthy of it*** er (sie) verdient es nicht, er (sie) ist es nicht wert
un·wrap auswickeln, auspacken
un·writ·ten ungeschrieben
un·yield·ing unnachgiebig
un·zip den Reißverschluss (*gen*) aufmachen
up 1. *adv* herauf, hinauf, aufwärts, nach oben, hoch, in die Höhe; oben; ***up there*** dort oben; ***jump up and down*** hüpfen; ***walk up and down*** auf und ab gehen, hin und her gehen; ***up to*** bis zu; ***be up to s.th.*** F et. vorhaben, et. im Schilde führen; ***not to be up to s.th.*** e-r Sache nicht gewachsen sein; ***it's up to you*** das liegt bei dir; **2.** *prp* herauf, hinauf; oben auf (*dat*); ***up the river*** flussaufwärts; **3.** *adj* nach oben (gerichtet), Aufwärts…; ASTR aufgegangen; ECON gestiegen; *time*: abgelaufen, um; aufgestanden, F auf; ***the up train*** der Zug nach London; ***be up and about*** F wieder auf den Beinen sein; ***what's up?*** F was ist los?; **4.** F *v/t Angebot*, *Preis etc* erhöhen; **5.** ***the ups and downs*** F die Höhen und Tiefen *pl* (***of life*** des Lebens)
up-and-com·ing aufstrebend, vielversprechend
up·bring·ing Erziehung *f*
up·com·ing bevorstehend
up·coun·try landeinwärts; im Landesinneren
up·date 1. auf den neuesten Stand bringen; aktualisieren; **2.** Lagebericht *m*
up·end hochkant stellen
up·grade *j-n* befördern
up·heav·al *fig* Umwälzung *f*
up·hill aufwärts, bergan; bergauf führend; *fig* mühsam
up·hold *Rechte etc* schützen, wahren; JUR *Urteil* bestätigen
up·hol·ster *Möbel* polstern
up·hol·ster·er Polsterer *m*
up·hol·ster·y Polsterung *f*; Bezug *m*; Polsterei *f*
up·keep Instandhaltung(skosten *pl*) *f*; Unterhalt(ungskosten *pl*) *m*
up·land *mst pl* Hochland *n*
up·lift 1. *j-n* aufrichten, *j-m* Auftrieb geben; **2.** Auftrieb *m*
up·on → ***on***, ***once*** *1*
up·per obere(r, -s), Ober…;
up·per·most 1. *adj* oberste(r, -s), größte(r, -s), höchste(r, -s); ***be uppermost*** oben sein; *fig* an erster Stelle stehen; **2.** *adv* nach oben
up·right aufrecht, *a.* gerade, *fig a.* rechtschaffen
up·ris·ing Aufstand *m*
up·roar Aufruhr *m*
up·roar·i·ous lärmend, laut; schallend (*laughter*)
up·root ausreißen, entwurzeln; *fig j-n* he-

rausreißen (***from*** aus)
up·set umkippen, umstoßen, umwerfen; *Pläne etc* durcheinanderbringen, stören; *j-n* aus der Fassung bringen; ***the fish has upset me*** *or* ***my stomach*** ich habe mir durch den Fisch den Magen verdorben; ***be upset*** aufgeregt sein; aus der Fassung *or* durcheinander sein; gekränkt *or* verletzt sein
up·shot Ergebnis *n*
up·side down verkehrt herum; *fig* drunter und drüber; ***turn upside down*** umdrehen, *a. fig* auf den Kopf stellen
up·stairs 1. die Treppe herauf *or* hinauf, nach oben; oben; **2.** im oberen Stockwerk (gelegen), obere(r, -s)
up·start Emporkömmling *m*
up·state im Norden (e-s Bundesstaats)
up·stream fluss-, stromaufwärts
up·take: F ***be quick*** (***slow***) ***on the uptake*** schnell begreifen (schwer von Begriff sein)
up-to-date modern; aktuell, auf dem neuesten Stand
up·town in den Wohnvierteln; in die Wohnviertel
up·turn Aufschwung *m*
up·ward(s) aufwärts, nach oben
u·ra·ni·um CHEM Uran *n*
ur·ban städtisch, Stadt...
ur·ban·i·za·tion Verstädterung *f*
ur·chin Bengel *m*
urge 1. *j-n* drängen (***to do*** zu tun); drängen auf (*acc*); *a.* ***urge on*** *j-n* drängen, antreiben; **2.** Drang *m*, Verlangen *n*
ur·gen·cy Dringlichkeit *f*
ur·gent dringend; ***be urgent*** *a.* eilen
u·ri·nate urinieren
u·rine Urin *m*
urn Urne *f*; Großteemaschine *f*, Großkaffeemaschine *f*
us uns; ***all of us*** wir alle; ***both of us*** wir beide
us·age Sprachgebrauch *m*; Behandlung *f*; Verwendung *f*, Gebrauch *m*
use 1. *v/t* benutzen, gebrauchen, anwenden, verwenden; (ver)brauchen; ***use up*** auf-, verbrauchen; *v/i*: ***I used to live here*** ich habe früher hier gewohnt; **2.** Benutzung *f*, Gebrauch *m*, Verwendung *f*; Nutzen *m*; ***be of use*** nützlich *or* von Nutzen sein (***to*** für); ***it's no use*** *doing* es ist nutzlos *or* zwecklos *zu inf*; → ***milk*** *1*
used[1]: ***be used to s.th.*** an et. gewöhnt sein, et. gewohnt sein; ***be used to doing s.th.*** es gewohnt sein, et. zu tun
used[2] gebraucht
used car Gebrauchtwagen *m*
used car deal·er Gebrauchtwagenhändler(in)
use·ful nützlich
use·less nutzlos, zwecklos
us·er Benutzer(in); Verbraucher(in)
us·er-friend·ly benutzer- *or* verbraucherfreundlich
us·er in·ter·face EDP Benutzeroberfläche *f*
ush·er 1. Platzanweiser *m*; Gerichtsdiener *m*; **2.** *j-n* führen, geleiten (***into*** in *acc*; ***to*** zu)
ush·er·ette Platzanweiserin *f*
u·su·al gewöhnlich, üblich
u·su·al·ly (für) gewöhnlich, normalerweise
u·sur·er Wucherer *m*
u·su·ry Wucher *m*
u·ten·sil Gerät *n*
u·te·rus ANAT Gebärmutter *f*
u·til·i·ty Nutzen *m*; *pl* Leistungen *pl* der öffentlichen Versorgungsbetriebe
u·til·ize nutzen
ut·most äußerste(r, -s), größte(r, -s), höchste(r, -s)
u·to·pi·an utopisch
ut·ter[1] total, völlig
ut·ter[2] äußern, *Seufzer etc* ausstoßen, *Wort* sagen
U-turn MOT Wende *f*; *fig* Kehrtwendung *f*
u·vu·la ANAT (Gaumen)Zäpfchen *n*

V

V, v V, v *n*
va·can·cy freie *or* offene Stelle; ***vacancies*** Zimmer frei; ***no vacancies*** belegt
va·cant leer stehend, unbewohnt; frei (*seat etc*); frei, offen (*job*); *fig* leer (*expression, stare etc*)
va·cate *Hotelzimmer* räumen; *Stelle etc* aufgeben
va·ca·tion 1. Ferien *pl*, Urlaub *m*; *esp Br* UNIV Semesterferien *pl*; JUR Gerichtsferien *pl*; ***be on vacation*** im Urlaub sein, Urlaub machen; **2.** Urlaub machen, die Ferien verbringen
va·ca·tion·er, va·ca·tion·ist Urlauber(in)
vac·cin·ate MED impfen
vac·cin·a·tion MED (Schutz)Impfung *f*
vac·cine MED Impfstoff *m*
vac·il·late *fig* schwanken
vac·u·um 1. PHYS Vakuum *n*; **2.** F *Teppich, Zimmer etc* saugen
vacuum bot·tle Thermosflasche® *f*
vacuum clean·er Staubsauger *m*
vacuum flask *Br* Thermosflasche® *f*
vacuum-packed vakuumverpackt
vag·a·bond Vagabund *m*, Landstreicher(in)
va·ga·ry *mst pl* Laune *f*; wunderlicher Einfall
va·gi·na ANAT Vagina *f*, Scheide *f*
va·gi·nal ANAT vaginal, Scheiden…
va·grant Nichtsesshafte *m, f*, Landstreicher(in)
vague verschwommen; vage; unklar
vain eingebildet, eitel; vergeblich; ***in vain*** vergebens, vergeblich
val·en·tine Valentinskarte *f*
va·le·ri·an BOT, PHARM Baldrian *m*
val·et (Kammer)Diener *m*
val·id stichhaltig, triftig; gültig (***for two weeks*** zwei Wochen); JUR rechtsgültig, rechtskräftig; ***be valid*** *a.* gelten
va·lid·i·ty (JUR Rechts)Gültigkeit *f*; Stichhaltigkeit *f*, Triftigkeit *f*
val·ley Tal *n*
val·u·a·ble 1. wertvoll; **2.** *pl* Wertgegenstände *pl*, Wertsachen *pl*
val·u·a·tion Schätzung *f*; Schätzwert *m* (***on*** *gen*)
val·ue 1. Wert *m*; ***be of value*** wertvoll sein (***to*** für); ***get value for money*** reell bedient werden; **2.** *Haus etc* schätzen (***at*** auf *acc*); *j-n, j-s Rat etc* schätzen
val·ue-ad·ded tax *Br* ECON (ABBR ***VAT***) Mehrwertsteuer *f*
val·ue·less wertlos
valve TECH, MUS Ventil *n*; ANAT (*Herz- etc*) Klappe *f*
vam·pire Vampir *m*
van MOT Lieferwagen *m*, Transporter *m*; *Br* RAIL (geschlossener) Güterwagen
van·dal Wandale *m*, Vandale *m*
van·dal·ism Wandalismus *m*, Vandalismus *m*
van·dal·ize mutwillig beschädigen *or* zerstören
vane TECH (*Propeller- etc*)Flügel *m*; (*Wetter*)Fahne *f*
van·guard MIL Vorhut *f*
va·nil·la Vanille *f*
van·ish verschwinden
van·i·ty Eitelkeit *f*
vanity bag Kosmetiktäschchen *n*
vanity case Kosmetikkoffer *m*
van·tage·point Aussichtspunkt *m*; ***from my vantagepoint*** *fig* aus m-r Sicht
va·por·ize verdampfen; verdunsten (lassen)
va·po(u)r Dampf *m*, Dunst *m*
vapo(u)r trail AVIAT Kondensstreifen *m*
var·i·a·ble 1. variabel, veränderlich; unbeständig, wechselhaft; TECH einstellbar, regulierbar; **2.** MATH, PHYS Variable *f*, veränderliche Größe (*both a. fig*)
var·i·ance: ***be at variance with*** im Gegensatz *or* Widerspruch stehen zu
var·i·ant 1. abweichend, verschieden; **2.** Variante *f*
var·i·a·tion Abweichung *f*; Schwankung *f*; MUS Variation *f*
var·i·cose veins MED Krampfadern *pl*
var·ied unterschiedlich; abwechslungsreich
va·ri·e·ty Abwechslung *f*; Vielfalt *f*; ECON Auswahl *f*, Sortiment *n* (***of*** an *dat*); BOT, zo Art *f*; Varietee *n*; ***for a variety of reasons*** aus den verschiedensten Gründen
variety show Varieteevorstellung *f*
variety thea·ter (*Br* **thea·tre**) Varietee (-theater) *n*
var·i·ous verschieden; mehrere, verschiedene
var·nish 1. Lack *m*; **2.** lackieren
var·si·ty team SPORT Universitäts-, College-, Schulmannschaft *f*
var·y *v/i* sich (ver)ändern; variieren, auseinandergehen (*opinions etc*) (***on*** über *acc*); ***vary in size*** verschieden groß sein; *v/t* (ver)ändern; variieren

vase Vase *f*
vast gewaltig, riesig, (*area a.*) ausgedehnt, weit
vast·ly gewaltig, weitaus
vat (großes) Fass, Bottich *m*
VAT ABBR *of* ***value-added tax*** ECON Mehrwertsteuer *f*
vau·de·ville Varietee(theater) *n*
vault[1] ARCH Gewölbe *n*; *a. pl* Stahlkammer *f*, Tresorraum *m*; (Keller)Gewölbe *n*; Gruft *f*
vault[2] **1.** ***vault*** (***over***) springen über (*acc*); **2.** *esp* SPORT Sprung *m*
vault·ing horse *gymnastics*: Pferd *n*
vaulting pole SPORT Sprungstab *m*
VCR ABBR *of* ***video cassette recorder*** Videorekorder *m*, Videogerät *n*
veal GASTR Kalbfleisch *n*; ***veal chop*** Kalbskotelett *n*; ***veal cutlet*** Kalbsschnitzel *n*; ***roast veal*** Kalbsbraten *m*
veer (sich) drehen; MOT ausscheren; ***veer to the right*** das Steuer nach rechts reißen
veg·e·ta·ble **1.** *mst pl* Gemüse *n*; **2.** Gemüse…; Pflanzen…
veg·e·tar·i·an **1.** Vegetarier(in); **2.** vegetarisch
veg·e·tate (dahin)vegetieren
veg·e·ta·tion Vegetation *f*
ve·he·mence Vehemenz *f*, Heftigkeit *f*
ve·he·ment vehement, heftig
ve·hi·cle Fahrzeug *n*; *fig* Medium *n*
veil **1.** Schleier *m*; **2.** verschleiern (*a. fig*)
vein ANAT Vene *f*, Ader *f* (*a.* BOT, GEOL, *fig*); *fig* (*Charakter*)Zug *m*; Stimmung *f*
ve·loc·i·ty TECH Geschwindigkeit *f*
ve·lour(s) Velours *m*
vel·vet Samt *m*
vel·vet·y samtig
vend·er → ***vendor***
vend·ing ma·chine (Verkaufs-, Waren-)Automat *m*
vend·or (*Straßen*)Händler(in), (*Zeitungs-etc*)Verkäufer(in)
ve·neer **1.** Furnier *n*; *fig* Fassade *f*; **2.** furnieren
ven·e·ra·ble ehrwürdig
ven·e·rate verehren
ven·e·ra·tion Verehrung *f*
ve·no·re·al dis·ease MED Geschlechtskrankheit *f*
Ve·ne·tian **1.** Venezianer(in); **2.** venezianisch
Venetian blind (Stab)Jalousie *f*
ven·geance Rache *f*; ***take vengeance on*** sich rächen an (*dat*); ***with a vengeance*** mächtig, F wie verrückt
ve·ni·al entschuldbar, verzeihlich; REL lässlich

V

ven·i·son GASTR Wildbret *n*
ven·om ZO Gift *n*, *fig a.* Gehässigkeit *f*
ven·om·ous giftig, *fig a.* gehässig
ve·nous MED venös
vent **1.** *v/t s-m Zorn etc* Luft machen, *s-e Wut etc* auslassen, abreagieren (***on*** an *dat*); **2.** Schlitz *m* (*in a coat etc*); TECH (Abzugs)Öffnung *f*; ***give vent to*** *s-m Ärger etc* Luft machen
ven·ti·late (be)lüften; *fig* äußern
ven·ti·la·tion (Be)Lüftung *f*, Ventilation *f*
ven·ti·la·tor Ventilator *m*
ven·tri·cle ANAT Herzkammer *f*
ven·tril·o·quist Bauchredner(in)
ven·ture **1.** *esp* ECON Wagnis *n*, Risiko *n*; ECON Unternehmen *n*; → ***joint venture***; **2.** sich wagen; riskieren
ven·ue SPORT Austragungsort *m*
verb LING Verb *n*, Zeitwort *n*
verb·al mündlich; wörtlich, Wort…
ver·dict JUR (Urteils)Spruch *m*; *fig* Urteil *n*; ***bring in*** *or* ***return a verdict of*** (***not***) ***guilty*** JUR auf (nicht) schuldig erkennen
ver·di·gris Grünspan *m*
verge **1.** Rand *m* (*a. fig*); ***be on the verge of*** kurz vor (*dat*) stehen; ***be on the verge of despair*** (***tears***) der Verzweiflung (den Tränen) nahe sein; **2.** ***verge on*** *fig* grenzen an (*acc*)
ver·i·fy bestätigen; nachweisen; (über-)prüfen
ver·i·ta·ble wahr
ver·mi·cel·li Fadennudeln *pl*
ver·mi·form ap·pen·dix ANAT Wurmfortsatz *m*, Blinddarm *m*
ver·mil·i·on **1.** zinnoberrot; **2.** Zinnoberrot *n*
ver·min Ungeziefer *n*; Schädlinge *pl*; *fig* Gesindel *n*, Pack *n*
ver·min·ous voller Ungeziefer
ver·nac·u·lar Dialekt *m*, Mundart *f*; ***in the vernacular*** im Volksmund
ver·sa·tile vielseitig; vielseitig verwendbar
verse Versdichtung *f*; Vers *m*; Strophe *f*
versed: ***be*** (***well***) ***versed in*** beschlagen *or* bewandert sein in (*dat*)
ver·sion Version *f*; TECH Ausführung *f*; Darstellung *f* (*of an event*); Fassung *f* (*of a film etc*); Übersetzung *f*
ver·sus (ABBR ***v., vs.***) SPORT, JUR gegen
ver·te·bra ANAT Wirbel *m*
ver·te·brate ZO Wirbeltier *n*
ver·ti·cal vertikal, senkrecht
ver·ti·go MED Schwindel *m*; ***suffer from vertigo*** an *or* unter Schwindel leiden
verve Elan *m*, Schwung *m*
ver·y **1.** *adv* sehr; aller…; ***I very much hope that*** ich hoffe sehr, dass; ***the very***

best das Allerbeste; ***for the very last time*** zum allerletzten Mal; **2.** *adj* ***the very*** genau der *or* die *or* das; ***the very opposite*** genau das Gegenteil; ***the very thing*** genau das Richtige; ***the very thought of*** schon der *or* der bloße Gedanke an (*acc*)

ves·i·cle MED Bläschen *n*

ves·sel ANAT, BOT Gefäß *n*; Schiff *n*

vest Weste *f*; *Br* Unterhemd *n*; *kugelsichere* Weste

ves·ti·bule (Vor)Halle *f*

ves·tige *fig* Spur *f*

vest·ment Ornat *n*, Gewand *n*, Robe *f*

ves·try REL Sakristei *f*

vet[1] F Tierarzt *m*, Tierärztin *f*

vet[2] *esp Br* F überprüfen

vet[3] MIL F Veteran *m*

vet·e·ran **1.** MIL Veteran *m* (*a. fig*); **2.** altgedient; erfahren

veteran car *Br* Oldtimer *m* (*built before 1905*)

vet·e·ri·nar·i·an Tierarzt *m*, -ärztin *f*

vet·e·ri·na·ry tierärztlich

veterinary sur·geon *Br* Tierarzt *m*, Tierärztin *f*

ve·to **1.** Veto *n*; **2.** sein Veto einlegen gegen

vexed ques·tion leidige Frage

vi·a über (*acc*), via

vi·a·duct Viadukt *m*, *n*

vi·al (*esp* Arznei)Fläschchen *n*

vibes F Atmosphäre *f*

vi·brant kräftig (*color etc*); pulsierend (*city etc*)

vi·brate *v/i* vibrieren, zittern; flimmern; *fig* pulsieren; *v/t* in Schwingungen versetzen

vi·bra·tion Vibrieren *n*, Zittern *n*; *pl* F Atmosphäre *f*

vic·ar REL Pfarrer *m*

vic·ar·age Pfarrhaus *n*

vice[1] Laster *n*

vice[2] *esp Br* Schraubstock *m*

vice... Vize..., stellvertretend

vice squad Sittendezernat *n*, Sittenpolizei *f*; Rauschgiftdezernat *n*

vi·ce ver·sa: ***and vice versa*** und umgekehrt

vi·cin·i·ty Nähe *f*; Nachbarschaft *f*

vi·cious brutal; bösartig

vi·cis·si·tudes *das* Auf und Ab, *die* Wechselfälle *pl*

vic·tim Opfer *n*

vic·tim·ize (ungerechterweise) bestrafen, ungerecht behandeln; schikanieren

vic·to·ri·ous siegreich

vic·to·ry Sieg *m*

vid·e·o **1.** Video *n*; Videokassette *f*; F Videoband *n*; *esp Br* Videorekorder *m*, Videogerät *n*; ***on video*** auf Video; **2.** Video...; **3.** *esp Br* auf Video aufnehmen, aufzeichnen

video cam·e·ra Videokamera *f*

video cas·sette Videokassette *f*

video cas·sette re·cord·er → ***video recorder***

video clip Videoclip *m*

vid·eo·disk Bildplatte *f*

vid·e·o game Videospiel *n*

video li·brary Videothek *f*

video re·cord·er Videorekorder *m*, Videogerät *n*

video re·cord·ing Videoaufnahme *f*, Videoaufzeichnung *f*

video shop *Br*, **video store** Videothek *f*

vid·e·o·tape **1.** Videokassette *f*; Videoband *n*; **2.** auf Video aufnehmen, aufzeichnen

vid·e·o·text Bildschirmtext *m*

vie wetteifern (***with*** mit; ***for*** um)

Vi·en·nese **1.** Wiener(in); **2.** wienerisch, Wiener...

view **1.** Sicht *f* (***of*** auf *acc*); Aussicht *f*, (Aus)Blick *m* (***of*** auf *acc*); Ansicht *f* (*a.* PHOT), Meinung *f* (***about, on*** über *acc*); *fig* Überblick *m* (***of*** über *acc*); ***a room with a view*** ein Zimmer mit schöner Aussicht; ***be on view*** ausgestellt *or* zu besichtigen sein; ***be hidden from view*** nicht zu sehen sein; ***come into view*** in Sicht kommen; ***in full view of*** direkt vor *j-s* Augen; ***in view of*** *fig* angesichts (*gen*); ***in my view*** m-r Ansicht nach; ***keep in view*** et. im Auge behalten; ***with a view to*** *fig* mit Blick auf (*acc*); **2.** *v/t Haus etc* besichtigen; *fig* betrachten (***as*** als); *v/i* fernsehen

view·da·ta Bildschirmtext *m*

view·er Fernsehzuschauer(in), F Fernseher(in); TECH (*Dia*)Betrachter *m*

view·find·er PHOT Sucher *m*

view·point Gesichts-, Standpunkt *m*

vig·il (Nacht)Wache *f*

vig·i·lance Wachsamkeit *f*

vig·i·lant wachsam

vig·or·ous energisch; kräftig

vig·o(u)r Energie *f*

Vi·king **1.** Wikinger *m*; **2.** Wikinger...

vile gemein, niederträchtig; F scheußlich

vil·lage Dorf *n*

village green Dorfanger *m*

vil·lag·er Dorfbewohner(in)

vil·lain Bösewicht *m*, Schurke *m*; *Br* F Ganove *m*

vin·di·cate *j-n* rehabilitieren; *et.* rechtfertigen; *et.* Bestätigen

vin·dic·tive rachsüchtig, nachtragend

vine BOT (Wein)Rebe *f*; Kletterpflanze *f*
vin·e·gar Essig *m*
vine·grow·er Winzer *m*
vine·yard Weinberg *m*
vin·tage 1. Weinernte *f*, Weinlese *f*; GASTR Jahrgang *m*; **2.** GASTR Jahrgangs…; *fig* hervorragend, glänzend; ***a 1994 vintage*** ein 1994er Jahrgang *or* Wein
vin·tage car *esp Br* Oldtimer *m* (*built between 1919 and 1930*)
vi·o·la MUS Bratsche *f*
vi·o·late *Vertrag etc* verletzen, *a. Versprechen* brechen, *Gesetz etc* übertreten; *Ruhe etc* stören; *Grab etc* schänden
vi·o·la·tion Verletzung *f*, Bruch *m*, Übertretung *f*
vi·o·lence Gewalt *f*; Gewalttätigkeit *f*; Ausschreitungen *pl*; Heftigkeit *f*
vi·o·lent gewalttätig; gewaltsam; heftig
vi·o·let 1. BOT Veilchen *n*; **2.** violett
vi·o·lin MUS Geige *f*, Violine *f*
vi·o·lin·ist Geiger(in), Violinist(in)
VIP ABBR *of* ***very important person*** VIP *f*
VIP lounge AVIAT *etc* VIP-Lounge *f*; SPORT Ehrentribüne *f*
vi·per zo Viper *f*, Natter *f*
vir·gin 1. Jungfrau *f*; **2.** jungfräulich, unberührt (*both a. fig*)
Vir·go ASTR Jungfrau *f*; ***he*** (***she***) ***is*** (***a***) ***Virgo*** er (sie) ist Jungfrau
vir·ile männlich; potent
vi·ril·i·ty Männlichkeit *f*; Potenz *f*
vir·tu·al eigentlich, praktisch
vir·tu·al·ly praktisch, so gut wie
vir·tu·al re·al·i·ty EDP virtuelle Realität
vir·tue Tugend *f*; Vorzug *m*, Vorteil *m*; ***by*** *or* ***in virtue of*** aufgrund (*gen*), kraft (*gen*); ***make a virtue of necessity*** aus der Not e-e Tugend machen
vir·tu·ous tugendhaft
vir·u·lent MED (akut und) bösartig; schnell wirkend (*poison*); *fig* bösartig, gehässig
vi·rus MED Virus *n, m*
vi·sa Visum *n*, Sichtvermerk *m*
vis·cose Viskose *f*
vis·cous dickflüssig, zähflüssig
vise TECH Schraubstock *m*
vis·i·bil·i·ty Sicht *f*, Sichtverhältnisse *pl*, Sichtweite *f*
vis·i·ble sichtbar; (er)sichtlich
vi·sion Sehkraft *f*; Weitblick *m*; Vision *f*
vi·sion·a·ry 1. weitblickend; eingebildet, unwirklich; **2.** Fantast(in), Träumer(in); Seher(in)
vis·it 1. *v/t j-n* besuchen, *Schloss etc a.* besichtigen; *et.* inspizieren; *v/i*: ***be visiting*** auf Besuch sein (***with*** bei); ***visit with*** plaudern mit; **2.** Besuch *m*, Besichtigung *f* (***to*** *gen*); Plauderei *f*; ***for*** *or* ***on a visit*** auf Besuch; ***have a visit from*** Besuch haben von; ***pay a visit to*** *j-n* besuchen, *j-m* e-n Besuch abstatten; *Arzt* aufsuchen
vis·it·ing hours MED Besuchszeit *f*
vis·it·or Besucher(in), Gast *m*
vi·sor Visier *n*; Schirm *m*; MOT (*Sonnen*)-Blende *f*
vis·u·al Seh…; visuell
visual aids PED Anschauungsmaterial *n*, Lehrmittel *pl*
visual dis·play u·nit EDP Bildschirmgerät *n*, Datensichtgerät *n*
visual in·struc·tion PED Anschauungsunterricht *m*
vis·u·al·ize sich *et.* vorstellen
vi·tal vital, Lebens…; lebenswichtig; unbedingt notwendig; ***of vital importance*** von größter Wichtigkeit
vi·tal·i·ty Vitalität *f*
vit·a·min Vitamin *n*
vitamin de·fi·cien·cy Vitaminmangel *m*
vit·re·ous Glas…
vi·va·cious lebhaft, temperamentvoll
viv·id hell (*light*); kräftig, leuchtend (*color*); anschaulich (*description*); lebhaft (*imagination*)
vix·en zo Füchsin *f*
V-neck V-Ausschnitt *m*
V-necked mit V-Ausschnitt
vo·cab·u·la·ry Vokabular *n*, Wortschatz *m*; Wörterverzeichnis *n*
vo·cal Stimm…; F lautstark; MUS Vokal…, Gesang…
vocal cords ANAT Stimmbänder *pl*
vo·cal·ist Sänger(in)
vo·ca·tion Begabung *f* (***for*** für); Berufung *f*
vo·ca·tion·al Berufs…
vocational ed·u·ca·tion Berufsausbildung *f*
vocational guid·ance Berufsberatung *f*
vocational train·ing Berufsausbildung *f*
vogue Mode *f*; ***be in vogue*** Mode sein
voice 1. Stimme *f*; ***active voice*** LING Aktiv *n*; ***passive voice*** LING Passiv *n*; **2.** zum Ausdruck bringen; LING (stimmhaft) aussprechen
voiced LING stimmhaft
voice·less LING stimmlos
void 1. leer; JUR ungültig; ***void of*** ohne; **2.** (Gefühl *n* der) Leere *f*
vol ABBR *of* ***volume*** Bd., Band *m*
vol·a·tile cholerisch (*person*); explosiv (*situation etc*); CHEM flüchtig
vol·ca·no Vulkan *m*
vol·ley 1. Salve *f*; (*Geschoss- etc*)Hagel *m* (*a. fig*); *tennis*: Volley *m*, Flugball *m*; *soccer*: Volleyschuss *m*; **2.** *Ball* volley schie-

ßen
vol·ley·ball SPORT Volleyball *m*
volt ELECTR Volt *n*
volt·age ELECTR Spannung *f*
vol·u·ble redselig; wortreich
vol·ume Band *m*; Volumen *n*, Rauminhalt *m*; Umfang *m*, große Menge; Lautstärke *f*
vo·lu·mi·nous bauschig (*dress etc*); geräumig; umfangreich (*notes etc*)
vol·un·ta·ry freiwillig; unbezahlt
vol·un·teer 1. *v/i* sich freiwillig melden (***for*** zu) (*a.* MIL); *v/t Hilfe etc* anbieten; *et.* von sich aus sagen, F herausrücken mit; 2. Freiwillige *m, f*; freiwilliger Helfer
vo·lup·tu·ous sinnlich (*lips etc*); aufreizend (*gesture etc*); üppig (*body etc*); kurvenreich (*woman*)
vom·it 1. *v/t* erbrechen; *v/i* (sich er)brechen, sich übergeben; 2. Erbrochene *n*
vo·ra·cious unersättlich (*appetite etc*)
vote 1. Abstimmung *f* (***about, on*** über *acc*); (Wahl)Stimme *f*; Stimmzettel *m*; *a. pl* Wahlrecht *n*; ***vote of no confidence*** Misstrauensvotum *n*; ***take a vote on s.th.*** über et. abstimmen; 2. *v/i* wählen; ***vote for*** (***against***) stimmen für (gegen); ***vote on*** abstimmen über (*acc*); *v/t* wählen; *et.* bewilligen; ***vote out of office*** abwählen
vot·er Wähler(in)
vot·ing booth Wahlkabine *f*
vouch: ***vouch for*** (sich ver)bürgen für
vouch·er Gutschein *m*, Kupon *m*
vow 1. Gelöbnis *n*; Gelübde *n*; ***take a vow, make a vow*** ein Gelöbnis *or* Gelübde ablegen; 2. geloben, schwören (***to do*** zu tun)
vow·el LING Vokal *m*, Selbstlaut *m*
voy·age (See)Reise *f*
vul·gar vulgär, ordinär; geschmacklos
vul·ne·ra·ble *fig* verletzbar, verwundbar; verletzlich; anfällig (***to*** für)
vul·ture ZO Geier *m*

W

W, w W, w *n*
wad (*Watte- etc*)Bausch *m*; Bündel *n*; (*Papier- etc*)Knäuel *m, n*
wad·ding Einlage *f*, Füllmaterial *n*
wad·dle watscheln
wade *v/i* waten; ***wade through*** waten durch; F sich durchkämpfen durch, *et.* durchackern; *v/t* durchwaten
wa·fer (*esp* Eis)Waffel *f*; Oblate *f*; REL Hostie *f*
waf·fle[1] Waffel *f*
waf·fle[2] *Br* F schwafeln
waft *v/i* ziehen (*smell etc*); *v/t* wehen
wag 1. wedeln (mit); 2. ***with a wag of its tail*** schwanzwedelnd
wage[1] *mst pl* (Arbeits)Lohn *m*
wage[2]: ***wage (a) war against*** *or* ***on*** MIL Krieg führen gegen; *fig* e-n Feldzug führen gegen
wage earn·er Lohnempfänger(in); Verdiener(in)
wage freeze Lohnstopp *m*
wage ne·go·ti·a·tions Tarifverhandlungen *pl*
wage pack·et Lohntüte *f*
wage rise Lohnerhöhung *f*
wa·ger Wette *f*
wag·gle F wackeln (mit)
wag·gon *Br* → **wag·on** Fuhrwerk *n*, Wagen *m*; *Br* RAIL (offener) Güterwagen; (*Tee- etc*)Wagen *m*
wag·tail ZO Bachstelze *f*
wail 1. jammern; heulen (*siren, wind*); 2. Jammern *n*; Heulen *n*
wain·scot (Wand)Täfelung *f*
waist Taille *f*
waist·coat *esp Br* Weste *f*
waist·line Taille *f*
wait 1. *v/i* warten (***for, on*** auf *acc*); ***wait for s.o.*** *a.* j-n erwarten; ***keep s.o. waiting*** j-n warten lassen; ***wait and see!*** warte es ab!; ***wait on*** (*Br* ***at***) ***table*** bedienen, servieren; ***wait on s.o.*** j-n bedienen; ***wait up*** F aufbleiben (***for*** wegen); *v/t*: ***wait one's chance*** auf e-e günstige Gelegenheit warten (***to do*** zu tun); ***wait one's turn*** warten, bis man an der Reihe ist; 2. Wartezeit *f*; ***have a long wait*** lange warten müssen; ***lie in wait for s.o.*** j-m auflauern
wait·er Kellner *m*, Ober *m*; ***waiter, the check*** (*Br* ***bill***), ***please!*** (Herr) Ober,

bitte zahlen!
wait·ing Warten *n*; ***no waiting*** MOT Halt(e)verbot *n*
waiting list Warteliste *f*
waiting room MED *etc* Wartezimmer *n*; RAIL Wartesaal *m*
wait·ress Kellnerin *f*, Bedienung *f*; ***waitress, the check*** (*Br* ***bill***), ***please!*** Fräulein, bitte zahlen!
wake[1] *v/i a.* ***wake up*** aufwachen, wach werden; *v/t a.* ***wake up*** (auf)wecken; *fig* wachrufen, wecken
wake[2] MAR Kielwasser *n*; ***follow in the wake of*** *fig* folgen auf (*acc*)
wake·ful schlaflos
wak·en *v/i a.* ***waken up*** aufwachen, wach werden; *v/t a.* ***waken up*** (auf)wecken
walk 1. *v/i* (zu Fuß) gehen, laufen; spazieren gehen; wandern; *v/t Strecke* gehen, laufen; *j-n* bringen (***to*** zu; ***home*** nach Hause); *Hund* ausführen; *Pferd* im Schritt gehen lassen; ***walk away*** → ***walk off***; ***walk in*** hineingehen, hereinkommen; ***walk off*** fort-, weggehen; ***walk off with*** F abhauen mit; F *Preis etc* locker gewinnen; ***walk out*** hinausgehen; (unter Protest) den Saal *etc* verlassen; ECON streiken, in (den) Streik treten; ***walk out on s.o.*** F j-n verlassen, j-n im Stich lassen; ***walk up*** hinaufgehen, heraufkommen; ***walk up to s.o.*** auf j-n zugehen; ***walk up!*** treten Sie näher!; **2.** Spaziergang *m*; Wanderung *f*; Spazier-, Wanderweg *m*; ***go for a walk, take a walk*** e-n Spaziergang machen, spazieren gehen; ***an hour's walk*** e-e Stunde Fußweg *or* zu Fuß; ***from all walks of life*** *Leute* aus allen Berufen *or* Schichten
walk·a·way F Spaziergang *m*, leichter Sieg
walk·er Spaziergänger(in); Wanderer *m*, Wand(r)erin *f*; SPORT Geher(in); ***be a good walker*** gut zu Fuß sein
walk·ie-talk·ie Walkie-Talkie *n*, tragbares Funksprechgerät
walk·ing Gehen *n*, Laufen *n*; Spazierengehen *n*; Wandern *n*
walking pa·pers: ***get one's walking papers*** F den Laufpass bekommen
walking shoes Wanderschuhe *pl*
walking stick Spazierstock *m*
walking tour Wanderung *f*
Walk·man® Walkman® *m*
walk·out Auszug *m* (***by, of*** *e-r Delegation etc*); ECON Ausstand *m*, Streik *m*
walk·over → ***walkaway***
walk-up F (Miets)Haus *n* ohne Fahrstuhl; Wohnung *f or* Büro *n etc* in e-m Haus ohne Fahrstuhl
wall 1. Wand *f*; Mauer *f*; **2.** *a.* ***wall in*** mit e-r Mauer umgeben; ***wall up*** zumauern
wall cal·en·dar Wandkalender *m*
wall·chart Wandkarte *f*
wal·let Brieftasche *f*
wall·flow·er F Mauerblümchen *n*
wal·lop F *j-m* ein Ding verpassen; SPORT *j-n* erledigen, vernichten (***at*** in *dat*)
wal·low sich wälzen; *fig* schwelgen, sich baden (***in*** in *dat*)
wall·pa·per 1. Tapete *f*; **2.** tapezieren
wall-to-wall: ***wall-to-wall carpet(ing)*** Spannteppich *m*, Teppichboden *m*
wal·nut BOT Walnuss(baum *m*) *f*
wal·rus ZO Walross *n*
waltz 1. Walzer *m*; **2.** Walzer tanzen
wand (*Zauber*)Stab *m*
wan·der (herum)wandern, herumlaufen, umherstreifen; *fig* abschweifen; fantasieren
wane 1. ASTR abnehmen; *fig* schwinden; **2.** ***be on the wane*** *fig* im Schwinden begriffen sein
wan·gle F deichseln, hinkriegen; ***wangle s.th. out of s.o.*** j-m et. abluchsen; ***wangle one's way out of*** sich herauswinden aus
want 1. *v/t et.* wollen; *j-n* brauchen; *j-n* sprechen wollen; F *et.* brauchen, nötig haben; ***be wanted*** (*polizeilich*) gesucht werden (***for*** wegen); *v/i* wollen; ***I don't want to*** ich will nicht; ***he does not want for anything*** es fehlt ihm an nichts; **2.** Mangel *m* (***of*** an *dat*); Bedürfnis *n*, Wunsch *m*; Not *f*
want ad Kleinanzeige *f*
want·ed (*polizeilich*) gesucht
wan·ton mutwillig
war Krieg *m* (*a. fig*); *fig* Kampf *m* (***against*** gegen)
war·ble ZO trillern
ward 1. MED Station *f*; *Br* POL Stadtbezirk *m*; JUR Mündel *n*; **2.** ***ward off*** *Schlag etc* abwehren, *Gefahr etc* abwenden
war·den Aufseher(in); Heimleiter(in); (Gefängnis)Direktor(in)
ward·er *Br* Aufsichtsbeamte *m*, -beamtin *f*
war·drobe Kleiderschrank *m*; Garderobe *f*
ware·house Lager(haus) *n*
war·fare Krieg *m*; Kriegführung *f*
war·head MIL Spreng-, Gefechtskopf *m*
war·like kriegerisch; Kriegs...
warm 1. *adj* warm, *fig a.* herzlich; ***I am warm, I feel warm*** mir ist warm; **2.** *v/t a.* ***warm up*** wärmen, sich *die Hände etc* wärmen; *Motor* warm laufen lassen; *v/i a.* ***warm up*** warm *or* wärmer werden, sich erwärmen

warmth Wärme *f*
warm-up SPORT Aufwärmen *n*
warn warnen (***against, of*** vor *dat*); *j-n* verständigen
warn·ing Warnung *f* (***of*** vor *dat*); Verwarnung *f*; ***without warning*** ohne Vorwarnung
warning sig·nal Warnsignal *n*
warp sich verziehen *or* werfen
war·rant **1.** JUR (Durchsuchungs-, Haft- *etc*)Befehl *m*; **2.** *et.* rechtfertigen
warrant of ar·rest JUR Haftbefehl *m*
war·ran·ty ECON Garantie(erklärung) *f*; ***it's still under warranty*** darauf ist noch Garantie
war·ri·or Krieger *m*
war·ship Kriegsschiff *n*
wart MED Warze *f*
war·y vorsichtig
was *ich, er, sie, es* war; *passive*: *ich, er, sie, es* wurde
wash **1.** *v/t* waschen, sich *die Hände etc* waschen; *v/i* sich waschen; sich *gut etc* waschen (lassen); ***wash up*** *v/i Br* abwaschen, (das) Geschirr spülen; *v/t* anschwemmen, anspülen; ***wash one's dirty linen*** schmutzige Wäsche waschen; **2.** Wäsche *f*; MOT Waschanlage *f*, Waschstraße *f*; ***be in the wash*** in der Wäsche sein; ***give s.th. a wash*** et. waschen; ***have a wash*** sich waschen
wash·a·ble (ab)waschbar
wash-and-wear bügelfrei; pflegeleicht
wash·ba·sin *Br*, **wash·bowl** Waschbecken *n*
wash·cloth Waschlappen *m*
wash·er Waschmaschine *f*; TECH Unterlegscheibe *f*
wash·ing **1.** Wäsche *f*; **2.** Wasch…
wash·ing ma·chine Waschmaschine *f*
washing pow·der Waschpulver *n*, -mittel *n*
washing-up *Br* Abwasch *m*; ***do the washing-up*** den Abwasch machen
wash·room Toilette *f*
wasp ZO Wespe *f*
waste **1.** Verschwendung *f*; Abfall *m*; Müll *m*; ***waste of time*** Zeitverschwendung *f*; ***hazardous waste, special toxic waste*** Sondermüll *m*; ***special waste dump*** Sondermülldeponie *f*; **2.** *v/t* verschwenden, vergeuden; *j-n* auszehren; *v/i* ***waste away*** immer schwächer werden (*person*); **3.** überschüssig; Abfall…; brachliegend, öde; ***lay waste*** verwüsten
waste dis·pos·al Abfall-, Müllbeseitigung *f*; Entsorgung *f*
waste disposal site Deponie *f*
waste·ful verschwenderisch
waste gas Abgas *n*
waste pa·per Abfallpapier *n*; Altpapier *n*
waste·pa·per bas·ket Papierkorb *m*
waste pipe Abflussrohr *n*
watch **1.** *v/i* zuschauen; ***watch for*** warten auf (*acc*); ***watch out!*** pass auf!, Vorsicht!; ***watch out for*** Ausschau halten nach; sich in Acht nehmen vor (*dat*); *v/t* beobachten; zuschauen bei, sich *et.* ansehen; → ***television***; **2.** (*Armband-, Taschen-*)Uhr *f*; Wache *f*; ***keep watch*** Wache halten, wachen (***over*** über *acc*); ***be on the watch for*** Ausschau halten nach; auf der Hut sein vor (*dat*); ***keep (a) careful*** *or* ***close watch on*** genau beobachten, scharf im Auge behalten
watch·dog Wachhund *m*
watch·ful wachsam
watch·mak·er Uhrmacher(in)
watch·man Wachmann *m*, Wächter *m*
watch·tow·er Wach(t)turm *m*
wa·ter **1.** Wasser *n*; **2.** *v/t Blumen* gießen, *Rasen etc* sprengen; *Vieh* tränken; ***water down*** verdünnen, verwässern; *fig* abschwächen; *v/i* tränen (*eyes*); ***make s.o. 's mouth water*** j-m den Mund wässerig machen
wa·ter bird ZO Wasservogel *m*
wa·ter·col·o(u)r Wasser-, Aquarellfarbe *f*; Aquarellmalerei *f*; Aquarell *n*
wa·ter·course Wasserlauf *m*
wa·ter·cress BOT Brunnenkresse *f*
wa·ter·fall Wasserfall *m*
wa·ter·front Hafenviertel *n*; ***along the waterfront*** am Wasser entlang
wa·ter·hole Wasserloch *n*
wa·ter·ing can Gießkanne *f*
wa·ter jump SPORT Wassergraben *m*
wa·ter lev·el Wasserstand *m*
wa·ter lil·y BOT Seerose *f*
wa·ter·mark Wasserzeichen *n*
wa·ter·mel·on BOT Wassermelone *f*
wa·ter pol·lu·tion Wasserverschmutzung *f*
water po·lo SPORT Wasserball(spiel *n*) *m*
wa·ter·proof **1.** wasserdicht; **2.** *Br* Regenmantel *m*; **3.** imprägnieren
wa·ters Gewässer *pl*; Wasser *pl*
wa·ter·shed GEOGR Wasserscheide *f*; *fig* Wendepunkt *m*
wa·ter·side Ufer *n*
wa·ter ski·ing SPORT Wasserskilaufen *n*
wa·ter·tight wasserdicht, *fig a.* hieb- und stichfest
wa·ter·way Wasserstraße *f*
wa·ter·works Wasserwerk *n*; ***turn on the waterworks*** F zu heulen anfangen
wa·ter·y wäss(e)rig
watt ELECTR Watt *n*

wave 1. *v/t* schwenken; winken mit; *Haar* wellen, in Wellen legen; ***wave one's hand*** winken; ***wave s.o. aside*** j-n beiseitewinken; *v/i* winken; wehen (*flag etc*); sich wellen (*hair*); ***wave at s.o., wave to s.o.*** j-m zuwinken; **2.** Welle *f* (*a. fig*); Winken *n*
wave·length PHYS Wellenlänge *f* (*a. fig*)
wa·ver flackern; schwanken
wav·y wellig, gewellt
wax[1] 1. Wachs *n*; (*Ohren*)Schmalz *n*; **2.** wachsen; bohnern
wax[2] ASTR zunehmen
wax·en wächsern
wax·works Wachsfigurenkabinett *n*
wax·y wächsern
way 1. Weg *m*; Richtung *f*, Seite *f*; Entfernung *f*, Strecke *f*; Art *f*, Weise *f*; ***ways and means*** Mittel und Wege *pl*; ***way back*** Rückweg *m*, Rückfahrt *f*; ***way home*** Heimweg *m*; ***way in*** Eingang *m*; ***way out*** Ausgang *m*; ***be on the way to, be on one's way to*** unterwegs sein nach; ***by way of*** über (*acc*), via; *esp Br* statt; ***by the way*** übrigens; ***give way*** nachgeben; *Br* MOT die Vorfahrt lassen; ***in a way*** in gewisser Hinsicht; ***in no way*** in keiner Weise; ***lead the way*** vorangehen; ***let s.o. have his (own) way*** j-m s-n Willen lassen; ***lose one's way*** sich verlaufen *or* verirren; ***make way*** Platz machen (***for*** für); ***no way!*** F kommt überhaupt nicht in Frage!; ***out of the way*** ungewöhnlich; ***this way*** hierher; hier entlang; **2.** *adv* weit
way·bill ECON Frachtbrief *m*
way·lay *j-m* auflauern; *j-n* abfangen, abpassen
way·ward eigensinnig, launisch
we wir *pl*
weak schwach (***at, in*** in *dat*), GASTR *a.* dünn
weak·en *v/t* schwächen (*a. fig*); *v/i* schwächer werden; *fig* nachgeben
weak·ling Schwächling *m*, F Schlappschwanz *n*
weak·ness Schwäche *f*
weal Striemen *m*
wealth Reichtum *m*; *fig* Fülle *f* (***of*** von)
wealth·y reich
wean entwöhnen; ***wean s.o. from*** *or* ***off s.th.*** j-m et. abgewöhnen
weap·on Waffe *f* (*a. fig*)
wear 1. *v/t Bart, Brille, Schmuck etc* tragen, *Mantel etc a.* anhaben, *Hut etc a.* aufhaben; abnutzen, abtragen; ***wear the pants*** (*Br* ***trousers***) F die Hosen anhaben; ***wear an angry expression*** verärgert dreinschauen; *v/i* sich abnutzen, verschleißen; sich gut *etc* halten; ***s.th. to wear*** et. zum Anziehen; ***wear away*** (sich) abtragen *or* abschleifen; ***wear down*** (sich) abtreten (*stairs*), (sich) ablaufen (*heels*), (sich) abfahren (*tires*); abschleifen; *j-n* zermürben; ***wear off*** nachlassen (*pain etc*); ***wear on*** sich hinziehen (***all day*** über den ganzen Tag); ***wear out*** (sich) abnutzen *or* abtragen; *fig j-n* erschöpfen; **2.** *often in cpds* Kleidung *f*; *a.* ***wear and tear*** Abnutzung *f*, Verschleiß *m*; ***the worse for wear*** abgenutzt, verschlissen; F lädiert
wear·i·some ermüdend; langweilig; lästig
wear·y erschöpft, müde; ermüdend, anstrengend; ***be weary of s.th.*** F et. satthaben
wea·sel ZO Wiesel *n*
weath·er 1. Wetter *n*; Witterung *f*; **2.** *v/t* dem Wetter aussetzen; *fig Krise etc* überstehen; *v/i* verwittern
weath·er-beat·en verwittert
weath·er chart METEOR Wetterkarte *f*
weather fore·cast METEOR Wettervorhersage *f*; Wetterbericht *m*
weath·er·man *radio*, TV Wetteransager *m*
weath·er·proof 1. wetterfest; **2.** wetterfest machen
weath·er re·port METEOR Wetterbericht *m*
weather sta·tion METEOR Wetterwarte *f*
weather vane Wetterfahne *f*
weave weben; *Netz* spinnen; *Korb* flechten; ***weave one's way through*** sich schlängeln durch
weav·er Weber(in)
web Netz *n* (*a. fig*), Gewebe *n*; ZO Schwimmhaut *f*
wed heiraten
Wed(s) ABBR *of* ***Wednesday*** Mi., Mittwoch *m*
wed·ding 1. Hochzeit *f*; **2.** Hochzeits…, Braut…, Ehe…, Trau…
wed·ding ring Ehering *m*, Trauring *m*
wedge 1. Keil *m*; **2.** verkeilen, mit e-m Keil festklemmen; ***wedge in*** einkeilen, einzwängen
wed·lock: ***born in (out of) wedlock*** ehelich (unehelich) geboren
Wednes·day (ABBR ***Wed, Weds***) Mittwoch *m*; ***on Wednesday*** (am) Mittwoch; ***on Wednesdays*** mittwochs
wee[1] F klein, winzig; ***a wee bit*** ein (kleines) bisschen
wee[2] F **1.** Pipi machen; **2.** ***do*** *or* ***have a wee*** Pipi machen
weed 1. Unkraut *n*; **2.** jäten
weed·kill·er Unkrautvertilgungsmittel *n*
weed·y voll Unkraut; F schmächtig; F rückgratlos

week Woche *f*; ***week after week*** Woche um Woche; ***a week today, today week*** heute in e-r Woche *or* in acht Tagen; ***every other week*** jede zweite Woche; ***for weeks*** wochenlang; ***four times a week*** viermal die Woche; ***in a week('s time)*** in e-r Woche
week·day Wochentag *m*
week·end Wochenende *n*; ***on*** (*Br **at***) ***the weekend*** am Wochenende
week·end·er Wochenendausflügler(in)
week·ly 1. Wochen…; wöchentlich; **2.** Wochenblatt *n*, Wochen(zeit)schrift *f*, Wochenzeitung *f*
weep weinen (***for*** um *j-n*; ***over*** über *acc*); MED nässen
weep·ing wil·low BOT Trauerweide *f*
weep·y F weinerlich; rührselig
wee-wee F → ***wee²***
weigh *v/t* (ab)wiegen; *fig* abwägen (***against*** gegen); ***weigh anchor*** MAR den Anker lichten; ***be weighed down with*** *fig* niedergedrückt werden von; *v/i* … *Kilo etc* wiegen; ***weigh on*** *fig* lasten auf (*dat*)
weight 1. Gewicht *n*; Last *f* (*a. fig*); *fig* Bedeutung *f*; ***gain weight, put on weight*** zunehmen; ***lose weight*** abnehmen; **2.** beschweren
weight·less schwerelos
weight·less·ness Schwerelosigkeit *f*
weight lift·er SPORT Gewichtheber *m*
weight lift·ing SPORT Gewichtheben *n*
weight·y schwer; *fig* schwerwiegend
weir Wehr *n*
weird unheimlich; F sonderbar, verrückt
wel·come 1. *int* ***welcome back!, welcome home!*** willkommen zu Hause!; ***welcome to England!*** willkommen in England!; **2.** *v/t* begrüßen (*a. fig*), willkommen heißen; **3.** *adj* willkommen; ***you are welcome to do it*** Sie können es gerne tun; ***you're welcome!*** nichts zu danken!, keine Ursache!, bitte sehr!; **4.** Empfang *m*, Willkommen *n*; ***outstay*** *or* ***overstay one's welcome*** j-s Gastfreundschaft überstrapazieren *or* zu lange in Anspruch nehmen
weld TECH schweißen
wel·fare Wohl(ergehen) *n*; Sozialhilfe *f*; ***be on welfare*** Sozalhilfe beziehen
welfare state Wohlfahrtsstaat *m*
welfare work Sozialarbeit *f*
welfare work·er Sozialarbeiter(in)
well¹ 1. *adv* gut; gründlich; ***as well*** ebenso, auch; ***as well as …*** sowohl … als auch …; nicht nur …, sondern auch …; ***very well*** also gut, na gut; ***well done!*** bravo!; → ***off*** *1*; **2.** *int* nun, also; ***well, well!*** na so was!; **3.** *adj* gesund; ***feel well*** sich wohlfühlen
well² 1. Brunnen *m*; (*Öl*)Quelle *f*; (*Aufzugs- etc*)Schacht *m*; **2.** *a.* ***well out*** quellen (***from*** aus); ***tears welled*** (***up***) ***in their eyes*** die Tränen stiegen ihnen in die Augen
well-bal·anced ausgeglichen (*person*); ausgewogen (*diet*)
well-be·haved artig, gut erzogen
well·be·ing Wohl(befinden) *n*
well-dis·posed: ***be well-disposed towards s.o.*** j-m wohlgesinnt sein
well-done GASTR durchgebraten
well-earned wohlverdient
well-fed gut genährt
well-found·ed (wohl) begründet
well-in·formed gut unterrichtet; gebildet
well-known (wohl) bekannt
well-mean·ing wohlmeinend, gut gemeint
well-meant gut gemeint
well-off 1. wohlhabend, vermögend, bessergestellt; ***be well-off for*** gut versorgt sein mit; **2.** ***the well-off*** die Wohlhabenden *pl*
well-read belesen
well-timed (zeitlich) günstig, im richtigen Augenblick
well-to-do wohlhabend, reich
well-worn abgetragen; *fig* abgedroschen
Welsh 1. walisisch; **2.** LING Walisisch *n*; ***the Welsh*** die Waliser *pl*
welt Striemen *m*
wel·ter Wirrwarr *m*, Durcheinander *n*
wel·ter·weight SPORT Weltergewicht *n*; Weltergewichtler *m*
were *du* warst, *Sie* waren, *wir, sie* waren, *ihr* wart
west 1. West, Westen *m*; ***the West*** POL der Westen; die Weststaaten *pl*; **2.** *adj* westlich, West…; **3.** *adv* nach Westen, westwärts
west·er·ly West…, westlich
west·ern 1. westlich, West…; **2.** Western *m*
west·ward(s) westlich, nach Westen
wet 1. nass, feucht; **2.** Nässe *f*; **3.** nass machen, anfeuchten
weth·er ZO Hammel *m*
wet nurse Amme *f*
whack (knallender) Schlag; F Anteil *m*
whacked F fertig, erledigt
whack·ing 1. *Br* F Mords…; **2.** (Tracht *f*) Prügel *pl*
whale ZO Wal *m*
wharf Kai *m*
what 1. *pron* was; ***what about …?*** wie wärs mit …?; ***what for?*** wozu?; ***so***

W

what? na und?; ***know what's what*** F wissen, was Sache ist; **2.** *adj* was für ein(e), welche(r, -s); alle, die; alles, was
what·cha·ma·call·it F → ***whatsit***
what·ev·er **1.** *pron* was (auch immer); alles, was; egal, was; **2.** *adj* welche(r, -s) … auch (immer); ***no … whatever*** überhaupt kein(e) …
whats·it F Dings(bums, -da) *m, f, n*
what·so·ev·er → ***whatever***
wheat BOT Weizen *m*
whee·dle beschwatzen; ***wheedle s.th. out of s.o.*** j-m et. abschwatzen
wheel **1.** Rad *n*; MOT, MAR Steuer *n*; **2.** schieben, rollen; kreisen; ***wheel about, wheel (a)round*** herumfahren, herumwirbeln
wheel·bar·row Schubkarre(n *m*) *f*
wheel·chair Rollstuhl *m*
wheel clamp MOT Parkkralle *f*
wheeled mit Rädern; fahrbar; *in cpds* …räd(e)rig
wheeze keuchen, pfeifend atmen
whelp zo Welpe *m*, Junge *n*
when wann; als; wenn; obwohl; ***since when?*** seit wann?
when·ev·er wann auch (immer); jedes Mal, wenn
where wo; wohin; ***where … (from)?*** woher?; ***where … (to)?*** wohin?
where·a·bouts **1.** *adv* wo etwa; **2.** Verbleib *m*; Aufenthalt *m*, Aufenthaltsort *m*
where·as während, wohingegen
where·by wodurch, womit; wonach
where·u·pon worauf, woraufhin
wher·ev·er wo *or* wohin auch (immer); ganz gleich wo *or* wohin
whet *Messer etc* schärfen; *fig Appetit* anregen
wheth·er ob
whey Molke *f*
which welche(r, -s); der, die, das; was; ***which of you?*** wer von euch?
which·ev·er welche(r, -s) auch (immer); ganz gleich, welche(r, -s)
whiff Luftzug *m*; Hauch *m* (*a. fig* ***of*** von); Duft *m*, Duftwolke *f*
while **1.** Weile *f*; ***for a while*** e-e Zeit lang; **2.** *cj* während; obwohl; **3.** *mst* ***while away*** sich *die Zeit* vertreiben (***by doing s.th.*** mit et.)
whim Laune *f*
whim·per **1.** wimmern; zo winseln; **2.** Wimmern *n*; zo Winseln *n*
whim·si·cal wunderlich; launisch
whine **1.** zo jaulen; jammern (***about*** über *acc*); **2.** zo Jaulen *n*; Gejammer *n*
whin·ny zo **1.** wiehern; **2.** Wiehern *n*
whip **1.** Peitsche *f*; GASTR Creme *f*; **2.** *v/t* (aus)peitschen; GASTR schlagen; *v/i* sausen, flitzen, (*wind*) fegen
whipped cream Schlagsahne *f*, Schlagrahm *m*
whipped eggs Eischnee *m*
whip·ping (Tracht *f*) Prügel *pl*
whip·ping boy Prügelknabe *m*
whip·ping cream Schlagsahne *f*, Schlagrahm *m*
whir → ***whirr***
whirl **1.** wirbeln; ***my head is whirling*** mir schwirrt der Kopf; **2.** Wirbeln *n*; Wirbel *m* (*a. fig*); ***my head's in a whirl*** mir schwirrt der Kopf
whirl·pool Strudel *m*; Whirlpool *m*
whirl·wind Wirbelsturm *m*
whirr schwirren
whisk **1.** schnelle Bewegung; Wedel *m*; GASTR Schneebesen *m*; **2.** GASTR schlagen; ***whisk its tail*** zo mit dem Schwanz schlagen; ***whisk away*** *Fliegen etc* verscheuchen *or* wegscheuchen; *et.* schnell verschwinden lassen *or* wegnehmen
whis·ker zo Schnurr- *or* Barthaar *n*; *pl* Backenbart *m*
whis·k(e)y Whisky *m*
whis·per **1.** flüstern; **2.** Flüstern *n*; ***say s.th. in a whisper*** et. im Flüsterton sagen
whis·tle **1.** Pfeife *f*; Pfiff *m*; **2.** pfeifen
white **1.** weiß; **2.** Weiß(e) *n*; Weiße *m, f*; Eiweiß *n*
white bread Weißbrot *n*
white coffee *Br* Milchkaffee *m*, Kaffee *m* mit Milch
white-col·lar work·er (Büro)Angestellte *m, f*
white lie Notlüge *f*
whit·en weiß machen *or* werden
white·wash **1.** Tünche *f*; **2.** tünchen, anstreichen; weißen; *fig* beschönigen
whit·ish weißlich
Whit·sun Pfingstsonntag *m*; Pfingsten *n or pl*
Whit Sunday Pfingstsonntag *m*
Whit·sun·tide Pfingsten *n or pl*
whit·tle (zurecht)schnitzen; ***whittle away*** *Gewinn etc* allmählich aufzehren; ***whittle down*** et. reduzieren (***to*** auf *acc*)
whiz(z) F **1.** ***whiz by, whiz past*** vorbeizischen, vorbeidüsen; **2.** Ass *n*, Kanone *f* (***at*** in *dat*)
whiz kid F Senkrechtstarter(in)
who wer; wen; wem; welche(r, -s); der, die, das
who·dun·(n)it F Krimi *m*
who·ev·er wer *or* wen *or* wem auch (immer); egal, wer *or* wen *or* wem
whole **1.** *adj* ganz; **2.** *das* Ganze; ***the***

W

whole of London ganz London; ***on the whole*** im Großen (und) Ganzen
whole·heart·ed ungeteilt (*attention*), voll (*support*), ernsthaft (*effort etc*)
whole·heart·ed·ly uneingeschränkt, voll und ganz
whole·meal Vollkorn…; ***wholemeal bread*** Vollkornbrot *n*
whole·sale ECON **1.** Großhandel *m*; **2.** Großhandels…
wholesale mar·ket ECON Großmarkt *m*
whole·sal·er ECON Großhändler *m*
whole·some gesund
whole wheat → ***wholemeal***
whol·ly gänzlich, völlig
whoop 1. schreien, *esp* jauchzen; ***whoop it up*** F auf den Putz hauen; **2.** (*esp* Freuden)Schrei *m*
whoop·ee: F ***make whoopee*** auf den Putz hauen
whoop·ing cough MED Keuchhusten *m*
whore Hure *f*
why warum, weshalb; ***that's why*** deshalb
wick Docht *m*
wick·ed gemein, niederträchtig
wich·er·work Korbwaren *pl*
wick·et *cricket*: Tor *n*
wide 1. *adj* breit; weit offen, aufgerissen (*eyes*); *fig* umfangreich (*knowledge etc*), vielfältig (*interests etc*); **1.** *adv* weit; ***go wide*** danebengehen; ***go wide of the goal*** SPORT am Tor vorbeigehen
wide-an·gle lens PHOT Weitwinkelobjektiv *n*
wide-a·wake hellwach; *fig* aufgeweckt, wach
wide-eyed mit großen *or* aufgerissenen Augen; naiv
wid·en verbreitern; breiter werden
wide-o·pen weit offen, aufgerissen (*eyes*)
wide·spread weit verbreitet
wid·ow Witwe *f*
wid·owed verwitwet; ***be widowed*** verwitwet sein; Witwe(r) werden
wid·ow·er Witwer *m*
width Breite *f*; Bahn *f*
wield *Einfluss etc* ausüben
wife (Ehe)Frau *f*, Gattin *f*
wig Perücke *f*
wild 1. *adj* wild; stürmisch (*wind*, *applause etc*); außer sich (***with*** vor *dat*); verrückt (*idea etc*); ***make a wild guess*** einfach drauflosraten; ***be wild about*** (ganz) verrückt sein nach; **2.** *adv*: ***go wild*** ausflippen; ***let one's children run wild*** s-e Kinder machen lassen, was sie wollen; **3.** ***in the wild*** in freier Wildbahn; ***the wilds*** die Wildnis
wild·cat zo Wildkatze *f*
wild·cat strike ECON wilder Streik
wil·der·ness Wildnis *f*
wild·fire: ***spread like wildfire*** sich wie ein Lauffeuer verbreiten
wild·life Tier- und Pflanzenwelt *f*
wil·ful *Br* → ***willful***
will[1] *v/aux ich*, *du* will(st) *etc*; *ich* werde … *etc*
will[2] Wille *m*; Testament *n*; ***of one's own free will*** aus freien Stücken
will[3] durch Willenskraft erzwingen; JUR vermachen
will·ful eigensinnig; absichtlich, *esp* JUR vorsätzlich
will·ing bereit (***to do*** zu tun); (bereit)willig
will-o'-the-wisp Irrlicht *n*
wil·low BOT Weide *f*
wil·low·y *fig* gertenschlank
will·pow·er Willenskraft *f*
wil·ly-nil·ly wohl oder übel
wilt verwelken, welk werden
wi·ly gerissen, raffiniert
wimp F Schlappschwanz *m*
win 1. *v/t* gewinnen; ***win s.o. over*** *or* ***round to*** j-n gewinnen für; *v/i* gewinnen, siegen; ***OK, you win*** okay, du hast gewonnen; **2.** *esp* SPORT Sieg *m*
wince zusammenzucken (***at*** bei)
winch TECH Winde *f*
wind[1] **1.** Wind *m*; Atem *m*, Luft *f*; MED Blähungen *pl*; ***the wind*** MUS die Bläser *pl*; **2.** *j-m* den Atem nehmen *or* verschlagen; HUNT wittern
wind[2] **1.** *v/t* drehen (an *dat*); *Uhr etc* aufziehen; wickeln (***round*** um); *v/i* sich winden *or* schlängeln; ***wind back*** *Film etc* zurückspulen; ***wind down*** *Autofenster etc* herunterdrehen, -kurbeln; *Produktion etc* reduzieren; sich entspannen; ***wind forward*** *Film etc* weiterspulen; ***wind up*** *v/t Autofenster etc* hochdrehen, -kurbeln; *Uhr etc* aufziehen; *Versammlung etc* schließen (***with*** mit); *Unternehmen* liquidieren, auflösen; *v/i* F enden, landen; (*esp* s-e Rede) schließen (***by saying*** mit den Worten); **2.** Umdrehung *f*
wind·bag F Schwätzer(in)
wind·fall BOT Fallobst *n*; unverhofftes Geschenk; unverhoffter Gewinn
wind·ing gewunden
wind·ing stairs Wendeltreppe *f*
wind in·stru·ment MUS Blasinstrument *n*
wind·lass TECH Winde *f*
wind·mill Windmühle *f*
win·dow Fenster *n*; Schaufenster *n*; Schalter *m*
window clean·er Fensterputzer *m*
window dress·er Schaufensterdekora-

teur(in)
window dress·ing Schaufensterdekoration *f*; *fig* F Mache *f*
win·dow·pane Fensterscheibe *f*
win·dow seat Fensterplatz *m*
win·dow shade Rouleau *n*
win·dow-shop: ***go window-shopping*** e-n Schaufensterbummel machen
win·dow·sill Fensterbank *f*, -brett *n*
wind·pipe ANAT Luftröhre *f*
wind·screen *Br* MOT Windschutzscheibe *f*
windscreen wip·er *Br* MOT Scheibenwischer *m*
wind·shield MOT Windschutzscheibe *f*
windshield wip·er MOT Scheibenwischer *m*
wind·surf·ing SPORT Windsurfing *n*, Windsurfen *n*
wind·y windig; MED blähend
wine Wein *m*
wine cel·lar Weinkeller *m*
wine list Weinkarte *f*
wine mer·chant Weinhändler *m*
win·er·y Weinkellerei *f*
wine tast·ing Weinprobe *f*
wing zo Flügel *m*, Schwinge *f*; *Br* MOT Kotflügel *m*; AVIAT Tragfläche *f*; AVIAT MIL Geschwader *n*; *pl* THEA Seitenkulisse *f*
wing·er SPORT Außenstürmer(in), Flügelstürmer(in)
wink 1. zwinkern; ***wink at*** *j-m* zuzwinkern; *et.* geflissentlich übersehen; ***wink one's lights*** *Br* MOT blinken; **2.** Zwinkern *n*; ***I didn't get a wink of sleep last night, I didn't sleep a wink last night*** ich habe letzte Nacht kein Auge zugetan; → ***forty 1***
win·ner Gewinner(in), *esp* SPORT Sieger(in)
win·ning 1. einnehmend, gewinnend; **2.** *pl* Gewinn *m*
win·ter 1. Winter *m*; ***in (the) winter*** im Winter; **2.** überwintern; den Winter verbringen
winter sports Wintersport *m*
win·ter·time Winter *m*; Winterzeit *f*; ***in (the) wintertime*** im Winter
win·try winterlich; *fig* frostig
wipe (ab-, auf)wischen; ***wipe off*** ab-, wegwischen; ***wipe out*** auswischen; auslöschen, ausrotten; ***wipe up*** aufwischen
wip·er MOT (*Scheiben*)Wischer *m*
wire 1. Draht *m*; ELECTR Leitung *f*; Telegramm *n*; **2.** Leitungen verlegen in (*dat*) (*a.* ***wire up***); *j-m* ein Telegramm schicken; *j-m et.* telegrafieren
wire·less drahtlos, Funk…
wire net·ting Maschendraht *m*
wire-tap *j-n*, *j-s Telefon* abhören
wir·y *fig* drahtig
wis·dom Weisheit *f*, Klugheit *f*
wis·dom tooth Weisheitszahn *m*
wise weise, klug
wise·crack F **1.** Witzelei *f*; **2.** witzeln
wise guy F Klugscheißer *m*
wish 1. wünschen; wollen; ***wish s.o. well*** j-m alles Gute wünschen; ***if you wish (to)*** wenn du willst; ***wish for s.th.*** sich et. wünschen; **2.** Wunsch *m* (***for*** nach)
wish·ful think·ing Wunschdenken *n*
wish·y-wash·y F labb(e)rig, wäss(e)rig; *fig* lasch (*person*); verschwommen
wisp (*Gras-, Haar*)Büschel *n*
wist·ful wehmütig
wit Geist *m*, Witz *m*; geistreicher Mensch; *a. pl* Verstand *m*; ***be at one's wits' end*** mit s-r Weisheit am Ende sein; ***keep one's wits about one*** e-n klaren Kopf behalten
witch Hexe *f*
witch·craft Hexerei *f*
with mit; bei; vor (*dat*)
with·draw *v/t Geld* abheben (***from*** von); *Angebot etc* zurückziehen, *Anschuldigung etc* zurücknehmen; MIL *Truppen* zurückziehen, abziehen; *v/i* sich zurückziehen; zurücktreten (***from*** von)
with·draw·al Rücknahme *f*; *esp* MIL Abzug *m*, Rückzug *m*; Rücktritt *m* (***from*** von), Ausstieg *m* (***from*** aus); MED Entziehung *f*, Entzug *m*; ***make a withdrawal*** Geld abheben (***from*** von)
withdrawal cure MED Entziehungskur *f*
withdrawal symp·toms MED Entzugserscheinungen *pl*
with·er eingehen *or* verdorren *or* (ver)welken (lassen)
with·hold zurückhalten; ***withhold s.th. from s.o.*** j-m et. vorenthalten
with·in innerhalb (*gen*)
with·out ohne (*acc*)
with·stand *e-m Angriff etc* standhalten; *Beanspruchung etc* aushalten
wit·ness 1. Zeuge *m*, Zeugin *f*; ***witness for the defense*** (*Br* ***defence***) JUR Entlastungszeuge *m*, -zeugin *f*; ***witness for the prosecution*** JUR Belastungszeuge *m*, -zeugin *f*; **2.** Zeuge sein von *et.*; *et.* bezeugen, *Unterschrift* beglaubigen; ***witness box*** *Br*, **witness stand** JUR Zeugenstand *m*
wit·ti·cis·m geistreiche *or* witzige Bemerkung
wit·ty geistreich, witzig
wiz·ard Zauberer *m*; *fig* Genie *n* (***at*** in *dat*)
wiz·ened verhutzelt

W

wob·ble *v/i* wackeln, zittern (*a. voice*), schwabbeln; MOT flattern; *fig* schwanken; *v/t* wackeln an (*dat*)
woe·ful traurig; bedauerlich
wolf **1.** ZO Wolf *m*; ***lone wolf*** *fig* Einzelgänger(in); **2.** *a.* ***wolf down*** F *Essen* hinunterschlingen
wom·an Frau *f*
woman doc·tor Ärztin *f*
woman driv·er Frau *f* am Steuer
wom·an·ish weibisch
wom·an·ly fraulich; weiblich
womb ANAT Gebärmutter *f*
women's lib·ber F Emanze *f*
women's move·ment Frauenbewegung *f*
women's ref·uge *Br*, **women's shel·ter** Frauenhaus *n*
won·der **1.** neugierig *or* gespannt sein, gern wissen mögen; sich fragen, überlegen; sich wundern, erstaunt sein (***about*** über *acc*); ***I wonder if you could help me*** vielleicht können Sie mir helfen; **2.** Staunen *n*, Verwunderung *f*; Wunder *n*; ***do*** *or* ***work wonders*** wahre Wunder vollbringen, Wunder wirken (***for*** bei)
won·der·ful wunderbar, wundervoll
wont **1.** ***be wont to do s.th.*** et. zu tun pflegen; **2.** ***as was his wont*** wie es s-e Gewohnheit war
woo umwerben, werben um
wood Holz *n*; Holzfass *n*; *a. pl* Wald *m*, Gehölz *n*; ***touch wood!*** unberufen!, toi, toi, toi!; ***he can't see the wood for the trees*** er sieht den Wald vor lauter Bäumen nicht
wood·cut Holzschnitt *m*
wood·cut·ter Holzfäller *m*
wood·ed bewaldet
wood·en hölzern (*a. fig*), aus Holz, Holz…
wood·peck·er ZO Specht *m*
wood·wind: ***the woodwind*** MUS die Holzblasinstrumente *pl*, die Holzbläser *pl*; ***woodwind instrument*** Holzblasinstrument *n*
wood·work Holzarbeit *f*
wood·y waldig; BOT holzig
wool Wolle *f*
wool·(l)en **1.** wollen, Woll…; **2.** *pl* Wollsachen *pl*, Wollkleidung *f*
wool·(l)y **1.** wollig; *fig* schwammig; **2.** *pl* F Wollsachen *pl*
word **1.** Wort *n*; Nachricht *f*; Losung *f*, Losungswort *n*; Versprechen *n*; Befehl *m*; *pl* MUS *etc* Text *m*; ***have a word*** *or* ***a few words with s.o.*** mit j-m sprechen; **2.** *et.* ausdrücken, *Text* abfassen, formulieren
word·ing Wortlaut *m*
word or·der LING Wortstellung *f*
word pro·cess·ing EDP Textverarbeitung *f*
word pro·ces·sor EDP Textverarbeitungsgerät *n*
word·y wortreich, langatmig
work **1.** Arbeit *f*; Werk *n*; *pl* TECH Werk *n*, Getriebe *n*; ECON Werk *n*, Fabrik *f*; ***at work*** bei der Arbeit; ***be in work*** Arbeit haben; ***be out of work*** arbeitslos sein; ***go*** *or* ***set to work*** an die Arbeit gehen; **2.** *v/i* arbeiten (***at, on*** an *dat*); TECH funktionieren (*a. fig*); wirken; ***work to rule*** Dienst nach Vorschrift tun; *v/t j-n* arbeiten lassen; *Maschine etc* bedienen, *et.* betätigen; *et.* bearbeiten; bewirken, herbeiführen; ***work one's way*** sich durcharbeiten *or* durchkämpfen; ***work off*** *Schulden* abarbeiten; *Wut etc* abreagieren; ***work out*** *v/t* ausrechnen; *Aufgabe* lösen; *Plan etc* ausarbeiten; *fig* sich *et.* zusammenreimen; *v/i* gut gehen, F klappen; aufgehen; F SPORT trainieren; ***work up*** *Zuhörer etc* aufpeitschen, aufwühlen; *et.* ausarbeiten (***into*** zu); ***be worked up*** aufgeregt *or* nervös sein (***about*** wegen)
work·a·ble formbar; *fig* durchführbar
work·a·day Alltags…
work·a·hol·ic F Arbeitssüchtige *m, f*
work·bench TECH Werkbank *f*
work·book PED Arbeitsheft *n*
work·day Arbeitstag *m*; Werktag *m*; ***on workdays*** werktags
work·er Arbeiter(in); Angestellte *m, f*
work ex·pe·ri·ence Erfahrung *f*
work·ing werktätig; Arbeits…; ***working knowledge*** Grundkenntnisse *pl*; ***in working order*** in betriebsfähigem Zustand
working class Arbeiterklasse *f*
working day → ***workday***
working hours Arbeitszeit *f*; ***fewer working hours*** Arbeitszeitverkürzung *f*; ***reduced working hours*** Kurzarbeit *f*
work·ings Arbeits-, Funktionsweise *f*
work·man Handwerker *m*
work·man·like fachmännisch
work·man·ship fachmännische Arbeit
work of art Kunstwerk *n*
work·out F SPORT Training *n*
work·place Arbeitsplatz *m*; ***at the workplace*** am Arbeitsplatz
works coun·cil Betriebsrat *m*
work·sheet PED *etc* Arbeitsblatt *n*
work·shop Werkstatt *f*; Workshop *m*
work·shy arbeitsscheu
work·sta·tion EDP Bildschirmarbeitsplatz *m*
work-to-rule *Br* Dienst *m* nach Vorschrift

world 1. Welt *f*; ***all over the world*** in der ganzen Welt; ***bring into the world*** auf die Welt bringen; ***do s.o. a*** *or* ***the world of good*** j-m unwahrscheinlich guttun; ***mean all the world to s.o.*** j-m alles bedeuten; ***they are worlds apart*** zwischen ihnen liegen Welten; ***think the world of*** große Stücke halten von; ***what in the world ...?*** was um alles in der Welt ...?; 2. Welt...
world cham·pi·on SPORT Weltmeister *m*
world cham·pi·onship SPORT Weltmeisterschaft *f*
World Cup Fußballweltmeisterschaft *f*; *skiing*: Weltcup *m*
world-fa·mous weltberühmt
world lit·er·a·ture Weltliteratur *f*
world·ly weltlich; irdisch
world·ly-wise weltklug
world mar·ket ECON Weltmarkt *m*
world pow·er POL Weltmacht *f*
world rec·ord SPORT Weltrekord *m*
world trip Weltreise *f*
world war Weltkrieg *m*
world·wide weltweit; auf der ganzen Welt
worm 1. zo Wurm *m*; 2. *Hund etc* entwurmen; ***worm one's way through*** sich schlängeln *or* zwängen durch; ***worm o.s. into s.o.'s confidence*** sich in j-s Vertrauen einschleichen; ***worm s.th. out of s.o.*** j-m et. entlocken
worm-eat·en wurmstichig
worm's-eye view Froschperspektive *f*
worn-out abgenutzt, abgetragen; *fig* erschöpft
wor·ried besorgt, beunruhigt
wor·ry 1. beunruhigen; (sich) Sorgen machen; ***don't worry!*** keine Angst!, keine Sorge!; 2. Sorge *f*
worse schlechter, schlimmer; ***worse still*** was noch schlimmer ist; ***to make matters worse*** zu allem Übel
wors·en schlechter machen *or* werden, (sich) verschlechtern
wor·ship 1. Verehrung *f*; Gottesdienst *m*; 2. *v/t* anbeten, verehren; *v/i* den Gottesdienst besuchen
wor·ship·(p)er Anbeter(in), Verehrer(in); Kirchgänger(in)
worst 1. *adj* schlechteste(r, -s), schlimmste(r, -s); 2. *adv* am schlechtesten, am schlimmsten; 3. *der, die, das* Schlechteste *or* Schlimmste; ***at (the) worst*** schlimmstenfalls
wor·sted Kammgarn *n*
worth 1. wert; ***worth reading*** lesenswert; 2. Wert *m*
worth·less wertlos
worth·while lohnend; ***be worthwhile*** sich lohnen
worth·y würdig
would-be Möchtegern...
wound 1. Wunde *f*, Verletzung *f*; 2. verwunden, verletzen
wow *int* F wow!, Mensch!, toll!
wran·gle 1. (sich) streiten; 2. Streit *m*
wrap 1. *v/t a.* ***wrap up*** (ein)packen, (ein)wickeln (***in*** in *dat*); *et.* wickeln (***[a]round*** um); *v/i*: ***wrap up*** sich warm anziehen; 2. Umhang *m*
wrap·per (Schutz)Umschlag *m*
wrap·ping Verpackung *f*
wrapping pa·per Einwickel-, Pack-, Geschenkpapier *n*
wrath Zorn *m*
wreath Kranz *m*
wreck 1. MAR Wrack *n* (*a. fig*); 2. *Pläne etc* zunichtemachen; ***be wrecked*** MAR zerschellen; Schiffbruch erleiden
wreck·age Trümmer *pl* (*a. fig*), Wrackteile *pl*
wreck·er MOT Abschleppwagen *m*
wreck·ing com·pa·ny Abbruchfirma *f*
wrecking ser·vice MOT Abschleppdienst *m*
wren zo Zaunkönig *m*
wrench 1. MED sich *das Knie etc* verrenken; ***wrench s.th. from*** *or* ***out of s.o.'s hands*** j-m et. aus den Händen winden, j-m et. entwinden; ***wrench off*** *et.* mit e-m Ruck abreißen *or* wegreißen; ***wrench open*** aufreißen; 2. Ruck *m*; MED Verrenkung *f*; *Br* TECH Schraubenschlüssel *m*
wrest: ***wrest s.th. from*** *or* ***out of s.o.'s hands*** j-m et. aus den Händen reißen, j-m et. entreißen *or* entwinden
wres·tle *v/i* SPORT ringen (***with*** mit), *fig a.* kämpfen (***with*** mit); *v/t* SPORT ringen gegen
wres·tler SPORT Ringer *m*
wres·tling SPORT Ringen *n*
wretch *often* HUMOR Schuft *m*, Wicht *m*; *a.* ***poor wretch*** armer Teufel
wretch·ed elend; (tod)unglücklich; scheußlich; verdammt, verflixt
wrig·gle *v/i* sich winden; zappeln; ***wriggle out of*** *fig* F sich herauswinden aus; F sich drücken vor (*dat*); *v/t* mit *den Zehen* wackeln
wring *j-m die Hand* drücken; *die Hände* ringen; *den Hals* umdrehen; ***wring out*** *Wäsche etc* auswringen; ***wring s.o.'s heart*** j-m zu Herzen gehen
wrin·kle 1. Falte *f*, Runzel *f*; 2. runzeln; *Nase* krausziehen, rümpfen; faltig *or* runz(e)lig werden
wrist ANAT Handgelenk *n*

wrist·band Bündchen *n*, (Hemd)Manschette *f*; Armband *n*
wrist·watch Armbanduhr *f*
writ JUR Befehl *m*, Verfügung *f*
write schreiben; ***write down*** auf-, niederschreiben; ***write off*** *j-n*, ECON *et.* abschreiben; ***write out*** *Namen etc* ausschreiben; *Bericht etc* ausarbeiten; *j-m e-e Quittung etc* ausstellen
write pro·tec·tion EDP Schreibschutz *m*
writ·er Schreiber(in), Verfasser(in), Autor(in); Schriftsteller(in)
writhe sich krümmen *or* winden (***in, with*** vor *dat*)
writ·ing **1.** Schreiben *n*; (Hand)Schrift *f*; Schriftstück *n*; *pl* Werke *pl*; ***in writing*** schriftlich; **2.** Schreib…
writing case Schreibmappe *f*
writing desk Schreibtisch *m*
writing pad Schreibblock *m*
writing pa·per Briefpapier *n*, Schreibpapier *n*
writ·ten schriftlich
wrong **1.** *adj* falsch; unrecht; ***be wrong*** falsch sein, nicht stimmen; unrecht haben; falsch gehen (*watch*); ***be on the wrong side of forty*** über 40 (Jahre alt) sein; ***is anything wrong?*** ist et. nicht in Ordnung?; ***what's wrong with her?*** was ist los mit ihr?, was hat sie?; **2.** *adv* falsch; ***get wrong*** *j-n, et.* falsch verstehen; ***go wrong*** e-n Fehler machen; kaputtgehen; *fig* F schiefgehen; **3.** Unrecht *n*; ***be in the wrong*** im Unrecht sein; **4.** *j-m* unrecht tun
wrong·ful ungerechtfertigt; gesetzwidrig
wrong-way driv·er MOT F Geisterfahrer(in)
wrought i·ron Schmiedeeisen *n*
wrought-i·ron schmiedeeisern
wry süßsauer (*smile*); ironisch, sarkastisch (*humor etc*)
wt ABBR *of* ***weight*** Gew., Gewicht *n*
WWF ABBR *of* ***World Wide Fund for Nature*** WWF *m*
WYSIWYG ABBR *of* ***what you see is what you get*** EDP was du (*auf dem Bildschirm*) siehst, bekommst du (*auch ausgedruckt*)

X, Y

X, x X, x *n*
xen·o·pho·bi·a Fremdenhass *m*; Ausländerfeindlichkeit *f*
XL ABBR *of* ***extra large*** (***size***) extragroß
X·mas F → ***Christmas***
X-ray MED **1.** röntgen; **2.** Röntgenstrahl *m*; Röntgenaufnahme *f*, -bild *n*; Röntgenuntersuchung *f*
xy·lo·phone MUS Xylophon *n*
Y, y Y, y *n*
yacht MAR **1.** (Segel)Boot *n*; Jacht *f*; **2.** segeln; ***go yachting*** segeln gehen
yacht club Segelklub *m*, Jachtklub *m*
yacht·ing Segeln *n*, Segelsport *m*
Yan·kee F Yankee *m*, Ami *m*
yap kläffen; F quasseln
yard[1] (ABBR ***yd***) Yard *n* (*91, 44 cm*)
yard[2] Hof *m*; (*Bau-, Stapel- etc*)Platz *m*; Garten *m*
yard·stick *fig* Maßstab *m*
yarn Garn *n*; ***spin s.o. a yarn about*** j-m e-e abenteuerliche Geschichte *or* e-e Lügengeschichte erzählen von
yawn **1.** gähnen; **2.** Gähnen *n*
yeah F ja
year Jahr *n*; ***all the year round*** das ganze Jahr hindurch; ***year after year*** Jahr für Jahr; ***year in year out*** jahraus, jahrein; ***this year*** dieses Jahr; ***this year's*** diesjährige(r, -s)
year·ly jährlich
yearn sich sehnen (***for*** nach; ***to do*** danach, zu tun)
yearn·ing **1.** Sehnsucht *f*; **2.** sehnsüchtig
yeast Hefe *f*
yell **1.** schreien, brüllen (***with*** vor *dat*); ***yell at s.o.*** j-n anschreien *or* anbrüllen; ***yell*** (***out***) *et.* schreien, brüllen; **2.** Schrei *m*
yel·low **1.** gelb; F feig(e); **2.** Gelb *n*; ***at yellow*** MOT bei Gelb; **3.** (sich) gelb färben; gelb werden; vergilben
yel·low fe·ver MED Gelbfieber *n*
yel·low·ish gelblich
Yel·low Pag·es® TEL *die* Gelben Seiten *pl*, Branchenverzeichnis *n*
yel·low press Sensationspresse *f*
yelp **1.** (auf)jaulen; aufschreien; **2.** (Auf)Jaulen *n*; Aufschrei *m*
yes **1.** ja; doch; **2.** Ja *n*
yes·ter·day gestern; ***yesterday morning***

(***afternoon***) gestern Morgen (Nachmittag); ***the day before yesterday*** vorgestern
yet 1. *adv in questions*: schon; noch; (doch) noch; doch, aber; ***as yet*** bis jetzt, bisher; ***not yet*** noch nicht; **2.** *cj* aber, doch
yew BOT Eibe *f*
yield 1. *v/t Früchte* tragen; *Gewinn* abwerfen; *Resultat etc* ergeben, liefern; *v/i* nachgeben; ***yield to*** MOT *j-m* die Vorfahrt lassen; **2.** Ertrag *m*
yip·pee *int* F hurra!
yo·del 1. jodeln; **2.** Jodler *m*
yo·ga Joga *m, n*, Yoga *m, n*
yog·h(o)urt, yog·urt Jog(h)urt *m, n*
yoke Joch *n* (*a. fig*)
yolk (Ei)Dotter *m, n*, Eigelb *n*
you du, ihr, Sie; (*dat*) dir, euch, Ihnen; (*acc*) dich, euch, Sie; man
young 1. jung; **2.** zo Junge *pl*; ***with young*** zo trächtig; ***the young*** die jungen Leute *pl*, die Jugend
young·ster Junge *m*
your dein(e); *pl* euer, eure; Ihr(e) (*a. pl*)
yours deine(r, -s); *pl* euer eure(s); Ihre(r, -s) (*a. pl*); ***a friend of yours*** ein Freund von dir; ***Yours, Bill*** Dein Bill
your·self selbst; dir, dich, sich; ***by yourself*** allein
youth Jugend *f*; Jugendliche *m*
youth club Jugendklub *m*
youth·ful jugendlich
youth hos·tel Jugendherberge *f*
yuck·y F *contp* scheußlich
Yu·go·slav 1. jugoslawisch; **2.** Jugoslawe *m*, Jugoslawin *f*
Yu·go·sla·vi·a Jugoslawien *n*
yup·pie, yup·py ABBR *of* ***young upwardly-mobile*** *or* ***urban professional*** junger, aufstrebender *or* städtischer Karrieremensch, Yuppie *m*

Z

Z, z Z, z *n*
zap F *esp computer game etc*: abknallen, fertigmachen; MOT beschleunigen (***from … to …*** von … auf *acc* …); jagen, hetzen; TV *Fernbedienung* bedienen; TV zappen, umschalten; ***zap off*** abzischen; ***zap to*** düsen *or* jagen *or* hetzen nach
zap·per TV F Fernbedienung *f*
zap·py *Br* F voller Pep, schmissig, fetzig
zeal Eifer *m*
zeal·ot Fanatiker(in), Eiferer *m*, Eiferin *f*
zeal·ous eifrig; ***be zealous to do s.th.*** eifrig darum bemüht sein, et. zu tun
ze·bra zo Zebra *n*
ze·bra cross·ing *Br* Zebrastreifen *m*
zen·ith Zenit *m* (*a. fig*)
ze·ro 1. Null *f*; Nullpunkt *m*; ***20 degrees below zero*** 20 Grad unter Null; **2.** Null…
zero growth Nullwachstum *n*
zero in·terest: ***have zero interest in s.th.*** F null Bock auf et. haben
zero op·tion POL Nulllösung *f*
zest *fig* Würze *f*; Begeisterung *f*; ***zest for life*** Lebensfreude *f*
zig·zag 1. Zickzack *m*; **2.** Zickzack…; **3.** im Zickzack fahren, laufen *etc*, zickzackförmig verlaufen
zinc CHEM Zink *n*
zip[1] **1.** Reißverschluss *m*; **2.** ***zip the bag open*** (***shut***) den Reißverschluss der Tasche aufmachen (zumachen); ***zip s.o. up*** j-m den Reißverschluss zumachen
zip[2] **1.** Zischen *n*, Schwirren *n*; F Schwung *m*; **2.** zischen, schwirren; ***zip by, zip past*** vorbeiflitzen
zip code Postleitzahl *f*
zip fas·ten·er *esp Br* → ***zipper***
zip·per Reißverschluss *m*
zo·di·ac ASTR Tierkreis *m*; ***signs of the zodiac*** Tierkreiszeichen *pl*
zone Zone *f*
zoo Zoo *m*, Tierpark *m*
zo·o·log·i·cal zoologisch
zoological gar·dens Tierpark *m*, zoologischer Garten
zo·ol·o·gist Zoologe *m*, Zoologin *f*
zo·ol·o·gy Zoologie *f*
zoom 1. surren; F sausen; F *fig* in die Höhe schnellen; PHOT zoomen; ***zoom by, zoom past*** F vorbeisausen; ***zoom in on*** PHOT *et.* heranholen; **2.** Surren *n*; *a.* ***zoom lens*** PHOT Zoom *n*, Zoomobjektiv *n*

States of the Federal Republic of Germany

Baden-Württemberg ['ba:dən'vʏrtəmbɛrk] Baden-Württemberg
Bayern ['baɪɐn] Bavaria
Berlin [bɛr'li:n] Berlin
Brandenburg ['brandənbʊrk] Brandenburg
Bremen ['bre:mən] Bremen
Hamburg ['hambʊrk] Hamburg
Hessen ['hɛsən] Hesse
Mecklenburg-Vorpommern ['me:klənbʊrk'fo:ɐpɔmɐn] Mecklenburg-Western Pomerania
Niedersachsen ['ni:dɐzaksən] Lower Saxony
Nordrhein-Westfalen ['nɔrtraɪnvɛst'fa:lən] North Rhine-Westphalia
Rheinland-Pfalz ['raɪnlant'pfalts] Rhineland-Palatinate
Saarland ['za:ɐlant]: ***das Saarland*** the Saarland
Sachsen ['zaksən] Saxony
Sachsen-Anhalt ['zaksən'anhalt] Saxony-Anhalt
Schleswig-Holstein ['ʃle:svɪç'hɔlʃtaɪn] Schleswig-Holstein
Thüringen ['ty:rɪŋən] Thuringia

States of the Republic of Austria

Burgenland ['bʊrgənlant]: ***das Burgenland*** the Burgenland
Kärnten ['kɛrntən] Carinthia
Niederösterreich ['ni:dɐˀø:stəraɪç] Lower Austria
Oberösterreich ['o:bɐˀø:stəraɪç] Upper Austria
Salzburg ['zaltsbʊrk] Salzburg
Steiermark ['ʃtaɪɐmark]: ***die Steiermark*** Styria
Tirol [ti'ro:l] Tyrol
Vorarlberg ['fo:ɐˀarlbɛrk] Vorarlberg
Wien [vi:n] Vienna

Cantons of the Swiss Confederation

Aargau ['a:ɐgaʊ]: ***der Aargau*** the Aargau
Appenzell [apən'tsɛl] Appenzell
Basel ['ba:zəl] Basel, Basle
Bern [bɛrn] Bern(e)
Freiburg ['fraɪbʊrk], *French* **Fribourg** [fri'bu:r] Fribourg
Genf [gɛnf], *French* **Genève** [ʒə'nɛ:v] Geneva
Glarus ['gla:rʊs] Glarus
Graubünden [graʊ'bʏndən] Graubünden, Grisons
Jura ['ju:ra]: ***der Jura*** the Jura
Luzern [lu'tsɛrn] Lucerne
Neuenburg ['nɔʏənbʊrk], *French* **Neuchâtel** [nøʃa'tɛl] Neuchâtel
St. Gallen [zaŋkt 'galən] St Gallen, St Gall
Schaffhausen [ʃaf'haʊzən] Schaffhausen
Schwyz [ʃvi:ts] Schwyz
Solothurn ['zo:lotʊrn] Solothurn
Tessin [tɛ'si:n]: ***der Tessin*** the Ticino, *Italian* **Ticino** [ti'tʃi:no]: ***das Tessin*** the Ticino
Thurgau ['tu:ɐgaʊ]: ***der Thurgau*** the Thurgau
Unterwalden ['ʊntɐvaldən] Unterwalden
Uri ['u:ri] Uri
Waadt [va(:)t], *French* **Vaud** [vo] Vaud
Wallis ['valɪs], *French* **Valais** [va'lɛ]: ***das Valais*** the Valais, Wallis
Zug [tsu:k] Zug
Zürich ['tsy:rɪç] Zurich

Alphabetical List of the German Irregular Verbs

Infinitive – Present Tense – Past Tense – Past Participle

backen – backt/bäckt – backte – gebacken
bedingen – bedingt – bedang (bedingte) – bedungen (*conditional*: bedingt)
befehlen – befiehlt – befahl – befohlen
beginnen – beginnt – begann – begonnen
beißen – beißt – biss – gebissen
bergen – birgt – barg – geborgen
bersten – birst – barst – geborsten
bewegen – bewegt – bewog – bewogen
biegen – biegt – bog – gebogen
bieten – bietet – bot – geboten
binden – bindet – band – gebunden
bitten – bittet – bat – gebeten
blasen – bläst – blies – geblasen
bleiben – bleibt – blieb – geblieben
bleichen – bleicht – blich – geblichen
braten – brät – briet – gebraten
brauchen – braucht – brauchte – gebraucht (*v/aux* brauchen)
brechen – bricht – brach – gebrochen
brennen – brennt – brannte – gebrannt
bringen – bringt – brachte – gebracht
denken – denkt – dachte – gedacht
dreschen – drischt – drosch – gedroschen
dringen – dringt – drang – gedrungen
dürfen – darf – durfte – gedurft (*v/aux* dürfen)
empfehlen – empfiehlt – empfahl – empfohlen
erlöschen – erlischt – erlosch – erloschen
erschrecken – erschrickt/erschreckt – erschrak – erschrocken
essen – isst – aß – gegessen
fahren – fährt – fuhr – gefahren
fallen – fällt – fiel – gefallen
fangen – fängt – fing – gefangen
fechten – ficht – focht – gefochten
finden – findet – fand – gefunden
flechten – flicht – flocht – geflochten
fliegen – fliegt – flog – geflogen
fliehen – flieht – floh – geflohen
fließen – fließt – floss – geflossen
fressen – frisst – fraß – gefressen
frieren – friert – fror – gefroren
gären – gärt – gor (*esp fig* gärte) – gegoren (*esp fig* gegärt)
gebären – gebärt/gebiert – gebar – geboren
geben – gibt – gab – gegeben
gedeihen – gedeiht – gedieh – gediehen
gehen – geht – ging – gegangen
gelingen – gelingt – gelang – gelungen
gelten – gilt – galt – gegolten
genesen – genest – genas – genesen
genießen – genießt – genoss – genossen
geschehen – geschieht – geschah – geschehen
gewinnen – gewinnt – gewann – gewonnen
gießen – gießt – goss – gegossen
gleichen – gleicht – glich – geglichen
gleiten – gleitet – glitt – geglitten
glimmen – glimmt – glomm – geglommen
graben – gräbt – grub – gegraben
greifen – greift – griff – gegriffen
haben – hat – hatte – gehabt
halten – hält – hielt – gehalten
hängen – hängt – hing – gehangen
hauen – haut – haute (hieb) – gehauen
heben – hebt – hob – gehoben
heißen – heißt – hieß – geheißen
helfen – hilft – half – geholfen
kennen – kennt – kannte – gekannt
klingen – klingt – klang – geklungen
kneifen – kneift – kniff – gekniffen
kommen – kommt – kam – gekommen
können – kann – konnte – gekonnt (*v/aux* können)
kriechen – kriecht – kroch – gekrochen
laden – lädt – lud – geladen
lassen – lässt – ließ – gelassen (*v/aux* lassen)
laufen – läuft – lief – gelaufen
leiden – leidet – litt – gelitten
leihen – leiht – lieh – geliehen
lesen – liest – las – gelesen
liegen – liegt – lag – gelegen
lügen – lügt – log – gelogen
mahlen – mahlt – mahlte – gemahlen
meiden – meidet – mied – gemieden
melken – melkt – melkte (molk) – gemolken (gemelkt)
messen – misst – maß – gemessen
misslingen – misslingt – misslang – misslungen
mögen – mag – mochte – gemocht (*v/aux* mögen)
müssen – muss – musste – gemusst (*v/aux* müssen)
nehmen – nimmt – nahm – genommen
nennen – nennt – nannte – genannt
pfeifen – pfeift – pfiff – gepfiffen
preisen – preist – pries – gepriesen
quellen – quillt – quoll – gequollen
raten – rät – riet – geraten
reiben – reibt – rieb – gerieben
reißen – reißt – riss – gerissen
reiten – reitet – ritt – geritten

rennen - rennt - rannte - gerannt
riechen - riecht - roch - gerochen
ringen - ringt - rang - gerungen
rinnen - rinnt - rann - geronnen
rufen - ruft - rief - gerufen
salzen - salzt - salzte - gesalzen (gesalzt)
saufen - säuft - soff - gesoffen
saugen - saugt - sog - gesogen
schaffen - schafft - schuf - geschaffen
schallen - schallt - schallte (scholl) - geschallt (*for* ***erschallen*** *a.* erschollen)
scheiden - scheidet - schied - geschieden
scheinen - scheint - schien - geschienen
scheißen - scheißt - schiss - geschissen
scheren - schert - schor - geschoren
schieben - schiebt - schob - geschoben
schießen - schießt - schoss - geschossen
schinden - schindet - schund - geschunden
schlafen - schläft - schlief - geschlafen
schlagen - schlägt - schlug - geschlagen
schleichen - schleicht - schlich - geschlichen
schleifen - schleift - schliff - geschliffen
schließen - schließt - schloss - geschlossen
schlingen - schlingt - schlang - geschlungen
schmeißen - schmeißt - schmiss - geschmissen
schmelzen - schmilzt - schmolz - geschmolzen
schneiden - schneidet - schnitt - geschnitten
schrecken - schrickt/schreckt - schrak - *rare* geschrocken
schreiben - schreibt - schrieb - geschrieben
schreien - schreit - schrie - geschrie(e)n
schreiten - schreitet - schritt - geschritten
schweigen - schweigt - schwieg - geschwiegen
schwellen - schwillt - schwoll - geschwollen
schwimmen - schwimmt - schwamm - geschwommen
schwinden - schwindet - schwand - geschwunden
schwingen - schwingt - schwang - geschwungen
schwören - schwört - schwor - geschworen
sehen - sieht - sah - gesehen
sein - ist - war - gewesen
senden - sendet - sandte - gesandt
sieden - siedet - sott - gesotten
singen - singt - sang - gesungen
sinken - sinkt - sank - gesunken
sinnen - sinnt - sann - gesonnen
sitzen - sitzt - saß - gesessen
sollen - soll - sollte - gesollt (*v/aux* sollen)
spalten - spaltet - spaltete - gespalten (gespaltet)
speien - speit - spie - gespie(e)n
spinnen - spinnt - spann - gesponnen
sprechen - spricht - sprach - gesprochen
sprießen - sprießt - spross - gesprossen
springen - springt - sprang - gesprungen
stechen - sticht - stach - gestochen
stecken - steckt - steckte (stak) - gesteckt
stehen - steht - stand - gestanden
stehlen - stiehlt - stahl - gestohlen
steigen - steigt - stieg - gestiegen
sterben - stirbt - starb - gestorben
stinken - stinkt - stank - gestunken
stoßen - stößt - stieß - gestoßen
streichen - streicht - strich - gestrichen
streiten - streitet - stritt - gestritten
tragen - trägt - trug - getragen
treffen - trifft - traf - getroffen
treiben - treibt - trieb - getrieben
treten - tritt - trat - getreten
trinken - trinkt - trank - getrunken
trügen - trügt - trog - getrogen
tun - tut - tat - getan
verderben - verdirbt - verdarb - verdorben
verdrießen - verdrießt - verdross - verdrossen
vergessen - vergisst - vergaß - vergessen
verlieren - verliert - verlor - verloren
verschleißen - verschleißt - verschliss - verschlissen
verzeihen - verzeiht - verzieh - verziehen
wachsen - wächst - wuchs - gewachsen
wägen - wägt - wog (*rare* wägte) - gewogen (*rare* gewägt)
waschen - wäscht - wusch - gewaschen
weben - webt - wob - gewoben
weichen - weicht - wich - gewichen
weisen - weist - wies - gewiesen
wenden - wendet - wandte - gewandt
werben - wirbt - warb - geworben
werden - wird - wurde - geworden (worden*)
werfen - wirft - warf - geworfen
wiegen - wiegt - wog - gewogen
winden - windet - wand - gewunden
wissen - weiß - wusste - gewusst
wollen - will - wollte - gewollt (*v/aux* wollen)
wringen - wringt - wrang - gewrungen
ziehen - zieht - zog - gezogen
zwingen - zwingt - zwang - gezwungen

* only in connection with the past participles of other verbs, *e.g.* ***er ist gesehen worden*** he has been seen.

Examples of German Declension and Conjugation

A. Declension

Order of cases: *nom*, *gen*, *dat*, *acc*, *sg* and *pl*. - Compound nouns and adjectives (e.g. *Eisbär*, *Ausgang*, *abfällig* etc.) inflect like their last elements (*Bär*, *Gang*, *fällig*). *dem* = demonstrative, *imp* = imperative, *ind* = indicative, *perf* = perfect, *pres* = present, *pres p* = present participle, *rel* = relative, *su* = substantive;
the swung dash or tilde(~) represents the preceding word.

I. Nouns

1 Bild ~(e)s[1] ~(e) ~
Bilder[2] ~ ~n ~

[1] ***es only***: Geist, Geistes.
[2] **a, o, u 〉 ä, ö, ü:** Rand, Ränder; Haupt, Häupter; Dorf, Dörfer; Wurm, Würmer.

---

2 Reis* ~es ['-zəs] ~(e) ~
Reiser[1] ['-zɐ] ~ ~n ~

[1] **a, o 〉 ä, ö:** Glas, Gläser ['glɛːzɐ]; Haus, Häuser ['hɔʏzɐ]; Fass, Fässer; Schloss, Schlösser.
* Fass, Fasse(s).

---

3 Arm ~(e)s[1, 2] ~(e)[1] ~
Arme[3] ~ ~n ~

[1] ***without* e:** Billard, Billard(s).
[2] ***es only***: Maß, Maßes.
[3] **a, o, u 〉 ä, ö, ü:** Gang, Gänge; Saal, Säle; Gebrauch, Gebräuche [gə'brɔʏçə]; Sohn, Söhne; Hut, Hüte.

---

4 Greis[1]* ~es ['-zəs] ~(e) ~
Greise[2] ['-zə] ~ ~n ~

[1] **s 〉 ss:** Kürbis, Kürbisse(s).
[2] **a, o, u 〉 ä, ö, ü:** Hals, Hälse; Bass, Bässe; Schoß, Schöße; Fuchs, Füchse; Schuss, Schüsse.
* Ross, Rosse(s).

---

5 Strahl ~(e)s[1, 2] ~(e)[2] ~
Strahlen[3] ~ ~ ~

[1] ***es only***: Schmerz, Schmerzes.
[2] ***without* e:** Juwel, Juwel(s).
[3] Sporn, Sporen.

---

6 Lappen ~s ~ ~*
Lappen[1] ~ ~ ~

[1] **a, o 〉 ä, ö:** Graben, Gräben; Boden, Böden.

* ***Infinitives used as nouns have no*** *pl* : Geschehen, Befinden etc.

---

7 Maler ~s ~ ~
Maler[1] ~ ~n ~

[1] **a, o, u 〉 ä, ö, ü:** Vater, Väter; Kloster, Klöster; Bruder, Brüder.

---

8 Untertan ~s ~ ~
Untertanen[1, 2] ~ ~ ~

[1] ***with change of accent***: Pro'fessor, Profes'soren [-'soːrən]; 'Dämon ['dɛːmɔn], Dä'monen [dɛ'moːnən].
[2] *pl* **ien** [-jən]: Kolleg, Kollegien [-'leːgjən]; Mineral, Mineralien.

---

9 Studium ~s ~ ~
Studien[1, 2] ['-djən] ~ ~ ~

[1] **a *and* o(n) 〉 en:** Drama, Dramen; Stadion, Stadien.
[2] **on *and* um 〉 a:** Lexikon, Lexika; Neutrum, Neutra.

---

10 Auge ~s ~ ~
Augen ~ ~ ~

---

11 Genie ~s[1]* ~ ~
Genies[2]* ~ ~ ~

[1] ***without inflection***: Bouillon etc.
[2] *pl* **s *or* ta:** Komma, Kommas ***or*** Kommata; ***but***: 'Klima, Klimate [kli'maːtə] (3).
* ***s is pronounced***: [ʒe'niːs].

---

12 Bär* ~en[1] ~en[1] ~en[1]
Bären ~ ~ ~

[1] Herr, *sg mst* Herrn; Herz, *gen* Herzens, *acc* Herz.

* **...'log *as well as* ... 'loge** (13), e.g. Biolog(e).

13 Knabe ~n[1] ~n ~n
Knaben ~ ~ ~

[1] **ns:** Name, Namens.

14 Trübsal ~ ~ ~
Trübsale[1, 2, 3] ~ ~n ~

[1] **a, o, u 〉 ä, ö, ü:** Hand, Hände; Braut, Bräute; Not, Nöte; Luft, Lüfte; Nuss, Nüsse; **without e:** Tochter, Töchter; Mutter, Mütter.

[2] **s 〉 ss:** Kenntnis, Kenntnisse; Nimbus, Nimbusse.

[3] **is *or* us 〉 e:** Kultus, Kulte; ***with change of accent*:** Di'akonus, Dia'kone [-'koːnə].

15 Blume ~ ~ ~
Blumen ~ ~ ~

...ee: eː, *pl* eːən, *e.g.* I'dee, I'deen.

...ie { ***stressed syllable*:** iː, *pl* iːən, *e.g.* Batte'rie(n). ***unstressed syllable*:** jə, *pl* jən, *e.g.* Ar'terie(n).

16 Frau ~ ~ ~
Frauen[1, 2, 3] ~ ~ ~

[1] **in 〉 innen:** Freundin, Freundinnen.

[2] **a, is, os *and* us 〉 en:** Firma, Firmen; Krisis, Krisen; Epos, Epen; Genius, Genien; ***with change of accent*:** 'Heros, He'roen [he'roːən]; Di'akonus, Dia'konen [-'koːnən].

[3] **s 〉 ss:** Kirmes, Kirmessen.

II. Proper nouns

17 ***In general proper nouns have no*** *pl.*

The following form the *gen sg* ***with*** **s:**

1. ***Proper nouns without a definite article*:** Friedrichs, Paulas, (Friedrich von) Schillers, Deutschlands, Berlins;
2. ***Proper nouns, masculine and neuter*** (***except the names of countries***) ***with a definite article and an adjective*:** des braven Friedrichs Bruder, des jungen Deutschlands (Söhne).

After* s, sch, ß, tz, x, *and* z *the *gen sg* ***ends in* -ens** *or* '(***instead of ' it is more advisable to use the definite article or* von**), e.g. die Werke des [*or* von] Sokrates, Voß *or* Sokrates', Voß' [***not*** Sokratessens, ***seldom*** Vossens] Werke; ***but*:** die Umgebung von Mainz.

Feminine names ending in a consonant or the vowel* e *form the *gen sg* ***with*** **(en)s *or* (n)s; *in the*** *dat* ***and*** *acc sg* ***such names may end in* (e)n** (*pl* = **a**).

***If a proper noun is followed by a title, only the following forms are inflected*:**

1. ***the title when used*** with ***a definite article*:**
   der Kaiser Karl (der Große)
   des ~s ~ (des ~n)
   etc.
2. ***the*** (***last***) ***name when used*** with-out ***an article*:**
   Kaiser Karl (der Große)
   ~ ~s (des ~n) etc.
   (***but*:** Herrn Lehmanns Brief).

III. Adjectives and participles (also used as nouns*), pronouns, etc.

18

	m	*f*	*n*	*pl*	
a) gut	er[1, 2]	~e	~es	~e°	***without article, after prepositions, personal pronouns, and invariables***
	en**	~er	~en**	~er	
	em	~er	~em	~en	
	en	~e	~es	~e	

b) gut	e[1, 2]	~e	~e	~en	***with definite article*** (22) ***or with pronoun*** (21)
	en	~en	~en	~en	
	en	~en	~en	~en	
	en	~e	~e	~en	
c) gut	er[1, 2]	~e	~es	~en	***with indefinite article or with pronoun*** (20)
	en	~en	~en	~en	
	en	~en	~en	~en	
	en	~e	~es	~en	

[1] krass, krasse(r, ~s, ~st etc.).
[2] **a, o, u > ä, ö, ü *when forming the*** *comp* ***and*** *sup*: alt, älter(e, ~es etc.), ältest (der ~e, am ~en); grob, gröber(e, ~es etc.), gröbst (der ~e, am ~en); kurz, kürzer(e, ~es etc.), kürzest (der ~e, am ~en).

* e.g. Böse(r) *su*: der (die, eine) Böse, ein Böser; Böse(s) *n*: das Böse, ***without article*** Böses; ***in the same way*** Abgesandte(r) *su*, Angestellte(r) *su* etc.; ***in some cases the use varies.***

** ***Sometimes the*** *gen sg* ***ends in*** ~es ***instead of*** ~**en**: gutes (***or*** guten) Mutes sein.

° ***In*** böse, böse(r, ~s, ~st etc.) ***one e is dropped.***

The Grades of Comparison

The endings of the *comparative* ***and*** *superlative* ***are***:

	reich	schön	
comp	reicher	schöner	***inflected according to*** (18²).
sup	reichst	schönst	

After vowels (***except* e** [18°]) ***and after*** d, s, sch, ß, st, t, tz, x, y, z ***the*** *sup* ***ends in*** ~**est*, but in unstressed syllables after* d, sch *and* t *generally in*** ~**st**: blau, 'blau**est**; rund, 'rund**est**; rasch, 'rasch**est** etc.; ***but***: 'dringend, 'dringend**st**; 'närrisch, 'närrisch**st**; ge'eignet, ge'eignet**st**.

Note.– ***The adjectives ending in*** ~**el**, ~**en** (***except*** ~nen) ***and*** ~**er** (e.g. dunk**el**, eb**en**, heit**er**), ***and also the possessive adjectives*** unser ***and*** euer ***generally drop* e.**

Inflection:	~**e**	~**em**	~**en**	~**er**	~**es, and**
~**el** >	~le	~lem*	~len*	~ler	~les
~**en** >	~(e)ne	~(e)nem	~(e)nen	~(e)ner°	~(e)nes
~**er** >	~(e)re	~rem*	~ren*	~(e)rer°	~(e)res

* ***or*** ~elm, ~eln, ~erm, ~ern; e.g. **dunk|el:** ~le, ~lem (***or*** ~elm), ~len (***or*** ~eln), ~ler, ~les; **eb|en:** ~(e)ne, ~(e)nem etc.; **heit|er:** ~(e)re, ~rem (***or*** ~erm) etc.

° ***The inflected*** *comp* ***ends in*** ~ner ***and*** ~rer ***only***: eben, ebnere(r, ~s etc.); heiter, heitrere(r, ~s etc.); ***but*** *sup* ebenst, heiterst.

19

	1st pers. *m, f, n*	***2nd pers.*** *m, f, n*	***3rd pers.*** *m*	*f*	*n*
sg	ich	du	er	sie	es
	meiner*	deiner*	seiner*	ihrer	seiner*
	mir	dir	ihm	ihr	ihm°
	mich	dich	ihn	sie	es°
pl	wir	ihr		sie	(Sie)
	unser	euer		ihrer	(Ihrer)
	uns	euch		ihnen	(Ihnen)°
	uns	euch		sie	(Sie)°

* ***In poetry sometimes without inflection***: gedenke mein!; ***also*** es ***instead of*** seiner *n* (= *e-r Sache*): ich bin es überdrüssig.
° ***Reflexive form***: sich.

20

	m	*f*	*n*	*pl*
mein		~e	~	~e*
dein	es	~er	~es	~er
sein	em	~er	~em	~en
(k)ein	en	~e	~	~e

* ***The indefinite article*** ein ***has no*** *pl*. – ***In poetry*** mein, dein ***and*** sein ***may stand behind the*** *su* ***without inflection***: die Mutter (Kinder) mein, ***or as predicate***: *der Hut [die Tasche, das Buch] ist* mein; ***without*** *su*: meiner *m*, meine *f*, mein(e)s *n*, meine *pl* etc.: *wem gehört der Hut [die Tasche, das Buch]? es ist* meiner (meine, mein[e]s); ***or with definite article***: der (die, das) meine, *pl* die meinen (18b). ***Regarding*** unser ***and*** euer ***see note*** (18).

[1] **welche(r, s)** ***as*** *rel pron*: *gen sg* dessen, deren, *gen pl* deren, *dat pl* denen (23).

* ***Used as*** *su*, dies ***is preferable to*** dieses.

** manch, solch, welch ***frequently are uninflected***:

manch	gut**er**	(ein gut**er**)		Mann
solch	~**en**	(~**es**	~**en**)	~**es**
welch	~**em**	(~**em**	~**en**)	~**e**
		etc. (18)		

Similarly all:

all der (dies**er**, mein) Schmerz
~ des (~**es**, ~**es**) ~**es**

21

	m	*f*	*n*	*pl*
dies	er	~e	~es*	~e**
jen	es	~er	~es	~er[1]
manch	em	~er	~em	~en[1]
welch	en	~e	~es*	~e

[1] derjenige, derselbe – desjenigen, demjenigen, desselben, demselben etc. (18b).

22

m	*f*	*n*	*pl*	
der	die	das	die[1]	***definite article***
des	der	des	der	
dem	der	dem	den	
den	die	das	die	

[1] ***also*** derer, ***when used as*** *dem pron*
* ***also*** des.

23 Relative pronoun

m	*f*	*n*	*pl*
der	die	das	die
dessen*	deren	dessen*	deren[1]
dem	der	dem	denen
den	die	das	die

24

wer	was	jemand, niemand
wessen*	wessen	~(e)s
wem	–	~(em°)
wen	was	~(en°)

* ***also*** wes.
° ***preferably without inflection.***

B. Conjugation

In the conjugation tables (25–30) only the simple verbs may be found; in the alphabetical list of the German irregular verbs compound verbs are only included when no simple verb exists (e.g. **beginnen;** *ginnen* does not exist). In order to find the conjugation of any compound verb (with separable or inseparable prefix, regular or irregular) look up the respective simple verb.

Verbs with separable and stressed prefixes such as **'ab-, 'an-, 'auf-, 'aus-, 'bei-, be'vor-, 'dar-, 'ein-, em'por-, ent'gegen-, 'fort-, 'her-, he'rab-** etc. and also *'klar-[legen], 'los-[schießen], 'sitzen [bleiben], über'hand [nehmen]* etc. (but not the verbs derived from compound nouns as *be'antragen* or *be'ratschlagen* from *Antrag* and *Ratschlag* etc.) take the preposition **zu** (in the *inf* and the *pres p*) and the syllable **ge** (in the *pp* and in the passive voice) between the stressed prefix and their root.

Verbs with inseparable and unstressed prefixes such as **be-**, **emp-**, **ent-**, **er-**, **ge-**, **ver-**, **zer-** and generally **miss-** (in spite of its being stressed) take the preposition **zu** before the prefix and drop the syllable **ge** in the *pp* and in the passive voice. The prefixes **durch-**, **hinter-**, **über-**, **um-**, **unter-**, **voll-**, **wi(e)der-** are separable when stressed and inseparable when unstressed, e.g.

geben: *zu geben*, *zu gebend*; *gegeben*; *ich gebe*, *du gibst* etc.;

'abgeben: *'abzugeben*, *'abzugebend*; *'abgegeben*; *ich gebe* (*du gibst* etc.) *ab*;

ver'geben: *zu ver'geben*, *zu ver'gebend*; *ver'geben*; *ich ver'gebe*, *du ver'gibst* etc.;

'umgehen: *'umzugehen*, *'umzugehend*; *'umgegangen*; *ich gehe* (*du gehst* etc.) *um*;

um'gehen: *zu um'gehen*, *zu um'gehend*; *um'gangen*; *ich um'gehe*, *du um'gehst* etc.

The same rules apply to verbs with two prefixes, e.g.

zu'rückbehalten [see *halten*]: *zu'rückzubehalten*, *zu'rückzubehaltend*; *zu-'rückbehalten*; *ich behalte* (*du behältst* etc.) *zurück*;

wieder 'aufheben [see *heben*]: *wieder 'aufzuheben*, *wieder 'aufzuhebend*; *wieder 'aufgehoben*; *ich hebe* (*du hebst* etc.) *wieder auf*.

The forms in parentheses ( ) follow the same rules.

a) 'Weak' Conjugation

25 loben

pres ind	lobe	lobst	lobt
	loben	lobt	loben
pres subj	lobe	lobest	lobe
	loben	lobet	loben
pret ind and *subj*	lobte	lobtest	lobte
	lobten	lobtet	lobten

imp sg lob(e), *pl* lob(e)t, loben Sie; *inf pres* loben; *inf perf* gelobt haben; *pres p* lobend; *pp* gelobt (18; 29**).

26 reden

pres ind	rede	redest	redet
	reden	redet	reden
pres subj	rede	redest	rede
	reden	redet	reden
pret ind and *subj*	redete	redetest	redete
	redeten	redetet	redeten

imp sg rede, *pl* redet, reden Sie; *inf pres* reden; *inf perf* geredet haben; *pres p* redend; *pp* geredet (18; 29**).

27 reisen

pres ind	reise	rei(se)st*	reist
	reisen	reist	reisen
pres subj	reise	reisest	reise
	reisen	reiset	reisen
pret ind and *subj*	reiste	reistest	reisten
	reisten	reistet	reisten

imp sg reise, *pl* reist, reisen Sie; *inf pres* reisen; *inf perf* gereist sein *or now rare* haben; *pres p* reisend; *pp* gereist (18; 29**).

* **sch:** naschen, nasch(e)st; **ß:** spa-ßen, spaßt (spaßest); **tz:** ritzen, ritzt (ritzest); **x:** hexen, hext (hexest); **z:** reizen, reizt (reizest); faulenzen, faulenzt (faulenzest).

28 fassen

pres ind	fasse	fasst	(fassest)fasst
	fassen	fasst	fassen
pres subj	fasse	fassest	fasse
	fassen	fasset	fassen
pret ind and *subj*	fasste	fasstest	fasste
	fassten	fasstet	fassten

imp sg fasse (fass), *pl* fasst, fassen Sie; *inf pres* fassen; *inf perf* gefasst haben; *pres p* fassend; *pp* gefasst (18; 29**).

29 handeln

pres ind

handle*	handelst	handelt
handeln	handelt	handeln

pres subj

handle*	handelst	handle*
handeln	handelt	handeln

pret ind and *subj*

handelte	handeltest	handelte
handelten	handeltet	handelten

imp sg handle, *pl* handelt, handeln Sie; *inf pres* handeln; *inf perf* gehandelt haben; *pres p* handelnd; *pp* gehandet (18).

* ***Also*** handele; wandern, wand(e)re; bessern, bessere (bessre); donnern, donnere.

** ***Without* ge*, when the first syllable is unstressed,*** e.g. be'grüßen, be'grüßt; ent'stehen, ent'standen; stu'dieren, studiert (***not*** gestudiert); trom'peten, trom'petet (***also when preceded by a stressed prefix***: 'austrompeten, 'austrompetet, ***not*** 'ausgetrompetet). ***In some weak verbs the*** *pp* ***ends in*** en ***instead of*** t, e.g. mahlen, gemahlen. ***With the verbs*** brauchen, dürfen, heißen, helfen, hören, können, lassen, lehren, lernen, machen, mögen, müssen, sehen, sollen, wollen ***the*** *pp* ***is replaced by*** *inf* (***without*** ge), ***when used in connection with another*** *inf*, e.g. ich habe ihn singen hören, du hättest es tun können, er hat gehen müssen, ich hätte ihn laufen lassen sollen.

b) 'Strong' Conjugation

30 **fahren**

pres ind	fahre	fährst	fährt
	fahren	fahrt	fahren
pres subj	fahre	fahrest	fahre
	fahren	fahret	fahren
pret ind	fuhr	fuhr(e)st	fuhr
	fuhren	fuhrt	fuhren
pres subj	führe	führest	führe
	führen	führet	führen

imp sg fahr(e), *pl* fahr(e)t, fahren Sie; *inf pres* fahren; *inf perf* gefahren haben ***or*** sein;
pres p fahrend; *pp* gefahren (18; 29**).

German Weights and Measures

I Linear Measure

1 mm ***Millimeter*** millimeter, *Br* millimetre
= $^{1}/_{1000}$ meter (*Br* metre)
= 0.003 feet
= 0.039 inches

1 cm ***Zentimeter*** centimeter, *Br* centimetre
= $^{1}/_{100}$ meter (*Br* metre)
= 0.39 inches

1 dm ***Dezimeter*** decimeter, *Br* decimetre
= $^{1}/_{10}$ meter (*Br* metre)
= 3.94 inches

1 m ***Meter*** meter, *Br* metre
= 1.094 yards
= 3.28 feet
= 39.37 inches

1 km ***Kilometer*** kilometer, *Br* kilometre
= 1,000 meters (*Br* metres)
= 1,093.637 yards
= 0.621 (statute) miles

1 sm ***Seemeile*** nautical mile
= 1,852 meters (*Br* metres)

II Square Measure

1 mm² ***Quadratmillimeter*** square millimeter (*Br* millimetre)
= 0.0015 square inches

1 cm² ***Quadratzentimeter*** square centimeter (*Br* centimetre)
= 0.155 square inches

1 m² ***Quadratmeter*** square meter (*Br* metre)
= 1.195 square yards
= 10.76 square feet

1 a ***Ar*** are
= 100 square meters (*Br* metres)
= 119.59 square yards
= 1,076.40 square feet

1 ha ***Hektar*** hectare
= 100 ares
= 10,000 square meters (*Br* metres)
= 11,959.90 square yards
= 2.47 acres

1 km² ***Quadratkilometer*** square kilometer (*Br* kilometre)
= 100 hectares
= 1,000,000 square meters (*Br* metres)
= 247.11 acres
= 0.386 square miles

III Cubic Measure

1 cm³ ***Kubikzentimeter*** cubic centimeter (*Br* centimetre)
= 1,000 cubic millimeters (*Br* millimetres)
= 0.061 cubic inches

1 dm³ ***Kubikdezimeter*** cubic decimeter (*Br* decimetre)
= 1,000 cubic centimeters (*Br* centimetres)
= 61.025 cubic inches

1 m³ ***Kubikmeter***
1 rm ***Raummeter***
1 fm ***Festmeter*** } cubic meter (*Br* metre)
= 1,000 cubic decimeters (*Br* decimetres)
= 1.307 cubic yards
= 35.31 cubic feet

1 RT ***Registertonne*** register ton
= 2.832 m³
= 100 cubic feet

IV Measure of Capacity

1 l ***Liter*** liter, *Br* litre
= 10 deciliters (*Br* decilitres)
= 2.11 pints (*Am*)
= 8.45 gills (*Am*)
= 1.06 quarts (*Am*)
= 0.26 gallons (*Am*)
= 1.76 pints (*Br*)
= 7.04 gills (*Br*)
= 0.88 quarts (*Br*)
= 0.22 gallons (*Br*)

1 hl ***Hektoliter*** hectoliter, *Br* hectolitre
= 100 liters (*Br* litres)
= 26.42 gallons (*Am*)
= 2.84 bushels (*Am*)
= 22.009 gallons (*Br*)
= 2.75 bushels (*Br*)

V Weight

1 mg ***Milligramm*** milligram(me)
= $^{1}/_{1000}$ gram(me)
= 0.015 grains

1 g ***Gramm*** gram(me)
= $^{1}/_{1000}$ kilogram(me)
= 15.43 grains

1 Pfd ***Pfund*** pound (German)
= $^{1}/_{2}$ kilogram(me)
= 500 gram(me)s
= 1.102 pounds (1b)

1 kg ***Kilogramm***, ***Kilo*** kilogram(me)
= 1,000 gram(me)s
= 2.204 pounds (1b)

1 Ztr. ***Zentner*** centner
= 100 pounds (German)
= 50 kilogram(me)s
= 110.23 pounds (1b)
= 1.102 US hundredweights
= 0.98 British hundredweights

1 t ***Tonne*** ton
= 1,000 kilogram(me)s
= 1.102 US tons
= 0.984 British tons

Conversion Tables for Temperatures

°C (Celsius)	°F (Fahrenheit)
100	212
95	203
90	194
85	185
80	176
75	167
70	158
65	149
60	140
55	131
50	122
45	113
40	104
35	95
30	86
25	77
20	68
15	59
10	50
5	41
0	32
- 5	23
-10	14
-15	5
-17.8	0
-20	- 4
-25	-13
-30	-22
-35	-31
-40	-40
-45	-49
-50	-58

Clinical Thermometer

°C (Celsius)	°F (Fahrenheit)
42.0	107.6
41.8	107.2
41.6	106.9
41.4	106.5
41.2	106.2
41.0	105.8
40.8	105.4
40.6	105.1
40.4	104.7
40.2	104.4
40.0	104.0
39.8	103.6
39.6	103.3
39.4	102.9
39.2	102.6
39.0	102.2
38.8	101.8
38.6	101.5
38.4	101.1
38.2	100.8
38.0	100.4
37.8	100.0
37.6	99.7
37.4	99.3
37.2	99.0
37.0	98.6
36.8	98.2
36.6	97.9

Rules for Conversion

$$°F = \frac{9}{5}\,°C + 32$$

$$°C = (°F - 32)\frac{5}{9}$$

Numerals

Cardinal Numbers

0 null *nought, zero*
1 eins *one*
2 zwei *two*
3 drei *three*
4 vier *four*
5 fünf *five*
6 sechs *six*
7 sieben *seven*
8 acht *eight*
9 neun *nine*
10 zehn *ten*
11 elf *eleven*
12 zwölf *twelve*
13 dreizehn *thirteen*
14 vierzehn *fourteen*
15 fünfzehn *fifteen*
16 sechzehn *sixteen*
17 siebzehn *seventeen*
18 achtzehn *eighteen*
19 neunzehn *nineteen*
20 zwanzig *twenty*
21 einundzwanzig *twenty-one*
22 zweiundzwanzig *twenty-two*
30 dreißig *thirty*
31 einunddreißig *thirty-one*
40 vierzig *forty*
41 einundvierzig *forty-one*
50 fünfzig *fifty*
51 einundfünfzig *fifty-one*
60 sechzig *sixty*
61 einundsechzig *sixty-one*
70 siebzig *seventy*
71 einundsiebzig *seventy-one*
80 achtzig *eighty*
81 einundachtzig *eighty-one*
90 neunzig *ninety*
91 einundneunzig *ninety-one*
100 hundert *a* or *one hundred*
101 hunderteins *a hundred and one*
200 zweihundert *two hundred*
300 dreihundert *three hundred*
572 fünfhundertzweiundsiebzig *five hundred and seventy-two*
1000 tausend *a* or *one thousand*
1999 neunzehnhundertneunundneunzig *nineteen hundred and ninetynine*
2000 zweitausend *two thousand*
5044 TEL fünfzig vierundvierzig *five O* (or *zero*) *double four*
1 000 000 eine Million *one million*
2 000 000 zwei Millionen *two million*

Ordinal Numbers

1. erste *first* (*1st*)
2. zweite *second* (*2nd*)
3. dritte *third* (*3rd*)
4. vierte *fourth* (*4th*)
5. fünfte *fifth* (*5th*) *etc* .
6. sechste *sixth*
7. siebente *seventh*
8. achte *eighth*
9. neunte *ninth*
10. zehnte *tenth*
11. elfte *eleventh*
12. zwölfte *twelfth*
13. dreizehnte *thirteenth*
14. vierzehnte *fourteenth*
15. fünfzehnte *fifteenth*
16. sechzehnte *sixteenth*
17. siebzehnte *seventeenth*
18. achtzehnte *eighteenth*
19. neunzehnte *nineteenth*
20. zwanzigste *twentieth*
21. einundzwanzigste *twenty-first*
22. zweiundzwanzigste *twenty-second*
23. dreiundzwanzigste *twenty-third*
30. dreißigste *thirtieth*
31. einunddreißigste *thirty-first*
40. vierzigste *fortieth*
41. einundvierzigste *forty-first*
50. fünfzigste *fiftieth*
51. einundfünfzigste *fifty-first*
60. sechzigste *sixtieth*
61. einundsechzigste *sixty-first*
70. siebzigste *seventieth*
71. einundsiebzigste *seventy-first*
80. achtzigste *eightieth*
81. einundachtzigste *eighty-first*
90. neunzigste *ninetieth*
100. hundertste (*one*) *hundredth*
101. hundert(und)erste (*one*) *hundred and first*
200. zweihundertste *two hundredth*
300. dreihundertste *three hundredth*
572. fünfhundert(und)zweiundsiebzigste *five hundred and seventysecond*
1000. tausendste (*one*) *thousandth*
1970. neunzehnhundert(und)siebzigste *nineteen hundred and seventieth*
500 000. fünfhunderttausendste *five hundred thousandth*
1 000 000. millionste (*one*) *millionth*